The Thomas Guide

METROPOLITAN
BAY AREA

Table of Contents

Introduction	❖ Legend of Map Symbols	**ii**	INTRO
	❖ How to Use This Thomas Guide	**iii**	
	❖ Cities and Communities Index	**iv - vi**	
Area Pages	❖ Key to Map Pages	**vii**	AREA
	❖ Transit Map & Information	**viii - x**	
	❖ Airport Pages	**xi - xiii**	
	❖ Downtown Maps	**xiv - xvi**	
Map Pages	❖ Arterial Maps	**243 & 263**	MAP
	❖ Detail Maps	**509 - 895**	
Indexes	❖ List of Abbreviations	**896**	INDEX
	❖ Street Index	**897 - 1016**	
	❖ Points of Interest Index	**1017 - 1045**	

Thomas Bros. Maps®
Since 1915
1-800-899-MAPS
1-800-899-6277

Corporate Office & Showroom
17731 Cowan, Irvine, CA 92614 (714) 863-1984 or 1-888-826-6277
Thomas Bros. Maps® & Books
550 Jackson St., San Francisco, CA 94133 (415) 981-7520 or 1-800-969-3072
521 W. 6th St., Los Angeles, CA 90014 (213) 627-4018 or 1-888-277-6277
Customer Service: 1-800-899-6277
World Wide Web: www.thomas.com
e-mail: comments@thomas.com

———	Freeway
———	Interchange/Ramp
———	Highway
———	Primary Road
———	Secondary Road
———	Minor Road
-----	Restricted Road
-----	Alley
– – –	Unpaved Road
———	Tunnel
———	Toll Road
———	High Occupancy Veh. Lane
———	Stacked Multiple Roadways
·········	Proposed Road Under Const.
– – –	Proposed Freeway
———	Freeway Under Construction
←———	One–Way Road
←——→	Two–Way Road
·········	Trail, Walkway
▬▬▬	Stairs
–+–+–+–	Railroad
•–•–•–	Rapid Transit
∘–∘–∘–	Rapid Transit, Underground
– – –	City Boundary
▬▬▬	County Boundary
▬▬▬	State Boundary
▬▬▬	International Boundary
— — —	Military Base, Indian Resv.
———	River, Creek, Shoreline
– – –	Ferry

LEGEND OF MAP SYMBOLS

N
NORTH

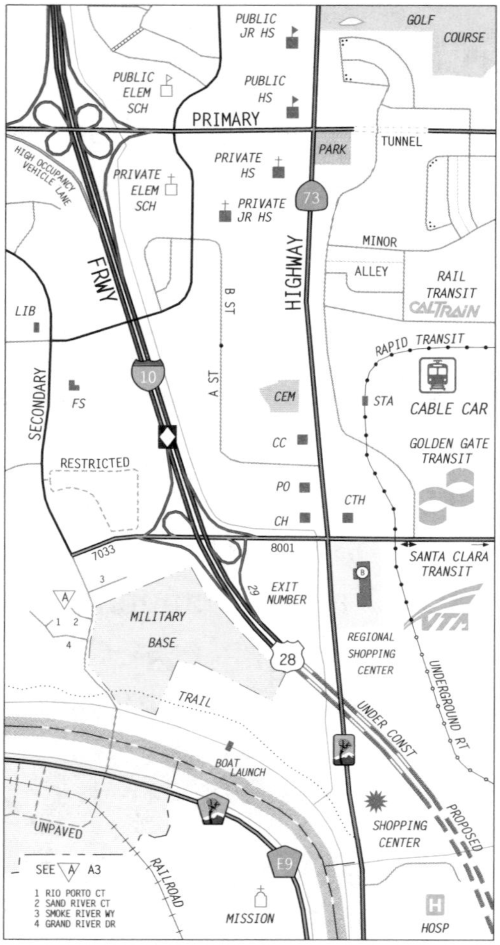

	Interstate
	Interstate (Business)
	U.S. Highway
	State Highway
	County Highway
	State Scenic Highway
	County Scenic Highway
◈	Carpool Lane
▽	Street List Marker
⋮	Street Name Continuation
•	Street Name Change
	Airport
–	Station (Train, Bus)
■	Building (see List of Abbreviations page)
⌐■	Building Footprint
⌂	Public Elementary School
▶	Public High School
⌂	Private Elementary School
✝	Private High School
✳	Shopping Center
▮	Fire Station
▯	Library
⌂	Mission
♆	Winery
▲	Campground
☼	Mountain
⊕	Section Corner
–	Boat Launch
✕	Gates, Locks, Barricades
☼	Lighthouse

INTRO

☐	County Seat	▨	Incorporated City	▨	Dam	▤	Parking Lot
	County	▨	City, County, State Park	▨	Point of Interest	▨	Structure Footprint
	Incorporated City	▨	National Forest, Park	▨	Golf Course, Country Club		Regional Shopping Center
	Incorporated City	▨	Water	▨	Cemetery	Ⓑ	Major Dept. Store (see List of Abbreviations page)
	Incorporated City	– – –	Intermittent Lake, Marsh	▨	Military Base		
	Incorporated City	▨	Dry Lake, Beach	▨	Airport		

Arterial Map Scale
1 Inch to 4 Miles

Miles
Kilometers

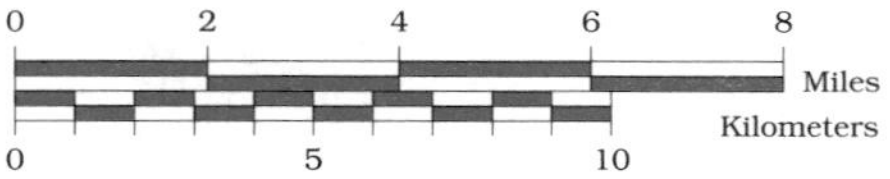

Arterial Grid Equivalents
1 Grid Equals:

1 Detail Page
4.5 x 3.5 Miles
1.125 x .875 Inches

Detail Map Scale
1 Inch to 1900 Feet

Miles
Kilometers

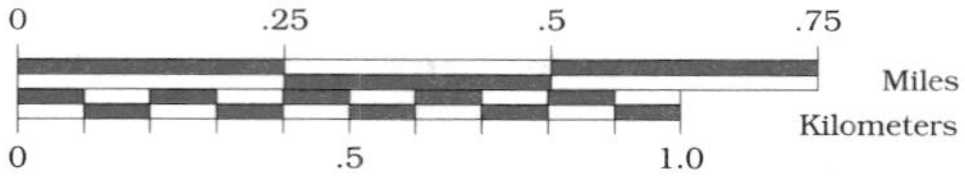

Detail Grid Equivalents
1 Grid Equals:

.5 x .5 Miles
2640 x 2640 Feet
1.4 x 1.4 Inches

How to Use this Street Guide & Directory

To Find a City or Community:

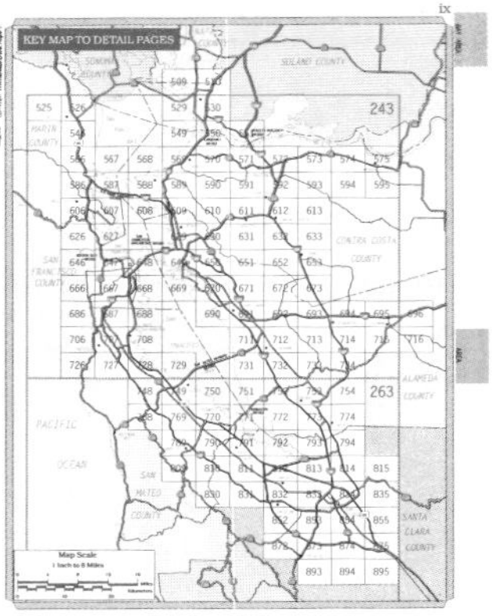

If you know the general area in which the city or community is located, start with the ***Key Map*** on Page vii, or ***Arterial Maps*** (Pages 243, 263), then turn to the ***Detail Page*** indicated. (Pages 509-895)

— OR —

Look up the city or community name in the ***Cities and Communities*** pages, located on Page iv - vi. The Detail Page is listed next to each name. Turn to the Detail Page indicated.

COMMUNITY NAME	ABBR.	ZIP	EST. POP.	PAGE
CHINATOWN		94108		648
FINANCIAL DIST		94104		648
NOB HILL		94108		648
NORTH BEACH		94133		648
NORTH WATERFRONT		94133		648
RUSSIAN HILL		94133		648
* SAN FRANCISCO	SF	94102	759,300	647
-- SAN FRANCISCO CO			759,300	647
SOUTH BEACH		94107		648
SOUTH OF MARKET		94103		648
TELEGRAPH HILL		94133		648

Thomas Bros. Maps® Page and Grid

The pages in this Thomas Guide® are part of our national Page and Grid layout and our new computer digital mapping system. Each page number in the Bay Area is unique, enabling you to have precise page information when looking up a city, community, or street address. We hope that you will use the Thomas Bros. Maps Page and Grid as a regular part of your business, and that it will be helpful to you as you navigate throughout the Bay Area.

Unique Page Number for Each Geographic Area

In order to eliminate the confusion associated with map pages that overlap and repeat between each different county or area, or for each new map book, *the Thomas Bros. Maps Page and Grid assigns a unique page number to each geographical area.*

Page numbers for each Thomas Bros. Maps street guide begin with the lowest map page number, and continue on through the highest number. Each map page is clearly marked in the upper outside corner of the page.

Grids are 1/2 Mile Square

The detail map Grids (shown in magenta on your map) are 1/2 mile square, and go from Grid A1 through Grid J7. This gives you the ability to quickly locate cities, streets, addresses, and points of interest. If you have any questions about the Thomas Bros. Maps Page and Grid, please call us at 1-800-899-6277 (800-899-MAPS).

To Find an Address:

1

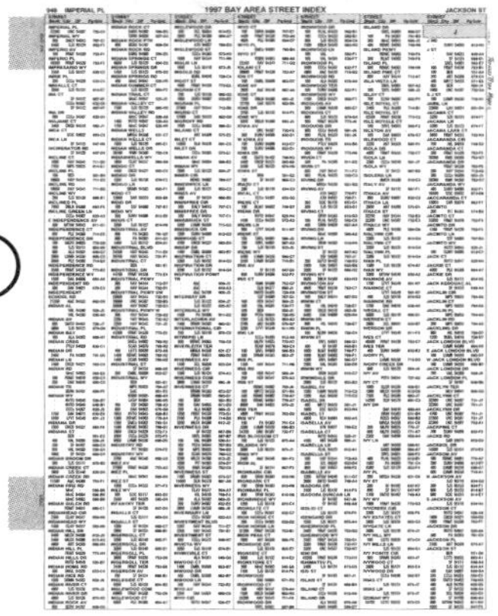

Look up the street name in the ***Street Index***. If there are multiple listings, choose the proper city and/or block address range.

2

JACKSON ST
550 SF 94133 648-A4

The index entry will include a ***Thomas Bros. Maps® Page and Grid*** where the street and address are located.

3

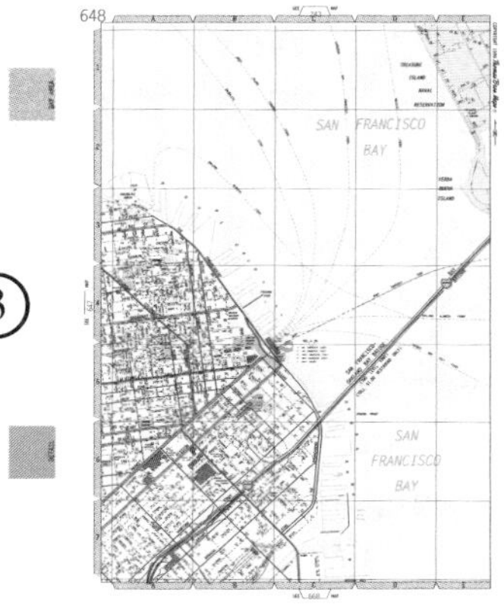

Turn to the page indicated.

4

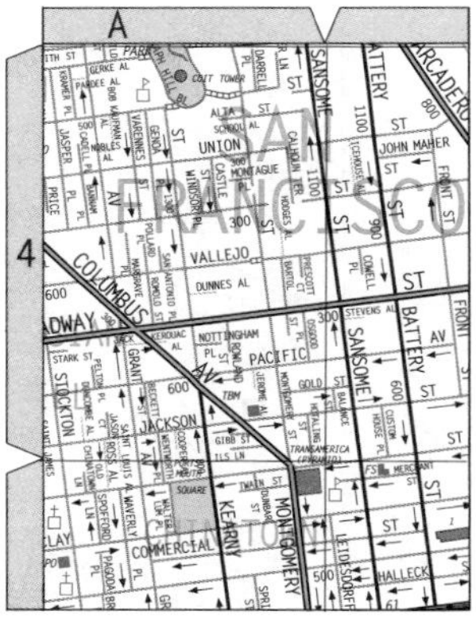

Locate the street by following the indicated ***Letter Column and Number Row*** until the two intersect. The street name is in this grid.

We Welcome Your Suggestions

Since 1915, Thomas Bros. Maps has been publishing mapping products, and is recognized as an industry leader. We believe that our best products and enhancements come from your suggestions. We also appreciate your corrections to the map or index. We welcome your suggestions and look forward to providing you with many fine mapping products in the future.

1998 METROPOLITAN BAY AREA CITIES AND COMMUNITIES

COMMUNITY NAME	ABBR.	ZIP CODE	EST. POP.	PAGE
* ALAMEDA	ALA	94501	76,300	669
-- ALAMEDA COUNTY	AlaC		1,375,900	649
ALAMO		94507		632
ALAMO SQUARE		94115		647
* ALBANY	ALB	94706	17,300	609
ALMONTE		94941		606
ALPINE HILLS		94025		810
ALTO		94941		606
ALUM ROCK		95127		834
ALVARADO		94587		731
ALVISO		95002		793
* AMERICAN CANYON	AMCN	94589	9,025	509
* ANTIOCH	ANT	94509	76,500	575
ANZA VISTA		94115		647
ASHLAND		94578		691
* ATHERTON	ATN	94027	7,375	790
AVON		94553		572
BALBOA TERRACE		94127		667
BAY FARM ISLAND		94502		669
BAY POINT		94565		573
BAYSHORE		94005		688
BAYVIEW		94124		668
BAYVIEW HEIGHTS		94124		688
BEL AIRE		94920		607
BEL MARIN KEYS		94949		526
* BELMONT	BLMT	94002	25,200	769
* BELVEDERE	BLV	94920	2,280	627
BENICIA	BEN	94510	27,350	551
* BERKELEY	BERK	94510	105,900	629
* BERNAL HEIGHTS		94110		667
BERRYESSA		95132		814
BLACKHAWK		94526		654
BLACK POINT		94945		526
* BRISBANE	BSBN	94005	3,210	688
BROADMOOR VILLAGE		94015		687
BROOKFIELD VILLAGE		94603		670
* BURLINGAME	BURL	94010	28,550	728
BURLINGAME HILLS		94010		728
CAMBRIAN VILLAGE		95124		873
* CAMPBELL	CMBL	95008	39,300	853
CANYON		94516		630
CARQUINEZ HEIGHTS		94590		550
CASTRO VALLEY		94546		691
CENTERVILLE		94536		752
CHINATOWN		94108		648
CLAREMONT		94705		630
CLARENDON HEIGHTS		94114		667
* CLAYTON	CLAY	94517	10,050	593
CLYDE		94520		572
* COLMA	CLMA	94014	1,240	687
* CONCORD	CNCD	94520	111,800	593
-- CONTRA COSTA COUNTY	CCCo		879,200	571
CORONA HEIGHTS		94114		667
* CORTE MADERA	CMAD	94925	8,750	606
COW HOLLOW		94123		647
CRAGMONT		94708		609
CROCKER AMAZON		94112		687
CROCKETT		94525		550
* CUPERTINO	CPTO	95014	44,800	852
* DALY CITY	DALY	94014	101,300	687
* DANVILLE	DNVL	94506	38,100	653
DEVONSHIRE		94070		769
DIABLO		94528		633
DIAMOND HEIGHTS		94131		667
DIMOND		94602		650
DOUGHERTY		94566		694
* DUBLIN	DBLN	94568	26,750	693
DUBOCE TRIANGLE		94114		667
EAST MENLO		94025		770
EASTMONT		94605		671
* EAST PALO ALTO	EPA	94303	25,050	791
EAST SAN JOSE		95127		835
* EL CERRITO	ELCR	94530	23,300	609
ELMHURST		94603		670
EL SOBRANTE		94803		569
EMERALD LAKE		94062		789
* EMERYVILLE	EMVL	94608	6,525	629
EUREKA VLY/DOLORES HTS		94114		667
EVERGREEN		95121		855
EXCELSIOR		94112		687
FARM HILLS		94061		789
FERNSIDE		94501		670
FINANCIAL DISTRICT		94104		648
FOREST HILL		94116		667
FOREST KNOLLS		94131		667
FOREST PARK		94611		630
* FOSTER CITY	FCTY	94404	29,750	749
* FREMONT	FRMT	94536	192,200	753
FRUITVALE		94601		650
GALLINAS		94903		566
GLEN PARK		94131		667
GLENWOOD		94901		567
GOLDEN GATE HEIGHTS		94122		667
GREENBRAE		94904		586
GREEN POINT		94945		526
HAIGHT-ASHBURY		94117		667
HARBOR POINT		94941		606
HAYES VALLEY		94103		667

* INDICATES INCORPORATED CITY

1998 METROPOLITAN BAY AREA CITIES AND COMMUNITIES

	COMMUNITY NAME	ABBR.	ZIP CODE	EST. POP.	PAGE
*	HAYWARD	HAY	94541	123,900	711
*	HERCULES	HER	94547	18,800	569
	HILL HAVEN		94920		607
*	HILLSBOROUGH	HIL	94010	11,350	748
	HILLSDALE		94403		749
	HOMESTEAD VALLEY		94941		606
	HUNTERS POINT		94124		668
	IGNACIO		94949		546
	INGLESIDE		94112		667
	INGLESIDE HEIGHTS		94112		667
	INGLESIDE TERRACE		94112		667
	IRVINGTON		94538		753
	JORDAN HTS/LAUREL HTS		94118		647
	KENSINGTON		94708		609
	KENTFIELD		94904		586
	KILKARE		94586		734
	KINGS MOUNTAIN		94062		789
	LADERA		94025		810
*	LAFAYETTE	LFYT	94549	23,600	611
	LAKE		94118		647
	LAKE SHORE		94132		686
	LAKESIDE		94132		667
*	LARKSPUR	LKSP	94939	11,750	586
	LINDA MAR		94044		726
	LINDENWOOD		94025		790
	LITTLE REED HEIGHTS		94920		607
*	LIVERMORE	LVMR	94550	67,800	696
	LONE MOUNTAIN		94118		647
*	LOS ALTOS	LALT	94022	28,000	811
*	LOS ALTOS HILLS	LAH	94022	7,975	811
*	LOS GATOS	LGTS	95030	29,700	873
	LOS RANCHITOS		94903		566
	LOS TRANCOS WOODS		94025		830
	MANZANITA		94941		606
	MARE ISLAND		94592		529
	MARINA		94123		647
	MARIN BAY		94901		567
	MARIN CITY		94965		626
--	MARIN COUNTY	MrnC		242,200	566
	MARIN VILLAGE		94947		526
	MARINWOOD		94903		546
*	MARTINEZ	MRTZ	94553	35,350	571
	MELROSE		94601		670
	MENLO OAKS		94025		790
*	MENLO PARK	MLPK	94025	30,550	790
	MERCED HEIGHTS		94112		687
	MERCED MANOR		94132		667
	MIDTOWN TERRACE		94131		667
*	MILLBRAE	MLBR	94030	21,450	728
	MILLSMONT		94619		651
*	MILL VALLEY	MLV	94941	13,900	606
*	MILPITAS	MPS	95035	61,200	794
	MIRALOMA PARK		94127		667
	MISSION BAY		94107		668
	MISSION DISTRICT		94110		667
	MISSION DOLORES		94110		667
	MISSION SAN JOSE		94538		753
	MISSION TERRACE		94112		667
	MONTE VISTA		95014		852
	MONTCLAIR		94611		650
	MONTEREY HEIGHTS		94127		667
*	MONTE SERENO	MSER	95030	3,360	873
*	MORAGA	MRGA	94556	16,350	631
*	MOUNTAIN VIEW	MTVW	94040	73,000	811
	MT DAVIDSON MANOR		94127		667
	MULFORD GARDENS		94577		690
--	NAPA COUNTY	NaCo		120,800	509
	NEW ALMADEN		95042		894
*	NEWARK	NWK	94560	40,450	752
	NILES		94536		753
	NOB HILL		94108		648
	NOE VALLEY		94114		667
	NORTH BEACH		94133		648
	NORTH FAIR OAKS		94063		770
	NORTH PANHANDLE		94117		647
	NORTH RICHMOND		94807		588
	NORTH WATERFRONT		94133		648
*	NOVATO	NVTO	94949	46,100	526
	OAK KNOLL		94605		671
*	OAKLAND	OAK	94601	388,100	649
	OAKMORE		94602		650
	OCEANVIEW		94112		687
*	ORINDA	ORIN	94563	16,900	610
	ORINDA VILLAGE		94563		610
	OUTER MISSION		94112		687
	PACHECO		94553		592
*	PACIFICA	PCFA	94044	39,650	727
	PACIFIC HEIGHTS		94115		647
*	PALO ALTO	PA	94301	59,900	791
	PALOMAR PARK		94062		769
	PARADISE CAY		94920		607
	PARK MERCED		94132		687
	PARKSIDE		94116		667
	PARNASSUS/ASHBURY HTS		94117		667
	PEACOCK GAP		94901		567
*	PIEDMONT	PDMT	94611	11,300	650
	PIEDMONT PINES		94611		650
	PINE LAKE PARK		94132		667

* INDICATES INCORPORATED CITY

1998 METROPOLITAN BAY AREA CITIES AND COMMUNITIES

COMMUNITY NAME	ABBR.	ZIP CODE	EST. POP.	PAGE
* PINOLE	PIN	94564	18,150	569
* PITTSBURG	PIT	94565	50,800	574
* PLEASANT HILL	PLHL	94523	31,450	592
* PLEASANTON	PLE	94566	59,800	714
PORT COSTA		94569		550
PORTOLA		94134		667
* PORTOLA VALLEY	PTLV	94028	4,470	810
PORTOLA VALLEY RANCH		94025		830
POTRERO HILL		94107		668
PRESIDIO HEIGHTS		94118		647
PRESIDIO OF SAN FRANCISCO		94129		647
RANCHO RINCONADA		95014		852
* REDWOOD CITY	RDWC	94061	73,200	770
REDWOOD SHORES		94065		749
REED		94920		607
RHEEM VALLEY		94556		631
* RICHMOND	RCH	94801	91,300	588
RICHMOND		94121		647
ROCKAWAY BEACH		94044		726
ROCKRIDGE		94618		630
RODEO		94572		549
* ROSS	ROSS	94957	2,260	586
ROSSMOOR LEISURE WORLD		94595		632
RUSSIAN HILL		94133		648
SAINT FRANCIS WOOD		94127		667
* SAN ANSELMO	SANS	94960	12,300	566
* SAN BRUNO	SBRN	94066	40,800	707
* SAN CARLOS	SCAR	94070	28,050	769
* SAN FRANCISCO	SF	94102	778,100	647
-- SAN FRANCISCO COUNTY			778,100	647
* SAN JOSE	SJS	95103	873,300	834
* SAN LEANDRO	SLN	94577	72,600	690
SAN LORENZO		94580		711
SAN MARIN		94945		525
* SAN MATEO	SMTO	94401	92,200	749
-- SAN MATEO COUNTY	SMCo		701,100	770
* SAN PABLO	SPAB	94806	25,900	588
SAN PEDRO TERRACE		94044		726
SAN QUENTIN		94964		587
* SAN RAFAEL	SRFL	94901	53,400	566
* SAN RAMON	SRMN	94583	41,950	673
* SANTA CLARA	SCL	95050	100,000	833
-- SANTA CLARA COUNTY	SCIC		1,653,100	893
SANTA RITA		94566		694
SANTA VENETIA		94903		566
SAN TOMAS		95008		853
* SARATOGA	SAR	95070	30,600	872
* SAUSALITO	SAUS	94965	7,725	627
SCOTTS CORNER		94586		734

COMMUNITY NAME	ABBR.	ZIP CODE	EST. POP.	PAGE
SEACLIFF		94121		647
SEMINARY		94619		670
SERRAMONTE		94015		707
SHARON HEIGHTS		94025		790
SHARP PARK		94044		707
SHEFFIELD VILLAGE		94605		671
SHERWOOD FOREST		94127		667
SILVER TERRACE		94124		668
SKY LONDA		94062		809
SLEEPY HOLLOW		94960		566
-- SOLANO COUNTY	SoLC		375,400	550
SOUTH BEACH		94107		648
SOUTH OF MARKET		94103		648
* SOUTH SAN FRANCISCO	SSF	94080	57,600	707
SOUTH SHORE		94501		669
SPRING TOWN		94550		696
STANFORD		94305		790
STONESTOWN		94132		687
STRAWBERRY MANOR		94941		606
SUNNYSIDE		94112		667
* SUNNYVALE	SUNV	94086	129,300	812
SUNSET		94122		666
SUNOL		94586		734
TAMALPAIS VALLEY		94941		626
TELEGRAPH HILL		94133		648
TEMESCAL		94609		629
TERRA LINDA		94903		566
THE HIGHLANDS		94402		748
THOUSAND OAKS		94707		609
* TIBURON	TBRN	94920	8,550	607
TRESTLE GLEN		94610		650
TWIN PEAKS		94131		667
* UNION CITY	UNC	94587	59,700	732
* VALLEJO	VAL	94590	110,500	530
VALLEJO HEIGHTS		94590		529
VALLEMAR		94044		727
VISITACION VALLEY		94134		688
VISTA VERDE		94025		830
* WALNUT CREEK	WLCK	94595	62,200	612
WESTBOROUGH		94080		707
WEST MENLO PARK		94025		790
WEST PORTAL		94127		667
WESTRIDGE		94025		810
WESTWOOD HIGHLANDS		94127		667
WESTWOOD PARK		94127		667
* WOODSIDE	WDSD	94062	5,475	789
WOODSIDE HIGHLANDS		94025		809
WOODSIDE HILLS		94062		789

*** INDICATES INCORPORATED CITY**

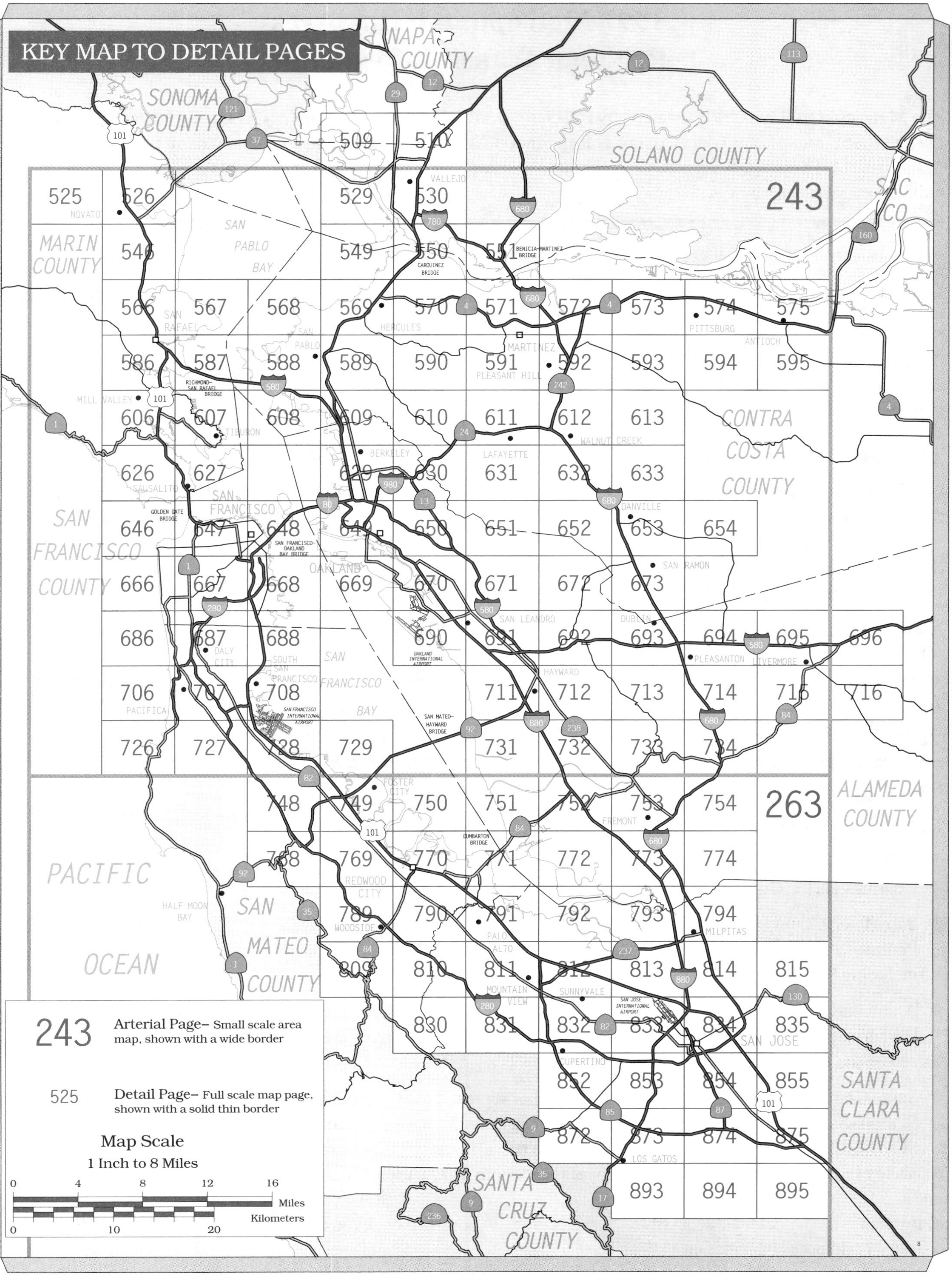
KEY MAP TO DETAIL PAGES
NAPA COUNTY
SONOMA COUNTY
SOLANO COUNTY
MARIN COUNTY
SAN PABLO BAY
SAN FRANCISCO COUNTY
CONTRA COSTA COUNTY
ALAMEDA COUNTY
SAN FRANCISCO BAY
PACIFIC OCEAN
SAN MATEO COUNTY
SANTA CLARA COUNTY
SANTA CRUZ COUNTY
SAC CO
NOVATO
VALLEJO
CARQUINEZ BRIDGE
BENICIA-MARTINEZ BRIDGE
HERCULES
PITTSBURG
ANTIOCH
MARTINEZ
PLEASANT HILL
SAN RAFAEL
SAN PABLO
RICHMOND-SAN RAFAEL BRIDGE
MILL VALLEY
TIBURON
BERKELEY
LAFAYETTE
WALNUT CREEK
SAUSALITO
GOLDEN GATE BRIDGE
SAN FRANCISCO
DANVILLE
SAN FRANCISCO-OAKLAND BAY BRIDGE
OAKLAND
SAN RAMON
SAN LEANDRO
DUBLIN
DALY CITY
SOUTH SAN FRANCISCO
OAKLAND INTERNATIONAL AIRPORT
PLEASANTON
LIVERMORE
HAYWARD
PACIFICA
SAN FRANCISCO INTERNATIONAL AIRPORT
SAN MATEO-HAYWARD BRIDGE
FOSTER CITY
FREMONT
DUMBARTON BRIDGE
REDWOOD CITY
HALF MOON BAY
WOODSIDE
PALO ALTO
MILPITAS
MOUNTAIN VIEW
SUNNYVALE
SAN JOSE INTERNATIONAL AIRPORT
SAN JOSE
CUPERTINO
LOS GATOS
243
263
509 510
525 526 529 530
546 549 550 551
566 567 568 569 570 571 572 573 574 575
586 587 588 589 590 591 592 593 594 595
606 607 608 609 610 611 612 613
626 627 629 630 631 632 633
646 647 648 649 650 651 652 653 654
666 667 668 669 670 671 672 673
686 687 688 690 691 692 693 694 695 696
706 707 708 711 712 713 714 715 716
726 727 728 729 731 732 733 734
748 749 750 751 752 753 754
768 769 770 771 772 773 774
789 790 791 792 793 794
809 810 811 812 813 814 815
830 831 832 833 834 835
852 853 854 855
872 873 874 875
893 894 895
101 121 37 29 12 113 160 680 780 4 580 242 1 24 980 13 80 280 238 92 880 84 82 35 237 130 85 87 9 17 236 ← route markers
243 Arterial Page– Small scale area map, shown with a wide border
525 Detail Page– Full scale map page, shown with a solid thin border
Map Scale
1 Inch to 8 Miles
0 4 8 12 16 Miles
0 10 20 Kilometers

1997 Metropolitan Bay Area Regional Transit Information

The Metropolitan Bay Area is serviced by CalTrain, BART, Golden Gate Transit (GGT), San Mateo County Transit District (SamTrans), Santa Clara County Transportation Agency (SCCTA), and Alameda-Contra Costa Transit District (AC Transit). These agencies offer trip-planning assistance and operate an extensive network of local and intercity public transportation services.

Personal Trip Planning

Contact your local agency (Monday - Friday) for information about route maps, timetables, and trip planning. Please have pen, paper, and the following information ready:

Your departure point (address or nearest cross streets)
Your destination (address or nearest cross streets)
Day and time you wish to travel

<u>Transit Information Numbers:</u>

Golden Gate Transit (GGT)

San Francisco County	(415) 923-2000
Marin County	(415) 455-2000
Sonoma County	(707) 541-2000
Hearing Impaired TDD	(415) 257-4554

Alameda-Contra Costa Transit District (AC Transit)
(Oakland, Hayward, Richmond, Fremont, and Newark areas)

Toll Free	(800) 559-INFO
Hearing Impaired (TDD)	(800) 448-9790

San Mateo County Transit District (SamTrans)

Toll Free	(800) 660-4BUS
	(800) 660-4287
Hearing Impaired (TDD)	(415) 508-6448

Santa Clara County Transportation Agency (SCCTA)

Direct	(408) 321-2300
Toll Free from 415 Area Code	(800) 894-9908
South County	(408) 683-4151
Hearing Impaired (TDD)	(408) 321-2330

Buses

There are several bus systems servicing the Metropolitan Bay Area:

- Golden Gate Transit (GGT) operates approximately 50 bus routes between San Francisco, Marin, and Sonoma Counties via the Golden Gate Bridge.
- San Mateo County Transit (SamTrans) operates more than 85 Express and Local Routes along the San Francisco Peninsula. Buses serve major residential and business areas, as well as transportation hubs along the Peninsula including San Francisco International Airport, CalTrains, and BART stations.
- Alameda-Contra Costa Transit (AC Transit) operates an extensive network of local, intercity express and transbay bus services in the East Bay, serving most cities and adjacent suburban areas including service to BART stations and across the Bay Bridge to San Francisco.
- Santa Clara Transit (SCCTA) offers 74 routes that serve the area, including extensions to the Menlo Park CalTrain Station (San Mateo County-SamTrans), and to the Fremont BART Station (Alameda County-BART-AC Transit). SCCTA also operates 10 Express and 4 Super Express bus routes linking residential areas of the County with Silicon Valley Industrial Centers. Major employers work with SCCTA to provide commuter services.

Many routes are wheelchair accessible. Some operate 24 hours a day, seven days a week. Please call your local transit district for additional information.

1998 Metropolitan Bay Area Regional Transit Information

Park and Ride

Park and Ride facilities, located throughout the Metropolitan Bay Area, are provided to encourage public transit use and ridesharing. For the location of Park and Ride lots, see the Points of Interest Index in this atlas, and look under the heading of "PARK & RIDE".

All Park and Ride lots may be used at no charge as a convenient meeting point for carpool and vanpool passengers. Many are served by buses and some offer special features such as passenger shelters, transit schedule signs, and bicycle lockers.

BART

Bay Area Rapid Transit (BART) lines are shown throughout this street guide. Please refer to the LEGEND page to see how BART lines are symbolized.

CalTrain

For information regarding fares, tickets, schedules, train/bus connections, or any questions and/or comments concerning CalTrain service, please call the following numbers Monday-Friday, 6:00 a.m. to 10:00 p.m.; Saturday, Sunday, and Holidays, 8:00 a.m. to 8:00 p.m.

Hotline .... (800) 660-4287 Hearing Impaired (TDD) ..... (415) 508-6448

Existing High Occupancy Vehicle (HOV) Lanes Summary

County	Route Description	Direction	Lane Miles	Occupancy	Days & Hours of Operation
Alameda	INT 880 - Marina Blvd to Whipple Rd	Southbound	9.2	2+	(M-F) 5:00-9:00 a.m.; 3:00-7:00 p.m.
Alameda	INT 880 - Whipple Rd to Rte 238 Connector	Northbound	7.3	2+	(M-F) 5:00-9:00 a.m.; 3:00-7:00 p.m.
Alameda	INT 80 - Rte 580 to Toll Plaza Meter (left side)	Westbound	1.2	3+	(M-F) 5:00-10:00 a.m.; 3:00-7:00 p.m.
Alameda	INT 80 - Powell St to Toll Plaza Meter (right side)	Westbound	2.0	3+	(M-F) 5:00-10:00 a.m.; 3:00-7:00 p.m. Buses daily: 24 Hours
Alameda	SR 92 - Clawiter Rd to Toll Plaza	Westbound	1.5	2+	(M-F) 5:00-10:00 a.m.; 3:00-6:00 p.m.
Alameda	SR 84 - Newark Blvd to Toll Plaza	Westbound	1.8	2+	(M-F) 5:00-10:00 a.m.; 3:00-6:00 p.m.
Contra Costa	INT 580 - Marine St to Central Av	Eastbound	4.9	2+	(M-F) 7:00-8:00 a.m.
Contra Costa	INT 580 - Central Av to Marine St	Westbound	5.3	2+	(M-F) 5:00-6:00 p.m.
Contra Costa	INT 680 - Dublin Blvd to Rudgear Rd	Northbound	14.5	2+	(M-F) 6:00-9:00 a.m.; 3:00-6:00 p.m.
Contra Costa	INT 680 - Rudgear Rd to Dublin Blvd	Southbound	14.5	2+	(M-F) 6:00-9:00 a.m.; 3:00-6:00 p.m.
Contra Costa	INT 80 - Central Av to Route 4	Eastbound	9.5	3+	(M-F) 5:00-10:00 a.m.; 3:00-7:00 p.m.
Ala/CC	INT 80 - Route 4 to Powell St	Westbound	14.1	3+	(M-F) 5:00-10:00 a.m.; 3:00-7:00 p.m.
Solano	INT 80 - At Carquinez Toll Plaza	Eastbound	0.2	3+	(M-F) 5:00-10:00 a.m.; 3:00-7:00 p.m.
San Mateo	US 101 - Whipple Av to SC County Line	Southbound	6.6	2+	(M-F) 5:00-9:00 a.m.; 3:00-7:00 p.m.
San Mateo	US 101 - SC County Line to Whipple Av	Northbound	6.6	2+	(M-F) 5:00-9:00 a.m.; 3:00-7:00 p.m.
Santa Clara	SR 85 - Route 237 to Route 280	Southbound	4.1	2+	(M-F) 5:00-9:00 a.m.; 3:00-7:00 p.m.
Santa Clara	SR 85 - Fremont Av to Route 237	Northbound	2.8	2+	(M-F) 5:00-9:00 a.m.; 3:00-7:00 p.m.
Santa Clara	US 101 - San Mateo Co. Line to Bernal Rd	Southbound	25.2	2+	(M-F) 5:00-9:00 a.m.; 3:00-7:00 p.m.
Santa Clara	US 101 - Bernal Rd to San Mateo Co. Line	Northbound	24.5	2+	(M-F) 5:00-9:00 a.m.; 3:00-7:00 p.m.
Santa Clara	SR 237 - Route 880 to Mathilda Av	Westbound	6.0	2+	(M-F) 5:00-9:00 a.m.
Santa Clara	SR 237 - Mathilda Av to Zanker Rd	Eastbound	5.7	2+	(M-F) 3:00-7:00 p.m.
Santa Clara	INT 280 - Magdalena Av to Meridian Av	Southbound	11.2	2+	(M-F) 5:00-9:00 a.m.; 3:00-7:00 p.m.
Santa Clara	INT 280 - Leland Av to Magdalena Av	Northbound	10.7	2+	(M-F) 5:00-9:00 a.m.; 3:00-7:00 p.m.
Marin	US 101 - 4.7 / 8.4	Southbound	3.7	2+	(M-F) 6:30-8:30 a.m.
Marin	US 101 - 4.0 / 7.5	Northbound	3.5	2+	(M-F) 4:30-7:30 p.m.
Marin	US 101 - 12.8 / 18.9	Southbound	6.1	2+	(M-F) 6:30-8:30 a.m.
Marin	US 101 - 12.8 / 18.9	Northbound	6.1	2+	(M-F) 4:30-7:00 p.m.

METROPOLITAN BAY AREA TRANSIT MAP

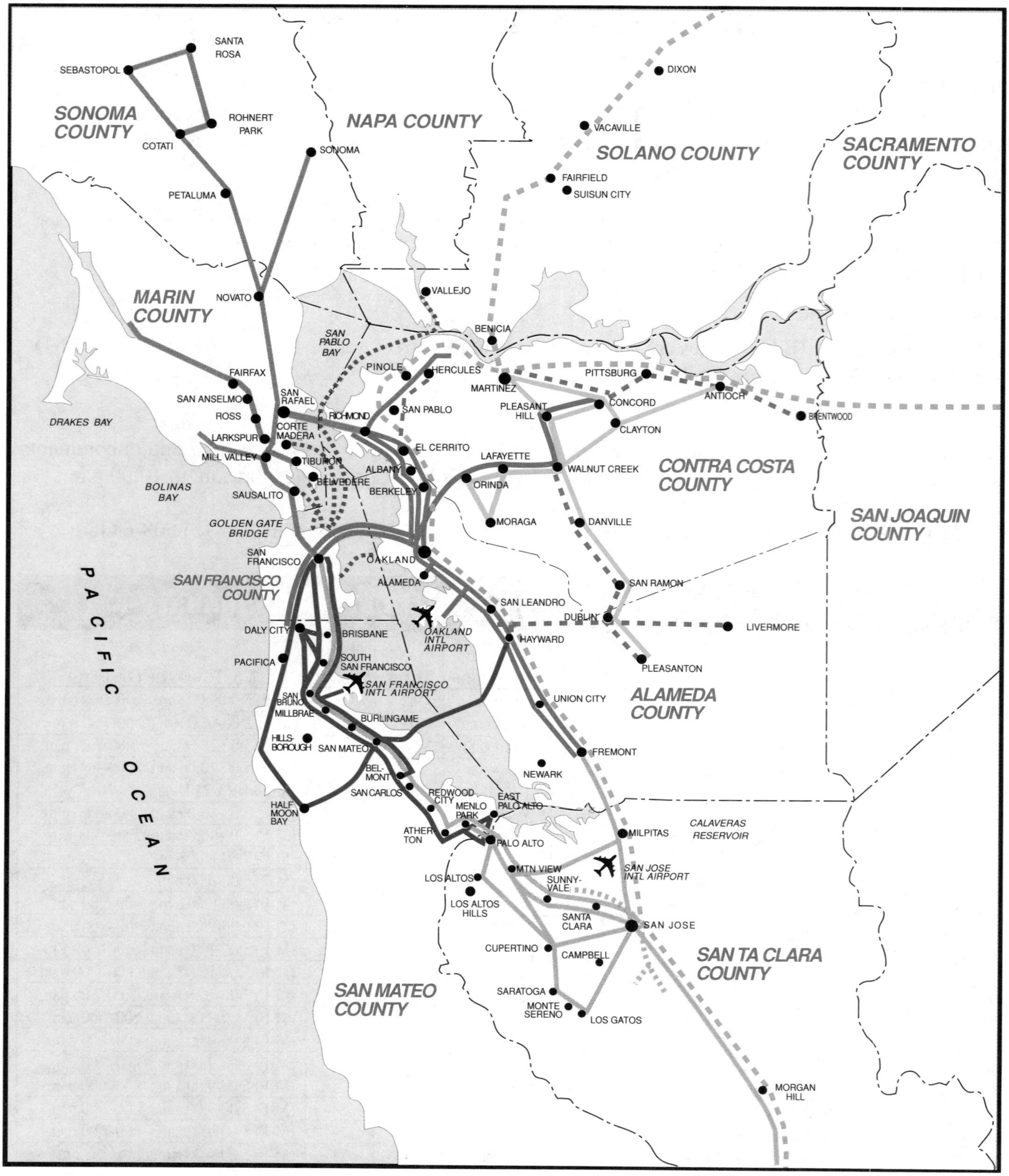

KEY TO TRANSIT MAP

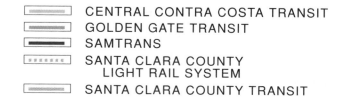

- AC TRANSIT
- AMTRAK
- BART
- BART EXPRESS BUS SERVICE
- CALTRAIN
- FERRY
- CENTRAL CONTRA COSTA TRANSIT
- GOLDEN GATE TRANSIT
- SAMTRANS
- SANTA CLARA COUNTY LIGHT RAIL SYSTEM
- SANTA CLARA COUNTY TRANSIT

SAN FRANCISCO INTERNATIONAL AIRPORT

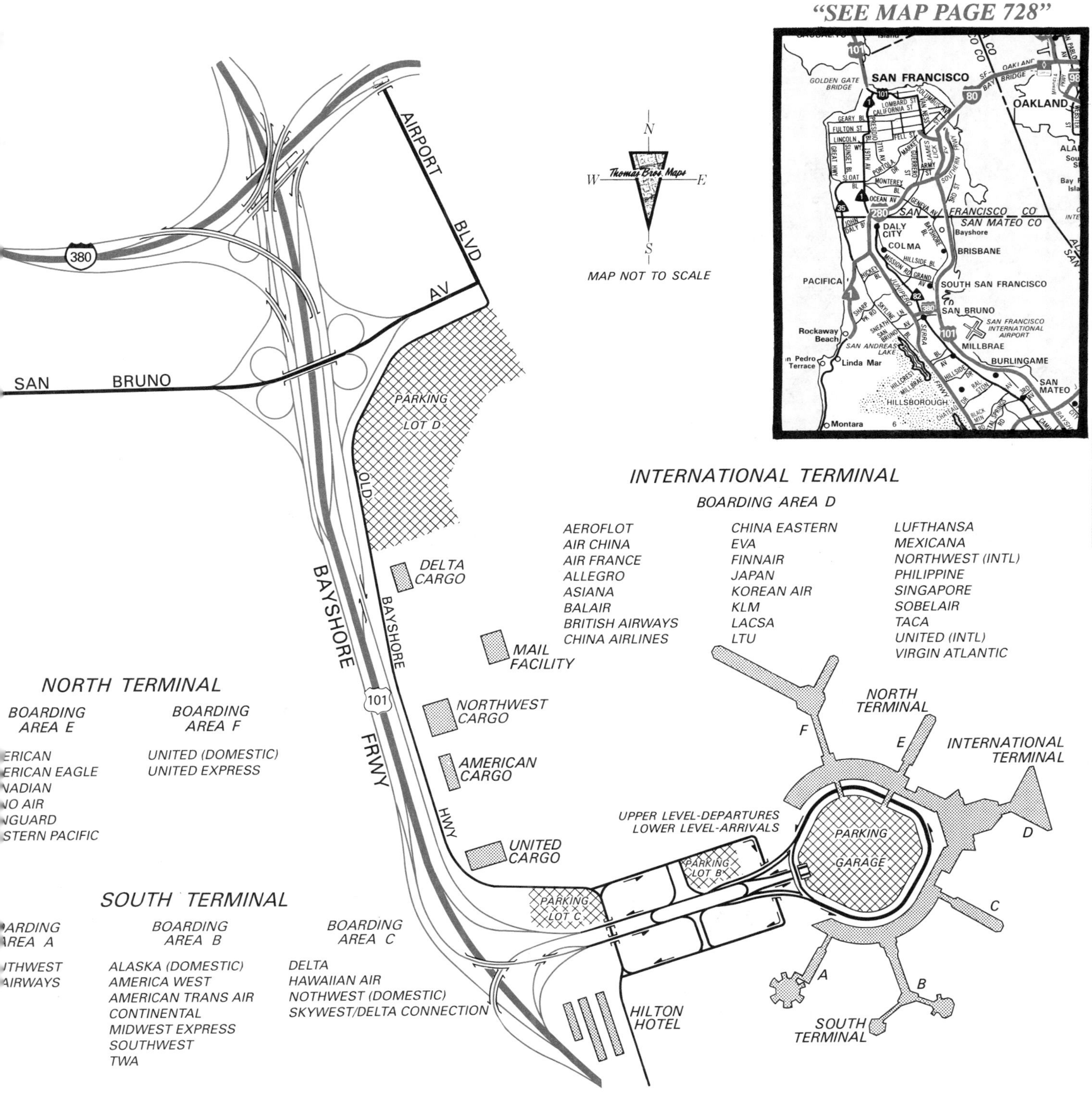
"SEE MAP PAGE 728"
SAN FRANCISCO
GOLDEN GATE BRIDGE
OAKLAND
LOMBARD ST
CALIFORNIA ST
GEARY BL
FULTON ST
LINCOLN WY
GREAT HWY
SUNSET BL
19TH AV
SLOAT BL
MONTEREY BL
OCEAN AV
SAN FRANCISCO CO
SAN MATEO CO
DALY CITY
Bayshore
COLMA
BRISBANE
PACIFICA
SOUTH SAN FRANCISCO
SAN BRUNO
SAN FRANCISCO INTERNATIONAL AIRPORT
Rockaway Beach
SAN ANDREAS LAKE
MILLBRAE
Linda Mar
BURLINGAME
SAN MATEO
HILLSBOROUGH
Montara
AIRPORT BLVD
380
SAN BRUNO AV
N
S
W
E
Thomas Bros Maps
MAP NOT TO SCALE
PARKING LOT D
OLD BAYSHORE HWY
BAYSHORE FRWY
101
DELTA CARGO
MAIL FACILITY
NORTHWEST CARGO
AMERICAN CARGO
UNITED CARGO
PARKING LOT C
PARKING LOT B
UPPER LEVEL-DEPARTURES
LOWER LEVEL-ARRIVALS
PARKING GARAGE
HILTON HOTEL
NORTH TERMINAL
INTERNATIONAL TERMINAL
SOUTH TERMINAL
A
B
C
D
E
F
INTERNATIONAL TERMINAL
BOARDING AREA D
AEROFLOT
AIR CHINA
AIR FRANCE
ALLEGRO
ASIANA
BALAIR
BRITISH AIRWAYS
CHINA AIRLINES
CHINA EASTERN
EVA
FINNAIR
JAPAN
KOREAN AIR
KLM
LACSA
LTU
LUFTHANSA
MEXICANA
NORTHWEST (INTL)
PHILIPPINE
SINGAPORE
SOBELAIR
TACA
UNITED (INTL)
VIRGIN ATLANTIC
NORTH TERMINAL
BOARDING AREA E
ERICAN
ERICAN EAGLE
NADIAN
NO AIR
NGUARD
STERN PACIFIC
BOARDING AREA F
UNITED (DOMESTIC)
UNITED EXPRESS
SOUTH TERMINAL
ARDING
REA A
THWEST
AIRWAYS
BOARDING AREA B
ALASKA (DOMESTIC)
AMERICA WEST
AMERICAN TRANS AIR
CONTINENTAL
MIDWEST EXPRESS
SOUTHWEST
TWA
BOARDING AREA C
DELTA
HAWAIIAN AIR
NOTHWEST (DOMESTIC)
SKYWEST/DELTA CONNECTION

OAKLAND INTERNATIONAL AIRPORT

"SEE MAP PAGE 690"

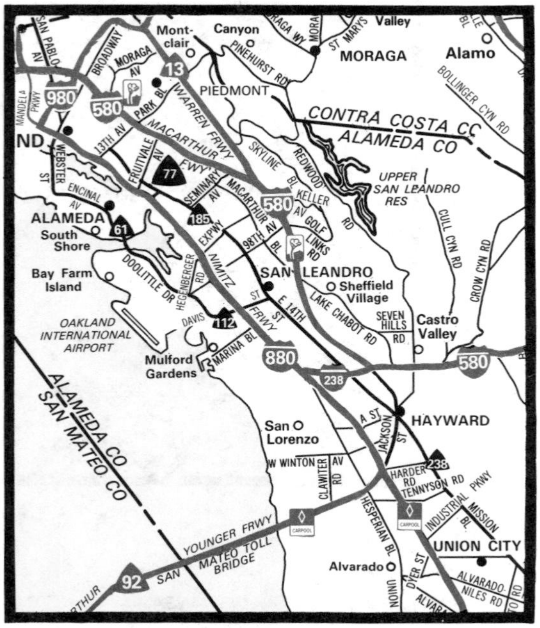
Montclair
Canyon
MORAGA
Alamo
PIEDMONT
CONTRA COSTA CO
ALAMEDA CO
UPPER SAN LEANDRO RES
ALAMEDA
South Shore
Bay Farm Island
OAKLAND INTERNATIONAL AIRPORT
SAN LEANDRO
Sheffield Village
Castro Valley
Mulford Gardens
San Lorenzo
HAYWARD
UNION CITY
Alvarado
ALAMEDA CO
SAN MATEO CO
YOUNGER FRWY
SAN MATEO TOLL BRIDGE
NIMITZ
MACARTHUR FWY
WARREN FRWY
980
580
13
77
185
61
112
880
238
92

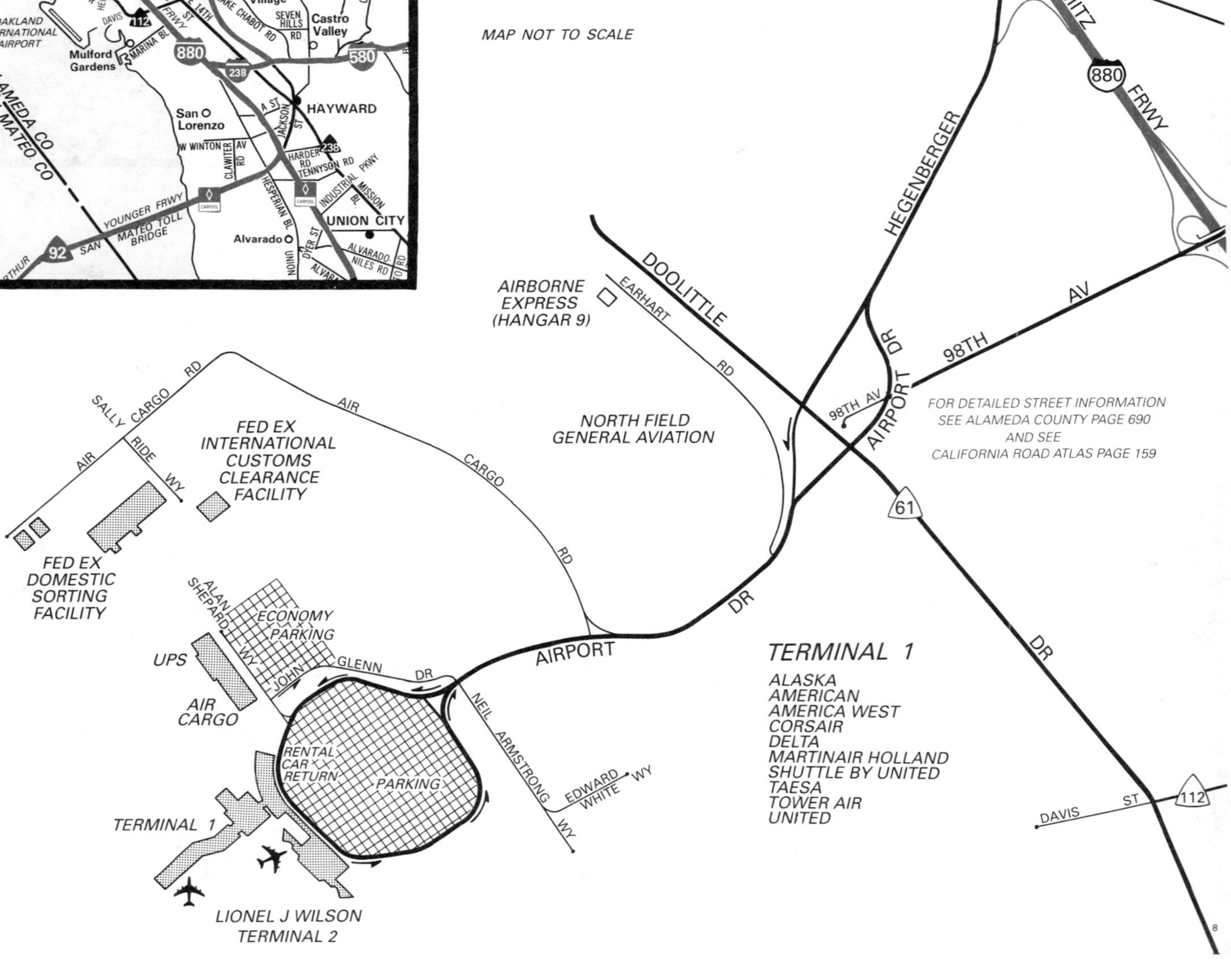
N
S
W
E
Thomas Bros. Maps
MAP NOT TO SCALE
COLISEUM WY
ENTERPRISE WY
RD
EDES AV
NIMITZ
880
FRWY
HEGENBERGER
DOOLITTLE
EARHART RD
AIRBORNE EXPRESS (HANGAR 9)
98TH AV
AIRPORT DR
98TH AV
FOR DETAILED STREET INFORMATION SEE ALAMEDA COUNTY PAGE 690 AND SEE CALIFORNIA ROAD ATLAS PAGE 159
61
NORTH FIELD GENERAL AVIATION
SALLY RIDE WY
AIR CARGO RD
FED EX INTERNATIONAL CUSTOMS CLEARANCE FACILITY
FED EX DOMESTIC SORTING FACILITY
ALAN SHEPARD WY
ECONOMY PARKING
JOHN GLENN DR
UPS
AIR CARGO
AIRPORT DR
NEIL ARMSTRONG WY
EDWARD WHITE WY
RENTAL CAR RETURN
PARKING
TERMINAL 1
LIONEL J WILSON TERMINAL 2
DR
TERMINAL 1
ALASKA
AMERICAN
AMERICA WEST
CORSAIR
DELTA
MARTINAIR HOLLAND
SHUTTLE BY UNITED
TAESA
TOWER AIR
UNITED
DAVIS ST
112

SAN JOSE INTERNATIONAL AIRPORT

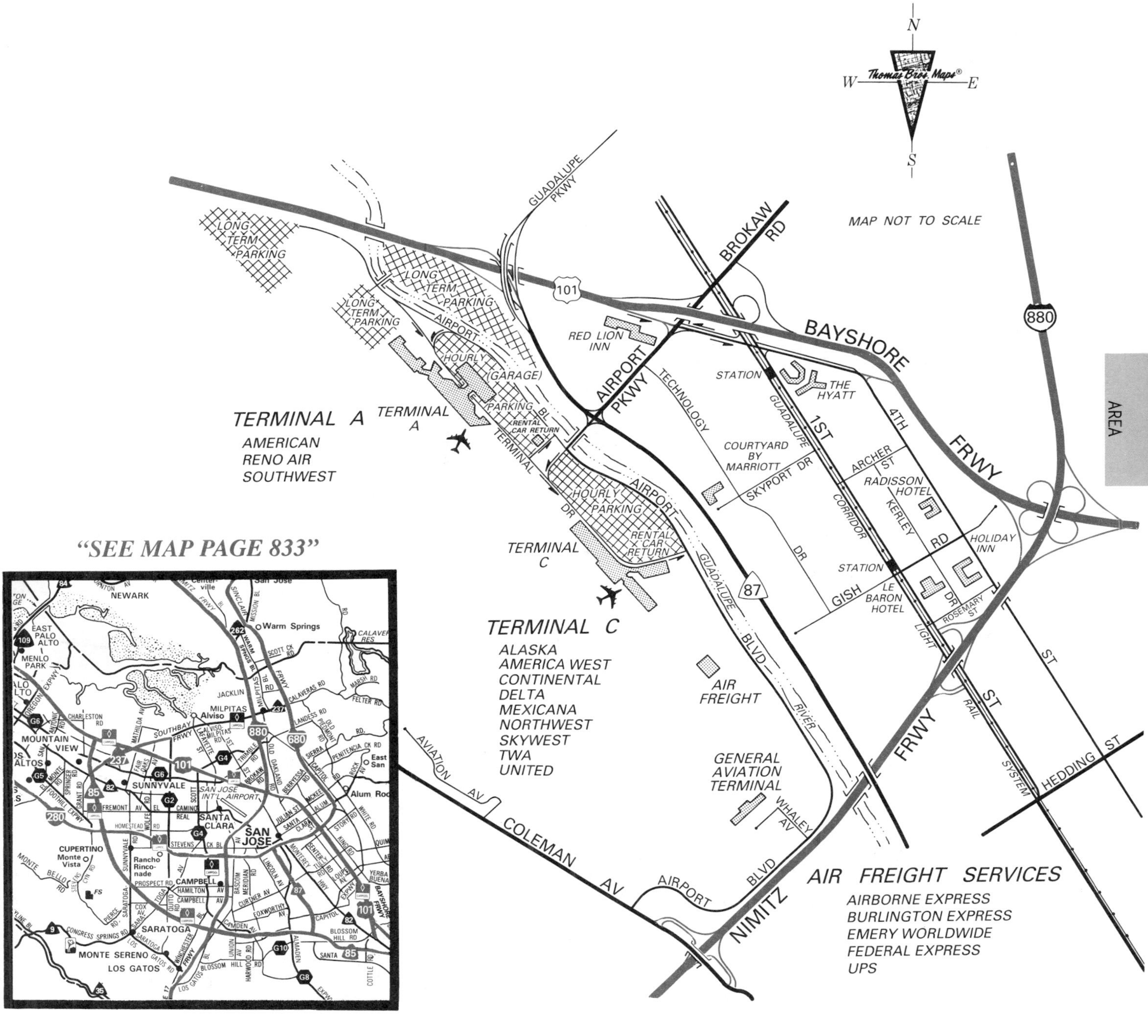
N
W
E
S
Thomas Bros. Maps®
MAP NOT TO SCALE
LONG TERM PARKING
LONG TERM PARKING
LONG TERM PARKING
GUADALUPE PKWY
BROKAW RD
101
880
BAYSHORE FRWY
RED LION INN
AIRPORT
HOURLY
(GARAGE)
PARKING
RENTAL CAR RETURN
AIRPORT PKWY
TECHNOLOGY DR
STATION
THE HYATT
GUADALUPE
1ST
4TH
TERMINAL A
AMERICAN
RENO AIR
SOUTHWEST
TERMINAL A
TERMINAL
DR
HOURLY PARKING
AIRPORT
RENTAL CAR RETURN
COURTYARD BY MARRIOTT
SKYPORT DR
ARCHER ST
RADISSON HOTEL
CORRIDOR
KERLEY
RD
HOLIDAY INN
TERMINAL C
STATION
GISH
LE BARON HOTEL
ROSEMARY ST
87
GUADALUPE
BLVD
TERMINAL C
ALASKA
AMERICA WEST
CONTINENTAL
DELTA
MEXICANA
NORTHWEST
SKYWEST
TWA
UNITED
AIR FREIGHT
RIVER
LIGHT RAIL SYSTEM
ST
ST
FRWY
HEDDING ST
AVIATION AV
GENERAL AVIATION TERMINAL
WHALEY AV
COLEMAN AV
AIRPORT BLVD
NIMITZ
AIR FREIGHT SERVICES
AIRBORNE EXPRESS
BURLINGTON EXPRESS
EMERY WORLDWIDE
FEDERAL EXPRESS
UPS

"SEE MAP PAGE 833"

NEWARK
Warm Springs
EAST PALO ALTO
MENLO PARK
MILPITAS
Alviso
MOUNTAIN VIEW
SUNNYVALE
SAN JOSE INT'L AIRPORT
SANTA CLARA
SAN JOSE
CUPERTINO
Monte Vista
Rancho Rinconada
CAMPBELL
SARATOGA
MONTE SERENO
LOS GATOS
Alum Rock
880
680
101
237
262
280
85
17
82
87
35
9

Downtown San Francisco

Points of Interest

1	Ana Hotel	E7
2	Chinatown	D4
3	Coit Tower	E3
4	Embarcadero Center	F5
5	Fairmont Hotel	D5
6	Fashion Institute	D7
7	Ferry Building–Embarcadero	G5
8	Fishermans Memorial Chapel	B1
9	Fishermans Wharf	B1
10	Four Seasons Clifton Hotel	C7
11	Geary Theatre	D7
12	Ghirardelli Square	A2
13	Golden Gateway Center	F4
14	Grand Hyatt San Francisco	D6
15	Holiday Inn–Financial District	E5
16	Holiday Inn–Union Square	D6
17	Hotel Nikko	D7
18	Howard Johnsons	B1
19	Hyatt Regency San Francisco	F5
20	Hyatt–Fishermans Wharf	B2
21	Hyatt–Park	F5
22	Jackson Square	E4
23	Justin Herman Plaza	F5
24	Lombard Street	B3
25	Mandarin Oriental Hotel	F5
26	Maritime Plaza	F5
27	Mark Hopkins Hotel	D6
28	Marriott–Fishermans Wharf	C2
29	Marriott–San Francisco	E7
30	Nob Hill	C6
31	Pan Pacific Hotel	D6
32	Parc Fifty Five Hotel	D7
33	Pier 39	D1
34	Ramada–Fishermans Wharf	B2
35	Raphael Hotel	D7
36	Ritz Carlton San Francisco	D6
37	San Francisco Art Institute	B3
38	San Francisco Centre	D7
39	San Francisco Hilton and Towers	D7
40	San Francisco National Maritime Museum	A2
41	San Francisco Visitors Bureau	F7
42	Sheraton Palace Hotel	E6
43	Sheraton–Fishermans Wharf	C2
44	Sir Francis Drake Hotel	D6
45	Stouffer Stanford Court Hotel	D6
46	The Anchorage	B2
47	The Cannery	B2
48	The Donatello	D7
49	Thomas Bros. Maps & Books	E4
50	Transamerica Building	E5
51	Transbay Transit Terminal	F6
52	Union Square	D7
53	Villa Florence Hotel	D7
54	Westin Saint Francis	D7

Map Scale

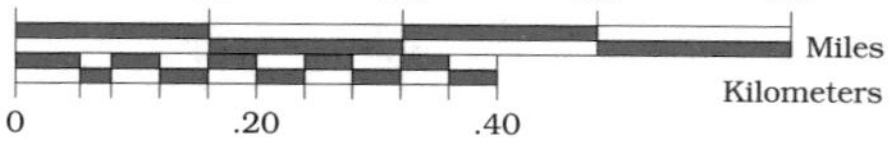

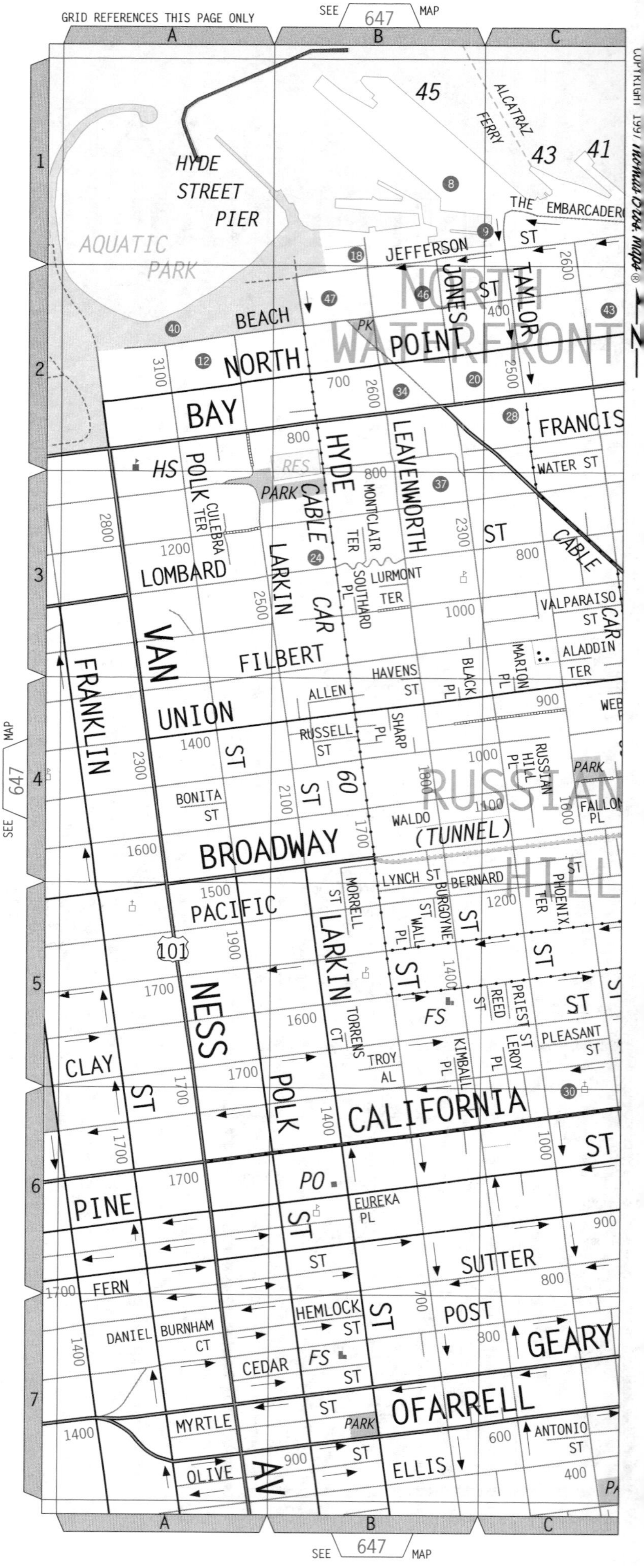

SEE 647 MAP
C
D
E
F
G
1
2
3
4
5
6
7
SEE 648 MAP
OAKLAND ALAMEDA FERRY
SAUSALITO FERRY
UNDERWATER WORLD
THE EMBARCADERO
BEACH ST
POWELL ST
NORTHPOINT CTR
ST
KEARNY ST
MONTGOMERY ST
MID
CHESTNUT
TELEGRAPH HILL
LOMBARD
GRANT
FS
LIB
GREENWICH
NORTH BEACH
ABLE
CAR
ALADDIN TER
PO
COLUMBUS AV
UNION
ALTA ST
SANSOME
BATTERY ST
FRONT
DAVIS
EMBARCADERO
WEBB PL
GREEN
VALLEJO
PARK
59
FALLON PL
1600
2600
PHOENIX
MASON
AV
POWELL
STOCKTON
JACKSON
GOLD ST
DRUMM
WASHINGTON
CODMAN PL
WETMORE
WAVERLY PL
CLAY
CHINATOWN
FINANCIAL DISTRICT
TRANSIT TRANSFER POINT
SPEAR ST
STEUART ST
SACRAMENTO
NOB HILL
MILES PL
QUINCY ST
CC
STA
BEALE
MAIN ST
FREMONT
BUSH
900
600
CROCKER GALLERIA
STEVENSON ST
BUS ONLY
MISSION
1ST
TAYLOR
BART
JESSIE
MUS
2ND
NATOMA
MINNA
TEHAMA
FOLSOM ST
HARRISON
4TH
3RD ST
CENTER FOR THE ARTS
EDDY ST
400
41
35
33
31
29
27
23
19
17
15
9
7
3
1
1/2

Downtown Oakland

Points of Interest

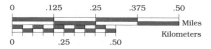

1	Alameda County Health Department	C6
2	Alameda County Welfare Building	C6
3	Alice Arts Center	D5
4	Asian Branch Library	C6
5	Bank of America Building	D4
6	BART Headquarters	D6
7	Broadway Building	C5
8	California Building	D5
9	Chinatown	D6
10	City Center	C5
11	Clorox Building	C5
12	County Administration Building	D6
13	Courthouse	E6
14	Dellums Train Station (Amtrak)	C7
15	Edoff Memorial Bandstand	E4
16	Financial Center Building	D5
17	Franklin Building	D5
18	H J Kaiser Convention Center	E6
19	Jack London Square	C7
20	Jack London Village	C7
21	Kaiser Center	D4
22	Labor Temple	D4
23	Laney College	E7
24	Macarthur Broadway Center	E2
25	Morgan Building	C5
26	Oakland Chamber of Commerce	C5
27	Oakland City Hall	C5
28	Oakland Convention Ctr & Vis Auth	C5
29	Oakland Federal Building	C5
30	Oakland Main Library	D6
31	Oakland Marriott City Center	C5
32	Oakland Museum of California	D6
33	Oakland Unified School Dist Admin	E6
34	Pacific Building	C4
35	Paramount Theatre	D4
36	Pardee Home Museum	C5
37	Storefront Museum	C5
38	The Ordway	D4
39	Trans Pacific Center	C5
40	Tribune Tower	C5
41	Veterans Building	E4
42	Victorian Row Old Oakland	C6
43	Waterfront Plaza Hotel	C7
44	Wells Fargo Building	C5
45	YMCA	D4
46	YWCA	D5

Map Scale

0 .125 .25 .375 .50 Miles

0 .25 .50 Kilometers

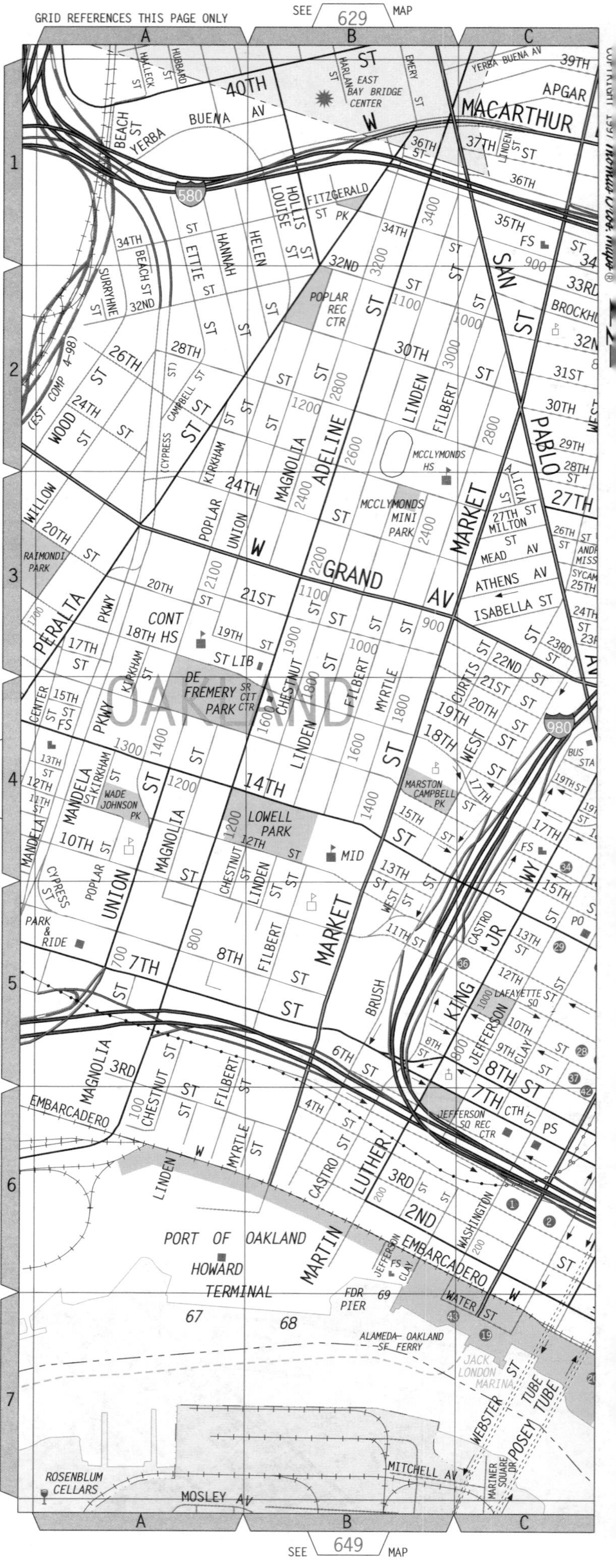

SEE 629 MAP

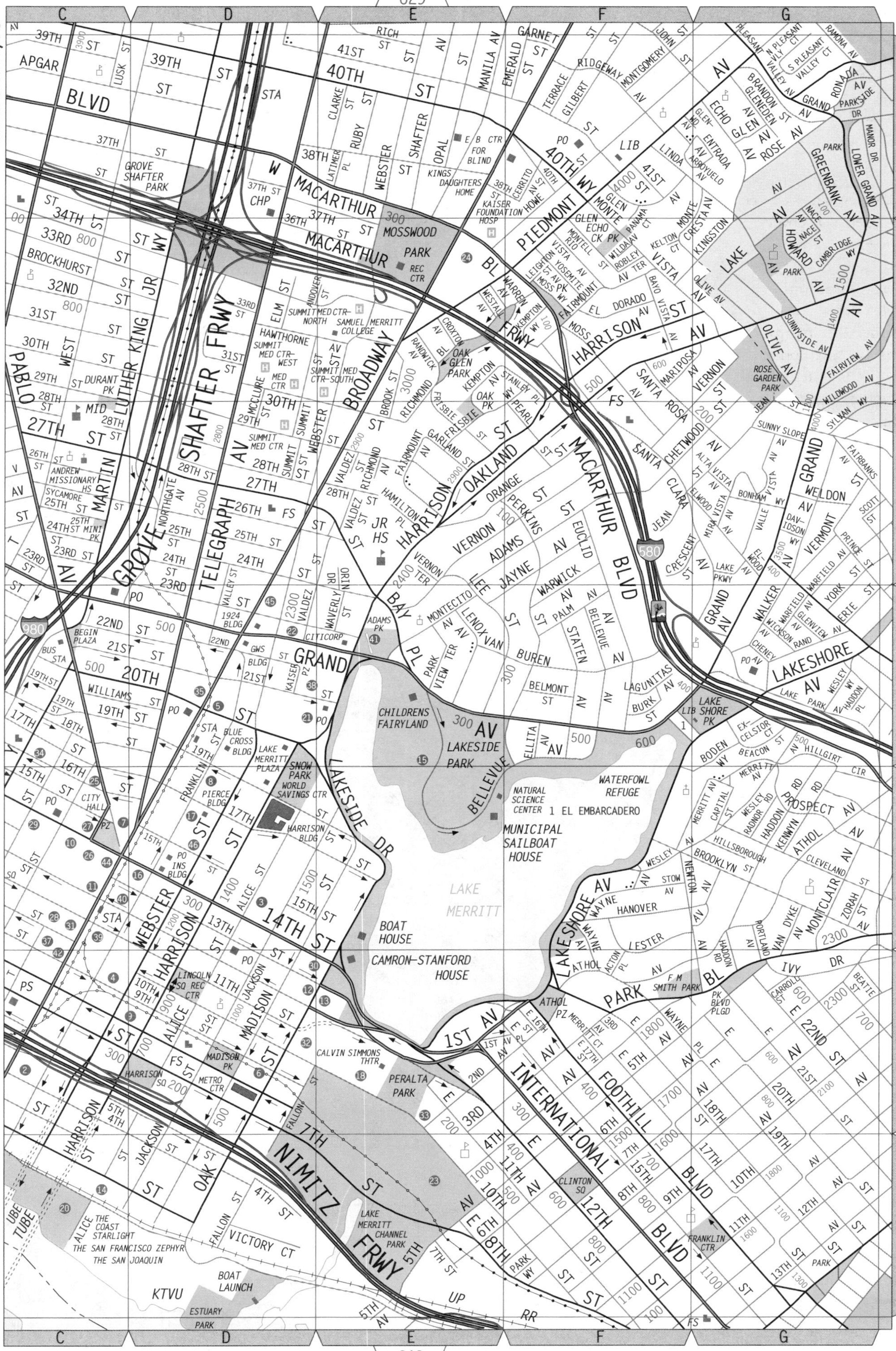
C
D
E
F
G
1
2
3
4
5
6
7
39TH ST
APGAR
BLVD
40TH ST
41ST ST
RICH ST
GARNET
MANILA AV
EMERALD ST
RIDGEWAY AV
MONTGOMERY
GILBERT ST
TERRACE
PLEASANT VALLEY
GRAND AV
RONADA AV
PARKSIDE DR
MANOR DR
LOWER GRAND AV
BRANDON ST
GLENEDEN AV
ECHO AV
GLEN AV
ROSE AV
GREENBANK AV
PARK
37TH ST
GROVE SHAFTER PARK
38TH ST
CLARKE ST
RUBY ST
WEBSTER ST
SHAFTER AV
OPAL ST
E/B CTR FOR BLIND
KINGS DAUGHTERS HOME
40TH WY
PIEDMONT AV
LIB
LINDA AV
41ST ST
GLEN ECHO CK PK
MONTE CRESTA AV
KINGSTON AV
LAKE AV
HOWARD AV
NACE AV
CAMBRIDGE WY
W MACARTHUR
CHP
MACARTHUR BL
MOSSWOOD PARK
REC CTR
KAISER FOUNDATION HOSP
34TH ST
33RD ST
BROCKHURST ST
32ND ST
31ST ST
30TH ST
29TH ST
28TH ST
27TH ST
DURANT PK
MID
PABLO
WEST ST
MARTIN LUTHER KING JR WY
SHAFTER FRWY
SUMMIT MED CTR-NORTH
SAMUEL MERRITT COLLEGE
HAWTHORNE
SUMMIT MED CTR-WEST
SUMMIT MED CTR-SOUTH
SUMMIT MED CTR
BROADWAY
OAK GLEN PARK
OAK PK
HARRISON ST
OAKLAND AV
MACARTHUR FRWY
EL DORADO
SANTA ROSA AV
VERNON ST
OLIVE AV
ROSE GARDEN PARK
SUNNYSIDE AV
FAIRVIEW AV
WILDWOOD AV
GRAND AV
ANDREW MISSIONARY HS
SYCAMORE
25TH ST
24TH ST
25TH ST MINI PK
23RD ST
GROVE
TELEGRAPH AV
NORTHGATE AV
26TH ST
FS
JR HS
VALDEZ ST
ORANGE ST
PERKINS ST
VERNON ST
ADAMS ST
JAYNE AV
EUCLID AV
WARWICK AV
MACARTHUR BLVD
580
SANTA CLARA AV
CHETWOOD ST
JEAN ST
CRESCENT ST
LAKE PKWY
BONHAM WY
WALKER AV
WELDON AV
VERMONT
WARFIELD AV
YORK ST
ERIE ST
SCOTT ST
980
PO
22ND ST
21ST ST
20TH ST
BUS STA
BEGIN PLAZA
1924 BLDG
CITICORP
GRAND AV
BAY PL
ADAMS PK
MONTECITO AV
LENOX AV
VAN BUREN AV
STATEN AV
BELLEVUE AV
BELMONT ST
LAGUNITAS AV
LAKE SHORE PK
LAKESHORE AV
WILLIAMS ST
19TH ST
18TH ST
17TH ST
16TH ST
15TH ST
CITY HALL
PZ
BLUE CROSS BLDG
LAKE MERRITT PLAZA
SNOW PARK
WORLD SAVINGS CTR
PIERCE BLDG
FRANKLIN ST
CHILDRENS FAIRYLAND
LAKESIDE PARK
BELLEVUE AV
NATURAL SCIENCE CENTER
1 EL EMBARCADERO
WATERFOWL REFUGE
MUNICIPAL SAILBOAT HOUSE
LAKESIDE DR
BODEN WY
EXCELSIOR AV
BEACON ST
HILLGIRT CIR
PROSPECT AV
HILLSBOROUGH ST
CLEVELAND AV
MONTCLAIR AV
HARRISON BLDG
PO INS BLDG
WEBSTER ST
HARRISON ST
ALICE ST
14TH ST
13TH ST
15TH ST
LAKE MERRITT
BOAT HOUSE
CAMRON-STANFORD HOUSE
LAKESHORE AV
HANOVER AV
LESTER AV
ATHOL AV
BROOKLYN AV
IVY DR
PARK BL
F M SMITH PARK
PK BLVD PLGD
LINCOLN SQ REC CTR
JACKSON ST
MADISON ST
MADISON PK
METRO CTR
HARRISON SQ
1ST AV
ATHOL PZ
INTERNATIONAL BLVD
FOOTHILL BLVD
22ND ST
21ST ST
20TH ST
19TH ST
18TH ST
17TH ST
CALVIN SIMMONS THTR
PERALTA PARK
NIMITZ FRWY
7TH ST
CLINTON SQ
12TH ST
10TH ST
11TH AV
FRANKLIN CTR
OAK ST
JACKSON ST
HARRISON ST
4TH ST
VICTORY CT
THE COAST STARLIGHT
THE SAN FRANCISCO ZEPHYR
THE SAN JOAQUIN
LAKE MERRITT CHANNEL PARK
BOAT LAUNCH
KTVU
ESTUARY PARK
UP RR

SEE 650 MAP

SEE 649 MAP

Downtown San Jose

Points of Interest

1	Chamber of Commerce	F5
2	Children's Discovery Museum	E6
3	City Hall	D2
4	Civic Auditorium	F5
5	Civic Center	D2
6	County Administration Bldg	D2
7	County Courthouse	E4
8	County Sheriff's Office	D1
9	Egyptian Museum & Planetarium	A5
10	Fairmont Hotel	F5
11	Holiday Inn	E6
12	Hotel De Anza	E5
13	Hotel Sainte Claire	F5
14	Library	F6
15	Museum of Art	F5
16	Pavilion at San Jose	F5
17	Peralta Adobe	E4
18	Performing Arts Center	E6
19	San Jose Arena	D5
20	San Jose Convention Center	F6
21	San Jose Hilton & Towers Hotel	F6
22	San Jose Hospital	G3
23	San Jose International Airport	B1
24	San Jose State University	G5
25	The Tech Museum of Innovation	F6
26	US Army Reserve Center	C2
27	Visitors Bureau	E6

Map Scale

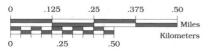

0 .125 .25 .375 .50 Miles
0 .25 .50 Kilometers

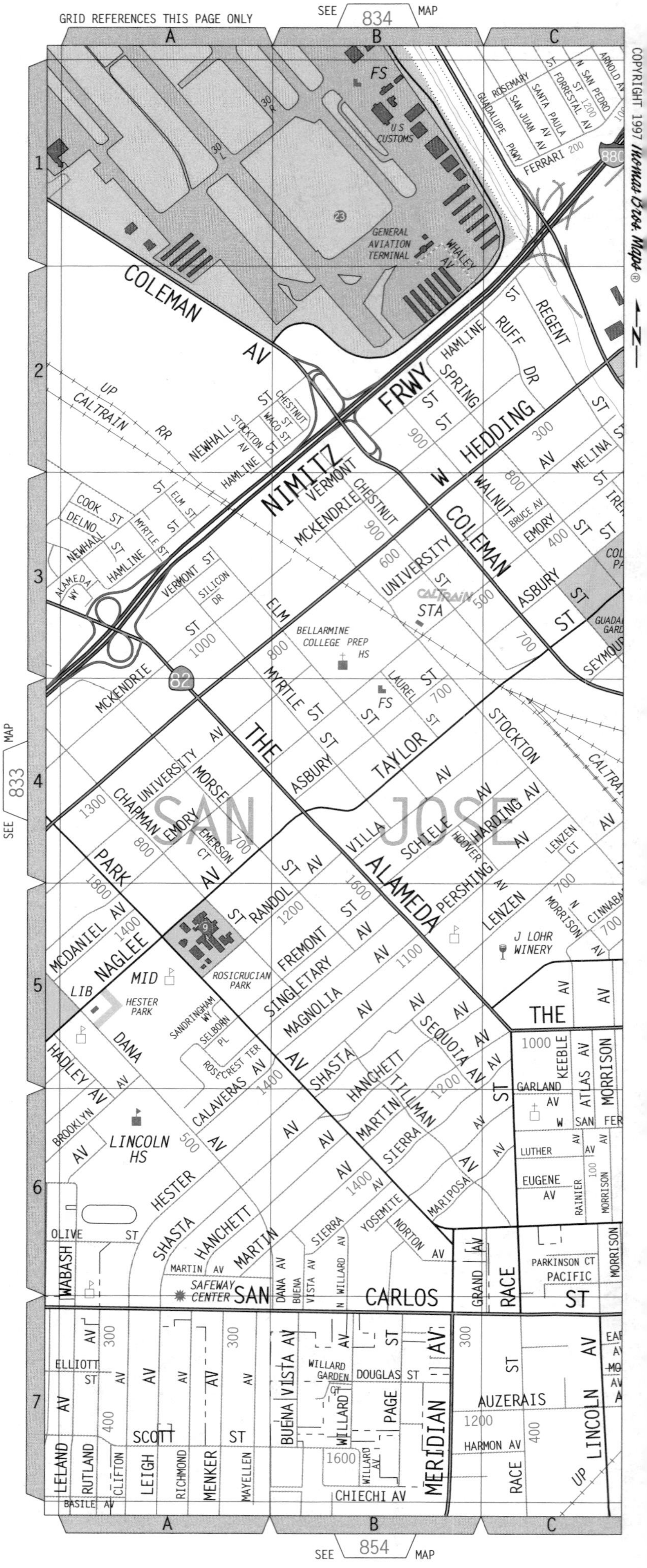

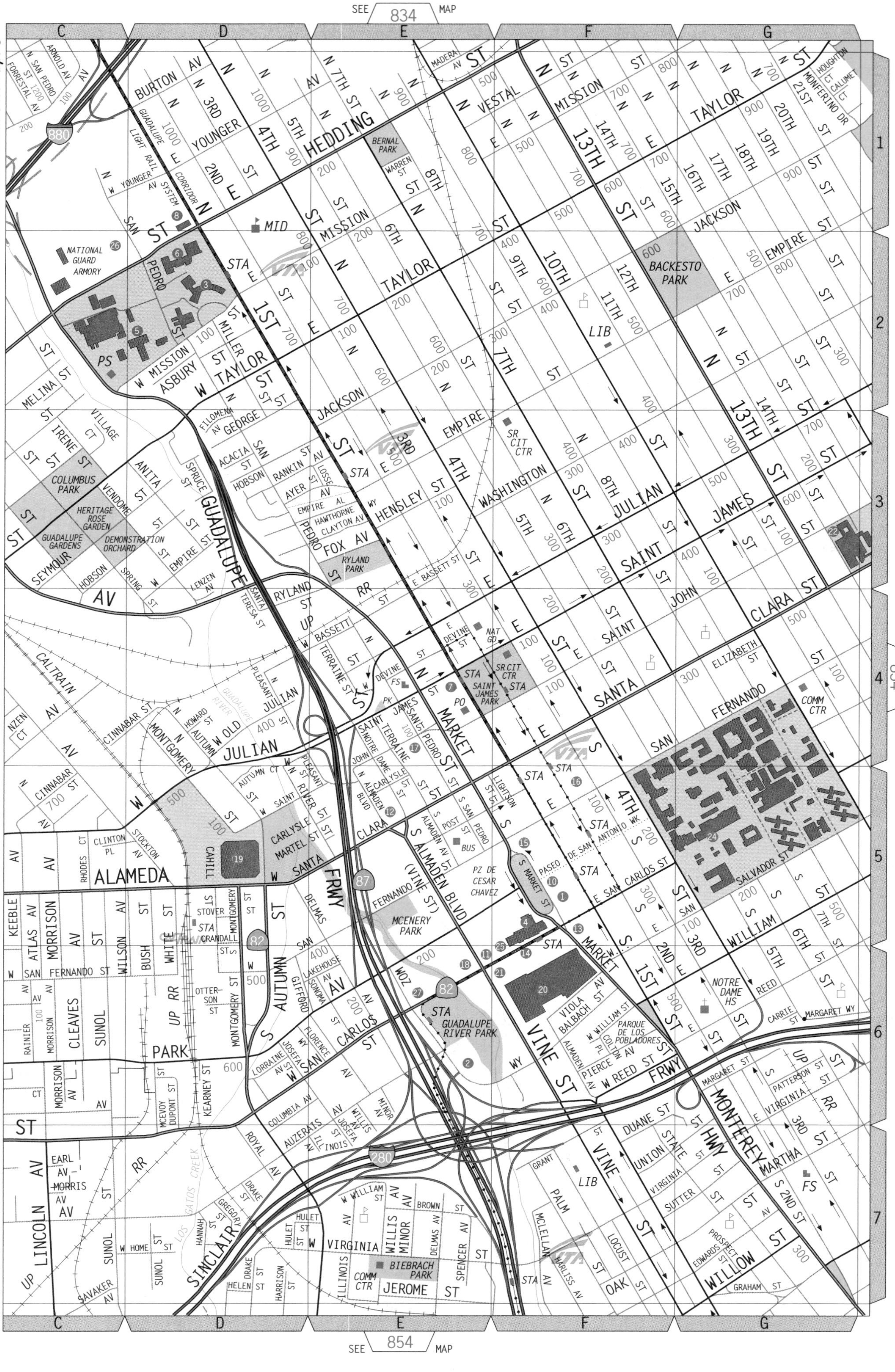
SEE 834 MAP
SEE 834 MAP
SEE 854 MAP
C
D
E
F
G
1
2
3
4
5
6
7
HEDDING
TAYLOR
JACKSON
EMPIRE
JULIAN
JAMES
SAINT JOHN
SANTA CLARA
SAN FERNANDO
WILLIAM
GUADALUPE
ALAMEDA
SAN CARLOS
VINE ST
MONTEREY HWY
SINCLAIR
LINCOLN AV
VIRGINIA
WILLOW
NATIONAL GUARD ARMORY
BERNAL PARK
BACKESTO PARK
COLUMBUS PARK
HERITAGE ROSE GARDEN
GUADALUPE GARDENS
DEMONSTRATION ORCHARD
RYLAND PARK
SAINT JAMES PARK
MCENERY PARK
GUADALUPE RIVER PARK
PZ DE CESAR CHAVEZ
PARQUE DE LOS POBLADORES
NOTRE DAME HS
BIEBRACH PARK
COMM CTR
SR CIT CTR
CALTRAIN
GUADALUPE LIGHT RAIL CORRIDOR SYSTEM

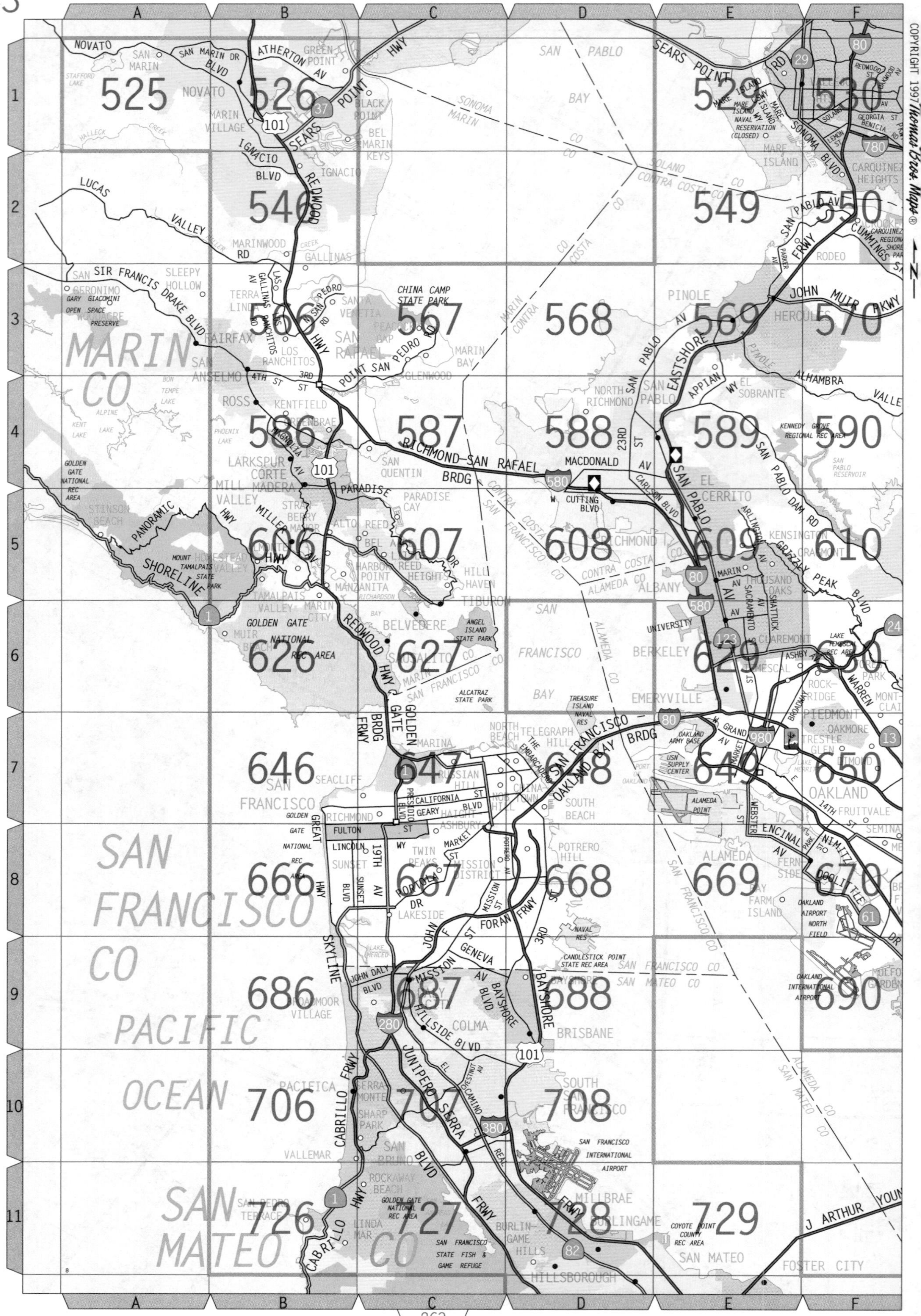

A B C D E F
1 2 3 4 5 6 7 8 9 10 11
525 526 529 530
546 549 550
566 567 568 569 570
586 587 588 589 590
606 607 608 609 610
626 627 629 630
646 647 648 649 650
666 667 668 669 670
686 687 688 690
706 707 708
726 727 728 729
NOVATO
SAN MARIN
SAN MARIN DR
ATHERTON AV
GREEN POINT
BLACK POINT
BEL MARIN KEYS
IGNACIO BLVD
REDWOOD
IGNACIO
SEARS POINT
LUCAS VALLEY RD
MARINWOOD
GALLINAS
SAN PABLO BAY
SONOMA MARIN
SOLANO CONTRA COSTA CO
MARE ISLAND
CARQUINEZ HEIGHTS
RODEO
SIR FRANCIS DRAKE BLVD
SLEEPY HOLLOW
TERRA LINDA
SANTA VENETIA
CHINA CAMP STATE PARK
SAN RAFAEL
FAIRFAX
SAN ANSELMO
MARIN CO
PINOLE
HERCULES
JOHN MUIR PKWY
EASTSHORE
SAN PABLO AV
APPIAN WY
EL SOBRANTE
ALHAMBRA VALLEY
ROSS
KENTFIELD
GREENBRAE
LARKSPUR
CORTE MADERA
RICHMOND-SAN RAFAEL BRDG
SAN QUENTIN
NORTH RICHMOND
MACDONALD AV
CUTTING BLVD
EL CERRITO
SAN PABLO DAM RD
KENNEDY GROVE REGIONAL REC AREA
MILL VALLEY
PARADISE DR
PARADISE CAY
STINSON BEACH
PANORAMIC HWY
SHORELINE HWY
MOUNT TAMALPAIS STATE PARK
GOLDEN GATE NATIONAL REC AREA
HOMESTEAD VALLEY
ALTO
REED
BEL AIRE
HARBOR POINT
MANZANITA
TIBURON
HILL HAVEN
RICHMOND
KENSINGTON
ALBANY
THOUSAND OAKS
GRIZZLY PEAK BLVD
TAMALPAIS VALLEY
MARIN CITY
MUIR BEACH
BELVEDERE
ANGEL ISLAND STATE PARK
SAUSALITO
SAN FRANCISCO BAY
BERKELEY
UNIVERSITY
CLAREMONT
ALCATRAZ STATE PARK
TREASURE ISLAND NAVAL RES
EMERYVILLE
ROCKRIDGE
PIEDMONT
OAKMORE
GOLDEN GATE BRDG
NORTH BEACH
TELEGRAPH HILL
THE EMBARCADERO
SAN FRANCISCO OAKLAND BAY BRDG
MARINA
RUSSIAN HILL
NOB HILL
CHINATOWN
SEACLIFF
SAN FRANCISCO
CALIFORNIA ST
GEARY BLVD
RICHMOND
FULTON ST
HAIGHT ASHBURY
SOUTH BEACH
OAKLAND ARMY BASE
USN SUPPLY CENTER
ALAMEDA POINT
OAKLAND
FRUITVALE
GOLDEN GATE NATIONAL REC AREA
LINCOLN WY
SUNSET
TWIN PEAKS
MISSION DISTRICT
POTRERO HILL
ALAMEDA
ENCINAL AV
NIMITZ
DOOLITTLE
BAY FARM ISLAND
OAKLAND AIRPORT NORTH FIELD
SAN FRANCISCO CO
PORTOLA DR
LAKESIDE
JOHN F FORAN FRWY
GENEVA AV
SKYLINE
CANDLESTICK POINT STATE REC AREA
SAN MATEO CO
JOHN DALY BLVD
MISSION ST
BAYSHORE BLVD
BROADMOOR VILLAGE
COLMA
HILLSIDE BLVD
BRISBANE
OAKLAND INTERNATIONAL AIRPORT
PACIFIC OCEAN
PACIFICA
SERRAMONTE
SHARP PARK
CABRILLO FRWY
JUNIPERO SERRA BLVD
EL CAMINO REAL
SOUTH SAN FRANCISCO
SAN FRANCISCO INTERNATIONAL AIRPORT
ALAMEDA CO
SAN BRUNO
VALLEMAR
ROCKAWAY BEACH
SAN PEDRO TERRACE
LINDA MAR
GOLDEN GATE NATIONAL REC AREA
MILLBRAE
BURLINGAME
BURLINGAME HILLS
SAN FRANCISCO STATE FISH & GAME REFUGE
HILLSBOROUGH
COYOTE POINT COUNTY REC AREA
SAN MATEO
J ARTHUR YOUNGER
FOSTER CITY
SAN MATEO CO
COPYRIGHT 1997 Thomas Bros. Maps ®

SEE 263 MAP

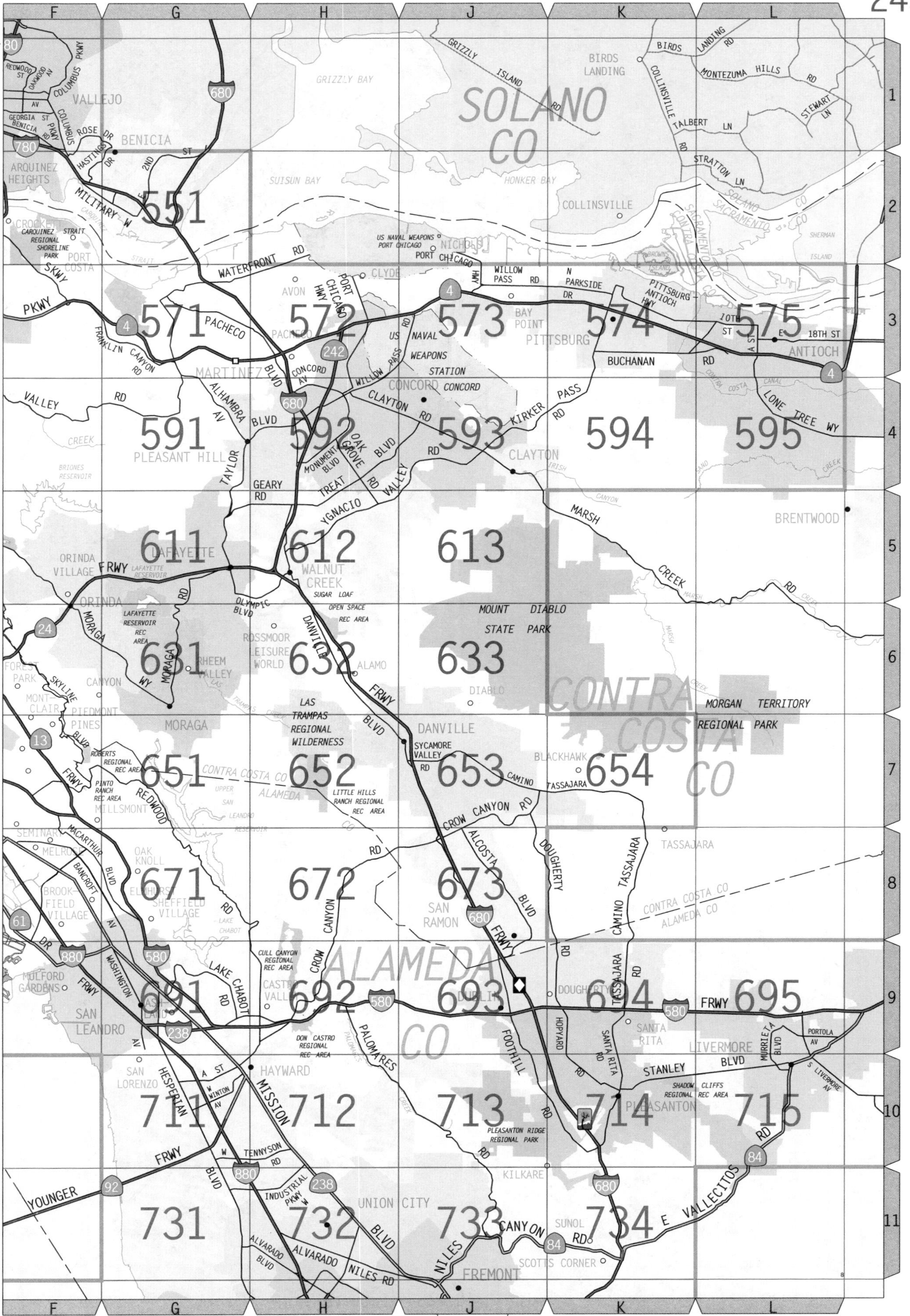
F G H J K L
1 2 3 4 5 6 7 8 9 10 11
551 571 572 573 574 575
591 592 593 594 595
611 612 613
631 632 633
651 652 653 654
671 672 673
691 692 693 694 695
711 712 713 714 715
731 732 733 734
SOLANO CO
CONTRA COSTA CO
ALAMEDA CO
VALLEJO
BENICIA
ARQUINEZ HEIGHTS
CROCKETT
CARQUINEZ STRAIT REGIONAL SHORELINE PARK
PORT COSTA
GRIZZLY BAY
SUISUN BAY
HONKER BAY
BIRDS LANDING
COLLINSVILLE
US NAVAL WEAPONS PORT CHICAGO
PORT CHICAGO
CLYDE
AVON
PACHECO
MARTINEZ
CONCORD
BAY POINT
PITTSBURG
ANTIOCH
CLAYTON
PLEASANT HILL
BRENTWOOD
LAFAYETTE
WALNUT CREEK
ORINDA VILLAGE
ORINDA
MOUNT DIABLO STATE PARK
ROSSMOOR LEISURE WORLD
ALAMO
DIABLO
RHEEM VALLEY
MORAGA
FOREST PARK
MONTCLAIR
PIEDMONT PINES
LAS TRAMPAS REGIONAL WILDERNESS
DANVILLE
SYCAMORE VALLEY
BLACKHAWK
MORGAN TERRITORY REGIONAL PARK
MILLSMONT
SEMINARY
MELROSE
OAK KNOLL
ELMHURST
SHEFFIELD VILLAGE
BROOKFIELD VILLAGE
SAN RAMON
TASSAJARA
MULFORD GARDENS
SAN LEANDRO
CASTRO VALLEY
DUBLIN
DOUGHERTY
SANTA RITA
LIVERMORE
PLEASANTON
SAN LORENZO
HAYWARD
DON CASTRO REGIONAL REC AREA
SHADOW CLIFFS REGIONAL REC AREA
PLEASANTON RIDGE REGIONAL PARK
KILKARE
UNION CITY
SUNOL
SCOTTS CORNER
FREMONT
680 780 80 4 242 24 13 61 880 580 238 84 92

SEE 263 MAP

SEE 243 MAP

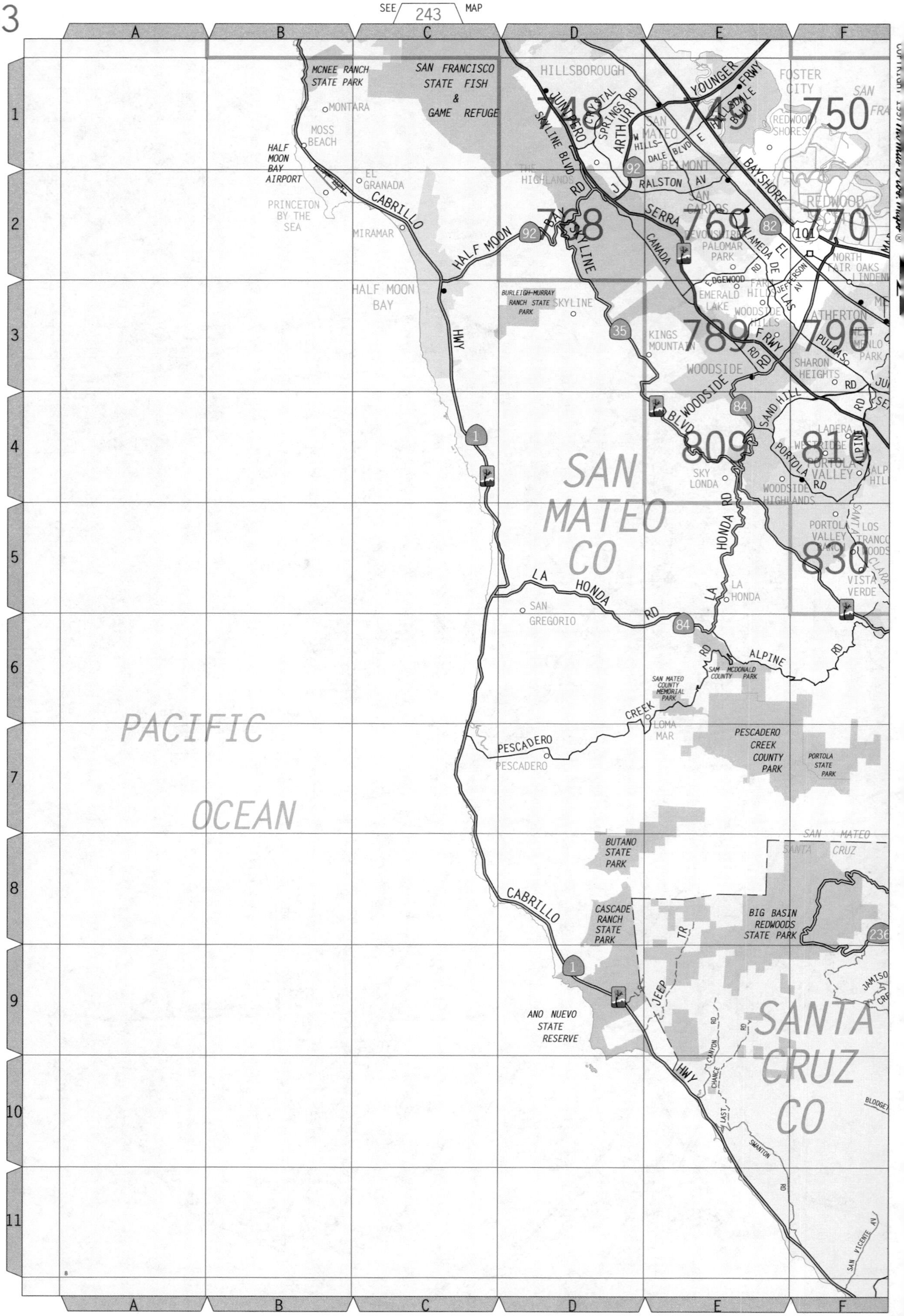
A
B
C
D
E
F
1
2
3
4
5
6
7
8
9
10
11
MCNEE RANCH STATE PARK
SAN FRANCISCO STATE FISH & GAME REFUGE
HILLSBOROUGH
FOSTER CITY
748
749
750
MONTARA
MOSS BEACH
HALF MOON BAY AIRPORT
EL GRANADA
PRINCETON BY THE SEA
MIRAMAR
THE HIGHLANDS
BELMONT
SAN MATEO
REDWOOD SHORES
REDWOOD
SAN CARLOS
768
769
770
CABRILLO
HALF MOON
SKYLINE BLVD
RALSTON AV
SERRA
CANADA
BAYSHORE
YOUNGER
FRWY
ALAMEDA DE LAS
DEVONSHIRE
PALOMAR PARK
NORTH FAIR OAKS
HALF MOON BAY
BURLEIGH-MURRAY RANCH STATE PARK
SKYLINE
EDGEWOOD
EMERALD LAKE
WOODSIDE HILLS
ATHERTON
KINGS MOUNTAIN
789
790
WOODSIDE
SHARON HEIGHTS
HWY
WOODSIDE
BLVD
SAND HILL
LADERA
WESTRIDGE
PORTOLA
PORTOLA VALLEY
809
810
SAN MATEO CO
SKY LONDA
WOODSIDE HIGHLANDS
PORTOLA VALLEY RANCH
LOS TRANCOS WOODS
830
VISTA VERDE
LA HONDA
LA HONDA RD
SAN GREGORIO
ALPINE
SAM MCDONALD COUNTY PARK
SAN MATEO COUNTY MEMORIAL PARK
CREEK
LOMA MAR
PESCADERO
PESCADERO CREEK COUNTY PARK
PORTOLA STATE PARK
PACIFIC
OCEAN
BUTANO STATE PARK
SAN MATEO
SANTA CRUZ
CABRILLO
CASCADE RANCH STATE PARK
BIG BASIN REDWOODS STATE PARK
ANO NUEVO STATE RESERVE
JEEP TR
SANTA CRUZ CO
CANYON RD
CHANCE
LAST
SWANTON RD
SAN VICENTE AV
BLODGETT
JAMISON

SEE 243 MAP

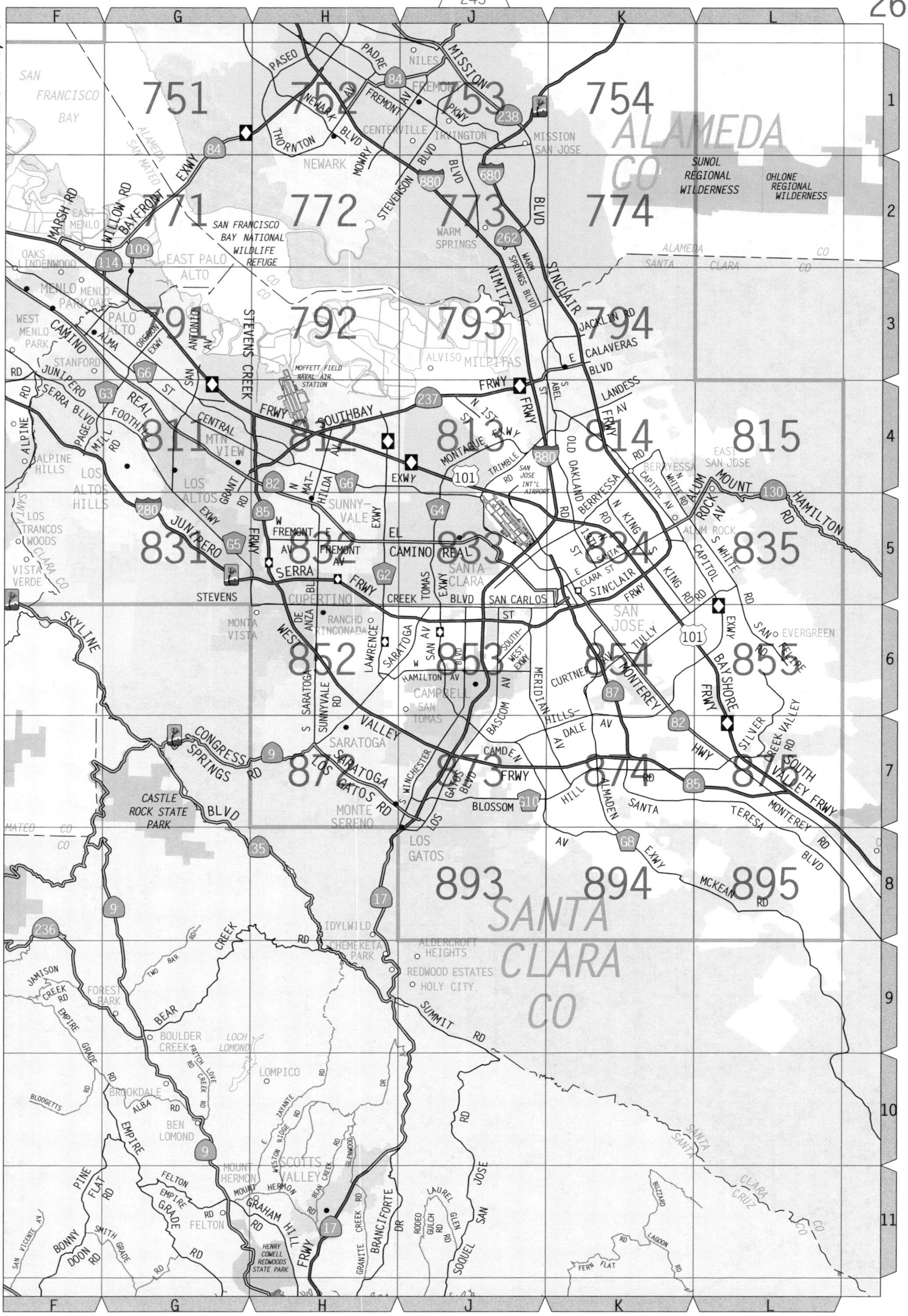
F
G
H
J
K
L
1
2
3
4
5
6
7
8
9
10
11
751
752
753
754
771
772
773
774
791
792
793
794
811
812
813
814
815
831
832
833
834
835
852
853
854
855
872
873
874
875
893
894
895
SAN FRANCISCO BAY
ALAMEDA CO
SANTA CLARA CO
SUNOL REGIONAL WILDERNESS
OHLONE REGIONAL WILDERNESS
SAN FRANCISCO BAY NATIONAL WILDLIFE REFUGE
NILES
FREMONT
CENTERVILLE
IRVINGTON
MISSION SAN JOSE
NEWARK
WARM SPRINGS
EAST MENLO
EAST PALO ALTO
OAKS LINDENWOOD
MENLO PARK
MENLO OAKS
WEST MENLO PARK
PALO ALTO
STANFORD
MOFFETT FIELD NAVAL AIR STATION
ALVISO
MILPITAS
MTN VIEW
LOS ALTOS
LOS ALTOS HILLS
ALPINE HILLS
LOS TRANCOS WOODS
VISTA VERDE
SUNNYVALE
SANTA CLARA
SAN JOSE INT'L AIRPORT
EAST SAN JOSE
SAN JOSE
EVERGREEN
STEVENS
CUPERTINO
MONTA VISTA
RANCHO RINCONADA
CAMPBELL
SAN TOMAS
SARATOGA
MONTE SERENO
LOS GATOS
CASTLE ROCK STATE PARK
IDYLWILD
CHEMEKETA PARK
ALDERCROFT HEIGHTS
REDWOOD ESTATES
HOLY CITY
FOREST PARK
BOULDER CREEK
LOCH LOMOND
LOMPICO
BROOKDALE
BEN LOMOND
MOUNT HERMON
SCOTTS VALLEY
FELTON
HENRY COWELL REDWOODS STATE PARK
SANTA CRUZ
NIMITZ FRWY
SINCLAIR FRWY
BAYSHORE FRWY
MONTEREY HWY
SOUTH VALLEY FRWY
EL CAMINO REAL
STEVENS CREEK BLVD
SKYLINE BLVD
CONGRESS SPRINGS RD
SUMMIT RD

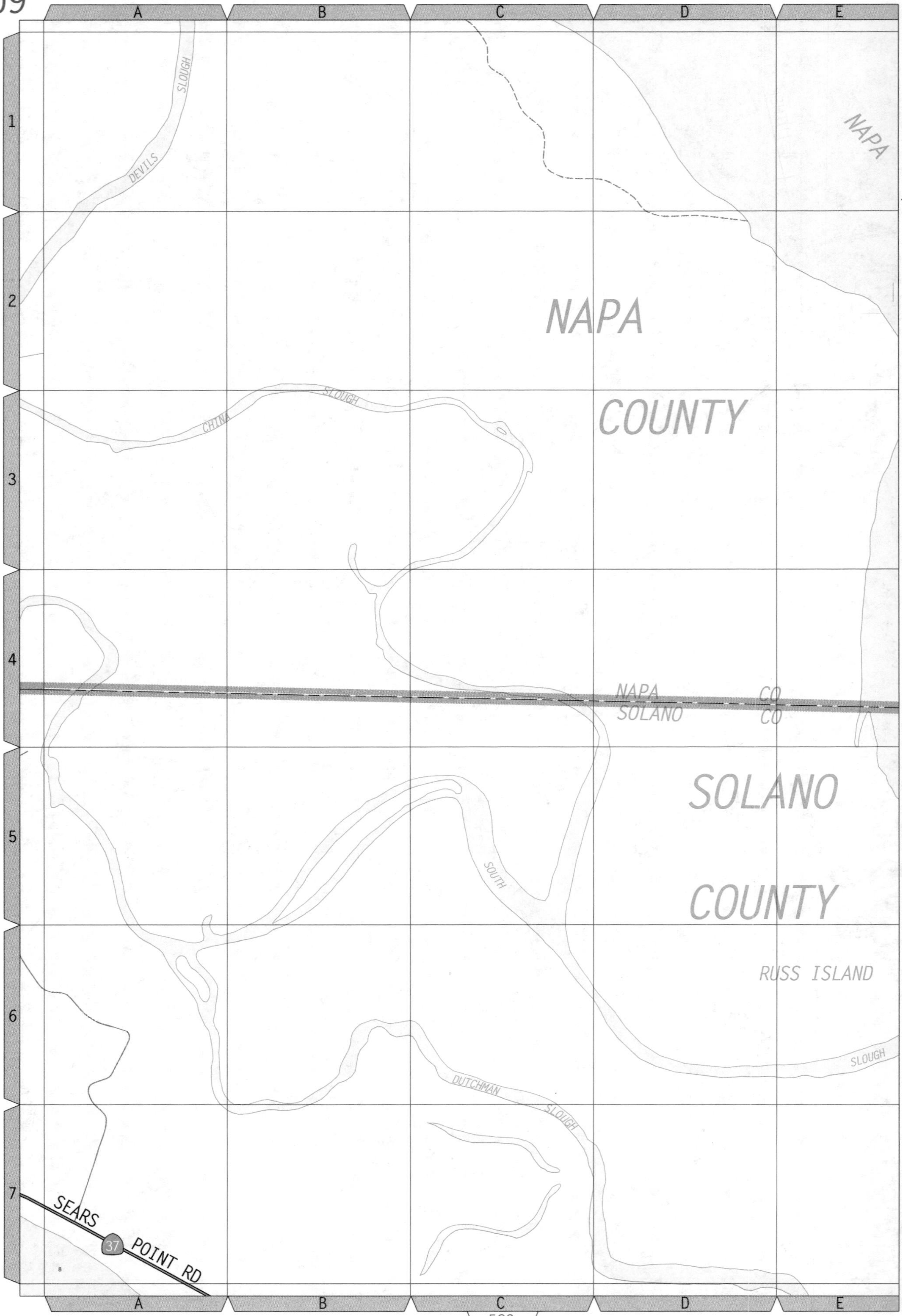

A
B
C
D
E
1
2
3
4
5
6
7
DEVILS SLOUGH
NAPA
NAPA COUNTY
CHINA SLOUGH
NAPA CO
SOLANO CO
SOLANO COUNTY
SOUTH
RUSS ISLAND
SLOUGH
DUTCHMAN SLOUGH
SEARS POINT RD
37

SEE 529 MAP

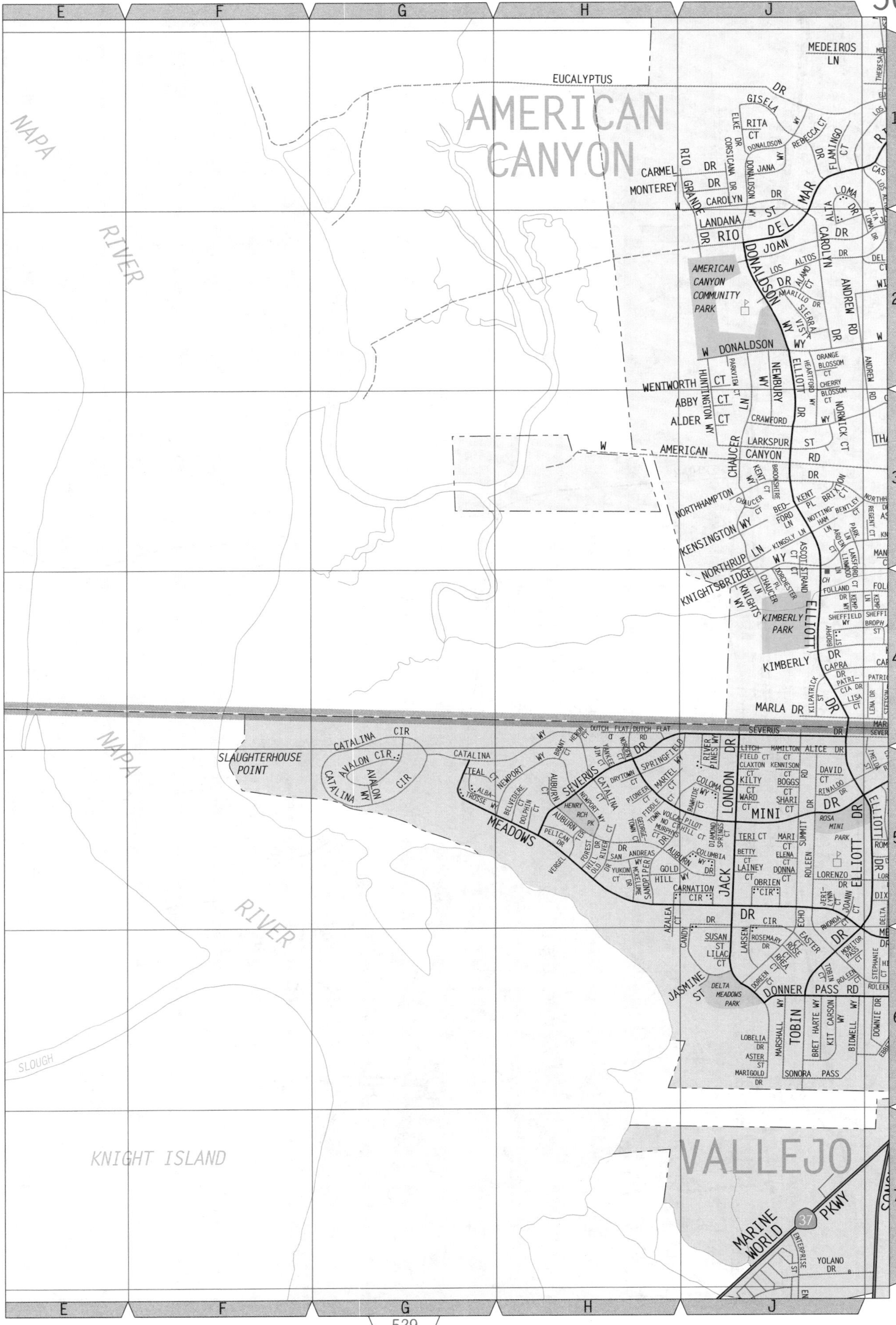
E
F
G
H
J
1
2
3
4
5
6
7
AMERICAN CANYON
VALLEJO
NAPA RIVER
NAPA RIVER
SLOUGH
KNIGHT ISLAND
SLAUGHTERHOUSE POINT
EUCALYPTUS
MEDEIROS LN
GISELA DR
RITA CT
REBECCA CT
FLAMINGO CT
DONALDSON WY
JANA
ELKE DR
CORSICANA DR
CARMEL DR
MONTEREY DR
CAROLYN ST
LANDANA DR
RIO GRANDE
RIO DEL MAR
LOMA DR
ALTA CT
JOAN DR
CAROLYN DR
LOS ALTOS DR
ALAMO CT
AMARILLO DR
SIERRA VISTA
ANDREW RD
AMERICAN CANYON COMMUNITY PARK
DONALDSON WY
W DONALDSON WY
WENTWORTH CT
HUNTINGTON WY
PARKVIEW CT
ABBY CT
ALDER CT
NEWBURY WY
ELLIOTT DR
HEARTFORD WY
ORANGE BLOSSOM CT
CHERRY BLOSSOM CT
NORWICK CT
CRAWFORD WY
LARKSPUR ST
W AMERICAN CANYON RD
CHAUCER WY
KENT CT
BROOKSHIRE
NORTHAMPTON
KENSINGTON WY
BEDFORD LN
KENT PL
BRIXTON CT
NOTTINGHAM
BENTLEY
REGENT CT
ARDEN CT
PARK LN
LANSFORD CT
LINWOOD
NORTHRUP LN
KINGSLY LN
ASCOT CT
STRAND CT
KNIGHTSBRIDGE WY
KNIGHTS LN
CHAUCER PL
DORCHESTER
FOLLAND DR
KEMP WY
SHEFFIELD WY
BROPHY ST
KIMBERLY PARK
KIMBERLY DR
ELLIOTT DR
CAPRA
PATRICIA DR
LISA CT
KILPATRICK ST
MARLA DR
SEVERUS DR
CATALINA CIR
AVALON CIR
AVALON WY
CATALINA
TEAL CT
ALBATROSSE
NEWPORT WY
BELVEDERE CT
DOLPHIN CT
AUBURN CT
SEVERUS
CATALINA
BRANT
HERON CT
DUTCH FLAT CT
DUTCH FLAT RD
JIM CT
YANKEE CT
NORDEN
DRYTOWN
SPRINGFIELD
MARTEL WY
PIONEER CT
FIDDLETOWN
VOLCANO
PILOT HILL CT
MURPHYS
DIAMOND SPRINGS CT
RIVER PINES WY
COLOMA WY
RAWHIDE WY
LONDON DR
HENRY
AUBURN
NEWPORT
PELICAN CT
MEADOWS
VERGEL
FOREST HILL
OLD RIVER
SAN ANDREAS
SANDPIPER
YUKON CT
MOKELUMNE
GEORGETOWN
COLUMBIA WY
GOLD HILL
CARNATION CIR
JACK DR
LITCHFIELD CT
HAMILTON CT
CLAXTON CT
KENNISON CT
ALICE DR
DAVID CT
RINALDO
KILTY CT
WARD CT
BOGGS CT
SHARI CT
MINI DR
ROSA MINI PARK
TERI CT
MARI CT
BETTY CT
ELENA CT
LAINEY
DONNA CT
OBRIEN CIR
SUMMIT
ROLEEN
LORENZO DR
JERI-LYNN
JOANN CT
ELLIOTT DR
AZALEA CT
CANDY
SUSAN ST
LILAC CT
LARSEN
ROSEMARY DR
ECHO
EASTER
RHONDA CT
MONITOR PASS
TOBIN CT
STEPHANIE
DOREEN CT
DONNER PASS RD
JASMINE ST
DELTA MEADOWS PARK
MARSHALL WY
TOBIN
BRET HARTE WY
KIT CARSON WY
BIDWELL WY
DOWNIE DR
LOBELIA DR
ASTER ST
MARIGOLD DR
SONORA PASS
MARINE WORLD PKWY
37
ENTERPRISE
YOLANO DR

SEE 510 MAP

SEE 529 MAP

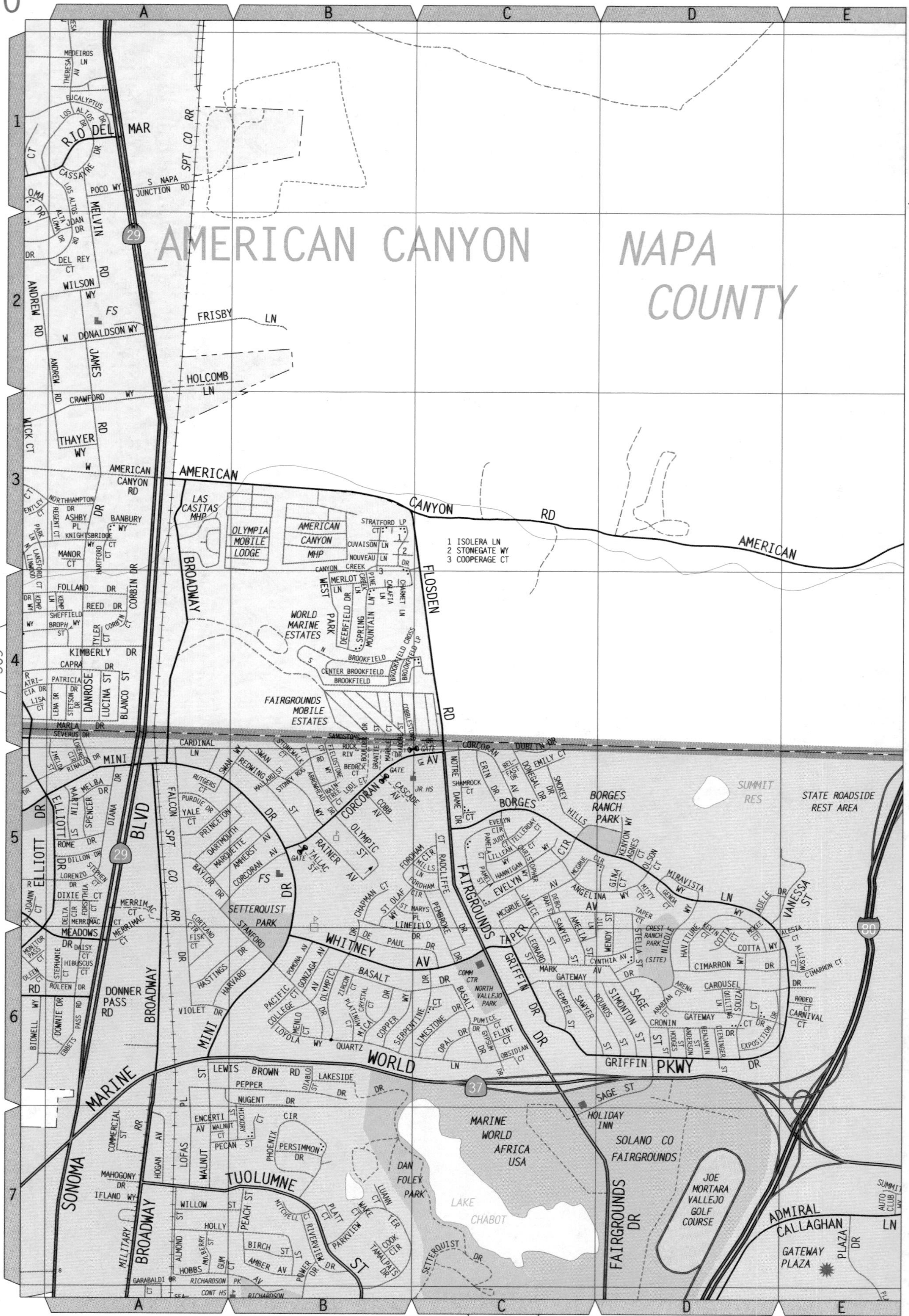
AMERICAN CANYON
NAPA COUNTY
RIO DEL MAR
S NAPA JUNCTION RD
SPT CO RR
MELVIN RD
DEL REY CT
WILSON WY
ANDREW RD
FS
FRISBY LN
W DONALDSON WY
JAMES RD
HOLCOMB LN
CRAWFORD WY
THAYER WY
W AMERICAN CANYON RD
AMERICAN CANYON RD
LAS CASITAS MHP
OLYMPIA MOBILE LODGE
AMERICAN CANYON MHP
BROADWAY
FLOSDEN RD
1 ISOLERA LN
2 STONEGATE WY
3 COOPERAGE CT
WORLD MARINE ESTATES
FAIRGROUNDS MOBILE ESTATES
KIMBERLY DR
MINI DR
CORCORAN AV
BORGES RANCH PARK
SUMMIT RES
STATE ROADSIDE REST AREA
ELLIOTT DR
SONOMA BLVD
SETTERQUIST PARK
WHITNEY AV
FAIRGROUNDS DR
MIRAVISTA LN
VANESSA ST
CREST RANCH PARK (SITE)
GATEWAY DR
DONNER PASS RD
MARINE WORLD PKWY
GRIFFIN DR
SAGE ST
HOLIDAY INN
MARINE WORLD AFRICA USA
SOLANO CO FAIRGROUNDS
LAKE CHABOT
DAN FOLEY PARK
JOE MORTARA VALLEJO GOLF COURSE
TUOLUMNE ST
ADMIRAL CALLAGHAN LN
GATEWAY PLAZA
A B C D E
1 2 3 4 5 6 7

SEE 509 MAP

SEE 530 MAP

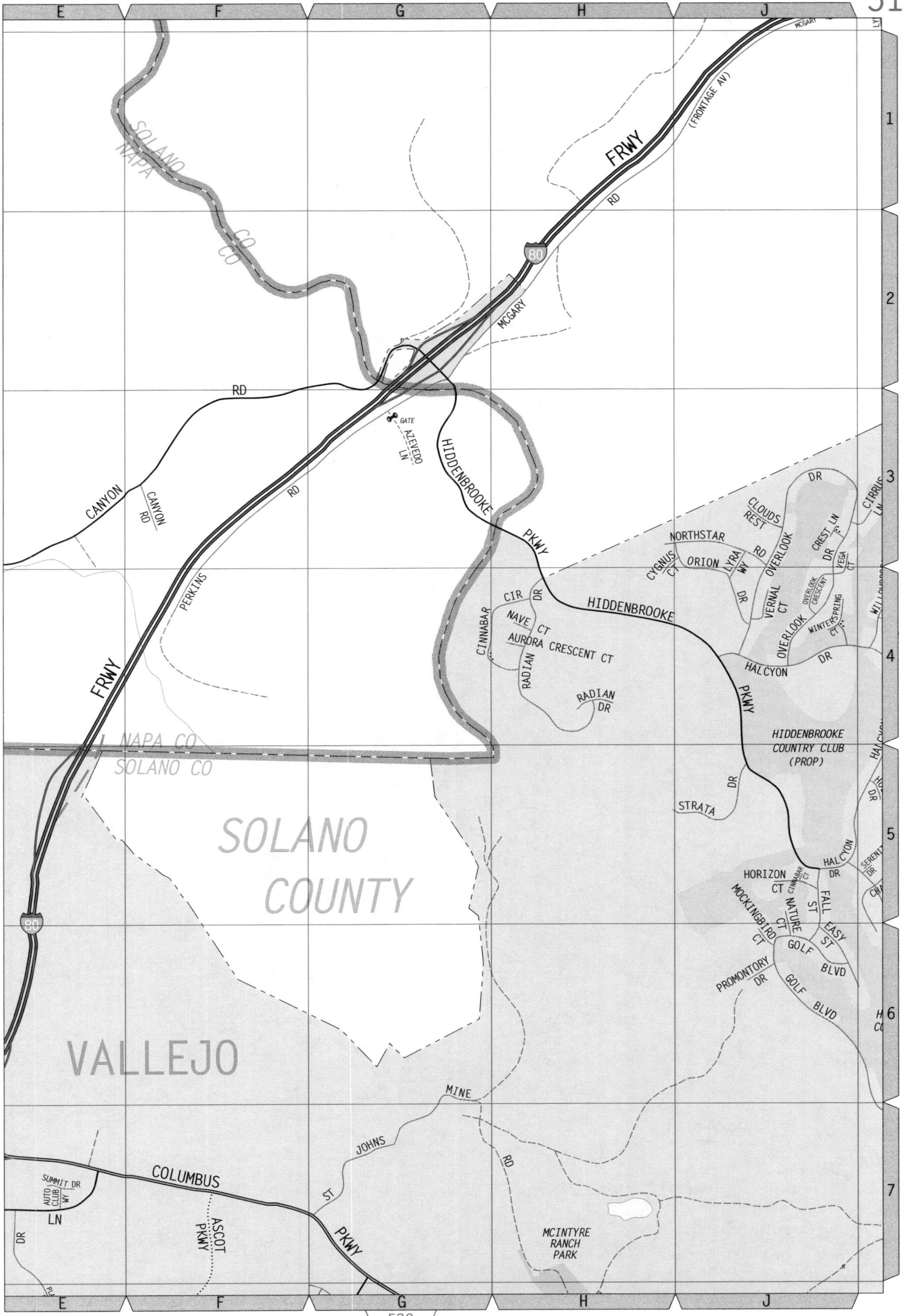
E
F
G
H
J
1
2
3
4
5
6
7
SOLANO
NAPA
CO
CO
FRWY
(FRONTAGE AV)
RD
MCGARY
80
MCGARY
RD
GATE
AZEVEDO LN
HIDDENBROOKE
CANYON
CANYON RD
RD
PERKINS
PKWY
NORTHSTAR
CLOUDS REST
DR
CIRRUS LN
CREST LN
DR
VEGA CT
CYGNUS CT
ORION
LYRA WY
RD
OVERLOOK
VERNAL CT
DR
OVERLOOK CRESCENT
SPRING
WINTER
CT
OVERLOOK
CIR
DR
HIDDENBROOKE
CINNABAR
NAVE CT
AURORA CRESCENT CT
RADIAN
HALCYON
DR
FRWY
RADIAN DR
PKWY
HIDDENBROOKE COUNTRY CLUB (PROP)
NAPA CO
SOLANO CO
DR
STRATA
SOLANO COUNTY
HALCYON
DR
HORIZON CT
CINNABAR CT
MOCKINGBIRD CT
NATURE CT
FALL ST
EASY ST
GOLF
BLVD
PROMONTORY DR
GOLF BLVD
80
VALLEJO
MINE
ST JOHNS
ST
RD
COLUMBUS
SUMMIT DR
AUTO CLUB WY
LN
DR
ASCOT PKWY
PKWY
MCINTYRE RANCH PARK

SEE 530 MAP

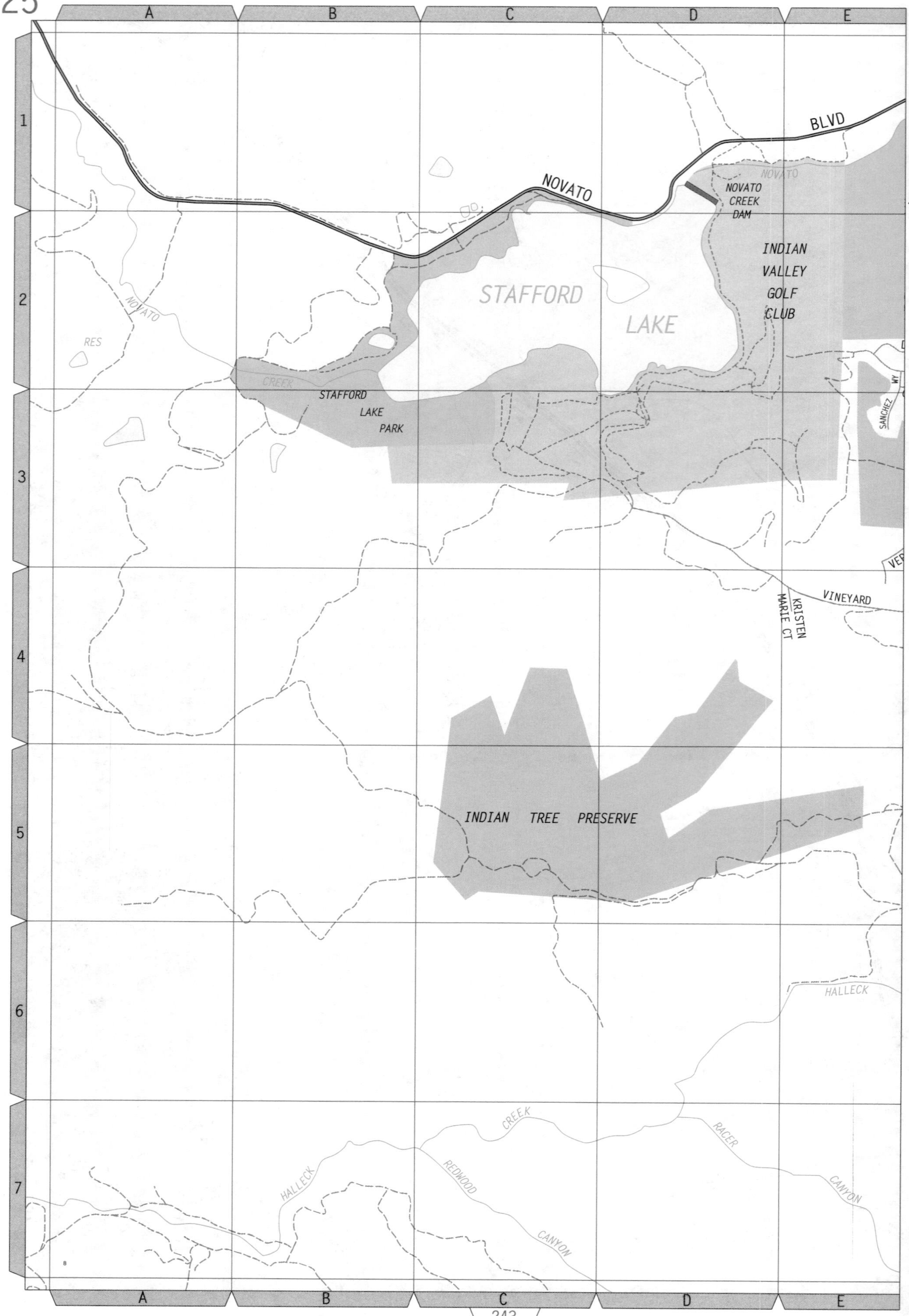
A
B
C
D
E
1
2
3
4
5
6
7
NOVATO
BLVD
NOVATO
NOVATO CREEK DAM
INDIAN VALLEY GOLF CLUB
STAFFORD LAKE
NOVATO
RES
CREEK
STAFFORD LAKE PARK
SANCHEZ
WY
VINEYARD
KRISTEN
MARIE CT
INDIAN TREE PRESERVE
HALLECK
CREEK
RACER
CANYON
HALLECK
REDWOOD
CANYON

SEE 243 MAP

E
F
G
H
J
1
2
3
4
5
6
7
SAN MARIN
NOVATO
MOUNT BURDELL PRESERVE
MT BURDELL PRESERVE
1 SAN DOMINGO WY
1 SAN CARLOS WY
2 JACINTO WY
LIONS PARK
LITTLE MOUNTAIN 806'
LITTLE MOUNTAIN OPEN SPACE PRESERVE
SEE A G1
1 SYCAMORE DR
2 JUNIPER PL
3 CEDAR PL
4 MAGNOLIA PL
5 ACACIA CT
6 TAMARACK PL
7 ALDER PL
8 SPRUCE PL
9 CONIFER PL
10 WALNUT CT
11 COTTONWOOD PL
12 PINYON PL
13 CITRUS PL
OHAIR PARK
VERISSIMO HILLS PRESERVE
SAN MARIN HS
MARIN MUSEUM OF THE AMERICAN INDIAN
MIWOK PARK
PIONEER PARK
THE SQUARE
MARIN HIGHLANDS PARK
INDIAN VALLEY PRESERVE
NOVATO BLVD
SAN MARIN DR
SAN CARLOS WY
SAN MIGUEL WY
SAN FELIPE WY
FELIZ DR
ESTADO WY
SAN ANDREAS DR
SUTRO AV
CENTER RD
WILSON AV
INDIAN VALLEY RD
SIMMONS LN
VIRGINIA AV
DARYL AV
TAURUS DR
TRISH DR
STASIA CT
OAK VALLEY DR
VERISSIMO DR
PALOMINO RD
REBELO LN
PINTO VALLEY LN
HORSE
WILD
SANTA MARIA DR
SANTA BLANCA
ROCA CT
EL DORADO CT
VIDA CT
PLATA CT
CABRO CT
TRUMBULL AV
MILL RD
VINEYARD RD
HATCH RD
SILVA LN
KNUTTE CT
SYL DOR LN
PILLSBURY LN
MCCLAY RD
SLOWDOWN CT
MAESTRO RD
LAUREL AV
TANGLEWOOD LN
SYOSSET LN
INDIAN SPRINGS RD
GAGE LN
BLOOM LN
WILDWOOD LN
INDIAN TRAIL CT
DEER TR
RANCH RD
BURNT H RANCH RD
OLD RANCH RD
EBRIGHT FIRE RD
RIDGE FIRE RD
SKY TRAIL FIRE RD
BROOKSIDE CT
MIWOK DR
KEENA LN
DOW LN
LESLIE CT
CANYON RD
RIDGE RD
HALF MOON RD
FORREST RD
LOVERS LN
NOVATO CREEK
AVICHI
ARROYO
CREEK
RES
800
2200
2000
2100
1800
600
200

SEE 526 MAP

SEE 243 MAP

SEE 525 MAP

A
B
C
D
E
1
2
3
4
5
6
7
MARIN COUNTY
NOVATO
MARIN VILLAGE
MOUNT BURDELL PRESERVE
RUSH CREEK OPEN SPACE PRESERVE
PARK & RIDE
CHERRY HILL
STAFFORD GROVE PARK
MARION PARK
DOWNTOWN NOVATO CENTER
LEE GARNER PARK
SUTTON PARK
OLIVE PARK
NOVATO FAIR
SLADE PARK
HILL PARK
NAVE CENTER
NOVATO COMMUNITY HOSPITAL
ARROYO AVICHI PARK
PARK & RIDES
VINTAGE OAKS AT NOVATO
NOVATO HS
LYNWOOD PARK
LYNWOOD HILL PARK
INDIAN VALLEY PRESERVE
INDIAN VALLEY COLLEGES
SAN MARIN DR
REDWOOD BLVD
REDWOOD HWY
S NOVATO BLVD
GRANT AV
DIABLO AV
HILL RD
ROWLAND BLVD
INDIAN VALLEY RD
IGNACIO BLVD
SUNSET PKWY
OLIVE AV
DE LONG AV
TAMALPAIS AV
SIMMONS LN
101

SEE 546 MAP

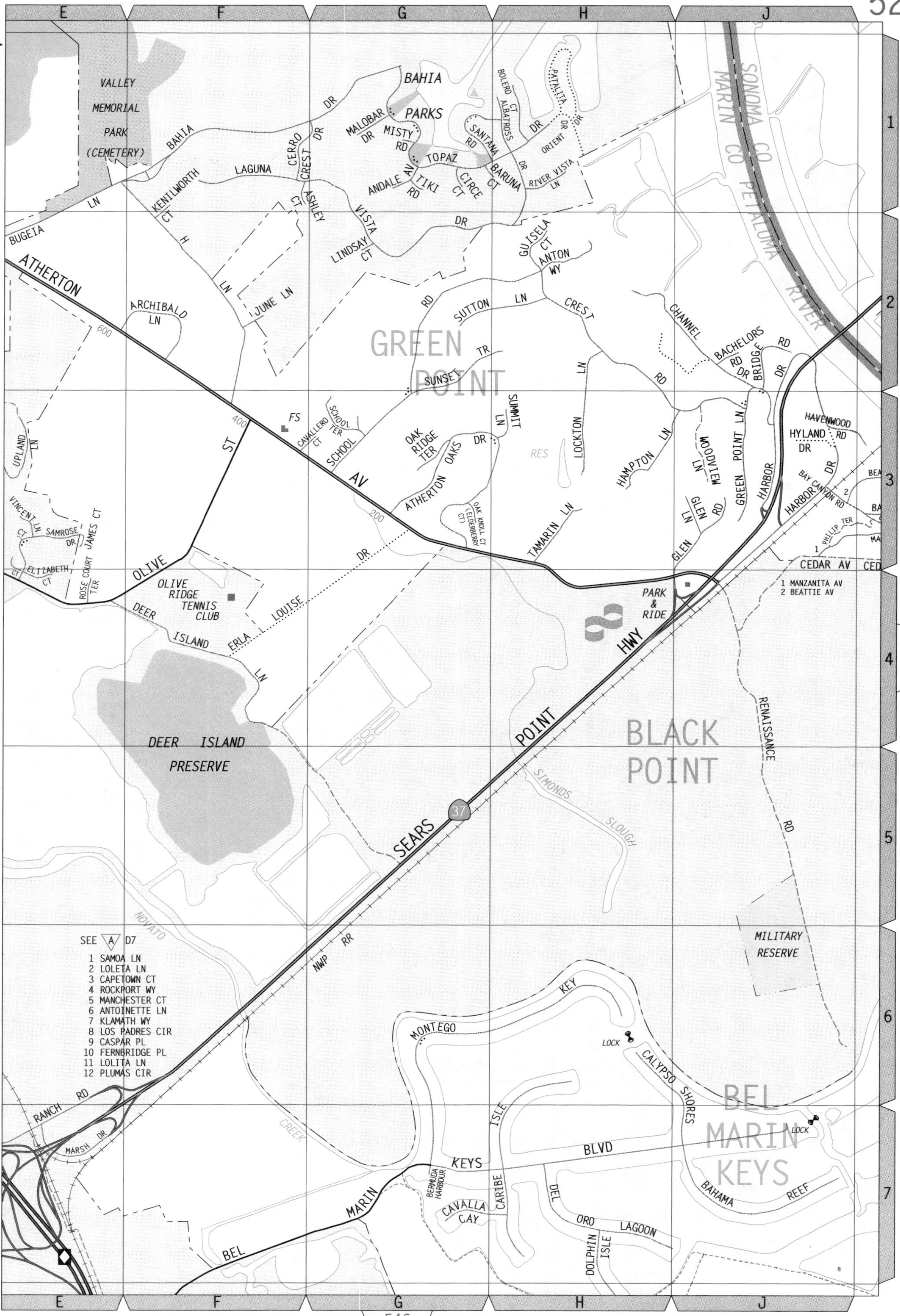
E
F
G
H
J
1
2
3
4
5
6
7
VALLEY MEMORIAL PARK (CEMETERY)
BAHIA
BAHIA PARKS
MALOBAR DR
MISTY RD
TOPAZ
ANDALE AV
TIKI RD
CIRCE CT
SANTANA RD
BARUNA CT
BOLERO CT
ALBATROSS DR
PATALITA DR
ORIENT DR
RIVER VISTA LN
LAGUNA
CERRO CREST DR
ASHLEY CT
VISTA DR
LINDSAY CT
KENILWORTH CT
BUGEIA LN
ATHERTON AV
ARCHIBALD LN
JUNE LN
GUISELA CT
ANTON WY
SUTTON LN
CREST RD
CHANNEL DR
BACHELORS RD
BRIDGE RD
GREEN POINT
SUNSET TR
SUMMIT LN
LOCKTON LN
RES
FS
CAVALLERO CT
SCHOOL TER
SCHOOL
OAK RIDGE TER
OAKS DR
ATHERTON OAKS
OAK KNOLL CT (ELDERBERRY CT)
TAMARIN LN
HAMPTON LN
WOODVIEW LN
GLEN LN
GLEN RD
GREEN POINT LN
HARBOR DR
HAVENWOOD
HYLAND RD
DR
BAY CANYON RD
PHILLIP TER
CEDAR AV
1 MANZANITA AV
2 BEATTIE AV
SONOMA CO
MARIN CO
PETALUMA RIVER
UPLAND LN
VINCENT CT
SAMROSE DR
JAMES CT
ELIZABETH CT
ROSE COURT TER
OLIVE ST
600
400
200
OLIVE RIDGE TENNIS CLUB
DEER ISLAND LN
ERLA
LOUISE DR
PARK & RIDE
SEARS POINT HWY
37
BLACK POINT
RENAISSANCE RD
SIMONDS SLOUGH
DEER ISLAND PRESERVE
NOVATO CREEK
NWP RR
MILITARY RESERVE
SEE A D7
1 SAMOA LN
2 LOLETA LN
3 CAPETOWN CT
4 ROCKPORT WY
5 MANCHESTER CT
6 ANTOINETTE LN
7 KLAMATH WY
8 LOS PADRES CIR
9 CASPAR PL
10 FERNBRIDGE PL
11 LOLITA LN
12 PLUMAS CIR
MONTEGO KEY
LOCK
CALYPSO SHORES
BEL MARIN KEYS
RANCH RD
MARSH DR
ISLE
BEL MARIN KEYS BLVD
BERMUDA HARBOUR
CAVALLA CAY
CARIBE
DEL ORO LAGOON
DOLPHIN ISLE
BAHAMA REEF

SEE 243 MAP
SEE 546 MAP

SEE 509 MAP

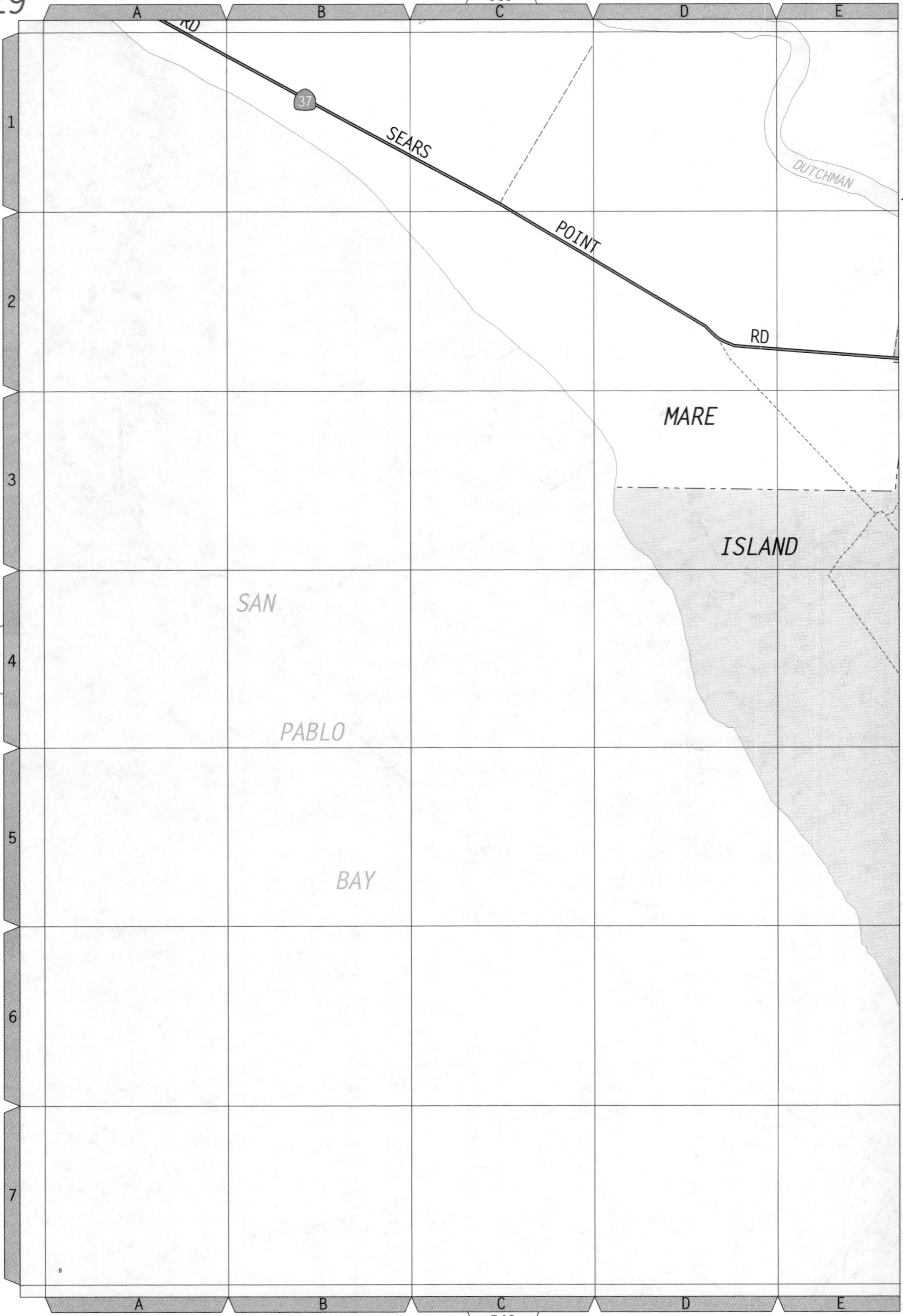
A
B
C
D
E
1
2
3
4
5
6
7
RD
37
SEARS
POINT
RD
DUTCHMAN
MARE
ISLAND
SAN
PABLO
BAY

SEE 243 MAP

SEE 549 MAP

SEE 509 MAP

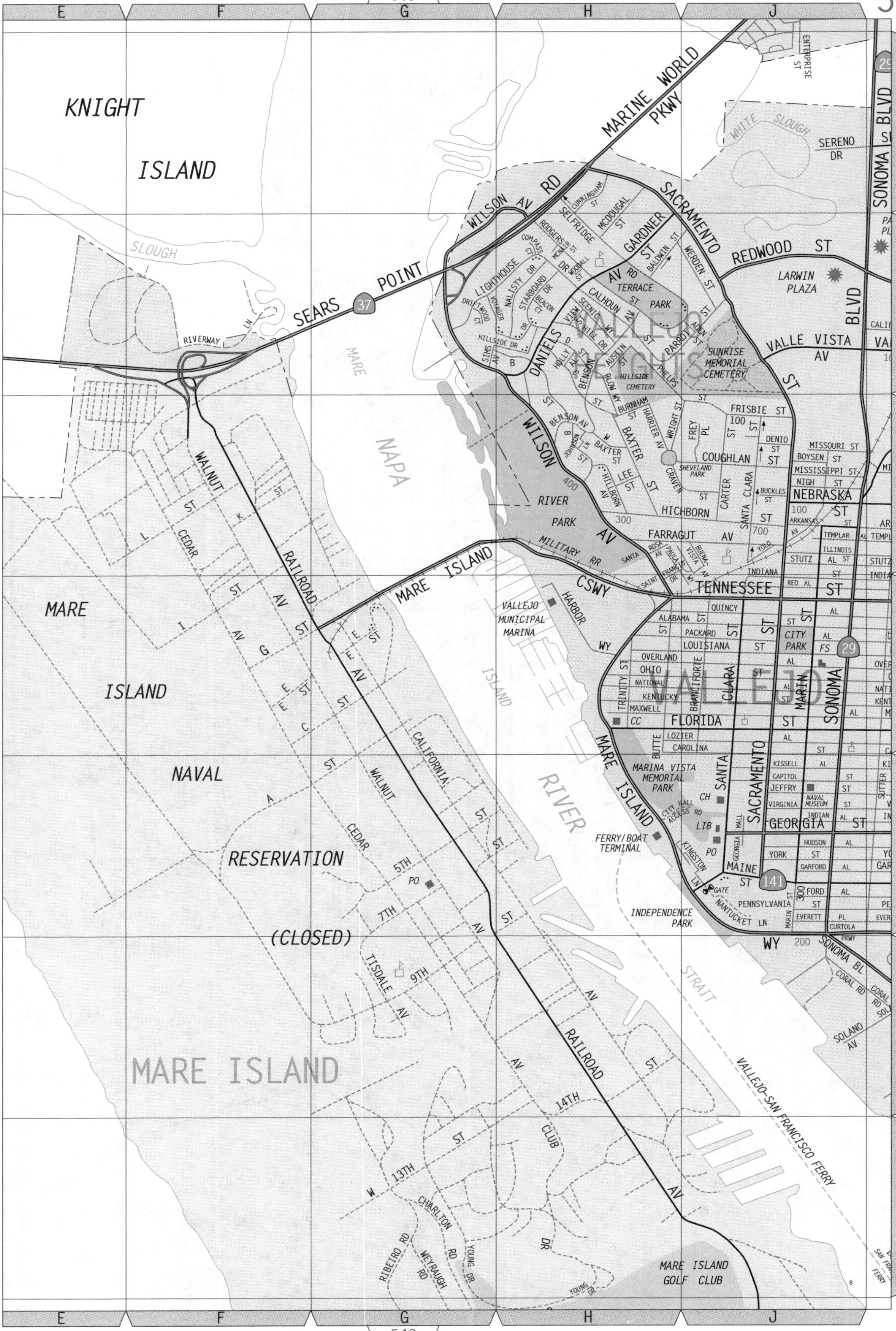
E
F
G
H
J
1
2
3
4
5
6
7
KNIGHT ISLAND
SLOUGH
MARINE WORLD PKWY
SEARS POINT RD
37
WILSON AV
RIVERWAY
LN
ENTERPRISE ST
WHITE SLOUGH
SERENO DR
SONOMA BLVD
29
SACRAMENTO ST
REDWOOD ST
LARWIN PLAZA
VALLE VISTA AV
VALLEJO HEIGHTS
SUNRISE MEMORIAL CEMETERY
HILLSIDE CEMETERY
TERRACE PARK
CUNNINGHAM ST
SELFRIDGE ST
MCDOUGAL ST
GARDNER ST
BALDWIN ST
WERDEN ST
RODGERS ST
COMPASS CT
MCNAIR ST
WOODALL ST
LIGHTHOUSE DR
NALISTY DR
STARBOARD DR
BEACON CT
DRIFTWOOD CT
VOYAGER CT
HILLSIDE DR
SIMS AV
DANIELS AV
CALHOUN ST
SCENIC VIEW
WILL DR
HOLLY
BENSON AV
AUSTIN ST
PARROTT ST
ALDEN ST
PHELPS ST
BURNHAM ST
BLOW WY
HARRIER AV
WRIGHT ST
FREY PL
BAXTER ST
JOHNSON LN
HILBORN AV
LEE ST
CRAVEN ST
SHEVELAND PARK
CARTER ST
SANTA CLARA ST
FRISBIE ST
DENIO ST
MISSOURI ST
BOYSEN ST
MISSISSIPPI ST
NIGH ST
BUCKLES ST
NEBRASKA ST
COUGHLAN ST
HICHBORN ST
ARKANSAS AV
TEMPLAR
ILLINOIS
STUTZ AL
INDIANA ST
YOLO
RIVER PARK
MILITARY RR
FARRAGUT AV
SANTA ROSA AV
PAUL AV
BUENA VISTA AV
SAINT FRANCIS DR
TENNESSEE ST
REO AL
MARE ISLAND CSWY
NAPA RIVER
MARE ISLAND STRAIT
VALLEJO MUNICIPAL MARINA
HARBOR WY
QUINCY
ALABAMA ST
PACKARD
LOUISIANA ST
OVERLAND
OHIO
NATIONAL
KENTUCKY
MAXWELL
TRINITY ST
BRANCIFORTE
CLARA
CITY PARK
FS
VALLEJO
MARIN ST
SONOMA
FLORIDA ST
CC
LOZIER
CAROLINA
BUTTE ST
KISSELL
CAPITOL
JEFFRY
VIRGINIA
NAVAL MUSEUM
INDIAN AL
GEORGIA ST
SACRAMENTO
SANTA
MARINA VISTA MEMORIAL PARK
CH
CITY HALL ACCESS RD
LIB
PO
FERRY/BOAT TERMINAL
KINGSTON LN
GEORGIA MALL
MAINE ST
141
HUDSON
YORK
GARFORD
GATE
PENNSYLVANIA
FORD
NANTUCKET LN
MARIN ST
EVERETT
PL
CURTOLA PKWY
INDEPENDENCE PARK
WY
SONOMA BL
CORAL RD
SOLANO AV
VALLEJO-SAN FRANCISCO FERRY
MARE ISLAND NAVAL RESERVATION (CLOSED)
MARE ISLAND
WALNUT AV
RAILROAD AV
CEDAR AV
L ST
K ST
I ST
G AV
E ST
C ST
A ST
CALIFORNIA ST
5TH ST
7TH ST
9TH
TISDALE AV
PO
14TH
13TH ST
W
CLUB DR
CHARLTON RD
RIBEIRO RD
WEYRAUGH RD
YOUNG DR
MARE ISLAND GOLF CLUB
100
200
300
400
700

SEE 530 MAP

SEE 549 MAP

SEE 510 MAP

A
B
C
D
E
1
2
3
4
5
6
7
SONOMA BLVD
BROADWAY
SERENO DR
REDWOOD ST
REDWOOD PKWY
VALLE VISTA AV
TUOLUMNE ST
FAIRGROUNDS DR
ADMIRAL CALLAGHAN LN
FRWY
TURNER
SOLANO COUNTY FAIRGROUNDS
DAN FOLEY PARK
MARINE WORLD AFRICA USA
VALLEJO CORNERS
KAISER FOUNDATION HOSP
SUTTER SOLANO MEDICAL CENTER
PARK PLACE
FIRST HOSP VALLEJO
VALLEJO HS
JR HS
HANS MEM PARK
NORTH HILLS CHRISTIAN HS
GREENFIELD AV
SKYLINE
FLEMING AV
TENNESSEE ST
NEBRASKA
ALAMEDA ST
AMADOR
MARIPOSA ST
HUMBOLDT ST
SPRINGS RD
GEORGIA ST
SOLANO AV
CURTOLA
BENICIA RD
WILSON PARK
LAKE DALWIGK
LAKE DALWIGK PARK
VALLEJO MOBILE ESTATES
LEMON ST
SONOMA BLVD
SHERIDAN ST
MAGAZINE ST
NAPA RIVER
VALLEJO-SAN FRANCISCO FERRY
WASHINGTON PARK
GRANT MAHONEY PARK
CHILDRENS WONDERLAND
GIBSON PK
HOGAN HS
REIGNIERD HS
CO BLDG
BEVERLY HILLS PARK
29
80
141
9

SEE 529 MAP

SEE 550 MAP

SEE 510 MAP

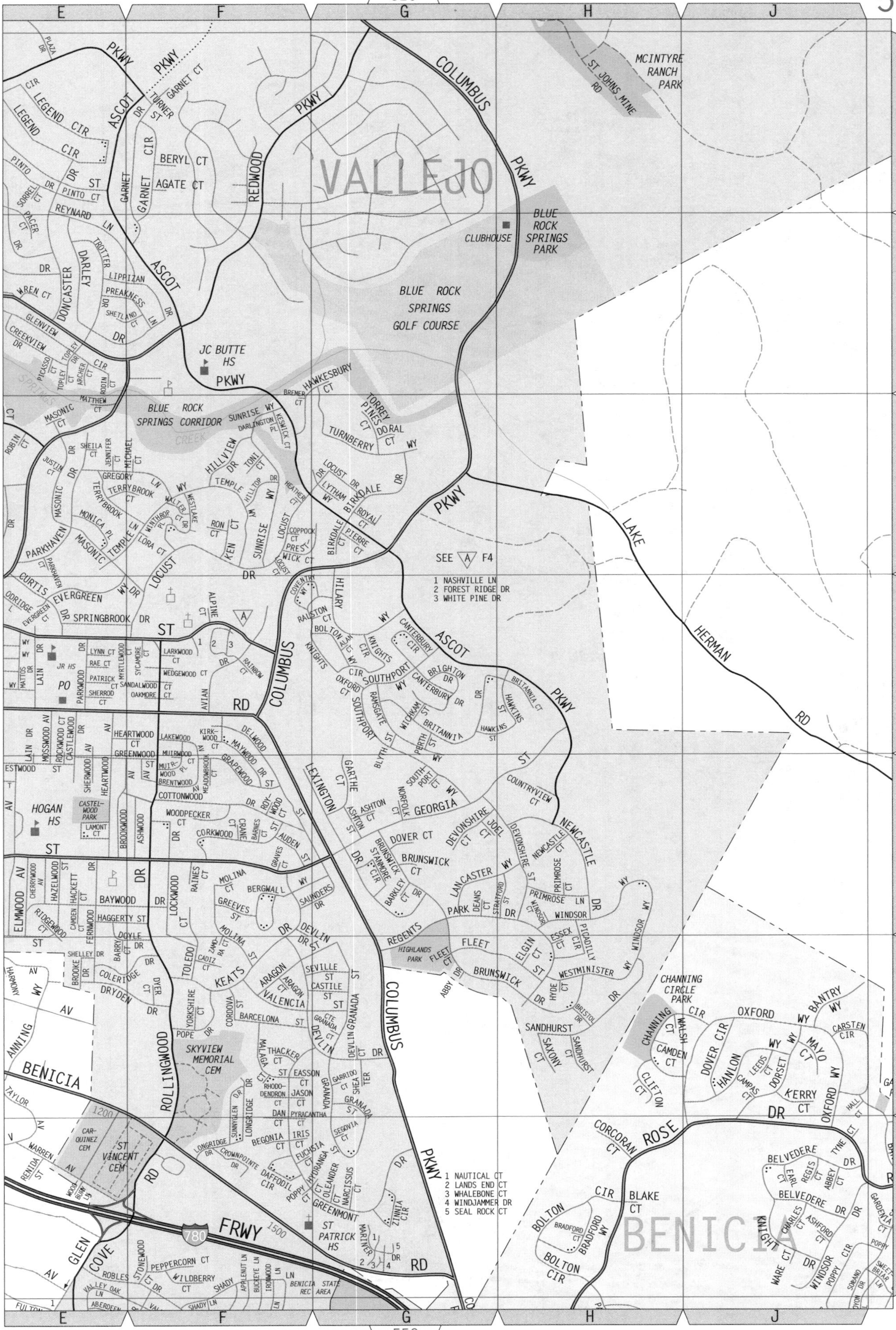
E
F
G
H
J
1
2
3
4
5
6
7
VALLEJO
BENICIA
COLUMBUS PKWY
ASCOT PKWY
REDWOOD
LAKE HERMAN RD
MCINTYRE RANCH PARK
ST JOHNS MINE RD
BLUE ROCK SPRINGS PARK
CLUBHOUSE
BLUE ROCK SPRINGS GOLF COURSE
JC BUTTE HS
BLUE ROCK SPRINGS CORRIDOR
CREEK
SEE A F4
1 NASHVILLE LN
2 FOREST RIDGE DR
3 WHITE PINE DR
JR HS
PO
HOGAN HS
CASTLEWOOD PARK
SKYVIEW MEMORIAL CEM
CARQUINEZ CEM
ST VINCENT CEM
ST PATRICK HS
BENICIA STATE REC AREA
HIGHLANDS PARK
CHANNING CIRCLE PARK
ROLLINGWOOD
BENICIA RD
GLEN COVE
FRWY
780
1 NAUTICAL CT
2 LANDS END CT
3 WHALEBONE CT
4 WINDJAMMER DR
5 SEAL ROCK CT
LEXINGTON
GEORGIA ST
NEWCASTLE
SOUTHPORT
BRUNSWICK
WINDSOR
OXFORD
ROSE DR
KNIGHT
BOLTON CIR
BLAKE CT
BELVEDERE DR
DEVLIN
KEATS
ARAGON
VALENCIA
TOLEDO
SPRINGBROOK DR
EVERGREEN
MASONIC
PARKHAVEN
TEMPLE
LOCUST DR
DOVER CT
DEVONSHIRE
LANCASTER
FLEET
WESTMINISTER
SANDHURST
CORCORAN CT
KERRY
MAYO CT
BANTRY WY
CARSTEN CIR

SEE 243 MAP

MAP

SEE 550 MAP

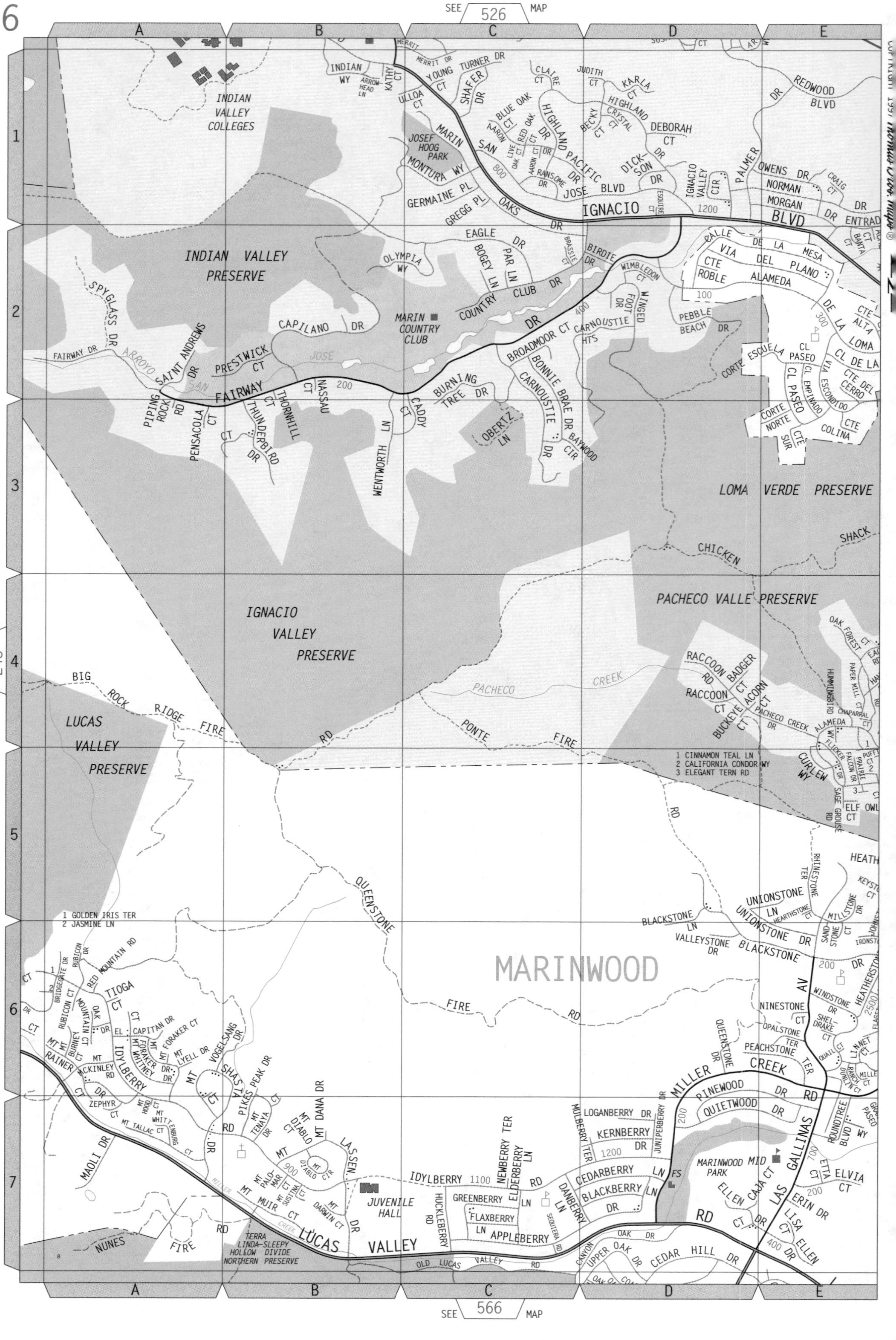
SEE 526 MAP
SEE 243 MAP
SEE 566 MAP
INDIAN VALLEY COLLEGES
INDIAN VALLEY PRESERVE
JOSEF HOOG PARK
MARIN COUNTRY CLUB
IGNACIO BLVD
SAN MARIN DR
JOSE BLVD
PACIFIC DR
HIGHLAND DR
REDWOOD BLVD
FAIRWAY DR
SPYGLASS DR
SAINT ANDREWS DR
PRESTWICK CT
CAPILANO DR
COUNTRY CLUB DR
BROADMOOR CT
CARNOUSTIE HTS
PEBBLE BEACH DR
BURNING TREE DR
OBERTIZ LN
WENTWORTH LN
CADDY CT
THORNHILL CT
THUNDERBIRD DR
PENSACOLA CT
PIPING ROCK RD
LOMA VERDE PRESERVE
CHICKEN SHACK
PACHECO VALLE PRESERVE
IGNACIO VALLEY PRESERVE
PACHECO CREEK
PONTE FIRE RD
BIG ROCK RIDGE FIRE RD
LUCAS VALLEY PRESERVE
1 CINNAMON TEAL LN
2 CALIFORNIA CONDOR WY
3 ELEGANT TERN RD
QUEENSTONE
1 GOLDEN IRIS TER
2 JASMINE LN
MARINWOOD
FIRE RD
MILLER CREEK RD
BLACKSTONE DR
UNIONSTONE DR
VALLEYSTONE DR
IDYLBERRY RD
JUVENILE HALL
MARINWOOD MID PARK
LAS GALLINAS AV
LUCAS VALLEY RD
OLD LUCAS VALLEY RD
TERRA LINDA–SLEEPY HOLLOW DIVIDE NORTHERN PRESERVE
NUNES FIRE RD
MAOLI DR
CEDAR HILL DR
UPPER OAK DR

SEE 526 MAP

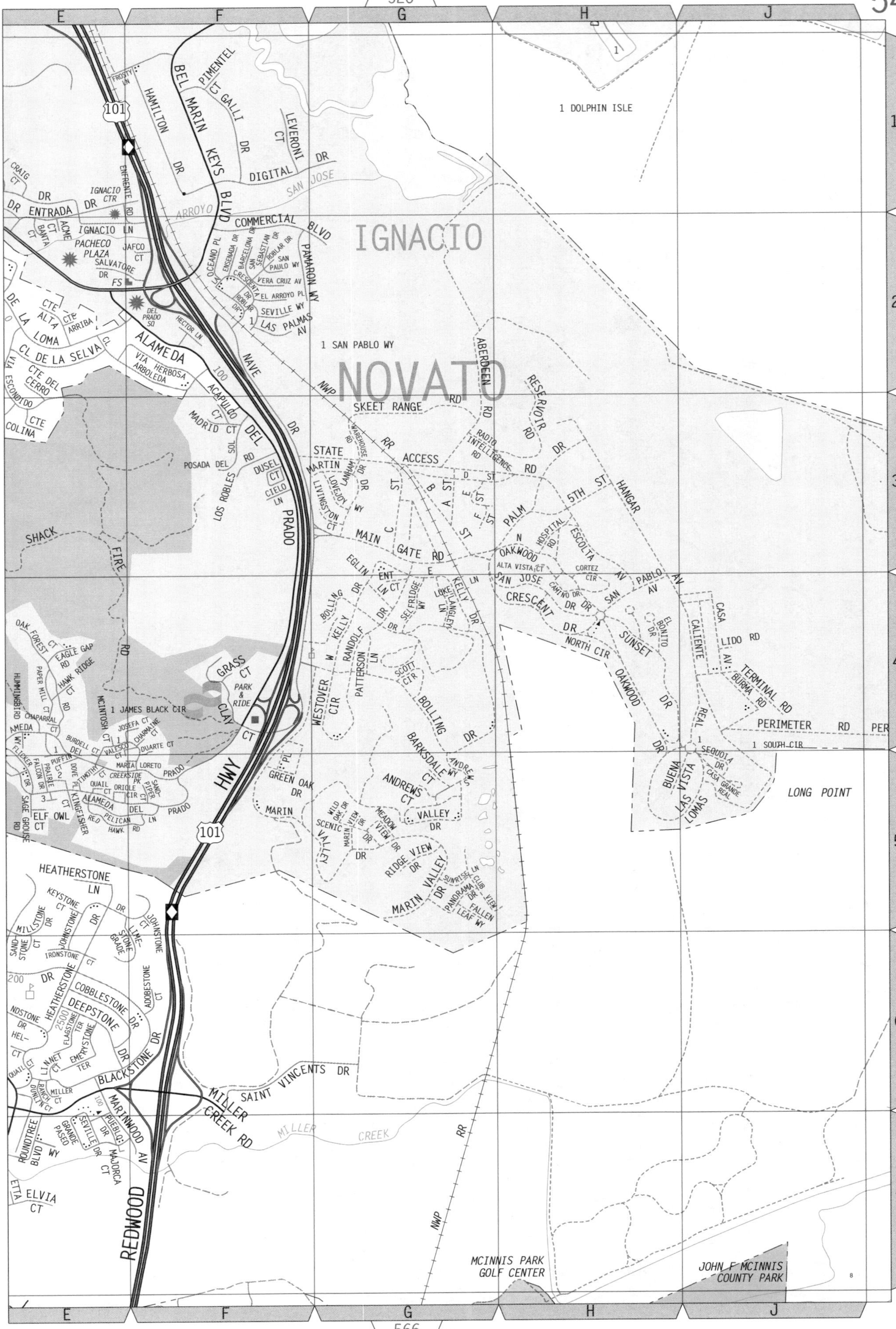
IGNACIO
NOVATO
1 DOLPHIN ISLE
BEL MARIN KEYS BLVD
HAMILTON DR
PIMENTEL CT
GALLI DR
LEVERONI CT
DIGITAL DR
SAN JOSE
ARROYO
COMMERCIAL BLVD
ENTRADA DR
IGNACIO LN
IGNACIO CTR
PACHECO PLAZA
SALVATORE DR
JAFCO CT
PAMARON WY
VERA CRUZ AV
EL ARROYO PL
SEVILLE WY
LAS PALMAS AV
1 SAN PABLO WY
ALAMEDA DEL PRADO
CL DE LA SELVA
VIA HERBOSA
HECTOR LN
NAVE DR
ACAPULCO CT
MADRID CT
SKEET RANGE RD
ABERDEEN RD
RESERVOIR RD
STATE ACCESS RD
RADIO INTELLIGENCE RD
MARTIN DR
LOS ROBLES
POSADA DEL SOL
DUSEL CT
CIELO LN
SHACK
FIRE RD
MAIN GATE RD
5TH ST
HANGAR
PALM
HOSPITAL RD
ESCOLTA AV
OAKWOOD
SAN PABLO AV
SAN JOSE
CRESCENT DR
NORTH CIR
SUNSET
EL BONITO
CALIENTE
CASA
LIDO RD
TERMINAL RD
BURMA RD
PERIMETER RD
1 SOUTH CIR
SEQUOIA DR
CASA GRANDE REAL
BUENA VISTA
LAS LOMAS
LONG POINT
KELLY DR
EGLIN LN
BOLLING DR
RANDOLF
PATTERSON LN
WESTOVER CIR
SCOTT CIR
BARKSDALE CT
ANDREWS CT
GREEN OAK DR
MARIN VALLEY DR
VALLEY DR
RIDGE VIEW DR
SUNRISE LN
FALLEN LEAF WY
PANORAMA DR
GRASS CT
CLAY CT
PARK & RIDE
1 JAMES BLACK CIR
OAK FOREST CT
EAGLE GAP RD
HAWK RIDGE CT
PAPER MILL CT
HUMMINGBIRD
CHAPARRAL CT
MCINTOSH CT
JOSEFA CT
CHARMAINE CT
DUARTE CT
MARIA LORETO
KINGFISHER
ELF OWL CT
PELICAN LN
SAGE GROUSE RD
HWY 101
HEATHERSTONE LN
KEYSTONE CT
MILLSTONE DR
JOHNSTONE DR
IRONSTONE CT
COBBLESTONE
DEEPSTONE DR
ADOBESTONE CT
BLACKSTONE DR
SAINT VINCENTS DR
MILLER CREEK RD
MILLER CREEK
MARINWOOD AV
ROUNDTREE BLVD
ELVIA CT
MAJORCA CT
REDWOOD
NWP RR
MCINNIS PARK GOLF CENTER
JOHN F MCINNIS COUNTY PARK
SEE 243 MAP

SEE 566 MAP

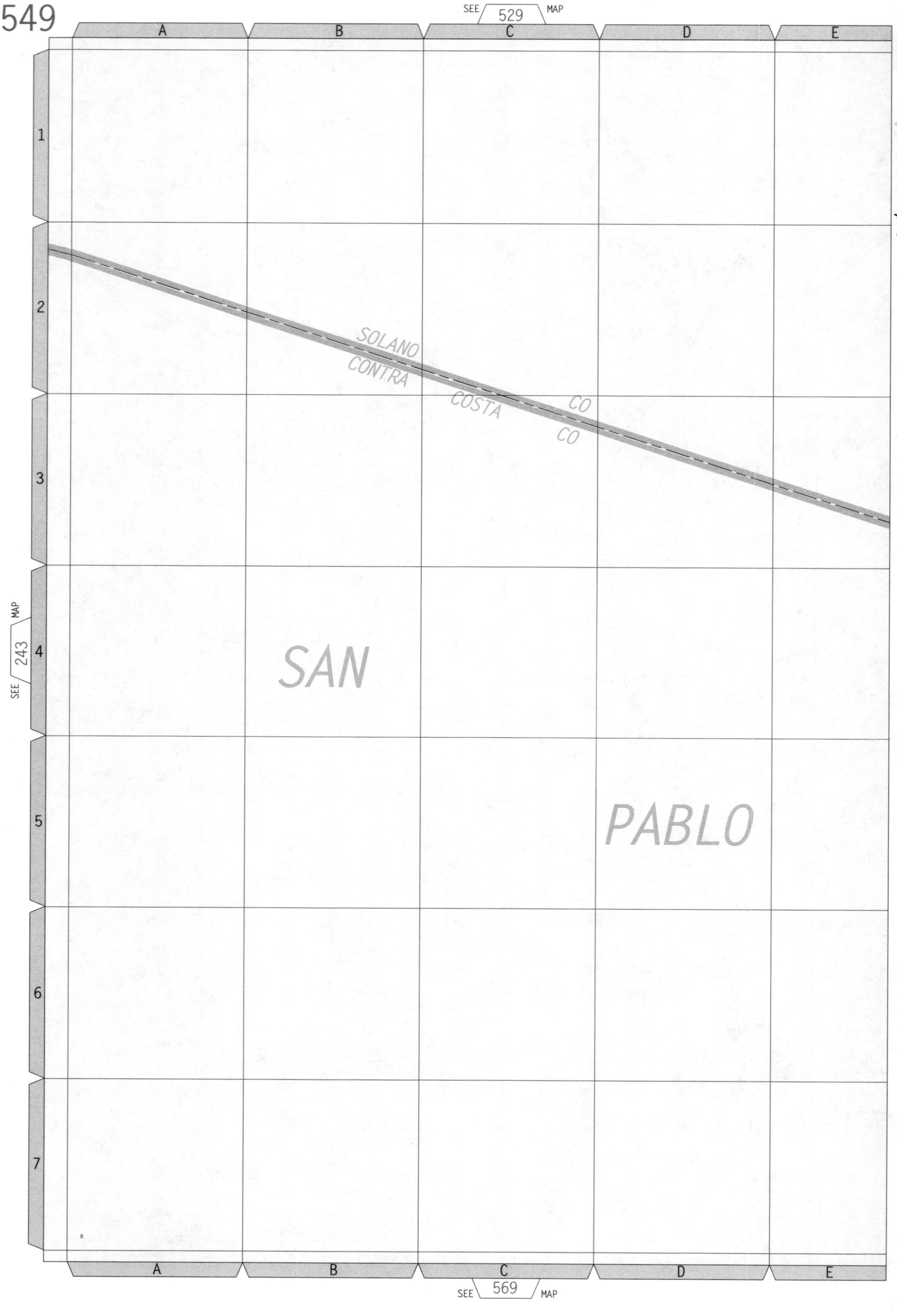
SEE 529 MAP
A
B
C
D
E
1
2
3
4
5
6
7
SOLANO
CONTRA
COSTA
CO
CO
SEE 243 MAP
SAN
PABLO
SEE 569 MAP

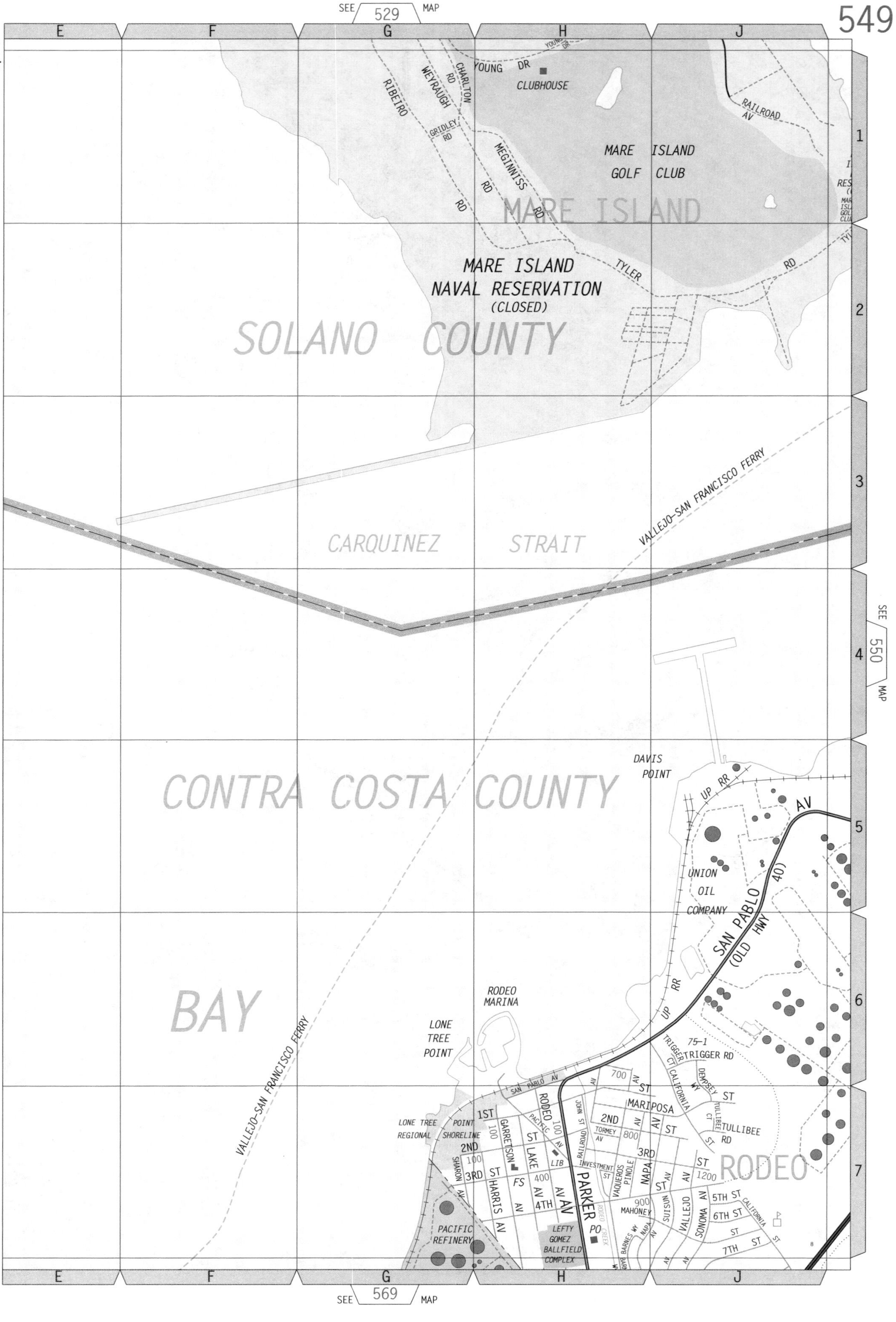
SEE 529 MAP
E
F
G
H
J
1
2
3
4
5
6
7
YOUNG DR
CLUBHOUSE
RIBEIRO
WEYRAUGH
CHARLTON RD
GRIDLEY RD
MEGINNISS RD
RD
RD
RAILROAD AV
MARE ISLAND GOLF CLUB
MARE ISLAND
MARE ISLAND NAVAL RESERVATION (CLOSED)
TYLER RD
SOLANO COUNTY
VALLEJO-SAN FRANCISCO FERRY
CARQUINEZ STRAIT
SEE 550 MAP
DAVIS POINT
UP RR
AV
UNION OIL COMPANY
SAN PABLO (OLD HWY 40)
CONTRA COSTA COUNTY
BAY
RODEO MARINA
LONE TREE POINT
UP RR
TRIGGER CT
75-1
TRIGGER RD
CALIFORNIA
DEMPSEY WY
ST
TULLIBEE CT
TULLIBEE RD
SAN PABLO AV
700
ST
MARIPOSA
RODEO AV
JOHN ST
2ND
AV
ST
TORMEY AV
800
3RD
LONE TREE POINT REGIONAL SHORELINE
1ST
100
GARRETSON
ST
PACIFIC
100
2ND
LAKE
LIB
RAILROAD
INVESTMENT ST
VAQUEROS
PINOLE
NAPA
ST
AV
AV
1200
RODEO
SHARON AV
3RD ST
HARRIS AV
FS
400
AV
4TH AV
AV
PARKER
900
MAHONEY
SUISUN
VALLEJO
SONOMA AV
5TH ST
6TH ST
CALIFORNIA ST
ST
7TH ST
PACIFIC REFINERY
LEFTY GOMEZ BALLFIELD COMPLEX
PO
RODEO CREEK
BARNES WY
NAPA
AV
AV
E
F
G
H
J
SEE 569 MAP

SEE 530 MAP

CARQUINEZ HEIGHTS
VALLEJO
MARE ISLAND NAVAL RESERVATION (CLOSED)
MARE ISLAND GOLF CLUB
NAPA RIVER
MARE ISLAND STRAIT
VALLEJO - SAN FRANCISCO FERRY
CARQUINEZ STRAIT LIGHTHOUSE
CALIFORNIA MARITIME ACADEMY
BEVERLY HILLS PARK
CARQUINEZ PARK
SWANZY RESERVOIR
MORROW COVE
SONOMA BLVD
MARITIME ACADEMY DR
FRWY
CARQUINEZ BRIDGE
($1.00 TOLL NORTH ONLY)
SOLANO CO
CONTRA COSTA CO
SOLANO
CARQUINEZ STRAIT
CARQUINEZ STRAIT TRAIL
SAN PABLO AV
(OLD HWY 40)
VISTA DEL RIO
CRESTVIEW
DOWRELIO DR
WANDA ST
LORING ST
WINSLOW ST
EDWARDS ST
POMONA ST
FLORA ST
JOHN SWETT HS
ALEXANDER PARK
CROCKETT
CROCKETT BLVD
UNION OIL COMPANY
SELBY RESERVOIR
OLD COUNTY RD
CUMMINGS SKWY
EASTSHORE FRWY
CONTRA COSTA COUNTY
596'
1 COLUMBUS AV
1 SUMMERSVILLE CT
2 BRIDGEVIEW PL
1 GLEN COVE RD

SEE 549 MAP

SEE 570 MAP

SEE 530 MAP

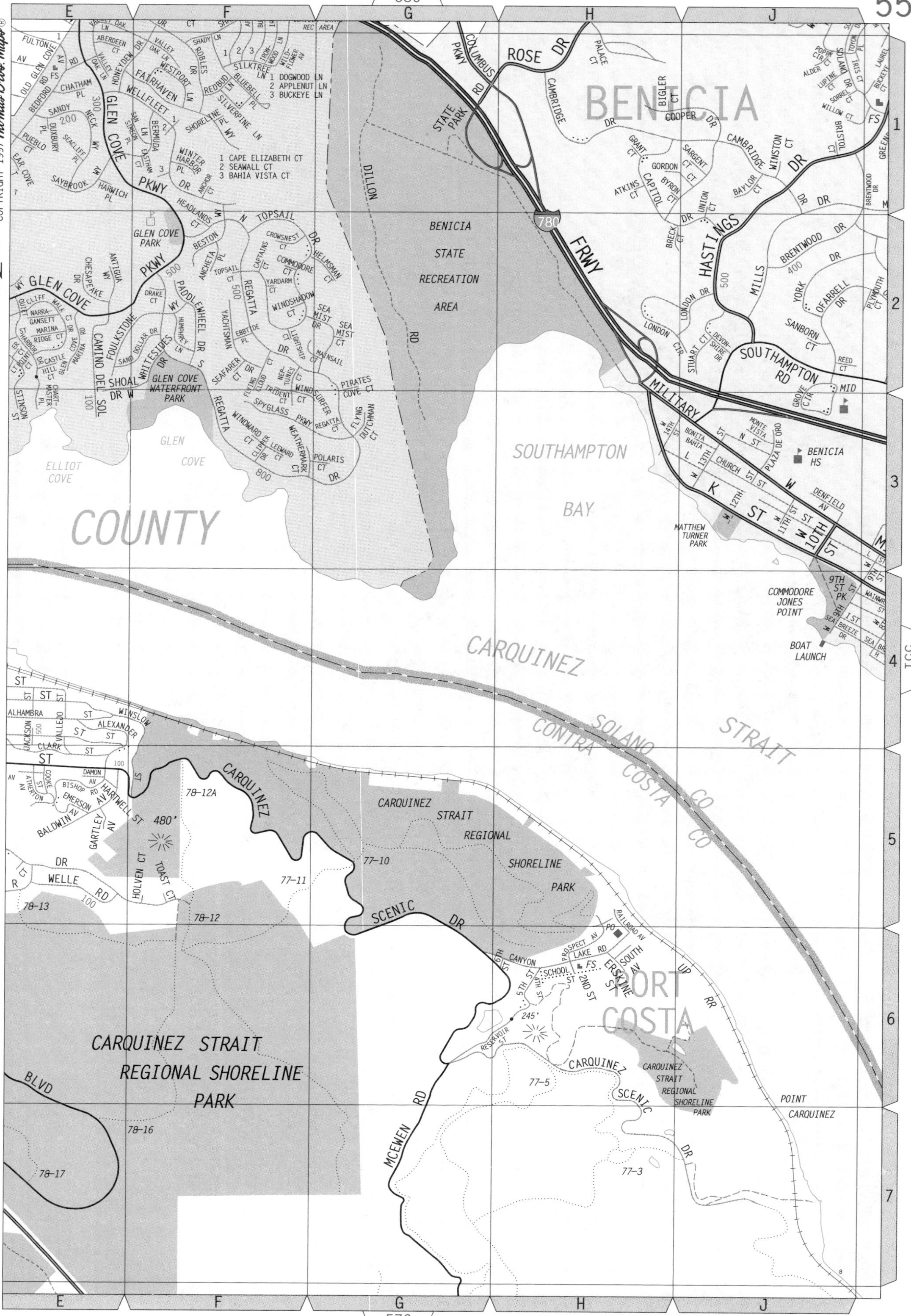
E
F
G
H
J
1
2
3
4
5
6
7
BENICIA
COUNTY
BENICIA STATE RECREATION AREA
SOUTHAMPTON BAY
GLEN COVE
ELLIOT COVE
GLEN COVE PARK
GLEN COVE WATERFRONT PARK
CARQUINEZ STRAIT
SOLANO CO
CONTRA COSTA CO
CARQUINEZ STRAIT REGIONAL SHORELINE PARK
PORT COSTA
POINT CARQUINEZ
COMMODORE JONES POINT
BOAT LAUNCH
MATTHEW TURNER PARK
BENICIA HS
9TH ST PK
780
FRWY
MILITARY
HASTINGS DR
SOUTHAMPTON RD
ROSE DR
COLUMBUS PKWY
STATE PARK RD
DILLON RD
CAMBRIDGE DR
GLEN COVE PKWY
CAMINO DEL SOL
REGATTA
K ST
W 10TH ST
SCENIC DR
CARQUINEZ SCENIC DR
MCEWEN RD
WELLE RD
WINSLOW ST
BLVD
1 DOGWOOD LN
2 APPLENUT LN
3 BUCKEYE LN
1 CAPE ELIZABETH CT
2 SEAWALL CT
3 BAHIA VISTA CT
480'
245'
78-12A
78-12
78-13
78-16
78-17
77-10
77-11
77-5
77-3

SEE 551 MAP

SEE 570 MAP

SEE 243 MAP

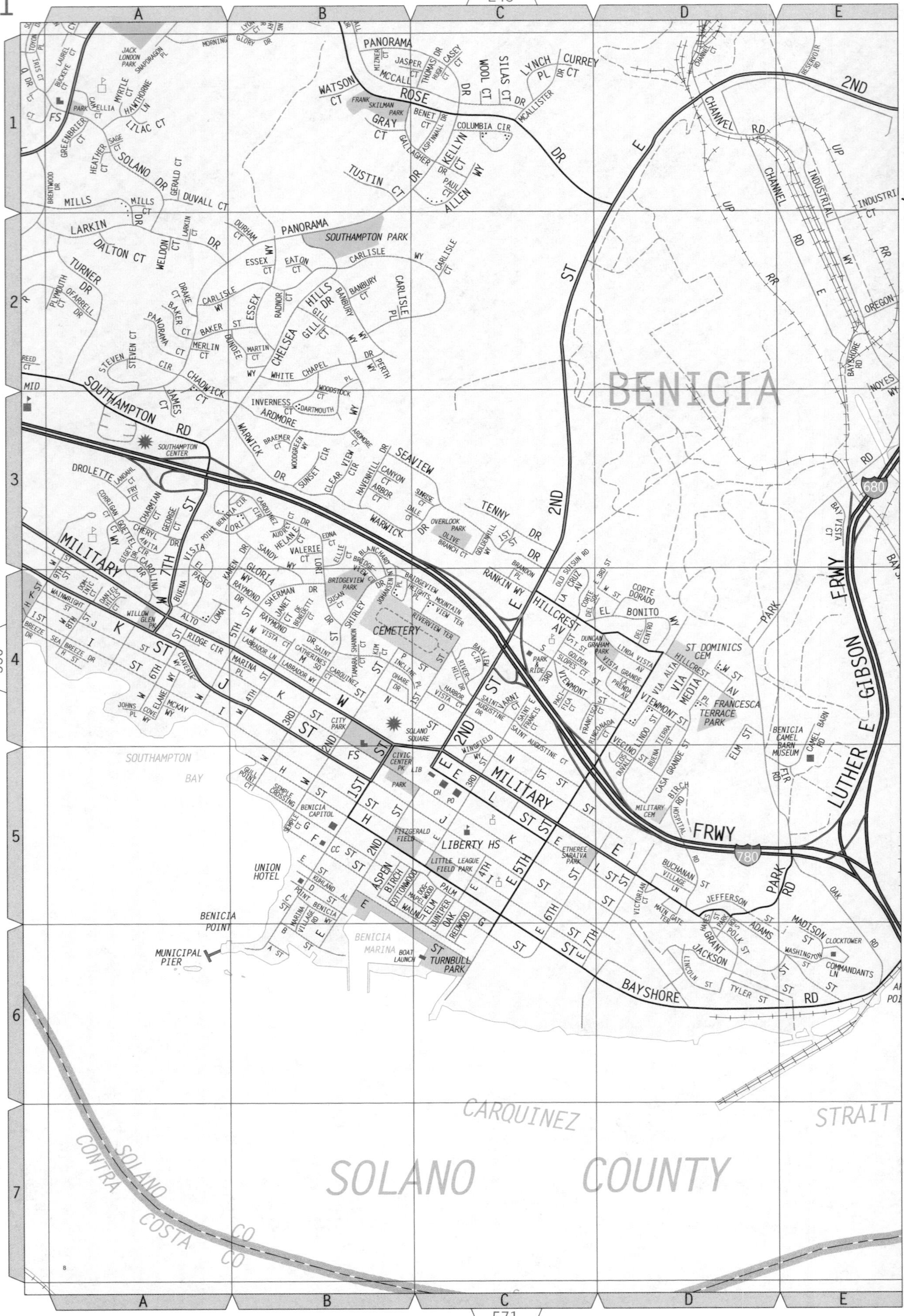
A
B
C
D
E
1
2
3
4
5
6
7
BENICIA
SOLANO COUNTY
CARQUINEZ STRAIT
CONTRA COSTA CO
SOLANO CO
SOUTHAMPTON BAY
SOUTHAMPTON PARK
SOUTHAMPTON RD
SOUTHAMPTON CENTER
PANORAMA DR
ROSE DR
MILITARY
E MILITARY
2ND ST
E 2ND ST
FRWY
780
680
LUTHER E GIBSON FRWY
BAYSHORE RD
PARK RD
INDUSTRIAL WY
CHANNEL RD
CEMETERY
ST DOMINICS CEM
MILITARY CEM
LIBERTY HS
CITY PARK
CIVIC CENTER PK
FITZGERALD FIELD
LITTLE LEAGUE FIELD PARK
BENICIA CAPITOL
UNION HOTEL
BENICIA POINT
MUNICIPAL PIER
BENICIA MARINA
BOAT LAUNCH
TURNBULL PARK
SOLANO SQUARE
BENICIA CAMEL BARN MUSEUM
FRANCESCA TERRACE PARK
OVERLOOK PARK
BRIDGEVIEW PARK
FRANK SKILMAN PARK
JACK LONDON PARK
WILLOW GLEN PK
PARK & RIDE
ETHEREE SARATIVA PARK
DUNCAN GRAHAM PARK
CLOCKTOWER
COMMANDANTS LN
JEFFERSON ST
MADISON ST
ADAMS ST
TYLER ST
GRANT
JACKSON
LINCOLN ST
WARWICK DR
SEAVIEW
TENNY DR
RANKIN WY
HILLCREST AV
CARLISLE WY
CHELSEA HILLS DR
WHITE CHAPEL
LARKIN DR
MILLS DR
DUVALL CT
SOLANO DR
TUSTIN CT
WATSON CT
CURREY CT
LYNCH PL
RIDGE CIR
BUENA VISTA
MARINA PL
CHADWICK CT
STEVEN CIR

SEE 550 MAP

SEE 571 MAP

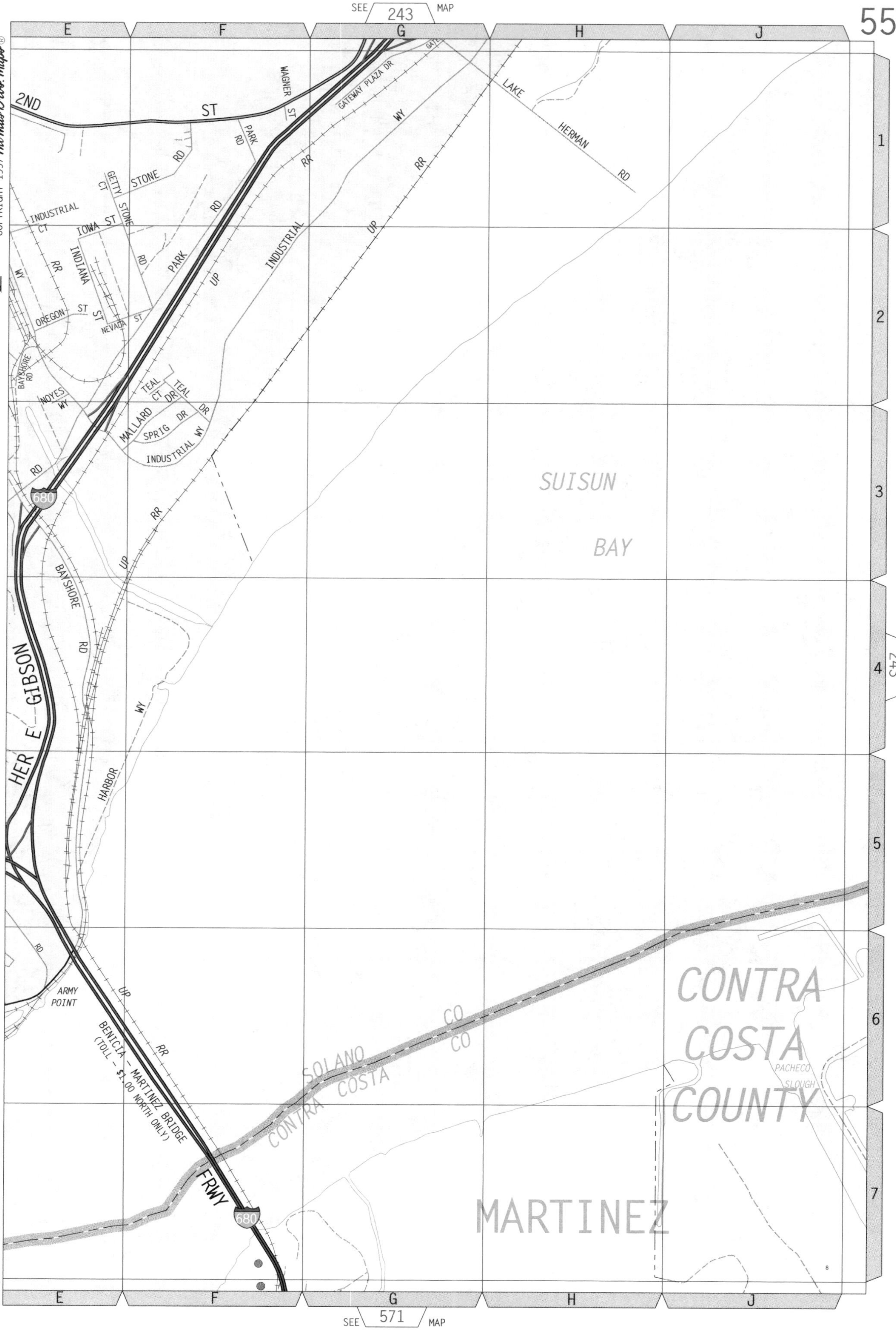
SEE 243 MAP
SEE 243 MAP
SEE 571 MAP
E F G H J
1 2 3 4 5 6 7
2ND ST
WAGNER ST
PARK RD
GATEWAY PLAZA DR
GATE
WY
LAKE
HERMAN
RD
STONE RD
GETTY CT
STONE
INDUSTRIAL CT
IOWA ST
INDIANA
RR
WY
PARK RD
UP RR
INDUSTRIAL WY
UP RR
OREGON ST
ST
NEVADA ST
BAYSHORE RD
NOYES WY
TEAL CT
TEAL DR
MALLARD DR
SPRIG DR
INDUSTRIAL WY
RD
680
SUISUN
BAY
BAYSHORE RD
UP RR
E GIBSON
HERE
WY
HARBOR
RD
ARMY POINT
UP RR
BENICIA - MARTINEZ BRIDGE
(TOLL - $1.00 NORTH ONLY)
FRWY
680
SOLANO CO
CONTRA COSTA CO
CONTRA COSTA
CONTRA
COSTA
COUNTY
PACHECO
SLOUGH
MARTINEZ

SEE 546 MAP

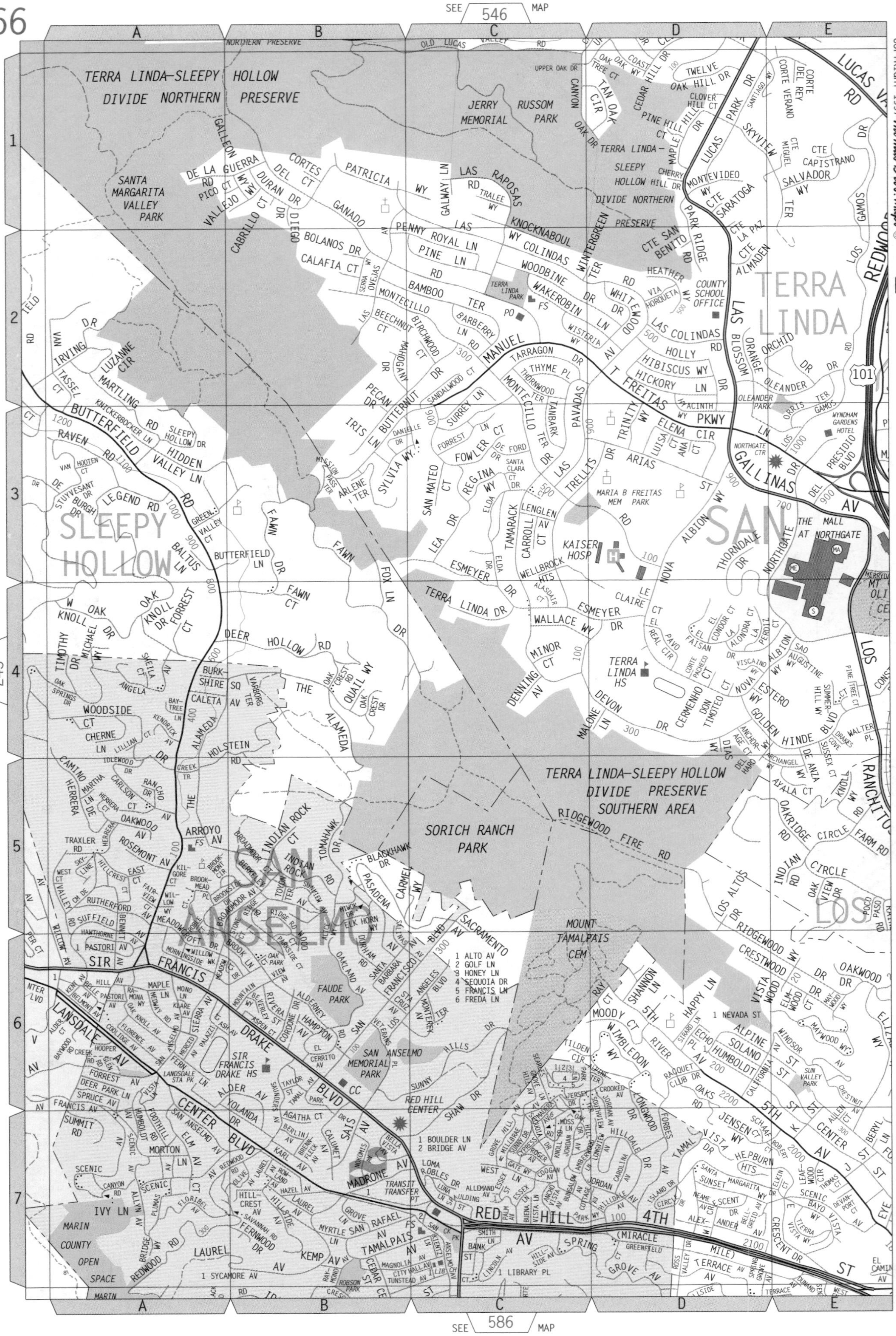
A
B
C
D
E
1
2
3
4
5
6
7
TERRA LINDA–SLEEPY HOLLOW DIVIDE NORTHERN PRESERVE
JERRY RUSSOM MEMORIAL PARK
TERRA LINDA–SLEEPY HOLLOW DIVIDE NORTHERN PRESERVE
SANTA MARGARITA VALLEY PARK
TERRA LINDA
SLEEPY HOLLOW
SAN
THE MALL AT NORTHGATE
TERRA LINDA–SLEEPY HOLLOW DIVIDE PRESERVE SOUTHERN AREA
SORICH RANCH PARK
SAN ANSELMO
MOUNT TAMALPAIS CEM
FAUDE PARK
SAN ANSELMO MEMORIAL PARK
SIR FRANCIS DRAKE HS
RED HILL CENTER
MARIN COUNTY OPEN SPACE
TERRA LINDA HS
KAISER HOSP
MARIA B FREITAS MEM PARK
COUNTY SCHOOL OFFICE
NORTHGATE CTR
WYNDHAM GARDENS HOTEL
OLEANDER PARK
SUN VALLEY PARK
TERRA LINDA PARK
LUCAS VALLEY RD
REDWOOD
101
MANUEL T FREITAS PKWY
LAS GALLINAS AV
DEL PRESIDIO BLVD
BUTTERFIELD RD
SIR FRANCIS DRAKE BLVD
CENTER BLVD
RED HILL AV
4TH ST
5TH AV
LOS RANCHITOS RD
RIDGEWOOD FIRE RD
1 ALTO AV
2 GOLF LN
3 HONEY LN
4 SEQUOIA DR
5 FRANCIS LN
6 FREDA LN
1 BOULDER LN
2 BRIDGE AV
1 NEVADA ST
1 SYCAMORE AV
1 LIBRARY PL
1 PASTORI AV
TRANSIT TRANSFER PT

SEE 243 MAP
SEE 586 MAP

SEE 546 MAP

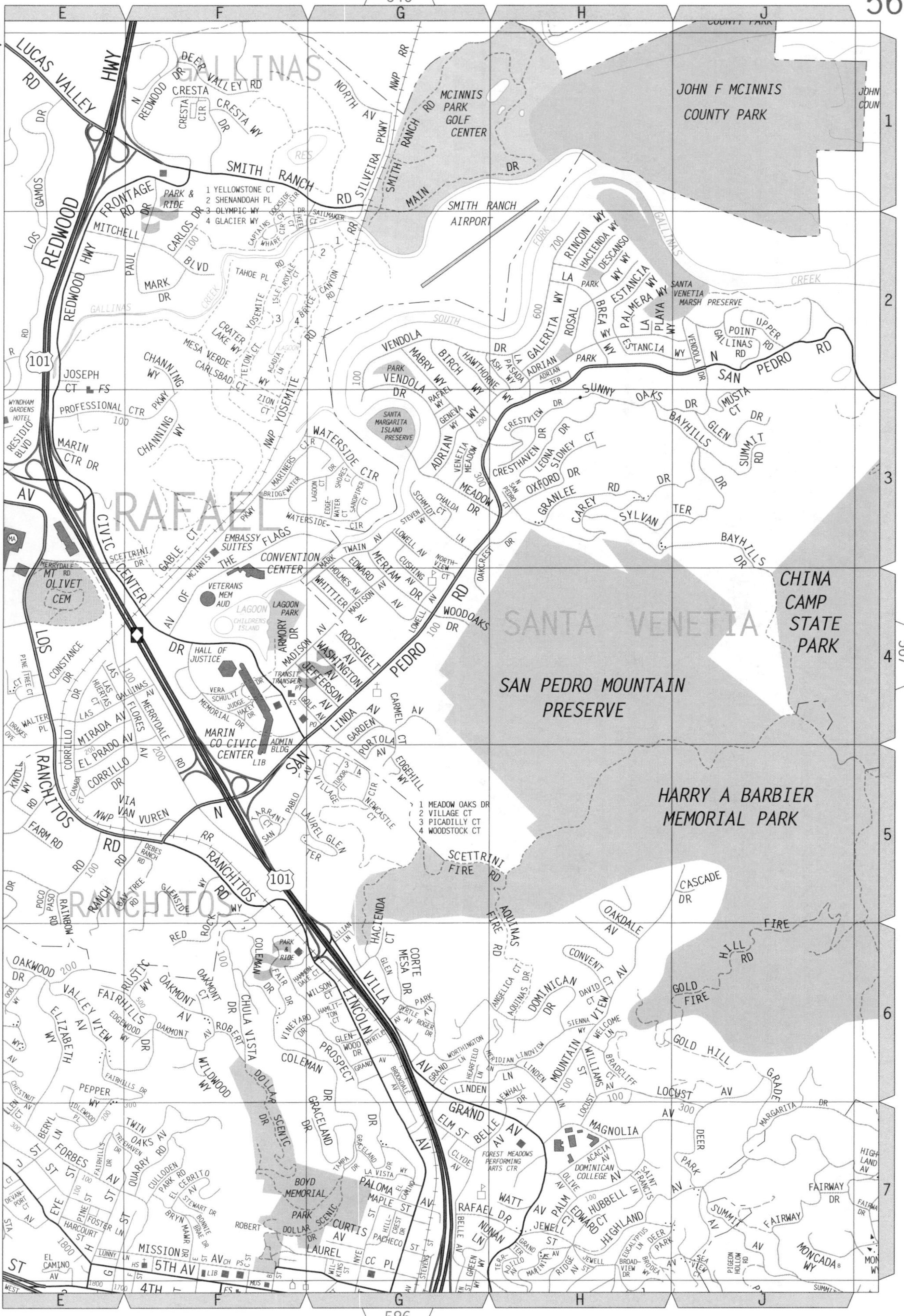
GALLINAS
LUCAS VALLEY RD
REDWOOD HWY
101
SMITH RANCH RD
MCINNIS PARK GOLF CENTER
JOHN F MCINNIS COUNTY PARK
SMITH RANCH AIRPORT
SANTA VENETIA MARSH PRESERVE
SANTA MARGARITA ISLAND PRESERVE
N SAN PEDRO RD
RAFAEL
CIVIC CENTER DR
EMBASSY SUITES
CONVENTION CENTER
VETERANS MEM AUD
LAGOON PARK
MT OLIVET CEM
HALL OF JUSTICE
MARIN CO CIVIC CENTER
SANTA VENETIA
CHINA CAMP STATE PARK
SAN PEDRO MOUNTAIN PRESERVE
HARRY A BARBIER MEMORIAL PARK
1 MEADOW OAKS DR
2 VILLAGE CT
3 PICADILLY CT
4 WOODSTOCK CT
1 YELLOWSTONE CT
2 SHENANDOAH PL
3 OLYMPIC WY
4 GLACIER WY
LOS RANCHITOS RD
RANCHITOS
SCETTRINI FIRE RD
AQUINAS FIRE RD
GOLD HILL FIRE RD
LINCOLN AV
GRAND AV
DOMINICAN COLLEGE
FOREST MEADOWS PERFORMING ARTS CTR
BOYD MEMORIAL PARK
MISSION AV
5TH AV
4TH ST

SEE 567 MAP

SEE 586 MAP

SEE 243 MAP

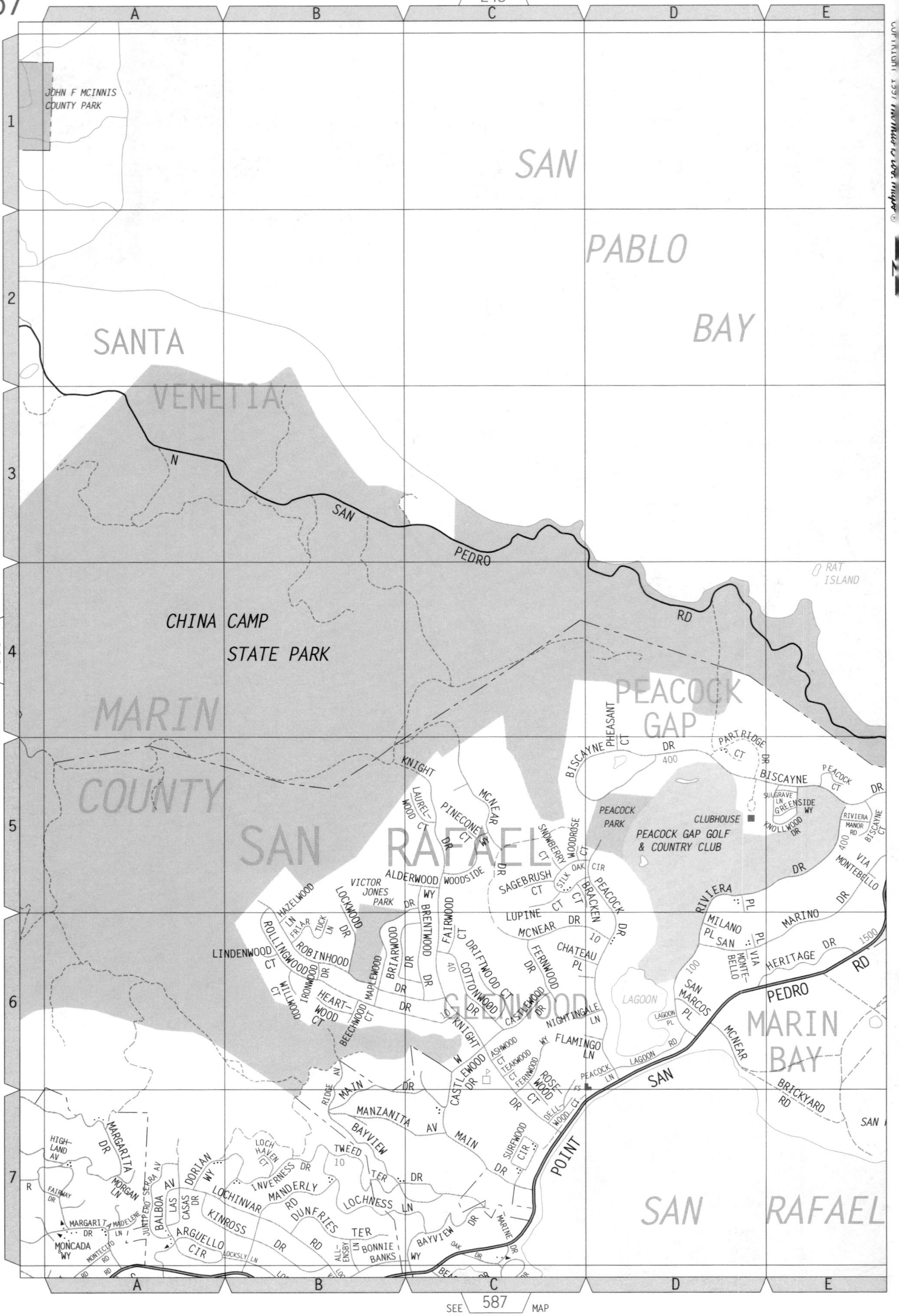
A
B
C
D
E
1
2
3
4
5
6
7
JOHN F MCINNIS COUNTY PARK
SAN
PABLO
BAY
SANTA
VENETIA
N
SAN
PEDRO
RD
RAT ISLAND
CHINA CAMP
STATE PARK
MARIN
COUNTY
SAN
RAFAEL
PEACOCK GAP
PEACOCK PARK
PEACOCK GAP GOLF & COUNTRY CLUB
CLUBHOUSE
BISCAYNE DR
PHEASANT CT
PARTRIDGE DR
CT
GREENSIDE WY
SULGRAVE LN
KNOLLWOOD DR
PEACOCK CT
RIVIERA MANOR RD
BISCAYNE CT
VIA MONTEBELLO
RIVIERA DR
MILANO PL
SAN MARINO DR
MARINO
HERITAGE DR
MONTE-BELLO
VIA
PL
SAN MARCOS PL
LAGOON
LAGOON PL
LAGOON RD
KNIGHT DR
LAUREL-WOOD CT
PINECONE CT
MCNEAR DR
WY
SNOWBERRY CT
WOODROSE CT
SILK OAK CIR
SAGEBRUSH CT
BRACKEN CT
PEACOCK DR
LUPINE CT
MCNEAR DR
CHATEAU PL
FERNWOOD DR
ALDERWOOD
WOODSIDE
VICTOR JONES PARK
HAZELWOOD LN
FRIAR LN
TUCK LN
LOCKWOOD DR
BRENTWOOD DR
FAIRWOOD CT
DRIFTWOOD CT
COTTONWOOD DR
BRIARWOOD DR
MAPLEWOOD DR
ROBINHOOD DR
ROLLINGWOOD DR
LINDENWOOD CT
IRONWOOD
WILLWOOD CT
HEART-WOOD CT
BEECHWOOD CT
GLENWOOD
CASTLEWOOD DR
NIGHTINGALE LN
FLAMINGO LN
KNIGHT DR
W
ASHWOOD CT
TEAKWOOD CT
FERNWOOD
ROSE-WOOD CT
PEACOCK LN
DELL-WOOD CT
SURFWOOD CIR
MAIN DR
RIDGE AV
MANZANITA AV
BAYVIEW TER
TWEED DR
LOCH HAVEN CT
INVERNESS DR
MANDERLY RD
LOCHINVAR
DUNFRIES
LOCHNESS LN
KINROSS DR
ARGUELLO CIR
LOCKSLY LN
ALL-ENSBY LN
BONNIE BANKS WY
BAYVIEW DR
OAK
MARINE DR
TER
RD
DORIAN WY
LAS CASAS DR
BALBOA AV
JUNIPERO SERRA AV
MARGARITA DR
MORGAN LN
HIGH-LAND AV
FAIRWAY DR
MARGARITA
MADELENE LN
MONCADA WY
MONTECITO RD
R
POINT SAN PEDRO RD
MCNEAR
BRICKYARD RD
MARIN BAY
SAN
400
10
40
100
1500

SEE 566 MAP

MAP

SEE 587 MAP

SEE 243 MAP

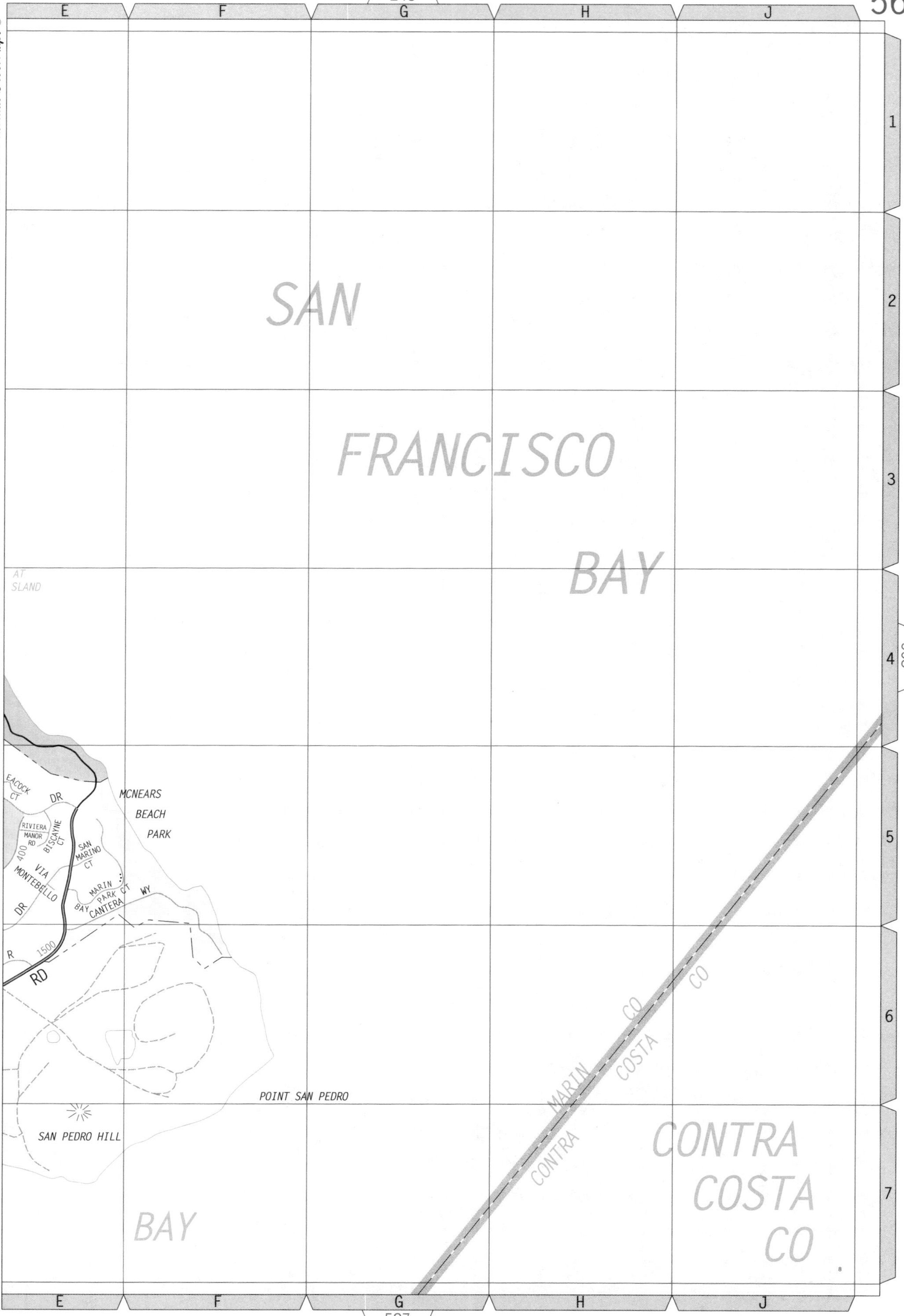
E
F
G
H
J
1
2
3
4
5
6
7
SAN
FRANCISCO
BAY
AT
SLAND
EACOCK
CT
DR
MCNEARS
BEACH
PARK
RIVIERA
MANOR
RD
BISCAYNE
CT
SAN
MARINO
CT
400
VIA
MONTEBELLO
DR
MARIN
PARK
CT
BAY
CANTERA
WY
R
1500
RD
POINT SAN PEDRO
SAN PEDRO HILL
BAY
MARIN
CO
CONTRA
COSTA
CO
CONTRA
CONTRA
COSTA
CO

SEE 568 MAP
SEE 587 MAP

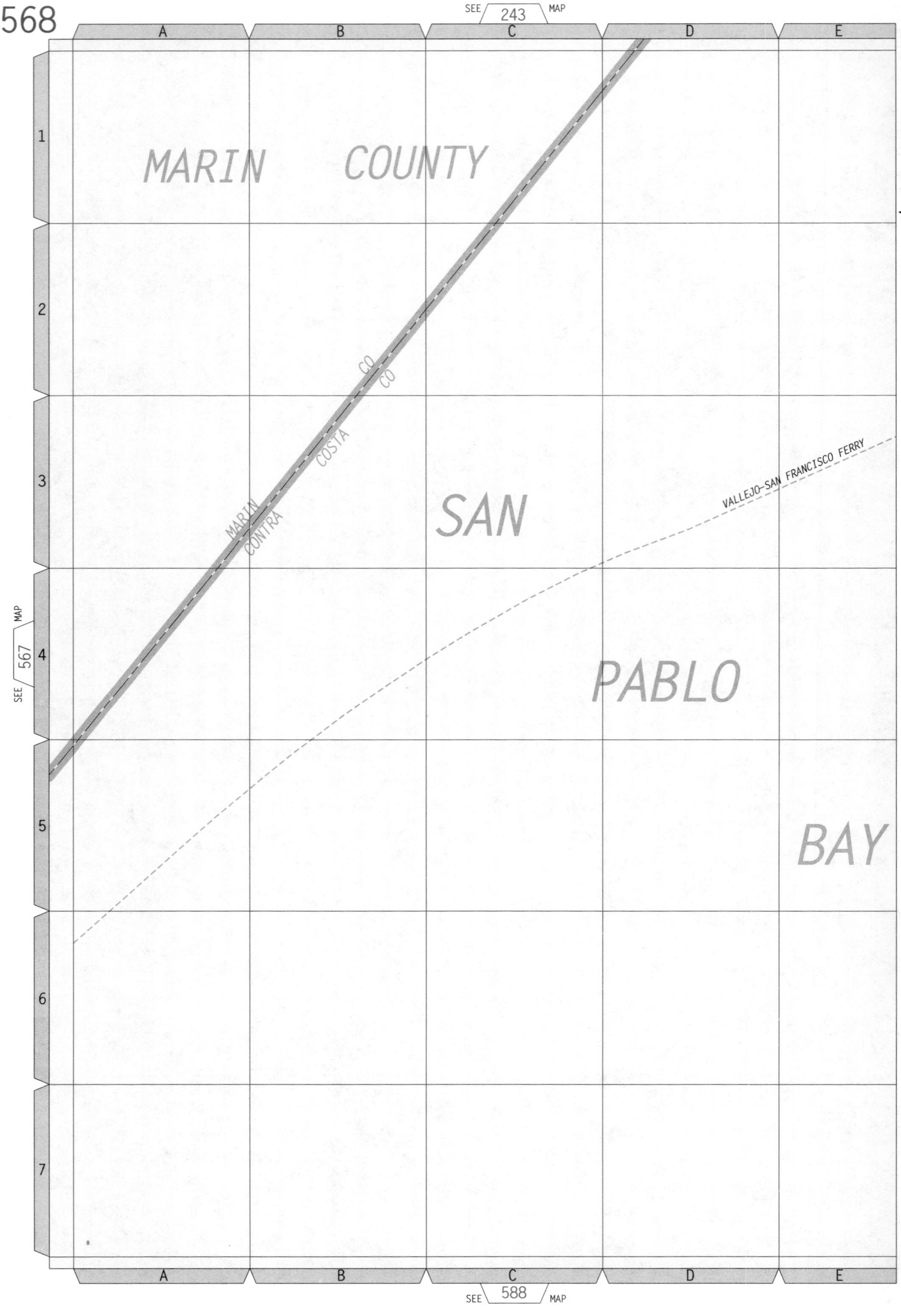
SEE 243 MAP
A
B
C
D
E
1
2
3
4
5
6
7
MARIN COUNTY
MARIN CO
CONTRA COSTA CO
SAN PABLO BAY
VALLEJO-SAN FRANCISCO FERRY
SEE 567 MAP
SEE 588 MAP

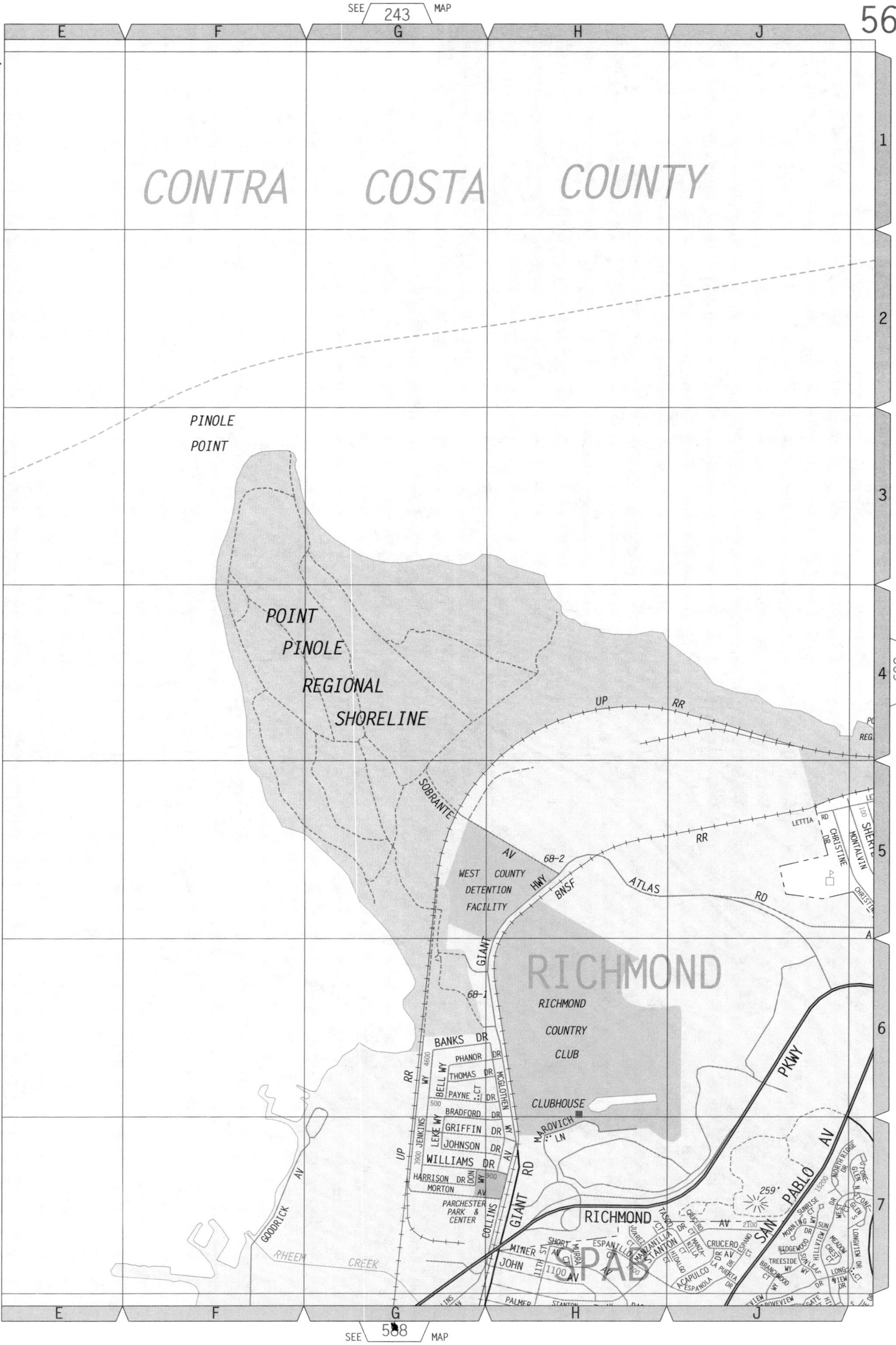
SEE 243 MAP
E
F
G
H
J
1
2
3
4
5
6
7
CONTRA COSTA COUNTY
PINOLE POINT
POINT PINOLE REGIONAL SHORELINE
SEE 569 MAP
UP RR
SOBRANTE AV
68-2
HWY
BNSF
RR
ATLAS RD
LETTIA
CHRISTINE DR
MONTALVIN
WEST COUNTY DETENTION FACILITY
GIANT
RICHMOND
68-1
RICHMOND COUNTRY CLUB
CLUBHOUSE
MAROVICH LN
BANKS DR
PHANOR DR
THOMAS DR
BELL WY
PAYNE CT
BRADFORD DR
GRIFFIN DR
JOHNSON DR
LEKE WY
JENKINS WY
WILLIAMS DR
HARRISON DR
MORTON AV
DON WY
MCGLOTHEN WY
UP RR
GIANT RD
PARCHESTER PARK & CENTER
COLLINS
PKWY
SAN PABLO AV
259'
RICHMOND AV
MINER AV
SHORT ST
JOHN AV
11TH ST
MURRA
ESPANILLO
STANTON
MANZANILLA
CRUCERO DR
ACAPULCO
ESPANOLA
TREESIDE WY
RIDGEWOOD
HILLVIEW
NORTH RIDGE DR
LONGVIEW DR
GOODRICK AV
RHEEM CREEK
PALMER
E
F
G
H
J
SEE 588 MAP

SEE 549 MAP

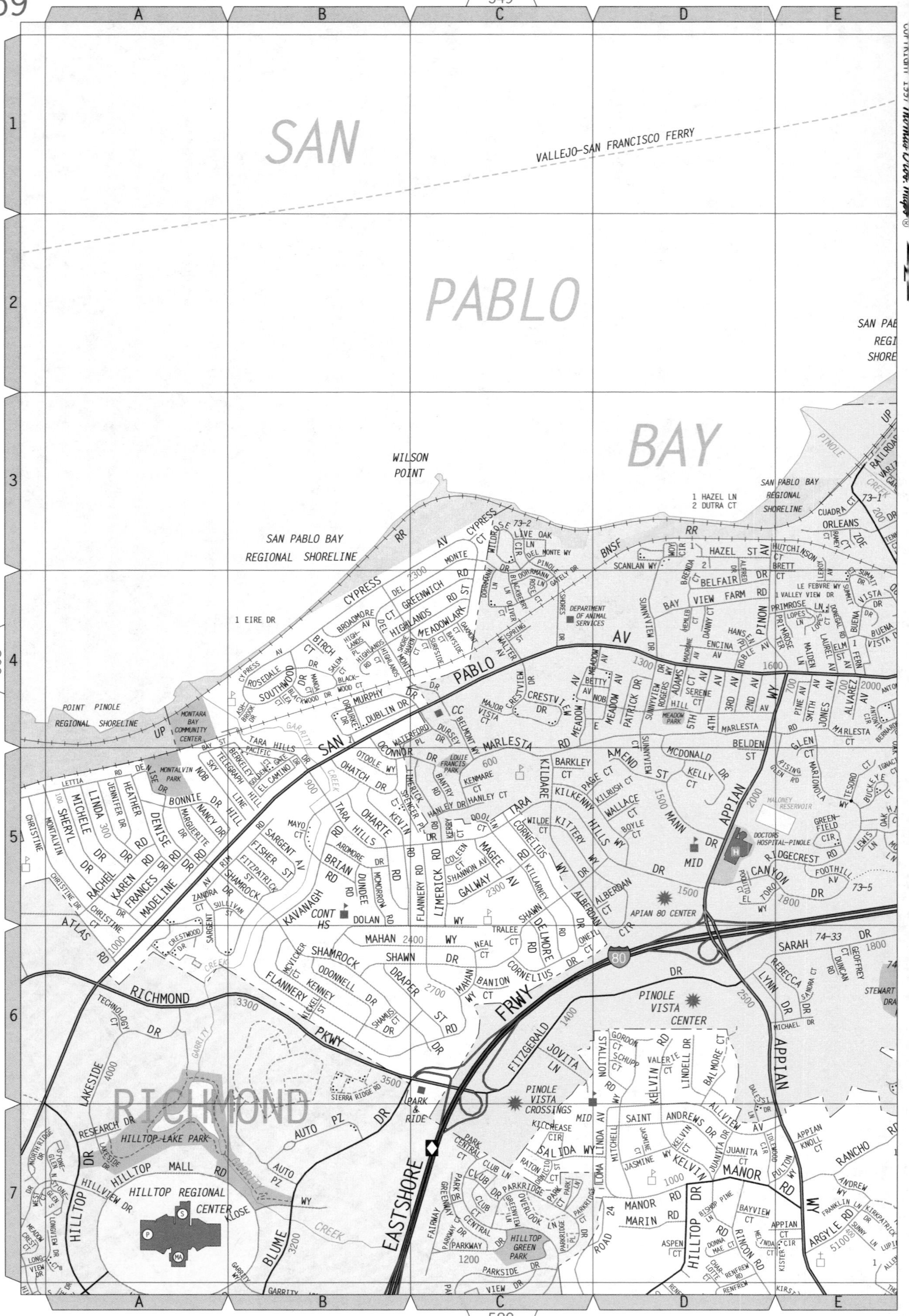
A
B
C
D
E
1
2
3
4
5
6
7
SAN
PABLO
BAY
VALLEJO-SAN FRANCISCO FERRY
WILSON
POINT
SAN PABLO BAY
REGIONAL SHORELINE
POINT PINOLE
REGIONAL SHORELINE
MONTARA BAY COMMUNITY CENTER
MONTALVIN PARK
1 EIRE DR
1 HAZEL LN
2 DUTRA CT
DEPARTMENT OF ANIMAL SERVICES
LOUIE FRANCIS PARK
MEADOW PARK
MALONEY RESERVOIR
DOCTORS HOSPITAL-PINOLE
APIAN 80 CENTER
PINOLE VISTA CENTER
PINOLE VISTA CROSSINGS
CONT HS
PARK & RIDE
RICHMOND
HILLTOP LAKE PARK
HILLTOP REGIONAL CENTER
HILLTOP GREEN PARK
SIERRA RIDGE RD
SAN PABLO AV
RICHMOND PKWY
EASTSHORE FRWY
APPIAN WY
ATLAS RD
HILLTOP DR
HILLTOP MALL RD
BLUME DR
FITZGERALD DR
MARLESTA RD
MANOR RD
GARRITY CREEK
PINOLE CREEK
CYPRESS AV
BNSF
RR
80

SEE 568 MAP

SEE 589 MAP

SEE 549 MAP

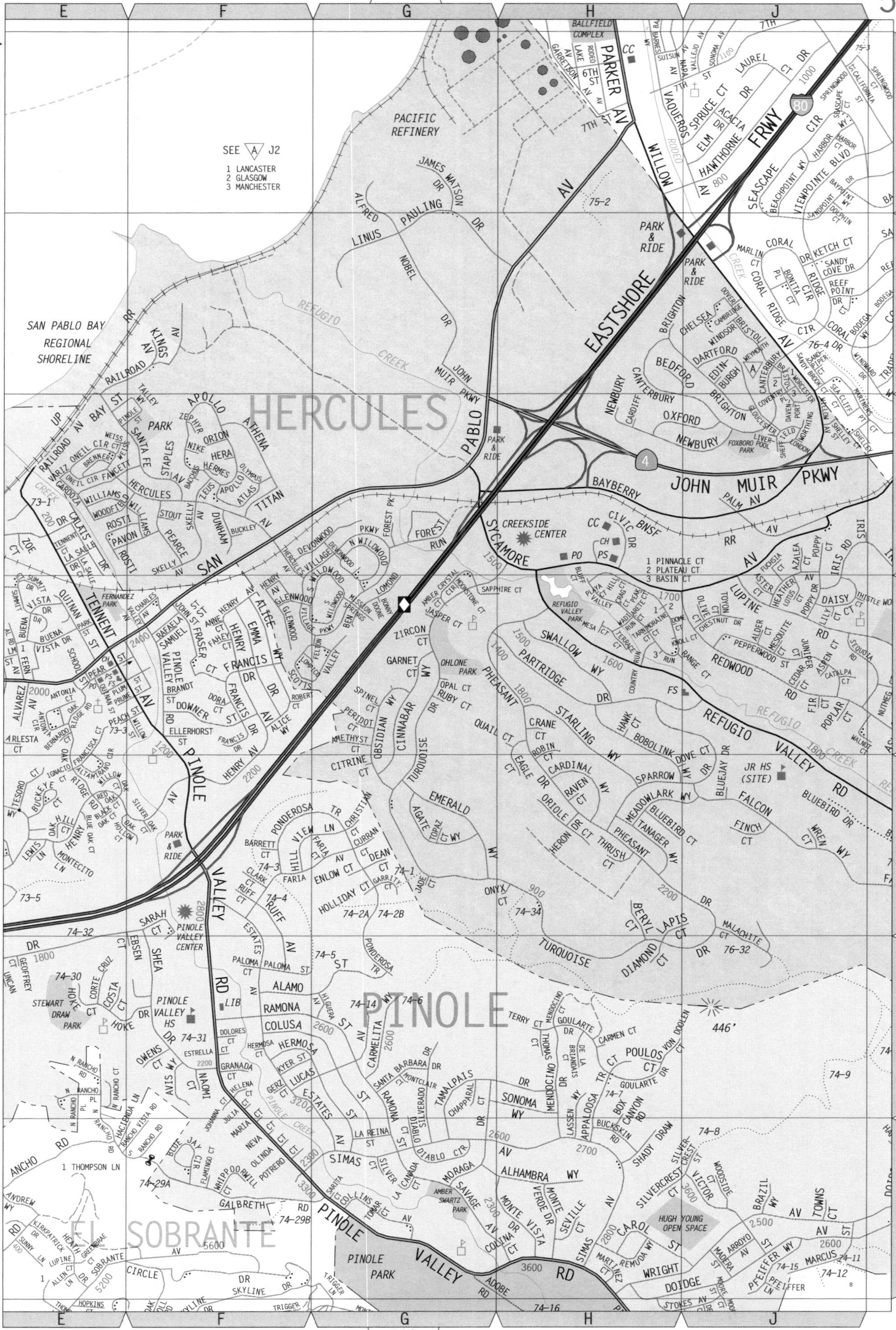
E
F
G
H
J
1
2
3
4
5
6
7
PACIFIC REFINERY
BALLFIELD COMPLEX
SEE A J2
1 LANCASTER
2 GLASGOW
3 MANCHESTER
SAN PABLO BAY REGIONAL SHORELINE
HERCULES
PINOLE
EL SOBRANTE
EASTSHORE FRWY
80
4
JOHN MUIR PKWY
PABLO AV
SAN PABLO AV
PARKER AV
WILLOW AV
REFUGIO CREEK
REFUGIO VALLEY RD
SYCAMORE AV
CREEKSIDE CENTER
PARK & RIDE
1 PINNACLE CT
2 PLATEAU CT
3 BASIN CT
REFUGIO VALLEY PARK
OHLONE PARK
JR HS (SITE)
FOXBORO POOL PARK
FERNANDEZ PARK
PINOLE VALLEY CENTER
PINOLE VALLEY RD
PINOLE VALLEY HS
STEWART DRAW PARK
PINOLE PARK
AMBER SWARTZ PARK
HUGH YOUNG OPEN SPACE
1 THOMPSON LN
TENNENT AV
TURQUOISE DR
APPIAN WY
446'
BNSF RR
RAILROAD AV

SEE 570 MAP

SEE 589 MAP

BAY AREA

MAP

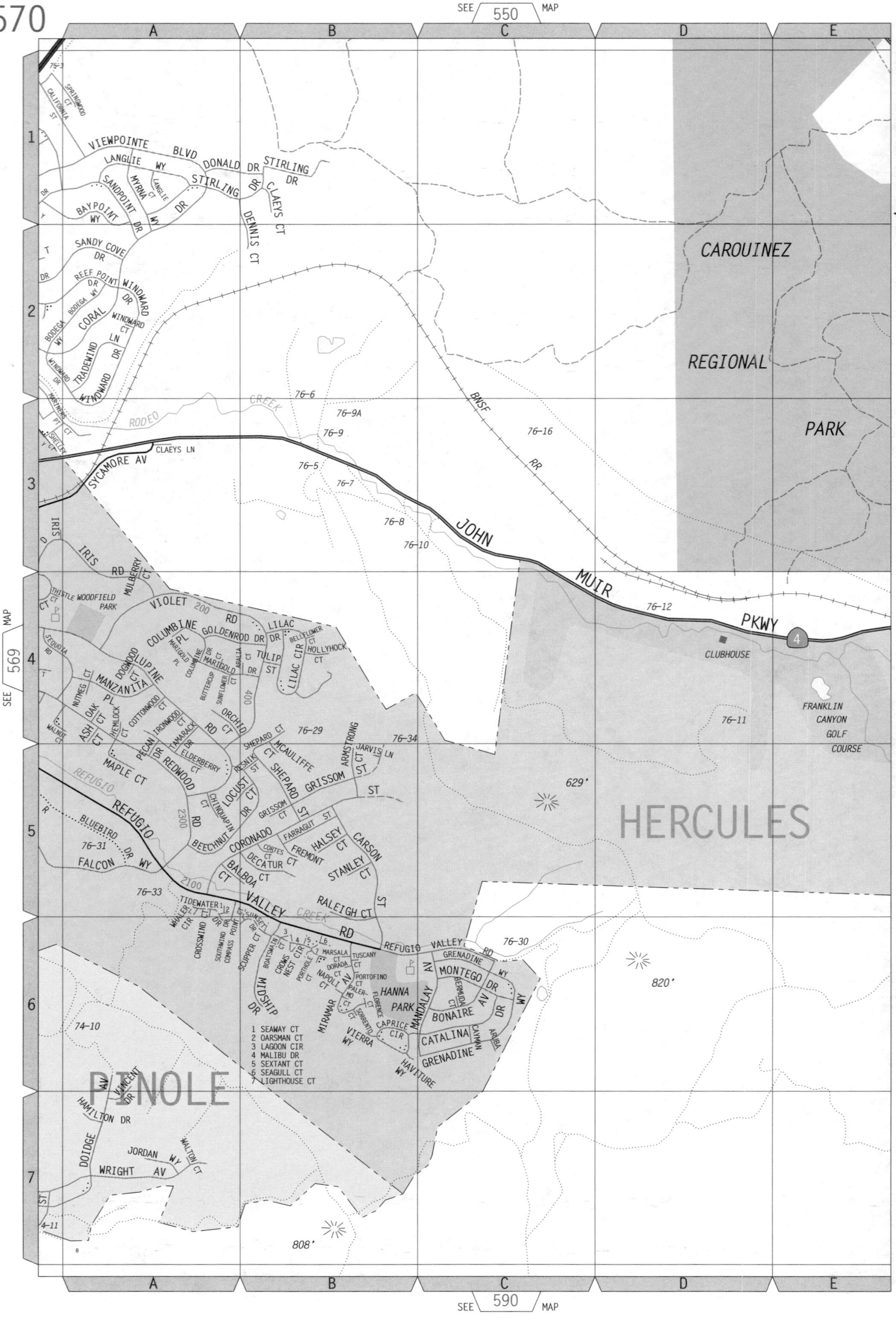
SEE 550 MAP
A
B
C
D
E
1
2
3
4
5
6
7
SEE 569 MAP
SEE 590 MAP
SPRINGWOOD CT
CALIFORNIA ST
VIEWPOINTE BLVD
LANGLIE WY
DONALD DR
STIRLING DR
STIRLING
MYRNA
LANGLIE CT
SANDPOINT DR
BAYPOINT WY
CLAEYS CT
DENNIS CT
SANDY COVE DR
REEF POINT DR
BODEGA WY
WINDWARD DR
CORAL
WINDWARD CT
TRADEWIND LN
WINDWARD DR
MARINERS PT
SHELLEY CT
RODEO CREEK
CLAEYS LN
SYCAMORE AV
BNSF RR
JOHN MUIR PKWY
4
CAROUINEZ REGIONAL PARK
CLUBHOUSE
FRANKLIN CANYON GOLF COURSE
IRIS RD
MULBERRY CT
THISTLE CT
WOODFIELD PARK
VIOLET RD
COLUMBINE PL
GOLDENROD DR
LILAC DR
BELLFLOWER CT
HOLLYHOCK CT
LILAC CIR
TULIP ST
SEQUOIA RD
MARIGOLD PL
MARIGOLD CT
AZALEA CT
BUTTERCUP CT
SUNFLOWER CT
ORCHID CT
DOGWOOD
LUPINE
MANZANITA
NUTMEG CT
OAK PL
ASH CT
WALNUT CT
HEMLOCK CT
COTTONWOOD CT
IRONWOOD CT
TAMARACK CT
PECAN DR
ELDERBERRY CT
REDWOOD RD
MAPLE CT
SHEPARD CT
MCAULIFFE CT
ARMSTRONG ST
JARVIS LN
GRISSOM ST
SHEPARD ST
RESNIK CT
LOCUST DR
CHINQUAPIN CT
BEECHNUT CT
GRISSOM CT
FARRAGUT ST
HALSEY CT
CARSON ST
CORONADO
CORTES CT
FREMONT CT
DECATUR CT
BALBOA CT
STANLEY CT
RALEIGH CT
REFUGIO VALLEY RD
REFUGIO CREEK
BLUEBIRD DR
FALCON WY
629'
HERCULES
TIDEWATER
WHALER CIR
CROSSWIND DR
SOUTHWIND DR
COMPASS POINT
SUNSET
SCUPPER CT
BOATSWAIN CT
CROWS NEST CIR
PORTHOLE CT
MIDSHIP DR
MARSALA CT
TUSCANY CT
DORADA CT
PORTOFINO CT
NAPOLI AV
PALERMO CT
FLORENCE CT
SORRENTO CT
MIRAMAR CT
VIERRA WY
HANNA PARK
CAPRICE CIR
MANDALAY AV
GRENADINE WY
MONTEGO DR
BERMUDA CT
BONAIRE AV
CATALINA CT
CAYMAN CT
ARUBA CT
GRENADINE
HAVITURE WY
820'
1 SEAWAY CT
2 OARSMAN CT
3 LAGOON CIR
4 MALIBU DR
5 SEXTANT CT
6 SEAGULL CT
7 LIGHTHOUSE CT
PINOLE
VINCENT DR
HAMILTON DR
DOIDGE AV
JORDAN WY
WALTON CT
WRIGHT AV
808'

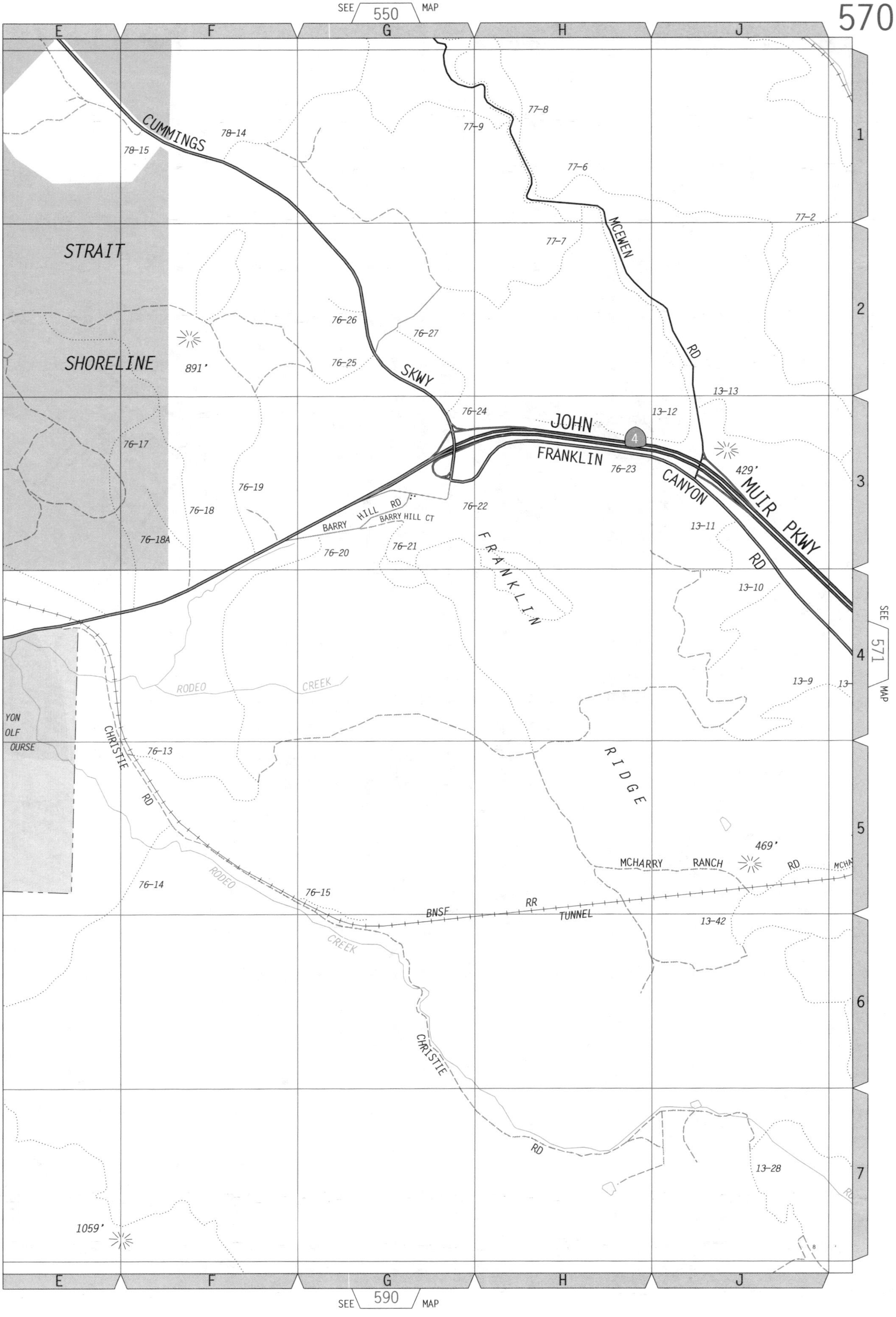
SEE 550 MAP
E
F
G
H
J
1
2
3
4
5
6
7
CUMMINGS
SKWY
78-14
78-15
77-8
77-9
77-6
77-7
77-2
MCEWEN
RD
STRAIT
SHORELINE
891'
76-26
76-27
76-25
13-13
13-12
76-24
JOHN
4
FRANKLIN
76-23
CANYON
RD
MUIR PKWY
429'
76-17
76-19
76-18
76-18A
BARRY HILL RD
BARRY HILL CT
76-22
76-20
76-21
13-11
FRANKLIN
13-10
SEE 571 MAP
13-9
13-
RODEO CREEK
YON
OLF
OURSE
CHRISTIE RD
76-13
RIDGE
469'
MCHARRY RANCH RD
MCHA
76-14
RODEO
76-15
BNSF RR TUNNEL
13-42
CREEK
CHRISTIE RD
13-28
1059'
SEE 590 MAP

SEE 551 MAP

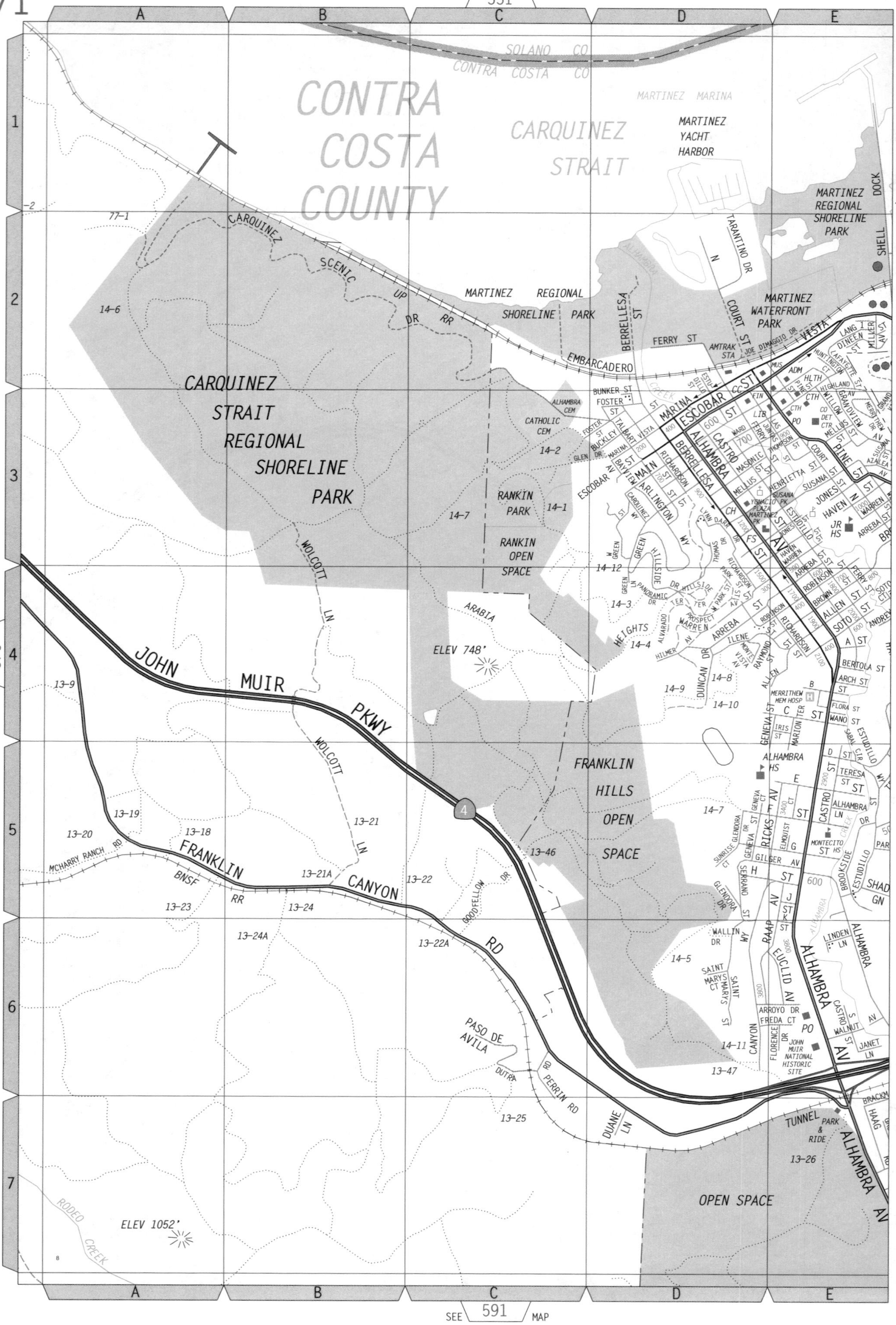
A B C D E
1 2 3 4 5 6 7
SOLANO CO
CONTRA COSTA CO
CONTRA COSTA COUNTY
CARQUINEZ STRAIT
MARTINEZ MARINA
MARTINEZ YACHT HARBOR
MARTINEZ REGIONAL SHORELINE PARK
DOCK
SHELL
CARQUINEZ SCENIC DR
UP RR
MARTINEZ REGIONAL SHORELINE PARK
MARTINEZ WATERFRONT PARK
TARANTINO DR
COURT ST
BERRELLESA ST
FERRY ST
AMTRAK STA
JOE DIMAGGIO DR
VISTA
EMBARCADERO
CARQUINEZ STRAIT REGIONAL SHORELINE PARK
ALHAMBRA CEM
CATHOLIC CEM
BUNKER ST
FOSTER
MARINA
ESCOBAR ST
ALHAMBRA
BERRELLESA
CASTRO
MAIN ST
ARLINGTON
ESCOBAR
RANKIN PARK
RANKIN OPEN SPACE
WOLCOTT LN
ARABIA
HEIGHTS
ELEV 748'
JOHN MUIR PKWY
4
WOLCOTT LN
FRANKLIN HILLS OPEN SPACE
MERRITHEW MEM HOSP
ALHAMBRA HS
JR HS
PINE
SUSANA
FRANKLIN CANYON RD
MCHARRY RANCH RD
BNSF RR
GOODFELLOW DR
PASO DE AVILA
OUTRA
PERRIN RD
DUANE LN
TUNNEL
PARK & RIDE
ALHAMBRA AV
OPEN SPACE
JOHN MUIR NATIONAL HISTORIC SITE
EUCLID AV
ELEV 1052'
RODEO CREEK
77-1
14-6
14-7
14-2
14-1
14-12
14-3
14-4
14-9
14-8
14-10
14-7
14-5
14-11
13-47
13-9
13-19
13-20
13-18
13-21
13-21A
13-22
13-23
13-24
13-24A
13-22A
13-46
13-25
13-26
SEE 570 MAP

SEE 591 MAP

SEE 551 MAP

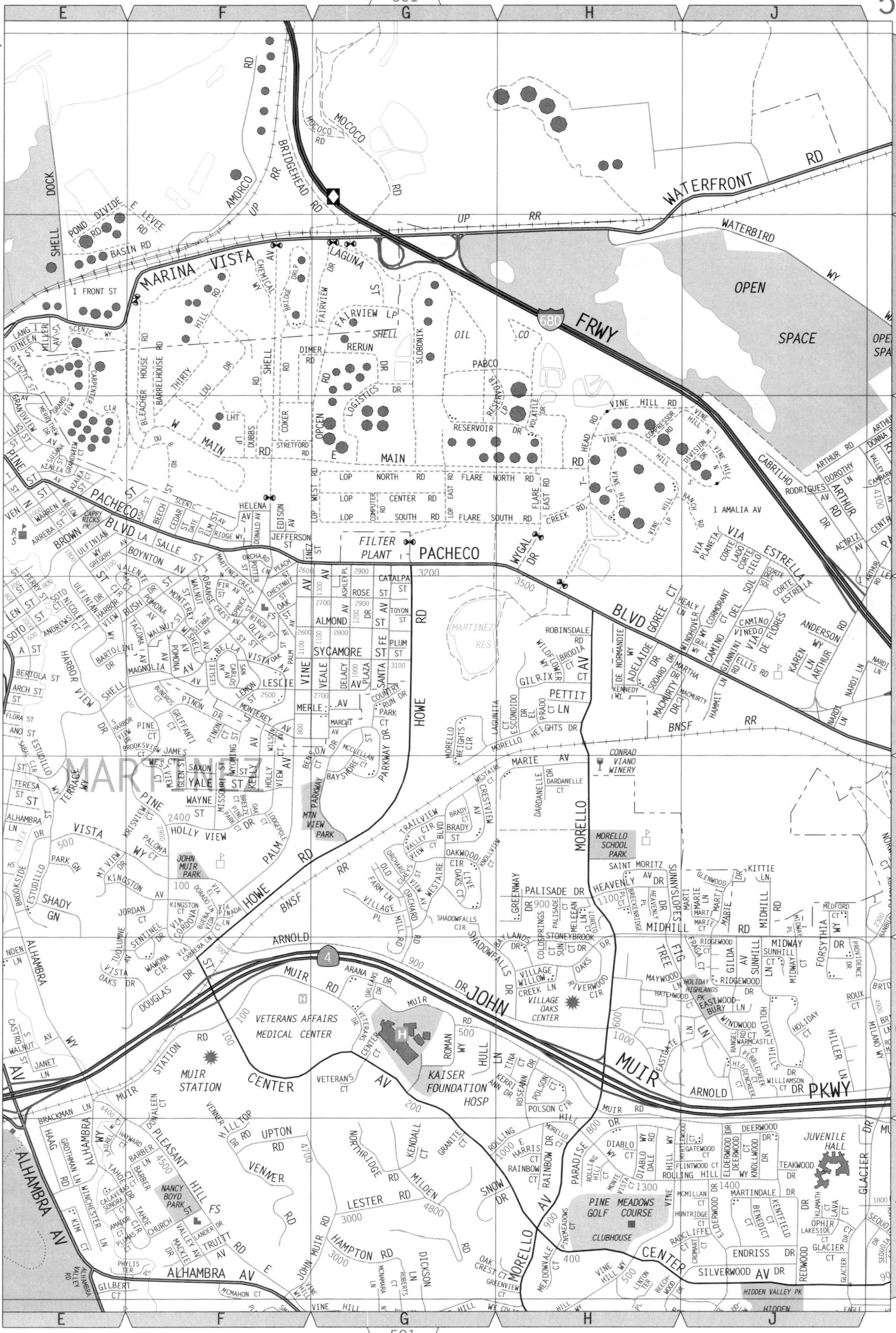
E
F
G
H
J
1
2
3
4
5
6
7
MARTINEZ
WATERFRONT RD
WATERBIRD WY
OPEN SPACE
680
FRWY
MARINA VISTA
BRIDGEHEAD RD
MOCOCO RD
UP RR
SHELL
DOCK
BASIN RD
1 FRONT ST
PACHECO BLVD
FILTER PLANT
PACHECO
MAIN
RESERVOIR DR
VINE HILL RD
CABRILHO
1 AMALIA AV
VIA ESTRELLA
MARTINEZ RES
BNSF RR
HOWE RD
MORELLO AV
CONRAD VIANO WINERY
MORELLO SCHOOL PARK
MTN VIEW PARK
JOHN MUIR PARK
ARNOLD DR
4
JOHN MUIR PKWY
VETERANS AFFAIRS MEDICAL CENTER
KAISER FOUNDATION HOSP
MUIR STATION
CENTER AV
VILLAGE OAKS CENTER
HOLIDAY HIGHLANDS PK
EASTWOOD BURY
NANCY BOYD PARK
PINE MEADOWS GOLF COURSE
CLUBHOUSE
JUVENILE HALL
HIDDEN VALLEY PK
ALHAMBRA AV
PLEASANT HILL RD
SILVERWOOD AV
GLACIER DR
VINE HILL WY

SEE 572 MAP

SEE 591 MAP

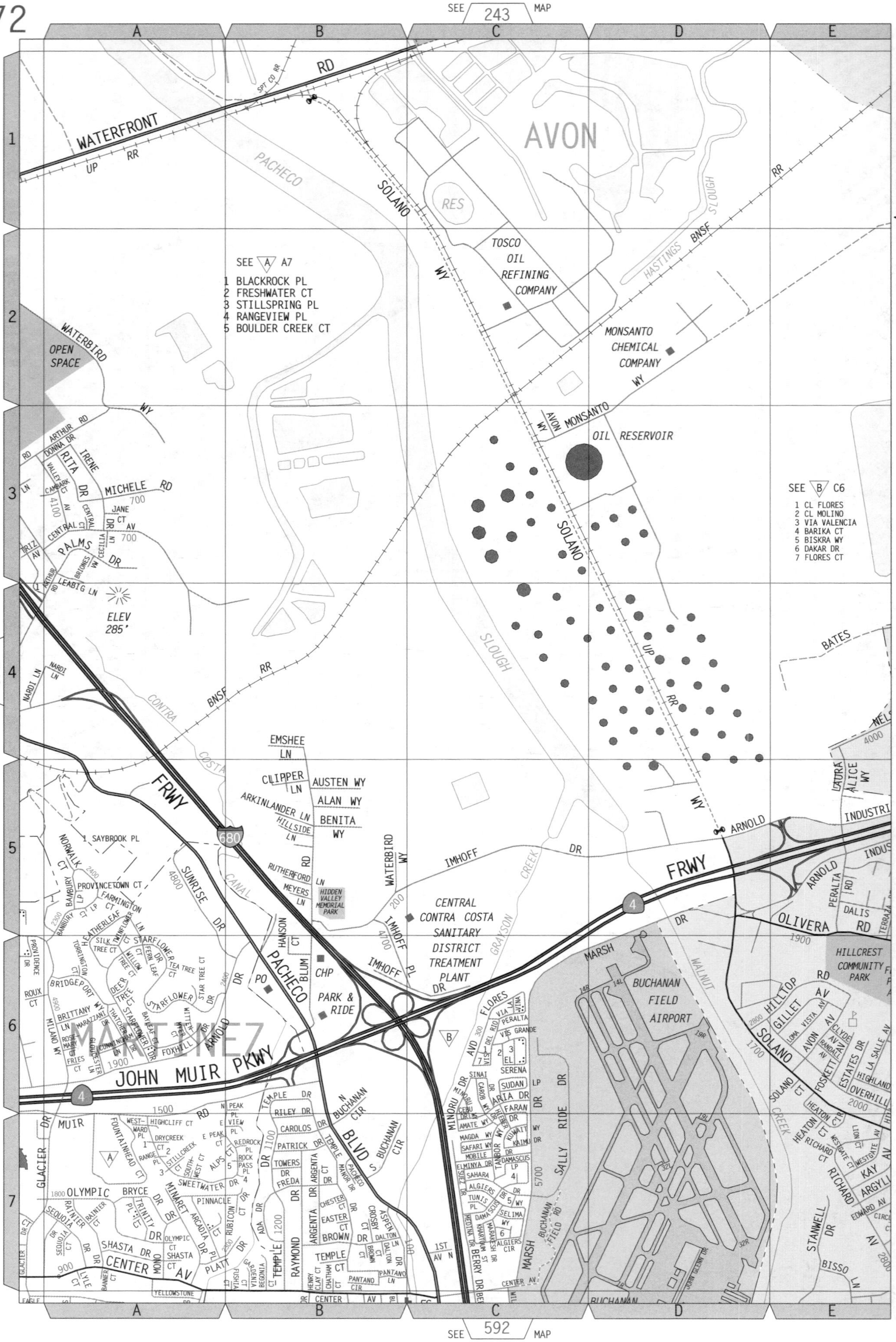
SEE 243 MAP
SEE 592 MAP
SEE 571 MAP
A
B
C
D
E
1
2
3
4
5
6
7
AVON
WATERFRONT RD
UP RR
SPT CO RR
PACHECO
SOLANO WY
RES
TOSCO OIL REFINING COMPANY
HASTINGS SLOUGH
BNSF RR
MONSANTO CHEMICAL COMPANY
MONSANTO WY
AVON WY
OIL RESERVOIR
SEE A A7
1 BLACKROCK PL
2 FRESHWATER CT
3 STILLSPRING PL
4 RANGEVIEW PL
5 BOULDER CREEK CT
SEE B C6
1 CL FLORES
2 CL MOLINO
3 VIA VALENCIA
4 BARIKA CT
5 BISKRA WY
6 DAKAR DR
7 FLORES CT
OPEN SPACE
WATERBIRD WY
ARTHUR RD
DONNA DR
RITA DR
IRENE
MICHELE RD
JANE CT
CENTRAL AV
PALMS DR
LEABIG LN
ELEV 285'
NARDI LN
CONTRA COSTA CANAL
SLOUGH
BATES
FRWY
680
EMSHEE LN
CLIPPER LN
AUSTEN WY
ARKINLANDER LN
ALAN WY
HILLSIDE LN
BENITA WY
RUTHERFORD LN
MEYERS LN
HIDDEN VALLEY MEMORIAL PARK
WATERBIRD WY
IMHOFF DR
IMHOFF PL
ARNOLD
UP RR
GRAYSON CREEK
CENTRAL CONTRA COSTA SANITARY DISTRICT TREATMENT PLANT
1 SAYBROOK PL
NORWALK CT
PROVINCETOWN CT
FARMINGTON CT
HEATHERLEAF LN
STARFLOWER CT
SUNRISE DR
HANSON CT
PACHECO BLVD
BLUM
CHP
PO
PARK & RIDE
MARSH DR
BUCHANAN FIELD AIRPORT
WALNUT CREEK
HILLCREST COMMUNITY PARK
INDUSTRIAL
OLIVERA RD
ARNOLD
PERALTA
DALIS
LAURA ALICE WY
NELSON
HILLTOP RD
GILLET AV
LOMA VISTA AV
AVON AV
SOLANO
CLYDE
FOSKETT AV
ESTATES DR
LA SALLE AV
HIGHLAND
OVERHILL
HEATON CIR
RICHARD CT
KAY AV
ARGYLE
EDWARD AV
STANWELL DR
BISSO LN
MARTINEZ
BRIDGEPORT
BRITTANY WY
ROUX CT
MILANO WY
FOXHILL
ARNOLD DR
JOHN MUIR PKWY
4
MUIR RD
FOUNTAINHEAD CT
HIGHCLIFF CT
DRYCREEK
STILLCREEK
ALPS CT
REDROCK PL
SWEETWATER
MINARET DR
PINNACLE
GLACIER DR
OLYMPIC
BRYCE
TRINITY PL
RAINIER
SEQUOIA CT
SHASTA DR
CENTER AV
LYLE CT
YELLOWSTONE
RUBICON CT
ARCADIA DR
PLATT DR
ADA DR
TEMPLE DR
RILEY DR
CAROLOS
PATRICK DR
TOWERS
FREDA
ARGENTA DR
CHESTER
EASTER CT
BROWN
RAYMOND DR
CROSBY
ASPEN
DALTON LN
PANTANO LN
N BUCHANAN CIR
BUCHANAN CIR
BLVD
TEMPLE MANOR DR
PACHECO MANOR DR
1ST AV N
FLORES
VIA DEL RIO
PERALTA
VIS GRANDE
SERENA
EL
SINAI
MINORU DR
CEBU
SUDAN
ARIA DR
FARAN
HEBRA
KAIMU DR
SAFARI WY
MOBILE
DAMASCUS
ALGIERS
SAHARA
TUNIS PL
SELIMA
MEDINA DR
KHARTOUM ST
BERRY DR
ALGIERS CIR
BUCHANAN FIELD RD
MARSH DR
SALLY RIDE DR
CENTER AV
JOHN GLENN DR
BUCHANAN
CENTER AV

SEE 243 MAP

UNITED STATES
NAVAL WEAPONS
STATION CONCORD
(PORT CHICAGO)
CLYDE
MALLARD
RESERVOIR
CLYDE PARK
DIABLO
CREEK
GOLF
COURSE
CLUBHOUSE
MEMORY
GARDENS
CEM
UNITED STATES
NAVAL WEAPONS
STATION CONCORD
CONCORD
HILLCREST
COMMUNITY
PARK
FERNANDO
PACHECO
ADOBE
SUN
TERRACE
PARK
BAYVIEW
CIRCLE
PARK
PARK
&
RIDE
JOHN F
BALDWIN PARK
WILLOW
PASS
COMMUNITY
PARK
PORT CHICAGO HWY
FRWY
WILLOW PASS RD
OLIVERA RD
INDUSTRIAL WY
BATES AV
ARNOLD INDUSTRIAL WY
SEE 573 MAP
SEE 592 MAP

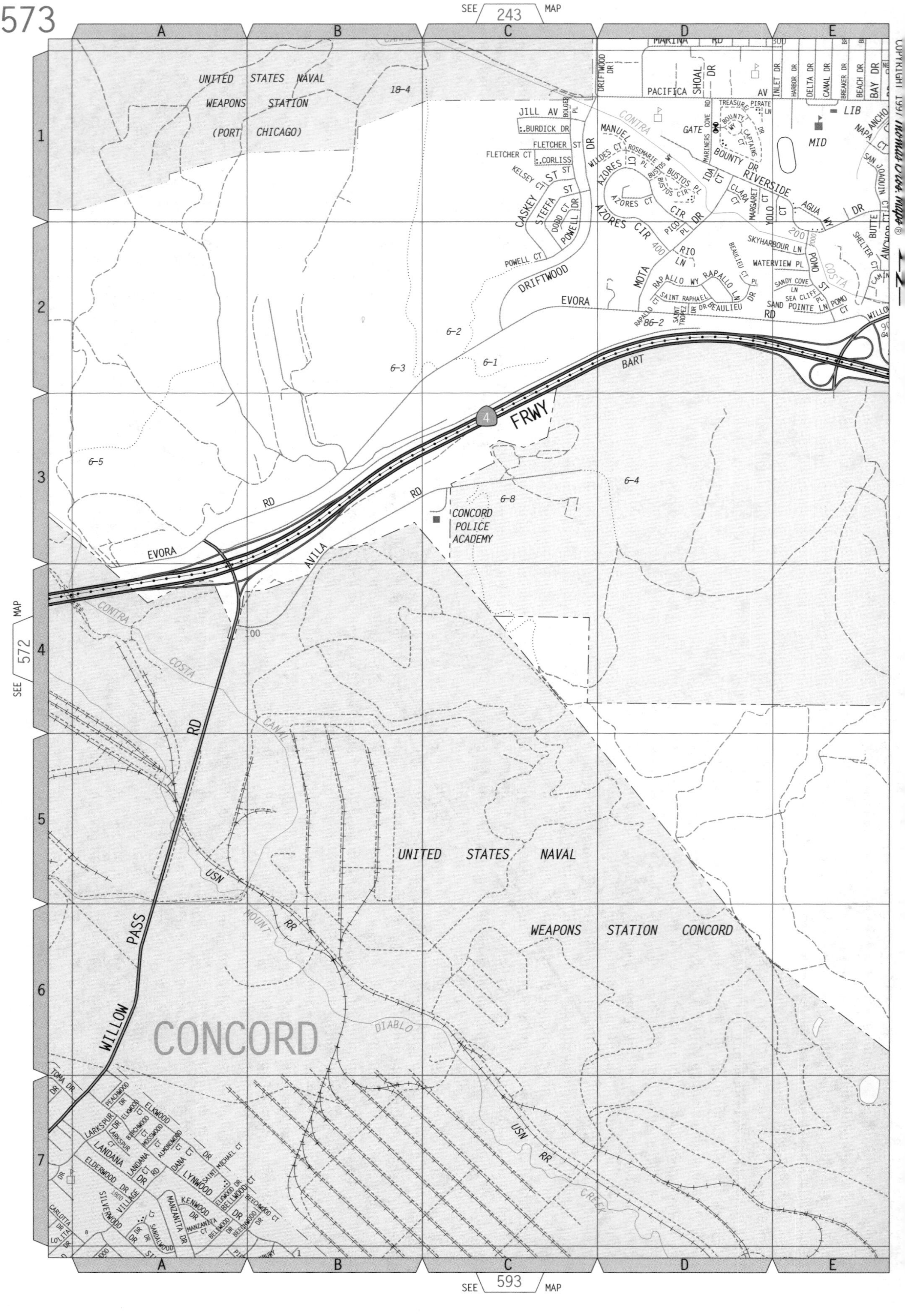
SEE 243 MAP
SEE 572 MAP
SEE 593 MAP
UNITED STATES NAVAL WEAPONS STATION (PORT CHICAGO)
UNITED STATES NAVAL WEAPONS STATION CONCORD
CONCORD
CONCORD POLICE ACADEMY
FRWY
BART
EVORA RD
AVILA RD
WILLOW PASS RD
CONTRA COSTA CANAL
USN RR
MOUNT DIABLO CREEK
MARINA RD
PACIFICA AV
SHOAL DR
DRIFTWOOD DR
JILL AV
BOLGER PL
BURDICK DR
FLETCHER ST
FLETCHER CT
CORLISS
KELSEY CT
CASKEY ST
STEFFA ST
DODD CT
POWELL DR
POWELL CT
MANUEL DR
WILDES CT
ROSEMARIE PL
AZORES CT
AZORES CIR
BUSTOS WY
BUSTOS PL
BUSTOS CIR
GATE
MARINERS COVE RD
TREASURE DR
PIRATE LN
BOUNTY WY
BOUNTY DR
CAPTAINS CT
IDA CT
CLARA CT
MARGARET CT
YOLO CT
RIVERSIDE DR
AGUA WY
PICO PL
RIO LN
MOTA DR
RAPALLO WY
RAPALLO LN
RAPALLO CT
SAINT RAPHAEL DR
SAINT TROPEZ DR
BEAULIEU CT
BEAULIEU DR
EVORA RD
SKYHARBOUR LN
WATERVIEW PL
SANDY COVE LN
SEA CLIFF PL
SAND POINTE LN
POMO ST
POMO CT
INLET DR
HARBOR DR
DELTA DR
CANAL DR
BREAKER DR
BEACH DR
BAY DR
LIB
MID
NAPA
ANCHOR
SAN JOAQUIN CT
BUTTE
SHELTER
COSTA
6-1
6-2
6-3
6-4
6-5
6-8
18-4
86-2
TOMA DR
PEACHWOOD DR
ELKWOOD CT
ELKWOOD DR
BIRCHWOOD CT
LARKSPUR DR
LARKSPUR CT
MOSSWOOD CT
ALMONDWOOD CT
LANDANA DR
LANDANA CT
DANA CT
ELDERWOOD DR
LYNWOOD DR
SAINT MICHAEL CT
SILVERWOOD DR
VILLAGE DR
KENWOOD DR
ELMWOOD DR
BELLWOOD CT
MANZANITA DR
MANZANITA CT
BEECHWOOD CT
BEECHWOOD DR
SANDALWOOD DR
CARLOTTA DR
LOLITA DR
A B C D E
1 2 3 4 5 6 7

SEE 243 MAP
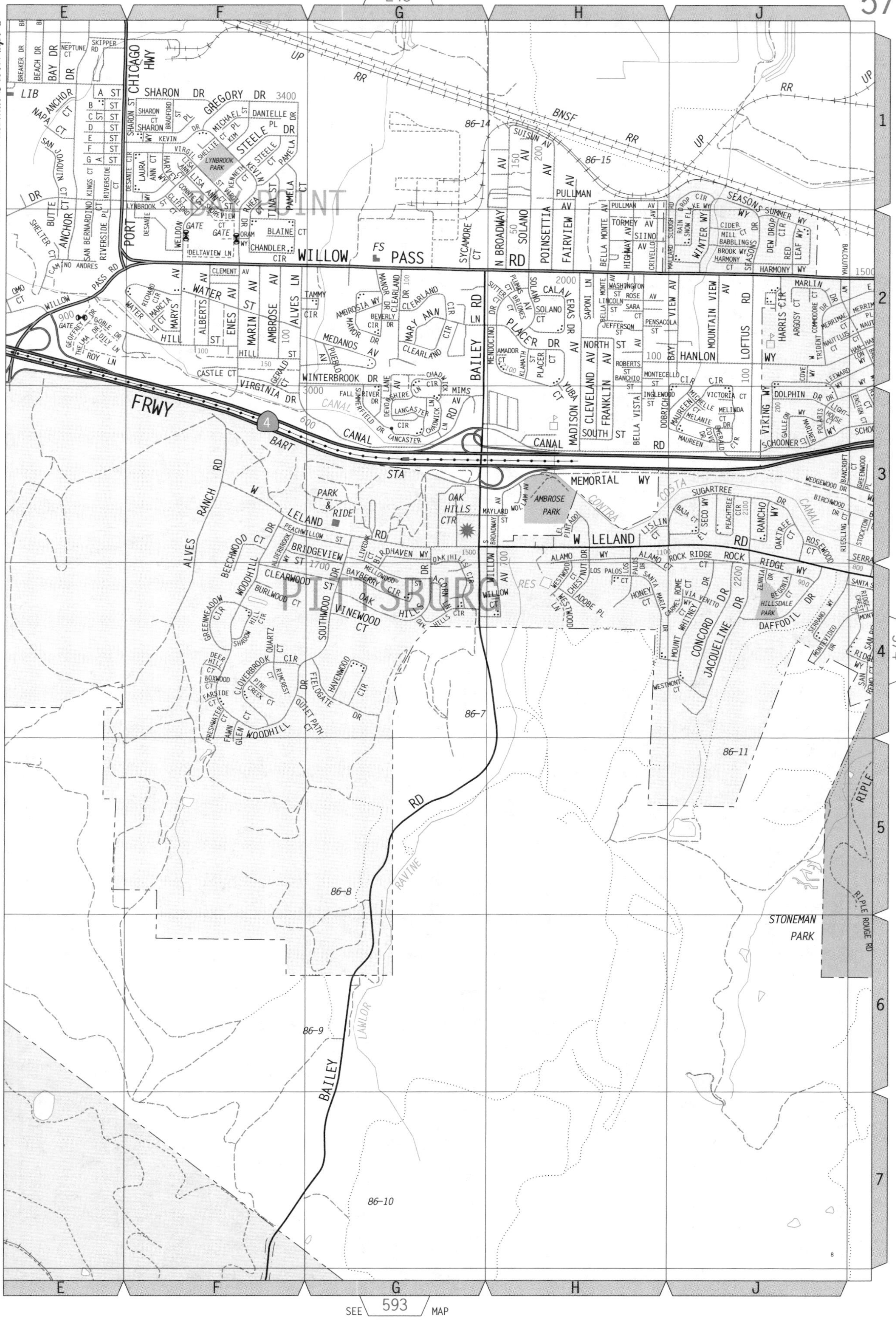
BAY POINT
PITTSBURG
WILLOW PASS RD
PORT CHICAGO HWY
FRWY
4
BART
STA
CANAL RD
W LELAND RD
MEMORIAL WY
BAILEY RD
RD
BAILEY
CONTRA COSTA CANAL
LAWLOR
RAVINE
RIPLE
ROUGE RD
STONEMAN PARK
AMBROSE PARK
LYNBROOK PARK
HILLSDALE PARK
OAK HILLS CTR
PARK & RIDE
FS
LIB
RES
BNSF RR
UP RR
86-14
86-15
86-7
86-8
86-9
86-10
86-11
SHARON DR
GREGORY DR
STEELE DR
WATER ST
MARIN AV
AMBROSE AV
ALVES LN
MEDANOS AV
CLEARLAND DR
MARY ANN LN
WINTERBROOK DR
VIRGINIA DR
CASTLE CT
N BROADWAY AV
SOLANO AV
POINSETTIA AV
FAIRVIEW AV
PULLMAN AV
CALAVERAS DR
PLACER DR
MADISON AV
CLEVELAND AV
FRANKLIN AV
BELLA VISTA AV
BAY VIEW AV
HANLON WY
MOUNTAIN VIEW DR
LOFTUS RD
HARRIS CIR
WINTER WY
SEASONS CIR
SUMMER WY
DOLPHIN DR
SCHOONER CT
VIKING DR
MARLIN DR
HARMONY CT
ROCK RIDGE RD
ROCK RIDGE WY
BRIDGEVIEW DR
CLEARWOOD DR
VINEWOOD CT
SOUTHWOOD DR
OAK HILLS CIR
ACORN LN
BAYBERRY CIR
DHAVEN WY
BEECHWOOD CT
WOODHILL DR
GREENMEADOW CIR
CLOVERBROOK CIR
HAVENWOOD CIR
FIELDGATE DR
QUIET PATH CT
ALVES RANCH RD
W LELAND RD
SUGARTREE DR
PEACHTREE CIR
RANCHO WY
OAKTREE CT
ROSEWOOD DR
CONCORD DR
JACQUELINE DR
MOUNT WHITNEY DR
DAFFODIL DR
WESTWOOD LN
CHESTNUT DR
ADOBE PL
ALAMO WY
HONEY CT
WESTMONT CT
SAN JOAQUIN CT
ANCHOR CT
BUTTE CT
SHELTER CT
CAMINO ANDRES
ROY LN
SEE 574 MAP
SEE 593 MAP

SEE 243 MAP

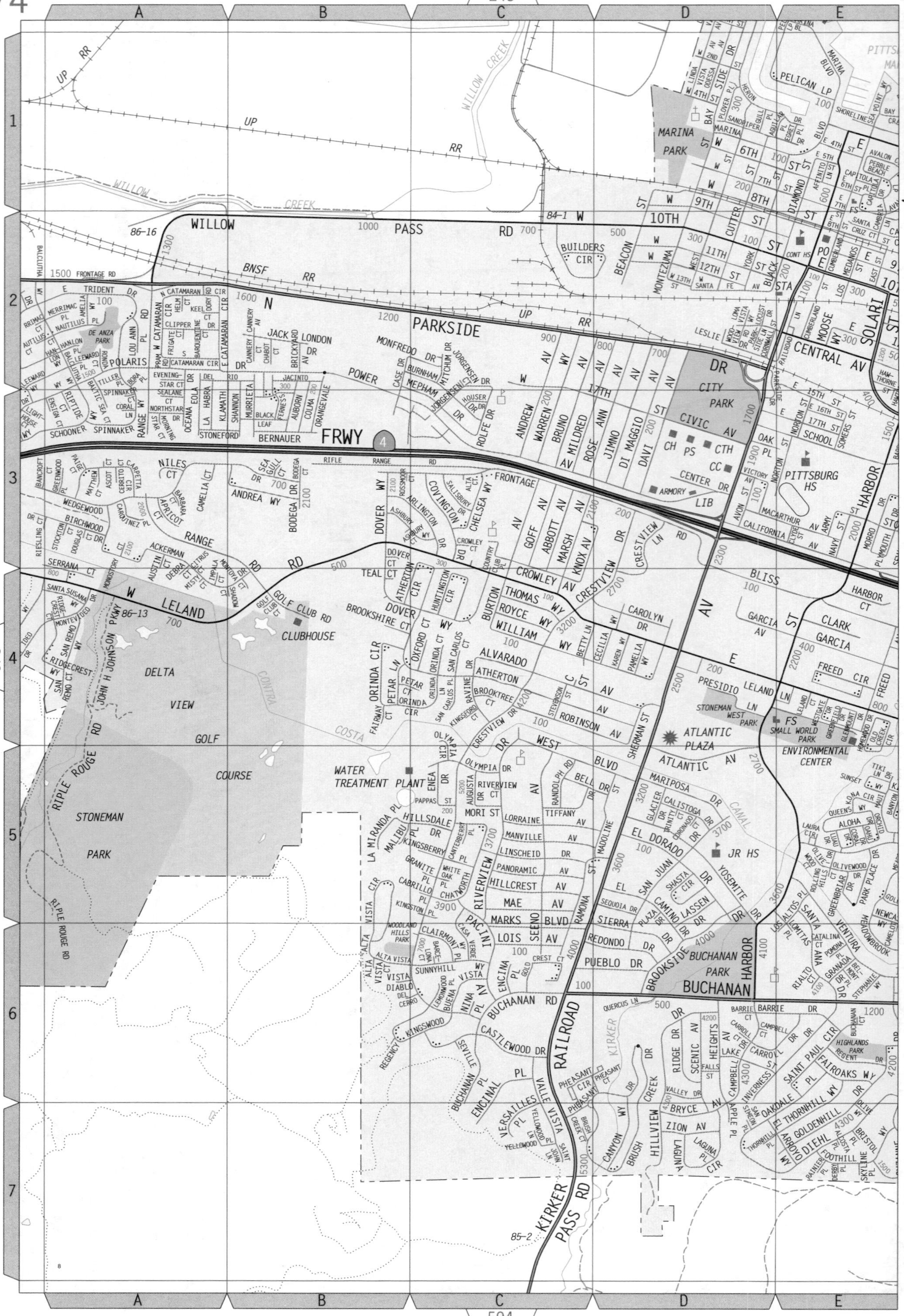

A
B
C
D
E
1
2
3
4
5
6
7
UP RR
WILLOW CREEK
WILLOW PASS RD
BNSF RR
N PARKSIDE DR
FRONTAGE RD
TRIDENT DR
DE ANZA PARK
POLARIS
JACK LONDON DR
MONFREDO DR
POWER
FRWY
4
SCHOONER
SPINNAKER
STONEFORD
BERNAUER
RIFLE RANGE RD
NILES CT
ANDREA WY
BODEGA DR
DOVER WY
COVINGTON
CHELSEA WY
RANGE RD
W LELAND RD
JOHN H JOHNSON PKWY
GOLF CLUB RD
CLUBHOUSE
DELTA VIEW GOLF COURSE
CONTRA COSTA CANAL
RIPLE ROUGE RD
STONEMAN PARK
WATER TREATMENT PLANT
WEST BLVD
ATLANTIC AV
ATLANTIC PLAZA
STONEMAN WEST PARK
SMALL WORLD PARK
ENVIRONMENTAL CENTER
FS
CROWLEY AV
CRESTVIEW DR
THOMAS WY
ROYCE WY
WILLIAM WY
ALVARADO
ATHERTON
ROBINSON AV
BLISS
GARCIA AV
CLARK
FREED CIR
PRESIDIO
LELAND LN
MARINA PARK
10TH ST
BUILDERS CIR
BEACON
MONTEZUMA
CUTTER
DIAMOND
CENTRAL AV
SOLARI ST
CITY PARK
CIVIC AV
CH
PS
CTH
CC
CENTER DR
ARMORY
LIB
PITTSBURG HS
HARBOR ST
CALIFORNIA AV
MACARTHUR
RAILROAD AV
17TH
ANDREW AV
WARREN AV
BRUNO AV
MILDRED AV
ROSE AV
ANN AV
JIMNO AV
DI MAGGIO AV
DAVI AV
GOFF AV
ABBOTT AV
MARSH AV
KNOX AV
MARIPOSA
EL DORADO
SAN JUAN
YOSEMITE DR
JR HS
HILLSDALE DR
MORI ST
LORRAINE
MANVILLE AV
LINSCHEID DR
PANORAMIC AV
HILLCREST AV
MAE AV
MARKS BLVD
LOIS AV
RIVERVIEW
PACINI
SEENO
RAMONA
MADOLINE
SIERRA
REDONDO
PUEBLO DR
BROOKSIDE DR
BUCHANAN PARK
BUCHANAN RD
HARBOR
KIRKER PASS RD
KIRKER CREEK
CASTLEWOOD DR
KINGSWOOD
ENCINAL PL
VALLE VISTA
VERSAILLES
HILLVIEW DR
ZION AV
BRYCE
CANYON WY
BRUSH CREEK
SCENIC AV
HEIGHTS
CAMPBELL
INVERNESS
OAKDALE
THORNHILL WY
GOLDENHILL
DIEHL
FOOTHILL
SAINT PAUL CIR
FAIROAKS WY
HIGHLANDS PARK
LOS ALTOS PL
SANTA ANA
RIALTO
VENTURA
GREENBRIAR
PARK PLACE DR
MEADOWBROOK
CATALINA
86-16
86-13
84-1
85-2

SEE 573 MAP

SEE 594 MAP

SEE 243 MAP

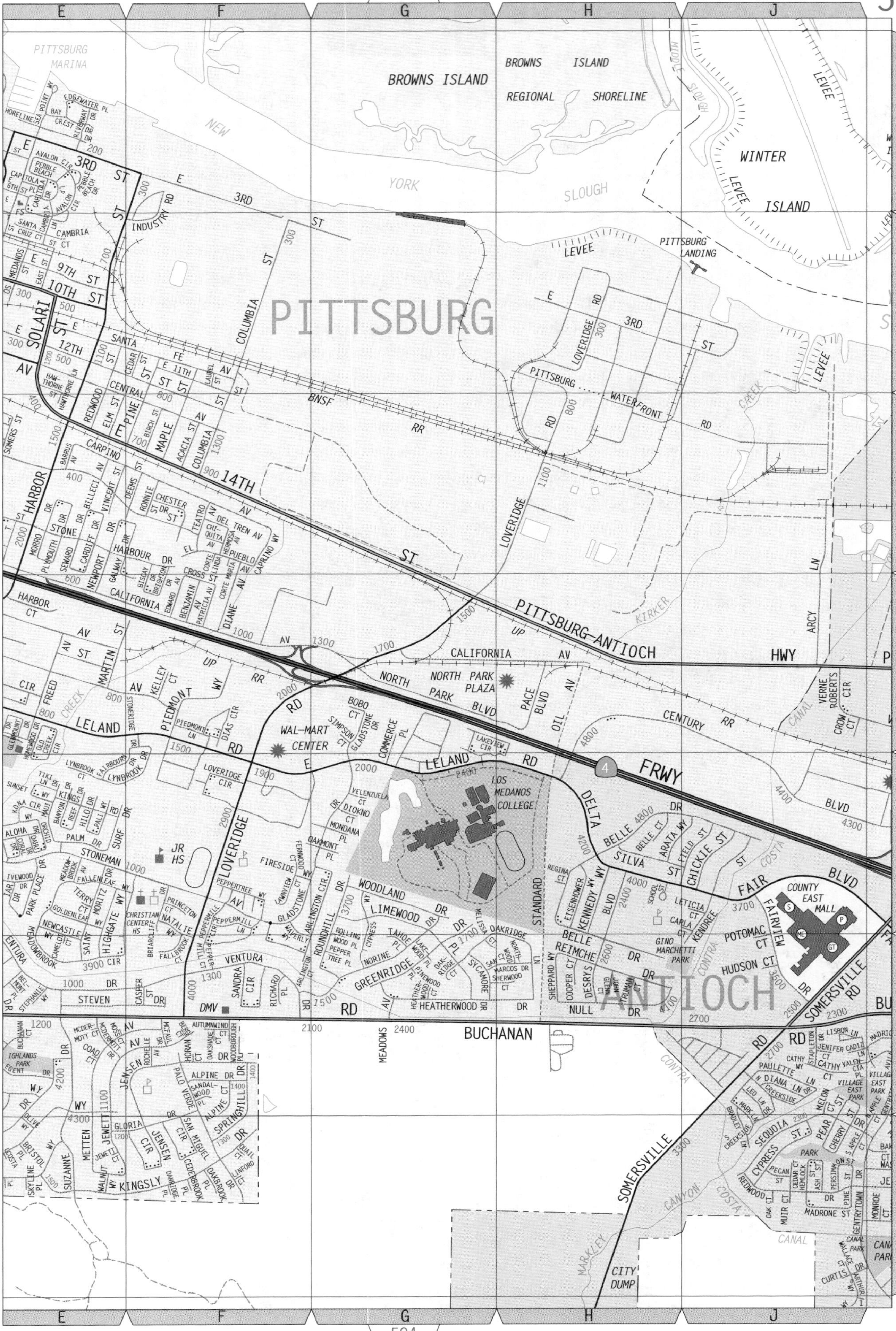
E
F
G
H
J
1
2
3
4
5
6
7
PITTSBURG MARINA
BROWNS ISLAND
BROWNS ISLAND REGIONAL SHORELINE
NEW YORK SLOUGH
MIDDLE SLOUGH
WINTER ISLAND
LEVEE
PITTSBURG LANDING
PITTSBURG
ANTIOCH
EDGEWATER PL
SEA POINT WY
HORELINE
BAY CREST
RIVERVIEW DR
AVALON CIR
PEBBLE BEACH
CAPITOLA
3RD ST
E 3RD ST
INDUSTRY RD
CAMBRIA CT
SANTA CRUZ CT
MEDANOS
9TH ST
10TH ST
SOLARI ST
12TH
SANTA FE
BNSF RR
COLUMBIA ST
CEDAR ST
E 11TH
LAUREL
CENTRAL
REDWOOD
ELM ST
PINE
BIRCH ST
MAPLE AV
ACACIA ST
HAWTHORNE
HARBOR ST
SOMERS ST
CARPINO
BARRUS AV
BILLECI AV
VINCENT ST
DEEMS
RONNIE
CHESTER DR
TEATRO
DEL TREN AV
CHIQUITA
PUEBLO
CAPRINO WY
14TH ST
STONE
CARDIFF DR
MORRO
PLYMOUTH
SEWARD
NEWPORT
HARBOUR DR
GALWAY
BRIGHTON
CROSS
CALIFORNIA AV
BENJAMIN
PATRICIA AV
DIANE AV
HARBOR CT
PITTSBURG WATERFRONT RD
LOVERIDGE RD
PITTSBURG-ANTIOCH HWY
KIRKER CREEK
ARCY LN
UP RR
VERNE ROBERTS CIR
CROW CT
CALIFORNIA AV
NORTH PARK BLVD
NORTH PARK PLAZA
PACE BLVD
OIL AV
CENTURY BLVD
FREED
MARTIN ST
KELLEY CT
PIEDMONT WY
DIAS CIR
LELAND RD
E LELAND RD
WAL-MART CENTER
BOBO CT
SIMPSON CT
GLADSTONE
COMMERCE PL
LAKEVIEW CIR
LYNBROOK CT
FAIRBOURN
LOVERIDGE CIR
DELTA FRWY
4
LOS MEDANOS COLLEGE
VELENZUELA
DIOKNO CT
MONDANA
OAKMONT PL
BELLE DR
ARATA WY
FIELD ST
CHICKIE ST
SILVA ST
COSTA
FAIR BLVD
COUNTY EAST MALL
FAIRVIEW DR
KINGS
HILO
PALM DR
SURF
STONEMAN
JR HS
FIRESIDE
FERNWOOD
WOODLAND
LIMEWOOD DR
PEPPERTREE
PRINCETON
NATALIE
CHRISTIAN CENTER HS
MEADOWBROOK
PEPPERMILL LN
GLADSTONE
ARLINGTON CIR
ROUNDHILL
TAHOE PL
MELISSA CT
OAKRIDGE
STANDARD
REGINA CT
EISENHOWER
KENNEDY WY
BLVD
SCHOOL
LETICIA CT
CARLA
KENDREE
POTOMAC CT
HUDSON CT
GINO MARCHETTI PARK
CONTRA
REIMCHE DR
COOPER CT
DESRYS
TRUMAN CT
SHEPPARD WY
GREENRIDGE
NORINE
SYCAMORE
SHERWOOD
VENTURA DR
SANDRA CIR
RICHARD PL
STEVEN
CASPER ST
DMV
HEATHERWOOD DR
NULL DR
BUCHANAN RD
MEADOWS
SOMERSVILLE RD
AUTUMNWIND
OAKSHADE
WOODBOROUGH
JENSEN
ALPINE DR
SANDALWOOD
SPRINGHILL DR
PALO VERDE
GLORIA CIR
SAN MIGUEL
CEDERBROOK
OAKBROOK
KINGSLY
METTEN
SUZANNE
JEWETT
BRISTOL
SKYLINE PL
LINFORD
QUAIL
LISBON LN
JENIFER
CATHY WY
PAULETTE
DIANA LN
CREEKSIDE
SEQUOIA ST
PEAR
CHERRY
CYPRESS
PECAN
CEDAR CT
HEMLOCK
PERSIMMON ST
REDWOOD
MADRONE ST
GENTRYTOWN
MONROE
VILLAGE EAST PARK
PARK
CANYON
MARKLEY
CITY DUMP
CANAL
CANAL PARK
CURTIS
ARTHUR

SEE 575 MAP
SEE 594 MAP

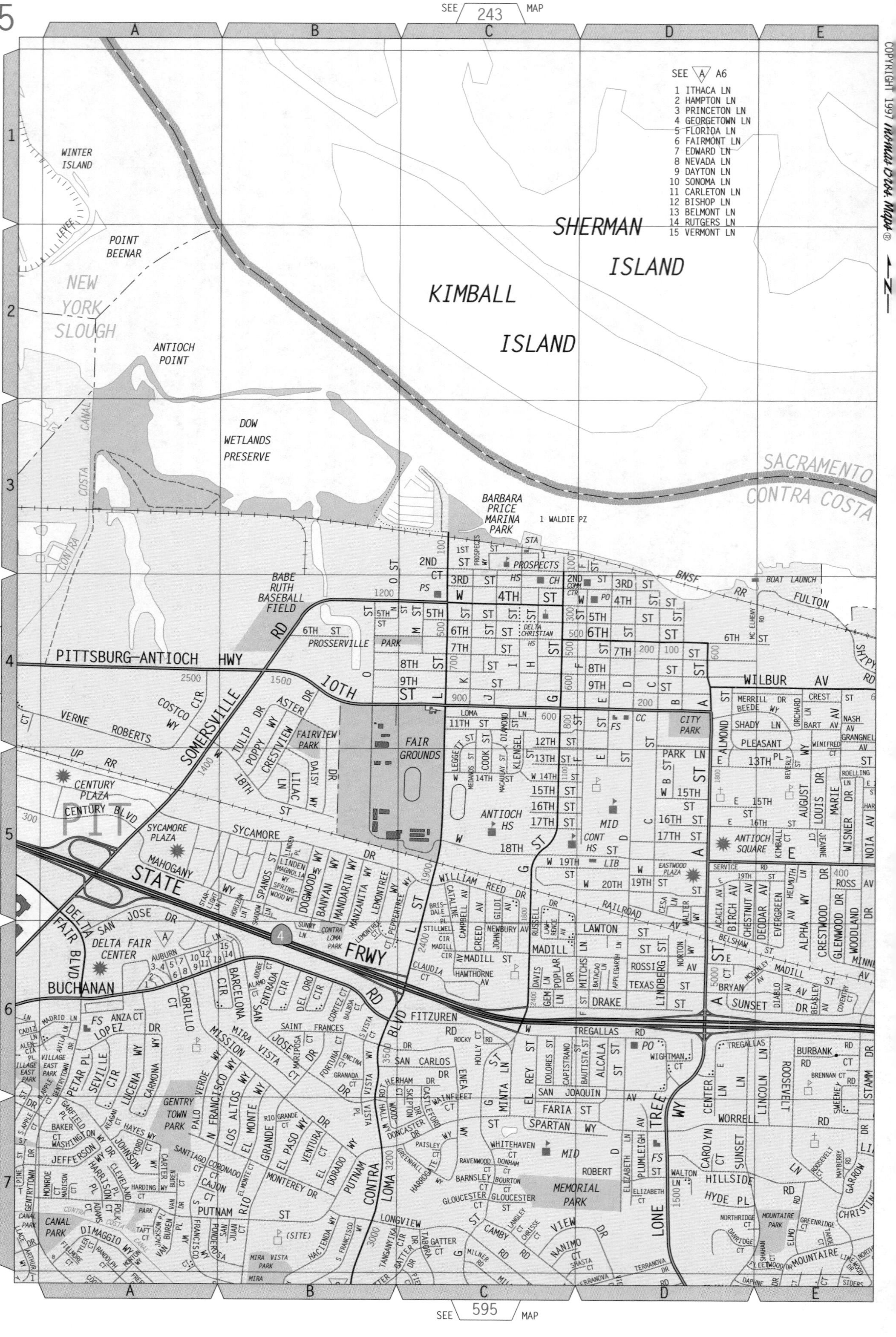
SEE 243 MAP
SEE 574 MAP
SEE 595 MAP
SEE A A6
1 ITHACA LN
2 HAMPTON LN
3 PRINCETON LN
4 GEORGETOWN LN
5 FLORIDA LN
6 FAIRMONT LN
7 EDWARD LN
8 NEVADA LN
9 DAYTON LN
10 SONOMA LN
11 CARLETON LN
12 BISHOP LN
13 BELMONT LN
14 RUTGERS LN
15 VERMONT LN
WINTER ISLAND
POINT BEENAR
LEVEE
NEW YORK SLOUGH
ANTIOCH POINT
DOW WETLANDS PRESERVE
CONTRA COSTA CANAL
SHERMAN ISLAND
KIMBALL ISLAND
SACRAMENTO
CONTRA COSTA
BARBARA PRICE MARINA PARK
1 WALDIE PZ
BABE RUTH BASEBALL FIELD
PROSSERVILLE PARK
PITTSBURG-ANTIOCH HWY
SOMERSVILLE RD
10TH ST
WILBUR AV
FULTON
BOAT LAUNCH
BNSF RR
COSTCO WY
VERNE ROBERTS CIR
UP RR
CENTURY PLAZA
CENTURY BLVD
PIT
FAIRVIEW PARK
FAIR GROUNDS
ANTIOCH HS
MID
CONT HS
LIB
CITY PARK
ANTIOCH SQUARE
SYCAMORE PLAZA
SYCAMORE DR
MAHOGANY WY
STATE FRWY
4
DELTA FAIR BLVD
DELTA FAIR CENTER
SAN JOSE DR
BUCHANAN RD
WILLIAM REED DR
RAILROAD AV
LAWTON
MADILL ST
DRAKE ST
TREGALLAS RD
FITZUREN RD
CONTRA LOMA BLVD
LONE TREE WY
GENTRY TOWN PARK
CANAL PARK
MEMORIAL PARK
MIRA VISTA PARK
WORRELL RD
HILLSIDE
HYDE PL
LONGVIEW
SPARTAN WY
SAN JOAQUIN
FARIA ST
EASTWOOD PLAZA
MOUNTAIRE PARK
MOUNTAIRE

SEE 243 MAP

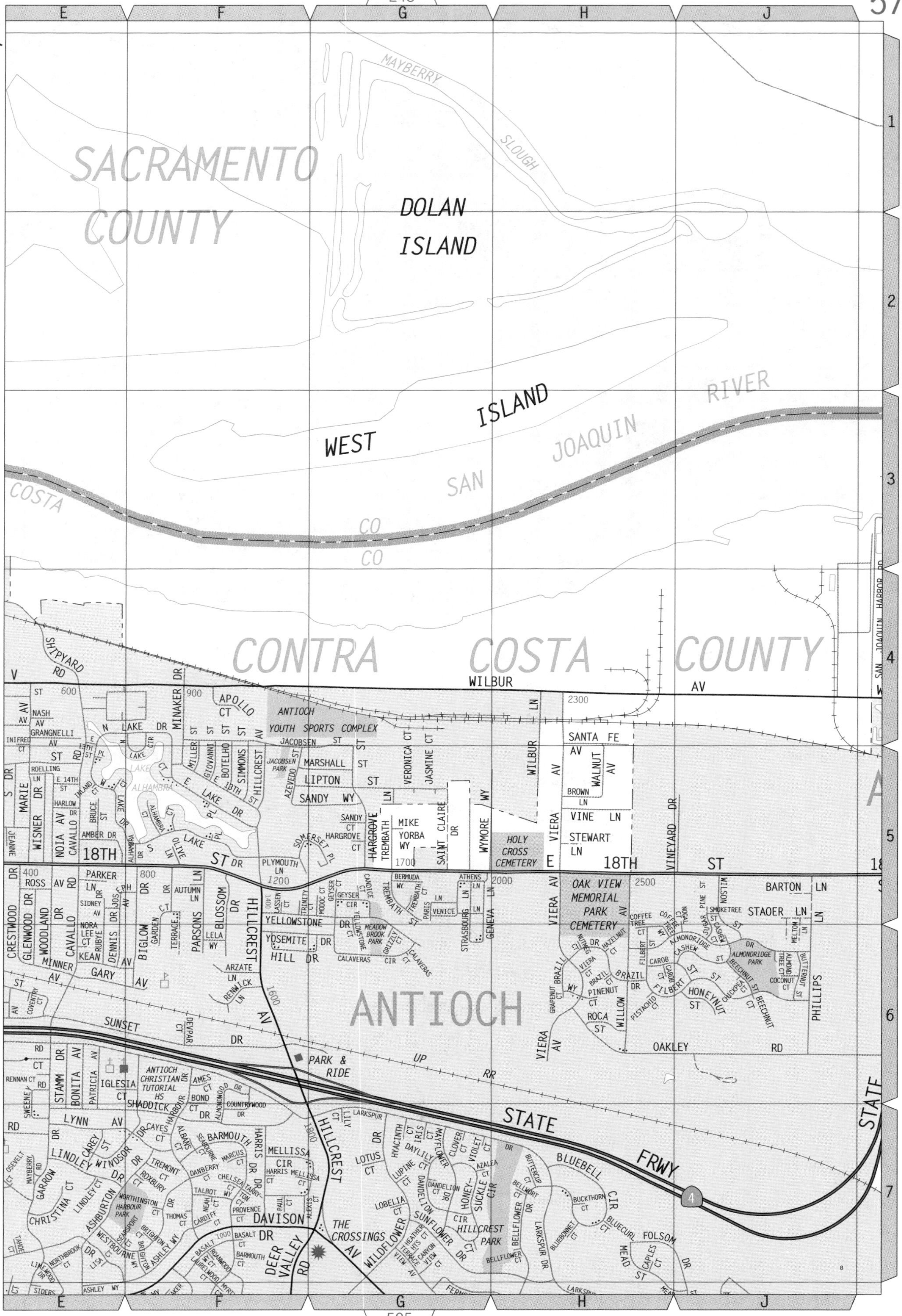
SACRAMENTO COUNTY
DOLAN ISLAND
MAYBERRY SLOUGH
WEST ISLAND
SAN JOAQUIN RIVER
COSTA
CO
CO
CONTRA COSTA COUNTY
ANTIOCH
WILBUR AV
18TH ST
SHIPYARD RD
MINAKER DR
APOLLO CT
ANTIOCH YOUTH SPORTS COMPLEX
JACOBSEN ST
MARSHALL ST
LIPTON ST
SANDY WY
HARGROVE CT
MIKE YORBA WY
SAINT CLAIRE DR
WYMORE WY
HOLY CROSS CEMETERY
VIERA AV
SANTA FE AV
WALNUT AV
BROWN LN
VINE LN
STEWART LN
VINEYARD DR
OAK VIEW MEMORIAL PARK CEMETERY
BARTON LN
STAOER LN
HILLCREST AV
YELLOWSTONE DR
YOSEMITE DR
HILL DR
CALAVERAS CIR
SUNSET DR
PARK & RIDE
UP RR
STATE FRWY
4
OAKLEY RD
PHILLIPS
BRAZIL DR
PINENUT CT
ROCA ST
WILLOW
HONEYNUT ST
BEECHNUT
ALMONDRIDGE PARK
LYNN AV
LINDLEY DR
WINDSOR DR
IGLESIA CT
SHADDICK
ANTIOCH CHRISTIAN TUTORIAL HS
BARMOUTH CT
MELLISSA CIR
DAVISON DR
DEER VALLEY RD
THE CROSSINGS
WILDFLOWER
SUNFLOWER DR
HILLCREST PARK
BLUEBELL CIR
FOLSOM DR
LARKSPUR DR
BELLFLOWER
WORTHINGTON HARBOUR PARK
CHRISTINA CT
GARROW
ASHBURTON
WESTBOURNE
ASHLEY WY
SIDERS

SEE 595 MAP

SEE 566 MAP

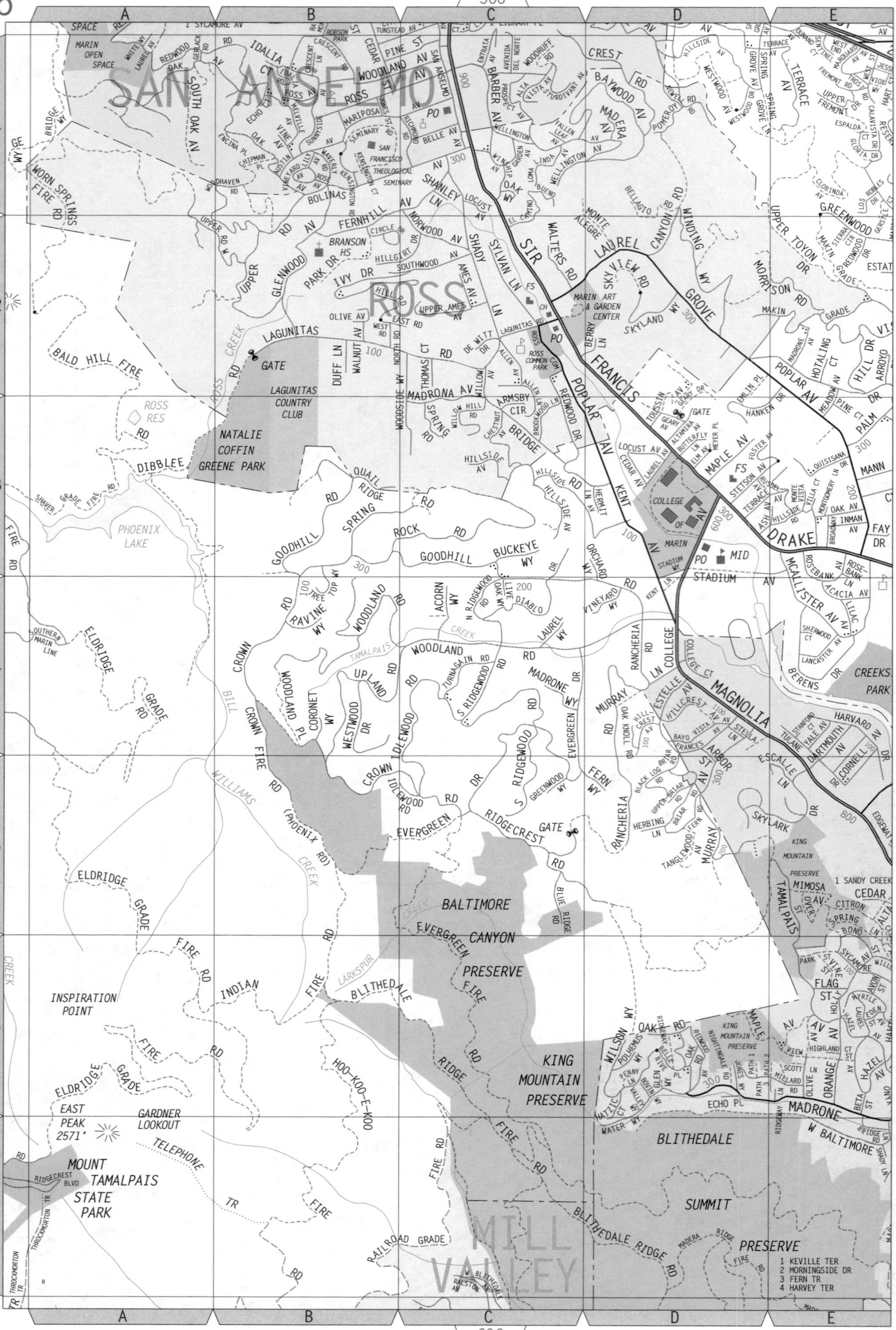
SAN ANSELMO
ROSS
MILL VALLEY
MARIN OPEN SPACE
SAN FRANCISCO THEOLOGICAL SEMINARY
BRANSON HS
MARIN ART & GARDEN CENTER
ROSS COMMON PARK
LAGUNITAS COUNTRY CLUB
NATALIE COFFIN GREENE PARK
ROSS RES
PHOENIX LAKE
COLLEGE OF MARIN
STADIUM AV
BALTIMORE CANYON PRESERVE
KING MOUNTAIN PRESERVE
BLITHEDALE SUMMIT PRESERVE
INSPIRATION POINT
EAST PEAK 2571'
GARDNER LOOKOUT
MOUNT TAMALPAIS STATE PARK
SIR FRANCIS DRAKE
MAGNOLIA
LAGUNITAS RD
POPLAR AV
SHADY LN
LAUREL GROVE
BALD HILL FIRE RD
ELDRIDGE GRADE
CROWN FIRE RD
INDIAN FIRE RD
HOO-KOO-E-KOO
TELEPHONE TR
RAILROAD GRADE
BLITHEDALE RIDGE RD
W BALTIMORE
MADRONE
EVERGREEN
RIDGECREST RD
CREEKSIDE PARK
1 KEVILLE TER
2 MORNINGSIDE DR
3 FERN TR
4 HARVEY TER
A B C D E
1 2 3 4 5 6 7

SEE 243 MAP

SEE 606 MAP

SEE 566 MAP

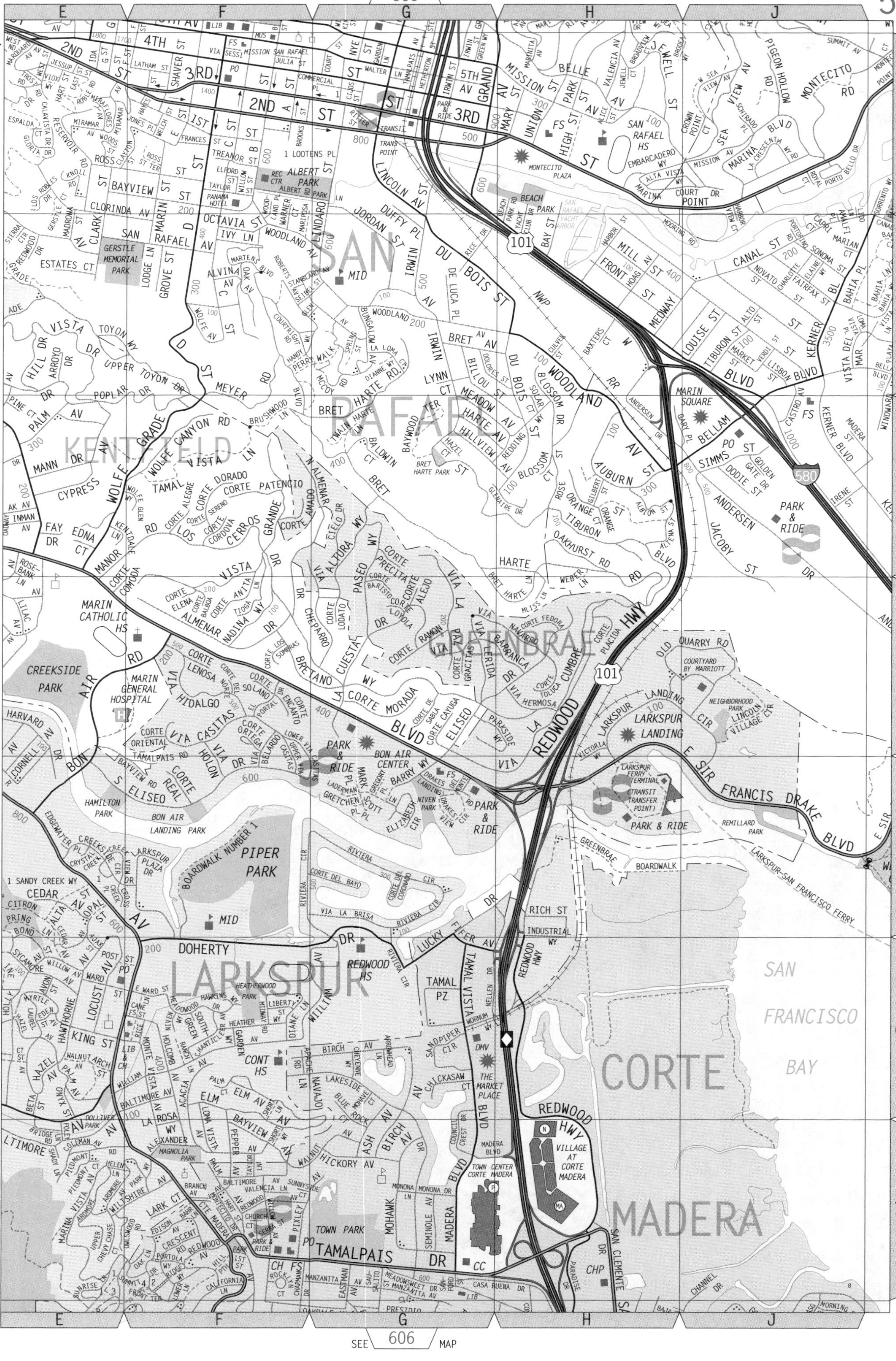
E
F
G
H
J
1
2
3
4
5
6
7
SAN RAFAEL
KENTFIELD
GREENBRAE
LARKSPUR
CORTE MADERA
SAN FRANCISCO BAY
2ND ST
3RD ST
4TH ST
5TH AV
LINCOLN AV
MISSION ST
GRAND AV
DU BOIS ST
IRWIN ST
WOODLAND AV
BRET HARTE RD
SIR FRANCIS DRAKE BLVD
REDWOOD HWY
TAMALPAIS DR
DOHERTY DR
MAGNOLIA AV
WOLFE GRADE
KERNER BLVD
CANAL ST
ANDERSEN DR
BELLAM BLVD
101
580
MARIN CATHOLIC HS
MARIN GENERAL HOSPITAL
CREEKSIDE PARK
PIPER PARK
LARKSPUR LANDING
LARKSPUR FERRY TERMINAL
BON AIR CENTER
MARIN SQUARE
ALBERT PARK
GERSTLE MEMORIAL PARK
BRET HARTE PARK
HAMILTON PARK
BON AIR LANDING PARK
REMILLARD PARK
TOWN PARK
MAGNOLIA PARK
VILLAGE AT CORTE MADERA
TOWN CENTER CORTE MADERA
THE MARKET PLACE
REDWOOD HS
CONT HS
SAN RAFAEL HS
COURTYARD BY MARRIOTT
LARKSPUR-SAN FRANCISCO FERRY
PARK & RIDE

SEE 587 MAP

SEE 606 MAP

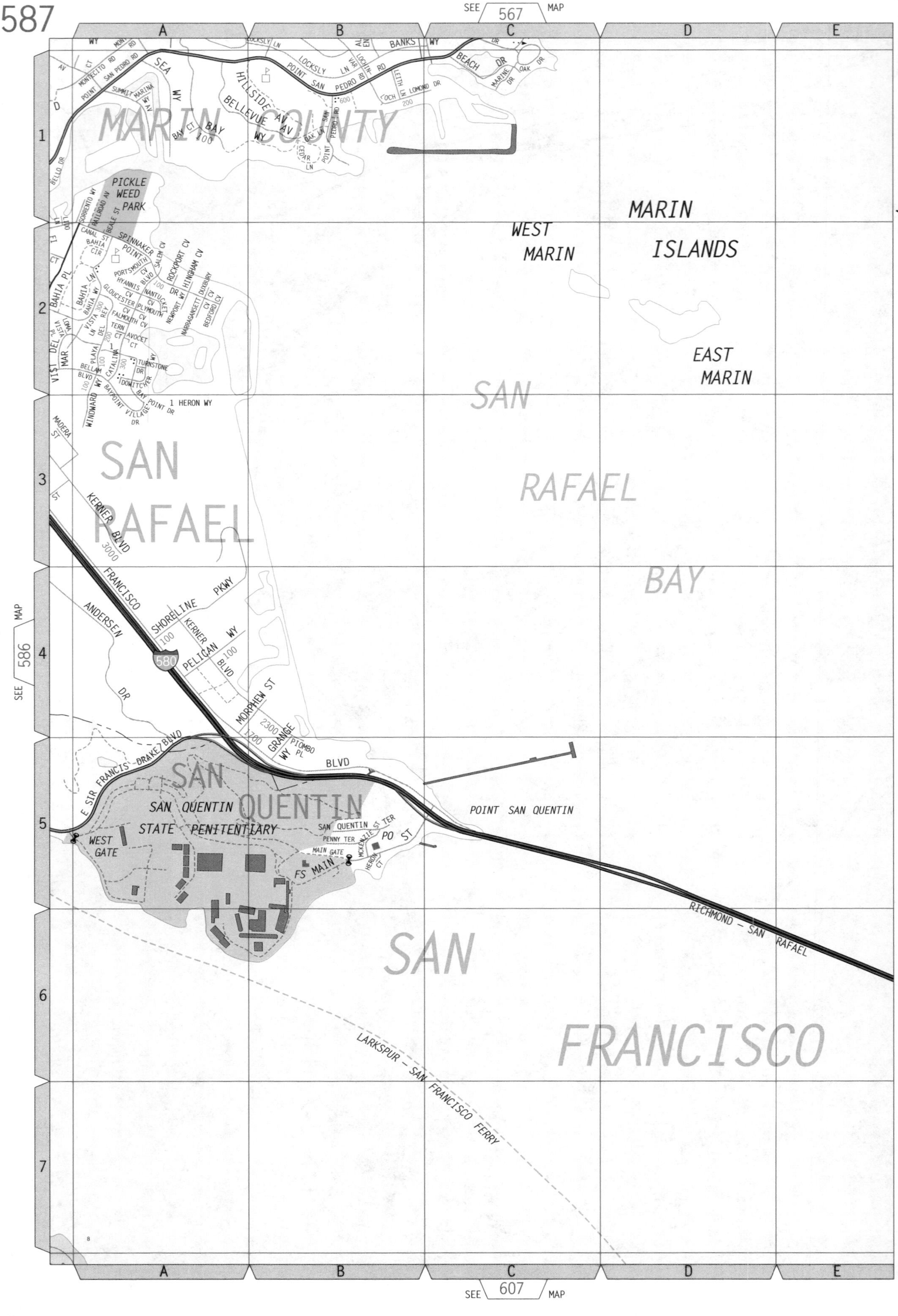

SEE 567 MAP
A
B
C
D
E
1
2
3
4
5
6
7
MARIN COUNTY
SEA WY
HILLSIDE AV
BELLEVUE AV
POINT SAN PEDRO RD
LOCKSLY LN
BANKS WY
BEACH DR
MARINE DR
OAK DR
LOCH LOMOND DR
LEITH LN
MONTECITO RD
SAN PEDRO RD
SUMMIT
MARINA WY
BAY WY
BAY CT
CEDAR LN
BELLO DR
PICKLE WEED PARK
SORRENTO WY
RAILROAD AV
BEALE ST
CANAL ST
BAHIA CIR
SPINNAKER POINT
PORTSMOUTH CV
HYANNIS CV
ROCKPORT CV
HINGHAM CV
SALEM CV
NANTUCKET CV
PLYMOUTH CV
GLOUCESTER CV
FALMOUTH CV
NEWPORT WY
NARRAGANSETT CV
DUXBURY CV
BEDFORD CV
TERN CT
AVOCET CT
TURNSTONE DR
DOWITCHER WY
BAHIA PL
BAHIA LN
BAHIA WY
VISTA DEL REY
PLAYA DEL MAR
VISTA DEL MAR
CATALINA BLVD
BELLAM BLVD
WINDWARD WY
BAYPOINT VILLAGE DR
BAY POINT DR
1 HERON WY
MADERA ST
WEST MARIN
MARIN ISLANDS
EAST MARIN
SAN RAFAEL
SAN RAFAEL BAY
KERNER BLVD
FRANCISCO BLVD
SHORELINE PKWY
PELICAN WY
ANDERSEN DR
580
MORPHEW ST
GRANGE WY
PTOMBO PL
E SIR FRANCIS DRAKE BLVD
SAN QUENTIN
SAN QUENTIN STATE PENITENTIARY
WEST GATE
SAN QUENTIN ST
PENNY TER
MAIN GATE
MAIN ST
MCKENZIE ST
HERON CT
PO ST
POINT SAN QUENTIN
RICHMOND - SAN RAFAEL
LARKSPUR - SAN FRANCISCO FERRY
SAN FRANCISCO
SEE 586 MAP
SEE 607 MAP

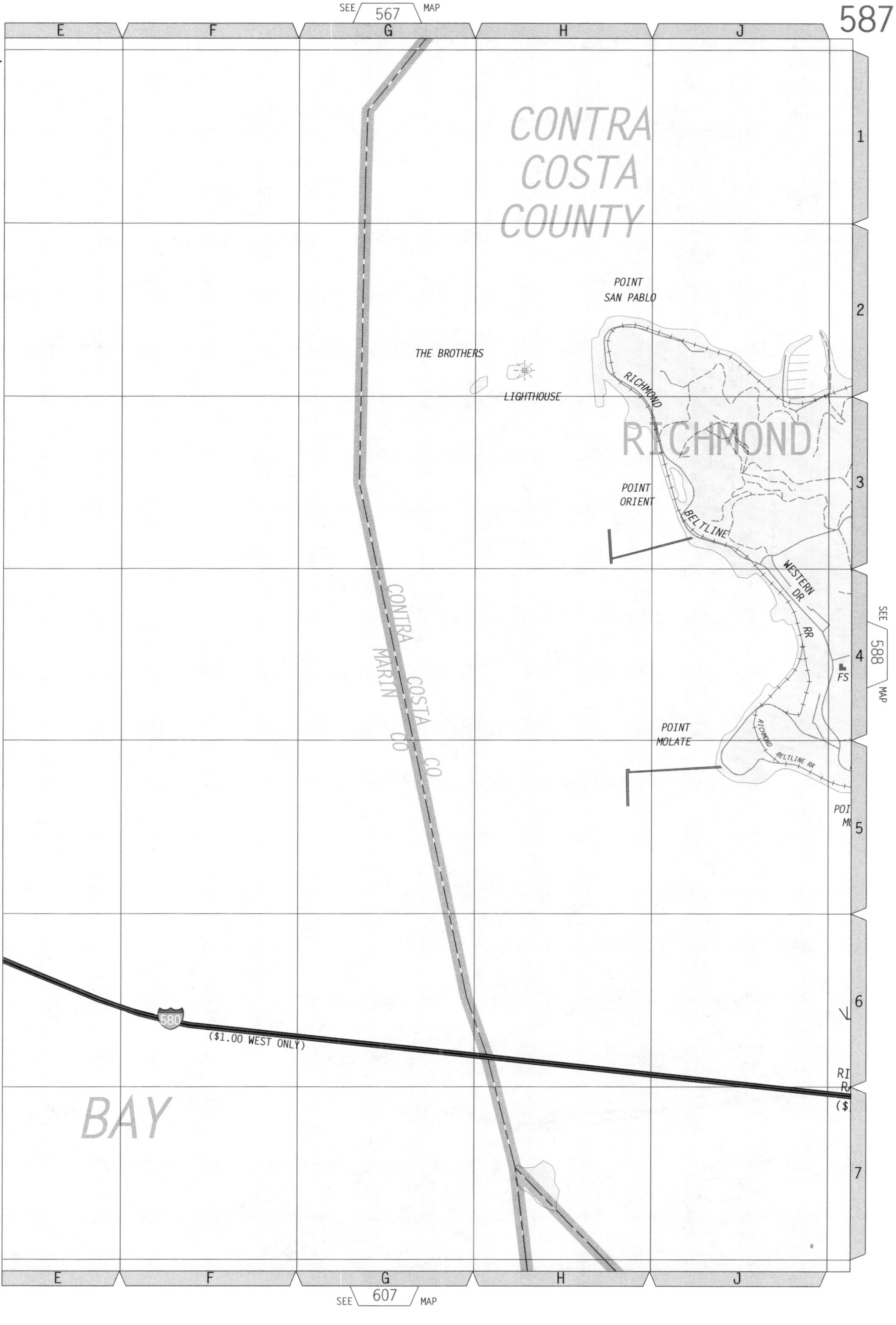
SEE 567 MAP
E
F
G
H
J
CONTRA COSTA COUNTY
POINT SAN PABLO
THE BROTHERS
LIGHTHOUSE
RICHMOND
RICHMOND
POINT ORIENT
BELTLINE
WESTERN DR
RR
CONTRA COSTA CO
MARIN CO
FS
POINT MOLATE
RICHMOND BELTLINE RR
580
($1.00 WEST ONLY)
BAY
1
2
3
4
5
6
7
SEE 588 MAP
SEE 607 MAP

SEE 568 MAP

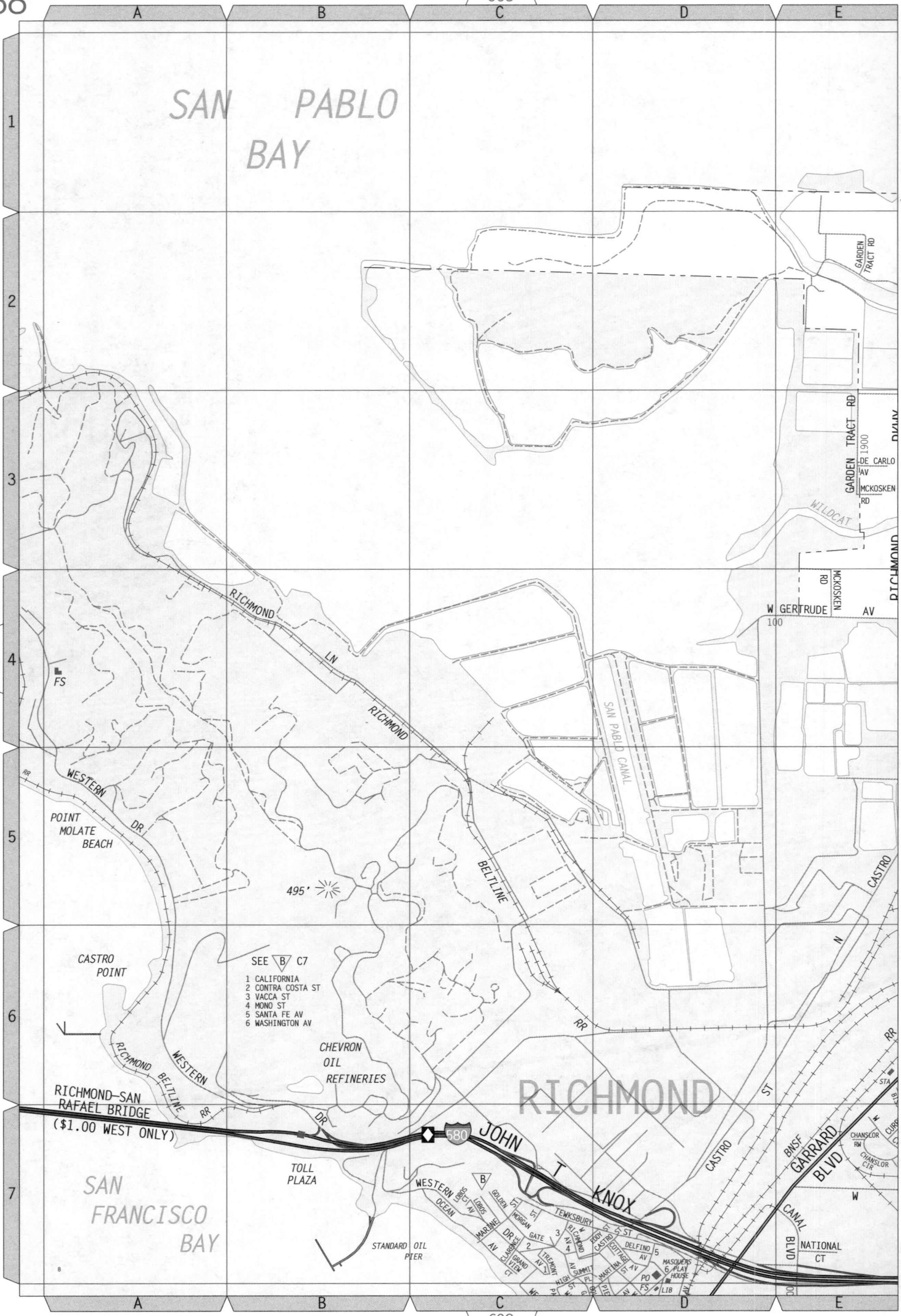
A
B
C
D
E
1
2
3
4
5
6
7
SAN PABLO BAY
GARDEN TRACT RD
GARDEN TRACT RD
1900
DE CARLO AV
MCKOSKEN RD
WILDCAT
PKWY
RICHMOND
MCKOSKEN RD
W GERTRUDE AV
100
RICHMOND LN
RICHMOND
FS
SAN PABLO CANAL
WESTERN DR
RR
POINT MOLATE BEACH
BELTLINE
495'
CASTRO
N
CASTRO POINT
SEE B C7
1 CALIFORNIA
2 CONTRA COSTA ST
3 VACCA ST
4 MONO ST
5 SANTA FE AV
6 WASHINGTON AV
CHEVRON OIL REFINERIES
RR
RICHMOND BELTLINE
WESTERN
RICHMOND
RICHMOND-SAN RAFAEL BRIDGE
($1.00 WEST ONLY)
RR
DR
580
JOHN T KNOX
ST
CASTRO
CASTRO ST
BNSF
GARRARD BLVD
CHANSLOR RW
CHANSLOR CIR
W
CANAL BLVD
NATIONAL CT
TOLL PLAZA
SAN FRANCISCO BAY
WESTERN
OCEAN
MARINE AV
DR
GATE
TEWKSBURY
DELFINO
MASQUERS PLAY HOUSE
PO
FS
LIB
STANDARD OIL PIER

A
B
C
D
E
SEE 587 MAP
SEE 608 MAP

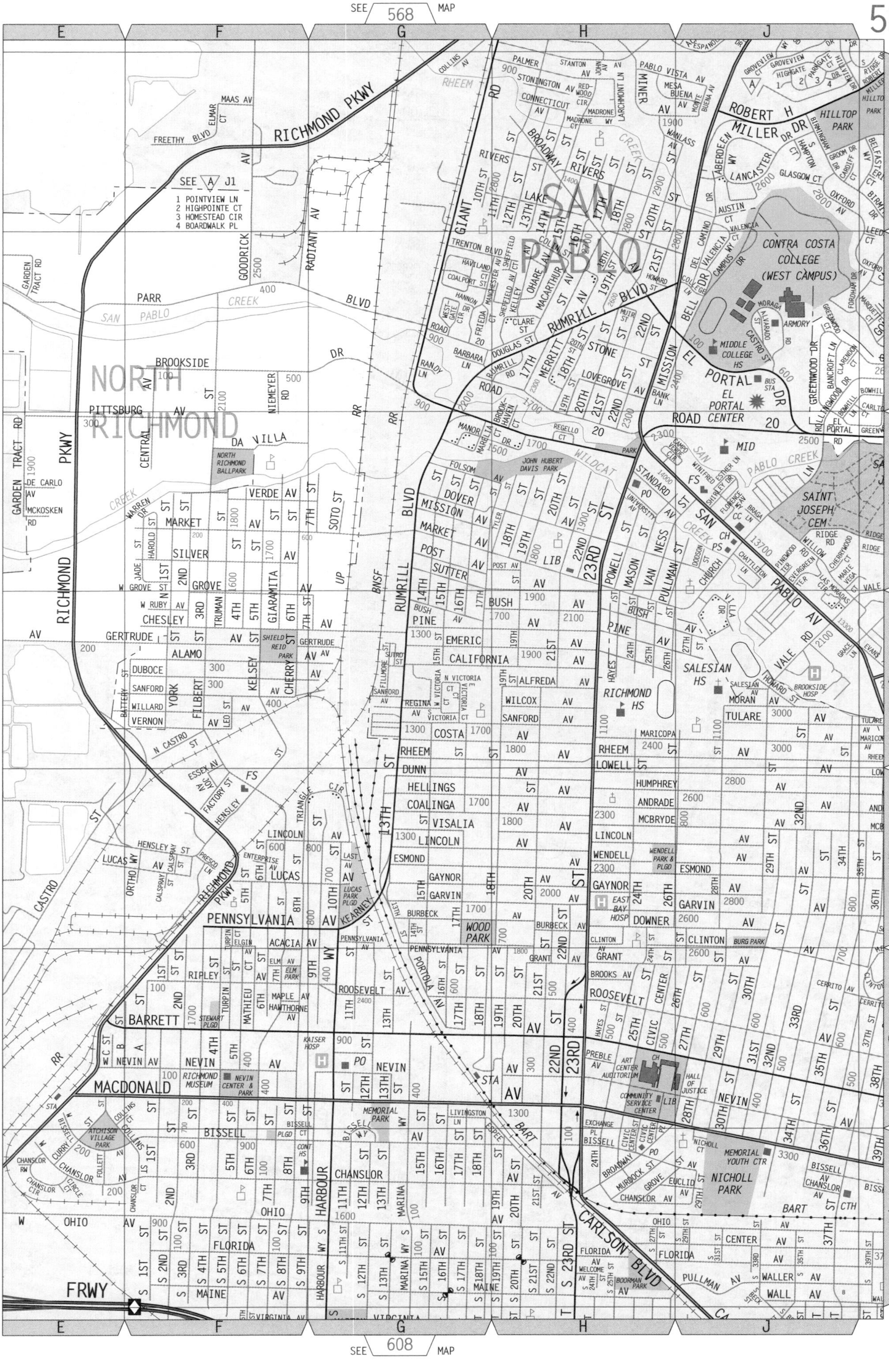
SEE 568 MAP
E
F
G
H
J
1
2
3
4
5
6
7
SEE 589 MAP
SEE 608 MAP
SAN PABLO
NORTH RICHMOND
RICHMOND PKWY
GIANT RD
RUMRILL BLVD
SAN PABLO AV
PARR BLVD
SAN PABLO CREEK
WILDCAT CREEK
BROOKSIDE DR
EL PORTAL DR
ROAD 20
23RD ST
13TH ST
MACDONALD AV
BARRETT AV
CARLSON BLVD
CUTTING BLVD
FRWY
CONTRA COSTA COLLEGE (WEST CAMPUS)
HILLTOP PARK
MIDDLE COLLEGE HS
EL PORTAL CENTER
JOHN HUBERT DAVIS PARK
NORTH RICHMOND BALLPARK
SHIELD REID PARK
SAINT JOSEPH CEM
SALESIAN HS
RICHMOND HS
BROOKSIDE HOSP
EAST BAY HOSP
KAISER HOSP
WOOD PARK
LUCAS PARK PLGD
WENDELL PARK & PLGD
BURG PARK
STEWART PLGD
RICHMOND MUSEUM
NEVIN CENTER & PARK
ATCHISON VILLAGE PARK
MEMORIAL PARK
ART CENTER AUDITORIUM
HALL OF JUSTICE
COMMUNITY SERVICE CENTER
CIVIC CENTER
MEMORIAL YOUTH CTR
NICHOLL PARK
BOORMAN PARK
BART
BNSF
UP
RR
SEE A J1
1 POINTVIEW LN
2 HIGHPOINTE CT
3 HOMESTEAD CIR
4 BOARDWALK PL

BAY AREA

MAP

SEE 569 MAP

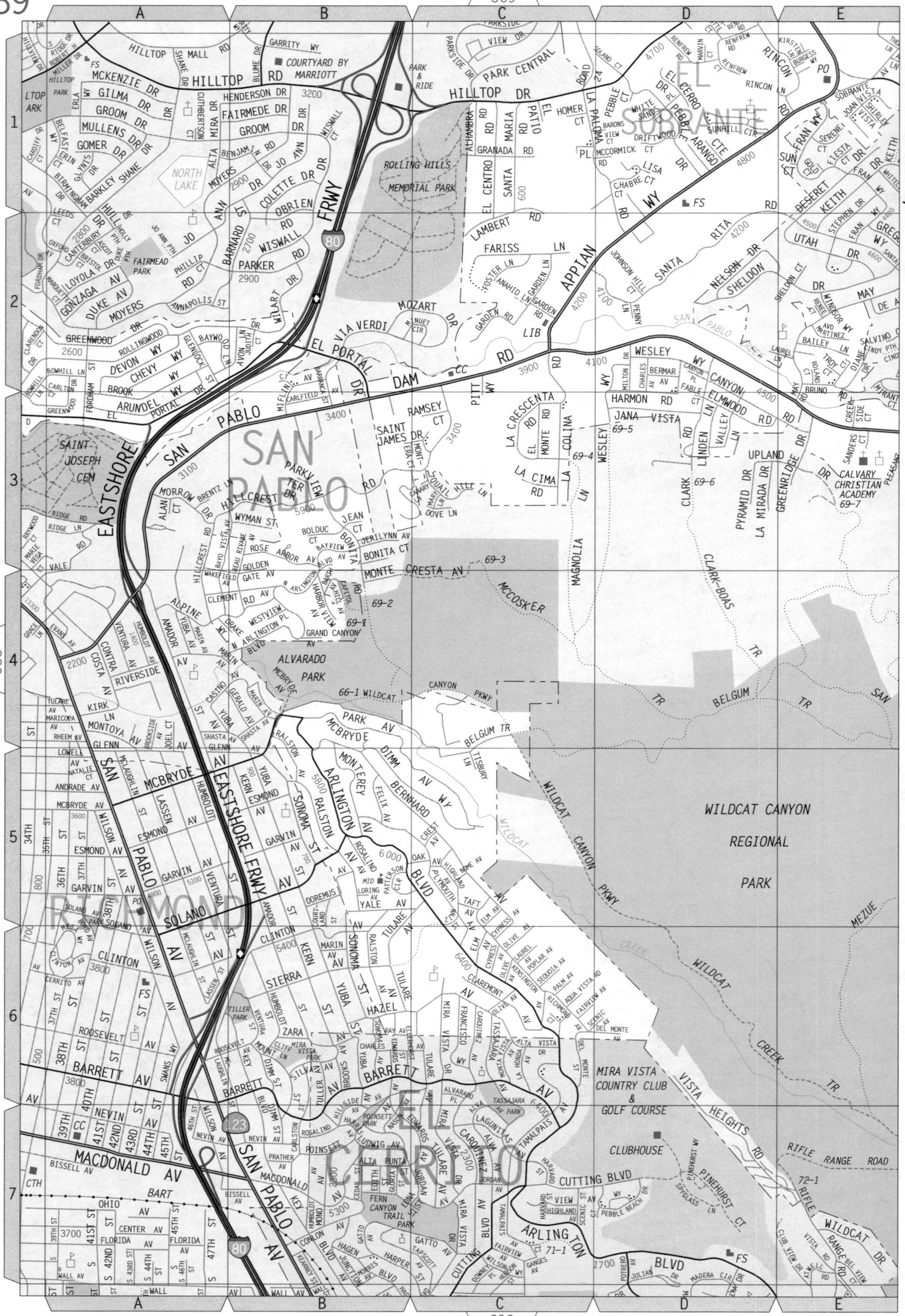
A
B
C
D
E
1
2
3
4
5
6
7
HILLTOP MALL RD
GARRITY WY
COURTYARD BY MARRIOTT
MCKENZIE DR
HILLTOP RD
HILLTOP DR
PARK & RIDE
PARK CENTRAL
ROLLING HILLS MEMORIAL PARK
NORTH LAKE
FAIRMEAD PARK
EL SOBRANTE
RINCON
APPIAN WY
FRWY
80
EL PORTAL DR
VIA VERDI
DAM RD
SAN PABLO
SAN PABLO DAM RD
EASTSHORE
SAINT JOSEPH CEM
WESLEY WY
CANYON
LA CRESCENTA
LA COLINA
MAGNOLIA LN
CLARK-BOAS
CALVARY CHRISTIAN ACADEMY
UPLAND
PYRAMID DR
LA MIRADA DR
GREENRIDGE DR
MONTE CRESTA AV
MCCOSKER
ALVARADO PARK
WILDCAT CANYON PKWY
BELGUM TR
SAN
WILDCAT CANYON REGIONAL PARK
MCBRYDE AV
ARLINGTON
EASTSHORE FRWY
SAN PABLO AV
RICHMOND
SOLANO AV
CLINTON AV
BARRETT AV
MACDONALD AV
BART
CUTTING BLVD
ARLINGTON BLVD
EL CERRITO
123
MIRA VISTA COUNTRY CLUB & GOLF COURSE
CLUBHOUSE
VISTA HEIGHTS RD
WILDCAT CREEK TR
MEZUE
RIFLE RANGE ROAD
WILDCAT RANGE DR
PINEHURST CT
TILLER PARK
FERN CANYON TRAIL PARK
CC
FS
PO
LIB
CTH

SEE 588 MAP

SEE 609 MAP

SEE 569 MAP

E
F
G
H
J
1
2
3
4
5
6
7
PINOLE
RICHMOND
PINOLE PARK
ALHAMBRA VALLEY RD
ADOBE RD
PINOLE VALLEY RD
SKYLINE DR
FORREST RD
SETTING SUN
INGROFF
PONY
FULL MOON DR
ROCKY RD
THUNDERHEAD CT
BLACK FEATHER DR
LONGHORN DR
MEADOWBROOK DR
MAYWOOD DR
MORWOOD DR
LA MOINE VALLEY VIEW PARK
MORNINGSIDE
HIDDEN SPRINGS CT
ROBERT WY
GREGORY WY
WESTWOOD CT
CLEARFIELD AV
HEAVENLY RIDGE
POWDER BOWL CT
SNOWDRIFT CT
SOFT SHADOW CT
DE ANZA HS
MAY
DE ANZA
SWEETWOOD DR
QUIET LN
SIMONI CT
PAMELA CT
AMEND RD
TRAVALINI CT
FS
SOBRANTE RIDGE REGIONAL PRESERVE
SILVER BELT DR
COACH DR
CARRIAGE DR
CUTTER LN
CONESTOGA WY
BUCKBOARD WY
SAN PABLO DAM RD
VALLEY VIEW RD
LA HONDA RD
AVILLA WY
FASCINATION CIR
RAIN CLOUD DR
SOLITUDE LN
RAIN CLOUD PARK
PINOLE RD
CASTRO RANCH RD
KIPLING RD
MAISON WY
OLINDA RD
NOTTINGHAM DR
HOOD DR
RIDGEVIEW CIR
ALLISON DR
ABBIE LN
HILLSIDE DR
HEIDE CT
PATRA DR
KENNEDY GROVE REGIONAL RECREATIONAL AREA
SAN PABLO RESERVOIR RECREATIONAL AREA
DAM
SAN PABLO RESERVOIR
SAN PABLO RIDGE
NIMITZ WY
NIMITZ TR
MEZUE TR
FIRE TRAIL 4
ROAD TR
HAVEY CANYON TR
WILDCAT CREEK TR
CONLON TR
EAGLES NEST TR

SEE 590 MAP

SEE 609 MAP

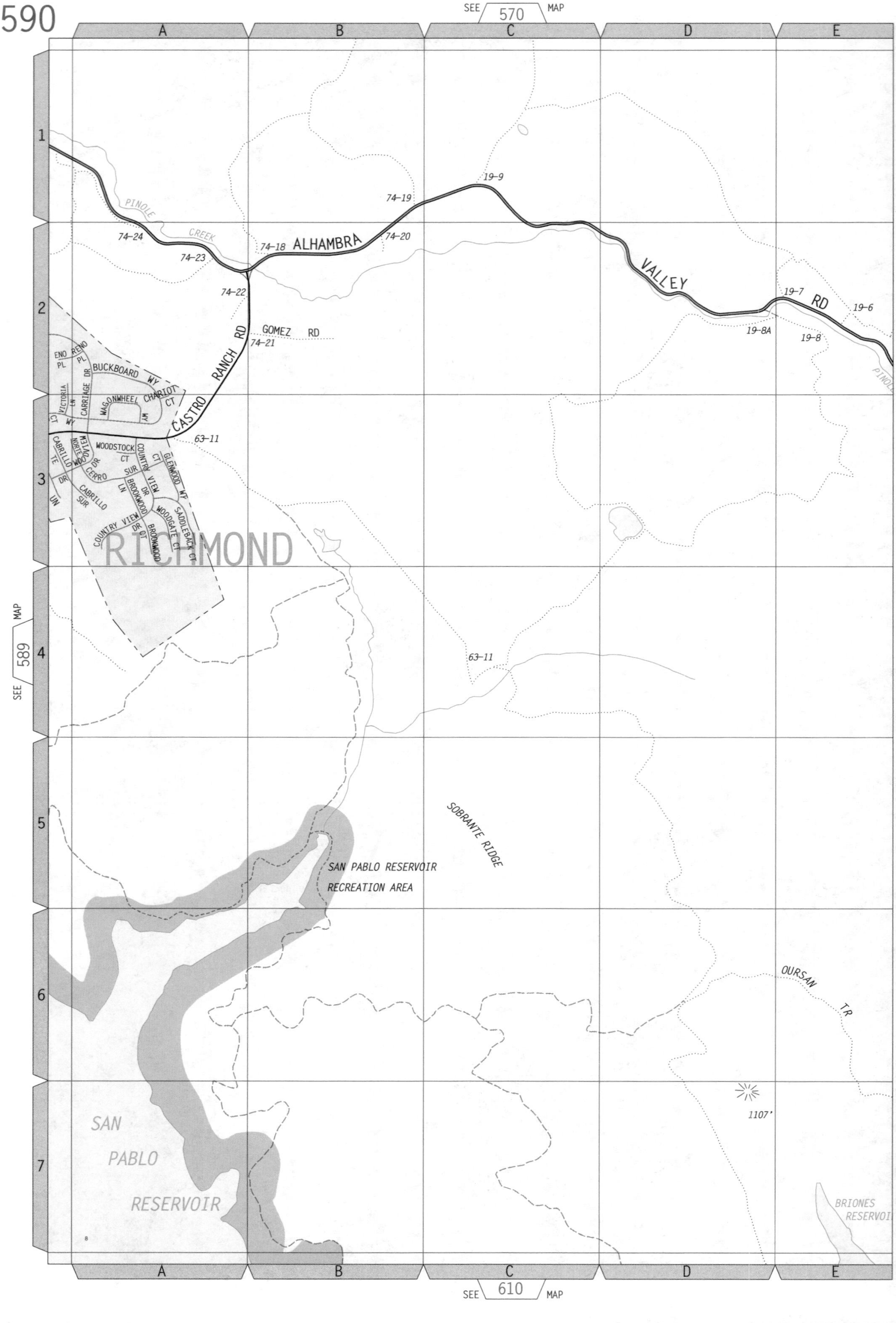
SEE 570 MAP
A
B
C
D
E
1
2
3
4
5
6
7
SEE 589 MAP
PINOLE CREEK
ALHAMBRA VALLEY RD
74-24
74-23
74-22
74-18
74-19
74-20
74-21
19-9
19-7
19-6
19-8A
19-8
PINOLE
GOMEZ RD
CASTRO RANCH RD
ENO PL
RENO PL
BUCKBOARD WY
CARRIAGE DR
VICTORIA LN
CT
WY
WAGONWHEEL WY
CHARIOT CT
CABRILLO TE
NORTE
WOODVIEW DR
WOODSTOCK CT
COUNTRY CT
GLENWOOD WY
CT
CERRO SUR
DR
LN
BROOKWOOD LN
COUNTRY VIEW DR
CABRILLO SUR
UN
WOODGATE CT
SADDLEBACK CT
COUNTRY VIEW DR
BROOKWOOD CT
63-11
RICHMOND
63-11
SOBRANTE RIDGE
SAN PABLO RESERVOIR
RECREATION AREA
OURSAN TR
1107'
SAN
PABLO
RESERVOIR
BRIONES
RESERVOI
SEE 610 MAP

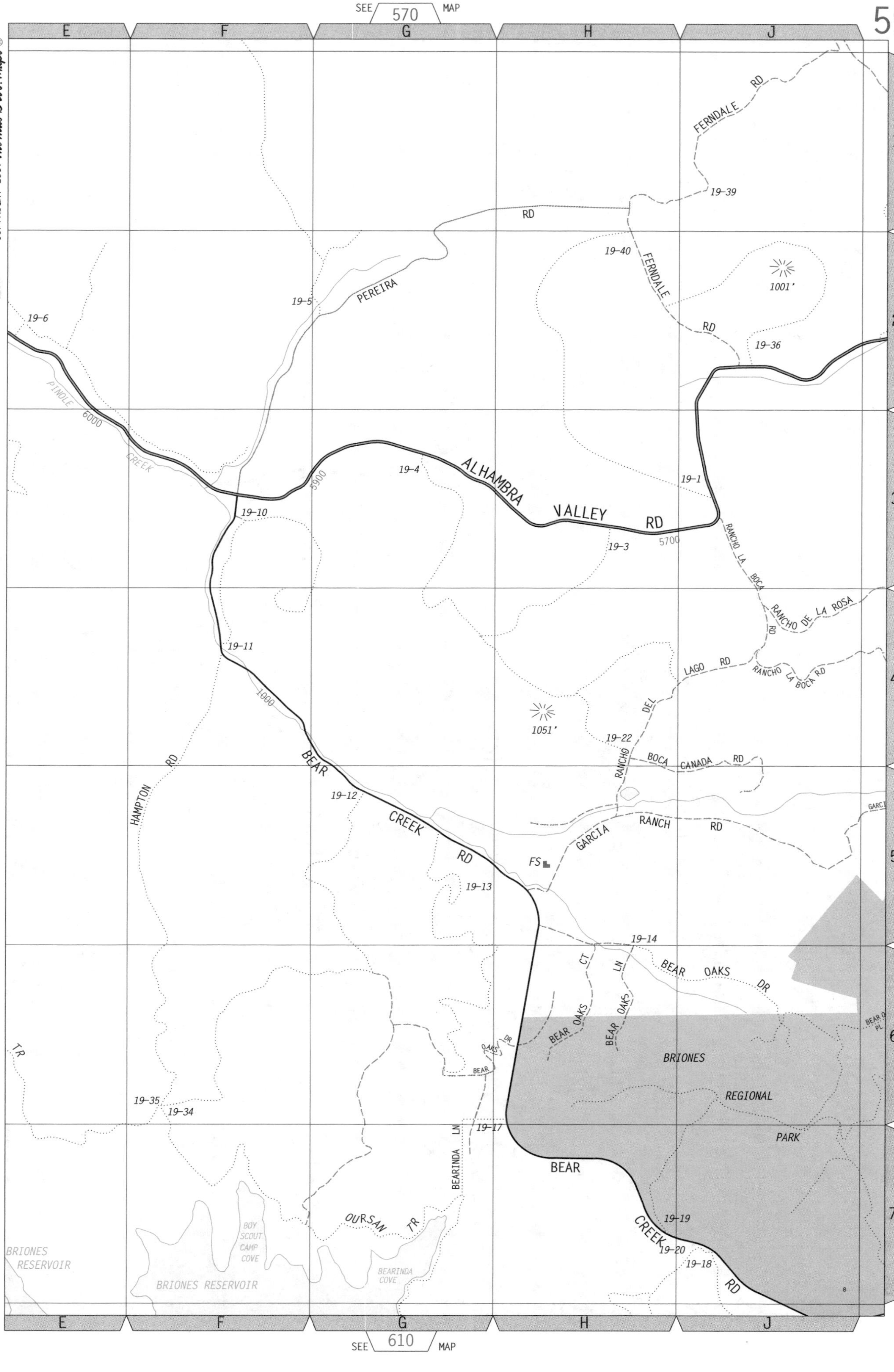
SEE 570 MAP
E
F
G
H
J
1
2
3
4
5
6
7
FERNDALE RD
19-39
RD
19-40
FERNDALE
RD
1001'
19-36
19-5
PEREIRA
19-6
PINOLE
6000
CREEK
19-4
ALHAMBRA VALLEY RD
5900
19-1
19-10
5700
19-3
RANCHO LA BOCA
RANCHO DE LA ROSA
RD
19-11
LAGO RD
RANCHO LA BOCA RD
SEE 591 MAP
1000
DEL
1051'
19-22
RANCHO
BOCA CANADA RD
BEAR
HAMPTON RD
19-12
CREEK
GARCIA RANCH RD
GARCIA
RD
FS
19-13
19-14
CT
LN
BEAR OAKS DR
BEAR OAKS
BEAR OAKS
BEAR OAKS PL
OAKS DR
BEAR
BRIONES
REGIONAL
PARK
TR
19-35
19-34
19-17
BEARINDA LN
BEAR
CREEK
RD
19-19
19-20
19-18
OURSAN TR
BOY SCOUT CAMP COVE
BRIONES RESERVOIR
BRIONES RESERVOIR
BEARINDA COVE
SEE 610 MAP

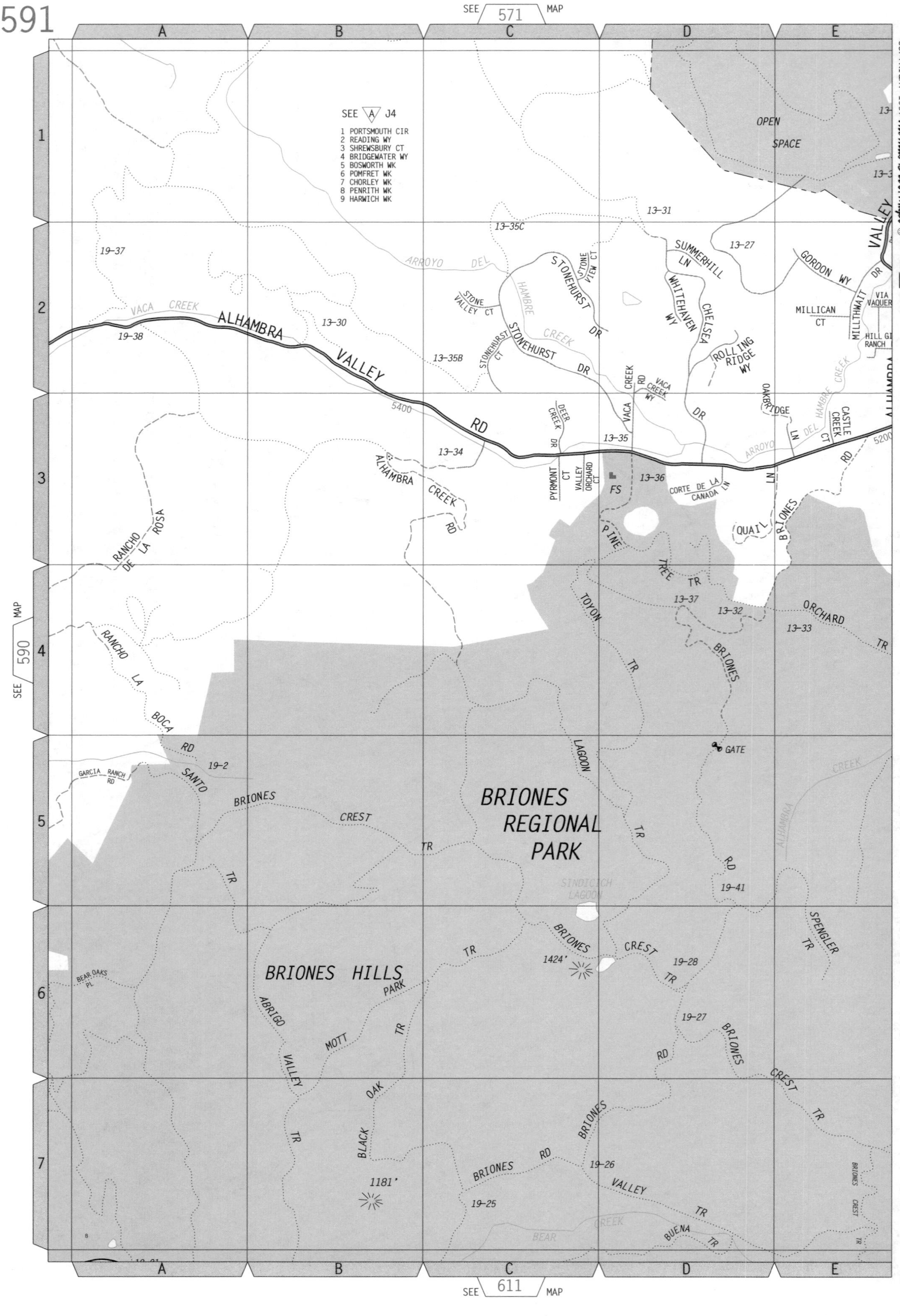
SEE 571 MAP
SEE 611 MAP
SEE 590 MAP
A
B
C
D
E
1
2
3
4
5
6
7
SEE A J4
1 PORTSMOUTH CIR
2 READING WY
3 SHREWSBURY CT
4 BRIDGEWATER WY
5 BOSWORTH WK
6 POMFRET WK
7 CHORLEY WK
8 PENRITH WK
9 HARWICH WK
OPEN SPACE
ALHAMBRA VALLEY RD
VACA CREEK
ARROYO DEL HAMBRE CREEK
STONEHURST DR
STONEHURST CT
STONE VALLEY CT
STONE VIEW CT
SUMMERHILL LN
WHITEHAVEN WY
CHELSEA
ROLLING RIDGE WY
GORDON WY
MILLICAN CT
MILLTHWAIT DR
VIA VAQUERO
HILL GIRT RANCH
VACA CREEK RD
VACA CREEK WY
DEER CREEK DR
OAKBRIDGE LN
CASTLE CREEK CT
PYRMONT CT
VALLEY ORCHARD CT
FS
CORTE DE LA CANADA LN
QUAIL
BRIONES
ALHAMBRA CREEK RD
RANCHO DE LA ROSA
PINE TREE TR
TOYON TR
ORCHARD TR
BRIONES RD
RANCHO LA BOCA RD
GARCIA RANCH RD
SANTO
BRIONES CREST TR
LAGOON TR
GATE
BRIONES REGIONAL PARK
SINDICICH LAGOON
SPENGLER TR
1424'
BRIONES HILLS
BEAR OAKS PL
ABRIGO VALLEY TR
MOTT PARK TR
BLACK OAK
1181'
BRIONES RD
BRIONES VALLEY TR
BEAR CREEK
BUENA TR
5400
5200
13-31
13-35C
13-27
19-37
13-30
19-38
13-35B
13-34
13-35
13-36
13-37
13-32
13-33
19-2
19-41
19-28
19-27
19-26
19-25

SEE 571 MAP
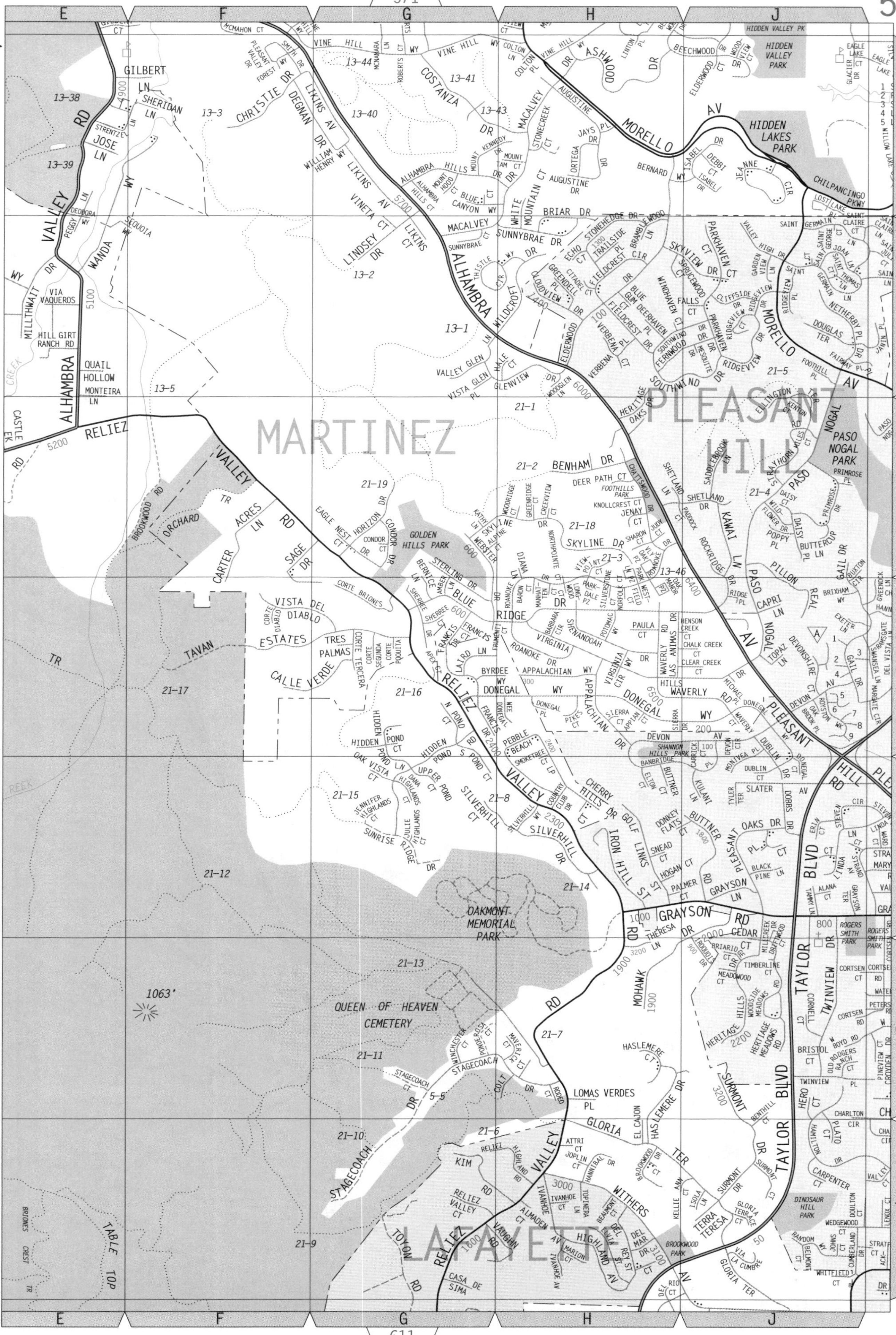

MARTINEZ
PLEASANT HILL
LAFAYETTE
E F G H J
1 2 3 4 5 6 7
ALHAMBRA AV
MORELLO AV
VINE HILL WY
RELIEZ VALLEY RD
PLEASANT HILL RD
TAYLOR BLVD
GRAYSON RD
CHILPANCINGO PKWY
HIDDEN VALLEY PARK
HIDDEN LAKES PARK
PASO NOGAL PARK
GOLDEN HILLS PARK
SHANNON HILLS PARK
OAKMONT MEMORIAL PARK
QUEEN OF HEAVEN CEMETERY
ROGERS SMITH PARK
DINOSAUR HILL PARK
BROOKWOOD PARK
FOOTHILLS PARK
1063'

SEE 592 MAP
SEE 611 MAP
BAY AREA
MAP

SEE 572 MAP

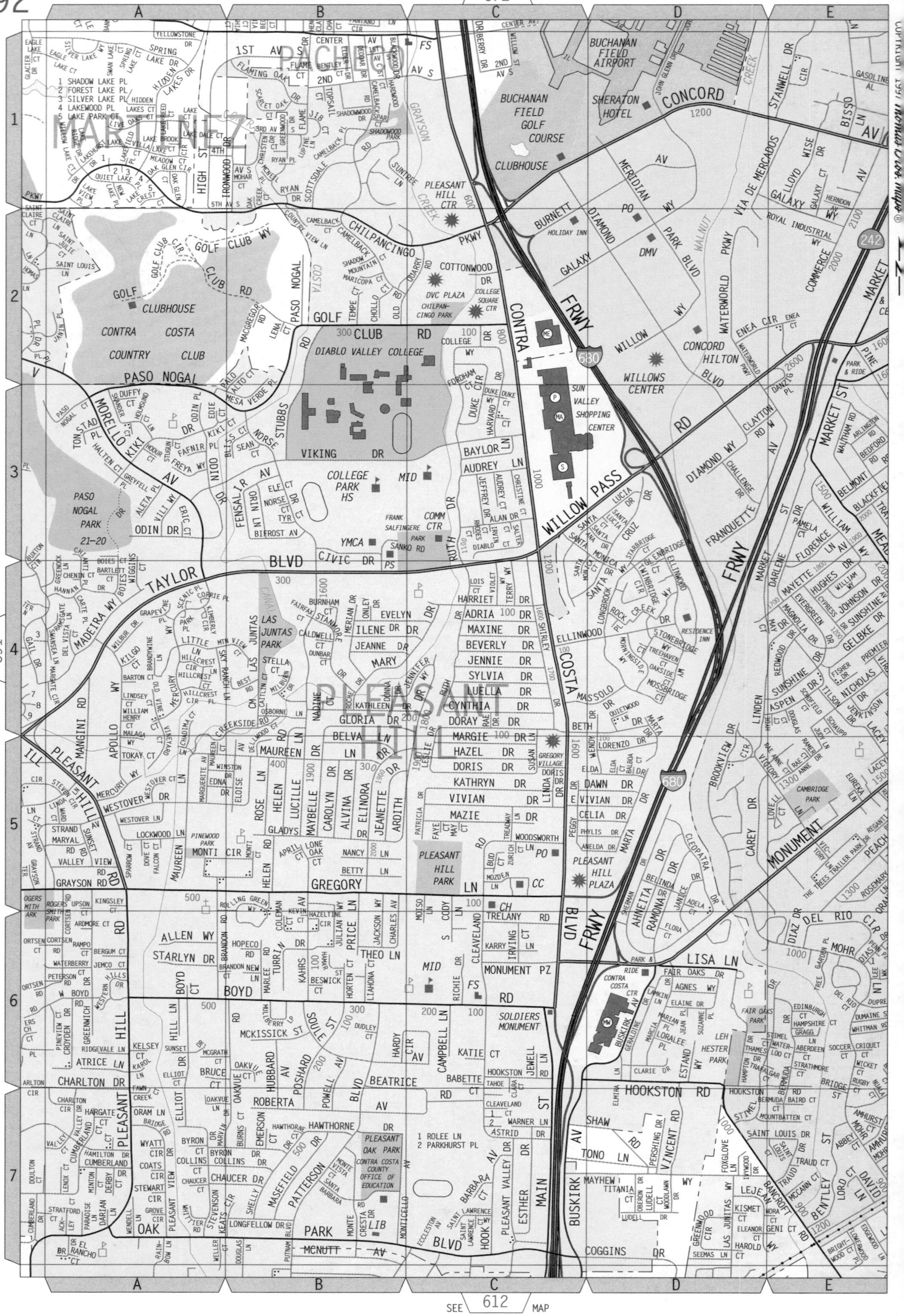

PACHECO
MARTINEZ
PLEASANT HILL
BUCHANAN FIELD AIRPORT
BUCHANAN FIELD GOLF COURSE
CLUBHOUSE
SHERATON HOTEL
CONCORD AV
PLEASANT HILL CTR
CHILPANCINGO PKWY
GOLF CLUB WY
CONTRA COSTA COUNTRY CLUB
GOLF CLUBHOUSE
PASO NOGAL
GOLF CLUB RD
DIABLO VALLEY COLLEGE
DVC PLAZA
CHILPANCINGO PARK
COLLEGE SQUARE CTR
SUN VALLEY SHOPPING CENTER
WILLOWS CENTER
CONCORD HILTON
WILLOW PASS RD
CONTRA COSTA FRWY
680
242
VIKING DR
COLLEGE PARK HS
PASO NOGAL PARK
YMCA
COMM CTR
TAYLOR BLVD
CIVIC DR
LAS JUNTAS PARK
RESIDENCE INN
GREGORY VILLAGE
GREGORY LN
PLEASANT HILL PARK
PLEASANT HILL PLAZA
MONUMENT BLVD
CAMBRIDGE PARK
CONTRA COSTA BLVD
SOLDIERS MONUMENT
BOYD RD
HOOKSTON RD
FAIR OAKS PARK
HESTER PARK
PLEASANT OAK PARK
CONTRA COSTA COUNTY OFFICE OF EDUCATION
OAK PARK BLVD
PLEASANT HILL RD
BUSKIRK AV
MAIN ST
1 ROLEE LN
2 PARKHURST PL
1 SHADOW LAKE PL
2 FOREST LAKE PL
3 SILVER LAKE PL
4 LAKEWOOD PL
5 LAKE PARK CT

SEE 591 MAP

SEE 612 MAP

SEE 572 MAP

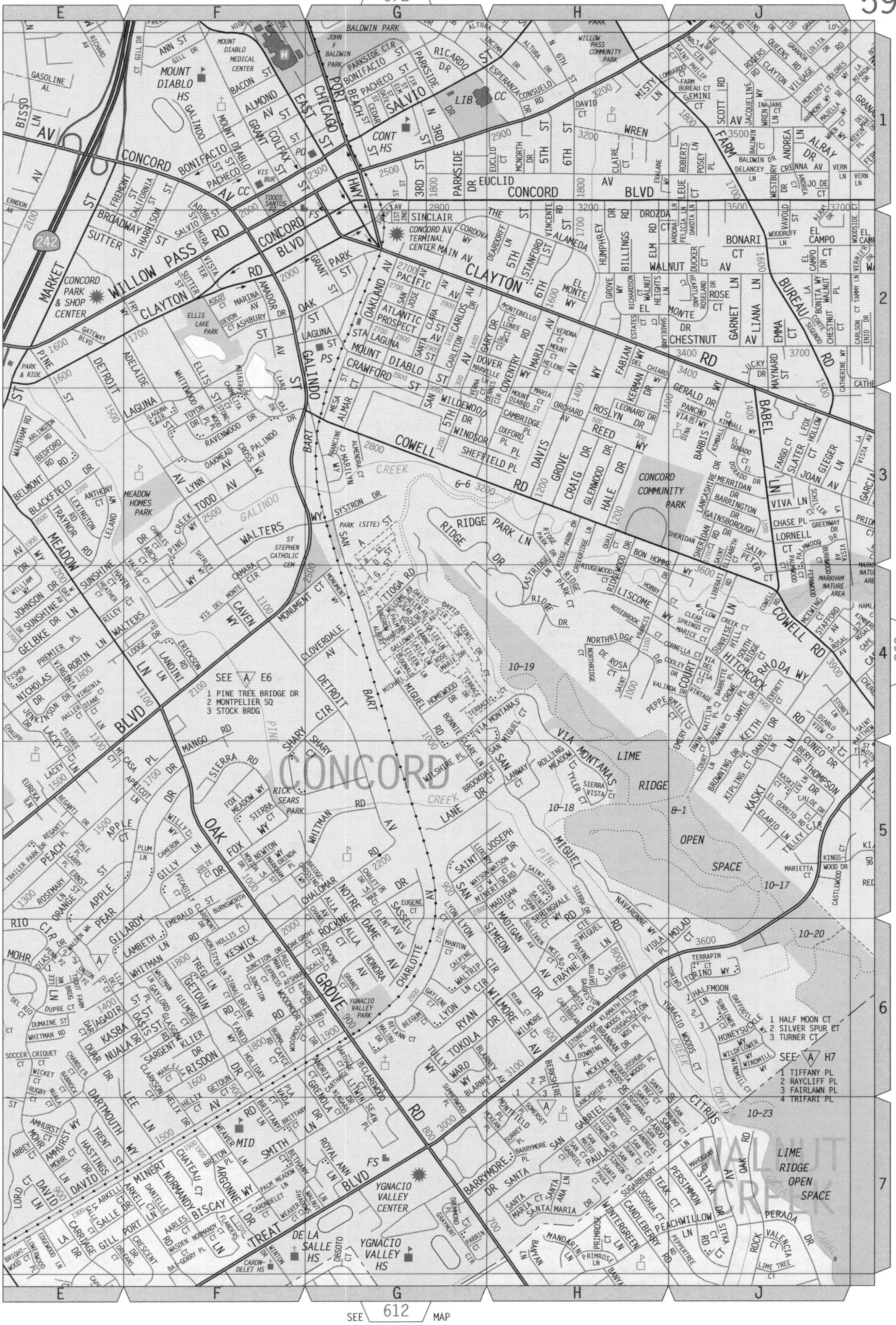
CONCORD
WALNUT CREEK
MOUNT DIABLO MEDICAL CENTER
MOUNT DIABLO HS
CONCORD PARK & SHOP CENTER
ELLIS LAKE PARK
MEADOW HOMES PARK
ST STEPHEN CATHOLIC CEM
CONCORD COMMUNITY PARK
MARKHAM NATURE AREA
LIME RIDGE OPEN SPACE
LIME RIDGE OPEN SPACE
RICK SEARS PARK
YGNACIO VALLEY PARK
YGNACIO VALLEY CENTER
YGNACIO VALLEY HS
DE LA SALLE HS
WILLOW PASS COMMUNITY PARK
BALDWIN PARK
CONCORD AV TERMINAL CENTER
CONT HS
MID
WILLOW PASS RD
CONCORD BLVD
CLAYTON RD
COWELL RD
YGNACIO VALLEY RD
OAK GROVE RD
TREAT BLVD
MONUMENT BLVD
GALINDO ST
SEE A E6
1 PINE TREE BRIDGE DR
2 MONTPELIER SQ
3 STOCK BRDG
1 HALF MOON CT
2 SILVER SPUR CT
3 TURNER CT
SEE A H7
1 TIFFANY PL
2 RAYCLIFF PL
3 FAIRLAWN PL
4 TRIFARI PL

SEE 593 MAP

SEE 612 MAP

BAY AREA

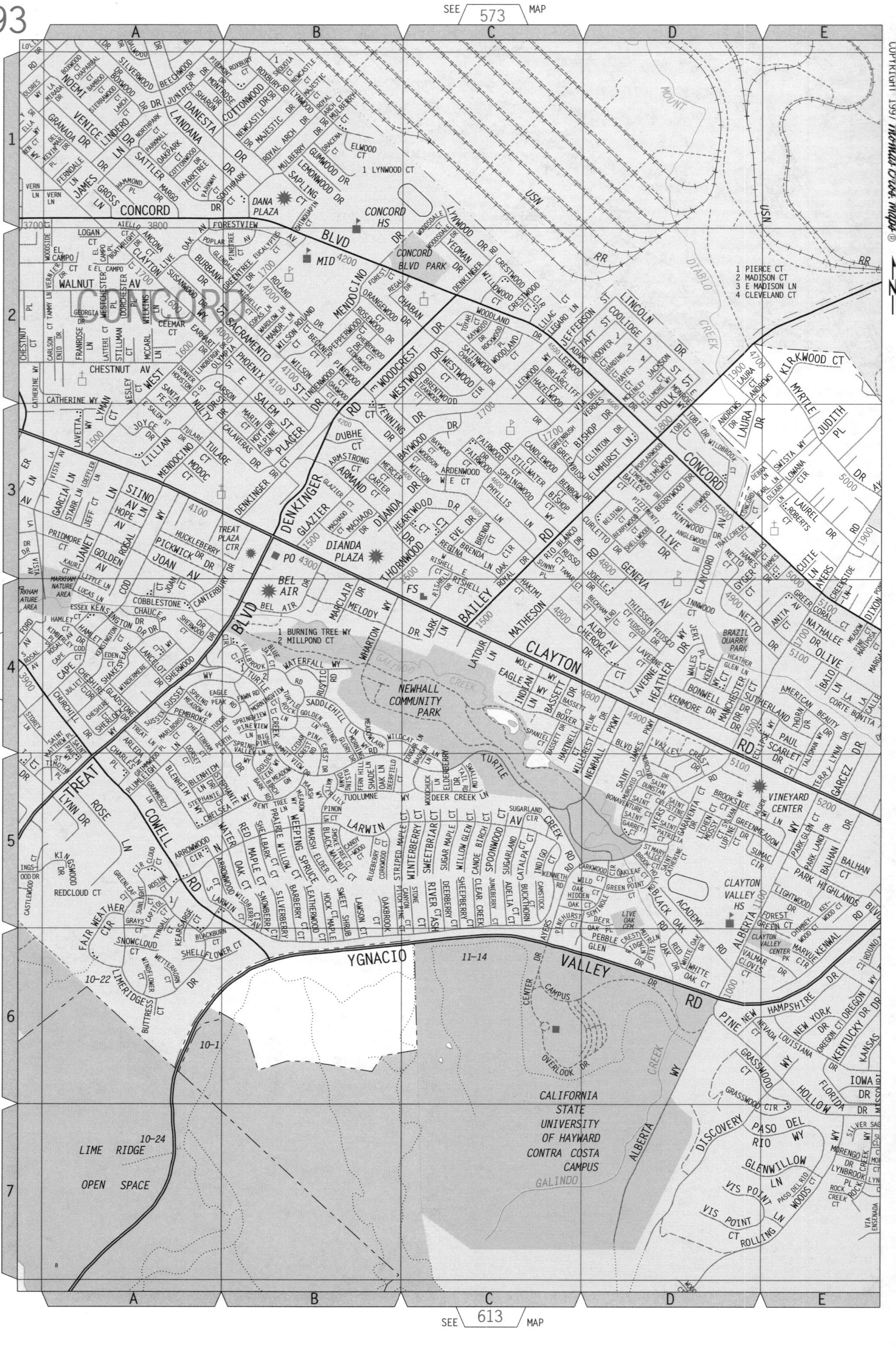
SEE 573 MAP
SEE 592 MAP
SEE 613 MAP
A B C D E
1 2 3 4 5 6 7
CONCORD
CONCORD BLVD
CLAYTON RD
DENKINGER RD
TREAT BLVD
COWELL RD
YGNACIO VALLEY RD
BAILEY RD
CONCORD HS
CONCORD BLVD PARK
DANA PLAZA
TREAT PLAZA CTR
DIANDA PLAZA
BEL AIR
NEWHALL COMMUNITY PARK
BRAZIL QUARRY PARK
VINEYARD CENTER
CLAYTON VALLEY HS
MARKHAM NATURE AREA
LIME RIDGE OPEN SPACE
CALIFORNIA STATE UNIVERSITY OF HAYWARD CONTRA COSTA CAMPUS
GALINDO CREEK
USN RR
1 BURNING TREE WY
2 MILLPOND CT
1 PIERCE CT
2 MADISON CT
3 E MADISON LN
4 CLEVELAND CT
1 LYNWOOD CT
COPYRIGHT 1997 Thomas Bros. Maps ®

MAP

SEE 573 MAP

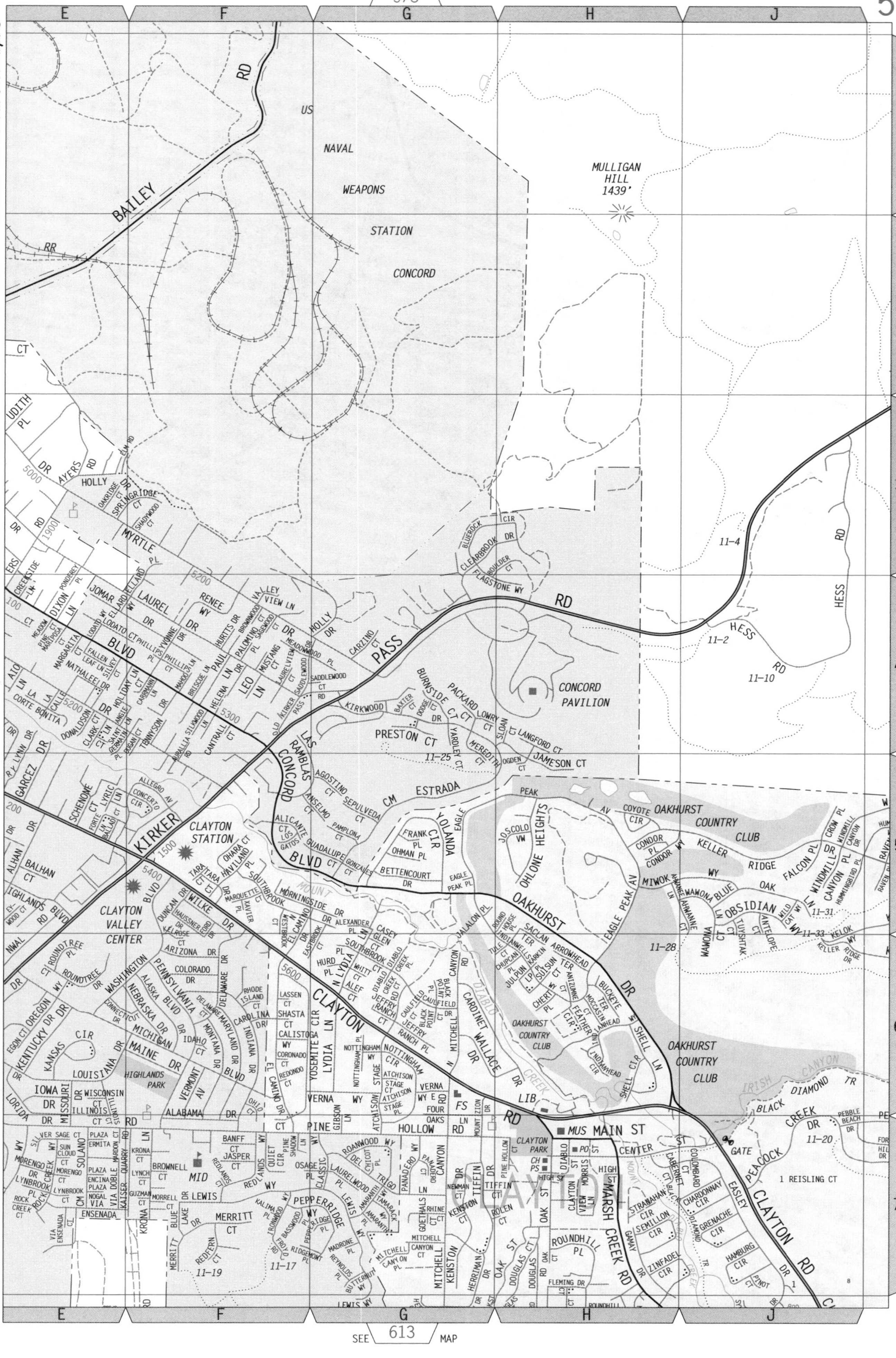
US NAVAL WEAPONS STATION CONCORD
BAILEY RD
RR
MULLIGAN HILL 1439'
CONCORD PAVILION
CONCORD BLVD
PASS RD
KIRKER PASS RD
HESS RD
CLAYTON STATION
CLAYTON VALLEY CENTER
OAKHURST COUNTRY CLUB
OAKHURST DR
CLAYTON RD
MARSH CREEK RD
MAIN ST
CENTER ST
PINE HOLLOW RD
EAGLE PEAK AV
KELLER RIDGE
BLACK DIAMOND TR
PEACOCK CREEK DR
IRISH CANYON
DIABLO CREEK
MOUNT DIABLO CREEK
HIGHLANDS PARK
CLAYTON PARK
CLAYTON
MID
FS
LIB
MUS
PO
CH
PS
YOLANDA CIR
ESTRADA
BETTENCOURT DR
PRESTON CT
KIRKWOOD
WASHINGTON BLVD
PENNSYLVANIA BLVD
LOUISIANA DR
IOWA DR
ALABAMA
MAINE DR
MICHIGAN
VERMONT AV
KENTUCKY DR
KANSAS CIR
LEWIS WY
MERRITT CT
PEPPERRIDGE WY
MITCHELL CANYON RD
CARDINET DR
WALLACE DR
LYDIA LN
NOTTINGHAM
ATCHISON STAGE
VERNA WY
FOUR OAKS
MYRTLE DR
HOLLY DR
LAUREL DR
AYERS RD
1 REISLING CT
11-2
11-4
11-10
11-17
11-19
11-20
11-25
11-28
11-31
11-33
E
F
G
H
J
1
2
3
4
5
6
7

SEE 594 MAP

SEE 613 MAP

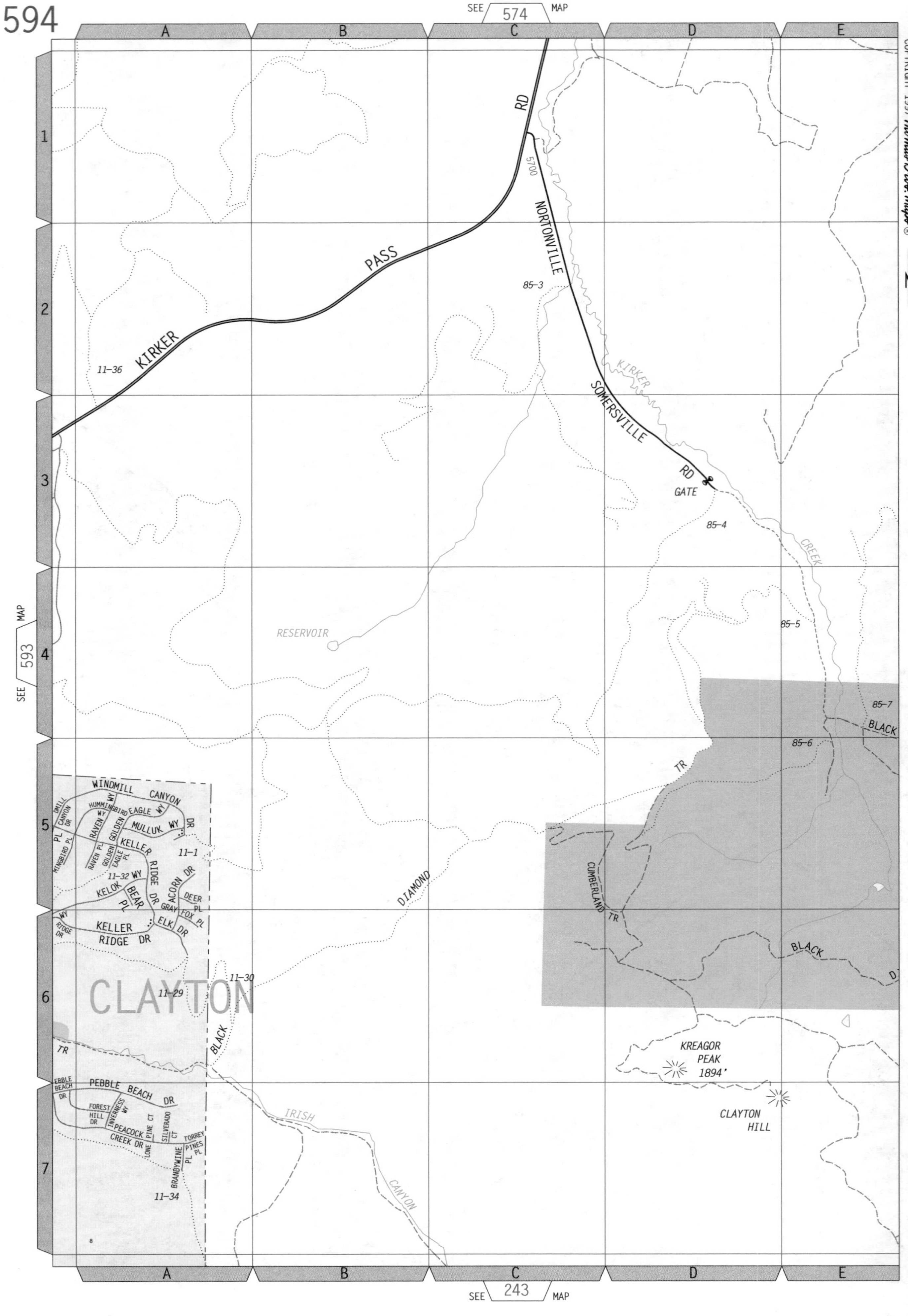

SEE 574 MAP
SEE 593 MAP
SEE 243 MAP
A
B
C
D
E
1
2
3
4
5
6
7
KIRKER
PASS
RD
5700
NORTONVILLE
SOMERSVILLE
RD
GATE
KIRKER
CREEK
85-3
85-4
85-5
85-6
85-7
11-36
RESERVOIR
BLACK
DIAMOND
TR
CUMBERLAND
TR
WINDMILL
CANYON
DR
HUMMINGBIRD
EAGLE
WY
MULLUK
WY
RAVEN
GOLDEN
KELLER
PL
MINGBIRD PL
RAVEN PL
GOLDEN EAGLE PL
11-1
11-32
KELOK
WY
RIDGE
DR
ACORN
DR
BEAR
PL
DEER
PL
GRAY
FOX
PL
ELK
DR
KELLER
RIDGE DR
CLAYTON
11-30
11-29
BLACK
TR
PEBBLE BEACH DR
FOREST HILL DR
INVERNESS WY
PEACOCK CREEK DR
LONE PINE CT
SILVERADO CT
TORREY PINES PL
BRANDYWINE PL
11-34
IRISH
CANYON
KREAGOR
PEAK
1894'
CLAYTON
HILL

SEE 574 MAP

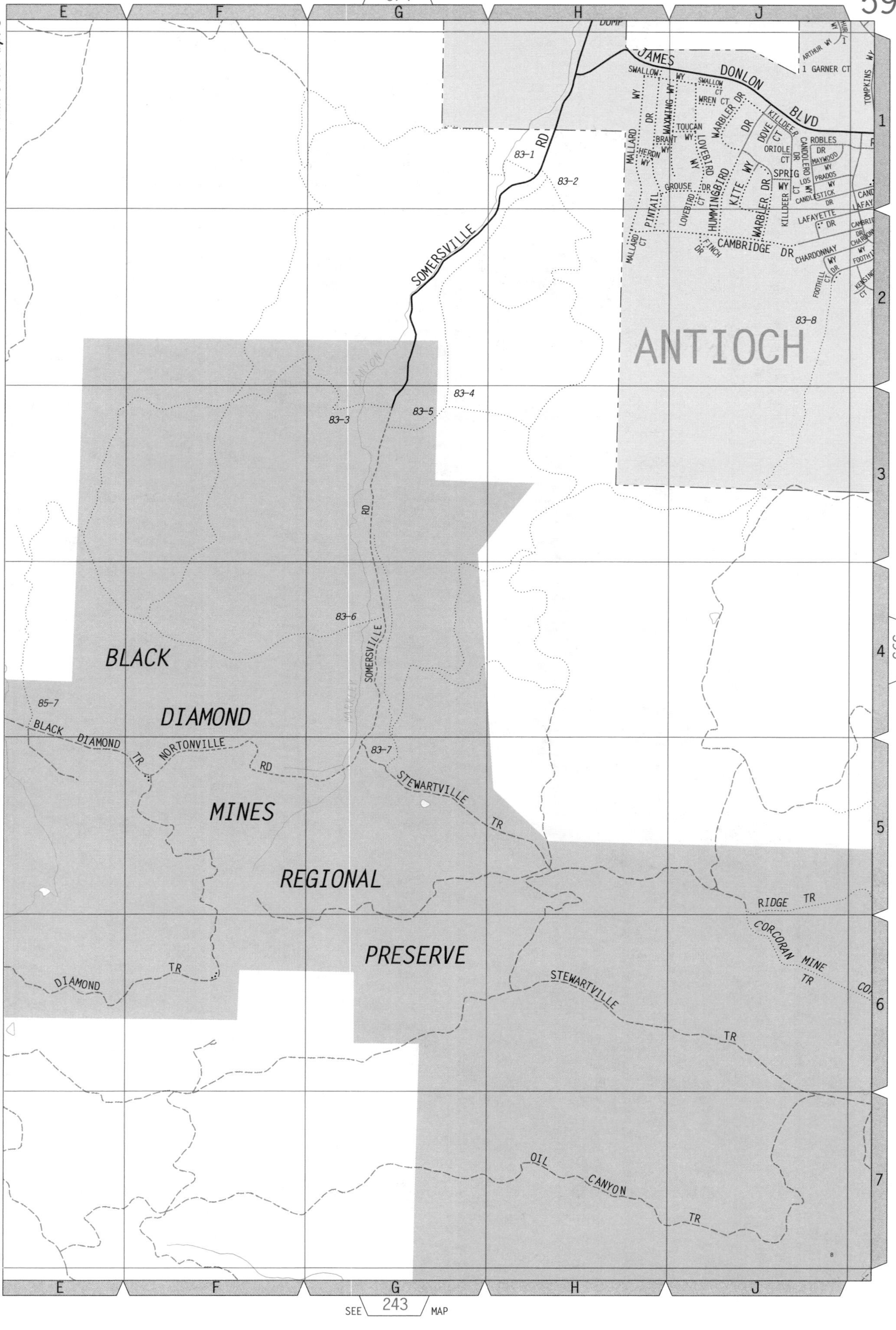
E
F
G
H
J
1
2
3
4
5
6
7
ANTIOCH
BLACK
DIAMOND
MINES
REGIONAL
PRESERVE
DUMP
JAMES DONLON BLVD
SOMERSVILLE RD
SWALLOW WY
SWALLOW CT
WREN CT
WARBLER DR
KILLDEER
TOUCAN
BRANT WY
HERON WY
MALLARD DR
WAXWING WY
LOVEBIRD
DOVE CT
ORIOLE CT
SPRIG WY
KITE WY
HUMMINGBIRD
GROUSE
PINTAIL
MALLARD CT
LOVEBIRD CT
FINCH DR
CAMBRIDGE DR
CANDOLERO
ROBLES
MAYWOOD
PRADOS
LOS
CANDLESTICK DR
LAFAYETTE DR
CHARDONNAY WY
FOOTHILL CT
FOOTHILL DR
ARTHUR WY
GARNER CT
TOMPKINS WY
83-1
83-2
83-3
83-4
83-5
83-6
83-7
83-8
85-7
CANYON
RD
SOMERSVILLE
MARKLEY
BLACK DIAMOND TR
NORTONVILLE RD
STEWARTVILLE TR
RIDGE TR
CORCORAN MINE TR
DIAMOND TR
OIL CANYON TR

SEE 595 MAP

SEE 243 MAP

BAY AREA

MAP

SEE 575 MAP

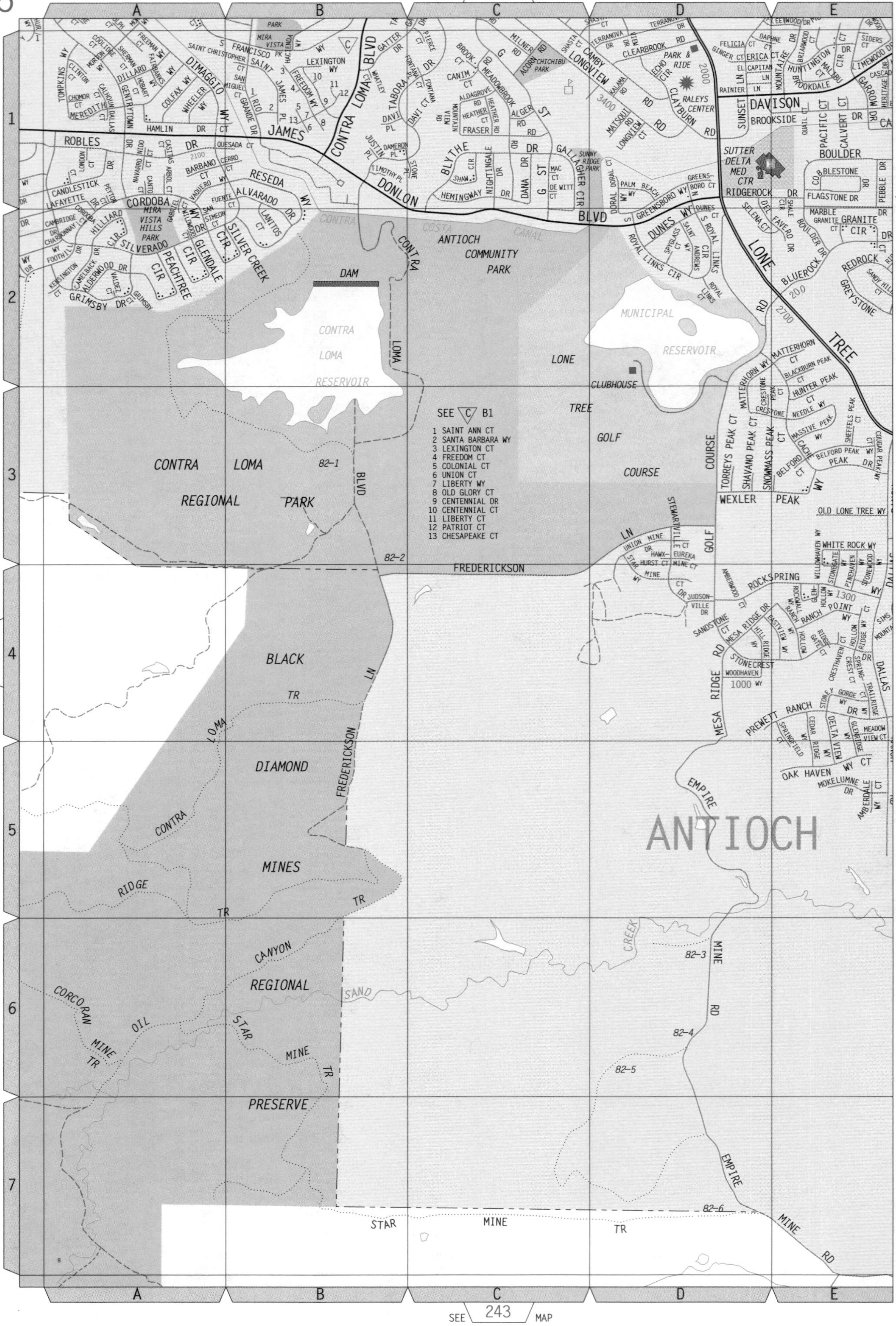
A
B
C
D
E
1
2
3
4
5
6
7
ROBLES DR
HAMLIN DR
JAMES
CONTRA LOMA BLVD
DONLON BLVD
DAVISON DR
BROOKSIDE
BOULDER
RIDGEROCK DR
SUTTER DELTA MED CTR
RALEYS CENTER
PARK & RIDE
CLAYBURN RD
LONGVIEW RD
CAMBY RD
CLEARBROOK
BLYTHE DR
GALLAGHER CIR
DIMAGGIO WY
LEXINGTON WY
FREEDOM WY
RESEDA
ALVARADO DR
CORDOBA
MIRA VISTA HILLS PARK
SILVERADO DR
PEACHTREE CIR
GLENDALE CIR
SILVER CREEK
GRIMSBY DR
CONTRA COSTA CANAL
ANTIOCH COMMUNITY PARK
DAM
CONTRA LOMA RESERVOIR
MUNICIPAL RESERVOIR
LONE TREE GOLF COURSE
CLUBHOUSE
LONE TREE RD
DUNES WY
ROYAL LINKS CIR
SEE C B1
1 SAINT ANN CT
2 SANTA BARBARA WY
3 LEXINGTON CT
4 FREEDOM CT
5 COLONIAL CT
6 UNION CT
7 LIBERTY WY
8 OLD GLORY CT
9 CENTENNIAL DR
10 CENTENNIAL CT
11 LIBERTY CT
12 PATRIOT CT
13 CHESAPEAKE CT
CONTRA LOMA REGIONAL PARK
82-1
82-2
FREDERICKSON LN
STEWARTVILLE LN
GOLF COURSE RD
WEXLER PEAK
OLD LONE TREE WY
ROCKSPRING
MESA RIDGE RD
PREWETT RANCH DR
OAK HAVEN WY
DALLAS
BLACK DIAMOND MINES REGIONAL PRESERVE
LOMA TR
CONTRA RIDGE TR
CANYON TR
CORCORAN MINE TR
OIL
STAR MINE TR
SAND CREEK
EMPIRE MINE RD
82-3
82-4
82-5
82-6
ANTIOCH
SEE 594 MAP

SEE 243 MAP

SEE 575 MAP

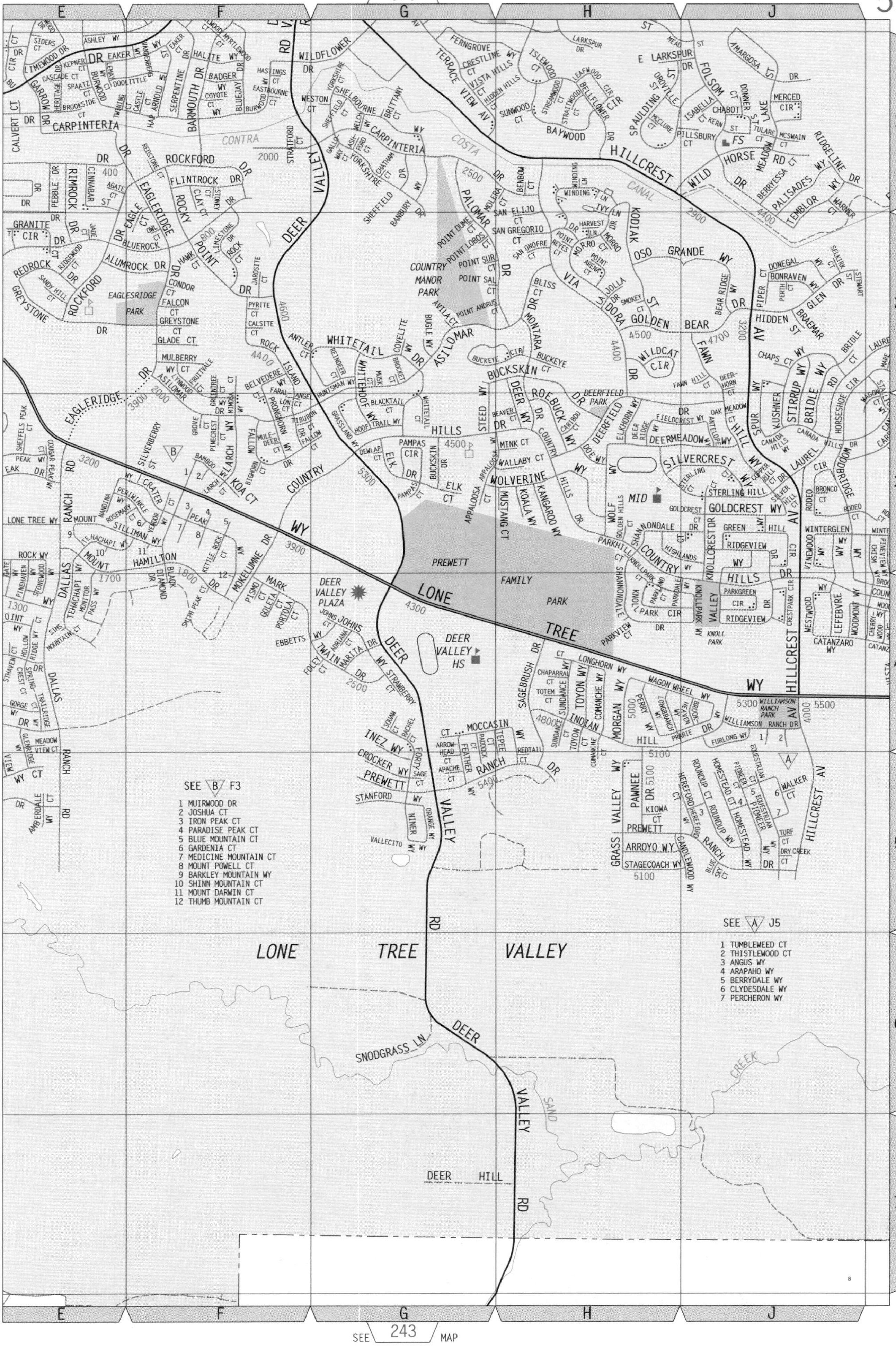
E
F
G
H
J
1
2
3
4
5
6
7
CONTRA COSTA CANAL
DEER VALLEY RD
HILLCREST AV
LONE TREE WY
LONE TREE VALLEY
PREWETT FAMILY PARK
DEER VALLEY PLAZA
DEER VALLEY HS
EAGLESRIDGE PARK
COUNTRY MANOR PARK
KNOLL PARK
WILLIAMSON RANCH PARK
DEER HILL
SNODGRASS LN
SAND CREEK
SEE B F3
1 MUIRWOOD DR
2 JOSHUA CT
3 IRON PEAK CT
4 PARADISE PEAK CT
5 BLUE MOUNTAIN CT
6 GARDENIA CT
7 MEDICINE MOUNTAIN CT
8 MOUNT POWELL CT
9 BARKLEY MOUNTAIN WY
10 SHINN MOUNTAIN CT
11 MOUNT DARWIN CT
12 THUMB MOUNTAIN CT
SEE A J5
1 TUMBLEWEED CT
2 THISTLEWOOD CT
3 ANGUS WY
4 ARAPAHO WY
5 BERRYDALE WY
6 CLYDESDALE WY
7 PERCHERON WY

SEE 243 MAP

SEE 586 MAP

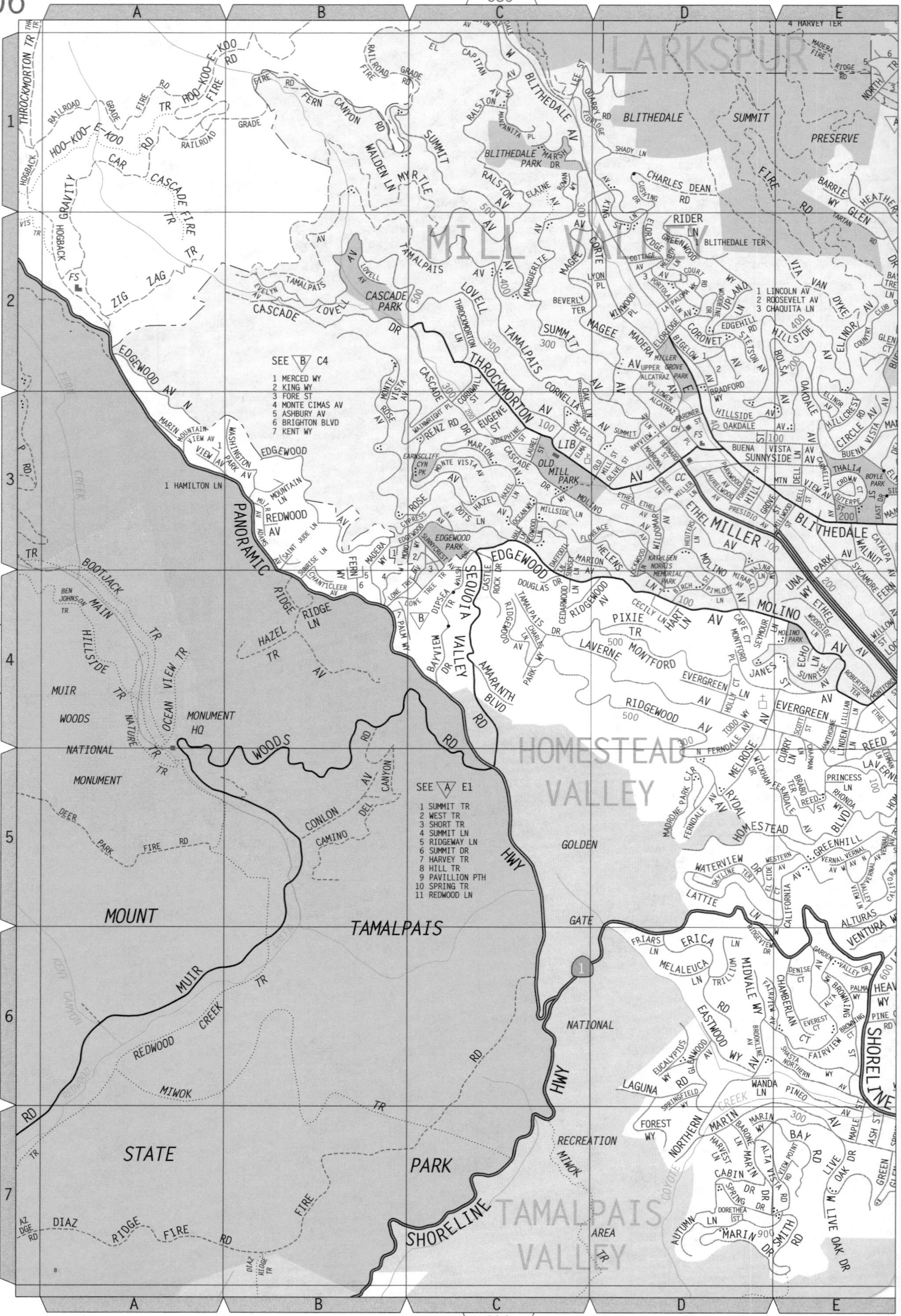
LARKSPUR
MILL VALLEY
BLITHEDALE SUMMIT PRESERVE
HOMESTEAD VALLEY
TAMALPAIS VALLEY
MUIR WOODS NATIONAL MONUMENT
MOUNT TAMALPAIS STATE PARK
GOLDEN GATE NATIONAL RECREATION AREA
MONUMENT HQ
CASCADE PARK
OLD MILL PARK
EDGEWOOD PARK
THROCKMORTON AV
BLITHEDALE AV
MILLER AV
EDGEWOOD AV
PANORAMIC HWY
SHORELINE HWY
SEQUOIA VALLEY DR
MOLINO AV
RIDGEWOOD AV
HOMESTEAD BLVD
MUIR WOODS RD
SEE B C4
1 MERCED WY
2 KING WY
3 FORE ST
4 MONTE CIMAS AV
5 ASHBURY AV
6 BRIGHTON BLVD
7 KENT WY
1 HAMILTON LN
SEE A E1
1 SUMMIT TR
2 WEST TR
3 SHORT TR
4 SUMMIT LN
5 RIDGEWAY LN
6 SUMMIT DR
7 HARVEY TR
8 HILL TR
9 PAVILLION PTH
10 SPRING TR
11 REDWOOD LN
1 LINCOLN AV
2 ROOSEVELT AV
3 CHAQUITA LN
1 BLITHEDALE TER
4 HARVEY TER
SEE 243 MAP

SEE 626 MAP

SEE 586 MAP

CORTE MADERA
MILL VALLEY GOLF COURSE
CAMINO ALTO PRESERVE
ALTO BOWL PRESERVE
TIBURON RIDGE PRESERVE
RING MOUNTAIN OPEN SPACE PRESERVE
TIBURON
ALTO
GRANADA PARK
SAN CLEMENTE PARK
PARADISE CENTER
STRAWBERRY MANOR
STRAWBERRY PARK
STRAWBERRY VILLAGE
RICHARDSON BAY AUDUBON CENTER
HARBOR POINT
GOLDEN GATE BAPTIST THEOLOGICAL SEMINARY
BOTHIN MARSH OPEN SPACE PRESERVE
SILVA ISLAND
MANZANITA
HELIPORT
RICHARDSON BAY
STRAWBERRY POINT
ALMONTE
TAMALPAIS HS
TAMALPAIS JUNCTION
BOTHIN MARSH
OPEN SPACE PRESERVE
DAPHNE FERNWOOD CEMETERY
MID BAYFRONT PARK
REC CTR
ENCHANTED KNOLLS PARK
FREEMAN PARK
BOYLE PARK
SAUSALITO CANAL
COYOTE CREEK
TRANSIT TRANSFER POINT
PARK & RIDE
HWY 101
131
1
REDWOOD HWY
SHORELINE HWY
CAMINO ALTO
CORTE MADERA AV
BLITHEDALE AV
MILLER AV
ALMONTE BLVD
TIBURON BLVD
PARADISE DR
SEMINARY DR
STRAWBERRY DR
1 SHERIDAN CT
SEE D J4
1 SALT LNDG
2 CAPTAINS LNDG
3 SEADRIFT LNDG
1 BLUEBIRD LN
2 COURTNEY LN
1 WEMBURY WY
SEE C G4
1 DICKENS CT
2 SANDBURG CT
3 WHITTIER CT
4 EMERSON DR
5 FIELDING CIR
6 COLERIDGE DR
E F G H J
1 2 3 4 5 6 7

SEE 607 MAP

SEE 626 MAP

SEE 587 MAP

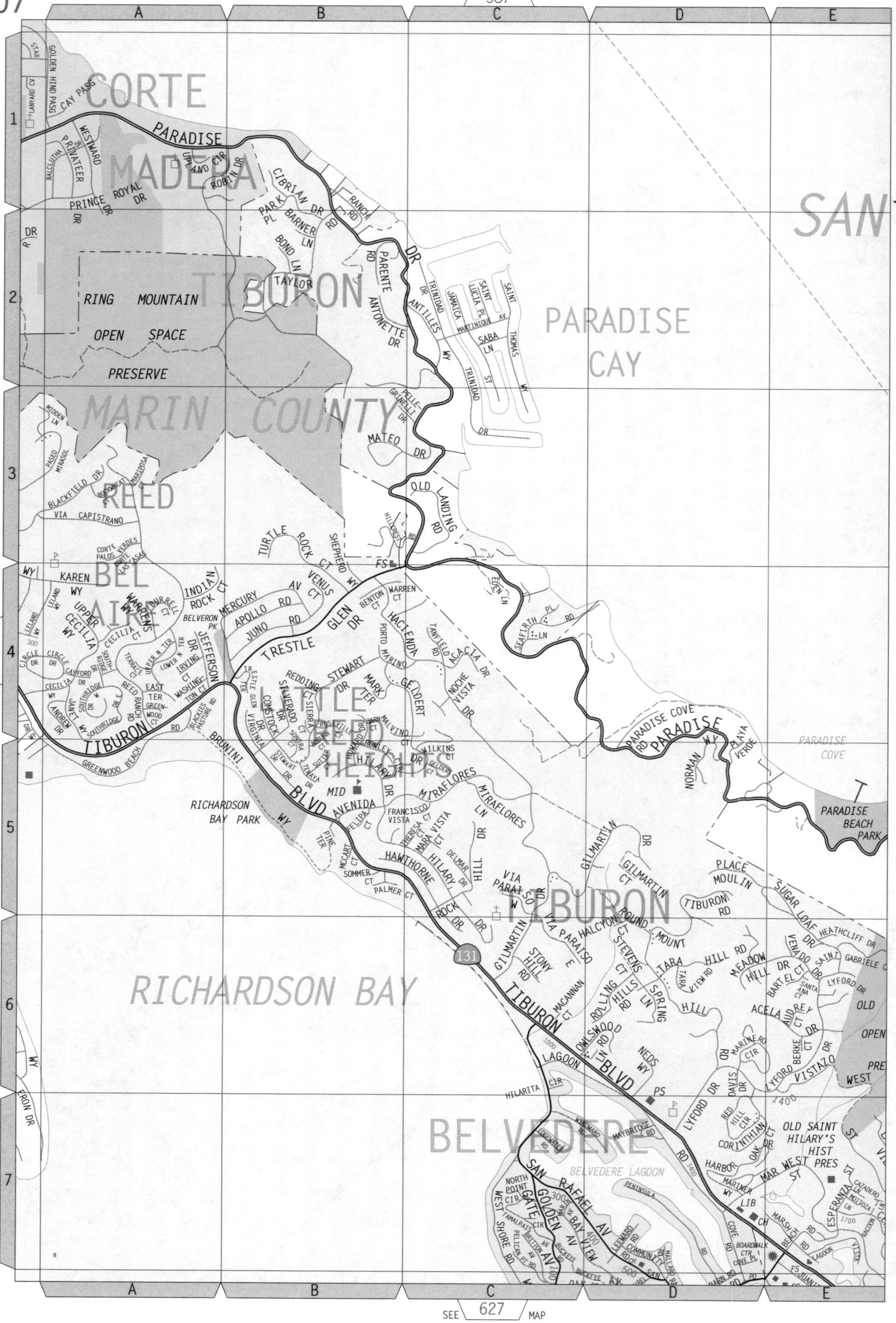
CORTE MADERA
PARADISE DR
TIBURON
RING MOUNTAIN OPEN SPACE PRESERVE
MARIN COUNTY
PARADISE CAY
SAN
REED
BEL AIRE
LITTLE REED HEIGHTS
RICHARDSON BAY PARK
RICHARDSON BAY
TIBURON BLVD
PARADISE COVE
PARADISE BEACH PARK
BELVEDERE
BELVEDERE LAGOON
OLD SAINT HILARY'S HIST PRES
OLD LANDING RD
TRESTLE GLEN DR
GREENWOOD BEACH RD
SAN RAFAEL AV
GOLDEN GATE AV
WEST SHORE RD
LYFORD DR
GILMARTIN DR
HILARY DR
MIRAFLORES
HAWTHORNE
ROUND MOUNT
TIBURON RD
SUGAR LOAF DR
MAR WEST ST
BEACH RD
131

SEE 606 MAP

SEE 627 MAP

SEE 587 MAP

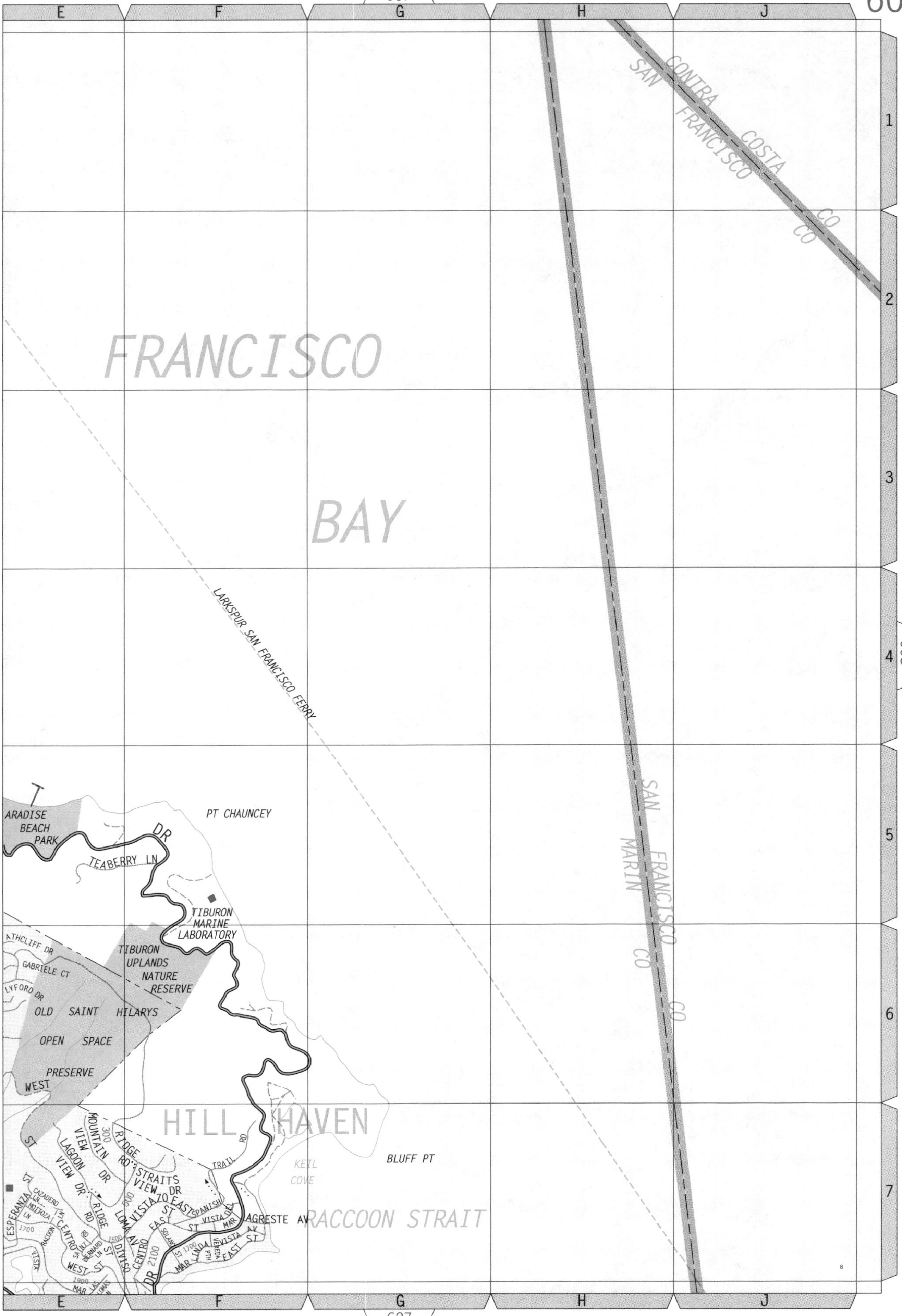
E
F
G
H
J
1
2
3
4
5
6
7
FRANCISCO
BAY
CONTRA COSTA CO
SAN FRANCISCO CO
LARKSPUR SAN FRANCISCO FERRY
SAN FRANCISCO CO
MARIN CO
PT CHAUNCEY
ARADISE BEACH PARK
DR
TEABERRY LN
TIBURON MARINE LABORATORY
ATHCLIFF DR
GABRIELE CT
LYFORD DR
TIBURON UPLANDS NATURE RESERVE
OLD SAINT HILARYS
OPEN SPACE
PRESERVE
WEST
ST
HILL HAVEN
MOUNTAIN VIEW
LAGOON VIEW DR
VIEW DR
RIDGE RD
300
TRAIL
RD
KEIL COVE
BLUFF PT
STRAITS VIEW DR
VISTAZO EAST
VISTAZO EAST ST
SPANISH TRAIL
VISTA DEL MAR
AGRESTE AV
RACCOON STRAIT
ESPERANZA
CAZADERO LN
MOLTOZA LN
CENTRO WEST
RIDGE RD
LOMA AV
DIVISO ST
CENTRO EAST
MAR LINDA
VISTA EAST ST
WEST ST
MAR LAS LOMAS
DR
1700
1900
2100

SEE 608 MAP

SEE 627 MAP

SEE 588 MAP

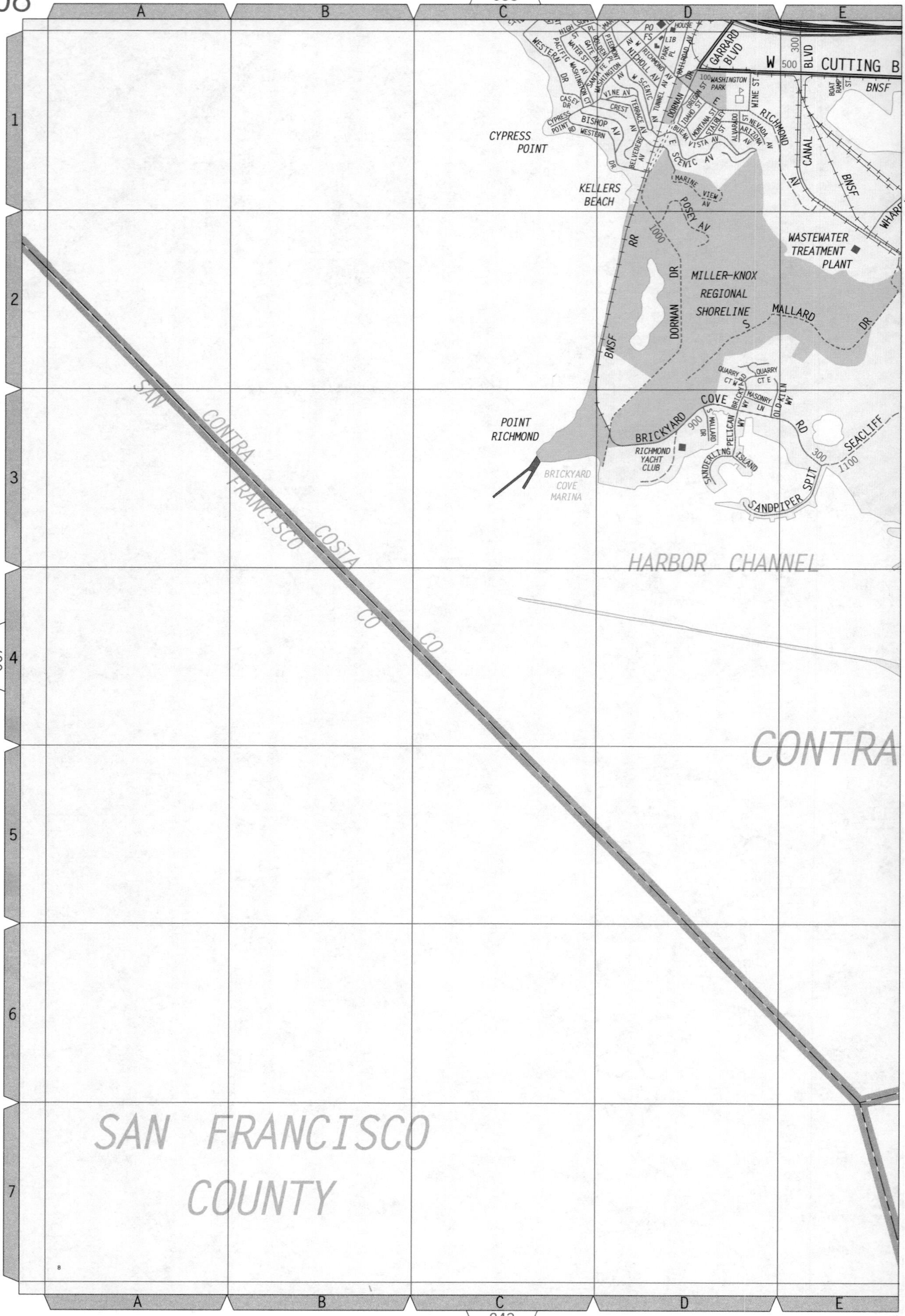
CYPRESS POINT
KELLERS BEACH
POINT RICHMOND
BRICKYARD COVE MARINA
MILLER-KNOX REGIONAL SHORELINE
WASTEWATER TREATMENT PLANT
RICHMOND YACHT CLUB
HARBOR CHANNEL
W CUTTING BLVD
GARRARD BLVD
WASHINGTON PARK
BRICKYARD COVE RD
DORNAN DR
S MALLARD DR
SANDPIPER SPIT
SEACLIFF
BNSF
CANAL BLVD
SAN FRANCISCO CO
CONTRA COSTA CO
CONTRA
SAN FRANCISCO COUNTY

SEE 607 MAP

SEE 243 MAP

SEE 588 MAP

RICHMOND
JOHN T KNOX FRWY
580
CUTTING BLVD
MARTIN LUTHER KING MEMORIAL PARK
VIRGINIA AV
POTRERO AV
HOFFMAN BLVD
WRIGHT AV
MEEKER AV
REGATTA BLVD
PIERSON AV
HALL AV
SCOTT AV
MARINA WY
HARBOUR WY
CARLSON BLVD
STEGE AV
ERLANDSON ST
HINKLEY AV
JOHNSON AV
FOOTHILL AV
SANTA FE CHANNEL
RICHMOND YACHT HARBOR
LAURITZEN CHANNEL
PARR-RICH CANAL
HARBOR CHANNEL
WHARF ST
CANAL BLVD
SEACLIFF DR
BNSF
RR
BOAT RAMP
MARINA PARK
ESPLANADE DR
SCHOONER DR
MELVILLE SQ
BAY ST
MARINA BAY PKWY
MARINA LAKES DR
SHORELINE CT
BAYSIDE DR
SEAGULL DR
SEA ISLE DR
SHOREWOOD CT
LAKESHORE CT
PENINSULA
SANDPOINT
HARBORVIEW DR
WATERVIEW DR
WINDWARD WY
SHIMADA FRIENDSHIP PARK
SOUTHWIND CIR
LIGHTHOUSE
BREAKERS
SEABREEZE
VINCENT PARK
RICHMOND MARINA BAY
FORD CHANNEL
UNIV OF CALIFORNIA RICHMOND FIELD STA
POINT ISABEL REGIONAL SHORELINE
SEAVER AV
46TH ST
RICHMOND INNER HARBOR
SHOAL POINT
SEE A J3
1 FARALLON CT
2 PROMONTORY DR
3 DEEPWATER CT
4 BAY HARBOR CT
5 MAINSAIL CT
6 WINDJAMMER CT
7 ROCKPORT CT
8 BAY HARBOR DR
COSTA COUNTY
CONTRA COSTA CO
ALAMEDA CO
ALAMEDA COUNTY

SEE 609 MAP

SEE 243 MAP

SEE 589 MAP

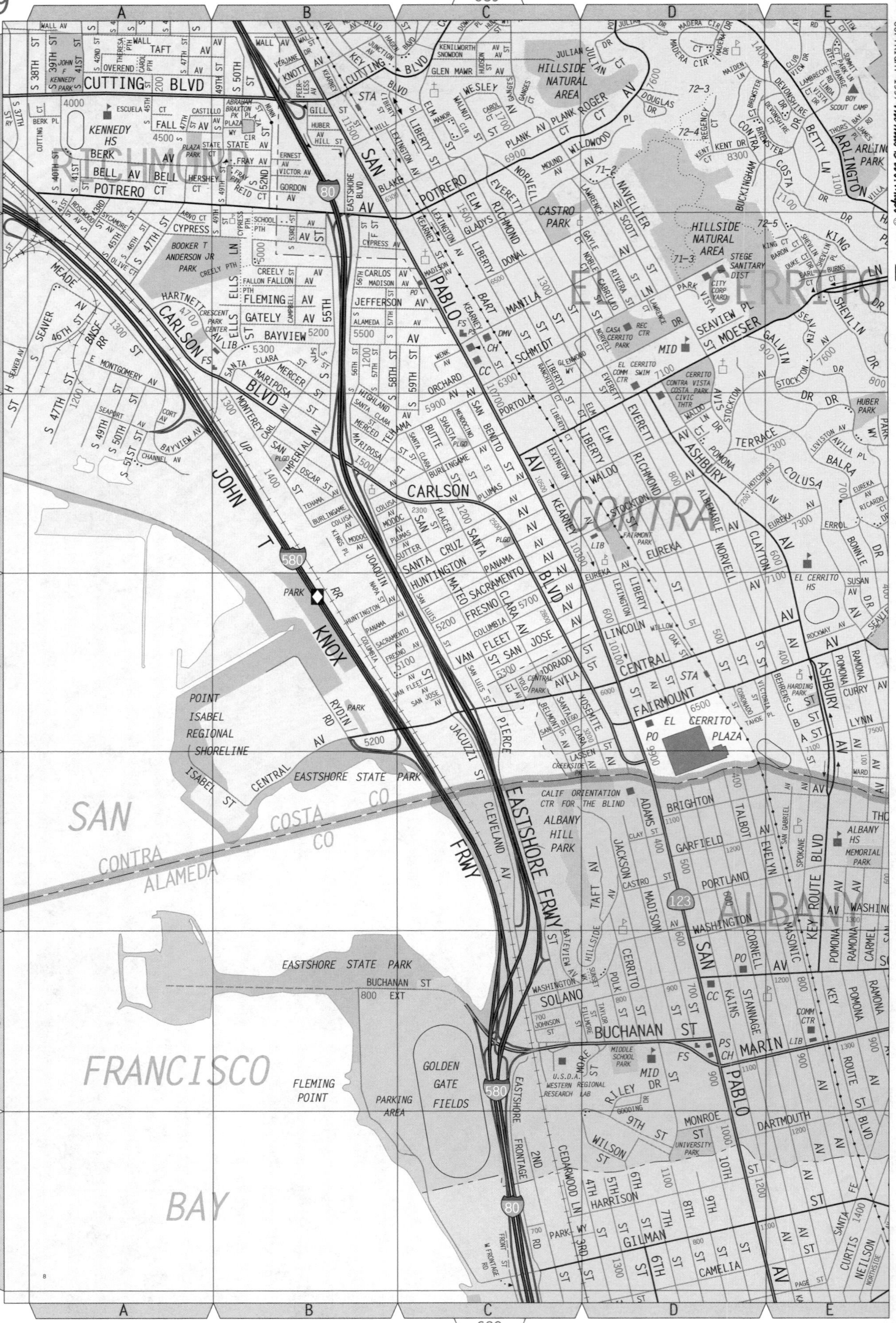
A
B
C
D
E
1
2
3
4
5
6
7
RICHMOND
EL CERRITO
CONTRA COSTA
ALBANY
SAN FRANCISCO BAY
CONTRA COSTA CO
ALAMEDA CO
CUTTING BLVD
POTRERO AV
SAN PABLO AV
CARLSON BLVD
JOHN T KNOX FRWY
EASTSHORE FRWY
KENNEDY HS
HILLSIDE NATURAL AREA
CASTRO PARK
BOOKER T ANDERSON JR PARK
POINT ISABEL REGIONAL SHORELINE
EASTSHORE STATE PARK
ALBANY HILL PARK
CALIF ORIENTATION CTR FOR THE BLIND
GOLDEN GATE FIELDS
FLEMING POINT
PARKING AREA
EL CERRITO HS
EL CERRITO PLAZA
ALBANY HS
MEMORIAL PARK
U.S.D.A. WESTERN REGIONAL RESEARCH LAB
MIDDLE SCHOOL PARK
UNIVERSITY PARK
FAIRMOUNT AV
CENTRAL AV
MOESER LN
ASHBURY AV
COLUSA AV
KEY ROUTE BLVD
BUCHANAN ST
SOLANO AV
MARIN AV
GILMAN ST
WASHINGTON AV
BRIGHTON AV
GARFIELD AV
PORTLAND AV
DARTMOUTH ST
MONROE ST
HARRISON ST
CAMELIA ST
EASTSHORE FRONTAGE RD
CLEVELAND AV
JACUZZI ST
PIERCE ST
ARLINGTON AV
BUCKINGHAM
SEAVIEW PL
TERRACE
STOCKTON AV
CREELY
FLEMING AV
GATELY AV
BAYVIEW AV
JEFFERSON AV
80
580
123

SEE 608 MAP

SEE 629 MAP

SEE 589 MAP

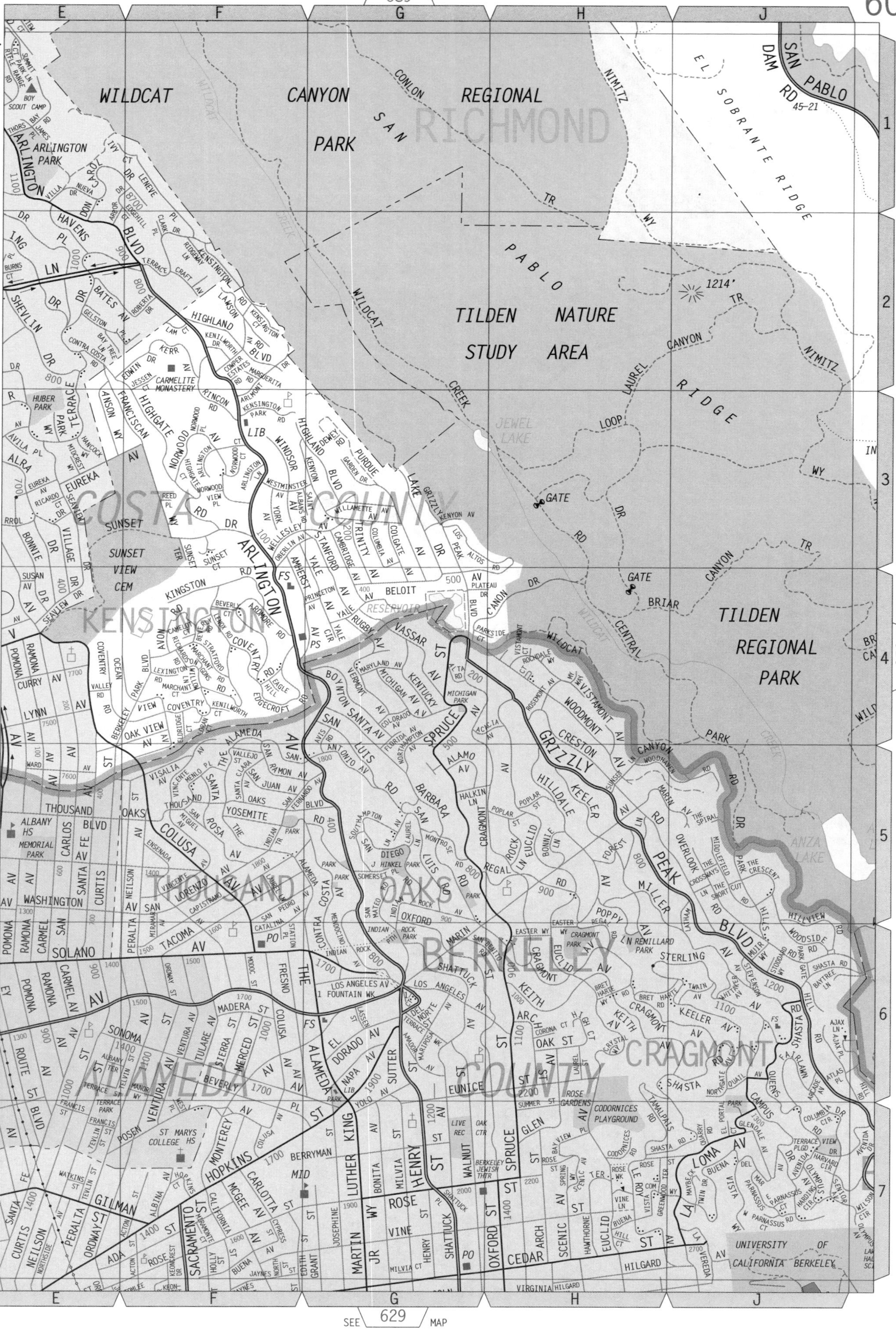
E
F
G
H
J
1
2
3
4
5
6
7
WILDCAT CANYON REGIONAL PARK
SAN PABLO RIDGE
RICHMOND
EL SOBRANTE RIDGE
SAN PABLO DAM RD
TILDEN NATURE STUDY AREA
NIMITZ WY
WILDCAT CREEK
JEWEL LAKE
CONLON TR
LAUREL CANYON TR
LOOP
CENTRAL PARK DR
GATE
1214'
TILDEN REGIONAL PARK
ANZA LAKE
CANYON TR
BRIAR
WILDCAT
ARLINGTON PARK
ARLINGTON BLVD
KENSINGTON
COSTA COUNTY
CARMELITE MONASTERY
HUBER PARK
SUNSET VIEW CEM
LIB
FS
PS
RESERVOIR
THOUSAND OAKS
BERKELEY
ALAMEDA COUNTY
CRAGMONT
GRIZZLY PEAK BLVD
SPRUCE ST
SHATTUCK AV
MARTIN LUTHER KING JR WY
SAN PABLO AV
SOLANO AV
COLUSA AV
HOPKINS ST
GILMAN ST
ROSE ST
VINE ST
CEDAR ST
HILGARD
EUCLID AV
MILLER AV
MICHIGAN PARK
LIVE OAK REC CTR
CODORNICES PLAYGROUND
ROSE GARDENS
ST MARYS COLLEGE HS
ALBANY HS
MEMORIAL PARK
TERRACE PARK
BERKELEY JEWISH THTR
PO
UNIVERSITY OF CALIFORNIA BERKELEY

SEE 610 MAP

SEE 629 MAP

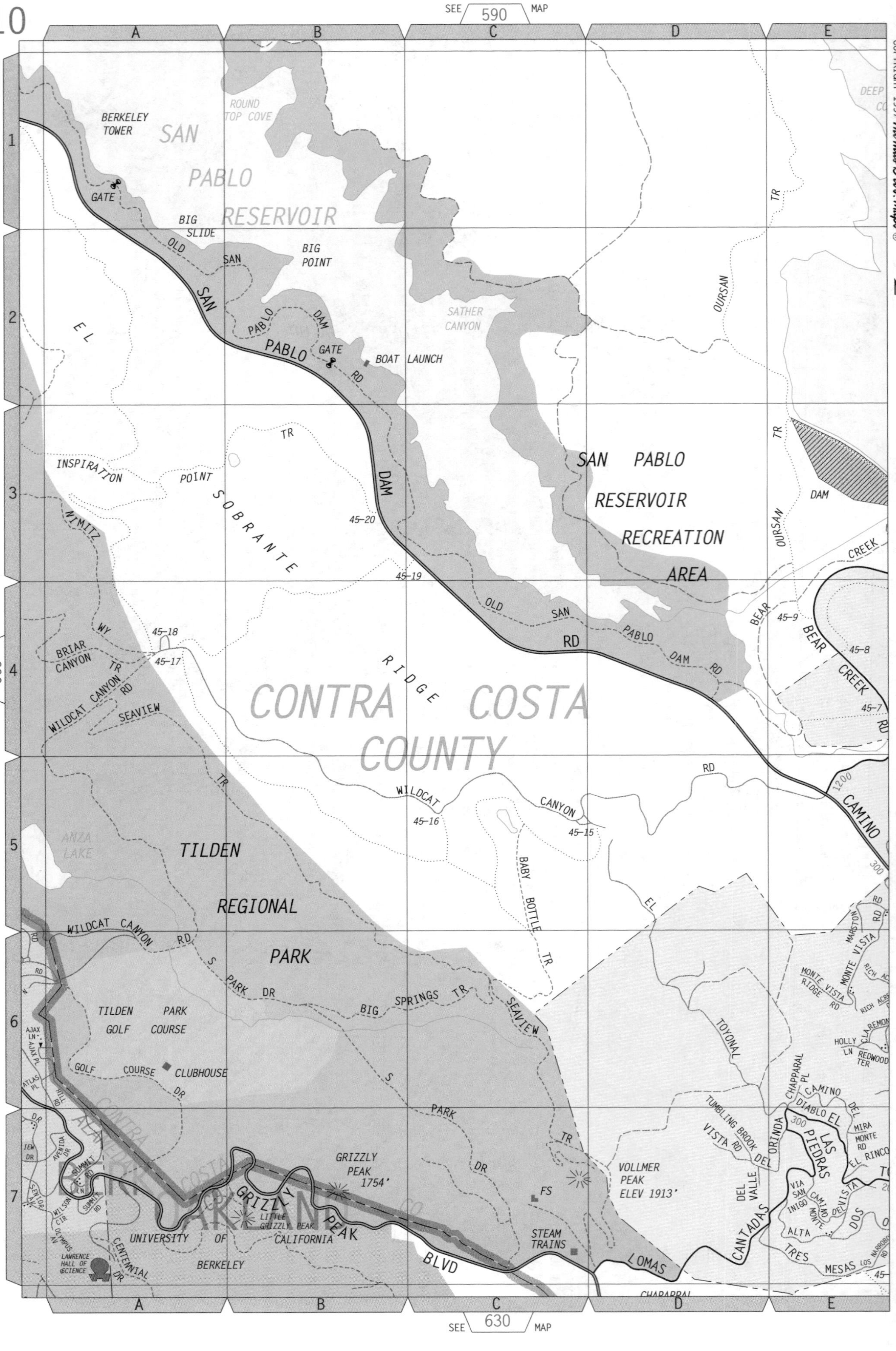
SEE 590 MAP
SEE 609 MAP
SEE 630 MAP
A
B
C
D
E
1
2
3
4
5
6
7
BERKELEY TOWER
SAN PABLO RESERVOIR
ROUND TOP COVE
GATE
BIG SLIDE
BIG POINT
OLD SAN PABLO DAM RD
SAN PABLO DAM RD
SATHER CANYON
BOAT LAUNCH
OURSAN
TR
EL
INSPIRATION POINT
SOBRANTE
RIDGE
NIMITZ WY
SAN PABLO RESERVOIR RECREATION AREA
DAM
CREEK
BEAR CREEK RD
45-20
45-19
45-18
45-17
45-9
45-8
45-7
45-16
45-15
BRIAR CANYON TR
WILDCAT CANYON RD
SEAVIEW
CONTRA COSTA COUNTY
RD
CAMINO
1200
300
ANZA LAKE
TILDEN REGIONAL PARK
BABY BOTTLE TR
EL
S PARK DR
BIG SPRINGS TR
SEAVIEW
TOYONAL
TILDEN PARK GOLF COURSE
GOLF COURSE DR
CLUBHOUSE
AJAX LN
AJAX PL
ATLAS PL
HILL RD
MARSTON
MONTE VISTA
MONTE VISTA RIDGE RD
RICH ACRES
CLAREMONT
HOLLY LN
REDWOOD TER
CHAPPARAL PL
CAMINO DEL DIABLO
EL CAMINO
TUMBLING BROOK
VISTA DEL ORINDA
LAS PIEDRAS
MIRA MONTE RD
EL RINCON
GRIZZLY PEAK 1754'
VOLLMER PEAK ELEV 1913'
LITTLE GRIZZLY PEAK
GRIZZLY PEAK BLVD
FS
STEAM TRAINS
DEL VALLE
CANTADAS
LOMAS
VIA SAN INIGO
CAMINO MONTE
DEL VISTA
ALTA
DOS
TRES MESAS
CHAPARRAL
UNIVERSITY OF CALIFORNIA
BERKELEY
OAKLAND
CONTRA COSTA CO
ALAMEDA CO
SUMMIT
SUMMIT RD
AVENIDA DR
WILSON CIR
SENIOR AV
OLYMPUS AV
CENTENNIAL DR
LAWRENCE HALL OF SCIENCE
DEEP

SEE 590 MAP

E
F
G
H
J
1
2
3
4
5
6
7
BRIONES
BRIONES REGIONAL PARK
DEEP COVE
PEREIRA COVE
TIN HOUSE COVE
OURSAN TR
BEAR CREEK TR
RESERVOIR
BLACK HILLS
CUTTER COVE
LITTLE JOHN COVE
BEAR CREEK RD
ORINDA
ORINDA VILLAGE
SAN PABLO CREEK
CAMINO PABLO
MINER RD
LAUTERWASSER CREEK
ORINDA COUNTRY CLUB
ORINDA SPORTS FIELD
CLUBHOUSE
LAKE CASCADE
ORINDA COMMUNITY PARK
PINE GROVE SPORTS FIELD
JFK UNIVERSITY
NORTH BAY ORINDA HS
LIB
COMM CTR
FS
PO
CH
FRWY
BART
24
SLEEPY HOLLOW LN
BEAR RIDGE RD
VAN RIPPER LN
DALEWOOD DR
DIABLO VIEW DR
SYCAMORE RD
TIGER TAIL CT
EL CAMINO DR
LAS VEGAS RD
HONEY HILL RD
CHARLES HILL RD
EL NIDO RANCH RD
MORAGA WY
ORINDA WY
SOUTHWOOD DR
DAVIS RD
MONTEREY TER
EL TOYONAL
LOMA VISTA DR
CANON DR
ARDILLA RD
ALTARINDA RD
GATE

SEE 611 MAP

SEE 630 MAP

BAY AREA

MAP

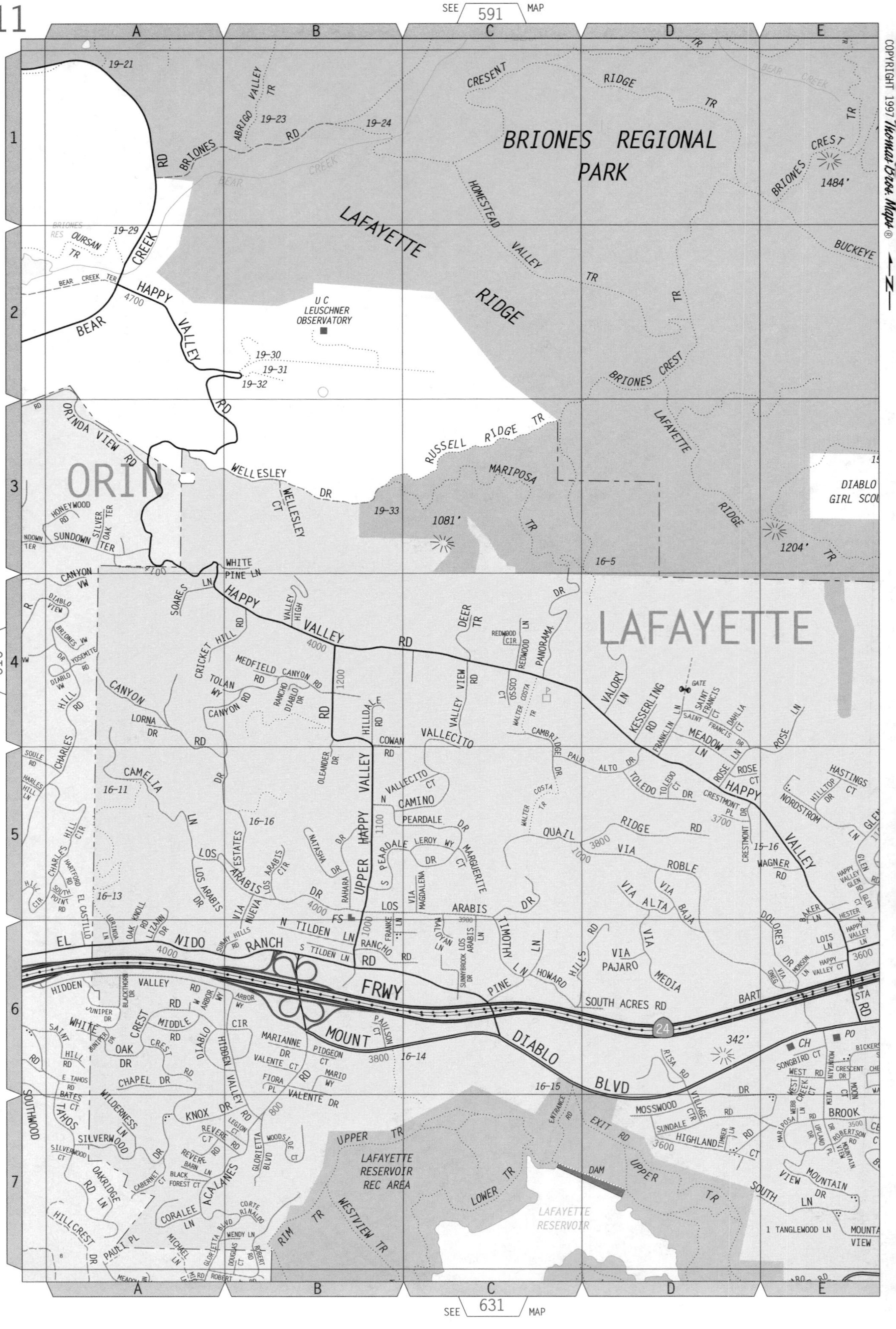

SEE 591 MAP
SEE 610 MAP
SEE 631 MAP
BRIONES REGIONAL PARK
LAFAYETTE RIDGE
UC LEUSCHNER OBSERVATORY
ORIN
LAFAYETTE
DIABLO GIRL SCOU
LAFAYETTE RESERVOIR REC AREA
LAFAYETTE RESERVOIR
BEAR CREEK RD
HAPPY VALLEY RD
BRIONES RD
ABRIGO VALLEY TR
CRESENT RIDGE TR
HOMESTEAD VALLEY TR
BRIONES CREST
BUCKEYE
RUSSELL RIDGE TR
MARIPOSA TR
LAFAYETTE RIDGE
WELLESLEY DR
WELLESLEY CT
ORINDA VIEW RD
HONEYWOOD RD
SUNDOWN TER
SILVER OAK TER
CANYON VW
WHITE PINE LN
SOARES LN
VALLEY HIGH
CRICKET HILL RD
MEDFIELD CANYON RD
TOLAN WY
CANYON RD
RANCHO DIABLO DR
UPPER HAPPY VALLEY RD
HILLDALE RD
COWAN RD
VALLECITO
VALLEY VIEW RD
DEER TR
REDWOOD CIR
REDWOOD LN
PANORAMA DR
COSSO CT
WALTER COSTA TR
CAMBRIDGE DR
PALO ALTO DR
TOLEDO DR
TOLEDO CT
VALORY LN
KESSERLING RD
GATE
FRANKLIN LN
SAINT FRANCIS CT
SAINT FRANCIS DR
DAHLIA CT
MEADOW LN
ROSE LN
ROSE CT
CRESTMONT PL
CRESTMONT DR
HASTINGS CT
HILLTOP DR
NORDSTROM LN
CAMELIA LN
LORNA DR
CANYON RD
OLEANDER DR
N VALLECITO CT
CAMINO
PEARDALE DR
S PEARDALE
LEROY WY
MARGUERITE CT
QUAIL RIDGE RD
VIA ROBLE
VIA ALTA
VIA BAJA
WAGNER RD
DOLORES DR
BAKER LN
HESTER LN
LOIS LN
LOS ESTATES
LOS ARABIS DR
LOS ARABIS CIR
VIA NUEVA
NATASHA DR
RAHARA DR
FS
N TILDEN LN
S TILDEN LN
RANCHO RD
FRANKE LN
VIA MAGDALENA
MALOYAN LN
LOS ARABIS CT
SUNNYBROOK DR
TIMOTHY LN
HOWARD LN
PINE LN
HILLS RD
VIA PAJARO
VIA MEDIA
SOUTH ACRES RD
BART
STA RD
24
EL NIDO RANCH RD
FRWY
MOUNT DIABLO BLVD
HIDDEN VALLEY RD
JUNIPER DR
WHITE OAK DR
CREST RD
MIDDLE RD
ARBOR WY
DIABLO RD
HIDDEN VALLEY CIR
MARIANNE DR
VALENTE CT
PIDGEON CT
PAULSON CT
FIORA PL
MARIO WY
VALENTE DR
CHAPEL DR
KNOX DR
WILDERNESS LN
SILVERWOOD DR
SILVERWOOD CT
SOUTHWOOD
TAHOS RD
BATES CT
OAKRIDGE LN
CABERNET CT
BLACK FOREST CT
REVERE CT
REVERE BARN LN
LEGION CT
GLORIETTA BLVD
WOODSIDE CT
ACALANES RD
CORALEE LN
CORTE RINALDO
WENDY LN
MICHAEL LN
PAULI PL
HILLCREST DR
UPPER TR
RIM TR
WESTVIEW TR
LOWER TR
DAM
ENTRANCE RD
EXIT RD
RISA RD
VILLAGE CTR
MOSSWOOD DR
SUNDALE RD
HIGHLAND RD
TIMBER LN
CH
PO
SONGBIRD CT
WEST RD
MOUNTAIN VIEW DR
BROOK
MARIPOSA LN
ROBERTSON CT
SOUTH LN
MOUNTAIN VIEW
1 TANGLEWOOD LN
1484'
1081'
1204'
342'

SEE 591 MAP

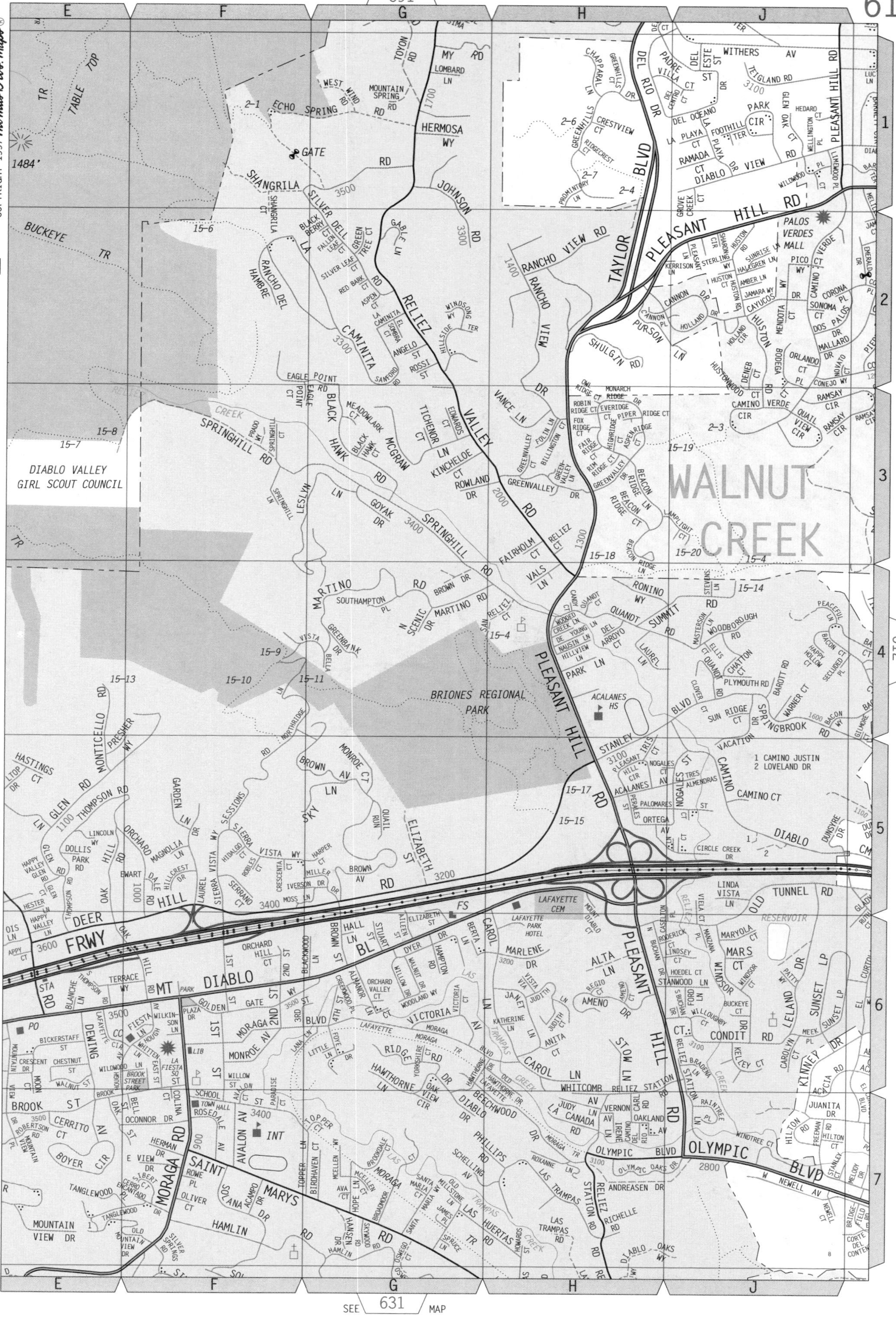
E
F
G
H
J
1
2
3
4
5
6
7
WALNUT
CREEK
DIABLO VALLEY
GIRL SCOUT COUNCIL
BRIONES REGIONAL
PARK
PALOS
VERDES
MALL
ACALANES
HS
LAFAYETTE
CEM
LAFAYETTE
PARK
HOTEL
RESERVOIR
INT
PO
LIB
FS
TOWN HALL
1484'
GATE
TABLE TOP
TR
BUCKEYE
TR
PLEASANT HILL RD
RELIEZ VALLEY RD
TAYLOR BLVD
DEL RIO DR
SPRINGHILL RD
RANCHO VIEW DR
DEER HILL RD
MT DIABLO BLVD
FRWY
OLD TUNNEL RD
OLYMPIC BLVD
SAINT MARYS RD
MORAGA RD
STANLEY BLVD
ECHO SPRING RD
HERMOSA WY
SHANGRILA RD
CAMINITA
MARTINO RD
ACALANES AV
CAMINO DIABLO
CAMINO CT
ELIZABETH ST
BROWN AV
1 CAMINO JUSTIN
2 LOVELAND DR

SEE 612 MAP

SEE 631 MAP

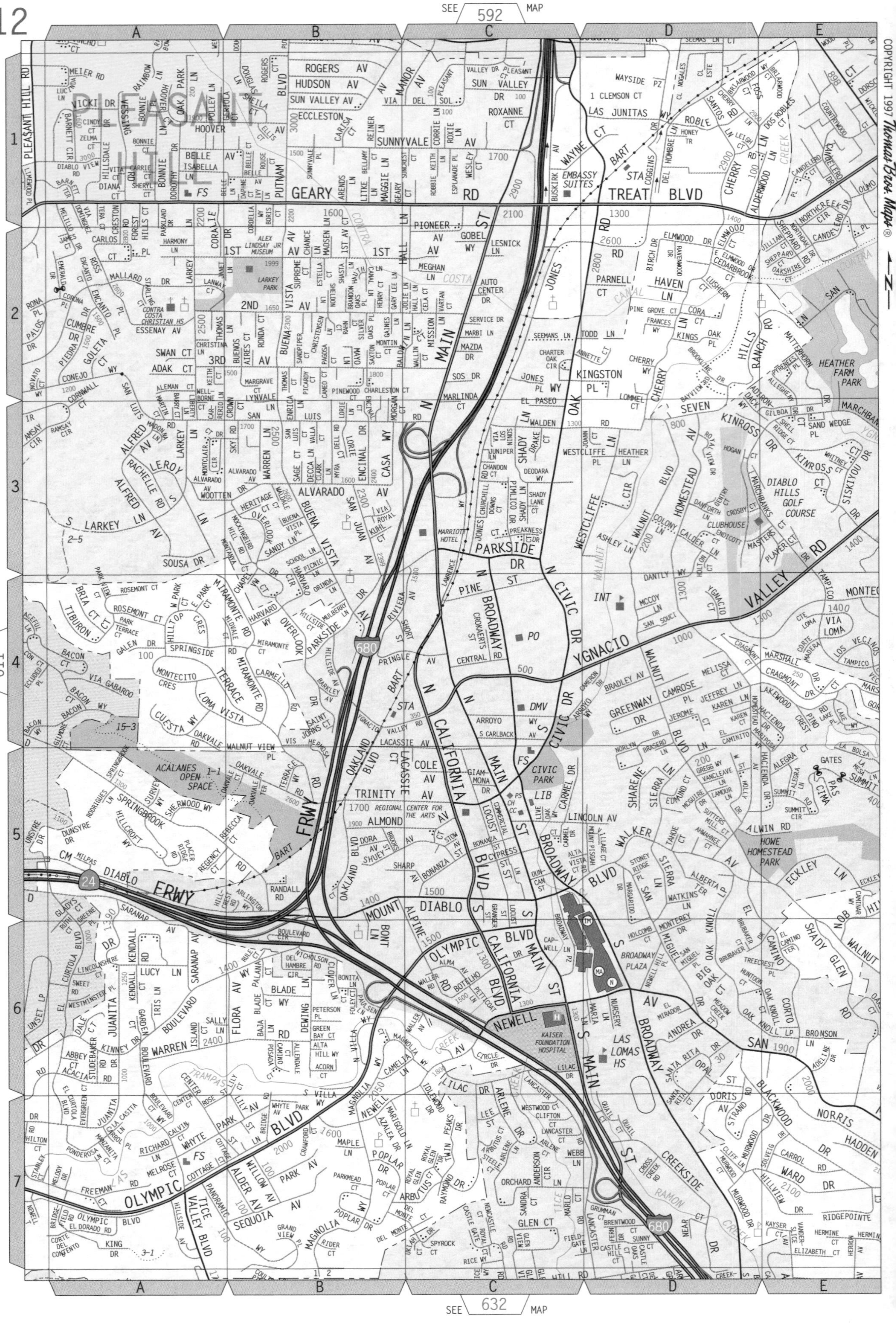
SEE 592 MAP
SEE 611 MAP
SEE 632 MAP
A B C D E
1 2 3 4 5 6 7
PLEASANT HILL
PLEASANT HILL RD
GEARY RD
TREAT BLVD
BUSKIRK AV
EMBASSY SUITES
BART STA
JONES RD
OAK RD
N MAIN ST
CONTRA COSTA CANAL
ALEX LINDSAY JR MUSEUM
LARKEY PARK
CONTRA COSTA CHRISTIAN HS
HEATHER FARM PARK
YGNACIO VALLEY RD
DIABLO HILLS GOLF COURSE
CLUBHOUSE
MARRIOTT HOTEL
PARKSIDE DR
CIVIC DR
BROADWAY
CALIFORNIA BLVD
CIVIC PARK
LIB
PO
DMV
ACALANES OPEN SPACE
REGIONAL CENTER FOR THE ARTS
HOWE HOMESTEAD PARK
DIABLO FRWY
MOUNT DIABLO BLVD
BROADWAY PLAZA
NEWELL AV
KAISER FOUNDATION HOSPITAL
LAS LOMAS HS
OLYMPIC BLVD
TICE VALLEY BLVD
S MAIN ST
SAN MIGUEL DR
BLACKWOOD DR
680
24
COPYRIGHT 1997 Thomas Bros. Maps ®

SEE 592 MAP

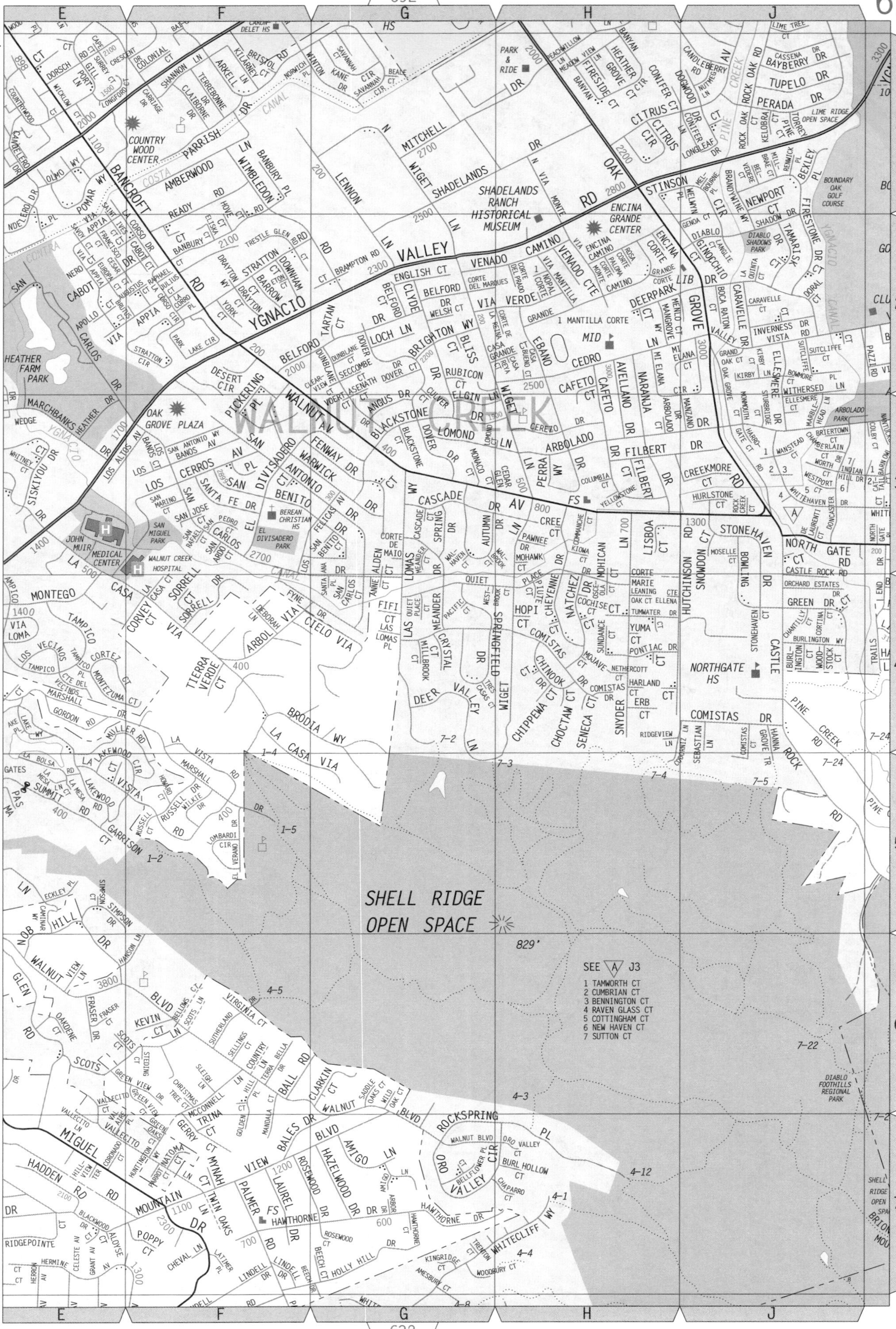
WALNUT CREEK
SHELL RIDGE OPEN SPACE
829'
COUNTRY WOOD CENTER
SHADELANDS RANCH HISTORICAL MUSEUM
ENCINA GRANDE CENTER
OAK GROVE PLAZA
HEATHER FARM PARK
JOHN MUIR MEDICAL CENTER
WALNUT CREEK HOSPITAL
SAN MIGUEL PARK
EL DIVISADERO PARK
BEREAN CHRISTIAN HS
NORTHGATE HS
CARONDELET HS
PARK & RIDE
DIABLO SHADOWS PARK
BOUNDARY OAK GOLF COURSE
LIME RIDGE OPEN SPACE
ARBOLADO PARK
DIABLO FOOTHILLS REGIONAL PARK
SHELL RIDGE OPEN SPACE
YGNACIO VALLEY RD
OAK GROVE RD
BANCROFT RD
WALNUT AV
N MITCHELL DR
SHADELANDS DR
STINSON
SAN CARLOS DR
NORTH GATE RD
CASTLE ROCK RD
PINE CREEK RD
ROCKSPRING PL
MOUNTAIN DR
MIGUEL
HADDEN RD
SEE A J3
1 TAMWORTH CT
2 CUMBRIAN CT
3 BENNINGTON CT
4 RAVEN GLASS CT
5 COTTINGHAM CT
6 NEW HAVEN CT
7 SUTTON CT
E F G H J
1 2 3 4 5 6 7

SEE 613 MAP

SEE 632 MAP

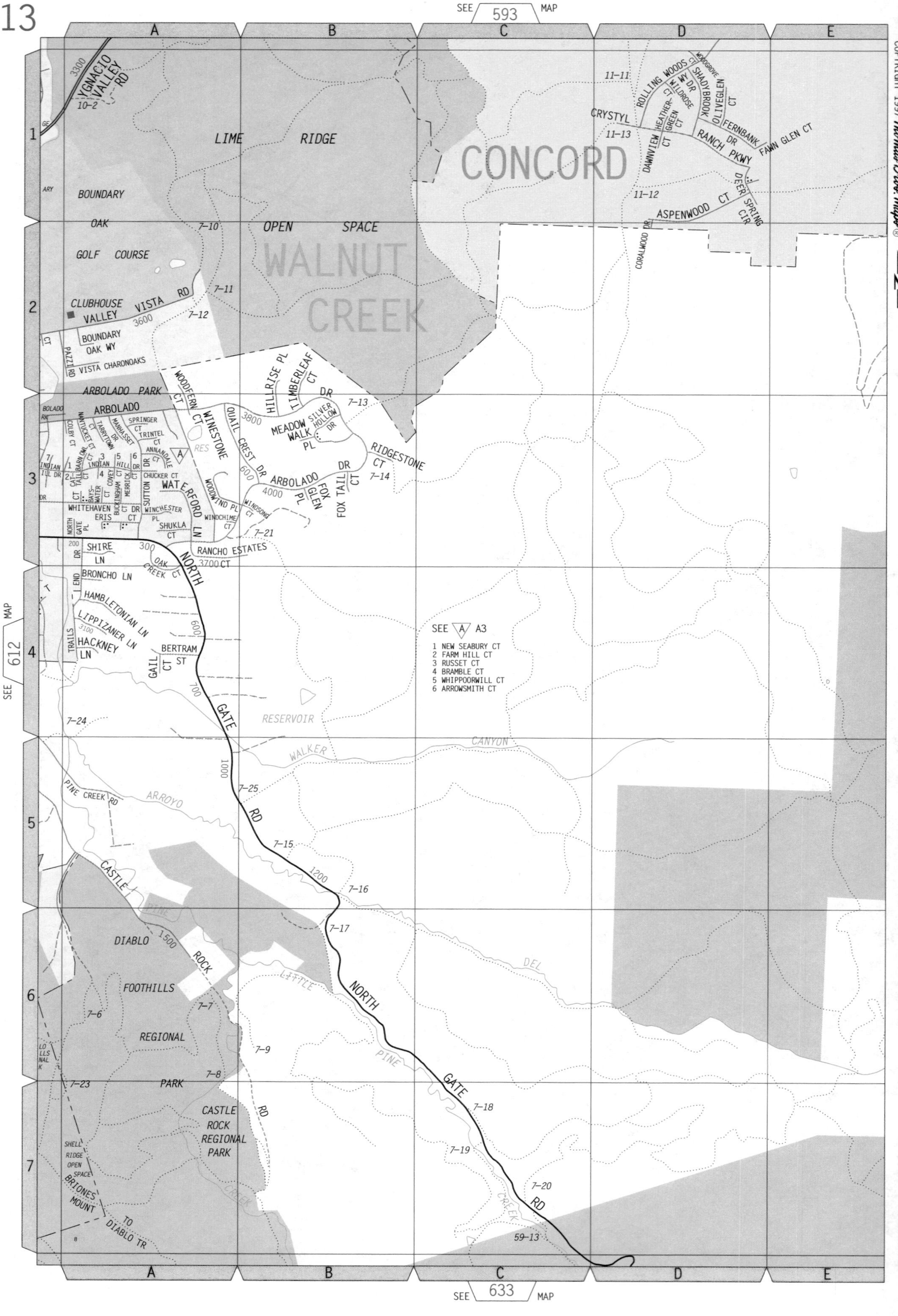
SEE 593 MAP
SEE 633 MAP
SEE 612 MAP
A
B
C
D
E
1
2
3
4
5
6
7
YGNACIO VALLEY RD
3300
10-2
LIME RIDGE
BOUNDARY OAK GOLF COURSE
OPEN SPACE
WALNUT CREEK
CONCORD
CLUBHOUSE
VALLEY VISTA RD
3600
BOUNDARY OAK WY
PAZZI RD
VISTA CHARONOAKS
ARBOLADO PARK
ARBOLADO
WOODFERN CT
WINESTONE
HILLRISE PL
TIMBERLEAF CT
DR
QUAIL CREST DR
3800
MEADOW WALK PL
SILVER HOLLOW DR
RIDGESTONE CT
ARBOLADO PL
4000
FOX GLEN
FOX TAIL CT
DR
RES
WATERFORD LN
WOODWIND PL
WINDCHIME CT
WINDSONG CT
RANCHO ESTATES
3700 CT
SPRINGER CT
TRINTEL CT
ANNANDALE
CHUCKER CT
SUTTON
WINCHESTER PL
SHUKLA CT
WHITEHAVEN
ERIS
BUCKINGHAM
MERRICK
COVEY
INDIAN
HILL
BARN OWL
NANTUCKET
TARRYTOWN
MANHASSET
COLBY CT
NORTH GATE PL
SHIRE LN
200
300
OAK CREEK CT
NORTH GATE RD
BRONCHO LN
HAMBLETONIAN LN
LIPPIZANER LN
3100
HACKNEY LN
TRAILS
BERTRAM ST
GAIL CT
600
700
1000
1200
1500
RESERVOIR
WALKER CANYON
PINE CREEK RD
ARROYO
CASTLE ROCK RD
PINE
DEL
LITTLE
CREEK
DIABLO FOOTHILLS REGIONAL PARK
CASTLE ROCK REGIONAL PARK
SHELL RIDGE OPEN SPACE
BRIONES MOUNT
TO DIABLO TR
ROLLING WOODS CT
WOODGROVE
SHADYBROOK
WY DR
WILDROSE
OLIVEGLEN CT
FERNBANK
HEATHER CT
GREEN CT
CRYSTYL
DAWNVIEW CT
RANCH PKWY
FAWN GLEN CT
DR
DEER SPRING CIR
ASPENWOOD CT
CORALWOOD DR
11-11
11-13
11-12
7-10
7-11
7-12
7-13
7-14
7-15
7-16
7-17
7-18
7-19
7-20
7-21
7-23
7-24
7-25
7-6
7-7
7-8
7-9
59-13
SEE A A3
1 NEW SEABURY CT
2 FARM HILL CT
3 RUSSET CT
4 BRAMBLE CT
5 WHIPPOORWILL CT
6 ARROWSMITH CT

SEE 593 MAP

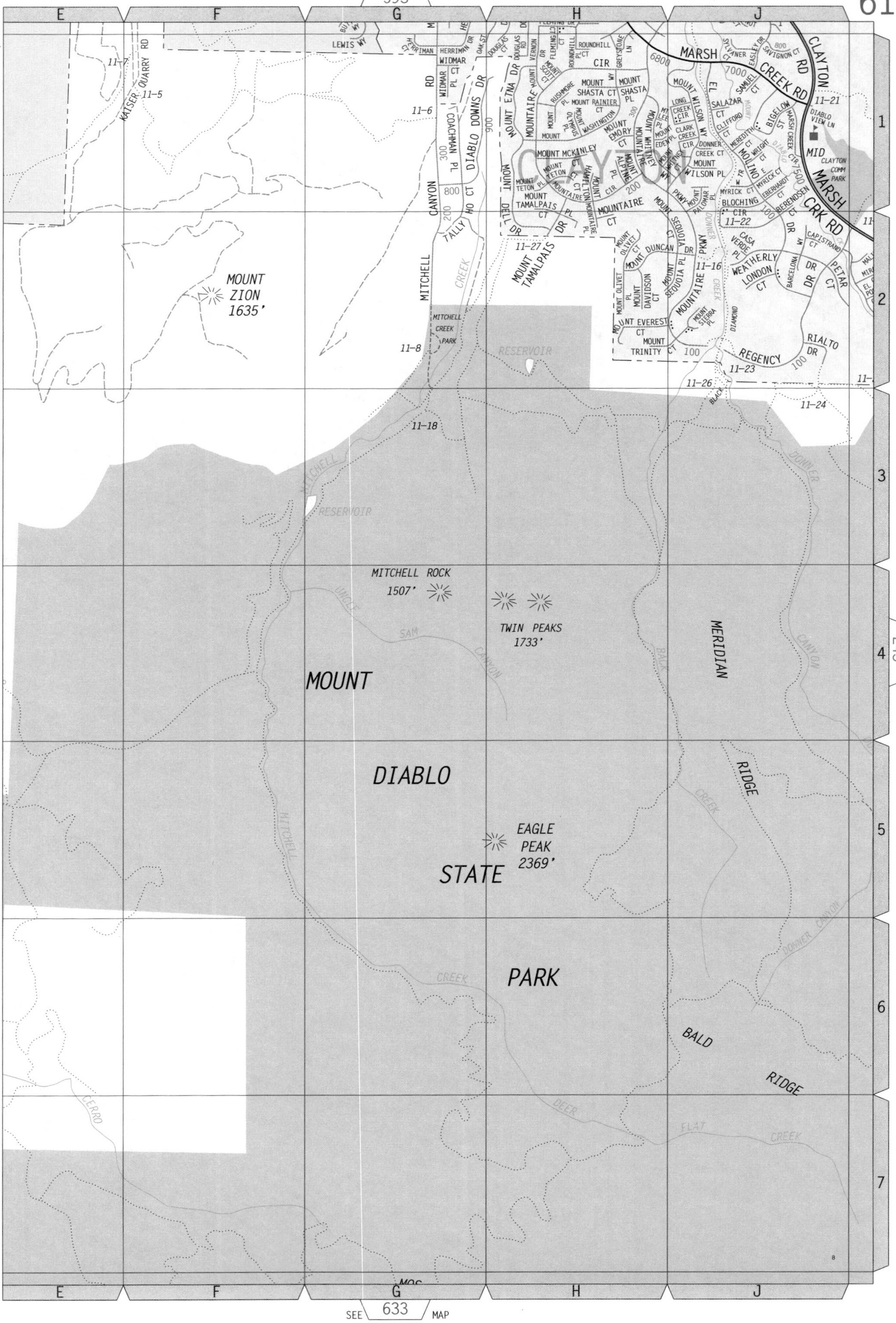
E F G H J
1 2 3 4 5 6 7
CLAYTON
MARSH CREEK RD
CLAYTON RD
MOUNT ZION
1635'
MITCHELL ROCK
1507'
TWIN PEAKS
1733'
EAGLE
PEAK
2369'
MOUNT
DIABLO
STATE
PARK
MERIDIAN
RIDGE
BALD
RIDGE
RESERVOIR
MITCHELL CANYON RD
MITCHELL CREEK PARK
UNCLE SAM CANYON
DEER FLAT CREEK
DONNER CANYON
KAISER QUARRY RD
DIABLO DOWNS DR
COACHMAN PL
TALLY HO CT
LEWIS WY
HERRIMAN DR
WIDMAR CT
MOUNT TAMALPAIS
MOUNT DELL DR
MOUNTAIRE
MOUNT WILSON PL
MOUNT SEQUOIA PL
REGENCY DR
RIALTO DR
WEATHERLY
LONDON CT
BLOCHING CT
MID CLAYTON COMM PARK
DIABLO VIEW LN
BIGELOW ST
SAMUEL CT
SALAZAR CT
CERRO
11-5
11-6
11-7
11-8
11-16
11-18
11-21
11-22
11-23
11-24
11-26
11-27

SEE 243 MAP

SEE 633 MAP

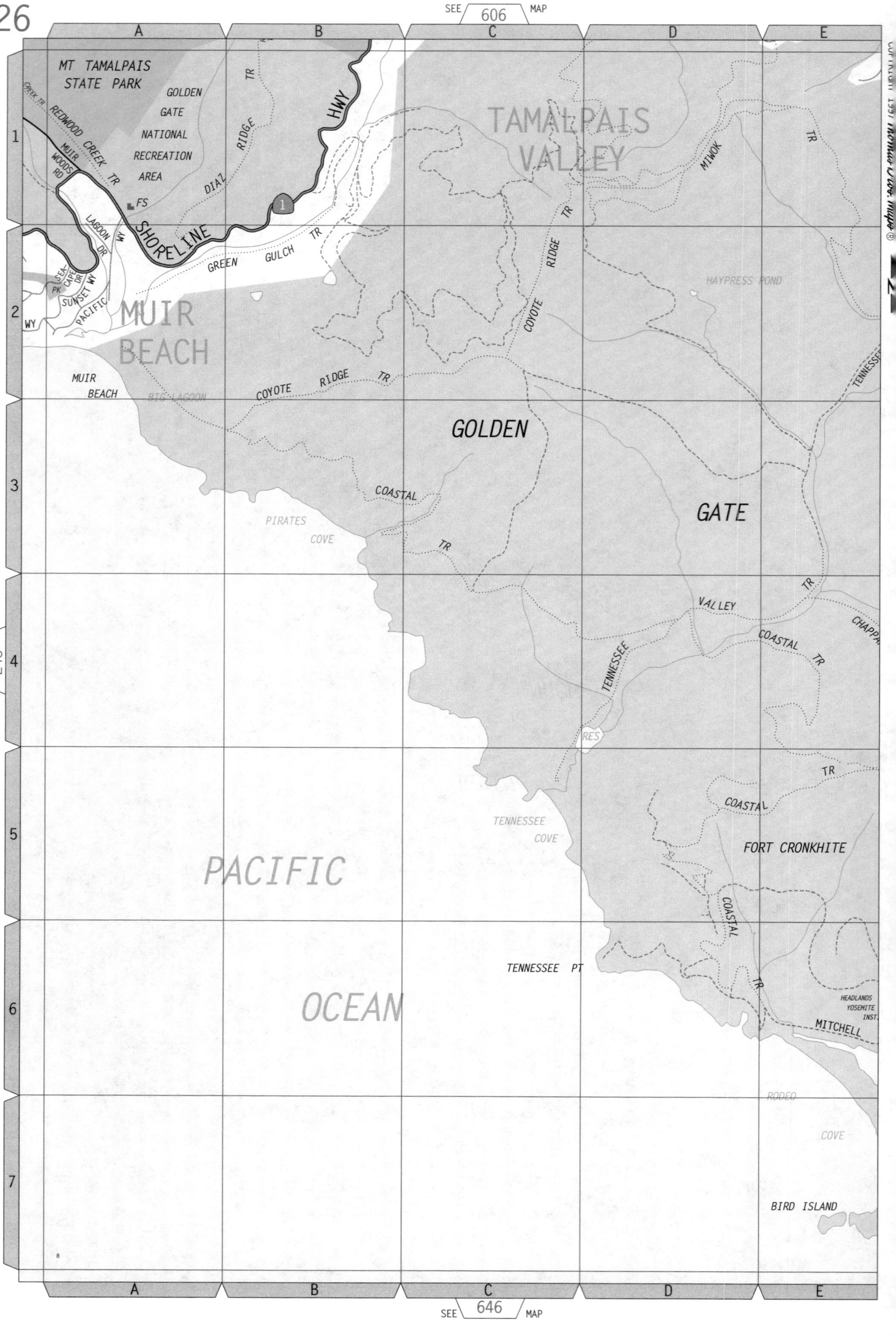
SEE 606 MAP
A
B
C
D
E
1
2
3
4
5
6
7
MT TAMALPAIS
STATE PARK
GOLDEN
GATE
NATIONAL
RECREATION
AREA
REDWOOD CREEK TR
CREEK TR
MUIR WOODS RD
FS
DIAZ RIDGE TR
HWY
1
SHORELINE
LAGOON DR
WY
SEA CAPE DR
PK
SUNSET WY
PACIFIC WY
GREEN GULCH TR
MUIR
BEACH
MUIR
BEACH
BIG LAGOON
TAMALPAIS
VALLEY
MIWOK
TR
COYOTE RIDGE TR
HAYPRESS POND
COYOTE RIDGE TR
TENNESSEE
GOLDEN
GATE
COASTAL TR
PIRATES
COVE
VALLEY TR
COASTAL TR
CHAPPA
TENNESSEE
RES
TR
COASTAL
FORT CRONKHITE
TENNESSEE
COVE
PACIFIC
OCEAN
COASTAL TR
TENNESSEE PT
HEADLANDS
YOSEMITE
INST
MITCHELL
RODEO
COVE
BIRD ISLAND
SEE 243 MAP
SEE 646 MAP

SEE 606 MAP

E
F
G
H
J
1
2
3
4
5
6
7
MARIN CITY
SAUSALITO
NATIONAL
RECREATION
AREA
FORT BAKER
FORT BERRY
COUNTYVIEW DR
DURANT
ASHTON WY LN
VISTA DE VALLE
VIA RECODO
CARRERA DR
VIOLA
RD
WY
VALLEY
OAKWOOD
ALTA AV
BURGESS CT
DUTTON CT
DRAKE AV
WALDO CT
PACHECO ST
EUREKA ST
LIB
COMM CTR
FS
TRANSIT TRANSFER PT
DONAHUE ST
TERNERS DR
FLEMINGS CT
TERRACE DR
COLE DR
DRAKE AV
REDWOOD
HWY
101
1
BRIDGEWAY
GATE 5 RD
GATE 6 RD
VARDA LANDING RD
HARBOR DR
PO
MARTIN LUTHER KING JR PARK
COLOMA
OLIMA
EBBTIDE AV
ROSS
EDEN ROC
STANFORD WY
SACRAMENTO AV
LOWER
BUTTE ST
CYPRESS PL
WILLOW LN
BUCHANAN DR
WILLIAM CT
DUNN LN
WATEREE
ANCHORAGE RD
TOMALES ST
MARINSHIP
MARIN-SHIP AV PK
WOODWARD AV
LINCOLN DR
NEVADA ST
MARIN AV
ARANA CIR
KENDELL CT
RODEO AV
TESTA ST
GORDON ST
SPRING HILL CIR
SPRING ST
TOYON CT
CURREY LN
CURREY CT
MIWOK TR
TENNESSEE
BOBCAT TR
CHAPPARAL TR
RODEO VALLEY TR
WOLFBACK RIDGE RD
TR
HEADLANDS INSTITUTE & YOSEMITE NATIONAL INSTITUTE
MITCHELL RD
BUNKER RD
RODEO VALLEY
MCCULLOUGH RD
COASTAL TR
SIMMONDS RD
VIS CTR
BODSWORTH RD
FIELD RD
CONZELMAN RD
RODEO LAGOON
COVE
BONITA COVE

SEE 627 MAP
SEE 646 MAP

MAP

SEE 607 MAP

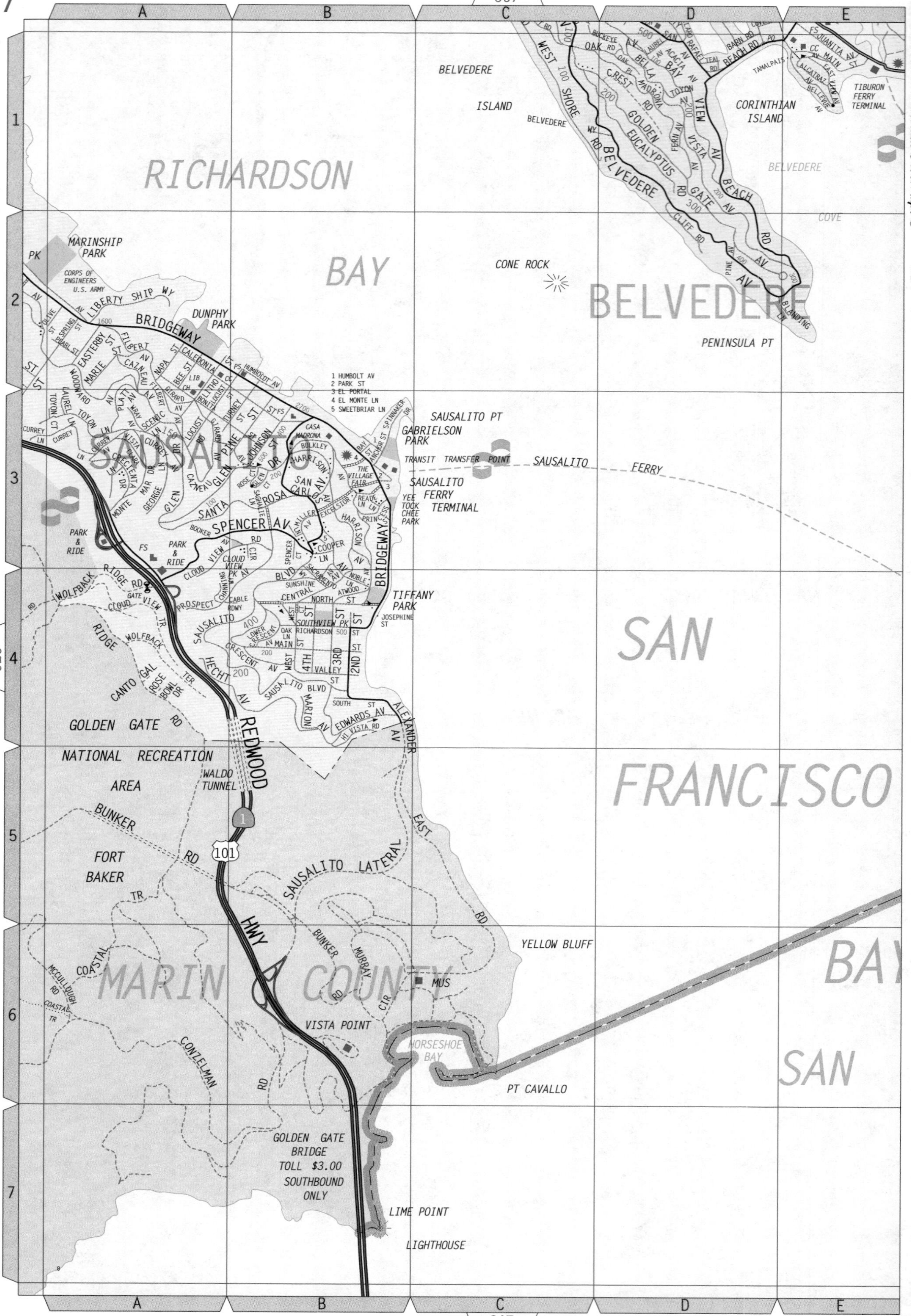
RICHARDSON BAY
BELVEDERE ISLAND
BELVEDERE
CORINTHIAN ISLAND
TIBURON FERRY TERMINAL
BELVEDERE COVE
CONE ROCK
PENINSULA PT
MARINSHIP PARK
CORPS OF ENGINEERS U.S. ARMY
DUNPHY PARK
LIBERTY SHIP WY
BRIDGEWAY
1 HUMBOLT AV
2 PARK ST
3 EL PORTAL
4 EL MONTE LN
5 SWEETBRIAR LN
SAUSALITO
SAUSALITO PT
GABRIELSON PARK
TRANSIT TRANSFER POINT
SAUSALITO FERRY
SAUSALITO FERRY TERMINAL
YEE TOCK CHEE PARK
SPENCER AV
PARK & RIDE
TIFFANY PARK
JOSEPHINE ST
SAN FRANCISCO BAY
WOLFBACK RIDGE RD
GOLDEN GATE NATIONAL RECREATION AREA
WALDO TUNNEL
REDWOOD HWY
101
1
BUNKER RD
FORT BAKER
SAUSALITO LATERAL
EAST RD
ALEXANDER AV
YELLOW BLUFF
MARIN COUNTY
MUS
VISTA POINT
HORSESHOE BAY
PT CAVALLO
CONZELMAN RD
GOLDEN GATE BRIDGE TOLL $3.00 SOUTHBOUND ONLY
LIME POINT
LIGHTHOUSE
SAN

SEE 626 MAP
SEE 647 MAP

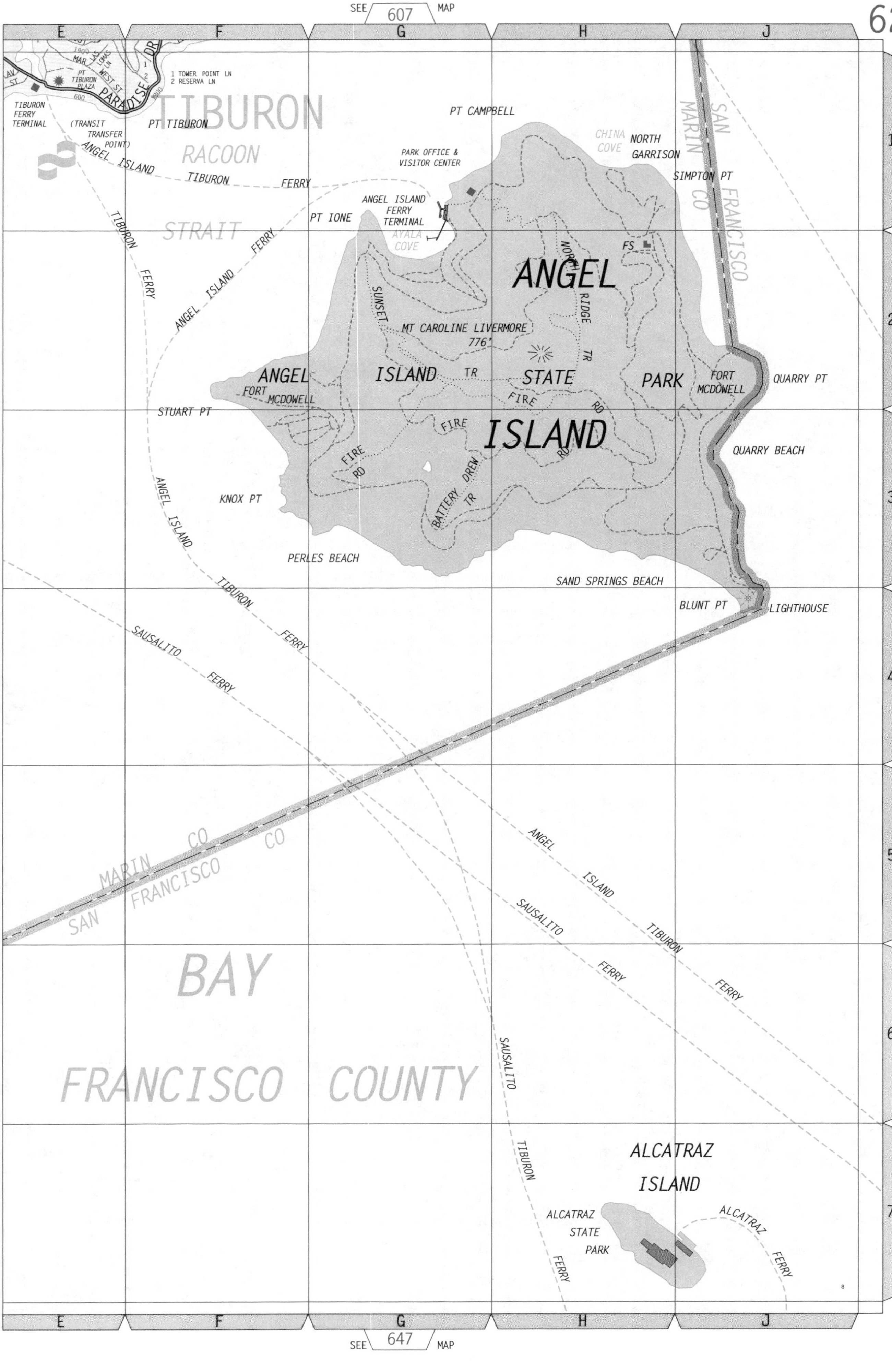
SEE 607 MAP
E
F
G
H
J
1
2
3
4
5
6
7
1 TOWER POINT LN
2 RESERVA LN
MAR LAS LOMAS
PT TIBURON PLAZA
WEST ST
PARADISE DR
TIBURON
TIBURON FERRY TERMINAL
(TRANSIT TRANSFER POINT)
PT TIBURON
RACOON
STRAIT
ANGEL ISLAND TIBURON FERRY
TIBURON FERRY
ANGEL ISLAND FERRY
PT CAMPBELL
CHINA COVE
NORTH GARRISON
PARK OFFICE & VISITOR CENTER
ANGEL ISLAND FERRY TERMINAL
AYALA COVE
PT IONE
SIMPTON PT
MARIN CO
SAN FRANCISCO
FS
ANGEL ISLAND
NORTH RIDGE TR
SUNSET TR
MT CAROLINE LIVERMORE
776'
ANGEL ISLAND STATE PARK
FORT MCDOWELL
QUARRY PT
STUART PT
FIRE RD
BATTERY DREW TR
QUARRY BEACH
KNOX PT
ANGEL ISLAND TIBURON FERRY
PERLES BEACH
SAND SPRINGS BEACH
BLUNT PT
LIGHTHOUSE
SAUSALITO FERRY
SEE 243 MAP
MARIN CO
SAN FRANCISCO CO
ANGEL ISLAND TIBURON FERRY
SAUSALITO FERRY
BAY
FRANCISCO COUNTY
SAUSALITO TIBURON FERRY
ALCATRAZ ISLAND
ALCATRAZ STATE PARK
ALCATRAZ FERRY
SEE 647 MAP

SEE 609 MAP

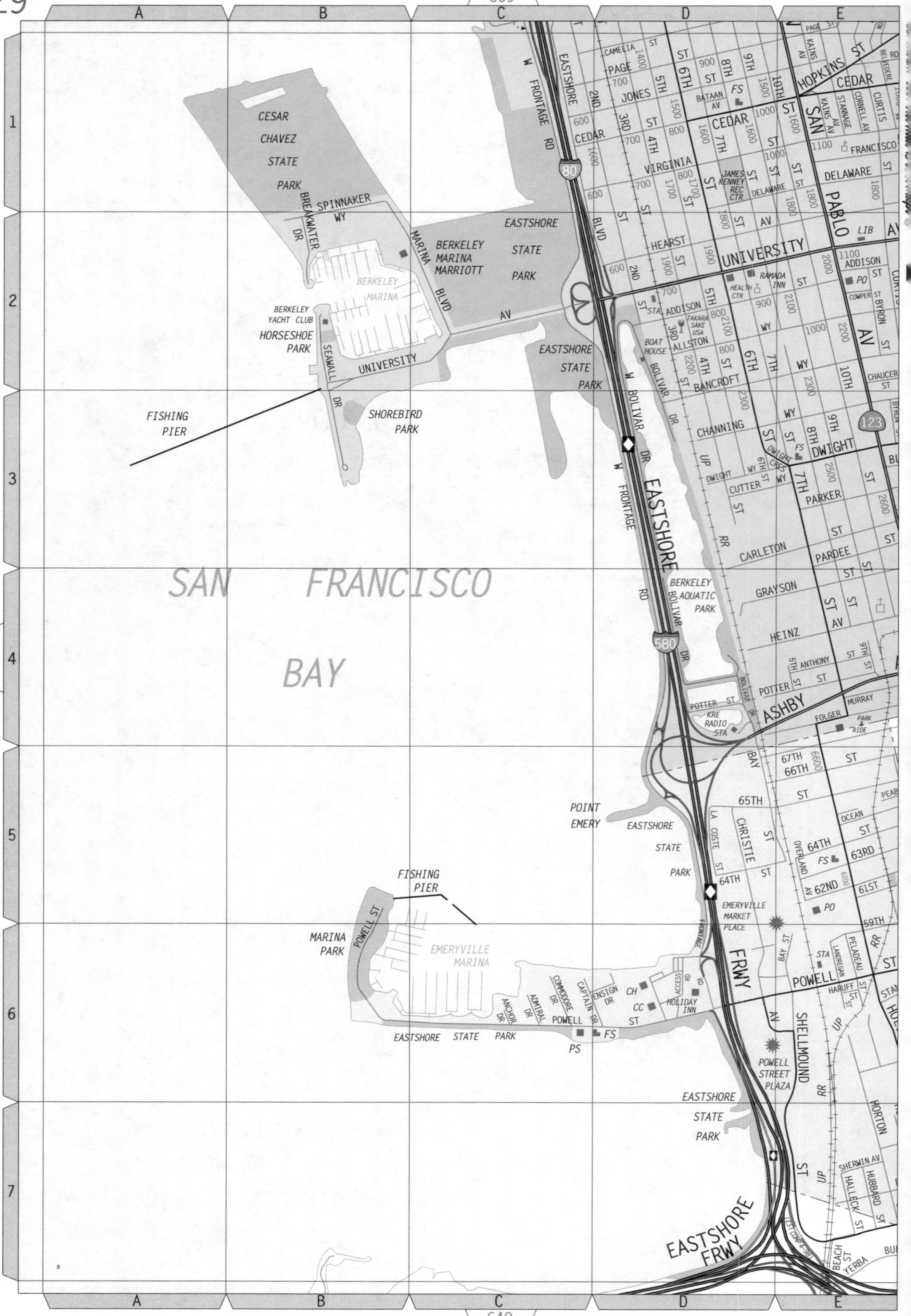

A B C D E
1 2 3 4 5 6 7
SAN FRANCISCO BAY
CESAR CHAVEZ STATE PARK
SPINNAKER WY
BREAKWATER DR
BERKELEY MARINA
BERKELEY YACHT CLUB
HORSESHOE PARK
SEAWALL DR
UNIVERSITY AV
MARINA BLVD
BERKELEY MARINA MARRIOTT
EASTSHORE STATE PARK
FISHING PIER
SHOREBIRD PARK
W FRONTAGE RD
EASTSHORE
80
580
123
EASTSHORE FRWY
W BOLIVAR DR
BOLIVAR DR
BERKELEY AQUATIC PARK
BOAT HOUSE
TAKARA SAKE USA
2ND
3RD
4TH
5TH
6TH
7TH
8TH
9TH
10TH
CAMELIA ST
PAGE ST
JONES ST
CEDAR ST
VIRGINIA ST
HEARST ST
ADDISON ST
ALLSTON WY
BANCROFT WY
CHANNING WY
DWIGHT WY
CUTTER ST
CARLETON ST
PARKER ST
PARDEE ST
GRAYSON ST
HEINZ AV
ANTHONY ST
POTTER ST
ASHBY
MURRAY
FOLGER
PARK & RIDE
KRE RADIO STA
BAY ST
67TH
66TH
65TH
64TH
63RD
62ND
61ST
59TH
LA COSTE ST
CHRISTIE ST
OVERLAND AV
OCEAN
POINT EMERY
EMERYVILLE MARKET PLACE
POWELL ST
POWELL STREET PLAZA
SHELLMOUND ST
HOLIDAY INN
ACCESS RD
FRONTAGE
MARINA PARK
EMERYVILLE MARINA
COMMODORE DR
CAPTAIN DR
ENSIGN DR
ADMIRAL DR
ANCHOR DR
CH
CC
PS
FS
PO
LIB
STA
JAMES KENNEY REC CTR
HEALTH CTR
RAMADA INN
HOPKINS ST
SAN PABLO AV
DELAWARE ST
FRANCISCO
BATAAN AV
KAINS AV
STANNAGE AV
CORNELL AV
CURTIS
COWPER ST
BYRON ST
CHAUCER ST
LANDREGAN
PELADEAU
HARUFF ST
HORTON
SHERWIN AV
HALLECK ST
HUBBARD ST
BEACH ST
YERBA
FRWY
UP
RR

SEE 243 MAP

SEE 649 MAP

SEE 609 MAP

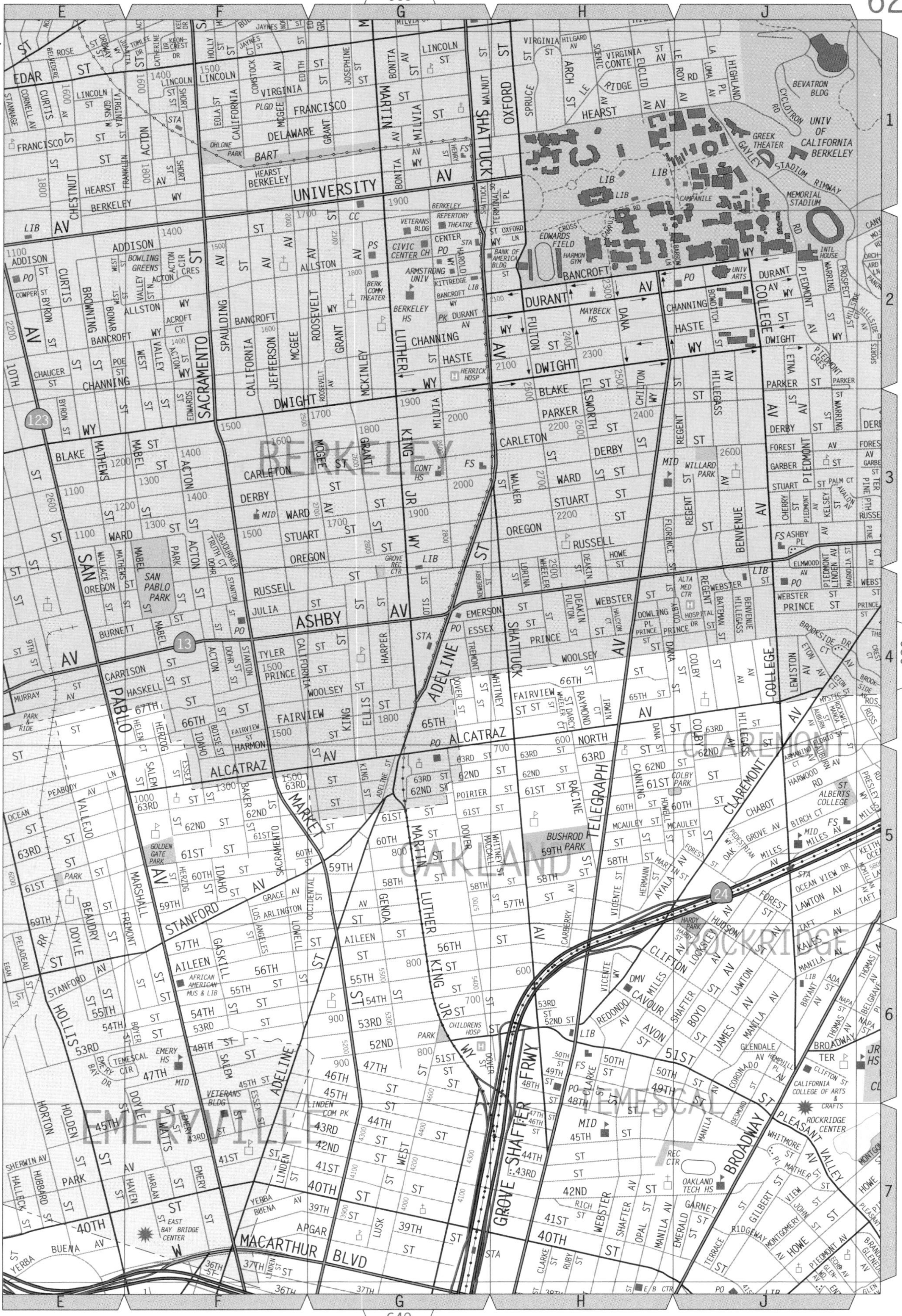
BERKELEY
OAKLAND
EMERYVILLE
CLAREMONT
ROCKRIDGE
TEMESCAL
UNIV OF CALIFORNIA BERKELEY
MEMORIAL STADIUM
GREEK THEATER
BEVATRON BLDG
EDWARDS FIELD
SAN PABLO PARK
BUSHROD PARK
UNIVERSITY AV
SHATTUCK AV
ASHBY AV
ALCATRAZ AV
TELEGRAPH AV
COLLEGE AV
SAN PABLO AV
ADELINE ST
MARTIN LUTHER KING JR WY
GROVE SHAFTER FRWY
MACARTHUR BLVD
BROADWAY
CLAREMONT AV
DWIGHT WY
BANCROFT WY
DURANT AV
STANFORD AV
40TH ST
CALIFORNIA COLLEGE OF ARTS & CRAFTS
ROCKRIDGE CENTER
EAST BAY BRIDGE CENTER
OAKLAND TECH HS
HERRICK HOSP
ALTA MED CTR
CHILDRENS HOSP
ST ALBERTS COLLEGE
AFRICAN AMERICAN MUS & LIB
E F G H J
1 2 3 4 5 6 7

SEE 630 MAP

SEE 649 MAP

SEE 610 MAP

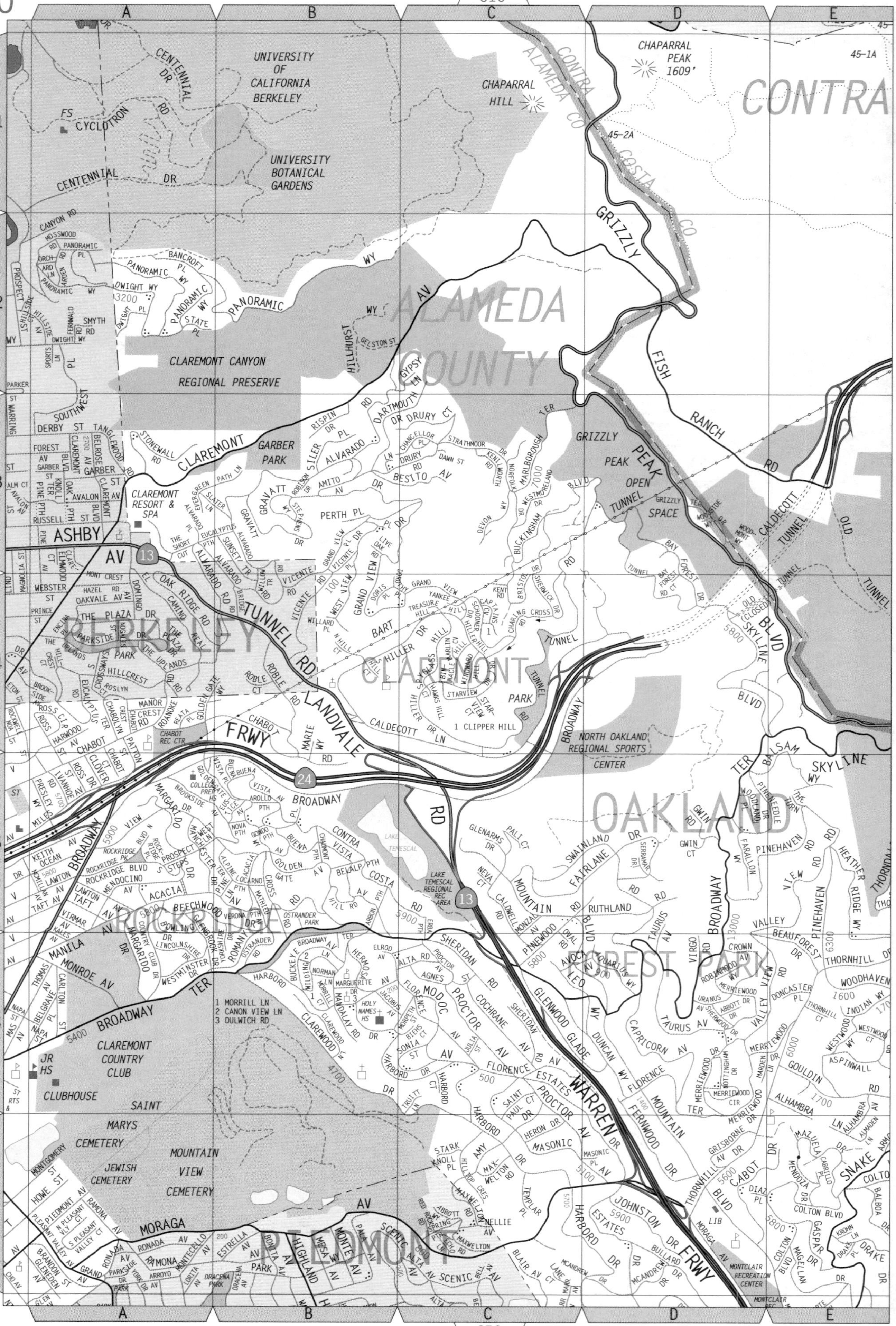
A
B
C
D
E
1
2
3
4
5
6
7
UNIVERSITY OF CALIFORNIA BERKELEY
UNIVERSITY BOTANICAL GARDENS
CHAPARRAL PEAK 1609'
CHAPARRAL HILL
CONTRA
ALAMEDA CO
CONTRA COSTA CO
CENTENNIAL DR
CYCLOTRON RD
GRIZZLY
ALAMEDA COUNTY
CLAREMONT CANYON REGIONAL PRESERVE
PANORAMIC WY
FISH RANCH RD
GRIZZLY PEAK OPEN SPACE
GRIZZLY PEAK BLVD
CLAREMONT AV
GARBER PARK
CLAREMONT RESORT & SPA
ASHBY AV
13
TUNNEL RD
BERKELEY
CALDECOTT TUNNEL
OLD TUNNEL RD
SKYLINE BLVD
CLAREMONT
PARK
1 CLIPPER HILL
LANDVALE RD
FRWY
24
BROADWAY
NORTH OAKLAND REGIONAL SPORTS CENTER
OAKLAND
LAKE TEMESCAL
LAKE TEMESCAL REGIONAL REC AREA
ROCKRIDGE
FOREST PARK
MOUNTAIN BLVD
BROADWAY TER
1 MORRILL LN
2 CANON VIEW LN
3 DULWICH RD
CLAREMONT COUNTRY CLUB
CLUBHOUSE
SAINT MARYS CEMETERY
JEWISH CEMETERY
MOUNTAIN VIEW CEMETERY
WARREN FRWY
MORAGA AV
PIEDMONT
MONTCLAIR RECREATION CENTER
SNAKE

SEE 629 MAP
SEE 650 MAP

SEE 610 MAP

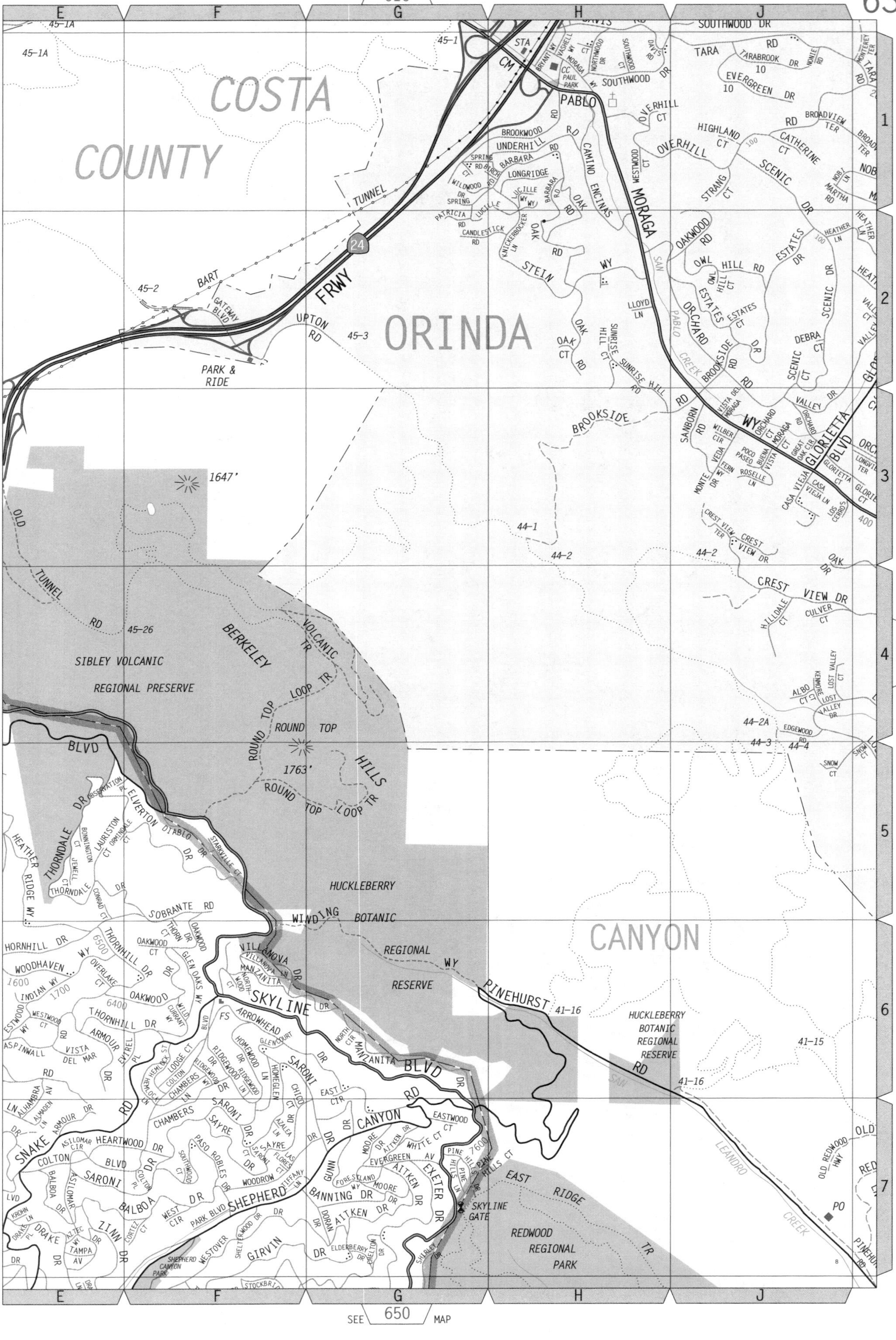
COSTA
COUNTY
ORINDA
CANYON
TUNNEL
BART
FRWY
24
GATEWAY BLVD
UPTON RD
PARK & RIDE
MORAGA WY
SAN PABLO CREEK
SOUTHWOOD DR
TARA RD
TARABROOK DR
EVERGREEN DR
OVERHILL CT
OVERHILL RD
HIGHLAND CT
CATHERINE CT
SCENIC DR
BROADVIEW TER
STRANG CT
CAMINO ENCINAS
OAK RD
UNDERHILL RD
BROOKWOOD RD
LONGRIDGE RD
BARBARA RD
LUCILLE WY
PATRICIA RD
CANDLESTICK RD
KNICKERBOCKER LN
STEIN WY
LLOYD LN
OAK CT
SUNRISE HILL RD
OAKWOOD RD
OWL HILL RD
ESTATES DR
ORCHARD RD
BROOKSIDE RD
DEBRA CT
SCENIC CT
VALLEY DR
GLORIETTA BLVD
SANBORN RD
MONTE VEDA DR
CASA VIEJA
CREST VIEW DR
HILLDALE CT
CULVER CT
LOST VALLEY DR
EDGEWOOD RD
SNOW CT
1647'
OLD TUNNEL RD
SIBLEY VOLCANIC REGIONAL PRESERVE
BERKELEY
VOLCANIC TR
ROUND TOP LOOP TR
ROUND TOP
1763'
HILLS
HUCKLEBERRY BOTANIC REGIONAL RESERVE
WINDING WY
PINEHURST RD
SAN LEANDRO CREEK
SKYLINE BLVD
THORNDALE DR
ELVERTON DR
DIABLO DR
SOBRANTE RD
HORNHILL DR
THORNHILL DR
OAKWOOD CT
WOODHAVEN WY
OVERLAKE CT
MANZANITA DR
ARROWHEAD DR
HOMEWOOD DR
SARONI DR
CANYON RD
SNAKE RD
ARMOUR DR
HEARTWOOD DR
COLTON BLVD
SHEPHERD CANYON RD
BALBOA DR
ASILOMAR DR
DRAKE DR
ZINN DR
GIRVIN DR
EXETER DR
AITKEN DR
BANNING DR
SKYLINE GATE
EAST RIDGE TR
REDWOOD REGIONAL PARK
OLD REDWOOD HWY
PO
SEE 631 MAP

SEE 650 MAP

SEE 611 MAP

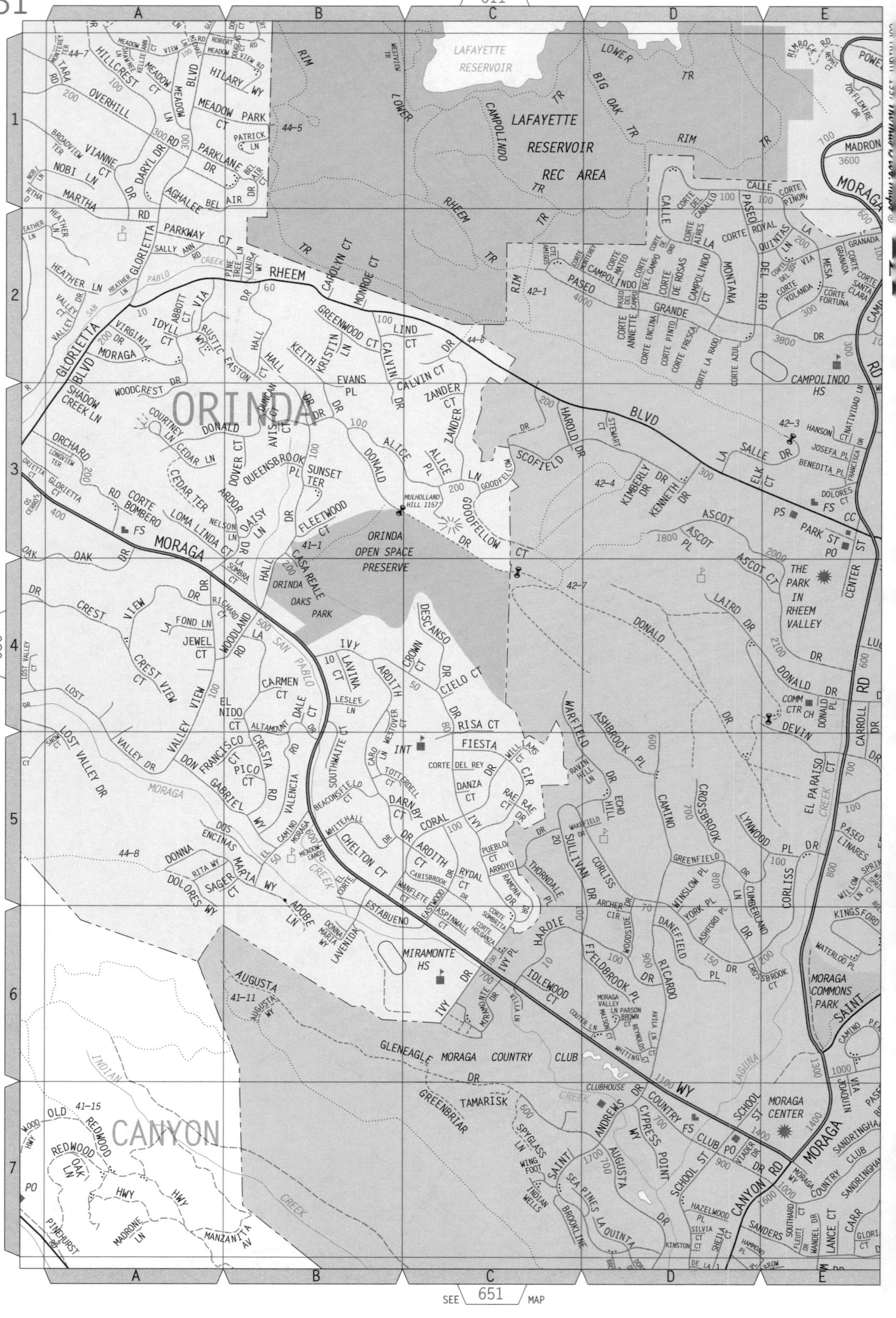

A B C D E
1 2 3 4 5 6 7
ORINDA
LAFAYETTE RESERVOIR
LAFAYETTE RESERVOIR REC AREA
ORINDA OPEN SPACE PRESERVE
ORINDA OAKS PARK
MULHOLLAND HILL 1157
CAMPOLINDO HS
MIRAMONTE HS
MORAGA COUNTRY CLUB
CLUBHOUSE
MORAGA CENTER
MORAGA COMMONS PARK
THE PARK IN RHEEM VALLEY
CANYON
INDIAN CREEK
LAGUNA CREEK
SAN PABLO CREEK
MORAGA CREEK
MORAGA WY
RHEEM BLVD
GLORIETTA BLVD
MORAGA RD
MORAGA BLVD
CANYON RD
ST MARYS RD
MORAGA CT
CAMINO PABLO
LOWER RIM TR
BIG OAK TR
RHEEM TR
CAMPOLINDO TR
PASEO GRANDE
CAMPOLINDO DR
DONALD DR
ASCOT DR
ASCOT CT
CAMINO RICARDO
CROSSBROOK DR
CORLISS DR
SULLIVAN DR
GLENEAGLE DR
GREENBRIAR
TAMARISK
SPYGLASS LN
SAINT ANDREWS DR
COUNTRY CLUB DR
CYPRESS POINT WY
AUGUSTA DR
SCHOOL ST
CARROLL DR
EL PARAISO CT
CREST VIEW DR
LOST VALLEY DR
DON GABRIEL WY
EL NIDO RANCH RD
VALLEY VIEW
WOODLAND RD
IVY DR
CORAL DR
ARDITH DR
CHELTON CT
ESTABUENO
LAVENIDA
ADOBE LN
DOLORES WY
SAGER CT
MARIA WY
DONNA MARIA WY
AUGUSTA DR
AUGUSTA WY
OLD REDWOOD HWY
REDWOOD OAK LN
MANZANITA AV
MADRONE LN
PINEHURST RD
HILLCREST CT
OVERHILL RD
MEADOW LN
MEADOW PARK CT
HILARY WY
PARKLANE DR
BEL AIR DR
AGHALEE RD
MARTHA RD
PARKWAY CT
SALLY ANN RD
HEATHER LN
IDYLL CT
VIRGINIA DR
WOODCREST DR
SHADOW CREEK LN
ORCHARD RD
CORTE BOMBERO
LOMA LINDA CT
OAK DR
NELSON CT
DAISY LN
ARDOR DR
QUEENSBROOK PL
SUNSET TER
FLEETWOOD CT
DOVER CT
CEDAR LN
CEDAR TER
COURTNEY LN
DUNCAN DR
EVANS PL
KEITH DR
KRISTIN LN
GREENWOOD CT
CAROLYN CT
MONROE CT
CALVIN DR
CALVIN CT
LIND CT
ZANDER DR
ZANDER CT
ALICE LN
ALICE PL
GOODFELLOW DR
GOODFELLOW CT
SCOFIELD DR
HAROLD DR
KIMBERLY DR
KENNETH DR
LA SALLE DR
ELK CT
PARK ST
CENTER ST
LAIRD DR
DEVIN DR
WARFIELD DR
ASHBROOK PL
RAVEN HILL LN
ECHO HILL
GREENFIELD DR
LYNWOOD PL
WINSLOW PL
YORK PL
ASHFORD PL
CUMBERLAND DR
DANEFIELD PL
FIELDBROOK PL
WOODSIDE DR
HARDIE DR
IDLEWOOD CT
THORNDALE PL
DESCANSO DR
CROWN CT
CIELO CT
RISA CT
FIESTA CIR
CORTE DEL REY
DANZA CT
RAE CT
LAVINA CT
LESLEE LN
SOUTHWAITE CT
BEACONSFIELD CT
WHITEHALL DR
DARNBY CT
CARMEN CT
DALE CT
CRESTA RD
PICO CT
VALENCIA RD
DOS ENCINAS
CAMINO MORAGA
MIRAMONTE DR
SANDERS DR
HAZELWOOD PL
SEA PINES LA QUINTA
BROOKLINE
INDIAN WELLS
WING FOOT
MADRON
POWELL
DONALD DR
42-1
42-3
42-4
42-7
44-5
44-6
44-7
44-8
41-1
41-11
41-15
FS
PO
PS
INT
COMM CTR
CH

SEE 630 MAP

SEE 651 MAP

SEE 611 MAP

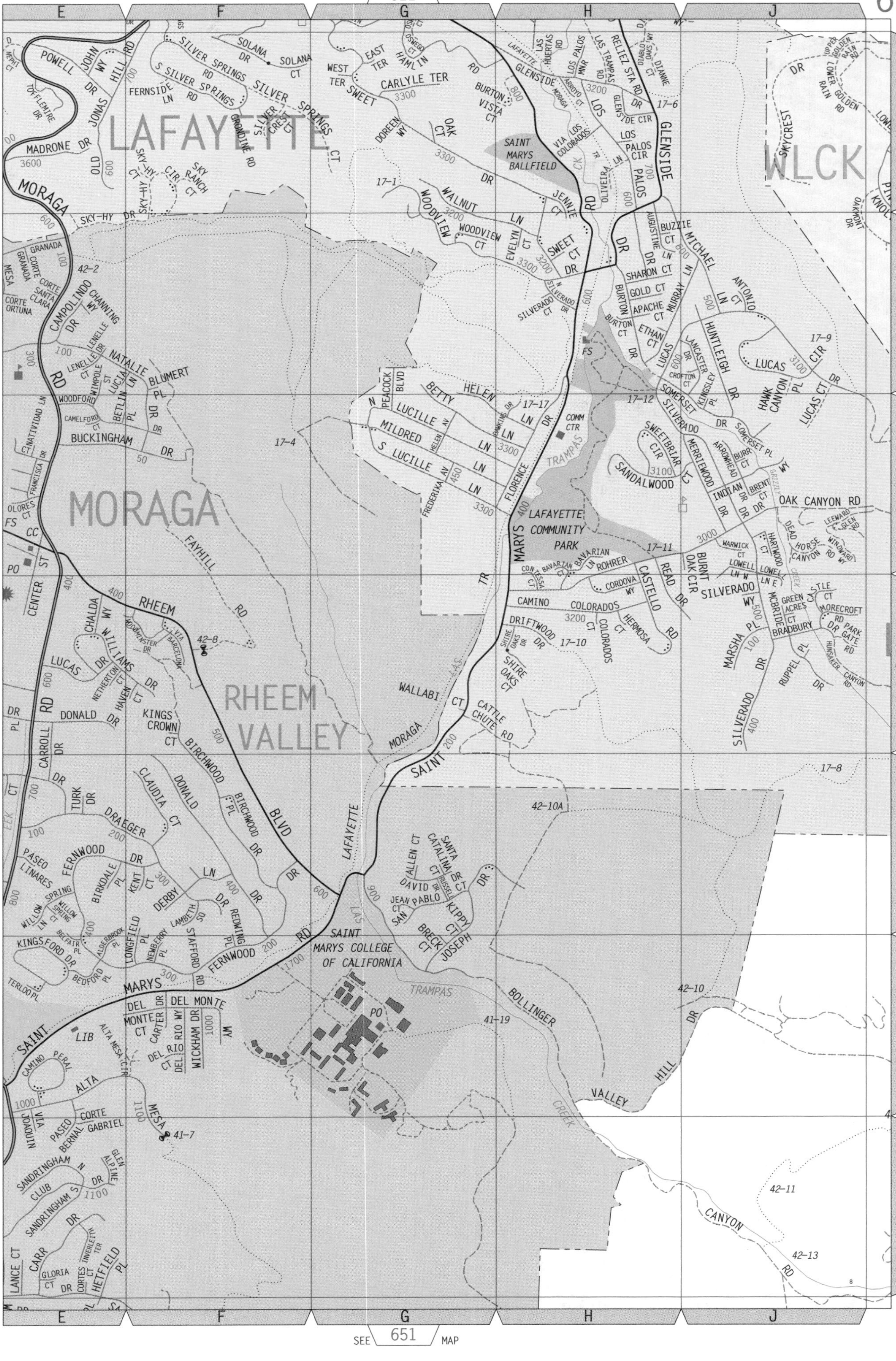
LAFAYETTE
MORAGA
RHEEM VALLEY
WLCK
SAINT MARYS BALLFIELD
LAFAYETTE COMMUNITY PARK
SAINT MARYS COLLEGE OF CALIFORNIA
COMM CTR
FS
PO
LIB
CC
MORAGA RD
SAINT MARYS RD
RHEEM BLVD
GLENSIDE DR
SILVER SPRINGS CT
S SILVER SPRINGS RD
SOLANA DR
CARLYLE TER
SWEET DR
WALNUT LN
WOODVIEW CT
JENNIE CT
BURTON DR
MICHAEL LN
HUNTLEIGH DR
LUCAS CIR
SILVERADO DR
OAK CANYON RD
HELEN LN
LUCILLE LN
MILDRED LN
S LUCILLE LN
FLORENCE DR
CAMINO COLORADOS
CASTELLO RD
HERMOSA RD
MCBRIDE DR
BRADBURY DR
MORAGA CT
CATTLE CHUTE RD
WALLABI CT
FAYHILL RD
WILLIAMS DR
DONALD DR
BIRCHWOOD DR
DRAEGER DR
FERNWOOD DR
CARROLL DR
KINGSFORD DR
BOLLINGER CANYON RD
HILL DR
VALLEY HILL DR
LAS TRAMPAS CREEK
CANYON RD
SANDRINGHAM N
SANDRINGHAM S
CAMINO PERAL
ALTA MESA DR
VIA JOAQUIN
PASEO BERNAL
CORTE GABRIEL
DEL MONTE DR
CAMPOLINDO DR
NATALIE DR
BUCKINGHAM DR
CENTER ST
17-1
17-4
17-6
17-8
17-9
17-10
17-11
17-12
17-17
42-2
42-8
42-10
42-10A
42-11
42-13
41-7
41-19
E
F
G
H
J
1
2
3
4
5
6
7

SEE 632 MAP

SEE 651 MAP

BAY AREA

MAP

SEE 612 MAP

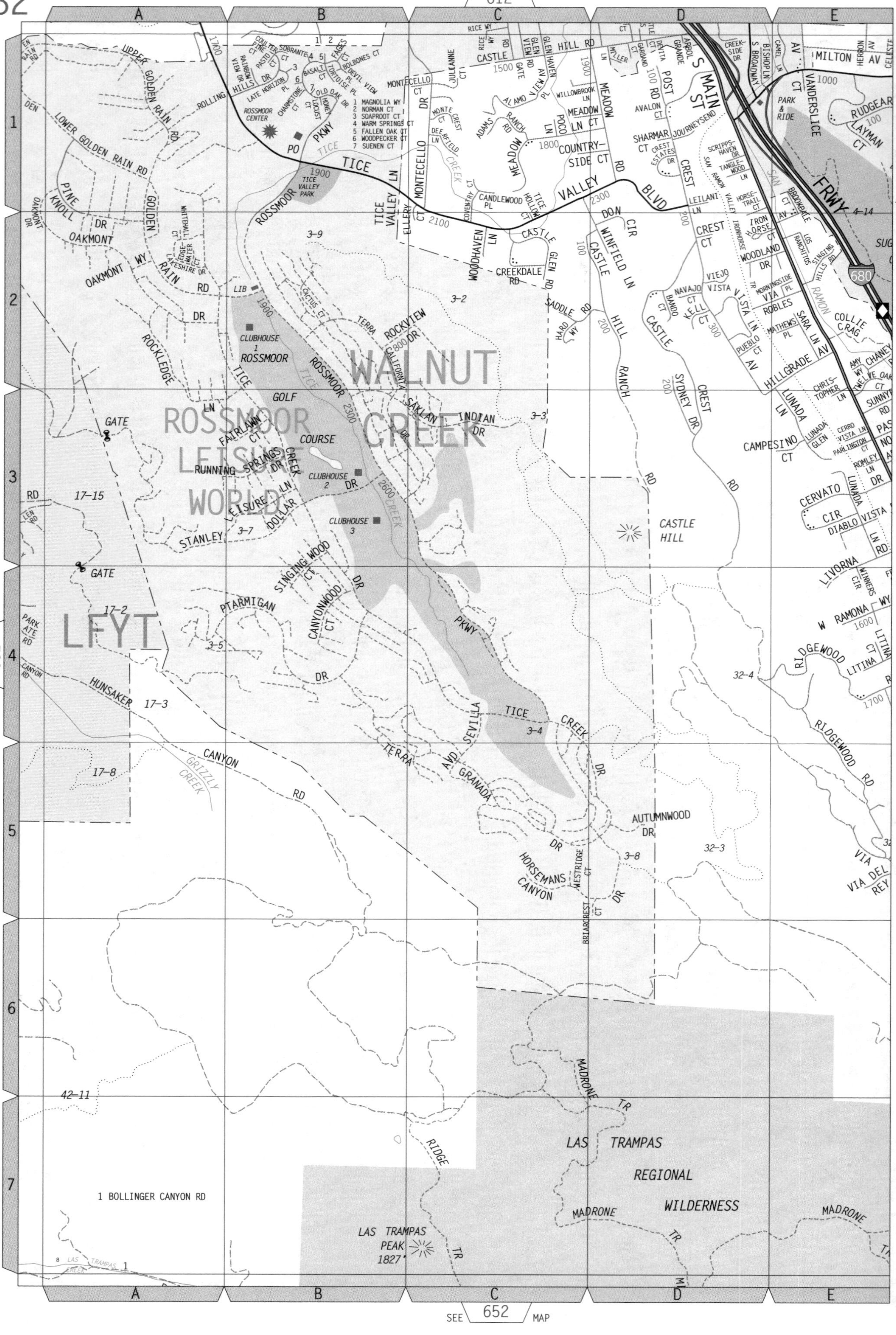

A
B
C
D
E
1
2
3
4
5
6
7
ROSSMOOR LEISURE WORLD
WALNUT CREEK
LFYT
GOLF COURSE
CLUBHOUSE 1 ROSSMOOR
CLUBHOUSE 2
CLUBHOUSE 3
ROSSMOOR CENTER
TICE VALLEY PARK
PARK & RIDE
CASTLE HILL
LAS TRAMPAS REGIONAL WILDERNESS
LAS TRAMPAS PEAK 1827'
1 BOLLINGER CANYON RD
1 MAGNOLIA WY
2 NORMAN CT
3 SOAPROOT CT
4 WARM SPRINGS CT
5 FALLEN OAK CT
6 WOODPECKER CT
7 SUENEN CT
UPPER GOLDEN RAIN RD
LOWER GOLDEN RAIN RD
GOLDEN RAIN RD
PINE KNOLL DR
OAKMONT DR
OAKMONT WY
ROCKLEDGE DR
ROLLING HILLS DR
ROSSMOOR PKWY
TICE CREEK DR
RUNNING SPRINGS DR
FAIRLAWN CT
LEISURE LN
DOLLAR DR
STANLEY DR
SINGING WOOD CT
CANYONWOOD CT
PTARMIGAN DR
ROCKVIEW DR
SAKLAN INDIAN DR
TERRA GRANADA DR
AVD SEVILLA
HORSEMANS CANYON DR
WESTRIDGE CT
BRIARCREST CT
AUTUMNWOOD DR
HUNSAKER CANYON RD
GRIZZLY CREEK
GATE
TICE VALLEY BLVD
TICE VALLEY LN
MONTECELLO DR
CASTLE HILL RD
CASTLE GLEN RD
CREEKDALE RD
WOODHAVEN LN
SADDLE RD
CASTLE HILL RANCH RD
WINFIELD LN
SYDNEY DR
CASTLE CREST RD
DON CIR
MEADOW RD
COUNTRYSIDE CT
S MAIN ST
CREST AV
SAN RAMON VALLEY BLVD
PUEBLO CT
VISTA LN
HILLGRADE AV
LUNADA LN
CAMPESINO CT
CERVATO CIR
DIABLO VISTA
LIVORNA RD
W RAMONA WY
RIDGEWOOD RD
LITINA CT
VIA DEL REY
MILTON AV
VANDERSLICE AV
RUDGEAR RD
FRWY
680
MADRONE TR
RIDGE TR
3-9
3-2
3-3
3-7
3-5
3-4
3-8
17-15
17-2
17-3
17-8
32-4
32-3
42-11
4-14

SEE 631 MAP

SEE 652 MAP

SEE 612 MAP

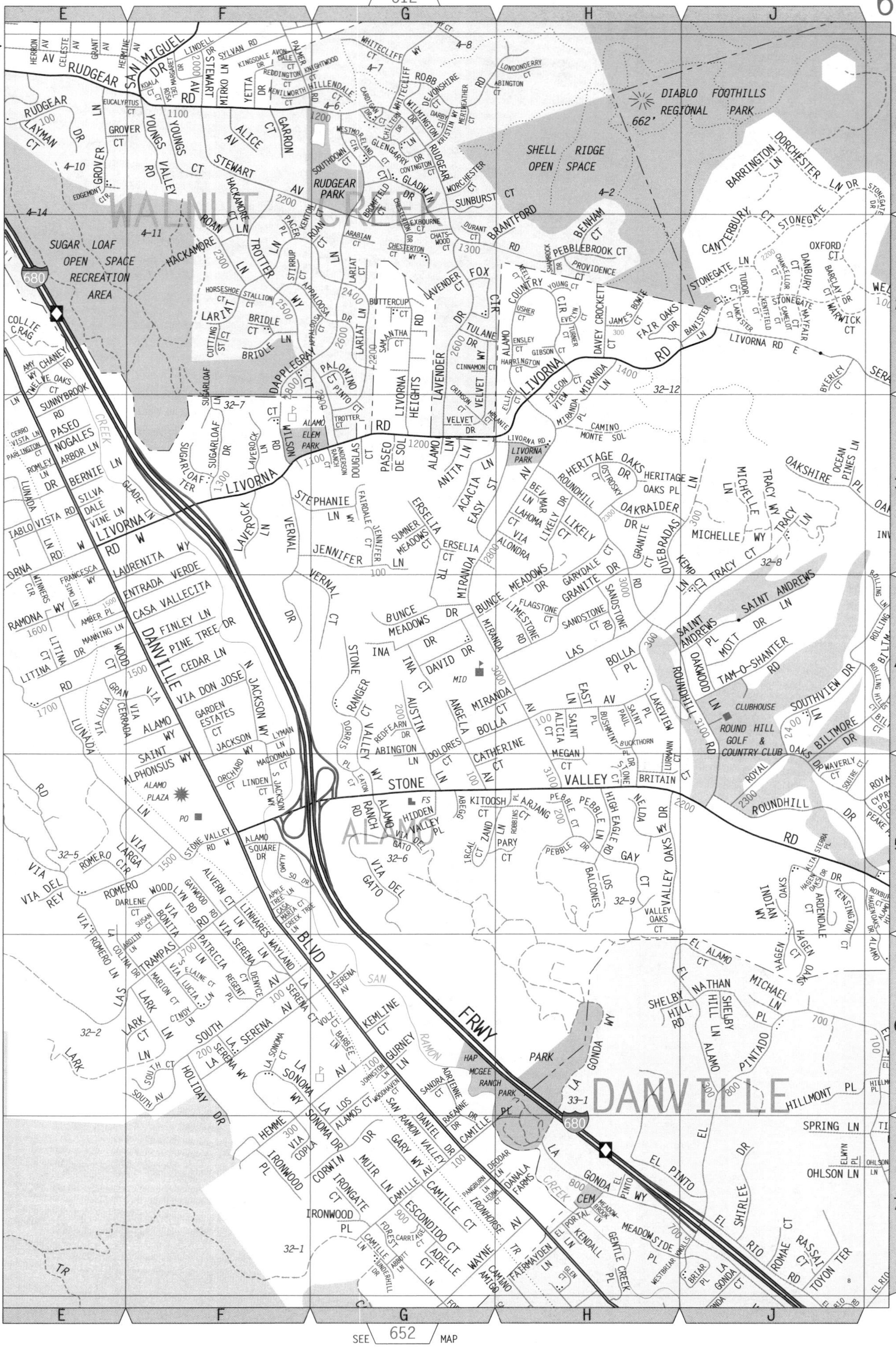
WALNUT CREEK
ALAMO
DANVILLE
DIABLO FOOTHILLS REGIONAL PARK
SHELL RIDGE OPEN SPACE
SUGAR LOAF OPEN SPACE RECREATION AREA
RUDGEAR PARK
LIVORNA PARK
ALAMO ELEM PARK
ALAMO PLAZA
ROUND HILL GOLF & COUNTRY CLUB
CLUBHOUSE
HAP MCGEE RANCH PARK
DANALA FARMS
CEM
PO
FS
MID
662'
RUDGEAR RD
SAN MIGUEL DR
STEWART AV
LIVORNA RD
LIVORNA RD W
LIVORNA RD E
DANVILLE BLVD
FRWY
STONE VALLEY RD
STONE VALLEY RD W
ROUNDHILL RD
MIRANDA AV
BOLLA AV
LAS TRAMPAS RD
SAN RAMON VALLEY BLVD
LA GONDA WY
EL PINTO
SAN RAMON CREEK
HILLMONT PL
SPRING LN
OHLSON LN
680

SEE 633 MAP

SEE 652 MAP

BAY AREA

MAP

SEE 613 MAP

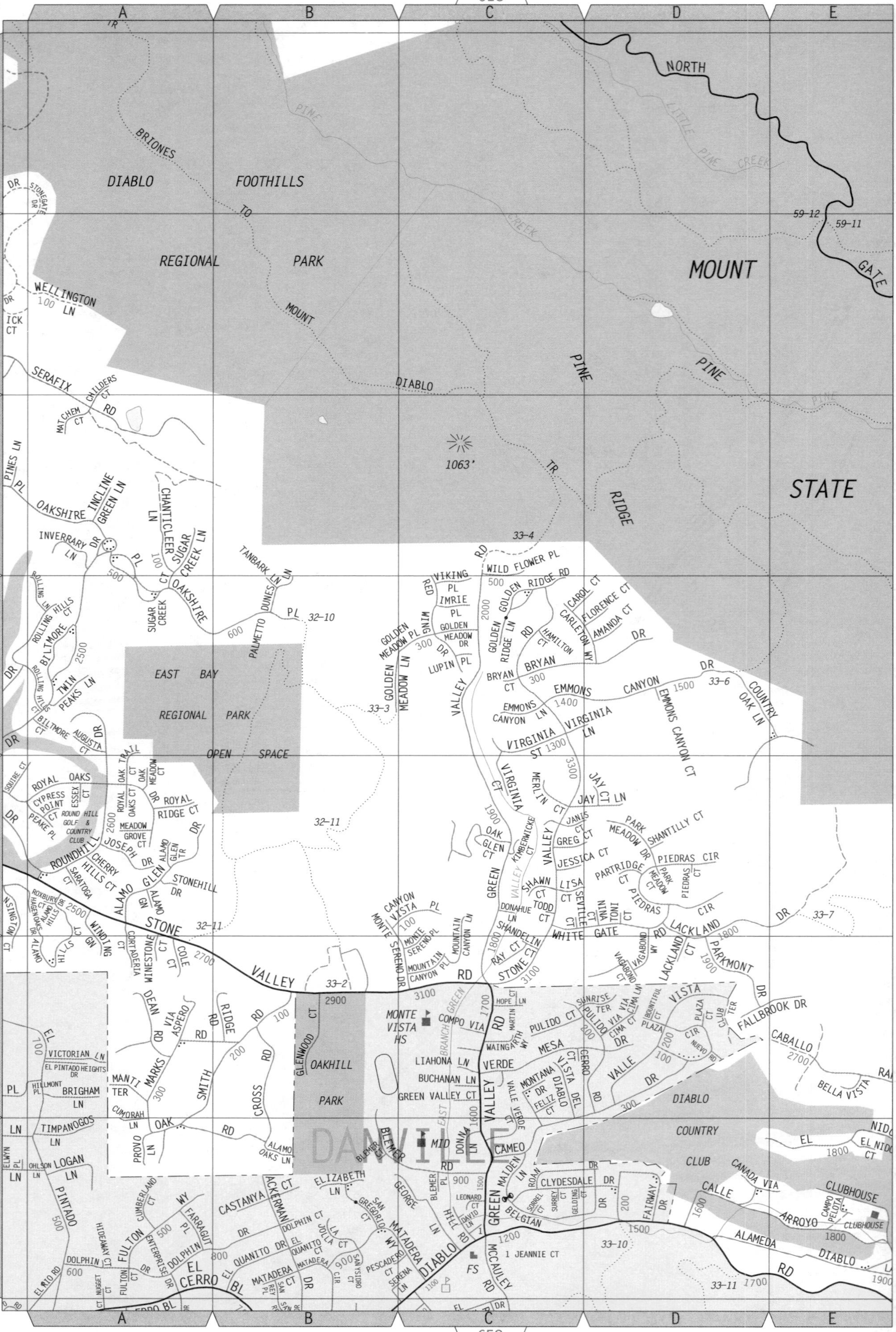
A
B
C
D
E
1
2
3
4
5
6
7
DIABLO FOOTHILLS
REGIONAL PARK
BRIONES TO MOUNT DIABLO TR
MOUNT
STATE
NORTH GATE
PINE RIDGE
PINE CREEK
LITTLE PINE CREEK
1063'
59-12
59-11
33-4
33-3
33-6
33-7
32-10
32-11
33-2
33-10
33-11
EAST BAY
REGIONAL PARK
OPEN SPACE
WELLINGTON LN
SERAFIX RD
CHILDERS CT
MATCHEM CT
PINES LN
PINES PL
OAKSHIRE PL
INCLINE GREEN LN
INVERRARY LN
CHANTICLEER LN
SUGAR CREEK LN
SUGAR CREEK CT
TANBARK LN
DUNES LN
PALMETTO
ROLLING HILLS CT
BILTMORE DR
TWIN PEAKS LN
AUGUSTA DR
ROYAL OAKS CT
CYPRESS POINT CT
ESSEX CT
ROUND HILL GOLF & COUNTRY CLUB
PEAKE PL
ROUNDHILL RD
MEADOW GROVE CT
ROYAL RIDGE CT
JOSEPH DR
CHERRY HILLS CT
SARATOGA
ALAMO GLEN DR
STONEHILL DR
STONE VALLEY RD
WINDING GN
CORTADERIA CT
WINESTONE CT
COLE CT
GOLDEN MEADOW LN
VIKING PL
IMRIE PL
GOLDEN MEADOW DR
LUPIN PL
WILD FLOWER PL
GOLDEN RIDGE RD
GOLDEN RIDGE LN
CAROL CT
FLORENCE CT
CARLETON WY
AMANDA CT
HAMILTON CT
BRYAN CT
EMMONS CANYON DR
EMMONS CANYON CT
COUNTRY OAK LN
VIRGINIA ST
VIRGINIA LN
VIRGINIA CT
MERLIN CT
JAY CT
JAY LN
JANIS CT
GREG CT
JESSICA CT
KIMBERWICKE CT
OAK GLEN CT
GREEN VALLEY RD
SHAWN CT
LISA CT
SEVILLE CT
TODD CT
DONAHUE LN
SHANDELIN CT
RAY CT
STONE CT
NINA CT
TONI CT
PARTRIDGE CT
PARK MEADOW DR
SHANTILLY CT
PIEDRAS CIR
WHITE GATE RD
LACKLAND DR
LACKLAND CT
PARKMONT DR
VAGABOND WY
CANYON VISTA PL
MONTE SERENO DR
MOUNTAIN CANYON PL
FALLBROOK DR
CABALLO
BELLA VISTA
DEAN RD
VIA ASPERO
RIDGE RD
SMITH RD
CROSS RD
MARKS RD
VICTORIAN LN
EL PINTADO HEIGHTS DR
HILLMONT DR
BRIGHAM LN
MANTI TER
CUMORAH LN
PROVO LN
OAK RD
TIMPANOGOS LN
LOGAN LN
ALAMO OAKS LN
GLENWOOD CT
OAKHILL PARK
MONTE VISTA HS
COMPO VIA
HOPE CT
MARTIN WY
WAINGARTH WY
PULIDO CT
SUNRISE TER
CIMA CT
VIA CIMA LN
BOUNTIFUL CT
VISTA PLAZA
CLUB TER
MESA VERDE
LIAHONA LN
BUCHANAN LN
GREEN VALLEY CT
MONTANA DR
VALLE VERDE CT
FELIZ CT
DIABLO VISTA
CERRO DEL
VALLE DR
DIABLO COUNTRY CLUB
DANVILLE
MID
BLEMER RD
DONNA LN
CAMEO
MAIDEN LN
CLYDESDALE DR
SORREL CT
SURREY CT
GELDING CT
FAIRWAY DR
CANADA VIA
CALLE ARROYO
CLUBHOUSE
CAMPO PELOTA
ALAMEDA DIABLO RD
EL NIDO CT
PINTADO
FULTON WY
CUMBERLAND CT
HIDEAWAY CT
ENTERPRISE DR
FARRAGUT PL
DOLPHIN DR
ACKERMAN CT
CASTANYA CT
ELIZABETH LN
DOLPHIN CT
LA JOLLA CT
SAN GREGORIO CT
SAN MATADERA WY
QUANITO DR
EL QUANITO CT
MATADERA DR
SAN YSIDRO CIR
PESCADERO CT
SERENA LN
GEORGE LN
HILL RD
LEONARD CT
DAVID CT
GREEN
BELGIAN
FS
1 JEANNIE CT
MCCAULEY RD
DIABLO RD
EL CERRO BL
EL RIO RD
ELWYN PL
OHLSON LN
NUGGET CT

SEE 632 MAP

SEE 653 MAP

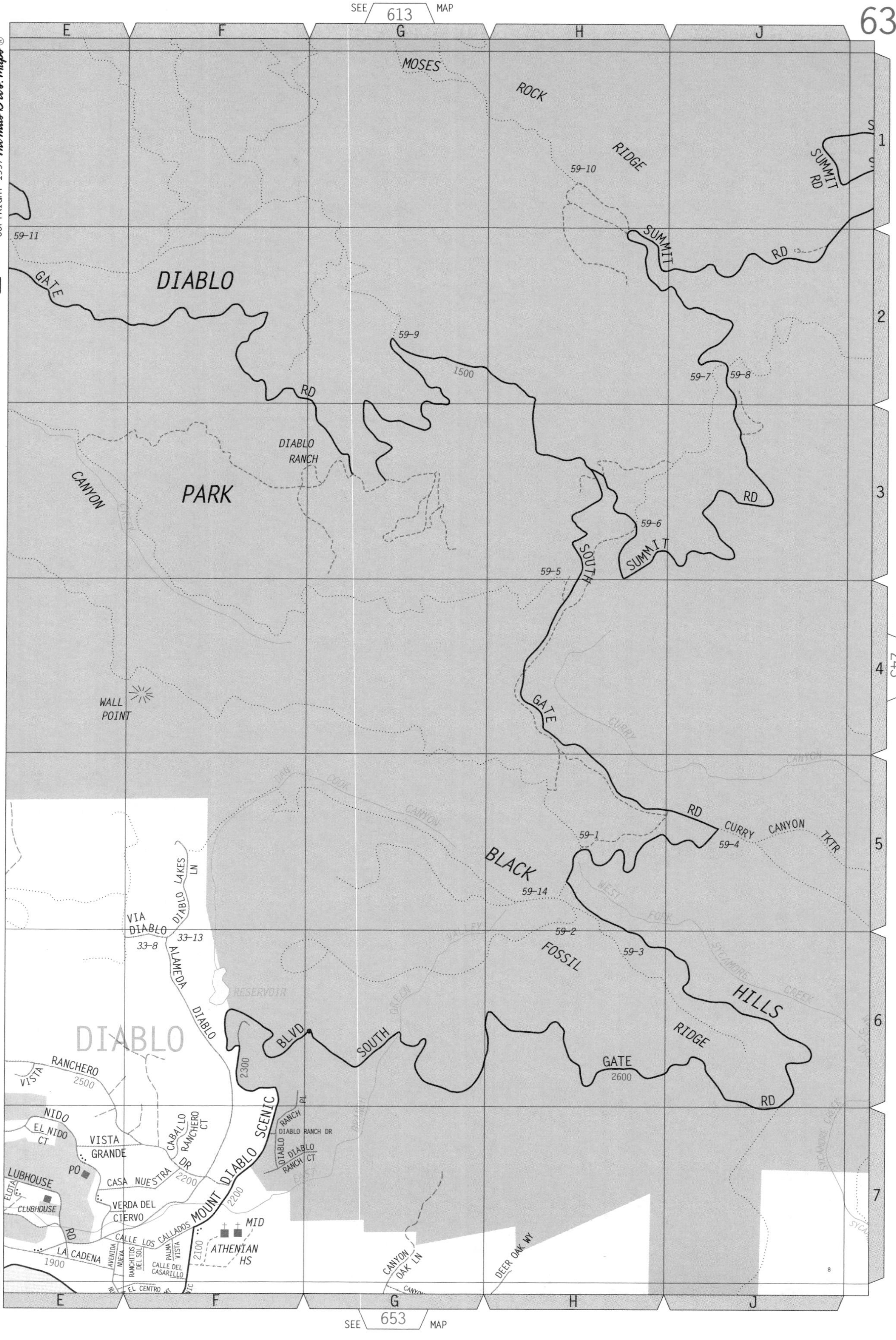
SEE 613 MAP
E
F
G
H
J
1
2
3
4
5
6
7
MOSES
ROCK
RIDGE
SUMMIT RD
59-10
59-11
GATE
DIABLO
SUMMIT
RD
59-9
1500
59-7
59-8
RD
DIABLO RANCH
CANYON
PARK
RD
59-6
SUMMIT
SOUTH
59-5
SEE 243 MAP
WALL POINT
GATE
CURRY
CANYON
DAN
COOK
CANYON
RD
CURRY
CANYON
TKTR
59-1
59-4
BLACK
59-14
WEST
FORK
DIABLO LAKES LN
VIA DIABLO
33-8
33-13
ALAMEDA
DIABLO
59-2
59-3
FOSSIL
VALLEY
SYCAMORE
CREEK
RESERVOIR
GREEN
HILLS
DIABLO
BLVD
SOUTH
2300
RIDGE
GATE
2600
RD
RANCHERO
VISTA
2500
NIDO
EL NIDO CT
VISTA
GRANDE
CABALLO
RANCHERO CT
MOUNT DIABLO SCENIC
RANCH PL
DIABLO RANCH DR
DIABLO RANCH CT
SYCAMORE CREEK
LUBHOUSE
PO
CASA NUESTRA
DR
2200
CLUBHOUSE
VERDA DEL CIERVO
2200
MID
RD
CALLE LOS CALLADOS
ATHENIAN HS
LA CADENA
1900
2100
CANYON OAK LN
DEER OAK WY
EL CENTRO
SEE 653 MAP

SEE 626 MAP

A B C D E

1 2 3 4 5 6 7

SEE 243 MAP

SEE 666 MAP

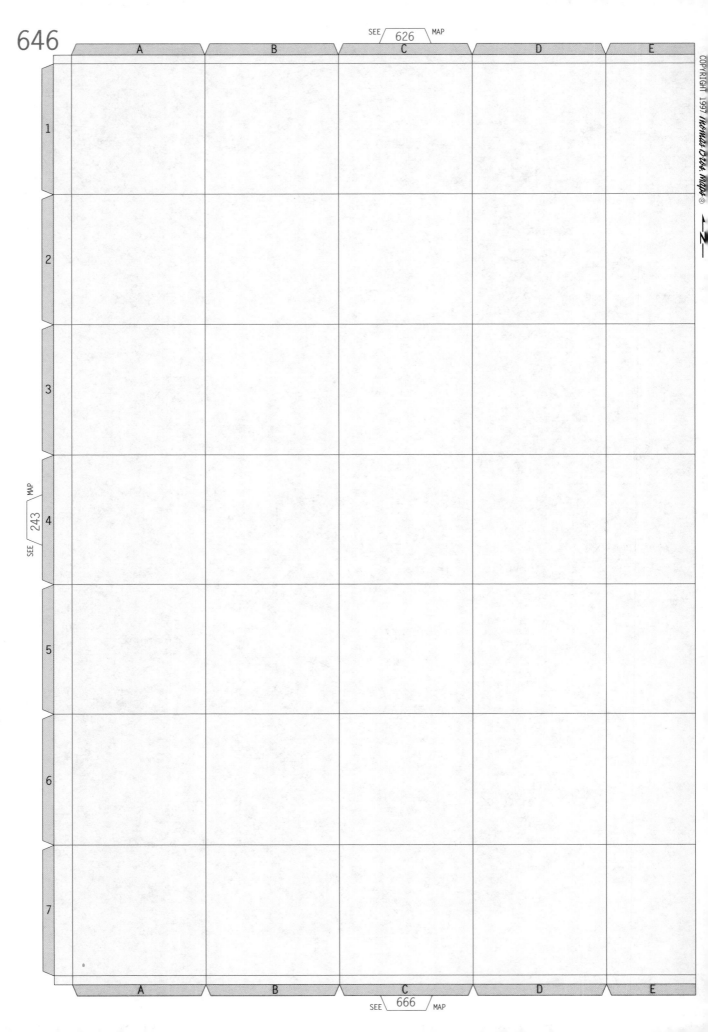

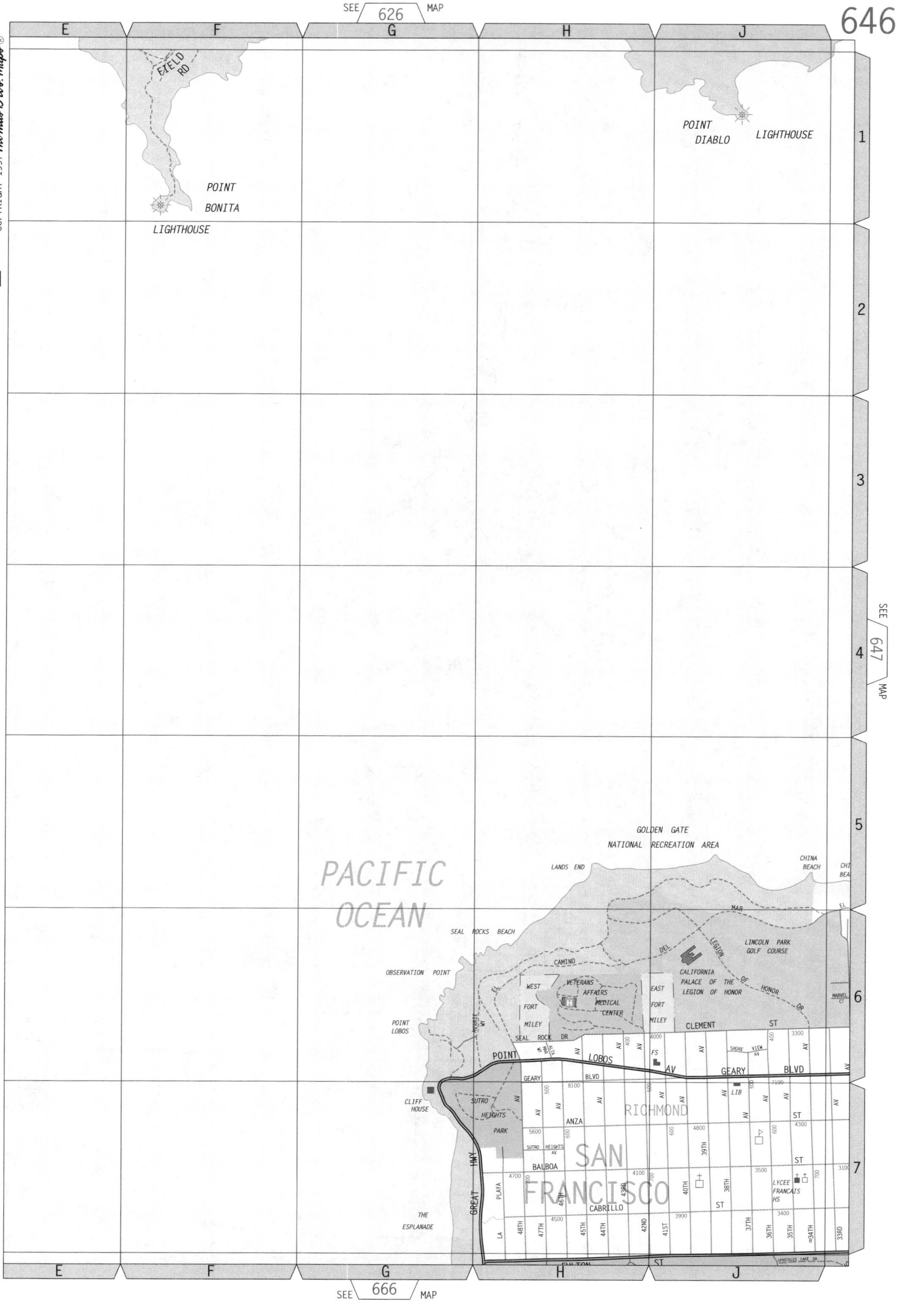
SEE 626 MAP
E
F
G
H
J
1
2
3
4
5
6
7
SEE 647 MAP
SEE 666 MAP
FIELD RD
POINT BONITA
LIGHTHOUSE
POINT DIABLO
LIGHTHOUSE
PACIFIC OCEAN
GOLDEN GATE NATIONAL RECREATION AREA
LANDS END
CHINA BEACH
SEAL ROCKS BEACH
OBSERVATION POINT
POINT LOBOS
CLIFF HOUSE
THE ESPLANADE
SUTRO HEIGHTS PARK
EL CAMINO DEL MAR
LEGION OF HONOR DR
LINCOLN PARK GOLF COURSE
CALIFORNIA PALACE OF THE LEGION OF HONOR
WEST FORT MILEY
EAST FORT MILEY
VETERANS AFFAIRS MEDICAL CENTER
MERRIE WY
SEAL ROCK DR
CLEMENT ST
POINT LOBOS AV
GEARY BLVD
ANZA ST
BALBOA ST
CABRILLO ST
FULTON ST
GREAT HWY
LA PLAYA
SUTRO HEIGHTS AV
SHORE VIEW AV
MARVEL CT
RICHMOND
SAN FRANCISCO
FS
LIB
LYCEE FRANCAIS HS
48TH
47TH
46TH
45TH
44TH
43RD
42ND
41ST
40TH
39TH
38TH
37TH
36TH
35TH
34TH
33RD
SPRECKLES LAKE DR

SEE 627 MAP

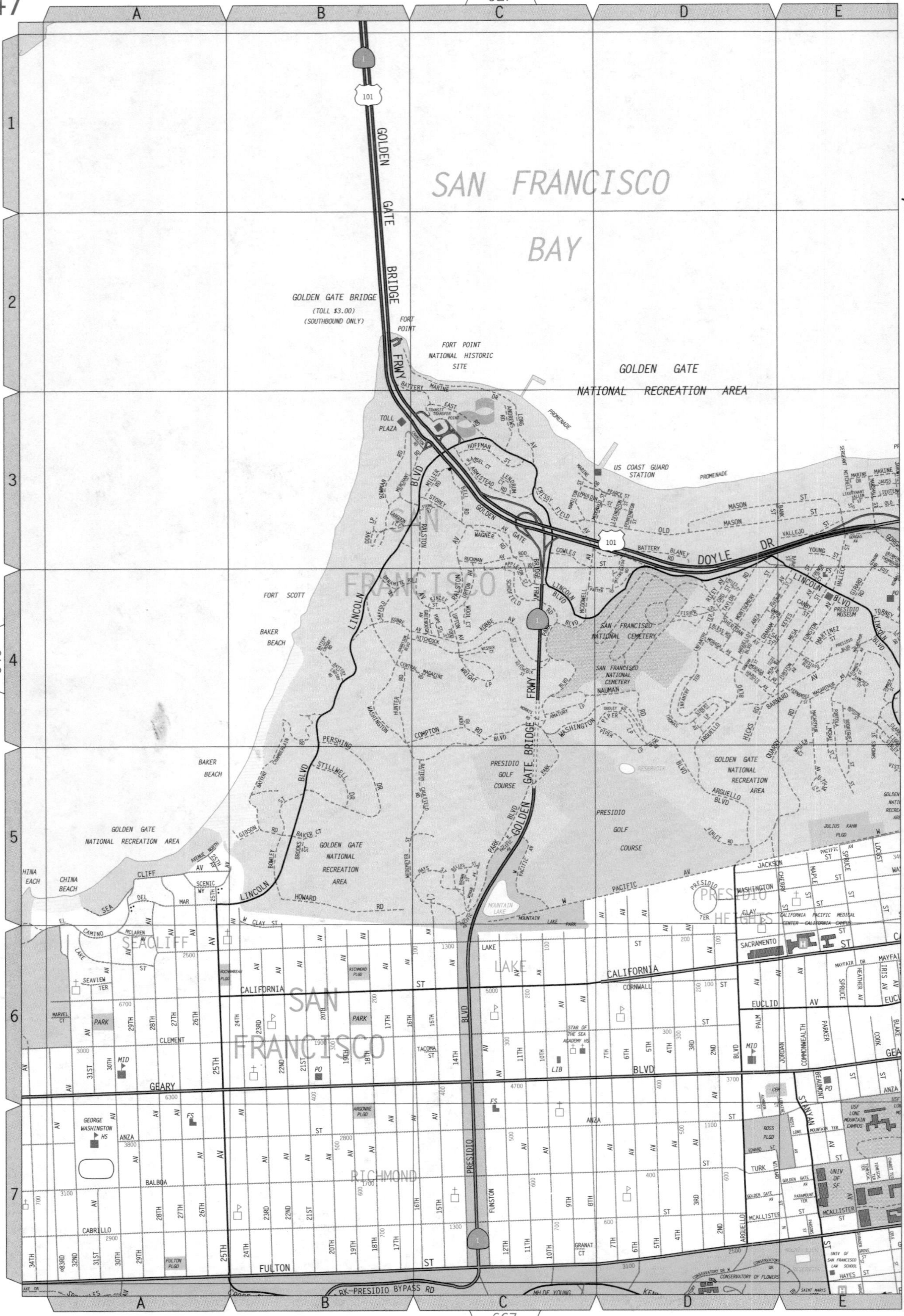
SAN FRANCISCO BAY
GOLDEN GATE BRIDGE
(TOLL $3.00)
(SOUTHBOUND ONLY)
GOLDEN GATE BRIDGE FRWY
FORT POINT
FORT POINT NATIONAL HISTORIC SITE
GOLDEN GATE NATIONAL RECREATION AREA
TOLL PLAZA
US COAST GUARD STATION
PROMENADE
SAN FRANCISCO
FORT SCOTT
BAKER BEACH
LINCOLN BLVD
DOYLE DR
SAN FRANCISCO NATIONAL CEMETERY
PRESIDIO MUSEUM
PRESIDIO GOLF COURSE
CHINA BEACH
SEACLIFF
LAKE
PRESIDIO HEIGHTS
RICHMOND
GEARY BLVD
CALIFORNIA ST
CLEMENT ST
FULTON ST
PARK PRESIDIO BYPASS RD
PRESIDIO BLVD
GEORGE WASHINGTON HS
STAR OF THE SEA ACADEMY HS
UNIV OF SF
USF LONE MOUNTAIN CAMPUS
CONSERVATORY OF FLOWERS
JULIUS KAHN PLGD
ROSS PLGD
ARGONNE PLGD
FULTON PLGD
RICHMOND PLGD
MOUNTAIN LAKE
STANYAN
ARGUELLO BLVD

SEE 646 MAP

SEE 667 MAP

SEE 627 MAP

E F G H J
1 2 3 4 5 6 7
SAN FRANCISCO BAY
SAUSALITO TIBURON FERRY
ALCATRAZ FERRY
SAN FRANCISCO MARITIME NATIONAL HISTORICAL PARK
MUNICIPAL PIER
GOLDEN GATE NATIONAL RECREATION AREA
PIER 1
PIER 2
PIER 3
SAINT FRANCIS YACHT CLUB
GOLDEN GATE YACHT CLUB
PROMENADE
HYDE STREET PIER
FISHERMANS WHARF
FISHERMANS MEMORIAL CHAPEL
AQUATIC PARK
SAN FRANCISCO NATIONAL MARITIME MUSEUM
THE CANNERY
THE ANCHORAGE
GHIRARDELLI SQUARE
FORT MASON CENTER
FORT MASON
MARINA
MARINA GREEN DR
MARINA BLVD
EXPLORATORIUM
PALACE OF FINE ARTS
SAN FRANCISCO
GEORGE R MOSCONE RECREATION CENTER
LOMBARD ST
LETTERMAN GENERAL HOSPITAL
PRESIDIO BLVD
GOLDEN GATE NATIONAL RECREATION AREA
COW HOLLOW
PACIFIC HEIGHTS
ALTA PLAZA
LAFAYETTE PARK
RUSSIAN HILL
SAN FRANCISCO ART INSTITUTE
COLUMBUS AV
VAN NESS AV
101
BROADWAY
UNIVERSITY OF THE PACIFIC
CALIFORNIA PACIFIC MEDICAL CEN HOSP
SAN FRANCISCO UNIVERSITY HS
CALIFORNIA ST
GEARY BLVD
JAPAN CENTER
UCSF MOUNT ZION HOSPITAL
HAMILTON SQUARE
JORDAN HEIGHTS/LAUREL HEIGHTS
KAISER PERMANENTE MEDICAL CENTER
JEFFERSON SQUARE
ANZA VISTA
USF LONE MOUNTAIN CAMPUS
UNIV OF SAN FRANCISCO
LONE MOUNTAIN
ALAMO SQUARE
CITY HALL
CIVIC CENTER
FEDERAL BUILDING
STATE BUILDING
MAIN LIBRARY
OPERA HOUSE
DAVIES SYMPHONY HALL
SAN FRANCISCO PERFORMING ARTS LIBRARY & MUSEUM
TRANSIT TRANS POINT
MARKET ST
MISSION ST
FELL ST
OAK ST
FULTON ST
GOLDEN GATE AV
TURK ST
DMV

SEE 648 MAP

SEE 667 MAP

SEE 243 MAP

A
B
C
D
E
1
2
3
4
5
6
7
SAN FRANCISCO BAY
TREASURE ISLAND NAVAL RESERVATION
TREASURE ISLAND MUSEUM
YERBA BUENA ISLAND
BAY BRIDGE
SAN FRANCISCO-OAKLAND BAY BRIDGE
(TWO LEVEL FRWY)
(TOLL $1.00 WESTBOUND ONLY)
TRANSBAY TUBE
BART
OAKLAND ALAMEDA FERRY
HARBOR BAY ISLE FERRY
ANGEL ISLAND
SAUSALITO
TIBURON
FERRY
LARKSPUR
SAN FRANCISCO
VALLEJO
OAKLAND
ALAMEDA
PIER 39
UNDERWATER WORLD
NORTH POINT
THE EMBARCADERO
TELEGRAPH HILL
NORTH BEACH
CHINATOWN
FINANCIAL DISTRICT
SAN FRANCISCO
SOUTH OF MARKET
SOUTH BEACH
SOUTH BEACH MARINA
CHINA BASIN
MISSION ROCK
RINCON POINT
FISHING PIER
JUSTIN HERMAN PLAZA
GOLDEN GATEWAY CENTER
FERRY BUILDING
UNION SQUARE
YERBA BUENA GARDENS
MOSCONE CONVENTION CENTER
FASHION INSTITUTE
HALL OF JUSTICE
CALTRAIN
1 ONE EMBARCADERO CENTER
2 TWO EMBARCADERO CENTER
3 THREE EMBARCADERO CENTER
4 FOUR EMBARCADERO CENTER
5 HYATT REGENCY
COLUMBUS AV
BROADWAY
CALIFORNIA
MARKET
MISSION
HOWARD
FOLSOM
HARRISON
BRYANT
BRANNAN
TOWNSEND
KING
EMBARCADERO
80
COPYRIGHT 1997 Thomas Bros. Maps ®
SEE 647 MAP
SEE 668 MAP

SEE 243 MAP

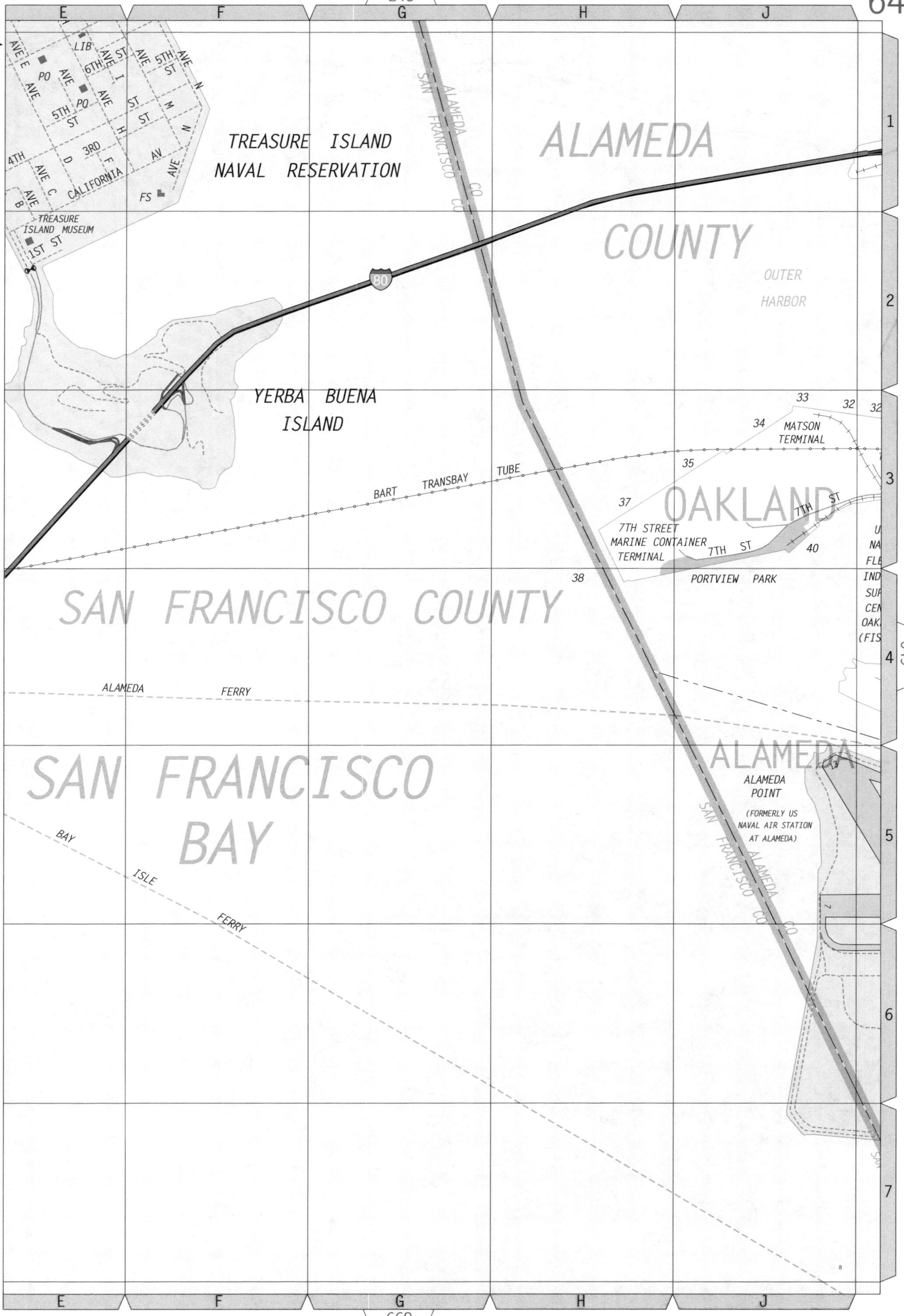
E
F
G
H
J
1
2
3
4
5
6
7
TREASURE ISLAND
NAVAL RESERVATION
TREASURE
ISLAND MUSEUM
LIB
PO
FS
1ST ST
3RD
4TH
5TH ST
6TH
CALIFORNIA
AVE B
AVE C
AVE D
AVE E
AVE F
AVE H
AVE I
AVE M
AVE N
YERBA BUENA
ISLAND
80
ALAMEDA
COUNTY
SAN FRANCISCO CO
ALAMEDA CO
OUTER
HARBOR
MATSON
TERMINAL
33
32
34
35
37
38
40
OAKLAND
7TH ST
7TH STREET
MARINE CONTAINER
TERMINAL
PORTVIEW PARK
BART
TRANSBAY
TUBE
SAN FRANCISCO COUNTY
ALAMEDA
FERRY
SAN FRANCISCO
BAY
BAY
ISLE
FERRY
ALAMEDA
ALAMEDA
POINT
(FORMERLY US
NAVAL AIR STATION
AT ALAMEDA)

SEE 649 MAP

SEE 668 MAP

SEE 629 MAP

SEE 648 MAP

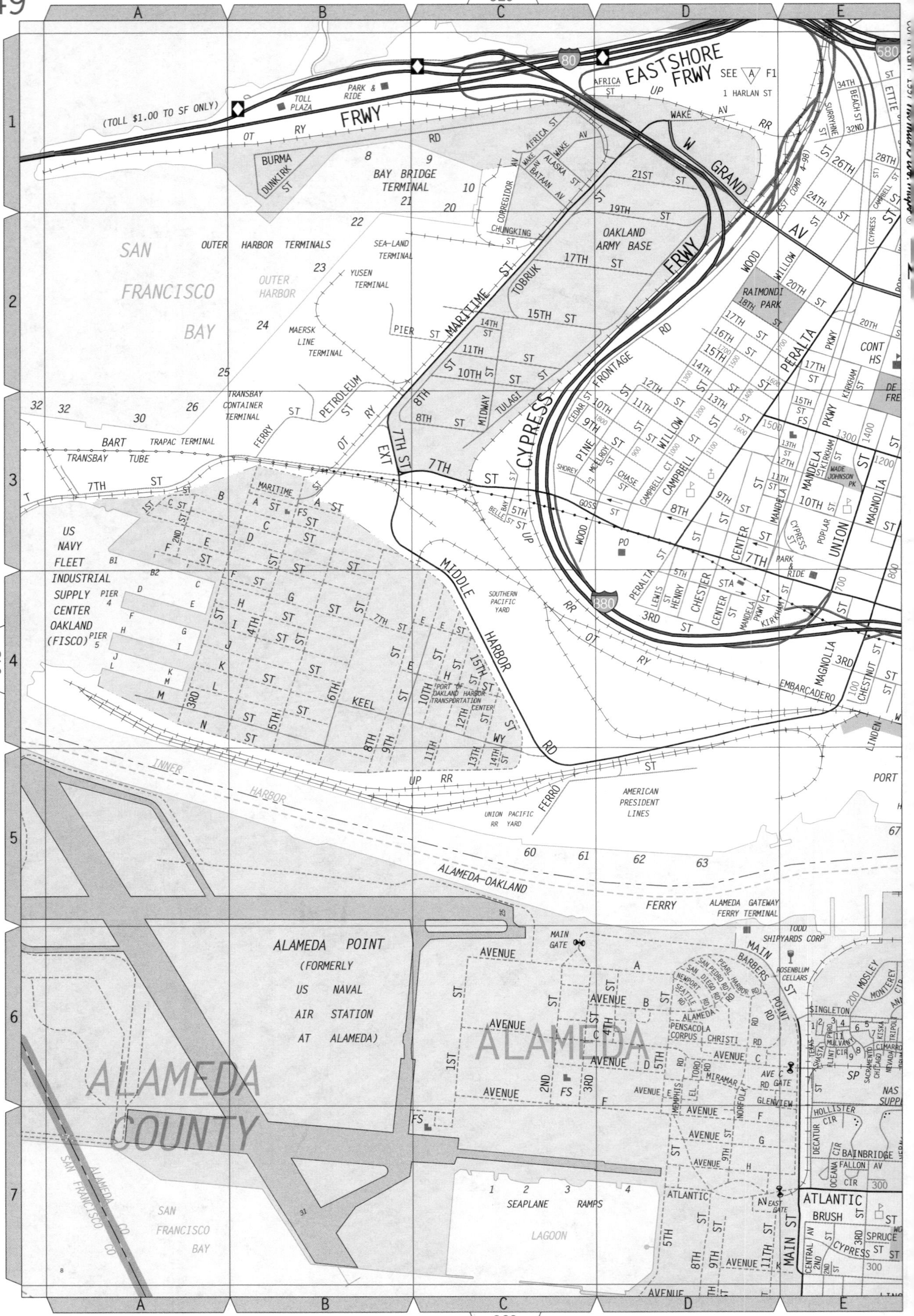
EASTSHORE FRWY
(TOLL $1.00 TO SF ONLY)
TOLL PLAZA
PARK & RIDE
BAY BRIDGE TERMINAL
OUTER HARBOR TERMINALS
SAN FRANCISCO BAY
OUTER HARBOR
SEA-LAND TERMINAL
YUSEN TERMINAL
MAERSK LINE TERMINAL
TRANSBAY CONTAINER TERMINAL
TRAPAC TERMINAL
BART TRANSBAY TUBE
OAKLAND ARMY BASE
RAIMONDI PARK
CYPRESS FRWY
MARITIME ST
W GRAND AV
US NAVY FLEET INDUSTRIAL SUPPLY CENTER OAKLAND (FISCO)
SOUTHERN PACIFIC YARD
MIDDLE HARBOR RD
PORT OF OAKLAND HARBOR TRANSPORTATION CENTER
INNER HARBOR
UNION PACIFIC RR YARD
AMERICAN PRESIDENT LINES
ALAMEDA-OAKLAND FERRY
ALAMEDA GATEWAY FERRY TERMINAL
TODD SHIPYARDS CORP
ROSENBLUM CELLARS
ALAMEDA POINT (FORMERLY US NAVAL AIR STATION AT ALAMEDA)
ALAMEDA
ALAMEDA COUNTY
SAN FRANCISCO CO
SEAPLANE RAMPS
LAGOON
SAN FRANCISCO BAY
MAIN GATE
EAST GATE
ATLANTIC AV
MAIN ST
EMBARCADERO
MAGNOLIA
MANDELA PKWY
PERALTA
UNION
WADE JOHNSON PK

SEE 669 MAP

SEE 629 MAP

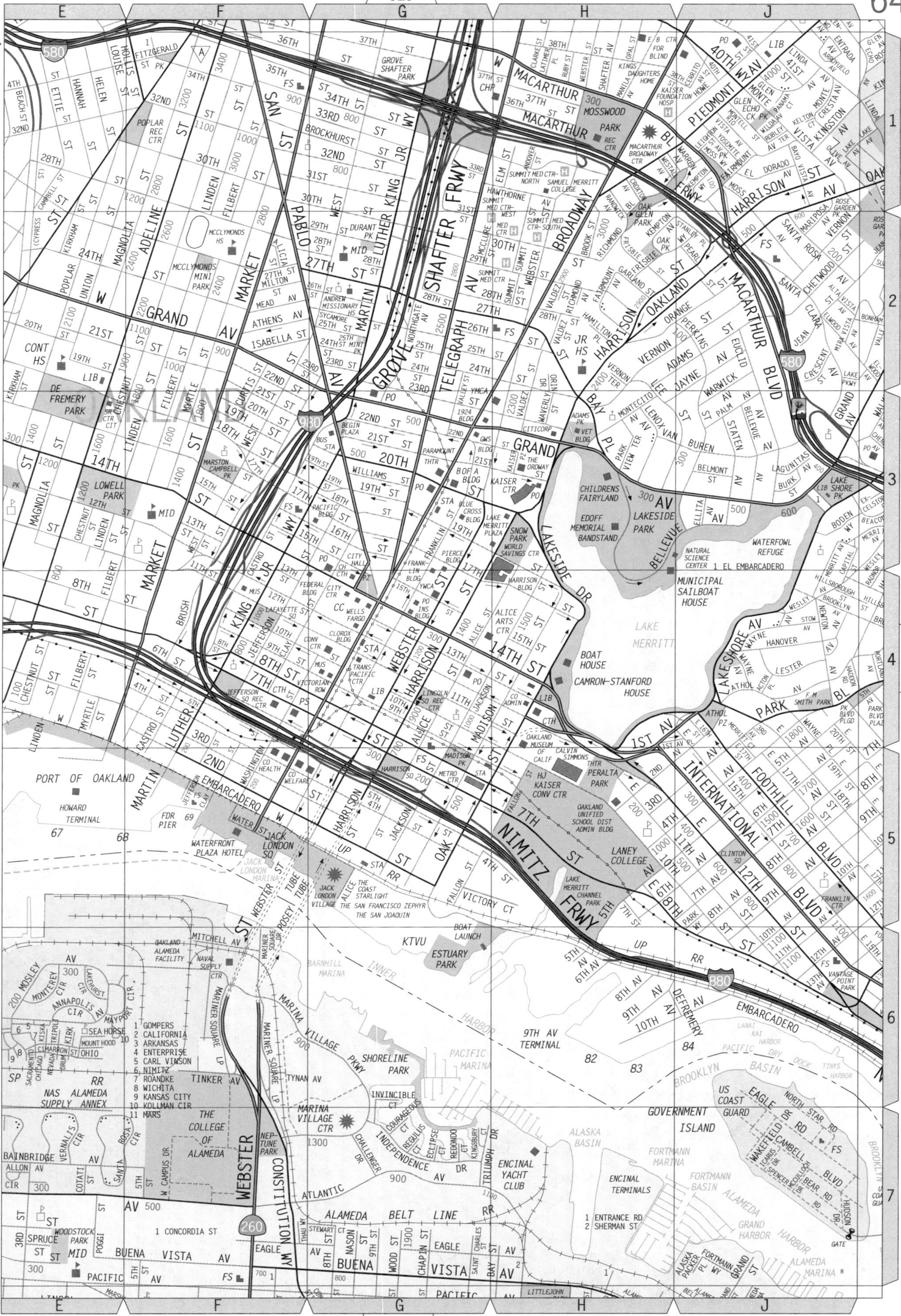
E
F
G
H
J
1
2
3
4
5
6
7
OAKLAND
580
980
880
260
MACARTHUR BLVD
MACARTHUR FRWY
BROADWAY
GRAND AV
TELEGRAPH AV
SHAFTER FRWY
SAN PABLO AV
MARKET ST
ADELINE ST
MARTIN LUTHER KING JR WY
NIMITZ FRWY
INTERNATIONAL BLVD
FOOTHILL BLVD
LAKESHORE AV
LAKESIDE DR
LAKE MERRITT
CHILDRENS FAIRYLAND
LAKESIDE PARK
EDOFF MEMORIAL BANDSTAND
NATURAL SCIENCE CENTER
1 EL EMBARCADERO
MUNICIPAL SAILBOAT HOUSE
WATERFOWL REFUGE
BOAT HOUSE
CAMRON-STANFORD HOUSE
OAKLAND MUSEUM OF CALIF
HJ KAISER CONV CTR
LANEY COLLEGE
PERALTA PARK
DE FREMERY PARK
LOWELL PARK
MOSSWOOD PARK
GROVE SHAFTER PARK
PORT OF OAKLAND
HOWARD TERMINAL
JACK LONDON SQ
JACK LONDON VILLAGE
WATERFRONT PLAZA HOTEL
FDR PIER
KTVU
ESTUARY PARK
INNER HARBOR
9TH AV TERMINAL
BROOKLYN BASIN
GOVERNMENT ISLAND
US COAST GUARD
ALASKA BASIN
FORTMANN MARINA
FORTMANN BASIN
ENCINAL TERMINALS
ENCINAL YACHT CLUB
ALAMEDA
GRAND HARBOR
ALAMEDA MARINA
PACIFIC MARINA
SHORELINE PARK
MARINA VILLAGE CTR
BARNHILL MARINA
NAS ALAMEDA SUPPLY ANNEX
THE COLLEGE OF ALAMEDA
WEBSTER ST
CONSTITUTION WY
ATLANTIC AV
ALAMEDA BELT LINE RR
BUENA VISTA AV
PACIFIC AV
1 GOMPERS
2 CALIFORNIA
3 ARKANSAS
4 ENTERPRISE
5 CARL VINSON
6 NIMITZ
7 ROANOKE
8 WICHITA
9 KANSAS CITY
10 KOLLMAN CIR
11 MARS
1 CONCORDIA ST
1 ENTRANCE RD
2 SHERMAN ST
67
68
69
82
83
84

SEE 650 MAP

SEE 669 MAP

SEE 630 MAP

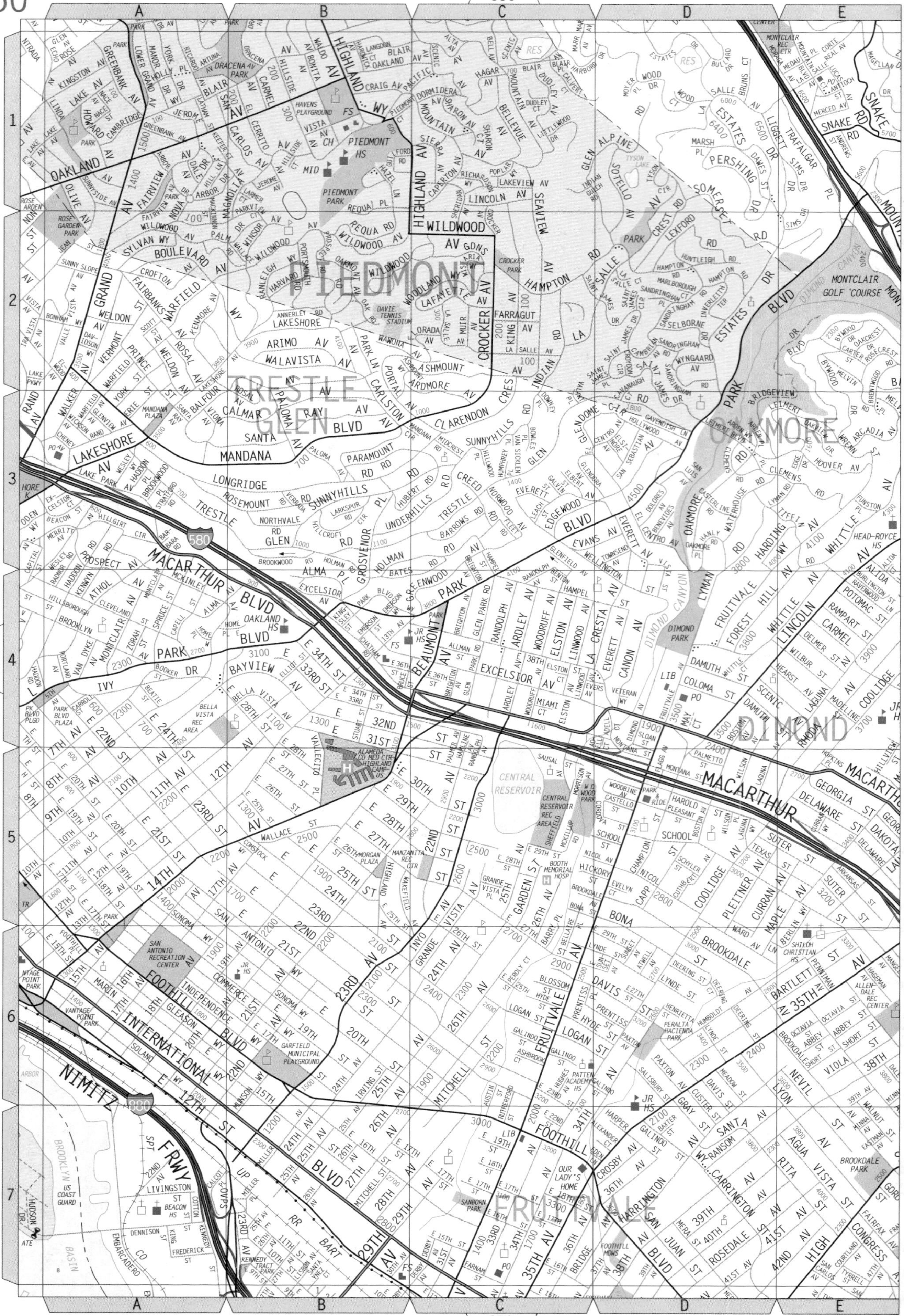
A
B
C
D
E
1
2
3
4
5
6
7
PIEDMONT
TRESTLE GLEN
OAKMORE
DIMOND
FRUITVALE
MACARTHUR BLVD
MACARTHUR
580
880
NIMITZ FRWY
INTERNATIONAL BLVD
FOOTHILL BLVD
GRAND AV
LAKESHORE AV
PARK BLVD
OAKLAND AV
HIGHLAND AV
MOUNTAIN BLVD
WARREN FRWY
MONTCLAIR GOLF COURSE
DIMOND CANYON
DIMOND PARK
CENTRAL RESERVOIR
PIEDMONT PARK
SAN ANTONIO RECREATION CENTER
GARFIELD MUNICIPAL PLAYGROUND
FRUITVALE AV
FRUITVALE
HIGH ST
35TH AV
29TH AV
23RD AV
14TH AV
E 12TH ST
WILDWOOD AV
LINCOLN AV
PARK BLVD
BEAUMONT AV
US COAST GUARD
BROOKLYN BASIN

SEE 649 MAP

SEE 670 MAP

SEE 630 MAP

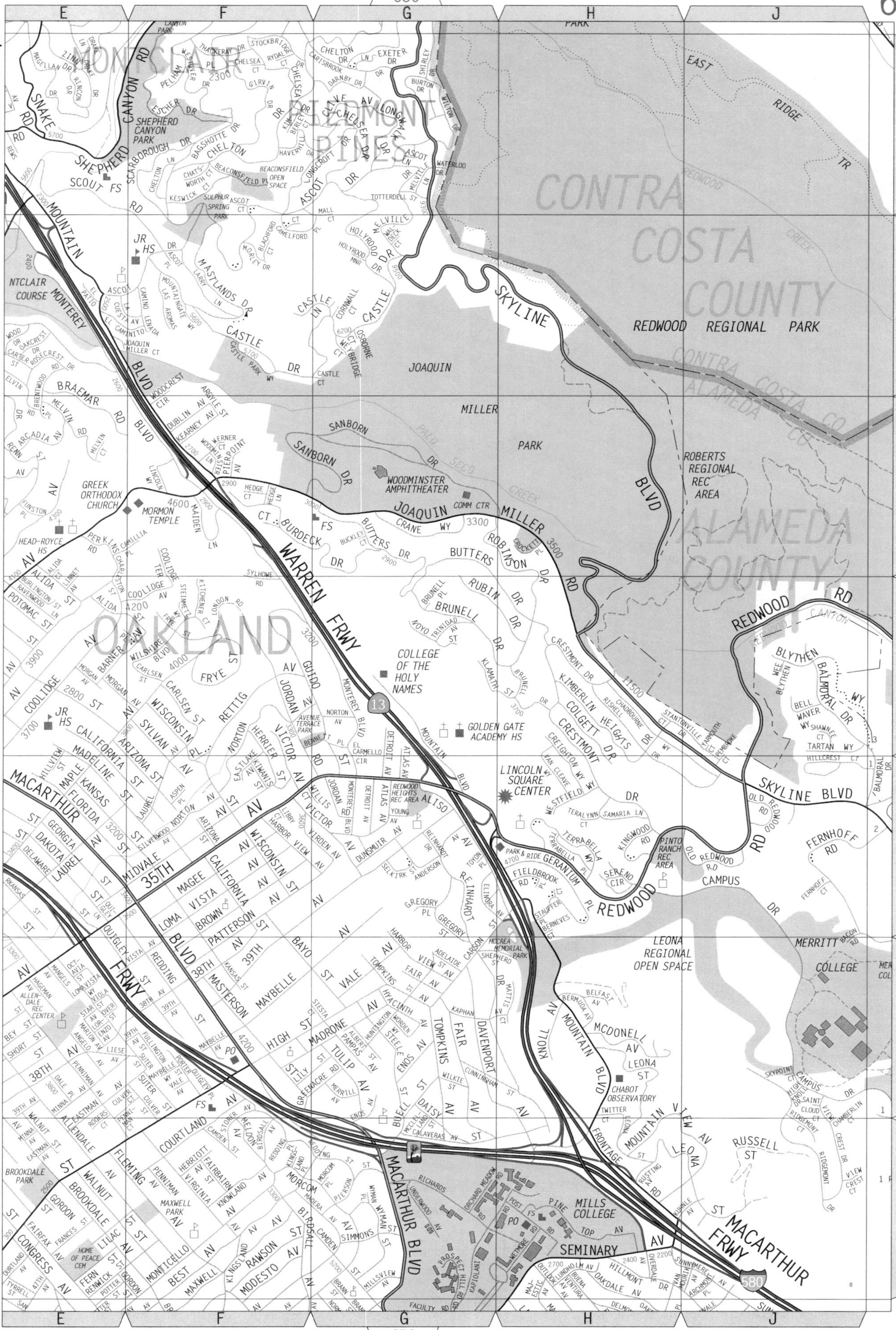
E
F
G
H
J
1
2
3
4
5
6
7
MONTCLAIR
PIEDMONT PINES
CONTRA COSTA COUNTY
ALAMEDA COUNTY
OAKLAND
REDWOOD REGIONAL PARK
JOAQUIN MILLER PARK
ROBERTS REGIONAL REC AREA
SHEPHERD CANYON PARK
WOODMINSTER AMPHITHEATER
GREEK ORTHODOX CHURCH
MORMON TEMPLE
HEAD-ROYCE HS
COLLEGE OF THE HOLY NAMES
GOLDEN GATE ACADEMY HS
LINCOLN SQUARE CENTER
REDWOOD HEIGHTS REC AREA
PINTO RANCH REC AREA
LEONA REGIONAL OPEN SPACE
MERRITT COLLEGE
CHABOT OBSERVATORY
MILLS COLLEGE
MCCREA MEMORIAL PARK
ALLENDALE REC CENTER
BROOKDALE PARK
MAXWELL PARK
HOME OF PEACE CEM
SKYLINE BLVD
JOAQUIN MILLER RD
WARREN FRWY
MOUNTAIN BLVD
MACARTHUR BLVD
MACARTHUR FRWY
35TH AV
REDWOOD RD
SHEPHERD CANYON RD
EAST RIDGE TR
CAMPUS DR
SEMINARY AV
13
580

SEE 651 MAP

SEE 670 MAP

BAY AREA

MAP

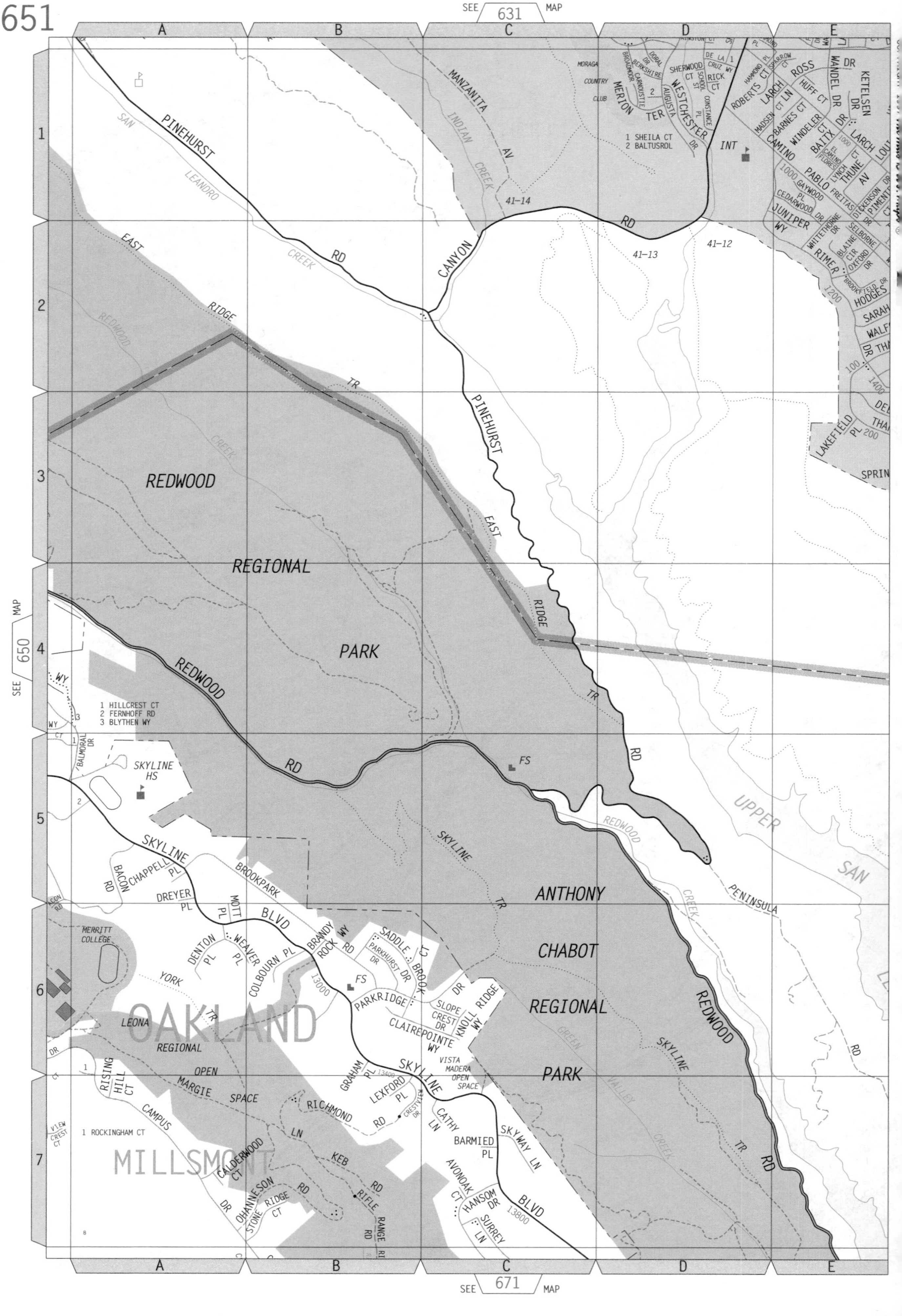
SEE 631 MAP
SEE 650 MAP
SEE 671 MAP
A
B
C
D
E
1
2
3
4
5
6
7
REDWOOD REGIONAL PARK
ANTHONY CHABOT REGIONAL PARK
OAKLAND
MILLSMONT
LEONA REGIONAL OPEN SPACE
VISTA MADERA OPEN SPACE
PINEHURST RD
CANYON RD
REDWOOD RD
SKYLINE BLVD
EAST RIDGE TR
SKYLINE TR
SAN LEANDRO CREEK
REDWOOD CREEK
INDIAN CREEK
UPPER SAN LEANDRO
GREEN VALLEY CREEK
PENINSULA
MANZANITA AV
MORAGA COUNTRY CLUB
INT
41-14
41-13
41-12
1 SHEILA CT
2 BALTUSROL
1 HILLCREST CT
2 FERNHOFF RD
3 BLYTHEN WY
1 ROCKINGHAM CT
SKYLINE HS
MERRITT COLLEGE
FS
BROOKPARK
CHAPPELL PL
BACON RD
DREYER PL
MOTT PL
WEAVER PL
DENTON PL
COLBOURN PL
BRANDY ROCK WY
SADDLE BROOK CT
PARKHURST DR
PARKRIDGE DR
SLOPE CREST DR
KNOLL RIDGE WY
CLAIREPOINTE WY
YORK TR
RISING HILL CT
MARGIE
CAMPUS
GRAHAM PL
LEXFORD PL
CRESTVIEW
RICHMOND RD
CATHY LN
BARMIED PL
SKYWAY LN
AVONOAK CT
HANSOM DR
SURREY LN
CALDERWOOD CT
OHANNESON DR
STONE RIDGE CT
KEB RD
RIFLE RANGE RD
BALMORAL DR
LAKEFIELD PL
MERION TER
WESTCHESTER
AUGUSTA
SHERWOOD CT
ROBERTS CT
ROSS
WANDEL DR
KETELSEN DR
LARCH
CAMINO PABLO
JUNIPER WY
RIMER
HODGES
13000
13400
13800
1000
1200

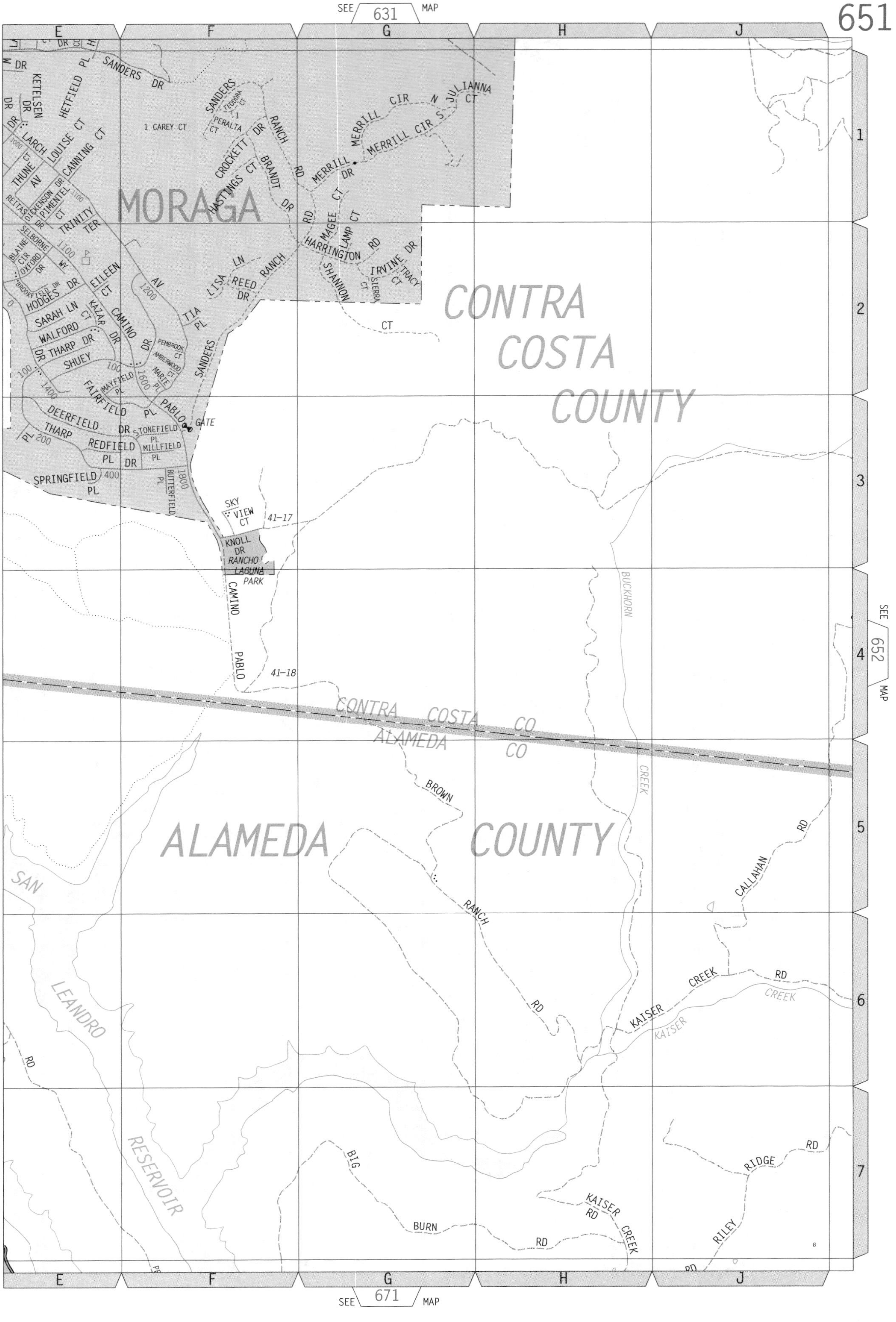
SEE 631 MAP
E
F
G
H
J
1
2
3
4
5
6
7
MORAGA
CONTRA COSTA COUNTY
ALAMEDA COUNTY
CONTRA COSTA CO
ALAMEDA CO
SANDERS DR
KETELSEN DR
HETFIELD PL
LARCH
LOUISE CT
CANNING CT
THUNE AV
DICKENSON DR
PIMENTEL CT
TRINITY TER
SELBORNE
BLAINE CIR
OXFORD DR
BROOKFIELD DR
HODGES DR
EILEEN CT
SARAH LN
WALFORD CT
KAZAR
THARP DR
SHUEY
CAMINO PABLO
MAYFIELD PL
FAIRFIELD PL
DEERFIELD DR
THARP PL
REDFIELD PL
STONEFIELD PL
MILLFIELD PL
SPRINGFIELD PL
BUTTERFIELD PL
PEMBROOK CT
AMBERWOOD CT
MARIE PL
TIA PL
1 CAREY CT
SANDERS CT
TEODORA CT
PERALTA CT
CROCKETT DR
HASTINGS CT
BRANDT DR
RANCH RD
MERRILL DR
MERRILL CIR N
MERRILL CIR S
JULIANNA CT
MAGEE CT
LAMP CT
HARRINGTON RD
SHANNON CT
IRVINE DR
TRACY CT
SIERRA CT
LISA LN
REED DR
RANCH
GATE
SKY VIEW CT
KNOLL DR
RANCHO LAGUNA PARK
41-17
41-18
BUCKHORN CREEK
BROWN RANCH RD
CALLAHAN RD
KAISER CREEK RD
KAISER CREEK
BIG BURN RD
KAISER CREEK RD
RIDGE RD
RILEY
SAN LEANDRO RESERVOIR
RD
SEE 652 MAP
SEE 671 MAP

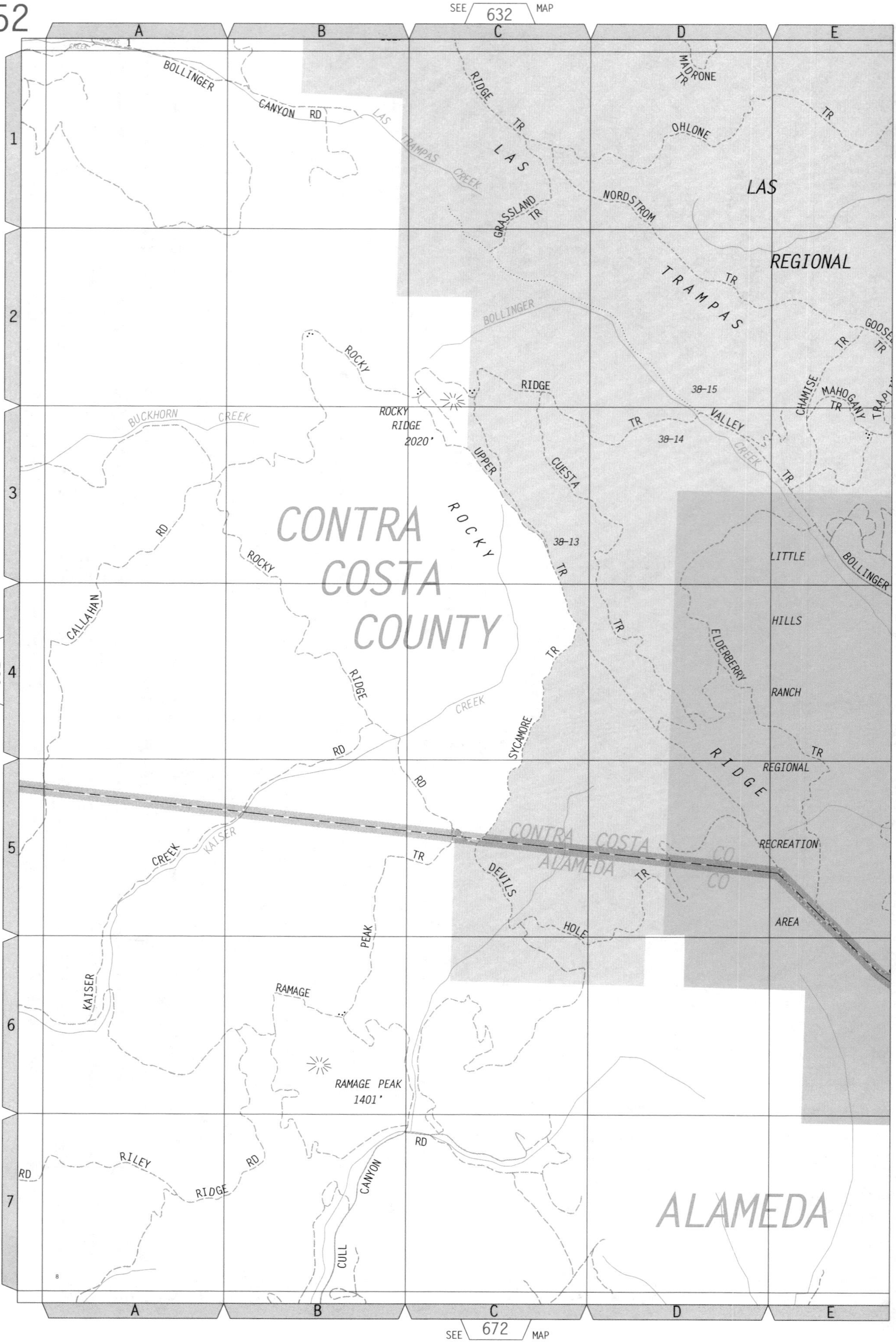
SEE 632 MAP
A
B
C
D
E
1
2
3
4
5
6
7
SEE 651 MAP
SEE 672 MAP
BOLLINGER CANYON RD
LAS TRAMPAS CREEK
RIDGE TR
MADRONE TR
OHLONE
TR
LAS
GRASSLAND TR
NORDSTROM
LAS
REGIONAL
TRAMPAS
TR
BOLLINGER
GOOSE
TR
ROCKY
RIDGE
38-15
CHAMISE
MAHOGANY TR
ROCKY RIDGE 2020'
BUCKHORN CREEK
TR
38-14
VALLEY
CREEK
UPPER
CUESTA
TR
RD
CONTRA COSTA COUNTY
ROCKY
ROCKY
38-13
TR
LITTLE
BOLLINGER
CALLAHAN
TR
HILLS
ELDERBERRY
TR
RIDGE
RANCH
CREEK
SYCAMORE
RD
RD
TR
REGIONAL
RIDGE
CONTRA COSTA
CO
ALAMEDA
CO
RECREATION
KAISER
CREEK
TR
DEVILS
TR
AREA
PEAK
HOLE
KAISER
RAMAGE
RAMAGE PEAK 1401'
RD
RILEY
RD
RD
RIDGE
CANYON
ALAMEDA
CULL

SEE 632 MAP

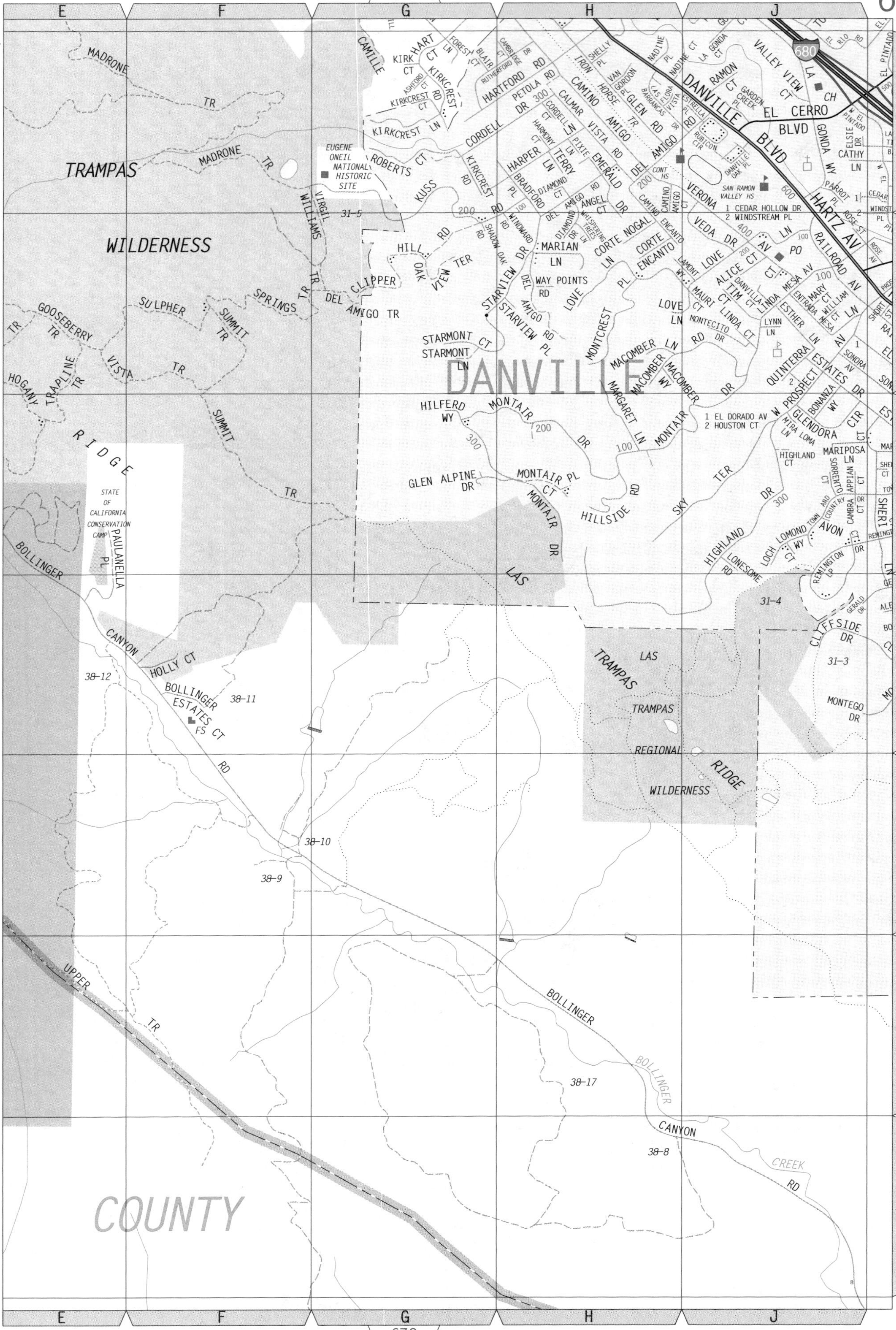
E
F
G
H
J
1
2
3
4
5
6
7
DANVILLE
COUNTY
TRAMPAS
WILDERNESS
RIDGE
LAS TRAMPAS
TRAMPAS
REGIONAL
RIDGE
WILDERNESS
MADRONE TR
MADRONE TR
EUGENE ONEIL NATIONAL HISTORIC SITE
VIRGIL WILLIAMS TR
SULPHER SPRINGS TR
SUMMIT TR
GOOSEBERRY TR
VISTA TR
TRAPLINE TR
HOGANY TR
SUMMIT TR
DEL AMIGO TR
STATE OF CALIFORNIA CONSERVATION CAMP
PAULANELLA PL
BOLLINGER CANYON RD
HOLLY CT
BOLLINGER ESTATES CT
FS
UPPER TR
BOLLINGER CANYON CREEK RD
BOLLINGER
38-12
38-11
38-10
38-9
38-17
38-8
31-5
31-4
31-3
DANVILLE BLVD
EL CERRO BLVD
HARTZ AV
RAILROAD AV
680
CAMILLE
KIRK CT
HART CT
FOREST LN
BLAIR CT
KIRKCREST RD
KIRKCREST LN
ASHFORD CT
CAMBRIDGE DR
RUTHERFORD DR
HARTFORD RD
PETOLA DR
CORDELL DR
ROBERTS CT
KUSS RD
KIRKCREST RD
HARPER LN
BRADFORD PL
HARMONY CT
CORDELL LN
TERRY LN
CALMAR VISTA RD
CAMINO AMIGO
IRON HORSE TR
SHELLY PL
VAN GORDON PL
GLEN RD
EMERALD DR
PIXIE LN
NADINE PL
NADINE CT
LAS BARRANCAS
LA FLORA
VISTA DR
ESTRELLA CT
RUBICON CIR
DEL AMIGO RD
CONT HS
SAN RAMON VALLEY HS
DANVILLE OAK PL
RAMON CT
LA GONDA CT
GARDEN CREEK PL
VALLEY VIEW CT
LA GONDA WY
CH
EL RIO RD
EL PINTADO
W EL PINTADO
ELSIE DR
CATHY LN
PARROT PL
ROSE ST
CEDAR
WINDSTREAM PL
1 CEDAR HOLLOW DR
2 WINDSTREAM PL
VERONA AV
CAMINO AMIGO
CAMINO ENCANTO
VEDA DR
LOVE LN
PO
HILL RD
OAK VIEW TER
SHADOW OAK DR
WINWARD DR
DEL AMIGO RD
DIAMOND CT
DIAMOND DR
WHISPERING TREES LN
ANGEL CT
CORTE NOGAL
CORTE ENCANTO
MARIAN LN
WAY POINTS RD
STARVIEW DR
DEL AMIGO RD
STARVIEW PL
LOVE LN
CLIPPER
STARMONT CT
STARMONT LN
MONTCREST PL
LAMONT WY
LOVE LN
ALICE CT
MAURI CT
TIM CT
DANVILLA CT
LINDA MESA AV
LINDA CT
MONTECITO DR
MARY CT
WILLIAM CT
ENTRADA MESA
ESTHER LN
LYNN LN
MACOMBER LN
MACOMBER WY
MACOMBER RD
MARGARET LN
QUINTERRA ESTATES DR
SONORA AV
W PROSPECT AV
BONANZA WY
GLENDORA CIR
1 EL DORADO AV
2 HOUSTON CT
MIRA LOMA LN
HILFERD WY
MONTAIR DR
MONTAIR PL
MONTAIR CT
MONTAIR DR
GLEN ALPINE DR
HILLSIDE RD
SKY TER
HIGHLAND DR
HIGHLAND CT
MARIPOSA LN
SORRENTO CT
APPIAN CT
CAMBRA CT
COUNTRY DR
TOWN AND
AVON WY
LOCH LOMOND WY
LONESOME RD
HIGHLAND RD
REMINGTON CT
REMINGTON LP
REMINGTON DR
SHERI
GERALD DR
CLIFFSIDE DR
MONTEGO DR
LAS
100
200
300
400
500
600

SEE 653 MAP

SEE 672 MAP

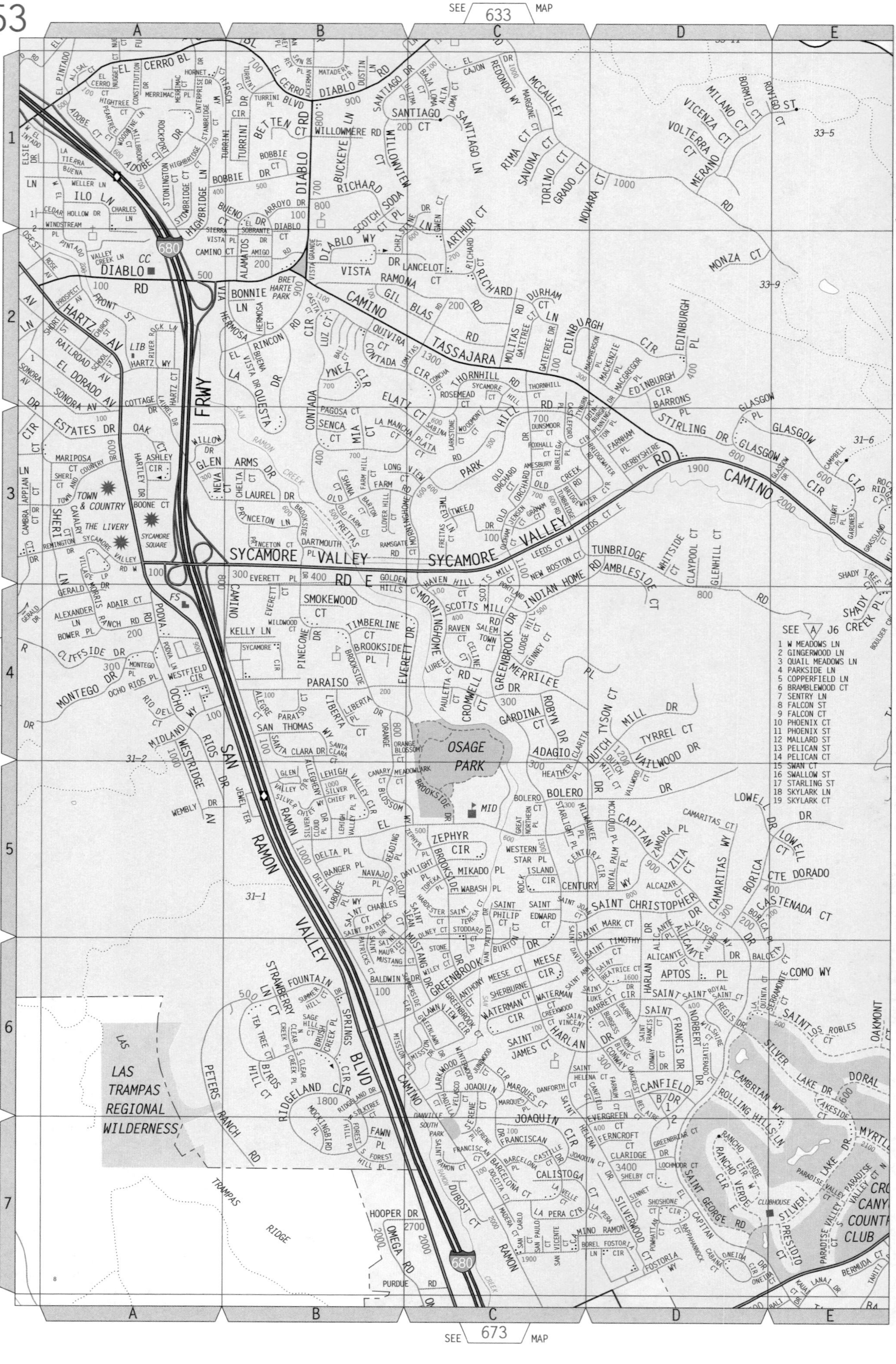
SEE 633 MAP
A
B
C
D
E
1
2
3
4
5
6
7
SEE 652 MAP
SEE 673 MAP
EL CERRO BL
DIABLO RD
CAMINO TASSAJARA
SYCAMORE VALLEY RD E
SYCAMORE VALLEY RD W
SAN RAMON VALLEY BLVD
CAMINO RAMON
FRWY
680
HARTZ AV
DIABLO
CC
LIB
FS
MID
TOWN & COUNTRY
THE LIVERY
SYCAMORE SQUARE
OSAGE PARK
LAS TRAMPAS REGIONAL WILDERNESS
TRAMPAS RIDGE
CROW CANYON COUNTRY CLUB
SAINT CHRISTOPHER DR
GREENBROOK DR
STIRLING DR
GLASGOW CIR
EDINBURGH CIR
SEE A J6
1 W MEADOWS LN
2 GINGERWOOD LN
3 QUAIL MEADOWS LN
4 PARKSIDE LN
5 COPPERFIELD LN
6 BRAMBLEWOOD CT
7 SENTRY LN
8 FALCON ST
9 FALCON CT
10 PHOENIX CT
11 PHOENIX ST
12 MALLARD ST
13 PELICAN ST
14 PELICAN CT
15 SWAN CT
16 SWALLOW ST
17 STARLING ST
18 SKYLARK LN
19 SKYLARK CT

SEE 633 MAP

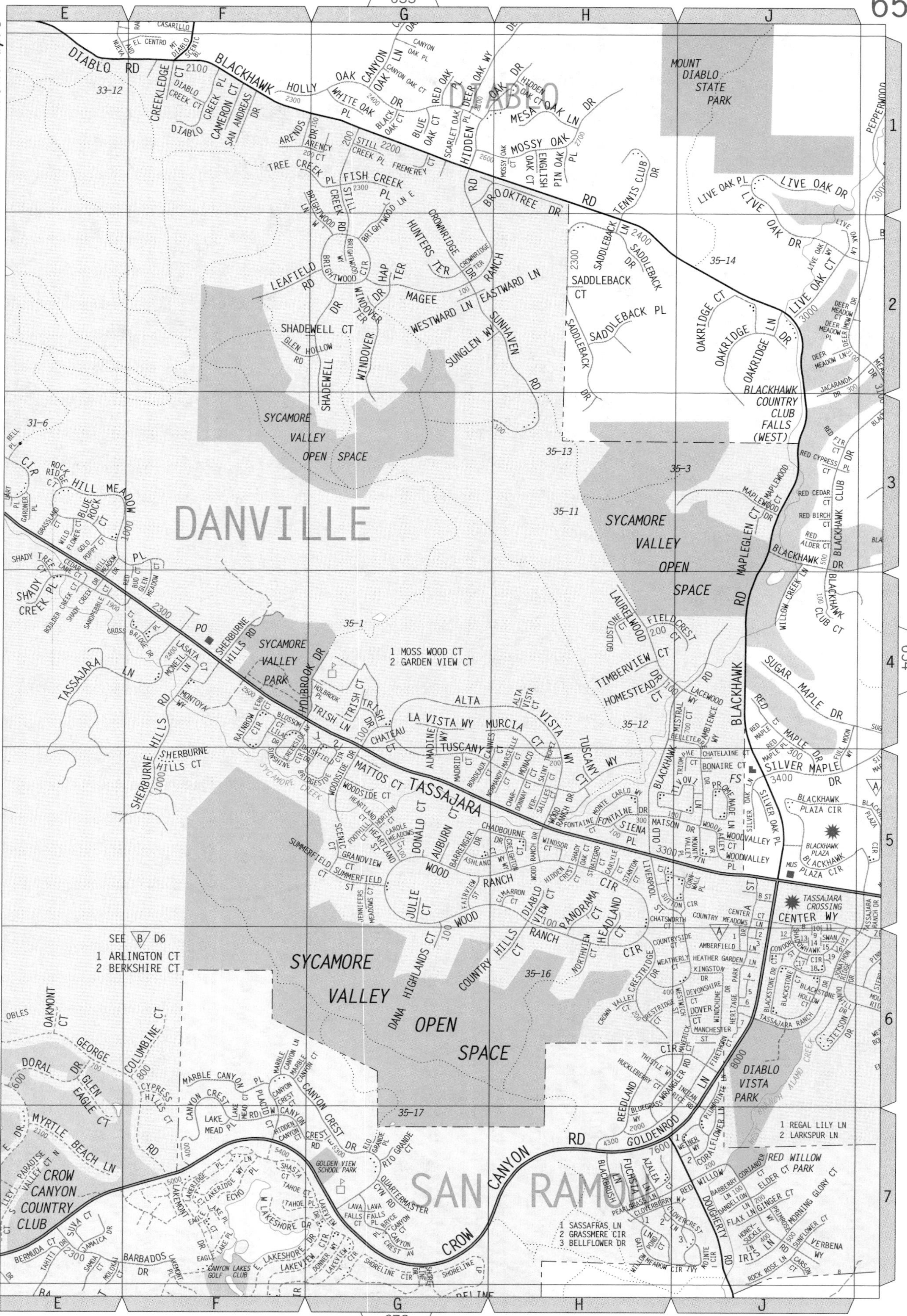
DANVILLE
SAN RAMON
DIABLO
MOUNT DIABLO STATE PARK
SYCAMORE VALLEY OPEN SPACE
SYCAMORE VALLEY PARK
BLACKHAWK COUNTRY CLUB FALLS (WEST)
DIABLO VISTA PARK
CROW CANYON COUNTRY CLUB
GOLDEN VIEW SCHOOL PARK
RED WILLOW PARK
BLACKHAWK PLAZA
TASSAJARA CROSSING
CANYON LAKES GOLF CLUB
DIABLO RD
BLACKHAWK RD
TASSAJARA RD
CROW CANYON RD
CAMINO TASSAJARA
DOUGHERTY RD
SHERBURNE HILLS RD
TASSAJARA LN
HOLBROOK DR
ALTA VISTA WY
LIVE OAK DR
MAPLEGLEN CT
SUGAR MAPLE DR
SILVER MAPLE DR
WOOD RANCH CIR
PANORAMA CIR
HEADLAND CT
COUNTRY HILLS CT
DANA HIGHLANDS CT
GOLDENROD LN
CANYON CREST DR
1 MOSS WOOD CT
2 GARDEN VIEW CT
SEE B D6
1 ARLINGTON CT
2 BERKSHIRE CT
1 REGAL LILY LN
2 LARKSPUR LN
1 SASSAFRAS LN
2 GRASSMERE CIR
3 BELLFLOWER DR
SEE 654 MAP
SEE 673 MAP

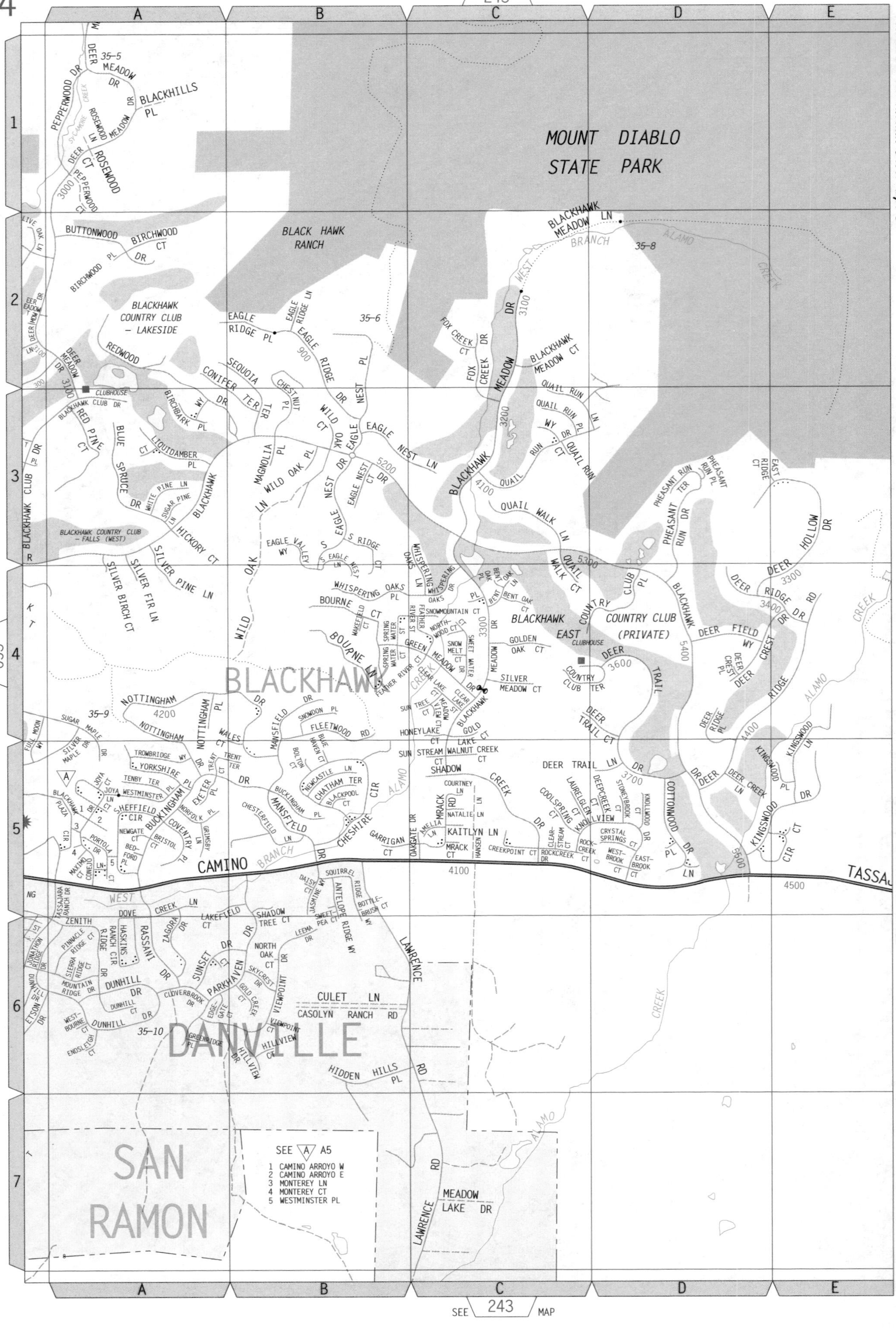
SEE 243 MAP
A
B
C
D
E
1
2
3
4
5
6
7
MOUNT DIABLO STATE PARK
BLACK HAWK RANCH
BLACKHAWK COUNTRY CLUB - LAKESIDE
BLACKHAWK COUNTRY CLUB - FALLS (WEST)
BLACKHAWK
BLACKHAWK EAST
COUNTRY CLUB (PRIVATE)
CLUBHOUSE
DANVILLE
SAN RAMON
CAMINO
TASSAJ
SEE 653 MAP
DEER MEADOW DR
BLACKHILLS PL
PEPPERWOOD DR
ROSEWOOD LN
ROSEWOOD CT
BUTTONWOOD
BIRCHWOOD CT
BIRCHWOOD PL
REDWOOD
SEQUOIA TER
CONIFER TER
CHESTNUT PL
EAGLE RIDGE PL
EAGLE RIDGE LN
EAGLE NEST PL
EAGLE NEST LN
BLACKHAWK MEADOW LN
BLACKHAWK MEADOW DR
BLACKHAWK MEADOW CT
FOX CREEK CT
FOX CREEK DR
QUAIL RUN PL
QUAIL RUN WY
QUAIL RUN DR
QUAIL WALK LN
QUAIL WALK CT
RED PINE CT
BLUE SPRUCE DR
LIQUIDAMBER PL
WHITE PINE LN
SUGAR PINE LN
HICKORY CT
BLACKHAWK DR
BLACKHAWK CLUB DR
SILVER PINE LN
SILVER FIR LN
SILVER BIRCH CT
MAGNOLIA PL
WILD OAK PL
WILD OAK LN
EAGLE VALLEY WY
S EAGLE RIDGE CT
WHISPERING OAKS PL
BOURNE CT
BOURNE LN
PHEASANT RUN DR
PHEASANT RUN PL
PHEASANT RUN TER
EAST RIDGE CT
DEER HOLLOW DR
DEER RIDGE DR
DEER FIELD WY
DEER CREST PL
DEER CREST RIDGE
DEER RIDGE PL
COUNTRY CLUB PL
COUNTRY CLUB TER
DEER TRAIL
DEER TRAIL CT
DEER TRAIL LN
DEER CREEK LN
KINGSWOOD DR
KINGSWOOD PL
KINGSWOOD CIR
GOLDEN OAK CT
SILVER MEADOW CT
SNOWMOUNTAIN CT
HONEYLAKE CT
GOLD LAKE CT
SUN STREAM
WALNUT CREEK CT
SHADOW CREEK
NOTTINGHAM DR
NOTTINGHAM PL
SUGAR MAPLE
SILVER MAPLE DR
FULL MOON WY
TROWBRIDGE WY
YORKSHIRE PL
TENBY TER
SHEFFIELD CIR
BUCKINGHAM
COVENTRY
EXETER CT
TRENT TER
WALES
MANSFIELD DR
SNOWDON PL
FLEETWOOD RD
BLUE HAVEN CT
BOLTON CT
NEWCASTLE LN
CHATHAM TER
BLACKPOOL CT
CHESHIRE CIR
CHESTERFIELD LN
GARRIGAN CT
OAKGATE DR
AMELIA LN
MRACK RD
NATALIE LN
KAITLYN LN
HANSEN LN
COURTNEY LN
CREEKPOINT CT
ROCKCREEK DR
CLEARSTREAM CT
COOLSPRING CT
LAURELGLEN CT
DEEPCREEK CT
STONEYBROOK CT
KNOLLVIEW
KNOLLWOOD DR
CRYSTAL SPRINGS CT
WESTBROOK CT
EASTBROOK CT
COTTONWOOD PL
COTTONWOOD LN
BLACKHAWK PLAZA CIR
PORTOLA
BEDFORD PL
NEWGATE CT
BRISTOL CT
GRIMSBY LN
NORFOLK PL
TASSAJARA RANCH DR
DOVE CREEK LN
LAKEFIELD CT
SHADOW TREE CT
DAISY CT
JASMINE WY
SQUIRREL RIDGE
BOTTLEBRUSH CT
ANTELOPE RIDGE WY
SWEET PEA CT
LEEMA CT
ZENITH RIDGE DR
PINNACLE RIDGE CT
SIERRA RIDGE CT
HASKINS RANCH CIR
RASSANI DR
ZAGORA DR
SUNSET DR
NORTH OAK CT
SKYCREST DR
VIEWPOINT DR
PARKHAVEN DR
GOLD CREEK CT
EDGE GATE CT
CLOVERBROOK DR
MOUNTAIN RIDGE DR
DUNHILL DR
DUNHILL CT
WESTBOURNE CT
ENDSLEIGH CT
JONATHON RIDGE
ETSON DR
GREENRIDGE PL
HILLVIEW DR
HILLVIEW CT
CULET LN
CASOLYN RANCH RD
LAWRENCE RD
HIDDEN HILLS PL
MEADOW LAKE DR
SEE A A5
1 CAMINO ARROYO W
2 CAMINO ARROYO E
3 MONTEREY LN
4 MONTEREY CT
5 WESTMINSTER PL
ALAMO CREEK
WEST BRANCH
35-5
35-6
35-8
35-9
35-10

MAP

SEE 243 MAP

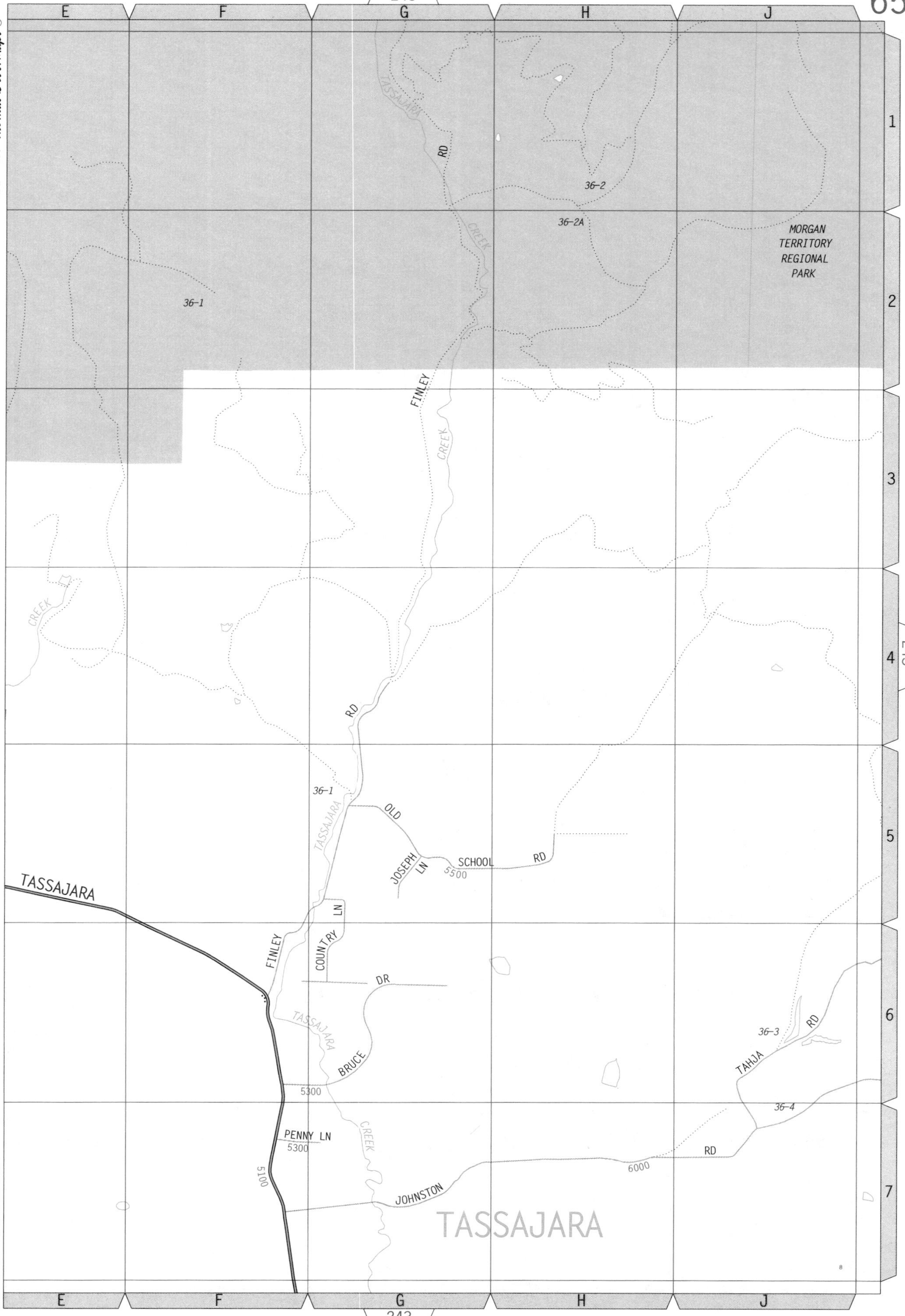
E
F
G
H
J
1
2
3
4
5
6
7
TASSAJARA
RD
CREEK
36-2
36-2A
MORGAN TERRITORY REGIONAL PARK
36-1
FINLEY
CREEK
CREEK
RD
36-1
TASSAJARA
OLD
SCHOOL
RD
JOSEPH LN
5500
TASSAJARA
COUNTRY LN
FINLEY
DR
TASSAJARA
BRUCE
5300
36-3
RD
TAHJA
36-4
PENNY LN
5300
CREEK
RD
6000
5100
JOHNSTON
TASSAJARA
8

SEE 243 MAP

SEE 243 MAP

SEE 646 MAP

A B C D E

1 2 3 4 5 6 7

SEE 243 MAP

A B C D E

SEE 686 MAP

SEE 646 MAP

E
F
G
H
J
1
2
3
4
5
6
7
PACIFIC OCEAN
THE ESPLANADE
GOLDEN GATE NATIONAL RECREATION AREA
OCEAN BEACH
GOLDEN GATE PARK
FULTON ST
DUTCH WINDMILL
JOHN F KENNEDY DR
47TH AV
CLUBHOUSE
GOLDEN GATE MUNICIPAL GOLF COURSE
SOCCER FIELDS
MURPHY WINDMILL
MARTIN LUTHER KING JR DR
S FORK DR
NORTH LAKE
CHAIN OF LAKES DR W
CHAIN OF LAKES DR E
BERCUT EQUITATION FIELD
ANGLERS LODGE
FLY CASTING POOL
MIDDLE LAKE
SOUTH LAKE
MIDDLE DR W
BUFFALO ENCLOSURE
GOLDEN GATE EQUESTRIAN CENTER
STADIUM
SENIOR CITIZEN CENTER
SPRECKELS LAKE
SPRECKELS LAKE DR
36TH AV
METSON
LINCOLN WY
GREAT HWY
LA PLAYA
IRVING ST
JUDAH ST
MUNI N CAR
KIRKHAM ST
LAWTON ST
MORAGA ST
NORIEGA ST
ORTEGA ST
PACHECO ST
QUINTARA ST
RIVERA ST
SANTIAGO ST
TARAVAL ST
MUNI L CAR
ULLOA ST
VICENTE ST
WAWONA ST
CUTLER AV
YORBA ST
YORBA LN
SUNSET
SAN FRANCISCO
SUNSET BLVD
FS
INDEPENDENCE HS
LIB
JOHN OCONNELL HS
MID
SUNSET COMMUNITY CENTER
SAINT IGNATIUS COLLEGE PREP HS
SOUTH SUNSET PLGD
PINO AL
48TH
47TH
46TH
45TH
44TH
43RD
42ND
41ST
40TH
39TH
38TH
37TH
36TH
35TH
34TH
SLOAT BLVD
SAN FRANCISCO ZOO
AVIARY
AFRICAN SCENE
HERBST RD
SKYLINE BLVD
UNITED STATES MILITARY RESERVE
ARMORY RD
FORT FUNSTON
35
LAKESHORE DR
LAKESIDE DR
HUNTINGTON DR
BERKSHIRE WY
BROOKHAVEN WY
COUNTRY CLUB DR
LAKE MERCED BLVD
BONNIE BRAE
OCEAN AV
GELLERT DR
MORNINGSIDE DR
CLEARFIELD DR
LAKE MERCED
HARDING RD
CLUBHOUSE
HARDING PARK MUNICIPAL GOLF COURSE

SEE 667 MAP

SEE 686 MAP

SEE 647 MAP

A
B
C
D
E
1
2
3
4
5
6
7
SAN FRANCISCO
GOLDEN GATE PARK
GOLDEN GATE PARK EQUESTRIAN CENTER & STADIUM
STOW LAKE
STRAWBERRY HILL
MH DE YOUNG MUSEUM
ASIAN ART MUSEUM
JAPANESE TEA GARDEN
MORRISON PLANETARIUM
STEINHART AQUARIUM
CALIFORNIA ACADEMY OF SCIENCES
STRYBING ARBORETUM
SAN FRANCISCO COUNTY FAIR BUILDING
CONSERVATORY OF FLOWERS
CHILDRENS PLGD
KEZAR STADIUM
MCLAREN LODGE
PARK-PRESIDIO BYPASS RD
CROSS OVER DR
JOHN F KENNEDY DR
MIDDLE DR
MARTIN LUTHER KING JR DR
LINCOLN WY
IRVING
JUDAH
KIRKHAM
LAWTON
MORAGA
NORIEGA
ORTEGA
PACHECO
QUINTARA
RIVERA
SANTIAGO
TARAVAL
ULLOA
VICENTE
WAWONA
SLOAT BLVD
OCEAN AV
19TH AV
SUNSET
SUNSET PLGD
SHRINERS HOSP FOR CRIPPLED CHILDREN
SUNSET RESERVOIR
ABRAHAM LINCOLN HS
PARKSIDE
MCCOPPIN SQUARE
LARSEN PARK
PARKSIDE SQUARE
UNIVERSITY OF CALIFORNIA SAN FRANCISCO MEDICAL CENTER
INTERIOR PARK BELT
MOUNT SUTRO
FOREST KNOLLS
GOLDEN GATE HEIGHTS
GRAND VIEW PARK
SUNSET HEIGHTS PARK
LAGUNA HONDA
LAGUNA HONDA HOSPITAL
FOREST HILL
MIDTOWN TERRACE
MIDTOWN TERRACE PLGD
YOUTH GUIDANCE CENTER
EDGEHILL MOUNTAIN PARK
MIRALOMA PARK
MOUNT DAVIDSON PARK
MOUNT DAVIDSON
SHERWOOD FOREST
WEST PORTAL
PORTOLA DR
SAINT FRANCIS WOOD
MONTEREY HEIGHTS
WESTWOOD HIGHLANDS
WESTWOOD PARK
BALBOA TERRACE
MOUNT DAVIDSON MANOR
APTOS PLGD
PINE LAKE PARK
SIGMUND STERN RECREATION GROVE
LUCKY LAKESHORE PLAZA
STONESTOWN
MERCED MANOR
ROLPH NICOL PARK
LOWELL HS
STONESTOWN GALLERIA
GOLDEN GATE NATIONAL RECREATION AREA
LAKE MERCED
HARDING PARK MUNICIPAL GOLF COURSE
SAN FRANCISCO STATE UNIVERSITY
SCHOOL OF THE ARTS HS
LAKESHORE
INGLESIDE TERRACE
INGLESIDE HEIGHTS
JUNIPERO SERRA BLVD
RIORDAN (BOYS) HS
SAN FRANCISCO CITY COLLEGE
HOLLOWAY AV
MONTEREY BLVD
WOODSIDE AV
CLARENDON AV
7TH AV
LAGUNA HONDA BLVD

SEE 666 MAP

SEE 687 MAP

SEE 647 MAP

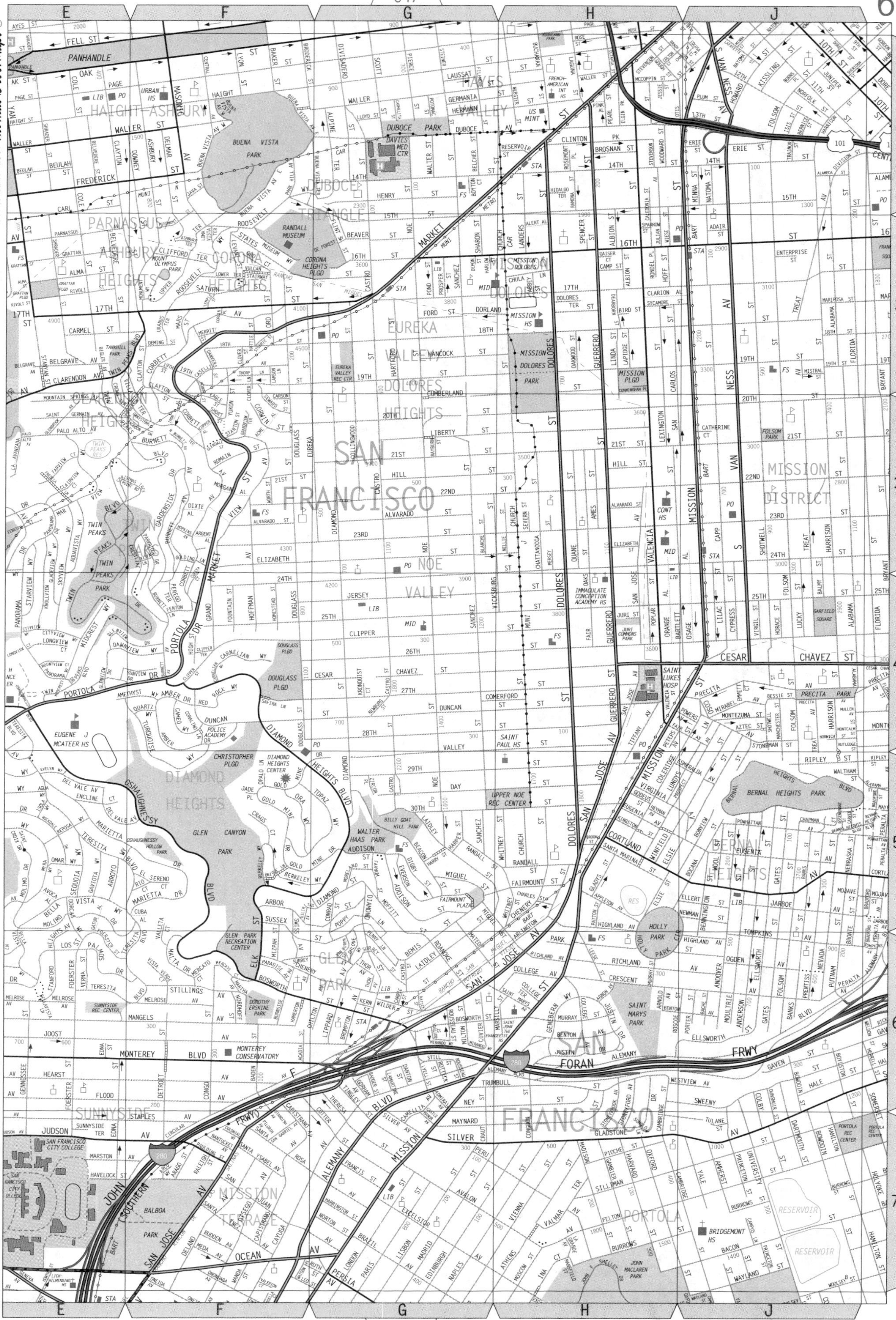
E
F
G
H
J
1
2
3
4
5
6
7
SAN FRANCISCO
HAIGHT-ASHBURY
PARNASSUS/ ASHBURY HEIGHTS
CORONA HEIGHTS
CLARENDON HEIGHTS
TWIN PEAKS
DUBOCE TRIANGLE
HAYES VALLEY
MISSION DOLORES
EUREKA VALLEY
DOLORES HEIGHTS
NOE VALLEY
MISSION DISTRICT
DIAMOND HEIGHTS
GLEN PARK
BERNAL HEIGHTS
SUNNYSIDE
MISSION TERRACE
PORTOLA
PANHANDLE
BUENA VISTA PARK
DUBOCE PARK
RANDALL MUSEUM
CORONA HEIGHTS PLGD
MISSION DOLORES PARK
TWIN PEAKS PARK
DOUGLASS PLGD
GLEN CANYON PARK
BERNAL HEIGHTS PARK
PRECITA PARK
HOLLY PARK
SAINT MARYS PARK
BALBOA PARK
JOHN MCLAREN PARK
SAN FRANCISCO CITY COLLEGE
SAINT LUKES HOSP
DAVIES MED CTR
MONTEREY BLVD
JOHN F FORAN FRWY
SOUTHERN FRWY
MARKET ST
MISSION ST
CESAR CHAVEZ ST
OCEAN AV
ALEMANY BLVD
SILVER AV
PORTOLA DR
101
280

SEE 668 MAP

SEE 687 MAP

SEE 648 MAP

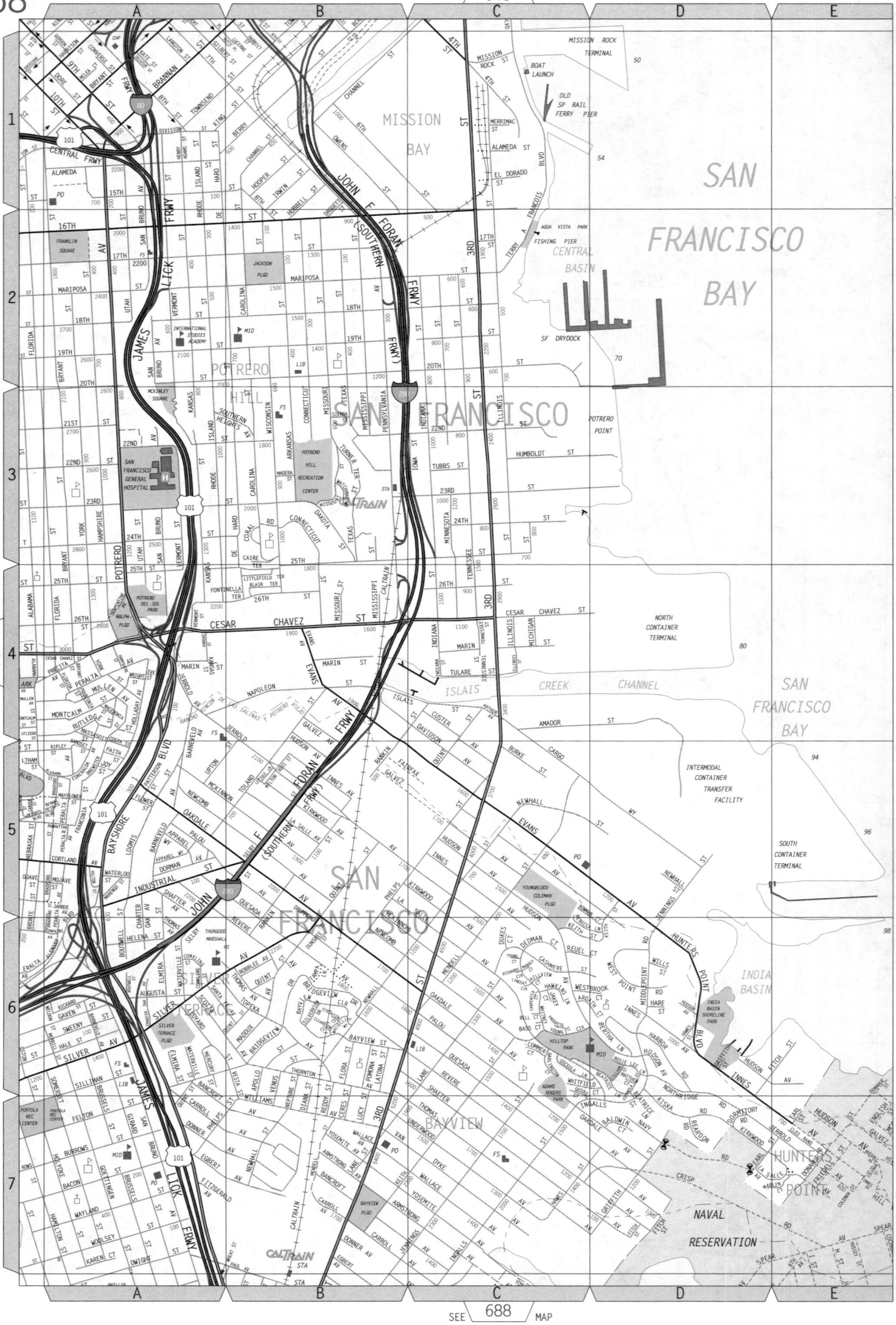
A
B
C
D
E
1
2
3
4
5
6
7
MISSION BAY
SAN FRANCISCO BAY
CENTRAL BASIN
SF DRYDOCK
POTRERO HILL
SAN FRANCISCO
POTRERO POINT
MISSION ROCK TERMINAL
BOAT LAUNCH
OLD SP RAIL FERRY PIER
AGUA VISTA PARK
FISHING PIER
NORTH CONTAINER TERMINAL
ISLAIS CREEK CHANNEL
INTERMODAL CONTAINER TRANSFER FACILITY
SOUTH CONTAINER TERMINAL
INDIA BASIN
INDIA BASIN SHORELINE PARK
HUNTERS POINT
NAVAL RESERVATION
BAYVIEW
SILVER TERRACE
JOHN F FORAN FRWY (SOUTHERN FRWY)
JAMES LICK FRWY
CENTRAL FRWY
BAYSHORE BLVD
CESAR CHAVEZ ST
3RD ST
EVANS AV
INDUSTRIAL ST
SILVER AV
SAN FRANCISCO GENERAL HOSPITAL
FRANKLIN SQUARE
MCKINLEY SQUARE
POTRERO HILL RECREATION CENTER
POTRERO DEL SOL PARK
JACKSON PLGD
INTERNATIONAL STUDIES ACADEMY
YOUNGBLOOD COLEMAN PLGD
HILLTOP PARK
ADAMS ROGERS PARK
BAYVIEW PLGD
SILVER TERRACE PLGD
PORTOLA REC CENTER
THURGOOD MARSHALL HS
CALTRAIN

SEE 667 MAP

SEE 688 MAP

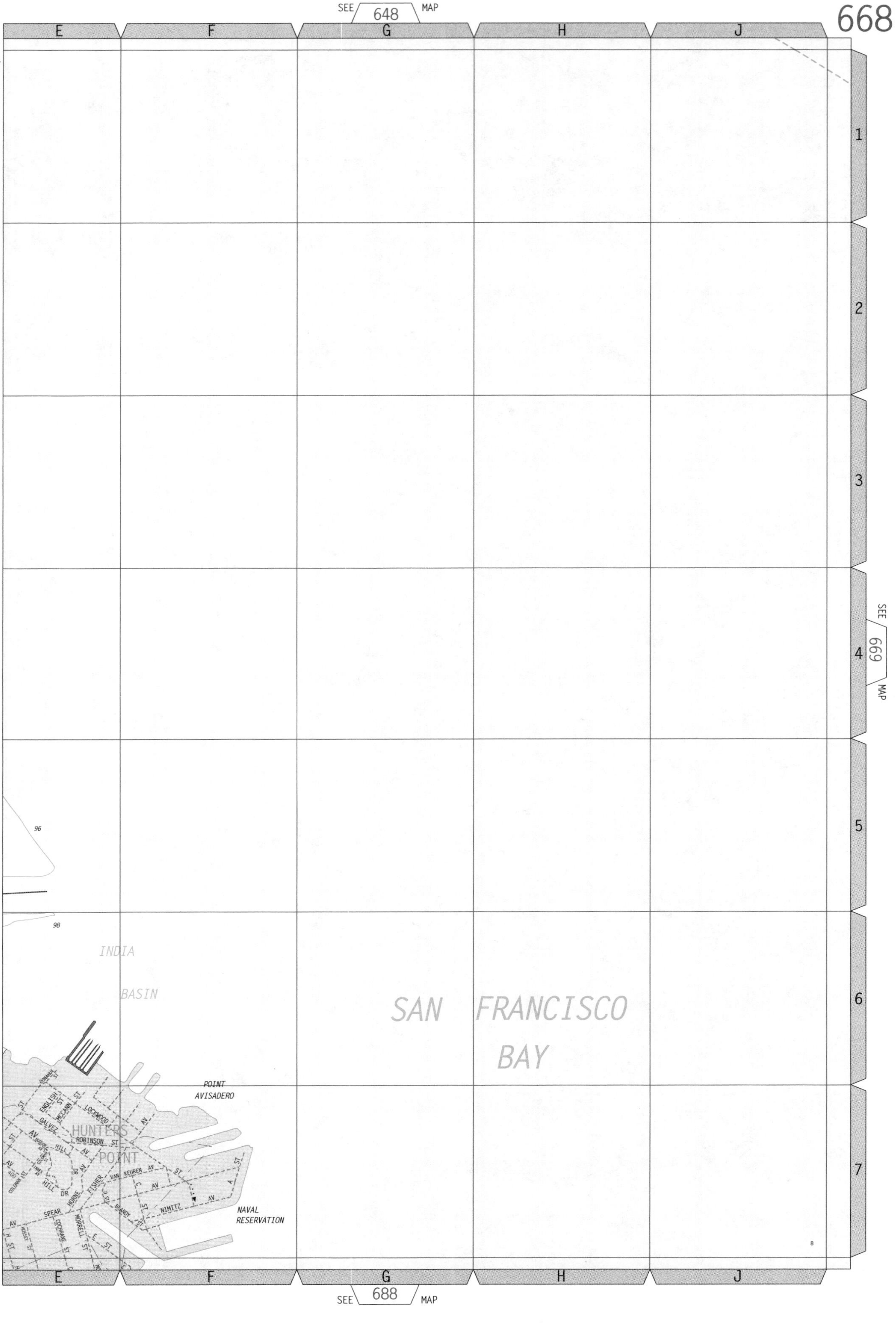
SEE 648 MAP
E
F
G
H
J
1
2
3
4
5
6
7
SEE 669 MAP
SEE 688 MAP
SAN FRANCISCO BAY
INDIA BASIN
HUNTERS POINT
POINT AVISADERO
NAVAL RESERVATION
ENGLISH ST
McCANN ST
LOCKWOOD ST
GALVEZ AV
ROBINSON ST
HILL DR
FISHER AV
HORNE AV
VAN KEUREN AV
NIMITZ AV
SPEAR AV
COCHRANE ST
MORRELL ST
96
98

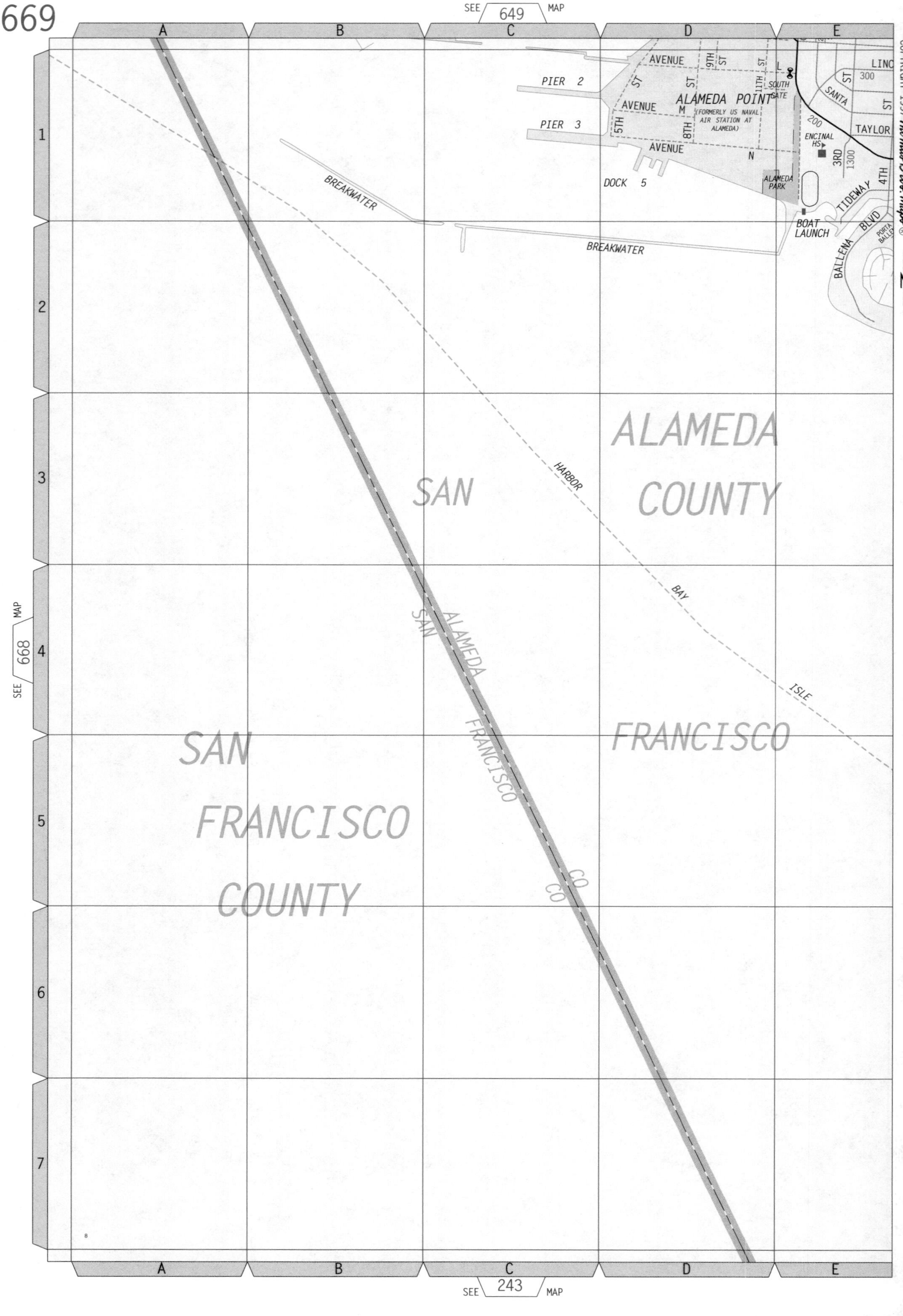
SEE 649 MAP
A
B
C
D
E
1
2
3
4
5
6
7
SEE 668 MAP
SEE 243 MAP
PIER 2
PIER 3
DOCK 5
AVENUE
AVENUE
AVENUE
M
N
L
5TH
ST
8TH
9TH
ST
11TH
ST
ALAMEDA POINT
(FORMERLY US NAVAL AIR STATION AT ALAMEDA)
SOUTH GATE
ENCINAL HS
ALAMEDA PARK
BOAT LAUNCH
BREAKWATER
BREAKWATER
LINC
300
SANTA
ST
TAYLOR
200
3RD
1300
4TH
TIDEWAY
BALLENA
BLVD
HARBOR
BAY
ISLE
ALAMEDA COUNTY
SAN
ALAMEDA
SAN
FRANCISCO
CO
CO
FRANCISCO
SAN FRANCISCO COUNTY

SEE 649 MAP

E
F
G
H
J
1
2
3
4
5
6
7
ALAMEDA
SOUTH SHORE
BAY FARM ISLAND
BAY
OAK
SAN LEANDRO CHANNEL
FERRY
FERRY TERMINAL
BALLENA BAY
ROBERT CROWN MEMORIAL STATE BEACH
CRAB COVE VISITORS CENTER
WASHINGTON PARK
LITTLEJOHN PARK
FRANKLIN PARK
RITTLER PARK
LONGFELLOW PARK
TILLMAN PARK
SHORELINE PARK
MASTICK SENIOR CENTER
ALAMEDA HS
ST JOSEPH NOTRE DAME HS
ALAMADA HOSP
ISLAND YACHT CLUB
SOUTH SHORE CTR
VET BLDG
LAGOON
PACIFIC AV
LINCOLN AV
HAIGHT AV
SANTA CLARA AV
TAYLOR AV
CENTRAL AV
WEBSTER ST
ENCINAL AV
OTIS DR
SHORE LINE DR
GRAND ST
PARK ST
BUENA VISTA AV
CLEMENT AV
CHESTNUT ST
WILLOW ST
WALNUT ST
OAK ST
SAN ANTONIO AV
SAN JOSE AV
CLINTON AV
SANDCREEK WY
FRANCISCAN WY
ROSEWOOD WY
WESTLINE DR
TIDEWAY DR
BALLENA BLVD
SEA VIEW PKWY
ISLAND DR
MECARTNEY RD
HARBOR BAY PKWY
NORTH LOOP RD
ADELPHIAN WY
MCDONNEL RD
SEE A G2
1 CHERRY WK
2 STORYBOOK WK
3 BLOSSOM WK
4 SAND BEACH PL
5 MEADOW WK
1 FERNDELL WK
2 YORKSHIRE PL
3 WHITEHALL PL
SEE B J6
1 VIA ALAMOSA
2 VIA CORTA
3 BURGNER AV
4 CHRISTENSEN CT
5 MILLINGTON CT
6 MONTEGO BAY
7 JERVIS BAY
8 INDIAN BAY
9 FUNDY BAY
10 ENCOUNTER BAY
11 BISCAY BAY

SEE 670 MAP

SEE 243 MAP

SEE 650 MAP

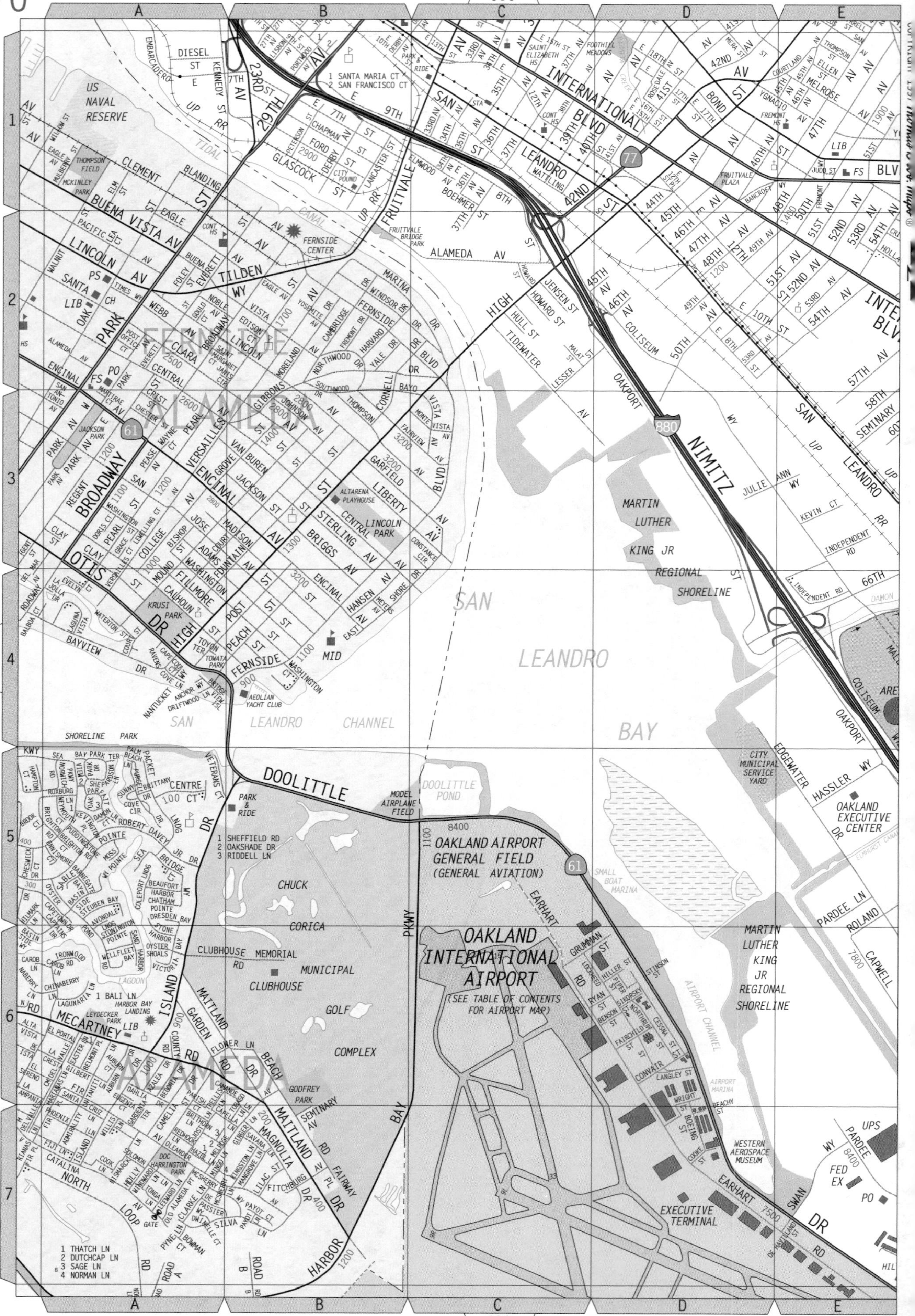

US NAVAL RESERVE
THOMPSON FIELD
MCKINLEY PARK
DIESEL ST
EMBARCADERO
KENNEDY ST
23RD AV
29TH AV
1 SANTA MARIA CT
2 SAN FRANCISCO CT
CLEMENT AV
BLANDING AV
BUENA VISTA AV
LINCOLN AV
PARK ST
TILDEN WY
FERNSIDE CENTER
FRUITVALE AV
FRUITVALE BRIDGE PARK
ALAMEDA AV
INTERNATIONAL BLVD
SAN LEANDRO ST
FOOTHILL MEADOWS
SAINT ELIZABETH HS
HIGH ST
FERNSIDE
ALAMEDA
JACKSON PARK
BROADWAY
ENCINAL AV
OTIS DR
KRUSI PARK
LINCOLN PARK
ALTARENA PLAYHOUSE
MID
AEOLIAN YACHT CLUB
SAN LEANDRO CHANNEL
SHORELINE PARK
SAN LEANDRO BAY
NIMITZ
MARTIN LUTHER KING JR REGIONAL SHORELINE
OAKPORT ST
COLISEUM WY
HEGENBERGER
DOOLITTLE DR
DOOLITTLE POND
MODEL AIRPLANE FIELD
1 SHEFFIELD RD
2 OAKSHADE DR
3 RIDDELL LN
CHUCK CORICA MUNICIPAL GOLF COMPLEX
CLUBHOUSE MEMORIAL RD
CLUBHOUSE
OAKLAND AIRPORT GENERAL FIELD (GENERAL AVIATION)
OAKLAND INTERNATIONAL AIRPORT
(SEE TABLE OF CONTENTS FOR AIRPORT MAP)
SMALL BOAT MARINA
AIRPORT CHANNEL
CITY MUNICIPAL SERVICE YARD
OAKLAND EXECUTIVE CENTER
EDGEWATER DR
HASSLER WY
PARDEE LN
ROLAND WY
CAPWELL DR
MARTIN LUTHER KING JR REGIONAL SHORELINE
ISLAND DR
MECARTNEY RD
LEYDECKER PARK
1 BALI LN
HARBOR BAY LANDING
ALAMEDA
GODFREY PARK
MAITLAND DR
MAGNOLIA DR
FITCHBURG AV
HARBOR BAY PKWY
FAIRWAY DR
DOC HARRINGTON PARK
CATALINA AV
NORTH LOOP RD
1 THATCH LN
2 DUTCHCAP LN
3 SAGE LN
4 NORMAN LN
EXECUTIVE TERMINAL
WESTERN AEROSPACE MUSEUM
EARHART RD
SWAN WY
UPS
FED EX
PO
A B C D E
1 2 3 4 5 6 7

SEE 669 MAP

SEE 690 MAP

SEE 650 MAP

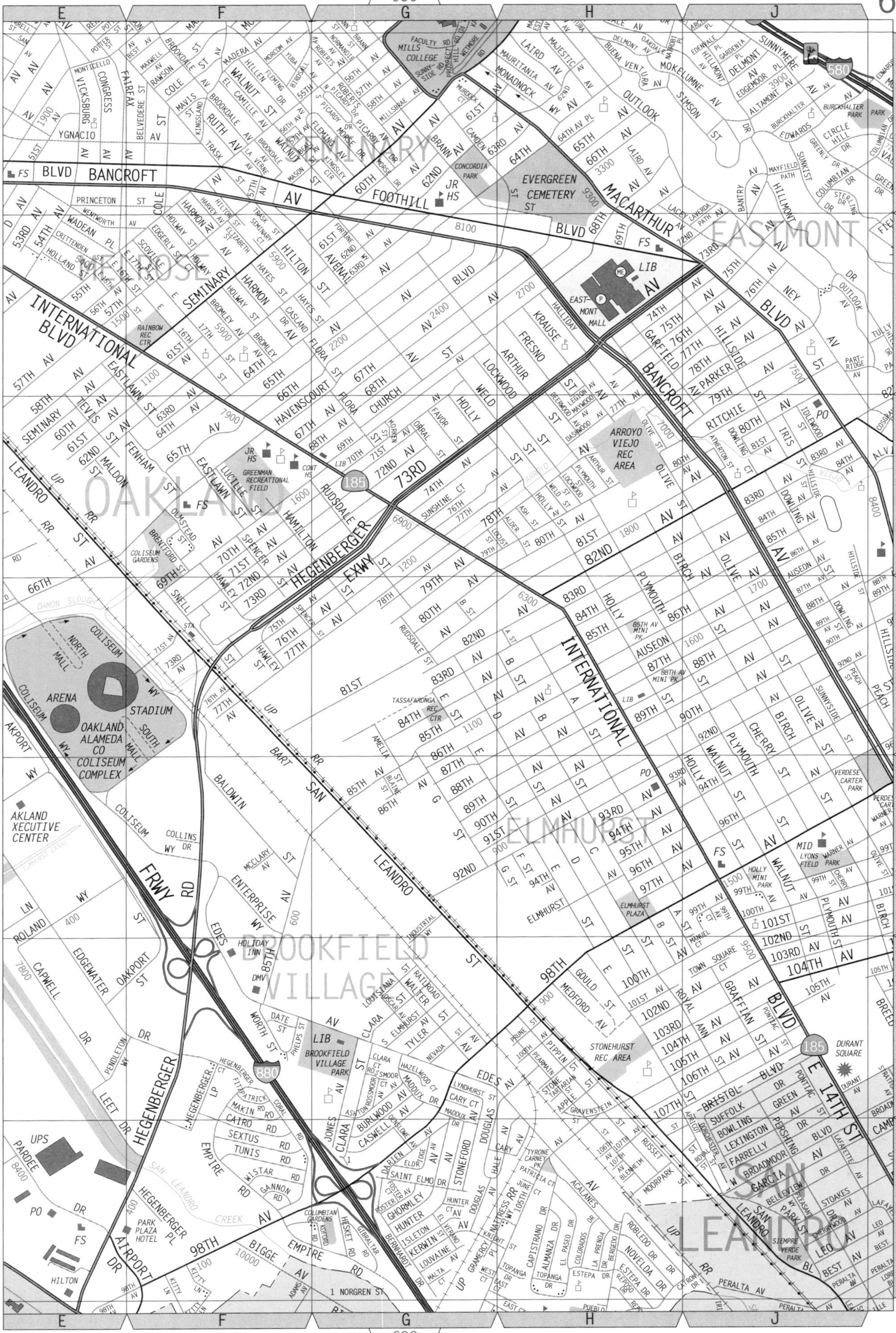
E
F
G
H
J
1
2
3
4
5
6
7
SEMINARY
MILLS COLLEGE
EVERGREEN CEMETERY
EASTMONT
EASTMONT MALL
MELROSE
OAKLAND
ELMHURST
BROOKFIELD VILLAGE
SAN LEANDRO
BANCROFT AV
FOOTHILL BLVD
MACARTHUR BLVD
SEMINARY AV
INTERNATIONAL BLVD
HEGENBERGER EXWY
73RD AV
BANCROFT AV
SAN LEANDRO ST
HEGENBERGER RD
NIMITZ FRWY
E 14TH ST
98TH AV
EDES AV
DOOLITTLE DR
OAKLAND ALAMEDA CO COLISEUM COMPLEX
ARENA
STADIUM
ARROYO VIEJO REC AREA
GREENMAN RECREATIONAL FIELD
RAINBOW REC CTR
TASSAFARONGA REC CTR
BROOKFIELD VILLAGE PARK
STONEHURST REC AREA
ELMHURST PLAZA
VERDESE CARTER PARK
LYONS FIELD
WARNER PARK
DURANT SQUARE
OAKLAND EXECUTIVE CENTER
HOLIDAY INN
PARK PLAZA HOTEL
HILTON
UPS
CONCORDIA PARK
BURCKHALTER PARK
COLISEUM GARDENS
580
880
185

SEE 671 MAP

SEE 690 MAP

SEE 651 MAP

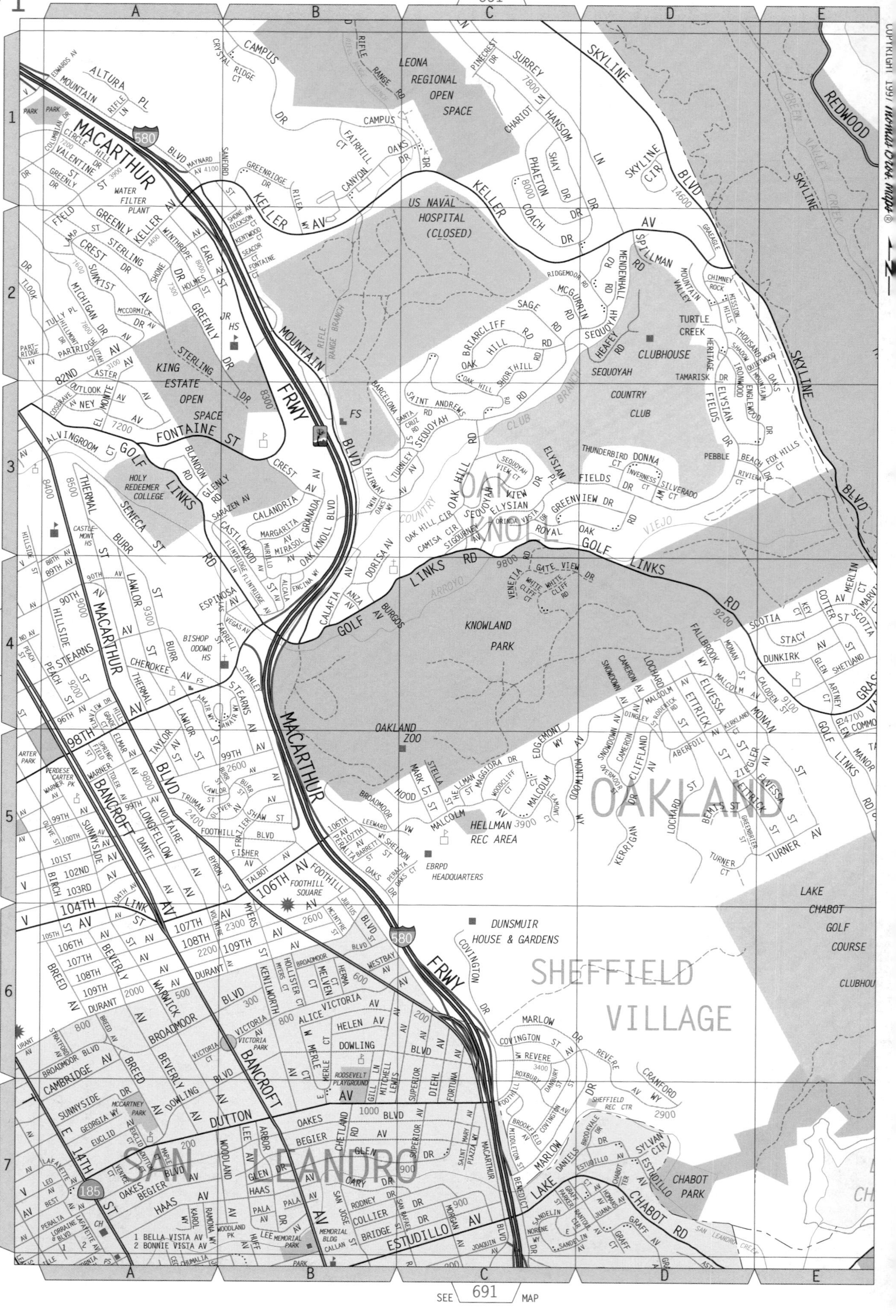

A B C D E
1 2 3 4 5 6 7
COPYRIGHT 1997 Thomas Bros. Maps ®
LEONA REGIONAL OPEN SPACE
US NAVAL HOSPITAL (CLOSED)
KING ESTATE OPEN SPACE
HOLY REDEEMER COLLEGE
SEQUOYAH COUNTRY CLUB
CLUBHOUSE
TURTLE CREEK
OAK KNOLL
KNOWLAND PARK
OAKLAND ZOO
OAKLAND
HELLMAN REC AREA
EBRPD HEADQUARTERS
DUNSMUIR HOUSE & GARDENS
SHEFFIELD VILLAGE
LAKE CHABOT GOLF COURSE
CHABOT PARK
SAN LEANDRO
FOOTHILL SQUARE
VICTORIA PARK
ROOSEVELT PLAYGROUND
MCCARTNEY PARK
MEMORIAL PARK
SHEFFIELD REC CTR
WATER FILTER PLANT
BISHOP ODOWD HS
MACARTHUR FRWY
MACARTHUR BLVD
580
185
SKYLINE BLVD
REDWOOD
KELLER AV
MOUNTAIN BLVD
GOLF LINKS RD
FONTAINE ST
98TH AV
BANCROFT AV
104TH AV
106TH AV
FOOTHILL BLVD
DUTTON AV
ESTUDILLO AV
E 14TH ST
CHABOT RD
LAKE CHABOT RD
BROADMOOR BLVD
1 BELLA VISTA AV
2 BONNIE VISTA AV

SEE 670 MAP

SEE 691 MAP

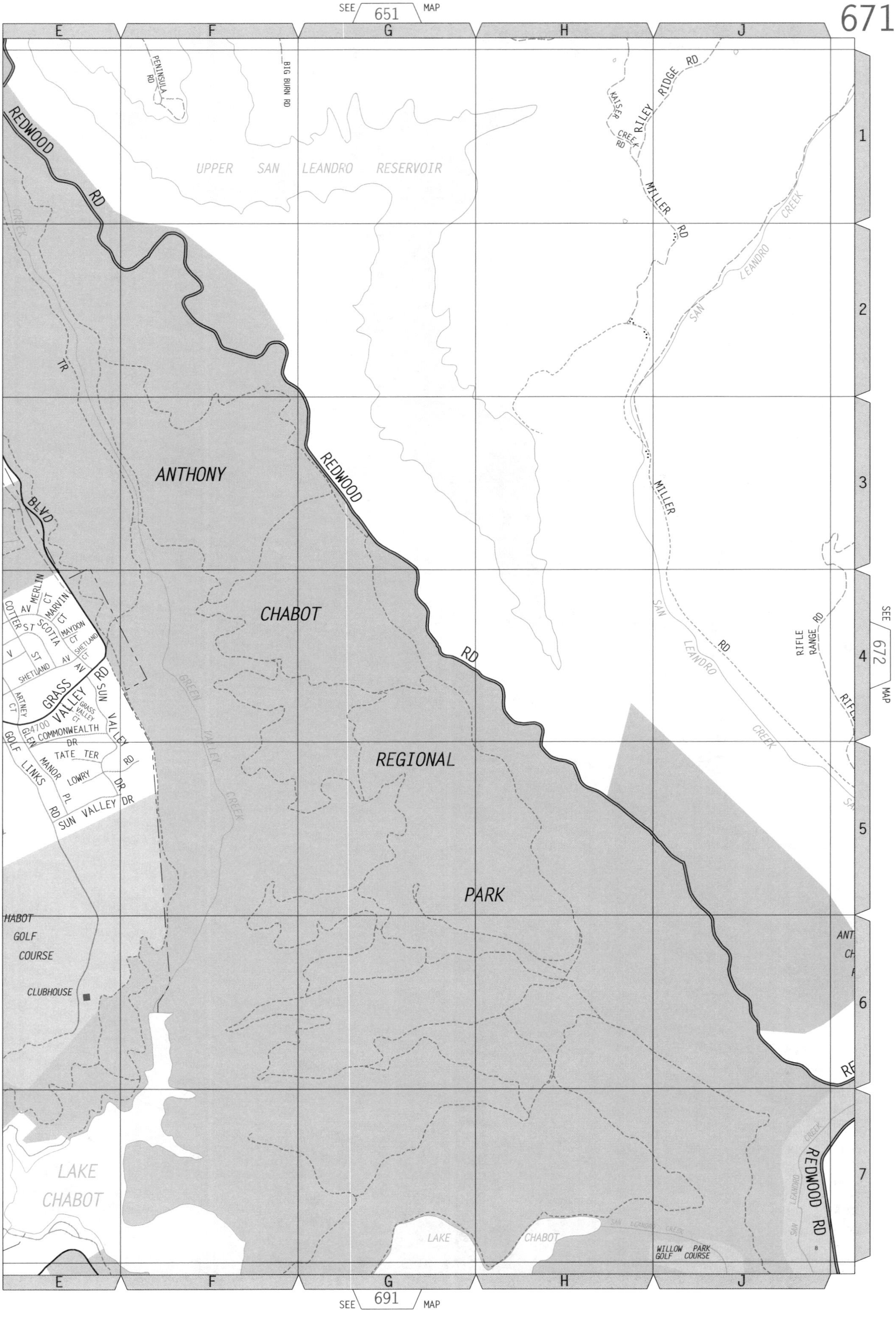
SEE 651 MAP
E
F
G
H
J
PENINSULA RD
BIG BURN RD
RILEY RIDGE RD
KAISER CREEK RD
MILLER RD
UPPER SAN LEANDRO RESERVOIR
REDWOOD RD
CREEK
SAN LEANDRO CREEK
TR
ANTHONY
CHABOT
REGIONAL
PARK
BLVD
MILLER
MERLIN CT
COTTER
AV
MARVIN CT
ST
SCOTIA
MAYDON CT
SHETLAND CT
V
ST
SHETLAND
AV
AV
GRASS VALLEY RD
ARTNEY CT
GRASS VALLEY CT
SUN VALLEY
4700
GLEN
COMMONWEALTH DR
TATE TER
RD
GOLF LINKS
MANOR
LOWRY
DR
PL
RD
SUN VALLEY DR
GREEN VALLEY CREEK
SAN LEANDRO CREEK
RD
RIFLE RANGE RD
SEE 672 MAP
RIFLE
HABOT GOLF COURSE
CLUBHOUSE
ANT
CH
LAKE CHABOT
LAKE CHABOT
SAN LEANDRO CREEK
WILLOW PARK GOLF COURSE
REDWOOD RD
SAN LEANDRO CREEK
1
2
3
4
5
6
7
SEE 691 MAP

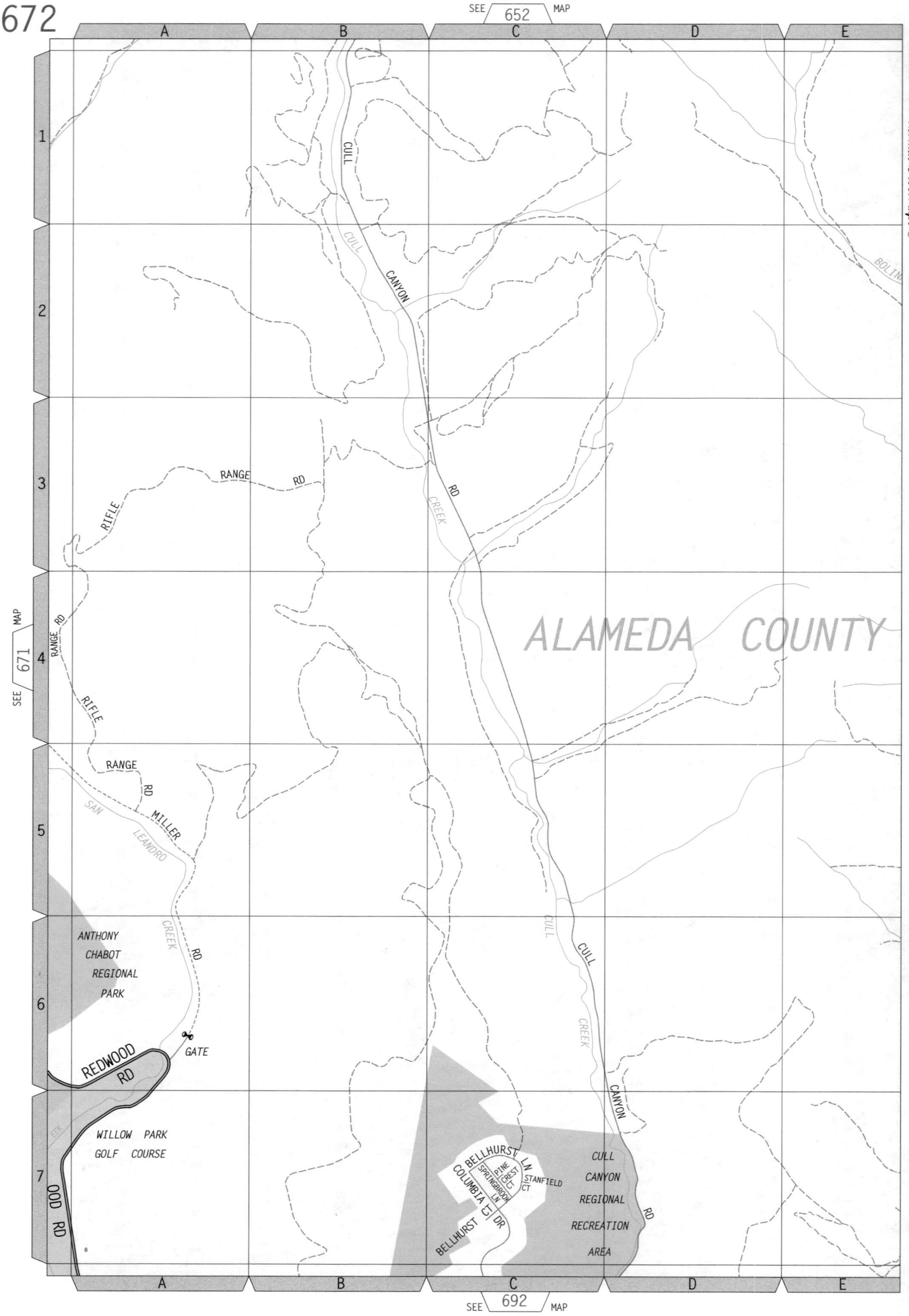
SEE 652 MAP
SEE 671 MAP
SEE 692 MAP
A
B
C
D
E
1
2
3
4
5
6
7
CULL CANYON RD
CULL CREEK
BOLIN
RIFLE RANGE RD
ALAMEDA COUNTY
MILLER RD
SAN LEANDRO CREEK
ANTHONY CHABOT REGIONAL PARK
GATE
REDWOOD RD
OOD RD
WILLOW PARK GOLF COURSE
BELLHURST LN
BELLHURST CT
SPRINGBROOK LN
PINE CREST CT
STANFIELD CT
COLUMBIA DR
CULL CANYON REGIONAL RECREATION AREA

SEE 652 MAP

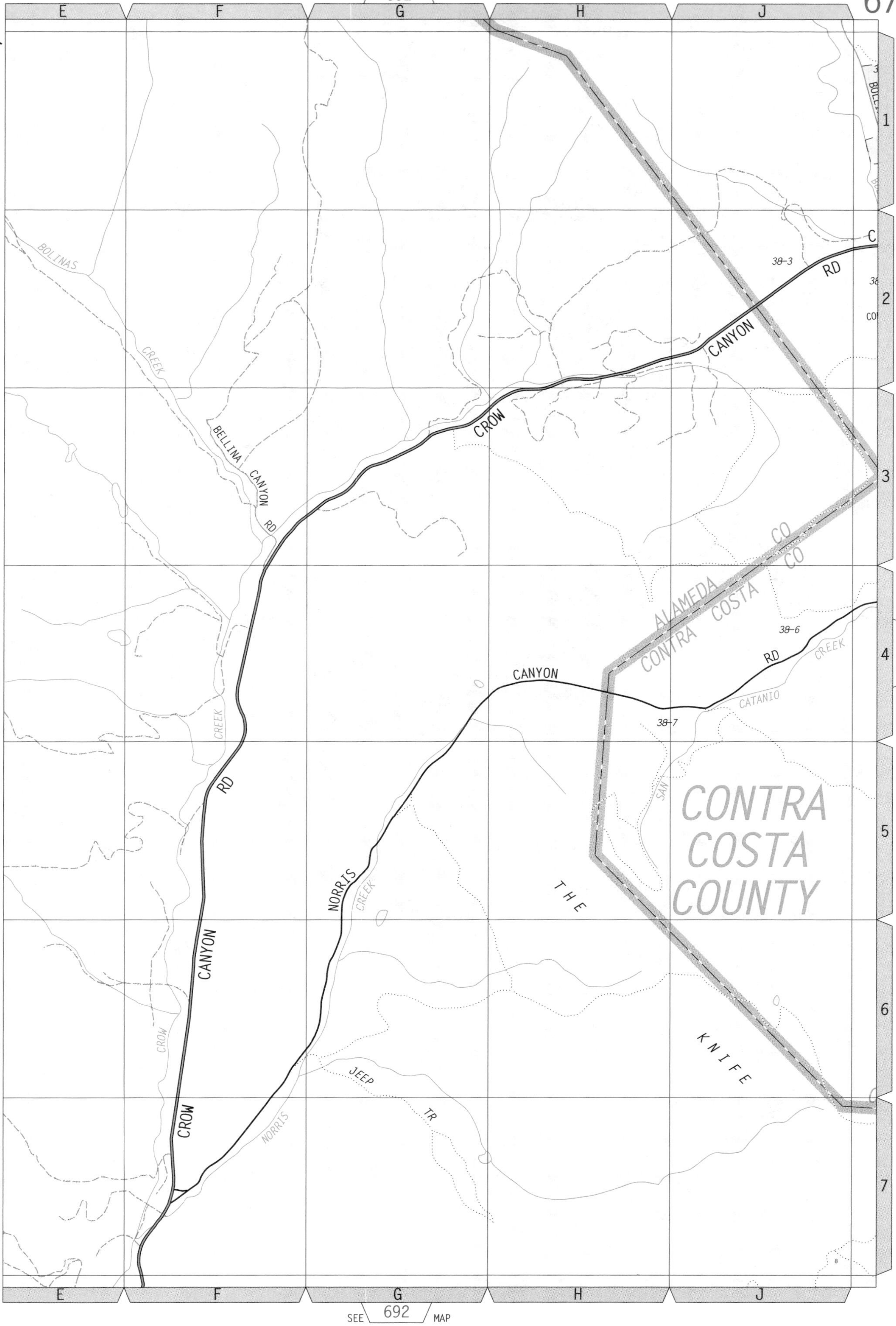
E
F
G
H
J
1
2
3
4
5
6
7
BOLINAS
CREEK
BELLINA CANYON RD
CROW CANYON RD
CROW CANYON RD
38-3
38-6
38-7
CANYON RD
NORRIS
CREEK
CATANIO CREEK
SAN
ALAMEDA CO
CONTRA COSTA CO
CONTRA COSTA CO
CONTRA COSTA COUNTY
THE KNIFE
JEEP TR
NORRIS
CROW
CREEK

SEE 673 MAP

SEE 692 MAP

SEE 653 MAP

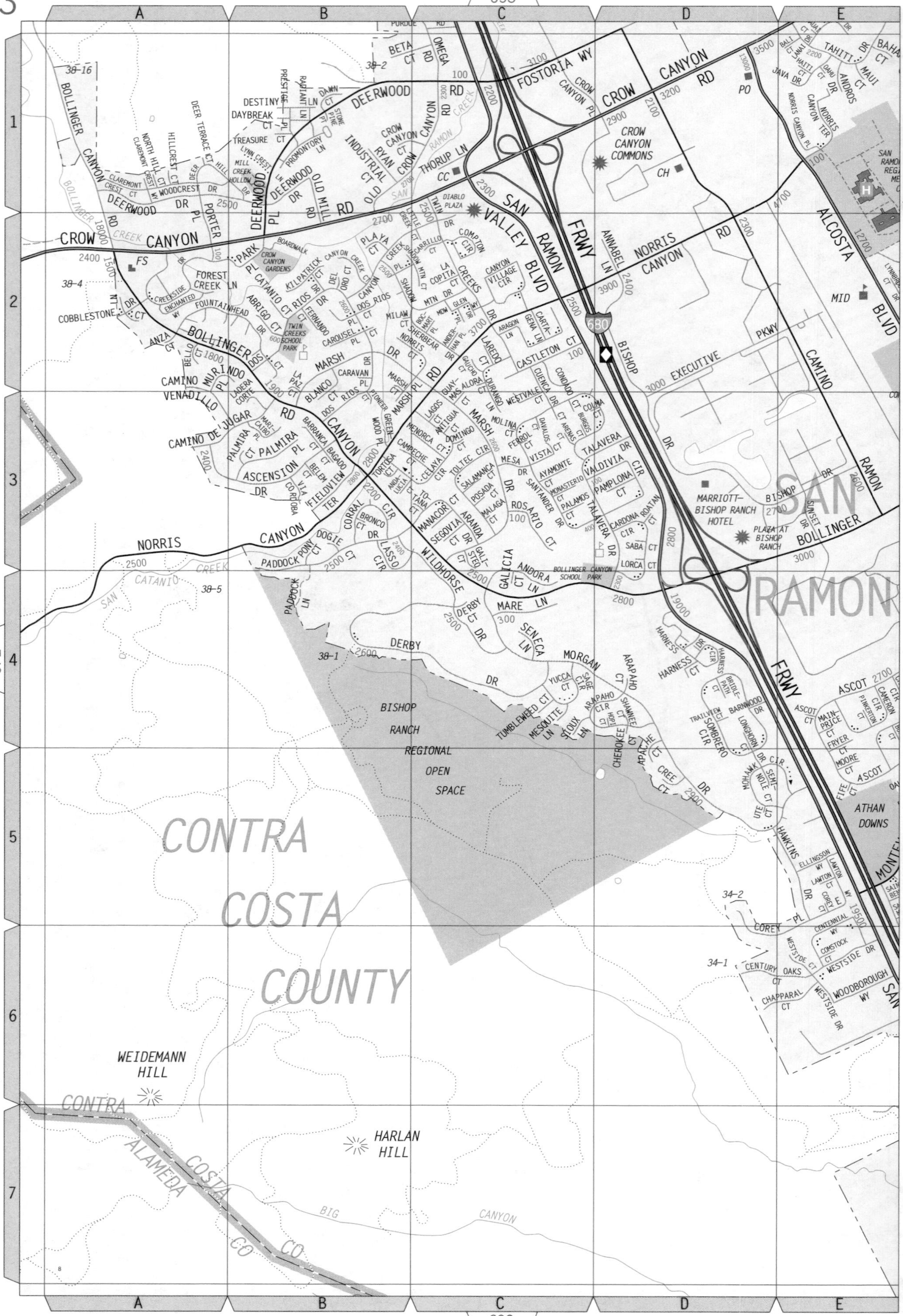

A
B
C
D
E
1
2
3
4
5
6
7
CROW CANYON RD
BOLLINGER CANYON RD
DEERWOOD DR
DEERWOOD RD
SAN RAMON VALLEY BLVD
SAN RAMON FRWY
680
NORRIS CANYON RD
BISHOP DR
EXECUTIVE PKWY
CAMINO RAMON
ALCOSTA BLVD
FOSTORIA WY
CROW CANYON PL
CROW CANYON COMMONS
THORUP LN
OLD CROW CANYON RD
INDUSTRIAL CT
RYAN CT
OLD MILL RD
PROMONTORY LN
DESTINY
DAYBREAK CT
TREASURE CT
DEER TERRACE CT
HILLCREST CT
NORTH HILL CT
CLAREMONT CREST CT
WOODCREST DR
PORTER DR
FOREST CREEK LN
FOUNTAINHEAD
COBBLESTONE CT
ANZA CT
CAMINO MURINDO
CAMINO VENADILLO
CAMINO DE JUGAR
PALMIRA
ASCENSION DR
FIELDVIEW TER
BARRANCA
MARSH DR
MARSH CREEK
CASTLETON CT
LAREDO
WESTVALE
MOLINA
VALDIVIA CIR
PAMPLONA CT
TALAVERA DR
ROSARIO
SEGOVIA
ARANDA
WILDHORSE
GALICIA
ANDORA LN
BOLLINGER CANYON SCHOOL PARK
TWIN CREEKS SCHOOL PARK
CROW CANYON GARDENS
MARE LN
SENECA LN
DERBY DR
MORGAN DR
ARAPAHO CT
HARNESS DR
TUMBLEWEED CT
MESQUITE LN
SIOUX LN
CHEROKEE CT
APACHE CT
CREE CT
SOMBRERO CIR
LONGHORN
HAWKINS DR
ASCOT DR
ASCOT CT
ATHAN DOWNS
COREY PL
WESTSIDE DR
CENTURY OAKS CT
CHAPPARAL CT
WOODBOROUGH WY
MARRIOTT-BISHOP RANCH HOTEL
PLAZA AT BISHOP RANCH
SAN RAMON
BISHOP RANCH REGIONAL OPEN SPACE
CONTRA COSTA COUNTY
WEIDEMANN HILL
HARLAN HILL
CONTRA COSTA CO
ALAMEDA CO
BIG CANYON
PO
CH
CC
FS
MID

SEE 672 MAP

SEE 693 MAP

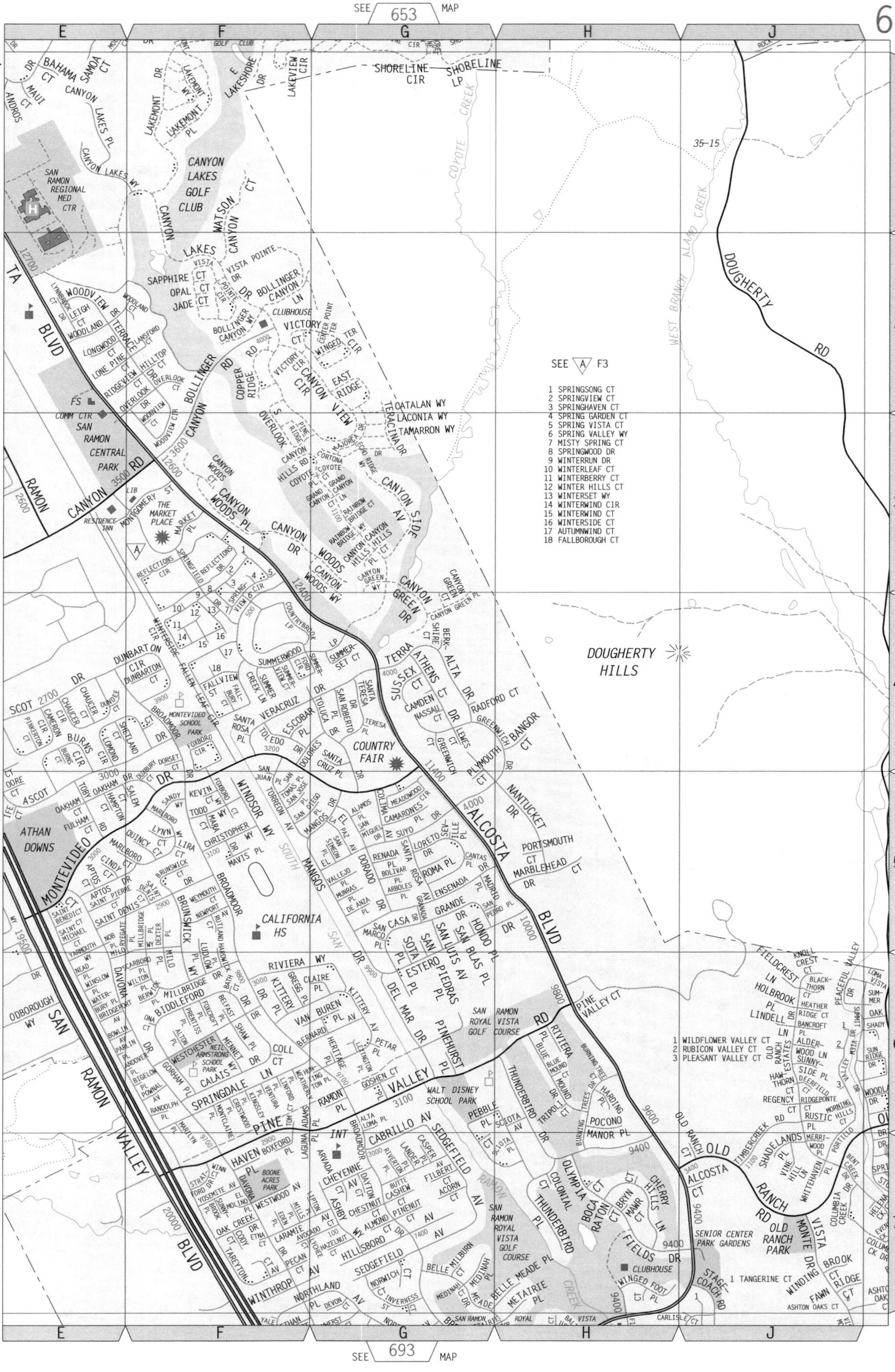
SEE 653 MAP
SEE 693 MAP
SEE 243 MAP
SHORELINE CIR
SHORELINE LP
CANYON LAKES GOLF CLUB
SAN RAMON REGIONAL MED CTR
SAN RAMON CENTRAL PARK
COMM CTR
THE MARKET PLACE
RESIDENCE INN
BOLLINGER CANYON RD
CANYON LAKES DR
ALCOSTA BLVD
SAN RAMON VALLEY BLVD
DOUGHERTY RD
DOUGHERTY HILLS
COYOTE CREEK
WEST BRANCH ALAMO CREEK
MONTEVIDEO DR
ATHAN DOWNS
COUNTRY FAIR
CALIFORNIA HS
MONTEVIDEO SCHOOL PARK
WESTCHESTER NEIL ARMSTRONG SCHOOL PARK
PINE VALLEY RD
WALT DISNEY SCHOOL PARK
SAN RAMON ROYAL VISTA GOLF COURSE
BOONE ACRES PARK
OLD RANCH RD
OLD RANCH PARK
SENIOR CENTER PARK GARDENS
CLUBHOUSE
STAGE COACH RD
SEE A F3
1 SPRINGSONG CT
2 SPRINGVIEW CT
3 SPRINGHAVEN CT
4 SPRING GARDEN CT
5 SPRING VISTA CT
6 SPRING VALLEY WY
7 MISTY SPRING CT
8 SPRINGWOOD DR
9 WINTERRUN DR
10 WINTERLEAF CT
11 WINTERBERRY CT
12 WINTER HILLS CT
13 WINTERSET WY
14 WINTERWIND CIR
15 WINTERWIND CT
16 WINTERSIDE CT
17 AUTUMNWIND CT
18 FALLBOROUGH CT
1 WILDFLOWER VALLEY CT
2 RUBICON VALLEY CT
3 PLEASANT VALLEY CT
1 TANGERINE CT

SEE 666 MAP

A B C D E

1 2 3 4 5 6 7

SEE 243 MAP

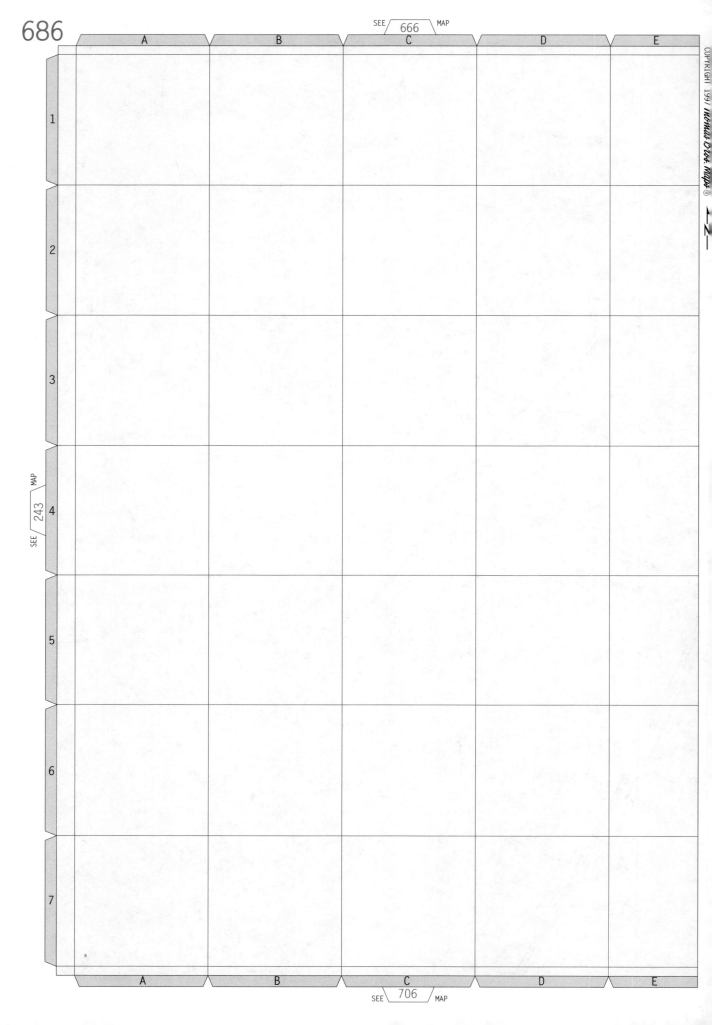

SEE 706 MAP

SEE 666 MAP

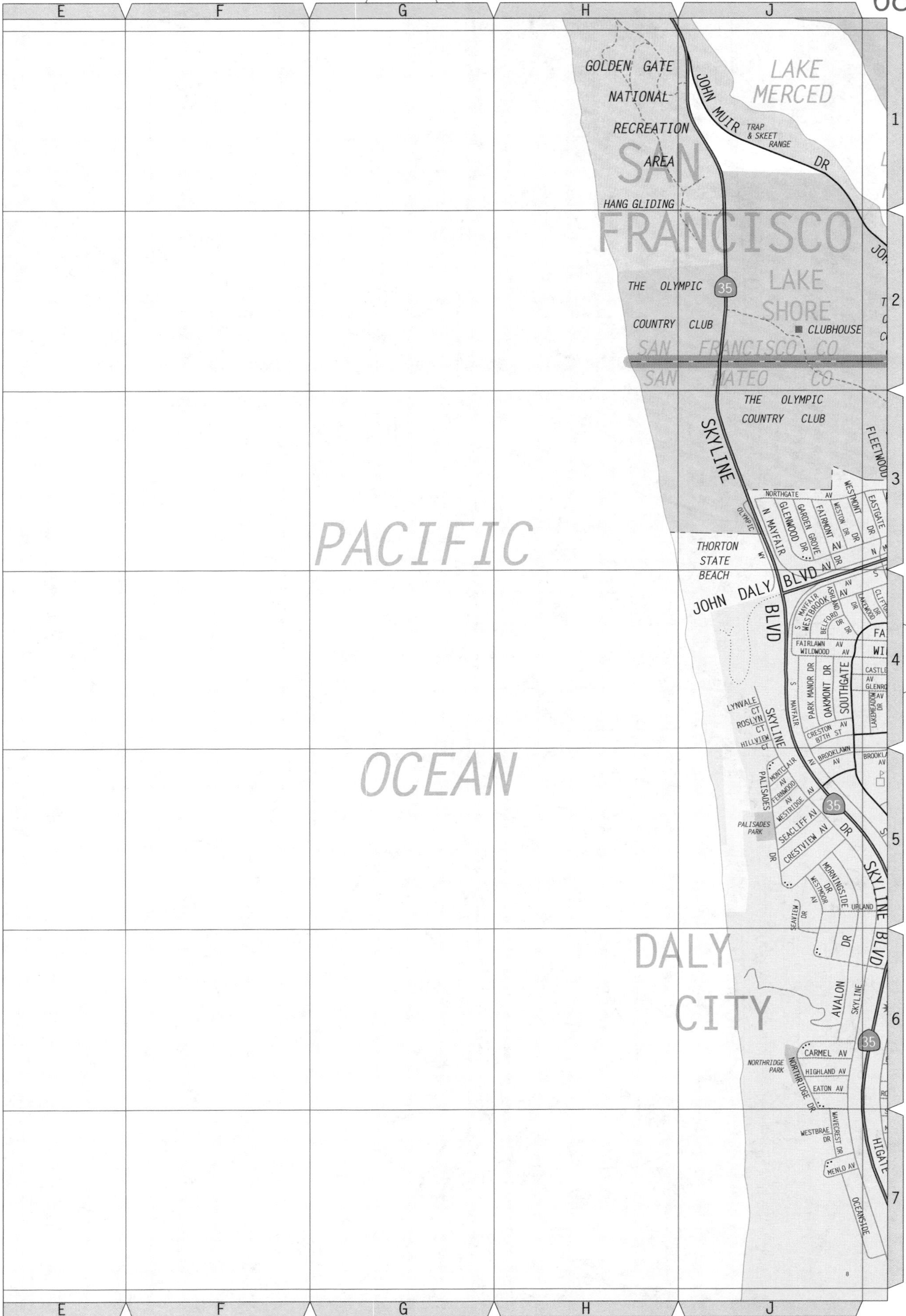
E
F
G
H
J
1
2
3
4
5
6
7
GOLDEN GATE NATIONAL RECREATION AREA
LAKE MERCED
JOHN MUIR DR
TRAP & SKEET RANGE
SAN FRANCISCO
HANG GLIDING
THE OLYMPIC COUNTRY CLUB
LAKE SHORE
CLUBHOUSE
SAN FRANCISCO CO
SAN MATEO CO
SKYLINE
FLEETWOOD
NORTHGATE AV
WESTMONT
EASTGATE
OLYMPIC WY
N MAYFAIR
GLENWOOD DR
GARDEN GROVE
FAIRMONT AV
WESTON DR
PACIFIC
OCEAN
THORTON STATE BEACH
JOHN DALY BLVD
WESTBROOK
ASHLAND
BELFORD DR
FAIRLAWN AV
WILDWOOD AV
PARK MANOR DR
OAKMONT DR
SOUTHGATE
S MAYFAIR
CRESTON AV
87TH ST
BROOKLAWN AV
LYNVALE CT
ROSLYN CT
HILLVIEW CT
SKYLINE
MONTCLAIR AV
FERNWOOD AV
WESTRIDGE AV
SEACLIFF AV
CRESTVIEW AV
PALISADES DR
PALISADES PARK
35
SKYLINE DR
SKYLINE BLVD
MORNINGSIDE DR
WESTMOOR AV
URLAND
SEAVIEW DR
DALY CITY
AVALON DR
CARMEL AV
HIGHLAND AV
EATON AV
NORTHRIDGE PARK
NORTHRIDGE DR
WESTBRAE DR
WAVECREST DR
MENLO AV
OCEANSIDE
HIGATE

SEE 687 MAP

SEE 706 MAP

SEE 667 MAP

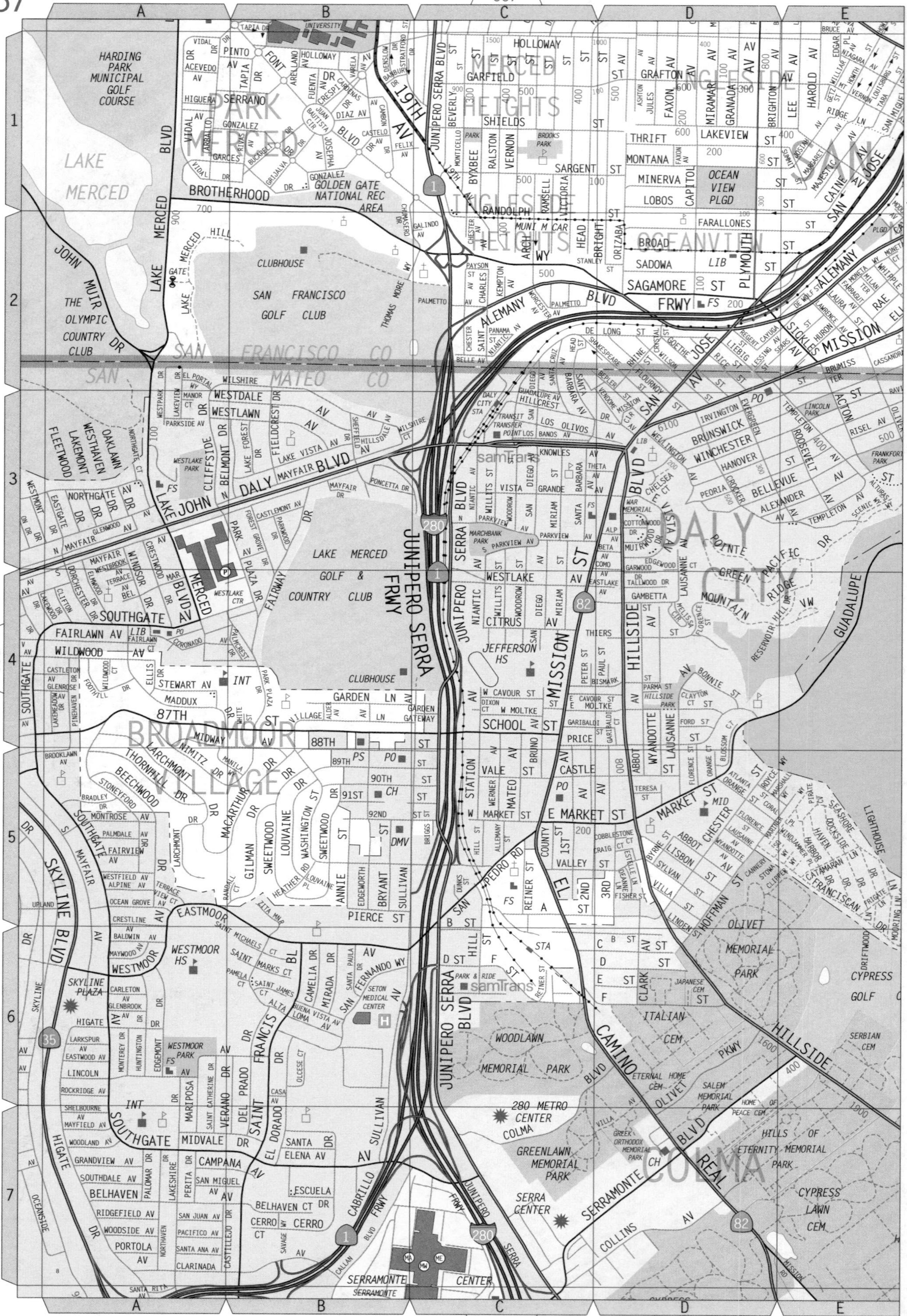
A
B
C
D
E
1
2
3
4
5
6
7
HARDING PARK MUNICIPAL GOLF COURSE
LAKE MERCED
PARK MERCED
MERCED HEIGHTS
INGLESIDE HEIGHTS
OCEANVIEW
INGLESIDE
GOLDEN GATE NATIONAL REC AREA
BROTHERHOOD
JOHN MUIR DR
THE OLYMPIC COUNTRY CLUB
CLUBHOUSE
SAN FRANCISCO GOLF CLUB
SAN FRANCISCO CO
SAN MATEO CO
LAKE MERCED BLVD
JUNIPERO SERRA BLVD
19TH AV
ALEMANY BLVD
SAN JOSE AV
MISSION ST
OCEAN VIEW PLGD
BROOKS PARK
JOHN DALY BLVD
WESTLAKE PARK
LAKE MERCED GOLF & COUNTRY CLUB
JUNIPERO SERRA FRWY
DALY CITY
JEFFERSON HS
HILLSIDE BLVD
GUADALUPE
SOUTHGATE AV
87TH ST
BROADMOOR VILLAGE
SCHOOL ST
E MARKET ST
SKYLINE BLVD
WESTMOOR HS
SKYLINE PLAZA
SETON MEDICAL CENTER
WOODLAWN MEMORIAL PARK
OLIVET MEMORIAL PARK
ITALIAN CEM
CYPRESS GOLF
SERBIAN CEM
HILLS OF ETERNITY MEMORIAL PARK
CYPRESS LAWN CEM
280 METRO CENTER COLMA
GREENLAWN MEMORIAL PARK
SERRA CENTER
COLMA
EL CAMINO REAL
SERRAMONTE BLVD
SERRAMONTE CENTER
CABRILLO FRWY
SAINT FRANCIS BLVD
WESTMOOR PARK
COLLINS AV
LIGHTHOUSE
FRANCISCAN
samTrans
1
35
82
280

SEE 686 MAP

SEE 707 MAP

SEE 667 MAP

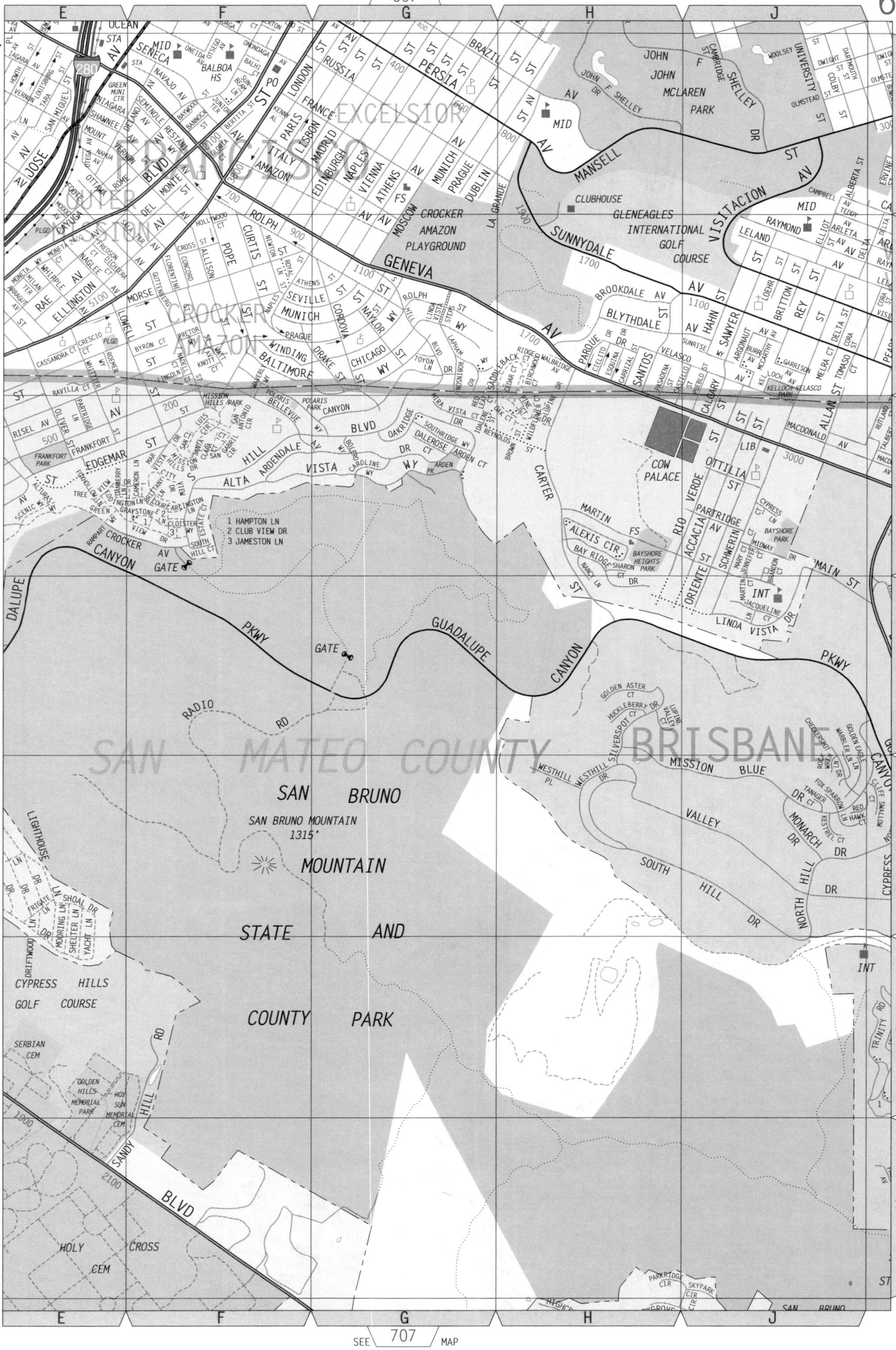
E
F
G
H
J
1
2
3
4
5
6
7
SAN FRANCISCO
EXCELSIOR
OUTER MISSION
CROCKER AMAZON
CROCKER AMAZON PLAYGROUND
JOHN MCLAREN PARK
GLENEAGLES INTERNATIONAL GOLF COURSE
CLUBHOUSE
BALBOA HS
GENEVA AV
MANSELL ST
SUNNYDALE AV
VISITACION AV
MISSION ST
PERSIA AV
COW PALACE
BAYSHORE HEIGHTS PARK
BAYSHORE PARK
FRANKFORT PARK
KELLOCH VELASCO PARK
MISSION HILLS PARK
POLARIS PARK
1 HAMPTON LN
2 CLUB VIEW DR
3 JAMESTON LN
GATE
GUADALUPE CANYON PKWY
RADIO RD
SAN MATEO COUNTY
BRISBANE
SAN BRUNO MOUNTAIN STATE AND COUNTY PARK
SAN BRUNO MOUNTAIN
1315'
MISSION BLUE DR
SOUTH HILL DR
NORTH HILL DR
VALLEY DR
CYPRESS HILLS GOLF COURSE
SERBIAN CEM
GOLDEN HILLS MEMORIAL PARK
HOY SUN MEMORIAL CEM
HOLY CROSS CEM
SANDY HILL RD
BLVD
INT
LIB
FS
MID

SEE 688 MAP

SEE 707 MAP

SEE 668 MAP
SEE 687 MAP
SEE 708 MAP
A
B
C
D
E
1
2
3
4
5
6
7
SAN FRANCISCO
BAYVIEW
BAYVIEW HEIGHTS
VISITACION VALLEY
HUNTERS POINT
NAVAL RESE
SOUTH BASIN
CANDLESTICK POINT
NATURE AREA
3COM PARK
(CANDLESTICK PARK)
HOME OF SF GIANTS & 49ERS
CANDLESTICK POINT STATE RECREATION AREA
BAYVIEW PARK
GILMAN PARK
EXECUTIVE PARK BLVD
HARNEY WY
JAMESTOWN AV EX
HUNTERS POINT EXWY
JAMES LICK FRWY
101
BAYSHORE FRWY
BAYSHORE BLVD
GENEVA AV
SUNNYDALE AV
MANSELL ST
3RD ST
CALTRAIN STA
PHILLIP BURTON & SALA HS
BAYSHORE
SAN MATEO COUNTY
BRISBANE
GUADALUPE CANYON PKWY
CALTRAIN
TUNNEL AV
INDUSTRIAL WY
VALLEY DR
LAGOON
LAGOON WY
SIERRA POINT PKWY
GUADALUPE CANAL
SIERRA POINT
MARINA BLVD
MARINA
SAN
SAN BRUNO MOUNTAIN STATE AND COUNTY PARK
1 SAN MATEO LN
2 PLACER WY
PARK & RIDE
samTrans

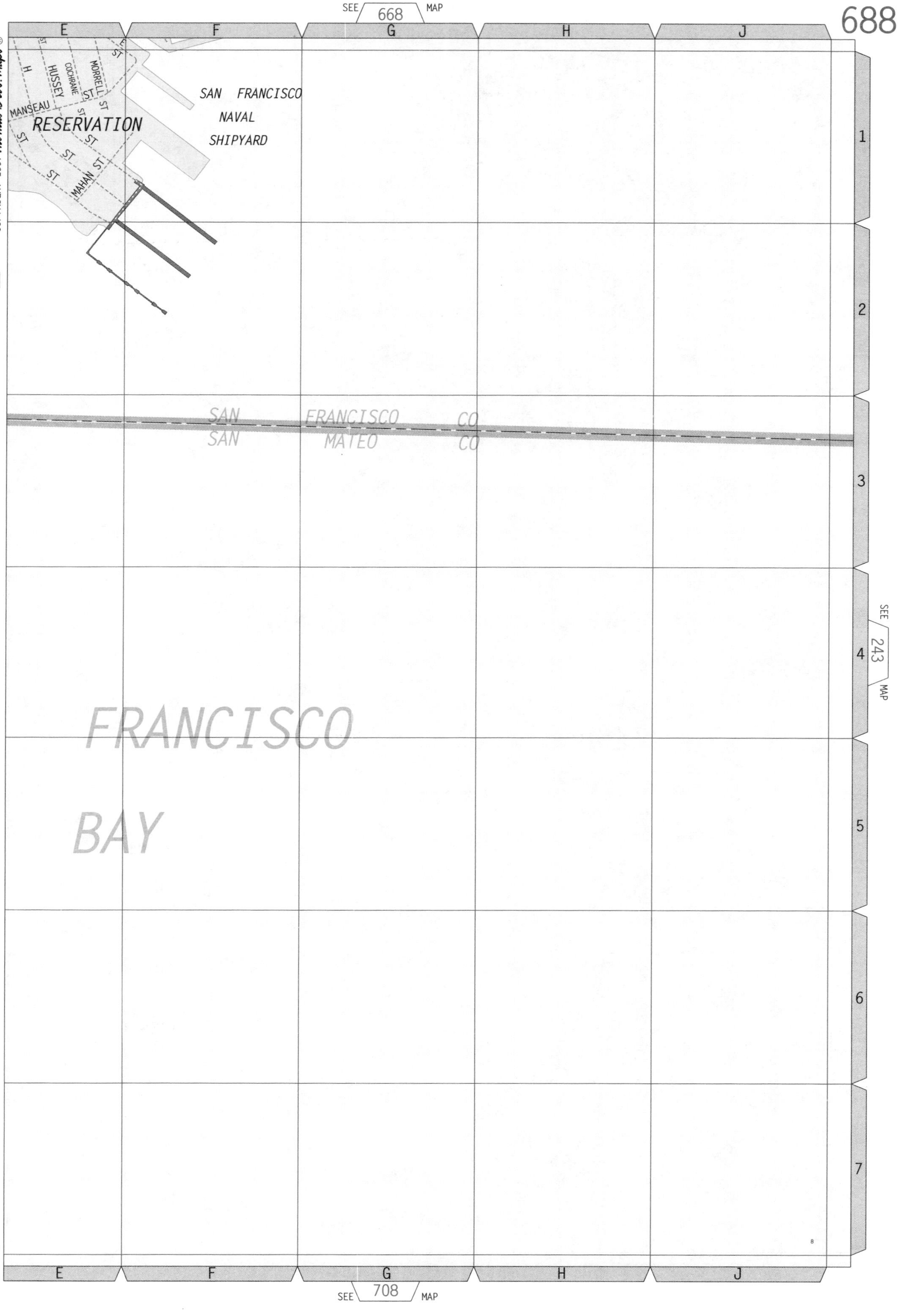
SEE 668 MAP
E
F
G
H
J
H
HUSSEY
COCHRANE
MORRELL ST
MANSEAU
ST
RESERVATION
MAHAN ST
SAN FRANCISCO
NAVAL
SHIPYARD
SAN FRANCISCO CO
SAN MATEO CO
FRANCISCO
BAY
1
2
3
4
5
6
7
SEE 243 MAP
SEE 708 MAP

SEE 670 MAP

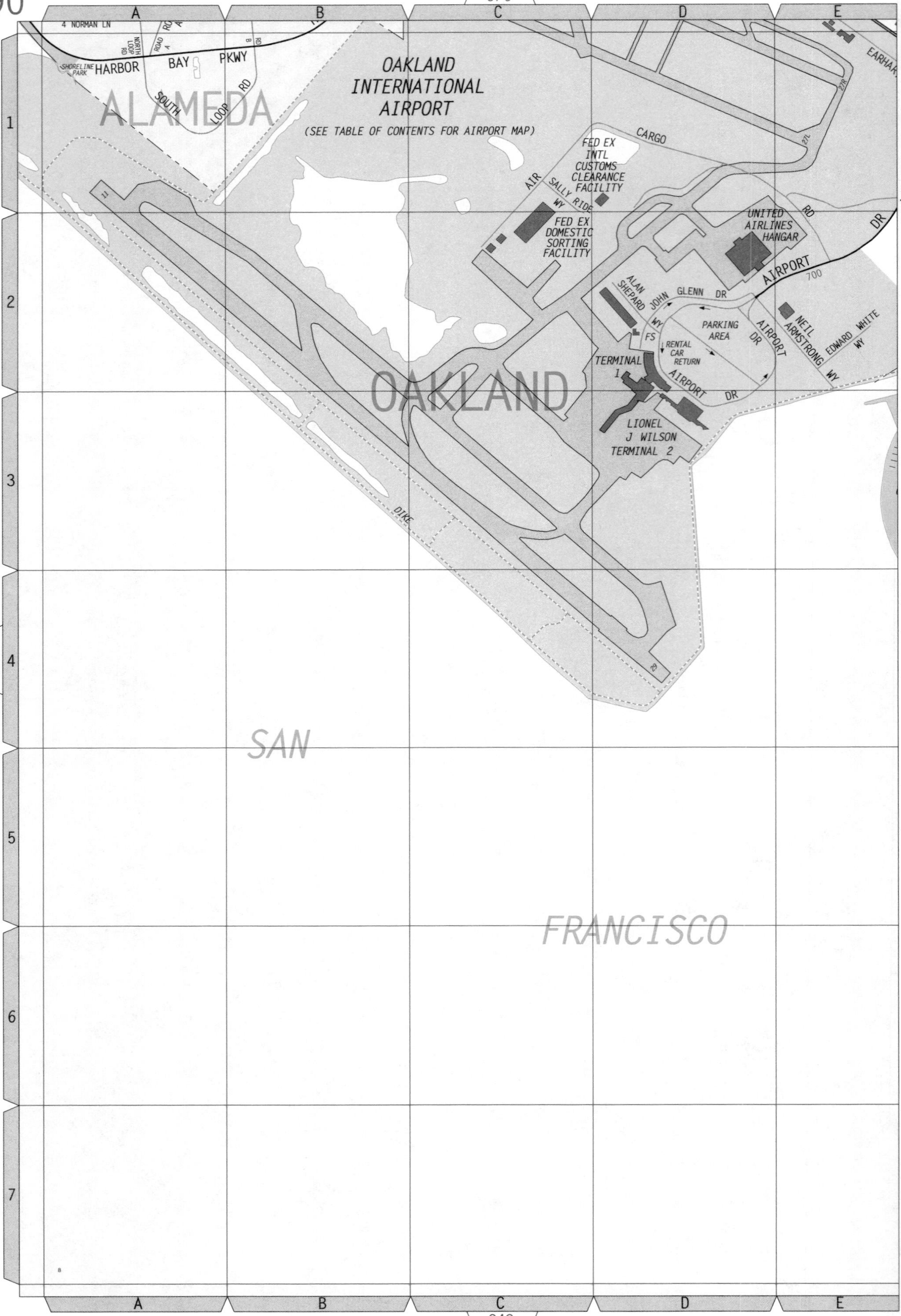

A
B
C
D
E
1
2
3
4
5
6
7
4 NORMAN LN
NORTH LOOP RD
ROAD A
ROAD B
SHORELINE PARK
HARBOR
BAY
PKWY
SOUTH
LOOP
RD
ALAMEDA
OAKLAND
INTERNATIONAL
AIRPORT
(SEE TABLE OF CONTENTS FOR AIRPORT MAP)
FED EX
INTL
CUSTOMS
CLEARANCE
FACILITY
CARGO
AIR
SALLY RIDE
WY
FED EX
DOMESTIC
SORTING
FACILITY
UNITED
AIRLINES
HANGAR
EARHART
RD
DR
AIRPORT
700
ALAN
SHEPARD
JOHN
GLENN
DR
WY
FS
PARKING
AREA
RENTAL
CAR
RETURN
AIRPORT
DR
NEIL
ARMSTRONG
EDWARD
WHITE
WY
WY
TERMINAL
1
AIRPORT
DR
OAKLAND
LIONEL
J WILSON
TERMINAL 2
DIKE
RD
SAN
FRANCISCO

SEE 243 MAP

SEE 243 MAP

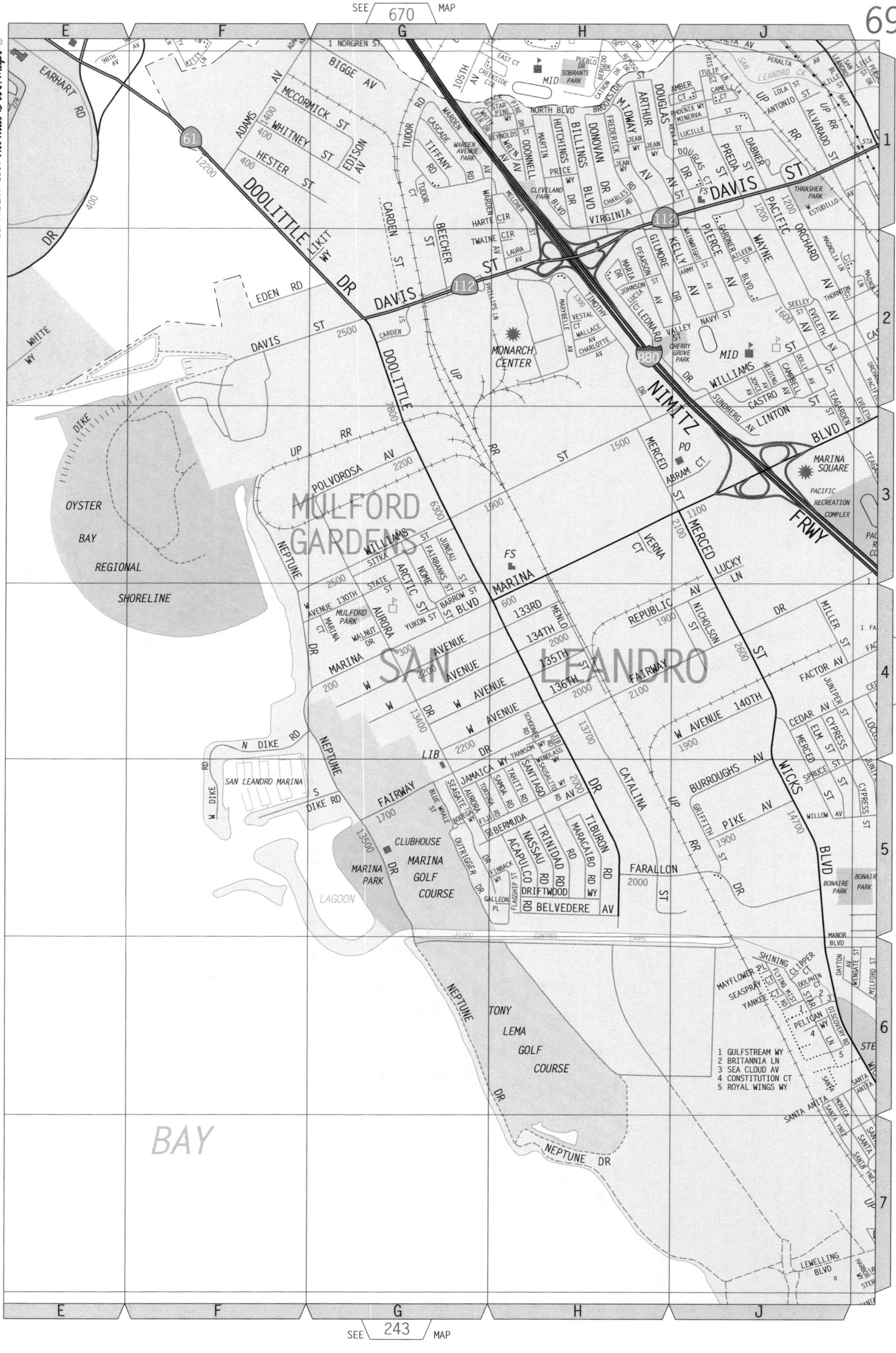
SEE 670 MAP
E
F
G
H
J
1
2
3
4
5
6
7
SEE 691 MAP
SEE 243 MAP
MULFORD GARDENS
SAN LEANDRO
OYSTER BAY REGIONAL SHORELINE
BAY
LAGOON
SAN LEANDRO MARINA
MARINA PARK
CLUBHOUSE
MARINA GOLF COURSE
TONY LEMA GOLF COURSE
MONARCH CENTER
MARINA SQUARE
PACIFIC RECREATION COMPLEX
CLEVELAND PARK
THRASHER PARK
CHERRY GROVE PARK
MULFORD PARK
BONAIRE PARK
SOBRANTE PARK
NIMITZ FRWY
880
112
61
DOOLITTLE DR
DAVIS ST
EDEN RD
MARINA BLVD
WICKS BLVD
MERCED ST
NEPTUNE DR
FAIRWAY DR
N DIKE RD
S DIKE RD
W DIKE RD
FLOOD CONTROL CANAL
LEWELLING BLVD
MANOR BLVD
UP RR
1 GULFSTREAM WY
2 BRITANNIA LN
3 SEA CLOUD AV
4 CONSTITUTION CT
5 ROYAL WINGS WY

SEE 671 MAP

SAN LEANDRO
SAN LORENZO
NIMITZ FRWY
MACARTHUR FRWY
HESPERIAN BLVD
WASHINGTON AV
E 14TH ST
BANCROFT AV
MARINA BLVD
FLORESTA BLVD
HALCYON DR
LEWELLING BLVD
GRANT AV
LAKE CHABOT RD
DAVIS ST
ESTUDILLO AV
SAN LEANDRO HS
SAN LEANDRO HOSP
LINCOLN HS
PACIFIC REC COMPLEX
WASHINGTON MANOR PARK
STENZEL PARK
BAYFAIR MALL
GREENHOUSE MARKETPLACE
ARROYO HS
CATHOLIC CEMETERY
VENCOR HOSPITAL
SEE A B2
1 CLARIDGE PL
2 LIMEHOUSE LN
3 WIMBLEDON PL
SEE B B4
1 AVANSINO ST
2 MORTENSEN RD
3 WEDGEWOOD ST
SEE C C5
1 MILLSTREAM DR
2 EBB TIDE ST

SEE 690 MAP

SEE 711 MAP

SEE 671 MAP

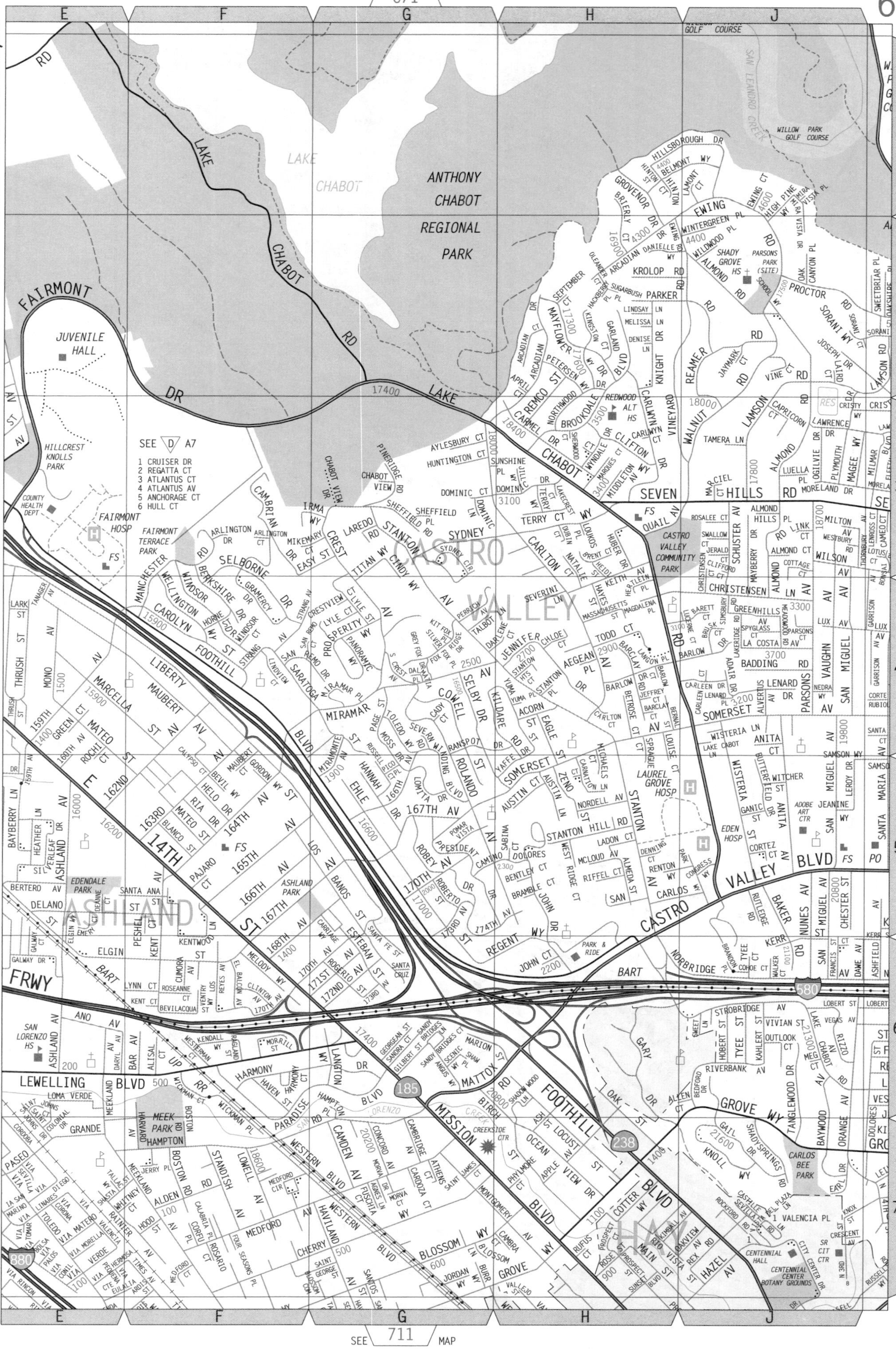
ANTHONY
CHABOT
REGIONAL
PARK
LAKE
CHABOT
LAKE CHABOT RD
FAIRMONT DR
JUVENILE HALL
HILLCREST KNOLLS PARK
COUNTY HEALTH DEPT
FAIRMONT HOSP
FAIRMONT TERRACE PARK
SEE D A7
1 CRUISER DR
2 REGATTA CT
3 ATLANTUS CT
4 ATLANTUS AV
5 ANCHORAGE CT
6 HULL CT
CASTRO
VALLEY
CASTRO VALLEY COMMUNITY PARK
SEVEN HILLS RD
SHADY GROVE HS
PARSONS PARK (SITE)
REDWOOD ALT HS
WILLOW PARK GOLF COURSE
SAN LEANDRO CREEK
LAUREL GROVE HOSP
EDEN HOSP
ADOBE ART CTR
CASTRO VALLEY BLVD
FOOTHILL BLVD
ASHLAND
EDENDALE PARK
ASHLAND PARK
SAN LORENZO HS
LEWELLING BLVD
MEEK PARK
HAMPTON
MISSION BLVD
CREEKSIDE CTR
PARK & RIDE
BART
FRWY
580
185
238
880
GROVE WY
CARLOS BEE PARK
CENTENNIAL HALL
CENTENNIAL CENTER BOTANY GROUNDS
CITY CTR
HAY
E 14TH ST
GARRISON
SAN MIGUEL AV
STANTON AV
GRANDE
PARADISE BLVD
WESTERN BLVD
CAMDEN AV
ATHENS
MEDFORD AV
CHERRY
BLOSSOM WY
JORDAN WY

SEE 692 MAP

SEE 711 MAP

SEE 672 MAP

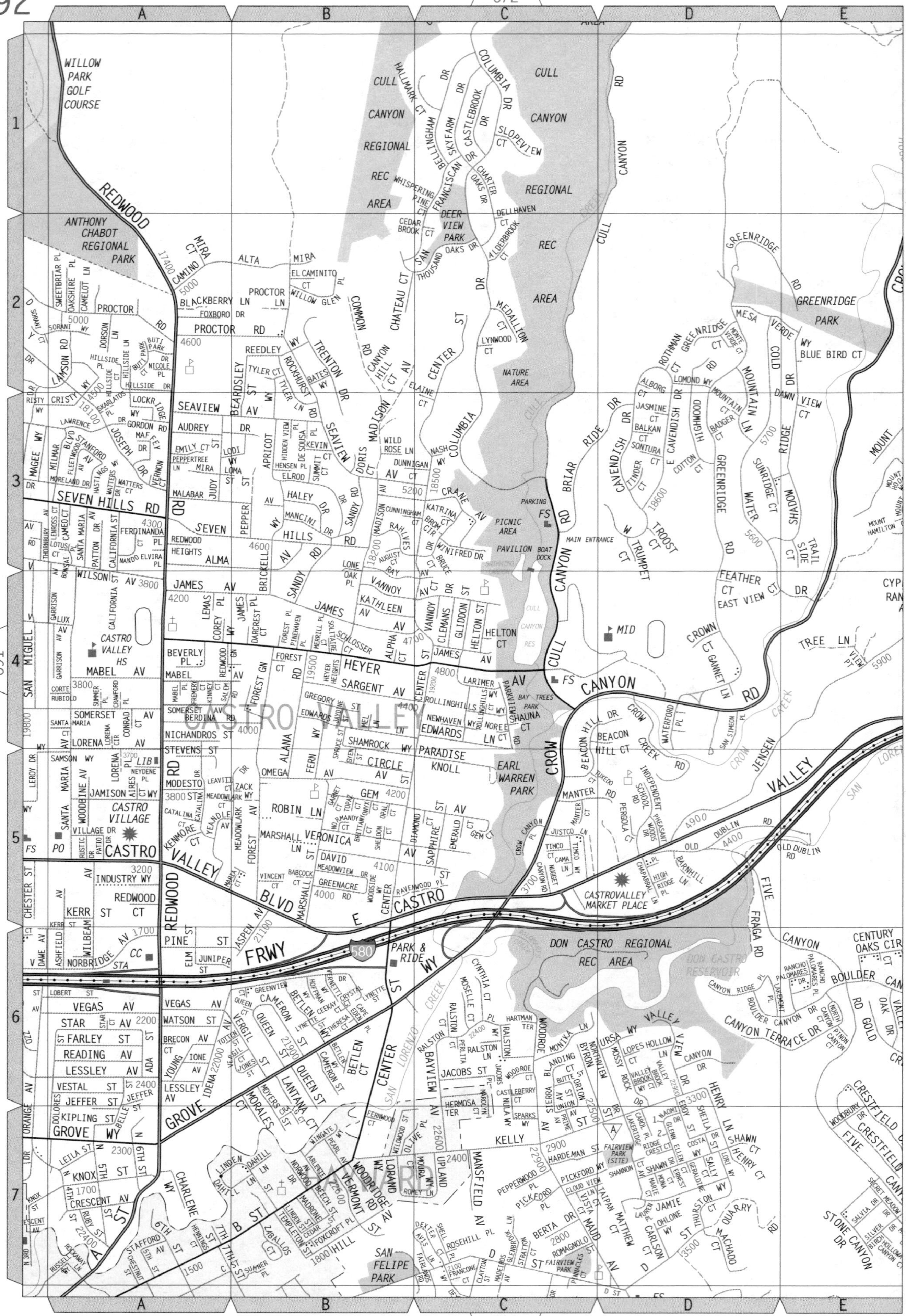

A
B
C
D
E
1
2
3
4
5
6
7
WILLOW PARK GOLF COURSE
ANTHONY CHABOT REGIONAL PARK
CULL CANYON REGIONAL REC AREA
GREENRIDGE PARK
CASTRO VALLEY
CASTRO VALLEY HS
CASTRO VILLAGE
CASTROVALLEY MARKET PLACE
EARL WARREN PARK
DON CASTRO REGIONAL REC AREA
DON CASTRO RESERVOIR
SAN FELIPE PARK
NATURE AREA
PICNIC AREA
PAVILION
MAIN ENTRANCE
CULL CANYON RES
DEER VIEW PARK
BAY TREES PARK
CENTURY OAKS CIR
PARK & RIDE
REDWOOD RD
SEVEN HILLS RD
CASTRO VALLEY BLVD
E CASTRO VALLEY BLVD
CULL CANYON RD
CROW CANYON RD
GROVE WY
CENTER ST
HEYER AV
JAMES AV
PROCTOR RD
SEAVIEW AV
MADISON AV
FIVE CANYON
GREENRIDGE RD
DUBLIN RD
OLD DUBLIN RD
FRWY 580
KELLY
MANSFIELD AV
HAYWARD

SEE 691 MAP

SEE 712 MAP

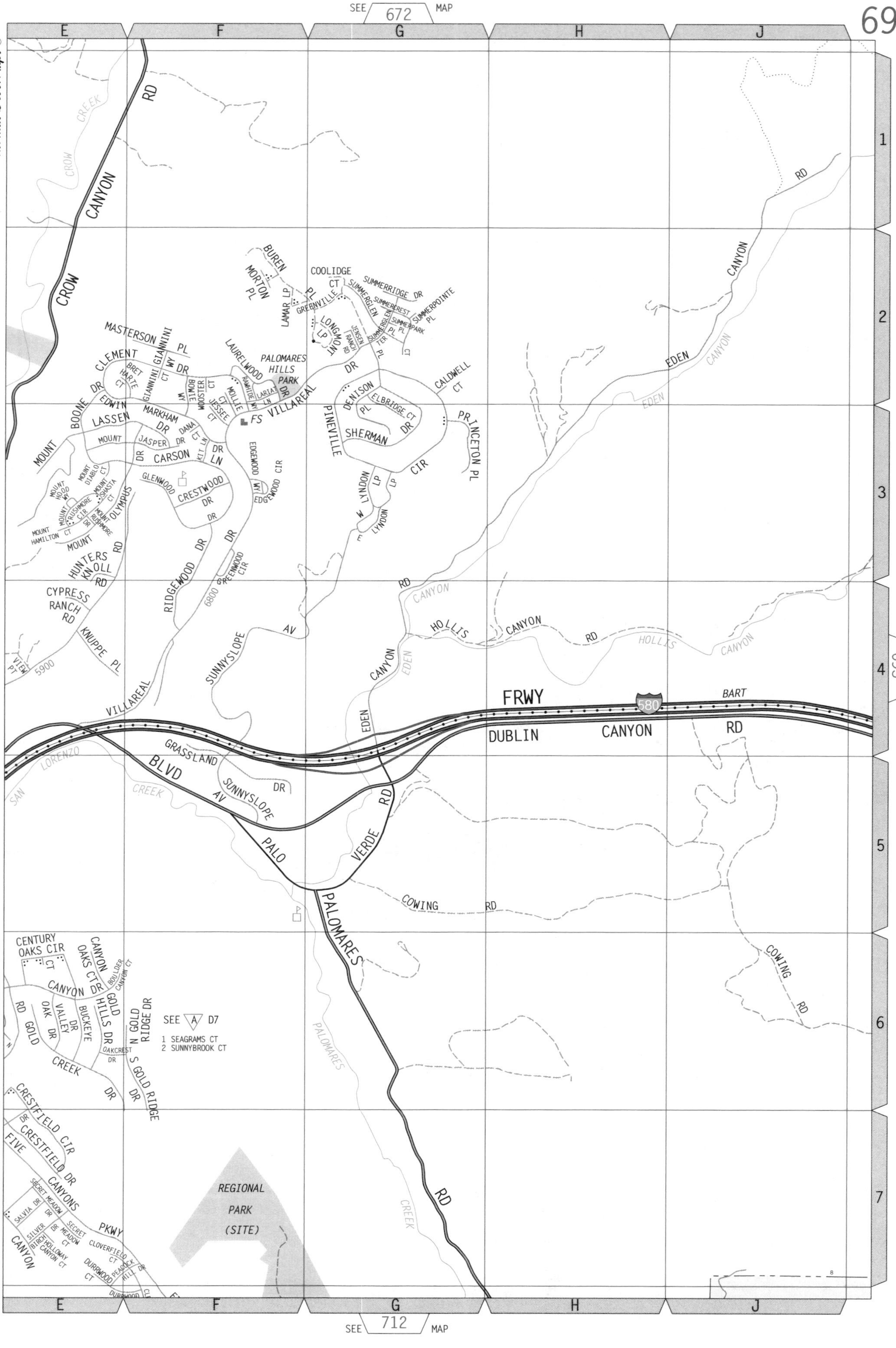
SEE 672 MAP
E
F
G
H
J
1
2
3
4
5
6
7
CROW CANYON RD
CROW CREEK
BUREN
MORTON PL
LAMAR LP
PL
COOLIDGE CT
GREENVILLE
SUMMERGLEN CT
SUMMERRIDGE DR
SUMMERCREST
SUMMERPOINTE PL
SUMMERPARK PL
SUMMERGLEN TER
LONGMONT LP
JENSEN RANCH RD
CT
PL
MASTERSON PL
GIANNINI DR
GIANNINI CT
WY
CLEMENT
BRET HARTE CT
LAURELWOOD
PALOMARES HILLS PARK
BOWIE WY
WOOSTER CT
MOLLIE
RAWHIDE WY
LARIAT LN
DR
JESSEE CT
FS
VILLAREAL DR
DENISON
ELBRIDGE CT
PL
CALDWELL CT
PINEVILLE
SHERMAN DR
PRINCETON PL
CIR
EDWIN
BOONE
LASSEN
MARKHAM DR
DANA CT
MOUNT
JASPER DR
CARSON
KIT LN
DR LN
EDGEWOOD WY
EDGEWOOD CIR
GLENWOOD
CRESTWOOD DR
DR
LYNDON LP
LP
W
E
LYNDON
MOUNT DIABLO CT
MOUNT SHASTA CT
MOUNT HOOD WY
RUSHMORE CIR
MOUNT RUSHMORE CT
OLYMPUS
MOUNT HAMILTON CT
MOUNT
HUNTERS KNOLL RD
RD
RIDGEWOOD DR
GREENWOOD CIR
6800
CYPRESS RANCH RD
KNUPPE PL
VIEW PT
5900
SUNNYSLOPE AV
VILLAREAL
EDEN CANYON RD
EDEN CANYON
CANYON
RD
HOLLIS CANYON RD
HOLLIS CANYON
EDEN
FRWY
580
BART
DUBLIN CANYON RD
SEE 693 MAP
SAN LORENZO CREEK
GRASSLAND DR
BLVD
SUNNYSLOPE AV
PALO VERDE RD
COWING RD
PALOMARES
CENTURY OAKS CIR
CT
CANYON OAKS CT
BOULDER CANYON CT
CANYON DR
GOLD HILLS DR
N GOLD RIDGE DR
RD
GOLD
OAK DR
VALLEY DR
BUCKEYE
OAKCREST DR
S GOLD RIDGE
CREEK DR
SEE A D7
1 SEAGRAMS CT
2 SUNNYBROOK CT
CRESTFIELD CIR
CRESTFIELD DR
FIVE CANYONS PKWY
SECRET MEADOW DR
SALVIA DR
SILVER BIRCH DR
HOLLOWAY CANYON CT
SECRET MEADOW CT
CLOVERFIELD CT
DURWOOD CT
PEACOCK HILL DR
DURWOOD
SAN CANYON
REGIONAL PARK (SITE)
PALOMARES RD
PALOMARES CREEK
SEE 712 MAP

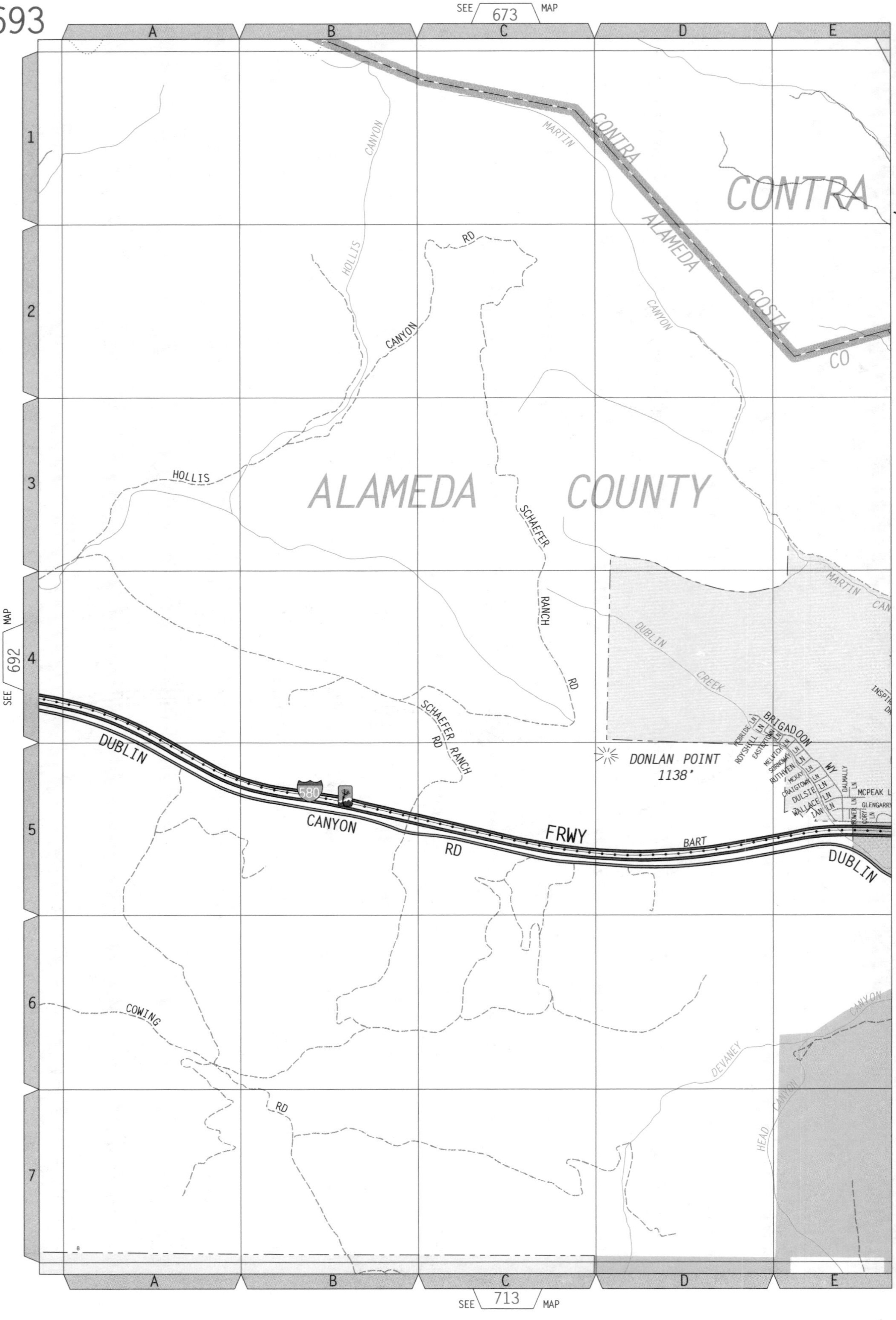
SEE 673 MAP
A
B
C
D
E
1
2
3
4
5
6
7
SEE 692 MAP
SEE 713 MAP
CANYON
MARTIN
CONTRA
ALAMEDA
COSTA
CO
CONTRA
RD
HOLLIS
CANYON
CANYON
HOLLIS
ALAMEDA
COUNTY
SCHAEFFER
RANCH
RD
MARTIN
CAN
DUBLIN
CREEK
INSPIR
DR
SCHAEFFER
RD
RANCH
MCBRIDE LN
ROYSHILL LN
EASTERTOWN LN
BRIGADOON
WY
MELVICH LN
SORNOWAY LN
RUTHVEN LN
MCKAY LN
CRAIGTOWN LN
DULSIE LN
WALLACE LN
IAN LN
DALMALLY LN
MCPEAK L
GLENGARRY
BOWER LN
CORY LN
DONLAN POINT
1138'
DUBLIN
580
CANYON
RD
FRWY
BART
DUBLIN
COWING
RD
DEVANEY
CANYON
HEAD
CANYON

SEE 673 MAP

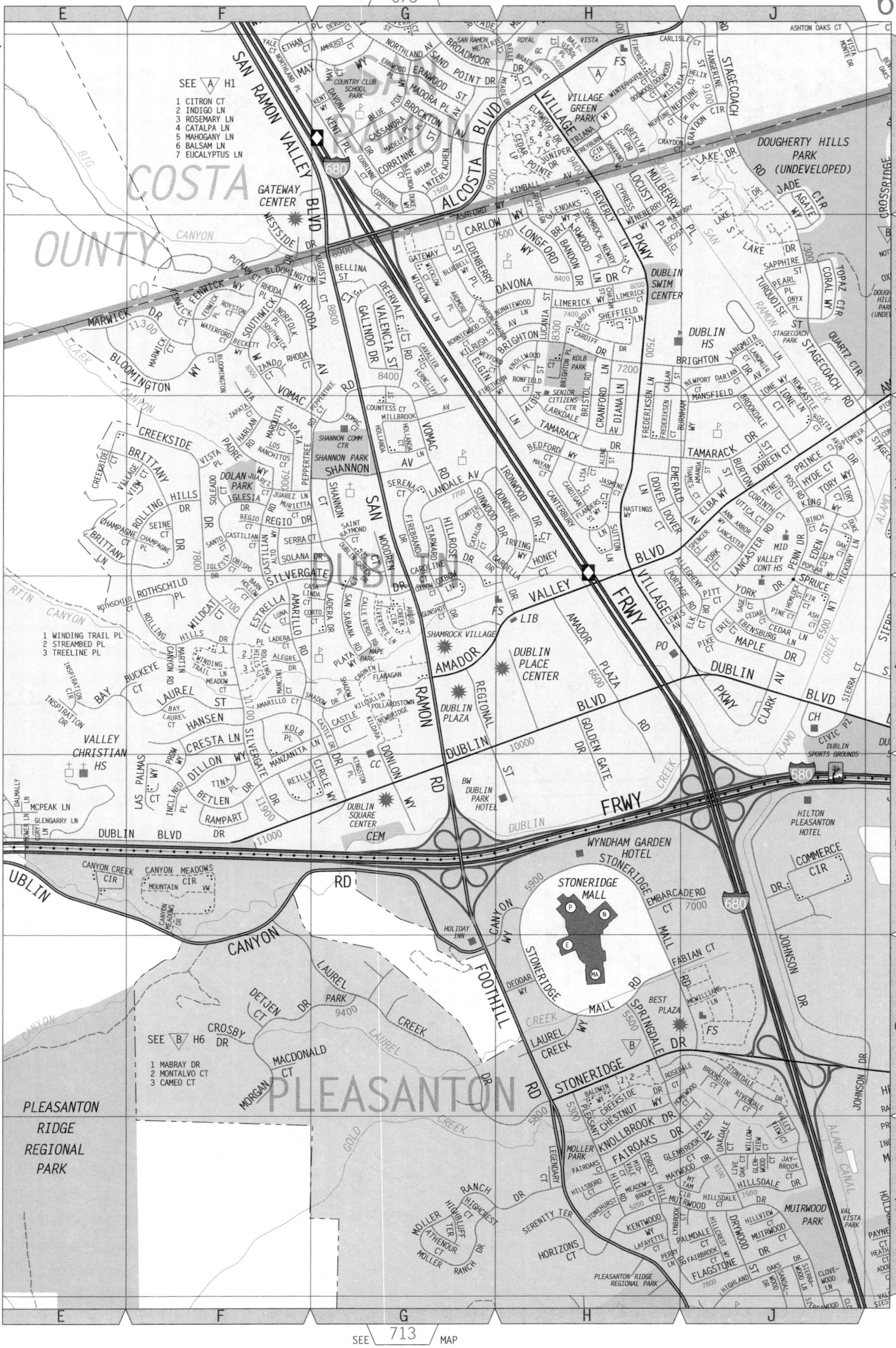

E
F
G
H
J
1
2
3
4
5
6
7
SAN RAMON
COSTA
COUNTY
DUBLIN
PLEASANTON
SEE A H1
1 CITRON CT
2 INDIGO LN
3 ROSEMARY LN
4 CATALPA LN
5 MAHOGANY LN
6 BALSAM LN
7 EUCALYPTUS LN
SAN RAMON VALLEY BLVD
ALCOSTA BLVD
VILLAGE PKWY
GATEWAY CENTER
DOUGHERTY HILLS PARK (UNDEVELOPED)
DUBLIN SWIM CENTER
DUBLIN HS
KOLB PARK
SENIOR CITIZENS CTR
SHANNON COMM CTR
SHANNON PARK
DOLAN PARK
DUBLIN PLACE CENTER
DUBLIN PLAZA
SHAMROCK VILLAGE
VALLEY CHRISTIAN HS
1 WINDING TRAIL PL
2 STREAMBED PL
3 TREELINE PL
AMADOR VALLEY BLVD
DUBLIN BLVD
SAN RAMON RD
REGIONAL ST
AMADOR PLAZA RD
GOLDEN GATE DR
DUBLIN SQUARE CENTER
BW DUBLIN PARK HOTEL
DUBLIN SPORTS GROUNDS
CIVIC PZ
HILTON PLEASANTON HOTEL
DUBLIN FRWY
580
680
WYNDHAM GARDEN HOTEL
STONERIDGE MALL
STONERIDGE MALL RD
COMMERCE CIR
HOLIDAY INN
FOOTHILL RD
CANYON WY
JOHNSON DR
BEST PLAZA
CANYON MEADOWS CIR
CANYON CREEK CIR
DUBLIN CANYON RD
LAUREL CREEK DR
SEE B H6
1 MABRAY DR
2 MONTALVO CT
3 CAMEO CT
PLEASANTON RIDGE REGIONAL PARK
STONERIDGE DR
SPRINGDALE DR
MOLLER PARK
MUIRWOOD PARK
MOLLER RANCH DR
ALAMO CANAL

SEE 694 MAP

MAP

SEE 713 MAP

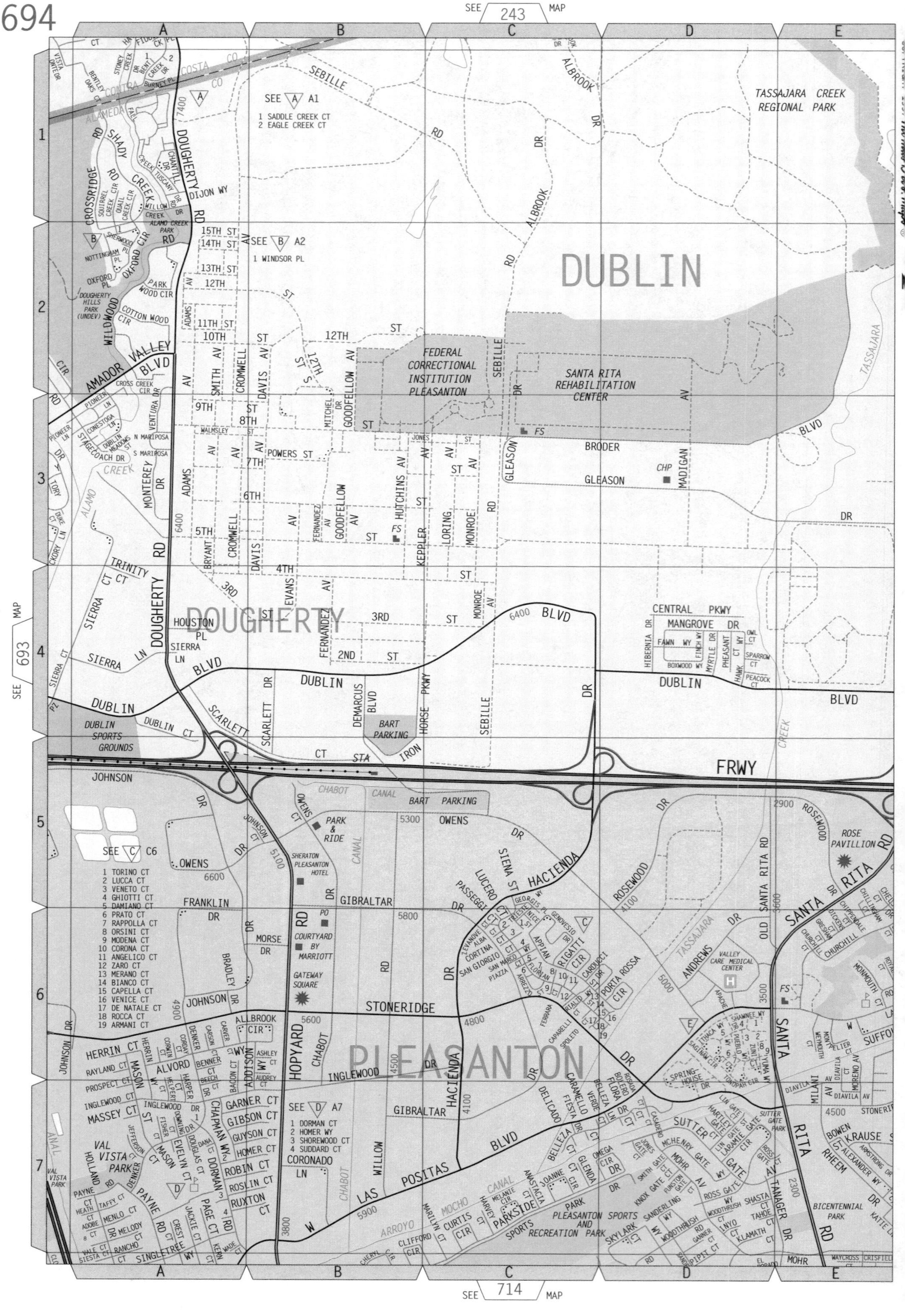
SEE 243 MAP
SEE 714 MAP
SEE 693 MAP
A B C D E
1 2 3 4 5 6 7
DUBLIN
PLEASANTON
DOUGHERTY
TASSAJARA CREEK REGIONAL PARK
FEDERAL CORRECTIONAL INSTITUTION PLEASANTON
SANTA RITA REHABILITATION CENTER
DOUGHERTY HILLS PARK (UNDEV)
DUBLIN SPORTS GROUNDS
BART PARKING
PARK & RIDE
SHERATON PLEASANTON HOTEL
COURTYARD BY MARRIOTT
GATEWAY SQUARE
VALLEY CARE MEDICAL CENTER
ROSE PAVILLION
VAL VISTA PARK
PLEASANTON SPORTS AND RECREATION PARK
BICENTENNIAL PARK
ALAMO CREEK PARK
SPRING-HOUSE
SEE A A1
1 SADDLE CREEK CT
2 EAGLE CREEK CT
SEE B A2
1 WINDSOR PL
SEE C C6
1 TORINO CT
2 LUCCA CT
3 VENETO CT
4 GHIOTTI CT
5 DAMIANO CT
6 PRATO CT
7 RAPPOLLA CT
8 ORSINI CT
9 MODENA CT
10 CORONA CT
11 ANGELICO CT
12 ZARO CT
13 MERANO CT
14 BIANCO CT
15 CAPELLA CT
16 VENICE CT
17 DE NATALE CT
18 ROCCA CT
19 ARMANI CT
SEE D A7
1 DORMAN CT
2 HOMER WY
3 SHOREWOOD CT
4 SUDDARD CT
DOUGHERTY RD
DUBLIN BLVD
AMADOR VALLEY BLVD
HOPYARD RD
STONERIDGE DR
HACIENDA DR
W LAS POSITAS BLVD
SANTA RITA RD
OWENS DR
JOHNSON DR
GIBRALTAR DR
TASSAJARA CREEK
ARROYO MOCHO CANAL
CHABOT CANAL
FRWY
GLEASON DR
BRODER BLVD
CENTRAL PKWY
ALBROOK DR
SEBILLE RD
CHP
FS

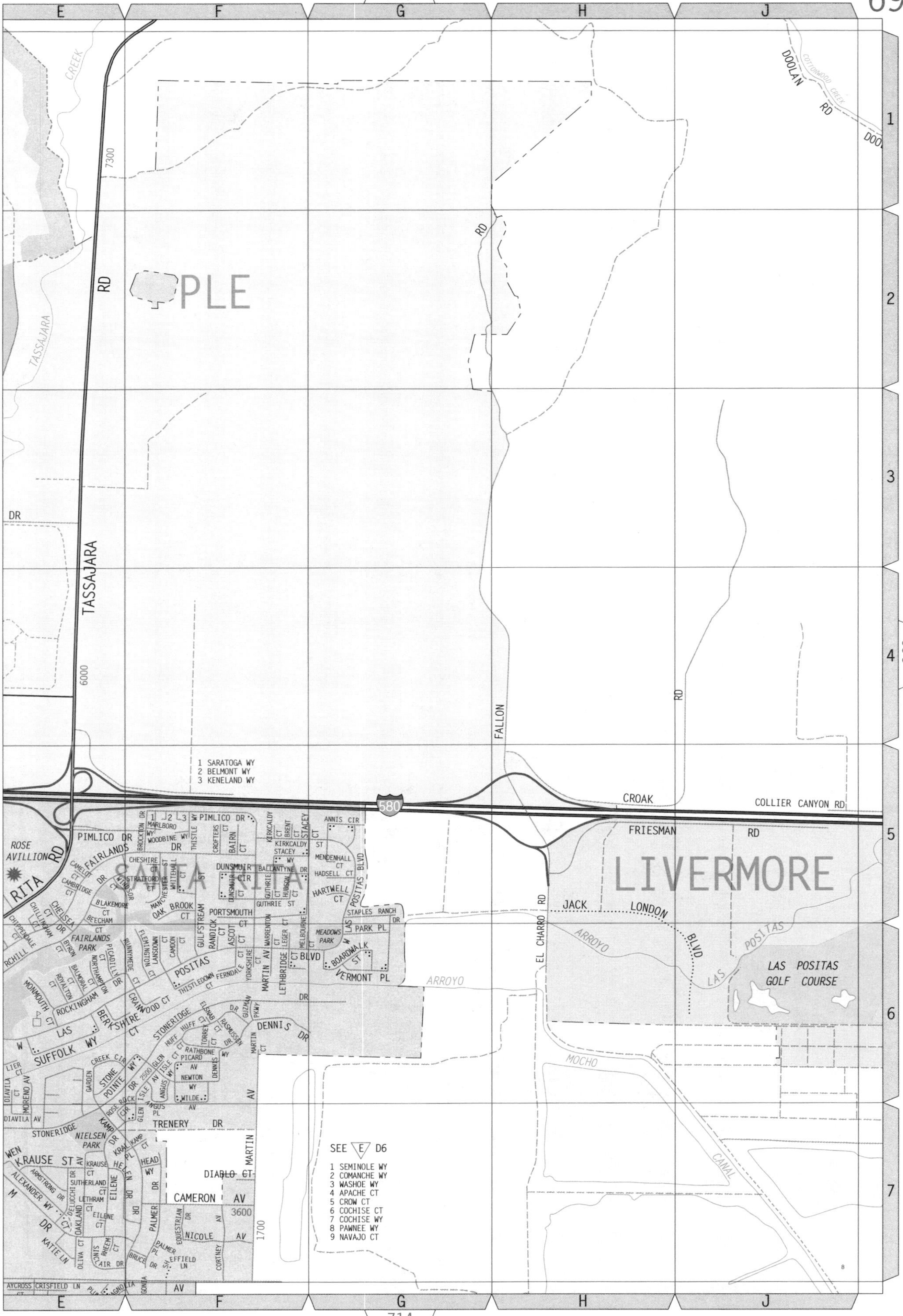
SEE 243 MAP
SEE 714 MAP
SEE 695 MAP
BAY AREA
MAP
E
F
G
H
J
1
2
3
4
5
6
7
DOOLAN RD
COTTONWOOD CREEK
CREEK
TASSAJARA RD
TASSAJARA
7300
6000
PLE
RD
DR
FALLON RD
RD
1 SARATOGA WY
2 BELMONT WY
3 KENELAND WY
580
CROAK
COLLIER CANYON RD
FRIESMAN RD
LIVERMORE
SANTA RITA
ROSE AVILLION
RITA RD
PIMLICO DR
FAIRLANDS
JACK LONDON BLVD
EL CHARRO RD
ARROYO LAS POSITAS
LAS POSITAS GOLF COURSE
LAS POSITAS BLVD
ARROYO
MOCHO
CANAL
PORTSMOUTH
POSITAS
SUFFOLK WY
BERKSHIRE
STONERIDGE
DENNIS DR
TRENERY DR
KRAUSE ST
CAMERON AV
NICOLE AV
PALMER DR
DIABLO CT
MARTIN AV
3600
1700
SEE E D6
1 SEMINOLE WY
2 COMANCHE WY
3 WASHOE WY
4 APACHE CT
5 CROW CT
6 COCHISE CT
7 COCHISE WY
8 PAWNEE WY
9 NAVAJO CT
VERMONT PL
BOARDWALK ST
MEADOWS PARK
STAPLES RANCH DR
HARTWELL CT
ROCKINGHAM
NIELSEN PARK
FAIRLANDS PARK
STONEPOINTE WY
DIAVILA AV
ALEXANDER WY
CRISFIELD LN

SEE 243 MAP
SEE 694 MAP
SEE 715 MAP
A
B
C
D
E
1
2
3
4
5
6
7
DOOLAN
RD
DOOLAN
RD
CREEK
COTTONWOOD
COLLIER CANYON RD
CANYON
COLLIER
RD
CANYON
COLLIER
LAS POSITAS COLLEGE
LIVERMORE
TRIAD DR
PKWY
N CANYONS
CONSTITUTION DR
INDEPENDENCE DR
COLLIER
CANYON RD
2600
1400
COLLIER CANYON CT
580
LAS
BLVD
KITTY HAWK RD
NISSEN DR
EARHART WY
ARMSTRONG ST
LINDBERGH AV
KITTY HAWK RD
ARROYO
PARK & RIDE
AIRWAY
LAS POSITAS GOLF COURSE
CLUBHOUSE DR
TERMINAL CIR
AIRWAY
E
AIRWAY BLVD
200
LIVERMORE MUNICIPAL AIRPORT
RUTAN DR
W JACK LONDON BLVD
KITTY HAWK RD
RICKENBACKER CIR
RICKENBACKER PL
RUTAN CT
BOEING CT
WRIGHT BROTHERS AV
ZEPPELIN DR
E JACK LONDON BLVD
SHASTA ST
LOGAN ST
TRINITY CIR
TOIYABE CT
TAMALPAIS AV
GARDEN COM
TANAGER WY
YELLOWSTONE WY
LN
DR
TETON CT
YOSEMITE PL
CARLSBAD CT
EVERGLADES DR
OLYMPIC WY
SWAN PL
HAGEMANN LN
JUNCO AV
GULL WY
FINCH WY
RD
CEDAR DR
300
YOSEMITE AV
CASCADE AV
SWAN EGRET RD
CURLEW
TANAGER
SWALLOW
TEAL CT
SWALLOW CT
KINGLET RD
STARLING AV
HEMLOCK CT
MAYTEN DR
BUCKEYE
THRASHER AV
PELICAN CT
OLIVINA AV
SUTTER ST
SADDLEBACK CIR
SPLITRAIL CT
STETSON WY
CORRAL CT
MONTECITO CIR
COLUSA WY
MENDOCINO RD
DEL NORTE
MODOC CT
HUMBOLDT
ALAMEDA WY
DR
HENRY PARK
HANOVER ST
COVINGTON WY
HUNTINGTON WY
BETHAL PL
TIFFIN ST
WILTON
SAYBROOK
YORK WY
RD
ARLINGTON RD
HANOVER
ASBURY
KENT CT
SHELBURNE
BRISTOL
SALEM CT
CHASE CT
MURRIETA
DOVER WY
CAROLINE CT
BROOKFIELD DR
BRIGHTON
400
BLVD
TROY ST
LAKEHURST RD
NORFOLK
WY
500
ZERMATT ST
ROMA CT
ROMA ST
LUCERNE
TURINO CT
RAVENNA ST
PLACENZA ST
SANDPIPER
FIRENZA ST
DR
1500
1300
1600
1100
HA

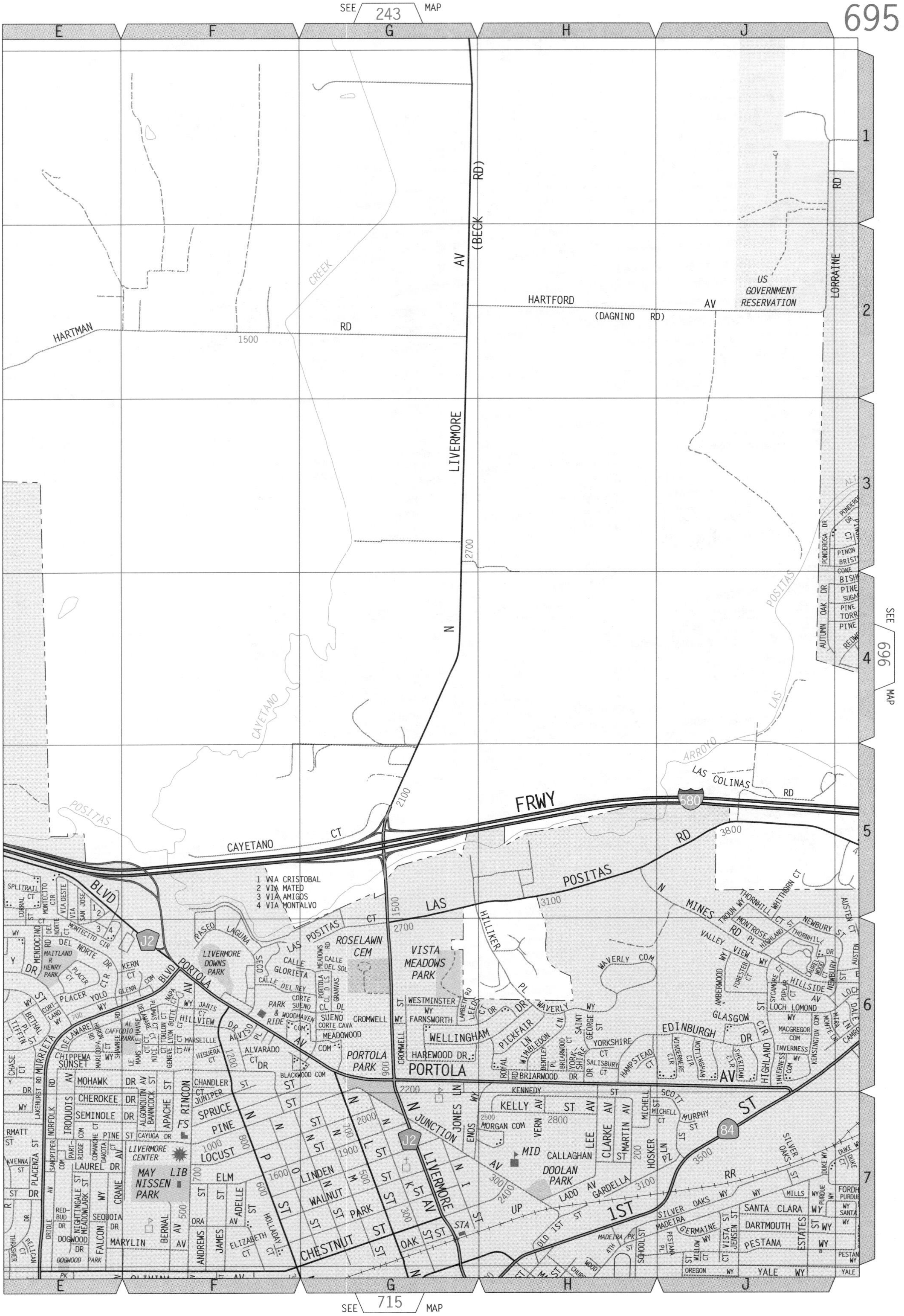
SEE 243 MAP
E
F
G
H
J
1
2
3
4
5
6
7
HARTMAN RD
1500
CREEK
LIVERMORE AV (BECK RD)
HARTFORD AV (DAGNINO RD)
US GOVERNMENT RESERVATION
LORRAINE RD
2700
N LIVERMORE AV
CAYETANO
POSITAS
ARROYO LAS POSITAS
LAS COLINAS RD
FRWY
580
CAYETANO CT
2100
3800
LAS POSITAS RD
3100
1 VIA CRISTOBAL
2 VIA MATED
3 VIA AMIGOS
4 VIA MONTALVO
BLVD
J2
PORTOLA BLVD
LIVERMORE DOWNS PARK
ROSELAWN CEM
VISTA MEADOWS PARK
HILLIKER PL
WAVERLY COM
N MINES RD
VALLEY VIEW WY
PARK & RIDE
WESTMINSTER WY
FARNSWORTH
WELLINGHAM DR
HAREWOOD DR
PORTOLA PARK
PORTOLA AV
EDINBURGH DR
GLASGOW
HIGHLAND
MURRIETA
PLACER
DELAWARE
ALVARADO
MOHAWK DR
CHEROKEE DR
SEMINOLE DR
PINE ST
LIVERMORE CENTER
MAY NISSEN PARK
LIB
SPRUCE
LOCUST
ELM
LINDEN
WALNUT
CHESTNUT ST
JUNCTION
KELLY ST
MID
CALLAGHAN
DOOLAN PARK
LADD AV
GARDELLA
1ST ST
SCOTT
MURPHY ST
84
SILVER OAKS WY
SANTA CLARA WY
DARTMOUTH WY
PESTANA
ESTATES
YALE WY
OREGON
MARYLIN AV
OLIVINA AV
SEE 696 MAP
SEE 715 MAP

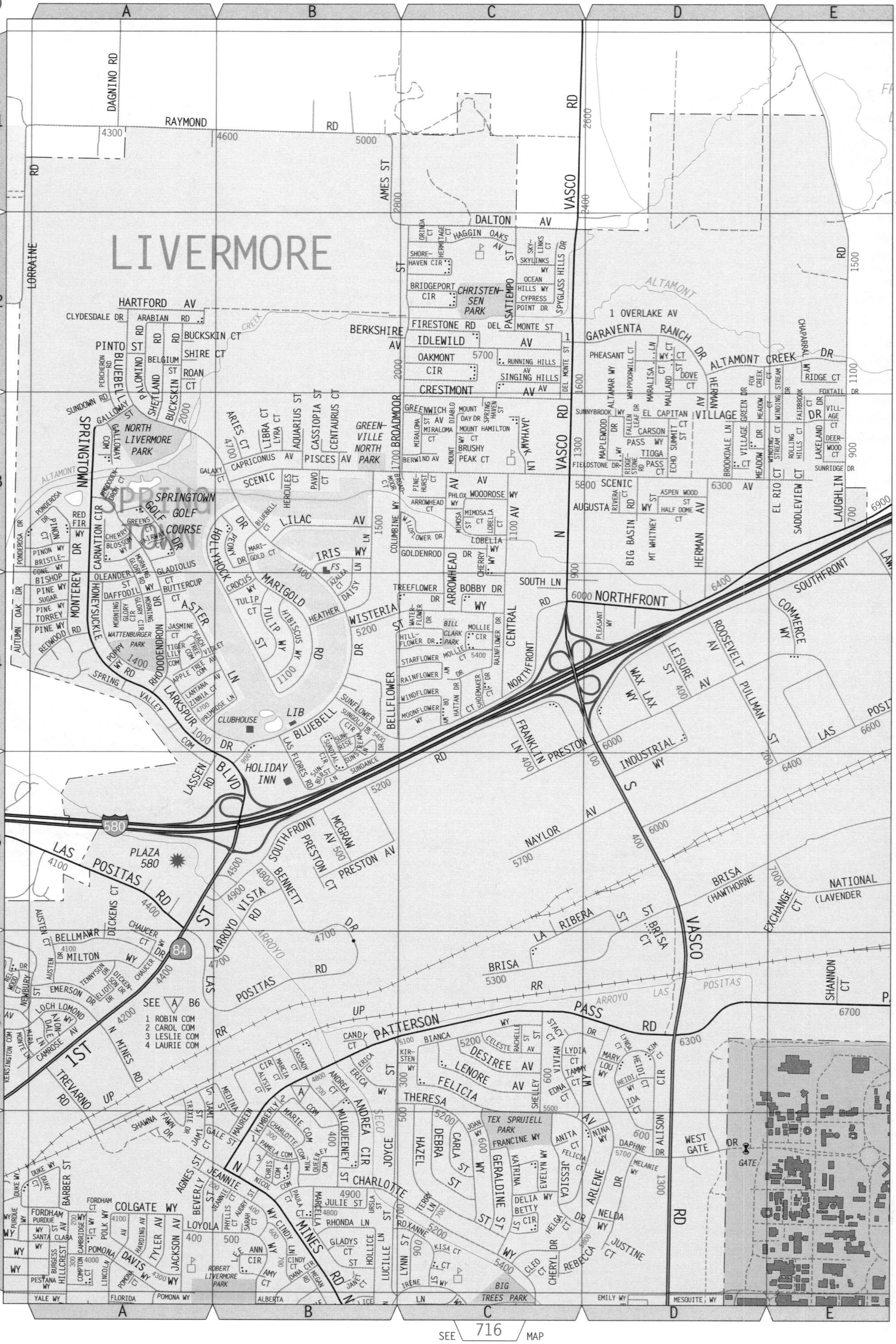
A
B
C
D
E
1
2
3
4
5
6
7
LIVERMORE
RAYMOND RD
DAGNINO RD
LORRAINE RD
VASCO RD
AMES ST
DALTON AV
HARTFORD AV
CLYDESDALE DR
ARABIAN RD
BUCKSKIN CT
PINTO ST
BLUEBELL
PALOMINO RD
SHETLAND
BELGIUM ST
SHIRE CT
ROAN CT
BUCKSKIN
PERCHERON RD
SUNDOWN RD
GALLOWAY
SPRINGTOWN
NORTH LIVERMORE PARK
SPRINGTOWN GOLF COURSE
ALTAMONT CREEK
ARIES CT
LIBRA CT
LYRA CT
AQUARIUS ST
CASSIOPIA ST
CENTAURUS CT
CAPRICONUS AV
PISCES AV
PAVO CT
HERCULES CT
GALAXY CT
SCENIC AV
LILAC AV
IRIS WY
HOLLYHOCK
MARIGOLD
TULIP
HIBISCUS WY
HEATHER
WISTERIA DR
GREENVILLE NORTH PARK
BROADMOOR ST
BERKSHIRE AV
IDLEWILD AV
OAKMONT CIR
CRESTMONT AV
FIRESTONE RD
DEL MONTE ST
BRIDGEPORT CIR
CHRISTENSEN PARK
PASATIEMPO
HAGGIN OAKS AV
SHOREHAVEN CIR
ORINDA CT
HERMITAGE CT
SKYLINKS
SPYGLASS HILLS DR
OCEAN HILLS WY
CYPRESS POINT DR
RUNNING HILLS
SINGING HILLS
GREENWICH
MIRALOMA
MOUNT DIABLO
MOUNT HAMILTON
BRUSHY PEAK CT
JAYHAWK LN
BERWIND AV
PHLOX
WOODROSE WY
ARROWHEAD
MIMOSA CT
LOBELIA
GOLDENROD DR
TREEFLOWER DR
BOBBY DR
BILL CLARK PARK
MOLLIE CIR
STARFLOWER
RAINFLOWER
WINDFLOWER
MOONFLOWER
BELLFLOWER
CENTRAL
NORTHFRONT RD
SOUTH LN
GARAVENTA RANCH RD
1 OVERLAKE AV
ALTAMONT CREEK DR
PHEASANT CT
HERMAN AV
VILLAGE
EL CAPITAN
CARSON PASS WY
TIOGA PASS
ECHO SUMMIT CT
FIELDSTONE DR
SUNNYBROOK WY
SCENIC AV
AUGUSTA
RIVERA
ASPEN WOOD
HALF DOME CT
BIG BASIN
MT WHITNEY
SADDLEVIEW CT
EL RIO CT
LAUGHLIN RD
CHAPARRAL
RIDGE CT
FOXTAIL DR
SUNRIDGE DR
LAKELAND
SOUTHFRONT
COMMERCE WY
ROOSEVELT AV
LEISURE ST
WAX LAX WY
PULLMAN ST
LAS POSITAS
INDUSTRIAL WY
PRESTON
FRANKLIN LN
NAYLOR AV
BRISA ST
LA RIBERA
NATIONAL (LAVENDER)
BRISA (HAWTHORNE)
EXCHANGE CT
SHANNON CT
580
PLAZA 580
LAS POSITAS RD
SOUTHFRONT RD
MCGRAW AV
PRESTON AV
BENNETT
ARROYO VISTA
ARROYO
LAS POSITAS RD
1ST ST
84
HOLIDAY INN
CLUBHOUSE
LIB
LASSEN RD
BLVD
LARKSPUR
SPRING VALLEY COM
LAS FLORES RD
SUNFLOWER
SUNDANCE
BELLMAWR
MILTON WY
DICKENS CT
CHAUCER
EMERSON DR
LOCH LOMOND
CAMROSE AV
N MINES RD
TREVARNO RD
UP RR
PATTERSON PASS RD
SEE A B6
1 ROBIN COM
2 CAROL COM
3 LESLIE COM
4 LAURIE COM
CANDY CT
BIANCA
DESIREE AV
LENORE
FELICIA AV
THERESA
TEX SPRUELL PARK
FRANCINE WY
ANDREA CIR
MULQUEENEY ST
CHARLOTTE
JOYCE
HAZEL
DEBRA
CARLA ST
GERALDINE ST
JESSICA
ARLENE
NELDA WY
JUSTINE CT
REBECCA CT
CHERYL DR
ALISON CIR
WEST GATE DR
GATE
DAPHNE
COLGATE WY
AGNES ST
JEANNIE
BEVERLY
LOYOLA
JACKSON AV
TYLER AV
DAVIS
POMONA
ROBERT LIVERMORE PARK
BIG TREES PARK
YALE WY
FLORIDA
POMONA WY
ALBERTA
EMILY WY
MESQUITE WY
MINES RD

SEE 695 MAP
SEE 716 MAP

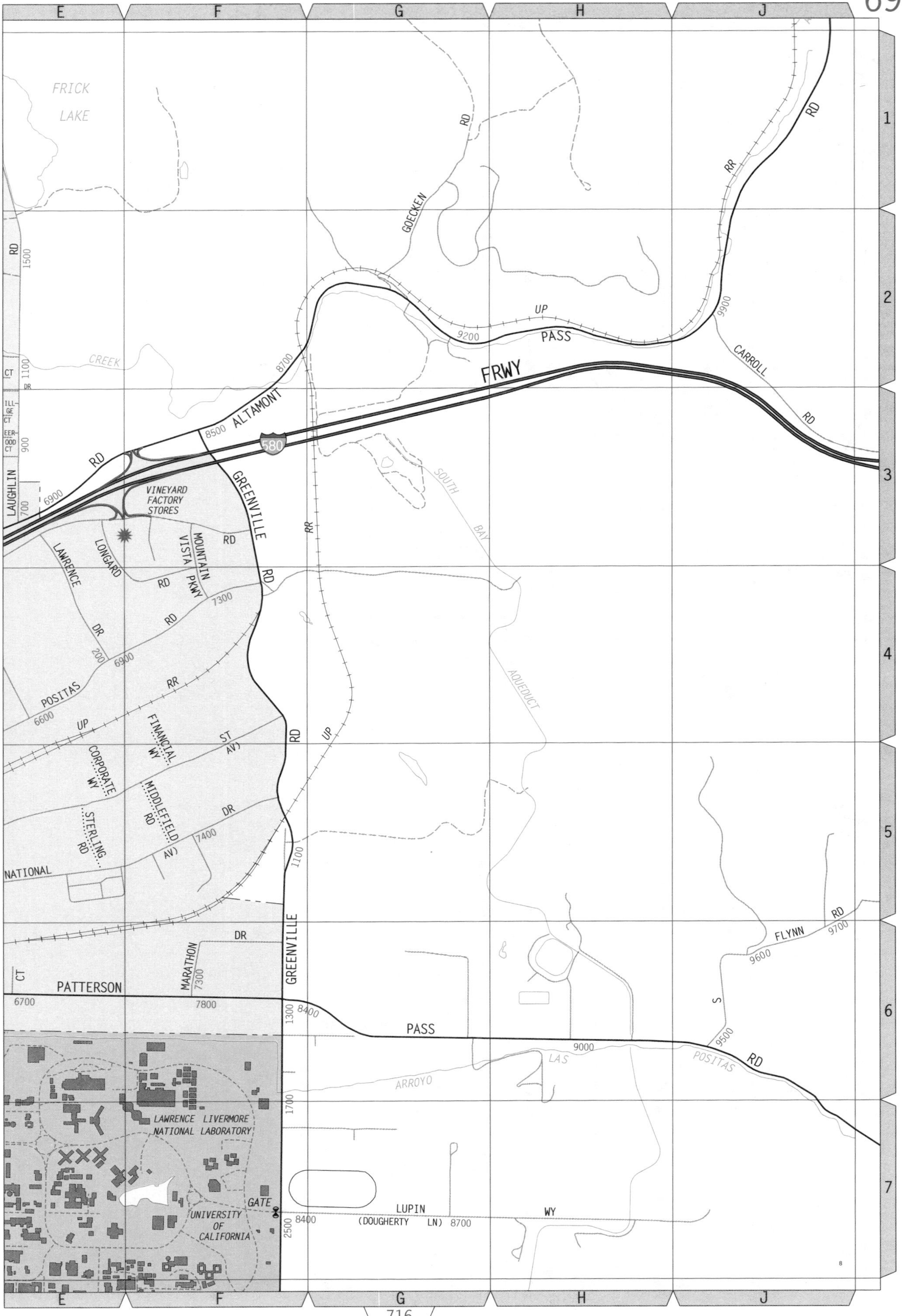
E
F
G
H
J
1
2
3
4
5
6
7
FRICK
LAKE
RD
GOECKEN
RD
RR
RD
1500
UP
9200
PASS
9900
CARROLL
RD
CREEK
1100
CT
DR
8700
FRWY
ALTAMONT
8500
580
RD
LAUGHLIN
900
700
6900
VINEYARD
FACTORY
STORES
GREENVILLE
RD
SOUTH
BAY
RR
LAWRENCE
LONGARD
MOUNTAIN
VISTA
PKWY
RD
RD
7300
RD
DR
200
6900
POSITAS
6600
RR
UP
FINANCIAL
WY
ST
AV)
RD
UP
AQUEDUCT
CORPORATE
WY
MIDDLEFIELD
RD
DR
STERLING
RD
7400
AV)
NATIONAL
1100
DR
MARATHON
7300
GREENVILLE
CT
PATTERSON
6700
7800
1300
8400
PASS
9000
LAS
POSITAS
ARROYO
RD
9500
S
FLYNN
RD
9600
9700
1700
LAWRENCE LIVERMORE
NATIONAL LABORATORY
GATE
UNIVERSITY
OF
CALIFORNIA
2500
8400
LUPIN
(DOUGHERTY
LN)
8700
WY
8

SEE 716 MAP

SEE 686 MAP

A B C D E

1
2
3
4
5
6
7

SEE 243 MAP

8

A B C D E

SEE 726 MAP

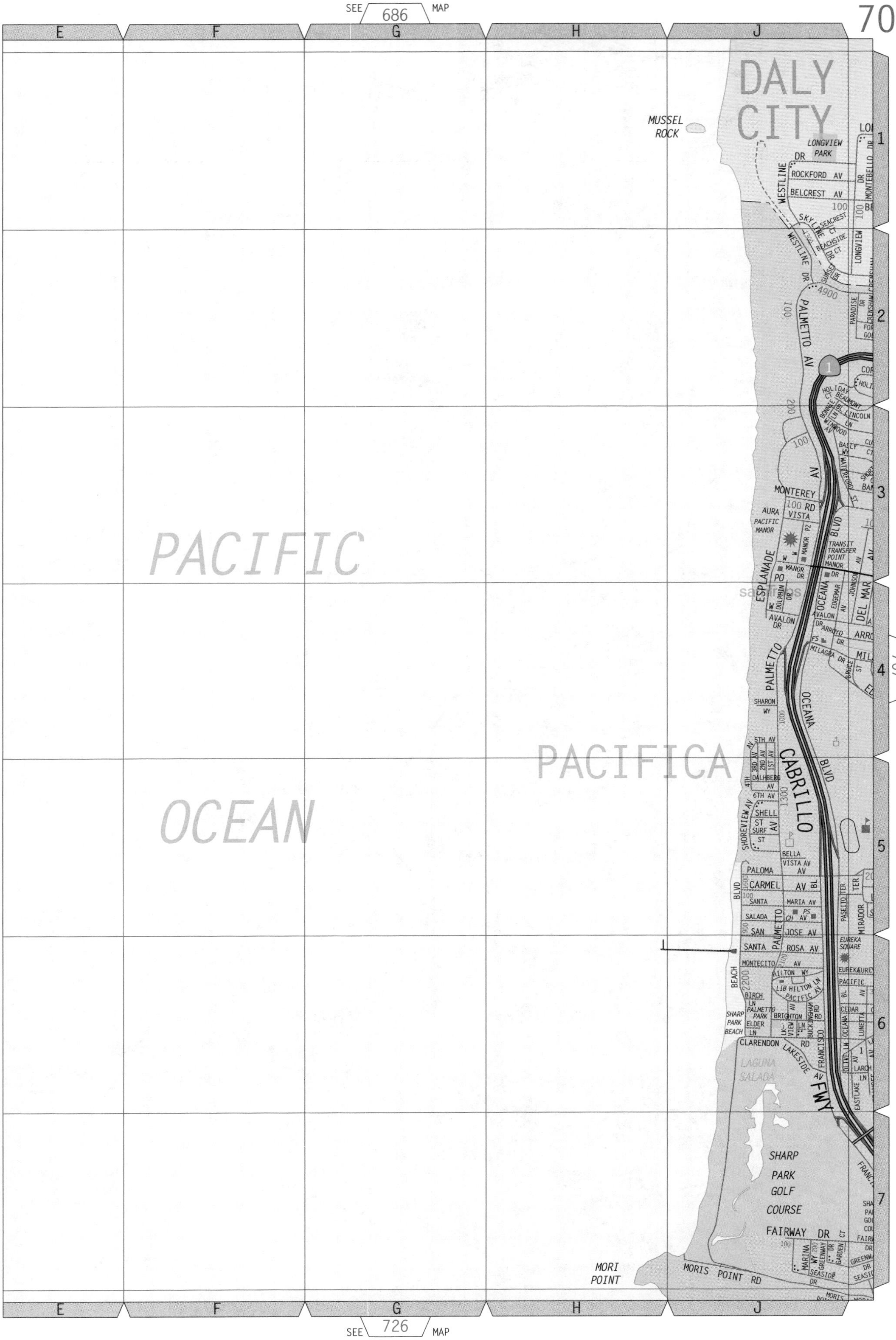
SEE 686 MAP
E
F
G
H
J
1
2
3
4
5
6
7
DALY CITY
MUSSEL ROCK
LONGVIEW PARK
DR
WESTLINE
ROCKFORD AV
BELCREST AV
MONTEBELLO DR
SKYLINE
SEACREST
BEACHSIDE CT
WESTLINE DR
SUNSET DR
LONGVIEW
4900
PARADISE DR
CRENSHAW
PALMETTO AV
HOLIDAY CT
BEAUMONT BL
BONNIE
LINCOLN LN
WINWOOD
BALLY WY
WATERFORD
MONTEREY RD
VISTA
AURA
PACIFIC MANOR
TRANSIT TRANSFER POINT
MANOR DR
ESPLANADE
PO
DOLPHIN DR
OCEANA
EDGEMAR
JOHNSON
DEL MAR
AVALON DR
ARROYO DR
MILAGRA DR
BRUCE ST
PACIFIC
PACIFICA
OCEAN
SEE 707 MAP
SHARON WY
OCEANA BLVD
CABRILLO
5TH AV
3RD AV
2ND AV
1ST AV
4TH AV
DALHBERG AV
6TH AV
SHOREVIEW AV
SHELL ST
SURF ST
BELLA VISTA AV
PALOMA AV
CARMEL AV
SANTA MARIA AV
SALADA AV
SAN JOSE AV
SANTA ROSA AV
BLVD
PASEITO TER
MIRADOR TER
EUREKA SQUARE
MONTECITO AV
HILTON WY
LIB HILTON LN
PACIFIC AV
BEACH BLVD
BIRCH LN
PALMETTO PARK
BRIGHTON RD
BUCKINGHAM RD
SHARP PARK BEACH
ELDER LN
LK VIEW LN
CLARENDON RD
LAKESIDE AV
FRANCISCO
CEDAR
LUNETTA
OLIVE LN
LARCH LN
EASTLAKE
LAGUNA SALADA
FWY
SHARP PARK GOLF COURSE
FAIRWAY DR
MARINA WY
GREENWAY DR
GARDEN CT
SEASIDE DR
MORI POINT
MORIS POINT RD
SEE 726 MAP

SEE 687 MAP

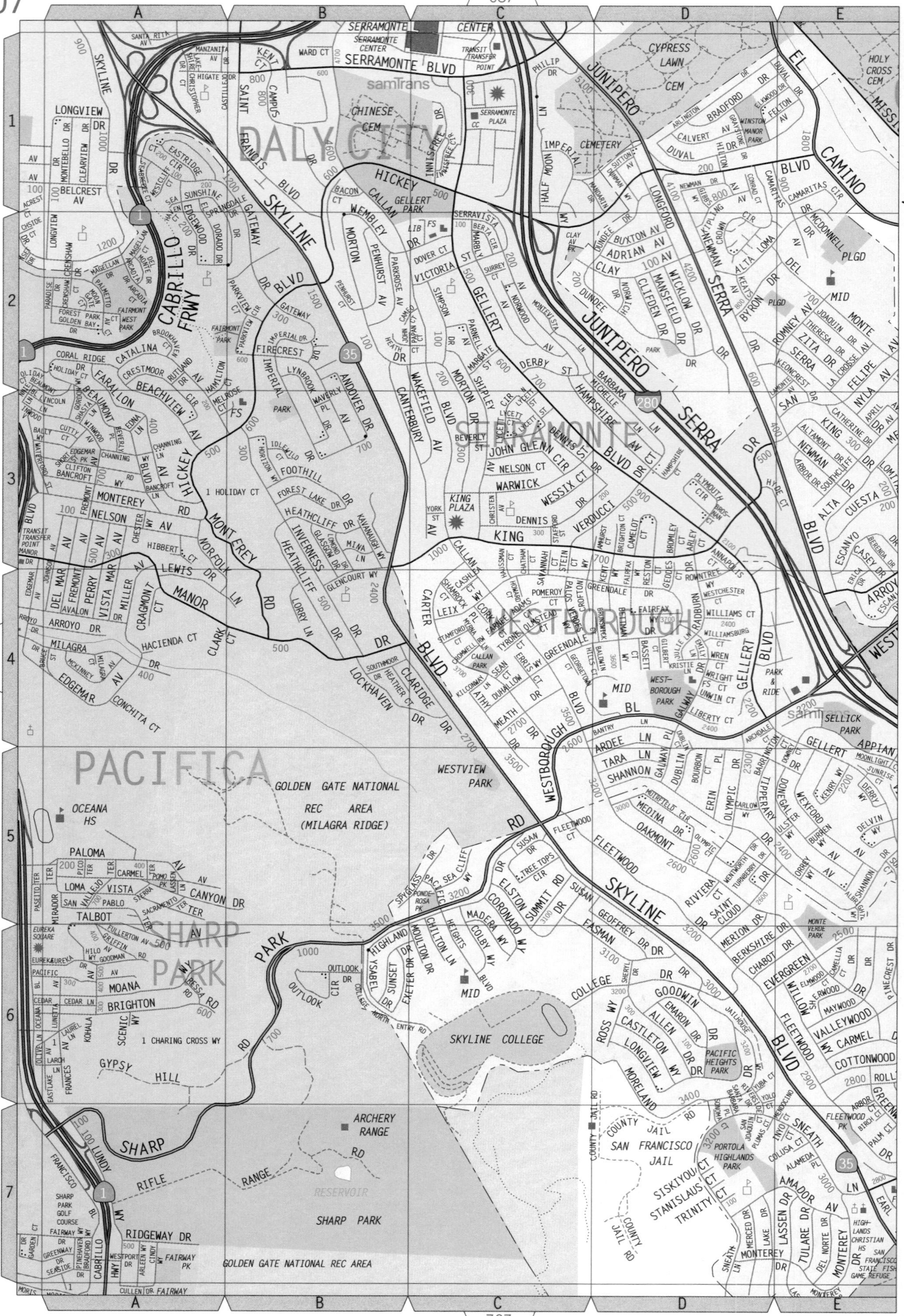

DALY CITY
SERRAMONTE
WESTBOROUGH
PACIFICA
SHARP PARK
SERRAMONTE CENTER
SERRAMONTE BLVD
CHINESE CEM
CYPRESS LAWN CEM
HOLY CROSS CEM
CEMETERY
JUNIPERO SERRA BLVD
EL CAMINO
SKYLINE BLVD
CABRILLO FRWY
HICKEY BLVD
GELLERT BLVD
KING DR
WESTBOROUGH BLVD
SHARP PARK RD
MONTEREY RD
MANOR DR
IMPERIAL PARK
GELLERT PARK
KING PLAZA
WEST-BOROUGH PARK
SELLICK PARK
WESTVIEW PARK
GOLDEN GATE NATIONAL REC AREA (MILAGRA RIDGE)
OCEANA HS
SKYLINE COLLEGE
COUNTY JAIL
SAN FRANCISCO JAIL
PORTOLA HIGHLANDS PARK
PACIFIC HEIGHTS PARK
MONTE VERDE PARK
ARCHERY RANGE
RIFLE RANGE RD
RESERVOIR
SHARP PARK
SHARP PARK GOLF COURSE
GOLDEN GATE NATIONAL REC AREA
HIGHLANDS CHRISTIAN HS
SAN FRANCISCO STATE FISH GAME REFUGE
GYPSY HILL
1 HOLIDAY CT
1 CHARING CROSS WY

SEE 706 MAP

SEE 727 MAP

SEE 687 MAP

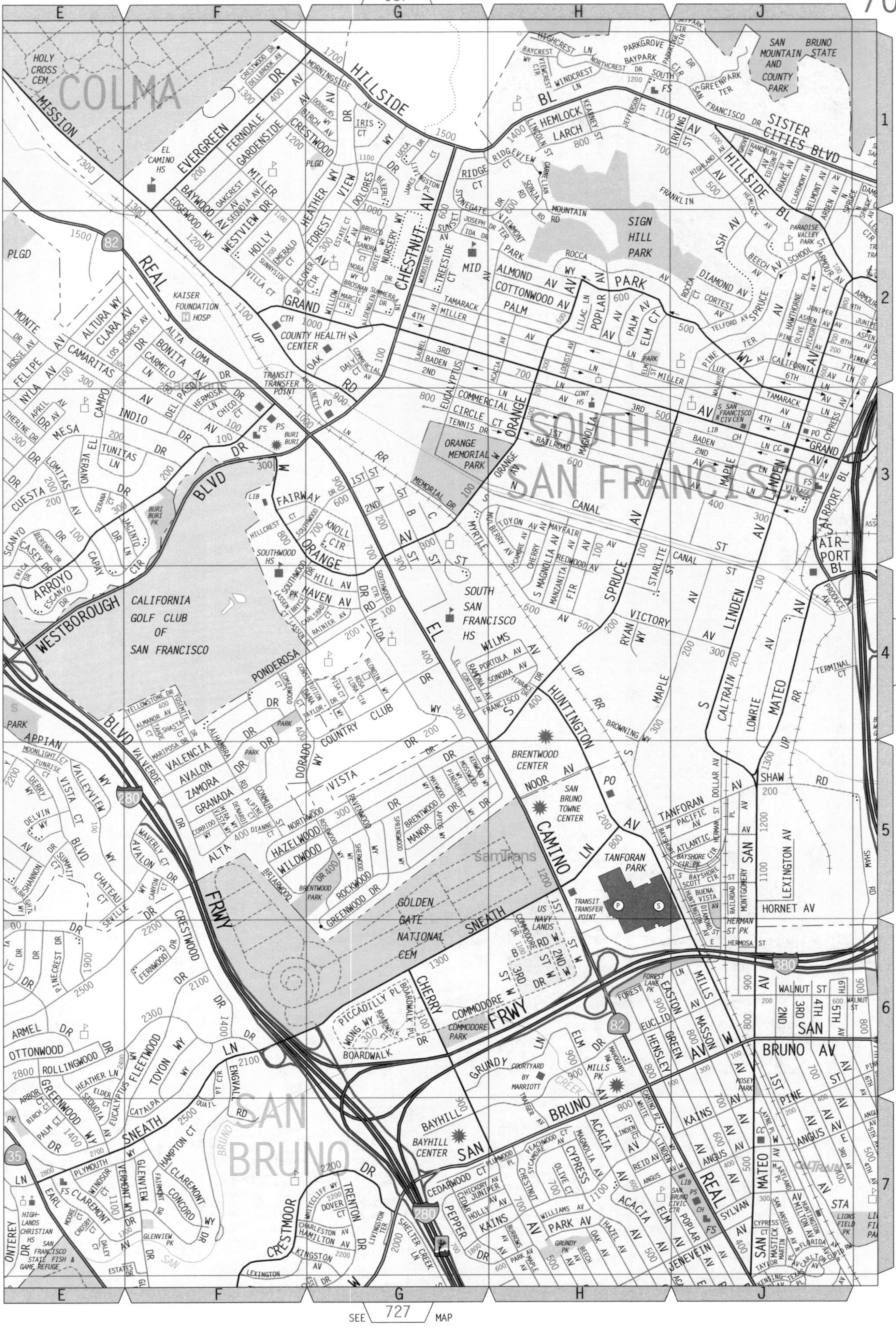
COLMA
HOLY CROSS CEM
SAN BRUNO MOUNTAIN STATE AND COUNTY PARK
SIGN HILL PARK
SOUTH SAN FRANCISCO
KAISER FOUNDATION HOSP
COUNTY HEALTH CENTER
TRANSIT TRANSFER POINT
BURI BURI
ORANGE MEMORIAL PARK
SOUTH SAN FRANCISCO HS
SOUTHWOOD HS
EL CAMINO HS
CALIFORNIA GOLF CLUB OF SAN FRANCISCO
BRENTWOOD CENTER
SAN BRUNO TOWNE CENTER
TANFORAN PARK
GOLDEN GATE NATIONAL CEM
US NAVY LANDS
COMMODORE PARK
COURTYARD BY MARRIOTT
MILLS PK
BAYHILL CENTER
SAN BRUNO
SAN BRUNO CIVIC CTR
HIGHLANDS CHRISTIAN HS
SAN FRANCISCO STATE FISH & GAME REFUGE
LIONS FIELD PK
HILLSIDE BL
SISTER CITIES BLVD
MISSION
GRAND AV
EL CAMINO REAL
WESTBOROUGH BLVD
SKYLINE BLVD
JUNIPERO SERRA FRWY
AIRPORT BL
LINDEN AV
SPRUCE AV
CHESTNUT AV
HUNTINGTON AV
SAN MATEO AV
SAN BRUNO AV
SNEATH LN
CRESTMOOR DR
CALTRAIN
SOUTHERN PACIFIC RR

SEE 708 MAP
SEE 727 MAP

SEE 688 MAP
SEE 707 MAP
SEE 728 MAP
A
B
C
D
E
1
2
3
4
5
6
7
SAN BRUNO MOUNTAIN STATE AND COUNTY PARK
SOUTH SAN FRANCISCO DR
SISTER CITIES BLVD
BAYSHORE BLVD
BAYSHORE FRWY
SHORELINE CT
OYSTER COVE MARINA
OYSTER POINT
OYSTER POINT MARINA
OYSTER POINT BLVD
OYSTER POINT PARK
GULL RD
MARINA BLVD
SOUTH SAN FRANCISCO
SAN
RANDOLPH AV
AIRPORT BLVD
TRANSIT TRANSFER POINT
samTrans
LINDEN AV
DUBUQUE AV
CALTRAIN WY
THE GATEWAY
GATEWAY BLVD
ECCLES AV
ROZZI PL
CARLTON CT
FORBES BLVD
KAUFFMANN CT
POINT SAN BRUNO BLVD
POINT SAN BRUNO PARK
GRANDVIEW DR
INDUSTRIAL WY
STA
CALTRAIN
EMBASSY SUITES SOUTH SAN FRANCISCO
ROEBLING RD
UP RR
CABOT RD
CABOT CT
E GRAND AV
ALLERTON AV
HARBOR WY
POINT SAN BRUNO
SYLVESTER RD
BAKER ST
ASSOCIATED RD
W HARRIS AV
HARRIS CT
E HARRIS AV
MITCHELL AV
FS
LAWRENCE AV
LITTLEFIELD AV
KIMBALL WY
SWIFT AV
MICHELLE CT
HASKINS WY
E JAMIE CT
RAMADA INN SAN FRANCISCO
WONDERCOLOR LN
HOLIDAY INN SAN FRANCISCO INTERNATIONAL AIRPORT NORTH
WATTIS WY
UTAH AV
COLMA CREEK SERVICE RD
COREY WY
SAN BRUNO CANAL
BEST WESTERN GROSVENOR HOTEL
MARCO WY
AIRPORT BLVD
BELLE AIR RD
BEACON ST
N ACCESS RD
SHAW RD
380
COAST GUARD RD
FLYING TIGERS
SF COM COLLEGE AIRPORT SCHOOL
UNITED MAINTENANCE
GATE
SEAPLANE HARBOR
USCG AIR STATION
SAN FRANCISCO INTERNATIONAL AIRPORT (SEE TABLE OF CONTENTS FOR AIRPORT MAP)
SAN BRUNO AV
7TH & WALNUT PARK
WALNUT ST
5TH AV
6TH AV
ECONOMY PARKING
7TH AV PARK
MCDONNELL RD
AMERICAN HANGAR
DELTA CARGO
MAIL FACILITY
BUTLER AVIATION
AIRPORT ENG & MAINT
LIONS FIELD PARK
LIONS FIELD PK
101

SEE 688 MAP
E
F
G
H
J
1
2
3
4
5
6
7
FRANCISCO
BAY
SEE 243 MAP
SEE 728 MAP

SEE 691 MAP

SEE 243 MAP

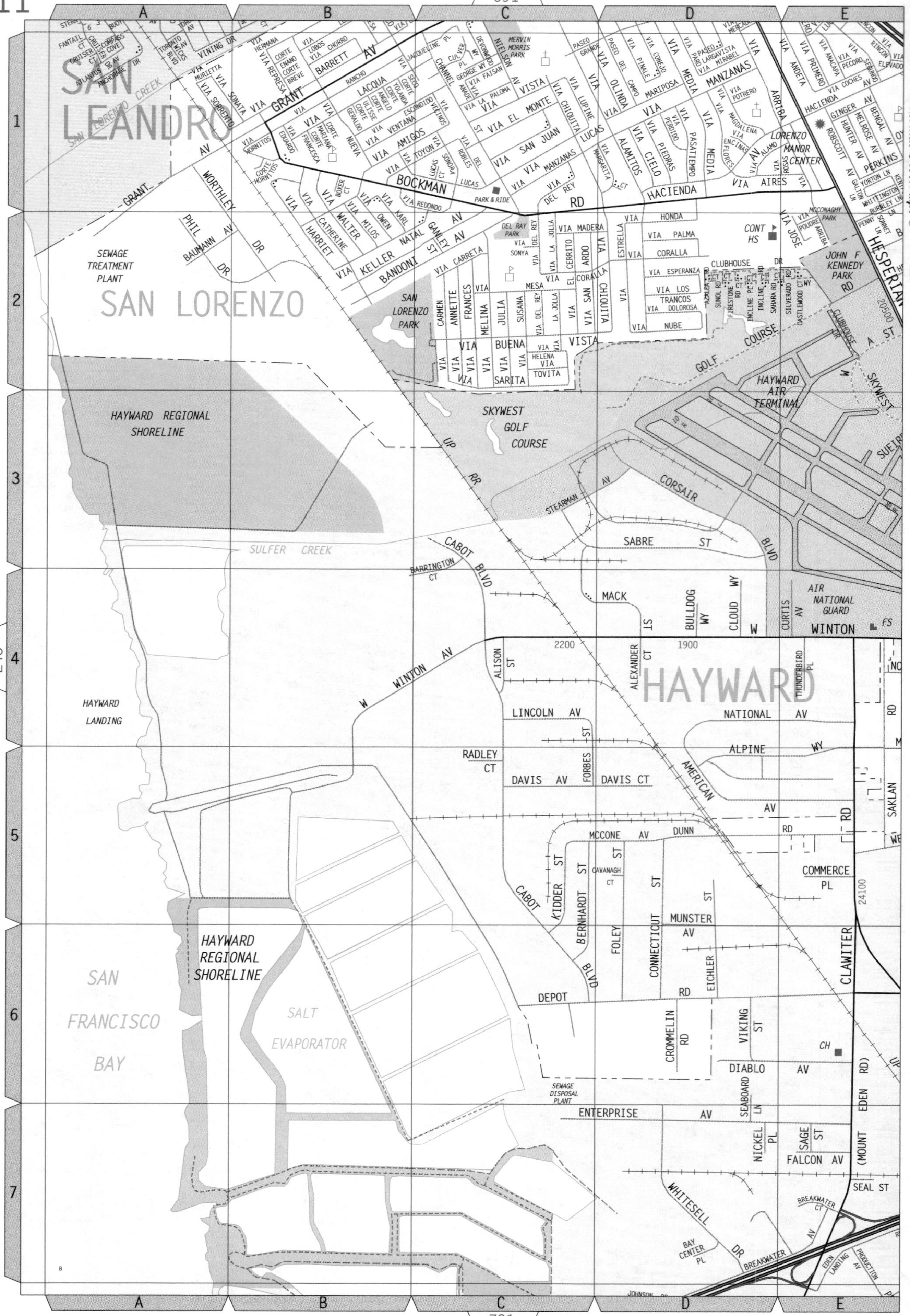
SAN LEANDRO
SAN LORENZO
HAYWARD
SEWAGE TREATMENT PLANT
SAN LORENZO PARK
HAYWARD REGIONAL SHORELINE
SKYWEST GOLF COURSE
HAYWARD AIR TERMINAL
JOHN F KENNEDY PARK
AIR NATIONAL GUARD
SULFER CREEK
SAN LORENZO CREEK
HAYWARD LANDING
SAN FRANCISCO BAY
SALT EVAPORATOR
SEWAGE DISPOSAL PLANT
MERVIN MORRIS PARK
DEL RAY PARK
LORENZO MANOR CENTER
CONT HS
PARK & RIDE
GRANT AV
BOCKMAN RD
HACIENDA
HESPERIAN
WORTHLEY DR
BAUMANN AV
KELLER
BANDONI ST
GANLEY AV
VIA BUENA VISTA
GOLF COURSE
CLUBHOUSE DR
CORSAIR BLVD
SABRE ST
CABOT BLVD
BARRINGTON CT
MACK ST
BULLDOG WY
CLOUD WY
CURTIS AV
W WINTON AV
ALISON ST
ALEXANDER CT
THUNDERBIRD PL
LINCOLN AV
NATIONAL AV
ALPINE WY
RADLEY CT
DAVIS AV
FORBES ST
DAVIS CT
AMERICAN
MCCONE AV
DUNN RD
KIDDER ST
BERNHARDT ST
CAVANAGH CT
FOLEY ST
CONNECTICUT ST
MUNSTER AV
EICHLER ST
COMMERCE PL
SAKLAN RD
CLAWITER RD
DEPOT RD
CROMMELIN RD
VIKING ST
DIABLO AV
ENTERPRISE AV
SEABOARD LN
NICKEL PL
SAGE ST
FALCON AV
SEAL ST
(MOUNT EDEN RD)
WHITESELL DR
BAY CENTER PL
BREAKWATER AV
BREAKWATER CT
EDEN LANDING RD
PRODUCTION AV
UP RR
2200
1900
20500
24100
A
B
C
D
E
1
2
3
4
5
6
7

SEE 731 MAP

SEE 691 MAP

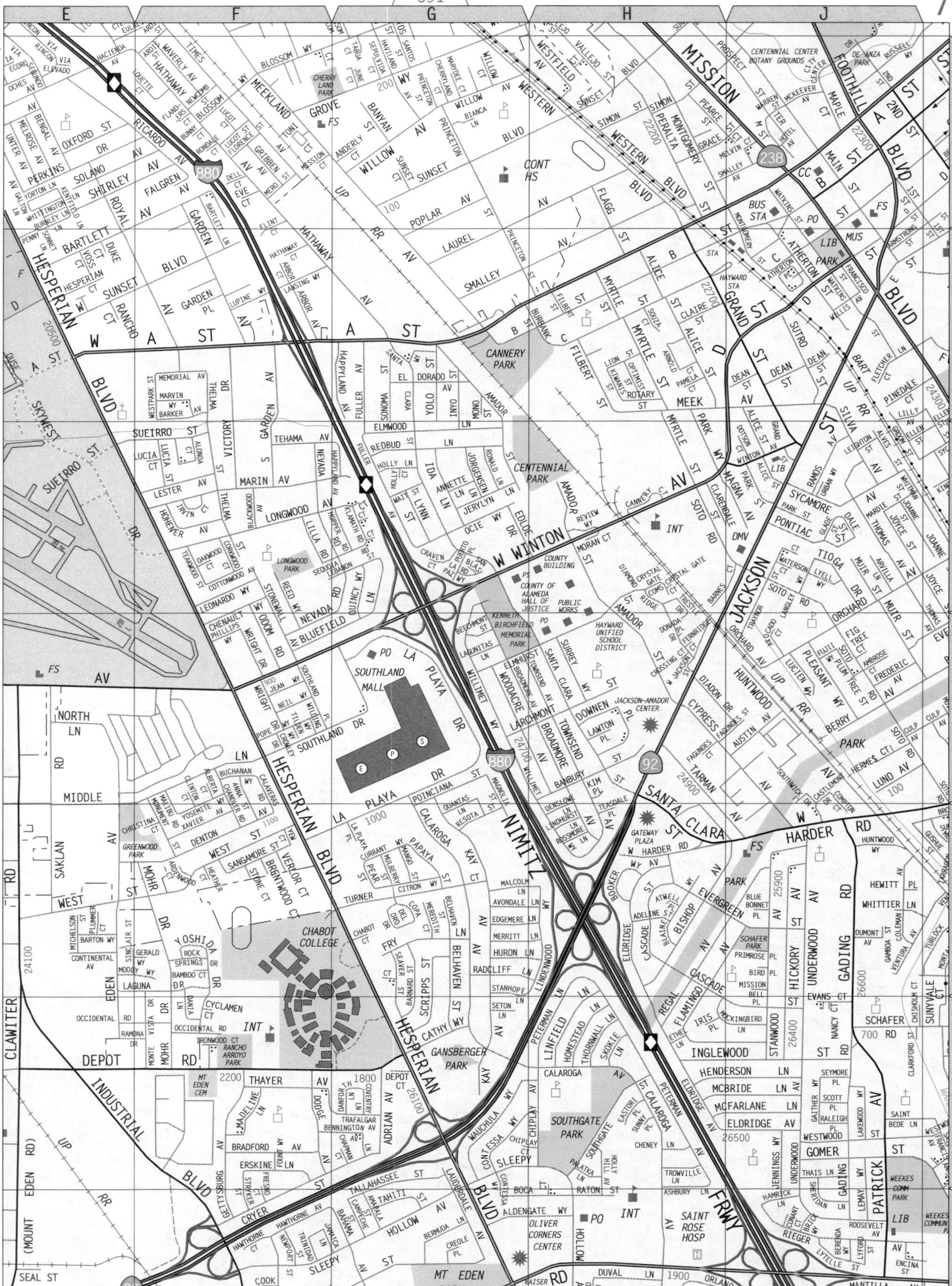
E
F
G
H
J
1
2
3
4
5
6
7
HESPERIAN BLVD
W A ST
MISSION BLVD
FOOTHILL BLVD
JACKSON ST
NIMITZ FRWY
W WINTON AV
SANTA CLARA ST
HARDER RD
W TENNYSON RD
INDUSTRIAL BLVD
INDUSTRIAL PKWY
CLAWITER RD
DEPOT RD
WESTERN BLVD
GROVE WY
SUNSET BLVD
ORCHARD AV
SKYWEST DR
SUEIRRO ST
CANNERY PARK
CENTENNIAL PARK
LONGWOOD PARK
SOUTHLAND MALL
CHABOT COLLEGE
GANSBERGER PARK
RANCHO ARROYO PARK
MT EDEN CEM
SOUTHGATE PARK
MT EDEN PARK
WEEKES COMM PARK
PALMA CEIA PARK
GREENWOOD PARK
CHERRY LAND PARK
LIB PARK
CONT HS
COUNTY BUILDING
COUNTY OF ALAMEDA HALL OF JUSTICE
PUBLIC WORKS
HAYWARD UNIFIED SCHOOL DISTRICT
KENNETH BIRCHFIELD MEMORIAL PARK
JACKSON-AMADOR CENTER
GATEWAY PLAZA
OLIVER CORNERS CENTER
SAINT ROSE HOSP
KAISER FOUNDATION HOSPITAL
HAYWARD STA
BUS STA
CENTENNIAL CENTER BOTANY GROUNDS
DE ANZA PARK
880
238
92

SEE 712 MAP

SEE 731 MAP

SEE 692 MAP

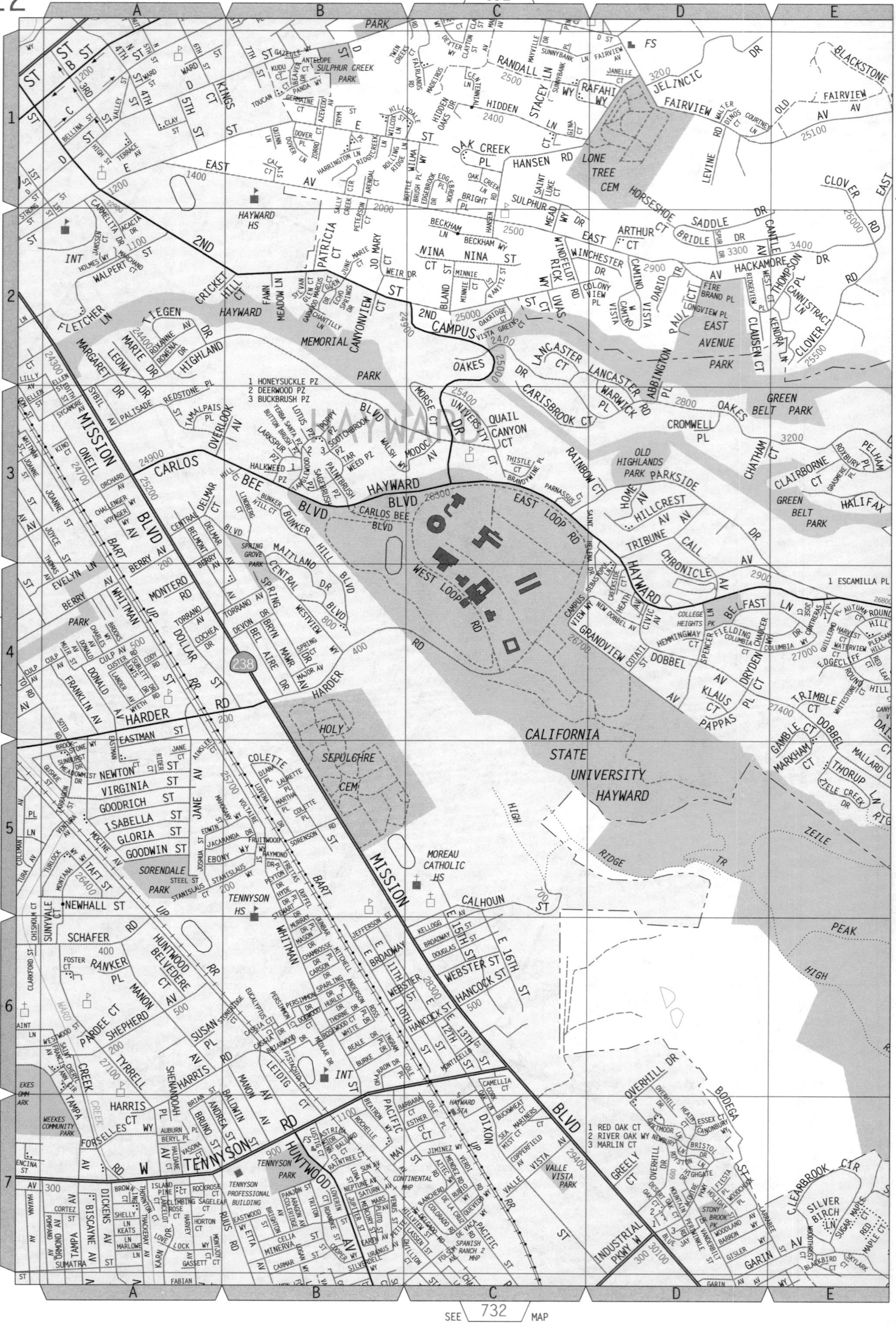

A
B
C
D
E
1
2
3
4
5
6
7
HAYWARD
CALIFORNIA STATE UNIVERSITY HAYWARD
MISSION BLVD
HAYWARD BLVD
CARLOS BEE BLVD
CAMPUS DR
2ND ST
EAST AV
HARDER RD
W TENNYSON RD
INDUSTRIAL PKWY W
HUNTWOOD AV
DIXON ST
JANE AV
WHITMAN ST
BART
UP RR
238
HAYWARD MEMORIAL PARK
EAST AVENUE PARK
GREEN BELT PARK
SULPHUR CREEK PARK
LONE TREE CEM
HOLY SEPULCHRE CEM
HAYWARD HS
TENNYSON HS
MOREAU CATHOLIC HS
TENNYSON PARK
SORENDALE PARK
WEEKES COMMUNITY PARK
VALLE VISTA PARK
SPRING GROVE PARK
TENNYSON PROFESSIONAL BUILDING
FS
INT
HAYWARD STA
SPANISH RANCH 2 MHP
CONTINENTAL MHP
1 HONEYSUCKLE PZ
2 DEERWOOD PZ
3 BUCKBRUSH PZ
1 ESCAMILLA PL
1 RED OAK CT
2 RIVER OAK WY
3 MARLIN CT
CALHOUN ST
HIGH RIDGE
ZEILE CREEK DR
OVERHILL DR
BODEGA
CLEARBROOK CIR
GARIN AV
FAIRVIEW AV
BLACKSTONE
JELINCIC DR
HACKAMORE
OAKES
HANSEN RD
RANDALL LN
HARRIS RD
SCHAFER RD
NEWHALL ST
SUSAN PL

SEE 711 MAP

SEE 732 MAP

SEE 692 MAP

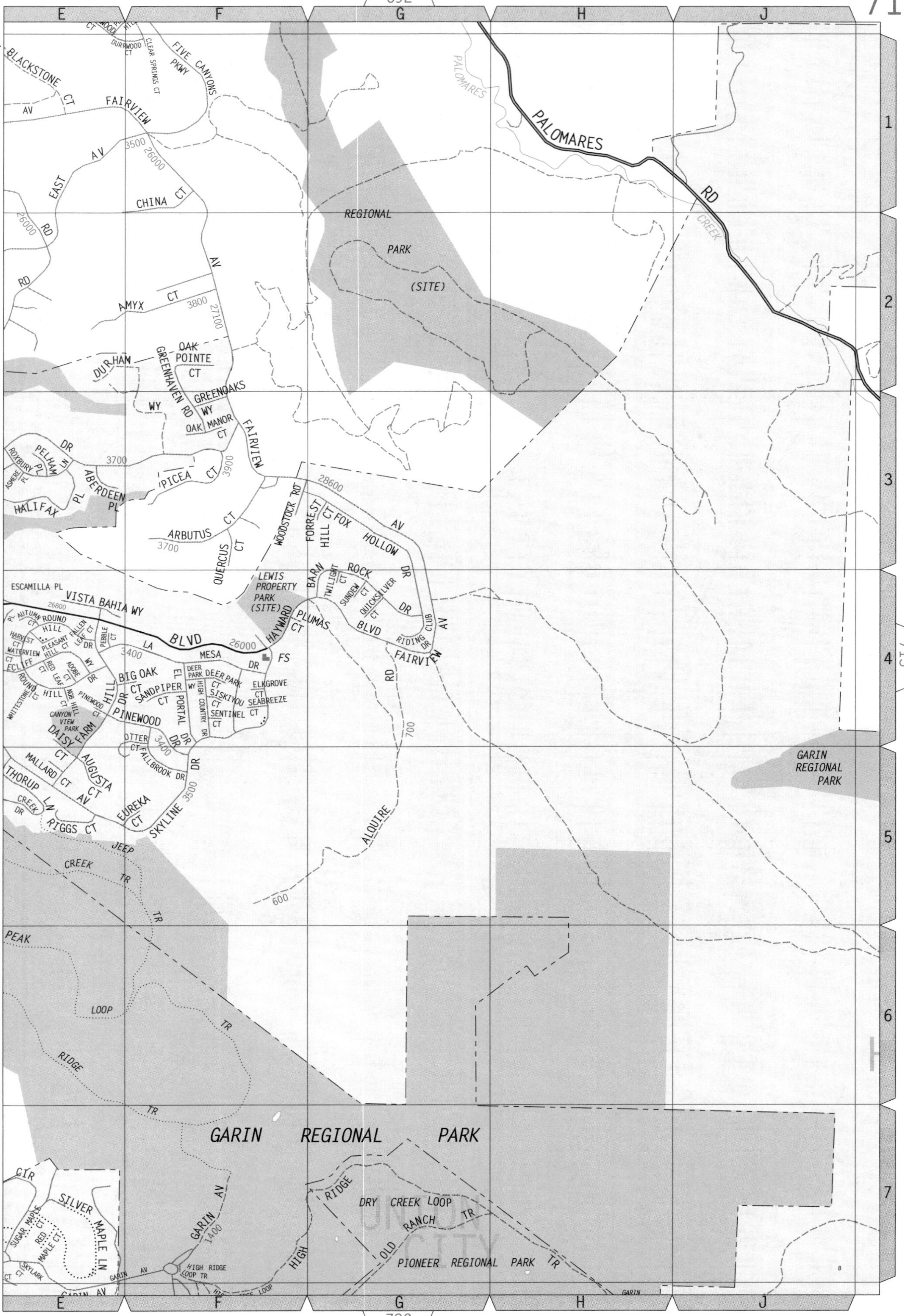

E
F
G
H
J
1
2
3
4
5
6
7
BLACKSTONE CT
FAIRVIEW AV
FIVE CANYONS PKWY
CLEAR SPRINGS CT
DURRWOOD CT
PALOMARES
PALOMARES RD
CREEK
EAST AV
3500
26000
CHINA CT
RD
REGIONAL PARK (SITE)
AMYX CT
3800
27100
OAK POINTE CT
DURHAM
GREENHAVEN RD
GREENOAKS WY
WY
OAK MANOR CT
FAIRVIEW
PELHAM PL
DR
LN
ROXBURY PL
ASMERE PL
3700
PICEA CT
3900
ABERDEEN PL
HALIFAX
PL
28600
WOODSTOCK RD
FORREST HILL CT
FOX HOLLOW DR
AV
ARBUTUS CT
3700
QUERCUS CT
ESCAMILLA PL
VISTA BAHIA WY
LEWIS PROPERTY PARK (SITE)
BARN
TWILIGHT CT
ROCK
SUNDEW CT
QUICKSILVER CT
DR
26800
AUTUMN
ROUND HILL
HARVEST CT
WATERVIEW
PLEASANT HILL CT
FALLEN LEAF CT
PEBBLE CT
BLVD
26000
HAYWARD BLVD
PLUMAS CT
RIDING CLUB AV
LA
3400
MESA DR
FS
FAIRVIEW
RD
BIG OAK CT
DEER PARK CT
ELKGROVE CT
SANDPIPER CT
EL PORTAL DR
HIGH COUNTRY DR
SISKIYOU CT
SEABREEZE CT
SENTINEL CT
WHITESTONE CT
NOB HILL
PINEWOOD CT
CANYON VIEW PARK
PINEWOOD DR
DAISY FARM CT
OTTER CT
3400
FALLBROOK DR
700
GARIN REGIONAL PARK
MALLARD CT
AUGUSTA CT
THORUP LN
CREEK DR
RIGGS CT
EUREKA CT
SKYLINE DR
3500
ALQUIRE RD
600
JEEP
CREEK TR
TR
PEAK
LOOP
TR
RIDGE
TR
GARIN REGIONAL PARK
CIR
SILVER MAPLE LN
SUGAR MAPLE CT
RED MAPLE CT
SKYLARK CT
GARIN AV
1400
HIGH RIDGE LOOP TR
RIDGE
DRY CREEK LOOP
RANCH TR
OLD
HIGH
PIONEER REGIONAL PARK
TR
UNION CITY
GARIN

SEE 713 MAP

MAP

SEE 732 MAP

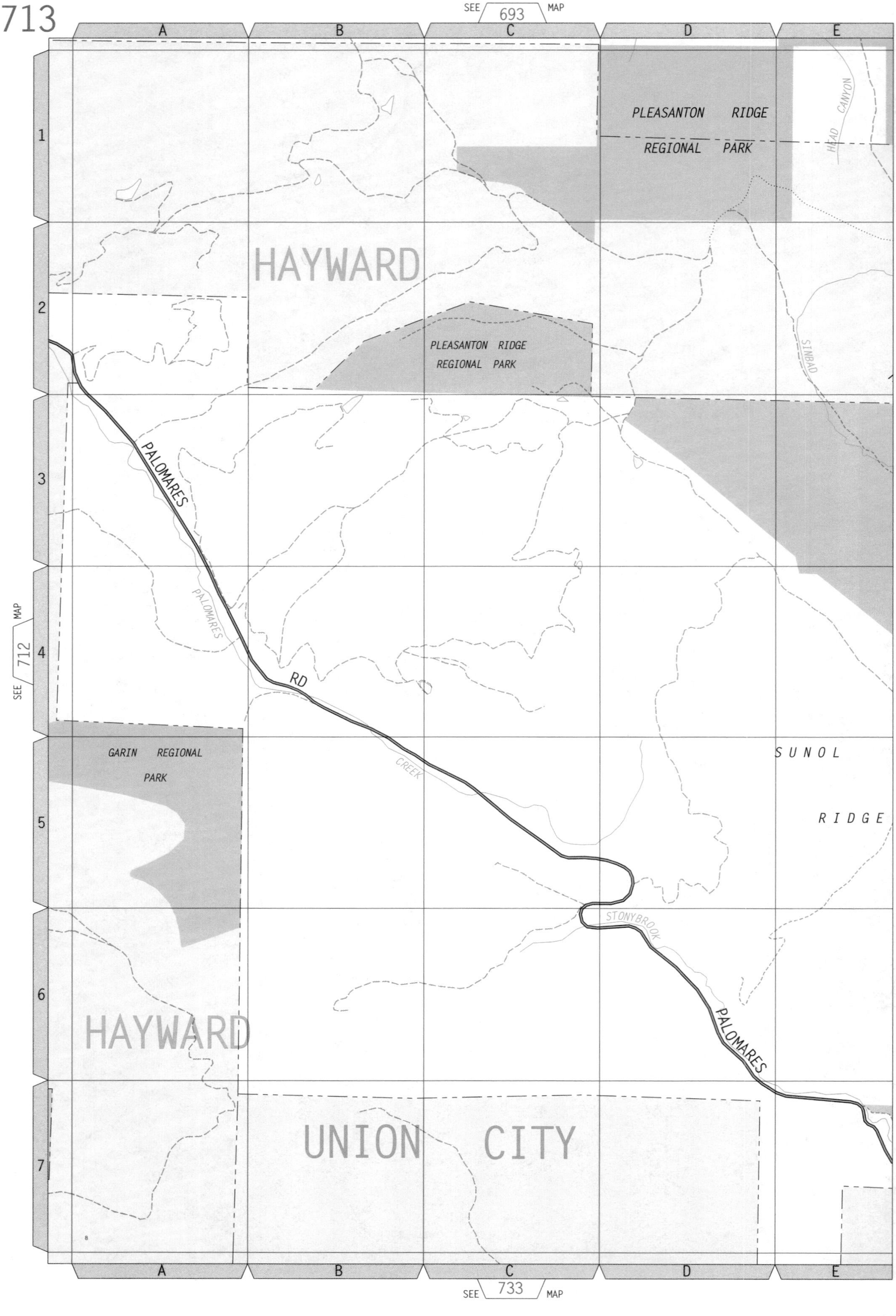
SEE 693 MAP
A
B
C
D
E
1
2
3
4
5
6
7
PLEASANTON RIDGE REGIONAL PARK
HEAD CANYON
HAYWARD
PLEASANTON RIDGE REGIONAL PARK
SINBAD
PALOMARES
PALOMARES
RD
CREEK
SEE 712 MAP
GARIN REGIONAL PARK
SUNOL
RIDGE
STONYBROOK
PALOMARES
HAYWARD
UNION CITY
SEE 733 MAP

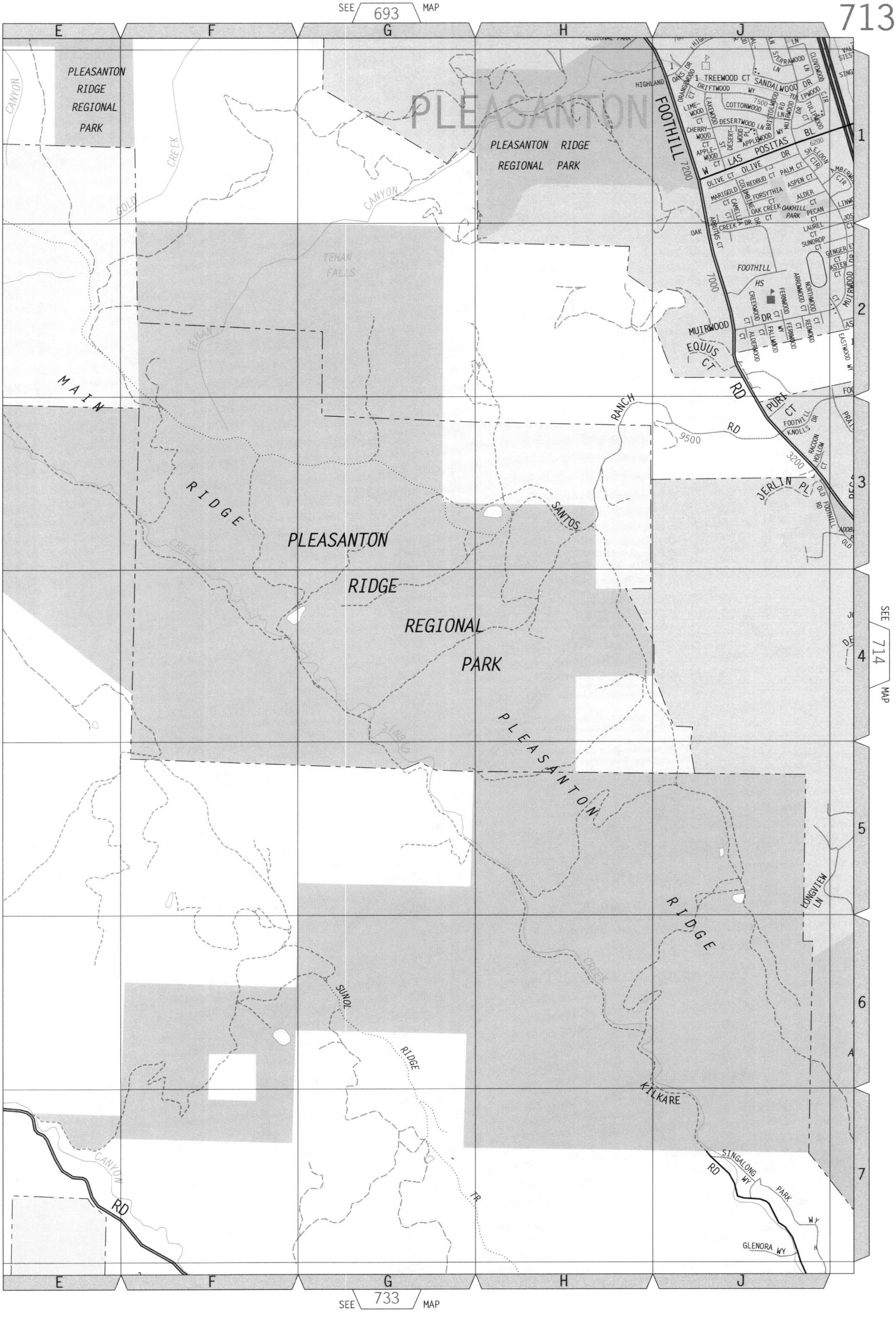
SEE 693 MAP
E
F
G
H
J
PLEASANTON RIDGE REGIONAL PARK
PLEASANTON
PLEASANTON RIDGE REGIONAL PARK
FOOTHILL
RD
HIGHLAND
LAS POSITAS
BL
W
OLIVE
FOOTHILL HS
MUIRWOOD
EQUUS CT
RANCH
RD
9500
JERLIN PL
OLD FOOTHILL RD
GOLD
CREEK
CANYON
TEHAN FALLS
TEHAN
MAIN
RIDGE
PLEASANTON
RIDGE
REGIONAL
PARK
SANTOS
PLEASANTON
RIDGE
CREEK
SUNOL
RIDGE
TR
KILKARE
RD
SINGALONG WY
PARK WY
GLENORA WY
LONGVIEW LN
CANYON
RD
SEE 714 MAP
1
2
3
4
5
6
7
SEE 733 MAP

BAY AREA

SEE 694 MAP

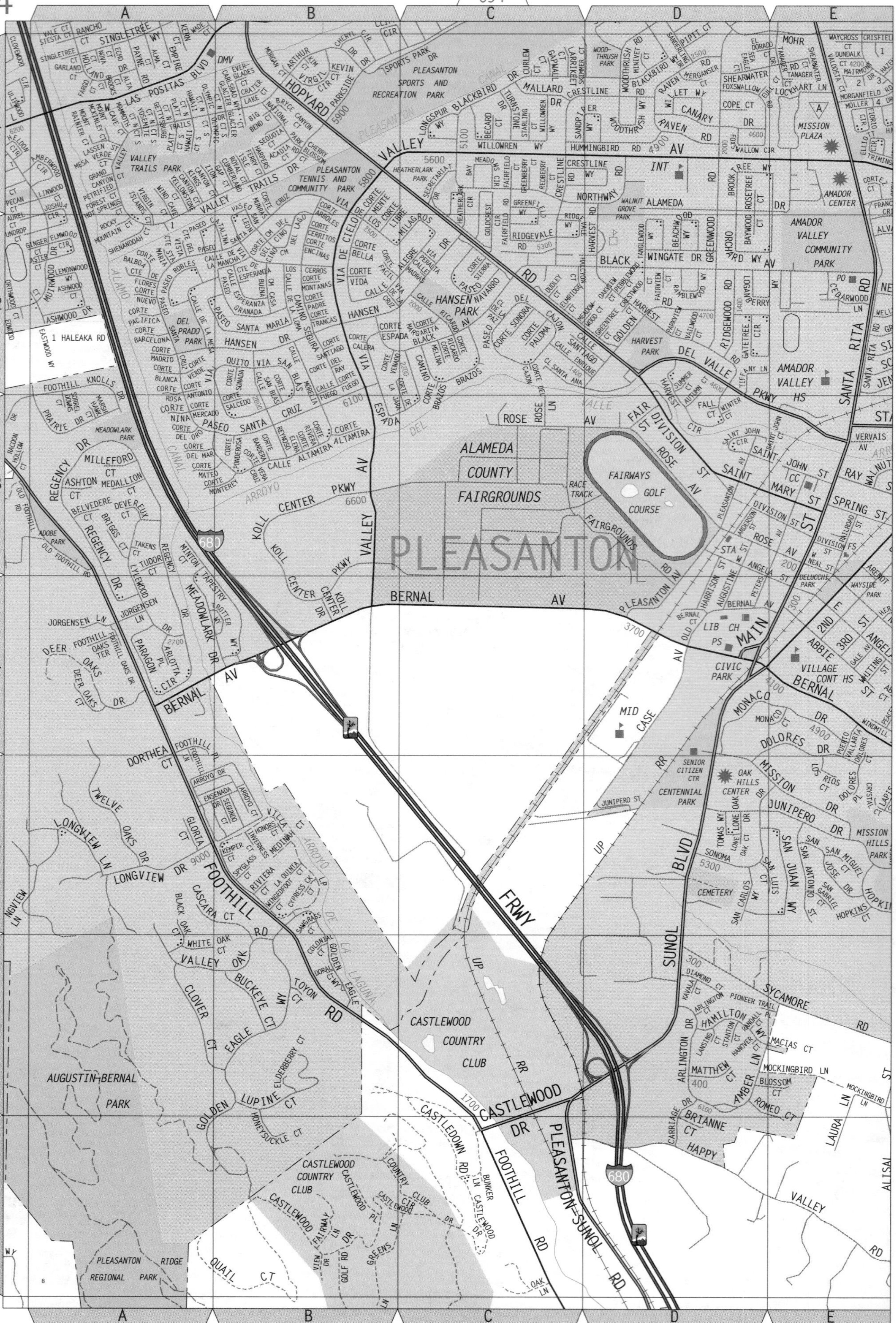
PLEASANTON
ALAMEDA COUNTY FAIRGROUNDS
FAIRWAYS GOLF COURSE
RACE TRACK
PLEASANTON SPORTS AND RECREATION PARK
PLEASANTON TENNIS AND COMMUNITY PARK
VALLEY TRAILS PARK
DEL PRADO PARK
HANSEN PARK
HARVEST PARK
MEADOWLARK PARK
ADOBE PARK
AMADOR VALLEY COMMUNITY PARK
AMADOR VALLEY HS
AMADOR CENTER
MISSION PLAZA
VILLAGE CONT HS
CIVIC PARK
MID CASE
SENIOR CITIZEN CTR
CENTENNIAL PARK
OAK HILLS CENTER
MISSION HILLS PARK
CEMETERY
CASTLEWOOD COUNTRY CLUB
AUGUSTIN BERNAL PARK
PLEASANTON RIDGE REGIONAL PARK
HOPYARD RD
VALLEY AV
SANTA RITA RD
KOLL CENTER PKWY
BERNAL AV
FOOTHILL RD
SUNOL BLVD
MAIN ST
DEL VALLE PKWY
BLACK AV
FRWY
CASTLEWOOD DR
PLEASANTON-SUNOL RD
LAS POSITAS BLVD
VALLEY TRAILS DR
ARROYO DEL VALLE
ARROYO DE LA LAGUNA
ALAMO CANAL
PLEASANTON CANAL
680
A B C D E
1 2 3 4 5 6 7

SEE 713 MAP

SEE 734 MAP

MAP

SEE 694 MAP

E
F
G
H
J
1
2
3
4
5
6
7
SEE A E1
1 COTTERELL CT
2 LIGHTLAND CT
3 HAYFORD CT
4 APPERSON WY
5 DANBURY PARK DR
SEE B G3
1 PASAS ST
2 SEVA ST
3 CIRVELA ST
4 SAINT THOMAS WY
5 SAINT FRANCIS WY
BUSCH RD
VALLEY AV
UP RR
BOULDER ST
QUARRY LN
SERPENTINE LN
KOLLIN ST
NEVIS ST
SANTA RITA RD
SILVER ST
SCHOOL ST
JENSEN ST
STANLEY BLVD
CID WY
ALVARADO ST
TRIMINGHAM DR
SHADOW CLIFFS REGIONAL RECREATION AREA
BERNAL AV
WASHINGTON ST
CALIFORNIA AV
WYOMING ST
UTAH ST
DEL VALLE PKWY
ARROYO DEL VALLE
VINEYARD AV
VINEYARD MOBILE VILLA
HACIENDA MHP
VISTA GRANDE
EL CAPITAN DR
LIBERTY DR
BADGER DR
TIOGA
VISTA DIABLO
MARGO LN
CLARA LN
PIETRONAVE LN
FOX BROUGH CT
GRAY FOX CIR
EAGLE CT
EAGLET CT
RED FEATHER DR
TOKAY CT
RHINE WY
BERATLIS PL
ZINFANDEL RD
NAVALLE CT
MATARO CT
VINTNER WY
ARBOR DR
CRELLIN
CATAWBA CT
MONTEVINO
AMOROSO CT
VICTORIA RIDGE CT
SYLVANER DR
CHARDONNAY DR
MADEIRA CT
CHABLIS CT
MALBEC CT
TANNET CT
RIESLING DR
PALOMINO DR
CONCORD
TOURIGA
KOTTINGER DR
KOTTINGER VILLAGE PARK
KOTTINGER PARK
ZWISSIG CT
MAVIS DR
ADAMS WY
SPRING ST
1ST ST
RAY ST
WALNUT DR
VERVAIS AV
NEAL ST
ANGELA ST
ABBIE ST
BONITA AV
MIRADOR DR
BONDE CT
GENEVIEVE PL
ROSELMA PL
HEARST DR
CASTERSON CT
REMILLARD CT
GRANT CT
BENEDICT CT
SMALLWOOD CT
CRESPI CT
BRANDY CT
BORDEAUX ST
GRILLO CT
AMANDA PL
BRAXTON PL
MIDDLETON PL
LIVINGSTON
MISSION HILLS PARK
HOPKINS DR
LUND RANCH RD
MINNIE ST
BYRD LN
MOCKINGBIRD LN
ALISAL ST
RD
SEE 715 MAP

SEE 734 MAP

BAY AREA

MAP

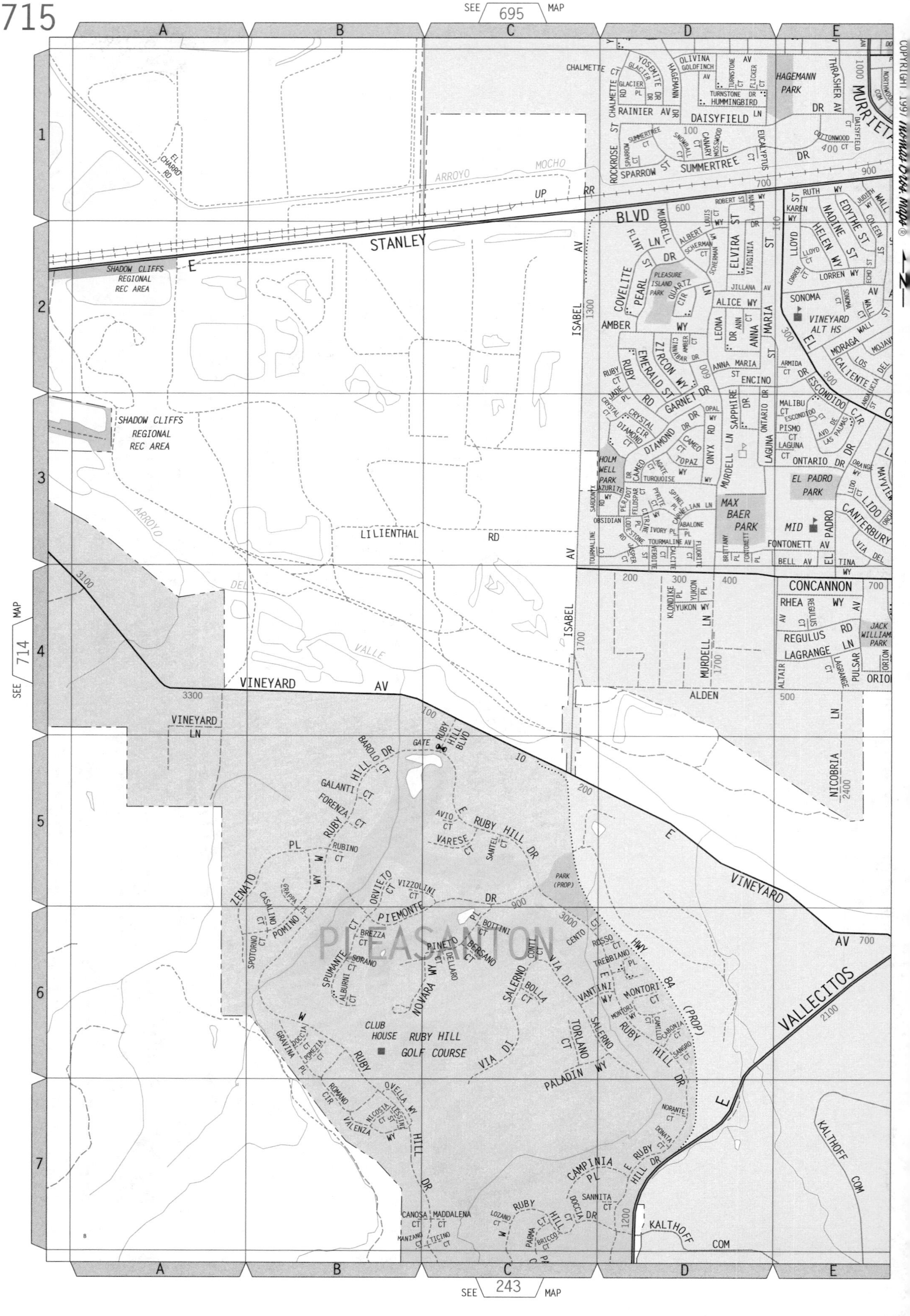
SEE 695 MAP
SEE 714 MAP
SEE 243 MAP
A
B
C
D
E
1
2
3
4
5
6
7
COPYRIGHT 1997 Thomas Bros. Maps ®
SHADOW CLIFFS REGIONAL REC AREA
SHADOW CLIFFS REGIONAL REC AREA
EL CHARRO RD
ARROYO MOCHO
UP RR
E STANLEY BLVD
ISABEL AV
LILIENTHAL RD
ARROYO DEL VALLE
VINEYARD AV
VINEYARD LN
E VINEYARD AV
VALLECITOS
E VALLECITOS
HWY 84 (PROP)
PLEASANTON
RUBY HILL BLVD
GATE
RUBY HILL DR
E RUBY HILL DR
CLUB HOUSE
RUBY HILL GOLF COURSE
PARK (PROP)
BAROLO DR
GALANTI CT
FORENZA CT
RUBY W WY
PL
RUBINO CT
AVIO CT
VARESE CT
SANTEL CT
ZENATO
CASALINO
GRAPPA PL
POMINO CT
SPOTORNO CT
ORVIETO CT
VIZZOLINI CT
PIEMONTE DR
BREZZA CT
BOTTINI CT
PINETO CT
BIERSANO
DELLARO
SORANO
SPUMANTE CT
ALBURNI CT
NOVARA W WY
CONTI CT
VIA DI SALERNO
SALERNO CT
BOLLA CT
CENTO CT
ROSSO CT
TREBBIANO PL
VANTINI WY
MONTORI CT
CAMILLO CT
CABONIA CT
SANGRO CT
TORLANO CT
PALADIN WY
GRAVINA PL
DOCCIA CT
POMEZIA CT
ROMANO CIR
OVELLA WY
NICOSIA CT
LESSINI ST
VALENZA WY
NORANTE CT
DONATA CT
CAMPINIA PL
SANNITA CT
DOCCIA DR
LOZANO CT
PARMA CT
BRICCO CT
CANOSA CT
MADDALENA CT
MANZANO CT
TICINO CT
KALTHOFF COM
CHALMETTE CT
YOSEMITE DR
GLACIER RD
OLIVINA AV
GOLDFINCH
HAGEMANN DR
TURNSTONE CT
FLICKER CT
HUMMINGBIRD
HAGEMANN PARK
THRASHER AV
MURRIETA
RAINIER AV
DAISYFIELD LN
DAISYFIELD
ROCKROSE ST
SPARROW ST
SUMMERTREE ST
SUMMERTREE CT
SNOWBALL CT
CANARY CT
EUCALYPTUS CT
COTTONWOOD CT
RUTH WY
KAREN WY
JUDITH WY
NADINE ST
EDYTHE ST
HELEN WY
COLEEN ST
LLOYD CT
LORREN WY
MURDELL LN
FLINT ST
ALBERT DR
SCHERMAN WY
ELVIRA ST
VIRGINIA
JILLANA AV
PLEASURE ISLAND PARK
QUARTZ CIR
COVELITE
PEARL
AMBER WY
ALICE WY
LEONA
ANNA
MARIA ST
ANNA MARIA ST
SONOMA AV
VINEYARD ALT HS
MORAGA
MOJAVE
RUBY RD
EMERALD ST
ZIRCON WY
CIMMARON DR
ENCINO
ARMIDA DR
ESCONDIDO CIR
CALIENTE
JADE
CRYSTAL CIR
DIAMOND DR
GARNET DR
OPAL WY
SAPPHIRE DR
LAGUNA DR
ONTARIO DR
MALIBU CT
PISMO CT
LAGUNA CT
AVD DE LAS PALMAS
ORANGE
MAYVIEW
HOLM WELL PARK
CAMEO
TOPAZ
TURQUOISE
ONYX RD
AZURITE
EL PADRO PARK
LIDO
CANTERBURY
MAX BAER PARK
MID
SPINEL
CORNELIAN LN
OBSIDIAN
IVORY PL
ABALONE
TOURMALINE
FONTONETT AV
BELL AV
EL PADRO
TINA WY
VIA DEL
CONCANNON
RHEA WY
REGULUS RD
KLONDIKE PL
YUKON WY
JACK WILLIAMS PARK
LAGRANGE LN
ALTAIR
PULSAR
ORION
ALDEN
NICOBRIA LN
MURDELL LN

SEE 695 MAP

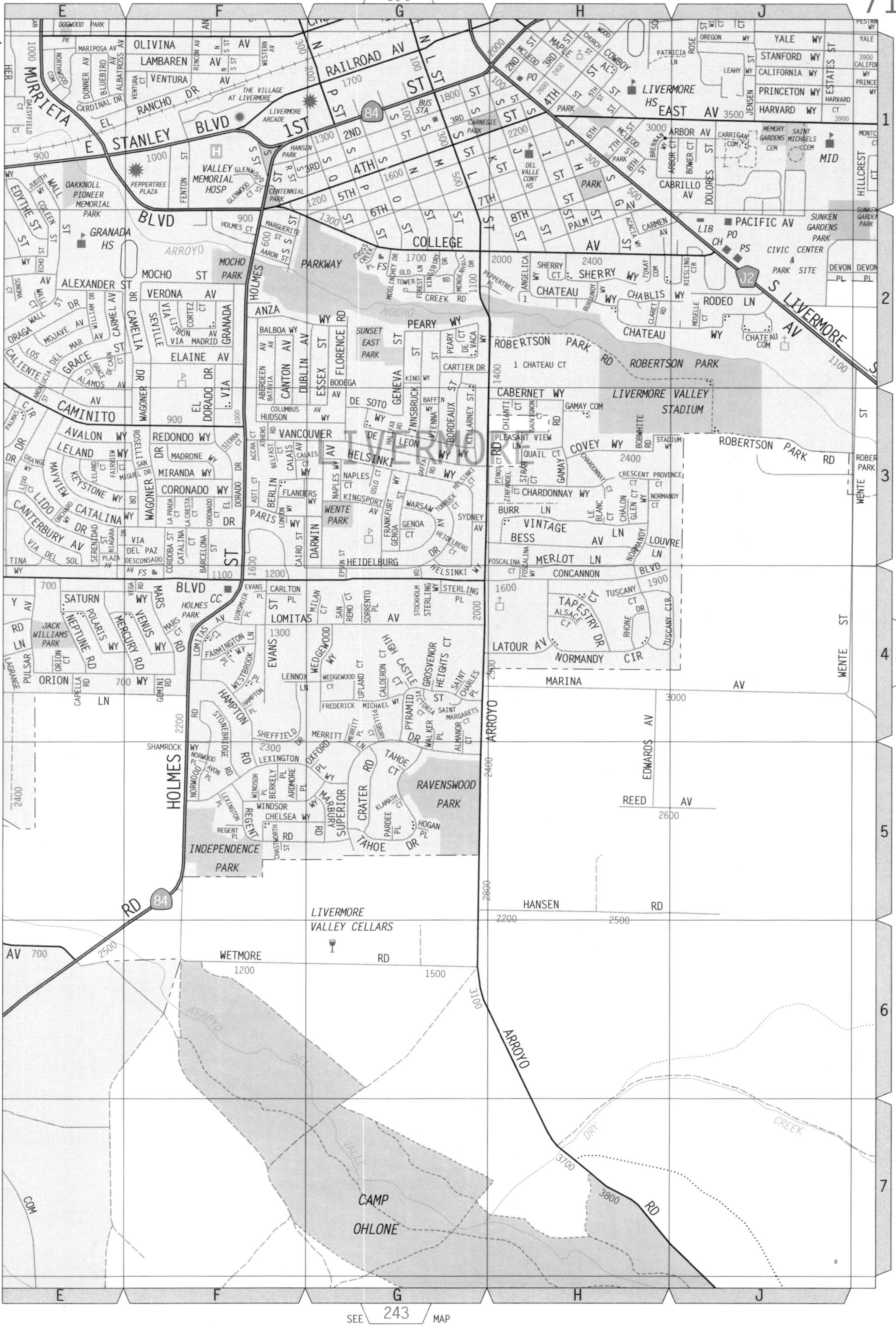
E
F
G
H
J
1
2
3
4
5
6
7
LIVERMORE
STANLEY BLVD
MURRIETA
RAILROAD AV
1ST ST
2ND ST
3RD ST
4TH ST
5TH ST
6TH ST
7TH ST
8TH ST
EAST AV
COLLEGE AV
HOLMES ST
ARROYO RD
CONCANNON BLVD
S LIVERMORE AV
PACIFIC AV
ROBERTSON PARK RD
ROBERTSON PARK
LIVERMORE VALLEY STADIUM
CHATEAU WY
SHERRY WY
PEARY WY
HELSINKI WY
HEIDELBURG DR
VANCOUVER WY
DE SOTO WY
LOMITAS AV
LATOUR AV
NORMANDY CIR
MARINA AV
EDWARDS AV
REED AV
HANSEN RD
WETMORE RD
WENTE ST
TAHOE DR
LEXINGTON WY
VINTAGE LN
BESS AV
MERLOT LN
COVEY WY
CABERNET WY
VALLEY MEMORIAL HOSP
PEPPERTREE PLAZA
OAKKNOLL PIONEER MEMORIAL PARK
GRANADA HS
MOCHO PARK
MOCHO ST
PARKWAY
SUNSET EAST PARK
WENTE PARK
HOLMES PARK
JACK WILLIAMS PARK
RAVENSWOOD PARK
INDEPENDENCE PARK
LIVERMORE VALLEY CELLARS
CAMP OHLONE
ARROYO DEL VALLE
DRY CREEK
LIVERMORE HS
LIVERMORE ARCADE
THE VILLAGE AT LIVERMORE
DEL VALLE CONT HS
CARNEGIE PARK
MEMORY GARDENS CEM
SAINT MICHAELS CEM
CARRIGAN COM
CIVIC CENTER & PARK SITE
SUNKEN GARDENS PARK
CHATEAU COM
GAMAY COM
OLIVINA AV
LAMBAREN AV
VENTURA AV
RANCHO DR
ALEXANDER ST
VERONA AV
ELAINE AV
CAMINITO AV
AVALON WY
LELAND WY
REDONDO WY
MIRANDA WY
CORONADO WY
CATALINA DR
CANTERBURY AV
SATURN WY
ORION WY
YALE WY
STANFORD WY
CALIFORNIA WY
PRINCETON WY
HARVARD WY
ARBOR AV
CABRILLO AV
DEVON PL
RODEO LN
PALM AV
84
J2

SEE 716 MAP

SEE 243 MAP

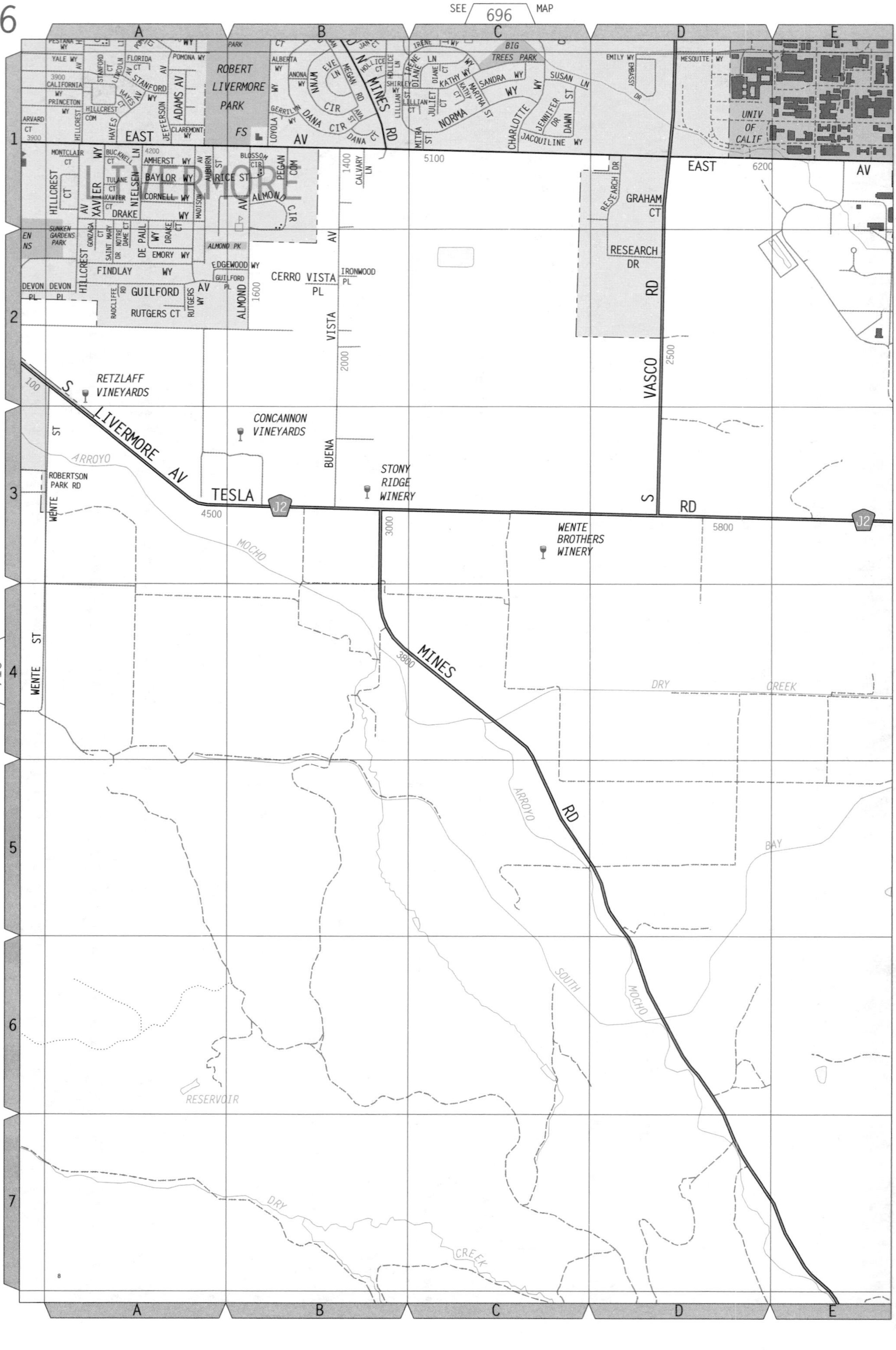
SEE 696 MAP
SEE 715 MAP
A
B
C
D
E
1
2
3
4
5
6
7
LIVERMORE
ROBERT LIVERMORE PARK
FS
EAST AV
4200
5100
6200
N MINES RD
BIG TREES PARK
UNIV OF CALIF
MESQUITE WY
EMILY WY
EMBASSY DR
RESEARCH DR
GRAHAM CT
VASCO RD
S VASCO RD
2500
YALE WY
CALIFORNIA WY
PRINCETON WY
ARVARD CT
3900
HILLCREST
STANFORD
LINCOLN AV
FLORIDA CT
HAYES AV
JEFFERSON AV
ADAMS AV
POMONA WY
CLAREMONT WY
ALBERTA WY
ANONA WY
GERRILYN WY
LOYOLA WY
WYNN CIR
EVE LN
MEGAN RD
DANA CIR
DANA CT
HOLLICE CT
SHIRLEY WY
LILLIAN CT
IRENE LN
DIANE CT
MITRA ST
JULIET CT
KATHY WY
MARTHA ST
SANDRA WY
NORMA WY
SUSAN LN
JENNIFER DR
DAWN ST
CHARLOTTE
JACQUILINE WY
MONTCLAIR CT
BUCKNELL CT
AMHERST WY
BAYLOR WY
TULANE CT
XAVIER AV
CORNELL WY
NIELSEN LN
DRAKE
MADISON
AUBURN WY
BLOSSOM CIR
RICE ST
PEGAN COM
ALMOND AV
ALMOND CIR
ALMOND PK
SUNKEN GARDENS PARK
GONZAGA CT
SAINT MARY DR
NOTRE DAME CT
DE PAUL WY
EMORY WY
FINDLAY WY
EDGEWOOD WY
GUILFORD CT
GUILFORD AV
RADCLIFFE RD
RUTGERS CT
RUTGERS WY
DEVON PL
CERRO VISTA PL
IRONWOOD PL
CALVARY LN
1400
1600
VISTA AV
2000
BUENA VISTA AV
RETZLAFF VINEYARDS
CONCANNON VINEYARDS
STONY RIDGE WINERY
WENTE BROTHERS WINERY
S LIVERMORE AV
100
ARROYO
ROBERTSON PARK RD
WENTE ST
TESLA RD
4500
5800
J2
3000
MINES RD
3800
ARROYO MOCHO
DRY CREEK
BAY
SOUTH
RESERVOIR
CREEK
8

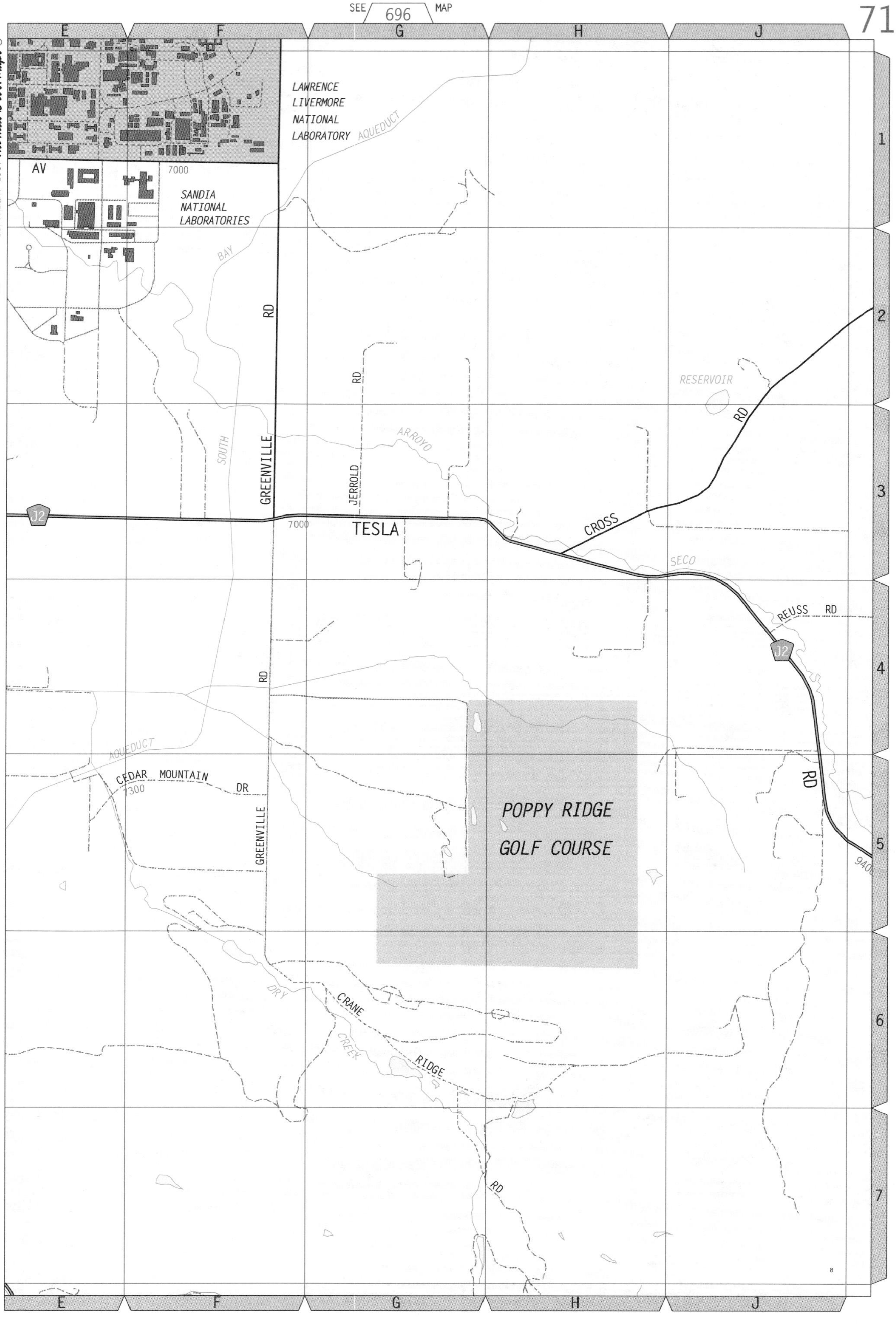

SEE 696 MAP
E
F
G
H
J
1
2
3
4
5
6
7
LAWRENCE
LIVERMORE
NATIONAL
LABORATORY
AQUEDUCT
AV
7000
SANDIA
NATIONAL
LABORATORIES
BAY
RD
SOUTH
GREENVILLE
RD
JERROLD
ARROYO
RESERVOIR
RD
CROSS
J2
7000
TESLA
SECO
REUSS RD
J2
RD
AQUEDUCT
CEDAR MOUNTAIN DR
7300
GREENVILLE
POPPY RIDGE
GOLF COURSE
RD
9400
DRY
CREEK
CRANE
RIDGE
RD

SEE 706 MAP

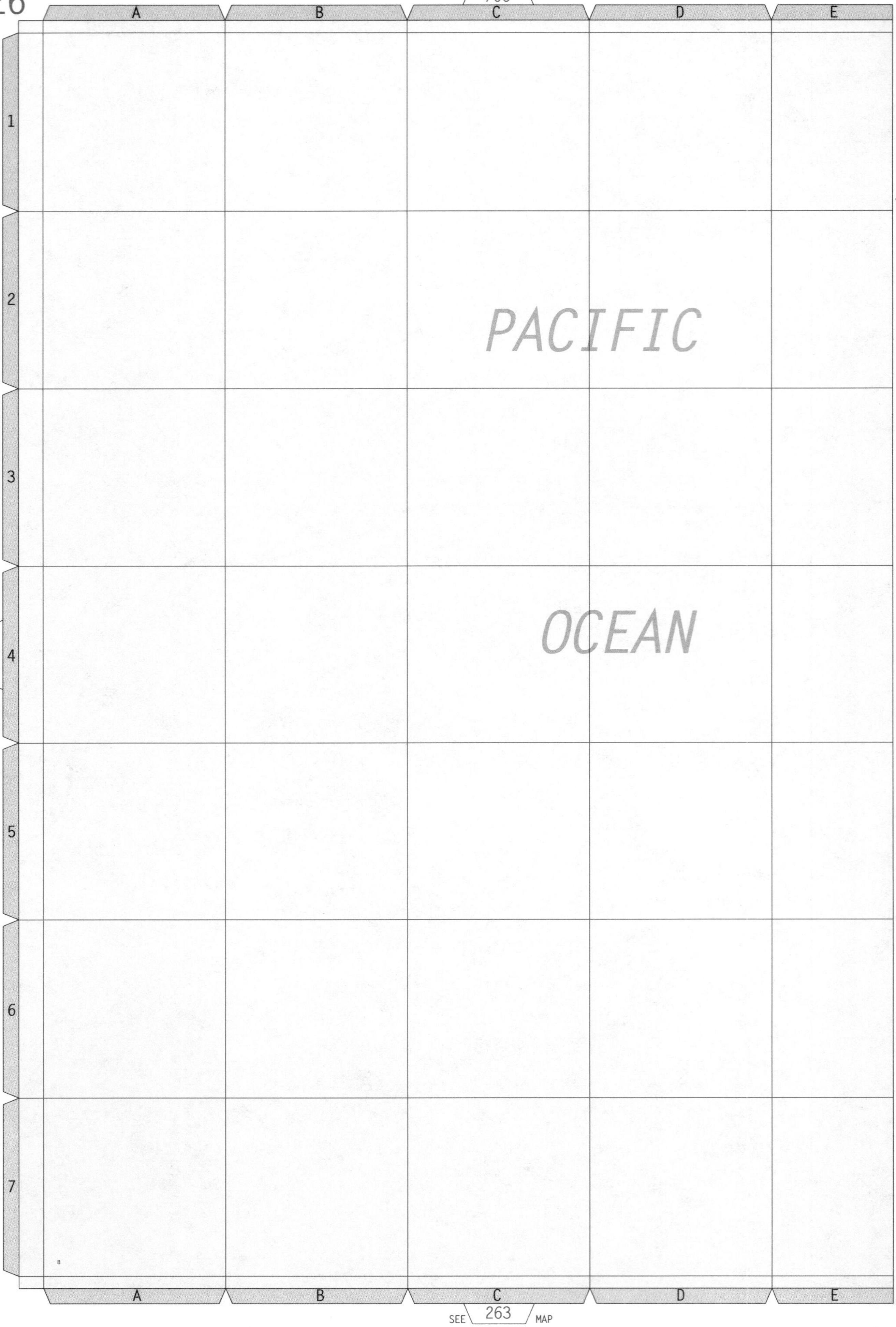

SEE 243 MAP
SEE 263 MAP

SEE 706 MAP
E
F
G
H
J
1
2
3
4
5
6
7
SEE 727 MAP
SEE 263 MAP
POINT
MORIS POINT RD
CALARA CREEK
COUNTY RD
HWY
400
SAN PEDRO BEACH
CABRILLO
1
ROCKAWAY BEACH
FASSLER AV
ROCKAWAY BEACH AV
ROBERTS RD
COAST LN
EBKEN ST
COPELAND ST
DONALDSON AV
HARVEY WY
OLD COUNTY RD
SAN MARLO WY
BAY VIEW RD
ODDSTAD WY
samTrans
PO
CRESPI DR
PARK & RIDE
CRESPI CENTER
PACIFICA
SHELTER COVE
SAN PEDRO ROCK
PEDRO POINT
SAN PEDRO TERRACE
SHELTER COVE RD
KENT
STANLEY AV
SAN PEDRO AV
GRAND AV
ATHENIAN WY
BELFAST AV
LINDA MAR
LINDA MAR BLVD
MONTEZUMA
SAN PEDRO TERRACE RD
ANZA DR
BALBOA WY
CERVANTES
DE SOLO DR
ENCANTO WY
ARGUELLO
FERNANDEZ
MARVILLA CIR
ESCALERO AV
CORONA DR
ALTA VISTA DR
ALTURA WY
CRESPI
SERENA
REGINA WY
SEVILLE DR
OVIEDO CT
ALCALA CT
TAPIS WY
VALENCIA
LA MIRADA DR
ODDSTAD PARK
DRIFTWOOD CIR
HINTON RANCH
BARCELONA DR
GRANADA DR
SANCHEZ ADOBE MUSEUM
WHITE FIELD
FS
BLVD
STANDISH DR
DELL RD
HERMOSA AV
ROSITA RD
PERALTA
BOWER RD
RIO VISTA DR
SERRA DR
SOLANO DR
GALVEZ DR
MONTE VERDE DR
PALOU DR
HIGGINS WY
ADOBE WY
SHAMROCK RANCH RD
HWY
SAN PEDRO MOUNTAIN RD
PEREZ DR
VALLEYWOOD DR
OAKWOOD CT
SPRINGWOOD WY
ALVISO CT
MALAVEAR CT
CELESTIAL CT
AVILA
DEVILS SLIDE
CABRILLO
MCNEE RANCH STATE PARK
SAN PEDRO VALLEY COUNTY PARK
1

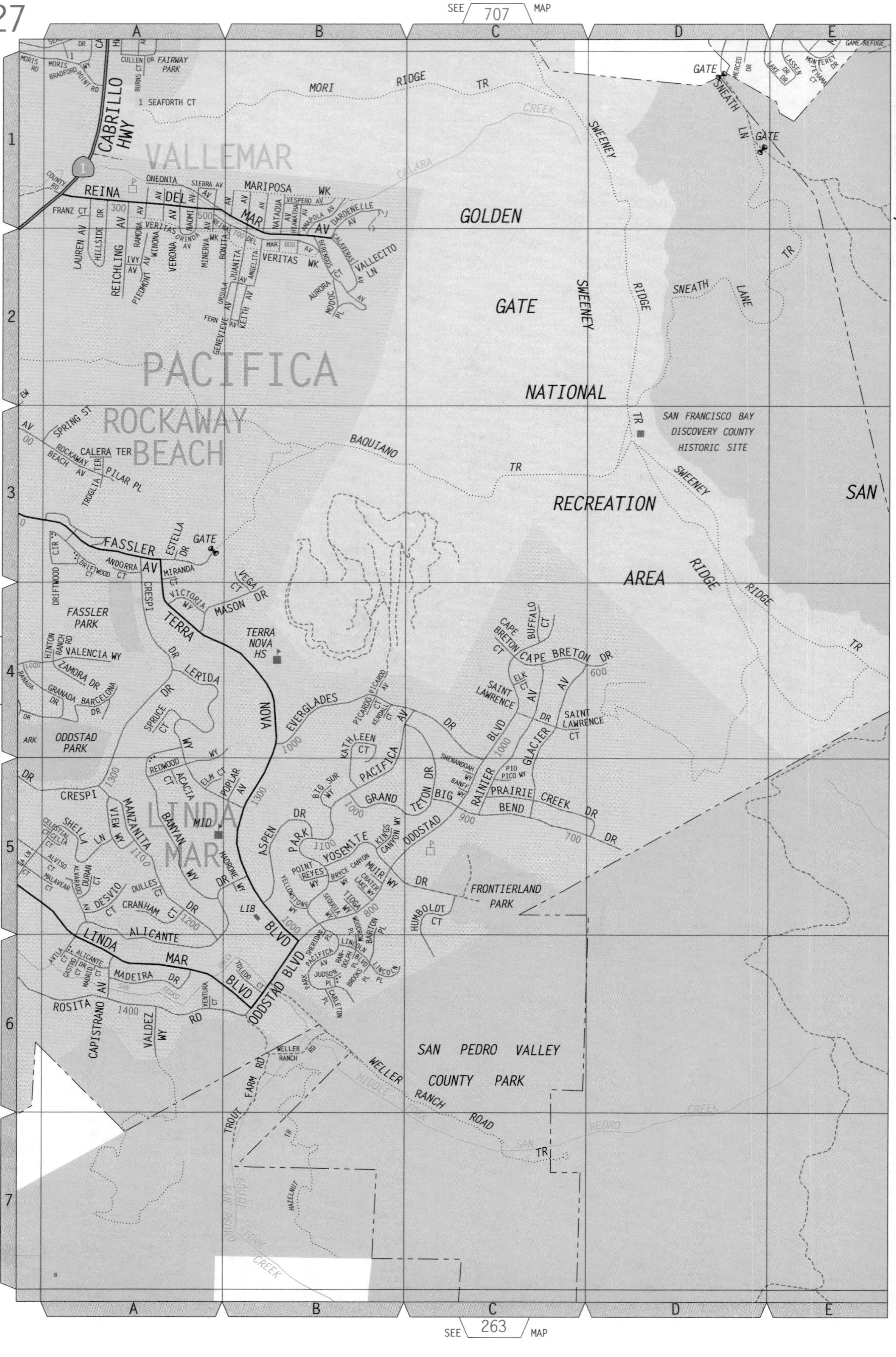
SEE 707 MAP
SEE 726 MAP
SEE 263 MAP
A
B
C
D
E
1
2
3
4
5
6
7
VALLEMAR
PACIFICA
ROCKAWAY BEACH
LINDA MAR
GOLDEN GATE NATIONAL RECREATION AREA
SAN PEDRO VALLEY COUNTY PARK
SAN FRANCISCO BAY DISCOVERY COUNTY HISTORIC SITE
FASSLER PARK
ODDSTAD PARK
FRONTIERLAND PARK
FAIRWAY PARK
TERRA NOVA HS
MID
LIB
CABRILLO HWY
REINA DEL MAR AV
MARIPOSA WK
ONEONTA
SIERRA AV
VESPERO AV
DARDENELLE
FRANZ CT
LAUREN AV
HILLSIDE DR
REICHLING AV
RAMONA AV
VERITAS WK
WINONA
VERONA
MINERVA WK
JUANITA
VERITAS WK
BERENDOS
CALAVERAS
VALLECITO LN
AURORA
MODOC
KEITH AV
URSULA
GENEVIEVE AV
1 SEAFORTH CT
MORI RIDGE TR
SWEENEY RIDGE
SNEATH LN
SNEATH LANE
GATE
BAQUIANO TR
SPRING ST
CALERA TER
ROCKAWAY BEACH AV
PILAR PL
TROGLIA TER
FASSLER AV
ESTELLA DR
ANDORRA CT
DRIFTWOOD CT
DRIFTWOOD CIR
MIRANDA
VEGA CT
VICTORIA WY
MASON DR
CRESPI DR
TERRA NOVA BLVD
LERIDA
VALENCIA WY
HINTON RANCH
ZAMORA DR
GRANADA DR
BARCELONA DR
SPRUCE DR
REDWOOD WY
ACACIA CT
ELM CT
POPLAR AV
EVERGLADES DR
KATHLEEN CT
PICARDO
KENDALL CT
PACIFICA AV
CAPE BRETON DR
CAPE BRETON CT
BUFFALO CT
ELK CT
SAINT LAWRENCE AV
SAINT LAWRENCE CT
GLACIER AV
RAINIER BLVD
SHENANDOAH WY
BANFF WY
PIO PICO WY
PRAIRIE CREEK DR
BIG BEND
TETON DR
GRAND
BIG SUR WY
ASPEN DR
PARK
YOSEMITE DR
KINGS CANYON WY
ODDSTAD BLVD
POINT REYES WY
BRYCE CANYON WY
CRATER LAKE WY
MUIR WY
YELLOWSTONE WY
SEQUOIA WY
TIOGA
HUMBOLDT CT
SHEILA LN
MANZANITA DR
VIEW WY
BANYAN WY
MADRONE
ALVISO
ALVARADO
DURAN
DESVIO CT
DULLES CT
CRANHAM CT
MALAVEAR
ALICANTE DR
LINDA MAR BLVD
MADEIRA DR
TOLEDO CT
VENTURA CT
ROSITA RD
CAPISTRANO AV
VALDEZ WY
SHERIDAN
LINCOLN PL
BARTON PL
JUDSON PL
CARLETON
BROOKS PL
WELLER RANCH
TROUT FARM RD
WELLER RANCH ROAD
MIDDLE FORK
SAN PEDRO CREEK
SOUTH FORK SAN PEDRO CREEK
HAZELNUT
TR
SAN

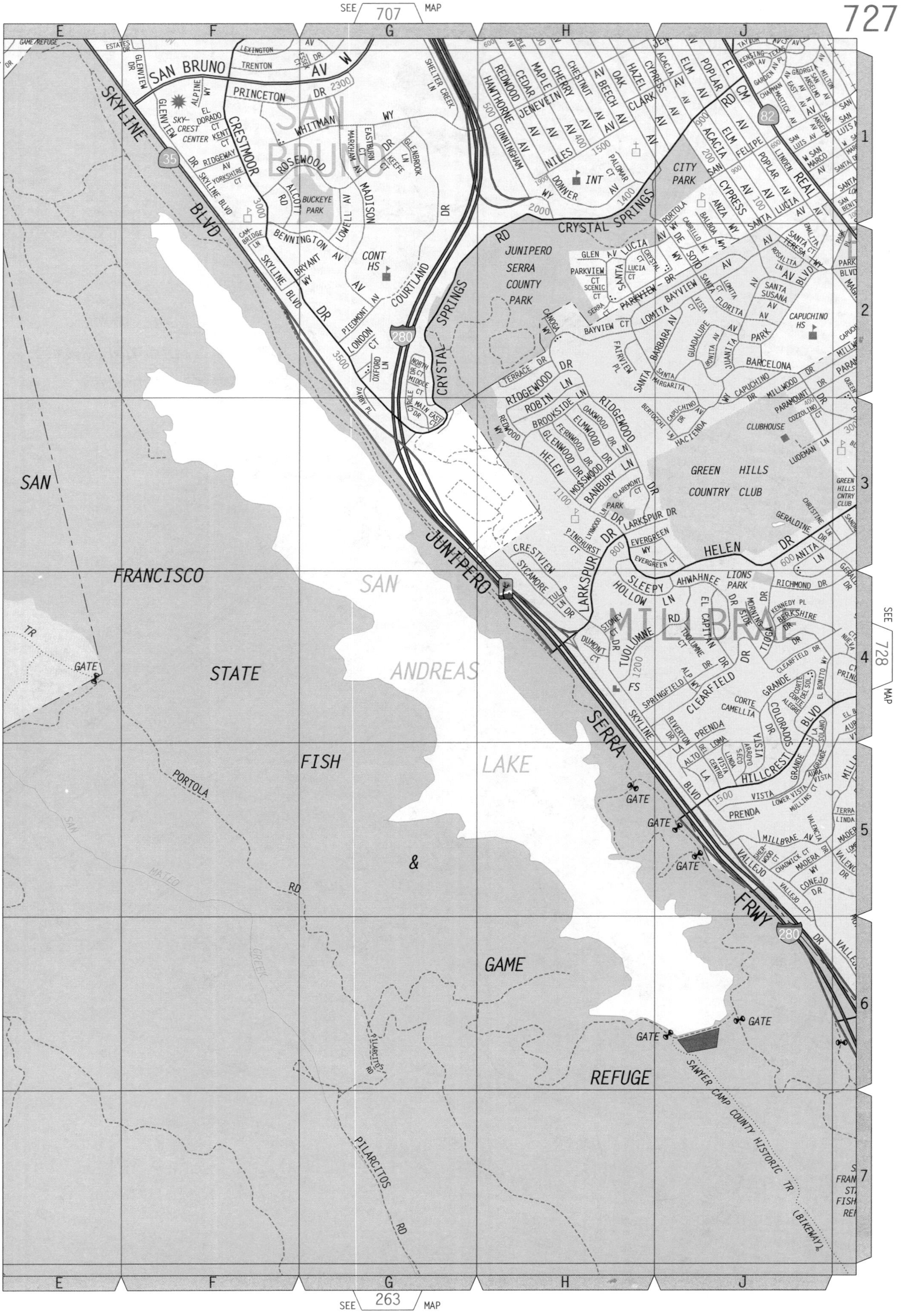
SEE 707 MAP
E
F
G
H
J
1
2
3
4
5
6
7
SAN BRUNO
SKYLINE BLVD
SAN BRUNO AV W
PRINCETON DR
CRESTMOOR
WHITMAN WY
ROSEWOOD
BUCKEYE PARK
MADISON
BENNINGTON AV
CONT HS
COURTLAND
CRYSTAL SPRINGS RD
JUNIPERO SERRA COUNTY PARK
CITY PARK
INT
PARKVIEW DR
BAYVIEW
CAPUCHINO HS
BARCELONA
RIDGEWOOD DR
GREEN HILLS COUNTRY CLUB
CLUBHOUSE
HELEN DR
LARKSPUR DR
LIONS PARK
MILLBRAE
SAN FRANCISCO STATE FISH & GAME REFUGE
SAN ANDREAS LAKE
JUNIPERO SERRA FRWY
PORTOLA RD
PILARCITOS RD
SAWYER CAMP COUNTY HISTORIC TR (BIKEWAY)
GATE
REFUGE
EL CM REAL
HILLCREST BLVD
MILLBRAE AV
SEE 728 MAP
SEE 263 MAP

SEE 708 MAP

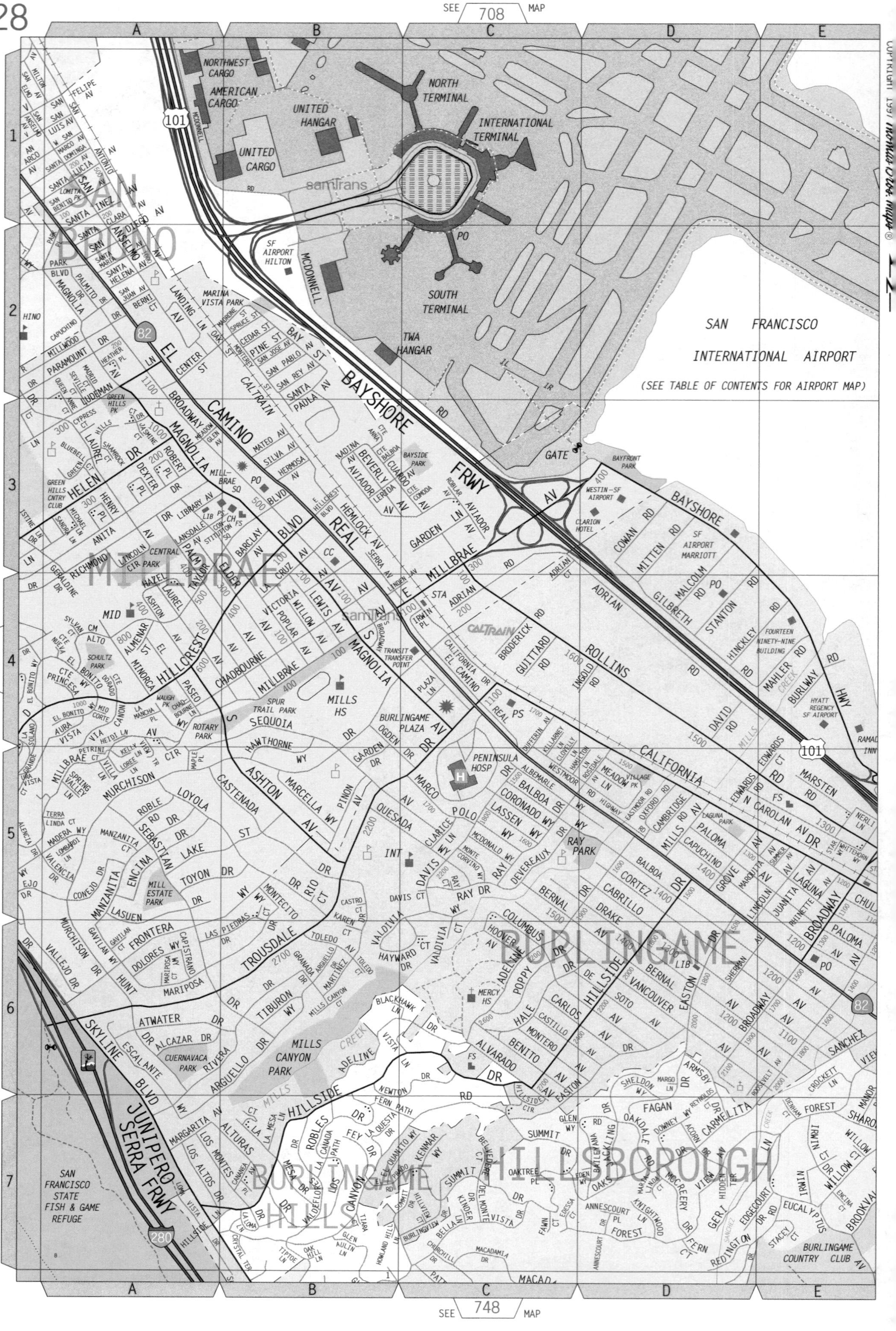
SAN FRANCISCO
INTERNATIONAL AIRPORT
(SEE TABLE OF CONTENTS FOR AIRPORT MAP)
NORTH TERMINAL
INTERNATIONAL TERMINAL
SOUTH TERMINAL
NORTHWEST CARGO
AMERICAN CARGO
UNITED HANGAR
UNITED CARGO
TWA HANGAR
SF AIRPORT HILTON
SAN BRUNO
MILLBRAE
BURLINGAME
HILLSBOROUGH
BURLINGAME HILLS
BAYSHORE FRWY
EL CAMINO REAL
JUNIPERO SERRA FRWY
SKYLINE BLVD
MILLS HS
MILLS ESTATE PARK
MILLS CANYON PARK
CUERNAVACA PARK
SCHULTZ PARK
SPUR TRAIL PARK
ROTARY PARK
RAY PARK
BAYSIDE PARK
BAYFRONT PARK
PENINSULA HOSP
MERCY HS
BURLINGAME PLAZA
WESTIN-SF AIRPORT
CLARION HOTEL
SF AIRPORT MARRIOTT
HYATT REGENCY SF AIRPORT
FOURTEEN NINETY-NINE BUILDING
TRANSIT TRANSFER POINT
GREEN HILLS CNTRY CLUB
SAN FRANCISCO STATE FISH & GAME REFUGE
BURLINGAME COUNTRY CLUB
GATE
CALTRAIN
samTrans
101
82
280
A
B
C
D
E
1
2
3
4
5
6
7

SEE 727 MAP

SEE 748 MAP

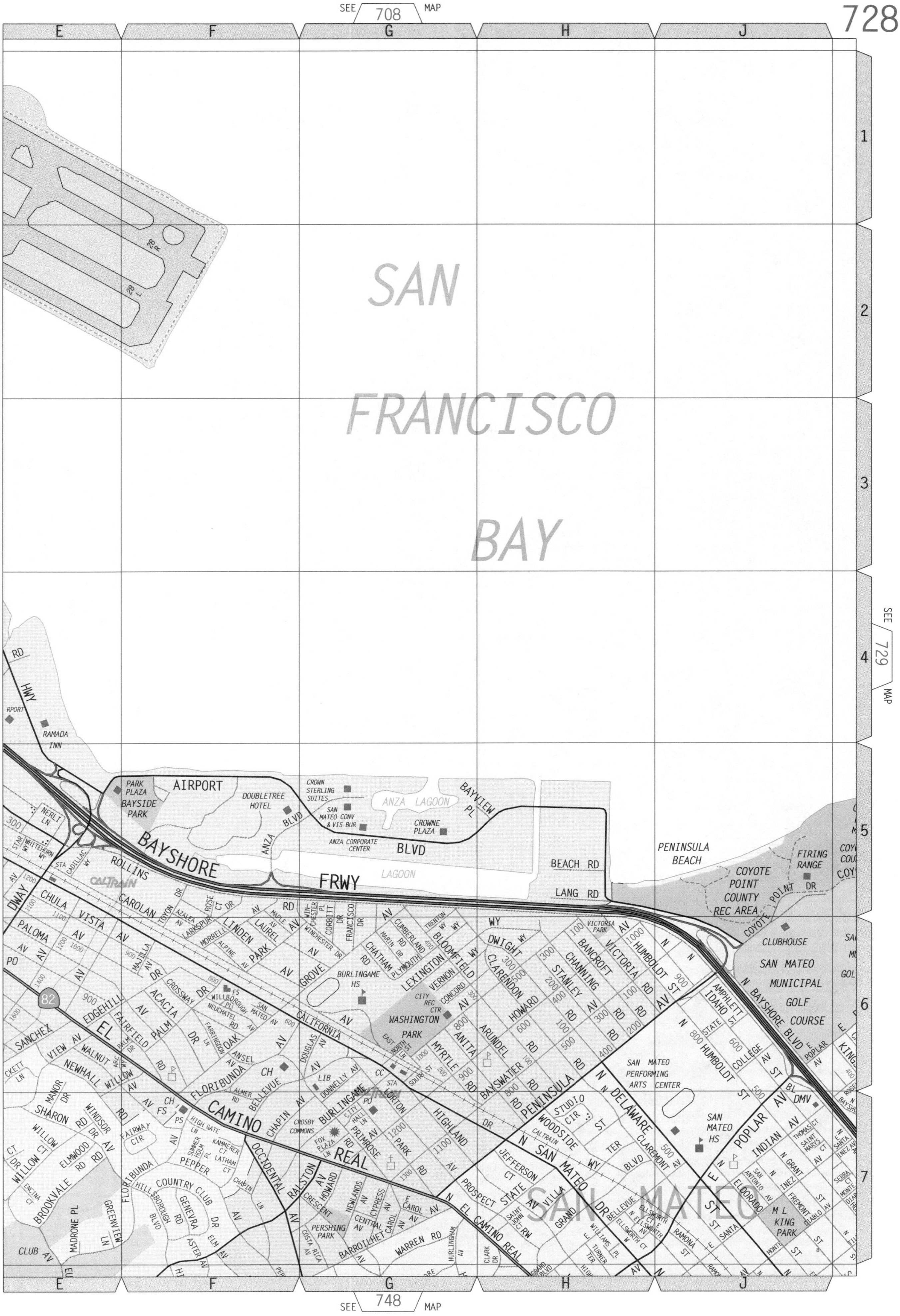

SEE 708 MAP
SEE 729 MAP
SEE 748 MAP
E
F
G
H
J
1
2
3
4
5
6
7
SAN FRANCISCO BAY
28 R
28 L
RD
HWY
RAMADA INN
PARK PLAZA
BAYSIDE PARK
AIRPORT
DOUBLETREE HOTEL
BLVD
CROWN STERLING SUITES
SAN MATEO CONV & VIS BUR
ANZA LAGOON
CROWNE PLAZA
ANZA CORPORATE CENTER
BLVD
BAYVIEW PL
ANZA
LAGOON
BAYSHORE
FRWY
BEACH RD
LANG RD
PENINSULA BEACH
COYOTE POINT COUNTY REC AREA
FIRING RANGE
COYOTE POINT DR
CLUBHOUSE
SAN MATEO MUNICIPAL GOLF COURSE
N BAYSHORE BLVD
NERLI LN
STAR WHITEHORN WY
CADILLAC WY
ROLLINS
CALTRAIN
CAROLAN
CHULA VISTA AV
PALOMA AV
TOYON DR
AZALEA
LARKSPUR DR
ROSE CT
MORRELL
ALPINE
LINDEN
LAUREL
PARK
MAPLE AV
WINCHESTER PL
WINCHESTER DR
CORBITT DR
FRANCISCO DR
GROVE
BURLINGAME HS
CHATHAM RD
CUMBERLAND
MARIN DR
PLYMOUTH
LEXINGTON
TRENTON WY
BLOOMFIELD
VERNON
CONCORD
WASHINGTON PARK
CITY REC CTR
DWIGHT
CLARENDON
HOWARD
STANLEY
BANCROFT
CHANNING
VICTORIA PARK
VICTORIA
HUMBOLDT ST
AMPHLETT
IDAHO ST
STATE
COLLEGE
POPLAR AV
DMV
82
EL CAMINO REAL
EDGEHILL
FAIRFIELD
ACACIA
PALM
CROSSWAY
WILLBOROUGH PL
NEUCHATEL
SAN MATEO AV
FARRINGDON LN
OAK
ANSEL
FLORIBUNDA
CALIFORNIA
DOUGLAS AV
DONNELLY AV
LIB
CH
BELLEVUE
ALMER RD
CHAPIN AV
BURLINGAME
PRIMROSE
CITY HALL
PO
LORTON
HIGHLAND
MYRTLE
ANITA
ARUNDEL
BAYSWATER
PENINSULA
EAST NORTH LN
SOUTH
SANCHEZ
VIEW AV
WALNUT
NEWHALL
WILLOW
MANOR DR
SHARON
WINDSOR
ELMWOOD RD
BROOKVALE
ENCINA CT
MADRONE PL
GREENVIEW LN
CLUB AV
FAIRWAY CIR
HIGH GATE LN
SUMMER HOLM PL
KAMMERER CT
LATHAM CT
PEPPER
COUNTRY CLUB DR
HILLSBOROUGH BLVD
GENEVRA RD
ASTER AV
ELM
OCCIDENTAL
CROSBY COMMONS
FOX PLAZA LN
RALSTON AV
CRESCENT
HOWARD
NEWLANDS
CYPRESS
CENTRAL
CAROL
PERSHING PARK
COSTA RICA AV
BARROILHET
WARREN RD
HURLINGHAM AV
CLARK DR
SAN MATEO PERFORMING ARTS CENTER
STUDIO CIR
WOODSIDE
N SAN MATEO DR
JEFFERSON
PROSPECT
STATE
SAINT JOHN CT
VILLA
GRAND
BELLEVUE
ELLSWORTH
DELAWARE
CLAREMONT AV
TER
BLVD
SAN MATEO HS
ELDORADO
SAN ANTONIO AV
INDIAN AV
GRANT
INEZ
FREMONT
M L KING PARK
DIABLO
RAMONA ST
SANTA
SAN MATEO
N EL CAMINO REAL

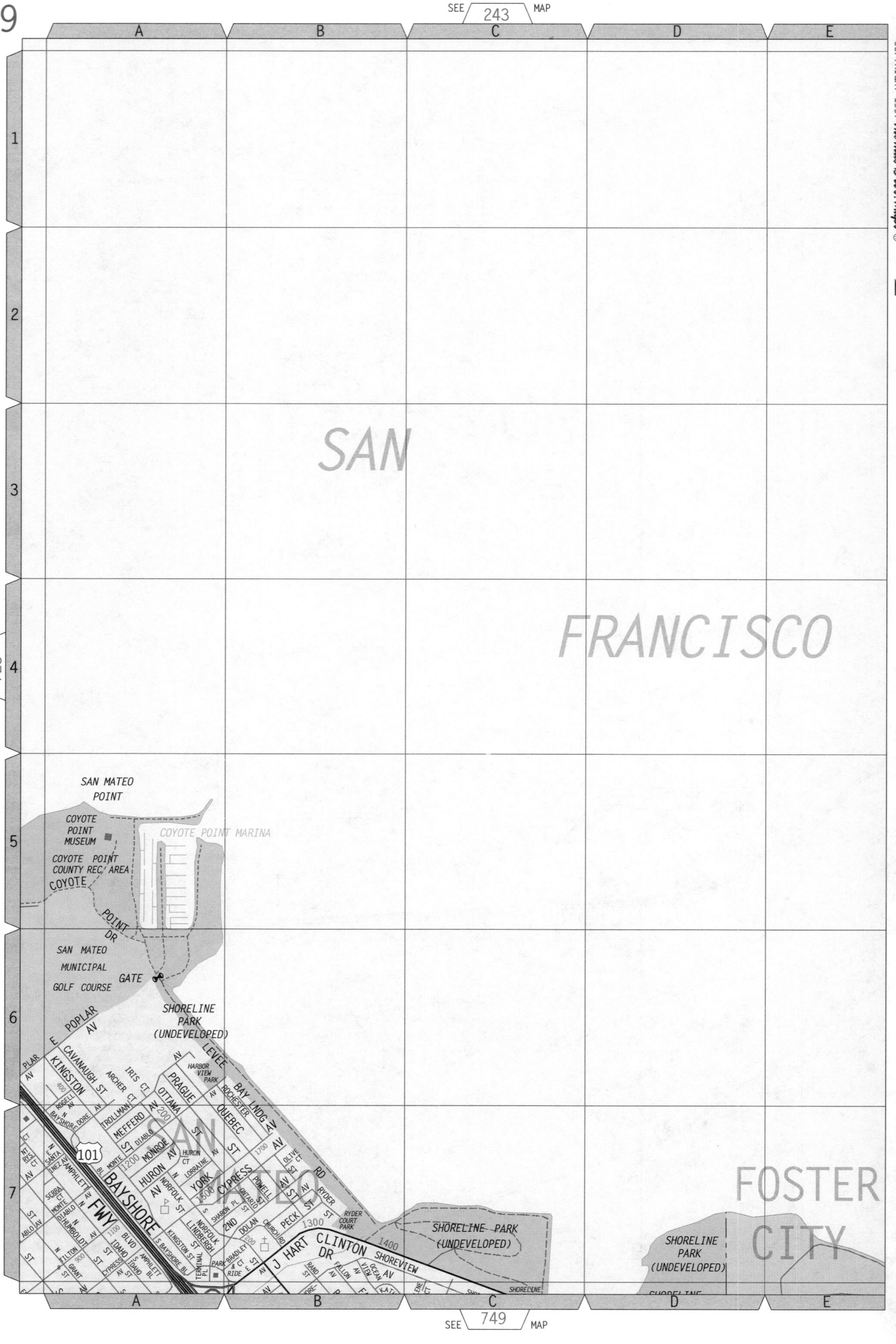
SEE 243 MAP
A
B
C
D
E
1
2
3
4
5
6
7
SEE 728 MAP
SAN
FRANCISCO
SAN MATEO POINT
COYOTE POINT MUSEUM
COYOTE POINT MARINA
COYOTE POINT COUNTY REC AREA
COYOTE
POINT
DR
SAN MATEO MUNICIPAL GOLF COURSE
GATE
SHORELINE PARK (UNDEVELOPED)
E POPLAR AV
PLAR AV
CAVANAUGH ST
KINGSTON ST
ARCHER CT
IRIS CT
HARBOR VIEW PARK
LEVEE
BAY LNDG
PRAGUE
OTTAWA
ROCHESTER
QUEBEC
TROLLMAN
MEFFERD
DIABLO
MONROE
HURON
AV
AV
HURON CT
LORRAINE
NORFOLK
YORK
CYPRESS
POWELL
OLIVE CT
RD
RYDER
RYDER COURT PARK
SAN
MATEO
101
BAYSHORE
FWY
N BAYSHORE
DORE
AMPHLETT
SERRA
MONTE
DIABLO
HUMBOLDT
IDAHO
TILTON
GRANT
CYPRESS
KINGSTON
S BAYSHORE BL
LINDBERGH
SHARON PL
TERMINAL
2ND
DOLAN
CHURCHILL
PECK
PARK & RIDE
BRADLEY CT
J HART CLINTON DR
SHOREVIEW AV
RAND
FALLON
VIEW
OCEAN
1100
1200
1300
1400
1500
1700
200
400
900
SHORELINE PARK (UNDEVELOPED)
SHORELINE
SHORELINE PARK (UNDEVELOPED)
FOSTER
CITY
SEE 749 MAP

SEE 243 MAP

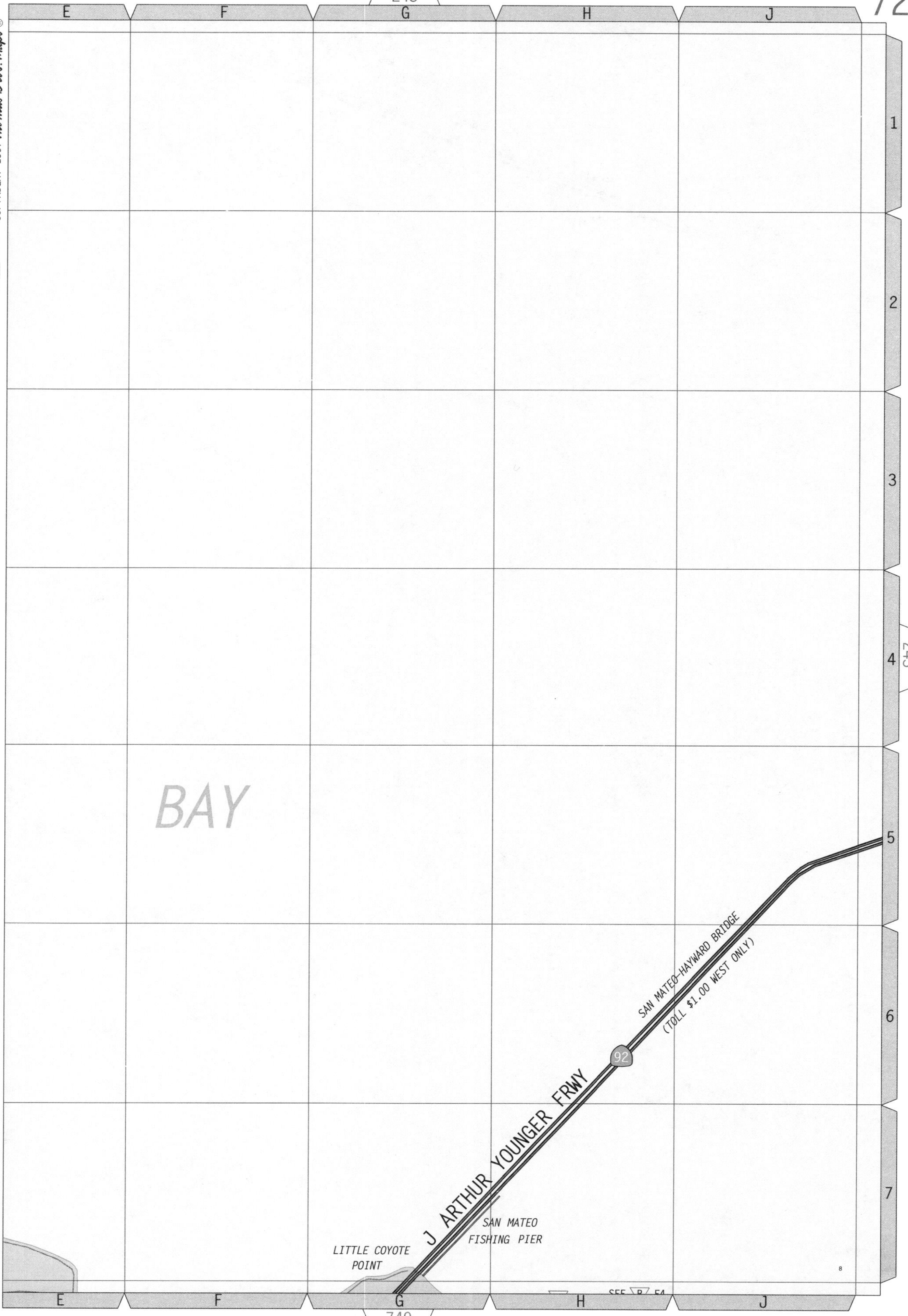
E
F
G
H
J
1
2
3
4
5
6
7
BAY
SAN MATEO-HAYWARD BRIDGE
(TOLL $1.00 WEST ONLY)
92
J ARTHUR YOUNGER FRWY
SAN MATEO
FISHING PIER
LITTLE COYOTE
POINT

SEE 243 MAP

SEE 749 MAP

BAY AREA

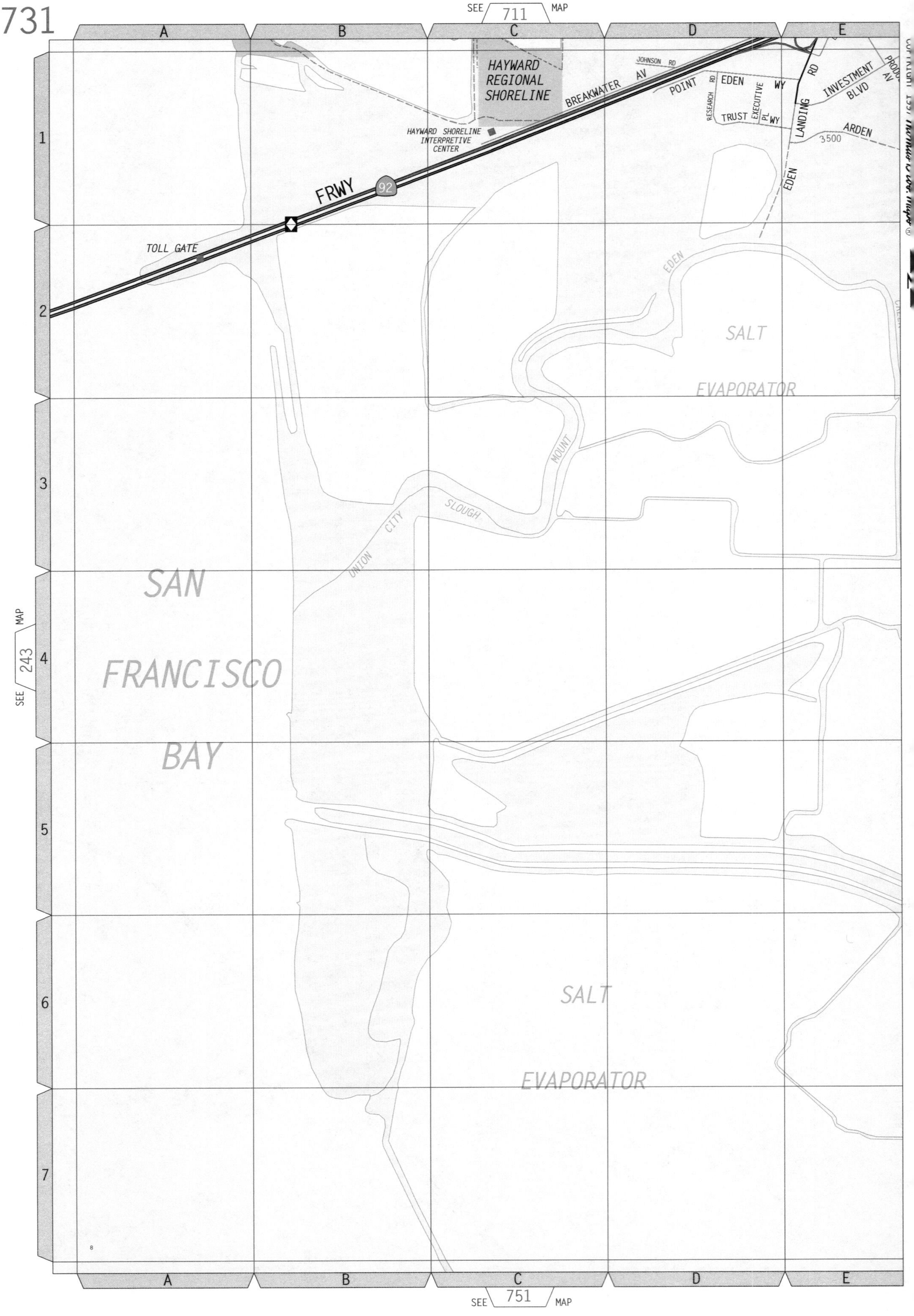

SEE 711 MAP
A
B
C
D
E
1
2
3
4
5
6
7
HAYWARD REGIONAL SHORELINE
HAYWARD SHORELINE INTERPRETIVE CENTER
JOHNSON RD
BREAKWATER AV
POINT EDEN WY
RESEARCH RD
EXECUTIVE PL
TRUST WY
LANDING RD
INVESTMENT BLVD
ARDEN
3500
EDEN
FRWY
92
TOLL GATE
SALT EVAPORATOR
MOUNT EDEN
UNION CITY SLOUGH
SAN FRANCISCO BAY
SEE 243 MAP
SALT EVAPORATOR
SEE 751 MAP

MAP

SEE 711 MAP

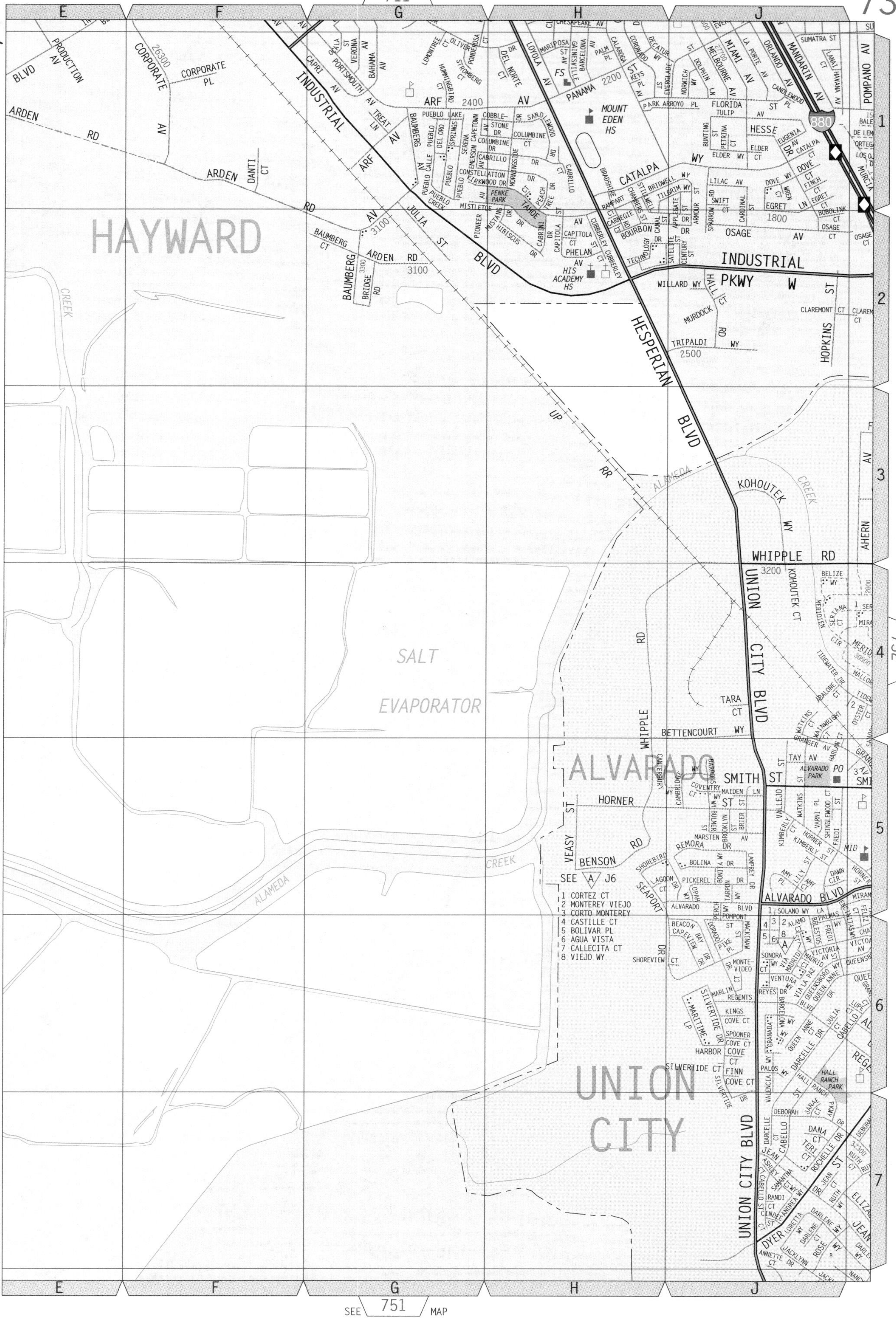
E
F
G
H
J
1
2
3
4
5
6
7
HAYWARD
SALT
EVAPORATOR
ALVARADO
UNION
CITY
INDUSTRIAL PKWY W
HESPERIAN BLVD
UNION CITY BLVD
INDUSTRIAL BLVD
WHIPPLE RD
ARDEN RD
ALVARADO BLVD
SMITH ST
ALAMEDA CREEK
UP RR
MOUNT EDEN HS
HIS ACADEMY HS
PENKE PARK
ALVARADO PARK
HALL RANCH PARK
CORPORATE AV
PRODUCTION AV
ARF AV
CATALPA WY
OSAGE AV
TRIPALDI WY
KOHOUTEK WY
BETTENCOURT WY
HORNER ST
BENSON RD
VEASY ST
SEE A J6
1 CORTEZ CT
2 MONTEREY VIEJO
3 CORTO MONTEREY
4 CASTILLE CT
5 BOLIVAR PL
6 AGUA VISTA
7 CALLECITA CT
8 VIEJO WY

SEE 732 MAP

BAY AREA

MAP

SEE 751 MAP

SEE 712 MAP

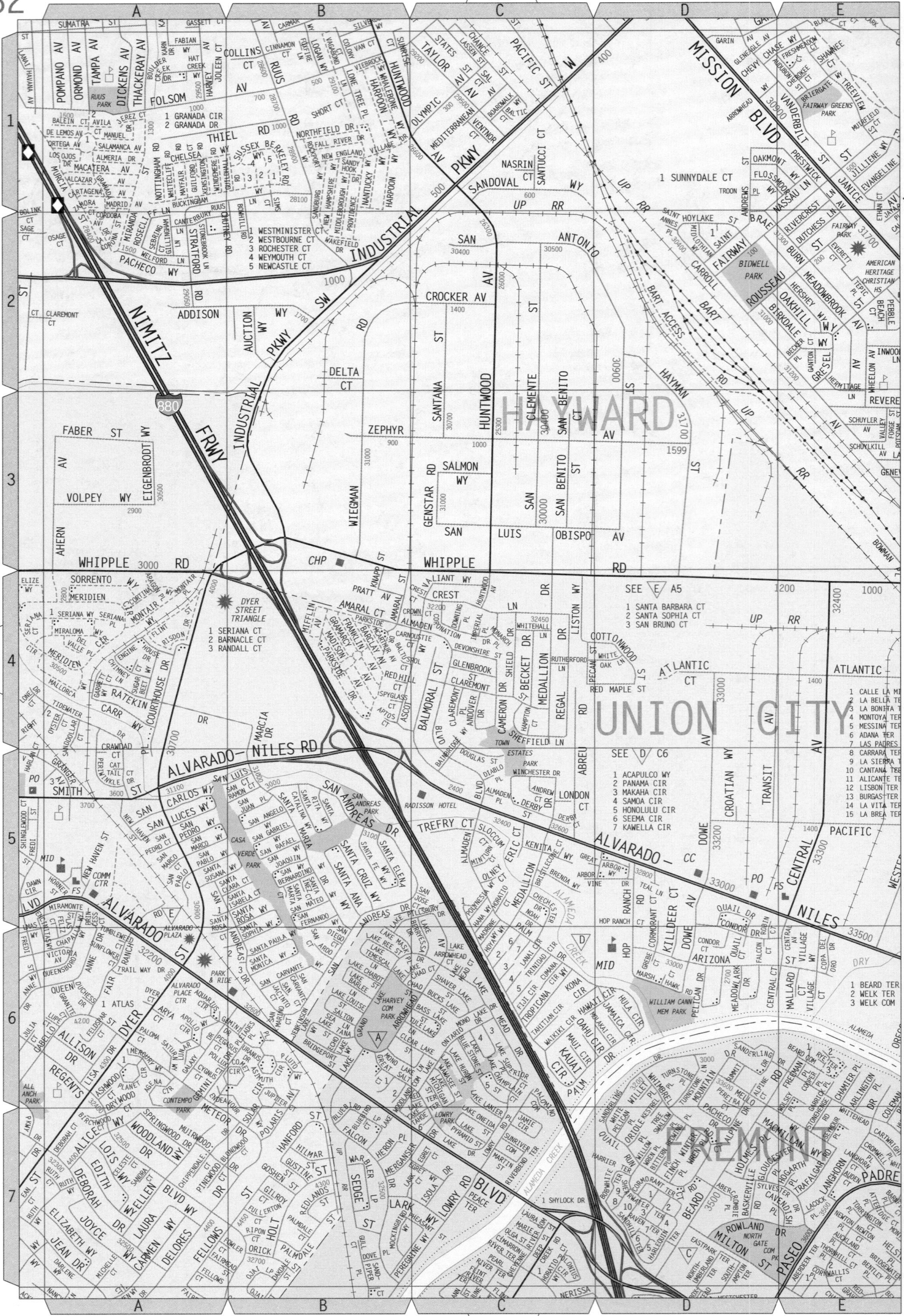
HAYWARD
UNION CITY
FREMONT
NIMITZ FRWY
880
INDUSTRIAL PKWY
INDUSTRIAL PKWY SW
MISSION BLVD
WHIPPLE RD
ALVARADO-NILES RD
ALVARADO BLVD
DYER ST
SMITH ST
HUNTWOOD AV
SAN ANTONIO ST
CROCKER AV
ZEPHYR
SAN LUIS OBISPO AV
ADDISON
FOLSOM AV
THIEL RD
PACHECO WY
SANDOVAL WY
UP RR
BART
BIDWELL PARK
RUUS PARK
DYER STREET TRIANGLE
HARVEY COM PARK
WILLIAM CANN MEM PARK
CONTEMPO PARK
RADISSON HOTEL
ALVARADO PLAZA
ALAMEDA CREEK
AMERICAN HERITAGE CHRISTIAN HS
FAIRWAY PARK
FAIRWAY GREENS PARK
1 GRANADA CIR
2 GRANADA DR
1 WESTMINISTER CT
2 WESTBOURNE CT
3 ROCHESTER CT
4 WEYMOUTH CT
5 NEWCASTLE CT
1 SERIANA CT
2 BARNACLE CT
3 RANDALL CT
SEE E A5
1 SANTA BARBARA CT
2 SANTA SOPHIA CT
3 SAN BRUNO CT
SEE D C6
1 ACAPULCO WY
2 PANAMA CIR
3 MAKAHA CIR
4 SAMOA CIR
5 HONOLULU CIR
6 SEEMA CIR
7 KAWELLA CIR
1 CALLE LA MI
2 LA BELLA TER
3 LA BONITA TER
4 MONTOYA TER
5 MESSINA TER
6 ADANA TER
7 LAS PADRES
8 CARRARA TER
9 LA SIERRA T
10 CANTANA TER
11 ALICANTE TE
12 LISBON TER
13 BURGAS TER
14 LA VITA TER
15 LA BREA TE
1 BEARD TER
2 WELK TER
3 WELK COM
1 SUNNYDALE CT
1 ATLAS
1 SHYLOCK DR

SEE 731 MAP
SEE 752 MAP

SEE 712 MAP

GARIN REGIONAL PARK
DRY CREEK PIONEER REGIONAL PARK
HAY
JORDON POND
CHAPEL OF THE CHIMES MEMORIAL CEM
AMERICAN HERITAGE CHRISTIAN HS
EL RANCHO VERDE ALT HS
DECOTO
MASONIC HOME FOR ADULTS
SEVEN HILLS PARK
CHARLES F KENNEDY PARK
JAMES LOGAN HS
UNION CITY MARKETPLACE
EL MERCADO PLAZA
ARROYO PARK
QUARRY LAKES REGIONAL PARK
NILES
MISSION BLVD
WHIPPLE RD
DECOTO RD
ALVARADO NILES RD
NILES BLVD
PADRE PKWY
OLD RANCH TR
HIGH RIDGE LOOP TR
SEE C D7
1 THRUSH TER
2 DOWITCHER TER
3 FULMAR TER
4 FOXSWALLOW TER
5 AVOCET TER
6 KINGLET TER
7 GANNET TER
8 GOLDFINCH TER
9 GOLDFINCH TER
10 CARDINAL TER
SEE B E7
1 CHAMBERLAIN TER
2 CHAUCER DR
3 WARWICK CT
4 WINCHESTER PL
SEE A B6
1 JACANA LAKE CT
2 SHOVLER LAKE CT
3 LAKE CANDLEWOOD ST
4 LAKE ERIE ST
5 LAKE GARRISON ST
6 GREAT SALT LAKE TER
1 CALLE LA MIRADA COM
2 LA BELLA TER
3 LA BONITA TER
4 MONTOYA TER
5 MESSINA TER
6 ADANA TER
7 LAS PADRES TER
8 CARRARA TER
9 LA SIERRA TER
10 CANTANA TER
11 ALICANTE TER
12 LISBON TER
13 BURGAS TER
14 LA VITA TER
15 LA BREA TER
1 DONOSO PZ
2 CORONA PZ
3 CAMINO PZ
4 BOLERO PZ
5 AURORA PZ
1 BEARD TER
2 WELK TER
3 WELK COM
SEE 733 MAP

SEE 752 MAP

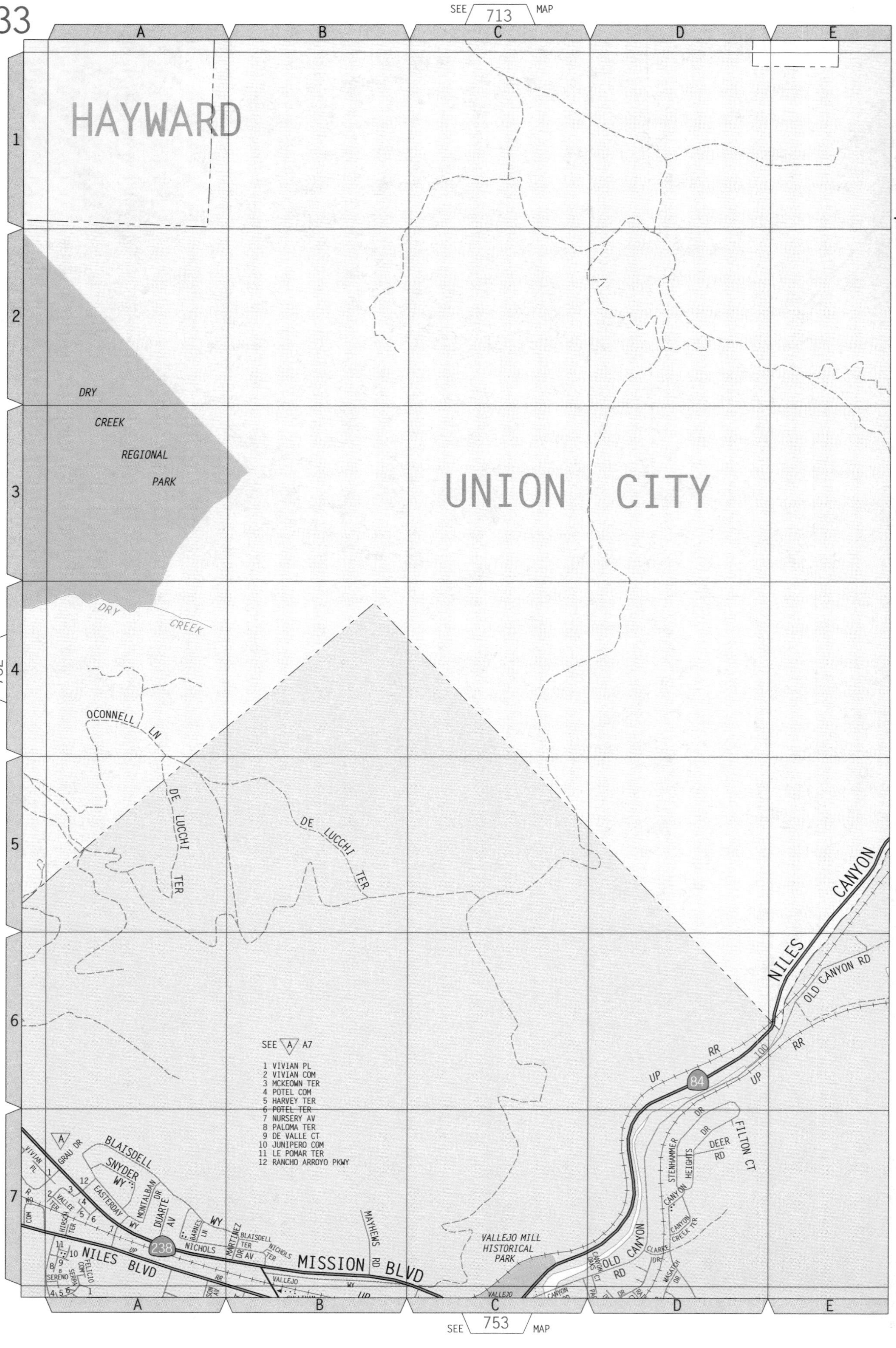
SEE 713 MAP
SEE 732 MAP
SEE 753 MAP
A
B
C
D
E
1
2
3
4
5
6
7
HAYWARD
UNION CITY
DRY CREEK REGIONAL PARK
DRY CREEK
OCONNELL LN
DE LUCCHI TER
NILES CANYON
OLD CANYON RD
UP RR
84
100
SEE A A7
1 VIVIAN PL
2 VIVIAN COM
3 MCKEOWN TER
4 POTEL COM
5 HARVEY TER
6 POTEL TER
7 NURSERY AV
8 PALOMA TER
9 DE VALLE CT
10 JUNIPERO COM
11 LE POMAR TER
12 RANCHO ARROYO PKWY
BLAISDELL
GRAU DR
SNYDER WY
EASTERDAY WY
MONTALBAN DR
DUARTE AV
VIVIAN PL
VALLEE TER
HIRSCH TER
BARNES LN
NICHOLS
MARTINEZ DR
BLAISDELL TER
NICHOLS TER
238
NILES BLVD
MISSION BLVD
MAYHEWS RD
VALLEJO
VALLEJO MILL HISTORICAL PARK
SERENO
FELICIO COM
SERPA COM
FILTON CT
DEER RD
STENHAMMER DR
HEIGHTS DR
CANYON HEIGHTS DR
CANYON CREEK TER
CANYON OAKS CT
OLD CANYON RD
CLARKE DR
WASATCH DR

SEE 713 MAP

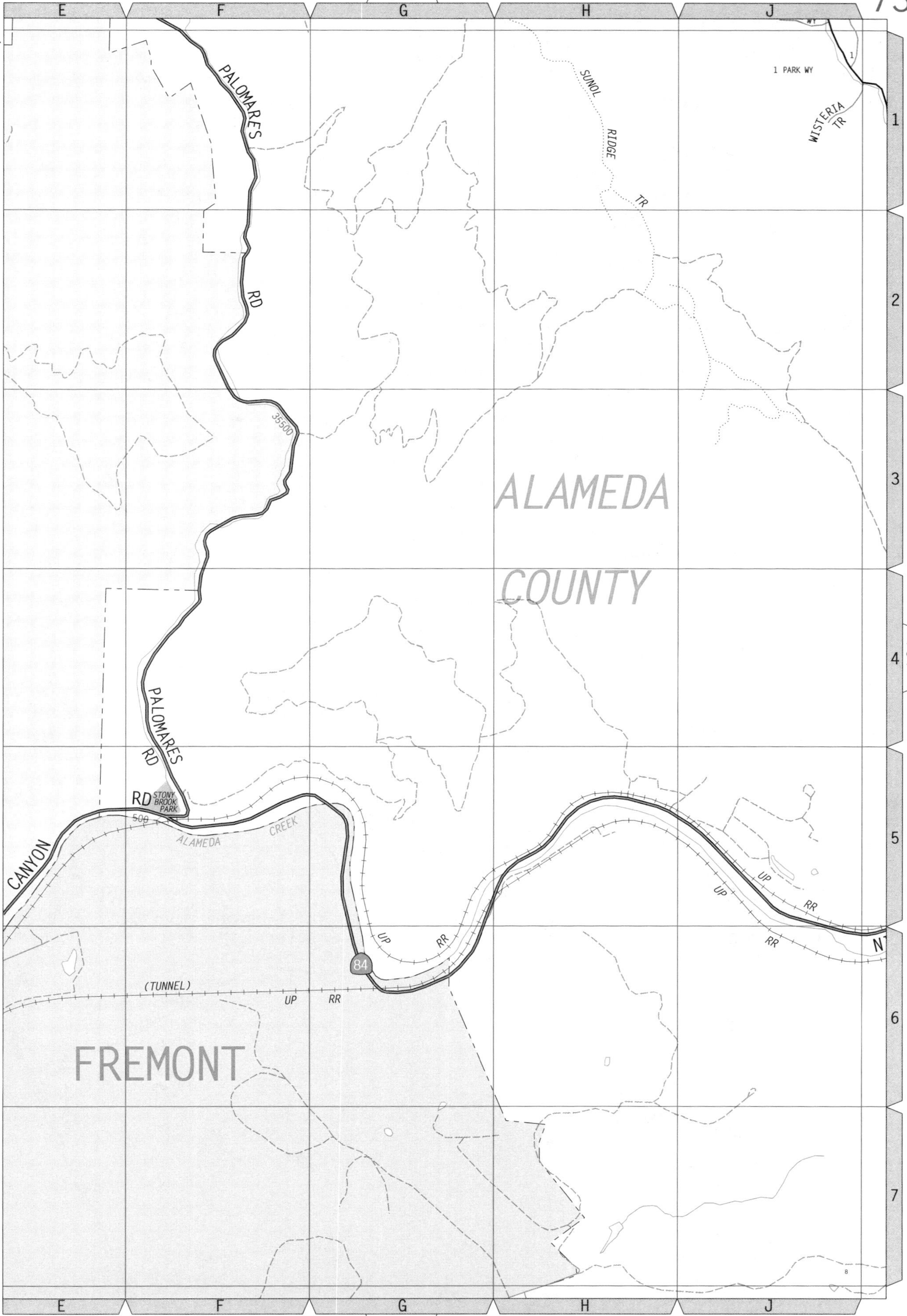
E
F
G
H
J
1
2
3
4
5
6
7
PALOMARES
RD
35500
PALOMARES
RD
RD
STONY BROOK PARK
500
ALAMEDA CREEK
CANYON
84
(TUNNEL)
UP RR
UP RR
UP RR
UP RR
SUNOL RIDGE TR
1 PARK WY
WISTERIA TR
ALAMEDA
COUNTY
FREMONT
NT

SEE 734 MAP
SEE 753 MAP

BAY AREA
MAP

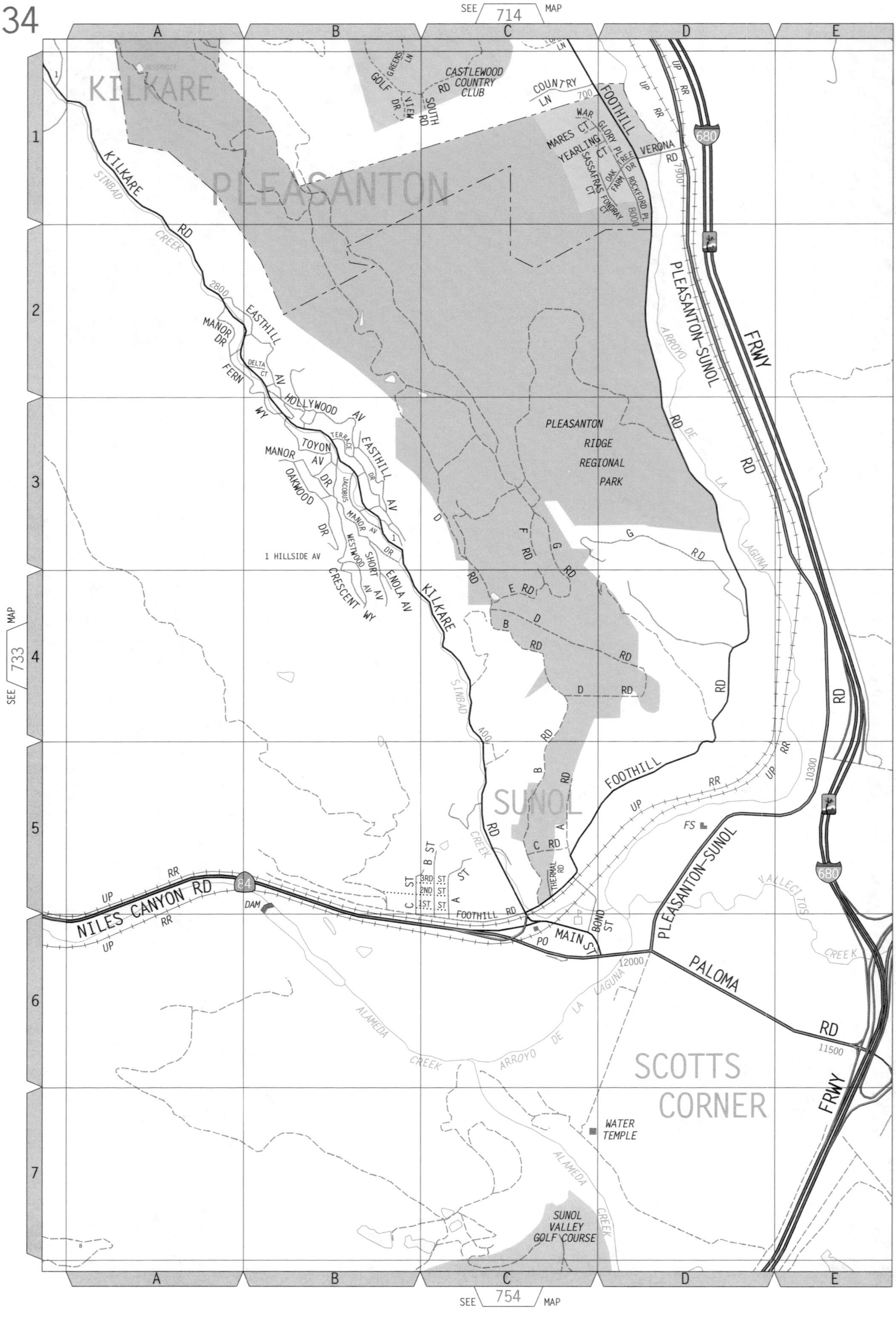
SEE 714 MAP
SEE 733 MAP
SEE 754 MAP
A
B
C
D
E
1
2
3
4
5
6
7
KILKARE
PLEASANTON
SUNOL
SCOTTS CORNER
CASTLEWOOD COUNTRY CLUB
PLEASANTON RIDGE REGIONAL PARK
SUNOL VALLEY GOLF COURSE
WATER TEMPLE
KILKARE RD
SINBAD CREEK
EASTHILL
MANOR DR
DELTA CT
FERN WY
HOLLYWOOD AV
TERRACE
EASTHILL DR
EASTHILL AV
TOYON AV
MANOR DR
OAKWOOD DR
JACOBUS
MANOR AV
WESTWOOD
SHORT AV
ENOLA AV
CRESCENT WY
1 HILLSIDE AV
GOLF VIEW DR
GREENS LN
SOUTH RD
COUNTRY LN
FOOTHILL RD
WAR
MARES CT
YEARLING CT
GLORY PL
TREE
SASSAFRAS CT
OAK FARM DR
FONDRAY CT
ROCKFORD PL
VERONA RD
PLEASANTON-SUNOL RD
ARROYO DE LA LAGUNA
FRWY
680
UP RR
D RD
F RD
G RD
E RD
B RD
C RD
A RD
THERMAL RD
NILES CANYON RD
84
DAM
C ST
B ST
3RD ST
2ND ST
1ST ST
A ST
FOOTHILL RD
PO
MAIN ST
BOND ST
FS
PALOMA RD
VALLECITOS CREEK
ALAMEDA CREEK
2800
400
700
7900
8000
10300
11500
12000

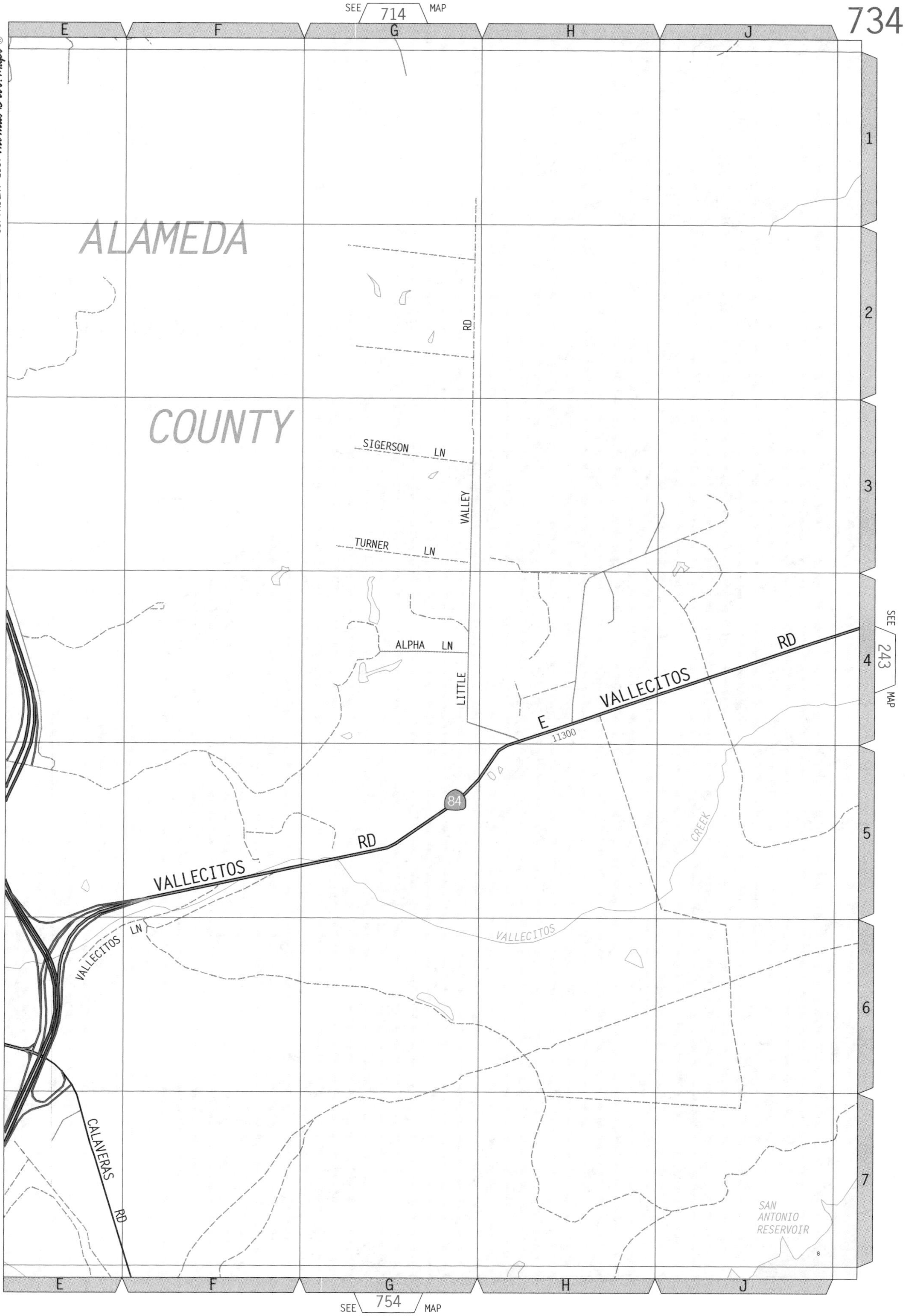
SEE 714 MAP
E
F
G
H
J
1
2
3
4
5
6
7
ALAMEDA
COUNTY
SIGERSON LN
TURNER LN
ALPHA LN
LITTLE VALLEY RD
E VALLECITOS RD
11300
84
VALLECITOS RD
VALLECITOS LN
CREEK
VALLECITOS
CALAVERAS RD
SAN ANTONIO RESERVOIR
SEE 243 MAP
SEE 754 MAP

BAY AREA

MAP

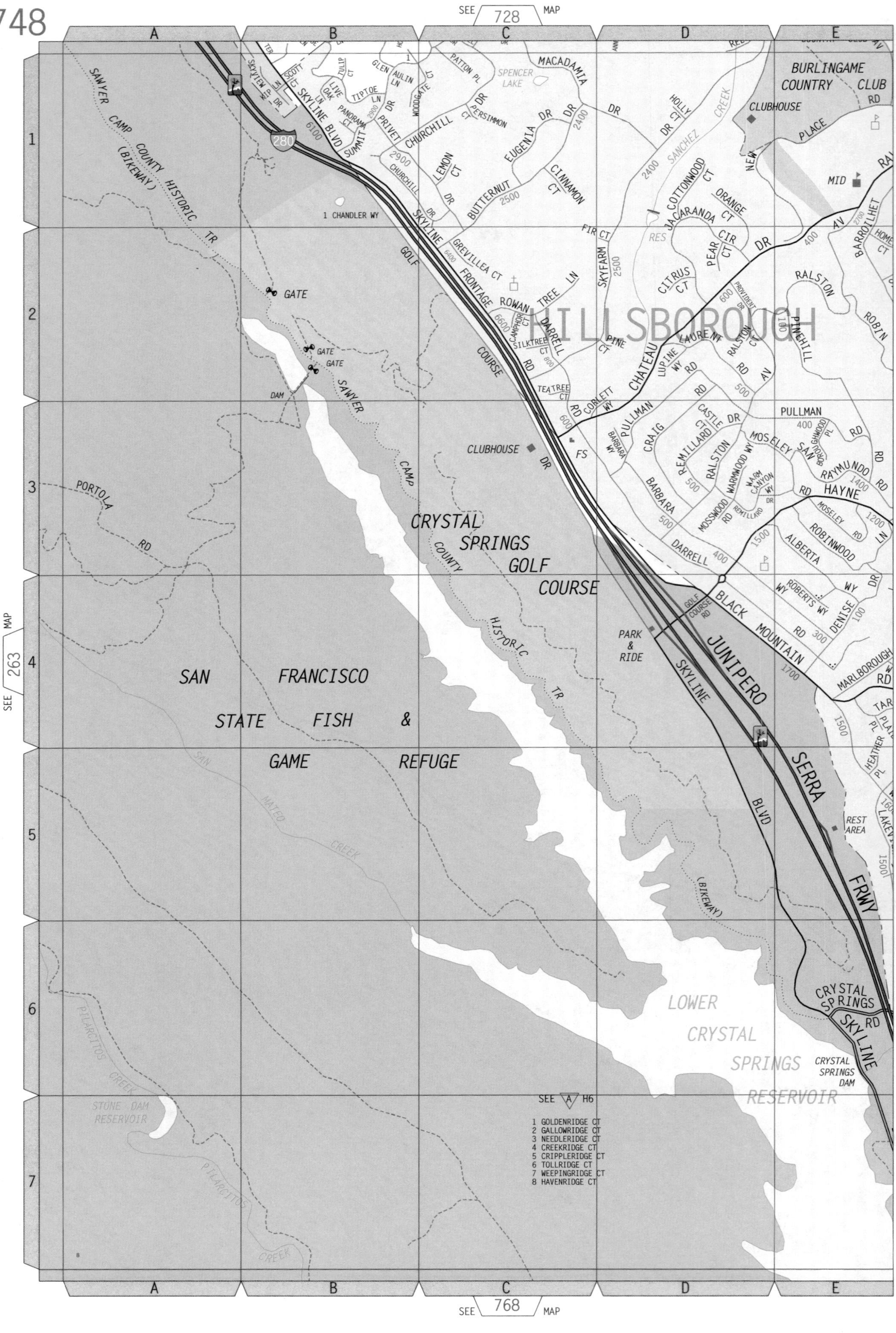
SEE 728 MAP
SEE 768 MAP
SEE 263 MAP
A B C D E
1 2 3 4 5 6 7
HILLSBOROUGH
SAN FRANCISCO STATE FISH & GAME REFUGE
CRYSTAL SPRINGS GOLF COURSE
BURLINGAME COUNTRY CLUB
CLUBHOUSE
LOWER CRYSTAL SPRINGS RESERVOIR
CRYSTAL SPRINGS DAM
STONE DAM RESERVOIR
SPENCER LAKE
SAWYER CAMP COUNTY HISTORIC TR
(BIKEWAY)
CRYSTAL COUNTY HISTORIC TR
PORTOLA RD
JUNIPERO SERRA FRWY
SKYLINE BLVD
GOLF COURSE DR
SKYLINE FRONTAGE RD
BLACK MOUNTAIN RD
CRYSTAL SPRINGS RD
SAN MATEO CREEK
PILARCITOS CREEK
SANCHEZ CREEK
GATE
DAM
PARK & RIDE
REST AREA
FS
RES
MID
1 CHANDLER WY
MACADAMIA
CHURCHILL DR
EUGENIA DR
CINNAMON CT
BUTTERNUT DR
LEMON CT
PERSIMMON
PRIVET DR
SUMMIT
TIPTOE LN
PANORAMA CT
LIVE OAK LN
SCOTT CT
GLEN AULIN LN
WOODGATE CT
PATTON PL
GREVILLEA CT
ROWAN DR
DARRELL RD
TREE LN
SILKTREE CT
TEATREE CT
CAMPHOR
CORLETT WY
CHATEAU DR
PINE CT
LUPINE WY
LAURENT RD
RALSTON AV
PINEHILL
ROBIN
SKYFARM
CITRUS CT
PEAR CT
JACARANDA CIR
COTTONWOOD CT
ORANGE CT
HOLLY DR
FIR CT
PULLMAN
CRAIG
REMILLARD CT
CASTLE DR
BARBARA WY
RALSTON
WARMWOOD WY
MOSSWOOD RD
WARM CANYON WY
MOSELEY RD
HAYNE RD
RAYMUNDO DR
ROBINWOOD
ALBERTA
ROBERTS WY
DENISE
MARLBOROUGH RD
BARROILHET AV
HOME CT
PLACE
NEW
SEE A H6
1 GOLDENRIDGE CT
2 GALLOWRIDGE CT
3 NEEDLERIDGE CT
4 CREEKRIDGE CT
5 CRIPPLERIDGE CT
6 TOLLRIDGE CT
7 WEEPINGRIDGE CT
8 HAVENRIDGE CT
280

SEE 728 MAP

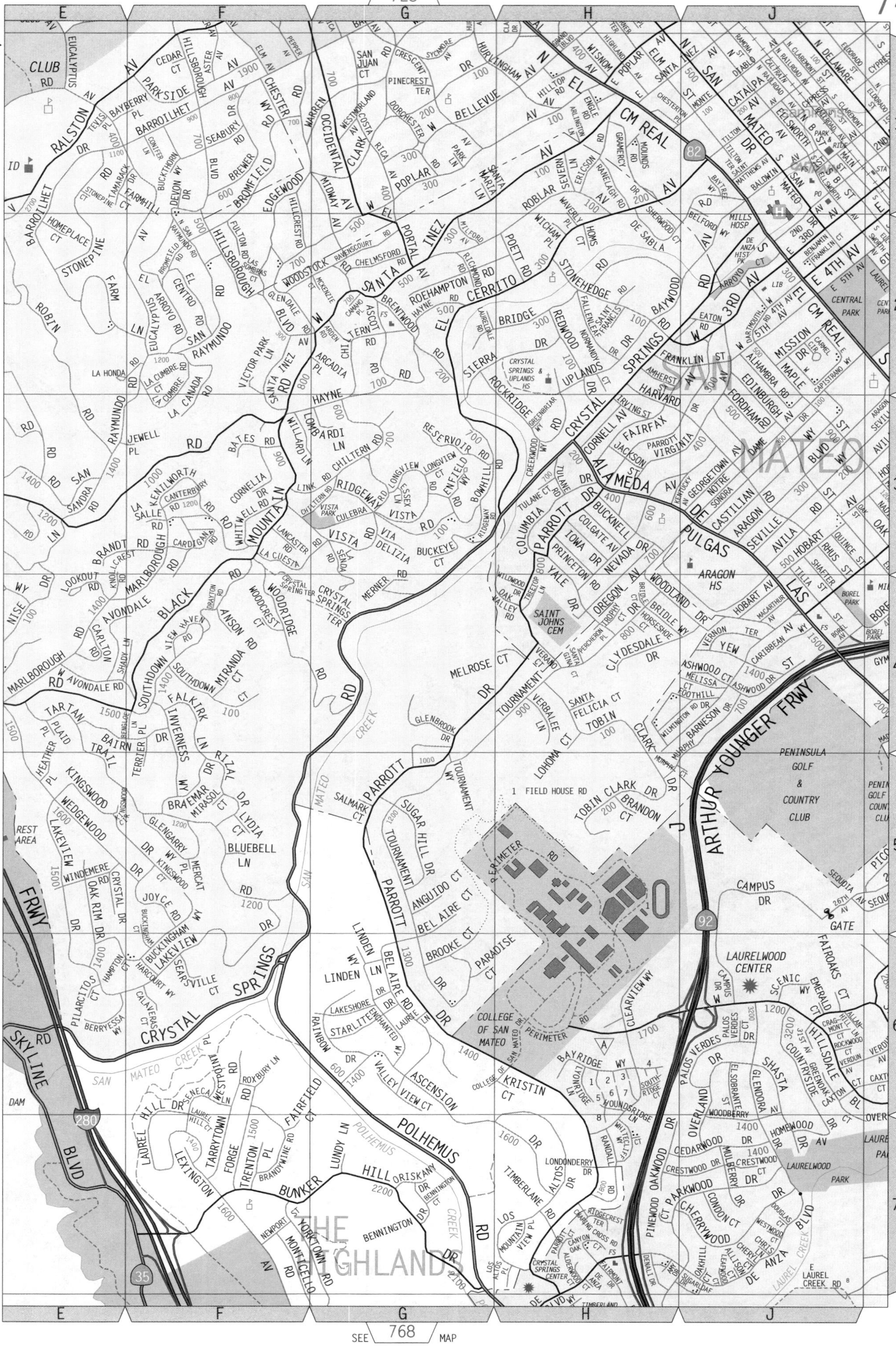
SAN MATEO
THE HIGHLANDS
COLLEGE OF SAN MATEO
PENINSULA GOLF & COUNTRY CLUB
CENTRAL PARK
LAURELWOOD CENTER
LAURELWOOD PARK
SAINT JOHNS CEM
ARAGON HS
MILLS HOSP
CRYSTAL SPRINGS & UPLANDS HS
CRYSTAL SPRINGS CENTER
REST AREA
SAN MATEO CREEK
POLHEMUS CREEK
LAUREL CREEK
ARTHUR YOUNGER FRWY
CRYSTAL SPRINGS RD
POLHEMUS RD
SKYLINE BLVD
EL CAMINO REAL
ALAMEDA DE LAS PULGAS
BLACK MOUNTAIN RD
HILLSDALE BL
PARROTT DR
EL CERRITO AV
SANTA INEZ AV
W 3RD AV
E 4TH AV
RALSTON AV
BUNKER HILL DR
DE ANZA BLVD
FIELD HOUSE RD
CAMPUS DR
GATE
82
92
280
35

SEE 749 MAP

SEE 768 MAP

SEE 729 MAP

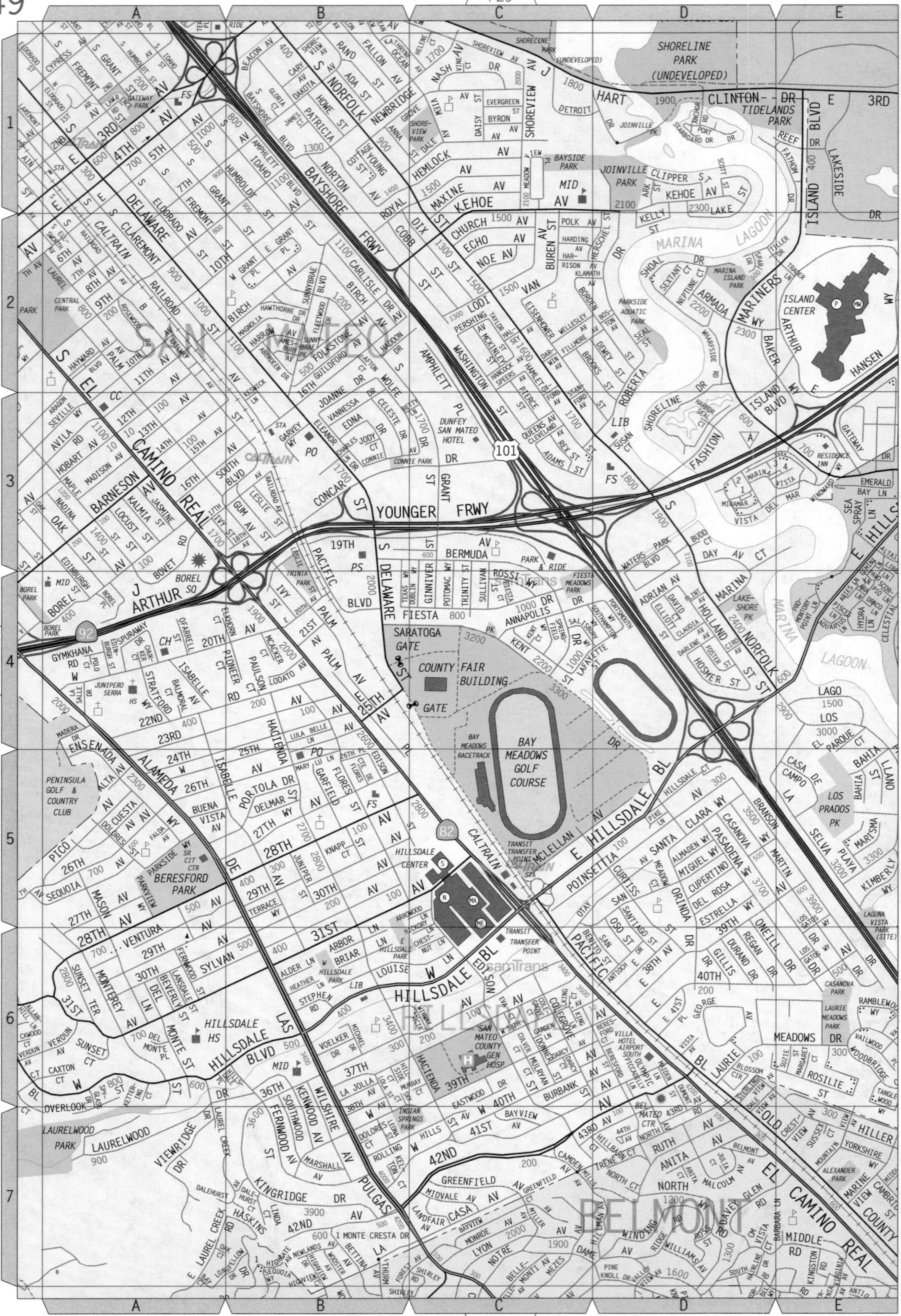
SHORELINE PARK (UNDEVELOPED)
TIDELANDS PARK
SAN MATEO
BAYSHORE FRWY
101
YOUNGER FRWY
J ARTHUR
92
EL CAMINO REAL
CALTRAIN
MARINA LAGOON
ISLAND CENTER
BAYSIDE PARK
JOINVILLE PARK
CENTRAL PARK
DUNFEY SAN MATEO HOTEL
BOREL SQ
SARATOGA GATE
COUNTY FAIR BUILDING
BAY MEADOWS GOLF COURSE
BAY MEADOWS RACETRACK
PENINSULA GOLF & COUNTRY CLUB
BERESFORD PARK
HILLSDALE CENTER
HILLSDALE HS
SAN MATEO COUNTY GEN HOSP
HILLSDALE
LAURELWOOD PARK
BELMONT
LOS PRADOS PK
E HILLSDALE BL
S DELAWARE
ALAMEDA DE LAS PULGAS
HILLSDALE BLVD
PACIFIC BLVD
S NORFOLK ST
MARINERS ISLAND BLVD
ISLAND BLVD
E 3RD AV
CLINTON DR
KEHOE AV
FASHION ISLAND BLVD
82

SEE 748 MAP

SEE 769 MAP

SEE 729 MAP

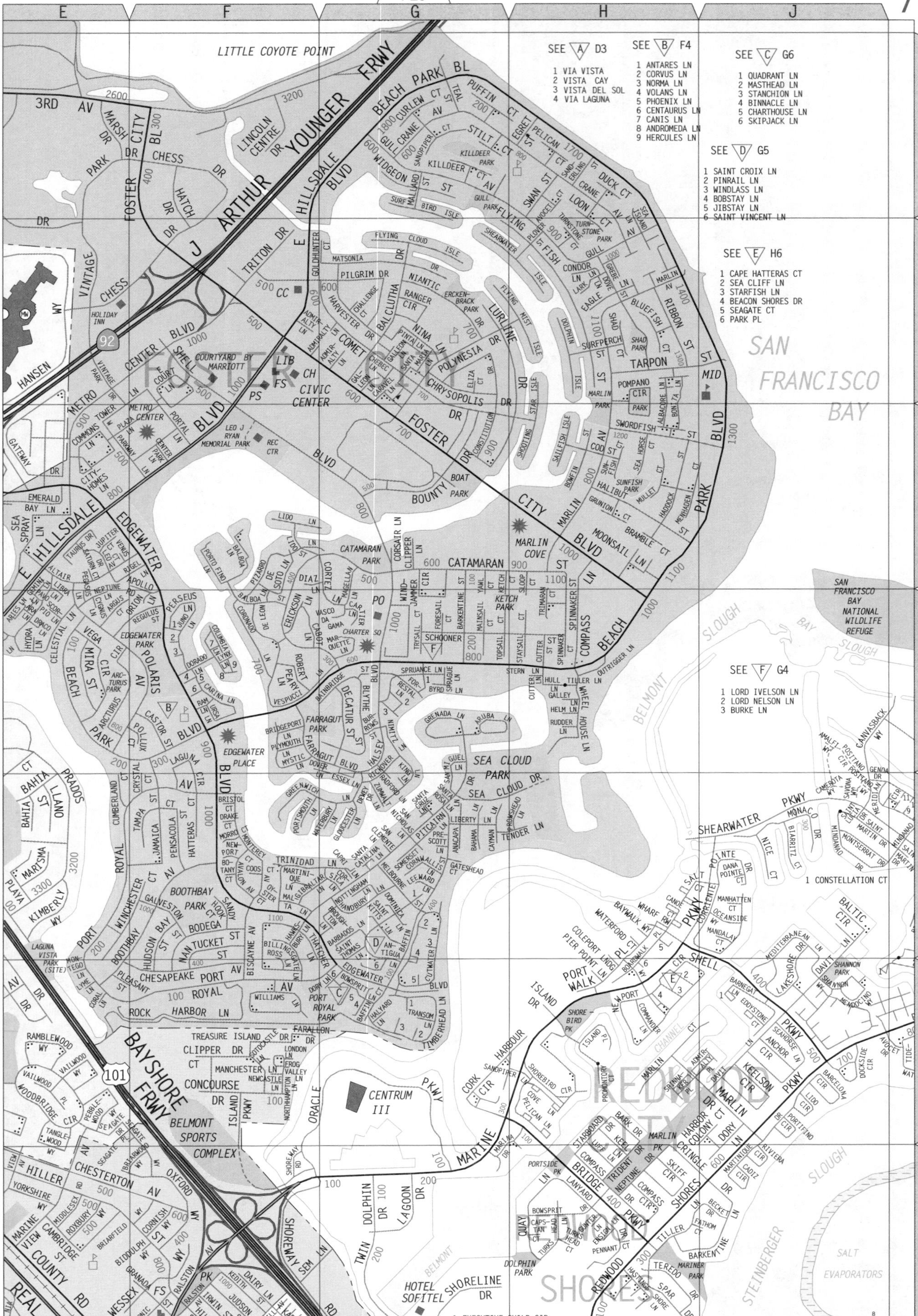
LITTLE COYOTE POINT
J ARTHUR YOUNGER FRWY
FOSTER CITY
SAN FRANCISCO BAY
SAN FRANCISCO BAY NATIONAL WILDLIFE REFUGE
BAYSHORE FRWY
REDWOOD CITY
REDWOOD SHORES
BELMONT SPORTS COMPLEX
CENTRUM III
HOTEL SOFITEL
SALT EVAPORATORS
SEE A D3
1 VIA VISTA
2 VISTA CAY
3 VISTA DEL SOL
4 VIA LAGUNA
SEE B F4
1 ANTARES LN
2 CORVUS LN
3 NORMA LN
4 VOLANS LN
5 PHOENIX LN
6 CENTAURUS LN
7 CANIS LN
8 ANDROMEDA LN
9 HERCULES LN
SEE C G6
1 QUADRANT LN
2 MASTHEAD LN
3 STANCHION LN
4 BINNACLE LN
5 CHARTHOUSE LN
6 SKIPJACK LN
SEE D G5
1 SAINT CROIX LN
2 PINRAIL LN
3 WINDLASS LN
4 BOBSTAY LN
5 JIBSTAY LN
6 SAINT VINCENT LN
SEE E H6
1 CAPE HATTERAS CT
2 SEA CLIFF LN
3 STARFISH LN
4 BEACON SHORES DR
5 SEAGATE CT
6 PARK PL
SEE F G4
1 LORD IVELSON LN
2 LORD NELSON LN
3 BURKE LN
1 CONSTELLATION CT
1 EXECUTIVE GUILD CIR

SEE 750 MAP

SEE 769 MAP

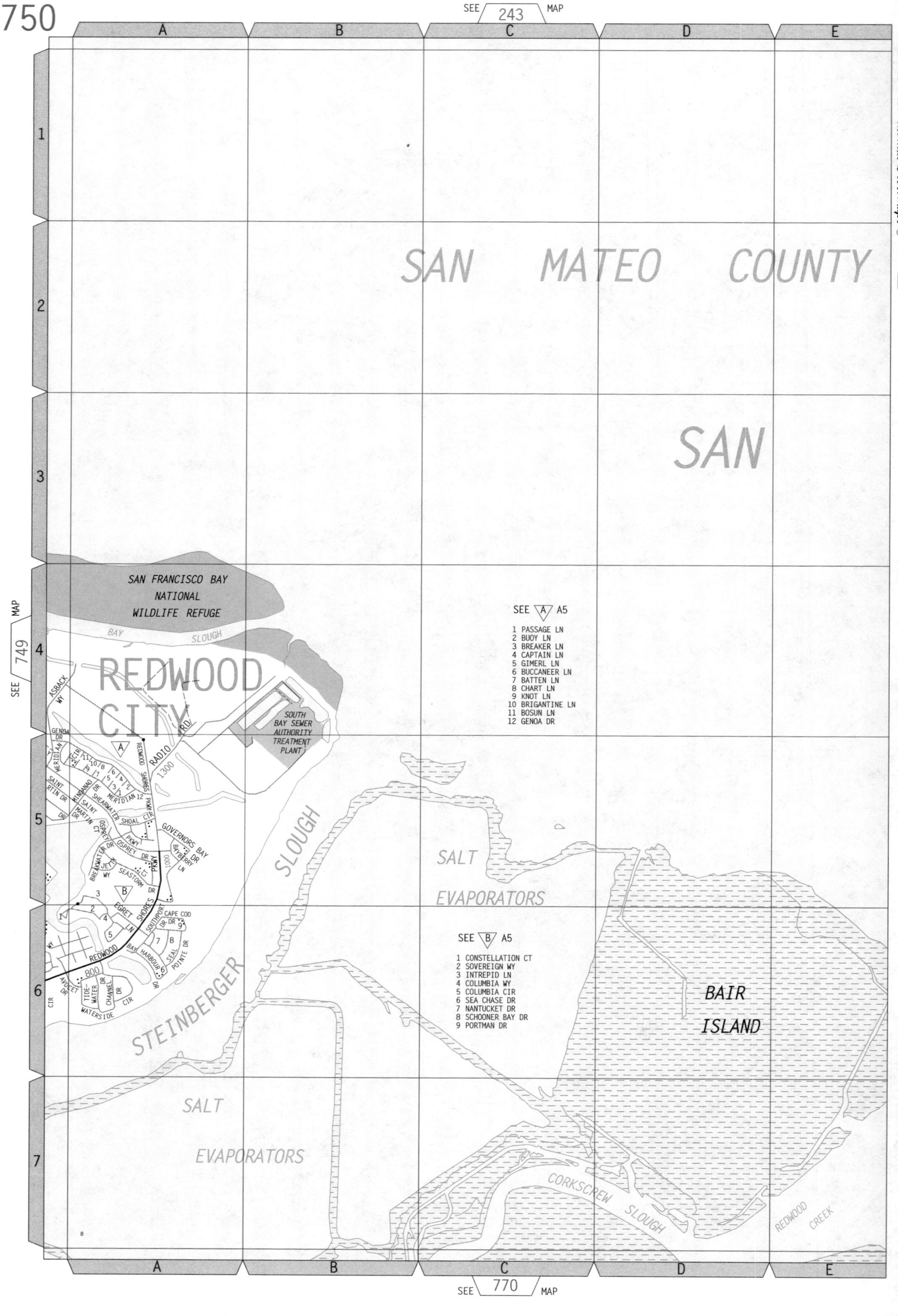
SEE 243 MAP
SEE 749 MAP
SEE 770 MAP
A B C D E
1 2 3 4 5 6 7
SAN MATEO COUNTY
SAN
SAN FRANCISCO BAY NATIONAL WILDLIFE REFUGE
BAY SLOUGH
REDWOOD CITY
SOUTH BAY SEWER AUTHORITY TREATMENT PLANT
RADIO RD
1300
REDWOOD SHORES PKWY
ASBACK WY
GENOA DR
MERIDIAN
MINDANAO DR
SAINT MARTIN DR
SHEARWATER
SHOAL CIR
GOVERNORS BAY DR
BAYBERRY LN
OSPREY DR
OSPREY CT
BREAKWATER DR
JETTY WY
SEASTORM DR
1000
EGRET LN
SHORES PKWY
SOUTHPORT DR
CAPE COD DR
SEAL POINTE DR
BAY HARBOUR DR
REDWOOD
800
AVOCET DR
TIDE-WATER DR
CHANNEL DR
CIR
WATERSIDE CIR
SLOUGH
STEINBERGER
SALT EVAPORATORS
SALT EVAPORATORS
BAIR ISLAND
CORKSCREW SLOUGH
REDWOOD CREEK
SEE A A5
1 PASSAGE LN
2 BUOY LN
3 BREAKER LN
4 CAPTAIN LN
5 GIMERL LN
6 BUCCANEER LN
7 BATTEN LN
8 CHART LN
9 KNOT LN
10 BRIGANTINE LN
11 BOSUN LN
12 GENOA DR
SEE B A5
1 CONSTELLATION CT
2 SOVEREIGN WY
3 INTREPID LN
4 COLUMBIA WY
5 COLUMBIA CIR
6 SEA CHASE DR
7 NANTUCKET DR
8 SCHOONER BAY DR
9 PORTMAN DR

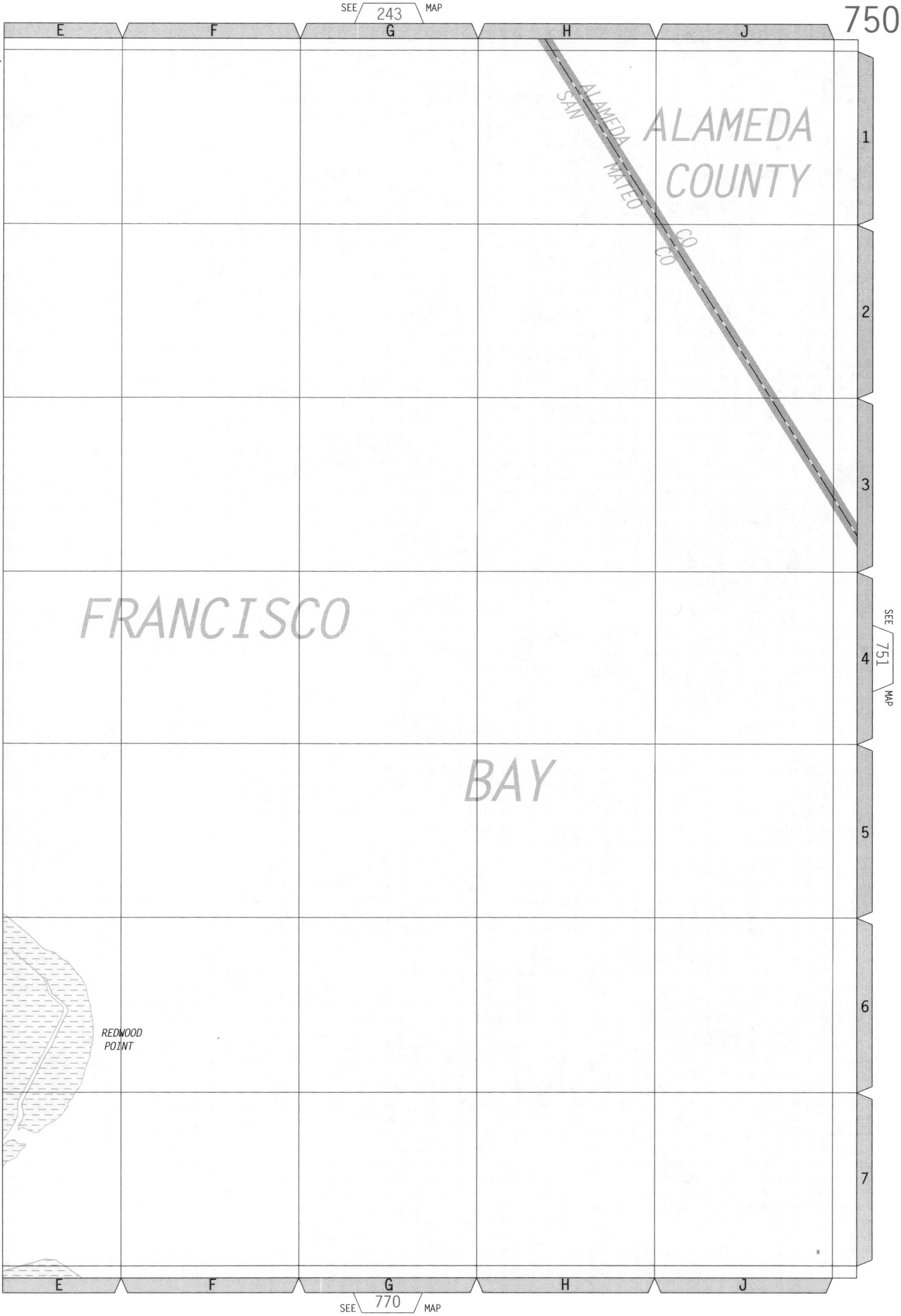

SEE 243 MAP
E
F
G
H
J
1
2
3
4
5
6
7
ALAMEDA COUNTY
ALAMEDA CO
SAN MATEO CO
FRANCISCO
BAY
SEE 751 MAP
REDWOOD POINT
SEE 770 MAP

SEE 731 MAP

SEE 750 MAP

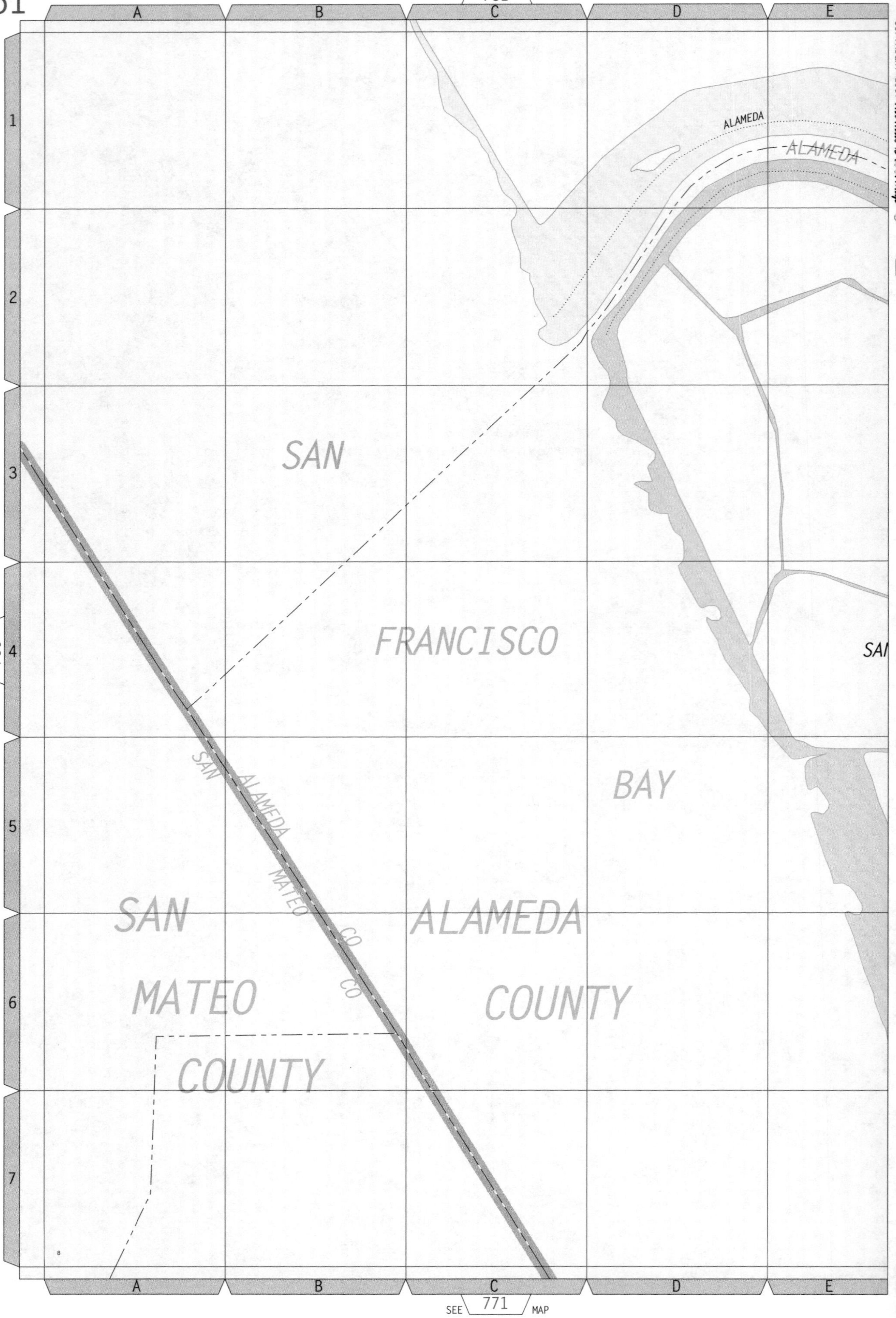

SEE 771 MAP

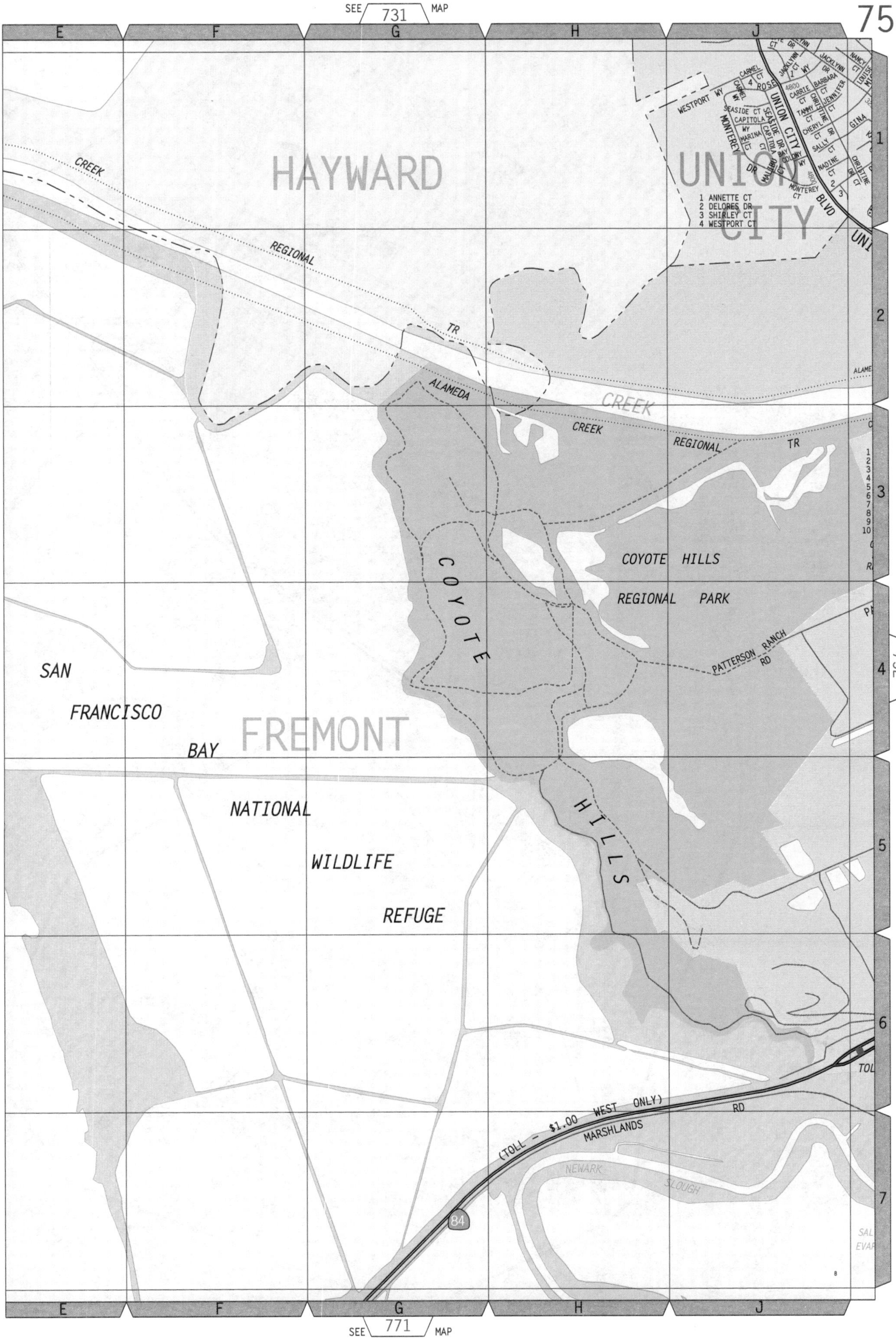
SEE 731 MAP
E
F
G
H
J
1
2
3
4
5
6
7
HAYWARD
UNION CITY
FREMONT
CREEK
REGIONAL
TR
ALAMEDA
CREEK
CREEK
REGIONAL
TR
WESTPORT WY
CARMEL
CARMEL WY
ROSE
SEASIDE CT
CAPITOLA
MARINA
MONTEREY
MALIBU
SEASIDE DR
CAPITOLA CT
BAY COLONY
UNION CITY BLVD
JACKLYNN
CARRIE
BARBARA
TAMMY CT
CHRISTINE
JENNIFER
CHERYL CT
SALLY CT
NADINE CT
GINA
NANCY
MONTEREY CT
1 ANNETTE CT
2 DELORES DR
3 SHIRLEY CT
4 WESTPORT CT
COYOTE HILLS REGIONAL PARK
COYOTE
HILLS
PATTERSON RANCH RD
SEE 752 MAP
SAN FRANCISCO BAY
NATIONAL WILDLIFE REFUGE
(TOLL - $1.00 WEST ONLY)
MARSHLANDS
RD
NEWARK
SLOUGH
84
SEE 771 MAP

SEE 732 MAP

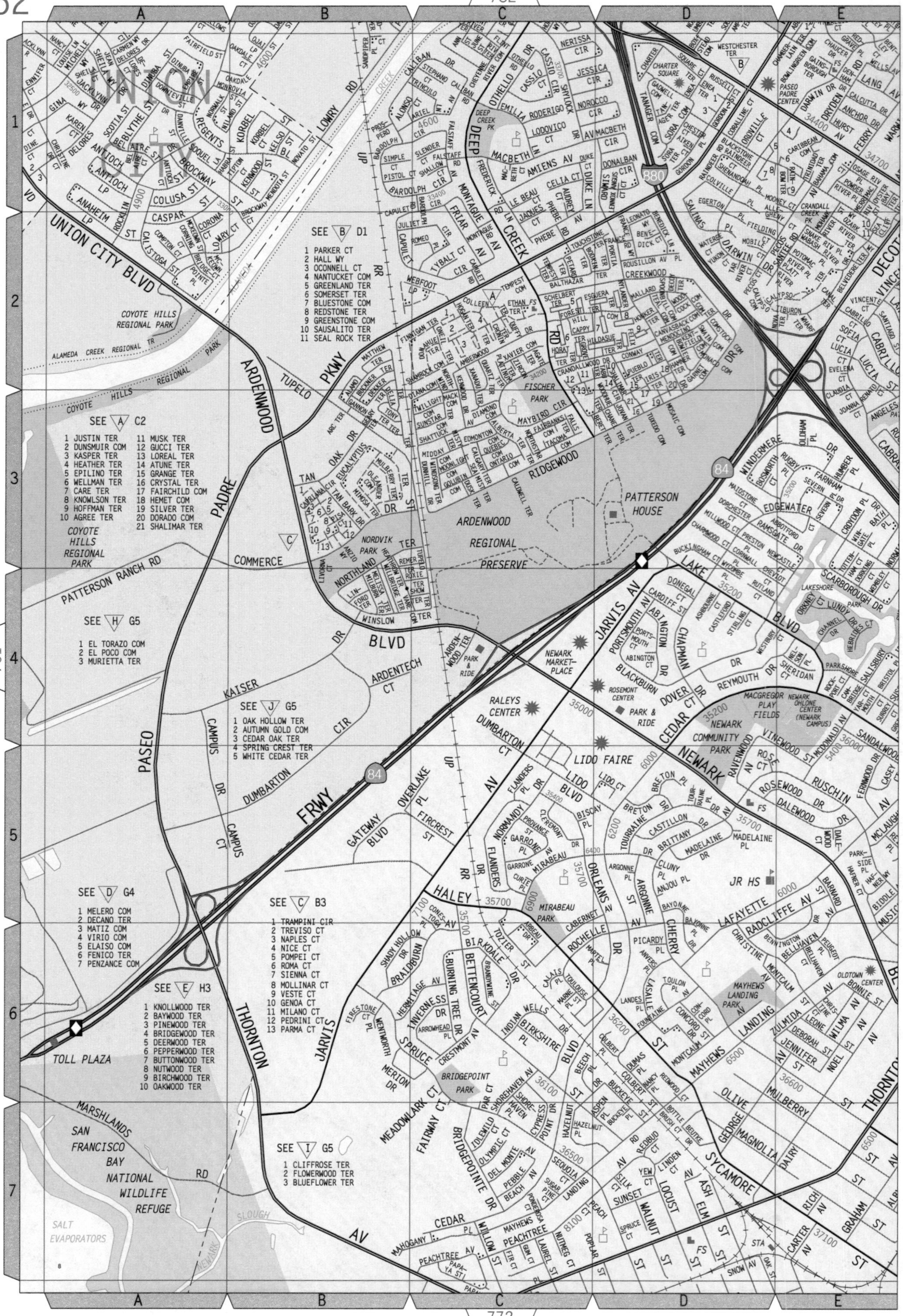
UNION CITY
UNION CITY BLVD
COYOTE HILLS REGIONAL PARK
ALAMEDA CREEK REGIONAL TR
COYOTE HILLS REGIONAL PARK
ARDENWOOD
PADRE
PASEO
PATTERSON RANCH RD
COMMERCE
TUPELO
PKWY
DEEP CREEK
FISCHER PARK
RIDGEWOOD
PATTERSON HOUSE
ARDENWOOD REGIONAL PRESERVE
NORTHLAND
WINSLOW
BLVD
KAISER
ARDENTECH CT
CAMPUS DR
DUMBARTON CIR
DUMBARTON FRWY
GATEWAY BLVD
OVERLAKE PL
FIRCREST ST
PARK & RIDE
NEWARK MARKET PLACE
RALEYS CENTER
ROSEMONT CENTER
JARVIS AV
CEDAR BLVD
LAKE
NEWARK BLVD
MACGREGOR PLAY FIELDS
NEWARK OHLONE CENTER (NEWARK CAMPUS)
NEWARK COMMUNITY PARK
LIDO FAIRE
MIRABEAU PARK
JR HS
MAYHEWS LANDING PARK
OLDTOWN CENTER
HALEY ST
THORNTON AV
BRIDGEPOINT PARK
TOLL PLAZA
MARSHLANDS RD
SAN FRANCISCO BAY NATIONAL WILDLIFE REFUGE
SALT EVAPORATORS
CEDAR BLVD
SYCAMORE
MULBERRY
OLIVE
MAGNOLIA
SEE A C2
1 JUSTIN TER
2 DUNSMUIR COM
3 KASPER TER
4 HEATHER TER
5 EPILINO TER
6 WELLMAN TER
7 CARE TER
8 KNOWLSON TER
9 HOFFMAN TER
10 AGREE TER
11 MUSK TER
12 GUCCI TER
13 LOREAL TER
14 ATUNE TER
15 GRANGE TER
16 CRYSTAL TER
17 FAIRCHILD COM
18 HEMET COM
19 SILVER TER
20 DORADO COM
21 SHALIMAR TER
SEE B D1
1 PARKER CT
2 HALL WY
3 OCONNELL CT
4 NANTUCKET COM
5 GREENLAND TER
6 SOMERSET TER
7 BLUESTONE COM
8 REDSTONE TER
9 GREENSTONE COM
10 SAUSALITO TER
11 SEAL ROCK TER
SEE H G5
1 EL TORAZO COM
2 EL POCO COM
3 MURIETTA TER
SEE J G5
1 OAK HOLLOW TER
2 AUTUMN GOLD COM
3 CEDAR OAK TER
4 SPRING CREST TER
5 WHITE CEDAR TER
SEE D G4
1 MELERO COM
2 DECANO TER
3 MATIZ COM
4 VIRIO COM
5 ELAISO COM
6 FENICO TER
7 PENZANCE COM
SEE C B3
1 TRAMPINI CIR
2 TREVISO CT
3 NAPLES CT
4 NICE CT
5 POMPEI CT
6 ROMA CT
7 SIENNA CT
8 MOLLINAR CT
9 VESTE CT
10 GENOA CT
11 MILANO CT
12 PEDRINI CT
13 PARMA CT
SEE E H3
1 KNOLLWOOD TER
2 BAYWOOD TER
3 PINEWOOD TER
4 BRIDGEWOOD TER
5 DEERWOOD TER
6 PEPPERWOOD TER
7 BUTTONWOOD TER
8 NUTWOOD TER
9 BIRCHWOOD TER
10 OAKWOOD TER
SEE I G5
1 CLIFFROSE TER
2 FLOWERWOOD TER
3 BLUEFLOWER TER

SEE 751 MAP
SEE 772 MAP

SEE 732 MAP

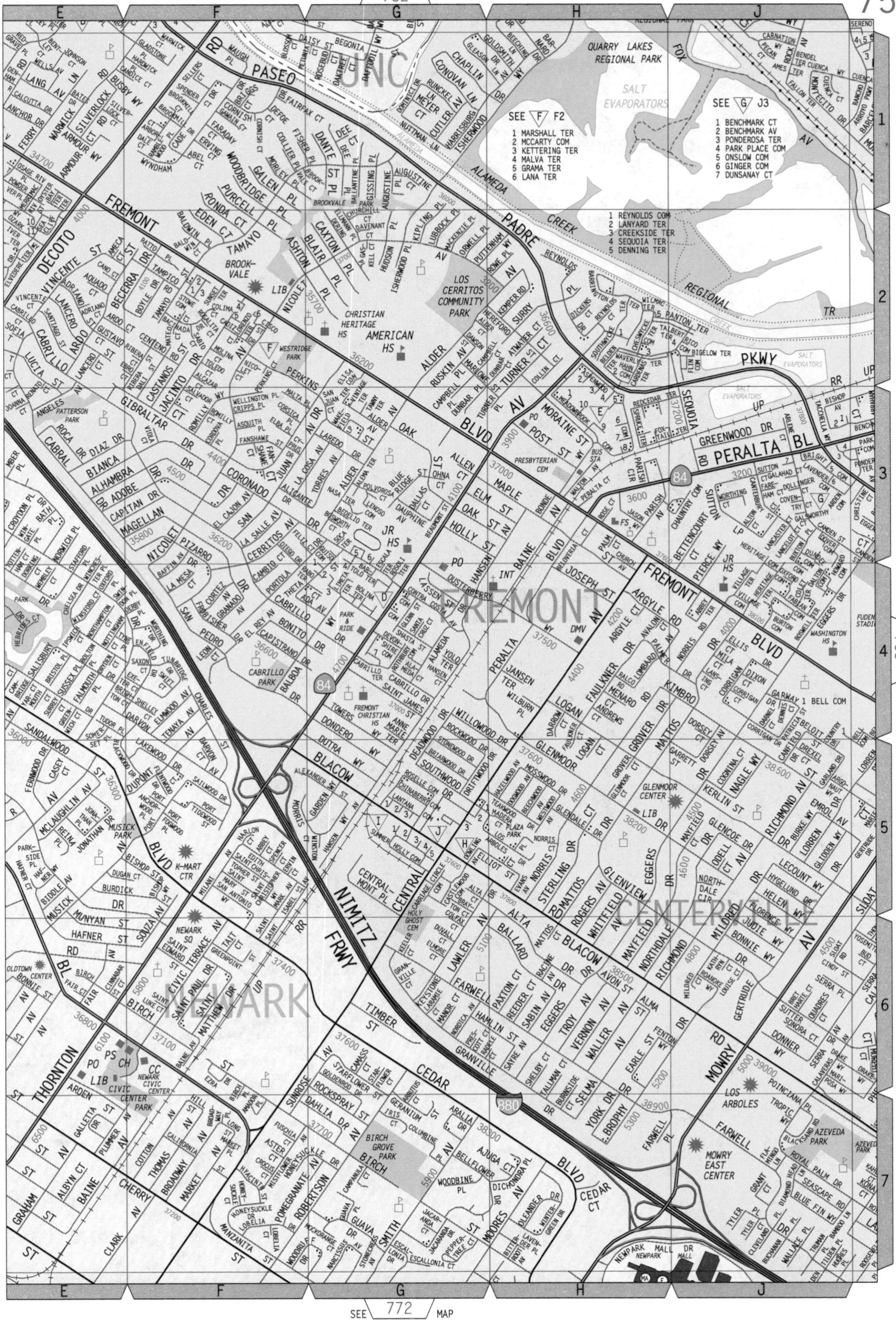
QUARRY LAKES REGIONAL PARK
SALT EVAPORATORS
SEE F F2
1 MARSHALL TER
2 MCCARTY COM
3 KETTERING TER
4 MALVA TER
5 GRAMA TER
6 LANA TER
SEE G J3
1 BENCHMARK CT
2 BENCHMARK AV
3 PONDEROSA TER
4 PARK PLACE COM
5 ONSLOW COM
6 GINGER COM
7 DUNSANAY CT
1 REYNOLDS COM
2 LANYARD TER
3 CREEKSIDE TER
4 SEQUOIA TER
5 DENNING TER
ALAMEDA CREEK REGIONAL TR
PASEO PADRE PKWY
FREMONT BLVD
DECOTO RD
PERALTA BL
BROOKVALE
LOS CERRITOS COMMUNITY PARK
CHRISTIAN HERITAGE HS
AMERICAN HS
WESTRIDGE PARK
PATTERSON PARK
PRESBYTERIAN CEM
FREMONT
JR HS
PARK & RIDE
DMV
CABRILLO PARK
FREMONT CHRISTIAN HS
WASHINGTON HS
1 BELL COM
GLENMOOR CENTER
MUSICK PARK
K-MART CTR
NEWARK SQ
NIMITZ FRWY
CENTERVILLE
HOLY GHOST CEM
BLACOW RD
MOWRY AV
NEWARK
OLDTOWN CENTER
NEWARK CIVIC CENTER
CIVIC CENTER PARK
BIRCH GROVE PARK
CEDAR BLVD
LOS ARBOLES
MOWRY EAST CENTER
AZEVEDA PARK
NEWPARK MALL
THORNTON AV
CHERRY ST
SLOAT

SEE 753 MAP

SEE 772 MAP

SEE 733 MAP

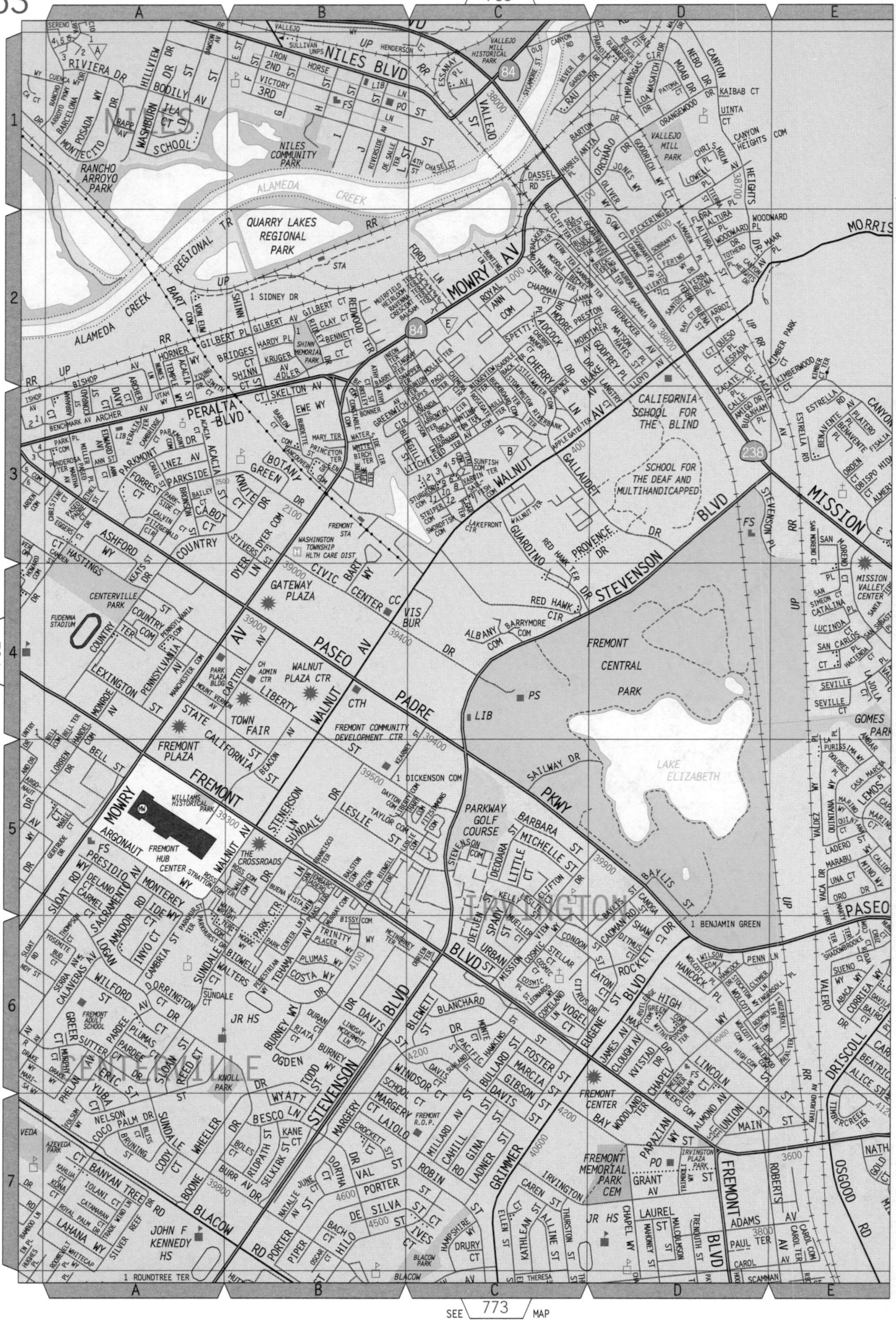
NILES
NILES BLVD
NILES COMMUNITY PARK
RANCHO ARROYO PARK
ALAMEDA CREEK
QUARRY LAKES REGIONAL PARK
VALLEJO MILL HISTORICAL PARK
VALLEJO MILL PARK
MOWRY AV
PERALTA BLVD
CALIFORNIA SCHOOL FOR THE BLIND
SCHOOL FOR THE DEAF AND MULTIHANDICAPPED
WASHINGTON TOWNSHIP HLTH CARE DIST
GATEWAY PLAZA
CENTERVILLE PARK
FUDENNA STADIUM
PASEO PADRE PKWY
WALNUT PLAZA CTR
TOWN FAIR
FREMONT PLAZA
FREMONT COMMUNITY DEVELOPMENT CTR
FREMONT CENTRAL PARK
LAKE ELIZABETH
FREMONT HUB CENTER
WILLIAMS HISTORICAL PARK
THE CROSSROADS
PARKWAY GOLF COURSE
IRVINGTON
STEVENSON BLVD
FREMONT BLVD
MISSION BLVD
MISSION VALLEY CENTER
GOMES PARK
CENTERVILLE
FREMONT ADULT SCHOOL
KNOLL PARK
FREMONT R.O.P.
FREMONT CENTER
FREMONT MEMORIAL PARK CEM
IRVINGTON PLAZA PARK
JOHN F KENNEDY HS
AZEVEDA PARK
BLACOW PARK
BLACOW RD
GRIMMER BLVD
DRISCOLL RD
OSGOOD RD

SEE 752 MAP
SEE 773 MAP

SEE 733 MAP

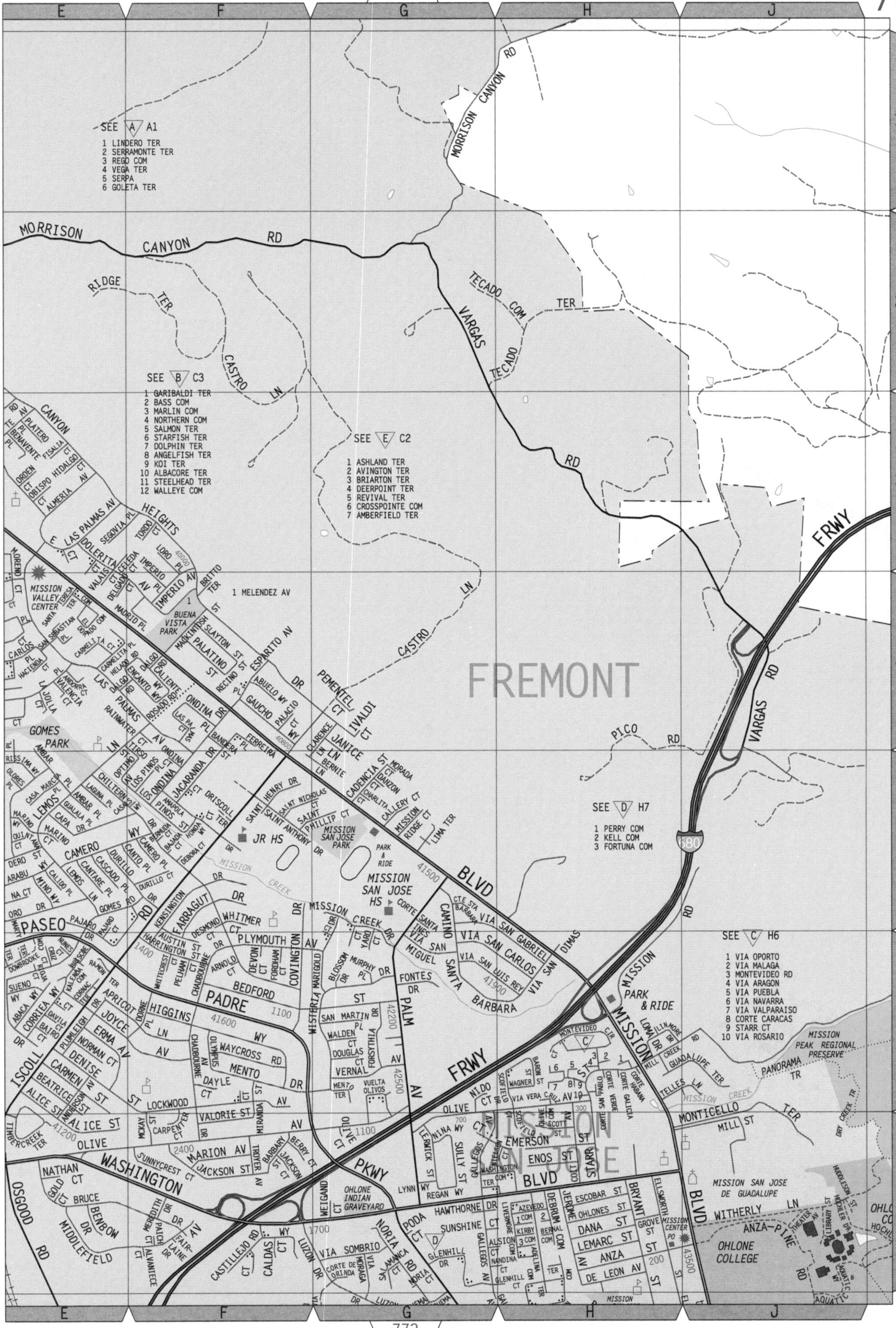
FREMONT
MISSION SAN JOSE
MORRISON CANYON RD
VARGAS RD
TECADO COM
CASTRO LN
RIDGE TER
FRWY
680
MISSION BLVD
PICO RD
SEE A A1
1 LINDERO TER
2 SERRAMONTE TER
3 REGO COM
4 VEGA TER
5 SERPA
6 GOLETA TER
SEE B C3
1 GARIBALDI TER
2 BASS COM
3 MARLIN COM
4 NORTHERN COM
5 SALMON TER
6 STARFISH TER
7 DOLPHIN TER
8 ANGELFISH TER
9 KOI TER
10 ALBACORE TER
11 STEELHEAD TER
12 WALLEYE COM
SEE E C2
1 ASHLAND TER
2 AVINGTON TER
3 BRIARTON TER
4 DEERPOINT TER
5 REVIVAL TER
6 CROSSPOINTE COM
7 AMBERFIELD TER
1 MELENDEZ AV
SEE D H7
1 PERRY COM
2 KELL COM
3 FORTUNA COM
SEE C H6
1 VIA OPORTO
2 VIA MALAGA
3 MONTEVIDEO RD
4 VIA ARAGON
5 VIA PUEBLA
6 VIA NAVARRA
7 VIA VALPARAISO
8 CORTE CARACAS
9 STARR CT
10 VIA ROSARIO
MISSION VALLEY CENTER
BUENA VISTA PARK
GOMES PARK
JR HS
MISSION SAN JOSE PARK
PARK & RIDE
MISSION SAN JOSE HS
MISSION CREEK
PASEO PADRE PKWY
WASHINGTON BLVD
OHLONE INDIAN GRAVEYARD
MISSION SAN JOSE DE GUADALUPE
OHLONE COLLEGE
MISSION PEAK REGIONAL PRESERVE
PANORAMA TR
MONTICELLO TER
HEIGHTS
ESPARITO AV
PEMENTEL CT
IVALDI CT
JANICE LN
PALM AV
OLIVE AV
PLYMOUTH AV
BEDFORD ST
HIGGINS LN
COVINGTON
MENTO DR
LOCKWOOD
VALORIE ST
ALICE ST
MARION AV
JACKSON ST
OSGOOD RD
MIDDLEFIELD DR
NATHAN CT
ANZA-PINE RD
WITHERLY LN
DE LEON AV
ANZA ST
LEMARC ST
DANA ST
OHLONES ST
ESCOBAR ST
BRYANT ST
HAWTHORNE DR
SUNSHINE DR
NORIA RD
LUZON DR
VIA SOMBRIO
CALDAS CT
CASTILLEJO RD
CAMINO SANTA BARBARA
VIA SAN GABRIEL
VIA SAN CARLOS
VIA SAN DIMAS
MISSION CENTER PO
E F G H J
1 2 3 4 5 6 7

SEE 754 MAP

SEE 773 MAP

SEE 734 MAP

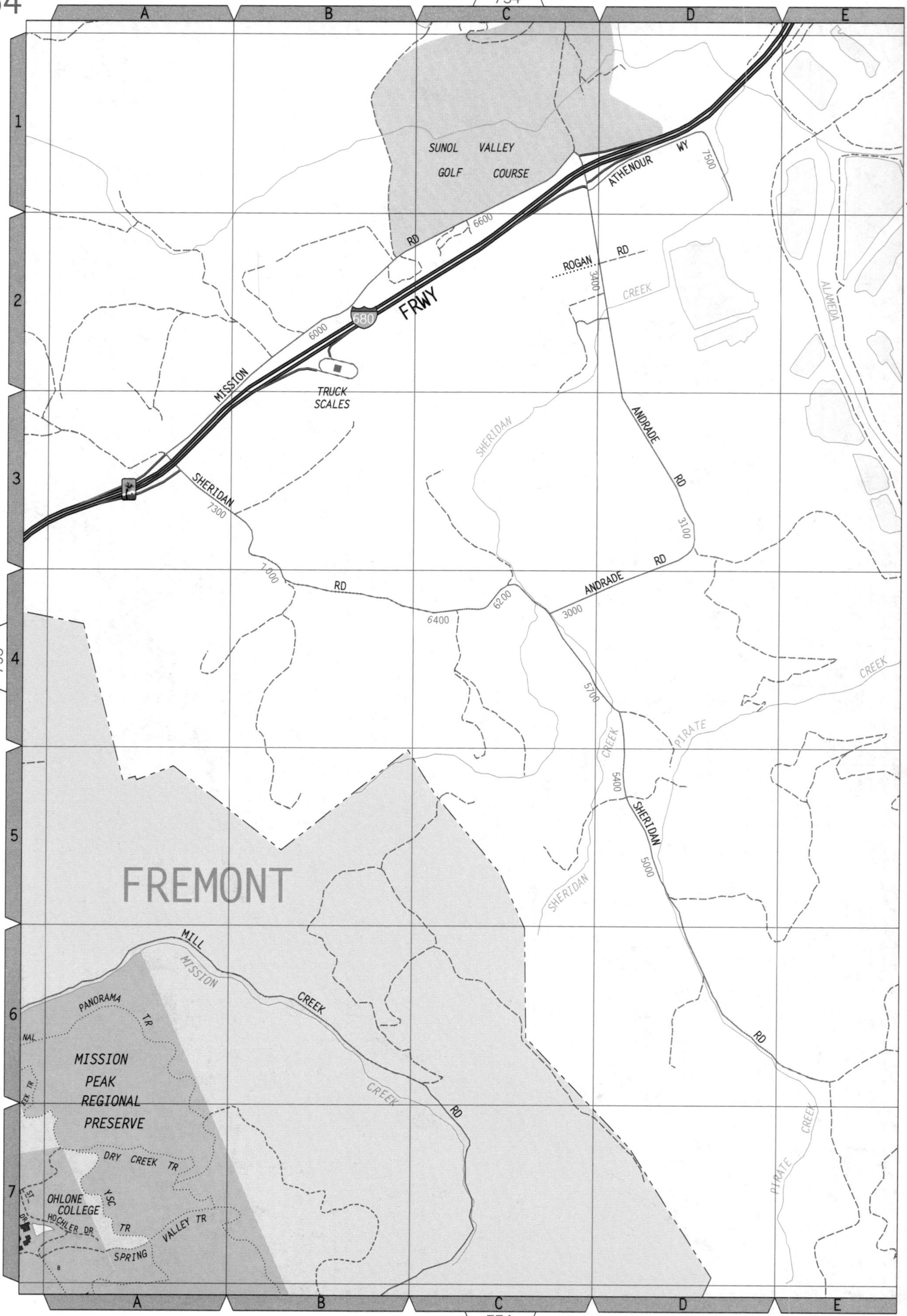
SUNOL VALLEY
GOLF COURSE
ATHENOUR WY
7500
MISSION RD
6600
6000
ROGAN RD
3400
CREEK
680
FRWY
TRUCK SCALES
ALAMEDA
SHERIDAN
ANDRADE RD
3100
SHERIDAN
7300
7000
RD
6400
6200
ANDRADE RD
3000
5700
CREEK
PIRATE
CREEK
5400
SHERIDAN
5000
SHERIDAN
FREMONT
MILL
MISSION
CREEK
RD
PANORAMA TR
MISSION
PEAK
REGIONAL
PRESERVE
CREEK
RD
DRY CREEK TR
OHLONE
COLLEGE
YSC
TR
HOCHLER DR
VALLEY TR
SPRING
RD
PIRATE
CREEK

SEE 753 MAP

SEE 774 MAP

SEE 734 MAP
E
F
G
H
J
1
2
3
4
5
6
7
INDIAN CREEK RD
INDIAN CREEK RD
INDIAN CREEK RD
SAN ANTONIO CREEK
SAN ANTONIO RESERVOIR
CALAVERAS RD
8700
8800
CREEK
CREEK
SOUTH FORK APPERSON CREEK
SEE 263 MAP
ALAMEDA CREEK
MAGUIRE PEAKS
SUNOL REGIONAL WILDERNESS
WELCH CREEK RD
WELCH CREEK
WELCH CREEK RD
CREEK
HAYFIELD RD
HAYNES GULCH
9100
SEE 774 MAP

SEE 748 MAP

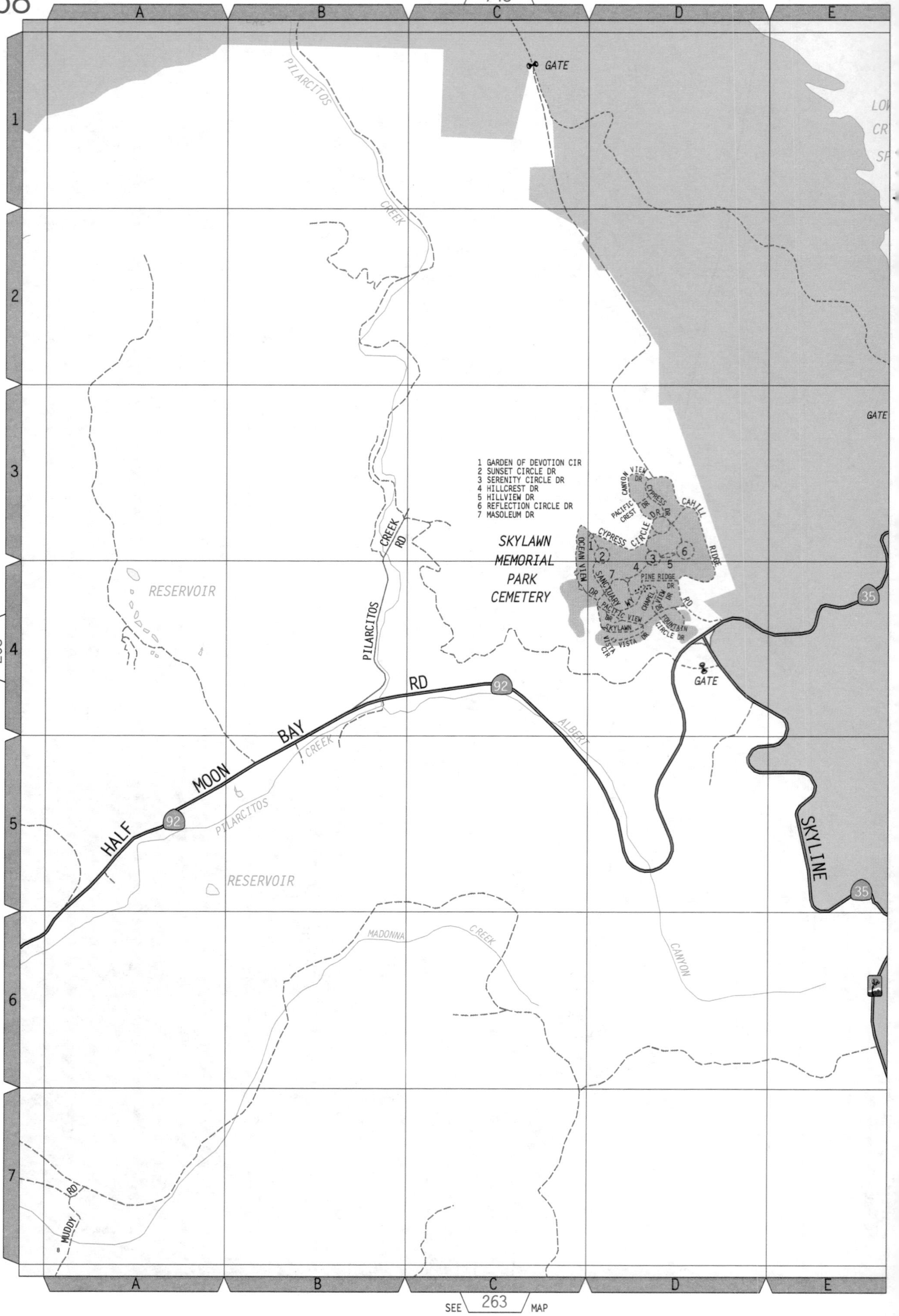
A
B
C
D
E
1
2
3
4
5
6
7
GATE
PILARCITOS
CREEK
1 GARDEN OF DEVOTION CIR
2 SUNSET CIRCLE DR
3 SERENITY CIRCLE DR
4 HILLCREST DR
5 HILLVIEW DR
6 REFLECTION CIRCLE DR
7 MASOLEUM DR
SKYLAWN MEMORIAL PARK CEMETERY
CANYON VIEW DR
CYPRESS DR
CAHILL RIDGE
PACIFIC CREST DR
CYPRESS CIRCLE DR
OCEAN VIEW DR
SANCTUARY WY
PINE RIDGE DR
CHAPEL VIEW DR
PACIFIC VIEW DR
SKYLAWN
FOUNTAIN CIRCLE DR
VISTA CIR
VISTA DR
RD
RESERVOIR
PILARCITOS CREEK RD
HALF MOON BAY RD
92
35
ALBERT
CANYON
SKYLINE
MADONNA CREEK
MUDDY RD

SEE 263 MAP

SEE 263 MAP

SEE 748 MAP

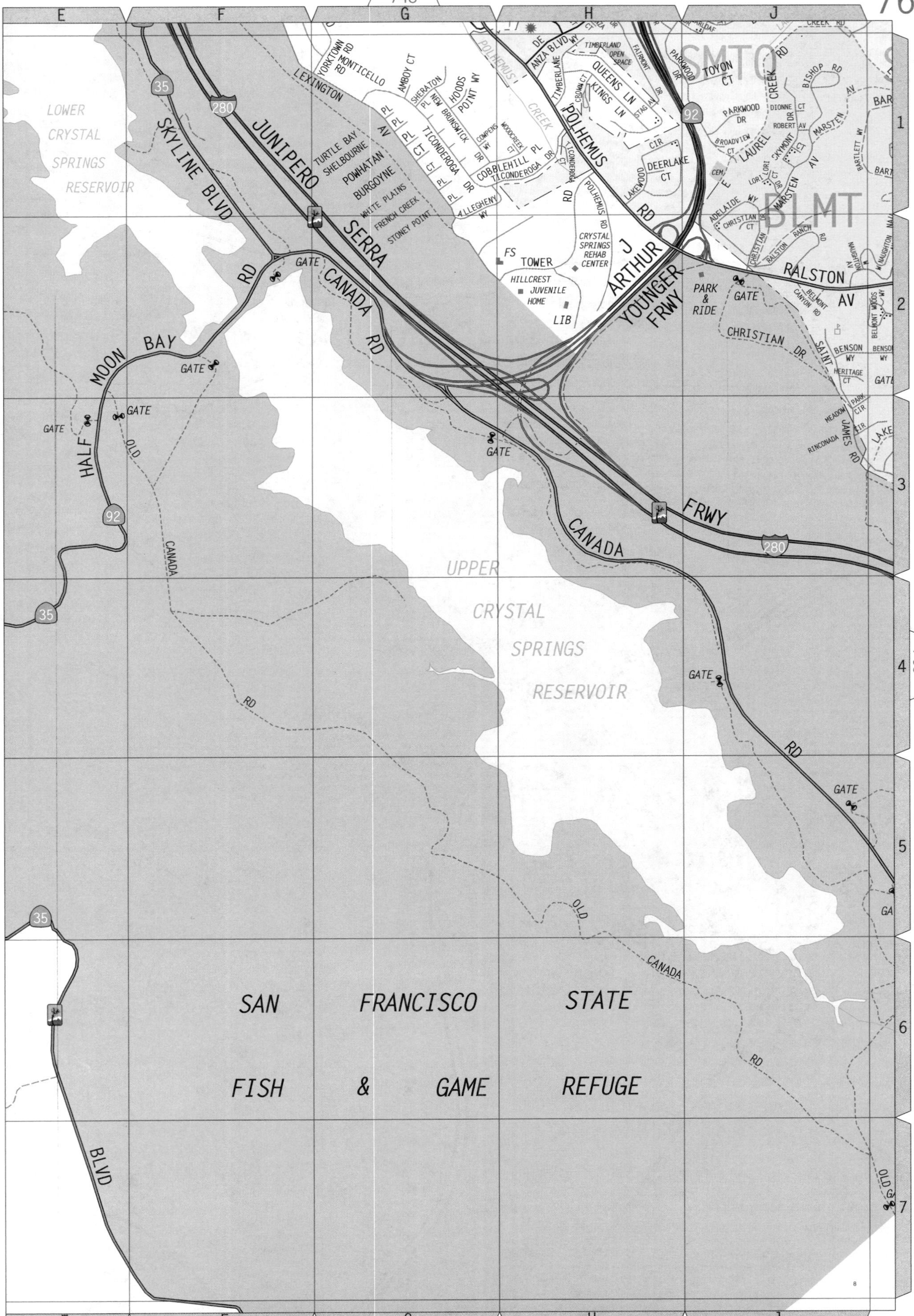
E
F
G
H
J
1
2
3
4
5
6
7
LOWER
CRYSTAL
SPRINGS
RESERVOIR
UPPER
CRYSTAL
SPRINGS
RESERVOIR
SAN FRANCISCO STATE
FISH & GAME REFUGE
SMTO
BLMT
JUNIPERO
SERRA
FRWY
280
35
92
SKYLINE BLVD
BLVD
HALF MOON BAY RD
CANADA RD
OLD CANADA RD
J ARTHUR YOUNGER FRWY
POLHEMUS RD
POLHEMUS CREEK
RALSTON AV
CHRISTIAN DR
LEXINGTON
YORKTOWN RD
MONTICELLO RD
AMBOY CT
SHERATON PL
NEW BRUNSWICK PL
HOODS POINT WY
TURTLE BAY
SHELBOURNE
POWHATAN
BURGOYNE
WHITE PLAINS
FRENCH CREEK
STONEY POINT
TICONDEROGA DR
COBBLEHILL PL
ALLEGHENY WY
ANZA BLVD
TIMBERLANE
TIMBERLAND OPEN SPACE
QUEENS LN
KINGS LN
DEERLAKE CT
LAKEWOOD
PARKWOOD DR
TOYON CT
LAUREL CREEK RD
BISHOP RD
MARSTEN AV
ADELAIDE WY
CHRISTIAN CT
RALSTON RANCH RD
FS
TOWER
HILLCREST JUVENILE HOME
LIB
CRYSTAL SPRINGS REHAB CENTER
PARK & RIDE
GATE
SAINT JAMES RD
BENSON WY
HERITAGE CT
RINCONADA
MEADOW PARK CIR

SEE 769 MAP

SEE 263 MAP

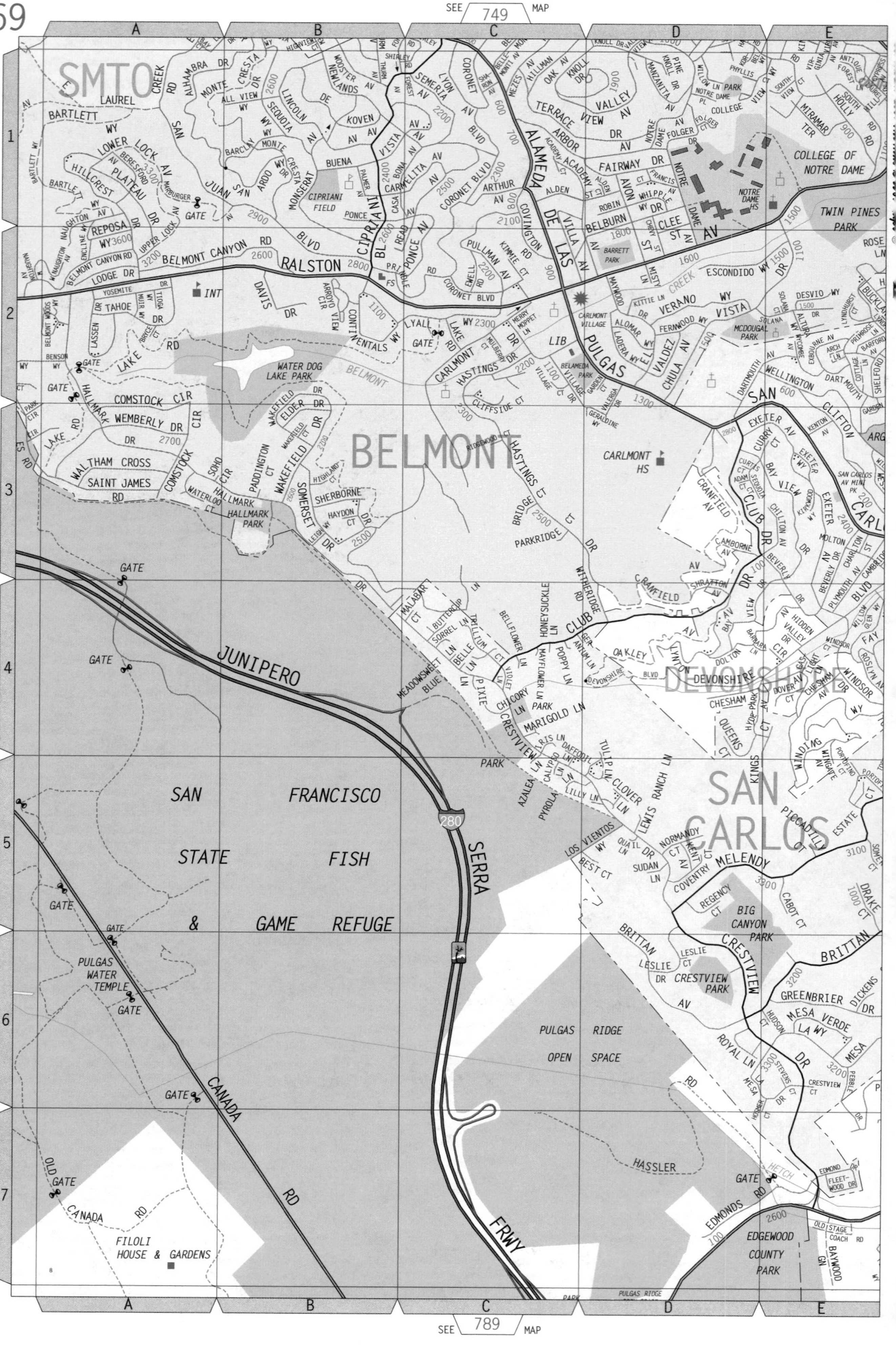
SEE 749 MAP
SEE 768 MAP
SEE 789 MAP
A
B
C
D
E
1
2
3
4
5
6
7
SMTO
BELMONT
SAN CARLOS
DEVONSHIRE
SAN FRANCISCO STATE FISH & GAME REFUGE
PULGAS RIDGE OPEN SPACE
WATER DOG LAKE PARK
COLLEGE OF NOTRE DAME
NOTRE DAME HS
TWIN PINES PARK
CARLMONT HS
CIPRIANI FIELD
BARRETT PARK
HALLMARK PARK
MCDOUGAL PARK
BELAMEDA PARK
BIG CANYON PARK
CRESTVIEW PARK
EDGEWOOD COUNTY PARK
FILOLI HOUSE & GARDENS
PULGAS WATER TEMPLE
CARLMONT VILLAGE
LIB
INT
FS
GATE
JUNIPERO SERRA FRWY
280
RALSTON AV
ALAMEDA DE LAS PULGAS
BELMONT CANYON RD
CANADA RD
OLD CANADA RD
CLUB DR
EDMONDS RD
HASSLER
CRESTVIEW DR
BRITTAN AV
MELENDY DR
SAN CARLOS AV
HASTINGS DR
CARLMONT DR
WITHERIDGE RD
LAUREL CREEK
BARTLETT WY
HALLMARK DR
COMSTOCK CIR
WEMBERLY DR
WALTHAM CROSS
SAINT JAMES RD
WAKEFIELD DR
SOMERSET DR
NOTRE DAME AV
VALLEY VIEW AV
FAIRWAY DR
ESCONDIDO WY
VERANO WY
VISTA
CHULA VISTA
WELLINGTON DR
EXETER AV
CRANFIELD AV
OAKLEY AV
DEVONSHIRE BLVD
CHESHAM AV
QUEENS CT
KINGS
PICCADILLY
WINDSOR DR
LEWIS RANCH LN
CLOVER LN
LOS VIENTOS WY
GREENBRIER DR
MESA VERDE
ROYAL LN
OLD STAGE COACH RD
BAYWOOD GN
FLEETWOOD DR

SEE 749 MAP

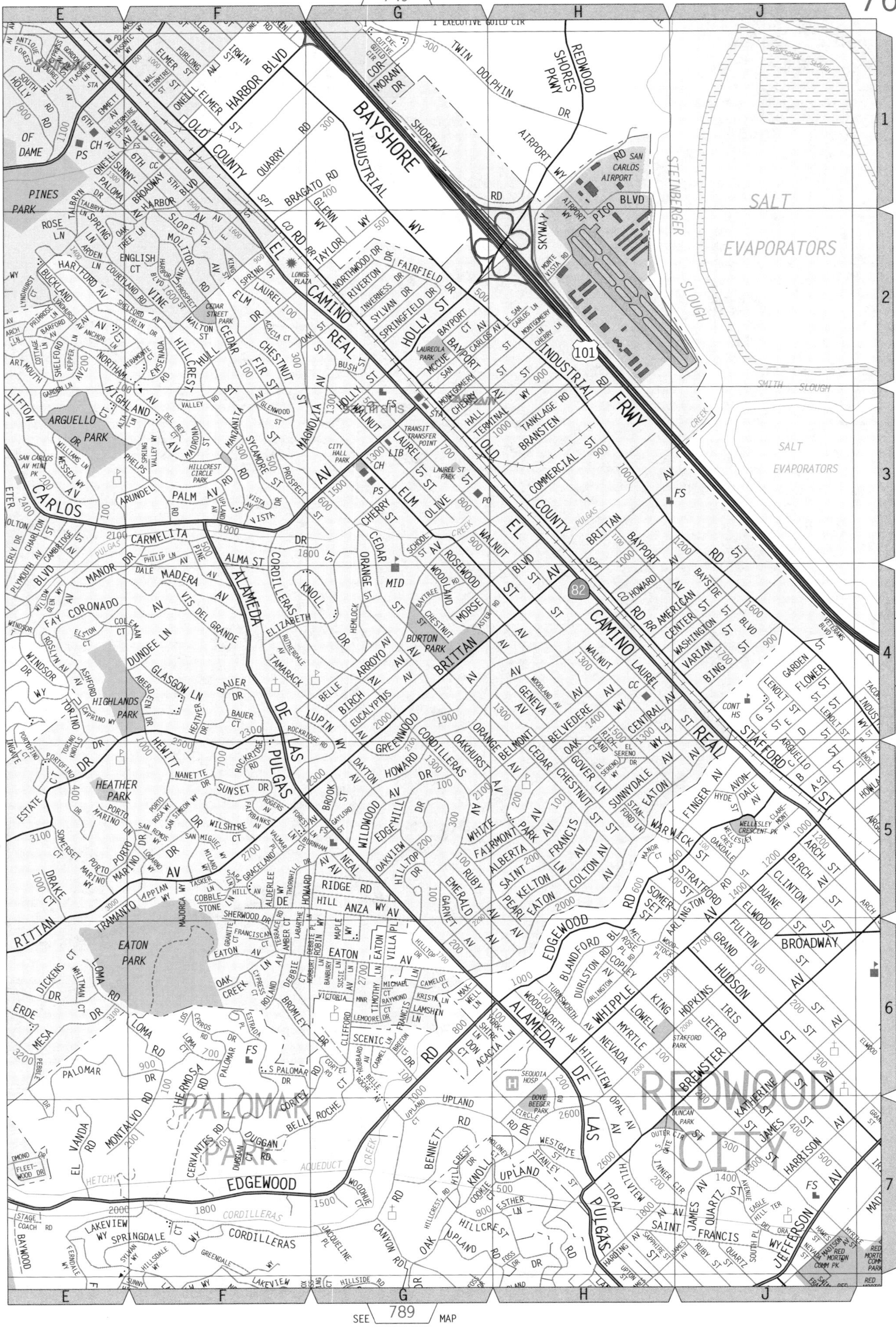
E
F
G
H
J
1
2
3
4
5
6
7
BAYSHORE
INDUSTRIAL
WY
HARBOR BLVD
OLD COUNTY RD
EL CAMINO REAL
INDUSTRIAL FRWY
101
82
REDWOOD SHORES PKWY
TWIN DOLPHIN DR
SHOREWAY RD
AIRPORT WY
SAN CARLOS AIRPORT
SKYWAY
SALT EVAPORATORS
STEINBERGER SLOUGH
SMITH SLOUGH
PINES PARK
ARGUELLO PARK
HIGHLANDS PARK
HEATHER PARK
EATON PARK
BURTON PARK
CEDAR STREET PARK
HILLCREST CIRCLE PARK
CITY HALL PARK
LAUREOLA PARK
STAFFORD PARK
DOVE BEEGER PARK
DUNCAN PARK
SEQUOIA HOSP
TRANSIT TRANSFER POINT
LONGS PLAZA
CARLOS
BRITTAN AV
ALAMEDA DE LAS PULGAS
EDGEWOOD RD
WHIPPLE AV
JEFFERSON AV
BROADWAY
STAFFORD
BRANSTEN
COMMERCIAL ST
PALOMAR PARK
REDWOOD CITY
HETCHY AQUEDUCT
CORDILLERAS CREEK
PULGAS CREEK

SEE 770 MAP

SEE 789 MAP

SEE 750 MAP

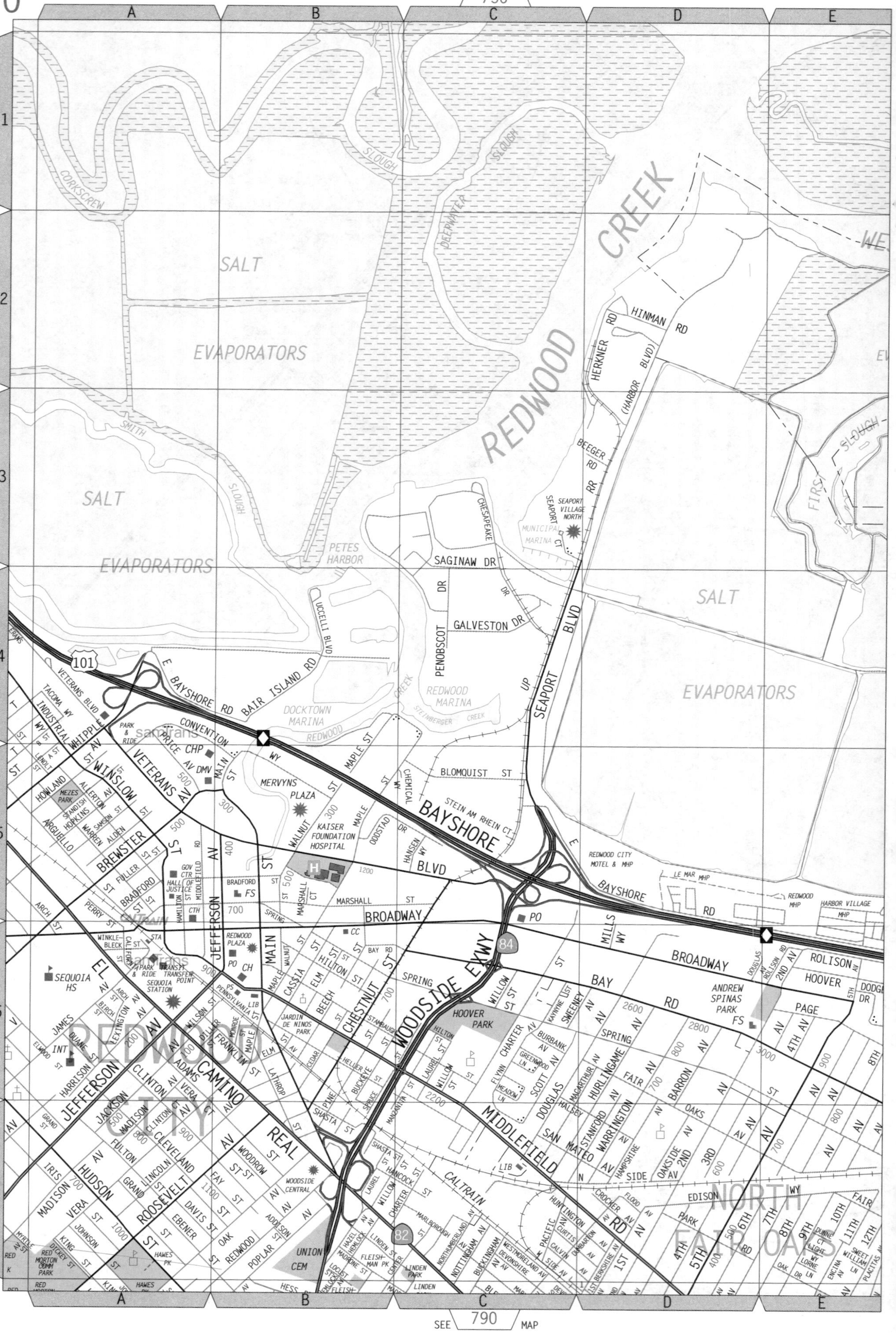
A
B
C
D
E
1
2
3
4
5
6
7
SALT
EVAPORATORS
SALT
EVAPORATORS
SALT
EVAPORATORS
CORKSCREW
SLOUGH
SMITH
SLOUGH
DEEPWATER SLOUGH
REDWOOD CREEK
FIRST SLOUGH
PETES HARBOR
HINMAN RD
HERKNER RD
(HARBOR BLVD)
BEEGER RD
SEAPORT CT
SEAPORT VILLAGE NORTH
MUNICIPAL MARINA
CHESAPEAKE DR
SAGINAW DR
GALVESTON DR
PENOBSCOT DR
SEAPORT BLVD
UP RR
UCCELLI BLVD
REDWOOD MARINA
DOCKTOWN MARINA
STEINBERGER CREEK
BAIR ISLAND RD
E BAYSHORE RD
101
VETERANS BLVD
CONVENTION WY
MAPLE ST
BLOMQUIST ST
CHEMICAL WY
STEIN AM RHEIN CT
BAYSHORE BLVD
E BAYSHORE RD
REDWOOD CITY MOTEL & MHP
LE MAR MHP
REDWOOD MHP
HARBOR VILLAGE MHP
MERVYNS PLAZA
KAISER FOUNDATION HOSPITAL
ODDSTAD DR
HANSEN WY
CHP
DMV
PARK & RIDE
samTrans
WHIPPLE AV
WINSLOW ST
VETERANS AV
INDUSTRIAL WY
TACOMA WY
HOWLAND
MEZES PARK
ALLERTON
STANDISH
HOPKINS
SAMSON
ARGUELLO
WARREN
ALDEN
BREWSTER AV
FULLER
BRADFORD ST
PERRY ST
ARCH ST
GOV CTR
HALL OF JUSTICE
MIDDLEFIELD RD
CTH
HAMILTON ST
JEFFERSON AV
MAIN ST
WALNUT ST
MARSHALL CT
MARSHALL ST
SPRING ST
BROADWAY
PO
84
WOODSIDE EXWY
MILLS WY
BROADWAY
REDWOOD PLAZA
CC
BAY RD
CH
SEQUOIA HS
SEQUOIA STATION
TRANSIT TRANSFER POINT
WINKLEBLECK
CALIFORNIA
EL CAMINO REAL
JAMES AV
DUANE ST
INT
HARRISON AV
LEXINGTON AV
BIRCH AV
JEFFERSON AV
REDWOOD CITY
CLINTON
ADAMS
WILSON ST
VERA AV
JACKSON AV
MADISON
CLEVELAND
FULTON
LINCOLN
ROOSEVELT AV
GRAND ST
HUDSON ST
IRIS
VERA
KING ST
JOHNSON
DICKEY ST
RED MORTON COMM PARK
HAWES PK
CASSIA
ELM ST
HILTON ST
BEECH
CHESTNUT ST
JARDIN DE NINOS PARK
FRANKLIN ST
LATHROP
SPRING
HOOVER PARK
WILLOW ST
LAUREL ST
CHARTER AV
BURBANK AV
SWEENEY AV
FLYNN AV
GREENWOOD LN
MEADOW LN
SCOTT ST
DOUGLAS AV
HALSEY
SAN MATEO AV
STANFORD AV
WARRINGTON AV
HURLINGAME AV
FAIR AV
BARRON AV
OAKS
MIDDLEFIELD RD
BAY RD
ANDREW SPINAS PARK
FS
ROLISON
HOOVER
PAGE
DODGE DR
2ND AV
4TH AV
8TH
SIDE AV
OAKSIDE AV
2ND
3RD
CALTRAIN
EDISON WY
NORTH FAIR OAKS
HUNTINGTON AV
PACIFIC AV
CALVIN AV
CURTIS
BARTON AV
1ST AV
4TH
5TH
6TH
7TH
8TH
9TH
10TH
11TH
12TH
CROCKER
FLOOD
PARK RD
LIB
WOODSIDE CENTRAL
UNION CEM
WOODROW ST
DAVIS ST
EBENER
OAK
REDWOOD
POPLAR AV
ADDISON AV
SHASTA
PINE
BUCKEYE
SPRUCE
HELLER ST
MANZANITA
HANCOCK ST
HAZEL AV
MADRONE
FLEISHMAN PK
LINDEN PARK
LINDEN ST
82
MARLBOROUGH
NORTHUMBERLAND AV
NOTTINGHAM AV
BUCKINGHAM AV
WESTMORELAND AV
DEVONSHIRE AV
HESS
A
B
C
D
E

SEE 769 MAP
SEE 790 MAP

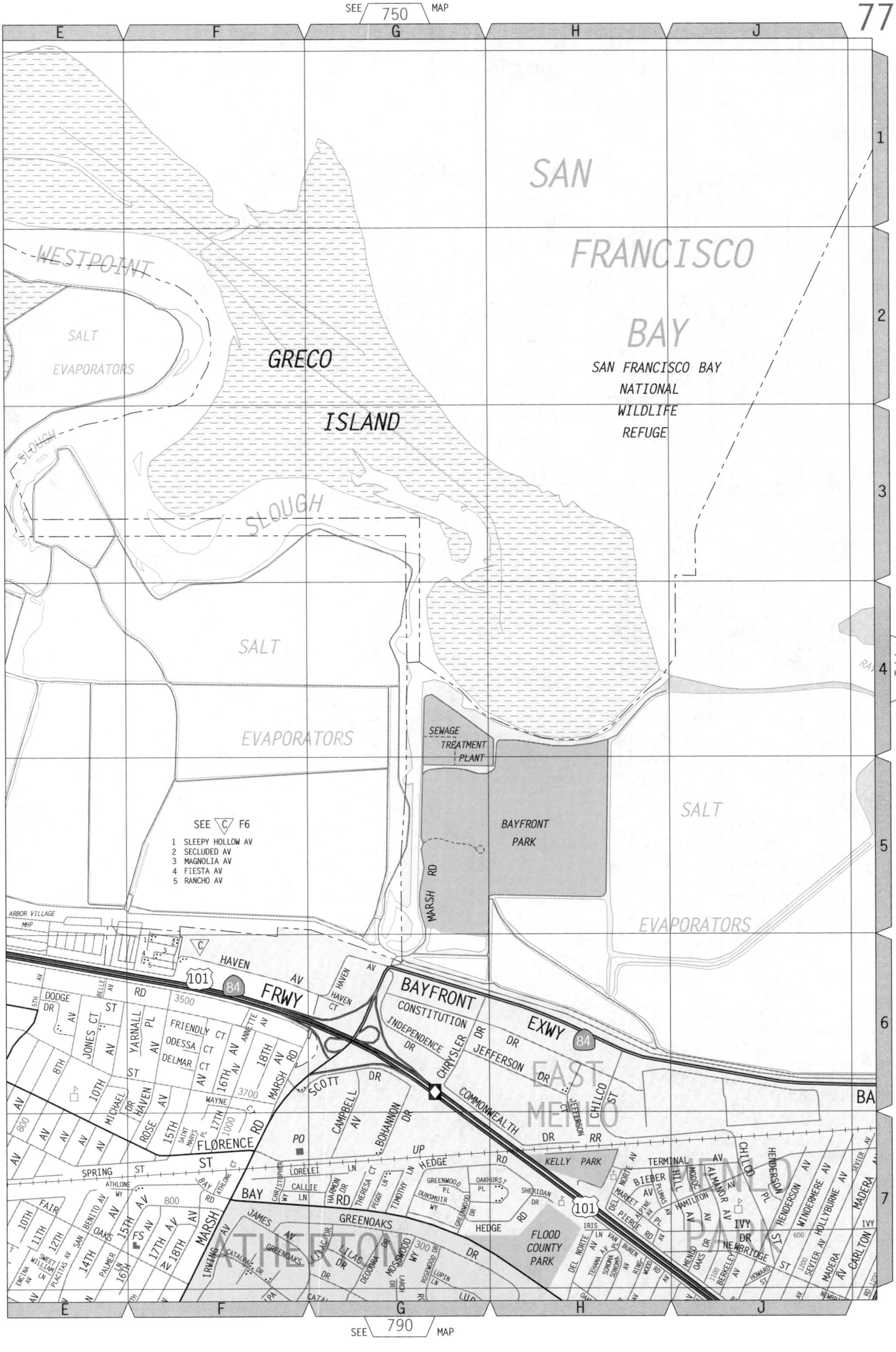

SEE 750 MAP
SEE 790 MAP
SEE 771 MAP
E
F
G
H
J
1
2
3
4
5
6
7
SAN FRANCISCO BAY
SAN FRANCISCO BAY NATIONAL WILDLIFE REFUGE
GRECO ISLAND
WESTPOINT SLOUGH
SLOUGH
SALT EVAPORATORS
SALT
EVAPORATORS
SEWAGE TREATMENT PLANT
BAYFRONT PARK
MARSH RD
SEE C F6
1 SLEEPY HOLLOW AV
2 SECLUDED AV
3 MAGNOLIA AV
4 FIESTA AV
5 RANCHO AV
ARBOR VILLAGE MHP
HAVEN AV
FRWY
BAYFRONT EXWY
CONSTITUTION DR
INDEPENDENCE DR
CHRYSLER DR
JEFFERSON DR
EAST MENLO
CHILCO ST
COMMONWEALTH DR
SCOTT DR
CAMPBELL AV
BOHANNON DR
KELLY PARK
TERMINAL AV
MENLO PARK
ATHERTON
FLOOD COUNTY PARK
FLORENCE ST
SPRING ST
BAY RD
GREENOAKS DR
MARSH RD
DODGE DR
JONES CT
YARNALL PL
FRIENDLY CT
ODESSA CT
DELMAR CT
MICHAEL DR
ROSE AV
HAVEN AV
WAYNE CT
HEDGE RD
LORELEI LN
CALLIE LN
JAMES AV
LILAC DR
MOSSWOOD WY
IRVING AV
DEL NORTE AV
IVY DR
NEWBRIDGE ST
HENDERSON AV
WINDERMERE AV
HOLLYBURNE AV
MADERA AV
CARLTON AV
SEVIER AV
BERKELEY AV
MENLO OAKS DR
ALMANOR AV
HAMILTON AV
BIEBER AV
PIERCE RD
SHERIDAN DR
OAKHURST PL
GREENWOOD PL
DUNSMUIR WY
TIMOTHY LN
PEGGY LN
THERESA CT
HARMON DR
CHRISTOPHER WY
ATHLONE WY
10TH AV
11TH AV
12TH AV
14TH AV
15TH AV
16TH AV
17TH AV
18TH AV
SAN BENITO AV
OAKS AV
PALMER LN
FAIR OAKS
PO
FS
3500
3700
800
1000
1200
600
300

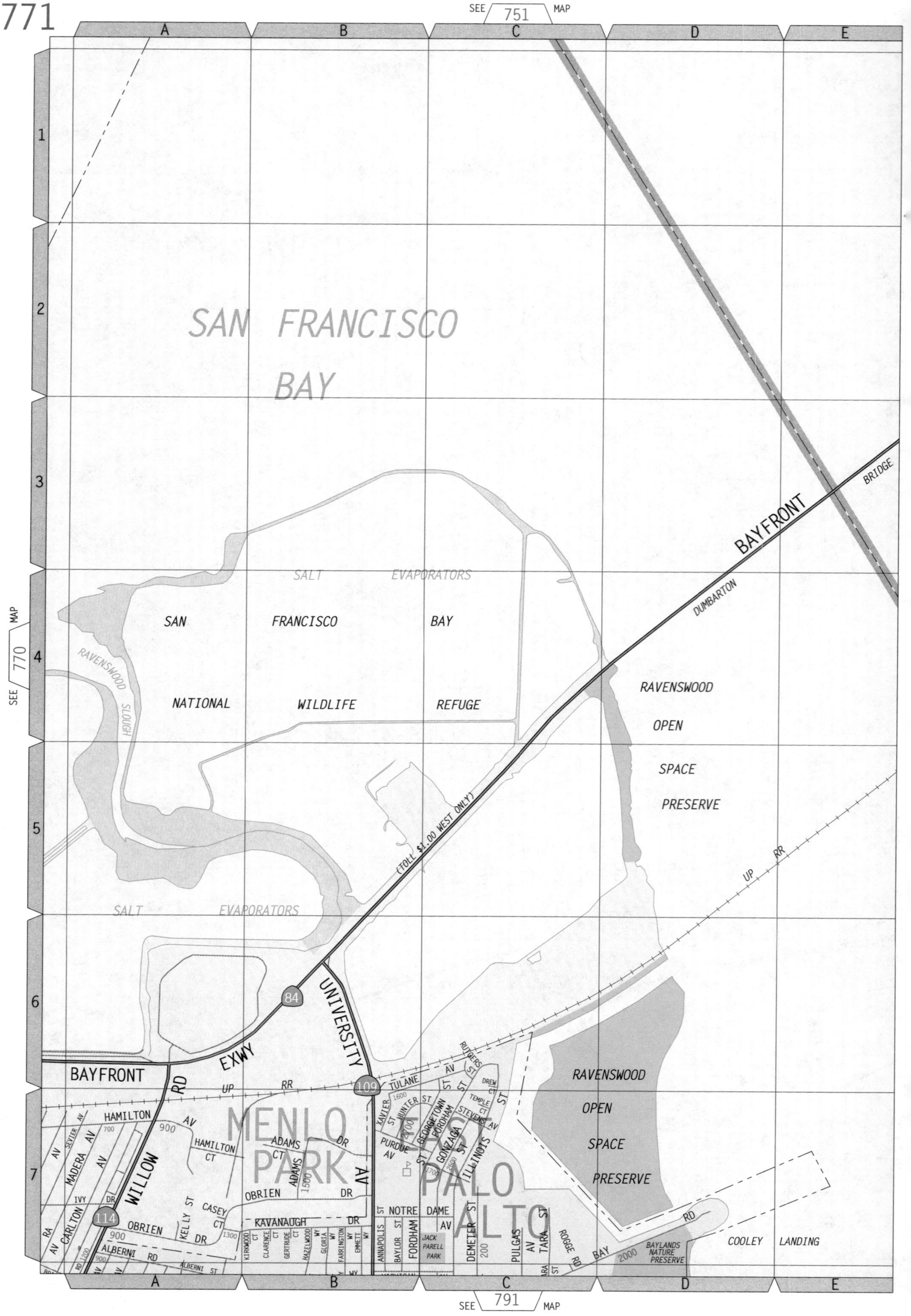
SEE 751 MAP
SEE 770 MAP
SEE 791 MAP
SAN FRANCISCO BAY
SALT EVAPORATORS
SAN FRANCISCO BAY NATIONAL WILDLIFE REFUGE
RAVENSWOOD SLOUGH
RAVENSWOOD OPEN SPACE PRESERVE
BAYFRONT
DUMBARTON
BRIDGE
(TOLL $1.00 WEST ONLY)
UP RR
SALT EVAPORATORS
84
UNIVERSITY
BAYFRONT EXWY
WILLOW RD
109
114
MENLO PARK
EAST PALO ALTO
HAMILTON AV
HAMILTON CT
ADAMS DR
ADAMS CT
OBRIEN DR
CASEY CT
KAVANAUGH DR
KELLY ST
ALBERNI RD
ALBERNI ST
CARLTON AV
MADERA AV
SEVIER AV
IVY
TULANE AV
RUTGERS ST
XAVIER ST
HUNTER ST
GEORGETOWN ST
FORDHAM ST
PURDUE AV
GONZAGA ST
ILLINOIS ST
STEVENS AV
TEMPLE CT
DREW CT
NOTRE DAME AV
ANNAPOLIS ST
BAYLOR ST
FORDHAM ST
JACK PARELL PARK
DEMETER ST
PULGAS AV
TARA ST
ROGGE RD
BAY RD
KIRKWOOD CT
CLARENCE CT
GERTRUDE CT
HAZELWOOD WY
GLORIA WY
FARRINGTON WY
EMMETT WY
BAYLANDS NATURE PRESERVE
COOLEY LANDING
RAVENSWOOD OPEN SPACE PRESERVE

SEE 751 MAP

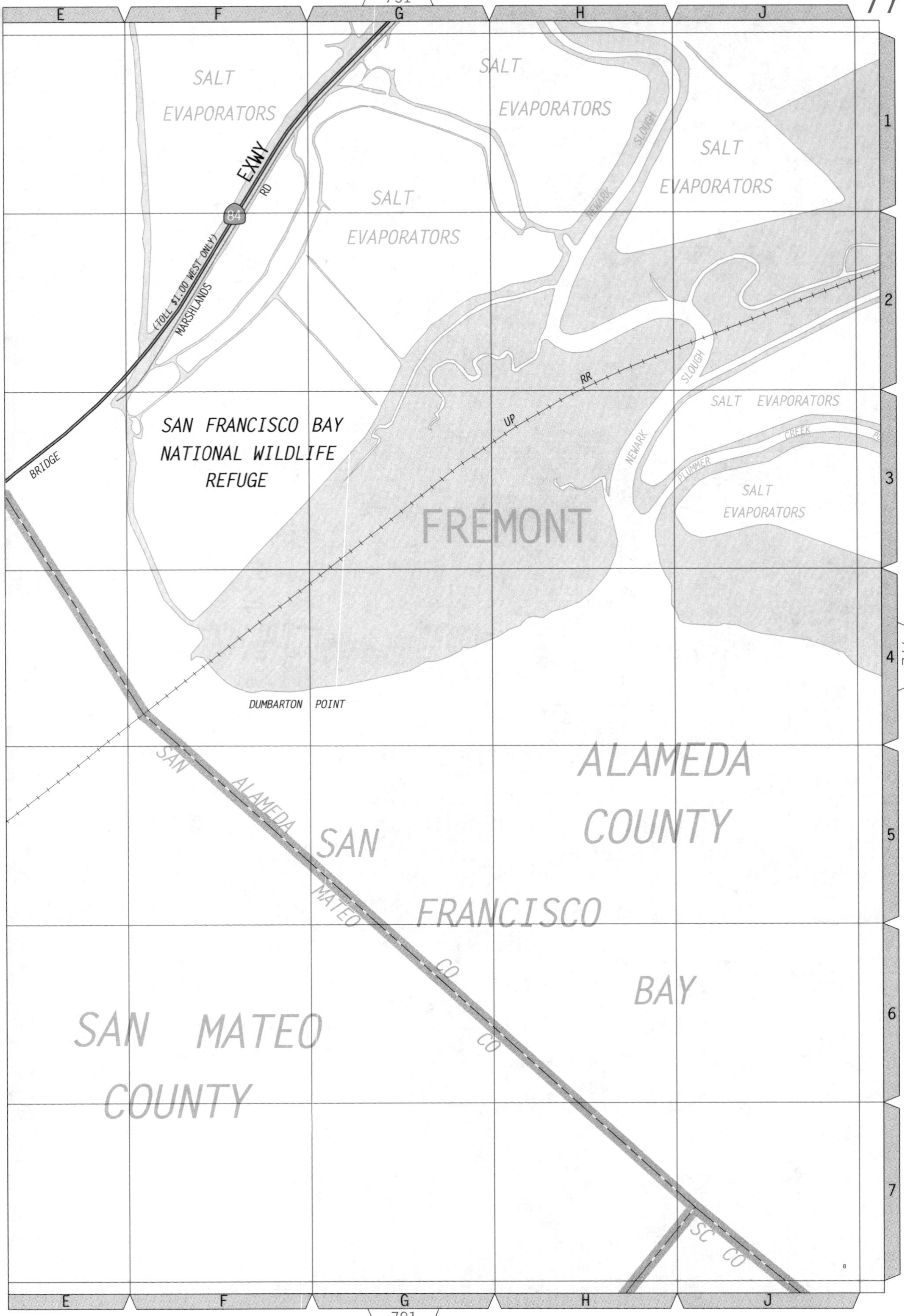
E
F
G
H
J
1
2
3
4
5
6
7
SALT EVAPORATORS
SALT EVAPORATORS
SALT EVAPORATORS
SALT EVAPORATORS
SALT EVAPORATORS
SALT EVAPORATORS
EXWY
84
RD
(TOLL $1.00 WEST ONLY)
MARSHLANDS
BRIDGE
NEWARK SLOUGH
NEWARK SLOUGH
PLUMMER CREEK
SAN FRANCISCO BAY NATIONAL WILDLIFE REFUGE
UP RR
FREMONT
DUMBARTON POINT
SAN ALAMEDA
SAN MATEO CO
CO
ALAMEDA COUNTY
SAN FRANCISCO BAY
SAN MATEO COUNTY
SC CO

SEE 772 MAP
SEE 791 MAP

SEE 752 MAP

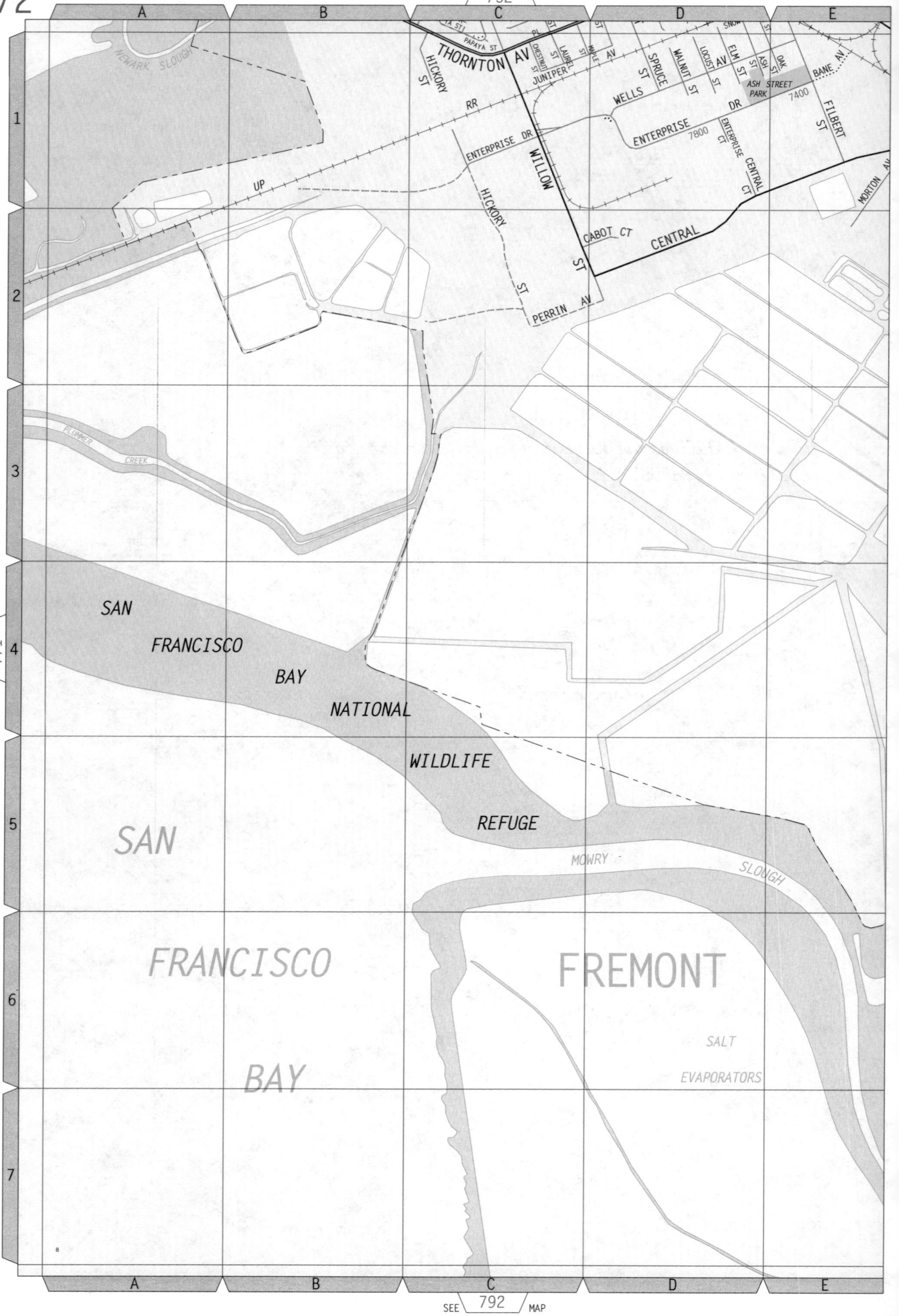
THORNTON AV
HICKORY ST
JUNIPER
WELLS ST
SPRUCE
WALNUT ST
LOCUST ST
ELM ST
ASH ST
OAK ST
ASH STREET PARK
BANE AV
7400
FILBERT ST
ENTERPRISE DR
7800
ENTERPRISE CT
CENTRAL CT
MORTON AV
WILLOW ST
RR
UP
HICKORY ST
CABOT CT
CENTRAL
PERRIN AV
NEWARK SLOUGH
PLUMMER CREEK
SAN FRANCISCO BAY NATIONAL WILDLIFE REFUGE
MOWRY SLOUGH
SAN FRANCISCO BAY
FREMONT
SALT EVAPORATORS

SEE 771 MAP

SEE 792 MAP

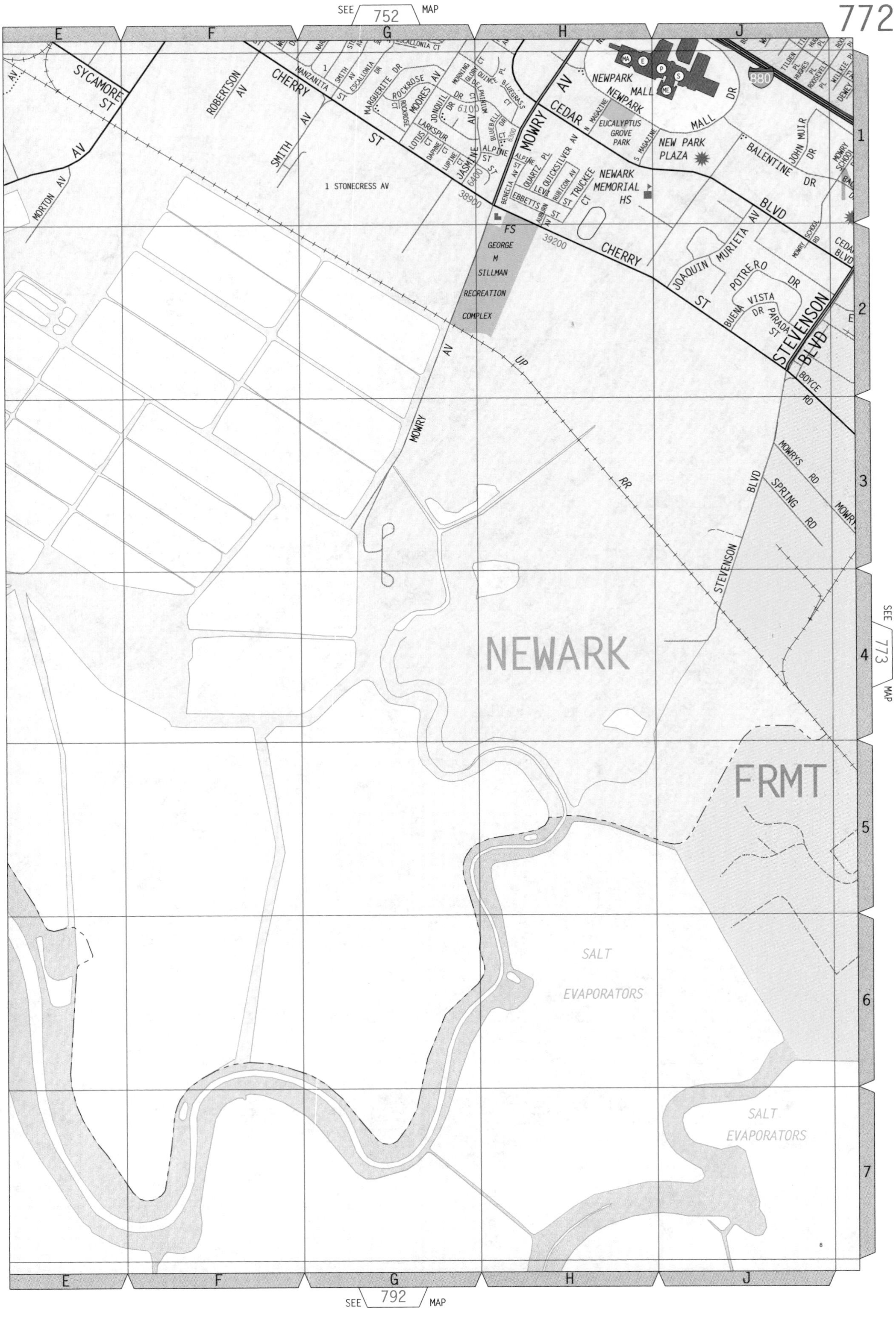
SEE 752 MAP
E
F
G
H
J
1
2
3
4
5
6
7
SYCAMORE ST
ROBERTSON AV
CHERRY ST
SMITH AV
MORTON AV
MANZANITA
MARGUERITE DR
ROCKROSE CT
MOORES AV
JONQUIL DR
LARKSPUR CT
LOTUS CT
JASMINE AV
MORNING GLORY CT
DELPHINIUM CT
BLUEGRASS CT
BLUEBELL DR
ALPINE ST
MOWRY AV
CEDAR BLVD
NEWPARK MALL
NEWPARK MALL DR
EUCALYPTUS GROVE PARK
NEW PARK PLAZA
880
BALENTINE DR
JOHN MUIR DR
MOWRY SCHOOL RD
QUARTZ PL
QUICKSILVER AV
RUBICON AV
TRUCKEE CT
EBBETTS
AUBURN AV
BENECIA AV
NEWARK MEMORIAL HS
1 STONECRESS AV
38900
39200
6100
6300
6400
FS
GEORGE M SILLMAN RECREATION COMPLEX
JOAQUIN MURIETA AV
POTRERO DR
BUENA VISTA DR
PARADA ST
STEVENSON BLVD
BOYCE RD
MOWRYS RD
SPRING RD
UP RR
NEWARK
FRMT
SALT EVAPORATORS
SALT EVAPORATORS
SEE 773 MAP
SEE 792 MAP

SEE 753 MAP

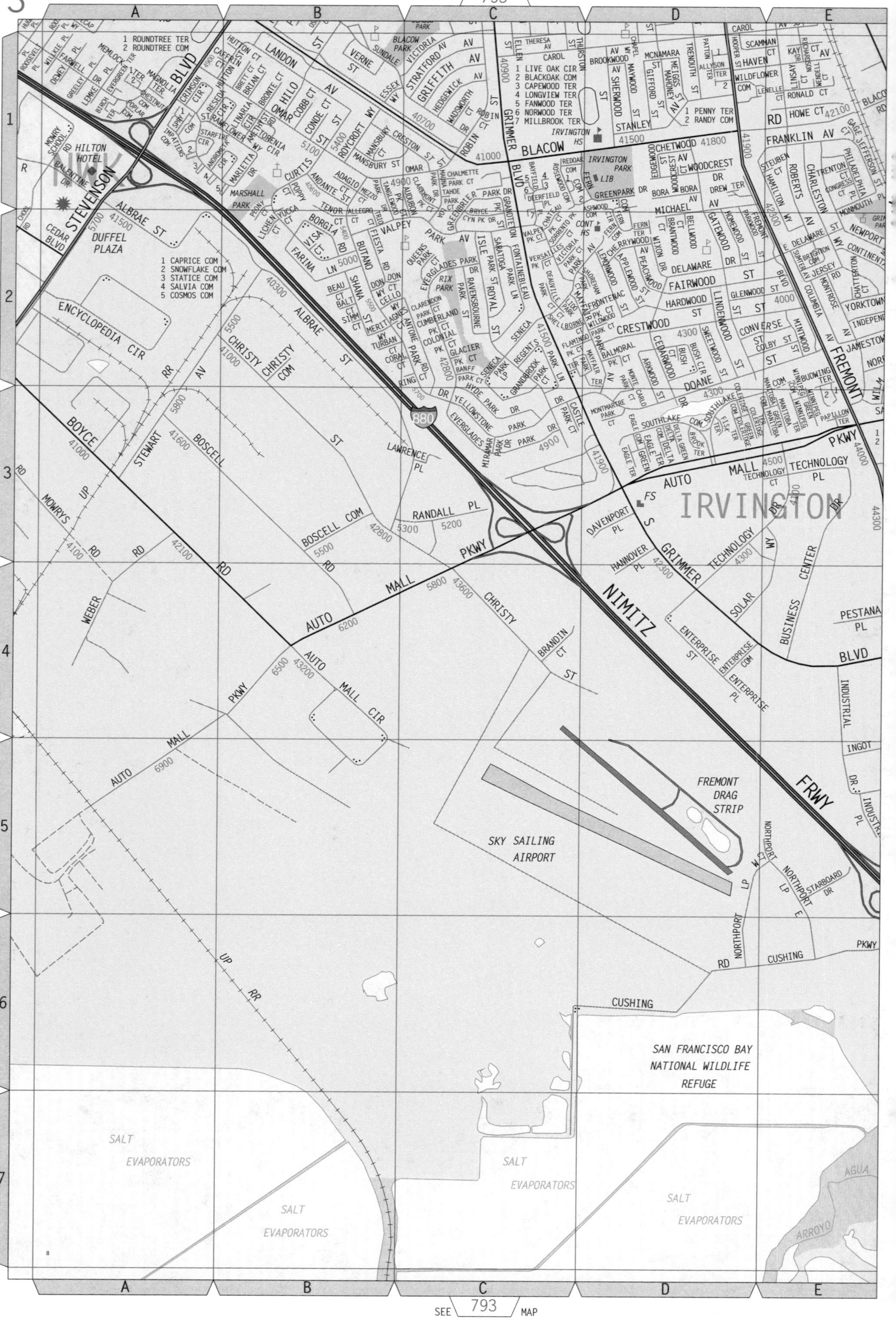
A
B
C
D
E
1
2
3
4
5
6
7
1 ROUNDTREE TER
2 ROUNDTREE COM
1 LIVE OAK CIR
2 BLACKOAK COM
3 CAPEWOOD TER
4 LONGVIEW TER
5 FANWOOD TER
6 NORWOOD TER
7 MILLBROOK TER
1 PENNY TER
2 RANDY COM
1 CAPRICE COM
2 SNOWFLAKE COM
3 STATICE COM
4 SALVIA COM
5 COSMOS COM
STEVENSON BLVD
HILTON HOTEL
MOWRY SCHOOL
DUFFEL PLAZA
ALBRAE ST
ENCYCLOPEDIA CIR
BOYCE RD
STEWART AV
BOSCELL ST
CHRISTY ST
CHRISTY COM
MOWRYS RD
WEBER
UP RR
BOSCELL COM
RANDALL PL
LAWRENCE PL
AUTO MALL PKWY
AUTO MALL CIR
NIMITZ FRWY
880
BLACOW
GRIMMER BLVD
FREMONT BLVD
IRVINGTON
IRVINGTON HS
IRVINGTON PARK
LIB
FS
MARSHALL PARK
RIX PARK
BLACOW PARK
TECHNOLOGY DR
BUSINESS CENTER DR
ENTERPRISE ST
SOLAR WY
BRANDIN CT
PESTANA PL
INDUSTRIAL
FREMONT DRAG STRIP
SKY SAILING AIRPORT
NORTHPORT LP
CUSHING PKWY
SAN FRANCISCO BAY NATIONAL WILDLIFE REFUGE
SALT EVAPORATORS
AGUA
ARROYO

SEE 772 MAP

SEE 793 MAP

SEE 753 MAP

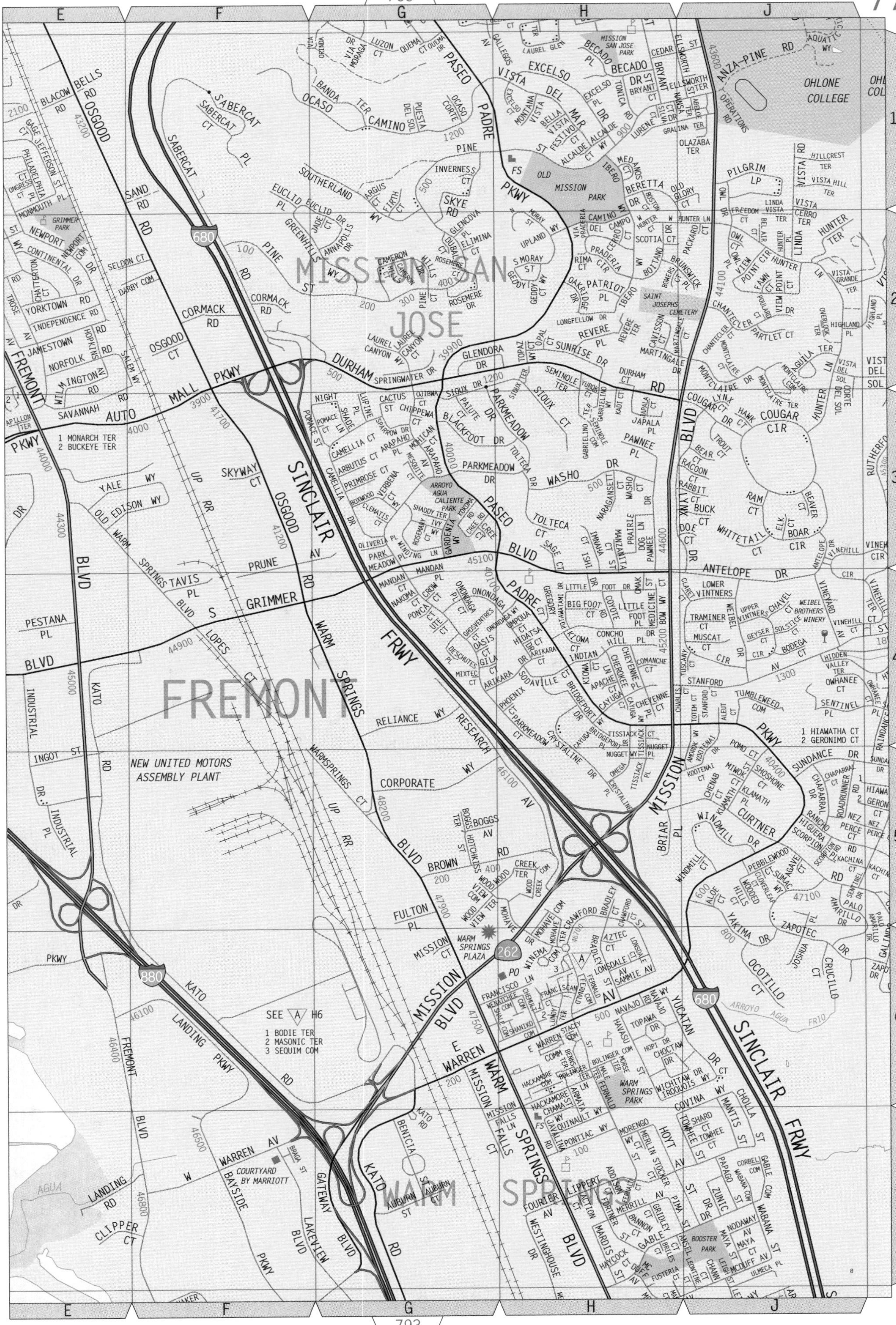
MISSION SAN JOSE
FREMONT
WARM SPRINGS
OHLONE COLLEGE
OLD MISSION PARK
SAINT JOSEPHS CEMETERY
ARROYO AGUA CALIENTE PARK
NEW UNITED MOTORS ASSEMBLY PLANT
WARM SPRINGS PLAZA
WARM SPRINGS PARK
BOOSTER PARK
GRIMMER PARK
WEIBEL BROTHERS WINERY
COURTYARD BY MARRIOTT
SINCLAIR FRWY
MISSION BLVD
PASEO PADRE PKWY
DURHAM RD
AUTO MALL PKWY
OSGOOD RD
GRIMMER BLVD
WARM SPRINGS BLVD
FREMONT BLVD
WARREN AV
KATO RD
1 MONARCH TER
2 BUCKEYE TER
1 HIAWATHA CT
2 GERONIMO CT
SEE A H6
1 BODIE TER
2 MASONIC TER
3 SEQUIM COM
SEE 774 MAP
E
F
G
H
J
1
2
3
4
5
6
7

SEE 793 MAP

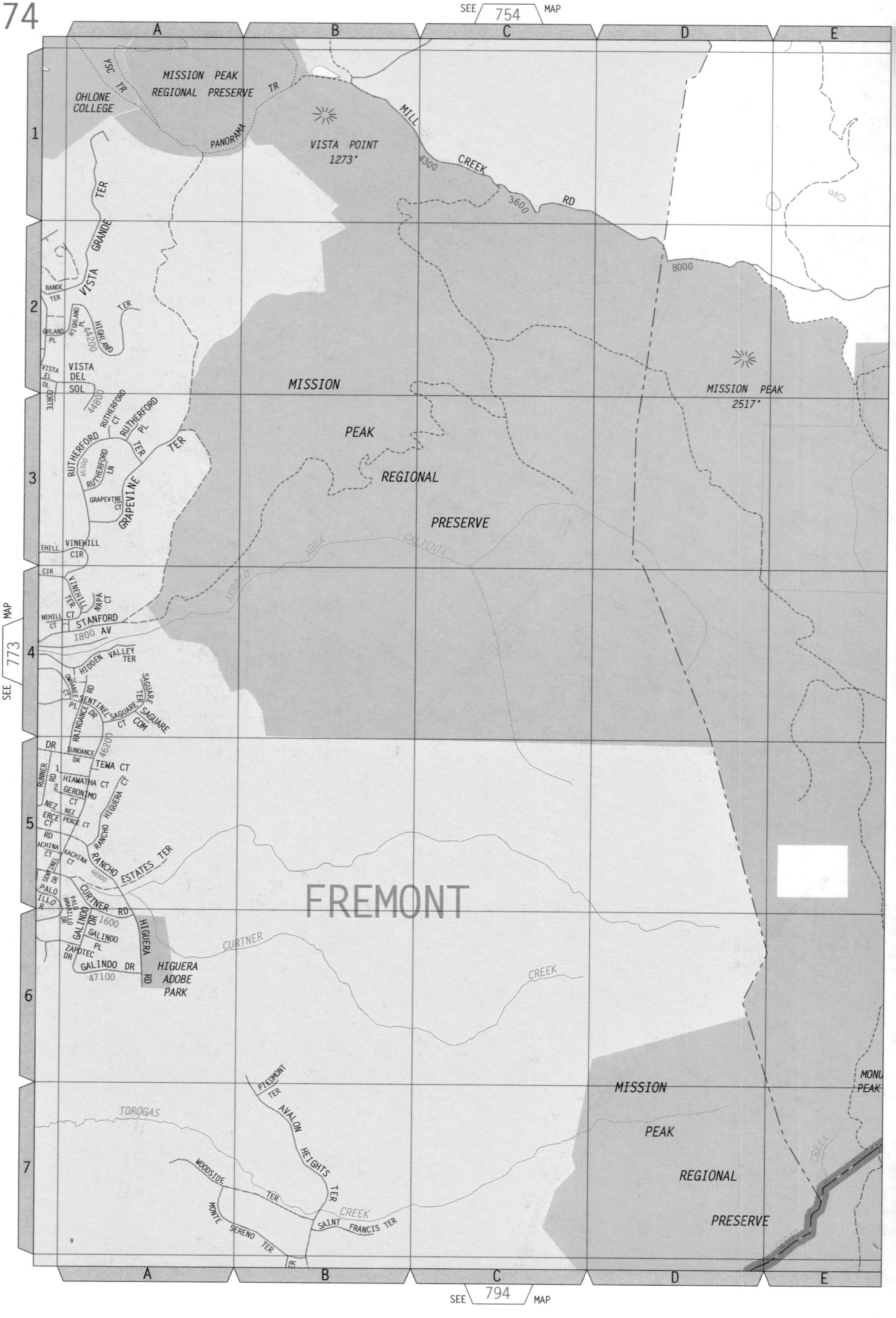
SEE 754 MAP
SEE 773 MAP
SEE 794 MAP
A
B
C
D
E
1
2
3
4
5
6
7
MISSION PEAK REGIONAL PRESERVE
OHLONE COLLEGE
PANORAMA TR
VISTA POINT 1273'
MILL CREEK RD
4300
3600
8000
VISTA GRANDE TER
RANDE TER
HIGHLAND PL
HIGHLAND TER
44200
VISTA DEL SOL
CORTE
44800
RUTHERFORD CT
RUTHERFORD PL
RUTHERFORD TER
RUTHERFORD LN
45300
GRAPEVINE CT
GRAPEVINE TER
VINEHILL CIR
VINEHILL TER
NAPA CT
STANFORD AV
1800
HIDDEN VALLEY TER
MISSION PEAK REGIONAL PRESERVE
MISSION PEAK 2517'
ARROYO AGUA CALIENTE
SAGUARE TER
SAGUARE CT
SAGUARE COM
SENTINEL DR
RAINDANCE DR
SUNDANCE DR
46200
TEWA CT
HIAWATHA CT
GERONIMO CT
RUNNER RD
NEZ PERCE CT
HIGUERA CT
RANCHO HIGUERA CT
KACHINA CT
RANCHO ESTATES TER
46900
PALO AMARILLO DR
CURTNER RD
1600
GALINDO DR
GALINDO PL
ZAPOTEC DR
47100
HIGUERA RD
HIGUERA ADOBE PARK
FREMONT
CURTNER CREEK
TOROGAS CREEK
PIEDMONT TER
AVALON HEIGHTS TER
WOODSIDE TER
MONTE SERENO TER
SAINT FRANCIS TER
MISSION PEAK REGIONAL PRESERVE
MONU PEAK

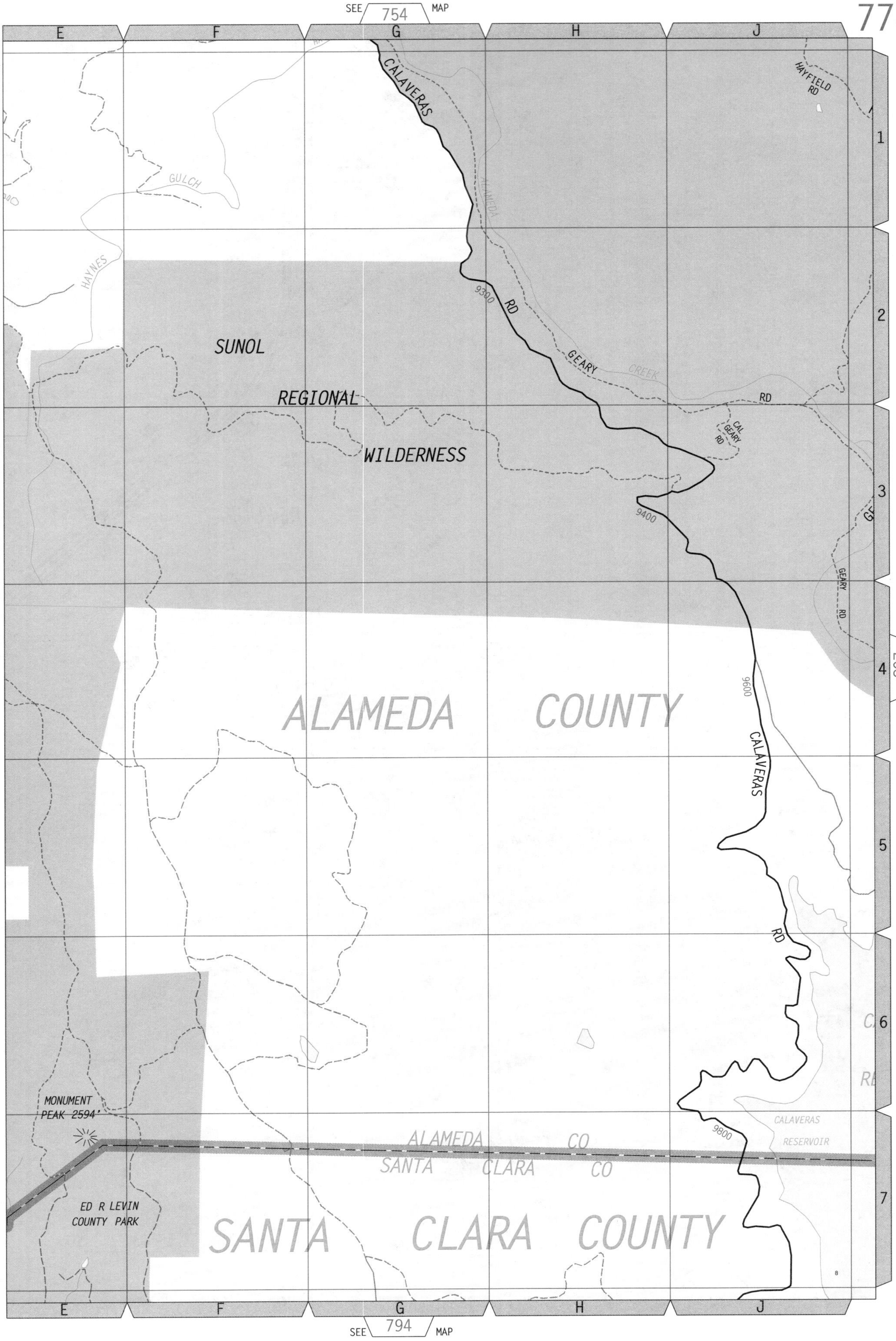
SEE 754 MAP
E
F
G
H
J
1
2
3
4
5
6
7
CALAVERAS
HAYFIELD RD
GULCH
ALAMEDA
HAYNES
9300
RD
SUNOL
REGIONAL
WILDERNESS
GEARY
CREEK
RD
CAL GEARY RD
9400
GEARY RD
SEE 263 MAP
9600
ALAMEDA COUNTY
CALAVERAS
RD
MONUMENT PEAK 2594'
9800
CALAVERAS
RESERVOIR
ALAMEDA CO
SANTA CLARA CO
ED R LEVIN COUNTY PARK
SANTA CLARA COUNTY
SEE 794 MAP

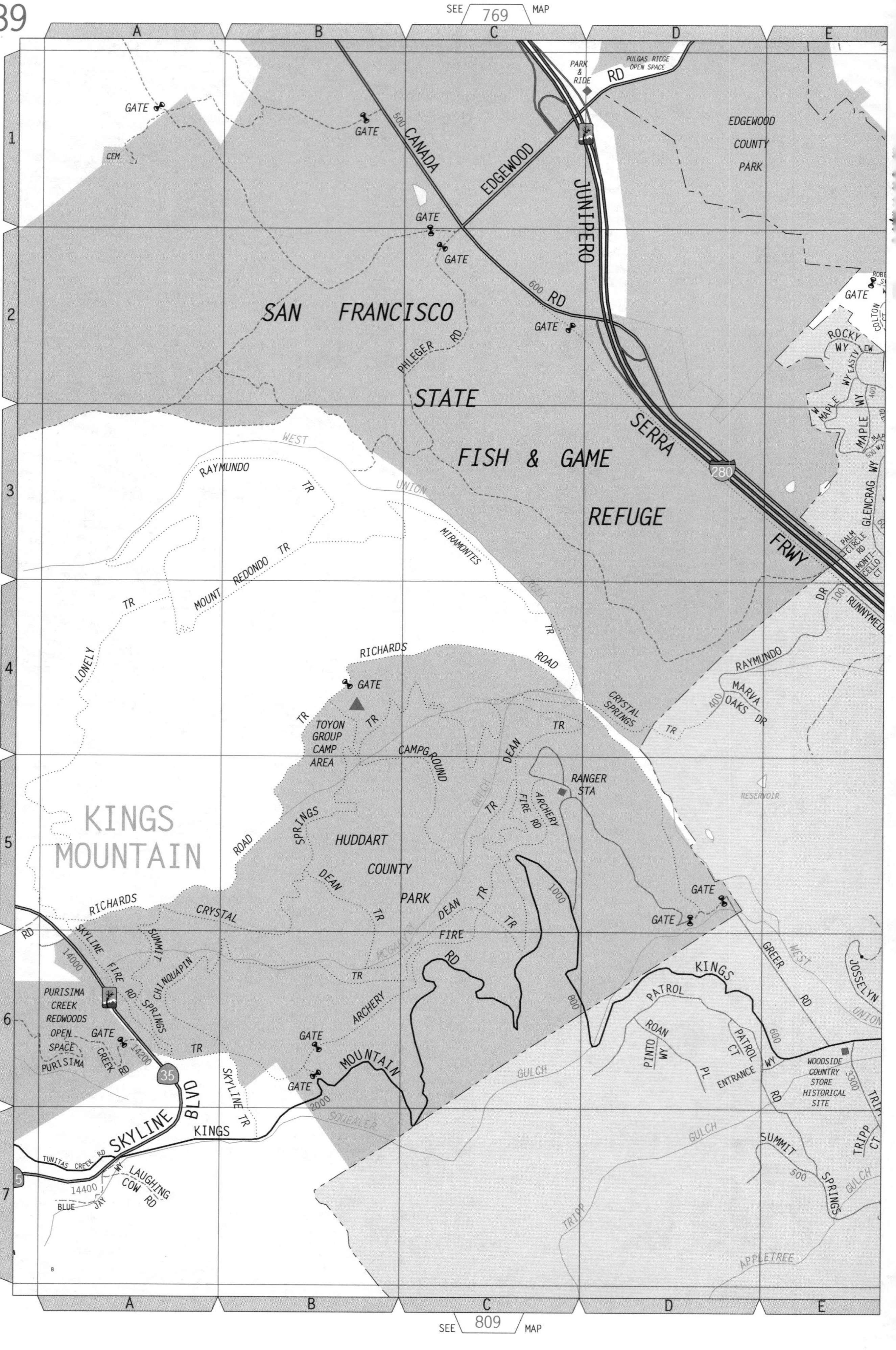
SEE 769 MAP
SEE 263 MAP
SEE 809 MAP
A
B
C
D
E
1
2
3
4
5
6
7
SAN FRANCISCO
STATE
FISH & GAME
REFUGE
EDGEWOOD
COUNTY
PARK
PULGAS RIDGE
OPEN SPACE
PARK & RIDE
CANADA
RD
EDGEWOOD
JUNIPERO
SERRA
FRWY
280
PHLEGER RD
GATE
CEM
WEST
UNION
CREEK
RAYMUNDO TR
MOUNT REDONDO TR
MIRAMONTES
LONELY TR
RICHARDS ROAD
CRYSTAL SPRINGS TR
TOYON
GROUP
CAMP
AREA
CAMPGROUND
DEAN TR
RANGER STA
ARCHERY FIRE RD
GULCH
HUDDART
COUNTY
PARK
KINGS
MOUNTAIN
RESERVOIR
RAYMUNDO
MARVA OAKS DR
RUNNYMEDE
DR
ROCKY WY
MAPLE WY
GLENCRAG WY
PALM CIRCLE RD
MONTICELLO CT
COLTON
GREER RD
JOSSELYN
KINGS MOUNTAIN RD
PATROL RD
PATROL CT
ROAN PL
PINTO WY
ENTRANCE WY
WOODSIDE
COUNTRY
STORE
HISTORICAL
SITE
TRIPP CT
SUMMIT SPRINGS
TRIPP
APPLETREE
SQUEALER
PURISIMA
CREEK
REDWOODS
OPEN
SPACE
PURISIMA CREEK RD
SKYLINE FIRE RD
SUMMIT SPRINGS
CHINQUAPIN
ARCHERY TR
MCGARVEY
SKYLINE TR
SKYLINE BLVD
35
TUNITAS CREEK RD
LAUGHING COW RD
BLUE JAY WY
14000
14200
14400
500
600
400
100
1000
800
2000
3300

SEE 769 MAP

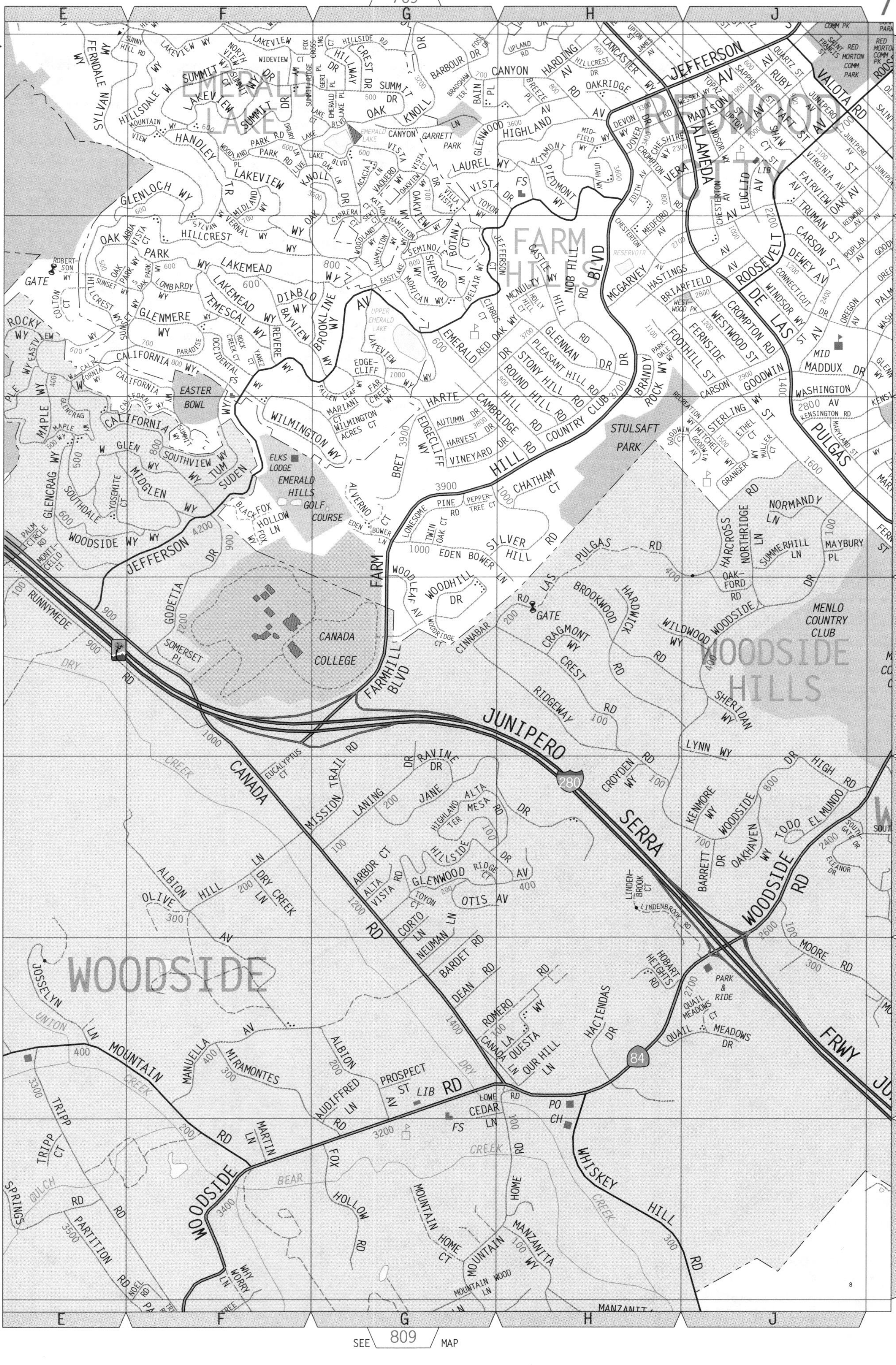
E
F
G
H
J
1
2
3
4
5
6
7
EMERALD LAKE
REDWOOD CITY
FARM HILLS
WOODSIDE HILLS
WOODSIDE
STULSAFT PARK
MENLO COUNTRY CLUB
CANADA COLLEGE
EMERALD HILLS GOLF COURSE
ELKS LODGE
EASTER BOWL
EMERALD LAKE
UPPER EMERALD LAKE
RESERVOIR
GARRETT PARK
RED MORTON COMM PARK
PARK & RIDE
JEFFERSON AV
ALAMEDA DE LAS PULGAS
ROOSEVELT AV
JUNIPERO SERRA FRWY
280
84
FARM HILL BLVD
FARMHILL BLVD
CANADA RD
WOODSIDE RD
WHISKEY HILL RD
MOUNTAIN HOME RD
MOUNTAIN HOME CT
MOUNTAIN WOOD LN
MANZANITA WY
HOME RD
CEDAR LN
PROSPECT ST
ALBION AV
AUDIFFRED LN
MIRAMONTES RD
MANUELLA AV
MOUNTAIN RD
UNION CREEK
BEAR CREEK
DRY CREEK
JOSSELYN LN
TRIPP RD
TRIPP CT
SPRINGS GULCH RD
PARTITION RD
WHY WORRY LN
FOX HOLLOW RD
OLIVE HILL LN
ALBION HILL LN
DRY CREEK LN
MISSION TRAIL RD
EUCALYPTUS CT
LANING DR
JANE DR
RAVINE DR
HIGHLAND TER
ALTA MESA DR
HILLSIDE DR
GLENWOOD AV
RIDGE CT
OTIS AV
ARBOR CT
ALTA VISTA RD
TOYON CT
CORTO LN
NEUMAN LN
BARDET RD
DEAN RD
ROMERO RD
LA QUESTA WY
OUR HILL LN
HACIENDAS DR
HOBART HEIGHTS RD
QUAIL MEADOWS DR
QUAIL MEADOWS CT
LINDENBROOK CT
LINDENBROOK RD
MOORE RD
BARRETT DR
OAKHAVEN WY
KENMORE WY
TODO EL MUNDO
HIGH RD
CROYDEN WY
LYNN WY
SHERIDAN WY
RIDGEWAY RD
CRAGMONT WY
CREST RD
BROOKWOOD RD
HARDWICK RD
WILDWOOD WY
WOODSIDE DR
OAKFORD RD
HARCROSS NORTHRIDGE LN
NORMANDY LN
SUMMERHILL LN
MAYBURY PL
LAS PULGAS RD
CINNABAR
WOODRIDGE CT
WOODLEAF AV
WOODHILL DR
EDEN BOWER LN
SILVER HILL RD
TWIN OAK CT
LONESOME PINE RD
PEPPERTREE CT
CHATHAM CT
ALVERNO CT
BLACK FOX HOLLOW LN
GODETIA DR
SOMERSET PL
RUNNYMEDE RD
JEFFERSON AV
WOODSIDE WY
SOUTHDALE WY
GLENCRAG WY
YOSEMITE CT
MIDGLEN WY
SOUTHVIEW WY
TUM SUDEN WY
CALIFORNIA WY
MAPLE WY
ROCKY WY
GATE
HILLCREST WY
SUNSET WY
GLENMERE WY
TEMESCAL WY
LAKEMEAD WY
DIABLO WY
BAYVIEW WY
BROOKLINE WY
REVERE WY
OCCIDENTAL WY
WILMINGTON WY
WILMINGTON ACRES CT
MARIANI CT
EDGECLIFF WY
FAR CREEK WY
HARTE
BRET HARTE
AUTUMN DR
HARVEST DR
VINEYARD DR
CAMBRIDGE RD
ROUND HILL RD
STONY HILL RD
PLEASANT HILL RD
GLENNAN DR
RED OAK WY
EMERALD HILL RD
COUNTRY CLUB DR
BRANDY ROCK WY
CASTLE HILL RD
NOB HILL RD
MCNULTY WY
HOLLY CT
JEFFERSON CT
BELAIR WY
BOTANY CT
SHEPARD WY
MOHICAN WY
SEMINOLE WY
HAMILTON WY
OAKVIEW WY
VAQUERO WY
LAUREL WY
VISTA DR
TOYON WY
PIEDMONT WY
ALTAMONT WY
HIGHLAND AV
GLENWOOD AV
CANYON
GARRETT
OAK KNOLL DR
SUMMIT DR
LAKEVIEW WY
LAKEVIEW DR
HANDLEY TR
GLENLOCH WY
HILLCREST WY
PARK WY
SYLVAN WY
FERNDALE WY
HILLSDALE WY
MIDLAND WY
VERNAL WY
KNOLL DR
CREST DR
HILLWAY
BARBOUR DR
HARDING AV
OAKRIDGE AV
LANCASTER WY
MCGARVEY AV
HASTINGS
BRIARFIELD
MEDFORD AV
CHESTERTON AV
EDITH AV
VERA AV
CHESHIRE WY
CROMPTON WY
DOVER DR
DEVON WY
MADISON AV
EUCLID AV
CARSON ST
DEWEY AV
TRUMAN ST
WINDSOR WY
CONNECTICUT DR
OREGON AV
WESTWOOD ST
FERNSIDE ST
CROMPTON RD
FOOTHILL ST
CARSON
GOODWIN AV
STERLING WY
ETHEL CT
MITCHELL WY
GRANGER WY
MID MADDUX DR
WASHINGTON AV
KENSINGTON RD
JUNIPERO AV
VALOTA RD
QUARTZ ST
RUBY ST
SAPPHIRE ST
TOPAZ ST
TAFT ST
SHAW AV
VIRGINIA AV
FAIRVIEW AV
OAK AV
LIB
FS
PO
CH
GATE

SEE 790 MAP

SEE 809 MAP

SEE 770 MAP

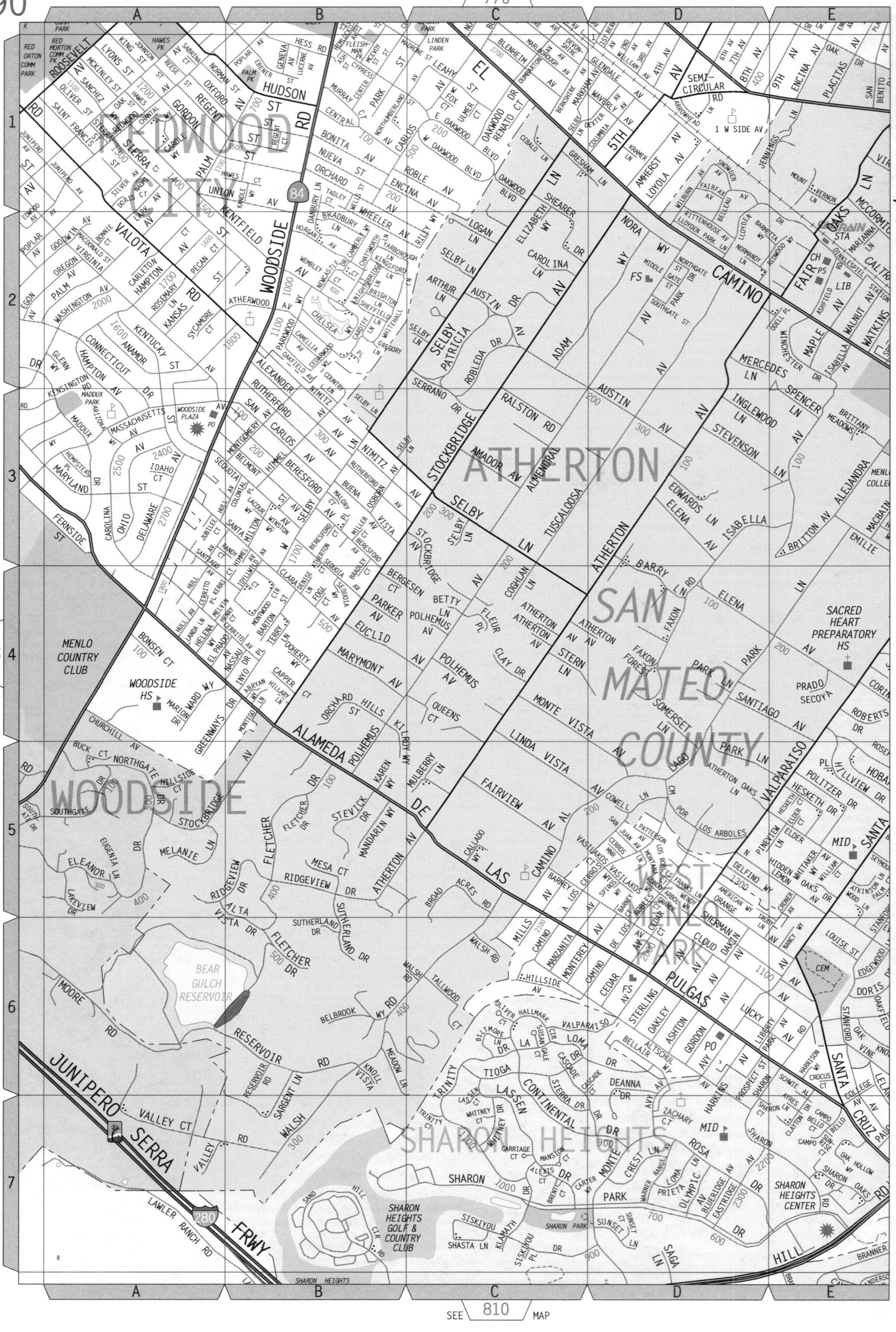
A
B
C
D
E
1
2
3
4
5
6
7
REDWOOD CITY
ATHERTON
SAN MATEO COUNTY
WOODSIDE
WEST MENLO PARK
SHARON HEIGHTS
MENLO COUNTRY CLUB
WOODSIDE HS
WOODSIDE PLAZA
SACRED HEART PREPARATORY HS
BEAR GULCH RESERVOIR
SHARON HEIGHTS GOLF & COUNTRY CLUB
SHARON HEIGHTS CENTER
WOODSIDE RD
ALAMEDA DE LAS PULGAS
EL CAMINO
JUNIPERO SERRA FRWY
SELBY LN
VALPARAISO AV
MIDDLEFIELD RD
ATHERTON AV
FLETCHER DR
RESERVOIR RD
SAND HILL RD
VALOTA RD
HUDSON ST
STOCKBRIDGE AV
WALSH RD
SHARON PARK DR
MENLO COUNTRY CLUB
SELBY LN
MARSH RD
RIDGEVIEW DR
MOORE RD
CEM

SEE 789 MAP

SEE 810 MAP

SEE 770 MAP

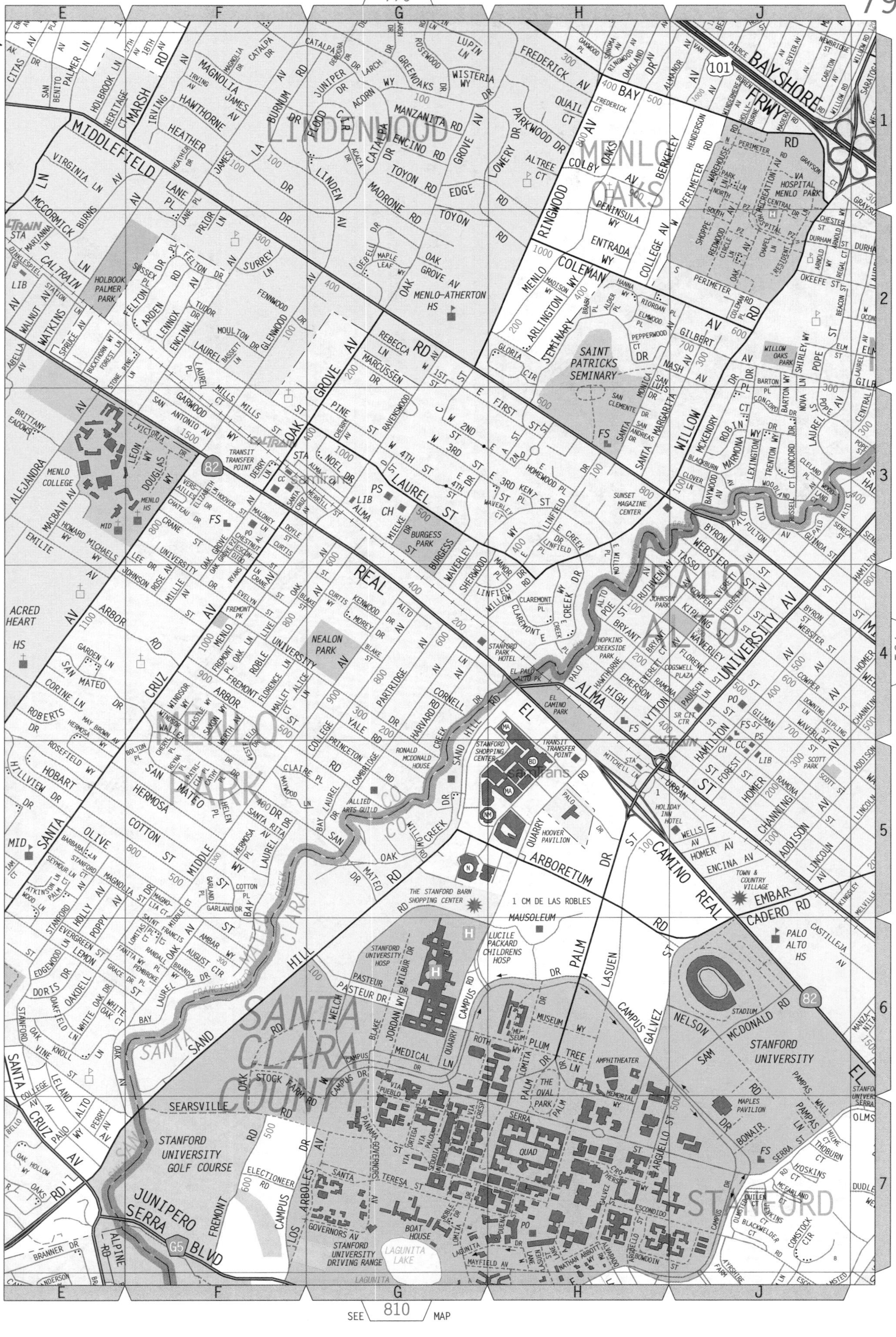
LINDENWOOD
MENLO OAKS
MENLO PARK
PALO ALTO
SANTA CLARA COUNTY
STANFORD
MIDDLEFIELD RD
BAYSHORE FRWY
101
82
G5
EL CAMINO REAL
UNIVERSITY AV
WILLOW RD
ALMA ST
SAND HILL RD
JUNIPERO SERRA BLVD
SANTA CRUZ AV
OAK GROVE AV
RINGWOOD AV
COLEMAN AV
PALM DR
ARBORETUM DR
CAMPUS DR
EMBARCADERO RD
VA HOSPITAL MENLO PARK
MENLO-ATHERTON HS
SAINT PATRICKS SEMINARY
MENLO COLLEGE
SACRED HEART HS
HOLBOOK PALMER PARK
BURGESS PARK
NEALON PARK
STANFORD SHOPPING CENTER
STANFORD PARK HOTEL
EL CAMINO PARK
HOLIDAY INN HOTEL
TOWN & COUNTRY VILLAGE
PALO ALTO HS
THE STANFORD BARN SHOPPING CENTER
STANFORD UNIVERSITY HOSP
LUCILE PACKARD CHILDRENS HOSP
MAUSOLEUM
STANFORD UNIVERSITY
STANFORD UNIVERSITY GOLF COURSE
STANFORD UNIVERSITY DRIVING RANGE
LAGUNITA LAKE
MAPLES PAVILION
STADIUM
QUAD
THE OVAL PARK
SUNSET MAGAZINE CENTER
HOPKINS CREEKSIDE PARK
JOHNSON PARK
ALLIED ARTS GUILD
RONALD MCDONALD HOUSE
HOOVER PAVILION
SAN FRANCISQUITO CREEK

SEE 791 MAP

SEE 810 MAP

BAY AREA

MAP

SEE 771 MAP

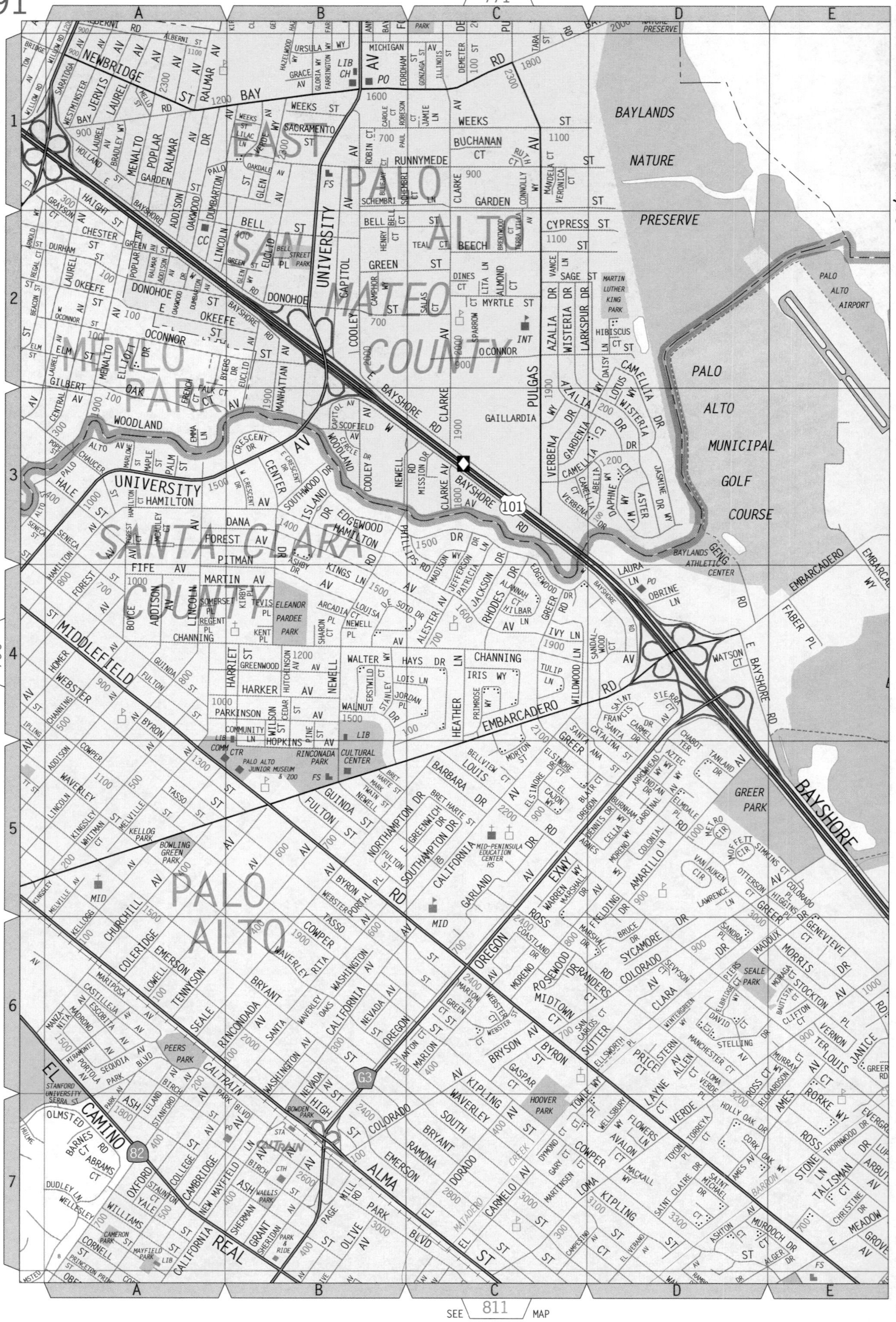
A
B
C
D
E
1
2
3
4
5
6
7
EAST PALO ALTO
SAN MATEO COUNTY
MENLO PARK
SANTA CLARA COUNTY
PALO ALTO
BAYLANDS NATURE PRESERVE
PALO ALTO AIRPORT
PALO ALTO MUNICIPAL GOLF COURSE
BAYLANDS ATHLETIC CENTER
MARTIN LUTHER KING PARK
ELEANOR PARDEE PARK
RINCONADA PARK
CULTURAL CENTER
PALO ALTO JUNIOR MUSEUM & ZOO
GREER PARK
SEALE PARK
PEERS PARK
HOOVER PARK
BOWLING GREEN PARK
KELLOG PARK
CAMERON PARK
MAYFIELD PARK
BOWDEN PARK
WALLIS PARK
MID-PENINSULA EDUCATION CENTER HS
STANFORD UNIVERSITY
CALTRAIN
BAYSHORE
UNIVERSITY AV
EMBARCADERO RD
MIDDLEFIELD RD
OREGON EXWY
EL CAMINO REAL
ALMA ST
CALIFORNIA AV
101
82
G3

SEE 790 MAP

SEE 811 MAP

SEE 771 MAP

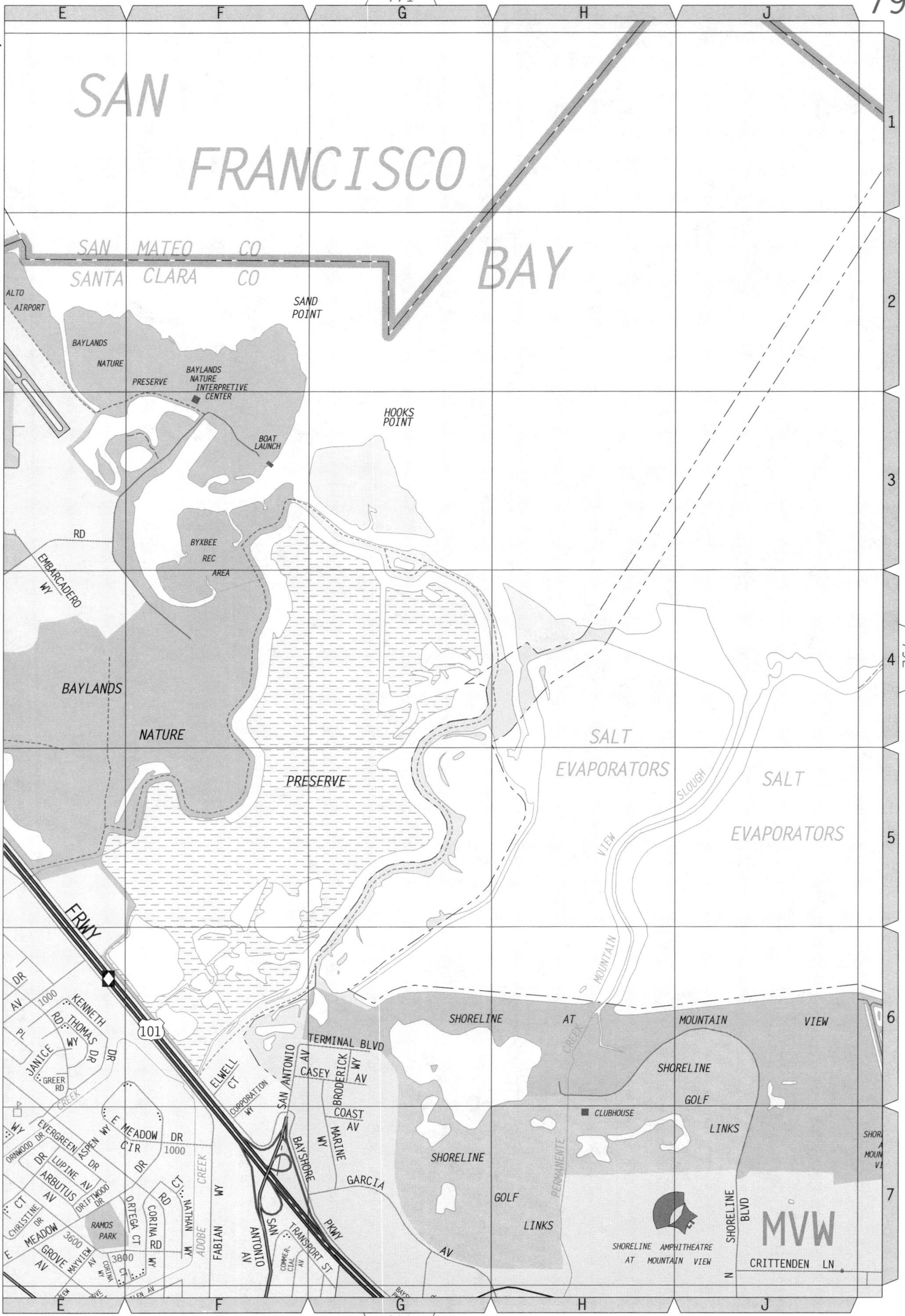
E
F
G
H
J
1
2
3
4
5
6
7
SAN FRANCISCO BAY
SAN MATEO CO
SANTA CLARA CO
ALTO AIRPORT
SAND POINT
BAYLANDS NATURE PRESERVE
BAYLANDS NATURE INTERPRETIVE CENTER
HOOKS POINT
BOAT LAUNCH
RD
EMBARCADERO WY
BYXBEE REC AREA
BAYLANDS NATURE PRESERVE
SALT EVAPORATORS
SALT EVAPORATORS
SLOUGH
VIEW
MOUNTAIN
FRWY
101
SHORELINE AT MOUNTAIN VIEW
SHORELINE GOLF LINKS
CLUBHOUSE
SHORELINE GOLF LINKS
CREEK
PERMANENTE
TERMINAL BLVD
CASEY AV
BRODERICK WY
COAST AV
MARINE WY
SAN ANTONIO AV
ELWELL CT
CORPORATION WY
BAYSHORE PKWY
GARCIA AV
DR
AV
PL
1000
KENNETH DR
THOMAS DR
RD
WY
JANICE
GREER RD
CREEK
E MEADOW DR
CIR
1000
EVERGREEN
ASPEN WY
WY
ORNWOOD DR
DR
LUPINE AV
ARBUTUS AV
DRIFTWOOD DR
CT
CHRISTINE DR
MEADOW
GROVE AV
MAYVIEW AV
3600
3800
RAMOS PARK
ORTEGA CT
CORINA RD
RD
CT
NATHAN WY
ADOBE CREEK
FABIAN WY
SAN ANTONIO AV
COMMERCIAL AV
TRANSPORT ST
SHORELINE AMPHITHEATRE AT MOUNTAIN VIEW
MVW
SHORELINE BLVD
N
CRITTENDEN LN

SEE 792 MAP

SEE 811 MAP

SEE 772 MAP

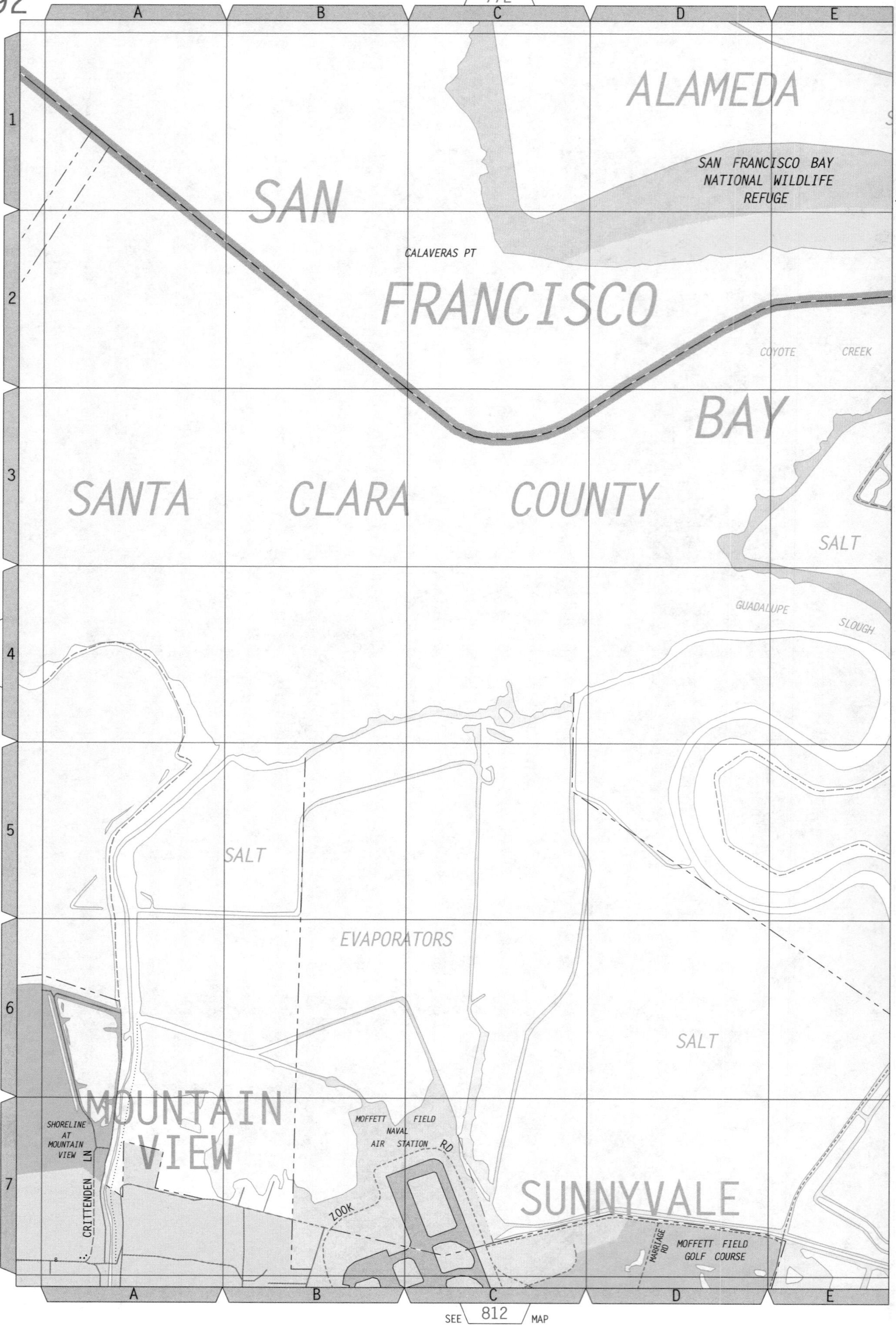
A
B
C
D
E
1
2
3
4
5
6
7
ALAMEDA
SAN FRANCISCO BAY
NATIONAL WILDLIFE
REFUGE
SAN
CALAVERAS PT
FRANCISCO
COYOTE
CREEK
BAY
SANTA
CLARA
COUNTY
SALT
GUADALUPE
SLOUGH
SALT
EVAPORATORS
SALT
MOUNTAIN
VIEW
SHORELINE
AT
MOUNTAIN
VIEW
CRITTENDEN
LN
MOFFETT
FIELD
NAVAL
AIR
STATION
RD
ZOOK
SUNNYVALE
MARRIAGE
RD
MOFFETT FIELD
GOLF COURSE

SEE 791 MAP

SEE 812 MAP

SEE 772 MAP

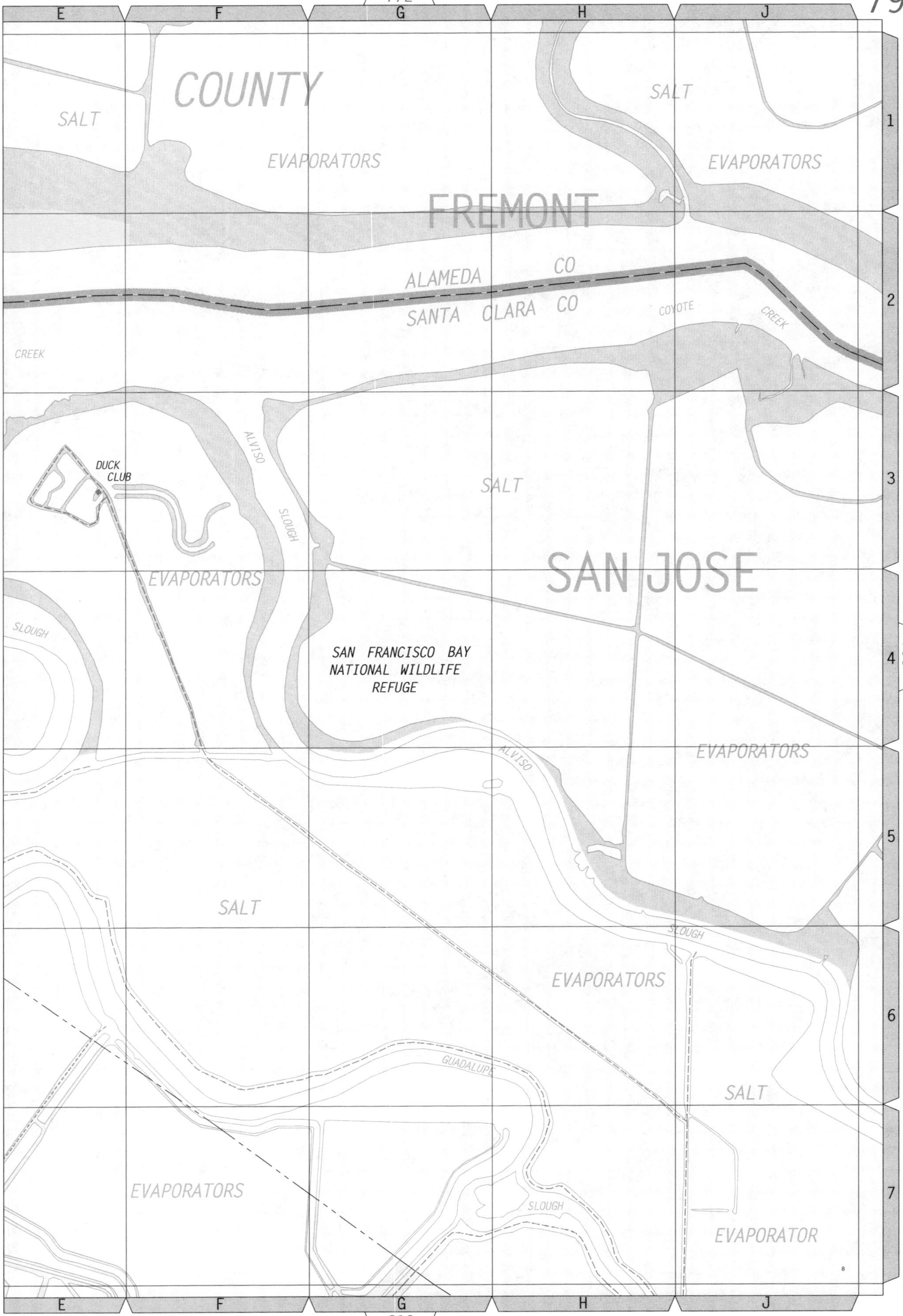
E
F
G
H
J
1
2
3
4
5
6
7
COUNTY
SALT
EVAPORATORS
SALT
EVAPORATORS
FREMONT
ALAMEDA CO
SANTA CLARA CO
COYOTE
CREEK
CREEK
ALVISO
SLOUGH
DUCK CLUB
SALT
SAN JOSE
EVAPORATORS
SLOUGH
SAN FRANCISCO BAY
NATIONAL WILDLIFE
REFUGE
ALVISO
EVAPORATORS
SALT
SLOUGH
EVAPORATORS
GUADALUPE
SALT
EVAPORATORS
SLOUGH
EVAPORATOR

SEE 793 MAP

SEE 812 MAP

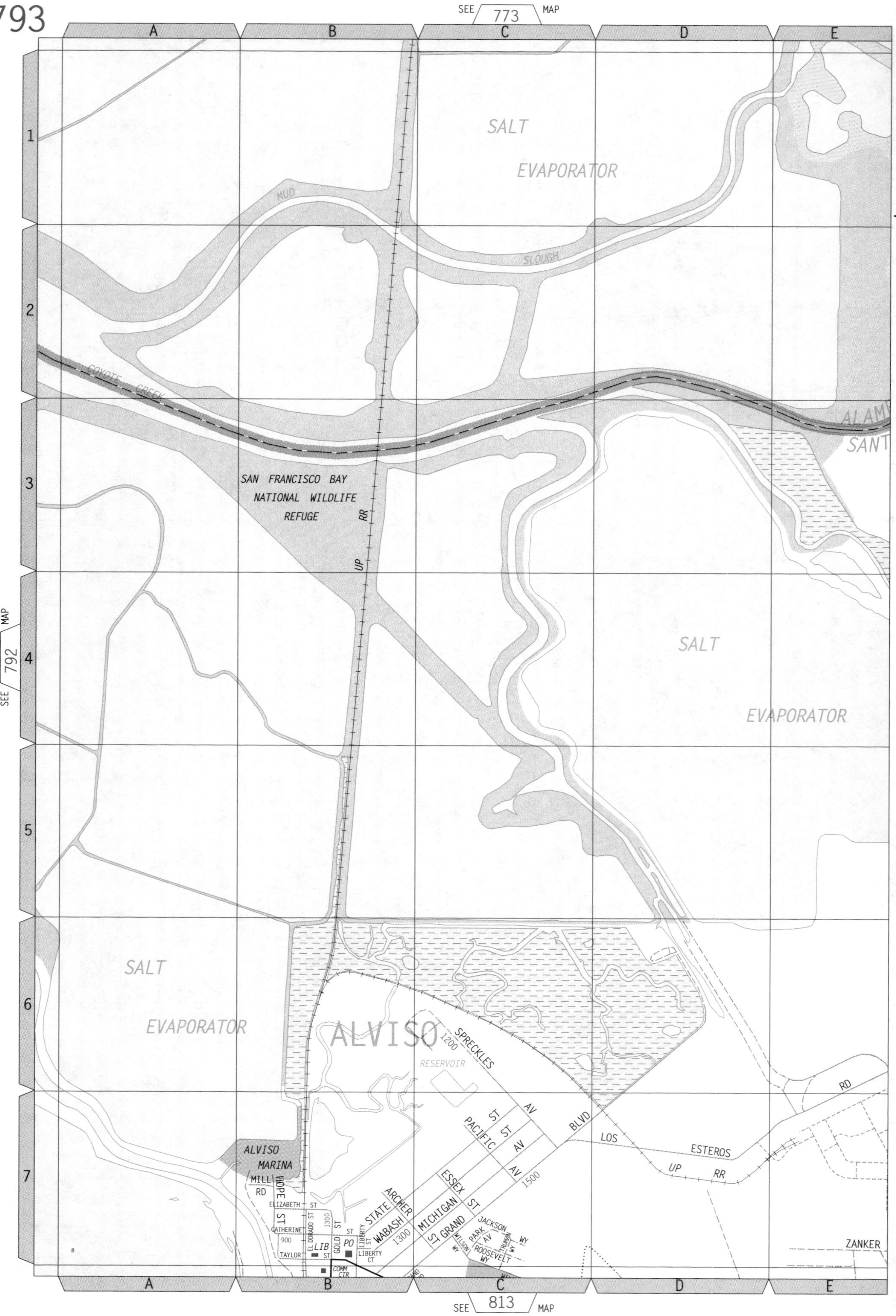
SEE 773 MAP
A
B
C
D
E
1
2
3
4
5
6
7
SEE 792 MAP
SALT
EVAPORATOR
MUD
SLOUGH
COYOTE
CREEK
ALAMI
SANT
SAN FRANCISCO BAY
NATIONAL WILDLIFE
REFUGE
UP
RR
SALT
EVAPORATOR
SALT
EVAPORATOR
ALVISO
SPRECKLES
1200
RESERVOIR
AV
ST
PACIFIC
ST
AV
BLVD
LOS
ESTEROS
RD
UP
RR
AV
1500
ESSEX
ST
MICHIGAN
ARCHER
STATE
WABASH
1300
GRAND
ST
JACKSON
PARK
AV
TRUMAN
WY
WY
WILSON
WY
ROOSEVELT
WY
ALVISO
MARINA
MILL
RD
HOPE
ST
ELIZABETH
ST
EL DORADO
ST
1300
GOLD
ST
LIBERTY
ST
ST
CATHERINE
900
TAYLOR
LIB
PO
LIBERTY
CT
COMM
CTR
ZANKER
SEE 813 MAP

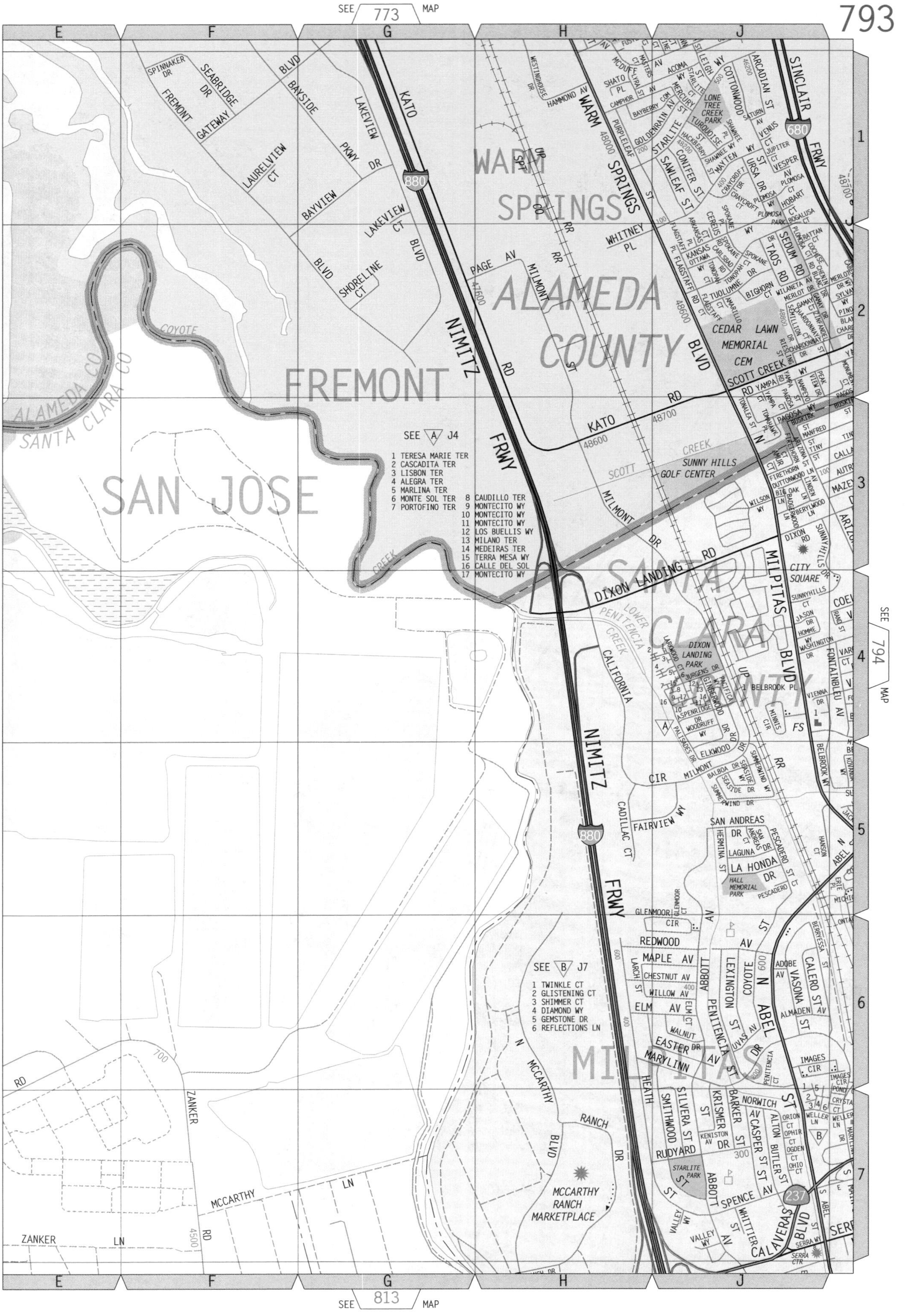
SEE 773 MAP
SEE 813 MAP
SEE 794 MAP
E
F
G
H
J
1
2
3
4
5
6
7
FREMONT
SAN JOSE
WARM SPRINGS
ALAMEDA COUNTY
SANTA CLARA COUNTY
MILPITAS
ALAMEDA CO
SANTA CLARA CO
COYOTE CREEK
NIMITZ FRWY
SINCLAIR FRWY
KATO RD
WARM SPRINGS BLVD
MILPITAS BLVD
DIXON LANDING RD
SCOTT CREEK RD
MILMONT DR
CALIFORNIA CIR
FAIRVIEW WY
CADILLAC CT
N MCCARTHY BLVD
RANCH DR
MCCARTHY LN
ZANKER RD
ZANKER LN
CALAVERAS BLVD
N ABEL ST
LAKEVIEW BLVD
BAYSIDE PKWY
SHORELINE CT
LAURELVIEW CT
BAYVIEW DR
GATEWAY
SEABRIDGE DR
SPINNAKER DR
FREMONT BLVD
PAGE AV
WHITNEY PL
HAMMOND AV
CEDAR LAWN MEMORIAL CEM
SUNNY HILLS GOLF CENTER
LONE TREE CREEK PARK
DIXON LANDING PARK
HALL MEMORIAL PARK
STARLITE PARK
CITY SQUARE
MCCARTHY RANCH MARKETPLACE
LOWER PENITENCIA CREEK
SAN ANDREAS DR
LA HONDA DR
LAGUNA
PESCADERO ST
REDWOOD AV
MAPLE AV
CHESTNUT AV
WILLOW AV
ELM AV
WALNUT
EASTER AV
MARYLINN DR
ABBOTT AV
PENITENCIA ST
LEXINGTON ST
COYOTE DR
HEATH
SILVERA ST
SMITHWOOD ST
KRISMER DR
BARKER ST
NORWICH
RUDYARD DR
SPENCE AV
VALLEY WY
WHITTIER ST
SEE A J4
1 TERESA MARIE TER
2 CASCADITA TER
3 LISBON TER
4 ALEGRA TER
5 MARLINA TER
6 MONTE SOL TER
7 PORTOFINO TER
8 CAUDILLO TER
9 MONTECITO WY
10 MONTECITO WY
11 MONTECITO WY
12 LOS BUELLIS WY
13 MILANO TER
14 MEDEIRAS TER
15 TERRA MESA WY
16 CALLE DEL SOL
17 MONTECITO WY
SEE B J7
1 TWINKLE CT
2 GLISTENING CT
3 SHIMMER CT
4 DIAMOND WY
5 GEMSTONE DR
6 REFLECTIONS LN
880
680
237

SEE 774 MAP

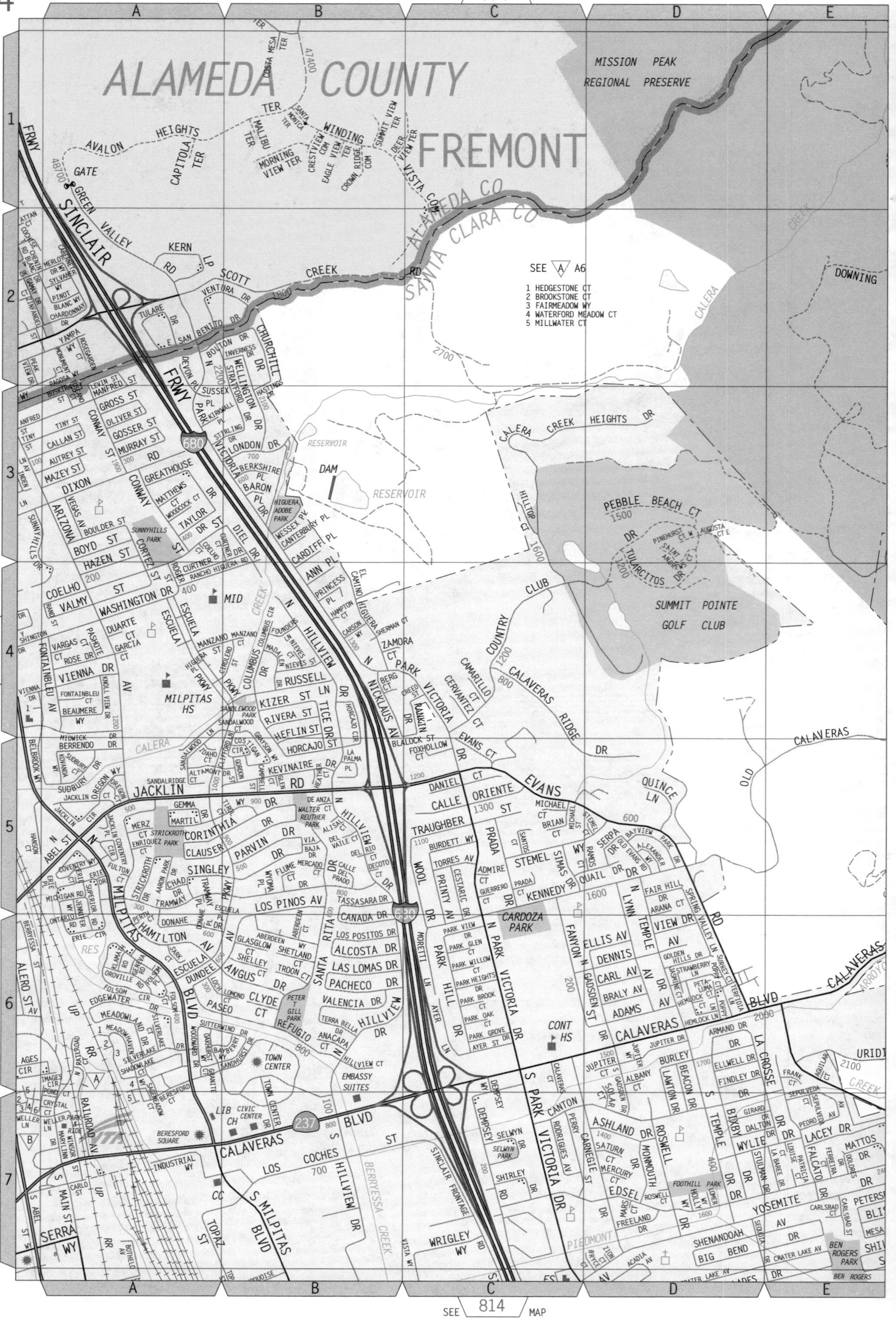

A
B
C
D
E
1
2
3
4
5
6
7
ALAMEDA COUNTY
FREMONT
MISSION PEAK REGIONAL PRESERVE
ALAMEDA CO
SANTA CLARA CO
SEE A A6
1 HEDGESTONE CT
2 BROOKSTONE CT
3 FAIRMEADOW WY
4 WATERFORD MEADOW CT
5 MILLWATER CT
AVALON HEIGHTS
GATE
CAPITOLA TER
COSTA MESA TER
SANTA MONICA TER
MALIBU TER
MORNING VIEW TER
CRESTVIEW COM
EAGLE VIEW TER
WINDING
CROWN RIDGE COM
SUMMIT VIEW TER
DEER VIEW TER
VISTA COM
FRWY
SINCLAIR
GREEN VALLEY
KERN
RD
LP
SCOTT
CREEK
VENTURA DR
TULARE DR
E SAN BENITO DR
CHURCHILL
WELLINGTON DR
BOULTON DR
INVERNESS
STRATFORD
DEVON PL
SUSSEX PL
KIRKWALL
STIRLING
LONDON DR
BERKSHIRE
BARON PL
VICTORIA
PARK
680
RESERVOIR
DAM
HIGUERA ADOBE PARK
WESSEX PL
CANTERBURY PL
CARDIFF PL
ANN PL
PRINCESS
EL CAMINO HIGUERA
HAMPTON CT
CARSON
SHERMAN CT
ZAMORA
CALERA CREEK HEIGHTS DR
HILLTOP
PEBBLE BEACH CT
PINEHURST CT
AUGUSTA CT
SAINT ANDREWS
TULARCITOS DR
CLUB
SUMMIT POINTE GOLF CLUB
COUNTRY
CAMARILLO CT
CERVANTEZ CT
CALAVERAS RIDGE DR
CALAVERAS
DOWNING
OLD
QUINCE LN
YAMPA WY
ROSEGARDEN
PAGOSA WY
LEVIN ST
MANFRED
GROSS ST
OLIVER ST
GOSSER ST
MURRAY ST
TINY ST
CALLAN ST
AUTREY ST
MAZEY ST
DIXON
CONWAY
GREATHOUSE
MATTHEWS CT
WOODCOCK CT
TAYLOR
DR ST
DIEL DR
ARIZONA
VEGAS AV
BOULDER ST
SUNNYHILLS PARK
BOYD ST
HAZEN ST
CORTEZ ST
ROGER
RANCHO HIGUERA RD
CURTNER
SUNNYHILLS
COELHO
VALMY
WASHINGTON DR
ESCUELA
MID
CREEK
DUARTE CT
GARCIA CT
VARGAS
ROSE DR
FONTAINEBLEU AV
VIENNA DR
KNOLL VIEW DR
BEAUMERE
MILPITAS HS
MANZANO
COLUMBUS
FOUNDERS
NIEVES CT
HIGUERA
PKWY
RUSSELL
KIZER ST
RIVERA ST
HEFLIN ST
TICE DR
HORCAJO ST
HORCAJO CT
HILLVIEW
NICKLAUS AV
BERG CT
CREED ST
RANKIN DR
BLALOCK ST
FOXHOLLOW CT
EVANS CT
MIDWICK
BERRENDO DR
CALERA
BELBROOK WY
SUDBURY
OREGON WY
JACKLIN
SANDALRIDGE CT
KEVINAIRE DR
LA PALMA PL
DANIEL CT
CALLE ORIENTE
EVANS
MICHAEL CT
BRIAN CT
TRAUGHBER
GEMMA
MARTIL
DE ANZA
WALTER REUTHER PARK
ABEL ST
MERZ
STRICKROTH
ENRIQUEZ PARK
CORINTHIA
CLAUSER
PARVIN
SINGLEY
LOS PINOS AV
TASSASARA DR
CANADA DR
WOOL
BURDETT WY
TORRES AV
PRADA
ADMIRE CT
STEMEL WY
SIMAS DR
KENNEDY
CARDOZA PARK
QUAIL DR
SERPA
LYNN
TEMPLE
FAIR HILL DR
ARANA CT
VIEW DR
SPRING VALLEY LN
RD
MILPITAS
HAMILTON
DONAHE
ESCUELA
DUNDEE
ANGUS
CLYDE
PASEO
REFUGIO
PETER T GILL PARK
SANTA RITA
LOS POSITOS DR
ALCOSTA DR
LAS LOMAS DR
PACHECO
VALENCIA DR
HILLVIEW
ANACAPA
MORETTI LN
PARK HILL
AYER
N PARK VICTORIA DR
FANYON
GADSDEN ST
ELLIS AV
DENNIS
CARL AV
BRALY AV
ADAMS
CONT HS
CALAVERAS
BLVD
CALAVERAS
MEADOWLAND DR
EDGEWATER CIR
OROVILLE
RR
UP
ALERO ST
TOWN CENTER
EMBASSY SUITES
LIB
CH
CIVIC CENTER
BERESFORD SQUARE
237
CALAVERAS
LOS COCHES
ST
INDUSTRIAL WY
CC
S MILPITAS BLVD
TOPAZ ST
HILLVIEW DR
BERRYESSA CREEK
SINCLAIR FRONTAGE
WRIGLEY WY
DEMPSEY
SELWYN
SHIRLEY
CANTON
PERRY
RODRIGUES AV
CARNEGIE ST
S PARK VICTORIA DR
ASHLAND DR
SATURN
MERCURY
EDSEL
FREELAND
ROSWELL
MONMOUTH
LAWTON DR
BEACON DR
BURLEY
JUPITER
FOOTHILL PARK
TEMPLE
BIXBY
WYLIE
ELLWELL DR
FINDLEY DR
LA CROSSE
DALTON
LACEY DR
FALCATO
MATTOS
YOSEMITE
AV
DR
SHENANDOAH
BIG BEND
BEN ROGERS PARK
PIEDMONT
URIDIAS
RAILROAD AV
SERRA WY
S MAIN ST
S ABEL

SEE 793 MAP

SEE 814 MAP

SEE 774 MAP

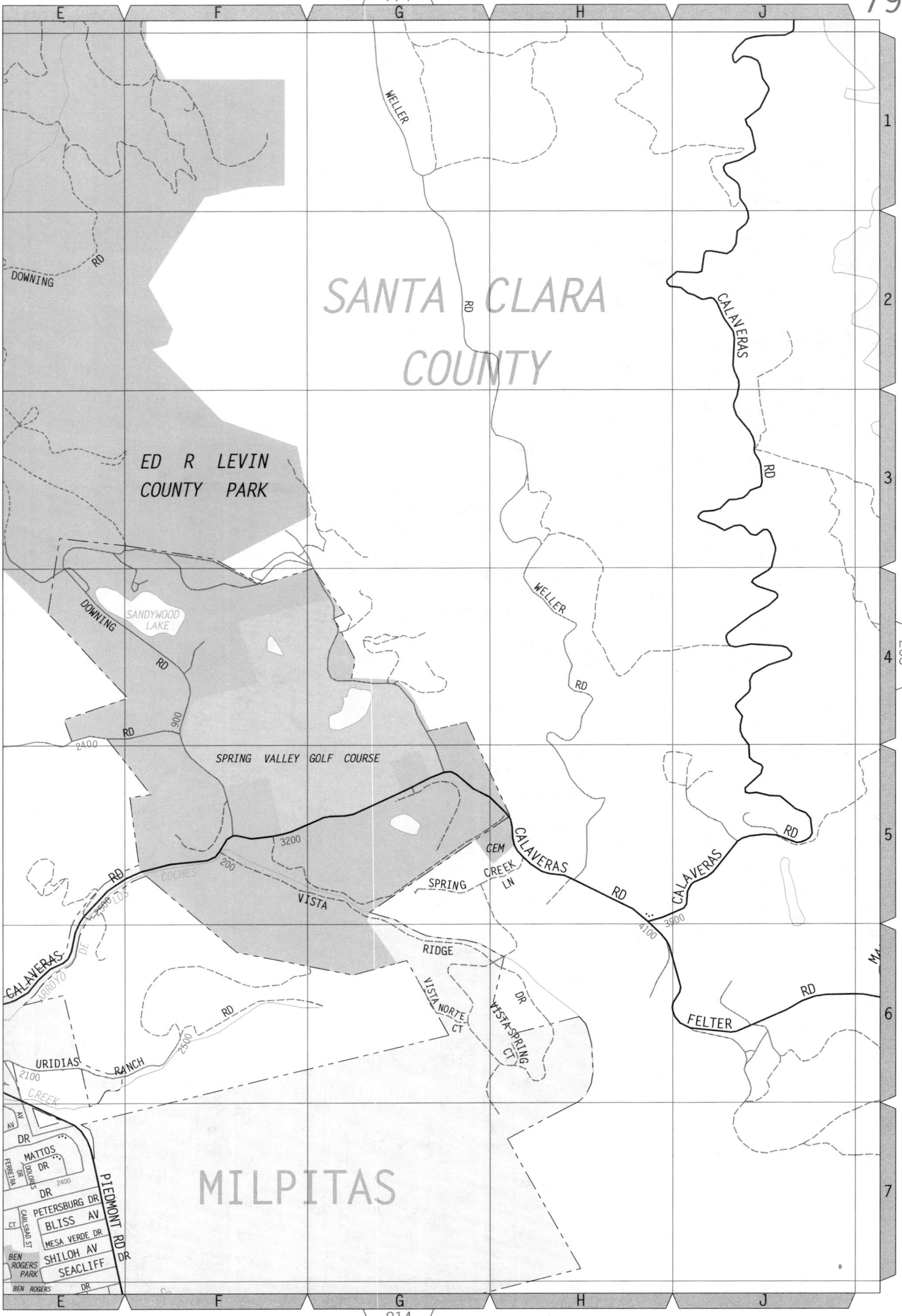
E
F
G
H
J
1
2
3
4
5
6
7
SANTA CLARA COUNTY
ED R LEVIN COUNTY PARK
SPRING VALLEY GOLF COURSE
SANDYWOOD LAKE
MILPITAS
WELLER RD
WELLER RD
CALAVERAS RD
CALAVERAS RD
CALAVERAS RD
CALAVERAS RD
DOWNING RD
DOWNING RD
CEM
SPRING CREEK LN
VISTA RIDGE DR
VISTA NORTE CT
VISTA SPRING CT
ARROYO DE LOS COCHES
FELTER RD
URIDIAS RANCH RD
CREEK
PIEDMONT RD
MATTOS DR
FERREIRA DR
DOLORES DR
PETERSBURG DR
BLISS AV
CARLSBAD ST
CT
MESA VERDE DR
SHILOH AV
SEACLIFF DR
BEN ROGERS PARK
BEN ROGERS DR
AV
DR
900
2400
3200
200
2500
2100
4100
3900
2400

SEE 263 MAP

SEE 814 MAP

SEE 789 MAP

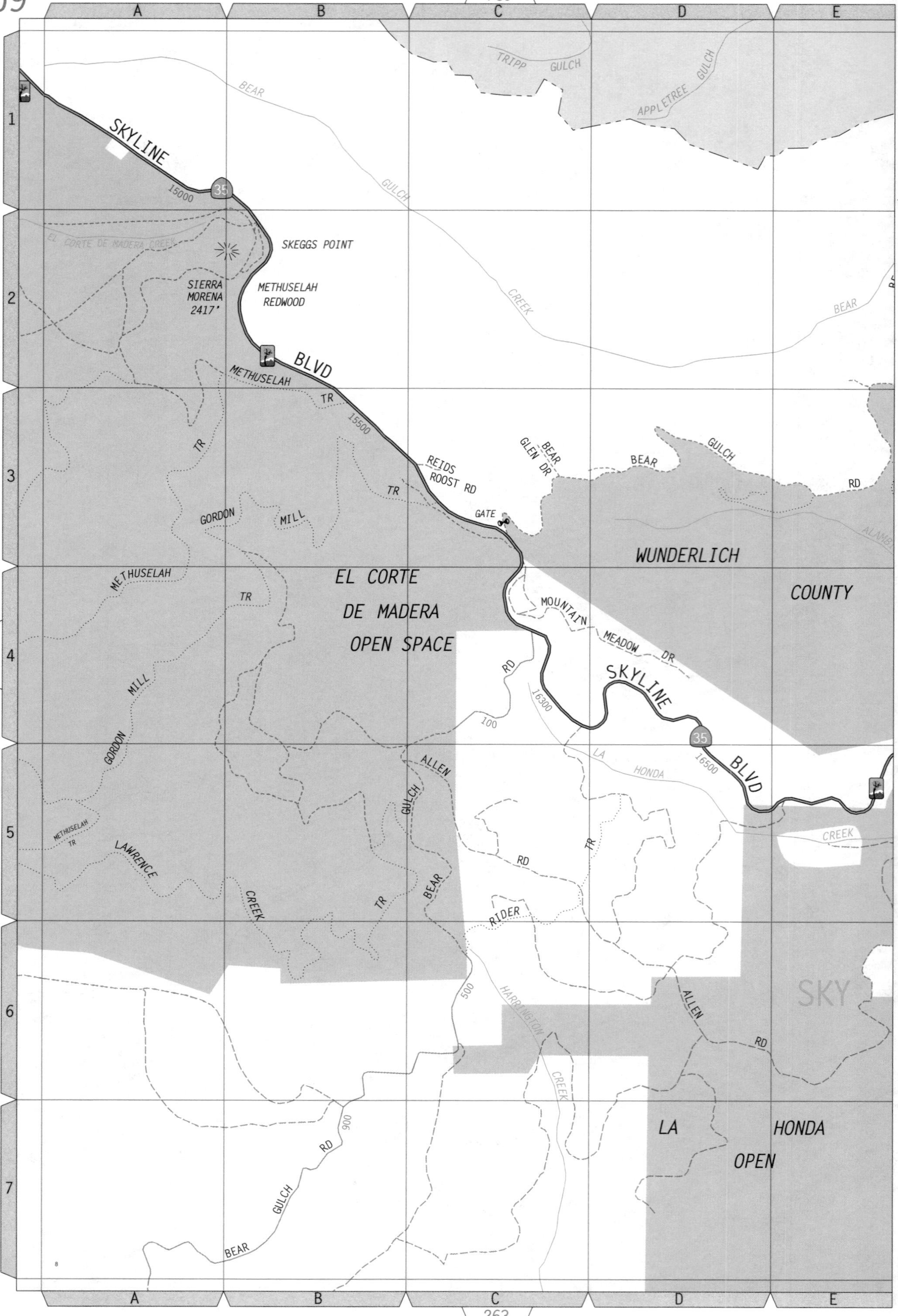
A
B
C
D
E
1
2
3
4
5
6
7
SKYLINE
BLVD
35
15000
15500
16300
16500
TRIPP GULCH
APPLETREE GULCH
BEAR GULCH CREEK
EL CORTE DE MADERA CREEK
SKEGGS POINT
SIERRA MORENA 2417'
METHUSELAH REDWOOD
METHUSELAH TR
REIDS ROOST RD
BEAR GLEN DR
BEAR GULCH RD
GATE
WUNDERLICH COUNTY
EL CORTE DE MADERA OPEN SPACE
GORDON MILL TR
LAWRENCE CREEK
MOUNTAIN MEADOW DR
LA HONDA CREEK
ALLEN RD
BEAR GULCH RD
RIDER RD
HARRINGTON CREEK
SKY
LA HONDA OPEN
100
500
900
ALAMB
8

SEE 263 MAP

SEE 263 MAP

SEE 789 MAP

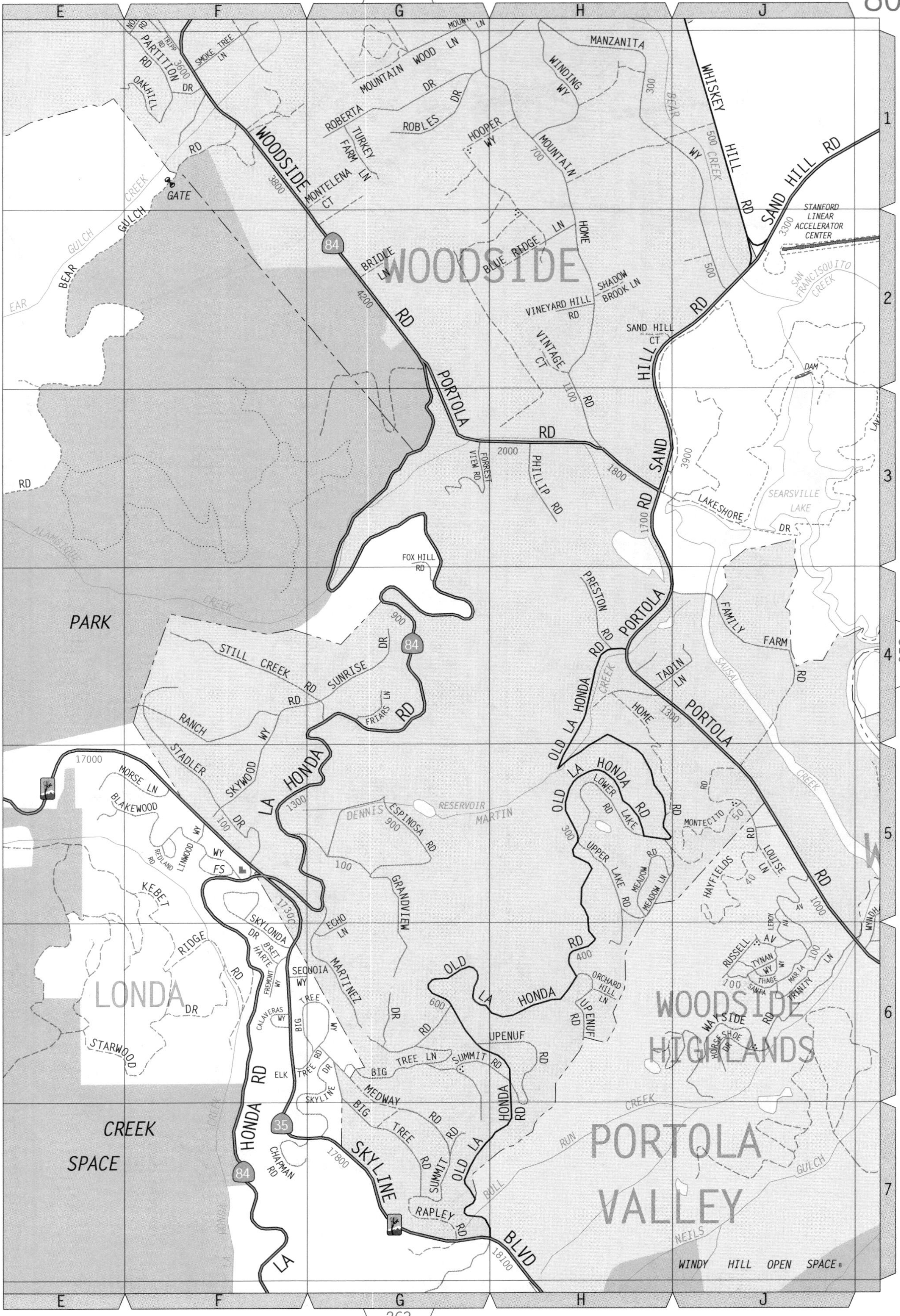
E
F
G
H
J
1
2
3
4
5
6
7
WOODSIDE
WOODSIDE HIGHLANDS
PORTOLA VALLEY
LONDA
PARK
CREEK
SPACE
WOODSIDE RD
PORTOLA RD
SAND HILL RD
WHISKEY HILL RD
LA HONDA RD
OLD LA HONDA RD
SKYLINE BLVD
MANZANITA
WINDING WY
MOUNTAIN HOME RD
MOUNTAIN WOOD LN
ROBERTA DR
ROBLES DR
TURKEY FARM LN
HOOPER WY
MONTELENA CT
BLUE RIDGE LN
BRIDLE LN
VINEYARD HILL RD
SHADOW BROOK LN
VINTAGE CT
SAND HILL CT
STANFORD LINEAR ACCELERATOR CENTER
SAN FRANCISQUITO CREEK
BEAR CREEK
BEAR GULCH RD
GATE
SMOKE TREE LN
PARTITION RD
OAKHILL DR
FORREST VIEW RD
PHILLIP RD
LAKESHORE DR
SEARSVILLE LAKE
DAM
FOX HILL RD
PRESTON RD
FAMILY FARM RD
SAUSAL CREEK
TADIN LN
STILL CREEK RD
SUNRISE DR
FRIARS LN
RANCH RD
SKYWOOD WY
STADLER DR
MORSE LN
BLAKEWOOD
REDLAND
LINWOOD WY
FS
KEBET RIDGE RD
SKYLONDA DR
BRET HARTE
FREMONT WY
SEQUOIA WY
CALAVERAS WY
BIG TREE WY
ELK TREE RD
DENNIS ESPINOSA RD
MARTIN RESERVOIR
GRANDVIEW DR
ECHO LN
MARTINEZ DR
LOWER LAKE RD
UPPER LAKE RD
MEADOW RD
MEADOW LN
MONTECITO RD
HAYFIELDS RD
LOUISE LN
ORCHARD HILL LN
UPENUF RD
BIG TREE LN
SUMMIT RD
MEDWAY RD
SKYLINE
CHAPMAN RD
RAPLEY RD
RUSSELL AV
LEROY AV
TYNAN WY
THAGE WY
SANTA MARIA
TRINITY LN
WAYSIDE
HORSESHOE DR
STARWOOD DR
ALAMBIQUE CREEK
BULL RUN CREEK
NEILS GULCH
LA HONDA CREEK
WINDY HILL OPEN SPACE
84
35

SEE 810 MAP

SEE 263 MAP

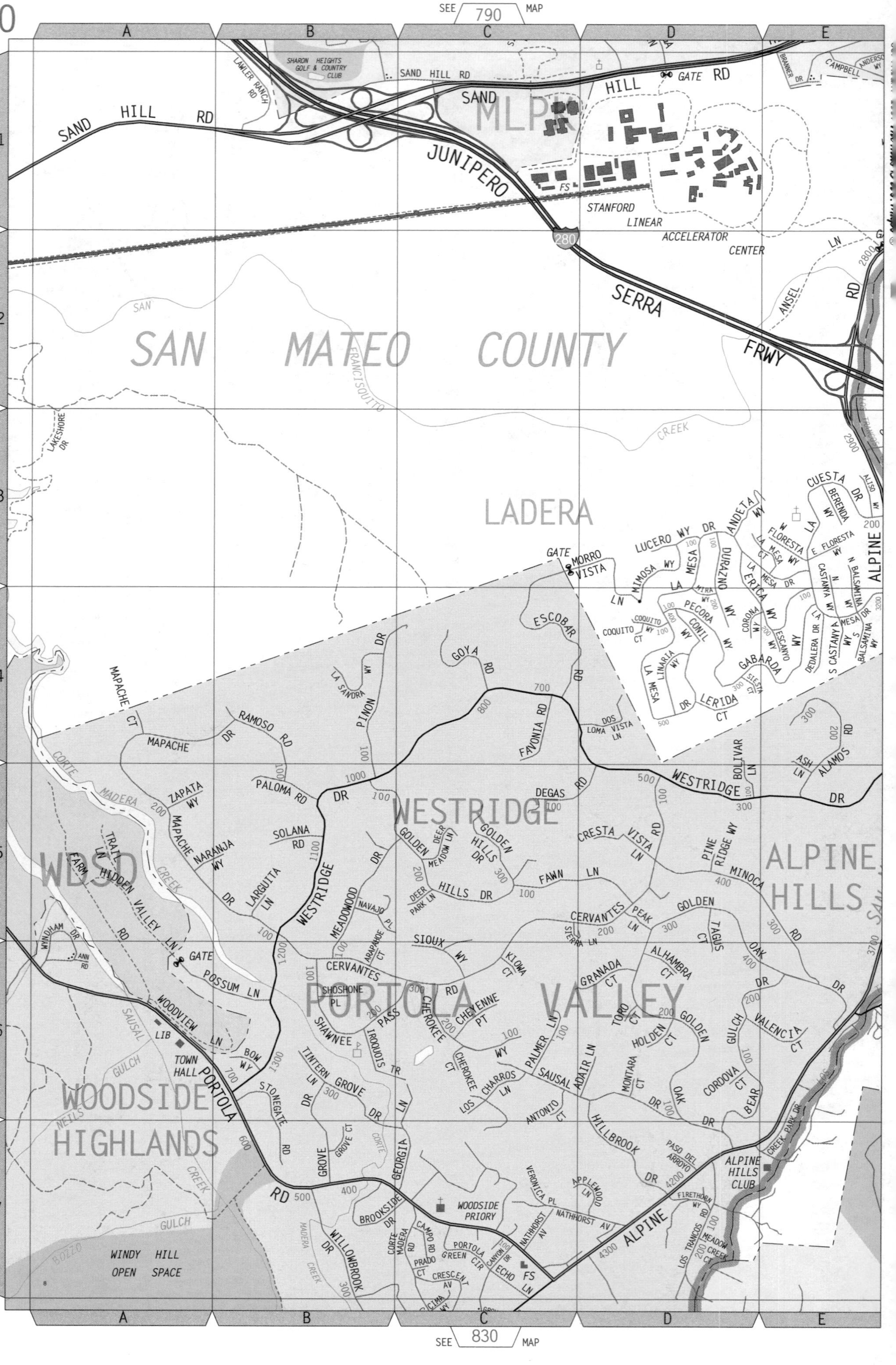
SEE 790 MAP
SEE 830 MAP
SEE 809 MAP
A
B
C
D
E
1
2
3
4
5
6
7
SHARON HEIGHTS GOLF & COUNTRY CLUB
LAWLER RANCH RD
SAND HILL RD
GATE
MLPK
JUNIPERO
280
SERRA
FRWY
STANFORD LINEAR ACCELERATOR CENTER
FS
CAMPBELL
ANSEL
SAN MATEO COUNTY
SAN FRANCISQUITO CREEK
LAKESHORE DR
LADERA
MORRO VISTA
LUCERO WY
LA MESA DR
ANDETA WY
CUESTA DR
BERENDA WY
ALPINE
MIMOSA WY
DURAZNO WY
ERICA WY
PECORA WY
COQUITO CT
CONIL WY
CORONA WY
ESCANYO WY
GABARDA WY
LINARIA WY
LERIDA CT
SIESTA CT
DEDALERA DR
ESCOBAR RD
GOYA RD
FAVONIA RD
DOS LOMA VISTA LN
MAPACHE CT
MAPACHE DR
RAMOSO RD
LA SANDRA WY
PINON DR
PALOMA RD
ZAPATA WY
NARANJA WY
SOLANA RD
LARGUITA LN
WESTRIDGE DR
WESTRIDGE
DEGAS RD
BOLIVAR LN
ASH LN
ALAMOS RD
CORTE MADERA CREEK
WDSD
FARM LN
TRAIL
HIDDEN VALLEY LN
MEADOWOOD DR
NAVAJO PL
GOLDEN HILLS DR
DEER MEADOW LN
DEER PARK LN
CRESTA VISTA RD
PINE RIDGE WY
MINOCA RD
ALPINE HILLS
FAWN LN
CERVANTES RD
PEAK LN
GOLDEN OAK DR
TAGUS CT
SIERRA LN
SIOUX WY
ARAPAHOE CT
KIOWA CT
WYNDHAM DR
ANN RD
POSSUM LN
WOODVIEW LN
LIB
TOWN HALL
BOW WY
PORTOLA VALLEY
SHOSHONE PL
SHAWNEE PASS
IROQUOIS TR
CHEROKEE CT
CHEYENNE PT
GRANADA CT
ALHAMBRA CT
TORO CT
HOLDEN CT
PALMER LN
ADAIR LN
MONTARA CT
VALENCIA CT
GULCH DR
CORDOVA CT
BEAR
SAUSAL GULCH
WOODSIDE HIGHLANDS
NEILS GULCH
PORTOLA RD
STONEGATE RD
TINTERN LN
GROVE DR
GROVE CT
GEORGIA LN
LOS CHARROS LN
ANTONIO CT
HILLBROOK DR
PASO DEL ARROYO
CREEK PARK DR
ALPINE HILLS CLUB
WINDY HILL OPEN SPACE
BOZZO GULCH
BROOKSIDE DR
WILLOWBROOK DR
MADERA CREEK
CORTE MADERA
CAMPO RD
PRADO CT
PORTOLA GREEN CIR
CRESCENT AV
CIMA WY
CANYON DR
ECHO LN
FS
WOODSIDE PRIORY
VERONICA PL
APPLEWOOD LN
NATHHORST AV
FIRETHORN WY
LOS TRANCOS RD
MEADOW CREEK CT

SEE 790 MAP
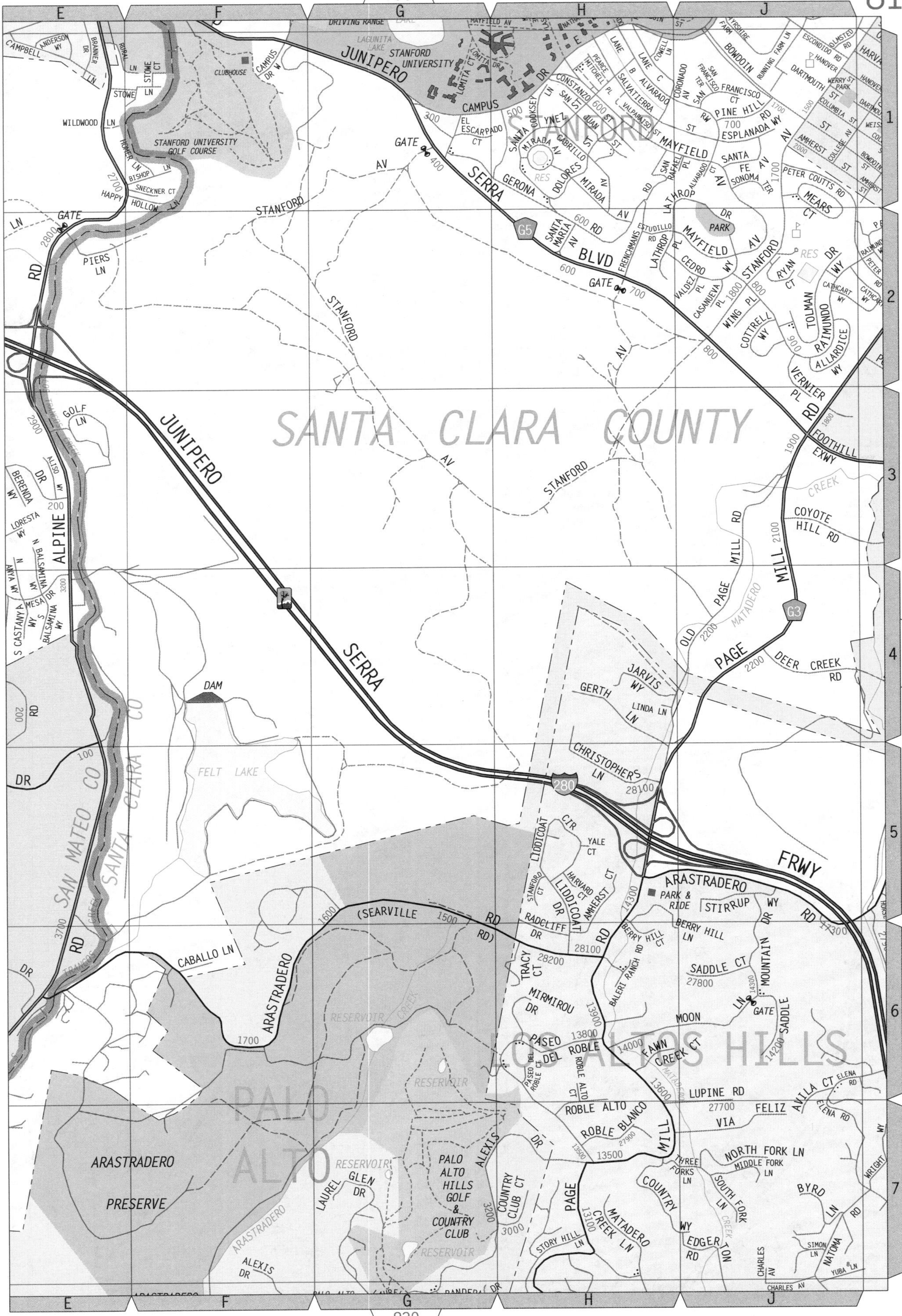
SANTA CLARA COUNTY
STANFORD
STANFORD UNIVERSITY
LAGUNITA LAKE
DRIVING RANGE
STANFORD UNIVERSITY GOLF COURSE
CLUBHOUSE
CAMPUS DR W
CAMPUS DR
JUNIPERO SERRA BLVD
JUNIPERO SERRA FRWY
280
G5
G3
GATE
STANFORD AV
MAYFIELD AV
ALPINE RD
PAGE MILL RD
OLD PAGE MILL RD
FOOTHILL EXWY
ARASTRADERO RD
(SEARVILLE RD)
COYOTE HILL RD
DEER CREEK RD
MATADERO CREEK
FELT LAKE
DAM
SAN MATEO CO
SANTA CLARA CO
LOS ALTOS HILLS
PALO ALTO
ARASTRADERO PRESERVE
PALO ALTO HILLS GOLF & COUNTRY CLUB
RESERVOIR
PARK & RIDE
CHRISTOPHERS LN
LIDDICOAT CIR
LIDDICOAT DR
YALE CT
HARVARD CT
AMHERST CT
STANFORD CT
RADCLIFF DR
STIRRUP WY
BERRY HILL LN
BERRY HILL CT
SADDLE CT
SADDLE MOUNTAIN DR
BALERI RANCH RD
MOON LN
FAWN CREEK CT
PASEO DEL ROBLE
ROBLE ALTO
ROBLE BLANCO
LUPINE RD
VIA FELIZ
AVILA CT
ELENA RD
NORTH FORK LN
MIDDLE FORK LN
THREE FORKS LN
SOUTH FORK LN
COUNTRY WY
EDGERTON RD
BYRD LN
NATOMA RD
CHARLES AV
SIMON LN
YUBA LN
WRIGHT WY
COUNTRY CLUB CT
ALEXIS DR
LAUREL GLEN DR
STORY HILL LN
MATADERO CREEK LN
TRACY CT
MIRMIROU DR
CABALLO LN
GERTH LN
JARVIS WY
LINDA LN
GOLF LN
BERENDA WY
ALISO WY
LORESTA WY
N BALSAMINA WY
S BALSAMINA WY
ANYA WY
MESA WY
S CASTANYA WY
PIERS LN
HAPPY HOLLOW LN
BISHOP LN
SNECKNER CT
HOMER LN
WILDWOOD LN
STOWE LN
STOWE CT
RURAL LN
CAMPBELL LN
ANDERSON WY
BRANNER DR
COMITA CT
EL ESCARPADO CT
SANTA YNEZ ST
COOKSEY LN
MIRADA AV
CABRILLO AV
DOLORES ST
GERONA RD
SANTA MARIA AV
CONSTANZO ST
SAN JUAN ST
PEARCE MITCHELL PL
SALVATIERRA ST
ALVARADO ROW
LANE B
LANE C
LANE E
CORONADO AV
SAN FRANCISCO TER
SAN FRANCISCO CT
PINE HILL RD
ESPLANADA WY
SANTA FE AV
SONOMA TER
SAN RAFAEL PL
LATHROP PL
LATHROP DR
FRENCHMANS RD
ESTUDILLO RD
CEDRO WY
VALDEZ PL
CASANUEVA PL
WING PL
COTTRELL WY
RYAN CT
TOLMAN DR
RAIMUNDO WY
ALLARDICE WY
VERNIER PL
CATHCART WY
MEARS CT
PETER COUTTS RD
BOWDOIN ST
DARTMOUTH
HANOVER ST
AMHERST ST
COLUMBIA ST
COLLEGE AV
ESCONDIDO RD
OLMSTED RD
RUNNING FARM LN
AYRSHIRE FARM LN
WERRY PARK
HARVARD
PARK
RES
SEE 811 MAP
SEE 830 MAP

SEE 791 MAP

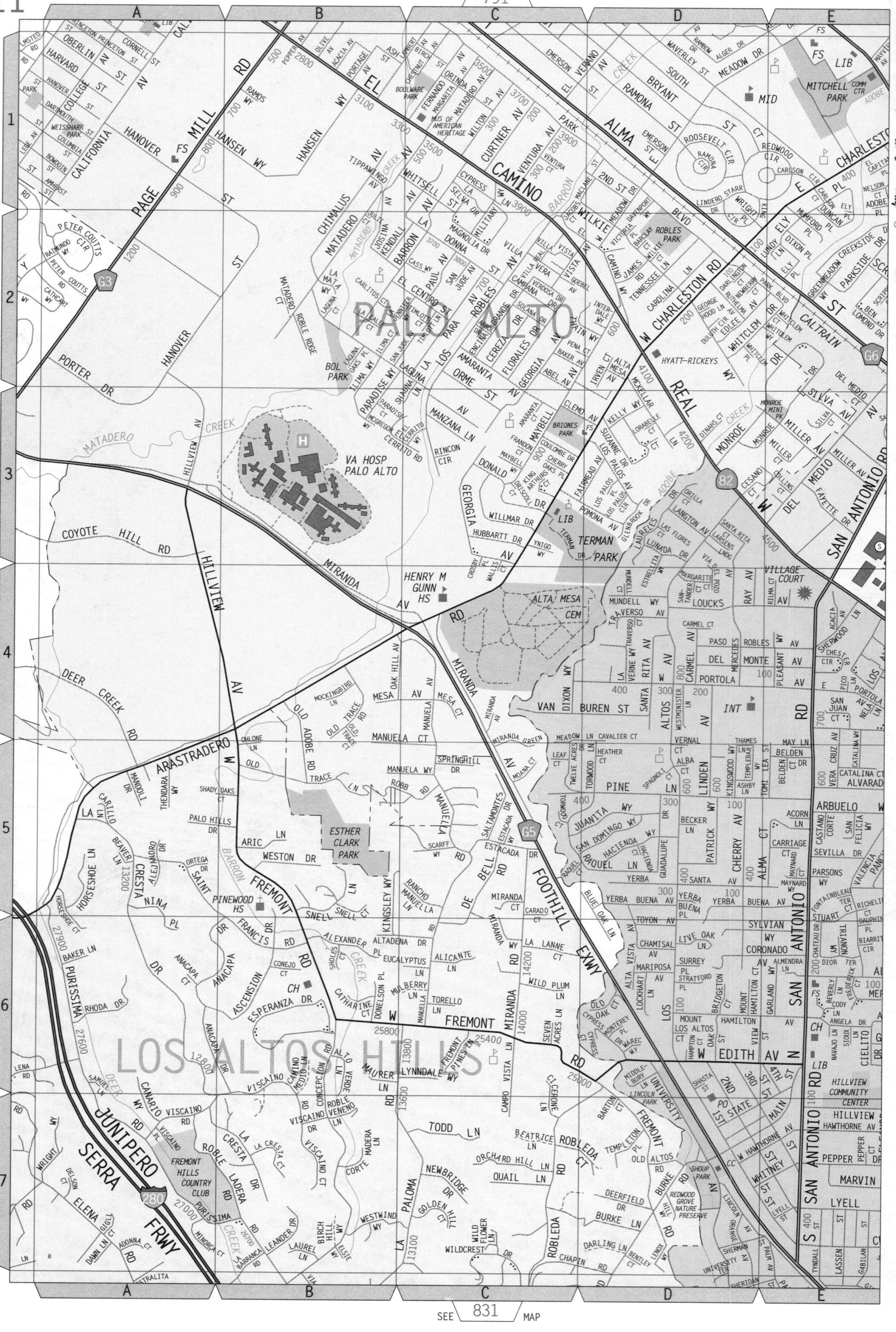
PALO ALTO
LOS ALTOS HILLS
VA HOSP PALO ALTO
HENRY M GUNN HS
ALTA MESA CEM
TERMAN PARK
ESTHER CLARK PARK
BOL PARK
ROBLES PARK
MITCHELL PARK
BOULWARE PARK
BRIONES PARK
MONROE MINI PK
HYATT-RICKEYS
MUS OF AMERICAN HERITAGE
VILLAGE COURT
PINEWOOD HS
FREMONT HILLS COUNTRY CLUB
REDWOOD GROVE NATURE PRESERVE
SHOUP PARK
LINCOLN PARK
HILLVIEW COMMUNITY CENTER
EL CAMINO REAL
ALMA ST
PAGE MILL RD
HANOVER ST
FOOTHILL EXWY
ARASTRADERO RD
HILLVIEW AV
MIRANDA AV
COYOTE HILL RD
DEER CREEK RD
PORTER DR
W CHARLESTON RD
SAN ANTONIO RD
W FREMONT RD
JUNIPERO SERRA FRWY
MATADERO CREEK
BARRON CREEK
ADOBE CREEK
CALTRAIN
G3
G5
G6
82
280
A
B
C
D
E
1
2
3
4
5
6
7

SEE 810 MAP

SEE 831 MAP

SEE 791 MAP

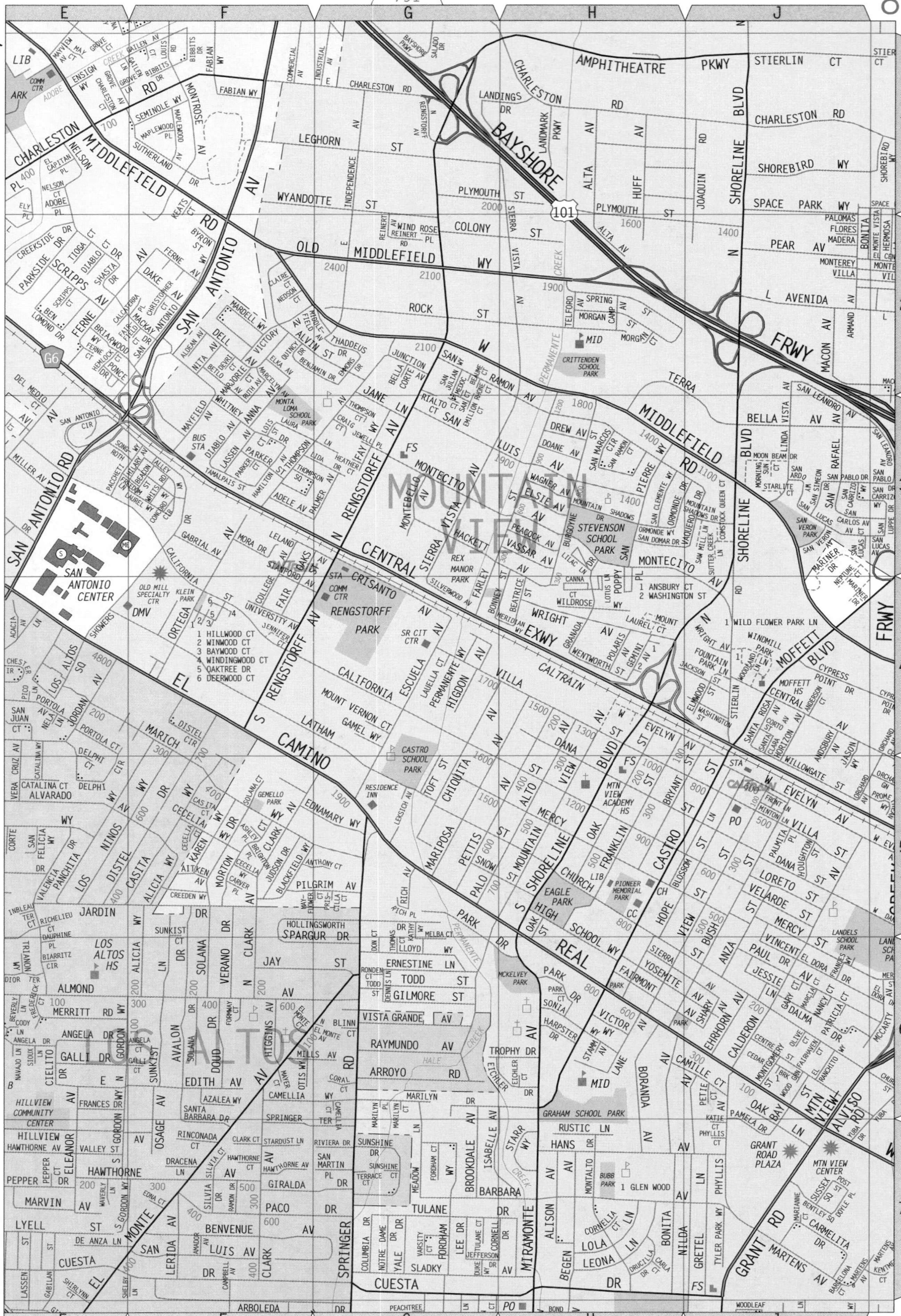
MOUNTAIN VIEW
LOS ALTOS
AMPHITHEATRE PKWY
CHARLESTON RD
BAYSHORE FRWY
101
MIDDLEFIELD RD
OLD MIDDLEFIELD WY
SAN ANTONIO RD
CENTRAL EXWY
EL CAMINO REAL
N RENGSTORFF AV
S RENGSTORFF AV
SHORELINE BLVD
N SHORELINE BLVD
MOFFETT BLVD
CASTRO ST
GRANT RD
ALVISO RD
CALTRAIN
SAN ANTONIO CENTER
RENGSTORFF PARK
CRITTENDEN SCHOOL PARK
STEVENSON SCHOOL PARK
CASTRO SCHOOL PARK
EAGLE PARK
PIONEER MEMORIAL PARK
GRAHAM SCHOOL PARK
MCKELVEY PARK
LANDELS SCHOOL PARK
GRANT ROAD PLAZA
MTN VIEW CENTER
LOS ALTOS HS
HILLVIEW COMMUNITY CENTER
MTN VIEW ACADEMY HS
MOFFETT HS
G6

SEE 812 MAP

SEE 831 MAP

SEE 792 MAP

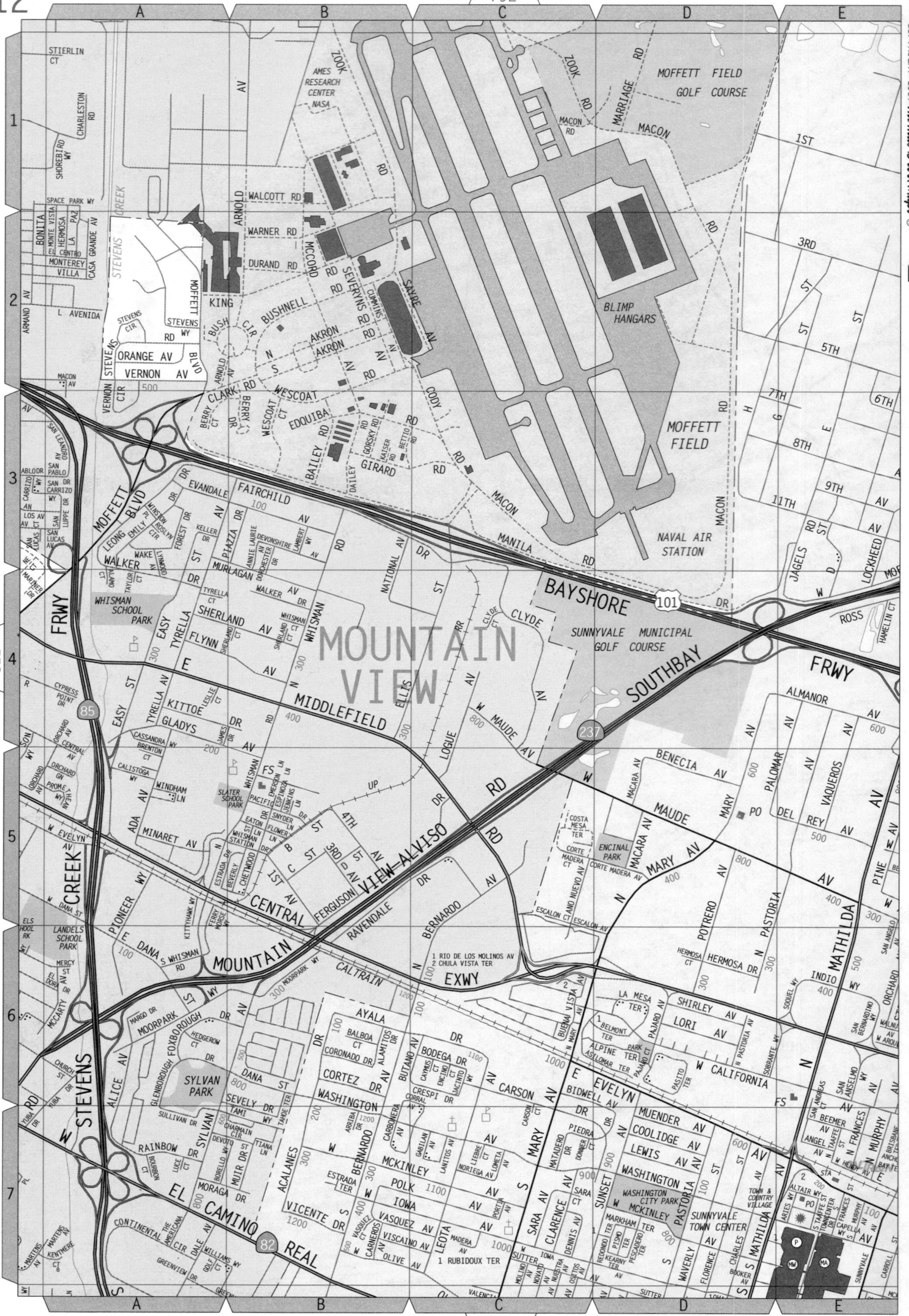
A
B
C
D
E
1
2
3
4
5
6
7
MOFFETT FIELD GOLF COURSE
AMES RESEARCH CENTER NASA
BLIMP HANGARS
MOFFETT FIELD
NAVAL AIR STATION
MOUNTAIN VIEW
SUNNYVALE MUNICIPAL GOLF COURSE
WHISMAN SCHOOL PARK
SLATER SCHOOL PARK
LANDELS SCHOOL PARK
SYLVAN PARK
ENCINAL PARK
WASHINGTON CITY PARK
SUNNYVALE TOWN CENTER
TOWN & COUNTRY VILLAGE
WHISMAN STATION
BAYSHORE FRWY
SOUTHBAY FRWY
STEVENS CREEK FRWY
MOFFETT BLVD
MIDDLEFIELD RD
CENTRAL EXWY
MOUNTAIN VIEW ALVISO RD
EL CAMINO REAL
W EVELYN AV
W MAUDE AV
N MATHILDA AV
W CALIFORNIA AV
N MARY AV
N PASTORIA AV
N WHISMAN RD
STIERLIN CT
CHARLESTON RD
SHOREBIRD WY
SPACE PARK WY
VERNON AV
ORANGE AV
MACON RD
MANILA DR
ZOOK RD
MARRIAGE RD
CALTRAIN
1 RIO DE LOS MOLINOS AV
2 CHULA VISTA TER
1 RUBIDOUX TER
85
101
237
82

SEE 811 MAP

SEE 832 MAP

SEE 792 MAP

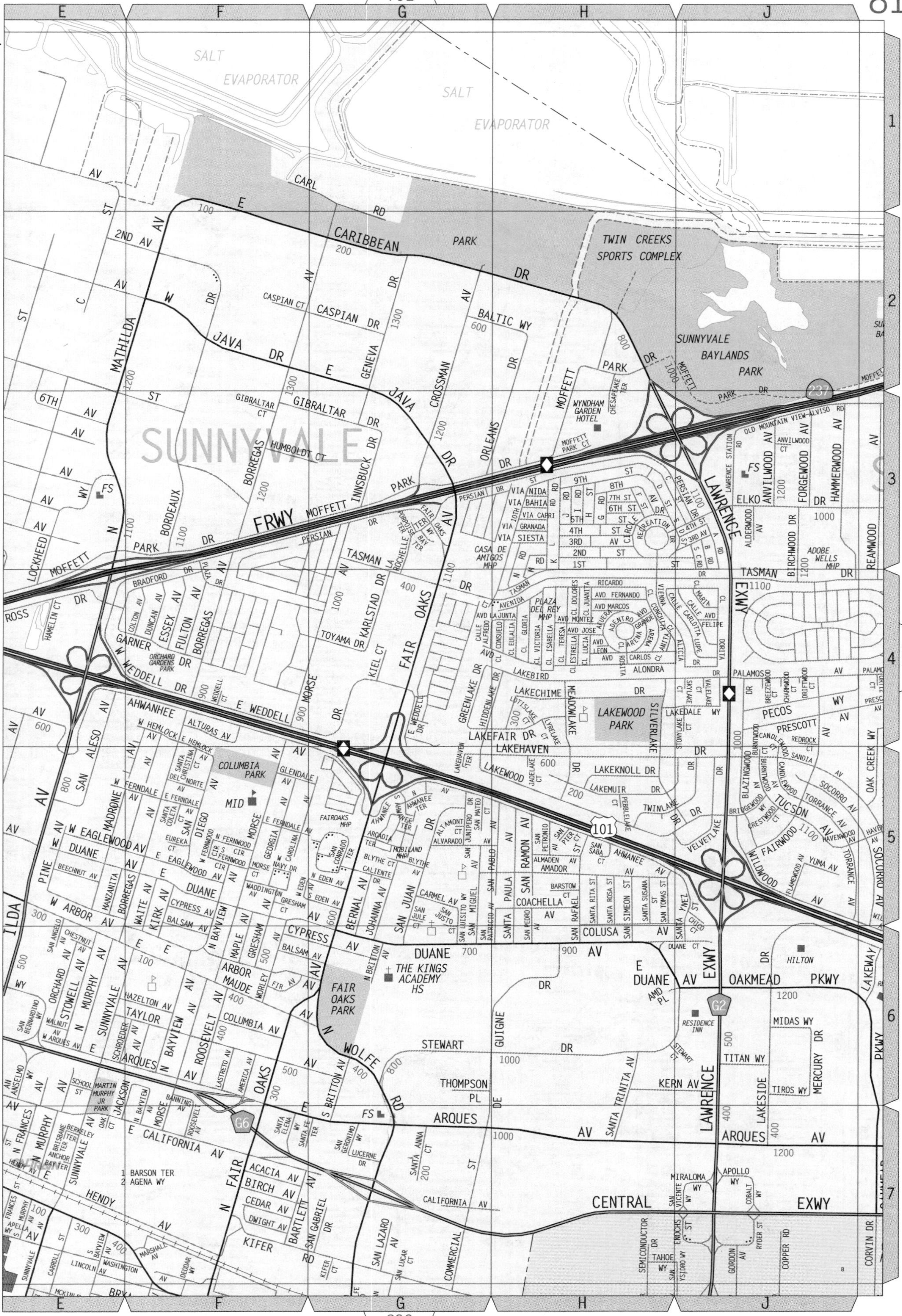
E
F
G
H
J
1
2
3
4
5
6
7
SALT EVAPORATOR
SALT EVAPORATOR
SUNNYVALE
TWIN CREEKS SPORTS COMPLEX
SUNNYVALE BAYLANDS PARK
WYNDHAM GARDEN HOTEL
CARIBBEAN DR
E CARIBBEAN PARK DR
CARL RD
JAVA DR
E JAVA DR
W JAVA DR
MOFFETT PARK DR
MOFFETT FRWY
MOFFETT PARK CT
CASPIAN CT
CASPIAN DR
BALTIC WY
GIBRALTAR CT
GIBRALTAR DR
HUMBOLDT CT
BORREGAS AV
BORDEAUX DR
GENEVA DR
CROSSMAN AV
ORLEANS DR
INNSBUCK DR
N MATHILDA AV
LOCKHEED
2ND AV
6TH AV
PERSIAN DR
TASMAN DR
FAIR OAKS AV
KARLSTAD DR
KIEL CT
TOYAMA DR
CASA DE AMIGOS MHP
PLAZA DEL REY MHP
ADOBE WELLS MHP
LAWRENCE EXWY
LAWRENCE STATION RD
OLD MOUNTAIN VIEW-ALVISO RD
ANVILWOOD AV
FORGEWOOD AV
HAMMERWOOD AV
ELKO DR
BIRCHWOOD DR
REAMWOOD
FS
237
101
G2
G6
ORCHARD GARDENS PARK
GARNER DR
W WEDDELL DR
E WEDDELL DR
AHWANHEE AV
ALTURAS AV
W HEMLOCK AV
COLUMBIA PARK
GLENDALE AV
MID
LAKEBIRD DR
LAKECHIME DR
LAKEWOOD PARK
LAKEFAIR DR
LAKEHAVEN DR
LAKEWOOD DR
LAKEKNOLL DR
LAKEMUIR DR
SILVERLAKE DR
LAKEDALE WY
PALAMOS AV
PECOS WY
PRESCOTT AV
TUCSON AV
SOCORRO AV
OAK CREEK WY
FAIROAKS MHP
MOBILAND MHP
W EAGLEWOOD AV
DUANE AV
E DUANE AV
W ARBOR AV
CYPRESS AV
COLUSA AV
SAN RAMON AV
SAN JUAN AV
BERNAL AV
JOHANNA AV
THE KINGS ACADEMY HS
FAIR OAKS PARK
OAKMEAD PKWY
HILTON
RESIDENCE INN
MIDAS WY
TITAN WY
MERCURY DR
KERN AV
TIROS WY
LAKESIDE DR
STEWART DR
GUIGNE DR
THOMPSON PL
WOLFE RD
ARQUES AV
E ARQUES AV
W ARQUES AV
CALIFORNIA AV
E CALIFORNIA AV
CENTRAL EXWY
SANTA TRINITA AV
SUNNYVALE AV
MURPHY AV
N FAIR OAKS AV
ACACIA AV
BIRCH AV
CEDAR AV
DWIGHT AV
KIFER RD
HENDY AV
BARTLETT AV
SAN GABRIEL DR
SAN LAZARO AV
COMMERCIAL ST
SEMICONDUCTOR DR
TAHOE WY
GORDON AV
COPPER RD
CORVIN DR
MARTIN MURPHY JR PARK
1 BARSON TER
2 AGENA WY
AMD PL

SEE 813 MAP
SEE 832 MAP

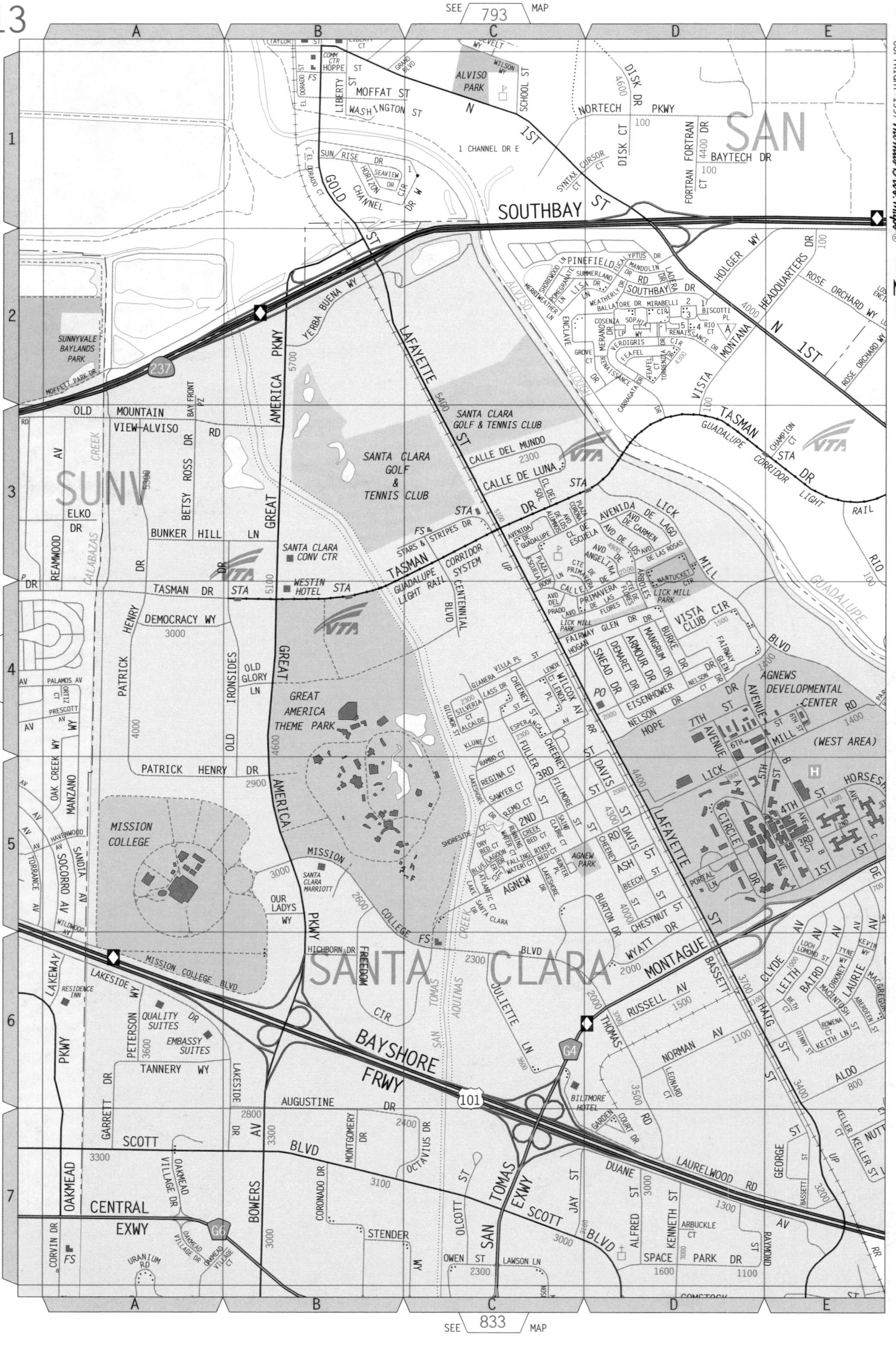
SEE 793 MAP
SEE 812 MAP
SEE 833 MAP
A
B
C
D
E
1
2
3
4
5
6
7
SAN
SUNV
SANTA CLARA
SUNNYVALE BAYLANDS PARK
ALVISO PARK
SANTA CLARA GOLF & TENNIS CLUB
SANTA CLARA CONV CTR
WESTIN HOTEL
GREAT AMERICA THEME PARK
MISSION COLLEGE
SANTA CLARA MARRIOTT
AGNEW PARK
LICK MILL PARK
AGNEWS DEVELOPMENTAL CENTER
(WEST AREA)
RESIDENCE INN
QUALITY SUITES
EMBASSY SUITES
BILTMORE HOTEL
SOUTHBAY FRWY
BAYSHORE FRWY
CENTRAL EXWY
SAN TOMAS EXWY
MONTAGUE EXWY
237
101
G4
G6
N 1ST ST
GOLD ST
MOFFAT ST
WASHINGTON ST
LIBERTY ST
HOPPE ST
TAYLOR ST
EL DORADO ST
SCHOOL ST
NORTECH PKWY
DISK DR
DISK CT
FORTRAN DR
FORTRAN CT
BAYTECH DR
CURSOR CT
SYNTAX CT
1 CHANNEL DR E
SUNRISE DR
HORIZON CIR
SEAVIEW CT
CHANNEL DR W
EL DORADO CT
PINEFIELD RD
MANDOLIN DR
SOUTHBAY DR
LADERA DR
HOLGER WY
HEADQUARTERS DR
ROSE ORCHARD WY
VISTA MONTANA
TASMAN DR
GUADALUPE CORRIDOR LIGHT RAIL
CHAMPION CT
STA
VTA
ALVISO SLOUGH
YERBA BUENA WY
GREAT AMERICA PKWY
LAFAYETTE ST
MOFFETT PARK DR
OLD MOUNTAIN VIEW-ALVISO RD
BAY FRONT PZ
BETSY ROSS DR
ELKO DR
BUNKER HILL LN
REAMWOOD AV
CALABAZAS CREEK
PATRICK HENRY DR
DEMOCRACY WY
IRONSIDES
OLD GLORY LN
OLD IRONSIDES DR
CALLE DEL MUNDO
CALLE DE LUNA
STARS & STRIPES DR
GUADALUPE LIGHT RAIL CORRIDOR SYSTEM
CENTENNIAL BLVD
LICK MILL BLVD
VISTA CLUB CIR
FAIRWAY GLEN DR
HOGAN DR
SNEAD DR
DEMARET DR
ARMOUR DR
MANGRUM DR
BURKE DR
EISENHOWER DR
NELSON DR
HOPE DR
WILCOX AV
CHENEY ST
FULLER ST
FILLMORE ST
DAVIS ST
3RD ST
2ND ST
ASH ST
BEECH ST
CHESTNUT ST
BURTON DR
WYATT DR
AGNEW RD
LAKESHORE DR
MISSION COLLEGE BLVD
OUR LADYS WY
HICHBORN DR
FREEDOM CIR
JULIETTE LN
RUSSELL AV
NORMAN AV
THOMAS RD
LEONARD CT
BASSETT ST
HAIG ST
CLYDE AV
LEITH AV
BAIRD AV
LAURIE AV
ALDO AV
LAKEWAY DR
LAKESIDE DR
PETERSON WY
TANNERY WY
LAKESIDE PKWY
OAKMEAD PKWY
GARRETT DR
AUGUSTINE DR
SCOTT BLVD
BOWERS AV
MONTGOMERY DR
OCTAVIUS DR
CORONADO DR
STENDER WY
OLCOTT ST
OWEN ST
LAWSON LN
JAY ST
ALFRED ST
KENNETH ST
ARBUCKLE CT
SPACE PARK DR
DUANE AV
LAURELWOOD RD
GEORGE ST
RAYMOND AV
KELLER ST
CORVIN DR
URANIUM RD
OAKMEAD VILLAGE DR
MANZANO WY
OAK CREEK WY
SOCORRO AV
SANDIA AV
TORRANCE AV
PALAMOS AV
PRESCOTT
HAVENWOOD
WILDWOOD
FS
PO

SEE 793 MAP

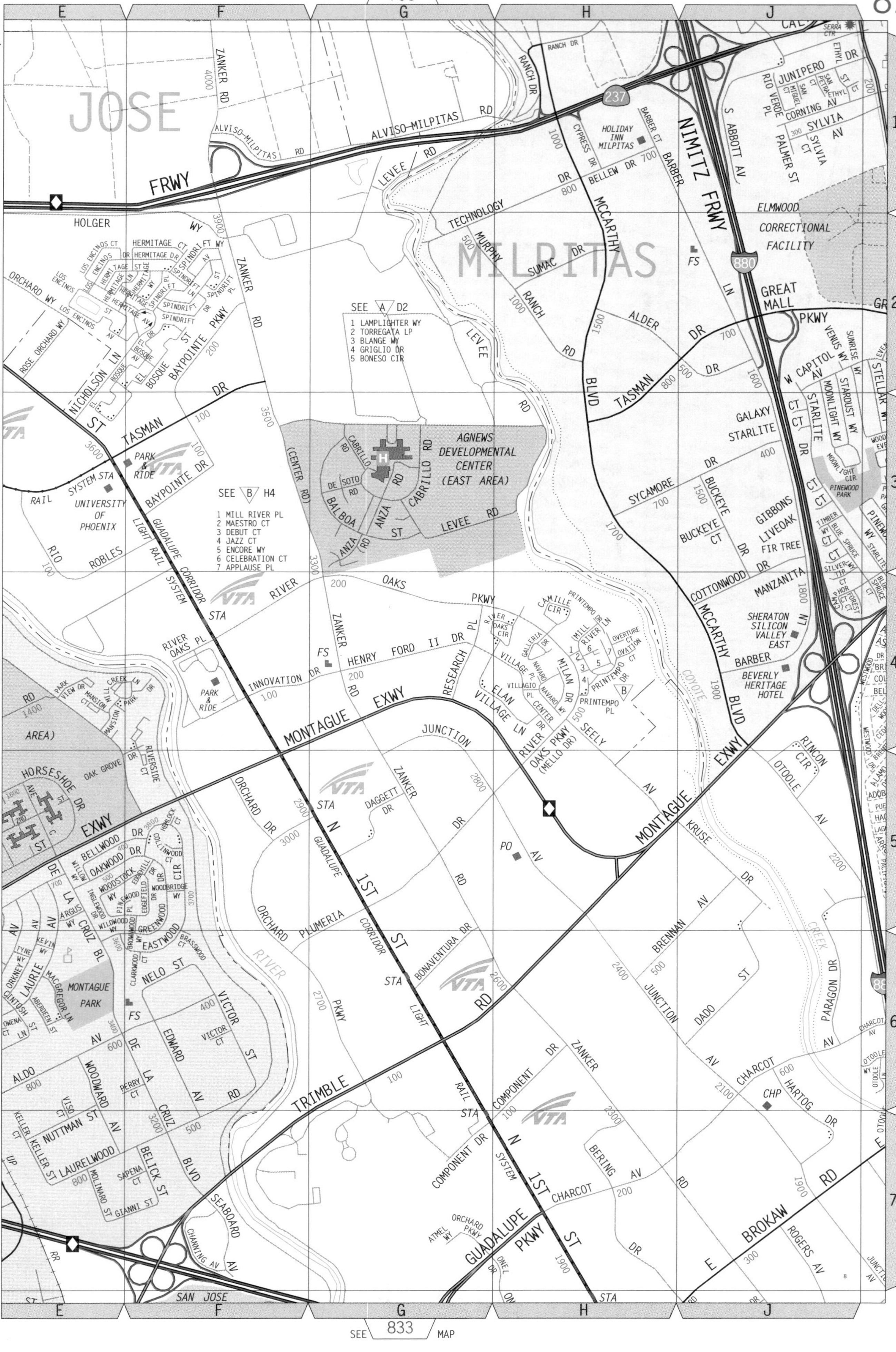

E
F
G
H
J
1
2
3
4
5
6
7
JOSE
MILPITAS
ALVISO-MILPITAS RD
FRWY
237
NIMITZ FRWY
880
ZANKER RD
RANCH DR
LEVEE RD
HOLIDAY INN MILPITAS
BARBER CT
BARBER LN
CYPRESS DR
BELLEW DR
TECHNOLOGY DR
MURPHY RANCH RD
SUMAC DR
McCARTHY BLVD
ALDER DR
S ABBOTT AV
RIO VERDE PL
JUNIPERO
CORNING AV
SYLVIA AV
SYLVIA CT
PALMER ST
ETHYL DR
SERRA CTR
CALAVERAS
ELMWOOD CORRECTIONAL FACILITY
FS
GREAT MALL PKWY
TASMAN DR
W CAPITOL AV
VENUS WY
SUNRISE WY
STARDUST WY
MOONLIGHT WY
STARLITE DR
STELLAR WY
GALAXY CT
STARLITE CT
PINEWOOD PARK
SYCAMORE DR
BUCKEYE DR
BUCKEYE CT
GIBBONS
LIVEOAK
FIR TREE DR
COTTONWOOD DR
MANZANITA
HOLGER WY
HERMITAGE CT
HERMITAGE DR
LOS ENCINOS CT
ORCHARD WY
ROSE ORCHARD WY
SPINDRIFT
NICHOLSON LN
BOSQUE
BAYPOINTE PKWY
BAYPOINTE DR
ST TASMAN DR
PARK & RIDE
SYSTEM STA
RAIL
UNIVERSITY OF PHOENIX
RIO ROBLES
SEE A D2
1 LAMPLIGHTER WY
2 TORREGATA LP
3 BLANGE WY
4 GRIGLIO DR
5 BONESO CIR
(CENTER RD)
CABRILLO RD
DE SOTO RD
BALBOA
ANZA ST
AGNEWS DEVELOPMENTAL CENTER (EAST AREA)
SEE B H4
1 MILL RIVER PL
2 MAESTRO CT
3 DEBUT CT
4 JAZZ CT
5 ENCORE WY
6 CELEBRATION CT
7 APPLAUSE PL
GUADALUPE CORRIDOR LIGHT RAIL SYSTEM
RIVER OAKS PKWY
STA
RIVER OAKS PL
CAMILLE CIR
PRINTEMPO DR
HENRY FORD II DR
RESEARCH PL
INNOVATION DR
VILLAGE CENTER DR
ELAN VILLAGE LN
MILAN DR
OVERTURE CT
OVATION CT
PRINTEMPO PL
SEELY AV
RIVER OAKS PKWY (MELLO DR)
COYOTE
SHERATON SILICON VALLEY EAST
BEVERLY HERITAGE HOTEL
BARBER
MONTAGUE EXWY
JUNCTION AV
RINCON CIR
OTOOLE AV
KRUSE DR
HORSESHOE DR
OAK GROVE DR
RIVERSIDE CT
BELLWOOD DR
OAKWOOD DR
WOODSTOCK
WOODBRIDGE WY
EASTWOOD
GREENWOOD
ORCHARD DR
DAGGETT DR
GUADALUPE
N 1ST ST
PO
PLUMERIA
BONAVENTURA DR
BRENNAN AV
DADO ST
CRUZ BL
MONTAGUE PARK
NELO ST
VICTOR ST
VICTOR CT
EDWARD AV
RIVER
PARAGON DR
CHARCOT AV
HARTOG DR
CHP
ALDO AV
WOODWARD AV
PERRY CT
DE LA CRUZ BLVD
NUTTMAN ST
KELLER ST
LAURELWOOD
BELICK ST
SAPENA CT
GIANNI ST
TRIMBLE RD
COMPONENT DR
BERING AV
CHARCOT
SEABOARD AV
CHANNING AV
SAN JOSE
GUADALUPE PKWY
ORCHARD PKWY
ATMEL WY
E BROKAW RD
ROGERS AV
SEE 814 MAP

SEE 833 MAP

BAY AREA

MAP

SEE 794 MAP

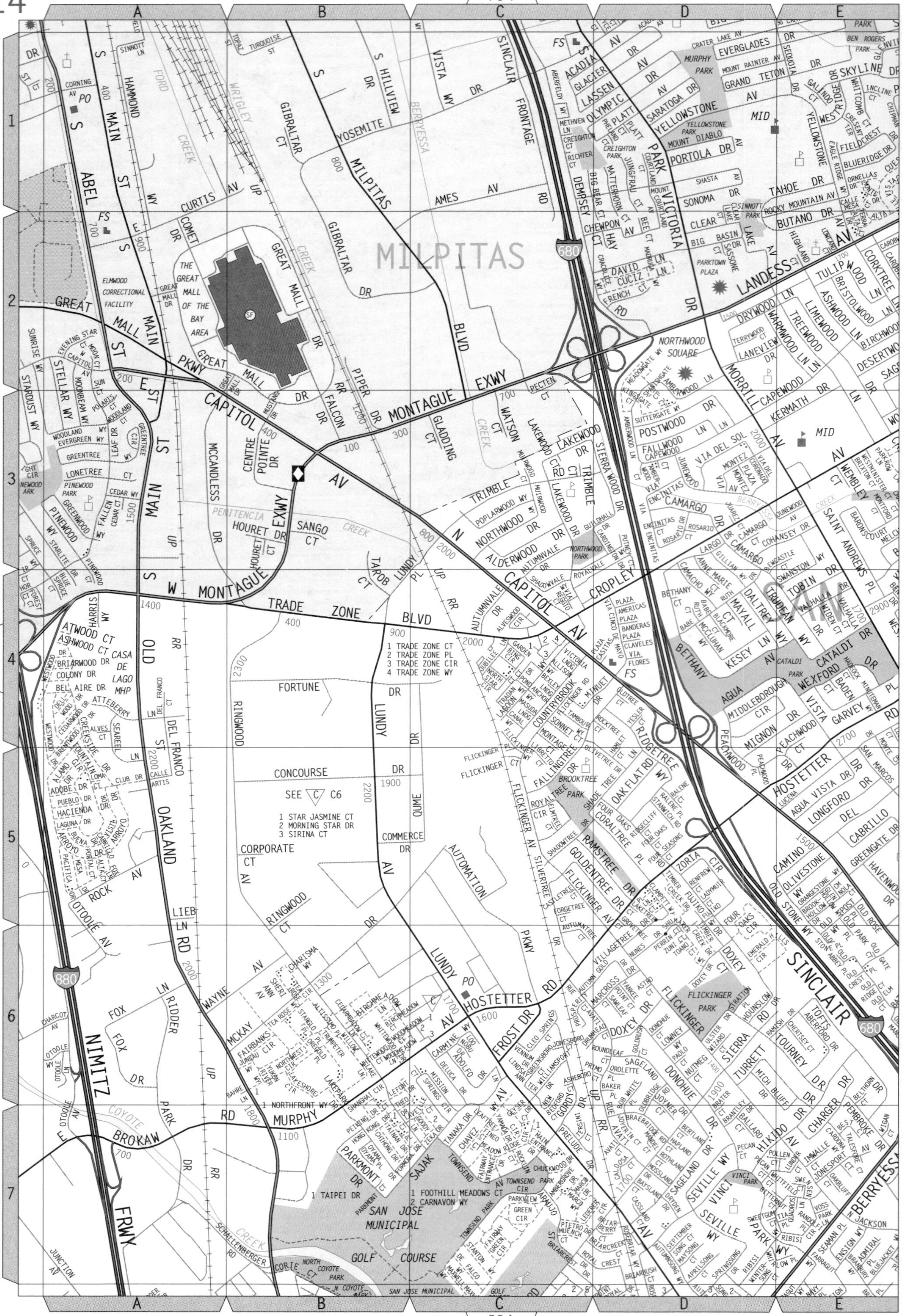
MILPITAS
THE GREAT MALL OF THE BAY AREA
ELMWOOD CORRECTIONAL FACILITY
NORTHWOOD SQUARE
PARKTOWN PLAZA
MURPHY PARK
YELLOWSTONE PARK
CREIGHTON PARK
NORTHWOOD PARK
BROOKTREE PARK
FLICKINGER PARK
VINCI PARK
BETHANY PARK
SAN JOSE MUNICIPAL GOLF COURSE
NORTH COYOTE PARK
MONTAGUE EXWY
CAPITOL AV
TRADE ZONE BLVD
GREAT MALL PKWY
LANDESS AV
HOSTETTER RD
BERRYESSA RD
SINCLAIR FRWY
NIMITZ FRWY
OLD OAKLAND RD
LUNDY AV
MURPHY AV
BROKAW RD
S MAIN ST
S ABEL ST
S MILPITAS BLVD
1 TRADE ZONE CT
2 TRADE ZONE PL
3 TRADE ZONE CIR
4 TRADE ZONE WY
SEE C6
1 STAR JASMINE CT
2 MORNING STAR DR
3 SIRINA CT
1 NORTHFRONT WY
1 TAIPEI DR
1 FOOTHILL MEADOWS CT
2 CARNAVON WY
CASA DE LAGO MHP

SEE 813 MAP

SEE 834 MAP

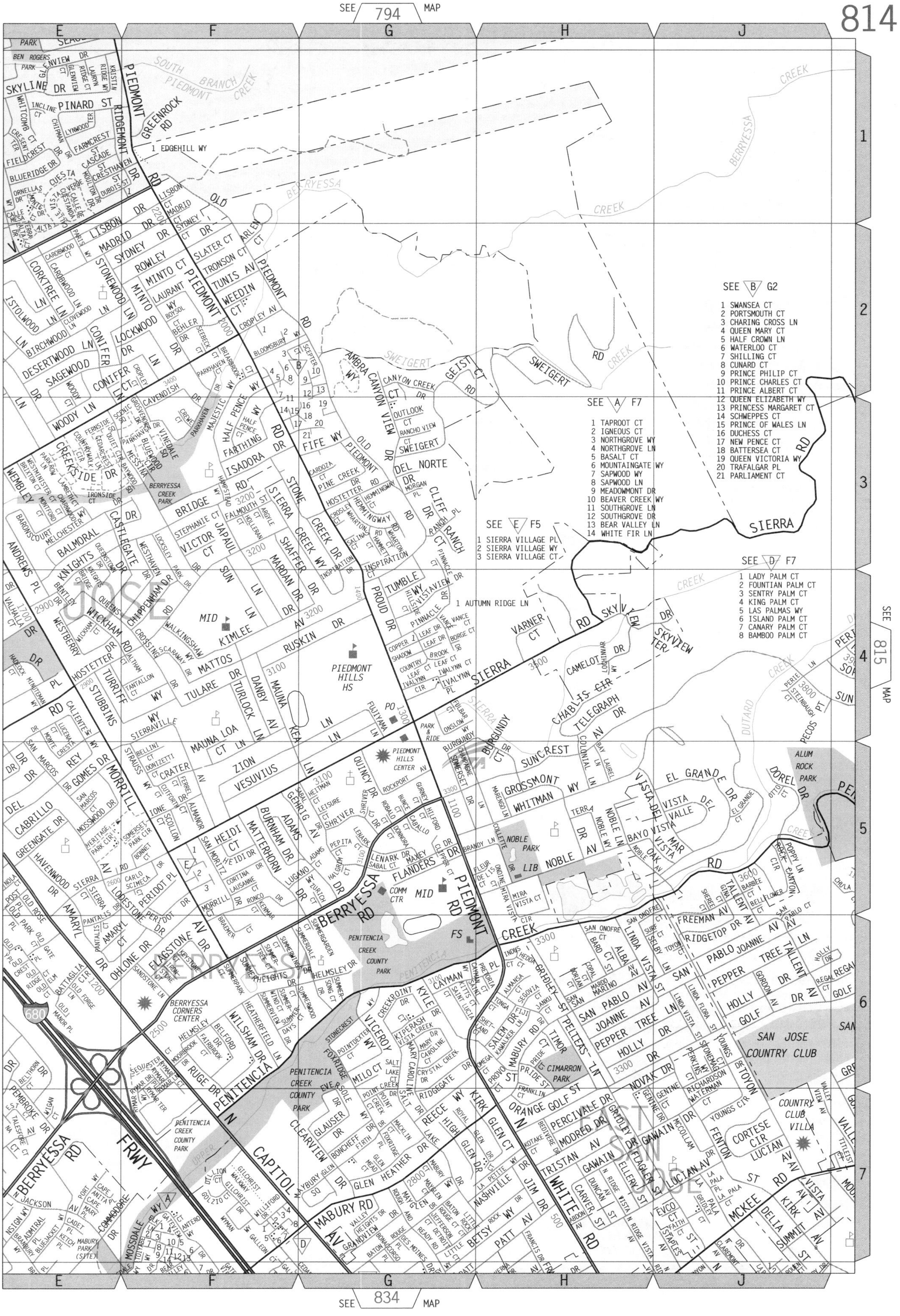
SEE 794 MAP
SEE 834 MAP
SEE 815 MAP
E
F
G
H
J
1
2
3
4
5
6
7
SEE B G2
1 SWANSEA CT
2 PORTSMOUTH CT
3 CHARING CROSS LN
4 QUEEN MARY CT
5 HALF CROWN LN
6 WATERLOO CT
7 SHILLING CT
8 CUNARD CT
9 PRINCE PHILIP CT
10 PRINCE CHARLES CT
11 PRINCE ALBERT CT
12 QUEEN ELIZABETH WY
13 PRINCESS MARGARET CT
14 SCHWEPPES CT
15 PRINCE OF WALES LN
16 DUCHESS CT
17 NEW PENCE CT
18 BATTERSEA CT
19 QUEEN VICTORIA WY
20 TRAFALGAR PL
21 PARLIAMENT CT
SEE A F7
1 TAPROOT CT
2 IGNEOUS CT
3 NORTHGROVE WY
4 NORTHGROVE LN
5 BASALT CT
6 MOUNTAINGATE WY
7 SAPWOOD WY
8 SAPWOOD LN
9 MEADOWMONT DR
10 BEAVER CREEK WY
11 SOUTHGROVE LN
12 SOUTHGROVE DR
13 BEAR VALLEY LN
14 WHITE FIR LN
SEE E F5
1 SIERRA VILLAGE PL
2 SIERRA VILLAGE WY
3 SIERRA VILLAGE CT
SEE D F7
1 LADY PALM CT
2 FOUNTIAN PALM CT
3 SENTRY PALM CT
4 KING PALM CT
5 LAS PALMAS WY
6 ISLAND PALM CT
7 CANARY PALM CT
8 BAMBOO PALM CT
1 EDGEHILL WY
1 AUTUMN RIDGE LN
SOUTH BRANCH PIEDMONT CREEK
BERRYESSA CREEK
SWEIGERT CREEK
PIEDMONT RD
SIERRA RD
BERRYESSA RD
CAPITOL AV
WHITE RD
PENITENCIA CREEK RD
MORRILL AV
PIEDMONT HILLS HS
PIEDMONT HILLS CENTER
BERRYESSA CREEK PARK
PENITENCIA CREEK COUNTY PARK
BERRYESSA CORNERS CENTER
ALUM ROCK PARK
NOBLE PARK
CIMARRON PARK
SAN JOSE COUNTRY CLUB
COUNTRY CLUB VILLA
MABURY PARK (SITE)
EAST SAN JOSE
SAN JOSE
BERRYESSA
680
FRWY
MCKEE RD
ALUM ROCK AV
SKYLINE DR
PINARD ST
LISBON DR
MADRID DR
SYDNEY DR
ROWLEY DR
STONEWOOD LN
CONIFER LN
LOCKWOOD DR
SAGEWOOD DR
DESERTWOOD LN
BIRCHWOOD LN
CREEKSIDE DR
WEMBLEY DR
ANDREWS DR
BALMORAL DR
KNIGHTSBRIDGE DR
CASTLEGATE DR
WICKHAM DR
HOSTETTER RD
RUSKIN DR
KIMLEE DR
MATTOS DR
TULARE DR
MAUNA KEA LN
ZION AV
VESUVIUS LN
SUNCREST AV
GROSSMONT DR
WHITMAN WY
VISTA DEL MAR
NOBLE AV
FLANDERS DR
SHRIVER DR
SAN PABLO AV
JOANNE AV
PEPPER TREE LN
HOLLY DR
GOLF DR
ORANGE GOLF ST
PERCIVALE DR
TRISTAN AV
GAWAIN DR
LUCIAN AV
CORTESE CIR
FENTON AV
TOYON AV
PELLIER LN
KIRK AV
CLEARVIEW DR
GLEN HEATHER DR
MABURY RD
NASHVILLE DR
BETSY WY
JIM DR
PATT AV
CAPITOL AV
BERRYESSA RD

SEE 263 MAP

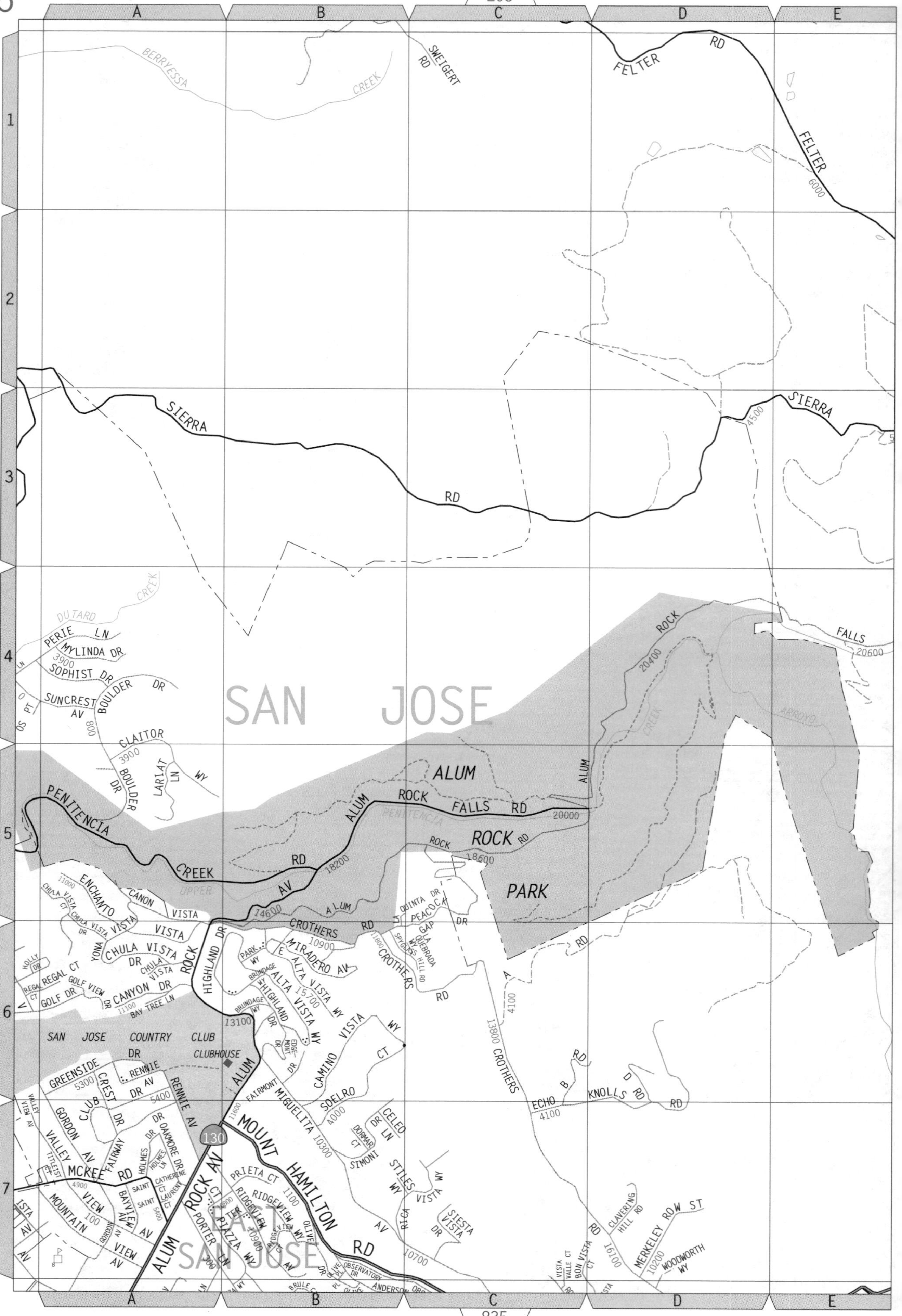
SAN JOSE
EAST SAN JOSE
ALUM ROCK FALLS RD
ALUM ROCK PARK
SIERRA RD
FELTER RD
PENITENCIA CREEK RD
ALUM ROCK AV
MOUNT HAMILTON RD
CROTHERS RD
SAN JOSE COUNTRY CLUB
CLUBHOUSE
MCKEE RD
130

SEE 814 MAP

SEE 835 MAP

SEE 263 MAP

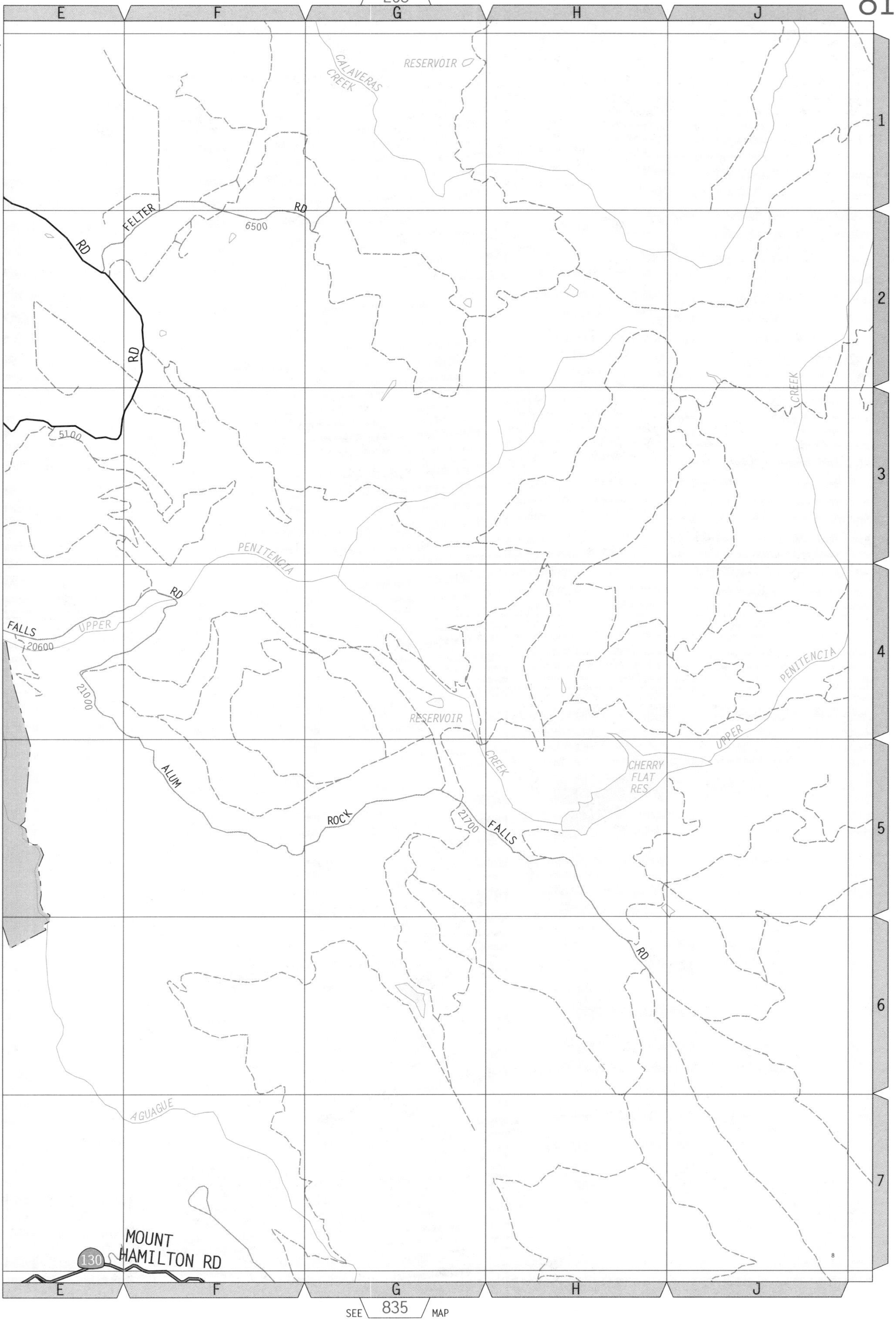
E
F
G
H
J
1
2
3
4
5
6
7
RESERVOIR
CALAVERAS CREEK
FELTER RD
RD
6500
RD
5100
PENITENCIA
RD
FALLS
UPPER
20600
21000
RESERVOIR
CREEK
CHERRY FLAT RES
UPPER
PENITENCIA
CREEK
ALUM
ROCK
21700
FALLS
RD
AGUAGUE
MOUNT HAMILTON RD
130

SEE 835 MAP

SEE 810 MAP

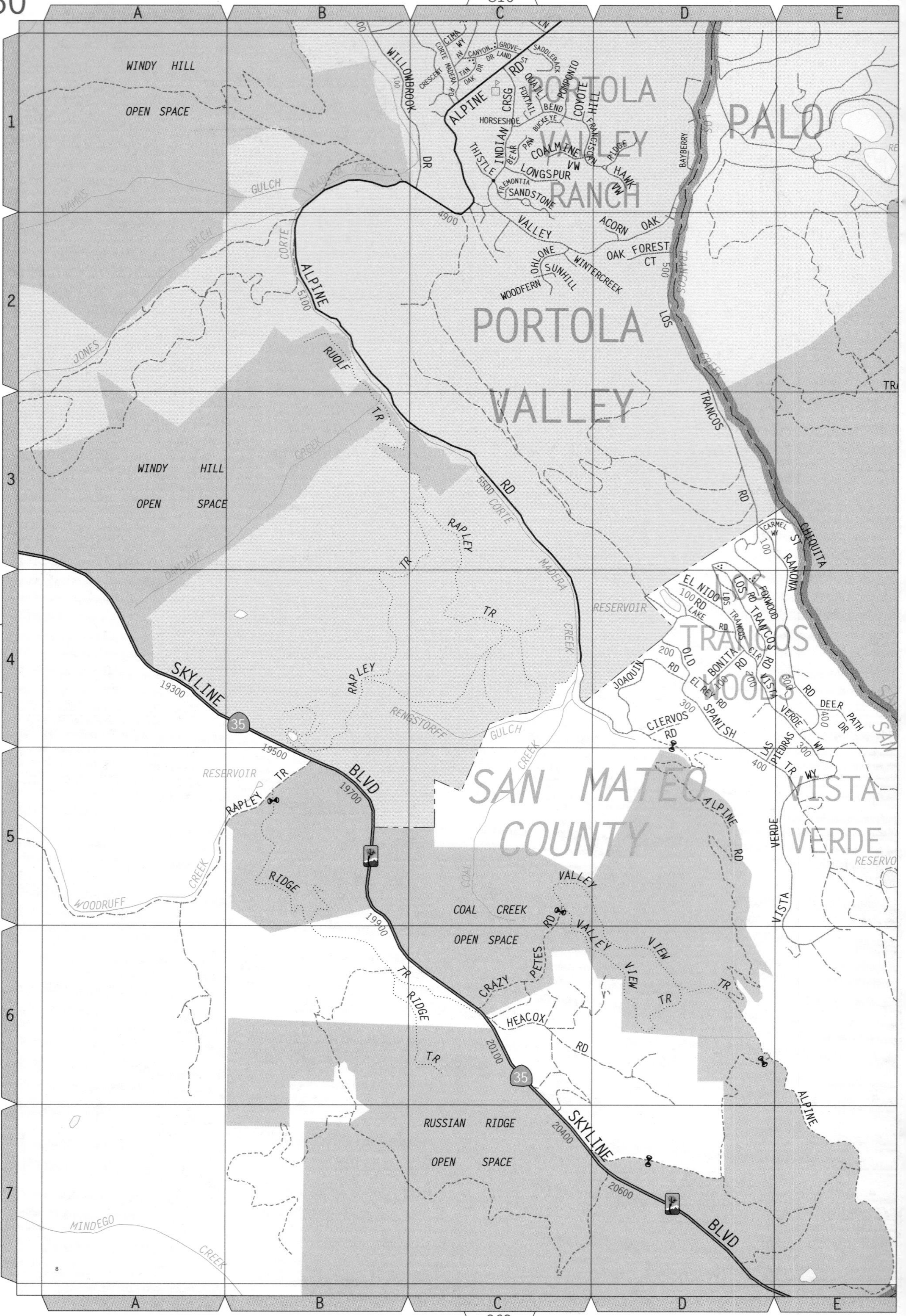
WINDY HILL
OPEN SPACE
PORTOLA VALLEY RANCH
PALO
PORTOLA
VALLEY
WINDY HILL
OPEN SPACE
LOS TRANCOS WOODS
SAN MATEO
COUNTY
VISTA VERDE
COAL CREEK
OPEN SPACE
RUSSIAN RIDGE
OPEN SPACE
ALPINE RD
SKYLINE BLVD
35
WILLOWBROOK DR
LOS TRANCOS RD
CORTE MADERA CREEK
RAPLEY RIDGE TR
RUOLF TR
JONES GULCH
RENGSTORFF GULCH
COAL CREEK
WOODRUFF CREEK
MINDEGO CREEK
HEACOX RD
CRAZY PETES RD
VALLEY VIEW TR
RESERVOIR
19300
19500
19700
19900
20100
20400
20600
4900
5100
5500

SEE 263 MAP

SEE 263 MAP

SEE 810 MAP

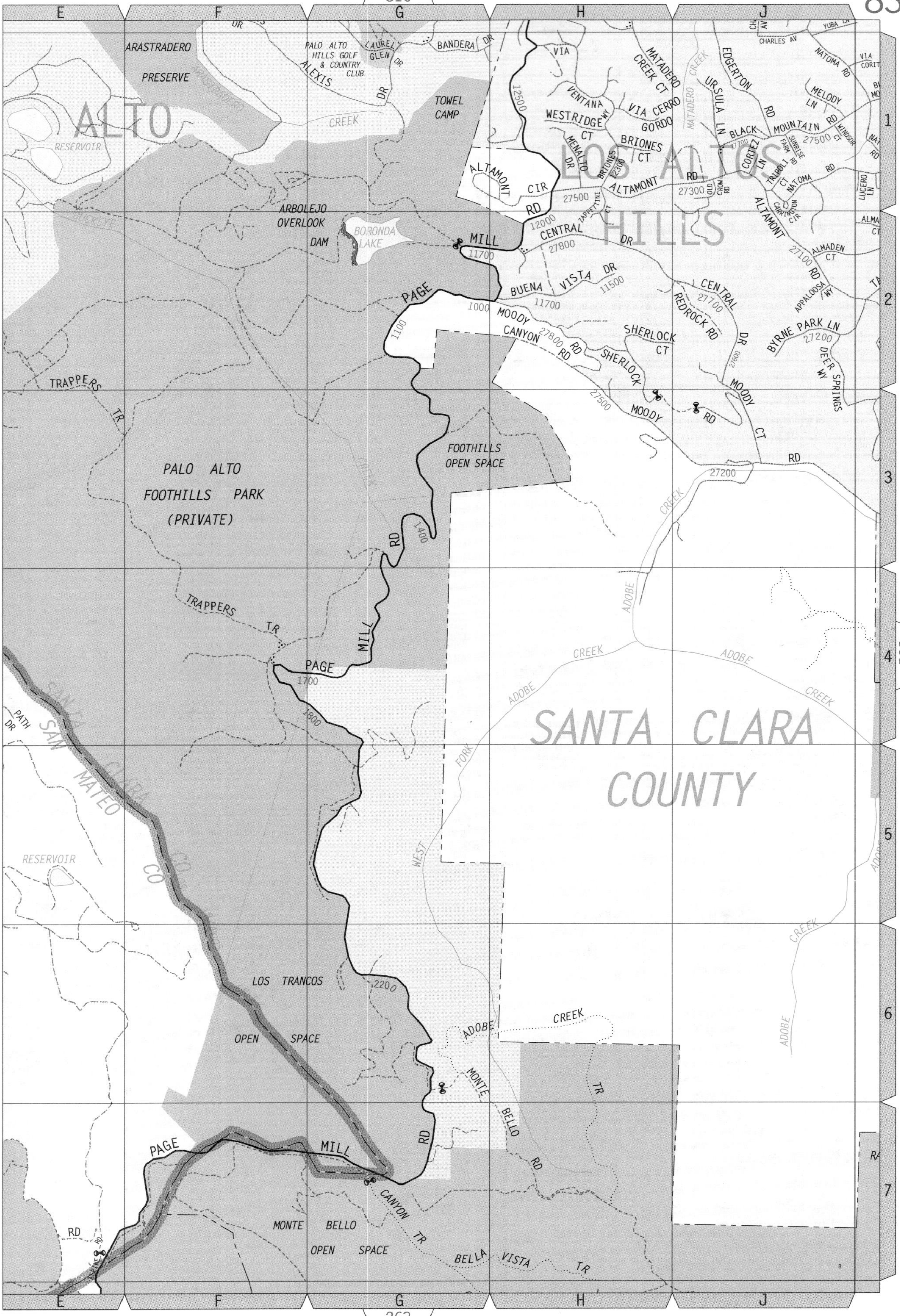
E
F
G
H
J
1
2
3
4
5
6
7
ARASTRADERO
PRESERVE
ALTO
RESERVOIR
PALO ALTO HILLS GOLF & COUNTRY CLUB
LAUREL GLEN DR
ALEXIS DR
BANDERA DR
TOWEL CAMP
CREEK
ARBOLEJO OVERLOOK
DAM
BORONDA LAKE
BUCKEYE
LOS ALTOS HILLS
VIA
MATADERO CREEK CT
EDGERTON RD
URSULA LN
CHARLES AV
NATOMA RD
YUBA LN
MELODY LN
VENTANA WY
WESTRIDGE CT
VIA CERRO GORDO
BRIONES CT
MENALTO DR
BLACK MOUNTAIN RD
CORTEZ LN
TRIPOLI CT
NATOMA RD
LUCERO LN
ALTAMONT CIR
ALTAMONT RD
CENTRAL DR
BUENA VISTA DR
MILL
PAGE
MOODY CANYON RD
SHERLOCK CT
SHERLOCK
MOODY RD
REDROCK RD
CENTRAL DR
MOODY CT
ALTAMONT
ALMADEN CT
APPALOOSA WY
BYRNE PARK LN
DEER SPRINGS WY
TRAPPERS TR
PALO ALTO FOOTHILLS PARK (PRIVATE)
FOOTHILLS OPEN SPACE
PAGE MILL RD
ADOBE CREEK
SANTA CLARA COUNTY
SANTA CLARA
SAN MATEO CO
WEST FORK
RESERVOIR
LOS TRANCOS OPEN SPACE
MONTE BELLO RD
MONTE BELLO OPEN SPACE
CANYON TR
BELLA VISTA TR

SEE 831 MAP

SEE 263 MAP

SEE 811 MAP

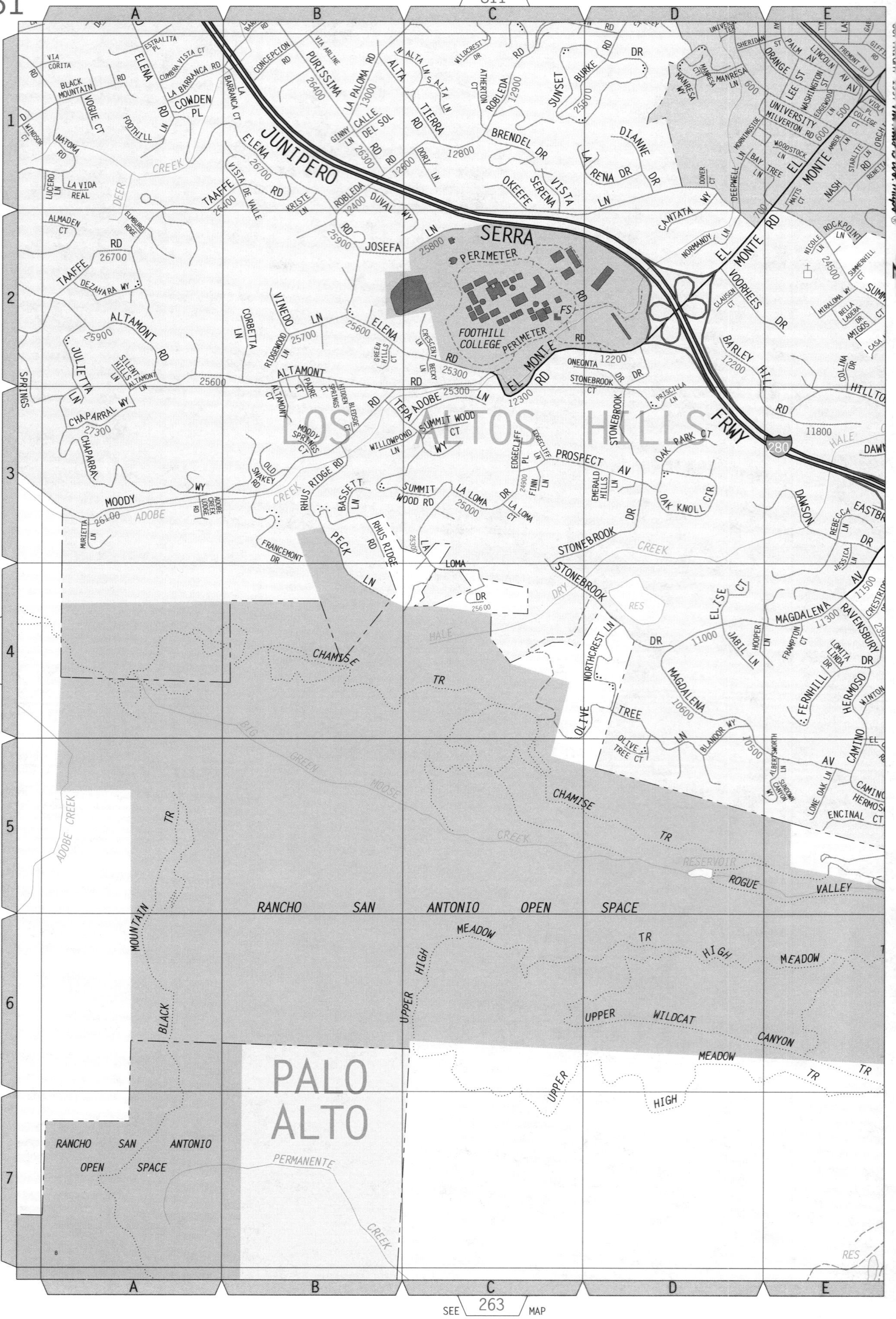
LOS ALTOS HILLS
PALO ALTO
RANCHO SAN ANTONIO OPEN SPACE
JUNIPERO SERRA FRWY
280
FOOTHILL COLLEGE
PERIMETER
FS
EL MONTE RD
ALTAMONT RD
MOODY RD
ADOBE CREEK
ROBLEDA RD
JOSEFA LN
ELENA RD
VINEDO LN
CORBETTA LN
JULIETTA LN
CHAPARRAL WY
TAAFFE RD
DEZAHARA WY
ALMADEN CT
ELMBURG RIDGE
LUCERO LN
LA VIDA REAL
NATOMA RD
WINDSOR CT
VIA CORITA
BLACK MOUNTAIN RD
VOGUE CT
FOOTHILL LN
ESTRALITA PL
CUMBRE VISTA CT
LA BARRANCA RD
COWDEN PL
CONCEPCION RD
PURISSIMA RD
VIA ARLINE
LA PALOMA RD
CALLE DEL SOL
GINNY LN
ALTA TIERRA RD
BRENDEL DR
SUNSET DR
BURKE RD
DIANNE DR
LA RENA LN
OKEEFE LN
SERENA VISTA
CANTATA WY
MANRESA LN
UNIVERSITY AV
MILVERTON RD
VOORHEES DR
BARLEY HILL RD
PROSPECT AV
STONEBROOK DR
OAK PARK CT
OAK KNOLL CIR
EDGECLIFF PL
LA LOMA DR
SUMMIT WOOD RD
RHUS RIDGE RD
PECK LN
BASSETT LN
TEPA WY
ADOBE LN
WILLOWPOND CT
MOODY SPRINGS CT
FRANCEMONT DR
MAGDALENA AV
NORTHCREST LN
OLIVE TREE LN
BLANDOR WY
ELISE CT
JABIL LN
RAVENSBURY AV
FERNHILL DR
HERMOSO
DAWSON
REBECCA DR
CHAMISE TR
HALE CREEK
DRY CREEK
BIG GREEN MOOSE CREEK
RESERVOIR
ROGUE VALLEY
HIGH MEADOW TR
UPPER HIGH MEADOW TR
UPPER WILDCAT CANYON
BLACK MOUNTAIN TR
PERMANENTE CREEK
DEER CREEK
ENCINAL CT
LONE OAK LN
RES

SEE 830 MAP

SEE 263 MAP

SEE 811 MAP

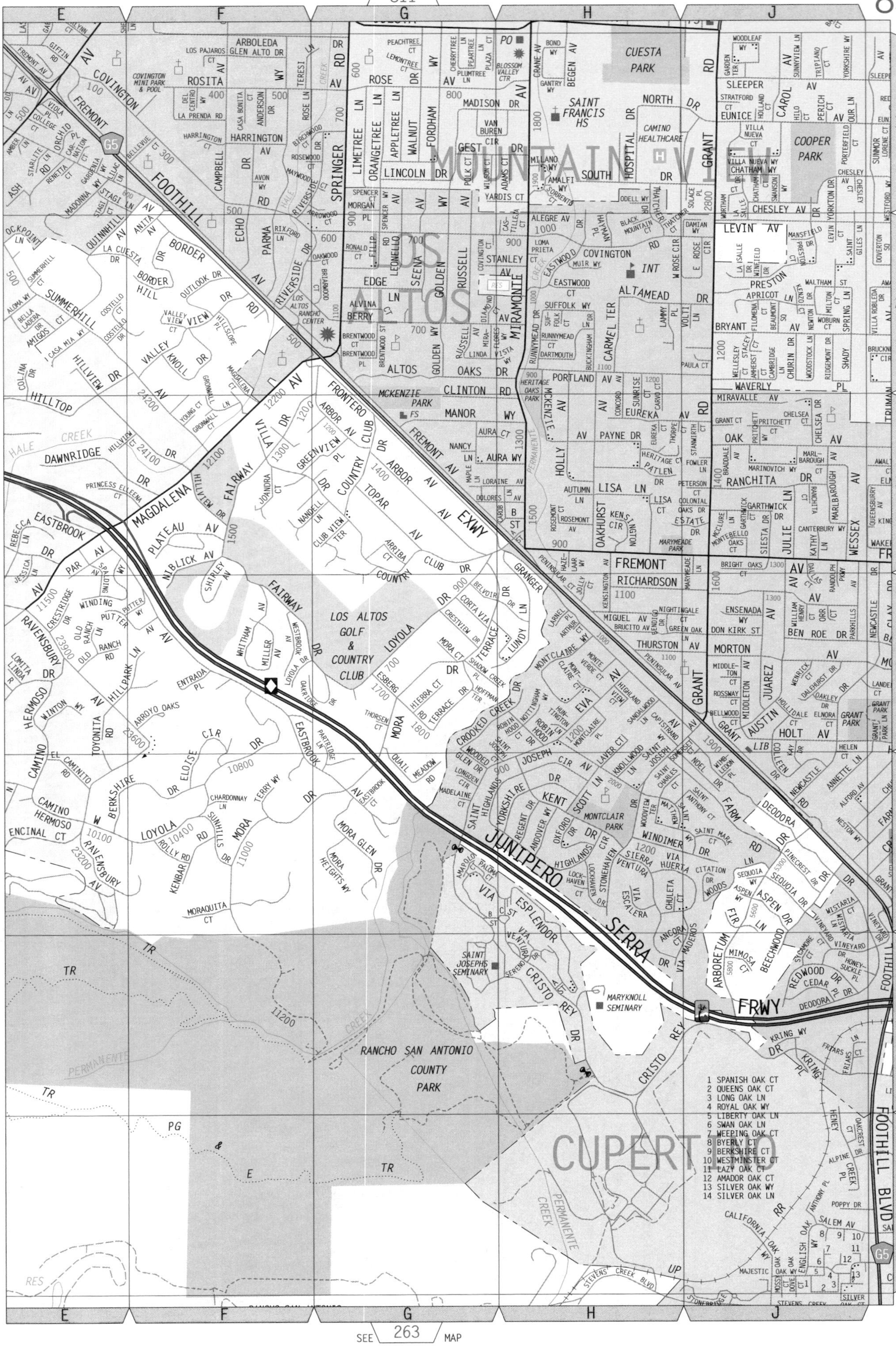
E
F
G
H
J
1
2
3
4
5
6
7
MOUNTAIN VIEW
LOS ALTOS
CUPERTINO
CUESTA PARK
COOPER PARK
SAINT FRANCIS HS
CAMINO HEALTHCARE
MCKENZIE PARK
LOS ALTOS GOLF & COUNTRY CLUB
MONTCLAIR PARK
GRANT PARK
MARYMEADE PARK
COVINGTON MINI PARK & POOL
LOS ALTOS RANCHO CENTER
BLOSSOM VALLEY CTR
SAINT JOSEPHS SEMINARY
MARYKNOLL SEMINARY
RANCHO SAN ANTONIO COUNTY PARK
FOOTHILL EXWY
FOOTHILL BLVD
JUNIPERO SERRA FRWY
FREMONT AV
GRANT RD
MAGDALENA AV
HALE CREEK
PERMANENTE CREEK
STEVENS CREEK BLVD
CRISTO REY DR
1 SPANISH OAK CT
2 QUEENS OAK CT
3 LONG OAK LN
4 ROYAL OAK WY
5 LIBERTY OAK LN
6 SWAN OAK LN
7 WEEPING OAK CT
8 BYERLY CT
9 BERKSHIRE CT
10 WESTMINSTER CT
11 LAZY OAK CT
12 AMADOR OAK CT
13 SILVER OAK WY
14 SILVER OAK LN

SEE 832 MAP

SEE 263 MAP

SEE 812 MAP

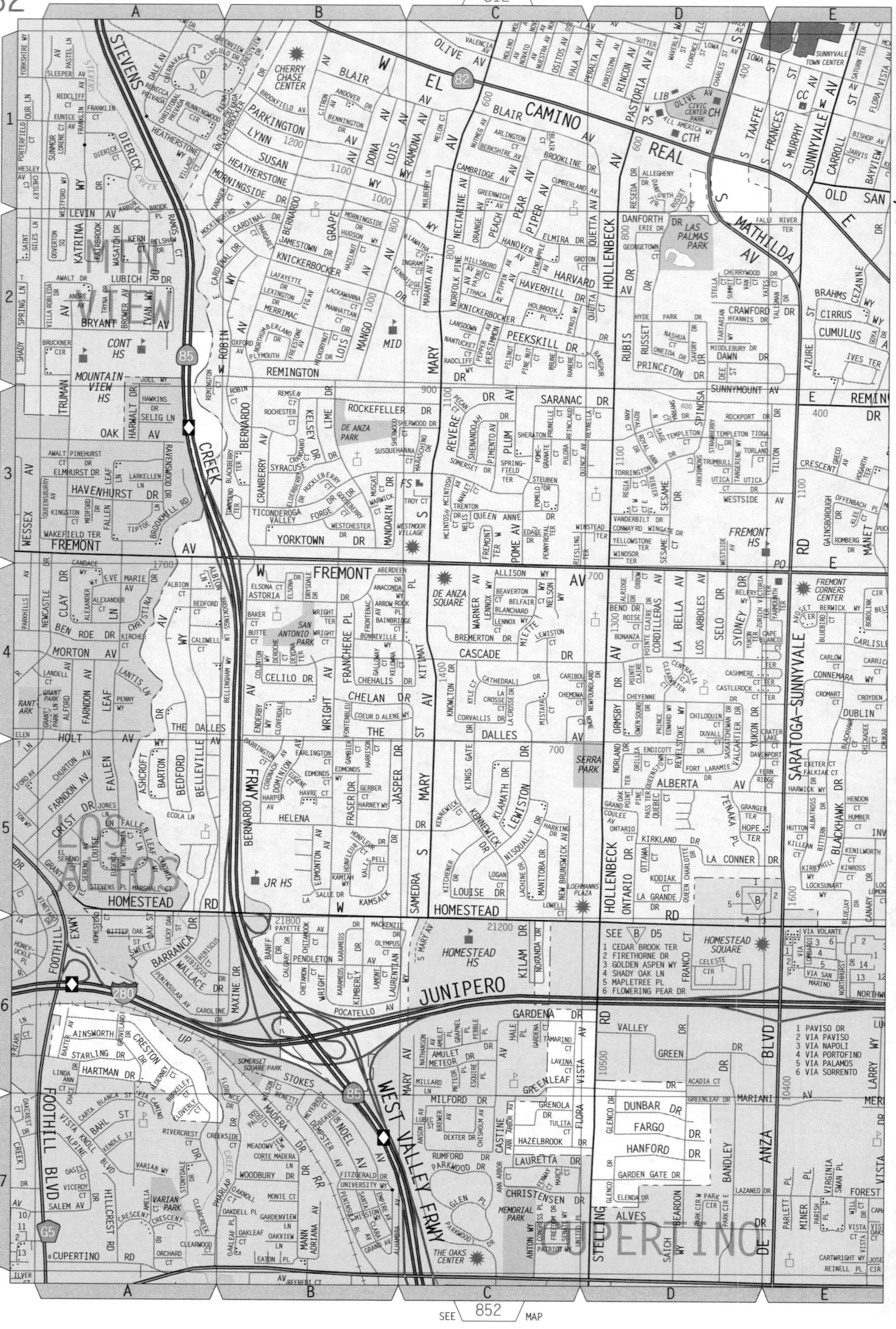
A
B
C
D
E
1
2
3
4
5
6
7
STEVENS CREEK
EL CAMINO REAL
OLIVE AV
BLAIR AV
PARKINGTON AV
LYNN AV
SUSAN AV
HEATHERSTONE WY
MORNINGSIDE DR
CHERRY CHASE CENTER
KNICKERBOCKER DR
JAMESTOWN DR
CARDINAL DR
BERNARDO AV
GRAPE AV
DONA AV
LOIS AV
RAMONA AV
MARY AV
NECTARINE AV
PEACH AV
PEAR AV
PIPER AV
ELMIRA DR
HARVARD AV
HAVERHILL DR
PEEKSKILL DR
QUETTA AV
HOLLENBECK AV
PASTORIA AV
CIVIC CENTER PARK
LIB
PS
CH
CTH
CC
MATHILDA AV
LAS PALMAS PARK
DANFORTH DR
RUSSET DR
PRINCETON DR
REMINGTON DR
SUNNYMOUNT AV
S TAAFFE ST
S FRANCES ST
S MURPHY AV
SUNNYVALE AV
CARROLL ST
BAYVIEW AV
OLD SAN FRANCISCO RD
SUNNYVALE TOWN CENTER
CRAWFORD DR
CIRRUS
CUMULUS
IVES TER
MTN VIEW
CONT HS
MOUNTAIN VIEW HS
TRUMAN AV
OAK AV
BRYANT AV
KATRINA WY
LEVIN AV
DIERICK WY
MID
ROCKEFELLER DR
DE ANZA PARK
SARANAC DR
REVERE AV
PLUM AV
WESTSIDE AV
FREMONT HS
FREMONT AV
WESSEX AV
HAVENHURST DR
YORKTOWN DR
TICONDEROGA VALLEY
FORGE DR
MANDARIN DR
WESTMOOR VILLAGE
QUEEN ANNE DR
DE ANZA SQUARE
SARATOGA-SUNNYVALE RD
FREMONT CORNERS CENTER
ALLISON WY
CASCADE DR
BREMERTON DR
DALLES AV
CELILO DR
CHELAN DR
THE DALLES AV
SAN ANTONIO PARK
FRANCHERE PL
KITIMAT PL
HOLLENBECK AV
CORDILLERAS AV
LA BELLA AV
LOS ARBOLES AV
SELO DR
SYDNEY DR
YUKON DR
DUBLIN WY
SERRA PARK
ALBERTA AV
KIRKLAND DR
LA CONNER DR
ONTARIO DR
HOMESTEAD RD
BELLEVILLE WY
ASHCROFT AV
BEDFORD AV
FALLEN LEAF LN
LOS ALTOS
HELENA DR
KAMSACK DR
JASPER DR
JR HS
LOEHMANNS PLAZA
BLACKHAWK DR
SEE B D5
1 CEDAR BROOK TER
2 FIRETHORNE DR
3 GOLDEN ASPEN WY
4 SHADY OAK LN
5 MAPLETREE PL
6 FLOWERING PEAR DR
HOMESTEAD SQUARE
HOMESTEAD HS
JUNIPERO SERRA FRWY
FOOTHILL EXWY
FOOTHILL BLVD
CRIST DR
BARRANCA DR
PENINSULAR AV
CAROLINE DR
MAXINE DR
POCATELLO AV
AINSWORTH DR
CRESTON DR
STARLING DR
HARTMAN DR
SOMERSET SQUARE PARK
STOKES ST
WEST VALLEY FRWY
MILFORD DR
GREENLEAF DR
VISTA DR
VALLEY GREEN DR
DE ANZA BLVD
MARIANI AV
DUNBAR DR
FARGO DR
HANFORD DR
GARDEN GATE DR
BANDLEY DR
STELLING RD
ALVES DR
CHRISTENSEN DR
HAZELBROOK DR
MEMORIAL PARK
CUPERTINO
THE OAKS CENTER
VARIAN PARK
CUPERTINO RD
HILLCREST RD
MCCLELLAN RD
1 PAVISO DR
2 VIA PAVISO
3 VIA NAPOLI
4 VIA PORTOFINO
5 VIA PALAMOS
6 VIA SORRENTO
85
280
82
G5
SEE 831 MAP

SEE 852 MAP

SEE 812 MAP

SUNNYVALE
SANTA CLARA
EL CAMINO REAL
82
LAWRENCE EXWY
G2
SERRA FRWY
280
WOLFE RD
FREMONT AV
HOMESTEAD RD
KIFER RD
EVELYN AV
REED AV
MONROE ST
REMINGTON DR
PRUNERIDGE AV
STEVENS CREEK
CALTRAIN
LAWRENCE STA
PAVLINA PLAZA
WOLFE-REED CENTER
BRALY PARK
PONDEROSA PARK
LA HACIENDA CTR
COMM CTR
SUNKEN GARDENS GOLF COURSE
RADISSON HAUS INN
LAWRENCE SQUARE
PANAMA PARK
MID
ORTEGA PARK
RAYNOR PARK
PARK & RIDE
VTA
DMV
EARL J CARMICHAEL PARK
HOMESTEAD CTR
LAWRENCE STATION CTR
CUPERTINO VILLAGE
COURTYARD BY MARRIOTT
VALLCO FASHION PARK
PORTAL PARK
JENNY STRAND PARK
MAYWOOD PARK
MACHADO PARK
SAINT LAWRENCE ACADEMY HS
CALABAZAS CREEK
SARATOGA CREEK
1 W EVELYN TER
2 EVELYN TER
3 E EVELYN TER
1 W GARLAND TER
2 N GARLAND TER
3 E GARLAND TER
1 CROCUS CT
2 DAHLIA CT
1 MIRAVERDE CT
2 MIRAMESA CT
3 MIRA PLAZA CT
SEE C H4
1 GAZDAR CT
2 KARINA WY
3 EUROPE WY
4 SARITA WY
5 BRACH WY
6 CASA CT
SEE A E6
1 NORTHBROOK SQ
2 NORTHWEST SQ
3 NORTHSEAL SQ
4 NORTHSKY SQ
5 NORTHPOINT WY
6 NORTHSHORE SQ
7 NORTHWIND SQ
8 NORTHCREST SQ
9 NORTHFIELD SQ
10 NORTHVIEW SQ
11 NORTHRIDGE SQ
12 NORTHOAK SQ
13 NORTHCOVE SQ
14 NORTHGLEN SQ
SEE D A1
1 CARLOS PRIVADA
2 ANA PRIVADA
3 MARIA PRIVADA
1 DOMINICAN DR

SEE 833 MAP

SEE 852 MAP

SEE 813 MAP

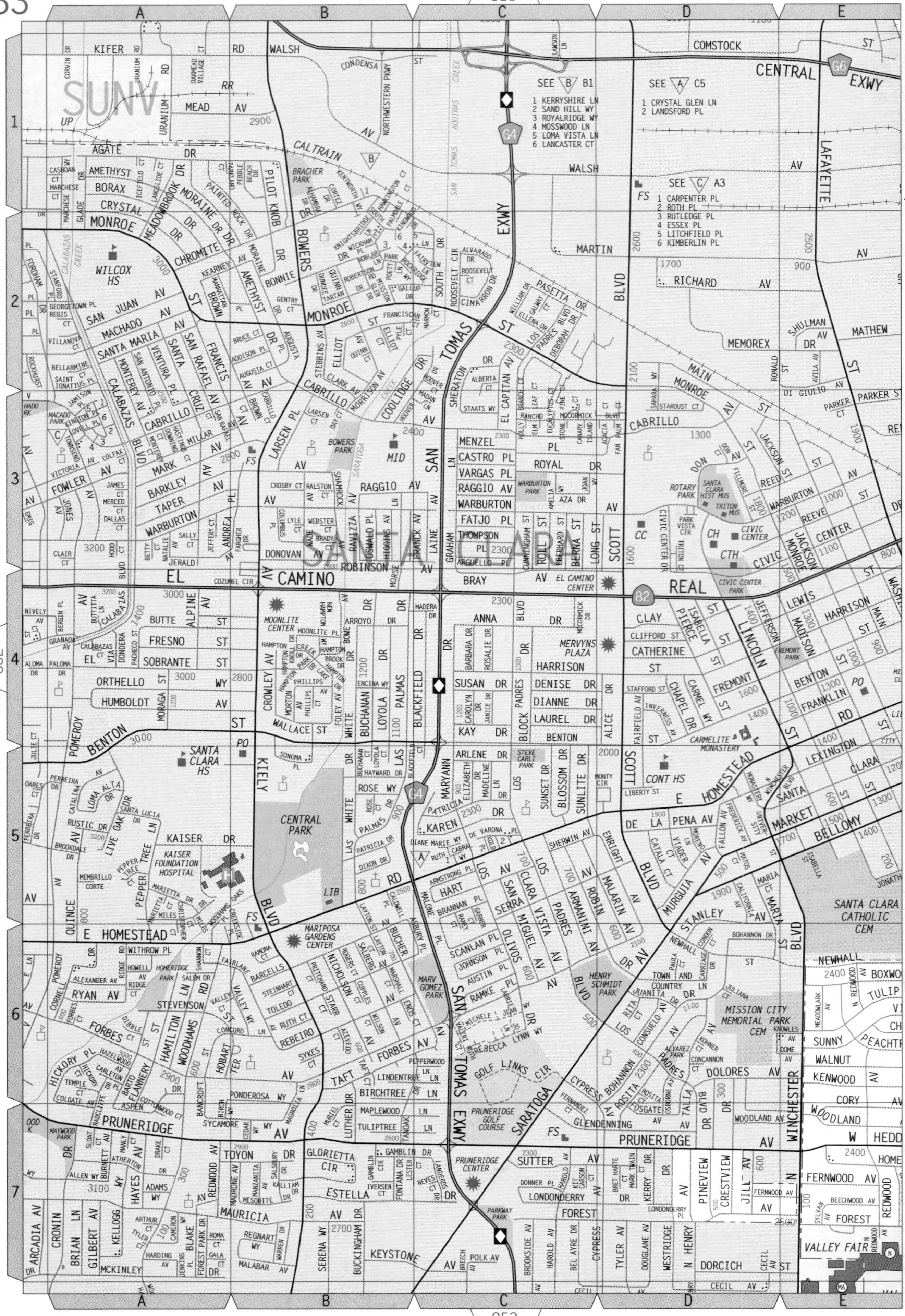
A
B
C
D
E
1
2
3
4
5
6
7
SUNV
SANTA CLARA
KIFER RD
WALSH
COMSTOCK
CENTRAL EXWY
G6
G4
82
SEE B B1
1 KERRYSHIRE LN
2 SAND HILL WY
3 ROYALRIDGE WY
4 MOSSWOOD LN
5 LOMA VISTA LN
6 LANCASTER CT
SEE A C5
1 CRYSTAL GLEN LN
2 LANDSFORD PL
SEE C A3
1 CARPENTER PL
2 ROTH PL
3 RUTLEDGE PL
4 ESSEX PL
5 LITCHFIELD PL
6 KIMBERLIN PL
CALTRAIN
MEAD AV
AGATE DR
AMETHYST
BORAX
CRYSTAL
MONROE
MEADOWBROOK DR
MORAINE DR
CHROMITE
PILOT KNOB
BRACHER PARK
BOWERS
WILCOX HS
SAN JUAN AV
MACHADO AV
SANTA MARIA AV
CALABAZAS BLVD
CABRILLO AV
MILLAR AV
FOWLER
BARKLEY
TAPER
WARBURTON
EL CAMINO REAL
BUTTE ST
FRESNO ST
SOBRANTE ST
ORTHELLO WY
HUMBOLDT AV
BENTON ST
POMEROY
SANTA CLARA HS
KAISER DR
KAISER FOUNDATION HOSPITAL
E HOMESTEAD
CENTRAL PARK
KIELY BLVD
LIB
MOONLITE CENTER
MARIPOSA GARDENS CENTER
RYAN AV
STEVENSON
FORBES AV
PRUNERIDGE AV
TOYON DR
MAURICIA
KEYSTONE AV
SAN TOMAS EXWY
LAWRENCE EXWY
MARTIN
RICHARD AV
MEMOREX DR
SHULMAN
MATHEW
LAFAYETTE
PASETTA DR
SCOTT BLVD
EL CAPITAN AV
MENZEL PL
CASTRO PL
VARGAS PL
RAGGIO AV
BOWERS PARK
MID
WARBURTON PARK
EL CAMINO CENTER
ROTARY PARK
SANTA CLARA HIST MUS
TRITON MUS
CIVIC CENTER
CIVIC CENTER PARK
CC
CH
CTH
MERVYNS PLAZA
CLAY
CATHERINE ST
HARRISON
LINCOLN
JACKSON ST
MONROE
FREMONT PARK
BENTON
FRANKLIN
LEXINGTON
CARMELITE MONASTERY
CONT HS
HOMESTEAD
SANTA CLARA
MARKET
BELLOMY
DE LA PENA AV
MURGUIA
STANLEY AV
SANTA CLARA CATHOLIC CEM
NEWHALL
HENRY SCHMIDT PARK
MISSION CITY MEMORIAL PARK CEM
MARV GOMEZ PARK
GOLF LINKS CIR
PRUNERIDGE GOLF COURSE
PRUNERIDGE CENTER
SARATOGA
DOLORES AV
WINCHESTER BLVD
VALLEY FAIR
FOREST
PINEVIEW
CRESTVIEW
DORCICH ST
SUTTER AV
LONDONDERRY
PARKWAY PARK
POLK AV
FS
PO

SEE 832 MAP

SEE 853 MAP

SEE 813 MAP

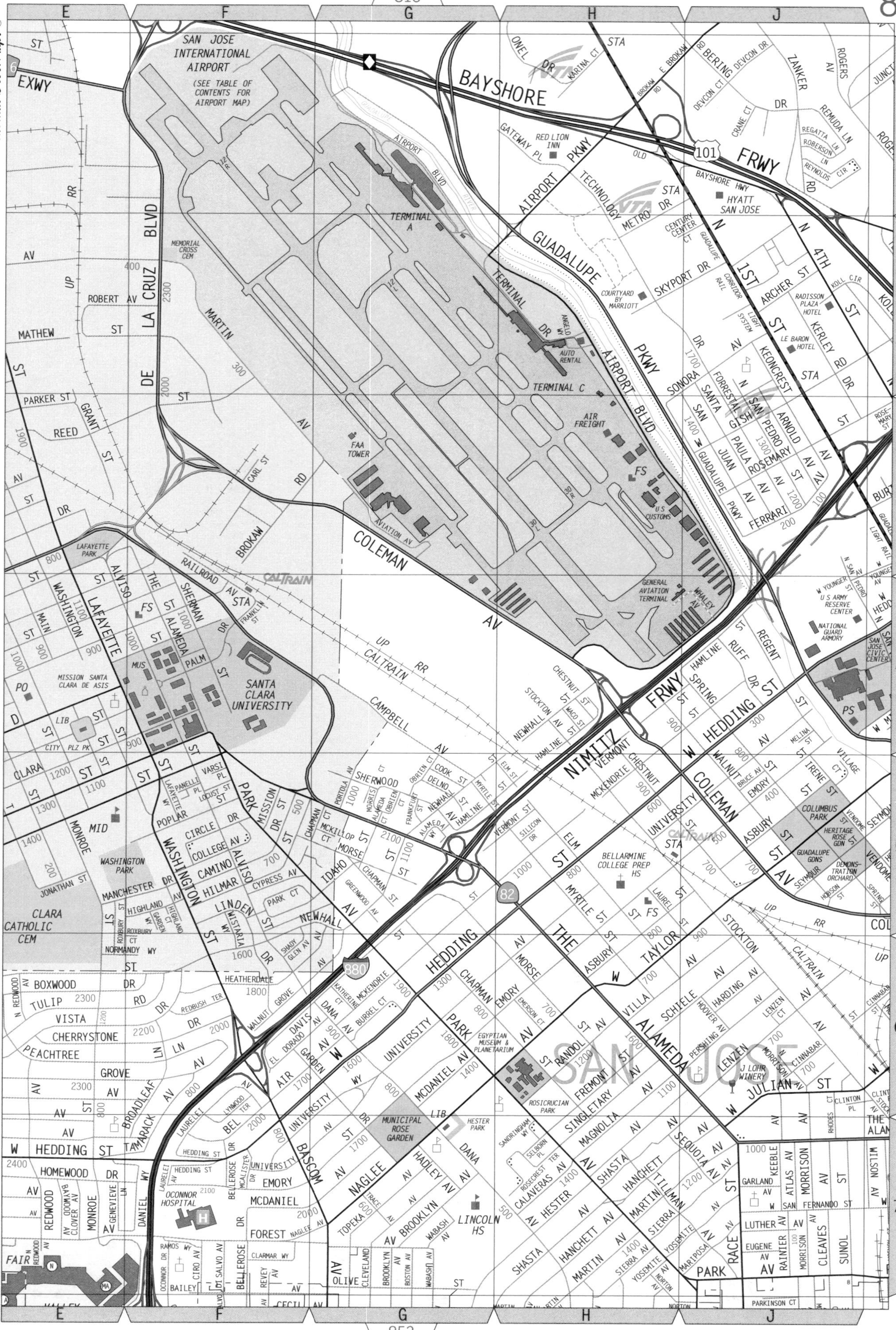

SAN JOSE INTERNATIONAL AIRPORT
(SEE TABLE OF CONTENTS FOR AIRPORT MAP)
TERMINAL A
TERMINAL C
AIR FREIGHT
FAA TOWER
U S CUSTOMS
GENERAL AVIATION TERMINAL
AUTO RENTAL
BAYSHORE FRWY
101
GUADALUPE PKWY
AIRPORT BLVD
AIRPORT PKWY
COLEMAN AV
DE LA CRUZ BLVD
MARTIN AV
BROKAW RD
NIMITZ FRWY
880
82
THE ALAMEDA
W HEDDING ST
SANTA CLARA UNIVERSITY
MISSION SANTA CLARA DE ASIS
MEMORIAL CROSS CEM
CLARA CATHOLIC CEM
LAFAYETTE PARK
WASHINGTON PARK
CALTRAIN
UP RR
RED LION INN
HYATT SAN JOSE
COURTYARD BY MARRIOTT
RADISSON PLAZA HOTEL
LE BARON HOTEL
U S ARMY RESERVE CENTER
NATIONAL GUARD ARMORY
SAN JOSE CIVIC CENTER
COLUMBUS PARK
HERITAGE ROSE GDN
GUADALUPE GDNS
DEMONSTRATION ORCHARD
BELLARMINE COLLEGE PREP HS
EGYPTIAN MUSEUM & PLANETARIUM
ROSICRUCIAN PARK
MUNICIPAL ROSE GARDEN
HESTER PARK
LINCOLN HS
OCONNOR HOSPITAL
J LOHR WINERY
SAN JOSE
E F G H J
1 2 3 4 5 6 7

SEE 834 MAP

SEE 853 MAP

SEE 814 MAP

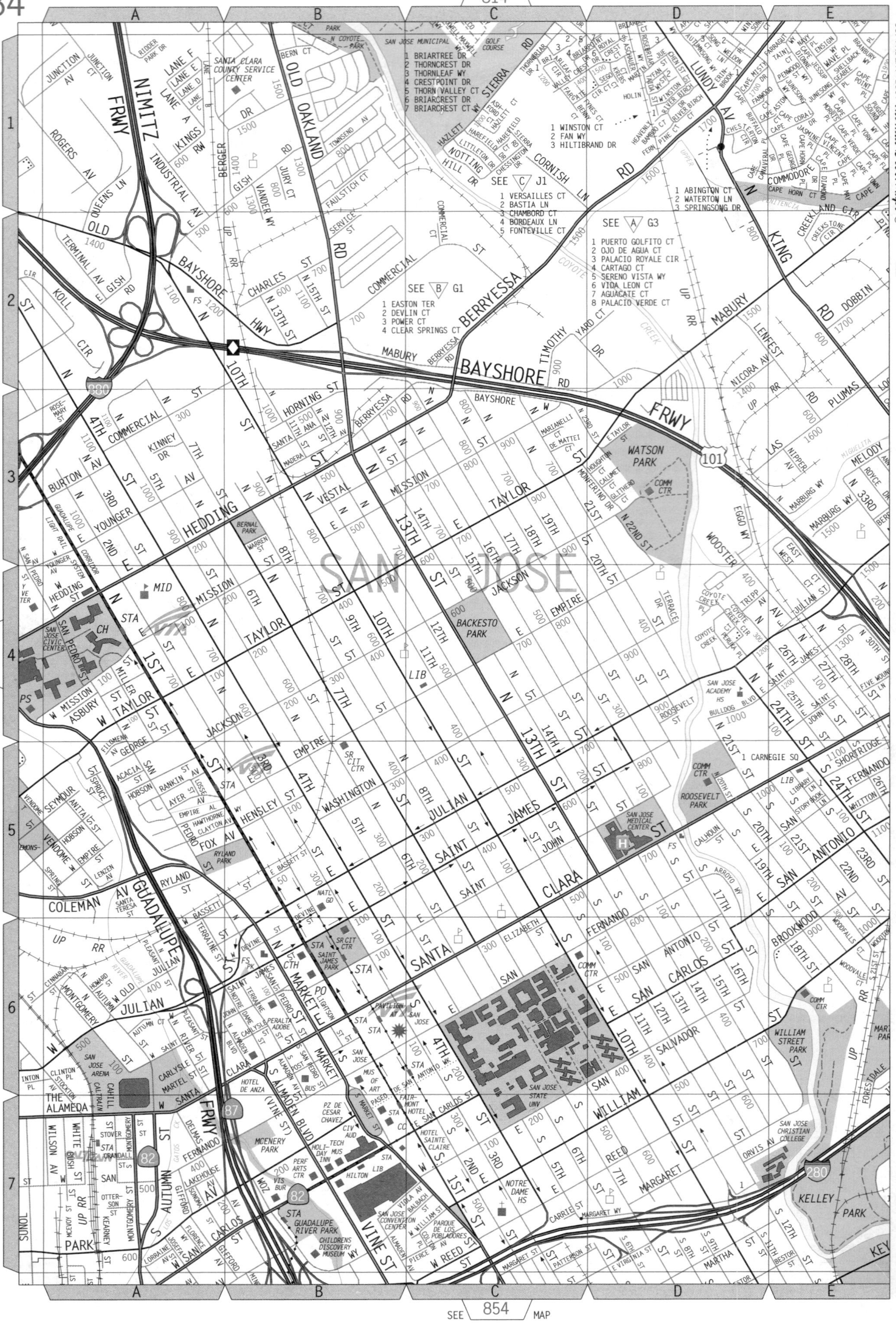
A
B
C
D
E
1
2
3
4
5
6
7
SAN JOSE
NIMITZ FRWY
OLD OAKLAND RD
BAYSHORE FRWY
BERRYESSA RD
GUADALUPE FRWY
SANTA CLARA ST
SAN JOSE MUNICIPAL GOLF COURSE
1 BRIARTREE DR
2 THORNCREST DR
3 THORNLEAF WY
4 CRESTPOINT DR
5 THORN VALLEY CT
6 BRIARCREST DR
7 BRIARCREST CT
1 WINSTON CT
2 FAN WY
3 HILTIBRAND DR
SEE C J1
1 VERSAILLES CT
2 BASTIA LN
3 CHAMBORD CT
4 BORDEAUX LN
5 FONTEVILLE CT
1 ABINGTON CT
2 WATERTON LN
3 SPRINGSONG DR
SEE A G3
1 PUERTO GOLFITO CT
2 OJO DE AGUA CT
3 PALACIO ROYALE CIR
4 CARTAGO CT
5 SERENO VISTA WY
6 VIDA LEON CT
7 AGUACATE CT
8 PALACIO VERDE CT
SEE B G1
1 EASTON TER
2 DEVLIN CT
3 POWER CT
4 CLEAR SPRINGS CT
1 CARNEGIE SQ
SANTA CLARA COUNTY SERVICE CENTER
WATSON PARK
BACKESTO PARK
BERNAL PARK
ROOSEVELT PARK
SAN JOSE MEDICAL CENTER
SAN JOSE STATE UNV
SAN JOSE ACADEMY HS
SAN JOSE CIVIC CENTER
SAINT JAMES PARK
RYLAND PARK
WILLIAM STREET PARK
KELLEY PARK
SAN JOSE CHRISTIAN COLLEGE
GUADALUPE RIVER PARK
SAN JOSE ARENA
MCENERY PARK
SAN JOSE CONVENTION CENTER
CHILDRENS DISCOVERY MUSEUM
NOTRE DAME HS
PERALTA ADOBE
THE ALAMEDA
880
101
87
82
280

SEE 833 MAP

SEE 854 MAP

SEE 814 MAP

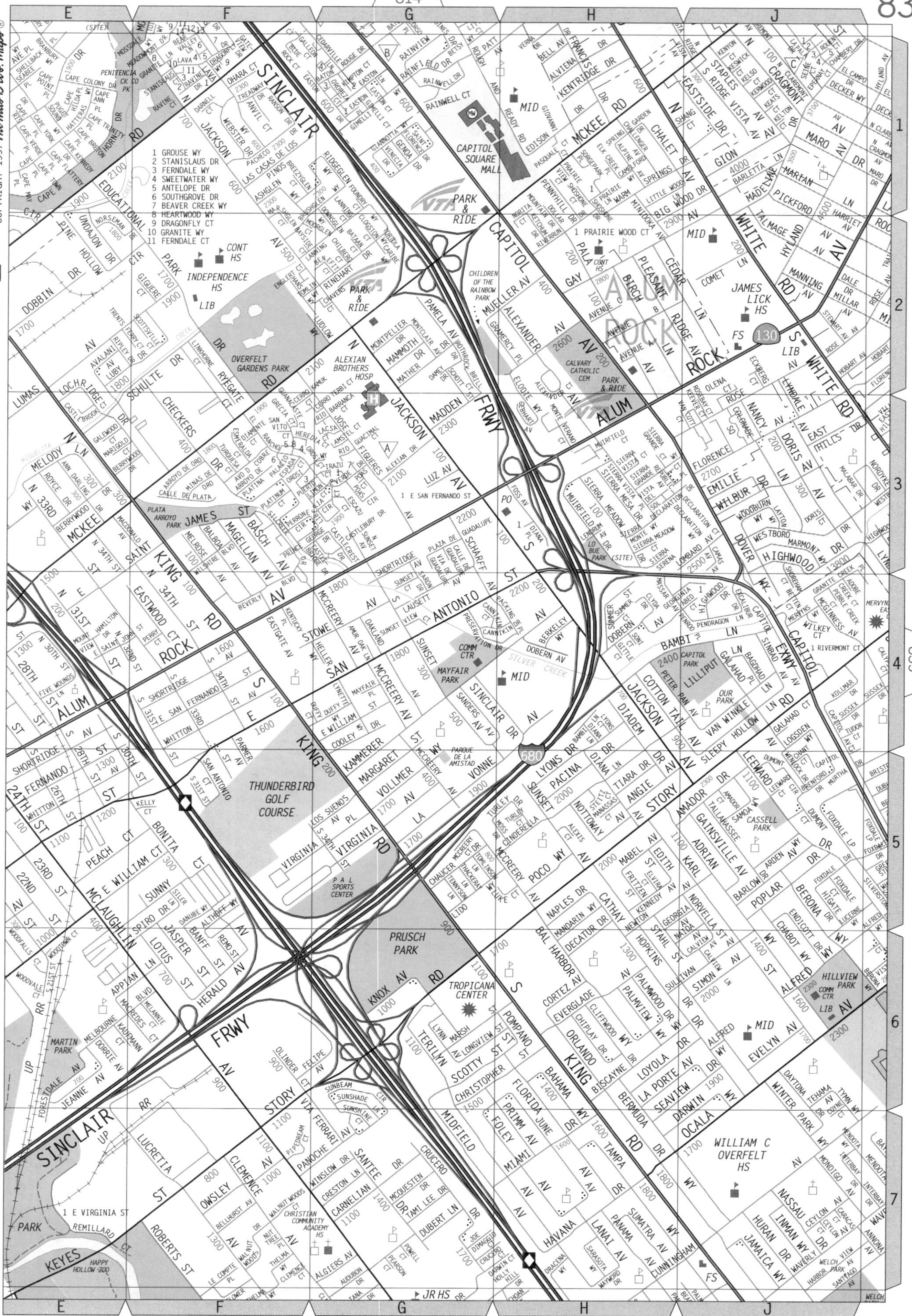
E
F
G
H
J
1
2
3
4
5
6
7
SINCLAIR
FRWY
CAPITOL
CAPITOL SQUARE MALL
PARK & RIDE
CHILDREN OF THE RAINBOW PARK
ALUM ROCK
ALUM ROCK AV
MCKEE RD
WHITE RD
JAMES LICK HS
INDEPENDENCE HS
OVERFELT GARDENS PARK
ALEXIAN BROTHERS HOSP
CALVARY CATHOLIC CEM
PLATA ARROYO PARK
KING RD
SAN ANTONIO ST
MAYFAIR PARK
COMM CTR
CAPITOL EXWY
CAPITOL PARK
OUR PARK
THUNDERBIRD GOLF COURSE
PAL SPORTS CENTER
PRUSCH PARK
TROPICANA CENTER
STORY RD
HILLVIEW PARK
MARTIN PARK
WILLIAM C OVERFELT HS
CHRISTIAN COMMUNITY ACADEMY HS
HAPPY HOLLOW ZOO
KEYES
1 E VIRGINIA ST
1 E SAN FERNANDO ST
1 RIVERMONT CT
1 PRAIRIE WOOD CT
1 GROUSE WY
2 STANISLAUS DR
3 FERNDALE WY
4 SWEETWATER WY
5 ANTELOPE DR
6 SOUTHGROVE DR
7 BEAVER CREEK WY
8 HEARTWOOD WY
9 DRAGONFLY CT
10 GRANITE WY
11 FERNDALE CT
680
130

SEE 835 MAP

SEE 854 MAP

SEE 815 MAP

SEE 834 MAP

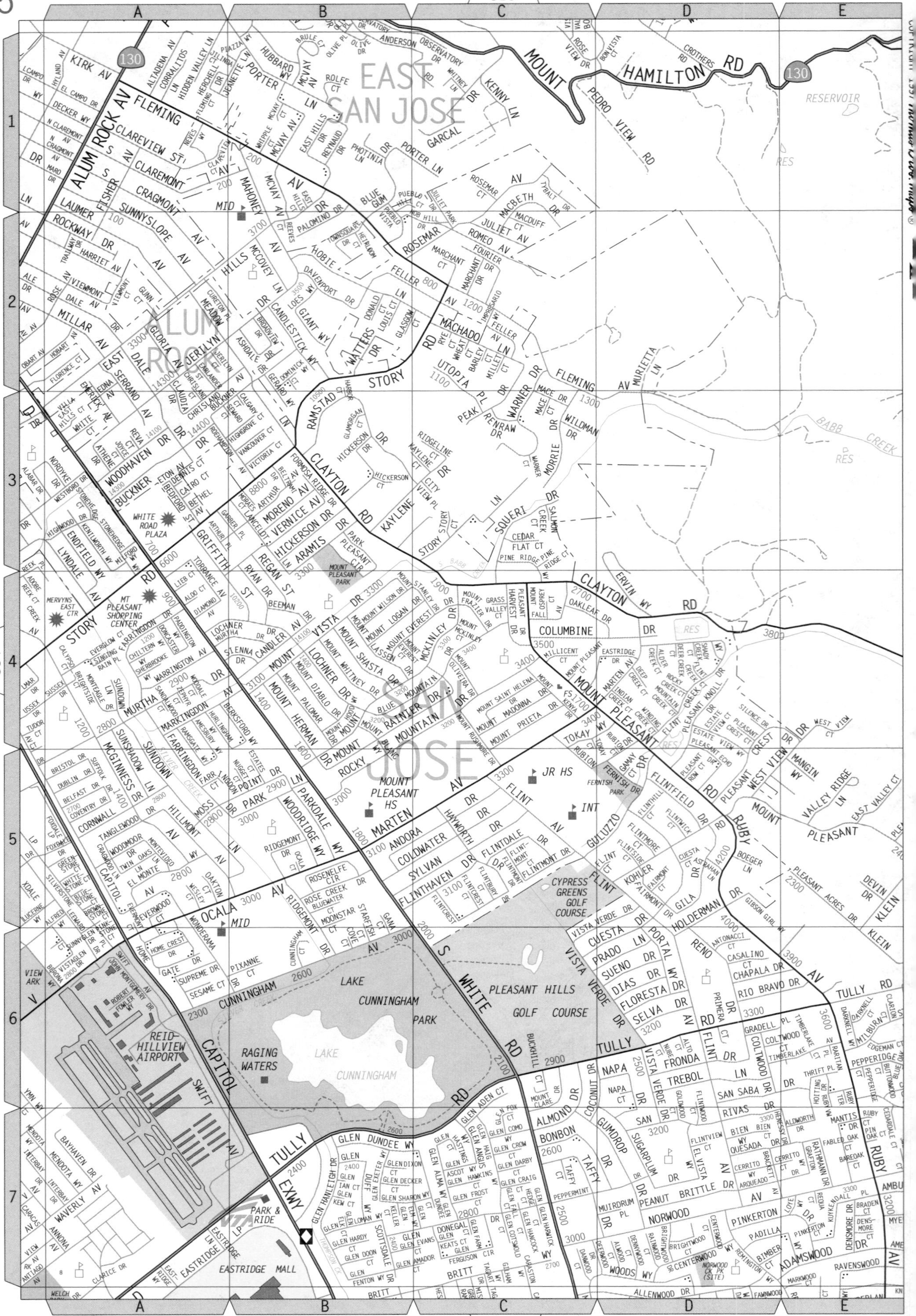

A
B
C
D
E
1
2
3
4
5
6
7
EAST SAN JOSE
ALUM ROCK
SAN JOSE
MOUNT HAMILTON RD
130
ALUM ROCK AV
FLEMING AV
STORY RD
CLAYTON RD
S WHITE RD
CAPITOL EXWY
TULLY RD
MOUNT PLEASANT RD
RUBY AV
MARTEN AV
OCALA AV
CUNNINGHAM AV
WHITE ROAD PLAZA
MT PLEASANT SHOPPING CENTER
MERVYNS EAST CTR
MOUNT PLEASANT PARK
MOUNT PLEASANT HS
JR HS
INT
MID
FERNISH PARK
CYPRESS GREENS GOLF COURSE
PLEASANT HILLS GOLF COURSE
LAKE CUNNINGHAM PARK
LAKE CUNNINGHAM
RAGING WATERS
REID-HILLVIEW AIRPORT
EASTRIDGE MALL
PARK & RIDE
RESERVOIR
BABB CREEK
RES

SEE 855 MAP

SEE 815 MAP

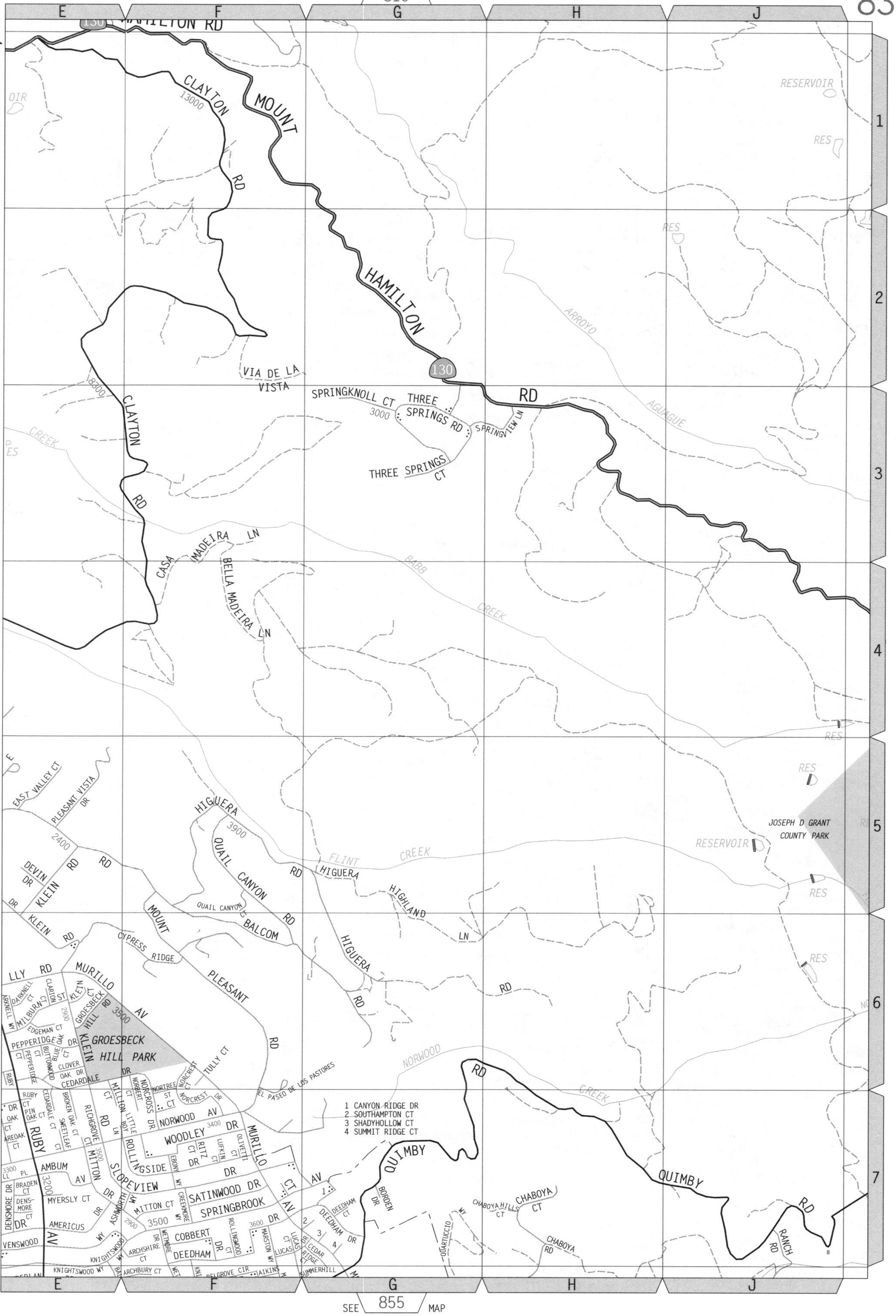
MOUNT HAMILTON RD
CLAYTON RD
VIA DE LA VISTA
SPRINGKNOLL CT
THREE SPRINGS RD
SPRINGVIEW LN
THREE SPRINGS CT
ARROYO AGUAGUE
CASA MADEIRA LN
BELLA MADEIRA LN
BABB CREEK
RESERVOIR
RES
JOSEPH D GRANT COUNTY PARK
EAST VALLEY CT
PLEASANT VISTA DR
HIGUERA RD
QUAIL CANYON RD
QUAIL CANYON CT
BALCOM
FLINT CREEK
HIGHLAND LN
DEVIN DR
KLEIN RD
MOUNT PLEASANT RD
CYPRESS RIDGE
MURILLO AV
GROESBECK HILL PARK
GROESBECK HILL RD
TULLY CT
NORWOOD CREEK
EL PASEO DE LOS PASTORES
NORWOOD AV
WOODLEY DR
QUIMBY RD
1 CANYON RIDGE DR
2 SOUTHAMPTON CT
3 SHADYHOLLOW CT
4 SUMMIT RIDGE CT
RUBY AV
AMBUM AV
SLOPEVIEW DR
SATINWOOD DR
SPRINGBROOK AV
COBBERT DR
DEEDHAM DR
BORDEN DR
CHABOYA HILLS CT
CHABOYA RD
RANCH RD
KNIGHTSWOOD WY
ARCHBURY CT
SUMMERHILL

SEE 855 MAP

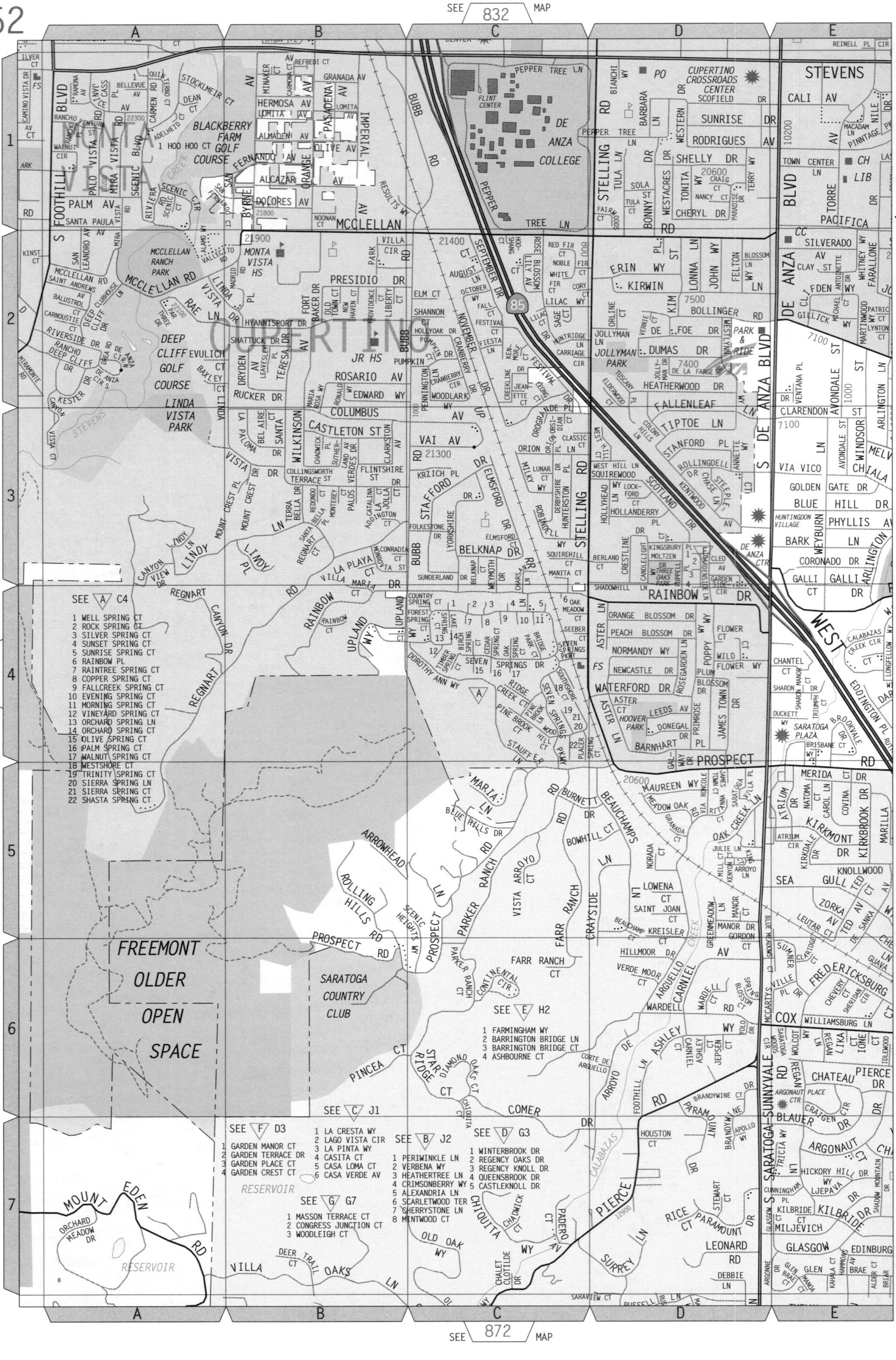
SEE 832 MAP
SEE 872 MAP
SEE 263 MAP
A
B
C
D
E
1
2
3
4
5
6
7
MONTA VISTA
CUPERTINO
STEVENS
BLACKBERRY FARM GOLF COURSE
DE ANZA COLLEGE
FLINT CENTER
CUPERTINO CROSSROADS CENTER
McCLELLAN RANCH PARK
MONTA VISTA HS
DEEP CLIFF GOLF COURSE
LINDA VISTA PARK
JR HS
JOLLYMAN PARK
PARK & RIDE
HOOVER PARK
HUNTINGDON VILLAGE
DE ANZA CTR
SARATOGA PLAZA
ARGONAUT PLACE
FREEMONT OLDER OPEN SPACE
SARATOGA COUNTRY CLUB
RESERVOIR
S FOOTHILL BLVD
McCLELLAN RD
STEVENS CREEK BLVD
S DE ANZA BLVD
SARATOGA SUNNYVALE RD
STELLING RD
BUBB RD
PROSPECT RD
RAINBOW DR
REGNART CANYON DR
BOLLINGER RD
PIERCE RD
MOUNT EDEN RD
COX AV
CHATEAU DR
FREDERICKSBURG DR
KIRKMONT DR
WEST VALLEY FWY
SEE A C4
1 WELL SPRING CT
2 ROCK SPRING CT
3 SILVER SPRING CT
4 SUNSET SPRING CT
5 SUNRISE SPRING CT
6 RAINBOW PL
7 RAINTREE SPRING CT
8 COPPER SPRING CT
9 FALLCREEK SPRING CT
10 EVENING SPRING CT
11 MORNING SPRING CT
12 VINEYARD SPRING CT
13 ORCHARD SPRING LN
14 ORCHARD SPRING CT
15 OLIVE SPRING CT
16 PALM SPRING CT
17 WALNUT SPRING CT
18 WESTSHORE CT
19 TRINITY SPRING CT
20 SIERRA SPRING LN
21 SIERRA SPRING CT
22 SHASTA SPRING CT
SEE E H2
1 FARMINGHAM WY
2 BARRINGTON BRIDGE LN
3 BARRINGTON BRIDGE CT
4 ASHBOURNE CT
SEE C J1
SEE F D3
1 GARDEN MANOR CT
2 GARDEN TERRACE DR
3 GARDEN PLACE CT
4 GARDEN CREST CT
1 LA CRESTA WY
2 LAGO VISTA CIR
3 LA PINTA WY
4 CASITA CT
5 CASA LOMA CT
6 CASA VERDE AV
SEE B J2
1 PERIWINKLE LN
2 VERBENA WY
3 HEATHERTREE LN
4 CRIMSONBERRY WY
5 ALEXANDRIA LN
6 SCARLETWOOD TER
7 CHERRYSTONE LN
8 MINTWOOD CT
SEE D G3
1 WINTERBROOK DR
2 REGENCY OAKS DR
3 REGENCY KNOLL DR
4 QUEENSBROOK DR
5 CASTLEKNOLL DR
SEE G G7
1 MASSON TERRACE CT
2 CONGRESS JUNCTION CT
3 WOODLEIGH CT

SEE 832 MAP

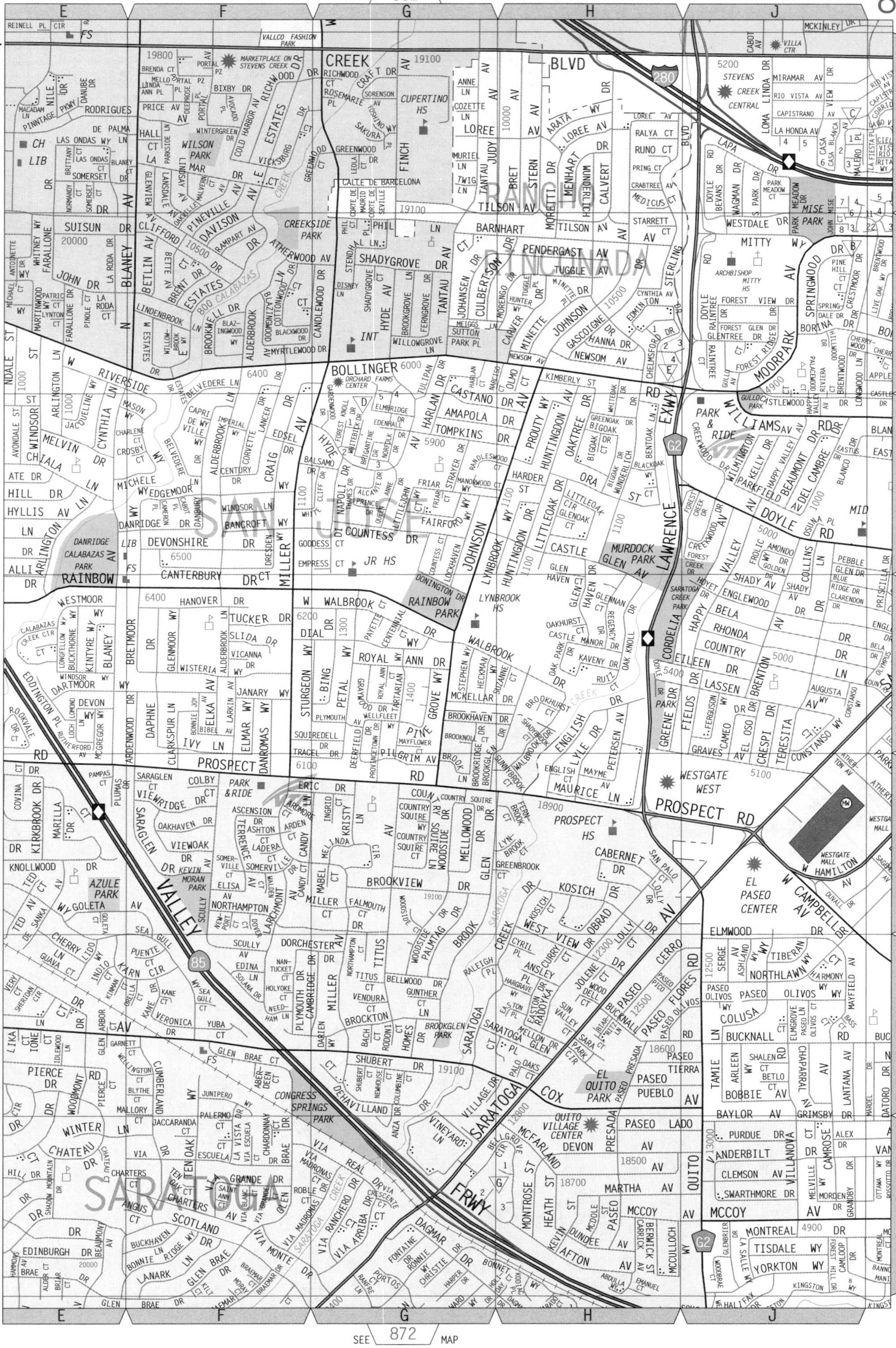

E
F
G
H
J
1
2
3
4
5
6
7
STEVENS CREEK BLVD
280
VALLCO FASHION PARK
MARKETPLACE ON STEVENS CREEK
STEVENS CREEK CENTRAL
CUPERTINO HS
WILSON PARK
CREEKSIDE PARK
RANCHO RINCONADA
ARCHBISHOP MITTY HS
MISE PARK
BOLLINGER
ORCHARD FARMS CENTER
INT
GULLO PARK
PARK & RIDE
WILLIAMS RD
LAWRENCE EXWY
G2
SAN JOSE
DANRIDGE CALABAZAS PARK
LIB
FS
MURDOCK GLEN PARK
JR HS
RAINBOW PARK
LYNBROOK HS
SARATOGA CREEK PARK
PROSPECT RD
WESTGATE WEST
WESTGATE MALL
PROSPECT HS
EL PASEO CENTER
AZULE PARK
MORAN PARK
VALLEY
85
BROOKGLEN PARK
EL QUITO PARK
CONGRESS SPRINGS PARK
QUITO VILLAGE CENTER
SARATOGA
FRWY
MILLER AV
SARATOGA AV
COX AV
QUITO RD
W CAMPBELL AV

SEE 853 MAP

SEE 872 MAP

SEE 833 MAP

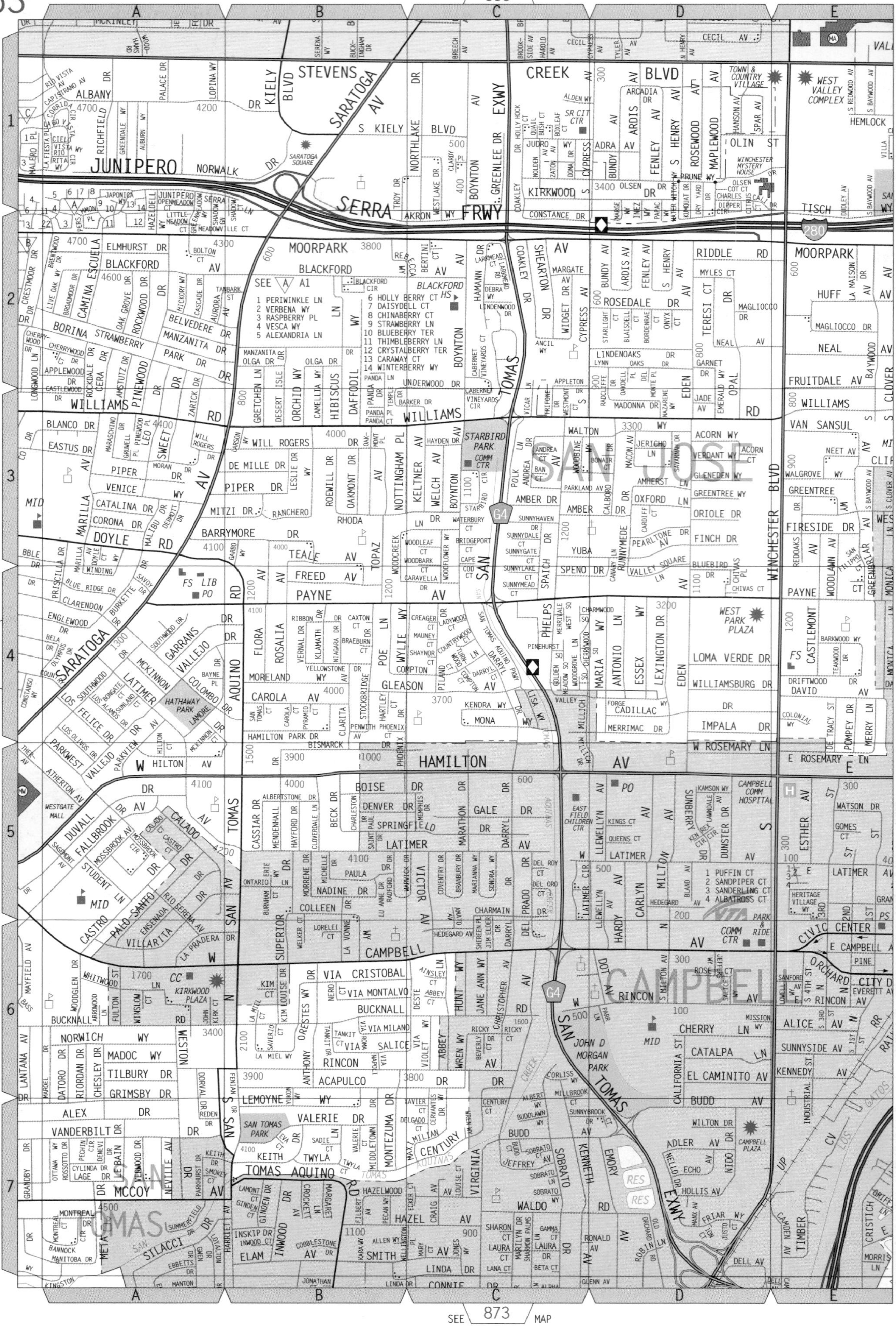

SAN JOSE
CAMPBELL
STEVENS CREEK BLVD
SARATOGA AV
JUNIPERO SERRA FRWY
280
MOORPARK AV
WILLIAMS RD
HAMILTON AV
CAMPBELL AV
SAN TOMAS EXWY
SAN TOMAS AQUINO RD
WINCHESTER BLVD
PAYNE AV
DOYLE RD
BLACKFORD AV
KIELY BLVD
BOYNTON AV
SARATOGA SQUARE
WEST VALLEY COMPLEX
TOWN & COUNTRY VILLAGE
WINCHESTER MYSTERY HOUSE
BLACKFORD HS
STARBIRD PARK COMM CTR
WEST PARK PLAZA
HATHAWAY PARK
WESTGATE MALL
KIRKWOOD PLAZA
SAN TOMAS PARK
JOHN D MORGAN PARK
CAMPBELL PLAZA
CAMPBELL COMM HOSPITAL
HERITAGE VILLAGE
G4
SEE A A1
1 PERIWINKLE LN
2 VERBENA WY
3 RASPBERRY PL
4 VESCA WY
5 ALEXANDRIA LN
6 HOLLY BERRY CT
7 DAISYDELL CT
8 CHINABERRY CT
9 STRAWBERRY LN
10 BLUEBERRY TER
11 THIMBLEBERRY LN
12 CRYSTALBERRY TER
13 CARAWAY CT
14 WINTERBERRY WY
1 PUFFIN CT
2 SANDPIPER CT
3 SANDERLING CT
4 ALBATROSS CT

SEE 852 MAP

SEE 873 MAP

SEE 833 MAP

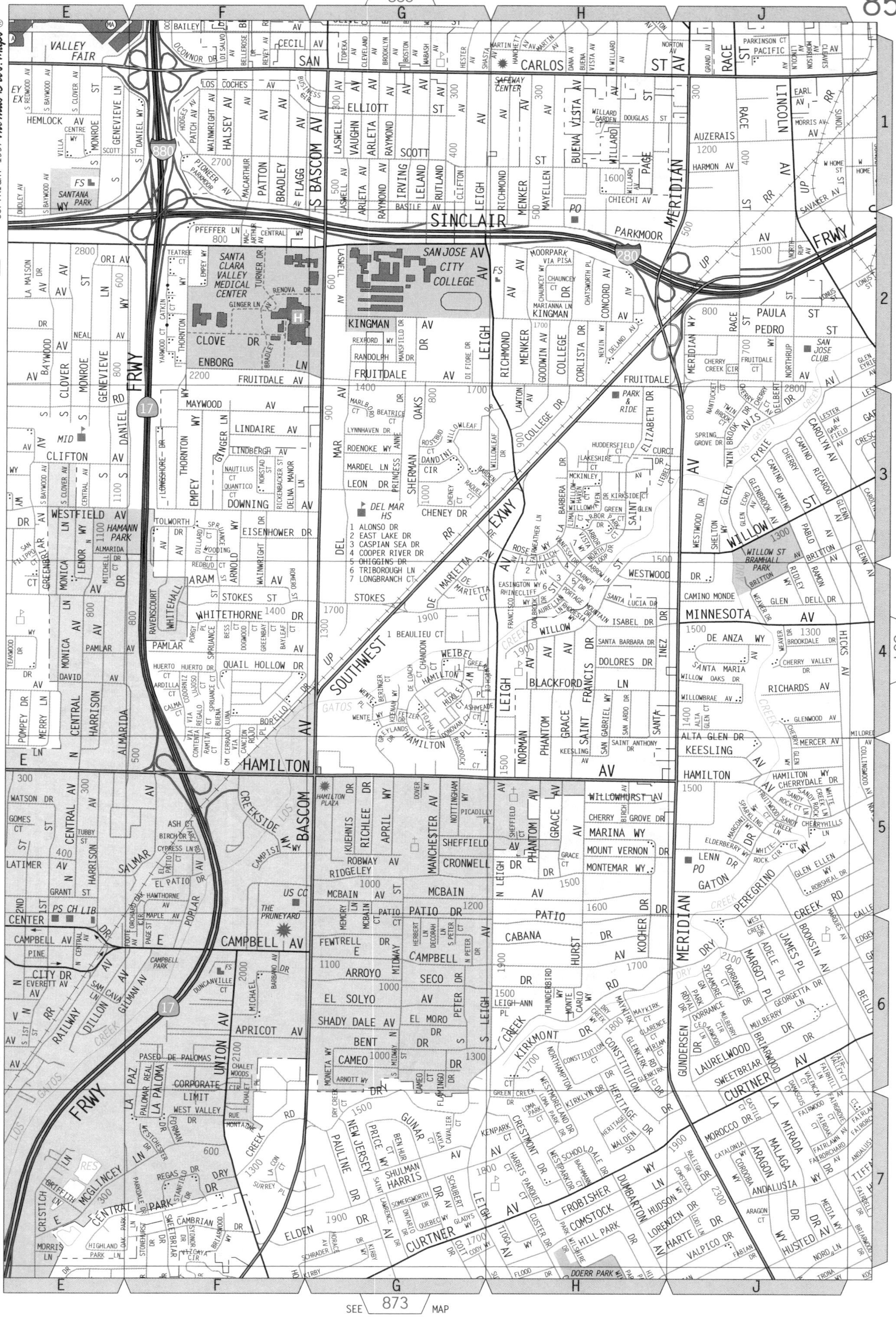
E
F
G
H
J
1
2
3
4
5
6
7
VALLEY FAIR
SANTANA PARK
SAN CARLOS
SINCLAIR FRWY
PARKMOOR AV
MERIDIAN AV
S BASCOM AV
SANTA CLARA VALLEY MEDICAL CENTER
SAN JOSE CITY COLLEGE
SAFEWAY CENTER
AUZERAIS
LINCOLN AV
RACE ST
SAN JOSE CLUB
PARK & RIDE
KINGMAN AV
FRUITDALE AV
CLOVE DR
ENBORG LN
FRWY
MAYWOOD AV
LINDAIRE AV
DEL MAR HS
1 ALONSO DR
2 EAST LAKE DR
3 CASPIAN SEA DR
4 COOPER RIVER DR
5 OHIGGINS DR
6 TRIBOROUGH LN
7 LONGBRANCH CT
SOUTHWEST EXWY
LEIGH AV
HAMANN PARK
WESTFIELD AV
WILLOW ST
WILLOW ST BRAMHALL PARK
MINNESOTA AV
HAMILTON AV
HAMILTON PLAZA
THE PRUNEYARD
CAMPBELL AV
CAMPBELL PARK
CENTER
CURTNER AV
DOERR PARK
KIRKMONT DR
FROBISHER WY
LAURELWOOD DR
PEREGRINO WY
LOS GATOS CREEK
FRWY

SEE 854 MAP

SEE 873 MAP

SEE 834 MAP

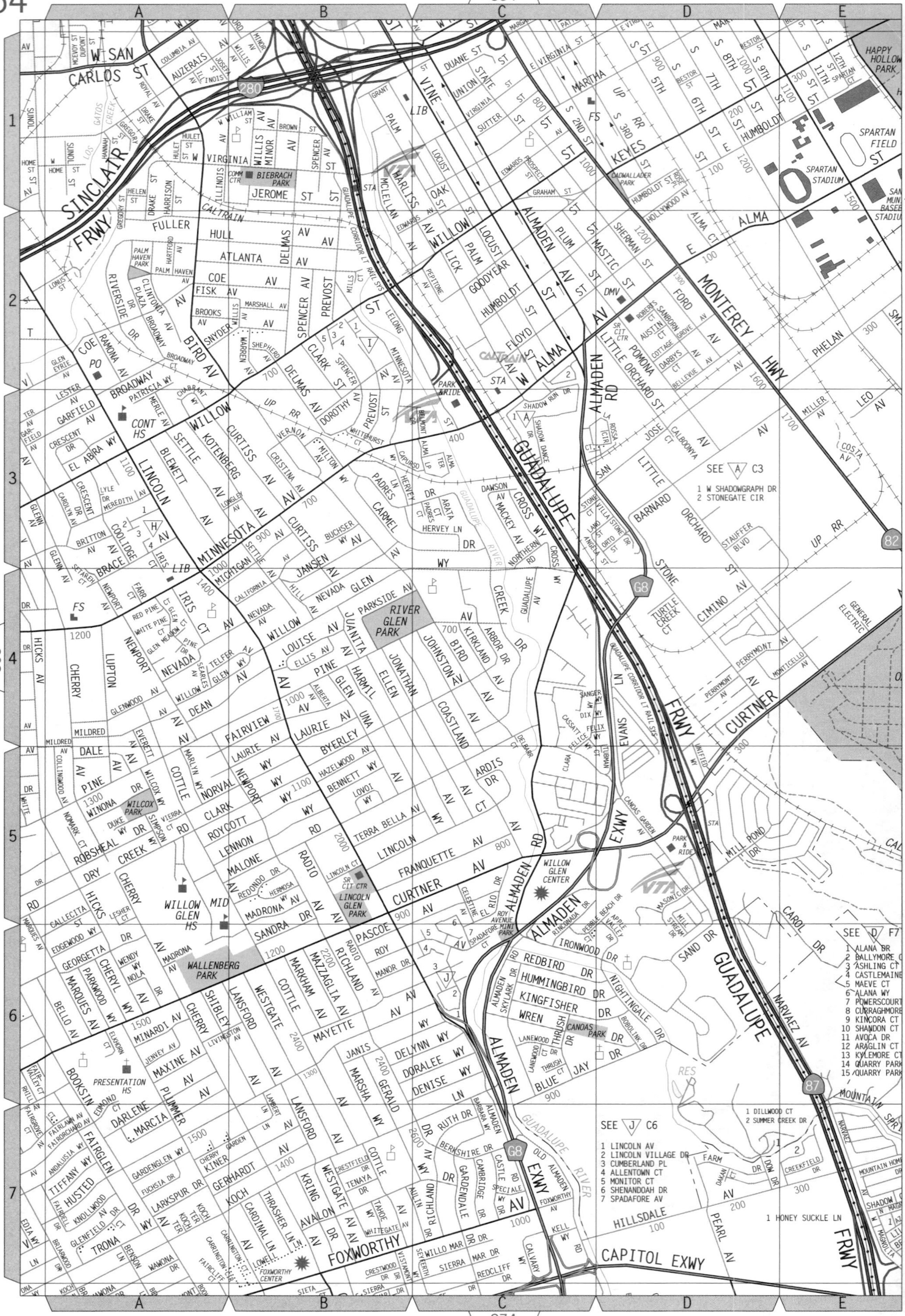
SINCLAIR FRWY
GUADALUPE FRWY
MONTEREY HWY
ALMADEN EXWY
CAPITOL EXWY
CURTNER AV
FOXWORTHY AV
MINNESOTA AV
WILLOW ST
LINCOLN AV
ALMA AV
HAPPY HOLLOW PARK
SPARTAN FIELD
SPARTAN STADIUM
BIEBRACH PARK
PALM HAVEN PARK
RIVER GLEN PARK
WILCOX PARK
LINCOLN GLEN PARK
WALLENBERG PARK
CANOAS PARK
WILLOW GLEN CENTER
FOXWORTHY CENTER
WILLOW GLEN HS
CONT HS
PRESENTATION HS
SEE A C3
1 W SHADOWGRAPH DR
2 STONEGATE CIR
SEE D F7
1 ALANA BR
2 BALLYMORE C
3 ASHLING CT
4 CASTLEMAINE
5 MAEVE CT
6 ALANA WY
7 POWERSCOURT
8 CURRAGHMORE
9 KINCORA CT
10 SHANDON CT
11 AVOCA DR
12 ARAGLIN CT
13 KYLEMORE CT
14 QUARRY PARK
15 QUARRY PARK
SEE J C6
1 LINCOLN AV
2 LINCOLN VILLAGE DR
3 CUMBERLAND PL
4 ALLENTOWN CT
5 MONITOR CT
6 SHENANDOAH DR
7 SPADAFORE AV
1 DILLWOOD CT
2 SUMMER CREEK DR
1 HONEY SUCKLE LN

SEE 853 MAP

SEE 874 MAP

SEE 834 MAP

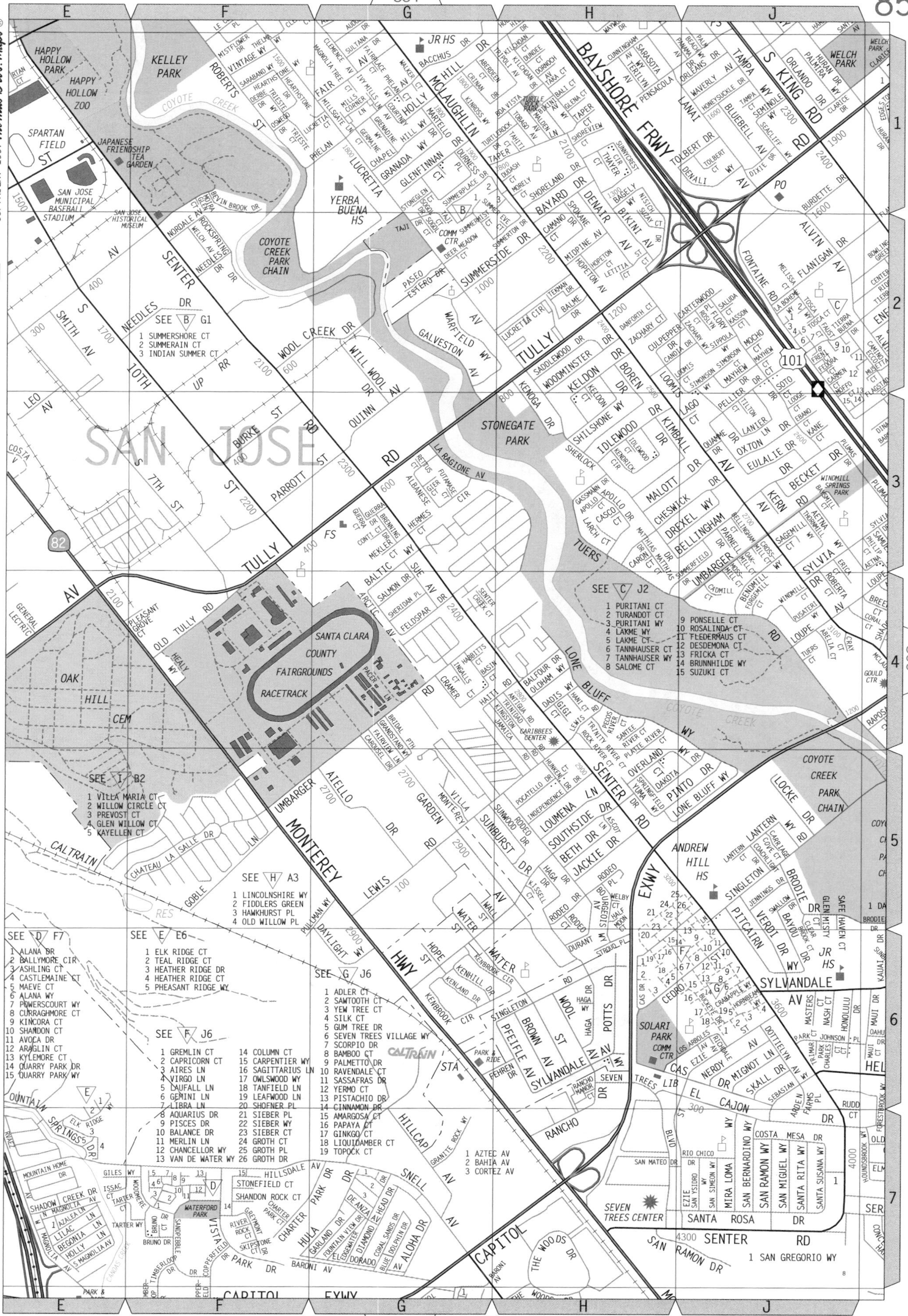
E F G H J
SAN JOSE
HAPPY HOLLOW PARK
HAPPY HOLLOW ZOO
KELLEY PARK
COYOTE CREEK
SPARTAN FIELD
JAPANESE FRIENDSHIP TEA GARDEN
SAN JOSE MUNICIPAL BASEBALL STADIUM
SAN JOSE HISTORICAL MUSEUM
COYOTE CREEK PARK CHAIN
YERBA BUENA HS
JR HS
COMM CTR
BAYSHORE FRWY
S KING RD
WELCH PARK
PO
TULLY RD
SENTER RD
MONTEREY HWY
STONEGATE PARK
SANTA CLARA COUNTY FAIRGROUNDS
RACETRACK
OAK HILL CEM
CALTRAIN
ANDREW HILL HS
SOLARI PARK COMM CTR
SEVEN TREES CENTER
SEVEN TREES LIB
CAPITOL EXWY
WATERFORD PARK
WINDMILL SPRINGS PARK
GARIBBEES CENTER
GOULD CTR
FS
STA
PARK & RIDE
SEE B G1
1 SUMMERSHORE CT
2 SUMMERAIN CT
3 INDIAN SUMMER CT
SEE C J2
1 PURITANI CT
2 TURANDOT CT
3 PURITANI WY
4 LAKME WY
5 LAKME CT
6 TANNHAUSER CT
7 TANNHAUSER WY
8 SALOME CT
9 PONSELLE CT
10 ROSALINDA CT
11 FLEDERMAUS CT
12 DESDEMONA CT
13 FRICKA CT
14 BRUNNHILDE WY
15 SUZUKI CT
SEE I B2
1 VILLA MARIA CT
2 WILLOW CIRCLE CT
3 PREVOST CT
4 GLEN WILLOW CT
5 KAYELLEN CT
SEE H A3
1 LINCOLNSHIRE WY
2 FIDDLERS GREEN
3 HAWKHURST PL
4 OLD WILLOW PL
SEE D F7
1 ALANA DR
2 BALLYMORE CIR
3 ASHLING CT
4 CASTLEMAINE CT
5 MAEVE CT
6 ALANA WY
7 POWERSCOURT WY
8 CURRAGHMORE CT
9 KINCORA CT
10 SHANDON CT
11 AVOCA DR
12 ARAGLIN CT
13 KYLEMORE CT
14 QUARRY PARK DR
15 QUARRY PARK WY
SEE E E6
1 ELK RIDGE CT
2 TEAL RIDGE CT
3 HEATHER RIDGE DR
4 HEATHER RIDGE CT
5 PHEASANT RIDGE WY
SEE G J6
1 ADLER CT
2 SAWTOOTH CT
3 YEW TREE CT
4 SILK CT
5 GUM TREE DR
6 SEVEN TREES VILLAGE WY
7 SCORPIO DR
8 BAMBOO CT
9 PALMETTO DR
10 RAVENDALE CT
11 SASSAFRAS DR
12 YERMO CT
13 PISTACHIO DR
14 CINNAMON DR
15 AMARGOSA CT
16 PAPAYA CT
17 GINKGO CT
18 LIQUIDAMBER CT
19 TOPOCK CT
SEE F J6
1 GREMLIN CT
2 CAPRICORN CT
3 AIRES LN
4 VIRGO LN
5 LAUFALL LN
6 GEMINI LN
7 LIBRA LN
8 AQUARIUS DR
9 PISCES DR
10 BALANCE DR
11 MERLIN LN
12 CHANCELLOR WY
13 VAN DE WATER WY
14 COLUMN CT
15 CARPENTIER WY
16 SAGITTARIUS LN
17 OWLSWOOD WY
18 TANFIELD LN
19 LEAFWOOD LN
20 SHOFNER PL
21 SIEBER PL
22 SIEBER WY
23 SIEBER CT
24 GROTH CT
25 GROTH PL
26 GROTH DR
1 AZTEC AV
2 BAHIA AV
3 CORTEZ AV
1 SAN GREGORIO WY
SEE 855 MAP

SEE 874 MAP

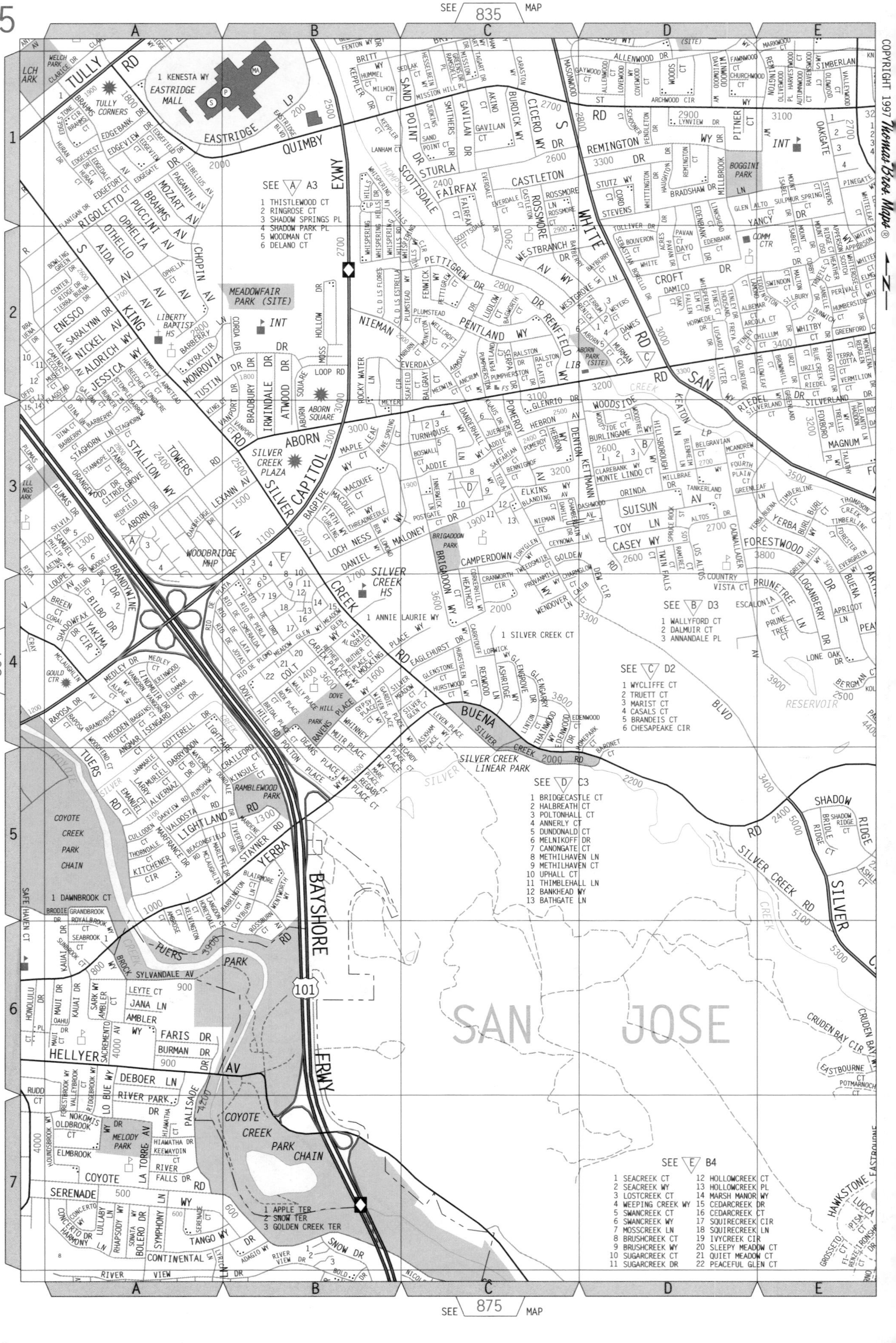
SEE 835 MAP
SEE 875 MAP
SEE 854 MAP
COPYRIGHT 1997 Thomas Bros. Maps ®
SAN JOSE
EASTRIDGE MALL
1 KENESTA WY
TULLY CORNERS
MEADOWFAIR PARK (SITE)
LIBERTY BAPTIST HS
SILVER CREEK PLAZA
WOODBRIDGE MHP
SILVER CREEK HS
BRIGADOON PARK
ABORN PARK (SITE)
ABORN SQUARE
BOGGINI PARK
COMM CTR
SILVER CREEK LINEAR PARK
RAMBLEWOOD PARK
COYOTE CREEK PARK CHAIN
MELODY PARK
RESERVOIR
GOULD CTR
TULLY RD
QUIMBY RD
CAPITOL EXWY
ABORN RD
SILVER CREEK RD
WHITE RD
SAN FELIPE RD
BAYSHORE FRWY
YERBA BUENA RD
HELLYER AV
101
SEE A A3
1 THISTLEWOOD CT
2 RINGROSE CT
3 SHADOW SPRINGS PL
4 SHADOW PARK PL
5 WOODMAN CT
6 DELANO CT
SEE B D3
1 WALLYFORD CT
2 DALMUIR CT
3 ANNANDALE PL
SEE C D2
1 WYCLIFFE CT
2 TRUETT CT
3 MARIST CT
4 CASALS CT
5 BRANDEIS CT
6 CHESAPEAKE CIR
SEE D C3
1 BRIDGECASTLE CT
2 HALBREATH CT
3 POLTONHALL CT
4 ANNERLY CT
5 DUNDONALD CT
6 MELNIKOFF DR
7 CANONGATE CT
8 METHILHAVEN LN
9 METHILHAVEN CT
10 UPHALL CT
11 THIMBLEHALL LN
12 BANKHEAD WY
13 BATHGATE LN
SEE E B4
1 SEACREEK CT
2 SEACREEK WY
3 LOSTCREEK CT
4 WEEPING CREEK WY
5 SWANCREEK CT
6 SWANCREEK WY
7 MOSSCREEK LN
8 BRUSHCREEK CT
9 BRUSHCREEK WY
10 SUGARCREEK CT
11 SUGARCREEK DR
12 HOLLOWCREEK CT
13 HOLLOWCREEK PL
14 MARSH MANOR WY
15 CEDARCREEK DR
16 CEDARCREEK CT
17 SQUIRECREEK CIR
18 SQUIRECREEK LN
19 IVYCREEK CIR
20 SLEEPY MEADOW CT
21 QUIET MEADOW CT
22 PEACEFUL GLEN CT
1 APPLE TER
2 SNOW TER
3 GOLDEN CREEK TER
1 DAWNBROOK CT
1 ANNIE LAURIE WY
1 SILVER CREEK CT

SEE 835 MAP

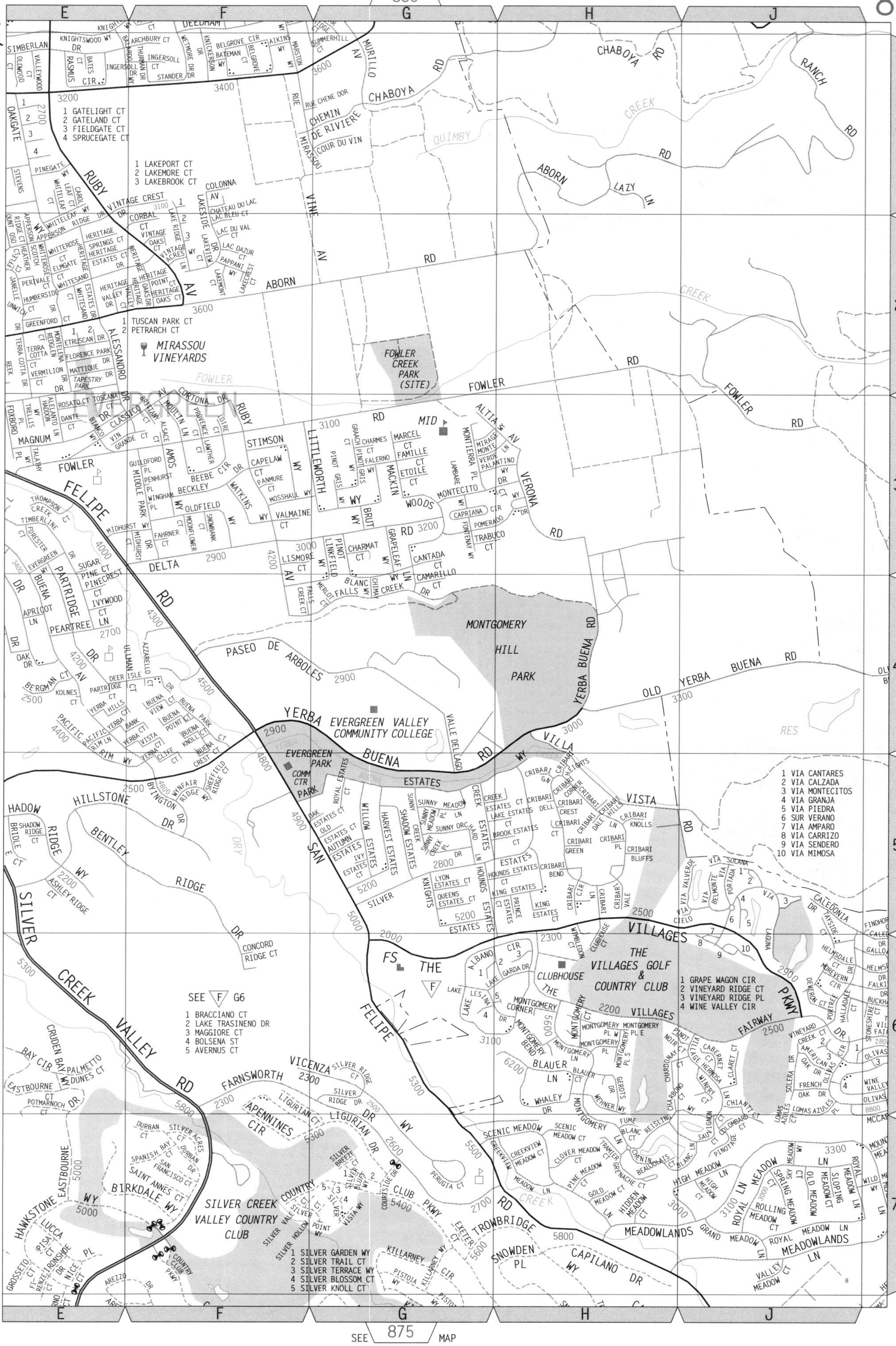
E
F
G
H
J
1
2
3
4
5
6
7
CHABOYA RD
RANCH RD
ABORN RD
LAZY LN
QUIMBY
CREEK
MURILLO AV
VINE AV
RUBY AV
MIRASSOU VINEYARDS
FOWLER CREEK PARK (SITE)
FOWLER RD
MID
VERONA RD
DELTA RD
MONTGOMERY HILL PARK
YERBA BUENA RD
OLD YERBA BUENA RD
RES
EVERGREEN VALLEY COMMUNITY COLLEGE
EVERGREEN PARK
COMM CTR PARK
SAN FELIPE RD
VILLA VISTA RD
HILLSTONE DR
BENTLEY RIDGE DR
SILVER CREEK VALLEY RD
THE VILLAGES PKWY
THE VILLAGES GOLF & COUNTRY CLUB
CLUBHOUSE
FS
FAIRWAY
SILVER CREEK VALLEY COUNTRY CLUB
FARNSWORTH DR
TROWBRIDGE WY
MEADOWLANDS LN
CAPILANO DR
1 GATELIGHT CT
2 GATELAND CT
3 FIELDGATE CT
4 SPRUCEGATE CT
1 LAKEPORT CT
2 LAKEMORE CT
3 LAKEBROOK CT
1 TUSCAN PARK CT
2 PETRARCH CT
1 VIA CANTARES
2 VIA CALZADA
3 VIA MONTECITOS
4 VIA GRANJA
5 VIA PIEDRA
6 SUR VERANO
7 VIA AMPARO
8 VIA CARRIZO
9 VIA SENDERO
10 VIA MIMOSA
1 GRAPE WAGON CIR
2 VINEYARD RIDGE CT
3 VINEYARD RIDGE PL
4 WINE VALLEY CIR
SEE F G6
1 BRACCIANO CT
2 LAKE TRASINENO DR
3 MAGGIORE CT
4 BOLSENA ST
5 AVERNUS CT
1 SILVER GARDEN WY
2 SILVER TRAIL CT
3 SILVER TERRACE WY
4 SILVER BLOSSOM CT
5 SILVER KNOLL CT

SEE 875 MAP

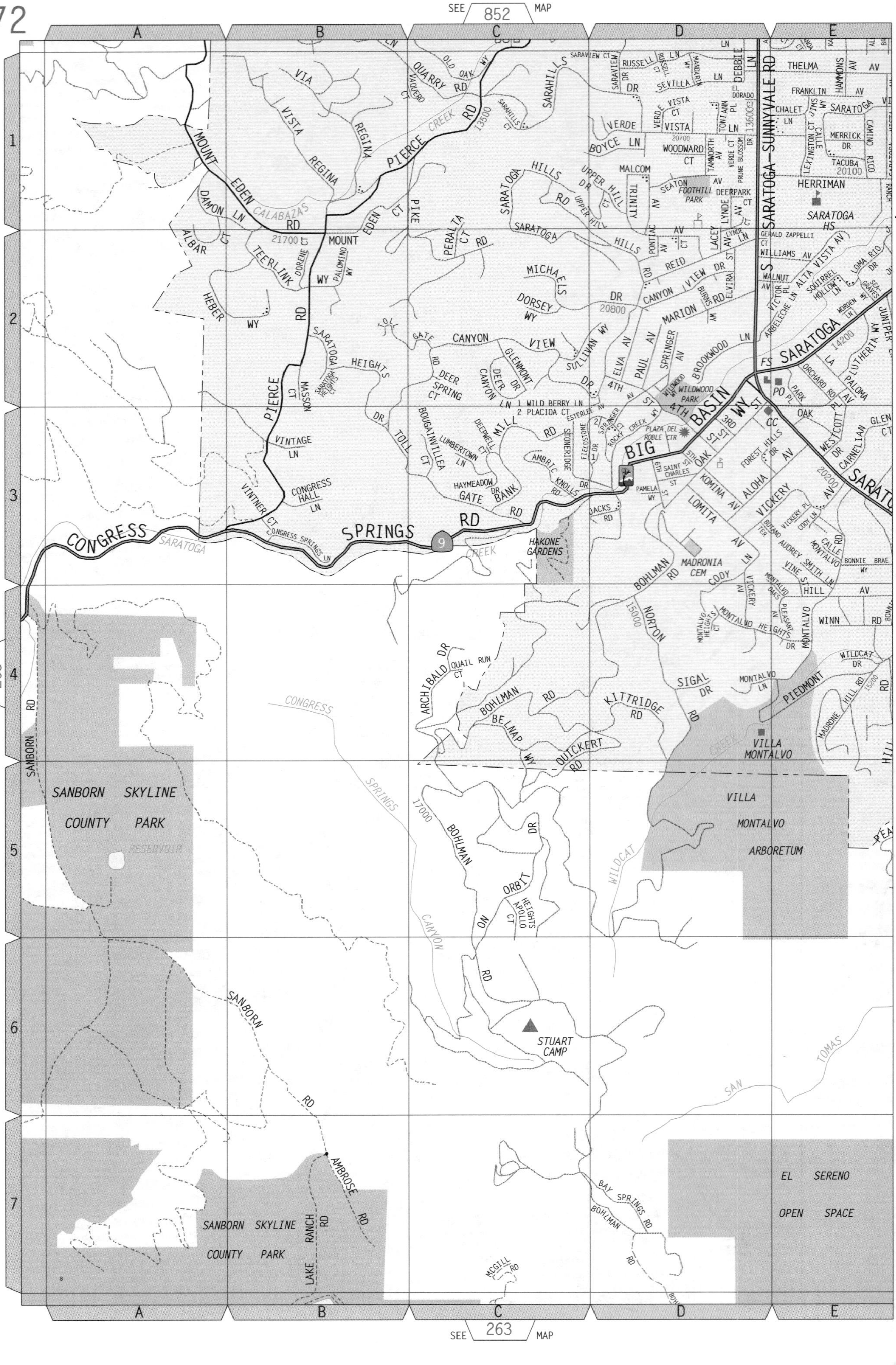
SEE 852 MAP
SEE 263 MAP
SEE 263 MAP
A
B
C
D
E
1
2
3
4
5
6
7
COPYRIGHT 1997 Thomas Bros. Maps ®
MOUNT EDEN RD
PIERCE RD
VIA VISTA
REGINA
QUARRY RD
OLD OAK WY
VAQUERO CT
SARAHILLS
SARAHILLS CT
SARAVIEW CT
RUSSELL LN
SEVILLA
VERDE
VISTA
BOYCE LN
WOODWARD CT
MALCOM
FOOTHILL PARK
SARATOGA HILLS RD
UPPER HILL DR
SARATOGA-SUNNYVALE RD
S SARATOGA-SUNNYVALE RD
THELMA AV
HAMMONS
FRANKLIN AV
CHALET LN
SARATOGA
MERRICK DR
TACUBA
HERRIMAN
SARATOGA HS
DAMON LN
CALABAZAS
ALBAR CT
TEERLINK WY
MOUNT EDEN CT
PIKE
PERALTA CT
HEBER WY
DORENE CT
PALOMINO WY
MICHAELS
DORSEY WY
CANYON VIEW DR
REID
MARION
SARATOGA HEIGHTS DR
TOLL GATE
CANYON VIEW
DEER SPRING CT
DEER CANYON LN
GLENMONT DR
SULLIVAN WY
ELVA AV
PAUL AV
SPRINGER AV
BROOKWOOD LN
WILDWOOD PARK
4TH ST
BIG BASIN WY
SARATOGA
PO
CC
OAK
MASON CT
VINTAGE LN
CONGRESS HALL LN
VINTNER CT
BOUGAINVILLEA CT
LUMBERTOWN LN
DEEPWELL LN
MILL RD
STONERIDGE
HAYMEADOW DR
GATE
BANK
AMBRIC KNOLLS RD
PLAZA DEL ROBLE CTR
CONGRESS SPRINGS RD
SARATOGA CREEK
CONGRESS SPRINGS LN
HAKONE GARDENS
JACKS RD
PAMELA WY
6TH ST
SAINT CHARLES ST
KOMINA AV
ALOHA AV
FOREST HILLS DR
LOMITA AV
VICKERY AV
MADRONIA CEM
BOHLMAN RD
CODY LN
NORTON RD
HILL AV
MONTALVO HEIGHTS DR
MONTALVO RD
WINN RD
SIGAL DR
KITTRIDGE RD
ARCHIBALD DR
QUAIL RUN CT
BELNAP WY
QUICKERT RD
PIEDMONT
WILDCAT DR
MADRONE HILL RD
VILLA MONTALVO
VILLA MONTALVO ARBORETUM
SANBORN RD
SANBORN SKYLINE COUNTY PARK
RESERVOIR
CONGRESS SPRINGS CANYON
BOHLMAN DR
ORBIT DR
APOLLO HEIGHTS CT
ON ORBIT
STUART CAMP
SAN TOMAS
WILDCAT
AMBROSE RD
LAKE RANCH RD
SANBORN SKYLINE COUNTY PARK
BAY SPRINGS RD
BOHLMAN RD
MCGILL RD
EL SERENO OPEN SPACE

SEE 852 MAP

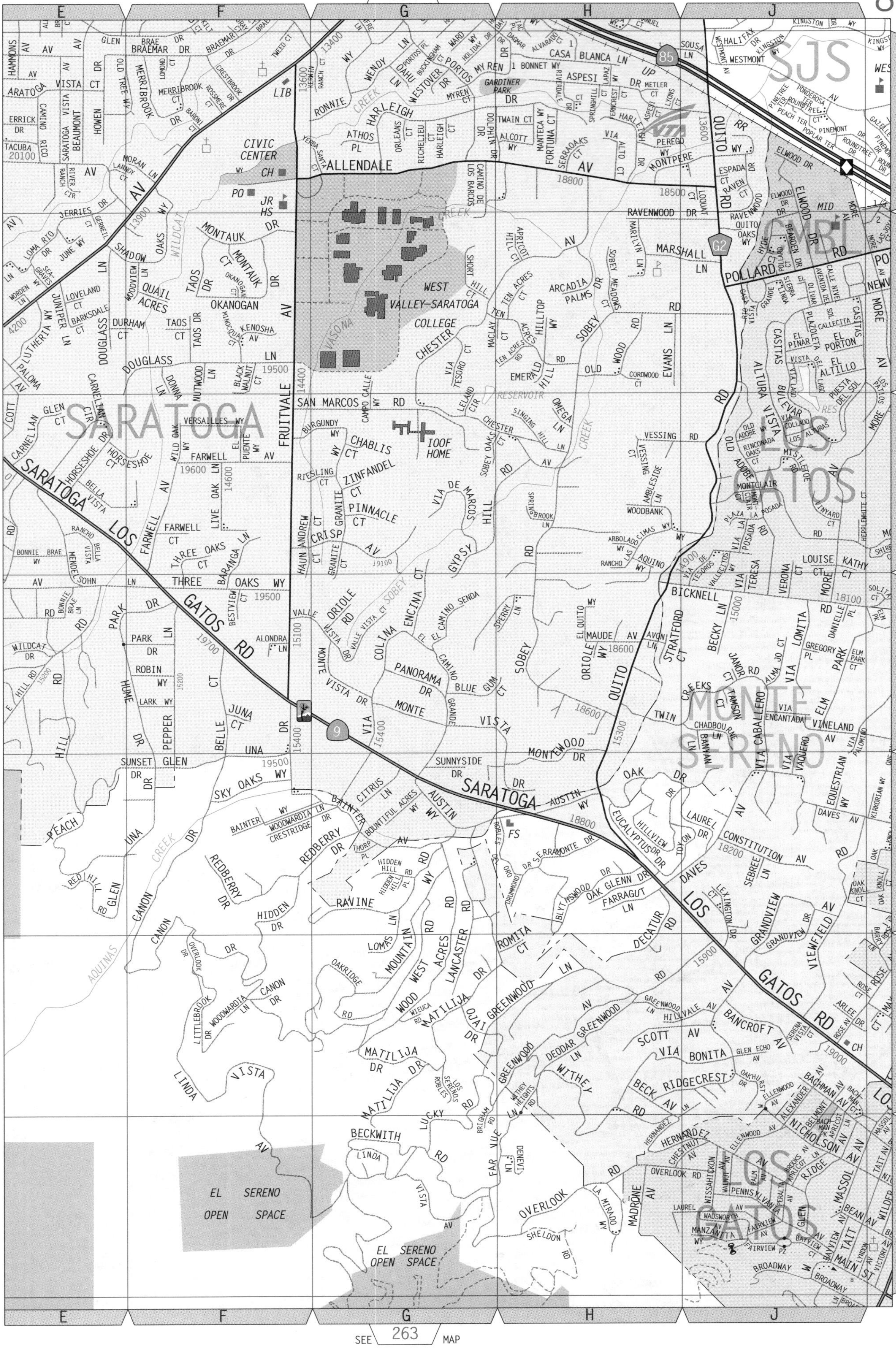
E
F
G
H
J
1
2
3
4
5
6
7
SARATOGA
LOS GATOS
MONTE SERENO
SJS
CMBL
CIVIC CENTER
CH
PO
LIB
JR HS
WEST VALLEY-SARATOGA COLLEGE
IOOF HOME
GARDINER PARK
FS
PZ
EL SERENO OPEN SPACE
EL SERENO OPEN SPACE
ALLENDALE AV
FRUITVALE AV
SARATOGA AV
SARATOGA LOS GATOS RD
LOS GATOS RD
QUITO RD
POLLARD RD
BICKNELL RD
SOBEY RD
CHESTER AV
SAN MARCOS RD
MONTE VISTA DR
MONTEWOOD DR
SARATOGA AV
THREE OAKS WY
DOUGLASS LN
MONTAUK DR
MARSHALL LN
RAVENWOOD DR
HARLEIGH DR
VIA CABALLERO
CONSTITUTION AV
GREENWOOD LN
OVERLOOK RD
BECKWITH
LINDA VISTA AV
MATILIJA DR
BROADWAY
MAIN ST
RESERVOIR
VASONA CREEK
WILDCAT CREEK
SOBEY CREEK
AQUINAS CREEK
85
9
G2

SEE 873 MAP

BAY AREA

MAP

SEE 263 MAP

SEE 853 MAP

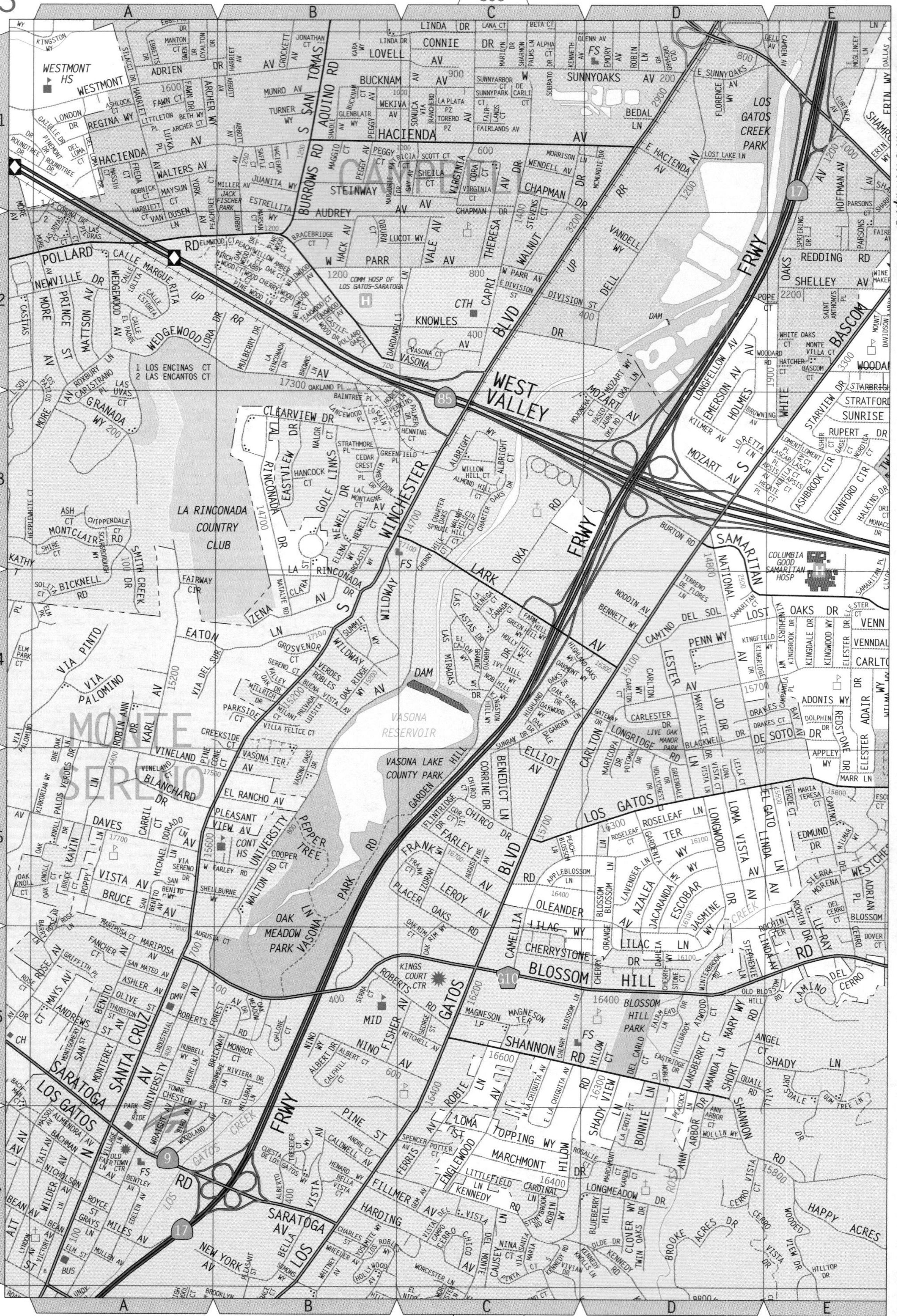

CAMPBELL
MONTE SERENO
WESTMONT HS
LOS GATOS CREEK PARK
LA RINCONADA COUNTRY CLUB
VASONA RESERVOIR
VASONA LAKE COUNTY PARK
OAK MEADOW PARK
BLOSSOM HILL PARK
COMM HOSP OF LOS GATOS-SARATOGA
COLUMBIA GOOD SAMARITAN HOSP
KINGS COURT CTR
WEST VALLEY FRWY
WINCHESTER BLVD
SARATOGA LOS GATOS RD
SANTA CRUZ AV
BLOSSOM HILL RD
LOS GATOS BLVD
HACIENDA AV
POLLARD RD
LARK AV
SAMARITAN DR
SHANNON RD
UNIVERSITY AV
BASCOM AV
DAM
MID
CONT HS
CTH
DMV
FS
BUS
PARK & RIDE
OLD TOWN CTR

SEE 872 MAP

SEE 893 MAP

SEE 853 MAP

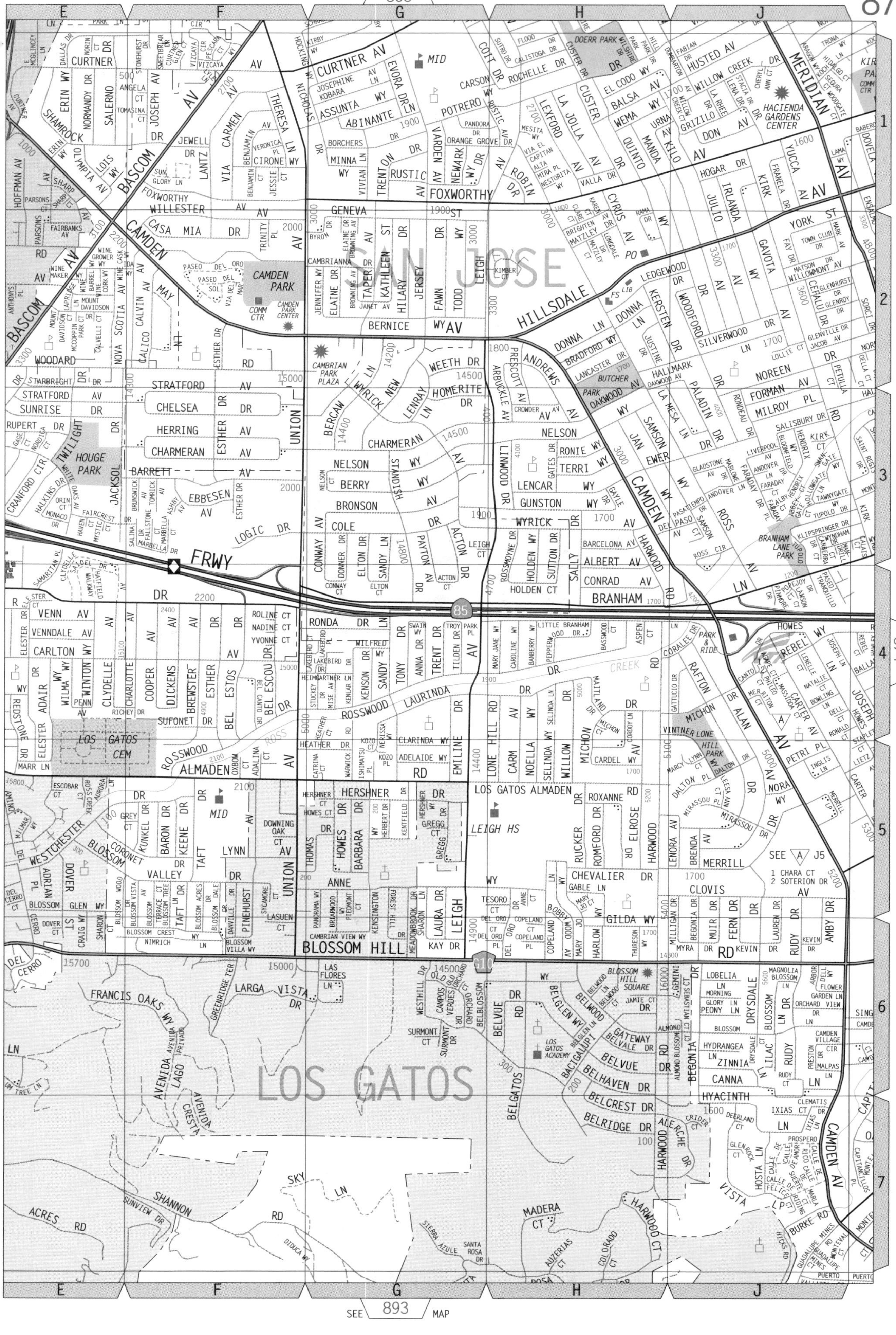
E
F
G
H
J
1
2
3
4
5
6
7
SAN JOSE
LOS GATOS
CURTNER AV
MERIDIAN AV
BASCOM AV
CAMDEN AV
HILLSDALE AV
FOXWORTHY AV
UNION AV
BRANHAM LN
ALMADEN RD
BLOSSOM HILL RD
CAMDEN PARK
HOUGE PARK
LOS GATOS CEM
DOERR PARK
HACIENDA GARDENS CENTER
CAMBRIAN PARK PLAZA
BUTCHER PARK
BRANHAM LANE PARK
VINTNER LONE HILL PARK
BLOSSOM HILL SQUARE
LEIGH HS
LOS GATOS ACADEMY
LEIGH AV
SHANNON RD
SKY LN
HARWOOD RD
FRWY
85
G10
SEE A J5
1 CHARA CT
2 SOTERION DR

SEE 874 MAP

SEE 893 MAP

SEE 854 MAP

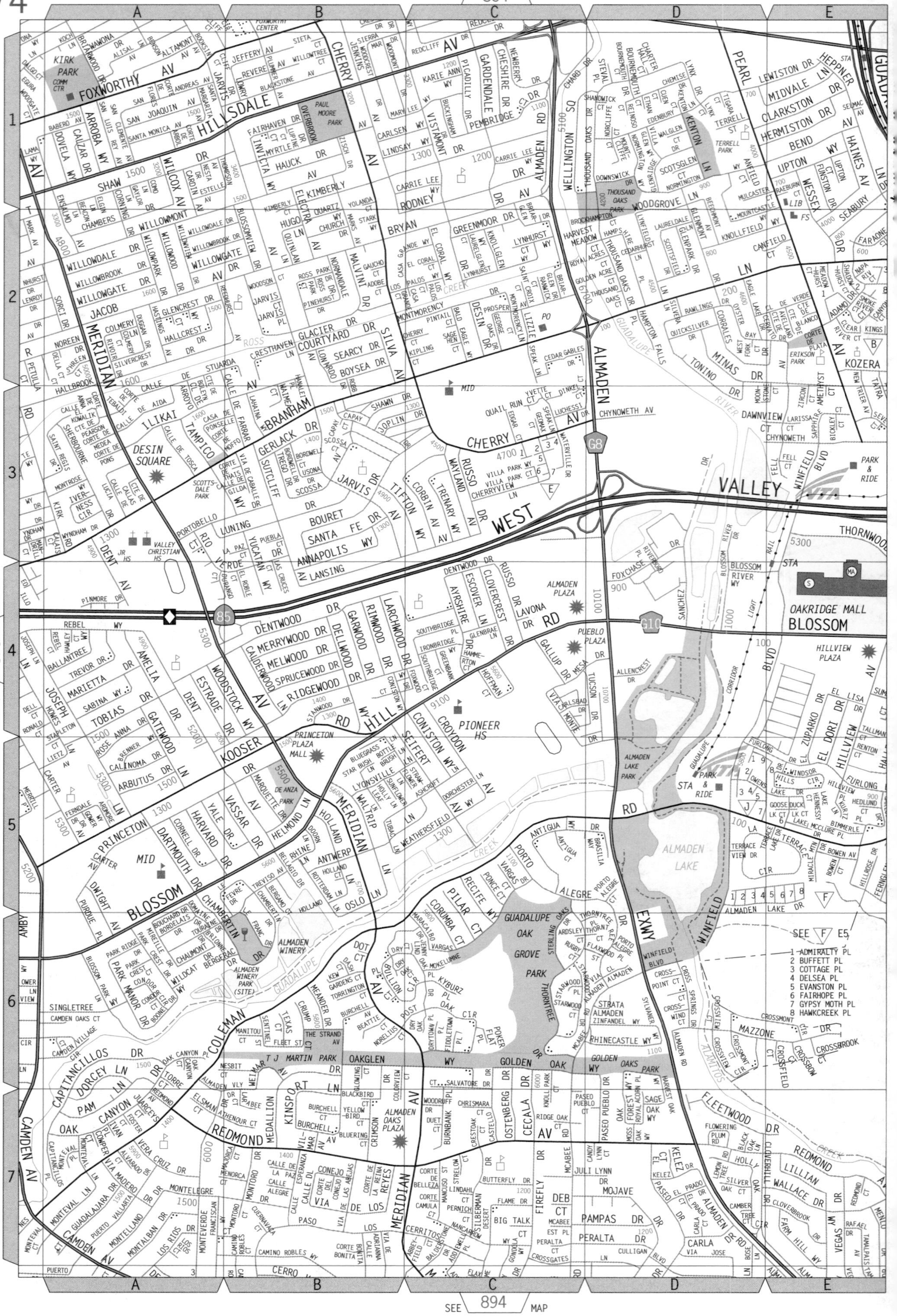
A
B
C
D
E
1
2
3
4
5
6
7
HILLSDALE
FOXWORTHY
CHERRY
ALMADEN
MERIDIAN
BRANHAM
WEST
VALLEY
BLOSSOM
OAKRIDGE MALL
HILLVIEW PLAZA
PIONEER HS
PRINCETON PLAZA MALL
KOOSER
ALMADEN LAKE
ALMADEN LAKE PARK
GUADALUPE OAK GROVE PARK
T J MARTIN PARK
OAKGLEN
GOLDEN OAK
REDMOND
CAMDEN AV
COLEMAN
ALMADEN EXWY
ALMADEN WINERY
ALMADEN OAKS PLAZA
DESIN SQUARE
ALMADEN PLAZA
PUEBLO PLAZA
VALLEY CHRISTIAN HS
KIRK PARK
PAUL MOORE PARK
THOUSAND OAKS PARK
TERRELL PARK
DE ANZA PARK
GUADALUPE RIVER
WINFIELD BLVD
CAPITANCILLOS
MERIDIAN AV
SEE F E5
1 ADMIRALTY PL
2 BUFFETT PL
3 COTTAGE PL
4 DELSEA PL
5 EVANSTON PL
6 FAIRHOPE PL
7 GYPSY MOTH PL
8 HAWKCREEK PL

SEE 873 MAP

SEE 894 MAP

SEE 854 MAP

CAPITOL EXWY
GUADALUPE
MONTEREY HWY
SNELL AV
BRANHAM LN
CHYNOWETH AV
FRWY 85
HILL RD
SANTA TERESA BLVD
BLOSSOM HILL RD
SAN JOSE
MALL
GUNDERSON HS
SANTA TERESA HS
SUNRISE PLAZA
DOWNER SQUARE
SANTA TERESA SQUARE
FOOTHILL PARK
VISTA PARK
COMANCHE PARK
PARKVIEW 3 PARK
DANNA ROCK PARK
COY PARK
PLAYA DEL REY PARK
PEARLWOOD PARK
MEADOWS PARK
SEE B E2
1 COLUMBIA RIVER CT
2 BLACK RIVER CT
3 CAPITOL REEF CT
4 POWDERBORN CT N
5 POWDERBORN CT S
6 PINTO RIVER CT
7 DURANGO RIVER CT
8 NOYO RIVER CT
9 JOSEPH SPECIALE DR
SEE C G3
1 DON CORRELLI CT
2 DON CORRELLI WY
3 DON MATEO CT
4 DON EDMONDO CT
5 DON DIABLO CT
6 DON RODOLFO CT
7 DON EDGARDO CT
8 DON MARCO CT
9 DON DIEGO CT
SEE D J2
1 PATH WY
2 SADDLE BROOK DR
3 FRONTIER TRAIL DR
4 CANYON TRAIL WY
5 PONY PASS CIR
6 BROKEN ARROW DR
7 BEAR CLAW WY
8 INDIAN RIVER DR
9 LITTLE BEAR WY
10 SADDLE TREE CT
11 RAINDANCE CT
12 ARCHBOW CT
13 INDIAN RIVER CT
14 LOST TRAIL CT
15 RIVER TRAIL CT
SEE E C3
1 ROBERTSVILLE CT
2 ILLIAD CT
3 ODYSSEY CT
4 CLAYCOMB CT
5 MARLENE CT
6 VILLA PARK LN
7 NORMA JEAN WY
SEE G H3
1 DON ANDRES WY
2 DON BASILLO CT
3 DON BASILLO WY
4 DON ALFONSO CT
5 DON ALFONSO WY
6 DON PEDRO CT
7 DON GIOVANNI CT
8 DON FERNANDO WY
9 DON SEVILLE CT
10 DON CARLOS CT
11 DON ANDRES CT
12 DON PIZARRO CT
13 DON MARCELLO CT
14 DON MANRICO CT
15 DON DEL MONICO CT
16 DON ENRICO CT
17 DON OCTAVIO CT
18 DON RICARDO CT
19 DON SCALA CT
SEE H J4
1 CARERA CT
2 ISDLIO CT
3 SEAN CT
4 KANDICE CT
5 DUSTIN CT
6 OCCIDENTAL CT
7 HESTIN CT
8 RALT CT
9 DUNIGAN CT
10 WALSH CT
11 FRAN CT
12 BRINDOS CT
SEE I J3
1 MACAW PL
2 MACAW WY
3 MACAW LN
4 BANANA GROVE LN
5 HEAVENLY VALLEY CT
6 JACANA LN
7 PELICAN CT
8 OSTRICH CT
9 MYNA CT
10 JACANA CT
11 CENTERHART CT
12 PEACH GROVE CT
13 PLUM GROVE CT
14 PERSIMMON GROVE CT
15 PISTACHIO GROVE CT
16 TEAK GROVE CT
17 MAPLE GROVE CT
SEE K F4
1 BRIAR RIDGE DR
2 BIRCH RIDGE CIR
3 PALM RIDGE LN
4 SUN RIDGE LN
5 WIND RIDGE LN
6 ROSE RIDGE LN
7 RUSTIC RIDGE CIR
8 DEER RIDGE CIR
SEE J D5
1 LAKE CROWLEY PL
2 MONO LAKE CT
3 BRIDGEPORT LAKE DR
4 LAKE SHASTA CT
5 LAKE TAHOE CT
6 EASTMAN LAKE DR
7 LAKE MANOR DR
8 LAKE ALMANOR DR
9 LAKE ISABELLA WY
SEE A G1
1 MEADOWSIDE CT
2 GOLDEN LEAF CT
3 SHADOW WOOD CT
4 BARONI GREEN DR

SEE 875 MAP

SEE 894 MAP

BAY AREA

MAP

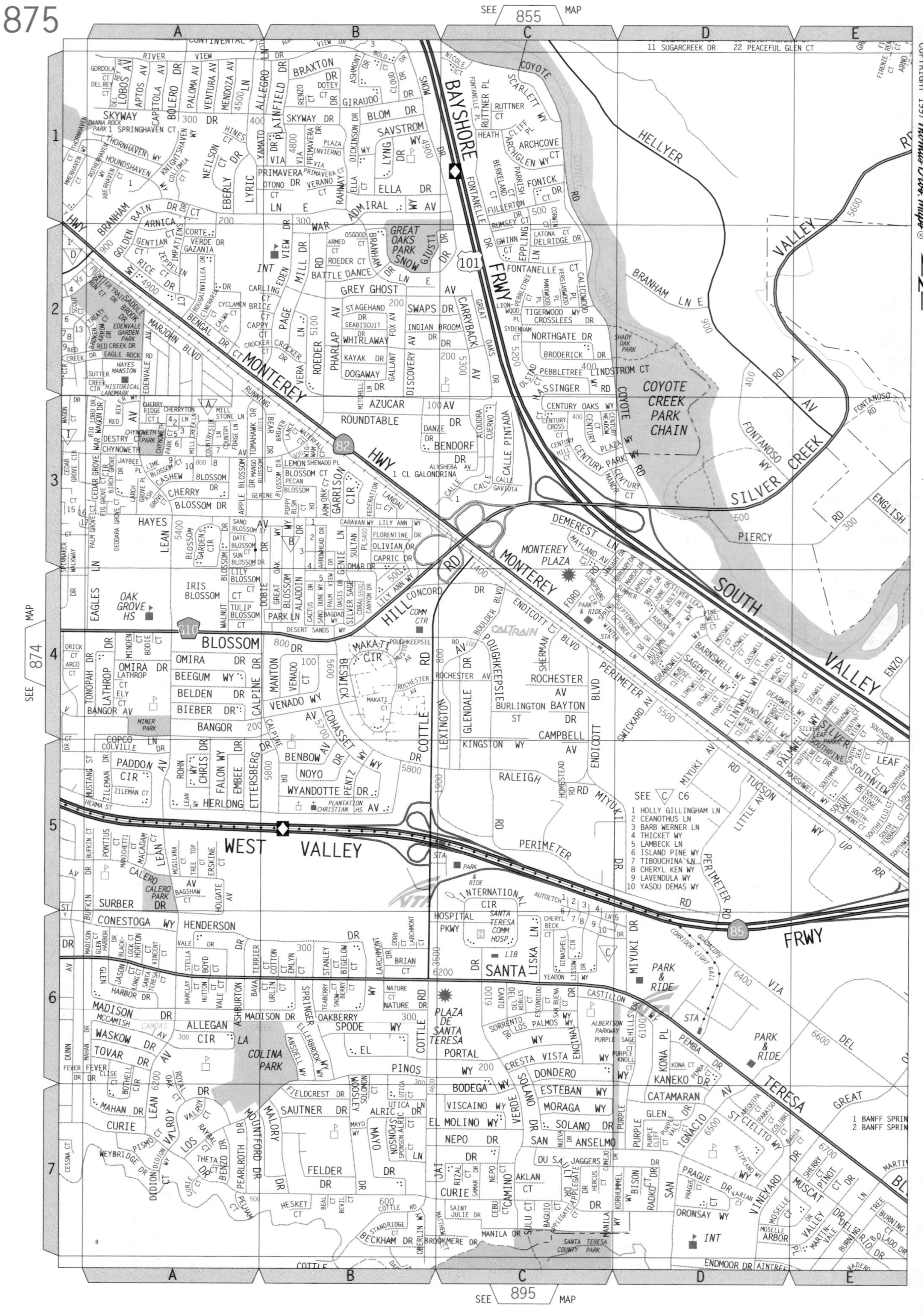
SEE 855 MAP
SEE 874 MAP
SEE 895 MAP
A
B
C
D
E
1
2
3
4
5
6
7
BAYSHORE FRWY
101
MONTEREY HWY
82
BLOSSOM HILL RD
610
WEST VALLEY FRWY
85
SANTA TERESA BLVD
SOUTH VALLEY FRWY
SILVER CREEK VALLEY RD
HELLYER AV
COYOTE CREEK PARK CHAIN
GREAT OAKS PARK SNOW
MONTEREY PLAZA
OAK GROVE HS
PLAZA DE SANTA TERESA
LA COLINA PARK
MINER PARK
CALERO PARK
SANTA TERESA COUNTY PARK
EDENVALE GARDEN PARK
HAYES MANSION HISTORICAL LANDMARK
SHADY OAK PARK
PLANTATION CHRISTIAN HS
SANTA TERESA COMM HOSP
HOSPITAL PKWY
INTERNATIONAL CIR
CALTRAIN
PARK & RIDE
BRANHAM LN
BRANHAM LN E
SKYWAY DR
SANTA TERESA
CONESTOGA WY
HENDERSON
COTTLE RD
SAN IGNACIO AV
GUADALUPE CORRIDOR LIGHT RAIL
SEE C C6
1 HOLLY GILLINGHAM LN
2 CEANOTHUS LN
3 BARB WERNER LN
4 THICKET WY
5 LAMBECK LN
6 ISLAND PINE WY
7 TIBOUCHINA LN
8 CHERYL KEN WY
9 LAVENDULA WY
10 YASOU DEMAS WY
11 SUGARCREEK DR
22 PEACEFUL GLEN CT
1 BANFF SPRIN
2 BANFF SPRIN
COPYRIGHT 1997

SEE 855 MAP

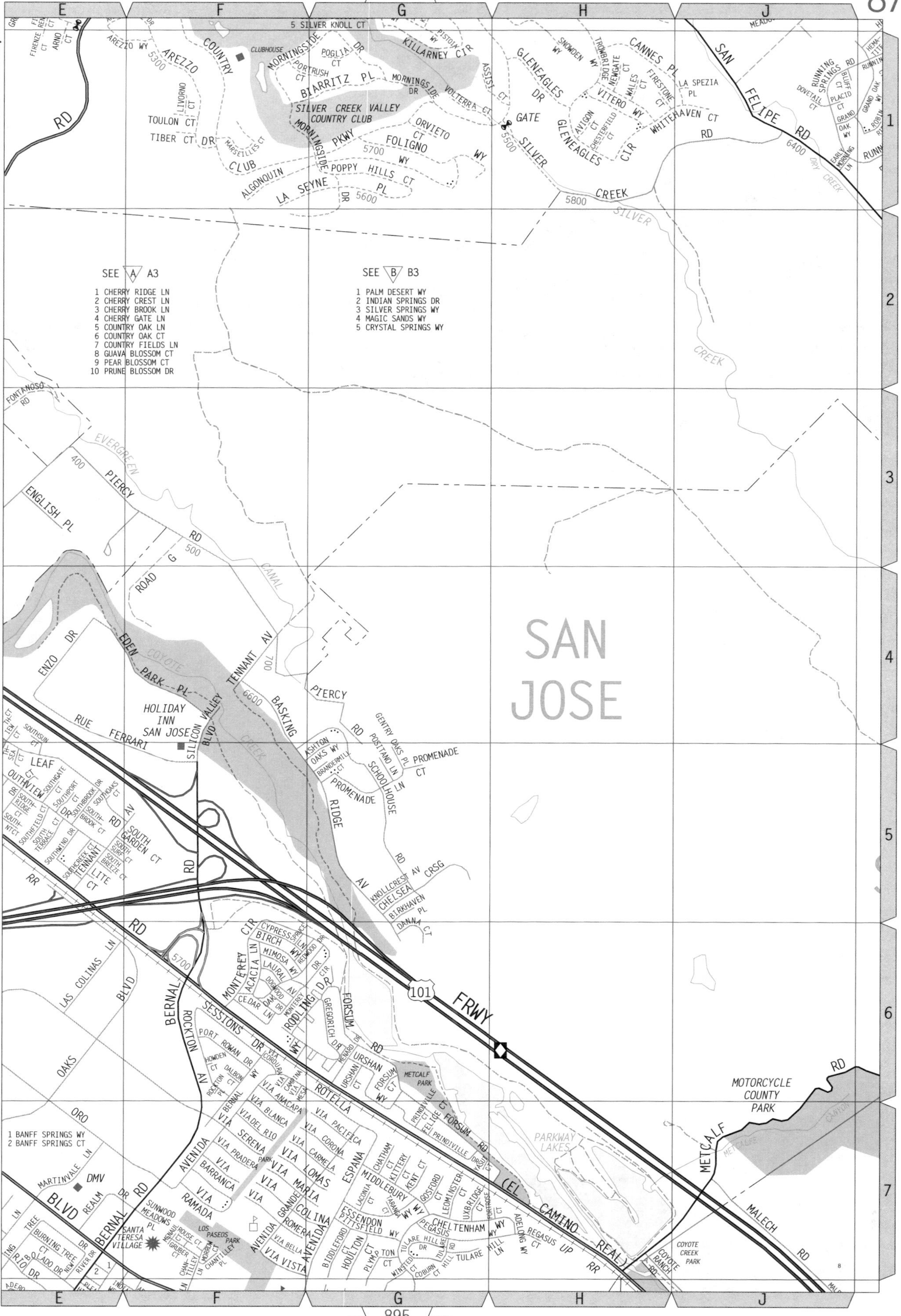
E F G H J
1 2 3 4 5 6 7
5 SILVER KNOLL CT
KILLARNEY CIR
SAN FELIPE RD
SILVER CREEK VALLEY COUNTRY CLUB
CLUBHOUSE
COUNTRY CLUB DR
AREZZO WY
MORNINGSIDE DR
BIARRITZ PL
POGLIA DR
PORTRUSH CT
VOLTERRA CT
GLENEAGLES DR
SILVER GATE
GLENEAGLES CIR
VITERO WY
CANNES PL
WHITEHAVEN CT
LA SPEZIA PL
FIRESTONE CT
TROWBRIDGE
NEWGATE CT
WALES CT
AVIGON CT
CHESTERFIELD CT
SNOWDEN WY
ASSISI CT
ORVIETO CT
FOLIGNO WY
POPPY HILLS CT
LA SEYNE PL
ALGONQUIN
TOULON CT
TIBER CT
LIVORNO CT
MARSEILLES CT
SILVER CREEK RD
RUNNING SPRINGS
DOVETAIL CT
PLACID CT
GRAND OAK WY
EARLY MORNING LN
SEE A A3
1 CHERRY RIDGE LN
2 CHERRY CREST LN
3 CHERRY BROOK LN
4 CHERRY GATE LN
5 COUNTRY OAK LN
6 COUNTRY OAK CT
7 COUNTRY FIELDS LN
8 GUAVA BLOSSOM CT
9 PEAR BLOSSOM CT
10 PRUNE BLOSSOM DR
SEE B B3
1 PALM DESERT WY
2 INDIAN SPRINGS DR
3 SILVER SPRINGS WY
4 MAGIC SANDS WY
5 CRYSTAL SPRINGS WY
CREEK
FONTANOSO RD
EVERGREEN
PIERCY RD
ENGLISH PL
CANAL
ROAD G
ENZO DR
EDEN PARK PL
COYOTE CREEK
TENNANT AV
BASKING RIDGE AV
PIERCY RD
HOLIDAY INN SAN JOSE
RUE FERRARI
SILICON VALLEY BLVD
SAN JOSE
GENTRY OAKS PL
POSITANO LN
SCHOOLHOUSE LN
PROMENADE CT
ASHTON OAKS WY
BRANDERMILL CT
PROMENADE
KNOLLCREST AV
CHELSEA
BIRKHAVEN PL
DANNA CT
CRSG
LEAF
SOUTH GARDEN CT
TENNANT
LITE CT
RR
RD
CYPRESS
BIRCH
MIMOSA WY
LAUREL
ACACIA LN
MONTEREY CIR
DOGWOOD
CEDAR LN
RODLING DR
GREGORICH DR
FORSUM RD
101
FRWY
LAS COLINAS LN
BLVD
BERNAL RD
ROCKTON AV
SESSIONS DR
PORT ROWAN DR
OAKS
ORO
1 BANFF SPRINGS WY
2 BANFF SPRINGS CT
MARTINVALE LN
DMV
BLVD
REALM DR
SANTA TERESA VILLAGE
SUNWOOD MEADOWS PL
LOS PASEOS PARK
AVENIDA RAMADA
VIA BLANCA
VIA ANACAPA
VIA SERENA
VIA PRADERA
VIA BARRANCA
VIA MARIA
VIA LOMAS
VIA COLINA
VIA ROMERA
VIA BELLA
VIA VISTA
VIA PACIFICA
VIA CORONA
VIA CARMELA
ROTELLA
URSHAN
METCALF PARK
FORSUM CT
ESPANA
CHATHAM CT
KITTERY CT
KENT CT
MIDDLEBURY WY
GOSFORD CT
LEOMINSTER CT
UXBRIDGE
ESSENDON CT
PITTSFIELD WY
CHELTENHAM WY
TULARE HILL DR
TULARE
HOULTON CT
BIDDLEFORD
WINSTED CT
COBURN CT
ADELONG WY
REGASUS CT
PRINDIVILLE CT
PARKWAY LAKES
EL CAMINO REAL
UP RR
MOTORCYCLE COUNTY PARK
METCALF RD
MALECH RD
COYOTE CREEK PARK
COYOTE RANCH RD

SEE 895 MAP

SEE 873 MAP

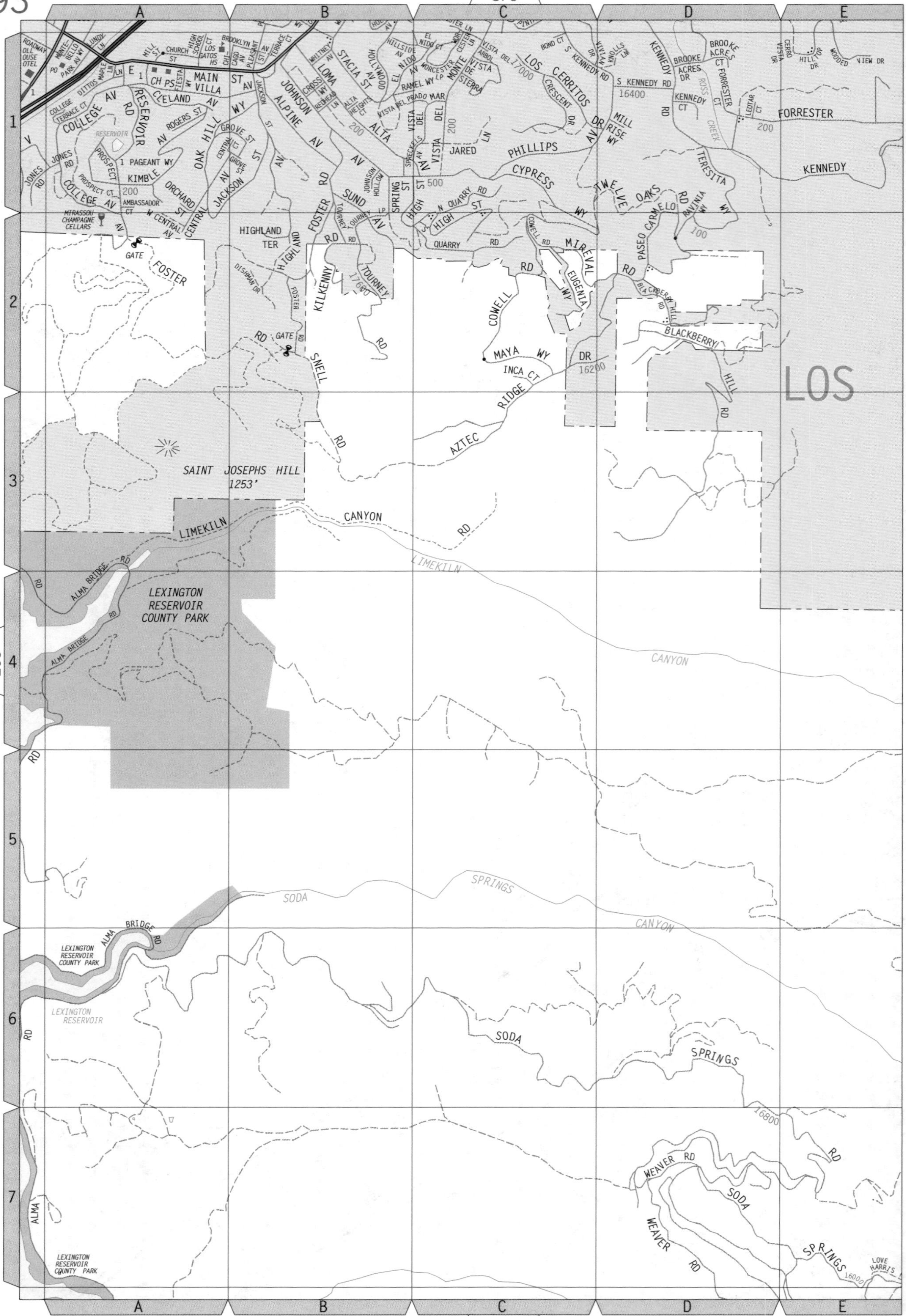

A
B
C
D
E
1
2
3
4
5
6
7
MAIN ST
VILLA AV
COLLEGE AV
RESERVOIR RD
CLELAND AV
ROGERS ST
OAK HILL WY
JOHNSON AV
ALPINE AV
LOMA ALTA AV
STACIA ST
HOLLYWOOD AV
EL NIDO
VISTA DEL MONTE
LOS CERRITOS DR
S KENNEDY RD
KENNEDY RD
BROOKE ACRES DR
FORRESTER RD
KENNEDY
PHILLIPS AV
CYPRESS WY
JARED LN
TWELVE OAKS
TERESITA WY
PASEO CARMELO
RAVINIA
MIREVAL RD
EUGENIA WY
COWELL
MAYA WY
INCA CT
RIDGE DR
AZTEC
BLACKBERRY HILL RD
LOS
HIGHLAND TER
FOSTER RD
KILKENNY
TOURNEY
SUND AV
SPRING ST
HIGH ST
N QUARRY RD
QUARRY RD
GATE
SNELL RD
MIRASSOU CHAMPAGNE CELLARS
SAINT JOSEPHS HILL 1253'
LIMEKILN CANYON RD
ALMA BRIDGE RD
LEXINGTON RESERVOIR COUNTY PARK
LEXINGTON RESERVOIR
SODA SPRINGS CANYON
SODA SPRINGS RD
WEAVER RD
ALMA
LOVE HARRIS
SEE 263 MAP

SEE 263 MAP

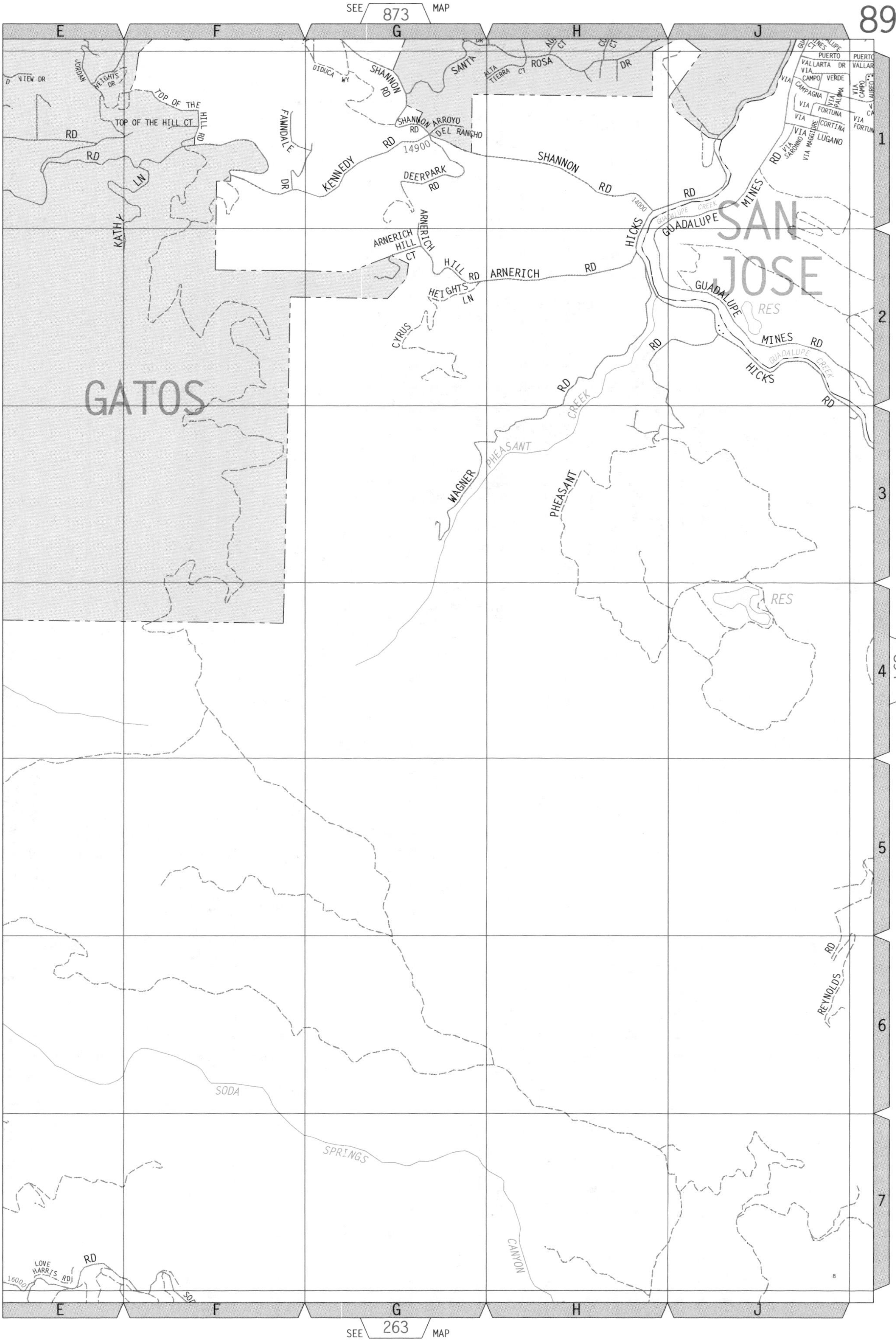
SEE 873 MAP
E
F
G
H
J
1
2
3
4
5
6
7
SEE 894 MAP
SEE 263 MAP
GATOS
SAN JOSE
SHANNON RD
SANTA ROSA DR
ALTA TIERRA CT
DIDUCA WY
FAWNDALE DR
TOP OF THE HILL RD
TOP OF THE HILL CT
HEIGHTS DR
JORDAN
VIEW DR
KATHY LN
KENNEDY RD
SHANNON RD
ARROYO DEL RANCHO
14900
DEERPARK RD
ARNERICH HILL CT
ARNERICH HILL RD
ARNERICH RD
HEIGHTS LN
CYRUS
HICKS RD
14000
GUADALUPE MINES RD
GUADALUPE CREEK
RES
WAGNER RD
PHEASANT CREEK
PHEASANT
VALLARTA DR
PUERTO
VIA CAMPAGNA
VIA VERDE
VIA PALOMA
VIA FORTUNA
VIA CORTINA
VIA LUGANO
VIA SARONNO
VIA MAGGIORE
VIA CAMPO AUREO
REYNOLDS RD
SODA SPRINGS CANYON
LOVE HARRIS RD
16000

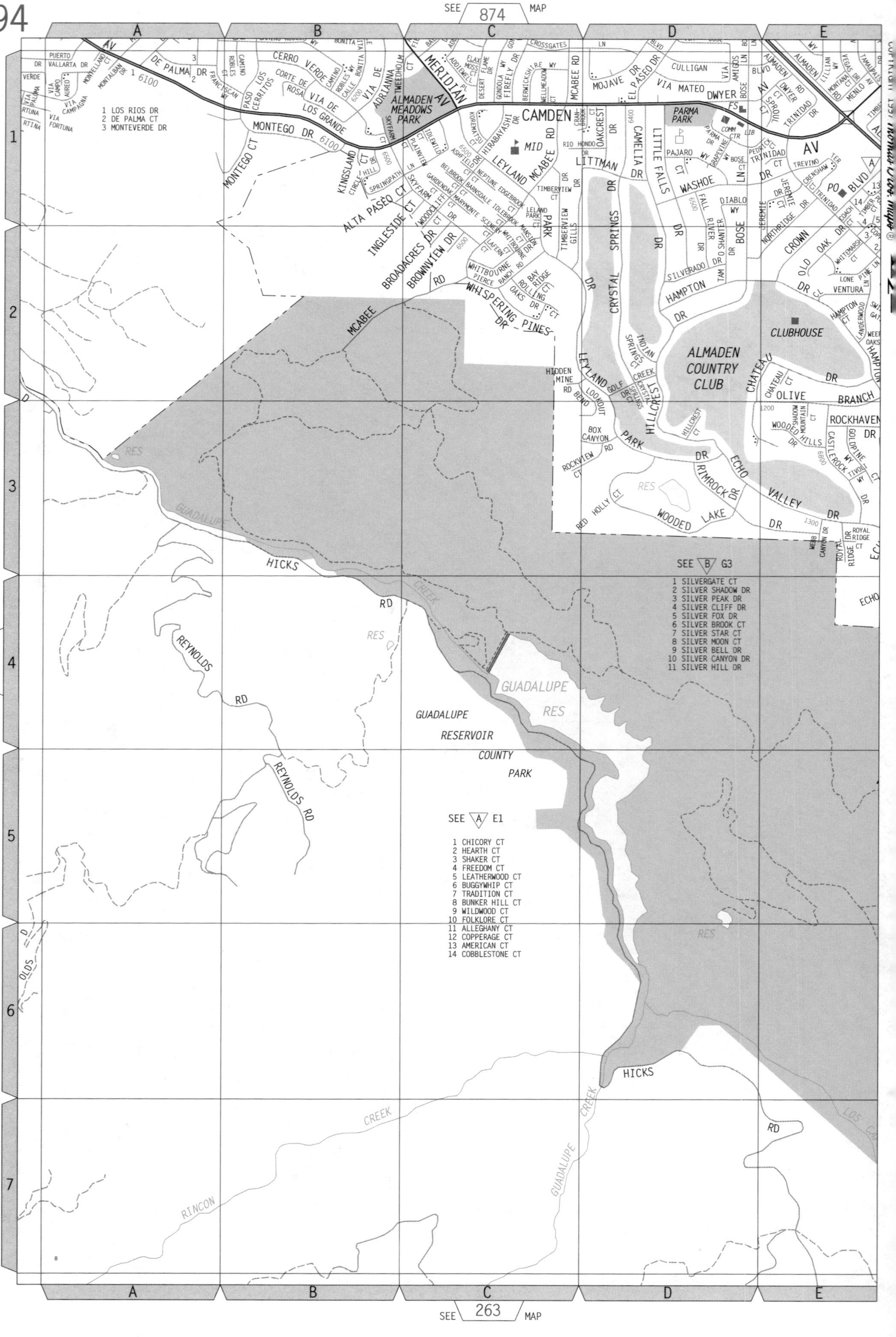
SEE 874 MAP
SEE 893 MAP
SEE 263 MAP
A
B
C
D
E
1
2
3
4
5
6
7
CAMDEN AV
MERIDIAN AV
ALMADEN MEADOWS PARK
PARMA PARK
ALMADEN COUNTRY CLUB
CLUBHOUSE
MID
DE PALMA DR
CERRO VERDE
MONTEGO DR
VIA DE LOS GRANDE
LEYLAND PARK DR
MCABEE RD
CRYSTAL SPRINGS DR
CAMELIA DR
LITTLE FALLS DR
LITTMAN DR
WASHOE DR
HAMPTON DR
CROWN
OLIVE BRANCH
ROCKHAVEN
ECHO VALLEY DR
RIMROCK DR
WOODED LAKE DR
WHISPERING PINES DR
BROADACRES DR
BROWNVIEW DR
INGLESIDE CT
ALTA PASEO CT
KINGSLAND CT
MONTEGO CT
VIA MATEO
DWYER
MOJAVE DR
EL PASEO DR
CULLIGAN
TRINIDAD
PO BLVD
ALMADEN BLVD
1 LOS RIOS DR
2 DE PALMA CT
3 MONTEVERDE DR
SEE B G3
1 SILVERGATE CT
2 SILVER SHADOW DR
3 SILVER PEAK DR
4 SILVER CLIFF DR
5 SILVER FOX DR
6 SILVER BROOK CT
7 SILVER STAR CT
8 SILVER MOON CT
9 SILVER BELL DR
10 SILVER CANYON DR
11 SILVER HILL DR
SEE A E1
1 CHICORY CT
2 HEARTH CT
3 SHAKER CT
4 FREEDOM CT
5 LEATHERWOOD CT
6 BUGGYWHIP CT
7 TRADITION CT
8 BUNKER HILL CT
9 WILDWOOD CT
10 FOLKLORE CT
11 ALLEGHANY CT
12 COPPERAGE CT
13 AMERICAN CT
14 COBBLESTONE CT
GUADALUPE RESERVOIR COUNTY PARK
GUADALUPE RES
GUADALUPE CREEK
HICKS RD
REYNOLDS RD
RINCON CREEK
LOS GATOS
RES
OLDS

SEE 874 MAP

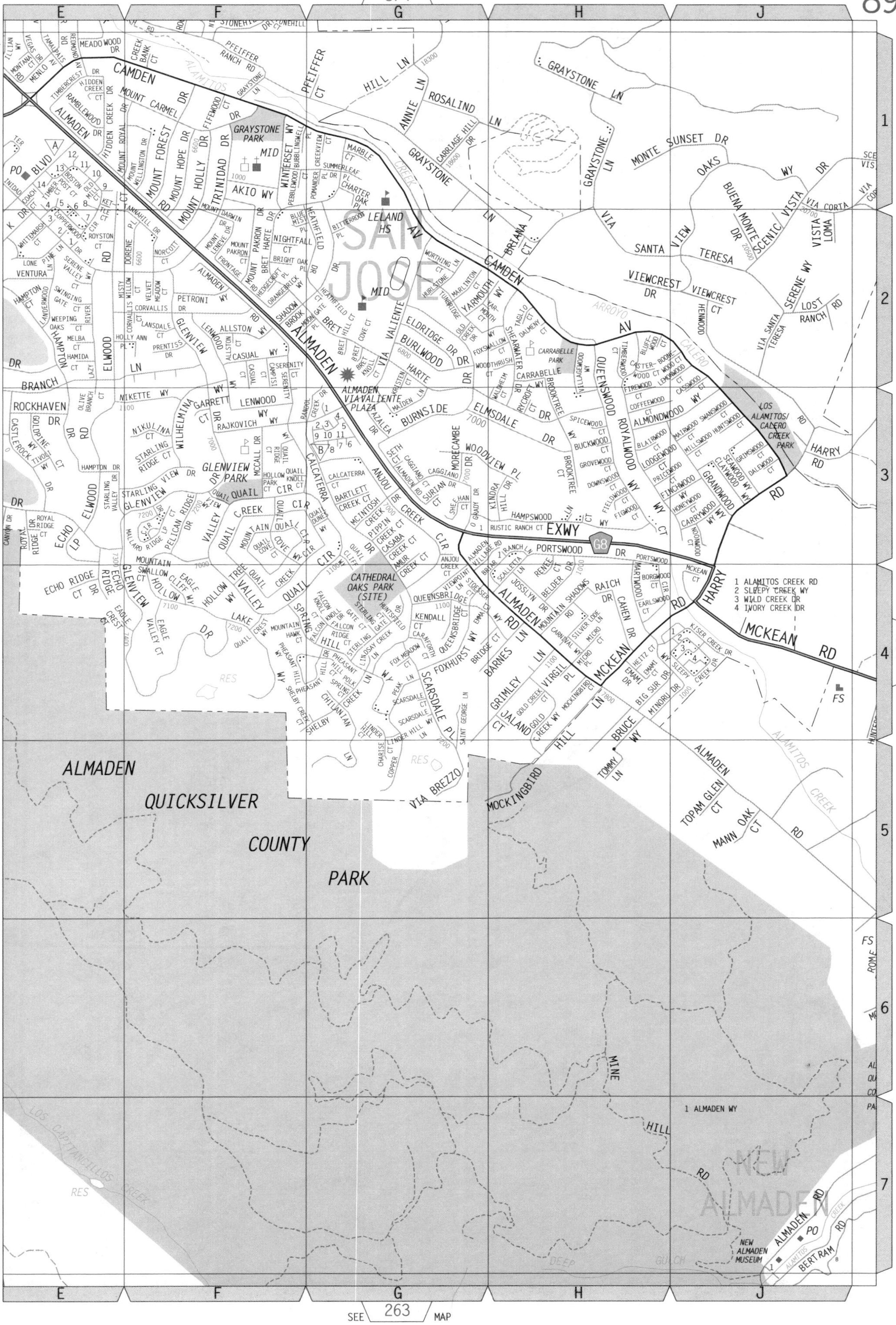

E
F
G
H
J
1
2
3
4
5
6
7
SAN JOSE
CAMDEN
ALMADEN
ALMADEN EXWY
G8
MCKEAN RD
HARRY RD
GRAYSTONE LN
GRAYSTONE PARK
LELAND HS
MID
CARRABELLE PARK
GLENVIEW PARK
ALMADEN VIA VALIENTE PLAZA
CATHEDRAL OAKS PARK (SITE)
LOS ALAMITOS/ CALERO CREEK PARK
ALMADEN QUICKSILVER COUNTY PARK
MINE HILL RD
NEW ALMADEN
NEW ALMADEN MUSEUM
PO
FS
RES
LOS CAPITANCILLOS CREEK
ALAMITOS CREEK
ARROYO CALERO
DEEP GULCH
1 ALAMITOS CREEK RD
2 SLEEPY CREEK WY
3 WILD CREEK DR
4 IVORY CREEK DR
1 ALMADEN WY

SEE 895 MAP

SEE 263 MAP

BAY AREA

MAP

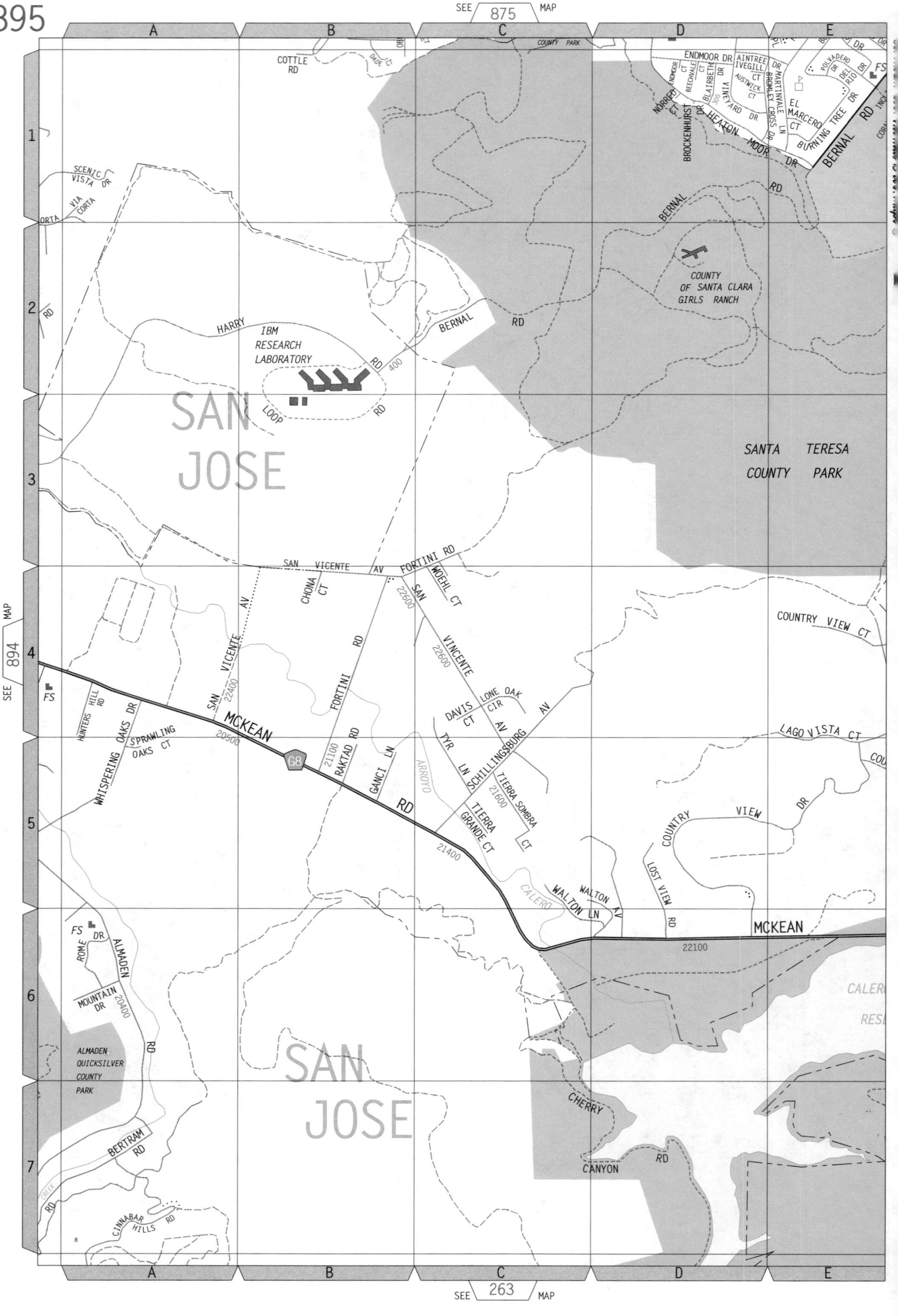
SEE 875 MAP
SEE 894 MAP
SEE 263 MAP
A
B
C
D
E
1
2
3
4
5
6
7
COTTLE RD
DADE CT
COUNTY PARK
ENDMOOR DR
AINTREE DR
IVEGILL CT
ENDMOOR CT
BEECHVALE CT
BLAIRBETH DR
AUSTWICK CT
MARTINVALE LN
BROMLEY CROSS DR
NORRED CT
BROCKENHURST DR
HEATON MOOR DR
VINEYARD DR
POLVADERO DR
DEL RIO DR
EL MARCERO CT
BURNING TREE DR
BERNAL RD
FS
SCENIC VISTA DR
VIA CORTA
ORTA
RD
BERNAL RD
COUNTY OF SANTA CLARA GIRLS RANCH
HARRY RD
IBM RESEARCH LABORATORY
400
BERNAL
LOOP RD
SAN JOSE
SANTA TERESA COUNTY PARK
SAN VICENTE AV
FORTINI RD
WOEHL CT
CHONA CT
SAN VICENTE AV
22400
22600
SAN VINCENTE AV
22600
FORTINI RD
COUNTRY VIEW CT
FS
HUNTERS HILL RD
WHISPERING OAKS DR
SPRAWLING OAKS CT
MCKEAN RD
20500
G8
21100
RAKTAD RD
GANCI LN
ARROYO
DAVIS CT
LONE OAK CIR
SCHILLINGSBURG AV
TYR LN
TIERRA SOMBRA CT
21600
TIERRA GRANDE CT
21400
LAGO VISTA CT
COUNTRY VIEW DR
LOST VIEW RD
WALTON AV
WALTON LN
CALERO
MCKEAN
22100
FS
ROME DR
ALMADEN RD
MOUNTAIN DR
20400
ALMADEN QUICKSILVER COUNTY PARK
SAN JOSE
CALERO
RESE
CHERRY CANYON RD
BERTRAM RD
CREEK
RD
CINNABAR HILLS RD

SEE 875 MAP

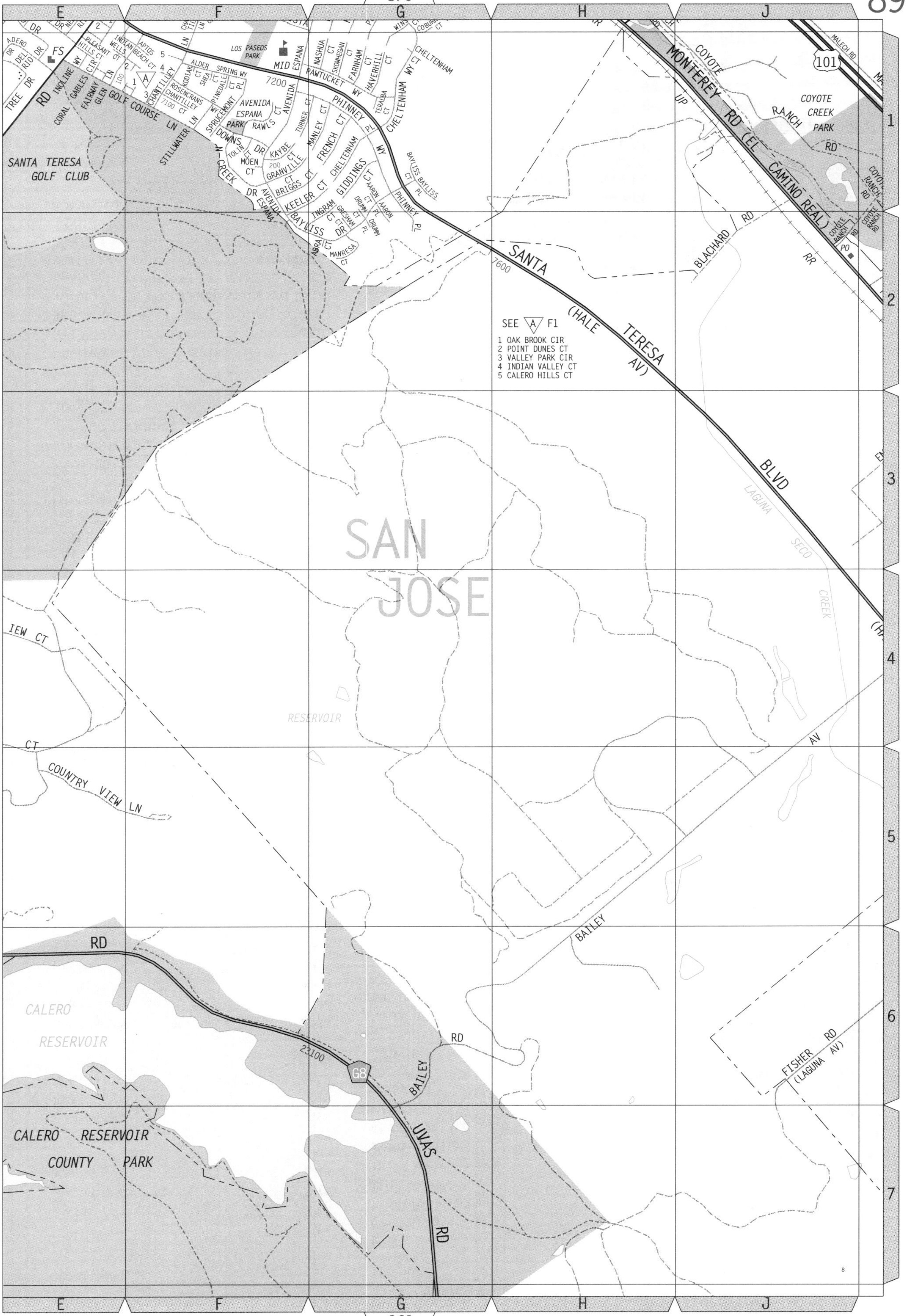

E
F
G
H
J
1
2
3
4
5
6
7
SANTA TERESA GOLF CLUB
GOLF COURSE LN
STILLWATER LN
LOS PASEOS PARK
MID ESPANA
AVENIDA ESPANA PARK
NASHUA CT
SKOWHEGAN CT
FARNHAM CT
HAVERHILL CT
PAWTUCKET WY
PHINNEY PL
CHELTENHAM WY
CHELTENHAM
TERALBA CT
TURNER CT
MANLEY CT
FRENCH CT
CHELTENHAM
GIDDINGS CT
KAYBE CT
GRANVILLE
BRIGGS CT
KEELER CT
INGRAM CT
GRESHAM CT
DRUMM CT
AARON CT
BAYLISS DR
MANRESA CT
ABRA CT
BAYLISS PL
PHINNEY PL
DOWNS DR
MOEN CT
TOLIN CT
SPRUCEMONT
PINEDALE CT
ROSENCRANS CT
CHANTILLEY
ALDER SPRING WY
INCLINE WY
CORAL GABLES CIR
FAIRWAY GLEN
PLEASANT HILLS CT
INDIAN WELLS CT
APTOS BEACH CT
TREE DR
FS
7200
7600
SANTA TERESA BLVD
(HALE AV)
MONTEREY RD (EL CAMINO REAL)
COYOTE
101
MALECH RD
COYOTE CREEK RANCH PARK
RANCH RD
COYOTE RANCH RD
PO
BLACHARD RD
RR
UP
SEE A F1
1 OAK BROOK CIR
2 POINT DUNES CT
3 VALLEY PARK CIR
4 INDIAN VALLEY CT
5 CALERO HILLS CT
SAN JOSE
LAGUNA SECO CREEK
RESERVOIR
IEW CT
CT
COUNTRY VIEW LN
BAILEY AV
RD
CALERO RESERVOIR
23100
G8
BAILEY RD
UVAS RD
CALERO RESERVOIR COUNTY PARK
FISHER RD
(LAGUNA AV)

SEE 263 MAP

LIST OF ABBREVIATIONS

PREFIXES AND SUFFIXES

AL .... ALLEY
ARC .... ARCADE
AV, AVE .... AVENUE
AVCT .... AVENUE COURT
AVD .... AVENIDA
AVDR .... AVENUE DRIVE
AVEX .... AVENUE EXTENSION
BLEX .... BOULEVARD EXTENSION
BL, BLVD .... BOULEVARD
BLCT .... BOULEVARD COURT
BRCH .... BRANCH
BRDG .... BRIDGE
BYPS .... BYPASS
CIDR .... CIRCLE DRIVE
CIR .... CIRCLE
CL .... CALLE
CLJ .... CALLEJON
CM .... CAMINO
CMTO .... CAMINITO
COM .... COMMON
CORR .... CORRIDOR
CRES .... CRESCENT
CRLO .... CIRCULO
CRSG .... CROSSING
CSWY .... CAUSEWAY
CT .... COURT
CTAV .... COURT AVENUE
CTE .... CORTE
CTO .... CUT OFF
CTR .... CENTER
CUR .... CURVE
CV .... COVE
D .... DE
DIAG .... DIAGONAL
DR .... DRIVE
DVDR .... DIVISION DRIVE
EXAV .... EXTENSION AVENUE
EXBL .... EXTENSION BOULEVARD
EXRD .... EXTENSION ROAD
EXST .... EXTENSION STREET
EXT .... EXTENSION
EXWY .... EXPRESSWAY
FRWY .... FREEWAY
GDNS .... GARDENS
GN .... GLEN
GRN .... GREEN
HWY .... HIGHWAY
JCT .... JUNCTION
LN .... LANE
LNDG .... LANDING
LP .... LOOP
LS .... LAS, LOS
MNR .... MANOR
MTWY .... MOTORWAY
OH .... OUTER HIGHWAY
OVL .... OVAL
OVPS .... OVERPASS
PAS .... PASEO
PK .... PARK
PKWY .... PARKWAY
PL .... PLACE
PLZ, PZ .... PLAZA
PT .... POINT
PTH .... PATH
RD .... ROAD
RDEX .... ROAD EXTENSION
RDGE .... RIDGE
RW .... ROW
SKWY .... SKYWAY
SQ .... SQUARE
ST .... STREET
STAV .... STREET AVENUE
STCT .... STREET COURT
STDR .... STREET DRIVE
STEX .... STREET EXTENSION
STLN .... STREET LANE
STLP .... STREET LOOP
STPL .... STREET PLACE
STXP .... STREET EXPRESSWAY
TER .... TERRACE
TFWY .... TRAFFICWAY
THWY .... THROUGHWAY
TKTR .... TRUCKTRAIL
TPKE .... TURNPIKE
TR .... TRAIL
TUN .... TUNNEL
UNPS .... UNDERPASS
VIS .... VISTA
VW .... VIEW
WK .... WALK
WY .... WAY
WYPL .... WAY PLACE

DIRECTIONS

E .... EAST
KPN .... KEY PENINSULA NORTH
KPS .... KEY PENINSULA SOUTH
N .... NORTH
NE .... NORTHEAST
NW .... NORTHWEST
S .... SOUTH
SE .... SOUTHEAST
SW .... SOUTHWEST
W .... WEST

DEPARTMENT STORES

BN .... BLOOMINGDALES
BN .... THE BON MARCHE
D .... DIAMONDS
FN .... FREDERICK & NELSON
G .... GOLDWATERS
GT .... GOTTSCHALKS
H .... HARRIS
IM .... I MAGNIN
L .... LAMONTS
MA .... MACY'S
ME .... MERVYN'S
MF .... MEIER & FRANK
MW .... MONTGOMERY WARD
N .... NORDSTROM
NM .... NEIMAN-MARCUS
P .... J C PENNEY
RM .... ROBINSONS MAY
S .... SEARS
SF .... SAKS FIFTH AVENUE
W .... WEINSTOCKS

BUILDINGS

CC .... CHAMBER OF COMMERCE
CH .... CITY HALL
CHP .... CALIFORNIA HIGHWAY PATROL
COMM CTR .... COMMUNITY CENTER
CON CTR .... CONVENTION CENTER
CONT HS .... CONTINUATION HIGH SCHOOL
CTH .... COURT HOUSE
DMV .... DEPT OF MOTOR VEHICLES
FAA .... FEDERAL AVIATION ADMIN
FS .... FIRE STATION
HOSP .... HOSPITAL
HS .... HIGH SCHOOL
INT .... INTERMEDIATE SCHOOL
JR HS .... JUNIOR HIGH SCHOOL
LIB .... LIBRARY
MID .... MIDDLE SCHOOL
MUS .... MUSEUM
PO .... POST OFFICE
PS .... POLICE STATION
SR CIT CTR .... SENIOR CITIZENS CENTER
STA .... STATION
THTR .... THEATER
VIS BUR .... VISITORS BUREAU

OTHER COMMON ABBREVIATIONS

BCH .... BEACH
BLDG .... BUILDING
CEM .... CEMETERY
CK .... CREEK
CO .... COUNTY
CTR .... CENTER
COMM .... COMMUNITY
EST .... ESTATE
HIST .... HISTORIC
HTS .... HEIGHTS
LK .... LAKE
MDW .... MEADOW
MED .... MEDICAL
MEM .... MEMORIAL
MHP .... MOBILE HOME PARK
MT .... MOUNT
MTN .... MOUNTAIN
NATL .... NATIONAL
PKG .... PARKING
PLGD .... PLAYGROUND
RCH .... RANCH
RCHO .... RANCHO
REC .... RECREATION
RES .... RESERVOIR
RIV .... RIVER
RR .... RAILROAD
SPG .... SPRING
STA .... SANTA
VLG .... VILLAGE
VLY .... VALLEY
VW .... VIEW

STREET Block City ZIP Pg-Grid

A

A RD
- SUNV 94089 812-J3
100 AlaC 94586 734-C5
4100 SCIC 95127 815-C6
A ST
- BEN 94510 551-B6
- CCCo 94565 573-E1
- CNCD 94518 592-G3
- CPTO 95014 831-H6
- NVTO 94949 546-G3
- OAK 94625 649-B3
- VAL 94592 529-F5
- CNCD 94520 572-G3
- HAY 94541 711-J1
- LALT 94024 831-H3
- SSF 94080 707-G3
- SCIC 94024 831-H3
100 AlaC 94586 734-C5
100 MLPK 94025 790-H3
100 RDWC 94063 769-J5
100 SMCo 94014 687-C5
100 RDWC 94063 770-A5
200 AlaC 94541 711-G2
300 DNVL 94506 653-J5
400 CLMA 94014 687-C5
400 RCH 94801 588-F6
400 DALY 94014 687-C5
500 MRTZ 94553 571-E4
600 ANT 94509 575-D4
600 UNC 94587 732-F4
600 SF 94124 668-F7
700 SRFL 94901 586-F1
800 CCCo 94525 550-A5
1200 HAY 94541 712-A1
1300 HAY 94541 692-A7
1300 AlaC 94546 692-A7
7100 ELCR 94530 609-E4
8200 OAK 94621 670-H4
9000 OAK 94603 670-H5
W A ST
- AlaC 94541 711-F2
- HAY 94541 711-E2
AARLES CT
2400 WLCK 94598 592-F7
AARON CT
- NVTO 94949 546-C1
7500 SJS 95139 895-G1
AARON DR
- NVTO 94949 546-C1
AARON PL
7500 SJS 95139 895-G1
AARON ST
1200 LVMR 94550 715-F2
AARON PARK DR
700 MPS 95035 794-A5
ABACA WY
2300 FRMT 94539 753-E6
ABALONE CT
3500 UNC 94587 731-J4
ABALONE PL
200 LVMR 94550 715-D3
ABBEY AV
1400 SLN 94579 691-A6
ABBEY CT
- CCCo 94595 612-A6
600 BEN 94510 530-J7
1400 CNCD 94518 592-E7
3800 SJS 95008 853-C6
5200 NWK 94560 752-F5
ABBEY LN
200 SJS 95008 853-C6
2100 CMBL 95008 853-C6
ABBEY ST
- SF 94114 667-H2
2600 OAK 94619 650-E6
ABBEY TER
4000 FRMT 94536 752-J4
ABBEYFIELD CT
6200 SJS 95120 874-C7
ABBEYGATE CT
4500 SJS 95124 873-J3
ABBIE CT
600 PLE 94566 714-E4
ABBIE LN
- CCCo 94803 589-H4
ABBIE ST
100 PLE 94566 714-E4
ABBINGTON PL
25900 HAY 94542 712-D3
ABBOT AV
- DALY 94014 687-D5
ABBOTFORD CT
5000 NWK 94560 752-D3
ABBOTT AV
100 MPS 95035 793-J6
900 CMBL 95008 873-B1
2100 PIT 94565 574-C3
S ABBOTT AV
- MPS 95035 813-J1
ABBOTT CT
- ORIN 94563 631-A2
ABBOTT DR
- OAK 94611 630-D6
ABBOTT LN
- CCCo 94507 632-G7
ABBOTT WY
- PDMT 94618 630-C7
ABBY CT
- AMCN 94589 509-H3
ABBY DR
700 VAL 94591 530-G6
ABBY WOOD CT
100 LGTS 95030 873-B2
ABDON AV
14000 SCIC 95127 814-H7
14000 SJS 95127 814-H7
ABDULLA WY
14000 SAR 95070 852-H7
ABED CT
2500 SJS 95116 834-J4
ABEGG
- CCCo 94507 632-G5
ABEL AV
4100 PA 94306 811-C2
ABEL CT
35200 FRMT 94536 752-F1
N ABEL ST
- MPS 95035 794-A5
- MPS 95035 793-J6
S ABEL ST
- MPS 95035 793-J7
100 MPS 95035 814-A1
ABELIA CT
3000 SJS 95121 854-J4
ABELIA WY
100 EPA 94303 791-D3
ABELOE TER
43700 FRMT 94539 773-J1
ABERCROMBIE PL
33800 FRMT 94555 732-D7
ABERDEEN AV
900 LVMR 94550 715-F3
ABERDEEN CT
100 VAL 94591 550-E1
600 MPS 95035 794-B6
1300 CNCD 94518 592-E6
1800 SJS 95122 854-G1
12800 SAR 95070 852-F6
ABERDEEN DR
100 SCAR 94070 769-F4
900 SUNV 94087 832-B4
1300 SMTO 94402 749-B2
ABERDEEN PL
26900 HAY 94542 712-E3
ABERDEEN RD
- NVTO 94949 546-G2
ABERDEEN ST
3500 SCL 95054 813-E6
ABERDEEN TER
34100 FRMT 94555 732-E7
ABERDEEN WY
500 MPS 95035 794-B6
2300 RCH 94806 588-J1
ABERFELDY WY
1200 MPS 95035 814-C1
ABERFOIL AV
4200 OAK 94605 671-D5
ABERFORD DR
1200 SJS 95131 814-E6
ABERHAVEN CT
- SJS 95111 875-A1
ABINANTE LN
1900 SJS 95124 873-G1
ABINGTON CT
1700 SJS 95131 834-D1
2100 WLCK 94596 632-G1
5600 NWK 94560 752-D4
ABINGTON DR
5500 NWK 94560 752-D4
ABINGTON LN
- CCCo 94507 632-G5
ABORN CT
2800 SJS 95148 855-D2
ABORN RD
1500 SJS 95121 855-A3
2900 SJS 95122 855-B3
3000 SJS 95148 855-F2
3300 SJS 95135 855-H1
3500 SCIC 95135 855-H1
ABORN SQUARE LOOP RD
2900 SJS 95121 855-B3
ABRA CT
200 SJS 95139 895-G2
ABRAHAM ST
37800 FRMT 94536 753-A3
ABRAM CT
1600 SLN 94577 690-H3
ABRAMS CT
- SCIC - 791-A7
ABREU RD
- UNC 94587 732-C5
ABRIGO CT
600 SRMN 94583 673-B2
ABRIGO VALLEY TR
- CCCo - 591-B6
- CCCo - 611-B1
ABRYAN WY
2000 SMCo 94061 790-B4
ABUELO WY
40800 FRMT 94539 753-F4
ACACIA AV
- BLV 94920 627-D1
- PA 94306 811-B1
- BERK 94708 609-G4
- LKSP 94939 586-F6
- MrnC 94904 586-E4
- SRFL 94901 566-H7
100 SBRN 94066 727-J1
200 SSF 94080 707-H2
400 SBRN 94066 707-H7
700 RCH 94801 588-F5
800 SUNV 94086 812-F7
900 LALT 94022 811-E4
1900 ANT 94509 575-D6
5800 OAK 94618 630-A5
ACACIA CT
- PCFA 94044 727-A5
100 SCAR 94070 769-F2
500 NVTO 94945 525-E2
2000 SCL 95050 833-D3
38200 FRMT 94536 753-A3
ACACIA DR
- ATN 94027 790-G1
- ORIN 94563 610-F6
- TBRN 94920 607-C4
700 BURL 94010 728-F6
800 CCCo 94572 569-J1
1200 HAY 94541 712-A2
2200 CNCD 94520 572-F6
ACACIA LN
- SMCo 94062 769-G6
- SMCo 94062 789-G1
200 CCCo 94507 632-G3
900 SJS 95138 875-F6
ACACIA RD
2700 CCCo 94595 612-A6
2700 CCCo 94595 611-J7
ACACIA ST
100 SJS 95110 834-A5
1300 PIT 94565 574-F3
1400 SLN 94579 691-A4
38000 FRMT 94536 753-A2
ACACIA WY
- VAL 94591 530-D6
900 LVMR 94550 715-H2
ACADEMY AV
900 BLMT 94002 769-C1
ACADEMY CT
700 BLMT 94002 769-C1
ACADEMY RD
5000 CNCD 94521 593-D5
ACADIA AV
1100 MPS 95035 814-C1
1200 MPS 95035 794-D7
ACADIA CT
6000 PLE 94588 714-B1
20600 CPTO 95014 832-D6
ACADIA LN
300 SRFL 94903 566-F2
ACADIA ST
100 SF 94131 667-F6
ACALANES AV
3100 LFYT 94549 611-H5
ACALANES DR
100 SUNV 94086 812-B7
10500 OAK 94603 670-H7
ACALANES RD
800 LFYT 94549 611-A7
ACAMPO DR
800 LFYT 94549 611-F7
ACAPULCO CT
- NVTO 94949 546-F2
ACAPULCO DR
1700 SPAB 94806 568-J7
3700 SJS 95008 853-B6
ACAPULCO RD
14100 SLN 94577 690-H5
ACAPULCO WY
100 UNC 94587 732-D5
ACCACIA ST
- DALY 94014 687-J3
ACCESS RD
- EMVL 94608 629-D6
N ACCESS RD
100 SSF 94080 708-A5
ACCRA CT
1200 LVMR 94550 715-F3
ACELA DR
- TBRN 94920 607-D6
ACEVEDO AV
- SF 94132 687-A1
ACKERMAN DR
800 DNVL 94526 653-B1
800 DNVL 94526 633-B7
2100 PIT 94565 574-A3
ACKLEY CT
- PLHL 94523 592-A7
ACME AL
- SF 94114 667-F3
ACME CT
1000 NVTO 94949 546-E2
ACOMA WY
200 FRMT 94539 793-J1
ACORN
- PTLV 94028 830-D2
ACORN AL
1400 SF 94109 647-J5
ACORN CT
- CCCo 94595 612-B6
- NVTO 94949 546-D4
700 SRMN 94583 673-G7
3100 SJS 95117 853-D3
ACORN DR
- CLAY 94517 594-A5
- HIL 94010 728-D7
ACORN LN
- LALT 94022 811-E5
100 PIT 94565 573-G4
ACORN RD
3100 ANT 94509 595-C1
ACORN ST
2600 AlaC 94546 691-H4
ACORN WY
- ATN 94027 790-G1
- MrnC 94904 586-C4
3100 SJS 95117 853-D3
ACROFT CT
1400 BERK 94702 629-F2
ACTION CT
100 FRMT 94539 773-H7
ACTON CIR
- BERK 94702 629-F2
ACTON CRES
1400 BERK 94702 629-F2
ACTON CT
14800 SCIC 95124 873-G4
ACTON DR
14500 SCIC 95124 873-G3
ACTON PL
200 OAK 94606 649-J4
ACTON ST
- BERK 94706 609-F7
- SF 94112 687-E3
- DALY 94014 687-E3
1300 BERK 94702 609-F7
1400 BERK 94702 629-F1
ACTRIZ AV
400 CCCo 94553 571-J3
ADA AV
100 MTVW 94043 812-A5
36700 FRMT 94536 752-F4
ADA CT
- SF 94109 647-J6
ADA DR
300 CCCo 94553 572-B7
ADA ST
200 OAK 94618 629-J6
700 SMTO 94401 749-B1
1300 BERK 94702 609-E7
1400 BERK 94703 609-E7
21700 AlaC 94546 692-A6
ADAGIO CT
4900 FRMT 94538 773-B1
ADAGIO DR
300 DNVL 94526 653-C4
ADAGIO WY
600 SJS 95111 855-B7
ADAIR CT
- DNVL 94526 653-A4
ADAIR DR
19600 AlaC 94546 691-J4
ADAIR LN
- PTLV 94028 810-D6
ADAIR ST
- SF 94103 667-J2
ADAIR WY
4900 SJS 95124 873-E4
ADAK CT
- WLCK 94596 612-A2
ADALINA CT
5200 SJS 95124 873-F5
ADAM CT
- SCAR 94070 769-D3
ADAM WY
- ATN 94027 790-C2
ADAMO CT
4700 SJS 95136 874-E2
ADAMO DR
4600 SJS 95136 874-E2
ADAMS AV
- DBLN 94568 694-A2
- MrnC 94965 606-B3
700 LVMR 94550 716-A1
1000 SLN 94577 690-F1
1400 MPS 95035 794-D6
1700 SLN 94577 670-F7
3600 FRMT 94538 753-D7
ADAMS CT
- NVTO 94947 526-B5
700 PIN 94564 569-D4
1100 SJS 95132 814-G5
1300 MLPK 94025 771-B7
1900 MTVW 94040 831-H1
2500 SSF 94080 707-C4
3100 ANT 94509 575-A7
ADAMS DR
- EPA 94303 771-B7
1100 SJS 95132 814-F5
1500 MLPK 94025 771-B7
1500 MLPK 94303 771-B7
4500 CNCD 94521 593-C2
ADAMS PL
100 SRMN 94583 673-F6
ADAMS ST
- BEN 94510 551-D6
- ELCR 94530 609-D5
- VAL 94590 550-B1
100 NVTO 94947 526-B5
200 OAK 94610 649-H2
400 ALB 94706 609-D5
500 RDWC 94062 770-A6
600 RDWC 94061 770-A6
1700 SMTO 94403 749-C3
2800 ALA 94501 670-A3
ADAMS WY
300 PLE 94566 714-F3
3000 SCL 95051 833-A7
ADAMS RANCH RD
100 CCCo 94595 632-C1
ADAMSWOOD DR
3100 SJS 95148 835-E7
ADANA TER
- UNC 94587 732-E4
ADASON DR
900 SLN 94578 691-D4
ADCOCK DR
38600 FRMT 94536 753-C2
ADCOCK PL
38600 FRMT 94536 753-C2
ADDIEWELL PL
1300 SJS 95120 874-C7
1300 SJS 95120 894-C1
ADDINGTON CT
21500 CPTO 95014 852-B3
ADDISON AV
100 PA 94301 790-J5
300 PA 94301 791-A4
2000 EPA 94303 791-A2
ADDISON CT
200 FRMT 94539 773-H7
ADDISON PL
2800 SCL 95051 833-B2
ADDISON ST
- SF 94131 667-G5
600 BERK 94804 629-D2
1100 BERK 94702 629-E2
1300 RDWC 94061 770-B7
1500 BERK 94703 629-E2
1900 BERK 94704 629-E2
ADDISON WY
1700 HAY 94544 732-A2
4300 PLE 94588 694-B7
ADELA CT
100 PLHL 94523 592-D5
ADELAIDE DR
- CCCo 94553 571-H4
ADELAIDE ST
1500 CNCD 94520 592-F2
4300 OAK 94619 650-G6
ADELAIDE WY
1900 SJS 95124 873-G5
3200 BLMT 94002 768-J2
ADELE AV
2300 MTVW 94043 811-F3
ADELE CT
- SF 94133 648-A4
ADELE DR
100 VAL 94589 510-D5
ADELE PL
1900 SJS 95125 853-J6
ADELE ST
200 NVTO 94947 526-C5
ADELHEID CT
10000 CPTO 95014 852-A1
ADELIA CT
4400 CNCD 94521 593-C5
ADELINA COM
43300 FRMT 94539 753-H7
ADELINA TER
43500 FRMT 94539 753-H7
43500 FRMT 94539 773-H1
ADELINE DR
1500 BURL 94010 728-C6
1500 SMCo 94010 728-B6
ADELINE ST
- OAK 94607 649-F2
800 HAY 94544 711-H5
2800 BERK 94703 629-G4
2800 OAK 94608 649-F1
3200 OAK 94608 629-G5
4200 EMVL 94608 629-F6
ADELL CT
3300 OAK 94602 650-D4
ADELLE CT
- CCCo 94507 632-G7
ADELLE ST
300 LVMR 94550 695-F7
500 LVMR 94550 715-F1
ADELONG WY
- SJS 95139 875-H7
ADELPHIAN WY
200 ALA 94502 669-H6
ADEN ST
- VAL 94590 529-J2
ADENTRO ARENA
- SUNV 94089 812-H4
ADIRONDACK WY
500 WLCK 94598 612-D2
ADIT CT
100 VAL 94591 550-C1
ADLER AV
100 CMBL 95008 853-D7
ADLER CT
1100 FRMT 94536 753-B2
3600 SJS 95111 854-G6
ADMIRAL AV
- SF 94112 667-G6
ADMIRAL DR
- EMVL 94608 629-C6
ADMIRAL PL
2000 SJS 95133 814-E7
ADMIRAL CALLAGHAN DR
300 VAL 94591 530-C2
ADMIRAL CALLAGHAN LN
- VAL 94591 530-D2
900 VAL 94591 510-D7
ADMIRALITY LN
1100 ALA 94502 670-A7
ADMIRALTY LN
1100 FCTY 94404 749-F2
ADMIRALTY PL
- RDWC 94065 749-J6
6000 SJS 95123 874-E6
ADMIRE CT
1300 MPS 95035 794-C5
ADOBE AV
100 MPS 95035 793-J6
ADOBE CT
- NVTO 94945 526-A1
- DNVL 94526 653-A1
1400 SJS 95118 874-B2
2700 ANT 94509 575-B6
6800 PLE 94588 694-A7
27800 HAY 94542 712-E4
ADOBE DR
- CNCD 94520 572-F6
200 SJS 95131 814-A5
600 DNVL 94526 653-A1
1300 PCFA 94044 726-H6
35800 FRMT 94536 752-E3
ADOBE LN
- ORIN 94563 631-B5
25400 LAH 94022 831-C3
ADOBE PL
400 PA 94306 811-E1
1100 PIT 94565 573-H4
ADOBE RD
1200 PIN 94564 569-G7
1200 PIN 94564 589-H1
ADOBE ST
100 VAL 94589 510-B5
2000 CNCD 94520 592-F1
ADOBE CREEK CT
1000 SJS 95127 834-J4
ADOBE CREEK LODGE RD
- LAH 94022 831-A3
ADOBE RIVER CT
4600 SJS 95136 874-E2
ADOBESTONE CT
200 MrnC 94903 546-F6
ADOLFO DR
1500 SJS 95131 814-C6
ADOLPH SUTRO CT
- SF 94131 667-E3
ADONIS CT
800 SUNV 94086 832-G1
ADONIS WY
2400 SJS 95124 873-E4
ADONNA CT
27100 LAH 94022 811-A7
ADRA AV
3400 SCIC 95117 853-D1
3400 SJS 95117 853-D1
ADRAGNA CT
4400 SJS 95136 874-H1
ADRIA DR
100 PLHL 94523 592-C4
ADRIAN AV
100 SSF 94080 707-D2
1300 SMTO 94403 749-D4
26100 HAY 94545 711-G6
ADRIAN CT
- BURL 94010 728-C4
ADRIAN PL
100 LGTS 95032 873-E5
ADRIAN RD
200 MLBR 94030 728-C4
1500 BURL 94010 728-D4
ADRIAN TER
- MrnC 94903 566-H2
ADRIAN WY
- MrnC 94903 566-H2
1100 SJS 95122 834-J5
ADRIANA AV
10000 CPTO 95014 832-B7
ADRIANA CT
5100 ANT 94509 595-G4
ADRIANO CT
4200 FRMT 94536 752-E2
ADRIANO ST
35100 FRMT 94536 752-E2
ADRIATIC WY
3700 SCL 95051 832-H4
ADRIEN DR
1500 CMBL 95008 873-A1
ADRIENNE DR
1000 CCCo 94507 632-G6
ADRIENNE ST
600 NVTO 94945 526-C4
ADVENT AV
1300 SLN 94579 691-A6
AEGEAN PL
- AlaC 94546 691-H4
AERIAL WY
- SF 94116 667-C3
AETNA WY
2800 SJS 95121 854-J3
2800 SJS 95121 855-A3
AFFINITO LN
- PIT 94565 574-E1
AFRICA ST
- OAK 94607 649-C1
- OAK 94649 649-C1
AFSHAR CT
1900 CNCD 94518 592-F6
AFTON AV
18600 SAR 95070 852-H7
AFTON CT
- SMTO 94402 749-B2
6000 SJS 95123 874-E5
AFUERA ARENA
- SUNV 94089 812-H4
AGADIR ST
1600 CNCD 94518 592-E6
AGAPE CT
4900 SJS 95118 873-J4
AGATE AL
600 SF 94109 647-J5
AGATE CT
- VAL 94591 530-F1
- LVMR 94550 715-D3
400 ANT 94509 595-E1
2600 SCL 95051 832-J1
AGATE DR
2700 SCL 95051 833-A1
3200 SCL 95051 832-J1
AGATE TER
34300 FRMT 94555 752-C2
AGATE WY
100 HER 94547 569-G5
7900 DBLN 94568 693-J1
AGATHA CT
- SANS 94960 566-B7
AGATHA WY
3900 SJS 95136 874-E1
AGAVE CT
- FRMT 94539 773-J5
AGENA CIR
4300 UNC 94587 732-A6
AGENA WY
100 SUNV 94086 812-F7
AGHALEE
- ORIN 94563 631-A1
AGNES CT
100 VAL 94589 510-D5
5600 FRMT 94538 773-B2
AGNES LN
20600 AlaC 94541 691-G7
AGNES ST
- LVMR 94550 696-A7
- OAK 94618 630-C6
AGNES WY
100 PLHL 94523 592-D6
900 PA 94303 791-C5
AGNEW RD
2000 SCL 95054 813-C5
AGNON AV
- SF 94112 667-H6
AGOSTINO CT
5400 CNCD 94521 593-G5
AGREE TER
34600 FRMT 94555 752-A3
AGRESTE AV
2500 TBRN 94920 607-F7
2500 MrnC 94920 607-F7
AGUA WY
- SF 94127 667-E5
200 CCCo 94565 573-E1
AGUACATE CT
100 SJS 95116 834-D2
AGUA VISTA
4400 UNC 94587 731-H6
AGUA VISTA CT
- SMCo 94062 789-F2
AGUA VISTA DR
2600 SJS 95132 814-D3
AGUA VISTA ST
3800 OAK 94601 650-E7
AGUILA TER
44700 FRMT 94539 773-J2
AGUILAR CT
2100 MPS 95035 794-E6
AGUILAR PL
300 PIT 94565 574-D1
AHERN AV
29900 UNC 94587 732-A3
AHERN CT
3300 RCH 94803 589-F1
AHERN WY
- SF 94103 648-A7
AHLERS CT
- SF 94123 647-G4
AHNEITA DR
2000 PLHL 94523 592-D6
AHWAHNEE CT
600 WLCK 94596 612-D5
AHWAHNEE DR
800 MLBR 94030 727-J4
AHWANEE AV
600 SUNV 94086 812-G5
AHWANEE LN
300 CLAY 94517 593-H5
N AHWANEE TER
- SUNV 94086 812-G5
S AHWANEE TER
- SUNV 94086 812-G5
AHWANHEE AV
100 SUNV 94086 812-F4
AHWANNE CT
300 CLAY 94517 593-H5
AIDA AV
2600 SJS 95122 855-A2
AIELLO CT
1700 CNCD 94519 593-A2
AIELLO DR
2700 SJS 95111 854-G5
AIKEN CT
34300 FRMT 94555 752-D1
AIKINS WY
3500 SJS 95148 855-F1
AILEEN ST
500 OAK 94609 629-G6
800 OAK 94608 629-F6
1000 LFYT 94549 611-G5
1200 SLN 94577 690-J2
AINSLEE CT
500 HAY 94544 712-A5
AINSLEY CT
3800 SJS 95008 853-C6
AINSWORTH DR
10200 CPTO 95014 832-A6
10500 SCIC 94024 832-A6
AINTREE DR
6800 SJS 95119 895-D1
AIR CARGO RD
- OAK 94621 690-C1
AIRES CT
3700 AlaC 94546 692-A5
AIRES LN
400 SJS 95111 854-F6
AIRPORT BLVD
- BURL 94010 728-F5
- SMTO 94401 728-F5
- SSF 94080 707-J3
400 SSF 94080 708-A2
1100 SJS 95110 833-G1
S AIRPORT BLVD
- SMCo 94128 708-A5
100 SSF 94080 707-A5
100 SSF 94080 708-A4
AIRPORT DR
- OAK 94603 670-E7
- OAK 94621 670-E7
100 OAK 94603 690-D2
100 OAK 94621 690-D2
AIRPORT PKWY
- SJS 95110 833-H2
AIRPORT WY
400 SCAR 94070 769-H1
600 RDWC 94065 769-H1
AIRWAY BLVD
100 LVMR 94550 695-B6
E AIRWAY BLVD
200 LVMR 94550 695-D5
300 AlaC 94550 695-D5
AITKEN AV
2100 MTVW 94040 811-F5
AITKEN DR
6500 OAK 94611 630-G7
AJAX DR
700 SUNV 94086 832-F1
AJAX PL
- BERK 94708 609-J6
AJAX ST
- LKSP 94939 586-E5
AJUGA CT
38400 NWK 94560 752-G7
AKINO CT
2800 SJS 95148 855-C1
AKIO WY
1000 SJS 95120 894-F1
AKLAN CT
300 SJS 95119 875-C7
N AKRON RD
- SCIC 94035 812-B2
- SCIC 94043 812-B2
S AKRON RD
- SCIC 94035 812-B2
- SCIC 94043 812-B2
AKRON WY
3700 SJS 95117 853-B2
ALABAMA DR
5500 CNCD 94521 593-F7
ALABAMA ST
- VAL 94590 529-H4
100 SF 94103 667-J2
300 SF 94110 667-J2
500 VAL 94590 530-A4
800 SF 94110 668-A5
1400 SF 94110 667-J4
ALADDIN AV
600 SLN 94577 691-A3
ALADDIN DR
5400 SJS 95123 875-B4
ALADDIN TER
- SF 94133 647-J4
ALAMATOS DR
100 DNVL 94526 653-B2
ALAMEDA AV
1500 ALA 94501 669-H2
2300 ALA 94501 670-A2
3200 OAK 94601 670-C2
5500 RCH 94804 609-B2
5500 ELCR 94530 609-B2
ALAMEDA CT
2100 SJS 95126 833-G5
37000 FRMT 94536 752-G4
ALAMEDA DR
400 LVMR 94550 695-E6
4400 FRMT 94536 752-G4
4700 PLE 94566 714-D1
ALAMEDA PL
- SBRN 94066 707-E7
ALAMEDA RD
- ALA 94501 649-D6
ALAMEDA ST
- VAL 94590 530-A4
300 SF 94107 668-C1
1700 SF 94103 668-A1
2200 SF 94103 667-J1
2500 VAL 94589 530-A1
ALAMEDA WY
2000 SJS 95126 833-G5
ALAMEDA DE LA LOMA
- NVTO 94949 546-D2
- MrnC 94949 546-D2
ALMDA D LS PULGAS
- SMCo 94062 789-H1
- ATN 94027 790-B4
- RDWC 94062 769-H6
100 BLMT 94002 749-A5
100 SMCo 94062 769-H6
200 SMTO 94402 748-H3
200 BLMT 94002 769-C1
400 RDWC 94062 789-J1
400 SCAR 94070 769-F4
400 SMCo 94062 769-H6
600 RDWC 94061 789-H1
1700 SMTO 94403 749-A5
1700 SMTO 94403 748-H3
1800 RDWC 94061 790-B4
1800 WDSD 94062 790-B4
2000 SMCo 94062 790-B4
2100 SMCo 94061 790-B4
3000 SMCo 94025 790-B4
3700 MLPK 94025 790-B4
ALAMEDA DEL PRADO
- NVTO 94949 546-F2
- MrnC 94949 546-F2
ALAMEDA DIABLO
1600 CCCo 94526 633-F6
ALAMEDA MARINA DR
- ALA 94501 669-J1

STREET
Block City ZIP Pg-Grid

ALAMITOS DR
100 SUNV 94086 812-B6
ALAMITOS CREEK RD
1000 SJS 95120 894-J4
ALAMO AV
- BERK 94708 609-G5
- CCCo 94801 588-F4
200 RCH 94801 588-F4
ALAMO CT
- AMCN 94589 509-J2
500 MTVW 94043 812-A4
1000 PIT 94565 573-H3
2700 ANT 94509 575-B6
4400 UNC 94587 731-J6
ALAMO DR
600 SJS 95123 874-G4
600 SJS 95131 814-A5
ALAMO GN
- CCCo 94526 633-A5
ALAMO LN
- CCCo 94507 632-G3
- WLCK 94596 632-G3
ALAMO ST
2400 PIN 94564 569-F6
4400 UNC 94587 731-J6
ALAMO TER
5400 FRMT 94555 752-B3
ALAMO WY
- CPTO 95014 852-A2
1100 PIT 94565 573-H3
1500 CCCo 94507 632-F4
ALAMO COUNTRY CIR
- CCCo 94507 632-H2
ALAMO GLEN DR
- CCCo 94507 633-A5
- CCCo 94526 633-A5
ALAMO GLEN TR
- CCCo 94507 633-A5
ALAMO HILLS CT
100 CCCo 94507 633-A5
ALAMO HILLS DR
100 CCCo 94507 633-A5
ALAMO OAKS LN
- CCCo 94526 633-B7
- DNVL 94526 633-B7
ALAMO RANCH RD
100 CCCo 94507 632-G5
ALAMOS PL
200 SRMN 94583 673-G5
ALAMOS RD
- PTLV 94028 810-E5
ALAMO SQUARE DR
- CCCo 94507 632-F5
ALAMO VIEW PL
1900 CCCo 94595 632-C1
ALAN AV
4900 SJS 95124 873-J4
ALAN CT
- SPAB 94806 589-A3
100 VAL 94591 530-G4
ALAN DR
- PLHL 94523 592-C3
ALAN PTH
3400 RCH 94803 589-E1
ALAN WY
- CCCo 94553 572-B5
ALANA CT
800 PLHL 94523 591-J5
ALANA DR
400 SJS 95136 854-E6
ALANA RD
19500 AlaC 94546 692-B5
ALANA WY
- BSBN 94005 688-B2
- SJS 95136 854-E6
- SF 94134 688-B2
ALANNAH CT
- PA 94303 791-C4
ALAN SHEPARD WY
- OAK 94621 690-D2
ALASDAIR CT
- SRFL 94903 566-C4
ALASKA DR
5500 CNCD 94521 593-F6
ALASKA ST
- OAK 94607 649-C1
ALASKA PACKER PL
- ALA 94501 649-J7
ALBA CT
200 LALT 94022 811-D5
800 SCIC 95127 814-H6
4100 PLE 94588 694-C6
ALBACORE LN
100 FCTY 94404 749-H3
ALBACORE TER
- FRMT 94536 753-F3
ALBANESE CIR
600 SJS 95111 854-G3
ALBANS CT
1100 ANT 94509 575-F7
ALBANY COM
39400 FRMT 94538 753-C4
ALBANY CT
1500 MPS 95035 794-D6
ALBANY DR
100 SJS 95129 853-A1
ALBANY ST
31900 HAY 94544 732-E3
ALBANY TER
1500 ALB 94706 609-E6
ALBAR CT
13900 SAR 95070 872-A1
ALBATROSS AV
100 LVMR 94550 715-E1
300 LVMR 94550 695-F7
ALBATROSS CT
- CMBL 95008 853-D5
ALBATROSS DR
600 NVTO 94945 526-H1
1500 SUNV 94087 832-E5
ALBATROSSE WY
100 VAL 94589 509-G5
ALBEMAR CT
3100 SJS 95148 855-D2
ALBEMARLE ST
400 ELCR 94530 609-D3
ALBEMARLE WY
1500 BURL 94010 728-C5
ALBERDAN CIR
1000 PIN 94564 569-C5
ALBERDAN CT
1200 PIN 94564 569-D5
ALBERNI ST
1000 EPA 94303 791-A1
ALBERNI ST Rt#-114
900 EPA 94303 771-A7
ALBERT
- CNCD 94518 592-G4
ALBERT AV
1700 SJS 95124 873-H4
ALBERT CT
100 LGTS 95032 873-B6
ALBERT DR
200 LGTS 95032 873-B6
ALBERT LN
- MLV 94941 606-G2
ALBERT ST
4300 OAK 94619 650-G6
ALBERT WY
200 LVMR 94550 715-D2
600 CMBL 95008 853-C7
ALBERTA AV
100 SCAR 94070 769-H5
500 SUNV 94087 832-D5
1700 SJS 95125 854-B4
ALBERTA CT
2300 SCL 95050 833-C2
24100 HAY 94545 711-F4
ALBERTA ST
- SF 94134 687-J1
ALBERTA TER
- WLCK 94596 612-D5
34400 FRMT 94555 752-C3
ALBERTA WY
200 LVMR 94550 716-B1
300 HIL 94010 748-E3
500 CNCD 94521 593-D6
ALBERTO WY
400 LGTS 95032 873-B7
ALBERT PARK LN
1000 SRFL 94901 586-F1
ALBERTS AV
- CCCo 94565 573-F2
ALBERTSTONE DR
4000 SJS 95130 853-B5
ALBERTSWORTH LN
10400 LAH 94024 831-E5
ALBINA AV
- BERK 94706 609-F7
ALBION AV
100 WDSD 94062 789-F5
200 AlaC 94580 691-D6
ALBION CT
300 NVTO 94947 526-D7
500 SJS 95136 874-F1
1200 SUNV 94024 832-A4
ALBION DR
500 SJS 95136 874-E1
ALBION LN
1200 SUNV 94024 832-A4
ALBION ST
- MrnC 94901 586-H3
- SF 94103 667-H2
100 SF 94110 667-H2
ALBO CT
- ORIN 94563 630-J4
ALBORG CT
5400 AlaC 94552 692-D2
ALBRAE ST
40000 FRMT 94538 773-A1
ALBRIGHT CT
- LGTS 95030 873-C3
ALBRIGHT WY
- LGTS 95030 873-C3
2500 SSF 94080 707-E5
ALBROOK DR
- DBLN 94568 694-C1
ALBURNI CT
- PLE 94566 715-B6
ALBY CT
1600 SJS 95124 873-J3
ALBYN CT
37200 NWK 94560 752-E7
ALCALA AV
9500 OAK 94605 671-B4
ALCALA CT
- PCFA 94044 726-J5
ALCALA ST
2700 ANT 94509 575-D6
ALCALDE CT
500 FRMT 94539 773-H1
ALCALDE ST
2100 SCL 95054 813-C4
ALCALDE WY
500 FRMT 94539 773-H1
ALCANTE DR
6000 SJS 95129 852-G3
ALCATRAZ AV
- BLV 94920 627-E1
- TBRN 94920 627-E1
300 OAK 94618 629-G5
400 OAK 94609 629-G5
1200 OAK 94608 629-F5
1200 BERK 94702 629-F5
1300 BERK 94703 629-G5
2700 BERK 94705 629-G5
ALCATRAZ FERRY
- SF - 627-J7
- SF 94133 647-J1
ALCAZAR AV
1400 HAY 94544 732-A1
21700 CPTO 95014 852-B1
21900 SCIC 95014 852-B1
ALCAZAR CT
400 DNVL 94526 653-D5
35800 FRMT 94536 752-F2
ALCAZAR DR
3000 BURL 94010 728-A6
5800 SJS 95123 874-G5
ALCOSTA BLVD
8900 SRMN 94583 693-G1
9300 SRMN 94583 673-E1
ALCOSTA CT
100 SRMN 94583 673-J7
ALCOSTA DR
700 MPS 95035 794-B6
ALCOSTA PL
4300 PIT 94565 574-E7
ALCOTT RD
200 SBRN 94066 727-F1
ALCOTT WY
18400 SAR 95070 872-H1
ALDAGROVE RD
3300 ANT 94509 595-C1
ALDEA ST
8000 DBLN 94568 693-H3
ALDEAN AV
300 MTVW 94043 811-F2
ALDEN CT
- WLCK 94598 612-G3
1200 BLMT 94002 769-D1
ALDEN LN
200 LVMR 94550 715-D4
200 AlaC 94550 715-D4
ALDEN RD
100 AlaC 94541 691-F7
ALDEN ST
200 RDWC 94063 770-A5
500 VAL 94590 530-A7
1800 BLMT 94002 769-C1
ALDEN WY
3500 SJS 95117 853-C1
ALDENGATE WY
2000 HAY 94545 711-G7
ALDENGLEN DR
100 SSF 94080 707-G2
ALDER AV
- CCCo 94595 612-B7
- FRMT 94536 752-G2
- SANS 94960 566-A6
100 SMCo 94015 687-B4
ALDER CT
- AMCN 94589 509-H3
- FRFX 94930 566-A6
100 HER 94547 569-J4
500 BEN 94510 550-J1
7400 PLE 94588 713-J1
13400 SAR 95070 852-E7
36500 FRMT 94536 752-G2
ALDER DR
500 MPS 95035 813-H2
ALDER LN
400 SMTO 94403 749-B6
ALDER PL
- MLPK 94025 790-H2
200 NVTO 94945 525-E2
ALDER ST
- SF 94134 688-A1
7800 OAK 94621 670-H3
ALDER TER
36500 FRMT 94536 752-G3
ALDER WY
1400 CNCD 94521 593-D5
ALDERBROOK CT
5800 AlaC 94552 692-C2
ALDERBROOK LN
800 CPTO 95014 852-F2
1000 SJS 95129 852-F3
ALDERBROOK PL
200 MRGA 94556 631-E6
ALDERBROOK WY
2200 PIT 94565 573-F4
ALDER CREEK CT
1600 SJS 95148 835-D4
ALDERLEE WY
- SCAR 94070 769-F5
ALDERNEY CT
22100 SCIC 94024 832-A6
ALDERNEY RD
- SANS 94960 566-B6
ALDER SPRING WY
7100 SJS 95139 895-F1
ALDERWOOD AV
1200 SUNV 94089 812-J3
ALDERWOOD CT
1800 SMTO 94402 748-H7
4000 PLE 94588 713-J2
ALDERWOOD DR
2400 ANT 94509 595-A2
2500 SJS 95132 814-C3
ALDERWOOD LN
- CCCo 94596 612-D1
- SRMN 94583 673-J6
ALDERWOOD RD
- CCCo 94596 612-D1
ALDERWOOD WY
- SRFL 94901 567-B5
ALDO AV
400 SCL 95054 813-E6
ALDO CT
14000 SJS 95127 835-A4
ALDRICH AL
- SF 94105 648-B6
ALDRICH WY
1500 SJS 95121 855-A2
ALDWORTH DR
2700 SJS 95148 835-E7
ALEF CT
- CLAY 94517 593-G6
ALEGRA CT
- WLCK 94598 612-E5
ALEGRA LN
100 WLCK 94598 612-E5
ALEGRA TER
400 MPS 95035 793-G3
ALEGRE AV
1000 LALT 94024 831-H1
ALEGRE CT
- DNVL 94526 653-B4
ALEGRE DR
11500 DBLN 94568 693-F4
ALEJANDRA AV
- MLPK 94027 790-E3
- ATN 94027 790-E3
ALEJANDRO DR
26800 LAH 94022 811-A5
ALELANTO LN
3100 SJS 95135 855-E3
ALEMA TER
4300 FRMT 94536 752-G3
ALEMAN CT
- WLCK 94596 612-A2
ALEMANY BLVD
- SF 94110 668-A6
- SF 94110 667-H6
- SF 94124 668-A6
800 SF 94112 667-G6
1900 SF 94112 687-E2
3200 SF 94132 687-C2
ALENE ST
7800 DBLN 94568 693-H3
ALERCHE DR
100 LGTS 95032 873-H7
ALERT AL
- SF 94114 667-H2
ALESIA CT
100 VAL 94589 510-E6
ALESSANDRO DR
3000 SJS 95135 855-E2
ALESTER AV
600 PA 94303 791-C4
ALETA PL
500 PLHL 94523 592-A3
ALEUT CT
200 FRMT 94539 773-J4
ALEX DR
4400 SJS 95130 853-A7
4600 SJS 95130 852-J7
ALEXANDER AV
- DALY 94014 687-D3
- LKSP 94939 586-F7
- SJS 95116 834-H2
- SRFL 94901 566-D7
- SAUS 94965 627-B4
- MrnC 94965 627-B4
100 SMCo 94061 790-B2
200 LGTS 95030 872-J7
200 MSER 95030 872-J7
3000 SCL 95051 833-A6
ALEXANDER CT
- PLE 94588 694-E7
- SJS 95116 834-H2
1600 LALT 94024 832-A4
3400 OAK 94601 650-C7
21000 HAY 94545 711-D4
ALEXANDER LN
- DNVL 94526 653-A4
ALEXANDER PL
300 CLAY 94517 593-G5
26200 LAH 94022 811-B6
ALEXANDER RD
- BSBN 94005 688-A7
ALEXANDER ST
100 CCCo 94525 550-E4
700 LVMR 94550 715-E2
37000 FRMT 94536 752-F5
ALEXANDER WY
400 MPS 95035 794-D5
1600 LALT 94024 832-A4
2100 PLE 94588 694-E7
ALEXANDRIA LN
4800 SJS 95129 853-B2
ALEXANDRIA ST
15000 SLN 94579 691-C6
ALEXIAN DR
2100 SJS 95116 834-G3
ALEXIS CIR
500 DALY 94014 687-H3
ALEXIS CT
- MLPK 94025 790-C7
900 SJS 95116 834-H5
1500 ANT 94509 575-F7
ALEXIS DR
3100 PA 94304 830-F1
3100 PA 94304 810-F7
3200 LAH 94022 810-G7
ALFONSO DR
3200 CNCD 94518 592-H6
ALFORD AV
1800 LALT 94024 832-A4
1900 LALT 94024 831-J5
ALFRED AV
900 WLCK 94596 612-A3
ALFRED DR
200 PIN 94564 569-D3
ALFRED ST
3000 SCL 95054 813-D7
ALFRED WY
2300 SJS 95122 834-J6
2400 SJS 95122 835-A6
ALFREDA AV
1800 SPAB 94806 588-H4
ALFRED NOBEL DR
- HER 94547 569-G1
ALGER DR
400 PA 94306 791-D7
400 PA 94306 811-D1
ALGER RD
3200 ANT 94509 595-C1
ALGIERS AV
1000 SJS 95122 834-G7
ALGIERS CIR
100 CCCo 94553 572-C7
ALGIERS WY
100 CCCo 94553 572-C7
ALGONQUIN AV
900 LVMR 94550 695-F7
ALGONQUIN WY
5600 SJS 95138 875-F1
ALHAMBRA AV
100 VAL 94591 530-D7
400 MRTZ 94553 571-D3
5500 MRTZ 94553 591-G2
5900 OAK 94611 630-E7
5900 CCCo 94553 591-G2
5900 PLHL 94523 591-G2
6000 PLHL 94553 591-G2
10000 CPTO 95014 832-B7
ALHAMBRA CT
- ANT 94509 575-F5
- PTLV 94028 810-D6
ALHAMBRA DR
1700 ANT 94509 575-F5
2600 BLMT 94002 749-B7
2600 BLMT 94002 769-A1
2700 SCL 95051 833-B1
4500 FRMT 94536 752-E3
ALHAMBRA LN
600 MRTZ 94553 571-E5
1600 OAK 94611 630-E6
ALHAMBRA RD
400 SSF 94080 707-F4
500 SMTO 94402 748-J2
700 CCCo 94803 589-C1
ALHAMBRA ST
- SF 94123 647-F4
300 CCCo 94525 550-E4
ALHAMBRA WY
600 MRTZ 94553 571-E6
2600 PIN 94564 569-H7
ALHAMBRA CREEK RD
- CCCo 94553 591-B3
ALHAMBRA HILLS CT
5600 MRTZ 94553 591-G1
ALHAMBRA HILLS DR
- MRTZ 94553 591-G1
ALHAMBRA VALLEY RD
500 CCCo - 590-B2
500 PIN 94564 589-H1
500 CCCo 94564 589-H1
4900 MRTZ 94553 571-E7
4900 MRTZ 94553 591-E3
4900 CCCo 94553 591-A2
5600 CCCo 94553 590-G3
ALICANTE CT
200 DNVL 94526 653-D6
1800 CNCD 94521 593-F5
ALICANTE DR
1000 DNVL 94526 653-D5
1100 PCFA 94044 727-A6
36300 FRMT 94536 752-F3
ALICANTE LN
25900 LAH 94022 811-C6
ALICANTE PL
200 DNVL 94526 653-D6
ALICANTE TER
- UNC 94587 732-E5
ALICE AV
- CMBL 95008 853-E6
400 MTVW 94043 812-A7
800 SLN 94577 671-B6
2100 WLCK 94596 632-F1
ALICE CT
100 DNVL 94526 652-J2
ALICE DR
1100 SCL 95050 833-D4
1800 VAL 94589 509-J5
ALICE LN
100 CCCo 94803 589-E1
100 ORIN 94563 631-B3
900 MLPK 94025 790-F4
ALICE PL
- ORIN 94563 631-C3
ALICE ST
- OAK 94607 649-G4
- SRFL 94901 586-H1
700 NVTO 94945 526-C4
1200 OAK 94612 649-G4
22500 HAY 94541 711-H2
24100 HAY 94544 711-J3
41100 FRMT 94539 753-E6
ALICE WY
- SANS 94960 566-B6
300 LVMR 94550 715-D2
900 SUNV 94087 832-G4
2500 PIN 94564 569-F4
4400 UNC 94587 732-A7
ALICE EASTWOOD CAMP RD
- MrnC 94965 606-A2
ALICIA ST
2700 OAK 94607 649-F2
ALICIA WY
200 LALT 94022 811-F5
ALIDA CT
- OAK 94602 650-E3
ALIDA ST
2400 OAK 94602 650-E3
ALIDA WY
300 SSF 94080 707-G4
300 SMCo 94080 707-G4
ALISAL AV
1500 SJS 95125 874-A1
ALISAL CT
400 DNVL 94526 653-A1
800 MPS 95035 794-B5
16800 AlaC 94580 691-F6
ALISAL ST
6000 AlaC 94566 714-E7
6000 AlaC 94586 714-E7
ALISO AV
3800 OAK 94619 650-G5
ALISO WY
- SMCo 94028 810-E3
ALISON AV
1500 MTVW 94040 811-H7
ALISON CIR
600 LVMR 94550 696-D7
ALISON ST
22900 HAY 94545 711-C4
ALKAE CT
1200 SJS 95121 855-A4
ALLA AV
900 CNCD 94518 592-G5
ALLA CT
900 CNCD 94518 592-G6
ALL AMERICA WY
700 SUNV 94086 832-D1
ALLAN ST
400 DALY 94014 687-J3
400 SF 94134 687-J3
ALLANHILL LN
3100 SMTO 94403 748-J6
ALLARDICE WY
800 SCIC 94305 810-J2
ALLBROOK CIR
6000 PLE 94588 694-A6
ALLEGAN CIR
300 SJS 95123 875-A6
ALLEGHANY CT
6500 SJS 95120 894-C6
ALLEGHENY CT
34600 FRMT 94555 752-D2
ALLEGHENY DR
500 WLCK 94598 612-E2
600 SUNV 94087 832-D1
1000 DNVL 94526 653-B4
6900 DBLN 94568 693-H3
ALLEGHENY WY
2200 SMCo 94402 768-G2
ALLEGRO AV
1500 CNCD 94521 593-F5
ALLEGRO CT
4800 FRMT 94538 773-B2
ALLEGRO LN
4500 SJS 95111 875-B1
ALLEMAND AV
- SANS 94960 566-C7
ALLEMANY ST
- DALY 94014 687-C5
ALLEN AV
- ROSS 94957 586-C2
5600 SJS 95123 874-F5
ALLEN CT
- SRFL 94901 566-E7
100 MRGA 94556 631-G5
700 PA 94303 791-D6
1500 AlaC 94546 691-H6
ALLEN CT
3300 SCL 95051 832-J7
36900 FRMT 94536 752-G3
ALLEN DR
- SBRN 94066 707-D6
ALLEN LN
- ROSS 94957 586-C2
- CCCo 94803 569-E7
ALLEN RD
200 SMCo 94062 809-C5
ALLEN ST
- SF 94109 647-J4
200 MRTZ 94553 571-E4
ALLEN WY
- BEN 94510 551-C2
100 PLHL 94523 592-A6
1000 CMBL 95008 853-B7
3100 SCL 95051 833-A7
3200 SCL 95051 832-J7
ALLENCREST DR
11700 SJS 95118 874-D4
ALLENDALE AV
3500 OAK 94619 650-E7
18400 SAR 95070 872-G1
ALLENDALE CT
- CCCo 94595 612-B6
ALLENSBY LN
- SRFL 94901 567-B7
- SRFL 94901 587-B1
ALLENTOWN CT
2300 SJS 95125 854-D7
ALLENWOOD CT
2900 SJS 95148 855-D1
ALLENWOOD DR
3000 SJS 95148 855-D1
ALLERTON AV
300 SSF 94080 708-B3
ALLERTON ST
400 RDWC 94063 770-A5
ALLEY WY
- MTVW 94040 811-F3
ALLINE ST
41100 FRMT 94538 753-C7
41100 FRMT 94538 773-C1
ALLISON CT
100 VAL 94589 510-E6
3400 SMTO 94403 748-J7
ALLISON DR
32200 UNC 94587 732-A6
ALLISON LN
5400 RCH 94803 589-F3
ALLISON ST
- SF 94112 687-F2
ALLISON WY
700 SUNV 94087 832-C4
1800 SJS 95131 814-C4
ALLMAN ST
1300 OAK 94602 650-C4
ALLSTON CT
1100 SJS 95120 894-F2
ALLSTON WY
- SF 94127 13-D5
700 BERK 94804 629-D2
1100 BERK 94702 629-E2
1100 SJS 95120 894-F2
1500 BERK 94703 629-F2
2000 BERK 94704 629-F2
ALLVIEW AV
700 CCCo 94803 569-D7
ALL VIEW WY
2600 BLMT 94002 769-B1
ALLYN AV
- SANS 94960 566-A7
ALLYSON TER
4000 FRMT 94538 773-D1
ALMA AV
600 OAK 94610 650-A4
1300 WLCK 94596 612-C6
4300 AlaC 94546 692-A3
W ALMA AV
- SJS 95110 854-C2
200 SJS 95125 854-C2
ALMA CT
- LALT 94022 811-E5
1300 SJS 95112 854-D2
3900 PLE 94588 714-A1
ALMA LN
- MLPK 94025 790-F3
ALMA LP
1400 SJS 95125 854-C3
ALMA PL
800 OAK 94610 650-B4
ALMA ST
- MLPK 94025 790-G3
- PA 94301 790-H4
- SF 94117 667-E2
200 SF 94117 667-E2
1100 PA 94301 791-B7
1500 PA 94306 791-B7
2000 SCAR 94070 769-F3
3000 PA 94306 811-D1
3900 MTVW 94040 811-D1
38600 FRMT 94536 752-H6
E ALMA ST
- SJS 95112 854-D2
ALMA TER
1500 SJS 95125 854-C3
ALMA BRIDGE RD
17200 SCIC 95030 893-A4
ALMADEN AV
100 MPS 95035 793-J6
400 SJS 95110 834-B7
500 SJS 95110 854-C1
800 SUNV 94086 812-H5
21800 CPTO 95014 852-B1
S ALMADEN AV
- SJS 95113 834-B6
ALMADEN BLVD
32000 UNC 94587 732-C5
N ALMADEN BLVD
100 SJS 95110 834-B6
100 SJS 95113 834-B6
S ALMADEN BLVD
- SJS 95113 834-B6
- SJS 95110 834-B6
ALMADEN CT
- LFYT 94549 591-H7
500 SF 94118 647-D6
26700 LAH 94022 830-J2
26800 LAH 94022 831-A2
ALMADEN EXWY
Rt#-G8
1500 SJS 95125 854-C6
3300 SJS 95118 854-C6
3300 SJS 95136 854-C6
3500 SJS 95118 874-D2
3500 SJS 95136 874-D2
4000 SJS 95118 854-C7
4000 SJS 95136 854-C7
5900 SJS 95120 874-D2
6600 SJS 95120 894-F2
8900 SJS 95123 874-D2
ALMADEN LN
5900 OAK 94611 630-E7
ALMADEN PL
2400 UNC 94587 732-C5
38700 FRMT 94536 753-D2
ALMADEN RD
1300 SJS 95110 854-C3
1300 SJS 95125 854-C3
3300 SJS 95118 874-C1
5900 SJS 95118 874-D6
6500 SJS 95120 894-E1
18800 SCIC 95120 894-J5
19700 SCIC 95120 895-A6
ALMADEN WY
200 SMTO 94403 749-D5
21700 SCIC 95120 894-J7
ALMADEN LAKE DR
900 SJS 95123 874-D5
ALMADEN VALLEY DR
1400 SJS 95120 874-A6
ALMADEN VILLAGE RD
1100 SJS 95120 894-G3
ALMADINE WY
100 DNVL 94506 653-G5
ALMA JO CT
15100 MSER 95030 872-J4
ALMANOR AV
400 SSF 94080 707-F4
600 SUNV 94086 812-E4
1000 MLPK 94025 790-H1
1100 MLPK 94025 770-J7
ALMANOR CT
900 LFYT 94549 611-G6
1300 SJS 95132 814-F5
2500 LVMR 94550 715-G5
ALMANOR LN
900 LFYT 94549 611-G6
ALMANSA CT
3200 SJS 95127 814-H6
ALMANZA DR
400 OAK 94603 670-H7
ALMAR CT
1200 CNCD 94518 592-G3
ALMARIDA DR
500 CMBL 95008 853-F5
1000 CMBL 95128 853-E3
1100 SJS 95128 853-E3
ALMEDA ST
20400 AlaC 94546 691-H5
ALMENAR DR
- MrnC 94904 586-F4
N ALMENAR DR
200 MrnC 94904 586-F3
200 LKSP 94904 586-F3
ALMENAR ST
800 MLBR 94030 728-A4
ALMENDRA AV
200 LGTS 95030 873-A7
ALMENDRA CT
1100 CNCD 94518 592-G3
ALMENDRA LN
- LALT 94022 811-E6
ALMENDRAL AV
- ATN 94027 790-C3
ALMER RD
500 BURL 94010 728-F7
ALMERIA AV
100 FRMT 94539 753-E3
ALMERIA DR
700 SJS 95123 874-F5
1400 HAY 94544 732-A1
ALMOND AV
- LALT 94022 811-E6
600 LALT 94024 811-E6
700 SSF 94080 707-H2
1100 LVMR 94550 716-B2
1500 AlaC 94550 716-B2
1700 WLCK 94596 612-B5
2000 CNCD 94520 592-F1
3700 FRMT 94538 753-D7
ALMOND CIR
4600 LVMR 94550 716-B1
ALMOND CT
- EPA 94303 791-C2
- NVTO 94947 526-D7
300 SRMN 94583 673-G7
1500 WLCK 94596 612-C5
3700 AlaC 94546 691-J3
ALMOND DR
2500 SJS 95148 835-C7
ALMOND RD
17300 AlaC 94546 691-J2
ALMOND ST
300 VAL 94589 510-A7
900 ANT 94509 575-D5
2600 CCCo 94553 571-G4
ALMOND BLOSSOM CT
100 LGTS 95032 873-J6
ALMOND BLOSSOM LN
1600 SJS 95124 873-H6
1700 LGTS 95032 873-H6
ALMOND HILL CT
100 LGTS 95030 873-C3
ALMOND HILLS PL
3800 AlaC 94546 691-J3
ALMONDRIDGE DR
2600 ANT 94509 575-H6
ALMOND TREE CT
3100 ANT 94509 575-J6
ALMONDWOOD CT
1800 CNCD 94519 573-A7
ALMONDWOOD DR
1200 ANT 94509 575-F7
ALMONDWOOD WY
700 SJS 95120 894-H3
ALMONTE BLVD
100 MrnC 94941 606-F6
100 MLV 94941 606-F5
ALOE CT
46900 FRMT 94539 773-J5

STREET Block City ZIP Pg-Grid

ALOHA
200 PIT 94565 574-E5
ALOHA AV
- SF 94122 667-C3
14500 SAR 95070 872-D3
ALOHA DR
200 SJS 95136 854-G7
300 SLN 94578 691-C5
ALOMAR WY
1100 BLMT 94002 769-D2
ALONDA CT
800 HAY 94541 711-F3
ALONDRA LN
15100 SAR 95070 872-F4
ALONSO CT
4600 FRMT 94555 752-B1
ALONSO DR
1100 SJS 95126 853-G3
ALORA CT
300 SRMN 94583 673-C3
ALOYSE CT
2300 CCCo 94596 612-E7
ALP AV
- DALY 94014 687-D3
ALP WY
- MLBR 94030 727-J4
ALPHA CT
600 CMBL 95008 873-C1
3700 AlaC 94546 692-B4
ALPHA LN
1200 AlaC 94586 734-G4
ALPHA ST
- SF 94134 688-A2
ALPHA WY
1800 ANT 94509 575-E6
ALPINE AV
- DALY 94015 687-A5
- LGTS 95032 893-B1
200 SJS 95127 834-H1
800 BURL 94010 728-F6
1100 MLPK 94025 770-H7
1300 SCL 95051 833-A4
ALPINE CT
- MRTZ 94553 591-G3
- PIT 94565 574-F7
- VAL 94591 530-F4
300 SSF 94080 707-F5
3100 FRMT 94555 732-D6
ALPINE DR
1300 PIT 94565 574-F6
1500 CNCD 94521 593-B3
3100 FRMT 94555 732-D7
10100 CPTO 95014 832-A7
22500 CPTO 95014 831-J7
ALPINE RD
- SCIC 94028 830-E4
- SMCo 94020 830-D5
- PTLV 94028 810-D7
- PTLV 94028 830-C1
- SMCo 94028 810-E3
- SMCo 94028 830-D5
300 SMCo 94025 810-E3
1100 WLCK 94596 612-B5
2400 SMCo 94025 790-E7
2400 MLPK 94025 790-E7
2500 MLPK 94025 810-E3
5400 SPAB 94806 589-A4
5700 CCCo 94806 589-A4
ALPINE ST
100 SRFL 94901 566-D6
39000 NWK 94560 772-H1
ALPINE TER
- OAK 94618 630-B5
- SANS 94960 566-C6
- SF 94117 667-G1
900 SUNV 94086 812-C6
ALPINE WY
100 SBRN 94066 727-F1
1900 HAY 94545 711-D5
ALPS CT
2200 MRTZ 94553 572-A7
ALQUIRE PKWY
600 HAY 94544 712-D7
ALQUIRE RD
600 HAY 94544 712-G5
700 HAY 94542 712-G5
ALRAY DR
1700 CNCD 94519 592-J1
ALRIC CT
300 SJS 95123 875-B7
ALRIC DR
300 SJS 95123 875-B7
ALRIDGE DR
1300 SUNV 94087 832-D4
ALRO AV
4800 CNCD 94521 593-D4
ALRO CT
1500 CNCD 94521 593-D4
ALSACE CT
- LVMR 94550 715-H4
- SJS 95135 855-F3
ALSION CT
700 FRMT 94539 753-G7
ALTA AV
- MrnC 94965 606-G7
- PDMT 94611 630-C7
- PDMT 94611 650-C1
- MrnC 94965 626-G1
300 SAUS 94965 626-H2
500 SMTO 94403 749-A5
500 MrnC 94965 627-A4
500 SAUS 94965 627-A4
800 MTVW 94043 811-H1
ALTA CT
- PIT 94565 574-C3
2200 SJS 95131 814-A5
4000 PLE 94588 714-A1
37700 FRMT 94536 752-G5
ALTA DR
37800 FRMT 94536 752-H5
ALTA LN
- SCAR 94070 769-E3
3200 LFYT 94549 611-H6
N ALTA LN
13000 LAH 94022 831-C1
S ALTA LN
13000 LAH 94022 831-C1
ALTA RD
- BERK 94708 609-G4
100 OAK 94618 630-C6
ALTA ST
- LKSP 94939 586-E5

ALTA ST
- SF 94133 648-A4
ALTA TER
- CMAD 94925 606-G1
ALTA WY
- CMAD 94925 606-G1
500 MrnC 94965 606-E6
ALTADENA AV
3900 SCIC 95127 835-A1
ALTADENA DR
26000 LAH 94022 811-B6
ALTA GLEN CT
1500 SJS 95125 853-J4
ALTA GLEN DR
1500 SJS 95125 853-J4
ALTA HACIENDAS
100 ORIN 94563 610-G4
ALTA HEIGHTS CT
100 LGTS 95032 893-B1
ALTA HILL WY
- CCCo 94595 612-B6
ALTAIR AV
600 FCTY 94404 749-E3
1800 LVMR 94550 715-E4
ALTAIR WY
300 SUNV 94086 812-E7
ALTA LOMA
- BEN 94510 551-A4
ALTA LOMA AV
100 DALY 94015 687-B6
ALTA LOMA CT
- DNVL 94526 653-C1
ALTA LOMA DR
- AMCN 94589 510-A1
- AMCN 94589 509-J2
100 SSF 94080 707-D2
ALTA LOMA PL
500 SRMN 94583 673-G6
ALTA MAR WY
- SF 94121 646-H6
ALTAMAR WY
1500 LVMR 94550 696-D3
ALTAMEAD DR
1100 LALT 94024 831-H2
ALTA MESA
1000 MRGA 94556 631-E6
ALTA MESA AV
4100 PA 94306 811-D2
ALTA MESA CIR
- MRGA 94556 631-E6
ALTA MESA DR
100 SSF 94080 707-E3
ALTA MESA RD
100 WDSD 94062 789-G5
ALTAMIRA AV
- MrnC 94904 586-D3
ALTA MIRA DR
1000 SCL 95051 832-J4
2900 RCH 94806 589-A1
ALTA MIRA PL
1800 SJS 95124 873-H1
ALTAMIRANO CIR
1100 PIN 94564 569-E5
ALTAMONT AV
- MLV 94941 606-F3
1500 SJS 95125 874-A1
3700 OAK 94605 670-J1
ALTAMONT CIR
27700 SCIC 94022 830-G1
ALTAMONT CT
800 SUNV 94086 812-G5
12100 LAH 94022 831-B2
ALTAMONT DR
300 SSF 94080 707-E3
400 MPS 95035 794-A5
ALTAMONT LN
27100 LAH 94022 831-A3
ALTAMONT RD
2000 AlaC 94578 691-D3
25300 LAH 94022 831-A2
26600 LAH 94022 830-H1
ALTAMONT WY
3500 RDWC 94062 789-H1
ALTAMONT CREEK DR
- LVMR 94550 696-D2
ALTAMONT PASS RD
8500 AlaC 94550 696-F3
ALTAMOUNT DR
- ORIN 94563 631-B4
ALTA PASEO CT
6500 SJS 95120 894-B2
ALTA PUNTA DR
- VAL 94591 550-D1
ALTA PUNTA ST
5600 ELCR 94530 589-B7
ALTARINDA CIR
- ORIN 94563 610-J6
E ALTARINDA DR
- ORIN 94563 610-H6
ALTARINDA RD
- ORIN 94563 610-H7
ALTA SIERRA PL
2300 CCCo 94507 632-J5
ALTA TIERRA CT
100 LGTS 95032 893-H1
ALTA TIERRA RD
12800 LAH 94022 831-B1
ALTA VISTA
- ORIN 94563 610-E7
3000 ALA 94502 669-J6
3900 PIT 94565 574-B6
ALTA VISTA AV
- MLV 94941 606-E3
- SANS 94960 586-C1
100 LALT 94022 811-D6
300 OAK 94610 649-J2
13900 SAR 95070 872-E2
ALTA VISTA CIR
3800 PIT 94565 574-B6
ALTA VISTA CT
- NVTO 94949 546-H3
- PIT 94565 574-B6
400 DNVL 94506 653-H4
1100 WLCK 94596 612-C5
ALTA VISTA DR
100 ATN 94027 790-A5
200 SMCo 94080 707-F5
300 SSF 94080 707-F5
600 PCFA 94044 726-J4
6400 ELCR 94530 589-C6
ALTA VISTA RD
100 WDSD 94062 789-G5

ALTA VISTA RD
700 MrnC 94965 606-D7
ALTA VISTA TER
1600 SF 94133 647-J4
ALTA VISTA WY
- SMCo 94014 687-F3
- SRFL 94901 586-H1
- DALY 94014 687-F3
- MrnC 94901 586-H1
100 DNVL 94506 653-G4
15700 SCIC 95127 815-B6
E ALTA VISTA WY
15700 SCIC 95127 815-B6
15800 SJS 95127 815-B6
ALTENA ST
- MrnC 94901 586-H3
ALTER LN
- NVTO 94945 526-B2
ALTHAM CT
1500 SJS 95132 814-F4
ALTHOFF WY
1300 SJS 95116 834-F6
ALTIA AV
- SJS 95135 855-G3
ALTIPLANO WY
700 PIN 94564 569-E4
6700 SJS 95119 875-D7
ALTISSIMO PL
- SJS 95131 814-B6
ALTO AV
- SANS 94960 566-C6
ALTO CT
2500 SJS 95148 835-D6
ALTO LN
- MLPK 94025 790-G4
ALTO ST
- SRFL 94901 586-J2
ALTO WY
7700 DBLN 94568 693-F3
ALTO LOMA
100 MLBR 94030 727-J5
ALTON AV
- SF 94116 667-D4
ALTON CT
3300 FRMT 94536 752-J3
ALTON PL
- SRMN 94583 673-F6
ALTON ST
- MPS 95035 793-J7
ALTOS OAKS DR
700 LALT 94024 831-G2
ALTO VERDE LN
12700 LAH 94022 811-B6
ALTREE CT
- ATN 94027 790-H1
ALTSCHUL AV
900 MLPK 94025 790-D6
1000 SMCo 94025 790-D6
ALTURA DR
1900 CNCD 94519 572-G7
1900 CNCD 94519 592-H1
ALTURA PL
400 FRMT 94536 753-D2
7200 OAK 94605 671-A1
ALTURA ST
38700 FRMT 94536 753-D2
ALTURA WY
- SRFL 94901 586-G3
- MrnC 94904 586-G3
- SSF 94080 707-E2
- LKSP 94904 586-G3
900 PCFA 94044 726-J4
1500 BLMT 94002 769-E2
ALTURAS AV
200 SUNV 94086 812-F4
ALTURAS DR
100 SMCo 94010 728-A7
1500 BURL 94010 728-B7
ALTURAS WY
- DALY 94014 687-E3
400 MrnC 94941 606-E6
ALTURA VISTA
100 LGTS 95030 872-J2
ALUM ROCK AV
11600 SCIC 95127 815-B6
14600 SJS 95127 815-B6
ALUM ROCK AV
Rt#-130
1100 SJS 95116 834-E4
3400 SJS 95127 834-H3
3500 SCIC 95127 834-H3
5900 SCIC 95127 834-H3
6900 SJS 95127 835-A1
8900 SCIC 95127 815-A7
ALUMROCK DR
500 ANT 94509 595-E2
ALUM ROCK RD
16100 SJS 95127 815-B5
ALUM ROCK FALLS RD
18200 SJS 95127 815-D5
18200 SJS 95132 815-B5
20400 SCIC 95127 815-F5
20400 SCIC 95132 815-F5
20600 SCIC 95140 815-F5
ALVA AV
2200 ELCR 94530 589-C7
ALVANIECE CT
42400 FRMT 94539 753-F7
ALVARADO AV
- LALT 94022 811-E5
- MLV 94941 606-E3
- PIT 94565 574-C4
200 VAL 94590 530-A2
700 SUNV 94086 812-G5
1200 PCFA 94044 727-A5
1300 BURL 94010 728-C6
1400 SMCo 94010 728-C6
1500 WLCK 94596 612-A3
ALVARADO BLVD
- UNC 94545 731-J5
31500 UNC 94587 731-J5
32100 UNC 94587 732-A5
32700 FRMT 94555 732-A5
ALVARADO CT
700 SCIC 94305 810-J1
1600 LVMR 94550 695-F6
5900 SJS 95120 874-A7
13400 SAR 95070 872-H1
ALVARADO DR
2000 ANT 94509 595-B1
2300 SCL 95051 833-C2
ALVARADO PL
- OAK 94705 630-A3

ALVARADO PL
6100 ELCR 94530 589-C6
ALVARADO RD
- BERK 94705 630-A3
- OAK 94705 630-A3
ALVARADO RW
500 SCIC 94305 790-H7
500 SCIC 94305 810-H1
ALVARADO ST
- BSBN 94005 688-A6
- SF 94110 667-H3
- SPAB 94806 588-J2
200 RCH 94801 608-D1
400 SF 94114 667-F3
700 SLN 94577 690-J1
1100 SLN 94577 691-A2
3400 SLN 94578 691-A3
4000 PLE 94566 714-E2
ALVARADO TER
100 MRTZ 94553 571-D4
ALVARADO-NILES RD
31100 UNC 94587 732-A5
35200 FRMT 94536 732-C5
ALVAREZ AV
700 PIN 94564 569-E4
ALVERN CT
100 CCCo 94507 632-F5
ALVERNAZ DR
1100 SJS 95121 855-A5
ALVERNO CT
- RDWC 94061 789-G3
ALVERTUS AV
19600 AlaC 94546 691-J4
ALVES CT
1100 SJS 95131 814-A4
ALVES DR
20500 CPTO 95014 832-D7
ALVES LN
- CCCo 94565 573-F2
ALVES ST
24200 HAY 94544 711-J3
ALVES RANCH RD
- CCCo - 573-F3
- PIT - 573-F3
- PIT 94565 573-F3
ALVESWOOD CIR
2400 SJS 95131 814-C4
ALVIENA DR
2900 SCIC 95133 834-H1
ALVIN AV
2400 SJS 95121 854-J2
2600 SJS 95121 855-A2
ALVIN ST
2400 MTVW 94043 811-F2
ALVINA AV
- SRFL 94901 586-F2
ALVINA CT
700 LALT 94024 831-G2
ALVINA DR
1900 PLHL 94523 592-B5
ALVINGROOM CT
2600 OAK 94605 671-A3
ALVISO CT
- PCFA 94044 726-J5
- PCFA 94044 727-A5
200 DNVL 94526 653-D6
ALVISO PL
1600 LVMR 94550 695-F6
ALVISO ST
- SF 94132 687-C1
- SF 94127 667-C7
- SJS 95050 833-F5
- SCL 95050 833-E3
500 SCL 95050 833-F5
1100 SJS 95126 833-F5
ALVISO WY
300 DNVL 94526 653-D5
ALVISO-MILPITAS RD
- MPS 95035 813-G1
1500 SJS 95134 813-F1
1500 SCIC 95134 813-G1
ALVORD WY
6100 PLE 94588 694-A6
ALWIN RD
- WLCK 94598 612-D5
ALWOOD CT
2800 SJS 95148 835-D7
ALYSHEBA AV
200 SJS 95111 875-B3
ALYSIA CT
- LVMR 94550 696-B6
ALYSSUM CT
- NVTO 94945 526-B2
AMADOR AV
- ATN 94027 790-C3
100 SBRN 94066 707-E7
400 LALT 94024 811-F7
800 SUNV 94086 812-H5
1100 BERK 94707 609-G6
1500 CNCD 94520 592-F2
AMADOR CT
- CCCo 94565 573-H2
300 PLE 94566 714-F3
600 MRTZ 94553 571-E7
2300 SJS 95122 834-J5
AMADOR DR
2200 SJS 95122 834-J5
AMADOR PL
6000 NWK 94560 752-F7
AMADOR RD
4300 FRMT 94538 753-A6
AMADOR ST
- SF 94124 668-C4
- VAL 94590 530-B4
600 RCH 94805 589-B5
1000 SPAB 94805 589-A4
1000 SPAB 94806 589-A4
22500 HAY 94541 711-G2
24000 HAY 94544 711-H3
AMADOR OAK CT
10000 CPTO 95014 831-J7
AMADOR PLAZA RD
6600 DBLN 94568 693-H4
AMADOR VALLEY BLVD
6500 DBLN 94568 694-A2
6800 DBLN 94568 693-G4
AMADOR VALLEY CT
6500 DBLN 94568 693-G4
AMALCO WY
700 UNC 94587 732-G5
AMALFI PL
- SRFL 94901 586-J1

AMALFI WY
400 RDWC 94065 749-J4
1900 MTVW 94040 831-H1
AMALIA AV
4100 CCCo 94553 572-A4
4100 CCCo 94553 571-J4
AMANDA CT
- CCCo 94526 633-D4
AMANDA DR
700 SJS 95136 874-E1
AMANDA LN
- NVTO 94945 525-H2
100 LGTS 95032 873-D6
AMANDA PL
4700 PLE 94566 714-F5
AMANDA ST
7200 DBLN 94568 693-J3
AMAPALA ST
26600 HAY 94545 711-G7
AMAPOLA AV
100 PCFA 94044 727-B2
AMAPOLA CT
41000 FRMT 94539 753-F5
AMAPOLA DR
5800 SJS 95129 852-G3
40800 FRMT 94539 753-F5
AMAPOLO CT
23800 CPTO 95014 831-G5
AMARAL CIR
400 PLE 94566 714-F3
AMARAL CT
2400 HAY 94587 732-B4
2400 UNC 94587 732-B4
AMARAL ST
31900 HAY 94587 732-B4
31900 UNC 94587 732-B4
AMARANTA AV
4000 PA 94306 811-C2
AMARANTA CT
4100 PA 94306 811-C3
AMARANTH BLVD
600 MrnC 94941 606-C4
AMARANTH PL
5700 CNCD 94521 593-G7
AMARANTH WY
1200 CNCD 94521 593-G7
AMARGOSA CT
400 SJS 95111 854-G7
AMARGOSA DR
4200 ANT 94509 595-J1
AMARILLO AV
900 PA 94303 791-D5
AMARILLO CT
11600 DBLN 94568 693-F4
48700 FRMT 94539 793-J2
AMARILLO DR
- AMCN 94589 509-J2
AMARILLO RD
7300 DBLN 94568 693-F4
AMARYL CT
2500 SJS 95132 814-E6
AMARYL DR
2400 SJS 95132 814-E5
AMATE WY
200 CCCo 94553 572-C7
AMATO AV
- CMBL 95008 853-C5
AMATURY LP
400 SF 94129 647-C4
AMAZON AV
- SF 94112 687-F1
AMBAR PL
40500 FRMT 94539 753-E4
AMBAR WY
300 MLPK 94025 790-F6
AMBASSADOR CT
200 LGTS 95032 893-A1
AMBER AV
200 VAL 94589 510-B7
AMBER CT
- HER 94547 569-G4
- NVTO 94947 525-G4
- SCAR 94070 769-F6
500 LVMR 94550 715-D2
1200 SLN 94577 690-H1
AMBER DR
- SF 94131 667-F4
500 ANT 94509 575-E5
3400 SJS 95117 853-C3
AMBER ISLE
500 ALA 94501 669-G2
AMBER LN
- CCCo 94549 611-J2
500 MRTZ 94553 591-G4
800 LALT 94024 831-E1
6100 PLE 94566 714-D6
6400 AlaC 94566 714-D6
AMBER PL
- CCCo 94507 632-E4
AMBER WY
100 LVMR 94550 715-D2
AMBERDALE CT
5200 ANT 94509 595-E5
AMBERDALE WY
5200 ANT 94509 595-E5
AMBERFIELD LN
- DNVL 94506 653-J6
AMBERFIELD TER
600 FRMT 94536 753-G3
AMBERGROVE DR
1400 SJS 95131 814-C7
AMBER OAK CT
100 LGTS 95030 873-B2
AMBER VALLEY DR
100 ORIN 94563 610-J3
AMBERWOOD CIR
4100 PLE 94588 714-A1
4100 PLE 94588 713-J1
AMBERWOOD CT
- MRGA 94556 651-F2
2000 SJS 95132 814-D3
4000 ANT 94509 595-D4
AMBERWOOD DR
5000 FRMT 94555 752-C2
AMBERWOOD LN
- SANS 94960 566-C7
- WLCK 94598 612-F1
2000 SJS 95132 814-D2
AMBERWOOD WY
500 LVMR 94550 695-J6
AMBIENCE WY
600 DNVL 94506 653-J4

AMBLER CT
3900 SJS 95111 855-A6
AMBLER WY
3900 SJS 95111 855-A6
AMBLESIDE CT
- DNVL 94526 653-D3
AMBLESIDE LN
18600 SAR 95070 872-H3
AMBOY CT
- SMCo 94402 768-G1
AMBOY DR
500 SJS 95136 874-F2
AMBRA WY
3400 SJS 95132 814-G2
AMBRIC KNOLLS RD
14600 SAR 95070 872-C3
AMBROSE AV
- CCCo 94565 573-F2
AMBROSE CT
300 HAY 94544 711-J4
4000 SJS 95121 855-A5
AMBROSE RD
17000 SCIC 95070 872-B7
AMBROSIA WY
- CCCo 94565 573-G2
AMBUM AV
3400 SJS 95148 835-E7
AMBY DR
5400 SJS 95124 873-J6
AMD PL
- SUNV 94086 812-H6
AMECA CT
4100 FRMT 94536 752-E2
AMELIA AV
32000 HAY 94544 732-F2
AMELIA CT
10100 CPTO 95014 832-A7
AMELIA DR
5100 SJS 95118 874-A4
AMELIA LN
300 CCCo 94506 654-C5
AMELIA ST
100 VAL 94589 510-C5
8300 OAK 94621 670-G4
AMELIA WY
- PIT 94565 574-A2
1800 SCL 95050 833-C3
AMEND CT
200 CCCo 94803 589-G2
AMEND RD
5200 CCCo 94803 589-G2
5200 RCH 94803 589-H3
AMEND ST
1000 PIN 94564 569-D5
AMENO CT
1000 LFYT 94549 611-H6
AMENO DR
3200 LFYT 94549 611-H6
AMENO RD
3100 CNCD 94519 572-H7
AMERICA AV
300 SUNV 94086 812-F6
AMERICAN AV
2000 HAY 94545 711-D5
AMERICAN CT
6500 SJS 95120 894-C6
AMERICAN ST
800 SCAR 94070 769-H4
AMERICAN WY
1300 SMCo 94025 790-D5
AMERICAN BEAUTY CT
5100 CNCD 94521 593-E4
AMERICAN BEAUTY DR
1500 CNCD 94521 593-E4
AMERICAN CANYON RD
- AMCN 94589 510-A3
- NaCo 94589 510-A3
1800 VAL 94589 510-D3
W AMERICAN CYN RD
- AMCN 94589 509-H3
- AMCN 94589 510-A3
- NaCo 94589 509-H3
AMERICAN OAK DR
8600 SJS 95135 855-J6
AMERICUS DR
3300 SJS 95148 835-E7
AMES AV
- ROSS 94957 586-C2
700 MPS 95035 814-C1
700 PA 94303 791-D7
AMES CT
800 PA 94303 791-E6
1100 ANT 94509 575-F6
AMES ST
- SF 94110 667-H3
2800 LVMR 94550 696-B1
AMES TER
36400 FRMT 94536 752-J1
AMESBURY AV
600 SMTO 94402 749-B2
AMESBURY CT
- DNVL 94526 653-C3
1900 WLCK 94596 612-G7
1900 WLCK 94596 632-G1
AMESBURY WY
1400 SJS 95127 835-A4
AMETHYST CT
100 HER 94547 569-G4
5000 SJS 95136 874-E3
AMETHYST DR
2100 SCL 95051 833-A1
AMETHYST RD
5200 FRMT 94538 773-B1
AMETHYST WY
- SF 94131 667-E4
AMHERST AV
- SMCo 94063 790-D1
100 VAL 94589 510-B5
100 CCCo 94708 609-F3
AMHERST CT
- SRMN 94583 693-G1
1200 SLN 94579 691-A4
3500 MTVW 94040 831-J2
14100 LAH 94022 810-H5
AMHERST DR
19600 CPTO 95014 832-F7
AMHERST LN
3200 SJS 95117 853-D3
AMHERST ST
- SF 94134 667-J7
200 SMTO 94402 748-H2
2000 PA 94306 810-J1

AMHERST WY
4200 LVMR 94550 716-A1
AMHURST CT
- DALY 94015 707-D3
900 CNCD 94518 592-E7
AMHURST WY
1500 CNCD 94518 592-E7
AMICITA AV
- MLV 94941 606-E4
AMIENS AV
4400 FRMT 94555 752-C1
AMIGO LN
- CCCo 94596 612-G7
AMIGO RD
100 DNVL 94526 653-B2
AMIGOS CT
24400 SCIC 94024 831-E2
24400 LAH 94024 831-E2
AMITO AV
1000 OAK 94705 630-B3
AMITY AL
600 SF 94109 647-J6
AMONDO DR
5000 SJS 95129 852-J3
AMORCO RD
400 MRTZ 94553 571-F1
AMOROK WY
- FRMT 94539 773-J5
AMOROSO CT
2900 PLE 94566 714-H3
AMOS WY
4000 SJS 95135 855-F3
AMPHITHEATRE PKWY
- MTVW 94043 811-H1
AMPHLETT BLVD
- SMTO 94401 729-A7
- SMTO 94401 749-B1
600 SMTO 94402 749-B1
N AMPHLETT BLVD
- SMTO 94401 729-A7
200 SMTO 94401 728-J6
AMPHLETT PL
1600 SMTO 94402 749-C2
AMSTEL CT
2100 SJS 95116 834-G3
AMSTUTZ DR
900 SJS 95129 853-A3
AMULET DR
21200 CPTO 95014 832-C6
AMULET PL
10600 CPTO 95014 832-C6
AMUR CT
2000 MPS 95035 793-J3
AMUR CREEK CT
1100 SJS 95120 894-G4
AMUR OAK LN
100 SJS 95116 834-G4
AMY CT
3800 UNC 94587 731-J5
4600 LVMR 94550 696-B7
AMY DR
- SMTO 94403 748-H7
5600 OAK 94618 630-C7
AMY PL
3800 UNC 94587 731-J5
AMY WY
2400 CCCo 94507 632-E2
AMYX CT
3800 AlaC 94542 712-E2
ANA CT
- SRFL 94903 566-D3
ANACAPA CT
700 MPS 95035 794-B6
12900 LAH 94022 811-A6
ANACAPA DR
26300 LAH 94022 811-A6
ANACAPA LN
600 FCTY 94404 749-G5
ANACONDA WY
900 SUNV 94087 832-B4
ANAHEIM LP
5000 UNC 94587 752-A1
ANAHEIM ST
5000 UNC 94587 752-A2
ANAHID LN
- CCCo 94803 589-C2
ANAIR WY
- OAK 94605 671-A4
ANAMOR ST
1600 RDWC 94061 790-A2
ANA PRIVADA
1100 MTVW 94040 832-H6
ANASTACIA CT
3200 PLE 94588 694-C7
ANCHETA PL
100 VAL 94591 550-F2
ANCHOR CIR
500 RDWC 94065 749-J6
ANCHOR CT
100 CCCo 94565 573-E1
100 VAL 94591 550-F1
ANCHOR DR
- CCCo 94565 573-E2
- EMVL 94608 629-C6
34500 FRMT 94555 752-E1
ANCHOR LN
- SCAR 94070 769-E2
ANCHOR RD
400 SMTO 94404 749-D1
ANCHOR ST
- SAUS 94965 627-B3
ANCHOR WY
300 ALA 94501 670-A4
1800 SJS 95131 814-C4
ANCHORAGE CT
- SLN 94579 691-F3
- SRFL 94903 566-D4
ANCHORAGE DR
- SLN 94579 691-A7
- SLN 94579 711-A1
ANCHORAGE RD
- SAUS 94965 626-H1
ANCHOR BAY TER
100 SUNV 94086 812-E7
ANCHO VISTA AV
- SANS 94960 566-C7
ANCIL WY
3500 SJS 95117 853-C2
ANCONA CT
1700 CNCD 94519 593-A2
ANCORA CT
2200 LALT 94024 831-H6

STREET
Block City ZIP Pg-Grid

ANCRUM CT
3000 SJS 95148 855-C2
ANDALE AV
600 NVTO 94945 526-G1
ANDALUCIA CT
3700 SRMN 94583 673-C3
ANDALUCIA ST
1000 LVMR 94550 715-E3
ANDALUSIA WY
1500 SJS 95125 854-A7
1500 SJS 95125 853-J7
ANDANTE ST
40600 FRMT 94538 773-B1
ANDERHAN PL
3700 SRMN 94583 673-C2
ANDERLY CT
100 AlaC 94541 711-G1
ANDERSEN DR
700 SRFL 94901 586-H3
800 SRFL 94901 587-A4
ANDERSON AV
2600 FRMT 94539 753-E7
4300 OAK 94619 650-G5
ANDERSON CIR
- WLCK 94595 612-C7
ANDERSON CT
- MTVW 94043 811-J4
ANDERSON DR
700 LALT 94024 831-F1
ANDERSON PL
27600 HAY 94544 712-B6
ANDERSON RD
100 ALA 94502 669-H5
10200 SCIC 95127 815-B7
10200 SCIC 95127 835-B1
ANDERSON ST
- SF 94110 667-J6
100 VAL 94589 510-D6
400 PLE 94566 714-D3
ANDERSON WY
- MLPK 94025 790-E7
- MLPK 94025 810-E1
100 CCCo 94553 571-J4
ANDERSON RANCH CT
- CCCo 94507 632-G3
ANDETA WY
100 SMCo 94028 810-D3
ANDORA DR
3100 SJS 95148 835-B5
ANDORA LN
300 SRMN 94583 673-C4
ANDORRA CT
- PCFA 94044 727-A3
40400 FRMT 94539 753-E4
ANDOVER DR
300 PCFA 94044 707-B2
1100 SUNV 94087 832-B1
2400 UNC 94587 732-C4
ANDOVER LN
1600 SJS 95124 873-J3
ANDOVER PL
- SRMN 94583 673-F6
ANDOVER ST
- SF 94110 667-J6
300 OAK 94609 649-H1
15000 SLN 94579 691-B6
ANDOVER WY
900 LALT 94024 831-H5
ANDRADE AV
2300 RCH 94804 588-H5
3500 RCH 94804 589-A5
3600 RCH 94805 589-A5
ANDRADE RD
3000 AlaC 94586 754-D3
ANDRE AV
1100 MTVW 94040 832-A2
ANDRE CT
100 LGTS 95032 873-B7
ANDREA CIR
300 LVMR 94550 696-B6
ANDREA CT
1700 CNCD 94519 592-J1
3500 SJS 95117 853-C3
4800 LVMR 94550 696-B6
ANDREA DR
100 WLCK 94596 612-D6
1000 SJS 95117 853-C3
ANDREA LN
1800 CNCD 94519 592-J1
ANDREA PL
1600 SCL 95051 833-B3
ANDREA ST
27600 HAY 94544 712-A7
ANDREA WY
700 PIT 94565 574-B3
4700 UNC 94587 731-J7
ANDREASEN DR
3100 LFYT 94549 611-H7
ANDREW AV
- PIT 94565 574-C3
ANDREW CT
2400 UNC 94587 732-C5
14800 SAR 95070 872-F3
ANDREW DR
- TBRN 94920 607-A4
ANDREW RD
- AMCN 94589 510-A2
100 AMCN 94589 509-J2
ANDREW WY
500 CCCo 94803 569-E7
ANDREWS AV
1800 SJS 95124 873-H2
ANDREWS CT
- NVTO 94949 546-G5
1900 CCCo 94521 593-D2
16100 MSER 95030 873-A6
37800 FRMT 94536 752-H4
ANDREWS DR
900 MRTZ 94553 571-E4
1800 CCCo 94521 593-D3
3600 PLE 94588 694-D6
ANDREWS RD
- SF 94129 647-C3
ANDREWS ST
100 LGTS 95030 873-A6
300 LVMR 94550 695-F7
300 LVMR 94550 715-F1
300 MSER 95030 873-A6
2100 OAK 94611 650-E1
ANDREWS WY
- NVTO 94949 546-G5

STREET
Block City ZIP Pg-Grid

ANDRIX CT
800 CNCD 94518 592-G6
ANDROMEDA LN
800 FCTY 94404 749-H1
ANDROMETA CIR
5400 FRMT 94538 773-A1
ANDROS DR
300 SRMN 94583 673-E1
ANDSBURY AV
200 MTVW 94043 811-J5
ANELDA DR
- PLHL 94523 592-C5
ANFIELD CT
4000 SJS 95136 874-D1
ANGEL AV
300 SUNV 94086 812-E7
ANGEL CT
- DNVL 94526 652-H1
- NVTO 94947 525-J3
100 LGTS 95032 873-D6
4500 ANT 94509 595-F3
ANGELA AV
- MrnC 94960 566-A4
- SANS 94960 566-A4
100 CCCo 94507 632-G4
ANGELA CT
300 LALT 94022 811-F6
2200 SJS 95008 873-E1
ANGELA DR
- LALT 94022 811-E6
ANGELA PL
4000 PLE 94566 714-F4
ANGELA ST
1600 SJS 95125 854-C3
E ANGELA ST
100 PLE 94566 714-E4
W ANGELA ST
400 PLE 94566 714-D3
ANGELES AV
4500 FRMT 94536 752-E3
ANGELFISH TER
- FRMT 94536 753-F3
ANGELICA CT
- NVTO 94947 525-G4
- SRFL 94901 566-H6
ANGELICA WY
1000 LVMR 94550 715-H2
ANGELICO CT
5100 PLE 94588 694-A6
ANGELINA DR
3400 SCL 95051 832-J4
ANGELINA WY
100 VAL 94589 510-C5
ANGEL
ISLAND-TIBURON FER
- MrnC - 627-F3
- SF - 627-H5
- SF - 648-B1
- TBRN - 627-E1
ANGELITA AV
100 PCFA 94044 727-B2
ANGELL CT
- SCIC - 791-A7
- SCIC 94305 790-J7
ANGELO AV
3700 OAK 94619 650-E6
ANGELO ST
3300 LFYT 94549 611-G2
ANGELO WY
- SJS 95110 833-H2
ANGIE AV
2100 SJS 95116 834-H5
ANGIE LN
- CNCD 94521 593-E4
ANGLEWOOD DR
4700 CNCD 94521 593-D3
ANGLO AL
- SF 94116 667-B4
ANGMAR CT
1100 SJS 95121 855-A5
ANGUIDO CT
- HIL 94402 748-G5
ANGUS AV E
200 SBRN 94066 707-J7
500 SBRN 94066 708-A7
ANGUS AV W
- SBRN 94066 707-H7
ANGUS CT
19900 SAR 95070 852-E7
34200 FRMT 94555 752-D1
ANGUS DR
300 MPS 95035 794-B6
2100 WLCK 94598 612-G3
ANGUS PL
3500 PLE 94588 694-F6
ANGUS WY
- PLE 94588 694-F6
5100 ANT 94509 595-J6
20600 AlaC 94541 691-G6
ANITA AV
300 SCIC 94024 831-F2
800 BLMT 94002 749-D7
19700 AlaC 94546 691-J5
ANITA CIR
700 BEN 94510 551-A3
ANITA CT
- BLMT 94002 749-D7
900 LFYT 94549 611-H6
1700 CNCD 94521 593-E4
3200 AlaC 94546 691-J4
5500 LVMR 94550 696-C7
38300 FRMT 94536 753-C1
ANITA DR
200 MLBR 94030 728-A3
ANITA LN
- CCCo 94507 632-G3
- WLCK 94596 632-G3
500 MLBR 94030 728-A3
500 MLBR 94030 727-J3
ANITA RD
- BURL 94010 728-G6
ANITA ST
400 SJS 95110 834-A5
ANIZUMNE CT
700 CLAY 94517 593-H6
ANJOU PL
35900 NWK 94560 752-D5
ANJOU CREEK CIR
7000 SJS 95120 894-G3
ANJOU CREEK CT
7100 SJS 95120 894-G3

STREET
Block City ZIP Pg-Grid

ANKENY ST
- SF 94134 688-A1
ANN CT
100 VAL 94590 550-C2
300 LVMR 94550 715-D2
38100 FRMT 94536 753-A3
ANN PL
600 MPS 95035 794-B4
ANN PTH
- RCH 94803 589-F1
ANN RD
- PTLV 94028 810-A6
ANN ST
100 FRMT 94555 732-C7
100 FRMT 94555 752-C1
2100 CNCD 94520 572-F7
2100 CNCD 94520 592-F1
2500 FRMT 94536 753-A3
ANNA AV
300 MTVW 94043 811-F3
ANNA DR
1900 SCL 95050 833-C4
4800 SJS 95124 873-G4
ANNA ST
900 SMTO 94401 749-B1
24300 HAY 94545 711-F4
ANNABEL LN
- SRMN 94583 673-D2
ANNALISA DR
2500 CCCo 94520 572-G3
ANNA MARIA ST
100 LVMR 94550 715-D2
ANNANDALE CT
3600 WLCK 94598 613-A3
ANNANDALE PL
3400 SJS 95121 855-D4
ANNAPOLIS CIR
2000 ALA 94501 649-E6
ANNAPOLIS CT
3800 SSF 94080 707-D3
ANNAPOLIS DR
1000 SMTO 94403 749-C4
2100 FRMT 94539 773-G2
ANNAPOLIS ST
2500 EPA 94303 791-B1
2500 EPA 94303 771-B7
3200 RCH 94806 589-A2
ANNAPOLIS TER
- SF 94118 647-E7
ANNAPOLIS WY
1300 SJS 95118 874-B4
ANN ARBOR AV
10300 CPTO 95014 832-C7
10300 SCIC 95014 832-C7
ANN ARBOR CT
100 LGTS 95032 873-D7
10200 CPTO 95014 832-C7
ANN ARBOR DR
100 LGTS 95032 873-D7
ANN ARBOR WY
6900 DBLN 94568 693-J3
ANN DARLING DR
300 SJS 95133 834-E3
ANNE CT
- CCCo 94598 612-G4
- NVTO 94945 526-A2
1800 SJS 95124 873-H5
2600 PIN 94564 569-F4
ANNE LN
19100 SCIC 95014 852-G1
ANNE WY
100 LGTS 95032 873-G5
1800 SJS 95124 873-G5
ANNE MARIE CT
1800 SJS 95132 814-D3
ANNE MARIE TER
37200 FRMT 94536 752-G4
ANNERLEY RD
1000 OAK 94610 650-B2
1000 PDMT 94610 650-B2
ANNERLY CT
2000 SJS 95121 855-C5
ANNESCOURT DR
- HIL 94010 728-D7
ANNESCOURT PL
- HIL 94010 728-D7
ANNETTE AV
300 VAL 94591 530-D6
1200 RDWC 94063 770-F6
ANNETTE CT
- CCCo 94596 612-C2
4800 UNC 94587 751-J1
ANNETTE LN
300 HAY 94541 711-G3
1900 LALT 94024 831-J5
ANNETTE WY
1000 CPTO 95014 852-D3
ANNIE LN
18500 SCIC 95120 894-G1
ANNIE ST
- SF 94105 648-A6
- SF 94103 648-A6
1500 SMCo 94015 687-B5
1500 DALY 94015 687-B5
ANNIE LAURIE AV
- MTVW 94043 812-B3
ANNIE LAURIE WY
1600 SJS 95121 855-B4
ANNIS CIR
3600 PLE 94588 694-G5
ANNIS RD
100 BSBN 94005 688-B7
ANNONA AV
2200 SJS 95122 835-A7
ANO AV
200 AlaC 94580 691-E6
ANONA WY
- LVMR 94550 716-B1
ANO NUEVO AV
400 SUNV 94086 812-C5
ANSBURY CT
1000 MTVW 94043 811-H4
ANSDELL WY
6100 SJS 95123 875-B6
ANSEL AV
600 BURL 94010 728-F6
ANSEL CT
47700 FRMT 94539 773-H7
ANSEL LN
- SMCo 94025 810-E2
ANSELMO CT
5400 CNCD 94521 593-F5

STREET
Block City ZIP Pg-Grid

ANSHEN CT
800 SUNV 94086 832-F2
ANSLEY PL
18800 SAR 95070 852-H6
ANSON AV
10300 CPTO 95014 832-C7
ANSON PL
- SF 94108 648-A5
ANSON RD
- HIL 94010 748-F4
ANSON WY
- CCCo 94707 609-E2
ANTARES LN
800 FCTY 94404 749-H1
ANTELOPE CT
- CLAY 94517 593-J5
1700 HAY 94541 712-B1
ANTELOPE DR
2300 SJS 95133 834-F1
45400 FRMT 94539 773-J4
ANTELOPE WY
4600 ANT 94509 595-J3
ANTELOPE RIDGE WY
400 DNVL 94506 654-B5
ANTERO WY
800 SJS 95133 814-F7
ANTHONY CT
- NVTO 94947 525-G3
100 DNVL 94526 653-C6
1800 MTVW 94040 811-F5
2300 CNCD 94520 592-E3
ANTHONY DR
2000 SJS 95008 853-B6
ANTHONY PL
10200 CPTO 95014 831-J7
ANTHONY ST
- SF 94105 648-B5
800 BERK 94804 629-E4
ANTIGUA CT
400 SRMN 94583 673-C3
5800 SJS 95120 874-C5
ANTIGUA DR
5800 SJS 95120 874-C5
ANTIGUA LN
1400 FCTY 94404 749-G5
ANTIGUA RD
2700 SJS 95111 854-H4
ANTIGUA WY
100 VAL 94591 550-E2
5700 SJS 95120 874-C5
ANTILLES WY
- MrnC 94920 607-B2
ANTIOCH CT
2000 OAK 94611 650-E1
32900 UNC 94587 752-A1
ANTIOCH DR
- SMTO 94403 749-D6
ANTIOCH LP
4900 UNC 94587 752-A1
ANTIOCH ST
4900 UNC 94587 752-A1
6100 OAK 94611 650-E1
ANTIQUE FOREST LN
- BLMT 94002 769-E1
ANTLER CT
- ANT 94509 595-F2
ANTOINETTE DR
10500 CPTO 95014 852-E2
ANTOINETTE LN
200 NVTO 94947 526-E6
800 SSF 94080 707-F2
ANTON CT
400 PA 94301 791-B6
ANTON WY
- MrnC 94945 526-H2
10000 CPTO 95014 832-C7
ANTONACCI CT
3300 SJS 95148 835-D6
ANTONE CT
14300 SLN 94578 691-C3
ANTONE RD
5600 FRMT 94538 773-C2
ANTONETTE AV
- SRFL 94901 586-F2
ANTONETTE DR
- TBRN 94920 607-B2
ANTONIA CIR
800 PIN 94564 569-E4
ANTONIA CT
700 PIN 94564 569-E4
ANTONIO CT
- PTLV 94028 810-C7
500 LFYT 94549 631-J2
ANTONIO LN
1300 SJS 95117 853-D4
1400 SCIC 95117 853-D4
ANTONIO ST
- SF 94102 647-J6
700 SLN 94577 690-J1
ANTWERP LN
1200 SJS 95118 874-B5
ANVERS PL
36100 NWK 94560 752-D6
ANVIL CT
600 SJS 95133 834-F1
ANVILWOOD AV
1200 SUNV 94089 812-J3
ANVILWOOD CT
1000 SUNV 94089 812-J3
ANZA AV
9700 OAK 94605 671-B4
ANZA BLVD
100 BURL 94010 728-F5
ANZA CT
100 SRMN 94583 673-A2
2700 ANT 94509 575-A6
ANZA DR
900 PCFA 94044 726-H4
13000 SAR 95070 852-G7
ANZA RD
- SJS 95134 813-G3
ANZA ST
- SF 94129 647-D4
100 FRMT 94539 753-H7
100 SF 94118 647-E6
400 MTVW 94041 811-J6
500 SF 94118 647-C7
2600 SF 94121 647-A7
4200 SF 94121 646-H7
ANZA WY
100 SBRN 94066 727-J1
300 SLN 94578 691-B5

STREET
Block City ZIP Pg-Grid

ANZA WY
1200 LVMR 94550 715-F2
ANZA-PINE RD
100 FRMT 94539 753-J7
200 FRMT 94539 773-J1
ANZAVISTA AV
- SF 94115 647-F7
ANZIO WY
34300 FRMT 94555 752-B3
APACHE CT
- PLE 94588 694-G7
- SRMN 94583 673-D5
300 FRMT 94539 773-H4
600 SJS 95123 874-G5
3200 LFYT 94549 631-H2
5000 ANT 94509 595-G5
APACHE DR
- PLE 94588 694-D6
APACHE RD
- CMAD 94925 586-F6
APACHE ST
1000 LVMR 94550 695-F7
APENNINES CIR
5100 SJS 95138 855-F6
APEX CT
- MRTZ 94553 591-G4
APGAR ST
600 OAK 94609 629-F7
800 OAK 94608 629-F7
APOLLO
200 HER 94547 569-F3
APOLLO CIR
4200 UNC 94587 732-A6
APOLLO CT
- ANT 94509 575-F4
100 NVTO 94947 525-H3
500 VAL 94591 530-E6
1800 WLCK 94598 612-E2
2600 SJS 95121 854-H3
APOLLO DR
2600 SJS 95121 854-H3
APOLLO RD
- TBRN 94920 607-B4
700 FCTY 94404 749-E3
APOLLO ST
- SF 94124 668-B6
APOLLO WY
200 PLHL 94523 592-A5
1200 SUNV 94086 812-J7
12900 SAR 95070 852-D7
APOLLO HEIGHTS CT
13000 SCIC 95070 872-C5
APPALACHIAN DR
100 MRTZ 94553 591-H4
200 PLHL 94523 591-H4
APPALACHIAN WY
300 CCCo 94549 591-H4
300 MRTZ 94553 591-H4
APPALOOSA CT
2500 WLCK 94596 632-G2
2800 PIN 94564 569-H6
4700 ANT 94509 595-G3
APPALOOSA DR
500 CCCo 94507 632-F2
500 WLCK 94596 632-F2
APPALOOSA TR
2600 PIN 94564 569-H7
APPALOOSA WY
4500 ANT 94509 595-G3
27000 LAH 94022 830-J2
APPAREL WY
- SF 94124 668-A5
APPERSON WY
2000 PLE 94566 714-F1
APPERSON RIDGE CT
3100 SJS 95148 855-E1
APPERSON RIDGE DR
3000 SJS 95148 855-E2
APPIAN CT
- CCCo 94803 569-D7
- DNVL 94526 652-J3
- MRTZ 94553 591-H4
APPIAN LN
1000 SJS 95116 834-E6
APPIAN ST
3800 PLE 94588 694-C6
APPIAN WY
- SSF 94080 707-E4
100 UNC 94587 732-J5
400 CCCo 94803 589-C2
400 CCCo 94803 569-D6
700 PIN 94564 569-D5
2900 SCAR 94070 769-F5
5000 RCH 94803 589-C2
APPIAN KNOLL CT
- CCCo 94803 569-E7
APPLAUSE PL
600 SJS 95134 813-F3
APPLE AV
1100 AlaC 94541 691-H7
1200 HAY 94541 691-H7
APPLE CT
1000 CNCD 94518 592-E5
N APPLE CT
2900 ANT 94509 575-A7
2900 ANT 94509 574-J7
S APPLE CT
3000 ANT 94509 574-J7
APPLE DR
1200 CNCD 94518 592-E5
APPLE PL
4300 PIT 94565 574-D7
APPLE ST
800 OAK 94603 670-H6
APPLE TER
700 SJS 95111 855-B7
APPLEBERRY DR
500 MrnC 94903 546-C7
APPLE BLOSSOM DR
5300 SJS 95123 875-A3
APPLEBLOSSOM LN
16400 SCIC 95032 873-C5
APPLEGARTH LN
2400 ANT 94509 575-D6
APPLEGATE CT
6400 SJS 95119 875-C7
APPLEGATE DR
6400 SJS 95119 875-C7
APPLEGATE ST
2100 HAY 94545 731-J2
APPLE GATE TER
38900 FRMT 94536 753-C3

STREET
Block City ZIP Pg-Grid

APPLEGATE WY
- ALA 94502 669-H5
APPLENUT LN
100 VAL 94591 530-F7
100 VAL 94591 550-F1
APPLETON AV
- SF 94110 667-H5
APPLETON DR
3500 SJS 95117 853-C2
APPLETON ST
- SF 94129 647-C3
APPLE TREE COM
4600 LVMR 94550 696-A4
APPLE TREE DR
20000 CPTO 95014 832-E7
APPLE TREE LN
- CCCo 94507 632-F5
APPLETREE LN
1800 MTVW 94040 831-G1
APPLE VALLEY DR
800 SJS 95125 854-D5
APPLEWOOD CT
7900 PLE 94588 713-J1
APPLEWOOD DR
4600 SJS 95129 853-A2
APPLEWOOD LN
- PTLV 94028 810-C7
APPLEWOOD ST
42600 FRMT 94538 773-D2
APPLEWOOD WY
7900 PLE 94588 713-J1
APPLEY WY
2400 SJS 95124 873-E5
APRICOT AV
800 CMBL 95008 853-F6
APRICOT CT
2100 PIT 94565 574-A3
APRICOT LN
100 LGTS 95030 872-J7
200 MTVW 94040 831-J2
1000 CNCD 94518 592-E5
2500 SJS 95121 855-E4
41200 FRMT 94539 753-E6
APRICOT ST
10700 OAK 94603 670-J6
10700 SLN 94577 670-J6
APRICOT WY
17800 AlaC 94546 692-B3
APRICOT HILL CT
14000 SAR 95070 872-H2
APRIL AV
100 SSF 94080 707-E3
APRIL CT
- PLHL 94523 592-B5
17700 AlaC 94546 691-H2
APRIL DR
100 SJS 95138 875-D4
APRIL WY
300 CMBL 95008 853-G5
APRILSONG CT
1700 SJS 95131 814-D7
APSIS AV
2400 SJS 95124 873-D3
APSIS CT
2300 SJS 95124 873-E3
APTOS AV
- SF 94127 667-C6
4500 SJS 95111 875-A1
APTOS CT
100 SRMN 94583 673-E5
2400 UNC 94587 732-B4
APTOS DR
2800 SRMN 94583 673-E5
APTOS PL
200 DNVL 94526 653-D6
APTOS WY
100 SSF 94080 707-G5
APTOS BEACH CT
7100 SJS 95139 895-F1
AQUA ST
- SLN 94578 691-C5
AQUADO CT
35200 FRMT 94536 752-E2
AQUARIUS CIR
4100 UNC 94587 732-A6
AQUARIUS DR
500 SJS 95111 854-F7
AQUARIUS LN
600 FCTY 94404 749-E4
AQUARIUS ST
1700 LVMR 94550 696-B3
AQUARIUS WY
900 OAK 94611 630-D6
AQUATIC WY
800 FRMT 94539 753-J7
800 FRMT 94539 773-J1
AQUA VISTA
- ORIN 94563 610-J5
AQUA VISTA DR
- SRFL 94901 586-J1
AQUA VISTA RD
1400 CCCo 94805 589-C6
2500 ELCR 94530 589-C6
AQUAVISTA WY
- SF 94131 667-E3
AQUILA AV
4000 SJS 95124 873-E3
AQUINAS DR
- SRFL 94901 566-H6
AQUINAS FIRE RD
- SRFL 94901 566-H5
AQUINO WY
18600 SAR 95070 872-H3
ARA LN
600 FCTY 94404 749-E4
ARABIA HTS
- CCCo 94553 571-C4
- MRTZ 94553 571-C4
ARABIAN CT
- WLCK 94596 632-G2
100 VAL 94589 510-D6
5900 SJS 95123 874-J5
ARABIAN RD
4300 LVMR 94550 696-A2
ARABIAN ST
400 SJS 95123 874-J5
ARAGLIN CT
4000 SJS 95136 854-E6
ARAGO ST
- SF 94112 667-F7
ARAGON AV
28400 HAY 94544 712-B7

STREET
Block City ZIP Pg-Grid

ARAGON BLVD
- SMTO 94401 749-A3
- SMTO 94402 749-A3
- SMTO 94402 748-J3
ARAGON CT
100 VAL 94591 530-F6
1000 PCFA 94044 726-J5
2500 SJS 95125 853-J7
ARAGON LN
3800 SRMN 94583 673-C2
ARAGON PL
30200 UNC 94587 732-A4
ARAGON ST
100 VAL 94591 530-F6
ARAGON WY
2400 SJS 95125 853-J7
2700 SJS 95125 873-J1
ARAK CT
1100 PLE 94566 714-G4
ARALIA CT
100 HER 94547 570-B4
ARALIA DR
38200 NWK 94560 752-G7
ARAM AV
300 CMBL 95128 853-F4
300 SJS 95128 853-F4
ARAM CT
- NVTO 94947 526-B4
ARAMIS DR
3200 SJS 95127 835-B3
ARAMON CT
800 PLE 94566 714-H3
ARANA CIR
- SAUS 94965 626-J2
ARANA CT
1700 MPS 95035 794-D6
ARANA DR
100 MRTZ 94553 571-G6
ARANDA DR
2500 SRMN 94583 673-C3
ARAPAHO AV
2000 FRMT 94539 773-G3
ARAPAHO CIR
100 SRMN 94583 673-C4
ARAPAHO CT
- SRMN 94583 673-D4
ARAPAHO DR
5700 SJS 95123 874-H5
ARAPAHO PL
2000 FRMT 94539 773-G3
ARAPAHO WY
5200 ANT 94509 595-J6
ARAPAHOE CT
- PTLV 94028 810-B6
ARASTRADERO RD
200 PA 94304 811-A5
200 LAH 94022 811-A5
400 PA 94306 811-A5
1500 PA 94304 810-F6
1700 SCIC 94304 810-H5
1700 PTLV 94028 810-F6
9600 SCIC 94304 811-A5
16000 LAH 94022 810-H5
ARATA CT
1500 SJS 95125 854-C3
ARATA WY
2200 ANT 94509 574-H5
18800 SCIC 95014 852-H1
ARAUJO ST
1300 SJS 95131 814-C7
ARBALLO DR
200 SF 94132 687-A1
ARBEAU DR
7100 NWK 94560 752-C6
ARBELECHE LN
20400 SAR 95070 872-D2
ARBOL CT
2200 ANT 94509 595-A1
ARBOL DR
4000 PA 94306 811-C2
ARBOL LN
- SF 94115 647-F7
ARBOLADO CT
- ORIN 94563 610-J6
3000 WLCK 94598 612-H3
ARBOLADO DR
- WLCK 94598 612-H3
3300 WLCK 94598 613-A3
3600 CCCo 94598 613-B3
4000 CCCo - 613-B3
ARBOLADO WY
18500 SAR 95070 872-H3
ARBOLEDA DR
300 LALT 94024 831-F1
ARBOLES PL
700 SRMN 94583 673-G5
ARBOL GRANDE
1900 WLCK 94595 612-D7
1900 WLCK 94595 632-D1
ARBOL GRANDE CT
- SMCo 94025 790-D5
ARBOL VIA
400 CCCo 94598 612-F4
400 WLCK 94598 612-F4
ARBON PTH
- OAK 94618 630-B5
ARBOR AV
1200 SCIC 94024 831-G3
1900 BLMT 94002 769-C1
3000 LVMR 94550 715-H1
21900 AlaC 94541 711-F2
E ARBOR AV
200 SUNV 94086 812-F6
W ARBOR AV
100 SUNV 94086 812-E5
ARBOR CIR
- NVTO 94947 525-J3
ARBOR CT
100 SBRN 94066 707-E7
100 WDSD 94062 789-G5
300 BEN 94510 551-B3
800 LVMR 94550 715-J1
1200 MTVW 94040 832-A1
3500 PLE 94566 714-G4
21600 AlaC 94541 711-F2
ARBOR DR
- CCCo 94596 612-G7
- PDMT 94610 650-A1
300 SSF 94080 707-E3
600 SLN 94577 671-B7
1600 SJS 95125 854-C4
3100 PLE 94566 714-G4

STREET Block City ZIP Pg-Grid

ARBOR DR
8600 ELCR 94530 609-E2
ARBOR LN
100 SMTO 94403 749-B6
1400 CCCo 94507 632-E3
ARBOR RD
- MLPK 94025 790-E4
ARBOR ST
- LKSP 94939 586-D4
- SF 94131 667-F5
1700 ALA 94501 669-H1
ARBOR WY
- LFYT 94549 611-B6
W ARBOR WY
- LFYT 94549 611-A6
ARBOR CREEK CIR
7600 DBLN 94568 693-G4
ARBORDALE CT
35100 FRMT 94536 752-F1
ARBOR DELL WY
5600 SJS 95124 873-J6
ARBORETUM DR
5200 SCIC 94024 831-J6
5300 LALT 94024 831-J6
ARBORETUM RD
300 PA 94304 790-H5
400 SCIC 94305 790-H5
ARBOR PARK CT
1300 SJS 95126 853-H3
ARBOR PARK DR
1300 SJS 95126 853-H3
ARBOR VALLEY DR
100 SJS 95119 875-D7
ARBOR VALLEY PL
200 SJS 95119 875-E7
ARBOR VINE DR
32800 UNC 94587 732-C5
ARBOR VISTA WY
1100 SJS 95126 853-H3
ARBUCKLE AV
3700 SJS 95124 873-H2
ARBUCKLE CT
1500 SCL 95054 813-D7
ARBUELO WY
- LALT 94022 811-E5
ARBUTUS AV
600 SUNV 94086 832-F1
3500 PA 94303 791-E7
ARBUTUS CT
- WLCK 94595 612-C7
2000 FRMT 94539 773-G3
3700 AlaC 94542 712-F3
4400 PLE 94588 713-J1
5600 NWK 94560 752-G7
ARBUTUS DR
1500 CCCo 94595 612-B7
1500 SJS 95118 874-A5
1500 WLCK 94595 612-B7
ARC RD
200 CMBL 95008 853-F5
ARC TER
- FRMT 94555 752-B3
ARC WY
1500 BURL 94010 728-E6
ARCADE AV
- BERK 94708 609-J6
ARCADIA AV
- SCL 95051 832-J7
4300 OAK 94602 650-E3
ARCADIA CT
100 PCFA 94044 707-A2
2200 MRTZ 94553 572-A7
ARCADIA DR
- DALY 94015 707-A2
- PCFA 94044 707-A2
3300 SJS 95117 853-D1
3300 SCIC 95117 853-D1
ARCADIA PL
- HIL 94010 748-G2
1400 PA 94303 791-B4
2200 MRTZ 94553 572-A7
ARCADIA TER
600 SUNV 94086 812-G5
ARCADIAN CT
3500 AlaC 94546 691-H2
ARCADIAN DR
3300 AlaC 94546 691-H2
ARCADIAN ST
46200 FRMT 94539 793-J1
ARCADIA PALMS DR
14000 SAR 95070 872-H2
ARCH CT
1100 CNCD 94520 592-F3
ARCH LN
- SCAR 94070 769-E2
ARCH ST
- BERK 94707 609-H6
- LKSP 94939 586-E6
- RDWC 94062 769-J5
- SF 94132 687-C2
100 RDWC 94062 770-A5
500 MRTZ 94553 571-E4
1600 BERK 94709 609-H7
1600 BERK 94708 609-H6
1800 BERK 94709 629-H1
ARCHANGEL WY
- SRFL 94903 566-D5
ARCHBOW CT
4700 SJS 95136 874-H3
ARCHBURY CT
3200 SJS 95148 855-F1
ARCHCLIFF CT
700 HAY 94544 732-E2
ARCHCOVE CT
400 SJS 95111 875-C1
ARCHDALE CT
2200 SSF 94080 707-D4
ARCHER AV
1900 FRMT 94536 753-A3
ARCHER CIR
- MRGA 94556 631-D5
ARCHER CT
- VAL 94591 530-E2
- SMTO 94401 729-A6
1500 CMBL 95008 873-A1
38000 FRMT 94536 753-A2
ARCHER ST
- SJS 95112 833-J2
1300 SJS 95002 793-B7
ARCHER WY
1100 CMBL 95008 873-A1
ARCHERY CT
- CCCo 94803 589-G4
ARCHERY WY
4000 CCCo 94803 589-G4
ARCHERY FIRE RD
- SMCo 94062 789-C5
ARCHERY FIRE TR
- SMCo 94062 789-B6
ARCHGLEN WY
400 SJS 95111 875-C1
ARCHIBALD DR
15400 SCIC 95070 872-C4
ARCHIBALD LN
- MrnC 94945 526-F2
ARCHMONT PL
3900 OAK 94605 650-J7
ARCHSHIRE CT
3200 SJS 95148 835-F7
ARCHWOOD CIR
2900 SJS 95148 855-D1
ARCO CT
300 SJS 95123 874-J4
ARCO WY
- SF 94112 667-F7
ARCOLA CT
3100 SJS 95148 855-D2
ARCTIC AV
2500 SJS 95111 854-G4
ARCTIC ST
1900 SLN 94577 690-G3
ARCTURUS CIR
800 FCTY 94404 749-E4
ARCY LN
- PIT 94565 574-J4
ARDATH CT
- SF 94124 668-C6
ARDEE LN
2400 SSF 94080 707-D5
ARDEN AV
100 SSF 94080 707-J2
ARDEN COM
3000 FRMT 94536 753-A3
3000 FRMT 94536 752-J3
ARDEN CT
- DALY 94014 687-G3
- RDWC 94061 770-A7
- RDWC 94061 790-A1
200 AMCN 94589 509-J3
19500 SAR 95070 852-F5
ARDEN LN
1400 BLMT 94002 769-E2
ARDEN PL
4300 OAK 94602 650-D3
ARDEN RD
- BERK 94704 630-A2
200 MLPK 94025 790-F2
300 HIL 94010 748-G2
3100 HAY 94545 731-E1
ARDEN ST
37000 NWK 94560 752-E6
ARDEN WY
1400 OAK 94602 650-D3
2300 SJS 95122 834-J5
ARDENDALE CT
- CCCo 94507 632-J5
ARDENDALE DR
- DALY 94014 687-F3
ARDEN FARMS PL
3900 SJS 95111 854-J7
ARDENTECH CT
6000 FRMT 94555 752-B4
ARDENWOOD BLVD
34100 FRMT 94555 752-B2
34100 UNC 94587 752-B2
ARDENWOOD CT
24500 HAY 94545 711-F5
ARDENWOOD CT E
1600 CNCD 94521 593-C3
ARDENWOOD CT W
1600 CNCD 94521 593-C3
ARDENWOOD DR
1500 SJS 95129 852-F5
ARDENWOOD TER
5700 FRMT 94555 752-C4
ARDENWOOD WY
- SF 94132 667-C6
ARDILLA CT
2500 SJS 95128 853-F4
ARDILLA RD
- ORIN 94563 610-F6
ARDIS AV
300 SJS 95117 853-D2
300 SCIC 95117 853-D1
ARDIS DR
2000 SJS 95125 854-C5
ARDIS ST
- AlaC 94580 691-F7
- AlaC 94580 711-F1
- AlaC 94541 691-F7
- AlaC 94541 711-F1
ARDITH CT
100 ORIN 94563 631-C5
ARDITH DR
100 ORIN 94563 631-B4
1700 PLHL 94523 592-B5
ARDITH LN
- CCCo 94507 632-E6
ARDLEY AV
3500 OAK 94602 650-C4
ARDMORE AV
- LKSP 94939 586-E7
1000 OAK 94610 650-B2
ARDMORE CT
- PLHL 94523 592-A6
100 BEN 94510 551-B3
19500 SAR 95070 852-F5
ARDMORE DR
1200 SLN 94577 691-D2
2500 CCCo 94806 569-B5
ARDMORE PL
1400 LVMR 94550 715-F5
8500 DBLN 94568 693-G2
ARDMORE RD
- CCCo 94707 609-F4
ARDMORE ST
8400 DBLN 94568 693-G2
ARDMORE WY
100 BEN 94510 551-B3
5300 SJS 95118 874-A5
ARDO CT
35300 FRMT 94536 752-E2
ARDO ST
4000 FRMT 94536 752-E2
ARDOR DR
- ORIN 94563 631-A3
ARDORA LN
1700 CNCD 94519 592-J2
ARDSLEY CT
1100 SJS 95120 874-C6
ARELIOUS WALKER DR
2800 SF 94124 688-C1
ARELLANO AV
- SF 94132 687-B1
ARENA CT
100 VAL 94589 510-D6
ARENA ST
1500 SLN 94579 691-A7
ARENAS CT
- SRMN 94583 673-C3
ARENCY CT
200 DNVL 94506 653-F1
ARENDAL CT
24300 AlaC 94541 712-B1
ARENDS DR
100 DNVL 94506 653-F1
ARENDS LN
- WLCK 94596 612-B1
ARENDT WY
- PLE 94566 714-E3
AREQUIPA CT
200 SJS 95119 875-D7
ARETE CT
- HER 94547 569-H4
AREZZO DR
5200 SJS 95138 855-E7
5200 SJS 95138 875-F1
AREZZO WY
5200 SJS 95138 875-E1
ARF AV
2300 HAY 94545 731-G1
ARGENT AL
- SF 94131 667-F3
ARGENTA CT
900 CCCo 94553 572-B7
ARGENTA DR
2100 SJS 95130 852-J6
900 CCCo 94553 572-B7
ARGONAUT AV
- SF 94134 687-J2
ARGONAUT CT
4200 FRMT 94536 753-A5
20200 SAR 95070 852-E7
ARGONAUT DR
20100 SAR 95070 852-E7
ARGONAUT WY
38700 FRMT 94536 752-J5
38700 FRMT 94536 753-A5
39000 FRMT 94538 753-A5
ARGONNE DR
1700 CNCD 94518 592-F7
1700 WLCK 94598 592-F7
13400 SAR 95070 852-D7
ARGONNE PL
35800 NWK 94560 752-D5
ARGONNE ST
15500 SLN 94579 691-B7
35800 NWK 94560 752-D5
ARGOSY CT
- PIT 94565 573-J2
ARGUELLO AV
100 VAL 94591 530-D7
ARGUELLO BLVD
- SF 94118 647-D7
300 SF 94129 647-D7
300 SF 94129 647-D4
500 PCFA 94044 726-H4
800 SF 94117 647-D7
1200 SF 94117 667-D2
1200 SF 94122 667-D2
1200 SF 94143 667-D2
ARGUELLO CIR
- SRFL 94901 567-A7
ARGUELLO DR
700 SLN 94578 691-B4
2700 BURL 94010 728-A6
ARGUELLO PL
2300 SCL 95050 833-C3
ARGUELLO ST
300 RDWC 94063 769-J4
500 SCIC 94305 790-H7
800 RDWC 94063 770-A5
ARGUS CT
- ALA 94502 669-J6
800 FCTY 94404 749-E4
1800 FRMT 94539 773-G1
ARGUS WY
600 SCL 95054 813-E5
ARGYLE CT
1500 SJS 95132 814-F3
4100 FRMT 94536 752-H4
ARGYLE RD
5100 CCCo 94803 569-E7
37600 FRMT 94536 752-H4
ARGYLE ST
2200 AlaC 94578 691-F3
2700 OAK 94602 650-F2
ARGYLL AV
2700 CNCD 94520 572-E7
ARIA DR
200 CCCo 94553 572-C6
ARIAS ST
200 SRFL 94903 566-D3
ARIC LN
26300 LAH 94022 811-B5
ARIEL AV
4400 FRMT 94555 752-C1
ARIEL CT
400 SJS 95123 874-J5
ARIEL DR
400 SJS 95123 874-J5
ARIES CT
4700 LVMR 94550 696-B3
ARIES LN
- NVTO 94947 525-F3
700 FCTY 94404 749-E4
ARIES WY
100 SUNV 94086 812-E7
ARIKARA CT
700 FRMT 94539 773-H4
ARIKARA DR
800 FRMT 94539 773-G4
ARIMO AV
600 OAK 94610 650-B2
ARIZONA AV
200 RCH 94801 608-D1
1100 MPS 95035 794-A3
1900 MPS 95035 793-J3
ARIZONA DR
5500 CNCD 94521 593-F6
ARIZONA ST
3000 OAK 94602 650-E4
33000 UNC 94587 732-D6
ARIZONA WY
1900 RDWC 94061 790-A3
ARJANG CT
- CCCo 94507 632-H5
ARK DR
900 SLN 94578 691-D4
ARK ST
1600 SMTO 94403 749-D1
ARKANSAS
3000 ALA 94501 649-F6
ARKANSAS PL
48400 FRMT 94539 793-J1
ARKANSAS ST
- SF 94107 668-B3
100 VAL 94590 529-J3
300 VAL 94590 530-A3
3200 OAK 94602 650-E5
ARKELL CT
1900 WLCK 94598 592-E7
ARKELL RD
1000 WLCK 94598 592-E7
1300 WLCK 94598 612-F1
ARKINLANDER LN
100 CCCo 94553 572-B5
ARKWOOD ST
43200 FRMT 94538 773-D2
ARLEDA LN
4300 CNCD 94521 593-A4
ARLEE DR
18000 MSER 95030 872-J6
ARLEEN AV
1300 SUNV 94087 832-F4
ARLEEN WY
700 PCFA 94044 707-A7
700 PCFA 94044 727-A1
ARLEN CT
3700 SJS 95132 814-F2
ARLENE CT
- WLCK 94595 612-C7
37700 FRMT 94536 752-J3
ARLENE DR
100 WLCK 94595 612-C6
2300 SCL 95050 833-C5
ARLENE LN
- WLCK 94595 612-C7
ARLENE PL
4700 PLE 94566 714-E5
ARLENE TER
100 SRFL 94903 566-B3
ARLENE WY
800 NVTO 94947 526-D7
800 NVTO 94947 546-D1
5400 LVMR 94550 696-D7
ARLETA AV
- SF 94134 688-A2
- SF 94134 687-J2
300 SCIC 95128 853-G1
ARLETTE AV
22500 HAY 94541 692-B7
ARLEY CT
- DALY 94015 707-D3
ARLINGTON AV
- BERK 94707 609-F3
- CCCo 94530 609-F3
- CCCo 94707 609-F3
- CCCo 94708 609-F3
800 ELCR 94530 609-F3
800 OAK 94608 629-F5
ARLINGTON BLVD
900 ELCR 94530 609-E1
1400 ELCR 94530 589-C7
5400 SPAB 94806 589-B5
5800 CCCo 94805 589-B5
N ARLINGTON BLVD
5400 SPAB 94806 589-B4
5500 CCCo 94806 589-B4
5500 RCH 94806 589-B4
ARLINGTON CIR
- NVTO 94949 526-C7
500 NVTO 94947 526-C7
3700 PIT 94565 574-F5
ARLINGTON CT
- CCCo 94707 609-F3
- NVTO 94947 526-C7
- PIT 94565 574-F6
300 DNVL 94526 653-E6
400 PLE 94566 714-D6
900 SUNV 94087 832-C1
2300 AlaC 94578 691-F3
ARLINGTON DR
- SSF 94080 707-D1
- PIT 94565 574-B3
2200 AlaC 94578 691-F3
6300 PLE 94566 714-D6
ARLINGTON ISL
600 ALA 94501 669-G2
ARLINGTON LN
- DALY 94014 687-F3
- CCCo 94708 609-F3
300 SMTO 94402 748-H1
1000 SJS 95129 852-E3
ARLINGTON PL
2700 FRMT 94555 732-E7
ARLINGTON RD
200 RDWC 94062 769-H6
1000 LVMR 94550 695-D6
2300 CNCD 94520 592-E3
ARLINGTON ST
- SF 94131 667-H6
ARLINGTON WY
- WLCK 94595 612-B5
- SMCo 94025 790-H2
- MLPK 94025 790-H2
700 MRTZ 94553 571-D3
ARLMONT DR
- CCCo 94708 609-F3
ARLOTTA PL
2500 PLE 94588 714-A4
ARMADA WY
2200 SMTO 94404 749-D2
ARMAND AV
- MTVW 94043 811-J2
ARMAND DR
1700 MPS 95035 794-D6
4200 CNCD 94521 593-B3
ARMANI CT
5200 PLE 94588 694-A6
ARMANINI AV
600 SCL 95050 833-C5
ARMANINO CT
- OAK 94618 629-J5
ARMATA ST
47100 FRMT 94539 773-H6
ARMDALE CT
3000 SJS 95148 855-C2
ARMED CT
300 SJS 95111 875-B2
ARMIDA CT
400 LVMR 94550 715-E2
ARMISTEAD RD
1200 SF 94129 647-C3
ARMITAGE ST
1000 ALA 94502 669-J6
ARMONK CT
5300 SJS 95123 875-B3
ARMORY DR
- SRFL 94903 566-F4
ARMORY RD
- SF 94132 666-H6
ARMOUR AV
200 SSF 94080 708-A2
200 SSF 94080 707-J2
ARMOUR CT
34900 FRMT 94555 752-E1
ARMOUR DR
4600 SCL 95054 813-D4
6600 OAK 94611 630-E6
ARMOUR ST
28200 HAY 94545 731-J2
ARMOUR WY
34800 FRMT 94555 752-E1
ARMSBY CIR
- ROSS 94957 586-C3
ARMSBY DR
1200 HIL 94010 728-D6
1200 BURL 94010 728-D6
ARMSTEAD CT
2800 SJS 95121 855-A2
ARMSTRONG AV
1200 SF 94124 688-C1
1300 SF 94124 668-B7
1500 NVTO 94945 526-C2
1500 MrnC 94945 526-C2
ARMSTRONG CT
100 HER 94547 570-B5
1600 CNCD 94521 593-B3
ARMSTRONG DR
2100 PLE 94588 694-E7
ARMSTRONG PL
2400 SCL 95050 833-C5
ARMSTRONG ST
1000 HAY 94541 712-A1
1000 HAY 94541 711-J2
2400 LVMR 94550 695-C5
ARMY ST
100 PIT 94565 574-E3
1300 SLN 94577 690-J2
ARNERICH RD
14000 SCIC 95032 893-H2
ARNERICH HILL CT
14500 LGTS 95032 893-G2
14500 SCIC 95032 893-G2
ARNERICH HILL RD
14500 SCIC 95032 893-G1
ARNICA CT
4900 SJS 95111 875-A2
ARNO CT
- SJS 95138 875-E1
4700 RCH 94804 609-A2
ARNOLD AV
- MTVW 94043 812-B2
- SCIC 94043 812-A2
- SF 94110 667-H6
1200 SJS 95110 833-J3
ARNOLD CT
3700 FRMT 94539 753-F6
22700 HAY 94541 711-H2
ARNOLD DR
700 MRTZ 94553 571-F6
1700 MRTZ 94553 572-A6
ARNOLD WY
700 MLPK 94025 790-J2
800 SJS 95128 853-F4
ARNOLD INDUSTRL PL
1700 CNCD 94520 572-E5
ARNOLD INDUSTRL WY
1700 CNCD 94520 572-F4
1700 CCCo 94553 572-D5
1700 CCCo 94520 572-F4
ARNOTT WY
1000 CMBL 95008 853-G6
AROLLO PTH
- OAK 94618 630-B5
ARONIA LN
- NVTO 94945 526-B2
ARPEGGIO AV
4200 SJS 95136 874-G1
ARQUEADO DR
3200 SJS 95148 835-D7
ARQUES AV
1200 SUNV 94086 812-J7
E ARQUES AV
100 SUNV 94086 812-E6
W ARQUES AV
100 SUNV 94086 812-E6
ARRAN CT
500 SUNV 94087 832-E4
ARREBA ST
- MRTZ 94553 571-E3
ARREZZO ST
5200 PLE 94588 694-C6
ARRIBA CT
1500 SCIC 94024 831-G3
ARRIBA DR
200 SUNV 94086 812-B7
ARROBA WY
3000 SJS 95118 874-A1
ARROW LN
1500 SJS 95126 853-H4
ARROWHEAD AV
1000 LVMR 94550 696-C4
ARROWHEAD CT
400 VAL 94589 510-B4
5000 ANT 94509 595-G5
5400 LVMR 94550 696-C3
ARROWHEAD DR
100 SJS 95123 874-H6
100 VAL 94589 510-B5
500 LFYT 94549 631-J3
1600 OAK 94611 630-F6
5400 SJS 95123 875-B4
ARROWHEAD LN
- CMAD 94925 586-G6
- NVTO 94949 546-B1
- SMCo 94063 790-D1
21300 SCIC 95070 852-B5
ARROWHEAD PL
7700 NWK 94560 752-C6
ARROWHEAD TER
900 CLAY 94517 593-H6
ARROWHEAD WY
500 HAY 94544 732-D1
1000 PA 94303 791-D5
ARROWOOD CT
600 LALT 94024 831-F1
ARROWOOD LN
100 SMTO 94403 749-B5
2000 SJS 95130 853-A6
ARROW ROCK PL
900 SUNV 94087 832-B4
ARROWSMITH CT
600 WLCK 94598 613-C4
ARROWTAIL TER
1000 FRMT 94536 753-C3
ARROWWOOD CIR
4300 CNCD 94521 593-A5
ARROWWOOD CT
3900 PLE 94588 713-J2
4400 CNCD 94521 593-A5
ARROYO AV
- SANS 94960 566-A5
- PDMT 94611 630-A7
200 SLN 94577 691-A1
1100 SCAR 94070 769-G4
2500 PIN 94564 569-J7
ARROYO CT
- SMTO 94402 748-J2
700 LFYT 94549 631-H1
2100 PLE 94588 714-B5
ARROYO DR
- MrnC 94904 586-E2
- ORIN 94563 631-C5
- SSF 94080 707-E4
- MRGA 94556 631-C5
100 DNVL 94526 653-B1
100 SJS 95131 814-A5
200 PCFA 94044 707-A4
200 PCFA 94044 706-J4
300 MRTZ 94553 571-D6
2400 SCL 95051 833-B4
8000 PLE 94588 714-A5
ARROYO LN
- NVTO 94947 526-B5
17900 SAR 95070 852-D5
ARROYO RD
700 LALT 94024 811-G6
1100 LVMR 94550 715-H5
1500 AlaC 94550 715-H5
2300 AlaC 94550 715-H6
ARROYO WY
- SF 94127 667-E5
100 SJS 95112 834-D5
1200 WLCK 94596 612-C4
5100 ANT 94509 595-H5
ARROYO DE ARGUELLO
12300 SAR 95070 852-D6
ARROYO DEL RANCHO
500 LGTS 95032 893-G1
ARROYO DE ORO
1700 SJS 95116 834-F3
ARROYO DE PLATINA
1800 SJS 95116 834-F3
ARROYO GRANDE WY
100 LGTS 95030 873-C4
ARROYO OAKS
11500 SCIC 94024 831-F4
ARROYO SECO
- MLBR 94030 727-J5
ARROYO SECO DR
1000 CMBL 95008 853-G6
1500 SCIC 95125 853-G6
ARROYO VIEW CIR
- BLMT 94002 769-B2
ARROYO VISTA RD
4700 LVMR 94550 696-B6
ARROYUELO AV
4200 OAK 94611 649-J1
ARROZ PL
200 FRMT 94536 753-D2
ARTHUR AV
600 SF 94124 668-C4
600 SLN 94577 690-H1
2100 BLMT 94002 769-C1
3200 SJS 95127 835-B3
ARTHUR CT
200 DNVL 94526 653-C2
2900 AlaC 94541 712-D2
3000 SCL 95051 833-A7
11700 LALT 94024 831-H4
ARTHUR DR
5800 PLE 94588 714-B1
ARTHUR LN
- ATN 94027 790-C2
ARTHUR PL
1100 SJS 95127 835-A3
ARTHUR RD
- CCCo 94553 571-J3
400 CCCo 94553 572-A3
ARTHUR ST
400 NVTO 94947 526-B5
6400 OAK 94605 670-H2
6900 OAK 94621 670-H3
ARTHUR WY
2300 ANT 94509 574-J7
2300 ANT 94509 594-J1
ARTHUR E HANSEN WY
1900 SMTO 94404 749-E2
ARTUNA AV
- PDMT 94611 650-A1
ARUBA
100 HER 94547 570-C6
ARUBA LN
900 FCTY 94404 749-G4
ARUNDEL CT
4900 SJS 95136 874-F2
ARUNDEL RD
- BURL 94010 728-H6
- SCAR 94070 769-E3
ARUNDEL WY
2800 CCCo 94806 589-A3
ARVADA CT
100 SRMN 94583 673-G7
ARVILLA LN
24800 HAY 94544 711-J3
ARYA CT
32000 UNC 94587 732-A6
ARZATE LN
2100 ANT 94509 575-F6
ASBURY CT
400 LVMR 94550 695-E6
1200 SLN 94579 691-A4
ASBURY PL
700 SCL 95051 833-B5
ASBURY ST
- SJS 95110 834-A4
300 SJS 95110 833-J5
700 SJS 95126 833-H6
ASBY BAY
100 ALA 94502 669-J6
ASCENSION DR
1400 SMCo 94402 748-G6
2400 SRMN 94583 673-B3
19600 SAR 95070 852-F5
26300 LAH 94022 811-B6
ASCHAUER CT
1100 SJS 95131 834-D1
ASCOT CT
- OAK 94611 650-F1
- SRMN 94583 673-E4
100 MRGA 94556 631-D3
300 AMCN 94589 509-J3
1800 CNCD 94520 592-F2
2100 PIT 94565 574-A3
3100 PLE 94588 694-F6
3100 RCH 94806 589-A2
ASCOT DR
1800 MRGA 94556 631-D3
2600 SRMN 94583 673-E4
5400 OAK 94611 650-F1
ASCOT LN
- OAK 94611 650-G1
3000 SJS 95111 854-H5
ASCOT PKWY
- VAL 94591 510-F7
1700 VAL 94591 530-E1
ASCOT PL
- MRGA 94556 631-D3
5500 OAK 94611 650-F2
ASCOT RD
300 HIL 94010 748-G2
ASCOT WY
2400 UNC 94587 732-B4
ASENATH CT
2100 WLCK 94598 612-G3
ASH AV
- CMAD 94925 586-G7
- MrnC 94904 586-D3
- SANS 94960 566-A6
600 SSF 94080 707-J2
ASH CT
100 HER 94547 570-A5
100 LGTS 95030 873-A3
600 CMBL 95008 853-F5
6800 DBLN 94568 693-J4
ASH LN
100 PTLV 94028 810-E4
300 CCCo 94803 589-E1
ASH ST
- RDWC 94061 790-B1
300 SF 94102 647-H7
400 PA 94306 811-B1
400 MrnC 94965 606-E7
1200 AlaC 94541 691-H7
1400 MRTZ 94553 571-F3
1800 PA 94306 791-A7
1800 SCL 95054 813-D5
3000 CNCD 94520 572-F6
3100 ANT 94509 574-J7
7800 OAK 94621 670-H3
36700 NWK 94560 752-D7
37100 NWK 94560 772-D1
ASH WY
100 MrnC 94903 566-H2
ASHBOURNE CT
5300 NWK 94560 752-D4
10700 SCIC 95014 852-C6
ASHBOURNE DR
600 SUNV 94087 832-F4
ASHBROOK CIR
4000 SJS 95124 873-E3
ASHBROOK CT
2900 OAK 94601 650-C6
ASHBROOK DR
1900 CCCo 94806 569-B4
ASHBROOK PL
- MRGA 94556 631-D4
ASHBURTON DR
3000 ANT 94509 575-E7
3200 ANT 94509 595-E1
6000 SJS 95123 875-A6
ASHBURY AV
- ALB 94706 609-E4
- ELCR 94530 609-D3
- MrnC 94965 606-B3
ASHBURY CT
- PIT 94565 574-B3
ASHBURY DR
1500 CNCD 94520 592-F2
ASHBURY LN
1600 HAY 94545 711-H6
ASHBURY ST
- SF 94117 647-E7
200 SF 94117 667-F1
ASHBURY TER
- SF 94117 667-F2
ASHBURY WY
- PIT 94565 574-B3
ASHBY AV
- SJS 95124 873-F3
ASHBY AV Rt#-13
1200 BERK 94702 629-F4
1200 BERK 94804 629-D4
1300 BERK 94703 629-F4
2100 BERK 94705 629-F4
2800 BERK 94705 630-A3
ASHBY DR
700 PA 94301 791-B3

STREET Block City ZIP Pg-Grid

ASHBY LN
100 LALT 94022 811-D5
ASHBY PL
200 AMCN 94589 510-A3
2700 BERK 94705 629-J3
ASHBY WY
9600 SRMN 94583 673-G7
ASHCROFT LN
1200 SJS 95118 874-C5
ASHCROFT WY
1100 SUNV 94087 832-A5
ASHDALE DR
1800 CNCD 94519 572-J7
10200 SCIC 95127 835-B2
ASHEBORO CT
1400 SJS 95131 814-C6
ASHER CT
3900 SJS 95124 873-E3
ASHFIELD AV
20800 AlaC 94546 692-A6
ASHFIELD CT
6500 SJS 95120 894-C1
ASHFIELD RD
- ATN 94027 790-E2
ASHFORD AV
- MLV 94941 606-F3
300 SCAR 94070 769-E4
ASHFORD CT
- CCCo 94507 652-G1
600 BEN 94510 530-J7
1200 SJS 95131 834-C1
2300 ANT 94509 595-G1
ASHFORD PL
- MRGA 94556 631-D6
ASHFORD WY
7500 DBLN 94568 693-G2
38100 FRMT 94536 753-A3
ASHGLEN WY
2300 SJS 95133 834-F1
ASH GROVE CT
100 SJS 95123 875-A3
ASHLAND AV
16000 AlaC 94580 691-E5
ASHLAND CT
1000 DNVL 94506 653-G5
ASHLAND DR
- DALY 94015 686-J4
1400 MPS 95035 794-D7
ASHLAND TER
500 FRMT 94536 753-G3
ASHLAND WY
- DNVL 94506 653-G5
1900 SJS 95130 852-J6
ASHLER AV
- LGTS 95030 873-A6
ASHLEY CIR
200 DNVL 94526 653-A3
ASHLEY CT
- NVTO 94945 526-F1
4700 UNC 94587 731-J7
6000 PLE 94588 694-B6
12800 SAR 95070 852-D6
ASHLEY LN
- WLCK 94596 612-D3
ASHLEY PL
- CCCo 94553 571-G4
1000 MTVW 94040 811-F5
ASHLEY WY
3100 ANT 94509 575-F7
3100 ANT 94509 595-E1
20500 SAR 95070 852-D6
32200 UNC 94587 731-J7
ASHLEY RIDGE CT
4700 SJS 95138 855-E5
ASHLING CT
- SJS 95136 854-E6
ASHLOCK CT
1100 CMBL 95008 873-A1
ASHMEADE CT
1800 SJS 95125 853-G4
ASHMONT DR
4800 SJS 95111 875-B1
ASHMOUNT AV
1000 OAK 94610 650-C2
1200 PDMT 94610 650-C2
ASHMOUNT WY
- OAK 94610 650-B2
ASHRIDGE LN
3800 SJS 95121 855-C4
ASHTON AV
- MLBR 94030 728-A4
- SF 94112 687-D1
200 SF 94112 667-D7
200 SF 94132 667-D7
200 SF 94127 667-D7
300 OAK 94603 670-G6
500 PA 94306 791-D7
2000 SMCo 94025 790-D6
S ASHTON AV
- MLBR 94030 728-B5
1800 BURL 94010 728-B5
ASHTON CT
- VAL 94591 530-G5
3400 PA 94306 791-D7
7500 PLE 94588 714-A3
19600 SAR 95070 852-F5
ASHTON LN
300 MrnC 94965 626-F1
ASHTON PL
35700 FRMT 94536 752-F2
ASHTON ST
100 VAL 94591 530-G5
ASHTON OAKS CT
- SRMN 94583 673-J7
ASHTON OAKS WY
700 SJS 95138 875-G5
ASHWOOD AV
800 VAL 94591 530-F5
ASHWOOD COM
4400 FRMT 94538 773-D2
ASHWOOD CT
- SJS 95131 814-A4
- SRFL 94901 567-C6
1300 SMTO 94402 748-J4
4400 UNC 94587 732-A6
7300 PLE 94588 714-A2
ASHWOOD DR
1400 MRTZ 94553 591-H1
1400 SMTO 94402 748-J4
3600 PLE 94588 714-A2
ASHWOOD LN
- SF 94131 667-D3
2000 SJS 95132 814-E2
ASHWORTH WY
3000 SJS 95148 835-E7
ASILOMAR CIR
- OAK 94611 630-E7
ASILOMAR DR
1900 OAK 94611 630-E7
2000 ANT 94509 595-F2
ASILOMAR TER
900 SUNV 94086 812-C6
ASIMUTH CIR
4100 UNC 94587 732-B6
ASKHAM PLACE CT
1700 SJS 95121 855-C4
ASPEN
- BEN 94510 551-B5
ASPEN AV
200 SSF 94080 708-A2
200 SSF 94080 707-J2
21100 AlaC 94546 692-B6
ASPEN CT
- CCCo 94803 569-D7
- LFYT 94549 611-G2
- SANS 94960 566-B6
- SolC 94591 550-E1
100 HER 94547 569-J4
4800 SJS 95124 873-H4
7400 PLE 94588 713-J1
ASPEN DR
100 CCCo 94553 572-B7
100 CCCo 94553 592-E4
100 NVTO 94945 525-G1
1100 CNCD 94520 592-E4
1200 PCFA 94044 727-B5
2900 SCL 95051 833-A7
22800 SCIC 94024 831-J5
ASPEN PL
4000 OAK 94602 650-F5
7600 NWK 94560 752-D7
ASPEN WY
400 SCIC 94024 831-J5
800 PA 94303 791-E7
ASPENRIDGE CT
1900 WLCK 94596 611-H3
ASPENRIDGE DR
200 MPS 95035 793-J4
ASPENWOOD COM
37100 FRMT 94536 752-H2
ASPENWOOD CT
- CNCD - 613-D1
ASPEN WOOD ST
6400 LVMR 94550 696-D3
ASPESI CT
18600 SAR 95070 872-H1
ASPESI DR
18500 SAR 95070 872-H1
ASPINWALL CT
- ORIN 94563 631-C6
ASPINWALL DR
- BEN 94510 551-C1
ASPINWALL RD
6000 OAK 94611 630-E6
ASQUITH PL
36000 FRMT 94536 752-F3
ASSAY CT
100 VAL 94591 530-C7
ASSISI CT
5800 SJS 95138 875-G1
ASSOCIATED RD
100 SSF 94080 708-A3
ASSUNTA WY
1900 SJS 95124 873-G1
ASTER AV
- HIL 94010 728-F7
- HIL 94010 748-F1
900 SUNV 94086 832-G1
8200 OAK 94605 671-A2
ASTER CT
- MLV 94941 606-F3
100 HER 94547 569-J4
900 SUNV 94086 832-G1
1400 CPTO 95014 852-D4
7400 PLE 94588 714-A2
37600 NWK 94560 752-F7
ASTER DR
1300 ANT 94509 575-B4
ASTER LN
1100 LVMR 94550 696-A4
1200 CPTO 95014 852-D4
ASTER RD
100 SCAR 94070 769-G4
ASTER ST
900 VAL 94589 509-J6
ASTER WY
100 EPA 94303 791-D3
ASTI CT
1200 LVMR 94550 715-F3
ASTOR CT
1700 SLN 94577 671-D7
1700 SLN 94577 691-D1
ASTOR DR
1800 SLN 94577 691-D1
ASTOR ST
2400 UNC 94587 732-G7
ASTORIA DR
900 SUNV 94087 832-B4
ASTRAHAN LN
2200 SJS 95148 835-D5
ASTRID DR
100 PLHL 94523 592-C7
ASTRIDA DR
- HAY 94544 712-B7
ASTRO CT
1900 SJS 95131 814-D6
ATALAYA TER
- SF 94117 647-F7
ATCHISON STAGE CT
- CLAY 94517 593-G6
ATCHISON STAGE PL
- CLAY 94517 593-G6
ATCHISON STAGE RD
- CLAY 94517 593-G7
ATHENA
500 HER 94547 569-F3
ATHENE CT
3100 CNCD 94519 572-G7
ATHENE DR
2100 CNCD 94519 572-G7
10200 SCIC 95127 835-A3
ATHENIAN WY
400 PCFA 94044 726-G4
ATHENOUR CT
- PLE 94586 693-G7
1400 SJS 95120 874-A7
ATHENOUR WY
7500 AlaC 94586 754-D1
ATHENS AV
800 OAK 94607 649-F2
ATHENS CT
20900 AlaC 94541 691-G7
ATHENS DR
5000 SRMN 94583 673-G4
ATHENS LN
1800 ANT 94509 575-G5
ATHENS RD
1200 LVMR 94550 715-F3
ATHENS ST
- SF 94112 667-H7
300 SF 94112 687-G1
ATHERTON AV
- ATN 94027 790-C4
- MrnC 94945 526-E2
- PIT 94565 574-C4
- NVTO 94945 526-E2
- CCCo 94525 550-E5
4700 SJS 95130 853-A5
4700 SJS 95130 852-J5
4800 SJS 95129 852-J4
ATHERTON CIR
- PIT 94565 574-B4
ATHERTON CT
100 SMCo 94061 790-B4
12800 LAH 94022 831-C1
ATHERTON DR
3000 SCL 95051 833-A7
ATHERTON PL
22600 HAY 94541 711-J2
ATHERTON ST
1000 VAL 94590 530-C7
8000 OAK 94605 670-J3
22500 HAY 94541 711-J2
ATHERTON OAKS DR
- MrnC 94945 526-G3
ATHERTON OAKS LN
- ATN 94027 790-D5
ATHERWOOD AV
- RDWC 94061 790-B2
6300 CPTO 95014 852-F2
ATHERWOOD PL
- RDWC 94061 790-B2
ATHLONE CT
- SMCo 94025 770-F7
ATHLONE WY
- SMCo 94025 770-E7
ATHOL AV
100 OAK 94606 649-J4
400 OAK 94606 650-A4
600 OAK 94610 650-A4
ATHOS PL
19300 SAR 95070 872-G1
ATHY CT
38500 FRMT 94536 753-B2
ATHY DR
3500 SSF 94080 707-C4
ATHY ST
38500 FRMT 94536 753-B3
ATKINS CT
500 BEN 94510 550-H1
ATKINSON LN
1000 MLPK 94025 790-E5
ATLANTA AV
300 SJS 95125 854-A2
ATLANTA ST
500 DALY 94014 687-D5
ATLANTIC AV
- SBRN 94066 707-J5
100 ALA 94501 649-E7
100 PIT 94565 574-D5
ATLANTIC CT
1700 UNC 94587 732-D4
4200 SCL 95054 813-C5
ATLANTIC ST
1100 UNC 94587 732-E4
2700 CNCD 94518 592-G2
ATLANTUS AV
- SLN 94579 691-F3
- SLN 94579 711-A1
ATLANTUS CT
- SLN 94579 691-F3
ATLAS
- UNC 94587 732-A6
300 HER 94547 569-F3
ATLAS AV
- SJS 95126 833-J7
3700 OAK 94619 650-G4
ATLAS PL
- BERK 94708 610-A6
ATLAS RD
5600 RCH 94806 568-H5
6000 RCH 94806 569-A5
6100 CCCo 94806 569-A5
ATMEL WY
- SJS 95131 813-G7
ATRICE LN
700 PLHL 94523 592-A6
ATRIUM CIR
12200 SAR 95070 852-E5
ATRIUM DR
12000 SAR 95070 852-E5
ATTEBERRY LN
1400 SJS 95131 814-A4
ATTERIDGE CT
34300 FRMT 94555 732-E7
ATTERIDGE PL
34200 FRMT 94555 732-E7
ATTRI CT
- CCCo 94549 591-H7
ATTRIDGE AL
- SF 94133 647-J4
ATUNE TER
5000 FRMT 94555 752-A3
ATWATER CT
3400 FRMT 94536 752-H2
ATWATER DR
2900 BURL 94010 728-A6
ATWELL AV
2800 OAK 94601 650-D6
ATWELL PL
25800 HAY 94544 711-H5
ATWELL RD
1400 ELCR 94530 589-E7
1400 ELCR 94530 609-E1
ATWOOD AV
- SAUS 94965 627-B4
ATWOOD CT
- SJS 95131 814-A4
100 LGTS 95032 873-D6
ATWOOD DR
2900 SJS 95121 855-B3
2900 SJS 95122 855-B3
AUBURN
200 PIT 94565 574-B3
AUBURN AV
- NWK 94560 772-H1
1000 SLN 94579 691-B5
6000 OAK 94618 629-J4
AUBURN CT
- DNVL 94506 653-G5
- TBRN 94920 607-B5
700 VAL 94589 509-H5
800 FRMT 94538 773-G7
1000 ALA 94502 670-A6
19600 CPTO 95014 832-F7
AUBURN DR
100 VAL 94589 509-H5
1000 ALA 94502 670-A6
19600 CPTO 95014 832-F7
AUBURN LN
2500 ANT 94509 575-A6
AUBURN PL
- HAY 94544 712-A7
AUBURN ST
- SF 94133 647-J4
100 MrnC 94901 586-H3
1000 LVMR 94550 716-A1
1100 FRMT 94538 773-G7
AUBURN WY
200 SJS 95129 853-A1
AUCKLAND CT
34300 FRMT 94555 732-E7
AUCKLAND PL
34200 FRMT 94555 732-E7
AUCTION WY
29900 HAY 94544 732-B2
AUDEN CT
34100 FRMT 94555 732-E7
AUDEN ST
100 VAL 94591 530-F5
AUDIFFRED LN
100 WDSD 94062 789-G6
AUDREY AV
900 CMBL 95008 873-B2
AUDREY CT
- TBRN 94920 607-E6
800 PLHL 94523 592-C3
1700 BEN 94510 551-B3
6000 PLE 94588 694-B6
34100 FRMT 94555 752-C1
AUDREY DR
4700 AlaC 94546 692-A3
AUDREY LN
- PLHL 94523 592-C3
AUDREY SMITH LN
- SAR 95070 872-E3
AUDRY ST
- LVMR 94550 696-B7
AUDUBON CT
600 HAY 94544 732-E1
AUDUBON DR
1000 SJS 95122 834-G7
AUDUBON ST
27600 HAY 94544 732-E1
AUDUBON PARK CT
3800 FRMT 94539 773-E3
5300 FRMT 94538 773-B1
AUGHINBAUGH WY
200 ALA 94502 669-J5
AUGUST CIR
300 MLPK 94025 790-F6
AUGUST CT
5000 AlaC 94546 692-B3
AUGUST DR
5600 SJS 95138 875-D4
AUGUST LN
7900 CPTO 95014 852-C2
AUGUST WY
1200 ANT 94509 575-E5
AUGUSTA AL
- SF 94133 648-A4
AUGUSTA CT
- CCCo 94507 633-A4
- LGTS 95030 873-A6
800 CNCD 94518 592-H6
2800 SCL 95051 833-B2
3400 HAY 94542 712-E5
8700 DBLN 94568 693-G2
AUGUSTA CT E
1500 MPS 95035 794-D3
AUGUSTA DR
500 MRGA 94556 631-B6
800 MRGA 94556 651-D1
3700 PIT 94565 574-C5
AUGUSTA PL
2100 SCL 95051 833-B2
AUGUSTA ST
- SF 94124 668-A6
AUGUSTA WY
- MRGA 94556 631-B6
4900 SJS 95129 852-J4
6100 LVMR 94550 696-C3
AUGUSTINE AV
15700 LGTS 95032 873-C5
AUGUSTINE CT
35700 FRMT 94536 752-G1
AUGUSTINE DR
100 MRTZ 94553 591-H1
2400 SCL 95054 813-B6
AUGUSTINE LN
600 LFYT 94549 631-H1
AUGUSTINE PL
35700 FRMT 94536 752-G2
AUGUSTINE ST
4500 PLE 94566 714-D4
AUGUSTUS CT
400 WLCK 94598 612-E2
AULIN DR
2900 SJS 95125 854-B7
AURA CT
900 LALT 94024 831-G3
AURA WY
1400 LALT 94024 831-G3
AURALLIA RD
1700 CNCD 94521 593-F5
AURA VISTA
- MLBR 94030 727-J5
- PCFA 94044 706-J3
- MLBR 94030 728-A4
AURELIA WY
14600 AlaC 94578 691-E2
AURELIAN LN
1400 SJS 95126 853-H4
AURORA AV
700 SJS 95129 853-A2
AURORA CT
- PCFA 94044 727-B2
AURORA DR
1500 SLN 94577 690-G4
AURORA LN
100 LGTS 95032 873-E5
AURORA PZ
100 UNC 94587 732-J5
AURORA TER
38600 FRMT 94536 753-D2
AURORA CRESCENT CT
- VAL 94591 510-H4
AUSEON AV
1600 OAK 94621 670-H4
1700 OAK 94605 670-J4
AUSTEN CT
700 LVMR 94550 696-A5
AUSTEN WY
- CCCo 94553 572-B5
600 LVMR 94550 696-A6
AUSTIN AV
- ATN 94027 790-C2
- HAY 94544 711-J4
- SANS 94960 586-B1
1600 LALT 94024 831-J4
AUSTIN CT
- ORIN 94563 610-J6
- RCH 94806 588-J1
- SPAB 94806 588-J1
100 SJS 95110 854-D2
2100 PIT 94565 574-A4
2300 AlaC 94546 691-H5
AUSTIN LN
- CCCo 94507 632-G4
19600 AlaC 94546 691-H5
AUSTIN PL
2400 SCL 95050 833-C6
AUSTIN ST
- OAK 94601 650-C7
- SF 94109 647-H5
- VAL 94590 529-H2
1200 FRMT 94539 753-F5
AUSTIN WY
18400 SCIC 95030 872-G5
18400 MSER 95030 872-H5
18800 SAR 95070 872-G5
AUSTWICK CT
6900 SJS 95119 895-D1
AUTO DR
1600 SF 94122 667-D3
AUTO PZ
3200 RCH 94806 569-B7
AUTO CENTER DR
- WLCK 94596 612-C2
AUTO CLUB WY
- VAL 94591 510-E7
AUTOETCH LN
- SJS 95119 875-C5
AUTO MALL CIR
43200 FRMT 94538 773-B4
AUTO MALL PKWY
3800 FRMT 94539 773-E3
4000 FRMT 94538 773-D3
AUTOMATION PKWY
1600 SJS 95131 814-C5
AUTREY ST
100 MPS 95035 794-A3
AUTUMN CT
400 SJS 95110 834-A6
1100 PLE 94566 714-D3
27700 HAY 94542 712-E4
AUTUMN DR
700 WLCK 94598 612-G3
3800 RDWC 94061 789-G3
AUTUMN LN
- SJS 95138 875-D4
800 ANT 94509 575-F5
800 MrnC 94965 606-D7
1000 LALT 94024 831-H3
N AUTUMN ST
- SJS 95113 834-A6
- SJS 95110 834-A6
S AUTUMN ST Rt#-82
- SJS 95110 834-A7
- SJS 95113 834-A7
AUTUMN ESTATES
2800 SJS 95135 855-G5
AUTUMN GOLD COM
- FRMT 94536 752-B4
AUTUMN GOLD DR
1900 SJS 95131 814-C6
AUTUMN OAK DR
1600 LVMR 94550 695-J4
AUTUMN RIDGE LN
1300 SJS 95132 814-G4
AUTUMNSONG WY
1100 SJS 95131 834-D1
1100 SJS 95131 814-D7
AUTUMNTREE CT
2000 SJS 95131 814-C6
AUTUMNVALE DR
2400 SJS 95131 814-C4
2500 SJS 95132 814-C4
AUTUMNWIND CT
- PIT 94565 574-F6
- SRMN 94583 673-H3
AUTUMNWOOD CT
3000 SJS 95148 855-E1
AUTUMNWOOD DR
- WLCK 94595 632-D5
AUZERAIS AV
400 SJS 95126 854-A1
700 SJS 95126 853-J1
AUZERIAS CT
100 LGTS 95032 873-H7
AVA CT
800 LFYT 94549 611-G7
AVA ST
1100 LVMR 94550 716-B1
AVALANI AV
400 SJS 95133 834-E2
AVALON AV
- SF 94112 667-G7
800 LFYT 94549 611-F7
1000 FCTY 94404 749-F5
2900 BERK 94705 629-J3
2900 BERK 94705 630-A3
AVALON CIR
100 VAL 94589 509-G5
200 PIT 94565 574-E1
AVALON CT
- CCCo 94595 632-D1
800 LFYT 94549 611-F7
3100 PA 94306 791-D7
4100 FRMT 94536 752-H4
AVALON DR
- DALY 94015 686-J6
- LALT 94022 811-F6
100 PCFA 94044 706-J4
200 PCFA 94044 707-A4
200 SSF 94080 707-F5
1100 SJS 95125 854-B7
W AVALON DR
100 PCFA 94044 706-J4
AVALON WY
100 VAL 94589 509-G5
700 LVMR 94550 715-E3
AVALON HEIGHTS TER
- FRMT 94539 774-B7
47400 FRMT 94539 794-A1
AVANSINO ST
3700 SLN 94578 691-B3
AVATI CT
1700 SJS 95131 814-D7
AVELLANO DR
3000 WLCK 94598 612-H2
AVENAL AV
5700 OAK 94605 670-G2
AVENIDA DR
- BERK 94708 609-J7
- BERK 94708 610-A7
AVENIDA ABETOS
300 SJS 95123 874-H3
AVENIDA ALMENDROS
5300 SJS 95123 874-H3
AVENIDA ALONDRA
600 SUNV 94089 812-H4
AVENIDA ARBOLES
300 SJS 95123 874-H3
AVENIDA CARLOS
- SUNV 94089 812-H4
AVENIDA CRESTA
16200 LGTS 95032 873-F7
AVENIDA DE ANGELINA
4900 SCL 95054 813-D3
AVENIDA DE CARMEN
4900 SCL 95054 813-D3
AVENIDA DE COBRE
1800 SJS 95116 834-F3
AVENIDA DE GUADALUPE
2300 SCL 95054 813-C3
AVENIDA DE LAGO
4900 SCL 95054 813-D3
AVENIDA DE LA FLORES
2100 SCL 95054 813-D4
AVENIDA DE LA PALMAS
1100 LVMR 94550 715-E3
AVENIDA DE LA ROSAS
1900 SCL 95054 813-D3
AVENIDA DE LO ALUMNOS
2200 SCL 95054 813-C3
AVENIDA DE LO ARBOLES
4800 SCL 95054 813-D3
AVENIDA DEL PRADO
- SCL 95054 813-C4
AVENIDA DEL ROBLE
300 SJS 95123 874-H3
AVENIDA DEL SOL
100 LGTS 95030 872-J2
AVENIDA DE ORINDA
- ORIN 94563 610-G7
AVENIDA ESPANA
- SJS 95139 875-G7
100 SJS 95139 895-F1
AVENIDA FELIPE
- SUNV 94089 812-J4
AVENIDA FERNANDO
- SUNV 94089 812-H4
AVENIDA FLORES
300 CCCo 94553 572-C6
AVENIDA GRANDE
- SUNV 94089 812-H4
- SJS 95139 875-F7
AVENIDA JOSE
- SUNV 94089 812-H4
AVENIDA LAGO
16100 LGTS 95032 873-F6
16300 SCIC 95032 873-F6
AVENIDA LA JUNTA
- SUNV 94089 812-G4
AVENIDA LEON
- SUNV 94089 812-H4
AVENIDA MANZANOS
300 SJS 95123 874-H3
AVENIDA MARCOS
- SUNV 94089 812-H4
AVENIDA MARTINEZ
- CCCo 94803 589-E2
AVENIDA MIRAFLORES
100 TBRN 94920 607-C5
AVENIDA MONTEZ
- SUNV 94089 812-H4
AVENIDA NOGALES
300 SJS 95123 874-H3
AVENIDA NUEVA
1500 CCCo 94506 653-E1
1500 CCCo 94526 653-E1
1500 CCCo 94526 633-E7
AVENIDA PALMAS
300 SJS 95123 874-H3
AVENIDA PINOS
300 SJS 95123 874-H3
AVENIDA PRIVADO
16100 LGTS 95032 873-F6
AVENIDA RICARDO
600 SUNV 94089 812-H4
AVENIDA ROTELLA
6800 SJS 95139 875-G6
AVENIDA SEVILLA
- WLCK 94595 632-C5
AVENUE A
- ALA 94501 649-D6
2700 SJS 95127 834-H2
2700 SCIC 95127 834-H2
3800 SCL 95134 813-D5
4300 SCL 95054 813-D5
AVENUE B
- ALA 94501 649-D6
- SF 94130 648-E1
2700 SJS 95127 834-H2
2700 SCIC 95127 834-H2
3800 SCL 95134 813-E5
4300 SCL 95054 813-E5
AVENUE C
- ALA 94501 649-C6
- SF 94130 648-E1
2700 SCIC 95127 834-H2
3800 SCL 95134 813-E5
AVENUE D
- ALA 94501 649-D6
- SF 94130 648-E1
AVENUE DEL NORTE
- SANS 94960 566-C7
- SANS 94960 586-C1
AVENUE DEL ORA
400 RDWC 94062 769-J7
AVENUE E
- ALA 94501 649-D6
- SF 94130 648-E1
AVENUE F
- ALA 94501 649-D7
AVENUE G
- ALA 94501 649-D7
AVENUE H
- ALA 94501 649-D7
AVENUE K
- ALA 94501 649-D7
AVENUE L
- ALA 94501 669-D1
AVENUE M
- ALA 94501 669-D1
AVENUE N
- ALA 94501 669-D1
AVENUE NORTH
- SF 94121 647-A5
AVENUE OF THE FLAGS
100 SRFL 94903 566-F4
AVENUE OF THE PALMS
- SF 94130 648-E1
AVERNUS CT
3400 SJS 95135 855-F6
AVERY CT
4900 SJS 95136 874-F2
AVERY LN
200 LGTS 95030 873-A6
AVERY ST
- SF 94115 647-G6
AVIADOR AV
- MLBR 94030 728-B3
AVIAN DR
100 VAL 94591 530-F4
AVIATION AV
- SCL 95050 833-G3
- SJS 95050 833-G3
1200 SJS 95110 833-G3
1200 SCL 95110 833-G3
AVICHI KNOLL DR
- NVTO 94947 526-B5
AVIGON CT
5800 SJS 95138 875-H1
AVILA AV
2100 SCL 95050 833-E2
AVILA CT
- HAY 94544 732-A1
1300 PCFA 94044 727-A6
4300 ANT 94509 595-G2
13100 LAH 94022 810-J7
AVILA LN
- MRGA 94556 631-D6
- ANT 94509 575-A6
AVILA PL
700 ELCR 94530 609-E3
AVILA RD
- PIT 94565 573-B4
- SMTO 94402 749-A3
100 CCCo 94520 573-B4
100 CNCD 94520 573-B4
100 CCCo - 573-B4
200 SMTO 94402 748-J3
AVILA ST
- SF 94123 647-F3
5800 ELCR 94530 609-C4
AVINGTON RD
100 ALA 94502 669-J5
AVINGTON TER
500 FRMT 94536 753-G3
AVIO CT
- PLE 94566 715-C5
AVIS CT
- ORIN 94563 631-B3
AVIS DR
800 ELCR 94530 609-D2
1100 SJS 95126 853-J3
AVIS LN
23000 AlaC 94541 692-C7
AVIS RD
- BERK 94707 609-G4
AVIS WY
3100 PIN 94564 569-F6
AVOCA AL
- SF 94127 667-E5
AVOCA AV
5900 OAK 94611 630-C6
AVOCA DR
4000 SJS 95136 854-E6
AVOCADO CT
- HAY 94544 711-J4
100 SRMN 94583 673-F7
AVOCADO PL
10100 CPTO 95014 852-F1
AVOCET CT
- SRFL 94901 587-A2
200 FCTY 94404 749-H2
AVOCET DR
- RDWC 94065 749-J6
200 RDWC 94065 750-A6

STREET / Block City ZIP Pg-Grid

AVOCET TER
3800 FRMT 94555 732-J3
AVON
- DNVL 94526 652-J3
AVON AV
- MLV 94941 606-F3
1000 SLN 94579 691-A5
2800 CNCD 94520 572-E6
AVON CT
4200 SJS 95136 874-G1
7200 DBLN 94568 693-J3
AVON LN
3000 CCCo 94806 589-B2
18500 MSER 95030 872-H4
18500 SAR 95070 872-H4
AVON PL
2400 LVMR 94550 715-F5
AVON RD
- CCCo 94707 609-F4
AVON ST
- LKSP 94939 586-E6
100 PIT 94565 574-D3
400 OAK 94618 629-H6
900 BLMT 94002 769-D1
38500 FRMT 94536 752-H6
AVON WY
- CCCo 94553 572-C3
500 LALT 94024 831-F1
2800 SF 94132 667-B6
AVONDALE AV
- RDWC 94062 769-J5
AVONDALE CT
900 WLCK 94596 632-F1
AVONDALE LN
300 LVMR 94550 696-A6
1000 HAY 94545 711-G5
AVONDALE LNDG
- ALA 94502 670-A6
AVONDALE RD
1200 HIL 94010 748-E4
W AVONDALE RD
- HIL 94010 748-E4
AVONDALE ST
1000 SJS 95129 852-E3
AVONOAK CT
- OAK 94619 651-C7
- OAK 94605 651-C7
AVOSET TER
1300 SUNV 94087 832-E4
AVY AV
1800 MLPK 94025 790-D6
1800 SMCo 94025 790-D6
AWALT CT
1500 LALT 94024 832-A3
AWALT DR
1100 MTVW 94040 832-A2
AYALA AV
5700 OAK 94609 629-H5
AYALA CT
- SRFL 94903 566-E5
AYALA DR
1100 SUNV 94086 812-B6
AYAMONTE CT
- SRMN 94583 673-C3
AYER AV
- SJS 95110 834-A5
AYER LN
- MPS 95035 794-C6
AYER ST
1200 MPS 95035 794-C6
AYERS RD
1300 CNCD 94521 593-D5
1800 CCCo 94521 593-E3
AYLESBURY CT
3100 AlaC 94546 691-G3
AYRES LN
- MLPK 94025 790-E7
AYRSHIRE DR
5300 SJS 95118 874-C4
AYRSHIRE FARM LN
- SCIC 94305 790-J7
AZA DR
2100 SCL 95050 833-C3
AZALEA AV
900 BURL 94010 728-F5
1400 MRTZ 94553 571-E3
AZALEA CT
- HAY 94541 711-D2
100 HER 94547 569-J3
100 VAL 94589 509-H6
1400 MRTZ 94553 571-E3
2800 ANT 94509 575-G7
5300 LVMR 94550 696-B4
AZALEA DR
- MLV 94941 606-F3
800 SUNV 94086 832-G1
1000 ALA 94502 670-A6
1900 CCCo 94595 612-B7
6900 SJS 95120 894-G3
AZALEA LN
- SRMN 94583 653-H7
- OAK 94611 630-F7
- SCAR 94070 769-C5
600 SJS 95136 854-E7
AZALEA RD
17900 HAY 94541 711-D2
AZALEA WY
400 LALT 94022 811-F6
16100 SCIC 95032 873-D5
AZALIA DR
100 EPA 94303 791-C2
AZARA PL
600 SUNV 94086 832-F1
AZELIA CT
2900 UNC 94587 732-F7
AZEVEDO AV
23900 AlaC 94541 712-B1
AZEVEDO COM
500 FRMT 94539 753-H7
AZEVEDO CT
600 SCL 95051 833-B6
AZEVEDO LN
- NaCo 94589 510-G3
AZEVEDO ST
1200 ANT 94509 575-F5
AZORES CIR
400 CCCo 94565 573-D1
AZORES CT
200 CCCo 94565 573-D1
AZTEC AV
100 SJS 95136 854-G7
AZTEC CT
600 FRMT 94539 773-H6
AZTEC RD
29000 HAY 94544 712-C7
AZTEC ST
- SF 94110 667-J4
AZTEC WY
- OAK 94611 630-E7
2400 PA 94303 791-D5
AZTEC RIDGE DR
16200 LGTS 95032 893-C3
16200 SCIC 95032 893-C3
16200 SCIC 95030 893-C3
AZUCAR AV
- SJS 95111 875-B2
AZUL WY
2200 PLE 94566 714-G3
AZULE AV
600 SJS 95123 874-G5
AZURE ST
800 SUNV 94087 832-E2
AZURITE WY
- LVMR 94550 715-C3
AZZARELLO CT
4400 SJS 95121 855-F4

B

B RD
- SUNV 94089 812-J3
100 AlaC 94586 734-C4
15000 SCIC 95127 815-C6
B RD W
800 SBRN 94066 707-H6
B ST
- CCCo 94525 550-A5
- CCCo 94565 573-E1
- CNCD 94518 592-G3
- CNCD 94520 572-J3
- DALY 94014 687-C6
- MTVW 94043 812-B5
- NVTO 94949 546-G3
- OAK 94625 649-A3
- DNVL 94506 653-J5
- VAL 94590 529-H2
100 AlaC 94586 734-C5
100 HAY 94541 711-J1
100 MRTZ 94553 571-E4
100 RDWC 94063 769-J5
100 SSF 94080 707-G3
100 BEN 94510 551-B6
200 SMCo 94014 687-C6
300 ANT 94509 575-D4
300 CLMA 94014 687-D6
300 RDWC 94063 770-A4
400 RCH 94801 588-F6
400 SRFL 94901 586-F1
500 UNC 94587 732-F4
900 LALT 94024 831-H3
1100 SRFL 94901 566-F7
1100 HAY 94541 712-A1
1400 HAY 94541 692-B7
7100 ELCR 94530 609-E4
7600 CPTO 95014 831-G5
8000 OAK 94621 670-G4
9000 OAK 94603 670-H5
N B ST
- SMTO 94401 748-J1
S B ST
100 SMTO 94401 748-J1
300 SMTO 94401 749-A2
1200 SMTO 94402 749-A2
BABBLING BROOK WY
200 PIT 94565 573-J2
BABCOCK CT
3700 AlaC 94546 692-B5
BABEL LN
1200 CNCD 94518 592-J3
1200 CNCD 94521 592-J3
BABERO AV
1600 SJS 95118 874-A1
BABE RUTH CT
1800 SJS 95132 814-D4
BABE RUTH DR
2700 SJS 95132 814-D4
BABETTE CT
200 PLHL 94523 592-C6
BABY BOTTLE TR
- CCCo 94563 610-C5
- CCCo 94708 610-C5
BACA VISTA
- NVTO 94945 525-J2
BACCHARIS PL
- MrnC 94920 606-J4
BACCHUS
- HER 94547 569-F3
BACCHUS DR
1100 SJS 95122 854-G1
BACH CT
4700 FRMT 94538 753-B7
12700 SAR 95070 852-G6
BACHE ST
- SF 94110 667-J6
BACHELORS RD
- MrnC 94945 526-J2
BACHMAN AV
100 LGTS 95030 873-A7
300 LGTS 95030 872-J6
400 MSER 95030 872-J6
BACHMAN CT
16100 LGTS 95030 872-J6
BACHMANN CT
2400 SJS 95124 853-H7
BACIGALUPI DR
100 LGTS 95032 873-H6
BACINADA CT
4100 FRMT 94536 752-F2
BACINADA DR
4000 FRMT 94536 752-F2
BACON CT
- DALY 94015 707-B1
- LFYT 94549 612-A4
- LFYT 94549 611-J4
4400 PLE 94588 694-A7
BACON PL
34400 FRMT 94555 732-E7
BACON RD
5300 OAK 94619 651-A5
5300 OAK 94619 650-J6
BACON ST
- SF 94124 668-A7
- SF 94134 668-A7
600 SF 94134 667-J7
2200 CNCD 94520 592-F1
BACON WY
1100 LFYT 94549 612-A4
1100 LFYT 94549 611-J4
BADDING RD
3300 AlaC 94546 691-J4
BADEN AV
100 SSF 94080 707-G2
BADEN CT
1600 SJS 95132 814-E4
BADEN ST
- SF 94131 667-F6
BADGER CT
- NVTO 94949 546-D4
5800 AlaC 94552 692-D3
BADGER DR
3000 PLE 94566 714-H2
BADGER LN
1200 CNCD 94521 593-C5
BADGER ST
- SF 94112 667-G6
BADGER WY
900 ANT 94509 595-F1
BADGERWOOD LN
1900 MPS 95035 793-J3
BAFFIN AV
4700 FRMT 94536 752-F4
BAFFIN CT
- FCTY 94404 749-G6
BAFFIN ST
100 FCTY 94404 749-G5
BAFFIN WY
1200 LVMR 94550 715-G3
BAGADO CT
500 SRMN 94583 673-B3
BAGDAD WY
- SJS 95123 875-B4
BAGDHAD PL
800 SJS 95116 834-J4
BAGELY WY
1300 SJS 95122 854-H1
BAGGINS CT
1200 SJS 95121 855-A4
BAGPIPE WY
1600 SJS 95121 855-B3
BAGSHAW CT
300 SJS 95123 875-A5
BAGSHOTTE DR
5800 OAK 94611 650-F1
BAGUIO CT
6400 SJS 95119 875-C7
BAGWORTH CT
3100 SJS 95148 855-C2
BAHAMA AV
26600 HAY 94545 711-G7
27400 HAY 94545 731-G1
BAHAMA COM
34600 FRMT 94555 752-E1
BAHAMA CT
100 SRMN 94583 673-E1
BAHAMA LN
600 FCTY 94404 749-G5
BAHAMA WY
1400 SJS 95122 834-H6
BAHAMA REEF
- MrnC 94949 526-J7
BAHIA
1800 SMTO 94403 749-E5
BAHIA AV
100 SJS 95136 854-G7
BAHIA CIR
100 SRFL 94901 587-A2
BAHIA CT
200 SJS 95119 875-D7
BAHIA DR
400 NVTO 94945 526-F1
500 MrnC 94945 526-F1
BAHIA LN
200 SRFL 94901 587-A2
200 SRFL 94901 586-J2
BAHIA PL
200 SRFL 94901 587-A2
200 SRFL 94901 586-J2
BAHIA WY
- SRFL 94901 587-A2
300 SRFL 94901 586-J2
BAHIA VISTA CT
100 VAL 94591 550-F1
BAHL ST
22200 CPTO 95014 832-A7
BAHR LN
- CMAD 94925 586-F7
BAHRE LN
- SJS 95131 814-B6
BAI-GORRY PL
1000 WLCK 94598 592-F7
1000 WLCK 94598 612-F1
BAILEY AV
400 SJS 95141 895-H6
2200 SJS 95128 833-F7
2200 SCIC 95128 833-F7
BAILEY CT
2600 FRMT 94536 753-A3
4700 CNCD 94521 593-D3
BAILEY LN
- CCCo 94803 589-E2
BAILEY RD
- CNCD 94520 573-G7
- SCIC 94035 812-B3
- SCIC 94043 812-B3
100 CCCo 94565 573-G2
500 SJS 95141 895-G6
500 SJS 95139 895-G6
500 PIT 94565 573-G2
700 CCCo 94565 573-G2
900 CCCo - 573-G7
1500 CNCD 94521 593-C4
1800 CCCo 94521 593-E2
1900 CNCD 94520 593-E2
BAILEYANA RD
900 HIL 94010 728-D7
BAIN PL
700 RDWC 94062 789-G1
BAINBRIDGE AV
100 ALA 94501 649-E7
BAINBRIDGE CT
900 SUNV 94087 832-B4
BAINBRIDGE ST
600 FCTY 94404 749-G4
BAINBRIDGE WY
2400 UNC 94587 732-C5
BAINE AV
4000 FRMT 94536 752-H4
6000 NWK 94560 752-F6
BAINTER AV
19100 SAR 95070 872-G5
19100 SCIC 95030 872-G5
1930C SAR 95030 872-G5
BAINTER WY
19400 SCIC 95030 872-F5
BAINTREE PL
100 LGTS 95030 873-B2
BAIO LN
1600 CNCD 94521 593-E4
BAIRD AV
700 SCL 95054 813-E6
BAIRD CT
1300 CNCD 94518 592-E7
BAIR ISLAND RD
500 RDWC 94063 770-B4
BAIRN CT
3700 PLE 94588 694-F5
BAIRN DR
1400 HIL 94010 748-E4
BAIRO CT
41000 FRMT 94539 753-E6
BAITX DR
- MRGA 94556 651-E1
BAJA CT
- PIT 94565 573-J3
- CMAD 94925 606-H1
BAJA LN
- CCCo 94595 612-B6
BAJADA CT
900 FRMT 94539 753-F5
BAJA LOMA CT
- DNVL 94526 653-C1
BAKER AV
4100 PA 94306 811-C2
BAKER CT
300 BEN 94510 551-A2
1000 SUNV 94087 832-B4
1700 SF 94129 647-B5
2200 ANT 94509 575-A7
BAKER DR
3100 CNCD 94519 572-G7
BAKER LN
3600 LFYT 94549 611-E6
27800 LAH 94022 811-A6
BAKER PL
1900 SJS 95131 814-D6
BAKER RD
20700 AlaC 94546 691-J5
BAKER ST
- SF 94117 667-F1
100 SSF 94080 708-A3
200 BEN 94510 551-A2
200 SF 94117 647-F7
700 SF 94115 647-F5
2500 SF 94123 647-F5
2900 SF 94123 647-F3
3200 BERK 94702 629-F5
3200 OAK 94608 629-F5
BAKER WY
900 SMTO 94404 749-D2
BAL CT
1500 SLN 94578 691-D3
BALANCE DR
500 SJS 95111 854-F7
BALANCE ST
- SF 94133 648-B4
BALARDO WY
3000 SJS 95148 855-E1
BALBACH ST
- SJS 95110 834-C7
BALBOA AV
- SJS 95116 834-F3
- SRFL 94901 567-A7
- SRFL 94901 587-A1
- VAL 94591 530-D5
1000 BURL 94010 728-D5
BALBOA CT
100 HER 94547 570-A5
300 ALA 94501 669-J4
1200 SUNV 94086 812-B6
1600 PLHL 94523 592-D5
2700 ANT 94509 575-B6
BALBOA DR
100 MPS 95035 793-J5
5500 OAK 94611 630-E7
BALBOA LN
800 FCTY 94404 749-F3
BALBOA ST
- SJS 95134 813-G3
- SF 94118 647-A7
900 FCTY 94404 749-F4
1600 SF 94121 647-A7
3200 SF 94121 646-H7
BALBOA WY
100 SBRN 94066 727-J1
100 PCFA 94044 726-H4
1100 LVMR 94550 715-F2
1300 BURL 94010 728-C5
4600 FRMT 94536 752-F4
BALCETA AV
- SF 94127 667-D4
BALCETA CT
100 DNVL 94526 653-D6
BALCLUTHA DR
- CMAD 94925 607-A1
1100 FCTY 94404 749-G2
BALCLUTHA WY
- PIT 94565 573-J2
- PIT 94565 574-A2
BALCOM RD
3800 SCIC 95148 835-F6
BALD EAGLE WY
4300 SJS 95118 874-C2
BALDERSTONE DR
6200 SJS 95120 874-C7
BALD HILL FIRE RD
- MrnC 94904 586-A2
- MrnC 94930 586-A2
BALDWIN AV
- CCCo 94525 550-E5
- DALY 94015 687-A6
- SMTO 94401 748-J1
BALDWIN CT
- SF 94124 668-D7
- SRFL 94901 586-G3
- WLCK 94596 612-C2
1800 CNCD 94519 592-J1
3900 FRMT 94536 752-F2
BALDWIN DR
100 DNVL 94526 653-B6
1700 CNCD 94519 592-J1
3800 SCL 95051 832-H7
BALDWIN LN
2600 WLCK 94596 612-C2
BALDWIN PL
35400 FRMT 94536 752-F2
BALDWIN ST
- VAL 94590 529-H2
8100 OAK 94621 670-F5
24600 HAY 94544 712-A6
BALDWIN WY
- PLE 94588 693-H6
BALDWIN HILLS CT
3600 SSF 94080 707-D4
BALEIN CT
- HAY 94544 732-A1
BALENTINE DR
39600 NWK 94560 773-A1
39700 NWK 94560 772-J1
BALERI RANCH RD
14000 LAH 94022 810-H6
BALES CT
1700 CNCD 94521 593-D3
BALES DR
100 CCCo 94596 612-F7
BALFOUR AV
3600 OAK 94610 650-A3
BALFOUR DR
600 SJS 95111 854-H4
BALGRAY CT
3000 SJS 95148 855-C3
BALHAN CT
5200 CNCD 94521 593-E5
BALHAN DR
1300 CNCD 94521 593-E5
BAL HARBOR LN
2600 HAY 94545 711-F7
BAL HARBOR WY
1100 SJS 95122 834-H5
BALHI CT
- SF 94112 687-F1
BALI CT
600 SRMN 94583 673-E1
800 DNVL 94526 653-B2
1300 SJS 95122 854-H1
BALI LN
- ALA 94502 670-A6
BALKAN CT
5400 AlaC 94552 692-D3
BALL RD
- CCCo 94596 612-F6
BALLAD CT
1500 CNCD 94521 593-E5
BALLANTINE PL
35600 FRMT 94536 752-G1
BALLANTREE WY
1500 SJS 95118 874-A4
BALLANTYNE DR
3500 PLE 94588 694-F5
BALLARD CT
- HAY 94544 712-B7
1200 SJS 95131 814-D7
BALLARD DR
37900 FRMT 94536 752-H6
BALLATORE DR
100 SJS 95134 813-D2
BALLENA BLVD
1000 ALA 94501 669-E2
BALLEYBAY
- ALA 94502 669-J6
BALLY WY
400 PCFA 94044 707-A3
400 PCFA 94044 706-J3
BALLYMORE CIR
- SJS 95136 854-E6
BALME DR
2300 SJS 95122 854-H2
BALMORAL CT
2100 SMTO 94403 749-A4
3200 PLE 94588 694-E6
BALMORAL DR
3000 SJS 95132 814-E3
5600 OAK 94619 651-A5
5600 OAK 94619 650-J4
5600 OAK - 651-A5
BALMORAL ST
2400 UNC 94587 732-C4
BALMORAL WY
300 HAY 94544 732-E2
BALMORAL PARK CT
4500 FRMT 94538 773-D2
BALMORE CT
900 CCCo 94803 569-D6
900 PIN 94564 569-D6
BALMY ST
- SF 94110 667-J4
BALRA DR
- NVTO 94947 526-C6
400 ELCR 94530 609-E3
BALSA AV
1700 SJS 95124 873-H1
BALSA CT
700 UNC 94587 732-G3
2200 CNCD 94520 572-F5
BALSAM AV
300 SUNV 94086 812-F5
BALSAM LN
- SRMN 94583 693-F1
BALSAM TER
600 FRMT 94536 753-B2
BALSAM WY
6800 OAK 94611 630-E5
N BALSAMINA WY
100 SMCo 94028 810-E3
S BALSAMINA WY
200 SMCo 94028 810-E4
BALSAMO DR
6200 SJS 95129 852-F3
BALT CT
5500 FRMT 94538 773-B2
BALTHAZAR TER
4700 FRMT 94555 752-C2
BALTIC CIR
- RDWC 94065 749-J5
BALTIC CT
29800 HAY 94544 732-C1
BALTIC WY
400 SJS 95111 854-G4
600 SUNV 94089 812-G2
BALTIC SEA CT
300 PIT 94565 574-A2
BALTIMORE AV
- CMAD 94925 586-F7
- LKSP 94939 586-E6
W BALTIMORE AV
200 LKSP 94939 586-E7
BALTIMORE WY
- SF 94112 687-F2
100 DALY 94014 687-F2
BALTUS LN
- MrnC 94960 566-A3
BALTUSROL
- MRGA 94556 651-D1
BALTUSROL CT
- SRMN 94583 693-H1
2400 UNC 94587 732-B4
BALTUSROL PL
100 SRMN 94583 693-H1
BALUSTROL CT
22300 CPTO 95014 852-A2
BAMBI LN
2300 SJS 95116 834-H4
BAMBOO CT
500 SJS 95111 854-G6
1900 HAY 94545 711-F5
3700 CNCD 94519 593-A1
BAMBOO DR
700 SUNV 94086 832-F1
BAMBOO LN
5200 FRMT 94538 752-J7
BAMBOO TER
600 SRFL 94903 566-C2
BAMBOO WY
2100 ANT 94509 595-F3
BAMBOO PALM CT
- SJS 95133 814-J4
BAN CT
3500 SJS 95117 853-C3
BANANA GROVE LN
100 SJS 95123 874-J3
BANBERRY WY
4800 SJS 95124 873-H4
BANBRIDGE PL
- PLHL 94523 591-H5
BANBURY CT
100 BEN 94510 551-B2
600 WLCK 94598 612-F1
2300 MRTZ 94553 572-A5
BANBURY DR
- SF 94132 687-B1
BANBURY LN
700 MLBR 94030 727-H3
2700 SCAR 94070 769-G6
BANBURY LP
2300 MRTZ 94553 572-A5
BANBURY PL
2200 WLCK 94598 612-F1
BANBURY RD
2000 WLCK 94598 612-F2
BANBURY ST
400 HAY 94544 711-H4
BANBURY WY
- AMCN 94589 510-A3
- BEN 94510 551-B2
4000 ANT 94509 595-G2
BANCHIO ST
- CCCo 94565 573-H2
BANCROFT AV
200 SLN 94577 671-B6
1200 SLN 94577 691-B1
1400 SF 94124 668-A6
4200 OAK 94601 670-E1
5500 OAK 94605 670-H2
9000 OAK 94603 671-A5
10400 OAK 94603 670-H2
13600 SLN 94578 691-B1
18100 MSER 95030 872-J6
BANCROFT CT
1000 WLCK 94598 612-E1
1500 SLN 94578 691-D3
2100 PIT 94565 573-J3
BANCROFT LN
400 PCFA 94044 707-A3
2400 CCCo 94806 588-J2
BANCROFT PL
- SRMN 94583 673-J6
400 OAK 94704 630-A2
BANCROFT RD
- BURL 94010 728-H6
700 WLCK 94598 612-E1
800 WLCK 94598 592-E7
900 CNCD 94518 592-E7
900 WLCK 94596 592-E7
900 CCCo 94596 592-E7
BANCROFT ST
400 SCL 95051 833-A7
BANCROFT WY
200 PCFA 94044 707-A3
200 PCFA 94044 706-J3
600 BERK 94804 629-D3
1100 BERK 94702 629-E2
1400 OAK 94601 670-D1
1500 BERK 94703 629-F2
2000 BERK 94704 629-G2
2200 BERK 94720 629-H2
6200 SJS 95129 852-F3
BANDA TER
43200 FRMT 94539 773-G1
BANDERA DR
3100 PA 94304 830-G1
BANDERA ST
40800 FRMT 94539 753-F4
BANDLEY DR
10000 CPTO 95014 832-D7
BANDO CT
100 CCCo 94595 632-D2
BANDON DR
8400 DBLN 94568 693-H2
8800 SRMN 94583 693-H2
BANDONI AV
1500 AlaC 94580 711-B2
BANFF AV
2000 SLN 94579 691-A7
BANFF CT
5500 CNCD 94521 593-F7
BANFF DR
1700 SUNV 94087 832-B6
BANFF ST
600 SJS 95116 834-F6
BANFF WY
- PCFA 94044 727-C5
BANFF PARK CT
5000 FRMT 94538 773-C2
BANFF SPRINGS CT
7000 SJS 95139 875-E7
BANFF SPRINGS WY
100 SJS 95139 875-E7
BANGOR AV
- SJS 95123 875-A4
100 SJS 95123 874-J4
BANGOR CT
- SRMN 94583 673-H4
BANION CT
100 CCCo 94806 569-C6
BANISTER LN
600 CCCo 94507 632-J2
BANK LN
2300 SPAB 94806 588-H2
BANK ST
- SF 94129 647-E3
- SANS 94960 566-C7
BANKHEAD WY
2500 SJS 95121 855-C5
BANK MILL RD
21000 SAR 95070 872-C3
BANKS DR
500 RCH 94806 568-G6
BANKS ST
- SF 94110 667-J5
BANNAM PL
- SF 94133 648-A4
BANNCOCK ST
1000 LVMR 94550 695-F7
BANNECKER WY
800 SF 94102 647-H7
BANNER CT
2100 MRTZ 94553 572-A7
6100 SJS 95123 874-J6
BANNER DR
6100 SJS 95123 874-J6
BANNING AV
400 SUNV 94086 812-F6
BANNING DR
6600 OAK 94611 630-G7
BANNING WY
400 SolC 94591 530-E6
BANNISTER CT
200 ALA 94502 669-J6
BANNISTER WY
- ALA 94502 669-H6
BANNOCK CIR
4700 SJS 95130 853-A7
BANNOCK CT
900 CNCD 94518 592-E6
BANNOCK ST
- SF 94112 687-F1
BANNON CT
47600 FRMT 94539 773-H7
BANTA CT
600 SJS 95136 874-F2
1000 NVTO 94949 546-E2
BANTRY AV
3000 OAK 94605 670-J1
BANTRY CT
700 SUNV 94087 832-F4
BANTRY LN
2400 SSF 94080 707-D4
BANTRY RD
500 PIN 94806 569-C5
BANTRY WY
800 BEN 94510 530-J6
BANYAN CIR
500 WLCK 94598 612-H1
500 WLCK 94598 592-H7
BANYAN LN
600 WLCK 94598 592-H7
600 WLCK 94598 612-H1
15400 MSER 95030 872-J4
BANYAN ST
21500 AlaC 94541 711-G1
BANYAN WY
1000 PCFA 94044 727-A5
2100 ANT 94509 575-B5
BANYAN TREE CT
39500 FRMT 94538 753-A7
BANYAN TREE RD
39600 FRMT 94538 753-A7
BANYON DR
100 PIT 94565 574-E5
BAR AV
16700 AlaC 94580 691-F6
BARALAY PL
5100 SJS 95136 874-J3
BARANGA LN
14800 SAR 95070 872-F4
BARBADOS DR
2200 SRMN 94583 653-F7
BARBADOS LN
500 FCTY 94404 749-G5
BARBANO AV
- CMBL 95008 853-F6
BARBANO CT
2100 ANT 94509 595-A1
BARBARA AV
200 MTVW 94040 811-G7
BARBARA CIR
400 MRTZ 94553 591-H4
BARBARA CT
200 PLHL 94523 592-C7
300 HAY 94544 712-B7
600 SLN 94577 691-C1
2100 PIT 94565 574-A3
4200 PLE 94566 714-F4
4800 UNC 94587 751-J1
BARBARA DR
200 LGTS 95032 873-G5
1300 SCL 95050 833-C4
1900 PA 94303 791-C5
BARBARA LN
- BLMT 94002 749-E7
- MLPK 94025 790-E5
- SMCo 94070 769-D4
200 DALY 94015 707-D2
1000 SPAB 94806 588-G2
10100 CPTO 95014 852-D1
BARBARA RD
- ORIN 94563 630-H1
700 OAK 94610 650-A3

STREET
Block City ZIP Pg-Grid

BARBARA ST
39900 FRMT 94538 753-C5
BARBARA WY
300 HIL 94010 748-D3
2600 SJS 95125 854-C6
BARBAREE WY
- MrnC 94920 606-J5
BARBARY ST
42300 FRMT 94539 753-F7
BARBEE CT
15000 SCIC 95127 814-J5
BARBEE LN
- CCCo 94507 632-G6
BARBER AV
- SANS 94960 586-C1
100 ROSS 94957 586-C1
BARBER CT
- MRTZ 94553 571-F7
300 MPS 95035 813-H1
BARBER LN
- MRTZ 94553 571-F7
600 MPS 95035 813-H1
BARBER ST
100 LVMR 94550 696-A7
BARBERRY CT
1500 SJS 95121 855-A3
4400 CNCD 94521 593-B5
BARBERRY LN
100 SRMN 94583 653-J7
600 SRFL 94903 566-C2
1500 SJS 95121 855-A3
1700 SJS 95122 855-A2
BARBERS POINT RD
- ALA 94501 649-D6
BARBETTE PL
3600 CNCD 94518 592-J4
BARBIS WY
1300 CNCD 94518 592-J3
3500 CNCD 94519 592-J3
BARBOUR DR
- RDWC 94062 769-G7
600 RDWC 94062 789-G1
BARB WERNER LN
6100 SJS 95119 875-D5
BARCELLS AV
2600 SCL 95051 833-B6
BARCELONA AV
- SF 94115 647-F6
1700 SJS 95124 873-H3
27500 HAY 94545 711-H7
27700 HAY 94545 731-H1
BARCELONA CIR
- RDWC 94065 749-J6
2700 ANT 94509 575-B6
BARCELONA CT
- DNVL 94526 653-C7
- PIT 94565 574-C6
400 MTVW 94040 811-J7
BARCELONA DR
200 NVTO 94949 546-F2
400 FRMT 94536 753-A1
400 MLBR 94030 728-A3
400 MLBR 94030 727-J2
500 SBRN 94066 727-J2
1000 PCFA 94044 727-A4
1000 PCFA 94044 726-J4
BARCELONA PL
- DNVL 94526 653-C7
BARCELONA ST
200 VAL 94591 530-F6
1600 LVMR 94550 715-F4
8900 OAK 94605 671-B3
BARCELONA WY
- CLAY 94517 613-J2
4600 UNC 94587 731-J6
BARCLAY AV
- UNC 94587 732-B4
200 MLBR 94030 728-B3
BARCLAY CT
- CCCo 94507 632-J2
300 PA 94306 811-D2
2700 AlaC 94546 691-H4
6100 SJS 95123 875-A6
BARCLAY RD
2700 AlaC 94546 691-H4
BARCLAY WY
2600 BLMT 94002 769-B1
BARD ST
800 SCIC 95127 814-H6
800 SJS 95127 814-H6
BARDEN WY
1600 SJS 95128 853-G3
BARDET RD
100 WDSD 94062 789-G6
BARDOLPH CIR
33400 FRMT 94555 752-B1
BARDOLPH RD
4700 FRMT 94555 752-C1
BAREOAK CT
3300 SJS 95148 835-E7
BARETT CT
3100 AlaC 94546 691-J4
BARFORD AV
100 SCAR 94070 769-E2
BARIKA CT
- CCCo 94553 572-E3
BARINGTON DR
- VAL 94591 550-D2
BARK DR
400 RDWC 94065 749-H6
BARK LN
7000 SJS 95129 852-E3
BARKENTINE LN
400 RDWC 94065 749-H7
BARKENTINE ST
100 FCTY 94404 749-G4
BARKER AV
700 HAY 94541 711-F2
BARKER DR
3800 SJS 95117 853-B3
BARKER ST
100 MPS 95035 793-J7
BARKLEY AV
1900 WLCK 94596 612-B4
2600 SCL 95051 833-A3
BARKLEY CT
- VAL 94591 530-G5
900 PIN 94564 569-C5
BARKLEY DR
2900 RCH 94806 589-A1

BARKLEY MOUNTAIN WY
1500 ANT 94509 595-F5
BARKSDALE CT
- NVTO 94949 546-G4
14200 SAR 95070 872-E2
BARKWOOD WY
2900 SJS 95128 853-E4
BARLETTA LN
3100 SCIC 95127 834-J1
3100 SJS 95127 834-J1
BARLEY CT
3500 SJS 95127 835-C2
BARLEY HILL RD
12200 LAH 94024 831-D2
BARLOW AV
2200 SJS 95122 834-J5
BARLOW CT
1400 FRMT 94536 753-B3
19500 AlaC 94546 691-H4
BARLOW DR
2700 AlaC 94546 691-H4
BARMETTA WY
- ATN 94027 790-D2
BARMIED PL
- OAK 94619 651-C7
BARMOUTH CT
- ANT 94509 575-F7
BARMOUTH DR
3000 ANT 94509 575-F7
3200 ANT 94509 595-F1
BARN LN
- LFYT 94549 611-A7
BARN RD
- BLV 94920 607-D7
- BLV 94920 627-D1
- MrnC 94920 606-J4
BARNACLE CT
3500 UNC 94587 732-B4
3500 UNC 94587 731-J4
BARNARD AV
- SF 94129 647-D4
- SF 94129 647-E4
- SJS 95125 854-D3
BARNARD DR
35600 FRMT 94536 752-H1
35600 FRMT 94536 732-H7
BARNARD ST
2600 RCH 94806 589-B2
25400 HAY 94545 711-G6
36300 NWK 94560 752-E5
BARNEGAT LN
400 RDWC 94065 749-J6
BARNEGATE BAY
- ALA 94502 670-A5
BARNER AV
3900 OAK 94602 650-E4
BARNER LN
- TBRN 94920 607-B2
BARNER PL
- OAK 94602 650-E4
BARNES CT
- MRGA 94556 651-E1
- HAY 94544 711-H3
- SCIC - 791-A7
100 VAL 94591 530-F5
BARNES LN
- FRMT 94536 733-A7
1100 SJS 95120 894-G4
BARNES WY
500 CCCo 94572 549-H7
500 CCCo 94572 569-H1
BARNESON AV
- SMTO 94402 749-A3
300 SMTO 94402 748-J4
BARNETT CIR
1600 PLHL 94523 612-A1
BARNETT TER
100 PLHL 94523 612-A1
100 PLHL 94523 611-J1
BARNEVELD AV
- SF 94124 668-A5
700 SF 94134 668-A6
BARNEY AV
- ATN 94027 790-C5
- SMCo 94025 790-C5
BARNEY CT
- SMCo 94025 790-D5
BARNFIELD CT
34300 FRMT 94555 732-E7
BARNFIELD PL
34300 FRMT 94555 732-E7
BARNHART AV
18600 SCIC 95014 852-G2
BARNHART CT
10500 SCIC 95014 852-G2
BARNHART PL
7400 CPTO 95014 852-D4
BARNHILL LN
3700 AlaC 94552 692-D5
BARN HOLLOW CT
7700 DBLN 94568 693-F4
BARN OWL CT
600 WLCK 94598 613-A3
BARN ROCK DR
28500 HAY 94542 712-G4
BARNSDALE CT
6600 SJS 95120 894-C1
BARNSLEY CT
900 ANT 94509 575-C7
BARNSLEY WY
600 SUNV 94087 832-E4
BARNSWELL WY
5700 SJS 95138 875-D4
BARNWOOD DR
800 SRMN 94583 673-D4
BAROLO CT
- PLE 94566 715-B5
BARON CT
6500 MRTZ 94553 591-H4
7700 ELCR 94530 609-E2
BARON DR
5200 SJS 95124 873-F5
BARON PL
600 MPS 95035 794-B3
BARON ST
42600 FRMT 94539 753-H6
BARONE LN
- MrnC 94965 606-D7
BARONET CT
3900 SJS 95121 855-D5
3900 SJS 95121 855-D5

BARONI AV
100 SJS 95136 854-F7
100 SJS 95136 854-F7
BARONI CT
19900 SAR 95070 872-F1
19900 SAR 95070 872-F1
BARONI GREEN DR
300 SJS 95136 874-J7
300 SJS 95136 874-J7
BARON PARK CT
400 SJS 95136 874-F3
400 SJS 95136 874-F3
BARON PARK DR
4900 SJS 95136 874-G3
4900 SJS 95136 874-G3
BARONSCOURT WY
2900 SJS 95132 814-E3
2900 SJS 95132 814-E3
BARONS VIEW CT
- CCCo 94803 589-D1
BAROTT RD
1200 LFYT 94549 611-J4
BARQUENTINE CT
100 PIT 94565 574-A2
BARRANCA CT
400 SRMN 94583 673-B3
BARRANCA DR
10800 CPTO 95014 832-A6
10800 CPTO 95014 832-A6
BARRANCA ST
4100 CCCo 94803 589-B2
4100 RCH 94803 589-B2
BARRELHOUSE RD
- CCCo 94553 571-F3
BARRENGER DR
1000 DNVL 94506 653-G5
BARRETT AV
200 RCH 94801 588-F6
1600 RCH 94804 588-F6
2000 SJS 95124 873-F3
2000 SJS 95124 873-F3
3300 RCH 94805 588-F6
3600 RCH 94805 589-A6
5300 ELCR 94530 589-B6
BARRETT CIR
200 DNVL 94526 653-D6
BARRETT CT
- PIN 94564 569-F5
100 DNVL 94526 653-D6
BARRETT DR
- WDSD 94062 789-J5
BARRETT ST
2900 OAK 94605 671-B5
BARRI DR
700 SLN 94578 691-B4
BARRIE CT
- PIT 94565 574-D6
BARRIE DR
- PIT 94565 574-D6
BARRIE WY
- MLV 94941 606-E1
BARRINGTON CT
1100 SJS 95121 855-B5
1100 SJS 95121 855-B5
2200 SSF 94080 707-D5
2300 HAY 94545 711-B4
BARRINGTON DR
3700 CNCD 94518 592-J3
BARRINGTON LN
- CCCo - 632-J1
- CCCo 94507 632-J1
BARRINGTON TER
2600 FRMT 94536 752-H2
BARRINGTON BRIDGE CT
10800 SCIC 95014 852-C6
10800 SCIC 95014 852-C6
BARRINGTON BRIDGE LN
10800 SCIC 95014 852-C6
10800 SCIC 95014 852-C6
BARROILHET AV
- SMTO 94402 728-G7
- BURL 94010 728-G7
100 BURL 94010 748-F1
100 SMTO 94402 748-F1
200 HIL 94010 748-F1
BARROILHET DR
1100 HIL 94010 748-E2
BARRON AV
500 PA 94306 811-B2
500 PA 94306 811-B2
700 SMCo 94063 770-D6
BARRON WY
600 HAY 94544 712-D7
BARRONS PL
- DNVL 94526 653-D3
BARRONS WY
30800 UNC 94587 731-J5
BARROW CT
300 WLCK 94598 612-F2
2800 SJS 95121 855-A3
BARROW LN
- BERK 94720 629-H2
BARROW ST
2200 SLN 94577 690-G4
BARROWS RD
1300 OAK 94610 650-C3
BARRUS AV
1600 PIT 94565 574-E3
BARRY CT
- ALA 94502 669-H5
- WLCK 94596 612-A2
100 VAL 94591 530-E6
BARRY LN
- ATN 94027 790-D4
15900 MSER 95030 873-A5
BARRY PL
2700 OAK 94601 650-C6
BARRY WY
- LKSP 94939 586-G5
1000 FRMT 94536 753-B3
BARRY HILL CT
- CCCo - 570-G3
BARRY HILL RD
- CCCo - 570-G3
- CCCo 94553 570-G3
BARRYMORE COM
1900 FRMT 94538 753-C4
BARRYMORE DR
3000 CNCD 94518 592-G7
4000 SJS 95117 853-A3

BARRYMORE DR
4100 SJS 95129 853-A3
BARRYMORE PL
3100 CNCD 94518 592-H7
BARSON TER
300 SUNV 94086 812-F7
BARSTOW CT
900 SUNV 94086 812-H5
BART
- CNCD 94520 573-A4
BART AV
100 ANT 94509 575-E4
BART WY
2000 FRMT 94538 753-B4
BART ACCESS RD
- HAY 94544 732-D2
BARTEL CT
- TBRN 94920 607-E6
BARTH AV
- RCH 94806 589-B4
BARTLETT AV
200 SUNV 94086 812-F7
300 AlaC 94541 711-E2
BARTLETT CT
- PLHL 94523 592-A4
BARTLETT LN
20600 AlaC 94541 711-F1
BARTLETT PL
1000 PLE 94566 714-E5
BARTLETT ST
- SF 94110 667-J4
2300 OAK 94601 650-D6
2600 OAK 94602 650-D6
BARTLETT WY
3400 BLMT 94002 769-A1
3400 BLMT 94002 768-J1
BARTLETT CREEK CT
1100 SJS 95120 894-G3
BARTO ST
400 SCL 95051 833-A6
BARTOL ST
- SF 94133 648-A4
BARTOLINI DR
500 MRTZ 94553 571-E4
BARTOLO TER
4500 FRMT 94536 752-G4
BARTON CT
- PLHL 94523 592-A4
300 DNVL 94526 653-B3
13800 LAH 94022 811-D7
BARTON DR
200 FRMT 94536 753-C1
1400 SUNV 94087 832-A5
BARTON LN
1800 ANT 94509 575-J5
BARTON PL
- PCFA 94044 727-B6
100 MLPK 94025 790-J2
BARTON ST
1800 SMCo 94061 790-B4
BARTON WY
300 MLPK 94025 790-J3
1900 HAY 94545 711-E5
BARUNA CT
100 NVTO 94945 526-G1
BASALT CT
900 ANT 94509 575-F7
1900 WLCK 94595 632-B1
2300 SJS 95133 814-H3
BASALT DR
100 VAL 94589 510-B6
BASALT WY
800 ANT 94509 575-F7
BASCH AV
- SJS 95116 834-F3
BASCOM AV
- SCL 95128 833-F7
- SCL 95050 833-F7
- SJS 95050 833-F7
- SJS 95128 833-F7
100 SCIC 95128 833-F7
300 SJS 95128 853-G5
500 SCIC 95128 853-G5
700 SJS 95124 853-G5
700 SJS 95124 873-F1
1200 CMBL 95008 853-G5
1200 SJS 95125 853-G5
1500 CMBL 95125 853-G5
1800 CMBL 95128 853-G5
1800 SJS 95126 853-G5
2100 SJS 95008 853-G5
2500 SJS 95008 873-F1
2500 SCIC 95008 873-F1
2600 SCIC 95008 853-G5
S BASCOM AV
300 SJS 95128 853-G1
300 SCIC 95128 853-G1
3100 SJS 95124 873-E2
3100 SJS 95008 873-E2
3200 CMBL 95008 873-E2
3400 SCIC 95008 873-E2
3400 SCIC 95032 873-E2
BASCOM CT
100 CMBL 95008 873-E2
BASILE AV
1800 SJS 95128 853-G1
1800 SCIC 95128 853-G1
BASIN CT
- HER 94547 569-H4
500 SJS 95111 854-G4
BASIN RD
- MRTZ 94553 571-E2
BASIN SIDE WY
- ALA 94502 669-J6
- ALA 94502 670-A5
BASKERVILLE RD
3400 FRMT 94555 732-D7
BASKING RIDGE AV
6600 SJS 95138 875-F4
BASS COM
38800 FRMT 94536 753-F3
BASS CT
- SF 94124 668-C6
4800 SJS 95130 852-J6
BASSETT CT
3600 SSF 94080 707-D4
4800 CNCD 94521 593-C4
BASSETT DR
1400 CNCD 94521 593-C4
BASSETT LN
- ATN 94027 790-F2
25700 LAH 94022 831-B3

BASSETT ST
3100 SCL 95054 813-D6
E BASSETT ST
- SJS 95112 834-B5
W BASSETT ST
100 SJS 95110 834-A6
100 SJS 95113 834-A6
BASS LAKE ST
32700 FRMT 94555 732-C6
BASSWOOD AV
33100 UNC 94587 732-G3
BASSWOOD CT
4800 SJS 95124 873-H4
33000 UNC 94587 732-F3
BASSWOOD PL
1100 CNCD 94521 593-F7
BASTIA LN
- SJS 95127 834-C1
BATAAN AV
- OAK 94607 649-C1
900 BERK 94804 629-D1
BATAAN CT
400 SJS 95133 834-G2
BATACAO LN
300 ANT 94509 575-D6
BATAVIA AV
1000 LVMR 94550 715-F3
BATEMAN ST
3000 BERK 94705 629-J4
BATEMAN WY
3500 SJS 95148 855-F1
BATES AV
700 ELCR 94530 609-E2
1700 CCCo 94553 572-E4
1700 CNCD 94520 572-F3
2100 CCCo 94520 572-F3
BATES BLVD
- ORIN 94563 610-H7
- ORIN 94563 611-A7
BATES CT
100 ORIN 94563 611-A7
3000 SJS 95148 855-E1
BATES DR
34700 FRMT 94555 752-E1
BATES RD
- HIL 94010 748-F3
1200 OAK 94602 650-B4
1200 OAK 94610 650-B4
BATES WY
5100 AlaC 94546 692-B2
BATH CT
- SRMN 94583 673-F6
BATH PL
4900 NWK 94560 752-E3
BATHGATE LN
3400 SJS 95121 855-C5
BATON ROUGE CT
2800 SJS 95133 814-G7
BATON ROUGE DR
2400 SJS 95133 834-G1
2400 SCIC 95133 834-G1
2500 SJS 95133 814-G7
BATTAGLIA CIR
2400 SJS 95132 814-E6
BATTEN LN
- RDWC 94065 750-C4
BATTERSEA CT
1700 SJS 95132 814-J3
BATTERY ST
- SF 94104 648-B4
- SF 94111 648-B4
800 SF 94111 648-B3
1200 CCCo 94801 588-F4
BATTERY BLANEY RD
- SF 94129 647-D3
BATTERY CAULFIELD RD
- SF 94129 647-C5
BATTERY CHAMBERLAIN RD
- SF 94129 647-B5
BATTERY CROSBY RD
- SF 94129 647-B4
- SF 94129 647-B4
BATTERY DREW TR
- TBRN - 627-G3
BATTERY EAST RD
- SF 94129 647-B2
BATTLE DANCE DR
300 SJS 95111 875-B2
BAUER CT
800 SCAR 94070 769-F4
BAUER DR
800 SCAR 94070 769-F4
BAUMANN AV
2400 AlaC 94580 711-A2
BAUMBERG AV
2700 HAY 94545 731-G1
BAUMBERG CT
2700 HAY 94545 731-G2
BAUTISTA CT
900 PA 94303 791-E6
BAUTISTA ST
2700 ANT 94509 575-D6
43500 FRMT 94539 753-H7
BAVA CT
6100 SJS 95123 875-A6
BAVARIAN CT
500 LFYT 94549 631-H4
BAVARIAN LN
3100 LFYT 94549 631-H3
BAXLEY CT
22000 CPTO 95014 852-A2
BAXTER AL
- SF 94127 667-D6
BAXTER AV
10600 SCIC 94024 832-A6
BAXTER CT
1900 CNCD 94521 593-G4
BAXTER ST
100 VAL 94590 529-H3
2100 OAK 94601 650-D7
W BAXTER ST
100 VAL 94590 529-H3
BAXTERS CT
- SRFL 94901 586-H2
BAY CT
- SRFL 94901 587-A1
100 VAL 94591 530-E2
3300 BLMT 94002 749-A7
3300 BLMT 94002 769-A1

BAY DR
- CCCo 94565 573-E1
BAY LNDG
- SMTO 94401 729-B6
BAY PL
200 OAK 94610 649-H3
200 OAK 94612 649-H3
BAY RD
- MLPK 94025 770-F7
- ATN 94027 770-F7
300 ATN 94027 790-H1
300 MLPK 94025 790-H1
500 RDWC 94063 770-B6
500 SMCo 94025 790-H1
700 MrnC 94965 606-E7
900 EPA 94303 791-A1
1900 EPA 94303 771-D7
2200 SMCo 94063 770-B6
3700 SMCo 94025 770-F7
BAY ST
- SAUS 94965 627-B3
- SF 94111 648-A3
- SF 94133 648-A3
- SRFL 94901 586-H2
100 HER 94547 569-E3
100 MLBR 94030 728-B2
200 CCCo 94525 550-E4
300 SF 94133 647-H3
300 SJS 95123 874-J5
400 OAK 94607 649-C3
700 SF 94109 647-H3
800 MTVW 94041 811-J7
900 MTVW 94040 811-J7
1100 ALA 94501 669-G2
1100 SF 94123 647-G3
1600 CCCo 94806 569-A5
1800 ALA 94501 649-H7
4000 FRMT 94538 753-D7
6400 EMVL 94608 629-D5
6700 BERK 94804 629-D5
BAY TER
500 SUNV 94089 812-G3
BAY WY
- SRFL 94901 587-A1
BAYARD DR
1100 SJS 95122 854-H2
BAYBERRY
- PTLV 94028 830-D1
BAYBERRY AV
1500 HER 94547 569-H3
BAYBERRY CIR
2200 PIT 94565 573-G4
BAYBERRY COM
- FRMT 94539 793-H1
BAYBERRY CT
3000 SJS 95148 855-D2
BAYBERRY DR
3400 WLCK 94598 612-J1
BAYBERRY LN
900 RDWC 94065 750-A5
3000 SJS 95148 855-C2
15900 AlaC 94580 691-E5
BAYBERRY PL
- HIL 94010 748-E1
BAYBERRY WY
- MPS 95035 794-A6
BAY CANYON RD
- MrnC 94945 526-J3
BAY CENTER PL
3800 HAY 94545 711-D7
BAY COLONY WY
- UNC 94545 751-J1
BAY CREST DR
200 PIT 94565 574-E1
BAYCREST WY
1300 SSF 94080 707-H1
BAY EDGE RD
- ALA 94502 669-J6
BAYFAIR DR
- SLN 94578 691-D4
300 AlaC 94578 691-E4
BAYFAIR WY
1200 SLN 94578 691-D4
BAYFIELD PL
- FRMT 94538 773-C1
BAY FOREST CT
- OAK 94611 630-D4
BAY FOREST DR
- OAK 94611 630-D3
BAYFRONT DR
- RCH 94804 608-H2
BAYFRONT EXWY Rt#-84
- FRMT 94555 771-D3
- MLPK 94025 771-A6
- MLPK 94025 770-G6
- MLPK 94303 771-D3
BAY FRONT PZ
- SCL 95002 813-A3
BAY HARBOR CT
- RCH 94804 608-E3
BAY HARBOR DR
- RCH 94804 608-E3
BAY HARBOUR DR
800 RDWC 94065 750-A6
BAYHAVEN DR
2000 SJS 95122 835-A7
BAYHILL DR
800 SBRN 94066 707-G7
BAYHILLS DR
- MrnC 94903 566-H3
BAYHURST DR
- VAL 94591 550-D2
BAYLANDS DR
200 MRTZ 94553 571-H6
BAY LAUREL CT
- DBLN 94552 693-F4
BAY LAUREL DR
1100 MLPK 94025 790-F5
BAY LAUREL LN
1100 SJS 95132 814-H5
BAY LAUREL ST
- DBLN 94552 693-E4
- DBLN 94568 693-E4
BAYLEAF CT
800 SJS 95128 853-F4
4900 MRTZ 94553 572-A6
BAYLIS ST
2800 FRMT 94538 753-D5
BAYLISS CT
7400 SJS 95139 895-G1

BAYLISS DR
200 SJS 95139 895-F2
BAYLISS PL
7500 SJS 95139 895-G1
BAYLOR AV
1200 SLN 94579 691-A4
5100 SAR 95070 852-J7
18200 SJS 95130 852-J7
BAYLOR CT
500 BEN 94510 550-J1
BAYLOR DR
100 VAL 94589 510-A5
700 SCL 95051 832-J6
BAYLOR LN
- PLHL 94523 592-C3
BAYLOR ST
1700 UNC 94587 732-F6
2500 EPA 94303 791-B1
2500 EPA 94303 771-B7
BAYLOR WY
4200 LVMR 94550 716-A1
BAY MEADOWS CIR
2300 PLE 94566 714-C1
BAYNE PL
4300 SJS 95130 853-A4
BAYO ST
3800 OAK 94619 650-F6
BAYONNE DR
36000 NWK 94560 752-D5
BAYONNE PL
36000 NWK 94560 752-D5
BAYOU DR
3400 SJS 95111 854-J5
BAYO VISTA
1000 SJS 95132 814-H5
BAYO VISTA AV
- LKSP 94939 586-D4
- MrnC 94904 586-D4
- OAK 94611 649-J1
1500 CCCo 94806 589-A3
1600 SPAB 94806 589-A3
3000 ALA 94501 670-B2
BAYO VISTA WY
- SRFL 94901 566-E7
BAYPARK CIR
- SSF 94014 707-H1
BAY PARK TER
- ALA 94502 670-A5
BAY POINT DR
- SRFL 94901 587-A2
BAYPOINT WY
900 CCCo 94572 569-J1
900 CCCo 94572 570-A1
BAYPOINTE DR
100 SJS 95134 813-F3
BAYPOINTE PKWY
100 SJS 95134 813-F2
BAYPOINT VILLAGE DR
- SRFL 94901 587-A2
BAYPORT AV
500 SCAR 94070 769-G2
BAYPORT CT
- SCAR 94070 769-G2
BAY RIDGE CT
1300 SJS 95120 894-C2
BAY RIDGE DR
500 DALY 94014 687-H3
BAYRIDGE WY
1600 SMTO 94402 748-H6
N BAYSHORE W
600 SJS 95112 834-C3
BAYSHORE BLVD
- BSBN 94005 708-B1
- BSBN 94080 708-B1
- SSF 94080 708-B1
- SF 94134 688-A3
- SF 94124 668-A5
1700 SF 94124 688-A3
3000 BSBN 94005 688-A4
3000 DALY 94014 688-A3
N BAYSHORE BLVD
- SMTO 94401 729-A7
- SMTO 94401 728-J6
S BAYSHORE BLVD
- SMTO 94401 729-A7
500 SMTO 94401 749-B1
N BAYSHORE CIR
- SBRN 94066 707-H5
S BAYSHORE CIR
- SBRN 94066 707-J5
BAYSHORE FRWY U.S.-101
- BLMT - 749-B1
- BLMT - 769-G1
- BSBN - 688-B3
- BSBN - 708-B1
- BURL - 728-F5
- EPA - 791-E5
- EPA - 790-J1
- MLBR - 728-B2
- MLPK - 770-C5
- MLPK - 791-E5
- MLPK - 790-J1
- MTVW - 791-E5
- MTVW - 812-C4
- MTVW - 811-G1
- PA - 791-E5
- RDWC - 769-G1
- RDWC - 770-C5
- SCAR - 769-G1
- SCL - 813-B6
- SCIC - 812-C4
- SCIC - 855-B5
- SF - 688-B3
- SJS - 813-B6
- SJS - 834-C2
- SJS - 833-G1
- SJS - 855-B5
- SJS - 854-H1
- SJS - 875-C1
- SMCo - 708-A5
- SMCo - 728-B2
- SMCo - 769-G1
- SMTO - 729-A7
- SMTO - 728-F5
- SMTO - 749-B1
- SMTO - 749-B1
- SSF - 708-B1
- SUNV - 813-B6
- SUNV - 812-C4

STREET
Block City ZIP Pg-Grid

BAYSHORE HWY
- MLBR 94030 728-D3
1200 BURL 94010 728-D3
BAYSHORE PKWY
2100 MTVW 94043 791-F7
2100 MTVW 94043 811-G1
BAYSHORE RD
- BEN 94510 551-E2
E BAYSHORE RD
500 RDWC 94063 770-A4
800 EPA 94303 791-A1
1900 PA 94303 791-D4
3200 SMCo 94063 770-D5
W BAYSHORE RD
1200 EPA 94303 791-B2
1900 PA 94303 791-D4
BAYSHORE ST
700 MRTZ 94553 571-G5
BAYSIDE BLVD
1300 SCAR 94070 769-J4
BAYSIDE CT
- CCCo 94806 569-C4
- RCH 94804 608-J3
800 NVTO 94947 526-D7
2300 SJS 95133 834-F2
BAY SIDE DR
- PIT 94565 574-D1
BAYSIDE DR
- RCH 94804 608-J3
BAYSIDE PKWY
47000 FRMT 94538 773-F7
47000 FRMT 94538 793-F1
BAYSIDE TER
100 VAL 94591 550-D3
BAYSIDE VILLAGE PL
- SF 94107 648-C6
BAYSLAND CT
1300 SJS 95131 814-D7
BAYSMILL CT
2800 SJS 95121 854-J3
BAY SPRINGS RD
18500 SCIC 95070 872-D7
BAYSWATER AV
- BURL 94010 728-H7
1000 SMTO 94401 728-H7
BAYSWATER CT
700 WLCK 94598 613-A3
BAYTECH DR
100 SJS 95134 813-D1
BAYTON DR
- SJS 95193 875-C4
BAY TREE LN
- LALT 94022 831-D1
- MLV 94941 606-E2
- SCIC 95127 815-A6
700 ELCR 94530 609-E2
BAYTREE LN
- BERK 94708 609-J6
- SANS 94960 566-A4
BAY TREE RD
- MrnC 94903 566-E5
BAYTREE RD
100 SCAR 94070 769-G4
BAYTREE WY
- SMTO 94402 748-J1
BAY TREE HOLLOW
- MrnC 94945 526-D2
BAY VIEW AV
- CCCo 94565 573-J2
- BLV 94920 607-C7
- BLV 94920 627-D1
BAYVIEW AV
- LGTS 95030 872-J7
- LKSP 94939 586-F7
100 MLV 94941 606-D3
100 MRTZ 94553 571-D3
100 VAL 94590 530-C3
200 SCIC 95127 815-A7
200 SUNV 94086 832-E1
400 MLBR 94030 727-J2
900 OAK 94610 650-B4
1800 BLMT 94002 749-C7
4000 SMTO 94403 749-C7
4800 RCH 94804 609-B2
6100 CCCo 94806 589-B3
22400 AlaC 94541 692-C6
22500 HAY 94541 692-C6
N BAYVIEW AV
200 SUNV 94086 812-F6
S BAYVIEW AV
100 SUNV 94086 812-E7
BAYVIEW CIR
100 SF 94124 668-B6
1600 BEN 94510 551-C4
3800 CNCD 94520 572-G4
BAYVIEW CT
- LGTS 95030 872-J7
- MLBR 94030 727-H2
700 CCCo 94803 569-D7
2300 CNCD 94520 572-G5
BAY VIEW DR
- SCAR 94070 769-D3
200 SMCo 94070 769-D4
BAYVIEW DR
- FRMT 94538 793-G1
- MrnC 94901 587-C1
- MrnC 94901 567-B7
100 SRFL 94901 567-C7
100 MrnC 94941 606-C4
100 MrnC 94965 606-C4
800 ALA 94501 670-A4
2600 ALA 94501 669-J4
BAYVIEW PL
- BURL 94010 728-G5
1300 BERK 94708 609-H7
BAY VIEW RD
100 PCFA 94044 726-J3
BAYVIEW RD
- CCCo 94598 612-D3
- CCCo 94525 550-C5
- LKSP 94939 586-E4
- MrnC 94904 586-E4
BAYVIEW ST
- SF 94124 668-B6
- SRFL 94901 586-E1
BAYVIEW TER
- MrnC 94941 606-H4
BAYVIEW WY
700 SMCo 94062 789-F2
BAY VIEW FARM RD
1000 PIN 94564 569-D4
BAYVIEW PARK DR
400 MPS 95035 794-D5
BAYVIEW PARK RD
- SF 94124 688-B1
BAYVISTA CIR
200 MrnC 94965 606-G7
BAY VISTA CT
- BEN 94510 551-E3
BAYVISTA CT
- MrnC 94941 606-J4
BAYVISTA DR
- MrnC 94941 606-H3
- MrnC 94920 606-H3
BAYWALK RD
2800 ALA 94502 669-J6
BAYWALK WY
- RDWC 94065 749-H5
BAYWOOD AV
- HIL 94010 748-H2
- ROSS 94957 586-D1
- SMTO 94402 748-H2
100 MLPK 94025 790-J3
500 SJS 95128 833-E7
1200 SSF 94080 707-F1
21600 AlaC 94546 691-J7
S BAYWOOD AV
300 SJS 95128 853-E1
1200 CMBL 95128 853-E3
BAYWOOD CIR
- NVTO 94949 546-C3
3300 ANT 94509 595-H1
BAYWOOD CT
300 MTVW 94040 811-F4
1700 PLE 94566 714-D2
4200 CNCD 94521 593-C3
10500 CPTO 95014 832-F7
BAYWOOD DR
100 VAL 94591 530-E5
1600 CNCD 94521 593-C3
10400 CPTO 95014 832-F7
BAYWOOD GN
- SMCo 94062 769-E7
BAYWOOD LN
3000 CCCo 94806 589-A2
BAYWOOD RD
- FRFX 94930 566-A6
200 ALA 94502 669-J6
BAYWOOD SQ
1800 SJS 95132 814-E3
BAYWOOD ST
- SF 94112 687-F1
BAYWOOD TER
200 SRFL 94901 586-G3
3300 FRMT 94536 752-A6
BAYWOOD WY
- RCH 94804 608-H2
BEACH BLVD
1500 PCFA 94044 706-J6
BEACH DR
- CCCo 94565 573-E1
- MrnC 94901 587-C1
BEACH RD
- TBRN 94920 607-E7
- TBRN 94920 627-D1
100 BLV 94920 627-D1
200 ALA 94502 670-B6
300 BURL 94010 728-H5
BEACH ST
- SF 94133 648-A3
- SF 94133 647-H3
100 SF 94133 647-H3
600 SF 94109 647-H3
1000 VAL 94590 530-B6
1100 SolC 94590 530-B6
1500 OAK 94608 629-E7
1500 SF 94123 647-F3
1500 OAK 94608 649-E1
1900 CNCD 94519 592-G1
BEACH HEAD CT
- RCH 94804 608-H2
BEACH HEAD WY
- RCH 94804 608-H2
BEACHMONT DR
- SF 94132 667-B6
BEACH PARK BLVD
- FCTY 94404 749-G1
BEACH PARK RD
- SRFL 94901 586-H2
BEACHPOINT WY
900 CCCo 94572 569-J2
BEACHSIDE CT
- DALY 94015 706-J2
BEACHVIEW AV
100 PCFA 94044 707-A2
BEACHWOOD WY
1700 PLE 94566 714-D2
BEACHY ST
1000 OAK 94621 670-D7
BEACON AV
1200 SMTO 94401 749-B1
1400 SLN 94579 691-A6
3400 FRMT 94538 753-B5
BEACON CT
100 VAL 94590 529-H2
BEACON DR
- MPS 95035 794-D6
BEACON LN
3300 SJS 95118 874-A1
BEACON ST
- MTVW 94040 811-F3
100 SF 94131 667-G5
100 SSF 94080 708-A5
500 OAK 94610 650-A3
600 MLPK 94025 790-J2
800 PIT 94565 574-D2
BEACON BAY DR
- UNC 94545 731-J6
BEACON HILL CT
20400 AlaC 94552 692-D4
BEACON HILL DR
4700 AlaC 94552 692-C5
BEACON RIDGE CT
1900 WLCK 94596 611-H3
BEACON RIDGE LN
300 WLCK 94596 611-H3
BEACONSFIELD CT
- ORIN 94563 631-B5
BEACONSFIELD PL
2600 OAK 94611 650-F1
BEACONSFIELD RD
1100 SJS 95121 855-A5
BEACON SHORES DR
300 RDWC 94065 749-J2
BEAL AV
2600 OAK 94605 670-F1
BEAL CT
6400 SJS 95123 875-B7
BEALE CT
700 WLCK 94598 612-G1
BEALE DR
300 HAY 94544 712-B6
BEALE ST
- SF 94105 648-B5
- SRFL 94901 587-A2
400 SF 94107 648-B5
BEAN AV
200 LGTS 95030 873-A7
200 LGTS 95030 872-J7
BEAR CT
100 FRMT 94539 773-J3
BEAR PL
- CLAY 94517 594-A5
BEAR RD
- ALA 94501 649-J7
BEAR CLAW WY
- SJS 95136 874-H2
BEAR COVE CT
100 VAL 94591 550-E1
BEAR CREEK RD
- CCCo 94549 611-A2
- NVTO 94947 525-F4
1000 CCCo 94553 590-G4
1200 ORIN 94563 610-E4
1200 CCCo 94563 610-F2
1200 CCCo 94563 611-A2
1200 CCCo - 590-H7
BEAR CREEK TER
- CCCo 94563 611-A2
- CCCo 94563 610-G1
BEAR CREEK TR
- CCCo 94563 610-D4
- ORIN 94563 610-D4
BEARD COM
2800 FRMT 94555 732-E6
BEARD RD
2800 FRMT 94555 732-D7
BEARD TER
2800 FRMT 94555 732-E6
BEARDEN DR
1600 CMBL 95030 872-J2
BEARDON DR
10100 CPTO 95014 832-D7
10200 SCIC 95014 832-D7
BEARDSLEY ST
17800 AlaC 94546 692-B3
BEAR GLEN DR
- SMCo 94062 809-C3
BEAR GULCH DR
- PTLV 94028 810-D6
BEAR GULCH RD
- SMCo 94062 809-E2
- WDSD 94062 809-E2
BEARINDA LN
- CCCo - 590-G7
BEAR OAKS CT
- CCCo - 590-H6
BEAR OAKS DR
1400 CCCo - 590-G6
1400 CCCo 94553 590-H6
BEAR OAKS LN
- CCCo - 590-H6
BEAR OAKS PL
- CCCo - 591-A6
- CCCo - 590-J6
BEAR PAW
- PTLV 94028 830-C1
BEAR RIDGE RD
- ORIN 94563 610-F3
BEAR RIDGE TR
100 ORIN 94563 610-G3
BEAR RIDGE WY
3300 ANT 94509 595-J2
BEAR VALLEY LN
2300 SJS 95133 834-F1
2300 SJS 95133 814-H3
BEASLEY AV
2300 ANT 94509 575-E6
BEATIE ST
700 OAK 94606 650-A4
BEATRICE CT
2000 SJS 95128 853-G3
BEATRICE LN
- SF 94124 668-D6
26900 LAH 94022 811-C7
BEATRICE RD
400 PLHL 94523 592-B6
BEATRICE ST
100 MTVW 94043 811-H4
500 SLN 94579 691-C6
41100 FRMT 94539 753-E6
BEATRON WY
28200 HAY 94544 712-B7
BEATTIE AV
- MrnC 94945 526-J4
BEATTIE CT
1300 SJS 95120 874-B6
BEATTY AV
- BSBN 94005 688-A3
BEATTY ST
15000 SLN 94579 691-B6
BEAU CT
5500 FRMT 94538 773-B2
BEAUCHAMP CT
20800 SAR 95070 852-D5
BEAUCHAMPS LN
11900 SAR 95070 852-D5
BEAUDRY ST
5500 EMVL 94608 629-E5
BEAUFOREST DR
- OAK 94611 630-E6
BEAUFORT HARBOR
- ALA 94502 670-A5
BEAUJOLAIS CT
8400 SJS 95135 855-H7
BEAULIEU CT
400 CCCo 94565 573-D2
1200 SJS 95125 853-G4
BEAULIEU DR
1200 CCCo 94565 573-D2
BEAULIEU PL
- CCCo 94565 573-D2
BEAUME CT
400 MTVW 94043 811-G2
BEAUMERE WY
100 MPS 95035 794-A4
BEAUMONT AV
- SF 94118 647-E6
2700 OAK 94606 650-C4
3100 OAK 94602 650-C4
13200 SAR 95070 852-E7
13400 SAR 95070 872-E1
BEAUMONT BLVD
100 PCFA 94044 706-J2
200 PCFA 94044 707-A3
BEAUMONT CT
- LFYT 94549 591-H7
BEAUMONT DR
1000 SJS 95129 852-J3
BEAUMONT SQ
3300 MTVW 94040 831-J2
BEAUMONT ST
4200 FRMT 94536 752-G3
BEAU RIVAGE AV
1500 CCCo 94806 589-B4
BEAVEN DR
21700 CPTO 95014 832-B7
BEAVER CT
800 FRMT 94539 773-J3
4500 ANT 94509 595-G3
BEAVER DR
- HAY 94541 712-B1
BEAVER LN
26900 LAH 94022 811-A5
BEAVER ST
- SF 94114 667-G2
BEAVER CREEK WY
700 SJS 95133 814-H3
700 SJS 95133 834-F1
BEAVERTON CT
800 SUNV 94087 832-C4
BECADO DR
300 FRMT 94539 773-H1
BECADO PL
400 FRMT 94539 773-H1
BECARD CT
2100 UNC 94587 732-G7
2600 PLE 94566 714-C1
BECERRA DR
400 FRMT 94536 752-E2
BECK AV
18400 MSER 95030 872-H6
BECK DR
1600 SJS 95130 853-B5
S BECK ST
300 RCH 94804 608-J1
300 RCH 94804 588-J7
BECKER LN
400 LALT 94022 811-D5
BECKER PL
- HAY 94544 732-E2
BECKET DR
500 RDWC 94065 749-J7
1200 SJS 95121 854-J3
2400 UNC 94587 732-C4
BECKET TER
38500 FRMT 94536 753-C2
BECKETT ST
- SF 94133 648-A4
BECKETT WY
8600 DBLN 94568 693-F2
BECKHAM CT
4800 CNCD 94521 593-D4
BECKHAM DR
400 SJS 95123 875-B7
BECKHAM LN
2200 AlaC 94541 712-C2
BECKHAM WY
2200 AlaC 94541 712-C2
BECKLEY DR
3000 SJS 95135 855-F3
BECKNER CT
1600 CNCD 94521 593-B2
BECKWITH RD
19200 SCIC 95030 872-G7
BECKY CT
300 NVTO 94949 546-D1
BECKY LN
15000 MSER 95030 872-J4
25300 LAH 94022 831-C2
BEDAL LN
300 CMBL 95008 873-D1
BEDELIO TER
36500 FRMT 94536 752-G3
BEDFORD
100 HER 94547 569-H2
BEDFORD AV
1300 SUNV 94024 832-A5
1300 SUNV 94087 832-A5
BEDFORD CT
1200 SUNV 94024 832-A4
7400 DBLN 94568 693-H3
BEDFORD CV
- SRFL 94901 587-A2
BEDFORD DR
1800 AlaC 94546 691-J6
1800 HAY 94546 691-J6
BEDFORD LN
300 AMCN 94589 509-J3
BEDFORD PL
- CCCo 94506 654-A5
- SF 94133 648-A4
300 MRGA 94556 631-E6
BEDFORD RD
2300 CNCD 94520 592-E3
BEDFORD ST
700 FRMT 94539 753-F6
10000 SCIC 95127 835-A3
BEDFORD WY
7300 DBLN 94568 693-H3
BEDIVERE DR
600 SJS 95127 814-H7
BEDROCK CT
100 VAL 94589 510-B5
BEE CT
1000 MPS 95035 814-D2
BEE ST
300 SAUS 94965 627-A2
BEEBE CIR
4000 SJS 95135 855-F3
BEECH AV
400 SBRN 94066 727-H1
400 SSF 94080 707-J2
500 SBRN 94066 707-H7
BEECH CT
- CCCo 94596 612-G7
6300 PLE 94588 694-A7
BEECH DR
900 CCCo 94596 612-F7
900 CCCo 94596 632-G1
BEECH PL
36300 NWK 94560 752-C6
BEECH ST
100 RDWC 94063 770-B6
900 EPA 94303 791-C2
1300 MRTZ 94553 571-F3
1800 SCL 95054 813-D5
22600 HAY 94541 692-B7
BEECHAM CT
3400 PLE 94588 694-E5
BEECHER CT
2800 SJS 95121 855-A2
BEECHER ST
900 SLN 94577 690-G1
BEECH GROVE CT
5300 SJS 95123 874-J3
BEECHMONT AV
4200 SJS 95136 874-D1
BEECHMONT ST
500 HAY 94544 711-G4
BEECHNUT AV
200 SUNV 94086 812-E5
BEECHNUT CT
700 SRFL 94903 566-B2
3000 ANT 94509 575-J6
BEECHNUT DR
100 HER 94547 570-A5
BEECHNUT ST
3000 ANT 94509 575-J6
BEECHVALE CT
300 SJS 95119 895-D1
BEECHWOOD AV
700 VAL 94591 530-E5
1500 SLN 94579 691-A5
2400 SJS 95128 833-E7
4700 FRMT 94536 752-H5
BEECHWOOD CT
- PIT 94565 573-F4
- SRFL 94901 567-B6
3900 CNCD 94519 573-A7
BEECHWOOD DR
- OAK 94618 630-A5
700 DALY 94015 687-A5
800 SMCo 94015 687-A5
1400 MRTZ 94553 591-H1
1600 MRTZ 94553 571-J7
3200 LFYT 94549 611-G6
3800 CNCD 94519 593-A1
3900 CNCD 94519 573-A7
5300 SCIC 94024 831-J6
5300 LALT 94024 831-J6
BEEDE WY
- ANT 94509 575-D4
BEEGER RD
- RDWC 94063 770-C3
BEEGUM CT
2500 CNCD 94518 592-G6
BEEGUM WY
200 SJS 95123 875-A4
BEEKMAN PL
19800 CPTO 95014 832-F6
BEEMAN DR
10300 SJS 95127 835-B4
BEEMER AV
100 SUNV 94086 812-E7
BEGEN AV
1500 MTVW 94040 811-H7
1700 MTVW 94040 831-H1
BEGIER AV
- SLN 94577 671-A7
BEGONIA CT
100 MRTZ 94553 572-B7
100 VAL 94591 530-F7
400 SLN 94578 691-C4
1800 PLE 94588 714-F1
2200 PIT 94565 573-J4
BEGONIA DR
400 SLN 94578 691-C4
1000 ALA 94502 670-A6
5400 SJS 95124 873-J6
BEGONIA LN
600 SJS 95136 854-E7
BEGONIA ST
2500 UNC 94587 732-F7
2600 UNC 94587 752-G1
BEGONIA WY
600 SUNV 94086 832-F1
BEHLER DR
3500 SJS 95132 814-F2
BEHR AV
- SF 94131 667-D3
BEHRENS ST
100 ALB 94706 609-E4
100 ELCR 94530 609-E4
BEIDEMAN ST
- SF 94115 647-G6
BELA DR
4700 SJS 95129 853-A4
4700 SJS 95129 852-J4
BEL AIR AV
2000 SJS 95126 833-F7
2000 SJS 95128 833-F7
BEL AIR CT
- FRMT 94539 773-J2
- ORIN 94563 631-B1
BEL AIR DR
- ORIN 94563 631-A1
1400 CNCD 94521 593-B4
BELAIR WY
- RDWC 94062 789-G2
BEL AIRE CT
- HIL 94402 748-G6
200 DNVL 94526 653-D6
11000 CPTO 95014 852-B3
32700 UNC 94587 752-A1
BEL AIRE DR
100 SJS 95131 814-A4
25700 HAY 94542 712-B4
BEL AIRE RD
1300 SMCo 94402 748-G6
1400 HIL 94402 748-G6
BEL AIRE ST
32700 UNC 94587 752-A1
BELALP PTH
- OAK 94618 630-B5
BELANN CT
800 CNCD 94518 592-G6
BEL AYRE DR
100 SCL 95117 833-C7
BELBLOSSOM WY
200 LGTS 95032 873-G6
BELBROOK CT
6500 SJS 95120 894-C1
BELBROOK PL
- MPS 95035 793-J4
BELBROOK WY
- ATN 94027 790-B6
1100 MPS 95035 793-J5
BELBURN DR
1600 BLMT 94002 769-D2
BEL CANTO DR
4900 SJS 95124 873-F4
BELCHER ST
- SF 94114 667-G1
BELCREST AV
- DALY 94015 707-A1
100 DALY 94015 706-J1
BELCREST DR
100 LGTS 95032 873-H7
BELDEN CT
600 LALT 94022 811-E5
BELDEN DR
- LALT 94022 811-E5
200 SJS 95123 875-A4
BELDEN ST
- SF 94104 648-A5
1400 PIN 94564 569-D5
BELDEN TER
3200 FRMT 94536 752-H2
BELDER DR
1000 SJS 95120 894-H4
BELDING CT
1700 CNCD 94521 593-D3
BELDING ST
1300 SLN 94579 691-B7
BELEM CT
600 SRMN 94583 673-B3
BEL ESCOU DR
4900 SJS 95124 873-F4
4900 SJS 95124 873-F4
BEL ESTOS DR
4900 SJS 95124 873-F4
15100 SCIC 95124 873-F4
BELESTOS WY
4300 UNC 94587 731-J6
BELFAIR CT
700 SUNV 94087 832-C4
BELFAIR DR
1000 PIN 94564 569-D4
BELFAIR PL
400 MRGA 94556 631-E5
BELFAST AV
400 PCFA 94044 726-G4
4600 OAK 94619 650-H6
BELFAST CT
500 SUNV 94087 832-E4
1300 LVMR 94550 715-F3
BELFAST DR
100 VAL 94589 510-C5
2700 SJS 95127 835-A5
BELFAST LN
27000 HAY 94542 712-D4
BELFAST PL
- SRMN 94583 673-F6
BELFAST WY
3000 RCH 94806 589-A1
3000 RCH 94806 588-J1
BELFORD CT
- WLCK 94598 612-G2
4900 ANT 94509 595-E3
BELFORD DR
- DALY 94015 686-J4
1000 SJS 95132 814-F6
2000 WLCK 94598 612-F2
BELFORD WY
- SMTO 94402 748-J1
BELFORD PEAK WY
4800 ANT 94509 595-E3
BELFRY WY
500 SUNV 94087 832-D4
BELGATOS RD
100 LGTS 95032 873-H7
BELGIAN DR
100 DNVL 94526 633-C7
BELGIUM ST
- LVMR 94550 696-A2
BELGLEN LN
100 LGTS 95032 873-H6
BELGLEN WY
100 LGTS 95032 873-H6
BELGRAVE AV
- SF 94117 667-E2
200 SF 94117 667-E2
BELGRAVE PL
5300 OAK 94618 630-A6
BELGRAVIAN CT
2700 SJS 95121 855-D3
BELGROVE CIR
3200 SJS 95148 855-F1
BELGROVE CT
3300 SJS 95148 855-F1
BELGUM TR
- CCCo 94805 589-C5
- RCH 94805 589-D4
BELHAVEN AV
- DALY 94015 687-A7
BELHAVEN CT
- DALY 94015 687-B7
BELHAVEN DR
100 LGTS 95032 873-H6
BELHAVEN ST
25000 HAY 94545 711-G5
BELICK ST
3100 SCL 95054 813-F7
BELINDA CT
- SRMN 94583 693-G1
BELINDA DR
- PLHL 94523 592-D5
BELIZE WY
3000 UNC 94587 732-A4
3000 UNC 94587 731-J4
BELKNAP CT
1200 CPTO 95014 852-C4
BELKNAP DR
7800 CPTO 95014 852-C3
BELL AV
100 PDMT 94611 630-C7
100 PDMT 94611 650-C1
400 LVMR 94550 715-E3
2900 SCIC 95133 834-H1
4100 RCH 94804 609-A1
BELL COM
4100 FRMT 94536 753-A5
4100 FRMT 94536 752-J4
BELL CT
- EPA 94303 791-B2
- SF 94124 668-C6
4500 RCH 94804 609-A1
BELL DR
- PIT 94565 574-C5
BELL LN
300 MrnC 94965 606-F7
BELL RD
- SF 94129 647-C3
BELL ST
300 EPA 94303 791-B2
800 LFYT 94549 611-F7
38700 FRMT 94536 753-A5
BELL TER
4000 FRMT 94536 753-A4
BELL WY
4300 RCH 94806 568-G6
BELLA CORTE
400 MTVW 94043 811-G2
BELLADONNA CT
600 SUNV 94086 832-F1
BELLAGIO DR
5600 SJS 95118 874-B5
BELLAGIO RD
- ROSS 94957 586-D1
BELLAIR PL
- SF 94133 648-A3
BELLAIR WY
1100 MLPK 94025 790-D6
1100 SMCo 94025 790-D6
BELLAIRE PL
2700 OAK 94601 650-C6
BELLA LADERA DR
24500 LAH 94024 831-E2
BELLAM BLVD
- SRFL 94901 586-J3
300 SRFL 94901 587-A2
BELLA MADEIRA LN
- SCIC 95127 835-F3
BELLA MONTE AV
- CCCo 94565 573-H2
BELLAMY CT
1000 WLCK 94596 612-B1
BELLARMINE CT
3200 SCL 95051 833-A2
BELLA VISTA
- CCCo 94526 633-E6
500 FRMT 94539 773-H1
19900 SAR 95070 872-E3
BELLA VISTA AV
- BLV 94920 627-D1
- CCCo 94565 573-H3
- SANS 94960 566-B7
100 LGTS 95032 873-B7
800 CCCo 94553 571-F4
800 SLN 94577 671-A7
1000 OAK 94610 650-B4
3400 SCL 95051 832-J3
BELLA VISTA CT
100 LGTS 95032 873-B7
3400 SCL 95051 832-J3
BELLA VISTA DR
100 HIL 94010 728-C7
BELLAVISTA LN
- SF 94127 667-E6
- SF 94127 667-E6
BELLA VISTA WY
- SF 94127 667-E5
100 VAL 94590 530-B3
200 SF 94127 667-E6
BELLE AV
- FRFX 94930 566-A6
- RDWC 94063 770-E6
- SANS 94960 586-C1
- SF 94132 687-C2
- SRFL 94901 586-H1
100 PLHL 94523 612-A1
600 SRFL 94901 566-G7
1900 SCAR 94070 769-G4
BELLE CT
- PLHL 94523 612-B1
2200 ANT 94509 574-H5
15100 SAR 95070 872-F4
BELLE DR
3900 ANT 94509 574-H5
BELLE LN
100 PLHL 94523 612-B1
BELLE ST
- OAK 94607 649-C3
22000 AlaC 94546 692-A7
BELLE AIR RD
100 SSF 94080 708-A5
BELLEAU AV
- ATN 94027 790-D2
BELLEAU ST
1000 SLN 94579 691-B7
BELLE MEADE DR
9400 SRMN 94583 693-H1
9500 SRMN 94583 673-G7
BELLE MEADE PL
100 SRMN 94583 673-H7
BELLEMONTI AV
2000 BLMT 94002 749-C7
2000 BLMT 94002 769-C1
BELLE RIVE PL
- LKSP 94939 586-D6
BELLE ROCHE AV
- SMCo 94062 769-G6
BELLE ROCHE CT
- SMCo 94062 769-F7
BELLEROSE DR
300 SJS 95128 833-F7
500 SCIC 95128 833-F7
600 SCIC 95128 853-F1
800 SJS 95128 853-F1
BELLES ST
- SF 94129 647-C5
BELLETERRE DR
1000 DNVL 94506 653-H4
BELLEVIEW DR
100 SLN 94577 671-A7
100 SLN 94577 670-J7
BELLEVILLE WY
1200 SUNV 94024 832-A5
1200 SUNV 94087 832-A5
BELLE VISTA AV
100 PCFA 94044 706-J5

STREET Block City ZIP Pg-Grid

BELLEVUE AV
- BLV 94920 627-E1
- DALY 94014 687-D3
- PDMT 94611 650-C1
- SJS 95110 854-D3
- SRFL 94901 587-A1
- SF 94112 687-F3
300 OAK 94610 649-H3
1100 BURL 94010 728-F7
1500 HIL 94010 728-F7
22300 CPTO 95014 852-A1
E BELLEVUE AV
- SMTO 94401 728-H7
W BELLEVUE AV
- SMTO 94402 748-G1
BELLEVUE CT
300 LALT 94024 831-F1
BELLEW DR
700 MPS 95035 813-H1
BELLEZA DR
5600 PLE 94588 694-C7
BELLEZA LN
5600 PLE 94588 694-C6
BELLFLOWER AV
600 SUNV 94086 832-F2
BELLFLOWER CT
100 HER 94547 570-B4
1600 WLCK 94596 612-G7
2900 ANT 94509 575-G7
15000 SCIC 95127 814-J5
BELLFLOWER DR
100 SRMN 94583 653-H7
2800 ANT 94509 575-H7
3100 ANT 94509 595-H1
5700 NWK 94560 752-G7
BELLFLOWER LN
- SCAR 94070 769-C4
BELLFLOWER PL
1600 WLCK 94596 612-G7
BELLFLOWER ST
700 LVMR 94550 696-B4
BELLGROVE CIR
11800 SAR 95070 852-G7
BELLHAVEN AV
6000 NWK 94560 752-E6
BELLHAVEN CT
6100 NWK 94560 752-E6
BELLHURST AV
900 SJS 95122 834-F7
BELLHURST CT
6400 AlaC 94552 672-C7
BELLHURST LN
6500 AlaC 94552 672-C7
BELLINA ST
1200 HAY 94541 712-A1
8600 DBLN 94568 693-G2
BELLINA CANYON RD
- AlaC 94552 672-F3
BELLINGHAM CT
1100 SJS 95121 854-J3
BELLINGHAM DR
1000 SJS 95121 854-J3
5900 AlaC 94552 692-C1
BELLINGHAM WY
1300 SUNV 94087 832-B4
1400 SUNV 94024 832-B4
BELLINI CT
2800 SJS 95132 814-F5
BELLIS CT
700 SJS 95123 874-G6
BELLMAWR DR
4100 LVMR 94550 696-A6
BELLO AV
2000 SJS 95125 854-A6
BELLO CT
200 SRMN 94583 673-A2
BELLO RD
30600 AlaC 94544 712-E7
30600 AlaC 94544 732-E1
30600 HAY 94544 712-E7
30600 HAY 94544 732-E1
BELLOMO AV
900 SUNV 94086 832-F3
BELLOMY ST
700 SCL 95053 833-E5
700 SCL 95050 833-E5
1600 SCL 95128 833-E5
BELLOREID AV
- SRFL 94901 566-D7
BELLOWS CT
800 CCCo 94596 612-F6
800 WLCK 94598 612-F6
BELLS RD
2000 FRMT 94539 773-E1
BELLVIEW CT
2100 PA 94303 791-C5
BELL WAVER WY
- OAK 94619 650-J4
BELLWOOD CT
1300 LALT 94024 831-J4
3900 CNCD 94519 573-A7
42600 FRMT 94538 773-D2
BELLWOOD DR
400 SCL 95054 813-E5
3900 CNCD 94519 573-A7
3900 CNCD 94519 593-A1
19100 SAR 95070 852-G6
BELLWORT CT
2800 ANT 94509 575-H7
BEL MAR AV
- DALY 94015 687-A4
BEL MARIN KEYS BLVD
100 NVTO 94949 546-F1
400 NVTO 94949 526-F7
500 MrnC 94949 526-F7
BELMONT AV
- FRFX 94930 566-A6
- SF 94117 667-E2
100 SMCo 94061 790-B3
100 SSF 94080 707-J2
200 LGTS 95030 872-J7
300 MSER 95030 872-J7
800 BLMT 94002 749-D7
1100 SCAR 94070 769-H5
1100 SolC 94591 530-E7
3200 ELCR 94530 609-C4
3300 RCH 94804 609-C4
25100 HAY 94542 712-A3
BELMONT CT
- PLHL 94523 591-J7
BELMONT DR
- DALY 94015 687-B3
400 SJS 95125 854-C3
BELMONT LN
2600 ANT 94509 575-D1
BELMONT PL
900 PIT 94565 574-E6
1000 ALA 94502 670-A6
BELMONT RD
1500 CNCD 94520 592-E3
BELMONT ST
300 OAK 94610 649-J3
BELMONT TER
900 SUNV 94086 812-D6
BELMONT WY
700 PIN 94564 569-C4
3800 PLE 94588 694-F5
4400 AlaC 94546 691-H1
BELMONT CANYON RD
2500 BLMT 94002 769-A2
2800 BLMT 94002 768-J2
BELMONT WOODS WY
2900 BLMT 94002 769-A2
BELNAP WY
15400 SAR 95070 872-C4
15400 SCIC 95070 872-C4
BELOIT AV
400 CCCo 94708 609-G4
BELOIT ST
38600 FRMT 94536 752-J4
BELOVERIA CT
4000 FRMT 94536 752-H4
BELRIDGE DR
100 LGTS 95032 873-H7
BELROSE AV
2700 BERK 94705 630-A3
BELSHAW DR
1300 MTVW 94040 832-A2
BELSHAW ST
- ANT 94509 575-D6
BELTHORN CT
2200 SJS 95131 814-E6
BELTRAMI DR
1100 SJS 95127 835-B3
BELVA LN
200 PLHL 94523 592-B5
BELVALE DR
100 LGTS 95032 873-H6
BELVEDERE AV
- RCH 94801 608-D1
- SCAR 94070 769-H5
- BLV 94920 627-D1
1500 BERK 94702 629-E1
2200 SLN 94577 690-H5
BELVEDERE CT
- BURL 94010 728-C7
100 VAL 94589 509-H5
100 WLCK 94598 612-J1
7500 PLE 94588 714-A3
27000 HAY 94544 712-A6
BELVEDERE DR
- MrnC 94941 606-H4
600 BEN 94510 530-J7
4200 SJS 95129 853-A2
BELVEDERE LN
1000 SJS 95129 852-F3
BELVEDERE ST
- SF 94117 667-E1
- SRFL 94901 586-J2
5200 OAK 94601 670-F1
BELVEDERE TER
34900 FRMT 94555 752-E2
BELVEDERE WY
- BLV 94920 627-C1
4400 ANT 94509 595-F2
BEL VIEW CT
8400 ELCR 94530 589-E7
BELVOIR DR
1600 SCIC 94024 831-G4
BELVUE DR
- LGTS 95032 873-H6
BELWOOD CT
100 LGTS 95032 873-H6
BELWOOD LN
100 LGTS 95032 873-H6
BELWOOD GATEWAY
- LGTS 95032 873-H6
BEMIS ST
- SF 94131 667-G6
4200 OAK 94605 671-D5
BENAVENTE AV
39400 FRMT 94539 753-E3
BENAVENTE PL
39500 FRMT 94539 753-E3
BENBOW AV
200 SJS 95123 875-B5
BENBOW CT
4000 ANT 94509 595-H1
4600 CNCD 94521 593-C3
BENBOW DR
41900 FRMT 94539 753-E7
BENCHMARK AV
1900 FRMT 94536 753-A3
2400 FRMT 94536 752-J1
BENCHMARK CT
37800 FRMT 94536 752-J1
BEND AV
700 SJS 95136 874-E1
BEND DR
600 SUNV 94087 832-D4
BENDEL TER
36400 FRMT 94536 752-J1
BENDIGO DR
1700 LALT 94024 831-H4
BENDMILL WY
1000 SJS 95121 854-J4
BENDORF DR
100 SJS 95111 875-B3
BENECIA AV
1000 SUNV 94086 812-D5
6200 NWK 94560 772-H1
BENEDICK CT
4500 FRMT 94555 752-D2
BENEDICK LN
34300 FRMT 94555 752-D2
BENEDICT CT
- ALA 94502 669-H6
100 MRTZ 94553 571-J7
1200 SLN 94577 691-C1
1300 PLE 94566 714-G5
BENEDICT DR
1300 SLN 94577 671-C7
1300 SLN 94577 691-C1
1300 SLN 94605 671-C7
1300 OAK 94605 671-C7
BENEDICT LN
15400 LGTS 95032 873-C5
BENEDITA PL
- MRGA 94556 631-E3
BENEFIT CT
400 SJS 95133 834-G2
BENET CT
- BEN 94510 551-C1
BENETTI CT
21800 CPTO 95014 832-B7
BENEVIDES AV
4600 OAK 94602 650-D3
BENGAL AL
- SF 94127 667-D5
BENGAL AV
18200 AlaC 94541 711-E1
BENGAL CT
5100 SJS 95111 875-A2
BENGAL DR
5000 SJS 95111 875-A2
BENGLOE LN
- HIL 94010 748-F4
BENHAM CT
2300 WLCK 94596 632-H2
BENHAM DR
200 MRTZ 94553 591-H3
BEN HUR CT
2300 SJS 95124 853-G7
BENICIA RD
- VAL 94590 530-B6
100 SolC 94590 530-B6
500 SolC 94591 530-E6
600 VAL 94591 530-E6
BENICIA ST
47000 FRMT 94538 773-G7
BENITA WY
- CCCo 94553 572-B5
BENITO AV
1300 BURL 94010 728-C6
BENJAMIN AV
200 PIT 94565 574-F4
2800 SJS 95124 873-F1
BENJAMIN CT
2900 SJS 95124 873-F1
BENJAMIN DR
2400 MTVW 94043 811-F2
3100 RCH 94806 589-A1
BENJAMIN GRN
2900 FRMT 94538 753-D6
BENJAMIN ST
100 VAL 94589 510-D6
BENJAMIN FRANKLIN CT
- SMTO 94401 748-J2
BEN JOHNSON TR
- MrnC 94965 606-A4
BEN LOMOND
- HER 94547 569-G4
BEN LOMOND DR
4000 PA 94306 811-E2
BEN LOMOND WY
3300 SJS 95121 855-B3
BENNER CT
6300 PLE 94588 694-A6
BENNETT AV
200 VAL 94590 530-A6
3400 SCL 95051 832-J7
BENNETT CT
1100 FRMT 94536 753-B2
BENNETT DR
4700 LVMR 94550 696-B5
BENNETT PL
4300 OAK 94602 650-F4
BENNETT RD
- RDWC 94062 769-G7
BENNETT WY
1000 SJS 95125 854-B5
3300 CNCD 94519 572-G7
16300 LGTS 95032 873-D4
BENNIGHOF CT
2100 SJS 95121 855-C3
BENNINGTON AV
2300 SBRN 94066 727-F2
BENNINGTON CT
- SMCo 94402 748-G7
3200 WLCK 94598 612-H6
BENNINGTON DR
- SMCo 94402 748-G7
1100 SUNV 94087 832-B1
6000 NWK 94560 752-D6
BENNINGTON LN
2300 HAY 94545 711-F6
BENNINGTON ST
- SF 94110 667-J5
BENNIT AV
- SANS 94960 566-A5
BENNS TER
47000 FRMT 94539 773-H6
BENNY CT
1100 SJS 95131 834-C1
BEN ROE DR
1400 LALT 94024 831-J4
1500 LALT 94024 832-A4
BENSON AV
- VAL 94590 529-H2
BENSON CIR
200 MLV 94941 606-G2
BENSON CT
2600 MRTZ 94553 571-F5
BENSON LN
2500 SJS 95125 854-A7
2600 SJS 95125 874-A1
BENSON RD
31200 UNC 94587 731-H5
BENSON ST
1000 OAK 94621 670-D6
BENSON WY
2800 BLMT 94002 769-A2
2800 BLMT 94002 768-J2
BENT DR
1000 CMBL 95008 853-G6
BENT CREEK DR
2000 SRMN 94583 673-J7
2200 SRMN 94583 694-A1
BENTHILL CT
- CCCo 94549 591-J7
BENTLEY AV
- LGTS 95030 873-A7
BENTLEY CT
- CCCo 94553 592-B1
200 AMCN 94589 509-J3
2300 AlaC 94546 691-H5
26000 LAH 94022 811-D7
34500 FRMT 94555 752-E1
BENTLEY DR
1800 SJS 95132 814-E4
BENTLEY PL
600 LVMR 94550 695-H6
34400 FRMT 94555 732-E7
BENTLEY SQ
100 MTVW 94040 811-J7
BENTLEY ST
1200 CNCD 94518 592-E7
BENTLEY OAKS CT
4600 OAK 94602 650-D3
BENTLEY RIDGE DR
- SJS 95138 855-E5
BENT OAK CT
- CCCo 94506 654-C4
BENTOAK CT
1100 SJS 95129 852-H3
BENT OAK LN
1400 CCCo 94506 654-C4
BENTOAK LN
1000 SJS 95129 852-H3
BENT OAK PL
400 CCCo 94506 654-C4
BENTON AV
- SF 94110 667-H6
- SF 94112 667-H6
BENTON CT
1600 SUNV 94087 832-H5
BENTON LN
1900 NVTO 94945 526-A2
BENTON ST
400 SCL 95050 833-C4
1200 ALA 94501 669-H1
1400 OAK 94602 650-C4
1600 SUNV 94087 832-H5
2400 SCL 95051 833-A5
3300 CNCD 94519 572-G6
3300 SCL 95051 832-H5
BENT TREE LN
1300 CNCD 94521 593-B5
BENVENUE AV
300 LALT 94024 811-F7
2500 BERK 94704 629-J3
2700 BERK 94705 629-J3
6400 OAK 94618 629-J4
BENZO DR
6300 SJS 95123 875-A7
BEPLER ST
- DALY 94014 687-D2
BERATLIS PL
- PLE 94566 714-H4
BERCAW LN
14200 SJS 95124 873-G3
14200 SCIC 95124 873-G3
BERDINA RD
4000 AlaC 94546 692-A4
BERENDA DR
100 SSF 94080 707-E3
BERENDA WY
- SMCo 94028 810-E3
27400 HAY 94544 711-J7
BERENDOS AV
100 PCFA 94044 727-B2
BERENDSEN CT
900 CLAY 94517 613-J1
BERENS DR
- MrnC 94904 586-E4
BERESFORD AV
100 SMCo 94061 790-B3
100 RDWC 94061 790-B3
3400 BLMT 94002 769-A1
BERESFORD CT
- SMCo 94061 790-B3
- SMTO 94403 749-D6
100 MPS 95035 794-A7
BERESFORD PL
- SMCo 94061 790-B3
BERESFORD ST
3800 SMTO 94403 749-D6
BERET TER
34700 FRMT 94555 752-C3
BERETTA DR
43900 FRMT 94539 773-H1
BERG CT
1100 MPS 95035 794-B4
1300 PIT 94565 574-F6
BERGAMO CT
5600 SJS 95118 874-B5
BERGEDO DR
200 OAK 94603 690-H1
200 OAK 94603 670-H7
BERGEN PL
800 SF 94109 647-H3
BERGER DR
1400 SJS 95112 834-B1
BERGERAC DR
1400 SJS 95118 874-A6
BERGESEN CT
- ATN 94027 790-B4
BERGIN PL
1400 SCL 95051 833-A4
BERGMAN CT
2500 SJS 95121 855-E4
BERGUM CT
- PLHL 94523 592-A6
BERGWALL WY
- VAL 94591 530-F5
BERING DR
1800 SJS 95112 833-J1
2000 SJS 95131 813-H7
2100 SJS 95131 833-J1
BERINGER CT
1400 SJS 95125 853-G4
BERK AV
500 RCH 94804 609-A1
BERK PL
- RCH 94804 609-A1
BERKE CT
- TBRN 94920 607-E6
BERKELAND CT
4900 SJS 95111 875-C1
BERKELEY
100 CCCo 94806 569-B4
BERKELEY AV
- ORIN 94563 610-E6
- SANS 94960 566-B5
500 SMCo 94025 790-H1
1000 MLPK 94025 790-H1
1100 MLPK 94025 770-J7
BERKELEY COM
38400 FRMT 94536 753-B2
BERKELEY CT
22100 SCIC 94024 832-A7
BERKELEY RD
29000 HAY 94544 732-B1
BERKELEY TER
100 SUNV 94086 812-E7
BERKELEY WY
- SF 94131 667-F5
1200 BERK 94702 629-E2
1500 BERK 94703 629-F1
1900 BERK 94704 629-F1
2200 SJS 95116 834-H4
BERKELEY PARK BLVD
200 CCCo 94707 609-E4
BERKELY PL
1300 LVMR 94550 715-F5
BERKSFORD WY
1400 SJS 95127 835-A4
BERKSHIRE
- MRGA 94556 651-D1
BERKSHIRE AV
- LVMR 94550 696-B2
- SMCo 94063 790-C1
200 SMCo 94063 770-D7
900 SUNV 94087 832-C1
BERKSHIRE CT
100 SRMN 94583 673-G4
200 DNVL 94526 653-E6
3100 PLE 94588 694-E6
10000 CPTO 95014 831-J7
BERKSHIRE DR
700 MLBR 94030 728-A4
700 MLBR 94030 727-J4
1100 SJS 95125 854-C7
2600 SBRN 94066 707-D6
10200 SCIC 94024 831-E5
15900 AlaC 94578 691-F3
BERKSHIRE PL
600 MPS 95035 794-B3
700 CNCD 94518 592-H6
BERKSHIRE RD
- ALA 94502 669-J5
BERKSHIRE WY
- SF 94132 666-J6
BERLAND CT
7600 CPTO 95014 852-D3
BERLIN AV
- SANS 94960 566-B7
BERLIN WY
1300 LVMR 94550 715-F3
3000 OAK 94602 650-E6
BERMAR AV
4300 CCCo 94803 589-D2
BERMUDA AV
2200 SLN 94577 690-H5
4300 OAK 94619 650-H6
BERMUDA CT
100 HER 94547 570-C6
900 FRMT 94539 753-F5
900 SUNV 94086 832-G1
1200 CNCD 94518 592-D7
3400 SRMN 94583 653-E7
BERMUDA DR
400 SMTO 94403 749-C3
900 CNCD 94518 592-E7
BERMUDA LN
100 VAL 94591 550-F1
2300 HAY 94545 711-G7
BERMUDA WY
1500 SJS 95122 834-H6
1700 ANT 94509 575-G5
BERMUDA HARBOUR
- MrnC 94949 526-G7
BERN CT
900 SJS 95112 834-B1
BERNA ST
1600 SCL 95050 833-C3
BERNAL AV
300 LVMR 94550 695-F7
300 LVMR 94550 715-F1
600 SUNV 94086 812-G6
1000 BURL 94010 728-C5
3400 AlaC 94566 714-G2
3400 PLE 94566 714-G2
3800 AlaC 94566 714-E4
7700 AlaC 94588 714-A4
7700 PLE 94588 714-A4
BERNAL COM
500 FRMT 94539 753-H7
BERNAL CT
300 PLE 94566 714-D4
BERNAL RD
- SJS 95119 875-F6
- SJS 95138 875-F6
100 SJS 95139 875-F6
100 SJS 95139 895-E1
100 SJS 95119 895-E1
200 SCIC 95119 895-C2
500 SJS 95120 895-C2
BERNAL ST
19600 AlaC 94546 691-H4
BERNAL WY
- SJS 95119 875-F7
- SJS 95139 875-F7
BERNAL HEIGHTS BLVD
- SF 94110 668-A5
- SF 94110 667-J5
BERNARD AV
3000 SRMN 94583 673-F6
BERNARD LN
- MLV 94941 606-D3
BERNARD ST
- MLV 94941 606-D3
- SF 94133 647-J4
100 SF 94109 647-J4
BERNARD WY
1400 MRTZ 94553 591-H1
BERNARDO AV
500 SUNV 94087 832-B2
1600 CPTO 95014 832-B5
N BERNARDO AV
100 MTVW 94086 812-C6
100 MTVW 94043 812-C6
S BERNARDO AV
100 MTVW 94041 812-B7
100 SUNV 94086 812-B7
BERNARDO CT
900 PIN 94564 569-E4
BERNAUER
100 PIT 94565 574-B3
BERNEVES CT
- OAK 94619 650-H5
BERNHARD AV
5800 CCCo 94805 589-B5
BERNHARDT DR
9800 OAK 94603 670-G7
BERNHARDT ST
23000 HAY 94545 711-C6
BERNI CT
- MLBR 94030 728-A2
BERNICE LN
- MRTZ 94553 591-G3
BERNICE ST
- SF 94103 667-J1
BERNICE WY
1800 SJS 95124 873-G2
32000 HAY 94544 732-F2
BERNIE LN
1400 CCCo 94507 632-E3
41100 FRMT 94539 753-G5
BERONA WY
1400 SJS 95122 834-J5
1600 SJS 95122 835-A6
BERRELLESA ST
100 MRTZ 94553 571-D2
BERRENDO DR
- MPS 95035 794-A5
BERRY AV
100 HAY 94542 712-A3
200 HAY 94544 712-A4
500 HAY 94544 711-J4
600 LALT 94024 831-G2
BERRY CT
600 SCIC 94043 812-A3
1800 FRMT 94539 753-F7
BERRY DR
- CCCo 94553 592-C1
- CCCo 94553 572-C7
600 SCIC 94043 812-B3
BERRY LN
- ROSS 94957 586-D2
BERRY ST
- SF 94107 648-B7
200 SF 94107 668-B1
BERRY WY
3500 SCL 95051 832-J2
14500 SJS 95124 873-G3
14500 SCIC 95124 873-G3
BERRYBROOK HOLLOW
- ORIN 94563 610-F3
BERRYDALE WY
5200 ANT 94509 595-J6
BERRYESSA CT
4300 ANT 94509 595-J1
BERRYESSA RD
600 SJS 95112 834-B3
900 SJS 95133 834-C2
1200 SJS 95131 834-C2
1800 SJS 95133 814-G5
1800 SJS 95131 814-E7
2200 SCIC 95133 814-G5
2400 SJS 95132 814-G5
BERRYESSA ST
600 MPS 95035 793-J6
BERRYESSA WY
- HIL 94010 748-E6
BERRY HILL CT
14100 LAH 94022 810-H5
BERRY HILL LN
14100 LAH 94022 810-H6
BERRYMAN ST
1800 BERK 94703 609-F7
1900 BERK 94709 609-F7
BERRYWOOD CT
1700 CNCD 94521 593-D3
BERRYWOOD DR
1600 SJS 95133 834-E3
1700 CNCD 94521 593-D3
BERSANO CT
- PLE 94566 715-C6
BERTA CIR
- DALY 94015 707-C2
BERTA DR
2800 AlaC 94541 692-C7
BERTA LN
3200 LFYT 94549 611-G6
BERTERO AV
15900 AlaC 94580 691-E5
BERTHA LN
- SF 94124 668-D6
BERTIE MINOR LN
- SF 94115 647-E2
BERTINI CT
3700 SJS 95117 853-C2
BERTITA ST
100 SF 94112 687-F1
BERTLAND CT
1300 SJS 95131 814-D7
BERTOCCHI LN
- MLBR 94030 727-H3
BERTOLA ST
500 MRTZ 94553 571-E4
BERTRAM CT
3000 CNCD 94520 572-F6
BERTRAM RD
21000 SCIC 95120 895-A7
21400 SCIC 95120 894-J7
BERTRAM ST
- CCCo 94598 613-A4
BERWICK PL
- SF 94103 648-A7
100 SRMN 94583 673-F6
BERWICK ST
13100 SAR 95070 852-H7
BERWICK WY
100 SUNV 94087 832-E4
BERWICKSHIRE WY
6400 SJS 95120 894-C1
BERWIND AV
5500 LVMR 94550 696-C3
BERYL AV
200 MrnC 94941 606-F6
BERYL CT
- VAL 94591 530-F1
100 HER 94547 569-H5
BERYL DR
4100 CNCD 94518 592-J5
BERYL LN
- SRFL 94901 566-E7
BERYL PL
700 HAY 94544 712-A7
BERYLWOOD LN
- MPS 95035 793-J3
BESCO DR
39800 FRMT 94538 753-B7
BESITO AV
1100 OAK 94705 630-B3
BESS AV
2000 LVMR 94550 715-H3
BESS CT
1300 SJS 95128 853-F4
BESSIE ST
- SF 94110 667-J4
BEST AV
100 SLN 94577 670-J7
100 SLN 94577 671-A7
2400 OAK 94601 670-F1
2600 OAK 94619 650-F7
2600 OAK 94619 670-F1
BEST CT
700 SCAR 94070 769-D5
2100 SJS 95131 814-E7
BEST RD
500 PLHL 94523 592-B4
BESTON WY
100 VAL 94591 550-F2
BESTOR ST
200 SJS 95112 854-D1
400 SJS 95112 834-E7
BESTVIEW CT
15300 SAR 95070 872-F4
BESWICK CT
- PLHL 94523 592-B6
BESWICK DR
5600 SJS 95123 875-B4
BETA AV
- DALY 94014 687-D3
BETA CT
- SRMN 94583 673-B1
600 CMBL 95008 853-C7
BETA ST
- LKSP 94939 586-E6
BETH CT
3600 SCL 95054 813-E6
BETH DR
- PLHL 94523 592-C4
400 SJS 95111 854-H5
BETH WY
1500 CMBL 95008 873-A1
BETHAL PL
600 LVMR 94550 695-E6
BETHANY AV
1700 SJS 95132 814-D4
BETHANY CT
1800 SJS 95132 814-D4
2000 CNCD 94518 592-F7
BETHANY LN
800 CNCD 94518 592-F7
BETHANY ST
14600 SLN 94579 691-A5
BETHEL AV
10000 SCIC 95127 835-A3
BETLEN CT
2700 AlaC 94546 692-B6
BETLEN DR
11200 DBLN 94568 693-F5
BETLEN WY
22100 AlaC 94546 692-B6
BETLIN AV
800 CPTO 95014 852-F2
BETLIN PL
- MRGA 94556 631-E3
BETLO AV
2400 MTVW 94043 811-F2
2500 PA 94306 811-F2
BETLO CT
5000 SJS 95130 852-J6
BETROSE CT
19600 AlaC 94546 691-H4
BETSY WY
2800 SJS 95133 834-G1
2800 SJS 95133 814-G7
BETSY ROSS DR
5200 SCL 95054 813-A3
BETTE AV
800 CPTO 95014 852-F2
BETTEN CT
- DNVL 94526 653-B1
1000 SJS 95127 834-J4
BETTENCOURT CT
3900 FRMT 94536 752-J3
BETTENCOURT DR
5600 CLAY 94517 593-G5
BETTENCOURT ST
35700 NWK 94560 752-C6
BETTENCOURT WY
4300 UNC 94587 731-H4
BETTINA AV
2200 BLMT 94002 749-B7
2200 BLMT 94002 769-B1
4200 SMTO 94403 749-B7
BETTIO RD
- SCIC 94035 812-B3
BETTMAN WY
3600 SSF 94080 707-D4
BETTY AV
800 PIN 94564 569-C4
1200 SLN 94578 691-D4
BETTY CIR
5400 LVMR 94550 696-C7
BETTY CT
100 VAL 94589 509-J5
700 SUNV 94086 832-F2
1600 SCL 95051 833-A3
BETTY LN
- ATN 94027 790-C4
- NVTO 94947 526-A4
- SMTO 94402 749-C3
200 PLHL 94523 592-B5
3300 LFYT 94549 631-G2
3300 PIT 94565 574-C4
8400 ELCR 94530 609-E1
BEULAH ST
- SF 94117 667-E1
100 SF 94117 667-E1
BEUTKE DR
36500 NWK 94560 752-D7

BEVANS DR 1998 BAY AREA STREET INDEX BLOGETT LN 907

BAY AREA

STREET
Block City ZIP Pg-Grid

BEVANS DR
400 SJS 95129 852-J1
BEVERLEY WY
- SANS 94960 566-B6
BEVERLY AV
100 SLN 94577 671-A6
200 MLBR 94030 728-B3
400 OAK 94603 671-A6
BEVERLY BLVD
1700 SJS 95116 834-F4
BEVERLY CIR
- CCCo 94565 573-G2
BEVERLY CT
- CCCo 94707 609-F4
- SSF 94080 707-G1
200 CMBL 95008 853-C6
8400 DBLN 94568 693-H2
BEVERLY DR
- SCAR 94070 769-E3
- VAL 94591 530-D7
100 PLHL 94523 592-C4
200 SMCo 94070 769-E4
3000 CCCo 94565 573-G2
BEVERLY LN
100 LALT 94022 811-E6
8400 DBLN 94568 693-H1
BEVERLY PL
- PCFA 94044 707-A3
1600 ALB 94706 609-F6
1600 BERK 94706 609-F6
1600 BERK 94707 609-F6
4100 AlaC 94546 692-A4
BEVERLY RD
- CCCo 94707 609-F4
BEVERLY ST
- DALY 94015 707-C3
- MTVW 94043 812-B5
- SF 94132 687-C1
300 LVMR 94550 696-A7
1200 ANT 94509 575-E5
3000 SMTO 94403 749-A6
BEVERLY TER
- MLV 94941 606-C2
BEVIL CT
6400 SJS 95123 875-B7
BEVIL WY
16300 AlaC 94578 691-F5
BEVILACQUA CT
4200 PLE 94566 714-E4
BEVILACQUA ST
900 AlaC 94580 691-F6
BEVIN BROOK DR
1700 SJS 95112 854-F1
BEVMAR LN
- CCCo 94507 632-H3
BEWCASTLE CT
2900 SJS 95132 814-D4
BEXLEY LNDG
1800 SJS 95131 814-C4
BEXLEY PL
100 WLCK 94598 612-J1
BEYER CT
- NVTO 94945 526-A2
BIANCA DR
4500 FRMT 94536 752-E3
BIANCA LN
- AlaC 94541 711-G1
BIANCA WY
5100 LVMR 94550 696-C6
BIANCHI WY
10000 CPTO 95014 852-D1
BIANCO CT
5100 PLE 94588 694-A6
BIANCO WY
3400 SJS 95135 855-E3
BIARRITZ CIR
200 LALT 94022 811-E6
BIARRITZ CT
500 RDWC 94065 749-J5
12600 SAR 95070 852-H6
BIARRITZ LN
12600 SAR 95070 852-H6
BIARRITZ PL
5500 SJS 95138 875-F1
BIBBITS DR
3900 PA 94303 811-F1
3900 PA 94303 791-F7
BIBEL AV
6400 SJS 95129 852-F4
BICKERSTAFF ST
3600 LFYT 94549 611-E6
BICKLEY CT
5100 SJS 95136 874-E3
BICKNELL RD
600 LGTS 95030 873-A4
18000 MSER 95030 873-A4
18000 MSER 95030 872-H4
18000 LGTS 95030 872-H4
BIDDLE AV
5800 NWK 94560 752-E5
BIDDLEFORD CT
100 SJS 95139 875-G7
BIDDLEFORD DR
2800 SRMN 94583 673-F6
BIDDULPH WY
500 BLMT 94002 749-E7
BIDWELL AV
900 SUNV 94086 812-C6
BIDWELL DR
3900 FRMT 94538 753-B5
BIDWELL WY
- VAL 94589 509-J6
BIEBER AV
1100 MLPK 94025 770-H7
BIEBER DR
200 SJS 95123 875-A4
BIEHS CT
- OAK 94618 630-C6
BIEN CT
3300 SJS 95148 835-D7
BIEN WY
3300 SJS 95148 835-D7
BIEN VENIDA
- ORIN 94563 610-G6
BIFROST AV
400 PLHL 94523 592-B3
BIG BASIN DR
1400 MPS 95035 814-D2
BIG BASIN RD
1000 LVMR 94550 696-D3
BIG BASIN WY Rt#-9
14300 SAR 95070 872-D3

BIG BEAR CT
100 RCH 94803 589-G3
900 MPS 95035 814-C1
BIG BEND CT
6000 PLE 94588 714-B1
BIG BEND DR
600 PCFA 94044 727-C5
1500 MPS 95035 794-D7
BIG BURN RD
- AlaC 94546 651-G7
- AlaC 94546 671-F1
BIGELOW AV
- MLV 94941 606-D2
BIGELOW CT
6000 SJS 95123 875-B6
BIGELOW PL
- SRMN 94583 673-F6
BIGELOW ST
200 CLAY 94517 613-J1
BIGELOW TER
- FRMT 94536 752-J2
BIG FOOT CT
500 FRMT 94539 773-H4
BIGGE AV
10000 OAK 94603 670-F7
10000 SLN 94577 670-F7
10400 SLN 94577 690-G1
BIGGS CT
600 SJS 95136 874-F2
BIGHORN CT
4500 ANT 94509 595-F3
48700 FRMT 94539 793-J2
BIGLER AV
- SF 94117 667-E2
BIGLER CT
500 BEN 94510 550-H1
BIGLOW DR
1800 ANT 94509 575-F6
BIG OAK CT
- WLCK 94596 612-D6
3400 HAY 94542 712-E4
BIGOAK CT
1000 SJS 95129 852-H3
BIGOAK DR
5500 SJS 95129 852-H3
BIG OAK LN
- MPS 95035 793-J3
BIG OAK TR
- LFYT 94549 631-D1
BIG PINE LN
4400 CNCD 94521 593-B4
BIG ROCK RIDGE FIRE RD
200 MrnC 94903 546-A4
600 NVTO 94949 546-A4
BIG SPRINGS TR
- CCCo 94708 610-B6
BIG SUR DR
1000 SJS 95120 894-H4
BIG SUR WY
- PCFA 94044 727-B5
BIG TALK CT
1200 SJS 95120 874-C7
BIG TREE LN
- WDSD 94062 809-G6
- SMCo 94062 809-G6
BIG TREE RD
- SMCo 94062 809-G7
- WDSD 94062 809-G7
BIG TREE WY
- SMCo 94062 809-F6
BIG WOOD DR
2900 SJS 95127 834-H2
BIKINI AV
1900 SJS 95122 854-H1
BILBO CT
1300 SJS 95121 855-A4
BILBO DR
3000 SJS 95121 855-A4
BILICH PL
10100 CPTO 95014 832-F7
BILLECI AV
1600 PIT 94565 574-E3
BILLINGS BLVD
600 SLN 94577 690-H1
BILLINGS RD
1700 CNCD 94519 592-H2
BILLINGSGATE LN
200 FCTY 94404 749-F5
BILLINGTON CT
- LFYT 94549 611-H3
BILLOU ST
- SRFL 94901 586-G2
BILLY LN
2200 CNCD 94520 572-F5
BILLYS LN
- CMAD 94925 606-E1
BILTMORE CT
200 CCCo 94507 633-A4
BILTMORE DR
2400 CCCo 94507 633-A4
2400 CCCo 94507 632-J4
BILTMORE LN
- MLPK 94025 790-C6
BIMBER CT
3100 SJS 95148 835-D7
BIMMERLE PL
900 SJS 95123 874-E5
BINFORD RD
8000 MrnC 94945 526-C1
8000 NVTO 94945 526-C1
BING CT
2500 UNC 94587 732-F7
BING DR
800 SCL 95051 832-J5
1300 SJS 95129 852-G4
BING PL
2400 UNC 94587 732-F7
BING ST
900 SCAR 94070 769-J4
BINGHAM CT
5300 SJS 95123 874-J3
BINNACLE LN
100 FCTY 94404 749-J1
BINNACLE HILL
- OAK 94618 630-C4
BIRCH
- BEN 94510 551-B5
- ORIN 94563 630-G1
BIRCH AV
- CMAD 94925 586-G6
400 SMTO 94402 749-B2

BIRCH AV
800 SUNV 94086 812-F7
1200 SSF 94080 707-F1
1600 SJS 95125 853-H5
1600 SCIC 95125 853-H5
1900 ANT 94509 575-D6
1900 SCAR 94070 769-G4
2700 CNCD 94520 572-F7
BIRCH CT
100 SBRN 94066 707-E7
2100 CCCo 94806 569-B4
5800 OAK 94618 629-J5
6700 DBLN 94568 693-J3
BIRCH DR
- CCCo 94596 612-D2
1600 CMBL 95008 853-F5
BIRCH LN
- PCFA 94044 706-J6
- SCIC 95127 834-H2
BIRCH PL
6000 NWK 94560 752-F7
BIRCH RD
- BEN 94510 551-D5
BIRCH ST
- MLV 94941 606-D4
- RDWC 94062 769-J5
100 VAL 94589 510-B7
400 RDWC 94062 770-A6
500 SF 94102 647-H7
1300 PIT 94565 574-F3
1800 PA 94306 791-A6
2400 CCCo 94553 571-F4
3300 PA 94306 811-C1
8000 OAK 94621 670-H3
9000 OAK 94603 671-A5
9300 OAK 94603 670-J4
14300 SLN 94579 691-A4
20800 AlaC 94541 691-G6
36700 NWK 94560 752-E6
BIRCH TER
5700 FRMT 94538 773-A1
BIRCH WY
- MrnC 94903 566-G2
400 SCL 95051 833-A7
6200 SJS 95138 875-F6
BIRCHBARK PL
100 CCCo 94506 654-A3
BIRCH BARK RD
4300 CNCD 94521 593-B5
BIRCHBARK WY
- CCCo 94506 654-A3
BIRCH CREEK DR
200 PLE 94566 714-F3
BIRCH GROVE DR
5300 SJS 95123 875-A3
BIRCH HILL WY
26600 LAH 94022 811-B7
BIRCHMEADOW CT
1300 SJS 95131 814-B6
BIRCHMEADOW LN
1300 SJS 95131 814-B6
BIRCH RIDGE CIR
100 SJS 95123 874-G7
BIRCH SPRING CT
11600 CPTO 95014 852-C4
BIRCHTREE LN
2600 SCL 95051 833-B6
BIRCH WOOD CT
100 LGTS 95030 873-A2
BIRCHWOOD CT
- SF 94134 687-H2
600 CCCo 94506 654-A2
600 LALT 94024 831-F1
700 SRFL 94903 566-C2
3900 CNCD 94519 573-A7
4500 UNC 94587 732-A7
BIRCHWOOD DR
- NVTO 94947 526-D6
200 MRGA 94556 631-F4
800 PIT 94565 574-A3
800 PIT 94565 573-J3
1200 SUNV 94089 812-J4
BIRCHWOOD LN
3200 SJS 95132 814-E2
BIRCHWOOD PL
- CCCo 94506 654-A2
- MRGA 94556 631-F5
BIRCHWOOD TER
3500 FRMT 94536 752-A6
BIRD AV
300 SJS 95126 854-A2
400 LGTS 95030 873-A7
500 SJS 95125 854-A2
BIRD CT
600 NVTO 94947 526-A4
BIRD PL
700 HAY 94544 711-J5
BIRD ST
- SF 94110 667-H2
BIRDHAVEN CT
800 LFYT 94549 611-G7
BIRDHAVEN WY
1600 PIT 94565 573-G4
BIRDIE DR
- NVTO 94949 546-D2
BIRDSALL AV
2800 OAK 94619 670-F1
2900 OAK 94619 650-F7
BIRDS HILL CT
1700 DNVL 94526 653-B6
BIRDS NEST CT
- MrnC 94920 606-H3
BIRDSONG LN
- CCCo 94803 589-F3
BIRKDALE CT
100 VAL 94591 530-G3
BIRKDALE DR
200 VAL 94591 530-G3
7300 NWK 94560 752-C6
BIRKDALE PL
- MRGA 94556 631-E5
BIRKDALE WY
5000 SJS 95138 855-E7
31000 HAY 94544 732-D2
BIRKENSHAW PL
4500 SJS 95136 874-F2
BIRKHAVEN PL
- SJS 95138 875-G5
BIRKSHIRE PL
36200 NWK 94560 752-C6
BIRMINGHAM CT
4800 SJS 95136 874-G2

BIRMINGHAM DR
2900 RCH 94806 589-A1
2900 RCH 94806 588-J1
4800 SJS 95136 874-G2
BIRMINGHAM RD
- SF 94129 647-E3
BISCAY BAY
100 ALA 94502 669-H7
BISCAY DR
2000 PIT 94565 574-F4
BISCAY PL
35500 NWK 94560 752-C5
BISCAY WY
2500 WLCK 94598 592-F7
BISCAYNE AV
400 FCTY 94404 749-F6
27700 HAY 94544 712-A7
BISCAYNE CT
100 SRFL 94901 567-E5
BISCAYNE DR
- SRFL 94901 567-C5
BISCAYNE WY
1700 SJS 95122 834-H6
BISCOTTI PL
4000 SJS 95134 813-D2
BISHOP AV
100 RCH 94801 608-C1
300 SUNV 94086 832-E1
400 HAY 94544 711-H5
1900 FRMT 94536 753-A3
2400 FRMT 94536 752-J3
BISHOP CT
100 NVTO 94945 526-E3
4600 CNCD 94521 593-C3
37800 FRMT 94536 753-A3
BISHOP DR
1600 CNCD 94521 593-C3
2400 SRMN 94583 673-D2
BISHOP LN
- WLCK 94596 632-D1
- SMCo 94025 810-F1
2500 ANT 94509 575-D1
BISHOP RD
- CCCo 94525 550-E5
1900 BLMT 94002 768-J1
BISHOP ST
- SF 94134 688-A1
1100 ALA 94501 670-A3
36600 NWK 94560 752-E5
BISHOP WY
5500 NWK 94560 752-F5
BISHOP PINE LN
- CCCo 94803 569-D7
BISHOP PINE WY
4100 LVMR 94550 696-A4
4100 LVMR 94550 695-J4
BISKRA WY
100 CCCo 94553 572-E3
BISMARCK DR
1000 CMBL 95008 853-B5
1000 SJS 95130 853-B5
1000 SJS 95008 853-B5
BISMARCK LN
1100 ALA 94502 670-A7
BISMARK ST
- DALY 94014 687-C4
BISON CT
6500 SJS 95119 875-D7
BISSELL AV
- RCH 94801 588-F7
- RCH 94804 588-H7
3500 RCH 94805 588-J7
3700 RCH 94805 589-A7
W BISSELL AV
- RCH 94801 588-E6
BISSELL CT
- RCH 94801 588-F6
BISSELL WY
800 RCH 94801 588-G7
BISSO LN
2300 CNCD 94520 592-E1
2400 CNCD 94520 572-E7
BISSY COM
39700 FRMT 94538 753-B6
BITTERN DR
1300 SUNV 94087 832-E5
BITTERN PL
3500 FRMT 94555 732-D7
BITTERNUT CT
1100 SJS 95131 814-D7
BITTER OAK ST
22100 CPTO 95014 832-A6
22100 LALT 95014 832-A6
BITTERROOT AV
5900 NWK 94560 752-H7
BITTERROOT PL
6700 SJS 95120 894-G2
BIVAR CT
1600 PLE 94566 714-E1
BIXBY DR
100 MPS 95035 794-D7
19700 CPTO 95014 852-F1
BLACHARD RD
600 SJS 95139 895-J2
600 SCIC 95139 895-J2
BLACHFORD CT
- OAK 94611 650-F2
BLACK AV
4300 PLE 94566 714-C2
BLACK PL
2000 SF 94133 647-J4
BLACK BERRY CT
- LFYT 94549 611-F2
BLACKBERRY LN
400 PIN 94564 569-C4
500 MrnC 94903 546-D7
3700 AlaC 94546 692-A2
BLACKBERRY TER
1100 SUNV 94087 832-B3
BLACKBERRY HILL RD
15000 LGTS 95032 893-D2
15000 SCIC 95032 893-D2
BLACKBIRD CT
- HAY 94544 712-E7
6000 SJS 95120 874-B7
BLACKBIRD DR
5100 PLE 94566 714-C1
BLACKBIRD WY
2400 PLE 94566 714-D1
BLACKBRUSH LN
100 SRMN 94583 653-H7

BLACKBURN AV
100 MLPK 94025 790-J3
BLACKBURN CT
4500 CNCD 94518 593-A6
BLACKBURN DR
35100 NWK 94560 752-D4
BLACKBURN TER
- PCFA 94044 726-G4
BLACKBURN PEAK CT
4700 ANT 94509 595-E2
BLACK DIAMOND DR
4600 ANT 94509 595-F3
BLACK DIAMOND ST
500 PIT 94565 574-D2
BLACK DIAMOND TR
- CCCo - 594-E4
- CCCo - 613-J3
- CCCo 94517 613-J3
- CLAY 94517 594-E6
- CLAY 94517 593-H7
- CLAY 94517 613-J3
BLACK FEATHER DR
3600 RCH 94803 589-G2
BLACKFIELD CT
1000 SCL 95051 833-C5
BLACKFIELD DR
- MrnC 94941 606-J4
- MrnC 94920 606-J4
- TBRN 94920 606-J4
200 TBRN 94920 607-A3
1100 SCL 95051 833-C4
2000 CNCD 94520 592-E3
BLACKFIELD WY
1000 MTVW 94040 811-F5
BLACKFOOT CT
700 SJS 95123 874-H6
BLACKFOOT DR
1500 FRMT 94539 773-G3
BLACKFORD AV
3700 SJS 95117 853-B2
4000 SJS 95129 853-A2
BLACKFORD CIR
4100 SJS 95117 853-B2
BLACKFORD LN
1600 SCIC 95125 853-H4
1600 SJS 95125 853-H4
BLACK FOREST CT
- LFYT 94549 611-A7
BLACK FOX WY
- RDWC 94061 789-F3
- WDSD 94062 789-F3
BLACK HAWK CT
1400 LFYT 94549 611-G3
BLACKHAWK CT
1400 SUNV 94087 832-E5
5600 SJS 95123 874-H4
BLACKHAWK DR
- MrnC 94960 566-B5
- SANS 94960 566-B5
1500 SUNV 94087 832-E5
5000 CCCo 94506 653-J3
5000 CCCo 94506 654-A3
BLACKHAWK LN
- SMCo 94010 728-B6
BLACK HAWK RD
3400 LFYT 94549 611-G3
BLACKHAWK RD
2100 DNVL 94506 653-J4
2100 CCCo 94506 653-F1
BLACKHAWK CLUB CT
- CCCo 94506 653-J4
BLACKHAWK CLUB DR
500 CCCo 94506 653-J3
500 CCCo 94506 654-A3
BLACKHAWK MDW CT
4200 CCCo 94506 654-C2
BLACKHAWK MDW DR
3100 CCCo 94506 654-C3
BLACKHAWK MDW LN
- CCCo 94506 654-C2
BLACKHAWK MDW PL
4200 CCCo 94506 654-C4
BLACKHAWK PLAZA CIR
3400 CCCo 94506 654-A5
3800 CCCo 94506 653-J5
BLACKHILLS PL
- CCCo - 654-A1
BLACKIES PASTURE RD
400 TBRN 94920 607-A4
BLACK JOHN RD
100 NVTO 94945 526-C1
BLACK LEAF
300 PIT 94565 574-B3
BLACKLOCK CT
6000 SJS 95123 875-A6
BLACK LOG RD
- MrnC 94904 586-D5
BLACKMORE CT
1800 SJS 95132 814-D4
BLACK MOUNTAIN CT
900 LALT 94024 831-H2
BLACK MOUNTAIN RD
800 HIL 94010 748-D4
1600 SMCo 94010 748-D4
27100 LAH 94022 830-J1
27600 LAH 94022 831-A1
BLACKOAK COM
4500 FRMT 94538 773-C1
BLACK OAK CT
- CCCo 94506 653-G1
1300 PIN 94564 569-E5
2100 PLE 94588 714-A5
BLACK OAK LN
- NVTO 94947 526-A5
6100 SJS 95120 874-D7
BLACK OAK RD
5000 CNCD 94521 593-D5
BLACK OAK TR
- CCCo - 591-B7
BLACKOAK WY
5400 SJS 95129 852-H3
BLACK PINE DR
500 SLN 94577 690-G1
BLACK PINE LN
1100 PLHL 94523 591-J5
BLACK POINT CT
600 CLAY 94517 593-G6
BLACK POINT PL
700 CLAY 94517 593-G6

BLACKPOOL CT
100 CCCo 94506 654-B5
BLACKPOOL LN
2400 SLN 94577 691-B2
BLACKPOOL PL
2200 SLN 94577 691-B2
BLACK RIVER CT
4600 SJS 95136 874-G2
BLACKROCK PL
2200 MRTZ 94553 572-B2
BLACKSAND RD
5000 FRMT 94538 752-J7
BLACKSTONE AV
1400 SJS 95118 874-B1
BLACKSTONE CT
- AlaC 94542 712-E1
- SF 94123 647-H4
400 WLCK 94598 612-G3
400 DNVL 94506 653-J6
BLACKSTONE DR
- MrnC 94903 546-D6
100 DNVL 94506 653-J6
1900 WLCK 94598 612-G3
BLACKSTONE LN
- MrnC 94903 546-D6
BLACKSTONE WY
34300 FRMT 94555 752-D1
BLACKSTONE HLLW CT
- DNVL 94506 653-J6
BLACKTAIL CT
2500 ANT 94509 595-G3
BLACKTHORN CT
- SRMN 94583 673-J6
BLACKTHORN DR
- LFYT 94549 611-A6
BLACK WALNUT CT
4400 CNCD 94521 593-B5
14400 SAR 95070 872-F2
BLACKWELDER CT
100 SCIC 94305 790-J7
BLACKWELL DR
300 LGTS 95032 873-D5
BLACKWOOD AV
22600 HAY 94541 711-F3
BLACKWOOD COM
1700 LVMR 94550 695-F6
BLACKWOOD CT
- CCCo 94806 569-B4
2300 CCCo 94596 612-E7
BLACKWOOD DR
- CCCo 94553 592-B1
2000 CCCo 94596 612-D6
2000 CCCo 94806 569-B4
6300 CPTO 95014 852-F2
36400 NWK 94560 752-E5
BLACKWOOD LN
1000 LFYT 94549 611-G6
BLACOW CT
3900 PLE 94566 714-F1
BLACOW RD
2000 FRMT 94539 773-E1
37000 FRMT 94536 752-G5
39000 FRMT 94538 752-H6
39300 FRMT 94538 753-A7
40100 FRMT 94538 773-C1
BLACOW ST
4000 PLE 94566 714-F1
BLADE CT
- CCCo 94595 612-B6
BLADE WY
- CCCo 94595 612-B6
BLAINE CIR
- MRGA 94556 651-E2
BLAINE CT
- CCCo 94565 573-F2
BLAINE ST
8500 OAK 94621 670-G5
BLAINE WY
600 HAY 94544 711-H5
BLAIR AV
- PDMT 94611 650-A1
800 SUNV 94087 832-B1
800 OAK 94611 630-C7
800 OAK 94611 650-C1
BLAIR CT
- DNVL 94526 652-G1
700 SUNV 94087 832-C1
900 PA 94303 791-C5
BLAIR PL
- PDMT 94611 650-C1
- OAK 94611 650-C1
35700 FRMT 94536 752-F2
BLAIR TER
- SF 94107 668-B4
BLAIRBETH DR
300 SJS 95119 895-D1
BLAIRBURRY WY
500 SJS 95123 874-G4
BLAIRMORE CT
4000 SJS 95121 855-B5
BLAIRWOOD CT
700 SJS 95120 894-H3
BLAIRWOOD LN
- SF 94131 667-D3
BLAISDELL CT
700 SJS 95117 853-D2
BLAISDELL TER
- FRMT 94536 733-B7
BLAISDELL WY
- FRMT 94536 733-A7
BLAKE AV
- SCL 95051 833-A7
200 FRMT 94536 753-C3
BLAKE CT
- BEN 94510 530-H7
BLAKE ST
- SF 94118 647-E6
400 MLPK 94025 790-F4
1100 BERK 94702 629-E3
1500 BERK 94703 629-E3
1900 BERK 94704 629-H3
6300 ELCR 94530 609-B1
BLAKEMORE CT
3400 PLE 94588 694-E5
BLAKE WILBUR DR
900 SCIC 94305 790-G6
900 PA 94304 790-G6
BLAKEWOOD WY
- SMCo 94062 809-E5
BLALOCK ST
1000 MPS 95035 794-B5

BLANC CT
1100 PLE 94566 714-G4
BLANCA DR
- NVTO 94947 525-G4
BLANCHARD DR
17500 MSER 95030 873-A5
BLANCHARD LN
300 BEN 94510 551-B3
BLANCHARD ST
40100 FRMT 94538 753-C6
BLANCHARD WY
700 SUNV 94087 832-C4
BLANCHE LN
900 LFYT 94549 611-E6
BLANCHE ST
- SF 94114 667-G3
400 HAY 94544 732-F2
BLANCO CT
400 SRMN 94583 673-B3
BLANCO DR
4600 SJS 95129 853-A3
4700 SJS 95129 852-J3
BLANCO ST
400 AMCN 94589 510-A4
16300 AlaC 94578 691-F5
BLAND AV
100 CMBL 95008 853-D5
BLAND ST
24800 AlaC 94541 712-C2
BLANDFORD BLVD
800 RDWC 94062 769-H6
BLANDING AV
2100 SJS 95121 855-C3
2300 ALA 94501 670-A1
BLANDING CT
2900 AlaC 94541 692-C6
BLANDING LN
- BLV 94920 627-D2
BLANDON RD
3200 OAK 94605 671-A3
BLANDOR WY
10500 LAH 94024 831-D5
BLANDY ST
- SF 94124 668-E7
BLANEY AV
1000 SJS 95129 852-E4
N BLANEY AV
800 CPTO 95014 852-F2
10000 CPTO 95014 832-F6
BLANEY CT
10300 CPTO 95014 852-E1
BLANGE WY
- SJS 95134 813-G2
BLANKEN AV
- SF 94134 688-A2
BLARNEY AV
800 CNCD 94518 592-G6
BLARNEY CT
2600 CNCD 94518 592-G7
BLAUER CT
6200 SJS 95135 855-H6
BLAUER DR
20100 SAR 95070 852-E7
BLAUER LN
6200 SJS 95135 855-H6
BLAZINGWOOD AV
800 CPTO 95014 852-F2
BLAZINGWOOD DR
900 SUNV 94089 812-J5
BLAZINGWOOD WY
19700 CPTO 95014 852-F2
BLEACHER HOUSE RD
- CCCo 94553 571-F3
- MRTZ 94553 571-F3
BLEDSOE CT
- LAH 94022 831-B3
BLEMER CT
- DNVL 94526 633-B7
BLEMER PL
- DNVL 94526 633-C7
BLEMER RD
900 DNVL 94526 633-B7
BLENHEIM AV
2700 SMCo 94063 790-C1
BLENHEIM LN
3400 SJS 95121 855-D3
BLENHEIM ST
700 OAK 94603 670-H7
BLENHEIM WY
4300 CNCD 94521 593-A5
BLENHIEM LN
1200 CNCD 94521 593-A5
BLEWETT AV
1100 SJS 95125 854-A3
BLEWETT ST
4100 FRMT 94538 753-C6
BLINN CT
600 LALT 94024 811-G6
BLISS AV
- PIT 94565 574-D4
2100 MPS 95035 794-E7
BLISS CT
- ANT 94509 595-H2
- PLHL 94523 592-B3
200 WLCK 94598 612-G2
500 SJS 95136 874-F1
39600 FRMT 94538 753-A7
BLISS RD
- SF 94129 647-D4
BLITHEDALE AV
800 MLV 94941 606-F4
E BLITHEDALE AV
- MLV 94941 606-E3
W BLITHEDALE AV
- MLV 94941 606-C1
400 MLV 94941 586-C7
BLITHEDALE TER
- MLV 94941 606-D2
BLITHEDALE RDG RD
- LKSP 94939 586-C7
- MLV 94941 586-C7
- MrnC 94904 586-C7
BLITHEDALE RIDGE FIRE RD
- MrnC 94904 586-B6
- MrnC 94965 586-B6
BLOCHING CIR
700 CLAY 94517 613-J1
BLOCK DR
1100 SCL 95050 833-C4
BLOGETT LN
800 NVTO 94945 526-B3

INDEX

STREET
Block City ZIP Pg-Grid

BLOM DR
500 SJS 95111 875-B1
BLOMQUIST ST
300 RDWC 94063 770-C5
BLONDIN WY
400 SMCo 94080 707-G4
400 SSF 94080 707-G4
BLONDWOOD CT
4300 UNC 94587 732-A7
BLOOM LN
- MrnC 94947 525-H6
BLOOMFIELD DR
4200 SJS 95124 873-J3
BLOOMFIELD RD
- BURL 94010 728-G6
BLOOMINGTON CT
8600 DBLN 94568 693-F2
BLOOMINGTON WY
11300 DBLN 94568 693-E2
BLOOMSBURY WY
3600 SJS 95132 814-F2
BLOSSOM AV
5600 SJS 95123 874-H5
BLOSSOM CIR
100 SMTO 94403 749-D6
1200 LVMR 94550 716-B1
BLOSSOM COM
- AlaC 94541 691-G7
- AlaC 94541 711-G1
BLOSSOM CT
- DALY 94014 687-D5
100 DNVL 94506 653-F4
100 SRFL 94901 586-H3
600 PLE 94566 714-D6
2800 UNC 94587 752-F1
20600 AlaC 94541 711-F1
BLOSSOM DR
- MrnC 94901 586-H2
- SRFL 94901 586-H2
700 FRMT 94539 753-G6
800 SCL 95050 833-C5
1800 ANT 94509 575-F6
BLOSSOM LN
100 MTVW 94041 811-H5
800 AlaC 94541 691-G7
20500 CPTO 95014 852-D2
BLOSSOM ST
3000 OAK 94601 650-C6
BLOSSOM WK
- ALA 94501 669-G3
BLOSSOM WY
- AlaC 94541 711-F1
300 AlaC 94541 691-G7
500 SLN 94577 691-B2
5400 SJS 95123 875-B4
BLOSSOM ACRES DR
5400 SJS 95124 873-F6
BLOSSOM CREST WY
2100 SJS 95124 873-F6
BLOSSOM DALE DR
5400 SJS 95124 873-F6
BLOSSOM GARDENS CIR
5400 SJS 95123 875-A3
BLOSSOM GLEN WY
100 LGTS 95124 873-E5
100 SJS 95124 873-E5
100 LGTS 95032 873-E5
BLOSSOM HILL RD Rt#-G10
- LGTS 95030 873-C6
- SJS 95123 874-E4
100 SJS 95111 875-A4
200 SJS 95138 875-A4
400 LGTS 95032 873-C6
400 SCIC 95123 874-E4
700 SJS 95123 875-A4
1000 SJS 95193 875-A4
1400 SJS 95124 874-A6
1400 SJS 95124 873-F6
1600 SJS 95118 874-A6
15800 SCIC 95032 873-C6
BLOSSOM PARK LN
5600 SJS 95124 874-A6
5600 SJS 95118 874-A6
BLOSSOM RIVER DR
1000 SJS 95123 874-D4
BLOSSOM RIVER WY
1000 SJS 95123 874-D4
BLOSSOM TERRACE CT
5400 SJS 95124 873-F6
BLOSSOM TREE LN
5400 SJS 95124 873-F6
BLOSSOM VALLEY DR
200 LGTS 95032 873-E5
200 SJS 95124 873-E5
300 LGTS 95124 873-E5
BLOSSOMVIEW DR
3500 SJS 95118 874-B1
BLOSSOM VILLA WY
200 SJS 95124 873-F6
200 LGTS 95032 873-F6
BLOSSOM VISTA AV
5400 SJS 95124 873-F6
BLOSSOM WOOD DR
5400 SJS 95124 873-E6
BLUEBELL AV
2200 SJS 95122 854-J1
BLUEBELL CIR
2700 ANT 94509 575-H7
BLUEBELL CT
- NWK 94560 772-H1
- MLBR 94030 728-A3
1500 LVMR 94550 696-B3
BLUEBELL DR
900 LVMR 94550 696-A2
BLUEBELL LN
- HIL 94010 748-F5
BLUEBELL PL
100 VAL 94591 550-F1
BLUEBELL WY
900 SUNV 94086 832-G1
7600 DBLN 94568 693-G2
BLUE BELLE LN
- SCAR 94070 769-C4
BLUEBERRY CT
4400 CNCD 94521 593-B5
BLUEBERRY TER
500 SJS 95129 853-B2
BLUEBERRY HILL
100 LGTS 95032 873-D7
BLUEBIRD AV
100 LVMR 94550 715-E1
1000 SCL 95051 832-H5
BLUE BIRD CT
5800 AlaC 94552 692-E2
BLUEBIRD CT
100 HER 94547 569-H5
100 VAL 94591 530-E3
1300 SUNV 94087 832-E4
32800 FRMT 94555 732-B7
BLUEBIRD DR
- HER 94547 569-J5
- HER 94547 570-A5
3100 SJS 95117 853-D4
BLUEBIRD LN
- MrnC 94920 606-H3
BLUEBIRD LP
32800 FRMT 94555 732-B7
BLUEBONNET CT
2900 ANT 94509 575-H7
BLUEBONNET DR
900 SUNV 94086 832-G1
BLUE BONNET PL
400 HAY 94544 711-J5
BLUE CANYON CT
100 MRTZ 94553 591-G1
BLUE CANYON WY
100 MRTZ 94553 591-G1
BLUE CORAL TER
- FRMT 94536 753-C2
BLUE CREEK CT
3200 SJS 95135 855-E2
BLUECURL CT
2800 ANT 94509 575-H7
BLUE DOLPHIN DR
3600 SJS 95136 854-G7
BLUEFIELD CT
500 SJS 95136 874-F1
BLUEFIELD DR
200 SJS 95136 874-G1
BLUEFIELD LN
500 HAY 94541 711-F4
BLUE FIN WY
39300 FRMT 94538 752-J7
BLUEFISH CT
300 FCTY 94404 749-H2
BLUEFLOWER TER
- FRMT 94536 752-B7
BLUE FOX WY
7400 SRMN 94583 693-G1
BLUEGILL ST
- FRMT 94536 753-B3
BLUEGRASS CT
38800 NWK 94560 772-H1
BLUEGRASS LN
5600 SJS 95118 874-B5
BLUEGRASS WY
- SRMN 94583 653-H7
BLUE GUM CT
- PLHL 94523 591-H2
15100 SAR 95070 872-G4
BLUE GUM DR
3900 SCIC 95127 835-B1
BLUE HAVEN CT
- CCCo 94506 654-B4
BLUE HILL DR
6900 SJS 95129 852-E3
BLUE HILLS DR
21200 SCIC 95070 852-C5
21300 SAR 95070 852-C5
BLUEJACKET WY
2000 SJS 95133 814-E7
BLUE JAY CIR
2100 PIN 94564 569-F7
BLUE JAY CT
1200 CNCD 94521 593-B4
BLUEJAY CT
700 EPA 94303 791-B1
BLUE JAY DR
500 HAY 94544 712-D7
900 SCIC 95125 854-C6
900 SJS 95125 854-C6
BLUEJAY DR
100 HER 94547 569-J5
1600 SUNV 94087 832-E6
3300 ANT 94509 575-F7
3300 ANT 94509 595-F1
10900 CPTO 95014 832-E6
BLUE JAY WY
- SMCo 94062 789-A7
BLUE LAGOON DR
2300 SCL 95054 813-C5
BLUE LAKE DR
1100 CNCD 94521 593-F7
BLUE MEADOWS CT
12400 SAR 95070 852-E5
BLUE MIST PL
1000 SJS 95120 894-F2
BLUE MOUND CT
200 SRMN 94583 673-H6
BLUE MOUND DR
9600 SRMN 94583 673-H6
BLUE MOUNTAIN CT
1900 ANT 94509 595-F5
BLUE MOUNTAIN DR
3200 SJS 95127 835-B4
BLUE OAK CT
- NVTO 94949 546-C1
1300 PIN 94564 569-E5
2000 CCCo 94506 653-G1
2700 SJS 95148 835-E6
BLUE OAK LN
300 CLAY 94517 593-G6
300 SCIC 94306 811-D5
BLUERIDGE AV
2300 MLPK 94025 790-D7
BLUE RIDGE DR
100 MRTZ 94553 591-G4
4600 SJS 95129 853-A4
4700 SJS 95129 852-J4
BLUERIDGE DR
2000 MPS 95035 814-E1
BLUE RIDGE LN
- WDSD 94062 809-G2
BLUE RIDGE RD
- MrnC 94904 586-C5
BLUE RIDGE ST
4200 FRMT 94536 752-G3
BLUERING CT
6000 SJS 95120 874-B7
BLUEROCK CIR
2100 CNCD 94521 593-G3
BLUE ROCK CT
- CMAD 94925 586-G6
- DNVL 94526 653-E3
2500 SJS 95133 834-F1
BLUEROCK CT
300 ANT 94509 595-E2
BLUEROCK DR
200 ANT 94509 595-E2
BLUE SAGE DR
700 SUNV 94086 832-F1
BLUE SKY CT
5200 ANT 94509 595-J5
BLUE SPRUCE CT
1700 MPS 95035 814-A4
BLUE SPRUCE DR
600 CCCo 94506 654-A3
BLUE SPRUCE WY
1700 MPS 95035 813-J3
BLUESTONE COM
34500 FRMT 94555 752-B2
BLUESTONE CT
2500 SJS 95122 835-A5
BLUEWATER CT
3000 SJS 95148 835-B5
BLUE WHALE ST
- SLN 94577 690-G5
BLUEWOOD CIR
1900 SJS 95132 814-F3
BLUEWOOD CT
1700 CNCD 94521 593-D3
BLUFF CT
- SJS 95135 875-J1
- HER 94547 569-H3
BLUFFWOOD CT
6800 SJS 95120 894-H2
BLUM RD
- MRTZ 94553 572-B6
4400 CCCo 94553 572-B6
BLUME DR
3200 RCH 94806 589-B1
3200 RCH 94806 569-B7
3400 CCCo 94806 569-B7
BLUMERT PL
- MRGA 94556 631-F2
BLUXOME ST
- SF 94107 648-B7
BLYTH ST
- VAL 94591 530-G5
BLYTHDALE AV
- SF 94134 687-H2
BLYTHE AV
600 SUNV 94086 812-G5
BLYTHE CT
600 SUNV 94086 812-G5
19900 SAR 95070 852-F6
BLYTHE DR
3200 ANT 94509 595-C1
BLYTHE ST
1100 FCTY 94404 749-G4
4800 UNC 94587 752-A1
BLYTHEN WY
- AlaC - 650-J4
- OAK 94619 651-A4
- OAK 94619 650-J4
BLYTHSWOOD DR
18500 SCIC 95030 872-H5
18600 MSER 95030 872-H5
BOAR CIR
100 FRMT 94539 773-J3
BOARDMAN PL
- SF 94103 648-A7
BOARDWALK
- SRMN 94583 673-B2
BOARDWALK CT
100 SBRN 94066 707-G6
BOARDWALK DR
100 SBRN 94066 707-G6
BOARDWALK PL
- RCH 94806 588-F1
100 SBRN 94066 707-G6
700 RDWC 94065 749-H6
BOARDWALK ST
3000 PLE 94588 694-G6
BOARDWALK WY
- RDWC 94065 749-H6
100 HAY 94544 732-C1
BOARDWALK NUMBER 1
- LKSP 94939 586-F5
BOAT RAMP ST
- RCH 94804 608-E1
BOATSWAIN CT
300 HER 94547 570-B6
BOATWRIGHT DR
3900 CNCD 94519 593-A2
BOA VISTA DR
1200 SJS 95122 854-H1
BOBBIE AV
5000 SJS 95130 852-J6
BOBBIE CT
- DNVL 94526 653-B1
BOBBIE DR
400 DNVL 94526 653-A1
BOBBY DR
5500 LVMR 94550 696-C4
BOBBYWOOD AV
5400 SJS 95124 873-H5
BOBO CT
1400 PIT 94565 574-G4
BOBOLINK CIR
500 SUNV 94087 832-E4
BOBOLINK CT
1700 HAY 94545 731-J2
BOBOLINK DR
2500 SJS 95125 854-D6
BOBOLINK RD
- ORIN 94563 610-F5
BOBOLINK WY
100 HER 94547 569-H4
BOBSTAY LN
600 FCTY 94404 749-J1
BOBWHITE AV
1300 SUNV 94087 832-E4
BOB WHITE PL
1400 SJS 95131 814-D7
BOBWHITE RD
1700 LVMR 94550 715-H3
BOBWHITE TER
3600 FRMT 94555 732-D7
BOCA CANADA RD
1800 CCCo 94553 590-H4
BOCANA ST
- SF 94110 667-J5
BOCA RATON CT
- SRMN 94583 673-H7
300 WLCK 94598 612-J2
26800 HAY 94545 711-H6
BOCA RATON ST
1800 HAY 94545 711-G7
BOCKMAN RD
600 AlaC 94580 711-B1
BOCMART PL
3700 SRMN 94583 673-C2
BODEGA AV
1500 LVMR 94550 715-G3
BODEGA CT
- FRMT 94539 773-J4
1600 WLCK 94596 611-J2
2100 PIT 94565 574-B3
BODEGA DR
1100 SUNV 94086 812-C6
2100 PIT 94565 574-B3
BODEGA PL
1300 WLCK 94596 611-J2
BODEGA ST
- VAL 94591 550-E2
300 FCTY 94404 749-F5
29200 AlaC 94544 712-D6
29200 HAY 94544 712-D6
BODEGA WY
- SLN 94577 690-G5
300 SJS 95119 875-C7
800 CCCo 94572 569-J2
800 CCCo 94572 570-A2
BODEN WY
500 OAK 94610 649-J3
BODIE CT
5600 SJS 95123 875-A4
BODIE TER
46900 FRMT 94539 773-F6
BODILY AV
36800 FRMT 94536 753-A1
BODKIN TER
34300 FRMT 94555 752-C2
BODMIN AV
1000 SLN 94579 691-B5
BODSWORTH RD
- MrnC 94965 626-F6
BOEGER LN
3500 SJS 95148 835-D5
BOEHMER ST
3600 OAK 94601 670-C1
BOEING CT
5100 NWK 94560 752-E4
BOEING ST
8100 OAK 94621 670-D7
BOGALUSA CT
600 FRMT 94539 793-J2
BOGEY LN
- NVTO 94949 546-C2
BOGGS AV
800 FRMT 94539 773-G5
BOGGS CT
100 VAL 94589 509-J5
BOGGS TER
800 FRMT 94539 773-G5
BOHANNON DR
1900 SCL 95050 833-D6
3800 MLPK 94025 770-G7
BOHLMAN RD
14700 SAR 95070 872-C4
16400 SCIC 95070 872-C5
BOIES CT
- PLHL 94523 592-A3
BOIES DR
2900 PLHL 94523 592-A4
BOISE CT
600 SUNV 94087 832-D4
BOISE DR
3900 CMBL 95008 853-B5
3900 SJS 95130 853-B5
BOISE ST
3200 BERK 94702 629-F4
BOITANO DR
44100 FRMT 94539 773-H2
BOLADO DR
6900 SJS 95119 875-E7
BOLANOS DR
- SRFL 94903 566-B2
BOLBONES CT
1900 WLCK 94595 632-B1
BOLD CT
600 SJS 95111 875-B1
BOLD DR
600 SJS 95111 875-B1
BOLDUC CT
100 CCCo 94806 589-B3
BOLERO AV
2000 HAY 94545 711-H7
BOLERO CT
- DNVL 94526 653-C5
700 NVTO 94945 526-H1
3000 PLE 94588 694-D6
BOLERO DR
300 DNVL 94526 653-C5
4500 SJS 95111 855-A7
4500 SJS 95111 875-A1
BOLERO PZ
100 UNC 94587 732-J5
BOLERO WY
- DALY 94014 687-G3
BOLES CT
4700 FRMT 94538 753-B7
BOLGER PL
- CCCo 94565 573-C1
BOLINA DR
4200 UNC 94587 731-J5
BOLINA TER
36900 FRMT 94536 752-G4
BOLINAS AV
- SANS 94960 586-B1
- ROSS 94957 586-B1
BOLINAS ST
- MrnC 94941 606-G6
BOLINGER COM
400 FRMT 94539 773-H6
BOLINGER TER
300 FRMT 94539 773-H6
BOLIVAR DR
- BERK 94804 629-D2
600 SJS 95123 874-G5
W BOLIVAR DR
- BERK 94804 629-D2
BOLIVAR LN
100 PTLV 94028 810-D5
BOLIVAR PL
800 SRMN 94583 673-G5
4400 UNC 94587 731-H6
BOLLA AV
- CCCo 94507 632-G4
BOLLA CT
3200 PLE 94566 715-C6
BOLLA PL
400 CCCo 94507 632-H4
BOLLING DR
100 NVTO 94949 546-G4
BOLLINGER RD
5800 SJS 95014 852-D2
5800 SCIC 95014 852-G2
6000 CPTO 95014 852-D2
6400 SJS 95129 852-D2
BOLLINGER CANYON LN
500 SRMN 94583 673-F2
BOLLINGER CANYON RD
- CCCo - 632-A7
- CCCo - 672-J1
900 MRGA 94556 631-H6
1100 CCCo - 631-H6
1100 CCCo - 652-A1
1500 SRMN 94583 673-A2
18000 CCCo 94583 673-A1
18400 CCCo - 673-A1
18400 SRMN - 673-A1
BOLLINGER CANYON WY
600 SRMN 94583 673-F2
BOLLINGER ESTATES CT
- CCCo - 652-F4
BOLSA AV
- MLV 94941 606-D2
BOLSENA ST
3300 SJS 95135 855-F6
BOLTON CIR
800 BEN 94510 530-H7
BOLTON CT
- CCCo 94506 654-B5
600 SJS 95129 853-A2
BOLTON DR
800 MPS 95035 794-A2
BOLTON PL
- MLPK 94025 790-F5
BOLTON WY
100 VAL 94591 530-G4
BONA ST
2700 OAK 94601 650-C5
BONACCORSO PL
600 SJS 95133 814-G7
BONAIR
200 SCIC 94305 790-J7
BONAIR CT
3400 SJS 95117 853-D3
BON AIR RD
- LKSP 94939 586-E5
100 MrnC 94904 586-E5
BONAIRE AV
100 HER 94547 570-C6
BONAIRE CT
300 DNVL 94506 653-J5
BONANZA CT
600 SUNV 94087 832-D4
BONANZA ST
1500 WLCK 94596 612-C5
BONANZA WY
300 DNVL 94526 652-J3
BONAR ST
2000 BERK 94702 629-E2
BONARI CT
3500 CNCD 94519 592-J2
BONAVENTURA DR
2600 SJS 95134 813-G6
BONBON DR
2600 SJS 95148 835-C7
BONCHEFF DR
2700 SJS 95133 814-G7
BOND CT
100 LGTS 95032 893-C1
1100 ANT 94509 575-F6
BOND LN
- TBRN 94920 607-B2
BOND ST
- LKSP 94939 586-E5
800 SCL 95051 832-J6
4200 OAK 94601 670-D1
12200 AlaC 94586 734-C6
BOND WY
700 MTVW 94040 831-H1
BONDE CT
700 PLE 94566 714-F4
BONDE WY
3700 FRMT 94536 752-H3
BONESO CIR
4100 SJS 95134 813-G2
BONFACIO ST
2600 CNCD 94519 572-G7
2600 CNCD 94519 592-G1
BONFIELD CT
7500 DBLN 94568 693-H2
BONGATE CT
1400 SJS 95130 853-A4
BONHAM WY
400 OAK 94610 650-A2
BON HOMME WY
3600 CNCD 94518 592-H3
BONIFACIO ST
- SF 94107 648-B6
1900 CNCD 94520 592-F1
2600 CNCD 94519 592-G1
BONITA
- MTVW 94043 811-J2
BONITA AV
- PDMT 94611 630-B7
- RDWC 94061 790-B1
100 PCFA 94044 727-B2
100 PDMT 94611 650-B1
200 SJS 95116 834-F5
200 SSF 94080 707-F2
400 PLE 94566 714-F4
600 MLBR 94030 727-J2
900 MTVW 94040 811-H7
1200 BERK 94709 609-G7
1600 BERK 94709 629-G1
1900 BERK 94704 629-G1
2700 ANT 94509 575-E7
BONITA AV
3400 SCL 95051 832-J2
BONITA CT
- CCCo 94595 612-B6
100 CCCo 94572 569-J2
500 VAL 94591 530-D6
3400 SCL 95051 832-J2
6300 RCH 94806 589-B3
BONITA LN
- ORIN 94563 610-F7
100 FCTY 94404 749-H3
1200 CCCo 94595 612-B6
1200 WLCK 94595 612-B6
BONITA PL
- CCCo 94572 569-J2
BONITA RD
100 SMCo 94028 830-D4
1400 RCH 94806 589-B3
1500 CCCo 94806 589-B3
BONITA ST
- SAUS 94965 627-A3
- SF 94109 647-H4
BONITA WY
31200 UNC 94587 731-J5
BONITA BAHIA
1300 BEN 94510 550-J3
BONITO DR
36600 FRMT 94536 752-F4
BONNER AV
- FRMT 94538 753-B3
1000 FRMT 94536 753-B3
BONNET CT
1300 SJS 95132 814-F5
BONNET WY
13400 SAR 95070 852-G7
13500 SAR 95070 872-H1
BONNEVILLE WY
900 SUNV 94087 832-B4
BONNEY ST
100 MTVW 94043 811-G4
BONNIE CT
- PLHL 94523 612-A1
1400 RDWC 94061 790-A2
BONNIE DR
100 CCCo 94806 569-A5
400 ELCR 94530 609-E3
2500 SCL 95051 833-B2
BONNIE LN
- BERK 94708 609-H5
- PCFA 94044 706-J3
100 DNVL 94526 653-B2
2900 PLHL 94523 612-A1
16300 LGTS 95032 873-D7
BONNIE PL
- PLHL 94523 612-A1
BONNIE ST
400 DALY 94014 687-D4
36500 NWK 94560 752-E6
BONNIE WY
38800 FRMT 94536 752-J6
BONNIE BANKS WY
- SRFL 94901 587-B1
- SRFL 94901 567-B7
- MrnC 94901 567-B7
BONNIE BRAE DR
- NVTO 94949 546-C2
- SRFL 94901 566-F7
BONNIE BRAE LN
- SF 94132 666-J6
20100 SAR 95070 872-E4
BONNIE BRAE WY
20000 SAR 95070 872-E3
BONNIE CLARE LN
900 CNCD 94518 592-G4
BONNIE JOY AV
1500 SJS 95129 852-F4
BONNIE RIDGE WY
19700 SAR 95070 852-F7
BONNIE VISTA AV
800 SLN 94577 671-A7
BONNIEWOOD CT
7700 DBLN 94568 693-G2
BONNIEWOOD LN
7500 DBLN 94568 693-H2
BONNINGTON CT
- OAK 94611 630-E5
BONNY DR
10100 CPTO 95014 852-D2
BONNY DOONE
- HER 94547 569-G4
BONRAVEN WY
5000 ANT 94509 595-J2
BONSAI PL
3900 AlaC 94546 692-A4
BONSEN CT
100 SMCo 94062 790-A4
BONT LN
1100 WLCK 94596 612-B6
BONVIEW ST
- SF 94110 667-J5
BON VISTA CT
10000 SCIC 95127 815-C7
10000 SCIC 95127 835-D1
BONWELL DR
5000 CNCD 94521 593-D4
BOOK LN
2100 SCL 95054 813-C4
BOOKER AV
- SAUS 94965 627-A3
300 SUNV 94086 812-D7
BOOKER ST
2500 OAK 94606 650-A4
BOOKER WY
25700 HAY 94544 711-H5
BOOKSIN AV
1800 SJS 95125 853-J6
2100 SJS 95125 854-A6
2800 SJS 95125 874-A1
BOONE CT
100 DNVL 94526 653-A3
BOONE DR
1500 SJS 95118 874-A4
4600 FRMT 94538 753-A7
6100 AlaC 94552 692-E3
BOONEWOOD CT
700 SJS 95120 894-J2
BOOTHBAY AV
100 FCTY 94404 749-E6
BOOTJACK TR
- MrnC 94965 606-A3
BORA PL
- PIT 94565 574-A2
BORA BORA AV
4200 FRMT 94538 773-D1
BORANDA AV
900 MTVW 94040 811-H6
BORAX DR
2400 SCL 95051 833-A1
BORCHERS DR
1900 SJS 95124 873-G1
BORDEAUX CT
- DNVL 94506 653-G5
BORDEAUX DR
1100 SUNV 94089 812-F3
BORDEAUX LN
- SJS 95127 834-C2
BORDEAUX PL
3400 PLE 94566 714-G4
BORDEAUX ST
1100 LVMR 94550 715-G3
1100 PLE 94566 714-G4
BORDELAIS DR
1400 SJS 95118 874-A6
BORDEN DR
3700 SCIC 95148 835-G7
BORDEN ST
1600 SMTO 94403 749-C2
BORDENRAE CT
700 SJS 95117 853-D2
BORDER RD
1000 SCIC 94024 831-F2
BORDER HILL DR
12600 SCIC 94024 831-F2
BORDWELL CT
- ALA 94502 669-J6
- SJS 95118 874-B3
BORDWELL DR
4700 SJS 95118 874-B3
BOREL AV
- SMTO 94402 749-A4
400 SMTO 94402 748-J4
BOREL LN
2000 DNVL 94526 653-C7
BOREL PL
- SMTO 94402 749-A4
BORELLO DR
2400 SJS 95128 853-F4
BORELLO WY
700 MTVW 94041 812-A7
BOREN DR
2400 SJS 95121 854-H2
BORGE CT
3400 SJS 95132 814-G4
BORGES CT
- NVTO 94947 526-A4
BORGES LN
100 VAL 94589 510-C5
BORGIA RD
5100 FRMT 94538 773-B2
BORGWOOD CT
800 SJS 95120 894-H4
BORICA DR
300 DNVL 94526 653-D5
BORICA PL
200 DNVL 94526 653-D5
BORICA ST
- SF 94127 667-C7
- SF 94132 687-C1
BORINA DR
4200 SJS 95129 853-A2
4600 SJS 95129 852-J2
BORIS CT
- WLCK 94596 612-B1
BORMIO CT
- DNVL 94506 653-D1
BORNEO CIR
5200 SJS 95123 874-J3
BOROUGHWOOD PL
- HIL 94010 748-E3
BORREGAS AV
500 SUNV 94086 812-F5
900 SUNV 94089 812-F3
BOSCELL COM
5500 FRMT 94538 773-B3
BOSCELL RD
41000 FRMT 94538 773-A3
BOSE CT
6500 SJS 95120 894-D1
BOSE LN
6300 SJS 95120 894-D1
6600 SJS 95120 874-D7
BOSTON AV
- SJS 95128 853-G1
- SCIC 95128 853-G1
- SCIC 95128 833-G7
1600 SMTO 94403 749-D2
3100 OAK 94602 650-D5
BOSTON CT
43900 FRMT 94539 773-H1
BOSTON RD
17100 AlaC 94541 691-F7
BOSTON POST CT
6500 SJS 95120 894-E1
BOSUN LN
- RDWC 94065 750-C4
BOSWALL CT
3200 SJS 95121 855-C3
BOSWELL TER
3700 FRMT 94536 752-J4
BOSWORTH CT
4900 NWK 94560 752-D3
36500 FRMT 94536 752-G3
BOSWORTH ST
- SF 94112 667-G6
500 SF 94131 667-G6
BOSWORTH WK
- PLHL 94523 591-B1
BOTANY CT
- RDWC 94062 789-G2
- SMCo 94062 789-G2
500 FCTY 94404 749-F5
BOTANY GRN
38400 FRMT 94536 753-B3
BOTELHO DR
1500 WLCK 94596 612-C6
BOTELHO ST
1200 ANT 94509 575-F5
BOTHELL CIR
6200 SJS 95123 875-A7
BOTHELO AV
100 MPS 95035 794-A7
BOTTINI CT
- PLE 94566 715-C6

STREET Block City ZIP Pg-Grid
BOTTLE BRUSH CT
36500 NWK 94560 752-D7
BOTTLEBRUSH CT
- DNVL 94506 654-B5
BOTTLE BRUSH LN
1300 SJS 95118 874-B5
BOTTLE BRUSH PL
24300 AlaC 94541 712-C1
BOUCHARD DR
1400 SJS 95118 874-A6
BOUGAINVILLEA CT
14600 SAR 95070 872-C3
BOUGAINVILLEA DR
5000 SJS 95111 875-A2
BOULDER BLVD
- SJS 95193 875-C4
BOULDER CT
5200 CNCD 94521 593-G4
BOULDER DR
200 ANT 94509 595-E1
300 VAL 94589 510-B5
700 SJS 95132 815-A4
BOULDER LN
- SANS 94960 566-C7
BOULDER ST
200 MPS 95035 794-A3
3400 PLE 94566 714-F2
BOULDER CANYON CT
- AlaC 94552 692-E6
BOULDER CANYON DR
- AlaC 94542 692-D6
- AlaC 94552 692-E6
BOULDER CREEK CT
- DNVL 94526 653-E4
2200 MRTZ 94553 572-B2
BOULDER CREEK DR
1100 HAY 94544 732-A1
BOULDER MTN WY
6500 SJS 95120 874-F7
BOULEVARD CIR
2300 WLCK 94595 612-B6
BOULEVARD CT
- CCCo 94595 612-A7
- NVTO 94947 526-A3
14800 AlaC 94578 691-D3
BOULEVARD TER
- NVTO 94947 526-A4
BOULEVARD WY
400 OAK 94610 650-A2
400 PDMT 94610 650-A2
1000 CCCo 94595 612-A6
1400 WLCK 94595 612-A6
BOUNDARY OAK WY
400 WLCK 94598 613-A2
BOUNTIFUL CT
100 DNVL 94526 633-D6
BOUNTIFUL ACRES WY
19100 SAR 95070 872-G5
BOUNTY DR
500 FCTY 94404 749-G3
600 CCCo 94565 573-D1
BOUNTY LN
- VAL 94590 550-B1
BOUNTY WY
- CCCo 94565 573-D1
BOURBON CT
800 MTVW 94041 812-A7
2300 SSF 94080 707-D5
BOURBON DR
2100 HAY 94545 731-H2
BOURET DR
1200 SJS 95118 874-B3
BOURGEOIS WY
3100 SJS 95111 854-H5
BOURNE CT
- CCCo 94506 654-B4
BOURNE LN
- CCCo 94506 654-B4
BOURNEMOUTH CT
3500 SJS 95136 874-D1
BOURNEMOUTH DR
3500 SJS 95136 874-D1
BOURTON CT
800 ANT 94509 575-C7
BOUTWELL ST
- SF 94124 668-A6
BOUVERON CT
2800 SJS 95148 855-D2
BOUWINA CT
1100 CNCD 94518 592-J4
BOVET RD
- SMTO 94402 749-A4
BOVIN WY
- LKSP 94939 586-D6
BOW WY
- PTLV 94028 810-B6
BOWDITCH ST
2300 BERK 94704 629-J2
BOWDOIN ST
- SF 94134 667-J6
600 SF 94134 688-A1
700 SCIC 94305 790-H7
900 SCIC 94305 810-J1
2000 PA 94306 810-J1
2200 PA 94306 811-A1
BOWE AV
1400 SCL 95051 833-B4
BOWEN AV
800 SJS 95123 874-E5
BOWEN CT
5900 SJS 95123 874-E5
BOWEN ST
4400 PLE 94588 694-E7
BOWER CT
800 LVMR 94550 715-J1
BOWER LN
- DBLN 94568 693-E5
BOWER PL
- DNVL 94526 653-A4
BOWER RD
800 PCFA 94044 726-H5
BOWERS AV
1700 SCL 95051 833-B2
2900 SCL 95051 813-B7
3000 SCL 95054 813-B7
BOWERS CT
44100 FRMT 94539 773-H2
BOWFIN ST
300 FCTY 94404 749-H3
BOWHILL CT
20900 SAR 95070 852-C5
BOWHILL LN
2700 CCCo 94806 588-J3
2700 CCCo 94806 589-A2
BOWHILL RD
- HAY 94544 732-B1
700 HIL 94010 748-G3
BOWIE COM
34700 FRMT 94555 752-D2
BOWIE WY
6600 AlaC 94552 692-F2
BOWLES PL
- OAK 94610 650-C3
BOWLEY ST
- SF 94129 647-B5
BOWLIN AV
2800 SRMN 94583 673-E6
BOWLING DR
- OAK 94618 630-A5
BOWLING LN
1600 SJS 95118 873-J4
BOWLING GREEN
100 SLN 94577 670-J7
BOWLING GREEN CT
3100 WLCK 94598 612-J4
BOWLING GREEN DR
- SF - 667-D1
1600 SJS 95121 855-A2
2800 WLCK 94598 612-J3
BOWLINGREEN COM
34100 FRMT 94555 752-E1
BOWMAN CT
- SF 94124 668-C5
3500 ALA 94502 670-A7
BOWMAN DR
100 VAL 94591 530-D4
BOWMAN PL
- HAY 94544 732-E3
BOWMAN RD
- SF 94129 647-B3
BOWMORE CT
3300 WLCK 94598 612-J2
BOWSPRIT DR
300 RDWC 94065 749-H7
BOWSPRIT LN
100 FCTY 94404 749-G6
BOX CANYON RD
1300 SJS 95120 894-D3
2600 PIN 94564 569-H6
BOXER BLVD
4800 CNCD 94521 593-C4
BOXER CT
1900 AlaC 94580 711-B1
BOXFORD PL
- SRMN 94583 673-F7
BOXLEAF CT
400 SJS 95117 853-C1
BOXSTEAD COM
3900 FRMT 94555 752-D1
BOXWOOD AV
1400 SLN 94579 691-A5
BOXWOOD CT
- PIT - 573-F4
3700 CNCD 94519 573-F4
3700 CNCD 94519 593-A1
BOXWOOD DR
1800 CNCD 94519 593-A1
1800 CNCD 94519 573-A7
2200 SJS 95128 833-E6
2400 SCL 95128 833-E6
BOXWOOD WY
- DBLN 94568 694-D4
2000 FRMT 94539 773-G3
BOYCE AV
800 PA 94301 791-A4
BOYCE LN
20700 SAR 95070 872-C1
BOYCE RD
- FRMT 94538 772-J2
41500 FRMT 94538 773-A3
BOYD AV
700 RCH 94805 589-A5
4500 OAK 94618 629-J6
BOYD CT
- PLHL 94523 592-A6
6000 SJS 95123 875-A6
BOYD RD
- PLHL 94523 592-A6
W BOYD RD
700 PLHL 94523 592-A6
700 PLHL 94523 591-J6
BOYD ST
200 MPS 95035 794-A3
BOYER CIR
3500 LFYT 94549 611-E7
BOYER ST
5300 OAK 94608 629-F6
BOYLE CT
1500 PIN 94564 569-D5
BOYLE DR
4100 FRMT 94536 752-F2
BOYLSTON ST
- SF 94134 667-J6
BOYNTON AV
300 SJS 95117 853-C1
400 BERK 94707 609-G4
400 CCCo 94707 609-G4
1900 MRTZ 94553 571-E3
BOYSEA DR
1400 SJS 95118 874-B2
BOYSEN ST
100 VAL 94590 529-J3
BOYSOL CT
3500 SJS 95132 814-F2
BOYTON CT
- SF 94114 667-G1
BRABO TER
200 MrnC 94941 606-E5
BRACCIANO CT
3200 SJS 95135 855-F6
BRACE AV
1100 SJS 95125 854-A4
BRACEBRIDGE CT
1100 CMBL 95008 873-B2
BRACH WY
3600 SCL 95051 832-H4
BRACKEN CT
- SRFL 94901 567-C5
BRACKETT AV
2800 SJS 95148 835-D7
BRACKMAN LN
500 MRTZ 94553 571-E7
BRADBURY DR
500 LFYT 94549 631-J4
2900 SJS 95122 855-B3
BRADBURY LN
200 RDWC 94061 790-B2
BRADCLIFF CT
- SRFL 94901 566-H6
BRADDALE AV
1400 LALT 94024 831-J3
BRADDOCK CT
1600 SJS 95125 853-G5
BRADEN CT
3300 SJS 95148 835-E7
BRADENA LN
3100 LFYT 94549 611-J6
BRADFORD AV
2400 HAY 94545 711-F6
BRADFORD CT
900 BEN 94510 530-H7
BRADFORD DR
- SSF 94080 707-D1
100 SUNV 94089 812-F4
500 RCH 94806 568-G6
BRADFORD PL
500 DNVL 94526 652-H1
BRADFORD ST
- SF 94110 668-A5
200 RDWC 94063 770-A5
500 CCCo 94565 573-F1
BRADFORD WY
- MLV 94941 606-D2
700 PCFA 94044 707-A7
700 UNC 94587 732-G5
700 PCFA 94044 727-A1
900 BEN 94510 530-H7
1700 SJS 95124 873-H2
BRADHOFF AV
1900 SLN 94577 691-B1
BRADLEY AV
- WLCK 94596 612-D4
300 SCIC 95128 853-F1
300 SJS 95128 853-F1
700 NVTO 94947 526-A4
BRADLEY CT
- SMCo 94061 790-B4
1400 SMTO 94401 729-B7
46500 FRMT 94539 773-H5
BRADLEY DR
900 SMCo 94015 687-A5
900 DALY 94015 687-A5
4900 PLE 94588 694-A6
BRADLEY LN
- ANT 94509 574-J6
BRADLEY ST
14300 SLN 94579 691-A4
46600 FRMT 94539 773-H6
BRADLEY WY
1000 EPA 94303 791-A1
BRADRICK DR
400 SLN 94578 691-C5
BRADSHAW DR
3000 SJS 95148 855-D1
BRADSHAW TER
- RDWC 94062 789-G1
BRADSHIRE RD
28200 HAY 94545 731-H1
BRADWELL CT
100 SJS 95138 875-E4
BRADY CT
600 MRTZ 94553 571-G5
2600 SCL 95051 833-B3
BRADY PL
- MLPK 94025 790-H2
BRADY ST
- SF 94103 667-H1
600 MRTZ 94553 571-G5
BRAEBRIDGE RD
1300 SJS 95131 814-D7
BRAE BURN AV
30500 HAY 94544 732-D2
BRAEBURN CT
- SRMN 94583 693-H1
3900 SJS 95130 853-B4
BRAEMAR CT
19500 SAR 95070 852-F7
BRAEMAR DR
- HIL 94010 748-F5
19500 SAR 95070 852-F7
19500 SAR 95070 872-F1
BRAEMAR RD
2000 OAK 94602 650-E2
BRAEMAR ST
4500 ANT 94509 595-J2
BRAEMER CT
100 BEN 94510 551-B3
1100 SJS 95132 814-F5
BRAGA LN
2600 SPAB 94806 588-J3
BRAGA ST
- FRMT 94538 773-F7
BRAGATO RD
400 SMCo 94002 769-F1
BRAHMS AV
2500 SJS 95122 855-A1
BRAHMS CT
1900 SJS 95122 855-A1
BRAHMS WY
100 SUNV 94087 832-E2
BRAIDBURN AV
7200 NWK 94560 752-B6
BRALY AV
1500 MPS 95035 794-D6
BRAMBLE CT
300 FCTY 94404 749-H3
700 WLCK 94598 613-C4
2300 AlaC 94546 691-H5
BRAMBLEWOOD CT
- DNVL 94506 653-E4
BRAMBLEWOOD LN
100 PLHL 94523 591-H2
BRAMPTON CT
2100 WLCK 94598 612-G2
BRAMPTON RD
2200 WLCK 94598 612-G2
BRANBURY DR
100 CMBL 95008 853-C5
BRANBURY WY
900 SJS 95133 834-E1
1000 SJS 95133 814-E7
BRANCH AV
- LKSP 94939 586-F7
BRANCHWOOD CT
2400 RCH 94806 568-J7
BRANCIFORTE ST
500 VAL 94590 529-J4
BRANDEIS CT
2900 SJS 95148 855-D4
BRANDERMILL CT
700 SJS 95138 875-G5
BRANDIN CT
5000 FRMT 94538 773-C4
BRANDON CT
- DALY 94014 687-J4
- HIL 94402 748-H5
300 PLHL 94523 592-A6
BRANDON PL
100 BEN 94510 551-C3
2600 AlaC 94546 691-J6
BRANDON RD
- PLHL 94523 592-A6
BRANDON ST
- PDMT 94611 630-A7
1700 OAK 94611 630-A7
BRANDON WY
300 MLPK 94025 790-F6
BRANDON OAKS PL
- WLCK 94596 612-B2
BRANDT DR
- MRGA 94556 651-F1
BRANDT RD
1300 HIL 94010 748-E3
BRANDT ST
2500 PIN 94564 569-F4
BRANDY CT
3400 PLE 94566 714-G4
BRANDY LN
1000 SJS 95132 814-G5
BRANDYBUCK WY
1100 SJS 95121 855-A4
BRANDY ROCK WY
- OAK 94619 651-B6
3600 RDWC 94061 789-H3
BRANDYWINE CT
12900 SAR 95070 852-D6
BRANDYWINE DR
3000 SJS 95121 855-A3
12800 SAR 95070 852-D7
BRANDYWINE LN
400 PLHL 94523 592-A4
BRANDYWINE PL
- CLAY 94517 594-A7
- HAY 94542 712-C3
BRANDYWINE RD
1500 SMCo 94402 748-F7
BRANDYWINE ST
35900 NWK 94560 752-C6
BRANDYWINE WY
100 WLCK 94598 612-J1
BRANHAM LN
100 SJS 95136 874-G2
500 SCIC 95136 874-G2
1300 SJS 95118 874-B3
1700 SJS 95124 874-B3
2000 SJS 95118 873-H4
2000 SJS 95124 873-H4
14800 SCIC 95124 873-H4
BRANHAM LN E
100 SJS 95111 875-A2
400 SJS 95138 875-D2
BRANN ST
5300 OAK 94619 650-G7
5300 OAK 94619 670-G1
5500 OAK 94605 670-G1
BRANNAN PL
700 CNCD 94518 592-H6
2400 SCL 95050 833-C5
BRANNAN ST
- SF 94103 668-A1
- SF 94107 648-B7
700 SF 94103 648-B7
BRANNER DR
- SMCo 94025 790-E7
- SMCo 94025 810-E1
2300 MLPK 94025 790-E7
2300 MLPK 94025 810-E1
BRANSON DR
3400 SMTO 94403 749-D5
BRANSTEN RD
800 SCAR 94070 769-H3
BRANT CT
100 VAL 94589 509-H5
BRANT WY
- ANT 94509 594-H1
BRANTFORD
2300 WLCK 94596 632-G2
BRANTLEY DR
1900 SJS 95131 814-D7
BRANTWOOD CT
42600 FRMT 94538 773-D2
BRASERO LN
- WLCK 94596 612-D5
BRASILIA WY
5800 SJS 95120 874-D5
BRASSIE CT
- NVTO 94949 546-C2
BRASSWOOD CT
400 SCL 95054 813-F6
BRATER CT
1900 SJS 95131 814-D7
BRAUN CT
- MrnC 94965 606-G7
BRAXTON DR
600 SJS 95111 875-B1
BRAXTON PL
4800 PLE 94566 714-F5
BRAY AV
2000 SCL 95050 833-C4
BRAYTON CT
37700 FRMT 94536 752-G5
BRAZIL AV
- SF 94112 667-G7
600 SF 94112 687-G1
1100 SF 94134 687-G1
BRAZIL CT
2500 ANT 94509 575-H6
BRAZIL DR
2200 ANT 94509 575-H6
BRAZIL WY
3700 PIN 94564 569-J7
BREAKER DR
- CCCo 94565 573-E1
BREAKER LN
- RDWC 94065 750-C4
BREAKERS BLVD
- RCH 94804 608-J3
BREAKWATER AV
3500 HAY 94545 711-D7
3900 HAY 94545 731-C1
BREAKWATER CT
3400 HAY 94545 711-E7
BREAKWATER DR
- RDWC 94065 750-A5
- BERK 94804 629-B1
BRECK CT
- MRGA 94556 631-G5
500 BEN 94510 550-H2
BRECKENRIDGE CT
1100 MRTZ 94553 571-H5
BRECKENRIDGE PL
300 MRTZ 94553 571-H5
BRECKENRIDGE ST
1000 SLN 94579 691-B7
BRECON CT
100 SMCo 94062 769-G6
2500 AlaC 94546 692-A6
BREECH AV
100 SCL 95051 833-C7
100 SCL 95051 853-C1
BREED AV
100 SLN 94577 671-A6
10500 OAK 94603 671-A6
BREEN CT
3000 SJS 95121 855-A4
BREEN PL
- SF 94102 647-J6
BREEZE PL
800 RDWC 94062 789-H1
BREEZEWALK DR
100 VAL 94591 550-E2
BREEZEWOOD CT
1100 SUNV 94089 812-J4
BREEZYGLEN CT
500 SJS 95133 834-F1
BREHAUT CT
- ALA 94502 669-J6
BREMER CT
- VAL 94591 530-F2
BREMERTON DR
800 SUNV 94087 832-C4
BRENDA AV
5300 SJS 95124 873-J5
BRENDA CIR
4600 CNCD 94521 593-C3
BRENDA CT
200 PIN 94564 569-D4
1500 CNCD 94521 593-C3
19900 CPTO 95014 852-F1
BRENDA WY
32600 UNC 94587 732-C5
BRENDA LEE DR
600 SJS 95123 874-H7
BRENDEL DR
12800 LAH 94022 831-C1
BRENFORD DR
2500 SJS 95122 834-J5
BRENNAN AV
500 SJS 95131 813-H6
BRENNAN CT
300 ANT 94509 575-E6
BRENNAN WY
800 LVMR 94550 715-H1
BRENNER
100 HER 94547 569-E3
BRENNER WY
1500 SJS 95118 874-A5
BRENNFLECK AV
- SANS 94960 566-B7
BRENNING DR
2400 SJS 95111 854-G3
BRENT CT
- LFYT 94549 631-J3
- MLPK 94025 790-C7
3100 AlaC 94546 691-H3
3500 PLE 94588 694-F5
BRENT DR
800 CPTO 95014 852-F2
BRENTFORD ST
6700 OAK 94621 670-F3
BRENTON AV
1200 SJS 95129 852-J4
BRENTON CT
100 MTVW 94043 812-A5
BRENTWOOD AV
- SF 94127 667-D6
800 VAL 94591 530-F5
3300 RCH 94803 589-F2
BRENTWOOD CIR
4200 CNCD 94521 593-C2
BRENTWOOD CT
700 LALT 94024 831-G2
1500 WLCK 94595 612-D7
2200 EPA 94303 791-C2
24700 HAY 94545 711-F5
BRENTWOOD DR
- SJS 95131 814-A5
- SRFL 94901 567-C6
- SSF 94080 707-G5
400 BEN 94510 550-J2
400 BEN 94510 551-A1
600 SJS 95129 853-A2
600 SJS 95129 852-J3
BRENTWOOD PL
700 LALT 94024 831-G2
1800 OAK 94602 650-E3
BRENTWOOD RD
200 HIL 94010 748-G2
1800 OAK 94602 650-E3
BRENTWOOD ST
1200 LALT 94024 831-G2
BRENTZ LN
1800 SPAB 94806 589-A3
BRET AV
- SRFL 94901 586-G2
10000 SCIC 95014 852-H1
BRET CT
- NVTO 94947 526-B4
BRETANO WY
- MrnC 94904 586-F4
300 LKSP 94904 586-F4
BRET COVE CT
100 SJS 95120 894-G2
BRET HARTE
- SMCo 94020 809-F6
BRET HARTE CT
100 SCL 95050 833-D7
BRET HARTE CT
4700 FRMT 94538 752-J6
6500 AlaC 94552 692-E2
BRET HARTE DR
3600 RDWC 94061 789-G3
6600 SJS 95120 894-F2
BRET HARTE LN
- SRFL 94901 586-G3
BRET HARTE RD
- BERK 94708 609-H6
- MrnC 94901 586-G3
100 SRFL 94901 586-G3
BRET HARTE ST
1800 PA 94303 791-B5
BRET HARTE TER
- SF 94133 647-J3
BRET HARTE WY
- BERK 94708 609-H6
100 VAL 94589 509-J6
BRET HILL CT
100 SJS 95120 894-G2
BRET KNOLL CT
100 SJS 95120 894-G2
BRETMOOR WY
1100 SJS 95129 852-F4
BRETON DR
35400 NWK 94560 752-D5
BRETON PL
2600 WLCK 94598 592-F7
6000 NWK 94560 752-D5
BRETT CT
1400 PIN 94564 569-D4
5000 FRMT 94538 773-B1
BREWER AV
10400 CPTO 95014 832-C7
BREWER DR
600 HIL 94010 748-F1
BREWSTER AV
300 RDWC 94063 770-A5
900 RDWC 94062 770-A5
1200 RDWC 94062 769-J6
2700 SMCo 94062 769-J6
4900 SJS 95124 873-F4
15000 SCIC 95124 873-F4
BREWSTER CT
1300 ELCR 94530 609-D1
BREWSTER DR
1100 ELCR 94530 609-D1
BREWSTER ST
- SF 94110 668-A5
BREZZA CT
- PLE 94566 715-B6
BRIA CT
100 CCCo 94596 612-A4
BRIAN CT
- SRMN 94583 693-G1
300 SJS 95123 875-B6
1400 MPS 95035 794-C5
5000 FRMT 94538 773-B1
BRIAN LN
- SCL 95051 833-A7
BRIAN RD
2400 CCCo 94806 569-B5
BRIAN ST
400 HAY 94544 712-A7
BRIANA CT
900 SJS 95120 894-H2
BRIANNE CT
300 PLE 94566 714-D7
BRIAR CT
13400 SAR 95070 852-E7
BRIAR DR
200 MRTZ 94553 591-H2
BRIAR LN
100 SMTO 94403 749-B6
BRIAR PL
100 DNVL 94526 632-J7
46200 FRMT 94539 773-H5
BRIAR RD
- MrnC 94904 586-D5
- LKSP 94939 586-D5
BRIARBERRY CT
1200 SJS 95131 814-D7
BRIARBROOK CT
3500 SJS 95132 814-F2
BRIARBUSH CT
1700 SJS 95131 814-D7
BRIAR CANYON TR
- CCCo - 610-A4
- CCCo 94708 609-H4
- CCCo 94708 610-A4
BRIARCLIFF CT
600 SCL 95051 832-J6
4300 CNCD 94521 593-C2
BRIARCLIFF DR
600 SJS 95123 874-G5
3700 PIT 94565 574-F6
BRIARCLIFF RD
4300 OAK 94605 671-C2
BRIARCLIFF TER
- SF 94132 667-B5
BRIARCREEK CT
1200 SJS 95131 814-C7
BRIARCREST CT
1600 SJS 95131 834-C1
6100 WLCK 94595 632-D6
BRIARCREST DR
1200 SJS 95131 834-C1
1200 SJS 95131 814-C7
BRIARFIELD AV
2500 RDWC 94061 789-H2
BRIARFIELD WY
400 BLMT 94002 749-E7
BRIARGLEN DR
3900 SJS 95118 874-C1
BRIARIDGE CT
200 PLHL 94523 591-J6
BRIARLEAF CIR
1200 SJS 95131 834-C1
BRIARPOINT DR
1600 SJS 95131 834-C1
BRIAR RANCH LN
600 SJS 95120 894-G4
BRIAR RIDE DR
5300 AlaC 94552 692-C3
BRIAR RIDGE DR
5600 SJS 95123 874-G7
BRIARTON TER
500 FRMT 94536 753-G3
BRIARTREE DR
1400 SJS 95131 834-C1
BRIARWOOD CT
- CCCo 94596 612-E1
- NVTO 94947 526-D7
500 LVMR 94550 695-H6
1100 LALT 94024 831-G2
3500 ANT 94509 575-E7
3500 ANT 94509 595-E1
BRIARWOOD DR
- SRFL 94901 567-B6
100 HAY 94544 712-B6
200 SJS 95131 814-A4
400 SSF 94080 707-F5
1700 SCL 95051 832-J3
2100 SJS 95125 853-J6
2500 LVMR 94550 695-H6
2600 SJS 95125 854-A7
2700 SJS 95125 874-A1
2800 SJS 95118 874-A1
37400 FRMT 94536 752-G5
BRIARWOOD LN
8400 DBLN 94568 693-H2
BRIARWOOD WY
- BLMT 94002 749-E7
100 LGTS 95032 873-G6
700 SCIC 95008 853-F7
1100 CCCo 94596 612-D1
4100 PA 94306 811-E2
BRICCO CT
- PLE 94566 715-C7
BRICE CT
100 SJS 95111 875-A2
BRICK WY
27200 HAY 94544 711-J7
BRICKELL WY
18500 AlaC 94546 692-B4
BRICKWAY
- LGTS 95030 873-B6
BRICKYARD AV
200 PIT 94565 574-B2
BRICKYARD CV
- MrnC 94941 606-J6
BRICKYARD WY
1200 RCH 94801 608-D3
BRICKYARD COVE RD
300 RCH 94801 608-D3
BRIDAL PTH
- SJS 95111 854-G4
BRIDAL PLACE CT
3600 SJS 95121 855-B4
BRIDGE AV
- SANS 94960 566-C7
1800 OAK 94601 650-C7
BRIDGE CT
- BLMT 94002 769-C3
- VAL 94591 530-E4
7100 SJS 95120 894-G4
BRIDGE DR
700 SLN 94577 671-B7
BRIDGE DRLP
- MRTZ 94553 571-F2
BRIDGE PKWY
- RDWC 94065 749-H7
BRIDGE RD
- BERK 94705 630-B4
- HIL 94010 748-H2
- LKSP 94939 586-E7
- MrnC 94945 526-J2
- ROSS 94957 586-C3
- MrnC 94904 586-C3
100 PLHL 94523 592-A7
400 CCCo 94595 612-B7
3400 HAY 94545 731-G2
N BRIDGE RD
- MrnC 94965 606-H7
- MrnC 94965 626-H1
BRIDGE ST
1400 CNCD 94518 592-E6
BRIDGE WY
- MrnC 94930 586-A1
- SANS 94960 566-A7
BRIDGECASTLE CT
2000 SJS 95121 855-C5
BRIDGECROSSING WY
900 CNCD 94518 592-F5
BRIDGEFIELD RD
200 CCCo 94595 612-A7
BRIDGEGATE DR
- MrnC 94903 546-A6
BRIDGEHEAD RD
- MRTZ 94553 571-F1
- MRTZ 94553 551-F7
BRIDGE PARK CT
11500 CPTO 95014 852-C4
BRIDGEPOINTE DR
36300 NWK 94560 752-C7
BRIDGEPOINTE PL
4900 UNC 94587 752-A2
BRIDGEPORT AV
2800 SRMN 94583 673-E6
BRIDGEPORT CIR
5500 LVMR 94550 696-C2
BRIDGEPORT CT
3600 SJS 95117 853-C3
BRIDGEPORT DR
45500 FRMT 94539 773-H4
BRIDGEPORT LN
600 FCTY 94404 749-F4
BRIDGEPORT PL
45700 FRMT 94539 773-H4
BRIDGEPORT ST
32400 FRMT 94555 732-B6
BRIDGEPORT WY
2200 MRTZ 94553 572-A6
BRIDGEPORT LAKE DR
5800 SJS 95123 874-G7
BRIDGES CT
1400 FRMT 94536 753-A2
BRIDGESIDE CIR
- DNVL 94506 653-F5
BRIDGET DR
700 SJS 95136 874-E1
BRIDGETON CT
100 LALT 94022 811-D6
BRIDGEVIEW CT
- CCCo 94525 550-C4
300 BEN 94510 551-B3
BRIDGEVIEW DR
- SF 94124 668-B6
4300 OAK 94602 650-D3
BRIDGE VIEW ISL
3300 ALA 94501 670-A4

STREET Block City ZIP Pg-Grid

BRIDGEVIEW PL
100 VAL 94591 550-D2
BRIDGEVIEW ST
1700 PIT 94565 573-F3
BRIDGEVIEW HGTS PL
- BEN 94510 551-B4
BRIDGEWATER CIR
600 DNVL 94526 653-C3
BRIDGEWATER DR
- SRFL 94903 566-F3
BRIDGEWATER PL
34400 FRMT 94555 732-E7
BRIDGEWATER RD
500 DNVL 94526 653-C3
BRIDGEWATER WY
- PLHL 94523 591-B1
BRIDGEWAY
- MrnC 94941 626-J1
- MrnC 94965 626-J1
- SAUS 94965 626-J1
1200 SAUS 94965 627-A2
BRIDGEWOOD TER
3400 FRMT 94536 752-A6
BRIDGEWOOD WY
900 SUNV 94089 812-J5
BRIDLE CT
- HIL 94402 748-H4
500 WLCK 94596 632-F2
4800 ANT 94509 595-J2
BRIDLE DR
3000 AlaC 94541 712-D2
BRIDLE LN
- WDSD 94062 809-G2
2600 WLCK 94596 632-F2
BRIDLE WY
1000 HIL 94402 748-H4
4900 ANT 94509 595-J3
5800 SJS 95123 874-J5
BRIDLEPATH CT
- SRMN 94583 673-D4
BRIDLE RIDGE CT
5000 SJS 95138 855-E5
BRIDLEWOOD CT
100 VAL 94591 530-D2
BRIDWELL WY
2100 HAY 94545 731-H1
BRIER ST
31000 UNC 94587 731-J5
BRIERGATE WY
600 HAY 94544 732-E1
BRIERLY CT
16900 AlaC 94546 691-H1
BRIERTOWN CT
3400 WLCK 94598 612-J3
BRIGADOON WY
- DBLN 94552 693-D4
- DBLN 94568 693-D4
3200 SJS 95121 855-C3
BRIGANTINE DR
6100 SJS 95129 852-G3
BRIGANTINE LN
- RDWC 94065 750-C4
BRIGANTINE RD
100 VAL 94591 550-E2
BRIGGS AV
3200 ALA 94501 670-B3
BRIGGS CT
200 SJS 95139 895-F1
2700 PLE 94588 714-A3
3200 FRMT 94536 752-F1
BRIGGS ST
1500 SMCo 94015 687-C5
1500 DALY 94015 687-C5
BRIGHAM LN
400 DNVL 94526 633-A6
BRIGHAM RD
16200 SCIC 95030 872-G7
BRIGHT COM
37800 FRMT 94536 753-A3
37800 FRMT 94536 752-J3
BRIGHT PL
2100 AlaC 94541 712-C1
BRIGHT ST
- SF 94132 687-D2
BRIGHTEN AV
1700 SJS 95124 873-H2
BRIGHT OAK PL
1000 SJS 95120 894-F2
BRIGHT OAKS CT
1300 LALT 94024 831-J3
BRIGHTON
100 HER 94547 569-H2
BRIGHTON AV
- SF 94112 687-D1
200 SF 94112 667-D7
1100 ALB 94706 609-D5
3500 OAK 94602 650-C3
BRIGHTON BLVD
- MrnC 94965 606-B3
BRIGHTON COM
43000 FRMT 94538 773-E2
BRIGHTON CT
- DALY 94015 707-D3
200 ALA 94502 670-A5
1000 ANT 94509 575-F7
7400 DBLN 94568 693-H2
36200 NWK 94560 752-E4
BRIGHTON DR
- VAL 94591 530-G4
2000 PIT 94565 574-F4
6800 DBLN 94568 693-H2
BRIGHTON LN
200 RDWC 94061 790-B2
BRIGHTON PL
1000 MTVW 94040 811-F5
7400 DBLN 94568 693-H2
BRIGHTON RD
- ALA 94502 669-J5
- ALA 94502 670-A5
100 PCFA 94044 706-J6
200 PCFA 94044 707-A6
BRIGHTON ST
28400 HAY 94544 712-B7
BRIGHTON WY
400 LVMR 94550 695-D7
2200 WLCK 94598 612-G2
3200 ANT 94509 575-F7
BRIGHTSIDE CT
1100 SJS 95127 835-A4
BRIGHTWOOD CIR
- DNVL 94506 653-G2

BRIGHTWOOD CT
1000 WLCK 94598 592-E7
3100 SJS 95148 835-D7
BRIGHTWOOD DR
2800 SJS 95148 835-D7
BRIGHTWOOD LN E
100 DNVL 94506 653-G2
BRIGHTWOOD LN W
- DNVL 94506 653-F1
BRIGHTWOOD WY
- DNVL 94506 653-G2
BRILES CT
47700 FRMT 94539 773-H7
BRILL CT
100 SJS 95116 834-G2
BRINDOS CT
- SJS 95123 874-F7
BRINK CT
900 CNCD 94518 592-F6
BRIONES CT
- CCCo 94565 573-H2
27600 LAH 94022 830-H1
BRIONES RD
- CCCo - 591-C7
- CCCo - 611-A1
- CCCo 94553 591-E3
BRIONES VW
- CCCo 94553 572-A3
- ORIN 94563 611-A4
BRIONES WY
12300 LAH 94022 830-H1
BRIONES CREST TR
- CCCo - 591-A5
- CCCo - 611-E1
BRIONES TO MOUNT DIABLO TR
- CCCo - 613-A7
- WLCK 94596 613-A7
- WLCK 94596 612-J7
2000 CCCo - 633-A1
2000 CCCo 94526 633-A1
BRIONNE DR
5600 SJS 95118 874-A6
BRISA CT
- LVMR 94550 696-D5
BRISA ST
5300 LVMR 94550 696-D5
BRISBANE CT
7100 SJS 95129 852-E4
BRISBANE TER
100 SUNV 94086 812-E7
BRISBANE WY
7100 SJS 95129 852-E4
BRISCOE
1900 FRMT 94539 753-E6
BRISCOE LN
1800 CNCD 94521 593-F4
BRISDALE PL
- ANT 94509 575-C5
BRISTLECONE CT
2200 UNC 94587 732-C5
BRISTLECONE DR
2200 CCCo 94803 589-F4
2200 RCH 94803 589-F4
BRISTLECONE WY
4000 LVMR 94550 695-J3
4100 LVMR 94550 696-A3
BRISTOL
100 HER 94547 569-J2
BRISTOL BLVD
100 SLN 94577 670-J6
BRISTOL CT
- PLHL 94523 591-J6
200 CCCo 94506 654-A5
500 BEN 94510 550-J1
500 FCTY 94404 749-F5
500 LVMR 94550 695-E6
1000 WLCK 94598 612-F1
3100 RCH 94806 589-A2
BRISTOL DR
- VAL 94591 530-H6
600 HAY 94544 712-D7
2700 SJS 95127 835-A5
6800 OAK 94705 630-C4
BRISTOL PL
200 PIT 94565 574-E7
300 MrnC 94965 606-F7
5200 NWK 94560 752-E4
BRISTOL RD
7800 DBLN 94568 693-H3
BRISTOL WY
- RDWC 94061 789-J3
- RDWC 94061 790-A3
BRISTOLWOOD LN
2100 SJS 95132 814-E2
BRISTOLWOOD RD
4300 PLE 94588 713-J1
BRITAIN CT
200 CCCo 94507 632-H5
BRITANNIA CT
100 VAL 94591 530-H4
BRITANNIA DR
400 VAL 94591 530-G4
BRITANNIA LN
2000 SLN 94579 690-J6
BRITHORN LN
3400 ALA 94502 670-A7
BRITT CT
- ALA 94502 669-J6
BRITT WY
2400 SJS 95148 855-B1
2500 SJS 95148 835-C7
BRITTAN AV
800 SCAR 94070 769-H3
BRITTANY AV
6000 NWK 94560 752-D5
BRITTANY CT
- SJS 95135 855-F3
800 CNCD 94518 592-F7
2400 ANT 94509 595-G1
10200 CPTO 95014 852-E1
20100 AlaC 94546 692-B5
BRITTANY DR
- ALA 94502 670-A5
9200 DBLN 94568 693-E3
BRITTANY LN
- DALY 94014 687-F3
800 CNCD 94518 592-F7
2200 MRTZ 94553 572-A6
8000 DBLN 94568 693-E3
10800 AlaC 94552 693-E3

BRITTANY PL
300 LVMR 94550 715-D3
BRITTANY MEADOWS
- ATN 94027 790-E3
BRITTO TER
300 FRMT 94539 753-F4
BRITTON AV
- BLV 94920 607-C7
- BLV 94920 627-C1
100 ATN 94027 790-E3
300 SUNV 94086 832-F1
1100 SJS 95125 854-A3
1200 SJS 95125 853-J4
N BRITTON AV
500 SUNV 94086 812-G6
S BRITTON AV
300 SUNV 94086 812-G7
BRITTON CT
- NVTO 94947 525-J3
BRITTON ST
- SF 94134 687-J2
BRITWELL CT
4400 SJS 95136 874-F2
BRIXHAM WY
100 PLHL 94523 591-J4
BRIXTON CT
200 AMCN 94589 509-J3
1800 SJS 95132 814-E3
BROAD ST
- SF 94112 687-D2
200 SF 94132 687-D2
BROADACRES DR
6500 SJS 95120 894-B2
BROAD ACRES RD
- ATN 94027 790-C5
BROADLEAF LN
800 SJS 95128 833-F7
BROADMOOR
- MRGA 94556 631-D7
- MRGA 94556 651-D1
BROADMOOR AV
- SANS 94960 566-A5
2700 CNCD 94520 572-E7
2700 CNCD 94520 592-E1
BROADMOOR BLVD
- SLN 94577 671-A6
900 SLN 94577 670-J6
W BROADMOOR BLVD
100 SLN 94577 670-J7
BROADMOOR CT
- NVTO 94949 546-C2
- SRMN 94583 693-H1
100 SANS 94960 566-B5
800 LFYT 94549 611-G7
1600 LVMR 94550 696-B3
BROADMOOR DR
- SF 94132 667-C7
700 SJS 95129 853-A2
9400 SRMN 94583 693-G1
9500 SRMN 94583 673-F4
BROADMOOR ST
1700 LVMR 94550 696-B3
BROADMOOR VW
3000 OAK 94605 671-B5
BROADMORE AV
2100 CCCo 94806 569-B4
24200 HAY 94544 711-G4
BROADVIEW CT
- SRFL 94901 586-H1
3500 SMTO 94403 768-J1
BROADVIEW DR
- SRFL 94901 566-H7
- SRFL 94901 586-H1
10300 SCIC 95127 835-B2
BROADVIEW TER
- ORIN 94563 631-A1
- ORIN 94563 630-J1
BROADWAY
- MLBR 94030 728-A2
- MrnC 94904 586-E3
- OAK 94607 649-H2
- RCH 94804 588-H7
- RDWC 94063 770-B6
- VAL 94590 530-A4
- LGTS 95030 872-J7
300 ALA 94501 669-J4
300 ALA 94501 670-A2
300 SF 94133 648-A4
500 HAY 94544 712-B6
700 WLCK 94596 612-C5
800 BLMT 94002 769-F1
900 SF 94133 647-H4
1000 BURL 94010 728-D6
1000 SJS 95125 854-A2
1100 SF 94109 647-H4
1200 OAK 94612 649-H2
1700 VAL 94589 530-A1
2700 RDWC 94062 770-B5
2800 OAK 94611 630-C4
2800 OAK 94611 649-H2
2800 RDWC 94062 769-J6
3000 AMCN 94589 510-A3
3000 NaCo 94589 510-A3
3000 VAL 94589 510-A6
3900 OAK 94611 629-H7
5000 OAK 94618 630-A5
5200 OAK 94618 629-J7
BROADWAY Rt#-61
900 ALA 94501 670-A3
N BROADWAY
1300 WLCK 94596 612-C4
S BROADWAY
- CCCo 94596 612-D6
- WLCK 94596 632-D1
- MLBR 94030 728-B4
600 WLCK 94596 612-D6
BROADWAY AV
1000 SPAB 94806 588-H1
6100 NWK 94560 752-F7
N BROADWAY AV
- CCCo 94565 573-H2
S BROADWAY AV
600 CCCo 94565 573-H3
600 PIT 94565 573-H3
BROADWAY CT
1000 SJS 95125 854-A2
BROADWAY PL
- NWK 94560 752-F7
BROADWAY PZ
1100 WLCK 94596 612-C5
BROADWAY ST
- SF 94111 648-A4

BROADWAY ST
500 HAY 94544 712-C6
1500 CNCD 94520 592-E1
2000 SF 94115 647-H4
W BROADWAY ST
- SF 94129 647-F5
BROADWAY TER
5200 OAK 94618 629-J6
5300 OAK 94618 630-A6
5400 OAK 94611 630-D6
BROCASTLE WY
100 LGTS 95030 873-B4
BROCK WY
3900 SJS 95111 855-A6
3900 SCIC 95111 855-A6
BROCKENHURST DR
300 SJS 95119 895-D1
BROCKET CT
2400 ANT 94509 595-G2
BROCKHAMPTON CT
1000 SJS 95136 874-C2
BROCKHURST ST
600 OAK 94609 649-F1
800 OAK 94608 649-F1
BROCKTON AV
9500 SRMN 94583 693-G1
BROCKTON DR
3700 PLE 94588 694-F5
BROCKTON LN
19100 SAR 95070 852-G6
BROCKWAY CT
33000 UNC 94587 752-B2
BROCKWAY ST
32900 UNC 94587 752-A1
BRODEA WY
- SRFL 94901 566-H7
- SRFL 94901 586-H1
BRODER BLVD
- DBLN 94568 694-C3
BRODERICK DR
400 SJS 95111 875-C2
BRODERICK RD
- BURL 94010 728-C4
BRODERICK ST
100 SF 94117 667-F1
300 SF 94117 647-F6
900 SF 94115 647-F6
2600 SF 94123 647-F4
3000 SF 94123 647-F3
BRODERICK WY
2700 MTVW 94043 791-G7
BRODIA CT
- MRTZ 94553 571-H4
BRODIA WY
100 CCCo 94598 612-F4
BRODIE DR
3300 SJS 95111 854-J5
3400 SJS 95111 855-A5
BROKAW RD
- SJS 95131 833-H1
- SJS 95110 833-H1
- SJS 95112 833-H1
200 SCL 95050 833-F3
E BROKAW RD
100 SJS 95112 833-H1
100 SJS 95131 833-H1
200 SJS 95112 813-J7
200 SJS 95131 813-J7
600 SJS 95112 814-A7
600 SJS 95131 814-A7
BROKEN ARROW DR
5000 SJS 95136 874-H2
5000 SJS 95136 875-A2
BROKEN LANCE CT
5200 SJS 95136 875-B3
BROKEN OAK CT
2800 SJS 95148 835-E7
BROM CIR
5200 AlaC 94546 692-C3
BROM LN
- ORIN 94563 610-G3
BROMFIELD CT
2200 WLCK 94596 632-G2
BROMFIELD RD
600 SMTO 94402 748-F1
700 HIL 94010 748-F2
BROMLEY AV
5900 OAK 94621 670-F2
BROMLEY CT
- DALY 94015 707-D3
BROMLEY DR
- SCAR 94070 769-F6
- SMCo 94062 769-F6
BROMLEY PL
- SF 94115 647-G5
BROMLEY CROSS DR
200 SJS 95119 895-D1
BROMPTON AV
- SF 94131 667-G6
BRONCHO LN
3100 CCCo 94598 613-A4
BRONCO CT
- SRMN 94583 673-B3
5000 ANT 94509 595-J3
BRONSON AV
14500 SCIC 95124 873-G3
BRONSON LN
800 CCCo 94596 612-E6
800 WLCK 94596 612-E6
BRONSON ST
38300 FRMT 94536 753-A3
BRONTE CT
5000 FRMT 94538 773-B1
BRONTE ST
- SF 94110 667-J6
BROOK CT
3100 ANT 94509 595-C1
BROOK LN
- SANS 94960 566-A6
19000 SAR 95070 852-G5
BROOK PL
1300 MTVW 94040 832-A2
BROOK ST
- SF 94110 667-H5
100 SCAR 94070 769-G5
2000 CNCD 94520 572-E6
3000 OAK 94611 649-H2
3500 LFYT 94549 611-E7
BROOK TER
- FRMT 94538 773-D3
BROOK WY
2800 CCCo 94806 589-A3

BROOKBANK RD
- ORIN 94563 610-G4
BROOKCREST WY
- ANT 94509 595-J4
BROOKDALE AV
- SF 94134 687-H2
- SRFL 94901 566-G6
- CCCo 94595 632-E2
1200 MTVW 94040 811-G7
2800 OAK 94602 650-C5
2800 OAK 94601 650-C5
3500 OAK 94619 650-E7
4800 OAK 94601 670-F1
4800 OAK 94619 670-F1
5500 OAK 94605 670-F1
BROOKDALE BLVD
3300 AlaC 94546 691-H3
BROOKDALE CIR
3600 ANT 94509 595-E1
BROOKDALE CT
- LVMR 94550 696-D3
- CCCo 94595 632-E1
- LFYT 94549 611-G7
2900 CNCD 94518 592-G5
3500 ANT 94509 575-E7
3500 ANT 94509 595-E1
7300 DBLN 94568 693-J3
BROOKDALE DR
1400 SJS 95125 853-J4
3200 SCL 95051 833-A5
3300 SCL 95051 832-J5
BROOKDALE LN
- LVMR 94550 696-D3
BROOKE CIR
- MLV 94941 606-G4
BROOKE CT
- HIL 94402 748-G6
BROOKE DR
- NVTO 94947 525-F4
400 VAL 94591 530-E6
W BROOKE DR
- NVTO 94947 525-F4
- MrnC 94947 525-F4
BROOKE ACRES CT
16200 LGTS 95032 893-D1
BROOKE ACRES DR
16200 LGTS 95032 873-D7
16200 LGTS 95032 893-D1
BROOK ESTATES CT
3000 SJS 95135 855-G5
N BROOKFIELD
300 AMCN 94589 510-B4
S BROOKFIELD
500 AMCN 94589 510-B4
BROOKFIELD AV
1200 SUNV 94087 832-B1
3000 OAK 94605 671-C7
BROOKFIELD DR
- MRGA 94556 651-E6
500 LVMR 94550 695-E7
BROOKFIELD LP
900 AMCN 94589 510-B4
BROOKFIELD CROSS
900 AMCN 94589 510-B4
BROOK GLEN DR
- SJS 95129 852-G6
12100 SAR 95070 852-G6
BROOKGLEN DR
1300 SJS 95129 852-G5
11800 SAR 95070 852-G5
BROOKGROVE LN
800 CPTO 95014 852-G2
BROOKHAVEN CT
- PCFA 94044 707-A2
2200 SPAB 94806 588-H2
BROOKHAVEN DR
19000 SAR 95070 852-G4
BROOKHAVEN WY
- SF 94132 666-J6
BROOKHEAVEN WY
5000 ANT 94509 595-J4
BROOK HOLLOW CT
5000 CNCD 94521 593-D5
BROOKHOLLOW DR
- SJS 95132 814-E5
BROOKHURST CT
5600 SJS 95129 852-H4
BROOKINGS LN
- SUNV 94024 832-A4
BROOKLAWN AV
- DALY 94015 687-A5
- DALY 94015 686-J5
BROOK LEAF CT
3300 SJS 95132 814-G4
BROOKLINE
100 MRGA 94556 631-C7
BROOKLINE AV
500 MrnC 94965 606-D6
BROOKLINE DR
- CCCo 94598 612-D2
800 SUNV 94087 832-C1
BROOKLINE WY
3900 SMCo 94062 789-F2
BROOKLYN AV
- LGTS 95032 893-A1
- SJS 95126 833-G7
300 SJS 95128 833-G7
600 OAK 94606 649-J4
600 OAK 94606 650-A4
1200 SCIC 95128 833-G7
1400 SCIC 95128 853-G1
BROOKLYN PL
- SF 94108 648-A5
BROOKLYN ST
- UNC 94587 731-J5
BROOKMEAD CT
- SANS 94960 566-A5
BROOKMEAD PL
- SANS 94960 566-A5
BROOKMERE DR
300 SJS 95123 875-B7
BROOKMILL CT
3400 FRMT 94536 752-F1
BROOKMILL DR
3400 FRMT 94536 752-F1
BROOKMILL RD
1400 LALT 94024 832-A3
BROOKMONT CIR
- SANS 94960 566-B5
BROOKNOLL CT
19100 SAR 95070 852-G4

BROOKPARK RD
12500 OAK 94619 651-A5
BROOKRIDGE DR
11800 SAR 95070 852-G5
BROOKS AV
200 LGTS 95030 872-J7
500 SJS 95125 854-A2
2300 RCH 94804 588-H6
2600 ELCR 94530 589-B6
BROOKS CT
4000 PLE 94588 714-A1
BROOKS PL
- PCFA 94044 727-B6
BROOKS ST
- SF 94129 647-B5
800 SRFL 94901 586-F1
1500 WLCK 94596 612-B5
1700 SMTO 94403 749-C2
BROOKS WY
25400 HAY 94544 712-A4
BROOKSHIRE CT
- PIT 94565 574-B4
300 AMCN 94589 509-J3
BROOKSIDE AV
- BERK 94705 629-J4
- BERK 94705 630-A5
- SCL 95117 833-C7
- SCL 95117 853-C1
1100 SPAB 94805 589-A5
6100 OAK 94618 630-A5
BROOKSIDE CT
- BERK 94705 629-J4
- NVTO 94947 525-J4
- SANS 94960 566-B6
400 ANT 94509 595-E1
5100 CNCD 94521 593-D5
5300 PLE 94588 693-J6
BROOKSIDE DR
- SANS 94960 566-A5
100 ANT 94509 595-D1
100 BERK 94705 629-J4
100 CCCo 94801 588-F2
100 PTLV 94028 810-B7
600 DNVL 94526 653-B3
800 SPAB 94806 588-F2
900 RCH 94801 588-F2
3200 MRTZ 94553 571-E5
3700 PIT 94565 574-D6
BROOKSIDE LN
800 MLBR 94030 727-H3
5100 CNCD 94521 593-D5
BROOKSIDE PL
100 DNVL 94526 653-B4
BROOKSIDE RD
- ORIN 94563 630-J2
BROOKSIDE ST
1300 SLN 94577 690-H1
BROOKSTONE CT
- MPS 95035 794-C2
BROOKSTONE WY
- HAY 94544 712-A5
100 HAY 94544 711-J5
BROOKSVIEW CT
700 MRTZ 94553 571-E4
BROOKTREE CT
- PIT 94565 574-C4
7100 SJS 95120 894-H3
BROOKTREE DR
- DNVL 94506 653-G1
BROOKTREE WY
1800 PLE 94566 714-D1
7000 SJS 95120 894-H2
BROOKVALE CT
35600 FRMT 94536 752-F1
BROOKVALE DR
1100 SLN 94577 671-D7
1500 SJS 95129 852-E4
BROOKVALE RD
1800 HIL 94010 728-E7
BROOKVIEW CIR
700 CNCD 94520 592-D4
BROOKVIEW DR
1100 CNCD 94520 592-D5
19000 SAR 95070 852-G5
BROOKWELL DR
10700 CPTO 95014 852-F2
BROOKWOOD AV
300 SJS 95116 834-E6
800 VAL 94591 530-E5
4300 FRMT 94538 773-D1
BROOKWOOD CT
- CCCo 94549 591-H7
5400 RCH 94803 590-A3
BROOKWOOD DR
3200 CCCo 94549 591-H7
BROOKWOOD LN
- ROSS 94957 586-C3
5300 RCH 94803 590-A3
20500 SAR 95070 872-D2
BROOKWOOD PL
600 OAK 94610 650-A3
BROOKWOOD RD
- CCCo 94553 591-F3
- ORIN 94563 630-H1
100 WDSD 94062 789-H4
1000 OAK 94610 650-B3
BROPHY DR
4900 FRMT 94536 752-H7
BROPHY ST
100 AMCN 94589 509-J4
100 AMCN 94589 510-A4
BROSNAN CT
100 SSF 94080 707-G2
500 DALY 94015 707-G2
BROSNAN ST
- SF 94103 667-H1
BROTHERHOOD WY
500 SF 94132 687-A1
BROUGHTON LN
500 FCTY 94404 749-G5
BROWER AV
3300 MTVW 94040 832-A2
BROWN AV
1000 LFYT 94549 611-F5
2000 SCL 95051 833-A2
3600 OAK 94619 650-F5
12900 SCIC 95111 854-H6
BROWN CT
- CCCo 94553 572-B7
- NVTO 94947 526-B6
1200 SLN 94579 691-A5
2000 SCL 95051 833-B3

BROWN DR
- NVTO 94947 526-A6
100 CCCo 94553 572-B7
1000 LFYT 94549 611-G4
BROWN LN
1800 CCCo 94509 575-H5
BROWN RD
200 FRMT 94539 773-G5
BROWN ST
- DALY 94014 687-H3
- SF 94129 647-C5
200 MRTZ 94553 571-E3
300 SJS 95125 854-B1
1000 LFYT 94549 611-G6
1100 ALA 94502 669-J6
BROWNELL CT
- CNCD 94521 593-F7
BROWNHILL CT
3200 SJS 95135 855-E2
BROWNING AV
200 SCIC 95008 873-D3
3100 SJS 95124 873-G2
BROWNING CT
500 MrnC 94965 606-E6
27800 HAY 94544 712-A7
BROWNING DR
4000 CNCD 94518 592-J5
BROWNING ST
500 MrnC 94965 606-E6
2100 BERK 94702 629-E2
BROWNING WY
100 VAL 94590 530-B7
400 SSF 94080 707-H4
BROWN RANCH RD
- AlaC 94546 651-G5
- CCCo - 651-G5
BROWNS LN
14300 LGTS 95030 873-B2
BROWNSTONE CT
2500 SJS 95122 835-A5
BROWNVIEW DR
6500 SJS 95120 894-C2
BROWNWOOD CT
1800 CNCD 94521 593-F4
BROWNWOOD WY
3600 SCL 95054 813-F6
BRUBAKER CT
- WLCK 94596 612-D6
BRUBAKER DR
- WLCK 94596 612-D6
BRUCE AV
- SF 94112 667-E7
- SF 94112 687-E1
400 SJS 95110 833-J5
17600 LGTS 95030 873-A5
17600 MSER 95030 873-A5
BRUCE CT
- PLHL 94523 592-A6
2800 SCL 95051 833-B2
5100 AlaC 94546 692-C3
15800 MSER 95030 873-A5
BRUCE DR
800 PA 94303 791-D6
2400 FRMT 94539 753-E7
5300 PLE 94588 694-F7
5300 CCCo 94506 654-G6
BRUCE ST
100 PCFA 94044 707-A4
1600 ANT 94509 575-E5
3500 OAK 94602 650-B4
BRUCE WY
1100 SCIC 95120 894-H5
BRUCITO AV
1100 LALT 94024 831-H4
BRUCKNER CIR
1100 MTVW 94040 832-A2
BRULE CT
14900 SCIC 95127 835-B1
BRUMISS TER
- DALY 94014 687-E2
BRUNDAGE WY
10900 SCIC 95127 815-B6
BRUNELL DR
3200 OAK 94602 650-G4
BRUNELL PL
- OAK 94602 650-G4
BRUNETTI LN
- SLN 94578 691-C5
BRUNING ST
39600 FRMT 94538 753-A7
BRUNINI WY
- TBRN 94920 607-A4
BRUNNHILDE WY
1500 SJS 95121 854-J4
BRUNO AV
- DALY 94014 687-C5
- PIT 94565 574-C3
BRUNO CT
- SJS 95136 854-F7
- CCCo 94803 589-E2
BRUNO DR
- SJS 95136 854-F7
BRUNO RD
4700 CCCo 94803 589-E2
BRUNO ST
900 NVTO 94945 526-B3
27600 HAY 94544 712-A7
BRUNS CT
5900 OAK 94611 650-D1
BRUNSWICK AV
4400 SJS 95124 873-F3
BRUNSWICK CIR
15400 SLN 94579 691-A7
BRUNSWICK CT
- VAL 94591 530-G5
3700 SSF 94080 707-D4
9900 SRMN 94583 673-F5
BRUNSWICK DR
300 VAL 94591 530-G5
BRUNSWICK PL
100 FRMT 94539 773-H2
BRUNSWICK RD
100 ALA 94502 669-J5
BRUNSWICK ST
- SF 94112 687-D3
700 DALY 94014 687-D3
2200 CNCD 94520 572-G4
BRUNSWICK WY
9800 SRMN 94583 673-F5
BRUSCO WY
900 SSF 94080 707-G2

BRUSH PL 1998 BAY AREA STREET INDEX BYINGTON DR 911

BAY AREA

STREET
Block City ZIP Pg-Grid

BRUSH PL
- SF 94103 648-A7
BRUSH ST
100 ALA 94501 649-E7
200 OAK 94607 649-F4
1200 OAK 94612 649-F4
BRUSH CREEK CT
- PIT 94565 574-C7
BRUSHCREEK CT
1600 SJS 95121 855-D7
BRUSH CREEK DR
1100 PIT 94565 574-D7
BRUSH CREEK PL
1600 DNVL 94526 653-B6
BRUSHCREEK WY
1600 SJS 95121 855-D7
BRUSHGLEN WY
2300 SJS 95133 834-F2
BRUSHWOOD LN
- SRFL 94901 586-F3
BRUSHY PEAK CT
5500 LVMR 94550 696-C3
BRUSK CT
19300 AlaC 94546 691-J4
BRUSSELS ST
- SF 94134 668-A6
1100 SF 94134 688-A1
BRUT WY
4200 SJS 95135 855-G3
BRUTUS CT
400 WLCK 94598 612-E2
BRYAN AV
- ANT 94509 575-D6
400 SUNV 94086 832-E1
1100 SJS 95118 874-B2
BRYAN CT
- CCCo 94526 633-C4
BRYAN DR
300 CCCo 94526 633-C4
BRYAN LN
- NVTO 94945 526-A2
BRYANT AL
- SF 94133 648-A4
BRYANT AV
- DBLN 94568 694-A4
100 MTVW 94040 831-J2
700 MTVW 94040 832-A2
5300 OAK 94618 629-J6
BRYANT CT
300 FRMT 94539 773-H1
300 PA 94301 790-H4
BRYANT ST
- SF 94105 648-C6
100 MTVW 94041 811-H5
100 PA 94301 790-H4
100 SF 94107 648-B6
800 SF 94103 648-B7
900 SF 94103 668-A1
1000 PA 94301 791-B6
1500 DALY 94015 687-B5
1700 SF 94110 668-A2
2500 PA 94306 791-C7
3200 PA 94306 811-D1
43300 FRMT 94539 773-H1
43300 FRMT 94539 753-H7
BRYANT WY
- ORIN 94563 630-H1
100 SBRN 94066 727-G2
900 SUNV 94087 832-G4
BRYCE AV
- PIT 94565 574-D7
200 SSF 94080 707-F4
BRYCE CT
- BLMT 94002 769-A2
500 MPS 95035 794-D7
BRYCE DR
800 SJS 95123 874-F4
2100 MRTZ 94553 572-A7
BRYCE CANYON CT
100 SRMN 94583 653-G7
5900 PLE 94588 714-B1
BRYCE CANYON PL
- SRMN 94583 653-G7
BRYCE CANYON RD
100 SRFL 94903 566-F2
BRYCE CANYON WY
- PCFA 94044 727-B5
BRYCE CANYON PK DR
4800 FRMT 94538 773-C2
BRYN MAWR AV
25700 HAY 94542 712-B4
BRYN MAWR CT
- SRMN 94583 673-H7
BRYN MAWR DR
- SRFL 94901 566-F7
BRYSON AV
500 PA 94306 791-C6
BUBB RD
800 CPTO 95014 852-C1
BUBBLINGWELL PL
6600 SJS 95120 894-F1
BUCARELI DR
- SF 94132 687-B1
BUCCANEER CT
- CMAD 94925 606-J1
BUCCANEER LN
- RDWC 94065 750-C4
N BUCHAN DR
1000 LFYT 94549 611-H6
S BUCHAN DR
900 LFYT 94549 611-J6
N BUCHANAN CIR
400 CCCo 94553 572-B7
S BUCHANAN CIR
- CCCo 94553 572-B7
BUCHANAN CT
- EPA 94303 791-C1
100 SAUS 94965 626-J2
1000 SCL 95051 833-B5
4200 PIT 94565 574-E6
BUCHANAN DR
- SAUS 94965 626-J2
1100 SCL 95051 833-B4
BUCHANAN LN
- DNVL 94526 633-C6
BUCHANAN PL
4300 PIT 94565 574-C7
5400 FRMT 94538 752-J7
BUCHANAN RD
100 PIT 94565 574-C6
1100 ANT 94509 575-A6
2000 CCCo - 574-G6

BUCHANAN RD
2000 CCCo 94565 574-G6
2100 ANT 94509 574-G6
BUCHANAN ST
- SF 94102 667-H1
400 SF 94102 647-H7
600 SF 94115 647-G6
700 ALB 94706 609-D6
700 BEN 94510 551-D5
800 ALB 94804 609-D6
1400 NVTO 94947 526-B5
2800 SF 94123 647-G4
3100 SF 94123 647-G3
BUCHANAN WY
1100 HAY 94545 711-F4
BUCHANAN FIELD RD
- CCCo 94520 572-C7
- CCCo 94553 572-C7
BUCHANAN STREET EXT
800 ALB 94804 609-B6
BUCHER AV
500 SCL 95051 833-B6
BUCHSER WY
800 SJS 95125 854-B3
BUCK CT
100 FRMT 94539 773-J3
100 WDSD 94062 790-A5
BUCKBOARD COM
38700 FRMT 94536 753-C2
BUCKBOARD WY
4700 RCH 94803 589-J3
4800 RCH 94803 590-A2
BUCKBRUSH PZ
- HAY 94542 712-B3
BUCKELEW ST
- MrnC 94965 606-G7
- MrnC 94965 626-G1
BUCKEYE
- PTLV 94028 830-C1
BUCKEYE AV
- OAK 94618 630-B6
BUCKEYE CIR
- ANT 94509 595-G2
BUCKEYE CT
- ANT 94509 595-H2
- DBLN 94552 693-F4
- LFYT 94549 611-J6
- HIL 94010 748-G3
- NVTO 94949 546-D4
500 BEN 94510 551-A1
800 MPS 95035 813-J3
900 SUNV 94086 832-G2
1500 PIN 94564 569-E5
1900 PLE 94588 714-B6
BUCKEYE DR
- AlaC 94542 692-E6
- AlaC 94552 692-E6
500 LVMR 94550 695-E7
500 SJS 95111 854-J6
1500 MPS 95035 813-J3
BUCKEYE LN
- DNVL 94526 653-B1
100 VAL 94591 530-F7
100 VAL 94591 550-F1
BUCKEYE PL
7500 NWK 94560 752-D7
BUCKEYE RD
- BLV 94920 607-C7
- BLV 94920 627-C1
BUCKEYE ST
- RDWC 94063 770-B6
36400 NWK 94560 752-D6
BUCKEYE TER
- CLAY 94517 593-H6
43600 FRMT 94538 773-E3
BUCKEYE TR
300 CCCo - 611-E2
300 LFYT 94549 611-E2
BUCKEYE WY
- MrnC 94904 586-C3
BUCKHAVEN LN
19800 SAR 95070 852-F7
BUCKHILL CT
2500 SJS 95148 835-C6
BUCKINGHAM AV
- SMCo 94063 790-C1
- SMCo 94063 770-C7
BUCKINGHAM BLVD
6800 OAK 94705 630-C3
BUCKINGHAM CT
- HIL 94010 748-F5
700 WLCK 94598 613-A3
19100 SAR 95070 872-G1
35000 NWK 94560 752-D3
BUCKINGHAM DR
- MRGA 94556 631-E3
100 SCL 95051 833-B7
100 SCL 95051 853-B1
1000 LALT 94024 831-H2
3300 SJS 95118 874-C1
4100 CCCo 94506 654-A5
8300 ELCR 94530 609-D2
BUCKINGHAM PL
800 CCCo 94506 654-B5
BUCKINGHAM RD
300 PCFA 94044 706-J6
BUCKINGHAM WY
100 SF 94132 667-B7
1200 HIL 94010 748-F6
1300 HAY 94544 732-A1
BUCKINGHAM PARK CIR
400 SJS 95136 874-G1
BUCKLAND AV
700 SCAR 94070 769-E2
700 BLMT 94002 769-E2
BUCKLAND CT
- SCAR 94070 769-E2
BUCKLES ST
- VAL 94590 529-J3
BUCKLEY
100 HER 94547 569-F3
BUCKLEY CT
- OAK 94602 650-G3
BUCKLEY ST
100 MRTZ 94553 571-D3
3600 SCL 95051 832-H3
BUCKNALL RD
1600 CMBL 95008 853-A6
2000 SJS 95008 853-A6
4300 SJS 95130 853-A6
4500 SJS 95130 852-J6

BUCKNALL RD
18500 SAR 95070 852-H6
BUCKNAM AV
800 CMBL 95008 873-B1
BUCKNAM CT
1100 CMBL 95008 873-B1
BUCKNELL CT
1000 LVMR 94550 716-A1
BUCKNELL DR
400 SMTO 94402 748-H3
BUCKNER DR
3400 SCIC 95127 835-A3
3400 SJS 95127 835-A3
BUCKNER TER
5400 FRMT 94555 752-B3
BUCKSKIN CT
4400 LVMR 94550 696-A2
BUCKSKIN DR
4400 ANT 94509 595-G2
BUCKSKIN PL
100 VAL 94591 530-D2
BUCKSKIN RD
2000 LVMR 94550 696-A3
2800 PIN 94564 569-H7
BUCKS LAKE ST
32600 FRMT 94555 732-C6
BUCKTHORN CT
2900 ANT 94509 575-H7
4400 CNCD 94521 593-C5
BUCKTHORN PL
- CCCo 94507 632-H4
BUCKTHORN WY
- ATN 94025 790-E2
- HIL 94010 748-F1
- MLPK 94025 790-E2
BUCKTHORNE WY
1300 SJS 95129 852-E4
BUCKWHEAT CT
- TBRN 94920 607-A3
600 HAY 94544 712-C7
BUCKWOOD CT
800 SJS 95120 894-H3
BUD CT
- PLHL 94523 592-C5
39100 FRMT 94538 753-A6
BUDD AV
- CMBL 95008 853-C7
BUDD CT
600 CMBL 95008 853-C7
1500 SMTO 94403 749-D3
BUDDLAWN WY
600 CMBL 95008 853-C7
BUDGE ST
15500 SLN 94579 691-B7
BUDWING TER
4000 FRMT 94538 773-E2
BUEL AV
400 PCFA 94044 726-J2
BUELL ST
3700 OAK 94619 650-G7
3700 OAK 94613 650-G7
BUENA AV
1700 BERK 94703 609-F7
BUENA CREST CT
2600 SJS 95121 855-F5
BUENA KNOLL CT
2600 SJS 95121 855-F4
BUENA LUNA
1400 SJS 95128 853-F4
BUENA MONTE DR
20500 SCIC 95120 894-J1
BUENA PARK CT
4300 SJS 95121 855-F4
BUENA POINT CT
2600 SJS 95121 855-F4
BUENA TIERRA ST
1800 BEN 94510 551-D5
BUENA VENTURA AV
6100 OAK 94605 650-H7
6100 OAK 94605 670-H1
BUENA VIDA CT
200 MRTZ 94553 571-F5
BUENA VIEW CT
- SJS 95121 855-F4
BUENA VISTA
- BEN 94510 551-A4
- NVTO 94947 525-J3
- ORIN 94563 630-J3
- PIT 94565 574-C6
200 NVTO 94949 546-H5
39500 FRMT 94538 753-B5
BUENA VISTA AV
- MLV 94941 606-E2
- RCH 94801 608-D1
- SBRN 94066 707-J5
100 CMAD 94925 606-G1
100 SUNV 94086 812-C6
200 DALY 94015 687-B6
300 SCIC 95126 853-H1
300 SJS 95126 853-H1
400 SMCo 94061 790-B3
400 SMTO 94403 749-A5
400 ALA 94501 649-G7
1300 ALA 94501 669-J1
1400 AlaC 94550 716-B3
2100 ALA 94501 670-A1
2100 SLN 94577 691-B2
2200 WLCK 94596 612-B2
2300 BLMT 94002 769-B1
2700 CCCo 94596 612-B3
5600 OAK 94618 630-B5
17100 LGTS 95030 873-B4
BUENAVISTA AV
- VAL 94590 529-J3
BUENA VISTA AV E
- SF 94117 667-F1
BUENA VISTA AV W
- SF 94117 667-F1
BUENA VISTA DR
- NWK 94560 772-J2
- DNVL 94526 653-B2
100 PIN 94564 569-E4
100 SJS 95131 814-A5
11500 LAH 94022 830-H2
BUENA VISTA LN
- SANS 94960 566-C7
BUENA VISTA PL
- OAK 94618 630-B5
700 WLCK 94596 612-B3
BUENA VISTA TER
- SF 94117 667-G2

BUENA VISTA WY
2500 BERK 94708 609-H7
BUENO CT
- DNVL 94526 653-A1
BUENOS AIRES CT
2600 WLCK 94596 612-B2
BUFFALO CT
- PCFA 94044 727-C4
BUFFETT PL
6000 SJS 95123 874-E6
BUFKIN CT
5800 SJS 95123 875-A5
BUFKIN DR
5900 SJS 95123 875-A6
BUGATTI CT
400 SJS 95123 874-H3
BUGEIA LN
600 MrnC 94945 526-E2
600 NVTO 94945 526-E2
BUGGYWHIP CT
6600 SJS 95120 894-C5
BUGLE WY
2600 ANT 94509 595-G2
BUIDA CT
- CMAD 94925 606-F1
BUILDERS CIR
- PIT 94565 574-C2
BULKLEY AV
- SAUS 94965 627-B3
BULLARD DR
6000 OAK 94611 630-D7
6100 OAK 94611 650-D1
BULLARD ST
4100 FRMT 94538 753-C6
BULLDOG BLVD
1000 SJS 95116 834-D4
BULLDOG WY
21500 HAY 94545 711-D4
BULLION CIR
1300 SJS 95120 874-B6
BULLION CT
1400 SJS 95120 874-B6
BULLION PL
1400 SJS 95120 874-B6
BULMER ST
4700 UNC 94587 731-J5
BUNCE CT
1100 SJS 95132 814-G5
BUNCE MEADOWS DR
- CCCo 94507 632-G4
BUNDROS CT
2300 MRTZ 94553 571-F4
BUNDY AV
300 SJS 95117 853-D2
300 SCIC 95117 853-D1
BUNGALOW AV
- SANS 94960 566-C7
- SRFL 94901 586-G2
BUNKER CT
2800 SJS 95121 855-A2
BUNKER LN
- AlaC 94566 714-C7
BUNKER RD
- MrnC 94965 627-A5
- MrnC 94965 626-F6
BUNKER ST
200 MRTZ 94553 571-D3
BUNKER HILL BLVD
25300 HAY 94542 712-B3
BUNKER HILL CT
6600 SJS 95120 894-C5
25300 HAY 94542 712-B3
BUNKER HILL DR
2000 SMCo 94402 748-F7
2500 SMCo - 748-F7
BUNKER HILL LN
2800 SCL 95054 813-A3
BUNNY CT
200 AlaC 94541 711-F1
BUNTING LN
- FRMT 94536 753-C2
BUNTING ST
27900 HAY 94545 731-J1
BUOY CT
- SLN 94579 691-A7
BUOY LN
- RDWC 94065 750-C4
BURBANK AV
- RDWC 94063 770-C6
- SMTO 94403 749-C6
BURBANK CT
300 ANT 94509 575-E6
BURBANK DR
800 SCL 95051 832-J5
4000 CNCD 94521 593-A2
BURBANK RD
300 ANT 94509 575-E6
BURBANK ST
1300 ALA 94501 669-G1
22500 HAY 94541 711-H2
BURBECK AV
1300 RCH 94801 588-G5
BURCHELL AV
5800 SJS 95120 874-B6
BURCHELL CT
5900 SJS 95120 874-B7
BURCKHALTER AV
3900 OAK 94605 670-J1
BURDECK CT
- OAK 94602 650-F3
BURDECK DR
2900 OAK 94602 650-F3
BURDELL CT
- NVTO 94949 546-E4
BURDETT WY
1100 MPS 95035 794-C5
BURDETTE COM
- FRMT 94536 753-B3
BURDETTE DR
1600 SJS 95121 854-J1
BURDETTE ST
38300 FRMT 94536 753-B3
BURDICK DR
500 CCCo 94565 573-C1
BURDICK ST
36600 NWK 94560 752-E5
BURDICK WY
2800 SJS 95148 855-C1
BUREN PL
3700 AlaC 94552 692-F2
BURGAS TER
- UNC 94587 732-E5

BURGER CT
500 PLE 94566 714-G3
BURGESS CT
- MrnC 94965 606-G7
- MrnC 94965 626-G1
100 DNVL 94526 653-D6
BURGESS DR
300 MLPK 94025 790-G4
BURGESS ST
200 LVMR 94550 696-A7
BURGESS WY
- CCCo 94803 589-E1
BURGNER AV
2800 ALA 94502 669-H7
BURGOS AV
9700 OAK 94605 671-B4
BURGOS CT
- SRMN 94583 673-C3
BURGOYNE CT
- SMCo 94402 768-G1
BURGOYNE ST
- SF 94109 647-J5
300 MTVW 94043 811-H3
BURGUNDY CT
1200 SJS 95132 814-H5
BURGUNDY DR
3200 PLE 94566 714-G3
3300 SJS 95132 814-G5
BURGUNDY WY
1100 LVMR 94550 715-H2
19400 SAR 95070 872-F3
BURK ST
400 OAK 94610 649-J3
BURKE DR
300 HAY 94544 712-B6
4500 SCL 95054 813-D4
BURKE LN
1100 FCTY 94404 749-J4
13200 LAH 94022 811-D7
BURKE RD
13100 LAH 94022 831-C1
13300 LAH 94022 811-D7
16700 LGTS 95032 873-J7
16700 SJS 95120 873-J7
16700 SJS 95124 873-J7
BURKE ST
- SF 94124 668-C5
400 SJS 95112 854-F3
BURKE WY
4300 FRMT 94536 752-J5
BURKETTE DR
1200 SJS 95129 853-A4
BURKHART AV
900 SLN 94579 691-A6
BURKSHIRE SQ
- SANS 94960 566-A4
BURL CT
2800 SJS 95121 855-E3
BURL WY
2700 SJS 95121 855-E3
BURLEIGH PL
200 DNVL 94526 653-C3
BURLEY DR
1600 MPS 95035 794-D6
BURL HOLLOW CT
1800 WLCK 94596 612-H7
BURLINGAME AV
100 BURL 94010 728-G7
5100 RCH 94804 609-B3
BURLINGAME WY
2600 SJS 95121 855-D3
BURLINGTON CT
1000 WLCK 94598 612-J4
BURLINGTON ST
- SJS 95193 875-C4
2400 OAK 94602 650-E4
BURLINGTON WY
3000 WLCK 94598 612-J4
BURLINGVIEW DR
2700 BURL 94010 728-C7
BURLWAY RD
700 BURL 94010 728-E4
BURLWOOD AV
300 OAK 94603 670-G7
BURLWOOD CT
- PIT 94565 573-F4
BURLWOOD DR
- SF 94127 667-E6
900 SJS 95120 894-G2
BURMA RD
- NVTO 94949 546-J4
100 OAK 94607 649-B1
100 OAK 94649 649-B1
900 CNCD 94518 592-F6
BURMAN DR
900 SJS 95111 855-A6
BURNBANK PL
6000 SJS 95120 874-C7
BURNETT AV
- SF 94131 667-F3
300 SCL 95051 833-A7
900 SF 94131 667-F4
1000 CNCD 94520 592-C2
N BURNETT AV
- SF 94131 667-F3
BURNETT DR
20900 SAR 95070 852-C5
BURNETT ST
1200 BERK 94702 629-E4
BURNETTE ST
2900 VAL 94591 530-D5
BURNEY PL
600 SRMN 94583 694-A1
BURNEY WY
4300 FRMT 94538 753-B6
BURNHAM CT
- SCAR 94070 769-F5
- PLHL 94523 592-B4
100 CMBL 95008 853-B5
BURNHAM DR
1000 PIT 94565 574-B2
1100 SJS 95132 814-F5
BURNHAM PL
- FRMT 94539 753-D3
BURNHAM ST
- VAL 94590 529-H3
BURNHAM WY
2400 PA 94303 791-D5
7400 DBLN 94568 693-J3
31300 HAY 94544 732-E2
BURNING TREE CT
400 SRMN 94583 673-H6

BURNING TREE CT
6900 SJS 95119 875-E7
BURNING TREE DR
- NVTO 94949 546-C2
200 SJS 95119 875-E7
200 SJS 95119 895-E1
35800 NWK 94560 752-C6
BURNING TREE WY
- CNCD 94521 593-B4
BURNING TREES DR
3200 SRMN 94583 673-H7
BURNLEY LN
500 AlaC 94541 711-E1
BURNLEY WY
1100 SCL 95051 832-H4
1100 SUNV 94087 832-H4
BURNS AV
100 ATN 94027 790-E2
BURNS CIR
500 SRMN 94583 673-E4
BURNS CT
- SRMN 94583 673-E4
100 PLHL 94523 592-B7
800 PCFA 94044 727-A1
7800 ELCR 94530 609-E2
BURNS PL
- SF 94103 667-J1
BURNS WY
14200 SAR 95070 872-D2
BURNSIDE AV
- SF 94131 667-F6
BURNSIDE CT
1900 CNCD 94521 593-G4
5300 FRMT 94536 752-H7
BURNSIDE DR
6800 SJS 95120 894-G3
BURNSWORTH PL
- CNCD 94518 592-F5
BURNT OAK CIR
- LFYT 94549 631-J3
BURNT RIDGE FIRE RD
- MrnC 94946 525-F6
BURNTWOOD AV
1000 SUNV 94089 812-J5
BURNTWOOD CT
1100 SUNV 94089 812-J5
BURR AV
- SF 94134 687-J2
39800 FRMT 94538 753-B7
BURR CT
- LFYT 94549 631-J3
BURR LN
2000 LVMR 94550 715-H3
BURR ST
9000 OAK 94605 671-A3
BURR WY
21400 AlaC 94541 691-G7
BURREL CT
1400 SJS 95126 833-G6
BURRELL CT
- TBRN 94920 607-A4
BURREN WY
2900 SSF 94080 707-E5
BURRITT ST
- SF 94108 648-A5
BURROUGHS AV
1900 SLN 94577 690-J5
BURROWS AV
600 SBRN 94066 707-H7
BURROWS RD
1200 CMBL 95008 873-B2
BURROWS ST
- SF 94134 668-A7
600 SF 94134 667-H7
900 FCTY 94404 749-G4
2000 SF 94112 667-H7
BURRWOOD CT
3800 CNCD 94521 592-J3
BURTON AV
- SJS 95110 834-A3
- SJS 95112 834-A3
2100 PIT 94565 574-C4
BURTON COM
3800 FRMT 94536 752-J4
BURTON CT
100 DNVL 94526 653-C6
3200 LFYT 94549 631-H2
BURTON DR
600 LFYT 94549 631-H2
2800 OAK 94611 650-G1
3900 SCL 95054 813-D5
BURTON RD
16100 LGTS 95032 873-D3
BURTON ST
7200 DBLN 94568 693-J3
BURTON VISTA CT
- LFYT 94549 631-G1
BURWOOD WY
500 ANT 94509 595-E1
BUSBY AV
- SLN 94579 691-A7
BUSBY WY
34800 FRMT 94555 752-E1
BUSCH RD
4600 AlaC 94588 714-G1
4600 PLE 94588 714-G1
4600 PLE 94566 714-G1
BUSH AV
1100 SolC 94591 550-E1
1300 SPAB 94806 588-G4
2300 RCH 94806 588-H4
BUSH CIR
- SCIC 94043 812-A2
4400 FRMT 94538 773-D2
BUSH CT
43200 FRMT 94538 773-D2
BUSH ST
- SF 94111 648-A5
- SJS 95126 834-A7
100 MTVW 94041 811-J6
100 SF 94104 648-A5
300 SF 94108 648-A5
700 SF 94102 648-A5
800 SF 94108 647-F6
800 SF 94102 647-F6
900 MRTZ 94553 571-F4
900 SF 94109 647-F6
1100 SCAR 94070 769-G2
1200 CCCo 94553 571-F4
1900 SF 94115 647-F6

BUSHMINT PL
- CCCo 94507 632-H4
BUSHNELL RD
- SCIC 94035 812-B2
- SCIC 94043 812-B2
BUSINESS CIR
2200 SJS 95128 853-F1
BUSINESS CENTER DR
4000 FRMT 94538 773-E4
BUSKIRK AV
- CCCo 94596 592-C7
2400 PLHL 94523 592-D6
2900 CCCo 94596 612-C1
3000 PLHL 94523 612-C1
3100 PLHL 94596 592-D6
BUSKIRK ST
100 MPS 95035 793-J3
200 MPS 95035 794-A3
BUSS ST
- VAL 94590 530-C5
200 VAL 94591 530-C5
BUSTOS CIR
500 CCCo 94565 573-D1
BUSTOS PL
500 CCCo 94565 573-D1
BUSTOS WY
500 CCCo 94565 573-D1
BUTANO AV
100 SUNV 94086 812-B6
BUTANO CT
6100 SJS 95123 874-G6
BUTANO DR
1600 MPS 95035 814-E2
BUTANO TER
14700 SAR 95070 872-D3
BUTANO PARK DR
5300 FRMT 94538 773-B2
BUTCHER DR
3400 SCL 95051 832-J5
BUTI PARK CT
17600 AlaC 94546 692-A2
BUTI PARK DR
4900 AlaC 94546 692-A2
BUTLER AV
- SSF 94080 708-A2
1200 SLN 94579 691-A4
BUTLER ST
- MPS 95035 793-J7
BUTTE AV
3000 SRMN 94583 673-G7
BUTTE CT
100 CCCo 94565 573-E2
1000 SUNV 94087 832-B4
1100 LVMR 94550 695-F6
BUTTE PL
- SF 94103 668-A1
BUTTE ST
300 VAL 94590 529-H5
600 SAUS 94965 626-J2
1600 RCH 94804 609-C3
2800 SCL 95051 833-A4
2900 AlaC 94541 692-C6
BUTTERCUP CT
- CCCo 94507 632-G2
100 HER 94547 570-A4
1500 LVMR 94550 696-A4
2800 ANT 94509 575-H7
BUTTERCUP LN
- SCAR 94070 769-C4
400 PLHL 94523 591-J3
BUTTERFIELD DR
100 NVTO 94945 526-B1
20000 AlaC 94546 691-J4
BUTTERFIELD LN
- MrnC 94960 566-A3
BUTTERFIELD PL
400 MRGA 94556 651-F3
BUTTERFIELD RD
400 MrnC 94960 566-A3
1000 SANS 94960 566-A3
BUTTERFLY DR
1200 SJS 95120 874-C7
BUTTERFLY LN
- MrnC 94904 586-D3
BUTTERNUT CT
700 UNC 94587 732-G3
BUTTERNUT DR
700 SRFL 94903 566-B3
2400 HIL 94010 748-C1
BUTTERNUT ST
3000 ANT 94509 575-J6
BUTTERNUT WY
1100 CNCD 94521 593-G7
BUTTERS DR
2700 OAK 94602 650-G3
BUTTITTA LN
1400 SCL 95051 833-A4
BUTTNER CT
1800 PLHL 94523 591-H5
BUTTNER RD
1800 PLHL 94523 591-J5
BUTTON BRUSH PZ
- HAY 94542 712-B3
BUTTONWOOD CT
2700 SJS 95148 835-E6
BUTTONWOOD DR
500 CCCo 94506 654-A2
BUTTONWOOD TER
3500 FRMT 94536 752-A6
BUTTRESS CT
4500 CNCD 94518 593-A6
BUXTON AV
100 SSF 94080 707-D2
BUXTON CIR
100 PLHL 94523 591-J4
BUXTON COM
38000 FRMT 94536 752-J3
BUXTON PL
38000 FRMT 94536 752-J3
BUZZIE CT
600 LFYT 94549 631-H2
BYERLEY AV
700 SJS 95125 854-B5
BYERLEY CT
- CCCo 94507 632-J2
BYERLY CT
100 VAL 94591 530-E1
10100 CPTO 95014 831-J7
BYERS DR
1900 MLPK 94025 791-A2
BYINGTON DR
4800 SJS 95121 855-F5

INDEX

STREET
Block City ZIP Pg-Grid

BYINGTON DR
4800 SJS 95138 855-F5
BYINGTON ST
- SF 94115 647-G6
BYRD LN
800 FCTY 94404 749-G4
1000 AlaC 94566 714-E6
13000 LAH 94022 810-J7
BYRDEE WY
600 CCCo 94549 591-G4
BYRNE AV
10000 CPTO 95014 852-B1
10300 SCIC 95014 852-B1
BYRNE ST
100 DALY 94014 687-D5
100 SMCo 94014 687-D5
BYRNE PARK LN
27100 LAH 94022 830-J2
BYRON AV
1800 SMTO 94401 749-C1
BYRON CIR
- MLV 94941 606-G4
BYRON CT
- PLHL 94523 592-A7
- SF 94112 687-F2
500 BEN 94510 550-H1
3400 PLE 94588 694-E6
BYRON DR
- PLHL 94523 592-A7
800 SSF 94080 707-D2
1900 SJS 95124 873-G2
BYRON ST
100 PA 94301 790-J3
100 VAL 94590 530-A3
600 PA 94306 811-F2
1100 PA 94301 791-A4
2100 BERK 94702 629-E2
2700 PA 94306 791-C6
10300 OAK 94603 671-A5
22500 AlaC 94541 692-C6
BYWOOD DR
1900 OAK 94602 650-E2
BYXBEE ST
- SF 94132 687-C1

C

C RD
12200 AlaC 94586 734-C5
S C RD
- SUNV 94089 812-J3
C ST
- CCCo 94525 550-A5
- CCCo 94565 573-E1
- CNCD 94520 572-J3
- CPTO 95014 831-H5
- MTVW 94043 812-B5
- OAK 94625 649-A3
- SF - 668-F7
- SF 94124 668-F7
- VAL 94592 529-F4
- MRTZ 94553 571-E4
- SRFL 94901 586-F1
- VAL 94590 529-H2
100 AlaC 94586 734-B5
100 BEN 94510 551-B5
100 CCCo 94553 592-B1
100 HAY 94541 711-H2
100 MLPK 94025 790-G3
100 RDWC 94063 769-J5
200 SSF 94080 707-G3
300 ANT 94509 575-D4
300 CLMA 94014 687-D6
300 RDWC 94063 770-A4
300 UNC 94587 732-F4
400 RCH 94801 588-E6
900 NVTO 94949 546-G3
1000 HAY 94541 712-A1
1100 SRFL 94901 566-F7
1100 SUNV 94089 812-E2
1500 HAY 94541 692-A7
4300 PIT 94565 574-C4
7100 ELCR 94530 609-E4
9200 OAK 94603 670-H5
CABALLO CT
1100 SJS 95132 814-G5
CABALLO LN
- SCIC 94304 810-F6
CABALLO RANCHERO CT
2200 CCCo 94526 633-F7
CABALLO RANCHERO DR
2200 CCCo 94526 633-E6
CABANA CT
300 DNVL 94526 653-D7
CABANA DR
1600 SCIC 95125 853-H6
CABELLO CT
4800 UNC 94587 731-J7
CABELLO ST
4200 UNC 94587 732-A6
4200 UNC 94587 731-J7
CABERNET AV
6700 NWK 94560 752-C6
CABERNET CT
- LFYT 94549 611-A7
- ORIN 94563 611-A7
100 CLAY 94517 593-H7
4200 PLE 94566 714-F4
8200 SJS 95135 855-J6
CABERNET DR
18700 SAR 95070 852-H5
CABERNET WY
2000 LVMR 94550 715-H3
48800 FRMT 94539 794-A2
CABERNET VINEYARDS CIR
3600 SJS 95117 853-C2
CABERNET VINEYARDS CT
900 SJS 95117 853-C2
CABIN DR
700 MrnC 94965 606-D7
CABLE RDWY
- SAUS 94965 627-A4
CABONIA CT
- PLE 94566 715-D6
CABOOSE PL
200 DNVL 94526 653-B5
CABOT AV
- SCL 95051 852-J1
CABOT BLVD
22600 HAY 94545 711-C3
CABOT CT
400 SSF 94080 708-B3
500 WLCK 94598 612-F2
800 SCAR 94070 769-E5
2500 FRMT 94536 753-A3
8400 NWK 94560 772-C2
CABOT DR
1800 WLCK 94598 612-E2
5600 OAK 94611 630-D7
CABOT LN
800 FCTY 94404 749-F4
CABOT PL
1100 SJS 95129 852-F3
CABOT RD
400 SSF 94080 708-B3
CABRAL AV
5800 SJS 95123 874-F5
CABRAL DR
35000 FRMT 94536 752-E3
CABRILHO DR
4000 CCCo 94553 571-J3
CABRILLO AV
600 SCIC 94305 810-H1
1000 BURL 94010 728-D5
1200 SCL 95050 833-D3
1300 SJS 95132 814-E5
2400 SCL 95051 833-B2
2900 LVMR 94550 715-H1
3000 SRMN 94583 673-G7
3300 SCL 95051 832-J3
CABRILLO CT
- SRFL 94903 566-B2
2000 SCL 95051 833-B3
2300 HAY 94545 731-H1
2700 ANT 94509 575-A6
35000 FRMT 94536 752-E2
CABRILLO DR
100 VAL 94591 530-D7
800 SJS 95131 814-A5
2300 HAY 94545 731-G1
35100 FRMT 94536 752-E2
CABRILLO FRWY Rt#-1
- DALY - 687-B7
- DALY - 707-A2
- PCFA - 706-J4
100 PCFA - 707-A2
2100 DALY - 687-B7
CABRILLO HWY Rt#-1
- PCFA 94044 707-A7
- SMCo - 726-F6
100 PCFA 94044 727-A1
100 PCFA 94044 726-H3
CABRILLO PL
- OAK 94611 630-E7
300 PIT 94565 574-B5
CABRILLO RD
2000 SJS 95134 813-G3
CABRILLO ST
- SF 94118 647-A7
1200 ELCR 94530 609-D2
1600 SF 94121 647-A7
3200 SF 94121 646-H7
CABRILLO TER
37000 FRMT 94536 752-G4
CABRILLO WY
100 SBRN 94066 727-J1
CABRILLO NORTE
5500 RCH 94803 589-J3
CABRILLO SUR
5500 RCH 94803 589-J3
5500 RCH 94803 590-A3
CABRINI DR
28300 HAY 94545 731-H2
CABRO CT
1000 NVTO 94947 525-G5
CACHE PEAK DR
4700 ANT 94509 595-E3
CACTUS CT
- WLCK 94595 632-B2
CACTUS DR
5500 SJS 95123 875-B4
CACTUS ST
2200 FRMT 94539 773-G3
CADBURRY CT
500 SJS 95123 874-G4
CADDY CT
- NVTO 94949 546-C3
CADE DR
3200 FRMT 94536 752-F1
CADELL PL
- SF 94133 648-A4
CADENCIA ST
- FRMT 94539 753-G5
CADET PL
900 SJS 95133 814-E7
CADILLAC CT
900 MPS 95035 793-H5
CADILLAC DR
3100 SJS 95117 853-D4
CADILLAC WY
1000 BURL 94010 728-E5
CADIZ CIR
- RDWC 94065 749-J7
CADIZ CT
- PCFA 94044 726-J4
100 VAL 94591 530-F6
4100 FRMT 94536 752-F2
CADIZ DR
5800 SJS 95123 874-F5
35800 FRMT 94536 752-F2
CADIZ LN
- ANT 94509 575-A6
2800 ANT 94509 574-J6
CADLONI CT
300 VAL 94591 530-D2
CADLONI LN
100 VAL 94591 530-D2
CADMAN RD
3100 FRMT 94538 753-D6
CADMILL CT
2800 SJS 95121 854-J4
CADWALLADER AV
3500 SJS 95121 855-D3
CADWELL CT
100 SJS 95138 875-D4
CADY CT
2400 AlaC 94578 691-G4
CAFETO CT
100 WLCK 94598 612-H3
CAFETO DR
3000 WLCK 94598 612-H2
CAFFRIN CT
40000 FRMT 94538 773-A1
CAGGIANO CT
1000 SJS 95120 894-G3
CAGGIANO DR
1000 SJS 95120 894-G3
CAHALAN AV
5600 SJS 95123 874-G4
CAHALAN CT
700 SJS 95123 874-G4
CAHEN DR
7100 SJS 95120 894-H4
CAHILL ST
- SJS 95110 834-A6
- SJS 95113 834-A6
4300 FRMT 94538 753-C7
CAHILL RIDGE RD
- SMCo - 768-D3
CAIN LN
800 NVTO 94945 526-C3
CAINE AV
- SF 94112 687-E1
CAIRE TER
- SF 94107 668-B3
CAIRO CT
10000 SCIC 95127 835-A3
CAIRO RD
100 OAK 94603 670-F7
100 OAK 94621 670-F7
CAIRO ST
1600 LVMR 94550 715-F4
CAITLIN CT
- PLHL 94523 592-B4
CAJA CT
- MrnC 94903 546-D7
CAJON CT
1500 ANT 94509 575-A7
CALABAZAS BLVD
1300 SCL 95051 833-A2
CALABAZAS CT
1300 SCL 95051 833-A4
CALABAZAS CREEK CIR
6900 SJS 95129 852-E4
CALABRIA PL
19100 AlaC 94541 691-F7
CALADO AV
100 CMBL 95008 853-A5
400 SJS 95130 853-A5
CALADO CT
1600 CMBL 95008 853-A5
CALAFIA AV
3500 OAK 94605 671-B4
CALAFIA CT
- SRFL 94903 566-B2
CALAFIA LN
- AMCN 94589 510-B4
CALAIS AV
1300 LVMR 94550 715-F3
CALAIS CT
1400 LVMR 94550 715-F3
1700 AlaC 94541 712-B1
4700 SJS 95124 874-A3
CALAIS DR
200 PIN 94564 569-E3
2800 SRMN 94583 673-F6
CALAIS PL
7100 NWK 94560 752-C6
CALANDRIA
3400 OAK 94605 671-B3
CALAROGA AV
24600 HAY 94545 711-G5
27700 HAY 94545 731-H1
CALAVERAS AV
100 PCFA 94044 727-B2
1400 SJS 95126 833-H7
4500 FRMT 94538 753-A6
4600 FRMT 94538 752-J6
4800 OAK 94619 650-G7
CALAVERAS BLVD
1100 MPS 95035 794-D6
CALAVERAS BLVD Rt#-237
100 MPS 95035 794-A7
100 MPS 95035 793-J7
CALAVERAS CIR
1900 ANT 94509 575-G6
CALAVERAS CT
- HIL 94010 748-F6
- MPS 95035 794-C6
600 MRTZ 94553 571-E7
1900 ANT 94509 575-G6
CALAVERAS DR
1900 CCCo 94565 573-H2
4100 CNCD 94521 593-B3
CALAVERAS RD
- SCIC - 774-J4
- SCIC 95035 774-J4
2000 MPS 95035 794-E6
3600 SCIC 95035 794-H5
3900 SCIC 95140 794-J2
8500 AlaC 94586 734-E7
8500 AlaC 94586 754-F2
9100 AlaC 94586 774-G1
24300 HAY 94545 711-F4
CALAVERAS ST
- VAL 94590 530-C4
CALAVERAS WY
- SMCo 94020 809-F6
1000 VAL 94590 530-C3
CALAVERAS RIDGE DR
800 MPS 95035 794-C4
CALAVISTA DR
- SRFL 94901 586-E1
CALBOONYA CT
1600 SJS 95125 854-D3
CALBORO DR
1000 SJS 95117 853-D3
CALCATERRA CT
1100 SJS 95120 894-G3
CALCATERRA DR
7000 SJS 95120 894-G3
CALCATERRA PL
300 PA 94306 811-E2
CALCITE CT
- LVMR 94550 715-D3
CALCOT PL
1000 OAK 94606 650-A7
CALCOTT CT
3000 FRMT 94555 732-E7
CALCUTTA DR
34500 FRMT 94555 752-E1
CALDAS CT
42700 FRMT 94539 753-F7
CALDECOTT LN
100 OAK 94618 630-B4
200 OAK 94611 630-B4
CALDER LN
1100 WLCK 94598 612-D3
CALDERON AV
100 MTVW 94041 811-J6
CALDERON CT
- LVMR 94550 715-G4
CALDERWOOD CT
4800 OAK 94605 651-A7
CALDERWOOD LN
5200 SJS 95118 874-B4
CALDWELL AV
200 LGTS 95032 873-B7
1000 VAL 94591 530-D5
CALDWELL CT
- PLHL 94523 592-B4
1200 SUNV 94024 832-A4
7800 AlaC 94552 692-G2
CALDWELL PL
700 SCL 95051 833-B5
CALDWELL RD
600 OAK 94611 630-C5
CALDWELL TER
5100 FRMT 94555 752-C3
CALEB CT
2100 SJS 95121 855-C4
CALEB PL
500 HAY 94544 732-E2
CALEDONIA DR
7900 SJS 95135 855-J5
CALEDONIA ST
- SAUS 94965 627-A2
- SF 94103 667-H2
CALERA TER
800 PCFA 94044 727-A3
CALERA CREEK HEIGHTS DR
1600 MPS 95035 794-C3
CALERO AV
200 SJS 95123 874-F5
700 SJS 95123 875-A5
CALERO ST
600 MPS 95035 793-J6
CALERO HILLS CT
7100 SJS 95139 895-H2
CALETA AV
- SANS 94960 566-A4
CALFHILL CT
- LGTS 95032 873-B6
CALGARY CT
10100 SCIC 95127 835-B3
CALGARY DR
1700 SUNV 94087 832-B6
CALGARY LN
2100 CNCD 94520 572-F5
CALGARY ST
- SF 94134 687-J3
- DALY 94014 687-J3
15500 SLN 94579 691-A7
15500 SLN 94579 711-A1
CALGARY TER
34400 FRMT 94555 752-C3
CAL GEARY RD
- AlaC 94586 774-J3
CALHOUN CT
2300 ANT 94509 595-A1
CALHOUN ST
- VAL 94590 529-H2
700 HAY 94544 712-C5
800 SJS 95116 834-D5
2500 ALA 94501 670-A4
CALHOUN TER
- SF 94133 648-A4
CALI AV
20400 CPTO 95014 852-E1
CALIBAN DR
33400 FRMT 94555 752-B1
CALIBAN RD
33600 FRMT 94555 752-C1
CALICO AV
3300 SJS 95124 873-F2
3600 SCIC 95124 873-F2
CALICO CT
700 SUNV 94086 832-F1
CALICO LN
- NVTO 94947 525-H3
CALICOWOOD PL
5100 SJS 95111 875-C2
CALIDA DR
4900 SJS 95136 874-F2
CALIDO PL
40800 FRMT 94539 753-E5
CALIENTA REAL
- NVTO 94949 546-H4
CALIENTE AV
500 LVMR 94550 715-E2
CALIENTE CIR
200 SLN 94578 691-C5
CALIENTE DR
200 SLN 94578 691-C4
600 SUNV 94086 812-G5
CALIENTE RD
8300 CCCo 94803 589-F1
CALIENTE WY
1400 SJS 95132 814-E4
40500 FRMT 94539 753-F4
CALIENTE REAL
- NVTO 94949 546-J4
CALIFORNIA
600 RCH 94801 588-B6
3000 ALA 94501 649-F6
CALIFORNIA AV
- VAL 94592 529-G4
- MrnC 94941 606-E5
- ORIN 94563 610-E6
- PA 94301 791-B6
- PLE 94566 714-F2
- SF 94130 648-E2
- SRFL 94901 566-D6
100 PA 94306 791-A7
100 SSF 94080 708-A3
100 SLN 94577 671-A7
100 SLN 94577 691-A1
200 PIT 94565 574-D3
200 SSF 94080 707-J2
400 SCL 95050 833-D5
500 PA 94305 791-A7
700 PA 94303 791-C5
700 PA 94306 811-A1
700 PA 94304 811-A1
900 SJS 95125 854-B4
900 SUNV 94086 812-G7
1300 SPAB 94806 588-G4
1600 PA 94305 811-A1
1700 SCIC 94305 811-A1
E CALIFORNIA AV
100 SUNV 94086 812-F7
W CALIFORNIA AV
100 SUNV 94086 812-D6
900 MrnC 94941 606-E5
N CALIFORNIA BLVD
1300 WLCK 94596 612-C4
S CALIFORNIA BLVD
1100 WLCK 94596 612-C6
CALIFORNIA CIR
1200 MPS 95035 793-H4
CALIFORNIA DR
- BURL 94010 728-C4
- MLBR 94030 728-C4
CALIFORNIA LN
- CMAD 94925 586-F7
CALIFORNIA ST
- CCCo 94572 549-J6
- RDWC 94063 770-A6
- VAL 94590 530-A2
- SF 94111 648-A5
200 CMBL 95008 853-D7
300 SF 94104 648-A5
500 MTVW 94041 811-G4
600 SF 94108 648-A5
700 CCCo 94572 569-J1
900 CCCo 94572 570-A1
1000 SF 94108 647-E6
1200 SF 94109 647-E6
1300 BERK 94703 609-F7
1400 BERK 94703 629-F1
1800 CNCD 94520 592-F2
1900 MTVW 94040 811-F3
2100 SF 94115 647-E6
2800 OAK 94602 650-E4
3300 SF 94118 647-E6
3300 OAK 94608 629-F4
3500 OAK 94619 650-F5
3500 SF 94118 647-D6
5500 SF 94121 647-B6
18800 AlaC 94546 692-A3
37300 NWK 94560 752-F7
39300 FRMT 94538 753-A4
CALIFORNIA WY
500 RDWC 94062 789-E2
600 SMCo 94062 789-E2
700 WDSD 94062 789-E3
3800 LVMR 94550 715-J1
3900 LVMR 94550 716-A1
W CALIFORNIA WY
500 RDWC 94062 789-E3
500 WDSD 94062 789-E3
CALIFORNIA CONDOR WY
- NVTO 94949 546-D5
CALIFORNIA OAK WY
10000 CPTO 95014 831-J7
CALINOMA DR
1500 SJS 95118 874-A5
CALISTOGA CIR
400 FRMT 94536 732-H6
CALISTOGA CT
- DNVL 94526 653-C7
CALISTOGA DR
200 PIT 94565 574-D5
1800 SJS 95124 873-H1
CALISTOGA ST
4900 UNC 94587 752-A2
CALISTOGA WY
- MTVW 94043 812-A5
5600 CLAY 94517 593-F6
CALL AV
26500 HAY 94542 712-D3
CALLA DR
700 SUNV 94086 832-F2
CALLADO WY
- ATN 94027 790-C5
CALLAGHAN ST
3000 LVMR 94550 695-H7
CALLAHAN RD
- AlaC 94546 652-A4
- AlaC 94546 651-J5
- CCCo - 652-A4
CALLAN AV
- SLN 94577 691-B1
500 SLN 94577 671-B7
CALLAN BLVD
- DALY 94015 687-B7
3500 SSF 94080 707-C3
4000 DALY 94015 707-B1
CALLAN PL
- ALA 94502 669-H5
CALLAN ST
100 MPS 95035 794-A3
7700 DBLN 94568 693-H2
CALLE ALEGRE
1400 SJS 95120 874-B7
2600 PLE 94566 714-C2
CALLE ALFREDO
- SUNV 94089 812-G4
CALLE ALICIA
- SUNV 94089 812-H4
CALLE ALMADEN
5900 SJS 95120 874-D6
CALLE ALOUDRA
5400 SJS 95111 875-C3
CALLE ALTAMIRA
900 PLE 94566 714-B3
CALLE AMIGO DR
- FRMT 94539 753-D3
CALLE ANITA
- SUNV 94089 812-H4
CALLE ARBOLEDA
300 MrnC 94949 546-F2
600 NVTO 94949 546-F2
CALLE ARROYO
1600 CCCo 94526 633-E7
CALLE ARTIS
700 SJS 95131 814-A5
CALLE BONITA
6200 SJS 95120 874-B7
6200 SJS 95120 894-B1
CALLE CARLOTTA
- SUNV 94089 812-J4
CALLECITA
100 LGTS 95030 872-J2
CALLECITA CT
4400 UNC 94587 731-H6
CALLECITA ST
1400 SJS 95125 854-A6
CALLE CONCHITA
- SUNV 94089 812-H4
CALLE CONSUELO
- SUNV 94089 812-H4
CALLE CUERVO
200 SJS 95111 875-C3
CALLE DE AIDA
1500 SJS 95118 874-A3
CALLE DE AMOR
6000 SJS 95124 873-J7
CALLE DE ARROYO
4300 SJS 95118 874-A2
CALLE DE BARCELONA
19300 SCIC 95014 852-G1
CALLE DE CUESTANDA
1200 MPS 95035 814-E1
CALLE DE ESCUELA
4900 SCL 95054 813-C3
CALLE DE FARRAR
4300 SJS 95118 874-B3
CALLE DE FELICE
6000 SJS 95124 873-J7
CALLE DE GILDA
1400 SJS 95118 874-B3
CALLE DE GUADALUPE
- SJS 95116 834-G3
CALLE DE LA LOMA
2700 PLE 94566 714-B2
CALLE DE LA MANCHA
6500 PLE 94566 714-B2
CALLE DE LA MESA
200 MrnC 94949 546-E2
2700 PLE 94566 714-A2
CALLE DE LA PAZ
1400 SJS 95120 874-B7
1900 PLE 94566 714-C2
CALLE DE LA SELVA
200 MrnC 94949 546-E2
CALLE DE LAS ESTRELLA
2900 SJS 95148 855-C2
CALLE DE LAS FLORES
2900 SJS 95148 855-B2
CALLE DE LAS GRANVAS
- LVMR 94550 695-G6
CALLE DEL CASARILLO
- CCCo 94526 633-F7
CALLE DEL CONEJO
6100 SJS 95120 874-B7
CALLE DEL MUNDO
2300 SCL 95054 813-C3
CALLE DEL PRADO
600 MPS 95035 794-B5
CALLE DEL REY
- LVMR 94550 695-F6
CALLE DEL SOL
- LVMR 94550 695-G6
5100 SCL 95054 813-C3
26300 LAH 94022 831-B1
CALLE DEL SUENO
- LVMR 94550 695-G6
CALLE DE LUCIA
4700 SJS 95124 874-A3
CALLE DE LUNA
2200 SCL 95054 813-C3
CALLE DE PLATA
1700 SJS 95116 834-F3
CALLE DE PRIMAVERA
2000 SCL 95054 813-C4
CALLE DE PROSPERO
1600 SJS 95124 873-J7
CALLE DE RICO
6000 SJS 95124 873-J7
CALLE DE STUARDA
1500 SJS 95118 874-A2
CALLE DE SUERTE
6000 SJS 95124 873-J7
CALLE DE TOSCA
4500 SJS 95118 874-A3
CALLE DE VERDE
800 SJS 95136 874-E2
CALLE DOLORES
- SUNV 94089 812-H4
CALLE DORITA
- SUNV 94089 812-J4
CALLE EL KOWALIK
1600 SJS 95124 874-A3
CALLE EL PADRE
100 LGTS 95030 873-A2
CALLE EMPINADO
1000 MrnC 94949 546-E2
CALLE ENRIQUE
1400 PLE 94566 714-C2
CALLE ESPERANZA
6000 SJS 95120 874-B7
6400 PLE 94566 714-B2
CALLE ESTE
- WLCK 94596 612-D1
CALLE ESTORIA
100 LGTS 95030 873-A2
CALLE ESTRELLA
- SUNV 94089 812-H4
CALLE EULALIA
- SUNV 94089 812-H4
CALLE FLORES
300 CCCo 94553 572-C6
CALLE FUEGO
6200 PLE 94566 714-B2
CALLE GALONDRINA
- SJS 95111 875-C3
CALLE GAVIOTA
300 SJS 95111 875-C3
CALLE GLORIA
- SUNV 94089 812-H4
CALLE GLORIETA
- LVMR 94550 695-F6
CALLE ISABELLA
- SUNV 94089 812-H4
CALLE JUANITA
- SUNV 94089 812-H4
CALLE LA MESA
100 MRGA 94556 631-E2
CALLE LA MIRADA COM
- UNC 94587 732-E4
CALLE LA MONTANA
100 MRGA 94556 631-D2
CALLE LOLITA
200 LGTS 95030 873-A2
CALLE LOS CALLADOS
2000 CCCo 94526 633-F7
CALLE LUCIA
- SUNV 94089 812-H4
CALLE LUPE
1000 SUNV 94089 812-J4
CALLE MADRAS
2500 PLE 94566 714-C2
CALLE MARGUERITA
100 LGTS 95030 873-A2
CALLE MARIA
- SUNV 94089 812-J4
CALLE MESA ALTA
2000 MPS 95035 814-E2
CALLE MOLINO
300 CCCo 94553 572-C6
CALLE MONTALVO
20200 SAR 95070 872-E3
CALLE MORELIA
2600 PLE 94566 714-B2
CALLE NIVEL
100 LGTS 95030 872-J2
CALLE NOGALES
100 WLCK 94596 612-D1
CALLE ORIENTE
1100 MPS 95035 794-C5
CALLE PASEO
900 MrnC 94949 546-E2
CALLE PINTADA
5400 SJS 95111 875-C3
CALLE REYNOSO
2600 PLE 94566 714-B3
CALLE RICARDO
2000 PLE 94566 714-C2
CALLE ROSITA
- SUNV 94089 812-H4
CALLERY CT
- FRMT 94539 753-G5
CALLE SANTA ANA
1500 PLE 94566 714-C2
CALLE SANTIAGO
1500 PLE 94566 714-C2
CALLE TACUBA
13600 SAR 95070 872-E1
CALLE TERESA
- SUNV 94089 812-H4
CALLE VENTURA
1100 SJS 95120 894-E2
CALLE VERDE
900 MRTZ 94553 591-F4
CALLE VERDE RD
7500 DBLN 94568 693-G4
CALLE VICTORIA
- SUNV 94089 812-H4
CALLE VISTA VERDE
2100 MPS 95035 814-E1
CALLIE LN
- MLPK 94025 770-F7
CALMA CT
2500 SJS 95128 853-F4
CALMAR AV
600 OAK 94610 650-A3
CALMAR VISTA RD
600 DNVL 94526 652-H1
CALMOR AV
5600 SJS 95123 874-F4
CALMOR CT
5600 SJS 95123 874-F5
CALODEN ST
9900 OAK 94605 671-D4
CALOOSA CT
1700 SJS 95131 814-D7
CALPELLA DR
500 SJS 95136 874-F2
CALPINE DR
5600 SJS 95123 875-B4
CALPINE PL
2700 CNCD 94518 592-G6
CALSITE CT
100 ANT 94509 595-F2
CALSPRAY ST
700 RCH 94801 588-F5
CALUMET AV
- SANS 94960 566-B7
CALUMET CT
1000 SJS 95112 834-D3
CALVARY LN
1400 AlaC 94550 716-B1
CALVARY WY
- SJS 95118 854-C7
CALVELLI CT
3500 SJS 95124 873-E2
CALVERT AV
- SSF 94080 707-D1
CALVERT CT
- OAK 94611 650-C1
- PDMT 94611 650-C1
200 SCL 95051 832-J7
300 ANT 94509 595-E1
CALVERT DR
200 SCL 95051 832-J7
10100 SJS 95014 852-H1
10100 SCIC 95014 852-H1
CALVIEW AV
2000 SJS 95122 834-J6
CALVIEW LN
1400 SJS 95122 834-J6
CALVIN AV
2800 SMCo 94063 770-C7
3200 SJS 95124 873-F2
3600 SCIC 95124 873-F2
CALVIN CT
- CCCo 94595 612-A7
- ORIN 94563 631-B2
2800 FRMT 94536 753-A3
CALVIN DR
- ORIN 94563 631-B2
CALWA CT
5000 SJS 95111 875-A2
CALYPSO COM
4500 FRMT 94555 752-D2
CALYPSO CT
1100 SJS 95127 835-A4

STREET Block	City	ZIP	Pg-Grid
CALYPSO CT			
16200	AlaC	94578	691-F4
CALYPSO LN			
-	SCAR	94070	769-C5
CALYPSO TER			
4200	FRMT	94555	752-D2
CALYPSO SHORES			
-	MrnC	94949	526-H6
CALZAR DR			
3000	SJS	95118	874-A1
CAMA LN			
-	NVTO	94947	526-D7
3500	AlaC	94552	692-C5
CAMACHO WY			
1800	SJS	95132	814-D3
CAMAHO PL			
-	HIL	94010	748-G2
CAMANO CT			
1100	SJS	95122	854-H2
CAMANOE LN			
3400	ALA	94502	670-A6
CAMARA CIR			
2500	CNCD	94520	592-F4
CAMARDA CT			
20100	CPTO	95014	832-E7
CAMARGO CT			
2900	SJS	95132	814-D3
CAMARGO DR			
1700	SJS	95132	814-D3
CAMARILLO CT			
1000	MPS	95035	794-C4
3200	SJS	95135	855-G4
CAMARITAS AV			
-	SSF	94080	707-D1
CAMARITAS CIR			
800	SSF	94080	707-E1
CAMARITAS CT			
100	DNVL	94526	653-D5
CAMARITAS WY			
300	DNVL	94526	653-D5
CAMARONES PL			
3300	SRMN	94583	673-G5
CAMAS AV			
400	SJS	95116	834-J3
CAMASS CT			
5600	NWK	94560	752-G6
CAMBARK CT			
100	CCCo	94553	572-A3
100	CCCo	94553	571-J3
CAMBELL BLVD			
-	ALA	94501	650-A7
CAMBERLY WY			
400	RDWC	94061	790-B2
CAMBER TREE CT			
1100	SJS	95120	874-D7
CAMBIO CT			
4600	FRMT	94536	752-F4
CAMBON DR			
-	SF	94132	687-B1
CAMBORNE AV			
-	SMCo	94070	769-D3
-	SCAR	94070	769-D3
CAMBRA CT			
-	DNVL	94526	652-J3
21300	AlaC	94541	691-H7
CAMBRIA CT			
-	PIT	94565	574-E2
CAMBRIA LN			
-	PIT	94565	574-E2
CAMBRIA ST			
4300	FRMT	94538	753-A6
CAMBRIAN AV			
-	PDMT	94611	650-D2
CAMBRIAN DR			
500	SCIC	95008	853-F7
800	SJS	95008	853-F7
15800	AlaC	94578	691-F3
CAMBRIAN WY			
500	DNVL	94526	653-D6
CAMBRIANNA DR			
1900	SJS	95124	873-F2
CAMBRIAN VIEW WY			
100	LGTS	95032	873-G6
CAMBRIDGE			
-	HER	94547	569-J2
CAMBRIDGE AV			
-	SLN	94577	671-A7
200	CCCo	94708	609-G3
200	PA	94306	791-A7
600	MLPK	94025	790-G5
900	SUNV	94087	832-C1
20500	AlaC	94541	691-G7
CAMBRIDGE CT			
-	FRMT	94536	753-A3
-	DNVL	94526	652-H1
100	NVTO	94947	526-C6
300	LVMR	94550	696-A7
3600	PLE	94588	694-E5
5300	NWK	94560	752-E4
CAMBRIDGE DR			
500	BEN	94510	550-H1
500	SCL	95051	832-J6
1100	LFYT	94549	611-C4
1700	ALA	94501	670-B2
2300	ANT	94509	594-J2
2300	ANT	94509	595-A2
2800	SJS	95125	854-C7
12500	SAR	95070	852-G6
CAMBRIDGE HTS			
-	NVTO	94947	526-C6
CAMBRIDGE LN			
100	SBRN	94066	727-F2
3500	MTVW	94040	831-J2
CAMBRIDGE PL			
3200	CNCD	94518	592-H3
CAMBRIDGE RD			
600	RDWC	94061	789-G3
1100	BURL	94010	728-D5
CAMBRIDGE ST			
-	SCAR	94070	769-E3
-	SF	94134	667-H7
-	SF	94112	667-H7
500	BLMT	94002	749-E7
600	SF	94134	687-J1
1000	NVTO	94947	526-B5
CAMBRIDGE WY			
-	PDMT	94611	650-A1
200	LVMR	94550	696-A7
4200	UNC	94587	731-J5
CAMBY RD			
2900	ANT	94509	575-C7
3100	ANT	94509	595-D1
CAMDEN AV			
700	CMBL	95008	853-E7
700	CMBL	95008	873-E1
1000	SJS	95120	894-E1
1000	SCIC	95008	873-E1
1300	SJS	95008	873-E1
1800	SCIC	95124	873-E2
1800	SJS	95120	873-J7
1800	SJS	95124	873-E2
4200	SJS	95118	873-H3
4300	SMTO	94403	749-C7
6000	SJS	95120	874-A7
19600	AlaC	94541	691-G7
CAMDEN CT			
100	SRMN	94583	673-G4
100	VAL	94591	530-E5
800	BEN	94510	530-H6
CAMDEN RD			
400	ALA	94501	669-H3
CAMDEN ST			
4400	OAK	94619	650-F7
5400	OAK	94619	670-G1
5900	OAK	94605	670-G1
37800	FRMT	94536	753-A3
37800	FRMT	94536	752-J3
CAMDEN OAKS CT			
1500	SJS	95124	874-A6
CAMDEN VILLAGE CIR			
1500	SJS	95124	874-A6
1500	SJS	95124	873-J6
CAMDEN VILLAGE CT			
5700	SJS	95124	874-A6
CAMDON CT			
3100	PLE	94588	694-F6
CAMEL LN			
2000	WLCK	94596	612-E7
2000	WLCK	94596	632-E1
CAMELBACK CT			
-	PLHL	94523	592-B2
CAMELBACK DR			
2300	ANT	94509	595-A2
CAMELBACK PL			
8100	PLHL	94523	592-B1
CAMELBACK RD			
100	CCCo	94553	592-B1
100	PLHL	94523	592-B1
CAMEL BARN RD			
-	BEN	94510	551-E5
CAMELFORD CT			
-	MRGA	94556	631-E3
-	OAK	94611	650-F2
CAMELFORD PL			
-	OAK	94611	650-F2
CAMELFORD WY			
200	SJS	95127	834-H1
CAMELIA CT			
2100	PIT	94565	574-A3
CAMELIA DR			
100	DALY	94015	687-B6
700	LVMR	94550	715-F2
1000	ALA	94502	670-A7
6400	SJS	95120	894-D1
CAMELIA LN			
-	LFYT	94549	611-A5
100	CCCo	94595	612-B6
CAMELIA ST			
600	BERK	94804	629-D1
700	BERK	94804	609-D7
1000	BERK	94702	609-D7
CAMELLIA AV			
-	SF	94112	667-G7
100	RDWC	94061	790-B2
CAMELLIA CT			
-	EPA	94303	791-C3
100	SBRN	94066	707-E6
400	BEN	94510	551-A1
600	HAY	94544	712-C6
600	LALT	94024	811-G6
1100	SLN	94577	690-J1
2200	FRMT	94539	773-G3
4300	PLE	94588	713-J1
CAMELLIA DR			
1100	EPA	94303	791-D2
44300	FRMT	94539	773-G3
CAMELLIA TER			
100	LGTS	95032	873-C6
16100	SCIC	95032	873-C6
CAMELLIA WY			
500	LALT	94024	811-F6
900	SJS	95117	853-B3
CAMELOT CT			
-	CCCo	94507	632-J2
-	CCCo	94707	609-F4
-	DALY	94015	707-D3
-	SCAR	94062	769-G6
3600	PLE	94588	694-E5
4100	PIT	94565	574-E6
CAMELOT DR			
15100	SCIC	95132	814-H4
CAMELOT LN			
17700	AlaC	94546	692-A2
CAMEO CT			
-	PLE	94588	693-F6
-	DALY	94015	707-B2
-	WLCK	94596	612-B2
300	CMBL	95008	853-G7
1300	LVMR	94550	715-D3
18800	AlaC	94546	692-A3
CAMEO DR			
-	LVMR	94550	715-D3
100	DNVL	94526	633-C7
1400	CMBL	95008	853-G6
1400	SJS	95129	852-J4
CAMEO WY			
-	SF	94131	667-F4
CAMERO PL			
40900	FRMT	94539	753-F5
CAMERO WY			
900	FRMT	94539	753-E5
CAMERON AV			
3600	PLE	94588	694-F7
3600	AlaC	94588	694-F7
10700	OAK	94605	671-D4
CAMERON CIR			
300	SRMN	94583	673-E4
CAMERON CT			
-	DNVL	94506	653-F1
1800	CNCD	94518	592-F5
CAMERON DR			
-	WLCK	94596	612-D4
2400	UNC	94587	732-C4
CAMERON LN			
-	DALY	94014	687-F3
CAMERON PL			
1100	SJS	95129	852-F3
CAMERON ST			
21900	AlaC	94546	692-B6
CAMERON WY			
-	SF	94124	688-C1
3000	SCL	95051	833-A7
CAMERON HILLS CT			
1800	FRMT	94539	773-G2
CAMERON HILLS DR			
43700	FRMT	94539	773-G2
CAMEROTA WY			
400	RDWC	94065	749-J5
CAMILLE			
900	CCCo	94507	652-G1
CAMILLE AV			
100	CCCo	94507	632-G7
CAMILLE CIR			
400	SJS	95134	813-H4
CAMILLE CT			
100	CCCo	94507	632-G7
300	MTVW	94040	811-H6
CAMILLE LN			
900	CCCo	94507	632-G7
CAMILLE PL			
-	CCCo	94507	632-G7
-	DNVL	94526	632-G7
CAMILLIA PL			
-	OAK	94602	650-E3
CAMILLO CT			
-	PLE	94566	715-D6
CAMINA ESCUELA			
600	SJS	95129	853-A2
CAMINAR WY			
100	CCCo	94596	612-E5
100	WLCK	94596	612-E5
CAMINO CT			
-	DNVL	94526	653-A2
-	LFYT	94549	611-J5
CAMINO DR			
200	NVTO	94949	546-H4
500	SCL	95050	833-F5
CAMINO PZ			
100	UNC	94587	732-J5
700	SBRN	94066	707-H6
CAMINO AL LAGO			
200	ATN	94027	790-C5
200	SMCo	94025	790-C5
CAMINO A LOS CERROS			
-	ATN	94027	790-C5
-	SMCo	94027	790-C5
1800	SMCo	94025	790-C5
CAMINO ALTA MIRA			
4900	AlaC	94546	692-B2
CAMINO ALTO			
-	MLBR	94030	728-A4
-	MLV	94941	606-F2
100	VAL	94590	530-B3
300	CMAD	94925	606-F2
N CAMINO ALTO			
-	VAL	94590	530-B3
700	VAL	94589	530-B1
CAMINO ALTO CT			
200	MLV	94941	606-F4
CAMINO AMIGO			
600	DNVL	94526	652-H1
800	DNVL	94526	632-G7
CAMINO AMIGO CT			
100	DNVL	94526	652-H2
CAMINO ANDRES			
-	CCCo	94565	573-E2
CAMINO ARROYO E			
300	CCCo	94506	654-A5
CAMINO ARROYO W			
300	CCCo	94506	654-A5
CAMINO BRAZOS			
2100	PLE	94566	714-C2
CAMINO CASA BUENA			
2700	PLE	94566	714-B2
CAMINO CERRADO			
1500	SJS	95128	853-F5
CAMINO COLORADOS			
3100	LFYT	94549	631-H4
CAMINO DE HERRERA			
-	SANS	94960	566-A5
CAMINO DE JUGAR			
2400	CCCo	94583	673-A3
2400	SRMN	94583	673-A3
CAMINO DE LAS ROBLES			
-	PA	94301	790-H5
CAMINO DEL CAMPO			
600	FRMT	94539	773-H2
CAMINO DEL CANYON RD			
100	MrnC	94965	606-B5
CAMINO DEL CERRO			
100	LGTS	95032	873-E5
100	SCIC	95032	873-E6
CAMINO DEL CINO			
3000	PLE	94566	714-B2
CAMINO DEL DIABLO			
-	ORIN	94563	610-E6
CAMINO DEL LAGO			
6200	PLE	94566	714-B2
CAMINO DEL MONTE			
-	ORIN	94563	610-E7
CAMINO DE LOS BARCOS			
13900	SAR	95070	872-G1
CAMINO DE LOS ROBLES			
-	ATN	94027	790-D6
1800	SMCo	94025	790-D6
CAMINO DEL REY			
2600	SJS	95132	814-E5
CAMINO DEL RIO			
900	LFYT	94549	611-H7
CAMINO DEL SOL			
-	CCCo	94553	571-J4
100	VAL	94591	550-E3
16100	LGTS	95032	873-D4
CAMINO DEL VALLE			
1000	ALA	94502	670-A6
1100	ALA	94502	669-J7
CAMINO DIABLO			
2500	CCCo	94596	612-A5
2500	LFYT	94549	612-A5
2500	LFYT	94549	611-J5
2600	WLCK	94596	612-A5
2900	WLCK	94595	612-A5
CAMINO DOLORES			
2200	AlaC	94546	691-H5
CAMINO DON MIGUEL			
-	ORIN	94563	610-F5
CAMINO ECCO			
2600	SJS	95121	855-A2
CAMINO ENCANTO			
100	DNVL	94526	652-H2
CAMINO ENCINAS			
-	ORIN	94563	630-H1
CAMINO ESTRADA			
1800	CNCD	94521	593-G5
CAMINO HERMOSO			
23200	LAH	94024	831-E4
CAMINO JUSTIN			
-	LFYT	94549	611-J5
CAMINO LAS JUNTAS			
100	PLHL	94523	592-B4
CAMINO LENADA			
-	ORIN	94563	610-G6
2600	OAK	94611	650-F2
CAMINO MEDIO LN			
12700	LAH	94022	811-B6
CAMINO MONDE			
1500	SJS	95125	853-J4
CAMINO MONTE SOL			
-	CCCo	94507	632-H3
CAMINO NOLA CT			
-	SJS	95132	814-E5
CAMINO PABLO			
-	ORIN	94563	630-H1
-	ORIN	-	630-H1
-	ORIN	94563	610-F6
-	ORIN	-	610-F6
100	CCCo	-	610-F6
300	CCCo	94563	610-F6
1000	MRGA	94556	651-F3
1000	SJS	95125	853-J3
2100	CCCo	-	651-F4
CAMINO PERAL			
1300	MRGA	94556	631-E6
CAMINO POR LOS ARBOLES			
700	ATN	94027	790-D5
CAMINO POSADA			
-	CCCo	94595	612-B6
CAMINO POSADA CT			
-	CCCo	94595	612-B6
CAMINO RAMON			
800	DNVL	94526	653-B5
1000	SJS	95125	853-J4
2000	SRMN	94583	653-D7
2000	SRMN	94583	673-E3
2100	DNVL	94526	673-E3
CAMINO RICARDO			
600	MRGA	94556	631-D6
1000	SJS	95125	853-J3
CAMINO RICO			
13600	SAR	95070	872-E1
CAMINO ROBLES CT			
1400	SJS	95120	874-B7
1400	SJS	95120	894-B1
CAMINO ROBLES WY			
1300	SJS	95120	874-B7
1300	SJS	95120	894-B1
CAMINO SANTA BARBARA			
41900	FRMT	94539	753-G6
CAMINO SEGURA			
2600	PLE	94566	714-B2
CAMINO SOBRANTE			
-	ORIN	94563	610-G5
CAMINO SOLANO			
1100	CNCD	94521	593-E7
CAMINO TASSAJARA			
-	CCCo	-	654-E5
1000	DNVL	94526	653-C2
2400	DNVL	94506	653-G5
3300	CCCo	94506	653-G5
3400	DNVL	94506	654-E5
3400	CCCo	94506	654-E5
CAMINO VALLECITO			
1100	LFYT	94549	611-C4
CAMINO VENADILLO			
2700	SRMN	94583	673-A2
CAMINO VERDE			
900	WLCK	94596	611-J2
CAMINO VERDE CIR			
900	WLCK	94596	611-J3
CAMINO VERDE DR			
6000	SJS	95119	875-C7
CAMINO VINEDO			
4000	CCCo	94553	571-J4
CAMINO VISTA			
25500	AlaC	94541	712-D2
W CAMINO VISTA			
25600	AlaC	94541	712-D2
CAMINO VISTA CT			
-	BLMT	94002	749-D7
CAMINO VISTA WY			
15900	SCIC	95127	815-B6
CAMISA CIR			
-	OAK	94605	671-C3
CAMLOOP DR			
2600	SJS	95130	852-J7
CAMP AV			
700	MTVW	94043	811-H2
CAMP ST			
-	SF	94110	667-H2
CAMPANA AV			
200	DALY	94015	687-A7
CAMPANA DR			
4000	PA	94306	811-C2
CAMPANULA CT			
6000	NWK	94560	752-G7
CAMPANULA PL			
4800	LGTS	95124	873-E4
CAMPAS CT			
-	BEN	94510	530-J6
CAMPBELL AV			
-	SCL	95050	833-G4
-	SJS	95193	875-C5
-	SF	94134	687-J1
-	SF	94134	688-A1
100	ANT	94509	575-C6
100	VAL	94590	530-C5
500	LALT	94024	811-F7
500	LALT	94024	831-F1
1100	SJS	95126	833-G4
1200	SCL	95126	833-G4
1800	SLN	94577	690-J2
4000	MLPK	94025	770-G7
E CAMPBELL AV			
-	CMBL	95008	853-E6
1500	SCIC	95125	853-G6
W CAMPBELL AV			
-	CMBL	95008	853-C6
1800	SJS	95008	853-C6
3900	SJS	95130	853-A6
4600	SJS	95130	852-J5
5100	SJS	95129	852-J5
CAMPBELL CT			
-	NVTO	94947	525-J4
-	PIT	94565	574-D6
800	OAK	94607	649-D3
3500	FRMT	94536	752-G2
CAMPBELL DR			
4200	PIT	94565	574-D6
CAMPBELL LN			
-	MLPK	94025	810-E1
-	MLPK	94025	790-E7
200	PLHL	94523	592-C6
CAMPBELL PL			
-	DNVL	94526	653-E3
3700	FRMT	94536	752-G3
CAMPBELL ST			
700	OAK	94607	649-E1
900	MPS	95035	794-B5
1000	RCH	94804	609-B2
CAMPECHE CT			
2600	SRMN	94583	673-B3
CAMPECHE ST			
26000	HAY	94545	711-G7
CAMPERDOWN WY			
1900	SJS	95121	855-C3
CAMPESINO AV			
200	PA	94306	791-C7
CAMPESINO CT			
1600	CCCo	94507	632-D3
CAMPGROUND TR			
-	SMCo	94062	789-B5
CAMPHOR AV			
100	FRMT	94539	793-H1
CAMPHOR CT			
-	HIL	94010	748-C2
1800	MPS	95035	813-J4
CAMPHOR WY			
700	EPA	94303	791-B2
CAMPINIA PL			
-	PLE	94566	715-C7
CAMPISI CT			
6800	SJS	95120	894-F2
CAMPISI WY			
800	CMBL	95008	853-F5
CAMPO RD			
100	PTLV	94028	810-C7
CAMPO BELLO			
-	MLPK	94025	790-E7
CAMPO BELLO CT			
-	MLPK	94025	790-E7
CAMPO CALLE WY			
14400	SAR	95070	872-G3
CAMPOLINDO CT			
-	MRGA	94556	631-D2
CAMPOLINDO DR			
3700	MRGA	94556	631-D2
CAMPOLINDO TR			
-	LFYT	94549	631-C1
CAMPO PELOTA			
-	CCCo	94526	633-E7
CAMPOS VERDES			
100	LGTS	95032	873-G6
CAMPO VERDE CIR			
-	SPAB	94806	588-H3
CAMPO VISTA LN			
13800	LAH	94022	811-C7
CAMPTON PL			
-	SF	94108	648-A5
CAMPUS CIR			
-	SF	94132	667-B7
CAMPUS CT			
8200	FRMT	94555	752-A5
CAMPUS DR			
-	CNCD	94521	593-C6
-	NVTO	94945	526-B1
100	SCIC	94305	790-G6
800	DALY	94015	707-B1
800	SCIC	94305	810-J1
1200	BERK	94708	609-J6
2600	SMTO	94403	748-J5
2700	SPAB	94806	588-J2
8000	FRMT	94555	752-A4
11800	OAK	94619	650-J5
13200	OAK	94605	651-A7
13500	OAK	94619	651-A7
13600	OAK	94605	671-B1
24900	HAY	94541	712-C2
24900	HAY	94542	712-C2
24900	AlaC	94541	712-C2
E CAMPUS DR			
-	NVTO	94945	526-C1
W CAMPUS DR			
-	ALA	94501	649-F7
200	NVTO	94945	526-B1
CAMPUS DR E			
300	SCIC	94305	810-G1
700	SCIC	94305	790-H7
CAMPUS DR W			
100	SCIC	94305	790-F7
900	SCIC	94305	810-F1
900	SCIC	94304	810-F1
CAMPUS LN			
-	SF	94134	667-J7
CAMPUS VIEW WY			
26800	HAY	94542	712-C4
CAMROSE AV			
2100	SJS	95130	852-J7
4000	LVMR	94550	696-A6
4000	LVMR	94550	695-J6
CAMROSE PL			
100	WLCK	94596	612-D4
100	WLCK	94598	612-D4
CAMSTOCK CT			
4400	CNCD	94521	593-C5
CANADA CT			
-	SRFL	94903	566-E5
CANADA DR			
700	MPS	95035	794-B6
CANADA LN			
1400	WDSD	94062	789-G6
CANADA RD			
-	SMCo	94062	768-H3
-	SMCo	94070	768-H3
200	SMCo	94062	769-A6
200	SMCo	94070	769-A6
200	SMCo	94402	768-H3
500	SMCo	94062	789-C1
500	SMCo	94070	789-C1
800	WDSD	94062	789-F4
CANADA RD Rt#-92			
-	SMCo	-	768-G2
-	SMCo	94402	768-G2
-	SMCo	94062	768-G2
CANADA HILLS DR			
5000	ANT	94509	595-J3
CANADA HILLS WY			
-	ANT	94509	595-J3
CANADA VIA			
100	CCCo	94526	633-D7
CANAL BLVD			
200	RCH	94804	588-E7
300	RCH	94804	608-E2
500	RCH	94801	608-E1
CANAL DR			
-	CCCo	94565	573-E1
CANAL LN			
-	WLCK	94596	612-B2
CANAL RD			
600	CCCo	94565	573-G3
CANAL ST			
-	SRFL	94901	587-A2
-	SRFL	94901	586-J2
2200	HAY	94545	731-H2
N CANAL ST			
300	SSF	94080	707-H3
S CANAL ST			
300	SSF	94080	707-J3
CANAL TER			
34900	FRMT	94555	752-E2
CANAL WY			
1800	SJS	95131	814-C4
CANANEA AV			
3100	BURL	94010	728-B7
CANANEA PL			
-	BURL	94010	728-B7
CANARIO WY			
12700	LAH	94022	811-A6
CANARY CT			
-	DNVL	94526	653-B5
-	LVMR	94550	715-D1
2100	UNC	94587	732-G6
CANARY DR			
1600	SUNV	94087	832-E6
4600	PLE	94566	714-D1
CANARY LN			
-	RCH	94803	589-B3
1200	SJS	95117	853-D4
CANARY ISLAND CT			
2000	SCL	95050	833-C3
CANARY PALM CT			
-	SJS	95133	814-J4
CANBERRA CT			
4700	SJS	95124	873-J3
CANBERRA DR			
1600	SJS	95124	873-J3
CANBY ST			
-	SF	94129	647-E4
CANDACE WY			
1600	LALT	94024	832-A4
CANDELERO CT			
1600	WLCK	94598	612-E1
CANDELERO DR			
1300	WLCK	94598	612-E1
CANDELERO PL			
100	WLCK	94598	612-E1
CANDIA DR			
1100	SJS	95121	854-H2
CANDICE CT			
-	FRMT	94555	752-E1
1800	ANT	94509	575-G5
CANDLE TER			
-	ORIN	94563	610-J3
CANDLEBERRY RD			
300	WLCK	94598	612-J1
400	WLCK	94598	592-H7
CANDLELIGHT WY			
1100	CPTO	95014	852-D3
CANDLER AV			
14000	SJS	95127	835-B4
CANDLESTICK CT			
2300	ANT	94509	595-A1
CANDLESTICK DR			
2300	ANT	94509	595-A1
2400	ANT	94509	594-J1
CANDLESTICK RD			
-	ORIN	94563	630-G2
CANDLESTICK WY			
500	SJS	95127	835-B2
CANDLEWOOD AV			
1000	SUNV	94089	812-J5
CANDLEWOOD CT			
1100	SUNV	94089	812-J4
4600	CNCD	94521	593-C3
6300	CPTO	95014	852-F2
CANDLEWOOD DR			
600	CPTO	95014	852-F2
CANDLEWOOD PL			
-	CCCo	94595	632-C1
27900	HAY	94545	731-J1
CANDLEWOOD WY			
5200	ANT	-	595-H5
5200	ANT	94509	595-H5
CANDOLERO WY			
2400	ANT	94509	594-J1
CANDY CT			
1200	LFYT	94549	611-H4
4900	LVMR	94550	696-B6
12200	SAR	95070	852-F5
CANDY DR			
-	VAL	94589	509-J6
CANDY LN			
12000	SAR	95070	852-F5
CANDY LYNN CT			
6100	SJS	95120	874-D7
CANDYWOOD CT			
4500	CNCD	94521	593-B5
CANE ST			
400	LKSP	94939	586-F6
CANELLI CT			
3600	PLE	94566	714-G3
CANFIELD CT			
200	DNVL	94526	653-D6
800	SJS	95136	874-D2
CANFIELD DR			
3400	DNVL	94526	653-D6
4200	FRMT	94536	752-J5
CANIM CT			
3200	ANT	94509	595-C1
CANIM RD			
3200	ANT	94509	595-C1
CANIS LN			
800	FCTY	94404	749-H1
CANMORE CT			
2300	SJS	95136	874-J3
CANNA CT			
1500	MTVW	94043	811-H4
CANNA LN			
1600	SJS	95124	873-J6
CANNERY AV			
200	PIT	94565	574-B2
CANNERY CT			
-	HAY	94544	711-H3
200	PIT	94565	574-B2
CANNERY SQ			
-	DALY	94014	687-D5
CANNES CT			
-	DNVL	94506	653-G5
CANNES PL			
-	SJS	95138	875-H1
CANNIKIN CT			
200	SJS	95116	834-G4
CANNIKIN DR			
200	SJS	95116	834-G4
CANNING CT			
-	MRGA	94556	651-E1
CANNING ST			
5800	OAK	94609	629-H5
CANNISTRACI LN			
25700	AlaC	94541	712-E2
CANNON CT			
-	NVTO	94947	526-A5
CANNON DR			
1800	WLCK	94596	611-H2
CANNON PL			
1900	WLCK	94596	611-H2
CANO CT			
35200	FRMT	94536	752-E2
CANOAS GARDEN AV			
2100	SJS	95125	854-D5
2400	SCIC	95125	854-D5
CANOE CT			
200	RDWC	94065	749-H5
CANOE BIRCH CT			
4300	CNCD	94521	593-C5
CANOGA ST			
40300	FRMT	94538	753-D5
CANOGA WY			
-	MLBR	94030	727-H2
CANON AV			
3700	OAK	94602	650-D4
CANON DR			
-	ORIN	94563	610-F6
2300	CCCo	94708	609-H4
15500	SCIC	95030	872-F5
CANONBURY WY			
700	HAY	94544	712-D7
CANONGATE CT			
3300	SJS	95121	855-C5
CANON VIEW LN			
-	OAK	94618	630-B6
CANON VISTA			
11000	SJS	95127	815-A5
11000	SCIC	95127	815-A5
CANOSA CT			
-	PLE	94566	715-B7
CANTADA CT			
3200	SJS	95135	855-G3
CANTANA TER			
-	UNC	94587	732-E5
CANTARE PL			
40900	FRMT	94539	753-E5
CANTAS PL			
100	SRMN	94583	673-G5
CANTATA WY			
25200	LAH	94022	831-D2
CANTERA WY			
200	SRFL	94901	567-E5
CANTERBERRY PL			
3800	PIT	94565	574-C5
CANTERBURY			
1000	HER	94547	569-H2
CANTERBURY AV			
-	DALY	94015	707-B2
600	LVMR	94550	715-E3
CANTERBURY CIR			
-	VAL	94591	530-G4
CANTERBURY CT			
-	CCCo	94507	632-J2
3200	FRMT	94536	752-J3
6300	SJS	95129	852-F3
7600	DBLN	94568	693-H3
CANTERBURY DR			
-	VAL	94591	530-G4
1300	CNCD	94521	593-A4
2800	RCH	94806	589-A2
CANTERBURY LN			
-	HAY	94544	732-A2
7500	DBLN	94568	693-H3
CANTERBURY PL			
600	MPS	95035	794-B3
CANTERBURY RD			
1200	HIL	94010	748-F3
CANTERBURY ST			
37600	FRMT	94536	752-J3
CANTERBURY WY			
-	UNC	94587	731-H5
1500	LALT	94024	831-J3
CANTLE AV			
25500	AlaC	94541	712-D2
CANTO CT			
2200	ANT	94509	595-A1
CANTO DR			
4900	SJS	95124	873-J4
4900	SJS	95118	873-J4
CANTO PL			
40900	FRMT	94539	753-E5
CANTO GAL			
-	SAUS	94965	627-A4
CANTON AV			
1000	LVMR	94550	715-F3
CANTON DR			
500	SJS	95123	874-H4
1200	MPS	95035	794-C7

STREET
Block City ZIP Pg-Grid

CANTRALL CT
1700 CNCD 94521 593-F5
CANVASBACK COM
4700 FRMT 94555 752-D2
CANVASBACK WY
1000 RDWC 94065 749-J4
1400 RDWC 94065 750-A4
CANYON CT
- SSF 94080 707-F5
300 BEN 94510 551-B3
CANYON DR
- SF 94112 687-G3
- DALY 94014 687-G3
100 PTLV 94028 810-C7
200 PTLV 94028 830-C1
500 PCFA 94044 707-A5
1600 PIN 94564 569-D5
3700 AlaC 94541 692-D6
11000 SCIC 95127 815-A6
CANYON LN
- RDWC 94062 789-G1
- SMCo 94062 789-G1
CANYON PL
- CCCo 94803 589-D2
CANYON RD
- BERK 94704 630-A2
- BERK 94720 630-A2
- CCCo - 651-C2
- SANS 94960 566-A7
- ROSS 94957 586-D2
400 MRGA 94556 651-C2
500 NVTO 94947 526-A5
600 NVTO 94947 525-J4
600 RDWC 94062 789-H1
600 MrnC 94947 525-J4
700 RDWC 94062 769-G7
800 SMCo 94062 769-G7
1500 MRGA 94556 631-D7
2500 NaCo 94589 510-F3
2800 BURL 94010 728-B7
2800 SMCo 94010 728-B7
3900 LFYT 94549 611-A4
4500 CCCo 94803 589-D2
4700 RCH 94803 589-D2
27500 PA 94304 830-H2
27500 SCIC 95014 830-H2
CANYON VW
- ORIN 94563 610-J4
- ORIN 94563 611-A4
CANYON WY
3000 PIT 94565 574-D7
3700 MRTZ 94553 571-D6
7600 PLE 94588 693-H5
CANYON CREEK CIR
- PLE 94586 693-E5
CANYON CREEK CT
200 SRMN 94583 673-B2
CANYON CREEK DR
400 AMCN 94589 510-B4
400 NaCo 94589 510-B4
2700 SRMN 94583 673-B2
3400 SJS 95132 814-G2
CANYON CREEK TER
900 FRMT 94536 733-D7
CANYON CREST AV
2000 SRMN 94583 653-G7
CANYON CREST CT
100 SRMN 94583 653-F6
CANYON CREST DR
5000 SRMN 94583 653-F6
CANYON CREST RD E
4200 SRMN 94583 653-F7
CANYON CREST RD W
4000 SRMN 94583 653-F7
CANYON GREEN CT
- SRMN 94583 673-G3
CANYON GREEN DR
1000 SRMN 94583 673-G3
CANYON GREEN PL
100 SRMN 94583 673-G4
CANYON GREEN WY
- SRMN 94583 673-G3
CANYON HEIGHTS COM
- FRMT 94536 753-D1
CANYON HEIGHTS DR
37900 FRMT 94536 733-D7
38400 FRMT 94536 753-D1
39200 FRMT 94539 753-E3
CANYON HILL CT
3700 AlaC 94546 692-B2
CANYON HILLS CT
- SRMN 94583 673-G3
CANYON HILLS PL
- SRMN 94583 673-G3
CANYON HILLS RD
1000 SRMN 94583 673-F3
CANYON LAKE RD
- CCCo - 550-H6
CANYON LAKES DR
2000 SRMN 94583 673-F1
CANYON LAKES PL
200 SRMN 94583 673-E1
CANYON LAKES WY
100 SRMN 94583 673-E1
CANYON MEADOWS CIR
- PLE 94586 693-F5
- PLE 94588 693-F5
CANYON MEADOWS DR
- PLE 94586 693-F5
CANYON OAK CT
- CCCo 94506 653-G1
1800 SMTO 94402 748-H7
CANYON OAK DR
- SRFL 94903 566-C1
- SRFL 94903 546-D7
CANYON OAK LN
2100 CCCo 94506 633-G7
2100 CCCo 94506 653-G1
CANYON OAK PL
- CCCo 94506 653-G1
CANYON OAKS CT
- AlaC 94552 692-E6
38100 FRMT 94536 733-D7
38100 FRMT 94536 753-D1
CANYON OAKS DR
500 OAK 94605 671-B1
CANYON RIDGE DR
3800 SJS 95148 835-G7
CANYON RIDGE PL
- AlaC 94542 692-D6
- AlaC 94552 692-D6

CANYON RIVER CT
4700 SJS 95136 874-E2
N CANYONS PKWY
500 LVMR 94550 695-C5
CANYON SIDE AV
1100 SRMN 94583 673-G3
CANYON TERRACE DR
3700 AlaC 94542 692-D6
3700 AlaC 94552 692-D6
CANYON TRAIL WY
4800 SJS 95136 874-H2
CANYON VIEW CIR
100 SRMN 94583 673-F2
CANYON VIEW CT
2800 ANT 94509 575-G7
3400 SJS 95132 814-G3
CANYONVIEW CT
24800 HAY 94541 712-B2
CANYON VIEW DR
- SMCo - 768-D3
1500 SJS 95132 814-G2
20500 SAR 95070 872-C2
22100 CPTO 95014 852-A3
CANYON VILLAGE CIR
1000 SRMN 94583 673-C2
CANYON VISTA CT
10800 CPTO 95014 852-A2
CANYON VISTA PL
100 CCCo 94526 633-B5
CANYONWOOD CT
- WLCK 94595 632-B4
CANYON WOODS CT
- SRMN 94583 673-F3
CANYON WOODS DR
100 SRMN 94583 673-F3
CANYON WOODS PL
- SRMN 94583 673-F3
CANYON WOODS WY
200 SRMN 94583 673-G3
CAPA DR
40700 FRMT 94539 753-E5
CAPARELLI CT
5200 PLE 94588 694-C6
CAPAY CIR
- SSF 94080 707-E3
CAPAY CT
4600 SJS 95118 874-B3
CAPAY DR
4600 SJS 95118 874-B3
CAPE CT
300 MrnC 94941 606-D4
1700 WLCK 94598 612-E1
CAPE ANITA PL
900 SJS 95133 814-E7
CAPE ANN PL
1900 SJS 95133 834-E1
CAPE ASTON CT
1700 SJS 95133 834-D1
CAPE BLANCO CT
500 SUNV 94087 832-D4
CAPE BRETON CT
- PCFA 94044 727-C4
CAPE BRETON DR
600 PCFA 94044 727-C4
CAPE BRETON PL
800 SJS 95133 834-E1
CAPE BUFFALO DR
900 SJS 95133 834-D1
CAPE CANAVERAL PL
900 SJS 95133 834-D1
CAPE COD CT
- ALA 94501 670-A4
1200 CNCD 94521 593-A4
3600 SJS 95117 853-C3
CAPE COD DR
400 SLN 94578 691-C5
800 RDWC 94065 750-A6
CAPE COD WY
1200 CNCD 94521 593-A4
CAPE COLONY DR
800 SJS 95133 834-E1
CAPE CORAL DR
1700 SJS 95133 834-E1
CAPE DIAMOND DR
800 SJS 95133 834-E1
CAPE EDEN PL
22000 AlaC 94546 692-B6
CAPE ELIZABETH CT
100 VAL 94591 550-F1
CAPE FLATTERY PL
800 SJS 95133 834-E1
CAPE GEORGE PL
900 SJS 95133 834-E1
CAPE HATTERAS CT
- RDWC 94065 749-J2
CAPE HATTERAS WY
1700 SJS 95133 834-E1
CAPE HILDA PL
1900 SJS 95133 834-E1
CAPE HORN CT
1700 SJS 95133 834-E1
CAPE HORN DR
1700 SJS 95133 834-E1
CAPE HORN PL
1700 SJS 95133 834-E1
CAPE JASMINE PL
1700 SJS 95133 834-E1
CAPE JESSUP DR
900 SJS 95133 834-E1
CAPE KENNEDY DR
800 SJS 95133 834-E1
CAPELAW CT
3100 SJS 95135 855-F3
CAPELL ST
500 OAK 94606 650-A4
500 OAK 94610 650-A4
CAPELLA CT
3500 PLE 94588 694-A6
CAPELLA LN
3400 ALA 94502 670-A7
CAPELLA RD
2100 LVMR 94550 715-E4
CAPELLA WY
200 SUNV 94086 812-E7
CAPE MARY PL
900 SJS 95133 814-E7
CAPE MAY PL
800 SJS 95133 834-E1
CAPE MISTY DR
1700 SJS 95133 834-D1
CAPE MORRIS PL
900 SJS 95133 834-E1

CAPE POINT PL
900 SJS 95133 834-E1
CAPERTON AV
- PDMT 94611 650-C1
CAPETOWN AV
2500 HAY 94545 731-G1
CAPETOWN CT
300 NVTO 94947 526-E6
CAPETOWN DR
100 ALA 94502 669-J5
300 ALA 94502 670-A5
CAPE TOWN PL
800 SJS 95133 834-E1
CAPE TRINITY PL
800 SJS 95133 834-E1
CAPE VERDE PL
800 SJS 95133 834-E1
CAPEVIEW DR
- UNC 94545 731-J6
CAPE VINCENT PL
800 SJS 95133 834-E1
CAPEWOOD CT
2900 SJS 95132 814-D3
CAPEWOOD LN
2800 SJS 95132 814-D3
CAPEWOOD TER
4500 FRMT 94538 773-C1
CAPE YORK PL
800 SJS 95133 834-E1
CAPILAND DR
- VAL 94590 530-B3
CAPILANO DR
- NVTO 94949 546-B2
5700 SJS 95138 855-H7
CAPISTRANO AV
- SF 94112 667-F7
1300 PCFA 94044 727-A6
1500 BERK 94707 609-F5
4800 SJS 95129 853-A1
4800 SJS 95129 852-J1
CAPISTRANO CT
- CLAY 94517 613-J2
CAPISTRANO DR
400 OAK 94603 670-H7
2200 SCL 95051 832-J2
36600 FRMT 94536 752-F4
CAPISTRANO PL
100 LGTS 95030 873-A3
CAPISTRANO ST
2700 ANT 94509 575-C6
CAPISTRANO WY
600 SMTO 94402 748-J2
1800 BURL 94010 728-A6
23000 LALT 94024 831-H4
E CAPISTRANO WY
500 SMTO 94402 748-J2
W CAPISTRANO WY
700 SMTO 94402 748-J2
CAPITAL ST
400 OAK 94606 649-J4
400 OAK 94610 649-J4
CAPITAN DR
4600 FRMT 94536 752-E3
CAPITANCILLOS DR
1500 SJS 95120 874-A7
CAPITANCILLOS PL
1600 SJS 95120 874-A7
CAPITOL AV
- SF 94112 687-D1
- SJS 95116 834-J4
- SJS 95127 834-H2
200 SCIC 95127 834-H2
400 SJS 95133 834-H2
600 SCIC 95133 834-H2
1100 SF 94112 667-D7
1700 SJS 95127 835-A5
1800 SJS 95148 835-A5
1900 EPA 94303 791-B2
3000 FRMT 94538 753-B4
E CAPITOL AV
200 MPS 95035 814-A2
700 SJS 95132 814-A2
N CAPITOL AV
700 SJS 95133 814-F7
700 SCIC 95133 814-F7
900 SJS 95132 814-C4
1700 SJS 95131 814-C4
W CAPITOL AV
100 MPS 95035 814-A2
200 MPS 95035 813-J2
CAPITOL CT
1200 SJS 95127 834-J5
4400 CNCD 94518 593-A5
CAPITOL DR
500 BEN 94510 550-H1
CAPITOL EXWY
100 SJS 95136 854-D7
200 SJS 95136 874-F1
700 SJS 95127 834-J4
700 SJS 95116 834-J4
1000 SJS 95111 854-G7
1000 SJS 95122 834-J4
1000 SCIC 95111 854-G7
1200 SJS 95121 854-G7
1300 SJS 95127 835-A6
1300 SJS 95122 835-A6
1300 SJS 95121 855-B3
1800 SJS 95148 835-A6
2300 SJS 95122 855-B3
2300 SJS 95148 855-B3
CAPITOL ST
300 VAL 94590 529-J5
600 VAL 94590 530-A5
CAPITOLA AV
4500 SJS 95111 875-A1
CAPITOLA CT
- UNC 94545 751-J1
28300 HAY 94545 731-H2
CAPITOLA DR
- PIT 94565 574-E1
CAPITOLA PL
- PIT 94565 574-E1
CAPITOLA ST
2500 HAY 94545 731-H2
CAPITOLA TER
- FRMT 94539 794-A1
CAPITOLA WY
- UNC 94545 751-J1
900 SCL 95051 832-J5
CAPITOL HILL AV
1500 RCH 94806 589-B4
1500 CCCo 94806 589-B4

CAPITOL REEF CT
4500 SJS 95136 874-G2
CAPITOL VILLAGE CIR
200 SJS 95136 874-G1
CAPLES CT
- ANT 94509 575-H7
CAPP ST
- SF 94103 667-J3
100 SF 94110 667-J3
2900 OAK 94602 650-D5
CAPPER CT
- SMCo 94061 790-B4
CAPPY CT
- SJS 95111 875-A2
CAPPY TER
4900 FRMT 94555 752-C2
CAPRA DR
600 AMCN 94589 510-A4
600 AMCN 94589 509-J4
CAPRA WY
- SF 94123 647-F3
CAPRI AV
27200 HAY 94545 711-F7
27200 HAY 94545 731-G1
CAPRI CT
- SRFL 94901 586-J2
CAPRI DR
1100 CMBL 95008 873-C2
14100 LGTS 95030 873-C2
CAPRI LN
- PLHL 94523 591-J4
500 FCTY 94404 749-G5
CAPRI WY
6500 SJS 95129 852-F3
CAPRIANA CIR
3200 SJS 95135 855-G3
5900 FRMT 94555 752-B3
CAPRIC DR
400 SJS 95123 875-B3
CAPRICE CIR
100 HER 94547 570-B6
CAPRICE COM
5600 FRMT 94538 773-A2
CAPRICONUS AV
4700 LVMR 94550 696-B3
CAPRICORN AV
100 OAK 94611 630-D6
CAPRICORN CT
400 SJS 95111 854-F6
18500 AlaC 94546 691-J3
CAPRINO WY
300 SCAR 94070 769-E4
900 PIT 94565 574-F3
CAPSTAN CT
300 RDWC 94065 749-H7
CAPTAIN DR
- EMVL 94608 629-C6
CAPTAIN LN
- RDWC 94065 750-C4
CAPTAINS CT
100 VAL 94591 550-F2
500 CCCo 94565 573-D1
CAPTAINS CV
- OAK 94618 630-C4
- OAK 94705 630-C4
CAPTAINS DR
- ALA 94502 669-J5
- ALA 94502 670-A5
CAPTAINS LNDG
- MrnC 94920 606-H3
CAPTAINS COVE DR
100 SRFL 94903 566-F2
CAPUCHINO AV
900 BURL 94010 728-D5
CAPUCHINO DR
- MLBR 94030 728-A2
500 MLBR 94030 727-J3
CAPULET CIR
33800 FRMT 94555 752-B2
CAPULET RD
- FRMT 94555 752-C2
CAPURSO WY
1400 SJS 95125 854-B3
CAPWELL DR
7800 OAK 94621 670-E6
CAPWELL LN
1300 WLCK 94596 612-C6
CARACAS CT
2100 SJS 95122 834-J7
CARADO CT
25700 LAH 94022 811-C5
CARAMELLO CT
3100 PLE 94588 694-C6
CARASTON WY
2600 SJS 95148 835-C7
2600 SJS 95148 855-C1
CARAVAN PL
- SRMN 94583 673-B2
CARAVAN WY
- SJS 95123 875-B3
CARAVEL LN
700 FCTY 94404 749-G2
CARAVELLA DR
3700 SJS 95117 853-B4
CARAVELLE CT
3200 WLCK 94598 612-J2
CARAVELLE DR
300 WLCK 94598 612-J2
CARAWAY CT
4500 SJS 95129 853-B2
CARBERRY AV
5600 OAK 94609 629-H6
CARBONERA AV
100 SUNV 94086 812-B7
CARD AL
- SF 94133 648-A4
CARDEL WY
1700 SJS 95032 873-H5
CARDEN ST
- SLN 94577 690-G1
CARDENAS AV
- SF 94132 687-B1
CARDENAS TER
3100 FRMT 94536 752-H2
CARDIFF
100 HER 94547 569-H3
CARDIFF CT
- ANT 94509 575-F7
100 RCH 94806 588-J1
1100 SJS 95117 853-D3
8100 DBLN 94568 693-H2

CARDIFF DR
1900 PIT 94565 574-E3
8000 DBLN 94568 693-H2
CARDIFF LN
1000 RDWC 94061 790-B2
CARDIFF PL
600 MPS 95035 794-B4
CARDIFF ST
35000 NWK 94560 752-D4
CARDIGAN BAY
100 ALA 94502 669-J6
CARDIGAN CT
1100 WLCK 94596 632-G1
7600 DBLN 94568 693-H3
CARDIGAN DR
700 SUNV 94087 832-F4
1100 WLCK 94596 632-G1
CARDIGAN RD
1200 HIL 94010 748-F3
CARDIGAN ST
7600 DBLN 94568 693-H3
CARDIN AV
3300 SJS 95118 874-A1
CARDINAL CT
300 MrnC 94965 606-F7
2400 CNCD 94520 572-G5
CARDINAL DR
700 LVMR 94550 715-E1
3500 CNCD 94520 572-G6
E CARDINAL DR
900 SUNV 94087 832-A2
W CARDINAL DR
800 SUNV 94087 832-B2
CARDINAL LN
100 LGTS 95032 873-C7
100 VAL 94589 510-A4
2600 SJS 95125 854-B7
CARDINAL RD
200 MrnC 94965 606-F7
CARDINAL ST
28200 HAY 94545 731-J2
CARDINAL TER
3700 FRMT 94555 732-J3
CARDINAL WY
100 HER 94547 569-H5
1000 PA 94303 791-D5
CARDINET DR
5900 CLAY 94517 593-G6
CARDINGTON DR
2000 SJS 95132 814-D3
CARDONA CIR
300 SRMN 94583 673-D3
CARDONA WY
1200 SJS 95131 814-E7
CARDOZA
100 HER 94547 569-E3
CARDOZA CT
3400 SJS 95132 814-G3
20900 AlaC 94541 691-G7
CARDUCCI DR
- PLE 94588 694-C6
CARE TER
34300 FRMT 94555 752-A3
CAREN ST
4400 FRMT 94538 753-C7
CARERA CT
- SJS 95123 874-F6
CAREY CT
- MRGA 94556 651-F1
CAREY DR
- MrnC 94903 566-H3
1100 CNCD 94520 592-D5
CAREY ST
3000 ANT 94509 575-E7
CARGO WY
- SF 94124 668-C5
CARIBBEAN COM
4000 FRMT 94555 752-E1
CARIBBEAN CT
800 CNCD 94518 592-H6
E CARIBBEAN DR
200 SUNV 94089 812-G2
CARIBBEAN WY
600 SMTO 94402 748-J4
CARIBE ISL
- MrnC 94949 526-H7
CARIBE WY
300 SJS 95133 834-G2
CARIBOU CT
700 SUNV 94087 832-C4
4400 ANT 94509 595-H3
CARICK PLACE WY
3500 SJS 95121 855-B4
CARILLO LN
13400 LAH 94022 811-A5
CARINA LN
800 FCTY 94404 749-F4
CARISA CT
- NVTO 94945 525-H1
- WLCK 94596 612-B1
CARISBROOK CT
2500 HAY 94542 712-C3
CARISBROOK DR
- ORIN 94563 631-C5
2700 OAK 94611 650-G1
CARISBROOK LN
- OAK 94611 650-G1
CARL AV
1300 VAL 94590 530-C3
1500 MPS 95035 794-D6
5300 RCH 94804 609-B3
CARL RD
- SUNV 94089 812-F1
800 LFYT 94549 611-H7
CARL ST
- SF 94117 667-E1
100 SF 94117 667-E2
300 SCL 95050 833-F3
400 SF 94143 667-E2
CARLA CT
500 MTVW 94040 811-H7
1100 SJS 95120 874-D7
4000 ANT 94509 574-H5
CARLA DR
1100 SJS 95120 874-D7
CARLA ST
600 LVMR 94550 696-C7
S CARLBACK AV
1200 WLCK 94596 612-C4
CARLEEN CT
19600 AlaC 94546 691-J4

CARLEEN DR
3000 AlaC 94546 691-J4
CARLESTER DR
200 LGTS 95032 873-D4
CARLETON AV
- DALY 94015 687-A6
CARLETON CT
1600 RDWC 94061 790-A2
CARLETON DR
1300 CNCD 94518 592-G2
CARLETON LN
2600 ANT 94509 575-D1
CARLETON PL
- PCFA 94044 727-B6
3000 SCL 95051 833-A6
CARLETON ST
700 BERK 94804 629-D3
800 BERK 94702 629-F3
900 BERK 94703 629-F3
1900 BERK 94704 629-H3
CARLETON WY
500 CCCo 94526 633-C4
CARLFIELD AV
3500 CCCo 94803 589-B3
CARLILE DR
800 NVTO 94945 526-C3
CARLING CT
100 SJS 95111 875-A2
CARLISLE CT
- BEN 94510 551-C2
- SRMN 94583 673-H7
- SRMN 94583 693-J1
CARLISLE DR
1100 SMTO 94402 749-B2
CARLISLE PL
100 BEN 94510 551-B2
CARLISLE WY
- BEN 94510 551-A2
100 SUNV 94087 832-E4
CARLITOS CT
3700 PA 94306 811-B2
CARLMONT DR
2100 BLMT 94002 769-C2
E CARLO ST
- MPS 95035 794-A7
CARLOS AV
100 RDWC 94061 790-B1
1300 BURL 94010 728-C6
5500 ELCR 94530 609-B2
5500 RCH 94804 609-B2
CARLOS CT
- WLCK 94596 612-A2
CARLOS DR
100 SRFL 94903 566-F2
CARLOS PL
- WLCK 94596 612-A2
CARLOS BEE BLVD
24900 HAY 94542 712-A3
CARLO SCIMECA CT
2600 SJS 95132 814-F5
CARLO SCIMECA DR
2600 SJS 95132 814-F5
CARLOS PRIVADA
1100 MTVW 94040 832-H6
CARLOTTA AV
1200 BERK 94707 609-F7
1300 BERK 94703 609-F7
CARLOTTA CIR
100 MrnC 94941 606-H4
CARLOTTA CT
700 SJS 95136 874-E1
CARLOTTA DR
1800 CNCD 94519 573-A7
1800 CNCD 94519 572-J7
CARLOW CT
100 SUNV 94087 832-E4
CARLOW WY
2900 SSF 94080 707-D5
7500 DBLN 94568 693-G2
CARLSBAD CT
- SSF 94080 707-F4
200 SRFL 94903 566-F2
600 LVMR 94550 695-C7
600 MPS 95035 794-E7
3500 PLE 94588 714-B1
CARLSBAD DR
1100 SJS 95118 874-C4
CARLSBAD RD
48500 FRMT 94539 793-J2
CARLSBAD ST
500 MPS 95035 794-E7
CARLSBAD WY
3600 PLE 94588 714-B1
CARLSEN ST
2800 OAK 94602 650-F4
CARLSEN WY
1300 SJS 95118 874-B1
CARLSON
300 VAL 94590 530-B6
CARLSON AV
- SANS 94960 566-A5
CARLSON BLVD
- RCH 94801 588-H7
100 RCH 94804 588-H7
400 RCH 94804 608-J1
1000 RCH 94804 609-A2
2900 ELCR 94530 609-C3
CARLSON CIR
3700 PA 94306 811-E1
CARLSON CT
- SANS 94960 566-A5
1600 CNCD 94519 593-A2
3800 PA 94306 811-E1
23500 AlaC 94541 692-D7
CARLSON ST
300 VAL 94590 530-B6
300 SolC 94590 530-B6
CARLSTON AV
600 OAK 94610 650-B2
CARLSTON ST
300 RCH 94805 589-B7
CARLTON AV
100 LGTS 95032 873-D5
200 SBRN 94066 707-J7
200 SBRN 94066 727-J1
800 MLPK 94025 771-A7
1100 MLPK 94025 790-J1
1200 MLPK 94025 770-J7
15000 SCIC 95124 873-E4
15000 SJS 95124 873-E4
15600 LGTS 95124 873-E4
18000 AlaC 94546 691-H3

CARLTON CT
200 LGTS 95032 873-D4
400 SSF 94080 708-B3
2700 CCCo 94806 589-A2
2700 CCCo 94806 588-J2
19500 AlaC 94546 691-H4
CARLTON PL
1300 LVMR 94550 715-F4
CARLTON RD
1400 HIL 94010 748-E4
CARLTON ST
5400 OAK 94618 630-A6
CARLTON WY
200 LGTS 95032 873-D4
CARL VINSON
4000 ALA 94501 649-F6
CARLWYN CT
3700 AlaC 94546 691-H3
CARLWYN DR
18300 AlaC 94546 691-H2
CARLYLE CT
- DNVL 94506 653-H5
CARLYLE ST
300 HAY 94544 732-F3
CARLYLE TER
3300 LFYT 94549 631-G1
CARLYN AV
- CMBL 95008 853-D5
CARLYSLE AV
3600 SCL 95051 832-H6
CARLYSLE ST
100 SJS 95113 834-B6
200 SJS 95110 834-A6
CARM AV
5000 SJS 95124 873-H5
5100 SJS 95032 873-H5
CARMAR ST
300 HAY 94544 712-B7
500 HAY 94544 732-B1
CARMEL AV
- PCFA 94044 706-J5
- DALY 94015 686-J6
100 ELCR 94530 609-E6
200 PDMT 94611 650-B1
200 PCFA 94044 707-A5
500 ALB 94706 609-E6
700 LVMR 94550 715-E2
700 SUNV 94086 812-G5
800 LALT 94022 811-D4
CARMEL CIR
500 SMTO 94402 748-J2
CARMEL CT
- UNC 94545 751-J1
- MrnC 94903 566-G4
- NVTO 94945 526-B2
800 SLN 94578 691-C5
900 LALT 94022 811-D4
1200 WLCK 94596 612-C5
2200 PIT 94565 573-J4
39000 FRMT 94538 753-A5
CARMEL DR
- NVTO 94945 526-B2
100 AMCN 94589 509-H1
1400 SJS 95125 854-B3
1400 WLCK 94596 612-C5
2000 CNCD 94520 572-E6
2300 PA 94303 791-D4
2500 SBRN 94066 707-E6
17800 AlaC 94546 691-H3
CARMEL LN
- SMCo 94062 769-G6
CARMEL ST
- SF 94117 667-E2
2400 OAK 94602 650-E4
CARMEL TER
1200 LALT 94024 831-H2
CARMEL WY
- UNC 94545 751-J1
- MrnC 94960 566-B5
100 SMCo 94028 830-D3
1100 SCL 95050 833-D4
3700 SLN 94578 691-B5
CARMELITA AV
- MLV 94941 606-E3
1100 BURL 94010 728-D7
1900 HIL 94010 728-D7
2500 BLMT 94002 769-B1
CARMELITA CT
1400 CNCD 94520 592-F2
40400 FRMT 94539 753-E4
CARMELITA DR
100 MTVW 94040 811-J7
1800 SCAR 94070 769-F3
23900 HAY 94541 712-A1
CARMELITA PL
200 FRMT 94539 753-E4
CARMELITA ST
- SF 94117 667-G1
CARMELITA WY
2500 PIN 94564 569-G6
CARMELLO RD
- CCCo 94596 612-B4
- WLCK 94596 612-B4
CARMELO LN
200 SSF 94080 707-F2
CARMEN AV
900 LVMR 94550 715-H2
CARMEN CT
- PIN 94564 569-H6
- NVTO 94945 525-J1
- ORIN 94563 631-B4
1400 SJS 95121 854-J2
4600 UNC 94587 732-A7
4600 UNC 94587 752-A1
CARMEN LN
- CCCo 94803 589-E3
CARMEN RD
10000 CPTO 95014 852-A1
CARMEN ST
41100 FRMT 94539 753-E6
CARMEN WY
4500 UNC 94587 732-A7
4600 UNC 94587 752-A1
CARMINE WY
1400 SJS 95131 814-C6
CARMONA CT
10000 CPTO 95014 852-B1
CARMONA WY
2800 ANT 94509 575-A7
CARNABY CT
4500 SJS 95136 874-E2

CARNATION CIR — 1998 BAY AREA STREET INDEX — CASTRO ST 915

STREET
Block City ZIP Pg-Grid

CARNATION CIR
100 VAL 94589 509-H5
1700 LVMR 94550 696-A3
CARNATION CT
200 PLE 94566 714-F3
800 LALT 94024 831-E1
2600 AlaC 94546 691-H5
CARNATION LN
19700 AlaC 94546 691-H5
CARNATION WY
35600 FRMT 94536 752-J1
35700 FRMT 94536 732-J7
CARNAVON WY
1400 SJS 95131 814-C7
CARNEGIE CT
2400 HAY 94545 731-H2
CARNEGIE DR
- MPS 95035 794-D7
CARNEGIE SQ
- SJS 95116 834-D5
CARNELIAN CIR
14500 SAR 95070 872-E2
CARNELIAN DR
1100 SJS 95122 834-G7
CARNELIAN LN
1400 LVMR 94550 715-D3
CARNELIAN RD
100 SSF 94080 707-H1
CARNELIAN WY
- SF 94131 667-F4
- SF 94131 667-F4
CARNELIAN GLEN CT
14500 SAR 95070 872-E3
CARNEROS AV
400 SUNV 94086 812-B7
CARNFORTH CT
1100 SJS 95120 894-G4
CARNIEL AV
12700 SAR 95070 852-D6
CARNIEL CT
12800 SAR 95070 852-D6
CARNIVAL CT
100 VAL 94589 510-E6
CARNIVAL WY
7200 SJS 95120 894-H4
CARNOT DR
1500 SJS 95126 853-H4
CARNOUSITE DR
- NVTO 94949 546-C3
CARNOUSTIE
- MRGA 94556 651-D1
CARNOUSTIE CT
2500 UNC 94587 732-B4
22300 CPTO 95014 852-A2
CARNOUSTIE DR
- NVTO 94949 546-C2
CARNOUSTIE HTS
- NVTO 94949 546-C2
CARO LN
- ORIN 94563 631-B5
CAROB CT
2700 ANT 94509 575-H6
CAROB LN
100 ALA 94502 669-J6
100 ALA 94502 670-A6
1500 LALT 94024 831-H3
CAROB ST
2700 ANT 94509 575-H6
CAROB WY
- NVTO 94945 526-B1
200 CCCo 94553 572-C6
CAROBE CT
500 UNC 94587 732-G3
CAROBWOOD CT
3400 SJS 95132 814-E2
CAROBWOOD LN
2100 SJS 95132 814-E2
CAROL AV
1500 BURL 94010 728-G7
2000 MTVW 94040 831-J1
3600 FRMT 94538 773-C1
4300 FRMT 94538 753-D7
E CAROL AV
- BURL 94010 728-G7
CAROL COM
- LVMR 94550 696-A6
41500 FRMT 94538 753-E7
CAROL CT
200 CCCo 94526 633-C4
7000 ELCR 94530 609-C1
CAROL DR
2400 SCIC 95125 854-E5
2400 SJS 95125 854-E5
2700 SCIC 95136 854-E5
CAROL LN
900 LFYT 94549 611-H6
12000 SAR 95070 852-E5
CAROL PL
3700 AlaC 94541 692-D7
CAROL PTH
- RCH 94804 609-A1
CAROL ST
3700 PIN 94564 569-H7
CAROL TER
41600 FRMT 94538 753-E7
CAROLA AV
900 SJS 95130 853-B4
CAROLA CT
4100 SJS 95130 853-B4
CAROLAN AV
200 BURL 94010 728-E5
N CAROLAN AV
1300 BURL 94010 728-D5
CAROLE CT
700 EPA 94303 791-B1
CAROLE WY
1500 RDWC 94061 790-A1
CAROLE MEADOWS CT
100 DNVL 94506 653-G5
CAROLINA AV
- SANS 94960 566-D7
600 SUNV 94086 812-F5
2400 RDWC 94061 790-A3
CAROLINA DR
- BEN 94510 551-A3
1400 CLAY 94517 593-F6
1400 CNCD 94521 593-F6
CAROLINA LN
- ATN 94027 790-C2
200 PA 94306 811-D2
CAROLINA ST
- SF 94107 668-B2
100 SF 94103 668-B2
100 VAL 94590 529-H4
600 VAL 94590 530-A5
2200 VAL 94591 530-D5
CAROLINE CT
1100 LVMR 94550 695-D6
7900 DBLN 94568 693-G4
CAROLINE DR
22000 CPTO 95014 832-A6
CAROLINE ST
1200 ALA 94501 669-G2
CAROLINE WY
- DALY 94014 687-G3
4800 SJS 95124 873-H4
CAROL LEAF CT
3100 SJS 95148 855-E1
CAROL LEE DR
10100 CPTO 95014 832-E7
CAROLOS DR
100 CCCo 94553 572-B7
CAROLYN AV
1000 SJS 95125 853-J3
1000 SJS 95125 854-A3
CAROLYN CT
- LFYT 94595 611-J6
- ORIN 94563 631-B2
500 SUNV 94086 832-E1
2900 ANT 94509 575-D7
CAROLYN DR
- AMCN 94589 509-J2
- PIT 94565 574-D4
1100 SCL 95050 833-C4
1900 PLHL 94523 592-B5
W CAROLYN DR
100 AMCN 94589 509-J1
CAROLYN LN
- MrnC 94941 606-F5
CAROLYN ST
15900 AlaC 94578 691-F4
CAROLYN WY
2000 NVTO 94945 525-J1
CARON CT
900 SJS 95121 854-H3
CARONDELET CT
2600 CNCD 94518 592-F7
CAROUSEL CT
- SRMN 94583 673-B2
CAROUSEL DR
- SJS 95111 854-G4
100 VAL 94589 510-D6
CAROUSEL PL
- SRMN 94583 673-B2
CARPENTER CIR
- CCCo 94553 571-E2
CARPENTER CT
- PLHL 94523 591-J7
- SF 94124 668-C6
2300 FRMT 94539 753-F7
CARPENTER PL
2000 SCL 95051 833-D1
CARPENTIER ST
900 SLN 94577 691-A1
CARPENTIER WY
400 SJS 95111 854-F6
CARPETTA CIR
800 PIT 94565 574-A3
CARPINO AV
500 PIT 94565 574-E3
CARPINTERIA DR
2000 ANT 94509 595-E1
CARQUINEZ AV
2000 ELCR 94530 589-C7
2600 CCCo 94805 589-C6
CARQUINEZ CIR
- BEN 94510 551-B3
CARQUINEZ CT
200 BEN 94510 551-B4
CARQUINEZ PL
2100 PIT 94565 574-A3
CARQUINEZ ST
100 SolC 94590 530-C6
CARQUINEZ WY
600 MRTZ 94553 571-D3
1800 CCCo 94525 550-C4
CARQUINEZ SCENIC DR
- CCCo 94525 550-F5
- MRTZ 94553 571-B2
- CCCo 94553 571-B2
- CCCo - 550-F5
CARR DR
- MRGA 94556 631-E7
CARR ST
- SF 94124 688-B1
CARR WY
30600 UNC 94587 732-A4
CARRABELLE WY
900 SJS 95120 894-H2
CARRAGATA DR
- SJS 95134 813-D3
CARRARA TER
- UNC 94587 732-E5
CARRERA CT
- SMCo 94062 789-G2
CARRERA DR
300 MrnC 94965 606-F7
300 MrnC 94965 626-F1
CARRERIO LN
- WLCK 94596 612-A3
CARRIAGE CIR
7700 CPTO 95014 852-C2
CARRIAGE CT
- CCCo 94507 632-G7
- LALT 94022 811-E5
- MLPK 94025 790-C7
CARRIAGE DR
300 SCL 95050 833-D6
1300 WLCK 94598 592-E7
1500 WLCK 94598 612-F1
5000 RCH 94803 589-J2
5000 RCH 94803 590-A3
6300 PLE 94566 714-D7
CARRIAGE WY
- ANT 94509 595-J3
16800 AlaC 94578 691-G5
CARRIAGE CIRCLE COM
37600 FRMT 94536 752-G5
CARRIAGE COVE CT
3300 SJS 95111 854-J5
CARRIAGE HILL DR
18600 SCIC 95120 894-G1
CARRICK AV
13100 SAR 95070 852-H7
CARRICK CT
- PLHL 94523 591-J5
500 SUNV 94087 832-E4
CARRIE CT
- PLHL 94523 612-A1
4800 UNC 94587 751-J1
CARRIE ST
- SF 94131 667-G6
100 SJS 95112 834-C7
CARRIE LEE WY
1100 SJS 95118 874-B1
CARRIGAN COM
3600 LVMR 94550 715-J1
CARRIL CT
15500 MSER 95030 873-A5
CARRILLO CT
400 SRMN 94583 673-C2
CARRILLO DR
3400 SLN 94578 691-B4
CARRILLO WY
900 SLN 94578 691-B4
CARRINGTON CIR
- SJS 95125 854-A7
27200 LAH 94022 830-J1
CARRINGTON CT
- SJS 95125 854-A7
- SJS 95125 874-B1
CARRINGTON ST
3600 OAK 94601 650-D7
CARRINGTON WY
- OAK 94601 650-D7
CARRISON ST
1100 BERK 94702 629-E4
CARRIZAL ST
- SF 94134 687-H2
CARRMANN LN
- CNCD 94521 593-F4
CARROL PL
100 CCCo 94595 612-A7
CARROL RD
2100 CCCo 94596 612-E7
9900 AlaC 94550 696-J2
CARROLL AV
700 SF 94124 688-C1
1200 SF 94124 668-A7
30400 HAY 94544 732-D2
CARROLL CT
- PIT 94565 574-D6
- SRFL 94903 566-C3
CARROLL DR
- PIT 94565 574-D6
600 MRGA 94556 631-E5
CARROLL ST
- VAL 94590 530-B4
100 SUNV 94086 812-E7
200 SUNV 94086 832-E1
2200 OAK 94606 650-A4
CARRYBACK AV
5200 SJS 95111 875-C2
CARRYDUFF WY
3700 SJS 95121 855-C4
CARRYWOOD WY
4100 SJS 95118 874-C2
CARSON CT
- SRMN 94583 653-J7
100 SUNV 94086 812-C7
4600 PLE 94588 694-A6
CARSON DR
300 HAY 94544 712-B6
800 SUNV 94086 812-C6
CARSON LN
18800 AlaC 94552 692-F3
CARSON ST
- SF 94114 667-F3
100 HER 94547 570-B5
1200 RDWC 94061 789-J2
4000 CNCD 94521 593-A2
4000 OAK 94619 650-G6
CARSON WY
900 MPS 95035 794-B4
2700 SJS 95124 873-G1
CARSON PASS WY
6000 LVMR 94550 696-D3
CARSTEN CIR
700 BEN 94510 530-J6
CARTA BLANCA ST
22200 CPTO 95014 832-A7
CARTAGENA AV
1400 HAY 94544 732-A1
CARTAGENA LN
500 SRMN 94583 673-C2
CARTAGO CT
200 SJS 95116 834-D2
CARTE PL
- PLHL 94523 592-A4
CARTER AV
- SJS 95118 874-A5
4800 SJS 95118 873-J4
7300 NWK 94560 752-E7
CARTER CT
- CCCo 94803 589-F3
4200 CNCD 94521 593-B3
CARTER DR
900 MRGA 94556 631-F6
3500 SSF 94080 707-C4
CARTER ST
200 VAL 94590 529-J3
500 DALY 94014 687-H3
500 SF 94134 687-H3
600 SMCo 94014 687-H3
1700 OAK 94602 650-E2
CARTER WY
- MLPK 94025 790-C7
300 SCL 95051 832-J7
2900 ANT 94509 575-A7
CARTER ACRES LN
800 MRTZ 94553 591-F4
CARTERWOOD PL
1300 SJS 95121 854-J2
CARTHAGE CT
800 CNCD 94518 592-G6
CARTHAGE DR
2400 CNCD 94518 592-G6
CARTIER DR
1800 LVMR 94550 715-G2
CARTIER LN
900 FCTY 94404 749-G4
CARTWRIGHT PL
34100 FRMT 94555 732-E7
CARTWRIGHT WY
20200 CPTO 95014 832-E7
CARVER CT
4500 PLE 94588 694-A6
CARVER DR
10500 SCIC 95014 852-H2
10700 CPTO 95014 852-H2
CARVER PL
1100 MTVW 94040 811-F5
CARVER ST
- SF 94110 667-J5
500 SCIC 95127 814-H7
500 SJS 95127 814-H7
CARVO CT
1300 LALT 94024 831-H3
CARY AV
600 OAK 94603 670-G7
1200 SMTO 94401 749-B1
CARY CT
- OAK 94603 670-G6
CARY DR
600 SLN 94577 671-B7
CARZINO CT
1900 CNCD 94521 593-G4
CAS DR
3500 SJS 95111 854-H6
CASA AV
- NVTO 94949 546-J4
- DALY 94015 687-B6
CASA CT
1300 SCL 95051 832-H4
CASA WY
- SF 94123 647-G3
2400 WLCK 94596 612-B3
CASABA CREEK CT
1100 SJS 95120 894-G3
CASA BLANCA AV
400 SJS 95129 852-J1
CASA BLANCA LN
18600 SAR 95070 872-H1
CASA BONA AV
2300 BLMT 94002 769-B1
CASA BONITA CT
700 LALT 94024 831-F1
CASA BUENA DR
- CMAD 94925 586-G7
500 CMAD 94925 606-H1
CASA BUENO CT
2500 WLCK 94598 612-H2
CASA DE CAMPO
3100 SMTO 94403 749-E5
CASA DE PONSELLE
1500 SJS 95118 874-A3
CASADERO CT
3000 PLE 94588 694-D7
CASA DE SIMA
- LFYT 94549 591-G7
CASA GRANDE
100 LGTS 95030 872-J2
CASA GRANDE AV
- MTVW 94043 812-A2
CASA GRANDE CT
2500 WLCK 94598 612-G2
3700 SJS 95121 855-C4
CASA GRANDE DR
3200 SRMN 94583 673-G5
CASA GRANDE PL
- SRMN 94583 673-G6
2100 BEN 94510 551-D4
CASA GRANDE ST
1800 BEN 94510 551-D5
CASA GRANDE WY
3900 SJS 95118 874-B2
CASA GRANDE REAL
200 NVTO 94949 546-J5
CASA LINDA CT
11700 DBLN 94568 693-F4
CASALINO CT
- PLE 94566 715-B5
3400 SJS 95148 835-D6
CASA LOMA CT
400 SJS 95129 852-B7
CASALS CT
2800 SJS 95148 855-D4
CASALS WY
- FRMT 94539 753-E5
CASA MADEIRA LN
4300 SCIC 95127 835-F4
CASA MARCIA PL
1000 FRMT 94539 753-E5
CASA MARIA CT
- CCCo 94507 632-F5
CASA MIA DR
2000 SJS 95124 873-F2
CASA MIA WY
12400 SCIC 94024 831-E2
12400 LAH 94024 831-E2
CASANOVA DR
800 SLN 94578 691-C5
3500 SMTO 94403 749-D5
CASA NUESTRA
2000 CCCo 94526 633-E7
CASANUEVA PL
900 SCIC 94305 810-J2
CASA REALE
200 ORIN 94563 631-B3
CASA REYA CT
2500 WLCK 94598 612-H2
CASA VALLECITA
1300 CCCo 94507 632-F4
CASA VERDE AV
4900 SJS 95129 852-B7
CASA VERDE PL
- CLAY 94517 613-J2
CASA VERDE WY
- PIT 94565 574-C6
CASA VIEJA
- ORIN 94563 630-J3
CASA VIEJA LN
100 ORIN 94563 630-J3
CASA VIEW DR
- SJS 95129 852-J1
CASCADE AV
- LVMR 94550 695-D7
- VAL 94589 510-B5
CASCADE CT
- SMTO 94401 729-A7
700 WLCK 94598 612-G3
1000 MLPK 94025 790-C6
3700 ANT 94509 595-E1
CASCADE DR
- MLV 94941 606-B2
- SRFL 94901 566-J5
500 SUNV 94087 832-C4
700 SJS 95129 853-A2
1000 MLPK 94025 790-C6
2000 WLCK 94598 612-G3
CASCADE LN
- ORIN 94563 610-H6
CASCADE RD
400 SLN 94577 690-G1
CASCADE ST
2200 MPS 95035 814-E1
25700 HAY 94544 711-H5
CASCADE TER
- SUNV 94087 832-D4
CASCADE WK
- SF 94116 667-C3
CASCADE WY
- MLV 94941 606-C3
CASCADITA TER
400 MPS 95035 793-G3
CASCADO PL
40900 FRMT 94539 753-E5
CASCARA CT
2100 PLE 94588 714-A5
CASCO CT
2600 SJS 95121 854-H3
CASE AV
5000 PLE 94566 714-D4
5000 AlaC 94566 714-D4
CASE DR
200 PIT 94565 574-B2
CASELLI AV
- SF 94114 667-F2
CASELTON PL
- LFYT 94549 611-J6
CASEY AV
2500 MTVW 94043 791-F6
CASEY CT
- BEN 94510 551-C1
- MLPK 94025 771-A7
36200 NWK 94560 752-E5
CASEY DR
100 SSF 94080 707-E3
500 RCH 94801 608-C1
CASEY WY
2600 SJS 95121 855-D3
CASEY GLEN CT
- CLAY 94517 593-G5
CASHDAN CT
3300 SCL 95051 833-A1
CASHEW CT
500 SRMN 94583 673-G7
2900 ANT 94509 575-J5
CASHEW ST
2800 ANT 94509 575-J6
CASHEW WY
800 FRMT 94536 732-J7
CASHEW BLOSSOM DR
- SJS 95123 875-A3
CASHLEA CT
2600 SSF 94080 707-C4
CASHMERE CT
500 SUNV 94087 832-D4
CASHMERE ST
- SF 94124 668-C6
CASHMERE TER
- SUNV 94087 832-D4
CASINO AV
5600 SPAB 94806 589-A4
CASITA CT
400 LALT 94022 811-F5
400 SJS 95129 852-B7
800 DNVL 94526 653-B2
CASITA WY
400 LALT 94022 811-F5
CASITAS AV
100 SF 94127 667-D5
CASITAS CT
2100 ANT 94509 595-A1
CASITAS BULEVAR
100 LGTS 95030 872-J2
CASKEY ST
700 CCCo 94565 573-C2
CASLAND DR
6200 OAK 94621 670-F2
6200 OAK 94605 670-F2
CASOLYN RANCH RD
1200 DNVL 94506 654-B6
CASPAR PL
100 NVTO 94947 526-E6
CASPAR ST
4900 UNC 94587 752-A1
CASPER PL
200 SRMN 94583 673-G7
CASPER ST
- MPS 95035 793-J7
4100 PIT 94565 574-F6
CASPIAN CT
100 SUNV 94089 812-F2
CASPIAN DR
200 SUNV 94089 812-G2
CASPIAN SEA DR
11700 DBLN 94568 693-G4
CASS PL
10100 CPTO 95014 852-A1
CASS WY
3700 PA 94306 811-C2
CASSADAY CT
600 SJS 95136 874-E1
CASSADY CT
- LVMR 94550 696-B6
CASSADY ST
200 VAL 94590 530-B4
CASSANDRA CT
- SF 94112 687-E2
CASSANDRA PL
100 SRMN 94583 693-G1
CASSANDRA WY
- MTVW 94043 812-A4
CASSATT WY
500 SJS 95125 854-C4
CASSAYRE DR
- AMCN 94589 510-A1
CASSENA DR
3400 WLCK 94598 612-J1
CASSIA CT
- HAY 94544 712-B6
CASSIA DR
100 HAY 94544 712-B6
CASSIA ST
400 RDWC 94063 770-B6
CASSIA WY
1000 SUNV 94087 832-G2
CASSIAR DR
1600 SJS 95130 853-B5
CASSIO CIR
33700 FRMT 94555 752-C1
CASSIO CT
4300 FRMT 94555 752-C1
CASSIOPIA ST
1800 LVMR 94550 696-B3
CASSLAND CT
1300 SJS 95131 814-D7
CASSWELL CT
100 SJS 95138 875-D4
CASSWOOD CT
700 SJS 95120 894-J3
CASTANO DR
5800 SJS 95129 852-G2
CASTANO CORTE
500 LALT 94022 811-E5
CASTANOS ST
4200 FRMT 94536 752-F3
CASTANYA CT
400 DNVL 94526 633-B7
N CASTANYA WY
100 SMCo 94028 810-E3
S CASTANYA WY
200 SMCo 94028 810-E4
CASTELLO DR
6000 SJS 95120 874-C7
CASTELLO RD
300 LFYT 94549 631-H3
CASTELLO ST
2500 OAK 94602 650-D5
CASTELLO WY
2500 SCL 95051 832-J1
CASTELO AV
- SF 94132 687-B1
CASTENADA AV
- SF 94116 667-D4
200 SF 94116 667-D4
CASTENADA CT
300 DNVL 94526 653-D5
CASTENADA DR
200 MLBR 94030 728-A5
1800 BURL 94010 728-A5
CASTERLINE RD
1700 OAK 94602 650-D3
CASTERSON CT
4100 PLE 94566 714-F5
CASTERWOOD CT
700 SJS 95120 894-H2
CASTILE CT
2300 SJS 95125 853-J7
CASTILE ST
100 VAL 94591 530-F6
CASTILIAN CT
11600 DBLN 94568 693-F3
CASTILIAN RD
7600 DBLN 94568 693-F4
CASTILIAN WY
100 SMTO 94402 748-J3
CASTILLE CT
- DNVL 94526 653-C7
4400 UNC 94587 731-H6
CASTILLE LN
22000 HAY 94541 691-J7
CASTILLEJA AV
1400 PA 94301 791-A6
1400 PA 94301 790-J6
1500 PA 94306 791-A6
CASTILLEJA CT
900 LALT 94024 831-H2
CASTILLEJO CT
42700 FRMT 94539 753-F7
CASTILLEJO DR
- DALY 94015 687-A7
100 DALY 94015 707-A1
CASTILLEJO RD
2100 FRMT 94539 753-F7
CASTILLEJO WY
2000 FRMT 94539 753-F7
CASTILLO AV
200 RCH 94804 609-A1
1300 BURL 94010 728-C6
CASTILLO ST
- DALY 94014 687-H2
- SF 94134 687-H2
CASTILLON DR
6100 NWK 94560 752-D5
CASTILLON WY
100 SJS 95119 875-C6
CASTINE AV
10300 CPTO 95014 832-C7
CASTLE CT
- CCCo 94565 573-F2
- HIL 94010 748-D3
- OAK 94611 650-G2
100 LFYT 94549 631-J4
200 NVTO 94945 526-E3
600 ANT 94509 595-F1
11700 DBLN 94568 693-G4
CASTLE DR
2800 SJS 95125 854-C7
5600 OAK 94611 650-G2
7200 DBLN 94568 693-G4
CASTLE LN
- OAK 94611 650-F2
CASTLE ST
- DALY 94014 687-C5
- SF 94133 648-A4
900 SLN 94578 691-C4
CASTLE WY
1100 MLPK 94025 790-F4
CASTLEBAR PL
- ALA 94502 669-H5
CASTLEBERRY CT
2700 AlaC 94541 692-C6
CASTLEBRIDGE DR
- SJS 95116 834-G3
CASTLEBROOK CT
1700 SJS 95133 834-E3
CASTLEBROOK DR
5900 AlaC 94552 692-C1
CASTLEBURY DR
1900 SJS 95116 834-G3
CASTLE CREEK CT
- CCCo 94553 591-E3
CASTLECREST DR
- SJS 95116 834-G3
CASTLE CREST RD
- CCCo 94595 632-D2
300 CCCo 94507 632-D2
CASTLEDOWN RD
- AlaC 94566 714-C6
CASTLEFORD CIR
100 DNVL 94526 653-C2
CASTLEFORD CT
5300 NWK 94560 752-D4
CASTLEFORD DR
2800 ANT 94509 575-C6
CASTLEFORD PL
- DNVL 94526 653-C2
CASTLEGATE DR
1700 SJS 95132 814-E3
CASTLE GATE RD
- WLCK 94595 612-C7
- WLCK 94595 632-C1
CASTLE GLEN AV
5400 SJS 95129 852-H3
CASTLE GLEN RD
200 CCCo 94595 632-C2
CASTLE HILL CT
- VAL 94591 550-E2
- WLCK 94595 612-D7
- WLCK 94595 632-D1
CASTLE HILL RD
600 RDWC 94061 789-H2
1500 CCCo 94595 632-C1
1500 WLCK 94595 632-C1
1800 WLCK 94595 612-D7
CASTLE HILL RCH RD
100 CCCo 94595 632-C2
CASTLEKNOLL DR
6100 SJS 95129 852-C7
CASTLEMAINE CT
- SJS 95136 854-E6
CASTLE MANOR AV
- SF 94112 667-G7
CASTLE MANOR DR
5400 SJS 95129 852-H4
CASTLEMONT AV
- DALY 94015 687-B3
1200 SJS 95128 853-E4
CASTLEMONT DR
- HAY 94544 711-J4
CASTLE OAKS CT
1800 WLCK 94595 612-D7
1800 WLCK 94595 632-D1
CASTLE PARK CT
43300 FRMT 94538 773-C3
CASTLE PARK WY
- OAK 94611 650-F2
CASTLE ROCK CT
- WLCK 94598 612-J3
CASTLEROCK CT
500 SUNV 94087 832-D4
CASTLE ROCK DR
- MrnC 94941 606-C4
CASTLEROCK DR
6800 SJS 95120 894-E3
CASTLE ROCK RD
- WLCK 94598 612-J4
300 CCCo 94598 612-J4
900 CCCo 94598 613-A5
900 WLCK 94598 613-A5
CASTLEROCK TER
500 SUNV 94087 832-D4
CASTLETON AV
- DALY 94015 687-A4
- DALY 94015 686-J4
CASTLETON CT
100 SRMN 94583 673-C2
2500 SJS 95148 855-C1
CASTLETON DR
2500 SJS 95148 855-C1
CASTLETON ST
21500 CPTO 95014 852-B3
CASTLETON TER
1300 SUNV 94087 832-H4
CASTLETON WY
100 SBRN 94066 707-D6
1000 SUNV 94087 832-H4
CASTLETREE CT
1700 SJS 95131 814-C5
CASTLEWOOD COM
5000 FRMT 94536 752-G5
CASTLEWOOD CT
4000 CNCD 94518 593-A5
4000 CNCD 94518 592-J5
4900 SJS 95129 852-J2
18000 HAY 94541 711-E2
CASTLEWOOD DR
- PIT 94565 574-C6
- SRFL 94901 567-C6
- AlaC 94566 714-B7
800 LGTS 95030 873-B2
900 VAL 94591 530-E5
4600 SJS 95129 853-A3
4600 SJS 95129 852-J2
6800 PLE 94566 714-C7
6800 PLE 94588 714-C7
6800 AlaC 94588 714-C7
W CASTLEWOOD DR
- SRFL 94901 567-C7
- MrnC 94901 567-C7
CASTLEWOOD PL
- AlaC 94566 714-B7
CASTLEWOOD ST
8900 OAK 94605 671-A3
CASTLEWOOD WY
18000 HAY 94541 711-E2
CASTOR ST
800 FCTY 94404 749-F4
CASTRO AV
- SRFL 94901 586-J3
CASTRO CT
- BURL 94010 728-B5
300 CMBL 95008 853-A5
1300 PCFA 94044 727-A6
CASTRO DR
1700 CMBL 95008 853-A6
1700 SJS 95130 853-A6
CASTRO LN
- FRMT 94539 753-F2
CASTRO PL
2300 SCL 95050 833-C3
CASTRO ST
- SF 94114 667-G2
- SLN 94577 691-A2
- SF 94117 667-G2
100 MTVW 94041 811-H5

BAY AREA
INDEX

916 CASTRO ST 1998 BAY AREA STREET INDEX CHADBOURNE AV

BAY AREA

STREET Block City ZIP Pg-Grid

CASTRO ST
100 RCH 94801 588-D7
200 OAK 94607 649-F4
500 MRTZ 94553 571-D3
900 ALB 94706 609-D5
1000 MTVW 94040 811-H5
1100 SLN 94577 690-J2
1100 OAK 94612 649-F4
1600 SF 94131 667-G3
1700 SF 94131 667-G4
2600 SPAB 94806 588-J2
33100 UNC 94587 732-F3
N CASTRO ST
- CCCo 94801 588-F4
100 RCH 94801 588-F4
S CASTRO ST
4100 MRTZ 94553 571-E6
CASTRO RANCH RD
1200 CCCo 94803 589-H4
1400 RCH 94803 589-H4
2500 RCH 94803 590-A3
2900 CCCo - 590-A3
E CASTRO VALLEY BL
3300 AlaC 94552 692-B5
3300 AlaC 94542 692-B5
3700 AlaC 94546 692-B5
CASTRO VALLEY BLVD
- AlaC 94541 691-H6
3200 AlaC 94546 692-A5
3500 AlaC 94546 691-H6
CASUAL CT
- NVTO 94947 525-F3
6800 SJS 95120 894-F2
CASUAL WY
1100 SJS 95120 894-F2
CASWELL AV
300 OAK 94603 670-G7
300 OAK 94603 670-G7
CATALA CT
600 SCL 95050 833-D5
CATALAN WY
300 SRMN 94583 673-G2
CATALDI DR
2900 SJS 95132 814-E4
CATALINA AV
100 PCFA 94044 707-A2
1800 BERK 94707 609-F6
3000 ALA 94502 669-J7
3100 SCL 95051 833-A5
3100 ALA 94502 670-A7
CATALINA BLVD
- SRFL 94901 587-A2
CATALINA CIR
500 VAL 94589 509-G5
CATALINA CT
- LALT 94022 811-E5
100 VAL 94589 509-H5
800 PIT 94565 574-E6
1500 LVMR 94550 715-F3
3700 AlaC 94546 692-A5
11200 CPTO 95014 852-B3
CATALINA DR
100 HER 94547 570-C6
600 LVMR 94550 715-E3
4500 SJS 95129 853-A3
20000 AlaC 94546 692-A5
CATALINA PL
40000 FRMT 94539 753-E4
CATALINA ST
13700 SLN 94577 690-H5
CATALINA WY
200 VAL 94589 509-G5
600 LALT 94022 811-E5
CATALINE AV
- ANT 94509 575-C5
CATALON CT
7600 DBLN 94568 693-G3
CATALONIA WY
1600 SJS 95125 853-J7
CATALPA AV
- MLV 94941 606-E3
200 SMTO 94401 748-J1
CATALPA CT
100 HER 94547 569-J4
1700 HAY 94545 731-J1
4400 CNCD 94521 593-C5
CATALPA DR
- ATN 94027 770-F7
- ATN 94027 790-F1
CATALPA LN
- CMBL 95008 853-D6
- SRMN 94583 693-F1
CATALPA ST
3100 CCCo 94553 571-G4
CATALPA WY
1800 HAY 94545 711-H7
2300 SBRN 94066 707-F7
E CATAMARAN CIR
100 PIT 94565 574-A2
N CATAMARAN CIR
100 PIT 94565 574-A2
S CATAMARAN CIR
200 PIT 94565 574-A2
W CATAMARAN CIR
100 PIT 94565 574-A2
CATAMARAN CT
39600 FRMT 94538 753-A7
CATAMARAN LN
- DALY 94014 687-E5
CATAMARAN ST
300 FCTY 94404 749-G3
6500 SJS 95119 875-D7
CATANIO CT
500 SRMN 94583 673-B2
CATANZARO WY
5000 ANT 94509 595-J4
CATAWBA CT
3100 PLE 94566 714-H4
CATHARINE CT
26200 LAH 94022 811-B6
CATHAY DR
1100 SJS 95122 834-H5
CATHCART WY
1000 SCIC 94305 811-A2
1000 SCIC 94305 810-J2
CATHEDRAL DR
700 SUNV 94087 832-C4
CATHERINE CT
- CCCo 94507 632-G5
- SF 94110 667-J3
100 ORIN 94563 630-J1
CATHERINE DR
300 SSF 94080 707-E3
1400 BERK 94702 629-F1
CATHERINE ST
900 SJS 95002 793-B7
1600 SCL 95050 833-D4
CATHERINE WY
1500 CNCD 94519 593-A2
1500 CNCD 94519 592-J3
CATHY CT
2500 ANT 94509 574-J6
CATHY LN
- DNVL 94526 653-A1
- DNVL 94526 652-J1
- OAK 94619 651-C7
CATHY PL
- MLPK 94025 790-F5
CATHY WY
1300 HAY 94545 711-G6
2600 ANT 94509 574-J6
CATKIN CT
800 SJS 95128 853-F2
CATRINA CT
5100 SJS 95124 873-G5
CATRON DR
- OAK 94603 670-H7
100 OAK 94603 690-H1
CAT TAIL CT
3500 UNC 94587 732-A5
CATTAIL CT
700 WLCK 94598 613-A3
CATTLE CHUTE RD
- LFYT 94549 631-G4
CAUDILLO TER
400 MPS 95035 793-H3
CAULFIELD CT
500 CLAY 94517 593-G6
CAULFIELD DR
5700 CLAY 94517 593-G6
CAUSEY LN
200 LGTS 95032 873-C7
CAVALIER CT
400 LALT 94022 811-D4
1800 SJS 95124 853-G7
8400 DBLN 94568 693-G2
CAVALIER LN
8200 DBLN 94568 693-G2
CAVALLA CAY
- MrnC 94949 526-G7
CAVALLERO CT
- MrnC 94945 526-F3
CAVALLO RD
900 ANT 94509 575-E5
CAVALRY CT
- DNVL 94526 653-A3
CAVANAGH CT
2700 HAY 94545 711-C5
CAVANAUGH CT
- PDMT 94610 650-D3
CAVANAUGH ST
300 SMTO 94401 729-A6
CAVEN WY
1100 CNCD 94520 592-F4
CAVENDISH DR
3300 SJS 95132 814-F3
E CAVENDISH DR
18600 AlaC 94552 692-D3
W CAVENDISH DR
18500 AlaC 94552 692-D3
CAVENDISH LN
- OAK 94602 650-D3
CAVENDISH PL
34000 FRMT 94555 732-D7
CAVISSON CT
44400 FRMT 94539 773-H2
CAVORETTO LN
- CCCo 94803 589-F4
CAVOUR ST
300 OAK 94618 629-H6
E CAVOUR ST
- DALY 94014 687-C4
W CAVOUR ST
- DALY 94014 687-C4
CAXTON CT
3200 SMTO 94403 749-A6
3200 SMTO 94403 748-J6
3900 SJS 95130 853-B4
CAXTON PL
35700 FRMT 94536 752-G2
CAY PASG
- CMAD 94925 607-A1
CAYCE CT
900 CNCD 94518 592-F6
CAYES CT
1000 ANT 94509 575-F7
CAYETANO CT
- AlaC 94550 695-F5
CAYFORD DR
- TBRN 94920 607-A4
CAYMAN
- HER 94547 570-C6
CAYMAN LN
600 FCTY 94404 749-G5
CAYMAN PL
3100 SJS 95127 814-G6
CAYMAN WY
900 SJS 95127 814-G6
CAYMUS CT
100 SUNV 94086 812-C6
CAYUCOS DR
1500 WLCK 94596 611-J2
1600 CCCo 94549 611-J2
CAYUGA AV
- SF 94112 687-D2
1300 SF 94112 667-F7
CAYUGA CT
600 SJS 95123 874-H7
45700 FRMT 94539 773-H4
CAYUGA DR
600 SJS 95123 874-H7
900 LVMR 94550 695-F7
CAYUGA PL
- FRMT 94539 773-H4
CAYUGA WY
300 FRMT 94539 773-H4
CAZADERO LN
- TBRN 94920 607-E7
CAZNEAU AV
- SAUS 94965 627-A2
CEANOTHUS LN
6200 SJS 95119 875-D5
CEBALO LN
- ATN 94027 790-C1
CEBU CT
6400 SJS 95119 875-C7
CEBU DR
200 CCCo 94553 572-C7
CECALA DR
6000 SJS 95120 874-C7
CECELIA CT
500 LALT 94022 811-F5
1000 SLN 94577 671-A7
1000 SLN 94577 691-A1
CECELIA LN
- NVTO 94947 525-H2
CECELIA WY
2000 LALT 94022 811-F5
2000 MTVW 94040 811-F5
CECIL AV
- SCIC 95128 853-F1
- SJS 95128 853-F1
3100 SCL 95117 833-D7
3100 SCL 95117 853-C1
CECILIA AV
2200 SF 94116 667-C4
CECILIA CT
- TBRN 94920 607-A4
CECILIA LN
- CCCo 94553 572-A3
CECILIA WY
- TBRN 94920 607-A4
200 MrnC 94920 606-J4
200 TBRN 94920 606-J4
3200 PIT 94565 574-D4
CECILY LN
- MrnC 94941 606-D4
CEDAR AV
- LKSP 94939 586-E5
- NVTO 94945 526-J3
- MrnC 94904 586-D3
100 MrnC 94945 526-J3
400 SBRN 94066 727-H1
400 VAL 94592 529-F3
500 SBRN 94066 707-G7
800 SUNV 94086 812-F7
1300 SLN 94579 690-J4
1600 SLN 94579 691-A4
2000 SMCo 94025 790-D6
CEDAR BLVD
6500 NWK 94560 752-D5
38800 NWK 94560 772-H1
39800 NWK 94560 773-A2
CEDAR CT
- DALY 94014 687-H2
- SF 94134 687-H2
- HIL 94010 748-F1
- MPS 95035 814-A3
- SMCo 94025 790-D6
100 HER 94547 569-J4
1000 CCCo 94525 550-D5
3000 PLHL 94523 591-J5
3100 ANT 94509 574-J7
5500 NWK 94560 752-H7
6900 DBLN 94568 693-J4
CEDAR DR
300 LVMR 94550 695-D7
CEDAR LN
- SRFL 94901 587-B1
- ORIN 94563 631-A3
- SCIC 95127 834-H2
- WDSD 94062 789-G7
200 PCFA 94044 707-A6
200 PCFA 94044 706-J6
1400 CCCo 94507 632-F4
6200 SJS 95138 875-F6
6800 DBLN 94568 693-J4
CEDAR PL
600 NVTO 94945 525-E2
800 SSF 94080 708-A2
1400 LALT 94024 831-J6
CEDAR ST
- RDWC 94063 770-B6
- SANS 94960 566-B7
- SCAR 94070 769-F2
- SF 94109 647-H6
- SANS 94960 586-B1
100 FRMT 94539 773-H1
100 VAL 94591 530-D5
300 MLBR 94030 728-B2
600 BERK 94804 629-C1
600 OAK 94607 649-C3
700 BERK 94702 629-E1
800 ALA 94501 669-J3
900 BERK 94703 629-E1
1100 PA 94301 791-B4
1100 PIT 94565 574-F2
1400 MRTZ 94553 571-F3
1800 HAY 94541 692-B7
1900 BERK 94709 629-E1
2000 CNCD 94519 592-G1
2000 BERK 94709 609-H7
2300 ELCR 94530 589-B7
2400 BERK 94708 609-H7
CEDAR TER
- ORIN 94563 631-A3
CEDAR WY
- MPS 95035 814-A3
400 SCL 95051 833-B7
CEDARBERRY LN
500 MrnC 94903 546-C7
CEDAR BROOK
100 MTVW 94041 811-J6
CEDAR BROOK CT
5700 AlaC 94552 692-B2
CEDARBROOK CT
- CCCo 94596 612-D2
CEDAR BROOK TER
20500 CPTO 95014 832-D6
CEDARCREEK CT
1600 SJS 95121 855-D7
CEDARCREEK DR
3400 SJS 95121 855-D7
CEDARCREST LN
3100 SJS 95132 814-E3
CEDAR CREST PL
100 LGTS 95030 873-B3
CEDAR CREST RD
4400 CNCD 94521 593-B4
CEDARDALE CT
2800 SJS 95148 835-E6
CEDARDALE DR
3400 SJS 95148 835-E7
CEDAR FLAT CT
3500 SJS 95127 835-C3
CEDAR GABLES DR
1100 SJS 95118 874-C2
CEDARGATE LN
100 SJS 95136 874-J3
CEDAR GLEN CT
500 WLCK 94598 612-H3
CEDAR GROVE CIR
5300 SJS 95123 875-A3
5300 SJS 95123 874-J3
CEDAR HILL DR
400 SRFL 94903 566-D1
400 SRFL 94903 546-D7
CEDAR HOLLOW DR
200 DNVL 94526 653-A1
200 DNVL 94526 652-J1
CEDARHURST LN
- SJS 95136 874-D2
CEDAR LANE CT
100 DNVL 94526 653-E3
CEDARMEADOW CT
1300 SJS 95131 814-B6
CEDARMEADOW LN
1700 SJS 95131 814-B6
CEDAR MOUNTAIN DR
7300 AlaC 94550 716-E5
CEDAR OAK TER
- FRMT 94536 752-B4
CEDAR POINTE LP
- SRMN 94583 693-H1
CEDAR RIDGE CT
3000 SJS 95148 835-G7
CEDAR RIDGE WY
5100 ANT 94509 595-E4
CEDAR SPRING CT
11500 CPTO 95014 852-C4
CEDAR TREE CT
10500 CPTO 95014 832-E7
CEDAR TREE LN
20000 CPTO 95014 832-E6
CEDARVILLE LN
700 SCIC 95133 834-F1
700 SJS 95133 834-F1
CEDARWOOD CT
1600 SBRN 94066 707-G7
4200 CNCD 94521 593-B2
CEDARWOOD DR
- SJS 95131 814-A4
1100 MRGA 94556 651-E1
1400 SMTO 94403 748-H7
43100 FRMT 94538 773-D2
CEDARWOOD LN
- MrnC 94941 606-C4
- NVTO 94947 526-D6
1200 BERK 94804 609-C7
1400 PLE 94566 714-E2
2100 SJS 95125 853-J6
CEDARWOOD WY
1100 RDWC 94061 790-B2
CEDERBROOK PL
- PIT 94565 574-F7
CEDRO AV
- SF 94127 667-C7
CEDRO LN
2500 WLCK 94598 612-H2
CEDRO ST
300 SJS 95111 854-H6
CEDRO WY
700 SCIC 94305 810-J2
CEEKAY CT
3700 AlaC 94546 692-B6
CEEMAR CT
- CNCD 94519 593-A2
CEFALU DR
3600 SJS 95124 873-J2
CELA CT
- WLCK 94596 612-C2
CELAYA CIR
2600 SRMN 94583 673-C3
CELEBRATION CT
600 SJS 95134 813-F3
CELEDA CT
100 FRMT 94539 753-E4
CELEO LN
10600 SCIC 95127 815-B7
CELESTE AV
2000 CCCo 94596 612-E7
2000 CCCo 94596 632-E1
5300 LVMR 94550 696-C6
CELESTE CIR
20600 CPTO 95014 832-D6
CELESTE CT
- NVTO 94947 525-G2
32400 UNC 94587 732-A7
CELESTE DR
1600 SMTO 94402 749-B3
CELESTIAL CT
- PCFA 94044 727-A5
CELESTIAL LN
600 FCTY 94404 749-E4
CELESTINE AV
2200 SJS 95125 854-C5
CELIA CT
- PCFA 94044 727-A5
4500 FRMT 94555 752-C1
CELIA DR
- PLHL 94523 592-C5
CELIA ST
200 HAY 94544 712-B7
CELIA WY
900 PA 94303 791-D5
CELILO DR
1000 SUNV 94087 832-B4
CELINE CT
- DNVL 94526 653-C4
CELLO WY
5600 FRMT 94538 773-B2
CENTAURUS CT
1700 LVMR 94550 696-B3
CENTAURUS LN
800 FCTY 94404 749-H1
CENTENNIAL AV
800 ALA 94501 669-G1
CENTENNIAL BLVD
4900 SCL 95054 813-C4
CENTENNIAL CT
- ANT 94509 595-C3
1300 SJS 95129 852-G4
CENTENNIAL DR
- BERK 94708 610-A7
- BERK 94720 610-A7
CENTENNIAL DR
- BERK 94720 630-A1
- OAK 94708 610-A7
- OAK 94720 610-A7
- OAK 94720 630-A1
3500 ANT 94509 595-C3
CENTENNIAL LN
- AlaC 94541 712-C1
CENTENNIAL WY
2700 SRMN 94583 673-E6
CENTENO RD
35500 FRMT 94536 752-F2
CENTER AV
- MRTZ 94553 571-F6
900 MRTZ 94553 572-A7
1800 CCCo 94553 572-C7
1800 CCCo 94553 592-B1
1800 MRTZ 94553 592-B1
2600 RCH 94804 588-J7
3400 RCH 94804 589-A7
CENTER BLVD
- FRFX 94930 566-A6
100 SANS 94960 566-A6
CENTER CT
- DNVL 94506 654-A6
- DNVL 94506 653-J5
- CCCo 94595 612-A7
900 MRTZ 94553 571-G6
CENTER DR
- CNCD 94521 593-C6
- PIT 94565 574-D3
500 PA 94301 791-B3
CENTER LN
2900 ANT 94509 575-D7
CENTER RD
1500 NVTO 94947 526-A4
1800 NVTO 94947 525-E2
2500 MrnC 94947 525-E2
3100 SJS 95134 813-F3
CENTER ST
- MLBR 94030 728-A2
- RDWC 94063 770-B7
- SRFL 94901 566-E7
- RDWC 94061 770-B7
100 RDWC 94061 790-B1
300 OAK 94607 649-D4
400 CCCo 94595 612-A6
400 MRGA 94556 631-E4
800 SCAR 94070 769-H4
1900 BERK 94704 629-G2
5900 CLAY 94517 593-H7
17000 AlaC 94546 692-C4
19100 AlaC 94552 692-C2
22100 AlaC 94541 692-B6
22500 HAY 94541 692-B6
CENTER WY
- DNVL 94506 653-J5
CENTER BROOKFIELD
400 AMCN 94589 510-B4
CENTERHART CT
5200 SJS 95123 874-F7
CENTER PARK LN
500 FCTY 94404 749-F3
CENTER POINT TER
- SRMN 94583 673-G2
CENTER RIDGE DR
1600 SJS 95121 855-A2
CENTERWOOD CT
2800 SJS 95148 835-D7
CENTERWOOD WY
3000 SJS 95148 835-D7
CENTO CT
- PLE 94566 715-C6
CENTRAL AV
- LGTS 95032 893-A2
- MTVW 94043 811-J4
- PIT 94565 574-E2
- RDWC 94061 790-B1
- SAUS 94965 627-B4
- SF 94117 667-F1
100 ALA 94501 649-E7
100 BURL 94010 728-G7
100 VAL 94590 530-B5
100 ALA 94501 669-E1
200 SUNV 94086 812-A4
200 SUNV 94086 832-E1
300 MLPK 94025 791-A3
400 SF 94117 647-F7
500 CCCo 94553 572-A3
500 CCCo 94553 571-J3
600 MTVW 94043 812-A4
700 LVMR 94550 696-C4
900 SF 94115 647-F7
1100 SCAR 94070 769-H4
2200 ALA 94501 670-A2
2600 UNC 94587 732-E5
4000 FRMT 94536 752-G5
4800 CCCo 94801 588-F3
4900 RCH 94804 609-D4
5300 NWK 94560 752-G5
5400 ELCR 94530 609-D4
6400 NWK 94560 772-D2
15200 SLN 94578 691-C4
CENTRAL AV Rt#-61
700 ALA 94501 669-G1
N CENTRAL AV
- CMBL 95008 853-E5
1000 CMBL 95008 853-E3
1100 SJS 95128 853-E3
W CENTRAL AV
- LGTS 95032 893-A1
CENTRAL BLVD
800 HAY 94542 712-A3
CENTRAL CT
- LGTS 95032 893-A1
- MrnC 94920 606-H3
400 SLN 94578 691-D5
2600 UNC 94587 732-D6
4000 CCCo 94553 572-A3
37200 NWK 94560 772-D1
CENTRAL DR
- MLPK 94025 790-J1
- MrnC 94920 606-H3
27600 LAH 94022 830-H2
CENTRAL EXWY Rt#-G6
- MTVW 94041 812-B5
- MTVW 94043 812-B5
- MTVW 94086 812-B5
- PA 94306 811-G3
- SCL 94086 812-H7
- SCL 95051 812-H7
CENTRAL EXWY Rt#-G6
- SUNV 94086 813-A7
- SUNV 94086 812-H7
100 MTVW 94043 811-G3
700 SCL 95050 833-D1
700 SCL 95054 833-D1
800 MTVW 94041 811-G3
800 SCL 95054 833-D1
2000 MTVW 94040 811-G3
2400 SCL 95051 833-D1
2700 SCL 95051 813-A7
2700 SCL 95054 813-A7
3000 SUNV 95054 813-A7
CENTRAL FRWY U.S.-101
- SF - 647-H7
- SF - 668-A1
- SF - 667-J1
CENTRAL PKWY
- DBLN 94568 694-D4
CENTRAL RD
1400 WLCK 94596 612-C4
CENTRAL WY
600 SCIC 95128 853-F2
2200 SJS 95128 853-F2
CENTRALIA CT
500 SUNV 94087 832-D4
CENTRAL MAGAZINE RD
- SF 94129 647-C4
CENTRALMONT PL
37400 FRMT 94536 752-G5
CENTRAL PARK DR
500 CCCo 94708 609-H4
2100 CMBL 95008 853-E7
2100 SJS 95008 853-E7
CENTRE CT
100 ALA 94502 670-A5
CENTRE ST
- MTVW 94041 811-J6
CENTRE POINTE DR
1400 MPS 95035 814-B3
CENTRO WY
900 MrnC 94941 606-E5
CENTRO EAST ST
2000 TBRN 94920 627-F1
2000 TBRN 94920 607-F7
CENTRO WEST ST
1700 TBRN 94920 607-E7
1800 TBRN 94920 627-E1
CENTURY BLVD
4300 PIT 94565 575-A5
4300 PIT 94565 574-H4
4800 ANT 94509 574-H4
CENTURY CIR
300 DNVL 94526 653-C5
CENTURY CT
800 CMBL 95008 853-C7
CENTURY DR
- MrnC 94941 606-J7
300 CMBL 95008 853-C7
3400 SJS 95008 853-C7
6400 SJS 95129 852-F3
CENTURY PL
- SF 94104 648-B5
CENTURY ST
28400 HAY 94545 731-J2
CENTURY WY
700 DNVL 94526 653-C5
CENTURY CENTER CT
- SJS 95110 833-H2
CENTURY CROSS CT
400 SJS 95111 875-C3
CENTURY HILL CT
5400 SJS 95111 875-C3
CENTURY MANOR CT
5500 SJS 95111 875-C3
CENTURY MEADOW CT
5400 SJS 95111 875-C3
CENTURY OAKS CIR
3700 AlaC 94552 692-E6
CENTURY OAKS CT
400 SJS 95111 875-C3
2600 SRMN 94583 673-D6
3700 AlaC 94552 692-E6
CENTURY OAKS WY
400 SJS 95111 875-C3
CENTURY PARK WY
5400 SJS 95111 875-C3
CENTURY PLAZA WY
5400 SJS 95111 875-C3
CERA DR
900 SJS 95129 853-A3
CERES ST
- SF 94124 668-B7
1100 CCCo 94525 550-D5
CEREUS CT
48400 FRMT 94539 793-J1
CEREZA DR
700 PA 94306 811-C2
1000 PLE 94566 714-G3
CEREZO DR
100 WLCK 94598 612-H3
CERMENHO CT
- SRFL 94903 566-D4
CERRITO AV
100 RDWC 94061 790-A4
100 SMCo 94061 790-A4
3500 RCH 94805 589-A6
3500 RCH 94805 588-J6
3800 OAK 94611 649-J1
CERRITO CT
2100 PIT 94565 574-A3
3300 SJS 95148 835-D7
3600 LFYT 94549 611-E7
CERRITO PL
- SMCo 94061 790-A4
CERRITO ST
700 ALB 94706 609-D6
CERRITO WY
3200 SJS 95148 835-D7
CERRITOS AV
- SF 94127 667-C7
4500 FRMT 94536 752-F3
CERRO CT
- DNVL 94526 633-C6
300 DALY 94015 687-B7
2000 ANT 94509 595-A1
43900 FRMT 94539 773-H2
CERRO DR
- DALY 94015 687-B7
CERRO CHICO
200 LGTS 95032 873-C7
CERRO CREST DR
100 NVTO 94945 526-F1
CERRO ENCANTADO
- LFYT 94549 611-E7
CERRO KAMUK CT
2100 SJS 95116 834-F3
CERRO NORTE
5500 RCH 94803 589-J3
5500 RCH 94803 590-A3
CERROS MNR
- SMCo 94025 790-D5
CERRO SUR
5300 RCH 94803 590-A3
CERRO TERBI CT
2100 SJS 95116 834-G3
CERRO VERDE
1300 SJS 95120 894-B1
CERRO VISTA
3000 ALA 94502 669-J6
CERRO VISTA CT
15900 LGTS 95032 873-D7
CERRO VISTA DR
15900 LGTS 95032 873-D7
15900 LGTS 95032 893-E1
CERRO VISTA LN
2400 CCCo 94507 632-E3
CERRO VISTA PL
4800 AlaC 94550 716-B2
CERVANTES BLVD
- SF 94123 647-F3
CERVANTES RD
100 PTLV 94028 810-C5
100 SMCo 94062 769-F7
CERVANTES WY
1100 PCFA 94044 726-H4
2200 SJS 95008 853-C7
CERVANTEZ CT
1000 MPS 95035 794-C4
CERVATO CIR
1500 CCCo 94507 632-E3
CERVATO DR
1500 CCCo 94507 632-E3
CESA LN
- ANT 94509 575-D5
CESANO CT
400 PA 94306 811-D3
CESAR CT
500 WLCK 94598 612-E2
CESAR CHAVEZ ST
500 SF 94107 668-A4
500 SF 94124 668-A4
2700 SF 94110 668-A4
2900 SF 94110 668-A4
2900 SF 94110 667-J4
3800 SF 94131 667-G4
CESSNA CT
6300 SJS 95123 874-J7
CESSNA ST
7600 OAK 94621 670-D6
CESTARIC DR
400 MPS 95035 794-C5
CEYLON AV
1900 SJS 95122 834-J7
CEYLON CT
2100 SJS 95122 834-J7
CEYNOWA LN
- SJS 95121 855-C3
CEZANNE DR
600 SUNV 94086 832-E2
800 SUNV 94087 832-E2
CHABAN DR
4100 CNCD 94521 593-B2
CHABLIS CIR
3500 SJS 95132 814-H4
CHABLIS CT
- FRMT 94539 773-J4
3200 PLE 94566 714-G3
19300 SAR 95070 872-G3
CHABLIS WY
2500 LVMR 94550 715-H2
CHABOLYN TER
5900 BERK 94618 630-A4
5900 OAK 94618 630-A4
CHABOT CT
200 PIT 94565 574-B2
1500 HAY 94545 711-G5
5800 OAK 94618 630-A4
CHABOT DR
2600 SBRN 94066 707-D6
4500 PLE 94588 694-B6
CHABOT RD
5800 OAK 94618 629-J5
5900 OAK 94618 630-B4
CHABOT ST
4100 ANT 94509 595-J1
CHABOT TER
- SF 94118 647-E7
1600 SLN 94577 671-D7
2400 PA 94303 791-D4
CHABOT VW
18500 AlaC 94546 691-G3
CHABOT WY
1400 SJS 95122 834-J5
CHABOT CREST
5900 OAK 94618 630-A4
6000 BERK 94618 630-A4
CHABOT VIEW DR
- AlaC 94578 691-G3
CHABOYA CT
4200 SCIC 95148 835-H7
CHABOYA RD
3800 SJS 95148 855-G1
4000 SCIC 95148 855-H1
4000 SCIC 95148 835-H7
CHABOYA HILLS CT
4200 SCIC 95148 835-G7
CHABRANT WY
900 SJS 95125 854-A3
CHABRE CT
500 CCCo 94803 589-D1
CHACE DR
10400 CPTO 95014 832-A7
10500 SCIC 94024 832-A7
CHAD DR
300 MPS 95035 794-A5
CHADBOURN CT
1400 PLE 94566 714-G4
CHADBOURNE AV
- MLBR 94030 728-A4

INDEX

STREET Block City ZIP Pg-Grid

CHADBOURNE CT
- DNVL 94506 653-H5
CHADBOURNE DR
- DNVL 94506 653-G5
41500 FRMT 94539 753-F6
CHADBOURNE LN
1100 MLBR 94030 728-A4
18300 MSER 95030 872-J4
CHADBOURNE WY
- OAK 94619 650-H4
CHADIMA CT
- PLHL 94523 592-A5
CHADIMA LN
300 PLHL 94523 592-A5
CHADWICK CIR
1000 CCCo 94565 573-G2
CHADWICK CT
- MLBR 94030 727-J5
200 BEN 94510 551-A2
21100 SAR 95070 852-C7
CHADWICK LN
600 CCCo 94565 573-G3
CHADWICK PL
11100 CPTO 95014 852-B3
CHAIN OF LKS DR E
- SF - 666-J1
CHAIN OF LKS DR W
- SF - 666-H1
CHALDA CT
- MrnC 94903 566-G3
CHALDA WY
400 MRGA 94556 631-E4
CHALET AV
100 SJS 95127 834-H1
CHALET DR
900 CNCD 94518 592-G5
CHALET LN
20300 SAR 95070 872-E1
CHALET PL
100 CMBL 95008 853-F7
CHALET CLOTILDE DR
13400 SAR 95070 852-C7
CHALET WOODS CIR
100 CMBL 95008 853-F6
CHALK CREEK CT
100 MRTZ 94553 591-J4
CHALLENGE CT
100 FCTY 94404 749-G2
CHALLENGE DR
1600 CNCD 94520 592-D3
CHALLENGER AV
200 SJS 95127 834-H1
CHALLENGER DR
2000 ALA 94501 649-G7
CHALLENGER WY
800 HAY 94544 712-A3
CHALMETTE CT
- LVMR 94550 715-C1
CHALMETTE RD
200 LVMR 94550 715-D1
CHALMETTE PARK CT
4800 FRMT 94538 773-C1
CHALOMAR RD
2000 CNCD 94518 592-G5
CHALON GLEN CT
1900 LVMR 94550 715-H3
CHAMA WY
100 FRMT 94539 773-H7
CHAMBERLAIN AV
- NVTO 94947 526-A5
CHAMBERLAIN CT
- NVTO 94947 526-A5
3300 WLCK 94598 612-J3
CHAMBERLAIN DR
3500 SJS 95121 855-C3
CHAMBERLAIN TER
34100 FRMT - 752-E1
34100 FRMT 94555 732-J4
34100 FRMT 94555 752-E1
CHAMBERLAN CT
800 MrnC 94965 606-E6
CHAMBERLIN CT
4300 OAK 94619 650-J7
CHAMBERS DR
1500 SJS 95118 874-A2
6800 OAK 94611 630-F7
CHAMBERS LN
- OAK 94611 630-F7
CHAMBERS ST
28300 HAY 94545 731-H1
CHAMBERTIN DR
5600 SJS 95118 874-A5
CHAMBERY DR
- SJS 95127 834-J1
CHAMBORD CT
- SJS 95127 834-C2
CHAMBOSSE DR
300 HAY 94544 712-B6
CHAMIER PL
2800 FRMT 94555 732-E6
CHAMISAL AV
300 LALT 94022 811-D6
CHAMISE TR
- CCCo - 652-E3
CHAMPAGNE CT
11200 DBLN 94568 693-E3
CHAMPAGNE LN
1100 SJS 95132 814-G5
CHAMPAGNE PL
11300 DBLN 94568 693-F3
CHAMPION CT
100 SJS 95134 813-E3
CHAMPION ST
3000 OAK 94602 650-D5
CHAMPLAIN ST
- HAY 94544 732-E3
CHANCE LN
- WLCK 94596 612-B2
CHANCE ST
29200 HAY 94544 732-C1
CHANCELLOR CT
- CCCo 94507 632-J2
CHANCELLOR PL
- OAK 94705 630-C3
CHANCELLOR WY
3300 SJS 95111 854-F7
CHANDLER AV
800 RCH 94804 608-F2
CHANDLER CIR
3400 CCCo 94565 573-F2
CHANDLER CT
900 CNCD 94518 592-E6
1300 LVMR 94550 695-F6
5700 SJS 95123 874-J4
CHANDLER RD
24300 HAY 94545 711-F4
CHANDLER WY
- SMCo 94010 728-B7
- SMCo 94010 748-B1
CHANDON CT
500 WLCK 94596 612-C3
1300 SJS 95125 853-G4
CHANEL CT
900 CNCD 94518 592-G5
CHANEL TER
34700 FRMT 94555 752-D3
CHANEY RD
1300 CCCo 94507 632-E2
CHANN CT
48000 FRMT 94539 773-J7
CHANNEL AV
5100 RCH 94804 609-A3
CHANNEL CT
- BEN 94510 551-D1
CHANNEL DR
- CMAD 94925 606-J1
- RDWC 94065 750-A6
- CMAD 94925 586-J7
200 MrnC 94945 526-H2
5200 NWK 94560 752-E4
6200 SJS 95123 874-J7
CHANNEL DR E
- SJS 95002 813-C1
CHANNEL DR W
- SJS 95002 813-B1
CHANNEL LNDG
200 MrnC 94920 606-J4
CHANNEL RD
- BEN 94510 551-D1
CHANNEL RD E
- BEN 94510 551-D1
CHANNEL ST
- SF 94107 648-C7
- SF 94107 668-B1
15800 AlaC 94580 711-C1
CHANNING AV
100 PA 94301 790-J5
400 PA 94301 791-A4
1300 PA 94303 791-C4
2500 SJS 95131 813-F7
CHANNING CIR
800 BEN 94510 530-H6
CHANNING CT
2200 CNCD 94520 572-F6
CHANNING LN
500 PCFA 94044 707-A3
CHANNING RD
- BURL 94010 728-H6
CHANNING WY
- MRGA 94556 631-E2
- SAUS 94965 627-A4
200 ALA 94502 669-J5
200 SRFL 94903 566-F2
300 PCFA 94044 707-A3
1100 BERK 94804 629-D3
1200 BERK 94702 629-E3
1300 BERK 94703 629-G2
1900 BERK 94704 629-G2
CHANSLOR AV
2400 RCH 94801 588-G7
2700 RCH 94804 588-H7
3500 RCH 94805 588-J7
W CHANSLOR AV
- RCH 94801 588-E7
CHANSLOR CIR
- RCH 94801 588-E7
CHANSLOR CT
- RCH 94801 588-F7
CHANSLOR RW
- RCH 94801 588-E7
CHANT CT
2500 SJS 95122 834-J5
CHANTAL WY
- RDWC 94061 790-A1
CHANTECLER CT
- FRMT 94539 773-J2
CHANTECLER DR
- FRMT 94539 773-J2
CHANTEL CT
6800 SJS 95129 852-E4
CHANTICLEER AV
- LKSP 94939 586-F6
- MrnC 94965 606-B4
CHANTICLEER LN
100 CCCo 94507 633-A3
CHANTILL DR
7700 DBLN 94568 694-A1
CHANTILLEY CT
7100 SJS 95139 895-F1
CHANTILLEY LN
100 SJS 95139 875-F7
100 SJS 95139 895-F1
CHANTILLEY PL
200 SJS 95139 875-F7
CHANTILLY CT
900 WLCK 94598 612-J4
CHANTILLY LN
24700 HAY 94541 712-B2
CHAPALA DR
3400 SJS 95148 835-D6
CHAPALLA WY
4200 UNC 94587 732-A6
CHAPARRAL AV
2200 SJS 95130 852-J6
CHAPARRAL CT
- NVTO 94949 546-E4
3700 CNCD 94519 593-A1
5000 ANT 94509 595-H4
46500 FRMT 94539 773-J5
CHAPARRAL DR
46400 FRMT 94539 773-J5
CHAPARRAL LN
22000 AlaC 94552 692-D5
CHAPARRAL PL
4100 AlaC 94552 692-D5
CHAPARRAL WY
1400 LVMR 94550 696-E2
27300 LAH 94022 831-A3
CHAPARRO CT
1800 WLCK 94596 612-H7
CHAPEL AV
1200 SLN 94579 691-A6
CHAPEL CT
15100 SLN 94579 691-B6
CHAPEL DR
- LFYT 94549 611-A6
- MrnC 94941 606-H6
1100 SCL 95050 833-D4
CHAPEL LN
- MLPK 94025 790-J2
CHAPEL VW
- WLCK 94596 612-B4
CHAPEL WY
40400 FRMT 94538 753-D7
41100 FRMT 94538 773-D1
CHAPELHAVEN CT
- SJS 95111 874-J1
CHAPEL HILL WY
900 SJS 95122 854-G1
CHAPEL VIEW DR
- SMCo - 768-D4
CHAPIN AV
1400 BURL 94010 728-F7
CHAPIN LN
100 BURL 94010 728-F7
400 HIL 94010 728-F7
CHAPIN RD
25500 LAH 94022 811-C7
CHAPIN ST
1600 ALA 94501 669-G1
1700 ALA 94501 649-G7
CHAPLIN DR
35500 FRMT 94536 752-G1
CHAPMAN AV
- SSF 94080 708-A2
300 SBRN 94066 727-J1
CHAPMAN CT
100 VAL 94589 510-B5
500 SCL 95050 833-F5
26300 HAY 94545 711-G6
38600 FRMT 94536 753-C2
CHAPMAN DR
200 CMAD 94925 586-F7
200 CMAD 94925 606-F1
400 CMBL 95008 873-C1
5300 NWK 94560 752-D4
CHAPMAN LN
200 MrnC 94941 606-E4
CHAPMAN RD
- SMCo 94020 809-F7
14200 SLN 94578 691-B4
CHAPMAN ST
- SF 94110 667-J5
500 SJS 95126 833-G5
2800 OAK 94601 670-B1
CHAPMAN WY
4200 PLE 94588 694-A7
CHAPPARAL CT
2600 PIN 94564 569-G7
2600 SRMN 94583 673-D6
CHAPPARAL LN
1700 CCCo 94549 611-H1
CHAPPARAL PL
- ORIN 94563 610-E6
CHAPPELL PL
5600 OAK 94619 651-A5
CHAPS CT
4900 ANT 94509 595-J2
CHAQUITA LN
- MLV 94941 606-D2
CHARA CT
4900 SJS 95118 873-J5
CHARBONO CT
8300 SJS 95135 855-H6
CHARCOT AV
100 SJS 95131 814-A6
100 SJS 95131 813-J6
CHARD DR
4000 SJS 95136 874-C1
CHARDONAY CT
8000 SJS 95135 855-H6
CHARDONNAY CIR
300 CLAY 94517 593-J7
CHARDONNAY CT
- DNVL 94506 653-H5
1900 LVMR 94550 715-H3
19500 SAR 95070 852-F7
48800 FRMT 94539 793-J2
CHARDONNAY DR
400 FRMT 94539 793-J2
500 FRMT 94539 794-A2
2900 PLE 94566 714-G3
CHARDONNAY LN
- NVTO 94947 525-H4
10500 SCIC 94024 831-F5
CHARDONNAY PL
3200 PLE 94566 714-G3
CHARDONNAY WY
2000 LVMR 94550 715-H3
2300 ANT 94509 595-A2
2300 ANT 94509 594-J2
CHARGER DR
2000 SJS 95131 814-E7
CHARING CROSS LN
3400 SJS 95132 814-J2
CHARING CROSS RD
1800 SMCo 94402 748-H7
1800 SMTO 94402 748-H7
6600 OAK 94618 630-C4
6600 OAK 94705 630-C4
CHARING CROSS WY
200 PCFA 94044 707-A6
200 PCFA 94044 706-J6
CHARIOT CT
100 RCH 94803 590-A3
CHARIOT LN
5200 OAK 94605 671-C1
CHARISE CT
1200 SJS 95120 894-G5
CHARISMA WY
1200 SJS 95131 814-B6
CHARLENE CT
6700 SJS 95129 852-E3
CHARLENE WY
22400 AlaC 94546 692-A7
CHARLES AV
100 SUNV 94086 812-D7
100 PLHL 94523 592-B6
2500 PIN 94564 569-F4
3900 CCCo 94803 589-D2
5700 ELCR 94530 589-B6
25400 HAY 94544 712-A4
28000 LAH 94022 810-J7
28000 LAH 94022 830-J1
CHARLES CT
100 VAL 94591 530-D3
600 BEN 94510 530-J7
1100 CNCD 94520 592-F3
CHARLES LN
- SMTO 94402 749-B3
100 DNVL 94526 653-A1
500 MrnC 94941 606-C4
CHARLES PL
4300 CNCD 94521 593-A4
CHARLES RD
1600 SLN 94577 690-H1
CHARLES ST
- LGTS 95032 873-B7
100 SF 94131 667-H5
400 SUNV 94086 832-D1
600 SJS 95112 834-B2
36400 NWK 94560 752-F4
CHARLES CALI DR
500 SJS 95117 853-D1
CHARLES DEAN RD
- MLV 94941 606-D1
CHARLES HILL CIR
- ORIN 94563 611-A5
- ORIN 94563 610-J5
CHARLES HILL LN
- ORIN 94563 610-J5
CHARLES HILL PL
- ORIN 94563 610-J6
CHARLES HILL RD
- ORIN 94563 610-J6
- ORIN 94563 611-A5
CHARLESTON AV
2200 SBRN 94066 707-F7
CHARLESTON CT
600 WLCK 94596 612-B2
700 PA 94303 811-E1
CHARLESTON DR
1600 SJS 95130 853-B5
1600 CMBL 95008 853-B5
CHARLESTON RD
1200 MTVW 94043 811-H1
2000 MTVW 94043 812-A1
E CHARLESTON RD
100 PA 94306 811-E1
700 PA 94303 811-E1
900 PA 94303 811-G1
900 MTVW 94043 811-G1
W CHARLESTON RD
100 PA 94306 811-D2
CHARLESTON ST
2500 OAK 94602 650-E3
CHARLESTON WY
42500 FRMT 94538 773-E1
CHARLESTOWN PL
- SF 94105 648-B6
CHARLITA CT
41300 FRMT 94539 753-G5
CHARLOTTE AV
1900 SLN 94577 690-H2
2100 CNCD 94518 592-G6
15000 SCIC 95124 873-F4
CHARLOTTE COM
300 LVMR 94550 696-B7
CHARLOTTE CT
- CCCo 94803 569-D7
- CCCo 94803 589-D1
CHARLOTTE DR
- SRFL 94901 586-J2
CHARLOTTE WY
4700 LVMR 94550 696-B7
5500 LVMR 94550 716-C1
CHARLTON CIR
700 PLHL 94523 592-A7
700 PLHL 94523 591-J6
CHARLTON CT
- SF 94123 647-G4
CHARLTON DR
700 PLHL 94523 592-A6
CHARLTON RD
- VAL 94592 529-G7
- VAL 94592 549-G1
CHARLTON ST
- SCAR 94070 769-E3
CHARMAIN CIR
600 MTVW 94041 812-A7
CHARMAIN DR
600 CMBL 95008 853-C5
CHARMAINE CT
- NVTO 94949 546-F4
CHARMAT CT
3200 SJS 95135 855-G3
CHARMERAN AV
1800 SJS 95124 873-F3
14500 SCIC 95124 873-F3
CHARMES CT
3200 SJS 95135 855-G3
CHARMET LN
- AMCN 94589 510-B4
CHARMGLOW CT
2100 SJS 95121 855-C4
CHARMIAN CT
1400 BEN 94510 551-A3
CHARMSTONE CT
1900 WLCK 94595 632-B1
CHARMWOOD CT
1100 SUNV 94089 812-J4
35000 NWK 94560 752-D3
CHARMWOOD SQ
1300 SJS 95117 853-C4
CHARNWOOD CT
1800 SJS 95132 814-E3
CHARSAN LN
11400 CPTO 95014 852-C4
CHART LN
- RDWC 94065 750-C4
CHARTER ST
- RDWC 94063 770-C6
800 SMCo 94063 770-C6
CHARTER HALL CT
3500 SJS 95136 874-D1
CHARTER OAK AV
- SF 94124 668-A6
CHARTER OAK CIR
100 WLCK 94596 612-C2
CHARTER OAK PL
6600 SJS 95120 894-G1
CHARTER OAKS CIR
100 LGTS 95030 873-C3
CHARTER OAKS DR
200 LGTS 95030 873-C3
5800 AlaC 94552 692-C1
CHARTER PARK CT
3600 SJS 95136 854-F7
CHARTER PARK DR
3500 SJS 95136 854-F7
CHARTERS AV
19600 SAR 95070 852-F7
CHARTERS CT
19900 SAR 95070 852-E7
CHARTER SQUARE TER
34100 FRMT 94555 752-D1
CHARTHOUSE LN
- FCTY 94404 749-J1
CHARTMASTER PL
300 VAL 94591 550-E2
CHASE CT
- SF 94103 667-H1
200 FRMT 94536 753-C1
600 LVMR 94550 695-E6
CHASE PL
1300 CNCD 94518 592-J3
CHASE ST
- VAL 94590 530-B5
1200 NVTO 94945 526-C3
1700 OAK 94607 649-D3
CHASLEY CT
- CCCo 94520 572-G2
CHASTWORTH ST
- LVMR 94550 715-F5
CHATAM ST
8300 DBLN 94568 693-H2
CHATEAU COM
1300 LVMR 94550 715-J2
CHATEAU CT
- DNVL 94506 653-G4
- SSF 94080 707-E5
1900 WLCK 94596 592-F7
2100 LVMR 94550 715-H2
6800 SJS 95120 894-E2
17600 AlaC 94552 692-B2
20100 SAR 95070 852-E7
CHATEAU DR
- LALT 94022 811-E6
- MLPK 94025 790-F3
400 HIL 94010 748-D2
1100 SJS 95120 894-D2
20000 SAR 95070 852-E6
CHATEAU PL
- SRFL 94901 567-C6
CHATEAU WY
2100 LVMR 94550 715-H2
CHATEAU DU LAC
- SJS 95148 855-F1
CHATEAU LA SALLE DR
100 SJS 95111 854-F5
CHATEAU PARK CT
4600 FRMT 94538 773-C2
CHATELAINE CT
400 DNVL 94506 653-J5
CHATELI CT
800 PLE 94566 714-G3
CHATHAM CT
- SJS 95139 875-G7
100 CCCo 94553 572-B7
100 CCCo 94553 592-B1
300 MTVW 94040 831-J1
2400 ANT 94509 595-G1
3800 RDWC 94061 789-H3
3900 SSF 94080 707-C4
26400 HAY 94542 712-D3
CHATHAM PL
- SF 94108 648-A5
100 VAL 94591 550-E1
CHATHAM RD
400 BURL 94010 728-G6
1100 OAK 94610 650-B4
1300 OAK 94602 650-B4
CHATHAM TER
200 CCCo 94506 654-B5
CHATHAM WY
100 MTVW 94040 831-J1
CHATHAM POINTE
- ALA 94502 670-A5
CHATSWOOD CT
- WLCK 94596 632-G2
CHATSWORTH CT
- DNVL 94506 653-H5
- OAK 94611 650-F1
CHATSWORTH LN
400 RDWC 94061 790-B2
CHATSWORTH PL
600 SJS 95128 853-H2
CHATTANOOGA ST
- SF 94114 667-H3
CHATTERTON CT
43200 FRMT 94538 773-E2
CHATTLETON LN
2700 SPAB 94806 588-J3
CHATTON CT
1200 LFYT 94549 611-J4
CHATTSWOOD DR
6200 MRTZ 94553 591-H3
CHATWORTH
3700 PIT 94565 574-C5
CHAUCER CIR
400 SRMN 94583 673-E4
CHAUCER CT
- MLV 94941 606-G4
- SRMN 94583 673-E4
100 PLHL 94523 592-A7
300 AMCN 94589 509-J3
4300 LVMR 94550 696-A5
CHAUCER DR
- PLHL 94523 592-A7
1700 SJS 95116 834-G5
3100 FRMT 94555 732-J4
3600 FRMT - 752-E1
3600 FRMT 94555 752-E1
4100 CNCD 94521 593-A4
CHAUCER LN
500 AMCN 94589 509-J3
CHAUCER ST
- MLPK 94025 791-A3
400 PA 94301 791-A3
1100 BERK 94702 629-E2
CHAUCER WY
- HAY 94542 712-D4
800 LVMR 94550 696-A6
CHAUMONT DR
1500 SJS 95118 874-A6
CHAUMONT PTH
- OAK 94618 630-B5
CHAUNCEY CT
600 SJS 95128 853-H2
CHAUNCEY WY
600 SJS 95128 853-H2
CHAUNTRY COM
37500 FRMT 94536 752-H3
CHAVEL CT
- FRMT 94539 773-J4
CHAVES AV
- SF 94127 667-E5
CHAVEZ CT
1400 SJS 95131 814-C7
CHAVEZ WY
1300 SJS 95131 814-C7
CHAVOYA DR
20100 CPTO 95014 832-E7
CHEBEC LN
700 FCTY 94404 749-G2
CHECHESTER DR
32200 UNC 94587 732-C5
CHECKERS DR
- SJS 95116 834-F3
400 SJS 95133 834-F3
CHECKERSPOT DR
- BSBN 94005 687-J4
CHEDA LN
100 NVTO 94947 526-D7
CHEDA KNOLLS DR
- NVTO 94947 526-D7
CHEENEY ST
4000 SCL 95054 813-C4
CHEHALIS DR
900 SUNV 94087 832-B4
CHELAN DR
900 SUNV 94087 832-B4
CHELMSFORD DR
18400 SCIC 95014 852-H2
CHELMSFORD RD
500 HIL 94010 748-G2
CHELSEA
1000 HER 94547 569-J2
CHELSEA CRSG
- SJS 95138 875-G5
CHELSEA CT
- OAK 94611 650-F1
- DALY 94014 687-D3
1200 ANT 94509 575-F7
1300 LALT 94024 831-J3
3600 PLE 94588 694-E5
CHELSEA DR
1300 LALT 94024 831-J3
2400 OAK 94611 650-G1
3500 PLE 94588 694-E5
5000 NWK 94560 752-E4
5100 CCCo 94553 591-D2
15000 SCIC 95124 873-F3
CHELSEA PL
- SF 94108 648-A5
CHELSEA WY
- HAY 94544 732-A1
- PIT 94565 574-C3
100 RDWC 94061 790-B2
1200 CNCD 94521 593-A5
1300 LVMR 94550 715-F5
CHELSEA HILLS DR
- BEN 94510 551-B2
CHELTA CT
- DNVL 94526 653-B3
CHELTENHAM CT
100 SJS 95139 895-G1
4300 CNCD 94521 593-A4
CHELTENHAM PL
100 SJS 95139 895-G1
CHELTENHAM WY
- SJS 95139 875-G7
100 SJS 95139 895-G1
CHELTON CT
- ORIN 94563 631-B5
CHELTON DR
5600 OAK 94611 650-F1
6500 OAK 94611 630-G7
CHELTON LN
- OAK 94611 650-F1
CHEMEKETA CT
700 SJS 95123 874-G4
CHEMEKETA DR
600 SJS 95123 874-G4
CHEMICAL WY
- MRTZ 94553 571-F2
- RDWC 94061 770-C5
CHEMIN DE RIVIERE
3500 SJS 95148 855-F1
CHEMISE DR
900 SJS 95136 874-D1
CHEMOWA CT
700 SUNV 94087 832-C4
CHEMULT COM
46800 FRMT 94539 773-H6
CHEN ST
1100 SJS 95131 834-D1
CHENAB CT
400 FRMT 94539 773-J5
CHENAULT WY
800 HAY 94541 711-F4
CHENERY ST
- SF 94131 667-H5
CHENEY AV
400 OAK 94610 650-A3
CHENEY CT
1600 SJS 95128 853-G3
CHENEY DR
1700 SJS 95128 853-G3
CHENEY LN
1600 HAY 94545 711-H6
CHENIN CT
- PLHL 94523 592-A4
CHENIN BLANC DR
- FRMT 94539 793-J2
CHENIN BLANC LN
8400 SJS 95135 855-H7
CHERIS CT
5300 SJS 95123 874-J3
CHERIS DR
100 SJS 95123 874-J3
CHERNE LN
- SANS 94960 566-A4
CHEROKEE AV
2500 OAK 94605 671-A4
CHEROKEE CT
- PTLV 94028 810-C6
- SRMN 94583 673-D5
600 HAY 94544 732-E1
5000 CNCD 94521 593-C4
CHEROKEE DR
800 LVMR 94550 695-E7
4800 CNCD 94521 593-C4
CHEROKEE LN
45500 FRMT 94539 773-H4
CHEROKEE WY
100 PTLV 94028 810-C6
CHERRY AV
100 SSF 94080 707-H4
200 LALT 94022 811-D5
300 MLPK 94025 790-G3
400 SBRN 94066 727-H1
500 SBRN 94066 707-G6
900 SJS 95126 853-J2
1000 SJS 95125 853-J3
1200 SJS 95125 854-A4
3000 SJS 95118 854-A6
3000 SJS 95118 874-B1
CHERRY CT
- NVTO 94945 526-D2
900 SJS 95126 853-J3
1300 SJS 95118 874-B2
CHERRY LN
- CMBL 95008 853-D6
800 SCAR 94070 769-H2
900 SCL 95051 832-J5
2500 WLCK 94596 612-D3
2500 CCCo 94596 612-D1
20100 SAR 95070 852-E6
38500 FRMT 94536 753-C2
CHERRY ST
- FRMT 94538 772-H2
- SF 94118 647-D5
500 VAL 94590 530-B7
600 NVTO 94945 526-C2
900 SCAR 94070 769-G3
1300 RCH 94801 588-F4
2200 SLN 94577 691-B2
2800 BERK 94705 629-J3
2900 ANT 94509 574-J7
9000 OAK 94603 670-J4
35800 NWK 94560 752-D5
38900 NWK 94560 772-F1
CHERRY WK
- ALA 94501 669-G3
CHERRY WY
- CCCo 94596 612-D2
100 AlaC 94541 691-F7
5700 LVMR 94550 696-C4
CHERRY BLOSSOM CT
- AMCN 94589 509-J2
2800 PLE 94588 714-B1
CHERRY BLOSSOM DR
- SJS 95123 875-A3
CHERRY BLOSSOM LN
- LGTS 95032 873-C6
15600 SCIC 95032 873-D6
CHERRY BLOSSOM WY
2600 UNC 94587 732-F7
4300 LVMR 94550 696-A3
CHERRY BROOK LN
5200 SJS 95136 875-E2
CHERRY CANYON RD
23000 SCIC 95120 895-C7
23000 SJS 95120 895-C7
CHERRY CREEK CIR
800 SJS 95126 853-J2
CHERRY CREST LN
- SJS 95136 875-E2
CHERRYDALE DR
1400 SJS 95125 853-J5
CHERRY GARDEN LN
1400 SJS 95125 854-A7
CHERRY GATE LN
5200 SJS 95136 875-E2
CHERRY GLEN WY
1500 SJS 95125 853-J4
CHERRY GROVE DR
1600 SJS 95125 853-H5
1600 SCIC 95125 853-H5
CHERRY HILL CT
100 LGTS 95030 873-C4
CHERRY HILL DR
- SRFL 94903 566-D1
CHERRY HILLS CT
- CCCo 94507 633-A5
- CCCo 94549 591-H5
- SRMN 94583 673-H7
CHERRY HILLS DR
2400 CCCo 94549 591-H5
CHERRY HILLS LN
9400 SRMN 94583 673-H7
CHERRYHILLS LN
1700 SJS 95125 853-J5
CHERRYLAND CT
21600 AlaC 94541 711-G1
CHERRY MANOR CT
400 FRMT 94536 753-C2
CHERRY OAKS PL
4100 PA 94306 811-C3
CHERRY RIDGE CT
- SJS 95136 875-A3
CHERRY RIDGE LN
- SJS 95136 875-E2
CHERRYSTONE CT
100 LGTS 95032 873-D6
CHERRYSTONE DR
800 LGTS 95032 873-C6
2000 SJS 95128 833-E6
CHERRYSTONE LN
4800 SJS 95129 852-B7
CHERRYTON LN
- SJS 95136 875-A3
CHERRYTREE LN
1700 MTVW 94040 831-G1
10300 CPTO 95014 832-E7
CHERRY VALLEY DR
1400 SJS 95125 853-J4
CHERRYVIEW LN
1100 SJS 95118 874-C3
CHERRYWOOD AV
100 SLN 94577 671-A7
100 SLN 94577 670-J7
700 VAL 94591 530-E5
4300 FRMT 94538 773-D2
CHERRY WOOD CT
100 LGTS 95030 873-B2
CHERRYWOOD CT
- SPAB 94806 588-J3
900 SJS 95129 853-A2

STREET Block City ZIP Pg-Grid

CHERRYWOOD CT
4200 CNCD 94521 593-B2
7900 PLE 94588 713-J1
CHERRYWOOD DR
500 SUNV 94087 832-D2
1400 SMTO 94403 748-H7
1500 MRTZ 94553 571-H7
1500 MRTZ 94553 591-H1
2400 UNC 94587 732-F7
4600 SJS 95129 853-A2
4600 SJS 95129 852-J2
CHERRYWOOD SQ
1300 SJS 95117 853-D4
CHERT PL
800 CLAY 94517 593-H6
CHERTSEY CT
1300 SJS 95131 814-E6
CHERYL CIR
3200 PLE 94588 714-B1
CHERYL CT
3400 SMTO 94403 748-J7
4800 UNC 94587 751-J1
CHERYL DR
700 BEN 94510 551-A3
1300 LVMR 94550 696-C7
20600 CPTO 95014 852-D1
CHERYL PL
- MLPK 94025 790-F5
CHERYL WY
2100 SJS 95125 854-A6
CHERYL ANN CIR
900 HAY 94544 712-A6
CHERYL ANN CT
2700 SJS 95124 873-J1
CHERYL BECK CT
- SJS 95119 875-C6
CHERYL BECK DR
100 SJS 95119 875-C6
CHERYL KEN WY
- SJS 95119 875-D5
CHESAPEAKE AV
300 FCTY 94404 749-F6
2100 HAY 94545 711-H7
CHESAPEAKE CIR
2600 SJS 95148 855-D4
CHESAPEAKE CT
3700 ANT 94509 595-C3
CHESAPEAKE DR
100 VAL 94591 550-E2
300 RDWC 94063 770-C3
CHESAPEAKE TER
1300 SUNV 94089 812-H3
CHESBRO AV
5400 SJS 95123 874-G4
CHESHAM AV
100 SMCo 94070 769-D4
100 SCAR 94070 769-D4
CHESHIRE CIR
1000 CCCo 94506 654-B5
CHESHIRE CT
- ALA 94502 669-J5
1200 CNCD 94521 593-A4
2400 SLN 94577 691-B2
3800 PLE 94588 694-F5
CHESHIRE DR
3200 SJS 95118 874-C1
4100 CNCD 94521 593-A4
CHESHIRE PL
2300 SLN 94577 691-B2
CHESHIRE WY
600 SUNV 94087 832-E4
2300 RDWC 94061 789-H1
CHESLEY AV
- CCCo 94801 588-F4
100 RCH 94801 588-F4
300 MTVW 94040 831-J1
1100 SPAB 94806 588-F4
1100 SPAB 94801 588-F4
CHESLEY CT
- VAL 94591 530-D5
500 MTVW 94040 831-J1
CHESLEY DR
2100 SJS 95130 853-A7
CHESLEY ST
- SF 94103 648-A7
CHESS DR
- SMTO 94404 749-E2
1100 FCTY 94404 749-F1
CHESSINGTON DR
1200 SJS 95131 834-C1
CHESSON ST
- RCH 94804 608-E1
CHESTER AV
- SF 94132 687-C2
13900 SAR 95070 872-G2
CHESTER CIR
- LALT 94022 811-E4
CHESTER CT
- CCCo 94553 572-B7
34300 FRMT 94555 752-D1
CHESTER DR
600 PIT 94565 574-F3
CHESTER ST
- LGTS 95030 873-A6
- SMCo 94014 687-D5
- DALY 94014 687-D5
100 MLPK 94025 791-A2
300 OAK 94607 649-D4
300 MLPK 94025 790-J2
2600 ALA 94501 670-A3
20800 AlaC 94546 691-J5
CHESTER WY
- HIL 94010 748-F1
300 PCFA 94044 707-A3
700 SMTO 94402 748-F1
CHESTERFIELD CT
5800 SJS 95138 875-H1
CHESTERFIELD LN
900 CCCo 94506 654-B5
CHESTERTON AV
300 BLMT 94002 749-E7
800 RDWC 94061 789-H2
CHESTERTON CIR
1600 SJS 95133 834-D1
CHESTERTON CT
1200 WLCK 94507 632-G2
1200 WLCK 94596 632-G2
CHESTERTON DR
1600 WLCK 94507 632-G1
2300 WLCK 94596 632-G1
CHESTERTON PL
200 SMTO 94401 748-H1

CHESTERTON WY
2300 WLCK 94507 632-G2
2300 WLCK 94596 632-G2
CHESTNUT AV
- LGTS 95030 872-H7
- ROSS 94957 586-C3
- SRFL 94901 566-E6
- SSF 94080 707-G2
100 SUNV 94086 812-E6
200 PA 94306 791-C7
200 PA 94306 811-C1
400 MPS 95035 793-H6
400 SBRN 94066 727-H1
500 SBRN 94066 707-H7
1900 ANT 94509 575-D6
3400 CNCD 94519 592-J2
3800 CNCD 94519 593-A2
3800 CNCD 94521 593-A2
CHESTNUT COM
5600 FRMT 94538 773-A1
CHESTNUT CT
200 SRMN 94583 673-G7
1600 CNCD 94519 592-J2
CHESTNUT DR
100 HER 94547 569-J4
2100 PIT 94565 573-H4
CHESTNUT LN
100 SMTO 94403 749-C6
CHESTNUT PL
- CCCo 94506 654-B2
CHESTNUT ST
- SCAR 94070 769-F2
- SF 94111 648-A3
100 OAK 94607 649-E3
100 RDWC 94063 770-B6
100 SF 94133 648-A3
400 VAL 94590 530-A7
500 SF 94133 647-F4
700 SJS 95110 833-H4
800 ALA 94501 669-H2
900 SF 94109 647-F4
1000 MLPK 94025 790-F3
1300 CCCo 94553 571-F4
1300 SF 94123 647-F4
1500 BERK 94702 629-E2
1600 SCL 95054 813-D5
1800 LVMR 94550 695-G7
2800 OAK 94608 649-E3
3600 LFYT 94549 611-E6
22500 HAY 94541 692-A7
22500 HAY 94541 712-A1
37000 NWK 94560 772-C1
CHESTNUT WY
7600 PLE 94588 693-H7
CHESTNUT PARK CT
400 SJS 95136 874-G2
CHESWICK CT
200 ALA 94502 669-J5
CHESWICK DR
900 SJS 95121 854-H3
CHESWYCKE COM
2900 FRMT 94536 752-H2
CHESWYCKE TER
2900 FRMT 94536 752-H2
CHETAMON CT
1700 SUNV 94087 832-B6
CHETLAND RD
600 SLN 94577 671-B7
CHETWOOD AV
4200 FRMT 94538 773-D1
CHETWOOD DR
- MTVW 94043 812-B5
CHETWOOD ST
400 OAK 94610 649-J2
CHEVAL LN
200 CCCo 94596 612-F7
CHEVALIER DR
1700 SJS 95124 873-H5
CHEVERY CT
12500 SAR 95070 852-E6
CHEVIOT CT
35300 NWK 94560 752-D4
CHEVY ST
800 BLMT 94002 769-D1
CHEVY WY
2900 CCCo 94806 589-A2
CHEVY CHASE CT
- LKSP 94939 586-E7
CHEVY CHASE WY
600 HAY 94544 732-D1
CHEWPON AV
1200 MPS 95035 814-C2
CHEYENNE AV
2900 SRMN 94583 673-G7
CHEYENNE CT
- FRMT 94539 773-H4
2500 WLCK 94598 612-H4
CHEYENNE DR
500 SUNV 94087 832-D4
700 WLCK 94598 612-H4
CHEYENNE LN
400 SJS 95123 874-H5
CHEYENNE PL
45500 FRMT 94539 773-H4
CHEYENNE PT
- PTLV 94028 810-C6
CHEYENNE WY
- CMAD 94925 586-G6
CHEYENNE RIVER COM
4000 FRMT 94555 732-C7
4300 FRMT - 752-C1
4300 FRMT 94555 752-C1
CHIALA LN
6800 SJS 95129 852-E3
CHIANTI CT
1200 PLE 94566 714-G4
1400 LVMR 94550 715-H3
8300 SJS 95135 855-J6
CHIANTI PL
100 PLHL 94523 592-A3
CHICAGO
4000 ALA 94501 649-E6
CHICAGO AV
- LGTS 95032 893-B1
CHICAGO WY
- SF 94112 687-G2
CHICKADEE CT
1400 SUNV 94087 832-E5
CHICKASAW CT
- CMAD 94925 586-G6
500 SJS 95123 874-H6

CHICKEN SHACK FIRE RD
- NVTO 94949 546-D3
CHICKIE ST
2000 ANT 94509 574-J5
CHICKPEA CT
3000 ANT 94509 575-J6
CHICO CT
- OAK 94611 630-F6
- PCFA 94044 726-J4
- SSF 94080 707-F3
1000 SUNV 94086 812-J5
CHICO DR
700 SLN 94578 691-B4
CHICO ST
100 VAL 94591 530-C7
CHICOINE AV
31000 HAY 94544 732-E1
CHICORY CT
1100 SJS 95120 894-C5
CHICORY LN
- SCAR 94070 769-C4
CHICOT PL
1200 CNCD 94521 593-G7
CHIECHI AV
500 SJS 95126 853-H1
CHIHONG DR
1400 SJS 95131 814-B7
CHILANIAN LN
1200 SJS 95120 894-G4
CHILBERG CT
400 SJS 95133 834-G2
CHILCO ST
1200 MLPK 94025 770-H7
CHILD ST
- SF 94133 648-A3
CHILDERS CT
- CCCo - 633-A3
- CCCo 94507 633-A3
CHILES CT
5000 SJS 95136 874-F2
CHILES DR
4900 SJS 95136 874-F2
CHILLINGHAM CT
3600 PLE 94588 694-E5
CHILLUM CT
3100 SJS 95148 855-D2
CHILMARK LN
- ALA 94502 669-J6
CHILOQUIN CT
500 SUNV 94087 832-D4
CHILPANCINGO PKWY
- PLHL 94523 592-B2
200 CCCo 94523 592-B2
1900 MRTZ 94553 591-J1
1900 MRTZ 94553 592-B2
CHILTERN DR
1100 WLCK 94596 632-G1
40700 FRMT 94539 753-E5
CHILTERN RD
600 HIL 94010 748-G2
CHILTERN WY
2900 SJS 95127 835-A4
CHILTON AV
- SCAR 94070 769-E3
- SF 94131 667-F6
CHILTON LN
3800 SBRN 94066 707-C5
CHILTON WY
2500 BERK 94704 629-H3
CHIMALUS AV
500 PA 94306 811-B2
CHIMAY WY
3000 SJS 95135 855-G4
CHIMERA CIR
38500 FRMT 94536 753-C2
CHIMNEY CT
3100 UNC 94587 732-A4
CHIMNEY LN
30600 UNC 94587 732-A4
CHIMNEY ROCK
- OAK 94605 671-D2
CHIMNEYWOOD CT
1300 CNCD 94521 593-E5
CHINA CT
4000 AlaC 94542 712-F1
CHINABERRY COM
- FRMT 94536 752-G5
CHINABERRY CT
400 SJS 95129 853-B2
CHINABERRY LN
100 ALA 94502 669-J6
100 ALA 94502 670-A6
CHINOOK CT
2500 WLCK 94598 612-H4
2700 UNC 94587 732-F7
CHINOOK DR
2500 WLCK 94598 612-H4
CHINOOK LN
400 SJS 95123 874-H5
CHINQUAPIN CT
100 HER 94547 570-A5
1800 CNCD 94519 593-B2
CHINQUAPIN TR
- SMCo 94062 789-A6
CHIPLAY AV
26500 HAY 94545 711-H6
CHIPLAY CT
2000 HAY 94545 711-G6
CHIPLAY DR
1300 SJS 95122 834-H6
CHIPMAN DR
900 MPS 95035 814-E1
CHIPMAN PL
- SANS 94960 586-B1
CHIPPENDALE CT
100 LGTS 95030 873-A3
3500 PLE 94588 694-E5
4400 UNC 94587 732-A7
CHIPPENDALE DR
4300 UNC 94587 732-B7
CHIPPENHAM DR
3000 SJS 95132 814-F4
CHIPPEWA CT
1000 WLCK 94598 612-H4
1900 FRMT 94539 773-G3
CHIPPEWA WY
700 LVMR 94550 695-E6
CHIQUITA AV
200 MTVW 94041 811-G5
800 PIT 94565 574-F3

CHIQUITA CT
12800 SAR 95070 852-C6
CHIQUITA ST
- SMCo 94028 830-E3
CHIQUITA WY
21000 SAR 95070 852-C7
CHIRCO CT
16700 LGTS 95032 873-C5
CHIRCO DR
16600 LGTS 95032 873-C5
CHISHOLM AV
10400 CPTO 95014 832-C7
CHISHOLM CT
26500 HAY 94544 711-J6
CHITAMOOK CT
1700 SUNV 94087 832-B6
CHIVAS CT
3100 SJS 95117 853-D4
CHIVAS PL
3100 SJS 95117 853-D4
CHLOE CT
1000 CNCD 94518 592-J5
2800 AlaC 94546 691-H4
CHLOE DR
4200 CNCD 94518 592-J5
CHOCTAW CT
600 SJS 95123 874-H6
1000 WLCK 94598 612-H4
CHOCTAW DR
600 FRMT 94539 773-H6
600 SJS 95123 874-G6
CHOLLA ST
47400 FRMT 94539 773-J6
CHOLLO CT
100 PLHL 94523 592-B2
CHOMOR CT
2400 ANT 94509 595-A1
CHONA CT
21400 SCIC 95120 895-B4
CHOPIN AV
2600 SJS 95122 855-A2
CHOPIN DR
700 SUNV 94087 832-F3
CHORLEY WK
- PLHL 94523 591-B1
CHRIS COM
300 LVMR 94550 696-B7
CHRIS DR
5800 SJS 95123 875-A5
CHRIS LN
3400 SMTO 94403 748-J7
CHRISHOLM PL
38600 FRMT 94536 753-D1
CHRISLAND AV
14400 SCIC 95127 835-A3
CHRISLAND CT
3000 CNCD 94520 572-F6
10200 SCIC 95127 835-A2
CHRISMARA CT
1200 SJS 95120 874-C7
CHRISSE CT
3000 ANT 94509 575-C7
CHRISTEN AV
- DALY 94015 707-C3
CHRISTEN DR
- CCCo 94553 592-B1
100 PLHL 94523 592-B1
100 PLHL 94553 592-B1
CHRISTENSEN CT
- ALA 94502 669-H7
19100 AlaC 94546 691-J4
CHRISTENSEN DR
21000 CPTO 95014 832-C7
CHRISTENSEN LN
- WLCK 94596 612-B2
3300 AlaC 94546 691-J4
CHRISTIAN CT
- BLMT 94002 768-J2
2400 PIN 94564 569-G5
CHRISTIAN DR
3900 BLMT 94002 768-J2
3900 SMCo 94070 768-J2
CHRISTIE AV
5700 EMVL 94608 629-D5
CHRISTIE DR
100 MRTZ 94553 591-F1
13300 SAR 95070 852-G7
CHRISTIE RD
- HER - 570-E4
1000 CCCo 94553 570-G6
1000 CCCo - 570-E4
CHRISTINA CT
300 PLE 94566 714-F3
400 ANT 94509 575-E7
1400 HAY 94545 711-E5
CHRISTINA DR
1600 LALT 94024 832-A4
CHRISTINA LN
- WLCK 94596 612-A2
CHRISTINE CT
- CCCo 94806 569-A5
800 PLHL 94523 592-C3
3000 FRMT 94536 753-A3
4800 UNC 94587 752-A1
36500 NWK 94560 752-E6
CHRISTINE DR
100 CCCo 94806 569-A5
100 CCCo 94806 568-J5
600 DNVL 94526 653-B2
700 PA 94303 791-E7
4800 UNC 94587 751-J1
32500 UNC 94587 752-A1
CHRISTINE LN
- MLBR 94030 728-A3
- MLBR 94030 727-J3
CHRISTINE ST
36200 NWK 94560 752-D6
CHRISTMAS TREE CT
- CCCo 94596 612-F6
CHRISTMAS TREE POINT RD
100 SF 94131 667-E3
CHRISTOBAL PRIVADA
1200 MTVW 94040 832-A1
CHRISTOPHER AV
- CMBL 95008 853-C6
CHRISTOPHER CT
- CCCo 94803 589-F2
- DALY 94015 707-A1
- NVTO 94947 525-G3
800 SCL 95051 833-A5
4100 PA 94306 811-F2

CHRISTOPHER DR
- SF 94131 667-D3
CHRISTOPHER LN
- CCCo 94507 632-E2
CHRISTOPHER ST
1500 SJS 95122 834-G6
CHRISTOPHER WY
100 VAL 94589 510-C5
900 MLPK 94025 770-F7
3100 SRMN 94583 673-F5
CHRISTOPHERS LN
28100 LAH 94022 810-H5
CHRISTY COM
6000 FRMT 94538 773-B2
CHRISTY ST
41000 FRMT 94538 773-B2
CHROMITE DR
2600 SCL 95051 833-A2
CHRONICLE AV
2700 HAY 94542 712-D3
CHRYSLER DR
1100 MLPK 94025 770-G6
CHRYSOPOLIS DR
800 FCTY 94404 749-G2
CHUCKER CT
- WLCK 94598 613-A3
CHUCKWOOD DR
1300 SJS 95131 814-C7
CHUGACH WDS PL
3400 CNCD 94518 592-H6
CHUKAR CT
1400 SUNV 94087 832-E5
CHUKKER CT
100 SMTO 94403 749-A4
CHULA LN
- SF 94114 667-H2
CHULA VISTA
11000 SCIC 95127 815-A6
CHULA VISTA AV
900 BURL 94010 728-E5
CHULA VISTA CT
11300 SCIC 95127 815-A5
CHULA VISTA DR
- SRFL 94901 566-F6
1000 BLMT 94002 769-D2
11000 SCIC 95127 815-A5
CHULA VISTA TER
1000 SUNV 94086 812-C6
CHULETA CT
2100 LALT 94024 831-H5
CHUMALIA ST
- SLN 94577 691-A1
CHUMASERO DR
- SF 94132 687-B1
CHUNGKING ST
- OAK 94607 649-C2
CHUPCAN PL
400 CLAY 94517 593-H6
CHURCH AV
1400 SLN 94579 691-A6
1500 SMTO 94401 749-C2
37400 FRMT 94536 752-H3
CHURCH CT
- CMAD 94925 586-F7
CHURCH DR
1400 SJS 95118 874-B2
CHURCH LN
1800 SPAB 94806 588-J3
2500 CCCo 94806 588-J3
CHURCH RD
- SMTO 94401 729-B7
CHURCH ST
- SF 94117 667-H3
- DNVL 94526 653-A2
- SF 94114 667-H3
- MTVW 94041 811-H5
100 LGTS 95032 893-A1
100 MRTZ 94553 571-F7
100 MTVW 94041 812-A6
200 LVMR 94550 695-H7
200 LVMR 94550 715-H1
1100 BEN 94510 550-J3
1300 SF 94131 667-H3
1400 SF 94131 667-H5
1600 OAK 94605 670-G3
1600 OAK 94621 670-G3
CHURCHILL AV
- PA 94301 790-A4
- PA 94301 791-A6
- SMCo 94062 790-A4
- PA - 790-A4
- PA 94306 791-A6
- WDSD 94062 790-A4
CHURCHILL CT
3300 FRMT 94536 752-G2
3500 PLE 94588 694-E6
CHURCHILL DR
2100 MPS 95035 794-B2
2700 HIL 94010 728-C7
2700 HIL 94010 748-B1
3900 PLE 94588 694-E6
4100 CNCD 94521 593-A4
CHURCHILL ST
15000 SLN 94579 691-B6
CHURCHILL DOWNS CT
500 WLCK 94596 612-C3
CHURCHILL PARK DR
400 SJS 95136 874-F3
CHURCHWOOD CT
3100 SJS 95148 855-D1
CHURIN DR
3400 MTVW 94040 831-J2
CHURTON AV
1900 LALT 94024 832-A5
CHUTNEY RD
- HAY 94544 732-B1
CHYNOWETH AV
100 SJS 95136 874-D3
300 SCIC 95136 874-G3
500 SJS 95123 874-G3
700 SJS 95123 875-A3
700 SJS 95136 875-A3
CHYNOWETH PARK CT
5200 SJS 95136 875-A3
CIBRIAN DR
- TBRN 94920 607-B1
CICERO WY
2800 SJS 95148 855-C1
CICERONE LN
13800 LAH 94022 811-C6
CID WY
4000 PLE 94566 714-E2

CIDER MILL CT
- PIT 94565 573-J2
CIELITO DR
- LALT 94022 811-E6
- SF 94134 687-H2
CIELITO WY
6600 SJS 95119 875-D7
CIELO CT
- ORIN 94563 631-C4
CIELO DR
- LKSP 94904 586-G3
CIELO LN
- NVTO 94949 546-F3
CIELO VIA
100 CCCo 94598 612-F4
100 WLCK 94598 612-F4
CIELO VISTA WY
4700 SJS 95129 853-A1
CIERVOS RD
- SMCo 94028 830-D4
CIJOS ST
900 SRFL 94901 586-G1
CIMA DR
100 VAL 94589 530-C1
CIMA WY
- PTLV 94028 810-C7
- PTLV 94028 830-B1
CIMARRON CT
- DNVL 94506 653-H5
1000 VAL 94589 510-E6
CIMARRON DR
100 VAL 94589 510-D6
2300 SCL 95051 833-C2
CIMARRON ST
4000 ALA 94501 649-E6
CIMARRON RIVER CT
- SJS 95136 874-E2
CIMARRON RIVER TER
- FRMT 94555 732-C7
CIMINO AV
300 SJS 95125 854-D4
CINDEE ST
4700 UNC 94587 731-J7
CINDERELLA LN
1800 SJS 95116 834-H5
CINDY CT
- PLHL 94523 612-A1
300 SRMN 94583 673-E5
2900 RCH 94803 589-E2
4700 LVMR 94550 696-B7
CINDY LN
- CCCo 94507 632-F6
600 LVMR 94550 696-B7
CINDY PTH
2900 RCH 94803 589-E2
CINDY WY
700 PCFA 94044 707-A7
18700 AlaC 94546 691-G3
CINERARIA CT
5000 SJS 95111 875-A2
CINNABAR CIR
- VAL 94591 510-G4
CINNABAR CT
- VAL 94591 510-J5
5900 NWK 94560 752-E6
CINNABAR DR
500 LVMR 94550 715-D2
CINNABAR RD
200 WDSD 94062 789-G4
CINNABAR ST
500 SJS 95110 834-A6
700 SJS 95126 833-J6
3900 ANT 94509 595-E1
CINNABAR WY
100 HER 94547 569-G4
CINNABAR HILLS RD
10000 SCIC 95120 895-A7
10000 SJS 95120 895-A7
CINNAMON CT
- HIL 94010 748-C1
700 HAY 94544 732-B1
1200 WLCK 94596 632-G2
CINNAMON DR
500 SJS 95111 854-G7
CINNAMON TEAL LN
- NVTO 94949 546-D5
CIPRIANI BLVD
2100 BLMT 94002 749-C7
2100 BLMT 94002 769-B2
CIRCE CT
- NVTO 94945 526-G1
CIRCLE AV
- MLV 94941 606-E3
4200 AlaC 94546 692-B5
CIRCLE CT
- RCH 94801 588-E7
700 SSF 94080 707-G3
2700 CNCD 94520 572-E7
CIRCLE DR
- SANS 94960 566-D7
- SBRN 94066 727-G3
- SRFL 94901 566-D7
- SUNV 94089 812-H3
- ROSS 94957 586-B2
- TBRN 94920 607-A4
- TBRN 94920 606-J4
100 CCCo 94595 612-C6
600 EPA 94303 791-B3
700 SCL 95050 833-F5
700 SCL 95134 813-D5
5500 CCCo 94803 569-F7
CIRCLE LN
- MLPK 94025 790-J2
CIRCLE RD
- MrnC 94903 566-E5
- RDWC 94062 769-H7
CIRCLE WY
- MrnC 94941 606-E5
11500 DBLN 94568 693-F5
CIRCLE CREEK CT
1000 LFYT 94549 611-J5
CIRCLE CREEK DR
1000 LFYT 94549 611-J5
CIRCLE CREEK LN
1000 LFYT 94549 611-J5
CIRCLE HILL DR
6500 SJS 95120 894-B1
7200 OAK 94605 671-A1
7400 OAK 94605 670-J1
CIRCULAR AV
200 SF 94131 667-F7
600 SF 94112 667-F7

CIRO AV
100 SCIC 95128 833-F7
100 SJS 95128 833-F7
1400 SMTO 94403 749-D4
CIROLERO ST
1300 MPS 95035 794-B4
CIRONE WY
2000 SJS 95124 873-F1
CIRRUS CT
- RDWC 94061 789-G2
CIRRUS WY
100 SUNV 94087 832-E2
CIRVELA ST
2100 PLE 94566 714-G1
CISCO ST
4100 FRMT 94536 752-F2
CITADEL CT
- PLHL 94523 591-H2
CITATION DR
- LALT 94024 831-J5
CITRINE CT
100 HER 94547 569-G5
CITRINE PL
1500 LVMR 94550 715-D3
CITRON AV
- LKSP 94939 586-E5
700 SUNV 94087 832-B1
CITRON CT
- SRMN 94583 693-F1
CITRON WY
1000 HAY 94545 711-G5
CITRUS AV
- DALY 94014 687-C4
700 CNCD 94518 592-J7
3300 WLCK 94598 612-H1
3500 WLCK 94598 592-J7
CITRUS CIR
3000 WLCK 94598 612-H1
CITRUS CT
- HIL 94010 748-D2
500 SJS 95117 853-D2
2100 PIT 94565 574-A4
CITRUS DR
40400 FRMT 94538 753-C6
CITRUS LN
19100 SAR 95070 872-G5
CITRUS PL
700 NVTO 94945 525-E2
CITRUS GROVE CT
1500 SJS 95121 855-A3
CITY CENTER DR
- HAY 94541 711-J1
22000 HAY 94541 691-J7
CITY HALL AV
- SANS 94960 566-B7
CITY HALL LN
1300 BURL 94010 728-G7
CITY HALL ACCESS RD
- VAL 94590 529-H5
CITYHOMES LN
- FCTY 94404 749-E3
CITY VIEW DR
- DALY 94014 687-F3
CITY VIEW PL
1200 SJS 95127 835-C3
CITYVIEW DR
- SF 94131 667-E4
- SF 94131 667-E4
CIVIC AV
- PIT 94565 574-D3
2400 HAY 94542 712-D4
CIVIC DR
100 HER 94547 569-H3
300 PLHL 94523 592-B3
1100 WLCK 94596 612-C4
N CIVIC DR
300 WLCK 94596 612-C4
CIVIC LN
1300 BLMT 94002 769-F1
CIVIC PZ
100 DBLN 94568 693-J4
CIVIC CENTER DR
- SRFL 94903 566-E3
- CMBL 95008 853-E6
800 SCL 95050 833-D3
39000 FRMT 94538 753-B4
CIVIC CENTER PZ
300 RCH 94804 588-H7
CIVIC CENTER ST
200 RCH 94804 588-H6
CIVIC TERRACE AV
5700 NWK 94560 752-F6
CLAEYS CT
1100 CCCo 94572 570-B1
CLAEYS LN
100 CCCo 94572 570-A3
CLAEYS ST
400 MRTZ 94553 571-G5
CLAIBORNE DR
1100 WLCK 94598 612-F1
CLAIR CT
3300 SCL 95051 833-A3
CLAIRBORNE CT
26900 HAY 94542 712-E3
CLAIRE CT
- NVTO 94949 546-C1
1800 CNCD 94519 592-H1
2500 MTVW 94043 811-F2
CLAIRE PL
300 MLPK 94025 790-F5
600 SRMN 94583 673-F6
CLAIRE ST
500 HAY 94541 711-H2
CLAIRE WY
- TBRN 94920 606-J4
CLAIREPOINTE WY
13100 OAK 94619 651-B6
CLAIRMONT PL
- PIT 94565 574-C6
CLAIRVIEW CT
- SF 94131 667-E3
CLAITOR WY
3900 SJS 95132 815-A5
CLAMPETT CT
1500 SJS 95131 814-D5
CLAMPETT LN
1500 SJS 95131 814-D5
CLAMPETT PL
1500 SJS 95131 814-D5
CLAMPETT WY
1500 SJS 95131 814-D5

BAY AREA

STREET
Block City ZIP Pg-Grid

CLARA AV
- SSF 94080 707-E2
CLARA CT
- OAK 94603 670-G6
400 CCCo 94565 573-D1
2500 PLHL 94523 592-C7
CLARA DR
700 PA 94303 791-D6
CLARA LN
700 PLE 94566 714-H3
CLARA ST
100 SF 94107 648-A7
300 OAK 94603 670-G7
600 OAK 94621 670-G6
14800 SCIC 95030 873-B4
14800 MSER 95030 873-B4
CLARA FELICE WY
500 SJS 95125 854-C5
CLARA VISTA AV
600 SCL 95050 833-C5
CLARDY PL
500 SJS 95117 853-C1
CLARE CT
1800 SJS 95124 873-H1
CLARE ST
2400 SPAB 94806 588-H2
CLAREBANK WY
2500 SJS 95121 855-D3
CLAREMONT AV
- ORIN 94563 610-E6
- RDWC 94062 769-J5
- SCL 95051 832-J7
100 SSF 94080 707-J1
100 VAL 94590 530-C2
2600 OAK 94618 629-J5
3600 BERK 94705 629-J5
3900 BERK 94705 630-A3
4800 OAK 94705 630-A3
5100 OAK 94609 629-J5
6300 CCCo 94805 589-C6
N CLAREMONT AV
- SCIC 95127 835-A1
- SCIC 95127 834-J1
100 SCIC 95127 814-J7
S CLAREMONT AV
- SCIC 95127 835-A1
200 SJS 95127 835-A1
CLAREMONT BLVD
- SF 94127 667-C5
2800 BERK 94705 630-A3
CLAREMONT CT
- MLBR 94030 727-H3
2200 HAY 94545 732-A2
2200 HAY 94545 731-J2
CLAREMONT DR
1000 CNCD 94518 592-F5
1200 SBRN 94066 707-E7
CLAREMONT PL
- MLPK 94025 790-H4
2400 UNC 94587 732-C4
CLAREMONT ST
32200 UNC 94587 732-C4
N CLAREMONT ST
- SMTO 94401 728-H7
500 SMTO 94401 748-J1
S CLAREMONT ST
100 SMTO 94401 749-A2
100 SMTO 94401 748-J1
400 SMTO 94402 749-A2
CLAREMONT WY
300 MLPK 94025 790-H4
4300 LVMR 94550 716-A1
CLAREMONT CREST
- BERK 94705 630-A3
CLAREMONT CREST CT
2400 SRMN 94583 673-A1
CLAREMONT CREST WY
- SRMN 94583 673-A1
CLAREMONT PARK CT
4800 FRMT 94538 773-C1
CLARENCE AV
200 SUNV 94086 812-C7
CLARENCE CT
- EPA 94303 771-B7
1700 SJS 95124 853-H6
CLARENCE LN
100 FRMT 94539 753-F5
CLARENCE PL
- SF 94107 648-B7
CLARENCE ST
200 RCH 94801 588-C7
CLARENDALE ST
24100 HAY 94544 711-H3
CLARENDON AV
- SF 94117 667-E2
- SF 94114 667-E2
100 SF 94114 667-E3
100 SF 94117 667-E3
100 SF 94131 667-E3
400 SF 94116 667-E3
CLARENDON CRES
900 OAK 94610 650-C3
CLARENDON CT
2700 CCCo 94806 588-J2
CLARENDON DR
4600 SJS 95129 853-A4
4700 SJS 95129 852-J4
CLARENDON RD
- BURL 94010 728-H6
- PCFA 94044 706-J6
200 PCFA 94044 707-A6
CLARENDON ST
7000 SJS 95129 852-E3
CLARENDON PARK CT
5400 FRMT 94538 773-C2
CLARET CT
600 PLE 94566 714-G3
8200 SJS 95135 855-J6
45500 FRMT 94539 773-H4
CLARET RD
1200 LVMR 94550 715-H2
CLAREVIEW CT
200 SJS 95127 835-A1
CLAREVIEW ST
- SCIC 95127 835-A1
100 SJS 95127 835-A1
CLAREWOOD CT
800 CNCD 94518 592-G6
CLAREWOOD DR
4300 OAK 94618 630-B6
4300 OAK 94611 630-B6

CLAREWOOD LN
- OAK 94618 630-B6
CLARICE DR
1700 SJS 95122 854-J1
1800 SJS 95122 855-A1
1900 SJS 95122 835-A7
CLARICE LN
2000 BURL 94010 728-C5
CLARIDGE CT
20300 SAR 95070 852-E6
CLARIDGE DR
600 PCFA 94044 707-C4
3400 DNVL 94526 653-D7
CLARIDGE PL
2200 SLN 94577 691-A3
CLARIE DR
100 PLHL 94523 592-D6
CLARINADA AV
500 DALY 94015 687-A7
CLARINDA WY
1900 SJS 95124 873-G5
CLARION AL
- SF 94110 667-H2
CLARION CT
2700 SJS 95148 835-E6
CLARITA
100 DNVL 94526 653-C4
CLARITA AV
1400 SJS 95130 853-B4
1500 SJS 95008 853-B4
CLARITA CT
- NVTO 94947 525-G3
CLARK AV
- LALT 94024 811-F7
300 DALY 94014 687-D6
300 CLMA 94014 687-D6
900 SBRN 94066 727-H1
1000 MTVW 94040 811-F5
2000 SCL 95051 833-B2
6300 DBLN 94568 693-J4
6500 NWK 94560 752-E7
N CLARK AV
200 LALT 94022 811-F6
300 MTVW 94040 811-F6
CLARK CT
- CNCD 94521 593-E4
- PCFA 94044 707-A4
500 LALT 94024 811-F7
2700 PIN 94564 569-F5
CLARK DR
- SMTO 94402 748-G1
- SMTO 94402 728-H7
100 VAL 94591 530-D3
CLARK LN
1600 CNCD 94521 593-E4
2500 WLCK 94596 612-B3
CLARK PL
900 ELCR 94530 609-F2
CLARK RD
- MTVW 94043 812-A3
- SCIC 94043 812-A3
3800 CCCo 94803 589-D3
CLARK ST
- SRFL 94901 586-E2
200 CCCo 94525 550-E5
400 PIT 94565 574-E4
1100 SJS 95125 854-B2
CLARK WY
1100 SJS 95125 854-A5
CLARK-BOAS TR
- CCCo 94803 589-D3
- RCH 94803 589-D3
- RCH 94805 589-D3
CLARK CREEK CIR
- CLAY 94517 613-J1
CLARKE AV
200 LVMR 94550 695-H7
1800 EPA 94303 791-C1
CLARKE DR
800 FRMT 94536 733-D7
CLARKE LN
1100 ALA 94502 670-A7
CLARKE ST
- SF 94129 647-E4
1100 SLN 94577 691-A1
3800 OAK 94609 629-H6
3800 OAK 94609 649-H1
5100 OAK 94618 629-H6
CLARKFORD ST
26700 HAY 94544 711-J6
CLARKIN CT
300 CCCo 94596 612-G6
CLARKSON CT
900 CNCD 94518 592-F6
CLARKSPUR LN
1500 SJS 95129 852-F5
CLARKSTON AV
11000 CPTO 95014 852-B3
CLARKSTON DR
700 SJS 95136 874-D1
CLARKWOOD CT
400 SCL 95054 813-F6
CLARMAR WY
2000 SJS 95128 833-F7
CLASSIC CT
21000 CPTO 95014 852-C3
CLASSIC WY
1200 CNCD 94521 593-G7
CLASSICO AV
- SJS 95135 855-E3
CLATTON CT
100 VAL 94591 530-D3
CLAUDE LN
- SF 94108 648-A5
CLAUDIA AV
1300 SMTO 94403 749-D4
CLAUDIA CT
- CNCD 94519 572-G6
200 MRGA 94556 631-F5
1000 ANT 94509 575-C6
4600 FRMT 94536 752-E3
CLAUDIA DR
2900 CNCD 94519 572-F7
10200 SCIC 95127 835-A2
CLAUSEN CT
12800 LAH 94024 831-D2
25800 AlaC 94541 712-D2
CLAUSER DR
400 MPS 95035 794-A5
CLAUSING AV
700 NVTO 94945 526-C4

CLAUSING CT
- NVTO 94945 526-C4
CLAVERIE WY
- BEN 94510 551-A4
CLAVERING HILL RD
4100 SCIC 95127 815-D7
CLAWITER RD
- HAY 94545 731-E1
22900 AlaC 94545 711-E6
22900 HAY 94545 711-E6
CLAXTON CT
100 VAL 94589 509-J5
CLAY AV
- SSF 94080 707-D2
CLAY CT
- NVTO 94949 546-F4
900 ANT 94509 595-F1
1100 FRMT 94536 753-B2
CLAY DR
- ATN 94027 790-C4
1500 LALT 94024 832-A4
CLAY ST
- OAK 94607 649-F4
100 SF 94111 648-A5
100 VAL 94591 530-D4
700 SF 94108 648-A5
1000 ALB 94706 609-D5
1100 SF 94108 647-H5
1200 OAK 94612 649-F4
1300 SF 94109 647-H5
1400 HAY 94541 712-A1
1500 SCL 95050 833-D4
2200 SF 94115 647-E5
2500 ALA 94501 670-A3
3400 SF 94118 647-E5
3600 SF 94118 647-D5
20300 CPTO 95014 852-E2
W CLAY ST
- SF 94121 647-B6
CLAYBURN LN
1100 SJS 95121 855-B6
CLAYBURN RD
3400 ANT 94509 595-D1
CLAYCOMB CT
1100 SJS 95118 874-G3
CLAYCORD AV
1500 CNCD 94521 593-D4
CLAYPOOL CT
- DNVL 94526 653-D3
CLAYTON AV
- SJS 95110 834-A5
400 ELCR 94530 609-D3
CLAYTON CT
- DALY 94014 687-D4
1100 NVTO 94945 526-B3
CLAYTON DR
2100 MLPK 94025 790-E7
CLAYTON RD
1100 SJS 95127 835-B3
1500 CNCD 94520 592-F2
1900 CNCD 94519 592-G2
1900 CNCD 94518 592-G2
2700 SCIC 95127 835-F1
3100 SJS 95148 835-E4
3500 CNCD 94521 592-G2
3500 CNCD 94519 593-C4
3500 CNCD 94521 593-C4
5400 CLAY 94517 593-G6
6800 CLAY 94517 613-J1
CLAYTON RD W
1500 CNCD 94520 592-D3
CLAYTON ST
- SF 94117 647-E7
- SRFL 94901 586-E1
200 SF 94117 667-E1
1200 SF 94114 667-F2
CLAYTON WY
1600 CNCD 94521 593-A2
1600 CNCD 94519 593-A2
1800 CNCD 94521 593-J1
1900 CNCD 94519 572-J7
CLAYTON VIEW LN
900 CLAY 94517 593-H7
CLAYWOOD WY
6900 SJS 95120 894-J3
CLEARBROOK CIR
29800 HAY 94544 712-E7
CLEAR BROOK CT
- SJS 95111 854-J5
CLEARBROOK DR
5200 CNCD 94521 593-G3
CLEARBROOK RD
- ANT 94509 595-D1
CLEAR CREEK CT
100 MRTZ 94553 591-H4
4400 CNCD 94521 593-C5
CLEARCREEK CT
22000 CPTO 95014 832-A7
N CLEAR CREEK PL
1600 DNVL 94526 653-B6
S CLEAR CREEK PL
1700 DNVL 94526 653-B6
CLEARFIELD AV
3300 RCH 94803 589-F2
CLEARFIELD DR
- SF 94132 667-A6
600 MLBR 94030 728-A4
600 MLBR 94030 727-J4
CLEAR LAKE AV
1400 MPS 95035 814-D2
CLEAR LAKE CT
- CCCo 94506 654-C4
1100 MPS 95035 814-D1
CLEAR LAKE ST
600 CCCo 94506 654-C4
32700 FRMT 94555 732-B6
CLEARLAND CIR
2800 CCCo 94565 573-G2
CLEARLAND DR
100 CCCo 94565 573-G2
CLEAR PARK CIR
200 SJS 95136 874-H2
CLEAR PARK PL
4300 SJS 95136 874-H1
CLEARPOINTE DR
- VAL 94591 550-D1
CLEAR RIVER CT
4700 SJS 95136 874-E2
CLEAR SPRINGS CT
- AlaC 94542 712-F1
2400 SJS 95133 834-B2
3700 CNCD 94518 592-J4

CLEARSTREAM CT
- CCCo 94506 654-C5
CLEAR VIEW CIR
2000 BEN 94510 551-B3
CLEARVIEW CT
- SF 94124 668-B6
2000 WLCK 94598 612-G2
CLEARVIEW DR
- DALY 94015 707-A1
100 VAL 94591 550-D2
400 LGTS 95030 873-B3
500 SCIC 95030 873-B3
700 SJS 95133 814-F7
1600 SLN 94577 691-D1
CLEARVIEW WY
3000 SMTO 94402 748-H6
CLEAR WATER CT
4600 RCH 94803 589-G1
CLEARWATER CT
500 SUNV 94087 832-D4
CLEARWOOD CT
22000 CPTO 95014 832-A7
CLEARWOOD ST
1700 PIT 94565 573-F4
CLEARY CT
- SF 94109 647-H6
CLEAVELAND CT
- PLHL 94523 592-C7
CLEAVELAND RD
- PLHL 94523 592-C6
CLEAVES AV
- SJS 95126 833-J7
200 SCIC 95126 833-J7
200 SCIC 95126 853-J1
CLEE ST
1600 BLMT 94002 769-D2
CLELAND AV
- LGTS 95032 893-A1
CLELAND PL
- MLPK 94025 790-J3
CLEMANS DR
19000 AlaC 94546 692-C4
CLEMATIS CT
2000 FRMT 94539 773-G3
CLEMATIS DR
1000 SUNV 94086 832-H2
1600 SJS 95124 873-J7
CLEMENCE AV
1200 SJS 95122 834-F7
1400 SJS 95122 854-G1
CLEMENCE CT
1400 SJS 95122 834-F7
CLEMENS RD
1700 OAK 94602 650-D3
CLEMENT AV
- CCCo 94565 573-F2
1700 ALA 94501 669-J1
2000 ALA 94501 670-A1
5700 CCCo 94806 589-A4
CLEMENT DR
3700 AlaC 94552 692-E2
CLEMENT ST
- SF 94118 647-A6
1600 SF 94121 647-A6
3200 SF 94121 646-J6
CLEMENTE CT
- NVTO 94945 525-J1
CLEMENTINA ST
- SF 94105 648-A7
300 SF 94103 648-A7
700 SF 94103 647-J7
CLEMO AV
4100 PA 94306 811-C3
CLEMSON AV
18200 SAR 95070 852-J7
CLEMSON CT
- WLCK 94596 612-D1
CLEO AV
20600 CPTO 95014 852-D3
CLEO CT
5400 LVMR 94550 696-C7
CLEO ST
- NVTO 94947 526-C5
CLEOPATRA DR
- PLHL 94523 592-D5
CLEO RAND AV
100 SF 94124 668-E7
CLEO SPRINGS CT
1600 SJS 95131 814-C6
CLEREMONT DR
35400 NWK 94560 752-C5
CLEVELAND AV
- SJS 95126 833-G7
100 CCCo 94565 573-H3
100 SJS 95128 833-G7
100 SCIC 95128 833-G7
100 SCIC 95128 853-G1
200 MrnC 94941 606-F6
600 ALB 94804 609-C5
700 ALB 94706 609-C5
1300 SMTO 94403 749-C3
CLEVELAND CT
200 MrnC 94941 606-F6
1800 CNCD 94521 593-D2
CLEVELAND PL
3000 ANT 94509 575-A7
5400 FRMT 94538 752-J7
CLEVELAND ST
- SF 94103 648-A7
500 RDWC 94062 770-A7
600 RDWC 94061 770-A7
600 OAK 94606 650-A4
1900 SLN 94577 691-C1
CLIFDEN CT
200 SSF 94080 707-D2
CLIFDEN WY
20300 CPTO 95014 852-E2
CLIFF DR
1400 SJS 95132 814-G3
CLIFF LN
- CCCo 94596 612-D7
500 RCH 94805 589-B6
CLIFF RD
- BLV 94920 627-D2
CLIFFLAND AV
10900 OAK 94605 671-D5
CLIFFORD AV
- SMCo 94062 769-G6
200 SCAR 94070 769-G6
CLIFFORD CIR
3200 PLE 94588 694-B7

CLIFFORD CT
200 CLAY 94517 613-J1
400 CCCo 94565 573-F1
3500 AlaC 94546 691-J3
6600 CPTO 95014 852-F2
CLIFFORD DR
6500 CPTO 95014 852-F2
CLIFFORD LN
1000 MPS 95035 794-B5
CLIFFORD ST
1800 SCL 95050 833-D4
CLIFFORD TER
- SF 94117 667-F2
CLIFFROSE TER
- FRMT 94536 752-B7
CLIFFSIDE CT
- BLMT 94002 769-C3
CLIFFSIDE DR
- DALY 94015 687-A3
300 DNVL 94526 653-A4
300 DNVL 94526 652-J4
800 PLHL 94523 591-J2
CLIFF SWALLOW CT
- BSBN 94005 688-A5
CLIFF WALK DR
- VAL 94591 550-E2
CLIFFWOOD AV
27500 HAY 94545 711-H7
27500 HAY 94545 731-H1
CLIFFWOOD DR
1300 SJS 95122 834-H6
CLIFTON AV
- LGTS 95030 872-J7
200 SCAR 94070 769-E3
300 SCIC 95128 853-G1
300 SJS 95128 853-G1
400 CMBL 95128 853-E3
CLIFTON CT
- WLCK 94595 612-D4
800 BEN 94510 530-H6
3200 PA 94303 791-E6
3300 FRMT 94538 753-C5
CLIFTON DR
- DALY 94015 687-A4
CLIFTON RD
200 PCFA 94044 707-A3
200 PCFA 94044 706-J3
CLIFTON ST
- OAK 94618 629-H6
CLIFTON WY
18300 AlaC 94546 691-H3
CLIMBING ROSE CT
700 HAY 94544 712-A7
CLINTON AV
600 RCH 94805 589-A6
1300 ALA 94501 669-H2
2300 RCH 94804 588-H5
3300 RCH 94805 588-J5
3400 SCL 95051 832-J7
5700 CCCo 94805 589-B6
16800 AlaC 94578 691-F6
CLINTON CT
- RDWC 94061 770-A7
900 PLE 94566 714-F4
2300 ANT 94509 595-A1
24100 HAY 94545 711-F4
CLINTON DR
1700 CNCD 94521 593-D3
CLINTON PK
100 SF 94103 667-H1
CLINTON PL
700 SJS 95126 834-A6
700 SJS 95126 833-J6
CLINTON RD
800 LALT 94024 831-G3
CLINTON ST
- RDWC 94062 769-J5
400 RDWC 94062 770-A6
600 RDWC 94061 770-A6
CLINTONIA AV
800 SJS 95125 854-A2
CLIPPER CT
- FRMT 94538 773-E7
100 BLMT 94002 749-F6
1100 SJS 95132 814-G5
2000 SLN 94579 690-J6
CLIPPER DR
- ALA 94502 669-J5
100 BLMT 94002 749-F6
100 PIT 94565 574-A2
100 VAL 94591 550-F3
CLIPPER LN
100 CCCo 94553 572-B5
900 FCTY 94404 749-G3
CLIPPER ST
- SF 94131 667-G4
- SF 94114 667-G4
700 SF 94114 667-F4
700 SF 94131 667-F4
2300 SMTO 94403 749-D1
CLIPPER TER
800 SF 94114 667-F4
CLIPPER WY
- DALY 94014 687-D5
CLIPPER HILL
- OAK 94618 630-C4
CLIPPER HILL RD
500 DNVL 94526 652-G2
600 CCCo - 652-G2
CLISE CT
400 SJS 95123 875-A6
CLIVE AV
6200 OAK 94611 650-G1
CLOGSTON CT
400 SJS 95133 834-G2
CLOISTER WY
- DALY 94014 687-F3
CLORINDA AV
- SRFL 94901 586-E1
CLOS DUVALL
- BEN 94510 551-D5
CLOTILDA CT
- MrnC 94941 606-H4
CLOUD AV
900 MLPK 94025 790-D6
900 SMCo 94025 790-D6
CLOUD CT
4300 CNCD 94518 593-A5
CLOUD DR
4800 SJS 95111 875-B1
CLOUD WY
21300 HAY 94545 711-D4

CLOUDS REST
- VAL 94591 510-J3
CLOUD VIEW CIR
- SAUS 94965 627-B3
CLOUDVIEW DR
1400 PLHL 94523 591-H2
CLOUD VIEW LN
2900 AlaC 94541 692-C7
CLOUD VIEW RD
- SAUS 94965 627-A4
CLOUD VIEW TR
- SAUS 94965 627-A4
- MrnC 94965 627-A4
CLOUGH AV
3700 FRMT 94538 753-D6
CLOVE DR
2200 SCIC 95128 853-F2
CLOVELLY LN
1100 BURL 94010 728-C5
CLOVER AV
500 SJS 95128 833-E7
S CLOVER AV
300 SJS 95128 853-E1
1100 CMBL 95128 853-E3
CLOVER CIR
- SSF 94080 707-F2
CLOVER CT
1200 LFYT 94549 611-J4
1900 PLE 94588 714-A6
2700 ANT 94509 575-G7
2900 UNC 94587 732-F7
CLOVER DR
5700 OAK 94618 630-A5
CLOVER LN
- SCAR 94070 769-D5
- SF 94114 667-F3
100 MLPK 94025 790-J3
1200 CCCo 94595 612-B6
1200 WLCK 94595 612-B6
CLOVER RD
25500 AlaC 94542 712-E1
CLOVER ST
- SF 94114 667-F2
2400 UNC 94587 732-F7
CLOVER WY
100 LGTS 95032 873-D7
CLOVERBERRY WY
100 SRMN 94583 653-H7
CLOVERBROOK CIR
- PIT 94565 573-F4
CLOVERBROOK DR
500 DNVL 94506 654-A6
1000 SJS 95120 874-E7
CLOVERCREST DR
5300 SJS 95118 874-C4
CLOVERCREST LN
400 SRMN 94583 653-H7
CLOVERDALE AV
2500 CNCD 94518 592-G4
CLOVERDALE CT
1400 SUNV 94087 832-B4
CLOVERDALE LN
1600 SJS 95130 853-B5
CLOVERFIELD CT
- AlaC 94542 692-E7
CLOVER HILL CT
- SRFL 94903 566-D1
100 DNVL 94526 653-B3
CLOVERHILL DR
6100 SJS 95120 874-E7
CLOVERLEAF CT
46800 FRMT 94539 773-J5
CLOVERLY CT
22000 SCIC 94024 832-A7
CLOVER MEADOW CT
- SJS 95135 855-H7
CLOVER OAK DR
3400 SJS 95148 835-E6
CLOVEWOOD LN
3200 SJS 95132 814-E2
4300 PLE 94588 693-J7
4300 PLE 94588 713-J1
CLOVIS AV
1600 SJS 95124 873-J5
CLOVIS CT
5200 CNCD 94521 593-D6
CLUB CT
1200 RCH 94803 569-C7
CLUB DR
- VAL 94592 529-H7
- SCAR 94070 769-D3
200 SMCo 94070 769-D3
300 BLMT 94002 769-C4
1200 RCH 94803 569-C7
5400 SCIC 95127 815-A7
5400 SJS 95131 814-A5
CLUB LN
1300 RCH 94803 569-C7
CLUB TER
100 DNVL 94526 633-D6
100 CCCo 94526 633-D6
CLUB VW
- NVTO 94949 546-G5
CLUBHOUSE CT
4000 SJS 95135 855-H6
CLUBHOUSE DR
900 HAY 94541 711-E2
900 LVMR 94550 695-B5
CLUBHOUSE LN
10600 CPTO 95014 852-A2
CLUBHOUSE RD
1600 CCCo 94526 633-E7
CLUBHOUSE
MEMORIAL RD
- ALA 94502 670-A6
CLUB VIEW DR
- DALY 94014 687-F3
1300 ELCR 94530 609-E1
1300 ELCR 94530 589-E7
CLUB VIEW TER
11900 SCIC 94024 831-G3
CLUNY PL
35800 NWK 94560 752-D5
CLYDA DR
2500 SJS 95116 834-H4
CLYDE AV
- SRFL 94901 566-G7
300 MTVW 94043 812-C4
700 SCL 95054 813-E6
1900 CNCD 94520 572-E6
CLYDE CT
400 MTVW 94043 812-C4

CLYDE CT
500 MPS 95035 794-B6
CLYDE DR
100 WLCK 94598 612-G2
CLYDE ST
- SF 94107 648-B7
100 PIT 94565 574-E3
CLYDE BANK CT
1100 SUNV 94087 832-H4
CLYDELLE AV
4700 SJS 95124 873-E4
15200 SCIC 95124 873-E4
CLYDESDALE AV
5900 SJS 95123 874-J5
CLYDESDALE DR
- LVMR 94550 696-A2
100 DNVL 94526 633-C7
100 VAL 94591 530-E1
700 HIL 94402 748-H4
CLYDESDALE WY
5200 ANT 94509 595-J6
CLYMER CT
2700 CNCD 94519 572-H6
CLYMER LN
2500 FRMT 94538 753-D6
COACH CT
- RCH 94803 589-J2
1100 SJS 95120 894-E1
COACH DR
5100 RCH 94803 589-J2
8000 OAK 94605 671-C1
COACH LN
700 VAL 94589 530-D1
COACH RD
- MLV 94941 606-G2
COACHELLA AV
800 SUNV 94086 812-H5
COACHLIGHT DR
3300 SJS 95111 854-J5
COACHMAN PL
800 CCCo 94517 613-G1
COACHWOOD TER
- ORIN 94563 610-H3
COAD CT
1100 PIT 94565 574-E6
COAKLEY DR
400 SJS 95117 853-C2
COALBROOK DR
1600 SJS 95126 853-H4
COALINGA AV
1300 RCH 94801 588-G5
COALMINE VW
- PTLV 94028 830-C1
COALPORT ST
1000 SPAB 94806 588-G2
COAST AV
2600 MTVW 94043 791-G7
COAST LN
200 PCFA 94044 726-J2
COASTAL TR
- MrnC 94965 627-A6
COAST GUARD RD
- SMCo 94128 708-B5
- SSF 94080 708-B5
COASTLAND AV
1700 SJS 95125 854-C4
COASTLAND DR
700 PA 94303 791-C6
COAST OAK WY
- SRFL 94903 546-D7
- SRFL 94903 566-D1
COATS CIR
100 PLHL 94523 592-A7
COBALT WY
300 SUNV 94086 812-J7
COBB AV
100 VAL 94589 510-B5
COBB CT
5000 FRMT 94538 773-B1
COBB ST
1100 SMTO 94401 749-B2
COBBERT DR
3500 SJS 95148 835-F7
COBBLEHILL PL
2100 SMCo 94402 768-G1
COBBLER CT
4800 PLE 94566 714-F4
COBBLESTONE CT
- DALY 94014 687-C5
- SRMN 94583 673-A2
1300 CNCD 94521 593-A4
5900 CCCo 94803 589-G4
6500 SJS 95120 894-C6
COBBLESTONE DR
100 SRMN 94583 673-A2
100 MrnC 94903 546-E6
200 ANT 94509 595-E1
1200 CMBL 95008 853-B7
2400 HAY 94545 731-G1
4100 CNCD 94521 593-A4
35500 FRMT 94536 732-H6
COBBLESTONE LN
- BLMT 94002 769-E1
- SCAR 94070 769-F5
100 SRMN 94583 673-A2
300 VAL 94589 510-B4
COBURN CT
- SJS 95139 875-G7
800 SLN 94578 691-B2
COCHEA DR
700 HAY 94544 712-A4
COCHISE CT
- PLE 94588 694-G7
600 FRMT 94539 793-J2
900 WLCK 94598 612-H4
COCHISE WY
- PLE 94588 694-G7
COCHRANE AV
4900 OAK 94618 630-C6
COCHRANE ST
- SF 94124 668-E7
- SF 94124 688-E1
COCONUT CT
3000 ANT 94509 575-J6
COCONUT DR
2500 SJS 95148 835-C7
COCO PALM DR
4800 FRMT 94538 753-A7
5300 FRMT 94538 773-A1
COD ST
800 FCTY 94404 749-H3

INDEX

STREET
Block City ZIP Pg-Grid

CODMAN PL
100 SF 94108 648-A5
CODORNICES RD
- BERK 94708 609-H7
CODORNIZ LN
1100 WLCK 94598 612-H5
CODY CT
- SRMN 94583 673-F7
3600 SCL 95051 832-H7
4800 FRMT 94538 753-A7
CODY LN
- LALT 94022 811-E6
14700 SAR 95070 872-E3
S CODY LN
100 PLHL 94523 592-C6
CODY RD
- SCIC 94035 812-C2
500 HAY 94544 712-A4
CODY WY
1800 SJS 95124 853-G7
COE AV
400 SJS 95125 854-A2
1200 SLN 94579 691-A4
COELHO CT
400 MPS 95035 794-A3
COELHO DR
15700 AlaC 94578 691-E5
15700 SLN 94578 691-E5
15800 AlaC 94580 691-E5
COELHO ST
100 MPS 95035 794-A4
COEUR D ALENE WY
900 SUNV 94087 832-B4
COFFEE TREE CT
2600 ANT 94509 575-H5
COFFEE TREE WY
2600 ANT 94509 575-H5
COFFEEWOOD CT
700 SJS 95120 894-H3
COFFEY CT
700 SJS 95123 874-F5
COGGINS DR
100 CCCo 94596 592-C7
100 CCCo 94596 612-D1
100 PLHL 94523 592-C7
COGHLAN LN
- ATN 94027 790-C4
COGNINA CT
4300 FRMT 94536 752-J5
COHANSEY DR
2900 SJS 95132 814-D3
COHASSET WY
5700 SJS 95123 875-B4
COHEN PL
- SF 94109 647-J6
COHOE CT
2600 AlaC 94546 691-J6
COIT AV
43000 FRMT 94539 753-H7
COIT DR
2500 SJS 95124 853-G7
2500 SJS 95124 873-G1
COKER RD
- CCCo 94553 571-F3
- MRTZ 94553 571-F3
COLA BALLENA
400 ALA 94501 669-E1
COLBERT PL
36200 NWK 94560 752-D6
COLBERT ST
36300 NWK 94560 752-D6
COLBOURN PL
5600 OAK 94619 651-B6
COLBY AV
- MrnC 94941 606-E5
900 SMCo 94025 790-H1
10100 CPTO 95014 832-F7
COLBY CT
600 WLCK 94598 613-A3
19700 SAR 95070 852-F5
COLBY ST
- SF 94134 667-J6
400 AlaC 94580 691-D5
400 SLN 94578 691-D5
600 SF 94134 687-J1
2900 BERK 94705 629-J4
4100 FRMT 94538 773-D2
5900 OAK 94618 629-J4
5900 OAK 94609 629-J4
COLBY WY
3800 SBRN 94066 707-C6
COLD HARBOR AV
10100 CPTO 95014 852-F1
COLDSPRINGS CT
200 MRTZ 94553 571-H6
COLD WATER DR
5500 AlaC 94552 692-D2
COLDWATER DR
3100 SJS 95148 835-B5
COLE AV
1600 WLCK 94596 612-C5
COLE CT
- CCCo 94526 633-A6
COLE DR
- MrnC 94965 626-H1
14500 SCIC 95124 873-G3
14900 SJS 95124 873-G3
COLE PL
28100 HAY 94544 712-B6
COLE ST
- SF 94117 647-E7
200 SF 94117 667-E1
2400 OAK 94601 670-F1
COLEEN CT
- CCCo 94806 569-C5
COLEEN ST
100 LVMR 94550 715-E1
COLEGROVE CT
- SMTO 94403 749-C6
COLEGROVE ST
3600 SMTO 94403 749-C6
COLEMAN AV
- LKSP 94939 586-E7
400 SCL 95110 833-G3
400 SJS 95110 833-G3
600 MLPK 94025 790-H2
800 SMCo 94025 790-H2
900 SJS 95110 834-A5
1200 SCL 95050 833-G3
26000 HAY 94544 711-J5
COLEMAN CT
- SCAR 94070 769-E4

STREET
Block City ZIP Pg-Grid

COLEMAN CT
400 PLHL 94523 592-B6
COLEMAN DR
100 SRFL 94901 566-F6
COLEMAN PL
- MLPK 94025 790-J2
2800 FRMT 94555 732-E7
COLEMAN RD
- SJS 95123 874-A6
1100 SJS 95120 874-A6
COLEMAN ST
2700 SF 94124 668-E7
3000 SF 94124 668-E7
COLEPORT LNDG
- ALA 94502 670-A5
- RDWC 94065 749-H5
COLERAINE CT
600 SUNV 94087 832-E4
COLERIDGE AV
100 PA 94301 791-A6
28400 HAY 94544 712-B7
COLERIDGE COM
100 FRMT 94538 773-D2
COLERIDGE DR
- MLV 94941 606-H6
100 VAL 94591 530-E6
COLERIDGE GRN
100 FRMT 94538 773-D3
COLERIDGE ST
- SF 94110 667-H5
COLERIDGE TER
100 FRMT 94538 773-D3
COLET TER
3600 FRMT 94536 752-J4
COLETTE DR
3000 RCH 94806 589-B1
COLETTE PL
600 HAY 94544 712-B5
COLETTE ST
26500 HAY 94544 712-B5
COLFAX CT
3100 SCL 95051 833-A3
37700 FRMT 94536 752-G5
COLFAX DR
400 SJS 95123 874-J4
COLFAX ST
1700 CNCD 94519 592-F1
1700 CNCD 94520 592-F1
COLFAX WY
2100 ANT 94509 595-A1
COLGATE AV
200 CCCo 94708 609-G3
400 SMTO 94402 748-H3
3200 SCL 95051 833-A6
COLGATE DR
33500 UNC 94587 732-F5
COLGATE ST
14400 SLN 94579 691-A4
COLGATE WY
4100 LVMR 94550 696-A7
COLGETT DR
- OAK 94619 650-H4
COLIBRI CT
200 SJS 95119 875-D7
COLIMA AV
10100 SRMN 94583 673-G5
COLIMA CT
4100 FRMT 94536 752-F2
COLIN PL
- SF 94102 647-J6
COLIN ST
1400 SPAB 94806 588-H2
COLINA CT
900 LFYT 94549 611-F7
2400 PIN 94564 569-G7
COLINA DR
12200 LAH 94024 831-E2
COLIN P KELLY JR ST
- SF 94107 648-C6
COLINTON WY
1300 SUNV 94087 832-B4
COLISEUM WY
4300 OAK 94601 670-D2
5800 OAK 94621 670-E4
COLL CT
- SRMN 94583 673-F6
COLLEEN CT
- NVTO 94947 525-J3
600 SJS 95123 874-H7
COLLEEN DR
600 SJS 95123 874-F6
1800 LALT 94024 831-J4
COLLEEN TER
34100 FRMT 94555 752-C2
COLLEEN WY
600 CMBL 95008 853-B5
COLLEGE AV
- LGTS 95032 893-A1
- SF 94112 667-H6
100 MTVW 94040 811-F4
100 VAL 94589 510-B6
200 PA 94306 791-A7
600 MLPK 94025 790-G5
600 SMCo 94025 790-H2
700 LKSP 94939 586-D4
700 SCL 95050 833-F5
700 MrnC 94904 586-D4
900 PA 94306 811-A1
1000 ALA 94501 670-A3
1000 SMTO 94401 728-J6
1200 LVMR 94550 715-G2
1400 PA 94306 810-J1
2300 BERK 94704 629-J2
2700 BERK 94705 629-J4
2700 OAK 94618 629-J4
COLLEGE CT
- LKSP 94939 586-D4
700 LALT 94024 831-E1
1400 UNC 94587 732-F5
COLLEGE DR
- PLHL 94523 592-C2
300 SJS 95128 853-H2
2800 SBRN 94066 707-C6
COLLEGE LN
2300 SPAB 94806 588-J2
COLLEGE ST
100 AlaC 94580 691-D6
COLLEGE TER
- SF 94112 667-H6
COLLEGE WY
- PLHL 94523 592-C2

STREET
Block City ZIP Pg-Grid

COLLEGE NORTH ENTRY RD
3400 SBRN 94066 707-B6
COLLEGE OF SAN MATEO DR
100 SMCo 94402 748-G6
3300 SMTO 94402 748-G6
COLLEGE TERRACE CT
- LGTS 95032 893-A1
COLLEGE VIEW WY
- BLMT 94002 769-D1
COLLETTE DR
1000 SJS 95132 814-H5
COLLIE CRAG
- CCCo 94595 632-E2
COLLIER DR
700 SLN 94577 671-B7
COLLIER PL
35400 FRMT 94536 752-F1
COLLIER CANYON CT
- LVMR 94550 695-C5
COLLIER CANYON RD
2100 LVMR 94550 695-C5
3000 AlaC 94550 695-C2
7900 AlaC 94550 694-J5
COLLIN CT
3400 FRMT 94536 752-H2
COLLINGSWORTH ST
21700 CPTO 95014 852-B3
COLLINGWOOD AV
1600 SJS 95125 854-A5
COLLINGWOOD ST
- SF 94114 667-G3
COLLINS AV
- RCH 94806 588-G1
800 CLMA 94014 687-D7
1300 CLMA 94014 707-C1
2300 PIN 94564 569-G7
3400 SPAB 94806 568-H7
3400 RCH 94806 568-H7
COLLINS CT
- RCH 94801 588-E6
100 PLHL 94523 592-A7
900 HAY 94544 732-A1
4300 MTVW 94040 811-E3
COLLINS DR
- PLHL 94523 592-A7
8000 OAK 94621 670-F5
COLLINS LN
1200 SJS 95129 852-J4
COLLINS ST
- SF 94118 647-E6
100 RCH 94801 588-E6
COLLINWOOD CT
400 SCL 95054 813-F5
COLLOMIA CT
300 SJS 95111 875-A1
COLMA
200 PIT 94565 574-B3
COLMA BLVD
- CLMA 94014 687-C7
COLMA CT
- SRMN 94583 673-C3
COLMA CREEK SERV RD
- SSF 94080 708-A4
COLMERY CT
4000 SJS 95118 874-A2
COLMERY LN
1600 SJS 95118 874-A2
COLOMA ST
- SAUS 94965 626-J1
2100 OAK 94602 650-D4
COLOMA WY
100 VAL 94589 509-J5
COLOMBARD CT
200 CLAY 94517 593-J7
8300 SJS 95135 855-J7
COLOMBO DR
4200 SJS 95130 853-A4
4300 SJS 95129 853-A4
COLON AV
- SF 94112 667-D6
300 SF 94127 667-D6
COLONADE SQ
100 SJS 95127 834-J3
COLONIAL CT
- SRMN 94583 673-H7
2200 WLCK 94598 612-F1
3700 ANT 94509 595-C3
7900 PLE 94588 714-B6
COLONIAL DR
- AlaC 94580 691-E7
COLONIAL LN
900 PA 94303 791-D5
1100 SJS 95132 814-H4
COLONIAL PL
- SMCo 94061 790-B3
COLONIAL WY
- SF 94112 667-F7
3000 SJS 95128 853-E4
COLONIAL OAKS DR
1200 LALT 94024 831-H3
COLONIAL PARK CT
5200 FRMT 94538 773-C2
COLONNA AV
- SJS 95148 855-F1
COLONY CT
29000 HAY 94544 712-B7
29000 HAY 94544 732-B1
COLONY DR
200 SJS 95131 814-A4
COLONY LN
- CMAD 94925 606-F1
- WLCK 94598 612-D3
COLONY ST
1900 MTVW 94043 811-G2
COLONY WY
- CMAD 94925 606-F1
COLONY COVE DR
400 SJS 95123 874-G3
COLONY CREST DR
400 SJS 95123 874-G3
COLONY FIELD DR
5300 SJS 95123 874-G3
COLONY GREEN DR
5300 SJS 95123 874-G3
COLONY HILLS LN
1000 CPTO 95014 852-D3
COLONY KNOLL DR
400 SJS 95123 874-G3

STREET
Block City ZIP Pg-Grid

COLONY PARK CIR
5400 SJS 95123 874-G3
COLONY VIEW PL
2700 AlaC 94541 712-C2
COLORADO AV
- BERK 94707 609-G4
100 PA 94306 791-D6
100 PA 94301 791-B7
700 PA 94303 791-D6
COLORADO CT
100 LGTS 95032 873-H7
COLORADO DR
5500 CNCD 94521 593-F6
COLORADO PL
1000 PA 94303 791-E5
COLORADO RD
29100 HAY 94544 712-C7
COLORADOS CT
300 LFYT 94549 631-H4
COLORADOS DR
- MLBR 94030 727-J4
500 OAK 94603 670-H7
COLORVIEW CT
5900 SJS 95120 874-B7
COLT CT
100 VAL 94590 530-A7
200 CCCo 94549 591-H6
COLT WY
1300 SJS 95121 855-B4
COLTER PL
6000 SJS 95123 874-G6
COLTON AV
100 SCAR 94070 769-H5
1000 SUNV 94089 812-F4
COLTON BLVD
5600 OAK 94611 630-F6
COLTON CT
- RDWC 94062 789-E2
- SMCo 94062 789-E2
COLTON LN
- MRTZ 94553 591-H1
COLTON PL
- MRTZ 94553 591-H1
- OAK 94611 630-F7
500 SJS 95110 834-C7
COLTON ST
- SF 94103 667-H1
COLTWOOD CT
3400 SJS 95148 835-D6
COLTWOOD DR
2700 SJS 95148 835-D6
COLUMBIA AV
- SMCo 94063 790-D1
100 MrnC 94941 606-F5
200 CCCo 94708 609-G3
500 SJS 95126 854-A1
500 SUNV 94086 812-F6
2300 RCH 94804 609-B4
43200 FRMT 94538 773-E2
COLUMBIA CIR
- BEN 94510 551-C1
- BERK 94708 609-J7
800 RDWC 94065 750-C6
COLUMBIA CT
- WLCK 94598 612-H3
27000 HAY 94542 712-D4
COLUMBIA DR
600 SMTO 94402 748-H3
1600 MTVW 94040 811-G7
16500 AlaC 94552 692-C1
18000 AlaC 94552 672-C7
COLUMBIA LN
800 FCTY 94404 749-F4
COLUMBIA ST
1100 PIT 94565 574-F2
2000 PA 94306 810-J1
2200 PA 94306 811-A1
COLUMBIA WY
100 VAL 94589 509-J5
800 RDWC 94065 750-C6
27000 HAY 94542 712-D4
COLUMBIA CREEK DR
500 SRMN 94583 673-J7
COLUMBIAN DR
3300 OAK 94605 671-A1
3500 OAK 94605 670-J1
COLUMBIA RIVER CT
4600 SJS 95136 874-G2
COLUMBIA SQUARE ST
- SF 94103 648-A7
COLUMBINE AV
1100 SUNV 94086 832-H2
COLUMBINE CT
800 DNVL 94526 653-F6
2400 HAY 94545 731-H1
19200 SAR 95070 852-G6
COLUMBINE DR
100 HER 94547 570-A4
2500 HAY 94545 731-G1
3500 SJS 95148 835-C4
3500 SJS 95127 835-C4
4300 PLE 94588 713-J1
COLUMBINE LN
- NVTO 94947 526-D7
COLUMBINE PL
200 HER 94547 570-A4
38200 NWK 94560 752-G7
COLUMBINE WY
1400 LVMR 94550 696-B3
COLUMBUS AV
- SF 94111 648-A4
- SF 94133 648-A4
- SF 94133 648-A4
300 SF 94133 647-J3
700 SF 94133 647-J3
1200 LVMR 94550 715-F3
1300 BURL 94010 728-C5
1300 SF 94109 647-J3
1800 CCCo 94525 550-C5
21200 CPTO 95014 852-B3
COLUMBUS CIR
1300 MPS 95035 794-B4
COLUMBUS DR
1000 MPS 95035 794-B4
COLUMBUS PKWY
- BEN 94510 550-G1
- BEN 94591 530-G6
- BEN 94591 550-G1
- SolC 94591 550-G1
1500 VAL 94591 510-E7
1900 VAL 94591 530-G1
2500 SolC 94591 530-G6

STREET
Block City ZIP Pg-Grid

COLUMBUS PL
2700 SCL 95051 833-B3
COLUMN CT
3200 SJS 95111 854-F6
COLUSA AV
200 BERK 94707 609-F5
200 CCCo 94707 609-E3
200 ELCR 94530 609-E3
300 CCCo 94706 609-E3
900 SUNV 94086 812-H5
5200 RCH 94804 609-B3
COLUSA CT
100 SBRN 94066 707-D7
COLUSA PL
- SF 94103 667-J1
COLUSA ST
800 VAL 94590 530-B5
2400 PIN 94564 569-F6
4900 UNC 94587 752-A1
COLUSA WY
400 LVMR 94550 695-E6
1900 SJS 95130 852-J6
COLVILLE DR
300 SJS 95123 874-J5
300 SJS 95123 875-A5
25500 HAY 94544 711-J4
33000 UNC 94587 752-A2
COLVILLE PL
34400 FRMT 94555 752-D1
COMANCHE CT
- FRMT 94539 773-H4
800 LVMR 94550 695-E7
5100 ANT 94509 595-H5
5600 SJS 95123 874-H4
COMANCHE DR
5600 SJS 95123 874-H5
COMANCHE WY
- PLE 94588 694-G7
5000 ANT 94509 595-H4
COMBS LN
100 VAL 94590 530-C3
COMER DR
20900 SAR 95070 852-C7
COMERFORD ST
- SF 94131 667-G4
COMERWOOD CT
400 SSF 94080 707-F4
COMET CIR
4200 UNC 94587 732-B6
COMET DR
100 MPS 95035 814-A2
600 FCTY 94404 749-G2
COMET LN
2900 SJS 95127 834-J2
COMISTAS CT
- WLCK 94598 612-J5
COMISTAS DR
2000 WLCK 94598 612-H4
COMMANCHE CT
700 WLCK 94598 612-H3
COMMANDANTS LN
- BEN 94510 551-E6
COMMANDER LN
300 RDWC 94065 749-H6
COMMER CT
- SF 94124 668-C6
COMMERCE AV
2000 CNCD 94520 592-E2
COMMERCE CIR
7000 PLE 94588 693-J5
COMMERCE DR
1900 SJS 95131 814-B5
5700 FRMT 94555 752-B3
7000 PLE 94588 693-J5
COMMERCE PL
2100 HAY 94545 711-E5
2100 PIT 94565 574-G5
COMMERCE WY
400 LVMR 94550 696-E4
1500 OAK 94606 650-A6
COMMERCIAL AV
300 SSF 94080 707-G2
900 PA 94303 791-F7
900 PA 94303 811-F1
COMMERCIAL BLVD
- NVTO 94949 546-F2
COMMERCIAL CIR
5000 CCCo 94520 572-G3
COMMERCIAL CT
1000 SJS 95112 834-C1
COMMERCIAL LN
1300 WLCK 94596 612-C5
COMMERCIAL PL
800 SRFL 94901 586-F1
COMMERCIAL ST
- VAL 94589 510-A7
100 SUNV 94086 812-G7
100 SJS 95112 834-B2
400 SF 94111 648-A5
700 SF 94108 648-A5
900 SCAR 94070 769-H3
1000 SJS 95133 834-B2
COMMODORE CT
- PIT 94565 573-J2
100 VAL 94591 550-F2
COMMODORE DR
- EMVL 94608 629-C6
100 RCH 94804 608-H2
1100 SBRN 94066 707-H5
1600 SJS 95133 834-E1
2000 SJS 95133 814-E7
2100 SCIC 95133 814-E7
COMMODORE DR W
800 SBRN 94066 707-G6
COMMON RD
17300 AlaC 94546 692-B2
COMMONS LN
- FCTY 94404 749-E3
COMMONWEALTH AV
- SF 94118 647-E6
COMMONWEALTH DR
100 MLPK 94025 770-G6
4600 OAK 94605 671-E5
COMMUNITY LN
1100 PA 94301 791-A4
COMMUNITY RD
- BLV 94920 607-D7
- BLV 94920 627-D1
COMO AV
- DALY 94014 687-C3
COMO LN
3300 SJS 95118 874-A1
COMO WY
400 DNVL 94526 653-E6

STREET
Block City ZIP Pg-Grid

COMPASS CIR
500 RDWC 94065 749-H7
COMPASS CT
100 VAL 94590 529-H2
COMPASS CV
- SLN 94579 711-A1
COMPASS DR
400 RDWC 94065 749-H7
COMPASS LN
900 FCTY 94404 749-H4
COMPASS POINT CT
200 HER 94547 570-A6
COMPONENT DR
100 SJS 95131 813-G7
COMPO VIA
- DNVL 94526 633-C6
COMPRESSOR RD
- CCCo 94553 571-H3
COMPTON CIR
- MLV 94941 606-G2
100 SRMN 94583 673-C2
COMPTON CT
3600 SJS 95130 853-C4
4000 LVMR 94550 696-A7
25500 HAY 94544 711-J4
33000 UNC 94587 752-A2
COMPTON LN
3600 SJS 95130 853-B4
COMPTON RD
- SF 94129 647-C4
COMPUTER RD
- CCCo 94553 571-G3
COMSTOCK CIR
- SCIC 94305 790-J7
2500 BLMT 94002 769-A3
COMSTOCK COM
34700 FRMT 94555 752-D2
COMSTOCK CT
100 VAL 94589 530-B1
1500 BERK 94703 629-F1
2700 SRMN 94583 673-E6
COMSTOCK DR
500 TBRN 94920 607-B4
COMSTOCK LN
1700 SJS 95124 853-H7
COMSTOCK ST
700 SCL 95054 833-D1
COMSTOCK WY
1500 OAK 94606 650-B5
1800 SJS 95124 853-J7
COMSTOCK QUEEN CT
- MTVW 94043 811-J3
CONANT CT
27200 HAY 94544 711-J7
CONCANNON BLVD
900 LVMR 94550 715-E4
CONCANNON CT
300 SCL 95050 833-D6
CONCAR DR
- SMTO 94402 749-B3
CONCEPCION RD
12200 LAH 94022 831-B1
12300 LAH 94022 811-B7
CONCERTO CIR
5300 CNCD 94521 593-F5
CONCERTO DR
4400 SJS 95111 855-A7
CONCERTO WY
4400 SJS 95111 855-A7
CONCHA CT
500 DNVL 94526 653-C2
CONCHITA CT
- NVTO 94947 525-G4
- PCFA 94044 707-A4
CONCHO DR
- FRMT 94539 773-H4
CONCORD AV
700 SJS 95128 853-H2
1000 PLHL 94520 592-D1
1000 CNCD 94520 592-D1
1000 CCCo 94520 592-D1
1300 LALT 94024 831-H3
20200 AlaC 94541 691-G7
CONCORD BLVD
2200 CNCD 94520 592-F2
2300 CNCD 94519 592-H1
3700 CNCD 94519 593-A1
4000 CNCD 94521 593-D3
4800 CCCo 94521 593-D3
5500 CLAY 94517 593-F4
CONCORD CIR
- MTVW 94040 811-F3
CONCORD CT
- NVTO 94947 525-H3
1800 CNCD 94521 593-D3
CONCORD DR
- SJS 95123 875-B4
- SJS 95193 875-B4
200 MLPK 94025 790-J3
2200 PIT 94565 573-J4
CONCORD LN
2800 SCL 95051 833-A6
CONCORD PL
600 PLE 94566 714-G4
36300 NWK 94560 752-D6
CONCORD ST
- SF 94112 687-F2
100 VAL 94591 530-D5
700 PLE 94566 714-G4
36300 NWK 94560 752-D6
CONCORD WY
600 BURL 94010 728-G6
2700 SBRN 94066 707-F7
CONCORDIA ST
1600 ALA 94501 669-F1
1700 ALA 94501 649-F7
CONCORD RIDGE CT
- SJS 95138 855-F6
CONCOURSE DR
- SF 94118 667-C1
100 BLMT 94002 749-F6
1900 SJS 95131 814-B5
CONDADO CT
- SRMN 94583 673-C2
CONDE CT
5000 FRMT 94538 773-B1
CONDENSA ST
2500 SCL 95051 833-B1
CONDIT CT
900 LFYT 94549 611-J6
CONDIT RD
900 LFYT 94549 611-J6

STREET
Block City ZIP Pg-Grid

CONDON CT
- SMTO 94403 748-J7
300 SCL 95050 833-D6
CONDON ST
40200 FRMT 94538 753-C6
CONDOR CIR
5700 SJS 95118 874-A6
CONDOR CT
- DNVL 94506 653-J6
700 MRTZ 94553 591-G3
800 ANT 94509 595-F2
2700 UNC 94587 732-D6
5700 SJS 95118 874-A6
CONDOR DR
700 MRTZ 94553 591-G3
33100 UNC 94587 732-D6
CONDOR LN
900 FCTY 94404 749-H2
CONDOR PL
- CLAY 94517 593-H5
CONDOR ST
- DNVL 94506 653-J6
CONDOR WY
- CLAY 94517 593-H5
1500 SUNV 94087 832-E5
CONEJO CT
500 CCCo 94506 654-A5
26500 LAH 94022 811-B6
CONEJO DR
- MLBR 94030 728-A5
100 MLBR 94030 727-J5
200 SJS 95119 875-C7
4300 CCCo 94506 654-A5
CONEJO LN
- CCCo 94506 654-A5
CONEJO WY
1100 WLCK 94596 612-A2
1300 WLCK 94596 611-J2
CONESTOGA LN
6500 DBLN 94568 694-A3
CONESTOGA PL
35600 NWK 94560 752-C5
CONESTOGA WY
300 SJS 95123 874-J6
300 SJS 95123 875-A6
5300 RCH 94803 589-J2
CONGDON ST
- SF 94112 667-H7
CONGO ST
- SF 94131 667-F6
500 SF 94127 667-F6
CONGRESS AV
4500 OAK 94601 650-E7
4700 OAK 94601 670-E1
CONGRESS CT
3600 FRMT 94538 773-E1
CONGRESS PL
10000 CPTO 95014 832-C7
CONGRESS WY
20600 AlaC 94546 691-J5
CONGRESS HALL LN
21700 SAR 95070 872-B3
CONGRESS JUNCTION CIR
18900 SAR 95070 852-B7
CONGRESS SPRINGS LN
21700 SAR 95070 872-B3
CONGRESS SPRINGS RD Rt#-9
20900 SAR 95070 872-A3
21900 SCIC 95070 872-A3
CONIFER CT
300 WLCK 94598 612-H1
1900 SJS 95132 814-E2
CONIFER LN
- HIL 94010 748-F1
- WLCK 94598 612-J1
1900 SJS 95132 814-E2
CONIFER PL
300 NVTO 94945 525-E2
CONIFER ST
48200 FRMT 94539 793-J1
CONIFER TER
200 CCCo 94506 654-A2
CONIL WY
300 SMCo 94028 810-D4
CONISTON CT
1300 SJS 95118 874-B4
CONISTON WY
5600 SJS 95118 874-C4
CONKLING ST
- SF 94124 668-A6
CONLIN CT
400 SJS 95123 874-J5
CONLON AV
200 MrnC 94965 606-B5
6100 ELCR 94530 589-B7
CONLON TR
- CCCo 94708 609-G1
- RCH 94805 589-F7
- RCH 94805 609-G1
CONMUR ST
200 SSF 94080 707-F5
CONNECTICUT AV
1000 SPAB 94806 588-H1
CONNECTICUT DR
1000 RDWC 94061 789-J2
1500 RDWC 94061 790-A2
5500 CNCD 94521 593-E6
CONNECTICUT ST
- SF 94107 668-B3
23000 HAY 94545 711-D6
CONNEMARA WY
100 SUNV 94087 832-E4
CONNIE AV
600 SMTO 94402 749-B3
CONNIE CT
- CCCo 94565 573-F1
CONNIE DR
700 CMBL 95008 873-C1
CONNOLLY AV
15700 AlaC 94578 691-E5
15700 SLN 94578 691-E5
15700 AlaC 94580 691-E5
CONNOLLY WY
2300 EPA 94303 791-C1
CONOVAN LN
35500 FRMT 94536 752-G1
CONOW ST
100 CMAD 94925 586-H7
100 CMAD 94925 606-H1

STREET
Block City ZIP Pg-Grid

CONRAD AV
1700 SJS 95124 873-H4
CONRAD CT
- OAK 94611 630-E5
- SSF 94080 707-D1
19900 AlaC 94546 692-A4
CONRAD ST
- SF 94131 667-G5
38000 FRMT 94536 753-A3
CONRADIA CT
21500 CPTO 95014 852-B3
CONSERVATORY DR E
- SF 94117 647-D7
- SF 94117 667-D1
CONSERVATORY DR W
- SF - 647-D7
- SF - 667-D1
CONSTABLE COM
- FRMT 94536 753-B3
CONSTANCE CIR
3300 ALA 94501 670-B3
CONSTANCE DR
- SRFL 94903 566-E4
- VAL 94590 550-C1
3500 SJS 95117 853-C2
CONSTANCE PL
300 MRGA 94556 651-D1
CONSTANSO CT
1500 SJS 95129 852-J4
CONSTANSO WY
- SF 94132 667-A6
1400 SJS 95129 852-J4
CONSTANZO ST
500 SCIC 94305 810-H1
CONSTELLATION CT
800 RDWC 94065 750-A5
800 RDWC 94065 749-J5
CONSTELLATION DR
2400 HAY 94545 731-G1
CONSTITUTION AV
18000 MSER 95030 872-J5
CONSTITUTION CT
1800 SJS 95124 853-H6
2000 SLN 94579 690-J6
CONSTITUTION DR
- CMAD 94925 606-J2
100 MLPK 94025 770-G6
400 DNVL 94526 653-A1
800 FCTY 94404 749-G3
2100 SJS 95124 853-H6
2800 LVMR 94550 695-B5
CONSTITUTION SQ
300 MLBR 94030 728-B3
CONSTITUTION WY
400 SMCo 94080 707-F4
400 SSF 94080 707-F4
1600 ALA 94501 669-F1
1700 ALA 94501 649-F7
CONSUELO AV
2200 SCL 95050 833-D6
CONSUELO RD
2900 CNCD 94519 592-H1
CONTADA CIR
500 DNVL 94526 653-B2
CONTER CT
7700 DBLN 94568 693-G3
CONTESSA CT
200 LFYT 94549 631-H3
6300 SJS 95123 874-J7
CONTESSA WY
26700 HAY 94545 711-G6
CONTI CT
500 SJS 95111 854-G3
3100 PLE 94566 715-C6
CONTINENTAL AV
2000 HAY 94545 711-E5
CONTINENTAL CIR
700 MTVW 94040 812-A7
21400 SAR 95070 852-C6
CONTINENTAL DR
500 SJS 95111 855-A7
900 MLPK 94025 790-C6
43000 FRMT 94538 773-E2
CONTINENTALS WY
1000 BLMT 94002 769-B2
CONTRA COSTA AV
700 BERK 94707 609-G6
1300 SPAB 94806 589-A4
37000 FRMT 94536 752-G4
CONTRA COSTA BLVD
500 PLHL 94523 592-C2
800 CNCD 94520 592-C2
1400 CNCD 94523 592-C2
CONTRA COSTA COM
- FRMT 94536 752-G4
CONTRA COSTA DR
800 ELCR 94530 609-D1
CONTRA COSTA PL
- OAK 94618 630-B5
CONTRA COSTA RD
800 ELCR 94530 609-E2
5900 OAK 94618 630-B5
CONTRA COSTA ST
- RCH 94801 588-B6
- VAL 94590 530-B5
CONTRA LOMA BLVD
- ANT - 595-B2
- CCCo - 595-B2
2800 ANT 94509 595-B1
3000 ANT 94509 575-B7
CONTRA LOMA TR
- CCCo - 595-A5
CONTRERAS PL
3200 HAY 94542 712-E4
CONVAIR ST
1000 OAK 94621 670-D6
CONVENT CT
- SRFL 94901 566-H6
CONVENTION WY
300 RDWC 94063 770-A4
CONVERSE ST
- SF 94103 668-A1
4100 FRMT 94538 773-D2
CONWAY AV
14800 SCIC 95124 873-G4
CONWAY CT
100 DNVL 94526 653-D6
14700 SCIC 95124 873-G4
CONWAY DR
300 DNVL 94526 653-D6
CONWAY RD
600 SUNV 94087 832-D3

STREET
Block City ZIP Pg-Grid

CONWAY ST
1600 MPS 95035 794-A3
CONWAY TER
4900 FRMT 94555 752-D2
CONZELMAN RD
- MrnC 94965 627-A6
- MrnC 94965 626-F7
COOGAN AV
- SANS 94960 566-C7
COOK CIR
100 VAL 94589 510-B7
COOK LN
3300 ALA 94502 670-A7
COOK PL
2700 HAY 94545 711-F7
COOK ST
- SF 94118 647-E6
1100 ANT 94509 575-C5
1100 SJS 95126 833-G5
COOKE ST
- CCCo 94525 550-E5
1000 OAK 94621 670-D7
COOKIE CT
100 SMCo 94062 769-G7
COOKSEY LN
700 SCIC 94305 810-H1
COOLEY AV
1900 EPA 94303 791-B2
COOLEY DR
1700 SJS 95116 834-G5
3700 CNCD 94518 592-H4
COOLIDGE AV
- FRFX 94930 566-A6
800 SUNV 94086 812-D7
1100 SJS 95125 854-A3
2000 OAK 94601 650-D5
2800 OAK 94602 650-D5
COOLIDGE CT
2200 ANT 94509 595-A1
3700 AlaC 94552 692-G2
COOLIDGE DR
2000 SCL 95051 833-B3
COOLIDGE ST
4500 CNCD 94521 593-D2
COOLIDGE TER
- OAK 94602 650-F3
COOLSPRING CT
100 CCCo 94506 654-C5
COOPER AL
- SF 94108 648-A4
COOPER AV
15000 SCIC 95124 873-F4
COOPER CT
100 LGTS 95030 873-B5
2600 ANT 94509 574-H6
COOPER DR
500 BEN 94510 550-H1
3300 SCL 95051 832-J2
COOPER LN
- SAUS 94965 627-B3
COOPER PL
2800 FRMT 94555 732-E6
COOPER WY
200 HAY 94544 712-B7
COOPERAGE CT
- AMCN 94589 510-C3
COOPER RIVER DR
1100 SJS 95126 853-G3
COOS CT
500 FCTY 94404 749-F5
COPA DEL ORO DR
2500 UNC 94587 732-E6
24900 HAY 94545 711-G5
COPAL CT
800 SCIC 95127 814-H6
COPAS LN
- CNCD 94521 593-B2
COPCO LN
200 SJS 95123 875-A4
COPE CT
4600 PLE 94566 714-D1
COPELAND CT
5400 SJS 95124 873-H6
COPELAND LN
3800 FRMT 94538 753-C6
5400 SJS 95124 873-H6
COPELAND PL
5500 SJS 95124 873-H6
COPELAND ST
400 PCFA 94044 726-J2
COPLEY AV
- RDWC 94062 769-H6
COPPER AL
- SF 94114 667-F3
COPPER RD
2900 SCL 95051 812-J7
2900 SCL 95051 832-J1
COPPER WY
100 VAL 94589 510-B6
COPPERAGE CT
6500 SJS 95120 894-C6
COPPERFIELD AV
300 HAY 94544 712-C7
COPPERFIELD DR
4200 SJS 95136 854-F7
4200 SJS 95136 874-F1
COPPERFIELD LN
- DNVL 94506 653-E4
COPPER HILL CT
4800 ANT 94509 595-J3
COPPER LEAF DR
3300 SJS 95132 814-G4
COPPER PEAK LN
1100 SJS 95120 894-G5
COPPER RIDGE RD
- SRMN 94583 673-F2
COPPER SPRING CT
11500 CPTO 95014 852-A4
COPPERWOOD CIR
6500 SJS 95120 894-E1
COPPOCK CT
100 VAL 94591 530-F3
COQUITO CT
- SMCo 94028 810-D4
COQUITO WY
100 SMCo 94028 810-D4
CORA CT
- CCCo 94596 612-D2
1200 CMBL 95008 873-C1
CORA ST
- SF 94134 688-A2
- SF 94134 687-J2

STREET
Block City ZIP Pg-Grid

CORAL AV
1500 SLN 94578 691-D3
CORAL CT
600 LALT 94024 811-G6
3000 SJS 95121 855-A4
5100 CNCD 94521 593-E4
5600 FRMT 94538 773-B2
CORAL DR
- ORIN 94563 631-C5
200 PIT 94565 574-E5
700 CCCo 94572 569-J2
700 CCCo 94572 570-A2
CORAL LN
- PIT 94565 574-A3
- FCTY 94404 749-E6
CORAL PL
- DALY 94014 687-D5
CORAL RD
- VAL 94590 529-J6
- SF 94107 668-B3
- VAL 94590 530-A6
9200 OAK 94603 670-F6
CORAL WY
7600 DBLN 94568 693-J2
CORAL CANYON DR
5500 SJS 95123 875-B4
CORAL DELL WK
- ALA 94501 669-H3
CORALEE DR
1700 SJS 95124 873-H4
CORALEE LN
4000 LFYT 94549 611-A7
CORALFLOWER LN
2000 SRMN 94583 653-J7
CORAL GABLES CIR
200 SJS 95139 895-E1
CORALIE DR
400 WLCK 94596 612-A2
CORALINO LN
- SF 94131 667-F4
CORALLINE CT
4000 FRMT 94555 752-D1
CORAL REEF PL
1200 ALA 94501 669-G2
CORAL REEF RD
300 ALA 94501 669-G3
CORAL RIDGE CIR
700 CCCo 94572 569-J2
CORAL RIDGE DR
300 PCFA 94044 707-A2
CORAL SANDS DR
3600 SJS 95136 854-G7
CORALTREE PL
1600 SJS 95131 814-C5
CORALWOOD DR
- CNCD - 613-D2
CORALWOOD WY
5700 SJS 95123 874-F5
CORBAL CT
3100 SJS 95148 855-F2
CORBEL COM
- FRMT 94539 773-J7
CORBETT AV
- SF 94114 667-F2
700 SF 94131 667-F4
CORBETT CT
15200 SLN 94578 691-D5
CORBETTA LN
12400 LAH 94022 831-B2
CORBIN AV
4900 SJS 95118 874-C3
CORBIN CT
300 AMCN 94589 510-A4
CORBIN DR
- AMCN 94589 510-A4
CORBIN PL
- SF 94114 667-F2
CORBITT DR
500 BURL 94010 728-G6
CORBY DR
3100 SJS 95148 855-E2
CORCEL CT
16700 LGTS 95032 873-C5
CORCORAN AV
400 VAL 94589 510-B5
CORCORAN CT
800 BEN 94510 530-H7
CORCORAN MINE TR
- CCCo - 595-A6
- CCCo - 594-J6
CORD CT
2900 SJS 95148 855-D1
CORDA DR
2800 SJS 95122 855-B2
CORDAY CT
4600 PLE 94588 694-A6
CORDELIA AV
1100 SJS 95129 852-H4
CORDELIA ST
- SF 94133 648-A4
CORDELIA WY
- WLCK 94596 612-B2
CORDELL CT
700 DNVL 94526 652-H1
CORDELL DR
300 DNVL 94526 652-G1
CORDILLERAS AV
600 SCAR 94070 769-F3
1300 SUNV 94087 832-D4
CORDILLERAS CT
- SMCo 94062 769-F7
CORDILLERAS RD
900 SMCo 94062 769-F7
900 RDWC 94062 769-F7
CORDOBA AV
1400 HAY 94544 732-A2
CORDOBA CT
2200 ANT 94509 595-A1
CORDOBA ST
1600 LVMR 94550 715-F4
CORDOBA WY
2100 ANT 94509 595-A1
2400 SJS 95125 853-J7
CORDONE DR
- SANS 94960 566-B6
CORDOVA CT
- PTLV 94028 810-D6
CORDOVA PL
4400 FRMT 94536 752-F3
CORDOVA ST
- SF 94112 687-G2
100 VAL 94591 530-F6

STREET
Block City ZIP Pg-Grid

CORDOVA ST
500 DALY 94014 687-G2
2400 OAK 94602 650-D5
CORDOVA WY
100 CNCD 94519 592-G2
3100 LFYT 94549 631-H4
CORDOY LN
5000 SJS 95124 873-H5
5100 SJS 95032 873-H5
CORDWOOD CT
14300 SAR 95070 872-H2
COREY CT
- SRMN 94583 673-E5
COREY PL E
2600 SRMN 94583 673-D6
COREY WY
300 SSF 94080 708-A4
19200 AlaC 94546 692-A4
CORFU PL
19000 AlaC 94541 691-F7
CORIANDER CT
100 SRMN 94583 653-J7
CORIE CT
1100 SJS 95112 814-B7
CORINA CT
3800 PA 94303 791-F7
CORINA WY
3700 PA 94303 791-E7
3800 PA 94303 811-E1
CORINE LN
1300 MLPK 94025 790-E4
CORINTH CT
7000 DBLN 94568 693-J3
CORINTHIA CT
- NVTO 94947 526-D6
CORINTHIA DR
400 MPS 95035 794-A5
CORINTHIAN CT
- TBRN 94920 607-D7
CORK PL
3700 SSF 94080 707-C4
CORK RD
- ALA 94502 669-J5
CORKERHILL WY
3600 SJS 95121 855-C3
CORK HARBOUR CIR
400 RDWC 94065 749-G6
CORK OAK LN
28600 HAY 94544 712-C6
CORK OAK WY
3300 PA 94303 791-D7
CORKTREE LN
2000 SJS 95132 814-E2
CORKWOOD CT
100 SJS 95136 874-H1
4400 CNCD 94521 593-B5
22700 HAY 94541 711-F3
CORKWOOD ST
100 VAL 94591 530-F5
CORLETT WY
- HIL 94010 748-C3
CORLISS DR
- MRGA 94556 631-D5
CORLISS ST
600 CCCo 94565 573-C1
CORLISS WY
500 CMBL 95008 853-C6
CORLISTA DR
700 SJS 95128 853-H2
CORMACK RD
2500 FRMT 94539 773-F2
CORMORANT CT
- CCCo 94553 571-J4
1500 SUNV 94087 832-E5
2700 UNC 94587 732-D6
CORMORANT DR
- BLMT 94002 769-G1
- RDWC 94065 769-G1
CORMORANT TER
33700 FRMT 94555 732-D7
CORNAC TER
41000 FRMT 94539 753-E6
CORNELIA AV
- MLV 94941 606-C2
CORNELIA CT
600 MTVW 94040 811-H7
CORNELIA DR
- HIL 94010 748-F3
CORNELIUS DR
2600 CCCo 94806 569-C5
CORNELL AV
- LKSP 94939 586-E5
300 HAY 94544 732-F3
400 ALB 94706 609-D5
400 SMTO 94402 748-H3
1100 BERK 94706 609-D5
1300 BERK 94702 609-D5
1400 BERK 94702 629-E1
CORNELL CT
- PLHL 94523 591-J6
CORNELL DR
600 SCL 95051 833-A6
1600 ALA 94501 670-B3
1600 MTVW 94040 811-H7
5400 SJS 95118 874-A5
CORNELL RD
- MLPK 94025 790-G4
CORNELL ST
500 AlaC 94580 691-D5
2000 PA 94306 791-A7
2200 PA 94306 811-A1
CORNELL WY
4200 LVMR 94550 716-A1
CORNELLA CT
3700 CNCD 94518 592-H4
CORNFLOWER CT
1000 SUNV 94086 832-H2
CORNING AV
- MPS 95035 814-A1
100 MPS 95035 813-J1
CORNING CT
33000 UNC 94587 752-A2
CORNING DR
3300 SJS 95118 874-A1
CORNISH CT
3300 FRMT 94536 752-F1
CORNISH DR
35200 FRMT 94536 752-F1
CORNISH LN
11900 SJS 95131 834-C1
CORNISH WY
400 BLMT 94002 749-F7

STREET
Block City ZIP Pg-Grid

CORNWALL CT
- OAK 94611 650-G2
800 SUNV 94087 832-G4
1300 WLCK 94596 612-A3
CORNWALL DR
2700 SJS 95127 835-A5
CORNWALL PL
- DNVL 94506 653-J5
35200 NWK 94560 752-D3
CORNWALL ST
- MLV 94941 606-C3
- PIT 94565 574-D2
- SF 94118 647-D6
CORNWALL WY
- SLN 94577 691-B2
CORNWALLIS CT
34300 FRMT 94555 732-E7
CORNWALLIS LN
600 FCTY 94404 749-G5
CORNWALLIS PL
34200 FRMT 94555 732-E7
CORONA CT
- NVTO 94945 525-J1
800 PCFA 94044 726-J4
2300 BERK 94708 609-H6
4900 UNC 94587 752-A2
5100 PLE 94588 694-A6
CORONA DR
600 PCFA 94044 726-J4
4500 SJS 95129 853-A3
CORONA PL
1300 WLCK 94596 611-J2
1300 WLCK 94596 612-A2
CORONA PZ
100 UNC 94587 732-J5
CORONA ST
- SF 94127 667-C7
- SF 94132 687-C1
CORONA WY
100 SMCo 94028 810-D4
CORONACH AV
1500 SUNV 94087 832-B5
CORONADO AV
- OAK 94611 629-J6
- DALY 94015 687-A4
- LALT 94022 811-D6
- SCAR 94070 769-E4
600 SCIC 94305 810-H1
4900 OAK 94618 629-J6
5100 OAK 94609 629-J6
CORONADO CT
- CCCo 94596 612-E7
- NVTO 94945 525-H1
- PIT 94565 574-D5
1000 LVMR 94550 715-F3
1500 ANT 94509 575-A7
5500 CLAY 94517 593-F6
CORONADO DR
1200 SUNV 94086 812-B6
2900 SCL 95054 813-B7
7000 SJS 95129 852-E3
36100 FRMT 94536 752-F3
CORONADO LN
700 FCTY 94404 749-F4
5900 PLE 94588 694-B7
CORONADO ST
- SF 94124 688-B2
200 HER 94547 570-A5
300 ELCR 94530 609-D4
27400 HAY 94545 711-H7
27500 HAY 94545 731-H1
CORONADO WY
900 LVMR 94550 715-F3
1600 BURL 94010 728-C5
3700 SBRN 94066 707-C5
CORONATION DR
2500 UNC 94587 732-C4
CORONEL AV
900 VAL 94591 530-D7
900 VAL 94591 550-D1
CORONET AV
- MLV 94941 606-D2
CORONET BLVD
2100 BLMT 94002 769-C1
CORONET DR
200 LGTS 95032 873-E5
200 LGTS 95124 873-E5
200 SJS 95124 873-E5
CORONET WY
- MrnC 94904 586-B4
CORPORATE AV
26200 HAY 94545 711-E7
26300 HAY 94545 731-F1
CORPORATE CT
2000 SJS 95131 814-B5
CORPORATE PL
100 VAL 94590 530-A6
3100 HAY 94545 731-F1
CORPORATE WY
- LVMR 94550 696-E5
800 FRMT 94539 773-G5
CORPORATE LIMIT
600 CMBL 95008 853-F7
CORPORATION WY
1000 PA 94303 791-F7
CORPUS CHRISTI RD
100 ALA 94501 649-D6
CORRAL AV
100 SUNV 94086 812-B6
CORRAL CIR
100 SRMN 94583 673-B3
CORRAL ST
- LVMR 94550 695-E5
CORRALES DR
4700 SJS 95136 874-D2
CORRALITOS LN
14800 SCIC 95127 835-A1
CORREGIDOR AV
- OAK 94607 649-C2
CORRIDA CIR
4600 SJS 95129 853-A1
CORRIDO WY
400 SSF 94080 707-F5
CORRIE LN
1100 WLCK 94596 612-C1
CORRIE PL
800 PLHL 94523 592-A4
CORRIEA CT
41000 FRMT 94539 753-E6
CORRIEA WY
2400 FRMT 94539 753-E6

STREET
Block City ZIP Pg-Grid

CORRIENTE POINTE DR
800 RDWC 94065 749-J5
CORRIGAN CT
- BEN 94510 551-A3
38200 FRMT 94536 752-J4
CORRIGAN DR
4100 FRMT 94536 752-J4
CORRILLO DR
- SRFL 94903 566-E5
CORRINE DR
15400 LGTS 95032 873-C5
CORRINE ST
500 HAY 94544 732-E2
CORRINNE CT
100 SRMN 94583 693-G1
CORRINNE PL
7500 SRMN 94583 693-G1
CORRINNE ST
7500 SRMN 94583 693-G1
CORSAIR BLVD
20300 HAY 94545 711-D3
CORSAIR LN
900 FCTY 94404 749-G3
CORSICA LN
1200 FCTY 94404 749-G5
CORSICA PL
36000 FRMT 94536 752-F3
CORSICANA DR
100 AMCN 94589 509-J1
CORT AV
- RCH 94804 609-A3
CORTADERIA CT
- CCCo 94526 633-A5
CORTA VIA
1600 SCIC 94024 831-G4
CORTE AIRES
- MRGA 94556 631-D2
CORTE ALEGRE
- MLBR 94030 727-J4
- MrnC 94904 586-F3
CORTE ALEJO
- LKSP 94904 586-G4
CORTE ALMADEN
- SRFL 94903 566-D2
CORTE ALTA
- MrnC 94949 546-E2
CORTE ALTAMIRA
6100 PLE 94566 714-B3
CORTE AMADO
- MrnC 94904 586-F3
- LKSP 94904 586-F3
CORTE AMIGOS
- MRGA 94556 631-C2
CORTE ANGELO
15800 AlaC 94580 711-B1
CORTE ANITA
100 MrnC 94904 586-F4
CORTE ANNA
- MLBR 94030 728-B3
CORTE ANNETTE
- MRGA 94556 631-D2
CORTE ANTONIO
6900 PLE 94566 714-A2
CORTE ARANGO
400 CCCo 94803 589-D1
CORTE ARBOLES
5900 PLE 94566 714-B1
CORTE ARRIBA
- MrnC 94949 546-E2
CORTE AZUL
- MRGA 94556 631-D2
CORTE BALBOA
- MLBR 94030 728-B3
100 MrnC 94904 586-F4
7100 PLE 94566 714-A2
CORTE BANDERA
2700 PLE 94566 714-B3
CORTE BARCELONA
6900 PLE 94566 714-A2
CORTE BARISTO
- LKSP 94904 586-G4
CORTE BELLA
2500 PLE 94566 714-B2
CORTE BLANCA
7000 PLE 94566 714-A2
CORTE BOMBERO
- ORIN 94563 631-A3
CORTE BONITA
1300 SJS 95120 874-B7
CORTE BRAZOS
5800 PLE 94566 714-C3
CORTE BREVE
1800 AlaC 94580 711-B1
CORTE BRIONES
800 MRTZ 94553 591-G4
CORTE CALERA
6000 PLE 94566 714-B2
CORTE CAMELLIA
- MLBR 94030 727-J4
CORTE CAMULA
6100 SJS 95120 874-C7
CORTE CAPISTRANO
- SRFL 94903 566-E1
CORTE CARACAS
42900 FRMT 94539 753-H6
CORTE CAVA
- LVMR 94550 695-G6
CORTE CAYUGA
- MrnC 94904 586-G4
CORTE CERRITOS
5800 PLE 94566 714-B2
CORTE CIELO
- CCCo 94553 571-J3
CORTE COLINA
200 MrnC 94949 546-E3
CORTE COMODA
- MLBR 94030 728-C3
- MrnC 94904 586-E4
CORTE CORDOVA
- MrnC 94904 586-F3
CORTE CRUZ
1900 PIN 94564 569-E6
CORTE DE ANNA
1600 SJS 95124 874-A3
CORTE DE ARBOL
3100 SJS 95118 874-A1
CORTE DE ARGUELLO
12800 SAR 95070 852-C6
CORTE DE AVELLANO
4700 SJS 95136 874-E2

STREET
Block City ZIP Pg-Grid

CORTE DE BELLEZA
6100 SJS 95120 874-C7
CORTE DE BLANCO
800 SJS 95136 874-E2
CORTE DE BOLEYN
4300 SJS 95118 874-A2
CORTE DE CALLAS
1600 SJS 95124 874-A3
CORTE DE CERVATO
4700 SJS 95136 874-E2
CORTE DE FLORES
2000 SCL 95054 813-D4
2600 SMTO 94403 749-B5
3000 SJS 95118 874-A1
6800 PLE 94566 714-A2
CORTE DE LA JARA
2300 PLE 94566 714-C3
CORTE DE LA REINA
200 WLCK 94598 612-H2
6100 SJS 95120 874-B7
CORTE DEL BAYO
- LKSP 94939 586-G5
CORTE DEL CABALLO
- MRGA 94556 631-D2
CORTE DEL CAJON
5500 PLE 94566 714-C2
CORTE DEL CAMPO
- MRGA 94556 631-D2
CORTE DEL CERRO
200 MrnC 94949 546-E2
CORTE DEL CINO
3100 PLE 94566 714-B2
CORTE DEL CONEJO
6100 SJS 95120 874-B7
CORTE DEL CONTENTO
- CCCo 94595 612-A7
- CCCo 94595 611-J7
CORTE DEL CORONADO
- LKSP 94939 586-G5
CORTE DEL MAR
7000 PLE 94566 714-A3
CORTE DEL MARQUES
2500 WLCK 94598 612-G2
CORTE DEL NORTE
- LKSP 94939 586-F4
CORTE DEL ORO
7000 PLE 94566 714-A3
CORTE DEL PRADO
100 WLCK 94598 612-H2
CORTE DEL RAY
6100 PLE 94566 714-B2
CORTE DEL REY
- ORIN 94563 631-C5
- SRFL 94903 566-E1
CORTE DEL SOL
- BEN 94510 551-C4
- CCCo 94553 571-J4
- MLBR 94030 727-J4
- MRGA 94556 631-E2
900 FRMT 94539 773-J3
CORTE DEL VECINOS
1300 WLCK 94598 612-E4
CORTE DEL VISTA
6700 PLE 94566 714-A2
CORTE DE MADRID
10400 SCIC 95014 852-G1
CORTE DE MAIO
- WLCK 94598 612-G3
CORTE DE MEDEA
1600 SJS 95124 874-A3
CORTE DE MOFFO
1500 SJS 95118 874-A3
CORTE DE ORINDA
1700 FRMT 94539 753-G7
CORTE DE ORO
- MRGA 94556 631-D2
CORTE DE PEARSON
1500 SJS 95124 874-A3
CORTE DE PLATA
800 SJS 95136 874-E2
CORTE DE PONS
1600 SJS 95124 874-A3
CORTE DE PRIMAVERA
2000 SCL 95054 813-C3
CORTE DE ROSA
1400 SJS 95120 894-B1
CORTE DE ROSAS
- MRGA 94556 631-D2
CORTE DE SABLA
- MrnC 94904 586-G4
CORTE DE SEVILLE
10400 SCIC 95014 852-G2
CORTE DE TEBALDI
4200 SJS 95118 874-A3
CORTE DE THAIS
1400 SJS 95118 874-B3
CORTE DIABLO
900 MRTZ 94553 591-F4
CORTE DORADO
- BEN 94510 551-D4
- MLBR 94030 728-A4
- MrnC 94904 586-F3
400 DNVL 94526 653-E5
CORTE ELENA
100 MrnC 94904 586-F4
2600 PLE 94566 714-B3
CORTE ELLENA
- WLCK 94598 612-H4
CORTE ENANO
1800 AlaC 94580 711-B1
CORTE ENCANTO
- LKSP 94939 586-F4
- DNVL 94526 652-H2
CORTE ENCINA
- MRGA 94556 631-D2
CORTE ENCINAS
6000 PLE 94566 714-B2
CORTE ENRICO
15500 AlaC 94580 691-C7
CORTE ESCUELA
400 MrnC 94949 546-D2
CORTE ESPADA
5900 PLE 94566 714-B2
CORTE ESPERANZA
6300 PLE 94566 714-B2
CORTE ESTRELLA
- CCCo 94553 571-J4
CORTE EULALIA
- AlaC 94580 691-E7
- AlaC 94580 711-E1
CORTE FACIL
2500 PLE 94566 714-B2

STREET Block City ZIP Pg-Grid

CORTE FEDORA
- LKSP 94904 586-H4
CORTE FORTUNA
- MRGA 94556 631-E2
CORTE FRANCESCA
15800 AlaC 94580 711-B1
CORTE FRESCA
- MRGA 94556 631-D2
CORTE FUEGO
6200 PLE 94566 714-B2
CORTE GABRIEL
300 MRGA 94556 631-E7
CORTE GALICIA
42900 FRMT 94539 753-H6
CORTE GERALDO
15800 AlaC 94580 711-B1
CORTE GRACITAS
- LKSP 94904 586-G4
CORTE GRANADA
- MRGA 94556 631-E2
1400 VAL 94591 530-G6
CORTE HABANA
42900 FRMT 94539 753-H6
CORTE HOLGANZA
- ORIN 94563 631-C6
CORTE HORNITOS
2100 AlaC 94580 711-B1
CORTE LADO
- CCCo 94553 571-J3
CORTE LA PAZ
- SRFL 94903 566-D2
CORTE LA RADO
- MRGA 94556 631-D2
CORTE LAS CASAS
- TBRN 94920 607-A4
CORTE LENOSA
- LKSP 94939 586-F4
CORTE LIBRE
5700 PLE 94566 714-B2
CORTE LINDA
100 PIT 94565 574-F4
CORTE LODATO
- MrnC 94904 586-G4
CORTE LOMA
1300 WLCK 94598 612-E4
CORTE LOS SOMBRAS
- MrnC 94904 586-F4
CORTE LOYOLA
- LKSP 94904 586-G4
CORTE MADERA
1300 WLCK 94598 612-E4
CORTE MADERA AV
- CMAD 94925 586-F7
- MLV 94941 606-D2
200 CMAD 94925 606-F1
900 SUNV 94086 812-D5
CORTE MADERA CT
900 SUNV 94086 812-C5
CORTE MADERA LN
12600 LAH 94022 811-B7
21800 CPTO 95014 832-B7
CORTE MADERA RD
100 PTLV 94028 830-C1
100 PTLV 94028 810-C7
CORTE MADRID
6900 PLE 94566 714-A2
CORTE MARGARITA
5800 PLE 94566 714-C2
CORTE MARIA
100 PIT 94565 574-F3
CORTE MARIANA
15800 AlaC 94580 711-B1
CORTE MARIE
2700 WLCK 94598 612-H4
CORTE MATEO
- MRGA 94556 631-D2
6900 PLE 94566 714-A3
CORTE MELINA
2200 PLE 94566 714-C2
CORTE MENTE
5800 PLE 94566 714-B1
CORTE MERCADO
6900 PLE 94566 714-A3
CORTE MESA DR
- SRFL 94901 566-G6
CORTE MIGUEL
- SRFL 94903 566-E1
2900 CNCD 94518 592-H6
CORTE MONTANAS
6000 PLE 94566 714-B2
CORTE MONTEREY
- MRGA 94556 631-C2
6900 PLE 94566 714-A3
CORTE MORADA
- MrnC 94904 586-G4
CORTE MUNRAS
6800 PLE 94566 714-B1
CORTE NINA
7000 PLE 94566 714-A3
CORTE NOGAL
- DNVL 94526 652-H2
CORTE NORTE
400 MrnC 94949 546-E3
CORTE NUEVA
- MLBR 94030 728-A4
CORTE NUEVO
6800 PLE 94566 714-A2
CORTE ORIENTAL
- LKSP 94939 586-F4
CORTE ORTEGA
- LKSP 94939 586-F4
CORTE PACHECO
- SRFL 94903 566-D4
CORTE PACIFICA
6900 PLE 94566 714-A2
CORTE PADRE
6100 PLE 94566 714-B2
CORTE PALOMA
5400 PLE 94566 714-C2
CORTE PALOS VERDES
- TBRN 94920 607-A3
CORTE PATENCIO
- MrnC 94904 586-F3
CORTE PINON
- MRGA 94556 631-E1
CORTE PINTO
- MRGA 94556 631-D2
CORTE PLACIDA
- LKSP 94904 586-H4
CORTE PONDEROSA
2700 PLE 94566 714-B3

CORTE POQUITA
6700 MRTZ 94553 591-G4
CORTE PRECITA
- LKSP 94904 586-G3
CORTE PRINCESA
- MLBR 94030 728-A4
CORTE RAMON
- LKSP 94904 586-G4
CORTE REAL
- LKSP 94939 586-F5
CORTE REAL AV
1900 OAK 94611 650-E1
CORTE RICARDO
2100 PLE 94566 714-C2
CORTE RINALDO
3800 LFYT 94563 611-B7
3800 LFYT 94549 611-B7
CORTE RIVERA
2500 PLE 94566 714-B3
CORTE ROBLE
- MrnC 94949 546-D2
CORTE ROSA
7000 PLE 94566 714-A2
CORTE ROYAL
- MRGA 94556 631-D2
CORTE RUBIOLO
3600 AlaC 94546 692-A4
CORTES AV
- SF 94116 667-C4
CORTES CT
- MRGA 94556 631-E7
- SRFL 94903 566-B1
100 HER 94547 570-B5
CORTE SALCEDO
6800 PLE 94566 714-B3
CORTE SAN BENITO
- SRFL 94903 566-D2
CORTE SAN BLAS
2700 PLE 94566 714-B2
CORTE SAN FERNANDO
- TBRN 94920 606-J3
CORTE SAN PABLO
200 FRMT 94539 753-H6
CORTE SANTA
BARBARA
41900 FRMT 94539 753-G5
CORTE SANTA CLARA
- MRGA 94556 631-E2
CORTE SANTA INES
41800 FRMT 94539 753-G5
CORTE SANTA MARIA
6700 PLE 94566 714-A2
CORTE SANTIAGO
6100 PLE 94566 714-B2
CORTE SARATOGA
- SRFL 94903 566-D1
CORTESE CIR
3100 SJS 95127 814-J7
CORTE SEGUNDA
6700 MRTZ 94553 591-G4
CORTE SEGUNDO
3600 CNCD 94519 592-J2
CORTE SERENO
- MrnC 94904 586-F3
CORTESI AV
500 SSF 94080 707-J2
CORTE SIERRA
5500 PLE 94566 714-C2
CORTE SOLANO
- LKSP 94939 586-F4
CORTE SOMBRITA
- ORIN 94563 631-C6
CORTE SONADA
6800 PLE 94566 714-B2
CORTE SONORA
5500 PLE 94566 714-C2
CORTE SUENO
- LVMR 94550 695-F6
CORTE SUR
400 MrnC 94949 546-E3
CORTE TERCERA
6700 MRTZ 94553 591-G4
CORTE TOLUCA
- LKSP 94904 586-H4
CORTE TRANCAS
6100 PLE 94566 714-B2
CORTE ULISSE
15800 AlaC 94580 711-B1
CORTE VENADO
5900 PLE 94566 714-B2
CORTE VERA CRUZ
2700 PLE 94566 714-B3
CORTE VERANO
- SRFL 94903 546-E7
- SRFL 94903 566-E1
CORTE VERDE
6900 PLE 94566 714-A2
42900 FRMT 94539 753-H6
CORTE VERDE DR
5000 SJS 95111 875-A2
CORTE VIDA
2600 PLE 94566 714-B2
CORTE YOLANDA
- MRGA 94556 631-E2
15800 AlaC 94580 711-B1
CORTEZ AV
100 SJS 95136 854-G7
1000 BURL 94010 728-D5
1700 SJS 95122 834-H6
4700 FRMT 94536 752-F4
CORTEZ CIR
100 NVTO 94949 546-H3
CORTEZ CT
- OAK 94611 630-F7
800 LVMR 94550 715-F2
1400 WLCK 94598 612-E4
1800 PLE 94566 714-E1
2700 ANT 94509 575-B6
2700 AlaC 94546 691-J5
4300 UNC 94587 731-H5
CORTEZ DR
1200 SUNV 94086 812-B6
2600 SCL 95051 833-B1
CORTEZ LN
800 FCTY 94404 749-G3
12900 LAH 94022 830-J1
CORTEZ RD
- SMCo 94062 769-F7
CORTEZ ST
1100 HAY 94544 712-A7
1500 MPS 95035 794-A3

CORTINA CT
900 WLCK 94598 612-J4
4100 PLE 94588 694-C6
CORTINA DR
2900 SJS 95132 814-F5
CORTINA WY
2800 UNC 94587 732-A4
CORTLAND AV
- SF 94110 667-H5
1400 SF 94110 668-A5
1600 SF 94124 668-A5
CORTLAND CIR
200 VAL 94589 510-A5
CORTLAND WY
800 LVMR 94550 695-E6
CORTNEY AV
1500 PLE 94588 694-F7
CORTO CT
11600 DBLN 94568 693-F4
CORTO LN
- WDSD 94062 789-G6
CORTO SQ
600 RCH 94804 608-H1
CORTO ST
700 MTVW 94043 811-J4
CORTO MONTEREY
4400 UNC 94587 731-H6
CORTONA DR
- SJS 95135 855-F2
100 SRMN 94583 673-G3
CORTSEN CT
100 PLHL 94523 592-A6
100 PLHL 94523 591-J6
CORTSEN RD
100 PLHL 94523 592-A6
300 PLHL 94523 591-J6
CORUM CT
2400 UNC 94587 732-F6
CORUMBA CT
5800 SJS 95120 874-C5
CORVALLIS CT
1100 SJS 95120 894-F2
CORVALLIS DR
800 SUNV 94087 832-C4
1100 SJS 95120 894-F2
CORVALLIS ST
14000 SLN 94579 691-A4
CORVETTE DR
1000 SJS 95129 852-F3
CORVEY CT
1400 CCCo 94598 612-E4
1400 WLCK 94598 612-E4
CORVIN DR
2900 SCL 95051 813-A7
2900 SCL 95051 833-A1
CORVUS LN
800 FCTY 94404 749-H1
CORWIN CT
4700 PLE 94588 694-A6
5000 SJS 95111 875-C1
CORWIN DR
- CCCo 94507 632-F7
CORWIN ST
- SF 94114 667-F3
CORY AV
2300 SJS 95128 833-E7
CORY CT
21000 CPTO 95014 852-C2
CORY LN
- DBLN 94568 693-E5
COSENZA LP
4200 SJS 95134 813-D2
COSGRAVE AV
2800 OAK 94605 671-A3
COSMIC CT
3700 FRMT 94538 753-C6
COSMIC PL
3800 FRMT 94538 753-C6
COSMIC WY
3500 FRMT 94538 753-C6
COSMO PL
- SF 94109 647-J6
COSMOS COM
5500 FRMT 94538 773-A2
COSO AV
- SF 94110 667-J4
COSSO CT
- LFYT 94549 611-C4
COSTA AV
- SJS 95112 854-E3
1300 RCH 94801 588-G4
1300 SPAB 94806 588-G4
COSTA CT
2000 PIN 94564 569-E6
COSTA DR
3200 AlaC 94541 692-D7
COSTA ST
- SF 94110 668-A5
COSTA WY
39700 FRMT 94538 753-B6
COSTA MESA DR
300 SJS 95111 854-J7
COSTA MESA TER
- FRMT 94539 794-B1
400 SUNV 94086 812-C5
COSTANZA DR
100 MRTZ 94553 591-G1
COSTA RICA AV
100 BURL 94010 728-G7
100 BURL 94010 748-G1
300 SMTO 94402 748-G1
300 HIL 94010 748-G1
COSTCO WY
- ANT 94509 575-A4
COSTELLA ST
15000 SLN 94579 691-A6
COSTELLO CT
300 SCIC 94024 831-E2
COSTELLO DR
300 SCIC 94024 831-E2
COSTIGAN CIR
500 MPS 95035 794-B5
COT CT
- SJS 95117 853-D1
COTATI ST
2000 ALA 94501 649-E7
2100 HAY 94542 712-D4
COTELLA CT
- ALA 94502 669-J7
COTSWALD CT
1100 SUNV 94087 832-H4

COTTA CT
400 VAL 94589 510-D6
COTTA WY
100 VAL 94589 510-D6
COTTAGE AV
- MLV 94941 606-D2
- RCH 94801 588-D7
- SANS 94960 566-C7
1600 SRFL 94901 566-C7
COTTAGE CT
- CCCo 94595 612-A7
3700 AlaC 94546 691-J3
COTTAGE DR
- DNVL 94526 653-A2
COTTAGE LN
- CCCo 94595 612-A7
- SCAR 94070 769-E2
COTTAGE PL
6000 SJS 95123 874-E6
COTTAGE RW
- SF 94115 647-G6
COTTAGE ST
1400 ALA 94501 669-H1
COTTAGE GROVE AV
- SJS 95110 854-D2
1400 SMTO 94401 749-B1
COTTER ST
- SF 94112 667-G7
10700 OAK 94605 671-E4
COTTER WY
1100 HAY 94541 691-H7
COTTERELL CT
2000 PLE 94566 714-F1
COTTERELL DR
1200 SJS 95121 855-A5
COTTINGHAM CT
- WLCK 94598 612-H6
COTTLE AV
1500 SJS 95125 854-A5
COTTLE RD
- SJS 95193 875-B5
700 SJS 95123 875-B5
1800 SJS 95119 875-B5
6400 SCIC 95123 895-B1
COTTON AV
6100 NWK 94560 752-F7
COTTON CT
6000 SJS 95123 875-B6
18400 AlaC 94552 692-D3
COTTON PL
- MLPK 94025 790-F5
COTTON ST
300 MLPK 94025 790-F5
1000 OAK 94606 650-A7
COTTON TAIL AV
700 SJS 95116 834-H4
COTTONWOOD
- BEN 94510 551-B5
COTTONWOOD AV
700 SSF 94080 707-H2
800 HAY 94541 711-F3
COTTON WOOD CIR
6500 DBLN 94568 694-A2
COTTONWOOD CT
- HIL 94010 748-D1
100 HER 94547 570-A4
400 LVMR 94550 715-E1
2900 SCL 95051 833-A6
6300 CPTO 95014 852-F2
COTTONWOOD DR
- PLHL 94523 592-C2
- DALY 94014 687-D3
- SRFL 94901 567-C6
100 VAL 94591 530-F5
400 MPS 95035 813-J4
800 CPTO 95014 852-F2
2400 SBRN 94066 707-E6
3700 CNCD 94519 593-A1
3800 CCCo 94506 654-D5
COTTONWOOD LN
100 CCCo 94506 654-D5
7500 PLE 94588 713-J1
COTTONWOOD PL
- NVTO 94945 525-E2
100 CCCo 94506 654-D5
COTTONWOOD ST
1700 UNC 94587 732-C4
48200 FRMT 94539 793-J1
COTTRELL WY
900 SCIC 94305 810-J2
COTY WY
200 SJS 95136 874-G1
COUCH ST
100 VAL 94590 530-A3
500 VAL 94589 530-A3
COUGAR CIR
44900 FRMT 94539 773-J3
COUGAR DR
- FRMT 94539 773-J3
COUGAR LN
1200 CNCD 94521 593-B5
COUGAR PEAK CT
4900 ANT 94509 595-E3
COUGAR PEAK WY
- ANT 94509 595-E3
COUGHLAN ST
100 VAL 94590 529-J3
COULOMBE DR
4100 PA 94306 811-C3
COULTER PINE CT
1800 WLCK 94595 632-B1
COUNCIL CREST DR
- CMAD 94925 586-G7
COUNTESS CT
1100 SJS 95129 852-G4
7900 DBLN 94568 693-G3
COUNTESS DR
5900 SJS 95129 852-G3
COUNTESS ST
8300 DBLN 94568 693-G2
COUNTRY COM
38600 FRMT 94536 753-A4
COUNTRY DR
2000 FRMT 94536 753-A3
4100 FRMT 94536 752-J5
COUNTRY ISL
500 ALA 94501 669-G2
COUNTRY LN
- NVTO 94945 525-J2
- SMCo 94061 790-B2
- VAL 94590 550-C2
700 AlaC 94566 734-C1

COUNTRY LN
900 CCCo 94596 612-F6
1000 CCCo 94506 654-G6
4700 SJS 95129 852-J4
COUNTRY RUN
- HER 94547 569-H4
COUNTRY TER
38600 FRMT 94536 753-A4
COUNTRY WY
13300 LAH 94022 810-H7
COUNTRYBROOK
2400 SJS 95131 814-C4
COUNTRYBROOK LP
- SRMN 94583 673-F4
COUNTRY CLUB CIR
- AlaC 94566 714-B7
COUNTRY CLUB CT
3000 PA 94304 810-H7
COUNTRY CLUB DR
- HIL 94010 728-F7
- MLV 94941 606-E2
- NVTO 94949 546-C2
- SF 94132 666-J6
- ORIN 94563 631-A3
100 SSF 94080 707-G4
200 SMCo 94080 707-G4
700 MRGA 94556 631-D7
1000 CCCo 94549 591-H5
1000 MPS 95035 794-C4
1200 SCIC 94024 831-G3
3600 RDWC 94061 789-H3
5500 OAK 94618 630-A5
COUNTRY CLUB PKWY
5300 SJS 95138 855-F7
5300 SJS 95138 875-F1
COUNTRY CLUB PL
- PIT 94565 574-C3
- ORIN 94563 610-G7
3400 CCCo 94506 654-C4
COUNTRY CLUB TER
3400 CCCo 94506 654-C4
COUNTRY FIELDS LN
- SJS 95136 875-E2
COUNTRY FORGE LN
5200 SJS 95136 875-A3
COUNTRY HILLS CT
- DNVL 94506 653-G6
COUNTRY HILLS DR
4500 ANT 94509 595-F3
COUNTRY LEAF CT
3300 SJS 95132 814-G4
COUNTRY MEADOWS LN
200 DNVL 94506 653-J5
COUNTRY OAK CT
5200 SJS 95136 875-E2
COUNTRY OAK LN
- CCCo 94526 633-D4
- SJS 95136 875-E2
COUNTRY RUN DR
900 MRTZ 94553 571-G4
COUNTRYSIDE CT
- CCCo 94595 632-D1
- DNVL 94506 653-H6
COUNTRYSIDE DR
3200 SMTO 94403 748-J6
COUNTRYSIDE LN
5200 SJS 95136 875-A3
COUNTRY SPRING CT
11500 CPTO 95014 852-C4
COUNTRY SQUIRE CT
12100 SAR 95070 852-G5
COUNTRY SQUIRE DR
12100 SAR 95070 852-G5
COUNTRY SQUIRE LN
12000 SAR 95070 852-G5
COUNTRY SQUIRE WY
12100 SAR 95070 852-G5
COUNTRY VIEW CT
22600 SCIC 95119 895-E4
22600 SCIC 95139 895-E4
22600 SCIC 95120 895-E4
COUNTRYVIEW CT
100 VAL 94591 530-H5
COUNTRY VIEW DR
5300 RCH 94803 590-A3
22500 SCIC 95120 895-D5
22600 SCIC 95139 895-D5
COUNTRY VIEW LN
300 PLHL 94523 592-B1
22500 SCIC 95120 895-E5
COUNTRY VISTA CT
3900 SJS 95121 855-D4
COUNTRYWALK CIR
2700 SJS 95132 814-E3
COUNTRYWOOD CT
1600 WLCK 94598 612-E1
3600 SJS 95130 853-C4
COUNTRYWOOD DR
2700 ANT 94509 575-F7
COUNTY RD
- ALA 94502 670-A6
- SMCo 94062 789-A5
200 PCFA 94044 727-A1
200 PCFA 94044 726-J2
COUNTY ST
- DALY 94014 687-C5
COUNTY JAIL RD
- SMCo 94044 707-D7
COUNTYVIEW DR
300 MrnC 94965 626-E1
300 MrnC 94965 606-F7
COURAGEOUS CT
- ALA 94501 649-G7
COUR DU VIN
3500 SJS 95148 855-G1
COURT E
- DALY 94014 687-F3
COURT LN
700 CNCD 94518 592-J4
E COURT LN
- FCTY 94404 749-F2
COURT RD
- MLV 94941 606-D2
1000 NVTO 94945 526-B3
COURT ST
300 ALA 94501 670-A3
1000 SRFL 94901 586-G1
N COURT ST
- MRTZ 94553 571-D2
COURT ST N
500 MRTZ 94553 571-E3
COURTHOUSE DR
3100 UNC 94587 732-A4

COURTHOUSE PL
3100 UNC 94587 732-A4
COURTLAND AV
1000 MPS 95035 814-D1
1900 OAK 94601 670-D1
2200 OAK 94601 650-E7
2900 OAK 94619 650-F7
COURTLAND CT
900 MPS 95035 814-D1
COURTLAND DR
200 SBRN 94066 727-G2
2700 CNCD 94520 572-E7
COURTLAND RD
1600 BLMT 94002 769-E2
COURTLAND ST
600 RCH 94805 589-B5
COURTNEY AV
1700 SJS 95122 854-G1
COURTNEY LN
- AlaC 94542 712-D1
- CCCo 94506 654-C5
- MrnC 94920 606-H3
- ORIN 94563 631-A3
COURTRIGHT RD
100 SRFL 94901 586-F2
COURTSIDE DR
5200 SJS 95138 855-G7
COURTYARD DR
1400 SJS 95118 874-B2
COUTER LN
- MRGA 94556 631-C6
COVE CT
300 SLN 94578 691-C6
2000 SJS 95148 835-B6
COVE LN
- RDWC 94065 749-H6
COVE PL
- BLV 94920 607-D7
COVE RD
- ALA 94502 669-J5
- BLV 94920 607-D7
- BLV 94920 627-D1
COVE WY
- PIT 94565 573-J2
- CCCo 94565 573-J2
500 BEN 94510 551-A4
COVELITE LN
200 LVMR 94550 715-D2
COVELITE WY
2400 ANT 94509 595-G2
COVENTRY CIR
800 MPS 95035 794-A5
COVENTRY CT
- ANT 94509 575-E6
100 SCAR 94070 769-D5
800 SUNV 94087 832-F4
1900 CCCo 94595 632-C2
3300 FRMT 94536 752-J3
4300 UNC 94587 731-J5
COVENTRY DR
100 CMBL 95008 853-C5
3200 SJS 95127 835-A5
COVENTRY LN
- SF 94127 667-E6
26100 HAY 94545 711-G6
COVENTRY PL
- HER 94547 569-J3
400 CCCo 94506 654-A5
COVENTRY RD
200 CCCo 94707 609-E4
1200 CNCD 94518 592-H3
COVENTRY WY
100 VAL 94591 530-F4
800 MPS 95035 794-A5
4200 UNC 94587 731-J5
COVEWOOD CT
2900 SJS 95148 855-D1
COVEY CT
700 WLCK 94598 613-A3
COVEY WY
2400 LVMR 94550 715-H3
COVINA AV
- SJS 95123 874-J5
COVINA CT
12000 SAR 95070 852-E5
COVINA WY
700 FRMT 94539 773-H7
COVINGTON CT
100 SJS 95136 874-H1
900 LALT 94024 831-G2
1100 WLCK 94596 632-G1
COVINGTON DR
- OAK 94605 671-C6
- PIT 94565 574-C3
41500 FRMT 94539 753-F6
COVINGTON RD
100 LALT 94024 831-E1
800 BLMT 94002 769-C1
COVINGTON ST
- OAK 94605 671-C6
COVINGTON WY
500 LVMR 94550 695-E6
COWAN RD
800 BURL 94010 728-D3
3900 LFYT 94549 611-B4
COWBARN LN
- NVTO 94947 526-D7
COWBOY AL
400 LVMR 94550 715-H1
COWDEN PL
13100 LAH 94022 831-A1
COWELL LN
- ATN 94027 790-D5
400 SCIC 94305 810-H1
COWELL PL
- SF 94111 648-B4
- SF 94111 648-B4
COWELL RD
2700 CNCD 94518 592-G3
3900 CNCD 94521 592-J4
4000 CNCD 94518 593-A5
4000 CNCD 94521 593-A5
4500 CCCo 94518 593-A5
4500 CCCo 94521 593-A5
14600 LGTS 95032 893-C2
16000 SCIC 95032 893-C2
COWELL ST
16500 AlaC 94578 691-G4
COWING RD
8200 AlaC 94542 693-A6
8200 AlaC 94542 692-G5

COWLES ST
- SF 94129 647-C3
COWPENS WY
- SMCo 94402 768-G1
COWPER AV
- CCCo 94708 609-F2
- CCCo 94805 609-F2
COWPER CT
1500 SJS 95120 874-A7
3400 PA 94306 791-D7
COWPER ST
100 PA 94301 790-J4
800 PA 94301 791-A5
1100 BERK 94702 629-E2
2500 PA 94306 791-C7
COX AV
18500 SAR 95070 852-E6
COY DR
100 SJS 95123 874-J3
COYNE CT
2100 SJS 95122 834-J7
COYOTE CIR
2000 CLAY 94517 593-H5
COYOTE CT
- SRMN 94583 673-G3
900 ANT 94509 595-F1
COYOTE PL
- SRMN 94583 673-F3
COYOTE RD
400 SJS 95111 855-A7
700 SJS 95111 875-C1
700 SCIC 95111 875-C2
700 SCIC 95111 855-A7
45300 FRMT 94539 773-H4
COYOTE ST
600 MPS 95035 793-J6
COYOTE CREEK CIR
300 SJS 95116 834-D4
COYOTE CREEK CT
1200 SJS 95116 834-D4
COYOTE CREEK PL
1200 SJS 95116 834-D4
COYOTE HILL
- PTLV 94028 830-C1
COYOTE HILL RD
3100 SCIC 94304 810-J3
3100 PA 94304 811-A3
3100 SCIC 94304 811-A3
COYOTE POINT DR
1600 SMTO 94401 728-J6
1700 SMTO 94401 729-A5
COYOTE RANCH RD
5800 SCIC 95137 875-H7
5800 SCIC 95137 895-J1
5900 SJS 95137 895-J2
5900 SCIC 95137 895-J2
COZETTE LN
19100 SCIC 95014 852-G1
COZUMEL CIR
2800 SCL 95051 833-A4
COZY CT
500 SJS 95123 874-J7
COZY DR
500 SJS 95123 874-J6
COZZOLINO CT
- MLBR 94030 727-J3
CRABAPPLE WY
500 SJS 95111 854-J6
CRABTREE AV
18600 SCIC 95014 852-H1
CRACOLICE WY
1200 MPS 95035 814-D2
CRAFT AV
800 ELCR 94530 609-F2
14600 SLN 94578 691-D3
CRAFT DR
10000 CPTO 95014 852-G1
CRAG CT
- HER 94547 569-H4
CRAGMONT AV
- SF 94116 667-C4
400 BERK 94708 609-H5
N CRAGMONT AV
- SCIC 95127 835-A1
- SCIC 95127 834-J1
S CRAGMONT AV
- SCIC 95127 835-A1
200 SJS 95127 835-A1
CRAGMONT CT
- CCCo 94598 612-D4
- PCFA 94044 707-A4
- SMTO 94403 748-J6
CRAGMONT DR
100 CCCo 94598 612-E4
CRAGMONT WY
- WDSD 94062 789-H4
CRAGS CT
- SF 94131 667-F5
CRAGWOOD LN
1500 SJS 95127 835-A5
CRAIG AV
- PDMT 94611 650-B1
600 CMBL 95008 853-C7
CRAIG CT
300 DALY 94014 687-C5
500 NVTO 94949 546-E1
2300 MTVW 94043 811-G3
2500 AlaC 94546 692-B7
20600 CPTO 95014 852-D1
CRAIG DR
1000 SJS 95129 852-F3
1200 CNCD 94518 592-H3
CRAIG RD
500 HIL 94010 748-D3
CRAIG ST
38200 FRMT 94536 753-A3
CRAIG WY
100 LGTS 95032 873-E6
CRAIGEN CIR
20200 SAR 95070 852-E6
CRAIGTOWN LN
- DBLN 94552 693-E5
CRAILFORD CT
1300 SJS 95121 855-B5
CRAMER CT
2700 SJS 95111 854-G4
CRAN PL
- SF 94117 647-G7
CRANBERRY AV
1100 SUNV 94087 832-B3
CRANBERRY CIR
7900 CPTO 95014 852-C2

STREET Block City ZIP Pg-Grid

CRANBERRY DR
900 CPTO 95014 852-C2
CRANBROOK CT
6400 SJS 95120 894-D1
CRANBROOK ST
15500 SLN 94579 691-A7
15600 SLN 94579 711-A1
CRANBROOK WY
2200 CNCD 94520 572-F5
CRANDALL ST
500 SJS 95110 834-A7
CRANDALLWOOD DR
4900 FRMT 94555 752-C2
CRANDANO CT
1100 SUNV 94087 832-B3
CRANE AV
600 FCTY 94404 749-G1
600 LVMR 94550 695-E7
1700 MTVW 94040 831-H1
5100 AlaC 94546 692-C3
CRANE CT
- ORIN 94563 610-G3
100 ALA 94502 669-J5
100 VAL 94591 530-F5
100 HER 94547 569-H4
1600 SJS 95112 833-J1
CRANE ST
- SF 94124 688-B1
900 MLPK 94025 790-F3
CRANE TER
- ORIN 94563 610-G3
38700 FRMT 94536 753-D2
CRANE WY
3200 OAK 94602 650-G3
CRANE RIDGE RD
5400 AlaC 94550 716-G6
CRANFIELD AV
- BLMT 94002 769-D4
- SMCo 94002 769-D3
- SMCo 94070 769-D3
- BLMT 94070 769-D3
600 SCAR 94070 769-D3
CRANFORD CIR
4000 SJS 95124 873-E3
CRANFORD LN
7800 DBLN 94568 693-H3
CRANFORD WY
11700 OAK 94605 671-D6
CRANHAM CT
- PCFA 94044 727-A5
CRANLEIGH DR
- SF 94132 667-C6
CRANSTON RD
- SF 94129 647-C3
CRANWOOD CT
3100 PLE 94588 694-F6
CRANWORTH CIR
2000 SJS 95121 855-C4
CRATER LN
2800 SJS 95132 814-F5
CRATER RD
2600 LVMR 94550 715-G5
CRATER LAKE AV
1500 MPS 95035 794-E7
1500 MPS 95035 814-D1
CRATER LAKE CT
500 SUNV 94087 832-D4
6100 PLE 94588 714-B1
CRATER LAKE WY
- PCFA 94044 727-B5
200 SRFL 94903 566-F2
CRATER PEAK WY
1800 ANT 94509 595-F3
CRAUT ST
100 SF 94112 667-G7
CRAVEN CT
400 HAY 94541 711-G3
CRAVEN ST
100 VAL 94590 529-H3
CRAVENS CT
300 SJS 95133 834-G2
CRAWDAD CT
3500 UNC 94587 732-A5
CRAWFORD CT
- CCCo 94595 612-B7
46600 FRMT 94539 773-H6
CRAWFORD DR
500 SUNV 94087 832-D2
CRAWFORD PL
3700 AlaC 94546 692-A4
CRAWFORD ST
2700 CNCD 94518 592-G2
46700 FRMT 94539 773-H6
CRAWFORD WY
- AMCN 94589 510-A3
100 AMCN 94589 509-J3
CRAY CT
3000 SJS 95121 854-J4
CRAYCROFT CT
48400 FRMT 94539 793-J1
CRAYCROFT DR
300 FRMT 94539 793-J1
CRAYDON CIR
9000 SRMN 94583 693-J1
CRAYDON CT
- SRMN 94583 693-H1
CRAYSIDE LN
12200 SAR 95070 852-D6
CRAZY PETES RD
- SMCo 94028 830-C6
CREAGER CT
3700 SJS 95130 853-C4
CRECIENTA DR
- SAUS 94965 627-A3
CRECIENTA LN
- SAUS 94965 627-A3
CREE CT
- SRMN 94583 673-D5
600 SJS 95123 874-H6
700 WLCK 94598 612-H3
1400 FRMT 94539 773-G3
CREE DR
600 SJS 95123 874-H6
CREE RD
1400 FRMT 94539 773-G3
CREED AV
100 ANT 94509 575-C6
CREED RD
800 OAK 94610 650-C3
CREED ST
1100 MPS 95035 794-C4

CREEDEN WY
2100 LALT 94022 811-F5
2100 MTVW 94040 811-F5
CREEDON CIR
200 ALA 94502 669-H5
CREEK DR
600 MLPK 94025 790-G5
E CREEK DR
100 MLPK 94025 790-H3
N CREEK DR
200 SJS 95139 895-F1
CREEK LN
- MLV 94941 606-D3
E CREEK PL
- MLPK 94025 790-H4
CREEK RD
- CCCo 94553 571-H3
100 FRFX 94930 566-A6
100 SANS 94960 566-A6
1700 LVMR 94550 715-G2
27400 HAY 94544 712-A6
CREEK TR
- SANS 94960 566-A5
CREEK BANK CT
6500 SJS 95120 894-F1
CREEK BED CT
2200 SCL 95054 813-C5
CREEKDALE RD
100 CCCo 94595 632-C2
CREEK ESTATES
5100 SJS 95135 855-G5
CREEK ESTATES CT
3000 SJS 95135 855-G5
CREEKFIELD DR
600 SJS 95136 854-E7
CREEKLAND CIR
700 SJS 95133 834-E2
CREEKLEDGE CT
- DNVL 94506 653-F1
CREEKLINE DR
7800 CPTO 95014 852-C2
CREEKMORE CT
600 WLCK 94598 612-J3
CREEKMORE WY
3100 SJS 95148 835-F7
CREEK PARK DR
- PTLV 94028 810-E7
CREEKPOINT CT
4100 CCCo 94506 654-C5
CREEKPOINT DR
2900 SJS 95133 814-G6
CREEKRIDGE CT
- SMTO 94402 748-C7
CREEKRIDGE LN
- CNCD 94518 592-H4
CREEKSIDE AV
1000 DNVL 94506 653-F5
CREEKSIDE CIR
10500 OAK 94603 690-G1
CREEKSIDE CT
- CMAD 94925 606-H2
- NVTO 94945 526-A2
100 CCCo 94803 589-E3
2400 HAY 94542 712-D4
11200 DBLN 94568 693-E3
17300 MSER 95030 873-A4
22000 CPTO 95014 832-A7
CREEKSIDE DR
- PLE 94588 693-H6
- SRMN 94583 673-A2
- LKSP 94939 586-E5
100 PA 94306 811-E2
1300 WLCK 94596 612-D7
1400 WLCK 94596 632-D1
2700 SJS 95132 814-E3
3100 SJS 95131 814-A4
3300 SLN 94578 691-C5
7700 DBLN 94568 693-F3
N CREEKSIDE DR
- ANT 94509 574-J6
S CREEKSIDE DR
- ANT 94509 574-J7
CREEKSIDE LN
1800 CNCD 94521 593-E4
CREEKSIDE PL
700 SCL 95051 833-A5
CREEKSIDE RD
400 PLHL 94523 592-A5
CREEKSIDE TER
37100 FRMT 94536 752-H2
CREEK SIDE WY
- MrnC 94920 606-H3
CREEKSIDE WY
700 CMBL 95008 853-F5
CREEKSTONE CIR
1700 SJS 95133 834-E2
CREEK TREE LN
- CCCo 94507 632-F5
CREEK VIEW CIR
- LKSP 94939 586-E5
CREEKVIEW CT
6300 MRTZ 94553 591-H3
6600 SJS 95120 894-G1
CREEKVIEW DR
100 VAL 94591 530-E2
CREEKVIEW MDW CT
- SJS 95135 855-H7
CREEKVIEW MDW LN
- SJS 95135 855-H7
CREEKWOOD CT
- DNVL 94526 653-C6
3100 PLE 94588 713-J2
CREEKWOOD DR
1000 SJS 95129 852-J3
4600 FRMT 94555 752-D2
CREEKWOOD PL
900 LFYT 94549 611-G6
CREEKWOOD WY
- HIL 94010 748-H3
CREELY AV
5000 RCH 94804 609-B2
CREELY PTH
5000 RCH 94804 609-A2
CREIGHTON CT
1200 MPS 95035 814-C1
CREIGHTON PL
3300 SCL 95051 832-J2
CREIGHTON WY
100 DNVL 94506 653-H5
300 OAK 94619 650-H4
CRELLIN RD
800 PLE 94566 714-G4

CRENNA AV
3600 CNCD 94519 592-J1
CRENSHAW CT
100 PCFA 94044 707-A2
6500 SJS 95120 894-E1
CRENSHAW DR
- DALY 94015 707-A2
- PCFA 94044 707-A2
CREOLE PL
26900 HAY 94545 711-G7
CRESCENDO AV
4100 SJS 95136 874-G1
CRESCENT AV
- SAUS 94965 627-A4
- SF 94112 667-H6
- SF 94110 667-H6
100 BURL 94010 728-G7
100 PTLV 94028 810-C7
100 PTLV 94028 830-C1
100 SUNV 94087 832-E3
400 SMTO 94402 728-G7
400 SMTO 94402 748-G1
1400 AlaC 94546 691-J7
1400 AlaC 94546 692-A7
CRESCENT CT
- CPTO 95014 832-A7
- NVTO 94947 526-A3
100 VAL 94591 530-D4
2600 LVMR 94550 715-H3
3600 LFYT 94549 611-E6
17000 LGTS 95032 893-C1
E CRESCENT DR
- SRFL 94901 566-E7
500 PA 94301 791-B3
W CRESCENT DR
- SRFL 94901 566-D7
500 PA 94301 791-B3
CRESCENT LN
- SANS 94960 586-B1
25400 LAH 94022 831-C2
CRESCENT RD
- CMAD 94925 586-F7
100 SANS 94960 586-B1
10000 CPTO 95014 832-A7
CRESCENT ST
400 OAK 94610 649-J2
CRESCENT TER
- FRMT 94536 753-B2
600 SUNV 94087 832-E3
CRESCENT WY
900 AlaC 94586 734-B3
CRESCENTA CT
1100 LFYT 94549 611-F5
CRESCIO CT
- SF 94112 687-E2
CRESENT TER
1000 MPS 95035 814-E1
CRESENT RIDGE TR
- CCCo - 611-C1
CRESPI CT
3500 PLE 94566 714-G5
4000 SLN 94578 691-C5
CRESPI DR
- SF 94132 687-B1
500 PCFA 94044 726-H3
800 SLN 94578 691-C5
1000 PCFA 94044 727-A3
1100 SUNV 94086 812-C6
1400 SJS 95129 852-J5
CREST AV
- CCCo 94595 632-D1
- RCH 94801 608-D1
400 CCCo 94507 632-D1
1500 CCCo 94805 589-C5
2500 AlaC 94578 691-G3
7600 OAK 94605 671-A2
18100 AlaC 94546 691-G3
N CREST AV
2200 CCCo 94553 571-F4
S CREST AV
2200 CCCo 94553 571-F4
2500 AlaC 94578 691-G4
2500 AlaC 94546 691-G4
CREST CT
- CCCo 94595 632-D2
2600 UNC 94587 732-C4
4000 PLE 94588 694-A7
CREST DR
300 SCIC 95127 815-A6
400 SMCo 94062 789-G1
CREST LN
- VAL 94591 510-J3
2300 MLPK 94025 790-D7
32200 UNC 94587 732-C4
CREST RD
- SANS 94960 566-C7
- SANS 94960 586-D1
- BLV 94920 627-D1
- LFYT 94549 611-A6
- MrnC 94945 526-H2
- PDMT 94611 650-D2
- ROSS 94957 586-D1
100 WDSD 94062 789-H4
CREST ST
200 ANT 94509 575-E4
CRESTA CIR
- SRFL 94903 566-F1
CRESTA DR
100 SRFL 94903 566-F1
CRESTA LN
11300 DBLN 94568 693-F5
CRESTA WY
- SRFL 94903 566-F1
CRESTA BLANCA
- ORIN 94563 610-F6
CRESTA BLANCA CT
3000 PLE 94566 714-H4
CRESTA VISTA DR
- SF 94127 667-D6
CRESTA VISTA LN
500 PTLV 94028 810-D5
CRESTA VISTA WY
200 SJS 95119 875-C6

CRESTBROOK DR
19600 SAR 95070 872-F1
CREST ESTATES DR
- CCCo 94595 632-D1
CRESTFIELD CIR
- AlaC 94542 692-E6
CRESTFIELD DR
- AlaC 94542 692-E7
1300 SJS 95125 854-B7
CRESTHAVEN CT
5000 ANT 94509 595-E4
CRESTHAVEN DR
- MrnC 94903 566-H3
CRESTHAVEN LN
1400 SJS 95118 874-B2
CRESTHAVEN ST
2200 MPS 95035 814-E1
CRESTLAKE DR
- SF 94132 667-A5
500 SF 94116 667-A5
CRESTLINE AV
- DALY 94015 687-A5
CRESTLINE CT
2800 ANT 94509 595-G1
CRESTLINE DR
- SF 94131 667-F3
1100 CPTO 95014 852-D3
CRESTLINE RD
1800 PLE 94566 714-C1
CRESTLINE WY
5200 PLE 94566 714-C1
CRESTMONT AV
5500 LVMR 94550 696-C2
7600 NWK 94560 752-C6
CRESTMONT DR
- OAK 94619 650-H4
- SF 94131 667-D3
- SF 94122 667-D3
- OAK 94602 650-H4
1100 LFYT 94549 611-D5
1800 SJS 95124 853-H7
CRESTMONT PL
3700 LFYT 94549 611-D5
CRESTMOOR CIR
100 PCFA 94044 707-A2
CRESTMOOR CT
700 SJS 95129 852-J2
CRESTMOOR DR
600 SJS 95129 852-J2
2100 SBRN 94066 707-F7
2600 SBRN 94066 727-F1
CRESTOAK CT
6000 SJS 95120 874-C7
CRESTON AV
- DALY 94015 686-J4
CRESTON DR
10200 CPTO 95014 832-A6
10400 SCIC 94024 832-A6
CRESTON LN
1100 SJS 95122 834-G7
CRESTON RD
600 BERK 94708 609-H4
2800 WLCK 94596 612-A2
CRESTON ST
40700 FRMT 94538 773-B1
CRESTONE NEEDLE WY
4700 ANT 94509 595-D3
CRESTONE PEAK CT
4700 ANT 94509 595-D3
CRESTPARK CIR
5000 ANT 94509 595-J4
CRESTPOINT DR
1200 SJS 95131 834-C1
CRESTRIDGE CT
- DNVL 94506 653-H6
CRESTRIDGE DR
100 DNVL 94506 653-H6
11400 SCIC 94024 831-E4
19400 SCIC 95030 872-F5
CREST RIDGE LN
1100 CNCD 94521 593-D6
CRESTVIEW
- CCCo 94525 550-C5
CRESTVIEW AV
- DALY 94015 686-J5
500 BLMT 94002 749-E7
600 MRTZ 94553 571-G5
CRESTVIEW COM
- FRMT 94539 794-B1
CREST VIEW CT
- ORIN 94563 631-A4
CRESTVIEW CT
- CCCo 94549 611-H1
100 SCAR 94070 769-E6
2400 AlaC 94578 691-F4
CREST VIEW DR
- ORIN 94563 631-A4
100 ORIN 94563 630-J3
CRESTVIEW DR
- OAK 94619 651-B7
- MrnC 94903 566-H3
- SJS 95117 833-D7
100 SCAR 94070 769-C4
200 SCL 95050 833-D7
600 SMCo 94070 769-D6
700 MLBR 94030 727-H3
700 PIN 94564 569-C4
1000 MTVW 94040 832-B1
1200 ANT 94509 575-B5
1600 SCIC 94024 831-G4
2100 PIT 94565 574-C4
CRESTVIEW LN
2100 PIT 94565 574-D3
CREST VIEW TER
- ORIN 94563 630-J3
CRESTWELL WK
- SF 94122 667-C3
CRESTWOOD CIR
4400 CNCD 94521 593-C2
CRESTWOOD CT
900 SUNV 94089 812-J5
1400 SMTO 94403 748-J7
1800 CNCD 94521 593-C2
5000 PLE 94566 714-D2
CRESTWOOD DR
- CCCo 94806 569-A6
- DALY 94015 687-A3
- SRFL 94901 566-D6
1000 SSF 94080 707-F1
1300 SJS 95118 854-B7
1400 SBRN 94066 707-F5
1500 SMTO 94403 748-H7

CRESTWOOD DR
1800 ANT 94509 575-E6
6400 AlaC 94552 692-F3
CRESTWOOD PL
200 SRMN 94583 673-F6
CRESTWOOD ST
4000 FRMT 94538 773-D2
CREWE CT
1800 SJS 95132 814-F3
CRIBARI BEND
5400 SJS 95135 855-H5
CRIBARI CIR
5300 SJS 95135 855-H5
CRIBARI CT
5400 SJS 95135 855-H5
CRIBARI GN
5300 SJS 95135 855-H5
CRIBARI HTS
5300 SJS 95135 855-H5
CRIBARI LN
5000 SJS 95135 855-H5
CRIBARI PL
5000 SJS 95135 855-H5
CRIBARI BLUFFS
5000 SJS 95135 855-H5
CRIBARI CORNER
5200 SJS 95135 855-H5
CRIBARI CREST
5300 SJS 95135 855-H5
CRIBARI DALE
5200 SJS 95135 855-H5
CRIBARI DELL
5300 SJS 95135 855-H5
CRIBARI HILLS
5300 SJS 95135 855-H5
CRIBARI KNOLLS
5100 SJS 95135 855-H5
CRIBARI VALE
5000 SJS 95135 855-H5
CRICKET HILL CT
- HAY 94541 712-A2
CRICKET HILL RD
- LFYT 94549 611-A4
CRICKLEWOOD DR
- NVTO 94947 526-D7
CRIDER CT
100 LGTS 95032 873-J7
CRIMSON CIR
5400 FRMT 94538 773-A1
CRIMSON CT
1200 WLCK 94596 632-G2
CRIMSON DR
5900 SJS 95120 874-B7
CRIMSONBERRY WY
500 SJS 95129 852-B7
CRINAN DR
1800 SJS 95122 854-G1
CRINGLE DR
500 RDWC 94065 749-H7
CRIPPLERIDGE CT
- SMTO 94402 748-C7
CRIPPS PL
36000 FRMT 94536 752-F3
CRIQUET CT
1500 CNCD 94518 592-E6
CRISANTO AV
1900 MTVW 94040 811-G3
CRISFIELD LN
4100 PLE 94566 714-E1
CRISP AV
19100 SAR 95070 872-G3
CRISP RD
- SF 94124 668-D7
CRISSY FIELD AV
- SF 94129 647-C3
CRIST DR
1900 LALT 94024 832-A5
CRIST ST
2500 ALA 94501 670-A3
CRISTICH LN
- CMBL 95008 853-E7
CRISTINA AV
1200 SJS 95125 854-B3
CRISTOBAL WY
4000 PLE 94566 714-E2
CRISTO REY DR
22500 CPTO 95014 831-H6
22500 SCIC 94024 831-H6
22900 LALT 94024 831-H6
23700 SCIC 95014 831-H6
CRISTY WY
4400 AlaC 94546 692-A3
4400 AlaC 94546 691-J3
CRITTENDEN LN
- MTVW 94043 791-J7
2000 MTVW 94043 792-A7
CRITTENDEN ST
5400 OAK 94601 670-E2
CRIVELLO AV
- CCCo 94565 573-H2
CROAK RD
3400 AlaC 94568 694-H5
3400 DBLN 94568 694-H5
CROATIAN WY
33200 UNC 94587 732-D5
CROCE CT
4200 PLE 94566 714-F4
CROCKER AV
- DALY 94014 687-D3
- PDMT 94611 650-C1
100 PDMT 94610 650-C2
200 OAK 94610 650-C2
900 SMCo 94014 687-E3
1400 HAY 94544 732-C2
2800 SMCo 94063 770-D7
CROCKER CT
- SJS 95111 875-A2
CROCKER DR
- SJS 95111 875-B2
CROCKER WY
2200 SCL 95051 832-J2
2500 ANT 94509 595-G5
CROCKETT AV
600 CMBL 95008 853-E7
900 CMBL 95008 873-B1
CROCKETT BLVD
1300 CCCo 94525 550-D5
1500 CCCo - 550-D5
CROCKETT CT
4500 FRMT 94538 753-B7
CROCKETT DR
- MRGA 94556 651-F1

CROCKETT LN
1700 HIL 94010 728-E6
CROCKETT PL
5100 OAK 94602 650-H3
CROCKETT ST
40100 FRMT 94538 753-B7
CROCUS CT
- SMCo 94025 790-E6
1000 SUNV 94086 832-H2
37600 NWK 94560 752-F7
CROCUS DR
600 SLN 94578 691-C4
4400 SJS 95136 874-F2
CROCUS WY
5100 LVMR 94550 696-B4
CROFT DR
2700 SJS 95148 855-D2
CROFTERS CT
3700 PLE 94588 694-F5
CROFTON AV
400 OAK 94610 650-A2
400 PDMT 94610 650-A2
CROFTON CT
600 LFYT 94549 631-H2
CROFTON WY
3800 SSF 94080 707-C4
CROKAERTS ST
2000 WLCK 94596 612-C4
CROLLS GARDEN CT
100 ALA 94501 669-F1
CROLONA HGTS DR
- CCCo 94525 550-D4
CROMART CT
100 SUNV 94087 832-E4
2000 MRTZ 94553 571-J7
CROMMELIN RD
25000 AlaC 94545 711-D6
CROMPTON RD
600 RDWC 94061 789-H1
CROMWELL AV
- DBLN 94568 694-A2
CROMWELL CT
- DNVL 94526 653-C4
CROMWELL PL
3000 HAY 94542 712-D3
34100 FRMT 94555 732-E7
CROMWELL RW
2600 SSF 94080 707-C4
CROMWELL ST
900 LVMR 94550 695-G6
CROMWELL WY
2200 LVMR 94550 695-G6
CRONER AV
1700 MLPK 94025 790-E5
1700 SMCo 94025 790-E5
CRONIN
- DBLN 94568 693-G4
CRONIN CT
100 VAL 94589 510-D6
CRONIN DR
- SCL 95051 833-A7
800 VAL 94589 510-D6
CRONIN TER
34200 FRMT 94555 752-C2
CRONWELL DR
1900 CMBL 95008 853-G5
1900 SCIC 95125 853-G5
CROOK ST
- SF 94129 647-E3
CROOKED AV
- SANS 94960 566-D6
CROOKED CREEK DR
11400 LALT 94024 831-G4
CROPLEY AV
2500 SJS 95132 814-F2
CROPLEY CT
3300 SJS 95132 814-F2
CROSBY AV
1900 OAK 94601 650-D7
CROSBY CT
- CCCo 94553 572-B7
- WLCK 94598 612-D3
100 SBRN 94066 707-E7
2700 SCL 95051 833-B3
6700 SJS 95129 852-E3
CROSBY DR
9600 PLE 94586 693-F6
CROSBY PL
600 SLN 94579 691-B5
4100 PA 94306 811-C4
CROSBY ST
14700 SLN 94579 691-B5
CROSLEY CT
3300 SJS 95132 814-G3
CROSS RD
100 CCCo 94526 633-B6
100 OAK 94618 630-B5
3000 AlaC 94550 716-H3
CROSS ST
- SF 94112 687-F2
800 PIT 94565 574-F3
CROSS WY
- LGTS 95032 893-B1
1500 SJS 95125 854-C3
2500 CNCD 94520 592-F3
CROSSBOW CT
1000 SJS 95120 874-E6
CROSS BRIDGE CT
- DNVL 94526 653-F4
CROSS BRIDGE DR
200 DNVL 94526 653-E4
CROSS BRIDGE PL
- DNVL 94526 653-F4
CROSSBROOK CT
- SJS 95120 874-E6
800 MRGA 94556 631-D6
CROSSBROOK DR
700 MRGA 94556 631-D5
CROSS CAMPUS RD
- BERK 94720 629-H2
CROSS CREEK CIR
- DBLN 94568 694-A2
CROSS CREEK PL
- LKSP 94939 586-E5
1500 LVMR 94550 715-G2
CROSS CREEK RD
1500 WLCK 94596 612-D7
CROSS CREEK WY
- NVTO 94945 526-E3
CROSSFIELD CT
6000 SJS 95120 874-E6

CROSSGATES LN
1200 SJS 95120 874-C7
CROSSING CT
- HAY 94544 711-H4
CROSSLEES DR
400 SJS 95111 875-C2
CROSSMAN AV
1200 SUNV 94089 812-G3
CROSSMILL CT
2800 SJS 95121 854-J3
CROSSMONT CIR
5900 SJS 95120 874-D6
5900 SCIC 95120 874-D6
CROSSMONT CT
6000 SJS 95120 874-D6
CROSS OVER DR
300 SF - 647-A7
300 SF - 667-B1
CROSS OVER DR
Rt#-1
1000 SF - 667-B1
CROSSPOINT CT
1000 SJS 95120 874-D6
CROSSPOINTE COM
38400 FRMT 94536 753-G3
CROSSRIDGE CT
600 ORIN 94563 610-H6
CROSSRIDGE PL
- ORIN 94563 610-H6
CROSSRIDGE RD
7700 DBLN 94568 694-A2
CROSSRIDGE TER
- ORIN 94563 610-H6
CROSSROADS
700 NVTO 94947 526-D7
CROSS SPRINGS CT
1000 SJS 95120 874-D6
CROSS SPRINGS DR
1000 SJS 95120 874-D6
CROSSVIEW CIR
6000 SJS 95120 874-D6
CROSSVIEW CT
5900 SJS 95120 874-D6
CROSSWAY RD
700 BURL 94010 728-F6
S CROSSWAYS
- BERK 94705 630-A4
CROSSWIND CT
100 HER 94547 570-A6
1000 SJS 95120 874-D6
CROTHERS RD
10200 SCIC 95127 815-C6
10200 SJS 95127 815-B6
16400 SCIC 95127 835-D1
CROTHERS WY
300 SCIC 94305 790-H7
CROW CT
- PLE 94588 694-G7
- ANT 94509 574-J4
400 SJS 95123 874-H4
1600 FRMT 94539 773-G4
1600 SUNV 94087 832-E5
CROW LN
5600 SJS 95123 874-H4
CROW PL
100 CLAY 94517 593-J5
CROW CANYON CT
- SRMN 94583 673-B1
CROW CANYON PL
2000 SRMN 94583 673-C1
4600 AlaC 94552 692-C5
CROW CANYON RD
2300 CCCo 94583 673-A2
2300 CCCo 94583 672-G3
2400 SRMN 94583 673-D1
3200 DNVL 94526 673-D1
3500 SRMN 94583 653-G7
3500 DNVL 94526 653-G7
3700 AlaC 94552 692-E2
7600 AlaC 94552 672-G3
8000 DNVL 94506 653-G7
CROW CREEK RD
- AlaC 94552 692-D4
CROWDER AV
1800 SJS 95124 873-H3
CROWE PL
1000 CNCD 94518 592-J4
CROWLEY AV
100 PIT 94565 574-C3
1100 SCL 95051 833-B4
CROWLEY CT
- PIT 94565 574-C3
CROWLEY DR
24300 HAY 94545 711-F4
CROWN AV
6200 OAK 94611 630-D6
CROWN BLVD
6500 SJS 95120 894-E2
CROWN CIR
- SSF 94080 707-D2
CROWN CT
- MLV 94941 606-E3
- SMCo 94402 768-H1
- SMTO 94402 768-H1
- ORIN 94563 631-C4
1200 WLCK 94596 612-B3
2600 UNC 94587 732-C4
5400 AlaC 94552 692-D4
CROWN DR
1300 ALA 94501 669-F2
CROWN RD
100 MrnC 94904 586-B4
CROWN TER
- SF 94114 667-E2
CROWN FIRE RD
100 MrnC 94904 586-B4
CROWN POINT CT
- MrnC 94901 586-J1
- SRFL 94901 586-J1
CROWNPOINTE DR
100 VAL 94591 530-F7
CROWN RIDGE COM
- FRMT 94539 794-B1
CROWNRIDGE DR
- DNVL 94506 653-G1
CROWNRIDGE TER
- DNVL 94506 653-G2
CROWN VALLEY CT
- DNVL 94506 653-H6
CROWS NEST CIR
300 HER 94547 570-B6

STREET Block City ZIP Pg-Grid

CROWSNEST CT
100 VAL 94591 550-F2
CROWS NEST WY
1000 RCH 94803 589-H3
CROXTON AV
- OAK 94611 649-H1
CROYDEN CT
500 SUNV 94087 832-E4
2400 SLN 94577 691-B2
CROYDEN DR
200 PLHL 94523 592-A6
CROYDEN PL
2200 SLN 94577 691-B2
CROYDEN WY
100 WDSD 94062 789-H5
CROYDON AV
5600 SJS 95118 874-C4
CROYDON CIR
- PDMT 94611 650-D2
CROYDON PL
4900 NWK 94560 752-E3
CRSTAL COVE CT
- RCH 94804 608-J3
CRUCERO AV
1900 SPAB 94806 568-J7
CRUCERO CT
- SPAB 94806 568-J7
1400 SJS 95122 834-G7
CRUCERO DR
1300 SJS 95122 834-G7
CRUCERO ST
- VAL 94591 550-D1
CRUCILLO CT
47100 FRMT 94539 773-J6
CRUDEN BAY CIR
5000 SJS 95138 855-E6
CRUDEN BAY WY
5000 SJS 95138 855-E6
CRUISER CT
- SLN 94579 711-A1
CRUISER DR
- SLN 94579 691-F3
- SLN 94579 711-A1
CRUMP CT
5800 SJS 95120 874-B6
CRUZ CT
40800 FRMT 94539 753-E6
CRYER ST
2200 HAY 94545 711-F7
CRYSTAL AV
2300 CNCD 94520 572-F7
CRYSTAL CIR
- HER 94547 569-G4
1100 LVMR 94550 715-D3
CRYSTAL CT
- MPS 95035 794-A7
- MrnC 94920 606-H3
100 NVTO 94949 546-D1
100 SBRN 94066 727-H2
100 VAL 94589 510-B6
600 PLE 94566 714-E5
900 FCTY 94404 749-F5
1000 WLCK 94598 612-G4
1100 LVMR 94550 715-D3
3700 AlaC 94546 692-B6
CRYSTAL DR
1400 HIL 94010 748-E5
2400 SCL 95051 833-A1
CRYSTAL LN
600 PLE 94566 714-E5
CRYSTAL ST
- SF 94112 687-D2
CRYSTAL TER
- SMCo 94010 728-B7
4900 FRMT 94555 752-A3
CRYSTAL WY
- BERK 94708 609-H6
CRYSTALBERRY TER
500 SJS 95129 853-B2
CRYSTAL CREEK
- LKSP 94939 586-E5
CRYSTAL CREEK DR
2900 SJS 95133 814-G6
CRYSTAL GATE COMS
- HAY 94544 711-H3
CRYSTAL GATE CT
- HAY 94544 711-H3
CRYSTAL GLEN LN
800 SCL 95050 833-D1
CRYSTALINE DR
400 FRMT 94539 773-H4
CRYSTALINE PL
400 FRMT 94539 773-H5
CRYSTAL RIDGE CT
5000 OAK 94605 671-A1
CRYSTAL SPRING TER
- HIL 94010 748-F4
CRYSTAL SPRINGS CT
600 CCCo 94506 654-D5
6700 SJS 95120 894-D2
CRYSTAL SPRINGS DR
6400 SJS 95120 894-D2
CRYSTAL SPRINGS RD
- HIL 94010 748-H3
- SMTO 94402 748-H3
600 SBRN 94066 727-H1
1200 SMCo 94402 748-E6
1800 SMCo 94010 748-E6
1900 SMCo - 748-E6
2800 SMCo 94030 727-G3
CRYSTAL SPRINGS TER
- HIL 94010 748-G4
CRYSTAL SPRINGS TR
- SMCo 94062 789-D4
- WDSD 94062 789-D4
CRYSTAL SPRINGS WY
- SJS 95123 875-G2
CRYSTYL RANCH PKWY
- CNCD - 613-C1
CTE D L CANADA LN
- CCCo 94553 591-D3
CUADRA CT
2200 PIN 94564 569-E3
CUARDO AV
200 MLBR 94030 728-B3
CUBA AL
- SF 94127 667-F5
CUBBERLEY CT
28300 HAY 94545 731-H2
CUBBERLEY ST
28300 HAY 94545 731-H2

STREET Block City ZIP Pg-Grid

CUCIZ LN
1300 MPS 95035 814-D2
CUEN CT
3600 SJS 95136 874-D1
CUENCA CT
- SRMN 94583 673-C3
36600 FRMT 94536 752-J1
CUENCA DR
2400 SRMN 94583 673-C2
CUENCA WY
600 FRMT 94536 752-J1
600 FRMT 94536 753-A1
CUERNAVACA CT
1400 SJS 95120 874-B7
CUERNAVACA CIRCULO
1200 MTVW 94040 832-A1
CUESTA AV
600 SMTO 94403 749-A5
CUESTA CT
- SF 94131 667-F4
3500 SJS 95148 835-D5
CUESTA DR
- LALT 94022 811-E7
100 MTVW 94040 811-G7
100 SSF 94080 707-E3
300 LALT 94024 811-E7
2100 MPS 95035 814-E1
3200 SJS 95148 835-C6
CUESTA TR
- CCCo - 652-C3
CUESTA WY
- CCCo 94596 612-A4
CUESTA DE LOS GATOS WY
100 LGTS 95032 873-B7
CULBERTSON DR
10000 SCIC 95014 852-G2
CULEBRA RD
800 HIL 94010 748-G3
CULEBRA TER
- SF 94109 647-H3
CULET LN
3900 DNVL 94506 654-B6
CULL CANYON RD
- AlaC 94546 652-B7
10200 AlaC 94552 692-D2
11200 AlaC 94552 672-B1
20000 AlaC 94552 652-B7
CULLEN DR
400 PCFA 94044 727-A1
CULLIGAN BLVD
1000 SJS 95120 894-D1
1100 SJS 95120 874-D7
CULLODEN CT
1000 SJS 95121 855-A5
CULLODEN PARK RD
- SRFL 94901 566-F7
CULP AV
200 HAY 94544 712-A4
200 HAY 94544 711-J4
CULPEPPER DR
1200 SJS 95121 854-H2
CULVER CT
- ORIN 94563 631-A4
- ORIN 94563 630-J4
- SMTO 94403 749-C6
2200 WLCK 94598 612-G2
3000 OAK 94619 650-E6
CULVER PL
1300 AlaC 94580 711-C1
CULVER ST
- SRFL 94901 586-H2
4100 OAK 94619 650-F6
CULVERT DR
6200 SJS 95123 874-J7
CUMANA CIR
500 UNC 94587 732-C6
CUMBERLAND AV
800 SUNV 94087 832-C1
1000 SLN 94579 691-A5
CUMBERLAND CT
- DNVL 94526 633-A7
200 ALA 94502 669-J5
700 PLHL 94523 592-A7
900 FCTY 94404 749-E5
CUMBERLAND DR
400 PLHL 94523 591-J7
500 PLHL 94523 592-A7
12700 SAR 95070 852-F6
CUMBERLAND LN
- MRGA 94556 631-D5
CUMBERLAND PL
1000 SJS 95125 854-D7
CUMBERLAND RD
400 BURL 94010 728-G6
CUMBERLAND ST
- SF 94110 667-G2
200 SF 94114 667-G2
300 PIT 94565 574-E2
CUMBERLAND TR
- CCCo - 594-C5
CUMBERLAND WY
200 ALA 94502 669-J5
CUMBERLAND GAP CT
3400 PLE 94588 714-B1
CUMBERLAND PARK CT
5400 FRMT 94538 773-C2
CUMBRA VISTA CT
13000 LAH 94022 831-A1
CUMBRE DR
- WLCK 94596 612-A2
CUMBRIAN CT
3200 WLCK 94598 612-H6
CUMMINGS SKWY
- CCCo 94525 550-C6
- CCCo 94553 570-F1
CUMMINS AV
- SCIC 94035 812-B2
- SCIC 94043 812-B2
CUMORA AV
16600 AlaC 94580 691-F6
CUMORAH LN
- CCCo 94526 633-A6
CUMULUS AV
100 SUNV 94087 832-E2
CUNARD CT
3400 SJS 95132 814-J2
CUNEO CT
1100 CNCD 94518 592-J5
CUNEO DR
3700 CNCD 94518 592-J4
3900 CNCD 94518 593-A5

STREET Block City ZIP Pg-Grid

CUNNINGHAM AV
1500 SJS 95122 854-H1
1500 SJS 95122 834-H7
2100 SJS 95148 835-A6
2100 SJS 95122 835-A6
CUNNINGHAM CT
2000 SJS 95148 835-B6
5100 AlaC 94546 692-B3
CUNNINGHAM LN
2000 MRTZ 94553 572-A6
CUNNINGHAM PL
- SF 94110 667-H2
20400 SAR 95070 852-D7
CUNNINGHAM ST
- VAL 94590 529-H1
1600 SCL 95050 833-C4
4600 OAK 94619 650-G6
CUNNINGHAM WY
400 SBRN 94066 727-H1
CUPERTINO RD
22200 CPTO 95014 832-A7
CUPERTINO WY
200 SMTO 94403 749-D5
CUPID RW
100 SBRN 94066 707-J7
CUPPLES CT
600 SCL 95051 833-B6
CURCI DR
1400 SJS 95126 853-H3
CURETON PL
300 SCIC 95127 835-A2
300 SJS 95127 835-A2
CURIE CT
6400 SJS 95123 875-A7
CURIE DR
200 SJS 95119 875-C7
200 SCIC 95119 875-C7
300 SJS 95123 874-J7
400 SJS 95123 875-A7
CURIE PL
6700 NWK 94560 752-C5
CURLETTO DR
1700 CNCD 94521 593-D3
CURLEW CT
200 FCTY 94404 749-G1
2700 PLE 94566 714-C1
CURLEW RD
400 LVMR 94550 695-D7
CURLEW WY
- NVTO 94949 546-E5
CURLING CT
3200 SJS 95121 855-B3
CURRAGHMORE CT
4000 SJS 95136 854-E6
CURRAN AV
3000 OAK 94602 650-D5
CURRAN CT
2500 PIN 94564 569-G5
CURRAN WY
3400 OAK 94602 650-E5
CURRANT WY
900 HAY 94545 711-G5
CURRENT DR
6200 SJS 95123 874-J7
CURREY AV
- SAUS 94965 627-A3
CURREY CT
- BEN 94510 551-C1
CURREY LN
200 SAUS 94965 626-J3
200 SAUS 94965 627-A3
CURRY AV
200 VAL 94590 530-C5
7400 ELCR 94530 609-E4
CURRY CT
- SCAR 94070 769-D3
12400 SAR 95070 852-H6
CURRY LN
200 MrnC 94941 606-E5
CURRY ST
100 RCH 94801 588-E7
CURRY CANYON TKTR
2200 CCCo - 633-J5
CURSOR CT
- SJS 95134 813-C1
CURTIS AV
- SRFL 94901 566-G7
900 SCL 95051 832-J5
2800 SMCo 94063 770-C7
21300 HAY 94545 711-E4
E CURTIS AV
- MPS 95035 814-A2
CURTIS CIR
3200 PLE 94588 694-C7
CURTIS CT
- SCAR 94070 769-D3
CURTIS DR
- ANT 94509 575-A7
- ANT 94509 574-J7
100 VAL 94591 530-E4
CURTIS ST
- BERK 94706 609-E7
- SF 94112 687-F2
400 ALB 94706 609-E5
400 CCCo 94706 609-E5
800 MLPK 94025 790-F3
1300 BERK 94702 609-E7
1300 BERK 94702 629-E1
2000 OAK 94607 649-F3
5000 FRMT 94538 773-B1
CURTIS WY
700 MLPK 94025 790-G4
CURTISS AV
1100 SJS 95125 854-A3
CURTISS ST
3100 SMTO 94403 749-D5
CURTNER AV
- CMBL 95008 873-E1
100 SJS 95125 854-B5
200 PA 94306 811-C1
200 SCIC 95125 854-D4
300 SCIC 95008 873-E1
500 SJS 95008 873-G1
1600 SJS 95125 853-J7
1700 SJS 95124 853-G7
2000 SJS 95124 873-G1
CURTNER CT
400 MPS 95035 794-A3
CURTNER DR
400 MPS 95035 794-A4
CURTNER RD
100 FRMT 94539 774-A5

STREET Block City ZIP Pg-Grid

CURTNER RD
100 FRMT 94539 773-J5
CURTNER GLEN CT
2600 SJS 95008 873-F1
CURTOLA PKWY
- VAL 94590 529-J5
- VAL 94590 530-A5
400 SolC 94590 530-A5
CUSHING AV
- MrnC 94903 566-G3
CUSHING DR
- MLV 94941 606-D1
CUSHING PKWY
4300 FRMT 94538 773-E6
CUSHING RD
4600 FRMT 94538 773-D6
CUSTER AV
1400 SF 94124 668-C4
CUSTER DR
2500 SJS 95124 853-H7
2500 SJS 95124 873-H1
CUSTER RD
400 HAY 94544 712-A4
CUSTER ST
3500 OAK 94601 650-D6
CUSTOM HOUSE PL
- SF 94111 648-B4
CUTFORTH CT
1300 SJS 95132 814-F5
CUTHBERT AV
3100 OAK 94602 650-D5
CUTHBERTSON CT
3100 RCH 94806 589-A1
CUTIE LN
1800 CCCo 94521 593-E3
CUTLER AV
2700 FRMT 94536 752-G1
3600 SF 94116 666-H5
CUTTER LN
400 FCTY 94404 749-H4
5200 RCH 94803 589-J2
CUTTER ST
300 FCTY 94404 749-H4
800 PIT 94565 574-D2
CUTTER WY
800 BERK 94804 629-D3
CUTTING BLVD
100 RCH 94804 608-G1
2000 ELCR 94530 589-C7
3800 RCH 94804 609-A1
5800 ELCR 94530 609-B1
W CUTTING BLVD
- RCH 94801 608-E1
100 RCH 94804 608-E1
CUTTING CT
- RCH 94804 609-A1
- WLCK 94596 632-F2
CUTTING ST
2400 WLCK 94596 632-F2
CUTTY CT
300 PCFA 94044 707-A3
CUTWATER LN
500 FCTY 94404 749-G6
CUVAISON LN
- AMCN 94589 510-B3
CUVIER ST
- SF 94112 667-G6
CYCLAMEN CT
- SJS 95111 875-A2
1900 HAY 94545 711-F6
CYCLOTRON RD
- BERK 94709 629-J1
- BERK 94720 629-J1
- BERK 94720 630-A1
- OAK 94720 630-A1
CYGNUS CT
- VAL 94591 510-H4
32300 UNC 94587 732-A6
CYGNUS LN
600 FCTY 94404 749-E4
CYLINDA DR
3400 SJS 95130 853-A7
CYNTHIA AV
100 VAL 94589 510-C6
18600 SCIC 95014 852-H2
CYNTHIA CT
22100 AlaC 94541 692-C6
CYNTHIA DR
- PLHL 94523 592-C4
CYNTHIA LN
1000 SJS 95129 852-E3
CYNTHIA WY
2000 LALT 94024 832-A5
CYPRESS AV
- MLV 94941 606-B3
- MrnC 94904 586-E3
- SCL 95117 833-D7
- SCL 95117 853-D1
100 SBRN 94066 727-J1
100 SCL 95050 833-F5
100 SolC 94590 530-B6
200 SSF 94080 707-J3
300 SUNV 94086 812-F5
400 MLBR 94030 727-J1
400 SBRN 94066 707-H7
400 SMTO 94401 748-J1
500 SSF 94080 708-A2
600 SMTO 94401 749-A1
800 BLMT 94002 769-E1
800 NVTO 94947 526-B4
900 SMTO 94401 729-A7
1500 BURL 94010 728-G7
1500 CCCo 94805 589-C6
2000 CCCo 94806 569-B4
4500 RCH 94804 609-A2
5200 ELCR 94530 609-B2
24800 HAY 94544 711-H4
S CYPRESS AV
300 SJS 95117 853-C2
400 SCIC 95117 853-D1
CYPRESS CT
- CCCo 94806 569-C3
- DALY 94014 687-J3
- MLBR 94030 728-A3
- NVTO 94947 526-B3
- SBRN 94066 707-J7
- SCAR 94070 769-F6
400 LALT 94022 811-D6
8300 DBLN 94568 693-H1
10500 CPTO 95014 832-F6
CYPRESS DR
- SMCo - 768-D3

STREET Block City ZIP Pg-Grid

CYPRESS DR
300 LALT 94022 811-D6
300 MPS 95035 813-H1
1200 CNCD 94520 592-E4
10400 CPTO 95014 832-F7
CYPRESS FRWY I-880
- EMVL - 629-D7
- OAK - 629-E7
- OAK - 649-C3
CYPRESS LN
- BSBN 94005 688-A5
- DALY 94014 687-J3
500 CMBL 95008 853-F5
500 PA 94306 811-C1
6200 SJS 95138 875-F6
CYPRESS PL
- SAUS 94965 626-J1
CYPRESS PTH
- RCH 94804 609-B2
CYPRESS RD
- SANS 94960 566-C7
CYPRESS RDGE
2500 SCIC 95148 835-E6
CYPRESS ST
- SF 94110 667-J4
100 ALA 94501 649-E7
100 RDWC 94061 790-B1
600 OAK 94607 649-E2
1100 EPA 94303 791-C2
1400 WLCK 94596 612-C5
1400 BERK 94703 609-F7
2300 ANT 94509 574-J7
2600 OAK 94608 649-E2
14300 SLN 94579 690-J4
14400 SLN 94579 691-A5
CYPRESS WY
3700 PIT 94565 574-G6
16100 LGTS 95032 893-C1
CYPRESS CIRCLE DR
- SMCo - 768-D3
CYPRESS CREEK CT
7800 PLE 94588 714-B5
CYPRESS HILLS CT
200 DNVL 94526 653-F6
CYPRESS HOLLOW DR
- MrnC 94920 606-J4
CYPRESS PARK CT
400 SJS 95136 874-F1
CYPRESS POINT CT
- CCCo 94507 633-A5
CYPRESS POINT DR
200 MTVW 94043 812-A4
200 MTVW 94043 811-J4
5900 LVMR 94550 696-C2
36300 NWK 94560 752-C7
CYPRESS POINT RD
600 RCH 94801 608-C1
CYPRESS POINT WY
100 MRGA 94556 631-D7
CYPRESS RANCH RD
- AlaC 94552 692-E4
CYPRUS DR
36200 FRMT 94536 752-F3
CYRIL PL
18900 SAR 95070 852-H6
CYRIL MAGIN ST
- SF 94102 648-A6
CYRUS AV
3000 SJS 95124 873-H1
CYRUS PL
- SF 94109 647-J4
CYRUS HEIGHTS LN
17200 SCIC 95032 893-G2

D

D RD
1000 AlaC 94586 734-C3
15000 SCIC 95127 815-D6
D ST
- CCCo 94565 573-E1
- CNCD 94518 592-G3
- CNCD 94520 572-J3
- MTVW 94043 812-B5
- NVTO 94949 546-G3
- OAK 94625 649-B3
- SF 94124 668-E7
- SUNV 94089 812-H3
- SRFL 94901 586-F2
- UNC 94587 732-F4
- VAL 94590 529-H2
100 BEN 94510 551-B5
100 DALY 94014 687-C6
100 RDWC 94063 769-J4
200 ANT 94509 575-D4
200 FRMT 94536 753-A1
300 CLMA 94014 687-D6
300 HAY 94541 711-J1
300 HAY 94544 711-J2
300 MLPK 94025 790-G3
500 MRTZ 94553 571-E5
1000 HAY 94541 712-A1
1700 AlaC 94541 712-B1
1800 AlaC 94541 692-C7
9000 OAK 94603 670-H5
9900 OAK 94621 670-G4
S D ST
- SUNV 94089 812-J3
DABNER ST
- SLN 94577 690-J1
DADE CT
6400 SJS 95123 875-B7
6400 SJS 95123 895-B1
DADIS WY
600 SJS 95111 854-H4
DADO ST
600 SJS 95131 813-J6
DAFFODIL CIR
100 VAL 94591 530-F7
DAFFODIL CT
700 SUNV 94086 832-F2
DAFFODIL DR
2200 PIT 94565 573-J4
DAFFODIL LN
- MLV 94941 606-C3
- SCAR 94070 769-C4
DAFFODIL WY
700 CNCD 94518 592-J6
700 SJS 95117 853-B3
2600 UNC 94587 732-G7
2600 UNC 94587 752-G1
4300 LVMR 94550 696-A4

STREET Block City ZIP Pg-Grid

DAGGETT AV
100 UNC 94587 732-G5
DAGGETT DR
- SJS 95134 813-G5
DAGGETT ST
- SF 94107 668-B2
DAGMAR CT
700 SJS 95136 874-E1
DAGMAR DR
19000 SAR 95070 872-H1
19000 SAR 95070 852-G7
DAGNINO RD
3800 AlaC 94550 696-A1
DAHILL CT
3500 SJS 95121 855-C3
DAHILL LN
1700 HAY 94541 692-A7
DAHLIA CT
- LFYT 94549 611-D4
500 SLN 94578 691-C4
1100 SUNV 94086 832-H2
DAHLIA DR
100 ALA 94502 670-A6
1100 SUNV 94086 832-H2
37600 NWK 94560 752-F7
DAHLIA WY
15900 SCIC 95032 873-D6
15900 LGTS 95032 873-D6
DAILEY AV
700 SJS 95123 874-F4
DAILEY RD
- SCIC 94035 812-B3
- SCIC 94043 812-B3
DAILY CT
1500 SLN 94577 691-D2
DAILY DR
1200 SLN 94577 691-D2
DAIMLER CT
5300 SJS 95123 874-H3
DAIRY AV
6100 NWK 94560 752-D7
DAIRY LN
- BLMT 94002 749-F7
DAISY CT
- DNVL 94506 654-B5
100 HER 94547 569-J4
100 VAL 94589 510-A6
600 PLHL 94523 591-J3
1000 SUNV 94086 832-H2
2900 UNC 94587 732-F7
3300 HAY 94542 712-E4
DAISY LN
- ORIN 94563 631-B3
400 EPA 94303 791-D2
1300 LVMR 94550 696-B4
DAISY PL
500 PLHL 94523 591-J3
DAISY ST
900 SMTO 94401 749-C1
2900 UNC 94587 732-F7
4700 OAK 94619 650-G6
34800 UNC 94587 752-F1
DAISY WY
1400 ANT 94509 575-B5
DAISYDELL CT
400 SJS 95129 853-B2
DAISYFIELD CT
500 LVMR 94550 715-E1
DAISYFIELD DR
100 DNVL 94506 653-F5
100 LVMR 94550 715-D1
DAISY MAE CT
- NVTO 94947 525-J3
DAKAN CT
3100 SJS 95136 854-D7
DAKAR DR
100 CCCo 94553 572-E3
DAKE AV
4100 PA 94306 811-F2
DAKIN AV
1900 SMCo 94025 790-D6
DAKOTA AV
1200 SMTO 94401 749-B1
DAKOTA CT
800 LVMR 94550 695-E7
DAKOTA DR
600 SJS 95111 854-H5
DAKOTA LN
1700 CNCD 94519 592-J2
DAKOTA ST
- SF 94107 668-B3
3000 OAK 94602 650-E5
DALBON CT
6900 SJS 95119 875-F6
DALE AV
100 PDMT 94610 650-A1
100 SCAR 94070 769-F3
900 MTVW 94040 812-A7
1100 MTVW 94040 832-A1
1300 SJS 95125 854-A5
1500 SMTO 94401 749-C1
1900 SMTO 94403 749-C1
DALE CT
- CCCo 94595 612-A6
- ORIN 94563 631-B4
100 VAL 94591 530-D3
300 BEN 94510 551-B3
DALE DR
- SCIC 95127 835-A2
- SCIC 95127 834-J2
DALE PL
- SF 94102 647-J6
1000 CNCD 94518 592-E5
3800 OAK 94619 650-E6
DALE RD
400 MRTZ 94553 571-H7
DALE ST
24600 HAY 94544 711-J3
DALE WY
1200 PCFA 94044 726-G4
DALEHURST AV
700 SMTO 94403 749-A7
DALEHURST CT
3900 SMTO 94403 749-B7
DALEHURST DR
1600 LALT 94024 831-J4
DALEROSE CT
- DALY 94014 687-G3
DALESSI DR
1800 PIN 94564 569-D6
DALESSI LN
1800 PIN 94564 569-D6

STREET Block City ZIP Pg-Grid

DALE VIEW AV
500 BLMT 94002 749-D7
DALEWOOD CT
700 SJS 95120 894-J3
36100 NWK 94560 752-E5
DALEWOOD DR
300 ORIN 94563 610-H3
35700 NWK 94560 752-D5
DALEWOOD WY
- SF 94127 667-D5
DALEY CT
100 SBRN 94066 707-E7
DALGO RD
100 FRMT 94539 753-E4
DALHBERG AV
- PCFA 94044 706-J5
DALI ST
4200 FRMT 94536 752-F3
DALIS DR
- CNCD 94520 572-E5
DALLAS CT
1600 LALT 94024 831-J3
2300 ANT 94509 595-A1
3100 SCL 95051 833-A3
4200 FRMT 94536 752-G3
DALLAS DR
200 SCIC 95008 873-E1
DALLAS RANCH RD
4600 ANT 94509 595-E4
DALMA DR
- MTVW 94041 811-J6
DALMALLY LN
- DBLN 94568 693-E5
DALMATIA PL
- AlaC 94546 691-G4
DALMENY CT
6800 SJS 95120 894-H2
DALMUIR CT
2500 SJS 95121 855-D4
DALTON AV
5400 LVMR 94550 696-C2
5800 AlaC 94550 696-C2
DALTON COM
3500 FRMT 94536 752-J4
DALTON CT
- CCCo 94553 572-B7
400 BEN 94510 551-A2
33700 UNC 94587 732-E5
DALTON DR
1600 SJS 95124 873-J5
1700 MPS 95035 794-D7
DALTON LN
100 CCCo 94553 572-B7
DALTON PL
1800 SJS 95124 873-J5
DALTON WY
1600 UNC 94587 732-E6
DALTREY WY
1700 SJS 95132 814-D4
DALY CT
- SSF 94080 707-G2
DAMASCUS CT
2300 SJS 95125 853-J6
DAMASCUS DR
100 CCCo 94553 572-C7
DAMASCUS LP
100 CCCo 94553 572-C7
DAMERON PL
3500 ANT 94509 595-B1
DAMEY DR
2300 SJS 95116 834-G2
DAMIAN WY
900 LALT 94024 831-J2
DAMIANO CT
5100 PLE 94588 694-A5
DAMICO DR
2900 SJS 95148 855-D2
DAMON AV
- CCCo 94525 550-E5
DAMON CT
- ALA 94502 670-A5
DAMON LN
13900 SAR 95070 872-A1
13900 SCIC 95070 872-A1
DAMONTE CT
- SSF 94080 708-A1
DAMUTH ST
2000 OAK 94602 650-D4
DAN CT
100 VAL 94591 530-F6
DANA AV
- SJS 95128 853-H1
- SJS 95126 853-H1
- SJS 95126 833-G6
- SJS 95128 833-G7
1100 PA 94301 791-A3
1400 PA 94303 791-A3
DANA CIR
700 LVMR 94550 696-B7
700 LVMR 94550 716-B1
DANA CT
- SSF 94080 707-F4
3900 CNCD 94519 573-A7
4600 UNC 94587 731-J7
4900 LVMR 94550 716-B1
6300 PLE 94588 694-A7
6500 AlaC 94552 692-F3
DANA DR
3500 ANT 94509 595-C1
DANA ST
100 MTVW 94041 811-H4
300 FRMT 94539 753-H7
800 MTVW 94041 812-B6
900 SUNV 94086 812-B6
2300 BERK 94704 629-H2
2700 BERK 94705 629-H4
3100 OAK 94609 629-H4
E DANA ST
100 MTVW 94041 812-A6
W DANA ST
100 MTVW 94041 812-A5
DANA HIGHLANDS CT
- CCCo - 591-G5
100 DNVL 94506 653-G6
DANALA FARMS
- CCCo 94507 632-H7
DANA POINTE CT
- RDWC 94065 749-J5
DANBERRY CT
1100 ANT 94509 575-F7
DANBERRY LN
- DALY 94014 687-E3

Thomas Bros. Maps ® COPYRIGHT 1997

STREET Block City ZIP Pg-Grid

DANBERRY LN
2100 MrnC 94903 546-C7
DANBROOK CT
- ALA 94502 669-J5
- ALA 94502 670-A5
DANBURY CT
- CCCo 94507 632-J2
DANBURY DR
1000 SJS 95129 852-F3
DANBURY LN
- RDWC 94061 790-B2
DANBURY ST
- OAK 94605 671-C7
DANBURY PARK DR
1700 PLE 94566 714-F1
DANBY AV
1300 SJS 95132 814-F4
DANDELION CIR
2800 ANT 94509 575-G7
DANDELION CT
2800 ANT 94509 575-G7
DANDELION LN
200 SRMN 94583 653-J7
DANDERHALL WY
3100 SJS 95121 855-C3
DANDINI CIR
1800 SJS 95128 853-G3
DANEFIELD PL
- MRGA 94556 631-D6
DANESTA DR
1700 CNCD 94519 593-A1
DANFORTH CT
100 DNVL 94526 653-C6
1200 SJS 95121 854-H2
DANFORTH DR
600 SUNV 94087 832-D1
DANFORTH LN
1100 WLCK 94598 612-D3
26100 HAY 94545 711-G6
DANFORTH TER
700 SUNV 94087 832-D1
DANIA LN
25000 HAY 94545 711-F5
DANIEL CT
1200 MPS 95035 794-C5
DANIEL DR
100 CCCo 94507 632-G7
DANIEL LN
1100 CNCD 94518 592-J5
DANIEL WY
500 SJS 95128 833-F7
3700 SCL 95051 832-H7
S DANIEL WY
300 SJS 95128 853-F1
DANIEL BURNHAM CT
- SF 94109 647-H6
DANIEL HILLS CT
1100 BEN 94510 551-A4
DANIELLE CT
1800 WLCK 94598 592-F7
DANIELLE DR
100 SRFL 94903 566-B3
DANIELLE PL
3400 CCCo 94565 573-F1
15000 MSER 95030 872-J4
DANIELLE WY
4100 AlaC 94546 691-H2
DANIEL MALONEY DR
1700 SJS 95121 855-B3
DANIELS AV
- VAL 94590 529-H2
DANIELS DR
1500 SLN 94577 671-C7
DANMANN AV
1200 PCFA 94044 726-G4
DANNA CT
- SJS 95138 875-G6
DANNY CT
300 PIN 94564 569-D4
DANRIDGE CT
- ANT 94509 575-D7
DANRIDGE DR
6500 SJS 95129 852-E3
DANRIDGE PL
- PIT 94565 574-F7
DANROMAS WY
1500 SJS 95129 852-F5
DANROSE DR
100 AMCN 94589 510-A3
100 VAL 94589 510-A4
DANTE AV
9900 OAK 94603 671-A5
DANTE CT
2900 SJS 95135 855-E3
DANTE PL
35500 FRMT 94536 752-G1
DANTI CT
26500 HAY 94545 731-F1
DANTLY WY
200 WLCK 94598 612-D4
DANTON ST
- SF 94112 667-G6
DANUBE DR
10100 CPTO 95014 852-E1
DANUBE WY
1300 SJS 95116 834-F5
DANVERS ST
- SF 94114 667-F2
DANVILLA CT
100 DNVL 94526 652-J2
DANVILLE BLVD
600 DNVL 94526 652-H1
800 DNVL 94526 632-F4
900 CCCo 94507 632-F4
1900 CCCo 94595 632-F4
1900 WLCK 94595 632-F4
DANVILLE DR
200 LGTS 95032 873-F6
DANVILLE ST
32900 UNC 94587 752-A1
DANVILLE OAK PL
- DNVL 94526 652-J1
DANWOOD CT
2800 SJS 95148 835-C7
DANZA CT
100 ORIN 94563 631-C5
DANZE DR
100 SJS 95111 875-B3
DANZIG PZ
- CNCD 94520 592-E3
DANZON CT
41300 FRMT 94539 753-G5

DAPHNE CT
- EPA 94303 791-D3
- ORIN 94563 610-J5
100 ANT 94509 595-D1
100 PLHL 94523 612-B1
6400 NWK 94560 772-G1
DAPHNE DR
1200 SJS 95129 852-F4
5700 LVMR 94550 696-D7
DAPHNE WY
- EPA 94303 791-D3
DAPPLE DR
100 VAL 94591 530-E2
DAPPLEGRAY CT
600 WLCK 94596 632-F2
DAPPLEGRAY LN
2100 WLCK 94596 632-F3
DAR CT
900 CNCD 94518 592-E6
DARBY COM
- FRMT 94539 773-E2
DARBY CT
2100 WLCK 94596 632-G1
DARBY PL
100 SBRN 94066 727-G2
DARBYS CT
100 SJS 95110 854-D2
DARCELLE CT
4600 UNC 94587 731-J7
DARCELLE DR
4500 UNC 94587 731-J6
DARCREST CT
19300 AlaC 94546 692-B4
DARCY AV
- SMTO 94403 749-C6
DARCY CT
- SMTO 94403 749-C6
6400 OAK 94609 629-H4
DARDANELLE CT
100 MRTZ 94553 571-H5
DARDANELLE DR
100 MRTZ 94553 571-H5
DARDANELLI LN
100 LGTS 95030 873-B2
DARDENELLE AV
100 PCFA 94044 727-B1
DARIAN CT
6900 DBLN 94568 693-J2
DARIAN LN
- PLHL 94523 592-A7
DARIEN AV
300 OAK 94603 670-G7
DARIEN WY
- SF 94127 667-C6
12700 SAR 95070 852-G6
DARIO TR
25500 AlaC 94541 712-D2
DARIUS CT
1500 SLN 94577 691-D2
DARIUS WY
2600 SLN 94577 691-D2
14600 AlaC 94578 691-D2
DARKNELL CT
3500 SJS 95148 835-E6
DARKNELL WY
2700 SJS 95148 835-E6
DARLENE AV
1300 SMTO 94403 749-D4
1400 SJS 95125 854-A7
DARLENE CT
- CCCo 94507 632-E5
2700 AlaC 94546 691-G4
4700 UNC 94587 731-J7
DARLENE DR
1400 CNCD 94520 592-E4
DARLENE WY
32300 UNC 94587 731-J7
32300 UNC 94587 732-A7
DARLEY DR
100 VAL 94591 530-E2
DARLING LN
13400 LAH 94022 811-D7
DARLINGTON CT
4200 PA 94306 811-D2
DARLINGTON PL
- VAL 94591 530-F3
DARNBY CT
- ORIN 94563 631-B5
DARNBY DR
2700 OAK 94611 650-G1
DARNEL CT
38400 FRMT 94536 752-J4
DARNELL CT
2300 SJS 95133 834-F1
DARRELL PL
- SF 94133 648-A4
DARRELL RD
200 HIL 94010 748-C2
DARRINGTON CT
1000 SUNV 94087 832-B5
DARROW CT
4500 FRMT 94536 752-H4
DARRYDOON CT
1200 SJS 95121 855-A5
DARRYL CT
3600 SJS 95130 853-C4
DARRYL DR
- CMBL 95008 853-C5
1300 SJS 95130 853-C4
1500 CMBL 95130 853-C4
DARTFORD
100 HER 94547 569-J2
DARTMOOR LN
600 HAY 94544 712-D7
DARTMOOR WY
6400 SJS 95129 852-E4
DARTMOUTH
100 VAL 94589 510-A5
DARTMOUTH AV
- LKSP 94939 586-E5
- SCAR 94070 769-D2
1200 SLN 94579 691-A4
33700 UNC 94587 732-F5
DARTMOUTH DR
- OAK 94705 630-B3
5400 SJS 95118 874-A5
DARTMOUTH LN
1000 LALT 94024 831-H2
DARTMOUTH PL
- DNVL 94526 653-B3
100 BEN 94510 551-B3

DARTMOUTH RD
100 SMTO 94402 748-J2
DARTMOUTH ST
- SF 94134 667-J7
600 SF 94134 687-J1
900 SF 94134 688-A1
1100 ALB 94706 609-D7
2000 PA 94306 810-J1
2100 PA 94306 811-A1
DARTMOUTH WY
900 CNCD 94518 592-E6
3800 LVMR 94550 695-J7
3900 LVMR 94550 696-A7
DARTSHIRE CT
1400 SUNV 94087 832-G4
DARTSHIRE WY
700 SUNV 94087 832-F4
DARVON AV
36200 NWK 94560 752-E4
DARVON CT
36600 NWK 94560 752-F5
DARWIN AV
1300 LVMR 94550 715-G3
1500 SMTO 94403 749-C2
DARWIN CT
1300 SJS 95122 834-G7
DARWIN DR
3000 FRMT 94555 732-E7
3400 FRMT 94555 752-E1
DARWIN ST
2300 HAY 94545 711-F7
DARWIN WY
1700 SJS 95122 834-H7
DARYL AV
- MrnC 94947 525-E2
16700 AlaC 94580 691-E6
DARYL DR
- ORIN 94563 631-A1
DASH CT
5800 SJS 95120 874-B6
DASHELLE HAMMETT ST
- SF 94108 648-A5
DASHWOOD AV
2200 OAK 94605 670-H3
2400 SJS 95121 855-C3
DASSEL RD
- FRMT 94536 753-C1
DATE ST
1400 MRTZ 94553 571-F3
2000 CNCD 94519 592-G1
9100 OAK 94603 670-F6
DATE BLOSSOM CT
5400 SJS 95123 875-A3
DATORO DR
2100 SJS 95130 853-A7
DAUPHINE AV
36800 FRMT 94536 752-G3
DAUPHINE PL
200 LALT 94022 811-E6
DAVALOS CT
- SRMN 94583 673-C3
DAVENANT CT
3400 FRMT 94536 752-G2
DAVENPORT
- HER 94547 569-J3
DAVENPORT AV
4400 OAK 94619 650-G6
4900 OAK 94613 650-G6
DAVENPORT CT
- SRFL 94901 566-E7
500 SUNV 94087 832-D5
DAVENPORT DR
500 SJS 95127 835-B2
DAVENPORT PL
4700 FRMT 94538 773-D3
DAVENPORT WY
200 PA 94306 811-D2
DAVES AV
17500 MSER 95030 873-A5
17700 LGTS 95030 873-A5
17800 MSER 95030 872-J5
18200 SCIC 95030 872-H5
DAVEY CROCKETT CT
200 CCCo 94507 632-H2
DAVEY GLEN RD
- BLMT 94002 749-D7
DAVI AV
- PIT 94565 574-D3
DAVI CT
3500 ANT 94509 595-C1
DAVI PL
3500 ANT 94509 595-B1
DAVID AV
300 CMBL 95008 853-E4
1200 CNCD 94518 592-E7
2800 SJS 95128 853-E4
3000 SJS 95008 853-E4
3100 PA 94303 791-D6
DAVID CIR
100 CNCD 94518 592-G4
DAVID CT
- NVTO 94947 526-A4
- SRFL 94901 566-H6
100 VAL 94589 509-J5
2300 SMTO 94403 749-D4
3100 PA 94303 791-D6
3200 CNCD 94519 592-H1
DAVID DR
- MRGA 94556 631-G5
- CNCD 94518 592-G4
300 CCCo 94507 632-G4
DAVID LN
- DNVL 94526 633-C7
1200 CNCD 94518 592-E7
1300 MPS 95035 814-D2
DAVID RD
900 BURL 94010 728-D4
DAVID ST
4100 AlaC 94546 692-B5
DAVIDOR LN
- NVTO 94945 526-A2
DAVIDSON AV
1400 SF 94124 668-C4
DAVIDSON ST
500 NVTO 94945 526-D4
DAVIDSON WY
- OAK 94610 650-A2
DAVIDWOOD WY
2900 SJS 95148 855-D1
DAVILA CT
41000 FRMT 94539 753-E6

DA VILLA
500 CCCo 94801 588-F3
500 CCCo 94801 588-F3
D AVILLA WY
5300 CCCo 94803 589-F3
DAVIS AV
- DBLN 94568 694-B3
1200 CNCD 94518 592-H3
1300 CNCD 94519 592-H3
2300 HAY 94545 711-C5
DAVIS CT
- BURL 94010 728-B5
2200 HAY 94545 711-D5
22600 SCIC 95120 895-C4
40200 FRMT 94538 753-C6
DAVIS DR
- BLMT 94002 769-B2
- TBRN 94920 607-D7
1500 BURL 94010 728-C5
DAVIS LN
2400 ANT 94509 575-C6
DAVIS RD
- ORIN 94563 610-H7
- ORIN 94563 630-H1
DAVIS ST
- SF 94111 648-B4
600 SLN 94577 690-F2
700 SF 94111 648-B4
1100 RDWC 94061 770-A7
1200 SJS 95126 833-F6
3000 OAK 94601 650-C6
4000 SCL 95054 813-D5
39800 FRMT 94538 753-B6
DAVIS ST Rt#-112
- SLN 94577 690-J1
200 SLN 94577 691-A1
DAVIS WY
4100 LVMR 94550 696-A7
DAVISON AV
10400 CPTO 95014 852-F2
DAVISON DR
- ANT 94509 595-D1
700 ANT 94509 575-F7
DAVIT LN
600 RDWC 94065 749-J6
DAVONA DR
8200 DBLN 94568 693-H2
8800 SRMN 94583 693-G1
9600 SRMN 94583 673-E6
DAVY CT
38000 FRMT 94536 753-A3
DAWE AV
21100 AlaC 94546 691-J6
DAWES CT
- NVTO 94947 526-B5
2800 SJS 95148 855-D2
DAWES ST
1400 NVTO 94947 526-B5
6500 OAK 94611 650-D1
DAWKINS DR
500 LFYT 94549 631-H3
DAWN CIR
31100 UNC 94587 731-J5
DAWN CT
1300 SRMN 94583 673-B1
DAWN DR
- PLHL 94523 592-C5
500 SUNV 94087 832-D2
DAWN LN
300 MrnC 94965 606-F7
12100 LAH 94022 811-A7
DAWN PL
- MLV 94941 606-E2
DAWN ST
- OAK 94705 630-C3
1600 LVMR 94550 716-C1
DAWNBROOK CT
3700 SJS 95111 855-A5
DAWNRIDGE DR
24200 LAH 94024 831-E3
DAWN VIEW CT
5700 AlaC 94552 692-D3
DAWNVIEW CT
- CNCD - 613-D1
900 SJS 95136 874-D3
DAWNVIEW DR
- SF 94131 667-E4
DAWSON AV
400 SJS 95125 854-C3
36500 FRMT 94536 733-A7
36500 FRMT 94536 753-A1
DAWSON DR
300 SCL 95051 832-H7
11600 LAH 94024 831-E3
DAWSON PL
- SF 94108 648-A5
100 VAL 94591 530-C7
DAWSON ST
36500 FRMT 94536 752-G2
DAY AV
1500 SMTO 94403 749-D3
W DAY AV
1200 CNCD 94520 592-E4
DAY CT
2600 SCL 95051 833-B3
DAY ST
- SF 94110 667-G5
100 SF 94131 667-G5
DAYBREAK CT
300 CCCo 94583 673-B1
300 SRMN 94583 673-B1
DAYLE CT
2200 FRMT 94539 753-F6
DAYLIGHT PL
200 DNVL 94526 653-B5
DAYLIGHT WY
2900 SJS 95111 854-G6
DAYLILY CT
2800 ANT 94509 575-G7
DAYO CT
2800 SJS 95148 855-D2
DAYTON AV
300 SCL 95051 832-J7
1100 SCAR 94070 769-G5
1300 ALA 94501 669-H2
1400 SLN 94579 691-A6
1800 SLN 94579 690-J6
DAYTON COM
39600 FRMT 94538 753-B5
DAYTON CT
100 SRMN 94583 673-G7
800 CNCD 94518 592-H6

DAYTON CT
1500 SLN 94579 691-A6
DAYTON LN
2600 ANT 94509 575-D1
DAYTONA DR
1800 SJS 95122 834-J6
DEAD HORSE CYN RD
- LFYT 94549 631-J3
DEADWOOD DR
4600 FRMT 94536 752-G5
DEAKIN ST
2900 BERK 94705 629-H3
3200 OAK 94609 629-H4
DEAN AV
1100 SJS 95125 854-A4
DEAN CT
2600 PIN 94564 569-G5
22000 CPTO 95014 852-A1
DEAN RD
100 CCCo 94526 633-A6
100 WDSD 94062 789-G6
DEAN ST
500 HAY 94541 711-J2
DEAN TR
- SMCo 94062 789-B5
DEAN LESHER DR
2500 CCCo 94520 572-G2
DEANNA DR
1000 MLPK 94025 790-D6
DEANNE CT
16200 AlaC 94580 691-E5
DEANNE LN
300 DALY 94014 687-D5
DEANS CT
100 VAL 94591 530-G5
DEANS PLACE WY
3700 SJS 95121 855-B4
DE ANZA AV
100 SCAR 94070 769-F5
100 SJS 95136 854-G7
100 RDWC 94062 769-F5
100 SCAR 94062 769-F5
DE ANZA BLVD
1400 SMTO 94403 748-J7
1800 SMTO 94402 768-H1
1900 SMTO 94402 748-J7
10000 CPTO 95014 832-E7
10000 CPTO 95014 852-E2
S DE ANZA BLVD
- SJS 95129 852-D3
1300 CPTO 95014 852-D3
DE ANZA CIR N
22200 CPTO 95014 852-A2
DE ANZA CIR S
22200 CPTO 95014 852-A2
DE ANZA CT
- SMTO 94402 748-H7
800 MPS 95035 794-B5
DE ANZA DR
100 VAL 94589 530-B1
100 VAL 94590 530-B1
2900 RCH 94803 589-E2
DE ANZA LN
200 LALT 94022 811-E7
DE ANZA PL
3200 SRMN 94583 673-G5
DE ANZA WY
- SRFL 94903 566-E4
1500 SJS 95125 853-J4
DEARBORN ST
- SF 94110 667-H2
32400 HAY 94544 732-F3
DEARDORFF LN
1600 CNCD 94519 592-H2
DEARWELL WY
- SJS 95138 875-D4
DEAUVILLE PARK CT
42700 FRMT 94538 773-C2
DEB CT
1300 SJS 95120 874-C7
DEBBI CT
1500 MRTZ 94553 591-J1
DEBBIE CT
2700 SCAR 94070 769-F6
DEBBIE LN
- BLMT 94002 749-D7
- BLMT 94002 769-D1
13400 SAR 95070 872-D1
20600 SAR 95070 852-D7
DEBBIE PL
2600 SCAR 94070 769-F6
DEBELL DR
- ATN 94027 790-G2
DE BELL RD
14300 LAH 94022 811-C5
DE BENEDETTI CT
1400 BEN 94510 551-B4
DEBES RANCH RD
- MrnC 94903 566-F5
DEBOER LN
700 SJS 95111 855-A6
DE BOOM ST
- SF 94107 648-C6
DEBORA CT
900 FRMT 94539 753-F5
DEBORAH CT
100 NVTO 94949 546-D1
4600 UNC 94587 732-A7
DEBORAH DR
2200 SCL 95050 833-C2
32200 UNC 94587 731-J7
32300 UNC 94587 732-A7
DEBORAH LN
400 CCCo 94598 612-F4
DEBORAH ST
36500 NWK 94560 752-E6
DEBRA CT
- ORIN 94563 630-J2
2100 PIT 94565 574-A4
DEBRA LN
1800 CCCo 94521 593-D3
5400 RCH 94803 589-F4
DEBRA ST
500 LVMR 94550 696-C7
DEBRA WY
3600 SJS 95117 853-C2
DEBRUM COM
43300 FRMT 94539 753-H7
DE BURGH DR
- MrnC 94960 566-A3

DEBUT CT
800 SJS 95134 813-F3
DE CAEN CT
900 LVMR 94550 715-E2
DECANO TER
36600 FRMT 94536 752-A5
DE CARLI CT
900 CMBL 95008 873-C1
DE CARLO AV
500 CCCo 94801 588-E3
500 RCH 94801 588-E3
DECATUR CT
100 HER 94547 570-B5
DECATUR DR
1800 SJS 95122 834-H6
DECATUR RD
18400 MSER 95030 872-H6
18400 SCIC 95030 872-H6
DECATUR ST
- SF 94103 668-A1
1100 FCTY 94404 749-G4
2100 ALA 94501 649-E7
DECATUR WY
27500 HAY 94545 711-H7
27500 HAY 94545 731-H1
DECCA LN
2500 WLCK 94596 612-B3
DECKER AL
100 SF 94103 648-A7
DECKER WY
- SCIC 95127 835-A1
- SCIC 95127 834-J1
DECLARATION CT
100 SJS 95116 834-H3
DECLARATION DR
2500 SJS 95116 834-H3
DECLARATION WY
100 SJS 95116 834-H3
DECORAH LN
- CMBL 95008 853-G6
DECOTO CT
900 MPS 95035 794-B5
DECOTO RD
3000 FRMT 94555 732-F7
3000 UNC 94587 732-F7
3000 FRMT 94536 732-F7
3000 FRMT 94555 752-E2
3000 FRMT 94536 752-E2
DECOY TER
34400 FRMT 94555 752-D2
DEDALERA DR
200 SMCo 94028 810-E4
DEDMAN CT
- SF 94124 668-C6
DEE CT
3100 FRMT 94536 752-G1
DEE PL
35500 FRMT 94536 752-G1
DEE ST
800 SUNV 94087 832-D2
DEEDHAM CT
3800 SJS 95148 835-G7
DEEDHAM DR
3500 SJS 95148 835-F7
DEEMS RD
- SF 94129 647-D4
DEEMS ST
1600 PIT 94565 574-F3
DEEP CLIFF DR
10600 CPTO 95014 852-A2
DEEP CREEK CT
1800 SJS 95148 835-D4
DEEPCREEK CT
300 CCCo 94506 654-D5
DEEP CREEK RD
4000 FRMT 94555 732-C7
4100 FRMT - 752-C1
4100 FRMT 94555 752-C1
DEEP PURPLE WY
5400 SJS 95123 874-F3
DEEPROSE PL
10100 CPTO 95014 852-F1
DEEPSTONE DR
100 MrnC 94903 546-E6
DEEPWATER CT
- RCH 94804 608-E3
DEEPWELL CT
21000 SAR 95070 872-C3
DEEPWELL LN
- LALT 94022 831-D1
DEER AV
- SolC 94590 550-A1
700 VAL 94590 530-A7
700 VAL 94590 550-A1
DEER CT
500 SJS 95123 874-H4
DEER PL
- CLAY 94517 594-A5
DEER RD
1100 FRMT 94536 733-D7
DEER RUN
- CMAD 94925 606-H1
5400 RCH 94803 589-J3
DEER TR
- MrnC 94947 525-J6
- LFYT 94549 611-C4
DEER WY
4500 ANT 94509 595-H2
DEERBERRY CT
4000 CNCD 94521 593-C5
DEER CANYON LN
14400 SAR 95070 872-C2
DEER CREEK CT
1700 SJS 95148 835-D4
DEER CREEK DR
900 CCCo 94553 591-C3
DEER CREEK LN
- CCCo 94506 654-D5
4500 CNCD 94521 593-C5
DEER CREEK RD
3400 SCIC 94304 810-J4
3400 PA 94304 810-J4
3400 PA 94304 811-A4
DEER CREST DR
3500 CCCo 94506 654-D4
DEER CREST PL
- CCCo 94506 654-D4
DEERFIELD CT
- SRMN 94583 673-J6
1300 CNCD 94521 593-B5
DEERFIELD DR
200 MRGA 94556 651-E3

DEERFIELD DR
700 AMCN 94589 510-B4
1500 SJS 95129 852-G5
4400 ANT 94509 595-H3
25500 LAH 94022 811-D7
DEERFIELD LN
- CCCo 94595 632-C1
- NVTO 94947 526-B5
DEERFIELD PL
- FRMT 94538 773-C1
DEER FIELD WY
4400 CCCo 94506 654-D4
DEERHAVEN PL
- PLHL 94523 591-H2
DEER HILL
- ANT - 595-G7
DEER HILL CT
- PIT - 573-F4
- PIT 94565 573-F4
300 MrnC 94941 606-H5
DEER HILL DR
- SRMN 94583 673-A1
DEER HILL RD
3200 LFYT 94549 611-E6
DEER HOLLOW CT
6500 SJS 95120 874-F7
DEER HOLLOW DR
3300 CCCo 94506 654-D4
6400 SJS 95120 874-F7
DEER HOLLOW RD
- MrnC 94960 566-A4
DEERHORN CT
4500 ANT 94509 595-J2
DEERING CT
- OAK 94601 650-D6
DEERING ST
3200 OAK 94601 650-D6
DEER ISLAND LN
300 MrnC 94945 526-F4
300 NVTO 94945 526-F4
DEER ISLE DR
2700 SJS 95121 855-E4
DEERLAKE CT
- SMTO 94402 768-H1
DEERLAND CT
5900 SJS 95124 873-J7
DEER MEADOW CT
- CCCo 94506 654-A2
- CCCo 94506 653-J2
900 SJS 95122 854-G2
DEER MEADOW DR
2700 CCCo - 654-A1
2900 CCCo 94506 654-A2
3000 CCCo 94506 653-J2
DEER MEADOW LN
- CCCo 94506 653-J2
100 PTLV 94028 810-C5
DEER MEADOW PL
- CCCo 94506 653-J2
DEERMEADOW WY
4400 ANT 94509 595-H3
DEER OAK PL
1000 CNCD 94521 593-D5
DEER OAK WY
2100 CCCo 94506 633-H7
2100 CCCo 94506 653-G1
DEER OAKS CT
- PLE 94588 714-A4
DEER OAKS DR
- PLE 94588 714-A4
DEER PARK AV
- SRFL 94901 566-H7
DEER PARK CT
3500 HAY 94542 712-F4
DEERPARK CT
300 WLCK 94598 612-H2
20500 SAR 95070 872-D1
DEERPARK DR
2800 WLCK 94598 612-H2
DEER PARK LN
- PTLV 94028 810-C5
- SANS 94960 566-A6
DEERPARK RD
17200 SCIC 95032 893-G1
DEER PARK WY
3500 HAY 94542 712-F4
DEER PARK FIRE RD
- MrnC 94965 606-A5
DEER PATH CT
200 MRTZ 94553 591-H3
DEER PATH DR
- SMCo 94028 830-E4
DEERPOINT TER
500 FRMT 94536 753-G3
DEER RIDGE CIR
100 SJS 95123 874-G7
DEER RIDGE DR
3400 CCCo 94506 654-D4
DEER RIDGE PL
100 CCCo 94506 654-D4
DEER RIDGE RD
4400 CCCo 94506 654-D5
DEER RIDGE WY
4500 ANT 94509 595-H3
DEER RUN CIR
- SJS 95136 874-J2
DEER SPRING CIR
- CNCD - 613-D1
DEER SPRING CT
14500 SAR 95070 872-C2
DEER SPRINGS WY
27200 LAH 94022 830-J2
DEER TERRACE CT
- SRMN 94583 673-A1
DEER TRAIL CT
3700 CCCo 94506 654-C4
13400 SAR 95070 852-B7
DEER TRAIL DR
3600 CCCo 94506 654-D4
DEER TRAIL LN
3800 CCCo 94506 654-C5
DEERTRAIL LN
300 MrnC 94965 606-E7
300 MrnC 94965 626-E1
DEER TREE CT
2400 MRTZ 94553 572-A6
DEERVALE CT
7700 DBLN 94568 693-G2
DEERVALE RD
8300 DBLN 94568 693-G2
DEER VALLEY LN
2100 WLCK 94598 612-G4

BAY AREA

STREET
Block City ZIP Pg-Grid

DEER VALLEY RD
- ANT - 595-G6
- CCCo - 595-G6
100 SRFL 94903 566-F1
3300 ANT 94509 575-F7
3300 ANT 94509 595-F2
DEER VIEW TER
- FRMT 94539 794-B1
DEERWOOD AV
7300 OAK 94605 670-H2
DEERWOOD CT
- LVMR 94550 696-E3
300 MTVW 94040 811-F4
2100 MRTZ 94553 571-J7
DEERWOOD DR
1500 MRTZ 94553 571-J7
2400 SRMN 94583 673-A1
2800 SJS 95148 835-C7
DEERWOOD PL
100 SRMN 94583 673-B2
DEERWOOD PZ
- HAY 94542 712-B3
DEERWOOD RD
- DNVL 94526 673-B1
100 SRMN 94583 673-B1
100 CCCo 94583 673-B1
DEERWOOD TER
3400 FRMT 94536 752-A6
DE FALCO WY
1300 SJS 95131 814-C7
DEFOE CT
3200 FRMT 94536 752-F1
DE FOE DR
7400 CPTO 95014 852-D2
DE FORD DR
- SRFL 94903 566-C3
DE FOREST WY
- SF 94114 667-G2
DEFREMERY AV
900 OAK 94606 649-J6
DEGAS RD
100 PTLV 94028 810-C5
DEGNAN DR
5300 MRTZ 94553 591-F1
DE GUIGNE DR
300 SUNV 94086 812-G7
DE HARO ST
- SF 94107 668-B3
- SF 94103 668-A3
DEHAVILLAND CT
19400 SAR 95070 852-G6
DEHAVILLAND DR
19100 SAR 95070 852-G6
DE HAVILLAND ST
100 OAK 94621 670-D7
DEHON ST
- SF 94114 667-G2
DEKKER TER
5400 FRMT 94555 752-B3
DE KOVEN AV
2400 BLMT 94002 769-B1
DE LA BRIANDAIS CT
- PIN 94564 569-H6
DE LA CRUZ BLVD
- SJS 95054 813-F6
- SJS 95110 813-F6
500 SCL 95054 813-E5
500 SJS 95131 813-F6
1700 SCL 95050 833-F2
2500 SJS 95050 833-F2
2900 SJS 95054 833-F2
2900 SJS 95110 833-F2
DE LA CRUZ RD
29100 HAY 94544 712-C7
DE LA CRUZ WY
1400 MRGA 94556 651-D1
DELACY AV
1000 CCCo 94553 571-G4
DE LA FARGE DR
7400 CPTO 95014 852-D2
DE LA GUERRA RD
- SRFL 94903 566-A1
DEL AMIGO RD
- DNVL 94526 652-H1
DEL AMIGO TR
- CCCo - 652-G2
DELANCEY LN
3600 CNCD 94519 592-J1
DELANCEY ST
500 SF 94107 648-C6
DELAND AV
700 SJS 95128 853-H2
DELANO AV
- SF 94112 667-F7
500 SF 94112 687-E1
DELANO CT
1300 SJS 95121 855-B2
39100 FRMT 94538 753-A5
DELANO ST
700 AlaC 94580 691-E5
1000 AlaC 94578 691-E5
DE LA PENA AV
1800 SCL 95050 833-D5
DELAROSA CT
2400 PIN 94564 589-J1
DEL ARROYO CT
1200 LFYT 94549 611-H4
DE LAURENTI CT
- WLCK 94598 612-J3
DELAWARE AV
700 SJS 95123 874-F4
2400 RDWC 94061 790-A3
DELAWARE CT
1300 LVMR 94550 695-F6
5500 CNCD 94521 593-F6
DELAWARE DR
1400 CNCD 94521 593-F6
3600 FRMT 94538 773-D2
DELAWARE ST
200 VAL 94590 530-A3
800 BERK 94804 629-D1
1100 BERK 94702 629-E1
1500 BERK 94703 629-F1
1900 BERK 94709 629-F1
2800 OAK 94602 650-E5
E DELAWARE ST
3600 FRMT 94538 773-E2
N DELAWARE ST
- SMTO 94401 748-J1
100 SMTO 94401 728-H6
S DELAWARE ST
- SMTO 94401 749-A1

S DELAWARE ST
400 SMTO 94402 749-A1
1900 SMTO 94403 749-B3
DELAWARE WY
700 LVMR 94550 695-E6
DELBARR CT
2000 SJS 95125 854-C4
DELBERT WY
900 SJS 95126 853-J3
DEL CAMBRE DR
1000 SJS 95129 852-J3
DEL CAMINO DR
2700 SPAB 94806 588-J2
2900 RCH 94806 588-J2
DEL CAMPO CIR
3400 SLN 94578 691-B4
DEL CANTO DR
6100 SJS 95119 875-C6
DEL CARLO CT
100 LGTS 95032 873-D6
DEL CASA DR
- MLV 94941 606-E3
DEL CENTRO
- BEN 94510 551-D4
100 MLBR 94030 727-J5
DEL CENTRO CT
100 CCCo 94549 611-H1
DEL CENTRO WY
700 LALT 94024 831-F1
DEL CERRO
- PIT 94565 574-B6
DEL CERRO CT
15800 LGTS 95032 873-E5
DEL CHIARO WY
3400 CNCD 94518 592-H2
3400 CNCD 94519 592-H2
DE LEMOS AV
1500 HAY 94544 732-A1
DE LEON AV
400 FRMT 94539 753-H7
DE LEON LN
900 FCTY 94404 749-F4
DE LEON WY
1500 LVMR 94550 715-G3
DEL ESTE ST
1800 CCCo 94549 611-J1
DEL FAVERO DR
4000 ANT 94509 595-D1
DELFINO AV
200 RCH 94801 588-D7
DELFINO WY
1300 MLPK 94025 790-D5
DEL FRANCO CT
2100 SJS 95131 814-A4
DEL FRANCO ST
2100 SJS 95131 814-A4
DELGADO CT
- FRMT 94539 753-E4
100 VAL 94591 530-D3
3700 SJS 95008 853-B7
DELGADO PL
- SF 94109 647-J4
DELGADO RD
29000 HAY 94544 712-C7
DEL GANADO RD
600 SRFL 94903 566-B1
DEL HAMBRE CIR
- WLCK 94595 612-B6
DEL HARO WY
- SRFL 94903 566-D5
DEL HOMBRE LN
2900 CCCo 94596 612-D1
2900 WLCK 94596 612-D1
DELIA ST
100 SCIC 95127 814-J7
DELIA TER
34100 FRMT 94555 752-B3
DELIA WY
5400 LVMR 94550 696-C7
DELICADO CT
3100 PLE 94588 694-C7
DEL JIUDICE CT
1600 SLN 94578 691-C3
DELL AV
400 MTVW 94043 811-F2
900 CMBL 95008 873-D1
900 CMBL 95008 853-D7
DELL CT
200 AlaC 94541 711-F1
1600 SJS 95118 873-J4
DELL LN
- MLV 94941 606-E3
DELL RD
800 PCFA 94044 726-H5
DELL ST
- MLV 94941 606-E3
DELLARO CT
- PLE 94566 715-C6
DELLBROOK AV
- SF 94131 667-E3
400 SSF 94080 707-F1
DELLHAVEN CT
17400 AlaC 94552 692-C2
DEL LOMA CT
4700 SJS 95008 873-A1
DEL LOMA DR
2800 SJS 95008 873-A1
2900 CMBL 95008 873-A1
DELLWOOD CT
- PLHL 94523 592-B5
- SRFL 94901 567-C7
DELLWOOD DR
- SJS 95131 814-A4
DELLWOOD WY
5200 SJS 95118 874-B4
DEL MAR AV
- BERK 94708 609-J7
200 VAL 94589 530-B1
400 PCFA 94044 707-A4
700 LVMR 94550 715-E2
700 NVTO 94947 526-A4
800 ALA 94501 669-J4
800 SJS 95128 853-G3
DELMAR AV
25000 HAY 94542 712-A3
DEL MAR CIR
- CCCo 94525 550-C5
3400 SLN 94578 691-B4
DEL MAR CT
- ORIN 94563 610-F5
DELMAR CT
- RDWC 94063 770-F6

DELMAR CT
25100 HAY 94542 712-A3
DEL MAR DR
3200 LFYT 94549 591-H7
3500 CNCD 94519 593-A1
9800 SRMN 94583 673-G6
DELMAR DR
- TBRN 94920 607-C5
DELMAR ST
- SF 94117 667-F1
DELMAR WY
200 SMTO 94403 749-B5
DELMAS AV
- SJS 95110 834-A7
- SJS 95113 834-A7
300 SJS 95126 834-A7
600 SJS 95125 854-B2
DEL MEDIO AV
- MTVW 94040 811-E3
DEL MEDIO CT
2700 MTVW 94040 811-E2
DELMER ST
2400 OAK 94602 650-E4
DELMONT AV
3600 OAK 94605 670-H1
DEL MONTE
- LKSP 94939 586-G5
DEL MONTE AV
- LALT 94022 811-D4
100 SSF 94080 707-E2
2000 SCL 95051 832-J2
6800 CCCo 94805 589-D6
8000 NWK 94560 752-C7
DEL MONTE CT
1500 MRGA 94556 631-F6
1800 CCCo 94595 612-B7
DEL MONTE DR
- HIL 94010 728-C7
- PCFA 94044 707-A2
100 CCCo 94595 612-B7
100 WLCK 94595 612-B7
300 PIN 94564 569-B4
2100 CCCo 94564 569-B4
2100 CCCo 94806 569-B4
2100 PIN 94806 569-B4
DEL MONTE PL
- SMTO 94403 749-A6
900 SJS 95117 853-D2
DEL MONTE ST
- SF 94112 687-F2
1900 LVMR 94550 696-C2
2700 CCCo 94805 589-C6
2700 ELCR 94530 589-C6
3000 SMTO 94403 749-A6
DEL MONTE WY
300 PIN 94564 569-C3
1600 MRGA 94556 631-F6
3400 SLN 94578 691-B4
DELMORE RD
2700 CCCo 94806 569-C5
DELNA MANOR LN
1000 SJS 95128 853-F3
DELNO ST
1000 SJS 95126 833-G5
DEL NORTE AV
200 SUNV 94086 812-F5
1000 MLPK 94025 770-H7
1000 MLPK 94025 790-H1
DEL NORTE CT
- BERK 94707 609-G6
1600 LVMR 94550 695-E6
27500 HAY 94545 731-H1
DEL NORTE DR
100 SBRN 94066 707-E7
700 LVMR 94550 695-E6
3400 SJS 95132 814-G3
DEL NORTE ST
2000 BERK 94707 609-G6
DELNORTE ST
700 VAL 94591 530-D4
DE LOACH CT
1300 SJS 95125 853-G4
DEL OCEANO DR
3100 CCCo 94549 611-H1
DE LONG AV
600 NVTO 94945 526-B3
DE LONG ST
- SF 94112 687-C2
500 DALY 94014 687-C2
DELORES CT
4600 UNC 94587 752-A1
DELORES DR
4300 UNC 94587 732-A7
4500 UNC - 752-A1
4500 UNC 94587 752-A1
4800 UNC 94587 751-J1
DEL ORO CIR
2700 ANT 94509 575-B6
DEL ORO CT
- SRMN 94583 673-B2
600 CMBL 95008 853-C5
5500 SJS 95124 873-G6
DEL ORO DR
5400 SJS 95124 873-H6
DEL ORO PL
5500 SJS 95124 873-G6
DEL ORO LAGOON
- MrnC 94949 526-H7
DEL PASO AV
1700 SJS 95124 873-H3
DEL PASO DR
- SSF 94080 707-F3
DELPHI CIR
200 LALT 94022 811-E5
DELPHI CT
200 LALT 94022 811-E4
DELPHINIUM CT
38700 NWK 94560 772-G1
DEL PLAYA
1000 PLE 94566 714-G3
DEL PRADO DR
- CMBL 95008 853-C6
- DALY 94015 687-B7
DEL PRESIDIO BLVD
900 SRFL 94903 566-E3
DEL REY AV
500 SUNV 94086 812-D5
4400 SJS 95111 875-A1
DEL REY CT
- AMCN 94589 510-A2
- LFYT 94549 591-H7
- SCAR 94070 769-F3

DEL REY CT
300 SJS 95111 875-A1
DEL REY ST
1800 LFYT 94549 591-H7
DELRIDGE DR
400 SJS 95111 875-C2
DEL RIO
- PIT 94565 574-A2
DEL RIO CIR
1300 CNCD 94518 592-E6
3400 SLN 94578 691-B4
DEL RIO CT
- CCCo 94549 591-H7
- CCCo 94549 611-H1
- MRGA 94556 631-F6
800 MPS 95035 794-B5
1300 CNCD 94518 592-E6
DEL RIO DR
1800 CCCo 94549 591-J7
1800 CCCo 94549 611-H1
6900 SJS 95119 875-E7
6900 SJS 95119 895-E1
DEL RIO WY
1000 MRGA 94556 631-F6
DEL ROBLES CT
6100 SJS 95119 875-C6
DEL ROSA CT
- CCCo 94596 632-F1
DEL ROSA WY
200 SMTO 94403 749-D5
DEL ROY CT
600 CMBL 95008 853-C5
DELSEA PL
6000 SJS 95123 874-E6
DEL SOL AV
300 PLE 94566 714-E4
DELSON CT
13100 LAH 94022 811-A7
DEL SUR AV
- SF 94127 667-E5
DEL SUR ST
100 VAL 94591 550-D1
300 VAL 94591 530-D7
DELTA CIR
100 VAL 94589 510-A5
DELTA COM
- FRMT 94538 773-D3
DELTA CT
1600 HAY 94544 732-B2
1800 AlaC 94586 734-B2
DELTA DR
- CCCo 94565 573-E1
DELTA GRN
- FRMT 94538 773-D3
DELTA PL
- SF 94102 648-A5
200 DNVL 94526 653-B5
DELTA RD
2900 SJS 95135 855-F3
DELTA ST
- SF 94134 687-J2
100 SF 94134 688-A1
DELTA TER
- FRMT 94538 773-D3
DELTA WY
1100 DNVL 94526 653-B5
DELTA FAIR BLVD
2700 ANT 94509 575-A5
3300 ANT 94509 574-H5
DELTAVIEW LN
1000 CCCo 94565 573-F2
DELTA VIEW WY
5100 ANT 94509 595-E4
DEL TREN AV
800 PIT 94565 574-F3
DEL TRIGO LN
5800 CNCD 94521 593-G7
5800 CLAY 94517 593-G7
DELUCA DR
1500 SJS 95131 814-C6
DE LUCA PL
- SRFL 94901 586-G2
DELUCCHI DR
2100 PLE 94588 694-E7
DE LUCCHI TER
- FRMT 94536 733-A5
- UNC 94587 733-A5
- UNC 94587 732-J5
DEL VAILE CT
3400 PLE 94588 694-F6
DEL VALE AV
- SF 94127 667-E5
DEL VALLE
- ORIN 94563 610-D7
DEL VALLE CIR
- CCCo 94803 589-F3
2800 SJS 95148 835-D7
DEL VALLE CT
200 PLE 94566 714-E3
DEL VALLE PKWY
3500 PLE 94566 714-D2
DEL VALLE PL
30500 UNC 94587 732-A4
DELVIN WY
2200 SSF 94080 707-E5
DEL VISTA CT
- PLHL 94523 592-A4
DELWOOD ST
1100 VAL 94591 530-F4
DELYNN WY
1100 SJS 95125 854-B6
DEMARCUS BLVD
- DBLN 94568 694-B4
DEMARET DR
4600 SCL 95054 813-D4
DE MARIETTA AV
1600 SJS 95126 853-G4
DE MARIETTA CT
1700 SJS 95126 853-G4
DE MATTEI CT
1000 SJS 95112 834-C3
DEMEREST LN
5400 SJS 95138 875-C3
DEMETER ST
100 EPA 94303 791-C1
200 EPA 94303 771-C7
DE MILLE DR
4100 SJS 95117 853-B3
4100 SJS 95129 853-B3
DEMING ST
- SF 94114 667-F2

DEMOCRACY WY
2900 SCL 95054 813-A4
DE MONTFORT AV
- SF 94112 667-D7
DEMPSEY RD
- MPS 95035 794-C7
400 MPS 95035 814-C1
DEMPSEY WY
- MPS 95035 794-C6
100 CCCo 94572 549-J6
DEMPSTER AV
10200 CPTO 95014 832-B7
DENA DR
2100 CNCD 94519 572-G7
DENAIR AV
2200 SJS 95122 854-H1
DENALI DR
- SMTO 94403 748-H7
DENALI WY
1500 SJS 95122 854-H1
DENARDI WY
300 SSF 94080 707-F5
DE NATALE CT
5200 PLE 94588 694-A6
DENEB CT
1300 WLCK 94596 611-J2
DENEVI DR
2400 SJS 95130 853-A7
DENEVI LN
16500 SCIC 95030 872-H7
DENFIELD AV
- BEN 94510 550-J3
DENHAM CT
- HIL 94010 728-E7
DENHAM DR
35500 FRMT 94555 752-E1
DENICIO ST
- CCCo 94803 569-C7
DENIO ST
100 VAL 94590 529-J3
DENISE CT
- NVTO 94945 526-C3
800 MrnC 94965 606-E6
DENISE DR
- CCCo 94806 569-A5
- HIL 94010 748-E4
2000 SCL 95050 833-C4
DENISE LN
400 SMCo 94061 790-B4
3800 AlaC 94546 691-H2
DENISE ST
41100 FRMT 94539 753-E6
DENISE WY
1100 SJS 95125 854-C6
DENISON AV
10100 CPTO 95014 832-F7
DENISON PL
7500 AlaC 94552 692-G3
DENKE DR
1000 ALA 94502 669-J6
DENKER DR
4100 PLE 94588 694-A6
DENKINGER CT
1500 CNCD 94521 593-B3
DENKINGER RD
1500 CNCD 94521 593-C2
DENLYN ST
1100 NVTO 94947 526-C6
DENNING AV
- SRFL 94903 566-C4
DENNING CT
2500 AlaC 94546 691-H5
DENNING TER
37000 FRMT 94536 752-H2
DENNIS AV
300 SUNV 94086 812-C7
1400 MPS 95035 794-D6
1500 SLN 94578 691-D3
DENNIS CIR
1300 CNCD 94518 592-H3
DENNIS CT
1100 CCCo 94572 570-B1
10100 SCIC 95127 835-A3
38400 FRMT 94536 752-J4
DENNIS DR
100 DALY 94015 707-C3
900 PA 94303 791-D5
2000 ANT 94509 575-E6
3400 PLE 94588 694-F6
DENNIS LN
1500 MTVW 94040 811-G6
DENNISON ST
1800 ALA 94501 650-A7
1800 OAK 94606 650-A7
DENNYWOOD CT
2800 SJS 95148 835-D7
DE NORMANDIE WY
100 CCCo 94553 571-H4
DENSLOW DR
- SF 94132 667-B7
100 SF 94132 687-B1
DENSLOWE AV
- OAK 94603 670-G6
DENSLOWE LN
600 HAY 94544 711-H5
DENSMORE CT
3300 SJS 95148 835-E7
DENSMORE DR
2800 SJS 95148 835-E7
DENT AV
4900 SJS 95118 874-A3
DENT RD
- SF 94129 647-C4
DENTON AV
1100 HAY 94545 711-F5
1400 AlaC 94545 711-F5
DENTON CT
100 VAL 94591 530-C7
DENTON PL
5600 OAK 94619 651-A6
DENTON WY
3200 SJS 95121 855-C3
DENTWOOD DR
1200 SJS 95118 874-B4
DENVER DR
1000 CMBL 95008 853-B5
DENVER ST
4000 CNCD 94521 593-A2
DENYCE CT
- CCCo 94507 632-F6
DEODAR AV
1900 ANT 94509 575-E6

DEODAR DR
100 CCCo 94553 592-B1
DEODAR LN
- CCCo 94507 632-G7
16200 MSER 95030 872-H6
DEODAR WY
200 SUNV 94086 812-F7
7700 PLE 94588 693-H6
DEODARA DR
10400 CPTO 95014 832-F7
DEODARA ST
3100 FRMT 94538 753-C5
DEODARA WY
- WLCK 94596 612-C3
DEODARA GROVE CT
5300 SJS 95123 875-A3
DEODORA DR
- ATN 94027 790-G1
- ATN 94027 770-G7
400 LALT 94024 831-J6
1200 SCIC 94024 831-J5
DEODORA WY
- CCCo 94553 591-E1
DE PALMA CT
1400 SJS 95120 894-A1
DE PALMA DR
1400 SJS 95120 894-A1
DE PALMA LN
20000 CPTO 95014 852-E1
DE PASSIER WY
3500 ALA 94502 670-A7
DE PAUL DR
100 VAL 94589 510-B6
DE PAUL PL
2200 SCL 95051 832-J2
DE PAUL WY
1200 LVMR 94550 716-A2
DEPOT CT
1800 HAY 94545 711-G6
DEPOT RD
1800 HAY 94545 711-C6
2300 AlaC 94545 711-C6
33300 UNC 94587 732-F4
DERBE DR
800 SJS 95122 854-F1
DERBY AV
300 OAK 94601 670-B1
1200 OAK 94601 650-C7
DERBY CT
- SRMN 94583 673-C4
400 PLHL 94523 592-A7
600 SJS 94087 832-E4
32400 UNC 94587 732-C5
DERBY DR
2500 SRMN 94583 673-B4
DERBY LN
100 MRGA 94556 631-F5
DERBY PL
4300 PIT 94565 574-E7
4900 NWK 94560 752-F4
DERBY ST
- DALY 94015 707-C2
- SF 94102 648-A6
1100 BERK 94702 629-F3
1500 BERK 94703 629-F3
1900 BERK 94704 629-H3
2100 BERK 94705 629-H3
2100 BERK 94705 630-A3
2100 BERK 94704 630-A3
32200 UNC 94587 732-C5
DERBYSHIRE DR
1000 CPTO 95014 852-C3
DERBYSHIRE PL
600 DNVL 94526 653-D3
DEREK DR
5000 SJS 95136 874-J3
DERING PL
35700 FRMT 94536 752-G2
DERMODY AV
15200 AlaC 94580 691-D5
DERMOTT DR
1100 SJS 95129 853-A3
DEROCHE CT
1300 SJS 94087 832-B4
DE ROSA CT
3600 CNCD 94518 592-H4
DE ROSE WY
1400 SJS 95126 853-G3
DERRY LN
500 MLPK 94025 790-F3
DERRY WY
2200 SSF 94080 707-E5
DE SABLA RD
- SMTO 94402 748-H2
- HIL 94010 748-H2
DE SALLE TER
300 FRMT 94536 753-B1
DESANIE CIR
3500 CCCo 94565 573-F1
DESANIE WY
- CCCo 94565 573-F2
DE SANKA AV
12300 SAR 95070 852-E6
DESCANSO DR
- ORIN 94563 631-C4
DESCANSO WY
800 MrnC 94903 566-H2
DESCHUTES PL
1400 FRMT 94539 773-G4
DESCONSADO AV
900 LVMR 94550 715-E3
DESDEMONA CT
1500 SJS 95121 854-J4
DESERET DR
3000 RCH 94803 589-E2
DESERT CIR
1900 WLCK 94598 612-F2
DESERT FLAME DR
6200 SJS 95120 874-C7
6300 SJS 95120 894-C1
DESERT ISLE DR
800 SJS 95117 853-B3
DESERT OAK CT
29600 HAY 94544 712-D7
DESERT SANDS WY
- SJS 95123 875-B4
DESERTWOOD LN
3200 SJS 95132 814-E2
7600 PLE 94588 713-J1
DESERTWOOD PL
4400 PLE 94588 713-J1

DE SILVA CT
- MrnC 94941 606-G5
40500 FRMT 94538 753-C7
DE SILVA DR
- MrnC 94941 606-H5
DE SILVA ST
4500 FRMT 94538 753-B7
DESIN DR
4300 SJS 95118 874-C2
DESIREE AV
5200 LVMR 94550 696-C6
DES MOINES PL
600 SJS 95133 814-G7
DESMOND CT
1100 FRMT 94539 753-F6
DESMOND ST
- SF 94134 688-A2
4900 OAK 94618 629-J7
DE SOLO DR
1100 PCFA 94044 726-H4
DE SOTO AV
1300 BURL 94010 728-D6
3600 SCL 95051 832-H7
DE SOTO CT
- ORIN 94563 610-J5
DESOTO CT
800 WLCK 94598 592-G7
DE SOTO DR
700 PA 94303 791-B4
2400 SJS 95124 873-D4
2400 LGTS 95032 873-D4
DE SOTO LN
900 FCTY 94404 749-F3
DE SOTO RD
- SJS 95134 813-G3
DE SOTO ST
- SF 94127 667-C7
- SF 94132 687-C1
DE SOTO WY
100 SBRN 94066 727-J2
600 MLBR 94030 727-J2
1500 LVMR 94550 715-G3
DE SOUSA PL
3700 AlaC 94546 692-B3
DESRYS BLVD
2400 ANT 94509 574-H6
DESTINY LN
200 CCCo 94583 673-B1
200 SRMN 94583 673-B1
DESTRY CT
100 SJS 95136 875-A3
DESVIO CT
- PCFA 94044 727-A5
DESVIO WY
1500 BLMT 94002 769-E2
DETJEN CT
6200 PLE 94586 693-F6
DETJEN ST
3600 FRMT 94538 753-C6
DE TRACY ST
1400 SJS 95128 853-E5
DETROIT AV
900 CNCD 94518 592-G4
1100 CNCD 94520 592-E2
4200 OAK 94619 650-G4
DETROIT CT
600 SJS 95133 814-G7
DETROIT DR
1700 SMTO 94404 749-C1
2000 SMTO 94403 749-C1
DETROIT ST
100 SF 94131 667-F6
100 SF 94112 667-F6
500 SF 94127 667-F6
DE VACA WY
- HAY 94544 712-C7
1800 LVMR 94550 715-G2
DE VALLE CT
36200 FRMT 94536 733-B7
DE VARONA PL
2300 SCL 95050 833-C5
DEVCON CT
100 SJS 95112 833-J1
DEVCON DR
200 SJS 95112 833-J1
DEVEREAUX DR
1600 BURL 94010 728-C5
DEVEREUX CT
2800 PLE 94588 714-A3
DEVERON CT
7500 SJS 95135 855-J6
DE VILLE WY
6500 SJS 95129 852-F3
DEVILS DROP CT
700 RCH 94803 589-G3
DEVILS HOLE TR
- AlaC 94546 652-C5
- AlaC 94546 652-C5
- CCCo - 652-C5
DEVIL VIEW PL
1900 WLCK 94595 632-B1
DEVIN DR
- MRGA 94556 631-E4
2300 SCIC 95148 835-E5
E DEVINE ST
- SJS 95112 834-B6
W DEVINE ST
- SJS 95113 834-B6
100 SJS 95110 834-B6
DEVITA CT
2000 WLCK 94595 632-D1
DEVLIN CT
600 SJS 95133 834-B2
1100 VAL 94591 530-G6
DEVLIN DR
1100 SolC 94591 530-F6
1100 VAL 94591 530-F5
DEVON AV
- PLHL 94523 591-H4
18500 SAR 95070 852-H7
DEVON CIR
- PLHL 94523 591-J4
DEVON CT
400 SRMN 94583 673-G7
1800 CNCD 94520 592-F2
41500 FRMT 94539 753-F6
DEVON DR
100 SRFL 94903 566-D4
600 HIL 94010 748-F1
900 HAY 94542 712-B4
DEVON PL
2100 MPS 95035 794-A2

INDEX

STREET
Block City ZIP Pg-Grid

DEVON PL
3900 LVMR 94550 716-A2
3900 LVMR 94550 715-J2
DEVON WY
2800 CCCo 94806 589-A2
3400 RDWC 94061 789-H1
6800 SJS 95129 852-E4
6900 OAK 94705 630-C3
DEVONA TER
1300 SUNV 94087 832-B4
DEVON PARK CT
5100 SJS 95136 874-F3
DEVONSHIRE AV
- MTVW 94043 812-B3
800 SLN 94579 691-A5
2700 SMCo 94063 770-C7
2700 SMCo 94063 790-C1
DEVONSHIRE BLVD
- SCAR 94070 769-D4
100 SMCo 94070 769-D4
DEVONSHIRE CIR
- SMCo 94070 769-E4
DEVONSHIRE COM
4500 FRMT 94536 752-G4
DEVONSHIRE CT
- DNVL 94506 653-J6
100 VAL 94591 530-G5
200 PLHL 94523 591-J4
1300 ELCR 94530 609-D1
2100 WLCK 94596 632-G1
DEVONSHIRE DR
- NVTO 94947 525-G2
1300 ELCR 94530 609-E1
1700 BEN 94510 550-J2
6300 SJS 95129 852-F3
DEVONSHIRE LN
- CCCo 94565 573-G3
DEVONSHIRE ST
100 VAL 94591 530-H5
32200 UNC 94587 732-C4
DEVONSHIRE WY
- SF 94131 667-D3
700 SUNV 94087 832-F4
DEVONWOOD
100 HER 94547 569-F3
DEVONWOOD WY
15900 AlaC 94580 691-C7
15900 AlaC 94580 711-C1
DEVOS CT
3400 SCL 95051 832-J3
DEVOTO ST
800 MTVW 94041 812-A7
DEVPAR CT
2400 ANT 94509 575-F6
DEVRI CT
2500 MTVW 94043 811-F2
DEW DROP CIR
- PIT 94565 573-J2
DEWEY AV
1200 RDWC 94061 789-J2
DEWEY BLVD
400 SF 94116 667-D4
400 SF 94127 667-D4
DEWEY DR
600 FCTY 94404 749-G5
DEWEY PL
5400 FRMT 94538 773-A1
DEWEY RD
- CCCo 94708 609-G3
DEWEY ST
1700 SMTO 94403 749-D2
15000 SLN 94579 691-B6
DEWEY WY
6200 SJS 95123 874-J7
DEWING AV
800 LFYT 94549 611-E6
DEWING LN
1100 WLCK 94595 612-B6
1200 CCCo 94595 612-B6
DE WITT CT
2100 UNC 94587 732-G7
3600 ANT 94509 595-C1
DE WITT DR
- ROSS 94957 586-C2
DEWITT RD
- SF 94129 647-E4
- SF 94129 647-E4
DEWLAP CT
2500 ANT 94509 595-G3
DE WOLF ST
- SF 94112 687-E2
DEXTER AV
- SMCo 94063 790-C1
DEXTER CT
2200 AlaC 94541 692-C7
DEXTER DR
5300 SJS 95123 874-J3
21300 CPTO 95014 832-C7
DEXTER PL
- MLBR 94030 728-A3
200 SRMN 94583 673-F5
DEXTER WY
2200 AlaC 94541 692-C7
2200 AlaC 94541 712-C1
DE YOUNG LN
3200 LFYT 94549 611-H4
DEZAHARA WY
26800 LAH 94022 831-A2
DHILLION CT
- HAY 94544 712-B7
DIABLO AV
- NVTO 94945 526-B4
200 MTVW 94043 811-F3
700 NVTO 94947 526-B4
2300 ANT 94509 575-E6
3000 HAY 94545 711-D6
DIABLO CIR
- LFYT 94549 611-A6
3300 PIN 94564 569-G7
DIABLO CT
- DNVL 94526 653-B2
- NVTO 94947 526-A4
- PLHL 94523 592-C3
300 PA 94306 811-C3
400 MRTZ 94553 571-H7
3200 PIN 94564 569-G6
3600 PLE 94588 694-F7
DIABLO DR
- OAK 94611 630-F5
- OAK 94611 630-F5
- CCCo 94611 630-F5
- MrnC 94904 586-C4

DIABLO DR
900 LFYT 94549 611-G7
DIABLO PL
2400 UNC 94587 732-C5
DIABLO RD
- DNVL 94526 653-B1
- DNVL 94526 633-C7
1000 DNVL 94526 633-C7
1500 DNVL 94506 633-C7
1500 CCCo 94526 633-C7
1700 DNVL 94506 653-E1
1700 CCCo 94526 653-E1
1900 CCCo 94506 653-E1
DIABLO ST
- VAL 94589 510-B6
100 DNVL 94526 653-A2
100 DNVL 94526 652-J2
1000 CLAY 94517 593-H7
DIABLO VW
- ORIN 94563 611-A4
DIABLO WY
- DNVL 94526 653-B2
400 MRTZ 94553 571-H7
700 SMCo 94062 789-F2
1200 SJS 95120 894-D1
DIABLO CREEK CT
- DNVL 94506 653-F1
300 CLAY 94517 593-G6
DIABLO CREEK PL
- DNVL 94506 653-F1
400 CLAY 94517 593-G6
DIABLO DOWNS DR
800 CCCo 94517 613-G1
DIABLO LAKES LN
- CCCo 94526 633-F5
DIABLO OAKS WY
- LFYT 94549 611-H7
- LFYT 94549 631-H1
DIABLO RANCH CT
2100 CCCo - 633-F7
DIABLO RANCH DR
2100 CCCo - 633-F7
DIABLO RANCH PL
2300 CCCo - 633-F7
DIABLO SHADOW DR
3000 WLCK 94598 612-J2
DIABLO VIEW CT
- DNVL 94506 653-H5
4200 CNCD 94518 592-J4
DIABLO VIEW DR
- ORIN 94563 610-J4
- ORIN 94563 611-A4
DIABLO VIEW LN
- CLAY 94517 613-J1
DIABLO VIEW RD
- PLHL 94523 612-A1
- PLHL 94523 611-J1
3000 CCCo 94549 611-J1
DIABLO VISTA RD
1500 CCCo 94507 632-E3
DIADEM DR
700 SJS 95116 834-H4
DIADON DR
24800 HAY 94544 711-H4
DIAL WY
5900 SJS 95129 852-F4
DIAMENTE CT
1800 SJS 95116 834-F3
DIAMOND AV
500 SSF 94080 707-J2
14000 SJS 95127 835-A4
DIAMOND BLVD
1900 CNCD 94520 592-C2
DIAMOND COM
5200 FRMT 94555 752-C3
DIAMOND CT
- DNVL 94526 652-H1
100 HER 94547 569-H6
300 PLE 94566 714-D6
1100 LALT 94024 831-G2
1200 LVMR 94550 715-D3
20000 AlaC 94546 692-C5
DIAMOND DR
- DNVL 94526 652-H2
- LVMR 94550 715-D3
DIAMOND ST
- SF 94114 667-G3
100 SBRN 94066 707-J5
800 ANT 94509 575-C4
1100 SF 94131 667-G3
1200 SF 94131 667-G5
DIAMOND WY
200 MPS 95035 793-H6
1200 CNCD 94520 592-D3
DIAMOND HEAD DR
3500 SJS 95136 854-G7
DIAMOND HEAD LN
5200 FRMT 94538 752-J7
DIAMOND HEAD PASG
- CMAD 94925 606-J1
DIAMOND HEIGHTS BLVD
5000 SF 94114 667-F4
5000 SF 94131 667-F4
DIAMOND OAKS CT
21200 SAR 95070 852-C6
DIAMOND RIDGE DR
24500 HAY 94544 711-H3
DIAMOND SPRINGS CT
100 VAL 94589 509-J5
DIANA AV
800 SJS 95116 834-H5
DIANA COM
5300 FRMT 94555 752-B3
DIANA CT
- PLHL 94523 612-A1
DIANA DR
200 VAL 94589 510-A5
DIANA LN
- ANT 94509 574-J6
700 SJS 95116 834-H4
6400 MRTZ 94553 591-H3
7800 DBLN 94568 693-H3
DIANA PL
600 HAY 94544 712-B5
2100 SJS 95116 834-H3
DIANA ST
- SF 94124 668-B7
DIANDA DR
1500 CNCD 94521 593-B3
DIANE AV
100 PIT 94565 574-F4

DIANE CT
1700 CNCD 94520 592-E4
5100 LVMR 94550 716-C1
DIANE DR
- CCCo 94803 589-E2
- RCH 94803 589-E2
DIANE LN
- LKSP 94939 586-E6
5100 LVMR 94550 716-C1
DIANE MARIE WY
2400 SCL 95050 833-B5
DIANNE CT
- LFYT 94549 631-H1
400 SSF 94080 707-F5
DIANNE DR
2000 SCL 95050 833-C4
12600 LAH 94022 831-D1
DIANNE WY
- SRFL 94901 586-G2
DIAPIAN BAY
100 ALA 94502 669-J6
DIAS CIR
100 PIT 94565 574-F4
DIAS CT
- CCCo 94803 589-G2
DIAS DR
- CNCD 94518 592-E6
3200 SJS 95148 835-D6
DIAS WY
- SRFL 94903 566-D4
DIAS DORADAS
- ORIN 94563 610-G5
DIAVILA AV
4200 PLE 94588 694-E7
DIAVILA CT
2800 PLE 94588 694-E6
DIAZ AV
- SF 94132 687-B1
DIAZ DR
- CNCD 94518 592-E6
4500 FRMT 94536 752-E3
DIAZ LN
900 FCTY 94404 749-F3
DIAZ PL
- OAK 94611 630-D7
DIAZ RIDGE TR
- MrnC 94965 606-B7
- MrnC 94965 626-A1
DIAZ RIDGE FIRE RD
- MrnC 94965 606-A7
DIBBLE CT
3000 SCL 95051 833-A6
DIBBLEE RD
- MrnC 94904 586-A3
- ROSS 94957 586-A3
DICHA AL
- SF 94118 647-E6
DICHIERA CT
- SF 94112 687-E2
DICHONDRA PL
5700 NWK 94560 752-H7
DICKENS AV
15000 SCIC 95124 873-F4
27700 HAY 94544 712-A7
28000 HAY 94544 732-A1
DICKENS CT
- MLV 94941 606-H6
- SCAR 94070 769-E6
900 LVMR 94550 696-A6
3000 FRMT 94536 752-H2
3500 PLE 94588 694-E6
DICKENSON COM
3400 FRMT 94538 753-B5
DICKENSON DR
- LVMR 94550 696-A6
- MRGA 94556 651-E1
DICKEY ST
900 RDWC 94061 770-A7
DICKINSON DR
4800 SJS 95111 875-B1
DICKINSON WY
600 SJS 95111 875-B1
DICKSON CT
4100 OAK 94605 671-B2
DICKSON DR
1100 NVTO 94949 546-D1
DICKSON LN
- MRTZ 94553 571-G7
- MRTZ 94553 591-G1
DIDION CT
6300 SJS 95123 875-A7
DIDION WY
6300 SJS 95123 875-A7
DIDUCA WY
14800 SCIC 95032 873-F7
14800 SCIC 95032 893-G1
DIEGO DR
- SRFL 94903 566-B1
36400 FRMT 94536 752-F3
DIEHL AV
400 SLN 94577 671-C7
DIEHL WY
300 PIT 94565 574-E7
DIEL DR
1500 MPS 95035 794-B3
DIENINGER ST
- VAL 94589 510-D6
DIERICX CT
22300 MTVW 94040 832-A1
DIERICX DR
2500 MTVW 94040 832-A1
DIESEL ST
2000 OAK 94606 670-A1
DI FIORE DR
800 SJS 95128 853-G2
DIGBY ST
- SF 94131 667-G5
DIGITAL DR
- NVTO 94949 546-F1
DI GIULIO AV
900 SCL 95050 833-E2
DIJON WY
6400 DBLN 94568 694-A1
N DIKE RD
- SLN 94577 690-F4
S DIKE RD
- SLN 94577 690-F5
W DIKE RD
100 SLN 94577 690-F5
DILETTA AV
1600 SLN 94578 691-D3

DILLARD CT
- SJS 95128 853-F3
DILLARD WY
2100 ANT 94509 595-A1
DILLER ST
- RDWC 94063 770-A6
DILLION CT
2500 SJS 95133 814-F7
DILLO ST
900 SLN 94578 691-D4
DILLON AV
- CMBL 95008 853-E6
DILLON DR
100 VAL 94589 510-A5
DILLON RD
- BEN 94510 550-G1
DILLON WY
11300 DBLN 94568 693-F5
DILLWOOD CT
800 SCIC 95136 854-D7
DILY LN
- CCCo 94565 573-E2
DI MAGGIO AV
- PIT 94565 574-D3
DIMAGGIO WY
3200 ANT 94509 595-A1
3400 ANT 94509 575-A7
DIMER RD
- CCCo 94553 571-F2
DIMM ST
400 RCH 94805 589-B6
DIMM WY
5900 CCCo 94805 589-B5
DIMOND AV
3400 OAK 94602 650-D4
DINA CT
1500 SJS 95121 855-A3
DINA DR
1400 CNCD 94518 592-J3
DINA LN
2700 SJS 95121 855-A3
DINAHS CT
600 PA 94306 811-D3
DI NAPOLI DR
1000 SJS 95129 852-G3
DINEEN ST
1400 MRTZ 94553 571-E2
DINES CT
- EPA 94303 791-C2
DINGLEY ST
4100 OAK 94605 671-D4
DINKEL CT
1100 SJS 95118 874-C3
DINKLESPIEL STATION LN
- ATN 94027 790-E2
DINNY ST
3500 SCL 95054 813-E6
DINUBA CT
32700 UNC 94587 752-A1
DINUBA ST
4600 UNC 94587 752-A1
DIOKNO CT
1400 PIT 94565 574-G5
DIONNE CT
- BLMT 94002 768-J1
DIONNE WY
900 SJS 95133 834-E1
DIOR TER
- LALT 94022 811-E6
DIPPER CIR
500 SJS 95117 853-D1
DIPPER CT
- RCH 94803 589-F2
DIPSEA TR
100 MrnC 94941 606-C4
100 MrnC 94965 606-C4
DI SALVO AV
100 SJS 95128 833-F7
200 SCIC 95128 833-F7
200 SCIC 95128 853-F1
DISCOVERY AV
5000 SJS 95111 875-B2
DISCOVERY RD
15100 SLN 94579 690-J6
DISCOVERY WY
1000 CNCD 94521 593-D7
DISHMAN DR
17600 LGTS 95032 893-B2
DISHONG ST
800 VAL 94590 530-A6
DISK CT
4600 SJS 95134 813-D1
DISK DR
4700 SJS 95134 813-D1
DISNEY LN
6100 CPTO 95014 852-G2
DISTEL CIR
300 LALT 94022 811-F4
DISTEL DR
400 LALT 94022 811-E5
DITMUS CT
40400 FRMT 94538 753-D6
DITTOS LN
- LGTS 95032 893-A1
DIVISADERO ST
- SF 94117 667-G1
- SF 94114 667-G1
400 SF 94117 647-F4
1000 SF 94115 647-F4
2700 SF 94123 647-F4
3100 SF 94123 647-F3
DIVISION DR
- CCCo 94553 571-J3
DIVISION ST
- SF 94103 668-A1
- SF 94107 668-A1
300 SF 94103 667-J1
400 CMBL 95008 873-C2
E DIVISION ST
600 LGTS 95030 873-C2
600 CMBL 95008 873-C2
DIVISO ST
200 TBRN 94920 607-E7
200 TBRN 94920 627-E1
DIX ST
1100 SMTO 94401 749-B2
DIX WY
500 SJS 95125 854-C4
DIXIE AL
- SF 94114 667-F3

DIXIE AL
- SF 94131 667-F3
DIXIE CT
100 VAL 94589 510-A5
DIXIE DR
1600 SJS 95122 854-J1
DIXON CT
- DALY 94014 687-C4
38200 FRMT 94536 752-J4
DIXON DR
2500 SCL 95051 833-B5
DIXON LN
1800 CCCo 94521 593-E4
DIXON PL
3800 PA 94306 811-E2
DIXON RD
- MPS 95035 793-J3
100 MPS 95035 794-A3
DIXON ST
29000 HAY 94544 712-C7
29000 HAY 94544 732-D1
DIXON WY
700 LALT 94022 811-C4
DIXON LANDING RD
- FRMT 94538 793-H4
- SJS 95002 793-H4
- MPS 95035 793-H4
1600 MPS 95002 793-H4
DOANE AV
1700 MTVW 94043 811-H3
DOANE ST
500 AlaC 94580 691-D5
4000 FRMT 94538 773-D3
DOBBEL AV
26100 HAY 94542 712-D4
DOBBIN DR
1700 SJS 95133 834-E2
DOBBS DR
- PLHL 94523 591-J5
DOBERN AV
2200 SJS 95116 834-H4
DOBIE DR
- SJS 95123 875-B4
DOBRICH CIR
700 CCCo 94565 573-H3
DOBSON CT
2900 FRMT 94555 732-E7
DOBSON WY
34300 FRMT 94555 732-E7
DOCCIA CT
2200 PLE 94566 715-B6
DOCKSIDE CIR
- RDWC 94065 749-J6
- SRFL 94903 566-F2
DOCKSIDE DR
- DALY 94014 687-E5
DODD CT
800 CCCo 94565 573-C2
DODGE AL
700 VAL 94590 530-A6
DODGE AV
25800 HAY 94545 711-F6
DODGE CT
5400 CNCD 94521 593-G4
DODGE DR
1000 RDWC 94063 770-E6
DODGE PL
- SF 94102 647-J6
DODIE ST
- SRFL 94901 586-J3
DODSON ST
1900 SPAB 94806 588-J3
DOE CT
100 FRMT 94539 773-J3
2600 CNCD 94519 572-H6
DOE WY
4500 ANT 94509 595-H3
DOGAWAY DR
100 SJS 95111 875-B2
DOGIE CT
- SRMN 94583 673-B3
DOGWOOD
- BEN 94510 551-C5
DOGWOOD AV
4700 FRMT 94536 752-H5
DOGWOOD CT
- NVTO 94947 526-D6
- SRMN 94583 693-H1
- WLCK 94598 612-J1
100 HER 94547 570-A4
200 HAY 94544 712-B6
800 SJS 95128 853-F4
DOGWOOD DR
100 WLCK 94598 612-J1
700 LVMR 94550 695-E7
6200 SJS 95138 875-F6
DOGWOOD LN
100 VAL 94591 550-F1
DOGWOOD PL
100 SRMN 94583 693-H1
DOGWOOD WY
2100 ANT 94509 575-B5
DOHERTY DR
200 LKSP 94939 586-F6
DOHERTY WY
100 SMCo 94061 790-B4
DOHR ST
2700 BERK 94702 629-F3
DOHRMANN LN
400 PIN 94564 569-C4
DOIDGE AV
2300 PIN 94564 569-H7
2300 PIN 94564 589-H1
2700 PIN 94564 570-A7
DOLAN AV
300 MrnC 94941 606-F7
1500 SMTO 94401 729-B7
DOLAN WY
2300 CCCo 94806 569-B5
DOLCITA CT
200 DNVL 94526 653-C7
DOLERITA AV
100 FRMT 94539 753-E3
DOLERITA CT
- FRMT 94539 753-E3
DOLLAR AV
100 SSF 94080 707-J5
DOLLAR ST
25800 HAY 94544 712-A4
DOLLAR MOUNTAIN DR
200 SJS 95127 834-H1

DOLLINGER CT
3200 FRMT 94536 752-J3
DOLLIS PARK RD
- LFYT 94549 611-E5
DOLLY AV
1800 SLN 94577 690-J2
DOLORES AV
- SCL 95128 833-D6
200 SLN 94577 691-B1
900 LALT 94024 831-G3
2200 SCL 95050 833-D6
4600 OAK 94602 650-D3
21800 CPTO 95014 852-B1
21800 SCIC 95014 852-B1
DOLORES CT
- CCCo 94507 632-G5
- MRGA 94556 631-E3
400 PLE 94566 714-E5
400 SMTO 94403 749-B7
2300 PIN 94564 569-F6
DOLORES DR
400 MPS 95035 794-E7
900 LFYT 94549 611-D5
1600 SCIC 95125 853-H4
3200 SRMN 94583 673-F4
4800 PLE 94566 714-D4
DOLORES PL
500 PLE 94566 714-E5
40500 FRMT 94539 753-E5
DOLORES ST
- SF 94114 667-H3
- SRFL 94901 586-G2
- SF 94103 667-H3
300 SF 94110 667-H3
700 SCIC 94305 810-H1
900 LVMR 94550 715-J1
1300 SF 94131 667-H3
1400 SF 94110 667-H5
1400 SF 94131 667-H5
2300 SMTO 94403 749-A5
2700 ANT 94509 575-C6
21500 AlaC 94546 692-A7
DOLORES TER
- SF 94110 667-H2
DOLORES WY
- ORIN 94563 631-A5
300 SSF 94080 707-G1
2900 BURL 94010 728-A6
3600 CNCD 94519 593-A1
3600 CNCD 94519 592-J1
DOLPHIN CT
100 VAL 94589 509-H5
800 DNVL 94526 633-B7
900 CCCo 94572 569-J1
2000 SLN 94579 690-J6
DOLPHIN DR
- RCH 94804 608-H2
- PIT 94565 573-J3
500 PCFA 94044 706-J4
600 DNVL 94526 633-A7
2400 SJS 95124 873-E4
13600 SAR 95070 872-H1
DOLPHIN ISL
- MrnC 94949 526-H7
- MrnC 94949 546-H1
300 FCTY 94404 749-H2
DOLPHIN LN
27700 HAY 94545 731-J1
DOLPHIN TER
1000 FRMT 94536 753-F3
DOLTON AV
100 SMCo 94070 769-D4
100 SCAR 94070 769-D4
DOMA DR
400 SJS 95117 853-C1
400 SCIC 95117 853-C1
DOMAINE DR
5600 SJS 95118 874-A5
DOME AV
1800 SCL 95050 833-E6
1800 SCL 95128 833-E6
DOME CT
- HER 94547 569-H4
DOMINGO AV
- BERK 94705 630-A4
DOMINGO CT
300 SRMN 94583 673-C3
DOMINIC CT
- BEN 94510 551-A4
2900 AlaC 94546 691-G3
DOMINIC DR
2300 NVTO 94947 525-G3
3100 AlaC 94546 691-G3
DOMINIC LN
18400 AlaC 94546 691-G3
DOMINICA LN
1400 FCTY 94404 749-G5
DOMINICAN DR
- SRFL 94901 566-H6
3500 SCL 95051 832-J6
DOMINICI DR
2700 FRMT 94536 752-G1
DOMINICK CT
3400 SJS 95127 835-B2
DOMINICK WY
3400 SJS 95127 835-B2
DOMINION AV
1500 SUNV 94087 832-B5
DON AV
1300 SCL 95050 833-D3
1600 SJS 95124 873-J1
DON CIR
- CCCo 94595 632-D2
DON CT
- SMCo 94062 769-G6
1600 MTVW 94022 811-G6
1600 MTVW 94040 811-G6
2000 SCL 95050 833-D3
5600 FRMT 94538 773-B2
DON WY
3800 RCH 94806 568-G7
5600 FRMT 94538 773-B2
DONA AV
700 SUNV 94087 832-B1
DONADA PL
- HAY 94544 711-H4
DONAHE DR
300 MPS 95035 794-A6
DONAHE PL
400 MPS 95035 794-A6
DONAHUE LN
- CCCo 94526 633-C5

DONAHUE ST
- MrnC 94965 606-G7
300 MrnC 94965 626-H1
700 SF 94124 668-E6
700 SF 94124 668-E7
700 SF 94124 688-C2
DONAHUE TER
34100 FRMT 94555 752-C2
DONAL AV
6500 ELCR 94530 609-C2
DONALBAN CIR
4500 FRMT 94555 752-D1
DONALD AV
1400 CCCo 94553 571-F3
14900 SLN 94578 691-D3
25400 HAY 94544 712-A4
DONALD CT
100 DNVL 94506 653-G5
3500 SJS 95127 835-B2
DONALD DR
- ORIN 94563 631-A3
100 MRGA 94556 631-D4
1200 CCCo 94572 570-A1
4100 PA 94306 811-C3
DONALD LN
- CNCD 94518 592-G4
DONALD PL
- MRGA 94556 631-E4
DONALDSON AV
400 PCFA 94044 726-J2
DONALDSON CT
1600 CNCD 94521 593-E4
DONALDSON WY
- AMCN 94589 509-J1
W DONALDSON WY
- AMCN 94589 510-A2
100 AMCN 94589 509-J2
DONALEEN CT
100 MRTZ 94553 571-F7
DON ALFONSO CT
5500 SJS 95123 874-E6
DON ALFONSO WY
300 SJS 95123 874-E6
DON ANDRES CT
400 SJS 95123 874-E6
DON ANDRES WY
5400 SJS 95123 874-E6
DONATA CT
- PLE 94566 715-D7
DON BASILLO CT
5400 SJS 95123 874-E6
DON BASILLO WY
300 SJS 95123 874-E6
DON CARLOS CT
400 SJS 95123 874-E6
DON CAROL DR
8600 ELCR 94530 609-E2
DONCASTER DR
100 VAL 94591 530-E2
700 WLCK 94598 612-J3
1000 ANT 94509 575-B7
DONCASTER PL
6100 OAK 94611 630-E6
DONCASTER WY
1200 SJS 95127 835-A4
DON CORRELLI CT
400 SJS 95123 874-H2
DON CORRELLI WY
5400 SJS 95123 874-H2
DONDEE WY
400 PCFA 94044 726-J2
DON DEL MONICO CT
400 SJS 95123 874-E7
DONDERO WY
200 SJS 95119 875-C6
37000 FRMT 94536 752-G4
DON DIABLO CT
400 SJS 95123 874-H2
DON DIEGO CT
5400 SJS 95123 874-H2
DON EDGARDO CT
400 SJS 95123 874-H2
DON EDMONDO CT
5400 SJS 95123 874-H2
DONEGAL AV
2300 SSF 94080 707-E5
DONEGAL CT
- PLHL 94523 591-J5
35000 NWK 94560 752-D4
DONEGAL DR
100 VAL 94589 510-C5
7500 CPTO 95014 852-D4
DONEGAL PL
- CCCo 94549 591-H4
- MRTZ 94553 591-H4
DONEGAL RD
- PIN 94564 569-E4
DONEGAL WY
- ANT 94509 595-J2
- MRTZ 94553 591-H4
- PLHL 94523 591-J4
400 CCCo 94549 591-G4
DONELSON PL
14100 LAH 94022 811-B6
DON ENRICO CT
5500 SJS 95123 874-E7
DON FERNANDO WY
400 SJS 95123 874-E6
DON GABRIEL WY
- ORIN 94563 631-A5
DON GIOVANNI CT
300 SJS 95123 874-E6
DONHAM CT
800 ANT 94509 575-C7
DONINGTON DR
1100 SJS 95129 852-G3
DONIZETTI CT
2800 SJS 95132 814-F5
DON JOSE WY
300 SJS 95123 874-H3
DON JUAN CIR
5300 SJS 95123 874-H4
DONKEY FLATS CT
- PLHL 94523 591-H5
DON KIRK ST
1300 LALT 94024 831-J4
DONLON WY
6500 DBLN 94568 693-G4
DON MANRICO CT
5400 SJS 95123 874-E7
DON MARCELLO CT
5400 SJS 95123 874-E7

STREET
Block City ZIP Pg-Grid

DON MARCO CT
400 SJS 95123 874-H2
DON MATEO CT
5400 SJS 95123 874-H2
DONNA CT
100 VAL 94589 509-J5
DONNA DR
500 CCCo 94553 572-A3
500 CCCo 94553 571-J3
1800 PLHL 94523 592-B4
DONNA LN
- DNVL 94526 633-C7
1700 SJS 95124 873-H2
14400 SAR 95070 872-F2
DONNA ST
1300 NVTO 94947 526-C5
14800 SLN 94578 691-D3
DONNA WY
- OAK 94605 671-D3
DONNA MAE CT
600 CCCo 94803 569-D7
DONNA MARIA WY
- ORIN 94563 631-A5
DONNELLY AV
1200 BURL 94010 728-G7
DONNER AV
100 LVMR 94550 715-E1
700 SF 94124 688-B1
1400 SF 94124 668-A7
1500 SBRN 94066 727-H1
DONNER CT
100 SUNV 94086 812-C7
4100 ANT 94509 595-J1
DONNER DR
14800 SCIC 95124 873-G4
DONNER PL
2300 SCL 95050 833-C7
DONNER ST
3700 SMTO 94403 749-C6
DONNER WY
400 SRMN 94583 653-G7
39000 FRMT 94538 752-J6
DONNER CREEK CT
- CLAY 94517 613-J1
DONNER PASS RD
800 VAL 94589 509-J6
1300 VAL 94589 510-A6
DONNORA CT
1100 SJS 95132 814-G5
DON OCTAVIO CT
5500 SJS 95123 874-E7
DONOHOE ST
100 MLPK 94025 791-A2
100 EPA 94303 791-A2
DONOHUE CT
1900 SJS 95131 814-D6
DONOHUE DR
1200 SJS 95131 814-D6
7400 DBLN 94568 693-G3
DONOSO PZ
100 UNC 94587 732-J5
DONOVAN AV
2600 SCL 95051 833-B3
DONOVAN CT
2000 SJS 95125 853-G4
DONOVAN DR
700 SLN 94577 690-H1
DON PEDRO CT
5500 SJS 95123 874-E6
DON PIZARRO CT
5400 SJS 95123 874-E6
DON RICARDO CT
5500 SJS 95123 874-E7
DON RODOLFO CT
5400 SJS 95123 874-H2
DON SCALA CT
5500 SJS 95123 874-E7
DON SEVILLE CT
400 SJS 95123 874-E6
DON TIMOTEO CT
- SRFL 94903 566-D4
DOOLAN RD
1400 AlaC 94550 695-A1
1400 LVMR 94550 695-B4
4500 AlaC 94550 694-J1
DOOLEY CT
- NVTO 94945 526-B2
DOOLIN CT
- CCCo 94806 569-C5
- PIN 94806 569-C5
DOOLITTLE DR
- SLN 94577 690-G2
DOOLITTLE DR Rt#-61
- ALA 94502 670-B5
7200 OAK 94621 670-B5
7200 OAK 94621 690-F1
9400 SLN 94577 690-F1
10100 OAK 94603 690-F1
DOOLITTLE WY
600 ANT 94509 595-E1
DOON CT
1100 SUNV 94087 832-H4
DOORN LN
5600 SJS 95118 874-B5
DORA AV
1900 WLCK 94596 612-B5
DORA CT
2500 PIN 94564 569-F4
DORADA CT
100 HER 94547 570-B6
DORADO COM
34700 FRMT 94555 752-A3
DORADO DR
31300 UNC 94545 731-J6
DORADO LN
800 FCTY 94404 749-F4
15500 MSER 95030 873-A5
DORADO TER
- SF 94112 667-D7
DORADO WY
300 SMCo 94080 707-F5
300 SSF 94080 707-F5
DORAL CT
- ANT 94509 595-D1
100 VAL 94591 530-G3
3300 WLCK 94598 612-J2
7900 PLE 94588 714-B6
DORAL DR
- MRGA 94556 631-D7
- MRGA 94556 651-D1
600 DNVL 94526 653-E6
DORAL WY
- ANT 94509 595-D2
DORALEE WY
1100 SJS 95125 854-B6
DORAN DR
6300 OAK 94611 630-G7
DORANTES AV
- SF 94116 667-C4
DORAY DR
- PLHL 94523 592-C4
DORCAS WY
- SF 94127 667-E5
DORCEY LN
1500 SJS 95120 874-A7
DORCHESTER AV
- SLN 94577 670-J7
DORCHESTER CT
35000 NWK 94560 752-D3
DORCHESTER DR
- DALY 94015 687-A3
- MTVW 94043 812-B4
19400 SAR 95070 852-F6
DORCHESTER LN
- CCCo - 632-J1
- CCCo 94507 632-J1
1200 SJS 95118 874-C5
DORCHESTER PL
300 AMCN 94589 509-J4
1600 CNCD 94519 593-A2
DORCHESTER RD
400 SMTO 94402 748-G1
DORCHESTER WY
- SF 94127 667-D5
DORCICH ST
- SCL 95050 833-D7
3100 SCL 95117 833-D7
DORE AV
1200 SMTO 94401 729-A7
DORE ST
- SF 94103 647-J7
- SF 94103 667-J1
300 SF 94103 668-A1
DOREEN CT
100 VAL 94589 509-J6
6800 DBLN 94568 693-J3
DOREEN ST
7200 DBLN 94568 693-J3
DOREEN WY
600 LFYT 94549 631-G1
DOREL DR
800 SJS 95132 814-J5
900 SCIC 95132 814-J5
DOREMUS AV
5600 RCH 94805 589-B5
5800 CCCo 94805 589-B5
DORENE CT
14100 SAR 95070 872-B2
DORENE PL
6600 SJS 95120 894-F2
DORETHEA CT
800 MrnC 94965 606-D7
DORI LN
26200 LAH 94022 831-C1
DORIAN CT
800 SCIC 95127 814-H6
DORIAN WY
- SRFL 94901 567-A7
DORIC AL
- SF 94108 648-A5
DORIS AV
- NVTO 94947 525-H4
200 SCIC 95127 834-J3
2000 CCCo 94596 612-D7
2000 WLCK 94596 612-D7
DORIS CT
- RDWC 94061 790-A1
1000 ALA 94501 670-A3
10300 SCIC 95127 834-J3
18500 AlaC 94546 692-B3
DORIS DR
- PLHL 94523 592-C5
1800 MLPK 94025 790-E6
DORIS PL
- OAK 94705 630-B4
DORISA AV
3600 OAK 94605 671-B4
DORKING CT
5000 NWK 94560 752-E4
DORLAND ST
- SF 94110 667-G2
200 SF 94114 667-G2
DORMAN AV
- SF 94124 668-A5
DORMAN CT
4200 PLE 94588 694-B7
DORMAN RD
4000 PLE 94588 694-A7
DORMAR CT
10600 SCIC 95127 815-B7
DORMER AV
3400 CNCD 94519 572-G6
DORMER CT
3400 CNCD 94519 572-G5
DORMIDERA AV
- PDMT 94611 650-C1
DORMITORY RD
- SF 94124 668-D7
DORN CT
6000 SJS 95123 875-B6
DORNAN DR
- RCH 94801 608-D1
DORNE PL
2000 FRMT 94539 753-F6
DORNOCH AV
1300 SJS 95122 854-H1
DOROTHY AV
400 SJS 95125 854-B3
1200 SLN 94578 691-C4
DOROTHY CT
- VAL 94590 550-C2
DOROTHY DR
2900 PLHL 94523 612-A1
DOROTHY LN
500 CCCo 94553 571-J3
DOROTHY PL
- OAK 94705 630-B3
DOROTHY ANN WY
11700 CPTO 95014 852-C4
DORRANCE CT
1900 SJS 95125 853-J6
DORRANCE DR
1700 SJS 95125 853-J6
DORRIE AV
700 SJS 95116 834-E6
DORRINGTON CT
39500 FRMT 94538 753-A6
DORRIS PL
1200 CCCo 94507 632-G4
DORSCH RD
2000 WLCK 94598 612-E1
DORSET CT
100 SRMN 94583 673-F4
4300 CNCD 94521 593-A4
DORSET LN
- MrnC 94941 606-G3
- MLV 94941 606-G3
DORSET WY
600 SUNV 94087 832-E4
800 BEN 94510 530-J6
DORSEY AV
4300 FRMT 94536 752-J5
DORSEY CT
38200 FRMT 94536 752-J4
DORSEY WY
21000 SAR 95070 872-C2
DORSON LN
17500 AlaC 94546 692-A2
DORTHA CT
40100 FRMT 94538 753-B7
DORTHEA CT
8000 PLE 94588 714-A5
DORVAL DR
2200 SJS 95130 853-A6
DORY LN
- FCTY 94404 749-F6
500 RDWC 94065 749-J6
DORY RD
- PIT 94565 574-A2
DOS ENCINAS
- ORIN 94563 631-A5
DOS LOMA VISTA LN
- PTLV 94028 810-D4
DOS OSOS
- ORIN 94563 610-E7
DOS PALOS CT
21800 CPTO 95014 832-B7
DOS PALOS DR
1400 WLCK 94596 612-A2
1400 WLCK 94596 611-J2
DOS POSOS
- ORIN 94563 610-G6
DOS RIOS CT
- SRMN 94583 673-B2
DOS RIOS DR
2400 SRMN 94583 673-B2
DOS RIOS PL
- SRMN 94583 673-B2
DOS ROBLES CT
- CCCo 94596 612-E1
DOT AV
- CMBL 95008 853-D6
DOT CT
1400 SJS 95120 874-B6
DOTEY CT
600 SJS 95111 875-B1
DOTS LN
- MLV 94941 606-C3
DOTSON CT
24000 HAY 94544 711-J3
DOTTIELYN AV
3700 SJS 95111 854-J6
DOUBLE ROCK ST
- SF 94124 688-C1
DOUD DR
- LALT 94022 811-F6
DOUGHERTY LN
8400 AlaC 94550 696-G7
DOUGHERTY RD
- CCCo 94583 653-J7
- CCCo 94583 673-J2
- PLE 94588 694-A4
- SRMN 94583 653-J7
- SRMN 94583 673-J2
5800 DBLN 94568 694-A1
7500 CCCo 94583 694-A1
7500 SRMN 94583 694-A1
DOUGLANE AV
100 SCL 95117 833-D7
DOUGLAS AV
400 OAK 94603 670-G7
400 RDWC 94063 770-D6
400 SMCo 94063 770-D6
1100 BURL 94010 728-G6
DOUGLAS CT
- NVTO 94947 526-A5
- ORIN 94563 611-B7
- ORIN 94563 631-B1
900 CLAY 94517 593-H7
900 CLAY 94517 613-H1
900 SLN 94577 690-J1
1100 CCCo 94507 632-G3
1100 CNCD 94520 592-E4
1600 FRMT 94539 753-G6
2100 PIT 94565 574-A3
3400 SMTO 94403 748-J7
4300 PLE 94588 694-A7
DOUGLAS DR
- MRTZ 94553 571-F6
600 MrnC 94941 606-C4
600 SLN 94577 690-H1
1500 ELCR 94530 609-D1
DOUGLAS LN
200 PLHL 94523 592-B7
200 PLHL 94523 612-B1
DOUGLAS RD
500 CLAY 94517 593-H7
500 CLAY 94517 613-H1
DOUGLAS ST
700 HAY 94544 712-C6
1400 SCIC 95126 853-H1
1400 SJS 95126 853-H1
2300 SPAB 94806 588-G2
2400 UNC 94587 732-C4
DOUGLAS TER
200 PLHL 94523 591-J2
DOUGLAS WY
- ATN 94027 790-F3
1200 SSF 94080 707-G1
DOUGLASS CT
100 VAL 94589 530-B1
DOUGLASS LN
14000 SAR 95070 872-E2
DOUGLASS ST
- SF 94114 667-F3
DOUGLASS ST
1000 SF 94131 667-F4
1100 SF 94131 667-F4
DOULTON CT
400 PLHL 94523 591-J7
DOVE CT
100 HER 94547 569-H5
500 PLHL 94523 592-A5
1700 HAY 94545 731-J1
3800 ANT 94509 594-J1
6400 LVMR 94550 696-D2
DOVE LN
- RCH 94803 589-C3
1000 FCTY 94404 749-H2
1400 SUNV 94087 832-E4
DOVE LP
- SF 94129 647-B3
DOVE PL
- FRMT 94555 732-B7
- NVTO 94949 546-E5
DOVE WY
1800 HAY 94545 731-J1
DOVE CREEK LN
100 DNVL 94506 654-A6
DOVE HILL RD
3400 SJS 95121 855-B4
DOVELA WY
3000 SJS 95118 874-A1
DOVE OAK CT
10000 CPTO 95014 831-J7
DOVER
800 HER 94547 569-J2
DOVER AV
1300 SPAB 94806 588-G3
DOVER CIR
800 BEN 94510 530-J6
DOVER COM
38000 FRMT 94536 752-J3
DOVER CT
- DALY 94015 707-C2
- DNVL 94506 653-J6
- ORIN 94563 631-B3
- SMCo 94070 769-E4
- VAL 94591 530-G5
100 LGTS 95032 873-E6
100 SBRN 94066 707-G7
800 LALT 94022 831-D1
2100 WLCK 94598 612-G2
2100 PIT 94565 574-B3
7200 DBLN 94568 693-H3
12400 SAR 95070 852-F5
35300 NWK 94560 752-D4
DOVER DR
100 WLCK 94598 612-G2
DOVER LN
1100 FCTY 94404 749-F4
7200 DBLN 94568 693-H3
24000 AlaC 94541 712-B1
DOVER PL
1600 AlaC 94541 712-B1
DOVER RD
3300 RDWC 94061 789-H1
DOVER ST
- SF 94107 648-C6
100 LGTS 95032 873-E5
3300 BERK 94703 629-G4
5100 OAK 94609 629-G5
DOVER WY
400 CMBL 95008 853-G5
400 LVMR 94550 695-E6
2100 PIT 94565 574-B3
3100 CNCD 94518 592-G2
10200 SCIC 95127 834-J3
DOVERTON SQ
2700 MTVW 94040 832-A2
DOVETAIL CT
- SJS 95135 875-J1
DOW CT
38600 FRMT 94536 753-D2
DOW DR
3000 SCIC 95136 854-D7
3000 SJS 95136 854-D7
DOW LN
- NVTO 94947 525-J4
DOW PL
- SF 94107 648-B6
DOWE AV
2700 UNC 94587 732-D5
DOWITCHER TER
3600 FRMT 94555 732-J3
DOWITCHER WY
- SRFL 94901 587-A2
DOWLING AV
4900 FRMT 94536 752-G5
DOWLING BLVD
300 SLN 94577 671-B6
DOWLING CT
8000 OAK 94605 670-J3
DOWLING PL
2400 BERK 94705 629-H4
DOWLING ST
8000 OAK 94605 670-J3
DOWNEN PL
300 HAY 94544 711-H4
DOWNER AV
2300 RCH 94804 588-H5
DOWNER ST
2500 PIN 94564 569-F4
DOWNEY CT
2200 SSF 94080 707-E5
DOWNEY PL
- OAK 94610 650-C3
1900 ELCR 94530 589-C7
1900 ELCR 94530 609-C1
DOWNEY ST
- SF 94117 667-F1
DOWNEY WY
- HIL 94010 728-D7
DOWNHAM CT
300 WLCK 94598 612-F2
DOWNIE DR
100 VAL 94589 510-A6
DOWNIEVILLE ST
32700 UNC 94587 752-A1
DOWNING AV
2200 SJS 95128 853-F3
2200 SCIC 95128 853-F3
DOWNING CT
1900 SCL 95051 833-A3
4400 PLE 94588 694-A7
DOWNING LN
700 PA 94301 790-J4
DOWNING PL
3300 CNCD 94518 592-H6
32200 UNC 94587 732-C4
DOWNING RD
800 MPS 95035 794-E4
1000 SCIC 95035 794-E2
DOWNING OAK CT
15000 LGTS 95032 873-F5
DOWNS DR
7200 SJS 95139 895-F1
DOWNS WY
1000 VAL 94591 530-D4
DOWNSGLEN WY
500 SJS 95133 834-G1
DOWNSWICK DR
1000 SJS 95136 874-D1
DOWNSWOOD CT
800 SJS 95120 894-H3
S DOWRELIO DR
- CCCo 94525 550-C4
DOXEY CT
1400 SJS 95131 814-D6
DOXEY DR
1900 SJS 95131 814-D6
DOYLE CT
4600 SJS 95129 853-A4
DOYLE DR
- SF 94123 647-E3
- SF 94129 647-E3
100 VAL 94591 530-E6
1400 SJS 95129 852-H4
DOYLE DR U.S.-101
- SF 94129 647-D3
- SF 94129 647-E3
DOYLE PL
1100 MTVW 94040 811-J7
DOYLE RD
400 SJS 95129 852-J1
4500 SJS 95129 853-A3
DOYLE ST
1000 MLPK 94025 790-F3
4400 EMVL 94608 629-E6
DRACENA AV
100 PDMT 94611 630-B7
100 PDMT 94611 650-B1
DRACENA CT
3900 CNCD 94519 593-B1
DRACENA LN
400 LALT 94022 811-F7
DRACENA ST
2200 HAY 94545 711-H7
DRACENA WY
1800 SJS 95122 834-H7
DRACO LN
600 FCTY 94404 749-E4
DRAEGER DR
100 MRGA 94556 631-E5
DRAGONFLY CT
700 SJS 95133 834-F2
DRAGONFLY WY
700 SJS 95133 834-F1
DRAKE AV
- MrnC 94965 606-H7
100 SSF 94080 707-J1
200 MrnC 94965 626-G1
1000 BURL 94010 728-D5
1200 SLN 94579 691-A5
DRAKE CT
- WLCK 94596 612-C3
100 VAL 94591 550-F2
300 BEN 94510 551-A2
300 SCL 95051 833-A7
500 FCTY 94404 749-F5
1000 SCAR 94070 769-E5
4200 LVMR 94550 716-A2
19700 CPTO 95014 832-F6
DRAKE DR
1800 OAK 94611 630-E7
2000 OAK 94611 650-E1
19600 CPTO 95014 832-F6
DRAKE LN
- OAK 94611 650-E1
DRAKE PL
- OAK 94611 630-E7
DRAKE ST
- DALY 94014 687-G2
- SF 94112 687-G2
100 ANT 94509 575-D6
400 SJS 95126 854-A1
600 SJS 95125 854-A2
DRAKE WY
1400 CCCo 94806 589-A4
4000 LVMR 94550 716-A1
39300 FRMT 94538 753-A6
39300 FRMT 94538 752-J6
DRAKES CT
100 LGTS 95032 873-D4
DRAKES CV
- SRFL 94903 566-E4
DRAKES BAY AV
100 LGTS 95032 873-D4
DRAKES LANDING RD
- LKSP 94939 586-G5
DRAKES VIEW CIR
- LKSP 94939 586-G5
DRAKEWOOD LN
- NVTO 94947 526-B6
DRAKEWOOD PL
100 NVTO 94947 526-B6
DRAPER ST
2800 CCCo 94806 569-B6
DRAYTON CT
300 WLCK 94598 612-F2
DRAYTON RD
- HIL 94010 748-F4
DRAYTON WY
400 WLCK 94598 612-F2
DREA RD
10900 CPTO 95014 852-A2
DRESDEN BAY
- ALA 94502 670-A5
DRESDEN WY
1100 SJS 95129 852-F3
DREW AV
1700 MTVW 94043 811-H3
DREW CT
2800 EPA 94303 771-C6
DREW ST
500 AlaC 94580 691-D5
500 SLN 94578 691-D5
DREW TER
4000 FRMT 94538 773-D1
DREXEL CT
38600 FRMT 94536 752-J5
DREXEL WY
1000 SJS 95121 854-H3
27500 HAY 94545 711-H7
DREYER PL
5600 OAK 94619 651-A6
DRIFTER DR
6200 SJS 95123 874-J6
DRIFTWOOD AV
- NVTO 94945 526-A2
- NVTO 94945 525-J2
DRIFTWOOD CIR
- PCFA 94044 727-A4
DRIFTWOOD CT
- CCCo 94803 589-D1
- PCFA 94044 727-A3
- SRFL 94901 567-C6
- PLHL 94523 591-J6
100 VAL 94590 529-G2
1100 SUNV 94089 812-J4
DRIFTWOOD DR
100 CCCo 94565 573-D1
800 PA 94303 791-E7
2900 SJS 95128 853-E4
3200 LFYT 94549 631-H4
4700 FRMT 94536 752-G5
DRIFTWOOD LN
- DALY 94014 687-E6
300 ALA 94501 670-A4
DRIFTWOOD WY
2200 SLN 94577 690-H5
7500 PLE 94588 713-J1
DRISCOLL CT
600 PA 94306 811-C3
DRISCOLL RD
100 FRMT 94539 753-E6
DRISCOLL TER
41000 FRMT 94539 753-F5
DROLETTE WY
1300 BEN 94510 551-A3
DROZDA CT
- CNCD 94519 592-H2
DRUCILLA DR
500 MTVW 94040 811-H7
DRUM
4000 ALA 94501 649-E6
DRUMHEAD CT
1900 SJS 95131 814-C6
DRUMM CT
7400 SJS 95139 895-G1
DRUMM PL
7500 SJS 95139 895-G2
DRUMM ST
- SF 94111 648-B4
DRUMMOND AL
- SF 94124 668-B5
DRUMMOND DR
16200 SCIC 95030 872-H5
DRUMMOND PL
700 CNCD 94518 592-G7
DRURY CT
- OAK 94705 630-C3
4600 FRMT 94538 753-C7
DRURY LN
- OAK 94705 630-B3
500 SMCo 94062 789-F1
DRURY RD
1000 OAK 94705 630-C3
DRY BED CT
4200 SCL 95054 813-C5
DRY CREEK CT
2200 SJS 95008 853-G7
5200 ANT 94509 595-J5
DRYCREEK CT
2200 MRTZ 94553 572-A7
DRY CREEK LN
100 WDSD 94062 789-F5
DRY CREEK RD
1300 CMBL 95008 853-F7
1300 SJS 95125 854-A5
1300 SJS 95008 853-G7
1400 SJS 95125 853-J6
1400 SJS 95124 853-J6
1800 SCIC 95125 853-J6
DRY CREEK TR
- AlaC 94544 732-F1
- FRMT 94539 754-A7
- FRMT 94539 753-J7
- UNC 94587 732-F1
DRY CREEK WY
2000 SJS 95124 853-H6
DRYDEN AV
10800 CPTO 95014 852-B2
DRYDEN CT
2600 HAY 94542 712-D4
5100 NWK 94560 752-E4
DRYDEN DR
100 VAL 94591 530-E6
1300 SJS 95131 814-D7
DRYDEN RD
3600 FRMT 94555 752-E1
DRY OAK CT
5900 SJS 95120 874-B6
DRY OAK DR
5800 SJS 95120 874-B6
DRY OAK PL
5900 SJS 95120 874-C6
DRYSDALE CT
5700 SJS 95124 873-J6
DRYSDALE DR
100 LGTS 95032 873-E6
1300 SUNV 94087 832-B4
5400 SJS 95124 873-J6
DRYTOWN CT
100 VAL 94589 509-H5
DRYTOWN PL
5900 SJS 95120 874-C6
DRYWOOD CT
4400 UNC 94587 732-A7
DRYWOOD LN
3100 SJS 95132 814-D2
DRYWOOD ST
4700 PLE 94588 693-J7
DRY YARD DR
500 SJS 95117 853-D2
DU 8 RD
- CCCo 94553 571-F3
DUANE AV
600 SUNV 94086 812-G6
800 SCL 95054 813-D7
E DUANE AV
200 SUNV 94086 812-F5
W DUANE AV
100 SUNV 94086 812-E5
DUANE CT
1000 SUNV 94086 812-H6
DUANE LN
100 MRTZ 94553 571-D7
DUANE ST
- RDWC 94062 769-J5
- SJS 95110 854-C1
400 RDWC 94062 770-A6
DUAR DR
900 CNCD 94518 592-E6
DUARTE AV
- FRMT 94536 733-A7
DUARTE CT
- ALA 94502 669-J7
- NVTO 94949 546-F4
200 MPS 95035 794-A4
DUBAL CT
43800 FRMT 94539 773-G2
DUBANSKI DR
700 SJS 95123 874-F6
DUBBS RD
- CCCo 94553 571-F3
DUBERT LN
1300 SJS 95122 834-G7
DUBHE CT
4200 CNCD 94521 593-B3
DUBIN CT
18700 AlaC 94546 691-H3
DUBLIN AV
900 LVMR 94550 715-F2
5000 OAK 94602 650-F3
DUBLIN BLVD
- AlaC 94552 693-E5
- DBLN 94552 693-E5
6600 DBLN 94568 694-A4
8500 DBLN 94568 693-J4
11000 PLE 94588 693-E5
DUBLIN CT
- PLHL 94523 591-J5
3100 SSF 94080 707-D4
6400 DBLN 94568 694-A4
DUBLIN DR
- PLHL 94523 591-J4
100 VAL 94589 510-C4
2000 CCCo 94806 569-B4
2700 SJS 95127 835-A5
2900 SSF 94080 707-D5
DUBLIN ST
- SF 94112 687-G1
DUBLIN WY
500 SUNV 94087 832-E4
600 ALA 94502 669-J5
2000 SMTO 94403 749-C4
DUBLIN CANYON RD
7900 AlaC 94552 693-A4
7900 AlaC 94542 693-A4
9000 AlaC 94552 692-H4
9000 AlaC 94542 692-H4
10600 PLE 94588 693-E5
11000 PLE 94586 693-E5
11000 AlaC 94586 693-E5
11700 AlaC 94586 693-E5
DUBLIN GREEN CT
7700 DBLN 94568 693-G3
DUBLIN GREEN DR
11700 DBLN 94568 693-G3
DUBLIN MEADOWS ST
6900 DBLN 94568 694-A3
DUBOCE AV
- CCCo 94801 588-F4
- SF 94103 667-G1
100 RCH 94801 588-F4
300 SF 94102 667-G1
300 SF 94114 667-G1
300 SF 94117 667-G1
DU BOIS ST
100 SRFL 94901 586-G2
DUBOIS ST
2200 MPS 95035 814-E1
DUBOST CT
- DNVL 94526 653-C7
DUBUQUE AV
500 SSF 94080 708-A2
DUCHESS CT
3400 SJS 95132 814-J3
DUCHESS DR
4200 UNC 94587 732-A6
DUCK CT
200 FCTY 94404 749-H1
DUCKER CT
1700 CNCD 94519 592-J2
DUCKETT WY
1500 SJS 95129 852-E4
DUCK LAKE CT
800 SJS 95123 874-E5
DUDASH CT
1100 SJS 95122 854-H1
DUDLEY AV
- PDMT 94611 650-C1
500 SJS 95128 853-E2
DUDLEY CT
- PDMT 94611 650-C1
- PLHL 94523 592-B6
5400 PLE 94566 714-C2
DUDLEY LN
- SCIC - 791-A7
DUDLEY RD
- SF 94129 647-D4
DUENA ST
500 SCIC 94305 790-H7
DUESENBERG DR
5300 SJS 95123 874-G3
DUET CT
6000 SJS 95120 874-C7
DUFF CT
800 SUNV 94086 832-F2
DUFF LN
- ROSS 94957 586-B2
DUFFEL PL
27000 HAY 94544 712-B5
DUFFERIN AV
1100 BURL 94010 728-C5
DUFFY CT
- PLHL 94523 592-A3
200 SJS 95116 834-F4
DUFFY PL
- SRFL 94901 586-G1

BAY AREA

INDEX

Thomas Bros. Maps ® COPYRIGHT 1997

STREET Block City ZIP Pg-Grid

DUFFY TER
34200 FRMT 94555 752-C2
DUFFY WY
1700 SJS 95116 834-G4
DUGAN CT
1600 CNCD 94521 593-F5
36600 NWK 94560 752-E5
DUGGAN CT
- SMCo 94062 769-F7
DUGGAN DR
3900 SJS 95118 874-A2
DUGGAN RD
100 SMCo 94062 769-F7
DUHALLOW WY
2600 SSF 94080 707-C4
DUKE AV
2500 RCH 94806 589-A2
DUKE CIR
700 PLHL 94523 592-C3
DUKE CT
- PLHL 94523 592-C3
3300 SCL 95051 832-J6
3900 LVMR 94550 696-A7
4400 FRMT 94555 752-C1
6800 DBLN 94568 693-J3
7700 ELCR 94530 609-E2
19600 AlaC 94541 711-E2
DUKE LN
34100 FRMT 94555 752-C1
DUKE PTH
2600 RCH 94806 589-A2
DUKE WY
- PLHL 94523 592-C3
900 MTVW 94040 811-G7
1300 SJS 95125 854-A5
3900 LVMR 94550 696-A7
3900 LVMR 94550 695-J7
7500 SRMN 94583 693-G1
DUKES CT
- SF 94124 668-C6
DULCEY DR
4100 SJS 95136 874-G1
DULLES CT
1100 PCFA 94044 727-A5
DULSIE LN
- DBLN 94552 693-E5
DULUTH CIR
300 PA 94306 811-D2
DULWICH RD
- OAK 94618 630-B6
DUMAINE ST
1400 CNCD 94518 592-E6
DUMAS DR
7400 CPTO 95014 852-D2
DUMAS PL
7200 NWK 94560 752-D6
DUMBARTON AV
- SMCo 94063 790-C1
100 SMCo 94063 770-C7
2000 EPA 94303 791-A2
2500 SJS 95124 853-H7
2600 SJS 95124 873-J1
DUMBARTON CIR
7200 FRMT 94555 752-B5
DUMBARTON CT
35300 NWK 94560 752-C4
DUMBARTON ST
3500 CNCD 94519 572-G5
DUMONT AV
26200 HAY 94544 711-J5
DUMONT CIR
2400 SJS 95122 834-J5
DUMONT CT
- MLBR 94030 727-H4
2500 SJS 95122 834-J5
DUMONT ST
4200 SMTO 94403 749-D6
DUNAND AV
- SRFL 94901 566-E7
- SRFL 94901 586-E1
DUNBAR CT
- PLHL 94523 592-B4
3500 FRMT 94536 752-H2
DUNBAR DR
20600 SCIC 95014 832-D7
DUNBAR PL
3700 FRMT 94536 752-G3
27200 HAY 94544 712-B6
DUNBAR ST
- SF 94111 648-A5
DUNBARTON CIR
3900 SRMN 94583 673-E4
DUNBARTON CT
- SRMN 94583 673-F4
DUNBLANE CT
2100 WLCK 94598 612-G2
DUNBLANE DR
100 WLCK 94598 612-G2
DUNCAN AV
1000 SUNV 94089 812-F4
DUNCAN CT
- ORIN 94563 631-B3
DUNCAN DR
1400 CNCD 94521 593-F5
2300 MRTZ 94553 571-D4
DUNCAN PL
3800 PA 94306 811-E1
DUNCAN RD
2500 PIN 94564 569-E6
DUNCAN ST
- SF 94110 667-G4
200 SF 94131 667-F4
500 SCIC 95127 814-H7
500 SJS 95127 814-H7
1700 WLCK 94596 612-C5
DUNCAN WY
- OAK 94611 630-D6
DUNCANVILLE CT
700 CMBL 95008 853-F6
DUNCARDINE WY
700 SUNV 94087 832-F5
DUNCOMBE AL
- SF 94133 648-A4
DUNDALE DR
3700 SJS 95121 855-A5
DUNDALK CT
4200 PLE 94566 714-E1
DUNDEE AV
400 MPS 95035 794-A6
18700 SAR 95070 852-H7
DUNDEE COM
38000 FRMT 94536 752-J3
DUNDEE CT
- SRMN 94583 673-E4
1300 SJS 95122 854-H1
2400 SLN 94577 691-B2
3000 CNCD 94520 572-F6
DUNDEE DR
100 SSF 94080 707-C2
2500 SCL 95051 833-B2
DUNDEE LN
100 SCAR 94070 769-F4
DUNDEE RD
2600 CCCo 94806 569-B5
DUNDEE WY
200 BEN 94510 551-A2
DUNDONALD CT
3200 SJS 95121 855-C5
DUNES CT
- ANT 94509 595-D1
DUNES WY
- ANT 94509 595-D2
DUNFORD WY
900 SUNV 94087 832-G5
1000 SCL 95051 832-G5
DUNFRIES TER
- SRFL 94901 567-B7
DUNHAM
100 HER 94547 569-F3
DUNHILL CT
1000 DNVL 94506 654-A6
DUNHILL DR
600 DNVL 94506 653-J6
600 DNVL 94506 654-A6
34200 FRMT 94555 752-C3
DUNHOLME WY
500 SUNV 94087 832-E5
DUNIGAN CT
- SJS 95123 874-F7
DUNKIRK AV
4600 OAK 94605 671-E4
DUNKIRK ST
- OAK 94649 649-B1
DUNKS ST
- DALY 94014 687-C5
DUNLIN CT
- MrnC 94903 546-E6
DUNMAN WY
- SSF 94080 707-D1
DUNN AV
1300 RCH 94801 588-G5
5900 SJS 95123 874-J5
DUNN LN
- SAUS 94965 626-J2
DUNN RD
2200 AlaC 94545 711-D5
2200 HAY 94545 711-D5
DUNNE CT
- SMCo 94025 770-E7
DUNNES AL
- SF 94133 648-A4
DUNNIGAN CT
3700 AlaC 94546 692-B3
DUNNOCK WY
1300 SUNV 94087 832-E4
DUNRAVEN CT
600 SJS 95136 874-F2
DUNSANAY CT
3100 FRMT 94536 752-J1
DUNSBURRY CT
5500 SJS 95123 874-F4
DUNSBURRY WY
5500 SJS 95123 874-G3
DUNSHEE ST
- SF 94124 668-B6
DUNSMOOR CT
- DNVL 94526 653-C3
DUNSMUIR AV
4200 OAK 94619 650-G5
DUNSMUIR CIR
3600 PLE 94588 694-F5
DUNSMUIR COM
4900 FRMT 94555 752-A3
DUNSMUIR CT
3300 PLE 94588 694-F5
DUNSMUIR PL
1100 LVMR 94550 715-F4
DUNSMUIR ST
- SF 94134 667-J6
DUNSMUIR WY
100 MLPK 94025 770-G7
DUNSTER DR
300 CMBL 95008 853-D5
DUNSYRE DR
1100 LFYT 94549 611-J5
1100 CCCo 94596 611-J5
1100 CCCo 94596 612-A5
1100 LFYT 94549 612-A5
DUNWELL CT
100 SJS 95138 875-E4
DUNWICH CT
3100 SJS 95148 855-E2
DUPONT AV
5100 NWK 94560 752-F5
DUPONT ST
200 SJS 95126 854-A1
DUPRE CT
1400 CNCD 94518 592-E6
DUPURU DR
100 CCCo 94525 550-E5
DURAN CT
- PCFA 94044 727-A5
39800 FRMT 94538 753-B6
DURAN DR
- SRFL 94903 566-B1
DURAND DR
3900 SMTO 94403 749-D6
DURAND RD
- SCIC 94035 812-B2
- SCIC 94043 812-B2
DURANGO CT
5000 SJS 95118 874-A4
DURANGO LN
2600 SRMN 94583 673-C2
DURANGO RIVER CT
4700 SJS 95136 874-G2
DURANT AV
- SLN 94577 671-A6
- OAK 94605 671-A6
100 OAK 94603 671-A6
900 OAK 94603 670-J6
900 SLN 94577 670-J6
2000 BERK 94704 629-G2
3100 SJS 95111 854-H6
DURANT CT
1200 WLCK 94596 632-G2
DURANT WY
300 MrnC 94965 626-E1
DURAZNO WY
100 SMCo 94028 810-D3
DURBAN CT
5000 SJS 95138 855-F7
DURBAN DR
1900 SJS 95138 855-F7
DURHAM CT
- FRMT 94539 773-H2
300 BEN 94510 551-B2
300 DNVL 94526 653-C2
1000 SUNV 94087 832-H5
19900 SAR 95070 872-E2
DURHAM RD
- SANS 94960 566-B6
100 FRMT 94539 773-G2
DURHAM ST
100 MLPK 94025 791-A2
300 MLPK 94025 790-J2
DURHAM WY
26500 HAY 94542 712-E2
DURILLO CT
1000 FRMT 94539 753-F5
DURILLO DR
40900 FRMT 94539 753-E5
DURLANE CT
900 SUNV 94087 832-G5
DURLSTON RD
800 RDWC 94062 769-H6
DURNESS PL
1000 SJS 95122 854-G1
DURRWOOD CT
- AlaC 94542 692-E7
- AlaC 94542 712-E1
DURSEY DR
300 PIN 94806 569-C4
300 PIN 94564 569-C4
DURSHIRE WY
600 SUNV 94087 832-F5
DU SAULT DR
6400 SJS 95119 875-C7
DUSEL CT
- NVTO 94949 546-F3
DUSK TER
5100 FRMT 94555 752-C3
DUSTERBERRY WY
37000 FRMT 94536 752-G4
DUSTIN CT
- SJS 95123 874-F7
DUSTIN LN
- DNVL 94526 653-B1
DUTCHCAP LN
3400 ALA 94502 670-A7
DUTCHESS LN
300 HAY 94544 732-E2
DUTCH FLAT CT
200 VAL 94589 509-H4
DUTCH FLAT RD
100 VAL 94589 509-H4
DUTCH MILL CT
- DNVL 94526 653-D4
DUTCH MILL DR
1200 DNVL 94526 653-D5
DUTRA CT
200 PIN 94564 569-D3
DUTRA RD
100 CCCo 94553 571-C6
100 MRTZ 94553 571-C6
DUTRA WY
37000 FRMT 94536 752-G5
DUTTON AV
- SLN 94577 671-A7
1500 OAK 94605 671-A7
1500 SLN 94605 671-A7
DUTTON CT
- MrnC 94965 626-G1
- SLN 94577 671-A7
DUTTONWOOD LN
- MPS 95035 793-J3
DUVAL DR
- SSF 94080 707-D1
DUVAL LN
2000 HAY 94545 711-H7
DUVAL WY
26000 LAH 94022 831-B1
DUVALL CT
400 BEN 94510 551-A1
500 SUNV 94087 832-D4
37700 FRMT 94536 752-G6
DUVALL DR
1500 SJS 95130 853-A5
1700 SJS 95130 852-J5
DUXBURY CT
200 SRMN 94583 673-F5
DUXBURY CV
- SRFL 94901 587-A2
DUXBURY PL
100 VAL 94591 550-E1
DUZMAL AV
1000 SLN 94579 691-B7
DWIGHT AV
800 SUNV 94086 812-F7
5500 SJS 95118 874-A5
DWIGHT CRES
800 BERK 94804 629-D3
DWIGHT PL
500 OAK 94704 630-A2
DWIGHT RD
- BURL 94010 728-H6
DWIGHT ST
- SF 94134 668-A7
300 SF 94134 688-A1
700 SF 94134 687-J1
DWIGHT WY
100 VAL 94589 530-C1
1100 BERK 94702 629-E3
1100 BERK 94804 629-D3
1300 BERK 94703 629-F3
1900 BERK 94704 629-H2
3000 BERK 94704 630-A2
3200 OAK 94704 630-A2
DWINELLE CT
- ALA 94502 670-A7
DWYER AV
900 SJS 95120 894-D1
DWYER CT
6400 SJS 95120 894-E1
DYER COM
2400 FRMT 94536 753-B3
DYER CT
100 VAL 94591 530-F6
32200 UNC 94587 732-A6
DYER DR
1000 LFYT 94549 611-G6
DYER LN
2400 FRMT 94536 753-B4
DYER ST
2800 UNC 94587 732-A6
4700 UNC 94587 731-J7
DYMOND CT
400 PA 94306 791-C7
DYNAMITE RD
- SF 94129 647-B4
DYRTLE AV
- SRFL 94901 566-G6

E

E RD
12300 AlaC 94586 734-C4
E ST
- CCCo 94565 573-E1
- CNCD 94520 572-J3
- NVTO 94949 546-G3
- OAK 94625 649-A3
100 BEN 94510 551-B5
100 FRMT 94536 753-B1
100 MRTZ 94553 571-E5
100 RDWC 94063 769-J4
100 UNC 94587 732-F4
200 ANT 94509 575-D4
300 CLMA 94014 687-D6
300 SF 94124 668-E7
300 SF 94124 688-E1
600 SRFL 94901 586-F1
900 BLMT 94002 769-F2
900 HAY 94541 711-J2
1000 HAY 94541 712-A1
1000 SRFL 94901 566-F7
1100 SUNV 94089 812-E3
1400 AlaC 94541 712-B1
8500 OAK 94621 670-G4
9200 OAK 94603 670-H5
E E ST
- OAK 94625 649-C4
- VAL 94592 529-F4
E TER
- TBRN 94920 607-A4
EAGLE AV
600 ALA 94501 649-F7
1600 ALA 94501 669-J1
2100 ALA 94501 670-A1
EAGLE COM
- FRMT 94538 773-D3
EAGLE CT
100 HER 94547 569-H5
700 ANT 94509 595-F2
EAGLE DR
- NVTO 94949 546-C2
1600 SUNV 94087 832-E5
EAGLE GRN
- FRMT 94538 773-D3
EAGLE LN
1000 FCTY 94404 749-H2
EAGLE RD
- ALA 94501 649-J6
EAGLE ST
- SF 94114 667-F3
19500 AlaC 94546 691-H4
EAGLE TER
- FRMT 94538 773-D3
EAGLE WY
4800 CNCD 94521 593-C4
EAGLE CLIFF WY
7200 SJS 95120 894-F4
EAGLE CREEK CT
400 SRMN 94583 694-B1
EAGLE CREST CT
7300 SJS 95120 894-E4
EAGLE GAP CT
- NVTO 94949 546-E4
EAGLE GAP RD
- NVTO 94949 546-E4
EAGLEHAVEN CT
- SJS 95111 874-J1
EAGLE HILL
- CCCo 94707 609-F4
EAGLE HILL TER
- RDWC 94062 769-J7
EAGLEHURST DR
1700 SJS 95121 855-C4
EAGLE LAKE CT
- SRMN 94583 653-F7
1900 MRTZ 94553 592-A1
1900 MRTZ 94553 591-J1
EAGLE LAKE DR
4600 SJS 95136 874-D2
EAGLE LAKE PL
- SRMN 94583 653-F7
EAGLE NEST CT
400 MRTZ 94553 591-G3
1100 CCCo 94506 654-B3
EAGLE NEST DR
500 MRTZ 94553 591-G3
S EAGLE NEST DR
300 CCCo 94506 654-B3
EAGLE NEST LN
4000 CCCo 94506 654-B3
S EAGLE NEST LN
300 CCCo 94506 654-B3
EAGLE NEST PL
1000 CCCo 94506 654-B3
EAGLE PEAK AV
1800 CLAY 94517 593-G5
EAGLE PEAK PL
- CLAY 94517 593-G5
EAGLE PEAK RD
4300 CNCD 94521 593-A4
EAGLE POINT CT
1400 LFYT 94549 611-F3
EAGLE POINT RD
3500 LFYT 94549 611-F2
EAGLE RIDGE DR
900 CCCo 94506 654-B2
EAGLERIDGE DR
3900 ANT 94509 595-F1
EAGLE RIDGE LN
- CCCo 94506 654-B2
EAGLE RIDGE PL
- CCCo 94506 654-B2
EAGLE RIDGE WY
1000 MPS 95035 814-E1
EAGLE ROCK RD
- MrnC 94920 606-H3
4700 SJS 95136 874-J2
4800 SJS 95136 875-A2
EAGLES LN
5400 SJS 95123 875-A4
EAGLES NEST TR
- CCCo - 589-H7
- RCH 94805 589-H7
EAGLET CT
- PLE 94566 714-H4
EAGLE VALLEY CT
7100 SJS 95120 894-F4
EAGLE VALLEY WY
400 CCCo 94506 654-B3
EAGLE VIEW TER
- FRMT 94539 794-B1
E EAGLEWOOD AV
200 SUNV 94086 812-F5
W EAGLEWOOD AV
100 SUNV 94086 812-E5
EAKER CT
600 ANT 94509 595-F1
EAKER WY
500 ANT 94509 595-E1
EAMES CT
- NVTO 94947 525-H2
EARHART DR
4000 CNCD 94521 593-A2
EARHART RD
7200 OAK 94621 670-C5
7200 OAK 94621 690-E1
EARHART WY
300 LVMR 94550 695-B5
EARL AV
1000 SCIC 95126 853-J1
1700 SBRN 94066 707-E7
EARL CT
600 BEN 94510 530-J7
7700 ELCR 94530 609-E2
EARL DR
3400 SCL 95051 832-J2
22100 AlaC 94546 691-J7
EARL LN
1800 CCCo 94521 593-D3
EARL ST
700 SF 94124 668-C2
800 SF 94124 668-D7
7900 OAK 94605 671-A2
EARLANDER ST
10200 SCIC 95127 835-A2
EARLE ST
5000 FRMT 94536 752-H6
EARLINGTON CT
1000 SUNV 94087 832-B5
EARLSWOOD CT
7100 SJS 95120 894-H4
EARLY MORNING LN
- SJS 95135 875-J1
- SJS 95138 875-J1
EARLY RIVERS CT
2500 UNC 94587 732-F7
EARLY RIVERS PL
2400 UNC 94587 732-F7
EARTH AV
100 HAY 94544 712-B7
EASINGTON WY
1500 SJS 95126 853-H4
EASLEY DR
1000 CLAY 94517 613-J1
1000 CLAY 94517 593-J7
EASSON CT
100 VAL 94591 530-F6
EAST AV
200 SBRN 94066 727-J1
1400 AlaC 94541 712-C2
1400 HAY 94541 712-A1
3500 AlaC 94542 712-E1
3900 LVMR 94550 716-A1
4800 AlaC 94550 716-A1
EAST CIR
- OAK 94611 630-G6
EAST CT
- OAK 94603 670-G7
- OAK 94603 690-H1
- SBRN 94066 727-G3
- SANS 94960 566-A5
300 SJS 95116 834-E3
1100 NVTO 94945 526-B3
EAST DR
- MLV 94941 606-E3
EAST LN
100 CCCo 94507 632-H4
200 BURL 94010 728-G6
EAST RD
- MrnC 94965 627-C5
- ROSS 94957 586-B2
EAST ST
- SRFL 94901 586-E1
800 PIT 94565 574-E2
900 LFYT 94549 611-F6
1600 CNCD 94519 592-F1
1700 CNCD 94520 592-F1
2400 CNCD 94520 572-F7
EAST TER
- TBRN 94920 607-A4
3300 LFYT 94549 631-G1
EASTBOURNE CT
1100 ANT 94509 595-F1
5000 SJS 95138 855-E6
EASTBOURNE DR
5100 SJS 95138 855-E7
EASTBROOK AV
1600 SCIC 94024 831-F4
11000 LAH 94024 831-E3
EASTBROOK CT
- CLAY 94517 593-F6
800 CCCo 94506 654-D5
23200 SCIC 94024 831-G5
EASTBURN CT
100 SBRN 94066 727-G1
EASTER AV
400 MPS 95035 793-J6
EASTER CT
- CCCo 94553 572-B7
100 VAL 94589 509-J6
EASTER LN
1000 ALA 94502 670-A6
EASTER WY
- BERK 94708 609-H6
EASTERBY ST
500 SAUS 94965 627-A2
EASTERDAY WY
36000 FRMT 94536 733-A7
EASTERTOWN LN
- DBLN 94552 693-D5
EASTGATE AV
- SJS 95116 834-F4
2700 CNCD 94520 572-E7
EASTGATE DR
- DALY 94015 687-A3
EASTGATE LN
300 MRTZ 94553 571-H6
EASTHAM CT
100 VAL 94591 550-F1
EASTHILL AV
1500 AlaC 94586 734-A2
EAST HILLS CT
10400 SCIC 95127 835-B1
EAST HILLS DR
2900 SCIC 95127 834-J3
3000 SJS 95127 834-J3
3100 SCIC 95127 835-B1
3100 SCIC 95127 834-J3
3400 SJS 95127 835-B1
EASTLAKE AV
- DALY 94014 687-C4
- PCFA 94044 707-A6
4100 OAK 94602 650-F5
EAST LAKE DR
1500 SJS 95126 853-G3
EASTLAKE WY
3800 RDWC 94062 789-G2
3800 SMCo 94062 789-G2
EASTLAWN ST
5800 OAK 94621 670-E2
EAST LOOP RD
- HAY 94542 712-C3
- HAY 94544 712-C3
EASTMAN AV
100 CMAD 94925 586-G7
100 CMAD 94925 606-G1
2600 OAK 94619 650-E7
EASTMAN CT
26000 HAY 94544 712-A4
EASTMAN ST
- SF 94109 647-J4
- SF 94109 647-J4
200 HAY 94544 712-A5
EASTMAN LAKE DR
5900 SJS 95123 874-G7
EASTMOOR AV
- DALY 94015 687-A5
EASTMOOR RD
1100 BURL 94010 728-D5
EASTON AV
500 SBRN 94066 707-H6
EASTON CT
- ORIN 94563 631-B2
2500 SJS 95133 834-G1
EASTON DR
500 SJS 95133 834-F1
1500 BURL 94010 728-D6
2800 HIL 94010 728-C7
12500 SAR 95070 852-H6
EASTON LN
2500 SJS 95133 834-G1
2500 SCIC 95133 834-G1
EASTON PL
2500 SJS 95133 834-G1
18900 SAR 95070 852-H6
EASTON TER
2500 SJS 95133 834-B2
EASTORI PL
1600 HAY 94545 711-H6
EASTPARK TER
34000 FRMT 94555 732-D7
EAST RIDGE
- SRMN 94583 673-G2
EASTRIDGE AV
2200 MLPK 94025 790-D7
EASTRIDGE BLVD
2400 SJS 95122 855-B1
EASTRIDGE CIR
- PCFA 94044 707-A1
EAST RIDGE CT
- CCCo 94506 654-E3
EASTRIDGE CT
- PCFA 94044 707-A1
EASTRIDGE DR
100 LGTS 95032 873-D6
3500 SJS 95148 835-D4
EASTRIDGE LN
- CNCD 94518 592-H4
2200 SJS 95122 835-A7
EASTRIDGE LP
- SJS 95122 855-A1
200 SJS 95122 835-A7
EAST RIDGE TR
- AlaC - 651-A2
- CCCo - 630-H7
- CCCo - 651-A2
- CCCo - 650-J1
EASTRIDGE WY
2200 SJS 95122 835-A7
EASTSHORE BLVD
1400 BERK 94804 609-B1
1400 BERK 94804 629-C1
1600 ELCR 94530 609-B1
EAST SHORE DR
1200 ALA 94501 670-B4
EASTSHORE FRWY
I-80
- ALB - 609-C5
- BERK - 609-C5
- BERK - 629-D3
- CCCo - 549-J7
- CCCo - 550-B6
- CCCo - 569-H2
- CCCo - 589-A3
- ELCR - 609-C5
- EMVL - 629-D3
- HER - 569-H2
- OAK - 629-D7
- OAK - 649-D1
- PIN - 569-B7
- RCH - 569-B7
- RCH - 589-A3
- RCH - 609-C5
- SPAB - 589-A3
EASTSHORE FRONTAGE RD
1000 ALB 94804 609-C6
1000 BERK 94804 609-C6
EASTSIDE DR
200 SJS 95127 834-H1
200 SCIC 95127 834-H1
EASTUS DR
4600 SJS 95129 853-A3
4600 SJS 95129 852-J3
EAST VALLEY CT
3700 SCIC 95148 835-E5
EAST VIEW AV
- BLV 94920 627-E1
- TBRN 94920 627-E1
EAST VIEW CT
5500 AlaC 94552 692-D4
EASTVIEW DR
14500 LGTS 95030 873-B3
14700 SCIC 95030 873-B3
EASTVIEW WY
500 RDWC 94062 789-E2
500 SMCo 94062 789-E2
500 WDSD 94062 789-E2
4900 ANT 94509 595-D4
EASTWARD LN
- DNVL 94506 653-G2
EASTWOOD AV
- DALY 94015 687-A6
EASTWOOD CIR
3600 SCL 95054 813-F6
EASTWOOD CT
- OAK 94611 630-G7
- SJS 95116 834-F4
1000 LALT 94024 831-H2
3800 PLE 94588 714-A2
EASTWOOD DR
- ORIN 94563 631-C6
- SF 94112 667-D7
- SMTO 94403 749-C7
900 LALT 94024 831-H2
EASTWOOD ST
800 VAL 94591 530-D4
EASTWOOD WY
600 HAY 94544 712-B7
600 MrnC 94965 606-D6
3700 PLE 94588 714-A2
EASTWOODBURY LN
1400 MRTZ 94553 571-J6
EASY CT
- NVTO 94947 525-J3
EASY ST
- VAL 94591 510-J6
- MTVW 94043 812-A4
100 CCCo 94507 632-G3
16000 AlaC 94578 691-F3
EATON AV
- DALY 94015 686-J6
300 RDWC 94062 769-G6
300 RDWC 94070 769-G6
500 SCAR 94070 769-H5
2500 SCAR 94062 769-G6
EATON CT
- CCCo 94507 632-G5
200 BEN 94510 551-B2
40400 FRMT 94538 753-D6
EATON LN
400 MTVW 94043 812-B5
17100 MSER 95030 873-A4
EATON PL
- CPTO 95014 832-B7
- SF 94133 648-A4
EATON RD
200 SMTO 94402 748-J2
EATON VILLA PL
- SCAR 94062 769-G6
- RDWC 94062 769-G6
EBANO CT
1300 SJS 95121 854-J3
EBANO DR
200 WLCK 94598 612-H2
EBBESEN AV
2100 SJS 95124 873-F3
EBBETS PASS RD
100 VAL 94589 510-A6
EBBETTS DR
700 CMBL 95008 853-A7
700 CMBL 95008 873-A1
EBBETTS ST
39000 NWK 94560 772-H1
EBBETTS WY
5100 ANT 94509 595-F4
EBBTIDE AV
- SAUS 94965 626-H1
EBBTIDE PASG
- CMAD 94925 606-J1
- CMAD 94925 607-A1
EBBTIDE PL
100 VAL 94591 550-F2
EBB TIDE ST
14900 SLN 94578 691-C4
EBENER ST
1100 RDWC 94061 770-A7
1300 RDWC 94061 790-B1
EBENSBURG LN
6300 DBLN 94568 693-J4
EBERHARD ST
1600 SCL 95050 833-C3
EBERHARDT CT
800 CLAY 94517 613-J1
EBERLY DR
4900 SJS 95111 875-A1
EBKEN ST
300 PCFA 94044 726-J2
EBONY WY
200 HAY 94544 712-A5
2800 SJS 95148 835-F7
EBRIGHT FIRE RD
400 MrnC 94947 525-H6
600 MrnC 94946 525-H6
EBRO CT
35500 FRMT 94536 752-E2
EBSEN CT
1900 PIN 94564 569-F5
ECCLES AV
400 SSF 94080 708-B3
ECCLESTON AV
2700 PLHL 94523 592-C7
2700 WLCK 94596 592-C7
2800 WLCK 94596 612-B1
ECHO AV
- CMAD 94925 606-H1

BAY AREA
INDEX

STREET Block City ZIP Pg-Grid

ECHO AV
- OAK 94611 629-J7
- CMAD 94925 586-H7
100 CMBL 95008 853-D7
100 OAK 94611 650-A1
100 PDMT 94611 650-A1
1500 SMTO 94401 749-C2
ECHO CIR
- ANT 94509 595-D1
ECHO CT
- PLHL 94523 591-H2
- SANS 94960 586-B1
4200 PLE 94588 714-A1
ECHO DR
800 LALT 94024 831-F2
ECHO LN
- MLV 94941 606-E4
- PDMT 94618 630-C7
- WDSD 94062 809-G6
100 PTLV 94028 810-C7
ECHO LP
7100 SJS 95120 894-E3
ECHO PL
- LKSP 94939 586-D6
- SRFL 94901 566-D6
2000 SRMN 94583 653-F7
ECHO ST
500 LVMR 94550 715-E2
ECHO HAWK CT
500 RCH 94803 589-G3
ECHO HILL
- MRGA 94556 631-D5
ECHO KNOLLS RD
- SCIC 95140 815-C7
4100 SCIC 95127 815-C7
ECHO LAKE WY
3800 FRMT 94555 732-B6
ECHO RIDGE CT
1200 SJS 95120 894-E4
ECHO RIDGE DR
7100 SJS 95120 894-E4
ECHO RIDGE WY
300 SRMN 94583 673-G3
ECHO SPRING RD
3400 LFYT 94549 611-F1
ECHO SPRINGS DR
24700 HAY 94541 712-B2
ECHO SUMMIT RD
200 VAL 94589 509-J5
ECHO SUMMIT ST
1200 LVMR 94550 696-D3
ECHO VALLEY DR
1200 SJS 95120 894-D3
ECKBERG CT
- SJS 95127 834-J2
ECKER CT
600 CMBL 95008 853-C7
ECKER ST
- SF 94105 648-B5
ECKLEY LN
- WLCK 94596 612-E5
- CCCo 94596 612-E5
ECKLEY PL
- WLCK 94596 612-E5
ECLIPSE CT
- ALA 94501 649-G7
ECLIPSE WY
1500 CNCD 94521 593-D5
ECOLA LN
- SUNV 94087 832-A5
EDALE DR
700 SUNV 94087 832-C3
EDDINGTON LN
- DALY 94014 687-E3
EDDINGTON PL
1400 SJS 95129 852-E4
EDDY ST
- SF 94102 648-A6
100 RCH 94801 588-C7
200 SF 94102 647-F6
400 SF 94109 647-F6
1200 SF 94115 647-F6
23000 AlaC 94541 692-D6
EDDYSTONE CT
- RDWC 94065 749-J6
EDELEN AV
100 LGTS 95030 873-A7
EDELWEISS DR
400 SJS 95136 874-F2
EDEN AV
600 SJS 95117 853-D3
1500 CMBL 95117 853-D4
1500 CMBL 95008 853-D4
23300 HAY 94545 711-E6
23300 AlaC 94545 711-E6
N EDEN AV
500 SUNV 94086 812-G5
S EDEN AV
500 SUNV 94086 812-G5
W EDEN AV
500 SUNV 94086 812-F5
EDEN CT
500 SCL 95051 832-J6
4100 CNCD 94521 593-A4
35300 FRMT 94536 752-F2
EDEN DR
3400 SCL 95051 832-J6
EDEN LN
- OAK 94601 650-C7
4000 MrnC 94920 607-C4
EDEN PL
- SRMN 94583 673-F7
EDEN RD
- OAK 94603 690-F2
- SLN 94577 690-F2
EDEN ST
- LKSP 94939 586-E6
6800 DBLN 94568 693-J3
EDEN WY
- HIL 94010 728-D7
EDENBANK CT
2900 SJS 95148 855-D2
EDENBANK DR
3000 SJS 95148 855-D1
EDENBERRY PL
8500 DBLN 94568 693-G2
EDENBERRY ST
8700 DBLN 94568 693-G2
EDEN BOWER LN
900 RDWC 94061 789-G3
EDENBURY LN
900 SJS 95136 874-D1

EDEN CANYON RD
21100 AlaC 94552 692-J2
EDENHALL DR
6100 SJS 95129 852-G3
EDEN LANDING RD
25900 HAY 94545 711-E7
26000 HAY 94545 731-D1
EDEN PARK PL
5800 SJS 95138 875-E4
EDEN ROC DR
100 SAUS 94965 626-H1
EDENVALE AV
200 SJS 95111 875-A2
200 SJS 95136 875-A2
EDENVALE PL
3900 OAK 94605 670-J1
EDEN VIEW DR
4900 SJS 95111 875-B2
EDENWOOD CT
3800 SJS 95121 855-C4
EDENWOOD DR
3800 SJS 95121 855-C5
EDES AV
400 OAK 94603 670-G6
5800 OAK 94621 670-F5
EDESSA CT
- HIL 94010 728-C7
EDGAR CT
4900 SJS 95118 874-C3
EDGAR PL
- SF 94112 687-E1
EDGARDO PL
- SF 94133 648-A3
EDGE DR
4200 OAK 94602 650-E3
EDGE LN
700 LALT 94024 831-G2
EDGE RD
- ATN 94027 790-G1
EDGEBANK DR
1900 SJS 95122 855-A1
EDGEBROOK CT
6500 SJS 95120 894-C1
EDGEBROOK DR
24400 AlaC 94541 712-C1
EDGEBROOK PL
2100 AlaC 94541 712-C1
EDGECLIFF LN
12100 LAH 94022 831-C3
EDGECLIFF PL
12100 LAH 94022 831-C3
EDGECLIFF WY
300 SMCo 94062 789-G3
400 RDWC 94062 789-G3
27900 HAY 94542 712-E4
EDGECOURT DR
2100 HIL 94010 728-D7
EDGECREST DR
1900 SJS 95122 855-A1
EDGECROFT RD
- CCCo 94707 609-F4
EDGEDALE CT
2500 SJS 95122 855-A1
EDGEFIELD CT
2500 SJS 95122 855-A1
EDGEFIELD DR
3600 SCL 95054 813-F5
EDGEFORT CT
1900 SJS 95122 855-A1
EDGEGATE CT
- DNVL 94506 654-A6
EDGEGATE DR
2000 SJS 95122 855-A1
EDGEHILL CT
100 VAL 94589 530-B1
1700 SLN 94577 691-D1
8600 ELCR 94530 609-E1
EDGEHILL DR
100 SCAR 94070 769-G5
400 SCL 95054 813-F5
800 BURL 94010 728-E6
EDGEHILL RD
- MLV 94941 606-D2
1700 SLN 94577 691-D1
EDGEHILL WY
- MrnC 94903 566-G5
- SF 94127 667-D5
1200 MPS 95035 814-F1
EDGEMAN CT
3500 SJS 95148 835-E6
EDGEMAR AV
500 PCFA 94044 706-J4
600 PCFA 94044 707-A4
EDGEMAR ST
- DALY 94014 687-E3
EDGEMAR WY
- CMAD 94925 606-H1
EDGEMERE LN
1000 HAY 94545 711-G5
EDGEMONT AV
200 VAL 94590 530-C3
EDGEMONT CIR
- WLCK 94596 632-E1
EDGEMONT DR
- DALY 94015 687-A6
10900 SCIC 95127 815-B6
EDGEMONT WY
- OAK 94605 671-C5
EDGEMOOR PL
3900 OAK 94605 670-J1
EDGEMOOR ST
14900 SLN 94579 691-B6
EDGEMOOR WY
6300 SJS 95129 852-F3
EDGERLY ST
5500 OAK 94621 670-F2
EDGERTON RD
27400 LAH 94022 830-J1
27600 LAH 94022 810-J7
EDGESTONE CIR
1800 SJS 95122 855-A1
EDGEVIEW CT
2500 SJS 95122 855-A1
EDGEVIEW DR
1900 SJS 95122 855-A1
EDGEWATER BLVD
500 FCTY 94404 749-E3
EDGEWATER CT
- SRFL 94903 566-G3
1200 WLCK 94595 632-A2
EDGEWATER DR
- MPS 95035 794-A6

EDGEWATER DR
3500 SJS 95136 854-G7
5200 NWK 94560 752-D3
7100 OAK 94621 670-D4
EDGEWATER PL
- LKSP 94939 586-E5
- PIT 94565 574-E1
EDGEWATER RD
- BLV 94920 607-C7
EDGEWOOD AV
- MrnC 94941 606-C3
- MLV 94941 606-B3
100 SF 94117 667-E2
600 MrnC 94965 606-B3
4300 OAK 94602 650-C3
EDGEWOOD AV N
900 MrnC 94965 606-A2
900 MLV 94941 606-A2
EDGEWOOD CIR
20600 AlaC 94552 692-F3
EDGEWOOD CT
- DALY 94014 687-D3
EDGEWOOD DR
100 PCFA 94044 707-A1
1400 PA 94301 791-B3
1500 PA 94303 791-C3
EDGEWOOD LN
700 LALT 94022 831-E1
1800 MLPK 94025 790-E6
1900 WLCK 94598 592-E7
EDGEWOOD RD
- ORIN 94563 630-J4
- RDWC 94062 769-H6
300 HIL 94010 748-F1
300 SMTO 94402 748-F1
700 SMCo 94062 769-F7
2100 SMCo 94070 769-F7
2400 SMCo 94070 789-C1
2400 RDWC 94062 789-C1
2400 SMCo 94062 789-C1
EDGEWOOD ST
42200 FRMT 94538 773-D1
EDGEWOOD WY
- SRFL 94901 566-E6
1200 SSF 94080 707-F1
1500 SJS 95125 854-A6
4400 LVMR 94550 716-A2
6600 AlaC 94552 692-F3
EDGEWORTH AV
100 SMCo 94015 687-B5
400 DALY 94015 687-B5
EDIE CT
- PLHL 94523 592-A3
EDIE RD
- SF 94129 647-E4
EDINA LN
19700 SAR 95070 852-F6
EDINBURGH
100 HER 94547 569-J2
EDINBURGH CIR
100 DNVL 94526 653-C2
EDINBURGH CT
1300 CNCD 94518 592-E6
EDINBURGH DR
100 DNVL 94526 653-D2
3200 LVMR 94550 695-J6
20000 SAR 95070 852-E7
EDINBURGH PL
- DNVL 94526 653-D2
EDINBURGH ST
- SF 94112 667-G7
300 SF 94112 687-G1
500 SMTO 94402 748-J2
1200 SMTO 94402 749-A3
1800 SMTO 94403 749-A3
EDISON AV
- CMAD 94925 586-F7
100 SSF 94080 707-J1
400 SLN 94577 690-G1
1300 CCCo 94553 571-F3
EDISON CT
2600 ALA 94501 670-B2
EDISON DR
2800 SJS 95133 834-H1
2900 SCIC 95133 834-H1
EDISON ST
2600 SMTO 94403 749-C6
EDISON WY
3000 SMCo 94063 770-D7
3200 FRMT 94538 773-E3
3200 SMCo 94025 770-D7
EDITH AV
2400 RDWC 94061 789-H1
E EDITH AV
- LALT 94022 811-F6
W EDITH AV
- LALT 94022 811-D6
300 LAH 94022 811-D6
EDITH ST
- SF 94133 648-A4
1100 SJS 95122 834-H5
1400 BERK 94703 609-F7
1500 BERK 94703 629-F1
2300 ELCR 94530 589-B7
24300 HAY 94544 712-A3
37000 NWK 94560 752-F5
EDITH WY
32400 UNC 94587 732-A7
EDLEE AV
200 PA 94306 811-D2
EDLOE DR
24000 HAY 94541 711-G3
EDMINTON DR
18400 SCIC 95014 852-H2
EDMOND CT
1500 SJS 95125 854-A7
EDMOND DR
1500 SCAR 94070 769-E7
EDMONDS CT
1000 SUNV 94087 832-B5
EDMONDS RD
- SCAR 94070 769-D7
100 SMCo 94070 769-D7
EDMONDS WY
900 SUNV 94087 832-B5
EDMONTON
1900 SLN 94579 691-A7
EDMONTON AV
1600 SUNV 94087 832-B5
EDMONTON COM
5300 FRMT 94555 752-C3

EDMONTON WY
3600 CNCD 94520 572-G5
EDMUND CT
- WLCK 94596 612-D5
EDMUND DR
15800 LGTS 95032 873-E5
EDNA AV
- SCIC 95127 835-A3
EDNA CT
- MrnC 94904 586-E3
100 UNC 94587 732-E3
300 LALT 94022 811-F7
400 BEN 94510 551-B3
5500 LVMR 94550 696-C6
EDNA DR
500 PLHL 94523 592-A5
600 SMTO 94402 749-B3
EDNA LN
300 PCFA 94044 707-A3
EDNA ST
- SF 94112 667-E7
600 SF 94127 667-E7
2300 ELCR 94530 589-B7
14800 SLN 94578 691-C3
EDNAMARY WY
1700 MTVW 94040 811-F5
EDQUIBA RD
- SCIC 95035 812-B3
EDSEL DR
1100 MPS 95035 794-D7
6300 SJS 95129 852-F3
EDUCATIONAL PARK DR
300 SJS 95133 834-E1
EDWARD AV
- MrnC 94903 566-G3
200 PIT 94565 574-F4
2700 CNCD 94520 572-E7
3200 SCL 95054 813-F6
38000 FRMT 94536 753-A3
EDWARD CIR
900 VAL 94591 530-D4
EDWARD CT
- SRFL 94901 566-H7
EDWARD LN
2500 ANT 94509 575-D1
EDWARD ST
- SF 94118 647-D7
EDWARD WY
21500 CPTO 95014 852-B2
EDWARDS AV
- OAK 94605 671-A1
- SJS 95110 854-C1
- SAUS 94965 627-B4
2400 ELCR 94530 589-B6
2600 AlaC 94550 715-H5
3900 OAK 94605 670-J1
EDWARDS CT
- BURL 94010 728-E5
1400 LFYT 94549 611-G3
EDWARDS LN
- ATN 94027 790-D3
4200 AlaC 94546 692-B4
EDWARDS RD
1000 BURL 94010 728-D5
EDWARDS ST
200 CCCo 94525 550-E4
2300 BERK 94702 629-F3
EDWARD WHITE WY
- OAK 94621 690-E2
EDWIN DR
- CCCo 94707 609-E2
EDWIN WY
200 HAY 94544 712-A5
EDWIN MARKHAM DR
18700 AlaC 94552 692-E2
EDYTHE ST
100 LVMR 94550 715-E1
EGBERT AV
600 SF 94124 688-B1
1300 SF 94124 668-A7
EGERTON PL
34400 FRMT 94555 752-D1
EGGERS CT
38100 FRMT 94536 753-A3
EGGERS DR
3000 FRMT 94536 752-J4
5000 FRMT 94536 753-A3
EGGERS PZ
- MLV 94941 606-E4
EGGO WY
400 SJS 95116 834-D3
EGLIN LN
- NVTO 94949 546-G3
EGRET CT
- BEN 94510 551-G1
1700 HAY 94545 731-J1
4000 FRMT 94555 732-C7
EGRET DR
1300 SUNV 94087 832-F4
EGRET LN
800 RDWC 94065 750-A6
1800 HAY 94545 731-J1
EGRET PL
300 PIT 94565 574-E1
EGRET RD
400 LVMR 94550 695-D7
400 LVMR 94550 715-D1
EGRET ST
1000 FCTY 94404 749-H1
EGRET WY
- MrnC 94941 606-J6
33100 FRMT 94555 732-B7
EHLE ST
16400 AlaC 94578 691-G5
17000 AlaC 94546 691-G5
EHRHORN AV
600 MTVW 94041 811-J6
EICHLER CT
1200 MTVW 94040 811-H6
EICHLER DR
900 MTVW 94040 811-G6
EICHLER ST
23100 HAY 94545 711-D6
EIGENBRODT WY
30000 UNC 94587 732-A3
EILEEN CT
100 MRGA 94556 651-E2
EILEEN DR
5100 SJS 95129 852-H4
EILEEN LN
100 CNCD 94518 592-G4

EILENE CT
3900 PLE 94588 694-E7
EILENE DR
1900 PLE 94588 694-E7
EIRE DR
- CCCo 94806 569-B4
EISENHOWER DR
500 SJS 95128 853-F3
1400 SCL 95054 813-D4
EISENHOWER ST
1600 SMTO 94403 749-C2
EISENHOWER WY
4700 ANT 94509 574-H5
EL ABRA WY
1100 SJS 95125 854-A3
ELAIN PTH
- RCH 94803 589-F1
ELAINE AV
- MLV 94941 606-C1
800 LVMR 94550 715-F2
ELAINE CT
- CCCo 94507 632-F6
5300 AlaC 94546 692-B2
ELAINE DR
100 PLHL 94523 592-D6
3100 SJS 95124 873-G2
ELAINE WY
- SRFL 94901 586-J2
ELAISO COM
4400 FRMT 94536 752-A6
EL ALAMO
300 DNVL 94526 632-H6
EL ALAMO CT
400 DNVL 94526 632-J6
EL ALTILLO
100 LGTS 95030 872-J2
ELAM AV
1200 CMBL 95008 853-B7
ELANE WY
700 BEN 94510 551-A4
ELAN VILLAGE LN
300 SJS 95134 813-G4
ELARIO LN
4200 CNCD 94518 592-J5
EL ARROYO PL
600 NVTO 94949 546-F2
EL ARROYO RD
400 HIL 94010 748-F2
EL ARROYO WY
4300 PIT 94565 574-D7
ELATI CT
300 DNVL 94526 653-B2
ELBA PL
36000 FRMT 94536 752-F3
ELBA WY
7000 DBLN 94568 693-J3
EL BALCON AV
16800 AlaC 94578 691-F6
ELBERT ST
1000 OAK 94602 650-C3
EL BONITO DR
200 NVTO 94949 546-H4
EL BONITO WY
- BEN 94510 551-D4
- MLBR 94030 728-A4
200 MLBR 94030 727-J4
EL BOSQUE AV
200 SJS 95134 813-F2
EL BOSQUE DR
100 SJS 95134 813-E3
EL BOSQUE ST
100 SJS 95134 813-F2
ELBRIDGE CT
20900 AlaC 94552 692-G2
ELBRIDGE WY
800 PA 94303 791-D6
EL CAJON
- CCCo 94549 591-H7
EL CAJON AV
4500 FRMT 94536 752-F3
EL CAJON DR
200 SJS 95111 854-J6
900 DNVL 94526 633-C7
900 DNVL 94526 653-C1
EL CAJON WY
200 LGTS 95030 873-C4
900 PA 94303 791-C5
EL CAMILLE AV
5300 OAK 94619 670-F1
EL CAMINITO
- ORIN 94563 610-H6
- WLCK 94598 612-D4
100 LVMR 94550 715-E2
2500 OAK 94611 650-E2
EL CAMINITO AV
- CMBL 95008 853-D6
EL CAMINITO CT
5300 AlaC 94546 692-B2
EL CAMINITO RD
23500 LAH 94024 831-E5
EL CAMINO
- SRFL 94901 566-G7
1700 CCCo 94806 569-B5
EL CAMINO AV
- SRFL 94901 586-E1
- SRFL 94901 566-E7
EL CAMINO DR
- CMAD 94925 606-J1
100 PIT 94565 574-D5
1300 CLAY 94517 593-F6
N EL CAMINO DR
1500 CLAY 94517 593-F6
EL CAMINO TER
- CCCo 94596 612-E6
EL CAMINO WY
4000 PA 94306 811-C2
EL CAMINO BUENO
- ROSS 94957 586-C2
EL CAMINO CORTO
- WLCK 94596 612-D5
- CCCo 94596 612-D5
EL CAMINO DEL MAR
200 SF 94121 647-A5
2500 SF 94121 646-H6
EL CAMINO FLORES
- MRGA 94556 651-E1
EL CAMINO GRANDE
15100 SAR 95070 872-G4
EL CAMINO HIGUERA
1100 MPS 95035 794-B4
1300 SCIC 95035 794-B4

EL CAMINO MORAGA
- ORIN 94563 631-B5
EL CAMINO REAL
- BERK 94705 630-A4
- VAL 94590 530-B2
- MLBR 94030 728-C4
1700 BURL 94010 728-C4
5300 SJS 95111 875-C3
5500 SJS 95138 875-C4
5800 SJS 95139 875-H7
5800 SJS 95139 895-H1
5800 SJS 95137 875-H7
5800 SJS 95137 895-H1
5900 SCIC 95137 895-J2
EL CAMINO REAL Rt#-82
- BURL 94010 728-E6
- CLMA 94014 687-C5
- MLBR 94030 728-A2
- MLPK 94025 790-C1
- PA 94301 790-H4
- SCAR 94070 769-F2
- PA 94304 790-H4
100 ATN 94027 790-C1
100 BLMT 94002 749-D7
100 MTVW 94040 811-B1
100 SBRN 94066 727-J1
100 SSF 94080 707-G4
100 MTVW 94041 811-B1
100 SBRN 94066 707-G4
100 SMCo 94063 790-C1
200 DALY 94014 687-C5
200 SCIC 94305 790-H4
200 SMCo 94014 687-C5
200 PA 94305 790-H4
300 SCL 95050 833-A4
400 SCL 95053 833-A4
500 BLMT 94002 769-F2
500 HIL 94010 728-E6
700 CLMA 94014 707-E1
800 RDWC 94062 769-H3
800 RDWC 94062 770-A6
800 RDWC 94063 769-H3
800 RDWC 94063 770-A6
800 SMTO 94402 749-D7
1300 RDWC 94061 770-A6
1300 SMCo 94080 707-E1
1300 SBRN 94066 728-A2
1400 SCIC - 791-A6
1400 PA - 790-H4
1400 PA 94306 791-A6
1500 MLPK 94027 790-C1
1700 MLBR 94030 727-J1
1700 ATN 94025 790-C1
2400 PA 94305 791-A6
2400 SCL 95051 833-A4
2600 RDWC 94061 790-C1
2600 SMCo 94063 770-A6
2700 PA 94304 811-B1
2800 PA 94306 811-B1
3300 SCL 95051 832-J4
4300 LALT 94022 811-B1
E EL CAMINO REAL Rt#-82
- SCL 95051 832-G4
100 SUNV 94087 832-E2
100 SUNV 94086 832-G4
800 SCL 95087 832-G4
1100 SCL 94086 832-G4
N EL CAMINO REAL Rt#-82
- SMTO 94401 728-G7
- SMTO 94402 728-G7
100 SMTO 94402 748-H1
100 SMTO 94401 748-H1
800 BURL 94010 728-G7
S EL CAMINO REAL Rt#-82
- BLMT 94002 749-A2
- SMTO 94401 748-J2
- SMTO 94402 748-J2
500 SMTO 94402 749-A2
500 SMTO 94401 749-A2
2000 SMTO 94403 749-A2
W EL CAMINO REAL Rt#-82
- MTVW 94040 811-F4
- MTVW 94041 811-F4
100 SUNV 94086 832-C1
100 SUNV 94087 832-C1
100 MTVW 94040 812-A7
100 MTVW 94041 812-A7
300 SCIC 94087 832-C1
900 SUNV 94086 812-A7
1100 SUNV 94087 812-A7
1700 LALT 94022 811-F4
EL CAMINO SENDA
15000 SAR 95070 872-G4
EL CAMPANERO
- ORIN 94563 610-G5
EL CAMPO CT
100 VAL 94589 530-A1
3600 CNCD 94519 592-J2
3600 CNCD 94519 593-A2
E EL CAMPO CT
3800 CNCD 94519 593-A2
EL CAMPO DR
- SCIC 95127 835-A1
- SSF 94080 707-E3
100 SCIC 95127 834-J1
1600 CNCD 94519 592-J2
EL CAMPO PL
1700 CNCD 94519 593-A2
EL CAPITAN AV
- MLV 94941 606-C1
2000 SCL 95050 833-C3
EL CAPITAN CT
6300 LVMR 94550 696-D3
EL CAPITAN DR
- MrnC 94903 546-A6
400 DNVL 94526 653-D7
700 MLBR 94030 727-J4
2000 PLE 94566 714-H3
EL CAPITAN LN
- ANT 94509 595-D1
EL CAPITAN PL
400 PA 94306 811-E1
EL CARMELLO CIR
- OAK 94619 650-G4
EL CARMELO AV
100 PA 94306 791-C7

EL CASTILLO
- ORIN 94563 611-A5
EL CENTRO
- MTVW 94043 812-A2
100 CCCo 94526 653-F1
EL CENTRO AV
1000 OAK 94602 650-D3
EL CENTRO RD
400 HIL 94010 748-F2
600 CCCo 94803 589-C2
EL CENTRO ST
3700 PA 94306 811-B2
EL CERRITO AV
- SANS 94960 566-B6
- SMTO 94402 748-G2
- SRFL 94901 566-F7
100 PDMT 94611 650-B1
200 HIL 94010 748-G2
400 PDMT 94610 650-B1
EL CERRITO RD
3900 PA 94306 811-B3
4200 CNCD 94518 592-J5
EL CERRITO WY
1000 PA 94306 811-C3
EL CERRO BLVD
300 DNVL 94526 652-J1
500 DNVL 94526 653-A1
600 DNVL 94526 633-A7
EL CERRO CT
100 DNVL 94526 653-A1
EL CERRO DR
500 CCCo 94803 589-D1
EL CHARRO RD
- AlaC 94588 694-H6
- LVMR 94588 694-H6
600 AlaC 94550 715-A1
600 AlaC 94566 715-A1
EL CIDE CT
1200 MrnC 94941 606-D5
EL CODO WY
1700 SJS 95124 873-H1
EL CONDOR CT
- SRFL 94903 566-D4
EL CORAL CT
1300 SJS 95118 874-C2
EL CORAL WY
3900 SJS 95118 874-C2
EL CORTE
- ORIN 94563 631-B5
EL CORTEZ AV
300 SSF 94080 707-G4
EL CURTOLA BLVD
- CCCo 94596 612-A6
- CCCo 94596 611-J5
1000 CCCo 94595 612-A6
1000 LFYT 94595 612-A6
1200 LFYT 94549 611-J5
ELDA CT
- SRFL 94903 566-C3
1600 PLHL 94523 592-D5
ELDA DR
- PLHL 94523 592-C5
- SRFL 94903 566-C3
ELDAMAR CT
1200 SJS 95121 855-A4
ELDEN DR
600 SJS 95008 853-F7
1900 SJS 95124 853-F7
ELDER
- FRMT 94536 753-D1
ELDER AV
- MLBR 94030 728-A3
1100 MLPK 94025 790-E5
ELDER CT
- MLPK 94025 790-E5
100 SBRN 94066 707-E6
200 SRMN 94583 653-J7
500 SJS 95123 874-J7
1900 HAY 94545 731-J1
ELDER DR
- BLMT 94002 769-B3
100 CCCo 94553 592-B1
ELDER LN
- PCFA 94044 706-J6
ELDER WY
1900 HAY 94545 731-J1
ELDERBERRY CT
100 HER 94547 570-A5
1600 PLE 94588 714-B6
ELDERBERRY DR
- OAK 94611 630-G7
1200 SUNV 94087 832-B3
1300 CNCD 94521 593-C5
ELDERBERRY LN
2100 MrnC 94903 546-C7
ELDERBERRY TR
- CCCo - 652-D4
ELDERBERRY WY
600 SLN 94578 691-C4
1600 SJS 95125 853-J5
ELDERWOOD CT
1700 MRTZ 94553 591-J1
7600 CPTO 95014 852-D2
ELDERWOOD DR
- PLHL 94523 591-H2
400 MRTZ 94553 591-H2
1700 MRTZ 94553 571-J7
1800 CNCD 94519 573-A7
EL DIVISADERO AV
200 WLCK 94598 612-F3
EL DORA DR
- MTVW 94041 812-A6
- MTVW 94041 811-J6
EL DORADO AV
100 DNVL 94526 653-A2
100 DNVL 94526 652-J3
100 HAY 94541 711-G2
100 PA 94306 791-C7
100 SJS 95136 854-G7
500 OAK 94611 649-J1
1600 SJS 95126 833-F6
1900 BERK 94707 609-G6
EL DORADO COM
40200 FRMT 94539 753-E4
EL DORADO CT
- SJS 95002 813-B1
100 SBRN 94066 727-F1
1400 CNCD 94518 592-J3
2000 NVTO 94947 525-G4
4500 PLE 94566 714-D1
20500 SAR 95070 872-D1

BAY AREA INDEX

STREET
Block City ZIP Pg-Grid

EL DORADO DR
100 PIT 94565 574-D5
200 PCFA 94044 707-A1
300 DALY 94015 687-B7
1000 LVMR 94550 715-F3
1300 CNCD 94518 592-J3
10000 SRMN 94583 673-G5
EL DORADO LN
- ORIN 94563 610-F7
EL DORADO RD
100 CCCo 94595 612-A7
EL DORADO ST
- SF 94107 668-C1
100 VAL 94590 530-A4
1300 SJS 95002 793-B7
1500 SJS 95002 813-B1
5600 ELCR 94530 609-C4
N ELDORADO ST
- SMTO 94401 728-J7
- SMTO 94401 749-A1
- SMTO 94401 748-J1
S ELDORADO ST
200 SMTO 94401 749-A1
400 SMTO 94402 749-A1
EL DORADO WY
2900 ANT 94509 575-B7
EL DORI DR
5800 SJS 95123 874-E5
ELDRIDGE AV
- MLV 94941 606-C1
- OAK 94603 670-G7
25600 HAY 94544 711-H5
ELDRIDGE CT
- CCCo 94707 609-F4
600 NVTO 94947 526-C7
ELDRIDGE DR
6800 SJS 95120 894-G2
ELDRIDGE ST
500 NVTO 94947 526-C7
ELDRIDGE GRADE RD
- MrnC - 586-A4
ELDRIDGE GRADE FIRE RD
- MrnC 94965 586-A6
- MrnC - 586-A5
ELEANOR AV
- LALT 94022 811-E7
ELEANOR CT
400 WLCK 94596 592-D7
ELEANOR DR
- WDSD 94062 789-J5
100 WDSD 94062 790-A5
400 ATN 94027 790-A5
1600 SMTO 94402 749-B3
ELEANOR PL
500 HAY 94544 732-E2
ELEANOR WY
900 SUNV 94087 832-G4
ELECTIONEER RD
- SCIC 94305 790-F7
ELECTRA AV
3500 SJS 95118 874-B1
ELEGANT TERN RD
- NVTO 94949 546-D5
EL EMBARCADERO
500 OAK 94610 649-J3
ELENA AV
- ATN 94027 790-D3
ELENA CIR
- SRFL 94903 566-D3
ELENA CT
- NVTO 94945 525-J1
100 VAL 94589 509-J5
ELENA RD
25300 LAH 94022 831-A1
27000 LAH 94022 811-A7
27500 LAH 94022 810-J6
ELENA WY
100 LGTS 95030 873-B3
ELENA PRIVADA
1100 MTVW 94040 832-A1
ELENDA DR
20800 CPTO 95014 832-D7
20800 SCIC 95014 832-D7
EL ESCARPADO CT
400 SCIC 94305 810-G1
ELESTER CT
2300 SJS 95124 873-E4
ELESTER DR
4800 SJS 95124 873-E4
ELF CT
- PLHL 94523 592-B3
EL FAISAN DR
200 SRFL 94903 566-D4
ELFORD ST
- SRFL 94901 586-F1
ELF OWL CT
- NVTO 94949 546-E5
EL GATO LN
15500 LGTS 95032 873-E5
15500 SCIC 95032 873-E5
EL GAVILAN
- ORIN 94563 610-H5
EL GAVILAN CT
- ORIN 94563 610-J5
ELGIN AV
400 RCH 94801 588-F5
ELGIN CT
100 VAL 94591 530-H6
ELGIN LN
2300 WLCK 94598 612-G3
3300 SJS 95118 874-A1
7900 DBLN 94568 693-G2
ELGIN PK
- SF 94103 667-H1
ELGIN ST
600 AlaC 94578 691-E5
600 AlaC 94580 691-E6
ELGIN WY
800 AlaC 94580 691-E6
EL GRANDE CT
3600 SJS 95132 814-J5
EL GRANDE DR
3500 SJS 95132 814-J5
ELIM AL
- SF 94105 648-B5
ELIMINA CT
43800 FRMT 94539 773-G2
ELINOR AV
- MLV 94941 606-E2
ELINORA AV
4400 OAK 94619 650-G5

STREET
Block City ZIP Pg-Grid

ELINORA DR
1800 PLHL 94523 592-B5
ELIOT CT
- MLV 94941 606-G4
ELIOT DR
- LVMR 94550 696-A6
ELISA AV
19700 SAR 95070 852-F5
ELISA COM
4000 FRMT 94536 752-G2
ELISE CT
24200 LAH 94024 831-D4
ELISEO DR
- MrnC 94904 586-G4
- LKSP 94904 586-G4
S ELISEO DR
400 LKSP 94939 586-E5
ELISKA CT
600 WLCK 94598 612-F2
ELIZA CT
100 FCTY 94404 749-G2
ELIZABETH CIR
- LKSP 94939 586-G5
ELIZABETH CT
- NVTO 94945 526-E4
300 ANT 94509 575-D7
300 LVMR 94550 695-F7
1300 CCCo 94596 612-E7
ELIZABETH DR
900 SCL 95050 833-C5
ELIZABETH LN
- DNVL 94526 633-B7
700 MLPK 94025 790-F3
2900 ANT 94509 575-D7
ELIZABETH ST
- SF 94110 667-H3
300 SF 94114 667-F3
400 SJS 95112 834-C6
400 SJS 95113 834-C6
900 SJS 95002 793-B7
1000 LFYT 94549 611-G5
1700 SCAR 94070 769-F4
5700 OAK 94621 670-F2
5700 OAK 94605 670-F2
ELIZABETH WY
- ATN 94027 790-C2
- SRFL 94901 566-E6
600 HAY 94544 732-E2
900 SUNV 94087 832-G4
32400 UNC 94587 732-A7
32400 UNC 94587 731-J7
ELJA WY
800 SJS 95123 874-F5
ELK CT
- MRGA 94556 631-D3
- PCFA 94044 727-C4
4500 ANT 94509 595-G3
7100 DBLN 94568 693-J4
45200 FRMT 94539 773-J3
ELK DR
- CLAY 94517 594-A6
4300 ANT 94509 595-G3
ELK LN
2300 SJS 95133 814-F7
ELK ST
- SF 94131 667-F6
ELKA AV
1400 SJS 95129 852-F4
2400 MTVW 94043 811-F2
ELK CREEK PL
200 SJS 95127 834-H1
ELKE DR
100 AMCN 94589 509-J1
ELKGROVE CT
3600 HAY 94542 712-F4
ELKHART ST
- SF 94105 648-C6
ELKHORN CT
1900 SMTO 94403 749-A4
1900 SMTO 94402 749-A4
2200 SJS 95125 854-A6
ELK HORN WY
- SANS 94960 566-B5
ELKHORN WY
4500 ANT 94509 595-H3
ELKIN CT
- SRFL 94901 566-E7
ELKINS WY
2300 SJS 95121 855-C3
ELKO CT
15600 SLN 94579 691-B7
ELKO DR
1100 SUNV 94089 812-J3
1200 SUNV 94089 813-A3
ELK RIDGE CT
3000 SJS 95136 854-F6
ELK RIDGE WY
500 SJS 95136 854-E7
ELK TREE RD
- SMCo 94062 809-F6
ELKWOOD CT
3900 CNCD 94519 573-A7
ELKWOOD DR
- SSF 94080 707-D1
1100 MPS 95035 793-J5
1800 CNCD 94519 573-A7
ELLA CT
5000 SJS 95111 875-B1
ELLA DR
400 SJS 95111 875-B1
ELLARD PL
1800 CNCD 94521 593-F4
ELLARD WY
1800 CNCD 94521 593-E4
ELLEN AV
1700 SJS 95125 854-B4
ELLEN CT
- ORIN 94563 610-J6
300 MrnC 94903 546-D7
41100 FRMT 94538 753-C7
ELLEN DR
200 MrnC 94903 546-E7
ELLEN ST
700 HAY 94544 712-A3
700 HAY 94544 711-J3
4500 OAK 94601 670-E1
41100 FRMT 94538 753-C7
41100 FRMT 94538 773-C1
ELLEN WY
4300 UNC 94587 732-A7
ELLENA DR
2200 SCL 95050 833-C2

STREET
Block City ZIP Pg-Grid

ELLENWOOD AV
- LGTS 95030 872-J7
W ELLENWOOD AV
200 MSER 95030 872-J6
200 LGTS 95030 872-J6
ELLERBROOK WY
6100 SJS 95123 875-B6
ELLERHORST ST
2500 PIN 94564 569-F4
2600 ELCR 94530 589-B6
ELLERT ST
- SF 94110 667-J5
ELLERY CT
- CCCo 94595 632-C2
ELLERY PL
500 HAY 94544 732-E2
ELLERY ST
500 SCIC 95127 814-H7
500 SJS 95127 814-H7
ELLESMERE CT
3300 WLCK 94598 612-J3
ELLESMERE DR
400 WLCK 94598 612-J2
ELLIE CT
1700 BEN 94510 551-B3
ELLINGSON WY
2700 SRMN 94583 673-E5
ELLINGTON AV
- SF 94112 687-E2
ELLINGTON TER
2000 PLHL 94523 591-J3
ELLINWOOD DR
100 PLHL 94523 592-C4
ELLINWOOD WY
100 PLHL 94523 592-D3
ELLIOT AV
16500 LGTS 95032 873-C5
ELLIOT CT
- CCCo 94507 632-H3
- PLHL 94523 592-A6
2500 SCL 95051 833-B2
4900 FRMT 94536 752-H5
ELLIOT DR
- PLHL 94523 592-A7
ELLIOT ST
100 SF 94134 687-J2
2400 SCL 95051 833-B2
3200 OAK 94610 650-B4
37700 FRMT 94536 752-G5
ELLIOTT CIR
400 PLE 94566 714-E1
ELLIOTT DR
100 MLPK 94025 791-A2
900 VAL 94589 509-J5
900 VAL 94589 510-A5
1700 AMCN 94589 509-J2
ELLIOTT ST
1800 SCIC 95128 853-G1
2100 SJS 95128 853-G1
2300 SMTO 94403 749-D4
ELLIS AV
900 SJS 95125 854-B4
1500 MPS 95035 794-D6
ELLIS CT
- LFYT 94549 611-J4
- PLHL 94523 612-B1
38100 FRMT 94536 752-J4
ELLIS DR
800 SMCo 94015 687-A4
ELLIS RD
4000 CCCo 94553 571-J4
ELLIS ST
- SF 94102 648-A6
- SF 94108 648-A6
300 MTVW 94043 812-B4
300 SF 94102 647-H6
500 SF 94109 647-H6
600 MTVW 94043 812-B4
600 SCIC 94035 812-B4
1300 SF 94115 647-F6
1500 CNCD 94520 592-F2
2900 BERK 94703 629-G4
EL LISA DR
900 SJS 95123 874-E4
ELLITA AV
400 OAK 94610 649-J3
ELLMANN PL
35700 FRMT 94536 752-G1
ELLMAR OAKS CT
200 SJS 95136 874-G1
ELLMAR OAKS DR
3900 SJS 95136 874-G1
ELLMAR OAKS LP
3900 SJS 95136 874-G1
ELLS LN
1100 RCH 94804 609-B2
ELLS ST
1100 RCH 94804 609-B2
N ELLSWORTH AV
- SMTO 94401 728-H7
- SMTO 94401 748-J1
S ELLSWORTH AV
- SMTO 94401 748-J1
400 SMTO 94401 749-A2
ELLSWORTH CT E
400 SMTO 94401 728-H7
ELLSWORTH CT W
400 SMTO 94401 728-H7
ELLSWORTH PL
700 PA 94303 791-D6
ELLSWORTH ST
- SF 94110 667-J6
2300 BERK 94704 629-H2
2700 BERK 94705 629-H2
43300 FRMT 94539 773-H1
43300 FRMT 94539 753-H7
ELLSWORTH TER
100 FRMT 94539 773-H1
ELLWELL DR
1700 MPS 95035 794-D6
ELLYRIDGE CT
200 SJS 95123 874-J3
ELLYRIDGE DR
5400 SJS 95123 874-J3
ELM
- BEN 94510 551-C5
ELM AV
- LKSP 94939 586-F6
- MLV 94941 606-E3
- MrnC 94904 586-D3
- SANS 94960 566-A7
100 BURL 94010 748-F1

STREET
Block City ZIP Pg-Grid

ELM AV
100 SBRN 94066 727-J1
100 HIL 94010 748-F1
100 BURL 94010 728-F7
100 HIL 94010 728-F7
400 MPS 95035 793-H6
400 SBRN 94066 707-H6
700 RCH 94801 588-F6
1500 CCCo 94805 589-C5
ELM CT
- PCFA 94044 727-A5
100 SUNV 94086 832-F1
100 SANS 94960 566-A7
400 MPS 95035 793-J6
500 SSF 94080 707-H2
1000 ELCR 94530 609-D3
6700 DBLN 94568 693-J3
21400 CPTO 95014 852-C2
ELM DR
800 CCCo 94572 569-J1
1000 NVTO 94945 526-B3
ELM PK
15000 MSER 95030 873-A4
15000 MSER 95030 872-J4
ELM RD
- CNCD 94521 593-E3
1600 CNCD 94519 592-H1
ELM ST
- BEN 94510 551-D5
- LGTS 95030 873-A7
- SCAR 94070 769-F2
- SF 94102 647-H6
- SRFL 94901 566-G7
100 MLPK 94025 791-A2
100 RDWC 94063 770-B6
100 SMTO 94401 748-H1
300 MLPK 94025 790-J2
400 SSF 94080 707-H2
500 ELCR 94530 609-C1
600 SJS 95126 833-H5
1000 LVMR 94550 695-F7
1100 SF 94115 647-G7
1300 PIT 94565 574-E3
1400 MRTZ 94553 571-F3
1800 ALA 94501 670-A1
1800 PIN 94564 569-E4
2000 CNCD 94519 592-G1
3100 OAK 94609 649-H1
14300 SLN 94579 690-J4
21100 AlaC 94546 692-A6
36800 NWK 94560 752-D7
37000 FRMT 94536 752-G3
37200 NWK 94560 772-D1
ELMA ST
- MLV 94941 606-C3
ELMAR AV
9800 OAK 94603 671-A5
ELMAR CT
3000 RCH 94801 588-F1
ELMAR WY
1500 SJS 95129 852-F5
EL MARCERO CT
6900 SJS 95119 895-E1
ELMBRIDGE DR
6000 SJS 95129 852-G3
ELMBROOK WY
500 SJS 95111 855-A7
ELMBURG RDGE
100 LAH 94022 831-A2
ELMDALE PL
2600 PA 94303 791-D5
ELMER ST
1000 BLMT 94002 769-F1
1200 SMCo 94002 769-F1
ELMGATE CT
2100 SJS 95148 855-E2
ELMGROVE CT
5000 SJS 95130 852-J6
ELMGROVE LN
2000 SJS 95130 852-J6
ELMHURST AV
1000 OAK 94603 670-H5
3400 SCL 95051 832-J7
S ELMHURST AV
600 OAK 94603 670-G6
ELMHURST CT
100 SCL 95051 832-J7
ELMHURST DR
- SF 94132 667-C6
1500 LALT 94024 832-A3
4500 SJS 95119 853-A2
ELMHURST LN
1700 CNCD 94521 593-D3
ELMHURST ST
300 HAY 94544 711-G4
ELMINYA DR
100 CCCo 94553 572-C7
ELMIRA DR
800 SUNV 94087 832-C2
ELMIRA LN
- PLHL 94523 592-D7
ELMIRA ST
- SF 94124 668-A6
EL MIRADOR
- WLCK 94596 612-D6
EL MIRASOL PL
- SF 94132 667-A6
ELM LEAF CT
2000 SCL 95050 833-C3
ELMO RD
3000 ANT 94509 575-E7
EL MOLINO DR
- CLAY 94517 613-J1
EL MOLINO PL
100 SRMN 94583 673-F7
EL MOLINO WY
300 SJS 95119 875-B7
EL MONTE AV
- LALT 94024 831-E1
- LALT 94022 831-E1
100 VAL 94591 530-C7
900 MTVW 94040 811-E7
1500 MTVW 94022 811-E7
1500 LALT 94022 811-E7
2100 LALT 94024 811-E7
2900 OAK 94605 671-A3
N EL MONTE AV
- LALT 94022 811-G6
- LALT 94024 811-G6
EL MONTE CT
100 LALT 94022 811-F6
3000 ANT 94509 575-B7

STREET
Block City ZIP Pg-Grid

EL MONTE DR
3300 CNCD 94519 592-H2
EL MONTE LN
- SAUS 94965 627-B3
EL MONTE RD
- LALT 94024 831-D2
700 LALT 94022 831-D2
700 LAH 94024 831-D2
700 LAH 94022 831-D2
3900 CCCo 94803 589-C3
EL MONTE WY
100 CNCD 94519 592-H2
2700 SJS 95127 835-A5
2900 ANT 94509 575-B7
ELMORE CT
37700 FRMT 94536 752-G6
EL MORO DR
1200 CMBL 95008 853-G6
ELM PARK
15200 MSER 95030 872-J4
ELM PARK CT
15200 MSER 95030 872-J4
ELMQUIST CT
3100 MRTZ 94553 571-E5
ELMRIDGE CT
5300 PLE 94566 714-C2
ELMSDALE DR
7000 SJS 95120 894-G3
ELMSFORD CT
1100 CPTO 95014 852-C3
ELMSFORD DR
1100 CPTO 95014 852-C3
ELMTREE CT
1800 SJS 95131 814-C5
ELMVIEW DR
9700 OAK 94603 671-A4
ELMWOOD AV
700 VAL 94591 530-E5
2700 BERK 94705 629-J4
3000 OAK 94601 670-C1
5100 NWK 94560 752-F4
ELMWOOD CIR
7300 PLE 94588 714-A2
ELMWOOD CT
- CCCo 94596 612-D2
- NVTO 94945 526-C3
- SRFL 94901 566-E6
100 LGTS 95030 873-A2
100 SBRN 94066 707-E6
2900 BERK 94705 630-A3
ELMWOOD DR
- DALY 94015 687-A4
- SRMN 94583 693-H1
1100 CCCo 94596 612-D2
1100 MLBR 94030 727-H3
4900 SJS 95130 852-J6
E ELMWOOD DR
1100 CCCo 94596 612-D2
ELMWOOD LN
200 HAY 94541 711-G3
ELMWOOD PL
- MLPK 94025 790-H2
ELMWOOD RD
1800 HIL 94010 728-E7
4500 CCCo 94803 589-D3
ELMWOOD ST
100 MTVW 94043 811-J4
ELMWOOD WY
100 SF 94112 667-D7
ELNA DR
- VAL 94591 530-D3
EL NAVATO CIR
- NVTO 94945 526-C2
EL NIDO
1600 CCCo 94526 633-E7
EL NIDO AV
- LGTS 95032 893-B1
EL NIDO CT
- LGTS 95032 893-C1
- ORIN 94563 631-A4
100 CCCo 94526 633-E7
EL NIDO RD
100 SMCo 94028 830-D4
EL NIDO RANCH RD
3900 LFYT 94549 611-A6
4200 ORIN 94563 611-A6
4200 ORIN 94563 610-J6
ELNORA CT
1400 LALT 94024 831-J4
EL NOVATO CIR
- NVTO 94945 526-C2
EL NOVATO CT
- NVTO 94945 526-C2
ELODIE WY
- SJS 95116 834-H2
ELOISE AV
1800 PLHL 94523 592-B5
ELOISE CIR
10600 SCIC 94024 831-F5
EL OLIVAR
100 LGTS 95030 872-J2
EL OSO DR
1400 SJS 95129 852-J5
EL PADRO DR
1200 LVMR 94550 715-E3
EL PARAISO CT
- MRGA 94556 631-E5
EL PARQUE CT
1800 SMTO 94403 749-E5
EL PASEO
- BEN 94510 551-A3
- MLBR 94030 728-A4
- WLCK 94596 612-C3
3100 ALA 94502 669-J7
EL PASEO DR
400 OAK 94603 670-H7
6200 SJS 95120 874-D7
6300 SJS 95120 894-D1
EL PASEO DE LOS PASTORES
3600 SCIC 95148 835-F6
EL PASO WY
2900 ANT 94509 575-B7
EL PATIO
- OAK 94611 650-E2
- ORIN 94563 610-G3
- VAL 94590 530-B3
700 CCCo 94803 589-C1
EL PATIO CT
100 CMBL 95008 853-F5
EL PATIO DR
500 CMBL 95008 853-F5

STREET
Block City ZIP Pg-Grid

EL PAVO REAL CIR
- SRFL 94903 566-D4
EL PINAR
100 LGTS 95030 872-J2
EL PINTADO
- PIT 94565 573-H3
400 DNVL 94526 633-A6
400 DNVL 94526 653-A1
600 DNVL 94526 632-J7
W EL PINTADO
200 DNVL 94526 653-A1
300 DNVL 94526 652-J1
EL PINTADO HGTS DR
300 DNVL 94526 633-A6
EL PINTO
- DNVL 94526 632-H7
EL PLAZUELA WY
- SF 94127 667-C7
EL POCO COM
4800 FRMT 94536 752-A4
EL POCO PL
100 VAL 94589 530-B1
EL POLIN LP
- SF 94129 647-E5
EL PORTAL
- SAUS 94965 627-B3
100 DNVL 94526 632-H7
3100 ALA 94502 670-A6
EL PORTAL AV
300 HIL 94010 748-G2
300 SMTO 94402 748-G2
500 FRMT 94536 732-J7
EL PORTAL CT
- BERK 94708 609-J7
EL PORTAL DR
- CLAY 94517 613-J2
- LKSP 94939 586-F4
- SPAB 94806 588-J2
2500 CCCo 94806 589-A3
2500 CCCo 94806 588-J3
3400 CCCo 94803 589-B2
3600 RCH 94803 589-B2
27000 HAY 94542 712-F4
EL PORTAL WY
- DALY 94015 687-A2
200 SJS 95119 875-B6
300 SJS 95123 875-B6
EL PORTON
100 LGTS 95030 872-J2
EL PRADO AV
100 SRFL 94903 566-E5
200 SMCo 94061 790-A4
EL PRADO CT
- MRTZ 94553 571-H4
1100 SJS 95120 874-D7
EL PRADO DR
1100 SJS 95120 874-D7
EL PRADO RD
2700 BURL 94010 728-B7
EL PUEBLO AV
800 PIT 94565 574-F3
EL PUENTE WY
14500 SAR 95070 872-F3
EL PULGAR
- ORIN 94563 610-H5
EL QUANITO CT
800 DNVL 94526 633-B7
EL QUANITO DR
800 DNVL 94526 633-B7
EL QUANITO WY
- BURL 94010 728-B7
EL QUITO WY
15000 SAR 95070 872-H4
EL RANCHITO WY
600 MTVW 94041 811-J6
EL RANCHO AV
17300 MSER 95030 873-B5
EL RANCHO CT
- PLHL 94523 592-A7
EL RANCHO DR
- PLHL 94523 592-A7
700 LVMR 94550 715-E1
EL RANCHO VERDE CT
200 SJS 95116 834-G3
EL RANCHO VERDE DR
100 SJS 95116 834-F3
EL REY AV
4700 FRMT 94536 752-F4
EL REY PL
1800 CNCD 94519 572-J7
EL REY RD
- SMCo 94028 830-D4
EL REY ST
2700 ANT 94509 575-C7
EL RIBERO
- ORIN 94563 610-G6
EL RINCON
- ORIN 94563 610-E7
EL RINCON RD
800 DNVL 94526 653-B2
EL RIO CT
- LVMR 94550 696-E3
EL RIO DR
800 SJS 95125 854-C5
EL RIO RD
400 DNVL 94526 633-A7
400 DNVL 94526 632-J7
400 DNVL 94526 653-A1
400 DNVL 94526 652-J1
EL ROBLE CT
5000 SJS 95118 874-B4
ELROD AV
- OAK 94618 630-B6
ELROD DR
4900 AlaC 94546 692-B3
ELROSE AV
5000 SJS 95124 873-H5
5100 SJS 95032 873-H5
EL SECO WY
2100 PIT 94565 573-J3
EL SENDERO
100 VAL 94589 530-A1
EL SERENA
300 CCCo 94553 572-C6
EL SERENO
- ORIN 94563 610-G5
3100 ALA 94502 669-J6
EL SERENO AV
2000 LALT 94024 832-A5
EL SERENO CT
- LALT 94024 832-A5
- SF 94127 667-F5

STREET
Block City ZIP Pg-Grid

EL SERENO DR
- SCAR 94070 769-H5
700 SJS 95123 874-G6
EL SERENO WY
- SCAR 94070 769-H5
ELSIE AV
200 SLN 94577 691-B1
1700 MTVW 94043 811-H3
ELSIE DR
200 DNVL 94526 653-A1
200 DNVL 94526 652-J1
ELSIE ST
- SF 94110 667-H5
ELSIE WY
- LAH 94022 811-B7
ELSINORE AV
1000 OAK 94602 650-D3
ELSINORE CT
900 PA 94303 791-C5
ELSINORE DR
900 PA 94303 791-C5
ELSMAN CT
1400 SJS 95120 874-A7
ELSNAB CT
2800 PLE 94588 694-F6
EL SOBRANTE DR
200 DNVL 94526 653-B1
EL SOBRANTE ST
2700 SCL 95051 833-A4
3300 SMTO 94403 748-J6
EL SOLYO AV
1000 CMBL 95008 853-G6
EL SOMBRA CT
1500 LFYT 94549 611-G2
EL SOMBROSO DR
700 SJS 95123 874-G5
ELSONA CT
1300 SUNV 94087 832-B4
ELSONA DR
1300 SUNV 94087 832-B4
ELSTON AV
3700 OAK 94602 650-C4
ELSTON CT
- OAK 94602 650-C4
- SCAR 94070 769-E4
ELSTON DR
3600 SBRN 94066 707-C5
EL SUENO
- ORIN 94563 610-G5
EL SUYO DR
3200 SRMN 94583 673-G5
ELTON CT
- PLHL 94523 591-H5
14700 SCIC 95124 873-G4
ELTON DR
14800 SCIC 95124 873-G4
EL TORAZO COM
4800 FRMT 94536 752-A4
EL TORO CT
6100 SJS 95123 874-F6
EL TORO RD
100 ALA 94501 649-D6
EL TORO WY
1600 PIN 94564 569-D5
EL TOYONAL
- ORIN 94563 610-E7
500 CCCo 94563 610-D5
ELVA AV
14200 SAR 95070 872-D2
EL VANDA RD
- SMCo 94062 769-E7
EL VERANO
- ORIN 94563 610-J5
100 VAL 94590 530-B2
EL VERANO AV
100 PA 94306 811-C1
300 PA 94306 791-D7
EL VERANO DR
700 CCCo 94598 612-F5
EL VERANO ST
9800 OAK 94603 670-G7
EL VERANO WY
- SF 94127 667-D6
1500 BLMT 94002 769-D2
ELVERTON DR
6700 OAK 94611 630-F5
6800 CCCo 94611 630-F5
ELVESSA ST
10700 OAK 94605 671-D4
ELVIA CT
200 MrnC 94903 546-E7
ELVIA ST
3200 LFYT 94549 591-H7
ELVINA DR
15200 SLN 94579 691-A6
ELVIRA CT
1200 SJS 95122 834-H5
ELVIRA PL
4300 AlaC 94546 692-A3
ELVIRA ST
100 LVMR 94550 715-D2
14000 SAR 95070 872-D2
ELVIS DR
500 SJS 95123 874-J7
EL VISTA WY
2700 SJS 95148 835-D7
ELWELL CT
1000 PA 94303 791-F6
ELWOOD AV
300 OAK 94610 649-J2
300 OAK 94610 650-A2
ELWOOD CT
3900 CNCD 94519 593-B1
6600 SJS 95120 894-E1
ELWOOD DR
1300 CMBL 95030 872-J1
ELWOOD RD
6600 SJS 95120 894-E2
ELWOOD ST
- RDWC 94062 769-J5
- SF 94102 648-A6
300 RDWC 94062 770-A6
ELWYN PL
900 DNVL 94526 632-J7
ELY CT
200 SJS 95123 875-A4
ELY PL
100 PA 94306 811-E1
ELYSIAN PL
- OAK 94605 671-C3
ELYSIAN FIELDS DR
- OAK 94605 671-C3

STREET Block City ZIP Pg-Grid

EL ZUPARKO DR
5800 SJS 95123 874-E5
EMALITA CT
100 SBRN 94066 727-J2
EMAMI CT
7200 SJS 95120 894-H4
EMAMI DR
7200 SJS 95120 894-H4
EMANUEL CT
3600 SJS 95121 855-A5
18500 SAR 95070 852-H7
EMARON DR
100 SBRN 94066 707-D6
EMBARCADERO
- OAK 94606 649-J6
- OAK 94607 649-J6
100 MRTZ 94553 571-C2
1000 OAK 94606 650-A7
1800 OAK 94606 670-A1
39500 FRMT 94538 753-B5
EMBARCADERO W
300 OAK 94607 649-D4
EMBARCADERO CT
7000 PLE 94588 693-H5
EMBARCADERO RD
- SCIC 94305 790-J5
- PA 94301 790-J5
100 PA 94301 791-C4
700 PA 94303 791-C4
EMBARCADERO WY
- MrnC 94901 586-H1
- SRFL 94901 586-H1
2400 PA 94303 791-E3
EMBASSY DR
- LVMR 94550 716-D1
EMBEE DR
5800 SJS 95123 875-A5
EMBERS WY
1500 AlaC 94580 691-D6
1500 SLN 94579 691-D6
EMERALD AV
100 SCAR 94070 769-G5
800 SLN 94577 691-C1
7100 DBLN 94568 693-H3
EMERALD CIR
- VAL 94589 530-C1
EMERALD CT
- SMTO 94403 748-J6
- SSF 94080 707-F2
20000 AlaC 94546 692-C5
EMERALD DR
- DNVL 94526 652-H1
2800 WLCK 94596 612-A2
EMERALD LN
- SF 94132 667-A6
EMERALD ST
500 LVMR 94550 715-D2
1800 CNCD 94518 592-F6
4100 OAK 94609 629-J7
EMERALD WY
100 HER 94547 569-G5
900 SJS 95117 853-D3
EMERALD BAY LN
100 FCTY 94404 749-E3
EMERALD COVE DR
- CCCo 94565 573-J3
EMERALD HILL
14400 SAR 95070 872-H2
EMERALD HILL RD
600 RDWC 94061 789-G2
EMERALD HILLS CIR
2200 SJS 95131 814-D6
EMERALD HILLS LN
12000 LAH 94022 831-D3
EMERALD LAKE PL
- SMCo 94062 789-G1
EMERIC AV
1300 SPAB 94806 588-G4
2300 RCH 94806 588-G4
EMERICK AV
300 SCIC 95127 835-A2
300 SJS 95127 835-A2
EMERSON AV
- CCCo 94525 550-E5
1100 SCIC 95008 873-D3
2500 HAY 94545 731-G1
EMERSON CT
100 PLHL 94523 592-B7
700 FRMT 94539 753-G7
700 SJS 95126 833-H6
EMERSON DR
- MLV 94941 606-H6
4000 LVMR 94550 696-A6
EMERSON LN
100 MTVW 94043 812-B5
EMERSON ST
- SF 94118 647-E6
100 PA 94301 790-H4
400 FRMT 94539 753-H7
1100 PA 94301 791-A6
2000 BERK 94703 629-G4
2100 BERK 94705 629-G4
2500 PA 94306 791-B7
3100 PA 94306 811-C1
3600 OAK 94610 650-B4
EMERSON TER
- ALA 94501 669-H2
EMERSON WY
3700 OAK 94610 650-B4
EMERY CT
3700 CNCD 94518 592-J5
16300 AlaC 94580 691-E5
EMERY LN
- SF 94133 648-A4
EMERY ST
3800 EMVL 94608 629-F7
EMERY BAY DR
- EMVL 94608 629-E6
EMERYSTONE TER
200 MrnC 94903 546-E6
EMIG CT
1700 SCL 95051 832-J3
EMIL LN
- SF 94127 667-D6
EMILIA LN
33800 FRMT 94555 752-C1
EMILIE AV
- ATN 94027 790-E3
EMILIE DR
10500 SCIC 95127 834-J3
13200 SJS 95127 834-J3
EMILINE DR
5000 SJS 95124 873-G5
EMILIO CT
- CCCo 94803 589-F4
EMILY CT
100 VAL 94589 510-C5
4600 AlaC 94546 692-A3
EMILY DR
600 MTVW 94043 812-A3
EMILY LN
2400 SSF 94080 707-D4
EMILY WY
- LVMR 94550 716-D1
EMLIN PL
- MrnC 94904 586-D3
EMLYN CT
6000 SJS 95123 875-B6
EMMA CT
900 SJS 95120 894-G4
1600 CNCD 94519 592-J2
EMMA DR
2400 PIN 94564 569-F4
EMMA LN
100 MLPK 94025 791-A3
EMMA ST
- SF 94108 648-A5
EMMETT AV
800 BLMT 94002 769-E1
EMMETT CT
- SF 94110 667-J4
2200 SCL 95051 832-J2
EMMETT PL
3400 SCL 95051 832-J2
EMMETT WY
2500 EPA 94303 791-B1
2500 EPA 94303 771-B7
EMMONS DR
400 MTVW 94043 811-G2
EMMONS CANYON CT
- CCCo 94526 633-D4
EMMONS CANYON DR
1400 CCCo 94526 633-C4
EMMONS CANYON LN
100 CCCo 94526 633-C4
EMORY AV
500 CMBL 95008 853-D7
700 CMBL 95008 873-D1
EMORY ST
200 SJS 95110 833-J5
700 SJS 95126 833-H6
1700 SJS 95128 833-F7
EMORY WY
4200 LVMR 94550 716-A2
EMPEROR WY
1500 SUNV 94087 832-F5
EMPEY WY
600 SCIC 95128 853-F2
EMPIRE AL
- SJS 95110 834-A5
EMPIRE AV
10100 CPTO 95014 832-B7
EMPIRE CT
3900 PLE 94588 714-A1
EMPIRE RD
9100 OAK 94603 670-F7
EMPIRE ST
500 AlaC 94580 691-D6
4600 UNC 94587 752-A1
E EMPIRE ST
- SJS 95112 834-C4
W EMPIRE ST
200 SJS 95110 834-A5
EMPIRE MINE RD
- ANT 94509 595-D5
- CCCo - 595-D7
EMPRESS CT
6200 SJS 95129 852-F3
EMPRESS LN
- SF 94134 688-A2
EMROL AV
38700 FRMT 94536 752-J5
EMSHEE LN
- CCCo 94553 572-B4
ENA CT
- NVTO 94947 525-J3
ENBORG LN
2200 SCIC 95128 853-F2
ENCANTO AV
- SF 94115 647-F6
ENCANTO CT
1700 WLCK 94596 612-A2
ENCANTO PL
1500 WLCK 94596 612-A2
ENCANTO WY
200 FRMT 94539 753-E4
1100 PCFA 94044 726-H4
ENCERTI AV
- VAL 94589 510-A7
ENCHANTED WY
- SRMN 94583 673-A2
1300 SMCo 94402 748-G6
ENCHANTO VISTA
11000 SCIC 95127 815-A5
ENCIMA DR
1900 CNCD 94519 592-G1
ENCINA AV
- CMAD 94925 606-G1
- PA 94301 790-J5
200 RDWC 94061 790-B1
300 ATN 94027 790-E1
300 SMCo 94063 790-E1
500 SMCo 94025 770-E7
1000 PIN 94564 569-D4
ENCINA CT
- HIL 94010 728-E7
- NVTO 94945 526-C2
1100 ANT 94509 575-B6
15000 SAR 95070 872-G4
ENCINA DR
1200 MLBR 94030 728-A5
ENCINA PL
- BERK 94705 630-A4
- PIT 94565 574-C6
- SANS 94960 586-B1
ENCINA ST
1200 HAY 94544 712-A7
1200 HAY 94544 711-J7
ENCINA WY
2500 SCL 95051 833-B4
3400 OAK 94605 671-B4
ENCINA CAMINO
2800 WLCK 94598 612-H2
ENCINA CORTE
200 WLCK 94598 612-H2
ENCINA GRANDE DR
600 PA 94306 811-C2
ENCINAL AV
100 ATN 94027 790-F2
100 MLPK 94025 790-F2
100 MLPK 94027 790-F2
2600 ALA 94501 670-A3
ENCINAL AV Rt#-61
1300 ALA 94501 669-H2
2200 ALA 94501 670-A2
ENCINAL CT
600 WLCK 94596 612-B2
23200 LAH 94024 831-E5
ENCINAL DR
2400 WLCK 94596 612-B3
6100 SJS 95119 875-C6
ENCINAL PL
100 PIT 94565 574-C7
ENCINAL WK
- SF 94122 667-C3
ENCINITAS CT
2800 SJS 95132 814-D3
ENCINITAS WY
4200 UNC 94587 731-J5
4200 UNC 94587 732-A6
ENCINO CT
100 SUNV 94086 812-C6
ENCINO DR
300 LVMR 94550 715-D2
ENCINO RD
- ATN 94027 790-G1
ENCLAVE DR
- SJS 95134 813-C2
ENCLINE CT
- SF 94127 667-E5
ENCLINE WY
3700 BLMT 94002 769-A2
ENCORE WY
600 SJS 95134 813-F3
ENCOUNTER BAY
200 ALA 94502 669-H7
ENCYCLOPEDIA CIR
40400 FRMT 94538 773-A2
ENDEAVOR CV
- CMAD 94925 606-J2
ENDEAVOR DR
- CMAD 94925 606-J2
100 MrnC 94920 606-J2
ENDEAVOUR WY
32500 UNC 94587 732-A6
ENDERBY WY
1000 SUNV 94087 832-B4
ENDFIELD WY
10000 SCIC 95127 835-A3
ENDICOTT BLVD
1400 SJS 95193 875-C4
ENDICOTT CT
300 WLCK 94598 612-D3
ENDICOTT DR
500 SUNV 94087 832-D5
1400 SJS 95122 834-J5
ENDICOTT ST
14900 SLN 94579 691-B6
ENDMOOR CT
300 SJS 95119 895-D1
ENDMOOR DR
6700 SJS 95119 895-D1
ENDRISS DR
1600 MRTZ 94553 571-J7
ENDSLEIGH CT
700 DNVL 94506 654-A6
ENEA CIR
1400 CNCD 94520 592-D2
ENEA CT
- CNCD 94520 592-E2
4000 FRMT 94555 752-D1
ENEA DR
3600 PIT 94565 574-C5
ENEA TER
34300 FRMT 94555 752-D1
ENEA WY
2800 ANT 94509 575-C6
ENES AV
- CCCo 94565 573-F2
ENESCO AV
1600 SJS 95121 855-A2
1700 SJS 95122 855-A2
ENFIELD DR
5000 NWK 94560 752-F4
ENFIELD WY
700 HIL 94010 748-G3
ENFRENTE RD
300 NVTO 94949 546-E1
ENGINE HOUSE DR
30600 UNC 94587 732-A4
ENGLE RD
- SMTO 94402 748-H1
ENGLERT CT
300 SJS 95133 834-F2
ENGLEWOOD AV
16300 LGTS 95032 873-C7
16300 SCIC 95032 873-C7
ENGLEWOOD DR
4600 SJS 95129 853-A4
4600 SJS 95129 852-J4
10500 OAK 94605 671-D3
ENGLISH CT
- BLMT 94002 769-E2
- NVTO 94947 525-G3
1600 SJS 95129 852-H5
2200 WLCK 94598 612-G2
ENGLISH DR
1400 SJS 95129 852-H5
ENGLISH PL
400 SCIC 95138 875-E3
ENGLISH ST
- SF 94124 668-E7
ENGLISH OAK CT
2000 CCCo 94506 653-H1
ENGLISH OAK WY
10100 CPTO 95014 831-J7
ENGVALL RD
2300 SBRN 94066 707-F6
ENID DR
1600 CNCD 94519 593-A2
ENLOW CT
2600 PIN 94564 569-G5
ENNING AV
5600 SJS 95123 874-J4
ENNIS PL
- ALA 94502 669-J4
ENNISMORE CT
200 ALA 94502 670-A5
ENOCHS ST
3600 SCL 95051 812-J7
ENOLA AV
900 AlaC 94586 734-B4
ENOS AV
3600 OAK 94619 650-G6
ENOS CT
600 SCL 95051 833-B6
ENOS ST
400 FRMT 94539 753-H7
ENOS WY
500 LVMR 94550 695-G7
ENRICA LN
- WLCK 94596 612-B3
ENRIGHT AV
600 SCL 95050 833-D5
ENRIQUEZ CT
200 MPS 95035 794-A5
ENRIQUITA CT
700 SJS 95123 874-G5
ENSALMO AV
1600 SJS 95118 874-A1
ENSENADA AV
600 BERK 94707 609-F5
ENSENADA DR
100 NVTO 94949 546-F2
1500 CMBL 95008 853-A6
3200 SRMN 94583 673-G5
8000 PLE 94588 714-A5
ENSENADA RD
- SCAR 94070 769-F2
ENSENADA WY
1300 LALT 94024 831-J4
2100 SMTO 94403 749-A5
ENSIGN AV
1300 VAL 94590 530-C3
ENSIGN CT
300 PIT 94565 574-A3
ENSIGN DR
- EMVL 94608 629-C6
ENSIGN LN
300 RDWC 94065 749-H7
ENSIGN WY
700 PA 94303 811-E1
1900 SJS 95133 834-E1
1900 SJS 95133 814-E7
ENSLEY CT
- CCCo 94507 632-H2
ENT CT
- NVTO 94949 546-G4
ENTERPRISE
3000 ALA 94501 649-F6
ENTERPRISE AV
500 RCH 94801 588-F5
3300 HAY 94545 711-C7
ENTERPRISE COM
4500 FRMT 94538 773-D4
ENTERPRISE CT
3500 CNCD 94519 572-H5
37500 NWK 94560 772-D1
ENTERPRISE DR
- CMAD 94925 606-J2
400 DNVL 94526 653-A1
400 DNVL 94526 633-A7
7400 NWK 94560 772-C1
ENTERPRISE PL
4300 FRMT 94538 773-D4
ENTERPRISE ST
- SF 94110 667-J2
1000 VAL 94589 509-J7
1000 VAL 94589 529-J1
4300 FRMT 94538 773-D4
ENTERPRISE WY
8400 OAK 94621 670-F5
ENTERPRISE CONCOURSE
300 MrnC 94965 606-F7
ENTRADA AV
- OAK 94611 649-J1
ENTRADA CIR
2700 ANT 94509 575-B6
ENTRADA CT
4500 PLE 94566 714-E4
N ENTRADA CT
- SF 94127 667-C7
S ENTRADA CT
100 SF 94127 667-C7
ENTRADA DR
200 NVTO 94949 546-E1
4300 PLE 94566 714-E4
ENTRADA PL
11300 SCIC 94024 831-F4
ENTRADA PZ
200 UNC 94587 732-H5
ENTRADA WY
500 SMCo 94025 790-H2
ENTRADA CEDROS
5300 SJS 95123 874-H3
ENTRADA MESA
100 DNVL 94526 652-J2
ENTRADA OLEANDROS
5300 SJS 95123 874-H3
ENTRADA OLMOS
5200 SJS 95123 874-H3
ENTRADA VERDE
1400 CCCo 94507 632-E4
ENTRANCE RD
- LFYT 94549 611-C7
1800 ALA 94501 649-H7
1800 ALA 94501 669-H1
ENTRANCE WY
- WDSD 94062 789-D6
ENTRATA AV
- SANS 94960 586-C1
- SANS 94960 566-C7
ENZO DR
200 SJS 95138 875-E4
EOLA
- PIT 94565 574-A3
EOLA ST
1700 BERK 94703 629-F1
EPERNAY CT
- SJS 95127 834-J1
EPILINO TER
34300 FRMT 94555 752-A3
EPPINGER ST
- CCCo 94525 550-D4
EPPLING LN
5000 SJS 95111 875-C2
EPSON ST
1900 LVMR 94550 715-G4
EQUESTRIAN CT
- ANT 94509 595-J4
- MrnC 94945 526-D2
EQUESTRIAN DR
1700 PLE 94588 694-F7
EQUESTRIAN WY
- ANT - 595-J5
5100 ANT 94509 595-J5
15400 MSER 95030 872-J5
EQUUS CT
13000 PLE 94586 713-J2
13000 PLE 94588 713-J2
ERB CT
2700 WLCK 94598 612-H4
ERBA PTH
- OAK 94618 630-C5
ERIC CT
- PLHL 94523 592-A3
2100 UNC 94587 732-C5
3400 RCH 94803 589-F1
ERIC DR
19300 SAR 95070 852-F5
ERIC ST
39400 FRMT 94538 753-A6
ERICA CT
- NVTO 94947 525-G2
100 ANT 94509 595-D1
300 LVMR 94550 696-B6
2900 SJS 95121 854-J3
ERICA DR
300 SSF 94080 707-E4
900 SUNV 94086 832-G2
ERICA PL
500 HAY 94544 732-F2
ERICA RD
1000 MrnC 94965 606-D6
ERICA WY
100 SMCo 94028 810-D3
4900 LVMR 94550 696-B6
ERICKSON LN
800 FCTY 94404 749-F4
ERICKSON RD
1100 CNCD 94520 592-F4
ERICSON RD
100 HIL 94010 748-H1
100 SMTO 94402 748-H1
ERIE CIR
600 MPS 95035 794-A6
ERIE CT
700 MPS 95035 794-A5
4200 SCL 95054 813-C5
7000 DBLN 94568 693-J4
ERIE DR
300 MPS 95035 794-A5
600 SUNV 94087 832-D2
2300 CNCD 94519 572-G7
ERIE PL
100 HAY 94544 732-E3
700 MPS 95035 794-A5
ERIE ST
- SF 94103 667-J1
800 OAK 94610 650-A3
ERIE WY
200 CMBL 95008 853-B5
ERIN CT
- PLHL 94523 591-J5
2800 RCH 94806 589-A1
ERIN DR
- MrnC 94903 546-E7
100 VAL 94589 510-C5
ERIN PL
2300 SSF 94080 707-D5
ERIN WY
1000 SCIC 95008 873-E1
7500 CPTO 95014 852-D2
ERINBROOK PL
1700 SJS 95131 834-D1
ERINWOOD CT
1200 SJS 95121 855-A4
ERIS CT
3500 WLCK 94598 613-A3
ERKSON CT
- SF 94115 647-F6
ERLA WY
3000 RCH 94806 589-A1
ERLA LOUISE DR
- MrnC 94945 526-F4
200 NVTO 94945 526-F4
ERLANDSON ST
500 RCH 94804 608-J1
700 RCH 94804 609-A1
ERLIN DR
400 SCAR 94070 769-F2
ERMA AV
41200 FRMT 94539 753-E6
ERNEST AV
5200 ELCR 94530 609-B1
5200 RCH 94804 609-B1
ERNEST CT
23200 AlaC 94541 692-D7
ERNESTINE LN
1300 MTVW 94040 811-G6
ERNST ST
1000 CNCD 94518 592-E5
ERNWOOD PL
9600 SRMN 94583 693-G1
ERNWOOD ST
9500 SRMN 94583 693-G1
ERRIS CT
3600 SSF 94080 707-C4
ERROL DR
7400 ELCR 94530 609-E3
ERSELIA CT
- CCCo 94507 632-G3
ERSELIA TR
100 CCCo 94507 632-G3
ERSKINE CT
5800 SJS 95123 875-A5
ERSKINE LN
2400 HAY 94545 711-F6
ERSKINE ST
- CCCo - 550-H6
ERSTWILD CT
- PA 94303 791-B4
ERVIN CT
5200 NWK 94560 752-F5
ERVIN WY
11000 SCIC 95127 835-D4
ERVINE ST
- SF 94134 688-A1
ERVING CT
35200 FRMT 94536 752-F1
ESA DR
100 VAL 94591 530-D7
ESBERG RD
1700 SCIC 94024 831-G4
ESCALA TER
4400 FRMT 94536 752-G4
ESCALANTE WY
1600 BURL 94010 728-A6
ESCALERO AV
1000 PCFA 94044 726-H4
ESCALLE LN
- LKSP 94939 586-D5
ESCALLONIA CT
6200 NWK 94560 752-G7
ESCALLONIA DR
100 NVTO 94945 526-B2
6200 NWK 94560 752-G7
6200 NWK 94560 772-G1
ESCALON AV
900 SUNV 94086 812-C5
ESCALON CT
1000 SUNV 94086 812-C5
ESCALON DR
- MLV 94941 606-F3
ESCALONIA CT
2400 SJS 95121 855-D4
ESCAMILLA PL
3200 HAY 94542 712-E4
ESCANYO DR
- SSF 94080 707-E3
ESCANYO WY
100 SMCo 94028 810-E4
ESCAZU CT
100 SJS 95116 834-G3
ESCHER DR
5800 OAK 94611 650-F1
ESCOBAR AV
100 LGTS 95032 873-D5
16000 SCIC 95032 873-D5
ESCOBAR CT
100 LGTS 95032 873-E5
ESCOBAR PL
200 SRMN 94583 673-F4
ESCOBAR RD
100 PTLV 94028 810-C4
ESCOBAR ST
- MRTZ 94553 571-D3
300 FRMT 94539 753-H7
ESCOBITA AV
1500 PA 94306 791-A6
ESCOLTA AV
- NVTO 94949 546-H3
ESCOLTA WY
- SF 94116 667-A5
ESCONDIDO AV
- SF 94132 667-A6
ESCONDIDO CIR
500 LVMR 94550 715-E2
ESCONDIDO CT
600 LVMR 94550 715-E3
900 CCCo 94507 632-G7
6100 SJS 95119 875-C6
ESCONDIDO DR
100 MRTZ 94553 571-H4
ESCONDIDO LN
1100 MLPK 94025 790-F3
ESCONDIDO RD
600 SCIC 94305 790-H7
800 SCIC 94305 810-J1
ESCONDIDO WY
1500 BLMT 94002 769-D2
ESCOVER LN
5300 SJS 95118 874-C4
ESCUELA AV
100 MTVW 94040 811-G4
100 MTVW 94041 811-G4
ESCUELA CT
4500 RCH 94804 609-A1
ESCUELA DR
- DALY 94015 687-B7
ESCUELA PKWY
400 MPS 95035 794-A4
ESCUELA PL
600 MPS 95035 794-A5
ESGUERA TER
4800 FRMT 94555 752-C2
ESMERALDA AV
900 SF 94110 668-A5
900 SF 94110 667-H5
ESMERALDA CT
200 SJS 95116 834-F3
ESMEYER DR
- SRFL 94903 566-C3
ESMOND AV
1100 RCH 94801 588-G5
1700 RCH 94804 588-J5
3300 RCH 94805 588-J5
3400 RCH 94805 589-A5
ESPADA CT
- FRMT 94539 753-D2
13800 SAR 95070 872-J1
ESPADA PL
100 FRMT 94539 753-D2
ESPALDA CT
- SRFL 94901 586-E1
ESPANILLO CT
1600 SPAB 94806 568-H7
ESPANO CT
2200 SPAB 94806 568-J7
ESPANOLA DR
1700 SPAB 94806 568-J7
1900 SPAB 94806 588-J1
ESPANOLA ST
- SF 94124 668-D7
ESPARITO AV
- FRMT 94539 753-F4
ESPARITO PL
- FRMT 94539 753-F4
ESPEE AV
- RCH 94801 588-G6
ESPERANCA AV
2200 SCL 95054 813-C4
ESPERANZA DR
1900 CNCD 94519 572-G6
3000 CNCD 94519 592-G1
12800 LAH 94022 811-B6
ESPERANZA ST
100 TBRN 94920 607-E7
ESPINOSA AV
3100 OAK 94605 671-A4
ESPINOSA RD
900 WDSD 94062 809-G5
ESPINOZA LN
100 MTVW 94043 812-B5
ESPLANADA WY
700 SCIC 94305 810-J1
ESPLANADE
100 PCFA 94044 706-J4
ESPLANADE DR
1900 RCH 94804 608-G2
ESPLANADE PL
1000 WLCK 94596 612-C1
ESQUINA DR
- SF 94134 687-H2
ESQUIRE CT
- NVTO 94949 546-D1
ESQUIRE PL
10500 CPTO 95014 832-C6
ESSANAY AV
- FRMT 94536 753-C1
ESSANAY PL
37700 FRMT 94536 753-C1
ESSENAY AV
2000 WLCK 94596 612-A2
ESSENDON WY
- SJS 95139 875-G7
ESSER AV
1200 SLN 94579 691-A5
ESSEX AV
1000 RCH 94801 588-F5
1000 SUNV 94089 812-F4
ESSEX CT
- CCCo 94507 633-A5
100 SBRN 94066 727-G1
100 VAL 94591 530-H6
200 BEN 94510 551-B2
700 HAY 94544 712-D7
4000 CNCD 94521 593-A4
ESSEX LN
- SANS 94960 566-C7
100 HIL 94010 748-G3
1100 FCTY 94404 749-G5
ESSEX PL
1900 SCL 95051 833-D2
ESSEX ST
- SANS 94960 566-C7
- SF 94105 648-B6
100 CCCo 94520 572-G2
900 LVMR 94550 715-G3
1400 SJS 95002 793-C7
1900 BERK 94703 629-G4
2100 BERK 94705 629-G4
4300 EMVL 94608 629-F6
6400 OAK 94608 629-F5
ESSEX WY
- PCFA 94044 726-G4
200 BEN 94510 551-B2
1300 SCIC 95117 853-D4
1400 SJS 95117 853-D4
4800 FRMT 94538 773-B1
ESTABROOK CIR
2100 SLN 94577 691-B2
ESTABROOK ST
- SLN 94577 691-A2
ESTABUENO
- ORIN 94563 631-B6
ESTACADA DR
25800 LAH 94022 811-C5
ESTACADA WY
25800 LAH 94022 811-C5
ESTADO CT
- NVTO 94945 525-J1
ESTADO WY
400 NVTO 94945 526-A1
400 NVTO 94945 525-J1
ESTANCIA WY
700 MrnC 94903 566-H2
ESTAND WY
2400 PLHL 94523 592-D6
ESTATE CT
- SCAR 94070 769-E5
- SSF 94080 707-G2
600 DALY 94014 687-F3
ESTATE DR
1200 LALT 94024 831-H3
ESTATES AV
2600 PIN 94564 569-F5
ESTATES CT
- ORIN 94563 630-J2
- SRFL 94901 586-E2
1600 SJS 95127 835-B5
3300 CNCD 94519 592-H2
ESTATES DR
- DNVL 94526 653-A3
- NVTO 94947 525-H3
- ORIN 94563 630-J2
- PDMT 94611 650-D2
100 SBRN 94066 707-E7
100 OAK 94611 650-D1
100 DNVL 94526 652-J2
900 CPTO 95014 852-F2
1100 LFYT 94549 611-B5
2800 CNCD 94520 572-E6
5300 OAK 94618 630-C6
5800 OAK 94611 630-D7
E ESTATES DR
800 CPTO 95014 852-F1
W ESTATES DR
10700 CPTO 95014 852-F2
ESTATES RD
- CCCo 94708 609-F2
ESTATES ST
100 LVMR 94550 695-J7
400 LVMR 94550 715-J1
ESTATES TER
2000 FRMT 94539 774-A5
ESTATE VIEW CT
3500 SJS 95148 835-D4
ESTATE VIEW WY
2000 SJS 95148 835-D4
ESTEBAN ST
16900 AlaC 94541 691-G5
16900 AlaC 94578 691-G5
ESTEBAN WY
200 SJS 95119 875-C7
ESTELLA CT
- WLCK 94596 612-B2
ESTELLA DR
- PCFA 94044 727-A3
2500 SCL 95051 833-B7

BAY AREA

INDEX

STREET
Block City ZIP Pg-Grid

ESTELLE AV
- LKSP 94939 586-D4
- MrnC 94904 586-D4
1500 SJS 95118 874-A1
ESTELLE LN
200 DALY 94014 687-D5
ESTEPA DR
10700 OAK 94603 670-H7
ESTERBROOK CT
- ALA 94501 669-F1
ESTERLEE AV
14400 SAR 95070 872-C3
ESTERO AV
- SF 94127 667-C7
ESTERO DR
3200 SRMN 94583 673-G6
ESTERO WY
- SRFL 94903 566-D4
ESTHER AV
300 CMBL 95008 853-E5
ESTHER CT
200 HAY 94544 712-C7
ESTHER DR
1000 PLHL 94523 592-C7
4300 SCIC 95124 873-F2
4900 SJS 95124 873-F3
ESTHER LN
- SPAB 94806 588-J3
100 DNVL 94526 652-J2
700 SMCo 94062 769-H7
ESTON WY
- MLBR 94030 728-A5
- MLBR 94030 727-J5
ESTONIA CT
600 SJS 95123 874-G4
ESTRADA DR
- MTVW 94043 812-A5
ESTRADA LN
- CMAD 94925 606-H1
ESTRADA PL
- SMCo 94062 769-F6
ESTRADA TER
1200 SUNV 94086 812-B7
ESTRADE DR
5200 SJS 95118 874-A4
ESTRALITA PL
13100 LAH 94022 811-A7
13100 LAH 94022 831-A1
ESTRELLA AV
- PDMT 94611 630-B7
ESTRELLA CT
- NVTO 94945 525-J1
2300 PIN 94564 569-F6
11500 DBLN 94568 693-F4
ESTRELLA PL
- DNVL 94526 652-J1
ESTRELLA RD
100 FRMT 94539 753-E3
ESTRELLA WY
- NVTO 94945 525-J1
200 SMTO 94403 749-D6
ESTRELLITA WY
1000 LALT 94022 811-D4
1300 CMBL 95008 873-B1
ESTUDILLO AV
- SLN 94577 691-A1
100 OAK 94605 671-D7
100 SLN 94577 671-B7
W ESTUDILLO AV
100 SLN 94577 691-A1
1700 SLN 94577 690-J1
ESTUDILLO RD
700 SCIC 94305 810-H2
ESTUDILLO ST
400 MRTZ 94553 571-E3
ESTUDILLO WY
2900 MRTZ 94553 571-E4
ETHAN CT
- LFYT 94549 631-H2
300 SRMN 94583 693-F1
500 HAY 94544 732-E2
3600 SJS 95136 874-D1
ETHAN TER
34100 FRMT 94555 752-C2
ETHEL AV
- MLV 94941 606-D3
500 MrnC 94941 606-E4
ETHEL CT
- MLV 94941 606-D3
- RDWC 94061 789-J3
ETHEL LN
- MrnC 94941 606-E4
1300 HAY 94544 711-H6
ETHEL ST
2800 FRMT 94536 753-A3
ETHYL CT
100 MPS 95035 813-J1
ETHYL ST
300 MPS 95035 813-J1
ETNA CT
- SRMN 94583 673-F7
ETNA ST
2500 BERK 94704 629-J2
ETOILE CT
3300 SJS 95135 855-G3
ETON AV
3100 BERK 94705 629-J4
14100 SCIC 95127 835-A3
ETON CT
- BERK 94705 629-J4
300 WLCK 94598 612-F2
ETON WY
- MLV 94941 606-F3
900 SUNV 94087 832-G5
ETRUSCAN DR
- SJS 95135 855-E2
ETTA AV
28400 HAY 94544 712-B7
28600 HAY 94544 732-B1
ETTA CT
200 MrnC 94903 546-E7
ETTERSBERG DR
5800 SJS 95123 875-B5
ETTIE ST
2800 OAK 94608 649-E1
ETTRICK ST
10700 OAK 94605 671-D4
EUCALYPTUS AV
- SSF 94080 707-G3
100 HIL 94010 748-E1
600 HIL 94010 728-E7
700 NVTO 94947 525-H3
1900 SCAR 94070 769-G4
EUCALYPTUS CT
- LVMR 94550 715-D1
- WDSD 94062 789-F5
- WLCK 94596 632-E1
1700 CNCD 94521 593-B2
2000 SCL 95050 833-C3
27600 HAY 94544 712-B6
EUCALYPTUS DR
- AMCN 94589 510-A1
- SF 94132 667-B6
100 AMCN 94589 509-H1
300 SJS 95134 813-D2
600 NaCo 94589 509-H1
15700 SCIC 95030 872-H5
EUCALYPTUS LN
- SRFL 94901 566-H7
- SRMN 94583 693-F1
26000 LAH 94022 811-B6
EUCALYPTUS PTH
- OAK 94705 630-A3
EUCALYPTUS RD
- BERK 94705 630-A4
- BLV 94920 627-D1
- OAK 94618 630-A4
- OAK 94705 630-A4
EUCALYPTUS TER
34200 FRMT 94555 752-B3
EUCALYPTUS WY
600 MrnC 94965 606-D6
2400 SBRN 94066 707-E7
EUCALYPTUS KNOLLS
- MLV 94941 606-G5
EUCLID AV
- ATN 94027 790-B4
- SF 94115 647-E6
- SLN 94577 671-A7
- SF 94118 647-E6
100 SBRN 94066 707-H6
200 OAK 94610 649-J2
300 SF 94118 647-D6
500 BERK 94708 609-H5
1600 BERK 94709 609-H7
1600 BERK 94709 629-H1
1900 MLPK 94025 791-B3
2000 EPA 94303 791-B2
2100 RDWC 94061 789-J1
2700 RCH 94804 588-H7
2800 CNCD 94519 592-G1
3900 MRTZ 94553 571-E6
EUCLID CT
500 SLN 94577 671-A7
1800 CNCD 94519 592-H1
EUCLID DR
43500 FRMT 94539 773-F1
EUCLID PL
500 EPA 94303 791-B2
2300 FRMT 94539 773-F1
EUGENE AV
1000 SJS 95126 833-J7
EUGENE CT
1000 SUNV 94087 832-B5
2300 CNCD 94518 592-G5
EUGENE ST
- MLV 94941 606-C3
3500 FRMT 94538 753-C6
EUGENIA AV
- SF 94110 667-H5
1700 HAY 94545 731-J1
EUGENIA CT
3300 ALA 94502 670-A6
EUGENIA DR
- HIL 94010 748-C1
EUGENIA LN
- WDSD 94062 790-A5
EUGENIA WY
2000 LALT 94024 832-A5
16400 LGTS 95032 893-C2
16400 SCIC 95032 893-C2
EULALIE DR
2600 SJS 95121 854-J3
EULL CT
4500 PLE 94566 714-D1
EUNICE AV
100 MTVW 94040 831-J1
13100 MTVW 94040 832-A1
EUNICE ST
2000 BERK 94709 609-G6
2000 BERK 94707 609-G6
2300 BERK 94708 609-G6
EUREKA AV
- CCCo 94707 609-E3
1100 LALT 94024 831-H3
6300 ELCR 94530 609-D3
EUREKA CT
200 SUNV 94086 812-F5
1200 LALT 94024 831-H3
3400 HAY 94542 712-E5
EUREKA DR
200 PCFA 94044 707-A6
200 PCFA 94044 706-J6
EUREKA LN
1100 CNCD 94520 592-E5
EUREKA PL
- SF 94109 647-J5
EUREKA ST
- MrnC 94965 626-H1
- SF 94114 667-F3
EUREKA MINE CT
4900 ANT - 595-D3
EUROPA CT
500 WLCK 94598 612-E2
EUROPE WY
3600 SCL 95051 832-H4
EUROPEAN TER
- UNC 94587 732-G6
EUSTICE AV
- OAK 94618 630-B5
EUTERPE ST
- MLV 94941 606-E3
EVA AV
1200 LALT 94024 831-H4
EVA CT
- SMTO 94403 749-C6
2400 SJS 95008 853-B7
EVA ST
- SRFL 94901 586-G2
EVA TER
- SF 94117 647-G7
EVALANE WY
1800 CNCD 94519 592-H1
EVANDALE AV
- MTVW 94043 812-A3
EVANGELINE CT
6200 SJS 95123 874-G7
EVANGELINE DR
6100 SJS 95123 874-G6
EVANGELINE WY
500 HAY 94544 732-E1
EVANS AV
- DBLN 94568 694-B4
100 SolC 94590 530-B6
900 SF 94124 668-B4
1500 SPAB 94806 589-A4
1500 SPAB 94806 588-J4
2100 SF 94124 668-B4
4300 OAK 94602 650-C3
4900 FRMT 94536 752-H5
EVANS CT
- ALA 94502 669-H6
900 MPS 95035 794-C5
1000 HAY 94544 711-J6
EVANS LN
1800 SJS 95125 854-D5
14300 SAR 95070 872-H2
EVANS PL
- ORIN 94563 631-B3
1300 LVMR 94550 715-F4
EVANS RD
- MPS 95035 794-C5
- SCIC 95035 794-C5
EVANS ST
1900 LVMR 94550 715-F4
EVANSTON PL
6000 SJS 95123 874-E6
EVCO CT
3200 SJS 95127 814-J7
EVE CT
200 AlaC 94541 711-F1
EVE DR
1500 CNCD 94521 593-C3
EVE LN
1000 LVMR 94550 716-B1
EVE ST
- SF 94110 668-A4
EVELENA CT
4500 FRMT 94536 752-E2
EVELETH AV
1700 SLN 94577 690-J2
1900 SLN 94577 691-A2
EVELYN AV
- MLV 94941 606-B2
400 ALB 94706 609-D5
1100 BERK 94706 609-D5
1300 BERK 94702 609-D5
2000 SJS 95123 834-J6
E EVELYN AV
100 MTVW 94041 812-D6
100 SUNV 94086 812-D6
500 SUNV 94086 832-F1
W EVELYN AV
100 MTVW 94041 812-A5
200 MTVW 94041 811-H4
EVELYN CIR
100 VAL 94589 510-C5
EVELYN CT
- CCCo 94507 632-H2
600 LFYT 94549 631-H2
2600 ALA 94501 670-A4
2900 OAK 94602 650-D5
2900 OAK 94601 650-D5
4300 PLE 94588 694-A7
EVELYN DR
200 PLHL 94523 592-B4
EVELYN LN
400 HAY 94544 712-A4
400 HAY 94544 711-J4
EVELYN ST
900 MLPK 94025 790-F4
EVELYN TER
- SUNV 94086 832-H1
E EVELYN TER
1000 SUNV 94086 832-H1
W EVELYN TER
900 SUNV 94086 832-H1
EVELYN WY
- SF 94127 667-E5
100 SF 94127 667-E5
5400 LVMR 94550 696-C7
EVE MARIE AV
1600 LALT 94024 832-A4
EVENING SPRING CT
11500 CPTO 95014 852-A4
EVENING STAR CT
100 MPS 95035 814-A2
EVENINGSTAR CT
100 PIT 94565 574-A2
EVERDALE CT
2900 SJS 95148 855-C1
EVERDALE DR
2900 SJS 95148 855-C1
EVEREST CT
800 MrnC 94965 606-E6
EVERETT AL
600 VAL 94590 530-A5
EVERETT AV
100 PA 94301 790-H4
200 CMBL 95008 853-E6
800 OAK 94602 650-C3
1600 SJS 95125 854-A4
EVERETT CT
- DNVL 94526 653-B4
500 PA 94301 790-J4
1100 CNCD 94518 592-J4
31100 HAY 94544 732-E2
EVERETT DR
400 DNVL 94526 653-C4
EVERETT PL
300 DNVL 94526 653-B3
600 VAL 94590 529-J5
600 VAL 94590 530-A5
EVERETT ST
400 ELCR 94530 609-C1
1400 ALA 94501 670-A2
EVERGLADE AV
1700 SJS 95122 834-H6
EVERGLADE DR
- SF 94132 667-A6
EVERGLADE ST
1600 HAY 94545 711-J7
1600 HAY 94545 731-J1
EVERGLADES CT
6100 PLE 94588 714-B1
EVERGLADES DR
1000 PCFA 94044 727-B4
1500 MPS 95035 814-D1
EVERGLADES LN
400 LVMR 94550 695-D7
EVERGLADES PARK DR
4900 FRMT 94538 773-C2
EVERGLOW CT
2900 SJS 95127 835-A4
EVERGREEN AV
- DALY 94014 687-D3
- MLV 94941 606-D4
- MrnC 94941 606-D4
800 SLN 94577 691-C1
1800 ANT 94509 575-E6
6600 OAK 94611 630-G7
EVERGREEN CT
- CCCo 94595 612-A7
- MLBR 94030 727-H3
- VAL 94591 530-E4
400 DNVL 94526 653-D7
EVERGREEN DR
- MrnC 94904 586-B5
- ORIN 94563 630-J1
200 SSF 94080 707-F1
1200 CNCD 94520 592-E4
1900 SBRN 94066 707-D6
3500 PA 94303 791-E7
EVERGREEN LN
300 MrnC 94941 606-D4
EVERGREEN ST
600 MLPK 94025 790-E6
1800 SMTO 94401 749-C1
25600 HAY 94544 711-H5
EVERGREEN TER
1000 SPAB 94806 588-J3
5600 FRMT 94538 773-A1
EVERGREEN WY
100 MPS 95035 814-A3
100 VAL 94591 530-E4
900 MLBR 94030 727-H3
2800 SJS 95121 855-E3
EVERGREEN FIRE RD
- MrnC 94904 586-C5
EVERGREEN PATH LN
- OAK 94705 630-A3
EVERIDGE CT
1900 WLCK 94596 611-H3
EVERMONT CT
1900 SJS 95148 835-A5
1900 SJS 95127 835-A5
EVERS AV
1700 OAK 94602 650-C4
EVERSOLE DR
2700 SJS 95133 814-G7
EVERSON ST
- SF 94131 667-G5
EVERWOOD CT
1900 SJS 95148 835-A5
1900 SJS 95127 835-A5
EVIREL PL
- OAK 94611 630-E6
EVORA DR
2600 SJS 95124 873-G1
EVORA RD
4000 CCCo 94520 573-A3
4000 CCCo 94565 573-C2
EVULICH CT
22000 CPTO 95014 852-A2
EWART DALE
- LFYT 94549 611-E5
EWE WY
1300 FRMT 94536 753-B3
EWELL RD
2200 BLMT 94002 769-C2
EWER DR
1700 SJS 95124 873-H3
EWER PL
- SF 94108 648-A5
EWING CT
4600 AlaC 94546 691-J1
EWING DR
300 PLE 94566 714-F3
EWING RD
4400 AlaC 94546 691-J1
EWING TER
- SF 94118 647-E7
EXBOURNE AV
100 SCAR 94070 769-E2
EXBOURNE CT
1300 WLCK 94596 632-G2
EXCALIBUR DR
500 SJS 95116 834-J4
EXCELSIOR
- SAUS 94965 627-B3
EXCELSIOR AV
- SF 94112 667-G7
900 SF 94112 687-H1
1000 OAK 94610 650-B4
1300 OAK 94602 650-C4
EXCELSIOR CT
- OAK 94610 650-A3
EXCELSO CT
700 FRMT 94539 773-H1
EXCELSO DR
43500 FRMT 94539 773-H1
EXCELSO PL
43600 FRMT 94539 773-H1
EXCHANGE CT
500 LVMR 94550 696-E5
EXCHANGE PL
2300 RCH 94804 588-H6
EXECUTIVE PKWY
3000 SRMN 94583 673-D2
EXECUTIVE PL
26200 HAY 94545 731-D1
EXECUTIVE GUILD CIR
- BLMT 94002 749-G7
- BLMT 94002 769-G1
- RDWC 94065 749-G7
- RDWC 94065 769-G1
EXECUTIVE PARK BLVD
100 SF 94134 688-B2
EXETER AV
- SCAR 94070 769-D3
EXETER CT
100 SUNV 94087 832-E5
5900 SJS 95138 855-G7
36200 NWK 94560 752-E4
EXETER DR
3500 SBRN 94066 707-B6
6500 OAK 94611 630-G7
6500 OAK 94611 650-G1
EXETER LN
- PLHL 94523 592-A4
- PLHL 94523 591-J4
EXETER PL
600 CCCo 94506 654-A5
EXETER ST
- SF 94124 688-B1
EXETER WY
500 SCAR 94070 769-E3
EXIT RD
- LFYT 94549 611-D7
EXMOOR WY
900 SUNV 94087 832-G5
EXPOSITION DR
100 VAL 94589 510-D6
EXPRESS CT
900 CNCD 94518 592-F6
EYE ST
- SRFL 94901 566-E7
EZIE ST
300 SJS 95111 854-J6
EZRA DR
37300 NWK 94560 752-F6

F

F RD
1100 AlaC 94586 734-C3
F ST
- CCCo 94565 573-E1
- NVTO 94949 546-G3
- OAK 94625 649-A3
- SUNV 94089 812-H3
- MRTZ 94553 571-D5
- SRFL 94901 586-F1
100 BEN 94510 551-B5
100 DALY 94014 687-C6
100 FRMT 94536 753-B1
100 RDWC 94063 769-J4
100 UNC 94587 732-F4
100 SMCo 94014 687-C6
100 ANT 94509 575-D3
100 SRFL 94901 566-F7
200 CLMA 94014 687-D6
900 BLMT 94002 769-J4
900 SCAR 94070 769-J4
1500 ELCR 94530 609-B2
9200 OAK 94603 670-H5
FABER PL
2400 PA 94303 791-E4
FABER ST
2800 UNC 94587 732-A3
FABIAN COM
37800 FRMT 94536 752-J4
FABIAN CT
- NVTO 94947 525-G3
7000 PLE 94588 693-H6
FABIAN DR
1700 SJS 95124 853-J7
1700 SJS 95124 873-J1
FABIAN WY
100 CNCD 94519 592-H2
100 CNCD 94518 592-H2
1100 HAY 94544 732-A1
3700 PA 94303 791-F7
3700 PA 94303 811-F1
FABLE CT
4500 CCCo 94803 589-D2
FABLED OAK CT
3300 SJS 95148 835-E7
FACTOR AV
1400 SLN 94577 690-J4
1500 SLN 94577 691-A4
FACTORY ST
1000 RCH 94801 588-F5
FACULTY DR
200 VAL 94590 550-C2
FACULTY RD
5200 OAK 94613 670-G1
FAFNIR PL
- PLHL 94523 592-A3
FAGAN DR
- HIL 94010 728-D7
- BURL 94010 728-D7
FAGES CT
1900 WLCK 94595 632-B1
FAGUNDES CT
200 HAY 94544 711-H4
FAGUNDES ST
- HAY 94544 711-H4
FAHEY CT
2600 PIN 94564 569-F4
FAHRNER CT
2900 SJS 95135 855-F3
FAIR AV
- SF 94110 667-H4
900 SJS 95122 854-G1
4300 OAK 94619 650-G6
5800 NWK 94560 752-E6
FAIR CT
36700 NWK 94560 752-E6
FAIR DR
- SRFL 94901 566-F6
FAIR LN
- LGTS 95030 873-A7
FAIR ST
4700 PLE 94566 714-D3
FAIRBAIRN ST
4500 OAK 94619 650-F7
FAIRBANKS AV
100 SCAR 94070 769-F5
200 CMBL 95008 873-E2
400 OAK 94610 650-A2
FAIRBANKS CIR
- SJS 95131 814-B6
FAIRBANKS COM
5100 FRMT 94555 752-C3
FAIRBANKS ST
1900 SLN 94577 690-G3
FAIRBANKS WY
3600 ANT 94509 595-A1
FAIRBOURN DR
2200 PIT 94565 574-E5
FAIRBROOK CT
- LVMR 94550 696-E3
1000 SJS 95132 814-F6
7700 PLE 94588 693-J7
FAIRBROOK DR
1100 MTVW 94040 832-A2
FAIRCHILD COM
34700 FRMT 94555 752-A3
FAIRCHILD DR
- MTVW 94043 812-B3
FAIRCHILD ST
1000 OAK 94621 670-D6
FAIRCLIFF CT
2900 SJS 95125 854-A7
2900 SJS 95125 874-A1
FAIRCLIFF ST
30800 HAY 94544 732-E1
FAIRCREST DR
2200 SJS 95124 873-E3
FAIRDALE WY
- CCCo 94507 632-G3
FAIRDELL DR
2500 SJS 95125 854-A7
FAIRFAX AV
- ATN 94027 790-D1
300 SMTO 94402 748-H3
500 SF 94124 668-B5
2800 SJS 95148 855-C1
4500 OAK 94601 650-E7
4700 OAK 94601 670-E1
FAIRFAX CT
- PLHL 94523 592-B4
100 VAL 94591 530-D4
2800 SJS 95148 855-C1
3100 FRMT 94536 752-F1
FAIRFAX ST
- SRFL 94901 586-J2
FAIRFAX WY
3700 SSF 94080 707-D4
FAIRFIELD AV
900 SCL 95050 833-D4
2200 CNCD 94520 572-F7
FAIRFIELD CT
- SMCo 94402 748-F7
200 PA 94306 811-F2
2300 PLE 94566 714-C1
FAIRFIELD DR
200 SCAR 94070 769-G2
FAIRFIELD PL
100 MRGA 94556 651-E2
FAIRFIELD RD
700 BURL 94010 728-E6
2100 PLE 94566 714-C2
FAIRFIELD ST
32700 UNC - 752-A1
32700 UNC 94587 732-A7
32700 UNC 94587 752-A1
FAIRFIELD WY
- SF 94127 667-D7
FAIRFORD CT
1100 SJS 95129 852-G3
FAIRFORD WY
1100 SJS 95129 852-G3
FAIRGLEN DR
2200 SJS 95125 854-A7
FAIRGROUNDS DR
200 VAL 94589 530-D1
600 VAL 94589 510-C5
2300 NaCo 94589 510-C5
FAIRGROUNDS RD
- PLE 94566 714-C3
FAIRGROVE CT
2300 SJS 95125 853-J7
FAIRHAVEN
600 NVTO 94947 526-E7
FAIRHAVEN CT
- MTVW 94041 811-J6
1400 SJS 95118 874-B1
FAIRHAVEN DR
1400 SJS 95118 874-B1
FAIR HAVEN RD
300 ALA 94501 669-G3
FAIRHAVEN WY
100 VAL 94591 550-F1
FAIRHILL CT
5100 OAK 94605 671-B1
FAIR HILL DR
1700 MPS 95035 794-D5
FAIRHILL LN
2200 SJS 95125 853-J6
FAIRHILLS DR
- SRFL 94901 566-E6
FAIRHOLM CT
3200 LFYT 94549 611-H4
FAIRHOPE PL
6000 SJS 95123 874-E6
FAIRLAINE DR
3700 FRMT 94539 753-F7
FAIRLANDS AV
700 CMBL 95008 873-C1
FAIRLANDS CT
1100 CMBL 95008 873-C1
FAIRLANDS DR
3600 PLE 94588 694-E5
FAIRLANDS RD
23700 AlaC 94541 712-C1
FAIRLANE AV
600 SCL 95051 833-A6
FAIRLANE DR
6000 OAK 94611 630-C5
FAIRLAWN AV
- DALY 94015 686-J4
- DALY 94015 687-A4
1600 SJS 95125 854-A7
1600 SJS 95125 853-J7
FAIRLAWN CT
- WLCK 94595 632-A3
- DALY 94015 687-A4
2200 SJS 95125 854-A7
FAIRLAWN DR
- BERK 94708 609-J6
FAIRLAWN PL
700 CNCD 94518 592-J6
FAIRMAYDEN LN
- DNVL 94526 632-H7
FAIRMEAD AV
600 PA 94306 811-C3
FAIRMEAD LN
100 LGTS 95032 873-D6
FAIRMEAD ST
32700 UNC 94587 732-A7
FAIRMEADOW WY
100 MPS 95035 794-C2
FAIRMEDE DR
3100 RCH 94806 589-A1
FAIRMONT AV
100 SCAR 94070 769-G5
100 VAL 94590 530-C3
400 MTVW 94041 811-H6
FAIRMONT CT
2100 SJS 95148 835-D5
FAIRMONT DR
- DALY 94015 686-J3
1000 SBRN 94066 707-F7
1200 SLN 94578 691-D4
1300 AlaC 94578 691-E2
2000 SMTO 94402 748-H7
2000 SMTO 94402 768-H1
2100 SJS 95148 835-D5
15900 SCIC 95127 815-B7
FAIRMONT LN
2600 ANT 94509 575-D1
FAIRMOUNT AV
- OAK 94611 649-H2
300 OAK 94610 649-H2
6000 ELCR 94530 609-D4
FAIRMOUNT ST
- SF 94131 667-H5
FAIROAK CT
2400 SJS 95125 853-J7
FAIR OAKS AV
1000 ALA 94501 669-G1
1000 SUNV 94089 812-G4
2600 SMCo 94063 770-D6
3500 SMCo 94025 770-E7
N FAIR OAKS AV
100 SUNV 94086 812-F7
900 SUNV 94089 812-F7
S FAIR OAKS AV
100 SUNV 94086 832-F2
FAIROAKS CT
- SMTO 94403 748-J6
7900 PLE 94588 693-H7
FAIR OAKS DR
100 PLHL 94523 592-D6
700 CCCo 94507 632-H2
FAIROAKS DR
7600 PLE 94588 693-H7
FAIR OAKS LN
- ATN 94027 790-E2
FAIR OAKS ST
- SF 94110 667-H4
100 MTVW 94040 811-F4
FAIR OAKS WY
1200 SUNV 94089 812-G3
FAIROAKS WY
100 PIT 94565 574-E6
FAIRORCHARD AV
1600 SJS 95125 854-A7
1600 SJS 95125 853-J7
FAIRPLACE CT
1700 SJS 95122 854-G1
FAIR RANCH RD
4100 UNC 94587 732-A6
FAIR RIDGE CT
1900 WLCK 94596 611-H3
FAIRVALLEY CT
2200 SJS 95125 853-J6
FAIRVIEW AV
- ATN 94027 790-C5
- CCCo 94565 573-H2
- CMAD 94925 606-G1
- DALY 94015 687-A5
- LGTS 95030 872-J7
- PDMT 94610 650-A2
- VAL 94589 530-C2
- VAL 94590 530-C2
500 MrnC 94965 606-D6
1000 SJS 95125 854-B5
1100 RDWC 94061 789-J1
1500 CCCo 94805 589-C6
2900 ALA 94501 670-B3
6900 ELCR 94530 589-C7
24500 AlaC 94541 712-D1
24500 AlaC 94542 712-D1
27100 HAY 94542 712-G4
FAIRVIEW CT
- SANS 94960 566-A5
1300 LVMR 94550 715-E3
1500 PLE 94566 714-D2
FAIRVIEW DR
- MRTZ 94553 571-G2
3200 ANT 94509 574-J5
FAIRVIEW LN
- SJS 95111 854-G4
2400 SCL 95051 833-B2
FAIRVIEW LP
- CCCo 94553 571-G2
- MRTZ 94553 571-G2
FAIRVIEW PL
- MLBR 94030 727-H2
FAIRVIEW PZ
- LGTS 95030 872-J7
FAIRVIEW ST
100 DNVL 94506 653-G5
600 OAK 94609 629-H4
1400 BERK 94702 629-F4
1500 BERK 94703 629-F4
FAIRVIEW WY
300 MPS 95035 793-H5
FAIRWAY AV
3800 OAK 94605 671-B3
FAIRWAY CIR
600 HIL 94010 728-F7
17600 LGTS 95030 873-A4
17600 MSER 95030 873-A4
FAIRWAY CT
- PIT 94565 574-B4
4500 LVMR 94550 696-A3
8100 NWK 94560 752-C7
FAIRWAY DR
- DALY 94015 687-B4
- MLV 94941 606-E2
- MrnC 94901 566-J7
- NVTO 94949 546-A3
- ORIN 94563 610-F6
- SSF 94080 707-F3
100 MrnC 94901 567-A7
200 PCFA 94044 707-D7
200 CCCo 94526 633-D7
200 DNVL 94526 633-D7
300 PCFA 94044 707-A7
1100 RCH 94803 569-C7
1200 SCIC 94024 831-F3
1600 BLMT 94002 769-D1
1700 SLN 94577 690-H4
2500 SLN 94577 691-A4

STREET
Block City ZIP Pg-Grid

FAIRWAY DR
5300 SCIC 95127 815-A7
FAIRWAY LN
- AlaC 94566 714-B7
FAIRWAY PL
- PLHL 94523 592-A2
- PLHL 94523 591-J2
400 ALA 94502 670-B7
FAIRWAY ST
- HAY 94544 732-D2
FAIRWAY ENTRANCE DR
1300 SJS 95131 814-C7
FAIRWAY GLEN DR
2000 SCL 95054 813-C4
FAIRWAY GLEN LN
100 SJS 95139 895-E1
FAIRWAY GREEN CIR
1500 SJS 95131 814-C7
FAIR WEATHER CIR
1100 CNCD 94518 593-A6
FAIRWEATHER LN
1100 SJS 95126 853-H4
FAIRWOOD AV
900 SUNV 94089 812-J5
1600 SJS 95125 853-J7
FAIRWOOD CT
- SRFL 94901 567-C6
4300 CNCD 94521 593-C3
FAIRWOOD DR
1600 CNCD 94521 593-C3
FAIRWOOD ST
4000 FRMT 94538 773-D2
FAIRWOODS CT
20900 CPTO 95014 852-D1
FAITH CT
3200 SJS 95127 814-J7
FAITH ST
- SF 94110 668-A5
FALCATO DR
100 MPS 95035 794-E7
FALCON AV
1400 SUNV 94087 832-F4
3000 HAY 94545 711-E7
FALCON CT
- DNVL 94506 653-E4
- PLHL 94523 592-A5
800 ANT 94509 595-F2
1400 SUNV 94087 832-F5
2600 UNC 94587 732-D6
FALCON DR
- VAL 94589 510-A5
1200 MPS 95035 814-B3
3500 CNCD 94520 572-G5
32200 FRMT 94555 732-B7
FALCON PL
200 CLAY 94517 593-J5
FALCON ST
- DNVL 94506 653-E4
FALCON WY
100 HER 94547 569-J5
200 HER 94547 570-A5
400 LVMR 94550 695-E7
400 LVMR 94550 715-E1
FALCON KNOLL CT
7000 SJS 95120 894-G4
FALCON KNOLL DR
1100 SJS 95120 894-G4
FALCON RIDGE CT
7000 SJS 95120 894-G4
FALCON VIEW CT
- CCCo 94507 632-H3
FALDA AV
- SMTO 94403 749-A5
FALERNO WY
- SJS 95135 855-G3
FALGREN AV
300 AlaC 94541 711-F1
FALK CT
400 MLPK 94025 791-A3
FALKIAK CT
100 SUNV 94087 832-E5
FALKIRK LN
- HIL 94010 748-F4
FALL AV
1500 SJS 95127 835-C4
4500 RCH 94804 609-A1
FALL CT
4600 PLE 94566 714-D3
7900 CPTO 95014 852-C2
FALL ST
- VAL 94591 510-J5
FALLBOROUGH CT
- SRMN 94583 673-H3
FALLBROOK AV
1600 SJS 95130 853-A5
FALLBROOK CIR
4300 CNCD 94521 593-B4
FALLBROOK CT
3800 PIT 94565 574-F6
4300 CNCD 94521 593-B4
FALLBROOK DR
1800 CCCo 94526 633-D6
27900 HAY 94542 712-F5
FALLBROOK RD
4300 CNCD 94521 593-B4
FALLBROOK WY
10700 OAK 94605 671-D4
FALLBURY CT
100 SRMN 94583 673-F4
FALL CREEK RD
7900 DBLN 94568 694-A1
FALLCREEK SPRING CT
11500 CPTO 95014 852-A4
FALLEN LEAF AV
- ROSS 94957 586-C1
FALLEN LEAF CIR
500 SRMN 94583 673-F4
FALLEN LEAF CT
- LFYT 94549 611-G2
27700 HAY 94542 712-E4
FALLEN LEAF DR
1100 MPS 95035 814-A3
1400 LVMR 94550 696-D3
FALLENLEAF DR
100 HIL 94010 748-H2
FALLEN LEAF LN
1400 LALT 94024 832-A3
5200 CNCD 94521 593-E4
FALLENLEAF LN
7300 CPTO 95014 852-D3
7300 SJS 95129 852-D3
FALLEN LEAF TER
- ORIN 94563 610-J3
FALLEN LEAF WY
- NVTO 94949 546-G5
900 SMCo 94062 789-G2
FALLENLEAF WY
900 PIT 94565 574-E5
FALLEN OAK CT
1900 WLCK 94595 632-B1
3200 SJS 95148 855-D2
FALLINGTREE DR
2200 SJS 95131 814-C5
FALLING WATER CT
2300 SCL 95054 813-C5
FALLON AV
- ALA 94501 649-E7
500 SMTO 94401 729-B7
500 SMTO 94401 749-B1
600 SCL 95050 833-D5
5000 RCH 94804 609-B2
FALLON CIR
2000 ALA 94501 649-E7
FALLON PL
- SF 94133 647-J4
FALLON PTH
- RCH 94804 609-B2
FALLON RD
- AlaC 94588 694-H4
4200 DBLN 94568 694-H4
4200 AlaC 94568 694-H4
FALLON ST
100 OAK 94607 649-H5
FALLON TER
36400 FRMT 94536 752-J1
FALLOW CT
4500 ANT 94509 595-F3
FALLOW DR
4500 ANT 94509 595-F3
FALL RIVER DR
- CCCo 94565 573-G3
900 HAY 94544 732-B1
6500 SJS 95120 894-D1
FALL RIVER TER
500 SUNV 94087 832-D2
FALLS CT
700 PLHL 94523 591-H2
FALLS ST
- PIT 94565 574-D6
FALLS TER
34500 FRMT 94555 752-C3
FALLS CREEK CT
3000 SJS 95135 855-F4
FALLS CREEK DR
3100 SJS 95135 855-G4
FALLSTONE CT
4500 SJS 95124 873-F3
FALLVIEW ST
200 SRMN 94583 673-F4
FALLWOOD CT
4000 PLE 94588 713-J2
FALLWOOD LN
2800 SJS 95132 814-D3
FALMOUTH CT
19300 SAR 95070 852-G5
FALMOUTH CV
- SRFL 94901 587-A2
FALMOUTH PL
5200 NWK 94560 752-E4
FALMOUTH ST
- SF 94107 648-A7
3200 SJS 95132 814-F3
FALON WY
5800 SJS 95123 875-A5
FALSTAFF AV
4600 FRMT 94555 752-C1
FALSTAFF RD
33700 FRMT 94555 752-C1
FAMILLE CT
3300 SJS 95135 855-G3
FAMILY FARM RD
- WDSD 94062 809-J4
300 SMCo 94025 809-J4
FAMOSA PZ
200 UNC 94587 732-H5
FAN ST
1700 SJS 95131 834-D1
FAN WY
1700 SJS 95131 834-C1
FANCHER CT
100 LGTS 95030 873-A6
FANED WY
900 CNCD 94518 592-F6
FANITA WY
500 MLPK 94025 790-E6
FANNING WY
- SF 94116 667-C4
FAN PALM CT
2000 SCL 95050 833-D3
FANSHAWE CT
36100 FRMT 94536 752-F3
FANSHAWE ST
36100 FRMT 94536 752-F3
FANTAIL CT
- SLN 94579 711-A1
1500 SUNV 94087 832-F5
FANWOOD CT
1700 SJS 95133 834-D1
FANWOOD TER
41900 FRMT 94538 773-C1
FANYON ST
- MPS 95035 794-C6
FARADAY CT
1600 SJS 95124 873-J3
35200 FRMT 94536 752-F1
FARADAY DR
4300 SJS 95124 873-J3
FARADAY PL
4400 SJS 95124 873-J3
FARALLON AV
200 PCFA 94044 707-A2
FARALLON CT
- RCH 94804 608-E3
4400 ANT 94509 595-F3
FARALLON DR
100 VAL 94590 530-B2
300 BLMT 94002 749-F6
2000 SLN 94577 690-H5
FARALLON WY
6400 OAK 94611 630-D5
FARALLONE DR
10200 CPTO 95014 852-E2
FARALLONES ST
- SF 94112 687-D2
200 SF 94132 687-D2
FARAN DR
200 CCCo 94553 572-C7
FARAONE CT
4400 SJS 95136 874-E2
FARAONE DR
600 SJS 95136 874-E2
FAR CREEK WY
900 SMCo 94062 789-G2
FAREHAM CT
3200 FRMT 94536 752-J3
FARGATE CIR
1100 SJS 95131 834-C1
FARGHER DR
2800 SCL 95051 833-B3
FARGO AV
600 SLN 94579 691-B6
FARGO CT
1400 CNCD 94521 592-J3
4100 PLE 94588 714-A1
FARGO DR
20600 SCIC 95014 832-D7
FARGO PL
- SF 94103 648-A7
FARIA AV
2400 PIN 94564 569-F5
FARIA CT
2500 PIN 94564 569-F5
FARIA ST
500 ANT 94509 575-C7
FARINA LN
5100 FRMT 94538 773-B2
FARIS DR
900 SJS 95111 855-A6
FARIS ST
15500 SLN 94579 691-B7
FARISS LN
4000 CCCo 94803 589-C2
FARLEY RD
16400 SCIC 95032 873-C5
16500 LGTS 95032 873-C5
W FARLEY RD
17400 LGTS 95030 873-A5
FARLEY ST
100 MTVW 94043 811-G4
2200 AlaC 94546 692-A6
FARM DR
700 SJS 95136 854-D7
FARM LN
- HIL 94010 748-E2
- MRTZ 94553 571-G5
FARM RD
- MrnC 94903 566-E5
- LALT 94024 831-J5
100 PTLV 94028 810-A5
100 WDSD 94062 810-A5
FARM BUREAU CT
3500 CNCD 94519 592-J1
FARM BUREAU RD
1500 CNCD 94519 592-J1
FARMCREST ST
2200 MPS 95035 814-E1
FARM HILL BLVD
3500 RDWC 94061 789-G4
FARMHILL BLVD
4100 WDSD 94062 789-G4
FARM HILL CT
200 DNVL 94526 653-B3
700 WLCK 94598 613-C4
700 WLCK 94598 612-J3
FARMHILL CT
- HIL 94010 748-E1
FARM HILL DR
27800 HAY 94542 712-E4
FARM HILL WY
6300 SJS 95120 874-E7
14900 LGTS 95030 873-C4
FARMINGHAM WY
18400 SCIC 95014 852-C6
FARMINGTON CT
2400 MRTZ 94553 572-A5
FARMINGTON PL
2100 LVMR 94550 715-F4
FARMINGTON WY
1100 LVMR 94550 715-F4
FARNAM ST
3200 OAK 94601 650-C7
FARNDON AV
1800 LALT 94024 832-A4
FARNEE CT
2600 SSF 94080 707-C4
FARNHAM CT
100 SJS 95139 895-G1
FARNHAM DR
4700 NWK 94560 752-E3
FARNHAM PL
500 DNVL 94526 653-D3
FARNSWORTH DR
2300 LVMR 94550 695-G6
2300 SJS 95138 855-F6
FARNSWORTH LN
- SF 94117 667-E2
FARNSWORTH ST
14700 SLN 94578 691-B6
14700 SLN 94579 691-B6
FARNUM CT
300 DNVL 94526 653-D6
FARNUM ST
- SF 94131 667-G5
FARR CT
1300 SJS 95125 854-A4
FARRAGUT AV
- PDMT 94610 650-C2
- SF 94112 687-E2
100 VAL 94590 529-H3
FARRAGUT BLVD
900 FCTY 94404 749-F4
FARRAGUT DR
900 FRMT 94539 753-F6
FARRAGUT LN
18500 MSER 95030 872-H5
18500 SCIC 95030 872-H5
FARRAGUT PL
500 DNVL 94526 633-A7
FARRAGUT ST
100 HER 94547 570-B5
FARRAGUT WY
1900 SJS 95133 814-E7
1900 SJS 95133 834-E1
FARRELL ST
1300 VAL 94590 530-B5
9500 OAK 94605 671-B4
FARRELLY DR
100 SLN 94577 670-J7
FARRINGDON CT
1500 SJS 95127 835-A5
FARRINGDON DR
1200 SJS 95127 835-A4
FARRINGDON LN
700 BURL 94010 728-F6
FARRINGTON WY
2500 EPA 94303 791-B1
2500 EPA 94303 771-B7
FARROL AV
2000 UNC 94587 732-G7
FARROL CT
2400 UNC 94587 732-G7
FARR RANCH CT
12300 SAR 95070 852-C6
FARR RANCH RD
12100 SAR 95070 852-C6
FARSIDE CT
- PIT - 573-F4
FARTHING WY
3200 SJS 95132 814-F3
FARVIEW CT
- SF 94131 667-E3
FAR VUE LN
18900 SCIC 95030 872-H7
FARVUE ST
- NVTO 94947 525-J5
FARWELL AV
14600 SAR 95070 872-F3
FARWELL CT
14800 SAR 95070 872-F3
FARWELL DR
5400 FRMT 94538 773-A1
37600 FRMT 94536 752-G6
39000 FRMT 94538 752-J7
FARWELL PL
5300 FRMT 94536 752-H7
FASCINATION CIR
1200 RCH 94803 589-G3
FASHION ISLAND BLVD
- SMTO 94402 749-D3
1300 SMTO 94403 749-D3
1400 SMTO 94404 749-D3
FASMAN DR
3000 SBRN 94066 707-C5
FASSLER AV
300 PCFA 94044 726-J2
800 PCFA 94044 727-A3
FATHOM CT
400 RDWC 94065 749-H7
FATHOM DR
400 SMTO 94404 749-E1
FATJO PL
2300 SCL 95050 833-C3
FAULKNER CT
4500 FRMT 94536 752-H5
FAULKNER DR
4300 FRMT 94536 752-H4
FAULSTICH CT
800 SJS 95112 834-B1
FAUST CT
2600 SJS 95121 854-J2
FAVONIA RD
100 PTLV 94028 810-C4
FAVOR ST
7000 OAK 94621 670-G3
FAWCETT
100 HER 94547 569-E3
FAWN CT
- HIL 94010 728-C7
- MrnC 94960 566-B4
300 FRMT 94539 773-J2
1600 CMBL 95008 873-A1
FAWN DR
- LVMR 94550 696-A6
- MrnC 94960 566-B3
1100 CMBL 95008 873-A1
3000 SJS 95124 873-G2
FAWN LN
- CMAD 94925 606-H2
- PTLV 94028 810-C5
FAWN PL
- DNVL 94526 653-B7
FAWN RD
4400 CNCD 94521 593-B4
FAWN WY
- DBLN 94568 694-D4
FAWN CREEK CT
- PLHL 94523 592-A7
27800 LAH 94022 810-H6
FAWNDALE DR
15100 SCIC 95032 893-F1
FAWN GLEN CT
- CNCD - 613-D1
- PIT - 573-F5
FAWN HILL CT
4400 ANT 94509 595-H2
FAWN HILL WY
4400 ANT 94509 595-J2
FAWN MEADOW LN
24600 HAY 94541 712-B2
FAWN RIDGE CT
- SRMN 94583 673-J7
FAWNRIDGE CT
- NVTO 94945 526-A1
FAWNWOOD CT
3100 SJS 95148 855-D1
FAXON AV
- SF 94112 687-D1
400 SF 94112 667-D7
900 SF 94127 667-D7
FAXON RD
- ATN 94027 790-D4
FAXON FOREST
- ATN 94027 790-D4
FAY AV
- SCAR 94070 769-E4
- SMCo 94070 769-E4
FAY CT
100 UNC 94587 732-E3
FAY DR
- MrnC 94904 586-E3
1600 SJS 95124 873-J2
FAY ST
1100 RDWC 94061 770-A7
FAY WY
200 MTVW 94043 811-G3
FAYE CT
1900 PLHL 94523 592-C5
FAYE PARK DR
600 SJS 95136 874-E1
FAYETTE DR
2600 MTVW 94040 811-E3
FAYHILL RD
- MRGA 94556 631-F3
FEAFEL CT
4100 SJS 95134 813-D2
FEAFEL DR
4100 SJS 95134 813-D2
FEATHER CIR
1000 CLAY 94517 593-H6
FEATHER CT
- CLAY 94517 593-H6
5500 AlaC 94552 692-D4
FEATHER DR
900 PLE 94566 714-H4
FEATHER WY
5100 ANT 94509 595-G4
FEATHER RIVER CT
- CCCo 94506 654-B4
FEATHER RIVER ST
800 CCCo 94506 654-C4
FEBRUARY DR
100 SJS 95138 875-D4
FEDERAL ST
- SF 94107 648-B6
FEDERATION CT
5300 SJS 95123 875-B3
FEDORA CT
1400 SJS 95121 854-J2
FEDSCO CT
4800 CNCD 94521 593-D4
FEDSCO DR
5000 CNCD 94521 593-D4
FEHREN DR
13000 SCIC 95111 854-G6
13000 SJS 95111 854-G6
FELDER DR
6300 SJS 95123 875-B7
FELDSPAR CT
1600 LVMR 94550 715-D3
4300 UNC 94587 732-A6
FELDSPAR DR
400 SJS 95111 854-G4
FELICE CT
100 SJS 95138 875-G7
FELICIA AV
5100 LVMR 94550 696-C6
FELICIA CT
- ANT 94509 595-D1
1000 LVMR 94550 696-C7
FELICIA LN
1700 CNCD 94519 592-J2
FELICIO COM
200 FRMT 94536 733-A7
FELIPA CT
- TBRN 94920 607-B5
FELIPE AV
900 SJS 95122 834-F6
FELIX AV
- SF 94132 687-B1
6000 CCCo 94805 589-B5
FELIX TER
34400 FRMT 94555 752-D2
FELIX WY
500 SJS 95125 854-C4
FELIZ CT
100 DNVL 94526 633-C6
36400 FRMT 94536 752-F3
FELIZ DR
2100 NVTO 94945 525-J2
FELIZ RD
2000 NVTO 94945 526-A2
2000 NVTO 94945 525-J2
FELL AV
4800 SJS 95136 874-E3
FELL CT
900 SJS 95136 874-E3
FELL ST
- SF 94102 647-F7
700 SF 94117 647-F7
1600 SF 94117 667-E1
2000 SF 94117 667-E1
FELLA PL
- SF 94108 648-A5
FELLER AV
700 SJS 95127 835-B2
FELLOWS CT
32700 UNC 94587 732-A7
FELLOWS ST
4300 UNC 94587 732-A7
FELTER RD
4100 SCIC 95140 794-J6
4100 SCIC 95035 794-J6
5500 SCIC 95132 815-D1
5500 SCIC 95140 815-D1
FELTON
- HER 94547 569-F4
FELTON AV
- SSF 94080 707-D1
FELTON DR
100 MLPK 94025 790-F2
FELTON PL
100 MLPK 94025 790-F2
FELTON ST
- SF 94134 668-A7
500 SF 94134 667-H7
FELTON WY
10500 CPTO 95014 852-D2
FENHAM ST
6200 OAK 94621 670-F3
FENIAN DR
2200 SJS 95008 853-B6
FENICO TER
4400 FRMT 94536 752-A6
FENLEY AV
300 SCIC 95117 853-D1
600 SJS 95117 853-D2
FENNWOOD DR
- ATN 94027 790-F2
FENSALIR AV
400 PLHL 94523 592-B3
FENTON LN
- SF 94131 667-F4
FENTON ST
- LVMR 94550 715-F1
300 SJS 95127 814-J7
600 SCIC 95127 814-J7
FENTON WY
38700 FRMT 94536 752-H6
FENWAY CT
- WLCK 94598 612-G3
21000 CPTO 95014 832-C7
FENWAY DR
300 WLCK 94598 612-F3
FENWICK CT
11500 DBLN 94568 693-F2
FENWICK PL
11600 DBLN 94568 693-F2
FENWICK WY
2900 SJS 95148 855-C2
8600 DBLN 94568 693-F2
FERDINANDA PL
4300 AlaC 94546 692-A3
FERGUSON DR
100 MTVW 94043 812-B5
FERGUSON WY
1400 SJS 95129 852-J4
FERINO WY
100 FRMT 94536 753-D2
FERN AV
- BLV 94920 627-D1
- MLV 94941 606-E4
500 PIN 94564 569-E4
700 PCFA 94044 727-A2
FERN CIR
42500 FRMT 94538 773-D1
FERN COM
4400 FRMT 94538 773-C1
FERN CT
- HIL 94010 728-D7
100 DNVL 94506 653-F4
FERN DR
- WLCK 94595 612-D7
5400 SJS 95124 873-J6
FERN LN
- CMAD 94925 606-G1
- SANS 94960 566-A6
FERN PL
1600 VAL 94590 530-A4
FERN PTH
- SMCo 94010 728-B7
FERN RD
- MrnC 94904 586-D5
FERN ST
- SF 94109 647-H6
2400 OAK 94601 650-E7
5700 ELCR 94530 589-B7
FERN TER
4300 FRMT 94538 773-D2
FERN TR
- CMAD 94925 586-E7
FERN WY
- MrnC 94904 586-D5
- MrnC 94941 606-F6
- MrnC 94965 606-B3
- ORIN 94563 630-J3
1600 AlaC 94586 734-A2
19600 AlaC 94546 692-B5
FERNALD COM
46800 FRMT 94539 773-H6
FERNALD CT
47400 FRMT 94539 773-H7
FERNALD ST
46700 FRMT 94539 773-H6
FERNANDEZ AV
- DBLN 94568 694-B3
700 PIN 94564 569-E4
FERNANDEZ CT
400 SCL 95050 833-C6
FERNANDEZ ST
800 SF 94129 647-E4
FERNANDEZ WY
1100 PCFA 94044 726-H4
FERNANDO AV
200 PA 94306 811-C1
FERNANDO CT
400 SRMN 94583 673-B2
FERNANDO DR
500 NVTO 94945 526-D4
FERNBANK DR
- CNCD - 613-D1
FERNBRIDGE PL
400 NVTO 94947 526-E6
FERNBROOK CT
18900 SAR 95070 852-H5
FERN CANYON RD
- MLV 94941 606-B1
- MrnC 94965 606-B1
FERNCLIFF CT
8300 DBLN 94568 693-G2
FERNCREST CT
13600 SAR 95070 872-H1
FERNCROFT CT
500 DNVL 94526 653-D7
FERNDALE AV
200 MrnC 94941 606-D5
200 SSF 94080 707-F1
E FERNDALE AV
100 SUNV 94086 812-F5
N FERNDALE AV
300 MrnC 94941 606-D5
W FERNDALE AV
100 SUNV 94086 812-E5
FERNDALE CT
700 SJS 95133 834-F2
3000 PLE 94588 694-F6
FERNDALE DR
1500 SJS 95118 874-A5
FERNDALE LN
3900 CNCD 94519 593-A1
FERNDALE RD
- CCCo 94553 570-J7
- CCCo 94553 590-J1
FERNDALE WY
200 SMCo 94062 769-E7
200 SMCo 94062 789-E1
2300 SJS 95133 834-F1
FERNDELL WK
- ALA 94501 669-H3
FERNE AV
100 PA 94306 811-E2
FERNE CT
100 PA 94306 811-E2
FERNESS
300 PIT 94565 574-B3
FERNGLEN DR
5900 SJS 95123 874-E5
FERNGROVE DR
800 CPTO 95014 852-G2
FERNGROVE WY
3000 ANT 94509 575-G7
3000 ANT 94509 595-G1
FERNHILL AV
- ROSS 94957 586-B2
FERNHILL DR
23700 LAH 94024 831-E4
FERN HILL LN
1300 CNCD 94521 593-B5
FERNHOFF CT
- OAK 94619 650-J5
FERNHOFF RD
5400 OAK 94619 650-J5
5400 OAK 94619 651-A4
FERNISH DR
1900 SJS 95148 835-D5
FERN LEAF CT
2500 MRTZ 94553 572-A6
FERNLEAF DR
1000 SUNV 94086 832-G2
FERN PINE CT
1600 SJS 95131 834-D1
FERN RIDGE CT
500 SUNV 94087 832-D5
FERNRIDGE CT
- HAY 94544 711-H4
FERNSIDE BLVD
900 ALA 94501 670-B2
FERNSIDE LN
700 LFYT 94549 631-F1
FERNSIDE SQ
3100 SJS 95132 814-E3
FERNSIDE ST
- RDWC 94061 790-A3
- WDSD 94062 790-A3
1000 RDWC 94061 789-J2
1600 WDSD 94062 789-J2
FERNWALD RD
- BERK 94704 630-A2
FERNWOOD AV
- DALY 94015 686-J5
2500 SCL 95128 833-E7
2500 SJS 95117 833-D7
2500 SJS 95128 833-E7
N FERNWOOD CIR
300 SUNV 94086 812-F5
S FERNWOOD CIR
300 SUNV 94086 812-F5
W FERNWOOD CIR
600 SUNV 94086 812-F5
FERNWOOD CT
- PIT 94565 574-F5
2200 AlaC 94541 692-B7
3800 CNCD 94518 592-J4
4000 PLE 94588 713-J2
FERNWOOD DR
- SANS 94960 566-B7
- SBRN 94066 707-F6
- SF 94127 667-D6
- SRFL 94901 567-C6
100 MRGA 94556 631-E5
200 PLHL 94523 591-H2
1100 MLBR 94030 727-H3
1400 OAK 94611 630-D6
3300 VAL 94591 530-E6
5400 NWK 94560 752-E5
FERNWOOD ST
2800 SMTO 94403 749-A6
FERNWOOD WY
- SRFL 94901 567-C7
1700 BLMT 94002 769-D2
3900 PLE 94588 713-J2
FERRARA CT
5200 PLE 94588 694-C6
FERRARI AV
- SJS 95110 833-J3
FERREIRA CT
400 MPS 95035 794-E7
FERREIRA PL
40900 FRMT 94539 753-F4
FERREL CT
1300 SJS 95132 814-F5
FERRIS AV
16400 SCIC 95032 873-C7
16400 LGTS 95032 873-C7
FERRIS DR
1100 NVTO 94945 525-J2
1100 NVTO 94945 526-A1
FERRO CT
- ALA 94502 669-J7
FERRO ST
- OAK 94607 649-C5
FERROL CT
- SRMN 94583 673-C3
FERRUM CT
2900 SJS 95148 855-D2
FERRY LN
3500 FRMT 94555 752-E1
FERRY ST
300 MRTZ 94553 571-D2
700 OAK 94607 649-B3
FERRY MORSE WY
100 MTVW 94041 812-A6
FESTIVAL CT
7900 CPTO 95014 852-C2
FESTIVAL DR
7700 CPTO 95014 852-C2
10900 SCIC 95014 852-C2
FESTIVO CT
500 FRMT 94539 773-H1
FETZER DR
- SJS 95125 853-G4
FEVER DR
- SJS 95123 875-A6
- SJS 95123 874-J6
FEWTRELL DR
1000 CMBL 95008 853-G6
FEY DR
100 SMCo 94010 728-B7
FIDDLERS GRN
1200 SJS 95125 854-F5
FIDDLE TOWN CT
100 VAL 94589 509-H5
FIDDLETOWN PL
5900 SJS 95120 874-C6
FIELD RD
- MrnC 94965 626-F6

STREET
Block City ZIP Pg-Grid

FIELD ST
2000 ANT 94509 574-J5
3500 OAK 94605 671-A2
FIELDBROOK PL
- MRGA 94556 631-D6
4600 OAK 94619 650-H5
FIELDBROOK RD
4500 OAK 94619 650-H5
FIELDCREST CIR
1400 PLHL 94523 591-H2
FIELDCREST CT
200 DNVL 94506 653-H4
FIELDCREST DR
- DALY 94015 687-B3
400 SJS 95123 875-B7
1500 PLHL 94523 591-H2
2000 MPS 95035 814-E1
4300 CCCo 94803 589-F1
4300 RCH 94803 589-E1
FIELDCREST LN
- SRMN 94583 673-J6
FIELDCREST WY
4500 ANT 94509 595-H3
FIELDFAIR CT
1300 SUNV 94087 832-F4
FIELDGATE CT
3200 SJS 95148 855-E1
FIELDGATE DR
1600 PIT - 573-G4
1600 PIT 94565 573-G4
FIELDGATE LN
1600 WLCK 94595 612-D7
FIELD HOUSE RD
- SMTO 94402 748-H5
FIELDING CIR
- MLV 94941 606-H6
FIELDING CT
34600 FRMT 94555 752-D2
FIELDING DR
800 PA 94303 791-D6
27000 HAY 94542 712-D4
FIELDING ST
- SF 94133 648-A3
FIELDS DR
1400 SJS 95129 852-J4
FIELDSTONE CT
200 VAL 94589 510-B4
FIELDSTONE DR
300 FRMT 94536 732-J7
5900 LVMR 94550 696-C3
14600 SAR 95070 872-C3
FIELDSTONE WY
100 VAL 94589 510-B4
FIELDVIEW TER
2800 SRMN 94583 673-B3
FIELDWOOD CT
800 SJS 95120 894-H3
FIESTA AV
- SMCo 94063 770-F5
FIESTA CIR
100 ORIN 94563 631-C5
FIESTA CT
2000 SMTO 94403 749-C4
3100 RCH 94803 589-E1
FIESTA DR
500 SMTO 94403 749-B4
3000 PLE 94588 694-C7
FIESTA LN
- LFYT 94549 611-F6
7800 CPTO 95014 852-C2
FIESTA PL
600 HAY 94544 712-D7
FIESTA RD
5400 FRMT 94538 773-B2
FIESTA WY
- LGTS 95032 893-A1
FIFE AV
1000 PA 94301 791-A4
FIFE CT
- SRMN 94583 673-E5
FIFE WY
700 SUNV 94087 832-F5
3400 SJS 95132 814-G3
FIFER AV
- CMAD 94925 586-G5
FIFEWOOD CT
6500 SJS 95120 894-F1
FIFI CT
- CCCo 94598 612-G4
FIG AV
1000 SUNV 94087 832-B2
FIG GROVE CT
5300 SJS 95123 875-A3
FIG TREE CT
- NVTO 94947 525-J3
300 HAY 94544 711-J4
19800 CPTO 95014 832-F7
FIG TREE LN
- MRTZ 94553 571-H6
FIGUEROA DR
800 SLN 94578 691-A4
FIGWOOD CT
800 SJS 95120 894-H3
FIJI CIR
400 UNC 94587 732-C6
FIJI DR
800 SJS 95127 814-H6
FIJI LN
3100 ALA 94502 669-J7
3100 ALA 94502 670-A7
FIJI WY
2200 SLN 94577 690-G5
FILBERT AV
- SAUS 94965 627-A2
700 CMBL 95008 853-B7
FILBERT CT
600 SRMN 94583 673-G7
600 WLCK 94598 612-H3
FILBERT DR
2700 WLCK 94598 612-H3
FILBERT ST
100 OAK 94607 649-F3
200 SF 94133 648-A4
700 SF 94133 647-H4
1100 SF 94109 647-H4
1200 RCH 94801 588-F4
1500 SF 94123 647-H4
1800 SF 94123 647-F4
2600 ANT 94509 575-H6
2800 OAK 94608 649-F2
22500 HAY 94541 711-H2
37100 NWK 94560 772-E1

FILIP RD
700 LALT 94024 831-G2
FILLMER AV
- LGTS 95032 873-B7
FILLMORE AV
1600 SMTO 94403 749-C2
FILLMORE CT
2200 ANT 94509 575-A7
FILLMORE ST
- SF 94117 667-G1
400 SF 94117 647-G4
900 ALB 94706 609-C6
1100 SF 94115 647-G4
1300 SPAB 94806 588-G4
1800 SCL 95050 833-D3
2800 ALA 94501 670-A4
2800 SF 94123 647-G4
3100 SF 94123 647-G3
4300 SCL 95054 813-C5
FILLMORE WY
1800 CNCD 94521 593-D3
FILOMENA AV
100 SJS 95110 834-A5
FILOMENA CT
3300 MTVW 94040 831-J2
FILTON CT
1200 FRMT 94536 733-D7
FINANCIAL WY
- LVMR 94550 696-F4
FINBACK WY
- SLN 94577 690-H5
FINCH AV
10000 CPTO 95014 832-G7
10000 CPTO 95014 852-G1
10200 SCIC 95014 852-G1
FINCH CT
100 HER 94547 569-J5
1700 HAY 94545 731-J1
FINCH DR
- ANT 94509 594-J2
3200 SJS 95117 853-D3
FINCH PL
3500 FRMT 94555 732-D7
FINCH WY
- DBLN 94568 694-D4
300 LVMR 94550 695-D7
1500 SUNV 94087 832-F5
FINCHWELL CT
- SJS 95138 875-D4
FINCHWOOD WY
700 SJS 95120 894-H3
FINDLAY WY
4000 LVMR 94550 716-A2
FINDLEY DR
1700 MPS 95035 794-D6
FINEO CT
1400 SJS 95131 814-C7
FINGER AV
- RDWC 94062 769-J5
FINLEY LN
1400 CCCo 94507 632-F4
FINLEY RD
- SF 94129 647-D5
1100 CCCo 94506 654-G3
FINN LN
12000 LAH 94022 831-C3
FINN COVE CT
- UNC 94545 731-J6
FINNIGAN TER
34100 FRMT 94555 752-B2
FINOVINO CT
900 PLE 94566 714-H4
FIORA PL
4000 LFYT 94549 611-B6
FIORIO CIR
1900 PLE 94566 714-E1
FIR AV
100 SSF 94080 707-H4
500 SUNV 94086 812-F6
1500 AlaC 94578 691-D3
3100 ALA 94502 670-A6
FIR CT
- NWK 94560 752-C7
- HIL 94010 748-C1
100 HER 94547 569-J4
6800 DBLN 94568 693-J4
FIR LN
400 SCIC 94024 831-J5
FIR PL
1100 ALA 94502 670-A6
1100 ALA 94502 669-J7
FIR RD
- BEN 94510 551-E5
FIR ST
100 SCAR 94070 769-F2
2000 CNCD 94519 592-H1
2300 CCCo 94553 571-F4
FIRCREST CT
- SRMN 94583 693-H1
FIRCREST LN
9100 SRMN 94583 693-H1
9400 SRMN 94583 673-H7
FIRCREST ST
35300 NWK 94560 752-C5
FIRE RD
- MLV 94941 606-D1
- MrnC 94965 606-B7
- TBRN - 627-H2
FIREBIRD WY
1400 SUNV 94087 832-F4
FIREBRAND DR
7700 DBLN 94568 693-G3
FIRE BRAND PL
25600 AlaC 94541 712-D2
FIREBRICK TER
- UNC 94587 732-G6
FIRECREST AV
300 PCFA 94044 707-B2
FIREFLY DR
6200 SJS 95120 874-C7
6300 SJS 95120 894-C1
FIRENZA ST
500 LVMR 94550 695-E7
FIRENZE CT
- SJS 95138 855-E7
- SJS 95138 875-E1
FIRESIDE CT
500 WLCK 94598 612-H1
FIRESIDE DR
2900 SJS 95128 853-E3
FIRESIDE WY
- PIT 94565 574-F5

FIRESTONE CT
- SJS 95138 875-H1
200 WLCK 94598 612-J2
18000 HAY 94541 711-D2
35900 NWK 94560 752-B6
FIRESTONE DR
- CCCo 94507 632-H4
100 WLCK 94598 612-J1
FIRESTONE RD
5500 LVMR 94550 696-C2
17900 HAY 94541 711-D2
FIRETHORN CT
- SRMN 94583 653-J6
2000 MPS 95035 793-J3
FIRETHORN ST
- MPS 95035 793-J3
FIRETHORN WY
- DBLN 94568 693-G3
- PTLV 94028 810-D7
FIRETHORNE DR
11000 CPTO 95014 832-D6
FIRE TRAIL 4
- RCH 94805 589-E6
FIREWOOD CT
700 SJS 95120 894-H3
FIRLOCH AV
400 SUNV 94086 832-F1
E FIRST ST
500 MLPK 94025 790-H3
FIRTH CT
1000 SUNV 94087 832-H5
1800 FRMT 94539 773-G2
14900 SLN 94578 691-C5
FIRTH WY
3200 SJS 95121 855-B3
FIR TREE CT
300 MPS 95035 813-J3
FISALIA CT
200 FRMT 94539 753-E3
FISH AL
400 SF 94133 647-J3
FISHBURNE AV
5800 SJS 95123 874-F5
FISH CREEK PL
2300 DNVL 94506 653-G1
FISHER AL
- SF 94133 648-A4
FISHER AV
- SF 94124 668-E7
2600 OAK 94605 671-B5
4200 SCIC 95127 835-A2
16100 LGTS 95032 873-B6
FISHER CT
4500 PLE 94588 694-A7
FISHER DR
1600 CNCD 94520 592-E4
FISHER LP
- SF 94129 647-D4
FISHER PL
35500 FRMT 94536 752-F1
FISHER RD
200 SCIC 95037 895-J6
200 SJS 95141 895-J6
FISHER ST
400 DALY 94014 687-D5
2400 CCCo 94806 569-B5
FISHER HAWK DR
1300 SUNV 94087 832-F4
FISH RANCH RD
- CCCo - 630-D2
- OAK 94705 630-D2
FISK AV
500 SJS 95125 854-A2
FISK CT
100 VAL 94589 510-A6
14700 SLN 94579 691-A5
FISK TER
100 FRMT 94538 773-D3
FITCH ST
- SF 94124 668-E6
2600 SF 94124 688-C1
FITCHBURG AV
500 ALA 94502 670-B7
FITCHVILLE AV
1500 SJS 95126 853-H3
FITZGERALD AV
500 SF 94124 688-B1
1700 SF 94124 668-A7
FITZGERALD CIR
38300 FRMT 94536 753-A3
FITZGERALD DR
1400 PIN 94564 569-C6
1400 PIN 94803 569-C6
21500 CPTO 95014 832-B7
FITZGERALD ST
1300 OAK 94608 649-F1
FITZPATRICK DR
3100 CNCD 94519 572-G7
FITZPATRICK RD
200 OAK 94603 670-F6
FITZPATRICK ST
2400 CCCo 94806 569-B5
FITZSIMMONS COM
3400 FRMT 94538 753-C5
FITZUREN RD
900 ANT 94509 575-C6
FIVE CANYON RD
- AlaC 94542 692-D5
3700 AlaC 94552 692-D5
FIVE CANYONS PKWY
- AlaC 94542 692-E7
- AlaC 94542 712-F1
FIVE WOUNDS LN
1300 SJS 95116 834-E4
FJORD ST
14900 SLN 94578 691-C5
FLAG ST
- LKSP 94939 586-E6
FLAGG AV
400 SCIC 95128 853-F1
3300 OAK 94602 650-D5
FLAGG ST
22300 HAY 94541 711-H1
FLAGLER ST
500 SCIC 95127 814-H7
1800 SJS 95127 814-H7
FLAGSHIP ST
14400 SLN 94577 690-H5
FLAGSTAD CT
2700 SJS 95121 855-A3
FLAGSTAFF CT
48700 FRMT 94539 793-J2

FLAGSTAFF PL
48400 FRMT 94539 793-J2
FLAGSTAFF RD
48500 FRMT 94539 793-J2
FLAGSTONE CT
- CCCo 94507 632-H4
FLAGSTONE DR
- UNC 94587 732-G6
200 ANT 94509 595-E1
2500 SJS 95132 814-F6
7400 PLE 94588 693-J7
FLAGSTONE TER
200 MrnC 94903 546-E6
FLAGSTONE WY
2200 CNCD 94521 593-G3
FLAME CT
- CCCo 94553 592-B1
FLAME DR
- PLHL 94553 592-B1
100 CCCo 94553 592-B1
100 PLHL 94523 592-B1
FLAMEWOOD AV
900 SUNV 94089 812-J5
FLAMINGO AV
26100 HAY 94544 711-H6
FLAMINGO CT
- AMCN 94589 509-J1
2100 PIN 94564 569-F7
FLAMINGO DR
200 CMBL 95008 853-G7
3400 CNCD 94520 572-G6
FLAMINGO LN
- SRFL 94901 567-C6
5200 FRMT 94538 752-J7
FLAMINGO RD
200 MrnC 94965 606-F7
FLAMINGO WY
1400 SUNV 94087 832-F5
FLAMING OAK DR
300 PLHL 94523 592-B1
FLAMINGO PARK CT
4600 FRMT 94538 773-C2
FLANAGAN
- DBLN 94568 693-G4
FLANDERS CT
200 AlaC 94541 711-F1
1700 WLCK 94598 592-F7
FLANDERS DR
3100 SJS 95132 814-G5
6400 NWK 94560 752-C5
FLANDERS PL
6400 NWK 94560 752-C5
FLANDERS WY
1300 LVMR 94550 715-F3
7500 DBLN 94568 693-H3
FLANIGAN DR
1400 SJS 95121 854-J2
1500 SJS 95121 855-A2
FLANNERY RD
2600 CCCo 94806 569-C5
FLANNERY ST
500 SCL 95051 833-A7
FLARE EAST RD
- CCCo 94553 571-H3
FLARE NORTH RD
- CCCo 94553 571-G3
FLARE SOUTH RD
- CCCo 94553 571-G3
FLASHNER LN
900 BLMT 94002 769-E1
FLATER DR
3000 SJS 95148 855-C2
FLAT ROCK CIR
4900 SJS 95136 874-J2
FLAX LN
300 SRMN 94583 653-J7
FLAXBERRY LN
800 MrnC 94903 546-C7
FLAX MOSS CT
1200 SJS 95120 894-C1
FLAXWOOD ST
1100 SJS 95120 874-D6
FLEDERMAUS CT
1500 SJS 95121 854-J4
FLEET CT
- VAL 94591 530-G6
FLEET RD
1100 OAK 94602 650-C3
1100 OAK 94610 650-C3
FLEET ST
100 VAL 94591 530-G6
5800 SJS 95120 874-B6
FLEETWOOD AV
18400 AlaC 94546 692-A3
FLEETWOOD CT
- NVTO 94947 525-H3
- ORIN 94563 631-B3
100 SBRN 94066 707-C5
FLEETWOOD DR
- DALY 94015 687-A3
100 ANT 94509 575-D7
100 SCAR 94070 769-E7
800 SMTO 94402 749-B2
1000 SJS 95120 874-D7
2100 SBRN 94066 707-D5
3400 RCH 94803 589-E1
3900 SSF 94080 707-D5
FLEETWOOD RD
4400 CCCo 94506 654-B4
FLEMING AV
100 VAL 94590 530-C3
100 SJS 95127 835-A2
1200 SCIC 95127 835-C2
3800 RCH 94804 609-B2
4300 OAK 94619 650-E7
5000 OAK 94619 670-F1
5500 OAK 94605 670-F1
FLEMING AV E
400 VAL 94591 530-D3
FLEMING CT
- SJS 95127 835-A1
- CLAY 94517 593-H7
- CLAY 94517 613-H1
FLEMING DR
200 CLAY 94517 593-H7
FLEMING ST
15000 SLN 94579 691-B6
FLEMINGS CT
800 MrnC 94965 626-H1
FLEMINGTON CT
3200 PLE 94588 694-F6

FLETCHER CT
- CCCo 94565 573-C1
700 HAY 94544 711-J2
FLETCHER DR
- ATN 94027 790-B5
FLETCHER LN
800 HAY 94544 711-J2
900 HAY 94541 712-A2
900 HAY 94544 712-A2
FLETCHER ST
500 CCCo 94565 573-C1
FLEUR PL
- ATN 94027 790-C4
FLEUR DE LIS CT
3200 SJS 95132 814-G5
FLEUTI DR
- MRGA 94556 631-E7
FLICKER CT
200 LVMR 94550 715-D1
FLICKER DR
- NVTO 94949 546-E4
FLICKER WY
1300 SUNV 94087 832-F4
FLICKINGER AV
1100 SJS 95131 814-C5
FLICKINGER CT
1700 SJS 95131 814-C5
FLICKINGER PL
1700 SJS 95131 814-C5
FLICKINGER RD
1700 SJS 95131 814-C4
FLICKINGER WY
1800 SJS 95131 814-C4
FLIN COM
37200 FRMT 94536 752-J2
FLIN WY
800 SUNV 94087 832-F5
FLINT
3000 ALA 94501 649-E6
FLINT AV
900 CNCD 94518 592-G5
1400 SMTO 94403 749-D4
1800 SJS 95148 835-E6
2000 SCIC 95148 835-C5
FLINT CT
- NVTO 94949 526-B7
100 VAL 94589 510-C6
200 AlaC 94541 711-F2
3300 SJS 95148 835-D5
FLINT ST
- SF 94114 667-G2
100 LVMR 94550 715-D2
2900 UNC 94587 732-A4
FLINTBURY CT
2000 SJS 95148 835-C5
FLINT CREEK CT
1800 SJS 95148 835-D4
FLINT CREEK DR
3500 SJS 95148 835-D4
FLINT CREEK WY
1700 SJS 95148 835-D4
FLINTCREST CT
2000 SJS 95148 835-C5
FLINTCREST DR
2000 SJS 95148 835-C5
FLINTDALE DR
3200 SJS 95148 835-C5
FLINTFIELD DR
2000 SJS 95148 835-D5
FLINTHAVEN DR
3100 SJS 95148 835-B5
FLINTHILL CT
3400 SJS 95148 835-D5
FLINTMONT CT
3200 SJS 95148 835-C5
FLINTMONT DR
3200 SJS 95148 835-C5
FLINTMORE CT
2100 SJS 95148 835-D5
FLINTRIDGE AV
3200 OAK 94605 671-B4
FLINTRIDGE DR
15500 LGTS 95032 873-C5
FLINTRIDGE LN
8900 OAK 94605 671-B3
FLINT RIVER TER
200 FRMT - 752-C1
200 FRMT 94555 732-C7
200 FRMT 94555 752-C1
FLINTROCK DR
900 ANT 94509 595-F1
FLINTSHIRE ST
21500 CPTO 95014 852-B3
FLINTSIDE CT
2100 SJS 95148 835-D5
FLINTVIEW CT
3200 SJS 95148 835-D7
FLINTWELL CT
100 SJS 95138 875-D4
FLINTWELL WY
- SJS 95138 875-D4
FLINTWICK CT
2000 SJS 95148 835-D5
FLINTWOOD CT
1400 MRTZ 94553 571-H7
2600 SJS 95148 835-D6
FLINTWOOD DR
36600 NWK 94560 752-F5
FLOOD AV
- SF 94131 667-E6
200 SF 94112 667-E6
400 SF 94112 667-E6
2900 SMCo 94063 770-D7
FLOOD CIR
- ATN 94027 790-F1
FLOOD DR
1800 SJS 95124 873-H1
FLORA AV
100 CCCo 94595 612-B6
1200 SJS 95117 853-B4
1300 SJS 95130 853-B4
FLORA CT
- PLHL 94523 592-D6
3000 PLE 94588 694-D6
FLORA PL
400 FRMT 94536 753-D2
FLORA ST
- SF 94124 668-B6
500 MRTZ 94553 571-E4
1200 CCCo 94525 550-D5
6400 OAK 94621 670-G3
6400 OAK 94605 670-F2

FLORADA AV
- OAK 94610 650-C2
- PDMT 94610 650-C2
FLORALES DR
600 PA 94306 811-C2
FLORA VISTA
- DNVL 94526 652-H1
3000 ALA 94502 669-J6
FLORA VISTA AV
300 SUNV 94086 832-E1
3400 SCL 95051 832-J3
10300 SCIC 95014 832-C7
FLORENCE AV
- MLV 94941 606-C3
- SANS 94960 566-A6
- SPAB 94806 588-J3
100 OAK 94618 630-C6
2700 SJS 95127 834-J3
2800 SCIC 95127 834-J3
FLORENCE CT
100 CCCo 94526 633-D4
100 VAL 94589 530-B1
200 HER 94547 570-B6
3100 SJS 95127 835-A2
FLORENCE DR
400 LFYT 94549 631-H3
4100 MRTZ 94553 571-E6
10400 CPTO 95014 832-B6
FLORENCE LN
900 MLPK 94025 790-F4
1800 CNCD 94520 592-E4
FLORENCE RD
900 LVMR 94550 715-G2
FLORENCE ST
- FRMT 94536 732-J5
- AlaC 94541 711-F1
- DALY 94014 687-D4
- SF 94133 647-J4
100 SUNV 94086 812-D7
300 SUNV 94086 832-D1
300 UNC 94587 732-J5
400 PA 94301 790-J4
2800 BERK 94705 629-H3
3600 SMCo 94063 770-F7
3600 RDWC 94063 770-F7
FLORENCE TER
5500 OAK 94611 630-D6
FLORENCE WY
200 SJS 95110 834-A7
1000 CMBL 95008 873-D1
38800 FRMT 94536 752-J5
FLORENCE PARK DR
2900 SJS 95135 855-E2
FLORENTINE DR
500 SJS 95123 875-B3
FLORENTINE ST
- SF 94112 687-F2
FLORES
- MTVW 94043 811-J2
FLORES CT
300 CCCo 94553 572-E3
FLORES DR
1300 PCFA 94044 726-H4
FLORES ST
2200 SMTO 94403 749-B5
FLORESTA BLVD
200 SLN 94578 691-B4
FLORESTA DR
3200 SJS 95148 835-D6
E FLORESTA WY
100 SMCo 94028 810-E3
W FLORESTA WY
200 SMCo 94028 810-E3
FLORIAN ST
3500 PLE 94588 694-C6
FLORIBEL AV
- SANS 94960 566-A7
FLORIBUNDA AV
1200 BURL 94010 728-F7
1600 HIL 94010 728-F7
FLORIDA AV
- BERK 94707 609-G5
100 RCH 94804 588-F7
100 SBRN 94066 707-J7
1300 SJS 95122 834-H6
2800 RCH 94804 589-A7
FLORIDA CT
4100 LVMR 94550 716-A1
FLORIDA DR
5400 CNCD 94521 593-E6
FLORIDA LN
2500 ANT 94509 575-D1
FLORIDA ST
- SF 94103 667-J2
- VAL 94590 529-H4
300 SF 94110 667-J2
600 VAL 94590 530-A4
800 SF 94110 668-A4
1400 SF 94110 668-A4
1800 HAY 94545 731-J1
2300 VAL 94591 530-D4
2900 OAK 94602 650-E5
FLORIO ST
6200 OAK 94618 629-J4
FLORY DR
2400 SJS 95121 854-J2
FLOSDEN RD
2400 AMCN 94589 510-C3
2400 NaCo 94589 510-C3
FLOSSMOOR WY
30400 HAY 94544 732-D1
FLOURNOY ST
- DALY 94014 687-D2
100 SF 94112 687-D2
FLOWER CT
1300 CPTO 95014 852-D4
FLOWER LN
400 MTVW 94043 812-B5
500 ALA 94502 670-A6
FLOWER ST
- RDWC 94063 769-J4
- SF 94124 668-A5
FLOWER GARDEN LN
1600 SJS 95124 873-J6
FLOWERING PEAR DR
11000 CPTO 95014 832-D6
FLOWERING PLUM RD
6100 SJS 95120 874-D7
FLOWERS LN
3100 PA 94306 791-D7
FLOWERWOOD PL
1100 WLCK 94598 592-E7

FLOWERWOOD PL
1100 WLCK 94598 612-E1
FLOWERWOOD TER
- FRMT 94536 752-B7
FLOYD AV
1300 SUNV 94087 832-E4
FLOYD LN
2200 CNCD 94520 572-F5
FLOYD ST
- SJS 95110 854-C2
FLUME CT
700 MPS 95035 794-B5
700 SLN 94578 691-D5
FLUORITE CT
- LVMR 94550 715-D3
FLYING CLOUD CT
100 VAL 94591 550-F3
FLYING CLOUD ISL
100 FCTY 94404 749-G2
FLYING CLOUD CRSE
- CMAD 94925 606-J1
FLYING FISH ST
900 FCTY 94404 749-G1
FLYING MIST ISL
100 FCTY 94404 749-G2
FLYING MIST RD
15100 SLN 94579 690-J6
FLYNG DUTCHMAN CT
100 VAL 94591 550-G3
FLYNN AV
- MTVW 94043 812-A4
400 RDWC 94063 770-C6
S FLYNN RD
9200 AlaC 94550 696-J6
FOERSTER ST
- SF 94112 667-E6
400 SF 94127 667-E6
FOGL CT
- SMCo 94061 790-B4
FOLEY AV
1100 SCL 95051 833-B4
1400 SJS 95122 834-G7
FOLEY CT
- WLCK 94595 612-B6
5100 ANT 94509 595-F4
FOLEY LN
- LKSP 94939 586-E7
FOLEY ST
1600 ALA 94501 670-A2
23000 HAY 94545 711-D6
FOLGER AV
700 BERK 94804 629-E4
FOLGER CT
- BLMT 94002 769-D1
FOLGER DR
1500 BLMT 94002 769-D1
FOLIGNO WY
5700 SJS 95138 875-G1
FOLIN LN
- LFYT 94549 611-H3
FOLKESTONE DR
7900 CPTO 95014 852-C3
FOLKLORE CT
6600 SJS 95120 894-C5
FOLKSTONE AV
600 SMTO 94402 749-B2
FOLLAND DR
100 AMCN 94589 510-A4
200 AMCN 94589 509-J4
FOLLETT ST
100 RCH 94801 588-E7
FOLSOM AV
- HAY 94544 712-C7
100 HAY 94544 732-A1
1300 SPAB 94806 588-G3
1600 HAY 94544 731-J1
FOLSOM CIR
400 MPS 95035 794-A6
FOLSOM CT
400 MPS 95035 794-A6
4000 CNCD 94520 572-G3
FOLSOM DR
3900 ANT 94509 575-H7
3900 ANT 94509 595-J1
FOLSOM PL
100 MPS 95035 794-A6
FOLSOM ST
- SF 94105 648-B6
400 SF 94110 667-J4
600 SF 94107 648-B6
600 SF 94103 648-A7
1300 SF 94103 647-J7
1300 SF 94103 667-J1
2000 SF 94110 667-J4
FOLSUM WY
4900 FRMT 94538 753-A7
FONDRAY CT
8200 PLE 94586 734-D1
FONICK DR
400 SJS 95111 875-C1
FONT BLVD
- SF 94132 667-A7
200 SF 94132 687-B1
FONTAINBLEAU TER
300 LALT 94022 811-E5
FONTAINBLEU AV
1200 MPS 95035 794-A4
FONTAINBLEU CT
100 MPS 95035 794-A4
FONTAINE CT
300 DNVL 94506 653-H5
4100 OAK 94605 671-B2
FONTAINE DR
300 DNVL 94506 653-H5
13300 SAR 95070 852-G7
FONTAINE RD
2400 SJS 95121 854-J2
FONTAINE ST
7900 OAK 94605 671-A3
FONTAINEBLEAU PARK LN
42800 FRMT 94538 773-C2
FONTANA
- NVTO 94945 526-B2
FONTANA CT
3300 ANT 94509 595-C1
FONTANA DR
200 SCL 95051 833-B7
1000 ALA 94502 669-J6
FONTANA PL
3300 ANT 94509 595-B1

BAY AREA

INDEX

STREET
Block City ZIP Pg-Grid

FONTANELLE CT
400 SJS 95111 875-C2
FONTANELLE DR
300 SJS 95111 875-C1
FONTANELLE PL
4900 SJS 95111 875-C1
FONTANOSO WY
400 SJS 95138 875-D3
FONTENAY WY
- SJS 95135 855-G3
FONTENBLEU
1400 SUNV 94087 832-B4
FONTES DR
600 FRMT 94539 753-G6
FONTEVILLE CT
- SJS 95127 834-C2
FONTINELLA TER
- SF 94107 668-A4
FONTONETT AV
300 LVMR 94550 715-D3
FONTONETT PL
1500 LVMR 94550 715-D3
FOOTE AV
- CMBL 95008 853-E6
- SF 94112 687-E1
FOOTHILL AV
1500 PIN 94564 569-E5
2300 RCH 94804 608-H1
FOOTHILL BLVD
100 OAK 94606 649-J5
900 OAK 94606 650-A6
2300 OAK 94601 650-A6
3800 OAK 94601 670-G1
5500 OAK 94605 671-A5
5500 OAK 94605 670-G1
7500 SLN 94577 671-B5
10000 CPTO 95014 852-A1
15000 AlaC 94578 691-F4
17000 AlaC 94546 691-F4
17000 AlaC 94541 691-F4
FOOTHILL BLVD
Rt#-238
17200 AlaC 94546 691-H6
20800 AlaC 94541 691-H6
21000 HAY 94541 691-H6
21800 HAY 94541 711-J1
FOOTHILL BLVD
Rt#-G5
8100 CPTO 95014 832-A6
8100 LALT 94024 832-A6
8400 SCIC 94024 832-A6
8700 CPTO 94024 832-A6
FOOTHILL CT
- ANT - 594-J2
- CCCo - 594-J2
- DNVL 94506 653-G5
800 SJS 95123 874-F6
2400 ANT 94509 594-J2
FOOTHILL DR
100 VAL 94591 530-D1
600 PCFA 94044 707-B3
700 SJS 95123 874-E5
700 SMTO 94402 748-H4
900 SMCo 94015 687-A4
2300 ANT 94509 595-A2
2400 ANT 94509 594-J2
FOOTHILL EXWY
Rt#-G5
100 LALT 94022 811-C5
100 LALT 94022 831-F1
200 LALT 94024 831-F1
400 SCIC 94024 831-F1
2600 SCIC 94304 810-J3
2600 PA 94304 810-J3
2800 PA 94304 811-C5
2800 SCIC 94304 811-C5
4100 PA 94306 811-C5
4400 LALT 94024 832-A6
7100 CPTO 95014 832-A6
14000 LAH 94022 811-C5
14000 SCIC 94306 811-C5
FOOTHILL LN
- PLE 94588 714-A4
12100 LAH 94022 831-A1
12800 SAR 95070 852-D6
FOOTHILL PL
- PLE 94588 714-A4
- PLHL 94523 591-J2
1200 OAK 94606 650-A6
FOOTHILL RD
- SANS 94960 566-A7
1700 PLE 94588 693-G6
1700 PLE 94588 714-B5
2900 PLE 94588 713-J1
3200 AlaC 94588 713-J1
3700 PLE 94586 713-J1
7000 AlaC 94586 734-D5
7500 PLE 94586 693-G6
7500 AlaC 94566 734-C1
7500 PLE 94566 734-C1
7500 PLE 94566 734-C1
7800 AlaC 94566 714-C7
7900 AlaC 94586 693-G6
7900 AlaC 94588 714-B5
8000 AlaC 94588 693-G6
FOOTHILL ST
1100 RDWC 94061 789-H2
FOOTHILL WY
4200 PIT 94565 574-E7
5900 SLN 94605 671-C7
5900 OAK 94605 671-C7
FOOTHILL GLEN CT
6000 SJS 95123 874-F6
FOOTHILL GLEN DR
6000 SJS 95123 874-F6
FOOTHILL KNOLLS DR
7800 PLE 94588 714-A2
7900 PLE 94588 713-J3
FOOTHILL MEADOWS CT
1400 SJS 95131 814-C7
FOOTHILL OAKS DR
2800 PLE 94588 714-A4
FOOTHILL OAKS TER
7900 PLE 94588 714-A4
FOOTHILL PARK CIR
1600 CCCo 94549 611-J1
FOOTHILL PARK TER
- CCCo 94549 611-J1
FORBES AV
- SANS 94960 566-D7
- SRFL 94901 566-E7
FORBES AV
2100 SCL 95050 833-B6
2500 SCL 95051 833-A6
3200 SCL 95051 832-J6
FORBES BLVD
300 SSF 94080 708-B3
FORBES CT
3100 SCL 95051 833-A6
FORBES DR
6200 SJS 95123 874-J7
FORBES ST
21000 HAY 94545 711-C5
FORD AL
200 VAL 94590 529-J5
300 VAL 94590 530-A5
FORD AV
1400 SJS 95110 854-D2
FORD CT
2800 ANT 94509 575-A7
FORD DR
1400 CNCD 94521 593-F6
FORD LN
- FRMT 94536 753-B2
3100 LFYT 94549 611-J6
FORD RD
- SJS 95138 875-C4
FORD ST
- SF 94114 667-G2
400 DALY 94014 687-D4
2800 OAK 94601 670-B1
FORD WY
- NVTO 94947 526-C5
FORDHAM AV
1200 SLN 94579 691-A4
FORDHAM CIR
100 VAL 94589 510-B5
FORDHAM CT
- PLHL 94523 592-C3
1500 MTVW 94040 811-G7
4000 LVMR 94550 696-A7
41500 FRMT 94539 753-F6
FORDHAM DR
2000 SCL 95051 832-J2
2500 RCH 94806 589-A2
2500 RCH 94806 588-J2
FORDHAM RD
500 SMTO 94402 748-J2
FORDHAM ST
2300 CCCo 94806 589-A3
2300 SPAB 94806 589-A3
2400 EPA 94303 791-B1
2400 RCH 94806 589-A3
2500 EPA 94303 771-C7
FORDHAM WY
1100 MTVW 94040 811-G7
1600 MTVW 94040 831-G1
3900 LVMR 94550 696-A7
3900 LVMR 94550 695-J7
FORDWELL CT
- SJS 95138 875-D4
FORE ST
- MLV 94941 606-B3
FOREMAN LN
- MrnC 94941 606-H5
FOREMAST CV
- CMAD 94925 606-J1
FORENZA CT
- PLE 94566 715-B5
FORESAIL CT
200 FCTY 94404 749-G4
FOREST AV
- LGTS 95030 873-B6
100 PA 94301 790-J5
600 PA 94301 791-A3
1900 BLMT 94002 749-B7
2100 BLMT 94002 769-B1
2300 SJS 95050 833-E7
2300 SJS 95128 833-F7
2300 SCL 95128 833-F7
2400 SCL 95050 833-E7
2700 BERK 94705 629-J3
2800 BERK 94705 630-A3
3100 SCL 95128 833-E7
3100 SJS 95117 833-C7
3100 SCL 95117 833-C7
19500 AlaC 94546 692-B5
20000 CPTO 95014 832-E7
FOREST CT
1000 PA 94301 791-A3
1700 CNCD 94521 593-B2
1800 MPS 95035 813-J4
4300 AlaC 94546 692-B4
FOREST GN
4200 AlaC 94546 692-B4
FOREST LN
- BERK 94708 609-H5
- SBRN 94066 707-H6
- SCAR 94070 769-F5
100 MLPK 94025 790-E2
800 CCCo 94507 632-G7
800 CCCo 94507 652-G1
900 LVMR 94550 715-G2
FOREST PK
- HER 94547 569-G3
FOREST PL
3700 AlaC 94546 692-B4
FOREST RUN
500 HER 94547 569-G3
FOREST ST
400 OAK 94618 629-J5
FOREST WY
100 MRTZ 94553 591-F1
600 MrnC 94965 606-D7
FORESTBROOK WY
4000 SJS 95111 855-A7
FOREST CREEK DR
1100 SJS 95129 852-J3
FOREST CREEK LN
- SRMN 94583 673-A2
FORESTDALE AV
700 SJS 95116 834-E7
FORESTER CT
700 LVMR 94550 695-J6
3800 SJS 95121 855-E3
FOREST GLEN DR
5000 SJS 95129 852-J2
FOREST GREEN CT
5300 CNCD 94521 593-D5
FOREST GROVE DR
- DALY 94015 687-B3
FOREST HILL AV
3800 OAK 94602 650-D4
FOREST HILL COM
4900 FRMT 94555 752-C2
FOREST HILL DR
- CLAY 94517 594-A7
- CLAY 94517 593-J7
100 LGTS 95032 873-G5
300 VAL 94589 509-H5
2600 SJS 95130 852-J7
4900 PLE 94588 693-H7
N FOREST HILL PL
1800 DNVL 94526 653-B7
S FOREST HILL PL
1900 DNVL 94526 653-B7
FOREST HILLS CT
- WLCK 94596 612-A2
FOREST HILLS DR
20400 SAR 95070 872-D3
FOREST KNOLL DR
1000 SJS 95129 852-G3
FOREST KNOLLS DR
- SF 94131 667-E3
FOREST LAKE DR
600 PCFA 94044 707-B3
FOREST LAKE PL
2100 MRTZ 94553 592-A1
FORESTLAND WY
6600 OAK 94611 630-G7
FOREST PARK CT
200 PCFA 94044 707-A2
FOREST PARK DR
100 SCL 95051 833-A7
FOREST RIDGE DR
100 VAL 94591 530-G4
800 SJS 95129 852-J2
FOREST SIDE AV
- SF 94116 667-C5
- SF 94127 667-C5
FOREST SPRING CT
11500 CPTO 95014 852-C4
FOREST VIEW AV
- HIL 94010 728-D7
1500 BURL 94010 728-E7
FORESTVIEW AV
4000 CNCD 94521 593-A2
FOREST VIEW DR
- SF 94132 667-A6
200 SSF 94080 707-G2
5000 SJS 95129 852-J2
FORESTWOOD DR
3800 SJS 95121 855-D3
FORGE DR
18900 CPTO 95014 832-H6
FORGE RD
1400 SMCo 94402 748-F7
FORGEMILL CT
1000 SJS 95121 854-J4
FORGETREE CT
2000 SJS 95131 814-C5
FORGEWOOD AV
1200 SUNV 94089 812-J3
S FORK DR
1700 SF - 666-H1
FORMAN AV
1600 SJS 95124 873-J3
FORMAN DR
500 CMBL 95008 853-F7
FORMOSA DR
1200 SJS 95131 814-B7
FORMOSA RIDGE DR
3300 SJS 95127 835-B3
FORMWAY CT
100 LALT 94022 811-F6
FORNI DR
5000 CCCo 94520 572-F3
FORREST AV
- FRFX 94930 566-A6
- SANS 94960 566-A6
FORREST CT
- MrnC 94960 566-A4
2600 FRMT 94536 753-A3
FORREST LN
- SRFL 94903 566-C3
FORREST RD
- MrnC 94947 526-A5
- NVTO 94947 526-A5
- NVTO 94947 525-J5
7600 CCCo 94803 589-F1
FORREST ST
- MLV 94941 606-D3
FORRESTAL AV
1200 SJS 95110 833-J2
FORRESTAL LN
1100 FCTY 94404 749-G4
FORRESTER CT
200 LGTS 95032 893-D1
FORRESTER RD
200 LGTS 95032 893-D1
FORREST HILL CT
4100 HAY 94542 712-G3
FORREST VIEW RD
- WDSD 94062 809-G3
FORSELLES WY
1100 HAY 94544 712-A7
FORSUM CT
100 SJS 95138 875-G6
FORSUM RD
7200 SJS 95138 875-G6
FORSYTHIA CT
100 VAL 94589 510-A5
7700 PLE 94588 713-J1
FORSYTHIA DR
42200 FRMT 94539 753-G6
FORSYTHIA WY
2200 MRTZ 94553 571-J6
FORT BAKER DR
900 CPTO 95014 852-B2
FORTE LN
5300 CNCD 94521 593-E5
FORTINI RD
21100 SCIC 95120 895-B4
FORT LARAMIE DR
500 SUNV 94087 832-D5
FORTMANN WY
- ALA 94501 649-J7
FORTNER ST
47500 FRMT 94539 773-H7
FORTRAN CT
4400 SJS 95134 813-D1
FORTRAN DR
4400 SJS 95134 813-D1
FORTRESS ISL
600 ALA 94501 669-H2
FORTROSE CT
- SJS 95139 875-H7
FORT ROYAL PL
4600 SJS 95136 874-F2
FORTUNA AV
- SF 94115 647-F6
400 SLN 94577 671-C7
FORTUNA COM
600 FRMT 94539 753-H5
FORTUNA CT
2500 ANT 94509 575-B6
13600 SAR 95070 872-H1
FORTUNE DR
1700 SJS 95131 814-B4
FORTUNE WY
5900 OAK 94605 670-G2
FORTY NINER WY
2500 ANT 94509 595-G4
FOSCALINA CT
- LVMR 94550 715-H3
FOSCALINA WY
- LVMR 94550 715-H4
FOSGATE AV
2300 SCL 95050 833-D7
FOSKETT AV
2800 CNCD 94520 572-E6
FOSS AV
- SANS 94960 586-B1
- SJS 95116 834-H3
FOSS CT
- CCCo 94596 612-D1
FOSS DR
- RDWC 94062 789-G1
- RDWC 94062 769-H7
- SMCo 94062 769-H7
FOSTER AV
100 OAK 94603 670-G7
100 MrnC 94903 586-D3
FOSTER CT
- OAK 94603 670-G7
600 HAY 94544 712-A6
1500 SJS 95120 874-A7
FOSTER LN
- SRFL 94901 566-E7
4100 CCCo 94803 589-C2
FOSTER RD
100 LGTS 95032 893-B2
800 SCIC 95032 893-B2
18200 SCIC 95032 893-A2
FOSTER ST
- MRTZ 94553 571-C3
100 VAL 94591 530-D4
1000 ALA 94502 669-J6
2600 SMTO 94403 749-D4
40400 FRMT 94538 753-C6
FOSTER CITY BLVD
300 FCTY 94404 749-F2
FOSTORIA CIR
200 DNVL 94526 653-D7
FOSTORIA WY
3000 SRMN 94583 673-C1
3000 SRMN 94526 673-C1
3000 DNVL 94526 673-C1
3100 SRMN 94583 653-D7
3100 DNVL 94526 653-D7
FOULKSTONE WY
100 VAL 94591 550-E2
FOUNDERS LN
800 MPS 95035 794-B4
FOUNDRY CT
500 SJS 95133 834-G1
FOUNT WY
26100 HAY 94545 711-F6
FOUNTAIN CIR
100 SJS 95131 814-A4
FOUNTAIN ST
- SF 94114 667-F4
900 ALA 94501 670-A4
FOUNTAIN WK
- BERK 94707 609-G6
FOUNTAIN CIRCLE DR
- SMCo - 768-D4
FOUNTAINE AV
6500 NWK 94560 752-D6
FOUNTAINHEAD CT
- MRTZ 94553 572-A7
700 SRMN 94583 673-B2
FOUNTAINHEAD DR
600 SLN 94578 691-C5
2500 SRMN 94583 673-A2
FOUNTAIN PARK LN
800 MTVW 94043 811-J4
FOUNTAIN SPRINGS CIR
1300 DNVL 94526 653-B6
FOUNTAIN SPRINGS DR
1300 DNVL 94526 653-B6
FOUNTAIN VIEW DR
3700 SJS 95136 854-G7
FOUNTIAN PALM CT
- SJS 95133 814-J4
FOURIER AV
100 FRMT 94539 773-H7
FOURIER DR
800 SJS 95127 835-C2
FOUR OAKS CIR
1400 SJS 95131 814-D6
FOUR OAKS CT
2300 SJS 95131 814-D5
FOUR OAKS LN
5800 CLAY 94517 593-G6
FOUR OAKS RD
1400 SJS 95131 814-D5
FOUR SEASONS CT
2300 SJS 95131 814-D5
FOUR SEASONS PL
- AlaC 94541 691-F7
FOURTH PLAIN CT
2700 SJS 95121 855-D3
FOWLER AV
- SF 94127 667-E4
3100 SCL 95051 833-A3
3200 SCL 95051 832-J3
FOWLER CT
- SRFL 94903 566-C3
32700 UNC 94587 732-A7
FOWLER LN
1400 LALT 94024 831-J3
FOWLER RD
2800 SJS 95135 855-G2
3500 SCIC 95135 855-J2
FOX AV
- FRMT 94536 732-H7
- FRMT 94536 752-J1
- SJS 95110 834-A5
FOX CIR
2500 WLCK 94596 632-G2
FOX CT
- NVTO 94945 526-C4
W FOX CT
500 RDWC 94061 790-C1
FOX DR
1800 SJS 95131 814-A6
FOX LN
- MrnC 94960 566-B3
800 SJS 95131 814-A5
FOX RUN
600 ORIN 94563 610-H6
FOX WY
2000 CNCD 94518 592-F5
FOXBORO CIR
10000 SRMN 94583 673-F4
FOXBORO CT
300 SRMN 94583 673-F5
FOXBORO DR
5000 AlaC 94546 692-A2
FOXBORO PL
3200 SJS 95135 855-E3
FOXBORO WY
9900 SRMN 94583 673-F5
FOXBOROUGH DR
300 MTVW 94041 812-A6
FOX BROUGH CT
700 PLE 94566 714-H3
FOXCHASE DR
900 SJS 95123 874-D4
FOX CREEK CT
1400 LVMR 94550 696-D2
4000 CCCo 94506 654-C2
FOX CREEK DR
3100 CCCo 94506 654-C2
FOXCROFT PL
- SRMN 94583 673-F6
1800 HAY 94541 692-B7
FOX CROSSING CT
100 SMCo 94062 789-F1
FOXDALE CT
1500 SJS 95122 834-J5
FOXDALE DR
2400 SJS 95122 834-J5
2500 SJS 95122 835-A5
FOXDALE LP
1200 SJS 95122 835-A5
1200 SJS 95122 834-J5
FOXFIRE LN
28800 HAY 94544 732-B1
FOX GLEN PL
800 CCCo 94598 613-B3
FOXGLOVE DR
900 SUNV 94086 832-G2
FOXGLOVE LN
- CCCo 94596 592-D7
FOXHALL CT
- DNVL 94526 653-C3
FOXHALL LP
1900 SJS 95125 853-G4
FOXHILL DR
2200 MRTZ 94553 572-A6
FOX HILL RD
- SMCo 94062 809-G3
FOX HILLS CT
400 OAK 94605 671-E3
FOX HOLLOW
1400 CNCD 94521 592-J3
FOXHOLLOW CT
1100 MPS 95035 794-C5
FOX HOLLOW DR
28000 HAY 94542 712-G3
FOX HOLLOW LN
- RDWC 94061 789-F3
FOXHOLLOW LN
- DALY 94014 687-E3
FOX HOLLOW PL
- NVTO 94945 526-B1
FOX HOLLOW RD
100 WDSD 94062 789-G7
FOXHURST WY
1000 SJS 95120 894-G4
FOX MEADOW CT
1100 SJS 95120 894-G4
FOX MEADOW WY
1000 CNCD 94518 592-F5
FOX PLAZA LN
1400 BURL 94010 728-G7
FOX RIDGE CT
1900 WLCK 94596 611-H3
FOX RIDGE DR
- AlaC 94546 691-G4
FOXRIDGE PL
800 SJS 95133 814-G7
FOXRIDGE WY
800 SJS 95133 814-G6
FOX SPARROW LN
- BSBN 94005 687-J5
FOXSWALLOW CIR
1800 PLE 94566 714-D1
FOXSWALLOW CT
900 SJS 95120 894-G2
FOXSWALLOW RD
2000 PLE 94566 714-D1
FOXSWALLOW TER
3700 FRMT 94555 732-J3
FOXTAIL
- PTLV 94028 830-C1
FOX TAIL CT
- CCCo - 613-B3
FOXTAIL DR
- LVMR 94550 696-E3
600 SUNV 94086 832-F2
FOXTAIL TER
3200 FRMT 94536 752-J3
FOXWELL CT
- SJS 95138 875-D4
FOXWOOD DR
1200 SJS 95118 874-C4
FOXWOOD RD
100 SMCo 94028 830-D4
FOXWOOD WY
1200 SJS 95118 874-C4
FOXWORTHY AV
1000 SJS 95125 854-B7
1000 SJS 95136 854-C7
1000 SJS 95118 854-B7
FOXWORTHY AV
1200 SJS 95125 874-A1
1200 SJS 95118 874-A1
1500 SJS 95120 873-G1
1500 SJS 95125 873-G1
1500 SJS 95124 873-F1
FOYE DR
900 LFYT 94549 611-G6
FRAGA CT
400 MRTZ 94553 571-J6
FRAGA RD
3700 AlaC 94552 692-D5
FRAGRANT HARBOR CT
200 SJS 95123 874-J3
FRAMPTON CT
25600 LAH 94024 831-E4
FRAN CT
- SJS 95123 874-F7
FRAN WY
4100 RCH 94803 589-E1
FRANCE AV
- SF 94112 687-F1
FRANCE RD
4700 FRMT 94555 752-D2
FRANCE WY
34300 FRMT 94555 752-D2
FRANCEMONT DR
24800 LAH 94022 831-B3
FRANCES AV
- LKSP 94939 586-D4
- PCFA 94044 707-A6
- MrnC 94904 586-D4
N FRANCES AV
100 SUNV 94086 812-E7
FRANCES DR
200 LALT 94022 811-E6
FRANCES RD
1100 CCCo 94806 569-A5
FRANCES ST
- SRFL 94901 586-F1
2400 OAK 94601 650-E7
S FRANCES ST
100 SUNV 94086 812-E7
400 SUNV 94086 832-E1
FRANCES WY
- CCCo 94596 612-D2
400 MTVW 94041 811-J6
FRANCESCA WY
- CCCo 94507 632-E4
FRANCHERE PL
1300 SUNV 94087 832-B4
FRANCINE CT
1100 CNCD 94518 592-G3
FRANCINE WY
5300 LVMR 94550 696-C7
FRANCIS AV
- SANS 94960 566-A6
- FRFX 94930 566-A6
1600 BLMT 94002 769-D1
1900 SCL 95051 833-A2
FRANCIS CT
500 MRTZ 94553 591-G4
1700 BLMT 94002 769-D1
3100 AlaC 94546 691-J6
FRANCIS DR
300 SJS 95133 834-H1
300 SCIC 95133 834-H1
400 SJS 95133 814-H7
400 SCIC 95133 814-H7
500 MRTZ 94553 591-G4
500 CCCo 94549 591-G4
2500 PIN 94564 569-F4
FRANCIS LN
- SANS 94960 566-C6
200 RDWC 94070 769-G6
200 SCAR 94062 769-G6
200 SCAR 94070 769-G6
FRANCIS ST
- SF 94112 667-G7
1200 CCCo 94525 550-D5
1400 ALB 94706 609-E7
20900 AlaC 94546 691-J6
FRANCISCA CT
1000 PIN 94564 569-E5
1700 BEN 94510 551-C4
FRANCISCA DR
- MRGA 94556 631-E3
FRANCISCAN CT
- DNVL 94526 653-C7
200 FRMT 94539 773-H6
2400 SCL 95051 833-B2
2900 SCAR 94070 769-F6
6100 SJS 95120 874-A7
FRANCISCAN DR
- DALY 94014 687-E5
100 DNVL 94526 653-C7
100 VAL 94589 530-C1
FRANCISCAN RDGE
- PTLV 94028 830-C1
FRANCISCAN WY
- CCCo 94707 609-E3
- ELCR 94530 609-E3
1900 ALA 94501 669-H3
6100 SJS 95120 874-A7
6100 SJS 95120 894-A1
FRANCISCO AV
1100 SJS 95126 853-H4
FRANCISCO BLVD
300 SRFL 94901 586-H2
1100 SRFL 94901 587-A4
1600 PCFA 94044 706-J6
2200 PCFA 94044 707-A7
FRANCISCO CT
- ORIN 94563 631-A5
600 WLCK 94598 612-E2
S FRANCISCO CT
1600 ANT 94509 575-A7
FRANCISCO DR
100 SSF 94080 707-G4
500 BURL 94010 728-G6
FRANCISCO LN
- FRMT 94539 773-G6
FRANCISCO ST
- SF 94133 648-A3
400 SF 94133 647-J3
800 SF 94109 647-J3
1100 BERK 94702 629-E1
1200 BERK 94703 629-F1
1200 SF 94123 647-G3
1900 BERK 94709 629-F1
4000 PLE 94566 714-E1
22800 HAY 94541 711-J2
FRANCISCO WY
1900 CCCo 94805 589-C6
1900 ELCR 94530 589-C6
N FRANCISCO WY
2900 ANT 94509 575-A7
S FRANCISCO WY
3100 ANT 94509 575-A7
3100 ANT 94509 595-B1
FRANCISCO VISTA CT
- TBRN 94920 607-B5
FRANCIS OAKS WY
15200 LGTS 95032 873-E6
FRANCK AV
1600 SCL 95051 833-B3
FRANCO CT
10800 CPTO 95014 832-D6
FRANCONE CT
23800 AlaC 94541 692-C7
FRANCONIA ST
- SF 94110 668-A4
FRANDON CT
4100 PA 94306 811-C3
FRANELA DR
3000 SJS 95124 873-J1
FRANICISCO BLVD W
200 SRFL 94901 586-H2
FRANK AV
16700 LGTS 95032 873-C5
FRANK CT
2000 MPS 95035 794-E6
16900 LGTS 95032 873-C5
FRANK PL
5600 CLAY 94517 593-G5
FRANKE LN
3900 LFYT 94549 611-B6
FRANKFORT ST
- DALY 94014 687-E3
FRANKFURT ST
1100 SJS 95126 833-G5
FRANKFURT WY
1400 LVMR 94550 715-G3
FRANKLIN AV
- UNC 94587 732-B4
- SSF 94080 707-H1
200 CCCo 94565 573-H3
600 NVTO 94945 526-C4
3500 FRMT 94538 773-E1
13000 MTVW 94040 832-A1
20100 SAR 95070 872-E1
25400 HAY 94544 712-A4
FRANKLIN CT
700 SJS 95127 814-H6
22400 MTVW 94040 832-A1
FRANKLIN DR
4900 PLE 94588 694-A5
FRANKLIN LN
400 LVMR 94550 696-C4
600 CCCo 94803 569-E7
1200 LFYT 94549 611-D5
FRANKLIN ST
- OAK 94607 649-G3
- RDWC 94063 770-B6
- SF 94102 647-H4
100 MTVW 94041 811-H5
100 VAL 94591 530-D4
200 SMTO 94402 748-H2
400 SCL 95050 833-E4
700 SCL 95053 833-E4
900 SF 94109 647-H4
1200 OAK 94612 649-G3
1500 BERK 94702 629-F1
2400 SF 94123 647-H4
2600 SF 94123 647-H3
FRANKLIN CANYON RD
1400 MRTZ 94553 571-A5
1600 CCCo 94553 571-A5
2300 CCCo 94553 570-H3
FRANKS LN
1400 SMCo 94025 790-D5
FRANQUETTE AV
800 SJS 95125 854-B5
1200 CNCD 94520 592-D3
FRANROSE LN
1600 CNCD 94519 593-A2
FRANZ CT
100 PCFA 94044 727-A1
FRASCHINI CIR
5300 SJS 95123 874-H3
FRASER CT
- WLCK 94596 612-E6
2500 PIN 94564 569-F4
FRASER DR
- WLCK 94596 612-E6
1500 SUNV 94087 832-B5
FRASER RD
3200 ANT 94509 595-C1
FRATESSA CT
- SF 94134 688-A2
FRAY AV
4900 RCH 94804 609-B1
FRAY PTH
- RCH 94804 609-B1
FRAYNE CT
800 CNCD 94518 592-H6
FRAYNE LN
2800 CNCD 94518 592-H6
FRAZIER AV
2600 OAK 94605 671-B5
FREDA CT
300 MRTZ 94553 571-D6
1200 CMBL 95008 873-A1
FREDA DR
100 CCCo 94553 572-B7
FREDA LN
- SANS 94960 566-C6
FREDELA LN
- SF 94131 667-E3
FREDERIC AV
300 HAY 94544 711-J4
FREDERICK AV
- ATN 94027 790-H1
600 SCL 95050 833-D5
FREDERICK CT
- SMCo 94025 790-H1
100 LALT 94022 811-E6
FREDERICK LN
33900 FRMT 94555 752-C1
FREDERICK RD
700 SLN 94577 690-H1
4800 FRMT 94555 752-C1
FREDERICK ST
- SF 94117 667-E1

STREET
Block City ZIP Pg-Grid

FREDERICK ST
400 SF 94117 667-D1
2100 CNCD 94520 572-F7
2100 OAK 94606 650-A7
FREDERICK MICHAEL WY
1500 LVMR 94550 715-G4
FREDERICKSBURG CT
12200 SAR 95070 852-E6
FREDERICKSBURG DR
12100 SAR 95070 852-E6
FREDERICKSON LN
- ANT - 595-C4
- CCCo - 595-C4
FREDERIKA AV
400 LFYT 94549 631-G3
FREDERIKSEN CT
7500 DBLN 94568 693-H3
FREDERIKSEN LN
7400 DBLN 94568 693-H3
FREDI ST
31000 UNC 94587 731-J5
FREDSON CT
- NVTO 94947 525-J3
- SF 94112 687-E2
FREED AV
2100 PIT 94565 574-E4
3900 SJS 95117 853-B4
FREED CIR
1500 PIT 94565 574-E4
FREEDOM AV
15000 AlaC 94578 691-E3
FREEDOM CIR
3900 SCL 95054 813-B6
FREEDOM CT
100 FRMT 94539 773-J2
3600 ANT 94509 595-C3
6700 SJS 95120 894-C5
FREEDOM DR
21000 CPTO 95014 832-C7
FREEDOM LN
- MTVW 94040 811-E3
FREEDOM WY
3600 ANT 94509 595-B1
FREELAND DR
1400 MPS 95035 794-D7
FREELON ST
- SF 94107 648-B7
FREEMAN AV
14800 SCIC 95127 814-J6
14800 SJS 95127 814-J6
FREEMAN CT
- CCCo 94595 612-A7
- SF 94108 648-A5
2100 ANT 94509 595-A1
FREEMAN PL
2800 FRMT 94555 732-E6
FREEMAN RD
3300 CCCo 94595 611-J7
3300 LFYT 94549 611-J7
3400 CCCo 94595 612-A7
FREEMAN ST
- SF 94129 647-E4
FREESIA CT
600 SLN 94578 691-C4
FREESTONE AV
1000 SUNV 94087 832-B2
FREETHY BLVD
200 RCH 94801 588-F1
FRWY I-80
- OAK - 649-B1
- SF - 648-B7
- SF - 648-E4
- SF - 668-A1
- SolC - 550-D3
- SolC - 510-E4
- SolC - 530-D1
- VAL - 550-C2
- VAL - 510-E4
- VAL - 530-D1
FRWY I-238
- AlaC - 691-E6
- SLN - 691-E6
FRWY I-280
- DALY - 687-C2
- DALY - 707-C1
- SF - 687-D2
- SF - 687-E1
FRWY I-380
- SBRN - 708-A6
- SBRN - 707-H6
- SMCo - 708-A6
- SSF - 708-A5
FRWY I-580
- AlaC - 693-B5
- AlaC - 692-B6
- AlaC - 693-C5
- AlaC - 694-D5
- AlaC - 694-D5
- AlaC - 694-D5
- AlaC - 696-G2
- AlaC - 691-G6
- AlaC - 692-H4
- AlaC - 695-H5
- AlaC - 691-H6
- DBLN - 694-D5
- DBLN - 693-H5
- LVMR - 694-D5
- LVMR - 694-D5
- LVMR - 696-G2
- LVMR - 695-H5
- MrnC - 587-C5
- PLE - 693-C5
- PLE - 694-D5
- PLE - 693-H5
- SRFL - 587-A4
FRWY I-680
- AlaC - 714-C5
- AlaC - 714-C5
- AlaC - 714-C5
- AlaC - 714-C5
- AlaC - 734-D2
- AlaC - 734-D2
- AlaC - 754-B2
- AlaC - 753-J3
- BEN - 551-F7
- CCCo - 572-A5
- CCCo - 571-H2
- CCCo - 592-C2
- CCCo - 612-C1
- CCCo - 632-G6
FRWY I-680
- CNCD - 592-C2
- DBLN - 693-H4
- DNVL - 632-G6
- DNVL - 653-A3
- DNVL - 652-J1
- DNVL - 673-C2
- FRMT - 753-G6
- FRMT - 773-F1
- MRTZ - 551-F7
- MRTZ - 571-H2
- PLE - 693-H4
- PLE - 714-C5
- PLE - 714-C5
- PLE - 713-J1
- PLHL - 592-D6
- PLHL - 612-C1
- SRMN - 653-A3
- SRMN - 673-C2
- SRMN - 693-H4
- SolC - 551-F7
- WLCK - 612-B5
- WLCK - 632-E1
FRWY I-780
- BEN - 530-F7
- SolC - 530-F7
- VAL - 530-F7
- BEN - 551-D5
- BEN - 550-H2
FRWY Rt#-4
- ANT - 575-A5
- ANT - 574-H5
- CCCo - 573-C3
- CCCo - 572-D5
- CNCD - 573-C3
- CNCD - 572-H4
- PIT - 574-B3
- PIT - 573-C3
FRWY Rt#-17
- CMBL - 853-F3
- CMBL - 873-D2
- LGTS - 873-D3
- LGTS - 893-A1
- SCIC - 873-D2
- SJS - 853-F3
FRWY Rt#-24
- CCCo - 612-A5
- CCCo - 611-E6
- CCCo - 630-G2
- CCCo - 630-G2
- LFYT - 611-B6
- OAK - 629-H6
- OAK - 629-J5
- OAK - 630-B4
- OAK - 630-B4
- ORIN - 611-B6
- ORIN - 610-H6
- ORIN - 630-G2
- ORIN - 630-G2
- WLCK - 612-B5
FRWY Rt#-84
- FRMT - 752-B5
- NWK - 752-B5
4400 FRMT - 752-B5
FRWY Rt#-85
- CPTO - 852-C1
- SAR - 852-E5
- SCIC - 852-C2
- SJS - 852-D4
FRWY Rt#-92
- HAY - 711-H4
- HAY - 711-H5
- HAY - 731-B1
FRWY Rt#-242
- CNCD - 572-F6
- CNCD - 592-D4
- PLHL - 592-D4
FREITAS CT
300 DNVL 94526 653-C3
FREITAS DR
- MRGA 94556 651-E1
FREITAS PL
26800 HAY 94544 712-B5
FREITAS RD
400 DNVL 94526 653-B3
FREMEREY CT
400 DNVL 94506 653-G1
FREMERY CT
19600 AlaC 94546 692-A4
FREMONT AV
- SUNV 94087 832-A3
100 LALT 94022 831-E1
100 LALT 94024 831-E1
200 PCFA 94044 707-A3
800 SLN 94577 691-B4
800 SLN 94578 691-B4
1500 LALT 94024 832-A3
1700 SUNV 94024 832-A3
E FREMONT AV
500 SUNV 94087 832-E4
1000 SCIC 94087 832-E4
W FREMONT AV
500 SUNV 94087 832-B3
1200 SUNV 94024 832-B3
FREMONT BLVD
34000 FRMT 94555 732-D7
34000 FRMT - 752-E1
34000 FRMT 94555 752-E1
35000 FRMT 94536 752-E1
38200 FRMT 94536 753-A5
39000 FRMT 94538 753-A5
41500 FRMT 94538 773-D1
47000 FRMT 94538 793-F1
FREMONT BLVD Rt#-84
36800 FRMT 94536 752-H3
FREMONT CT
100 HER 94547 570-B5
FREMONT DR
1800 ALA 94501 670-B2
FREMONT PL
900 MLPK 94025 790-F4
FREMONT RD
- SRFL 94901 586-E1
500 SCIC 94305 790-F7
13400 LAH 94022 811-D7
W FREMONT RD
25000 LAH 94022 811-B5
FREMONT ST
- SF 94105 648-B5
100 VAL 94589 530-A1
500 MLPK 94025 790-F4
FREMONT ST
600 SCL 95050 833-D4
1100 SJS 95126 833-H6
1800 CNCD 94520 592-E1
5500 OAK 94608 629-E5
N FREMONT ST
- SMTO 94401 728-J7
- SMTO 94401 749-A1
S FREMONT ST
- SMTO 94401 749-A1
400 SMTO 94402 749-A1
FREMONT TER W
1200 SUNV 94087 832-C3
FREMONT WY
- SMCo 94020 809-F6
1700 OAK 94601 670-E1
FREMONTIA
- PTLV 94028 830-C1
FREMONT PINES LN
13800 LAH 94022 811-C6
FRENCH CT
- SF 94129 647-E4
100 SJS 95139 895-G1
400 MLPK 94025 791-A3
1300 MPS 95035 814-D2
FRENCH ST
2500 SCL 95051 832-J2
2500 SUNV 94086 832-J2
FRENCH CREEK PL
- SMCo 94402 768-G2
FRENCHMANS RD
700 SCIC 94305 810-H2
FRENCH OAK DR
8600 SJS 95135 855-J6
FRENI CT
1400 SJS 95121 854-J2
FRESHMEADOW CT
700 HAY 94544 732-E1
FRESHWATER CT
- PIT - 573-F5
2200 MRTZ 94553 572-B2
FRESNO AV
900 BERK 94707 609-F6
5100 RCH 94804 609-B4
FRESNO CT
26300 HAY 94545 711-F6
FRESNO ST
- SF 94133 648-A4
- VAL 94590 530-B4
2800 SCL 95051 833-A4
6800 OAK 94605 670-H2
FREY PL
- VAL 94590 529-J3
FREYA DR
2200 SJS 95148 855-D2
FREYA WY
500 PLHL 94523 592-A3
FRIAR AV
4800 FRMT 94555 752-C1
FRIAR CT
5700 CCCo 94803 589-G4
5900 SJS 95129 852-G3
FRIAR WY
100 CMBL 95008 853-D7
5800 SJS 95129 852-G3
FRIARS CT
2300 LALT 94024 831-J6
FRIARS LN
- MrnC 94965 606-D6
- WDSD 94062 809-G4
2300 LALT 94024 831-J6
FRIAR TUCK LN
- SRFL 94901 567-B6
FRICKA CT
2700 SJS 95121 854-J4
FRIEDA CT
100 VAL 94590 550-C1
2400 SPAB 94806 588-G2
FRIEDELL ST
900 SF 94124 668-E7
FRIENDLY CT
- RDWC 94063 770-F6
FRIENDLY LN
- NVTO 94945 526-A2
- NVTO 94945 525-J2
FRIES CT
2000 MRTZ 94553 572-A6
FRIESMAN RD
1600 LVMR 94588 694-H5
2000 LVMR 94550 694-H5
FRIGATE CT
200 PIT 94565 574-A2
FRIGATE LN
- DALY 94014 687-E5
FRISBEE CT
1500 CNCD 94520 592-E4
FRISBIE ST
100 OAK 94611 649-H2
100 VAL 94590 529-J3
FRISBIE WY
300 OAK 94611 649-H2
FRISBY LN
100 AMCN 94589 510-A2
100 NaCo 94589 510-A2
FRITZEN ST
1100 SJS 95122 834-H5
FROBISHER DR
36300 FRMT 94536 752-F4
FROBISHER WY
1700 SJS 95124 853-H7
FROG VALLEY LN
200 BLMT 94002 749-F6
FROLIC WY
1200 SJS 95129 852-J3
FRONDA DR
3200 SJS 95148 835-D6
FRONT LN
500 MTVW 94041 811-J5
FRONT ST
- BERK 94804 609-C7
- DNVL 94526 653-A2
- SF 94111 648-B4
- SRFL 94901 586-H2
800 SF 94111 648-B4
900 NVTO 94945 526-B3
1400 MRTZ 94553 571-E2
FRONT TER
- CMAD 94925 586-F7
FRONTAGE RD
- CCCo 94565 574-A2
- OAK 94607 649-C2
- OAK 94626 649-C2
FRONTAGE RD
- PIT 94565 574-C3
5500 OAK 94605 650-H7
5700 EMVL 94608 629-D5
6500 BERK 94804 629-D5
7000 NVTO 94945 526-C4
16500 SJS 95120 894-F2
W FRONTAGE RD
1300 BERK 94804 609-C7
1300 BERK 94804 629-C1
FRONTENAC AV
1300 SUNV 94087 832-B4
FRONTENAC PARK CT
4600 FRMT 94538 773-D2
FRONTERA WY
1200 MLBR 94030 728-A6
1200 BURL 94010 728-A6
FRONTERO AV
1400 SCIC 94024 831-G2
FRONTIER TRAIL DR
- SJS 95136 874-H2
2600 SJS 95136 875-A2
FROST CT
- MLV 94941 606-G4
FROST DR
1500 SJS 95131 814-C6
FROSTY LN
- NVTO 94949 546-E1
FROYD RD
1000 CNCD 94521 593-F7
FRUITDALE AV
1100 SCIC 95128 853-F2
1400 SJS 95128 853-E2
2300 SJS 95126 853-H2
FRUITDALE CT
1600 SJS 95126 853-J2
FRUITVALE AV
400 OAK 94601 670-B2
1300 OAK 94601 650-C6
2900 OAK 94602 650-D4
13600 SAR 95070 872-F3
FRUITVALE CT
- ANT 94509 595-F2
FRUITWOOD CT
1600 SJS 95125 853-J5
FRUITWOOD WY
500 HAY 94544 712-B5
FRUMENTI CT
500 MRTZ 94553 591-G4
FRY CT
1400 BEN 94510 551-A3
FRY LN
1300 HAY 94545 711-G5
FRY WY
- CNCD 94520 592-F2
FRYE ST
2800 OAK 94602 650-F4
FRYER CT
- SRMN 94583 673-E5
FUCHSIA CT
100 HER 94547 569-J3
100 VAL 94591 530-F7
FUCHSIA DR
1500 SJS 95125 854-A7
FUCHSIA LN
- SRMN 94583 653-H7
FUENTA AV
- SF 94132 687-B1
FUENTE CT
2100 ANT 94509 595-A1
FUJII WY
- HAY 94544 711-J4
FUJIKO DR
1500 SJS 95131 814-D5
FUJIKO WY
2100 SJS 95131 814-D5
FUJIYAMA LN
1300 SJS 95132 814-G4
FULBAR CT
1200 SJS 95132 814-G4
FULHAM CT
100 SRMN 94583 673-E5
FULLER AV
300 SJS 95125 854-A2
22300 HAY 94541 711-G2
FULLER ST
300 RDWC 94063 770-A5
4400 SCL 95054 813-C4
FULLERTON AV
400 PCFA 94044 707-A6
FULLERTON CT
500 SJS 95111 875-C1
32700 UNC 94587 732-B7
FULLERTON DR
400 SJS 95111 875-C1
FULLINGTON ST
4000 OAK 94619 650-F6
FULL MOON DR
4700 RCH 94803 589-G1
FULL MOON WY
400 CCCo 94506 653-J5
FULMAR TER
3700 FRMT 94555 732-J3
FULTON AV
700 SLN 94577 691-C1
700 VAL 94591 530-D7
900 SolC 94591 530-D7
1000 SUNV 94089 812-F4
1200 SolC 94591 550-E1
1300 VAL 94591 550-E1
FULTON CT
400 DNVL 94526 633-A7
400 SCL 95051 832-H7
700 MPS 95035 794-A5
FULTON PL
1000 FRMT 94539 773-G5
FULTON RD
400 SMTO 94402 748-F2
FULTON ST
- CMBL 95008 853-A6
- RDWC 94062 769-J6
100 PA 94301 790-J3
300 RDWC 94062 770-A7
600 PA 94301 791-A4
600 RDWC 94061 770-A7
800 SF 94117 647-F7
1700 PA 94303 791-B5
2100 SF 94117 647-B7
2200 BERK 94704 629-H2
2300 SF 94118 647-B7
2500 SF - 647-B7
FULTON ST
2700 BERK 94705 629-H4
4100 SF 94121 647-B7
5700 SF 94121 646-J7
5700 SF - 646-J7
5900 SF 94121 666-H1
5900 SF - 666-H1
FULTON WY
500 DNVL 94526 633-A7
800 CCCo 94803 569-D7
FULTON SHIPYARD RD
300 ANT 94509 575-E4
300 CCCo 94509 575-E4
FUME BLANC CT
8500 SJS 95135 855-H7
FUNDY BAY
100 ALA 94502 669-H7
FUNSTON AV
- SF 94118 647-C7
- SF 94129 647-E4
- SF 94129 647-E4
1200 SF 94122 667-C2
1800 SF 94116 667-C3
2100 SF 94116 667-C5
FUNSTON DR
4100 SJS 95136 874-E1
FUNSTON PL
2100 OAK 94602 650-E3
FUNSTON RD
- SF 94123 647-H3
FUNSTON GATE CT
4700 PLE 94566 694-D7
4700 PLE 94588 694-D7
FURLONG DR
800 SJS 95123 874-D5
FURLONG ST
1000 BLMT 94002 769-F1
FURLONG WY
5000 ANT 94509 595-J4
FUSCHIA CT
20500 AlaC 94541 691-G7
37600 NWK 94560 752-F7
FUSCHIA DR
1000 SUNV 94086 832-H2
FUSHIA CT
100 MRTZ 94553 572-B7
FUSTERIA CT
200 FRMT 94539 773-H7
200 FRMT 94539 793-H1
FUTAMASE CT
2400 SJS 95111 854-G3
FYNE DR
2800 WLCK 94598 612-F4
FYNES CT
1100 SJS 95131 834-C1

G

G RD
- SUNV 94089 812-H3
100 AlaC 94586 734-C3
G ST
- CCCo 94565 573-E1
- CNCD 94518 592-G4
- OAK 94625 649-B4
- VAL 94592 529-F4
- SRFL 94901 586-E1
- UNC 94587 732-F5
100 ANT 94509 575-C4
100 BEN 94510 551-B5
100 FRMT 94536 753-B1
100 MRTZ 94553 571-E3
100 RDWC 94063 769-J4
100 SRFL 94901 566-E7
1100 SUNV 94089 812-E3
3100 ANT 94509 595-C1
9200 OAK 94603 670-H5
9300 OAK 94621 670-G5
S G ST
700 LVMR 94550 715-H1
GABARDA WY
100 SMCo 94028 810-D4
GABILAN AV
200 SUNV 94086 812-C7
GABILAN ST
400 LALT 94022 811-E7
GABILAN WY
- SF 94132 667-B6
GABLE COM
47500 FRMT 94539 773-J7
GABLE CT
- SRFL 94903 566-F4
GABLE DR
- FRMT 94539 793-H1
100 FRMT 94539 773-H7
GABLE LN
- LFYT 94549 611-G2
1700 SJS 95124 873-H5
GABRIAL AV
2300 MTVW 94040 811-F3
GABRIEL CT
1200 SLN 94577 691-D2
2300 ANT 94509 595-A2
GABRIELINO TER
- FRMT 94539 773-H3
GABRIELINO WY
- FRMT 94539 773-H3
GADING RD
25800 HAY 94544 711-J5
N GADSDEN DR
- MPS 95035 794-D6
S GADSDEN DR
- MPS 95035 794-D6
GADWELL COM
34200 FRMT 94555 752-D1
GAGE CT
- FRMT 94538 773-E1
3900 SJS 95124 873-E3
GAGE LN
- MrnC 94947 525-H6
GAIL AV
500 SUNV 94086 832-F3
GAIL CT
- CCCo 94598 613-A4
GAIL DR
100 PLHL 94523 591-J4
100 PLHL 94523 592-A4
21400 AlaC 94546 691-J7
GAILEN AV
700 PA 94303 811-E1
800 PA 94303 791-F7
GAILEN CT
700 PA 94303 811-F1
GAILEN LN
700 PA 94303 811-E1
GAILLARDIA WY
1100 EPA 94303 791-C3
GAIL MEADOW CIR
200 SRMN 94583 653-H7
GAINES LN
700 WLCK 94596 612-B2
GAINESVILLE AV
27500 HAY 94545 711-H7
27700 HAY 94545 731-H1
GAINSBOROUGH CT
100 ALA 94502 669-J5
GAINSBOROUGH DR
1200 SUNV 94087 832-E3
3700 CNCD 94518 592-J3
GAINSBOROUGH TER
3600 FRMT 94555 752-E1
GAINSVILLE AV
1100 SJS 95122 834-J5
GAISER CT
- SF 94110 667-H2
GAITHER WY
26700 HAY 94544 711-J6
GALA CT
2900 SCL 95051 833-A7
GALAHAD AV
700 SJS 95116 834-J4
1100 SJS 95122 834-J4
GALAHAD CT
2500 SJS 95122 834-J4
3100 FRMT 94536 752-J3
GALANO PZ
200 UNC 94587 732-H5
GALANTI CT
- PLE 94566 715-B5
GALAXY CT
400 MPS 95035 813-J3
1800 LVMR 94550 696-A3
2100 CNCD 94520 592-E2
GALAXY DR
4100 UNC 94587 732-A6
GALAXY WY
1000 CNCD 94520 592-E1
GALBRETH RD
1900 PIN 94564 569-F7
2100 CCCo 94803 569-F7
GALE AV
4600 PLE 94566 714-E4
GALE DR
700 CMBL 95008 853-C5
GALE ST
4400 LVMR 94550 696-A7
GALEN DR
100 CCCo 94596 612-A4
400 SJS 95123 874-J7
GALEN PL
35400 FRMT 94536 752-F1
GALENA DR
2700 SJS 95121 855-A2
GALERITA WY
600 MrnC 94903 566-H2
GALEWOOD CIR
- SF 94131 667-D3
GALEWOOD CT
- SF 94131 667-D3
1700 SJS 95133 834-E3
GALICIA CT
- SRMN 94583 673-C4
GALILEE LN
- SF 94115 647-H6
GALINDO AV
- SF 94132 687-C2
GALINDO CT
800 MPS 95035 814-E1
8600 DBLN 94568 693-G2
GALINDO DR
8400 DBLN 94568 693-G2
47100 FRMT 94539 774-A6
GALINDO PL
1600 FRMT 94539 774-A6
GALINDO ST
1400 CNCD 94518 592-F2
1400 CNCD 94520 592-F1
2900 OAK 94601 650-C6
GALISTEO CT
100 SRMN 94583 673-C3
GALLAGHER CIR
3500 ANT 94509 595-C1
GALLAGHER DR
- BEN 94510 551-B1
GALLAGHER LN
- SF 94103 648-A6
GALLANT FOX AV
5100 SJS 95111 875-B2
GALLATIN DR
800 SCL 95051 832-J5
GALLAUDET DR
39300 FRMT 94536 753-C3
39300 FRMT 94538 753-C3
GALLEGOS AV
43000 FRMT 94539 753-G7
43000 FRMT 94539 773-G1
GALLEON CT
600 SJS 95133 814-F7
600 SJS 95133 834-F1
GALLEON LN
700 FCTY 94404 749-G2
GALLEON PL
2500 SLN 94577 690-G5
GALLEON WY
- PIT 94565 573-J3
- SRFL 94903 566-A1
GALLERIA DR
400 SJS 95134 813-H4
GALLETTA DR
6300 NWK 94560 752-E7
GALLEY LN
1000 FCTY 94404 749-H4
GALLI CT
300 LALT 94022 811-E6
7100 SJS 95129 852-E4
GALLI DR
- LALT 94022 811-E6
- NVTO 94949 546-F1
7000 SJS 95129 852-E4
GALLOWAY COM
2000 LVMR 94550 696-A3
GALLOWAY CT
1400 SUNV 94087 832-B4
GALLOWAY CT
2400 ANT 94509 595-G1
GALLOWAY DR
- CNCD 94518 592-G4
GALLOWAY ST
4100 LVMR 94550 696-A3
GALLOWRIDGE CT
- SMTO 94402 748-C7
GALLUP DR
2400 SCL 95051 833-B2
5600 SJS 95118 874-C4
GALSWORTHY CT
3300 FRMT 94536 752-J3
GALT ST
15200 SLN 94579 691-B6
GALTON LN
18600 AlaC 94541 711-E1
GALVESTON AV
2100 SJS 95122 854-G2
GALVESTON CT
800 CNCD 94518 592-H6
GALVESTON DR
100 RDWC 94063 770-C4
GALVESTON ST
1000 FCTY 94404 749-F5
GALVEZ AV
500 SF 94124 668-E7
600 SF 94124 668-B4
GALVEZ DR
1100 PCFA 94044 726-J5
GALVEZ ST
100 SCIC 94305 790-H6
GALVIN DR
800 ELCR 94530 609-D2
GALVIN ST
1000 OAK 94602 650-C3
GALWAY BAY
100 ALA 94502 669-J6
GALWAY CT
2300 SCL 95050 833-C2
16200 AlaC 94580 691-E6
GALWAY DR
700 AlaC 94580 691-E6
1600 CPTO 95014 852-D4
1900 PIT 94565 574-E4
2300 SSF 94080 707-D4
GALWAY LN
- SRFL 94903 566-C1
GALWAY PL
2400 SSF 94080 707-D5
GALWAY RD
2300 CCCo 94806 569-C5
GALWAY TER
100 FRMT 94536 732-J7
GAMAY COM
2300 LVMR 94550 715-H3
GAMAY CT
400 FRMT 94539 793-J2
700 PLE 94566 714-G4
3400 SJS 95148 835-D5
GAMAY DR
1100 CLAY 94517 593-H7
1100 CLAY 94517 613-H1
48800 FRMT 94539 793-J2
GAMAY RD
1400 LVMR 94550 715-H3
GAMBETTA ST
- DALY 94014 687-D4
GAMBIER CT
1500 SUNV 94087 832-B5
GAMBIER ST
- SF 94134 667-H7
GAMBLE CT
2600 HAY 94542 712-E5
GAMBLIN CIR
2600 SCL 95051 833-B7
GAMBLIN DR
2600 SCL 95051 833-B7
GAMBOA ST
26200 HAY 94544 711-J5
GAMEL WY
1900 MTVW 94040 811-G4
GAMMA CT
600 CMBL 95008 853-C7
GANA CT
2000 SJS 95148 835-B5
GANCI LN
21100 SCIC 95120 895-B5
GANGES AV
1900 ELCR 94530 589-C7
GANGES CT
7300 ELCR 94530 609-C1
GANGES ST
1700 ELCR 94530 609-C1
1900 ELCR 94530 589-C7
GANIC ST
2700 AlaC 94546 691-J5
GANLEY ST
17000 AlaC 94580 711-C2
GANNER CT
- PLE 94566 694-D7
GANNET LN
3700 AlaC 94552 692-D4
GANNET TER
33800 FRMT 94555 732-J3
GANNON RD
200 OAK 94603 670-F7
GANNON TER
34000 FRMT 94555 752-B3
GANTON CT
- HAY 94544 732-E2
GANTRY WY
700 MTVW 94040 831-H1
GAPWALL CT
2600 PLE 94566 714-C1
GAR TER
38900 FRMT 94536 753-C3
GARABALDI DR
100 VAL 94589 510-A7
GARATTI CT
4100 PLE 94566 714-E1
GARAVENTA CT
1400 CNCD 94521 593-D5
GARAVENTA DR
5100 CNCD 94521 593-D5
GARAVENTA RANCH DR
- LVMR 94550 696-D2
GARBER PL
1100 SJS 95127 835-A3
GARBER ST
2700 BERK 94705 629-J3
2800 BERK 94705 630-A3

BAY AREA

INDEX

938 GARBER ST 1998 BAY AREA STREET INDEX GIANNINI RD

STREET
Block City ZIP Pg-Grid

GARBER ST
3000 OAK 94705 630-A3
GARBO WY
1200 SJS 95117 853-B3
GARCAL DR
14900 SCIC 95127 835-C1
GARCES AV
5800 SJS 95123 874-F5
GARCES DR
- SF 94132 687-A1
GARCEZ DR
1500 CNCD 94521 593-E5
GARCIA AV
- SF 94127 667-D4
100 SLN 94577 670-J7
200 PIT 94565 574-D4
2300 MTVW 94043 791-G7
GARCIA CT
200 MPS 95035 794-A4
GARCIA LN
1400 CNCD 94521 593-A3
GARCIA ST
35100 UNC 94587 732-G7
GARCIA RANCH RD
1000 CCCo 94553 590-H5
1100 CCCo - 590-H5
1700 CCCo - 591-A5
GARDELLA DR
7500 DBLN 94568 693-G3
GARDELLA PZ
3000 LVMR 94550 695-H7
GARDEN AV
- MrnC 94903 566-G4
- ROSS 94957 586-C1
400 SBRN 94066 727-J1
2600 CNCD 94520 572-F7
2700 SJS 95111 854-G5
2800 SCIC 95111 854-G5
20400 AlaC 94541 711-F1
S GARDEN AV
22100 HAY 94541 711-F3
GARDEN COM
200 LVMR 94550 695-D7
GARDEN CT
- ANT 94509 575-F6
- BLMT 94002 769-D2
- NVTO 94947 526-B4
100 VAL 94591 530-D6
300 PCFA 94044 706-J7
1100 CCCo 94595 612-A6
GARDEN DR
- FRMT 94536 753-C1
- CCCo 94708 609-G3
700 SJS 95126 833-F6
700 SJS 95128 833-F6
1900 BURL 94010 728-B5
GARDEN LN
- SCAR 94070 769-E3
- SMCo 94015 687-B4
- SMTO 94403 749-C6
100 MLBR 94030 728-C3
200 LGTS 95032 873-C4
1100 LFYT 94549 611-F5
1100 SRFL 94901 586-G1
1300 MLPK 94025 790-E4
4000 CCCo 94803 589-C2
GARDEN PL
500 AlaC 94541 711-F2
GARDEN RD
- ALA 94502 670-A6
4100 CCCo 94803 589-C2
GARDEN ST
- RDWC 94063 769-J4
- SF 94115 647-F6
100 EPA 94303 791-A1
2700 OAK 94601 650-C5
GARDEN TER
2100 MTVW 94040 831-J1
GARDEN WY
- LKSP 94939 586-F6
- SCL 95050 833-F5
1300 ALA 94501 669-F1
5000 FRMT 94536 752-G5
GARDENA CT
10600 CPTO 95014 832-C6
GARDENA DR
21000 SCIC 95014 832-C6
21100 CPTO 95014 832-C6
GARDEN BING CIR
1900 SJS 95131 814-C4
GARDEN BING CT
1900 SJS 95131 814-C4
GARDEN COURT DR
- SCL 95054 813-D7
GARDEN CREEK CIR
2800 PLE 94588 694-E6
GARDEN CREEK PL
600 DNVL 94526 652-J1
GARDEN CREST CT
20600 CPTO 95014 852-B7
GARDENDALE DR
2700 SJS 95125 854-C7
3000 SJS 95118 854-C7
3100 SJS 95118 874-C1
GARDEN ESTATES CT
- CCCo 94507 632-F4
GARDEN GATE DR
20600 SCIC 95014 832-D7
GARDEN GATEWAY
- SMCo 94015 687-B4
- DALY 94015 687-B4
GARDENGLEN WY
1500 SJS 95125 854-A7
GARDEN GROVE DR
- DALY 94015 686-J3
GARDEN HILL DR
14900 LGTS 95030 873-C5
GARDENIA CT
- EPA 94303 791-D3
100 MRTZ 94553 572-B7
100 MRTZ 94553 592-B1
800 ANT 94509 595-F5
GARDENIA PL
3900 OAK 94605 670-J1
GARDENIA TER
1000 ALA 94502 670-A7
GARDENIA WY
100 EPA 94303 791-C3
800 LALT 94024 831-E1
1000 SUNV 94086 832-G2
15500 SCIC 95032 873-D5
44800 FRMT 94539 773-G3

GARDEN MANOR CT
20600 CPTO 95014 852-B7
GARDENOAK CT
6500 SJS 95120 894-C1
GARDEN OF DEVOTION CIR
- SMCo - 768-C3
GARDEN PLACE CT
20700 CPTO 95014 852-B7
GARDENSIDE AV
200 SSF 94080 707-F1
GARDENSIDE CIR
20600 CPTO 95014 852-D3
GARDENSIDE DR
- SF 94131 667-F3
GARDENSIDE LN
1100 CPTO 95014 852-D3
GARDEN TERRACE DR
11400 CPTO 95014 852-B7
GARDEN TRACT RD
1800 RCH 94801 588-E3
1900 CCCo 94801 588-E2
GARDEN VALLEY DR
500 MrnC 94965 606-E6
GARDEN VIEW CT
- DNVL 94506 653-G4
GARDEN VIEW LN
- PLHL 94523 591-J2
GARDENVIEW LN
21800 CPTO 95014 832-B7
GARDENWOOD DR
1000 SJS 95129 852-G2
GARDIE PLACE WY
3800 SJS 95121 855-B4
GARDINA CT
1200 DNVL 94526 653-C4
GARDINER AV
- SSF 94080 708-A2
GARDINER CT
- ORIN 94563 610-J4
GARDNER BLVD
1100 SLN 94577 690-J1
GARDNER PL
- DNVL 94526 653-E3
GARDNER ST
- VAL 94590 529-H2
- MLV 94941 606-D3
GARFIELD AV
1100 ALB 94706 609-D5
1100 SJS 95125 854-A3
1100 SJS 95125 853-J3
3200 ALA 94501 670-B3
7300 OAK 94605 670-H2
GARFIELD PL
2900 ANT 94509 575-A7
GARFIELD ST
- SF 94112 687-C1
- SF 94132 687-C1
1400 NVTO 94947 526-B5
2600 SMTO 94403 749-B5
GARFORD AL
500 VAL 94590 530-A5
500 VAL 94590 529-J5
GARIBALDI CT
- DALY 94014 687-D4
GARIBALDI PL
4100 PLE 94566 714-F4
GARIBALDI ST
- DALY 94014 687-C4
GARIBALDI TER
- FRMT 94536 753-F3
GARIN AV
500 HAY 94544 712-D7
500 HAY 94544 732-D1
1300 AlaC 94544 712-F7
GARLAND AV
600 SUNV 94086 832-F2
1000 SJS 95126 833-J7
GARLAND CT
2000 WLCK 94595 632-D1
6800 PLE 94588 714-A1
17500 AlaC 94546 691-H2
GARLAND DR
100 MLPK 94025 790-F5
700 PA 94303 791-C5
3700 SJS 95136 854-G7
4200 FRMT 94536 752-J5
GARLAND PL
- MLPK 94025 790-F5
GARLAND ST
- OAK 94611 649-H2
E GARLAND TER
600 SUNV 94086 832-F2
N GARLAND TER
600 SUNV 94086 832-F2
W GARLAND TER
600 SUNV 94086 832-F2
GARLAND WY
100 LALT 94022 811-E6
GARLINGTON CT
- SF 94124 668-C6
GARLOUGH DR
5800 SJS 95123 874-E5
GARLOUGH PL
900 SJS 95123 874-E5
GARNER CT
100 NVTO 94947 526-A6
700 SCL 95050 833-C5
2300 ANT 94509 594-J1
6200 PLE 94588 694-A7
GARNER DR
- NVTO 94947 526-A6
- NVTO 94949 526-A6
100 SUNV 94089 812-E4
GARNET AV
100 SCAR 94070 769-G5
GARNET CIR
- VAL 94591 530-F1
GARNET COM
4700 FRMT 94555 752-D2
GARNET CT
- VAL 94591 530-F1
100 HER 94547 569-G4
20000 AlaC 94546 692-B5
GARNET DR
- VAL 94591 530-F1
100 LVMR 94550 715-D3
3100 SJS 95117 853-D2
GARNET LN
1600 CNCD 94519 592-J2
GARNET ST
300 OAK 94609 629-J7

GARNET ST
300 OAK 94611 629-J7
GARNETT CT
19900 SAR 95070 852-E6
GARRANS DR
1300 SJS 95130 853-A4
1300 SJS 95129 853-A4
GARRARD BLVD
- RCH 94801 608-D1
- RCH 94804 608-D1
- RCH 94804 588-E7
- RCH 94801 588-E7
GARRETSON AV
- CCCo 94572 549-H7
400 CCCo 94572 569-H1
500 CCCo 94547 569-H1
GARRETT CT
1100 SJS 95120 894-F3
3200 UNC 94587 732-A4
GARRETT DR
3400 SCL 95054 813-A7
GARRETT ST
38200 FRMT 94536 752-J5
GARRETT WY
30700 UNC 94587 732-A4
GARRICK PL
2800 FRMT 94555 732-E6
GARRIDO CT
100 VAL 94591 530-G6
GARRIGAN CT
500 CCCo 94506 654-B5
GARRISON AV
- SF 94134 687-J2
19300 AlaC 94546 692-A4
GARRISON CIR
5200 SJS 95123 875-B3
GARRISON CT
- WLCK 94598 612-E5
GARRISON RD
700 RCH 94803 589-H3
GARRITY CT
2700 PIN 94564 569-G5
GARRITY WY
3100 RCH 94806 569-B7
3100 RCH 94806 589-B1
GARRON CT
- WLCK 94596 632-F1
GARRONE AV
6500 NWK 94560 752-C5
GARRONE PL
35500 NWK 94560 752-C5
GARROW DR
2700 ANT 94509 575-E7
3200 ANT 94509 595-E1
GARSIDE CT
600 SLN 94579 691-B5
GARTHE CT
- VAL 94591 530-G5
GARTHWICK CT
1300 LALT 94024 831-J3
GARTHWICK DR
1300 LALT 94024 831-J3
GARTLEY AV
- CCCo 94525 550-E5
GARVEY PL
1500 SJS 95132 814-E4
GARVEY WY
- SMTO 94402 749-B3
GARVIN AV
1300 RCH 94801 588-G5
2300 RCH 94804 588-J5
3300 RCH 94805 588-J5
3400 RCH 94805 589-A5
GARWAY DR
38400 FRMT 94536 752-J4
GARWOOD DR
- DALY 94014 687-D3
5300 SJS 95118 874-B4
GARWOOD WY
400 MLPK 94025 790-F3
GARWOOD GLEN DR
24700 HAY 94541 712-B2
GARY AV
500 ANT 94509 575-E6
800 SUNV 94086 832-F3
GARY CIR
100 VAL 94591 530-C7
GARY CT
100 MTVW 94041 811-J6
400 PA 94306 791-C7
GARY DR
1300 CNCD 94518 592-H2
21000 AlaC 94546 691-H6
21000 HAY 94546 691-H6
GARY PL
- SRFL 94901 586-H3
GARY WY
- CCCo 94507 632-G7
GARYDALE CT
100 CCCo 94507 632-H4
GARY LEE LN
- WLCK 94596 612-B2
GASCOIGNE DR
10500 SCIC 95014 852-H2
GASKELL CT
35900 FRMT 94536 752-G2
GASKILL ST
5300 OAK 94608 629-F6
GASLIGHT LN
- SMCo 94070 769-E4
GASOLINE AL
1400 CNCD 94520 592-E1
GASPAR CT
2700 PA 94306 791-C6
GASPAR DR
1800 OAK 94611 630-E7
GASSETT CT
1100 HAY 94544 712-A7
GASSMANN DR
2600 SJS 95121 854-H3
S GATE
- RDWC 94062 769-H7
W GATE WY
- SANS 94960 566-C7
GATE 5 RD
- SAUS 94965 626-J1
GATE 6 RD
- MrnC 94941 606-J7
- MrnC 94941 626-J1
GATE 6 1/2 RD
- MrnC 94941 606-H7
- MrnC 94941 626-H1

GATELAND CT
3200 SJS 95148 855-E1
GATELIGHT CT
3200 SJS 95148 855-E1
GATELY AV
5000 RCH 94804 609-B2
GATELY DR
400 PIN 94564 569-C4
GATES DR
4100 SJS 95124 873-H3
GATES ST
- SF 94110 667-J6
GATESHEAD CT
700 FCTY 94404 749-G5
GATETREE CIR
4500 PLE 94566 714-D2
GATETREE CT
100 DNVL 94526 653-C2
GATETREE DR
100 DNVL 94526 653-C2
GATEVIEW AV
600 ALB 94706 609-C5
GATEVIEW CT
- SF 94116 667-C4
800 SJS 95133 814-F7
GATE VIEW DR
- OAK 94605 671-C4
GATEVIEW DR
700 SJS 95133 814-F7
800 SJS 95133 834-F1
GATEWAY
- DBLN 94568 693-G2
GATEWAY AV
- SF 94130 648-D1
GATEWAY BLVD
- FRMT 94538 793-F1
- NWK 94560 752-B5
- ORIN 94563 630-F2
200 SSF 94080 708-A3
1800 CNCD 94520 592-E2
3400 FRMT 94538 773-G7
GATEWAY CT
100 VAL 94589 510-D6
GATEWAY DR
- DALY 94015 707-B1
- PCFA 94044 707-B1
100 LGTS 95032 873-D4
700 VAL 94589 510-C6
1800 SMTO 94404 749-E3
1800 FCTY 94404 749-E3
GATEWAY PL
1800 SJS 95110 833-G1
GATEWAY PLAZA DR
- BEN 94510 551-G1
GATEWOOD CT
1400 MRTZ 94553 571-J7
GATEWOOD LN
5200 SJS 95118 874-A4
GATEWOOD ST
42100 FRMT 94538 773-D2
GATON DR
1600 SJS 95125 853-J5
GATTER CT
800 ANT 94509 575-C7
GATTER DR
900 ANT 94509 575-C7
900 ANT 94509 595-B1
GATTO AV
6600 ELCR 94530 589-B7
GATTUCIO DR
4900 SJS 95124 873-J4
GATUN AL
- SF 94127 667-E5
GAUCHO CT
200 SRMN 94583 673-C2
1400 SJS 95118 874-B2
GAUCHO WY
40800 FRMT 94539 753-F4
GAUNDABERT LN
500 SJS 95136 874-F3
600 SCIC 95123 874-F3
GAVELLO AV
700 SUNV 94086 832-F2
GAVEN ST
- SF 94134 668-A6
200 SF 94134 667-J6
GAVILAN CT
- MLBR 94030 728-A6
2800 SJS 95148 855-C1
GAVILAN DR
2800 SJS 95148 855-C1
GAVILAN WY
1400 MLBR 94030 728-A6
GAVIOTA WY
- SF 94127 667-E5
GAVOTA AV
3100 SJS 95124 873-J2
GAWAIN CT
35200 FRMT 94536 752-F1
GAWAIN DR
3100 SJS 95127 814-H7
GAY AV
1200 CMBL 95008 873-C1
2700 SCIC 95127 834-H2
2800 SJS 95127 834-H2
GAY CT
100 CCCo 94507 632-H5
GAYLE CT
1300 ELCR 94530 609-D2
GAYLE DR
4200 SJS 95124 873-H3
GAYLENE CT
800 CNCD 94518 592-G6
GAYLEY RD
- BERK 94720 629-J1
GAYLOR LN
3300 SJS 95118 874-A1
GAYLORD PL
900 CNCD 94518 592-F6
GAYLORD ST
- SCAR 94070 769-G5
GAYNOR AV
1300 RCH 94801 588-G5
2300 RCH 94804 588-H5
GAYWOOD CT
3000 SJS 95148 855-C1
GAYWOOD PL
- MRGA 94556 651-E1
GAYWOOD RD
- CCCo 94507 632-F5
GAZANIA CT
- NVTO 94945 526-B2

GAZANIA DR
4900 SJS 95111 875-A2
GAZANIA TER
- FRMT 94536 753-D2
GAZDAR CT
1300 SCL 95051 832-H4
GAZELLE DR
2800 SJS 95008 873-A1
GAZELLE WY
1700 HAY 94541 712-B1
GEARY AV
- MrnC 94904 586-D3
GEARY BLVD
1100 SF 94109 647-E6
1500 SF 94115 647-E6
2700 SF 94118 647-E6
3100 SF 94118 647-A6
5300 SF 94121 647-A6
6900 SF 94121 646-H6
GEARY CT
- WLCK 94596 612-C1
GEARY DR
- MrnC 94904 586-D3
GEARY RD
- AlaC 94586 774-H2
1400 WLCK 94596 612-B1
1900 WLCK 94596 611-J1
1900 PLHL 94523 612-B1
1900 PLHL 94523 611-J1
GEARY ST
- SF 94108 648-A6
300 SF 94102 648-A6
400 SF 94102 647-J6
700 SF 94109 647-J6
GEARY TER
5300 FRMT 94555 752-B3
GEBHART AV
- SJS 95116 834-H3
GEDDES CT
3900 SSF 94080 707-D4
GEDDY CT
44000 FRMT 94539 773-H2
GEDDY WY
1000 FRMT 94539 773-H2
GEHRIG AV
1100 SJS 95132 814-F5
GEHRINGER DR
2200 CNCD 94520 572-F6
GEIST CT
1600 SJS 95132 814-G2
GELBKE LN
1700 CNCD 94520 592-E4
GELDERT CT
- TBRN 94920 607-C5
GELDERT DR
- TBRN 94920 607-B4
GELDING CT
- DNVL 94526 633-C7
GELLERT BLVD
300 DALY 94015 707-C2
2100 SSF 94080 707-D4
GELLERT DR
- SF 94132 666-J6
100 SF 94132 667-A6
GELSTON PL
700 ELCR 94530 609-E2
GELSTON ST
700 OAK 94705 630-B2
GEM AV
- LGTS 95032 873-C7
2200 UNC 94587 732-G7
4200 AlaC 94546 692-B5
GEM CT
20000 AlaC 94546 692-C5
GEM LN
2400 ANT 94509 575-C6
GEMINI AV
200 MTVW 94043 811-H4
GEMINI CT
100 LGTS 95032 873-J6
3500 CNCD 94519 592-J1
GEMINI DR
4100 UNC 94587 732-A6
GEMINI LN
700 FCTY 94404 749-E4
3400 SJS 95111 854-F6
GEMINI RD
2100 LVMR 94550 715-F4
GEMMA DR
300 MPS 95035 794-A5
GEMSTONE DR
200 MPS 95035 793-H6
GENEBERN WY
- SF 94112 667-H6
GENERAL ELECTRIC
- SJS 95125 854-E4
GENERAL KENNEDY AV
- SF 94129 647-E4
GENEVA AV
- HAY 94544 732-E3
- SF 94112 667-E7
- SF 94112 687-G2
500 RDWC 94061 790-B1
1300 SCAR 94070 769-H4
1600 SF 94134 687-G2
2100 DALY 94014 687-G2
3100 BSBN 94005 687-G2
3200 BSBN 94005 688-A3
3200 DALY 94014 688-A3
4800 CNCD 94521 593-D3
GENEVA CT
3200 MRTZ 94553 571-D5
GENEVA DR
1200 SUNV 94089 812-G2
3200 SCL 95051 832-J7
GENEVA LN
1800 ANT 94509 575-G6
GENEVA RD
200 MPS 95035 794-A6
GENEVA ST
1000 LVMR 94550 715-G3
1800 SJS 95124 873-G2
2700 MRTZ 94553 571-D5
GENEVA WY
- MrnC 94903 566-G3
GENEVE CT
1300 LVMR 94550 695-F6
GENEVIEVE AV
300 PCFA 94044 727-A2
GENEVIEVE CT
3100 PA 94303 791-E6

GENEVIEVE LN
500 SJS 95128 833-E7
S GENEVIEVE LN
300 SJS 95128 853-E1
GENEVIEVE PL
700 PLE 94566 714-F4
GENEVRA RD
- HIL 94010 728-F7
GENG RD
1700 PA 94303 791-D3
GENI CT
400 WLCK 94596 592-D7
GENIE LN
5400 SJS 95123 875-B4
GENINE CT
600 SJS 95127 814-J7
GENINE DR
500 SJS 95127 814-H7
GENNESSEE ST
- SF 94112 667-E6
400 SF 94127 667-E6
GENOA CT
- WLCK 94598 612-H2
100 VAL 94589 510-D5
1800 LVMR 94550 715-G3
6100 FRMT 94555 752-B6
GENOA DR
- RDWC 94065 749-J5
- RDWC 94065 750-C4
400 SJS 95133 834-G1
GENOA PL
100 SF 94133 648-A4
GENOA ST
1400 LVMR 94550 715-G3
5100 OAK 94608 629-G5
GENOVESIO DR
5600 PLE 94588 694-C6
GENSTAR RD
31000 HAY 94544 732-C3
GENTIAN CT
4900 SJS 95111 875-A2
GENTLE CREEK PL
700 DNVL 94526 632-H7
700 DNVL 94526 652-H1
GENTRY CT
400 WLCK 94598 612-D3
2700 SCL 95051 833-B2
GENTRY OAKS PL
6700 SJS 95138 875-G4
GENTRYTOWN DR
2700 ANT 94509 595-A1
3100 ANT 94509 575-A7
3300 ANT 94509 574-J7
GEOFFREY CT
2500 PIN 94564 569-E6
GEOFFREY DR
- CCCo 94565 573-E2
3100 SBRN 94066 707-D5
GEOMAX CT
4900 SJS 95118 874-C3
GEORGE AV
4100 SMTO 94403 749-D6
6400 NWK 94560 752-D7
GEORGE CIR
100 VAL 94591 530-D6
GEORGE CT
- SF 94124 668-C6
1400 BEN 94510 551-A3
GEORGE LN
- DNVL 94526 633-B7
- MLV 94941 606-G2
- SAUS 94965 627-A3
GEORGE ST
- SJS 95110 834-A5
900 NVTO 94945 526-B3
900 SCL 95054 813-E7
16100 LGTS 95032 873-C6
GEORGE WY
- AlaC 94580 711-C1
1000 AlaC 94541 691-G6
GEORGE HOOD LN
300 PA 94306 811-D2
GEORGE OAKS DR
4400 SJS 95118 874-C2
GEORGETOWN AV
300 SMTO 94402 748-J3
1200 SLN 94579 691-A5
GEORGETOWN CT
100 VAL 94589 509-H5
600 SUNV 94087 832-D2
3600 SSF 94080 707-C4
GEORGETOWN LN
2500 ANT 94509 575-D1
GEORGETOWN PL
3300 SCL 95051 833-A2
3300 SCL 95051 832-J2
GEORGETOWN ST
2700 EPA 94303 771-C7
GEORGETTA DR
1400 SJS 95125 854-A6
1500 SJS 95125 853-J6
GEORGIA AV
200 SBRN 94066 707-J7
200 SBRN 94066 727-J1
500 PA 94306 811-C3
600 SUNV 94086 812-F5
2000 SJS 95122 834-H5
GEORGIA DR
1600 CNCD 94519 593-A2
GEORGIA LN
100 PTLV 94028 810-C7
GEORGIA MALL
- VAL 94590 529-J5
GEORGIA ST
200 VAL 94590 529-J5
500 VAL 94590 530-B5
800 VAL 94591 530-D5
2800 OAK 94602 650-E5
GEORGIA WY
- SLN 94577 671-A7
GEORGINIA AV
400 SJS 95116 834-H4
GEORGIS PL
5700 PLE 94588 694-C5
GERALD AV
1200 SPAB 94806 589-B4
GERALD CT
- CCCo 94565 573-F2
400 BEN 94510 551-A1
GERALD DR
- CNCD 94518 592-J3

GERALD DR
- CNCD 94519 592-J3
100 DNVL 94526 653-A4
100 DNVL 94526 652-J4
GERALD WY
1900 HAY 94545 711-F5
2400 SJS 95125 854-B6
GERALDINE CT
23200 AlaC 94541 692-D7
GERALDINE DR
600 MLBR 94030 728-A3
600 MLBR 94030 727-J3
2300 PLHL 94523 592-D6
GERALDINE ST
500 LVMR 94550 696-C7
GERALDINE WY
1200 BLMT 94002 769-D3
GERALD ZAPPELLI CT
20400 SAR 95070 872-D2
GERANIUM LN
- SCAR 94070 769-C4
GERANIUM PL
4700 OAK 94619 650-H5
GERANIUM ST
38000 NWK 94560 752-G7
GERARD CT
500 PLE 94566 714-F4
GERARD WY
800 SJS 95127 835-B2
GERBER CT
900 SUNV 94087 832-B5
GERDTS DR
6200 SJS 95135 855-H6
GERHARDT AV
1400 SJS 95125 854-A7
GERI LN
2000 HIL 94010 728-D7
GERI PL
- SMCo 94062 789-G1
GERINE BLOSSOM DR
5300 SJS 95123 875-A3
GERIOLA CT
- PLHL 94523 612-B1
GERKE AL
- SF 94133 648-A4
GERLACK DR
1400 SJS 95118 874-B3
GERLACK RD
- SANS 94960 586-A1
GERMAINE CT
1700 AlaC 94541 712-B1
1800 SJS 95122 854-G1
GERMAINE PL
- NVTO 94949 546-C1
GERMAINE WY
3500 LVMR 94550 695-J7
GERMANIA ST
- SF 94117 667-G1
GERNEIL CT
14900 SAR 95070 872-E2
GERONA RD
400 SCIC 94305 810-H1
GERONIMO CT
1000 FRMT 94539 774-A5
1000 FRMT 94539 773-J4
GERONIMO DR
6100 SJS 95123 874-H6
GERRILYN WY
4600 LVMR 94550 716-B1
GERRY CT
200 CCCo 94596 612-F7
GERSTLE CT
- SRFL 94901 586-E2
GERTH LN
2200 LAH 94304 810-H4
GERTRUDE AV
200 CCCo 94801 588-E4
200 RCH 94801 588-F4
W GERTRUDE AV
- RCH 94801 588-E4
100 CCCo 94801 588-E4
GERTRUDE CT
- EPA 94303 771-B7
GERTRUDE DR
4300 FRMT 94536 753-A5
4300 FRMT 94536 752-J6
GERTRUDE LN
- NVTO 94947 525-G3
GERZ CT
2300 PIN 94564 569-F6
GEST DR
800 MTVW 94040 831-G1
GETOUN CT
1700 CNCD 94518 592-F6
GETOUN DR
900 CNCD 94518 592-F6
GETTY CT
- BEN 94510 551-E1
GETTYSBURG AV
25800 HAY 94545 711-F7
GETTYSBURG CT N
3700 PLE 94588 714-A1
GETTYSBURG CT S
3600 PLE 94588 714-A1
GETTYSBURG DR
500 SJS 95123 874-H4
GETZ ST
- SF 94112 687-E1
GEYSER CIR
1600 ANT 94509 575-G5
GEYSER CT
- FRMT 94539 773-J4
1800 ANT 94509 575-G5
GEYSER DR
1400 SJS 95131 814-C7
GHIOTTI CT
4000 PLE 94588 694-A5
GHORMLEY AV
100 OAK 94603 670-G7
GIAMMONA DR
1500 WLCK 94596 612-C5
GIANERA ST
2000 SCL 95054 813-C4
GIANNI ST
400 SCL 95054 813-E7
GIANNINI CT
6600 AlaC 94552 692-F2
GIANNINI DR
400 SCL 95051 832-H7
GIANNINI RD
- CCCo 94553 571-J4

BAY AREA
INDEX

STREET Block City ZIP Pg-Grid

GIANNINI WY
6700 AlaC 94552 692-F2
GIANNOTTA WY
400 SJS 95133 834-G1
GIANT HWY
4600 RCH 94806 568-G6
GIANT RD
900 SPAB 94806 588-G1
3200 SPAB 94806 568-H7
3500 RCH 94806 568-H7
GIANT WY
3400 SJS 95127 835-B2
GIANTS DR
3000 SF 94124 688-C1
GIARAMITA ST
1500 CCCo 94801 588-F4
GIBB ST
- SF 94111 648-A4
GIBBON CT
- SF 94129 647-F4
GIBBONS CT
400 MPS 95035 813-J3
GIBBONS DR
1400 ALA 94501 670-B3
GIBBS WY
900 SSF 94080 707-D1
GIBRALTAR CT
100 SUNV 94089 812-F3
600 MPS 95035 814-B1
36200 FRMT 94536 752-F3
GIBRALTAR DR
200 SUNV 94089 812-F3
500 MPS 95035 814-B2
4000 FRMT 94536 752-F3
5500 PLE 94588 694-B5
GIBRALTAR LN
500 FCTY 94404 749-F5
GIBRALTAR RD
9900 OAK 94603 670-G7
GIBSON AV
200 MrnC 94941 606-F6
3400 SCL 95051 832-J7
GIBSON CT
- CCCo 94507 632-H2
3500 SCL 95051 832-J7
6200 PLE 94588 694-A7
GIBSON LN
- CLAY 94517 593-G7
GIBSON RD
1700 SF 94129 647-B5
GIBSON ST
40400 FRMT 94538 753-C6
GIBSON GIRL WY
2300 SJS 95148 835-D5
2300 SCIC 95148 835-D5
GIDDINGS CT
100 SJS 95139 895-G1
GIEGER LN
1400 CNCD 94521 592-J3
GIER CT
700 SJS 95111 854-G3
GIFFIN RD
100 LALT 94022 831-E1
GIFFORD AV
100 SJS 95110 834-A7
300 SJS 95126 834-A7
GIFFORD ST
41600 FRMT 94538 773-D1
GIGEY DR
- BEN 94510 551-A3
GIGI CT
2800 SJS 95111 854-H4
GIGLI CT
12300 LAH 94022 811-A7
GIGUERE CT
600 SJS 95133 834-F2
GILA CT
1000 FRMT 94539 773-G4
GILA DR
3400 SJS 95148 835-D5
GILARDY DR
1700 CNCD 94518 592-E6
GILBERT AV
- SCL 95051 833-A7
100 MLPK 94025 791-A2
300 MLPK 94025 790-J2
1200 FRMT 94536 753-B2
GILBERT CT
100 MRTZ 94553 571-E7
1100 FRMT 94536 753-B2
3600 SSF 94080 707-D4
GILBERT DR
- MrnC 94941 606-H6
GILBERT LN
100 MRTZ 94553 591-F1
3100 ALA 94502 670-A6
GILBERT PL
1400 FRMT 94536 753-A2
GILBERT ST
- MrnC 94901 586-H3
- SF 94103 648-A7
- SF 94103 668-A1
1000 AlaC 94541 691-G6
4100 OAK 94611 629-J7
GIL BLAS RD
100 DNVL 94526 653-B2
GILBOA DR
1500 WLCK 94598 612-E3
GILBRETH RD
1500 BURL 94010 728-D4
GILCHRIST DR
800 SJS 95133 814-F7
GILCHRIST WALKWAY
800 SJS 95133 814-F7
GILDA AV
400 MRTZ 94553 571-J6
GILDA WY
1700 SJS 95124 873-H6
GILES WY
- SJS 95136 854-E7
GILGER AV
100 MRTZ 94553 571-D5
GILHAM WY
2700 SJS 95148 835-C7
GILL CT
100 BEN 94510 551-B2
2300 CNCD 94520 592-F1
GILL DR
2000 CNCD 94520 572-F7
2000 CNCD 94520 592-F1
GILL LN
500 SLN 94577 671-B7

GILL ST
5900 ELCR 94530 609-B1
GILL WY
100 BEN 94510 551-B2
GILLCREST AV
- SolC 94591 530-D7
400 SolC 94591 550-D1
400 VAL 94591 550-D1
GILLET AV
2800 CNCD 94520 572-E6
GILLETTE AV
- SF 94134 688-B2
GILLIAN WY
1800 SJS 95132 814-D3
GILLICK WY
20300 CPTO 95014 852-E2
GILLINGHAM LN
28900 HAY 94544 732-A2
GILLIS DR
3900 SMTO 94403 749-D6
GILLMOR ST
4700 SCL 95054 813-C4
GILL PORT CT
1800 WLCK 94598 612-E1
GILL PORT LN
2000 WLCK 94598 592-E7
2200 WLCK 94598 612-E1
GILLS DR
6500 SJS 95120 894-C2
GILLY LN
1800 CNCD 94518 592-F5
GILMA DR
2900 RCH 94806 589-A1
GILMAN AV
- CMBL 95008 853-E6
500 SF 94124 688-B1
GILMAN DR
1000 SMCo 94015 687-B5
1000 DALY 94015 687-B5
GILMAN ST
600 PA 94301 790-J4
700 BERK 94804 609-D7
1000 BERK 94706 609-E7
1000 BERK 94702 609-D7
GILMARTIN CT
- TBRN 94920 607-D5
GILMARTIN DR
- TBRN 94920 607-D5
GILMORE CT
- LFYT 94549 612-A4
900 CNCD 94518 592-F6
GILMORE DR
1200 SLN 94577 690-H2
GILMORE ST
1300 MTVW 94040 811-G6
GILRIX CT
- MRTZ 94553 571-H4
GILROY CT
32700 UNC 94587 732-B7
GILROY ST
- SF 94124 688-C2
GIMELLI CT
2500 SJS 95133 834-G1
GIMELLI WY
2500 SCIC 95133 834-G1
2500 SJS 95133 834-G1
GIMERL LN
- RDWC 94065 750-C4
GINA CT
- AlaC 94541 712-C1
100 VAL 94589 510-D5
12600 SCIC 95127 814-J5
GINA ST
4300 FRMT 94538 753-C7
GINA WY
4800 UNC 94587 752-A1
4800 UNC 94587 751-J1
GINASHELL CIR
6200 SJS 95119 875-C6
GINDEN CT
1400 CMBL 95008 853-B7
GINDEN DR
600 CMBL 95008 853-B7
GINGER AV
400 AlaC 94541 711-E1
GINGER COM
38100 FRMT 94536 752-J1
GINGER CT
- ANT 94509 595-D1
300 SRMN 94583 653-J7
7400 PLE 94588 714-A2
7400 PLE 94588 713-J2
GINGER LN
- ALA 94502 670-B7
900 SCIC 95128 853-F2
1000 SJS 95128 853-F3
GINGERWOOD DR
1100 MPS 95035 793-J4
GINGERWOOD LN
- DNVL 94506 653-E4
GINKGO CT
400 SJS 95111 854-G7
GINNEY CT
- DNVL 94526 653-C4
GINNIVER ST
2000 SMTO 94403 749-C4
GINNY LN
26300 LAH 94022 831-B1
GINOCCHIO CT
200 WLCK 94598 612-J2
GION AV
4000 SCIC 95127 834-J1
GIOVANNI CT
300 SJS 95133 834-H1
GIOVANNI ST
1200 ANT 94509 575-F5
GIRALDA DR
500 LALT 94024 811-F7
GIRARD AV
- SAUS 94965 627-A2
GIRARD DR
1700 MPS 95035 794-D7
GIRARD RD
- SolC 94035 812-B3
- SF 94129 647-E4
- SF 94129 647-E4
GIRARD ST
- SF 94134 668-A7
700 SF 94134 688-A1
GIRAUDO DR
500 SJS 95111 875-B1

GIRVIN DR
5900 OAK 94611 650-F1
6200 OAK 94611 630-F7
GISELA DR
100 AMCN 94589 509-J1
E GISH RD
- SJS 95112 834-B1
W GISH RD
- SJS 95110 833-J3
- SJS 95112 833-J3
GISLER WY
600 HAY 94544 712-D7
GISSING PL
35700 FRMT 94536 752-G1
GITTLE CT
600 SJS 95116 834-H4
GIUSTI DR
5100 SJS 95111 875-B2
GLACIER AV
1000 PCFA 94044 727-C4
GLACIER CT
1800 MRTZ 94553 571-J7
GLACIER CT N
3600 PLE 94588 714-B1
GLACIER CT S
3500 PLE 94588 714-B1
GLACIER DR
- MRTZ 94553 591-J1
- MRTZ 94553 571-J7
100 LVMR 94550 715-D1
300 MRTZ 94553 572-A7
1100 MPS 95035 814-C1
1400 SJS 95118 874-B2
3700 PIT 94565 574-D5
GLACIER PL
- LVMR 94550 715-D1
GLACIER WY
300 SRFL 94903 566-F2
GLACIER PARK CT
5100 FRMT 94538 773-C2
GLADDING CT
1500 MPS 95035 814-C3
GLADE CT
900 ANT 94509 595-F2
GLADE DR
2400 SCL 95051 833-A2
GLADE LN
- CCCo 94507 632-F3
GLADE ST
400 HAY 94544 711-J3
GLADEVIEW WY
- SF 94131 667-E4
GLADIOLA DR
800 SUNV 94086 832-F2
GLADIOLUS CT
1600 LVMR 94550 696-A4
GLADIOLUS LN
- SF 94132 667-C6
GLADSTONE AV
1700 SJS 95124 873-J3
GLADSTONE DR
- SF 94112 667-H7
2100 PIT 94565 574-G4
4200 CNCD 94521 593-A4
GLADSTONE PL
34500 FRMT 94555 732-E7
34600 FRMT 94555 752-F1
GLADWIN CT
2200 WLCK 94596 632-G1
GLADWIN DR
2200 WLCK 94596 632-G1
GLADYS AV
- BSBN 94005 688-B7
- MTVW 94043 812-A4
6500 ELCR 94530 609-C2
GLADYS CT
- LFYT 94595 612-A5
4900 LVMR 94550 696-B7
GLADYS DR
200 PLHL 94523 592-B5
GLADYS ST
- SF 94110 667-H5
GLADYS WY
1800 SJS 95124 853-G7
GLAMORGAN CT
3400 SJS 95127 835-B3
GLASCOCK ST
2800 OAK 94601 670-B1
GLASGLOW CT
400 MPS 95035 794-B6
GLASGOW
- HER 94547 569-F1
GLASGOW CIR
- DNVL 94526 653-D3
3600 LVMR 94550 695-J6
GLASGOW CT
2700 RCH 94806 588-J1
3500 SJS 95127 835-B2
13200 SAR 95070 852-E7
GLASGOW DR
- DNVL 94526 653-E3
400 PCFA 94044 707-B3
19900 SAR 95070 852-E7
GLASGOW LN
100 SCAR 94070 769-F4
GLASGOW PL
1000 DNVL 94526 653-D3
GLASGOW RD
900 CNCD 94518 592-F6
GLAUSER DR
2700 SJS 95133 814-G7
GLAZIER CT
4200 CNCD 94521 593-B3
GLAZIER DR
1500 CNCD 94521 593-B3
GLEASON AV
100 VAL 94590 530-C5
3500 SJS 95130 853-B4
GLEASON DR
- DBLN 94568 694-C3
GLEASON LN
35500 FRMT 94536 752-G1
GLEASON WY
1400 OAK 94606 650-A6
GLEN AV
- OAK 94611 649-J1
- SRFL 94901 586-F2
100 OAK 94611 650-A1
1100 BERK 94708 609-H7
1800 SBRN 94066 727-H2
2200 BERK 94709 609-H7

GLEN CT
- MLV 94941 606-E2
- SAUS 94965 627-B3
100 DNVL 94526 632-H7
100 WLCK 94595 612-C7
600 MPS 95035 794-B5
1000 LFYT 94549 611-E5
1700 PIN 94564 569-E5
GLEN DR
- MrnC 94903 566-J3
- SAUS 94965 627-A3
- MLV 94941 606-E1
500 SLN 94577 671-B7
700 MRTZ 94553 571-C3
GLEN LN
- MrnC 94945 526-J3
GLEN PKWY
- BSBN 94005 688-A7
GLEN PL
21200 CPTO 95014 832-C7
GLEN RD
- NVTO 94945 526-J3
- SANS 94960 566-A6
- MrnC 94945 526-J3
600 DNVL 94526 652-H1
800 DNVL 94526 632-H7
1000 LFYT 94549 611-E5
GLEN ST
700 MRTZ 94553 571-F5
GLEN WY
- LKSP 94939 586-D6
900 HIL 94010 728-C7
2000 EPA 94303 791-B1
W GLEN WY
600 WDSD 94062 789-E3
GLENA CT
1300 SJS 95122 854-H1
GLEN ADEN CT
2900 SJS 95148 835-C7
GLENAIRE DR
- SRFL 94901 586-G3
GLEN ALMA WY
2500 SJS 95148 835-C7
GLEN ALPINE
300 MRGA 94556 631-E7
GLEN ALPINE DR
- DNVL 94526 652-G3
GLEN ALPINE RD
- PDMT 94611 650-C1
100 OAK 94611 650-C1
GLEN ALTO CT
3000 SJS 95148 855-D1
GLEN ALTO DR
500 LALT 94024 831-F1
GLEN AMADOR CT
2700 SJS 95148 835-B7
GLEN ANGUS WY
2400 SJS 95148 835-C7
GLEN ARBOR CT
12700 SAR 95070 852-E6
GLEN ARMS DR
300 DNVL 94526 653-A3
GLENARMS DR
5900 OAK 94611 630-C5
GLEN ARTNEY CT
10900 OAK 94605 671-E4
GLEN ASCOT WY
2800 SJS 95148 835-C7
GLEN AULIN LN
100 SMCo 94010 728-B7
100 SMCo 94010 748-B1
GLENBAR AV
900 SUNV 94087 832-G5
GLENBLAIR WY
1100 CMBL 95008 873-B1
GLENBOROUGH DR
700 MTVW 94041 812-A7
GLEN BRAE CT
20400 SAR 95070 852-F6
GLEN BRAE DR
13000 SAR 95070 852-E7
19800 SAR 95070 872-E1
GLENBRAE LN
1200 SJS 95118 874-C4
GLENBRIDGE CT
100 PLHL 94523 592-D4
GLENBRIER DR
2600 SJS 95130 852-J7
GLENBROOK AV
- DALY 94015 687-A6
- SF 94114 667-E3
1000 SJS 95125 853-J3
GLENBROOK CT
2000 CNCD 94520 572-E6
7600 PLE 94588 693-H7
GLENBROOK DR
- HIL 94010 748-G4
600 PA 94306 811-D3
5500 OAK 94618 630-A5
GLENBROOK LN
100 SBRN 94066 727-G1
23600 AlaC 94541 692-C7
GLENBROOK ST
32200 UNC 94587 732-C4
GLENBURRY WY
500 SJS 95123 874-E3
GLENCO DR
10200 SCIC 95014 832-D7
GLENCOE CT
700 SUNV 94087 832-F4
GLENCOE DR
38600 FRMT 94536 752-J5
GLEN COMO WY
2900 SJS 95148 835-C7
GLEN COTSWOLD CT
2500 SJS 95148 835-C7
GLENCOURT
1000 OAK 94611 630-F6
GLENCOURT WY
300 PCFA 94044 707-B4
GLENCOVA PL
43800 FRMT 94539 773-G2
GLEN COVE PKWY
200 VAL 94591 550-E1
GLEN COVE RD
- SolC 94591 550-E1
100 SolC 94591 530-E7
100 VAL 94591 530-E7
100 VAL 94591 550-E1
GLEN COVE MARINA RD
- VAL 94591 550-E2

GLENCRAG WY
600 WDSD 94062 789-E3
GLEN CRAIG CT
2900 SJS 95148 835-C7
GLENCREST CT
1500 SJS 95118 874-A2
GLENCREST DR
1500 SJS 95118 874-A2
GLENCREST WY
1500 SJS 95118 874-A2
GLEN CROW CT
2900 SJS 95148 835-C7
GLENDA CT
3200 PLE 94588 694-C7
GLENDALE AV
300 OAK 94618 629-J6
400 SUNV 94086 812-F5
1300 BERK 94708 609-J7
3000 SMCo 94063 790-D1
4000 CNCD 94521 593-A2
GLENDALE CIR
2300 ANT 94509 595-A2
GLENDALE DR
- SJS 95193 875-C4
37900 FRMT 94536 752-H5
GLENDALE RD
300 HIL 94010 748-F2
300 SMTO 94402 748-F2
GLENDALE ST
- SF 94114 667-F3
GLEN DARBY CT
2900 SJS 95148 835-C7
GLEN DECKER CT
2800 SJS 95148 835-B7
GLEN DELL DR
1300 SJS 95125 853-J4
GLENDENNING AV
2300 SCL 95050 833-C7
GLEN DIXON CT
2800 SJS 95148 835-B7
GLENDOME CIR
700 OAK 94602 650-C3
GLEN DONEGAL DR
2700 SJS 95148 835-B7
GLEN DOON CT
2600 SJS 95148 835-B7
GLENDORA AV
1000 OAK 94602 650-C3
GLENDORA CIR
300 DNVL 94526 652-J3
GLENDORA CT
6200 SJS 95123 874-F6
GLENDORA DR
100 MRTZ 94553 571-D5
1400 SMTO 94403 748-J6
44100 FRMT 94539 773-G2
GLEN DUFF WY
2400 SJS 95148 835-B7
GLEN DUNDEE CT
2500 SJS 95148 835-C7
GLEN DUNDEE WY
2400 SJS 95148 835-B7
GLENEAGLE
- MRGA 94556 631-B6
GLENEAGLE AV
600 HAY 94544 712-E7
600 HAY 94544 732-D1
GLEN EAGLE CT
700 DNVL 94526 653-E6
GLENEAGLES CIR
5800 SJS 95138 875-H1
GLENEAGLES DR
5800 SJS 95138 875-H1
GLEN ECHO AV
1000 SJS 95125 853-J3
18300 MSER 95030 872-J6
GLENEDEN AV
- OAK 94611 629-J7
- OAK 94611 630-A7
GLENEDEN WY
3100 SJS 95117 853-D3
GLEN ELK CT
2600 SJS 95148 835-B7
GLEN ELLEN WY
1400 SJS 95125 853-J5
GLEN ELM WY
2400 SJS 95148 835-C7
GLEN EVANS CT
2800 SJS 95148 835-B7
GLEN EXETER WY
2400 SJS 95148 835-B7
GLEN EYRIE AV
1100 SJS 95125 854-A2
1100 SJS 95125 853-J3
GLEN FALL CT
2500 SJS 95148 835-C7
GLEN FARM CT
2400 SJS 95148 835-C7
GLEN FENTON WY
2600 SJS 95148 835-B7
GLEN FERGUSON CIR
2600 SJS 95148 835-C7
GLENFIELD AV
1300 OAK 94602 650-C3
GLENFIELD CT
1600 SJS 95125 854-A7
GLENFIELD DR
1600 SJS 95125 854-A7
GLENFINNAN CT
1000 SJS 95122 854-G1
GLENFINNAN DR
1000 SJS 95122 854-G1
GLEN FIRTH DR
2700 SJS 95133 814-G7
GLENFORD PARK CT
400 SJS 95136 874-F1
GLEN FOX CT
2400 SJS 95148 835-C7
GLEN FROST CT
2800 SJS 95148 835-C7
GLENGARRY DR
1100 WLCK 94596 632-G1
3800 SJS 95121 855-C4
GLENGARRY LN
- DBLN 94568 693-E5
1100 WLCK 94596 632-G1
GLENGARRY WY
- HIL 94010 748-F5
GLENGROVE WY
3800 SJS 95121 855-C4
GLEN HAIG WY
2400 SJS 95148 835-C7

GLEN HANCOCK CT
2500 SJS 95148 835-C7
GLEN HANLEIGH DR
2400 SJS 95148 835-B7
GLEN HARBOR DR
6000 SJS 95123 875-A6
GLEN HARDY CT
2600 SJS 95148 835-B7
GLEN HARWICK CT
2500 SJS 95148 835-C7
GLEN HASTINGS CT
2500 SJS 95148 835-C7
GLEN HAVEN AV
1800 WLCK 94595 612-C7
1800 WLCK 94595 632-C1
2000 CCCo 94595 632-C1
GLEN HAVEN CT
5600 SJS 95129 852-H3
GLEN HAVEN DR
1200 SJS 95129 852-H4
GLENHAVEN LN
100 SF 94131 667-D3
GLEN HAWKINS CT
2800 SJS 95148 835-C7
GLEN HEATHER DR
2700 SJS 95133 814-G7
GLEN HEDGE CT
2500 SJS 95148 835-C7
GLENHILL CT
- DNVL 94526 653-D4
700 FRMT 94539 753-G7
700 NVTO 94947 526-A4
GLENHILL DR
800 FRMT 94539 753-G7
GLEN HOLLOW RD
- DNVL 94506 653-F2
GLEN HOLLOW WY
- SJS 95132 814-E5
GLENHOLLOW WY
5000 ANT 94509 595-E4
GLENHURST DR
1600 SJS 95124 873-J2
GLEN IAN CT
2500 SJS 95148 835-B7
GLEN ISLE AV
2500 PLE 94588 694-F7
GLEN ISLE CT
4200 PLE 94588 694-F6
GLEN KEATS CT
2700 SJS 95148 835-C7
GLEN KELLER CT
2500 SJS 95148 835-B7
GLEN KEW CT
2500 SJS 95148 835-B7
GLENKIRK CT
2200 SJS 95124 853-H6
GLENKIRK DR
2100 SJS 95124 853-H6
GLENLOCH WY
600 SMCo 94062 789-E1
GLENLOCK ST
2400 CCCo 94806 589-A2
GLEN LOMAN WY
2600 SJS 95148 835-B7
GLENLY RD
3300 OAK 94605 671-A3
GLEN MANOR PL
11100 OAK 94605 671-E4
GLEN MAWR AV
6700 ELCR 94530 609-C1
GLEN MEAD CT
700 SJS 95133 814-G7
GLEN MEADOW CT
- DNVL 94526 653-F4
1100 SJS 95125 854-A4
GLENMERE WY
700 SMCo 94062 789-F2
GLENMONT DR
4100 SJS 95136 874-D1
21200 SAR 95070 872-C2
GLENMOOR CIR
400 MPS 95035 793-H6
GLENMOOR CT
500 MPS 95035 793-J6
4500 FRMT 94536 752-H5
GLENMOOR DR
37400 FRMT 94536 752-H5
GLENMOOR WY
1200 SJS 95129 852-F4
GLENMOUNT DR
2200 PIT 94565 574-E4
GLENN AV
400 CMBL 95008 873-C1
1100 SJS 95125 854-A3
1100 SJS 95125 853-J3
4900 SPAB 94805 589-A5
5400 SPAB 94806 589-A5
GLENN COM
1000 LVMR 94550 695-F6
GLENN ST
- VAL 94590 530-B4
4500 FRMT 94536 752-G4
GLENN WY
- SMCo 94002 769-G1
1500 RDWC 94061 790-A2
GLENNAN CT
5400 SJS 95129 852-H4
GLENNAN DR
500 RDWC 94061 789-H2
GLENN ELLEN DR
23000 AlaC 94541 692-D7
GLEN OAK CT
1600 CCCo 94549 611-J1
GLENOAK CT
5500 SJS 95129 852-H3
GLEN OAKS WY
6500 OAK 94611 630-F6
GLENOAKS WY
7300 DBLN 94568 693-H2
GLENORA WY
- AlaC 94586 713-J7
GLEN PARK AV
- SRFL 94901 566-G6
GLENPARK DR
4300 SJS 95136 874-D2
GLEN PARK RD
3500 OAK 94602 650-C4
GLEN PINE DR
1400 SJS 95125 854-A4
GLEN RIDGE AV
- LGTS 95030 872-J7

GLENRIDGE DR
900 SJS 95136 874-D1
GLENRIDGE WY
5100 ANT 94509 595-E4
GLENRIO DR
2500 SJS 95121 855-C3
GLENROCK CT
1600 SJS 95124 873-J7
GLENROSE AV
- DALY 94015 687-A4
- DALY 94015 686-J4
GLENROY DR
1600 SJS 95124 873-J2
GLEN SHARON WY
2800 SJS 95148 835-B7
GLENSIDE CIR
700 LFYT 94549 631-H1
GLENSIDE CT
2900 CNCD 94520 572-E6
GLENSIDE DR
600 LFYT 94549 631-H1
700 SJS 95123 874-G6
2800 CNCD 94520 572-E6
GLENSIDE WY
- MrnC 94903 566-F5
GLENSTONE CT
1700 SJS 95121 855-C4
GLENTREE CT
5100 SJS 95129 852-J2
GLENTREE DR
5000 SJS 95129 852-J2
GLEN UNA AV
1700 SJS 95125 854-B4
GLEN UNA DR
15400 SAR 95070 872-F5
15500 SCIC 95030 872-E5
15500 SAR 95030 872-F5
GLEN VALLEY CIR
- DNVL 94526 653-B5
GLENVIEW
- ALA 94501 649-D6
GLENVIEW AV
500 OAK 94610 650-A3
10300 CPTO 95014 852-F1
GLENVIEW CIR
100 VAL 94591 530-E2
GLENVIEW CT
800 MPS 95035 814-E1
GLENVIEW DR
- SF 94131 667-E4
100 MRTZ 94553 591-G2
200 SF 94131 667-E4
700 SBRN 94066 727-F1
900 SBRN 94066 707-F7
2100 MPS 95035 814-E1
6700 SJS 95120 894-F2
38200 FRMT 94536 752-H5
GLEN VIEW RD
1800 WLCK 94595 612-C7
1800 WLCK 94595 632-C1
GLENVILLE DR
1600 SJS 95124 873-J2
GLEN WILLOW CT
- SJS 95125 854-E5
GLENWILLOW LN
1100 CNCD 94521 593-D7
GLEN WOOD
800 MTVW 94041 811-H7
GLENWOOD
- HER 94547 569-F4
300 MRTZ 94553 571-J5
GLENWOOD AV
- OAK 94611 629-J7
- ROSS 94957 586-B2
100 ATN 94027 790-F2
100 DALY 94015 687-A3
100 WDSD 94062 789-G5
200 DALY 94015 686-J3
400 MLPK 94025 790-F2
600 MrnC 94965 606-D6
1100 SJS 95125 854-A4
1400 SJS 95125 853-J4
3500 RDWC 94062 789-G1
GLENWOOD CT
200 DNVL 94526 633-B6
1100 LVMR 94550 715-F1
5000 PLE 94588 693-J7
5400 RCH 94803 590-A3
GLENWOOD DR
- SRFL 94901 566-G6
1100 MLBR 94030 727-H3
1200 CNCD 94518 592-H3
1900 ANT 94509 575-E6
20100 AlaC 94552 692-F3
GLENWOOD ISL
- ALA 94501 669-H3
GLENWOOD ST
300 SCAR 94070 769-F3
800 VAL 94591 530-D4
1100 LVMR 94550 715-F1
4000 FRMT 94538 773-D2
GLENWOOD WY
- ELCR 94530 609-C2
5300 RCH 94803 590-A3
GLENWOOD GLADE
- OAK 94611 630-C6
GLIDDEN WY
4300 FRMT 94536 752-J5
GLIDDON ST
19000 AlaC 94546 692-C4
19100 AlaC 94552 692-C4
GLIDER DR
6100 SJS 95123 874-J7
GLISTENING CT
- MPS 95035 793-H6
GLITHERO CT
1000 SJS 95112 834-D3
GLOBE AL
- SF 94127 667-D6
GLORIA AV
300 SCIC 95127 835-A2
GLORIA CIR
- MLPK 94025 790-H2
GLORIA CT
- MRGA 94556 631-E7
- SF 94112 687-F1
- VAL 94590 550-C2
600 SMTO 94401 749-B1
2300 PLE 94588 714-A5
GLORIA DR
- SRFL 94901 586-E1
200 PLHL 94523 592-B4

STREET
Block City ZIP Pg-Grid

GLORIA DR
1200 PIT 94565 574-E7
GLORIA ST
100 HAY 94544 712-A5
2300 ELCR 94530 589-B7
GLORIA TER
3000 CCCo 94549 591-H7
3200 CCCo 94549 611-J1
GLORIA WY
500 BEN 94510 551-B3
2400 EPA 94303 791-B1
2500 EPA 94303 771-B7
GLORIA TERRACE CT
3100 CCCo 94549 591-J7
GLORIETTA BLVD
100 ORIN 94563 630-J3
100 ORIN 94563 631-A2
600 LFYT 94549 611-B7
3800 LFYT 94563 611-A7
4200 ORIN 94563 611-A7
GLORIETTA CIR
2700 SCL 95051 833-B7
GLORIETTA CT
- ORIN 94563 631-A3
- ORIN 94563 630-J3
GLOUCESTER
- HER 94547 569-J3
GLOUCESTER CT
900 ANT 94509 575-C7
1000 SUNV 94087 832-G5
GLOUCESTER CV
- SRFL 94901 587-A2
GLOUCESTER LN
600 FCTY 94404 749-G5
5000 MRTZ 94553 572-A6
GLOUCESTER PL
3300 FRMT 94555 732-D7
GLOUCESTER ST
800 ANT 94509 575-C7
GLOUCHESTER CT
5000 SJS 95136 874-F3
GLOVER ST
- SF 94109 647-J4
GLOWING CT
5900 SJS 95120 874-B7
GLYNIS DR
3000 RCH 94806 589-A1
GOBEL WY
- WLCK 94596 612-C2
GOBLE DR
- CCCo 94565 573-E2
GOBLE LN
- SJS 95111 854-F5
GODDESS CT
6200 SJS 95129 852-F3
GODETIA DR
900 WDSD 94062 789-F4
GODEUS ST
- SF 94110 667-H5
GODFREY PL
38800 FRMT 94536 753-D2
GODWIT CT
2100 UNC 94587 732-G7
GOEBEL AV
4100 PA 94306 811-C2
GOECKEN RD
- AlaC 94550 696-G2
GOETHALS CT
- CLAY 94517 593-G7
GOETHE ST
- DALY 94014 687-D2
- SF 94112 687-D2
GOETTEL CT
- BEN 94510 551-A3
GOETTINGEN ST
- SF 94134 668-A7
800 SF 94134 688-A1
GOFF AV
2100 PIT 94565 574-C3
GOHEEN CIR
100 VAL 94591 530-D3
GOING LN
700 NVTO 94947 525-H3
GOLD CT
3100 RCH 94803 589-E1
3200 FRMT 94539 753-E7
3200 LFYT 94549 631-H2
GOLD ST
- SCIC 95002 813-B1
- SF 94133 648-A4
1300 SJS 95002 793-B7
1500 SJS 95002 813-B1
GOLD CREEK CT
- DNVL 94506 654-B6
7200 SJS 95120 894-H4
GOLD CREEK DR
- AlaC 94542 692-E6
GOLD CREEK WY
7200 SJS 95120 894-H4
GOLDCREST CIR
2100 PLE 94566 714-C2
GOLD CREST CT
4000 PIT 94565 574-C6
GOLDCREST CT
4500 ANT 94509 595-H3
GOLDCREST WY
4600 ANT 94509 595-J3
GOLDEN AV
4000 CNCD 94521 593-A3
GOLDEN CT
- SF 94109 647-J5
GOLDEN DR
5000 SJS 95129 852-J3
GOLDEN RD
4700 PLE 94566 714-D2
GOLDEN WY
900 MTVW 94040 831-G2
1000 LALT 94024 831-G2
GOLDEN ACRE CT
1000 SJS 95136 874-C2
GOLDEN ASPEN WY
11000 CPTO 95014 832-D6
GOLDEN ASTER CT
- BSBN 94005 687-H4
GOLDEN BAY DR
200 PCFA 94044 707-A2
GOLDEN BEAR DR
4500 ANT 94509 595-H2
GOLDEN CREEK TER
700 SJS 95111 855-B7
GOLDEN DEW CIR
2100 SJS 95121 855-C3

GOLDEN EAGLE LN
- BSBN 94005 687-J4
GOLDEN EAGLE PL
6000 CLAY 94517 594-A5
GOLDEN EAGLE WY
6000 CLAY 94517 594-A5
7800 PLE 94588 714-B6
GOLDEN GATE
1700 CCCo 94806 569-B5
GOLDEN GATE AV
- BLV 94920 607-C7
- SF 94102 648-A6
- BLV 94920 627-D1
- SF 94102 647-F7
200 RCH 94801 588-C7
600 RCH 94801 608-C1
1000 SF 94115 647-F7
1200 SF 94117 647-F7
2200 SF 94118 647-F7
2500 SF 94118 647-D7
2500 SF 94117 647-E7
5000 OAK 94618 630-B5
5900 CCCo 94806 589-B4
GOLDEN GATE CT
100 CCCo 94806 569-B5
GOLDEN GATE DR
- SRFL 94901 586-J3
6600 DBLN 94568 693-H4
7000 SJS 95129 852-E3
15100 SLN 94579 691-C6
GOLDEN GATE PL
900 NVTO 94945 526-C2
GOLDEN GATE WY
3400 LFYT 94549 611-F6
5000 OAK 94618 630-A4
GOLDEN GATE BRG
FRWY U.S.-101
- SF - 627-B7
- SF - 647-B1
GOLDEN HILL CT
- CCCo 94596 612-F6
13600 LAH 94022 811-C7
GOLDENHILL DR
4200 PIT 94565 574-E7
GOLDEN HILL PL
100 CCCo 94596 612-F7
GOLDENHILL WY
2100 BEN 94510 551-C3
GOLDEN HILLS CT
100 DNVL 94526 653-B3
4500 ANT 94509 595-H3
GOLDEN HILLS DR
100 PTLV 94028 810-C5
1700 MPS 95035 794-D6
GOLDEN HIND PASG
- CMAD 94925 606-J1
100 CMAD 94925 586-J7
200 CMAD 94925 607-A1
GOLDEN HINDE BLVD
- SRFL 94903 566-D4
GOLDEN IRIS TER
- MrnC 94903 546-A6
GOLDEN LEAF CT
- SJS 95136 874-J7
GOLDEN LEAF WY
1300 CNCD 94521 593-B5
GOLDENLEAF WY
900 PIT 94565 574-E5
GOLDEN MEADOW DR
3000 CCCo 94526 633-C4
GOLDEN MEADOW LN
- CCCo 94526 633-B4
GOLDEN MEADOW PL
300 CCCo 94526 633-B4
GOLDEN MEADOW SQ
1400 SJS 95117 853-C4
GOLDEN OAK CT
700 SUNV 94086 832-F2
4200 CCCo 94506 654-C4
GOLDEN OAK DR
- PTLV 94028 810-D5
700 SUNV 94086 832-F2
GOLDEN OAK WY
1200 SJS 95120 874-C6
GOLDENRAIN AV
200 FRMT 94539 793-H1
GOLDEN RAIN CT
200 SJS 95111 875-A1
GOLDEN RAIN DR
- SJS 95111 875-A2
GOLDEN RAIN RD
- WLCK 94595 632-A1
GOLDENRIDGE CT
- SMTO 94402 748-C7
GOLDEN RIDGE LN
- CCCo 94526 633-C4
GOLDEN RIDGE RD
100 CCCo 94526 633-C4
GOLDENROD CT
800 SUNV 94086 832-F2
GOLDENROD DR
100 HER 94547 570-A4
5400 LVMR 94550 696-C3
37600 NWK 94560 752-G6
GOLDENROD LN
2000 SRMN 94583 653-H7
GOLDEN SLOPES CT
300 BEN 94510 551-C4
GOLDEN SPRINGS LN
1200 CNCD 94521 593-B4
GOLDEN STATE DR
3400 SCL 95051 832-J5
GOLDENTREE DR
1600 SJS 95131 814-C5
GOLDFIELD DR
5600 SJS 95123 874-J4
GOLDFINCH AV
200 LVMR 94550 715-D1
GOLDFINCH CT
- NVTO 94947 525-G4
GOLDFINCH TER
3700 FRMT 94555 732-J3
GOLDFINCH WY
1500 SUNV 94087 832-F5
GOLD HILL WY
100 VAL 94589 509-H5
GOLD HILL FIRE RD
- SRFL 94901 566-J6
100 SRFL 94901 567-A5
GOLD HILL GRADE
- MrnC 94901 566-J6
- SRFL 94901 566-J6

GOLD HILLS DR
- AlaC 94542 692-E6
GOLDHUNTER CT
100 FCTY 94404 749-G2
GOLDING LN
- SF 94131 667-F3
GOLD LAKE CT
400 CCCo 94506 654-C4
GOLD MEADOW CT
- SJS 95135 855-H7
GOLD MINE DR
- SF 94131 667-F5
GOLD MINER CT
- NVTO 94947 526-A4
GOLDPINE CT
6800 SJS 95120 894-E3
GOLDPINE WY
6800 SJS 95120 894-E3
GOLD POPPY CT
- DNVL 94526 653-E3
GOLDRIDGE CT
3200 SJS 95135 855-D2
N GOLD RIDGE DR
- AlaC 94542 692-F6
S GOLD RIDGE DR
- AlaC 94542 692-F6
GOLD RUN WY
100 SJS 95136 874-G1
GOLDRUSH CT
1400 SJS 95131 814-D6
GOLDSMITH DR
35500 FRMT 94536 752-G1
GOLDSTONE CT
- DNVL 94506 653-H4
GOLDWOOD CT
2600 SJS 95148 835-D6
GOLETA AV
- SF 94132 667-A6
12200 SAR 95070 852-E5
GOLETA CT
1400 WLCK 94596 612-A2
5100 ANT 94509 595-F4
12300 SAR 95070 852-E5
GOLETA TER
300 FRMT 94536 753-E1
GOLF AV
- SRFL 94903 566-F4
- MrnC 94903 566-F4
GOLF BLVD
- VAL 94591 510-J6
GOLF CT
1000 MTVW 94040 812-A7
GOLF DR
3100 SJS 95127 814-H7
3400 SCIC 95127 814-J6
3700 SCIC 95127 814-J6
4100 SCIC 95127 815-A6
4300 LVMR 94550 696-A3
GOLF LN
- SANS 94960 566-C6
- SCIC 94304 810-E3
- SMCo 94025 810-E3
GOLF RD
- AlaC 94566 714-B7
- AlaC 94566 734-B1
GOLF CLUB CIR
800 CCCo 94523 592-A2
GOLF CLUB CT
- PIT 94565 574-B4
GOLF CLUB RD
- PLHL 94523 592-B2
400 CCCo 94523 592-A2
2200 PIT 94565 574-B4
GOLF CLUB WY
600 CCCo 94523 592-A2
GOLF COURSE DR
- SMCo - 748-B2
- HIL - 748-B2
- SMCo 94010 748-B2
1200 CCCo 94708 610-A6
1200 OAK 94708 610-A6
3000 BERK 94708 610-A6
GOLF COURSE LN
7000 SJS 95139 895-E1
7000 SCIC 95119 895-E1
GOLF COURSE RD
1000 HAY 94541 711-D2
4600 ANT 94509 595-D3
4700 ANT - 595-D3
6600 SMCo 94010 748-D4
GOLF CREEK DR
1300 SJS 95120 894-D2
GOLF LINKS CIR
2200 SCL 95050 833-C6
GOLF LINKS DR
14600 LGTS 95030 873-B3
14800 SCIC 95030 873-B3
GOLF LINKS RD
8200 OAK 94605 671-A3
GOLF LINKS ST
200 PLHL 94549 591-H5
GOLF VIEW DR
400 SCIC 95127 815-A6
GOLUBIN COM
5400 FRMT 94555 752-C3
GOLZIO CT
2400 SJS 95133 814-F7
GOMER DR
2900 RCH 94806 589-A1
GOMER ST
1000 HAY 94544 711-J6
1100 HAY 94544 712-A6
GOMES CT
200 CMBL 95008 853-E5
GOMES DR
2600 SJS 95132 814-E5
GOMES RD
1400 FRMT 94539 753-E5
GOMEZ RD
- CCCo - 590-B2
GOMEZ WY
- MLV 94941 606-F5
GOMPERS
3000 ALA 94501 649-F6
GONDO PTH
- OAK 94618 630-B5
GONDOLA WY
6300 SJS 95120 874-C7
6300 SJS 95120 894-C1
GONSALVES CT
- ALA 94502 669-H5

GONZAGA AV
400 VAL 94589 510-B6
2800 RCH 94806 589-A2
GONZAGA CT
1200 LVMR 94550 716-A2
GONZAGA PL
3300 SCL 95051 832-J2
GONZAGA ST
2400 EPA 94303 791-C1
2500 EPA 94303 771-C7
GONZALES CT
5500 CNCD 94521 593-G5
GONZALEZ DR
- SF 94132 687-A1
GOODFELLOW AV
- DBLN 94568 694-B3
GOODFELLOW CT
- MRGA 94556 631-C3
- ORIN 94563 631-C3
GOODFELLOW DR
- MRGA 94556 631-C3
100 ORIN 94563 631-C3
200 CCCo 94553 571-C6
GOODHILL RD
100 MrnC 94904 586-B3
GOODING DR
800 ALB 94706 609-D6
800 ALB 94804 609-D6
GOODMAN RD
400 PCFA 94044 707-A6
GOODRICH ST
100 HAY 94544 712-A5
GOODRICH WY
38500 FRMT 94536 753-D1
GOODRICK AV
2500 RCH 94801 588-F2
2500 CCCo 94801 588-F2
3000 RCH 94801 568-F7
3000 RCH 94806 568-F7
GOODWIN AV
700 SJS 95128 853-H2
1900 RDWC 94061 789-J2
3000 RDWC 94061 790-A2
GOODWIN CT
- RDWC 94061 789-H3
GOODWIN DR
100 SBRN 94066 707-D6
GOODWIN ST
100 HAY 94544 712-A5
GOODY LN
1400 SJS 95131 814-C7
GOODYEAR ST
- SJS 95110 854-C2
GOOSEBERRY CT
1200 SUNV 94087 832-B3
GOOSEBERRY TR
- CCCo - 652-E2
GOOSE LAKE CT
800 SJS 95123 874-E5
GORDOLA CT
300 SJS 95111 875-A1
GORDON AV
300 SCIC 95127 815-A7
600 SCIC 95127 814-J6
800 BLMT 94002 769-E1
2000 SMCo 94025 790-D6
2900 SCL 95051 812-J7
2900 SCL 95051 832-J1
5200 ELCR 94530 609-B1
5200 RCH 94804 609-B1
GORDON CT
- CCCo 94803 569-D6
500 BEN 94510 550-H1
20500 SAR 95070 852-D6
GORDON PL
4300 FRMT 94555 752-D1
GORDON RD
100 CCCo 94598 612-E4
4600 AlaC 94546 692-A3
GORDON ST
- SF 94103 668-A1
- SAUS 94965 626-J2
1000 MPS 95035 794-B5
1200 RDWC 94061 790-A1
1300 VAL 94590 530-B5
4000 FRMT 94555 752-D1
4300 OAK 94601 650-E7
GORDON WY
100 PCFA 94044 707-A3
100 CCCo 94553 591-E2
16300 AlaC 94578 691-F5
N GORDON WY
- LALT 94022 811-E6
S GORDON WY
- LALT 94022 811-E7
GORDON MILL TR
- SMCo 94062 809-A3
GORDY DR
1500 SJS 95131 814-C7
GOREE CT
- CCCo 94553 571-H4
GORGAS AV
- SF 94129 647-E3
- SF 94129 647-E3
GORHAM AV
- SF 94112 667-G6
GORHAM PL
9700 SRMN 94583 673-F6
GORSKY RD
- SCIC 94035 812-B3
GOSFORD CT
- SJS 95139 875-G7
GOSHEN CT
300 SRMN 94583 673-G6
GOSHEN PL
100 SRMN 94583 673-G6
GOSHEN ST
32700 UNC 94587 732-B7
GOSS ST
1700 OAK 94607 649-C3
GOSSER ST
300 MPS 95035 794-A3
GOTHIC DR
- NVTO 94947 526-A4
GOUGH ST
- SF 94103 667-H1
- SF 94102 647-H4
100 SF 94102 667-H1
300 SF 94109 647-H4
2500 SF 94123 647-H4
2700 SF 94123 647-H3

GOULARTE DR
2700 PIN 94564 569-H6
GOULD CT
1600 ALA 94501 670-A2
GOULD ST
- SF 94124 688-B1
9800 OAK 94603 670-H6
GOULDIN RD
1600 OAK 94611 630-E6
GOVER LN
1500 SCAR 94070 769-H5
GOVERNORS AV
500 SCIC 94305 790-G7
GOVERNORS BAY DR
900 RDWC 94065 750-A5
GOWER DR
5300 SJS 95118 874-A5
GOYA DR
400 SUNV 94087 832-E2
GOYA RD
100 PTLV 94028 810-C4
GOYAK DR
3300 LFYT 94549 611-G3
GRAACH CT
4100 SJS 95135 855-G3
GRACE AV
100 EPA 94303 791-B1
900 OAK 94608 629-F5
1400 CMBL 95125 853-H5
1400 SCIC 95125 853-H5
GRACE CT
- SCIC 95125 853-H5
200 CMAD 94925 606-G1
700 HAY 94541 711-J1
700 LVMR 94550 715-E2
1000 ALA 94501 670-A3
GRACE DR
500 MLPK 94025 790-E6
GRACE LN
- MrnC 94941 606-F3
2100 SPAB 94806 588-J4
GRACE ST
- SF 94103 647-J7
600 LVMR 94550 715-E2
600 HAY 94544 711-H1
900 SLN 94578 691-D4
GRACELAND AV
2400 SCAR 94070 769-F5
GRACELAND DR
- SRFL 94901 566-G7
GRACELAND LN
- SCAR 94070 769-F5
GRACKLE CT
2100 UNC 94587 732-G7
GRACKLE WY
1500 SUNV 94087 832-F5
GRADELL PL
3300 SJS 95148 835-D6
GRADO CT
- DNVL 94526 653-C1
GRAEAGLE
- OAK 94605 671-D2
GRAFF AV
1300 SLN 94577 671-C7
1300 SLN 94577 691-D1
GRAFF CT
1600 SLN 94577 671-D7
GRAFFIAN ST
10200 OAK 94603 670-J6
GRAFTON AV
- SF 94112 687-D1
GRAFTON WY
2800 SJS 95148 835-E7
GRAGG LN
1300 CNCD 94518 592-E6
GRAHAM AV
6500 NWK 94560 752-E7
GRAHAM CT
700 DNVL 94526 653-C3
5900 LVMR 94550 716-D1
GRAHAM LN
1600 SCL 95050 833-C3
GRAHAM PL
- OAK 94619 651-B7
GRAHAM ST
- SF 94129 647-D4
- SF 94129 647-D4
100 SJS 95110 854-C1
4000 PLE 94566 714-E2
GRAHAM WY
1600 SLN 94578 691-D3
GRALINA TER
100 FRMT 94539 773-H1
GRAMA TER
4000 FRMT 94536 752-H1
GRAMARCY AV
- UNC 94587 732-B4
GRAMERCY DR
100 SMTO 94402 748-H1
15900 AlaC 94578 691-F4
GRAMERCY PL
100 SJS 95116 834-G2
300 OAK 94603 670-G7
GRAMMERCY LN
4300 CNCD 94521 593-A5
GRANADA AV
- SF 94112 687-D1
200 SF 94112 667-D7
3300 SCL 95051 833-A4
3300 SCL 95051 832-J4
9200 OAK 94605 671-B3
21600 CPTO 95014 852-B1
GRANADA CIR
28300 HAY 94544 732-A1
GRANADA CT
- PTLV 94028 810-D6
1100 ANT 94509 575-B6
2300 PIN 94564 569-F6
3300 SCL 95051 832-J4
20700 SAR 95070 852-D5
GRANADA DR
- PCFA 94044 727-A4
- CMAD 94925 606-J1
100 MTVW 94043 811-H4
100 SRMN 94583 673-G5
300 SSF 94080 707-F5
1000 PCFA 94044 726-J4
1500 BURL 94010 728-B6
1700 CNCD 94519 593-A1
1700 CNCD 94519 592-J1
1800 CNCD 94519 572-J7
4000 PIT 94565 574-E6

GRANADA DR
28400 HAY 94544 732-A1
GRANADA RD
4000 CCCo 94803 589-C1
GRANADA ST
800 BLMT 94002 749-E7
1000 BLMT 94002 769-F1
1000 VAL 94591 530-G6
GRANADA WY
100 LGTS 95030 873-A3
900 SJS 95122 854-G1
4700 UNC 94587 731-J6
GRANADO AV
4700 FRMT 94536 752-F4
GRANAT CT
- SF 94118 647-C7
GRAND AV
200 OAK 94612 649-H3
200 SJS 95126 853-J1
200 OAK 94610 649-J3
200 SCIC 95126 853-J1
300 SSF 94080 707-F2
600 SRFL 94901 586-G1
1200 OAK 94610 650-A2
1200 PDMT 94610 650-A2
1300 PCFA 94044 726-G4
1300 SRFL 94901 566-G6
1400 SLN 94577 691-C1
1500 PDMT 94611 650-A2
1500 PDMT 94611 630-A7
1600 OAK 94611 630-A7
1700 SLN 94577 671-C7
21500 CPTO 95014 832-B7
E GRAND AV
- SSF 94080 708-A3
- SSF 94080 707-J3
W GRAND AV
- OAK 94626 649-D1
- OAK 94649 649-D1
600 OAK 94612 649-D1
800 OAK 94607 649-D1
GRAND BLVD
- SMTO 94401 748-H1
- SMTO 94401 728-H7
1200 SJS 95002 793-C7
1200 SJS 95002 813-B1
GRAND CT
- SRFL 94901 566-G6
GRAND ST
- RDWC 94062 769-J6
300 ALA 94501 669-J1
400 RDWC 94062 770-A7
900 RDWC 94061 770-A7
2000 ALA 94501 649-J7
22500 HAY 94541 711-H2
24100 HAY 94544 711-J2
GRAND TER
- SRFL 94901 566-H7
GRANDBROOK WY
800 SJS 95111 855-A5
GRANDBROOK PARK CT
43100 FRMT 94538 773-C3
GRANDBY DR
2400 SJS 95130 852-J7
GRAND CANYON AV
5800 CCCo 94806 589-B4
GRAND CANYON CT
- SRMN 94583 673-F3
3900 PLE 94588 714-A1
GRAND CANYON LN
- SRMN 94583 673-G3
GRAND COULEE AV
600 SUNV 94087 832-D5
GRANDE CAMINO
2600 WLCK 94598 612-H2
GRANDE CORTE
2900 WLCK 94598 612-H2
GRANDE PASEO
- MrnC 94903 546-E7
GRANDE VISTA
- NVTO 94947 525-H2
GRANDE VISTA AV
2400 OAK 94601 650-C6
GRANDE VISTA PL
2300 OAK 94601 650-C5
GRAND FIR AV
500 SUNV 94086 832-F2
GRANDIN CT
300 SJS 95123 874-J4
GRAND LAKE DR
3000 FRMT 94555 732-B6
GRAND MEADOW LN
6300 SJS 95135 855-J7
GRAND OAK CT
400 WLCK 94598 612-J2
GRAND OAK WY
- SJS 95135 875-J1
GRANDPARK CIR
300 SJS 95136 874-G1
GRANDSTAND WY
- SJS 95111 854-G4
GRAND TETON DR
1000 PCFA 94044 727-B5
1500 MPS 95035 814-D1
GRANDTETON PARK ST
42400 FRMT 94538 773-C1
GRAND VIEW
- CCCo 94553 571-E3
GRAND VIEW AV
- SF 94114 667-F4
GRANDVIEW AV
- CCCo 94525 550-C5
- DALY 94015 687-A7
700 MRTZ 94553 571-E3
15800 MSER 95030 872-J6
26700 HAY 94542 712-C4
GRAND VIEW CT
500 RCH 94801 588-C7
GRANDVIEW CT
- DNVL 94506 653-G5
1400 MRTZ 94553 571-E3
GRAND VIEW DR
1100 OAK 94705 630-B4
1800 OAK 94618 630-C4
GRANDVIEW DR
- WDSD 94062 809-G5
400 SSF 94080 708-C3
2600 SCIC 95133 814-G7
2600 SJS 95133 814-G7
15800 MSER 95030 872-J6
GRAND VIEW PL
- CCCo 94595 612-B7

GRAND VIEW PL
- CCCo 94595 632-B1
1000 OAK 94705 630-B3
GRANDVIEW TER
- SF 94114 667-F3
GRANDWELL WY
- SJS 95138 875-D4
GRANDWOOD WY
6900 SJS 95120 894-J3
GRANEY CT
900 CNCD 94518 592-G6
GRANGE TER
4900 FRMT 94555 752-A3
GRANGE WY
100 SRFL 94901 587-B5
GRANGER AV
1700 SCIC 94024 831-H3
1700 LALT 94024 831-H3
30600 UNC 94587 731-J5
30800 UNC 94587 732-A5
GRANGER ST
- WLCK 94596 612-C5
GRANGER TER
500 SUNV 94087 832-D5
GRANGER WY
1500 RDWC 94061 789-J3
GRANGNELLI AV
300 ANT 94509 575-E4
GRANITE CIR
300 ANT 94509 595-E2
GRANITE CT
- MPS 95035 794-A6
- SCAR 94070 769-F6
300 ANT 94509 595-E2
900 MRTZ 94553 571-G7
2200 CCCo 94507 632-H3
4300 UNC 94587 732-A6
14900 SAR 95070 872-G4
GRANITE DR
2100 CCCo 94507 632-H4
GRANITE LN
2300 SJS 95133 834-F1
GRANITE PL
300 PIT 94565 574-B5
GRANITE ST
100 VAL 94589 510-B5
GRANITE WY
800 SJS 95133 834-F2
14600 SAR 95070 872-G3
GRANITE CREEK PL
2800 SJS 95127 834-J4
GRANITE ROCK WY
100 SJS 95136 854-G7
GRANLEE RD
- MrnC 94903 566-H3
GRANT AV
- SF 94108 648-A5
100 PA 94306 791-B7
500 AlaC 94580 691-C7
700 NVTO 94945 526-B3
1000 SF 94133 648-A4
1300 SF 94133 648-A3
1400 AlaC 94580 711-A1
2000 CCCo 94596 612-E7
2000 CCCo 94596 632-E1
2300 RCH 94801 588-H6
2500 RCH 94804 588-H6
GRANT CT
500 BEN 94510 550-H1
1300 LALT 94024 831-J3
4100 PLE 94566 714-G5
5300 FRMT 94538 752-J7
E GRANT PL
800 SMTO 94402 749-B2
W GRANT PL
800 SMTO 94402 749-B2
GRANT RD
1000 MTVW 94040 811-J7
1100 LALT 94024 831-J4
1100 MTVW 94040 831-J1
1100 SCIC 94040 831-J1
2200 LALT 94024 832-A5
GRANT ST
- FRMT 94538 753-D7
100 CMBL 95008 853-E5
200 SJS 95110 854-B1
300 VAL 94590 530-B7
700 BEN 94510 551-D6
900 VAL 94590 550-B1
1200 CNCD 94520 592-F1
1300 BERK 94703 609-G7
1400 BERK 94703 629-G1
1500 SCL 95050 833-E3
2200 CNCD 94520 572-E6
N GRANT ST
- SMTO 94401 729-A7
- SMTO 94401 749-A1
100 SMTO 94401 728-J7
S GRANT ST
- SMTO 94403 749-C3
- SMTO 94401 749-A1
400 SMTO 94402 749-A1
GRANT PARK LN
1800 LALT 94024 832-A4
1800 LALT 94024 831-J4
GRAN VIA
- CCCo 94507 632-E4
GRANVILLE AV
100 VAL 94591 530-D5
GRANVILLE CT
200 SJS 95139 895-F1
5300 FRMT 94536 752-G6
GRANVILLE DR
37600 FRMT 94536 752-G6
GRANVILLE WY
- SF 94127 667-D5
GRANZOTTO DR
3600 CNCD 94519 572-J7
3600 CNCD 94519 592-J1
GRAPE AV
600 SUNV 94087 832-B2
GRAPELEAF WY
4200 SJS 95135 855-G3
GRAPENUT CT
2200 ANT 94509 575-H6
GRAPEVINE CT
45400 FRMT 94539 774-A3
GRAPE VINE DR
500 PLE 94566 714-H3
GRAPEVINE PL
300 PLHL 94523 592-A4

STREET
Block City ZIP Pg-Grid

GRAPEVINE TER
2000 FRMT 94539 774-A3
GRAPEVINE WY
6500 SJS 95120 894-D1
GRAPE WAGON CIR
8700 SJS 95135 855-J6
GRAPEWOOD ST
100 VAL 94591 530-F5
GRAPNEL PL
10600 CPTO 95014 832-C6
GRAPPA PL
- PLE 94566 715-B5
GRASMERE PL
26900 HAY 94542 712-E3
GRASS CT
- NVTO 94949 546-F4
GRASSLAND CT
- DNVL 94526 653-E3
GRASSLAND DR
6000 AlaC 94552 692-F4
GRASSLAND TR
- CCCo - 652-C2
GRASSLAND WY
- ANT 94509 595-G3
GRASSMERE CIR
100 SRMN 94583 653-H7
GRASS VALLEY CT
- OAK 94605 671-E4
3400 SJS 95127 835-C4
GRASS VALLEY RD
4600 OAK 94605 671-E4
GRASS VALLEY WY
5100 ANT 94509 595-H5
GRASSWOOD CIR
5300 CNCD 94521 593-D6
GRASSWOOD CT
5200 CNCD 94521 593-D6
GRASSWOOD DR
3400 RCH 94803 589-F1
GRATTAN ST
- SF 94117 667-E2
200 SF 94117 667-E2
GRATTON WY
3000 CNCD 94520 572-F6
GRAU DR
100 FRMT 94536 733-A7
100 FRMT 94536 732-J7
GRAVATT DR
- OAK 94705 630-B3
GRAVENSTEIN ST
800 OAK 94603 670-H6
GRAVES AV
5000 SJS 95129 852-J5
GRAVES CT
100 VAL 94591 530-F5
GRAVINA PL
3400 PLE 94566 715-B6
GRAVITY CAR RD
- MrnC 94965 606-A2
GRAY CT
- BEN 94510 551-B1
GRAY ST
3500 OAK 94601 650-D6
GRAY FOX CIR
800 PLE 94566 714-H4
GRAY FOX CT
2800 PLE 94566 714-J4
GRAY FOX PL
- CLAY 94517 594-A5
GRAYMONT CIR
700 CNCD 94518 592-G7
GRAYMONT CT
2900 CNCD 94518 592-G7
GRAYS CT
4400 CNCD 94518 593-A5
GRAYS LN
- LGTS 95030 873-A7
GRAYSON CT
300 MLPK 94025 791-A1
300 MLPK 94025 790-J1
GRAYSON LN
700 PLHL 94523 591-J5
GRAYSON RD
700 PLHL 94523 591-H5
700 CCCo 94549 591-H5
800 PLHL 94523 592-A5
1000 PLHL 94549 591-H5
GRAYSON ST
700 BERK 94804 629-D4
GRAYSON TER
300 PLHL 94523 591-J5
GRAYSON WY
500 MPS 95035 794-B4
GRAYSTONE DR
- SSF 94080 707-D1
GRAYSTONE LN
- DALY 94014 687-E3
6600 SJS 95120 894-F1
6600 SCIC 95120 894-G1
GRAYSTONE TER
- SF 94114 667-F3
GRAYSTONE MDW CIR
6400 SJS 95120 874-F7
GRAYSTONE MDW DR
6400 SJS 95120 874-F7
GRAYWOOD DR
1400 SJS 95129 852-G4
GREAT HWY
- SF - 666-H4
500 SF 94121 646-G7
700 SF 94116 666-H4
700 SF 94122 666-H4
800 SF 94121 666-H4
1700 SF 94116 666-H5
2700 SF 94132 666-H6
GREAT AMERICA PKWY
- SCIC 95002 813-B3
- SJS 95002 813-B3
4100 SCL 95054 813-B3
GREAT ARBOR WY
32800 UNC 94587 732-C5
GREAT CIRCLE DR
- MrnC 94941 606-J6
GREATHOUSE DR
400 MPS 95035 794-A3
GREAT MALL DR
100 MPS 95035 814-A2
GREAT MALL PKWY
800 MPS 95035 813-J2
800 MPS 95035 814-A2
GREAT NORTHERN PL
100 DNVL 94526 653-C5

GREAT OAK CIR
- ORIN 94563 630-J3
GREAT OAK WY
5400 SJS 95123 875-B4
GREAT OAKS BLVD
- SJS 95119 875-E7
GREAT OAKS DR
5100 SJS 95111 875-C2
GREAT SALT LAKE CT
3800 FRMT 94555 732-B6
GREAT SALT LAKE DR
32700 FRMT 94555 732-B6
GREAT SALT LAKE TER
- FRMT 94555 732-H4
GREBE CT
33000 UNC 94587 732-D6
GREBE ST
1000 FCTY 94404 749-H2
GRECIA CT
300 SJS 95116 834-F3
GRECO AV
1000 SUNV 94087 832-E3
GREELEY PL
5400 FRMT 94538 773-A1
GREELY CT
600 HAY 94544 712-D7
GREEN AV
100 SSF 94080 708-A2
500 SBRN 94066 707-H6
GREEN CT
500 PA 94301 791-C6
1400 AlaC 94578 691-E4
GREEN LN
1000 MRTZ 94553 571-D4
GREEN RDGE
- DALY 94014 687-D4
GREEN ST
- SF 94111 648-A4
- MRTZ 94553 571-D3
100 MLPK 94025 791-A2
100 EPA 94303 791-B2
200 SF 94133 648-A4
700 SF 94133 647-F4
1000 SF 94109 647-F4
1500 SF 94123 647-F4
W GREEN ST
- MRTZ 94553 571-D3
GREEN WY
- SRFL 94901 566-G7
- SRFL 94901 586-G1
GREENACRE RD
3600 OAK 94619 650-F6
4000 AlaC 94546 692-B5
GREEN ACRES CT
- LFYT 94549 631-J4
GREENBANK AV
- PDMT 94611 650-A1
GREENBANK CT
5300 SJS 95118 874-C4
GREENBANK DR
100 LFYT 94549 611-G4
GREEN BAY CT
- CCCo 94595 612-B6
GREENBAY CT
800 SJS 95128 853-F4
GREENBERRY CT
2300 PLE 94566 714-C1
GREENBERRY LN
800 MrnC 94903 546-C7
GREENBRAE CT
- CCCo 94803 569-E7
GREENBRAE BOARDWLK
- CMAD 94904 586-H5
- CMAD 94925 586-H5
- MrnC 94925 586-H5
2100 LKSP 94904 586-H5
2100 MrnC 94904 586-H5
GREENBRIAR
100 MRGA 94556 631-C7
GREENBRIAR AV
1100 SJS 95128 853-E4
GREENBRIAR CT
400 DNVL 94526 653-D7
3000 SJS 95128 853-E4
GREENBRIAR DR
3700 PIT 94565 574-E5
GREENBRIAR WY
- HIL 94010 748-H3
GREENBRIER CT
400 BEN 94510 551-A1
GREENBRIER DR
1200 SCAR 94070 769-E6
GREENBRIER LN
31400 HAY 94544 732-E2
GREENBRIER RD
400 ALA 94501 669-H3
GREENBRIER ST
2100 CNCD 94520 572-F5
11300 OAK 94605 671-D5
GREENBRIER PARK DR
42300 FRMT 94538 773-C2
GREENBROOK CT
100 DNVL 94526 653-C6
18900 SAR 95070 852-G5
GREENBROOK DR
1100 DNVL 94526 653-C4
GREENBUSH CT
1700 CNCD 94521 593-C3
GREENBUSH DR
4600 CNCD 94521 593-C3
GREEN CREEK DR
1800 SJS 95124 853-H7
GREENDALE DR
100 LGTS 95032 873-D5
2100 SSF 94080 707-C4
GREENDALE WY
200 SJS 95129 853-A1
300 SMCo 94062 769-F7
GREENDELL PL
- PLHL 94523 591-H2
GREENE DR
1400 SJS 95129 852-H4
GREENE PL
- LFYT 94595 612-A6
GREENE ST
200 MrnC 94941 606-F6
GREENFIELD AV
- SANS 94960 566-D7
- SRFL 94901 566-D7
- VAL 94590 530-C2
200 SMTO 94403 749-C7

GREENFIELD CIR
1400 PIN 94564 569-E5
GREENFIELD CT
- MLV 94941 606-G3
- SANS 94960 566-D7
- SMTO 94403 749-C7
- VAL 94590 530-C2
- BLMT 94002 749-C7
GREENFIELD DR
- MRGA 94556 631-D5
2200 PIT 94565 574-E4
GREENFIELD PL
100 LGTS 95030 873-B3
GREENFIELD WY
5400 PLE 94566 714-C1
GREENFORD CT
3100 SJS 95148 855-E2
GREENGATE DR
2400 SJS 95132 814-E5
GREEN GLEN CT
1100 SJS 95126 853-H3
GREEN GLEN WY
400 MrnC 94965 606-E7
GREENHALL WY
3000 ANT 94509 575-C7
GREENHAVEN RD
4000 HAY 94542 712-F2
GREEN HILL CIR
4800 ANT 94509 595-J3
GREENHILL RD
900 MrnC 94941 606-E5
GREEN HILL WY
- ANT 94509 595-J3
100 LGTS 95030 873-C4
2500 SJS 95121 855-E4
GREENHILLS AV
3500 AlaC 94546 691-J4
GREEN HILLS CT
- MLBR 94030 728-A3
12000 LAH 94022 831-B2
GREENHILLS CT
1700 CCCo 94549 611-H1
GREEN HILLS DR
200 MLBR 94030 728-A3
GREENHILLS DR
3200 CCCo 94549 611-H1
GREENHILLS WY
43400 FRMT 94539 773-F2
GREENLAKE DR
300 SUNV 94089 812-G4
GREENLAND TER
4100 FRMT 94555 752-B2
GREENLAND WY
3200 SJS 95135 855-E2
GREENLAWN DR
1400 DNVL 94526 653-C6
GREENLEAF CT
4300 CNCD 94518 593-A5
GREENLEAF DR
20600 CPTO 95014 832-C7
20600 SCIC 95014 832-C7
GREENLEAF LN
2800 SJS 95121 855-D3
GREENLEE DR
3500 SJS 95117 853-C1
GREENLY DR
7000 OAK 94605 671-A1
7800 OAK 94605 670-J1
GREENMEADOW CIR
100 PIT 94565 573-F4
GREEN MEADOW DR
3300 CCCo 94506 654-B4
GREENMEADOW DR
5100 CNCD 94521 593-D5
GREENMEADOW LN
12400 SAR 95070 852-D6
GREENMEADOW WY
100 PA 94306 811-E2
500 SJS 95129 853-A2
GREENMONT DR
100 VAL 94591 530-F7
GREENMOOR DR
1100 SJS 95118 874-C2
GREENOAK CT
3000 SMTO 94403 748-J6
3100 SMTO 94403 749-A7
GREEN OAK DR
1000 NVTO 94949 546-F5
GREENOAK DR
5500 SJS 95129 852-H3
GREEN OAK LN
1200 LALT 94024 831-H4
GREEN OAK PL
1000 NVTO 94949 546-F4
GREEN OAKS CT
- WLCK 94596 612-F7
GREENOAKS DR
- ATN 94027 770-F7
100 ATN 94027 790-G1
GREENOAKS WY
4000 HAY 94542 712-F3
GREENOCK LN
100 PLHL 94523 592-A4
100 PLHL 94523 591-J4
GREENOUGH AV
- SF 94129 647-C4
GREENPARK COM
43100 FRMT 94538 773-D1
GREENPARK DR
41800 FRMT 94538 773-D1
GREENPARK TER
- SSF 94014 707-J1
GREENPARK WY
300 SJS 95136 874-G2
GREEN POINT CT
1000 CNCD 94521 593-D5
GREEN POINT LN
- MrnC 94945 526-J3
GREENPOINT ST
37100 NWK 94560 752-F6
GREENRIDGE CT
3100 ANT 94509 575-E7
6300 MRTZ 94553 591-H3
18500 AlaC 94552 692-D2
GREENRIDGE DR
1500 PIT 94565 574-G6
2100 RCH 94803 589-E3
2100 CCCo 94803 589-E3
8000 OAK 94605 671-B1
GREENRIDGE PL
- DNVL 94506 654-A6

GREENRIDGE RD
5200 AlaC 94552 692-D2
GREENRIDGE TER
16000 LGTS 95032 873-F6
GREENROCK RD
2500 MPS 95035 814-F1
GREENS CT
4400 LVMR 94550 696-A3
GREENS LN
- AlaC 94566 714-B7
- AlaC 94566 734-B1
GREENSBORO CT
- ANT 94509 595-D1
1500 SJS 95131 814-C6
GREENSBORO WY
- ANT 94509 595-D2
GREENSIDE DR
5300 SCIC 95127 815-A6
GREENSIDE WY
- SRFL 94901 567-E5
GREENSTONE COM
34600 FRMT 94555 752-B2
GREENSTONE CT
2500 SJS 95122 835-A5
GREENTREE CIR
- MPS 95035 814-A3
GREEN TREE CT
- LFYT 94549 611-G2
GREENTREE CT
2400 ANT 94509 595-F3
5100 PLE 94566 714-D2
GREENTREE DR
1600 CNCD 94521 593-B2
GREENTREE WY
- MPS 95035 814-A3
3000 SJS 95128 853-E3
3100 SJS 95117 853-D3
GREEN VALLEY CT
- DNVL 94526 633-B6
- MrnC 94960 566-A3
GREENVALLEY CT
- LFYT 94549 611-H3
GREENVALLEY DR
- WLCK 94596 611-H3
- LFYT 94549 611-H3
GREENVALLEY LN
- LFYT 94549 611-H3
GREEN VALLEY RD
1500 DNVL 94526 633-C7
1800 CCCo 94526 633-C5
48700 FRMT 94539 794-A1
48900 MPS 95035 794-A1
GREEN VIEW CT
400 CCCo 94596 612-F6
GREENVIEW CT
- SF 94131 667-E3
1200 MRTZ 94553 571-G7
21800 AlaC 94546 692-B6
GREEN VIEW DR
- DALY 94014 687-E3
400 CCCo 94596 612-E6
GREENVIEW DR
800 MTVW 94040 812-A7
800 MTVW 94040 832-A1
2700 AlaC 94546 692-B6
10300 OAK 94605 671-C3
GREENVIEW LN
- HIL 94010 728-E7
- RCH 94803 569-C7
GREENVIEW PL
600 SCIC 94024 831-F3
GREENVILLE PL
- AlaC 94552 692-F2
GREENVILLE RD
- AlaC 94550 696-F3
- LVMR 94550 696-F6
3100 AlaC 94550 716-F3
GREENWAY DR
- WLCK 94596 612-D4
200 PCFA 94044 707-A7
200 PCFA 94044 706-J7
300 MRTZ 94553 571-H5
1200 RCH 94803 569-C7
3800 CNCD 94521 592-J3
GREENWAYS DR
2100 SMCo 94062 790-A5
GREENWICH AV
900 SUNV 94087 832-C1
5500 LVMR 94550 696-C3
GREENWICH CIR
38600 FRMT 94536 753-B3
GREENWICH CT
100 SRMN 94583 673-G4
1300 SJS 95125 853-G4
2200 CCCo 94806 569-B4
5300 NWK 94560 752-E4
GREENWICH DR
100 PLHL 94523 592-A6
4000 SRMN 94583 673-G4
E GREENWICH DR
700 PA 94303 791-C5
GREENWICH LN
600 FCTY 94404 749-F5
GREENWICH RD
2200 CCCo 94806 569-B4
GREENWICH ST
100 SF 94111 648-A4
200 SF 94133 648-A4
700 SF 94133 647-G4
1100 SF 94109 647-G4
1500 SF 94123 647-G4
2300 SF 94123 647-F4
GREENWOOD AV
- SF 94112 667-D7
- SRFL 94901 586-E1
800 SMTO 94402 728-G7
800 SMTO 94402 748-G1
1000 PA 94301 791-B4
1000 SJS 95126 833-G5
1100 SCAR 94070 769-G5
3800 OAK 94602 650-C4
3800 OAK 94610 650-C4
15900 MSER 95030 872-H6
16100 SCIC 95030 872-H6
GREENWOOD CIR
100 WLCK 94596 592-D7
21000 AlaC 94552 692-F3
GREENWOOD COM
- BERK 94708 609-H7
GREENWOOD CT
- PLHL 94523 592-B1
- ORIN 94563 631-B2

GREENWOOD CT
- TBRN 94920 607-A4
2400 CCCo 94806 588-J2
10300 CPTO 95014 852-F1
GREENWOOD DR
- SSF 94080 707-G6
100 PLHL 94523 592-B1
100 CCCo 94553 592-B1
300 SCL 95054 813-F6
1000 MLPK 94025 770-G7
1000 NVTO 94947 526-D6
2400 CCCo 94806 589-A2
2400 CCCo 94806 588-J2
2900 FRMT 94536 752-J3
19300 CPTO 95014 852-G1
GREENWOOD LN
- RDWC 94063 770-C6
16000 MSER 95030 872-H6
16000 SCIC 95030 872-G6
GREENWOOD PL
- MLPK 94025 770-G7
- SRMN 94583 673-B3
2100 PIT 94565 574-A3
GREENWOOD RD
1200 PLE 94566 714-D2
2600 CCCo 94806 588-J2
15900 MSER 95030 872-H6
GREENWOOD ST
100 VAL 94591 530-E5
GREENWOOD TER
1400 BERK 94708 609-H7
GREENWOOD WY
- MLV 94941 606-D2
- MrnC 94904 586-C5
1400 SBRN 94066 707-E6
1500 MPS 95035 814-A3
GREENWOOD BAY DR
- MrnC 94920 606-J4
- MrnC 94941 606-J4
GREENWOOD BEACH RD
400 TBRN 94920 607-A5
GREENWOOD COVE DR
- MrnC 94920 606-J4
100 TBRN 94920 607-A5
100 TBRN 94920 606-J4
GREER AV
600 SLN 94579 691-C6
1700 CNCD 94521 593-E4
GREER CT
2200 UNC 94587 732-G7
4700 FRMT 94538 753-A6
GREER RD
100 SMCo 94062 789-D6
100 WDSD 94062 789-D6
500 PA 94303 791-C4
GREEVES ST
100 VAL 94591 530-F5
GREG CT
- CCCo 94526 633-C5
GREGG CT
200 LGTS 95032 873-G5
GREGG DR
200 LGTS 95032 873-G5
200 LGTS 95124 873-G5
1600 SJS 95124 873-G5
GREGG PL
- NVTO 94949 546-C1
400 SRMN 94583 673-F6
GREGG WY
- WLCK 94596 612-D5
GREGOR LN
- NVTO 94947 525-J3
GREGORICH DR
6900 SJS 95138 875-G6
GREGORY AV
1100 MRTZ 94553 571-E3
GREGORY CT
45400 FRMT 94539 773-H4
GREGORY DR
3400 CCCo 94565 573-F1
GREGORY LN
- PLHL 94523 592-B5
100 VAL 94591 530-E3
200 RDWC 94061 790-B2
GREGORY PL
- LKSP 94939 586-G5
- OAK 94619 650-G5
18200 MSER 95030 872-H4
GREGORY ST
400 SJS 95126 854-A1
500 SJS 95125 854-A2
4100 OAK 94619 650-G5
4300 AlaC 94546 692-B4
GREGORY WY
600 UNC 94587 732-H6
4500 RCH 94803 589-E2
GREMLIN CT
400 SJS 95111 854-F6
GRENACHE CIR
400 CLAY 94517 593-J7
GRENACHE CT
8400 SJS 95135 855-H7
GRENADA LN
800 FCTY 94404 749-G4
GRENADINE WY
100 HER 94547 570-C6
1800 SJS 95122 854-G1
GRENARD TER
- SF 94109 647-H4
GRENDA ST
15000 SLN 94579 691-C6
GRENNAN ST
- VAL 94591 530-D5
GRENOLA DR
800 CNCD 94518 592-G6
21000 SCIC 95014 832-C7
GRESEL ST
- HAY 94544 732-E2
GRESHAM AV
500 SUNV 94086 812-F6
GRESHAM CT
400 SUNV 94086 812-F5
4200 PLE 94588 694-E6
7400 SJS 95139 895-G1
GRESHAM LN
- ATN 94027 790-C1
GRETCHEN LN
- SJS 95117 853-B3
GRETCHEN PL
- LKSP 94939 586-G5
GRETEL LN
1200 MTVW 94040 811-J7

GREVILLEA CT
- HIL 94010 748-C2
GREY CT
2200 SJS 95124 873-E5
GREY EAGLE CT
- PLE 94566 714-H4
GREY FEATHER CIR
4900 SJS 95136 874-J3
GREYFELL PL
- PLHL 94523 592-A3
GREY FOX DR
- AlaC 94546 691-G4
GREY GHOST AV
200 SJS 95111 875-B2
GREYLANDS DR
1400 SJS 95125 853-G5
GREYLYN DR
600 SRMN 94583 693-H1
GREYMONT DR
3600 SJS 95136 854-F7
GREYSTONE CT
800 ANT 94509 595-F2
GREYSTONE DR
600 ANT 94509 595-E2
GREYSTONE LN
1400 CLAY 94517 593-H7
GREYSTONE TER
- ORIN 94563 610-H6
GRIBBEN AV
20700 AlaC 94541 711-F1
GRIDLEY CT
300 SJS 95127 814-J7
47600 FRMT 94539 773-H7
GRIDLEY RD
- VAL 94592 549-G1
GRIDLEY ST
300 SJS 95127 814-H6
400 SCIC 95127 814-H7
GRIFFANTI CT
2400 MRTZ 94553 571-F4
GRIFFIN AV
400 PCFA 94044 707-A6
GRIFFIN DR
500 RCH 94806 568-G7
900 VAL 94589 510-C6
GRIFFITH AV
4600 FRMT 94538 773-C1
GRIFFITH LN
100 CMBL 95008 853-E7
GRIFFITH PL
100 LGTS 95030 873-A6
GRIFFITH ST
900 SF 94124 668-D7
1000 SF 94124 688-C1
10000 SJS 95127 835-A3
14400 SLN 94577 690-J5
GRIGLIO DR
100 SJS 95134 813-G2
GRIJALVA DR
- SF 94132 687-B1
GRILLO CT
3700 PLE 94566 714-G4
GRIMLEY LN
1100 SJS 95120 894-H4
GRIMMER BLVD
40200 FRMT 94538 753-C7
40900 FRMT 94538 773-C1
S GRIMMER BLVD
43600 FRMT 94538 773-D3
44400 FRMT 94539 773-F4
GRIMMER TER
43000 FRMT 94538 773-C2
GRIMMWOOD PL
1200 CNCD 94521 593-A5
GRIMSBY CT
2300 ANT 94509 595-A2
2300 SJS 95130 852-J7
GRIMSBY DR
2300 ANT 94509 595-A2
4400 SJS 95130 853-A7
4800 SJS 95130 852-J7
GRIMSBY LN
500 CCCo 94506 654-A5
GRIMSWOOD CT
700 SJS 95120 894-J3
GRINNELL CT
300 SCL 95051 832-H7
GRISBORNE AV
5600 OAK 94611 630-D7
GRISSOM CT
100 HER 94547 570-B5
GRISSOM ST
200 HER 94547 570-B5
GRIZILO DR
1600 SJS 95124 873-J1
GRIZZLY CT
1900 ANT 94509 575-G6
GRIZZLY PEAK BLVD
- BERK 94708 610-B7
100 OAK 94708 610-B7
200 BERK 94708 609-G3
200 CCCo - 610-B7
200 CCCo 94708 609-G3
200 OAK 94704 610-B7
200 CCCo 94708 610-B7
2900 OAK 94720 610-D7
4800 OAK 94611 630-D1
4800 OAK 94705 630-D1
5000 CCCo - 630-D1
5000 OAK 94704 630-D1
5800 CCCo 94611 630-D1
GRIZZLY TERRACE DR
- CCCo - 630-D3
700 OAK 94611 630-D3
GROESBECK HILL RD
3600 SJS 95148 835-E6
GRONDINE RD
700 LFYT 94549 631-F1
GRONWALL CT
1200 SCIC 94024 831-F3
GRONWALL LN
1200 SCIC 94024 831-F2
GROOM DR
2700 RCH 94806 589-A1
2700 RCH 94806 588-J1
GROOM ST
24200 HAY 94544 711-J3
GROOT WY
2300 CNCD 94520 572-G5
GROSBEAK AV
1600 SUNV 94087 832-F5

GROSS LN
1800 CNCD 94519 593-A1
GROSS ST
300 MPS 95035 794-A3
GROSSETO CT
- SJS 95138 855-E7
GROSSMONT DR
3300 SJS 95132 814-H5
GROSVENOR CT
17200 MSER 95030 873-B4
GROSVENOR DR
1900 SJS 95132 814-F2
GROSVENOR PL
700 OAK 94610 650-B4
GROSVENOR HEIGHTS CT
2200 LVMR 94550 715-G4
GROSVENTRES CT
1300 FRMT 94539 773-G4
GROTE PL
- SF 94105 648-B6
GROTH CIR
1400 PLE 94566 714-E1
GROTH CT
3100 SJS 95111 854-F7
GROTH DR
500 SJS 95111 854-F7
GROTH PL
500 SJS 95111 854-F7
GROTHMAN LN
4500 MRTZ 94553 571-E7
GROTON CT
800 SUNV 94087 832-C2
GROUSE DR
- ANT 94509 594-H1
GROUSE WY
700 SJS 95133 834-F1
2200 UNC 94587 732-G7
GROVE AV
- CMAD 94925 586-F7
- CMAD 94925 606-F1
100 SSF 94080 707-J1
200 CCCo 94801 588-F3
1100 BURL 94010 728-D5
3700 PA 94303 791-E7
3800 PA 94303 811-E1
GROVE CIR
- BEN 94510 550-J3
100 PLHL 94523 592-A7
GROVE CT
- SJS 95134 813-C2
- PTLV 94028 810-B7
- PA 94303 811-E1
2500 ANT 94509 595-F3
GROVE DR
- PTLV 94028 810-B6
GROVE LN
- NVTO 94947 526-A3
- SANS 94960 566-B7
700 PA 94303 811-E1
GROVE ST
- LGTS 95032 893-A1
- MLV 94941 606-D3
- RCH 94804 588-H7
- SF 94102 647-G7
- SRFL 94901 586-F2
200 FRMT 94539 753-H7
800 SF 94117 647-E7
1300 ALA 94501 670-A3
2100 SF 94117 647-E7
W GROVE ST
100 CCCo 94801 588-F3
GROVE TER
34300 FRMT 94555 752-C2
GROVE WY
100 AlaC 94541 711-F1
500 AlaC 94541 691-H7
600 HAY 94541 691-H7
1200 CNCD 94518 592-H3
1400 AlaC 94546 691-J6
1400 CNCD 94519 592-H2
2300 AlaC 94546 692-A7
3700 AlaC 94552 692-A7
GROVE CREEK CT
- CCCo 94549 611-J2
GROVE HILL AV
- SANS 94960 566-C7
GROVELAND DR
10600 SCIC 94024 832-A6
GROVELAND ST
- PTLV 94028 830-C1
GROVENOR DR
16900 AlaC 94546 691-H1
GROVENOR LN
2100 CNCD 94520 572-F5
GROVER CT
- WLCK 94596 632-E1
4500 FRMT 94536 752-H5
GROVER DR
4300 FRMT 94536 752-H5
GROVER LN
100 WLCK 94596 632-E1
GROVE SHAFTER FRWY I-980
- OAK 94607 649-G2
- OAK 94609 649-G2
- OAK 94612 649-G2
GROVE SHAFTER FRWY Rt#-24
- OAK 94609 629-G7
- OAK 94609 649-G1
- OAK 94618 629-G7
GROVETREE CT
1500 SJS 95131 814-D5
GROVEVIEW CT
2400 RCH 94806 588-J1
GROVEVIEW DR
2500 RCH 94806 568-J7
2500 RCH 94806 588-J1
GROVEWOOD CT
800 SJS 95120 894-H3
GRUBER CT
7100 SJS 95139 875-F7
GRUBSTAKE PL
100 VAL 94591 530-C7
GRUMMAN CT
- WLCK 94595 612-D7
GRUMMAN ST
1000 OAK 94621 670-C6
GRUNDY LN
900 SBRN 94066 707-G6

STREET
Block City ZIP Pg-Grid

GRUNION CT
- FCTY 94404 749-H3
GRUNION TER
- FRMT 94536 753-B3
GRUWELL PL
1000 SJS 95129 853-A3
GUADALAJARA CT
1600 SJS 95120 874-A7
GUADALAJARA DR
1500 SJS 95120 874-A7
GUADALUPE AV
- DALY 94014 687-C2
600 MLBR 94030 727-J2
1700 SJS 95125 854-C4
GUADALUPE CT
5500 CNCD 94521 593-F5
GUADALUPE DR
500 LALT 94022 811-D5
GUADALUPE FRWY Rt#-87
- SCIC - 854-D6
- SCIC - 874-E1
- SJS - 834-A5
- SJS - 854-C3
- SJS - 874-E1
GUADALUPE PKWY
- SJS 95131 813-G7
- SJS 95131 833-H2
800 SJS 95110 833-H2
GUADALUPE TER
100 FRMT 94539 753-H6
GUADALUPE CANYON PKWY
- DALY 94014 687-E4
- BSBN 94005 688-A4
300 SMCo 94014 687-E4
300 BSBN 94005 687-E4
GUADALUPE MINES CT
6000 SJS 95120 873-J7
GUADALUPE MINES RD
6000 SJS 95120 873-J7
6600 SJS 95120 893-H2
GUALALA PL
40700 FRMT 94539 753-E5
GUANACASTE CT
200 SJS 95116 834-F2
GUARDINO DR
38900 FRMT 94536 753-C3
39000 FRMT 94538 753-C3
GUAVA CT
20100 SAR 95070 852-E6
GUAVA DR
38000 NWK 94560 752-G7
GUAVA PL
6100 NWK 94560 752-G7
GUAVA BLOSSOM CT
- SJS 95123 875-E2
GUAYMAS CT
600 SRMN 94583 673-C3
GUCCI TER
34600 FRMT 94555 752-A3
GUERRA CT
4200 SJS 95111 854-G3
GUERRA DR
500 SJS 95111 854-G3
GUERRERO CT
1300 MPS 95035 794-C5
GUERRERO ST
- SF 94103 667-H4
400 SF 94110 667-H4
1400 SF 94110 667-H4
GUIDO ST
3000 OAK 94602 650-F4
GUIFRIDA AV
300 SJS 95123 874-H4
GUIFRIDA CT
5400 SJS 95123 874-H4
GUILDFORD AV
500 SMTO 94402 749-B2
GUILDFORD PL
4100 SJS 95135 855-F3
GUILDHALL DR
2700 SJS 95132 814-C3
GUILDHALL RD
29000 HAY 94544 732-B1
GUILFORD AV
4000 LVMR 94550 716-A2
GUILFORD CT
28900 HAY 94544 732-A1
GUILFORD PL
4400 LVMR 94550 716-A2
GUILFORD RD
- PDMT 94611 650-B1
GUILLERMO PL
3200 HAY 94542 712-E4
GUINDA ST
300 PA 94301 790-J3
500 PA 94301 791-A4
1700 PA 94303 791-B5
GUISELA CT
- MrnC 94945 526-H2
GUISO COM
4500 FRMT 94536 752-G3
GUITTARD RD
- BURL 94010 728-C4
GULFSTREAM ST
3100 PLE 94588 694-F6
GULFSTREAM WY
2000 SLN 94579 690-J6
GULL AV
600 FCTY 94404 749-G1
GULL CT
33100 FRMT 94555 732-B7
GULL PL
300 PIT 94565 574-D1
GULL RD
700 SSF 94080 708-C2
GULL WY
200 LVMR 94550 695-D7
3800 CCCo 94553 571-J4
GULLO AV
900 SJS 95129 852-J2
GULL POINT CT
300 BEN 94510 551-B5
GULUZZO DR
3300 SJS 95148 835-C5
GUM CT
- NWK 94560 752-C7
100 VAL 94589 510-A7
GUM ST
1600 SMTO 94402 749-B3
GUMDROP DR
2500 SJS 95148 835-C7
GUM TREE CT
- NVTO 94947 525-H3
GUM TREE DR
3500 SJS 95111 854-G6
GUM TREE LN
15600 LGTS 95032 873-E6
GUMWOOD DR
1700 CNCD 94519 593-B1
GUNAR DR
2200 SJS 95124 853-G7
GUNDERSEN DR
2200 SJS 95125 853-J6
GUNN CT
100 SJS 95127 835-A2
GUNN DR
6600 OAK 94611 630-G7
GUNSHOT CT
7900 DBLN 94568 693-G4
GUNSTON WY
1700 SJS 95124 873-H3
1900 SCIC 95124 873-H3
GUNTER LN
300 RDWC 94065 749-H7
GUNTER WY
6200 SJS 95123 874-H6
GUNTHER CT
19100 SAR 95070 852-G6
GURDWARA RD
- FRMT 94536 732-J7
GURNARD TER
1000 FRMT 94536 753-C3
GURNEY CT
1100 SJS 95132 814-G5
GURNEY LN
- CCCo 94507 632-G6
GUSHUE ST
26000 HAY 94544 712-A5
GUSTAFSON CT
- NVTO 94947 525-G2
GUSTAVO CT
35300 FRMT 94536 752-E2
GUSTINE ST
32700 UNC 94587 732-B7
GUTHRIE CT
3300 PLE 94588 694-F5
GUTHRIE ST
3400 PLE 94588 694-F5
GUTTENBERG ST
- SF 94112 687-F2
300 DALY 94014 687-F2
GUY PL
- SF 94105 648-B6
GUYSON CT
6200 PLE 94588 694-A7
GUZMAN CT
- CNCD 94521 593-F7
GUZMAN PKWY
- PLE 94588 694-F6
GWEN CT
600 DNVL 94526 653-C2
GWEN DR
700 CMBL 95008 853-A7
800 CMBL 95008 873-A1
GWIN AV
- CNCD 94520 572-J3
GWIN CT
6400 OAK 94611 630-D5
GWIN RD
6400 OAK 94611 630-D5
GWINN CT
400 SJS 95111 875-C2
GYEN ST
19800 AlaC 94546 692-B5
GYGER CT
1700 CNCD 94521 593-D4
GYMKHANA RD
400 SMTO 94403 749-A4
GYPSUM DR
100 VAL 94589 510-C6
GYPSY LN
- OAK 94705 630-C2
GYPSY HILL RD
- PCFA 94044 707-A6
14600 SAR 95070 872-G4
GYPSY MOTH PL
6000 SJS 95123 874-E6
GYPSY PLACE CT
1600 SJS 95121 855-B4

H

H LN
- MrnC 94945 526-F2
- NVTO 94945 526-F2
H ST
- CNCD 94518 592-G4
- OAK 94625 649-B4
- SF 94124 688-E1
- SRFL 94901 566-E7
- SRFL 94901 586-E1
100 BEN 94510 551-A4
100 FRMT 94536 753-B1
200 MRTZ 94553 571-D5
300 ANT 94509 575-C4
300 SF 94124 668-E7
400 UNC 94587 732-G5
1100 SUNV 94089 812-D3
E H ST
- OAK 94607 649-C4
- OAK 94625 649-C4
S H ST
400 LVMR 94550 715-H1
HAAG RD
4400 MRTZ 94553 571-E7
HAAS AV
- SLN 94577 671-A7
HABBITTS CT
500 SJS 95111 854-G4
HACIENDA AV
- AlaC 94580 711-D1
- AlaC 94541 711-E1
300 CMBL 95008 873-A1
4500 SJS 95008 873-A1
E HACIENDA AV
200 CMBL 95008 873-D1
HACIENDA CIR
- ORIN 94563 610-F5
HACIENDA CT
- PCFA 94044 707-A4
- SRFL 94901 566-G6
300 LALT 94022 811-D5
1300 CMBL 95008 873-B1
3600 CNCD 94519 572-J7
40200 FRMT 94539 753-E4
HACIENDA DR
- TBRN 94920 607-B4
200 SJS 95131 814-A5
1000 WLCK 94598 612-D4
2900 CNCD 94519 572-G7
2900 CNCD 94519 592-G1
4100 PLE 94588 694-C5
4300 DBLN 94568 694-C5
HACIENDA LN
- CCCo 94803 569-E7
HACIENDA ST
2200 SMTO 94403 749-B4
HACIENDA WY
300 LALT 94022 811-D5
600 MLBR 94030 727-J3
700 MrnC 94903 566-H2
3300 ANT 94509 575-B7
3300 ANT 94509 595-B1
HACIENDAS DR
- WDSD 94062 789-H6
HACIENDAS RD
- ORIN 94563 610-G5
HACK AV
1400 CMBL 95008 873-B2
HACKAMORE COM
100 FRMT 94539 773-H6
HACKAMORE CT
2200 WLCK 94596 632-F1
HACKAMORE DR
3200 AlaC 94541 712-D2
3400 AlaC 94542 712-D2
HACKAMORE LN
- FRMT 94539 773-H6
500 WLCK 94596 632-F2
HACKBERRY PL
3900 AlaC 94546 691-H2
HACKBERRY ST
48200 FRMT 94539 793-J1
HACKETT AV
1600 MTVW 94043 811-G3
HACKETT CT
100 VAL 94591 530-E5
HACKNEY CT
5500 RCH 94803 589-J3
HACKNEY LN
3100 CCCo 94598 613-A4
5400 RCH 94803 589-J2
HADDEN RD
2100 CCCo 94596 612-E7
HADDOCK ST
800 FCTY 94404 749-H3
HADDON DR
900 SMTO 94402 749-B2
HADDON PL
700 OAK 94610 650-A3
HADDON RD
300 OAK 94606 649-J4
300 OAK 94606 650-A4
600 OAK 94610 650-A4
HADDON WY
3200 SJS 95135 855-E3
HADEOCK CT
1600 SJS 95132 814-E4
HADLEY AV
500 SJS 95126 833-G7
HADSELL CT
3300 PLE 94588 694-G5
HAFNER CT
36400 NWK 94560 752-E5
HAFNER ST
36400 NWK 94560 752-E6
HAFNER WY
5800 NWK 94560 752-E5
HAGA DR
3100 SJS 95111 854-H5
8900 SCIC 95111 854-H6
HAGA WY
10300 SCIC 95111 854-H6
HAGAR AV
100 PDMT 94611 650-C1
HAGEMAN AV
3500 OAK 94619 650-E6
HAGEMANN DR
100 LVMR 94550 715-D1
300 LVMR 94550 695-D7
HAGEN BLVD
6400 ELCR 94530 589-B7
6500 ELCR 94530 609-B1
HAGEN OAKS CT
- CCCo 94507 632-J5
HAGEN OAKS DR
- CCCo 94507 632-J5
2300 CCCo 94507 633-A5
HAGGERTY ST
100 VAL 94591 530-E5
HAGGIN OAKS AV
5500 LVMR 94550 696-C2
HAHN COM
- FRMT 94536 752-H2
HAHN ST
- SF 94134 687-J2
HAIG ST
3500 SCL 95054 813-E6
HAIGHT AV
100 ALA 94501 669-E1
HAIGHT ST
- SF 94102 667-F1
100 MLPK 94025 791-A1
400 SF 94117 667-F1
1800 SF 94117 667-E1
HAINES AV
4000 SJS 95136 874-E1
HAINLINE DR
400 BLMT 94002 749-D7
HAITI CT
500 SRMN 94583 673-E1
HAITI RD
500 SJS 95111 854-G4
HAKIMI CT
4700 CNCD 94521 593-C4
HALABUK CT
100 VAL 94591 530-D4
HALBREATH CT
3200 SJS 95121 855-C5
HALCYON CT
- TBRN 94920 607-C6
1800 PLE 94566 714-C2
3000 BERK 94705 629-H4
HALCYON DR
- VAL 94591 510-J4
2800 SLN 94578 691-C4
HALDANE CT
27700 HAY 94544 712-A7
HALE AV
400 OAK 94603 670-G7
7300 SJS 95139 895-H2
HALE CT
100 MRTZ 94553 591-H2
HALE DR
1200 CNCD 94518 592-H3
2100 BURL 94010 728-C6
HALE LN
- MLV 94941 606-C3
HALE PL
10600 CPTO 95014 832-C6
HALE ST
- SF 94134 668-A6
200 SF 94134 667-J6
400 PA 94301 791-A3
1200 VAL 94591 530-E3
HALEAKA RD
3400 PLE 94588 714-A2
HALEAKALA ST
3200 CNCD 94519 572-H7
HALEY CT
500 SJS 95123 874-J7
HALEY DR
4800 AlaC 94546 692-B3
HALEY ST
35500 NWK 94560 752-C5
HALF CROWN LN
3400 SJS 95132 814-J2
HALF DOME CT
6300 LVMR 94550 696-D3
HALF DOME DR
3100 PLE 94566 714-H3
HALF MOON CT
3200 SJS 95111 854-H5
3400 CNCD 94518 592-J6
HALF MOON LN
300 DALY 94015 707-C1
HALFMOON LN
700 CNCD 94518 592-J6
HALF MOON RD
- MrnC 94947 526-A5
- NVTO 94947 526-A5
- NVTO 94947 525-J5
HALF MOON BAY RD Rt#-92
2900 SMCo - 768-E3
2900 SMCo 94062 768-E3
HALFORD AV
1200 SCL 95051 832-H3
HALF PENCE CT
1800 SJS 95132 814-F3
HALF PENCE WY
1800 SJS 95132 814-F3
HALGRIM CT
3000 SJS 95132 814-G5
HALIBUT ST
1300 FCTY 94404 749-H3
HALIFAX DR
5100 SJS 95130 872-J1
HALIFAX PL
26800 HAY 94542 712-E3
HALIFAX RD
1200 LVMR 94550 715-G3
HALIFAX WY
3400 CNCD 94520 572-F5
HALITE WY
900 ANT 94509 595-F1
HALKIN LN
- BERK 94708 609-G5
HALKINS DR
4000 SJS 95124 873-E3
HALKWEED PZ
- HAY 94542 712-B3
HALL AV
1200 RCH 94804 608-G2
HALL CT
700 BEN 94510 530-J6
4000 PLE 94566 714-F1
19900 CPTO 95014 852-F1
HALL DR
- ORIN 94563 631-B2
HALL LN
100 WLCK 94596 612-C2
3400 LFYT 94549 611-G6
HALL RD
28700 HAY 94545 731-J2
HALL ST
900 SCAR 94070 769-G3
HALL WY
34300 FRMT 94555 752-B2
HALLADALE CT
7600 SJS 95135 855-J6
HALLAM ST
- SF 94103 648-A7
HALLBROOK DR
1500 SJS 95118 874-A3
1600 SJS 95124 873-J3
HALLCREST DR
1500 SJS 95118 874-A2
HALLECK DR
5700 SJS 95123 874-E5
HALLECK ST
- SF 94129 647-E4
- SF 94111 648-B5
100 SF 94104 648-B5
4000 EMVL 94608 629-E7
4000 OAK 94608 629-E7
HALLER CT
1600 CNCD 94520 592-E4
HALLGREN LN
- CCCo 94549 611-J2
HALLIDAY AV
6800 OAK 94605 670-H2
HALLIDAY ST
- VAL 94590 530-B4
HALLING WY
1200 PCFA 94044 726-G4
HALLMARK CIR
- MLPK 94025 790-C6
HALLMARK CT
5700 AlaC 94552 692-B1
HALLMARK DR
2400 BLMT 94002 769-A2
HALLMARK LN
1700 SJS 95124 873-H2
HALL RANCH PKWY
32200 UNC 94587 731-J6
HALSEY AV
300 SCIC 95128 853-F1
1400 SMTO 94403 749-C2
1500 SLN 94578 691-D3
2600 SMCo 94063 770-C6
HALSEY BLVD
900 FCTY 94404 749-G4
HALSEY CT
100 HER 94547 570-B5
HALTEN CT
- PLHL 94523 592-A3
HALYARD LN
300 FCTY 94404 749-G6
HAMANN DR
600 SJS 95117 853-C2
HAMAR ST
- PLHL 94523 592-B6
HAMBLETONIAN LN
3100 CCCo 94598 613-A4
HAMBURG CIR
500 CLAY 94517 593-J7
HAMELIN CT
900 SUNV 94089 812-E4
HAMERTON AV
- SF 94131 667-F6
HAMES CT
1700 CNCD 94521 593-E3
HAMES DR
4900 CNCD 94521 593-D3
HAMIDA CT
1200 SJS 95120 894-E2
HAMILTON AV
- CMBL 95008 853-J5
- PA 94301 790-J5
100 MLPK 94025 770-J7
100 MTVW 94043 811-F3
500 MPS 95035 794-A6
600 MLPK 94025 771-A7
700 PA 94301 791-A3
1400 SJS 95125 853-J5
1500 PA 94303 791-B3
1500 SCIC 95125 853-J5
1700 CMBL 95125 853-J5
2200 SBRN 94066 707-F7
2500 CNCD 94519 572-G6
E HAMILTON AV
- CMBL 95008 853-F5
800 SJS 95128 853-F5
800 CMBL 95128 853-F5
900 CMBL 95128 853-F5
900 SJS 95125 853-F5
W HAMILTON AV
- CMBL 95008 853-C5
1000 SJS 95130 853-C5
4700 SJS 95130 852-J5
4800 SJS 95129 852-J5
HAMILTON CT
- CCCo 94526 633-C4
- PA 94301 791-A3
- PCFA 94044 707-A3
- PLHL 94523 592-A7
- SRFL 94901 566-G6
100 VAL 94589 509-J5
900 MLPK 94025 771-A7
HAMILTON DR
- MLV 94941 606-G4
- NVTO 94949 546-F1
700 PLHL 94523 591-J7
800 PLHL 94523 592-A7
2700 PIN 94564 570-A7
HAMILTON LN
- MrnC 94965 606-A3
600 SCL 95051 833-A6
1100 BURL 94010 728-C5
HAMILTON PL
- OAK 94612 649-H2
- OAK 94611 649-H2
1400 SJS 95125 853-G4
HAMILTON ST
- SF 94129 647-C3
- SF 94134 667-J7
300 SF 94134 668-A7
500 RDWC 94063 770-A6
600 SF 94134 688-A1
6900 OAK 94621 670-F3
HAMILTON WY
400 PLE 94566 714-D6
1400 SJS 95125 853-J5
3700 RDWC 94062 789-G2
3700 SMCo 94062 789-G2
42600 FRMT 94538 773-D1
HAMILTON PARK DR
3900 SJS 95130 853-B4
HAMLET CT
2300 SJS 95131 814-D5
4000 CNCD 94521 593-A4
HAMLET DR
4000 CNCD 94521 593-A4
HAMLET ST
1700 SMTO 94403 749-C2
HAMLIN CT
2100 ANT 94509 595-A1
HAMLIN DR
2100 ANT 94509 595-A1
HAMLIN RD
3300 LFYT 94549 611-F7
3300 LFYT 94549 631-G1
HAMLIN ST
- SF 94109 647-J4
38300 FRMT 94536 752-G6
HAMLIN WY
500 SLN 94578 691-B4
HAMLINE AV
3200 OAK 94602 650-C5
HAMLINE ST
600 SJS 95110 833-J4
900 SJS 95126 833-G5
HAMMERTON CT
5300 SJS 95118 874-C4
HAMMERWOOD AV
1200 SUNV 94089 812-J3
HAMMETT CT
- SJS 95132 814-G3
HAMMIT LN
- CCCo 94553 571-J4
HAMMOND AV
- FRMT 94539 793-H1
HAMMOND PL
- MRGA 94556 631-D7
- MRGA 94556 651-D1
3600 CNCD 94519 593-A1
HAMMOND WY
600 MPS 95035 814-A1
HAMMONDALE CT
- SRFL 94901 566-G6
HAMMONS AV
13300 SAR 95070 852-E7
13400 SAR 95070 872-E1
HAMNER TER
- FRMT 94555 752-D2
HAMPEL ST
1100 OAK 94602 650-C3
HAMPSHIRE AV
- DALY 94015 707-C2
400 SMCo 94063 770-D7
HAMPSHIRE CT
200 DALY 94015 707-D3
1300 CNCD 94518 592-E6
HAMPSHIRE PL
4300 SJS 95136 874-D2
HAMPSHIRE ST
100 SF 94103 668-A1
200 VAL 94590 530-A3
300 SF 94110 668-A3
1500 SF 94110 668-A4
HAMPSHIRE WY
- NVTO 94945 526-A1
4600 FRMT 94538 753-C7
4600 FRMT 94538 773-C1
HAMPSTEAD CT
3300 LVMR 94550 695-H6
HAMPSTEAD WY
1700 SJS 95132 814-F3
HAMPSWOOD CT
900 SJS 95120 894-H3
HAMPSWOOD LN
900 SJS 95120 894-H3
HAMPSWOOD WY
800 SJS 95120 894-H3
HAMPTON AV
- SANS 94960 566-B6
1600 RDWC 94061 790-A2
HAMPTON CT
- ALA 94502 669-J5
- HIL 94010 748-E6
- LALT 94022 811-D6
100 SBRN 94066 707-F7
400 SRMN 94583 673-E5
900 MPS 95035 794-B4
1100 SJS 95120 894-E2
32300 UNC 94587 732-C4
S HAMPTON CT
3100 RCH 94806 588-J1
HAMPTON DR
1000 CNCD 94518 592-D6
1000 PLHL 94523 592-D6
1300 SUNV 94087 832-G4
6500 SJS 95120 894-D2
HAMPTON LN
- MrnC 94945 526-H3
1700 DALY 94014 687-F3
2500 ANT 94509 575-D1
HAMPTON PL
1300 LVMR 94550 715-F4
19000 AlaC 94541 691-G6
HAMPTON RD
- MRTZ 94553 571-G7
- PDMT 94611 650-D2
- PDMT 94610 650-C2
100 AlaC 94541 691-F7
1000 LFYT 94549 611-G6
2000 CCCo 94553 590-F5
2000 CCCo - 590-F5
2100 LVMR 94550 715-F4
HAMPTON BROOK DR
2600 SCL 95051 833-B4
HAMPTON CREEK DR
2700 SCL 95051 833-B4
HAMPTON FALLS PL
4600 SJS 95136 874-D2
HAMPTON KNOLL DR
1300 SCL 95051 833-B4
HAMPTON LAKE DR
1300 SCL 95051 833-B4
HAMPTON PARK DR
2700 SCL 95051 833-B4
HAMRICK CT
2800 SJS 95121 855-A2
HAMRICK LN
1400 HAY 94544 711-J7
HAMSHIRE CT
1000 SUNV 94087 832-H5
HANA WY
100 UNC 94587 732-C6
HANALEI PL
4400 SJS 95118 874-B2
HANCHETT AV
1100 SJS 95126 833-H7
1500 SJS 95128 833-H7
1500 SJS 95128 853-H1
HANCOCK AV
1300 SMTO 94403 749-C2
6100 SJS 95123 874-G6
HANCOCK CT
1000 PLE 94566 714-F5
2600 CNCD 94519 572-H6
14600 LGTS 95030 873-B3
HANCOCK DR
2800 FRMT 94538 753-D6
3700 SCL 95051 832-H7
HANCOCK PL
3100 FRMT 94538 753-D6
HANCOCK ST
- SF 94114 667-G2
500 HAY 94544 712-C6
600 NVTO 94945 526-C3
800 RDWC 94063 770-B7
HANCOCK WY
700 ELCR 94530 609-E3
HANDBURY LN
500 FCTY 94404 749-G5
HANDEL COM
4000 FRMT 94536 753-A5
HANDLEY TR
600 SMCo 94062 789-F1
HANDY WK
- SRFL 94901 586-F2
HANFORD AV
- CNCD 94518 592-G4
HANFORD DR
20600 SCIC 95014 832-D7
HANFORD ST
4100 UNC 94587 732-B7
HANGAR AV
- NVTO 94949 546-H3
HANI CT
2800 SJS 95111 854-H4
HANKEN DR
100 MrnC 94904 586-D3
HANLEY CT
500 PIN 94806 569-C5
HANLEY DR
400 PIN 94806 569-C5
HANLEY ST
100 SolC 94591 530-D7
HANLON PL
- PIT 94565 574-A2
HANLON WY
100 CCCo 94565 573-J2
300 PIT 94565 573-J2
800 BEN 94510 530-J6
1700 PIT 94565 574-A2
HANLY RD
3200 OAK 94602 650-D3
HANNA DR
18600 SCIC 95014 852-H2
HANNA TER
100 FRMT 94536 753-C2
HANNA WY
- MLPK 94025 790-H2
HANNA GROVE TR
- WLCK 94598 612-J4
HANNAH DR
16500 AlaC 94578 691-G5
HANNAH ST
400 SJS 95126 854-A1
2800 OAK 94608 649-E1
HANNAN DR
100 PLHL 94523 592-A4
HANNA RANCH RD
- NVTO 94945 526-E7
200 NVTO 94947 526-E7
HANNIBAL DR
1800 CCCo 94549 591-H7
HANNIGAN WY
100 VAL 94589 510-C5
HANNON DR
1000 SPAB 94806 588-G2
HANNOVER PL
4700 FRMT 94538 773-D4
HANNS AV
- VAL 94590 530-B3
HANNS LN
100 VAL 94590 530-C4
HANOVER AV
200 OAK 94606 649-J4
800 SUNV 94087 832-C2
HANOVER CT
- NVTO 94947 525-G2
6500 PLE 94566 714-D6
HANOVER DR
6300 SJS 95129 852-F4
HANOVER ST
- SF 94112 687-D3
400 DALY 94014 687-D3
400 LVMR 94550 695-D6
2000 PA 94306 811-A1
2000 PA 94306 810-J1
2200 PA 94304 811-A1
14600 SLN 94579 691-A4
HANS AV
200 MTVW 94040 811-H7
HANS WY
300 SJS 95133 834-F2
HANSELL DR
5300 SJS 95123 874-J3
HANSEN AV
1300 ALA 94501 670-B4
4100 FRMT 94536 752-G4
HANSEN CT
37100 FRMT 94536 752-G4
HANSEN DR
800 LFYT 94549 611-G7
5600 PLE 94566 714-B2
7000 DBLN 94568 693-F4
HANSEN LN
4100 CCCo 94506 654-C5
HANSEN PL
1300 PIN 94564 569-D4
HANSEN RD
- NVTO 94947 525-H4
2200 AlaC 94541 712-C1
2200 AlaC 94550 715-H5
HANSEN WY
600 PA 94304 811-A1
1000 RDWC 94063 770-C5
HANSOM DR
7500 OAK 94619 651-C7
7500 OAK 94605 651-C7
7600 OAK 94605 671-C1
HANSON AV
300 SJS 95117 853-D1
300 SCIC 95117 853-D1
HANSON CT
- MPS 95035 793-J5
- MRGA 94556 631-E3
100 CCCo 94553 572-B6
HANSON LN
- WLCK 94596 612-E6
HAP TER
- DNVL 94506 653-G2
HAP ARNOLD ST
500 ANT 94509 595-F1
HAPLAND CT
1300 SJS 95131 814-D7
HAPPY LN
- SRFL 94901 566-D6
HAPPY ACRES RD
100 LGTS 95032 873-E7
HAPPY HOLLOW CT
200 LFYT 94549 611-J4
HAPPY HOLLOW LN
- SMCo 94025 810-E1
HAPPYLAND AV
22300 HAY 94541 711-G2
HAPPY VALLEY AV
1000 SJS 95129 852-J3
HAPPY VALLEY CT
900 LFYT 94549 611-E6
HAPPY VALLEY LN
3600 LFYT 94549 611-E6

Thomas Bros. Maps ®
COPYRIGHT 1997 Thomas Bros. Maps

STREET
Block City ZIP Pg-Grid

HAPPY VALLEY RD
- AlaC 94586 714-D7
700 AlaC 94566 714-D7
800 PLE 94566 714-D7
3600 LFYT 94549 611-A4
4100 ORIN 94563 611-A2
4100 CCCo 94563 611-A2
4100 CCCo 94549 611-A2
HAPPY VLY GLEN RD
1000 LFYT 94549 611-E5
HARBOR BLVD
100 SMCo 94002 769-F1
700 BLMT 94002 769-F2
HARBOR CT
100 PIT 94565 574-E4
1000 CCCo 94572 569-J1
3400 SJS 95127 835-B2
HARBOR DR
- CCCo 94565 573-E1
- CMAD 94925 606-H1
- DALY 94014 687-E5
- MrnC 94945 526-J3
- SAUS 94965 626-J1
100 CMAD 94925 586-H7
HARBOR RD
- SF 94124 668-D6
200 ALA 94502 669-J5
HARBOR ST
- SRFL 94901 586-H2
300 PIT 94565 574-E3
HARBOR WY
- BEN 94510 551-E5
- SLN 94579 691-A7
- VAL 94590 529-H4
100 SSF 94080 708-A3
1000 CCCo 94572 569-J1
HARBOR BAY PKWY
1100 ALA 94502 670-B7
1100 OAK 94621 670-B7
1200 ALA 94502 690-A1
1300 ALA 94502 669-J7
HARBOR BAY ISLE FERRY
- ALA 94501 669-C3
- SF - 648-D5
- SF - 669-C3
HARBOR COLONY CT
500 RDWC 94065 749-H6
HARBOR COVE CT
- UNC 94545 731-J6
HARBOR COVE WY
- MrnC 94941 606-J4
HARBORD CT
- OAK 94618 630-C6
HARBORD DR
4300 OAK 94618 630-B6
5700 OAK 94611 630-C7
6000 OAK 94611 650-C1
6000 PDMT 94611 650-C1
HARBOR LIGHT RD
300 ALA 94501 669-G3
HARBOR OAK DR
- TBRN 94920 607-D7
HARBOR POINT DR
- MrnC 94941 606-J6
HARBOR SEAL CT
100 SMTO 94404 749-D3
HARBOR VIEW AV
1800 SJS 95122 835-A7
1800 SJS 95122 834-J7
3500 OAK 94619 650-F5
5900 CCCo 94806 589-B4
5900 RCH 94806 589-B4
HARBOR VIEW CT
- MrnC 94901 586-J1
HARBOR VIEW DR
900 MRTZ 94553 571-E4
HARBORVIEW DR
- RCH 94804 608-H3
2100 SLN 94577 691-D1
S HARBOR VIEW DR
800 MRTZ 94553 571-E4
HARBOR VISTA CT
100 BEN 94510 551-C4
HARBOUR DR
2700 ANT 94509 575-F7
HARBOUR WY
- RCH 94801 588-G7
HARBOUR WY S
- RCH 94804 588-G7
200 RCH 94804 608-G1
HARCOURT ST
- SRFL 94901 566-E7
HARCOURT WY
1300 HIL 94010 748-F6
HARCROSS RD
100 RDWC 94061 789-J3
100 WDSD 94062 789-J3
HARD WY
1200 CCCo 94595 632-C2
HARDEMAN ST
2900 AlaC 94541 692-C7
HARDER RD
- HAY 94544 712-A4
300 HAY 94542 712-B4
W HARDER RD
- HAY 94544 711-H5
500 HAY 94544 712-A5
HARDER ST
5700 SJS 95129 852-H3
HARDESTER CT
- DNVL 94526 653-C5
HARDIE AV
- SF 94129 647-D4
HARDIE DR
- MRGA 94556 631-C6
HARDIE PL
- SF 94108 648-A5
HARDIN ST
15200 SLN 94579 691-A6
HARDING AV
100 LGTS 95032 873-B7
300 LVMR 94550 696-A7
700 SJS 95126 833-J6
1800 RDWC 94062 769-H7
2000 SMTO 94403 749-C2
2000 SMCo 94062 769-H7
2300 RDWC 94062 789-H1
3000 SCL 95051 833-A7
HARDING CIR
- BERK 94708 609-J7
HARDING CT
1800 ANT 94509 575-A7
1800 CNCD 94521 593-D2
HARDING DR
- NVTO 94947 526-A6
HARDING PL
300 SRMN 94583 673-H6
HARDING RD
- SF 94132 666-J7
HARDING WY
1700 ANT 94509 575-A7
4000 OAK 94602 650-D3
HARDWICK AV
- PDMT 94611 650-B1
HARDWICK PL
200 SRMN 94583 673-F5
34800 FRMT 94555 752-F1
HARDWICK RD
100 WDSD 94062 789-H4
HARDWOOD CT
- PLHL 94523 592-B1
HARDWOOD ST
4200 FRMT 94538 773-D2
HARDY AV
- CMBL 95008 853-D6
HARDY CIR
100 PLHL 94523 592-B6
HARDY PL
1300 FRMT 94536 753-B2
HARDY ST
400 OAK 94618 629-J6
HARE ST
- SF 94124 668-D6
HAREFIELD CT
1300 SJS 95131 834-C1
HAREFIELD DR
1200 SJS 95131 834-C1
HAREWOOD DR
2300 LVMR 94550 695-G6
HARGATE CT
- PLHL 94523 592-A7
HARGRAVE WY
18900 SAR 95070 852-H6
HARGROVE CT
100 ANT 94509 575-G5
HARGROVE ST
1200 ANT 94509 575-G5
HARGUS AV
900 VAL 94591 530-E6
1000 SolC 94591 530-E6
HARKER AV
1000 PA 94301 791-B4
HARKING DR
700 SUNV 94087 832-C5
HARKINS AV
2100 SMCo 94025 790-D7
2100 MLPK 94025 790-D7
HARKLE RD
100 NVTO 94945 526-C4
HARKNESS AV
- SF 94134 688-A1
HARLAN CT
1000 SJS 95129 852-G2
30800 UNC 94587 731-J5
HARLAN DR
1000 SJS 95129 852-G3
1400 DNVL 94526 653-C6
HARLAN PL
- SF 94108 648-A5
HARLAN RD
11600 DBLN 94568 693-F3
HARLAN ST
- SLN 94577 691-A2
3300 OAK 94608 649-H1
3700 EMVL 94608 629-F7
HARLAND CT
2700 WLCK 94598 612-H4
HARLEIGH CT
13700 SAR 95070 872-G1
HARLEIGH DR
13600 SAR 95070 872-G1
HARLEM AL
- SF 94109 647-J6
HARLEQUIN TER
3700 FRMT 94555 732-D7
HARLISS AV
800 SJS 95110 854-B1
HARLON CT
5200 NWK 94560 752-F5
HARLOW DR
400 ANT 94509 575-E5
HARLOW ST
- SF 94114 667-G2
HARLOW WY
5400 SJS 95124 873-H6
HARMIL WY
1700 SJS 95125 854-B4
HARMON AV
- CMAD 94925 606-F1
900 SJS 95126 853-J1
5500 OAK 94621 670-F1
HARMON DR
900 MLPK 94025 770-G7
HARMON RD
3900 CCCo 94803 589-D2
HARMON ST
1200 BERK 94702 629-F5
1200 BERK 94703 629-F5
HARMONY CT
- DNVL 94526 652-H1
- PIT 94565 573-J2
600 AlaC 94541 691-F6
HARMONY DR
500 AlaC 94541 691-F6
HARMONY LN
- SolC 94591 530-E6
- WLCK 94596 612-A2
400 SJS 95111 855-A7
HARMONY WY
- PIT 94565 573-J2
3700 CNCD 94519 592-J1
4900 SJS 95130 852-J6
HARMS DR
1800 PLE 94566 714-E1
HARN CT
100 TBRN 94920 607-B4
HARNESS CIR
- SRMN 94583 673-D4
HARNESS CT
- SRMN 94583 673-D4
HARNESS DR
900 SRMN 94583 673-D4
HARNEY RD
- BSBN 94005 688-B3
- SF 94134 688-B3
HARNEY WY
- SF 94134 688-C2
- SF 94124 688-C2
900 SUNV 94087 832-B5
HAROLD AV
- SCL 95117 833-C7
- SCL 95117 853-C1
- SF 94112 687-E1
100 SCL 95050 833-C7
200 SF 94112 667-E7
14700 SLN 94578 691-C5
HAROLD CT
- WLCK 94596 592-D7
HAROLD DR
- MRGA 94556 631-C3
HAROLD RD
- SMCo 94014 688-B7
100 BSBN 94005 688-B7
HAROLD ST
1700 CCCo 94801 588-F3
2400 OAK 94602 650-D5
HAROLD WY
2200 BERK 94704 629-G2
HARPER AV
1000 SUNV 94087 832-B5
HARPER CT
- LFYT 94549 611-G5
4500 PLE 94588 694-A6
HARPER DR
13400 SAR 95070 852-G7
HARPER LN
300 DNVL 94526 652-H1
HARPER ST
- SF 94131 667-G5
2000 ELCR 94530 589-B7
2000 ELCR 94530 609-C1
2900 BERK 94703 629-G4
3400 OAK 94601 650-D7
HARPERS FERRY CT
3300 PLE 94588 714-B1
HARPOON WY
29200 HAY 94544 732-B1
HARPSTER DR
800 MTVW 94040 811-H6
HARRAN CIR
- ORIN 94563 610-J6
HARRIER AV
- VAL 94590 529-H3
HARRIER CT
1400 SUNV 94087 832-F4
HARRIER TER
3600 FRMT 94555 732-D7
HARRIET AV
- SCIC 95127 835-A2
- SCIC 95127 834-J2
500 CMBL 95008 853-B7
700 CMBL 95008 873-A1
HARRIET DR
- PLHL 94523 592-C4
HARRIET ST
- SF 94103 648-A7
400 SF 94103 668-B1
900 PA 94301 791-B4
HARRIET WY
- TBRN 94920 606-J4
HARRIETT CT
1300 CMBL 95008 873-A2
HARRINGTON AV
500 LALT 94024 831-F1
1800 OAK 94601 650-D7
HARRINGTON CT
- CCCo 94507 632-H2
400 LALT 94024 831-F1
HARRINGTON LN
24100 AlaC 94541 712-B1
HARRINGTON PL
24100 AlaC 94541 712-B1
HARRINGTON RD
- MRGA 94556 651-G2
HARRINGTON ST
- SF 94112 667-G7
1300 FRMT 94539 753-F6
HARRIS AV
100 CCCo 94572 549-H7
1800 SJS 95124 853-G7
2400 ELCR 94530 589-B7
E HARRIS AV
200 SSF 94080 708-A3
W HARRIS AV
100 SSF 94080 708-A4
HARRIS CIR
- PIT 94565 573-J2
100 CCCo 94565 573-J2
HARRIS CT
200 SSF 94080 708-A3
700 HAY 94544 712-A7
1400 ANT 94509 575-F7
2300 SJS 95124 853-H7
E HARRIS CT
1100 MRTZ 94553 571-H7
HARRIS DR
2800 ANT 94509 575-F7
HARRIS PL
- FRMT 94536 753-C1
- SF 94123 647-G4
HARRIS RD
200 HAY 94544 712-A6
HARRIS WY
100 VAL 94591 530-E4
2300 SJS 95131 814-A4
HARRISBURG AV
2100 FRMT 94536 752-G1
HARRIS HILL DR
- NVTO 94947 526-A4
- NVTO 94947 525-J4
HARRISON AV
- SAUS 94965 627-B3
- CMBL 95008 853-E5
100 RDWC 94062 770-A6
800 RDWC 94062 769-J7
2000 SMTO 94403 749-C2
HARRISON BLVD
- SF 94129 647-B4
- SF 94129 647-B4
HARRISON CT
- CCCo 94803 589-F2
- RCH 94803 589-F2
- NVTO 94947 526-B5
1500 SUNV 94087 832-B5
HARRISON DR
500 RCH 94806 568-G7
HARRISON PL
3000 ANT 94509 575-A7
HARRISON ST
- ALA 94501 649-G5
- OAK 94607 649-G4
- SF 94105 648-A7
600 SCL 95050 833-C4
600 SF 94107 648-A7
700 BERK 94804 609-D7
700 SJS 95125 854-A2
1000 SF 94103 648-A7
1000 SLN 94577 671-A7
1000 SLN 94577 691-A1
1100 BERK 94706 609-D7
1100 SF 94103 668-A1
1200 OAK 94612 649-H2
1300 SF 94103 667-J1
1600 CNCD 94520 592-F2
2000 SF 94110 667-J1
2400 OAK 94610 649-H2
2800 OAK 94611 649-J2
3000 SF 94110 667-J4
4600 PLE 94566 714-D4
HARRISON WY
- SMCo 94025 790-E6
HARROGATE CT
600 WLCK 94598 612-J3
HARROGATE WY
900 ANT 94509 575-C7
HARROW AV
600 SMTO 94402 749-B2
HARROW WY
600 SUNV 94087 832-E5
HARRY RD
600 SJS 95120 895-A2
600 SJS 95119 895-A2
20200 SJS 95120 894-J3
20300 SCIC 95120 894-J3
HARRY RD Rt#-G8
20400 SCIC 95120 894-J4
20400 SJS 95120 894-J4
HARRY ST
- SF 94131 667-G5
HART AV
100 CMAD 94925 586-F7
2300 SCL 95050 833-C5
HART COM
39600 FRMT 94538 753-C5
HART CT
900 CCCo 94507 652-G1
HART LN
- MrnC 94941 606-D4
HART ST
- SRFL 94901 586-E1
100 CMAD 94925 586-F7
HARTE AV
- SRFL 94901 586-G3
HARTE CIR
2100 SLN 94577 690-G1
HARTE DR
1700 SJS 95124 853-J7
HARTFORD AV
- AlaC 94550 695-H2
- LVMR 94550 695-H2
- SCAR 94070 769-E2
800 SJS 95125 854-A2
4200 LVMR 94550 696-A2
HARTFORD CT
100 AMCN 94589 510-A3
HARTFORD DR
1700 UNC 94587 732-E5
HARTFORD RD
- ORIN 94563 611-A5
100 DNVL 94526 632-H7
100 DNVL 94526 652-G1
HARTFORD ST
- SF 94114 667-G2
HARTLEY CT
1400 SJS 95130 853-B4
HARTLEY DR
600 DNVL 94526 653-A3
HARTLEY GATE CT
2700 PLE 94566 694-D7
HARTMAN DR
22300 SCIC 94024 832-A6
22300 CPTO 95014 832-A6
HARTMAN RD
1000 AlaC 94550 695-E2
HARTMAN TER
- AlaC 94541 692-C6
HARTNELL CT
1400 CNCD 94521 593-C5
HARTNELL ST
1600 UNC 94587 732-F6
HARTNETT AV
4700 RCH 94804 609-A2
HARTOG DR
1900 SJS 95131 813-J6
HARTWELL CT
3300 PLE 94588 694-G5
HARTWELL ST
- CCCo 94525 550-E5
HARTWOOD CT
- LFYT 94549 631-J3
HARTZ AV
100 DNVL 94526 652-J1
300 DNVL 94526 653-A2
HARTZ CT
- DNVL 94526 653-A2
HARTZ WY
700 DNVL 94526 653-A2
HARUFF ST
1400 EMVL 94608 629-E6
HARVARD
100 VAL 94589 510-A6
HARVARD AV
100 MrnC 94941 606-F5
200 SCL 95051 832-J6
600 MLPK 94025 790-G5
600 SUNV 94087 832-C2
16900 AlaC 94541 691-F6
HARVARD CIR
- BERK 94708 609-J7
2400 WLCK 94596 612-B3
HARVARD CT
- PLHL 94523 592-C3
3900 LVMR 94550 715-J1
14500 LAH 94022 810-H5
HARVARD DR
- LKSP 94939 586-E4
- PLHL 94523 592-C3
1800 ALA 94501 670-B2
5400 SJS 95118 874-A5
HARVARD RD
200 SMTO 94402 748-H2
1000 OAK 94610 650-B2
1000 PDMT 94610 650-B2
HARVARD ST
- SF 94134 667-H7
2000 PA 94306 811-A1
2000 PA 94306 810-J1
2300 ELCR 94530 589-C7
HARVARD WY
- CCCo 94596 612-B4
3800 LVMR 94550 715-J1
HARVEST CIR
1000 PLE 94566 714-D2
HARVEST CT
3200 HAY 94542 712-E4
HARVEST DR
1500 SJS 95127 835-C4
3800 RDWC 94061 789-G3
HARVEST LN
- ANT 94509 595-H2
- MrnC 94965 606-D7
HARVEST RD
1100 PLE 94566 714-D2
HARVESTER DR
600 FCTY 94404 749-G2
HARVEST ESTATES
5100 SJS 95135 855-G5
HARVEST MEADOW CT
1000 SJS 95136 874-C2
HARVEST OAK WY
6000 SJS 95120 874-D6
HARVESTWOOD CT
3000 SJS 95148 855-E1
HARVEY AV
5500 OAK 94601 670-F1
5500 OAK 94605 670-F1
5500 OAK 94621 670-F1
28000 HAY 94544 712-A7
28900 HAY 94544 732-A1
HARVEY CT
3200 PLE 94588 694-C7
HARVEY TER
- CMAD 94925 586-E7
- FRMT 94536 733-B6
HARVEY TR
- CMAD 94925 606-C5
200 CMAD 94925 586-F7
HARVEY WY
400 PCFA 94044 726-J2
500 CCCo 94565 573-F1
HARWALT DR
1300 LALT 94024 832-A3
HARWELL CT
5700 SJS 95138 875-D4
HARWICH PL
100 VAL 94591 550-E1
HARWICH WK
- PLHL 94523 591-B1
HARWICK WY
100 SUNV 94087 832-E5
HARWOOD AL
- SF 94133 648-A4
HARWOOD AV
6000 OAK 94618 629-J5
6200 OAK 94618 630-A4
HARWOOD CT
100 LGTS 95032 873-H7
HARWOOD RD
4500 SJS 95124 873-H3
5200 SJS 95032 873-H5
15000 LGTS 95032 873-H7
HASKELL ST
1200 BERK 94702 629-F4
HASKINS DR
3300 BLMT 94002 749-B7
3300 SMTO 94403 749-B7
HASKINS WY
100 SSF 94080 708-C4
HASKINS RANCH CIR
- DNVL 94506 654-A6
HASLEMERE CT
100 CCCo 94549 591-H6
HASLEMERE DR
100 CCCo 94549 591-H7
HASSINGER RD
400 SJS 95111 875-C3
HASSLER RD
- SMCo 94070 769-D7
HASSLER WY
- OAK 94621 670-E5
HASTE ST
1900 BERK 94704 629-G2
HASTINGS AV
2500 RDWC 94061 789-H2
3900 SJS 95118 874-A2
HASTINGS CT
- MRGA 94556 651-F1
1100 ANT 94509 595-F1
1900 SCL 95051 833-A3
3600 LFYT 94549 611-E5
38100 FRMT 94536 753-A3
HASTINGS DR
100 VAL 94589 510-A6
500 BEN 94510 550-J2
500 BEN 94510 551-A1
900 CNCD 94518 592-E7
900 MPS 95035 794-B3
2200 BLMT 94002 769-C2
HASTINGS ST
38200 FRMT 94536 753-A3
39000 FRMT 94538 753-A3
HASTINGS TER
- SF 94109 647-J4
HASTINGS WY
7400 DBLN 94568 693-H3
18400 AlaC 94546 692-A3
HASTINGS PARK CT
3900 SJS 95136 874-F1
HASTINGS SHORE LN
200 RDWC 94065 749-H7
HATCH DR
300 FCTY 94404 749-F1
HATCH RD
2000 MrnC 94947 525-G4
HATCHER CT
2200 CMBL 95008 873-E2
HATCHWOOD CT
1200 MRTZ 94553 571-H6
HAT CREEK WY
1100 HAY 94544 732-A1
HATFIELD WALKWAY
4700 SJS 95124 873-E4
HATHAWAY AV
19000 AlaC 94541 711-F1
20700 HAY 94541 711-F2
HATHAWAY CT
200 AlaC 94541 711-F2
600 SJS 95136 874-F2
HATTAN DR
700 LVMR 94550 696-C4
HATTERAS CT
1000 FCTY 94404 749-F5
HATTIE ST
- SF 94114 667-F2
HATZIC CT
- LKSP 94939 586-D7
HAUCK DR
1400 SJS 95118 874-B1
HAUGHTON DR
2800 SJS 95148 855-D1
HAUN CT
14900 SAR 95070 872-F4
HAUSSMAN CT
3900 SSF 94080 707-C4
HAUSSNER DR
5400 CNCD 94521 593-F5
HAUTH LN
500 WLCK 94596 612-B2
HAVANA AV
27600 HAY 94544 711-J7
27800 HAY 94544 731-J1
HAVANA DR
1500 SJS 95122 834-H7
HAVASU ST
47000 FRMT 94539 773-H6
HAVELOCK ST
- SF 94112 667-E7
HAVEN AV
- FRMT 94538 773-D1
700 SSF 94080 707-F4
800 RDWC 94063 770-H6
3500 MLPK 94025 770-G6
3500 SMCo 94063 770-F6
HAVEN CT
- MRGA 94556 631-E4
100 VAL 94591 530-D4
1100 CNCD 94520 592-E4
3700 MLPK 94025 770-G6
4100 SJS 95124 873-E3
HAVEN DR
- DALY 94014 687-E5
HAVEN LN
- CCCo 94596 612-D2
HAVEN PL
- SRMN 94583 673-F7
HAVEN ST
300 MRTZ 94553 571-E3
3700 EMVL 94608 629-E7
17500 AlaC 94541 691-F6
HAVEN HILL CT
100 DNVL 94526 653-C4
HAVENHILL DR
2000 BEN 94510 551-B3
HAVENHURST DR
1600 LALT 94024 832-A3
HAVENRIDGE CT
- SMTO 94402 748-C7
HAVENS PL
1000 ELCR 94530 609-E2
HAVENS ST
- SF 94109 647-J4
HAVENSCOURT BLVD
1400 OAK 94621 670-F3
2200 OAK 94605 670-F3
HAVENSIDE DR
100 SF 94132 667-A6
HAVENWOOD AV
1100 SUNV 94089 813-A5
1100 SUNV 94089 812-J5
HAVENWOOD CIR
- PIT - 573-G4
- PIT 94565 573-G4
HAVENWOOD DR
1300 SJS 95132 814-E5
HAVENWOOD RD
- MrnC 94945 526-J3
HAVERHILL CT
- NVTO 94947 525-G2
100 SJS 95139 895-G1
HAVERHILL DR
700 SUNV 94087 832-C2
2600 OAK 94611 650-F1
HAVEY CANYON TR
- RCH 94805 589-F7
HAVILAND AV
20000 AlaC 94541 691-G7
20800 AlaC 94541 711-G1
HAVILAND CT
- SPAB 94806 588-G2
1500 CLAY 94517 593-F5
HAVILAND PL
1500 CLAY 94517 593-F5
HAVITURE WY
100 HER 94547 570-B6
100 VAL 94589 510-D6
HAVRE CT
1000 SUNV 94087 832-B5
HAWAII CIR
100 UNC 94587 732-C6
HAWAII CT N
3700 PLE 94588 714-A1
HAWAII CT S
3600 PLE 94588 714-A1
HAWES CT
1500 RDWC 94061 790-A1
HAWES ST
600 RDWC 94061 769-J7
1200 RDWC 94061 790-A1
1200 SF 94124 668-C7
2300 SF 94124 688-B1
HAWK CT
- FRMT 94539 773-J3
100 HER 94547 569-H4
800 ANT 94509 595-F2
1400 SUNV 94087 832-F4
HAWK VW
- PTLV 94028 830-D1
HAWK WY
- DBLN 94568 694-D4
HAWK CANYON PL
- LFYT 94549 631-J3
HAWKCREEK PL
6000 SJS 95123 874-E6
HAWKESBURY CT
- VAL 94591 530-F2
HAWKHURST PL
1200 SJS 95125 854-F5
HAWKINGTON CT
2500 SCL 95051 833-B2
HAWKINS DR
1700 LALT 94024 832-A3
12900 SRMN 94583 673-D5
12900 CCCo 94583 673-D5
HAWKINS LN
- SF 94124 668-C6
HAWKINS ST
100 VAL 94591 530-G4
4100 FRMT 94538 753-C6
HAWKINS WY
- LKSP 94939 586-F6
HAWK RIDGE CT
- NVTO 94949 546-E4
HAWKRIDGE TER
- ORIN 94563 610-H6
HAWKSBURY LN
400 FCTY 94404 749-F5
HAWKS HILL CT
- OAK 94618 630-C4
HAWKSTONE WY
5000 SJS 95138 855-E7
HAWLEY CT
5000 SJS 95118 874-A4
HAWLEY ST
7600 OAK 94621 670-F3
HAWTHORN CT
- SRMN 94583 673-J6
HAWTHORNE AV
- LALT 94022 811-E7
- LKSP 94939 586-E6
- SANS 94960 566-A6
- VAL 94590 530-B3
100 PA 94301 790-H6
300 OAK 94609 649-G1
300 OAK 94611 649-G1
400 LALT 94024 811-F7
400 SBRN 94066 727-H1
400 SUNV 94086 832-F1
500 CMBL 95008 853-F5
700 RCH 94801 588-F6
900 ANT 94509 575-C6
2600 HAY 94545 711-F7
6000 LVMR 94550 696-D5
W HAWTHORNE AV
- LALT 94022 811-D7
HAWTHORNE CT
- CCCo 94596 612-G7
- PLHL 94523 592-B7
500 LALT 94024 811-F7
2700 HAY 94545 711-F7
HAWTHORNE DR
- ATN 94027 790-F1
- PLHL 94523 592-B7
600 CCCo 94596 612-F7
600 TBRN 94920 607-B5
700 CCCo 94572 569-J1
700 FRMT 94539 753-G7
900 LFYT 94549 611-G6
1000 SMTO 94402 749-B2
HAWTHORNE LN
- CMAD 94925 606-G1
- PIT 94565 574-E3
400 BEN 94510 551-A1
HAWTHORNE PL
600 SSF 94080 707-J2
HAWTHORNE ST
- SF 94105 648-B6
- SF 94103 648-B6
100 SF 94107 648-B6
200 MrnC 94941 606-E5
400 PIT 94565 574-E2
1200 ALA 94501 669-G2
HAWTHORNE TER
1400 BERK 94708 609-H7
2000 NVTO 94945 525-H1
HAWTHORNE WY
- SJS 95110 834-A5
100 MrnC 94903 566-G2
800 MLBR 94030 728-B5
HAWXHURST CT
4800 ANT - 595-D3
HAY CT
1000 MPS 95035 814-D2
HAYCOCK CT
100 FRMT 94539 773-H7
HAYDEN AV
800 NVTO 94945 526-C4
HAYDEN DR
3700 SJS 95117 853-C3
HAYDON CT
- BLMT 94002 769-B3
HAYES AV
- SJS 95193 875-A3
- SJS 95123 875-A3
200 SCL 95051 833-A7
600 LVMR 94550 716-A1
HAYES CT
700 LVMR 94550 716-A1
1800 CNCD 94521 593-D2
HAYES ST
- BEN 94510 551-D6
- NVTO 94947 526-B5
- SF 94102 647-E7
- SRFL 94901 586-F1
500 RCH 94804 588-H6
800 SF 94117 647-E7
1300 RCH 94806 588-H4
1600 SPAB 94806 588-H4
2100 SF 94117 647-E7
5900 OAK 94621 670-F2
5900 OAK 94605 670-F2
19000 AlaC 94546 691-H4
38800 FRMT 94536 753-D2
HAYES WY
2800 ANT 94509 575-A7
HAYFIELD RD
- AlaC 94586 754-J7
- AlaC 94586 774-J1
HAYFIELDS RD
- WDSD 94062 809-J5

STREET
Block City ZIP Pg-Grid

HAYFIELDS RD
- PTLV 94028 809-J5
HAYFORD CT
4200 PLE 94566 714-F1
HAYFORD DR
1600 SJS 95130 853-B5
HAYMAN AV
2900 VAL 94591 530-D5
HAYMAN PL
900 LALT 94024 831-H2
HAYMAN ST
31400 HAY 94544 732-D2
HAYMEADOW DR
21000 SAR 95070 872-C3
HAYNE RD
500 HIL 94010 748-G2
HAYS CT
- ALA 94502 669-H6
HAYS ST
- SF 94129 647-C5
1100 SLN 94577 691-A1
HAYWARD AV
- SMTO 94401 749-A2
HAYWARD BLVD
25800 HAY 94542 712-B3
HAYWARD CT
- BURL 94010 728-C6
W HAYWARD CT
- MRTZ 94553 571-E7
HAYWARD DR
2500 BURL 94010 728-B6
2500 SCL 95051 833-B5
HAYWORTH DR
1800 SJS 95148 835-C5
HAZEHURST CT
4100 PLE 94566 714-E1
HAZEL AV
- LKSP 94939 586-E6
- MLBR 94030 728-A4
- MLV 94941 606-C3
- RDWC 94061 770-B7
- SANS 94960 566-B7
300 SBRN 94066 727-H1
500 SBRN 94066 707-H7
900 CMBL 95008 853-B7
1000 HAY 94541 691-J7
1000 HAY 94541 711-J1
5600 RCH 94805 589-B6
5700 CCCo 94805 589-B6
6400 ELCR 94530 589-B6
HAZEL CT
- SRFL 94901 586-G3
HAZEL DR
100 PLHL 94523 592-C5
HAZEL LN
- MLV 94941 606-C3
- PIN 94564 569-D3
- PDMT 94611 650-B1
3400 ALA 94502 670-A7
HAZEL RD
- BERK 94705 630-A4
HAZEL ST
500 LVMR 94550 696-C7
1000 PIN 94564 569-D3
HAZEL TR
- MrnC 94965 606-B4
HAZELAAR WY
1600 LALT 94024 831-H3
HAZELBROOK DR
21000 SCIC 95014 832-C7
HAZELDELL WY
500 SJS 95129 853-A2
HAZELNUT CT
- SRMN 94583 673-G7
800 SUNV 94087 832-B2
2400 ANT 94509 575-H6
HAZELNUT DR
7500 NWK 94560 752-C7
HAZELNUT PL
7700 NWK 94560 752-C7
HAZELTINE CIR
100 PLHL 94523 592-B6
HAZELTON AV
200 SUNV 94086 812-E6
HAZELWOOD AV
- SF 94112 667-D6
200 SF 94127 667-D6
900 CMBL 95008 853-B7
1000 SJS 95125 854-B5
3000 SCL 95051 833-A6
4700 FRMT 94536 752-H5
HAZELWOOD CT
- OAK 94603 670-G6
HAZELWOOD DR
- SSF 94080 707-F5
700 CCCo 94596 612-G7
HAZELWOOD LN
- SRFL 94901 567-B6
4300 CNCD 94521 593-C2
HAZELWOOD PL
100 MRGA 94556 631-D7
HAZELWOOD ST
3000 VAL 94591 530-E5
HAZELWOOD WY
2500 EPA 94303 791-B1
2500 EPA 94303 771-B7
HAZEN ST
200 MPS 95035 794-A4
HAZLETT CT
1200 SJS 95131 834-C1
HAZLETT WY
1200 SJS 95131 834-C1
HEACOX RD
- SMCo 94028 830-C6
HEAD ST
- SF 94112 687-C2
200 SF 94132 687-C2
900 SF 94132 667-C7
900 SF 94127 667-C7
HEAD WY
4200 PLE 94588 694-F7
HEADLAND CT
- DNVL 94506 653-H6
HEADLANDS CT
100 VAL 94591 550-F1
HEADQUARTERS DR
- SJS 95134 813-E2
HEAFEY RD
4500 OAK 94605 671-D2
HEALD CT
600 CCCo 94525 550-E5

HEALD ST
- CCCo 94525 550-E4
HEALY LN
- CCCo 94553 571-H4
HEALY WY
2400 SJS 95111 854-F4
2400 SCIC 95111 854-F4
HEARFIELD LN
- SRFL 94901 566-G6
HEARST AV
- SF 94131 667-E6
300 SF 94112 667-E6
500 SF 94112 667-E6
600 BERK 94804 629-D2
1100 BERK 94702 629-E1
1500 BERK 94703 629-F1
1900 BERK 94704 629-H1
1900 BERK 94709 629-H1
2200 BERK 94720 629-H1
2400 OAK 94602 650-D4
HEARST DR
1000 PLE 94566 714-G4
HEARTFORD WY
100 AMCN 94589 509-J2
HEARTH CT
1100 SJS 95120 894-C5
HEARTHSTONE CT
- MrnC 94903 546-E5
HEARTHSTONE DR
1400 SJS 95122 854-F1
HEARTHSTONE WY
800 SJS 95122 854-F1
HEARTHWOOD CT
- SRFL 94901 567-B6
HEARTLAND CT
- DNVL 94506 653-G5
1600 CNCD 94519 592-J2
HEARTLAND ST
100 DNVL 94506 653-G5
HEARTWOOD AV
900 VAL 94591 530-E5
HEARTWOOD CT
100 VAL 94591 530-E4
4300 CNCD 94521 593-B3
HEARTWOOD DR
1500 CNCD 94521 593-C3
6500 OAK 94611 630-E7
HEARTWOOD WY
800 SJS 95133 834-F2
HEATH AV
- HAY 94542 712-D4
HEATH CT
- DALY 94015 707-B2
700 HAY 94544 712-D7
6800 PLE 94588 694-A7
HEATH DR
1900 CCCo 94803 569-E7
HEATH ST
- MPS 95035 793-H6
13000 SAR 95070 852-H7
HEATHCLIFF DR
- TBRN 94920 607-E6
300 PCFA 94044 707-B3
HEATH CLIFF PL
400 SJS 95111 875-C1
HEATHCOT CT
3600 SJS 95121 855-C4
HEATHER AV
- SF 94118 647-E6
100 HER 94547 569-J4
HEATHER CT
- BEN 94510 551-A1
100 VAL 94591 530-F3
400 LALT 94022 811-D5
600 PCFA 94044 707-B4
800 MPS 95035 794-B5
1100 CNCD 94520 592-E4
2300 MTVW 94043 811-G3
3400 ANT 94509 595-C1
14300 SJS 95124 873-G5
24600 HAY 94545 711-F5
HEATHER DR
- ATN 94027 790-F1
- CCCo 94806 569-A5
800 SCAR 94070 769-F4
1500 CNCD 94521 593-D4
1700 WLCK 94598 612-E3
1900 SJS 95124 873-F5
HEATHER LN
- MLV 94941 606-E1
- NVTO 94947 525-H3
- ORIN 94563 631-A2
- WLCK 94596 612-D3
- ORIN 94563 630-J2
100 PA 94303 791-C4
400 SMTO 94403 749-B6
900 AlaC 94580 691-E5
1100 LVMR 94550 696-B4
2500 SBRN 94066 707-E6
HEATHER PL
- HIL 94010 748-E5
- MLBR 94030 728-A2
200 DNVL 94526 653-C5
HEATHER RD
800 SMCo 94015 687-B5
3400 ANT 94509 595-C1
HEATHER TER
34100 FRMT 94555 752-A3
HEATHER WK
- ALA 94501 669-G2
HEATHER WY
- LKSP 94939 586-F6
- MLV 94941 606-E1
300 SSF 94080 707-G2
500 SRFL 94903 566-D2
HEATHERBRAY CT
400 SJS 95136 874-F2
HEATHERCREEK WY
6100 SJS 95123 874-H6
HEATHERDALE AV
1400 SJS 95050 833-F6
1400 SCL 95050 833-F6
1500 SJS 95126 833-F6
1500 SJS 95128 833-F6
HEATHERFIELD LN
1000 SJS 95132 814-F6
HEATHER GARDEN LN
- DNVL 94506 653-J6
HEATHER GLEN LN
5000 CNCD 94521 593-D4
HEATHERGREEN CT
- CNCD - 613-D1

HEATHER GROVE CT
500 WLCK 94598 612-H1
HEATHER HTS CT
2800 ANT 94509 575-G7
HEATHERKIRK CT
600 SJS 95123 874-H6
HEATHERLARK CIR
2400 PLE 94566 714-C2
HEATHERLEAF LN
2400 MRTZ 94553 572-A6
HEATHER RIDGE CT
- SRMN 94583 673-J6
3200 SJS 95136 854-F6
HEATHER RIDGE DR
3100 SJS 95136 854-F6
HEATHER RIDGE WY
6300 OAK 94611 630-E5
HEATHERSTONE DR
2500 MrnC 94903 546-E6
HEATHERSTONE LN
- MrnC 94903 546-E5
HEATHERSTONE WY
800 MTVW 94040 832-A1
900 SUNV 94087 832-B1
HEATHERTREE LN
500 SJS 95129 852-B7
HEATHERWOOD CT
- PIT 94565 574-G6
HEATHERWOOD DR
1600 PIT 94565 574-G6
7400 CPTO 95014 852-D2
HEATHFIELD CT
6700 SJS 95120 894-G2
HEATHFIELD DR
6600 SJS 95120 894-F1
HEATHROW LN
2400 SLN 94577 691-B2
HEATHROW TER
34400 FRMT 94555 752-B3
HEATON CIR
1900 CNCD 94520 572-E6
HEATON CT
1900 CNCD 94520 572-E7
HEATON MOOR DR
6700 SJS 95119 895-D1
6700 SCIC 95119 895-D1
HEAVENLY DR
1100 MRTZ 94553 571-H5
HEAVENLY PL
300 MRTZ 94553 571-H5
HEAVENLY WY
- MrnC 94941 606-E6
HEAVENLY BAMBOO CT
1700 SJS 95131 834-D1
HEAVENLY RIDGE LN
5100 RCH 94803 589-F2
HEAVENLY VALLEY CT
5300 SJS 95136 874-F7
HEBER WY
21700 SAR 95070 872-A2
HEBRIDES CT
5100 NWK 94560 752-E4
HEBRIDES WY
600 SUNV 94087 832-F5
HEBRON AV
2400 SJS 95121 855-C3
HEBRON CT
3200 SJS 95121 855-C3
15600 SLN 94579 691-A7
HECATE CT
2300 SJS 95124 873-D3
HECATE PL
2400 SJS 95124 873-D3
HECHT AV
- SAUS 94965 627-A4
HECKMAN WY
1300 SJS 95129 852-G4
HECTOR LN
- NVTO 94949 546-F2
HEDARO CT
3000 CCCo 94549 611-J1
HEDDA CT
3200 SJS 95127 814-H6
HEDDING ST
100 SJS 95110 833-F7
2200 SJS 95128 833-F7
E HEDDING ST
- SJS 95112 834-A3
2300 SJS 95133 834-A3
W HEDDING ST
- SJS 95110 834-A4
200 SJS 95110 833-J4
700 SJS 95126 833-G6
1700 SJS 95128 833-E7
2400 SCL 95128 833-E7
HEDEGARD AV
200 CMBL 95008 853-D5
HEDERA CT
1000 SUNV 94086 832-H2
HEDGE CT
2900 OAK 94602 650-F3
HEDGE LN
4900 OAK 94602 650-F3
HEDGE RD
100 MLPK 94025 770-G7
HEDGECROFT PL
1000 SJS 95120 894-F2
HEDGEROW CT
300 MTVW 94041 812-A6
HEDGESTONE CT
- MPS 95035 794-C2
HEDGEWICK AV
4600 FRMT 94538 773-C1
HEDLUND CT
900 SJS 95123 874-E5
HEFLIN ST
700 MPS 95035 794-B5
HEGENBERGER CT
- OAK 94621 670-F6
HEGENBERGER EXWY
300 OAK 94621 670-F4
HEGENBERGER LP
- OAK 94621 670-F7
HEGENBERGER PL
- OAK 94621 670-F7
HEGENBERGER RD
- OAK 94621 670-F7
HEIDE CT
2500 CCCo 94803 589-H4
HEIDELBERG CT
2000 LVMR 94550 715-G3

HEIDELBURG DR
1400 LVMR 94550 715-G4
HEIDI CT
800 LVMR 94550 696-D6
2900 SJS 95132 814-F5
HEIDI DR
2900 SJS 95132 814-F5
HEIDI LN
- MLBR 94030 728-A4
HEIDI ST
18900 AlaC 94546 691-H3
HEIDI WY
5800 LVMR 94550 696-D6
HEIGHTS AV
4200 PIT 94565 574-D6
HEIMGARTNER LN
1900 SJS 95124 873-F4
HEINZ AV
700 BERK 94804 629-D4
HEIRLOOM CT
600 SJS 95127 835-B2
HEIRLOOM TER
600 FRMT 94536 753-B2
HEITMAN CT
3100 SJS 95132 814-G5
HEITZ CT
7200 SJS 95120 894-H4
HELADO RD
200 FRMT 94539 753-E4
HELANE CT
- BEN 94510 551-B3
HELEN AV
- CNCD 94518 592-G4
200 MrnC 94941 606-F6
400 LFYT 94549 631-G3
900 SLN 94577 671-B6
900 SUNV 94086 832-H4
1000 SCL 95051 832-H4
1000 SCL 94086 832-H4
2400 VAL 94591 530-D4
HELEN CT
1900 LALT 94024 831-J5
6600 OAK 94608 629-F4
HELEN DR
200 MLBR 94030 728-A3
500 MLBR 94030 727-H3
3500 PLE 94588 694-E7
HELEN LN
- LKSP 94939 586-E7
3200 LFYT 94549 631-G2
HELEN PL
- MLPK 94025 790-F5
HELEN RD
1800 PLHL 94523 592-B5
HELEN ST
- SF 94109 647-J5
700 SJS 95125 854-A1
2800 OAK 94608 649-E1
HELEN WY
200 LVMR 94550 715-E2
38800 FRMT 94536 752-J5
HELENA AV
2400 CCCo 94553 571-F3
HELENA CT
2300 PIN 94564 569-F6
HELENA DR
700 SUNV 94087 832-B5
1800 CNCD 94521 593-F4
HELENA ST
- SF 94124 668-A6
HELENA WY
2000 SMCo 94061 790-A4
HELENE CT
1800 SMTO 94401 729-C7
1800 SMTO 94401 749-C1
3200 CNCD 94518 592-H2
HELENS LN
- MLV 94941 606-D3
HELGA CT
- LVMR 94550 696-C7
HELIX CT
- SRMN 94583 693-J1
1700 CNCD 94518 592-F7
HELIX DR
900 CNCD 94518 592-F6
HELLER ST
200 RDWC 94063 770-B6
HELLER WY
100 SJS 95116 834-G4
HELLINGS AV
1300 RCH 94801 588-G5
HELLMAN ST
10700 OAK 94605 671-C5
HELLYER AV
500 SJS 95111 855-A6
700 SCL 95111 855-A6
4700 SJS 95138 855-A6
4800 SCIC 95138 855-A6
4800 SJS 95138 875-D1
HELM CT
- FRMT 94536 732-J7
200 PIT 94565 574-A2
HELM LN
1000 FCTY 94404 749-H4
HELMOND LN
1400 SJS 95118 874-B5
HELMSDALE CT
7500 SJS 95135 855-J6
HELMSLEY DR
2600 SJS 95132 814-F6
HELMSMAN CT
100 VAL 94591 550-F2
HELMUTH LN
- ANT 94509 575-E5
HELO DR
16300 AlaC 94578 691-F5
HELPERT CT
4600 PLE 94588 694-A6
HELSINKI CT
1600 LVMR 94550 715-G3
HELSINKI WY
1400 LVMR 94550 715-G4
HELSTON PL
34400 FRMT 94555 732-E7
HELTON CT
5100 AlaC 94546 692-C4
HELTON ST
19000 AlaC 94546 692-C4
HEMET COM
34700 FRMT 94555 752-A3
HEMINGWAY DR
3200 ANT 94509 595-C1

HEMLEB CT
300 PIN 94564 569-D4
HEMLOCK AV
- RDWC 94061 770-B7
300 RDWC 94061 790-B1
400 SSF 94080 707-H1
500 MLBR 94030 728-B3
1400 SMTO 94401 749-C1
2200 CNCD 94520 572-F7
2800 SJS 95128 853-E1
E HEMLOCK AV
100 SUNV 94086 812-F4
W HEMLOCK AV
100 SUNV 94086 812-F4
HEMLOCK CT
- MPS 95035 794-D6
100 PA 94306 811-E2
100 HER 94547 570-A4
400 SCL 95054 813-F5
500 LVMR 94550 695-E7
HEMLOCK DR
33100 UNC 94587 732-G3
HEMLOCK LN
- MPS 95035 794-D6
- OAK 94611 630-F6
HEMLOCK ST
- SF 94109 647-H6
100 SCAR 94070 769-G4
600 SF 94115 647-H6
3100 ANT 94509 574-J7
6500 DBLN 94568 693-J4
7000 OAK 94611 630-F6
14300 SLN 94579 691-A4
HEMME AV
100 CCCo 94507 632-F7
HEMMINGWAY CT
- SJS 95132 814-G3
26900 HAY 94542 712-D4
HEMMINGWAY RD
- SJS 95132 814-G3
HEMPHILL PL
300 OAK 94618 629-J6
HEMPSTEAD PL
1700 RDWC 94061 790-A3
HEMWAY TER
- SF 94117 647-E7
HENARD WY
100 LGTS 95032 873-B7
HENDERSON AV
700 SUNV 94086 832-H4
1000 MLPK 94025 790-J1
1100 MLPK 94025 770-J7
1300 SUNV 94087 832-H4
HENDERSON CT
- FRMT 94536 753-B1
HENDERSON DR
300 SJS 95123 875-A6
3100 RCH 94806 589-A1
HENDERSON LN
1200 HAY 94544 711-H6
HENDERSON PL
- MLPK 94025 770-J7
HENDERSON RD
- CCCo 94520 572-F4
HENDON CT
500 SUNV 94087 832-E5
HENDRIX CT
4400 SJS 95124 873-J3
HENDRIX WY
4200 SJS 95124 873-J3
E HENDY AV
100 SUNV 94086 812-E7
W HENDY AV
100 SUNV 94086 812-E7
HENESSY DR
2700 SJS 95148 835-E7
HENEY CREEK PL
10300 CPTO 95014 831-J6
HENNING CT
100 LGTS 95030 873-C3
E HENNING CT
4200 CNCD 94521 593-B3
E HENNING DR
4200 CNCD 94521 593-B2
HENNINGS CT
22500 HAY 94541 692-A7
HENRIETTA AV
700 SUNV 94086 832-F2
HENRIETTA ST
400 MRTZ 94553 571-E3
3400 OAK 94601 650-D6
HENRY AV
- HER 94547 569-F4
1900 PIN 94564 569-F4
N HENRY AV
100 SCL 95117 833-D7
100 SCL 95117 853-D1
300 SJS 95117 833-D7
S HENRY AV
300 SJS 95117 853-D2
300 SCIC 95117 853-D1
HENRY CT
- EPA 94303 791-B2
- WLCK 94596 612-B2
1000 VAL 94591 530-D3
23200 AlaC 94541 692-D7
HENRY LN
23000 AlaC 94541 692-D6
HENRY PL
- MLBR 94030 728-A3
HENRY ST
- SF 94114 667-G1
300 OAK 94607 649-D4
300 VAL 94591 530-D3
1200 BERK 94709 609-G7
1900 BERK 94704 629-G1
HENRY ADAMS ST
- SF 94103 668-A1
HENRY CLAY CT
100 CCCo 94553 572-B7
100 CCCo 94553 592-B1
HENRY FORD II DR
200 SJS 95134 813-G4
HENSEN PL
3700 AlaC 94546 692-B3
HENSLEY AV
600 SBRN 94066 707-H6
HENSLEY ST
- SJS 95112 834-B5
900 RCH 94801 588-F5
HENSON CREEK CT
100 MRTZ 94553 591-J4

HENWOOD RD
20500 SJS 95120 894-J2
20500 SCIC 95120 894-J2
HEPBURN HTS
- SRFL 94901 566-D7
HEPPLEWHITE CT
100 LGTS 95030 872-J3
HEPPNER LN
3700 SJS 95136 874-E1
HERA
- HER 94547 569-F3
HERALD AV
1200 SJS 95116 834-F6
HERBERT DR
5200 SJS 95124 873-G5
5300 LGTS 95032 873-G5
HERBERT LN
- CMBL 95008 853-G6
HERBING LN
- MrnC 94904 586-D5
HERBST RD
3100 SF 94132 666-H6
HERCHELL DR
10800 SCIC 95127 835-A1
HERCULES AV
1000 HER 94547 569-E3
HERCULES CT
4900 LVMR 94550 696-B3
HERCULES LN
800 FCTY 94404 749-H1
HERCUS CT
6500 SJS 95119 875-C7
HEREDIA CT
300 SJS 95116 834-F3
HEREFORD CT
5100 ANT 94509 595-H5
HEREFORD ST
36500 FRMT 94536 752-H2
HEREFORD WY
5100 ANT 94509 595-J5
HERITAGE
- OAK 94605 671-D2
HERITAGE COM
38000 FRMT 94536 752-J3
HERITAGE CT
- ATN 94027 790-E1
- BLMT 94002 768-J2
- WLCK 94596 612-B3
1100 LALT 94024 831-H3
2300 SJS 95124 853-H7
HERITAGE DR
- SRFL 94901 567-E6
2200 SJS 95124 853-H6
3700 ANT 94509 595-E1
HERITAGE LN
200 PLE 94566 714-E4
HERITAGE PL
800 SRMN 94583 673-G6
HERITAGE TER
3700 FRMT 94536 752-J4
HERITAGE ESTS CT
3100 SJS 95148 855-E2
HERITAGE ESTS DR
3200 SJS 95148 855-E2
HERITAGE HILLS DR
2200 PLHL 94523 591-J6
HERITAGE OAKS CT
3200 SJS 95148 855-F2
HERITAGE OAKS DR
- PLHL 94523 591-H3
- PLHL 94553 591-H3
2300 CCCo 94507 632-H3
3400 SJS 95148 855-E2
HERITAGE OAKS PL
100 CCCo 94507 632-H3
HERITAGE PARK CIR
2600 SJS 95132 814-E5
HERITAGE PARK DR
100 DNVL 94506 653-J6
HERITAGE POINT CT
3200 SJS 95148 855-F2
HERITAGE SPRGS CT
3100 SJS 95148 855-E2
HERITAGE VALLEY CT
3400 SJS 95148 855-F2
HERITAGE VALLEY DR
3100 SJS 95148 855-E2
HERITAGE VLG WY
- CMBL 95008 853-E5
HERKNER RD
- RDWC 94063 770-D2
HERLONG AV
100 SJS 95123 875-A5
HERMA CT
300 SLN 94577 671-B6
HERMA ST
5600 SJS 95123 874-J5
5800 SJS 95123 875-A5
HERMAN AV
800 LVMR 94550 696-D2
HERMAN DR
3500 LFYT 94549 611-F7
HERMAN ST
1000 SBRN 94066 707-J5
HERMANN ST
- SF 94102 667-G1
200 SF 94117 667-G1
5700 OAK 94609 629-H5
HERMANOZ CT
1500 SLN 94578 691-D3
HERMES
700 HER 94547 569-F3
HERMES CT
100 HAY 94544 711-J4
600 SJS 95111 854-G3
HERMINA ST
1000 MPS 95035 793-J5
HERMINE AV
100 CCCo 94596 612-E7
1300 CCCo 94596 632-E1
HERMINE CT
1300 CCCo 94596 612-E7
HERMISTON DR
700 SJS 95136 874-D1
HERMIT LN
- MrnC 94904 586-D3
HERMITAGE AV
500 SJS 95134 813-E2
7500 NWK 94560 752-B6
HERMITAGE CT
500 SJS 95134 813-F2
5500 LVMR 94550 696-C2

HERMITAGE DR
500 SJS 95134 813-F2
HERMITAGE LN
- HAY 94544 732-E2
600 SJS 95134 813-E2
HERMITAGE PL
500 SJS 95134 813-E2
HERMITAGE ST
500 SJS 95134 813-E2
HERMITAGE WY
600 SJS 95134 813-F2
HERMOSA
- MTVW 94043 812-A2
HERMOSA AV
- MLBR 94030 728-B3
- OAK 94618 630-B6
- PIT 94565 574-F3
- VAL 94590 530-A2
100 VAL 94589 530-A2
1200 PCFA 94044 726-H5
21800 CPTO 95014 852-B1
HERMOSA CT
- DNVL 94526 653-B2
300 LFYT 94549 631-H4
900 SUNV 94086 812-D6
2300 PIN 94564 569-F6
HERMOSA DR
800 SUNV 94086 812-D6
HERMOSA LN
- SSF 94080 707-F3
HERMOSA PL
- MLPK 94025 790-F5
HERMOSA RD
- SMCo 94062 769-F7
HERMOSA ST
- SBRN 94066 707-J6
2400 PIN 94564 569-F6
HERMOSA TER
2500 HAY 94541 692-C7
HERMOSA WY
300 MLPK 94025 790-E4
1200 SJS 95125 854-B5
3300 LFYT 94549 611-G1
HERNANDEZ AV
- LGTS 95030 872-H7
- SF 94127 667-D4
400 MSER 95030 872-H7
HERNANDEZ LN
18400 MSER 95030 872-H7
HERNDON AV
2500 CNCD 94520 592-E1
HERO CT
- PLHL 94523 591-J6
HERON CT
- MrnC 94964 587-B5
100 VAL 94589 509-H4
HERON DR
- MrnC 94941 607-A7
- MrnC 94941 606-J6
100 HER 94547 569-H5
100 PIT 94565 574-D1
1500 SUNV 94087 832-F6
5800 OAK 94618 630-C7
HERON PL
4000 FRMT 94555 732-B7
HERON ST
- SF 94103 648-A7
HERON WY
- ANT 94509 594-H1
- SRFL 94901 587-A3
HERRERA CT
- SANS 94960 566-A5
HERRICK AV
300 SJS 95123 874-J4
HERRIER ST
3300 OAK 94602 650-F4
HERRIMAN AV
19900 SAR 95070 872-E1
HERRIMAN CT
- CLAY 94517 613-G1
HERRIMAN DR
5800 CLAY 94517 593-G7
5800 CLAY 94517 613-G1
HERRIN CT
6700 PLE 94588 694-A6
HERRIN WY
4600 PLE 94588 694-A6
HERRING AV
15100 SCIC 95124 873-F3
HERRING DR
- MrnC 94941 606-J6
HERRINGBONE WY
- UNC 94587 732-G6
HERRIOTT AV
3100 OAK 94619 650-F7
HERRON AV
2000 CCCo 94596 612-E7
2000 CCCo 94596 632-E1
HERSCHEL ST
1700 SMTO 94403 749-D2
HERSHEY CT
4700 RCH 94804 609-A1
HERSHEY WY
31000 HAY 94544 732-E2
HERSHNER CT
200 LGTS 95032 873-F5
HERSHNER DR
300 SJS 95124 873-G5
300 LGTS 95032 873-G5
HERSHNER WY
400 LGTS 95032 873-G5
HERTIAGE MEADOWS RD
3200 PLHL 94523 591-J6
HERTLEIN PL
3200 AlaC 94546 691-H4
HERVEY LN
1400 SJS 95125 854-B3
HERZOG ST
5900 OAK 94608 629-F4
HESKET CT
6400 SJS 95123 875-B7
HESKET RD
9800 OAK 94603 670-G7
HESKETH CT
- MLPK 94025 790-E5
HESKETH DR
- MLPK 94025 790-E5
HESPERIAN BLVD
14900 SLN 94578 691-D5
15400 AlaC 94580 691-D7
15500 SLN 94579 691-D5

1998 BAY AREA STREET INDEX

STREET
Block City ZIP Pg-Grid

HESPERIAN BLVD
16400 AlaC 94580 711-E2
18100 AlaC 94541 711-E2
19200 HAY 94541 711-E2
24000 HAY 94545 711-F4
24800 AlaC 94545 711-F4
27500 HAY 94545 731-H2
HESPERIAN CT
600 AlaC 94541 711-E2
HESS RD
- CCCo - 593-J4
1400 RDWC 94061 770-B7
1400 RDWC 94061 790-B1
HESSE DR
27900 HAY 94545 731-J1
HESSELBEIN WY
2600 SJS 95148 855-C1
HESTER AV
- SF 94134 688-B2
1100 SJS 95126 833-H7
1600 SJS 95128 833-H7
1700 SJS 95128 853-G1
HESTER LN
3600 LFYT 94549 611-E5
HESTER ST
400 SLN 94577 690-F1
HESTIN CT
- SJS 95123 874-F7
HETFIELD PL
- MRGA 94556 631-E7
- MRGA 94556 651-E1
HETHERTON ST
800 SRFL 94901 586-G1
HEUTERS LN
- MLV 94941 606-D3
HEWITT DR
1000 SCAR 94070 769-F4
HEWITT PL
100 HAY 94544 711-J5
HEYER AV
3700 AlaC 94546 692-B4
4800 AlaC 94552 692-B4
HEYER HTS
3700 AlaC 94546 692-B4
HEYMAN AV
- SF 94110 667-H5
HIAWATHA AV
100 PCFA 94044 727-B2
HIAWATHA CT
- FRMT 94539 773-J4
1000 FRMT 94539 774-A5
1000 SUNV 94087 832-F5
4300 SJS 95111 855-A7
HIAWATHA DR
700 SJS 95111 855-A7
HIBBARD ST
1600 ALA 94501 669-H1
HIBBERT CT
- PCFA 94044 707-A3
HIBERNIA DR
- DBLN 94568 694-D4
HIBERNIA WY
700 SUNV 94087 832-F5
HIBISCUS AV
35800 FRMT 94536 732-J7
HIBISCUS CT
400 EPA 94303 791-D2
22000 CPTO 95014 832-A6
35800 FRMT 94536 732-J7
HIBISCUS DR
2400 HAY 94545 731-H2
22000 CPTO 95014 832-A6
HIBISCUS LN
700 SJS 95117 853-B3
HIBISCUS WY
300 SRFL 94903 566-D2
1100 LVMR 94550 696-B4
HIBUSCUS CT
100 VAL 94589 510-A6
HICHBORN DR
- SCL 95054 813-B6
HICHBORN ST
300 VAL 94590 529-H3
HICKERSON CT
3500 SJS 95127 835-B3
HICKERSON DR
3200 SJS 95127 835-B3
HICKEY BLVD
100 PCFA 94044 707-A3
100 SSF 94080 707-B1
300 DALY 94015 707-B1
HICKORY AV
- CMAD 94925 586-G7
1500 SLN 94579 691-A5
1600 SBRN 94066 707-G7
25900 HAY 94544 711-J5
HICKORY CT
- CCCo 94506 654-A3
500 SCL 95051 833-A6
HICKORY DR
2200 CNCD 94520 572-F7
HICKORY LN
100 SMTO 94403 749-B6
300 SRFL 94903 566-D2
6800 DBLN 94568 693-J4
HICKORY PL
400 SCL 95051 833-A6
700 SSF 94080 707-J2
HICKORY ST
- SF 94102 647-H7
100 VAL 94589 510-B7
2600 OAK 94602 650-C5
37000 NWK 94560 772-C1
HICKORY WY
700 SJS 95129 853-A2
800 FRMT 94536 732-J7
HICKORY HILL WY
20200 SAR 95070 852-E7
HICKORYNUT CT
1000 SUNV 94087 832-B2
HICKOX RD
- NVTO 94947 525-H3
HICKS AV
1400 SJS 95125 853-J4
1700 SJS 95125 854-A5
HICKS RD
- SF 94129 647-D4
16700 LGTS 95032 873-J7
16700 LGTS 95032 893-J2
17300 SCIC 95032 893-H2
18000 SCIC 95032 894-B3
19400 SCIC 95120 894-B3
19600 SCIC 95030 894-B3
HIDALGO CT
- SPAB 94806 568-J7
200 FRMT 94539 753-E3
1100 LFYT 94549 611-F5
2900 SJS 95125 873-J1
HIDALGO TER
- SF 94103 667-H1
HIDATSA CT
800 FRMT 94539 773-H4
HIDDEN CT
24400 AlaC 94541 712-C1
HIDDEN DR
15800 SCIC 95030 872-F5
HIDDEN LN
- MrnC 94941 606-F6
- ORIN 94563 610-G3
HIDDEN TER
- HIL 94010 728-D7
HIDDENBROOKE PKWY
- NaCo 94589 510-G3
- SolC 94589 510-G3
- VAL 94591 510-H4
2500 VAL 94589 510-G3
HIDDEN CANYON CT
- SRMN 94583 653-F7
HIDDEN CREEK CT
6400 SJS 95120 894-E1
HIDDENCREEK CT
200 MRTZ 94553 571-J6
HIDDEN CREEK DR
6400 SJS 95120 894-E1
HIDDEN CREST CT
- DNVL 94506 653-H5
HIDDEN GLEN DR
5000 ANT 94509 595-J2
HIDDEN HILL PL
15700 SCIC 95030 872-G5
HIDDEN HILL RD
15700 SCIC 95030 872-G5
HIDDEN HILLS CT
2800 ANT 94509 595-G1
HIDDEN HILLS PL
- DNVL 94506 654-B6
HIDDENLAKE DR
300 SUNV 94089 812-G4
HIDDEN LAKES CT
2200 MRTZ 94553 592-A1
HIDDEN LAKES DR
600 MRTZ 94553 572-A7
600 MRTZ 94553 592-A1
HIDDEN MEADOW CT
6200 SJS 95135 855-H7
HIDDEN MINE RD
1300 SJS 95120 894-C2
HIDDEN OAK CT
- CCCo 94506 653-H1
1000 CNCD 94521 593-C5
HIDDEN OAK DR
2100 CCCo 94506 653-G1
HIDDEN OAKS DR
- NVTO 94945 526-A2
1100 MLPK 94025 790-E5
2300 AlaC 94541 712-C1
HIDDEN POND CT
- CCCo - 591-G4
HIDDEN POND LN
- CCCo - 591-G4
HIDDEN POND RD
2100 CCCo - 591-G5
2100 CCCo 94549 591-G5
HIDDEN SPRINGS CT
- LAH 94022 831-B2
3700 RCH 94803 589-G1
HIDDEN TRAIL LN
100 VAL 94591 530-D2
HIDDEN VALLEY DR
- SMCo 94070 769-E4
HIDDEN VALLEY LN
- MrnC 94960 566-A3
- PTLV 94028 810-A5
- WDSD 94062 810-A5
4000 SCIC 95127 835-A1
HIDDEN VALLEY PL
- CCCo 94507 632-G5
HIDDEN VALLEY RD
- ORIN 94563 610-J6
- LFYT 94549 611-B6
4100 ORIN 94563 611-A6
HIDDEN VALLEY TER
600 FRMT 94539 774-A4
600 FRMT 94539 773-J4
HIDDEN VIEW PL
3700 AlaC 94546 692-B3
HIDEAWAY CT
200 DNVL 94526 633-A7
HIEBER DR
200 CCCo 94553 572-C6
HIERRA CT
11500 SCIC 94024 831-G4
HIGATE DR
100 DALY 94015 687-A6
100 DALY 94015 707-A1
1500 SJS 95122 834-J5
HIGDON AV
100 MTVW 94041 811-G4
HIGGINS AV
- LALT 94022 811-F6
1600 SCL 95051 833-B3
HIGGINS PL
3000 PA 94303 791-E5
HIGGINS WY
1500 PCFA 94044 726-H5
1500 SMCo - 726-H5
41500 FRMT 94539 753-F6
HIGH COM
3400 FRMT 94538 753-D6
HIGH CT
1100 BERK 94708 609-H6
HIGH RD
- WDSD 94062 790-A5
800 WDSD 94062 789-J5
HIGH ST
- SRFL 94901 586-H1
- SF 94114 667-F4
- CCCo 94553 592-A1
100 MRTZ 94553 592-A1
200 PA 94301 790-H4
200 PLHL 94523 592-A1
300 ALA 94501 670-A4
300 OAK 94601 670-C2
400 RCH 94801 588-C7
400 RCH 94801 608-C1
2000 OAK 94601 650-E7
2100 PA 94301 791-B7
2600 OAK 94619 650-F6
5900 CLAY 94517 593-H7
17300 LGTS 95032 893-B2
22800 HAY 94541 712-A1
40600 FRMT 94539 753-D6
40700 FRMT 94538 753-D6
HIGHBLUFF TER
- PLE 94586 693-G7
HIGHBRIDGE CT
- DNVL 94526 653-A1
HIGHBRIDGE LN
700 DNVL 94526 653-A2
HIGH CASTLE CT
2200 LVMR 94550 715-G4
HIGHCLIFF CT
2200 MRTZ 94553 572-A7
HIGH COUNTRY DR
27900 HAY 94542 712-F4
HIGHCREST CT
- PLE 94586 693-G7
HIGHCREST LN
1200 SSF 94080 707-H1
HIGH EAGLE RD
- CCCo 94507 632-H5
HIGHGATE AV
2800 BLMT 94002 749-B7
HIGHGATE CT
- CCCo 94707 609-F3
HIGHGATE DR
2200 RCH 94806 588-J1
29500 HAY 94544 712-D7
HIGH GATE LN
- HIL 94010 728-F7
HIGHGATE RD
- CCCo 94707 609-F3
- ELCR 94530 609-F3
HIGHGATE WY
3900 PIT 94565 574-E6
HIGH GLEN DR
600 SJS 95133 814-G7
HIGHGROVE CT
14300 SCIC 95127 835-A3
HIGH KNOLL DR
4200 OAK 94619 650-J6
HIGHLAND AV
- SF 94131 667-H5
- BURL 94010 728-G7
- DALY 94015 686-J6
- LGTS 95032 893-B2
- MrnC 94901 567-A7
- MrnC 94901 566-J7
- PDMT 94611 630-B7
- SCAR 94070 769-E2
- SF 94110 667-H5
- SSF 94080 707-J1
100 PDMT 94611 650-B2
100 SRFL 94901 566-H7
300 SMTO 94401 728-G7
600 SMTO 94401 748-H1
1000 SCL 95050 833-F5
1000 VAL 94590 530-C3
1300 MRTZ 94553 571-E3
1900 LFYT 94549 591-H7
2400 OAK 94606 650-B5
3500 RDWC 94062 789-H1
5500 RCH 94804 609-B2
6200 CCCo 94805 589-C5
7200 ELCR 94530 589-C5
HIGHLAND BLVD
- CCCo 94530 609-F2
- CCCo 94708 609-F2
900 HAY 94542 712-A2
HIGHLAND CT
- LFYT 94549 611-D7
- BLMT 94002 769-B3
- DNVL 94526 652-J3
- LKSP 94939 586-E6
- ORIN 94563 630-J1
300 CCCo 94520 572-G1
1000 SCL 95050 833-F5
1200 SCAR 94070 769-B3
1300 MPS 95035 814-E2
HIGHLAND DR
300 DNVL 94526 652-J3
1000 NVTO 94949 546-C1
2000 CNCD 94520 572-E6
3100 SBRN 94066 707-B6
15700 SCIC 95127 815-A6
HIGHLAND LN
100 MrnC 94941 606-F5
HIGHLAND PL
1700 BERK 94709 629-J1
44100 FRMT 94539 774-A2
44100 FRMT 94539 773-J2
HIGHLAND RD
3600 LFYT 94549 611-D7
HIGHLAND ST
500 LVMR 94550 695-J6
HIGHLAND TER
100 WDSD 94062 789-G5
200 LGTS 95032 893-B2
44200 FRMT 94539 774-A2
HIGHLAND WY
300 PDMT 94611 650-B1
HIGHLAND OAKS DR
100 LGTS 95032 873-C4
7400 PLE 94588 693-F7
7500 PLE 94588 713-H1
HIGHLAND OAKS WY
100 LGTS 95032 873-C4
HIGHLAND PARK LN
2200 SJS 95008 853-E7
HIGHLANDS CIR
800 LALT 94024 831-G5
HIGHLANDS CT
200 CCCo 94806 569-B4
HIGHLANDS PL
200 CCCo 94806 569-B4
HIGHLANDS RD
2100 CCCo 94806 569-B4
HIGHLANDS WY
4800 ANT 94509 595-H3
HIGHLAND VIEW CT
1400 LALT 94024 831-H4
HIGH MEADOW CT
6200 SJS 95135 855-J7
HIGH MEADOW LN
3000 SJS 95135 855-H7
HIGH PINE WY
17000 AlaC 94546 691-J2
HIGHPOINTE CT
3200 RCH 94806 588-F1
HIGHRIDGE CT
1900 WLCK 94596 611-H3
HIGH RIDGE PL
4100 AlaC 94552 692-D5
HIGH RIDGE TR
- AlaC 94544 712-E6
- HAY 94544 712-C5
HIGH RIDGE LOOP TR
- AlaC 94544 712-F7
- AlaC 94544 732-F1
- UNC 94587 712-F7
- UNC 94587 732-F2
HIGH SCHOOL AV
2400 CNCD 94520 572-F7
2400 CNCD 94520 592-F1
HIGH SCHOOL CT
- LGTS 95032 893-A1
HIGH SCHOOL WY
800 MTVW 94041 811-H5
HIGHTREE CT
- DNVL 94526 653-A1
HIGHVIEW CT
600 SMTO 94403 749-B7
HIGHVIEW DR
4200 SMTO 94403 749-B7
4200 SMTO 94403 769-B1
HIGHWAY AV
- CCCo 94565 573-H2
HIGHWAY RD
1400 BURL 94010 728-D5
HIGHWOOD DR
2600 SJS 95116 834-J4
13500 SCIC 95127 834-J3
13800 SCIC 95127 835-A3
HIGHWOOD RD
5700 AlaC 94552 692-D3
HIGUERA AV
- SF 94132 687-A1
2900 PIN 94564 569-G6
HIGUERA CT
1200 LVMR 94550 695-F6
HIGUERA PL
1300 MPS 95035 794-A4
HIGUERA RD
3800 SCIC 95148 835-F5
HIGUERA HIGHLAND LN
3900 SCIC 95148 835-G5
HIKIDO DR
1900 SJS 95131 814-D7
HILARITA AV
- MLV 94941 606-E4
HILARITA CIR
- BLV 94920 607-C7
HILARY AV
- MTVW 94040 811-F3
HILARY DR
300 TBRN 94920 607-B5
3000 SJS 95124 873-G2
HILARY WY
- ORIN 94563 631-A1
100 VAL 94591 530-G4
HILBAR LN
500 PA 94303 791-C4
HILDASUE TER
4900 FRMT 94555 752-C2
HILDING AV
1800 SLN 94577 690-J2
HILFERD WY
- DNVL 94526 652-G3
HILFORD CT
1100 SJS 95132 814-G5
HILGARD AV
2300 BERK 94709 609-H7
2300 BERK 94709 629-H1
HILIRITAS AV
- SF 94131 667-F5
HILL AV
- FRFX 94930 566-A6
- SCAR 94070 769-F5
- SANS 94960 566-A6
700 SSF 94080 707-G4
1300 MLPK 94025 770-H7
1500 SJS 95125 854-B4
1800 HAY 94541 692-B7
1800 AlaC 94541 692-B7
20100 SAR 95070 872-E4
S HILL BLVD
- SF 94112 687-G2
300 DALY 94014 687-F3
HILL CT
- HAY 94542 712-A3
- HER 94547 569-H4
2500 BERK 94708 609-H7
N HILL CT
- OAK 94618 630-B4
S HILL CT
- OAK 94618 630-B4
HILL DR
- SF 94124 668-E7
- MrnC 94904 586-E2
100 VAL 94590 529-H2
1400 ANT 94509 575-F6
HILL LN
- PLHL 94523 592-A6
100 PDMT 94610 650-A1
18300 SJS 95120 874-G7
18300 SCIC 95120 874-G7
18400 SCIC 95120 894-G1
18400 SJS 95120 894-G1
HILL PTH
- CMAD 94925 586-F7
100 CMAD 94925 606-F1
HILL RD
- BERK 94708 609-J6
- NVTO 94947 526-A4
- ROSS 94957 586-B2
- BERK 94708 610-A6
100 DNVL 94526 633-C7
6100 OAK 94618 630-B5
HILL ST
- CCCo 94565 573-F2
- DALY 94014 687-C5
- MLV 94941 606-D3
- SF 94110 667-H3
- SMCo 94014 687-C5
300 SF 94114 667-G3
800 BLMT 94002 769-E1
6100 ELCR 94530 609-B1
37300 NWK 94560 752-F7
HILL TR
- CMAD 94925 586-E7
- CMAD 94925 606-C5
HILL WY
300 SCAR 94070 769-G5
13500 LAH 94022 811-D7
HILLARY LN
- SMCo 94061 790-B4
HILLBARN CT
4200 SMTO 94403 749-D7
HILLBORN AV
100 VAL 94590 529-H3
HILLBRIGHT CIR
5700 SJS 95123 874-J5
HILLBRIGHT CT
5700 SJS 95123 874-J5
HILLBRIGHT PL
500 SJS 95123 874-J5
HILLBROOK DR
- PTLV 94028 810-D6
100 LGTS 95032 873-D6
HILLCAP AV
200 SJS 95136 854-G7
200 SCIC 95136 854-G7
HILLCREST AV
- ANT - 595-J5
- BEN 94510 551-C4
- LKSP 94939 586-D4
- PIT 94565 574-C5
- SANS 94960 566-B7
100 LVMR 94550 696-A7
100 MrnC 94904 586-D4
400 LVMR 94550 716-A1
1200 ANT 94509 575-F5
2100 ANT 94509 595-H1
2600 HAY 94542 712-D3
HILLCREST BLVD
- SMCo - 727-J5
- MLBR 94030 728-A4
100 MLBR 94030 727-J5
E HILLCREST BLVD
- MLBR 94030 728-B3
HILLCREST CIR
200 PLHL 94523 592-A4
HILLCREST COM
4000 LVMR 94550 716-A1
HILLCREST CT
- BERK 94705 630-A4
- OAK 94619 651-A4
- OAK 94619 650-J5
- SANS 94960 566-A6
- SF 94127 667-E6
- SRMN 94583 673-A1
- SSF 94080 707-F1
200 PLHL 94523 592-A4
1000 LVMR 94550 716-A1
1300 SJS 95120 894-D3
HILLCREST DR
- SMCo - 768-C3
- DALY 94014 687-C3
- ORIN 94563 631-A1
- SRFL 94901 566-G7
100 ORIN 94563 611-A7
400 RDWC 94062 769-G7
400 RDWC 94062 789-H1
400 SMCo 94062 769-G7
1100 LFYT 94549 611-F5
1200 SJS 95120 894-D3
3400 BLMT 94002 769-A1
HILLCREST LN
- PLHL 94523 592-A4
HILLCREST PL
200 PLHL 94523 592-A4
HILLCREST RD
- WLCK 94595 612-B5
- BERK 94705 630-A4
- MLV 94941 606-E3
- SCAR 94070 769-F2
- MrnC 94920 607-B3
- TBRN 94920 607-B3
100 BERK 94618 630-A4
200 OAK 94618 630-A4
400 SMTO 94402 748-F1
500 SMCo 94062 769-G7
500 RDWC 94062 769-G7
1500 CCCo 94806 589-A3
1500 SPAB 94806 589-A3
3400 CCCo 94803 589-A3
3700 RCH 94803 589-A3
10000 CPTO 95014 832-A7
HILLCREST TER
600 FRMT 94539 773-J1
HILLCREST WY
400 SMCo 94062 789-E2
4800 PLE 94588 693-J7
HILLCROFT CIR
900 OAK 94610 650-B3
HILLCROFT WY
- CCCo 94596 612-A5
HILLDALE AV
- SANS 94960 566-D7
600 BERK 94708 609-H5
HILLDALE CT
- ORIN 94563 630-J4
HILLDALE DR
- SANS 94960 566-D7
HILLDALE RD
- LFYT 94549 611-B4
HILLDALE WY
400 MrnC 94941 606-E6
HILLEGASS AV
2500 BERK 94704 629-J2
2700 BERK 94705 629-J4
6000 OAK 94618 629-J4
HILLEN DR
5200 OAK 94619 670-F1
HILLENDALE CT
1000 WLCK 94596 632-F1
HILLER DR
- OAK 94618 630-B4
HILLER LN
1800 MRTZ 94553 571-J6
HILLER ST
100 BLMT 94002 749-E7
1000 BLMT 94002 769-F1
1000 OAK 94621 670-D6
HILLFLOWER DR
5300 LVMR 94550 696-C4
HILLGIRT CIR
600 OAK 94610 650-A3
HILLGIRT DR
- ROSS 94957 586-B2
HILL GIRT RANCH RD
100 CCCo 94553 591-E2
HILLGRADE AV
1500 CCCo 94507 632-D3
HILLGRADE CT
9700 OAK 94603 671-A4
HILLHURST WY
- OAK 94705 630-B2
HILLIARD CIR
2300 ANT 94509 595-A2
HILLIKER PL
1200 AlaC 94550 695-H6
1200 LVMR 94550 695-H6
HILLMAN AV
1700 BLMT 94002 749-D7
1900 BLMT 94002 769-C1
HILL MEADOW DR
- DNVL 94526 653-E3
HILL MEADOW PL
1000 DNVL 94526 653-E3
HILLMONT AV
1500 SJS 95127 835-A5
1800 SJS 95148 835-A5
HILLMONT DR
6100 OAK 94605 650-H7
6400 OAK 94605 670-J1
7700 OAK 94605 671-A2
HILLMONT PL
- DNVL 94526 633-A6
- DNVL 94526 632-J6
HILLMOOR DR
20700 SAR 95070 852-D6
HILL PARK DR
2500 SJS 95124 853-H7
2500 SJS 95124 873-H1
HILLPARK LN
11500 SCIC 94024 831-E4
HILLPOINT AV
- SF 94117 667-E2
HILL RIDGE WY
4900 ANT 94509 595-D4
HILLRISE PL
- CCCo 94598 613-B3
HILLROSE DR
5900 SJS 95123 874-E5
7500 DBLN 94568 693-G3
HILLSBORO AV
900 SUNV 94087 832-C2
7300 SRMN 94583 673-G7
HILLSBORO CT
7900 PLE 94588 693-H7
HILLSBOROUGH BLVD
300 HIL 94010 748-F1
300 SMTO 94402 748-F2
800 HIL 94010 728-F7
HILLSBOROUGH CT
2200 CNCD 94520 572-F6
HILLSBOROUGH DR
3400 CNCD 94520 572-F5
4400 AlaC 94546 691-H1
HILLSBOROUGH ST
600 OAK 94606 649-J4
600 OAK 94606 650-A4
HILLSBOROUGH WY
3400 SJS 95121 855-D3
HILLSDALE AV
- DALY 94015 687-B3
- SJS 95136 854-D7
- SCIC 95125 854-D7
200 SCL 95051 832-H7
500 SCIC 95136 854-F7
1000 SJS 95118 854-D7
1000 SJS 95118 874-A1
1600 SJS 95120 873-H2
1600 SJS 95124 873-H2
E HILLSDALE BLVD
- SMTO 94403 749-D5
600 FCTY 94404 749-F1
W HILLSDALE BLVD
- SMTO 94403 749-A6
800 SMTO 94403 748-J6
1700 SMTO 94402 748-J6
HILLSDALE CT
- SMTO 94403 749-D5
3700 SCL 95051 832-H6
7600 PLE 94588 693-J7
HILLSDALE DR
300 PIT 94565 574-B5
2900 PLHL 94523 612-A1
7500 PLE 94588 693-J7
HILLSDALE PL
- SMTO 94403 749-A6
HILLSDALE ST
1900 AlaC 94541 712-B1
HILLSDALE WY
200 SMCo 94062 769-F7
200 SMCo 94062 789-E1
HILLSIDE AV
- SRFL 94901 566-B7
- LGTS 95032 893-B1
- MLV 94941 606-E2
- MrnC 94904 586-E4
- SANS 94960 566-B7
- SRFL 94901 587-A1
- ROSS 94957 586-C3
100 PDMT 94611 630-A2
100 PDMT 94611 650-B1
100 SMCo 94025 790-C6
200 SRFL 94901 586-J1
700 ALB 94706 609-D6
1000 AlaC 94586 734-B3
1600 CCCo 94595 612-A7
2000 WLCK 94596 612-B4
2400 BERK 94704 630-A2
2800 CNCD 94520 572-E7
3700 LVMR 94550 695-J6
3900 LVMR 94550 696-A6
5400 ELCR 94530 589-B7
HILLSIDE BLVD
- DALY 94014 687-D4
100 SSF 94080 708-A2
100 SSF 94080 707-J1
1000 SMCo 94014 687-D4
1300 CLMA 94014 687-D6
1400 SMCo 94014 707-G1
1700 CLMA 94014 707-G1
1700 SSF 94080 687-D6
HILLSIDE CIR
1300 BURL 94010 728-C6
2000 SLN 94577 691-D1
HILLSIDE CT
- BERK 94704 629-J2
100 WDSD 94062 790-A5
400 PDMT 94611 650-B1
2200 CCCo 94596 612-B4
3300 SJS 95132 814-G4
3700 SMTO 94403 749-B6
4600 AlaC 94546 692-A3
35700 FRMT 94536 732-J7
HILLSIDE DR
100 WDSD 94062 789-G5
100 VAL 94590 529-G2
200 PCFA 94044 727-A2
1100 MRTZ 94553 571-D3
1500 BURL 94010 728-D6
1500 SMCo 94010 728-B7
2000 SLN 94577 691-D1
4600 AlaC 94546 692-A2
5900 CCCo 94803 589-H4
HILLSIDE LN
100 CCCo 94553 572-B5
3100 BURL 94010 728-A7
3100 SMCo 94010 728-A7
3700 AlaC 94546 692-A2
HILLSIDE PL
4600 AlaC 94546 692-A2
HILLSIDE RD
- ANT 94509 575-D7
- DNVL 94526 652-H3
- MrnC 94904 586-E3
500 RDWC 94062 789-G1
500 SMCo 94062 789-G1
HILLSIDE ST
7300 OAK 94605 671-A4
7300 OAK 94605 670-J2
9000 OAK 94603 671-A4
HILLSIDE TER
- LFYT 94549 611-G2
- MRTZ 94553 571-D4
HILLSLOPE PL
1100 SCIC 94024 831-F2
HILLSTONE DR
2100 SJS 95138 855-E5
HILLSWOOD DR
- NVTO 94947 526-B6
HILLTOP CRES
100 CCCo 94596 612-A4
5300 OAK 94618 630-C7
HILLTOP CT
- SRMN 94583 673-F2
1500 MPS 95035 794-C3
HILLTOP DR
- RDWC 94062 769-G6
- SCAR 94070 769-G5
100 LGTS 95032 873-E7
100 LGTS 95032 893-E1
100 VAL 94591 530-F3
1100 LFYT 94549 611-E5
2800 RCH 94806 569-A7
2800 RCH 94806 568-J6
2900 RCH 94806 589-C1
4100 CCCo 94803 589-C1
4100 RCH 94803 589-C1
4800 CCCo 94803 569-D7
11800 LAH 94024 831-E3
HILLTOP RD
- SMTO 94402 748-H1
- MRTZ 94553 571-F7
2800 CNCD 94520 572-E6
3100 RCH 94806 589-A1
HILLTOP WY
14200 SAR 95070 872-H2
HILLTOP MALL RD
1000 RCH 94806 569-A7
2100 RCH 94806 589-A1
HILLVALE AV
16100 MSER 95030 872-H6
HILLVIEW AV
- LALT 94022 811-E7
- RDWC 94062 769-H6
- SRFL 94901 586-G3
3200 PA 94304 811-A3
5800 SJS 95123 874-E5
HILLVIEW CT
- BURL 94010 728-C7
- DALY 94015 686-J5
- DNVL 94506 654-B6
- SF 94124 668-C6
800 MPS 95035 794-B6
3100 CNCD 94519 572-G7
7400 PLE 94588 693-J7
24200 LAH 94024 831-E3
HILLVIEW DR
- SMCo - 768-C3
- DNVL 94506 654-B6
100 VAL 94591 530-F3
100 FRMT 94536 733-A7
100 FRMT 94536 753-A1
1100 MLPK 94025 790-E5
1200 LVMR 94550 695-F6
1500 LAH 94024 831-E2
1500 SCIC 94024 831-F3
1700 SLN 94577 691-D1
2100 CCCo 94596 612-D7
3200 RCH 94806 588-J1
3200 RCH 94806 568-J7
3500 RCH 94806 569-A7
4200 PIT 94565 574-D7
18400 MSER 95030 872-H5
18400 SCIC 95030 872-H5
N HILLVIEW DR
100 MPS 95035 794-B4
S HILLVIEW DR
100 MPS 95035 794-B7
300 MPS 95035 814-B1
HILL VIEW LN
2400 PIN 94564 569-F5
HILLVIEW LN
3200 LFYT 94549 611-H4
HILLVIEW PL
- MLPK 94025 790-E5
- SJS 95123 874-E5
HILLVIEW RD
1100 BERK 94708 609-J5
HILLVIEW ST
3600 OAK 94602 650-E5

STREET
Block City ZIP Pg-Grid
HILLVIEW ST
28900 HAY 94544 712-B7
HILLVIEW TER
- CCCo 94596 612-E7
HILLWAY AV
- SF 94143 667-D2
- SF 94117 667-D2
HILLWAY DR
300 SMCo 94062 789-G1
HILLWOOD CT
300 MTVW 94040 811-F4
HILLWOOD DR
800 SJS 95129 852-J2
HILLWOOD PL
- OAK 94610 650-C3
HILMAR ST
500 SCL 95050 833-F5
32700 UNC 94587 732-B7
HILMER AV
100 MRTZ 94553 571-D4
HILO CT
2300 MTVW 94040 831-J1
HILO DR
- PIT 94565 574-E5
HILO ST
4500 FRMT 94538 753-B7
4800 FRMT 94538 773-B1
HILO WY
300 PCFA 94044 707-A6
HILOW CT
100 LGTS 95032 873-D6
HILOW RD
16300 SCIC 95032 873-C7
16400 LGTS 95032 873-C7
HILTIBRAND DR
1600 SJS 95131 834-C1
HILTON AV
- VAL 94591 530-D5
100 SSF 94080 707-D1
4300 SJS 95130 853-A5
HILTON CT
- CCCo 94595 611-J7
1500 SJS 95130 853-A5
HILTON LN
100 PCFA 94044 706-J6
HILTON RD
700 CCCo 94595 611-J7
HILTON ST
- SF 94124 668-A5
100 RDWC 94063 770-B6
2400 UNC 94587 732-E6
5500 OAK 94605 670-F1
HILTON WY
100 PCFA 94044 706-J6
HIMMEL AV
1100 SMCo 94061 790-B3
HIMMELMANN PL
- SF 94133 647-J4
HINCKLEY RD
800 BURL 94010 728-D4
HINES CT
300 SJS 95111 875-A1
HINGHAM CV
- SRFL 94901 587-A2
HINKLEY AV
2400 RCH 94804 608-H1
HINMAN RD
- RDWC 94063 770-D2
HINTON CT
16900 AlaC 94546 691-H1
HINTON ST
4400 AlaC 94546 691-H1
HINTON RANCH RD
- PCFA 94044 727-A4
HIRABAYASHI DR
6400 SJS 95120 894-C1
HIRSCH TER
200 FRMT 94536 733-A7
HIRSCH WY
800 DNVL 94526 653-A1
HITCHCOCK RD
3700 CNCD 94518 592-J4
HITCHCOCK ST
- SF 94129 647-C4
- SF 94129 647-C4
HI VISTA RD
100 SAUS 94965 627-B4
HOAD ST
900 SLN 94579 691-B7
HOAG AV
- SRFL 94901 586-H2
HOBART AL
- SF 94102 648-A5
- SF 94102 647-J5
HOBART AV
- SMTO 94402 749-A3
200 SMTO 94402 748-J3
1700 SJS 95127 834-J2
1700 SCIC 95127 834-J2
3900 SCIC 95127 835-A2
HOBART CT
600 FRMT 94539 793-J1
2200 ANT 94509 595-A1
HOBART ST
500 MLPK 94025 790-E5
HOBART TER
500 SCL 95051 833-A6
HOBART HEIGHTS RD
100 WDSD 94062 789-H6
HOBBS AV
100 VAL 94589 510-A7
HOBBY CT
3600 CNCD 94518 592-H4
HOBERT ST
21200 AlaC 94546 691-J6
HOBIE LN
500 SJS 95127 835-B2
HOBSON ST
- SJS 95110 834-A5
400 SJS 95110 833-J5
HOCHLER DR
- FRMT 94539 754-A7
- FRMT 94539 753-J7
HOCKING WY
2700 SJS 95124 873-F1
HOCK MAPLE CT
4400 CNCD 94521 593-B5
HODGES AL
- SF 94133 648-A4
HODGES AV
400 SCIC 95128 853-F1

STREET
Block City ZIP Pg-Grid
HODGES DR
- MrnC 94941 606-H5
100 MRGA 94556 651-E2
HODGES ST
100 VAL 94589 510-D6
HODUR CT
- PLHL 94523 592-A3
HOEDEL CT
1000 LFYT 94549 611-J6
HOFF ST
- SF 94110 667-H2
HOFFMAN AV
- SF 94114 667-F4
1200 CMBL 95008 873-E1
HOFFMAN BLVD
600 RCH 94804 608-F1
HOFFMAN CT
5600 SJS 95118 874-C4
HOFFMAN ST
- SF 94129 647-C3
- SMCo 94014 687-D5
- CLMA 94014 687-D5
300 DALY 94014 687-D5
HOFFMAN TER
800 SCIC 94024 831-G4
4800 FRMT 94555 752-A3
HOFFMAN WY
21800 AlaC 94546 692-B6
HOGAN AV
100 VAL 94589 510-A7
HOGAN CT
- PLHL 94549 591-H5
100 WLCK 94598 612-D3
HOGAN DR
1700 SCL 95054 813-C4
HOGAN PL
2700 LVMR 94550 715-G5
HOGAN TER
34200 FRMT 94555 752-C2
HOGAR DR
1700 SJS 95124 873-J1
HOGARTH PL
3300 FRMT 94555 732-E7
HOGARTH TER
400 SUNV 94087 832-E3
HOGBACK
- MrnC 94965 606-A2
HOGUE CT
20100 CPTO 95014 832-E7
HOHENER AV
800 HAY 94541 711-F3
HOITING DR
3400 SJS 95148 835-E6
HOKE CT
1800 PIN 94564 569-E6
HOKE DR
2000 PIN 94564 569-E6
HOKETT WY
6200 SJS 95123 874-G7
HOLBROOK DR
2000 DNVL 94506 653-F4
2100 CNCD 94519 572-G7
HOLBROOK LN
- ATN 94027 790-E1
HOLBROOK PL
- DNVL 94506 653-G4
- SRMN 94583 673-J6
700 SUNV 94087 832-C2
HOLCOMB AV
100 LKSP 94939 586-F6
HOLCOMB CT
- WLCK 94596 612-D6
HOLCOMB LN
100 AMCN 94589 510-A2
HOLDEN CT
- PTLV 94028 810-D6
14200 SCIC 95124 873-H4
HOLDEN ST
4000 EMVL 94608 629-E7
HOLDEN WY
14800 SCIC 95124 873-H4
HOLDERMAN DR
3300 SJS 95148 835-D6
3400 SCIC 95148 835-D6
HOLGATE AV
5900 SJS 95123 875-A6
HOLGER WY
- SJS 95134 813-D2
HOLIDAY CT
- PCFA 94044 707-A2
- PCFA 94044 706-J2
200 MRTZ 94553 571-J6
900 CNCD 94518 592-F6
13400 SAR 95070 852-H7
HOLIDAY DR
- CCCo 94507 632-F6
13400 SAR 95070 872-G1
HOLIDAY LN
- CNCD 94521 593-E4
HOLIDAY ST
29600 HAY 94544 712-D7
HOLIDAY HILLS DR
100 MRTZ 94553 571-J6
HOLIN WY
1700 SJS 95131 834-D1
HOLLADAY AV
100 SF 94110 668-A4
HOLLADAY CT
300 LVMR 94550 695-F7
HOLLAND CIR
1700 WLCK 94596 611-J2
HOLLAND CT
- SF 94103 648-A6
100 MTVW 94040 831-J1
1300 SJS 95118 874-B5
HOLLAND DR
- CCCo 94549 611-J2
1600 WLCK 94596 611-J2
4000 PLE 94588 714-A1
4400 PLE 94588 694-A7
HOLLAND LN
5600 SJS 95118 874-B5
HOLLAND ST
100 EPA 94303 791-A1
2300 SMTO 94403 749-D4
5300 OAK 94601 670-E2
HOLLANDA CT
8000 DBLN 94568 693-G3
HOLLANDA LN
8000 DBLN 94568 693-G3
HOLLANDERRY PL
7500 CPTO 95014 852-D3

STREET
Block City ZIP Pg-Grid
HOLLENBECK AV
600 SUNV 94087 832-D2
HOLLERAN CT
1500 SJS 95132 814-F3
HOLLICE CT
- LVMR 94550 716-B1
HOLLICE LN
- LVMR 94550 696-B7
- LVMR 94550 716-B1
HOLLIDALE CT
1400 LALT 94024 831-J4
HOLLIDAY CT
2700 PIN 94564 569-G5
HOLLINGSWORTH DR
500 MTVW 94022 811-F5
600 LALT 94022 811-F5
HOLLIS AV
100 CMBL 95008 853-D7
HOLLIS CT
1900 CNCD 94518 592-F6
HOLLIS ST
- SF 94115 647-G6
3200 OAK 94608 649-F1
3500 OAK 94608 629-E6
3800 EMVL 94608 629-E6
6600 BERK 94804 629-E6
HOLLIS CANYON RD
7400 AlaC 94552 692-G4
22900 AlaC 94552 693-A3
HOLLISTER AV
900 SF 94124 688-B1
HOLLISTER CIR
2100 ALA 94501 649-E7
HOLLISTER CT
200 SLN 94577 671-B6
HOLLOW LN
3700 AlaC 94541 692-D6
HOLLOWAY AV
- SF 94112 687-C1
900 SF 94132 687-B1
HOLLOWAY CANYON CT
- AlaC 94542 692-E7
HOLLOWCREEK CT
1600 SJS 95121 855-D7
HOLLOWCREEK PL
1600 SJS 95121 855-D7
HOLLOWGATE LN
4400 SJS 95124 873-J3
HOLLOW LAKE WY
7000 SJS 95120 894-F4
HOLLOW PARK CT
1100 SJS 95120 894-F3
HOLLOW RIDGE CT
5000 ANT 94509 595-E4
HOLLOW RIDGE WY
5000 ANT 94509 595-E4
HOLLOW TREE WY
7000 SJS 95120 894-F4
HOLLY AL
- VAL 94590 529-H2
HOLLY AV
- LKSP 94939 586-E6
200 SSF 94080 707-F2
1300 LALT 94024 831-H3
1600 SBRN 94066 707-G7
1700 MLPK 94025 790-E6
HOLLY CIR
1600 PLE 94566 714-F1
HOLLY CT
- CCCo - 652-F4
- HIL 94010 748-D1
300 MrnC 94941 606-D4
2700 ANT 94509 575-C6
22900 HAY 94541 711-G3
HOLLY DR
300 SRFL 94903 566-D2
1900 CNCD 94521 593-E3
2000 CCCo 94521 593-E3
3300 SCIC 95127 814-J6
3300 SJS 95127 814-J6
W HOLLY DR
1000 WLCK 94598 612-D5
HOLLY LN
- CCCo 94803 589-F2
100 ORIN 94563 610-E6
400 HAY 94541 711-G3
600 SJS 95136 854-E7
HOLLY PL
100 PDMT 94611 650-A1
HOLLY PTH
3100 RCH 94806 589-A2
HOLLY RD
700 BLMT 94002 769-E1
HOLLY ST
- RDWC 94065 769-G2
- SCAR 94002 769-G2
- SMCo 94002 769-G2
- SMCo 94070 769-G2
- WLCK 94598 612-D5
200 VAL 94589 510-A7
1000 ALA 94502 670-A7
1000 SCAR 94070 769-G2
1400 BERK 94703 609-F7
1400 BERK 94703 629-F1
7000 OAK 94621 670-G3
9000 OAK 94603 670-H5
37000 FRMT 94536 752-G3
HOLLY WY
400 MPS 95035 794-D7
HOLLY ANN PL
1100 SJS 95120 894-E2
HOLLY BERRY CT
400 SJS 95129 853-B2
HOLLY BRANCH CT
2000 SCL 95050 833-C3
HOLLYBURNE AV
- MLPK 94025 771-A7
1000 MLPK 94025 790-J1
1100 MLPK 94025 770-J7
HOLLYCREST DR
100 LGTS 95032 873-D5
HOLLY GILLINGHAM LN
6300 SJS 95119 875-D5
HOLLYHEAD LN
1100 CPTO 95014 852-D3
HOLLY HILL AV
26800 HAY 94545 711-H6
HOLLY HILL CT
700 RDWC 94061 789-H2
HOLLY HILL DR
800 CCCo 94596 612-G7

STREET
Block City ZIP Pg-Grid
HOLLY HILL DR
1000 SJS 95122 854-G1
1400 SJS 95122 834-H7
HOLLY HILL WY
100 LGTS 95030 873-C4
HOLLY HOCK CT
400 SJS 95117 853-C1
HOLLYHOCK CT
- MLV 94941 606-F3
100 HER 94547 570-B4
HOLLYHOCK DR
500 SLN 94578 691-C4
HOLLYHOCK ST
1000 LVMR 94550 696-A3
34800 UNC 94587 732-F7
HOLLY LEAF LN
5600 SJS 95118 874-B5
HOLLY OAK CIR
1100 SJS 95120 874-D7
HOLLY OAK DR
700 PA 94303 791-D7
2300 CCCo 94506 653-F1
HOLLYOAK DR
21400 CPTO 95014 852-C2
HOLLY OAK LN
- ALA 94502 669-J6
HOLLY PARK CIR
- SF 94110 667-H6
HOLLY VIEW CT
2500 MRTZ 94553 571-F5
HOLLY VIEW DR
2400 MRTZ 94553 571-F5
HOLLYWOOD AV
- LGTS 95032 873-B7
- SJS 95112 854-D2
- VAL 94591 530-D7
900 OAK 94602 650-D3
1300 AlaC 94586 734-B3
17000 LGTS 95032 893-B1
HOLLYWOOD CT
- SF 94112 687-F2
HOLMAN RD
1100 OAK 94610 650-B3
1300 OAK 94602 650-B3
HOLMES AV
100 MrnC 94903 566-G4
1000 SCIC 95008 873-D3
3700 OAK 94605 671-A2
HOLMES CT
- LVMR 94550 715-F2
HOLMES DR
- SCIC 95127 815-A7
HOLMES LN
- SCIC 95127 815-A7
HOLMES PL
3300 FRMT 94555 732-D7
HOLMES ST Rt#-84
300 LVMR 94550 715-F2
2200 AlaC 94550 715-F5
HOLMES WY
1000 HAY 94541 712-A2
HOLMSUND CT
- PLHL 94523 592-A3
HOLSTEIN RD
- SANS 94960 566-A4
HOLSTON RIVER CT
4700 SJS 95136 874-E2
HOLSTROM CIR
- NVTO 94947 525-H3
HOLT AV
1300 LALT 94024 831-J4
1500 LALT 94024 832-A4
HOLT ST
4300 UNC 94587 732-B7
HOLTON CT
200 WLCK 94598 612-D4
HOLVEN CT
- CCCo 94525 550-F5
HOLWAY CT
5700 OAK 94621 670-F2
HOLWAY ST
5500 OAK 94621 670-F2
HOLYCON CIR
4600 SJS 95136 874-H2
HOLYOKE CT
12600 SAR 95070 852-F6
HOLYOKE ST
- SF 94134 668-A7
- SF 94134 688-A1
HOLYROOD DR
2900 OAK 94611 650-G2
HOLYROOD MNR
- OAK 94611 650-G2
HOMANS AV
1400 SLN 94577 671-D7
HOME AV
2500 HAY 94542 712-D3
HOME PL E
- OAK 94610 650-A4
HOME PL W
- OAK 94610 650-A4
HOME RD
- WDSD 94062 809-H4
W HOME ST
800 SJS 95126 854-A1
800 SJS 95126 853-J1
HOME ACRES AV
100 SolC 94591 530-D6
100 VAL 94591 530-D6
HOME CREST DR
1800 SJS 95148 835-A6
HOME GATE DR
1700 SJS 95148 835-A6
HOMEGLEN LN
- OAK 94611 630-F6
HOMEPARK CT
3900 SJS 95121 855-D5
HOMEPLACE CT
- HIL 94010 748-E2
HOMER AV
- PA 94301 790-J5
400 PA 94301 791-A4
HOMER CT
- CCCo 94803 589-C1
6100 PLE 94588 694-A7
HOMER LN
- SMCo 94025 810-F1
HOMER ST
- SF 94103 648-A7
HOMER WY
6100 PLE 94588 694-B7

STREET
Block City ZIP Pg-Grid
HOMERITE DR
14500 SJS 95124 873-G3
14500 SCIC 95124 873-G3
HOMES DR
12700 SAR 95070 852-G6
HOMESTEAD AV
900 WLCK 94596 612-D3
1000 WLCK 94598 612-D4
1100 CCCo 94598 612-D4
HOMESTEAD BLVD
- MrnC 94941 606-D5
- MLV 94941 606-E5
HOMESTEAD CIR
2300 RCH 94806 588-F1
HOMESTEAD CT
- DNVL 94506 653-H4
5100 ANT 94509 595-J5
11000 CPTO 94024 832-A6
11000 LALT 94024 832-A6
HOMESTEAD LN
1200 HAY 94545 711-H6
HOMESTEAD RD
- SJS 95193 875-C5
600 SCL 95050 833-F4
600 SCL 95053 833-F4
1100 SUNV 94087 832-A5
2200 LALT 94024 832-A5
2300 CPTO 94024 832-A5
22000 CPTO 95014 832-A5
E HOMESTEAD RD
100 SCL 95051 832-G6
100 SUNV 94087 832-G6
900 SCL 95050 833-D5
2500 SCL 95051 833-A6
18800 CPTO 95014 832-G6
W HOMESTEAD RD
1100 CPTO 95014 832-C5
19500 SUNV 94087 832-C5
19900 SUNV 95014 832-C5
HOMESTEAD ST
- SF 94114 667-F4
HOMESTEAD WY
5100 ANT 94509 595-J5
HOMESTEAD VALLEY TR
- CCCo - 611-C1
HOMEWOOD AV
1200 SMTO 94403 748-J7
HOMEWOOD CT
- SF 94112 667-D7
7500 PLE 94588 693-H6
HOMEWOOD DR
100 CNCD 94518 592-G4
2200 SJS 95128 833-E7
2200 PIT 94565 574-E5
7000 OAK 94611 630-F6
E HOMEWOOD PL
- MLPK 94025 790-H3
HOMEWOOD ST
42700 FRMT 94538 773-D1
HOMME WY
- MPS 95035 793-J4
HOMS CT
- HIL 94010 748-H2
HONDA WY
700 FRMT 94539 753-F5
HONDO PL
- SRMN 94583 673-G5
HONEY CT
1000 PIT 94565 573-H4
7500 DBLN 94568 693-H3
HONEY LN
- SANS 94960 566-C6
HONEY TR
1100 CCCo 94596 612-D1
HONEYDALE CT
4000 SJS 95121 855-A5
HONEYDEW DR
100 VAL 94591 550-E1
HONEY HILL CT
- ORIN 94563 610-J5
HONEY HILL DR
- ORIN 94563 610-J5
HONEYLAKE CT
500 CCCo 94506 654-B4
HONEY LOCUST CT
1900 WLCK 94595 632-B1
HONEYNUT ST
2900 ANT 94509 575-J6
HONEYSUCKLE CIR
2800 ANT 94509 575-G7
HONEYSUCKLE CT
1600 PLE 94588 714-B6
2900 ANT 94509 575-G7
6300 NWK 94560 752-F7
HONEYSUCKLE DR
1600 SJS 95122 854-J1
6100 NWK 94560 752-F7
HONEY SUCKLE LN
3900 SJS 95136 854-D7
HONEYSUCKLE LN
- SCAR 94070 769-C4
400 SRMN 94583 653-J7
HONEYSUCKLE PL
1500 LALT 94024 831-J6
HONEYSUCKLE PZ
- HAY 94542 712-B2
HONEYSUCKLE RD
1400 LVMR 94550 696-A4
HONEYSUCKLE WY
3500 CNCD 94518 592-J6
HONEYWOOD CT
700 SJS 95120 894-J3
HONEYWOOD RD
- ORIN 94563 611-A3
HONFLEUR CT
900 SUNV 94087 832-B5
HONFLEUR DR
1600 SUNV 94087 832-B5
HONG KONG DR
1200 SJS 95131 814-B7
HONISTER LN
900 CNCD 94518 592-F6
HONKER TER
4800 FRMT 94555 752-D2
HONOLULU CIR
400 UNC 94587 732-D5
HONOLULU CT
3900 SJS 95111 854-J6
HONOLULU DR
3700 SJS 95111 854-J6

STREET
Block City ZIP Pg-Grid
HONORA AV
900 CNCD 94518 592-G6
HONORS CT
7800 PLE 94588 714-B5
HOOD CT
1600 SCL 95051 833-A3
HOOD ST
- AlaC 94541 691-F7
3100 OAK 94605 671-C5
HOODS POINT WY
- SMCo 94402 768-G1
HOOF TRAIL WY
2300 ANT 94509 595-G3
HOO HOO CT
22300 CPTO 95014 852-A1
HOOK AV
1000 PLHL 94523 592-C7
HOOKE LN
100 LGTS 95030 873-B3
HOOKER AL
- SF 94108 648-A5
HOO-KOO-E-KOO TR
- MrnC 94965 606-A1
HOO-KOO-E-KOO FIRE RD
- MrnC 94965 586-B6
- MrnC 94965 606-A1
HOOKSTON RD
- PLHL 94523 592-C6
- PLHL 94596 592-C6
1200 CNCD 94518 592-D6
HOOPER
- SANS 94960 566-A6
HOOPER DR
2700 SRMN 94583 653-B7
HOOPER LN
11100 LAH 94024 831-D4
HOOPER ST
100 SF 94107 668-B1
41500 FRMT 94538 753-D7
41500 FRMT 94538 773-D1
HOOPER WY
- WDSD 94062 809-G1
HOOSHANG CT
800 CPTO 95014 852-C2
HOOVER AV
500 SJS 95126 833-J6
1500 BURL 94010 728-C6
1900 OAK 94602 650-E3
1900 PLHL 94523 612-A1
HOOVER CT
1400 ALA 94501 669-F1
1800 CNCD 94521 593-D2
2100 PLHL 94523 612-A1
2100 SCL 95051 833-C2
HOOVER DR
2000 SCL 95051 833-B3
HOOVER ST
1200 MLPK 94025 790-F3
3000 RDWC 94063 770-E6
HOPE AV
4000 CNCD 94521 593-A3
HOPE DR
1400 SCL 95054 813-D4
HOPE LN
100 DNVL 94526 633-C6
800 LFYT 94549 611-G7
HOPE ST
100 MTVW 94041 811-H5
1200 SJS 95002 793-B7
3000 SCIC 95111 854-G6
3000 SJS 95111 854-G6
HOPE TER
500 SUNV 94087 832-D5
HOPECO RD
100 PLHL 94523 592-B6
HOPETON AV
2300 SJS 95122 854-H2
HOPETON CT
1200 SJS 95122 854-H2
HOPI CIR
6200 SJS 95123 874-H7
HOPI CT
- SRMN 94583 673-D4
2500 WLCK 94598 612-H4
6200 SJS 95123 874-H7
HOPI DR
700 FRMT 94539 773-H6
HOPKINS AV
- SF 94131 667-F3
500 RDWC 94063 770-A5
1000 RDWC 94062 769-J6
1000 RDWC 94063 769-J6
1100 PA 94301 791-B5
43500 FRMT 94538 773-E2
HOPKINS CT
- BERK 94706 609-F7
- CCCo 94803 589-E1
5400 PLE 94566 714-E5
HOPKINS DR
1100 SJS 95122 834-H6
HOPKINS PL
2800 OAK 94602 650-E5
HOPKINS ST
1100 BERK 94702 629-E1
1200 BERK 94702 609-F7
1500 BERK 94706 609-F7
1500 BERK 94703 609-F7
1600 BERK 94707 609-F7
28800 HAY 94545 731-J2
HOPKINS WY
800 PLE 94566 714-E5
HOPPE ST
1000 SJS 95002 813-B1
HOPPER RD
23000 HAY 94541 711-G3
HOP RANCH CT
33000 UNC 94587 732-D5
HOP RANCH RD
2600 UNC 94587 732-D6
HOPYARD RD
1200 PLE 94566 714-B1
1600 PLE 94588 714-B1
2500 PLE 94588 694-B7
HORACE AV
2500 SJS 95124 853-G7
HORACE ST
- SF 94110 667-J4
HORAN CT
1300 PIT 94565 574-F6
HORAT TER
4000 FRMT 94555 752-C2

STREET
Block City ZIP Pg-Grid
HORATIO CT
- UNC 94587 732-C5
4000 FRMT 94555 732-C5
HORATIO WY
4000 FRMT 94555 732-C7
HORCAJO CIR
900 MPS 95035 794-B4
HORCAJO ST
800 MPS 95035 794-B5
HORGAN AV
- RDWC 94061 790-B2
HORIZON AV
100 MTVW 94043 811-J5
HORIZON CIR
200 SJS 95002 813-B1
HORIZON CT
- VAL 94591 510-J5
1000 DNVL 94506 653-G5
HORIZON DR
700 MRTZ 94553 591-G3
HORIZON LN
1900 ANT 94509 575-B5
HORIZON WY
300 PCFA 94044 707-B3
HORIZONS CT
- PLE 94586 693-H7
HORNBEAM WY
500 SJS 95111 854-J6
HORNBLOWER CT
500 SJS 95136 874-F2
HORNE AV
- SF 94124 668-E7
HORNE ST
2000 AlaC 94578 691-F4
HORNER ST
3700 UNC 94587 731-H5
4800 UNC 94587 732-A5
HORNER WY
1600 FRMT 94536 753-A2
HORNET AV
200 SSF 94066 707-J5
HORNET CT
- DNVL 94526 653-A1
HORNET DR
800 DNVL 94526 653-A1
HORNING ST
400 SJS 95112 834-B3
HORSEMANS CANYON DR
5900 WLCK 94595 632-C5
HORSESHOE BEND
- PTLV 94028 830-C1
HORSESHOE CIR
- ANT 94509 595-J3
HORSESHOE CT
- HIL 94402 748-H4
- WLCK 94596 632-F2
2800 LAH 94022 811-A5
3000 AlaC 94541 712-D1
14500 SAR 95070 872-E3
HORSESHOE DR
- PTLV 94028 809-J6
3800 SCL 95134 813-E5
14500 SAR 95070 872-E3
HORSESHOE LN
27000 LAH 94022 811-A5
HORSETRAIL CT
400 CCCo 94595 632-D1
HORTEN CT
- PLHL 94523 592-B6
HORTON CT
700 HAY 94544 712-A7
6000 SJS 95123 875-A6
HORTON ST
4000 EMVL 94608 629-E6
4000 OAK 94608 629-E6
HORWEDEL DR
2800 SJS 95148 855-D2
HOSKER LN
- LVMR 94550 695-J7
HOSKINS CT
- SCIC 94305 790-J7
HOSMER CT
300 SCAR 94070 769-D7
HOSMER ST
2600 SMTO 94403 749-D4
HOSPITAL DR
100 VAL 94589 530-B1
2400 BERK 94705 629-J4
2500 MTVW 94040 831-H1
HOSPITAL PKWY
200 SJS 95119 875-B6
HOSPITAL PZ
- MLPK 94025 790-J2
HOSPITAL RD
- BEN 94510 551-D5
- NVTO 94949 546-H3
HOSTA LN
5900 SJS 95124 873-J7
HOSTETTER RD
1600 SJS 95131 814-C6
2300 SJS 95132 814-G3
HOTALING CT
- MrnC 94904 586-E2
HOTALING ST
- SF 94111 648-A4
HOTCHKIN DR
1600 NVTO 94947 526-B4
HOTCHKISS AV
7200 ELCR 94530 609-D3
HOTCHKISS ST
45800 FRMT 94539 773-G5
HOTEL AV
900 HAY 94541 711-J1
HOT SPRINGS CT
3800 PLE 94588 714-A2
HOUGH AV
900 LFYT 94549 611-F6
HOUGHTON CT
1000 SJS 95112 834-D3
HOUGHTON ST
200 MTVW 94041 811-J5
HOULTON CT
100 SJS 95139 875-G7
HOUNDSBROOK WY
4100 SJS 95111 855-A7
HOUNDS ESTATES
5200 SJS 95135 855-G5
HOUNDS ESTATES CT
3000 SJS 95135 855-G5
HOUNDSHAVEN WY
4400 SJS 95111 874-J1

STREET
Block City ZIP Pg-Grid

HOUNDSHAVEN WY
4700 SJS 95111 875-A1
HOUNDSRIDGE LN
- SMTO 94402 748-H6
HOUNSLOW DR
2100 SJS 95131 814-D6
HOURET CT
1700 MPS 95035 814-B4
HOURET DR
200 MPS 95035 814-B3
HOUSER DR
300 PIT 94565 574-C3
HOUSTON CT
300 DNVL 94526 652-J3
4000 CNCD 94521 593-A2
13000 SAR 95070 852-D7
HOUSTON PL
6100 DBLN 94568 694-A4
HOUSTON ST
- SF 94133 647-J3
HOVE CT
600 WLCK 94598 612-F1
HOWARD AV
- BURL 94010 728-H6
- VAL 94589 530-C2
- VAL 94590 530-C2
200 PDMT 94611 650-A1
900 SCAR 94070 769-H4
1000 SMTO 94401 728-H6
HOWARD COM
3300 FRMT 94536 752-J4
HOWARD CT
- CCCo 94598 612-F5
3800 SSF 94080 707-C4
HOWARD DR
100 TBRN 94920 607-B5
200 SCL 95051 832-H7
HOWARD RD
- SF 94129 647-B5
HOWARD ST
- SF 94105 648-B6
400 SJS 95110 834-A6
600 SF 94103 648-B6
1100 MLPK 94025 770-J7
1200 SF 94103 647-J7
1400 SF 94103 667-J1
2100 SPAB 94806 588-H2
2800 RCH 94804 588-J4
4300 OAK 94601 670-C2
HOWARD WY
- ATN 94027 790-E3
HOWARD HILLS RD
1000 LFYT 94549 611-C6
HOWARDS ST
3300 LFYT 94549 611-H7
HOWDEN CT
6900 SJS 95119 875-F6
HOWE CT
3600 FRMT 94538 773-E1
HOWE DR
1900 AlaC 94578 691-D2
1900 SLN 94577 691-D2
HOWE RD
- MRTZ 94553 571-G4
- CCCo 94553 571-G4
HOWE ST
700 SMTO 94401 749-B1
2300 BERK 94705 629-H4
3700 OAK 94611 649-J1
4100 OAK 94611 629-J7
4400 OAK 94611 630-A7
HOWELL AV
2900 SCL 95051 833-A6
HOWELL ST
5800 OAK 94609 629-H5
HOWEN DR
13500 SAR 95070 872-E1
HOWES CT
200 LGTS 95032 873-F5
HOWES DR
100 LGTS 95032 873-G5
HOWES LN
4900 SJS 95118 873-J4
5100 SJS 95118 874-A4
HOWLAND ST
200 RDWC 94063 769-J5
200 RDWC 94063 770-A5
HOWLAND HILL LN
- SMCo 94010 728-B7
HOWTH ST
- SF 94112 687-E1
400 SF 94112 667-E7
HOYA WY
400 UNC 94587 732-C6
HOYET DR
5200 SJS 95129 852-J4
HOYLAKE ST
30400 HAY 94544 732-D2
HOYT DR
1500 CNCD 94521 593-B3
HOYT ST
47400 FRMT 94539 773-H7
HOYTT CT
2300 PIN 94564 589-J1
H RANCH RD
- MrnC 94946 525-F6
HUBBARD AV
100 PLHL 94523 592-B7
200 SMCo 94062 769-G6
500 SCL 95051 832-H6
1200 SLN 94579 691-A5
HUBBARD ST
4000 EMVL 94608 629-E7
4000 OAK 94608 629-E7
HUBBARD WY
10700 SCIC 95127 835-B1
HUBBARTT DR
4100 PA 94306 811-C3
HUBBELL CT
- SRFL 94901 566-H7
HUBBELL ST
100 SF 94107 668-B1
HUBBELL WY
500 LGTS 95030 873-A6
HUBER AV
5900 ELCR 94530 609-B1
HUBER DR
18800 AlaC 94546 691-H3
HUBERT RD
1000 OAK 94610 650-B3
HUCKLEBERRY CT
- BSBN 94005 687-H4
500 SRMN 94583 653-H6
1000 SUNV 94087 832-B3
HUCKLEBERRY DR
4100 CNCD 94521 593-A3
HUCKLEBERRY RD
2000 MrnC 94903 546-C7
2000 SRFL 94903 546-C7
HUDDERSFIELD CT
1500 SJS 95126 853-H3
HUDDLESON ST
- FRMT 94539 753-J7
HUDSON AL
500 VAL 94590 530-A5
500 VAL 94590 529-J5
HUDSON AV
600 SF 94124 668-B4
600 SF 94124 668-E7
3100 WLCK 94596 612-B1
HUDSON BAY
100 ALA 94502 669-J6
HUDSON CT
1100 SCAR 94070 769-E6
3300 PLE 94588 694-F5
3400 ANT 94509 574-J6
HUDSON DR
- ALA 94501 649-J7
600 SCL 95051 832-H6
1700 SJS 95124 853-H7
HUDSON LN
200 SLN 94577 691-B2
HUDSON PL
3300 FRMT 94536 752-G2
HUDSON ST
- RDWC 94062 769-J6
300 OAK 94618 629-J5
500 RDWC 94062 770-A7
600 RDWC 94061 770-A7
1200 RDWC 94061 790-B1
1800 ELCR 94530 609-C1
1900 ELCR 94530 589-C7
HUDSON WY
800 SUNV 94087 832-B2
1300 LVMR 94550 715-F3
HUDSON BAY ST
200 FCTY 94404 749-F5
HUERTO CT
2500 SJS 95128 853-F4
HUERTO DR
2400 SJS 95128 853-F4
HUFF AV
900 MTVW 94043 811-H1
1100 SLN 94577 671-B7
2800 SJS 95128 853-E2
HUFF CT
- MRGA 94556 651-E1
3600 PLE 94588 694-F6
HUFF DR
2700 PLE 94588 694-F6
HUGH CT
- BEN 94510 551-C1
HUGH ST
100 SolC 94591 530-E7
HUGH WY
31300 HAY 94544 732-E2
HUGHES AV
2300 OAK 94601 650-C6
HUGHES DR
1800 CNCD 94520 592-E4
HUGHES PL
5400 FRMT 94538 753-A7
5400 FRMT 94538 752-J7
5400 FRMT 94538 772-J1
HUGO LN
1400 SJS 95118 874-B2
HUGO ST
- SF 94122 667-D2
HULA CIR
200 UNC 94587 732-D6
HULA DR
3500 SJS 95136 854-F7
HULBERT AL
- SF 94107 648-A7
HULET ST
500 SJS 95125 854-A1
HULL AV
300 SJS 95125 854-A2
1700 SMCo 94061 790-A3
HULL CT
- SLN 94579 691-F3
HULL DR
1200 SCAR 94070 769-F2
3000 RCH 94806 589-A1
HULL LN
1000 FCTY 94404 749-H4
1300 MRTZ 94553 571-G6
HULL ST
4300 OAK 94601 670-C2
HULL TER
- FRMT 94536 753-C3
HULME CT
- SCIC 94305 790-J7
HUMBER CT
500 SUNV 94087 832-E5
HUMBER PL
4800 NWK 94560 752-E3
HUMBERSIDE CT
3100 SJS 95148 855-E2
HUMBOLDT AV
- SANS 94960 566-A7
300 RCH 94805 589-B7
500 SAUS 94965 627-B2
1400 SPAB 94806 589-A4
2200 ELCR 94530 589-B7
2300 OAK 94601 650-D6
2500 OAK 94602 650-D6
2800 SCL 95051 833-A4
HUMBOLDT CT
- PCFA 94044 727-C5
200 SUNV 94089 812-F3
HUMBOLDT DR
2500 SLN 94577 691-D2
HUMBOLDT RD
- BSBN 94005 688-A6
HUMBOLDT ST
- BURL 94010 728-H6
- SJS 95110 854-C2
- SJS 95112 854-D1
- SMTO 94401 728-H6
100 SF 94107 668-C3
100 SRFL 94901 566-D6
600 RCH 94805 589-A5
700 VAL 94591 530-D4
1000 SPAB 94805 589-A5
E HUMBOLDT ST
- SJS 95112 854-D1
N HUMBOLDT ST
- SMTO 94401 729-A7
- SMTO 94401 728-J6
S HUMBOLDT ST
- SMTO 94401 729-A7
- SMTO 94401 749-A1
400 SMTO 94402 749-A1
HUMBOLDT WY
400 LVMR 94550 695-E6
HUMBOLT AV
- SAUS 94965 627-B3
HUME DR
15100 SAR 95070 872-F4
HUMEWICK WY
800 SUNV 94087 832-F5
HUMMEL CT
2400 SJS 95148 855-B1
HUMMINGBIRD CT
27700 HAY 94545 731-G1
HUMMINGBIRD DR
800 SJS 95125 854-C6
3800 ANT 94509 594-J2
HUMMINGBIRD LN
300 LVMR 94550 715-D1
1600 SUNV 94087 832-F5
HUMMINGBIRD PL
4000 CLAY 94517 593-J5
HUMMINGBIRD RD
4900 PLE 94566 714-C1
HUMMINGBIRD WY
- NVTO 94949 546-E4
4000 CLAY 94517 594-A5
4000 CLAY 94517 593-J5
HUMPHREY AV
2300 RCH 94804 588-H5
3400 RCH 94804 589-A5
HUMPHREY DR
1600 CNCD 94519 592-H2
HUMPHREY LN
100 VAL 94591 550-F2
HUMPHREY PL
- OAK 94610 650-C3
HUNE CT
- NVTO 94947 525-H3
HUNKEN DR
2900 SJS 95111 854-H5
HUNSAKER CANYON RD
- CCCo 94549 632-A4
500 LFYT 94549 632-A4
500 LFYT 94549 631-J4
HUNT DR
1600 BURL 94010 728-A6
HUNT WY
- CMBL 95008 853-C6
HUNTER AV
100 OAK 94603 670-G7
18000 AlaC 94541 711-E1
HUNTER CT
- OAK 94603 670-G7
100 VAL 94591 530-D1
W HUNTER CT
200 FRMT 94539 773-H2
HUNTER LN
300 FRMT 94539 773-J2
W HUNTER LN
100 FRMT 94539 773-J2
HUNTER PL
- SCL 95054 813-C5
44200 FRMT 94539 773-J2
HUNTER RD
- SF 94129 647-B4
HUNTER ST
2700 EPA 94303 771-B7
HUNTER TER
44100 FRMT 94539 773-J2
HUNTER WY
18800 SCIC 95014 852-H2
HUNTER PEAK CT
4700 ANT 94509 595-E3
HUNTERS LN
5800 CCCo 94803 589-G4
HUNTERS TER
- DNVL 94506 653-G2
HUNTERS HILL RD
20400 SCIC 95120 895-A5
HUNTERS KNOLL RD
3700 AlaC 94552 692-E4
HUNTERS POINT BLVD
- SF 94124 668-D6
HUNTERS POINT EXWY
- SF 94124 688-C2
HUNTERSTON PL
1000 CPTO 95014 852-C3
HUNTINGDON AV
1000 SJS 95129 852-H3
HUNTINGDON DR
1000 SJS 95129 852-H4
HUNTINGTON AV
200 SBRN 94066 728-A1
200 SBRN 94066 727-J1
200 SBRN 94066 707-J7
1300 SSF 94080 707-H4
2800 SMCo 94063 770-C7
5100 RCH 94804 609-B4
HUNTINGTON AV E
1000 SBRN 94066 707-J5
HUNTINGTON CIR
- PIT 94565 574-C4
38600 FRMT 94536 753-C3
HUNTINGTON COM
900 FRMT 94536 753-C3
HUNTINGTON CT
700 MRTZ 94553 571-E2
3100 AlaC 94546 691-G3
HUNTINGTON DR
- DALY 94015 687-A6
- SF 94132 666-J6
200 ANT 94509 595-E1
HUNTINGTON LN
2000 LALT 94024 831-H4
HUNTINGTON PL
- SRMN 94583 673-G6
HUNTINGTON ST
3800 OAK 94619 650-G6
HUNTINGTON TER
900 FRMT 94536 753-C3
HUNTINGTON WY
400 LVMR 94550 695-E6
700 AMCN 94589 509-J2
900 WLCK 94596 612-F7
900 CCCo 94596 612-F7
HUNTLEIGH DR
600 LFYT 94549 631-J2
HUNTLEIGH RD
- PDMT 94611 650-D2
HUNTOON CT
- WLCK 94596 612-D6
HUNTRIDGE CT
2000 MRTZ 94553 571-H7
HUNTRIDGE LN
7700 CPTO 95014 852-C2
HUNTSFIELD CT
7000 SJS 95120 894-G4
HUNTSMAN WY
2300 ANT 94509 595-G2
HUNTSWOOD CT
700 SJS 95120 894-J3
HUNTWOOD AV
2600 UNC 94587 732-C4
24800 HAY 94544 732-B1
24800 HAY 94587 732-C3
27400 HAY 94544 712-A6
30000 HAY 94544 711-J4
HUNTWOOD WY
- HAY 94544 711-J5
HURAN CT
2500 SJS 95122 855-A1
HURAN DR
2000 SJS 95122 834-J7
2100 SJS 95122 854-J1
2300 SJS 95122 855-A1
HURD PL
100 CLAY 94517 593-G6
HURLEY DR
300 HAY 94544 712-B6
HURLINGAME AV
400 SMCo 94063 770-D6
HURLINGHAM AV
400 SMTO 94402 728-G7
400 SMTO 94402 748-G1
HURLINGHAM WY
1400 SJS 95127 835-A4
HURLSTONE CT
2900 WLCK 94598 612-J3
HURLSTONE LN
900 SJS 95120 894-G2
HURON AV
- DALY 94014 687-E2
100 SMTO 94401 729-A7
400 SF 94112 687-E2
HURON CT
- SMTO 94401 729-A7
HURON DR
2100 CNCD 94519 572-G6
HURON LN
1100 HAY 94545 711-G5
HURON RD
- LVMR 94550 695-E6
HURST AV
1600 SCIC 95125 853-H6
2000 SJS 95125 853-H6
2000 CMBL 95125 853-H6
34500 FRMT 94555 752-E1
HURSTGLEN WY
3800 SJS 95121 855-C4
HURSTWOOD CT
1700 SJS 95121 855-C4
HURTTS DR
1900 CNCD 94521 593-F4
HUSSEY ST
- SF 94124 688-E1
300 SF 94124 668-E7
HUSTED AV
1100 SJS 95125 854-A7
1600 SJS 95124 873-J1
1600 SJS 95125 853-J7
1600 SJS 95125 873-J1
HUSTON CT
- CCCo 94549 611-J2
HUSTON RD
1300 WLCK 94596 611-J2
1400 CCCo 94549 611-J2
HUSTONWOOD CT
1700 WLCK 94596 611-J2
HUTCHINGS DR
600 SLN 94577 690-H1
HUTCHINS AV
- DBLN 94568 694-B3
HUTCHINSON AV
900 PA 94301 791-B4
HUTCHINSON CT
1400 PIN 94564 569-D3
2700 WLCK 94598 612-H4
HUTCHINSON RD
700 WLCK 94598 612-H4
HUTTON CT
100 SUNV 94087 832-E5
6100 SJS 95123 875-A6
40000 FRMT 94538 773-B1
HUTTON ST
5000 FRMT 94538 773-A1
HUXLEY CT
1800 SJS 95125 853-G4
HUXLEY PL
2800 FRMT 94555 732-E7
HYACINTH AV
4300 OAK 94619 650-G6
HYACINTH CT
2700 ANT 94509 575-G7
HYACINTH LN
1600 SJS 95124 873-J7
HYACINTH ST
37600 NWK 94560 752-F7
HYACINTH WY
300 SRFL 94903 566-D2
HYANNIS CV
- SRFL 94901 587-A2
HYANNIS DR
500 SUNV 94087 832-D2
HYANNISPORT DR
8000 CPTO 95014 852-B2
HYDE AV
800 CPTO 95014 852-G2
1000 SJS 95129 852-G3
HYDE CT
- DALY 94015 707-D3
100 VAL 94591 530-H6
1100 CNCD 94520 592-E4
1600 CMBL 95030 872-J2
6700 DBLN 94568 693-J3
HYDE DR
300 HAY 94544 712-B5
1500 CMBL 95030 872-J2
HYDE PL
100 ANT 94509 575-D7
HYDE ST
- RDWC 94062 769-J5
- SF 94102 647-J6
300 SF 94109 647-J4
1000 SLN 94577 691-A1
1900 SF 94109 647-J3
2800 SF 94133 647-J3
3000 OAK 94601 650-C6
HYDE PARK AV
100 SMCo 94070 769-D4
100 SCAR 94070 769-D4
HYDE PARK DR
400 SJS 95136 874-F3
600 SUNV 94087 832-D2
4900 FRMT 94538 773-C3
HYDRA LN
700 FCTY 94404 749-E4
HYDRANGA CT
100 VAL 94591 530-F7
HYDRANGEA CT
800 SUNV 94086 832-F2
HYDRANGEA LN
1600 SJS 95124 873-J6
HYGELUND DR
38700 FRMT 94536 752-J5
HYLAND AV
4300 SCIC 95127 834-J2
4600 SJS 95127 834-J2
4800 SCIC 95127 835-A1
HYLAND DR
- MrnC 94945 526-J3

I

I RD
- SUNV 94089 812-H3
I ST
- OAK 94625 649-B4
- VAL 94592 529-F4
- ANT 94509 575-C4
100 BEN 94510 551-A4
100 FRMT 94536 753-B1
200 SF 94124 688-E1
500 SF 94124 668-E7
800 BEN 94510 550-J4
900 UNC 94587 732-F5
N I ST
200 LVMR 94550 695-G7
S I ST
300 LVMR 94550 715-H1
IAN LN
- DBLN 94552 693-E5
- DBLN 94568 693-E5
IAN ST
1000 SLN 94578 691-C5
IBERIS CT
1000 SUNV 94086 832-H2
IBERO WY
43800 FRMT 94539 773-H1
ICARUS DR
- ALA 94501 649-J7
ICEFIELD CT
2600 SCL 95051 833-A1
ICEHOUSE AL
- SF 94111 648-B4
ICHABOD LN
- ORIN 94563 610-F3
IDA CT
- CCCo 94565 573-D1
5800 LVMR 94550 696-D6
IDA DR
700 SSF 94080 707-G2
3100 CNCD 94519 572-G7
IDA LN
23000 HAY 94541 711-G3
IDA ST
- SRFL 94901 586-E1
IDA WY
2000 SJS 95124 873-E2
IDAHO CT
900 MPS 95035 794-A5
1400 CNCD 94521 593-F6
2000 RDWC 94061 790-A3
IDAHO ST
- RCH 94801 608-D1
1100 SJS 95126 833-G5
1300 SCL 95050 833-G5
3200 BERK 94702 629-F4
3200 OAK 94608 629-F5
N IDAHO ST
- SMTO 94401 728-J6
200 SMTO 94401 729-A7
S IDAHO ST
400 SMTO 94402 749-B1
800 SMTO 94401 729-A7
800 SMTO 94401 749-A1
IDALENE ST
- DALY 94014 687-G3
IDALIA CT
- SANS 94960 586-B1
IDALIA RD
- SANS 94960 586-B1
IDE CT
39300 FRMT 94538 753-A5
IDENA AV
21800 AlaC 94546 692-A6
IDLEBROOK CT
6500 SJS 95120 894-C1
IDLEWILD AV
5500 LVMR 94550 696-C2
IDLEWILD CT
- PCFA 94044 707-B3
6500 SJS 95120 894-C1
8100 NWK 94560 752-C7
IDLEWOOD CIR
800 CCCo 94803 569-D7
IDLEWOOD CT
- MRGA 94556 631-C6
900 SJS 95121 854-H3
IDLEWOOD DR
- CCCo 94595 612-C6
- SANS 94960 566-A5
900 SJS 95121 854-H3
IDLEWOOD LN
12700 SAR 95070 852-E6
IDLEWOOD PL
- SRFL 94901 566-E7
IDLEWOOD RD
- MrnC 94904 586-C5
IDLEWOOD ST
8000 OAK 94605 670-J3
IDORA AV
- SF 94127 667-D4
- SolC 94590 530-C6
- VAL 94591 530-D6
IDYLBERRY RD
500 MrnC 94903 546-A6
IDYLL CT
- ORIN 94563 631-A2
IDYLLWILD AV
1800 SMCo 94061 790-B4
IDYLLWILD CT
300 SMCo 94061 790-B4
IFLAND WY
100 VAL 94589 510-A7
IGLESIA CT
600 ANT 94509 575-E6
IGLESIA DR
7900 DBLN 94568 693-F3
IGNACIO BLVD
300 NVTO 94949 526-B7
400 NVTO 94949 546-D1
1300 MrnC 94949 546-D1
IGNACIO CT
1000 PIN 94564 569-E5
IGNACIO LN
- NVTO 94949 546-E2
IGNACIO ST
- SF 94124 688-C2
IGNACIO VALLEY CIR
100 NVTO 94949 546-D1
IGNEOUS CT
2300 SJS 95133 814-H3
IKE CT
- NVTO 94945 526-B2
ILA CT
37100 FRMT 94536 753-A1
ILENE DR
200 PLHL 94523 592-B4
ILENE ST
300 MRTZ 94553 571-D4
ILIKAI AV
1400 SJS 95118 874-A3
ILIMA CT
800 PA 94306 811-B2
900 FRMT 94536 732-J7
ILIMA WY
900 PA 94306 811-B3
ILLIAD CT
1100 SJS 95118 874-G3
ILLINOIS AV
400 SJS 95126 854-A1
500 SJS 95125 854-A1
ILLINOIS CT
5500 CNCD 94521 593-E6
ILLINOIS ST
- SF 94107 668-C3
100 VAL 94590 529-J3
300 VAL 94590 530-A3
1600 SF 94124 668-C4
1600 SF 94124 668-C4
2400 EPA 94303 791-C1
2500 EPA 94303 771-C7
ILLSLEY CT
4400 SJS 95136 874-H1
ILO LN
300 DNVL 94526 653-A1
ILS LN
- SF 94111 648-A5
IMAGES CIR
- MPS 95035 793-J6
100 MPS 95035 794-A6
IMELDA ST
100 VAL 94589 510-A5
IMHOFF DR
100 CCCo 94553 572-C5
300 CCCo 94520 572-C5
IMHOFF PL
4700 CCCo 94553 572-B5
IMNAHA CT
45000 FRMT 94539 773-H3
IMPALA CT
2100 PIT 94565 574-A4
IMPALA DR
3100 SJS 95117 853-D4
IMPATIENS COM
5600 FRMT 94538 773-A1
IMPATIENS DR
5000 SJS 95111 875-A2
IMPERIAL AV
- SF 94123 647-H4
5200 RCH 94804 609-A3
10000 CPTO 95014 852-B1
10400 SCIC 95014 852-B1
IMPERIAL DR
200 PCFA 94044 707-B2
IMPERIAL PL
32200 UNC 94587 732-C4
IMPERIAL WY
300 DALY 94015 707-C1
6400 SJS 95129 852-F3
IMPERIO AV
100 FRMT 94539 753-F4
IMPERIO PL
40300 FRMT 94539 753-F3
IMPRESARIO WY
3500 SJS 95127 835-C2
IMRIE PL
200 CCCo 94526 633-C4
IMWALLE CT
2000 SJS 95131 814-E7
INA CT
- CCCo 94507 632-G4
- SF 94112 667-H7
- SF 94112 687-H1
INA DR
900 CCCo 94507 632-G4
INAJANE CT
3400 CNCD 94519 592-J1
INCA CT
100 VAL 94591 530-D7
16200 SCIC 95032 893-C2
INCA LN
- SF 94115 647-H6
INCINERATOR RD
- SF 94129 647-D4
INCLINE CT
1000 HAY 94541 711-D2
2100 MPS 95035 814-E1
INCLINE PL
100 BEN 94510 551-B4
18000 HAY 94541 711-D2
INCLINE RD
18000 HAY 94541 711-D2
INCLINE WY
200 SJS 95139 895-E1
INCLINED PL
7000 DBLN 94568 693-F5
INCLINE GREEN LN
- CCCo 94507 633-A3
E INDEPENDENCE AV
700 MTVW 94043 811-G1
INDEPENDENCE CT
800 PLE 94566 714-E5
INDEPENDENCE DR
100 MLPK 94025 770-G6
400 SJS 95111 854-H5
900 ALA 94501 649-G7
2800 LVMR 94550 695-C5
5000 PLE 94566 714-E5
INDEPENDENCE RD
3500 FRMT 94538 773-E2
INDEPENDENCE WY
1500 OAK 94606 650-A6
INDEPENDENT RD
500 OAK 94621 670-E3
INDEPENDENT SCHOOL RD
21200 AlaC 94552 692-D5
INDIAN AL
300 VAL 94590 529-J5
700 VAL 94590 530-A5
INDIAN AV
600 SMTO 94401 728-J7
5600 SJS 95123 874-G6
INDIAN BAY
100 ALA 94502 669-H7
INDIAN CRSG
- PTLV 94028 830-C1
INDIAN DR
2400 PA 94303 791-D5
INDIAN LN
1400 CNCD 94521 593-C4
INDIAN RD
- MrnC 94903 566-E5
100 PDMT 94610 650-C3
200 OAK 94610 650-C3
INDIAN TR
- BERK 94707 609-F5
INDIAN WY
- CCCo 94507 632-J5
100 NVTO 94949 526-B7
100 NVTO 94949 546-B1
1700 OAK 94611 630-E6
3100 LFYT 94549 631-J3
INDIANA DR
1300 CNCD 94521 593-F6
INDIANA ST
- BEN 94510 551-E2
400 VAL 94590 529-J4
500 SF 94107 668-C3
600 VAL 94590 530-A4
1600 SF 94124 668-C4
1700 SF 94124 668-C4
INDIAN BROOM DR
300 SJS 95111 875-B2
INDIAN CREEK CT
1800 SJS 95148 835-D4
INDIAN CREEK RD
11500 AlaC 94586 754-F1
INDIAN FIRE RD
- MrnC - 586-B6
- MrnC 94904 586-B6
- MrnC 94965 586-B6
INDIAN GULCH RD
- PDMT 94611 650-C1
INDIANHEAD CIR
2500 CLAY 94517 593-H6
INDIANHEAD WY
1400 CLAY 94517 593-H6
INDIAN HILL DR
3400 WLCK 94598 612-J3
3400 WLCK 94598 613-A3
4800 ANT 94509 595-H4
INDIAN HILL PL
- FRMT 94539 773-H4
INDIAN HILLS DR
- NVTO 94949 526-B7
INDIAN HOME RD
500 DNVL 94526 653-C4
INDIAN RICE RD
3300 SRMN 94583 653-J6
INDIAN RIVER CT
4800 SJS 95136 874-H3
INDIAN RIVER DR
4800 SJS 95136 874-H2
INDIAN ROCK AV
800 BERK 94707 609-G5
INDIAN ROCK CT
- SANS 94960 566-B5
- TBRN 94920 607-A4
INDIAN ROCK PTH
800 BERK 94707 609-G6
INDIAN ROCK RD
- SANS 94960 566-B5
INDIAN SPRINGS CT
6600 SJS 95120 894-D2
INDIAN SPRINGS DR
5400 SJS 95123 875-G2
INDIAN SPRINGS RD
400 MrnC 94947 525-H5
INDIAN SUMMER CT
1000 SJS 95122 854-F2
INDIAN TRAIL CT
- MrnC 94947 525-J5
INDIAN VALLEY CT
7100 SJS 95139 895-H2
INDIAN VALLEY RD
1400 NVTO 94947 526-A6
1500 MrnC 94947 526-A6
1500 MrnC 94947 525-H5
INDIAN WELLS
- MRGA 94556 631-C7
INDIAN WELLS CT
200 SJS 95139 895-E1

STREET
Block City ZIP Pg-Grid

INDIAN WELLS DR
36100 NWK 94560 752-C6
INDIANWELLS WY
1600 CLAY 94517 593-G6
INDIGO CT
4400 CNCD 94521 593-C5
INDIGO DR
4200 SJS 95136 874-F2
INDIGO LN
- SRMN 94583 693-F1
INDIO CT
12600 SAR 95070 852-E6
INDIO DR
100 SSF 94080 707-E3
INDIO WY
300 SUNV 94086 812-E6
INDUS CT
3200 SJS 95127 814-H6
INDUSTRIAL AV
800 PA 94303 791-G7
800 PA 94303 811-G1
1400 SJS 95112 834-A1
INDUSTRIAL BLVD
24500 HAY 94545 711-E6
26700 HAY 94545 731-F1
INDUSTRIAL CT
- BEN 94510 551-E1
INDUSTRIAL DR
44700 FRMT 94538 773-E4
INDUSTRIAL PKWY SW
29900 HAY 94544 732-B3
30000 UNC 94587 732-B3
30000 HAY 94587 732-B3
INDUSTRIAL PKWY W
300 HAY 94544 712-D7
300 HAY 94544 732-B2
2200 HAY 94545 732-B2
2200 HAY 94545 731-J2
INDUSTRIAL PL
45300 FRMT 94538 773-E5
INDUSTRIAL RD
- SMCo 94002 769-H2
- SCAR 94070 769-H2
400 LGTS 95030 873-A6
1400 RDWC 94063 769-H2
1400 SCAR 94063 769-H2
INDUSTRIAL ST
- SF 94124 668-A5
300 CMBL 95008 853-E7
INDUSTRIAL WY
- BEN 94510 551-E1
- BSBN 94005 688-A4
- LKSP 94904 586-H5
100 MPS 95035 794-A7
100 SSF 94080 708-A3
800 OAK 94603 670-G6
1000 NVTO 94945 526-B3
1300 RDWC 94063 770-A4
1500 SMCo 94002 769-G1
1500 RDWC 94063 769-G1
3900 CNCD 94520 572-F3
3900 CCCo 94520 572-F3
6000 LVMR 94550 696-D5
INDUSTRY RD
- PIT 94565 574-F2
INDUSTRY WY
3700 AlaC 94546 692-A5
INEZ AV
37900 FRMT 94536 753-A3
INEZ PL
100 MrnC 94941 606-H4
INEZ ST
1300 CCCo 94553 571-F3
INEZ WY
500 SCIC 95117 853-D2
2500 ANT 94509 595-G4
INFANTRY TER
- SF 94129 647-D4
- SF 94129 647-D4
INGALLS CT
2700 SJS 95111 854-G4
INGALLS ST
1200 SF 94124 668-C7
2500 SF 94124 688-C1
INGERSOLL CT
3200 SJS 95148 855-F1
INGERSOLL DR
3200 SJS 95148 855-E1
INGERSOLL PL
3000 FRMT 94538 753-D6
INGERSOLL TER
3100 FRMT 94538 753-E6
INGERSON AV
700 SF 94124 688-B1
INGLESIDE CT
6500 SJS 95120 894-B2
INGLEWOOD COM
40800 FRMT 94538 753-D6
INGLEWOOD CT
6800 PLE 94588 694-A7
INGLEWOOD DR
500 SCL 95054 813-E5
5900 PLE 94588 694-A7
INGLEWOOD LN
- ATN 94027 790-D3
INGLEWOOD ST
- CCCo 94565 573-H3
1000 HAY 94544 711-H6
INGLIS LN
1600 SJS 95118 873-J5
INGOLD RD
- BURL 94010 728-C4
INGOT ST
4000 FRMT 94538 773-E5
INGRAM CT
200 SJS 95139 895-G2
1000 SUNV 94087 832-B2
INGRAM PL
27900 HAY 94544 712-B6
INGRID CT
12000 SAR 95070 852-G5
INGROFF RD
7000 CCCo 94803 589-G1
INLAND CT
- ANT 94509 575-E5
INLET CT
14900 SLN 94578 691-C5
INLET DR
- CCCo 94565 573-E1
INMAN AV
- MrnC 94904 586-E3

INMAN WY
2000 SJS 95122 834-J7
INNER CIR
- RDWC 94062 769-H7
INNERWICK LN
3300 SJS 95121 855-C3
INNES AV
400 SF 94124 668-B5
400 SF 94124 668-E7
INNISFREE CIR
300 DALY 94015 707-C1
INNISFREE DR
300 DALY 94015 707-C1
INNOVATION DR
100 SJS 95134 813-F4
INNSBRUCK ST
1000 LVMR 94550 715-G3
INNSBUCK DR
1200 SUNV 94089 812-G3
INNWOOD CT
4700 CNCD 94521 593-D4
INSKIP DR
1400 CMBL 95008 853-B7
INSPIRATION CIR
- DBLN 94552 693-E4
INSPIRATION CT
3300 SJS 95132 814-G3
INSPIRATION DR
- DBLN 94552 693-E4
3200 SJS 95132 814-G4
INSPIRATION POINT TR
- CCCo - 609-J3
- CCCo - 610-A3
- CCCo 94708 609-J3
INTERBAY DR
2000 SJS 95122 835-A7
2000 SJS 95122 834-J7
INTERDALE WY
4100 PA 94306 811-D2
INTERLACHEN AV
7400 SRMN 94583 693-G1
INTERNATIONAL BLVD
100 OAK 94606 649-J5
1300 OAK 94606 650-A6
2300 OAK 94601 650-A6
INTERNATIONAL BLVD Rt#-185
3500 OAK 94601 670-C1
5500 OAK 94621 670-H4
9400 OAK 94603 670-H4
9400 SLN 94577 670-H4
INTERNATIONAL CIR
200 SJS 95119 875-C5
INTREPID LN
800 RDWC 94065 750-C6
INVERLEITH TER
- MRGA 94556 631-E7
- PDMT 94611 650-D2
INVERNESS AV
1100 SCL 95050 833-D4
INVERNESS CIR
1500 SJS 95124 874-A3
INVERNESS COM
3800 LVMR 94550 695-J6
INVERNESS CT
- SRMN 94583 673-G7
- SRMN 94583 693-G1
100 BEN 94510 551-B3
200 OAK 94605 671-D3
200 ALA 94502 669-J5
1200 FRMT 94539 773-G1
2100 PLE 94588 714-B5
3200 WLCK 94598 612-J2
INVERNESS DR
- SF 94132 667-A6
- SRFL 94901 567-B7
100 VAL 94589 530-A1
300 PCFA 94044 707-B3
700 MPS 95035 794-B2
900 SCAR 94070 769-G2
3200 WLCK 94598 612-J2
4200 PIT 94565 574-D7
7600 NWK 94560 752-C6
INVERNESS ST
7400 SRMN 94583 673-G7
15000 SLN 94579 691-A6
INVERNESS WY
- CLAY 94517 594-A7
- HIL 94010 748-F4
200 ALA 94502 669-J5
200 SUNV 94087 832-E5
3800 LVMR 94550 695-J6
INVERRARY LN
- CCCo 94507 633-A3
INVESTMENT BLVD
3300 HAY 94545 711-E7
3300 HAY 94545 731-E1
INVESTMENT ST
600 CCCo 94572 549-H7
INVICTA WY
3200 SJS 95118 874-B1
INVINCIBLE CT
- ALA 94501 649-G6
INWOOD CT
1400 CMBL 95008 853-B7
INWOOD DR
500 CMBL 95008 853-B7
INWOOD LN
300 HAY 94544 732-E2
INYO AV
2200 OAK 94601 650-C6
INYO CIR
- NVTO 94947 526-E7
INYO CT
100 SBRN 94066 707-E7
4400 FRMT 94538 753-A6
4600 PLE 94566 694-D7
INYO PL
- SMCo 94061 790-B4
INYO ST
- BSBN 94005 688-A6
22500 HAY 94541 711-G2
IOLANI CT
39600 FRMT 94538 753-A7
ION CT
100 CMBL 95008 853-D7
IONE AV
2600 AlaC 94546 692-A6
IONE CT
7200 DBLN 94568 693-J2
12700 SAR 95070 852-E6

IONE DR
2700 SJS 95132 814-F5
IONE WY
6800 DBLN 94568 693-J3
IOWA AV
- UNC 94587 732-F5
100 SUNV 94086 832-D1
W IOWA AV
400 SUNV 94086 832-D1
700 SUNV 94086 812-B7
IOWA DR
400 SMTO 94402 748-H3
5400 CNCD 94521 593-E6
6100 SJS 95123 874-H6
IOWA ST
- BEN 94510 551-E2
700 SF 94107 668-C3
IPSWICH CT
- NWK 94560 752-E4
IRAZU CT
200 SJS 95116 834-G3
IRCAL CT
- CCCo 94507 632-G5
IRENE CT
100 BLMT 94002 749-D7
IRENE DR
- NVTO 94947 525-H4
4100 CCCo 94553 572-A3
IRENE LN
900 LFYT 94549 611-H7
IRENE ST
100 SRFL 94901 586-J3
200 SRFL 94901 587-A3
700 SJS 95110 833-J5
IRENE WY
5100 LVMR 94550 696-C7
5100 LVMR 94550 716-B1
IRIS AV
- SF 94118 647-E6
600 SUNV 94086 832-F2
IRIS CT
- NWK 94560 752-G7
- SLN 94577 690-J1
- SMTO 94401 729-A6
- SSF 94080 707-G1
100 HER 94547 569-J3
100 VAL 94591 530-F7
500 BEN 94510 550-J1
800 PCFA 94044 726-H5
1300 SJS 95125 854-A3
2700 ANT 94509 575-G7
3200 LFYT 94549 611-H5
IRIS LN
- CCCo 94595 612-A6
- MLPK 94025 770-H7
- SCAR 94070 769-C4
100 SRFL 94903 566-B3
500 SRMN 94583 653-J7
IRIS PL
1100 HAY 94544 711-H6
IRIS RD
100 HER 94547 569-J4
200 HER 94547 570-A3
IRIS ST
- RDWC 94062 769-J6
100 MRTZ 94553 571-E4
500 RDWC 94062 770-A7
600 RDWC 94061 770-A7
8000 OAK 94605 670-J3
IRIS TER
4800 FRMT 94555 752-D2
IRIS WY
100 PA 94303 791-C4
5200 LVMR 94550 696-B3
34700 UNC 94587 732-F7
IRIS BLOSSOM CT
100 SJS 95123 875-A4
IRLANDA WY
3000 SJS 95124 873-J1
IRMA WY
2400 AlaC 94546 691-F3
IRON AL
- SF 94114 667-F3
IRONBARK CIR
600 ORIN 94563 610-H6
IRONBARK CT
700 ORIN 94563 610-H6
IRONBARK PL
800 ORIN 94563 610-H6
IRONBRIDGE WY
1200 SJS 95118 874-C4
IRONGATE CT
100 CCCo 94507 632-G7
IRON HILL ST
400 PLHL 94549 591-H5
IRON HORSE CT
300 CCCo 94595 632-D2
IRON HORSE LN
37200 FRMT 94536 753-B1
IRON HORSE PKWY
- DBLN 94568 694-B5
IRON PEAK CT
1900 ANT 94509 595-F5
IRONSHOE DR
- SJS 95138 855-E7
IRONSIDE CT
3000 SJS 95132 814-E3
IRONSTONE CT
200 MrnC 94903 546-E6
1100 SJS 95132 814-F6
IRONWOOD
- OAK 94605 671-D2
IRONWOOD CT
100 HER 94547 570-A4
7500 DBLN 94568 693-H3
25200 HAY 94545 711-F6
IRONWOOD DR
- SRFL 94901 567-B6
100 PLHL 94523 592-B1
100 CCCo 94553 592-B1
700 SJS 95125 854-C6
7500 DBLN 94568 693-H3
IRONWOOD LN
100 VAL 94591 530-F7
100 VAL 94591 550-F1
IRONWOOD PL
1000 CCCo 94507 632-F7
4900 AlaC 94550 716-B2
IRONWOOD RD
100 ALA 94502 670-A6
IRONWOOD TER
500 SUNV 94086 832-F2

IRONWOOD WY
1100 CNCD 94521 593-F7
IROQUOIS AV
900 LVMR 94550 695-E7
IROQUOIS CT
600 SJS 95123 874-G4
900 FRMT 94539 773-J6
IROQUOIS DR
900 CCCo 94549 591-J6
900 PLHL 94523 591-J6
IROQUOIS TR
- PTLV 94028 810-B6
IROQUOIS WY
600 FRMT 94539 773-H6
IRVEN CT
500 PA 94306 811-D2
IRVIN CT
800 HAY 94541 711-F3
900 PLHL 94523 592-C3
IRVINE DR
- MRGA 94556 651-G2
IRVING AV
- ATN 94027 770-F7
- ATN 94027 790-F1
300 SCIC 95128 853-G1
300 SJS 95128 853-G1
IRVING CT
- ORIN 94563 610-G3
100 PLHL 94523 592-C6
400 TBRN 94920 607-A4
IRVING DR
- MrnC 94960 566-A2
IRVING LN
- ORIN 94563 610-H4
IRVING ST
- SF 94143 667-A2
- SSF 94080 707-J1
- SF 94122 667-A2
200 SMTO 94402 748-H3
1800 OAK 94601 650-B6
3200 SF 94122 666-H2
IRVING WY
8000 DBLN 94568 693-H3
IRVINGTON AV
4000 FRMT 94538 753-C7
IRVINGTON ST
100 DALY 94014 687-D3
IRWIN CT
700 HIL 94010 728-F7
1000 CNCD 94518 592-J5
6400 OAK 94609 629-H4
IRWIN DR
800 HIL 94010 728-E7
IRWIN PL
100 MLBR 94030 728-C4
IRWIN ST
- SRFL 94901 586-G1
400 SF 94107 668-B1
1000 BLMT 94002 749-F7
1000 BLMT 94002 769-F1
1200 SRFL 94901 566-G7
2900 VAL 94591 530-D5
IRWIN WY
- ORIN 94563 610-G7
IRWINDALE DR
2900 SJS 95122 855-B3
ISABEL AV
1300 LVMR 94550 715-C2
1300 AlaC 94550 715-C2
ISABEL DR
400 MRTZ 94553 591-J1
1600 SCIC 95125 853-H4
ISABEL ST
4800 RCH 94804 609-A5
ISABELLA AV
- ATN 94027 790-E2
ISABELLA CT
- NVTO 94945 525-J1
4100 ANT 94509 595-J1
ISABELLA LN
- PLHL 94523 612-A1
ISABELLA ST
100 HAY 94544 712-A5
500 SCL 95050 833-D4
800 OAK 94607 649-F2
ISABELLE AV
1200 MTVW 94040 811-G7
2000 SMTO 94403 749-A4
ISADORA DR
3100 SJS 95132 814-F3
ISADORA DUNCAN LN
- SF 94102 648-A6
- SF 94102 647-J6
ISDLIO CT
- SJS 95123 874-F6
ISENGARD DR
1200 SJS 95121 855-A4
ISHERWOOD PL
3400 FRMT 94536 752-G2
ISHERWOOD WY
3100 FRMT 94536 752-G1
3300 FRMT 94536 732-H7
3300 UNC 94587 732-H7
ISHI DR
45200 FRMT 94539 773-H3
ISHIMATSU PL
5100 SJS 95124 873-G5
ISIS ST
- SF 94103 667-J1
ISLAIS ST
- SF 94124 668-B4
ISLAND CT
- CCCo 94595 612-A6
ISLAND DR
- ALA 94502 670-A6
- SANS 94960 566-D7
- SRFL 94901 566-D7
100 PA 94301 791-B3
300 MrnC 94941 606-J5
400 RDWC 94065 749-H6
ISLAND PKWY
- RDWC 94065 749-F6
300 BLMT 94002 749-F6
ISLAND PL
500 RDWC 94065 749-H6
ISLAND PALM CT
- SJS 95133 814-J4
ISLAND PINE CT
800 HAY 94544 712-A7
ISLAND PINE WY
6200 SJS 95119 875-D5

ISLA VISTA LN
- SRFL 94901 587-A2
100 SRFL 94901 586-J2
ISLAY CT
700 SUNV 94087 832-F5
ISLE ROYAL CT
3400 PLE 94588 714-B1
ISLE ROYAL ST
42500 FRMT 94538 773-C2
ISLE ROYALE CT
100 SRFL 94903 566-F2
ISLETON AV
100 OAK 94603 670-G7
ISLEWOOD CT
3200 ANT 94509 595-H1
ISOLA DR
4000 FRMT 94555 732-C7
ISOLA LN
3200 CCCo 94549 591-J7
ISOLA WY
- SF 94127 667-E5
ISOLERA LN
- AMCN 94589 510-C3
ISSAC CT
- SJS 95136 854-E7
ITALY AV
- SF 94112 687-F1
ITHACA AV
800 SUNV 94087 832-C2
ITHACA LN
2600 ANT 94509 575-D1
ITHACA ST
32200 HAY 94544 732-E3
32300 UNC 94587 732-E3
ITHACA WY
4600 PLE 94588 694-D6
IVALDI CT
300 FRMT 94539 753-G4
IVALYNN CIR
3500 SJS 95132 814-G4
IVALYNN CT
3300 SJS 95132 814-G4
IVALYNN PL
3300 SJS 95132 814-G4
IVAN PL
1500 SJS 95120 874-A7
IVAN WY
3300 MTVW 94040 832-A2
IVANHOE AV
1700 LFYT 94549 591-H7
IVANHOE CT
- LFYT 94549 591-H7
400 SJS 95136 874-G3
IVANHOE RD
5700 OAK 94618 630-A5
IVEGILL CT
6800 SJS 95119 895-D1
IVERSEN CT
2600 SCL 95051 833-B7
IVERSON DR
- LFYT 94549 611-F5
IVES CT
40500 FRMT 94538 753-C7
IVES TER
400 SUNV 94087 832-E2
IVORY PL
- LVMR 94550 715-D3
IVORY CREEK DR
900 SJS 95120 894-J4
IVY AV
- PCFA 94044 727-A2
IVY CT
1000 ELCR 94530 609-E1
7500 PLE 94588 693-J7
14200 SLN 94578 691-C3
IVY DR
- OAK 94610 650-A4
- ORIN 94563 631-B4
- ROSS 94957 586-B2
- MRGA 94556 631-C6
200 MLPK 94025 770-J7
600 MLPK 94025 771-A7
2200 OAK 94606 650-A4
IVY LN
- ANT 94509 595-H1
- SRFL 94901 586-F2
- SANS 94960 566-A7
400 PLHL 94523 612-B1
1900 PA 94303 791-C4
6300 SJS 95129 852-F4
IVY PL
200 MRGA 94556 631-C6
IVY ST
200 SF 94102 647-H7
1700 SMTO 94402 749-A3
IVY WY
1900 FRMT 94539 773-G3
IVYCREEK CIR
1500 SJS 95121 855-D7
IVY ESTATES CT
2800 SJS 95135 855-G5
IVYGATE LN
3000 SJS 95136 874-J3
IVY HILL WY
100 LGTS 95030 873-C4
IVY MILLS LN
1700 SJS 95122 854-G1
IVY POINTE CIR
500 SRMN 94583 653-J7
IVYWOOD CT
2800 SJS 95121 855-E4
IVYWOOD DR
- CCCo 94596 592-D7
IXIAS CT
1600 SJS 95124 873-J7
IXIAS LN
5700 SJS 95124 873-J7
IZORAH WY
15700 LGTS 95032 873-C5

J

J RD
- SUNV 94089 812-H3
J ST
- OAK 94625 649-A4
- SF 94124 688-D1
- SRFL 94901 566-E7
100 BEN 94510 551-A4
100 FRMT 94536 753-B1
200 ANT 94509 575-C4
400 MRTZ 94553 571-E5
800 BEN 94510 550-J4
1000 UNC 94587 732-G5
S J ST
100 LVMR 94550 715-H1
JABIL LN
23900 LAH 94024 831-D4
JACANA CT
5200 SJS 95123 874-F7
JACANA LN
5200 SJS 95123 874-F7
JACANA LAKE CT
3800 FRMT 94555 732-H4
JACARANDA CIR
700 HIL 94010 748-D2
JACARANDA CT
500 FRMT 94539 753-F5
38300 NWK 94560 752-G7
JACARANDA DR
- FRMT 94539 753-F5
200 HAY 94544 712-A5
300 CCCo 94506 654-A2
300 CCCo 94506 653-J3
38300 NWK 94560 752-G7
JACARANDA WY
400 SUNV 94086 832-F1
16100 SCIC 95032 873-D6
JACCARANDA CT
13000 SAR 95070 852-F7
JACINTO
200 PIT 94565 574-B2
JACINTO CT
35800 FRMT 94536 752-F3
JACINTO DR
4100 FRMT 94536 752-F3
JACINTO LN
- SSF 94080 707-E3
JACINTO WY
- NVTO 94945 525-J1
100 SUNV 94086 812-C6
JACK CT
- NVTO 94947 525-H4
JACKIE CT
4000 PLE 94588 694-A7
JACKIE DR
400 SJS 95111 854-H5
JACK KEROUAC AL
- SF 94133 648-A4
JACKLIN CIR
- MPS 95035 794-A5
JACKLIN CT
- MPS 95035 794-A5
JACKLIN PL
- MPS 95035 794-A5
JACKLIN RD
- MPS 95035 794-A5
JACKLING DR
900 HIL 94010 728-D7
1200 BURL 94010 728-D7
JACK LONDON AL
- SF 94107 648-B6
JACK LONDON BLVD
- LVMR 94588 694-H5
E JACK LONDON BLVD
100 LVMR 94550 695-D7
W JACK LONDON BLVD
100 LVMR 94550 695-B7
JACK LONDON DR
- PIT 94565 574-B2
600 VAL 94589 509-J5
JACKLYN TER
- MLV 94941 606-G5
JACKLYNN CT
32300 UNC 94587 731-J7
32300 UNC 94587 751-J1
JACKLYNN DR
4700 UNC 94587 751-J1
32300 UNC 94587 731-J7
32300 UNC 94587 752-A1
JACKPINE CT
700 SUNV 94086 832-F2
JACKS RD
20800 SAR 95070 872-D3
JACKSOL DR
14300 SJS 95124 873-E3
JACKSON AV
100 RDWC 94061 770-A7
200 SUNV 94086 812-E7
400 LVMR 94550 696-A7
600 LVMR 94550 716-A1
N JACKSON AV
- SJS 95116 834-G2
300 SJS 95133 834-F1
900 SJS 95133 814-E7
900 SCIC 95133 814-E7
S JACKSON AV
- SJS 95116 834-H4
JACKSON CT
- NVTO 94947 526-A6
1800 CNCD 94521 593-D2
1900 FRMT 94539 753-F7
JACKSON DR
- NVTO 94947 526-A6
500 PA 94303 791-C4
JACKSON PL
3100 ANT 94509 575-A7
JACKSON ST
- BEN 94510 551-D6
- LGTS 95032 893-A1
- SF 94111 648-A4
- SJS 95112 834-A4
100 OAK 94607 649-G4
300 CCCo 94525 550-E5
300 SMTO 94402 748-H3
400 ALB 94706 609-D5
400 SF 94133 648-A4
500 SCL 95050 833-D3
600 SF 94108 648-A4
800 MTVW 94043 811-H4
1000 SF 94133 647-F5
1000 SF 94108 647-F5
1200 OAK 94612 649-G4
1200 SF 94109 647-F5
2100 FRMT 94539 753-F7
2100 SF 94115 647-F5
2800 ALA 94501 670-B3
3300 SF 94118 647-E5
3500 SF 94118 647-D5
JACKSON ST Rt#-92
- HAY 94544 711-H4
- HAY 94541 711-H4

W JACKSON ST
- HAY 94544 711-H4
JACKSON WY
- SJS 95002 793-C7
100 PLHL 94523 592-B6
100 VAL 94591 530-E4
1400 CCCo 94507 632-F4
N JACKSON WY
- CCCo 94507 632-F4
S JACKSON WY
100 CCCo 94507 632-F5
JACOB AV
1500 SJS 95118 874-A2
1700 SJS 95124 874-A2
1700 SJS 95124 873-J2
JACOB CT
- NVTO 94945 526-E3
JACOBS CT
400 PA 94306 811-C2
JACOBS PL
3700 AlaC 94541 692-C6
JACOBS ST
2500 AlaC 94541 692-C6
JACOBSEN ST
900 ANT 94509 575-F5
JACOBUS AV
1000 AlaC 94586 734-B3
4600 OAK 94618 630-B6
JACOBY ST
500 SRFL 94901 586-J3
JACQUELINE CT
- DALY 94014 687-J4
JACQUELINE DR
2100 PIT 94565 573-J4
JACQUELINE LN
- DALY 94014 687-J4
JACQUELINE PL
- SMCo 94062 769-G7
1300 AlaC 94580 711-B1
JACQUELINE WY
1000 SJS 95129 852-E3
1800 CNCD 94519 592-J1
JACQUES DR
5900 SJS 95123 874-G6
JACQUILINE WY
5500 LVMR 94550 716-C1
JACUZZI ST
500 RCH 94804 609-C4
JADE AV
3200 SJS 95117 853-D3
JADE CIR
200 VAL 94590 550-B2
7800 DBLN 94568 693-J1
JADE CT
- NVTO 94945 526-B3
- SRMN 94583 673-F2
100 HER 94547 569-G5
400 ANT 94509 595-E2
2200 FRMT 94539 773-G2
JADE PL
- SF 94131 667-F5
600 LVMR 94550 715-D3
JADE ST
1600 CCCo 94801 588-F3
JADELAKE CT
800 SUNV 94089 812-H5
JAFCO CT
- NVTO 94949 546-E2
JAFFA RD
1300 LVMR 94550 715-G3
JAGELS RD
- SUNV 94089 812-E4
JAGGERS DR
200 SJS 95119 875-C7
JAI DR
300 SJS 95119 875-C7
JAILHOUSE WY
- SBRN 94066 707-D6
JAKEY CT
- SF 94124 668-C6
JALALON PL
- CLAY 94517 593-G6
JALAND CT
1100 SJS 95120 894-H4
JAMAICA CIR
200 UNC 94587 732-D6
JAMAICA DR
- SRMN 94583 653-E7
JAMAICA LN
26600 HAY 94545 711-F7
JAMAICA RD
2700 SJS 95111 854-G4
JAMAICA ST
100 MrnC 94920 607-C2
900 FCTY 94404 749-F5
JAMAICA WY
2000 SJS 95122 834-J7
2300 SLN 94577 690-G5
JAMARA WY
3100 CCCo 94549 611-J2
JAMES AV
- RDWC 94062 789-H1
- SMCo 94062 789-H1
- ATN 94027 770-F7
- ATN 94027 790-F1
- RDWC 94063 770-A6
- RDWC 94062 770-A6
600 RDWC 94062 769-J7
3700 FRMT 94538 753-D6
4200 AlaC 94546 692-A4
4900 AlaC 94552 692-C4
5200 OAK 94618 629-J6
JAMES CT
- MrnC 94945 526-E3
- WLCK 94596 612-A2
100 SSF 94080 707-G1
200 BEN 94510 551-A2
1300 SMTO 94401 749-B1
2100 MRTZ 94553 571-F4
3100 SCL 95051 833-A3
JAMES DR
200 MTVW 94043 812-A4
JAMES LN
3500 CNCD 94519 593-A1
JAMES PL
100 LFYT 94549 611-G7
1100 ELCR 94530 609-E1
1900 SJS 95125 853-J6
19200 AlaC 94546 692-B4
JAMES RD
- AMCN 94589 510-A2
400 PA 94306 811-D2

STREET Block City ZIP Pg-Grid

JAMES ST
300 LVMR 94550 695-F7
400 LVMR 94550 715-F1
JAMES BLACK CIR
- NVTO 94949 546-E4
JAMES BOWIE CT
300 CCCo 94507 632-H2
JAMES DONLON BLVD
- ANT 94509 594-J1
1100 ANT 94509 595-B1
JAMES LICK FRWY U.S.-101
- SF - 668-A6
- SF - 688-A1
JAMESON CT
1900 CNCD 94521 593-H5
JAMES RIVER RD
100 VAL 94591 550-D2
JAMESTON LN
- DALY 94014 687-F3
JAMESTOWN AV
800 SF 94124 688-B1
JAMESTOWN AVEX
700 SF 94124 688-C2
JAMES TOWN CT
12000 SAR 95070 852-D5
JAMES TOWN DR
1400 CPTO 95014 852-D4
JAMESTOWN DR
1100 SUNV 94087 832-B2
JAMESTOWN RD
3500 FRMT 94538 773-E2
JAMES WATSON DR
100 HER 94547 569-G1
JAMI CT
200 LVMR 94550 696-A7
JAMI ST
- LVMR 94550 696-A6
JAMIE CIR
33200 FRMT 94555 732-C7
JAMIE CT
100 LGTS 95032 873-H6
E JAMIE CT
400 SSF 94080 708-C4
JAMIE DR
1000 CNCD 94518 592-J4
JAMIE LN
800 EPA 94303 791-C1
JAMIE WY
3100 AlaC 94541 692-D7
JAMISON PL
2000 SCL 95051 833-A3
JAMISON WY
3400 AlaC 94546 692-A5
JAN CT
800 AlaC 94580 691-E5
JAN WY
- NVTO 94947 525-H3
4000 SJS 95124 873-H3
JANA LN
800 SJS 95111 855-A6
JANA WY
200 AMCN 94589 509-J1
JANAE CT
4500 UNC 94587 731-J7
JANARY WY
6300 SJS 95129 852-F4
JANA VISTA
4200 CCCo 94803 589-D3
JANE AV
26000 HAY 94544 712-A5
JANE CT
300 HAY 94544 712-A5
700 CCCo 94553 572-A3
JANE DR
100 WDSD 94062 789-G5
JANE LN
2300 MTVW 94043 811-G2
JANE ANN WY
- CMBL 95008 853-C6
JANELLE CT
3100 AlaC 94541 712-D1
JANELLE DR
3200 SJS 95148 855-E2
JANES ST
- MrnC 94941 606-D4
- MLV 94941 606-D4
JANET AV
1900 SJS 95124 873-G2
JANET CT
1400 BEN 94510 551-B4
4900 LVMR 94550 696-B7
JANET LN
- WLCK 94596 612-B2
600 MRTZ 94553 571-E6
900 LFYT 94549 611-H6
1300 CNCD 94521 593-A3
JANET WY
- TBRN 94920 607-A4
JANICE AV
500 HAY 94544 732-E1
22200 CPTO 95014 852-A1
JANICE DR
1100 SCL 95050 833-C4
2000 PLHL 94523 592-D5
JANICE LN
41200 FRMT 94539 753-G4
JANICE ST
100 VAL 94589 510-C5
JANICE WY
3400 PA 94303 791-E6
JANIN PL
- PLHL 94523 592-A2
- PLHL 94523 591-J2
JANIS CIR
2600 ALA 94501 670-A2
JANIS CT
- CCCo 94526 633-C5
1400 LVMR 94550 695-F6
JANIS WY
1100 SJS 95125 854-B6
JANKU CT
3200 SJS 95127 814-H6
JANMARIE CT
1100 SJS 95121 855-A5
JANOR CT
15200 MSER 95030 872-J4
JANSEN AV
800 SJS 95125 854-B4
JANSEN ST
- SF 94133 647-J4
JANSEN TER
37400 FRMT 94536 752-H4
JANSSEN CT
24000 HAY 94541 712-A2
JANUARY DR
100 SJS 95138 875-C4
JAPALA CT
- FRMT 94539 773-H3
JAPALA PL
44500 FRMT 94539 773-H3
JAPAUL LN
1400 SJS 95132 814-F3
JAPONICA WY
4600 SJS 95129 853-A1
JAQUES CT
4700 FRMT 94555 752-C2
JARBOE AV
600 SF 94110 667-J5
1200 SF 94110 668-A5
JARDIN DR
100 LALT 94022 811-E5
200 MTVW 94040 811-E5
JARED LN
- LGTS 95032 893-C1
JAROSITE CT
4200 ANT 94509 595-F2
J ARTHUR YOUNGER FRWY Rt#-92
- BLMT - 768-H2
- FCTY - 729-G7
- FCTY - 729-G7
- FCTY - 749-F2
- HIL - 748-J5
- SMCo - 748-J5
- SMCo - 768-H2
- SMCo - 768-H2
- SMTO - 749-A4
- SMTO - 749-F2
- SMTO - 749-F2
- SMTO - 748-J5
- SMTO - 748-J5
- SMTO - 768-H2
- SMTO - 768-H2
JARVIS AV
3000 SJS 95118 874-A1
5600 NWK 94560 752-D4
JARVIS CT
300 SUNV 94086 832-E1
1500 SJS 95118 874-B2
JARVIS LN
100 HER 94547 570-B5
JARVIS PL
1500 SJS 95118 874-B2
JARVIS WY
2000 LAH 94304 810-H4
JASMINE AV
6200 NWK 94560 772-G1
JASMINE CT
- MLBR 94030 728-A3
100 MPS 95035 794-D6
1000 CCCo 94803 569-D7
1300 ANT 94509 575-G5
1400 LVMR 94550 696-A4
5500 AlaC 94552 692-D3
7600 DBLN 94568 693-H3
JASMINE DR
800 SUNV 94086 832-F2
JASMINE LN
- MrnC 94903 546-A6
JASMINE ST
- VAL 94589 509-H6
1400 SMTO 94402 749-A3
JASMINE WY
100 EPA 94303 791-D3
200 DNVL 94506 654-B5
1000 CCCo 94803 569-D7
16100 SCIC 95032 873-D6
JASON CT
- SF 94133 648-A4
100 VAL 94591 530-F6
6100 SJS 95123 875-A6
JASON DR
- MPS 95035 793-J4
JASON WY
200 MTVW 94043 811-J5
37300 FRMT 94536 752-H3
JASPER CT
- BEN 94510 551-B1
- LVMR 94550 715-D3
100 HER 94547 569-G4
5500 CNCD 94521 593-F7
JASPER DR
1500 SUNV 94087 832-B5
JASPER PL
- SF 94133 648-A4
JASPER ST
600 SJS 95116 834-F6
JAUSS ST
- SF 94129 647-E3
JAVA DR
3400 SRMN 94583 673-D1
E JAVA DR
200 SUNV 94089 812-G3
W JAVA DR
100 SUNV 94089 812-F2
JAVA ST
- SF 94117 667-F1
JAVALINA RD
47200 FRMT 94539 773-H7
JAVOWITZ ST
- SF 94129 647-E3
JAY CT
- CCCo 94526 633-D5
JAY LN
100 CCCo 94526 633-C5
JAY ST
500 LALT 94022 811-F6
1700 ALA 94501 669-H1
3000 SCL 95054 813-C7
JAYAR PL
500 HAY 94544 732-E2
JAYBEE PL
100 SJS 95123 875-A3
JAYBROOK CT
7300 PLE 94588 693-J7
JAYDINE ST
19500 AlaC 94546 692-B4
JAYHAWK LN
1300 LVMR 94550 696-C3
JAYMARK CT
18000 AlaC 94546 691-J2
JAYNE AV
200 OAK 94610 649-J3
JAYNES ST
1600 BERK 94703 629-F1
1700 BERK 94703 609-F7
JAYS PL
1400 MRTZ 94553 591-H1
JAZZ CT
800 SJS 95134 813-F3
JEAN CT
- CCCo 94806 589-B3
- MRGA 94556 631-G5
4600 UNC 94587 731-J7
JEAN DR
- CNCD 94518 592-G4
32200 UNC 94587 731-J7
32300 UNC 94587 732-A7
32500 UNC 94587 752-A1
JEAN PL
100 PLHL 94523 592-D6
JEAN ST
300 MrnC 94965 606-F7
400 OAK 94610 649-J2
600 OAK 94610 650-A2
JEAN WY
- SF 94118 647-E6
900 HAY 94545 711-F4
1300 SLN 94577 690-H1
JEANETTE CT
7800 CPTO 95014 852-C2
JEANETTE DR
1900 PLHL 94523 592-B5
JEANETTE LN
14800 SCIC 95127 835-A1
JEANINE WY
3300 AlaC 94546 691-J5
JEANNE AV
700 SJS 95116 834-E6
JEANNE CIR
1700 MRTZ 94553 591-J1
JEANNE CT
- ANT 94509 575-E5
JEANNE DR
200 PLHL 94523 592-B4
JEANNIE CT
100 DNVL 94526 633-C7
4500 LVMR 94550 696-B7
JEANNIE WY
200 LVMR 94550 696-A7
JEEP TR
- AlaC 94544 712-E5
- AlaC 94552 672-G6
- HAY 94542 712-E5
- HAY 94544 712-E5
JEFF CT
1400 CNCD 94521 593-A3
JEFFER ST
2200 AlaC 94546 692-A6
JEFFERS WY
- CMBL 95008 853-D6
JEFFERSON AV
- MrnC 94903 566-F4
400 RDWC 94063 770-B6
600 LVMR 94550 696-A7
600 LVMR 94550 716-A1
1200 RDWC 94062 770-A7
1200 RDWC 94061 770-B6
1900 RDWC 94062 769-J7
1900 RDWC 94061 769-J7
2000 BERK 94703 629-F2
2500 RDWC 94062 789-H1
2500 RDWC 94061 789-H1
3800 SMCo 94062 789-H1
4100 WDSD 94062 789-E3
5500 RCH 94804 609-B2
5700 ELCR 94530 609-B2
JEFFERSON CT
- MLPK 94025 770-H6
- NVTO 94947 526-B6
600 SJS 95133 814-G7
800 SMTO 94401 728-H7
3700 RDWC 94061 789-G2
4600 PLE 94588 694-A7
JEFFERSON DR
100 MLPK 94025 770-G6
100 TBRN 94920 607-A4
500 PA 94303 791-C4
800 MTVW 94040 811-G7
JEFFERSON ST
- FRMT 94538 773-E1
- CCCo 94565 573-H2
- OAK 94607 649-F4
- SF 94133 647-J3
- SSF 94080 707-H1
200 SCL 95050 833-D4
500 HAY 94544 712-B6
500 SF 94109 647-J3
800 BEN 94510 551-D5
1100 SLN 94577 691-A1
1200 OAK 94612 649-F4
1400 SF 94123 647-F3
1800 CNCD 94521 593-C2
2500 CCCo 94553 571-F3
JEFFERSON WY
2100 ANT 94509 575-A7
2100 ANT 94509 574-J7
JEFFERY AV
1400 SJS 95118 874-B1
JEFFERY CT
1700 SCL 95051 833-A3
JEFFREY AV
600 CMBL 95008 853-C7
JEFFREY CT
- NVTO 94945 526-A2
2700 AlaC 94546 691-H4
JEFFREY DR
800 PLHL 94523 592-C3
JEFFREY LN
900 WLCK 94598 612-D4
JEFFRY ST
300 VAL 94590 529-J5
700 VAL 94590 530-A5
JEFFRY RANCH CT
100 CLAY 94517 593-G6
JEFFRY RANCH PL
200 CLAY 94517 593-G6
JELINCIC DR
3200 AlaC 94542 712-D1
JEMCO CT
- PLHL 94523 592-A6
JEN CT
3100 CNCD 94518 592-H2
JENAY CT
200 MRTZ 94553 591-H3
JENEVEIN AV
- SBRN 94066 727-H1
500 SBRN 94066 707-J7
JENIFER CT
2500 ANT 94509 574-J6
JENKINS AV
3000 SJS 95118 874-B1
JENKINS CT
- SCIC 94305 790-J7
JENKINS LN
100 MTVW 94043 812-B5
JENKINS PL
- SCL 95051 833-A7
JENKINS WY
3800 RCH 94806 568-G7
JENKINSON DR
1600 CNCD 94520 592-E4
JENKINSON LAKE WY
3800 FRMT 94555 732-B6
JENNIE CT
600 LFYT 94549 631-H1
JENNIE DR
- PLHL 94523 592-C4
JENNIFER CT
- NVTO 94947 525-J4
- CCCo 94507 632-G3
- DALY 94014 687-J4
100 VAL 94591 530-E3
300 MTVW 94040 811-F4
4800 UNC 94587 751-J1
JENNIFER DR
100 CCCo 94806 569-A5
1700 LVMR 94550 716-C1
2700 AlaC 94546 691-H4
JENNIFER LN
- CCCo 94507 632-G3
- NVTO 94947 525-J3
JENNIFER ST
36500 NWK 94560 752-E6
JENNIFER WY
200 PLHL 94523 592-C4
700 MPS 95035 794-A5
3000 SJS 95124 873-G2
JENNIFER HGHLNDS CT
- CCCo - 591-G5
JENNIFERS MDWS CT
1000 DNVL 94506 653-G5
JENNINGS AV
500 VAL 94591 530-D6
JENNINGS DR
600 SJS 95111 854-J5
JENNINGS LN
- ATN 94027 790-D1
JENNINGS ST
100 SF 94124 668-D6
2700 SF 94124 688-B1
JENNINGS WY
26800 HAY 94544 711-J7
JENNY LIND CT
5900 SJS 95120 874-C6
JENSEN CIR
900 PIT 94565 574-F7
JENSEN CT
400 DNVL 94526 653-C3
JENSEN DR
1000 PIT 94565 574-F6
JENSEN RD
4900 AlaC 94552 692-D5
JENSEN ST
- OAK 94601 670-C2
100 LVMR 94550 695-J7
400 LVMR 94550 715-J1
4000 PLE 94566 714-E2
JENSEN WY
- SRFL 94901 566-D7
JENSEN RANCH RD
6600 AlaC 94552 692-G2
JENVEY AV
1400 SJS 95125 854-A6
JEPSEN CT
12800 SAR 95070 852-D6
JERABEK CT
3900 SJS 95136 874-F1
JERALD AV
2900 SCL 95051 833-A3
JERALD CT
3500 AlaC 94546 691-J3
JEREMIE CT
6500 SJS 95120 894-E1
JEREMIE DR
6500 SJS 95120 894-E2
JEREZ CT
1300 HAY 94544 732-A1
JERI PL
5000 CNCD 94521 593-D4
JERICHO LN
3300 SJS 95117 853-D3
JERILYN CT
10200 SCIC 95127 835-A2
JERILYN DR
3400 SCIC 95127 835-A2
11700 SJS 95127 835-A2
JERILYNN AV
6300 RCH 94803 589-B3
6300 RCH 94806 589-B3
JERILYNN CT
100 VAL 94589 509-J5
JERILYNN DR
2300 CNCD 94519 572-G7
JERLIN PL
- PLE 94588 713-J3
JEROME AL
- SF 94133 648-A4
JEROME AV
- PDMT 94611 650-A1
100 PDMT 94610 650-B1
43300 FRMT 94539 753-H7
JEROME CT
- WLCK 94596 612-D4
JEROME ST
300 SJS 95125 854-B1
JERRIES DR
14000 SAR 95070 872-E2
JERROLD AV
400 SF 94124 668-A4
JERROLD RD
3600 AlaC 94550 716-G3
JERRY PL
17400 AlaC 94541 691-F7
JERSEY DR
500 SANS 94960 566-C6
JERSEY RD
3700 FRMT 94538 773-E2
JERSEY ST
- SF 94114 667-G4
500 VAL 94590 530-A6
JERVIS AV
1100 EPA 94303 791-A1
JERVIS BAY
100 ALA 94502 669-H7
JERYLYN LN
200 HAY 94541 711-G3
JESSEE CT
3700 AlaC 94552 692-F2
JESSE JAMES DR
500 SJS 95123 874-J7
JESSEN CT
- CCCo 94707 609-F2
JESSICA CIR
4300 FRMT 94555 752-C1
JESSICA CT
- CCCo 94526 633-C5
JESSICA DR
700 LVMR 94550 696-C7
JESSICA LN
11600 LAH 94024 831-E4
JESSICA WY
1600 SJS 95121 855-A2
JESSIE CT
2900 SJS 95124 873-F1
JESSIE LN
200 MTVW 94041 811-J6
JESSIE ST
- SF 94105 648-A6
100 SF 94103 648-A6
600 SF 94103 647-J7
1300 SF 94103 667-H1
JESSUP ST
- SRFL 94901 586-E1
JETER ST
- RDWC 94062 769-J6
JETTY WY
- RDWC 94065 750-A5
JEWEL CT
- ORIN 94563 631-A4
JEWEL TER
200 DNVL 94526 653-B5
JEWELL CT
- SRFL 94901 586-H1
6800 OAK 94611 630-E5
JEWELL DR
2100 SJS 95124 873-F1
JEWELL LN
2400 PLHL 94523 592-C6
JEWELL PL
- HIL 94010 748-F3
2300 MTVW 94043 811-G3
JEWELL ST
- SRFL 94901 586-H1
200 SRFL 94901 566-H7
JEWETT AV
900 PIT 94565 574-E7
JEWETT CT
- PIT 94565 574-E7
J HART CLINTON DR
1300 SMTO 94401 729-B7
1500 SMTO 94401 749-C1
1700 SMTO 94404 749-C1
JIB CT
- PLHL 94523 592-B1
- PLHL 94553 592-B1
JIB RD
17300 SLN 94577 690-H4
JIBSTAY LN
500 FCTY 94404 749-J1
JILINDA CT
10800 SCIC 95127 835-A1
JILL AV
500 CCCo 94565 573-C1
500 SJS 95117 833-D7
600 SCL 95050 833-D7
JILL LN
100 VAL 94589 510-D5
JILL WY
18300 AlaC 94546 691-H3
JILLANA AV
300 LVMR 94550 715-D2
JILLIAN CT
1200 WLCK 94598 612-E2
JILLIENE WY
500 HAY 94544 732-E1
JIM DR
500 SJS 95133 814-H7
JIM ELDER DR
- CMBL 95008 853-C6
JIMINEZ WY
100 HAY 94544 712-C7
JIMNO AV
- PIT 94565 574-D3
JIMS WY
13600 SAR 95070 872-E1
JO DR
100 LGTS 95032 873-D4
JOAN AV
- NVTO 94947 526-B4
3600 CNCD 94521 592-J3
3900 CNCD 94521 593-A3
JOAN CT
1300 CNCD 94521 593-A4
JOAN DR
- AMCN 94589 510-A2
- AMCN 94589 509-J2
1900 AlaC 94578 691-D2
JOAN TER
100 FRMT 94536 732-J7
JOAN WY
1800 SCL 95050 833-C3
5300 LVMR 94550 696-C7
JOANDRA CT
500 SCIC 94024 831-F3
JOANN CT
- WLCK 94596 612-D3
100 VAL 94589 509-J5
JO ANN DR
2700 RCH 94806 589-B1
JOANNA CT
4600 FRMT 94536 752-E3
JOANNE AV
3300 SCIC 95127 814-H6
3400 SJS 95127 814-J6
14800 SCIC 95127 814-J6
JOANNE CIR
3100 PLE 94588 694-C7
JOANNE DR
600 SMTO 94402 749-B3
JOANNE ST
24600 HAY 94544 712-A3
24600 HAY 94544 711-J3
JOAN VISTA
300 CCCo 94803 589-E1
JOAQUIN AV
100 SLN 94577 671-C7
100 SLN 94577 691-A1
JOAQUIN CIR
100 DNVL 94526 653-C7
JOAQUIN CT
- DNVL 94526 653-C7
JOAQUIN DR
100 DNVL 94526 653-C6
500 SSF 94080 707-E2
JOAQUIN RD
- SMCo 94028 830-D4
900 MTVW 94043 811-J1
JOAQUIN MILLER CT
- OAK 94611 650-E2
JOAQUIN MILLER RD
2900 OAK 94602 650-G3
3500 OAK 94619 650-G3
JOAQUIN MURIETA AV
- NWK 94560 772-J2
JO DE CT
3700 CNCD 94519 592-J1
JODIE LN
- CCCo 94803 589-G4
JODY CT
- SMTO 94402 749-B3
JOE DIMAGGIO CT
1400 SJS 95122 834-G7
JOE DIMAGGIO DR
- MRTZ 94553 571-D2
JOEL CT
100 VAL 94591 530-G5
1100 SPAB 94805 589-A4
JOEL WY
1700 LALT 94024 832-A2
JOELLE DR
4800 CNCD 94521 593-D3
JOHANNA AV
600 SUNV 94086 812-G6
JOHANNA CT
2200 PIN 94564 569-F7
JOHANSEN DR
10500 SCIC 95014 852-G2
JOHANSEN PL
- BEN 94510 551-B4
JOHN AV
900 SPAB 94806 568-H7
1100 SPAB 94806 588-H1
JOHN CT
2200 AlaC 94546 691-H6
JOHN DR
6600 CPTO 95014 852-E2
19900 AlaC 94546 691-H5
JOHN ST
- CCCo 94572 549-H7
- SF 94133 648-A4
100 OAK 94611 629-J7
700 PIN 94564 569-F4
JOHN WY
700 LFYT 94549 631-E1
800 CPTO 95014 852-D2
JOHN DALY BLVD
400 DALY 94014 687-A3
500 DALY 94015 687-A3
800 DALY 94015 686-J4
JOHN F FORAN FRWY I-280
- DALY - 687-C2
- DALY - 687-C4
- SF - 668-A6
- SF - 668-B1
- SF - 667-E7
- SF - 687-D2
- SF - 687-E1
JOHN F KENNEDY DR
- SF 94117 667-B1
- SF 94118 667-B1
200 SF - 667-A1
1200 SF - 666-H1
JOHN F SHELLEY DR
- SF 94134 667-H7
- SF 94134 687-H1
JOHN GILDI AV
100 ANT 94509 575-C6
JOHN GLENN CIR
- DALY 94015 707-C3
JOHN GLENN CT
2600 ANT 94509 574-H6
JOHN GLENN DR
- OAK 94621 690-D2
- CCCo 94520 592-D1
2100 CCCo 94520 572-D7
JOHN H JOHNSON PKWY
2200 PIT 94565 574-A4
JOHN KIRK CT
100 CMBL 95008 853-A6
JOHN MAHER ST
- SF 94111 648-B4
JOHN MISE CT
400 SJS 95129 852-J2
JOHN MONTGMRY DR
2500 SJS 95148 835-A6
JOHN MUIR DR
- NWK 94560 772-J1
100 SF 94132 687-A2
100 SMCo 94015 687-A2
600 SF 94132 686-J1
JOHN MUIR RD
4700 MRTZ 94553 571-F7
J MUIR PKWY Rt#-4
- CCCo - 571-A4
- CCCo - 572-A6
- CCCo - 570-C3
- HER - 570-C3
- MRTZ - 572-A6
- MRTZ - 571-G6
1500 HER 94547 569-H3
1800 CCCo 94572 569-H3
1800 CCCo 94572 570-C3
JOHN PAPAN CT
- DALY 94015 707-B2
JOHNS CT
- PLHL 94523 591-J7
2300 ANT 94509 595-G4
JOHNS PL
600 BEN 94510 551-A4
JOHNS WY
2400 ANT 94509 595-G4
JOHNSON AV
- LGTS 95032 893-B1
400 PCFA 94044 707-A4
1000 SJS 95129 852-G3
1500 SAR 95070 852-G3
2800 ALA 94501 670-B3
2900 RCH 94804 608-J1
10200 SCIC 95014 852-H2
JOHNSON CT
3500 FRMT 94555 752-E1
5300 PLE 94588 694-A5
JOHNSON DR
500 RCH 94806 568-G7
1800 ANT 94509 575-A7
1800 CNCD 94520 592-E4
5100 PLE 94588 694-A5
5100 PLE 94588 693-J6
JOHNSON LN
- VAL 94590 529-H3
JOHNSON PL
2400 SCL 95050 833-C6
JOHNSON RD
3300 LFYT 94549 611-G1
4100 HAY 94545 731-D1
JOHNSON ST
300 SAUS 94965 627-B3
700 ALB 94706 609-C6
900 RDWC 94061 770-A7
1000 RDWC 94061 790-A1
1100 MLPK 94025 790-F4
1400 NVTO 94947 526-B5
1500 SLN 94577 690-H2
1800 CCCo 94525 550-C4
JOHNSON HILL CT
- CCCo 94803 589-D2
JOHNSON HOLLOW
100 LGTS 95032 893-B1
JOHNSTON AV
1700 SJS 95125 854-C4
JOHNSTON DR
5900 OAK 94611 630-D7
JOHNSTON LN
- CCCo 94507 632-G6
JOHNSTON RD
5300 CCCo - 654-G7
5300 CCCo 94506 654-G7
JOHNSTONE CT
- MrnC 94903 546-F5
JOHNSTONE DR
- SF 94131 667-E2
200 MrnC 94903 546-E6
JOHN T KNOX FRWY I-580
- ALB - 609-B3
- RCH - 588-C7
- RCH - 608-H1
- RCH - 609-B3
JOICE ST
- SF 94108 648-A5
JOLEEN CT
900 HAY 94544 732-A1
JOLENE CT
12400 SAR 95070 852-H6
JOLIE LN
- WLCK 94596 612-C2
JO LIN CT
- CCCo 94803 589-F3
JOLLY CT
1600 LALT 94024 831-H4
JOLLYMAN DR
1000 CPTO 95014 852-D2
JOLLYMAN LN
10700 CPTO 95014 852-D2
JOMAR DR
5100 CNCD 94521 593-E4
JO MARY CT
24700 AlaC 94541 712-B2
JONATHAN AV
1700 SJS 95125 854-B4
JONATHAN CT
900 CMBL 95008 873-B1
JONATHAN DR
5400 NWK 94560 752-E5
JONATHAN PL
5400 NWK 94560 752-E5
JONATHAN ST
1300 SCL 95050 833-E5
JONATHAN WY
500 UNC 94587 732-G3
JONATHON RIDGE DR
400 DNVL 94506 654-A6
400 DNVL 94506 653-J6
JONES AV
300 OAK 94603 670-G7
700 PIN 94564 569-E4
1700 SCL 95051 833-A3
JONES CT
1000 RDWC 94063 770-E6
JONES LN
- LVMR 94550 695-G7
1600 LALT 94024 832-A5
JONES PL
- SRFL 94901 586-F1
500 WLCK 94596 612-C2
JONES RD
200 LGTS 95032 893-A1
2400 WLCK 94596 612-C2
2400 CCCo 94596 612-C2
JONES ST
- DBLN 94568 694-B3
- SANS 94960 586-B1
- SF 94102 647-J4
300 MRTZ 94553 571-E3
600 BERK 94804 629-D1
800 SF 94109 647-J4
900 SF 94108 647-J4
1100 BERK 94702 629-D1
1500 SF 94133 647-J4
1900 SF 94133 647-J3
1900 SF 94109 647-J3
2600 AlaC 94546 692-B6
JONES WY
- LKSP 94939 586-D6
800 CMBL 95008 853-C7
38500 FRMT 94536 753-D1

STREET — Block City ZIP Pg-Grid

JONESBORO CT
1500 SJS 95131 814-C6
JONES GATE CT
2800 PLE 94566 694-D7
JONESPORT AV
2000 SJS 95131 814-E7
JONESPORT CT
1100 SJS 95131 814-E7
JONQUIL DR
- NWK 94560 772-G1
4300 SJS 95136 874-F1
JOOST AV
- SF 94131 667-E6
400 SF 94127 667-E6
600 SF 94127 667-E6
JOPLIN CT
- CCCo 94549 591-H7
JOPLIN DR
1300 SJS 95118 874-B3
JORDAN AV
- LALT 94022 811-E4
- SANS 94960 566-D6
- SF 94118 647-E6
5600 ELCR 94530 589-C7
JORDAN CT
300 MRTZ 94553 571-E5
JORDAN PL
- PA 94303 791-B4
JORDAN RD
2900 OAK 94602 650-F4
3500 OAK 94619 650-G5
JORDAN ST
- SRFL 94901 586-G1
100 VAL 94591 550-C1
400 VAL 94591 530-C7
JORDAN WY
200 PA 94304 790-G6
200 SCIC 94305 790-G6
600 AlaC 94541 691-G7
2800 PIN 94564 570-A7
JORDAN HEIGHTS DR
15500 LGTS 95032 893-E1
JORGENSEN CT
- PIT 94565 574-C2
JORGENSEN DR
300 PIT 94565 574-C3
JORGENSEN LN
7700 PLE 94588 714-A4
23100 HAY 94541 711-G3
JORN CT
700 SJS 95123 874-G6
JOSCOLO VW
100 CLAY 94517 593-H5
JOSE CT
3200 HAY 94542 712-E4
JOSE LN
100 CCCo 94553 591-E1
JOSEFA CT
- NVTO 94949 546-E4
JOSEFA LN
25700 LAH 94022 831-B2
JOSEFA PL
- MRGA 94556 631-E3
JOSEFA ST
200 SJS 95110 834-A7
300 SJS 95126 834-A7
300 SJS 95126 854-A1
JOSE FIGUERES AV
- SJS 95116 834-G3
JOSEPH AV
600 ANT 94509 575-E5
2700 SJS 95008 873-F1
JOSEPH CIR
20100 CPTO 95014 832-E7
JOSEPH CT
- SRFL 94903 566-E2
JOSEPH DR
700 SSF 94080 707-G2
1800 MRGA 94556 631-G6
2500 CCCo 94507 633-A5
3700 AlaC 94546 692-A3
18300 AlaC 94546 691-J2
JOSEPH LN
5000 SJS 95118 874-A4
5000 SJS 95118 873-J4
5400 CCCo 94506 654-G5
JOSEPH ST
37300 FRMT 94536 752-H4
JOSEPHA AV
- SF 94132 687-B1
JOSEPHINE AV
1900 SJS 95124 873-G1
JOSEPHINE ST
- MLV 94941 606-C3
- SAUS 94965 627-B4
1100 BERK 94707 609-G7
1200 BERK 94703 609-G7
1400 BERK 94703 629-G1
JOSEPH SPECIALE DR
4500 SJS 95136 874-G3
JOSHUA CIR
7300 PLE 94588 714-A1
JOSHUA CT
600 WLCK 94598 592-H7
2700 ANT 94509 595-F5
JOSHUA PL
900 FRMT 94539 773-J6
JOSHUA ST
26500 HAY 94544 712-A5
JOSHUA WY
400 SUNV 94086 832-F1
JOSHUA WOODS PL
3300 CNCD 94518 592-H6
JOSIAH AV
- SF 94112 687-E1
JOSINA AV
600 PA 94306 811-B2
JOSSELYN LN
100 WDSD 94062 789-E6
JOSSLYN DR
7100 SJS 95120 894-H4
JOST LN
1000 ALA 94502 670-A7
JOURNEYSEND
- CCCo 94595 632-D1
JOVAN TER
34700 FRMT 94555 752-D3
JOVITA LN
- CCCo 94803 569-C6
- PIN 94803 569-C6
JOY AV
- BSBN 94005 688-B6
- RCH 94801 588-F5
JOY ST
- SF 94110 668-A5
JOYA CT
600 CCCo 94506 654-A5
JOYA LN
4000 CCCo 94506 654-A5
JOYCE AV
1800 SLN 94577 690-J2
41000 FRMT 94539 753-E6
JOYCE CT
10200 SCIC 95127 835-A3
JOYCE DR
4000 CNCD 94521 593-A3
JOYCE RD
- HIL 94010 748-F5
JOYCE ST
200 LVMR 94550 696-B7
1300 NVTO 94947 526-C5
24600 HAY 94544 712-A3
24600 HAY 94544 711-J3
JOYCE WY
300 MrnC 94941 606-F6
32400 UNC 94587 732-A7
JOYERIN CT
1400 SJS 95131 814-D7
JOYNER CT
1300 SJS 95131 814-D6
J T KNOX FRWY I-580
- RCH - 588-C7
- RCH - 608-H1
JUANA AV
100 SLN 94577 691-B1
E JUANA AV
100 SLN 94577 671-D7
W JUANA AV
100 SLN 94577 691-A1
JUAN BAUTISTA CIR
- SF 94132 687-B1
JUANITA AV
- MLV 94941 606-F4
100 PCFA 94044 727-B2
300 MLBR 94030 727-J2
1100 BURL 94010 728-E5
1600 SJS 95125 854-B4
1600 TBRN 94920 607-E7
1600 TBRN 94920 627-E1
JUANITA CT
- NVTO 94945 525-H1
100 VAL 94590 530-B2
900 CCCo 94803 569-D7
JUANITA DR
400 SCL 95050 833-D6
800 CCCo 94595 611-J7
800 CCCo 94803 569-D7
800 CCCo 94595 612-A6
JUANITA WY
- SF 94127 667-D5
300 LALT 94022 811-C5
1200 CMBL 95008 873-B1
1500 BERK 94702 629-E1
JUARCEYS CT
1500 SJS 95120 874-A7
JUAREZ AV
1600 LALT 94024 831-J4
JUAREZ CT
- SPAB 94806 568-H7
1900 SJS 95132 814-D3
11600 DBLN 94568 693-F3
JUAREZ LN
11700 DBLN 94568 693-F3
JUBILEE CT
- SMCo 94061 790-A3
JUBILEE LN
2400 SJS 95131 814-C4
JUDAH ST
- SF 94122 667-A2
2800 SF 94122 666-H2
JUDD ST
4900 OAK 94601 670-E1
JUDGE HALEY DR
- SRFL 94903 566-F4
JUDIE WY
38800 FRMT 94536 752-J6
JUDITH CT
200 NVTO 94949 546-C1
3000 CCCo 94806 589-B2
3200 LFYT 94549 611-H6
JUDITH LN
3200 LFYT 94549 611-H6
JUDITH PL
1900 CCCo 94521 593-E3
JUDITH ST
5400 SJS 95123 874-J4
JUDITH WY
- LVMR 94550 715-E1
JUDKINS CT
2700 SJS 95148 855-C1
JUDRO WY
3500 SJS 95117 853-C1
JUDSON AV
100 SF 94131 667-E7
100 SF 94112 667-E7
300 SF 94112 667-E7
JUDSON DR
1000 MTVW 94040 811-F5
JUDSON LN
- MrnC 94941 606-H5
JUDSON PL
- PCFA 94044 727-B6
JUDSON ST
1000 BLMT 94002 749-F7
JUDSONVILLE DR
4900 ANT - 595-D4
JUDY AV
10000 SCIC 95014 852-H1
JUDY CT
100 MRTZ 94553 591-H3
100 VAL 94589 510-C5
JUDY LN
1100 CNCD 94520 592-E4
3200 LFYT 94549 611-H7
JUDY ST
18000 AlaC 94546 692-A3
JUERGEN DR
3500 SJS 95121 855-C3
JULES AV
- SF 94112 687-D1
200 SF 94112 667-D7
JULES DR
- NVTO 94947 525-H3
JULIA AV
200 MrnC 94941 606-F6
JULIA CT
- BLMT 94002 749-D7
2300 PIN 94564 569-F7
4400 UNC 94587 731-J6
JULIA ST
- OAK 94618 630-C6
- SF 94103 647-J7
- SRFL 94901 586-F1
1500 BERK 94703 629-F4
28100 HAY 94545 731-G1
JULIAN AV
- SF 94103 667-H2
JULIAN CT
1700 ELCR 94530 609-D1
JULIAN DR
1600 ELCR 94530 589-D7
1600 ELCR 94530 609-C1
E JULIAN ST
- SJS 95112 834-C5
1000 SJS 95116 834-E4
W JULIAN ST
100 SJS 95113 834-A6
100 SJS 95110 834-A6
600 SJS 95126 833-J6
1000 SJS 95126 834-A6
JULIAN WY
100 PLHL 94523 592-B6
JULIANA CT
2000 SCL 95050 833-D6
JULIANNA CT
- MRGA 94556 651-G1
JULIANNE CT
- CCCo 94595 632-C1
JULIE CT
- DNVL 94506 653-G5
1000 SCL 95051 832-J5
1000 CNCD 94518 592-F5
3500 PA 94306 811-B2
4500 RCH 94803 589-E1
JULIE LN
1500 LALT 94024 831-J3
2300 SSF 94080 707-D4
12300 SAR 95070 852-D5
JULIE ST
4800 LVMR 94550 696-B7
JULIE ANN WY
600 OAK 94601 670-D3
600 OAK 94621 670-D3
JULIE HIGHLANDS CT
- CCCo - 591-G5
JULIET AV
800 SJS 95127 835-C2
JULIET CIR
33800 FRMT 94555 752-B2
JULIET CT
1200 CNCD 94521 593-A4
1300 LVMR 94550 716-C1
JULIETA ST
14600 SLN 94578 691-C3
JULIET PARK DR
700 SJS 95127 835-C1
JULIETTA LN
27100 LAH 94022 831-A2
JULIETTE LN
3600 SCL 95054 813-C6
JULI LYNN DR
1200 SJS 95120 874-C7
JULIO AV
2700 SJS 95124 873-J1
JULIUS CT
2000 WLCK 94598 612-F2
JULIUS ST
- SF 94133 648-A3
200 SLN 94577 671-B5
10800 OAK 94605 671-B5
JULPUN LP
600 CLAY 94517 593-H6
JULY DR
100 SJS 95138 875-D4
JUNA CT
19500 SAR 95070 872-F4
JUNCO AV
200 LVMR 94550 695-D7
JUNCTION AV
200 LVMR 94550 695-G7
1700 SJS 95112 834-A1
1700 SJS 95112 814-A7
1700 SJS 95112 813-H6
1800 SJS 95131 813-H6
2000 ELCR 94530 609-B1
2000 ELCR 94530 589-B7
2100 MTVW 94043 811-G2
2500 SJS 95134 813-G4
JUNCTION CT
900 CNCD 94518 592-F6
1700 SJS 95112 834-A1
JUNCTION DR
1900 CNCD 94518 592-F6
JUNE AV
1400 SJS 95122 834-H7
JUNE CT
- AlaC 94541 711-G1
10400 OAK 94603 670-H7
40000 FRMT 94538 753-B7
JUNE DR
100 SJS 95138 875-D4
JUNE LN
- MrnC 94945 526-F2
- NVTO 94945 526-F2
JUNE ST
100 FRMT 94555 752-C1
JUNE WY
14000 SAR 95070 872-E2
JUNEAU ST
1900 SLN 94577 690-G3
JUNEAU WY
- SJS 95131 814-B6
JUNEBERRY CT
100 SJS 95136 874-H1
4400 CNCD 94521 593-C5
JUNE MARIE CT
1800 AlaC 94541 712-B2
JUNESONG WY
900 SJS 95133 834-E1
1100 SJS 95131 834-E1
JUNEWOOD AV
1800 SJS 95132 814-D3
JUNEWOOD CT
- DNVL 94526 653-C6
JUNGFRAU CT
800 MPS 95035 814-D1
JUNIOR TER
- SF 94112 687-F1
JUNIPER
- BEN 94510 551-C6
JUNIPER AV
200 SSF 94080 708-A2
200 SSF 94080 707-J2
1600 SBRN 94066 707-G7
8000 NWK 94560 772-C1
JUNIPER CT
100 HER 94547 569-J4
400 SUNV 94086 832-G1
900 CCCo 94525 550-D5
JUNIPER DR
- ATN 94027 790-G1
- LFYT 94549 611-A6
- SRMN 94583 693-H1
- ORIN 94563 611-A6
3700 CNCD 94519 593-A1
3800 CNCD 94519 573-B7
JUNIPER LN
- WLCK 94596 612-C3
14100 SAR 95070 872-E2
JUNIPER PL
800 NVTO 94945 525-E1
JUNIPER ST
- SF 94103 667-J1
1000 LVMR 94550 695-F7
2800 SMTO 94403 749-B5
3500 AlaC 94546 692-A6
14200 SLN 94579 690-J4
14300 SLN 94579 691-A5
JUNIPER WY
- MRGA 94556 651-D1
JUNIPERBERRY DR
2200 MrnC 94903 546-D7
JUNIPERO AV
- RDWC 94061 789-J1
1200 RDWC 94061 790-A1
JUNIPERO COM
200 FRMT 94536 733-B7
JUNIPERO DR
100 MPS 95035 813-J1
600 PLE 94566 714-D5
JUNIPERO ST
- AlaC 94566 714-D5
- PLE 94566 714-D5
JUNIPERO WY
19600 SAR 95070 852-F6
JUNIPERO SERRA AV
- SRFL 94901 567-A7
JUNIPERO SERRA BLVD
- SF 94127 667-C7
- SF 94132 667-C7
400 SSF 94080 707-C1
900 SF 94132 687-C1
1800 DALY 94014 687-C6
2300 DALY 94015 687-C6
3700 CLMA 94014 687-C6
4200 DALY 94015 707-D1
5000 CLMA 94014 707-C1
JUNIPERO SERRA BLVD Rt#-1
- SF 94132 687-C4
JUNIPERO SERRA BLVD Rt#-G5
- MLPK 94025 790-F7
- SCIC 94305 790-F7
- SCIC 94304 790-F7
100 SCIC 94304 810-G1
100 SCIC 94305 810-G1
JUNIPERO SERRA FRWY I-280
- DALY - 687-C7
- DALY - 687-C7
- DALY - 707-C2
- HIL - 748-D4
- HIL - 748-D4
- LAH - 811-A7
- LAH - 810-F3
- LAH - 831-G5
- LALT - 831-G5
- MLBR - 728-A7
- MLBR - 727-G3
- MLPK - 810-C1
- PA - 810-F3
- SBRN - 707-C2
- SBRN - 727-G3
- SCL - 832-C6
- SCL - 852-H1
- SCIC - 810-F3
- SCIC - 832-C6
- SCIC - 831-G5
- SJS - 853-A1
- SJS - 852-H1
- SMCo - 728-A7
- SMCo - 728-A7
- SMCo - 727-G3
- SMCo - 727-G3
- SMCo - 748-D4
- SMCo - 748-D4
- SMCo - 769-A4
- SMCo - 768-F1
- SMCo - 768-F1
- SMCo - 768-F1
- SMCo - 789-D1
- SMCo - 789-D1
- SMCo - 790-A6
- SMCo - 810-C1
- SSF - 707-C2
- SUNV - 832-C6
- WDSD - 789-G4
- WDSD - 790-A6
- CPTO - 832-C6
JUNIPERO SERRA FRWY Rt#-1
- DALY - 687-C3
- DALY - 687-C3
- SF - 687-C3
JUNIPERO SERRA LN
4300 SJS 95129 853-A1
JUNO LN
800 FCTY 94404 749-F4
JUNO RD
- TBRN 94920 607-B4
JUPITER CT
- UNC 94587 732-B6
600 FRMT 94539 793-J1
800 FCTY 94404 749-E3
1400 MPS 95035 794-D6
JUPITER DR
1500 MPS 95035 794-D6
JUPITER ST
28600 HAY 94544 712-B7
JUPITER WY
1500 MPS 95035 794-D6
JURA WY
700 SUNV 94087 832-F5
JURGENS DR
200 MPS 95035 793-J4
JURI ST
- SF 94110 667-H4
JURY CT
800 SJS 95112 834-B1
JUSTCO LN
21000 AlaC 94552 692-C5
JUSTIN CIR
- ALA 94502 669-J5
JUSTIN CT
100 VAL 94591 530-E3
JUSTIN DR
- SF 94112 667-H6
JUSTIN PL
3600 ANT 94509 595-B1
JUSTIN TER
5000 FRMT 94555 752-A3
JUSTIN WY
3000 CNCD 94520 572-F6
JUSTINE CT
- LVMR 94550 696-D7
JUSTINE DR
3600 SJS 95124 873-H2
JUSTO CT
100 CMBL 95008 853-D7
JUTLAND AV
15400 SLN 94579 691-B7

K

K RD
- SUNV 94089 812-H3
K ST
- OAK 94625 649-A4
- VAL 94592 529-F3
- SRFL 94901 566-E7
100 BEN 94510 551-A4
200 ANT 94509 575-C4
400 MRTZ 94553 571-E6
900 BEN 94510 550-J3
N K ST
100 LVMR 94550 695-G7
100 LVMR 94550 715-G1
S K ST
100 LVMR 94550 715-G1
KACHINA CT
1000 FRMT 94539 774-A5
1000 FRMT 94539 773-J5
KADEN CT
- NVTO 94947 526-C6
KADEN DR
- NVTO 94947 526-C6
KADI CT
44500 FRMT 94539 773-H3
KAEHLER ST
1200 NVTO 94945 526-B2
KAHALA CT
13300 SAR 95070 852-E7
KAHLERT ST
21200 AlaC 94546 691-J6
KAHLUA CT
39500 FRMT 94538 753-A7
KAHRS AV
400 PLHL 94523 592-B6
KAIBAB CT
800 FRMT 94536 753-D1
KAIMU DR
100 CCCo 94553 572-C7
KAINS AV
100 SBRN 94066 707-G7
400 ALB 94706 609-D6
1100 BERK 94706 609-D6
1400 BERK 94702 609-D6
1400 BERK 94702 629-E1
KAISER DR
3000 SCL 95051 833-A5
6400 FRMT 94555 752-A4
KAISER PZ
2100 OAK 94612 649-H3
KAISER RD
- SCIC 94035 812-B3
KAISER CREEK RD
- AlaC 94546 652-A6
- AlaC 94546 651-H6
- AlaC 94546 671-H1
- CCCo - 652-A6
KAISER QUARRY RD
- CCCo - 613-E1
1100 CCCo - 593-F7
1100 CCCo 94521 593-F7
1100 CNCD 94521 593-F7
KAITLIN PL
3800 CNCD 94518 592-J4
KAITLYN LN
200 CCCo 94506 654-C5
KALAMA RD
- ANT 94509 595-D1
KALENDA COM
2100 FRMT 94539 753-E6
KALES AV
5400 OAK 94618 629-J6
5400 OAK 94618 630-A5
KALIMA PL
1100 CNCD 94521 593-F7
KALISPELL CT
1600 SUNV 94087 832-B5
KALLIAM DR
2800 SCL 95051 833-B7
KALMIA ST
1400 SMTO 94402 749-A3
KALTHOFF COM
- AlaC 94550 715-D7
- LVMR 94550 715-D7
KAMIAH WY
900 SUNV 94087 832-B5
KAMMERER AV
1700 SJS 95116 834-G5
KAMMERER CT
- HIL 94010 728-F7
KAMP CT
2200 PLE 94588 694-F7
KAMP DR
3400 PLE 94588 714-F1
3400 PLE 94566 714-F1
3500 PLE 94588 694-E7
KAMSACK DR
1600 SUNV 94087 832-B5
KAMSON WY
200 CMBL 95008 853-D5
KANDICE CT
- SJS 95123 874-F7
KANDLE WY
1100 RDWC 94061 790-B1
KANE CIR
800 WLCK 94598 612-G1
KANE CT
1300 SJS 95121 854-J3
4600 FRMT 94538 753-B7
19800 SAR 95070 852-F6
KANE DR
12600 SAR 95070 852-F6
KANEKO DR
6500 SJS 95119 875-D7
KANGAROO WY
2200 ANT 94509 595-H3
KANSAS CIR
1200 CNCD 94521 593-E6
KANSAS ST
100 SF 94103 668-A1
400 SF 94107 668-A3
1600 RDWC 94061 790-A2
1600 SF 94124 668-A4
1600 SF 94124 668-A4
3000 OAK 94602 650-E5
3500 OAK 94619 650-F6
KANSAS WY
100 FRMT 94539 793-J2
KANSAS CITY
3000 ALA 94501 649-F6
KAPHAN AV
4600 OAK 94619 650-G6
KAPIOLANI RD
3100 OAK 94613 650-G7
KAPLAN LN
- SF 94103 648-B6
KAPPA AV
1700 SLN 94579 691-A6
KARA RD
- ALA 94502 669-J5
KARA WY
900 CMBL 95008 853-B7
900 CMBL 95008 873-B1
KARAMEOS CT
1700 SUNV 94087 832-B6
KARAMEOS DR
1700 SUNV 94087 832-B6
KAREN CT
- BURL 94010 728-B5
- SF 94134 668-A7
- WLCK 94598 612-D4
- VAL 94590 550-C2
100 UNC 94587 752-A1
200 LGTS 95032 873-D7
1700 SJS 95124 873-H1
KAREN DR
400 BEN 94510 551-A4
2300 SCL 95050 833-C5
KAREN LN
- WLCK 94598 612-D4
100 CCCo 94553 571-J4
KAREN RD
- SMCo 94002 749-F7
- SMCo 94002 769-F1
1100 CCCo 94806 569-A5
KAREN WY
100 ATN 94027 790-B5
200 TBRN 94920 606-J3
300 TBRN 94920 607-A4
400 LVMR 94550 715-E1
1000 MTVW 94040 811-F5
3300 PIT 94565 574-D4
KARIE ANN WY
1200 SJS 95118 874-C1
KARINA CT
- SJS 95131 833-H1
KARINA WY
1300 SCL 95051 832-H4
KARKIN PL
- CLAY 94517 593-H6
KARL AV
- SANS 94960 566-B7
14700 LGTS 95030 873-A4
14700 MSER 95030 873-A4
KARL ST
1100 SJS 95122 834-J5
KARLA CT
400 NVTO 94949 546-D1
KARLSTAD DR
1000 SUNV 94089 812-G4
KARMEN CT
1300 SCL 95051 832-H4
KARN CIR
19900 SAR 95070 852-E6
KARN DR
28100 HAY 94544 712-A7
28100 HAY 94544 732-A1
KARO CT
800 SUNV 94086 832-F2
KAROL LN
- PLHL 94523 592-A6
KAROL WY
900 SLN 94577 671-A7
KARREN ST
2100 CNCD 94520 572-F7
KARRY LN
- PLHL 94523 592-C6
KASBA ST
1600 CNCD 94518 592-E6
KASKI CT
4100 CNCD 94518 592-J5
6100 SJS 95123 874-G6
KASKI LN
1000 CNCD 94518 592-J5
1100 CNCD 94518 593-A4
KASPER TER
34100 FRMT 94555 752-A3
KASSON CT
1300 SJS 95121 854-J2
KATAOKA CT
- SMCo 94062 789-G1
KATE ST
- SF 94103 668-A1
KATHERINE AV
500 RDWC 94062 769-J7
KATHERINE CT
900 SJS 95126 833-G6
KATHERINE LN
1000 LFYT 94549 611-H6
KATHLEAN ST
41000 FRMT 94538 753-C7
41000 FRMT 94538 773-C1
KATHLEEN AV
4800 AlaC 94546 692-B4
KATHLEEN CT
- PCFA 94044 727-B4
KATHLEEN DR
- NVTO 94947 525-F2
200 PLHL 94523 592-B4
KATHLEEN ST
3000 SJS 95124 873-G2
KATHRYN CT
4800 FRMT 94536 752-J6
KATHRYN DR
- PLHL 94523 592-C5
KATHRYNE AV
700 SMTO 94401 749-B1
KATHY CT
- NVTO 94949 546-B1
100 LGTS 95030 872-J3
100 UNC 94587 732-E3
1300 LVMR 94550 716-C1
KATHY LN
- MRTZ 94553 591-G3
1500 LALT 94024 831-J3
17200 LGTS 95032 893-E2
KATHY WY
1100 MTVW 94022 811-G6
1100 MTVW 94040 811-G6
5100 LVMR 94550 716-C1
KATHY ELLEN CT
100 VAL 94591 530-D2
KATHY ELLEN DR
100 VAL 94591 530-D3
KATIE CT
- PLHL 94523 592-C6
1100 MTVW 94040 811-J7
KATIE LN
4200 PLE 94588 694-E7
KATLAS CT
- NVTO 94945 525-J2
KATO RD
46800 FRMT 94538 773-E4
47600 FRMT 94538 793-G1
48700 FRMT 94539 793-H3
KATON CT
700 SUNV 94086 832-F2
KATRINA CT
- ORIN 94563 610-G3
5200 AlaC 94546 692-C3
KATRINA ST
700 LVMR 94550 696-C7
KATRINA WY
2500 MTVW 94040 832-A2
KATRINE CT
1000 SUNV 94087 832-G5
KAUAI CIR
300 UNC 94587 732-C6
KAUAI CT
300 SRMN 94583 653-E7
KAUAI DR
3700 SJS 95111 855-A6
KAUFFMANN CT
400 SSF 94080 708-C3
KAUFMANN CT
700 SJS 95116 834-E6
KAURI CT
3900 CNCD 94521 593-A3
KAVALA CT
6100 PLE 94566 714-D6
KAVANAGH RD
2500 CCCo 94806 569-B5
KAVANAUGH DR
1300 MLPK 94025 771-B7
1300 EPA 94303 771-B7
KAVANAUGH WY
200 PCFA 94044 707-B3
KAVENY DR
5400 SJS 95129 852-H4
KAVIN LN
15400 MSER 95030 873-A5
15700 LGTS 95030 873-A5
KAVON CT
- NVTO 94947 526-D6
KAWAI LN
- PLHL 94523 591-J3
KAWALKER LN
3100 SJS 95127 814-H6
KAWELLA CIR
400 UNC 94587 732-D5
KAY AV
2700 CNCD 94520 572-E7
24700 HAY 94545 711-G5
KAY CT
- FRMT 94538 773-E1
KAY DR
- VAL 94590 550-C2
1800 SJS 95124 873-G6
1900 LALT 94024 831-J5
2300 SCL 95050 833-C4
KAYAK DR
100 SJS 95111 875-B2
KAY ANN CT
500 CCCo 94803 589-F3
KAYBE CT
200 SJS 95139 895-F1
KAYELLEN CT
1100 SJS 95125 854-E5
KAYLA CT
2300 SJS 95124 853-G7
KAYLENE CT
1200 SJS 95127 835-B3
KAYLENE DR
3400 SJS 95127 835-B3
KAYNYNE ST
800 RDWC 94063 770-C6
800 SMCo 94063 770-C6
KAYSER CT
- CCCo 94596 612-E7
KAYWOOD DR
1700 CNCD 94521 593-C2

STREET
Block City ZIP Pg-Grid

KAZAR CT
- MRGA 94556 651-E2
KEAN AV
500 ANT 94509 575-E6
KEARNEY AV
2800 SCL 95051 833-A2
5000 OAK 94602 650-F3
KEARNEY ST
- SSF 94080 707-H1
200 SJS 95110 834-A7
400 ELCR 94530 609-B1
1200 RCH 94801 588-G5
3000 FRMT 94538 753-B5
KEARNY ST
- SF 94108 648-A5
300 SF 94104 648-A5
600 SF 94111 648-A5
900 SF 94133 648-A5
1200 SF 94133 648-A3
KEARNY TER
800 SUNV 94086 812-D7
KEARSARGE CT
4300 CNCD 94518 593-A6
KEATON LP
3300 SJS 95121 855-D2
KEATS AV
700 SSF 94080 707-D2
KEATS CIR
200 PLHL 94523 592-B7
KEATS CT
600 PA 94306 811-F2
3600 SCIC 95127 834-J1
KEATS DR
- MLV 94941 606-G4
300 VAL 94591 530-F6
KEATS LN
1000 HAY 94544 712-A7
KEATS ST
3100 FRMT 94536 753-A4
KEB RD
- OAK 94605 651-B7
KEBET RIDGE RD
- SMCo 94062 809-F5
KEDITH ST
1000 BLMT 94002 749-F7
KEEBLE AV
- SJS 95126 833-J7
KEEFE CT
100 SBRN 94066 727-G1
KEEFER CT
- PDMT 94610 650-A1
KEEL CT
- SRFL 94903 566-F2
100 PIT 94565 574-A2
KEEL LN
400 RDWC 94065 749-H6
KEEL WY
- OAK 94607 649-B4
- OAK 94625 649-B4
KEELER AV
700 BERK 94708 609-H5
KEELER CT
200 SJS 95139 895-F2
5200 FRMT 94536 752-G6
KEELSON CIR
500 RDWC 94065 749-J6
KEENA LN
- NVTO 94947 525-J4
KEENAN WY
1300 SJS 95125 853-G4
KEENE DR
5200 SJS 95124 873-F5
KEESLING AV
1500 SJS 95125 853-J5
1800 SCIC 95125 853-H5
KEEVER CT
- SJS 95127 834-J2
KEEWAYDIN CT
700 SJS 95111 855-A7
KEHOE AV
1200 SMTO 94401 749-C1
1800 SMTO 94403 749-D1
KEHOE CT
100 SJS 95136 874-J2
KEIL BAY
100 ALA 94502 669-J6
KEITH AV
300 PCFA 94044 727-B2
1000 BERK 94708 609-H6
3000 AlaC 94546 691-H4
5800 OAK 94618 630-A5
KEITH CT
600 WLCK 94596 612-A2
KEITH DR
- ORIN 94563 631-B2
1100 CNCD 94518 592-J5
1500 SJS 95008 853-B7
3000 RCH 94803 589-E2
4100 CMBL 95008 853-A7
KEITH LN
800 SCL 95054 813-E6
KEITH PTH
- RCH 94803 589-E1
KEITH ST
- SF 94124 668-C6
- SF 94124 688-B1
KELDON CT
1000 SJS 95121 854-H2
KELDON DR
1000 SJS 95121 854-H3
KELEZ CT
6200 SJS 95120 874-D7
KELEZ DR
1100 SJS 95120 874-D7
KELL COM
500 FRMT 94539 753-H5
KELL CT
100 CCCo 94595 632-D2
KELL WY
- SJS 95136 854-C7
KELLER AV
1500 AlaC 94580 711-B2
3700 OAK 94605 671-B1
3800 OAK 94627 671-B1
KELLER CT
3300 SCL 95054 813-E7
KELLER DR
500 MTVW 94043 812-A3
KELLER ST
3200 SCL 95054 813-E7
KELLER RIDGE DR
4500 CLAY 94517 593-J5

KELLER RIDGE DR
4800 CLAY 94517 594-A5
KELLEY AV
2500 SPAB 94806 588-H2
KELLEY CT
900 LFYT 94549 611-J6
2100 PIT 94565 574-F4
KELLIE ANN CT
- CCCo 94549 591-J7
- ORIN 94563 631-A1
KELLOCH AV
- SF 94134 687-J2
KELLOGG AV
100 PA 94301 791-A6
700 HAY 94544 712-C6
KELLOGG WY
- SCL 95051 833-A7
KELLY AV
600 MRTZ 94553 571-F5
600 CCCo 94553 571-F5
1200 SLN 94577 690-H2
KELLY CT
1200 PIN 94564 569-D5
1400 SJS 95116 834-F5
KELLY DR
1000 SJS 95129 852-J3
E KELLY DR
100 NVTO 94949 546-G4
W KELLY DR
100 NVTO 94949 546-G4
KELLY LN
- MLBR 94030 728-A5
100 DNVL 94526 653-B4
KELLY ST
- MLPK 94025 771-A7
1700 SMTO 94403 749-D2
2100 AlaC 94541 692-C7
2100 HAY 94541 692-C7
2500 LVMR 94550 695-H7
40000 FRMT 94538 753-C5
KELLY WY
500 PA 94306 811-D3
KELLYN CT
- BEN 94510 551-C1
KELOBRA CT
100 WLCK 94598 612-J1
KELOK WY
- CLAY 94517 594-A5
- CLAY 94517 593-J6
KELOWNA CT
1400 SUNV 94087 832-B4
KELROSE CT
5500 CNCD 94521 593-F6
KELSEY CT
- CCCo 94565 573-C1
- PLHL 94523 592-A6
KELSEY DR
1100 SUNV 94087 832-B3
KELSEY ST
1200 RCH 94801 588-F4
2800 BERK 94705 629-J3
KELSO CT
3600 SCIC 95127 834-J1
KELSO ST
4600 UNC 94587 752-B1
KELTNER AV
900 SJS 95117 853-C3
KELTON AV
100 SCAR 94070 769-H5
KELTON CT
- OAK 94611 649-J1
- SMTO 94403 749-B7
3600 SCIC 95127 834-J1
KELVIN CT
900 CCCo 94803 569-D7
KELVIN RD
600 CCCo 94803 569-D7
KELVINGTON CT
4000 SJS 95121 855-A5
KEMLINE CT
- CCCo 94507 632-G6
KEMP AV
- SANS 94960 566-B7
KEMP CT
- CCCo 94507 632-H3
KEMP LN
- CCCo 94507 632-J4
100 AMCN 94589 510-A4
KEMP WY
100 AMCN 94589 509-J4
KEMPER CT
7900 PLE 94588 714-B5
KEMPER RD
3000 FRMT 94536 752-H2
KEMPER ST
100 VAL 94589 510-C6
KEMPTON AV
- SF 94132 687-C2
3200 OAK 94611 649-H2
KEMPTON WY
3500 OAK 94611 649-J1
3500 OAK 94610 649-J1
KEN CIR
200 CMBL 95008 853-D5
KEN CT
100 VAL 94591 530-F3
KENBAR RD
10200 SCIC 94024 831-F5
KENBRIDGE CT
1000 SUNV 94087 832-B2
KENBROOK CIR
- SJS 95111 854-G6
KENDALL AV
- CCCo 94525 550-C5
500 PA 94306 811-B2
KENDALL CT
- PCFA 94044 727-B4
1100 SJS 95120 894-G1
1200 CCCo 94595 612-A6
4800 MRTZ 94553 571-G7
KENDALL DR
- SF 94129 647-E4
KENDALL LN
- DNVL 94526 632-H7
KENDALL RD
100 CCCo 94595 612-A6
KENDALL WY
600 AlaC 94541 691-F6
KENDELL CT
- SAUS 94965 626-J2
KENDLE ST
22200 CPTO 95014 832-A7

KENDON LN
700 NVTO 94947 525-H3
KENDRA LN
25800 AlaC 94541 712-E2
25900 AlaC 94542 712-E2
KENDRA WY
3600 SJS 95130 853-C4
KENDREE ST
2000 ANT 94509 574-J6
KENDRICK AV
- SANS 94960 566-A4
KENDRICK CIR
2600 SJS 95121 854-H3
KENELAND WY
3800 PLE 94588 694-F5
KENESTA WY
2300 SJS 95122 855-A1
KENHILL DR
3100 SJS 95111 854-G6
KENILWORTH AV
200 SLN 94577 671-B6
6700 ELCR 94530 609-C1
KENILWORTH CT
- CCCo 94707 609-F4
- NVTO 94945 526-F2
500 SUNV 94087 832-E5
900 WLCK 94596 632-F1
KENILWORTH DR
- CCCo 94708 609-F2
KENILWORTH RD
1200 HIL 94010 748-F3
7000 OAK 94705 630-C3
KENILWORTH WY
10200 SCIC 95127 835-A3
KENISTON AV
300 MPS 95035 793-J7
KENITA WY
32500 UNC 94587 732-C5
KENLAND WY
3100 SJS 95111 854-G6
KENLAR DR
4900 SJS 95124 873-G4
KENLEY WY
700 SUNV 94087 832-F5
KENMAR CT
1100 SJS 95132 814-F5
KENMAR WY
- BURL 94010 728-C7
KENMARE CT
500 PIN 94806 569-C5
KENMORE AV
300 SUNV 94086 832-F1
500 OAK 94610 650-A2
KENMORE CT
- ORIN 94563 630-J4
1000 CPTO 95014 852-C2
3700 AlaC 94546 692-A5
KENMORE DR
5000 CNCD 94521 593-D4
KENMORE WY
100 WDSD 94062 789-J5
KENNARD WY
900 SUNV 94087 832-G5
KENNEDY AV
- CMBL 95008 853-E6
2000 SJS 95122 834-H5
2300 UNC 94587 732-G7
KENNEDY CT
200 LGTS 95032 893-D1
KENNEDY DR
1300 MPS 95035 794-C5
KENNEDY PL
- MLBR 94030 727-J4
KENNEDY RD
14900 SCIC 95032 893-G1
15200 LGTS 95032 893-D1
16200 LGTS 95032 873-D7
16600 SCIC 95032 873-C7
S KENNEDY RD
16000 LGTS 95032 873-C7
16100 LGTS 95032 893-C1
KENNEDY ST
300 OAK 94606 670-A1
400 OAK 94606 650-A7
2600 LVMR 94550 695-H7
KENNEDY WY
2400 ANT 94509 574-H5
3800 CCCo 94553 571-H4
KENNEDY KNOLLS LN
100 LGTS 95032 873-D7
KENNET ST
31800 HAY 94544 732-E3
KENNETH AV
400 CMBL 95008 853-C7
700 CMBL 95008 873-C1
KENNETH CT
- CCCo 94565 573-F1
KENNETH DR
- MRGA 94556 631-D3
3300 PA 94303 791-E6
KENNETH RD
- CNCD 94521 593-C5
KENNETH ST
2900 SCL 95054 813-D7
KENNEWICK CT
800 SUNV 94087 832-C5
KENNEWICK DR
1500 SUNV 94087 832-C5
KENNEY CT
400 SUNV 94086 832-E1
KENNEY DR
2500 CCCo 94806 569-B6
KENNISON CT
100 VAL 94589 509-J5
KENNY AL
- SF 94112 687-F1
KENNY LN
10100 SCIC 95127 835-C1
KENOGA DR
2400 SJS 95121 854-H2
KENOSHA AV
19500 SAR 95070 872-F2
KENPARK CT
1800 SJS 95124 853-G7
KENRY WY
2200 SSF 94080 707-E5
KENSINGTON AV
400 SBRN 94066 727-J1
1100 SCL 95051 832-H5
1100 SUNV 94087 832-H5
1600 LALT 94024 831-H4
6300 CCCo 94805 589-C6

KENSINGTON CIR
1500 LALT 94024 831-H3
KENSINGTON COM
34200 FRMT 94555 752-C2
KENSINGTON CT
- SANS 94960 586-B1
700 CCCo 94708 609-F2
2300 CCCo 94507 632-J5
2400 ANT 94509 595-A2
4100 CNCD 94521 593-A4
KENSINGTON DR
800 FRMT 94539 753-F5
4000 CNCD 94521 593-A4
KENSINGTON RD
- CCCo 94708 609-F2
- RDWC 94061 790-A3
- SANS 94960 586-B1
800 CCCo 94805 609-F2
800 ELCR 94530 609-F2
2700 RDWC 94061 789-J3
28900 HAY 94544 732-A1
KENSINGTON WY
- SF 94127 667-D5
100 SJS 95124 873-G6
100 LGTS 95032 873-G6
300 AMCN 94589 509-J3
KENSINGTON PARK CT
400 SJS 95136 874-F1
KENSINGTON PARK RD
- CCCo 94708 609-F3
KENSON DR
4900 SJS 95124 873-G4
KENSTON CT
- CLAY 94517 593-G7
KENSTON DR
900 CLAY 94517 593-G7
KENT AV
- FRFX 94930 566-A6
- MrnC 94904 586-D3
700 SCAR 94070 769-D5
1100 SUNV 94087 832-H5
16300 AlaC 94578 691-F6
16300 AlaC 94580 691-F6
KENT CT
- DALY 94015 707-B1
- MRGA 94556 631-F5
- SJS 95139 875-G7
- SMTO 94403 749-C4
100 SBRN 94066 727-F1
400 LVMR 94550 695-E6
900 AlaC 94580 691-F6
8300 ELCR 94530 609-D1
KENT DR
1900 LALT 94024 831-H5
8300 ELCR 94530 609-D1
KENT LN
- MrnC 94904 586-D4
KENT PL
- MLPK 94025 790-H3
- PA 94301 791-B4
200 AMCN 94589 509-J3
200 SRMN 94583 693-G1
KENT RD
- OAK 94705 630-C4
100 PCFA 94044 726-G4
KENT ST
- SF 94133 647-J4
2200 SMTO 94403 749-C4
KENT WY
- AMCN 94589 509-J3
- MrnC 94965 606-B3
1500 CNCD 94521 593-D4
3800 SSF 94080 707-D4
7500 SRMN 94583 693-G1
KENTDALE LN
- MrnC 94904 586-E3
KENTFIELD AV
1300 RDWC 94061 790-A1
KENTFIELD COM
4700 FRMT 94555 752-D2
KENTFIELD CT
- CCCo 94507 632-J2
100 MRTZ 94553 571-J7
KENTFIELD DR
5200 SJS 95124 873-G5
5300 LGTS 95032 873-G5
KENTFIELD LN
18600 AlaC 94541 711-E1
KENTMERE CT
400 MTVW 94040 812-A7
KENTON AV
- SCAR 94070 769-E3
KENTON CT
700 PLHL 94523 591-J3
2200 WLCK 94596 632-F2
3700 SJS 95136 874-D1
KENTON LN
3800 SJS 95136 874-D1
KENTRIDGE DR
2900 SCIC 95133 834-H1
KENTUCKY AV
400 BERK 94707 609-G4
500 SMTO 94402 748-H3
KENTUCKY DR
1200 CNCD 94521 593-E6
KENTUCKY PL
- SJS 95116 834-F4
KENTUCKY ST
- VAL 94590 529-H4
700 VAL 94590 530-A4
1600 RDWC 94061 790-A2
KENTWOOD AV
1000 CPTO 95014 852-D3
1200 SJS 95129 852-D3
KENTWOOD CT
4100 OAK 94605 671-B2
KENTWOOD LN
1100 AlaC 94578 691-F6
KENTWOOD WY
7800 PLE 94588 693-H7
KENTWORTH WY
2600 SCL 95051 833-B1
KENWAL RD
1000 CNCD 94521 593-E6
KENWOOD AV
2200 SJS 95128 833-E6
2400 SCL 95128 833-E6
3600 SMTO 94403 749-B6
KENWOOD CT
100 NVTO 94945 526-C3
KENWOOD DR
500 MLPK 94025 790-G4

KENWOOD DR
1800 CNCD 94519 573-A7
34200 FRMT 94555 752-C2
KENWOOD ST
4800 UNC 94587 752-B1
KENWOOD WY
- SF 94112 667-D7
- SF 94127 667-D7
200 SSF 94080 707-G5
KENWYN RD
500 OAK 94606 650-A4
500 OAK 94610 650-A4
KENYON AV
- CCCo 94708 609-F3
800 SLN 94577 691-C1
KENYON CT
3600 SCIC 95127 834-J1
18000 SAR 95070 852-D5
KENYON DR
3300 SCL 95051 832-J6
KENYON WY
100 VAL 94589 510-D5
KENZO CT
3300 MTVW 94040 831-J2
KEONCREST AV
1200 SJS 95110 833-J2
KEONCREST DR
500 SSF 94080 707-E2
1400 BERK 94702 609-F7
1400 BERK 94702 629-F1
KEPNER CT
500 ANT 94509 595-E1
KEPPLER AV
- DBLN 94568 694-C4
KEPPLER CT
2700 SJS 95148 855-B1
KEPPLER DR
2500 SJS 95148 855-B1
KERLEY DR
1400 SJS 95112 833-J2
KERLIN ST
38400 FRMT 94536 752-J5
KERMAN DR
100 CNCD 94518 592-H3
KERMATH DR
3100 SJS 95132 814-D3
KERN AV
1100 SUNV 94086 812-H6
2700 SJS 95121 854-J3
KERN CT
900 LVMR 94550 695-F6
1200 MTVW 94040 832-A1
3900 PLE 94588 694-A7
3900 PLE 94588 714-A1
KERN LP
1700 FRMT 94539 794-A2
KERN ST
100 SF 94131 667-G6
600 ELCR 94530 589-B6
600 RCH 94805 589-B5
4100 ANT 94509 595-J1
KERNBERRY DR
500 MrnC 94903 546-D7
KERNER BLVD
2300 SRFL 94901 587-A3
3000 SRFL 94901 586-J2
KERR AV
- CCCo 94707 609-F2
KERR ST
2700 AlaC 94546 691-J6
3100 AlaC 94546 692-A5
KERRI CT
100 SMCo 94061 790-A4
KERRI ANN DR
1000 MRTZ 94553 571-H6
KERRIGAN DR
11000 OAK 94605 671-D5
KERRISON LN
- CCCo 94549 611-H2
KERRY AV
1000 SUNV 94087 832-H5
KERRY COM
100 FRMT 94536 732-J7
KERRY CT
- CCCo 94806 569-C5
800 BEN 94510 530-J6
KERRY DR
100 SCL 95050 833-D7
KERRYSHIRE LN
2600 SCL 95051 833-C1
KERSTEN DR
3400 SJS 95124 873-H2
KERWIN AV
100 OAK 94603 670-G7
KERWIN RANCH CT
19200 SAR 95070 872-G1
KERWOOD CT
3600 SCIC 95127 834-J1
KESEY LN
2700 SJS 95132 814-D4
KESSERLING RD
3800 LFYT 94549 611-D4
KESTER DR
10800 CPTO 95014 852-A2
KESTERSON
15000 SLN 94579 691-C6
KESTREL CT
- BSBN 94005 687-J5
KESTREL PL
3300 FRMT 94555 732-D7
KESWICK CT
- OAK 94611 650-F1
- VAL 94591 530-F3
3600 SCIC 95127 834-J1
KESWICK LN
400 SMTO 94402 749-B3
1900 CNCD 94518 592-F6
KETCH CT
100 FCTY 94404 749-G4
800 CCCo 94572 569-J2
KETCH DR
800 CCCo 94572 569-J2
KETCH PL
900 SJS 95133 814-E7
KETCHUM DR
200 SJS 95127 834-H2
KETELSEN DR
- MRGA 94556 651-E1
KETTERING CT
3400 SMTO 94403 749-A6
KETTERING TER
4000 FRMT 94536 752-H1

KETTLE CT
6600 SJS 95120 894-E1
KETTLE ROCK CT
1900 ANT 94509 595-F4
KETTMANN RD
3300 SJS 95121 855-D3
3500 SCIC 95121 855-D3
KEVILLE TER
- CMAD 94925 586-E7
100 LKSP 94939 586-E7
KEVILLE TR
- CMAD 94925 606-E1
100 LKSP 94939 606-E1
KEVIN CT
- PLHL 94523 592-B6
- WLCK 94596 612-F6
100 VAL 94589 510-D5
400 SRMN 94583 673-F5
600 OAK 94621 670-E3
3200 PLE 94588 714-B1
5000 AlaC 94546 692-B3
KEVIN DR
- CCCo 94565 573-F1
1600 SJS 95124 873-J6
KEVIN PL
3500 CNCD 94519 593-A1
3500 CNCD 94519 592-J1
KEVIN RD
2500 CCCo 94806 569-B5
KEVIN ST
13100 SAR 95070 852-H7
KEVIN WY
3700 SCL 95054 813-E6
KEVINAIRE DR
500 MPS 95035 794-B5
KEVINGTON PL
200 ALA 94502 670-A5
KEW GARDENS CT
1400 SJS 95120 874-B6
KEY AV
900 SF 94124 688-B1
KEY BLVD
300 RCH 94805 589-B6
1800 ELCR 94530 609-B1
2000 ELCR 94530 589-B7
KEY CT
- OAK 94605 671-E4
KEYES AL
- SF 94133 648-A4
KEYES AV
- SF 94129 647-E4
KEYES ST
- SJS 95112 854-D1
100 SJS 95112 834-E7
400 SJS 95112 834-E7
KEY LARGO CV
- CMAD 94925 606-J1
KEY LARGO CRSE
- CMAD 94925 606-J1
KEYMAR DR
5600 SJS 95123 874-J4
KEY ROUTE BLVD
500 ALB 94706 609-E6
1100 BERK 94706 609-E6
KEYS PL
2100 HAY 94545 731-H1
KEYSTONE AV
2500 SCL 95051 833-B7
KEYSTONE CT
300 MrnC 94903 546-E5
1100 SJS 95132 814-F6
KEYSTONE DR
5000 FRMT 94536 752-G6
KEYSTONE WY
- SF 94127 667-D7
- SF 94112 667-D7
800 LVMR 94550 715-E3
KEYWOOD CT
1300 CNCD 94521 593-E5
KEZAR DR
500 SF 94117 667-D1
KHARTOUM ST
100 CCCo 94553 572-C7
KIDDER ST
22900 HAY 94545 711-C5
KIEL CT
1000 SUNV 94089 812-G4
KIELY BLVD
- SCL 95051 833-B5
- SCL 95051 853-B1
300 SJS 95129 853-B1
S KIELY BLVD
500 SJS 95117 853-B1
4000 SJS 95129 853-B1
KIENTZ LN
- SANS 94960 566-C7
KIFER CT
100 SUNV 94086 812-G7
KIFER RD
600 SUNV 94086 812-F7
900 SUNV 94086 832-G1
1100 SCL 94086 832-G1
2800 SCL 95051 833-A1
3000 SUNV 94086 833-A1
3300 SCL 95051 832-G1
KIKI CT
400 PLHL 94523 592-A3
KIKI DR
400 PLHL 94523 592-A3
KILAM DR
10800 CPTO 95014 832-C6
KILARNEY LN
1100 WLCK 94598 612-F1
KILAUEA ST
3300 CNCD 94519 572-H6
KILBIRNIE CT
800 SUNV 94087 832-F5
KILBRIDE CT
20300 SAR 95070 852-E7
KILBRIDE DR
20000 SAR 95070 852-E7
KILBURN CT
500 CCCo 94520 572-G1
KILBURN ST
100 CCCo 94520 572-G1
KILCHOAN CT
1300 SJS 95122 854-H1
KILCHOAN WY
1800 SJS 95122 854-H1
KILCONWAY LN
2700 SSF 94080 707-C4

KILCREASE CIR
1200 CCCo 94803 569-C7
KILCULLIN
- DBLN 94568 693-G4
KILDARA
- DBLN 94568 693-G4
KILDARE AV
1000 SUNV 94087 832-H5
KILDARE RD
16500 AlaC 94546 691-G4
16500 AlaC 94578 691-G4
KILDARE WY
1100 PIN 94564 569-C5
KILGO CT
- PLHL 94523 592-A4
KILGORE CT
- SANS 94960 566-A5
KILKARE RD
- AlaC 94586 713-H6
200 AlaC 94586 734-A1
KILKENNY CT
- ALA 94502 669-J6
700 SUNV 94087 832-F5
KILKENNY PL
- ALA 94502 669-J5
KILKENNY RD
17600 LGTS 95032 893-B2
17600 SCIC 95032 893-B2
KILKENNY WY
900 PIN 94564 569-C5
KILLARNEY CIR
- SJS 95138 855-G7
- SJS 95138 875-G1
KILLARNEY CT
800 SUNV 94087 832-F5
KILLARNEY LN
1100 BURL 94010 728-C5
KILLARNEY PL
- ALA 94502 669-H5
KILLARNEY RD
2600 CCCo 94806 569-C5
KILLARNEY ST
1100 LVMR 94550 715-G3
KILLARNEY WY
- SJS 95138 855-G7
KILLDEER CT
200 FCTY 94404 749-G1
1700 SUNV 94087 832-F6
2700 UNC 94587 732-D6
3900 ANT 94509 594-J2
KILLDEER DR
3800 ANT 94509 594-J1
KILLEAN CT
100 SUNV 94087 832-E5
KILLORGLIN COM
35800 FRMT 94536 732-J7
KILLYBEGS RD
- ALA 94502 669-H5
KILMER AV
100 SCIC 95008 873-D3
KILMER CT
- MLV 94941 606-G4
KILO AV
2800 SJS 95124 873-H1
KILPATRICK CT
2500 SRMN 94583 673-B2
KILPATRICK DR
100 SRMN 94583 673-B2
KILPATRICK ST
600 AMCN 94589 509-J4
KILROY WY
- ATN 94027 790-B4
KILRUSH AV
7500 DBLN 94568 693-G2
KILRUSH CT
1300 PIN 94564 569-D5
KILT CT
19600 SAR 95070 852-F7
19600 SAR 95070 872-F1
KILTY CT
100 VAL 94589 509-J5
KIM CT
- BEN 94510 551-B4
- MRTZ 94553 571-E7
100 VAL 94591 530-D3
1400 CMBL 95008 853-B6
3300 PLE 94588 714-B1
5900 LVMR 94550 696-D6
KIM PL
500 HAY 94544 711-H4
KIM RD
3300 LFYT 94549 591-G7
KIM ST
400 CCCo 94565 573-F1
800 CPTO 95014 852-D2
KIMBALL AV
1100 HAY 94541 691-H7
9000 SRMN 94583 693-H1
KIMBALL CT
- ANT 94509 575-E5
1400 CNCD 94518 592-J3
KIMBALL DR
2600 SJS 95121 854-H3
KIMBALL PL
- SF 94109 647-J5
KIMBALL WY
100 SSF 94080 708-B4
3500 CNCD 94518 592-J3
KIMBER CT
300 FRMT 94539 753-E2
2800 SJS 95124 873-H2
KIMBER TER
300 FRMT 94539 753-E2
KIMBERLEY CT
- OAK 94611 650-F1
KIMBERLEY PL
4000 CNCD 94521 593-A4
4000 CNCD 94521 592-J4
KIMBERLIN PL
2000 SCL 95051 833-D2
KIMBERLIN HEIGHTS DR
- OAK 94619 650-H4
KIMBERLY CIR
800 PLHL 94523 592-A4
KIMBERLY COM
4500 LVMR 94550 696-B7
KIMBERLY CT
1400 SJS 95118 874-B2
31200 UNC 94587 731-J5
KIMBERLY DR
- MRGA 94556 631-D3

STREET
Block City ZIP Pg-Grid

KIMBERLY DR
100 AMCN 94589 510-A4
400 AMCN 94589 509-J4
1100 SJS 95118 874-B1
1700 SUNV 94087 832-B6
KIMBERLY ST
3800 UNC 94587 731-J5
5500 SJS 95129 852-H2
KIMBERLY WY
3300 SMTO 94403 749-E5
KIMBER PARK CT
200 FRMT 94539 753-E2
KIMBERWICKE CT
300 CCCo 94526 633-C5
KIMBERWOOD CT
200 FRMT 94539 753-E2
KIMBLE AV
- LGTS 95032 893-A1
KIMBRO ST
38000 FRMT 94536 752-H4
KIMLEE DR
3100 SJS 95132 814-F4
KIM LOUISE DR
- CMBL 95008 853-B6
100 SJS 95008 853-B6
KIMMIE CT
- BLMT 94002 769-C2
KIMPTON CT
2400 SJS 95133 834-G1
KINCHELOE CT
3300 LFYT 94549 611-G3
KINCORA CT
4000 SJS 95136 854-E6
KINDER LN
- HIL 94010 728-C7
KINDRA HILL DR
7000 SJS 95120 894-H3
KINER AV
1400 SJS 95125 854-A7
KING AV
- FRMT 94536 732-J6
- PDMT 94611 650-C2
100 PDMT 94610 650-C2
E KING AV
- FRMT 94536 732-J6
KING CT
- SMTO 94403 749-C6
1100 ELCR 94530 609-D2
1700 SJS 95122 855-A3
2100 SCL 95051 832-J2
18000 SAR 95070 852-D5
35100 FRMT 94536 732-J6
KING DR
200 CCCo 94595 612-A7
300 SSF 94080 707-E3
500 DALY 94015 707-C3
900 ELCR 94530 609-E2
1100 PCFA 94044 707-C3
KING LN
- MLV 94941 606-D1
700 FCTY 94404 749-G4
3800 SMTO 94403 749-C6
KING RD
- SCIC 94035 812-A2
- SCIC 94043 812-A2
N KING RD
- SJS 95116 834-F3
300 SJS 95133 834-D2
800 SCIC 95133 834-D2
S KING RD
- SJS 95116 834-F4
1100 SJS 95122 834-H6
2100 SJS 95122 854-J1
2400 SJS 95121 854-J1
2400 SJS 95122 855-A2
2400 SJS 95121 855-A2
KING ST
- LKSP 94939 586-E6
- MLV 94941 606-D1
- RDWC 94062 769-H6
- SF 94107 648-B7
400 SF 94107 668-A1
400 SF 94103 668-A1
800 OAK 94606 650-A7
900 RDWC 94061 770-A7
1100 RDWC 94061 790-A1
1600 BLMT 94002 769-F2
2900 BERK 94703 629-G4
3800 OAK 94608 629-G5
KING WY
- MLV 94941 606-B2
6400 DBLN 94568 693-J3
KING ARTHURS CT
4100 PA 94306 811-C3
KINGBROOK DR
4800 SJS 95124 873-E4
KINGDALE DR
4800 SJS 95124 873-E4
KING ESTATES
3000 SJS 95135 855-G5
KING ESTATES CT
5300 SJS 95135 855-H5
KINGFIELD WY
2400 SJS 95124 873-D4
KINGFISHER CT
- NVTO 94949 546-E5
KINGFISHER DR
800 SJS 95125 854-C6
KINGFISHER TER
1200 SCIC 94087 832-F4
1200 SUNV 94087 832-F4
KINGFISHER WY
1300 SUNV 94087 832-F4
KINGHURST WY
4800 SJS 95124 873-E4
KINGLET CT
1700 SUNV 94087 832-F6
34900 UNC 94587 732-G7
KINGLET RD
400 LVMR 94550 695-E7
400 LVMR 94550 715-E1
KINGLET TER
3800 FRMT 94555 732-J3
KINGMAN AV
1400 SJS 95128 853-G2
KING PALM CT
- SJS 95133 814-J4
KINGRIDGE CT
1900 WLCK 94596 612-G7
KINGRIDGE DR
3600 SMTO 94403 749-B7
4800 SJS 95124 873-D4
KINGS AV
- HER 94547 569-F2
KINGS CT
- SLN 94578 691-D2
- CCCo 94565 573-E1
100 SCAR 94070 769-D5
400 CMBL 95008 853-D5
22800 HAY 94541 712-A1
KINGS LN
1400 PA 94303 791-B4
2000 SMCo 94402 768-H1
KINGS PL
5200 RCH 94804 609-B3
KINGS RD
- BSBN 94005 688-A7
500 ALA 94501 669-F1
800 PIT 94565 574-E5
KINGS RW
600 SJS 95112 834-A1
KINGSBERRY PL
200 PIT 94565 574-B5
KINGSBURY CT
- ALA 94501 649-G7
7500 CPTO 95014 852-D3
KINGSBURY DR
800 LVMR 94550 715-G2
KINGSBURY PL
7400 CPTO 95014 852-D3
KINGS CANYON CT
3500 PLE 94588 714-A1
KINGS CANYON WY
- PCFA 94044 727-B5
KINGS COVE CT
- UNC 94545 731-J6
KINGS CROSS WY
500 SJS 95136 874-F3
KINGS CROWN CT
- MRGA 94556 631-F4
KINGSDALE DR
100 CCCo 94596 632-F1
100 WLCK 94596 632-F1
KINGSFORD CT
- PIT 94565 574-C4
KINGSFORD DR
400 MRGA 94556 631-E6
KINGSFORD LN
200 RDWC 94061 790-B2
KINGSGATE CT
2800 SJS 95132 814-D2
KINGS GATE DR
1400 SUNV 94087 832-C5
KINGSLAND AV
2400 OAK 94601 670-F1
2600 OAK 94619 670-F1
2700 OAK 94619 650-F7
KINGSLAND CT
6500 SJS 95120 894-B1
KINGSLAND PL
- OAK 94619 650-F7
KINGSLEY AV
100 PA 94301 790-J5
100 PA 94301 791-A5
KINGSLEY CIR
5700 OAK 94605 670-G1
KINGSLEY CT
100 PLHL 94523 592-A5
KINGSLEY PL
300 SRMN 94583 673-F6
3100 LFYT 94549 631-J3
KINGSLEY ST
3600 OAK 94610 650-B4
KINGSLEY WY
14400 LAH 94022 811-B6
KINGSLY DR
1200 PIT 94565 574-E7
KINGSLY LN
300 AMCN 94589 509-J3
KINGS MOUNTAIN RD
100 WDSD 94062 789-D6
600 SMCo 94062 789-A7
KINGS OAK PL
- CCCo 94596 612-D2
KINGSPARK DR
4100 SJS 95136 874-G1
KINGSPORT AV
1400 LVMR 94550 715-G3
KINGS RIVER CT
4700 SJS 95136 874-E2
KINGSROW
- CNCD 94518 592-G4
KINGSTON AV
300 MRTZ 94553 571-E5
700 OAK 94611 649-J1
700 PDMT 94611 649-J1
700 PDMT 94611 650-A1
2200 SBRN 94066 707-F7
2200 SBRN 94066 727-G1
KINGSTON CT
200 MRTZ 94553 571-F5
1600 LALT 94024 832-A3
KINGSTON DR
400 DNVL 94506 653-J6
KINGSTON LN
200 VAL 94590 529-J5
1000 ALA 94502 670-B7
KINGSTON PL
- CCCo 94596 612-C2
- PIT 94565 574-B5
7200 DBLN 94568 693-G5
KINGSTON RD
- CCCo 94707 609-F4
500 BLMT 94002 749-E7
2700 SJS 95111 854-G4
KINGSTON ST
- SF 94110 667-H5
- SMTO 94401 729-A6
KINGSTON WY
- SJS 95193 875-C4
200 WLCK 94596 612-C2
4800 SJS 95130 852-J7
4800 SJS 95130 873-A1
4800 SJS 95130 872-J1
17400 AlaC 94546 691-H2
KINGSTON HILL WY
200 LGTS 95030 873-C4
KINGSWOOD
- PIT 94565 574-B6
KINGSWOOD CIR
- HIL 94010 748-E5
100 CCCo 94506 654-D5
KINGSWOOD CT
200 CCCo 94506 654-E5
1400 HIL 94010 748-F5
KINGSWOOD DR
1500 HIL 94010 748-E5
4300 CNCD 94518 592-J5
4300 CNCD 94518 593-A5
4500 CCCo 94506 654-D5
KINGSWOOD LN
300 CCCo 94506 654-E5
KINGSWOOD PL
500 CCCo 94506 654-D5
KINGSWOOD WY
600 LALT 94022 811-D5
KINGTON PL
2000 SCL 95051 833-A3
KINGWOOD DR
2500 SCL 95051 833-B2
KINGWOOD RD
- OAK 94619 650-H5
KINGWOOD WY
4800 SJS 95124 873-E4
KINMAN CT
12600 SAR 95070 852-E6
KINNE BLVD
- CCCo 94520 572-G3
- CNCD 94520 572-G3
KINNEY CT
19600 AlaC 94546 692-A4
KINNEY DR
200 SJS 95112 834-A3
2600 CCCo 94595 611-J6
2700 CCCo 94595 612-A6
2700 LFYT 94595 612-A6
KINO CT
700 HAY 94544 712-A3
KINO WY
1600 LVMR 94550 715-G2
KINROSS CT
500 SUNV 94087 832-E5
1400 WLCK 94598 612-E3
KINROSS DR
- SRFL 94901 567-A7
100 SRFL 94901 587-B1
100 WLCK 94598 612-D3
KINROSS WY
1800 SJS 95122 854-G1
KINSPORT LN
1300 SJS 95120 874-B7
KINSTON CT
- MRGA 94556 631-D7
KINSULE CT
1300 SJS 95121 855-B5
KINTYRE WY
900 SUNV 94087 832-G5
1300 SJS 95129 852-E4
KINZEY ST
- SF 94129 647-C4
KIOWA CIR
600 SJS 95123 874-H6
KIOWA CT
- PTLV 94028 810-C6
2600 WLCK 94598 612-H3
5100 ANT 94509 595-H5
45500 FRMT 94539 773-H4
KIP LN
3300 BURL 94010 748-B1
KIPERASH CT
800 SJS 95133 814-G6
KIPERASH DR
2900 SJS 95133 814-G6
KIPLING AV
800 SSF 94080 707-D2
KIPLING CT
800 RCH 94803 589-H3
1000 CNCD 94518 592-J5
1300 SJS 95118 874-C2
KIPLING DR
- MLV 94941 606-G4
5800 RCH 94803 589-G3
KIPLING PL
3100 FRMT 94536 752-G2
KIPLING ST
200 PA 94301 790-J4
2200 AlaC 94546 692-A7
2600 PA 94306 791-C6
KIPPY CT
- MRGA 94556 631-G5
KIRBY COM
600 FRMT 94539 753-H7
KIRBY CT
400 WLCK 94598 612-J2
KIRBY LN
3100 WLCK 94598 612-J2
KIRBY PL
- PA 94301 791-B4
KIRBY WY
1900 SJS 95124 853-G7
1900 SJS 95124 873-F1
KIRBYHILL WY
100 SUNV 94087 832-E5
KIRCHER CT
1700 LALT 94024 832-A4
KIRK
4000 ALA 94501 649-E6
KIRK AV
- SCIC 95127 835-A1
100 SUNV 94086 812-F6
100 SJS 95127 835-A1
200 SJS 95127 814-J7
200 SCIC 95127 814-J7
KIRK CT
- CCCo 94507 652-G1
1600 SJS 95124 873-J3
KIRK LN
1300 SPAB 94805 589-A4
1300 SPAB 94806 589-A4
KIRK RD
3000 SJS 95124 873-J1
4400 SJS 95124 874-A3
KIRK TER
38500 FRMT 94536 753-C2
KIRKALDY CT
800 SUNV 94087 832-F5
KIRKBROOK DR
12000 SAR 95070 852-E5
KIRKCALDY CT
3600 PLE 94588 694-F5
KIRKCALDY ST
3100 PLE 94588 694-F5
KIRKCREST CT
- DNVL 94526 652-G1
- CCCo 94507 652-G1
KIRKCREST LN
900 DNVL 94526 652-G1
KIRKCREST RD
700 CCCo 94507 652-G1
700 DNVL 94526 652-G1
KIRKDALE DR
12200 SAR 95070 852-E5
KIRKER PASS RD
- CCCo - 594-A2
1500 CLAY 94517 593-F5
1500 CNCD 94521 593-F5
2100 CCCo - 593-F5
5300 CCCo - 574-C7
KIRK GLEN CT
600 SJS 95133 814-G7
KIRKHAM ST
- SF 94143 667-C2
100 SF 94122 667-A2
600 OAK 94607 649-E3
2900 SF 94122 666-H2
KIRKHAVEN CT
- SJS 95111 874-J1
KIRKLAND AV
1700 SJS 95125 854-C4
KIRKLAND CT
- OAK 94605 671-D4
KIRKLAND DR
600 SUNV 94087 832-D5
KIRKLYN DR
1800 SJS 95124 853-H7
KIRKMONT DR
1700 SJS 95124 853-H6
20200 SAR 95070 852-E5
KIRKORIAN WY
15500 MSER 95030 873-A5
KIRKPATRICK DR
- CCCo 94803 569-E7
KIRKSIDE CT
1100 SJS 95126 853-H3
KIRKWALL PL
600 MPS 95035 794-A3
KIRKWOOD AV
500 SF 94124 668-B5
KIRKWOOD CT
- CCCo 94521 593-E2
- EPA 94303 771-B7
100 VAL 94591 530-F4
KIRKWOOD DR
2400 HAY 94545 731-G1
3300 SJS 95117 853-C1
3400 SCIC 95117 853-C1
5400 CNCD 94521 593-G4
KIRKWOOD WY
- SCAR 94070 769-E3
KIRSTEN LN
100 CCCo 94803 589-E1
KIRSTEN WY
5100 LVMR 94550 696-C6
KIRWIN LN
7400 CPTO 95014 852-D2
KISA CT
5200 LVMR 94550 696-C7
KISER CREEK DR
900 SJS 95120 894-J4
KISKA
4000 ALA 94501 649-E6
KISKA CT
3300 CNCD 94519 572-H7
KISKA RD
- SF 94124 668-D7
KISMET CT
500 WLCK 94596 592-D7
KISSELL AL
300 VAL 94590 529-J5
500 VAL 94590 530-A5
KISSELL CT
3100 SJS 95111 854-H5
KISSLING ST
- SF 94103 667-J1
KISTER CIR
500 CCCo 94803 569-E7
KIT LN
6700 AlaC 94552 692-F3
KIT CARSON CT
100 SCL 95050 833-C7
KIT CARSON WY
- VAL 94589 509-J6
KITCHENER CIR
1000 SJS 95121 855-A5
KITCHENER CT
2800 OAK 94602 650-F4
KITCHENER DR
1600 SUNV 94087 832-C5
KITE WY
3900 ANT 94509 594-J1
KITE HILL LN
- MLV 94941 606-F3
KITE HILL RD
600 ORIN 94563 610-H6
KITE HILL TER
500 ORIN 94563 610-H6
KIT FOX PL
- AlaC 94546 691-G4
KITIMAT PL
1300 SUNV 94087 832-C4
KITOOSH CT
- CCCo 94507 632-G5
KITSAP CT
2500 SCL 95051 832-J1
KITTERY AV
3000 SRMN 94583 673-G6
KITTERY CT
- SJS 95139 875-G7
KITTERY PL
200 SRMN 94583 673-F6
KITTERY WY
900 PIN 94564 569-C5
KITTIE LN
- BLMT 94002 769-D2
1500 CCCo 94553 571-J5
KITTIWAKE RD
- ORIN 94563 610-F5
KITTOE DR
100 MTVW 94043 812-A4
KITTREDGE ST
2000 BERK 94704 629-G2
KITTREDGE TER
- SF 94118 647-E7
KITTRIDGE RD
15300 SAR 95070 872-D4
KITTY LN
9800 OAK 94603 670-F7
9800 OAK 94603 690-F1
KITTY HAWK PL
1900 ALA 94501 669-H3
KITTY HAWK RD
300 ALA 94501 669-H3
1200 LVMR 94550 695-B5
KITTYHAWK WY
100 MTVW 94041 812-A6
KIWANIS ST
3300 OAK 94602 650-F5
22800 HAY 94541 711-H2
KIZER ST
700 MPS 95035 794-B4
KLAMATH
100 PIT 94565 574-A3
KLAMATH AV
800 SCL 95051 832-J3
2000 SMTO 94403 749-C2
KLAMATH CT
300 MRTZ 94553 571-J7
500 HAY 94541 711-G3
2600 LVMR 94550 715-G5
4600 PLE 94566 694-D7
KLAMATH DR
1000 MLPK 94025 790-C7
1300 SJS 95130 853-B4
1500 SUNV 94087 832-C5
KLAMATH PL
500 FRMT 94539 773-J5
KLAMATH RD
200 MPS 95035 794-A6
23000 HAY 94541 711-G3
KLAMATH ST
100 CCCo 94565 573-H2
200 BSBN 94005 688-A6
3500 OAK 94602 650-G4
46100 FRMT 94539 773-J5
KLAMATH WY
- NVTO 94947 526-E6
KLAMATH WOODS PL
3400 CNCD 94518 592-H6
KLARE AV
- SANS 94960 566-A6
KLAUS CT
27000 HAY 94542 712-D4
KLAUS DR
3000 SJS 95121 855-C3
KLEE CT
700 SJS 95123 874-G6
1200 SUNV 94087 832-E3
KLEIN CT
3600 SJS 95148 835-E6
KLEIN RD
2400 SCIC 95148 835-E5
2800 SJS 95148 835-E6
KLENGEL ST
1100 ANT 94509 575-C5
KLIER DR
1700 CNCD 94518 592-F6
KLIPSPRINGER DR
1600 SJS 95124 873-J3
KLONDIKE PL
- LVMR 94550 715-D4
KLOSE WY
3100 RCH 94806 569-B7
KLUNE CT
2300 SCL 95054 813-C4
KNAPP CT
- SMTO 94403 749-B5
KNAPP ST
31700 HAY 94587 732-B4
KNICKERBOCKER DR
600 SUNV 94087 832-A1
KNICKERBOCKER LN
- MrnC 94960 566-A2
- ORIN 94563 630-H2
KNICKERSON DR
3000 SJS 95148 855-F1
KNIGHT CT
100 NVTO 94945 526-E3
KNIGHT DR
- SRFL 94901 567-C5
600 BEN 94510 530-J7
3800 AlaC 94546 691-H2
KNIGHT ST
10300 OAK 94603 670-G7
KNIGHTS CIR
100 VAL 94591 530-F4
KNIGHTS WY
- AMCN 94589 509-J4
KNIGHTS BRIDGE CT
3000 SJS 95132 814-E3
KNIGHTSBRIDGE CT
100 AMCN 94589 510-A3
KNIGHTSBRIDGE LN
- RDWC 94061 790-B2
2600 SCL 95051 833-B2
KNIGHTS BRIDGE RD
2900 SJS 95132 814-E4
KNIGHTSBRIDGE WY
200 AMCN 94589 510-A3
200 AMCN 94589 509-J3
KNIGHTS ESTATES
5200 SJS 95135 855-G5
KNIGHTSHAVEN WY
100 SJS 95111 875-A1
KNIGHTSWOOD WY
3100 SJS 95148 835-E7
3100 SJS 95148 855-E1
KNIGHTWOOD CT
1000 WLCK 94596 632-F1
KNIGHTWOOD LN
- HIL 94010 728-D7
KNOBCONE CT
2200 RCH 94803 589-F4
KNOBCONE DR
2200 RCH 94803 589-F4
KNOCKASH HILL ST
- SF 94127 667-D5
KNOCKNABOUL WY
600 SRFL 94903 566-C1
KNOLL AV
4200 OAK 94619 650-H6
KNOLL CIR
100 SSF 94080 707-G3
KNOLL CT
- HER 94547 569-H4
KNOLL DR
- CCCo - 651-F3
- MRGA 94556 651-F3
600 SCAR 94070 769-G4
2900 CNCD 94520 572-E6
12500 SCIC 94024 831-F2
KNOLL LN
- MrnC 94941 606-H4
KNOLL RD
- SANS 94960 566-C7
- SRFL 94901 586-E1
N KNOLL RD
- MrnC 94920 606-H3
- MrnC 94941 606-H3
S KNOLL RD
- MrnC 94941 606-H4
KNOLL WY
- MrnC 94903 566-E5
21500 AlaC 94546 691-J7
KNOLLBROOK DR
7600 PLE 94588 693-H7
KNOLLCREST AV
- SJS 95138 875-G5
KNOLL CREST CT
- SRMN 94583 673-J6
KNOLLCREST CT
200 MRTZ 94553 591-H3
4800 ANT 94509 595-J3
KNOLLCREST DR
4700 ANT 94509 595-J4
KNOLLCREST RD
- HIL 94010 748-E4
KNOLLFIELD WY
800 SJS 95136 874-D2
KNOLLGLEN WY
4000 SJS 95118 874-C2
KNOLLPARK CIR
4400 ANT 94509 595-H4
KNOLL PARK CT
6000 SJS 95120 874-C7
KNOLLPARK CT
- ANT 94509 595-H3
KNOLLPARK WY
- ANT 94509 595-J4
KNOLL RIDGE WY
- OAK 94619 651-C6
KNOLLS LN
16300 LGTS 95032 893-D1
KNOLLTOP CT
- NVTO 94945 526-E3
KNOLLTOP WY
- NVTO 94945 526-D3
KNOLLVIEW CT
600 MRTZ 94553 571-G5
KNOLL VIEW DR
1200 MPS 95035 794-A4
KNOLLVIEW DR
4200 CCCo 94506 654-C5
KNOLLVIEW WY
- SF 94131 667-E4
KNOLL VISTA
- ATN 94027 790-B6
KNOLLWELL WY
5700 SJS 95138 875-D4
KNOLLWOOD AV
1600 SJS 95125 854-A7
KNOLLWOOD CT
500 CCCo 94506 654-D5
KNOLLWOOD DR
- SRFL 94901 567-E5
2100 MRTZ 94553 571-J7
19900 SAR 95070 852-E5
KNOLLWOOD LN
1900 LALT 94024 831-H5
KNOLLWOOD PL
7500 DBLN 94568 693-H2
KNOLLWOOD TER
3500 FRMT 94536 752-A6
KNOT LN
- RDWC 94065 750-C4
KNOTT AV
6300 ELCR 94530 609-B1
KNOTT CT
- SF 94112 687-F2
KNOWLAND AV
3100 OAK 94619 650-F7
KNOWLES AV
- DALY 94014 687-C3
400 SCL 95128 833-D6
400 SCL 95050 833-D6
KNOWLES DR
100 LGTS 95030 873-C2
100 CMBL 95008 873-C2
KNOWLSON TER
4800 FRMT 94555 752-A3
KNOWLTON DR
1400 SUNV 94087 832-C4
KNOX AV
1000 SJS 95116 834-G6
1100 SJS 95122 834-G6
2100 PIT 94565 574-C4
KNOX DR
- LFYT 94549 611-A7
KNOX ST
1500 AlaC 94546 692-A7
1800 AlaC 94546 691-J7
KNOX GATE CT
4700 PLE 94588 694-D7
KNUPPE PL
21100 AlaC 94552 692-E4
KNUTE CT
38500 FRMT 94536 753-B3
KNUTTE CT
- MrnC 94947 525-H4
KOA CT
700 SUNV 94086 832-F2
2200 ANT 94509 595-F3
KOALA CT
- CCCo 94596 632-F1
KOALA WY
2200 ANT 94509 595-H3
KOBARA LN
1900 SJS 95124 873-G1
KOBBE AV
- SF 94129 647-C4
1300 SF 94129 647-B4
KOCH
- CNCD 94518 592-G4
KOCH LN
1100 SJS 95125 854-B7
1500 SJS 95125 874-A1
1600 SJS 95125 873-J1
KOCH RD
- CMAD 94925 606-H2
KOCH TER
1500 SJS 95125 854-A7
KOCHER DR
1800 SCIC 95125 853-H6
KODIAC PL
13400 SAR 95070 852-H7
13400 SAR 95070 872-H1
KODIAK CT
600 SUNV 94087 832-D5
7100 SJS 95139 895-F1
KODIAK ST
3100 ANT 94509 595-H1
KOFMAN CT
- ALA 94502 669-J5
KOFMAN PKWY
1600 ALA 94502 669-H5
KOFORD RD
9800 OAK 94603 670-G7
KOHALA AV
300 PCFA 94044 707-A6
KOHLER RD
3300 SJS 95148 835-D5
KOHNER CT
300 SCL 95050 833-D6
KOHOUTEK CT
29700 UNC 94587 731-J4
KOHOUTEK WY
29300 UNC 94587 731-J3
KOI TER
- FRMT 94536 753-F3
KOKOMA RD
1400 FRMT 94539 773-G3
KOLB PL
800 SCL 95050 833-C5
7200 DBLN 94568 693-F4
KOLL CIR
1400 SJS 95112 834-A2
1400 SJS 95112 833-J2
KOLL CENTER DR
- PLE 94566 714-B4
KOLL CENTER PKWY
6600 PLE 94566 714-B3
KOLLMAN CIR
2000 ALA 94501 649-F7
KOLLMAR DR
2700 SJS 95127 834-J4
KOLLN ST
700 PLE 94566 714-E1
KOLNES CT
2500 SJS 95121 855-E4
KOMINA AV
20500 SAR 95070 872-D3
KONA CIR
100 PIT 94565 574-E5
100 UNC 94587 732-C6
KONA CT
6500 SJS 95119 875-D6
39500 FRMT 94538 753-A7
KONA PL
- SJS 95119 875-D6
KOOSER RD
1300 SJS 95124 874-A5
1300 SJS 95118 874-A5
KOOTENAI CT
- FRMT 94539 773-J5
KOOTENAI DR
- FRMT 94539 773-J5
KORBEL CT
4600 UNC 94587 752-B1
KORBEL ST
4600 UNC 94587 752-B1
KORBEL WY
- BLMT 94002 749-D7
- BLMT 94002 769-D1
KOREMATSU CT
6400 SJS 95120 894-C1
KORHUMMEL WY
6500 SJS 95119 875-D7
KOSICH CT
12200 SAR 95070 852-H5
KOSICH DR
18600 SAR 95070 852-H5
KOTAKE CT
3100 SJS 95127 814-H7
KOTENBERG AV
1100 SJS 95125 854-A3
KOTTINGER DR
100 PLE 94566 714-E3
KOVANDA WY
1100 MPS 95035 794-A5
KOZERA DR
800 SJS 95136 874-E2
KOZO CT
5100 SJS 95124 873-G5
KOZO PL
5100 SJS 95124 873-G5
KRAFTILE RD
- FRMT 94536 732-H7
KRAL PL
3900 PLE 94588 694-E7
KRAMER LN
- SMCo 94063 790-D1
KRAMER PL
- SF 94133 648-A4
KRAMER ST
800 SLN 94579 691-B7
KRAUSE AV
6800 OAK 94605 670-H2
KRAUSE CT
4200 PLE 94588 694-E7
KRAUSE ST
4300 PLE 94588 694-E7
KRAUSGRILL PL
- SF 94133 648-A4
KREBS CT
1100 SJS 95131 834-D1
KREISLER CT
20700 SAR 95070 852-D5
KRING DR
2600 SJS 95125 854-B7
KRING PL
2400 LALT 94024 831-J6
KRING WY
1400 LALT 94024 831-J6
KRISMER ST
200 MPS 95035 793-J7
KRISTA LN
- SCAR 94062 769-G6
KRISTE LN
26000 LAH 94022 831-B2
KRISTEN CT
1000 SJS 95120 894-G3

STREET
Block City ZIP Pg-Grid

KRISTEN MARIE CT
- MrnC 94947 525-E4
KRISTIE LN
2300 SSF 94080 707-D4
KRISTIN CT
100 SMCo 94402 748-H6
KRISTIN LN
- NVTO 94945 526-A2
- NVTO 94945 525-J2
- ORIN 94563 631-B2
KRISTIN WY
1200 WLCK 94596 632-G1
KRISTINA CT
100 VAL 94591 530-D5
KRISTIN RIDGE WY
800 MPS 95035 814-E1
KRISTY CT
- NVTO 94947 526-A4
KRISTY LN
12000 SAR 95070 852-G5
KRISVIEW CT
700 MRTZ 94553 571-F5
KROHN LN
- OAK 94611 630-E7
KROLOP RD
4000 AlaC 94546 691-H2
KRONA CT
- CNCD 94521 593-F7
KRONA LN
1100 CNCD 94521 593-F7
KRONQUIST CT
- SF 94131 667-G4
KRUEGER DR
2200 CNCD 94520 572-F6
KRUGER AV
1200 FRMT 94536 753-B2
KRUSE DR
2100 SJS 95131 813-J5
KRZICH PL
21300 CPTO 95014 852-C3
KUDU CT
1700 HAY 94541 712-B1
KUEHNIS DR
300 CMBL 95008 853-G5
KUHL CT
- WLCK 94596 612-B3
KUHLAND AL
100 BEN 94510 551-B5
KUHNLE AV
4000 OAK 94605 650-H7
KULANI LN
- PLHL 94523 591-J5
KUMQUAT DR
500 SJS 95117 853-D2
KUNKEL DR
5200 SJS 95124 873-F5
KURTZ LN
5700 SJS 95123 874-E5
KUSHNER WY
4900 ANT 94509 595-J3
KUSS RD
100 DNVL 94526 652-G1
100 CCCo 94526 652-G1
KUWAIT WY
200 CCCo 94553 572-C7
KUYKENDALL PL
3300 SJS 95148 835-E7
KVISTAD DR
3700 FRMT 94538 753-D6
KYBURZ PL
5900 SJS 95120 874-C6
KYER ST
2400 PIN 94564 569-F6
KYLE CT
1400 SUNV 94087 832-C4
KYLE ST
700 SJS 95133 814-G6
700 SJS 95127 814-G6
KYLEMORE CT
4000 SJS 95136 854-E6
KYRA CIR
1700 SJS 95122 855-A2

L

L RD
- SUNV 94089 812-H3
L ST
- OAK 94625 649-A4
- VAL 94592 529-F3
100 ANT 94509 575-C4
300 FRMT 94536 753-B1
400 BEN 94510 551-A3
900 BEN 94510 550-J3
1000 CCCo 94509 575-C4
E L ST
200 BEN 94510 551-C5
N L ST
100 LVMR 94550 715-G1
200 LVMR 94550 695-G7
S L ST
- LVMR 94550 715-G1
LA ALONDRA CT
100 SRFL 94903 566-D4
LA AVANZADA
- SF 94131 667-E3
LA BARBERA DR
800 SJS 95126 853-H3
LA BAREE DR
300 MPS 95035 794-E7
LA BARRANCA CT
26800 LAH 94022 831-B1
LA BARRANCA RD
13000 LAH 94022 831-A1
13100 LAH 94022 811-B7
LABARTHE LN
- SCAR 94070 769-F6
LA BELLA AV
1300 SUNV 94087 832-D4
LA BELLA TER
- UNC 94587 732-E4
LA BICA WY
- SF 94127 667-E5
LA BOHEME WY
1400 SJS 95121 854-J2
LA BOLSA RD
- WLCK 94598 612-E5
LA BOLSITA
- ORIN 94563 610-F7
LA BONITA TER
- UNC 94587 732-E4
LA BONITA WY
1600 CNCD 94519 592-J2
LABRADOR LN
400 BEN 94510 551-B4
LABRADOR ST
2200 CNCD 94520 572-F5
LABRADOR WY
300 BEN 94510 551-B4
LA BREA ST
100 VAL 94591 530-C7
LA BREA TER
- UNC 94587 732-E5
LA BREA WY
- MrnC 94903 566-H2
LABURNUM DR
800 SUNV 94086 832-F3
LA BURNUM RD
- ATN 94027 790-F1
LA CADENA
600 VAL 94590 530-B2
LA CALLE
1900 CCCo 94526 633-E7
LA CALLE
1700 CNCD 94521 593-E4
LA CALLE CT
3600 PA 94306 811-B2
LA CAMINITA
1500 LFYT 94549 611-F2
LA CAMPANA
- ORIN 94563 610-H5
LA CAMPANIA
3100 ALA 94502 669-J6
LA CANADA CT
100 LGTS 95030 873-C4
2400 PIN 94564 569-G7
LA CANADA PTH
- SMCo 94010 728-B7
LA CANADA RD
1200 HIL 94010 748-F3
3200 LFYT 94549 611-H7
LA CANYADA DR
200 VAL 94591 530-C7
700 VAL 94591 550-C1
LA CASA AV
200 SMTO 94403 749-B7
LA CASA CT
1500 WLCK 94598 612-F4
LA CASA VIA
200 CCCo 94598 612-F4
300 WLCK 94598 612-E3
LA CASITA LN
- CCCo 94595 612-A7
LACASSIE AV
1500 WLCK 94596 612-B4
LACASSIE CT
- WLCK 94596 612-C5
LAC BLEU CT
- SJS 95148 855-F2
LAC DAZUR CT
- SJS 95148 855-F2
LAC DU VAL CT
- SJS 95148 855-F2
LACEWOOD WY
- DNVL 94506 653-J4
LACEY AV
6900 OAK 94605 670-H1
13900 SAR 95070 872-D2
LACEY CT
1500 CNCD 94520 592-E5
LACEY DR
2100 MPS 95035 794-E7
LACEY LN
1100 CNCD 94520 592-E4
LA CHESNAYE
- ORIN 94563 610-F2
LACHINE DR
1600 SUNV 94087 832-C5
E LA CHIQUITA AV
16400 SCIC 95032 873-C7
W LA CHIQUITA AV
16300 SCIC 95032 873-C7
LA CIENEGA AV
100 VAL 94589 530-B1
LA CIENEGA CT
100 LGTS 95030 873-C4
LA CIENEGA PL
- VAL 94589 530-B1
LA CIMA RD
3900 CCCo 94803 589-C3
LA CINTILLA
- ORIN 94563 610-G5
LACKAWANNA CT
1000 SUNV 94087 832-B2
LACKLAND CT
100 CCCo 94526 633-D6
LACKLAND DR
1800 CCCo 94526 633-D5
LACOCK PL
3300 FRMT 94555 732-E7
LA COLINA DR
100 CCCo 94507 632-E5
LA COLINA RD
3800 CCCo 94803 589-C3
LA CON CT
2000 SJS 95008 853-F7
LACONIA CT
- SJS 95139 875-G7
LACONIA WY
300 SRMN 94583 673-G3
LA CONNER DR
400 SUNV 94087 832-D5
LA COPITA CT
500 SRMN 94583 673-C2
LA CORONA CT
1900 CMBL 95030 873-A2
LA CORONA DR
1900 CMBL 95030 873-A1
LA CORONA ST
28800 HAY 94544 732-A2
LA CORRO PL
- WLCK 94598 612-F2
LA CORSO CIR
400 WLCK 94598 612-F2
LA CORSO CT
1900 WLCK 94598 612-F2
LA CORSO DR
500 WLCK 94598 612-E1
LA CORTE BONITA
5100 CNCD 94521 593-E4
LA COSA AV
4200 FRMT 94536 752-F3
LA COSTA AV
3600 AlaC 94546 691-J4
LA COSTA CT
- NVTO 94947 525-G4
LA COSTE ST
6400 EMVL 94608 629-D5
LACOUR WY
300 SMCo 94061 790-B3
LA CRESCENTA DR
- NVTO 94949 546-F2
LA CRESCENTA RD
3900 CCCo 94803 589-C3
LA CRESCENTA WY
- SRFL 94901 586-J1
LA CRESENDA
- VAL 94590 530-B3
LA CRESTA
3100 ALA 94502 669-J6
3100 ALA 94502 670-A6
LA CRESTA AV
3800 OAK 94602 650-D4
LA CRESTA CT
1500 LVMR 94550 715-F3
12600 LAH 94022 811-B7
LA CRESTA DR
12500 LAH 94022 811-A5
LA CRESTA RD
- ORIN 94563 631-B4
LA CRESTA WY
4700 SJS 95129 852-B7
LA CROIX CT
16500 LGTS 95032 873-D7
LA CROSSE AV
1100 CCCo 94507 632-H6
LA CROSSE CT
100 SSF 94080 707-E2
800 SUNV 94087 832-C4
LA CROSSE DR
- MPS 95035 794-D6
1400 SUNV 94087 832-C4
LA CRUZ AV
- BEN 94510 551-C4
- MLBR 94030 728-B4
LACSA CT
2100 SJS 95116 834-G3
LA CUESTA
- ORIN 94563 610-G6
LA CUESTA AV
2600 OAK 94611 650-E2
LA CUESTA DR
- MrnC 94904 586-G4
- LKSP 94904 586-G4
200 SMCo 94028 810-E3
800 SCIC 94024 831-E2
LA CUESTA RD
1000 HIL 94010 748-F3
LA CUMBRE CT
- HIL 94010 748-F2
LA CUMBRE RD
1200 HIL 94010 748-F3
LADD AV
2800 LVMR 94550 695-H7
LADDIE CT
2100 SJS 95121 855-C3
LADDIE WY
1900 SJS 95121 855-C3
S LADERA
600 RCH 94804 608-H1
LADERA CT
11500 DBLN 94568 693-F4
19600 SAR 95070 852-F5
LADERA DR
100 VAL 94591 530-D7
100 VAL 94591 550-D1
300 SJS 95134 813-D2
11600 DBLN 94568 693-G4
LADERA PZ
100 UNC 94587 732-J5
LADERA WY
600 PCFA 94044 726-H4
1100 BLMT 94002 769-D2
LADERA CORTE
800 SRMN 94583 673-B3
LADERMAN LN
- LKSP 94939 586-G5
LADERO ST
40600 FRMT 94539 753-E5
LADIS CT
800 SUNV 94086 832-G2
LADNER DR
5600 SJS 95123 874-J4
LADNER ST
4300 FRMT 94538 753-C7
LADON CT
2500 AlaC 94546 691-H5
LA DONNA ST
3600 PA 94306 811-C2
LADYMUIR CT
2200 SJS 95131 814-D5
LADY PALM CT
- SJS 95133 814-J4
LADYWOOD CT
1300 SJS 95130 853-C4
LA ENCINAL
- ORIN 94563 610-E7
LA ESPIRAL
- ORIN 94563 610-H5
LAFAYETTE AV
- HAY 94544 732-E3
- PDMT 94611 650-C2
- PDMT 94610 650-C2
200 SLN 94577 691-A1
200 SLN 94577 671-A7
600 SLN 94577 670-J7
5300 NWK 94560 752-D6
LAFAYETTE CIR
200 LFYT 94549 611-E6
LAFAYETTE CT
7800 PLE 94588 693-H7
LAFAYETTE DR
1100 SUNV 94087 832-B2
2200 ANT 94509 595-A2
2300 ANT 94509 594-J2
LAFAYETTE ST
- SF 94103 667-J1
300 SCL 95050 833-E1
600 MRTZ 94553 571-E2
600 SCL 95053 833-E4
800 ALA 94501 669-H2
1000 SMTO 94403 749-C4
2900 SCL 95054 833-E1
2900 SCL 95054 813-E7
3900 SCL 95134 813-D5
LAFAYETTE WY
400 SCL 95050 833-F5
LAFAYETTE MORAGA TR
- LFYT 94549 631-G5
- MRGA 94556 631-G5
3200 LFYT 94549 611-G6
LAFAYETTE RIDGE TR
- CCCo - 611-D3
- LFYT 94549 611-D3
LAFERN CT
6500 SJS 95120 894-C2
LA FERRERA TER
- SF 94133 648-A3
LA FIESTA PL
4800 SJS 95129 853-A1
LA FOND LN
- ORIN 94563 631-A4
LAGE DR
4600 SJS 95130 853-A7
LAGO
1500 SMTO 94403 749-E4
LAGO CT
1100 SJS 95121 854-J3
LA GOMA ST
- MLV 94941 606-E4
LA GONDA CT
- DNVL 94526 632-J7
- DNVL 94526 652-J1
LA GONDA WY
400 DNVL 94526 652-J1
500 DNVL 94526 632-H6
LAGOON CIR
300 HER 94547 570-B6
LAGOON CT
- UNC 94587 731-H5
- SRFL 94903 566-G3
LAGOON DR
- MrnC 94965 626-A1
- RDWC 94065 749-G7
LAGOON PL
- SRFL 94901 567-D6
LAGOON RD
- SRFL 94901 567-D6
- TBRN 94920 607-C6
- BLV 94920 607-C6
LAGOON TR
- CCCo - 591-C5
- CCCo 94553 591-C5
LAGOON WY
100 BSBN 94005 688-B5
2400 SJS 95131 814-C4
LAGOON VIEW DR
1700 TBRN 94920 607-E7
LAGOON VISTA
- TBRN 94920 607-E7
LAGORIA CT
- ALA 94502 669-J6
LAGOS CT
500 SRMN 94583 673-C3
LAGO VISTA CIR
4600 SJS 95129 853-A1
4700 SJS 95129 852-B7
LAGO VISTA CT
4600 SCIC 95120 895-E4
LA GRANDE AV
- SF 94112 667-H7
100 SF 94112 687-G2
LA GRANDE DR
600 SUNV 94087 832-D5
LAGRANGE CT
2100 LVMR 94550 715-E4
LAGRANGE LN
500 LVMR 94550 715-E4
LAGUNA AV
200 SCIC 95037 895-J6
200 SJS 95141 895-J6
900 BURL 94010 728-E5
3400 OAK 94602 650-E4
3500 PA 94306 811-B2
LAGUNA CIR
- PIT 94565 574-D7
900 FCTY 94404 749-F4
2000 CNCD 94520 592-F3
LAGUNA CT
400 LVMR 94550 715-E3
3400 SCL 95051 832-J3
3500 PA 94306 811-B2
LAGUNA DR
200 MPS 95035 793-J5
200 SJS 95131 814-A5
1900 HAY 94545 711-E5
2000 AlaC 94545 711-E5
LAGUNA PL
- PIT 94565 574-D7
9700 SRMN 94583 673-F7
40700 FRMT 94539 753-E5
LAGUNA RD
600 MrnC 94965 606-D6
LAGUNA ST
- SF 94102 667-H1
100 VAL 94591 530-C7
200 SF 94102 647-H6
800 LVMR 94550 715-D3
1000 SF 94115 647-G4
1200 SF 94109 647-H6
1600 CNCD 94520 592-F2
2200 MRTZ 94553 571-G2
2700 CNCD 94518 592-G2
2700 SF 94123 647-G4
3000 SF 94123 647-G3
LAGUNA WY
3200 OAK 94602 650-D5
LAGUNA HONDA BLVD
200 SF 94131 667-D4
200 SF 94116 667-D4
300 SF 94116 667-D4
400 SF 94127 667-D4
LAGUNA OAKS PL
3700 PA 94306 811-B2
LAGUNARIA LN
100 ALA 94502 670-A6
LAGUNA SECA CT
700 SJS 95123 874-G5
LAGUNA SECA WY
5800 SJS 95123 874-G5
LAGUNA VISTA
300 ALA 94501 670-A4
LAGUNA VISTA DR
2000 NVTO 94945 526-F1
2300 MrnC 94945 526-F1
LAGUNITA CT
- MRTZ 94553 571-H4
LAGUNITA DR
500 SCIC 94305 790-G7
LAGUNITAS AV
400 OAK 94610 649-J3
2500 ELCR 94530 589-C7
LAGUNITAS DR
- SF 94132 667-C6
LAGUNITAS LN
500 HAY 94544 711-G4
LAGUNITAS RD
- ROSS 94957 586-B2
LA HABRA
- PIT 94565 574-A3
LA HABRA ST
4800 UNC 94587 752-A1
LAHAINA WY
4400 SJS 95118 874-B3
LAHANA WY
39600 FRMT 94538 753-A7
LA HERNAN DR
200 SCL 95051 832-H7
LAHOMA CT
- CCCo 94507 632-H3
LA HONDA AV
2600 ELCR 94530 589-C6
5000 SJS 95129 852-J1
LA HONDA CT
- CCCo 94803 589-F3
LA HONDA DR
200 MPS 95035 793-J5
LA HONDA RD
1300 HIL 94010 748-E2
5100 CCCo 94803 589-F3
LA HONDA RD Rt#-84
300 WDSD 94062 809-F5
400 SMCo 94062 809-F7
1700 SMCo 94020 809-F5
1700 WDSD 94020 809-F5
LAIDLEY ST
- SF 94131 667-G5
LAILA LN
- CNCD 94518 592-G4
LAIN DR
- VAL 94591 530-E4
LAINE AV
1700 SCL 95051 833-C3
LAINEY CT
100 VAL 94589 509-J5
LAIOLO RD
40100 FRMT 94538 753-B7
LAIR CT
100 VAL 94591 530-D3
LAIRD AV
5900 OAK 94605 670-H1
LAIRD CT
18000 AlaC 94546 691-J2
LAIRD DR
- MRGA 94556 631-D4
LAIRD LN
600 CCCo 94549 591-G4
LA JENNIFER WY
800 PA 94306 811-B2
LA JOLLA AV
400 SMTO 94403 749-B6
2700 SJS 95124 873-H1
LA JOLLA CT
- DNVL 94526 633-B7
11200 CPTO 95014 852-B3
40400 FRMT 94539 753-E4
LA JOLLA DR
2600 ALA 94501 670-A4
2800 ANT 94509 595-H2
LA JOLLA ST
400 VAL 94591 550-D1
LAKE AV
- PDMT 94611 650-A1
100 CCCo 94572 549-H7
100 PDMT 94611 649-J1
500 CCCo 94572 569-H1
LAKE BLVD
2400 SMCo 94062 789-F1
5300 NWK 94560 752-D3
N LAKE CIR
- ANT 94509 575-F5
LAKE CT
- SMCo 94062 789-F1
300 MRTZ 94553 592-A1
E LAKE CT
- ANT 94509 575-F5
S LAKE CT
- ANT 94509 575-F5
W LAKE CT
- ANT 94509 575-E5
LAKE DR
- DBLN 94568 693-J2
- RCH 94805 609-G3
100 SBRN 94066 707-D7
100 SBRN 94066 727-D1
200 CCCo 94708 609-G3
E LAKE DR
- ANT 94509 575-F5
N LAKE DR
- DBLN 94568 693-J1
- ANT 94509 575-E4
S LAKE DR
- DBLN 94568 693-J2
- ANT 94509 575-F5
W LAKE DR
- ANT 94509 575-E5
LAKE PKWY
- OAK 94610 650-A2
LAKE PL
- WLCK 94598 612-E4
E LAKE PL
- ANT 94509 575-F5
S LAKE PL
- ANT 94509 575-F5
W LAKE PL
- ANT 94509 575-E5
LAKE RD
- SMCo 94028 830-D4
2200 BLMT 94002 769-A2
LAKE ST
- SF 94118 647-C6
- PIT 94565 574-D6
100 BSBN 94005 688-B7
1000 MLBR 94030 728-A5
1000 SPAB 94806 588-H1
1600 SF 94121 647-A6
1700 SMTO 94403 749-D1
LAKE WY
- WLCK 94598 612-E4
LAKE WY
- CCCo 94598 612-E4
LAKE ALBANO CIR
3100 SJS 95135 855-G6
LAKE ALMANOR DR
5800 SJS 95123 874-G7
LAKE ARROWHEAD AV
3100 FRMT 94555 732-B6
LAKE ARROWHEAD CT
32600 FRMT 94555 732-C6
LAKE BARLEE LN
32400 FRMT 94555 732-B6
LAKE BERRYESSA DR
32400 FRMT 94555 732-C5
LAKEBIRD CT
4800 SJS 95124 873-F4
LAKEBIRD DR
600 SUNV 94089 812-H4
1800 SJS 95124 873-G4
LAKEBIRD PL
4800 SJS 95124 873-G4
LAKE BLUE STONE ST
3100 FRMT 94555 732-C6
LAKE BROOK CT
300 MRTZ 94553 592-A1
LAKEBROOK CT
- SJS 95148 855-F1
LAKE CABOT LN
2900 AlaC 94546 691-J4
LAKE CANDLEWOOD ST
32900 FRMT 94555 732-H4
LAKE CHABOT RD
300 SLN 94577 671-C7
1600 SLN 94577 691-E1
1600 AlaC 94578 671-C7
1600 AlaC 94578 691-E1
17400 AlaC 94546 691-G2
LAKE CHABOT ST
32400 FRMT 94555 732-B6
LAKE CHAD CT
3400 FRMT 94555 732-B6
LAKE CHAD ST
32500 FRMT 94555 732-B6
LAKE CHAMPLAIN CT
33200 FRMT 94555 732-C6
LAKE CHAMPLAIN ST
33200 FRMT 94555 732-C6
LAKECHIME DR
300 SUNV 94089 812-H4
LAKE CREST CT
2200 MRTZ 94553 592-A1
LAKECREST CT
- SJS 95148 855-F2
18400 AlaC 94546 691-H3
LAKE CROWLEY PL
5800 SJS 95123 874-G7
LAKE DALE CT
300 MRTZ 94553 592-A1
LAKEDALE WY
900 SUNV 94089 812-H4
LAKE ERIE ST
32900 FRMT 94555 732-H4
LAKE ESTATES CT
3000 SJS 95135 855-G5
LAKEFAIR DR
600 SUNV 94089 812-G4
LAKEFIELD CT
- DNVL 94506 654-A5
LAKEFIELD PL
200 MRGA 94556 651-E3
2100 MRTZ 94553 592-A1
LAKE FOREST CT
- SF 94131 667-D3
LAKE FOREST DR
- DALY 94015 687-B3
LAKEFRONT CIR
38800 FRMT 94536 753-C3
LAKE GARDA DR
3100 SJS 95135 855-G6
LAKE GARRISON ST
33100 FRMT 94555 732-H4
LAKEHAVEN DR
600 SUNV 94089 812-H5
LAKEHAVEN TER
600 SUNV 94089 812-G5
LAKE HENNESSY CT
5900 SJS 95123 874-E5
LAKE HERMAN RD
- BEN 94510 551-H1
- SolC 94510 530-H3
- SolC 94510 551-H1
- VAL 94591 530-H3
LAKEHOUSE AV
400 SJS 95110 834-A7
LAKE HURON ST
32900 FRMT 94555 732-C6
LAKEHURST CIR
2000 ALA 94501 649-E6
LAKEHURST DR
2100 MRTZ 94553 592-A1
LAKEHURST RD
1000 LVMR 94550 695-E7
LAKE ISABELLA WY
900 SJS 95123 874-G7
LAKEKNOLL DR
700 SUNV 94089 812-H5
LAKELAND DR
- LVMR 94550 696-E3
LAKE LANIER PL
33100 FRMT 94555 732-C6
LAKE LESINA DR
3200 SJS 95135 855-G6
LAKE LOUISE ST
32400 FRMT 94555 732-B6
LAKE MANOR DR
5800 SJS 95123 874-G7
LAKE MASK PL
32400 FRMT 94555 732-B5
LAKE MCCLURE DR
800 SJS 95123 874-E5
LAKE MEAD CT
- SRMN 94583 653-F7
3200 FRMT 94555 732-C6
LAKE MEAD DR
3500 FRMT 94555 732-C6
LAKE MEAD PL
700 SRMN 94583 653-F7
LAKEMEAD WY
500 SMCo 94062 789-F2
3900 RDWC 94062 789-F2
LAKE MEADOW CIR
300 MRTZ 94553 592-A1
LAKE MEADOW CT
2200 MRTZ 94553 592-A1
LAKEMEADOW DR
- DALY 94015 687-A4
LAKE MERCED BLVD
- SF 94132 666-J6
- SF 94132 667-A7
- SF 94132 687-A3
100 DALY 94015 687-A3
100 SMCo 94015 687-A3
LAKE MERCED HILL
- SF 94132 687-A2
LAKE MICHIGAN ST
32900 FRMT 94555 732-C6
LAKEMONT CT
- SJS 95148 855-F2
LAKEMONT DR
- DALY 94015 687-A3
700 SRMN 94583 673-F1
3100 SRMN 94583 653-F7
LAKEMONT PL
- AlaC 94542 692-D6
- AlaC 94552 692-D6
700 SRMN 94583 653-F7
700 SRMN 94583 673-F1
LAKEMONT WY
700 SRMN 94583 673-F1
LAKEMORE CT
- SJS 95148 855-F1
LAKEMUIR DR
200 SUNV 94089 812-H5
LAKE ONEIDA ST
33100 FRMT 94555 732-C7
LAKE ONTARIO DR
3200 FRMT 94555 732-C6
LAKE PARK AV
400 OAK 94610 650-A3
LAKE PARK CT
2300 MRTZ 94553 592-A1
LAKEPARK DR
1600 SJS 95131 814-B6
LAKE PILLSBURY DR
3100 FRMT 94555 732-B6
LAKEPORT CT
- SJS 95148 855-F1
LAKE PYRAMID ST
33100 FRMT 94555 732-C7
LAKE RANCH RD
- SCIC 95070 872-B7
LAKE REE ST
32400 FRMT 94555 732-B6
LAKE REED CT
300 MRTZ 94553 592-A1
LAKERIDGE AV
23000 AlaC 94541 692-D7
LAKERIDGE CT
- SRMN 94583 653-F7
LAKE RIDGE DR
2100 MRTZ 94553 592-A1
LAKE RIDGE LN
- SJS 95148 855-F1
LAKERIDGE LN
- SRMN 94583 653-F7
LAKERIDGE PL
700 SRMN 94583 653-F7
LAKERIDGE RD
19200 AlaC 94546 691-J4
LAKERIDGE WY
200 SRMN 94583 653-F7
LAKE SANTA CLARA DR
4200 SCL 95054 813-C5
LAKE SHASTA CT
5900 SJS 95123 874-G7
LAKESHIRE CT
900 SJS 95126 853-H3
LAKESHIRE DR
200 DALY 94015 687-A7
500 DALY 94015 707-A1
1900 WLCK 94595 632-A2
LAKESHORE AV
1200 OAK 94606 649-J4
1200 OAK 94607 649-J4
2100 OAK 94610 649-J4
3000 OAK 94610 650-A2
LAKESHORE CIR
1300 SJS 95131 814-B6
LAKESHORE CT
- RCH 94804 608-H3
LAKESHORE DR
- SF 94132 666-J6
100 SMCo 94402 748-G6
700 RDWC 94065 749-J6
700 SMCo 94025 809-A3
1200 SMCo 94025 810-A3
4200 SCL 95054 813-C5
E LAKESHORE DR
4000 SRMN 94583 653-F7
5000 SRMN 94583 673-F1
W LAKESHORE DR
5000 SRMN 94583 653-F7
LAKESHORE PZ
- SF 94132 667-A6
LAKESIDE AV
100 PCFA 94044 706-J6
LAKESIDE CT
300 MRTZ 94553 571-J7
700 DNVL 94526 653-E6
LAKESIDE DR
- SJS 95148 855-F1
- CMAD 94925 586-G6
- OAK 94607 649-H3
- OAK 94612 649-H3
300 FCTY 94404 749-E1
400 SUNV 94086 812-J7
400 VAL 94589 510-B6
600 SUNV 94086 813-A6
2800 SCL 95054 813-A6
3800 RCH 94806 569-A7
LAKE SPRING CT
11500 CPTO 95014 852-C4
LAKE SUPERIOR CT
33200 FRMT 94555 732-C6
LAKE SUPERIOR PL
33100 FRMT 94555 732-C6
LAKE TAHOE CT
900 SJS 95123 874-G7
LAKE TAHOE TER
- FRMT 94555 732-C7
LAKE TANA ST
32400 FRMT 94555 732-B6

STREET Block	City	ZIP	Pg-Grid
LAKE TEMESCAL LN			
32300	FRMT	94555	732-B6
LAKE TRASINENO DR			
3100	SJS	95135	855-F6
LAKETREE CT			
1500	SJS	95131	814-D5
LAKEVIEW AV			
-	PDMT	94611	650-C1
-	SF	94112	687-D1
200	PCFA	94044	706-J6
LAKEVIEW BLVD			
47000	FRMT	94538	773-F7
47400	FRMT	94538	793-G1
LAKEVIEW CIR			
-	SRMN	94583	673-F1
1100	PIT	94565	574-G4
5200	SRMN	94583	653-F7
LAKEVIEW CT			
-	FRMT	94538	793-G2
-	SJS	95148	855-F2
-	NVTO	94947	526-D6
1800	SLN	94577	691-D1
LAKEVIEW DR			
-	DALY	94015	687-A3
100	WDSD	94062	790-A5
1000	HIL	94010	748-E5
2100	SLN	94577	691-D1
5000	SRMN	94583	653-G7
LAKEVIEW LN			
200	PCFA	94044	706-J6
LAKE VIEW PL			
1900	MRTZ	94553	592-A1
LAKEVIEW PL			
300	CCCo	94507	632-H4
1400	CNCD	94520	592-F3
LAKEVIEW RD			
100	MrnC	-	586-A4
LAKEVIEW WY			
100	SMCo	94062	769-E7
300	SMCo	94062	789-F1
800	RDWC	94062	789-G2
1000	RDWC	94061	789-G2
LAKE VILLA CT			
2200	MRTZ	94553	592-A1
LAKE VISTA AV			
-	DALY	94015	687-B3
LAKE WAWASEE ST			
32900	FRMT	94555	732-C6
LAKEWAY			
3000	SUNV	94086	813-A6
LAKEWOOD AV			
-	SF	94127	667-C7
100	VAL	94591	530-F4
LAKEWOOD CIR			
-	SMTO	94402	768-H1
400	WLCK	94598	612-E5
LAKEWOOD CT			
2100	SJS	95132	814-C3
36600	NWK	94560	752-F5
LAKEWOOD DR			
-	DALY	94015	687-A4
-	DALY	94015	686-J4
600	SUNV	94089	812-G5
1900	SJS	95132	814-C3
36500	NWK	94560	752-F5
LAKEWOOD PL			
1600	PIT	94565	574-G6
2200	MRTZ	94553	592-A1
LAKEWOOD RD			
100	WLCK	94598	612-E5
100	CCCo	94598	612-D4
LAKEWOOD ST			
4500	PLE	94588	713-J1
LAKEWOOD WY			
26700	HAY	94544	711-J6
LAKE WOODLAND COM			
-	FRMT	94555	732-B7
LAKME CT			
4000	SJS	95121	854-H4
LAKME WY			
1400	SJS	95121	854-H4
LA LANNE CT			
25600	LAH	94022	811-C6
LA LOMA AV			
1300	BERK	94708	609-J7
1700	BERK	94709	609-J7
1700	BERK	94709	629-J1
LA LOMA CT			
-	SRFL	94901	586-G2
24900	LAH	94022	831-C3
LA LOMA DR			
-	SMCo	94025	790-C6
-	MLPK	94025	790-C6
24900	LAH	94022	831-C3
25300	SCIC	94022	831-C3
LA LOMA LN			
100	SMCo	94010	728-B7
LALOR DR			
5700	SJS	95123	874-G5
LAM CT			
-	CCCo	94707	609-F2
-	CCCo	94530	609-F2
LAMA WY			
1600	SJS	95120	873-J1
LA MADRONAL			
-	ORIN	94563	610-F7
LA MAISON DR			
600	SJS	95128	853-E2
LA MANCHA CT			
500	DNVL	94526	653-B3
LA MANCHA PL			
-	MLBR	94030	728-A4
LA MAR CT			
2200	CNCD	94518	592-G5
19600	CPTO	95014	852-F1
LA MAR DR			
2200	CNCD	94518	592-G5
19600	CPTO	95014	852-F1
LAMAR LP			
3700	AlaC	94552	692-F2
LAMARTINE ST			
-	SF	94112	667-G6
LA MATA WY			
3500	PA	94306	811-B2
LAMBARE WY			
-	SJS	95135	855-G3
LAMBAREN AV			
800	LVMR	94550	715-F1
LAMBECK LN			
6100	SJS	95119	875-D5
LAMBERT AV			
200	PA	94306	791-C7
200	PA	94306	811-B1
LAMBERT CT			
2500	UNC	94587	732-F7
LAMBERT LN			
2500	SJS	95125	854-B6
LAMBERT PL			
2400	UNC	94587	732-F6
LAMBERT RD			
4000	CCCo	94803	589-C2
LAMBERT WY			
-	NVTO	94945	525-J1
500	MTVW	94043	812-B3
LAMBETH CT			
600	SUNV	94087	832-E5
2900	SJS	95132	814-E3
LAMBETH LN			
1700	CNCD	94518	592-F6
LAMBETH RD			
900	LVMR	94550	695-G6
LAMBETH SQ			
-	MRGA	94556	631-F5
LAMBRECHT CT			
8600	ELCR	94530	609-E1
LA MESA CT			
-	BURL	94010	728-B7
-	WLCK	94598	612-E5
400	SMCo	94028	810-D3
4700	FRMT	94536	752-F4
LA MESA DR			
100	SMCo	94010	728-B7
100	SMCo	94028	810-D3
1500	BURL	94010	728-B7
3100	SCAR	94070	769-D6
3400	HAY	94542	712-F4
LA MESA LN			
-	BURL	94010	728-B7
-	WLCK	94598	612-E5
3900	SJS	95124	873-H2
LA MESA TER			
900	SUNV	94086	812-D6
LA MIEL CT			
2000	SJS	95008	853-B6
LA MIEL WY			
2100	SJS	95008	853-B6
LA MIRADA DR			
900	PCFA	94044	726-J4
2100	RCH	94803	589-D3
2300	SJS	95125	853-J7
3600	CNCD	94519	593-A1
3600	CNCD	94519	592-J1
LA MIRADO WY			
-	SCIC	95030	872-H7
LA MIRANDA PL			
3800	PIT	94565	574-B5
LAMKIN LN			
-	PLHL	94523	592-D6
LAMMERHAVEN CT			
-	SJS	95111	874-J1
LAMMY PL			
1100	LALT	94024	831-H2
LAMOND CT			
3200	SJS	95148	855-D2
LAMONT AV			
700	NVTO	94945	526-C4
LAMONT CT			
100	VAL	94591	530-E5
1400	CMBL	95008	853-B7
1700	SUNV	94087	832-B6
16900	AlaC	94546	691-J1
LAMONT WY			
400	DNVL	94526	652-H2
LA MONTAGNE CT			
100	LGTS	95030	873-B3
LA MONTANITA CT			
100	VAL	94589	530-C1
LAMONTE AV			
200	SSF	94080	707-D3
LAMORE DR			
1400	SJS	95130	853-A4
LAMOUR LN			
-	WLCK	94598	612-D5
LAMOUREUX ST			
3700	SLN	94578	691-B4
LAMP CT			
-	MRGA	94556	651-G2
LAMP ST			
3400	OAK	94605	671-A2
LAMPLIGHT CT			
1800	WLCK	94596	611-H3
LAMPLIGHTER WY			
-	SJS	95134	813-G2
LAMPREY DR			
-	UNC	94587	731-J5
LAMSHIN LN			
-	SCAR	94062	769-G6
LAMSON LN			
-	SF	94114	667-F2
LAMSON RD			
17800	AlaC	94546	691-J3
18500	AlaC	94546	692-A2
LANA CT			
800	CMBL	95008	853-C7
LANA LN			
3400	LFYT	94549	611-F6
LANA TER			
4000	FRMT	94536	752-H1
LANAI AV			
1800	SJS	95122	834-H7
2000	SJS	95122	854-J1
LANAI CIR			
500	UNC	94587	732-C6
LANAI CT			
27800	HAY	94544	731-J1
LANAI DR			
3400	SRMN	94583	673-E1
3400	SRMN	94583	653-E7
LANARK CT			
1000	SUNV	94087	832-G5
LANARK LN			
19700	SAR	95070	852-F7
LANCASHIRE DR			
1200	CNCD	94518	592-J3
LANCASHIRE PL			
3300	CNCD	94518	592-H7
LANCASTER			
-	HER	94547	569-F1
LANCASTER AV			
-	MrnC	94904	586-E4
LANCASTER CIR			
-	CCCo	94565	573-G3
LANCASTER CT			
-	CCCo	94507	632-J2
-	WLCK	94595	612-C7
2300	HAY	94542	712-C2
2500	SCL	95051	833-C1
3500	FRMT	94536	752-J3
7000	DBLN	94568	693-J3
LANCASTER DR			
600	LFYT	94549	631-J2
1700	SJS	95124	873-H2
2300	SPAB	94806	588-J1
2300	RCH	94806	588-J1
LANCASTER LN			
-	SF	94132	666-J6
200	CCCo	94565	573-G3
LANCASTER RD			
100	WLCK	94595	612-C6
600	WLCK	94595	632-D1
1000	HIL	94010	748-F3
2400	HAY	94542	712-C2
6800	DBLN	94568	693-J3
15700	SAR	95070	872-G6
15700	SCIC	95030	872-G6
15700	MSER	95030	872-G6
LANCASTER ST			
300	OAK	94601	670-B1
LANCASTER WY			
100	VAL	94591	530-G5
400	RDWC	94062	789-H1
600	RDWC	94061	789-H1
LANCE CT			
-	MRGA	94556	631-E7
LANCELOT CT			
800	DNVL	94526	653-B2
3500	FRMT	94536	752-J3
27900	HAY	94544	712-A7
LANCELOT DR			
4200	CNCD	94521	593-A4
LANCELOT LN			
1100	SJS	95127	835-B3
LANCER DR			
900	CPTO	95014	852-F3
1000	SJS	95129	852-F3
LANCERO CT			
4400	FRMT	94536	752-E2
LANCERO ST			
35100	FRMT	94536	752-E2
LANCEWOOD PL			
100	LGTS	95030	873-B3
LANDA LN			
-	SMCo	94061	790-A4
LANDAHL CT			
-	BEN	94510	551-A3
LANDALE AV			
7500	DBLN	94568	693-G3
LANDANA CT			
3800	CNCD	94519	573-A7
LANDANA DR			
1700	CNCD	94519	593-A1
1700	CNCD	94519	573-A7
1800	CNCD	94519	572-J7
LANDANA ST			
100	AMCN	94589	509-J2
LANDAU CT			
5300	SJS	95123	875-B3
LANDELL CT			
1500	LALT	94024	832-A4
LANDER AV			
25600	HAY	94544	712-A4
LANDER DR			
-	MRTZ	94553	571-F7
LANDER PL			
200	SRMN	94583	673-G7
LANDEROS DR			
200	SCL	95051	833-C7
LANDERS ST			
-	SF	94114	667-H2
LANDERWOOD LN			
6600	SJS	95120	894-E2
LANDES PL			
36200	NWK	94560	752-D6
LANDESS AV			
1400	MPS	95035	814-D2
1400	SJS	95132	814-D2
LANDFAIR AV			
300	SMTO	94403	749-C7
LANDING LN			
1100	MLBR	94030	728-A2
LANDING PKWY			
46100	FRMT	94538	773-F6
LANDING RD			
4000	FRMT	94538	773-E7
LANDINGS DR			
1800	MTVW	94043	811-G1
LANDINI LN			
1100	CNCD	94520	592-F4
LANDMARK PKWY			
-	MTVW	94043	811-H1
LANDON AV			
40200	FRMT	94538	773-B1
LANDREGAN ST			
5600	EMVL	94608	629-E6
LANDS END CT			
100	VAL	94591	530-G7
LANDSFORD PL			
800	SCL	95050	833-D1
LANDSLIDE CT			
2600	SCL	95051	833-A1
LANDVALE RD Rt#-13			
-	OAK	94611	630-B4
300	OAK	94618	630-B4
LANE AV			
200	CCCo	94565	573-G3
900	MTVW	94040	811-H6
LANE CT			
-	OAK	94611	630-C7
LANE DR			
2800	CNCD	94518	592-G5
LANE PL			
-	ATN	94027	790-F1
LANE ST			
1000	BLMT	94002	769-F2
1100	SF	94124	668-C6
LANE A			
-	SCIC	94305	790-H7
1500	SJS	95112	834-A1
LANE B			
500	SCIC	94305	810-H1
1500	SJS	95112	834-A1
LANE C			
500	SCIC	94305	790-H7
500	SCIC	94305	810-H1
600	SJS	95112	834-A1
LANE D			
600	SJS	95112	834-A1
LANE E			
600	SJS	95112	834-A1
LANE F			
600	SJS	95112	834-A1
LANEVIEW DR			
3100	SJS	95132	814-D2
LANE W			
500	SCIC	94305	790-H7
LANEWOOD CT			
900	SJS	95125	854-C6
LANEWOOD DR			
900	SJS	95125	854-C6
LANFAIR CIR			
400	SJS	95136	874-F1
LANFAIR CT			
600	SJS	95136	874-F1
LANFAIR DR			
500	SJS	95136	874-F1
LANG AV			
34500	FRMT	94555	752-E1
LANG RD			
300	BURL	94010	728-H5
LANG ST			
1400	MRTZ	94553	571-E2
LANGDON CT			
-	SF	94129	647-B3
-	PDMT	94611	650-B1
4000	SJS	95121	855-A5
LANGFORD CT			
5500	CNCD	94521	593-H4
LANGHORN CT			
34100	FRMT	94555	732-E7
LANGHORN DR			
2700	FRMT	94555	732-E7
LANGLEY CT			
3000	ANT	94509	575-C7
LANGLEY LN			
-	NVTO	94949	546-G4
LANGLEY ST			
-	OAK	94621	670-D6
LANGLEY WY			
200	HAY	94544	711-J4
LANGLIE CT			
1100	CCCo	94572	570-A1
LANGLIE WY			
1000	CCCo	94572	570-A1
LANGMUIR CT			
7500	DBLN	94568	693-J2
LANGMUIR LN			
6800	DBLN	94568	693-J2
LANGON PL			
19300	AlaC	94546	691-H4
LANGPORT DR			
1600	SUNV	94087	832-E5
LANGPORT WY			
1600	SUNV	94087	832-E5
LANGTON AV			
200	LALT	94022	811-D3
LANGTON ST			
-	SF	94103	668-A1
-	SF	94103	648-A7
LANGTON WY			
500	AlaC	94541	691-G6
LANGTRY CT			
38900	FRMT	94536	753-D2
LANHAM CT			
2300	SJS	95148	855-B1
LANHAM DR			
-	NVTO	94949	546-G3
LANIER AV			
1600	SLN	94579	691-A7
LANIER LN			
2600	SJS	95121	854-J3
LANI KAI DR			
1300	CNCD	94520	592-F2
LANING DR			
100	WDSD	94062	789-G5
LANITOS AV			
200	SUNV	94086	812-C7
LANITOS CT			
2000	ANT	94509	595-B2
LANNING CT			
500	SJS	95133	834-G1
LANNING WY			
2300	SJS	95133	834-F2
LANNOY CT			
19900	SAR	95070	872-E1
LANO ST			
400	SJS	95125	854-C3
LA NOCHE CT			
-	NVTO	94945	525-J2
LA NORIA			
-	ORIN	94563	610-G6
LANSBERRY CT			
100	LGTS	95032	873-D6
LANSDALE AV			
-	FRFX	94930	566-A6
-	SF	94127	667-D5
-	SANS	94960	566-A6
300	MLBR	94030	728-A3
10300	CPTO	95014	852-F1
LANSDALE CT			
1100	SJS	95120	894-F2
LANSDALE ST			
3000	SMTO	94403	749-A6
LANSDOWN CT			
800	SUNV	94087	832-C2
3100	PLE	94588	694-F6
LANSFORD AV			
2200	SJS	95125	854-A6
LANSFORD CT			
-	SRMN	94583	673-F2
200	AMCN	94589	509-J3
LANSING AV			
1200	SJS	95118	874-B4
LANSING CT			
6500	PLE	94566	714-D6
38100	FRMT	94536	752-J4
LANSING ST			
-	SF	94105	648-B6
LANSING WY			
200	AlaC	94541	711-F2
LANTANA AV			
2100	SJS	95130	852-J6
4700	LVMR	94550	696-A4
LANTANA COM			
-	FRMT	94536	752-G5
LANTANA CT			
22100	AlaC	94546	692-B6
LANTANA DR			
900	SUNV	94086	832-G2
LANTERN CT			
3200	SJS	95111	854-J5
LANTERN WY			
3200	SJS	95111	854-J5
LANTIS LN			
1700	LALT	94024	832-A4
LANTZ AV			
2700	SJS	95124	873-F1
LANWAY CT			
-	WLCK	94596	612-A2
3000	CNCD	94518	592-H5
LANYARD CV			
-	CMAD	94925	606-J1
LANYARD DR			
400	RDWC	94065	749-H7
LANYARD TER			
37100	FRMT	94536	752-H2
LA ORINDA PL			
2000	CNCD	94518	592-F5
LAPA DR			
5000	SJS	95129	852-J1
LA PALA CT			
3300	SJS	95127	814-J7
LA PALA DR			
200	SJS	95127	814-J7
200	SJS	95127	834-J1
LA PALA PL			
3300	SJS	95127	814-J7
LA PALMA PL			
600	MPS	95035	794-B5
LA PALMAS WY			
4200	UNC	94587	731-J6
LA PALOMA			
-	CMBL	95008	853-F7
LA PALOMA AV			
20200	SAR	95070	872-E2
LA PALOMA DR			
11000	CPTO	95014	852-B3
LA PALOMA PL			
-	CCCo	94803	589-C1
LA PALOMA RD			
400	CCCo	94803	589-C1
13000	LAH	94022	831-B1
13000	LAH	94022	811-C7
LA PALOMA WK			
-	MLV	94941	606-D2
LA PARA AV			
700	PA	94306	811-C2
LA PASADA			
100	MrnC	94903	566-H2
LA PAZ			
-	MTVW	94043	812-A2
-	CMBL	95008	853-F7
LA PAZ AV			
10000	SRMN	94583	673-G5
LA PAZ CT			
300	SRMN	94583	673-B2
1400	SJS	95118	874-A3
LA PAZ ST			
-	VAL	94591	530-C7
LA PAZ WY			
24000	HAY	94541	711-G3
LAPAZ WY			
13500	SAR	95070	872-H1
LA PERA CIR			
200	DNVL	94526	653-C7
LA PERA CT			
-	DNVL	94526	653-D7
LA PERDIZ CT			
100	SRFL	94903	566-D4
LA PETITE WY			
-	SJS	95133	814-G7
LAPHAM WY			
-	SF	94112	687-G2
LAPIDGE ST			
-	SF	94110	667-H2
LA PINTA WY			
4700	SJS	95129	852-B7
LAPIS CT			
100	HER	94547	569-H5
LAPIS LN			
4900	PLE	94566	714-E5
LA PLATA PZ			
800	CMBL	95008	873-C1
LA PLAYA			
200	SF	94121	646-H7
800	SF	94121	666-H2
1200	SF	94122	666-H2
LA PLAYA CT			
3100	CCCo	94549	611-J1
21500	CPTO	95014	852-B3
LA PLAYA DR			
500	HAY	94545	711-G4
1700	CCCo	94549	611-J1
LA PLAYA PL			
24700	HAY	94545	711-G5
LA PLAYA WY			
800	MrnC	94903	566-H2
LA PLAZA			
-	ORIN	94563	610-G7
LA PORTE AV			
1700	SJS	95122	834-H6
27400	HAY	94545	711-H7
27700	HAY	94545	731-J1
LA PRADA CT			
1500	LVMR	94550	715-F3
LA PRADERA DR			
1500	CMBL	95008	853-A6
LA PRENDA			
-	MLBR	94030	727-J5
LA PRENDA AV			
-	BEN	94510	551-D4
LA PRENDA DR			
500	OAK	94603	670-H7
LA PRENDA RD			
400	LALT	94024	831-F1
LAPRIDGE LN			
3400	SJS	95124	873-E2
LA PUERTA DR			
100	SPAB	94806	568-J7
LAPU LAPU ST			
-	SF	94107	648-B6
LA PUNTA			
-	ORIN	94563	610-H5
LA PURISSIMA PL			
1100	FRMT	94539	753-E4
LA PURISSIMA WY			
40500	FRMT	94539	753-E5
LA QUEBRADA WY			
100	SJS	95127	815-C6
LA QUESTA DR			
100	DNVL	94526	653-B2
100	SMCo	94010	728-B7
LA QUESTA WY			
100	WDSD	94062	789-H6
LA QUINTA			
-	MRGA	94556	631-D7
LA QUINTA CT			
200	WLCK	94598	612-J2
400	DNVL	94526	653-D6
7800	PLE	94588	714-B5
LA QUINTA DR			
-	SJS	95127	815-B6
LARABEE CT			
5900	SJS	95120	874-B7
LA RAGIONE AV			
2400	SJS	95111	854-G3
LARAMIE AV			
2800	SRMN	94583	673-F7
LARAMIE CT			
5300	FRMT	94536	752-G6
LARAMIE GATE CIR			
2600	PLE	94566	694-D7
LARCH AV			
400	SSF	94080	707-H1
1000	MRGA	94556	631-D7
1000	MRGA	94556	651-E1
LARCH CT			
2600	SJS	95121	854-H3
2700	ANT	94509	595-F3
3700	CNCD	94519	593-A1
LARCH DR			
-	ATN	94027	770-G7
-	ATN	94027	790-G1
-	NVTO	94947	526-D7
LARCH LN			
-	MRGA	94556	651-D1
200	PCFA	94044	707-A6
200	PCFA	94044	706-J6
LARCH ST			
200	SF	94102	647-H6
500	MPS	95035	793-H6
LARCH WY			
2500	ANT	94509	595-F3
36000	FRMT	94536	732-J7
LARCH GROVE PL			
5300	SJS	95123	875-A3
LARCHMONT AV			
12200	SAR	95070	852-F6
LARCHMONT CT			
6000	SJS	95123	875-B6
LARCHMONT DR			
600	SMCo	94015	687-A4
6000	SJS	95123	875-B6
LARCHMONT ISL			
500	ALA	94501	669-G2
LARCHMONT LN			
3100	SPAB	94806	588-H1
LARCHMONT ST			
300	HAY	94544	711-G4
LARCHWOOD DR			
5200	SJS	95118	874-B4
LAREDO CT			
100	SRMN	94583	673-C2
LAREDO DR			
36300	FRMT	94536	752-G3
LAREDO RD			
18500	AlaC	94546	691-G3
LA REINA ST			
2400	PIN	94564	569-G7
LA RENA DR			
25100	LAH	94022	831-C1
LARGA VISTA DR			
14900	LGTS	95032	873-F6
LARGO DR			
2700	SJS	95132	814-D3
LARGUITA LN			
-	PTLV	94028	810-B5
LA RHEE DR			
2800	SJS	95124	873-J1
LARIAT CT			
-	WLCK	94596	632-G2
LARIAT LN			
600	SJS	95132	815-A5
2100	WLCK	94596	632-F2
6700	AlaC	94552	692-F2
LA RIBERA ST			
5500	LVMR	94550	696-C6
LARIMER WY			
4800	AlaC	94546	692-C4
LA RINCON WY			
-	VAL	94590	530-B3
LA RINCONADA DR			
100	MSER	95030	873-B4
100	LGTS	95030	873-B2
14200	SCIC	95030	873-B3
LARIOS CT			
6000	SJS	95123	874-G6
LARIOS WY			
6100	SJS	95123	874-G6
LARISSA CT			
900	SJS	95136	874-E3
LARK AV			
1600	RDWC	94061	790-A2
16300	LGTS	95032	873-C4
16500	LGTS	95030	873-C4
LARK CT			
-	LKSP	94939	586-F7
300	CCCo	94507	632-F6
1000	NVTO	94947	526-B5
4100	FRMT	94555	732-B7
LARK LN			
100	MrnC	94941	606-F6
200	CCCo	94507	632-E6
1000	FCTY	94404	749-H2
1400	CNCD	94521	593-C4
1700	SUNV	94087	832-F6
LARK ST			
13800	SLN	94578	691-D3
15100	AlaC	94578	691-D3
LARK WY			
1800	SAR	95070	872-F4
33100	FRMT	94555	732-B7
LARKDALE AV			
7200	DBLN	94568	693-H3
LARKELLEN LN			
700	LALT	94024	832-A3
LARKEY LN			
2200	WLCK	94596	612-A2
S LARKEY LN			
2200	WLCK	94596	612-A3
LARKIN AV			
1400	SJS	95129	852-F4
LARKIN CT			
300	BEN	94510	551-A2
LARKIN DR			
300	BEN	94510	551-A2
400	BEN	94510	550-J2
LARKIN ST			
-	SF	94102	647-J5
600	SF	94109	647-J5
2300	SF	94109	647-H4
LARKMEAD CT			
600	SJS	95117	853-C2
LARKMEAD RD			
600	SJS	95117	853-C2
LARKSPUR AV			
-	DALY	94015	687-A6
900	SUNV	94086	832-G2
LARKSPUR CT			
1800	CNCD	94519	573-A7
LARKSPUR DR			
-	SMCo	-	727-H4
300	EPA	94303	791-D2
800	MLBR	94030	727-H3
900	BURL	94010	728-F6
900	LVMR	94550	696-A4
1500	SJS	95125	854-A7
2700	ANT	94509	575-G7
2900	ANT	94509	595-H1
3800	CNCD	94519	573-A7
3800	CNCD	94519	572-J7
E LARKSPUR DR			
3900	ANT	94509	595-H1
LARKSPUR LN			
-	NVTO	94947	526-D7
2100	SRMN	94583	653-J7
LARKSPUR PZ			
-	HAY	94542	712-B3
LARKSPUR RD			
900	OAK	94610	650-B3
LARKSPUR ST			
-	AMCN	94589	509-J3
-	SRFL	94901	586-J2
38600	NWK	94560	772-G1
LARKSPUR-SAN FRANCISCO FERRY			
-	CMAD	-	587-B6
-	LKSP	-	586-J5
-	MrnC	-	587-B6
-	SF	-	607-F4
-	SF	-	627-J1
-	SF	-	648-C1
LARKSPUR LANDING CIR			
-	LKSP	94904	586-H4
LARKSPUR PLAZA DR			
-	LKSP	94939	586-F5
LARKSTONE CT			
-	DNVL	94526	653-C3
LARKWOOD CIR			
100	DNVL	94526	653-C6
LARKWOOD CT			
200	VAL	94591	530-F4
1000	CNCD	94521	593-C5
1500	MPS	95035	793-J4
LARMER CT			
300	PDMT	94610	650-B1
LARNEL PL			
11700	LALT	94024	831-H4
LA ROCHELLE TER			
1100	SUNV	94089	812-G4
LA RODA CT			
20000	CPTO	95014	852-E2
LA RODA DR			
10500	CPTO	95014	852-E2
LA ROSA WY			
-	LKSP	94939	586-F7
LA ROSSA CIR			
1500	SJS	95125	854-D3
LA ROSSA CT			
200	SJS	95125	854-D3
LARRABEE ST			
29800	HAY	94544	712-D7
LARRIKEET CT			
2500	PLE	94566	714-C1
LARRY CT			
3600	SJS	95121	855-A5
LARRY LN			
-	OAK	94611	650-F2
LARRY PL			
1000	CNCD	94518	592-E5
LARRY WY			
10500	CPTO	95014	832-E6
LARSEN CIR			
100	VAL	94589	509-J6
LARSEN CT			
2600	SCL	95051	833-B3
LARSEN PL			
1800	SCL	95051	833-B3
LARSENS LNDG			
100	LALT	94022	811-D3
LARSON WY			
1000	SJS	95117	853-B3
LARWIN AV			
1100	CNCD	94521	593-A5
N LARWIN AV			
-	CNCD	94518	593-B5
-	CNCD	94521	593-B5
S LARWIN AV			
4300	CNCD	94521	593-A5
LA SALLE AV			
-	OAK	94611	650-D1
-	PDMT	94611	650-D1
-	PDMT	94610	650-C2
200	SCL	95051	832-J7
600	SF	94124	668-B5
2800	CNCD	94520	572-E6
4500	FRMT	94536	752-F3
LA SALLE CT			
-	PDMT	94611	650-D2
300	PIN	94564	569-E3
1900	WLCK	94598	592-E7
LA SALLE DR			
-	MRGA	94556	631-D3
1000	SUNV	94087	832-B5
2000	SMTO	94403	749-A4
2100	WLCK	94598	592-E7
2300	PIN	94564	569-E3
2600	MTVW	94040	831-J2

LASALLE DR 1998 BAY AREA STREET INDEX LEGEND RD 955

Thomas Bros. Maps ®
COPYRIGHT 1997

BAY AREA

STREET
Block City ZIP Pg-Grid

LASALLE DR
36100 NWK 94560 752-D6
LA SALLE RD
- HIL 94010 748-F3
LA SALLE ST
1600 MRTZ 94553 571-F3
LA SALLE WY
2600 SJS 95130 852-J7
LA SANDRA WY
- PTLV 94028 810-B4
LAS ANIMAS DR
6600 MRTZ 94553 591-H4
LAS AROMAS
- ORIN 94563 610-H6
2600 OAK 94611 650-F2
LAS ASTAS DR
100 LGTS 95030 873-C4
LASATA CT
100 DNVL 94526 653-F4
LAS BARRANCAS DR
600 DNVL 94526 652-H1
LASCAR CT
2300 SJS 95124 873-E3
LASCAR PL
2400 SJS 95124 873-E3
LAS CASAS DR
- SRFL 94901 567-A7
LAS CASAS DE LOS PINOS
2300 SJS 95133 834-F1
LAS CASCADAS
- ORIN 94563 610-H6
LAS COLINAS LN
- SJS 95119 875-E6
LAS COLINAS RD
3600 AlaC 94550 695-J5
LAS COLINDAS RD
300 SRFL 94903 566-C1
LAS CRUCES CT
5000 SJS 95118 874-B3
LA SELVA
3000 SMTO 94403 749-E5
LA SELVA DR
3700 PA 94306 811-C1
LAS ENCANTOS CT
1900 CMBL 95030 873-A2
1900 CMBL 95030 872-J2
LA SENDA
- ORIN 94563 610-G5
LA SENDA RD
- HIL 94010 748-G3
LA SERENA AV
100 CCCo 94507 632-F6
LA SERENA CT
- CCCo 94507 632-F6
LA SERENA WY
- CCCo 94507 632-F6
LA SEYNE PL
5600 SJS 95138 875-F1
LAS FELIZ CT
4200 UNC 94587 732-A5
LAS FLORES AV
100 SRFL 94903 566-E4
LAS FLORES CT
- OAK 94611 630-F7
1100 LALT 94022 811-D3
LAS FLORES LN
14800 LGTS 95032 873-G6
LAS FLORES RD
700 LVMR 94550 696-B4
LAS GALLINAS AV
100 MrnC 94903 546-E7
100 SRFL 94903 566-D2
1000 SRFL 94903 546-E7
LAS HUERTAS CT
- SRFL 94903 566-E4
LAS HUERTAS RD
3300 LFYT 94549 611-G7
3300 LFYT 94549 631-H1
LA SIERRA TER
- UNC 94587 732-E5
LAS JOYAS CT
1900 CMBL 95030 873-A2
LAS JUNITAS WY
- CCCo 94596 612-D1
1100 WLCK 94596 612-D1
1300 WLCK 94596 592-D7
LAS JUNTAS ST
600 MRTZ 94553 571-D3
LASKIE ST
- SF 94103 647-J7
LAS LOMAS
200 NVTO 94949 546-J5
LAS LOMAS CT
2000 CNCD 94519 572-J6
LAS LOMAS DR
700 MPS 95035 794-B6
LAS LOMAS LN
100 TBRN 94920 607-E7
100 TBRN 94920 627-E1
LAS LOMAS PL
- CCCo 94598 612-G4
LAS LOMAS WY
- WLCK 94598 612-G4
200 CCCo 94598 612-G4
LAS LOMITAS DR
4500 PLE 94566 714-E4
LAS MESAS PTH
- ORIN 94563 610-F7
LAS MIRADAS DR
200 LGTS 95030 873-C4
LAS MORADAS CIR
- SPAB 94806 588-J3
LA SOLANO
- MLBR 94030 727-J4
LA SOMBRA CT
- ORIN 94563 631-B4
LAS ONDAS CT
20000 CPTO 95014 852-E1
LAS ONDAS WY
10300 CPTO 95014 852-E1
LA SONOMA CT
- CCCo 94507 632-F6
LA SONOMA DR
- CCCo 94507 632-G6
LA SONOMA WY
100 CCCo 94507 632-F6
LAS OVEJAS AV
700 SRFL 94903 566-B2
LAS PADRES TER
- UNC 94587 732-E4

LAS PALMAS AV
100 VAL 94589 530-B1
800 NVTO 94949 546-F2
40100 FRMT 94539 753-E4
E LAS PALMAS AV
- FRMT 94539 753-E3
LAS PALMAS CT
100 FRMT 94539 753-F4
11200 DBLN 94568 693-F5
E LAS PALMAS CT
39900 FRMT 94539 753-E3
LAS PALMAS DR
800 SCL 95051 833-B5
LAS PALMAS WY
- SJS 95133 814-J4
7300 DBLN 94568 693-F5
LAS PALOMAS
- ORIN 94563 610-H5
LAS PAVADAS AV
800 SRFL 94903 566-C3
LA SPEZIA PL
- SJS 95138 875-J1
LAS PIEDRAS
- ORIN 94563 610-E7
- SMCo 94028 830-D5
LAS PIEDRAS CT
- BURL 94010 728-B5
1600 CMBL 95030 873-A2
LAS PIEDRAS DR
2800 BURL 94010 728-A6
LAS PLUMAS AV
1500 SJS 95133 834-E3
W LAS POSITAS BLVD
3000 PLE 94588 694-E6
4400 PLE 94566 694-E6
6300 PLE 94588 714-A1
6900 PLE 94588 713-J1
LAS POSITAS CT
2000 LVMR 94550 695-F6
LAS POSITAS RD
2700 LVMR 94550 695-G5
2900 AlaC 94550 695-G5
3800 AlaC 94550 695-G5
3800 AlaC 94550 696-A5
4200 LVMR 94550 696-E4
LAS PULGAS RD
400 WDSD 94062 789-H4
LAS QUEBRADAS LN
- CCCo 94507 632-H4
LAS RAMBLAS
1800 CNCD 94521 593-F4
LAS RAPOSAS RD
1000 SRFL 94903 566-C1
LASS DR
2300 SCL 95054 813-C4
LASSEN AV
200 MTVW 94043 811-F3
1100 MPS 95035 814-C1
5000 SJS 95129 852-J4
LASSEN CT
- MLPK 94025 790-C7
600 SSF 94080 707-F4
1500 VAL 94591 530-D3
1800 ANT 94509 575-F5
5600 CLAY 94517 593-F6
LASSEN DR
100 SBRN 94066 707-E7
100 SBRN 94066 727-E1
400 MRTZ 94553 572-A7
900 MLPK 94025 790-C7
1000 BLMT 94002 769-A2
3800 PIT 94565 574-D5
LASSEN LN
- NVTO 94947 526-E7
1000 PCFA 94044 707-A5
LASSEN RD
900 LVMR 94550 696-A5
LASSEN ST
400 LALT 94022 811-E7
500 SSF 94080 707-F4
600 RCH 94805 589-A5
700 VAL 94591 530-D4
1000 BERK 94707 609-G6
1000 SPAB 94805 589-A5
5700 ELCR 94530 609-C5
6900 PLE 94588 714-A1
29000 HAY 94544 712-C7
29200 HAY 94544 732-C1
37000 FRMT 94536 752-G4
LASSEN WY
1600 BURL 94010 728-C5
2600 PIN 94564 569-H7
LASSENPARK CIR
300 SJS 95136 874-G2
LASSO CIR
200 SRMN 94583 673-B3
LAS SOMBRAS CT
400 SMTO 94402 748-F2
LAST AV
100 RCH 94801 588-G5
LAS TARDES CT
- NVTO 94945 525-J2
LAS TRAMPAS RD
- LFYT 94549 631-H1
700 LFYT 94549 611-H7
1500 CCCo 94507 632-E6
LASTRETO AV
300 SUNV 94086 812-F6
LASUEN CT
100 LGTS 95032 873-F6
LASUEN DR
800 SLN 94578 691-C5
1200 MLBR 94030 728-A5
LASUEN ST
100 SCIC 94305 790-H6
LAS UVAS CT
100 LGTS 95030 873-A2
LAS VEGAS AV
9500 OAK 94605 671-B4
LAS VEGAS CT
- ORIN 94563 610-J5
LAS VEGAS RD
- ORIN 94563 610-J5
LASWELL AV
300 SCIC 95128 853-G1
300 SJS 95128 853-G2
LATE HORIZON PL
1800 WLCK 94595 632-B1
LA TERRACE CIR
1000 SJS 95123 874-D5
LATHAM CT
- HIL 94010 728-F7

LATHAM LN
- BERK 94708 609-J6
LATHAM ST
- SRFL 94901 586-F1
100 PDMT 94611 650-A1
1200 MTVW 94041 811-F4
1900 MTVW 94040 811-F4
LATHROP AV
100 SF 94134 688-A2
LATHROP CT
5600 SJS 95123 875-A4
LATHROP DR
800 SCIC 94305 810-H2
5600 SJS 95123 875-A4
LATHROP PL
900 SCIC 94305 810-H2
LATHROP ST
- RDWC 94063 770-B6
LA TIERRA BUENA
300 DNVL 94526 653-A1
LATIMER AV
3900 CMBL 95008 853-B5
4100 SJS 95130 853-A4
4500 SJS 95129 853-A4
E LATIMER AV
100 CMBL 95008 853-E5
W LATIMER AV
- CMBL 95008 853-D5
LATIMER CIR
500 CMBL 95008 853-D5
LATIMER PL
- CCCo 94596 612-F7
3700 OAK 94609 649-H1
LATONA CT
400 SJS 95111 875-C2
LATONA ST
- SF 94124 668-B6
LA TORRE AV
4200 SJS 95111 855-A7
LATOUR AV
- LVMR 94550 715-H4
LATOUR LN
1400 CNCD 94521 593-C4
LATTERI CT
1600 CNCD 94519 593-A2
LATTIE LN
1200 MrnC 94941 606-D5
LAUDERDALE AV
26600 HAY 94545 711-G6
LAUELLA CT
200 MTVW 94041 811-G4
LAUFALL LN
400 SJS 95111 854-F6
LAUGHING COW RD
100 SMCo 94062 789-A7
LAUGHLIN RD
700 LVMR 94550 696-E3
800 AlaC 94550 696-E3
LAUMER AV
- SCIC 95127 835-A1
200 SJS 95127 835-A1
LAURA AV
2000 SLN 94577 690-H2
LAURA CIR
- PIT 94565 574-E5
LAURA CT
800 CMBL 95008 853-C7
1900 CCCo 94521 593-D2
LAURA DR
600 CMBL 95008 853-C7
4700 CCCo 94521 593-D3
5400 SJS 95124 873-G6
LAURA LN
100 PA 94303 791-D4
200 MTVW 94043 811-F3
6200 AlaC 94566 714-E7
LAURA ST
- SF 94112 687-E2
- FRMT 94555 732-C7
LAURA WY
100 ORIN 94563 631-B2
4500 UNC 94587 732-A7
LAURA ALICE WY
1000 CNCD 94520 572-E5
1000 CCCo 94520 572-E5
LAURA ANN CT
500 CCCo 94565 573-F1
LAURAL AV
6200 SJS 95138 875-F6
LAURANT WY
3500 SJS 95132 814-F2
LAUREL AV
- BLV 94920 627-D1
- LKSP 94939 586-E6
- MLBR 94030 728-A3
- MrnC 94904 586-D3
- SANS 94960 566-A7
100 AlaC 94541 711-G2
100 LGTS 95030 872-H7
100 MLPK 94025 790-J3
200 SSF 94080 707-G2
300 HAY 94541 711-G2
300 MrnC 94947 525-G5
400 PIN 94564 569-E4
400 MLPK 94025 791-A2
400 SANS 94960 586-A1
500 SMTO 94401 749-A2
700 BURL 94010 728-F6
800 BLMT 94002 769-E1
1000 EPA 94303 791-A1
1500 CCCo 94805 589-C6
3200 OAK 94602 650-E5
LAUREL CT
- MRTZ 94553 571-E7
500 BEN 94510 551-A1
800 CCCo 94572 569-J1
7400 PLE 94588 714-A1
7400 PLE 94588 713-J2
LAUREL DR
- CMAD 94925 606-G1
- DNVL 94526 653-A2
700 CCCo 94596 612-F7
700 LVMR 94550 695-E7
1000 LFYT 94549 611-F5
2000 SCL 95050 833-C4
4900 CCCo 94521 593-E3
5100 CNCD 94521 593-F4
18300 SCIC 95030 872-J5
LAUREL LN
- BERK 94707 609-F5
- SAUS 94965 627-A2
- CCCo 94803 589-D2

LAUREL LN
- RCH 94803 589-D2
400 PCFA 94044 707-A6
1200 LFYT 94549 611-H4
26600 LAH 94022 811-B7
LAUREL PL
- MLPK 94025 790-F2
- SRFL 94901 566-G7
LAUREL RD
- ANT 94509 595-J3
LAUREL ST
- ATN 94027 790-F2
- MLV 94941 606-C3
- RDWC 94063 770-C6
- SCAR 94070 769-F2
- VAL 94591 530-D6
- MLPK 94025 790-F2
- SF 94118 647-E5
100 SolC 94591 530-D6
700 SJS 95126 833-H5
800 ALA 94501 669-J3
1100 BERK 94708 609-H6
1100 PIT 94565 574-F2
4200 FRMT 94538 753-D7
36800 NWK 94560 752-C7
36900 NWK 94560 772-C1
LAUREL WY
- MTVW 94040 811-E3
- MrnC 94904 586-C4
300 MrnC 94965 606-E7
3700 RDWC 94062 789-G1
LAUREL CANYON CT
2000 FRMT 94539 773-G2
LAUREL CANYON TR
- CCCo 94708 609-H3
LAUREL CANYON WY
44000 FRMT 94539 773-G2
LAUREL CREEK DR
3400 SMTO 94403 749-A7
5800 PLE 94586 693-G6
E LAUREL CREEK RD
3000 SMTO 94403 749-A7
3000 BLMT 94002 749-A7
3100 SMTO 94403 769-A1
3100 BLMT 94002 769-A1
3500 SMTO 94403 768-J1
3500 BLMT 94002 768-J1
3500 SMTO 94403 748-J7
3500 BLMT 94002 748-J7
LAUREL CREEK WY
7600 PLE 94588 693-H6
8000 PLE 94586 693-H6
LAURELDALE LN
4400 SJS 95136 874-D2
LAURELDALE RD
- HIL 94010 748-G2
LAURELEI AV
100 SJS 95128 833-F7
LAURELES DR
1000 LALT 94022 811-D3
LAUREL GLEN COM
43400 FRMT 94539 753-H7
43500 FRMT 94539 773-H1
LAURELGLEN CT
200 CCCo 94506 654-C5
4000 SJS 95118 874-C2
LAUREL GLEN DR
800 PA 94304 830-G1
800 PA 94304 810-G7
LAUREL GLEN TER
- SRFL 94903 566-F5
500 FRMT 94539 753-H7
LAUREL GROVE AV
- MrnC 94904 586-D2
- ROSS 94957 586-D2
LAUREL HILL CT
- SMCo 94402 748-F6
LAUREL HILL DR
1200 SMCo 94402 748-F7
LAURELVIEW CT
- FRMT 94538 793-F1
1800 CNCD 94521 593-F4
LAURELWOOD AV
- MLV 94941 606-D3
LAURELWOOD CT
- SRFL 94901 567-C5
600 LVMR 94550 695-J6
800 ANT 94509 575-F7
800 ANT 94509 595-F1
LAURELWOOD DR
100 DNVL 94506 653-H4
700 SMTO 94403 749-A7
1600 SJS 95125 853-J6
19600 AlaC 94552 692-F2
LAURELWOOD PL
5700 CNCD 94521 593-G7
LAURELWOOD RD
300 SCL 95054 813-D7
LAUREN AV
- NVTO 94947 526-B4
200 PCFA 94044 727-A2
LAUREN DR
5400 SJS 95124 873-J6
LAUREN PL
3700 AlaC 94541 692-D7
LAURENCE CT
3000 CNCD 94520 572-F6
LAURENITA WY
1400 CCCo 94507 632-E4
LAURENT RD
500 HIL 94010 748-D2
LAURENTIAN WY
1700 SUNV 94087 832-B6
LAURETTA DR
21000 CPTO 95014 832-C7
LAURETTE PL
600 HAY 94544 712-B5
LAURIE AV
600 SCL 95054 813-E6
1000 SJS 95125 854-B4
LAURIE COM
4600 LVMR 94550 696-A6
LAURIE CT
- NVTO 94947 525-H3
LAURIE DR
- NVTO 94947 525-H3
LAURIE LN
- SMCo 94402 748-G6
LAURIE JO LN
500 SCL 95050 833-C6
LAURIE MEADOWS DR
- SMTO 94403 749-D6

LAURINA RD
- MLV 94941 606-F3
LAURINDA DR
1800 SJS 95124 873-G4
1800 SJS 95032 873-G4
LAURISTON CT
8000 OAK 94611 630-E5
LAURYN RIDGE CT
800 MPS 95035 814-E1
LAUSANNE AV
- DALY 94014 687-D4
LAUSANNE CT
2800 SJS 95132 814-F5
LAUSETT AV
2000 SJS 95116 834-G4
LAUSSAT ST
- SF 94102 667-G1
200 SF 94117 667-G1
LAVA CT
300 MRTZ 94553 571-J7
LAVA DR
2300 SJS 95133 834-F1
LAVA WY
600 SJS 95133 834-F1
LAVA FALLS CT
100 SRMN 94583 653-G7
LAVA FALLS PL
- SRMN 94583 653-G7
LAVAGETTO CT
- ALA 94502 669-J7
LAVEILLE CT
1200 SJS 95131 814-B7
LA VELLE CT
- DNVL 94526 653-C7
LAVENDER AV
7000 LVMR 94550 696-E5
LAVENDER COM
37900 FRMT 94536 752-J3
LAVENDER CT
2400 WLCK 94596 632-G2
LAVENDER DR
800 SUNV 94086 832-F3
2400 WLCK 94596 632-G3
LAVENDER LN
100 MrnC 94941 606-F6
16300 SCIC 95032 873-D5
LAVENDER PL
5900 NWK 94560 752-H7
LAVENDULA WY
6100 SJS 95119 875-D5
L AVENIDA
1000 MTVW 94043 812-A2
1000 MTVW 94043 811-J2
LAVENIDA
- ORIN 94563 631-B6
LAVER CT
1900 LALT 94024 831-H5
LAVERDA PTH
3400 OAK 94605 670-J2
LA VEREDA
1500 BERK 94708 609-J7
1600 BERK 94709 609-J7
1600 BERK 94709 629-J1
LA VERNE AV
5500 OAK 94605 670-F1
LAVERNE AV
- MrnC 94941 606-C4
LAVERNE CT
- SLN 94579 691-A6
1500 CNCD 94521 593-D4
LAVERNE DR
15200 SLN 94579 691-A6
LAVERNE LN
- MrnC 94941 606-E5
LA VERNE WY
800 LALT 94022 811-D4
LAVERNE WY
5400 CNCD 94521 593-D4
LAVEROCK LN
1200 CCCo 94507 632-F3
LAVETTA WY
1500 CNCD 94519 593-A3
1500 CNCD 94521 593-A3
LA VIDA REAL
12800 LAH 94022 831-A1
LA VINA
300 CCCo 94553 572-C6
LAVINA CT
- ORIN 94563 631-B4
21000 SCIC 95014 832-C6
LA VISTA AV
1200 CNCD 94521 593-A3
1200 CNCD 94521 592-J3
LA VISTA CT
- WLCK 94598 612-E5
13000 SAR 95070 852-F7
LA VISTA DR
13000 SAR 95070 852-F7
LA VISTA RD
300 CCCo 94598 612-F4
500 WLCK 94598 612-E5
LA VISTA WY
- DNVL 94506 653-G4
- SRFL 94901 566-G7
LA VITA TER
- UNC 94587 732-E5
LAVONA DR
- SJS 95118 874-C4
LA VONNE AV
1700 SJS 95116 834-G5
LA VONNE DR
- CMBL 95008 853-B6
LA VUELTA
- ORIN 94563 610-H6
- VAL 94590 530-B3
LAWLER AV
5000 FRMT 94536 752-G6
LAWLER RANCH RD
- SMCo 94025 789-J7
- SMCo 94025 790-A7
- SMCo 94025 810-B1
- WDSD 94062 790-A7
LAWLOR ST
8900 OAK 94605 671-A4
LAWNDALE AV
300 CMBL 95008 853-D5
1600 SLN 94579 691-A7
LAWNVIEW CIR
100 DNVL 94526 653-C6
LAWNVIEW CT
- PIT 94565 574-F5

LAWRENCE AV
- ANT 94509 575-C5
- SF 94112 687-E2
200 SSF 94080 708-B4
LAWRENCE CT
1100 ELCR 94530 609-D2
1900 SCL 95051 832-J3
LAWRENCE DR
- NVTO 94945 526-D3
200 LVMR 94550 696-E3
4200 AlaC 94546 691-J3
4400 AlaC 94546 692-A3
LAWRENCE EXWY Rt#-G2
- SAR 95070 852-H4
- SCL 95051 832-J6
- SCL 95051 852-H4
100 SUNV 94086 812-J7
300 SJS 95014 852-H4
300 SJS 95129 852-H4
300 SCIC 95014 852-H4
800 SUNV 94087 832-J6
1000 SUNV 94089 812-J3
1800 SAR 95129 852-H4
1900 SUNV 94086 832-J6
2900 SCL 95051 812-J7
LAWRENCE LN
900 PA 94303 791-D5
LAWRENCE PL
42600 FRMT 94538 773-B3
LAWRENCE RD
- ALA 94502 669-H6
800 SMTO 94401 749-A1
1000 DNVL 94506 654-C7
1000 CCCo 94506 654-B6
1700 SCL 95051 832-J3
LAWRENCE ST
1200 ELCR 94530 609-C1
LAWRENCE WY
2300 WLCK 94596 612-C4
LAWRENCE CREEK TR
- SMCo 94062 809-A5
LAWRENCE STATION RD
100 SUNV 94086 832-J1
1200 SUNV 94089 812-J3
LAWSON CT
1600 SJS 95118 873-J4
4400 CNCD 94521 593-B5
LAWSON LN
2200 SCL 95054 813-C7
2200 SCL 95054 833-C1
LAWSON RD
- CCCo 94708 609-F2
LAWTHER CT
4000 SJS 95135 855-F3
LAWTON AV
900 SJS 95128 853-H3
4500 OAK 94609 629-J6
5100 OAK 94618 629-J5
5500 OAK 94618 630-A5
LAWTON CT
- SRMN 94583 673-E5
LAWTON DR
- MPS 95035 794-D6
LAWTON PL
400 HAY 94544 711-H4
LAWTON ST
- SF 94122 667-C2
200 ANT 94509 575-D6
2700 SF 94122 666-H3
LAWTON WY
12900 SRMN 94583 673-E5
LAYMAN CT
- WLCK 94596 632-E1
LAYNE CT
700 PA 94303 791-D7
LAYNE PL
- SBRN 94066 707-J7
LAYTON CT
700 SCL 95051 833-B6
LAYTON ST
700 SCL 95051 833-B5
LAYTON WY
10400 SCIC 95127 834-J3
LAZANEO DR
20300 CPTO 95014 832-D7
LAZY LN
3800 SCIC 95135 855-H1
LAZY OAK CT
22500 CPTO 95014 831-J7
LAZY RIVER WY
6700 SJS 95120 894-E2
LDU DR
- CCCo 94553 571-F3
- MRTZ 94553 571-F3
LEA CT
200 CCCo 94806 569-B4
400 NVTO 94945 526-D4
1600 ALA 94501 670-A2
LEA DR
900 SRFL 94903 566-C3
1100 NVTO 94945 526-D4
LEABIG LN
- CCCo 94553 572-A3
LEACH ST
4300 OAK 94602 650-C3
LEAF CT
600 LALT 94022 811-C5
LEAFIELD RD
- DNVL 94506 653-F2
LEAFTREE CIR
1400 SJS 95131 814-C7
LEAFTREE CT
1400 SJS 95131 814-C7
LEAFWOOD CIR
- SRFL 94901 566-E7
3500 ANT 94509 595-H1
LEAFWOOD CT
3400 SMTO 94403 748-J7
LEAFWOOD DR
1300 NVTO 94947 526-C6
LEAFWOOD HTS
1100 NVTO 94947 526-C6
LEAFWOOD LN
3200 SJS 95111 854-F6
LEAHY ST
500 RDWC 94061 790-C1
LEAHY WY
3300 LVMR 94550 715-J1
LEAMONT CT
- OAK 94605 671-C5

LEAN AV
5300 SJS 95123 875-A3
LEAN WY
5900 SJS 95123 875-A5
LEANDER DR
12700 LAH 94022 811-B7
LEANING OAK CT
2700 WLCK 94598 612-H4
LEANNE LN
100 CNCD 94518 592-G4
LEATHERWOOD CT
4400 CNCD 94521 593-B5
6700 SJS 95120 894-C5
LEAVENWORTH ST
- SF 94102 647-J5
300 SF 94109 647-J5
1900 SF 94109 647-J3
2000 SF 94133 647-J3
LEAVESLEY PL
10800 CPTO 95014 852-B2
LEAVITT CT
4000 AlaC 94546 692-A5
LE BAIN DR
2300 SJS 95130 853-A7
LEBANON ST
500 HAY 94541 711-F3
LE BEAU CT
4600 FRMT 94555 752-C1
LE BLANC CT
- LVMR 94550 715-H3
LECH WALESA
- SF 94102 647-J7
LE CLAIRE CT
- SRFL 94903 566-D4
LE COMPTE PL
800 SJS 95122 834-F7
LE CONTE AV
700 SF 94124 688-B1
2300 BERK 94709 629-H1
LECOUNT WY
38700 FRMT 94536 752-J5
LEDERER CIR
1600 SJS 95131 814-C7
LEDGEWOOD DR
1700 SJS 95124 873-H2
LEDYARD ST
- SF 94124 668-A6
LEE AV
- SF 94112 687-E1
100 LVMR 94550 695-H7
200 SF 94112 667-E7
600 SLN 94577 671-B7
LEE DR
900 MLPK 94025 790-F3
1600 MTVW 94040 811-G7
LEE LN
900 CNCD 94518 592-E6
LEE ST
- MLV 94941 606-C1
- VAL 94590 529-H3
- WLCK 94595 612-C7
200 OAK 94610 649-H2
600 LALT 94022 831-E1
40900 FRMT 94538 753-D7
LEE WK
- CNCD 94518 592-E6
LEE ANN CIR
4500 LVMR 94550 696-B7
LEEDS AV
7500 CPTO 95014 852-D4
LEEDS CT
800 BEN 94510 530-J6
2500 LVMR 94550 695-G6
2800 RCH 94806 589-A2
LEEDS CT E
- DNVL 94526 653-C3
LEEDS CT W
- DNVL 94526 653-C3
LEEMA DR
1100 DNVL 94506 654-B6
LEESA ANN CT
5200 SJS 95124 873-J5
LEESE LN
2000 NVTO 94945 526-A1
2000 NVTO 94945 525-J1
LEESE ST
- SF 94110 667-H6
LEET DR
- OAK 94621 670-E6
LEEWARD CT
100 VAL 94591 550-F3
1100 SJS 95122 834-J5
LEEWARD DR
1100 SJS 95122 834-J5
1400 SJS 95122 835-A5
LEEWARD LN
1100 ALA 94502 670-A7
1400 FCTY 94404 749-G5
LEEWARD PL
100 PIT 94565 574-A2
LEEWARD RD
- BLV 94920 607-D7
LEEWARD ST
2600 HAY 94545 711-F7
LEEWARD WY
- PIT 94565 574-A2
- PIT 94565 573-J2
3000 OAK 94605 671-B5
LEEWARD GLEN RD
- LFYT 94549 632-A3
- LFYT 94549 631-J3
LEEWOOD PL
4300 CNCD 94521 593-C2
LEEWOOD WY
1700 CNCD 94521 593-C2
LE FEBVRE WY
1700 PIN 94564 569-E4
LEFEBVRE WY
4800 ANT 94509 595-J4
LE FEVRE DR
5500 SJS 95118 874-A5
LEFONT DR
1200 SJS 95131 814-B6
LE FRANC DR
5700 SJS 95118 874-B6
LEGARO LN
1700 CNCD 94521 593-C2
LEGEND CIR
1000 VAL 94591 530-E1
LEGEND RD
- MrnC 94960 566-A3

INDEX

STREET
Block City ZIP Pg-Grid

LEGENDARY CT
- PLE 94586 693-H7
LEGER CT
3000 PLE 94588 694-F6
LEGGETT ST
1100 ANT 94509 575-C5
LEGHORN ST
1900 PA 94043 811-F1
1900 MTVW 94043 811-F1
L E GIBSON FWY
I-680
- BEN 94510 551-E5
LEGION AV
2300 OAK 94605 670-H3
LEGION CT
- SF 94127 667-D7
4000 LFYT 94549 611-B7
LEGION OF HONOR DR
- SF 94121 646-J6
LE HAVRE CT
1300 LVMR 94550 695-F6
LEHIGH DR
3500 SCL 95051 832-J6
LEHIGH VALLEY CIR
1000 DNVL 94526 653-B5
LEHIGH VALLEY PL
100 DNVL 94526 653-B5
LEHMAN LN
100 MrnC 94941 606-E4
LEHNING WY
- BSBN 94005 688-A6
LEIDESDORFF ST
- SF 94104 648-B5
200 SF 94111 648-B5
LEIDIG CT
27600 HAY 94544 712-B6
LEIGH AV
300 SCIC 95128 853-G2
300 SJS 95128 853-G2
1000 SJS 95126 853-H2
1400 SJS 95125 853-H4
2000 CMBL 95008 853-G7
2000 SCIC 95125 853-G7
2200 SJS 95124 853-G7
2700 SJS 95124 873-G2
3500 SCIC 95124 873-G2
14400 SJS 95032 873-G6
14500 LGTS 95032 873-G6
N LEIGH AV
1500 SJS 95125 853-H5
1600 CMBL 95008 853-H5
1600 CMBL 95125 853-H5
1800 SCIC 95125 853-H5
S LEIGH AV
1800 CMBL 95008 853-H6
1800 SCIC 95125 853-H6
LEIGH CT
- SRMN 94583 673-E2
1200 CCCo 94596 612-D1
14400 SCIC 95124 873-G3
LEIGH ST
47900 FRMT 94539 793-J1
48100 FRMT 94539 773-J7
LEIGH WY
2600 BLMT 94002 769-B3
LEIGH-ANN PL
1900 SCIC 95125 853-H6
LEIGHTON ST
600 HAY 94544 711-J3
3700 OAK 94611 649-J1
LEIGHTON WY
900 SUNV 94087 832-G5
LEILA CT
15400 LGTS 95032 873-D5
LEILA ST
1900 AlaC 94546 692-A7
LEILANI LN
- CCCo 94595 632-D1
LEIMERT BLVD
1300 OAK 94602 650-D3
LEIMERT PL
1700 OAK 94602 650-D3
LEISURE CT
3100 SJS 95132 814-G5
LEISURE LN
- WLCK 94595 632-B3
- CCCo 94803 589-E3
LEISURE ST
400 LVMR 94550 696-D4
LEITH AV
800 SCL 95054 813-E6
LEITH LN
- SRFL 94901 587-B1
LEIX WY
2600 SSF 94080 707-C4
LEJEAN WY
400 WLCK 94596 592-D7
LEKE WY
3900 RCH 94806 568-G7
LEKSICH AV
600 MTVW 94041 811-G5
LELA WY
900 ANT 94509 575-F6
LELAND AV
- SF 94134 687-J2
100 SMCo 94025 790-E6
200 PA 94306 791-A7
300 SCIC 95128 853-G1
300 SF 94134 688-A2
300 SJS 95128 853-G1
2100 MTVW 94040 811-F3
LELAND CIR
14400 SAR 95070 872-G3
LELAND CT
- NVTO 94947 526-A4
800 LVMR 94550 715-E3
LELAND DR
900 LFYT 94549 611-J6
LELAND LN
100 PIT 94565 574-D4
LELAND RD
2200 PIT 94565 574-E4
E LELAND RD
100 PIT 94565 574-E4
W LELAND RD
- PIT 94565 574-A4
800 PIT 94565 573-F3
1400 CCCo 94565 573-F3
LELAND WY
100 TBRN 94920 607-A4
100 TBRN 94920 606-J4
700 LVMR 94550 715-E3

LELAND WY
2000 CNCD 94520 592-E3
LELAND PARK CT
6500 SJS 95120 894-C1
LELONG ST
1100 SJS 95110 854-B2
LE MANS CT
1300 LVMR 94550 695-F6
LEMARC ST
300 FRMT 94539 753-H7
LEMAS PL
19100 AlaC 94546 692-A4
LEMAY CT
500 ANT 94509 595-E1
LEMAY WY
500 ANT 94509 595-E1
27000 HAY 94544 711-J7
LEMKE PL
5400 FRMT 94538 773-A1
N LEMON AV
1100 MLPK 94025 790-E5
LEMON CT
- HIL 94010 748-C1
LEMON ST
100 VAL 94590 530-B6
400 MLPK 94025 790-E6
900 CCCo 94553 571-F4
1300 SolC 94590 530-B6
LEMON BLOSSOM CT
- SJS 95123 875-B3
LEMONTREE CT
1200 ANT 94509 575-B6
1700 MTVW 94040 831-G1
27400 HAY 94545 711-G7
27400 HAY 94545 731-G1
LEMON TREE RD
1100 SJS 95120 874-D7
LEMONTREE WY
2100 ANT 94509 575-B5
LEMONWOOD CT
700 SJS 95120 894-H2
LEMONWOOD DR
1700 CNCD 94519 593-B1
LEMONWOOD PL
- PIT 94565 574-C6
LEMONWOOD ST
42500 FRMT 94538 773-D2
LEMONWOOD WY
7300 PLE 94588 714-A2
LEMOORE DR
- SCAR 94070 769-G6
LEMOS LN
400 FRMT 94539 753-E5
LEMOYNE WY
2200 SJS 95008 853-B7
LENA CT
100 CCCo 94523 592-B2
LENA DR
- AMCN 94589 510-A4
2700 SJS 95124 873-J1
LENARD DR
3100 AlaC 94546 691-J4
LENARD PL
- AlaC 94546 691-J4
LENARK CT
1100 SJS 95132 814-G5
LENARK DR
3100 SJS 95132 814-G5
LENCAR WY
1700 SJS 95124 873-H3
LENDRUM AV
2300 SJS 95116 834-H3
LENDRUM CT
- SF 94129 647-C3
LENELLE CT
- MRGA 94556 631-E2
3800 FRMT 94538 773-D1
5000 SJS 95118 873-J4
LENELLE DR
- MRGA 94556 631-E2
LENEVE PL
900 ELCR 94530 609-F1
LENFEST RD
600 SJS 95133 834-D2
LENGLEN AV
- SRFL 94903 566-C3
LENN DR
1800 SJS 95125 853-J5
LENNON LN
100 WLCK 94598 612-G1
LENNON WY
1100 SJS 95125 854-A5
LENNOX AV
200 MLPK 94025 790-F2
LENNOX CT
800 SUNV 94087 832-C4
34200 FRMT 94555 752-D2
LENNOX LN
1300 LVMR 94550 715-F4
LENNOX WY
1300 SUNV 94087 832-C4
LENOLT ST
1300 RDWC 94063 770-A5
1400 RDWC 94063 769-J4
LENOR WY
1000 CMBL 95128 853-E4
LENORA AV
5300 SJS 95124 873-J5
LENORA RD
5400 RCH 94803 589-F4
LENORE AV
5100 LVMR 94550 696-C6
LENOSO COM
4300 FRMT 94536 752-G3
LENOX AV
200 OAK 94610 649-H3
LENOX CT
- SCL 95054 813-C4
400 PLHL 94523 592-A7
LENOX PL
- SCL 95054 813-C4
LENOX RD
- CCCo 94707 609-F4
LENOX WY
- SF 94127 667-C5
13400 LAH 94022 811-D7
LENRAY LN
14300 SCIC 95124 873-G3
LENROSS CT
18800 AlaC 94546 692-A3
LENWOOD WY
6800 SJS 95120 894-F2

LENZEN AV
300 SJS 95110 834-A5
500 SJS 95110 833-J6
700 SJS 95126 833-J6
LENZEN CT
400 SJS 95126 833-J6
LENZI LN
100 VAL 94591 530-D6
LEO AV
200 SJS 95112 854-E3
200 SLN 94577 670-J7
200 SLN 94577 671-A7
LEO CIR
- SSF 94080 708-A2
- SSF 94080 707-J2
LEO DR
600 FCTY 94404 749-E3
900 SJS 95129 853-A3
LEO LN
- ANT 94509 574-J6
- MrnC 94941 606-E6
1800 CNCD 94521 593-F4
LEO ST
- SF 94112 667-F7
1200 RCH 94801 588-F4
LEO WY
800 OAK 94611 630-C6
LEOLA CT
10300 CPTO 95014 852-G1
LEOMINSTER CT
- SJS 95139 875-G7
LEON CT
4800 FRMT 94536 752-F4
LEON DR
2000 SJS 95128 853-G3
LEON WY
- ATN 94027 790-F3
LEONA CT
100 CCCo 94507 632-G7
LEONA DR
- MrnC 94903 566-H3
400 LVMR 94550 715-D2
24400 HAY 94542 712-A2
LEONA LN
500 MTVW 94040 811-H7
LEONA ST
3900 SMTO 94403 749-B7
5500 OAK 94605 650-H6
5500 OAK 94619 650-H6
LEONA TER
- SF 94115 647-F6
LEONARD CT
- ALA 94502 669-J6
- DNVL 94526 633-C7
3300 SCL 95054 813-D6
LEONARD DR
100 CNCD 94518 592-H3
1300 SLN 94577 690-H2
LEONARD RD
20500 SAR 95070 852-D7
LEONARD ST
100 VAL 94589 510-C6
LEONARDO WY
800 HAY 94541 711-F3
LEONATO WY
4500 FRMT 94555 752-D2
LEONE ST
36500 NWK 94560 752-E6
LEONELLO AV
900 LALT 94024 831-G2
LEONG CT
7800 CPTO 95014 852-C2
LEONG DR
600 MTVW 94043 812-A3
LEONTINE CT
47800 FRMT 94539 773-J7
48000 FRMT 94539 793-J1
LEOTA AV
100 SUNV 94086 812-C7
LEOTAR CT
100 LGTS 95032 893-D1
LE POMAR TER
200 FRMT 94536 733-B7
LERIDA AV
- MLBR 94030 728-B3
300 LALT 94024 811-F7
LERIDA CT
- SMCo 94028 810-D4
LERIDA WY
1200 PCFA 94044 727-A4
LE ROY AV
1400 BERK 94708 609-H7
1600 BERK 94709 609-H7
1700 BERK 94709 629-J1
LEROY AV
- PTLV 94028 809-J6
300 PIN 94564 569-E4
16700 LGTS 95032 873-C5
LEROY DR
20000 AlaC 94546 691-J5
LEROY LN
800 WLCK 94596 612-A3
LEROY PL
- SF 94109 647-J5
LEROY WY
3900 LFYT 94549 611-C5
LERWICK CT
1100 SUNV 94087 832-H5
LERWICK ST
800 FRMT 94539 753-G7
LESHER CT
1400 SJS 95125 854-A5
LESLEE LN
100 ORIN 94563 631-B4
LESLIE AV
2300 CCCo 94553 571-F4
LESLIE COM
300 LVMR 94550 696-A6
3400 FRMT 94538 753-B5
LESLIE CT
- NVTO 94947 525-J3
200 MTVW 94043 812-A4
900 SCAR 94070 769-D6
LESLIE DR
- PIT 94565 574-D2
- SCAR 94070 769-D6
1000 SJS 95117 853-B3
1800 PLHL 94523 592-C5
LESLIE ST
1700 SMTO 94402 749-B3
39600 FRMT 94538 753-B5

LESLYN LN
- LFYT 94549 611-F3
LESNICK LN
1400 WLCK 94596 612-C2
LESSER ST
400 OAK 94601 670-C2
LESSING ST
- SF 94112 687-D2
LESSINI ST
3500 PLE 94566 715-B7
LESSLEY AV
2100 AlaC 94546 692-A6
2100 AlaC 94546 691-J6
LESTER AV
200 OAK 94606 649-J4
800 HAY 94541 711-F3
1100 SJS 95125 854-A3
1100 SJS 95125 853-J3
LESTER CT
300 SCL 95051 833-B7
LESTER LN
100 LGTS 95032 873-D4
LESTER RD
3000 MRTZ 94553 571-G7
LETHBRIDGE CT
2900 PLE 94588 694-F6
LETHRAM CT
4000 PLE 94588 694-E7
LETICIA CT
4000 ANT 94509 574-H5
LETITIA CT
1200 SJS 95122 854-H2
LETITIA ST
1200 SJS 95122 854-H2
LETTERMAN DR
- SF 94129 647-E4
- SF 94129 647-E4
LETTIA RD
1000 CCCo 94806 568-J5
1000 CCCo 94806 569-A5
LETTUCE LN
- SF 94124 668-B5
LEUE CT
- CNCD 94519 592-J1
LEUTAR CT
20300 SAR 95070 852-E5
LEV LN
1100 CNCD 94518 592-J5
LEVANT ST
- SF 94114 667-F2
LEVEE RD
- SCIC 95035 813-G1
- SJS 95134 813-G1
- SMTO 94401 729-A6
E LEVEE RD
- MRTZ 94553 571-F2
LEVEN PLACE WY
3900 SJS 95121 855-C4
LEVERONI CT
- NVTO 94949 546-F1
LEVI ST
39000 NWK 94560 772-H1
LEVIN AV
300 MTVW 94040 831-J2
800 MTVW 94040 832-A2
LEVIN CT
2700 MTVW 94040 831-J2
LEVIN ST
300 MPS 95035 794-A3
LEVINE RD
- AlaC 94541 712-D1
- AlaC 94542 712-D1
LEVISTON AV
7500 ELCR 94530 609-E3
LEWELLING BLVD
700 AlaC 94580 691-B7
800 SLN 94579 691-B7
2000 SLN 94579 690-J7
E LEWELLING BLVD
- AlaC 94580 691-E6
200 AlaC 94541 691-E6
LEWELLING CT
1000 ALA 94501 670-A3
LEWES CT
- SRMN 94583 673-G4
LEWIS AV
- MLBR 94030 728-B4
- SSF 94080 708-A2
400 SLN 94577 671-B7
800 SUNV 94086 812-D7
1000 SolC 94591 530-D7
1000 VAL 94591 530-D7
7200 DBLN 94568 693-H4
33200 UNC 94587 732-F5
LEWIS DR
25600 HAY 94544 712-A4
LEWIS LN
400 PCFA 94044 707-A4
1300 PIN 94564 569-E5
LEWIS RD
- SJS 95111 854-H4
200 SCIC 95111 854-G5
LEWIS ST
300 OAK 94607 649-D4
700 SCL 95050 833-E4
33100 UNC 94587 732-E4
LEWIS WY
5500 CNCD 94521 593-F7
5700 CNCD 94521 613-G1
LEWIS BROWN RD
100 VAL 94589 510-A6
LEWIS RANCH LN
- SCAR 94070 769-D5
LEWISTON AV
3100 BERK 94705 629-J4
LEWISTON CT
700 SUNV 94087 832-C4
LEWISTON DR
700 SJS 95136 874-D1
1300 SUNV 94087 832-C5
LEXANN AV
1500 SJS 95121 855-A3
LEXFORD AV
2700 SJS 95124 873-H1
LEXFORD PL
- OAK 94619 651-B7
LEXFORD RD
- PDMT 94611 650-D2
LEXINGTON AV
- SJS 95119 875-C5
- SJS 95193 875-C5
100 RDWC 94062 770-A6

LEXINGTON AV
100 SLN 94577 670-J7
200 HAY 94544 732-F3
300 SSF 94066 707-J5
400 ELCR 94530 609-B1
1400 SMCo 94402 748-F7
1500 SMCo 94402 768-F1
LEXINGTON CT
3600 ANT 94509 595-C3
13600 SAR 95070 872-E1
18300 MSER 95030 872-E1
LEXINGTON DR
100 VAL 94591 530-F5
200 MLPK 94025 790-J3
1100 SUNV 94087 832-B2
1400 SJS 95117 853-D4
18200 MSER 95030 872-J5
LEXINGTON PL
900 SRMN 94583 673-G6
2400 LVMR 94550 715-F5
LEXINGTON RD
200 CCCo 94707 609-F4
1300 CNCD 94520 592-E3
LEXINGTON ST
- SF 94110 667-H3
600 MPS 95035 793-J6
900 SCL 95050 833-E5
38600 FRMT 94536 753-A4
LEXINGTON WY
300 BURL 94010 728-G6
1200 LVMR 94550 715-F5
2400 SBRN 94066 707-F7
2400 SBRN 94066 727-F1
3400 ANT 94509 595-B1
LEYLAND PARK DR
6500 SJS 95120 894-C1
LEYTE CT
800 SJS 95111 855-A6
LEYTE ST
- CNCD 94520 572-H3
LEYTON CT
- MLV 94941 606-G3
LHT LP
- CCCo 94553 571-F3
LIAHONA CT
- PLHL 94523 592-B6
LIAHONA LN
1600 DNVL 94526 633-C6
LIANA LN
1600 CNCD 94519 592-J2
LIBBY CT
3500 OAK 94619 650-F5
LIBERATI RD
1100 CNCD 94518 592-J4
LIBERIA CIR
1900 SJS 95116 834-G3
LIBERTA CT
- DNVL 94526 653-B4
LIBERTA PL
- DNVL 94526 653-B4
LIBERTY AV
3200 ALA 94501 670-B3
LIBERTY COM
3400 FRMT 94538 753-B5
LIBERTY CT
- ELCR 94530 609-C3
- SJS 95002 793-B7
900 CPTO 95014 852-B2
2400 SSF 94080 707-D4
3500 ANT 94509 595-C3
LIBERTY DR
2900 PLE 94566 714-H3
LIBERTY LN
- WLCK 94596 612-A2
700 FCTY 94404 749-G5
LIBERTY ST
- LKSP 94939 586-F6
- SF 94110 667-G3
200 SF 94114 667-G3
400 ELCR 94530 609-B1
1400 SJS 95002 813-B1
1600 SJS 95002 793-B7
1900 SCL 95050 833-D5
15200 AlaC 94578 691-F4
39000 FRMT 94538 753-B4
LIBERTY WY
3500 ANT 94509 595-C3
LIBERTY OAK LN
22700 CPTO 95014 831-J7
LIBERTY PARK AV
2000 SMCo 94025 790-D6
LIBERTY SHIP WY
- SAUS 94965 627-A2
LIBRA CT
4800 LVMR 94550 696-B3
LIBRA DR
- NVTO 94947 525-F3
- MrnC 94947 525-F3
LIBRA LN
600 FCTY 94404 749-E3
3300 SJS 95111 854-F6
LIBRARY AV
200 MLBR 94030 728-A3
LIBRARY LN
1100 SJS 95116 834-E5
LIBRARY PL
- SANS 94960 566-C7
LIBRARY ST
- FRMT 94539 753-J7
LIBRETTO CT
1800 SJS 95131 814-C4
LICHEN CT
100 FRMT 94538 773-B2
1300 CNCD 94521 593-D5
LICK AV
1000 SJS 95110 854-C2
LICK PL
- SF 94108 648-A5
- SF 94104 648-A5
LICK MILL BLVD
3800 SCL 95134 813-D3
4200 SCL 95054 813-D3
LICK MILL RD
1400 SCL 95134 813-D5
1400 SCL 95054 813-D5
LIDA DR
2300 MTVW 94043 811-F3
LIDDICOAT CIR
14300 LAH 94022 810-H5
LIDDICOAT DR
14100 LAH 94022 810-H5

LIDO BLVD
35000 NWK 94560 752-C5
LIDO CIR
- RDWC 94065 749-J6
LIDO CT
1400 LVMR 94550 715-E3
6200 NWK 94560 752-D5
LIDO DR
600 LVMR 94550 715-E3
LIDO LN
- SRFL 94901 586-J1
900 FCTY 94404 749-F3
LIDO RD
- NVTO 94949 546-J4
LIDO ST
700 FCTY 94404 749-F3
LIDO WY
1700 SJS 95116 834-G5
12600 SAR 95070 852-E6
LIDO PARK CT
42800 FRMT 94538 773-C2
LIEB CT
14000 SJS 95127 835-A4
LIEB LN
1500 SJS 95131 814-A5
LIEBELT CT
1000 SJS 95126 853-H3
LIEBIG ST
- DALY 94014 687-D2
- SF 94112 687-D2
LIEBRE CT
200 SUNV 94086 812-C7
LIESE AV
3100 OAK 94619 650-E6
LIETZ AV
1500 SJS 95118 874-A5
1500 SJS 95118 873-J5
LIEUTENANT ALLEN ST
- SF 94129 647-E3
- SF 94129 647-E3
LIGGETT AV
700 SF 94129 647-E4
LIGGETT DR
6500 OAK 94611 650-D1
LIGHT WY
- SMCo 94025 770-E7
LIGHTFARE CT
3600 SJS 95121 855-A4
LIGHTHOUSE CT
300 HER 94547 570-B6
300 PIT 94565 573-J3
LIGHTHOUSE DR
100 VAL 94590 529-G2
LIGHTHOUSE LN
- DALY 94014 687-E5
- RCH 94804 608-H3
LIGHTLAND CT
1900 PLE 94566 714-F1
LIGHTLAND RD
1100 SJS 95121 855-A5
LIGHTSHIP CT
100 VAL 94591 550-F2
LIGHTSON ST
- SJS 95113 834-B6
LIGHTWOOD DR
5300 CNCD 94521 593-E5
LIGURIAN CT
5200 SJS 95138 855-F6
LIGURIAN DR
5100 SJS 95138 855-G7
LIKA CT
12700 SAR 95070 852-E6
LIKELY CT
300 CCCo 94507 632-H3
LIKELY DR
200 CCCo 94507 632-H3
LIKINS AV
5300 MRTZ 94553 591-G1
LIKINS CT
5700 MRTZ 94553 591-G2
LIKIT WY
- SLN 94577 690-G2
LILA LN
- CCCo 94803 589-F3
LILAC AV
- MrnC 94904 586-E4
5200 LVMR 94550 696-B3
28200 HAY 94545 731-J1
LILAC CIR
100 HER 94547 570-B4
LILAC CT
100 VAL 94589 509-J6
400 BEN 94510 551-A1
1800 CNCD 94521 593-C2
7800 CPTO 95014 852-C2
34800 UNC 94587 732-G7
LILAC DR
- ATN 94027 770-G7
100 DNVL 94506 653-F4
100 HER 94547 570-B4
1500 WLCK 94596 612-C6
1600 CCCo 94595 612-C6
1600 WLCK 94595 612-C6
LILAC LN
- MrnC 94941 606-F6
- SSF 94080 707-H2
300 EPA 94303 791-B1
600 SJS 95136 854-E7
800 LALT 94024 831-E1
1400 ANT 94509 575-B5
1500 MTVW 94043 811-H3
16100 SCIC 95032 873-D6
16300 LGTS 95032 873-D6
LILAC LP
35000 UNC 94587 732-G7
LILAC ST
- SF 94110 667-J4
900 ALA 94502 670-B7
2500 OAK 94601 650-E7
2600 OAK 94619 650-E7
34700 UNC 94587 732-F7
LILAC WY
700 SCIC 95032 873-C6
700 LGTS 95032 873-C6
800 CPTO 95014 852-C2
LILAC BLOSSOM LN
5600 SJS 95124 873-J6
LILA DEL CT
1000 CNCD 94518 592-E6
LILIAN LN
- SRFL 94901 566-G6

LILIENTHAL RD
- AlaC 94566 715-B3
- AlaC 94550 715-B3
LILLA RD
22900 HAY 94541 711-F3
LILLE ST
300 SLN 94577 691-A1
300 SLN 94577 690-J1
LILLEAN CT
200 VAL 94589 510-C5
LILLEAN WY
100 VAL 94589 510-C5
LILLIAN AV
1200 SLN 94578 691-C4
1300 SUNV 94087 832-F4
LILLIAN CT
- SANS 94960 566-A4
5100 LVMR 94550 716-B1
LILLIAN DR
4000 CNCD 94521 593-A3
LILLIAN LN
- MrnC 94941 606-E4
LILLIAN ST
- SF 94124 668-D6
1200 CCCo 94525 550-D5
1200 LVMR 94550 716-B1
LILLIAN WY
6200 SJS 95120 874-E7
6400 SJS 95120 894-E1
LILLICK DR
1100 SUNV 94087 832-H4
1100 SCL 95051 832-H4
LILLIPUT LN
2500 SJS 95116 834-J4
LILLY AV
700 HAY 94544 712-A2
700 HAY 94544 711-J2
LILLY LN
- SCAR 94070 769-C5
LILY AV
- SANS 94960 586-B1
800 CPTO 95014 852-C2
1000 SUNV 94086 832-H2
LILY CT
- CCCo 94595 612-B6
100 HER 94547 569-J4
2700 ANT 94509 575-G7
7800 CPTO 95014 852-C2
LILY ST
- CCCo 94595 612-B7
- SF 94102 647-H7
3600 OAK 94619 650-F6
31200 UNC 94587 731-J5
LILY ANN WY
400 SJS 95123 875-B3
LILY BLOSSOM CT
100 SJS 95123 875-A4
LIMA CT
1500 SJS 95126 853-H3
LIMA TER
- FRMT 94539 753-G5
LIME DR
1100 SUNV 94087 832-B3
LIME BLOSSOM CT
100 SJS 95123 875-A3
LIMEHOUSE LN
2400 SLN 94577 691-A3
LIMEKILN CANYON RD
16000 SCIC 95030 893-A3
LIMERICK CT
700 SUNV 94087 832-F5
7300 DBLN 94568 693-H2
LIMERICK LN
700 ALA 94502 669-J5
LIMERICK RD
400 PIN 94806 569-C5
400 CCCo 94806 569-C5
LIMERICK WY
7300 DBLN 94568 693-H2
LIMERIDGE DR
1100 CNCD 94518 593-A6
LIMESTONE DR
- UNC 94587 732-G6
100 VAL 94589 510-C6
4100 ANT 94509 595-F2
LIMESTONE RD
2900 CCCo 94507 632-H4
LIMESTONE GRADE
- MrnC 94903 546-E5
LIMETA TER
36800 FRMT 94536 752-G4
LIME TREE CT
3400 WLCK 94598 592-J7
LIMETREE LN
1800 MTVW 94040 831-G1
LIMEWELL CT
- SJS 95138 875-D4
LIMEWOOD CT
1700 CNCD 94521 593-D3
7900 PLE 94588 713-J1
LIMEWOOD DR
400 ANT 94509 575-E7
400 ANT 94509 595-E1
1900 SJS 95132 814-E2
4700 CNCD 94521 593-D3
LIMEWOOD PL
- PLHL 94523 611-J1
1500 PIT 94565 574-G5
LIMON ST
2100 PLE 94566 714-G3
LINARES AV
- SF 94116 667-D3
LINARIA CIR
40200 FRMT 94538 773-B1
LINARIA WY
- SMCo 94028 810-D4
LINBURN CT
2900 SJS 95148 855-B2
LINCOLN AV
- DALY 94015 687-A6
- MLV 94941 606-D2
- PDMT 94611 650-C1
- SANS 94960 566-C7
100 ALA 94501 669-E1
100 PA 94301 790-J5
100 RDWC 94061 770-A7
200 SJS 95126 853-J1
200 PA 94301 791-A4
300 LVMR 94550 696-A7
300 LVMR 94550 716-A1
400 SUNV 94086 812-E7
400 SCIC 95126 853-J1

STREET
Block City ZIP Pg-Grid

LINCOLN AV
500 LALT 94022 811-D7
600 RCH 94801 588-F5
600 SRFL 94901 586-G1
600 LALT 94022 831-E1
900 SJS 95126 854-A3
1000 SJS 95125 854-A3
1100 BURL 94010 728-D5
1100 WLCK 94596 612-C5
1200 SRFL 94901 566-G6
2000 RCH 94804 588-H5
2100 ALA 94501 670-A2
2100 SRFL 94903 566-G6
2300 HAY 94545 711-C4
2400 BLMT 94002 769-B1
3500 OAK 94602 650-E4
6400 ELCR 94530 609-D4
LINCOLN BLVD
- SF 94129 647-E4
- SF 94129 647-B4
100 SF 94121 647-B5
900 PCFA 94044 727-B6
LINCOLN CIR
400 MLBR 94030 728-A3
LINCOLN CT
- SANS 94960 566-C7
- SF 94112 687-F2
800 SJS 95125 854-B5
3700 FRMT 94538 753-D6
LINCOLN DR
- SAUS 94965 626-J2
1100 MTVW 94040 831-G1
4500 CNCD 94521 593-D2
LINCOLN LN
100 PCFA 94044 706-J3
200 PCFA 94044 707-A3
1500 ALA 94501 669-J1
2700 ANT 94509 575-E7
LINCOLN PL
900 PCFA 94044 727-B6
LINCOLN RD
700 VAL 94591 530-C5
LINCOLN RD E
- VAL 94591 550-C1
100 VAL 94591 530-C6
LINCOLN RD W
- VAL 94590 530-C6
- VAL 94590 550-C1
400 SolC 94590 530-C6
LINCOLN ST
- BEN 94510 551-D6
- SSF 94080 707-H1
- CCCo 94565 573-H2
400 SCL 95128 833-D4
400 SCL 95050 833-D4
1300 BERK 94702 629-E1
1500 BERK 94703 629-F1
2000 BERK 94709 629-G1
2000 EPA 94303 791-A2
40800 FRMT 94538 753-D6
LINCOLN WY
- SF 94122 667-A1
- SF 94117 667-C1
200 SF - 667-A1
3200 SF - 666-H2
3200 SF 94122 666-H2
3600 LFYT 94549 611-E5
4900 OAK 94602 650-F3
LINCOLN CENTRE DR
100 FCTY 94404 749-F1
LINCOLNSHIRE CT
- LFYT 94595 612-A6
LINCOLNSHIRE DR
- OAK 94618 630-A6
LINCOLNSHIRE WY
1100 SJS 95125 854-F5
LINCOLN VILLAGE CIR
100 LKSP 94904 586-J4
LINCOLN VILLAGE DR
2400 SJS 95125 854-D7
LIND CT
- ORIN 94563 631-B2
LINDA AV
- MrnC 94903 566-G4
- OAK 94611 649-J1
100 PDMT 94611 649-J1
100 PDMT 94611 650-A1
400 PDMT 94610 650-A1
15500 SCIC 95032 873-D5
15900 LGTS 95032 873-E6
LINDA CT
- DNVL 94526 652-J2
- NVTO 94947 525-G3
- PLHL 94523 591-J5
700 SMTO 94403 749-B7
LINDA DR
100 CCCo 94806 569-A5
800 CMBL 95008 873-B1
800 CMBL 95008 853-C7
1700 PLHL 94523 592-C5
35500 FRMT 94536 732-J7
LINDA LN
100 PLHL 94523 591-J5
100 PLHL 94523 592-A5
28000 LAH 94304 810-H4
LINDA ST
- SF 94110 667-H2
LINDA WY
300 MrnC 94965 606-F7
4400 PLE 94566 714-F4
LINDA ANN CT
22400 CPTO 95014 832-A6
LINDA ANN PL
10100 CPTO 95014 852-F1
LINDA FLORA ST
700 SCIC 95127 814-J6
LINDAHL CT
1300 SJS 95120 874-C7
LINDAIRE AV
2200 SCIC 95128 853-F3
2300 SJS 95128 853-F3
LINDA MAR BLVD
500 PCFA 94044 726-H4
1100 PCFA 94044 727-A6
LINDA MESA AV
- DNVL 94526 652-J2
100 DNVL 94526 653-A2
LINDARO ST
600 SRFL 94901 586-G2
LINDA VISTA
- ORIN 94563 610-G6
LINDA VISTA
100 MLBR 94030 727-J5
3000 ALA 94502 669-J6
LINDA VISTA AV
- ATN 94027 790-C4
- BEN 94510 551-D4
- TBRN 94920 607-F7
100 PIT 94565 574-D1
800 MTVW 94043 811-J3
19100 SCIC 95030 872-F6
LINDA VISTA DR
100 DALY 94014 687-J4
1300 ELCR 94530 609-E1
10700 CPTO 95014 852-A2
LINDA VISTA LN
3100 LFYT 94549 611-J5
LINDA VISTA PL
22000 CPTO 95014 852-B2
LINDA VISTA RD
44000 FRMT 94539 773-J2
LINDA VISTA ST
700 SCIC 95127 814-H6
LINDA VISTA TER
200 FRMT 94539 773-J1
LINDA VISTA WY
800 LALT 94024 831-G2
LINDA VISTA STEPS
- SF 94112 687-G2
LINDBERG CT
- HAY 94542 712-B3
LINDBERG ST
2100 ANT 94509 575-D6
LINDBERGH AV
200 LVMR 94550 695-C5
2200 SJS 95128 853-F3
LINDBERGH DR
1600 CNCD 94521 593-A2
LINDBERGH ST
- SMTO 94401 729-A7
200 SMTO 94401 749-B1
LINDELL DR
1000 CCCo 94803 569-D6
1100 CCCo 94596 612-E1
1100 CCCo 94596 612-F7
LINDELL LN
- SRMN 94583 673-J6
LINDEN AV
- ATN 94027 790-G1
- MLBR 94030 727-J1
- SSF 94080 707-J3
- SBRN 94066 727-J1
300 SBRN 94066 707-H7
600 LALT 94022 811-D5
700 BURL 94010 728-F6
700 MLBR 94030 728-B4
900 SSF 94080 708-A2
2900 BERK 94705 629-J4
S LINDEN AV
- SSF 94080 707-J4
300 SSF 94066 707-J4
300 SBRN 94066 707-J4
LINDEN CT
- CCCo 94507 632-F5
700 SBRN 94066 707-H7
7600 NWK 94560 752-D7
LINDEN DR
- SCL 95050 833-F5
1100 CNCD 94520 592-D4
1100 SJS 95126 833-F5
LINDEN LN
- MrnC 94941 606-E5
100 SMCo 94402 748-G6
100 SRFL 94901 566-G6
600 MRTZ 94553 571-E6
1900 MPS 95035 793-J3
3800 CCCo 94803 589-D3
LINDEN PL
1700 ANT 94509 575-B5
LINDEN ST
- SMCo 94014 687-D5
100 OAK 94607 649-E3
100 RDWC 94061 770-B7
200 SF 94102 647-H7
600 DALY 94014 687-D5
1500 ALA 94501 669-F1
1600 LVMR 94550 695-G7
2700 OAK 94608 649-F2
3700 OAK 94608 629-F7
22400 HAY 94541 692-A7
LINDEN WY
100 SMCo 94402 748-G5
300 AlaC 94566 714-G3
1700 ANT 94509 575-B5
LINDENBROOK CT
300 WDSD 94062 789-H5
LINDENBROOK LN
19800 CPTO 95014 852-F2
LINDENBROOK RD
200 WDSD 94062 789-H5
LINDENOAKS DR
3200 SJS 95117 853-D2
LINDENTREE LN
2600 SCL 95051 833-B6
LINDENWOOD CT
- SRFL 94901 586-B7
LINDENWOOD DR
1600 CNCD 94521 593-B2
3600 SJS 95117 853-C2
LINDENWOOD ST
43100 FRMT 94538 773-D2
LINDENWOOD WY
25100 HAY 94545 711-H5
LINDER HILL CT
1200 SJS 95120 894-G4
LINDER HILL LN
1200 SJS 95120 894-G4
LINDERO DR
3600 CNCD 94519 593-A1
3700 PA 94306 811-D1
LINDERO TER
200 FRMT 94536 753-E1
200 FRMT 94536 733-A7
LINDHURST LN
600 HAY 94544 711-H5
LINDLEY CT
3100 ANT 94509 575-E7
LINDLEY DR
400 ANT 94509 575-E7
LINDMUIR DR
3200 SJS 95121 855-A4
LINDO ST
1700 BEN 94510 551-D5
LINDSAY AV
10300 CPTO 95014 852-F1
LINDSAY CIR
- SF 94124 668-C6
LINDSAY CT
- NVTO 94945 526-G2
LINDSAY LN
3900 AlaC 94546 691-H2
LINDSAY WY
1300 SJS 95118 874-B1
LINDSAY ANN TER
1400 SJS 95131 814-C6
LINDSAY CREEK LN
7100 SJS 95120 894-G4
LINDSAY MCDERMOTT LN
39800 FRMT 94538 753-B6
LINDSEY CT
- PLHL 94523 592-A4
1000 LFYT 94549 611-H6
LINDSEY DR
100 MRTZ 94553 591-G2
LINDSTROM CT
500 SJS 95111 875-C2
LINDVIEW
- SRFL 94901 566-H6
LINDVIEW CT
- AlaC 94578 691-F4
LINDY LN
21600 CPTO 95014 852-A3
LINDY PL
11300 CPTO 95014 852-B3
LINFIELD DR
100 VAL 94589 510-B5
400 MLPK 94025 790-G4
E LINFIELD DR
100 MLPK 94025 790-H3
LINFIELD LN
1200 HAY 94545 711-H6
LINFIELD PL
300 MLPK 94025 790-H3
LINFORD CT
- PIT 94565 574-F7
LINFORD PL
500 SRMN 94583 673-F6
LINFORD TER
6100 FRMT 94555 752-B4
LIN GATE CT
2600 PLE 94566 694-D7
LIN GATE ST
4500 PLE 94566 694-D7
LINHARES LN
100 CCCo 94507 632-F5
LINK CT
3800 AlaC 94546 691-J3
LINK RD
900 HIL 94010 748-F3
LINK ST
10400 OAK 94603 671-A6
LINKFIELD WY
3000 SJS 95135 855-G3
LINKHORNE CT
300 SJS 95133 834-F2
LINKSHEAD CT
3100 SJS 95148 855-D1
LINMORE DR
- FRMT 94539 753-H6
LINNEA AV
700 AlaC 94580 691-E5
LINNELL AV
400 SLN 94578 691-C5
LINNET AV
4200 OAK 94602 650-E4
LINNET CT
- MrnC 94903 546-E6
1900 CNCD 94518 592-G6
LINNET LN
1700 SUNV 94087 832-F6
10600 CPTO 95014 832-F6
LINNET WY
1700 SUNV 94087 832-F6
LINSAY CT
42000 FRMT 94538 773-E1
LINSCHEID DR
- PIT 94565 574-C5
LINTON CT
3800 SJS 95121 855-C4
LINTON PL
1400 MRTZ 94553 591-H1
LINTON ST
1200 SLN 94577 690-J3
LINTON TER
1400 MRTZ 94553 571-H7
1400 MRTZ 94553 591-H1
LINUS PAULING DR
100 HER 94547 569-G2
LINWELL CT
- SJS 95138 875-D5
LINWOOD AV
3700 OAK 94602 650-C4
LINWOOD CT
7300 PLE 94588 714-A1
LINWOOD DR
4100 SJS 95124 873-H3
LINWOOD LN
200 AMCN 94589 509-J3
LINWOOD WY
- SMCo 94062 809-F5
800 SLN 94577 691-C1
LION CT
2900 CNCD 94520 572-E7
LION ST
300 HAY 94541 711-H2
LIONWOOD PL
400 SJS 95111 875-C2
LIPPARD AV
- SF 94131 667-G6
LIPPERT AV
100 FRMT 94539 773-H7
LIPPIZAN DR
100 VAL 94591 530-E2
LIPPIZANER LN
3100 CCCo 94598 613-A4
LIPTON PL
100 SRMN 94583 673-F7
LIPTON ST
1500 ANT 94509 575-F5
1700 CCCo 94509 575-F5
LIQUIDAMBAR WY
400 SUNV 94086 832-G1
LIQUIDAMBER CT
- CCCo 94506 654-A3
400 SJS 95111 854-G7
LIQUIDAMBER PL
700 CCCo 94506 654-A3
LIRA CT
800 SRMN 94583 673-F5
LISA CT
- CCCo 94803 589-D1
- AMCN 94589 509-J4
- MrnC 94903 546-E7
- CCCo 94526 633-C5
800 PCFA 94044 726-H5
1200 LALT 94024 831-H3
3100 ANT 94509 575-E7
7700 DBLN 94568 693-H3
LISA DR
4300 UNC 94587 732-A6
LISA LN
- MRGA 94556 651-F2
500 SJS 95134 813-C2
1100 LALT 94024 831-H3
2200 PLHL 94523 592-D6
LISA WY
600 SJS 95130 853-C4
600 CMBL 95008 853-C4
LISA ANN CT
500 CCCo 94565 573-F1
LISA ANN ST
400 CCCo 94565 573-F1
LISA LEE LN
100 CNCD 94518 592-G4
LISBOA CT
42100 FRMT 94538 773-C1
LISBON AV
800 OAK 94601 670-B1
900 OAK 94601 650-B7
900 LVMR 94550 715-F2
LISBON CT
3600 SJS 95132 814-F1
LISBON DR
3400 SJS 95132 814-E2
LISBON LN
- ANT 94509 574-J6
LISBON ST
- SF 94112 667-G7
- SRFL 94901 586-J2
400 SF 94112 687-F1
500 SMCo 94014 687-D5
500 DALY 94014 687-D5
LISBON TER
- UNC 94587 732-E5
400 MPS 95035 793-G3
LISCOME WY
3400 CNCD 94518 592-H4
LISKA LN
5900 SJS 95119 875-C6
LISLIN CT
1000 PIT 94565 573-H3
LISLIN WY
1400 VAL 94590 530-C2
LISMORE CT
3000 SJS 95135 855-F3
LISSOW DR
- SJS 95119 875-C6
LISTON WY
2400 UNC 94587 732-C4
LITA LN
- EPA 94303 791-C2
LITCHFIELD AV
1200 FRMT 94536 753-B3
LITCHFIELD CT
100 VAL 94589 509-J5
LITCHFIELD PL
2000 SCL 95051 833-D2
LITCHI GROVE CT
100 SJS 95123 874-J3
LITE CT
5900 SJS 95138 875-E5
LITHO ST
400 SAUS 94965 627-A3
LITINA CT
2800 CCCo 94507 632-E4
LITINA DR
1500 CCCo 94507 632-E4
LITKE LN
- WLCK 94596 612-B1
LITTLE AV
- SJS 95119 875-D5
LITTLE CT
3400 FRMT 94538 753-C5
LITTLE LN
500 PLHL 94523 592-A4
3400 LFYT 94549 611-G6
4000 CNCD 94521 593-A3
LITTLE BEAR WY
- SJS 95136 874-H2
LITTLE BOY LN
2600 SJS 95148 835-F7
LITTLE BRANHAM LN
1700 SJS 95124 873-H4
LITTLEBROOK DR
19000 SCIC 95030 872-F6
LITTLE CREEK CT
- SRMN 94583 673-B1
LITTLE CREEK LN
- NVTO 94945 526-B1
LITTLE FALLS DR
6400 SJS 95120 894-D1
LITTLEFIELD AV
200 SSF 94080 708-A4
LITTLEFIELD LN
16600 LGTS 95032 873-C7
16600 SCIC 95032 873-C7
LITTLEFIELD TER
- SF 94107 668-A4
LITTLE FOOT DR
100 FRMT 94539 773-H4
LITTLE FOOT PL
45300 FRMT 94539 773-H4
LITTLEJOHN WY
6100 SJS 95129 852-G3
LITTLEMEADOW CT
4400 SJS 95129 853-A2
LITTLEOAK CIR
1100 SJS 95129 852-H3
LITTLEOAK DR
1000 SJS 95129 852-H3
LITTLE ORCHARD ST
1400 SJS 95110 854-D2
1400 SJS 95125 854-D3
LITTLE PEAK CT
400 RCH 94803 589-G3
LITTLE RIVER CT
100 VAL 94591 550-E2
4700 SJS 95136 874-E2
LITTLE ROCK CT
2800 SJS 95133 814-G7
LITTLE ROCK DR
2800 SJS 95133 814-G7
LITTLETON DR
1200 SJS 95131 834-C1
LITTLETON PL
1600 CMBL 95008 873-A1
LITTLE VALLEY RD
6500 AlaC 94586 734-G4
LITTLEWOOD DR
- PDMT 94611 650-C1
LITTLE WOOD LN
2900 SJS 95127 834-H1
LITTLEWORTH WY
4100 SJS 95135 855-F3
LITTMAN DR
1200 SJS 95120 894-C1
LITTON CT
600 SUNV 94087 832-E5
LITWIN DR
800 CNCD 94518 592-G6
LIVE OAK AV
600 MLPK 94025 790-F4
1700 CNCD 94521 593-A2
LIVE OAK CIR
- CCCo 94803 589-F1
- CCCo 94803 569-G7
LIVE OAK CT
- NVTO 94949 546-C1
3000 CCCo 94506 653-J2
5100 PLE 94588 693-J7
LIVEOAK CT
- PIT 94565 573-G3
300 MPS 95035 813-J3
LIVE OAK DR
200 CCCo 94506 654-A2
200 CCCo 94506 653-J1
400 MrnC 94965 606-E7
900 SCL 95051 833-A5
W LIVE OAK DR
400 MrnC 94965 606-E7
LIVE OAK LN
- CCCo 94506 653-J2
- HIL 94010 748-B1
200 LALT 94022 811-D6
500 SMCo 94062 789-F1
700 PIN 94564 569-C3
14600 SAR 95070 872-F3
LIVE OAK PL
- CCCo 94506 653-J1
LIVE OAK RD
- OAK 94705 630-B3
LIVE OAK WY
- MrnC 94904 586-C4
- CCCo 94506 653-J2
700 SJS 95129 853-A2
1600 WLCK 94596 612-C5
LIVE OAKS CT
300 MRTZ 94553 592-A1
500 MRTZ 94553 571-G5
N LIVERMORE AV
1500 AlaC 94550 695-G3
4400 LVMR 94550 695-G3
N LIVERMORE AV Rt#-J2
5100 LVMR 94550 695-G7
5800 LVMR 94550 715-G1
S LIVERMORE AV Rt#-J2
- LVMR 94550 715-J2
1400 LVMR 94550 716-A3
1700 AlaC 94550 716-A3
LIVERMORE COM
600 FRMT 94539 753-H7
LIVERPOOL
- HER 94547 569-J3
LIVERPOOL AV
1600 SJS 95124 873-J3
LIVERPOOL ST
100 DNVL 94506 653-H5
LIVERPOOL WY
700 SUNV 94087 832-F5
LIVINGSTON AV
1300 PCFA 94044 726-G4
1400 SJS 95125 854-A6
LIVINGSTON CT
- NVTO 94949 546-G3
LIVINGSTON LN
1600 RCH 94801 588-G6
LIVINGSTON PL
100 SSF 94080 707-G1
4800 PLE 94566 714-F5
LIVINGSTON ST
- SF 94129 647-D3
2000 OAK 94606 650-A7
LIVINGSTON TER
2000 SBRN 94066 707-G7
LIVINGSTON WY
600 PLE 94566 714-F5
LIVORNA CT
34300 FRMT 94555 752-B4
LIVORNA RD
100 CCCo 94507 632-F3
900 WLCK 94596 632-H3
LIVORNA RD E
1900 CCCo 94507 632-J2
LIVORNA RD W
1500 CCCo 94507 632-E3
LIVORNA HEIGHTS RD
200 CCCo 94507 632-G3
LIVORNO CT
5400 SJS 95138 875-F1
LIZANN DR
1000 LFYT 94549 611-A6
LIZZIE LN
4400 SJS 95118 874-C2
LJEPAVA DR
20000 SAR 95070 852-E7
LLANO ST
3200 SMTO 94403 749-E5
LLEWELLYN AV
- CMBL 95008 853-D5
LLOYD AV
100 FRMT 94536 753-D2
400 SLN 94578 691-C5
LLOYD CT
300 LVMR 94550 715-E2
LLOYD LN
- ORIN 94563 630-H2
LLOYD ST
- SF 94117 667-G1
100 LVMR 94550 715-E2
LLOYD WY
1300 MTVW 94040 811-G6
LLOYDEN DR
- ATN 94027 790-D2
LLOYDEN PARK LN
300 ATN 94027 790-D2
LLOYD WISE DR
- CNCD 94520 592-E1
LOA DR
- FRMT 94536 753-D1
LOBELIA CT
- LVMR 94550 696-C3
2800 ANT 94509 575-G7
37800 NWK 94560 752-F7
LOBELIA DR
900 VAL 94589 509-J6
37800 NWK 94560 752-F7
LOBELIA LN
1600 SJS 95124 873-J6
LOBELIA WY
- LVMR 94550 696-C3
LOBERT ST
2200 AlaC 94546 692-A6
2200 AlaC 94546 691-J6
LOBOS AV
700 RCH 94801 588-C7
4500 SJS 95111 875-A1
LOBOS CT
700 RCH 94801 588-C7
LOBOS ST
- SF 94112 687-D1
200 SF 94132 687-D1
LOBO VISTA
100 NVTO 94945 525-J2
LO BUE WY
4100 SJS 95111 855-A7
LOCARNO PTH
- OAK 94618 630-B5
LOCARNO WY
1000 SCAR 94070 769-F5
LOCH LN
2200 WLCK 94598 612-G2
3800 SLN 94578 691-D5
LOCHARD ST
10700 OAK 94605 671-D4
LOCHBURRY CT
500 SJS 95123 874-G3
LOCH HAVEN CT
- SRFL 94901 567-B7
LOCHINVAR AV
1100 SUNV 94087 832-J5
3300 SCL 95051 832-J5
LOCHINVAR RD
- SRFL 94901 587-B1
- SRFL 94901 567-A7
LOCHINVAR WY
15100 SCIC 95132 814-H4
LOCH LOMOND CT
- DNVL 94526 652-J3
300 MPS 95035 794-A6
500 SUNV 94087 832-E5
LOCH LOMOND DR
- SRFL 94901 587-B1
LOCH LOMOND LN
1500 SJS 95129 852-E4
LOCH LOMOND ST
3700 SCL 95054 813-E6
LOCH LOMOND WY
100 DNVL 94526 652-J3
3800 LVMR 94550 695-J6
3900 LVMR 94550 696-A6
LOCHMOOR CT
600 DNVL 94526 653-D7
LOCHNER DR
1400 SJS 95127 835-A4
LOCHNESS CT
1000 SUNV 94087 832-G5
LOCHNESS LN
- SRFL 94901 567-B7
- MrnC 94901 567-B7
LOCH NESS WY
1700 SJS 95121 855-B3
LOCHRIDGE DR
300 SJS 95133 834-E3
LOCKE AV
34300 FRMT 94555 732-F7
LOCKE CT
- PLE 94566 714-G5
3000 FRMT 94555 732-F7
LOCKE DR
3100 SJS 95111 854-J5
LOCKE LN
- MLV 94941 606-E4
LOCKFORD CT
7500 CPTO 95014 852-D3
LOCKHART LN
100 LALT 94022 811-D6
4600 PLE 94566 714-E1
LOCKHAVEN CT
800 LALT 94024 831-H5
LOCKHAVEN DR
600 PCFA 94044 707-B4
800 LALT 94024 831-H5
LOCKHAVEN WY
1100 SJS 95129 852-G4
LOCKHEED ST
7200 OAK 94621 670-C6
LOCKHEED WY
1100 SUNV 94089 812-E4
LOCKRIDGE WY
4600 AlaC 94546 692-A3
LOCKSLEY AV
- SF 94122 667-D3
5100 OAK 94618 629-J6
LOCKSLEY PARK DR
1500 SJS 95132 814-F3
LOCKSLY LN
- SRFL 94901 567-A7
- SRFL 94901 587-B1
LOCKSUNART WY
100 SUNV 94087 832-E5
LOCKTON LN
- MrnC 94945 526-H3
LOCKWOOD AV
1900 FRMT 94539 753-F6
LOCKWOOD CT
41900 FRMT 94539 753-F6
LOCKWOOD DR
- SRFL 94901 567-B5
500 VAL 94591 530-F5
2000 SJS 95132 814-E2
LOCKWOOD LN
- MLV 94941 606-D4
100 PLHL 94523 592-A5
LOCKWOOD ST
- SF 94124 668-E7
6900 OAK 94621 670-G2
LOCUST AV
- LKSP 94939 586-E6
- MLV 94941 606-E3
- ROSS 94957 586-C1
- SRFL 94901 566-H6
- MrnC 94904 586-D3
300 SSF 94080 707-H2
LOCUST CT
100 HER 94547 570-A5
600 VAL 94591 530-F3
7000 DBLN 94568 693-H2
LOCUST DR
100 VAL 94591 530-F3
1200 PIT 94565 574-D2
LOCUST PL
8100 DBLN 94568 693-H1
LOCUST RD
600 SAUS 94965 627-A3
LOCUST ST
- SF 94118 647-E5
100 RDWC 94061 770-B7
100 RDWC 94061 790-B1
300 SAUS 94965 627-A3
600 SJS 95110 854-C1
700 SCL 95050 833-F5
1000 LVMR 94550 695-F7
1100 WLCK 94596 612-C5
1400 SMTO 94402 749-A3
7800 OAK 94621 670-G3
14300 SLN 94579 691-A4
20800 AlaC 94541 691-H7
21200 HAY 94541 691-H7
36700 NWK 94560 752-D7
37200 NWK 94560 772-D1
LODATO AV
- SMTO 94403 749-B4
- SMTO 94402 749-B4
LODATO CT
5100 CNCD 94521 593-E4
LODATO WY
1800 CNCD 94521 593-E4
LODESTONE DR
1200 SJS 95132 814-E5
LODESTONE RD
1600 LVMR 94550 715-D3
LODGE CT
- OAK 94611 630-F6
1300 SJS 95121 854-J3
LODGE DR
- CNCD 94520 592-E4
3400 BLMT 94002 769-A2
LODGE LN
- SRFL 94901 586-F2
LODGE HILL CT
- DNVL 94526 653-C4
LODGEPOLE CT
300 MRTZ 94553 571-F5
LODGEWOOD CT
700 SJS 95120 894-H3
LODI AV
1300 SMTO 94403 749-C2
1300 SMTO 94401 749-C2
LODI CT
100 VAL 94589 510-B5
LODI LN
2500 SJS 95124 853-J7
LODI WY
4800 AlaC 94546 692-A3
LODOVICO CT
4500 FRMT 94555 752-C1
LOEFFLER LN
1400 CNCD 94521 593-A3
LOEHR ST
- SF 94134 687-J2
LOES WY
3400 SJS 95127 835-B2
LOFAS PL
100 VAL 94589 510-A7
LOFTUS RD
- CCCo 94565 573-J2
LOGAN CT
800 SUNV 94087 832-C5
3800 CNCD 94519 593-A2
4500 FRMT 94536 752-H5
LOGAN DR
37600 FRMT 94536 752-H4
39000 FRMT 94538 753-A6
39000 FRMT 94538 752-H4
LOGAN LN
- ATN 94027 790-C2
600 DNVL 94526 633-A7
LOGAN ST
600 NVTO 94945 526-C3
800 LVMR 94550 695-D7
2600 OAK 94601 650-C6
LOGAN WY
28800 HAY 94544 712-B7
28800 HAY 94544 732-B1
LOGANBERRY DR
500 MrnC 94903 546-D7
3900 SJS 95121 855-E4
LOGANBERRY WY
1500 PLE 94566 714-D2
LOGIC DR
2000 SJS 95124 873-F3
LOGISTICS DR
- CCCo 94553 571-G3
LOGSDEN WY
2500 SJS 95122 834-J4
LOGUE AV
300 MTVW 94043 812-C5
LOHOMA CT
- HIL 94402 748-H5
LOIRE CT
- SJS 95135 855-F3
LOIS AV
- PIT 94565 574-C6
700 SUNV 94087 832-B1
LOIS CT
- MLV 94941 606-G3
100 PLHL 94523 592-C4

STREET
Block City ZIP Pg-Grid

LOIS LN
- LFYT 94549 611-E6
100 PA 94303 791-B4
100 VAL 94590 530-C3
600 CCCo 94803 589-F4
LOIS ST
300 MTVW 94043 811-F3
LOIS WY
1400 SCIC 95008 873-E1
32400 UNC 94587 732-A7
LOLA LN
600 MTVW 94040 811-H7
LOLA ST
- SLN 94577 690-J1
3700 SMTO 94403 749-B6
LOLETA LN
500 NVTO 94947 526-E6
LOLITA DR
3600 CNCD 94519 573-A7
3600 CNCD 94519 572-J7
3600 CNCD 94519 592-J1
LOLITA LN
500 NVTO 94947 526-E6
LOLLIE CT
1600 SJS 95124 873-J2
LOLLY CT
12400 SAR 95070 852-H6
LOLLY DR
12300 SAR 95070 852-H5
LOMA AV
- TBRN 94920 607-E7
LOMA CT
- SJS 95131 814-A5
700 SMCo 94062 769-F6
LOMA DR
- FRMT 94539 753-H6
LOMA LN
700 ANT 94509 575-C4
LOMA RD
- SCAR 94070 769-E6
- SMCo 94062 769-F6
- SCAR 94062 769-E6
LOMA ST
16700 SCIC 95032 873-C7
LOMA ALTA AV
- LGTS 95032 893-B1
LOMA ALTA DR
3100 SCL 95051 833-A5
LOMA LINDA AV
- ROSS 94957 586-C1
900 CCCo 94803 569-D7
LOMA LINDA CT
- ORIN 94563 631-A3
LOMA LINDA DR
- SJS 95129 852-J1
LOMA LINDA RD
- SRFL 94901 586-J1
LOMA PARK CT
2300 SJS 95124 853-H7
LOMA PARK DR
2200 SJS 95124 853-H7
LOMA PRIETA CT
1000 LALT 94024 831-H2
LOMA PRIETA DR
5900 SJS 95123 874-G6
LOMA PRIETA LN
2300 MLPK 94025 790-D7
LOMA RIO DR
14000 SAR 95070 872-E2
LOMA ROBLES DR
- SANS 94960 566-C7
LOMAS LN
15700 SCIC 95030 872-G6
LOMAS AZULES CT
8700 SJS 95135 855-J7
LOMAS AZULES PL
8600 SJS 95135 855-J6
LOMAS CANTADAS
- ORIN 94563 610-D7
100 CCCo - 610-D7
100 CCCo 94708 610-D7
LOMAS VERDES PL
3200 CCCo 94549 591-H6
LOMA VERDE
100 AlaC 94541 691-E6
100 AlaC 94580 691-E6
LOMA VERDE AV
100 PA 94306 791-C7
700 PA 94303 791-C7
LOMA VERDE DR
3100 SJS 95117 853-D4
LOMA VERDE PL
3100 PA 94303 791-D6
LOMA VISTA
- CCCo 94596 612-A4
- VAL 94590 530-B3
LOMA VISTA AV
- LKSP 94939 586-F6
2800 CNCD 94520 572-E6
3400 OAK 94619 650-F5
15500 SCIC 95032 873-D5
LOMA VISTA CT
100 LGTS 95032 873-D5
LOMA VISTA DR
- BURL 94010 728-A7
- ORIN 94563 610-F7
100 SMCo 94010 728-A7
LOMA VISTA LN
2400 SCL 95051 833-C1
LOMA VISTA PL
- SRFL 94901 586-J2
LOMA VISTA TER
- SF 94117 667-F2
- SF 94114 667-F2
300 PCFA 94044 707-A5
LOMA VISTA WY
1200 PIT 94565 574-D2
3300 OAK 94619 650-E6
LOMBARD AV
2500 SJS 95116 834-H3
4100 FRMT 94536 752-H4
LOMBARD LN
- LFYT 94549 611-G1
LOMBARD ST
- SF 94129 647-H4
- SF 94111 648-A3
100 SF 94133 648-A3
1300 SF 94109 647-H4
2600 SF 94123 647-H4
LOMBARD ST Rt#-1
500 SF 94133 647-J3
1000 SF 94109 647-J4
LOMBARD ST
U.S.-101
1400 SF 94123 647-F4
LOMBARDI CIR
200 CCCo 94598 612-F5
LOMBARDI LN
- MLBR 94030 728-A5
800 HIL 94010 748-G3
LOMBARDO CT
3400 CNCD 94519 592-H1
LOMBARDY LN
- ORIN 94563 610-G4
LOMBARDY WY
600 SMCo 94062 789-F2
LOMBA VISTA
- NVTO 94945 525-J2
LOMENT CT
2300 SJS 95124 873-E3
LOMENT PL
2400 SJS 95124 873-E3
LOMER WY
400 MPS 95035 794-D7
LOMETA AV
200 SUNV 94086 812-C7
LOMITA AV
- SF 94122 667-C3
300 SBRN 94066 727-H2
300 MLBR 94030 727-H2
20500 SAR 95070 872-D3
21600 CPTO 95014 852-B1
21800 SCIC 95014 852-B1
LOMITA CT
500 MLBR 94030 727-J2
600 SCIC 94305 810-G1
LOMITA DR
- MLV 94941 606-G3
- MrnC 94941 606-G3
500 SCIC 94305 790-H6
500 SCIC 94305 810-G1
1900 AlaC 94578 691-G5
LOMITA LINDA DR
25700 LAH 94024 831-E4
LOMITAS AV
100 SSF 94080 707-E3
1000 LVMR 94550 715-F4
LOMITAS CT
- MLPK 94025 790-F6
2000 LVMR 94550 715-F4
LOMITAS PL
600 PIT 94565 574-E5
LOMITAS RD
- DNVL 94526 653-B2
LOMMEL CT
- CCCo 94596 612-D2
LOMOND CIR
600 SRMN 94583 673-E4
LOMOND CT
- SRMN 94583 673-F4
2300 WLCK 94598 612-G3
13500 SAR 95070 872-F1
LOMOND DR
400 PCFA 94044 707-B3
LOMOND LN
2200 WLCK 94598 612-G3
LOMOND WY
18400 AlaC 94552 692-D2
LOMPICO
- HER 94547 569-F4
LOMPICO DR
600 SJS 95123 874-G4
LONARDO AV
4300 SJS 95118 874-B2
LONDON
- HER 94547 569-J3
LONDON AV
1100 SUNV 94087 832-H6
1700 SLN 94579 691-A7
LONDON CIR
1400 BEN 94510 550-H2
LONDON CT
- CLAY 94517 613-J2
100 SBRN 94066 727-G2
2300 ANT 94509 595-A1
32400 UNC 94587 732-C5
LONDON DR
500 BEN 94510 550-J2
600 MPS 95035 794-B3
4700 SJS 95008 873-A1
LONDON LN
200 BLMT 94002 749-F6
LONDON RD
2800 OAK 94602 650-F4
LONDON ST
200 SF 94112 667-G7
500 SF 94112 687-F1
LONDON WY
1600 LVMR 94550 715-F3
LONDONDERRY CT
2100 WLCK 94596 632-H1
LONDONDERRY DR
100 SMCo 94402 748-H7
700 SUNV 94087 832-F5
3300 SCL 95050 833-C7
LONDONDERRY PL
3300 SCL 95050 833-D7
LONDON PARK CT
400 SJS 95136 874-F1
LONE BLUFF WY
2600 SJS 95111 854-H4
LONEE CT
3100 CNCD 94518 592-H2
LONE HILL RD
5000 SJS 95124 873-H5
11000 SJS 95032 873-H5
LONELY TR
- SMCo 94062 789-A4
LONE MOUNTAIN TER
- SF 94118 647-E7
LONE OAK CIR
21800 SCIC 95120 895-C4
LONE OAK CT
- PLHL 94523 592-B5
300 PLE 94566 714-D5
LONE OAK DR
300 PLE 94566 714-D5
2400 SJS 95121 855-E4
LONE OAK LN
10400 LAH 94024 831-E5
LONE OAK PL
4900 AlaC 94546 692-B3
LONE PINE CT
- CLAY 94517 594-A7
LONE PINE CT
- SRMN 94583 673-E2
LONE PINE LN
1100 SJS 95120 894-E2
LONESOME RD
- DNVL 94526 652-J3
LONESOME PINE RD
3900 RDWC 94061 789-G3
LONE TREE AV
- MLV 94941 606-B4
100 MrnC 94965 606-B4
LONETREE CT
15500 SCIC 95032 873-D5
LONE TREE CT
- MPS 95035 814-A3
LONE TREE PL
29100 HAY 94544 732-B1
LONE TREE TR
- MrnC 94965 606-C4
- MLV 94941 606-C4
LONE TREE WY
1100 ANT 94509 575-D7
1800 ANT 94509 595-D2
LONG AV
- SF 94129 647-C3
LONG CT
6100 SJS 95123 875-A6
LONG ST
1600 SCL 95050 833-D3
37400 NWK 94560 752-F7
LONGACRE CT
2800 SJS 95121 855-A2
LONGARD RD
- LVMR 94550 696-E3
LONGBRANCH CT
1100 SJS 95126 853-G4
LONGBRANCH WY
5000 ANT 94509 595-H4
LONGBROOK WY
100 PLHL 94523 592-D4
LONG CREEK CIR
- CLAY 94517 613-J1
LONGCROFT DR
6300 OAK 94611 650-F1
LONGDALE DR
3100 SJS 95124 873-H2
LONGDEN CIR
2000 LALT 94024 831-G5
LONGFELLOW AV
1000 SCIC 95008 873-D3
9900 OAK 94603 671-A5
LONGFELLOW CT
6900 SJS 95129 852-E4
LONGFELLOW DR
- MLV 94941 606-G4
100 PLHL 94523 592-B7
600 FRMT 94539 773-H2
3100 BLMT 94002 749-A7
3100 BLMT 94002 769-A1
LONGFELLOW WY
1200 SJS 95129 852-E4
LONGFIELD PL
100 MRGA 94556 631-F6
LONGFORD CT
1500 WLCK 94598 612-E1
LONGFORD DR
- SSF 94080 707-D1
2700 SJS 95132 814-E5
LONGFORD WY
8400 DBLN 94568 693-H2
LONGHORN CT
- SRMN 94583 673-D4
3700 RCH 94803 589-G1
5000 ANT 94509 595-H4
LONGHORN DR
- SRMN 94583 673-D5
LONGHORN WY
5000 ANT 94509 595-H4
LONGLEAF DR
100 WLCK 94598 612-J1
LONGLEY AV
900 SJS 95125 854-A3
LONGMEADOW DR
100 LGTS 95032 873-D7
LONGMONT LP
3700 AlaC 94552 692-G2
LONG OAK LN
10000 CPTO 95014 831-J6
LONGRIDGE
- ORIN 94563 630-H1
LONGRIDGE DR
100 VAL 94591 530-F7
LONGRIDGE RD
200 LGTS 95032 873-D4
600 OAK 94610 650-A3
LONGSHORE DR
1000 SCIC 95128 853-F3
1000 SJS 95128 853-F3
LONGSPUR
- PTLV 94028 830-C1
LONGSPUR AV
1500 SUNV 94087 832-F5
LONGSPUR WY
2700 PLE 94566 714-C1
LONGVIEW AV
- SANS 94960 566-D7
LONG VIEW CT
- DNVL 94526 653-B3
LONGVIEW CT
- HIL 94010 748-G3
- SF 94131 667-E4
200 ANT 94509 595-D1
3300 RCH 94806 569-A7
LONGVIEW DR
- DALY 94015 707-A1
1900 SLN 94577 691-D1
2600 RCH 94806 569-A7
2600 RCH 94806 568-J7
2900 SBRN 94066 707-D6
9000 PLE 94588 714-A5
LONGVIEW LN
9900 PLE 94588 714-A5
9900 PLE 94588 713-J5
LONGVIEW PL
25600 AlaC 94541 712-D2
LONGVIEW RD
800 HIL 94010 748-G3
2700 ANT 94509 575-B7
3000 ANT 94509 595-C1
LONGVIEW ST
1600 SJS 95122 834-G6
LONGVIEW TER
200 ORIN 94563 631-A3
4500 FRMT 94538 773-C1
LONGWALK DR
6500 OAK 94611 650-G1
LONGWOOD AV
500 HAY 94541 711-F3
LONGWOOD CT
- SRMN 94583 673-E2
500 HAY 94541 711-G3
6500 MRTZ 94553 591-H4
LONGWOOD DR
- SRFL 94901 566-D6
- SANS 94960 566-D6
15500 SCIC 95032 873-D5
LONGWOOD LN
900 SJS 95129 852-J3
LONGWORTH
700 ORIN 94563 610-J4
LONNA LN
800 CPTO 95014 852-D2
LONSDALE AV
600 FRMT 94539 773-H6
LONSDALE CT
46800 FRMT 94539 773-H6
LONUS ST
800 SJS 95126 854-A2
800 SJS 95126 853-J2
LOO LN
1400 SJS 95131 814-C6
LOOKOUT BEND
6700 SJS 95120 894-D2
LOOKOUT DR
- VAL 94591 550-D2
LOOKOUT RD
- HIL 94010 748-E4
LOOMIS CT
2500 SJS 95121 854-H2
LOOMIS DR
2400 SJS 95121 854-H2
LOOMIS ST
- SF 94124 668-A5
LOON CT
200 FCTY 94404 749-H1
LOOP DR
- CCCo 94708 609-H3
LOOP RD
400 SJS 95120 895-B3
LOOTENS PL
900 SRFL 94901 586-F1
LOP CENTER RD
- CCCo 94553 571-G3
LOP EAST RD
- CCCo 94553 571-G3
LOPES CT
500 PIN 94564 569-E4
3200 AlaC 94541 692-D6
44900 FRMT 94538 773-F4
LOPES LN
500 PIN 94564 569-E4
LOPEZ AV
- SF 94116 667-D4
LOPEZ DR
1800 SLN 94578 691-C2
1900 ANT 94509 575-A6
LOPINA WY
- SJS 95129 853-A1
LOP NORTH RD
- CCCo 94553 571-G3
LOP SOUTH RD
- CCCo 94553 571-G3
LOP WEST RD
- CCCo 94553 571-G3
LOQUAT CT
13900 SAR 95070 872-J1
LOQUAT LN
2200 SLN 94577 691-B2
LORA CT
100 VAL 94591 530-F3
LORA DR
14200 LGTS 95030 873-A2
LORABELLE CT
4200 PA 94306 811-D3
LORAIN PL
100 LGTS 95030 873-B3
LORAINE AV
900 LALT 94024 831-G3
LORAINE CT
100 SF 94118 647-E6
LORALEE PL
100 PLHL 94523 592-D6
LORAN CT
- CCCo 94707 609-F4
LORAND WY
22700 HAY 94541 692-B7
LORCA CT
- SRMN 94583 673-D3
LORD CT
1200 CNCD 94518 592-E7
LORD IVELSON LN
1100 FCTY 94404 749-J4
LORD NELSON LN
1100 FCTY 94404 749-J4
LOREAL TER
34600 FRMT 94555 752-A3
LOREE AV
18500 SCIC 95014 852-G1
LOREE LN
- MLBR 94030 728-A5
LORELEI CT
1200 CMBL 95008 853-B6
LORELEI LN
- MLPK 94025 770-F7
LORENA AV
3500 AlaC 94546 692-A5
LORENA CIR
3700 AlaC 94546 692-A4
LORENA PL
20000 AlaC 94546 692-A5
LORENE CIR
100 VAL 94589 510-A4
LORENE CT
13000 MTVW 94040 832-A1
LORENZEN DR
1700 SJS 95124 853-H7
LORENZO AV
3200 OAK 94619 650-E6
15500 AlaC 94580 691-C7
LORENZO DR
100 PLHL 94523 592-D5
1400 VAL 94589 509-J5
1400 VAL 94589 510-A5
LORENZO TER
4000 FRMT 94536 752-F2
LORETO CT
200 MRTZ 94553 571-H5
LORETO DR
3300 SRMN 94583 673-G5
LORETO ST
200 MTVW 94041 811-J5
LORETTA LN
- SCIC 95008 873-D3
LORETTA WY
4700 UNC 94587 731-J7
LORI AV
800 SUNV 94086 812-D6
LORI CT
3200 BLMT 94002 768-J1
LORI DR
300 BEN 94510 551-A3
3200 BLMT 94002 768-J1
LORI LN
- SF 94131 667-E3
LORI WY
23200 AlaC 94541 692-D7
LORIE CT
100 WLCK 94596 612-B3
LORIE LN
- WLCK 94596 612-B3
LORINA ST
2900 BERK 94705 629-H3
LORINDA LN
1000 LFYT 94549 611-A5
LORING AV
- DBLN 94568 694-C3
- MrnC 94941 606-E5
400 CCCo 94525 550-E4
5800 CCCo 94805 589-B5
LORITA AV
- PDMT 94611 630-A7
LORNA DR
4100 LFYT 94549 611-A4
LORNE LN
- SMCo 94025 770-E7
LORNE WY
900 SUNV 94087 832-G5
LORNELL CT
3800 CNCD 94518 592-J3
LORO PL
40300 FRMT 94539 753-F3
LORRAINE AV
- PIT 94565 574-C5
500 SJS 95110 834-A7
1500 SMTO 94401 729-A7
LORRAINE BLVD
200 SLN 94577 671-A7
300 SLN 94577 690-J1
LORRAINE CT
- NVTO 94947 525-G2
LORRAINE RD
3200 LVMR 94550 695-J2
3200 AlaC 94550 695-J2
LORREN CT
400 LVMR 94550 715-E2
LORREN DR
4200 FRMT 94536 752-J5
4300 FRMT 94536 753-A5
LORREN WY
500 LVMR 94550 715-E2
LORRY CT
3400 CNCD 94520 572-F6
LORRY LN
100 PCFA 94044 707-B4
LORTON AV
- BURL 94010 728-G7
LORWICK WY
1800 SJS 95121 855-C4
LOS ALAMOS AV
600 LVMR 94550 715-E2
LOS ALAMOS CT
- CCCo 94507 632-G6
LOS ALAMOS DR
17800 SJS 95130 853-A4
LOS ALONDRAS CT
- NVTO 94945 526-B3
LOS ALTOS AV
- LALT 94022 811-D6
100 WLCK 94598 612-E3
LOS ALTOS CT
200 LALT 94022 811-D6
3800 SJS 95121 855-D3
LOS ALTOS DR
- AMCN 94589 510-A1
- SRFL 94901 566-D5
- AMCN 94589 509-J2
1500 BURL 94010 728-A7
1700 SMCo 94402 748-H7
2100 SMTO 94402 748-H7
2700 SJS 95121 855-D3
LOS ALTOS PL
- SMCo 94402 748-G7
3800 PIT 94565 574-D6
LOS ALTOS RD
- ORIN 94563 610-F5
200 CCCo 94708 609-G3
LOS ALTOS SQ
- LALT 94022 811-E4
LOS ALTOS WY
2900 ANT 94509 575-B7
LOS ALTURAS
100 LGTS 95030 872-J3
LOS AMIGOS DR
- ORIN 94563 610-E5
LOS ANGELES AV
1900 BERK 94707 609-G6
LOS ANGELES BLVD
100 SANS 94960 566-B6
200 MrnC 94901 566-B6
LOS ANGELES ST
5600 OAK 94608 629-F5
LOS ARABIS CIR
- LFYT 94549 611-B5
LOS ARABIS DR
3800 LFYT 94549 611-A5
LOS ARABIS LN
1000 LFYT 94549 611-C6
LOS ARBOLES
- ORIN 94563 610-G5
LOS ARBOLES AV
300 SJS 95111 854-J6
500 SCIC 94305 790-F7
1300 SUNV 94087 832-D4
LOS ARBOLES DR
37600 FRMT 94536 752-H5
LOS ARBOLES PL
4800 FRMT 94536 752-H5
LOS ARIBIS DR
3800 LFYT 94549 611-B5
LOS BALCONES
- CCCo 94507 632-H5
LOS BANOS AV
100 DALY 94014 687-C3
100 WLCK 94598 612-F3
LOS BANOS CT
- WLCK 94598 612-F3
LOS BANOS ST
16500 AlaC 94578 691-F5
17000 AlaC 94541 691-F5
LOS BUELLIS WY
1400 MPS 95035 793-H3
LOS CEDROS DR
- NVTO 94947 525-G3
LOS CERRITOS DR
- VAL 94589 530-B1
17000 LGTS 95032 893-C1
LOS CERROS
- ORIN 94563 630-J3
LOS CERROS AV
- WLCK 94598 612-F3
LOS CERROS DR
- MrnC 94904 586-F3
LOS CERROS PL
- WLCK 94598 612-F3
LOS CERROS RD
- SMCo 94062 769-F6
LOS CHARROS LN
- PTLV 94028 810-C6
LOS COCHES AV
2300 SCIC 95128 853-F1
2600 SJS 95128 853-F1
LOS COCHES ST
300 MPS 95035 794-B7
LOS CONEJOS
- ORIN 94563 610-F7
LOS DEDOS
- ORIN 94563 610-H5
LOS DIAS CT
- NVTO 94945 525-J2
LOS ENCINAS CT
1600 CMBL 95030 873-A2
1600 CMBL 95030 872-J1
LOS ENCINOS AV
300 SJS 95134 813-E2
LOS ENCINOS CT
300 SJS 95134 813-E2
LOS ENCINOS DR
300 SJS 95134 813-E2
LOS ENCINOS ST
300 SJS 95134 813-E2
LOS ESTEROS RD
700 SJS 95134 793-D7
700 SJS 95002 793-D7
LOS FELICAS AV
200 WLCK 94598 612-F3
LOS FELICE DR
17800 SJS 95130 853-A4
17900 SJS 95129 853-A4
LOS FLORES AV
- SSF 94080 707-E2
3600 CNCD 94519 572-J7
LOS GAMOS DR
1000 SRFL 94903 566-E2
LOS GAMOS RD
1000 SRFL 94903 566-E3
LOS GATOS
5400 CNCD 94521 593-F5
LOS GATOS AV
100 VAL 94589 530-C1
LOS GATOS BLVD
- SJS 95124 873-B7
- LGTS 95032 873-B7
15900 SCIC 95032 873-B7
LOS GATOS WY
400 SMTO 94403 749-E5
LOS GATOS ALMADEN RD
1600 SJS 95124 873-D5
1700 SJS 95032 873-G5
1900 LGTS 95032 873-D5
16000 SCIC 95032 873-D5
LOS HUECOS DR
600 SJS 95123 874-G6
LOS MEDANOS ST
800 PIT 94565 574-E2
LOS MONTES DR
100 SMCo 94010 728-A7
1500 BURL 94010 728-A7
LOS NARROBOS RD
- ORIN 94563 610-E7
LOS NINOS WY
400 LALT 94022 811-E5
LOS OJOS DR
1500 HAY 94544 732-A1
LOS OLIVOS AV
- DALY 94014 687-C3
LOS OLIVOS DR
500 SCL 95050 833-C5
17900 SJS 95130 853-A4
LOS PADRES BLVD
300 SCL 95050 833-C2
LOS PADRES CIR
- NVTO 94947 526-E6
LOS PAJAROS CT
400 LALT 94024 831-F1
LOS PALMOS DR
- SF 94127 667-E6
400 SF 94127 667-D6
LOS PALMOS WY
200 SJS 95119 875-C6
LOS PALOS AV
4200 PA 94306 811-D3
LOS PALOS CIR
3200 LFYT 94549 631-H1
4200 PA 94306 811-D3
LOS PALOS CT
1100 PIT 94565 573-H4
4100 SJS 95118 874-C2
LOS PALOS DR
- PIT 94565 573-H4
600 LFYT 94549 631-H1
LOS PALOS MNR
700 LFYT 94549 631-H1
LOS PALOS PL
4200 PA 94306 811-D3
LOS PALOS WY
1300 SJS 95118 874-B2
LOS PATIOS
100 LGTS 95030 873-A2
LOS PATIOS
100 LGTS 95030 872-J2
LOS PINOS AV
500 MPS 95035 794-B5
LOS PINOS PL
600 FRMT 94539 753-F5
LOS PINOS ST
40800 FRMT 94539 753-F5
LOS PINOS WY
300 SJS 95119 875-A7
300 SJS 95123 875-A7
LOS POSITOS DR
700 MPS 95035 794-B6
LOS PRADOS
3000 SMTO 94403 749-E4
LOS PRADOS WY
2400 ANT 94509 595-A1
2400 ANT 94509 594-J1
LOS RANCHITOS
- CCCo 94595 632-E2
LOS RANCHITOS CT
11600 DBLN 94568 693-F3
LOS RANCHITOS RD
- SRFL 94903 566-E4
100 MrnC 94903 566-E4
LOS REYES AV
16700 AlaC 94578 691-F6
LOS RIOS CT
400 PLE 94566 714-E5
1500 SJS 95120 874-A7
LOS RIOS DR
1400 SJS 95120 874-A7
1500 SJS 95120 894-A1
LOS ROBLES AV
600 PA 94306 811-C2
LOS ROBLES CT
- SMCo 94025 790-D5
600 DNVL 94526 653-E6
LOS ROBLES DR
- SRFL 94901 586-E1
100 SMCo 94010 728-B7
LOS ROBLES RD
- NVTO 94949 546-F3
LOS ROBLES WY
17000 LGTS 95032 873-B7
LOS SANTOS CT
100 VAL 94590 530-B2
LOSSE ST
500 SJS 95110 834-A5
LOS SERENOS ROBLES
16200 SCIC 95030 872-G6
LOS SUENOS AV
1600 SJS 95116 834-G5
LOSTCREEK CT
3200 SJS 95121 855-D7
LOST LAKE LN
- CMBL 95008 873-D1
LOST LAKE PL
1900 MRTZ 94553 591-J1
LOST OAKS DR
2300 SJS 95124 873-D4
LOST RANCH RD
7700 SCIC 95120 894-J2
LOS TRANCOS CIR
100 SMCo 94028 830-D4
LOS TRANCOS RD
- PA 94304 830-D2
- PTLV 94028 810-D7
100 PA 94304 810-D7
900 PTLV 94028 830-D2
900 SMCo 94028 830-D4
LOST TRAIL CT
- SJS 95136 874-H3
LOST VALLEY CT
- ORIN 94563 630-J4
LOST VALLEY DR
- ORIN 94563 631-A4
- ORIN 94563 630-J4
LOST VIEW RD
7700 SCIC 95120 895-D5
LOS VECINOS
1400 WLCK 94598 612-E4
LOS VIENTOS WY
100 SMCo 94070 769-C5
100 SCAR 94070 769-C5
LOTISLAKE CT
700 SUNV 94089 812-H4
LOTTIE BENNETT LN
- SF 94115 647-E5
LOTUS CT
- NVTO 94945 526-B2
100 HER 94547 569-J4
2700 ANT 94509 575-G7
3900 AlaC 94546 692-A3
6400 NWK 94560 772-G1
LOTUS LN
400 MTVW 94043 811-H4
LOTUS PZ
- HAY 94542 712-B3
LOTUS ST
600 SJS 95116 834-F6
LOTUS WY
100 EPA 94303 791-D3
LOU ANN PL
- PIT 94565 574-A2
LOUCKS AV
- LALT 94022 811-D4
LOUETTE CT
200 AlaC 94541 711-E1
LOUIS CT
200 LVMR 94550 715-D2
3500 SJS 95127 835-B2
LOUIS DR
500 NVTO 94945 526-D4
1300 ANT 94509 575-E5
LOUIS RD
1900 PA 94303 791-C5
3800 PA 94303 811-F1
LOUISA CT
1500 PA 94303 791-B4
LOUISBURG ST
100 SF 94112 687-E1
LOUISE AV
600 NVTO 94947 525-H4
900 SJS 95125 854-B4
LOUISE CT
- MRGA 94556 651-E1
100 LGTS 95030 872-J3
100 VAL 94590 530-B2
300 MPS 95035 794-E7
600 CMBL 95008 853-C7
4800 FRMT 94536 752-J6

STREET
Block City ZIP Pg-Grid

LOUISE CT
19700 AlaC 94546 691-H4
LOUISE DR
800 SUNV 94087 832-C5
LOUISE LN
100 PTLV 94028 809-J5
100 SMTO 94403 749-B6
2000 LALT 94024 832-A5
4700 UNC 94587 752-A1
LOUISE ST
- SRFL 94901 586-J2
1000 MLPK 94025 790-E6
1100 SLN 94578 691-D4
3000 OAK 94608 649-E1
LOUISIANA DR
1300 CNCD 94521 593-E6
LOUISIANA ST
100 VAL 94590 529-J4
600 OAK 94603 670-G6
600 VAL 94590 530-A4
LOUKOS PL
18700 AlaC 94546 691-H3
LOUMENA LN
400 SJS 95111 854-H5
LOUPE AV
900 SJS 95121 854-J4
1100 SJS 95121 855-A4
LOUVAINE AV
100 OAK 94603 670-G7
LOUVAINE DR
1700 SMCo 94015 687-B5
LOUVAINE PL
- SMCo 94015 687-B5
LOUVRE LN
2600 LVMR 94550 715-H3
LOVE LN
100 DNVL 94526 652-H2
LOVEBIRD CT
- ANT 94509 594-J2
LOVEBIRD WY
- ANT 94509 594-J1
LOVEGROVE AV
1900 SPAB 94806 588-H2
LOVE HARRIS RD
20000 SCIC 95030 893-E7
LOVEJOY WY
- NVTO 94949 546-G3
LOVELAND CT
14200 SAR 95070 872-E2
LOVELAND DR
1100 LFYT 94549 611-J5
LOVELL AV
- MLV 94941 606-B2
- SRFL 94901 586-G2
900 CMBL 95008 873-B1
LOVELL CT
1100 CNCD 94520 592-E5
LOVELL PL
2000 SCL 95051 833-A3
LOVE LOCK WY
1000 HAY 94544 712-A7
LOVERIDGE CIR
500 PIT 94565 574-F5
LOVERIDGE RD
200 PIT 94565 574-H2
LOVERIN CT
200 HAY 94544 712-B7
LOVERS LN
- NVTO 94947 525-J5
- NVTO 94947 526-A5
LOVEWOOD WY
2900 SJS 95148 855-D1
LOVOI WY
1000 SJS 95125 854-B5
LOWANA CIR
1800 CCCo 94521 593-E3
LOWE RD Rt#-84
- WDSD 94062 789-G6
LOWELL AV
- MrnC 94903 566-G3
100 PA 94301 791-A6
100 SBRN 94066 727-G2
200 MrnC 94941 606-F6
2300 RCH 94804 588-H5
3300 RCH 94804 589-A5
3500 SPAB 94805 589-A5
18600 AlaC 94541 691-F7
LOWELL CT
200 DNVL 94526 653-E5
700 SUNV 94087 832-C5
LOWELL DR
100 DNVL 94526 653-D5
200 SCL 95051 832-H7
LOWELL LN
- SJS 95125 854-B7
LOWELL LN E
200 LFYT 94549 631-J3
LOWELL LN W
300 LFYT 94549 631-J3
LOWELL PL
400 FRMT 94536 753-D1
LOWELL ST
- SF 94112 687-E2
- RDWC 94062 769-H6
300 DALY 94014 687-E2
5300 OAK 94608 629-F5
LOWELL WY
- CMBL 95008 853-E6
LOWENA CT
20700 SAR 95070 852-D5
LOWER DR
- MLV 94941 606-G2
LOWER LN
- CMAD 94925 586-F7
- CMAD 94925 606-F1
LOWER TER
- SF 94114 667-F2
LOWER TR
- LFYT 94549 611-C7
- LFYT 94549 631-C1
LOWER ALCATRAZ PL
- MLV 94941 606-D3
LOWER ANCHORAGE RD
100 SAUS 94965 626-H1
LOWER CRESCENT AV
- SAUS 94965 627-B4
LOWER GRAND AV
1600 PDMT 94611 650-A1
LOWER LAKE RD
100 WDSD 94062 809-H5
LOWER LOCK AV
3300 BLMT 94002 769-A1
LOWER N TER
- TBRN 94920 607-A4
LOWER NORTH TER
- TBRN 94920 607-A4
LOWER VIA CASITAS
- LKSP 94939 586-F4
LOWER VINTNERS CIR
300 FRMT 94539 773-J4
LOWER VISTA GRANDE
1200 MLBR 94030 727-J5
LOWERY DR
- ATN 94027 790-G1
LOWLAND CT
1300 MPS 95035 814-E2
LOWNEY WY
1900 SJS 95131 814-D6
LOWRIE AV
1300 SSF 94080 707-J4
LOWRY CT
4900 UNC 94587 752-A2
5500 CNCD 94521 593-G4
LOWRY DR
3000 SJS 95118 874-B1
LOWRY RD
3500 FRMT 94555 732-C7
4400 FRMT - 752-B1
4400 FRMT 94555 752-B1
4700 OAK 94605 671-E5
4900 UNC 94587 752-B1
LOYALTON DR
700 CMBL 95008 853-A7
700 CMBL 95008 873-A1
LOYE WY
2900 SJS 95148 835-E7
LOYOLA AV
- SMCo 94063 790-D1
27500 HAY 94545 711-H7
27600 HAY 94545 731-H1
LOYOLA CT
1000 SCL 95051 833-B5
LOYOLA DR
200 MLBR 94030 728-A5
500 SCIC 94024 831-F4
1100 SCL 95051 833-B4
1700 SJS 95122 834-H6
1800 BURL 94010 728-A5
2800 RCH 94806 589-A2
W LOYOLA DR
10100 SCIC 94024 831-F5
LOYOLA TER
- SF 94117 647-E7
LOYOLA WY
400 LVMR 94550 696-A7
700 LVMR 94550 716-B1
1000 VAL 94589 510-B6
LOZANO CT
- PLE 94566 715-C7
LOZIER AL
100 VAL 94590 529-H4
900 VAL 94590 530-A4
LUANN CT
100 VAL 94589 510-B7
LU ANNE DR
100 CMBL 95008 853-B5
LUAU DR
200 PIT 94565 574-E5
LUBBOCK PL
3100 FRMT 94536 752-G2
LUBEC ST
21400 CPTO 95014 832-C7
LUBICH DR
1200 MTVW 94040 832-A2
LUBY DR
1800 SJS 95133 834-E2
LUCANIA ST
8300 DBLN 94568 693-H2
LUCAS AV
400 RCH 94801 588-E5
2400 PIN 94564 569-F6
6500 OAK 94611 650-E1
LUCAS CIR
3100 LFYT 94549 631-J2
LUCAS CT
- LFYT 94549 631-J3
3000 SJS 95148 835-F7
16100 AlaC 94580 711-C1
LUCAS DR
- MRGA 94556 631-E4
600 LFYT 94549 631-H2
3600 SJS 95148 835-F7
LUCAS LN
1300 CNCD 94521 593-A4
LUCAS PARK DR
- SRFL 94903 566-D1
LUCAS VALLEY RD
400 MrnC 94903 546-B7
800 SRFL 94903 546-B7
1900 SRFL 94903 566-E1
1900 MrnC 94903 566-E1
LUCCA CT
4100 PLE 94588 694-A5
LUCCA DR
100 SSF 94080 707-G1
LUCCA PL
- SJS 95138 855-E7
LUCE CT
700 MTVW 94041 812-A7
LUCENA CT
1400 SJS 95132 814-E4
LUCENA DR
2600 SJS 95132 814-E5
LUCENA WY
2700 ANT 94509 575-A7
LUCERNE AV
500 RDWC 94061 790-B1
LUCERNE CT
3100 AlaC 94546 691-J4
LUCERNE DR
700 SUNV 94086 812-G7
LUCERNE ST
100 SF 94103 668-B1
800 LVMR 94550 695-E7
LUCERNE WY
2400 SJS 95122 834-J5
LUCERO CT
4200 PLE 94588 694-C5
LUCERO LN
12800 LAH 94022 831-A1
LUCERO WY
100 SMCo 94028 810-D3
LUCHESSI CT
1100 SJS 95118 874-D2
LUCHESSI DR
1100 SJS 95118 874-C3
LUCIA CT
100 SBRN 94066 727-H2
900 HAY 94541 711-E3
1400 SLN 94577 690-H2
35000 FRMT 94536 752-E2
LUCIA LN
- MRGA 94556 631-E3
LUCIA ST
21800 HAY 94541 711-F3
35100 FRMT 94536 752-E2
LUCIAN AV
3300 SJS 95127 814-J7
14000 SCIC 95127 814-J7
LUCIEN WY
24900 HAY 94544 711-J4
LUCILLE AV
20000 CPTO 95014 832-E6
LUCILLE LN
1600 PLHL 94523 592-B5
N LUCILLE LN
3300 LFYT 94549 631-G3
S LUCILLE LN
3300 LFYT 94549 631-G3
LUCILLE ST
700 LVMR 94550 696-B7
900 LVMR 94550 716-B1
1000 SLN 94577 690-J1
6600 OAK 94621 670-F3
LUCILLE WY
- ORIN 94563 630-H1
LUCINA ST
400 AMCN 94589 510-A4
LUCINDA CT
40100 FRMT 94539 753-E4
LUCINDA LN
- PLHL 94523 612-A1
- PLHL 94523 611-J1
LUCKY AV
900 SMCo 94025 790-D6
LUCKY DR
- CMAD 94925 586-G6
- MrnC 94939 586-G6
100 LKSP 94925 586-G6
100 LKSP 94939 586-G6
1500 CNCD 94519 592-J2
LUCKY LN
- SLN 94577 690-J3
LUCKY RD
16200 MSER 95030 872-G7
16200 SCIC 95030 872-G7
LUCKY ST
- SF 94110 667-J4
LUCKY OAK ST
10900 CPTO 95014 832-A6
11000 CPTO 94024 832-A6
LUCOT CT
20200 AlaC 94541 711-F1
LUCOT ST
- AlaC 94541 711-F1
LUCOT WY
1000 CMBL 95008 873-B2
LUCRETIA AV
1100 SJS 95122 834-F7
1400 SJS 95122 854-G1
1900 SCIC 95122 854-G1
LUCRETIA CIR
900 SJS 95122 854-H2
LUCRETIA CT
1600 SJS 95122 854-F1
LUCY LN
2500 CCCo 94595 612-A6
LUCY ST
- SF 94124 668-B7
LUDELL CT
3000 CCCo 94596 592-D7
LUDELL DR
100 CCCo 94596 592-D7
LUDEMAN LN
- MLBR 94030 728-A3
300 MLBR 94030 727-J3
LUDLOW AL
- SF 94127 667-D5
LUDLOW CT
3100 SJS 95148 855-C2
LUDLOW PL
200 SRMN 94583 673-F5
LUDLOW WY
300 SJS 95133 834-F2
LUDWIG AV
5500 ELCR 94530 589-B7
LUELLA DR
- PLHL 94523 592-C4
LUELLA PL
3900 AlaC 94546 691-J3
LUFF LN
400 RDWC 94065 749-H6
LUFKIN CT
3600 SJS 95148 835-F7
LUGANO WY
2900 SJS 95132 814-F5
LUIKA PL
1600 CMBL 95008 873-A1
LUISA CT
- SRFL 94903 566-D3
LUIZ FIRE RD
- MrnC 94903 546-A4
LUJOSO CT
1400 SJS 95128 853-F4
LUKE CT
1800 SJS 95116 834-H5
LUKE LN
- NVTO 94949 546-G4
LULA WY
- MLV 94941 606-G2
LULA BELLE LN
100 SMTO 94403 749-B4
LULLABY LN
4400 SJS 95111 855-A7
LULU AL
- SF 94127 667-E6
LUMBERTOWN LN
21100 SAR 95070 872-C3
LUNA AV
2000 AlaC 94578 691-E3
LUNA CT
11600 DBLN 94568 693-F4
LUNA DR
100 VAL 94591 530-D7
100 VAL 94591 550-D1
LUNA LN
- SANS 94960 566-C7
LUNA ST
28600 HAY 94544 712-B7
LUNADA CT
- MrnC 94901 587-A1
LUNADA DR
300 LALT 94022 811-D3
LUNADA GN
- CCCo 94507 632-E3
LUNADA LN
2400 CCCo 94507 632-E3
LUNADO CT
100 SF 94127 667-C7
LUNADO WY
- SF 94132 687-C1
- SF 94127 667-C7
LUNAR CT
7800 CPTO 95014 852-C3
LUNAR WY
4100 UNC 94587 732-A6
LUND AV
- HAY 94544 712-A4
- HAY 94544 711-J4
LUNDEEN ST
- SF 94123 647-E3
- SF 94129 647-E3
LUNDER CT
1900 SJS 95131 814-E7
LUNDHOLM AV
3600 OAK 94605 650-H7
LUND RANCH RD
1100 PLE 94566 714-F5
LUNDY AV
900 SJS 95133 834-D1
1100 SJS 95131 834-D1
1200 SJS 95131 814-B4
LUNDY DR
35600 NWK 94560 752-E4
LUNDY LN
- LGTS 95030 893-A1
- SMCo 94402 748-G7
100 PA 94306 811-D2
800 SCIC 94024 831-H4
LUNDY PL
500 SJS 95131 814-B4
500 MPS 95035 814-B4
LUNDY TER
46900 FRMT 94539 773-H6
LUNDY WY
100 PCFA 94044 707-A7
700 PCFA 94044 727-A1
LUNDYS LN
- SF 94110 667-H5
LUNETA CT
3900 SJS 95136 874-F1
LUNETA DR
4000 SJS 95136 874-F1
LUNETTA AV
200 PCFA 94044 707-A6
LUNING DR
1300 SJS 95118 874-A3
LUNNY LN
1700 SRFL 94901 566-E7
LUPE CT
32000 UNC 94587 732-A6
LUPIN LN
- ATN 94027 770-G7
- ATN 94027 790-G1
LUPIN PL
- CCCo 94526 633-C4
LUPIN WY
900 SCAR 94070 769-F4
8400 AlaC 94550 696-G7
LUPINE AV
- SF 94118 647-E6
3500 PA 94303 791-E7
LUPINE CIR
- NVTO 94947 526-D7
LUPINE CT
- CCCo 94803 569-E7
- SRFL 94901 567-C5
500 BEN 94510 550-J1
1300 CNCD 94521 593-D5
1400 SJS 95118 874-B1
2800 ANT 94509 575-G7
6400 NWK 94560 772-G1
7600 PLE 94588 714-B6
LUPINE DR
- DALY 94014 687-H3
- CMAD 94925 606-H1
1000 SUNV 94086 832-G2
LUPINE LN
100 PLHL 94523 592-B1
LUPINE PL
44200 FRMT 94539 773-G3
LUPINE RD
1800 HER 94547 569-J4
1900 HER 94547 570-A4
27700 LAH 94022 810-J6
LUPINE WY
- HIL 94010 748-D2
300 AlaC 94541 711-F2
LUPINE VALLEY CT
- BSBN 94005 687-H4
LUPTON AV
1400 SJS 95125 854-A4
LU-RAY DR
100 LGTS 95032 873-E5
LUREE CT
- DNVL 94526 653-C4
LURENE DR
100 FRMT 94539 773-H1
LURLINE DR
700 FCTY 94404 749-G2
LURLINE ST
- SF 94122 667-C2
LURMANN CT
- CCCo 94507 632-H5
LURMONT TER
- SF 94109 647-J4
LUSARDI DR
2200 SJS 95148 855-D2
LUSHERM CT
- CCCo 94596 612-D2
LUSK ST
- SF 94107 648-B7
3800 OAK 94608 629-G7
LUSTERLEAF DR
700 SUNV 94086 832-G2
LUSTIG CT
28200 HAY 94544 712-B7
LUTHER AV
1000 SJS 95126 833-J7
LUTHER DR
400 SCL 95051 833-B7
LUTHERIA WY
14200 SAR 95070 872-E2
LUVENA DR
26500 HAY 94544 712-B5
LUX AV
100 SSF 94080 708-A3
100 SSF 94080 707-J2
3700 AlaC 94546 691-J4
3700 AlaC 94546 692-A4
LUX CT
3900 SJS 95136 874-F1
LUXURY DR
800 CNCD 94518 592-G5
LUZ AV
2100 SJS 95116 834-G3
LUZ CT
800 DNVL 94526 653-B2
LUZANNE CIR
- MrnC 94960 566-A2
LUZON CT
43200 FRMT 94539 773-G1
LUZON DR
42800 FRMT 94539 753-F7
42800 FRMT 94539 773-G1
LWR GOLDEN RAIN RD
2400 WLCK 94595 632-A1
2700 WLCK 94595 631-J1
LYALL WY
2300 BLMT 94002 769-C2
LYCETT CIR
- DALY 94015 707-C3
LYCETT CT
- DALY 94015 707-C3
N LYCETT ST
100 DALY 94015 707-C3
S LYCETT ST
100 DALY 94015 707-C3
LYCHEE CT
- SRMN 94583 673-F7
LYDIA CT
- HIL 94010 748-F5
5600 LVMR 94550 696-C6
LYDIA LN
1300 CLAY 94517 593-G6
N LYDIA LN
1300 CLAY 94517 593-G6
LYELL ST
- LALT 94022 811-E7
- SF 94112 667-G6
- SF 94131 667-G6
LYELL WY
24600 HAY 94544 711-J3
LYFORD DR
- TBRN 94920 607-E6
LYFORD ST
27400 HAY 94544 711-J7
LYLE CT
2000 MRTZ 94553 572-A7
2400 AlaC 94578 691-G4
2700 SCL 95051 833-B3
LYLE DR
1500 SJS 95125 854-A3
1500 SJS 95129 852-H5
LYLE LN
700 SJS 95008 873-F1
LYLE ST
16100 AlaC 94546 691-G4
16100 AlaC 94578 691-G4
LYLEWOOD DR
2700 PLE 94588 714-A3
LYMAN CT
1500 CNCD 94521 593-A3
LYMAN LN
- CCCo 94507 632-F4
LYMAN RD
3700 OAK 94602 650-D3
LYME LN
- FCTY 94404 749-E6
LYMEHAVEN CT
- SJS 95111 874-J1
LYNBROOK CT
2200 PIT 94565 574-E5
5000 PLE 94588 693-H7
5400 CNCD 94521 593-E7
18900 SAR 95070 852-H5
LYNBROOK DR
300 PCFA 94044 707-B2
2200 PIT 94565 574-E5
LYNBROOK PL
5500 CNCD 94521 593-E7
LYNBROOK ST
100 CCCo 94565 573-F1
LYNBROOK WY
1100 SJS 95129 852-G4
LYNCH CT
- MRGA 94556 651-E1
- CNCD 94521 593-F7
LYNCH PL
- BEN 94510 551-C1
LYNCH ST
- SF 94109 647-J4
LYNDA CT
5800 LVMR 94550 696-D6
LYNDALE AV
100 SCIC 95127 834-J2
100 SJS 95127 834-J2
10000 SCIC 95127 835-A3
LYNDE AV
13800 SAR 95070 872-D1
LYNDE CT
20500 SAR 95070 872-D2
LYNDE ST
2800 OAK 94601 650-C6
LYNDHURST AV
100 SCAR 94070 769-E2
200 BLMT 94002 769-E2
LYNDHURST CT
- BLMT 94002 769-E2
LYNDHURST DR
- SF 94132 667-B7
LYNDHURST ST
9800 OAK 94603 670-G6
LYNDON AV
- LGTS 95030 872-J7
E LYNDON LP
- AlaC 94552 692-G3
W LYNDON LP
- AlaC 94552 692-G3
LYNETTE ST
3000 AlaC 94546 692-B6
LYNETTE WY
200 SJS 95116 834-G4
LYNFIELD LN
4200 SJS 95136 874-D2
LYNG DR
4900 SJS 95111 875-B1
LYNHURST CT
1100 SJS 95118 874-C2
LYNHURST WY
1100 SJS 95118 874-C2
LYNN AV
- MPS 95035 794-D5
400 ANT 94509 575-E7
1100 SJS 95122 834-G6
2000 LGTS 95032 873-F5
2500 CNCD 94520 592-F3
7300 ELCR 94530 609-E4
15000 SJS 95032 873-F5
15000 SJS 95124 873-F5
LYNN CT
- SRFL 94901 586-G2
100 VAL 94591 530-E4
900 AlaC 94580 691-E6
900 SRMN 94583 673-F5
LYNN DR
2500 PIN 94564 569-D6
4300 CNCD 94518 593-A5
LYNN LN
- DNVL 94526 652-J2
LYNN ST
900 LVMR 94550 696-C7
23200 HAY 94541 711-G3
LYNN WY
100 WDSD 94062 789-J4
900 FRMT 94539 753-G7
1000 SUNV 94087 832-B1
LYNNBROOK CT
- SRMN 94583 673-E2
LYNNBROOK DR
300 SRMN 94583 673-E2
LYNN CREST LN
- SRMN 94583 673-B1
LYNNDALE WY
25900 LAH 94022 811-C6
LYNN DARR DR
100 MRTZ 94553 571-D3
LYNNHAVEN DR
2000 SJS 95128 853-G3
LYNN OAKS DR
3200 SJS 95117 853-D2
LYNTON AV
100 SCAR 94070 769-D4
100 SMCo 94070 769-D4
LYNTON CT
20100 CPTO 95014 852-E2
LYNVALE CT
- DALY 94015 686-J4
LYNVALE LN
1800 WLCK 94596 612-B3
LYNVIEW DR
3000 SJS 95148 855-D1
LYNWOOD AV
600 MTVW 94043 812-A3
LYNWOOD CT
- NVTO 94947 526-D7
4000 CNCD 94519 593-B1
5600 AlaC 94552 692-C2
LYNWOOD DR
1100 NVTO 94947 526-C6
1600 CNCD 94521 593-C1
1700 CNCD 94519 593-B1
1700 CNCD 94519 573-A7
LYNWOOD LN
900 MLBR 94030 727-H3
LYNWOOD PL
- MRGA 94556 631-D5
LYNWOOD TER
2000 SJS 95128 833-F7
2200 MPS 95035 814-E1
LYNWOOD WY
2000 ANT 94509 595-F2
LYNX CT
100 FRMT 94539 773-J3
3700 SJS 95136 874-D1
LYNX DR
3500 SJS 95136 874-D1
44700 FRMT 94539 773-H3
LYNX LN
800 FCTY 94404 749-F4
LYNXWOOD CT
500 SUNV 94086 832-F1
LYON AV
1900 BLMT 94002 749-C7
2100 BLMT 94002 769-C1
3500 OAK 94601 650-D6
LYON CIR
2600 CNCD 94518 592-G6
LYON CT
- BEN 94510 551-B1
900 CNCD 94518 592-G5
1300 LVMR 94550 695-F6
LYON PL
- MLV 94941 606-C2
LYON ST
- SF 94117 667-F1
300 SF 94117 647-F7
800 SF 94115 647-F5
2300 SF 94129 647-F4
2500 SF 94123 647-F4
2900 SF 94123 647-E3
2900 SF 94129 647-F4
LYONBURRY PL
500 SJS 95123 874-G4
LYONCROSS WY
400 SJS 95123 874-J4
LYON ESTATES CT
2900 SJS 95135 855-G5
LYONRIDGE LN
- SMTO 94402 748-H6
LYONS CT
2200 SJS 95116 834-H4
18500 SAR 95070 872-H1
LYONS DR
2100 SJS 95116 834-H5
LYONS ST
1100 RDWC 94061 790-A1
LYONSVILLE LN
1300 SJS 95118 874-B5
LYRA CT
4900 LVMR 94550 696-B3
LYRA ST
48800 FRMT 94539 793-H1
LYRA WY
- VAL 94591 510-J4
LYRELAKE CT
700 SUNV 94089 812-H4
LYRIC LN
1500 CNCD 94521 593-E5
4700 SJS 95111 855-A7
4700 SJS 95111 875-A1
LYSETTE ST
- SF 94109 647-J5
LYTELLE ST
1300 HAY 94544 711-J7
LYTER WY
3200 SJS 95135 855-D2
LYTHAM WY
100 VAL 94591 530-G3
LYTTON AV
100 PA 94301 790-H4

M

M RD
- SUNV 94089 812-H4
M ST
- OAK 94625 649-A4
400 ANT 94509 575-C4
22300 HAY 94541 711-J1
N M ST
200 LVMR 94550 695-G7
S M ST
100 LVMR 94550 715-G1
W M ST
200 BEN 94510 551-B4
MAAR AV
400 FRMT 94536 753-D2
MAAR PL
500 FRMT 94536 753-D2
MAAS AV
500 RCH 94801 588-F1
MABEL AV
2000 SJS 95122 834-H5
3800 AlaC 94546 692-A4
MABEL CT
12200 SAR 95070 852-G5
MABEL PL
19700 AlaC 94546 692-A4
MABEL ST
2500 BERK 94702 629-F3
MABIE CT
5900 SJS 95123 874-F5
MABINI ST
- SF 94107 648-B6
MABRAY DR
- PLE 94588 693-F6
MABREY CT
- SF 94124 668-C6
MABRY WY
- MrnC 94903 566-G2
MABURY CT
2800 SJS 95133 814-G7
MABURY RD
600 SJS 95133 834-B2
1100 SJS 95112 834-D2
2400 SJS 95133 814-G7
3100 SJS 95127 814-H6
3200 SCIC 95127 814-H6
12200 SCIC 95133 834-D2
MAC CT
3500 ANT 94509 595-C1
MACADAM CT
5800 SJS 95123 875-A5
MACADAM LN
10100 CPTO 95014 852-E1
MACADAMIA DR
900 HIL 94010 728-C7
900 HIL 94010 748-C1
MACALVEY DR
- MRTZ 94553 591-H1
MACANNAN CT
- TBRN 94920 607-C6
MACARA AV
400 SUNV 94086 812-D5
MACARTHUR AV
- SF 94123 647-H3
- SF 94129 647-E4
100 PIT 94565 574-D3
300 SJS 95128 853-F1
300 SCIC 95128 853-F1
400 SMCo 94063 770-C6
600 SMTO 94402 748-J4
800 SF 94129 647-E4
2500 SPAB 94806 588-H2
MACARTHUR BLVD
- OAK 94610 649-J2
- OAK 94610 650-A3
200 OAK 94605 671-A4
200 SLN 94577 671-C7
200 SLN 94605 671-C7
1300 OAK 94602 650-E5
3500 OAK 94619 650-E5
4900 OAK 94613 650-G7
5400 OAK 94619 670-H1
5400 OAK 94605 650-G7
5400 OAK 94605 670-H1
5500 OAK 94613 670-H1
9000 OAK 94603 671-A4
W MACARTHUR BLVD
100 OAK 94611 649-H1
300 OAK 94609 649-H1
600 OAK 94609 629-F7
800 OAK 94608 629-F7
800 EMVL 94608 629-F7
MACARTHUR DR
500 SMCo 94015 687-B5
MACARTHUR FRWY
I-580
- AlaC - 691-G6
- EMVL - 629-D6
- OAK - 629-D7
- OAK - 650-J7
- OAK - 671-A1
- SLN - 671-A1
- SLN - 691-C1
MACATERA AV
1400 HAY 94544 732-A1
MACAULAY ST
1100 ANT 94509 575-C5
MACAW LN
200 SJS 95123 874-F7

STREET
Block City ZIP Pg-Grid

MACAW PL
200 SJS 95123 874-F7
MACAW WY
5200 SJS 95123 874-F7
MACBAIN AV
- ATN 94027 790-E3
MACBETH AV
4400 FRMT 94555 752-C1
MACBETH CIR
4300 FRMT 94555 752-D1
MACBETH CT
4600 FRMT 94555 752-C1
MACBETH DR
3700 SJS 95127 835-C2
MACCALL ST
5700 OAK 94609 629-G5
MACDONALD AV
- DALY 94014 687-J3
- RCH 94801 588-E6
- DALY 94014 688-A3
200 SJS 95116 834-E3
1600 RCH 94804 588-E6
3300 RCH 94805 588-E6
3700 RCH 94805 589-A7
5300 ELCR 94530 589-B7
MACDONALD CT
- CCCo 94507 632-F5
9500 PLE 94586 693-F6
MACDONALD ST
1400 RDWC 94061 790-A2
MACDUEE CT
1800 SJS 95121 855-B3
MACDUEE WY
1800 SJS 95121 855-B3
MACDUFF CT
900 SJS 95127 835-C2
MACE CT
3600 SJS 95127 835-C3
MACE DR
1200 SJS 95127 835-C3
MACEDONIA ST
- SF 94110 668-A4
MACGREGOR COM
3800 LVMR 94550 695-J6
MACGREGOR LN
3500 SCL 95054 813-E6
MACGREGOR PL
- DNVL 94526 653-D2
MACGREGOR RD
200 CCCo 94523 592-B2
MACHADO AV
3000 SCL 95051 833-A2
3300 SCL 95051 832-J2
3500 SUNV 94086 832-J2
MACHADO CT
1500 CNCD 94521 593-B3
24000 AlaC 94541 692-D7
MACHADO DR
4200 CNCD 94521 593-B3
MACHADO LN
1000 SJS 95127 835-C2
10000 SCIC 95127 835-C2
MACHIN AV
900 NVTO 94945 526-B3
MACIAS CT
700 PLE 94566 714-E6
MACINTOSH ST
3500 SCL 95054 813-E6
MACK COM
5200 FRMT 94555 752-C3
MACK ST
20100 HAY 94545 711-D4
MACKALL WY
3100 PA 94306 791-D7
MACKAY DR
4100 PA 94306 811-F2
MACKENZIE DR
300 SCL 95051 832-H7
900 SUNV 94087 832-B6
MACKENZIE PL
- DNVL 94526 653-D2
3100 FRMT 94536 752-G2
MACKEY AV
1500 SJS 95125 854-C3
MACKIE DR
- MRTZ 94553 571-F7
MACKINAW ST
31300 UNC 94545 731-J6
MACKINNON ST
100 PDMT 94610 650-A1
MACKINTOSH ST
100 FRMT 94539 753-F4
MACKIN WOODS LN
3200 SJS 95135 855-G3
MACKLIN CT
700 SJS 95133 814-G7
MACLANE ST
200 PA 94306 811-C1
MACLAY CT
6000 SJS 95123 874-E5
14300 SAR 95070 872-G2
MACLAY DR
900 SJS 95123 874-E5
MACMILLAN WY
33700 FRMT 94555 732-D7
MACMURTY CT
3800 CCCo 94553 571-H4
MACMURTY DR
100 CCCo 94553 571-H4
MACOMBER LN
- DNVL 94526 652-H2
MACOMBER RD
- DNVL 94526 652-H3
MACOMBER WY
- DNVL 94526 652-H2
MACON AV
1000 MTVW 94043 812-A2
1000 MTVW 94043 811-J2
1000 SJS 95117 853-D3
MACON RD
- SCIC 94035 812-C1
MACONDRAY LN
- SF 94133 647-J4
- SF 94109 647-J4
MACPHERSON PL
- DNVL 94526 653-D2
MACREDES CT
700 SJS 95116 834-E6
MADALEN DR
1200 MPS 95035 794-B4
MADAN LN
- SCL 95051 833-C3
MADDALENA CT
- PLE 94566 715-C7
MADDEN AV
2300 SJS 95116 834-G3
MADDUX AV
- SF 94124 668-B6
MADDUX DR
700 SMCo 94015 687-A4
900 PA 94303 791-D6
900 DALY 94015 687-A4
1400 RDWC 94061 789-J2
1500 RDWC 94061 790-A3
9600 OAK 94603 670-G6
MADEIRA DR
800 PLE 94566 714-G3
1400 PCFA 94044 727-A6
MADEIRA WY
2800 PLHL 94523 592-A4
2800 PLHL 94523 591-J4
3100 LVMR 94550 695-J7
MADEIROS AV
23800 AlaC 94541 692-C7
23800 AlaC 94541 712-C1
MADELAINE CT
2000 LALT 94024 831-G5
MADELAINE DR
6000 NWK 94560 752-D5
MADELAINE PL
6000 NWK 94560 752-D5
MADELENE LN
- MrnC 94901 567-A7
MADELIA PL
100 SRMN 94583 693-G1
MADELINE CT
- NVTO 94947 526-A4
MADELINE DR
3300 SCIC 95127 834-J1
3400 SJS 95127 834-J1
MADELINE LN
900 SCL 95050 833-C5
25800 HAY 94545 711-F6
MADELINE RD
1000 CCCo 94806 569-A5
MADELINE ST
2600 OAK 94602 650-E4
MADERA
- MTVW 94043 811-J2
MADERA AV
- ROSS 94957 586-D1
- SCAR 94070 769-F4
- SANS 94960 566-C7
400 SJS 95112 834-B3
400 SUNV 94086 812-C7
1000 MLPK 94025 790-J1
1200 MLPK 94025 771-A7
1200 MLPK 94025 770-J7
2700 OAK 94601 670-F1
2700 OAK 94619 670-F1
MADERA BLVD
- CMAD 94925 586-G7
MADERA CIR
1500 ELCR 94530 589-D7
1500 ELCR 94530 609-D1
MADERA CT
- DNVL 94526 653-C7
100 LGTS 95032 873-H7
1500 ELCR 94530 609-D1
37700 FRMT 94536 752-H5
MADERA DR
500 SMCo 94403 749-A4
500 SMTO 94403 749-A4
1500 ELCR 94530 609-D1
2400 SCL 95051 833-C4
8500 ELCR 94530 589-D7
10300 CPTO 95014 832-B7
MADERA LN
- ORIN 94563 610-F6
MADERA ST
- SF 94107 668-B3
- SRFL 94901 587-A3
- SRFL 94901 586-J3
1700 BERK 94707 609-F6
3800 PIN 94564 569-J7
MADERA WY
200 MLV 94941 606-B3
200 MrnC 94965 606-B3
1300 MLBR 94030 728-A5
1300 MLBR 94030 727-J5
3700 SBRN 94066 707-C5
MADERA DEL PRESIDIO DR
- CMAD 94925 606-H1
MADERA RIDGE FIRE RD
- CMAD 94925 606-E1
- LKSP 94939 586-D7
- LKSP 94939 606-E1
- MLV 94941 606-E1
MADIGAN AV
- DBLN 94568 694-D3
- VAL 94590 530-C5
800 CNCD 94518 592-H5
MADIGAN CT
2800 CNCD 94518 592-H5
MADILL CIR
- ANT 94509 575-C6
MADILL CT
- ANT 94509 575-D6
MADILL ST
- ANT 94509 575-C6
E MADILL ST
- ANT 94509 575-E6
MADISON AV
- UNC 94587 732-B4
- CCCo 94565 573-H3
- SMTO 94402 749-A3
100 MrnC 94903 566-G4
100 RDWC 94061 770-A7
100 SBRN 94066 727-G1
100 SRFL 94903 566-F4
1000 LVMR 94550 716-A1
1100 RDWC 94061 769-J7
1600 RDWC 94061 789-J1
5500 RCH 94804 609-B2
5700 ELCR 94530 609-C2
17300 AlaC 94546 692-B3
MADISON CT
- NVTO 94947 526-B6
400 SJS 95123 875-A6
1800 CNCD 94521 593-D2
3000 ANT 94509 575-A7
MADISON DR
300 SJS 95123 875-A6
800 MTVW 94040 831-G1
E MADISON LN
1800 CNCD 94521 593-D2
MADISON ST
- BEN 94510 551-E6
- SF 94112 667-H7
- SF 94134 667-H7
100 OAK 94607 649-G4
200 SCL 95050 833-E4
500 ALB 94706 609-D5
1200 OAK 94612 649-G4
2800 ALA 94501 670-A3
MADISON WY
- SMCo 94025 790-H2
500 PA 94303 791-C4
MADOC WY
4400 SJS 95130 853-A6
MADOLINE ST
- PIT 94565 574-D5
MADONNA DR
3300 SJS 95117 853-D3
MADONNA LN
500 WLCK 94596 612-A3
MADONNA WY
800 LALT 94024 831-E2
MADORA PL
100 SRMN 94583 693-G1
MADRID AV
1400 HAY 94544 732-A1
MADRID CT
- DNVL 94506 653-G5
- MLBR 94030 728-A2
- NVTO 94949 546-F3
1300 PCFA 94044 727-A6
3600 SJS 95132 814-F1
4400 UNC 94587 731-J6
MADRID DR
3400 SJS 95132 814-E2
MADRID LN
- ANT 94509 575-A6
MADRID PL
- FRMT 94539 753-E4
- SRMN 94583 673-G5
MADRID RD
10600 CPTO 95014 852-B2
MADRID ST
- SF 94112 667-G7
400 SF 94112 687-G1
MADRONA AV
- BLV 94920 627-D1
- ROSS 94957 586-C3
1200 SJS 95125 854-B5
MADRONA ST
- MLV 94941 606-D3
- SCAR 94070 769-F3
- SRFL 94901 586-E2
MADRONE AV
- LKSP 94939 586-E6
- MrnC 94904 586-E2
- SANS 94960 566-B7
- SF 94127 667-C5
- SSF 94080 708-A2
200 SCL 95051 833-B7
500 SUNV 94086 812-E5
600 PIN 94564 569-D4
3600 OAK 94619 650-G6
16500 LGTS 95030 872-H7
16600 SCIC 95030 872-H7
MADRONE CT
1300 SPAB 94806 588-H1
MADRONE DR
3600 LFYT 94549 631-E1
MADRONE LN
- CCCo - 631-A7
MADRONE PL
- HIL 94010 728-E7
- ORIN 94563 610-F7
5700 CNCD 94521 593-G7
MADRONE RD
- ATN 94027 790-G1
MADRONE ST
100 RDWC 94061 770-B7
200 RDWC 94061 790-C1
300 MLBR 94030 728-A2
1000 NVTO 94945 526-C3
3200 ANT 94509 574-J7
3700 HAY 94541 692-B7
MADRONE TR
- CCCo - 632-C6
- CCCo - 652-D1
- CCCo 94507 652-F1
- CCCo 94526 652-F1
MADRONE WY
- MrnC 94904 586-C4
- PCFA 94044 727-A5
100 UNC 94587 732-C6
900 LVMR 94550 715-F3
1400 SPAB 94806 588-H1
MADRONE HILL RD
15200 SAR 95070 872-E4
MADRONE PARK CIR
- MrnC 94941 606-D5
MADRONO AV
- CMAD 94925 606-G1
1500 PA 94306 791-A6
MADRONO CT
- CMAD 94925 606-G1
MADRUGA WY
1200 MPS 95035 814-D2
MADSEN CT
- MRGA 94556 651-D1
MADSEN LN
- WLCK 94596 612-B2
MAE AV
- PIT 94565 574-C5
MAE CT
- MrnC 94947 525-E2
MAESTRO CT
500 SJS 95134 813-F3
MAESTRO RD
- MrnC 94947 525-G5
MAEVE CT
- SJS 95136 854-E6
MAFFEY DR
18200 AlaC 94546 692-A3
N MAGAZINE
- NWK 94560 772-H1
S MAGAZINE
- NWK 94560 772-H1
MAGAZINE ST
500 VAL 94590 530-C7
700 VAL 94590 550-B1
900 VAL 94591 530-D7
1600 SolC 94591 550-D1
1600 VAL 94591 550-D1
MAGDA WY
200 CCCo 94553 572-C7
MAGDALENA AV
10200 LAH 94024 831-F3
11500 SCIC 94024 831-F3
12200 LALT 94024 831-F3
MAGDALENA CIR
1900 SCL 95051 832-H3
MAGDALENA CT
- MLV 94941 606-F1
12300 SCIC 94024 831-F2
MAGDALENA PL
3200 AlaC 94546 691-H4
MAGEE AV
- MLV 94941 606-C2
2600 CCCo 94806 569-C5
3600 OAK 94619 650-F5
MAGEE CT
- MRGA 94556 651-G2
MAGEE WY
18300 AlaC 94546 691-J3
MAGEE RANCH RD
100 DNVL 94506 653-G2
MAGELLAN AV
- SF 94116 667-D4
- SJS 95116 834-F3
200 SF 94116 667-C4
3600 SCL 95051 832-H7
MAGELLAN CT
400 PCFA 94044 707-A2
MAGELLAN DR
300 PCFA 94044 707-A2
1800 OAK 94611 630-E7
1900 OAK 94611 650-E1
35900 FRMT 94536 752-E3
MAGELLAN LN
800 FCTY 94404 749-G4
MAGGIE LN
200 WLCK 94596 612-B1
MAGGIO CT
1200 CMBL 95008 873-B1
MAGGIORA CT
- OAK 94605 671-C5
MAGGIORA DR
3000 OAK 94605 671-C5
MAGGIORE CT
3100 SJS 95135 855-F6
MAGIC SANDS WY
- SJS 95123 875-G2
MAGILL ST
100 VAL 94589 530-A1
MAGLIOCCO DR
2900 SJS 95117 853-D2
3000 SJS 95128 853-E2
MAGNA AV
24100 HAY 94544 711-J3
MAGNESON LP
100 LGTS 95032 873-C6
100 SCIC 95032 873-C6
MAGNESON TER
100 LGTS 95032 873-C6
MAGNOLIA AV
- SANS 94960 566-B7
- SMCo 94402 770-F5
- SRFL 94901 566-H7
- SSF 94080 707-H3
- CMAD 94925 586-D4
- LKSP 94939 586-D4
100 PDMT 94610 650-B2
100 MLBR 94030 728-A2
300 PDMT 94611 650-B2
700 SBRN 94066 707-H7
700 SBRN 94066 728-A2
700 SBRN 94066 727-J2
700 MLBR 94030 727-J2
800 CCCo 94553 571-F4
1100 SJS 95126 833-H7
1200 SCAR 94070 769-F3
N MAGNOLIA AV
- SJS 95136 854-E7
S MAGNOLIA AV
- MLBR 94030 728-B4
600 SJS 95136 854-E7
1800 BURL 94010 728-B4
W MAGNOLIA AV
3900 SJS 95136 854-E7
MAGNOLIA AV S
- SSF 94080 707-H4
MAGNOLIA CIR
1700 PLE 94566 714-E1
MAGNOLIA CT
- CCCo 94595 612-B6
900 SLN 94577 691-A2
900 SLN 94577 690-J2
1600 MLPK 94025 790-F5
MAGNOLIA DR
- ATN 94027 790-F1
300 ALA 94502 670-B7
600 SMTO 94402 749-B2
1200 CNCD 94520 592-E4
3800 PA 94306 811-C2
MAGNOLIA LN
- CCCo 94803 589-C4
- RCH 94803 589-C4
- RCH 94805 589-C4
400 SCL 95051 833-B7
1100 LFYT 94549 611-F5
1500 SLN 94577 690-J2
1500 SLN 94577 691-A2
MAGNOLIA PL
- CCCo 94506 654-B3
500 NVTO 94945 525-E2
MAGNOLIA ST
- SF 94123 647-G4
400 OAK 94607 649-E2
600 MLPK 94025 790-E5
2800 OAK 94608 649-E2
2900 BERK 94705 629-J4
3500 EMVL 94608 629-J4
3500 OAK 94608 629-J4
24700 HAY 94545 711-G4
36600 NWK 94560 752-D7
MAGNOLIA TER
5500 FRMT 94538 773-A1
MAGNOLIA WY
1100 ANT 94509 575-B5
1700 CCCo 94595 632-B1
1700 CCCo 94595 612-B6
MAGNOLIA BLOSSOM LN
1600 SJS 95124 873-J6
MAGNOLIA TREE CT
1700 SJS 95122 854-F1
MAGNUM DR
2900 SJS 95135 855-E3
MAGPIE LN
1500 SUNV 94087 832-F5
MAHAN DR
6100 SJS 95123 875-A6
MAHAN ST
600 SF 94124 688-E1
MAHAN WY
2300 CCCo 94806 569-B6
MAHER CT
100 VAL 94591 530-D3
MAHLER RD
800 BURL 94010 728-D4
MAHOGANY CT
3600 WLCK 94598 592-J7
MAHOGANY DR
- SRFL 94903 566-B2
700 SUNV 94086 832-G2
MAHOGANY LN
- SRMN 94583 693-F1
MAHOGANY PL
8500 NWK 94560 752-B7
MAHOGANY RW
700 SBRN 94066 707-H6
MAHOGANY ST
26400 HAY 94544 712-A5
MAHOGANY TR
- CCCo - 652-E2
MAHOGANY WY
900 ANT 94509 575-A5
MAHOGONY DR
100 VAL 94589 510-A7
MAHONEY AV
200 SJS 95127 835-B1
200 SCIC 95127 835-B1
MAHONEY ST
900 CCCo 94572 549-H7
41200 FRMT 94538 773-D1
41600 FRMT 94538 753-D7
MAHOO LN
1800 CNCD 94521 593-F4
MAIDEN LN
- UNC 94587 731-J5
- OAK 94602 650-F3
- SF 94108 648-A6
100 DNVL 94526 633-C7
500 PIN 94564 569-E4
4100 SMTO 94403 749-D6
6900 SJS 95120 894-G3
8500 ELCR 94530 609-D1
MAIDSTONE CT
35000 NWK 94560 752-D3
MAIN AV
1600 CNCD 94519 592-G2
MAIN DR
- SBRN 94066 727-G3
- MrnC 94901 567-B7
- SRFL 94901 567-C7
200 SRFL 94903 566-G1
E MAIN RD
- CCCo 94553 571-G3
W MAIN RD
- CCCo 94553 571-F3
MAIN ST
- SRFL 94901 587-B5
- SRFL 94964 587-B5
- BLV 94920 627-E1
- LALT 94022 811-E7
- MRTZ 94553 571-D3
- SF 94105 648-B5
- TBRN 94920 627-E1
- MrnC 94964 587-B5
100 BSBN 94005 688-A4
100 BSBN 94005 687-J3
100 PLE 94566 714-D4
100 SAUS 94965 627-B4
100 SMTO 94401 748-J1
200 RDWC 94063 770-B5
200 SMTO 94401 749-A1
600 SCL 95050 833-D2
1700 ALA 94501 649-E7
3100 PLHL 94523 592-C7
3700 FRMT 94538 753-D7
3800 FRMT 94539 753-D7
6000 CLAY 94517 593-H7
12200 AlaC 94586 734-C6
21700 HAY 94541 691-H7
22100 HAY 94541 711-J1
E MAIN ST
- LGTS 95032 893-A1
N MAIN ST
1300 WLCK 94596 612-C2
S MAIN ST
- MPS 95035 794-A7
100 MPS 95035 814-A1
1100 WLCK 94596 612-C6
1800 WLCK 94595 612-C6
1900 CCCo 94595 632-D1
1900 WLCK 94595 632-D1
W MAIN ST
100 LGTS 95030 872-J7
MAIN TR
- MrnC 94965 606-A3
MAINE AV
- RCH 94804 588-F7
MAINE DR
5500 CNCD 94521 593-F6
MAINE ST Rt#-141
100 VAL 94590 529-J5
300 VAL 94590 530-A5
MAIN ENTRANCE DR
1400 SJS 95131 814-C7
MAIN GATE RD
- NVTO 94949 546-G3
MAIN GATE TER
700 BEN 94510 551-D5
MAINPRICE CT
- SRMN 94583 673-E4
MAINSAIL CT
- RCH 94804 608-E3
100 VAL 94591 550-G2
200 FCTY 94404 749-G4
MAIRMONT DR
4200 PLE 94566 714-E1
MAIRWOOD CT
700 SJS 95120 894-J3
MAISON CT
- MRGA 94556 631-D6
MAISON DR
- DNVL 94506 653-H5
MAISON WY
800 RCH 94803 589-H3
MAITLAND DR
- ALA 94502 670-A6
1700 SJS 95124 873-H4
25500 HAY 94542 712-B3
MAITLAND RD
400 PCFA 94044 726-J2
MAJELLA WY
3700 CNCD 94519 592-J1
MAJESTIC AV
- SF 94112 687-E1
3600 OAK 94605 650-H7
5900 OAK 94605 670-H1
MAJESTIC CT
1900 SJS 95132 814-F2
4000 CNCD 94519 593-B1
MAJESTIC DR
3900 CNCD 94519 593-B1
MAJESTIC WY
500 SLN 94578 691-B5
1700 SJS 95132 814-F3
MAJESTIC OAK WY
22700 CPTO 95014 831-J7
MAJILLA AV
1100 BURL 94010 728-F6
MAJOR AV
900 HAY 94542 712-B4
MAJORCA CT
- MrnC 94903 546-E7
6000 SJS 95120 874-B7
MAJORCA DR
200 SRMN 94583 673-G3
MAJORCA WY
2800 SCAR 94070 769-F6
MAJOR VISTA CT
600 PIN 94564 569-C4
MAKAHA CIR
400 UNC 94587 732-D5
MAKATI CIR
5100 SJS 95123 875-B4
MAKATI CT
- SJS 95123 875-B4
MAKIN RD
200 OAK 94603 670-F6
MAKIN GRADE
- ROSS 94957 586-D2
- SRFL 94901 586-E2
- MrnC 94904 586-D2
MALABAR AV
2800 SCL 95051 833-B7
4500 AlaC 94546 692-A3
MALABAR CT
- SCAR 94070 769-C4
MALABAR DR
400 SJS 95127 834-J3
MALACHITE CT
100 HER 94547 569-J5
MALAGA CT
100 VAL 94591 530-F6
1000 PLE 94566 714-H4
2500 SRMN 94583 673-C3
MALAGA DR
2500 SJS 95125 853-J7
MALAGA ST
100 VAL 94591 530-F6
MALAGA WY
400 PLHL 94523 592-A5
MALARIN AV
600 SCL 95050 833-D5
MALAT ST
4600 OAK 94601 670-C2
MALAVEAR CT
- PCFA 94044 726-J5
- PCFA 94044 727-A5
MALBEC CT
500 PLE 94566 714-G3
MALCOLM AV
100 BLMT 94002 749-D7
3000 OAK 94605 671-D4
MALCOLM LN
900 HAY 94545 711-G5
MALCOLM RD
800 BURL 94010 728-D4
MALCOLMSON ST
41200 FRMT 94538 753-D7
MALCOM AV
13800 SAR 95070 872-D1
MALDEN AL
- SF 94105 648-B6
MALDEN AV
1900 SJS 95122 854-H1
MALDON ST
6200 OAK 94621 670-E3
MALE TER
47100 FRMT 94539 773-H6
MALECH RD
100 SJS 95138 875-J7
100 SCIC 95137 875-J7
100 SCIC 95137 895-J1
MALERO PL
4700 SJS 95129 852-J1
MALIBU CT
- UNC 94545 751-J1
200 ANT 94509 595-E1
400 LVMR 94550 715-E3
MALIBU DR
300 HER 94547 570-B6
800 CNCD 94518 592-G6
1100 SJS 95129 853-A3
MALIBU PL
3800 PIT 94565 574-B5
MALIBU RD
24000 HAY 94545 711-F4
MALIBU TER
- FRMT 94539 794-B1
MALL CT
- OAK 94611 650-G2
MALLARD COM
4600 FRMT 94555 752-D2
MALLARD CT
- ANT 94509 594-H2
1700 LVMR 94550 696-D2
2600 UNC 94587 732-E6
3300 HAY 94542 712-E5
MALLARD DR
- BEN 94510 551-E3
2000 WLCK 94596 612-A2
2000 WLCK 94596 611-J2
4000 CNCD 94520 572-G3
5300 PLE 94566 714-C1
S MALLARD DR
1300 RCH 94801 608-D2
1300 RCH 94804 608-D2
MALLARD RD
- BLV 94920 607-D7
- BLV 94920 627-D1
MALLARD ST
- DNVL 94506 653-E4
300 VAL 94589 510-B5
800 FCTY 94404 749-G1
1500 LVMR 94550 696-D3
MALLARD WY
- ANT 94509 594-H1
1400 SUNV 94087 832-G4
MALLARD RIDGE CIR
1400 SJS 95120 894-F3
MALLARD RIDGE CT
7100 SJS 95120 894-F3
MALLARD RIDGE DR
1400 SJS 95120 894-F3
MALLARD RIDGE LP
7200 SJS 95120 894-F3
MALLARD SLOUGH RD
- PIT 94565 573-H2
MALLET CT
1000 MLPK 94025 790-F4
MALLORCA WY
- SF 94123 647-G3
2900 UNC 94587 732-A4
2900 UNC 94587 731-J4
MALLORY CT
19900 SAR 95070 852-E6
MALOBAR DR
500 NVTO 94945 526-G1
MALONE LN
- SRFL 94903 566-C4
MALONE PL
2500 SCL 95050 833-C5
MALONE RD
700 SJS 95125 854-B5
MALONEY LN
600 MLPK 94025 790-F3
MALORY CT
- SMCo 94061 790-B3
MALORY DR
6200 SJS 95123 875-B7
MALOTT DR
900 SJS 95121 854-H3
MALOYAN LN
- LFYT 94549 611-C5
MALPAS LN
5700 SJS 95124 873-J6
MALTA CIR
- CNCD 94519 592-J1
MALTA CT
- OAK 94603 670-G7
MALTA DR
- SF 94131 667-F6
MALTA LN
1200 FCTY 94404 749-F5
MALTA PL
36000 FRMT 94536 752-F3
MALTON CT
3100 SJS 95148 855-E2
MALVA TER
4000 FRMT 94536 752-H1
MALVASIA CT
3100 PLE 94566 714-G3
MALVERN CT
10300 CPTO 95014 852-F1
MALVINA PL
- SF 94108 648-A5
- SF 94108 647-J5
MALVINI DR
3900 SJS 95118 874-B2
MALVINO CT
- TBRN 94920 607-B4
MAMMOTH DR
2300 SJS 95116 834-G2
MAMMOTH CAVE CT
3800 PLE 94588 714-A1
MANACOR CT
3700 SRMN 94583 673-C3
MANASSAS CT
2000 SJS 95116 834-H5
MANCHESTER
- HER 94547 569-F1
MANCHESTER AV
200 CMBL 95008 853-G5
2400 SPAB 94806 588-G2
MANCHESTER COM
3300 FRMT 94536 753-A4
MANCHESTER CT
- NVTO 94947 526-E6
1500 CNCD 94521 593-D4
3100 PA 94303 791-D6
MANCHESTER DR
1000 SCL 95050 833-E5
1500 CNCD 94521 593-D4
5900 OAK 94618 630-A5
MANCHESTER LN
100 BLMT 94002 749-F6
MANCHESTER RD
1900 AlaC 94578 691-F4
MANCHESTER ST
- SF 94110 667-J4
200 DNVL 94506 653-J6
3600 PLE 94588 694-F5
MANCINI CT
7400 DBLN 94568 693-F4
MANCINI DR
4800 AlaC 94546 692-B3
MANCUSO ST
6100 SJS 95120 874-C7
MANDA DR
2800 SJS 95124 873-H1
MANDALA CT
100 CCCo 94596 612-F7
MANDALAY AV
100 HER 94547 570-C6
MANDALAY CT
- RDWC 94065 749-J5
MANDALAY LN
1000 SF 94116 667-C3

STREET Block City ZIP Pg-Grid
MANDALAY RD
- OAK 94618 630-B6
MANDAN CT
1800 FRMT 94539 773-G4
MANDAN PL
1800 FRMT 94539 773-G4
MANDANA BLVD
400 OAK 94610 650-A3
MANDANA CIR
- OAK 94610 650-B3
MANDARIN AV
27500 HAY 94544 731-J1
27700 HAY 94544 711-J7
MANDARIN DR
300 DALY 94015 707-C1
1200 SUNV 94087 832-B3
MANDARIN LN
600 WLCK 94598 592-H7
MANDARIN WY
- ATN 94027 790-B5
1800 SJS 95122 834-H6
2100 ANT 94509 575-B5
13500 SAR 95070 872-D1
MANDEL CT
1800 SJS 95131 814-D7
MANDELA CT
1000 EPA 94303 791-C1
MANDELA PKWY
300 OAK 94607 649-D3
2600 OAK 94608 649-E3
MANDERLY RD
- SRFL 94901 587-B1
- SRFL 94901 567-B7
MANDOLI DR
13400 LAH 94022 811-A5
MANDOLIN DR
300 SJS 95134 813-D2
MANDRILL CT
4700 SJS 95124 873-J3
MANET DR
1000 SUNV 94087 832-E3
MANFRED ST
100 MPS 95035 793-J3
100 MPS 95035 794-A3
MANGELS AV
- SF 94131 667-F6
200 SF 94127 667-F6
500 SF 94127 667-D6
3500 OAK 94619 650-E6
MANGIN WY
2100 SCIC 95148 835-E5
MANGINI RD
- PLHL 94523 592-A5
MANGO AV
800 SUNV 94087 832-B2
MANGO RD
2000 CNCD 94518 592-F5
MANGO ST
24700 HAY 94545 711-G5
MANGO BLOSSOM CT
5300 SJS 95123 875-A3
MANGOS DR
9900 SRMN 94583 673-F5
MANGROVE AV
800 SUNV 94086 832-G3
MANGROVE DR
- DBLN 94568 694-D4
MANGROVE LN
1000 ALA 94502 670-B7
MANGROVE WY
300 WLCK 94598 612-H2
MANGRUM DR
4600 SCL 95054 813-D4
MANHASSET DR
600 WLCK 94598 613-A3
MANHATTAN AV
1900 EPA 94303 791-B3
MANHATTAN CT
1000 SUNV 94087 832-B2
MANHATTAN DR
100 VAL 94591 530-D4
MANHATTAN PL
2200 SCL 95051 833-A2
MANHATTEN CT
- RDWC 94065 749-J5
6500 MRTZ 94553 591-H4
MANICHETTI CT
5800 SJS 95123 875-A5
MANILA AV
3700 OAK 94609 649-H1
3800 OAK 94609 629-H7
5100 OAK 94618 629-J6
5400 OAK 94618 630-A6
6300 ELCR 94530 609-C2
MANILA DR
- MTVW 94035 812-C3
- MTVW 94043 812-C3
- SCIC 94035 812-C3
- SUNV 94089 812-C3
300 SJS 95119 875-C7
MANILA WY
600 SMCo 94015 687-A5
6400 SJS 95119 875-C7
MANITA CT
21000 CPTO 95014 852-C3
MANITOBA COM
- FRMT 94538 773-D2
MANITOBA DR
1600 SUNV 94087 832-C5
4700 SJS 95130 853-A7
MANITOBA GRN
200 FRMT 94538 773-E3
MANITOBA TER
100 FRMT 94538 773-E3
MANITOU CT
1700 SJS 95120 874-B6
MANLEY CT
100 SJS 95139 895-G1
MANLY CT
300 SCL 95051 833-A7
MANN AV
2100 UNC 94587 732-G7
MANN DR
- MrnC 94904 586-E3
1500 PIN 94564 569-D5
10000 CPTO 95014 832-B7
MANNING AV
- SJS 95127 834-J2
- SCIC 95127 834-J2
MANNING LN
1500 CCCo 94507 632-E4
MANN OAK CT
20000 SCIC 95120 894-J5
MANOA CT
- CCCo 94806 569-B4
20300 SAR 95070 852-E7
MANOA ST
6200 OAK 94618 629-J4
MANON AV
26800 HAY 94544 712-A6
MANOR AV
- PLHL 94523 592-C7
- WLCK 94596 592-C7
- WLCK 94596 612-C1
MANOR BLVD
500 SLN 94579 691-A6
1700 SLN 94579 690-J6
MANOR CIR
1700 ELCR 94530 609-C1
MANOR CT
- DALY 94015 687-A3
- RDWC 94062 769-H5
200 AMCN 94589 510-A3
5300 FRMT 94536 752-G6
12500 SAR 95070 852-D5
MANOR DR
- CCCo 94565 573-G2
- PDMT 94611 650-A1
- SF 94127 667-C7
100 MLV 94941 606-E3
100 PCFA 94044 706-J3
100 SCAR 94070 769-E4
100 SSF 94080 707-G5
200 PCFA 94044 707-A4
1000 AlaC 94586 734-A2
1100 SJS 95125 854-B6
1300 SPAB 94806 588-G3
1700 HIL 94010 728-E7
20500 SAR 95070 852-D5
E MANOR DR
- MLV 94941 606-E3
MANOR LN
1600 CNCD 94521 593-B2
MANOR PL
- MLPK 94025 790-H3
W MANOR PZ
400 PCFA 94044 706-J3
MANOR RD
- MrnC 94904 586-E3
700 CCCo 94803 569-D7
MANOR TER
- MLV 94941 606-E3
MANOR WY
- ALB 94706 609-F6
700 LALT 94024 831-G3
MANOR CREST
6700 OAK 94618 630-A4
MANORWOOD CT
5800 SJS 95129 852-G3
MANRESA CT
200 LALT 94022 831-D1
7500 SJS 95139 895-G2
MANRESA LN
200 LALT 94022 831-D1
MANRESA WY
500 LALT 94022 831-D1
600 LAH 94022 831-D1
MANSBURY CT
4900 FRMT 94538 773-B1
MANSBURY ST
4900 FRMT 94538 773-B1
MANSEAU ST
600 SF 94124 688-E1
MANSELL ST
- SF 94134 688-A1
400 SF 94134 687-H1
MANSFIELD AV
6800 DBLN 94568 693-J3
22800 AlaC 94541 692-C7
MANSFIELD DR
200 SSF 94080 707-D2
500 MTVW 94040 831-J2
700 SJS 95128 853-G2
4300 CCCo 94506 654-B5
MANSFIELD ST
- SF 94112 667-H7
MANSION CT
- MLPK 94025 790-C7
500 SCL 95134 813-E4
1300 SJS 95120 894-C2
MANSION PARK DR
400 SCL 95134 813-E4
MANTECA CT
6100 SJS 95123 874-G6
MANTECA WY
13600 SAR 95070 872-H1
MANTER CT
4600 AlaC 94552 692-C5
MANTER RD
20800 AlaC 94552 692-C5
MANTI TER
- CCCo 94526 633-A6
MANTILLA AV
1200 HAY 94544 712-A7
1200 HAY 94544 711-J7
MANTILLA CORTE
2600 WLCK 94598 612-H2
MANTIS DR
2800 SJS 95148 835-E7
MANTIS ST
47400 FRMT 94539 773-J6
MANTON CT
800 CNCD 94518 592-G6
1600 CMBL 95008 873-A1
MANTON DR
100 SJS 95123 875-B4
MANUEL CT
200 CCCo 94565 573-D1
1200 OAK 94603 670-J6
MANUEL DR
600 NVTO 94945 526-C4
1300 HAY 94544 732-A1
MANUELA AV
4100 PA 94306 811-C4
MANUELA CT
4200 PA 94306 811-B5
MANUELA WY
26000 PA 94306 811-B5
MANUELLA AV
300 WDSD 94062 789-F6
MANUELLA RD
4200 PA 94306 811-C5
4200 LAH 94022 811-C6
MANUEL T FREITAS PKWY
600 SRFL 94903 566-C2
MANVILLE AV
- PIT 94565 574-C5
MANX AV
700 CMBL 95008 853-D7
MANXWOOD PL
5100 SJS 95111 875-C2
MANZANA LN
4000 PA 94306 811-C3
MANZANA PL
1000 LFYT 94549 611-J6
MANZANILLA CT
- SPAB 94806 568-J7
MANZANILLA DR
1700 SPAB 94806 568-H7
MANZANITA AV
- CCCo - 631-A7
- MRGA 94556 631-A7
- MRGA 94556 651-C1
- DALY 94015 707-A1
- MrnC 94901 567-B7
- MrnC 94945 526-J4
- SF 94118 647-E6
100 SCAR 94070 769-F3
100 SSF 94080 707-H4
200 PA 94306 791-A6
200 SCL 95051 833-B7
400 CMAD 94925 586-F7
500 SUNV 94086 812-E5
700 CMAD 94925 606-G1
1500 SLN 94579 691-A5
1600 BLMT 94002 769-D1
2000 SMCo 94025 790-C6
MANZANITA CT
- CCCo 94595 612-A7
- MLBR 94030 728-A5
200 CMAD 94925 586-G7
200 CMAD 94925 606-G1
300 MPS 95035 813-J4
3900 CNCD 94519 573-A7
45100 FRMT 94539 773-H3
MANZANITA DR
- ORIN 94563 610-F5
100 VAL 94589 530-B2
100 VAL 94590 530-B2
1000 PCFA 94044 727-A5
1200 MLBR 94030 728-A6
1700 OAK 94611 630-F6
1800 CNCD 94519 593-A1
1800 CNCD 94519 573-A7
2100 CCCo - 630-G6
3900 SJS 95117 853-B2
4200 SJS 95129 853-A2
MANZANITA LN
11500 DBLN 94568 693-F5
MANZANITA PL
- MLV 94941 606-C1
100 HER 94547 570-A4
MANZANITA RD
- ATN 94027 790-G1
MANZANITA ST
- RDWC 94063 770-B7
2100 PLE 94566 714-G2
6200 NWK 94560 772-F1
37700 NWK 94560 752-F7
45000 FRMT 94539 773-H3
MANZANITA TER
- ORIN 94563 610-F5
MANZANITA WY
100 WDSD 94062 789-H7
100 WDSD 94062 809-H1
2100 ANT 94509 575-B6
18200 LGTS 95030 872-J7
MANZANO CT
- PLE 94566 715-B7
- NVTO 94945 525-J1
600 MPS 95035 794-B4
MANZANO DR
3000 WLCK 94598 612-J3
MANZANO ST
500 MPS 95035 794-A4
MANZANO WY
1100 SUNV 94089 813-A5
MAOLI DR
1600 MrnC 94903 546-A7
MAPACHE CT
- PTLV 94028 810-A4
MAPACHE DR
100 PTLV 94028 810-A4
MAPEL
- BEN 94510 551-B5
MAPLE AV
- ATN 94027 790-E2
- LKSP 94939 586-D6
- MrnC 94904 586-D3
- SSF 94080 707-J3
100 VAL 94591 530-D6
400 MPS 95035 793-H6
400 SBRN 94066 727-H1
500 CMBL 95008 853-F6
500 SBRN 94066 707-H7
500 SUNV 94086 812-F6
700 RCH 94801 588-F6
800 BURL 94010 728-F5
2400 CNCD 94520 572-F7
3000 OAK 94602 650-E5
S MAPLE AV
100 SSF 94080 707-H4
MAPLE CT
- HAY 94541 711-J1
- NVTO 94947 526-D6
100 HER 94547 570-A5
600 SLN 94577 671-A7
MAPLE DR
- NVTO 94945 526-D2
6500 DBLN 94568 693-J4
MAPLE LN
- CCCo 94595 612-B7
- SANS 94960 566-A6
1500 LALT 94024 831-G3
16700 LGTS 95032 893-A1
MAPLE PL
100 MLBR 94030 728-A5
MAPLE ST
- RDWC 94063 770-B5
- SF 94118 647-E5
- SRFL 94901 566-G7
100 LVMR 94550 695-H7
100 LVMR 94550 715-H1
400 MrnC 94965 606-E7
400 PA 94301 791-A3
500 SMTO 94402 748-J2
1000 SMTO 94402 749-A3
1000 PIT 94565 574-F3
37000 FRMT 94536 752-H3
37000 NWK 94560 752-H3
37000 NWK 94560 772-C1
MAPLE WY
- SCAR 94070 769-G6
400 WDSD 94062 789-E3
W MAPLE WY
400 WDSD 94062 789-E3
MAPLECREST CT
5500 SJS 95123 874-G4
MAPLEGLEN CT
- DNVL 94506 653-J3
MAPLE GROVE CT
5300 SJS 95123 874-F7
MAPLE HILL DR
- SRFL 94903 566-D1
MAPLE LEAF CT
2000 PLE 94588 714-F1
2000 PLE 94566 714-F1
3200 SJS 95121 855-B3
MAPLE LEAF DR
1400 PLE 94588 714-F1
MAPLE LEAF WY
- ATN 94027 790-G2
MAPLETREE PL
20500 CPTO 95014 832-D6
MAPLEWOOD AV
300 SJS 95117 853-D1
300 SCIC 95117 853-D1
700 PA 94303 811-F1
MAPLEWOOD CT
- DNVL 94506 653-J3
3800 CNCD 94519 573-A7
MAPLEWOOD DR
- DNVL 94506 653-J3
- SRFL 94901 567-B6
1400 LVMR 94550 696-D3
3800 CNCD 94519 573-A7
MAPLEWOOD LN
2600 SCL 95051 833-B7
MAPLEWOOD PL
700 PA 94303 811-F1
MAPLEWOOD ST
10600 CPTO 95014 832-F6
MARA CT
200 SRMN 94583 673-F5
MARABU WY
1500 FRMT 94539 753-E5
MARACAIBO DR
5800 SJS 95120 874-C6
MARACAIBO RD
14100 SLN 94577 690-H5
MARAKESH DR
100 CCCo 94553 572-C7
MARALISA CT
1600 LVMR 94550 696-D3
MARALISA LN
1700 LVMR 94550 696-D2
MARANTA AV
800 SUNV 94087 832-C2
MARASCHINO CT
2500 UNC 94587 732-F7
MARASCHINO DR
1000 SJS 95129 853-A3
1100 SUNV 94087 832-C3
MARASCHINO PL
2400 UNC 94587 732-F7
MARATHON DR
1500 CMBL 95008 853-C5
7300 LVMR 94550 696-F6
MARA VISTA CT
- TBRN 94920 607-C5
MARAZZANI DR
2000 MRTZ 94553 572-A6
MARBELLA CT
2200 SJS 95124 873-F3
MARBELLA DR
2200 SJS 95124 873-F3
MARBI LN
- WLCK 94596 612-C2
MARBLE CT
100 VAL 94589 510-B5
900 SJS 95120 894-G1
MARBLE DR
200 ANT 94509 595-E1
MARBLE CANYON CT
400 SRMN 94583 653-F6
MARBLE CANYON LN
500 SRMN 94583 653-F6
MARBLE CANYON PL
3000 SRMN 94583 653-F6
MARBLEHEAD CT
4000 SRMN 94583 673-H5
MARBLEHEAD DR
4000 SRMN 94583 673-H5
MARBLEHEAD LN
500 WLCK 94598 612-J2
MARBLY AV
- DALY 94015 707-C2
MARBURG WY
1500 SJS 95133 834-E3
N MARBURG WY
400 SJS 95133 834-E3
MARBURGER AV
3100 BLMT 94002 769-A1
MARBURY RD
2400 LVMR 94550 715-G5
MARCEL CT
3300 SJS 95135 855-G3
MARCELA AV
- SF 94116 667-D4
MARCELLA CT
900 CNCD 94518 592-F6
4800 LVMR 94550 696-B7
MARCELLA ST
600 LVMR 94550 696-B7
15700 AlaC 94578 691-E4
MARCELLA WY
200 MLBR 94030 728-B5
MARCELYN AV
2400 MTVW 94043 811-F2
MARCH DR
100 SJS 95138 875-D4
MARCHAND CT
24000 HAY 94541 712-A2
MARCHANT CT
- CCCo 94707 609-F4
3700 SJS 95127 835-C2
MARCHANT DR
3700 SJS 95127 835-C2
MARCHANT GDNS
- CCCo 94707 609-F4
MARCHBANKS CT
100 WLCK 94598 612-E3
MARCHBANKS DR
1400 WLCK 94598 612-D3
MARCHESE CT
3300 SCL 95051 833-A1
MARCHESE WY
2400 SCL 95051 833-A2
MARCHI AV
2800 MRTZ 94553 571-G4
2800 CCCo 94553 571-G4
MARCHMONT CT
200 LGTS 95032 873-D7
MARCHMONT DR
200 LGTS 95032 873-C7
16500 SCIC 95032 873-C7
MARCIA AV
1400 SJS 95125 854-A7
MARCIA CT
- CCCo 94565 573-F2
- LVMR 94550 696-B6
100 MTVW 94041 811-J6
MARCIA DR
2300 PLHL 94523 592-D6
30500 UNC 94587 732-B4
MARCIA ST
40400 FRMT 94538 753-C6
MARCIE CIR
- SSF 94080 707-G2
MARCIEL CT
18900 AlaC 94546 691-J3
MARCLAIR DR
1400 CNCD 94521 593-B4
MARCO DR
1600 SJS 95131 814-C7
MARCO WY
100 SSF 94080 708-A5
1600 SJS 95131 814-C7
MARCONI WY
1600 SJS 95125 853-J5
MARCO POLO WY
1600 BURL 94010 728-C5
MARCROSS DR
1900 SJS 95131 814-D6
MARCUS CT
1200 ANT 94509 575-F7
1800 HAY 94541 712-B2
MARCUS ST
3900 PIN 94564 569-J7
3900 CCCo - 569-J7
MARCUSE ST
1000 ALA 94502 669-J6
MARCUSSEN DR
1000 MLPK 94025 790-G2
MARCY CT
- NVTO 94947 526-A4
21000 CPTO 95014 832-C7
MARCY PL
- SF 94108 647-J5
MARCY LYNN CT
1700 SJS 95124 873-H5
MARDAN DR
1400 SJS 95132 814-F3
MARDEL LN
2000 SJS 95128 853-G3
MARDELL WY
2500 MTVW 94043 811-F2
MARDEN LN
5900 OAK 94611 630-D6
MARDENE CT
3800 SJS 95121 855-B5
MARDIE ST
500 HAY 94544 711-J3
MARDIS ST
47600 FRMT 94539 773-H7
MARDON CT
1100 CNCD 94521 593-E7
MARE LN
300 SRMN 94583 673-C4
MAR EAST ST
2100 TBRN 94920 607-F7
2300 MrnC 94920 607-F7
MAREE CT
6100 SJS 95123 874-G6
MARE ISLAND CSWY
- VAL 94592 529-G4
- VAL 94590 529-G4
MARE ISLAND WY
200 VAL 94590 529-H4
MARELIA CT
1400 SPAB 94806 588-G3
MARENGO LN
1100 SJS 95132 814-H5
MARENGO ST
- SF 94124 668-A5
MARE PLACE CT
3800 SJS 95121 855-B5
MARES CT
400 PLE 94566 734-C1
MARFRANCE DR
3800 SJS 95121 855-A5
MARGARET AV
- BSBN 94005 688-A7
- SF 94112 687-E1
MARGARET CT
100 VAL 94590 550-B1
300 CCCo 94565 573-D1
900 SUNV 94087 832-B2
1000 NVTO 94947 526-D7
4100 SMTO 94403 749-E6
MARGARET DR
- CCCo 94596 632-F1
24300 HAY 94542 712-A2
MARGARET LN
- DNVL 94526 652-H2
600 CMBL 95008 853-B7
5600 OAK 94618 630-A5
MARGARET ST
- SJS 95112 834-D7
1700 SJS 95116 834-G5
MARGARET WY
100 SJS 95112 834-C7
MARGARIDO DR
100 WLCK 94596 612-D5
5600 OAK 94618 630-A5
MARGARITA AV
200 PA 94306 811-C1
3100 BURL 94010 728-A7
3400 OAK 94605 671-B3
MARGARITA CT
1700 CNCD 94521 593-E4
MARGARITA DR
- MrnC 94901 587-A1
300 SRFL 94901 567-A7
300 MrnC 94901 566-J7
300 SRFL 94901 566-J7
MARGARITA TER
- NVTO 94947 526-D6
MARGARITE CT
200 LALT 94022 811-D4
MARGATE AV
3500 SJS 95117 853-C2
MARGATE CIR
- PLHL 94523 592-A4
MARGATE ST
- DALY 94015 707-C2
MARGE CT
100 UNC 94587 732-F4
MARGE WY
500 SCIC 95117 853-D2
MARGERY AV
1200 SLN 94578 691-C4
MARGERY CT
40100 FRMT 94538 753-B7
MARGERY DR
4000 FRMT 94538 753-B7
MARGIE DR
100 PLHL 94523 592-C5
MARGIE LN
- OAK 94605 651-A7
- OAK 94619 651-A7
MARGO DR
100 MTVW 94041 812-A6
1700 CNCD 94519 593-A1
MARGO LN
- HIL 94010 728-D6
900 PLE 94566 714-H3
MARGONE CT
- DNVL 94526 653-C1
MARGORY CT
- NVTO 94947 525-J3
MARGOT PL
1900 SJS 95125 853-J6
MARGRAVE CT
- WLCK 94596 612-B2
MARGRAVE PL
- SF 94133 648-A4
MARGUERITA RD
- CCCo 94708 609-F2
MARGUERITE AV
- MLV 94941 606-C2
1900 PLHL 94523 592-A5
MARGUERITE CT
1000 LFYT 94549 611-C5
MARGUERITE DR
- CCCo 94806 569-A5
- OAK 94618 630-B6
6100 NWK 94560 772-G1
MARGUERITE ST
1200 LVMR 94550 715-F2
MARI CT
100 VAL 94589 509-J5
MARIA AV
1300 CNCD 94518 592-H2
MARIA CT
- NVTO 94945 525-H1
400 SCL 95050 833-D5
2300 PIN 94564 569-F7
3200 CNCD 94518 592-H3
3700 AlaC 94546 692-A5
MARIA DR
1300 SLN 94577 690-H2
MARIA LN
800 SUNV 94086 832-F3
1400 WLCK 94596 612-D6
21100 SAR 95070 852-C5
MARIA ST
200 SCL 95050 833-D5
MARIA WY
1300 SJS 95117 853-D4
1500 SCIC 95117 853-D4
MARIALINDA CT
- HIL 94010 728-D7
MARIA LORETO CT
- NVTO 94949 546-E5
MARIAN CT
- SRFL 94901 586-J2
MARIAN LN
- SCIC 95127 834-J1
400 DNVL 94526 652-H2
MARIAN PL
100 PLHL 94523 592-D6
MARIANAS LN
1000 ALA 94502 670-A6
1100 ALA 94502 669-J7
MARIANELLI CT
1000 SJS 95112 834-C3
MARIANI AV
20300 CPTO 95014 832-D7
MARIANI CT
- SMCo 94062 789-G3
MARIANI DR
1600 SUNV 94087 832-F5
MARIANNA LN
- ATN 94027 790-E2
1500 SJS 95128 853-H2
MARIANNA WY
100 CMBL 95008 853-C5
MARIANNE CT
100 MTVW 94040 811-J7
MARIANNE DR
4000 LFYT 94549 611-B6
MARIA PRIVADA
1100 MTVW 94040 832-H6
MARIA ROSA WY
10900 CPTO 95014 852-B3
MARIA TERESA CT
100 LGTS 95032 873-E5
MARICAIBO PL
900 SRMN 94583 673-B3
MARICE CT
3700 CNCD 94518 592-J4
MARICH WY
200 LALT 94022 811-F4
1100 MTVW 94040 811-F4
MARICOPA AV
2300 RCH 94804 588-H4
2300 RCH 94806 588-H4
3400 RCH 94804 589-A4
3400 SPAB 94805 589-A4
MARICOPA CT
100 PLHL 94523 592-B2
800 LVMR 94550 695-E6
MARICOPA DR
100 LGTS 95032 873-D5
MARIE AV
800 MRTZ 94553 571-H5
900 ANT 94509 575-E5
MARIE COM
300 LVMR 94550 696-B7
MARIE CT
4200 FRMT 94536 753-A5
MARIE DR
24400 HAY 94542 712-A2
MARIE PL
- MRGA 94556 651-F2
MARIE ST
- FRMT 94555 732-C7
- SAUS 94965 627-A2
MARIE WY
5900 OAK 94618 630-B4
MARIETTA CT
- CNCD 94518 592-J5
800 SCL 95051 833-A6
MARIETTA DR
- SF 94127 667-E5
1500 SJS 95118 874-A4
2900 SCL 95051 833-A5
40000 FRMT 94538 773-B1
MARIE VEGA CT
- SPAB 94806 589-A3
- SPAB 94806 588-J3
MARIGOLD CT
600 FRMT 94539 753-G5
1000 SUNV 94086 832-H2
1500 LVMR 94550 696-B3
1700 SJS 95133 834-E3
7800 PLE 94588 713-J1
27300 HAY 94545 711-G7
MARIGOLD DR
100 HER 94547 570-A4
900 VAL 94589 509-J6
41600 FRMT 94539 753-G6
MARIGOLD LN
- CCCo 94595 612-B7
- SCAR 94070 769-C4
MARIGOLD PL
200 HER 94547 570-A4
MARIGOLD RD
1000 LVMR 94550 696-B4
MARILLA AV
1000 SJS 95129 853-A3
MARILLA CT
20100 SAR 95070 852-E5
MARILLA DR
12000 SAR 95070 852-E5
MARILYN CT
1200 MTVW 94040 811-G7
3200 PLE 94588 694-C7
3200 PLE 94588 714-C1
MARILYN DR
700 CMBL 95008 853-C7
900 MTVW 94040 811-G6
900 CMBL 95008 873-C1
MARILYN LN
14000 SAR 95070 872-H2
MARILYN PL
- VAL 94590 530-B3
- SRMN 94583 673-F6
1300 MTVW 94040 811-G7
MARILYN WY
1100 CNCD 94518 592-G3
MARIN AV
- BLV 94920 607-C7
- CCCo 94565 573-F2
- SAUS 94965 626-J2
200 MrnC 94965 606-D7
500 HAY 94541 711-F3
1000 ALB 94706 609-D6
1200 RCH 94805 589-B6
1200 SPAB 94806 589-A4
1600 ALB 94707 609-G6
1600 BERK 94707 609-G6
2300 BERK 94708 609-H5
MARIN CT
4100 CNCD 94521 593-B3
MARIN DR
400 BURL 94010 728-G6
700 MrnC 94965 606-D7
MARIN RD
800 CCCo 94803 569-D7
MARIN ST
- SRFL 94901 586-F2
200 VAL 94590 529-J4
600 SF 94124 668-C4
1400 SF 94124 668-A4
MARIN WY
- MrnC 94965 606-D7
1500 OAK 94606 650-A6
MARINA AV
1800 CNCD 94520 592-F2
2000 AlaC 94550 715-H4
MARINA BLVD
- MrnC 94901 586-J1
- PIT 94565 574-D1
- SF 94123 647-F3
- SSF 94080 708-C2
- SRFL 94901 586-J1
200 BERK 94804 629-B2
200 SLN 94577 690-G4
400 BSBN 94005 688-C7
1400 SLN 94577 691-A2
MARINA CT
- UNC 94545 751-J1
1500 SMTO 94403 749-D4
2000 SLN 94577 690-G4
MARINA DR
- RDWC 94065 749-G7
2800 ALA 94501 670-B2
MARINA PL
300 BEN 94510 551-B4
MARINA WY
- SRFL 94901 587-A1
100 NVTO 94947 526-C5
100 RCH 94801 588-G7
200 PCFA 94044 706-J7
1600 SCIC 95125 853-H5
MARINA WY S
- RCH 94804 608-G1

STREET
Block City ZIP Pg-Grid

MARINA WY S
100 RCH 94804 588-G7
MARINA BAY PKWY
900 RCH 94804 608-H2
S MARINA BAY PKWY
900 RCH 94804 608-H1
MARINA COURT DR
- MrnC 94901 586-H1
100 SRFL 94901 586-H1
MARINA GREEN DR
- SF 94123 647-F3
MARINA LAKES DR
- RCH 94804 608-H2
MARINA RIDGE CT
- VAL 94591 550-E2
MARINA VILLAGE PKWY
700 ALA 94501 649-F6
MARINA VILLAGE RD
300 BEN 94510 551-B6
MARINA VISTA
100 MRTZ 94553 571-F2
1500 SMTO 94404 749-D3
MARINA VISTA AV
- LKSP 94939 586-E7
200 CMAD 94925 586-E7
MARIN BAY PARK CT
- SRFL 94901 567-E5
MARIN CENTER DR
100 SRFL 94903 566-E3
MARINE DR
- SF 94129 647-C2
- SF 94129 647-E3
- MrnC 94901 567-C7
- MrnC 94901 587-C1
MARINE PKWY
100 RDWC 94065 749-G7
MARINE ST
200 RCH 94801 588-C7
MARINE WY
2600 MTVW 94043 791-G7
MARINER CT
- PIT 94565 573-J3
MARINER DR
- VAL 94591 530-G7
900 SCIC 94043 811-J3
MARINER WY
- DALY 94014 687-D5
- TBRN 94920 607-D7
MARINER GREEN CT
100 CMAD 94925 606-J1
MARINER GREEN DR
- CMAD 94925 606-J1
MARINERO CIR
- TBRN 94920 607-D6
MARINERS CIR
- SRFL 94903 566-F3
MARINERS CT
300 HAY 94544 712-C7
MARINERS PT
800 CCCo 94572 569-J2
800 CCCo 94572 570-A3
MARINERS COVE RD
- CCCo 94565 573-D1
MARINERS ISLAND BLVD
300 FCTY 94404 749-D2
300 SMTO 94404 749-D2
MARINERS POINT CT
800 CCCo 94572 570-A3
MARINER SQUARE DR
2500 ALA 94501 649-F6
MARINER SQUARE LP
- ALA 94501 649-F6
MARINE VIEW AV
- SMTO 94403 749-E7
- RCH 94801 608-D1
300 BLMT 94002 749-E7
MARINEVIEW DR
1800 SLN 94577 691-D1
MARINE WORLD PKWY Rt#-37
700 SolC 94589 529-H1
700 VAL 94589 529-H1
700 VAL 94590 529-H1
700 SolC 94589 509-J7
700 VAL 94589 509-J7
1400 VAL 94589 510-A6
1600 VAL 94591 510-A6
MARINITA AV
- SRFL 94901 586-H1
- SRFL 94901 566-H7
MARINO CT
40700 FRMT 94539 753-E5
MARINO WY
40600 FRMT 94539 753-E5
MARIN OAKS DR
200 NVTO 94949 546-C1
MARINOVICH WY
1300 LALT 94024 831-J3
MARINSHIP AV
900 SAUS 94965 626-J1
2000 SAUS 94965 627-A2
MARIN VALLEY DR
- NVTO 94949 546-F5
MARIN VIEW AV
- MrnC 94965 606-A3
MARIN VIEW DR
- NVTO 94949 546-G5
MARINWOOD AV
100 MrnC 94903 546-E6
MARIO WY
4000 LFYT 94549 611-B6
MARION AV
- MLV 94941 606-C3
- SAUS 94965 627-B4
400 PA 94301 791-C6
500 PA 94306 791-C6
700 PA 94303 791-C6
1700 NVTO 94945 526-A2
2200 FRMT 94539 753-F7
3700 OAK 94619 650-E6
MARION CT
- CCCo 94507 632-F6
- NVTO 94945 526-A3
400 ALA 94501 669-E1
1900 LFYT 94549 591-H7
5800 CCCo 94803 589-G4
MARION DR
- SMCo 94062 790-A4
MARION PL
- SF 94133 647-J4
600 PA 94301 791-C6
MARION RD
20500 SAR 95070 872-D2
MARION ST
20600 AlaC 94541 691-G6
MARION TER
2700 MRTZ 94553 571-E5
MARION WY
900 SUNV 94087 832-G4
5800 CCCo 94803 589-G4
MARION OAKS CT
- NVTO 94945 526-A3
MARIONOLA WY
1100 PIN 94564 569-E5
N MARIPOSA
6500 DBLN 94568 694-A3
S MARIPOSA
6500 DBLN 94568 694-A3
MARIPOSA AV
- LGTS 95030 873-A6
- SANS 94960 586-B1
100 DALY 94015 687-A7
200 MTVW 94041 811-G5
300 LALT 94022 811-D6
600 OAK 94610 649-J2
700 LVMR 94550 715-E1
1000 BERK 94707 609-G6
1100 SJS 95126 833-J7
1500 PA 94306 791-A6
MARIPOSA CT
- BURL 94010 728-A6
- DNVL 94526 653-A3
- TBRN 94920 607-A3
- LGTS 95030 873-A5
- DNVL 94526 652-J3
1700 CNCD 94521 593-E4
2800 ANT 94509 575-B6
MARIPOSA DR
100 PIT 94565 574-D5
400 SSF 94080 707-F5
2700 BURL 94010 728-A6
MARIPOSA LN
- NVTO 94947 526-D7
- ORIN 94563 610-F7
MARIPOSA RD
- SRFL 94901 586-F2
800 LFYT 94549 611-E7
MARIPOSA ST
- BSBN 94005 688-A6
- VAL 94590 530-C3
400 SF 94107 668-B2
700 CCCo 94572 549-H7
1200 RCH 94804 609-B2
2200 SF 94110 668-A2
2300 HAY 94545 731-H1
2700 SF 94110 667-J2
MARIPOSA TR
800 LFYT 94549 611-C3
MARIPOSA WK
- PCFA 94044 727-B1
MARIPOSA WY
- WLCK 94598 612-D4
39300 FRMT 94538 753-A6
39300 FRMT 94538 752-J6
MARISMA
3300 SMTO 94403 749-E5
MARIST CT
2900 SJS 95148 855-D4
MARITA DR
5100 ANT 94509 595-G4
MARITIME LP
4600 UNC 94545 731-J6
MARITIME ST
- OAK 94649 649-C2
600 OAK 94625 649-B3
600 OAK 94607 649-C2
700 OAK 94626 649-C2
MARITIME ACADEMY DR
100 VAL 94590 550-C1
MARJOHN BLVD
4900 SJS 95111 875-A2
MARJORIE CT
2400 MTVW 94043 811-F3
MARJORIE DR
900 CMBL 95008 873-B1
MARK AV
100 VAL 94589 510-C6
2800 SCL 95051 833-A3
3300 SJS 95124 873-J2
MARK CT
- CNCD 94520 572-E4
MARK DR
- SRFL 94903 566-F2
MARK LN
- ANT 94509 574-J6
- SF 94108 648-A5
MARK PL
- LKSP 94939 586-G5
MARK ST
10500 OAK 94605 671-C5
MARK TER
- TBRN 94920 607-B4
MARKET AV
- CCCo 94801 588-F3
1000 RCH 94806 588-G3
1100 SPAB 94806 588-G3
6200 NWK 94560 752-F7
MARKET PL
- NWK 94560 752-F7
200 MLPK 94025 770-H7
1000 SRMN 94583 673-F3
MARKET ST
- OAK 94607 649-F2
- SF 94105 648-A6
- SF 94111 648-A6
100 SRFL 94901 586-J2
500 SF 94104 648-A6
600 DALY 94014 687-D5
600 SF 94108 648-A6
600 SF 94103 648-A6
700 SCL 95053 833-D5
800 SF 94102 648-A6
800 SCL 95050 833-D5
1000 SF 94102 647-J7
1000 SF 94103 647-J7
1500 CNCD 94520 592-E2
1600 SF 94102 667-G2
1600 SF 94103 667-G2
1900 SF 94114 667-G2
2800 OAK 94608 649-F2
3400 OAK 94608 629-F5
3400 SF 94131 667-F4
6300 BERK 94702 629-F5
6300 BERK 94703 629-F5
E MARKET ST
- DALY 94014 687-C5
N MARKET ST
- SJS 95110 834-B6
- SJS 95113 834-B6
S MARKET ST
- SJS 95113 834-B6
300 SJS 95110 834-B7
S MARKET ST Rt#-82
300 SJS 95110 834-B7
W MARKET ST
- DALY 94014 687-C5
MARKHAM AV
- SMCo 94063 790-C1
400 SBRN 94066 727-G1
2200 SJS 95125 854-B6
MARKHAM CT
2600 HAY 94542 712-E5
MARKHAM ST
900 CNCD 94518 592-F5
MARKHAM TER
800 SUNV 94086 812-D7
MARKINGDON AV
2900 SJS 95127 835-A4
MARKS AV
3500 SJS 95118 874-B2
MARKS BLVD
- PIT 94565 574-C6
MARKS RD
100 CCCo 94526 633-A6
MARK TWAIN AV
100 MrnC 94903 566-G4
MARK TWAIN CT
100 SCL 95050 833-D7
MARK TWAIN DR
2100 ANT 94509 595-F4
MARK TWAIN ST
1800 PA 94303 791-B5
MARKWOOD CT
3100 SJS 95148 835-E7
MARLA CT
6100 SJS 95124 873-J7
MARLA DR
- AMCN 94589 510-A4
200 AMCN 94589 509-J4
MARLBAROUGH AV
1400 LALT 94024 831-J3
MARLBAROUGH CT
1400 LALT 94024 831-J3
MARLBORO CT
500 SRMN 94583 673-E5
1200 CNCD 94521 593-A4
2000 SJS 95128 853-G3
MARLBORO WY
2900 SRMN 94583 673-F5
3600 PLE 94588 694-F5
MARLBOROUGH AV
2600 SMCo 94063 770-C7
2700 SMCo 94063 790-C1
MARLBOROUGH CT
- PDMT 94611 650-D2
MARLBOROUGH RD
1100 HIL 94010 748-E4
MARLBOROUGH TER
7000 OAK 94705 630-C3
MARLEE RD
- PLHL 94523 592-B6
MARLENE CT
1500 SJS 95118 874-G3
MARLENE DR
3200 LFYT 94549 611-H6
MARLESTA CT
1700 PIN 94564 569-E4
MARLESTA RD
500 PIN 94806 569-C5
500 PIN 94564 569-C5
MARLETTE DR
3800 SJS 95121 855-A5
MARLIN AV
- MLV 94941 606-E3
600 FCTY 94404 749-H2
MARLIN COM
38800 FRMT 94536 753-F3
MARLIN CT
100 SF 94124 668-D7
200 CCCo 94572 569-J2
500 HAY 94544 712-D7
500 RDWC 94065 749-H6
2300 PIN 94564 589-J1
31400 UNC 94545 731-J6
MARLIN CV
- OAK 94618 630-C4
MARLIN DR
- PIT 94565 573-J2
500 RDWC 94065 749-J6
MARLINA TER
400 MPS 95035 793-G3
MARLINDA CT
- WLCK 94596 612-C3
MARLINTON CT
900 SJS 95120 894-G2
MARLO CT
- WLCK 94595 612-C7
MARLOW DR
- OAK 94605 671-C6
400 SLN 94605 671-C7
MARLOWE DR
4300 SJS 95124 873-J3
MARLOWE LN
1000 HAY 94544 712-A7
MARLOWE ST
400 PA 94301 791-A3
36600 FRMT 94536 752-G2
MARLYN WY
1700 SJS 95125 854-A5
MARMON CT
2400 SCL 95051 833-C2
MARMONA CT
200 MLPK 94025 790-J3
MARMONA DR
200 MLPK 94025 790-J3
MARMONT WY
13500 SCIC 95127 834-J3
MAR MONTE CT
100 VAL 94589 530-B2
100 VAL 94590 530-B2
MARNE AV
- SF 94127 667-D5
MARNE PL
7100 NWK 94560 752-C6
MARNE ST
15400 SLN 94579 691-B7
MARO DR
- SCIC 95127 835-A1
- SCIC 95127 834-J1
MAROEL DR
2100 SJS 95130 853-A7
MAROLYN CT
22700 HAY 94541 692-C6
MAROVICH LN
- RCH 94806 568-H7
MARQUARD AV
- SRFL 94901 586-E1
MARQUES AV
1900 SJS 95125 853-J5
2000 SJS 95125 854-A6
MARQUES CT
- DNVL 94526 653-C6
3400 AlaC 94546 691-H3
MARQUES PL
- DNVL 94526 653-C6
MARQUETTE
100 VAL 94589 510-A5
MARQUETTE CT
- CLAY 94517 593-F5
2600 RCH 94806 589-A2
MARQUETTE DR
5400 SJS 95118 874-B5
MARQUETTE LN
900 FCTY 94404 749-G4
MARQUETTE ST
3500 SCL 95051 832-J2
MARQUETTE WY
1000 SLN 94579 691-B5
MARQUITA AV
1100 BURL 94010 728-D5
MARQUITA CT
8000 DBLN 94568 693-F3
MARR AV
- OAK 94611 630-C7
- OAK 94611 650-C1
MARR LN
2300 SJS 95124 873-E5
MARRIAGE RD
- SCIC 94035 792-D7
- SCIC 94035 812-D1
MARS
3000 ALA 94501 649-F7
MARS AV
100 HAY 94544 712-B7
MARS CT
400 MPS 95035 794-D7
900 LVMR 94550 715-F4
3100 LFYT 94549 611-J6
MARS RD
200 LVMR 94550 715-F4
MARS ST
- CNCD 94519 572-H7
- SF 94114 667-F2
MARSALA CT
100 HER 94547 570-B6
600 PLE 94566 714-H3
MARSAN CT
1400 CMBL 95008 873-B1
MARSEILLE AV
900 LVMR 94550 695-F6
MARSEILLE CT
- DNVL 94506 653-H5
MARSEILLES CT
1600 SJS 95138 875-F1
MARSH AV
2100 PIT 94565 574-C3
MARSH CT
200 SRMN 94583 673-B2
MARSH DR
- NVTO 94945 526-E7
- MLV 94941 606-C1
100 FCTY 94404 749-E1
2500 SRMN 94583 673-B2
4900 CCCo 94520 572-C6
4900 CNCD 94520 572-C6
5700 CCCo 94553 572-C7
MARSH PL
- OAK 94611 650-D1
100 SRMN 94583 673-B3
MARSH RD
- TBRN 94920 607-E7
800 SMCo 94025 770-F6
800 ATN 94027 770-F6
900 MLPK 94025 770-G5
900 RDWC 94063 770-F6
900 SMCo 94063 770-F6
1000 SMCo 94063 790-F1
1000 ATN 94027 790-F1
1100 RDWC 94025 770-F6
MARSH RD Rt#-84
- MLPK 94025 770-F7
MARSH ST
1500 SJS 95122 834-G6
MARSHA PL
100 LFYT 94549 631-J4
MARSHA WY
2400 SJS 95125 854-B6
MARSHALL AV
400 SJS 95125 854-B2
400 SUNV 94086 812-F7
900 SMTO 94403 749-B7
MARSHALL CT
- CCCo 94598 612-E4
600 RDWC 94063 770-B5
600 SCL 95051 833-B6
1700 LALT 94024 832-A5
MARSHALL DR
200 CCCo 94598 612-E4
300 WLCK 94598 612-E4
800 PA 94303 791-C5
MARSHALL LN
3700 AlaC 94546 692-B5
18500 SAR 95070 872-H2
MARSHALL ST
- SF 94129 647-E3
200 RDWC 94063 770-B5
1500 ANT 94509 575-F5
5500 OAK 94608 629-F5
20000 AlaC 94546 692-B5
MARSHALL TER
4000 FRMT 94536 752-H1
MARSHALL WY
- DALY 94014 687-D5
- VAL 94589 509-J6
400 ALA 94501 669-E1
MARSH CREEK CIR
7200 CLAY 94517 613-J1
MARSH CREEK RD
6400 CLAY 94517 593-H7
6700 CLAY 94517 613-J1
MARSH ELDER CT
4300 CNCD 94521 593-B5
MARSHGLEN CT
2300 SJS 95133 834-F2
MARSH HAWK CT
3300 PLE 94588 714-A3
33000 UNC 94587 732-D6
MARSH HAWK RD
33000 UNC 94587 732-D6
MARSHLANDS RD
9000 FRMT 94555 752-A7
9000 NWK 94560 752-A7
10000 FRMT 94555 751-H7
10000 FRMT 94555 771-F2
MARSH MANOR WY
3500 SJS 95121 855-D7
MARSH MEADOW WY
4500 CNCD 94521 593-B5
MARSHWELL WY
5800 SJS 95138 875-D5
MARSILLY ST
- SF 94112 667-H6
MARSTEN AV
3500 BLMT 94002 769-A1
3500 BLMT 94002 768-J1
4100 UNC 94587 731-J5
MARSTEN RD
1200 BURL 94010 728-E5
MARSTON AV
- SF 94112 667-E7
MARSTON RD
- ORIN 94563 610-E6
MARSTON WY
3000 SJS 95148 835-F7
3000 SJS 95148 855-F1
MARTA DR
1600 PLHL 94523 592-D5
N MARTA DR
1500 PLHL 94523 592-D4
MARTEL CT
100 VAL 94589 509-H5
MARTEL PL
6700 NWK 94560 752-C6
MARTEL ST
300 SJS 95110 834-A7
MARTELL AV
14700 SLN 94578 691-C5
MARTELL CT
14700 SLN 94578 691-C5
MARTELLO DR
1800 SJS 95122 854-G1
MARTEN AV
3100 SJS 95148 835-D4
3100 SJS 95127 835-B5
MARTENS AV
100 MTVW 94040 811-J7
400 MTVW 94040 812-A7
MARTENS BLVD
- SRFL 94901 586-F2
MARTHA AV
- SF 94131 667-F6
18500 SAR 95070 852-H7
MARTHA DR
3800 CCCo 94553 571-H4
MARTHA LN
- SANS 94960 566-A5
MARTHA PL
600 HAY 94544 712-B5
MARTHA RD
- ORIN 94563 631-A1
- ORIN 94563 630-J1
MARTHA ST
- SJS 95112 854-C1
300 SJS 95112 834-D7
1300 LVMR 94550 716-C1
MARTI WY
200 SJS 95136 874-G1
MARTIL WY
300 MPS 95035 794-A5
MARTI MARIE CT
200 MRTZ 94553 571-J5
MARTI MARIE DR
300 MRTZ 94553 571-J5
MARTI MARIE LN
300 MRTZ 94553 571-J5
MARTIN AV
100 LVMR 94550 695-H7
200 SJS 95050 833-F2
200 SCL 95050 833-C2
300 SJS 95110 833-F2
1100 SJS 95126 833-H7
1200 PA 94301 791-A4
1500 PLE 94588 694-F6
1500 AlaC 94588 694-F7
1600 SUNV 94087 832-F5
1600 SJS 95128 833-H7
1600 SJS 95128 853-H1
MARTIN BLVD
600 SLN 94577 690-H1
MARTIN CT
- PLE 94588 694-F6
- DALY 94014 687-J4
- WLCK 94596 612-A2
- DNVL 94526 653-C6
200 BEN 94510 551-B2
MARTIN DR
- NVTO 94949 546-F3
3500 SMTO 94403 749-D5
MARTIN LN
- CCCo 94803 589-E3
- RCH 94803 589-E3
- WDSD 94062 789-F7
MARTIN PL
100 SBRN 94066 707-J7
MARTIN ST
- DALY 94014 687-H3
100 VAL 94589 510-A5
600 OAK 94609 629-H5
2100 PIT 94565 574-E4
33200 FRMT 94555 732-C7
MARTINA ST
- RCH 94801 608-D1
100 RCH 94801 588-D7
MARTIN CANYON RD
7600 DBLN 94568 693-F4
MARTINDALE DR
1600 MRTZ 94553 571-J7
MARTINEZ AL
1900 SLN 94577 691-A2
MARTINEZ AV
2300 CCCo 94553 571-F3
MARTINEZ CT
- NVTO 94945 525-H1
2300 PIN 94564 569-H7
MARTINEZ DR
- FRMT 94536 733-B7
2600 BURL 94010 728-B6
MARTINEZ RD
- WDSD 94062 809-G6
MARTINEZ ST
- SF 94129 647-E4
1300 SLN 94577 691-A1
MARTINGALE CT
44400 FRMT 94539 773-J2
MARTINGALE DR
100 FRMT 94539 773-H2
MARTINIQUE AV
200 MrnC 94920 607-C2
MARTINIQUE CT
600 SJS 95123 874-G4
MARTINIQUE DR
500 RDWC 94065 749-J7
MARTINIQUE LN
1200 FCTY 94404 749-F5
MARTIN JUE ST
1700 SJS 95131 834-D1
MARTIN LUTHER KING JR DR
- SF - 667-A1
300 SF 94118 667-B1
1200 SF - 666-H1
MARTIN LUTHER KING JR WY
- OAK 94607 649-F5
1200 BERK 94703 609-G7
1200 BERK 94709 609-G7
1200 OAK 94612 649-G2
1300 BERK 94703 629-G1
1300 BERK 94709 629-G1
1900 BERK 94704 629-G1
2700 BERK 94707 609-G7
2700 OAK 94609 649-G2
3300 OAK 94609 629-G5
3300 OAK 94608 629-G5
MARTINO RD
1000 LFYT 94549 611-G4
MARTINSEN CT
400 PA 94306 791-C7
MARTINVALE LN
100 SJS 95119 875-E7
100 SJS 95119 895-E1
MARTINWOOD WY
10600 CPTO 95014 852-E2
MARTIRAE CT
2400 ALA 94501 670-A2
MARTIS CT
5400 CCCo 94803 589-F3
MARTLING RD
- MrnC 94960 566-A2
MARTWOOD WY
7000 SJS 95120 894-H3
MARTY TER
40800 FRMT 94539 753-E5
MARVA OAKS DR
100 WDSD 94062 789-D4
MARVEL CT
- SF 94121 647-A6
MARVELLE LN
3100 CNCD 94518 592-G2
MAR VIEW WY
- SF 94131 667-E3
MARVILLA CIR
200 PCFA 94044 726-H4
MARVILLA PL
200 PCFA 94044 726-H4
MARVIN AV
- LALT 94022 811-E7
MARVIN CT
- CCCo 94803 589-D1
- OAK 94605 671-E4
MARVIN DR
100 PLHL 94523 592-A7
MARVIN WY
800 HAY 94541 711-F2
MAR VISTA DR
- DALY 94014 687-F3
MARVUE CIR
5200 CNCD 94521 593-E6
MAR WEST ST
1100 TBRN 94920 607-D7
1100 BLV 94920 607-D7
1700 TBRN 94920 627-E1
MARWICK CT
8800 DBLN 94568 693-F2
MARWICK DR
11300 DBLN 94568 693-E2
MARY AV
500 SUNV 94086 812-D5
10000 CPTO 95014 832-C7
N MARY AV
100 SUNV 94086 812-D5
S MARY AV
100 SUNV 94086 812-C7
400 SUNV 94086 832-C2
600 SUNV 94087 832-C2
10800 CPTO 95014 832-C6
MARY CT
- DALY 94014 687-J3
- DNVL 94526 652-J2
800 CMBL 95008 853-C7
MARY DR
1600 PLHL 94523 592-B4
MARY LN
- RCH 94803 589-C3
MARY ST
- SF 94103 648-A6
- SRFL 94901 586-H1
MARY TER
- FRMT 94536 753-B3
MARY WY
100 LGTS 95032 873-D6
MARYAL RD
300 PLHL 94523 592-A5
300 PLHL 94523 591-J5
MARY ALICE DR
100 LGTS 95032 873-D4
MARYANN DR
800 SCL 95050 833-C5
MARY ANN LN
2900 CCCo 94565 573-G2
MARYBELLE AV
1300 SLN 94577 690-H2
MARY CAROLINE CT
2900 SJS 95133 814-G6
MARY CAROLINE DR
800 SJS 95133 814-G6
MARYDEE CT
21600 AlaC 94546 711-G1
MARY EVELYN DR
600 SJS 95123 874-H7
MARY JANE LN
- NVTO 94947 525-J3
MARY JANE WY
4800 SJS 95124 873-H4
MARY JO CT
5400 SJS 95124 873-H5
MARY JO WY
5300 SJS 95124 873-H6
MARYLAND AV
- BERK 94707 609-G4
MARYLAND DR
1300 CNCD 94521 593-F6
MARYLAND PL
- SBRN 94066 707-J7
MARYLAND ST
1600 RDWC 94061 789-J3
1900 RDWC 94061 790-A3
MARY LEE WY
1200 SJS 95118 874-B1
MARYLIN AV
700 LVMR 94550 695-E7
MARYLINN DR
300 MPS 95035 794-A7
400 MPS 95035 793-H6
MARY LOU WY
5700 LVMR 94550 696-D6
MARY LU LN
100 SMTO 94403 749-B5
MARYMEADE LN
1600 LALT 94024 831-J4
MARYMONT AV
- ATN 94027 790-B4
MARYMONTE CT
6500 SJS 95120 894-C1
MARYOLA CT
3100 LFYT 94549 611-J6
MARYS AV
- CCCo 94565 573-F2
MARY-VIN LN
800 SCL 95051 832-J6
MASEFIELD DR
500 PLHL 94523 592-B7
MASOLEUM DR
- SMCo - 768-C3
MASON CIR
100 CNCD 94520 572-F4
MASON CT
6500 PLE 94588 694-A7
MASON DR
300 HAY 94544 712-B6
1100 PCFA 94044 727-B4
MASON LN
2600 SMTO 94403 749-A5
MASON ST
- SF 94129 647-D3
- SF 94102 648-A4
700 SF 94108 648-A4
1300 SF 94133 648-A4
1400 SF 94133 647-J4
1700 SF 94133 647-J3
1800 SPAB 94806 588-H3
2500 OAK 94605 670-F1
4600 PLE 94588 694-A6
MASON WY
6700 SJS 95129 852-E3
MASONIC AV
- SF 94118 647-F6
- SF 94115 647-F6
300 SF 94117 647-F6
500 ALB 94706 609-E5
600 SF 94117 667-F1
1100 BERK 94706 609-E5
5100 OAK 94618 630-C7
MASONIC CT
400 VAL 94591 530-E3
MASONIC DR
100 VAL 94591 530-E3
2400 SJS 95125 854-D5
MASONIC PL
- OAK 94618 630-D7
MASONIC ST
400 MRTZ 94553 571-D3
MASONIC TER
46900 FRMT 94539 773-F6
MASONIC WY
500 BLMT 94002 749-F7
600 BLMT 94002 769-E1
MASONRY LN
500 RCH 94801 608-D3
MASONWOOD ST
2700 SJS 95148 855-C1
MASSACHUSETTS AV
- RDWC 94061 789-J3
2500 RDWC 94061 790-A3
MASSACHUSETTS DR
4900 SJS 95136 874-F3
MASSACHUSETTS ST
2900 AlaC 94546 691-H4
MASSAR AV
500 SJS 95116 834-H4
MASSASOIT ST
- SF 94110 668-A4
MASSET PL
- SF 94103 648-B6
MASSEY CT
6800 PLE 94588 694-A7
MASSIDDA CT
1600 SJS 95118 873-J4
MASSIH CT
1200 CMBL 95008 873-A1
1300 SJS 95008 873-A1
MASSIVE PEAK WY
4800 ANT 94509 595-E3
MASSOL AV
- LGTS 95030 872-J7
200 LGTS 95030 873-A7

STREET
Block City ZIP Pg-Grid

MASSOLO DR
- PLHL 94523 592-C4
MASSON AV
600 SBRN 94066 707-J6
MASSON CT
14700 SAR 95070 872-B2
MASSON TERRACE CIR
18800 SAR 95070 852-B7
MASTERS CT
100 WLCK 94598 612-D3
3700 SJS 95111 854-J6
47800 FRMT 94539 773-H7
47800 FRMT 94539 793-H1
MASTERSON LN
1300 LFYT 94549 611-J4
MASTERSON PL
18700 AlaC 94552 692-E2
MASTERSON ST
4000 OAK 94619 650-F6
MASTHEAD LN
300 FCTY 94404 749-J1
MASTIC ST
1000 SJS 95110 854-C2
MASTICK AV
200 SBRN 94066 727-J1
300 SBRN 94066 707-J7
MASTICK CT
- ALA 94501 669-G1
MASTLANDS DR
2000 OAK 94611 650-F2
MASUDA LNDG
1800 SJS 95131 814-C4
MAT AV
300 SJS 95123 874-J5
MATADERA CIR
800 DNVL 94526 633-B7
800 DNVL 94526 653-B1
MATADERA CT
300 DNVL 94526 633-B7
MATADERA WY
900 DNVL 94526 633-B7
MATADERO AV
200 PA 94306 811-C1
MATADERO CT
800 PA 94306 811-B2
MATADERO DR
100 SUNV 94086 812-C7
MATADERO CREEK CT
28600 LAH 94022 830-H1
28600 LAH 94022 810-H7
MATADERO CREEK LN
28500 LAH 94022 810-H7
MATARO CT
1100 PLE 94566 714-H4
MATCHEM CT
- CCCo 94507 633-A3
MATEO AV
- DALY 94014 687-C5
- MLBR 94030 728-B3
MATEO CT
4100 FRMT 94536 752-F2
MATEO DR
- TBRN 94920 607-B3
MATEO ST
- SF 94131 667-G6
15800 AlaC 94578 691-E4
MATHER DR
2300 SJS 95116 834-G2
MATHER ST
200 OAK 94611 629-J7
MATHESON RD
1500 CNCD 94521 593-C4
MATHEW ST
300 SCL 95050 833-E2
MATHEWS PL
- CCCo 94507 632-D2
MATHEWS ST
2500 BERK 94702 629-E3
MATHIEU AV
6100 OAK 94618 630-B5
MATHIEU CT
500 RCH 94801 588-F6
N MATHILDA AV
100 SUNV 94086 812-E6
1100 SUNV 94089 812-E2
S MATHILDA AV
100 SUNV 94086 812-D7
300 SUNV 94086 832-D2
600 SUNV 94087 832-D2
MATILDA AV
- MLV 94941 606-F4
MATILIJA DR
15800 SCIC 95030 872-G6
15800 MSER 95030 872-G6
MATISSE CT
1200 SUNV 94087 832-E3
MATIZ COM
36700 FRMT 94536 752-A6
MATOS CT
1800 SCL 95050 833-D5
MATSON DR
1600 SJS 95124 873-J2
MATSON PL
38800 FRMT 94536 753-D2
MATSONIA DR
600 FCTY 94404 749-G2
MATSQUI RD
200 ANT 94509 595-D1
MATT DAVIS TR
- MrnC 94965 606-A2
MATTERHORN CT
900 MPS 95035 814-D1
4700 ANT 94509 595-E2
MATTERHORN DR
500 WLCK 94598 612-E2
1100 SJS 95132 814-F5
MATTERHORN WY
4700 ANT 94509 595-D3
MATTHEW CT
- VAL 94591 530-E3
- SF 94124 668-D6
400 PLE 94566 714-D6
2100 PIT 94565 574-A3
2300 AlaC 94541 692-D7
6400 SJS 95123 875-B7
MATTHEW TER
5200 FRMT 94555 752-B2
MATTHEWS CT
400 MPS 95035 794-A3
MATTHIAS CT
2700 SJS 95121 854-H3
MATTHIAS DR
2700 SJS 95121 854-H3
MATTIQUE DR
2900 SJS 95135 855-E2
MATTIS CT
4400 OAK 94619 650-H6
MATTOS AV
3000 SJS 95132 814-F4
MATTOS CT
100 DNVL 94506 653-G5
5000 FRMT 94536 752-H6
MATTOS DR
1100 VAL 94591 530-E4
2200 MPS 95035 794-E7
4000 FRMT 94536 752-H5
MATTOX RD
1000 AlaC 94541 691-G6
MATTS CT
900 LALT 94024 831-E1
MATTSON AV
200 LGTS 95030 873-A2
MATZLEY CT
3100 SJS 95124 873-H2
MATZLEY DR
1700 SJS 95124 873-H2
MAUBERT AV
15500 AlaC 94578 691-F4
MAUBERT CT
16300 AlaC 94578 691-F5
MAUD AV
200 SLN 94577 691-B1
22900 AlaC 94541 692-C7
23900 AlaC 94541 712-D1
MAUD ST
- AlaC 94541 712-D1
MAUDE AV
18600 SAR 95070 872-H4
E MAUDE AV
100 SUNV 94086 812-F6
W MAUDE AV
100 SUNV 94086 812-D5
800 MTVW 94043 812-C4
MAUI CIR
200 UNC 94587 732-C6
MAUI CT
200 SRMN 94583 673-E1
3900 SJS 95111 855-A6
MAUI DR
100 PIT 94565 574-E5
3800 SJS 95111 855-A6
MAULDIN ST
- SF 94129 647-C3
MAUNA KEA CT
3200 CNCD 94519 572-H7
MAUNA KEA LN
1300 SJS 95132 814-F4
MAUNA LOA CT
3000 SJS 95132 814-F5
MAUNA LOA PARK DR
4800 FRMT 94538 773-C1
MAUNEY CT
3700 SJS 95130 853-C4
MAUREEN AV
400 PA 94306 791-D7
MAUREEN CIR
100 CCCo 94565 573-J3
4500 LVMR 94550 696-B7
MAUREEN CT
- PLHL 94523 592-A5
MAUREEN LN
300 PLHL 94523 592-A5
MAUREEN ST
15400 SLN 94579 691-B7
MAUREEN WY
20700 SAR 95070 852-D5
MAURER LN
26100 LAH 94022 811-B6
MAURER WY
100 VAL 94591 530-E4
MAURI CT
- DNVL 94526 652-J2
MAURICE LN
1500 SJS 95129 852-H5
MAURICIA AV
2700 SCL 95051 833-A7
3200 SCL 95051 832-J7
MAURINE CT
100 VAL 94590 550-C1
MAURITANIA AV
5900 OAK 94605 670-H1
MAVERICK CT
- SRMN 94583 653-J6
300 CCCo 94549 591-H6
MAVIS CT
600 PLE 94566 714-G3
MAVIS DR
100 SRMN 94583 673-F5
200 PLE 94566 714-F3
MAVIS PL
100 SRMN 94583 673-F5
MAVIS ST
2400 OAK 94601 670-F1
MAX DR
40500 FRMT 94538 753-D6
MAXEY DR
1100 SJS 95132 814-G5
MAXIMILIAN DR
2200 SJS 95008 853-C7
MAXIMILLIAN AV
- SLN 94578 691-B4
MAXIMO CT
- CCCo 94506 654-A5
MAXINE AV
1400 SJS 95125 854-A6
1500 SMTO 94401 749-C2
MAXINE DR
100 PLHL 94523 592-C4
400 SUNV 94086 832-E1
10700 CPTO 95014 832-B6
MAXWELL AL
- VAL 94590 529-H4
600 VAL 94590 530-A4
MAXWELL AV
2400 OAK 94601 670-F1
2600 OAK 94619 650-F7
2600 OAK 94619 670-F1
MAXWELL LN
- MrnC 94941 606-F5
1200 RDWC 94062 769-G6
MAXWELL WY
1300 SJS 95131 834-C1
1400 SJS 95131 814-C7
MAXWELTON RD
- PDMT 94618 630-C7
5500 OAK 94618 630-C7
MAY CT
- PA 94303 811-E1
- HAY 94544 712-B7
- SRMN 94583 693-G1
1300 CNCD 94520 592-D4
1900 PLHL 94523 592-C5
3500 OAK 94602 650-D4
MAY DR
100 SJS 95138 875-D4
MAY LN
- LALT 94022 811-E5
3400 SJS 95124 873-F2
MAY RD
100 UNC 94587 732-G3
2400 CCCo 94803 589-E3
2500 RCH 94803 589-F1
MAY WY
7500 SRMN 94583 693-F1
MAYA CT
700 FRMT 94539 773-J7
MAYA ST
47700 FRMT 94539 773-J7
MAYA WY
16100 SCIC 95032 893-C2
MAYALL CT
1700 SJS 95132 814-D4
MAYAN CT
7800 DBLN 94568 693-H3
MAYBECK TWIN DR
- BERK 94708 609-J7
MAYBELL AV
600 PA 94306 811-C3
MAYBELL WY
4100 PA 94306 811-C3
MAYBELLE AV
3400 OAK 94619 650-F6
MAYBELLE DR
1800 PLHL 94523 592-B5
MAYBELLE WY
3300 OAK 94619 650-F6
MAYBERRY DR
19000 AlaC 94546 691-J4
MAYBERRY RD
3000 ANT 94509 575-E7
MAYBIRD CIR
34200 FRMT 94555 752-C3
MAYBRIDGE RD
- BLV 94920 607-D7
MAY BROWN AV
1100 MLPK 94025 790-E4
MAYBURY PL
100 WDSD 94062 789-J3
MAYBURY SQ
800 SJS 95133 814-G7
MAYDON CT
- OAK 94605 671-E4
MAYELLEN AV
300 SJS 95126 853-H2
MAYER CT
- LALT 94022 811-F6
MAYETTE AV
1100 SJS 95125 854-B6
1600 CNCD 94520 592-E4
MAYFAIR AV
100 VAL 94591 530-D4
500 SSF 94080 707-H3
2600 CNCD 94520 572-E7
2600 CNCD 94520 592-E1
N MAYFAIR AV
- DALY 94015 687-A3
500 DALY 94015 686-J3
S MAYFAIR AV
100 DALY 94015 687-A3
700 DALY 94015 686-J4
MAYFAIR CT
- CCCo 94507 632-J2
MAYFAIR DR
- DALY 94015 687-B3
- SF 94118 647-E6
100 SF 94118 647-E6
MAYFAIR PL
1800 SJS 95116 834-G4
MAYFAIR RD
28900 HAY 94544 732-A1
MAYFAIR PARK AV
42700 FRMT 94538 773-C2
MAYFAIR PARK TER
43000 FRMT 94538 773-D2
MAYFIELD AV
- DALY 94015 687-A7
100 MTVW 94043 811-F3
500 SCIC 94305 790-G7
500 SCIC 94305 810-H1
1900 SJS 95130 852-J6
MAYFIELD CT
4500 FRMT 94536 752-J5
4900 SJS 95130 852-J6
MAYFIELD DR
4600 FRMT 94536 752-H6
MAYFIELD PL
- MRGA 94556 651-E2
MAYFIELD PTH
- OAK 94605 670-J1
MAYFLOWER CT
1700 MTVW 94040 811-G5
5900 SJS 95129 852-G4
MAYFLOWER DR
2700 ANT 94509 575-G7
17100 AlaC 94546 691-H2
MAYFLOWER LN
- SCAR 94070 769-C4
MAYFLOWER PL
2000 SLN 94579 690-J6
MAYFLOWER ST
300 SF 94110 668-A5
MAYGLEN CT
2800 SJS 95133 814-G7
MAYGLEN WY
2800 SJS 95133 814-G7
MAYHEW CT
1300 SJS 95121 854-J2
MAYHEW DR
1200 SJS 95121 854-J2
MAYHEW WY
- CCCo 94596 592-C7
- PLHL 94596 592-C7
100 WLCK 94596 592-C7
MAYHEWS RD
- FRMT 94536 733-B7
MAYHEWS LANDING RD
5800 NWK 94560 752-D6
MAYKIRK CT
1700 SJS 95124 853-H6
MAYKIRK RD
2000 SJS 95124 853-H6
MAYLAND AV
5400 SJS 95138 875-C3
MAYLAND CT
- SJS 95138 875-C3
MAYLARD ST
- CCCo 94565 573-G3
MAYME AV
5400 SJS 95129 852-H5
MAYNARD AV
4100 OAK 94605 671-A1
MAYNARD CT
- LALT 94022 811-E5
MAYNARD ST
- SF 94112 667-G7
1500 CNCD 94519 592-J3
MAYNARD WY
- LALT 94022 811-E5
MAYO AV
100 VAL 94590 530-C5
MAYO CT
- BEN 94510 530-J6
2400 CCCo 94806 569-B5
MAYO DR
6200 SJS 95123 875-B7
MAYO LN
- WLCK 94596 612-B2
MAYO WY
300 SJS 95123 875-B7
MAYPORT CIR
2000 ALA 94501 649-E6
MAYS AV
16000 MSER 95030 873-A6
MAYSONG CT
1700 SJS 95131 814-D7
MAYSUN CT
1400 CMBL 95008 873-A1
MAYTEN DR
500 LVMR 94550 695-E7
MAYTEN WY
100 FRMT 94539 793-J1
MAYTEN GROVE CT
5300 SJS 95123 874-J3
MAYTEN TREE CT
700 SUNV 94086 832-G2
MAYVIEW AV
700 PA 94303 811-E1
700 PA 94303 791-E7
MAYVIEW WY
800 LVMR 94550 715-E3
MAYVILLE DR
23900 AlaC 94541 712-C1
MAYWOOD AV
- DALY 94015 687-A6
2200 SJS 95128 853-F3
2200 SCIC 95128 853-F3
2200 OAK 94605 670-H3
MAYWOOD CT
900 LALT 94024 831-F1
MAYWOOD DR
- SF 94127 667-D6
100 VAL 94591 530-F4
1000 BLMT 94002 769-D2
2300 SBRN 94066 707-E6
3400 RCH 94803 589-F2
7300 PLE 94588 693-H7
MAYWOOD LN
- MLPK 94025 790-F5
1000 MRTZ 94553 571-H6
MAYWOOD ST
41600 FRMT 94538 773-D1
MAYWOOD WY
- SRFL 94901 566-E6
200 SSF 94080 707-G5
2400 ANT 94509 594-J1
MAZDA DR
1400 WLCK 94596 612-C2
MAZEY ST
100 MPS 95035 794-A3
MAZIE DR
- PLHL 94523 592-C5
MAZUELA DR
5800 OAK 94611 630-E7
MAZZAGLIA AV
2200 SJS 95125 854-B6
MAZZONE DR
900 SJS 95120 874-D6
MCABEE RD
5900 SCIC 95120 894-C1
5900 SJS 95120 874-C6
6000 SJS 95120 894-C1
MCABEE ESTATES PL
1200 SJS 95120 874-C7
MCACKER CT
- SMTO 94402 749-B4
MCALISTER DR
700 SJS 95128 833-F7
MCALLISTER AV
- MrnC 94904 586-E3
MCALLISTER DR
- BEN 94510 551-C1
MCALLISTER ST
- SF 94102 647-F7
1000 SF 94117 647-F7
2500 SF 94117 647-E7
2600 SF 94118 647-D7
MCANDREW CT
2800 SJS 95121 855-D3
MCANDREW DR
5800 OAK 94611 630-D7
MCARTHUR AV
2500 UNC 94587 732-B4
MCAULEY CT
1000 PA 94301 791-A3
MCAULEY ST
400 OAK 94609 629-H5
MCAULIFFE CT
100 HER 94547 570-B5
MCBAIN AV
1000 CMBL 95008 853-G5
1600 SCIC 95125 853-G5
MCBAIN CT
100 CMBL 95008 853-G6
MCBRIDE DR
400 LFYT 94549 631-J4
MCBRIDE LN
- DBLN 94552 693-D5
1200 HAY 94544 711-H6
MCBRYDE AV
2300 RCH 94804 588-H5
3100 RCH 94805 588-H5
3100 RCH 94805 589-A5
3100 RCH 94804 589-A5
5400 SPAB 94805 589-B4
5800 RCH 94806 589-B4
5800 CCCo 94805 589-B4
MCCALL DR
- BEN 94510 551-B1
6900 SJS 95120 894-F3
MCCAMISH AV
400 SJS 95123 875-A6
MCCANDLESS DR
1300 MPS 95035 814-A3
MCCANN CT
1200 CNCD 94518 592-E7
MCCANN ST
- SF 94124 668-E7
MCCARL LN
1600 CNCD 94519 593-A2
MCCART CT
- TBRN 94920 607-B5
MCCARTHY AV
- SF 94134 687-J2
MCCARTHY BLVD
500 MPS 95035 813-H1
N MCCARTHY BLVD
500 MPS 95035 793-H6
MCCARTHY LN
- SCIC 95134 793-F7
- SJS 95134 793-F7
MCCARTY AV
500 MTVW 94041 812-A6
MCCARTY COM
35600 FRMT 94536 752-H1
MCCARTYSVILLE PL
12600 SAR 95070 852-E6
MCCAULEY RD
1000 DNVL 94506 653-C1
1000 DNVL 94526 633-C7
1000 DNVL 94526 653-C1
MCCLARY AV
600 OAK 94621 670-F5
MCCLAY RD
500 MrnC 94947 525-H5
500 NVTO 94947 525-J3
800 NVTO 94947 526-A3
MCCLAY RIVER PKWY
- NVTO 94947 525-J4
MCCLELLAN CT
2800 MRTZ 94553 571-G4
MCCLELLAN PL
10500 CPTO 95014 852-D2
MCCLELLAN RD
20500 CPTO 95014 852-A2
21800 SCIC 95014 852-B2
MCCLELLAND DR
1100 NVTO 94945 526-D4
MCCLELLAND ST
- OAK 94619 650-G7
MCCLOUD PL
300 DNVL 94526 653-D5
MCCLUHAN WY
1700 SJS 95132 814-D4
MCCLURE AV
500 SLN 94578 691-B4
MCCLURE CT
4200 ANT 94509 595-H1
MCCLURE LN
1300 LALT 94024 831-J3
MCCLURE ST
2900 OAK 94609 649-G2
MCCOLLAM DR
500 SJS 95127 814-J7
MCCONE AV
2600 HAY 94545 711-C5
MCCONNELL LN
- CCCo 94596 612-F6
MCCOPPIN ST
- SF 94103 667-H1
MCCOPPIN PARK CT
3500 SJS 95124 873-E2
MCCORD AV
- SCIC 94035 812-B2
- SCIC 94043 812-B2
MCCORMICK AV
8000 OAK 94605 671-A2
MCCORMICK DR
1500 SCL 95050 833-C4
MCCORMICK LN
- ATN 94027 790-E1
MCCORMICK RD
- CCCo 94803 589-D1
MCCORMICK ST
- SF 94109 647-J5
400 SLN 94577 690-F1
MCCOSKER TR
- RCH 94803 589-C4
- RCH 94805 589-C4
MCCOVEY LN
300 SJS 95127 835-B2
MCCOY AV
1500 CMBL 95008 853-A7
1500 CMBL 95130 853-A7
2000 SJS 95130 853-A7
3200 SJS 95130 852-J7
18200 SAR 95070 852-H7
MCCOY LN
1000 WLCK 94596 612-D4
MCCOY RD
- SRFL 94901 586-G2
MCCREERY AV
- SJS 95116 834-G4
MCCREERY CT
1800 SJS 95116 834-G5
MCCREERY DR
- HIL 94010 728-D7
MCCUE AV
900 SCAR 94070 769-G2
MCCULLOCH DR
- ALA 94501 649-J7
MCCULLOCH WY
13200 SAR 95070 852-H7
MCCULLOUGH RD
- MrnC 94965 627-A6
- MrnC 94965 626-J6
MCDANIEL AV
1400 SJS 95126 833-G6
1700 SJS 95128 833-F7
MCDERMOTT CT
4200 PIT 94565 574-E6
MCDERMOTT DR
4200 PIT 94565 574-E6
MCDOLE ST
13100 SAR 95070 852-H7
MCDOLE TER
38500 FRMT 94536 753-C2
MCDONALD AV
5300 NWK 94560 752-E5
MCDONALD DR
1100 PIN 94564 569-D5
MCDONALD ST
- SF 94129 647-D3
MCDONALD WY
1600 BURL 94010 728-C5
31500 HAY 94544 732-F2
MCDONELL AV
4800 OAK 94619 650-H6
MCDONNEL RD
300 ALA 94502 669-H6
MCDONNELL DR
700 SSF 94080 707-E2
MCDONNELL RD
- MLBR 94030 728-B2
- SMCo 94128 728-A1
- SMCo 94128 708-A6
MCDOUGAL ST
- VAL 94590 529-H2
MCDOWELL AV
- SF 94123 647-G3
- SF 94129 647-C4
MCDUFF AV
200 FRMT 94539 773-J7
200 FRMT 94539 793-H1
MC ELHENY RD
200 ANT 94509 575-D4
MCELLEN CT
800 LFYT 94549 611-G7
MCELLEN WY
800 LFYT 94549 611-G7
MCELROY CT
800 CNCD 94518 592-H6
MCELROY ST
800 OAK 94607 649-C3
MCEVOY ST
200 RDWC 94061 790-B1
200 SJS 95126 834-A7
200 SJS 95126 854-A1
200 SCIC 95126 854-A1
300 RDWC 94061 770-B7
MCEWEN RD
- CCCo - 550-G7
- CCCo 94553 570-H1
MCEWING CT
1200 CNCD 94521 592-J4
MCFARLAND AV
18500 SAR 95070 852-H7
MCFARLAND CT
- SCIC 94305 790-J7
MCFARLANE LN
1200 HAY 94544 711-H6
MCFAUL DR
4200 PIT 94565 574-F6
MCGARVEY AV
2100 RDWC 94061 789-H2
MCGARY RD
- SolC 94589 510-H2
- VAL 94589 510-H2
MCGEE AV
1300 BERK 94703 609-F7
1400 BERK 94703 629-F1
MCGILL RD
17000 SCIC 95070 872-C7
MCGILVRA CT
5800 SJS 95123 875-A5
MCGINLEY AV
2300 ANT 94509 575-D6
MCGINNESS AV
1000 SJS 95127 835-A4
1000 SJS 95127 834-J4
E MCGLINCEY LN
200 CMBL 95008 853-E7
700 CMBL 95008 873-E1
MCGLINCHEY DR
800 LVMR 94550 715-G2
MCGLOTHEN WY
3900 RCH 94806 568-H6
MCGRATH CT
500 PLHL 94523 592-A6
MCGRAW AV
500 LVMR 94550 696-B5
MCGRAW LN
3300 LFYT 94549 611-G3
MCGREGOR WY
1000 PA 94306 811-B3
1500 SJS 95129 852-E5
MCGRUE AV
100 VAL 94589 510-C5
MCGRUE CIR
400 VAL 94589 510-C5
MCGUIRE DR
- WLCK 94596 612-D5
MCGURRIN RD
8900 OAK 94605 671-C2
MCHARRY RANCH RD
300 CCCo 94553 570-H5
300 CCCo 94553 571-A5
MCHENRY GATE WY
4700 PLE 94566 694-D7
MCINERNEY TER
- FRMT 94538 753-B6
MCINNIS PKWY
- SRFL 94903 566-F4
MCINTOSH AV
1200 SUNV 94087 832-C3
MCINTOSH CT
- NVTO 94949 546-E4
1200 SUNV 94087 832-C3
MCINTOSH CREEK DR
1100 SJS 95120 894-G3
MCINTYRE ST
10800 OAK 94605 671-B6
MCKAY AV
1300 ALA 94501 669-F2
MCKAY DR
1100 SJS 95131 814-B6
1300 SCIC 95131 814-B6
MCKAY LN
- DBLN 94552 693-E5
MCKAY ST
41900 FRMT 94539 753-F7
MCKAY WY
- BEN 94510 551-A4
MCKEAN CT
7100 SJS 95120 894-J4
MCKEAN DR
3100 CNCD 94518 592-H6
MCKEAN PL
700 CNCD 94518 592-G7
MCKEAN RD
19500 SJS 95120 894-H4
MCKEAN RD Rt#-G8
19600 SJS 95120 894-J4
19600 SCIC 95120 894-J4
20000 SCIC 95120 895-A4
22200 SJS 95120 895-D6
23100 SJS 95141 895-D6
MCKEE CT
100 VAL 94589 510-D6
MCKEE RD
1500 SJS 95116 834-H1
1600 SJS 95133 834-H1
2800 SJS 95127 834-H1
3200 SCIC 95133 834-H1
3600 SCIC 95127 834-H1
4000 SCIC 95127 814-J7
4100 SJS 95127 814-J7
4800 SJS 95127 815-A7
4900 SCIC 95127 815-A7
MCKEEVER AV
1000 HAY 94541 711-J1
MCKELLAR DR
5600 SJS 95129 852-G4
MCKELLAR LN
4200 PA 94306 811-D2
MCKELUME DR
300 VAL 94589 509-H5
MCKENDRIE ST
300 SJS 95110 833-H5
800 SJS 95126 833-G6
MCKENDRY DR
100 MLPK 94025 790-J3
MCKENDRY PL
300 MLPK 94025 790-J3
MCKENZIE AV
1300 LALT 94024 831-H2
MCKENZIE CT
- HIL 94010 748-G2
MCKENZIE DR
2900 RCH 94806 589-A1
MCKENZIE ST
- MrnC 94964 587-B5
MCKENZIE WY
2200 CNCD 94520 572-F5
MCKEON CT
- NVTO 94947 525-J3
MCKEOWN CT
33100 UNC 94587 752-A2
MCKEOWN ST
33000 UNC 94587 752-A2
MCKEOWN TER
36000 FRMT 94536 733-B6
MCKILLOP CT
- SCL 95050 833-G5
MCKILLUP RD
2500 OAK 94602 650-C5
MCKINLEY AV
200 SUNV 94086 832-E1
700 OAK 94610 650-A4
1400 SJS 95126 853-H3
1500 SCIC 95126 853-H3
2100 BERK 94703 629-G2
E MCKINLEY AV
400 SUNV 94086 832-E1
W MCKINLEY AV
300 SUNV 94086 812-B7
MCKINLEY CT
500 SLN 94577 691-B2
1800 CNCD 94521 593-D2
MCKINLEY DR
2900 SCL 95051 833-A7
3300 SCL 95051 832-J7
MCKINLEY ST
1100 RDWC 94061 790-A1
1600 SMTO 94403 749-C2
MCKINNEY AV
100 PCFA 94044 707-A4
MCKINNON AV
1400 SF 94124 668-A5
MCKINNON CT
1500 SJS 95130 853-A5
MCKINNON DR
4200 SJS 95130 853-A4
MCKISSICK ST
100 PLHL 94523 592-B6
MCKOSKEN RD
- RCH 94801 588-E3
1400 CCCo 94801 588-E3
MCLAIN RD
100 BSBN 94005 688-B7
MCLANE ST
400 VAL 94590 530-A7
MCLAREN AV
- SF 94121 647-A6
MCLAREN PL
10100 CPTO 95014 832-F7
MCLAUGHLIN AV
200 SJS 95116 834-E5
900 SJS 95122 834-E5
1600 SJS 95122 854-G1
2400 SJS 95121 854-G1
3100 SJS 95121 855-A4
5400 NWK 94560 752-E5
MC LAUGHLIN ST
400 RCH 94805 589-A6
MCLAUGHLIN ST
600 RCH 94805 589-A6
1000 SPAB 94805 589-A5
MCLEA CT
- SF 94103 668-A1
MCLELLAN AV
- SMTO 94403 749-C5
700 SJS 95110 854-B1
MCLEOD ST
100 LVMR 94550 715-H1
MCLOUD AV
2400 AlaC 94546 691-H5
MCMAHON CT
200 MRTZ 94553 571-F7
MCMILLAN AV
5500 OAK 94618 630-A5
5500 OAK 94618 629-J5

STREET
Block City ZIP Pg-Grid

MCMILLAN CT
2000 MRTZ 94553 571-H7
MCMORROW RD
2600 CCCo 94806 569-B5
MCMURDIE DR
1200 CMBL 95008 873-D1
MCMURTY CT
- ALA 94502 669-H6
MCNAIR ST
- VAL 94590 529-H2
MCNAMARA LN
- MRTZ 94553 571-G7
- MRTZ 94553 591-G1
MCNAMARA ST
4100 FRMT 94538 773-D1
MCNEAR DR
- SRFL 94901 567-C5
MCNEAR BRICKYARD RD
200 MrnC 94901 567-D6
MCNEIL LN
- DNVL 94526 653-F4
MCNEIL PL
800 PLHL 94523 592-B1
MCNORTH DR
1800 CNCD 94519 592-H1
MCNULTY WY
3600 RDWC 94061 789-H2
MCNUTT AV
3100 WLCK 94596 592-B7
MCPEAK LN
- DBLN 94568 693-E5
MC PHERSON ST
1300 SCL 95051 832-J4
MCQUESTEN DR
1300 SJS 95122 834-G7
MCRAE RD
100 MrnC 94941 606-F5
MCRAE ST
- SF 94129 647-E4
MCSHERRY LN
- ALA 94502 670-A7
MCSHERRY WY
3500 ALA 94502 670-A7
MCSWAIN CT
4200 ANT 94509 595-J1
MCVAY AV
10400 SCIC 95127 835-B1
MCVAY CT
14800 SCIC 95127 835-B1
MCVICKER CT
2500 CCCo 94806 569-B6
MCWILLIAMS LN
- PLE 94588 693-J6
MEACHAM PL
- SF 94109 647-J6
MEAD AV
800 OAK 94607 649-F2
2900 SCL 95051 833-A1
MEAD ST
- ANT 94509 575-H7
- ANT 94509 595-H1
MEAD WY
24900 AlaC 94541 712-C2
MEADE AV
700 SF 94124 688-B1
MEADE ST
1300 RCH 94804 609-A2
5100 RCH 94804 608-J2
MEADOW AV
- MrnC 94904 586-E3
- SRFL 94901 586-G3
500 SCL 95051 832-H7
700 PIN 94564 569-C4
E MEADOW AV
700 PIN 94564 569-D4
E MEADOW CIR
1000 PA 94303 791-E7
MEADOW CT
- DBLN 94552 693-F4
- LVMR 94550 696-D3
- ORIN 94563 631-A1
- SANS 94960 566-A6
- SMTO 94403 749-D5
- CCCo 94595 632-C1
MEADOW DR
- LVMR 94550 696-D3
- MrnC 94903 566-G3
- MrnC 94941 606-G3
E MEADOW DR
100 PA 94306 811-D1
600 PA 94306 791-E7
700 PA 94303 791-E7
W MEADOW DR
100 PA 94306 811-D2
MEADOW GN
1300 CNCD 94521 593-B5
MEADOW LN
- ATN 94027 790-B6
- RDWC 94063 770-C6
- WDSD 94062 809-H5
- PTLV 94028 809-H5
100 ORIN 94563 631-A1
300 SCIC 95127 835-A2
300 SJS 95127 835-A2
600 LALT 94022 811-C4
1100 CNCD 94520 592-E3
1400 MTVW 94040 811-G7
1500 BURL 94010 728-D5
1700 CCCo 94595 632-C1
3700 LFYT 94549 611-D4
MEADOW RD
- MLV 94941 606-G3
- WDSD 94062 809-H5
1900 CCCo 94595 632-D1
MEADOW ST
3500 OAK 94601 650-D6
MEADOW WK
- ALA 94501 669-G3
MEADOWBROOK AV
3700 PIT 94565 574-E5
30700 HAY 94544 732-E2
MEADOWBROOK CIR
3800 PIT 94565 574-E5
MEADOWBROOK COM
36900 FRMT 94536 752-H3
MEADOWBROOK CT
100 VAL 94591 530-F5
7800 PLE 94588 693-H7
MEADOWBROOK DR
- SF 94132 667-A6
100 LGTS 95032 873-G6

MEADOWBROOK DR
2400 SCL 95051 833-A2
3100 CNCD 94519 572-G7
4400 RCH 94803 589-E1
MEADOWBROOK LN
- DNVL 94526 632-H7
MEADOWBROOK RD
3200 ANT 94509 595-C1
MEADOW CREEK CT
- PTLV 94028 810-D7
800 WLCK 94596 612-D6
MEADOW CREEK DR
100 CMAD 94925 606-H2
600 SJS 95136 874-E1
MEADOW CREST CT
2600 RCH 94806 568-J7
MEADOWCREST DR
- MLV 94941 606-G1
1100 CMAD 94925 606-G1
MEADOWCREST RD
- NVTO 94945 526-B1
MEADOWCROFT DR
- SANS 94960 566-A5
MEADOW DALE CT
400 SJS 95136 874-F1
MEADOWGATE WY
2100 SJS 95132 814-D2
MEADOW GLEN AV
- MLBR 94030 728-A3
MEADOW GLEN CT
1500 SJS 95121 855-B4
MEADOW GLEN DR
2600 SRMN 94583 673-C2
MEADOW GLEN PL
2600 SRMN 94583 673-C2
MEADOW GLEN WY
1400 SJS 95121 855-B4
2600 SRMN 94583 673-C2
MEADOW GROVE CT
- CCCo 94507 633-A5
MEADOWHAVEN WY
200 MPS 95035 794-A6
MEADOW HILL DR
- TBRN 94920 607-D6
MEADOWHURST CT
4500 SJS 95136 874-E2
MEADOW LAKE DR
- DNVL 94506 654-C7
MEADOWLAKE DR
200 SUNV 94089 812-H4
MEADOW LAKE ST
4000 ANT 94509 595-J1
4100 ANT 94509 575-J7
MEADOWLAND DR
- MPS 95035 794-A6
MEADOWLANDS CT
- ORIN 94563 631-B5
MEADOWLANDS LN
2900 SJS 95135 855-H7
MEADOWLARK AV
1200 SJS 95128 833-E6
MEADOWLARK CT
- DNVL 94526 653-B5
- NVTO 94947 525-G4
1400 LFYT 94549 611-G3
4000 AlaC 94546 692-A5
8100 NWK 94560 752-B7
MEADOWLARK DR
2600 PLE 94588 714-A4
2600 UNC 94587 732-D6
19900 AlaC 94546 692-B5
MEADOWLARK LN
1500 SUNV 94087 832-G5
MEADOWLARK ST
400 LVMR 94550 695-E7
600 LVMR 94550 715-E1
2200 CCCo 94806 569-C4
MEADOWLARK WY
100 HER 94547 569-H5
1200 CNCD 94521 593-B4
MEADOWMIST DR
25800 HAY 94544 712-A5
MEADOWMONT DR
2300 SJS 95133 834-E1
2300 SJS 95133 814-H3
MEADOW OAK RD
20700 SAR 95070 852-D5
MEADOW OAKS DR
- SRFL 94903 566-G5
MEADOWOOD CIR
100 SRMN 94583 673-G5
MEADOWOOD COM
- LVMR 94550 695-G6
MEADOWOOD CT
300 PLHL 94523 591-J6
MEADOWOOD DR
- LKSP 94939 586-F6
100 PTLV 94028 810-B5
900 SJS 95120 894-E1
MEADOWOOD RD
19200 AlaC 94546 691-J4
MEADOW PARK CIR
- BLMT 94002 769-A3
- BLMT 94002 768-J3
MEADOW PARK CT
- ORIN 94563 631-A1
- LFYT 94549 631-A1
MEADOW PINE CT
1700 CNCD 94521 593-E4
MEADOW RIDGE CIR
1300 SJS 95131 814-C7
MEADOW RIDGE DR
- CMAD 94925 606-H2
MEADOWS AV
4000 PIT 94565 574-G6
MEADOWS DR
100 VAL 94589 509-G5
1500 VAL 94589 510-A6
W MEADOWS LN
300 DNVL 94506 653-J5
MEADOWSIDE CT
- SJS 95136 874-J7
MEADOWSIDE PL
200 DNVL 94526 632-H7
MEADOWSWEET DR
600 CMAD 94925 586-G7
800 CMAD 94925 606-H2
MEADOWSWEET LN
- SCAR 94070 769-C4
MEADOWVALE CT
900 MRTZ 94553 571-H7

MEADOW VALLEY LN
1400 CMAD 94925 606-H2
MEADOW VIEW CT
- CCCo 94506 654-C4
1300 ANT 94509 595-E4
MEADOW VIEW DR
- NVTO 94949 546-G5
MEADOWVIEW DR
4000 AlaC 94546 692-B5
MEADOW VIEW LN
3100 WLCK 94598 612-H1
MEADOWVIEW LN
21800 CPTO 95014 832-B7
MEADOW VIEW PL
2100 SMTO 94403 749-C1
MEADOW VIEW RD
- ORIN 94563 631-A1
100 ORIN 94563 611-A7
MEADOWVILLE CT
4400 SJS 95129 853-A2
MEADOW WALK PL
- CCCo 613-B3
- CCCo 94598 613-B3
MEADOWWOOD CT
5200 PLE 94566 714-D2
MEADOWWOOD PL
5300 CNCD 94521 593-F4
MEADWELL CT
100 SJS 95138 875-D4
MEANDER CT
800 WLCK 94598 612-G3
MEANDER DR
800 WLCK 94598 612-G4
5800 SJS 95120 874-B6
MEARS CT
900 SCIC 94305 810-J1
MEATH DR
2600 SSF 94080 707-C4
MECARTNEY RD
2500 ALA 94502 669-H6
3000 ALA 94502 670-A6
MEDA AV
- SF 94112 667-F7
MEDA CT
200 MrnC 94941 606-H5
MEDA LN
200 MrnC 94941 606-H5
MEDALLION CT
5700 AlaC 94552 692-C2
7500 PLE 94588 714-A3
MEDALLION DR
1300 SJS 95120 874-B7
2100 HAY 94544 732-C4
2100 HAY 94587 732-C4
2100 UNC 94587 732-C4
MEDANOS AV
- CCCo 94565 573-G2
MEDANOS CT
- FRMT 94539 773-H1
MEDANOS ST
1100 ANT 94509 575-C5
MEDAU PL
6100 OAK 94611 650-E1
MEDBURN ST
100 CCCo 94520 572-G2
MEDEIRAS TER
300 MPS 95035 793-H3
MEDEIROS LN
100 AMCN 94589 509-J1
100 AMCN 94589 510-A1
MEDFIELD RD
1200 LFYT 94549 611-B4
MEDFORD AV
100 AlaC 94541 691-F7
2700 RDWC 94061 789-H2
9800 OAK 94603 670-H6
MEDFORD CIR
19600 AlaC 94541 691-F7
MEDFORD CT
4000 MRTZ 94553 571-J5
19200 AlaC 94541 691-F7
MEDFORD DR
1500 LALT 94024 832-A3
MEDIA WY
2600 SJS 95125 853-J7
MEDIAN WY
400 MrnC 94941 606-E6
MEDICAL LN
- SCIC 94305 790-G6
300 PA 94304 790-G6
MEDICAL PZ
100 NVTO 94947 526-A5
MEDICINE BOW CT
45300 FRMT 94539 773-H4
MEDICINE BOW WY
45300 FRMT 94539 773-H4
MEDICINE MTN CT
1900 ANT 94509 595-F5
MEDICUS CT
18600 SCIC 95014 852-H1
MEDINA DR
100 CCCo 94553 572-C7
2600 SBRN 94066 707-D5
MEDINA ST
- LVMR 94550 696-B6
MEDINAH CT
- SRMN 94583 673-G7
400 HAY 94544 732-F2
7800 PLE 94588 714-B5
MEDINAH PL
100 SRMN 94583 673-G7
MEDINAH ST
31300 HAY 94544 732-E2
MEDITERRANEAN AV
100 HAY 94544 732-C1
MEDITERRANEAN LN
200 RDWC 94065 749-J6
MEDLAR DR
27700 HAY 94544 712-B6
MEDLEY CT
1200 SJS 95121 855-A4
MEDLEY DR
1200 SJS 95121 855-A4
MEDOC CT
400 MTVW 94043 811-G3
MEDWAY RD
- SANS 94960 566-A6
- SMCo 94062 809-G6
- SRFL 94901 586-H2
- WDSD 94062 809-G6
MEDWIN CT
3000 SJS 95148 855-C2

MEEK AV
200 HAY 94541 711-H2
MEEK PL
- LFYT 94549 611-J6
- LFYT 94595 611-J6
MEEKER AV
1900 RCH 94804 608-H2
MEEKLAND AV
200 AlaC 94541 691-E6
9000 AlaC 94541 711-F1
16600 AlaC 94580 691-E6
21600 HAY 94541 711-F1
MEEKS COM
3800 FRMT 94538 753-D6
MEEKS TER
3800 FRMT 94538 753-D6
MEESE CIR
- DNVL 94526 653-C6
MEESE CT
100 DNVL 94526 653-C6
MEFFERD AV
1400 SMTO 94401 729-A7
MEG CT
2000 AlaC 94546 691-J6
MEG DR
4200 SJS 95136 874-F1
MEGAN CT
100 CCCo 94507 632-H5
MEGAN RD
800 LVMR 94550 696-B7
800 LVMR 94550 716-B1
MEGHAN LN
300 WLCK 94596 612-C2
MEGINNISS RD
- VAL 94592 549-H1
MEIER RD
- PLHL 94523 612-A1
MEIGGS LN
19000 SCIC 95014 852-G2
MEIGGS ST
41600 FRMT 94538 773-D1
MEISNER CT
- NVTO 94947 525-G3
MEISNER DR
- NVTO 94947 525-G3
MEKLER CT
500 SJS 95111 854-G3
MEL LN
3700 AlaC 94546 692-B4
MELALEUCA LN
1000 MrnC 94965 606-D6
MELANIE CIR
3200 PLE 94588 694-C7
MELANIE CT
2800 WLCK 94596 632-G3
MELANIE DR
300 CCCo 94565 573-J3
MELANIE LN
- ATN 94027 790-A5
MELANIE WY
- LVMR 94550 696-D7
MELANNIE CT
700 SJS 95116 834-F6
MELBA AV
- SF 94132 667-B6
MELBA CT
1200 SJS 95120 894-E2
1500 MTVW 94040 811-G6
1500 MTVW 94022 811-G6
MELBA DR
100 VAL 94589 510-A5
MELBOURNE AV
27600 HAY 94545 711-J7
27600 HAY 94545 731-J1
MELBOURNE BLVD
800 SJS 95116 834-E6
MELBOURNE CT
3000 PLE 94588 694-F6
MELBOURNE PL
3100 WLCK 94598 612-J1
MELBOURNE ST
1300 FCTY 94404 749-G5
MELCHER ST
800 SLN 94577 690-H1
MELCHESTER DR
2900 SJS 95132 814-E3
MELDON AV
4600 OAK 94619 650-F7
MELEEAN LN
- MRTZ 94553 571-H5
MELENDEZ AV
100 FRMT 94539 753-F4
MELENDY DR
2300 SCAR 94070 769-D5
MELERO COM
36600 FRMT 94536 752-A5
MELILLO DR
2800 WLCK 94596 612-A1
MELINA ST
200 SJS 95110 833-J4
MELINDA CIR
12100 SAR 95070 852-G5
MELINDA CT
400 CCCo 94565 573-J3
500 CCCo 94803 569-D7
MELISSA CIR
- DALY 94014 687-D4
MELISSA CT
- PIT 94565 574-G5
700 SMTO 94402 748-J4
1000 WLCK 94598 612-D4
2500 SJS 95121 854-J2
MELISSA LN
3800 AlaC 94546 691-H2
MELISSA TER
34400 FRMT 94555 752-B4
MELLISSA CIR
1400 ANT 94509 575-F7
MELLISSA CT
1500 ANT 94509 575-F7
MELLO DR
600 SJS 95134 813-H5
MELLO PL
10100 CPTO 95014 852-F1
MELLO ST
1100 EPA 94303 791-A1
MELLO WY
33600 FRMT 94555 732-D6
MELLON DR
18900 SAR 95070 852-H6
MELLOWOOD DR
12100 SAR 95070 852-G5

MELLOWOOD ST
1600 PIT 94565 573-G4
MELLUS ST
400 MRTZ 94553 571-D3
MELNIKOFF DR
3000 SJS 95121 855-C5
MELODY CT
6700 PLE 94588 694-A7
MELODY DR
3500 CCCo 94595 612-A7
4300 CNCD 94521 593-B4
MELODY LN
- ORIN 94563 610-F2
- MLV 94941 606-D2
1600 SJS 95133 834-E3
3800 SCL 95051 832-H6
12300 LAH 94022 830-J1
MELODY WY
16700 AlaC 94578 691-F6
17000 AlaC 94541 691-F6
MELON CT
700 SUNV 94087 832-C1
2900 ANT 94509 574-J6
MELRA CT
- SF 94134 687-J2
MELROSE AV
- SF 94127 667-E6
- SJS 95116 834-F3
- SF 94131 667-F6
200 MrnC 94941 606-D5
400 ALA 94502 670-A7
400 SF 94127 667-E6
4400 OAK 94601 670-E1
18000 AlaC 94541 711-E1
MELROSE CT
- CCCo 94565 612-A7
- HIL 94010 748-G4
- PCFA 94044 707-A3
MELROSE PL
- RDWC 94062 769-H6
MELTON LN
1800 ANT 94509 575-J6
MELVEN CT
300 SLN 94577 671-B6
MELVICH LN
- DBLN 94552 693-D5
MELVILLE AV
- SANS 94960 586-B1
100 PA 94301 791-A5
MELVILLE DR
6200 OAK 94611 650-G2
MELVILLE LN
6400 OAK 94611 650-G1
MELVILLE SQ
1200 RCH 94804 608-H2
MELVILLE WY
2400 SJS 95130 852-J7
MELVIN CT
- OAK 94602 650-E3
800 HAY 94541 711-H1
MELVIN DR
6800 SJS 95129 852-E3
MELVIN RD
- AMCN 94589 510-A1
1800 OAK 94602 650-E2
MELVIN HENRY CT
- SMCo 94061 790-A4
MELWOOD DR
1300 SJS 95118 874-B4
MEMBRILLO CORTE
3100 SCL 95051 833-A5
MEMLOCK TER
5500 FRMT 94538 773-A1
MEMOREX DR
900 SCL 95050 833-D2
MEMORIAL AV
600 HAY 94541 711-F2
MEMORIAL DR
- SRFL 94903 566-F4
800 SSF 94080 707-G3
MEMORIAL WY
- CCCo 94565 573-H3
- PIT 94565 573-H3
100 SCIC 94305 790-H7
MEMORY LN
100 CMBL 95008 853-G6
MEMPHIS DR
300 CMBL 95008 853-C5
MEMPHIS RD
100 ALA 94501 649-D7
MENALTO AV
1900 MLPK 94025 791-A2
2100 EPA 94303 791-A1
MENALTO DR
12200 LAH 94022 830-H1
MENARD CT
37800 FRMT 94536 752-H4
MENARD DR
100 SJS 95138 875-G6
MENAUL CT
100 SJS 95139 875-F7
MENDELL ST
- SF 94124 668-C6
MENDELSOHN LN
14800 SAR 95070 872-E3
MENDENHALL CT
3500 PLE 94588 694-G5
MENDENHALL DR
800 LVMR 94550 715-G2
1500 SJS 95130 853-B5
MENDENHALL RD
- OAK 94605 671-D2
MENDEZ RD
29000 HAY 94544 712-C7
MENDOCINO AV
800 BERK 94707 609-G5
5700 OAK 94618 630-A5
MENDOCINO CIR
1500 SLN 94579 691-A7
MENDOCINO CT
100 SBRN 94066 707-E7
1500 SLN 94579 691-A7
2700 PIN 94564 569-H6
MENDOCINO DR
1500 CNCD 94521 593-B2
2000 CCCo 94565 573-H2
2600 PIN 94564 569-H6
MENDOCINO LN
- NVTO 94947 525-G2
MENDOCINO RD
1500 LVMR 94550 695-E6

MENDOCINO ST
100 BSBN 94005 688-A6
100 VAL 94590 530-C4
1600 RCH 94804 609-C3
15300 SLN 94579 691-A6
MENDOCINO TER
4700 FRMT 94555 752-D2
MENDOCINO WY
100 RDWC 94065 749-J6
MENDOSA AV
- SF 94116 667-C4
MENDOTA CT
1600 WLCK 94596 611-J2
MENDOTA ST
4800 UNC 94587 752-B1
MENDOTA WY
1700 WLCK 94596 611-J2
2000 SJS 95122 834-J7
2000 SJS 95122 835-A7
MENDOZA AV
4500 SJS 95111 875-A1
MENDOZA CT
1500 PLE 94566 714-E1
MENDOZA DR
5800 OAK 94611 630-E7
MENHADEN CT
300 FCTY 94404 749-H3
MENHART DR
10200 SCIC 95014 852-H1
MENKER AV
300 SJS 95126 853-H2
300 SJS 95128 853-H2
MENLO AV
- DALY 94015 686-J7
600 MLPK 94025 790-F4
MENLO CT
100 VAL 94589 510-B6
300 WLCK 94598 612-H2
6700 PLE 94588 694-A7
MENLO DR
6300 SJS 95120 874-E7
6300 SJS 95120 894-E1
MENLO PL
- BERK 94707 609-F5
MENLO ST
13100 SLN 94577 690-H4
MENLO OAKS DR
200 SMCo 94025 790-H2
1000 MLPK 94025 770-J7
1000 MLPK 94025 790-H2
MENNET WY
9700 SRMN 94583 673-F6
MENORCA CT
1400 SJS 95120 874-A7
2600 SRMN 94583 673-B3
MENTO DR
1700 FRMT 94539 753-F6
MENTO TER
1600 FRMT 94539 753-G6
MENZEL PL
2000 SCL 95050 833-C3
MEPHAM DR
1000 PIT 94565 574-B2
MERA ST
3800 OAK 94601 650-D7
4000 OAK 94601 670-D1
MERANO CT
5100 PLE 94588 694-A6
MERANO DR
100 SJS 95134 813-D2
MERANO ST
- DNVL 94506 653-D1
MERCADO CT
600 MPS 95035 794-B5
MERCAT PL
- HIL 94010 748-F5
MERCATO CT
- SF 94131 667-F6
MERCED AV
- SANS 94960 566-A6
- SF 94127 667-D4
6100 OAK 94611 650-E1
MERCED CIR
4200 ANT 94509 595-J1
MERCED CT
3100 SCL 95051 833-A3
MERCED DR
- SBRN 94066 707-D7
- SBRN 94066 727-D1
MERCED ST
1000 BERK 94707 609-F6
1400 RCH 94804 609-B3
1800 SLN 94577 690-H3
14200 SLN 94579 690-J4
MERCED WY
- MLV 94941 606-B2
MERCEDES AV
800 LALT 94022 811-D4
MERCEDES LN
- ATN 94027 790-D2
MERCEDES WY
- SF 94127 667-C7
MERCER AV
1400 SJS 95125 853-J5
MERCER CT
4200 CNCD 94521 593-B3
MERCER ST
1200 RCH 94804 609-B2
MERCHANT RD
- SF 94129 647-B3
MERCHANT ST
400 SF 94111 648-B5
1800 CCCo 94525 550-C4
MERCURY AV
- TBRN 94920 607-B4
MERCURY CT
- PLHL 94523 592-A4
1400 MPS 95035 794-D7
MERCURY DR
400 SUNV 94086 812-J6
MERCURY RD
1900 LVMR 94550 715-E4
MERCURY ST
- SF 94124 668-A6
28600 HAY 94544 712-B7
48100 FRMT 94539 793-J1
MERCURY WY
100 PLHL 94523 592-A4
32200 UNC 94587 732-A6
MERCY ST
- MTVW 94041 812-A6
- MTVW 94041 811-H5

MEREDITH AV
1100 SJS 95125 854-A3
MEREDITH CT
300 CLAY 94517 613-J1
1900 CNCD 94521 593-G4
25200 HAY 94545 711-G5
MEREDITH DR
42000 FRMT 94539 753-F7
MEREDITH WY
2100 ANT 94509 595-A1
MERGANSER CT
4800 PLE 94566 714-D1
MERGANSER DR
3900 FRMT 94555 732-B7
MERIAM DR
- MrnC 94903 566-G3
MERIAN DR
1600 PLHL 94523 592-B4
MERIDA DR
20200 SAR 95070 852-E5
MERIDIAN
- RDWC 94065 749-J5
- RDWC 94065 750-A5
MERIDIAN AV
300 SCIC 95126 853-J2
300 SJS 95126 853-J2
600 SJS 95128 853-J2
1000 SJS 95125 853-J2
1200 SCIC 95125 853-J6
1900 SJS 95124 853-J6
2800 SJS 95124 873-J1
2800 SJS 95125 873-J1
4600 SJS 95120 873-J1
4700 SJS 95124 874-A2
4700 SJS 95118 874-A2
5800 SJS 95120 874-B7
6200 SJS 95120 894-C1
MERIDIAN LN
- SRFL 94901 566-G6
MERIDIAN WY
200 SJS 95126 853-J2
1800 MTVW 94043 811-G4
MERIDIAN PARK BLVD
2000 CCCo 94520 592-D1
2000 CNCD 94520 592-D1
MERIDIEN CIR
2900 UNC 94587 732-A4
30400 UNC 94587 731-J4
MERION DR
2600 SBRN 94066 707-D6
8000 NWK 94560 752-B6
MERION TER
100 MRGA 94556 651-D1
MERIT WY
5600 FRMT 94538 773-B2
MERIWEATHER CT
2100 WLCK 94596 632-G1
MERKELEY ROW ST
10200 SCIC 95127 815-D7
MERLE AV
800 CCCo 94553 571-F4
1000 SJS 95125 854-A3
E MERLE CT
400 SLN 94577 671-B7
W MERLE CT
400 SLN 94577 671-B6
MERLIN CT
- OAK 94605 671-E4
200 BEN 94510 551-A2
300 FRMT 94539 773-H7
1100 CCCo 94526 633-C5
MERLIN LN
500 SJS 95111 854-F7
MERLIN ST
- SF 94107 648-A7
MERLOT CT
600 PLE 94566 714-G3
3000 SJS 95135 855-G4
MERLOT DR
400 FRMT 94539 793-J2
600 FRMT 94539 794-A2
MERLOT LN
400 AMCN 94589 510-B4
2200 LVMR 94550 715-H4
MERNER RD
1000 HIL 94010 748-G4
MERO ST
- AlaC 94541 711-F1
MERRIBROOK CT
19800 SAR 95070 872-F1
MERRIBROOK DR
19700 SAR 95070 872-F1
MERRICK CT
700 WLCK 94598 613-A3
MERRICK DR
20200 SAR 95070 872-E1
MERRIDAN DR
3600 CNCD 94518 592-J3
MERRIE WY
- SF 94121 646-H6
MERRIEWOOD CIR
- OAK 94611 630-D6
MERRIEWOOD DR
500 LFYT 94549 631-J3
5500 OAK 94611 630-D6
MERRILEE PL
300 DNVL 94526 653-C4
MERRILL AV
100 FRMT 94539 773-H7
4500 OAK 94619 650-G6
MERRILL CIR N
- MRGA 94556 651-G1
MERRILL CIR S
- MRGA 94556 651-G1
MERRILL DR
- MRGA 94556 651-G1
100 ANT 94509 575-D4
1600 SJS 95124 873-J5
MERRILL LP
1600 SJS 95124 873-J5
1600 SJS 95118 873-J5
MERRILL PL
3700 AlaC 94546 692-B4
MERRILL ST
- SF 94134 668-A6
1000 MLPK 94025 790-F3
MERRIMAC CT
- DNVL 94526 653-A1
- PIT 94565 574-A2
- PIT 94565 573-J2
100 VAL 94589 510-A5

STREET
Block City ZIP Pg-Grid

MERRIMAC DR
1000 SUNV 94087 832-B2
3300 SJS 95117 853-D4
3400 CMBL 95008 853-D4
MERRIMAC PL
- PIT 94565 574-A2
700 DNVL 94526 653-A1
MERRIMAC ST
- SF 94107 668-C1
MERRIMAC RIVER ST
4000 FRMT 94555 752-E2
MERRIT DR
1500 NVTO 94949 526-B7
1500 NVTO 94949 546-C1
MERRITHEW DR
1000 MRTZ 94553 571-E3
MERRITON CT
1600 SJS 95124 873-J4
MERRITT AV
400 OAK 94606 649-J4
400 OAK 94610 649-J4
400 OAK 94610 650-A3
1700 SPAB 94806 588-H2
MERRITT CT
- OAK 94606 649-J4
5500 CNCD 94521 593-F7
MERRITT DR
5500 CNCD 94521 593-F7
19600 CPTO 95014 832-E7
MERRITT LN
1100 HAY 94545 711-G5
1500 LVMR 94550 715-G4
MERRITT PL
2500 LVMR 94550 715-G4
MERRITT RD
100 LALT 94022 811-E6
MERRITT ST
- SF 94114 667-F2
MERRIVALE WEST SQ
1300 SJS 95117 853-C4
MERRIWEATHER LN
400 SJS 95134 813-C2
MERRIWOOD PL
400 SRMN 94583 673-J7
MERRY LN
- CMAD 94925 606-F1
1400 SJS 95128 853-E5
MERRYDALE RD
- SRFL 94903 566-F4
MERRY MOPPET LN
2200 BLMT 94002 769-C2
MERRYWOOD DR
1400 SJS 95118 874-B4
MERSEY AV
1000 SLN 94579 691-A5
MERSEY ST
- SF 94114 667-H3
MERVYNS WY
2700 SJS 95127 834-J4
MERZ CT
200 MPS 95035 794-A5
MESA AV
- SF 94129 647-D4
- SF 94129 647-E4
- MLV 94941 606-F3
- PDMT 94611 630-B7
- SF 94116 667-D4
800 PA 94306 811-B4
MESA CT
- ATN 94027 790-B5
100 HER 94547 569-H4
800 PA 94306 811-C4
MESA DR
1100 SJS 95118 874-C4
1100 SJS 95131 814-A5
MESA ST
- VAL 94591 530-C7
1100 CNCD 94518 592-G3
MESA WY
500 RCH 94805 589-A6
MESA BUENA AV
1800 SPAB 94806 588-H1
MESA OAK CT
900 SUNV 94086 832-G2
MESA OAK LN
- CCCo 94506 653-H1
MESA RIDGE DR
4900 ANT 94509 595-D4
MESA RIDGE RD
- ANT - 595-D4
- ANT 94509 595-D4
MESA VERDE AV
100 VAL 94589 530-B1
MESA VERDE CT
3800 PLE 94588 714-A1
MESA VERDE DR
2000 MPS 95035 794-E7
MESA VERDE PL
500 PLHL 94523 592-B3
MESA VERDE WY
100 SCAR 94070 769-E6
300 SRFL 94903 566-F2
18400 AlaC 94552 692-D2
MESA VISTA CT
3700 SRMN 94583 673-C3
MESA VISTA DR
3700 SRMN 94583 673-C3
MESCALERO DR
5900 SJS 95123 874-H5
MESITA WY
1800 SJS 95124 873-H1
MESQUITE CT
100 HER 94547 569-J4
44500 FRMT 94539 773-G3
MESQUITE DR
- PLHL 94523 591-J2
2800 SCL 95051 833-B7
MESQUITE LN
- SRMN 94583 673-C4
MESQUITE PL
800 SUNV 94086 832-G2
MESQUITE WY
- LVMR 94550 716-D1
6000 LVMR 94550 696-D7
6000 AlaC 94550 696-D7
MESSINA DR
1600 SJS 95132 814-F3
MESSINA TER
- UNC 94587 732-E4
META DR
2500 SJS 95130 853-A7

METAIRIE CT
- SRMN 94583 693-G1
METAIRIE PL
100 SRMN 94583 673-H7
100 SRMN 94583 693-H1
METCALF RD
100 SJS 95138 875-J7
METEOR DR
21200 CPTO 95014 832-C6
32300 UNC 94587 732-A7
METEOR PL
10500 CPTO 95014 832-C6
METHILHAVEN CT
3300 SJS 95121 855-C5
METHILHAVEN LN
3300 SJS 95121 855-C5
METHUSELA TR
- SMCo 94062 809-A2
METHUSELAH TR
- SMCo 94062 809-A4
METHVEN LN
1200 MPS 95035 814-C1
METLER CT
18700 SAR 95070 872-H1
METRO CIR
1000 PA 94303 791-D5
METRO DR
- SJS 95110 833-H2
METRO CENTER BLVD
900 FCTY 94404 749-E3
METSON RD
- SF - 667-A1
METTEN AV
1000 PIT 94565 574-E7
MEYER CIR
3000 SJS 95121 855-B3
3000 SJS 95148 855-B3
MEYER CT
35600 FRMT 94536 752-G1
MEYER PL
- MrnC 94904 586-D3
MEYER PZ
- VAL 94590 530-A6
MEYER RD
- SRFL 94901 586-F2
MEYERHOLZ CT
21700 CPTO 95014 832-B7
MEYERS AV
3300 ALA 94501 670-B4
MEYERS CT
- NVTO 94947 526-A3
- NVTO 94947 525-J3
MEYERS DR
1600 UNC 94587 732-F6
MEYERS LN
100 CCCo 94553 572-B5
MEZES AV
1800 BLMT 94002 749-C7
1900 BLMT 94002 769-C1
MEZUE TR
- RCH 94805 589-E6
MEZZO CT
4800 FRMT 94538 773-B1
MIA CIR
4600 SJS 95136 874-H2
MIA CT
600 DNVL 94526 653-B3
MIAMI AV
27400 HAY 94545 711-H7
27600 HAY 94545 731-J1
MIAMI CT
1600 OAK 94602 650-C4
MIAMI DR
1600 SJS 95122 834-H7
MICA DR
100 VAL 94589 510-B6
MI CASA CT
1100 CNCD 94520 592-E5
MICHAEL
- CNCD 94518 592-G4
MICHAEL AV
4000 FRMT 94538 773-D2
MICHAEL CT
- SCAR 94070 769-G6
100 VAL 94591 530-F3
1400 MPS 95035 794-C5
20300 CPTO 95014 852-E2
MICHAEL DR
200 CMBL 95008 853-F6
1600 PIN 94564 569-D6
3400 RDWC 94063 770-E7
3500 SMTO 94403 749-B6
MICHAEL LN
- DNVL 94526 632-J6
- MLBR 94030 728-A3
- ORIN 94563 611-A7
- ORIN 94563 631-A1
- MLBR 94030 727-J3
500 LFYT 94549 631-J2
15600 MSER 95030 873-A5
MICHAEL PL
200 MRTZ 94553 591-J4
3400 CCCo 94565 573-F1
MICHAEL ST
600 MPS 95035 794-C5
MICHAEL WY
- SANS 94960 566-A4
- SCL 95051 832-J7
- MrnC 94960 566-A4
MICHAELS CT
19700 AlaC 94546 691-H4
MICHAELS DR
20800 SAR 95070 872-C2
MICHAELS WY
- ATN 94027 790-E3
MICH BLUFF DR
1200 SJS 95131 814-D6
MICHELANGELO DR
900 SUNV 94087 832-F3
MICHELE CIR
- NVTO 94947 525-F2
MICHELE CT
100 VAL 94591 530-D2
MICHELE DR
100 CCCo 94806 569-A5
MICHELE RD
600 CCCo 94553 572-A3
MICHELE WY
6700 SJS 95129 852-E3
MICHELE JEAN WY
2400 SCL 95050 833-C6

MICHELL CT
300 LVMR 94550 695-H7
MICHELL ST
200 LVMR 94550 695-H7
MICHELLE CT
200 SSF 94080 708-B4
500 CCCo 94565 573-J3
4000 CNCD 94521 593-B2
4600 UNC 94587 732-A7
4600 UNC 94587 752-A1
MICHELLE DR
200 CMBL 95008 853-B5
MICHELLE LN
- CCCo 94507 632-J3
300 DALY 94015 707-C2
MICHELLE ST
39900 FRMT 94538 753-C5
MICHELLE WY
- UNC 94587 751-J1
300 CCCo 94507 632-J3
4700 UNC 94587 752-A1
MICHELSON ST
24300 HAY 94545 711-E5
MICHIGAN AV
400 BERK 94707 609-G4
900 SJS 95125 854-A4
1200 SJS 95002 793-C7
1600 EPA 94303 791-B1
MICHIGAN BLVD
5400 CNCD 94521 593-F6
5500 CLAY 94517 593-F6
MICHIGAN DR
7800 OAK 94605 671-A2
MICHIGAN RD
200 MPS 95035 794-A5
MICHIGAN ST
- VAL 94590 530-A3
800 SF 94107 668-C4
1600 SF 94124 668-C4
MICHON CT
1700 SJS 95124 873-H4
MICHON DR
1700 SJS 95124 873-J4
1800 SJS 95032 873-H5
MICRO CT
1000 SJS 95120 894-H4
MICRO PL
1000 SJS 95120 894-H4
MIDAS WY
1200 SUNV 94086 812-J6
MIDCREST RD
500 OAK 94610 650-C3
MIDCREST WY
- SF 94131 667-E4
100 SF 94131 667-E4
700 ELCR 94530 609-E3
MIDDAY COM
5400 FRMT 94555 752-C3
MIDDEN LN
- TBRN 94920 607-A3
- TBRN 94920 606-J3
MIDDLE AV
600 MLPK 94025 790-F5
MIDDLE CT
- SBRN 94066 727-G2
- MLV 94941 606-G2
400 MLPK 94025 790-F6
MIDDLE DR E
- SF 94118 667-D1
MIDDLE DR W
- SF - 667-A1
- SF - 666-J1
MIDDLE LN
1500 HAY 94545 711-E5
1600 AlaC 94545 711-E5
MIDDLE RD
- LFYT 94549 611-A6
300 BLMT 94002 749-E7
700 BLMT 94002 769-E1
MIDDLEBOROUGH CIR
2600 SJS 95132 814-D4
MIDDLEBOROUGH WY
29300 HAY 94544 732-B2
MIDDLEBURY DR
500 SUNV 94087 832-D2
MIDDLEBURY LN
500 LALT 94022 811-D6
MIDDLEBURY WY
7200 SJS 95139 875-G7
MIDDLEFIELD AV
- MTVW 94043 811-G2
2300 FRMT 94539 753-E7
MIDDLEFIELD DR
- SF 94132 667-A6
MIDDLEFIELD RD
- LVMR 94550 696-F5
- ATN 94027 790-E1
100 PA 94301 790-E1
400 RDWC 94063 770-A5
500 MLPK 94025 790-E1
600 PA 94301 791-A4
900 BERK 94708 609-J5
1600 PA 94303 791-A4
2500 SMCo 94063 770-C7
2600 PA 94306 791-A4
3100 SMCo 94063 790-E1
3600 PA 94306 811-E1
3600 PA 94303 811-E1
E MIDDLEFIELD RD
- SUNV 94086 812-B4
- MTVW 94043 812-B4
700 MTVW 94086 812-B4
W MIDDLEFIELD RD
500 MTVW 94043 811-H3
2200 SCIC 94043 811-H3
MIDDLE FORK LN
13400 LAH 94022 810-J7
MIDDLE GATE ST
- ATN 94027 790-D2
MIDDLE HARBOR RD
1200 OAK 94607 649-C3
1600 OAK 94625 649-C3
MIDDLE PARK DR
4000 SJS 95135 855-F3
MIDDLEPOINT RD
- SF 94124 668-D6
MIDDLESEX RD
500 BLMT 94002 749-E7
MIDDLESEX ST
200 CCCo 94520 572-G1
MIDDLETON AV
1600 LALT 94024 831-J4

MIDDLETON AV
3400 AlaC 94546 691-H3
MIDDLETON CT
1300 LALT 94024 831-J4
MIDDLETON PL
4900 PLE 94566 714-F5
MIDDLETON ST
3000 OAK 94605 671-C7
3000 SLN 94605 671-C7
MIDDLETOWN DR
2200 SJS 95008 853-B7
MIDFIELD AV
1300 SJS 95122 834-G7
MIDFIELD WY
3600 RDWC 94062 789-H1
MIDGLEN WY
800 WDSD 94062 789-F3
MIDHILL DR
- MLV 94941 606-G2
MIDHILL RD
- CCCo 94553 571-J5
- MRTZ 94553 571-H5
MIDHURST CT
3100 SJS 95135 855-F3
MIDHURST WY
2900 SJS 95135 855-E3
MIDLAND RD
14600 AlaC 94578 691-E2
MIDLAND WY
100 DNVL 94526 653-A4
700 SMCo 94062 789-F2
MIDLOTHIAN WY
30400 HAY 94544 732-D2
MIDPINE AV
1200 SJS 95122 854-H2
MIDSHIP DR
100 HER 94547 570-B6
MIDTOWN CT
2700 PA 94303 791-C6
MIDVALE AV
300 SMTO 94403 749-C7
3400 OAK 94602 650-F5
MIDVALE CT
- CCCo 94596 612-A4
5300 PLE 94588 693-H7
MIDVALE DR
- DALY 94015 687-A7
MIDVALE LN
700 SJS 95136 874-E1
MIDVALE WY
500 MrnC 94965 606-D6
MIDWAY AV
- MrnC 94941 606-E5
400 SMTO 94402 748-G1
500 SMCo 94015 687-A4
600 SLN 94577 690-H1
MIDWAY BLVD
300 NVTO 94947 526-C7
MIDWAY CT
- DALY 94014 687-J3
500 MRTZ 94553 571-J6
1100 NVTO 94947 526-D7
MIDWAY DR
- DALY 94014 687-J3
100 MRTZ 94553 571-J5
MIDWAY PL
400 MRTZ 94553 571-J5
MIDWAY RD
- LKSP 94939 586-F6
MIDWAY ST
- SF 94133 648-A3
- VAL 94590 530-A6
300 OAK 94626 649-C3
N MIDWAY ST
- CMBL 95008 853-G6
S MIDWAY ST
200 CMBL 95008 853-G6
MIDWICK DR
- MPS 95035 794-A4
MI ELANA CIR
2800 WLCK 94598 612-H2
MI ELANA CT
- WLCK 94598 612-H2
MIELKE DR
400 MLPK 94025 790-G3
MIETTE WY
1300 SUNV 94087 832-C4
MIFFLIN AV
- UNC 94587 732-B4
MIFLIN AV
3500 CCCo 94803 589-B3
MIFLIN CT
4100 CCCo 94803 589-B2
MIGNON DR
2600 SJS 95132 814-D5
MIGNOT LN
400 SJS 95111 854-J6
MIGUEL AV
1100 LALT 94024 831-H4
MIGUEL ST
- SF 94131 667-G5
MIGUELITA AV
10100 SCIC 95127 815-B6
MIKADO PL
500 DNVL 94526 653-C5
MIKEMARY CT
2400 AlaC 94546 691-F3
MIKE YORBA WY
- CCCo 94509 575-G5
MILA CT
38100 FRMT 94536 752-J4
MILAGRA CT
- PCFA 94044 707-A4
MILAGRA DR
100 PCFA 94044 706-J4
200 PCFA 94044 707-A4
MILAN CT
1400 LVMR 94550 715-G4
MILAN DR
400 SJS 95134 813-H4
MILAN TER
- SF 94112 687-E2
MILANI AV
2700 PLE 94588 694-E7
5300 NWK 94560 752-F5
MILANI CT
100 LGTS 95030 873-B4
MILANO CT
- DNVL 94506 653-D1
5900 FRMT 94555 752-B6
MILANO PL
- SRFL 94901 567-D6

MILANO TER
300 MPS 95035 793-H3
MILANO WY
1900 MTVW 94040 831-H1
2700 SCAR 94070 769-F5
4800 MRTZ 94553 572-A6
4800 MRTZ 94553 571-J6
MILAW CT
- SRMN 94583 673-B2
MILBURN CT
- SRMN 94583 673-G7
MILBURN DR
1700 PLHL 94523 592-B4
MILBURN ST
3500 SJS 95148 835-E6
MILBURN TER
34400 FRMT 94555 752-B4
MILDEN RD
4800 MRTZ 94553 571-G7
MILDRED AV
- PIT 94565 574-C3
1100 SJS 95125 854-A4
MILDRED CT
4900 FRMT 94536 752-J6
MILDRED DR
4500 FRMT 94536 752-J6
MILDRED LN
3300 LFYT 94549 631-G3
MILDRED PL
500 HAY 94544 732-F2
MILDRED ST
2100 CNCD 94520 572-F7
MILES AV
- LGTS 95030 873-A7
5100 OAK 94618 629-J5
5600 OAK 94618 630-A5
MILES CT
600 PLHL 94523 591-J3
800 SCL 95051 833-A5
MILES DR
2900 SCL 95051 833-A5
MILES PL
- SF 94108 648-A5
MILES ST
- SF 94129 647-D4
MILEY ST
- SF 94123 647-F4
MILFORD AV
- HIL 94010 748-G2
MILFORD DR
21200 CPTO 95014 832-C7
MILFORD ST
15000 SLN 94579 691-A6
MILFORD WY
- SCIC 95127 835-A3
- SJS 95127 835-A3
MILHON CT
2600 SJS 95148 855-B1
MILITA ST
100 VAL 94590 530-B3
MILITARY E
200 BEN 94510 551-C5
MILITARY W
100 BEN 94510 551-A3
900 BEN 94510 550-H2
MILITARY WY
400 PA 94306 811-C2
MILJEVICH DR
20000 SAR 95070 852-E7
MILKY WY
900 CPTO 95014 852-C3
MILL CT
18000 SAR 95070 852-D5
MILL RD
- SJS 95002 793-B7
300 MRTZ 94553 571-G5
2000 NVTO 94947 525-G3
2000 MrnC 94947 525-G3
MILL ST
- LGTS 95032 893-A1
- SF 94134 688-A1
- SRFL 94901 586-H2
43400 FRMT 94539 753-J7
MILLAND CT
- MrnC 94941 606-H5
MILLAND DR
- MrnC 94941 606-H5
MILLAR AV
- SJS 95127 834-J2
- SCIC 95127 834-J2
- SCIC 95127 835-A2
2800 SCL 95051 833-A3
MILLARD AV
4300 FRMT 94538 753-C7
MILLARD LN
21400 CPTO 95014 832-C6
MILLARD RD
- LKSP 94939 586-E6
MILLAY PL
- MLV 94941 606-G4
MILLBRAE AV
- MLBR 94030 728-B4
- SANS 94960 566-C7
1300 MLBR 94030 727-J5
E MILLBRAE AV
- MLBR 94030 728-C4
MILLBRAE CIR
- MLBR 94030 728-A4
MILLBRAE CT
100 WLCK 94598 612-J1
MILLBRAE LN
200 LGTS 95030 873-B7
MILLBRAE WY
2700 SJS 95121 855-D3
MILLBRIDGE DR
2900 SRMN 94583 673-F6
MILLBRIDGE PL
2800 SRMN 94583 673-F5
MILLBROOK AV
7600 DBLN 94568 693-G3
MILLBROOK CT
- DNVL 94526 653-A1
500 CMBL 95008 853-C6
1000 WLCK 94598 612-G4
MILLBROOK DR
3000 SJS 95148 855-D1
MILLBROOK TER
4600 FRMT 94538 773-C1
MILLCREEK DR
2200 PLHL 94523 591-J6
MILL CREEK LN
500 SCL 95134 813-E4

MILL CREEK LN
5200 SJS 95136 875-A3
MILL CREEK RD
- FRMT 94539 753-H6
3600 FRMT 94539 754-A6
3600 AlaC 94586 774-B1
3600 FRMT 94539 774-B1
MILLEFORD CT
7500 PLE 94588 714-A3
MILLER AV
- MLV 94941 606-D3
- SAUS 94965 627-B3
- SJS 95112 854-E3
- MrnC 94941 606-D3
100 SSF 94080 707-F1
200 MRTZ 94553 571-E2
500 PCFA 94044 707-A4
500 VAL 94591 530-D5
600 CPTO 95014 852-F4
900 BERK 94708 609-H5
1000 SJS 95129 852-F4
1100 OAK 94601 650-B7
1400 CMBL 95008 873-B1
1600 BLMT 94002 749-C7
1600 SCIC 94024 831-F4
2600 MTVW 94040 811-E3
4200 PA 94306 811-E3
10300 SCIC 95014 852-F4
12000 SAR 95070 852-G6
MILLER CT
- SMCo 94061 790-B3
4300 PA 94306 811-E3
19400 SAR 95070 852-F5
MILLER DR
1000 LFYT 94549 611-G5
MILLER LN
- MLV 94941 606-D3
- SAUS 94965 627-B3
1900 CCCo 94595 632-D1
1900 WLCK 94595 632-D1
MILLER PL
- SF 94108 648-A5
1000 OAK 94601 650-B7
38000 FRMT 94536 753-A3
MILLER RD
- SF 94129 647-C3
7000 AlaC 94546 672-A5
7000 AlaC 94546 671-H1
MILLER ST
600 SJS 95110 834-A4
1200 ANT 94509 575-F5
2700 SLN 94577 690-J4
MILLER CREEK RD
200 MrnC 94903 546-F6
200 SRFL 94903 546-D7
MILLER RANCH CT
- MrnC 94903 546-E6
MILLET CT
3500 SJS 95127 835-C2
MILLFIELD PL
400 MRGA 94556 651-F3
MILLHAVEN PL
100 SJS 95111 874-J1
MILLICAN CT
- CCCo 94553 591-E2
MILLICENT CT
3500 SJS 95148 835-C4
MILLICH DR
500 CMBL 95008 853-C4
MILLICH LN
600 CMBL 95008 853-C4
1300 SJS 95117 853-C4
MILLIE AV
900 MLPK 94025 790-F4
MILLIGAN DR
5400 SJS 95124 873-J6
MILLINGTON CT
- ALA 94502 669-H7
MILLION CT
2600 SJS 95148 835-E6
MILLPOND CT
1200 CNCD 94521 593-B4
MILL POND DR
300 SJS 95125 854-D5
400 SCIC 95125 854-D5
MILLRICH DR
17300 LGTS 95030 873-B4
MILL RISE WY
17100 LGTS 95032 893-D1
MILL RIVER LN
400 SJS 95134 813-H4
MILL RIVER PL
400 SJS 95134 813-F3
MILLS AV
600 LALT 94022 811-F6
700 SBRN 94066 707-J6
1100 BURL 94010 728-D5
1700 BLMT 94002 749-C7
2000 SMCo 94025 790-C6
15900 AlaC 94580 691-E6
MILLS CT
400 BEN 94510 551-A1
900 SJS 95125 854-B2
1400 MLPK 94025 790-F3
MILLS DR
400 BEN 94510 550-J2
400 BEN 94510 551-A1
MILLS LN
100 VAL 94589 510-C5
MILLS PL
100 SRMN 94583 673-F7
MILLS ST
1200 MLPK 94025 790-F3
MILLS WY
1000 RDWC 94063 770-D6
3800 LVMR 94550 695-J7
MILLSBRAE AV
2900 OAK 94605 670-G1
MILLS CANYON CT
- BURL 94010 728-B6
MILLS CORNER LN
900 SJS 95122 854-G1
MILLSGATE LN
1700 SJS 95122 854-G1
MILLSIDE LN
- MLV 94941 606-C3
MILLSTONE DR
- MrnC 94903 546-E5
MILL STONE LN
- SJS 95136 875-A3
MILL STREAM DR
700 SJS 95125 854-D5

MILLSTREAM DR
400 SLN 94578 691-C4
MILLSVIEW AV
3200 OAK 94619 650-G7
MILLSWOOD CT
700 SJS 95120 894-J3
MILLTHWAIT DR
- CCCo 94553 591-E2
MILLWATER CT
100 MPS 95035 794-C2
MILLWOOD CT
35000 NWK 94560 752-D3
MILLWOOD DR
100 MLBR 94030 728-A2
300 MLBR 94030 727-J3
MILLWOOD ST
- MLV 94941 606-E3
MILMAR BLVD
18300 AlaC 94546 692-A3
MILMAR WY
100 LGTS 95032 873-E5
MILMONT DR
- FRMT 94538 793-H3
1700 MPS 95035 793-J5
MILMONT ST
- FRMT 94538 793-H2
MILNE CT
1400 CNCD 94521 593-D4
MILNER RD
3100 ANT 94509 575-C7
3100 ANT 94509 595-C1
MILO CT
800 SJS 95133 814-G6
MILO PL
200 SRMN 94583 673-F5
MILO WY
2800 SRMN 94583 673-E6
MILPAS
- CCCo 94596 612-A5
N MILPITAS BLVD
- MPS 95035 794-A5
1100 MPS 95035 793-J3
2000 FRMT 94539 793-J3
S MILPITAS BLVD
- MPS 95035 794-B7
100 MPS 95035 814-B1
MILROY PL
1600 SJS 95124 873-J3
MILTON AV
200 SBRN 94066 728-A1
200 SBRN 94066 727-J1
300 SBRN 94066 707-J7
1300 CCCo 94596 632-E1
1300 WLCK 94596 632-E1
4000 AlaC 94546 691-J3
N MILTON AV
- CMBL 95008 853-D5
S MILTON AV
400 CMBL 95008 853-D6
MILTON CT
3000 MTVW 94040 831-J2
MILTON DR
3800 CCCo 94803 589-D2
MILTON ST
- SF 94112 667-G6
800 OAK 94607 649-F2
1600 SMCo 94061 790-B3
33900 FRMT 94555 732-D7
33900 FRMT 94555 752-E1
MILTON WY
- LVMR 94550 696-A6
1200 SJS 95125 854-B3
MILTON ROSS ST
- SF 94124 668-B5
MILVERTON RD
600 LALT 94022 831-D1
MILVIA CT
- BERK 94709 609-G7
MILVIA ST
1200 BERK 94709 609-G7
1600 BERK 94709 629-G1
1900 BERK 94704 629-G3
2700 BERK 94703 629-G3
MILWAUKEE PL
200 DNVL 94526 653-C5
MIMOSA AV
- LKSP 94939 586-E5
MIMOSA CT
- LVMR 94550 696-C3
500 SCIC 94024 831-J6
2400 ANT 94509 595-F3
MIMOSA ST
1400 LVMR 94550 696-C3
MIMOSA TER
34200 FRMT 94555 752-B3
MIMOSA WY
100 SMCo 94028 810-D4
2400 ANT 94509 595-F3
6200 SJS 95138 875-F6
MIMS AV
100 CCCo 94565 573-G3
MINA LN
300 PCFA 94044 707-B3
MINAHAN WY
1400 VAL 94590 530-C3
MINAKER CT
10000 CPTO 95014 852-B1
MINAKER DR
900 ANT 94509 575-F4
MINARDI AV
1500 SJS 95125 854-A6
MINARET AV
200 MTVW 94043 812-A5
MINARET DR
2200 MRTZ 94553 572-A7
MINAS DR
4700 SJS 95136 874-D2
MINAS DE ORO
1700 SJS 95116 834-F3
MINDANAO DR
- RDWC 94065 749-J5
- RDWC 94065 750-A5
MINDEN CT
5600 SJS 95123 875-A4
MINDY WY
600 SJS 95123 874-J7
MINE HILL RD
20500 SCIC 95120 894-H6
MINER AV
900 SPAB 94806 568-H7
1200 SPAB 94806 588-H1

STREET
Block City ZIP Pg-Grid

MINER PL
10100 CPTO 95014 832-E7
MINER RD
- ORIN 94563 610-G4
MINERT RD
1200 WLCK 94598 592-F7
1200 CNCD 94518 592-G5
MINERVA AV
100 PCFA 94044 727-A2
MINERVA ST
- SF 94112 687-D1
200 SF 94132 687-D1
400 HAY 94544 712-B7
1000 SLN 94577 690-J1
MINES RD
3000 AlaC 94550 716-C4
N MINES RD
100 LVMR 94550 695-J5
100 LVMR 94550 696-A6
200 LVMR 94550 716-B1
MINETTE DR
10600 SCIC 95014 852-H2
MINETTE PL
10600 SCIC 95014 852-H2
MING CT
100 NVTO 94945 526-E4
MINGO LN
- ALA 94502 670-A7
MINI DR
100 VAL 94589 509-H4
100 NaCo 94589 509-H4
500 VAL 94589 510-A5
MINIDOKA AV
100 SJS 95127 834-H1
MINIVET CT
2400 PLE 94566 714-D1
MINK CT
4300 ANT 94509 595-H3
MINNA AV
2600 OAK 94619 650-E6
MINNA ST
- SF 94105 648-B6
100 SF 94103 648-B6
600 SF 94103 647-J7
1000 SF 94103 667-J1
MINNA WY
1900 SJS 95124 873-G1
MINNER AV
300 ANT 94509 575-E6
MINNESOTA AV
200 SJS 95125 854-B2
1300 SJS 95125 853-J4
MINNESOTA ST
500 SF 94107 668-C3
MINNIE CT
24900 AlaC 94541 712-C2
MINNIE ST
700 AlaC 94566 714-E6
700 PLE 94566 714-E6
2100 AlaC 94541 712-C2
MINNIS CIR
- MPS 95035 793-J4
MINO WY
40800 FRMT 94539 753-E5
MINOCA RD
- PTLV 94028 810-D5
MINOCQUA CT
19700 SAR 95070 872-F2
MINOR AV
400 SJS 95126 854-B1
500 SJS 95125 854-B1
MINOR CT
- SRFL 94903 566-C4
MINORCA CT
12500 LAH 94022 811-A7
MINORCA WY
- MLBR 94030 728-A4
MINORU DR
200 CCCo 94553 572-C7
1000 SJS 95120 894-H4
MINORU WY
200 CCCo 94553 572-C6
MINT ST
- SF 94103 648-A6
MINTA LN
2700 ANT 94509 575-C7
MINTO CT
3500 SJS 95132 814-F2
MINTO DR
1900 SJS 95132 814-F2
MINTON CT
400 PLHL 94523 592-A7
2800 PLE 94588 714-A3
MINTON LN
500 MTVW 94041 811-J5
MINTURN CT
32200 UNC 94587 732-C5
MINTURN ST
1500 ALA 94501 669-J1
MINTWOOD CT
4800 SJS 95129 852-B7
MINTWOOD DR
1700 CNCD 94521 593-D3
MINTWOOD ST
43200 FRMT 94538 773-E2
MINUET CIR
4000 RCH 94803 589-B2
MINUET DR
1800 SJS 95131 814-C4
MINUTEMAN WY
1500 SJS 95132 814-E4
MIO CORTE
- MLBR 94030 728-A4
MIRA CT
15900 AlaC 94546 692-A2
MIRA ST
100 FCTY 94404 749-E4
MIRA WY
- SMCo 94028 810-D4
MIRABEAU DR
6300 NWK 94560 752-C5
MIRABEL AV
- MLV 94941 606-D3
- SF 94110 667-J4
MIRABELLA AV
1000 NVTO 94945 526-B3
MIRABELLI CIR
- SJS 95134 813-D2
MIRACLE MOUNTAIN DR
5900 SJS 95123 874-E5
MIRADA AV
200 SRFL 94903 566-E5
600 SCIC 94305 810-H1
MIRADA DR
100 DALY 94015 687-B6
MIRADERO AV
15000 SCIC 95127 815-B6
16000 SJS 95127 815-B6
MIRADOR CT
700 PLE 94566 714-F4
MIRADOR DR
4200 PLE 94566 714-E5
MIRADOR TER
900 PCFA 94044 707-A6
MIRA FLORES
- ORIN 94563 610-J5
MIRAFLORES AV
- SRFL 94901 586-E1
MIRAFLORES LN
- TBRN 94920 607-C5
MIRAFLORES WY
1200 LALT 94024 831-G2
MIRAGE WY
3200 SJS 95135 855-G3
MIRA LOMA
- ORIN 94563 610-G6
100 VAL 94590 530-B2
MIRALOMA CT
5400 LVMR 94550 696-C3
MIRALOMA DR
- SF 94127 667-D5
MIRA LOMA LN
- DNVL 94526 652-J3
MIRA LOMA ST
4600 AlaC 94546 692-A3
MIRALOMA ST
1700 LVMR 94550 696-C3
MIRA LOMA WY
3900 SJS 95111 854-J7
MIRALOMA WY
1100 SUNV 94086 812-H7
2900 UNC 94587 732-A4
3000 UNC 94587 731-J4
12500 LAH 94024 831-E2
MIRAMAR
1400 SMTO 94404 749-D3
MIRAMAR AV
- HER 94547 570-B6
- SF 94112 687-D1
- SRFL 94901 586-E1
200 SF 94112 667-D7
800 BERK 94707 609-F6
1900 AlaC 94578 691-G4
2500 AlaC 94546 691-G4
4800 SJS 95129 852-J1
MIRAMAR PL
16200 AlaC 94578 691-G4
MIRAMAR RD
100 ALA 94501 649-D6
MIRAMAR TER
700 BLMT 94002 769-E1
MIRAMAR WY
1100 SUNV 94086 832-H3
3700 SCL 95051 832-H3
MIRAMAR PARK DR
43300 FRMT 94538 773-C3
MIRAMESA CT
3700 SCL 95051 832-H3
MIRAMONTE AV
100 PA 94306 791-A6
800 MTVW 94040 811-H7
900 LALT 94024 831-H2
1600 MTVW 94040 831-H2
1900 AlaC 94578 691-G5
MIRAMONTE CT
- CCCo 94596 612-B4
- SCAR 94070 769-F2
1300 BERK 94703 609-F7
MIRAMONTE DR
- MRGA 94556 631-C6
MIRA MONTE LN
300 LVMR 94550 696-A6
300 LVMR 94550 695-J6
MIRA MONTE RD
- ORIN 94563 610-E7
MIRAMONTE RD
- CCCo 94596 612-B4
MIRAMONTE ST
4200 UNC 94587 732-A5
4200 UNC 94587 731-J5
MIRAMONTES RD
100 WDSD 94062 789-F6
MIRAMONTES TR
- SMCo 94062 789-C3
MIRANDA AV
200 CCCo 94507 632-G4
3200 PA 94304 811-B4
4000 PA 94306 811-C4
MIRANDA CT
- ALA 94502 669-J7
- CCCo 94507 632-G4
- HIL 94010 748-F4
- NVTO 94947 526-A4
1500 PCFA 94044 727-A3
14400 LAH 94022 811-C5
MIRANDA GRN
800 PA 94306 811-C5
MIRANDA LN
300 CCCo 94507 632-H3
MIRANDA PL
200 CCCo 94507 632-H3
MIRANDA RD
14000 LAH 94022 811-C6
MIRANDA ST
1300 HAY 94544 732-A2
41900 FRMT 94539 753-F7
MIRANDA WY
900 LVMR 94550 715-F3
14300 LAH 94022 811-C5
MIRANDO WY
- SF 94112 667-G6
MIRANTE CT
2900 RCH 94803 589-E2
MIRA PLAZA CT
1900 SCL 95051 832-H3
MIRASOL AV
3400 OAK 94605 671-B4
MIRASOL CT
- HIL 94010 748-F5
6100 SJS 95123 874-F6
MIRASSOU DR
1600 SJS 95124 873-J5
MIRASSOU PL
1700 SJS 95124 873-J5
MIRAVALLE AV
1300 LALT 94024 831-J3
MIRAVERDE CT
3700 SCL 95051 832-H3
MIRA VISTA AV
500 OAK 94610 649-J2
MIRA VISTA CIR
3300 SJS 95132 814-H5
MIRA VISTA CT
- DALY 94014 687-G3
1300 ANT 94509 575-B6
3300 SJS 95132 814-H5
MIRA VISTA DR
1800 CCCo 94805 589-C6
2000 ELCR 94530 589-C7
4700 AlaC 94546 691-J1
MIRA VISTA PL
16900 AlaC 94546 691-J1
MIRA VISTA RD
10200 CPTO 95014 852-A1
MIRA VISTA TER
1700 CNCD 94520 592-F2
MIRA VISTA WY
300 SSF 94080 707-F5
MIRAVISTA WY
100 VAL 94589 510-D5
MIREILLE DR
5600 SJS 95118 874-A6
MIREVAL RD
16200 LGTS 95032 893-C2
16200 SCIC 95032 893-C2
16500 SCIC 95032 893-C2
MIRIAM CT
1700 SJS 95124 853-H6
MIRIAM ST
- DALY 94014 687-C3
MIRKO LN
- CCCo 94596 632-F1
MIRMIROU DR
13800 LAH 94022 810-H6
MISE AV
4900 SJS 95124 873-G4
MISSION AV
- MrnC 94901 586-J1
- SRFL 94901 586-H1
900 SRFL 94901 566-F7
1300 SPAB 94806 588-G3
MISSION BLVD
400 HAY 94544 732-F3
35200 FRMT 94536 732-F3
42400 FRMT 94539 753-H6
43300 FRMT 94539 773-H5
46700 FRMT 94538 773-H5
MISSION BLVD Rt#-185
17300 AlaC 94541 691-G6
19800 HAY 94541 691-G6
MISSION BLVD Rt#-238
20100 HAY 94541 691-H7
20100 HAY 94541 711-H1
23900 HAY 94544 711-H1
24200 HAY 94544 712-B5
24300 HAY 94542 712-A3
30100 HAY 94544 732-D1
33000 UNC 94587 732-G4
35100 FRMT 94536 732-G4
35500 FRMT 94536 733-B7
37300 FRMT 94536 753-E3
39000 FRMT 94539 753-E3
MISSION BLVD Rt#-262
46000 FRMT 94539 773-G6
46600 FRMT 94538 773-G6
MISSION CIR
- DALY 94014 687-D3
MISSION CT
- AlaC 94541 711-F1
400 FRMT 94539 773-G6
1000 VAL 94591 530-D3
MISSION DR
- PLE 94566 714-D5
- SMTO 94402 748-J2
100 EPA 94303 791-C3
100 MrnC 94941 606-J6
1000 ANT 94509 575-A6
1500 DNVL 94526 653-C6
MISSION LN
700 WLCK 94596 612-C2
MISSION PL
500 DNVL 94526 653-B6
MISSION RD
900 FRMT 94539 753-H6
900 SSF 94080 707-E1
1400 CLMA 94014 707-E1
5700 AlaC 94586 754-A3
7400 CLMA 94014 687-E7
MISSION ST
- SF 94105 648-A6
500 SCL 95050 833-F5
600 SF 94103 648-A6
1100 SF 94103 647-J7
1500 SF 94103 667-J3
2000 SF 94110 667-J3
3000 SF 94110 667-H5
3800 SF 94112 667-G7
4100 SF 94112 687-E2
5900 DALY 94014 687-E2
MISSION ST Rt#-82
6300 DALY 94014 687-C4
E MISSION ST
- SJS 95112 834-B3
W MISSION ST
100 SJS 95110 834-A4
MISSION WY
- CMBL 95008 853-D6
3900 SLN 94578 691-C5
21500 CPTO 95014 832-B7
MISSION BELL DR
2400 SPAB 94806 588-H2
MISSION BELL PL
700 HAY 94544 711-J5
MISSION BLUE DR
- BSBN 94005 688-A4
- BSBN 94005 687-H5
MISSION COLLEGE BLVD
2000 SCL 95054 813-B5
3000 SUNV 94089 813-A6
MISSION CREEK CT
600 FRMT 94539 753-G5
MISSION CREEK DR
41600 FRMT 94539 753-F5
MISSION FALLS CT
47000 FRMT 94539 773-G6
MISSION FALLS LN
100 FRMT 94539 773-G7
MISSION GLEN DR
2300 SCL 95051 833-B2
MISSION GREENS DR
2600 SJS 95148 855-C1
MISSION HILL PL
2700 SJS 95148 855-C1
MISSION HILLS
- OAK 94605 671-D2
MISSION HILLS DR
- DALY 94014 687-F3
MISSION PASS TER
- MrnC 94960 566-B3
- SRFL 94903 566-B3
MISSION RIDGE CT
- FRMT 94539 753-G5
MISSION ROCK ST
- SF 94107 668-C1
MISSION SPRINGS
- HER 94547 569-G4
MISSION SPRINGS CIR
1500 SJS 95131 814-C6
MISSION SPRINGS CT
1500 SJS 95131 814-C6
MISSION TRAIL RD
- WDSD 94062 789-G5
MISSION VIEW DR
3000 FRMT 94538 753-C6
MISSISSIPPI ST
- SF 94107 668-B3
100 VAL 94590 529-J3
300 VAL 94590 530-A3
MISSOURI DR
1200 CNCD 94521 593-E7
MISSOURI ST
- SF 94107 668-B3
- VAL 94590 529-J3
400 MRTZ 94553 571-F5
MISTAYA CT
1400 SUNV 94087 832-C4
MISTFLOWER AV
6000 NWK 94560 752-F7
MISTFLOWER DR
800 SJS 95122 854-F1
MISTLETOE DR
2400 HAY 94545 731-G1
MISTLETOE RD
200 LGTS 95030 872-J3
MISTRAL CT
700 DNVL 94506 653-J4
MISTRAL ST
- SF 94110 667-J2
MISTRAL WY
200 VAL 94591 550-E2
MISTY CT
100 VAL 94589 510-D5
2000 PIT 94565 574-A4
MISTY LN
1000 BLMT 94002 769-D2
3400 CNCD 94519 592-H1
MISTY RD
- NVTO 94945 526-G1
MISTY TER
- FRMT 94555 752-C3
MISTY GLEN CT
- SJS 95111 854-J5
MISTY SPRING CT
900 SRMN 94583 673-H3
MISTY WILLOW CT
6700 SJS 95120 894-F2
MITCHEL DR
- DBLN 94568 694-B3
MITCHELL AV
- ALA 94501 649-F6
100 SSF 94080 708-A4
400 SLN 94577 671-B7
16800 LGTS 95032 873-C6
MITCHELL BLVD
- SRFL 94903 566-E2
MITCHELL CT
100 VAL 94589 510-B7
1000 CMBL 95128 853-E4
MITCHELL DR
2700 WLCK 94598 612-G1
MITCHELL LN
400 PA 94301 790-H5
5200 SJS 95111 875-B3
MITCHELL PL
27400 HAY 94544 712-B6
MITCHELL RD
- MrnC 94965 626-E6
MITCHELL ST
1400 OAK 94601 650-B7
MITCHELL WY
900 CCCo 94803 569-D7
1400 RDWC 94061 789-J3
MITCHELL CANYON CT
5800 CLAY 94517 593-G7
MITCHELL CANYON PL
5800 CLAY 94517 593-G7
MITCHELL CANYON RD
- CCCo 94517 613-G2
500 CLAY 94517 613-G2
700 CLAY 94517 593-G7
N MITCHELL CYN RD
1400 CLAY 94517 593-G6
MITCHS LN
2400 ANT 94509 575-D6
MITCHUM DR
200 PIT 94565 574-C2
MITEY MITE LN
100 RCH 94803 589-F2
MITRA ST
1500 LVMR 94550 716-C1
MITTEN RD
800 BURL 94010 728-D3
MITTON CT
3500 SJS 95148 835-F7
MITTON DR
2900 SJS 95148 835-E7
MITTY WY
4900 SJS 95129 852-J2
MITZI DR
4100 SJS 95117 853-A3
MITZI DR
4100 SJS 95129 853-A3
MIWOK CT
400 FRMT 94539 773-J5
MIWOK DR
- NVTO 94947 525-J4
- SANS 94960 566-B5
6000 SJS 95123 874-H6
MIWOK WY
- MLV 94941 606-G5
3000 CLAY 94517 593-H5
MIXTEC CT
1200 FRMT 94539 773-G4
MIYUKI AV
- SJS 95119 875-D5
MIYUKI DR
1600 SJS 95193 875-C5
5700 SJS 95119 875-C5
MIZNER CT
- BEN 94510 551-B1
MIZPAH ST
- SF 94131 667-F6
MLISS LN
- SRFL 94901 586-H4
MOAB DR
38300 FRMT 94536 753-D1
MOANA CT
800 PA 94306 811-C5
MOANA WY
200 PCFA 94044 707-A6
200 PCFA 94044 706-J6
MOBILE CT
34600 FRMT 94555 752-D2
MOBILE DR
100 CCCo 94553 572-C7
MOCCASIN CT
1100 CLAY 94517 593-H6
5000 ANT 94509 595-G4
MOCCASIN ST
32700 UNC 94587 732-F3
MOCCASIN WY
5000 ANT 94509 595-G4
MOCHO CT
1300 SJS 95121 854-J2
MOCHO ST
900 LVMR 94550 715-F2
MOCINE AV
26000 HAY 94544 712-A5
MOCKINGBIRD CT
- VAL 94591 510-J5
- NVTO 94947 525-G4
1100 SJS 95120 894-H4
MOCKINGBIRD LN
700 AlaC 94566 714-E6
700 PLE 94566 714-D6
800 PA 94306 811-B4
800 SUNV 94087 832-A2
26400 HAY 94544 711-H6
MOCKINGBIRD PL
1800 DNVL 94526 653-B6
MOCKINGBIRD WY
4200 FRMT 94555 732-B7
MOCKINGBIRD HILL LN
1100 SJS 95120 894-G5
10600 SCIC 95120 894-G5
MOCKINGBIRD HILL RD
2500 WLCK 94596 612-B3
MOCKING PLACE WY
1600 SJS 95121 855-B4
MOCKORANGE CT
6200 NWK 94560 752-G7
MOCOCO RD
- MRTZ 94553 571-F1
100 MRTZ 94553 551-G7
MODENA CT
5200 PLE 94588 694-A6
MODESTO AV
2800 OAK 94619 650-F7
MODESTO ST
3800 AlaC 94546 692-A5
MODOC AV
- SF 94112 687-E1
100 OAK 94618 630-C6
1300 MLPK 94025 770-J7
5200 RCH 94804 609-B3
MODOC CT
500 SJS 95123 874-H6
1800 ANT 94509 575-G5
4100 CNCD 94521 593-A3
MODOC PL
- NVTO 94947 526-E7
200 PCFA 94044 727-B2
400 LVMR 94550 695-D6
MODOC RD
- ORIN 94563 610-G2
MODOC ST
700 VAL 94591 530-D4
900 BERK 94707 609-F6
MODOC WY
39600 FRMT 94538 753-B6
MODRED DR
3100 SJS 95127 814-H7
MOEN CT
7300 SJS 95139 895-F1
MOESER LN
6300 ELCR 94530 609-D2
MOFFAT ST
1000 SJS 95002 813-B1
MOFFETT BLVD
100 MTVW 94043 811-J4
400 SCIC 94043 811-J4
500 MTVW 94043 812-A3
500 SCIC 94043 812-A2
MOFFETT CIR
1000 PA 94303 791-D5
MOFFETT PARK CT
900 SUNV 94089 812-H3
MOFFETT PARK DR
200 SUNV 94089 812-J2
1300 SUNV 94089 813-A2
W MOFFETT PARK DR
100 SUNV 94089 812-E4
MOFFITT ST
- SF 94131 667-G5
MOFFO CT
1400 SJS 95121 854-J3
MOHAR CT
300 PLHL 94523 592-B1
MOHAVE COM
100 FRMT 94539 773-H6
MOHAVE CT
- CMAD 94925 586-G6
MOHAVE DR
46600 FRMT 94539 773-H5
MOHAVE TER
100 FRMT 94539 773-H6
MOHAWK AV
- CMAD 94925 586-G7
MOHAWK CIR
2700 SRMN 94583 673-D5
MOHAWK CT
2500 WLCK 94598 612-H3
MOHAWK DR
800 LVMR 94550 695-E6
1900 CCCo 94549 591-H6
2000 PLHL 94523 591-H6
5900 SJS 95123 874-H6
MOHAWK RIVER ST
4100 FRMT 94555 752-E2
MOHICAN CT
800 WLCK 94598 612-H4
1800 FRMT 94539 773-G3
MOHICAN DR
600 SJS 95123 874-H5
MOHICAN ST
32400 HAY 94544 732-F3
MOHICAN WY
800 RDWC 94062 789-G2
MOHR AV
- AlaC 94588 694-E7
3300 PLE 94588 694-D7
3700 PLE 94566 694-D7
4100 PLE 94566 714-E1
MOHR CT
1400 CNCD 94518 592-E7
MOHR DR
24400 AlaC 94545 711-F5
24400 HAY 94545 711-F5
MOHR LN
900 CNCD 94518 592-E6
1000 CNCD 94520 592-E6
MOIRA GLEN CT
1700 SJS 95112 854-F1
MOISO LN
100 PLHL 94523 592-C6
MOITOZA LN
100 TBRN 94920 607-E7
MOJAVE AV
600 LVMR 94550 715-E2
MOJAVE CT
900 WLCK 94598 612-H4
MOJAVE DR
6200 SJS 95120 874-D7
6200 SJS 95120 894-D1
MOJAVE ST
- SF 94110 668-A5
- SF 94110 667-J5
MOJONERA CT
100 LGTS 95030 873-C3
MOKELUMNE AV
6400 OAK 94605 670-H1
MOKELUMNE DR
1200 ANT 94509 595-F4
MOKELUMNE PL
1200 SJS 95120 874-C6
MOLAD CT
1000 CNCD 94518 592-J6
MOLAKAI CIR
200 UNC 94587 732-C6
MOLERA CT
4100 ANT 94509 595-G2
MOLIMO DR
- SF 94127 667-E5
200 SF 94127 667-E5
MOLINA CT
- SRMN 94583 673-C3
200 VAL 94591 530-F5
35800 FRMT 94536 752-F2
MOLINA ST
100 VAL 94591 530-F5
MOLINARO ST
3100 SCL 95054 813-E7
MOLINO AV
- MLV 94941 606-C3
300 MrnC 94941 606-D4
400 SUNV 94086 812-C7
400 SUNV 94086 832-C1
MOLITAS RD
100 DNVL 94526 653-C2
MOLITOR RD
1500 BLMT 94002 769-F2
MOLLER DR
4100 PLE 94566 714-E1
MOLLER RANCH DR
- PLE 94586 693-G7
MOLLIE CIR
5400 LVMR 94550 696-C4
MOLLIE CT
5600 LVMR 94550 696-C4
19700 AlaC 94552 692-F2
MOLLIE TER
- FRMT 94536 753-C2
MOLLINAR CT
6000 FRMT 94555 752-B6
MOLOKAI CT
- SRMN 94583 653-E7
MOLONEY CT
- SMCo 94062 769-H7
E MOLTKE ST
- DALY 94014 687-C4
W MOLTKE ST
- DALY 94014 687-C4
MOLTON AV
- SCAR 94070 769-E3
MOLTZEN DR
7400 CPTO 95014 852-D3
MONA WY
3500 SJS 95008 853-C4
3500 CMBL 95008 853-C4
3500 SJS 95130 853-C4
MONACO AV
400 UNC 94587 732-J5
MONACO COM
34700 FRMT 94555 752-D2
MONACO CT
- DNVL 94506 653-H5
100 PLE 94566 714-D4
600 WLCK 94598 612-G3
MONACO DR
100 RDWC 94065 749-J5
2300 SJS 95124 873-E3
4900 PLE 94566 714-D4
MONADNOCK WY
5900 OAK 94605 670-G1
MONA MARIE CT
23400 AlaC 94541 692-D7
MONAN ST
10900 OAK 94605 671-D4
MONARCH DR
- BSBN 94005 687-J5
MONARCH PL
2500 UNC 94587 732-C4
MONARCH TER
43600 FRMT 94538 773-E3
MONARCH RIDGE DR
500 WLCK 94596 611-H3
MONASTERIO CT
- SRMN 94583 673-C3
MONASTERY WY
700 SCL 95050 833-D5
MONCADA WY
- MrnC 94901 567-A7
- SF 94127 667-C6
- MrnC 94901 566-J7
MONDANA PL
1400 PIT 94565 574-G5
MONDIGO AV
2000 SJS 95122 834-J7
MONET CIR
4100 SJS 95136 874-H1
MONET PL
4300 SJS 95136 874-H1
MONETA CT
- SF 94112 687-E2
MONETA WY
- SF 94112 687-E2
200 CMBL 95008 853-G6
MONFERINO DR
600 SJS 95112 834-C3
MONFREDO DR
1000 PIT 94565 574-B2
MONICA LN
500 CMBL 95008 853-E4
700 SJS 95008 853-E4
1000 CMBL 95128 853-E4
MONICA PL
100 VAL 94591 530-E3
MONIKA LN
3200 AlaC 94541 692-C6
MONITOR CT
2200 SJS 95125 854-D7
MONITOR PASS CT
100 VAL 94589 509-J6
MONITOR PASS WY
5200 ANT 94509 595-E4
MONIVEA PL
- PLHL 94523 591-J5
MONKTON CT
3000 SJS 95148 855-C2
MONMOUTH CT
500 WLCK 94598 612-J2
3200 PLE 94588 694-E6
MONMOUTH DR
200 MPS 95035 794-D7
MONMOUTH PL
3600 FRMT 94538 773-E1
MONO AV
1500 AlaC 94578 691-E4
2200 ELCR 94530 589-B7
MONO DR
1900 MRTZ 94553 572-A7
MONO LN
- SANS 94960 566-A6
MONO ST
- BSBN 94005 688-A6
- SF 94114 667-F3
200 RCH 94801 588-B6
22700 HAY 94541 711-G2
MONO WY
100 SCL 95051 832-H7
W MONO WY
- MLV 94941 606-B3
MONO LAKE CT
5900 SJS 95123 874-G7
MONO LAKE DR
32700 FRMT 94555 732-C6
MONO LAKE LN
32700 FRMT 94555 732-B6
MONONA DR
- CMAD 94925 586-G7
MONONA LN
- CMAD 94925 586-G7
MONOSTORY CT
2100 PIT 94565 574-A4
MONROE AV
- DBLN 94568 694-C3
1300 SMTO 94401 729-A7
2000 BLMT 94002 749-C7
3400 LFYT 94549 611-F6
3700 FRMT 94536 753-A4
6000 OAK 94618 630-A6
MONROE CT
- LGTS 95030 873-B6
- NVTO 94947 526-B5
- ORIN 94563 631-B2
3000 ANT 94509 575-A7
3400 LFYT 94549 611-G5
MONROE DR
100 PA 94306 811-D3
100 MTVW 94040 811-D3
MONROE ST
- SUNV 94086 832-J2
- SCL 95050 833-D2
- SCL 95128 833-E5
100 RDWC 94063 770-B6
400 SJS 95128 833-E7
500 SJS 95050 833-E7
1000 ALB 94804 609-D7
1000 ALB 94706 609-D7
2300 SCL 95051 833-A2
3200 SCL 95051 832-J2
S MONROE ST
300 SJS 95128 853-E1
500 SJS 95050 853-E1
E MONROE WY
- CNCD 94521 593-D2
MONROVIA DR
1700 SJS 95122 855-A2
1800 SJS 95121 855-A2
MONROVIA ST
21500 CPTO 95014 852-B3
32900 UNC 94587 752-A1
MONSANTO WY
1700 CCCo 94553 572-C3

BAY AREA
INDEX

MONSERAT AV — 1998 BAY AREA STREET INDEX — MORGAN DR 967

BAY AREA

STREET — Block City ZIP Pg-Grid

MONSERAT AV
2300 BLMT 94002 769-B1
MONSON LN
- LFYT 94549 611-E6
MONTAGE CT
1800 SJS 95131 814-C4
MONTAGUE AV
500 SLN 94577 691-A3
4800 FRMT 94555 752-C1
MONTAGUE EXWY
- MPS 95035 814-B3
900 SJS 95132 814-B3
1300 SJS 95131 814-B3
1300 SJS 95131 813-H5
1300 MPS 95035 813-H5
MONTAGUE EXWY Rt#-G4
- SJS 95134 813-F5
400 SCL 95054 813-D6
400 SCL 95134 813-F5
600 MPS 95035 813-F5
600 SJS 95131 813-F5
1500 SCIC 95134 813-F5
W MONTAGUE EXWY
- MPS 95035 814-A4
MONTAGUE PL
- SF 94133 648-A4
MONTAGUE RD
4800 FRMT 94555 752-C2
MONTAIR CT
100 DNVL 94526 652-H3
MONTAIR DR
- DNVL 94526 652-G3
MONTAIR PL
- DNVL 94526 652-H3
2800 UNC 94587 732-A4
MONTAIR WY
2800 UNC 94587 732-A4
MONTALBAN DR
- FRMT 94536 733-A7
1400 SJS 95120 874-A7
1400 SJS 95120 894-A1
MONTALTO DR
1500 MTVW 94040 811-H7
MONTALVIN DR
- CCCo 94806 569-A5
400 CCCo 94806 568-J5
MONTALVO AV
- SF 94116 667-C4
MONTALVO CT
5400 PLE 94588 693-F6
MONTALVO DR
5900 SJS 95123 874-G6
MONTALVO LN
20400 SAR 95070 872-D4
MONTALVO RD
100 SMCo 94062 769-E7
14700 SAR 95070 872-E4
MONTALVO HTS CT
15200 SAR 95070 872-D4
MONTALVO HTS DR
20400 SAR 95070 872-D4
MONTALVO OAKS
20400 SAR 95070 872-D3
MONTANA CT
6400 SJS 95120 894-E1
MONTANA DR
100 DNVL 94526 633-C6
1000 PLE 94566 714-G3
1300 CNCD 94521 593-F6
MONTANA LN
- SMCo 94025 790-D5
MONTANA ST
- RCH 94801 608-D1
- SF 94112 687-D1
200 SF 94132 687-D1
1800 OAK 94602 650-D4
MONTANA WY
26400 HAY 94544 712-A5
MONTANA VISTA
600 FRMT 94539 773-H1
MONTANYA CT
100 WLCK 94596 612-B3
MONTARA CT
- PTLV 94028 810-D6
MONTARA DR
4400 ANT 94509 595-H2
MONTAUK CT
19600 SAR 95070 872-F2
MONTAUK DR
19500 SAR 95070 872-F2
MONTA VISTA AV
2600 ELCR 94530 589-C6
MONT BLANC CT
100 DNVL 94526 653-D6
MONTCALM AV
6200 NWK 94560 752-D6
MONTCALM ST
- SF 94110 668-A4
300 SF 94110 667-J4
MONTCLAIR AV
- DALY 94015 686-J5
200 SJS 95116 834-G2
400 OAK 94606 650-A4
600 OAK 94610 650-A4
MONTCLAIR CIR
1900 WLCK 94596 612-A3
MONTCLAIR CT
100 LGTS 95030 872-J3
1000 LVMR 94550 716-A1
1900 WLCK 94596 612-A3
2500 PIN 94564 569-G6
MONTCLAIR DR
300 SCL 95051 832-H7
1900 WLCK 94596 612-A3
MONTCLAIR RD
100 LGTS 95030 873-A3
200 LGTS 95030 872-J3
400 SAR 95070 872-J3
MONTCLAIR TER
- SF 94109 647-J3
MONTCLAIRE COM
100 FRMT 94539 773-J2
MONTCLAIRE CT
- FRMT 94539 773-J2
23200 LALT 94024 831-H4
MONTCLAIRE DR
100 FRMT 94539 773-J2
MONTCLAIRE PL
100 SRMN 94583 673-F6
1400 LALT 94024 831-H4
MONTCLAIRE TER
300 FRMT 94539 773-J2
MONTCLAIRE WY
11400 LALT 94024 831-H4
MONTCREST PL
400 DNVL 94526 652-H2
MONTE AV
- PDMT 94611 630-B7
MONTE CT
2000 MPS 95035 814-E1
21800 CPTO 95014 832-B7
40300 FRMT 94538 753-C6
MONTE DR
1100 MPS 95035 814-E1
MONTEAGLE DR
1200 SJS 95127 835-A4
MONTE ALEGRE
- ROSS 94957 586-C1
MONTEBELLO AV
100 MTVW 94043 811-G3
MONTEBELLO CT
3000 CNCD 94518 592-H2
MONTEBELLO DR
- DALY 94015 707-A1
MONTE BELLO RD
- PA 94304 830-G6
MONTEBELLO WY
- LGTS 95030 893-A1
MONTEBELLO OAKS CT
1500 LALT 94024 831-J3
MONTE BUENA AV
3200 SPAB 94806 588-J1
MONTE CARLO AV
300 UNC 94587 732-J5
MONTE CARLO WY
100 DNVL 94506 653-H5
1800 SCIC 95125 853-H6
MONTE CARLO PARK CT
4600 FRMT 94538 773-D2
MONTECELLO AV
- PDMT 94611 630-A7
MONTECELLO CT
300 CCCo 94595 632-B1
MONTECELLO DR
200 WLCK 94595 632-C1
200 CCCo 94595 632-C1
MONTECELLO ST
- CCCo 94565 573-H2
MONTECILLO RD
- SRFL 94903 566-B2
MONTE CIMAS AV
- MrnC 94965 606-B3
MONTECITO AV
- SF 94112 667-D6
100 OAK 94610 649-H3
100 PCFA 94044 706-J6
1200 MTVW 94043 811-G3
2200 OAK 94612 649-H3
MONTECITO CIR
1700 LVMR 94550 695-E5
MONTECITO CRES
100 CCCo 94596 612-A4
MONTECITO CT
- SJS 95135 855-G3
MONTECITO DR
- CMAD 94925 586-F7
- DNVL 94526 652-J2
300 CMAD 94925 606-F1
3200 SJS 95135 855-G3
36500 FRMT 94536 753-A1
36700 FRMT 94536 752-J1
MONTECITO LN
1300 PIN 94564 569-E5
MONTECITO RD
- MrnC 94901 586-J1
- WDSD 94062 809-J5
100 MrnC 94901 587-A1
100 MrnC 94901 567-A7
MONTECITO WY
300 MPS 95035 793-H4
1800 BURL 94010 728-B5
MONTE CORVINO WY
1600 BURL 94010 728-C5
MONTE CREST CT
- CCCo 94595 632-C1
MONTE CRESTA AV
- RCH 94803 589-B4
- RCH 94805 589-B4
- OAK 94611 649-J1
6300 RCH 94803 589-B4
MONTE CRESTA DR
- PLHL 94523 592-B7
- WLCK 94596 592-B7
2600 BLMT 94002 749-B7
2600 BLMT 94002 769-A1
MONTE CRESTA WY
2800 SJS 95132 814-E4
MONTE DIABLO AV
- SMTO 94401 748-J1
600 SMTO 94401 728-J7
900 SMTO 94401 729-A7
MONTEGO
1200 WLCK 94598 612-E4
MONTEGO BAY
100 ALA 94502 669-H7
MONTEGO CT
6400 SJS 95120 894-A1
MONTEGO DR
100 HER 94547 570-C6
200 DNVL 94526 653-A4
200 DNVL 94526 652-J4
2600 SJS 95120 894-B1
2600 SCIC 95120 894-B1
MONTEGO LN
- FCTY 94404 749-E6
- SMCo 94061 790-B4
MONTEGO PL
- DNVL 94526 653-A4
MONTEGO KEY
- MrnC 94949 526-G6
MONTEIRA LN
500 CCCo 94553 591-E2
MONTEITH DR
1300 VAL 94590 530-C3
MONTELEGRE DR
1400 SJS 95120 874-A7
MONTELENA CT
- WDSD 94062 809-G1
MONTELENA DR
3100 SJS 95135 855-E2
MONTE LINDO CT
2600 SJS 95121 855-D3
MONTELL ST
- OAK 94611 649-J1
MONTELLANO CT
1600 SJS 95120 894-A1
MONTELLANO DR
1500 SJS 95120 874-A7
MONTE MAR DR
- SAUS 94965 627-A3
MONTEMAR WY
1600 SCIC 95125 853-H5
MONTE MARIA AV
1300 NVTO 94947 526-B6
MONTERA CT
3700 CCCo 94803 589-B3
MONTEREY
- MTVW 94043 812-A2
- MTVW 94043 811-J2
MONTEREY AV
- SANS 94960 566-C6
400 LGTS 95030 873-A6
1000 BERK 94707 609-F7
1000 FCTY 94404 749-F5
1400 BERK 94706 609-F7
2000 SMCo 94025 790-C6
2100 MRTZ 94553 571-F4
2100 SCL 95051 833-A2
2100 CCCo 94553 571-F4
5900 CCCo 94805 589-B5
MONTEREY BLVD
- SF 94131 667-E6
400 SF 94127 667-E6
400 SF 94112 667-E6
600 SF 94127 667-C6
600 SF 94112 667-D6
2300 OAK 94611 650-E2
2400 OAK 94602 650-E2
3400 SLN 94578 691-B5
3500 OAK 94619 650-G5
MONTEREY CIR
900 SJS 95138 875-F6
2000 ALA 94501 649-E6
MONTEREY CT
- UNC 94545 751-J1
- CCCo 94506 654-B7
800 SLN 94578 691-B5
1900 SCL 95051 833-A3
3500 CNCD 94519 592-J1
11200 CPTO 95014 852-B3
MONTEREY DR
- UNC 94545 751-J1
- AMCN 94589 509-H1
- DALY 94015 687-A6
- MrnC 94920 606-J4
- WLCK 94596 612-D6
1000 ANT 94509 575-B7
1500 SBRN 94066 707-D7
1600 LVMR 94550 696-A4
1700 SBRN 94066 727-E1
6400 DBLN 94568 694-A3
MONTEREY HWY Rt#-82
- SJS 95111 854-F5
- SJS 95125 854-D2
200 SCIC 95111 854-F5
700 SJS 95112 854-D2
700 SJS 95110 854-D2
3700 SJS 95136 854-F5
4100 SJS 95136 874-H1
4100 SJS 95111 874-H1
4700 SJS 95136 875-A2
4700 SJS 95111 875-A2
5100 SJS 95123 875-A2
5200 SJS 95193 875-A2
MONTEREY LN
100 CCCo 94506 654-B7
MONTEREY PL
300 LALT 94022 811-D6
MONTEREY RD
100 PCFA 94044 706-J3
200 PCFA 94044 707-A3
5300 SJS 95111 875-C3
5500 SJS 95138 875-C3
5800 SJS 95139 875-C3
5800 SJS 95139 895-H1
5800 SJS 95137 875-C3
5800 SJS 95137 895-H1
5900 SCIC 95137 895-H1
MONTEREY ST
- MLBR 94030 728-B2
- VAL 94590 530-A3
100 BSBN 94005 688-A6
1300 RCH 94804 609-B3
2600 SMTO 94403 749-A6
MONTEREY TER
- ORIN 94563 611-A7
- ORIN 94563 610-J7
- ORIN 94563 631-A1
- SANS 94960 566-C6
MONTEREY WY
39200 FRMT 94538 753-A5
MONTEREY VIEJO
4400 UNC 94587 731-H5
MONTERO AV
1300 BURL 94010 728-C6
MONTERO RD
- HAY 94544 712-A4
MONTE ROSA DR
600 MLPK 94025 790-D7
600 MLPK 94025 810-D1
MONTE SERENO DR
1800 CCCo 94526 633-B5
MONTE SERENO PL
100 CCCo 94526 633-C6
MONTE SERENO TER
- FRMT 94539 774-A7
- FRMT 94539 794-B1
MONTE SOL TER
400 MPS 95035 793-G3
MONTE SUNSET DR
20700 SCIC 95120 894-H1
MONTEVAL CT
1600 SJS 95120 873-J7
MONTEVAL LN
1500 SJS 95120 874-A7
MONTEVAL PL
1500 SJS 95120 874-A7
MONTE VEDA DR
- ORIN 94563 630-J3
MONTE VERANO CT
- SJS 95116 834-H3
MONTE VERDE CT
1200 LALT 94024 831-H4
6000 AlaC 94552 692-D2
MONTE VERDE DR
900 PCFA 94044 726-J5
2300 PIN 94564 569-H7
5700 CCCo 94803 589-F1
MONTEVERDE DR
5900 SJS 95120 874-A7
6100 SJS 95120 894-A1
MONTE VERDE LN
3200 SJS 95135 855-G3
MONTE VERDE WY
100 VAL 94589 530-C1
MONTEVIDEO CIR
- FRMT 94539 753-H6
MONTEVIDEO CT
4700 UNC 94587 731-J6
42600 FRMT 94539 753-H6
MONTEVIDEO DR
2200 PIT 94565 574-A4
2200 PIT 94565 573-J4
2900 SRMN 94583 673-E5
MONTEVIDEO LN
1600 SJS 95127 835-A5
MONTEVIDEO RD
- FRMT 94539 753-J6
MONTEVIDEO WY
- SRFL 94903 566-D1
MONTE VILLA CT
100 CMBL 95008 873-E2
MONTEVINO DR
700 PLE 94566 714-H4
5800 SJS 95123 874-G5
MONTE VISTA
- MTVW 94043 812-A2
- MrnC 94904 586-E3
1200 BEN 94510 550-J3
MONTE VISTA AV
- ATN 94027 790-C4
- LKSP 94939 586-F6
- MLV 94941 606-B3
- NVTO 94947 525-J3
- OAK 94611 649-J1
- VAL 94590 530-B3
400 OAK 94610 649-J1
1200 MRTZ 94553 571-D4
3200 ALA 94501 670-C3
MONTE VISTA CT
- PLHL 94523 592-B7
1200 MRTZ 94553 571-H7
MONTE VISTA DR
- SF 94132 667-B6
2300 PIN 94564 569-H7
15400 SAR 95070 872-G4
24900 AlaC 94545 711-F6
MONTEVISTA LN
100 DALY 94015 707-C2
MONTE VISTA RD
- ORIN 94563 610-E6
100 SCAR 94070 769-H2
MONTE VISTA RIDGE RD
200 ORIN 94563 610-E6
MONTEWOOD DR
18600 SAR 95070 872-H5
MONTEZUMA CT
600 WLCK 94598 612-E4
MONTEZUMA DR
600 PCFA 94044 726-H4
2200 SJS 95008 853-B7
MONTEZUMA ST
- SF 94110 667-J4
800 PIT 94565 574-D2
MONTFIELD PL
700 CNCD 94518 592-H7
MONTFORD AV
- MrnC 94941 606-D4
- MLV 94941 606-D4
MONTFORD CT
1800 SJS 95132 814-E3
MONTFORD PL
300 MrnC 94941 606-D4
MONTFORD ST
- MLV 94941 606-E4
- MrnC 94941 606-E4
MONTGOMERY AV
900 SBRN 94066 707-J5
1200 SMCo 94061 790-B3
2500 CNCD 94519 572-G6
20900 AlaC 94541 691-G7
21500 HAY 94541 691-G7
21700 HAY 94541 711-H1
E MONTGOMERY AV
4800 RCH 94804 609-A2
MONTGOMERY BEND
6000 SJS 95135 855-H6
MONTGOMERY CT
6000 SJS 95135 855-H6
MONTGOMERY DR
3200 SCL 95054 813-B7
MONTGOMERY LN
800 SCAR 94070 769-H2
5400 SJS 95135 855-H6
MONTGOMERY PL
6100 SJS 95135 855-H6
34400 FRMT 94555 732-E7
MONTGOMERY PL E
6000 SJS 95135 855-H6
MONTGOMERY PL S
6000 SJS 95135 855-H6
MONTGOMERY PL W
6000 SJS 95135 855-H6
MONTGOMERY ST
- LGTS 95030 873-A6
- SF 94108 648-A5
- SF 94104 648-A5
- SF 94129 647-D4
100 SRMN 94583 673-E3
500 SF 94111 648-A5
800 MTVW 94041 811-J6
800 SF 94133 648-A4
900 SCAR 94070 769-G3
1100 SF 94133 648-A3
1600 SF 94111 648-A3
4100 OAK 94611 649-J2
4400 OAK 94611 630-A7
21800 HAY 94541 711-H1
MONTGOMERY ST Rt#-82
- SJS 95110 834-A7
N MONTGOMERY ST
100 SJS 95110 834-A6
S MONTGOMERY ST Rt#-82
- SJS 95110 834-A7
- SJS 95113 834-A7
MONTGOMERY CORNER
6000 SJS 95135 855-H6
MONTI CIR
400 PLHL 94523 592-A5
MONTI CT
- PLHL 94523 592-B5
MONTICELLO AV
100 PLHL 94523 592-B7
200 SJS 95125 854-D4
2300 OAK 94601 670-E1
2400 OAK 94601 650-F7
2600 OAK 94619 650-F7
MONTICELLO CT
- WDSD 94062 789-E3
MONTICELLO RD
1100 LFYT 94549 611-E5
1700 SMCo 94402 748-F7
1700 SMCo 94402 768-G1
MONTICELLO ST
- SF 94127 667-C7
- SF 94132 687-C1
600 HAY 94544 712-C6
MONTICELLO TER
100 FRMT 94539 753-H7
MONTICELLO WY
2400 SCL 95051 832-J2
MONTIERRA PL
3200 SJS 95135 855-G3
MONTIN CT
1600 WLCK 94596 612-B2
MONTIVIDEO CT
- SRMN 94583 673-E5
MONTJOY CT
28100 HAY 94544 712-A7
MONTMARTRE PARK CT
4600 FRMT 94538 773-D3
MONTMORENCY CT
4300 SJS 95118 874-C2
MONTMORENCY DR
1200 SJS 95118 874-B2
MONTORI CT
- PLE 94566 715-D6
MONTORI WY
- PLE 94566 715-D6
MONTORO CT
1400 SJS 95120 874-B7
MONTORO DR
6000 SJS 95120 874-B7
MONTOYA AV
1100 SPAB 94805 589-A4
MONTOYA CT
2100 PIT 94565 574-A3
MONTOYA TER
- UNC 94587 732-E4
MONTOYA WY
- DNVL 94526 653-F4
MONTPELIER CT
3100 PLE 94588 694-E6
MONTPELIER DR
2300 SJS 95116 834-G2
MONTPELIER SQ
- CNCD 94518 592-F4
MONTPERE WY
18300 SAR 95070 872-H1
MONTREAL CIR
3600 CNCD 94520 572-F5
MONTREAL CT
4700 SJS 95130 853-A7
MONTREAL DR
4700 SJS 95130 853-A7
4800 SJS 95130 852-J7
MONTREAL ST
15400 SLN 94579 691-A7
15500 SLN 94579 711-A1
MONTROSE AV
- DALY 94015 687-A5
700 PA 94303 811-F1
43200 FRMT 94538 773-E2
MONTROSE DR
1200 SLN 94577 691-D1
1700 CNCD 94519 593-A1
MONTROSE PL
3600 LVMR 94550 695-J6
MONTROSE RD
- BERK 94707 609-G5
MONTROSE ST
13000 SAR 95070 852-H7
MONTROSE WY
1600 SJS 95124 874-A3
MONTSERRAT DR
- RDWC 94065 749-J5
MONTURA WY
100 NVTO 94949 546-C1
MONTWOOD CIR
300 SMCo 94061 790-B4
MONTWOOD WY
- OAK 94605 671-C5
MONTY CIR
800 SCL 95050 833-C5
MONUMENT BLVD
1200 CNCD 94520 592-E5
2000 PLHL 94523 592-E5
MONUMENT CT
500 FRMT 94539 794-A2
2600 CNCD 94520 592-F4
MONUMENT PZ
- PLHL 94523 592-C6
MONUMENT ST
24000 HAY 94545 711-F4
MONUMENT WY
- CNCD 94518 592-G4
- CNCD 94520 592-G4
- SF 94117 667-F2
MONZA CT
- DNVL 94506 653-D2
- DNVL 94526 653-D2
MONZAL AV
5900 OAK 94611 630-C6
MOODY CT
- SRFL 94901 566-D6
26800 LAH 94022 830-J2
MOODY RD
25300 LAH 94022 831-A3
26200 LAH 94022 830-H3
26200 SCIC 95014 831-A3
26200 SCIC 95014 830-H2
MOODY WY
2200 HAY 94545 711-E5
MOODY SPRINGS CT
1200 LAH 94022 831-B3
MOON CT
900 LFYT 94549 611-E6
1100 MPS 95035 814-A2
MOON LN
14000 LAH 94022 810-H6
MOON BEAM DR
- MTVW 94043 811-J3
MOONBEAM WY
1100 MPS 95035 814-A2
MOONEY AV
700 AlaC 94578 691-E5
700 AlaC 94580 691-E5
MOONEY CT
34600 FRMT 94555 752-D1
MOONFLOWER CT
4100 SJS 95135 855-F3
MOONFLOWER WY
5300 LVMR 94550 696-C4
MOON GATE CT
- PCFA 94044 707-A2
MOON GATE PL
1000 SJS 95120 894-F2
MOON GLOW CT
700 SJS 95123 874-F3
MOONLIGHT CIR
1300 MPS 95035 813-J3
MOONLIGHT COM
5400 FRMT 94555 752-C3
MOONLIGHT CT
- SSF 94080 707-E5
MOONLIGHT WY
1100 MPS 95035 813-J2
MOONLITE PL
2600 SCL 95051 833-B4
MOONRAKER CT
100 VAL 94590 550-B2
MOONRAKER DR
100 VAL 94590 550-B1
MOONSAIL LN
1200 FCTY 94404 749-H3
MOONSTAR CT
3000 SJS 95148 835-B5
MOONSTONE CT
- HER 94547 569-G4
5000 SJS 95136 874-E2
MOORBROOK DR
2600 SJS 95132 814-F6
MOORE CT
- ALA 94502 669-J6
- SRMN 94583 673-E5
100 SBRN 94066 707-E7
2400 PIN 94564 569-J7
2400 PIN 94564 589-J1
MOORE DR
6600 OAK 94611 630-G7
38600 FRMT 94536 753-C2
MOORE PL
- SF 94109 647-J4
MOORE RD
100 WDSD 94062 789-J6
300 WDSD 94062 790-A6
MOORE ST
2400 PIN 94564 569-J7
MOORES AV
5600 NWK 94560 752-H7
6100 NWK 94560 772-G1
MOORGLEN CT
2300 SJS 95133 834-F2
MOORING LN
- DALY 94014 687-E6
MOORING RD
- SRFL 94901 586-H2
- MrnC 94901 586-H2
MOORLAND ST
200 VAL 94590 530-C2
400 VAL 94589 530-C2
MOORPARK AV
1500 SJS 95117 853-B2
2000 SJS 95128 853-E2
2200 SCIC 95128 853-E2
4200 SJS 95129 853-B2
4600 SJS 95129 852-J2
MOORPARK ST
800 OAK 94603 670-H7
MOORPARK WY
- MTVW 94041 812-A6
MOOSE WY
1200 PIT 94565 574-E2
MORA CT
1700 SCIC 94024 831-G4
MORA DR
700 SCIC 94024 831-G4
2200 MTVW 94040 811-F3
11200 SCIC 95014 831-F5
MORA LN
- NVTO 94947 526-A5
MORADA CT
41300 FRMT 94539 753-G5
MORADO WY
2200 PLE 94566 714-G2
MORAES CT
1100 SJS 95127 835-B3
MORAGA AV
- SF 94129 647-D4
- SF 94129 647-D4
100 OAK 94611 630-A7
100 PDMT 94611 630-A7
800 PDMT 94618 630-D7
900 OAK 94618 630-D7
5800 SJS 95123 874-F5
6100 OAK 94611 650-D1
MORAGA BLVD
3300 LFYT 94549 611-F6
MORAGA CT
- ORIN 94563 630-J3
900 PA 94303 791-E6
MORAGA DR
500 LVMR 94550 715-E2
700 SLN 94578 691-B4
800 MTVW 94041 812-A7
2500 PIN 94564 569-G7
MORAGA RD
100 MRGA 94556 631-E7
600 LFYT 94549 631-E1
700 LFYT 94549 611-F7
2600 SPAB 94806 588-J2
MORAGA ST
200 SF 94122 667-A3
1100 SCL 95051 833-A4
2800 SF 94122 666-H3
MORAGA TR
- LFYT 94549 611-G7
MORAGA WY
- ORIN 94563 630-H1
200 SJS 95119 875-C7
400 ORIN 94563 631-A3
700 MRGA 94556 631-E7
MORAGA VALLEY LN
- MRGA 94556 631-D6
MORAGA VIA
- ORIN 94563 631-A2
MORA GLEN DR
23100 SCIC 94024 831-G5
MORA HEIGHTS WY
23200 SCIC 94024 831-G5
MORAINE CT
- HER 94547 569-H4
MORAINE DR
2200 SCL 95051 833-A1
MORAINE ST
36900 FRMT 94536 752-H3
MORALES CT
22200 AlaC 94546 692-B6
MORAN AV
2800 RCH 94804 588-J4
MORAN CT
- HAY 94544 711-H3
MORAN DR
4300 SJS 95129 853-A3
MORAN LN
19900 SAR 95070 872-E1
MORAQUITA CT
- SCIC 94024 831-F5
MORAY CT
19500 SAR 95070 852-F7
19500 SAR 95070 872-F1
N MORAY ST
43800 FRMT 94539 773-H2
S MORAY ST
43900 FRMT 94539 773-H2
MORCOM AV
2800 OAK 94619 670-F1
2800 OAK 94619 650-F7
MORCOM PL
- OAK 94619 650-G7
MORDEN DR
4800 SJS 95130 852-J7
MORE AV
200 SJS 95030 872-J1
200 CMBL 95030 872-J1
200 CMBL 95030 873-A2
200 LGTS 95030 873-A2
500 LGTS 95030 872-J4
MORE ST
- ALB 94706 609-D6
MORECAMBE DR
7000 SJS 95120 894-G3
MORECROFT RD
500 LFYT 94549 631-J4
MORELAND DR
1600 ALA 94501 670-B2
3200 SBRN 94066 707-D6
3400 SMCo 94044 707-D6
4200 AlaC 94546 691-J3
4400 AlaC 94546 692-A3
MORELAND ST
100 SF 94131 667-G5
MORELAND WY
4000 SJS 95130 853-B4
MORELLO AV
- MRTZ 94553 571-H5
200 CCCo 94553 571-H5
1100 MRTZ 94553 591-H1
1200 PLHL 94523 591-H1
1900 CCCo 94523 592-A3
1900 PLHL 94523 592-A3
MORELLO CT
- MRTZ 94553 571-H7
2600 UNC 94587 732-F7
MORELLO HEIGHTS CIR
100 MRTZ 94553 571-G5
MORELLO HEIGHTS DR
- MRTZ 94553 571-G4
MORELY CT
1100 SJS 95122 854-H1
MORENGO CT
5500 CNCD 94521 593-E7
MORENGO DR
5400 CNCD 94521 593-E7
10600 SCIC 95014 852-H2
MORENGO WY
300 FRMT 94539 773-H7
MORENO AV
700 PA 94303 791-D5
2900 PLE 94588 694-E7
3200 SJS 95127 835-B3
MORENO LN
600 SCL 95050 833-D5
MORETTI DR
3200 CNCD 94519 572-G6
10200 SCIC 95014 852-H2
MORETTI LN
200 MPS 95035 794-C6
MOREVERN CIR
7500 SJS 95135 855-J6
MOREY DR
500 MLPK 94025 790-G4
MORGAN
600 RCH 94801 588-C7
MORGAN AL
- SF 94114 667-F3
- SF 94131 667-F3
MORGAN AV
1200 SLN 94577 691-C1
1500 SLN 94577 671-C7
2800 OAK 94602 650-E4
MORGAN COM
500 LVMR 94550 695-H7
MORGAN CT
100 VAL 94591 530-E1
1500 WLCK 94596 612-B3
1600 MTVW 94043 812-H2
3300 PLE 94588 714-B1
MORGAN DR
600 NVTO 94949 546-E1
2700 SRMN 94583 673-C4
2800 CCCo 94583 673-C4
9400 PLE 94586 693-F6

INDEX

STREET Block City ZIP Pg-Grid

MORGAN LN
- MrnC 94901 567-A7
MORGAN PL
700 LALT 94024 831-G1
3400 SJS 95132 814-G3
MORGAN ST
1500 MTVW 94043 811-H2
MORGAN WY
5000 ANT 94509 595-H4
MORGANFIELD CT
4100 PLE 94566 714-E1
MORGANFIELD RD
4200 PLE 94566 714-E1
MORI ST
200 PIT 94565 574-C5
MORIS POINT RD
100 PCFA 94044 706-J7
100 PCFA 94044 727-A1
100 PCFA 94044 726-J1
MORKEN ST
6900 OAK 94621 670-G3
MORLEY DR
2800 OAK 94611 650-F2
MORLEY PL
35400 FRMT 94536 752-F1
MORNING GLORY CIR
1300 LVMR 94550 696-A4
MORNING GLORY CT
500 SRMN 94583 653-J7
6000 NWK 94560 752-H7
6000 NWK 94560 772-H1
MORNING GLORY DR
- BEN 94510 551-A1
1200 CNCD 94521 593-B4
MORNING GLORY LN
1600 SJS 95124 873-J6
MORNING GLORY RD
1600 LVMR 94550 696-A3
MORNING HILLS CT
- SRMN 94583 673-J6
MORNINGHOME RD
500 DNVL 94526 653-C3
MORNINGSIDE
600 LALT 94022 831-D1
MORNINGSIDE AV
100 VAL 94590 530-B4
1100 SSF 94080 707-G1
MORNINGSIDE DR
- CMAD 94925 586-E7
- DALY 94015 686-J5
- SANS 94960 566-A6
- SF 94132 667-A6
- SF 94132 666-J6
100 CMAD 94925 606-F1
600 MLBR 94030 727-J4
1000 SUNV 94087 832-A1
3300 RCH 94803 589-G2
5500 CLAY 94517 593-F5
5500 SJS 95138 875-F1
27900 HAY 94545 731-H1
MORNINGSIDE PL
- CCCo 94595 632-D2
MORNINGSIDE WY
800 PLHL 94523 592-D4
MORNING SPRING CT
11500 CPTO 95014 852-A4
MORNING STAR CT
300 PIT 94565 574-A3
MORNING STAR DR
- SJS 95131 814-B5
MORNING STAR CRSE
- CMAD 94925 606-J1
MORNING SUN AV
- MrnC 94941 606-E5
MORNING SUN CT
- MTVW 94043 811-J3
MORNING SUN DR
2500 RCH 94806 568-J7
MORNINGVIEW CT
1300 CNCD 94521 593-B4
MORNING VIEW TER
- FRMT 94539 794-B1
MOROCCO DR
1600 SJS 95125 853-J7
MORPETH ST
5700 OAK 94618 630-B6
MORPHEW ST
100 SRFL 94901 587-A4
MORRELL AV
800 BURL 94010 728-F6
MORRELL CT
1100 CNCD 94521 593-F7
MORRELL ST
- SF 94109 647-J4
300 SF 94124 668-E7
300 SF 94124 688-E1
MORRENE DR
100 CMBL 95008 853-B5
MORRIE DR
3600 SJS 95127 835-C3
MORRILL AV
1100 SJS 95132 814-D2
MORRILL CT
- OAK 94618 630-B6
1100 SJS 95132 814-F5
MORRILL LN
- OAK 94618 630-B6
MORRILL ST
800 AlaC 94541 691-F6
MORRIS AV
1000 SJS 95126 853-J1
6500 ELCR 94530 589-B7
6500 ELCR 94530 609-B1
MORRIS CT
1600 SLN 94578 691-C3
2100 SJS 95126 833-G5
MORRIS DR
3100 PA 94303 791-E6
MORRIS LN
100 CMBL 95008 853-E7
MORRIS RD
- SF 94129 647-C4
MORRIS ST
- SF 94107 648-A7
900 CLAY 94517 593-H7
MORRIS WY
5000 FRMT 94536 752-F5
MORRISON AV
100 SJS 95126 833-J7
200 SCIC 95126 833-J7
200 SCIC 95126 853-J1
2000 SCL 95051 833-B3
3200 OAK 94602 650-C5
N MORRISON AV
- SJS 95126 833-J6
MORRISON LN
300 CMBL 95008 873-C1
MORRISON RD
- ROSS 94957 586-D2
MORRISON CANYON RD
- FRMT 94536 733-H7
- FRMT 94536 753-G1
- FRMT 94539 753-E2
1500 AlaC 94586 753-G1
1500 FRMT 94586 753-G1
1500 AlaC 94536 753-G1
MORRIS RANCH RD
200 DNVL 94526 653-A4
MORRO CT
500 FCTY 94404 749-F5
2900 ANT 94509 595-H2
MORRO DR
1900 PIT 94565 574-E3
2800 ANT 94509 595-H2
MORRO VISTA LN
100 SMCo 94028 810-C3
MORROW CT
- SJS 95139 875-F7
MORROW DR
5300 SPAB 94806 589-A3
MORSE AV
200 SUNV 94086 812-F5
900 SUNV 94089 812-F4
MORSE BLVD
1100 SCAR 94070 769-G4
MORSE CT
400 SUNV 94086 812-F5
25300 HAY 94542 712-C3
MORSE DR
5500 OAK 94605 670-G1
6000 PLE 94588 694-B6
MORSE LN
- SMCo 94062 809-E5
1600 SCL 95051 833-B4
MORSE ST
- SF 94112 687-F2
500 SJS 95126 833-G5
1800 SCL 95050 833-G5
MORSE TER
47100 FRMT 94539 773-H6
MORTENSEN RD
3700 SLN 94578 691-B3
MORTIMER AV
38900 FRMT 94536 753-C2
MORTON AV
500 RCH 94806 568-G7
1100 SCL 95051 833-B4
1300 LALT 94024 831-J4
1400 LALT 94024 832-A4
7200 NWK 94560 772-E1
MORTON CT
- MLV 94941 606-G2
1000 MTVW 94040 811-F5
MORTON DR
- DALY 94015 707-B2
MORTON LN
- SANS 94960 566-A7
MORTON PL
3700 AlaC 94552 692-F2
MORTON ST
- PA 94303 791-C5
700 SF 94129 647-E4
1300 ALA 94501 669-H1
MORTON WY
2100 ANT 94509 595-A1
2100 ANT 94509 575-A7
5600 SJS 95123 874-F4
MORVA CT
600 AlaC 94541 691-G7
MORVA DR
20500 AlaC 94541 691-G7
MORWOOD DR
4800 RCH 94803 589-F1
MOSAIC COM
34700 FRMT 94555 752-D3
MOSCOW ST
200 SF 94112 667-H7
300 SF 94112 687-G2
MOSELEY RD
300 HIL 94010 748-D3
MOSELLE CT
200 SJS 95119 875-D7
1300 LVMR 94550 715-J2
2800 WLCK 94598 612-J3
4000 PLE 94566 714-F4
22100 AlaC 94541 692-C6
MOSELLE DR
6700 SJS 95119 875-D7
MOSLEY AV
- ALA 94501 649-E6
MOSS AV
- OAK 94610 649-J1
- OAK 94611 649-J1
MOSS CT
1200 PIT 94565 574-E6
MOSS DR
800 SJS 95116 834-G5
16500 AlaC 94578 691-G4
MOSS LN
- LFYT 94549 611-F5
- SANS 94960 566-C7
MOSS ST
- SF 94103 648-A7
MOSS WY
100 OAK 94611 649-J1
MOSSBRIDGE CT
- PLHL 94523 592-D4
MOSSBRIDGE LN
- ORIN 94563 610-H3
MOSSBROOK AV
1700 SJS 95130 853-A5
MOSSBROOK CIR
4500 SJS 95130 853-A5
MOSSCREEK LN
3300 SJS 95121 855-D7
MOSSDALE WY
2300 SJS 95133 814-F7
2300 SJS 95133 834-E1
MOSSHALL WY
3100 SJS 95135 855-F3
MOSS HOLLOW DR
2800 SJS 95121 855-B2
2800 SJS 95122 855-B2
MOSSLAND DR
1300 SJS 95131 814-D7
MOSSMILL CT
2800 SJS 95121 854-J3
MOSS OAK WY
6100 SJS 95120 874-D7
MOSS POINT DR
2800 SJS 95127 835-A5
MOSS POINTE
- ALA 94502 670-A5
MOSSWELL CT
100 SJS 95138 875-D4
MOSSWOOD AV
- VAL 94591 530-E5
MOSS WOOD CT
- DNVL 94506 653-G4
MOSSWOOD CT
- LVMR 94550 715-D1
- NVTO 94947 525-G3
3900 CNCD 94519 573-A7
MOSSWOOD DR
2600 SJS 95132 814-E5
3600 LFYT 94549 611-D7
37600 FRMT 94536 752-H5
MOSSWOOD LN
800 MLBR 94030 727-H3
2400 SCL 95051 833-C1
MOSSWOOD RD
- BERK 94704 630-A2
- HIL 94010 748-D3
MOSSWOOD WY
- ATN 94027 770-G7
200 SSF 94080 707-G5
MOSSY CT
1300 CNCD 94521 593-D5
MOSSY OAK CT
- CCCo 94506 653-H1
10000 CPTO 95014 831-J7
MOSSY OAK DR
2600 CCCo 94506 653-H1
MOSSY ROCK DR
22500 AlaC 94541 692-D6
MOTA DR
500 CCCo 94565 573-D2
MOTT DR
- CCCo 94507 632-J4
MOTT PL
- OAK 94619 651-A5
MOTT PARK TR
- CCCo - 591-B6
MOULIN LN
- SJS 95135 855-F3
MOULTON DR
- ATN 94027 790-F2
1100 MPS 95035 814-E1
3800 SBRN 94066 707-C6
MOULTON ST
- SF 94123 647-G4
MOULTRIE ST
100 SF 94110 667-J6
MOUND AV
7100 ELCR 94530 609-C1
MOUND ST
800 ALA 94501 670-A4
MOUNDHAVEN CT
100 SJS 95111 874-J1
MOUNDS RD
- SMTO 94402 748-H1
MOUN REDONDO TR
- SMCo 94062 789-B3
MOUNT CT
1400 CNCD 94518 592-H2
MOUNT LN
- SF 94122 667-C3
MOUNT ST
400 RCH 94805 589-B6
MOUNTAIN AV
100 PDMT 94611 650-C1
MOUNTAIN BLVD
400 OAK 94611 630-C5
1800 OAK 94611 650-E1
2500 OAK 94602 650-E1
3600 OAK 94619 650-G4
4700 OAK 94605 650-H6
5400 OAK 94613 650-H6
5900 OAK 94605 671-A1
MOUNTAIN CT
5700 AlaC 94552 692-D3
MOUNTAIN DR
3000 FRMT 94555 732-D6
20300 SCIC 95120 895-A6
MOUNTAIN LN
- MrnC 94965 606-B3
18500 AlaC 94552 692-D2
MOUNTAIN RD
100 SSF 94080 707-H2
MOUNTAIN VW
- PLE 94586 693-F5
300 DALY 94014 687-D4
MOUNTAIN WY
19200 SCIC 95030 872-G6
MOUNTAIN CANYON LN
100 CCCo 94526 633-C6
MOUNTAIN CANYON PL
100 CCCo 94526 633-C6
MOUNTAIN CREEK CT
1800 SJS 95148 835-D4
MOUNTAINGATE WY
2400 SJS 95133 814-H3
2600 OAK 94611 650-F2
MOUNTAIN HAWK CT
- SJS 95120 894-F4
MOUNTAIN HOME CT
300 WDSD 94062 789-G7
MOUNTAIN HOME DR
500 SJS 95136 854-E7
MOUNTAIN HOME RD
- WDSD 94062 789-G7
400 WDSD 94062 809-H1
MOUNTAIN MEADOW DR
- SMCo 94062 809-C4
MOUNTAIN OAK CT
29600 HAY 94544 712-D7
MOUNTAIN QUAIL CIR
1100 SJS 95120 894-F3
MOUNTAIN RIDGE DR
300 DNVL 94506 654-A6
300 DNVL 94506 653-J6
MOUNTAIN SPRING RD
3400 LFYT 94549 611-G1
MOUNTAIN SPRINGS AV
- SF 94114 667-E3
- SF 94114 667-E3
MOUNTAIN VALLEY
- OAK 94605 671-D2
MOUNTAIN VALLEY PL
- DNVL 94506 653-J5
MOUNTAIN VIEW AV
- SMTO 94403 749-E7
- CCCo 94565 573-J2
- MLV 94941 606-A3
- MrnC 94965 606-A3
- SANS 94960 566-B6
- SCIC 95127 815-A7
- SRFL 94901 566-H6
- VAL 94590 530-C2
100 MTVW 94041 811-H5
200 SJS 95127 814-J7
400 BLMT 94002 749-E7
500 VAL 94589 530-C2
800 LALT 94024 811-H5
900 MTVW 94040 811-H5
4100 OAK 94605 650-H7
MOUNTAIN VIEW BLVD
1000 CCCo 94596 612-F7
MOUNTAIN VIEW CT
500 PLHL 94523 592-A4
MOUNTAIN VIEW DR
800 LFYT 94549 611-E6
1800 TBRN 94920 607-E7
2200 CNCD 94520 572-F7
MOUNTAIN VIEW PL
- LFYT 94549 611-E7
- SMCo 94402 748-H7
MOUNTAIN VIEW RD
3400 ANT 94509 595-C1
MOUNTAIN VIEW TER
- BEN 94510 551-C4
MOUNTAIN VIEW WY
500 SMCo 94062 789-F1
MOUNTAIN VISTA PKWY
- LVMR 94550 696-F3
MOUNTAIN WOOD LN
- WDSD 94062 789-G7
100 WDSD 94062 809-G1
MOUNTAIRE CIR
200 CLAY 94517 613-H1
MOUNTAIRE CT
- CLAY 94517 613-H2
MOUNTAIRE DR
3000 ANT 94509 575-E7
3500 ANT 94509 595-E1
MOUNTAIRE PKWY
100 CLAY 94517 613-H1
MOUNTAIRE PL
- CLAY 94517 613-H1
MOUNT ALPINE PL
- CLAY 94517 613-H1
MOUNTBATTEN CT
1200 CNCD 94518 592-D7
MOUNT BLANC WY
1600 SJS 95127 835-B4
MOUNT CARMEL DR
900 SJS 95120 894-F1
MOUNTCASTLE WY
4100 SJS 95136 874-D2
MOUNT CLARE DR
2900 SJS 95148 835-C7
MOUNTCLIFFE CT
3800 SJS 95136 874-D1
MOUNT CREST DR
11200 CPTO 95014 852-B3
MOUNT DARWIN CT
1500 ANT 94509 595-F3
MOUNT DARWIN DR
1000 SJS 95120 894-F2
MOUNT DAVIDSON CT
500 CLAY 94517 613-H2
3500 SJS 95124 873-E2
MOUNT DAVIDSON DR
2200 SJS 95124 873-E2
MOUNT DAY DR
5600 LVMR 94550 696-C3
MOUNT DELL DR
500 CLAY 94517 613-H1
MOUNT DIABLO AV
1400 MPS 95035 814-D1
MOUNT DIABLO BLVD
1200 WLCK 94595 612-C5
1200 WLCK 94596 612-C5
3200 LFYT 94549 611-H5
MOUNT DIABLO CT
3700 AlaC 94552 692-E3
MOUNT DIABLO DR
1400 SJS 95127 835-B4
MOUNT DIABLO ST
1400 CNCD 94520 592-F1
2700 CNCD 94518 592-G2
MOUNT DIABLO WY
1700 LVMR 94550 696-C3
MT DIABLO SCENIC BL
2000 CCCo 94506 633-F7
2000 CCCo 94506 653-F1
2000 CCCo 94526 633-F7
2000 CCCo 94526 653-F1
2200 CCCo - 633-F7
MOUNT DUNCAN DR
600 CLAY 94517 613-H2
MOUNT EDEN CT
21400 SAR 95070 872-B1
MOUNT EDEN PL
- CLAY 94517 613-H1
MOUNT EDEN RD
- HAY 94545 731-E1
21700 SAR 95070 872-B1
22300 SCIC 95070 872-B1
22900 SCIC 95070 852-A7
25100 HAY 94545 711-E7
MOUNT EMORY CT
- CLAY 94517 613-H1
MOUNT ETNA DR
100 CLAY 94517 613-H1
MOUNT EVEREST CT
100 CLAY 94517 613-H2
1500 SJS 95127 835-B4
MOUNT EVEREST DR
3200 SJS 95127 835-B4
MOUNTFORD DR
6200 SJS 95123 875-A7
MOUNT FOREST DR
6500 SJS 95120 894-F1
MOUNT FRAZIER DR
1400 SJS 95127 835-C4
MOUNT HAMILTON AV
- LALT 94022 811-D6
MOUNT HAMILTON CT
- CLAY 94517 613-H1
100 LALT 94022 811-D6
3700 AlaC 94552 692-E3
5600 LVMR 94550 696-C3
MOUNT HAMILTON DR
1600 ANT 94509 595-F3
MOUNT HAMILTON RD Rt#-130
- SCIC 95127 815-B7
- SCIC 95127 835-D1
- SCIC 95140 835-G2
1000 SCIC 95140 815-E7
MOUNT HAMILTON VIEW DR
1400 SJS 95116 834-E4
MOUNT HERMAN DR
1400 SJS 95127 835-B4
MOUNT HOLLY DR
6600 SJS 95120 894-F1
MOUNT HOOD
4000 ALA 94501 649-E6
MOUNT HOOD CIR
2100 CNCD 94519 572-H6
MOUNT HOOD CT
5600 MRTZ 94553 591-G1
MOUNT HOOD WY
3100 SJS 95127 835-B4
3700 AlaC 94552 692-E3
MOUNT HOPE DR
6600 SJS 95120 894-F1
MOUNT ISABEL CT
3100 SJS 95148 855-E1
MOUNT ISABEL DR
3100 SJS 95148 855-E1
MOUNT JASPER DR
18800 AlaC 94552 692-F3
MOUNT KENNEDY DR
100 MRTZ 94553 591-G1
MOUNT KENYA DR
1700 SJS 95127 835-C4
MOUNT LASSEN DR
1400 SJS 95127 835-B4
18600 AlaC 94552 692-E3
MOUNT LAUREL CT
- MTVW 94043 811-H4
MOUNT LEE PL
- CLAY 94517 613-H1
MOUNT LENEVE DR
6700 SJS 95120 894-F2
MOUNT LOGAN DR
3200 SJS 95127 835-B4
MOUNT MADONNA DR
3300 SJS 95127 835-C4
MOUNT MCKINLEY CT
- CLAY 94517 613-H1
3400 SJS 95127 835-C4
3900 PLE 94588 714-A1
MOUNT MCKINLEY DR
3100 SJS 95127 835-C4
MOUNT OLIVEIRA DR
1600 SJS 95127 835-C4
MOUNT OLIVET CT
600 CLAY 94517 613-H2
MOUNT OLIVET PL
500 CLAY 94517 613-H2
MOUNT OLYMPUS DR
6300 AlaC 94552 692-E3
MOUNT OLYMPUS PL
- CLAY 94517 613-H1
MOUNT OSO DR
3100 SJS 95148 855-E2
MOUNT PAKRON CT
6700 SJS 95120 894-F2
MOUNT PAKRON DR
6600 SJS 95120 894-F2
MOUNT PALOMAR DR
1400 SJS 95127 835-B4
MOUNT PALOMAR PL
300 CLAY 94517 613-J1
MOUNT PISGAH RD
1300 WLCK 94596 612-D5
MOUNT PLEASANT CT
3500 SJS 95148 835-C4
MOUNT PLEASANT DR
1500 SJS 95127 835-C4
1600 SJS 95148 835-C4
MOUNT PLEASANT RD
1600 SJS 95148 835-D4
1600 SJS 95127 835-D4
2200 SCIC 95148 835-E5
MOUNT POWELL CT
1900 ANT 94509 595-F3
MOUNT PRIETA DR
3400 SJS 95127 835-C4
MOUNT RAINIER AV
1500 MPS 95035 814-D1
MOUNT RAINIER CT
- CLAY 94517 613-H1
3900 PLE 94588 714-A1
MOUNT RAINIER DR
3100 SJS 95127 835-B4
MOUNT ROYAL DR
6500 SJS 95120 894-F1
MOUNT RUSHMORE CIR
3700 AlaC 94552 692-E3
MOUNT RUSHMORE DR
1700 SJS 95127 835-C4
MOUNT RUSHMORE PL
- CLAY 94517 613-H1
MOUNT SAINT HELENA DR
3400 SJS 95127 835-C4
MOUNT SCOTT CT
- CLAY 94517 613-H1
MOUNT SEQUOIA CT
400 CLAY 94517 613-J2
MOUNT SEQUOIA PL
300 CLAY 94517 613-H2
MOUNT SHASTA AV
1300 MPS 95035 814-D1
MOUNT SHASTA CT
100 CLAY 94517 613-H1
3700 AlaC 94552 692-E3
MOUNT SHASTA DR
1400 SJS 95127 835-B4
MOUNT SHASTA PL
- CLAY 94517 613-H1
MOUNT SIERRA PL
300 CLAY 94517 613-J2
MOUNT SILLIMAN WY
1600 ANT 94509 595-E3
MOUNT STANLEY DR
1400 SJS 95127 835-C4
MOUNT TAM CIR
5100 PLE 94588 693-J7
MOUNT TAM CT
100 MRTZ 94553 591-H1
MOUNT TAMALPAIS CT
- CLAY 94517 613-H1
MOUNT TAMALPAIS DR
400 CLAY 94517 613-H2
MOUNT TAMALPAIS PL
- CLAY 94517 613-H2
MOUNT TETON CT
- CLAY 94517 613-H1
MOUNT TETON PL
- CLAY 94517 613-H1
MOUNT TIBURON RD
- TBRN 94920 607-D6
MOUNT TRINITY CT
100 CLAY 94517 613-H2
MOUNT VERNON AV
- SF 94112 687-E1
39000 FRMT 94538 753-A4
MOUNT VERNON CT
1900 MTVW 94040 811-G4
MOUNT VERNON DR
100 CLAY 94517 593-H7
100 CLAY 94517 613-H1
1600 SCIC 95125 853-H5
MOUNT VERNON LN
- ATN 94027 790-E1
MOUNTVIEW CT
- SF 94131 667-E4
MOUNT VIEW DR
400 MRTZ 94553 571-E5
MOUNT VISTA DR
3100 SJS 95127 835-B4
MOUNT WASHINGTON WY
300 CLAY 94517 613-H1
MOUNT WELLINGTON DR
6500 SJS 95120 894-F1
MOUNT WHITNEY CT
- MrnC 94903 546-A6
- SRFL 94903 546-A6
- CLAY 94517 613-H1
MOUNT WHITNEY DR
1400 SJS 95127 835-B4
2200 PIT 94565 573-J4
MOUNT WHITNEY ST
1100 LVMR 94550 696-D3
MOUNT WHITNEY WY
- CLAY 94517 613-H1
MOUNT WILSON DR
3200 SJS 95127 835-B4
MOUNT WILSON PL
200 CLAY 94517 613-J1
MOUNT WILSON WY
- CLAY 94517 613-J1
MOUNT ZION DR
5800 CLAY 94517 593-G6
MTN SHADOWS DR
1200 MTVW 94043 811-H3
MTN SHADOWS RD
1000 SJS 95120 894-H4
MTN SPRINGS DR
100 SJS 95136 854-E6
MTN SWALLOW CT
7100 SJS 95120 894-F3
MTN VIEW-ALVISO RD Rt#-237
200 MTVW 94041 812-A6
500 MTVW 94043 812-A6
MOURA CT
- HAY 94541 692-C7
MOVIDA DR
1000 CNCD 94518 592-F5
MOWRY AV
4500 FRMT 94538 753-A5
4500 FRMT 94538 752-J6
4500 FRMT 94536 753-A5
4500 FRMT 94536 752-J6
5700 NWK 94560 752-J6
6200 NWK 94560 772-H1
MOWRY AV Rt#-84
- FRMT 94536 753-C2
- FRMT 94538 753-C2
MOWRYS RD
1300 FRMT 94538 773-A3
1300 FRMT 94538 772-J3
MOWRY SCHOOL RD
5600 NWK 94560 773-A1
5600 NWK 94560 772-J2
MOYER PL
- OAK 94611 650-D1
MOYERS RD
2500 RCH 94806 589-A1
MOYERS ST
22100 AlaC 94546 692-B6
MOZART AV
2600 SCIC 95032 873-D3
2600 SJS 95122 855-A1
16300 LGTS 95030 873-D2
MOZART CT
500 SUNV 94087 832-E3
MOZART DR
4000 RCH 94803 589-B2
MOZART ST
1500 ALA 94501 669-G1
MOZART WY
16400 LGTS 95030 873-D3
MOZDEN LN
- PLHL 94523 592-C5
MRACK CT
- CCCo 94506 654-C5
MRACK RD
100 CCCo 94506 654-C5
MUDDY RD
- SMCo - 768-A7
MUELLER AV
2400 SJS 95116 834-G2
MUELLER CT
40100 FRMT 94538 753-C6
MUENCH CT
1300 SJS 95131 814-C7
MUENDER AV
800 SUNV 94086 812-D7
MUIR AV
- MrnC 94965 606-B3
- PDMT 94610 650-C2
- SCL 95051 832-J7
MUIR CT
3200 ANT 94509 574-J7
MUIR DR
700 MTVW 94041 812-B7
5400 SJS 95124 873-J6
MUIR LN
100 CCCo 94507 632-G7
MUIR LP
- SF 94129 647-F4
MUIR RD
100 MRTZ 94553 571-F6
1000 MRTZ 94553 572-A7
1700 CCCo 94553 572-A7
MUIR ST
2000 SPAB 94806 588-H2
24800 HAY 94544 712-A4
24900 HAY 94544 711-J3
MUIR WY
- PCFA 94044 727-B5
- BERK 94708 609-J6
1000 BLMT 94002 769-A2
1000 LALT 94024 831-H2
MUIRDRUM PL
3000 SJS 95148 835-D7
MUIRFIELD CIR
2600 SBRN 94066 707-D5
MUIRFIELD CT
- SJS 95116 834-H3
700 HAY 94544 732-E1
MUIRFIELD DR
- SJS 95116 834-H3
MUIRFIELD LN
5100 CNCD 94521 593-D6
MUIRFIELD TER
600 FRMT 94536 753-B2
MUIRHOUSE PL
5200 SJS 95136 874-F3
MUIR PLACE CT
3800 SJS 95121 855-B4
MUIR STATION RD
- MRTZ 94553 571-E6
MUIRWOOD CT
- VAL 94591 530-F5
2100 SJS 95132 814-C3
7400 PLE 94588 693-J7
MUIRWOOD DR
- ANT 94509 595-F5
- DALY 94014 687-D3
3600 PLE 94588 713-J1
3700 PLE 94588 714-A2
4500 PLE 94588 693-H7
32500 UNC 94587 732-A7
MUIRWOOD PL
100 VAL 94591 530-F4
MUIRWOOD WY
2000 SJS 95132 814-C3
MUIR WOODS RD
- MrnC 94965 606-A6
300 MrnC 94965 626-A1
MULBERRY AV
100 SSF 94080 707-H3
MULBERRY CIR
2100 SJS 95125 853-J6
MULBERRY CT
- ANT 94509 595-F2
- BLMT 94002 769-C2
100 HER 94547 570-A4
1000 CNCD 94519 593-B1
7000 DBLN 94568 693-H2
MULBERRY DR
1700 SMTO 94403 748-J7
3800 CNCD 94519 593-B1
14200 LGTS 95030 873-B2
MULBERRY LN
- ATN 94027 790-C5
- CCCo 94596 612-B4
- WLCK 94596 612-B4
800 SUNV 94087 832-C1
1600 SJS 95125 853-J6
26000 LAH 94022 811-B6
MULBERRY PL
8100 DBLN 94568 693-H1
MULBERRY ST
100 VAL 94589 510-A7
1800 ALA 94501 670-A1
24700 HAY 94545 711-G5
36500 NWK 94560 752-D6
MULBERRY TER
2200 MrnC 94903 546-D7
34200 FRMT 94555 752-B3
MULBERRY WY
- ANT 94509 595-F2
MULCASTER CT
800 SJS 95136 874-D1
MULEDEER CT
4400 ANT 94509 595-F3
MULFORD AL
- SF 94108 647-J5
MULLBERRY LP
100 PLHL 94523 592-B6
MULLEN AV
- LGTS 95030 873-A7
- SF 94110 668-A4
200 SF 94110 667-J4
MULLENS DR
2900 RCH 94806 589-A1
MULLER CT
3000 RDWC 94061 789-J3
MULLER RD
300 WLCK 94598 612-E4
MULLER ST
- VAL 94590 530-C5
MULLET CT
300 FCTY 94404 749-H3
MULLINS CT
- MLBR 94030 727-J5
MULLUK WY
7000 CLAY 94517 594-A5
MULQUEENEY COM
4700 LVMR 94550 696-B7
MULQUEENEY ST
200 LVMR 94550 696-B7
MULRYAN CT
- SMTO 94403 749-C6
MULVANY CIR
- ALA 94501 649-E6

STREET
Block City ZIP Pg-Grid

MUMFORD PL
3800 PA 94306 811-E1
MUNDELL CT
1000 LALT 94022 811-D4
MUNDELL WY
300 LALT 94022 811-D4
MUNICH ST
100 SF 94112 687-G1
MUNRAS PL
3200 SRMN 94583 673-G5
MUNRO AV
1200 CMBL 95008 873-B1
MUNSON WY
1400 OAK 94606 650-B7
MUNSTER AV
3600 HAY 94545 711-D5
MUNYAN ST
36600 NWK 94560 752-E5
MURCHIO CT
1400 CNCD 94521 593-D5
MURCHIO DR
4900 CNCD 94521 593-D5
MURCHISON DR
500 MLBR 94030 728-A5
1400 BURL 94010 728-A5
MURCIA CT
200 DNVL 94506 653-G4
MURCIA ST
- HAY 94544 731-J1
28400 HAY 94544 732-A1
MURDELL LN
- LVMR 94550 715-D1
MURDOCH CT
3400 PA 94306 791-D7
MURDOCH DR
3400 PA 94306 791-D7
MURDOCK CT
- HAY 94545 731-J2
5900 OAK 94605 670-G1
MURDOCK ST
- RCH 94804 588-H7
MURGUIA AV
1900 SCL 95050 833-D5
MURIEL CT
400 SCL 95051 833-B7
1100 SJS 95121 855-A5
MURIEL LN
19100 SCIC 95014 852-G1
MURIETTA CT
11700 DBLN 94568 693-F3
MURIETTA LN
3700 SJS 95127 835-D2
11800 LAH 94022 831-A3
MURIETTA TER
37600 FRMT 94536 752-A4
MURILLO AV
3500 SCIC 95148 835-F7
3500 SJS 95148 835-E6
3700 SJS 95148 855-G1
9300 OAK 94605 671-B3
MURINDO PL
300 SRMN 94583 673-A2
MURLAGAN AV
- MTVW 94043 812-A3
MURMAN CT
2900 SJS 95148 855-D2
MURPHY AV
1100 SJS 95131 814-B7
N MURPHY AV
100 SUNV 94086 812-E6
S MURPHY AV
100 SUNV 94086 812-E7
400 SUNV 94086 832-E1
MURPHY CT
- SMTO 94402 748-H5
4800 FRMT 94538 753-A6
MURPHY DR
700 SMTO 94402 748-H5
900 HIL 94402 748-H5
2000 CCCo 94806 569-B4
MURPHY PL
41700 FRMT 94539 753-G6
MURPHY ST
3500 LVMR 94550 695-J7
MURPHY RANCH RD
500 MPS 95035 813-G2
MURPHYS CT
100 VAL 94589 509-H5
MURRA CT
- SPAB 94806 568-H7
MURRAY AV
- MrnC 94904 586-D5
200 LKSP 94939 586-D5
MURRAY CIR
- MrnC 94965 627-B6
MURRAY COM
4000 FRMT 94538 753-B6
MURRAY CT
- RDWC 94061 790-B1
- SMTO 94403 749-B6
MURRAY DR
300 HAY 94544 712-B6
MURRAY LN
- LKSP 94939 586-D4
- MrnC 94904 586-D4
600 LFYT 94549 631-H2
MURRAY ST
- SF 94112 667-H6
300 MPS 95035 794-A3
400 SF 94110 667-H6
900 BERK 94804 629-E4
MURRAY WY
3200 PA 94303 791-E6
MURRE LN
1500 SUNV 94087 832-G5
MURRIETA
- PIT 94565 574-B3
MURRIETA BLVD
900 LVMR 94550 715-E1
1000 LVMR 94550 695-E6
MURTHA DR
2800 SJS 95127 835-A4
2800 SJS 95127 834-J5
MURWOOD CT
100 CCCo 94596 612-D7
MURWOOD DR
1400 CCCo 94596 612-D7
MUSCAT CT
- FRMT 94539 773-J4
1200 SUNV 94087 832-B3
3300 PLE 94566 714-G4
MUSCAT DR
6700 SJS 95119 875-E7
MUSETTA CT
1500 SJS 95121 855-A2
MUSEUM WY
- SF 94114 667-F2
100 SCIC 94305 790-H6
MUSICK AV
5500 NWK 94560 752-E6
MUSK CT
2400 ANT 94509 595-G2
MUSK TER
34600 FRMT 94555 752-A3
MUSTA CT
- MrnC 94903 566-J3
MUSTANG CT
- DNVL 94526 653-B6
100 VAL 94591 530-E2
1800 CNCD 94521 593-F4
2200 ANT 94509 595-H3
MUSTANG DR
1100 DNVL 94526 653-C6
1300 MPS 95035 814-B3
2400 HAY 94545 731-H2
MUSTANG ST
300 SJS 95123 875-A5
300 SJS 95123 874-J5
MUSTO AV
- SJS 95123 875-B4
MUTH DR
- ORIN 94563 610-J6
MY RD
- LFYT 94549 611-G1
MYER PL
10100 CPTO 95014 832-E7
MYERS CT
200 SLN 94577 671-B6
MYERS ST
10600 OAK 94603 671-B5
MYERSLY CT
3400 SJS 95148 835-E7
MYLES CT
3200 SJS 95117 853-D2
MYLINDA DR
3900 SJS 95132 815-A4
MYNA CT
5200 SJS 95123 874-F7
MYNAH CT
- CCCo 94596 612-F7
MYRA DR
1700 SJS 95124 873-J6
MYRA WY
300 SF 94127 667-E5
400 SF 94127 667-E5
MYRA DELL RD
2500 WLCK 94596 612-B3
MYREN CT
19000 SAR 95070 872-G1
MYREN DR
13400 SAR 95070 872-G1
E MYRICK CT
500 CLAY 94517 613-J1
W MYRICK CT
600 CLAY 94517 613-J1
MYRNA LN
3700 SSF 94080 707-C4
MYRNA WY
1100 CCCo 94572 570-A1
MYRTLE AV
- LKSP 94939 586-E6
- MLV 94941 606-B1
- SRFL 94901 566-G6
500 SSF 94080 707-G3
1300 SJS 95118 874-B1
MYRTLE CT
400 BEN 94510 551-A1
MYRTLE DR
- DBLN 94568 694-D4
1100 SUNV 94086 832-H2
4700 CCCo 94521 593-E2
5000 CNCD 94521 593-F3
MYRTLE LN
- SANS 94960 566-B7
MYRTLE PL
1000 NVTO 94945 525-G1
MYRTLE RD
100 BURL 94010 728-G6
MYRTLE ST
- RDWC 94062 769-H6
- SF 94109 647-H6
100 OAK 94607 649-F3
600 RDWC 94061 769-J7
600 SJS 95126 833-G5
900 EPA 94303 791-C2
2800 OAK 94608 649-F3
22500 HAY 94541 711-H2
MYRTLE WK
- ALA 94501 669-H3
MYRTLE BEACH LN
2100 DNVL 94526 653-E7
MYRTLEWOOD CT
100 VAL 94591 530-E4
900 ANT 94509 595-F1
1400 MRTZ 94553 571-J7
MYRTLEWOOD DR
6300 CPTO 95014 852-F2
MYSTIC CT
4100 SJS 95124 873-E3
MYSTIC LN
600 FCTY 94404 749-F4
MYSTIC ST
6300 OAK 94618 629-J4
MY WAY
- BERK 94708 609-H4

N

N RD
- SUNV 94089 812-H4
N ST
- OAK 94625 649-A4
100 BEN 94510 551-B4
400 ANT 94509 575-B4
1200 BEN 94510 550-J3
N N ST
200 LVMR 94550 695-G7
S N ST
- LVMR 94550 715-G1
NABOR ST
400 SLN 94578 691-C4
NACE AV
- PDMT 94611 650-A1
NACE ST
- PDMT 94611 650-A1
NADELL CT
- SF 94112 687-F2
NADINA AV
400 MLBR 94030 728-B3
NADINA ST
1200 SMTO 94402 749-A3
NADINA WY
100 MrnC 94904 586-F4
NADINE CT
- DNVL 94526 652-H1
1800 PLHL 94523 592-B4
4800 UNC 94587 752-A1
4800 UNC 94587 751-J1
15000 SCIC 95124 873-F4
NADINE DR
1100 CMBL 95008 853-B5
NADINE PL
- DNVL 94526 652-H1
NADINE ST
100 LVMR 94550 715-E1
NAGLE WY
4300 FRMT 94536 752-J5
NAGLEE AV
- SF 94112 687-E2
1200 SJS 95128 833-F7
1300 SJS 95126 833-G7
NAHUA AV
- SF 94112 687-E1
NAIDA AV
2000 SJS 95122 834-H6
NAIROBI PL
3800 OAK 94605 670-H1
NAKAYAMA CT
- ALA 94502 669-H5
NAKOMA CT
1800 FRMT 94539 773-G4
NALISTY DR
100 VAL 94590 529-H2
NALOR CT
17200 LGTS 95030 873-B3
NAMPEYO ST
48900 FRMT 94539 793-J2
NANCARROW CT
1300 SJS 95120 874-C7
NANCARROW WY
1200 SJS 95120 874-C7
NANCY CT
100 MTVW 94041 811-J6
1000 HAY 94544 711-J6
20600 CPTO 95014 852-D1
32400 UNC 94587 731-J7
32400 UNC 94587 751-A1
32400 UNC 94587 751-J1
NANCY DR
- CCCo 94806 569-A5
- NVTO 94947 525-H4
NANCY LN
- DALY 94014 687-H3
100 SJS 95127 834-J3
200 PLHL 94523 592-B5
200 SCIC 95127 834-J3
800 LALT 94024 831-G3
NANCY PL
7200 NWK 94560 752-D6
NANCY ST
- LVMR 94550 715-D1
NANCY WY
- MLPK 94025 790-E6
NANDELL LN
600 SCIC 94024 831-F3
NANDINA CT
- NVTO 94945 526-B2
700 FRMT 94539 753-G7
NANDINA WY
1000 SUNV 94086 832-G2
1700 ANT 94509 595-E3
NANDO CT
4200 AlaC 94546 692-A3
NANETTE DR
2500 SCAR 94070 769-F5
NANIMO CT
100 ANT 94509 575-C7
NANSA CT
43700 FRMT 94539 773-H1
NANTUCKET AV
- SF 94112 667-F7
NANTUCKET CIR
- SCL 95054 813-D4
NANTUCKET COM
34500 FRMT 94555 752-B2
NANTUCKET CT
600 WLCK 94598 613-A3
800 SUNV 94087 832-C2
900 SJS 95126 853-J3
12600 SAR 95070 852-F6
NANTUCKET CV
100 SRFL 94901 587-A2
NANTUCKET DR
800 RDWC 94065 750-C6
10000 SRMN 94583 673-H5
NANTUCKET LN
100 VAL 94590 529-J5
NANTUCKET ST
400 FCTY 94404 749-F5
NANTUCKET WY
300 ALA 94501 670-A4
NANTUCKY WY
29200 HAY 94544 732-B1
NAOMI AV
100 PCFA 94044 727-A1
NAOMI CT
1600 RDWC 94061 790-A1
3100 PIN 94564 569-F6
4000 SJS 95136 874-E1
NAOMI DR
3200 AlaC 94541 692-D7
NAPA AV
100 CCCo 94572 549-H7
500 CCCo 94572 569-H1
1900 BERK 94707 609-G6
NAPA CT
- CCCo 94565 573-E1
1100 LVMR 94550 695-F6
1800 FRMT 94539 774-A4
3200 SJS 95148 835-D6
NAPA DR
3100 SJS 95148 835-D6
NAPA ST
300 SAUS 94965 627-A2
300 VAL 94590 530-A3
2100 RCH 94804 609-B4
6000 OAK 94618 629-J6
6000 OAK 94618 630-A6
S NAPA JUNCTION RD
100 AMCN 94589 510-A1
NAPA RIVER CT
4500 SJS 95136 874-E2
NAPIER LN
- SF 94133 648-A3
NAPLES CT
1500 LVMR 94550 715-G3
6000 FRMT 94555 752-B6
NAPLES DR
1800 SJS 95122 834-H5
NAPLES ST
- SF 94112 667-G7
300 SF 94112 687-G1
2500 HAY 94545 711-G7
NAPLES WY
1400 LVMR 94550 715-G3
NAPOLEON ST
- SF 94124 668-B4
NAPOLI CT
200 HER 94547 570-B6
NARAGANSETT CT
44800 FRMT 94539 773-H3
NARANJA DR
3000 WLCK 94598 612-H2
NARANJA WY
- PTLV 94028 810-A5
NARCISO CT
1000 SJS 95129 852-G2
NARCISSUS CT
100 VAL 94591 530-G7
900 SLN 94578 691-C4
NARDI LN
100 CCCo 94553 571-J4
200 CCCo 94553 572-A4
NARRAGANSETT CT
- VAL 94591 550-E2
NARRAGANSETT CV
- SRFL 94901 587-A2
NARVAEZ AV
3000 SJS 95125 854-D6
3200 SCIC 95136 854-D6
3600 SJS 95136 854-E7
4200 SJS 95136 874-E1
NASA TER
36500 FRMT 94536 752-G3
NASH AV
300 ANT 94509 575-E4
600 MLPK 94025 790-H2
NASH CT
3700 SJS 95111 854-J6
NASH DR
1700 SMTO 94401 749-C1
NASH RD
700 LALT 94024 831-E1
NASH WY
5300 AlaC 94546 692-C3
NASHUA CT
100 SJS 95139 895-G1
600 SUNV 94087 832-D2
NASHVILLE DR
2900 SJS 95133 814-G7
NASHVILLE LN
100 VAL 94591 530-G4
NASON AV
2500 ELCR 94530 589-B7
NASON ST
1700 ALA 94501 649-G7
1700 ALA 94501 669-G1
NASRIN CT
300 HAY 94544 732-C1
NASSAU CT
- NVTO 94949 546-B2
100 SRMN 94583 673-G4
NASSAU DR
2000 SJS 95122 834-J7
2000 SMCo 94061 790-B4
NASSAU LN
300 HAY 94544 732-D1
NASSAU RD
14100 SLN 94577 690-H5
NATALIE AV
1600 SCL 95051 833-A3
4700 FRMT 94538 753-B7
NATALIE CT
1600 SJS 95118 873-J4
3600 RCH 94805 589-A5
18900 AlaC 94546 691-H3
NATALIE DR
100 MRGA 94556 631-E2
NATALIE LN
400 CCCo 94506 654-C5
NATALIE WY
1200 PIT 94565 574-F5
NATALYE RD
14900 MSER 95030 873-B4
NATAQUA AV
100 PCFA 94044 727-B2
NATASHA DR
4000 LFYT 94549 611-B5
NATCHEZ CT
900 WLCK 94598 612-H4
NATCHEZ DR
900 WLCK 94598 612-H4
NATHALEE DR
5100 CNCD 94521 593-E4
NATHAN CT
3200 FRMT 94539 753-E7
3700 PA 94303 791-F7
NATHAN PL
- DNVL 94526 632-J6
NATHAN WY
3700 PA 94303 791-F7
NATHAN ABBOTT WY
- SCIC 94305 790-H7
NATHANSON AV
10500 CPTO 95014 832-C6
NATHHORST AV
100 PTLV 94028 810-C7
NATICK ST
- SF 94131 667-G6
NATIONAL AL
- VAL 94590 529-H4
600 VAL 94590 530-A4
NATIONAL AV
400 MTVW 94043 812-B4
1700 HAY 94545 711-D4
14800 SJS 95124 873-D3
14800 LGTS 95032 873-D3
NATIONAL CT
700 RCH 94804 588-E7
NATIONAL DR
7000 LVMR 94550 696-E5
NATIONAL PARK RD
3200 PLE 94588 714-B1
NATIVIDAD LN
- MRGA 94556 631-E3
NATOMA CT
900 WLCK 94596 612-F7
12000 SAR 95070 852-E5
NATOMA DR
700 SJS 95123 874-G5
1900 CNCD 94519 573-A7
1900 CNCD 94519 572-J6
NATOMA RD
27200 LAH 94022 830-J1
27500 LAH 94022 831-A1
28200 LAH 94022 810-J7
NATOMA ST
- SF 94105 648-B6
400 SF 94103 648-A7
600 SF 94103 647-J7
900 SF 94103 667-J1
NATTRESS WY
10400 OAK 94603 670-G7
NATURE CT
- VAL 94591 510-J5
300 SJS 95123 875-B6
NATURE DR
300 SJS 95123 875-B6
NAUGHTON AV
3800 BLMT 94002 769-A2
W NAUGHTON AV
3700 BLMT 94002 769-A2
3700 BLMT 94002 768-J2
NAUMAN RD
- SF 94129 647-D4
NAUSIN LN
3200 LFYT 94549 611-H4
NAUTICAL CT
100 VAL 94591 530-G7
NAUTILUS CT
- PIT 94565 574-A2
- PIT 94565 573-J2
2400 SJS 95128 853-F3
NAUTILUS DR
100 VAL 94591 550-D1
NAUTILUS PL
- PIT 94565 574-A2
NAUTILUS ST
1800 ALA 94501 669-H1
NAVAJO AV
- SF 94112 687-F1
NAVAJO CT
- PLE 94588 694-G7
- CCCo 94595 632-D2
600 SJS 95123 874-G4
NAVAJO LN
- CMAD 94925 586-G6
- LALT 94022 811-E6
NAVAJO PL
- PTLV 94028 810-B5
500 DNVL 94526 653-B5
NAVAJO RD
47000 FRMT 94539 773-H6
NAVAJO WY
600 FRMT 94539 773-H6
NAVALLE CT
1100 PLE 94566 714-H4
NAVARO PL
400 SJS 95134 813-H4
NAVARO WY
400 SJS 95134 813-H4
NAVARONNE WY
700 CNCD 94518 592-H5
NAVARRE DR
500 PCFA 94044 726-H4
NAVARRO CT
2100 ANT 94509 595-A1
NAVARRO DR
1300 SUNV 94087 832-G4
NAVE CT
- VAL 94591 510-H4
- NVTO 94947 526-B4
NAVE DR
5300 NVTO 94949 546-F2
NAVELLIER ST
1000 ELCR 94530 609-D1
NAVLET CT
1200 SUNV 94087 832-C3
NAVONE ST
100 VAL 94591 550-C1
W NAVY DR
600 SUNV 94086 812-F5
NAVY PL
1900 SJS 95133 834-E1
NAVY RD
- SF 94124 668-D7
NAVY ST
100 PIT 94565 574-E3
1300 SLN 94577 690-J2
NAYLOR AV
5700 LVMR 94550 696-C5
NAYLOR ST
- SF 94112 687-G2
NAZARENE WY
900 SJS 95117 853-D3
NAZARETH CT
600 SCL 95051 832-J6
NEAD PL
- SRMN 94583 673-E6
NEAH CT
1100 ANT 94509 575-F7
NEAL AV
700 SCAR 94070 769-G5
2700 SJS 95128 853-E2
3100 SJS 95117 853-D2
NEAL CT
- CCCo 94806 569-C6
4400 PLE 94566 714-F4
NEAL PL
700 PLE 94566 714-F4
NEAL ST
100 PLE 94566 714-E4
W NEAL ST
- PLE 94566 714-E3
NEAL TER
40800 FRMT 94538 753-E6
NEAME AV
- SRFL 94901 566-D7
NEAR CT
- WLCK 94596 612-D7
NEBO DR
700 FRMT 94536 753-D1
NEBRASKA DR
5500 CNCD 94521 593-E6
NEBRASKA ST
- SF 94110 667-J5
100 VAL 94590 529-J3
200 VAL 94590 530-A3
NECTARINE AV
800 SUNV 94087 832-C2
NEDRA WY
3500 AlaC 94546 691-J4
NEDS WY
- TBRN 94920 607-D6
NEDSON CT
2500 MTVW 94043 811-F2
NEEDHAM LN
19600 SAR 95070 852-F6
NEEDLERIDGE CT
- SMTO 94402 748-C7
NEEDLES DR
400 SJS 95112 854-E2
NEELY CT
- CCCo 94507 632-H2
NEET AV
2900 SJS 95128 853-E3
NEIDER LN
100 MrnC 94941 606-H4
NEIL WY
900 HAY 94545 711-F4
NEILA WY
- MrnC 94920 606-H3
NEIL ARMSTRONG WY
11100 OAK 94621 690-E2
NEILSON CT
300 SJS 95111 875-A1
NEILSON ST
900 BERK 94707 609-E5
1000 ALB 94706 609-E5
1200 BERK 94706 609-E7
1300 BERK 94702 609-E7
1300 BERK 94702 629-E1
NELA LN
700 LALT 94022 811-E4
NELDA WY
2100 CCCo 94507 632-H5
5600 LVMR 94550 696-D7
NELIS CT
1200 SUNV 94087 832-C3
NELLEN DR
100 CMAD 94925 586-G6
100 LKSP 94925 586-G6
300 LKSP 94904 586-G6
NELLIE AV
- PDMT 94618 630-C7
NELLIE ST
- SF 94114 667-H3
NELLO DR
500 CMBL 95008 853-D7
NELO ST
400 SCL 95054 813-F6
NELSON AV
- MLV 94941 606-F4
100 PCFA 94044 707-A3
3600 SF 94124 688-B1
4000 CNCD 94520 572-E4
NELSON CT
- DALY 94015 707-C3
1000 PLE 94566 714-E5
1400 SCL 95054 813-D4
3900 PA 94306 811-E1
14600 SCIC 95124 873-G3
NELSON DR
1600 SCL 95054 813-D4
3800 PA 94306 811-E1
4300 RCH 94803 589-D2
NELSON LN
- ORIN 94563 631-A3
NELSON PL
5300 NWK 94560 752-E4
NELSON RD
- SCIC 94305 790-J6
NELSON ST
1800 SLN 94579 691-A7
4600 FRMT 94538 753-A7
NELSON WY
1300 SUNV 94087 832-C4
1700 SJS 95124 873-H3
14700 SCIC 95124 873-G3
NEON TER
- FRMT 94536 753-B2
NEPHI CT
- LFYT 94549 631-E1
NEPO CT
6400 SJS 95119 875-C7
NEPO DR
6300 SJS 95119 875-C7
NEPTUNE AV
100 HAY 94544 712-B7
NEPTUNE CT
- CCCo 94565 573-E1
- SRMN 94583 693-H1
800 SMTO 94404 749-D2
900 SCIC 94043 811-J4
6600 SJS 95120 894-C1
NEPTUNE DR
400 RDWC 94065 749-H7
1600 SLN 94577 690-F3
13900 SLN 94579 690-G6
NEPTUNE LN
700 FCTY 94404 749-E4
NEPTUNE PL
100 SRMN 94583 693-H1
NEPTUNE RD
1900 LVMR 94550 715-E4
NEPTUNE ST
- SF 94124 668-B6
NEPTUNES CT
100 VAL 94591 550-F2
NERDY AV
300 SJS 95111 854-J6
NERISSA CIR
4200 FRMT 94555 752-C1
NERISSA WY
5000 SJS 95124 873-G5
NERLI LN
1200 BURL 94010 728-E5
NERO CT
1900 WLCK 94598 612-E2
2000 SJS 95008 853-B6
NESBIT CT
1400 SJS 95120 874-A6
NESTA DR
3300 SJS 95118 874-A1
NESTON WY
1500 LALT 94024 831-J5
NESTORITA WY
1800 SJS 95124 873-H1
NETHERBY DR
200 PLHL 94523 591-J2
NETHERBY PL
200 PLHL 94523 591-J2
NETHERCOTT CT
2600 WLCK 94598 612-H4
NETHERTON CT
- MRGA 94556 631-E4
NETTLE PL
1000 SUNV 94086 832-G3
NETTO CT
1700 CNCD 94521 593-D3
NETTO DR
4900 CNCD 94521 593-D4
NEUCHATEL AV
700 BURL 94010 728-F6
NEUMAN LN
- WDSD 94062 789-G6
NEVA CT
- DNVL 94526 653-A3
- OAK 94611 630-C5
2300 PIN 94564 569-F7
NEVADA
4000 ALA 94501 649-E6
NEVADA AV
100 PA 94301 791-B6
200 RCH 94801 608-D1
400 SMTO 94402 748-H3
700 SJS 95125 854-A4
NEVADA CT
5400 CNCD 94521 593-D6
NEVADA LN
2600 ANT 94509 575-D1
NEVADA RD
22500 HAY 94541 711-F3
NEVADA ST
- BEN 94510 551-E2
- RDWC 94062 769-H6
- SF 94110 667-J6
- SRFL 94901 566-D6
300 VAL 94590 530-A3
500 SAUS 94965 626-J2
600 OAK 94603 670-G6
600 RDWC 94061 769-J7
700 RDWC 94061 789-J1
2400 UNC 94587 732-E6
NEVES CT
2600 SCL 95051 833-C7
NEVES WY
3400 SJS 95127 835-A1
NEVIL ST
3600 OAK 94601 650-E6
NEVILLE AV
2400 SJS 95130 853-A7
NEVIN AV
100 RCH 94801 588-F6
400 RCH 94805 589-A7
1200 RCH 94804 588-J6
3300 RCH 94805 588-J6
W NEVIN AV
- RCH 94801 588-E6
NEVIN WY
700 SJS 95128 853-H2
NEVIS ST
4000 PLE 94566 714-E2
NEW CT
5600 SJS 95123 874-H4
NEW LN
100 PLHL 94523 592-B6
NEWARK BLVD
34800 FRMT 94555 752-D5
34900 NWK 94560 752-D5
NEWARK WY
2800 SJS 95124 873-G1
NEW BEDFORD CT
700 VAL 94591 550-E1
1500 SJS 95131 814-C7
NEW BEDFORD RD
100 VAL 94591 550-E1
NEWBERRY CT
4200 PA 94306 811-D2
NEWBERRY DR
3100 SJS 95118 874-C1
NEWBERRY PL
- MRGA 94556 631-F6
NEWBERRY ST
2900 BERK 94703 629-G4
NEWBERRY TER
- MrnC 94903 546-C7
NEW BOSTON CT
- DNVL 94526 653-C3
NEWBRIDGE
- DBLN 94568 693-G4
NEWBRIDGE AV
1200 SMTO 94401 749-B1
1900 SMTO 94401 729-C7
NEWBRIDGE DR
26000 LAH 94022 811-C7
NEWBRIDGE ST
100 MLPK 94025 770-J7
600 MLPK 94025 790-J1
800 MLPK 94025 791-A1
900 EPA 94303 791-A1
NEW BRUNSWICK AV
1500 SUNV 94087 832-C5
NEW BRUNSWICK DR
2000 SMCo 94402 768-G1
NEWBURG ST
- SF 94131 667-G4
NEWBURY
100 HER 94547 569-H3
NEWBURY AV
600 ANT 94509 575-C5
NEWBURY LN
600 HAY 94544 712-D7
NEWBURY ST
600 LVMR 94550 696-A6
600 LVMR 94550 695-J6
NEWBURY WY
200 AMCN 94589 509-J2

STREET Block City ZIP Pg-Grid

NEWCASTLE CT
- SRFL 94903 566-G5
200 RDWC 94061 790-B2
400 VAL 94591 530-H5
1800 WLCK 94595 612-C7
4000 CNCD 94519 593-B1
29000 HAY 94544 732-B2
35300 NWK 94560 752-D3
NEWCASTLE DR
100 VAL 94591 530-H5
300 RDWC 94061 790-B2
1600 LALT 94024 832-A4
1800 LALT 94024 831-J5
7500 CPTO 95014 852-D4
NEWCASTLE LN
100 BLMT 94002 749-F6
300 CCCo 94506 654-B5
7100 DBLN 94568 693-J2
NEWCASTLE RD
3900 CNCD 94519 593-B1
NEWCASTLE WY
900 PIT 94565 574-E5
NEWCOMB AV
1300 SF 94124 668-A5
NEWCOMB ST
- AlaC 94541 711-F1
NEW COMPTON CT
4900 SJS 95136 874-F2
NEW COMPTON DR
600 SJS 95136 874-F2
NEW DOBBEL AV
26600 HAY 94542 712-D4
NEW DORSET CT
600 SJS 95136 874-F2
NEWELL AV
100 LGTS 95030 873-B3
1200 WLCK 94596 612-C6
1600 CCCo 94595 612-B7
1900 WLCK 94595 612-C6
W NEWELL AV
1600 CCCo 94595 611-J7
NEWELL CT
- CCCo 94595 611-J7
100 LGTS 95030 873-B3
NEWELL PL
800 PA 94303 791-B4
NEWELL RD
- EPA 94303 791-B3
- ROSS 94957 586-D1
500 PA 94301 791-B4
500 PA 94303 791-B5
NEWELL ST
2100 SF 94133 647-J3
NEWELL HILL PL
1200 WLCK 94596 612-D6
NEW ENGLAND CT
5000 SJS 95136 874-F3
NEW ENGLAND VILLAGE DR
- HAY 94544 732-B1
NEWFOUNDLAND DR
1400 SUNV 94087 832-D4
NEWGATE CT
- SJS 95138 875-H1
300 CCCo 94506 654-A5
NEWHALL DR
- SRFL 94901 566-H7
NEWHALL PKWY
1400 CNCD 94521 593-D5
NEWHALL RD
700 BURL 94010 728-E6
700 HIL 94010 728-E6
NEWHALL ST
- HAY 94544 712-A5
- SF 94124 668-C5
200 HAY 94544 711-J5
500 SJS 95110 833-H4
800 SCL 95128 833-F5
800 SJS 95126 833-G5
900 SJS 95128 833-E6
1400 SCL 95050 833-F5
NEW HAMPSHIRE DR
1200 CNCD 94521 593-D6
NEW HAMPSHIRE WY
29200 HAY 94544 732-B2
NEW HAMPTON WY
1300 SCL 95051 833-B4
NEW HAVEN CT
600 WLCK 94598 612-H6
900 CPTO 95014 852-B2
NEW HAVEN ST
31000 UNC 94587 732-A5
NEWHAVEN WY
4500 AlaC 94546 692-C4
NEWHOUSE CT
19200 SAR 95070 852-G6
NEW IRELAND CT
600 SJS 95136 874-F2
NEW JERSEY AV
2300 SJS 95124 853-G7
2500 SJS 95124 873-G3
14200 SCIC 95124 873-G3
NEW LAKE PL
2300 MRTZ 94553 592-A1
NEWLANDS AV
600 SMTO 94403 749-B7
1500 BURL 94010 728-G7
2500 BLMT 94002 769-B1
NEWMAN CT
- CLAY 94517 593-G7
NEWMAN DR
300 SSF 94080 707-D1
NEWMAN ST
- SF 94110 667-H5
NEW MAYFIELD LN
200 PA 94306 791-A7
NEW MONTGOMERY ST
- SF 94105 648-B6
NEWPARK MALL DR
- NWK 94560 772-H1
5300 NWK 94560 752-H7
NEW PENCE CT
1700 SJS 95132 814-J3
NEW PLACE RD
- HIL 94010 748-D1
NEWPORT AV
1300 SJS 95125 854-A4
3000 SRMN 94583 673-F5
NEWPORT CIR
700 RDWC 94065 749-H6
NEWPORT COM
- FRMT 94538 773-E2
NEWPORT CT
500 FCTY 94404 749-F5
3200 WLCK 94598 612-J1
7000 DBLN 94568 693-J2
12400 SAR 95070 852-F5
NEWPORT DR
1900 PIT 94565 574-E4
42500 FRMT 94538 773-E2
NEWPORT RD
100 ALA 94501 649-D6
NEWPORT ST
2300 SMCo 94402 748-F7
26600 HAY 94545 711-F7
NEWPORT WY
- SRFL 94901 587-A2
400 VAL 94589 509-H5
NEW RAMSEY CT
4900 SJS 95136 874-F2
NEW RIVER DR
100 SJS 95119 875-E7
NEWRY PL
8400 DBLN 94568 693-H2
NEW SEABURY CT
600 WLCK 94598 613-C4
NEWSOM AV
18600 SCIC 95014 852-H2
NEWTON AV
- OAK 94606 649-J4
1900 SJS 95122 834-H6
NEWTON CT
34300 FRMT 94555 732-E7
NEWTON DR
100 SMCo 94010 728-B6
3300 MTVW 94040 831-J2
NEWTON PL
34200 FRMT 94555 732-E7
NEWTON ST
- SF 94112 687-F2
100 HAY 94544 712-A5
NEWTON WY
2000 CNCD 94518 592-F5
3700 PLE 94588 694-F6
NEW TRIER AV
5000 SJS 95136 874-E2
NEWVILLE DR
500 LGTS 95030 873-A2
NEW WORLD DR
4900 SJS 95136 874-F3
NEW YORK AV
100 LGTS 95032 873-A7
NEW YORK DR
1200 CNCD 94521 593-E6
NEY AV
7200 OAK 94605 671-A3
7700 OAK 94605 670-J2
NEY ST
- SF 94112 667-G6
NEYDENE PL
3700 AlaC 94546 692-A5
NEZ PERCE CT
1000 FRMT 94539 774-A5
1000 FRMT 94539 773-J5
NIAGARA AV
- SF 94112 687-E1
NIAGARA CT
800 CNCD 94518 592-G6
NIAGARA DR
1300 SJS 95130 853-B4
1700 LVMR 94550 715-E3
NIANTIC AV
- SF 94132 687-C2
400 DALY 94014 687-C3
NIANTIC DR
700 FCTY 94404 749-G2
NIBBI CT
- SF 94134 688-B2
NIBLICK AV
11700 SMCo 94024 831-F4
NICE CT
- SJS 95138 855-E7
500 RDWC 94065 749-J5
1300 LVMR 94550 695-F6
6000 FRMT 94555 752-B6
NICE ST
5600 PLE 94588 694-C6
NICHANDROS ST
3900 AlaC 94546 692-A4
NICHOLAS DR
1400 CNCD 94520 592-E4
2700 SJS 95124 873-F1
NICHOLL AV
- RCH 94801 608-D1
200 RCH 94801 588-D7
NICHOLL CT
2700 RCH 94804 588-J7
NICHOLS AV
36500 FRMT 94536 733-A7
NICHOLS TER
- FRMT 94536 733-B7
NICHOLS WY
- SF 94124 688-C1
NICHOLSON AV
200 LGTS 95030 873-A7
200 LGTS 95030 872-J7
300 MSER 95030 872-J7
500 SCL 95051 833-B6
NICHOLSON LN
- SJS 95134 813-E3
NICHOLSON RD
100 WLCK 94595 612-B6
NICHOLSON ST
2500 SLN 94577 690-J4
NICKEL AV
1500 SJS 95121 855-A2
NICKEL PL
25600 HAY 94545 711-D7
NICKEL ST
2600 CCCo 94806 569-B6
NICK GUST WY
400 PCFA 94044 726-H2
NICKLAUS AV
1000 MPS 95035 794-B4
NICOBRIA LN
2400 LVMR 94550 715-E5
NICOL AV
2600 OAK 94602 650-C5
NICOL COM
4700 LVMR 94550 696-B7
NICOLE AV
3600 PLE 94588 694-F7
NICOLE CT
4800 SJS 95111 875-C1
NICOLE LN
24600 LAH 94024 831-E2
NICOLE PL
3700 AlaC 94546 692-A2
NICOLE WY
100 VAL 94589 510-D6
NICOLET AV
3400 FRMT 94536 752-F2
NICOLET CT
35900 FRMT 94536 752-F2
NICOLETTE CT
1900 MRTZ 94553 571-E4
NICORA AV
1400 SJS 95133 834-D3
NICOSIA CT
1900 PLE 94566 715-B7
NIDER LN
- ORIN 94563 610-J4
NIDO AV
- SF 94115 647-F7
NIDO CT
2200 ANT 94509 595-A1
42900 FRMT 94539 753-G6
NIDO DR
300 CMBL 95008 853-D7
NIDUS CT
2000 UNC 94587 732-F6
NIELSEN CT
43100 FRMT 94539 753-H7
NIELSEN LN
1000 LVMR 94550 716-A1
NIELSON AV
15800 AlaC 94580 691-C7
15800 AlaC 94580 711-C1
NIEMAN BLVD
2900 SJS 95148 855-B2
3200 SJS 95121 855-B2
NIEMAN CT
2300 SJS 95121 855-C3
NIEMEYER RD
- CCCo 94801 588-F2
NIEVES CT
1200 MPS 95035 794-B4
NIEVES ST
800 MPS 95035 794-B4
NIGH ST
100 VAL 94590 529-J3
NIGHTFALL CT
1000 SJS 95120 894-F2
NIGHTHAWK TER
1600 SUNV 94087 832-G6
NIGHTINGALE AV
1600 SUNV 94087 832-G6
NIGHTINGALE CT
1200 LALT 94024 831-H4
34800 FRMT 94555 732-F7
NIGHTINGALE DR
2400 SJS 95125 854-D6
2600 SCIC 95125 854-D6
3500 ANT 94509 595-C1
NIGHTINGALE LN
- SRFL 94901 567-C6
NIGHTINGALE PL
3000 FRMT 94555 732-F7
NIGHTINGALE RD
- LKSP 94939 586-D6
NIGHTINGALE ST
400 LVMR 94550 695-E7
NIGHTOWL CT
- RCH 94803 589-F1
NIGHT SHADE LN
2300 FRMT 94539 773-G3
NIKE
600 HER 94547 569-F3
NIKETTE WY
1100 SJS 95120 894-E3
NIKULINA CT
1100 SJS 95120 894-F3
NILAND ST
4600 UNC 94587 752-A1
NILDA AV
1000 MTVW 94040 811-J7
NILE DR
10100 CPTO 95014 852-E1
NILES AV
1300 SBRN 94066 727-H1
NILES BLVD
35200 FRMT 94536 732-H7
35400 FRMT 94536 753-B1
36400 FRMT 94536 733-A7
NILES CT
700 PIT 94565 574-A3
NILES CANYON RD
4700 AlaC 94586 733-E6
NILES CANYON RD Rt#-84
- UNC 94587 733-E5
100 FRMT 94536 733-G5
200 FRMT 94536 753-C1
500 AlaC 94586 733-G5
12000 AlaC 94586 734-A6
NIMITZ
4000 ALA 94501 649-F6
NIMITZ AV
- RDWC 94061 790-B3
- SMCo 94061 790-B3
600 SF 94124 668-F7
NIMITZ DR
1000 SMCo 94015 687-A5
NIMITZ FRWY I-880
- AlaC - 691-D6
- AlaC - 711-G5
- FRMT - 732-A2
- FRMT - 752-G5
- FRMT - 773-D4
- FRMT - 772-J1
- FRMT - 793-G2
- HAY - 711-G5
- HAY - 732-A2
- HAY - 731-J1
- MPS - 793-H4
- MPS - 813-J1
- NWK - 752-G5
- NWK - 773-D4
- NWK - 772-J1
- OAK - 649-H5
- OAK - 650-A6
- OAK - 670-D3
- OAK - 690-H2
- SJS - 814-A6
- SJS - 813-J1
- SJS - 834-A1
NIMITZ FRWY I-880
- SJS - 833-H5
- SJS - 853-F1
- SLN - 691-A3
- SLN - 690-H2
- UNC - 732-A2
NIMITZ LN
1100 FCTY 94404 749-G4
NIMITZ TR
- RCH 94805 589-F5
NIMITZ WY
- CCCo - 589-H7
- CCCo - 610-A3
- CCCo 94708 609-J2
- CCCo 94708 610-A3
- RCH 94805 589-E4
- RCH 94805 609-H1
NIMRICH LN
2100 SJS 95124 873-F6
NINA CT
- MrnC 94941 606-J7
- CCCo 94526 633-D5
100 LGTS 95032 873-C7
1900 AlaC 94541 712-C2
NINA DR
- NVTO 94947 525-G4
NINA LN
700 FCTY 94404 749-G2
NINA PL
- PIT 94565 574-C6
26800 LAH 94022 811-A5
NINA ST
2100 AlaC 94541 712-C2
NINA WY
800 FRMT 94539 753-G7
5600 LVMR 94550 696-D7
NINESTONE CT
- MrnC 94903 546-E6
NINO AV
400 LGTS 95032 873-B6
NINO WY
200 LGTS 95032 873-B6
NIPPER AV
500 SJS 95133 834-E3
NISICH CT
1400 SJS 95122 854-H2
NISICH DR
1300 SJS 95122 854-H1
NISQUALLY DR
700 SUNV 94087 832-C5
NISSEN DR
2400 LVMR 94550 695-B5
NITA AV
300 MTVW 94043 811-F2
NIVEN WY
- LKSP 94939 586-F6
NOAH DR
32600 UNC 94587 732-C5
NOB PL
- SRMN 94583 673-E5
NOB HILL
- CCCo 94806 569-A5
NOB HILL AV
800 PIN 94564 569-C4
NOB HILL CIR
- SF 94108 648-A5
NOB HILL CT
28000 HAY 94542 712-E4
NOB HILL DR
200 WLCK 94596 612-E6
200 CCCo 94596 612-E6
10200 SJS 95127 835-B2
15100 SCIC 95127 835-B2
NOB HILL PL
- SF 94108 648-A5
NOB HILL RD
900 RDWC 94061 789-H2
NOB HILL WY
200 LGTS 95030 873-C4
NOBI LN
- ORIN 94563 631-A1
- ORIN 94563 630-J1
NOBILI AV
1600 SCL 95051 832-J2
NOBLE AV
1000 SJS 95132 814-H5
2500 ALA 94501 670-A2
14600 SCIC 95132 814-H5
NOBLE CT
100 LGTS 95032 873-D6
1300 ELCR 94530 609-D2
NOBLE LN
- SAUS 94965 627-B4
1000 SJS 95132 814-H5
1000 SCIC 95132 814-H5
NOBLE FIR CT
21100 CPTO 95014 852-C2
NOBLES AL
- SF 94133 648-A4
NOBU DR
1500 SJS 95131 814-C6
NOCHE VISTA
- TBRN 94920 607-C4
NODAWAY AV
600 FRMT 94539 773-J7
NODDIN AV
16300 LGTS 95032 873-D4
NOE AV
1500 SMTO 94401 749-C2
NOE ST
- SF 94114 667-G2
1200 SF 94131 667-G3
1300 SF 94131 667-G5
NOEL AV
6200 NWK 94560 752-E6
10200 CPTO 95014 832-B7
NOEL DR
100 MLPK 94025 790-G3
1900 LALT 94024 831-J5
NOEL RD
- WDSD 94062 789-F7
- WDSD 94062 809-F1
NOELLA WY
5000 SJS 95124 873-H5
5100 SJS 95032 873-H5
NOEMI DR
1800 CNCD 94519 593-A1
1800 CNCD 94519 592-J1
NOGAL CT
- ANT 94509 575-J5
NOGALES CT
- NVTO 94947 526-A3
NOGALES CT
- NVTO 94947 525-J3
3200 LFYT 94549 611-H5
NOGALES ST
- BERK 94705 630-A4
1100 LFYT 94549 611-J5
NOIA AV
1300 ANT 94509 575-E5
NOKOMIS AV
- SANS 94960 566-B7
NOKOMIS DR
500 SJS 95111 855-A7
NOLA DR
2100 SJS 95125 854-A6
NOLAN TER
3800 FRMT 94538 753-D7
NOLDEN AV
400 SJS 95117 853-C1
400 SCIC 95117 853-C1
NOMARK CT
1700 SJS 95125 854-A5
NOME AV
1600 CCCo 94805 589-C5
NOME CT
1400 SUNV 94087 832-D4
NOME ST
1800 SLN 94577 690-G3
NONIE RD
- ORIN 94563 630-J1
NOONAN CT
21600 CPTO 95014 852-B1
NOONWOOD CT
7000 SJS 95120 894-J3
NOOR AV
400 SSF 94080 707-H5
NOPAL CORTE
100 WLCK 94598 612-H2
NORA CT
400 WLCK 94596 592-D7
NORA WY
- ATN 94027 790-D2
900 SSF 94080 707-G2
1600 SJS 95124 873-J5
NORADA CT
20700 SAR 95070 852-D5
NORA LEE CT
- ANT 94509 575-E6
NORANDA DR
700 CPTO 95014 832-C6
700 SUNV 95014 832-C6
NORANTE CT
- PLE 94566 715-D7
NORBERT CT
2700 SJS 95148 835-F6
NORBRIDGE AV
1700 AlaC 94546 692-A6
2200 AlaC 94546 691-H6
NORBURT LN
10300 CPTO 95014 852-E1
NORCLIFFE CT
3700 SJS 95136 874-D1
NORCOTT CT
6700 SJS 95120 894-F2
NORCREST CT
2800 SJS 95148 835-F6
NORCREST DR
2800 SJS 95148 835-F7
NORCROSS CT
3600 SJS 95148 835-F7
NORCROSS DR
2600 SJS 95148 835-F6
NORD LN
1600 SJS 95125 853-J7
NORDALE AV
600 SJS 95112 854-F2
NORDELL AV
2500 AlaC 94546 691-H5
NORDEN CT
100 VAL 94589 509-H4
NORDHOFF ST
- SF 94131 667-F6
NORDICA AV
5300 FRMT 94536 752-G6
NORDICA CT
3900 SJS 95124 873-E3
NORDSTROM LN
3600 LFYT 94549 611-E5
NORDSTROM TR
- CCCo - 652-D1
NORDYKE DR
600 SJS 95127 835-A3
NOREE CT
4700 AlaC 94546 692-C4
NOREEN DR
1600 SJS 95124 874-A2
1600 SJS 95124 873-J2
NORELIUS CT
1300 SJS 95120 874-B6
NORENE WY
1300 SLN 94577 671-C7
NORFOLK CT
- VAL 94591 530-G5
6500 MRTZ 94553 591-H4
NORFOLK DR
300 PCFA 94044 707-A3
1000 SJS 95129 852-G3
6900 OAK 94705 630-C3
NORFOLK PL
500 CCCo 94506 654-A5
11800 DBLN 94568 693-F2
NORFOLK RD
100 ALA 94501 649-D7
900 LVMR 94550 695-E7
3500 FRMT 94538 773-E2
NORFOLK ST
- SF 94103 667-J1
N NORFOLK ST
1200 SMTO 94401 729-A7
S NORFOLK ST
1200 SMTO 94401 729-A7
1300 SMTO 94401 749-B1
1500 SMTO 94403 749-C1
NORFOLK PINE AV
800 SUNV 94087 832-C2
NORGREN ST
500 OAK 94603 670-G7
NORIA CT
41200 FRMT 94539 753-G7
NORIA RD
42900 FRMT 94539 753-G7
42900 FRMT 94539 773-G1
NORIEGA AV
1000 SUNV 94086 812-C7
NORIEGA ST
100 SF 94122 667-A3
2700 SF 94122 666-H3
NORIEGA WY
700 PCFA 94044 726-H4
NORIN CT
900 SCIC 95008 873-E1
NORINE DR
1500 PIT 94565 574-G6
NORITA CT
2700 SJS 95127 834-H2
NORLAND DR
600 SUNV 94087 832-D5
NORLYN DR
- WLCK 94596 612-D5
NORMA CT
- NVTO 94947 525-J3
NORMA LN
800 FCTY 94404 749-H1
NORMA WY
5100 LVMR 94550 716-C1
NORMA JEAN WY
1500 SJS 95118 874-G3
NORMAN AV
100 CCCo 94520 572-G2
1100 SCL 95054 813-D6
1400 SCIC 95125 853-H5
NORMAN CT
- CCCo 94595 632-B1
41200 FRMT 94539 753-E6
NORMAN DR
300 NVTO 94949 546-E1
1200 SUNV 94087 832-G4
NORMAN LN
- OAK 94618 630-B6
3500 ALA 94502 670-A7
NORMAN ST
1300 RDWC 94061 790-A1
NORMAN WY
- TBRN 94920 607-D5
NORMANDALE DR
3900 SJS 95118 874-B2
NORMANDIE AV
5300 OAK 94619 650-G7
5300 OAK 94619 670-G1
NORMANDIE TER
- SF 94115 647-F5
NORMANDY CIR
- LVMR 94550 715-H4
NORMANDY CT
- LVMR 94550 715-H3
- DNVL 94506 653-H5
- HIL 94010 748-H2
100 SCAR 94070 769-D5
2500 WLCK 94598 592-F7
10300 CPTO 95014 852-E1
20100 AlaC 94546 692-B5
NORMANDY DR
1000 SCIC 95008 873-E1
6300 NWK 94560 752-C5
NORMANDY LN
- ORIN 94563 610-F4
- WLCK 94598 592-F7
100 ATN 94027 790-D2
100 WDSD 94062 789-J3
12700 LAH 94022 831-D2
NORMANDY WY
1200 SCL 95128 833-E6
1200 SCL 95050 833-E6
1700 LVMR 94550 715-H3
7500 CPTO 95014 852-D4
NORMINGTON WY
800 SJS 95136 874-D1
NOROCCO CIR
4400 FRMT 94555 752-C1
NORRED CT
300 SJS 95119 895-D1
NORRIS CT
300 SRMN 94583 673-B2
4700 FRMT 94536 752-H5
NORRIS RD
2000 CCCo 94596 612-E7
4000 FRMT 94536 752-J4
NORRIS CANYON PL
100 SRMN 94583 673-E1
NORRIS CANYON RD
2100 CCCo 94583 672-G5
2100 CCCo 94583 673-A3
2800 SRMN 94583 673-D2
8900 AlaC 94552 672-G5
NORRIS CANYON TER
100 SRMN 94583 673-E1
NORSE CT
- PLHL 94523 592-B3
NORSE DR
1900 PLHL 94523 592-B3
NORSEMAN DR
1800 SJS 95133 834-E2
NORSTAD ST
1000 SJS 95128 853-F3
NORTECH PKWY
100 SJS 95134 813-C1
NORTH AV
- SRFL 94903 566-G1
NORTH BLVD
1800 SLN 94577 690-H1
NORTH CIR
- NVTO 94949 546-H4
- OAK 94611 630-G6
NORTH CT
- SBRN 94066 727-G2
1100 BLMT 94002 749-D7
NORTH DR
100 MTVW 94040 831-H1
NORTH LN
- ORIN 94563 610-F6
1400 AlaC 94545 711-E4
1400 HAY 94545 711-E4
NORTH MALL
- OAK 94621 670-E4
NORTH PZ
- MLPK 94025 790-J1
NORTH RD
- ROSS 94957 586-B2
800 SMTO 94403 749-D7
800 BLMT 94002 749-D7
1400 BLMT 94002 769-D1
NORTH ST
- BERK 94703 609-F7
- CCCo 94565 573-H2
NORTH ST
200 SAUS 94965 627-B4
400 OAK 94609 629-H5
1000 BURL 94010 728-G6
NORTH TR
- MLV 94941 606-E1
- CMAD 94925 606-E1
NORTHAM AV
- SCAR 94070 769-E2
NORTHAMPTON AV
- BERK 94707 609-G5
NORTHAMPTON CT
3200 PLE 94588 694-E6
5000 NWK 94560 752-E4
12500 SAR 95070 852-G6
NORTHAMPTON DR
700 PA 94303 791-B5
2100 SJS 95124 853-H6
19200 SAR 95070 852-F5
NORTHAVEN DR
300 DALY 94015 687-A7
NORTH BRIDGE BLVD
- MrnC 94941 626-J1
- SAUS 94965 626-H1
- MrnC 94965 626-H1
NORTHBROOK CT
500 ANT 94509 575-E7
NORTHBROOK SQ
20100 CPTO 95014 832-G6
NORTH CANYON CT
- AlaC 94542 692-E6
NORTHCOVE SQ
20100 CPTO 95014 832-G6
NORTHCREEK CIR
100 WLCK 94598 612-E2
NORTHCREEK PL
- WLCK 94598 612-E2
NORTHCREST DR
1200 SSF 94080 707-H1
NORTHCREST LN
24700 SCIC 94024 831-D4
NORTHCREST SQ
20000 CPTO 95014 832-G6
NORTHDALE CIR
38700 FRMT 94536 752-J5
NORTHDALE CT
6300 SJS 95123 874-J7
NORTHDALE DR
4500 FRMT 94536 752-H6
NORTHERN AV
500 MrnC 94965 606-E6
NORTHERN COM
38800 FRMT 94536 753-F3
NORTHERN RD
400 SJS 95125 854-C3
NORTHFIELD DR
900 HAY 94544 732-B1
NORTHFIELD SQ
10800 CPTO 95014 832-G6
NORTHFORDE DR
10700 CPTO 95014 832-F6
NORTH FORK LN
13400 LAH 94022 810-J7
NORTHFRONT RD
5800 LVMR 94550 696-C4
6900 AlaC 94550 696-D4
NORTHFRONT WY
- SJS 95131 814-B7
NORTHGATE AV
- BERK 94708 609-J6
- DALY 94015 687-A3
200 DALY 94015 686-J3
2200 OAK 94612 649-G2
NORTHGATE CT
- DALY 94015 687-A3
NORTHGATE DR
- SF 94127 667-D7
100 WDSD 94062 790-A5
400 SJS 95111 875-C2
500 SRFL 94903 566-E3
NORTH GATE PL
700 WLCK 94598 613-A3
NORTH GATE RD
1200 WLCK 94598 612-J3
200 WLCK 94598 613-A3
200 CCCo 94598 613-A3
1100 CCCo - 613-B6
1400 CCCo - 633-D1
NORTHGATE ST
100 ATN 94027 790-D2
NORTHGLEN SQ
20100 CPTO 95014 832-G6
NORTHGROVE LN
2300 SJS 95133 814-H3
NORTHGROVE WY
2300 SJS 95133 814-H3
NORTHHAMPTON DR
200 AMCN 94589 510-A3
200 AMCN 94589 509-J3
NORTHHAMPTON LN
100 BLMT 94002 749-F6
NORTH HILL CT
- SRMN 94583 673-A1
NORTH HILL DR
- BSBN 94005 688-A5
100 BSBN 94005 687-J5
NORTHHURST DR
10800 CPTO 95014 832-E6
NORTHLAKE DR
300 SJS 95117 853-C1
NORTHLAND AV
7400 SRMN 94583 693-G1
7500 SRMN 94583 673-G7
NORTHLAND PL
7500 SRMN 94583 673-F7
7600 SRMN 94583 693-F1
NORTHLAND TER
5800 FRMT 94555 752-B4
NORTHLAWN CT
4900 SJS 95130 852-J6
NORTHLAWN DR
4800 SJS 95130 852-J6
NORTH LOOP DR
900 SJS 95126 853-H4
NORTH LOOP RD
2100 ALA 94502 669-J7
2100 ALA 94502 670-A7
2100 ALA 94502 690-A1
NORTH OAK CT
- DNVL 94506 654-B6
NORTHOAK DR
200 WLCK 94598 612-E1

STREET Block City ZIP Pg-Grid

NORTHOAK SQ
10800 CPTO 95014 832-G6
NORTH PARK BLVD
- PIT 94565 574-G4
NORTHPARK CT
3700 CNCD 94519 593-A1
NORTH POINT CIR
- BLV 94920 607-C7
NORTH POINT ST
- SF 94133 648-A3
200 SF 94133 647-H3
700 SF 94109 647-H3
1500 SF 94123 647-F3
NORTHPOINT WY
10800 CPTO 95014 832-G6
NORTHPOINTE CT
6400 MRTZ 94553 591-H3
NORTHPORT CT
45100 FRMT 94538 773-E5
NORTHPORT LP E
45600 FRMT 94538 773-E5
NORTHPORT LP W
45300 FRMT 94538 773-D6
NORTHRIDGE CT
- ANT 94509 575-D7
1100 CNCD 94518 592-H4
NORTH RIDGE DR
3700 RCH 94806 568-J7
3700 RCH 94806 569-A7
NORTHRIDGE DR
- DALY 94015 686-J6
1100 CNCD 94518 592-H4
6500 SJS 95120 894-E2
NORTHRIDGE LN
- LFYT 94549 611-F4
100 WDSD 94062 789-J3
NORTHRIDGE RD
- SF 94124 668-D6
4800 MRTZ 94553 571-G7
NORTHRIDGE SQ
10800 CPTO 95014 832-G6
NORTH RIDGE TR
- TBRN - 627-H2
NORTHRUP AV
700 SJS 95126 853-J2
NORTHRUP LN
300 AMCN 94589 509-J3
NORTHRUP ST
700 SCIC 95126 853-J2
700 SJS 95126 853-J2
7600 OAK 94621 670-D6
NORTHSEAL SQ
10900 CPTO 95014 832-G6
NORTHSHORE SQ
10800 CPTO 95014 832-G6
NORTHSIDE AV
1300 BERK 94702 609-E7
1300 BERK 94702 629-E1
NORTHSKY SQ
10800 CPTO 95014 832-G6
NORTH STAR CIR
1900 SJS 95131 814-C4
NORTH STAR CT
2400 SJS 95131 814-C4
NORTHSTAR DR
100 PIT 94565 574-A3
NORTH STAR RD
- ALA 94501 649-J6
NORTHSTAR RD
- VAL 94591 510-H3
NORTHSTAR TER
34400 FRMT 94555 752-C3
NORTHUMBERLAND AV
- RDWC 94063 770-C7
- SMCo 94063 770-C7
300 RDWC 94061 790-B1
NORTHUMBERLAND DR
1100 SUNV 94087 832-B2
NORTHUMBERLAND TER
3700 FRMT - 752-D1
3700 FRMT 94555 732-D7
3700 FRMT 94555 752-D1
NORTHVALE RD
800 OAK 94610 650-B3
NORTH VIEW CT
2800 SF 94109 647-H3
NORTHVIEW CT
- DNVL 94506 653-H6
- MrnC 94903 566-G3
NORTHVIEW DR
22500 AlaC 94541 692-C6
NORTHVIEW SQ
10800 CPTO 95014 832-G6
NORTH VIEW WY
- SMCo 94062 789-F1
NORTHWAY RD
5100 PLE 94566 714-C1
NORTHWEST CIR
1800 SJS 95131 814-B6
NORTHWEST SQ
20100 CPTO 95014 832-G6
NORTHWESTERN PKWY
2700 SCL 95051 833-B1
NORTHWIND SQ
20000 CPTO 95014 832-G6
NORTHWIND TER
34200 FRMT 94555 752-C2
NORTHWOOD CIR
2100 CNCD 94520 572-E6
NORTHWOOD COM
100 LVMR 94550 715-E1
NORTHWOOD CT
- CCCo 94506 654-C4
- ORIN 94563 630-H1
- PIT 94565 574-H6
1700 OAK 94611 630-F6
3800 PLE 94588 713-J2
NORTHWOOD DR
- ORIN 94563 630-H1
- SF 94112 667-D6
100 SSF 94080 707-F5
1000 SCAR 94070 769-G2
2500 SJS 95132 814-C3
2800 ALA 94501 670-B2
3200 CNCD 94520 572-F5
3400 AlaC 94546 691-H3
20000 CPTO 95014 832-E6
NORTON AV
- SJS 95126 833-H7
- SJS 95126 853-H1
3900 OAK 94602 650-F5

NORTON RD
15000 SAR 95070 872-D4
NORTON ST
- SF 94112 667-G7
900 SMTO 94401 749-B1
1500 PIT 94565 574-E3
1600 SMTO 94403 749-B1
14900 SLN 94579 691-B6
NORTON WY
2100 ANT 94509 575-D6
3300 PLE 94566 714-G4
NORTONVILLE RD
5700 CCCo - 594-F5
NORTONVILLE SOMERSVILLE RD
5700 CCCo - 594-C1
NORTREE ST
3600 SJS 95148 835-F7
NORVAL WY
1100 SJS 95125 854-A5
NORVELL CT
1100 ELCR 94530 609-D2
NORVELL ST
400 ELCR 94530 609-C1
NORVELLA ST
1300 SJS 95122 834-J5
NORWALK CT
2500 MRTZ 94553 572-A5
NORWALK DR
4200 SJS 95129 853-A1
NORWALK ST
32900 UNC 94587 752-A1
NORWICH AV
200 MPS 95035 793-J7
10200 CPTO 95014 832-F7
NORWICH CT
- SRMN 94583 673-G7
NORWICH DR
200 SSF 94080 707-D2
NORWICH PL
1000 WLCK 94598 612-F1
4900 NWK 94560 752-E3
NORWICH RD
100 ALA 94502 670-A5
NORWICH ST
- SF 94110 667-J4
NORWICH WY
4400 SJS 95008 853-A6
4400 SJS 95130 853-A6
27800 HAY 94545 731-J1
NORWICK CT
- AMCN 94589 509-J3
NORWOOD AV
- CCCo 94707 609-F3
- DALY 94015 707-C2
- ROSS 94957 586-C1
1000 OAK 94602 650-C3
1000 OAK 94610 650-C3
3000 SJS 95148 835-D7
NORWOOD CT
100 CCCo 94707 609-F3
NORWOOD DR
22500 HAY 94541 692-B7
NORWOOD PL
- CCCo 94707 609-F3
1200 LVMR 94550 715-F5
NORWOOD RD
2200 LVMR 94550 715-F5
NORWOOD TER
4600 FRMT 94538 773-C1
NORWOOD VIEW PL
- CCCo 94707 609-F3
NOTA CT
100 VAL 94590 550-C1
NOTRE DAME AV
- SMTO 94402 748-J3
900 BLMT 94002 769-D1
900 CNCD 94518 592-G5
1600 EPA 94303 771-B7
1600 BLMT 94002 749-C7
NOTRE DAME CT
100 VAL 94589 510-C5
1200 LVMR 94550 716-A2
NOTRE DAME DR
100 VAL 94589 510-C5
1600 MTVW 94040 811-G7
3400 SCL 95051 832-J2
NOTRE DAME PL
- BLMT 94002 769-D1
NOTRE DAME ST
- SJS 95110 834-B6
- SJS 95113 834-B6
NOTTINGHAM AV
- SMCo 94063 770-C7
- SMCo 94063 790-C1
NOTTINGHAM CIR
- CLAY 94517 593-G6
400 LVMR 94550 695-J6
NOTTINGHAM CT
- ALA 94502 669-J5
5000 NWK 94560 752-E4
5600 CCCo 94803 589-G4
NOTTINGHAM DR
100 ALA 94502 669-J5
4200 CCCo 94506 654-A4
5700 CCCo 94803 589-G4
5700 OAK 94611 630-D6
NOTTINGHAM LN
200 AMCN 94589 509-J3
500 FCTY 94404 749-G5
NOTTINGHAM PL
- CLAY 94517 593-G6
- SF 94133 648-A4
200 CCCo 94506 654-A5
1000 SJS 95117 853-B3
6500 DBLN 94568 694-A2
NOTTINGHAM RD
28900 HAY 94544 732-A1
NOTTINGHAM WY
- CLAY 94517 593-G6
300 CMBL 95008 853-G5
1000 LALT 94024 831-H4
NOTTING HILL DR
1200 SJS 95131 834-C1
NOTTOWAY AV
2000 SJS 95116 834-H5
NOUVEAU LN
- AMCN 94589 510-B3
NOVA CT
4200 PLE 94588 714-A1
NOVA DR
- PDMT 94610 650-A2

NOVA LN
- NVTO 94945 525-J2
300 MLPK 94025 790-J3
NOVA PTH
- OAK 94618 630-B5
NOVA TER
34900 FRMT 94555 752-E2
NOVA ALBION WY
- SRFL 94903 566-D4
NOVAK DR
500 SJS 95127 814-H7
NOVARA CT
- DNVL 94526 653-C1
NOVARA WY
- PLE 94566 715-B6
NOVA SCOTIA AV
3400 SJS 95124 873-E2
14200 SCIC 95124 873-E2
NOVATO AV
400 SUNV 94086 812-C7
400 SUNV 94086 832-C1
NOVATO BLVD
1500 NVTO 94947 526-A3
1600 NVTO 94947 525-F1
1600 NVTO 94945 525-F1
2400 MrnC 94945 525-C1
2400 MrnC 94947 525-C1
S NOVATO BLVD
1300 NVTO 94947 526-A3
1400 NVTO 94945 526-A3
NOVATO CT
1400 WLCK 94596 611-J2
NOVATO ST
- SRFL 94901 586-J2
4600 UNC 94587 752-B1
NOVATO LANDING CT
700 NVTO 94945 526-C4
NOVELDA DR
10900 OAK 94603 670-H7
NOVEMBER DR
900 CPTO 95014 852-C2
NOYES WY
- BEN 94510 551-E3
NOYO DR
100 SJS 95123 875-B5
NOYO ST
3300 OAK 94602 650-G4
NOYO RIVER CT
4600 SJS 95136 874-G2
NUALA CT
900 CNCD 94518 592-E6
NUALA ST
1500 CNCD 94518 592-E6
NUBE CT
2500 SJS 95148 835-D6
NUESTRA AV
400 SUNV 94086 812-C7
400 SUNV 94086 832-C1
NUEVA AV
- SF 94134 688-B2
NUEVA DR
6300 SJS 95119 875-C7
NUEVA ST
- RDWC 94061 790-B1
NUEVO RD
100 DNVL 94526 633-D6
NUGENT DR
100 VAL 94589 510-B6
NUGENT LN
800 NVTO 94945 526-C3
NUGGET CT
500 DNVL 94526 633-A7
500 DNVL 94526 653-A1
1600 SJS 95127 835-B5
NUGGET PL
- FRMT 94539 773-H5
NUGGET WY
- FRMT 94539 773-H5
NUGGET CANYON RD
21900 AlaC 94541 692-C5
NULA WY
22600 AlaC 94541 692-C6
NULL DR
4100 ANT 94509 574-H6
NULTY DR
4000 CNCD 94521 593-A3
NUNAN LN
- SRFL 94901 566-G7
NUNES AV
20800 AlaC 94546 691-J5
NUNES CT
40800 FRMT 94539 753-E6
NUNES DR
2000 SJS 95131 814-D6
NUNES LN
- FRMT 94536 753-A2
NUNES FIRE RD
- SRFL 94903 546-A7
- MrnC 94903 546-A7
NUNN ST
5000 RCH 94804 609-B1
NURSERY AV
- FRMT 94536 733-B7
NURSERY LN
1400 WLCK 94596 612-D6
NURSERY WY
900 SSF 94080 707-G2
1700 PLE 94588 714-F1
NUTHATCH LN
1500 SUNV 94087 832-G5
NUTMEG AV
700 SUNV 94087 832-C1
NUTMEG CT
100 HER 94547 570-A4
1900 SJS 95131 814-D6
2300 ANT 94509 575-H6
36800 NWK 94560 752-C7
NUTMEG LN
3300 WLCK 94598 612-J1
NUTTAL OAK CT
700 SUNV 94086 832-G2
NUTTMAN LN
35600 FRMT 94536 752-G1
NUTTMAN ST
500 SCL 95054 813-E7
NUT TREE PL
1300 SJS 95122 834-F7
NUTWOOD LN
14400 SAR 95070 872-F3
NUTWOOD TER
3600 FRMT 94536 752-A6

NYE ST
1100 SRFL 94901 586-G1
1200 SRFL 94901 566-G7
NYLA AV
100 SSF 94080 707-E3
NYLANDER TER
34400 FRMT 94555 752-D2

O

O ST
100 BEN 94510 551-C4
100 ANT 94509 575-B4
N O ST
300 LVMR 94550 695-F7
S O ST
- LVMR 94550 715-G1
OAHU CIR
200 UNC 94587 732-C6
OAHU CT
400 SRMN 94583 673-E1
OAHU DR
200 PIT 94565 574-E5
700 SJS 95111 855-A6
OAHU LN
19100 SAR 95070 872-G1
OAK
- BEN 94510 551-C6
OAK AV
- SMCo 94025 790-F6
- BLV 94920 627-C1
- CCCo 94805 589-C5
- MrnC 94904 586-E3
- RDWC 94061 789-J1
- SANS 94960 586-A1
- SRFL 94901 586-F2
- SSF 94080 707-G2
200 RDWC 94061 790-A1
300 SBRN 94066 727-H1
500 SBRN 94066 707-H7
600 ROSS 94957 586-B1
1000 RDWC 94061 770-B7
1300 LALT 94024 831-H3
1500 LALT 94024 832-A3
1500 LALT 94040 832-A3
1500 LALT 94040 831-J3
1600 MLPK 94025 790-J2
1600 MTVW 94040 832-A3
S OAK AV
- SANS 94960 586-A1
OAK CIR
600 PLE 94566 714-E4
OAK CT
- CLAY 94517 593-H7
- DALY 94014 687-H3
- DNVL 94526 653-A3
- SUNV 94086 812-E7
100 HER 94547 570-A4
100 MLPK 94025 791-A3
200 ORIN 94563 630-H2
3200 BLMT 94002 749-A7
3200 ANT 94509 574-J7
3300 LFYT 94549 631-G1
6700 DBLN 94568 693-J3
OAK DR
- MrnC 94901 567-C7
- ORIN 94563 631-A4
- ORIN 94563 630-J3
- MrnC 94901 587-C1
900 SJS 95138 875-F6
3400 SMCo 94025 770-E7
3500 SMCo 94025 790-E1
3600 ATN 94027 790-E1
18300 MSER 95030 872-H5
18300 SCIC 95030 872-H5
OAK LN
- CCCo - 631-A7
- SRFL 94901 587-B1
- MLV 94941 606-C2
- MTVW 94040 811-J6
- ORIN 94563 610-H4
- CMAD 94925 586-F7
200 SAUS 94965 627-B4
300 AlaC 94566 714-C7
900 MLPK 94025 790-F4
OAK PL
- BLV 94920 627-D1
100 PIT 94565 574-D3
14300 SAR 95070 872-E3
OAK RD
- BEN 94510 551-E5
- SCIC 94305 790-F6
- LKSP 94939 586-D6
- ORIN 94563 630-H1
100 CCCo 94526 633-A7
100 PDMT 94610 650-B2
2500 CCCo 94596 612-C3
2500 WLCK 94596 612-C3
OAK ST
- AlaC 94541 691-H6
- HAY 94546 691-H6
- LALT 94022 811-D6
- MLBR 94030 728-A2
- MLV 94941 606-C3
- SF 94102 647-G7
- SJS 95110 854-C1
100 MTVW 94041 811-H5
100 OAK 94607 649-G5
200 VAL 94591 530-C7
500 ELCR 94530 609-D4
600 SF 94117 647-G7
800 ALA 94501 669-J3
800 LFYT 94549 611-E7
900 CLAY 94517 593-H7
900 CLAY 94517 613-G1
1000 ALA 94501 670-A2
1000 CCCo 94553 571-F4
1000 SF 94117 667-E1
1200 OAK 94612 649-G5
1200 SCAR 94070 769-F2
1200 SMTO 94402 749-A3
1200 SMTO 94402 748-J3
2000 LVMR 94550 695-G7
2000 SF 94117 667-E1
2100 CNCD 94520 592-F2
2300 BERK 94708 609-H6
14400 SAR 95070 872-D3
21300 AlaC 94546 691-H6
21300 HAY 94541 691-H6
36500 FRMT 94536 752-G3
37100 NWK 94560 752-D7
37100 NWK 94560 772-D1

OAK WY
- NVTO 94945 526-C3
- ROSS 94957 586-C1
OAK ARBOR RD
- ORIN 94563 610-G5
OAKBERRY WY
300 SJS 95123 875-B6
OAKBLUFF CT
1100 SJS 95131 814-E7
OAK BREEZE CT
400 MRTZ 94553 571-F5
OAKBRIDGE DR
3000 SJS 95121 855-A3
OAKBRIDGE LN
100 CCCo 94553 591-D2
OAK BROOK CIR
200 SJS 95139 895-H2
OAK BROOK CT
3700 PLE 94588 694-F5
OAKBROOK CT
4400 CNCD 94521 593-B5
OAK BROOK PL
- PLHL 94523 591-J4
OAKBROOK PL
- PIT 94565 574-F7
OAK CANYON CT
1400 SJS 95120 874-A6
OAK CANYON DR
1400 SJS 95120 874-A7
OAK CANYON PL
1400 SJS 95120 874-A6
17400 AlaC 94546 691-J2
OAK CANYON RD
2700 LFYT 94549 631-J3
2700 LFYT 94549 632-A3
OAK CREEK CT
100 PLHL 94523 592-B1
3600 CCCo 94598 613-A3
7700 PLE 94588 713-J1
OAK CREEK DR
1300 PA 94304 790-G5
2800 SRMN 94583 673-F7
7800 PLE 94588 713-J2
OAK CREEK LN
- AlaC 94541 712-C1
- SCAR 94070 769-F6
20500 SAR 95070 852-D5
OAK CREEK PL
2000 AlaC 94541 712-C1
OAK CREEK RD
- CCCo 94803 589-G4
OAK CREEK WY
1200 SUNV 94089 813-A5
OAKCREST AV
200 SSF 94080 707-F1
OAK CREST CT
- NVTO 94947 526-D6
1200 MRTZ 94553 571-G7
OAKCREST CT
100 DNVL 94526 653-D6
22600 CPTO 95014 831-J7
OAK CREST DR
100 MrnC 94960 566-B4
OAKCREST DR
- AlaC 94542 692-E6
- MrnC 94903 566-G4
1900 OAK 94602 650-E2
6400 SJS 95120 894-D1
OAK CREST RD
- MrnC 94960 566-B4
OAKDALE AV
- MLV 94941 606-E2
- SRFL 94901 566-H5
300 CMAD 94925 606-F1
400 EPA 94303 791-B1
1000 SF 94124 668-A5
5900 OAK 94605 650-H7
6000 OAK 94605 670-H1
OAKDALE CT
5100 PLE 94588 693-J7
32800 UNC 94587 752-A1
OAK DALE DR
200 LGTS 95032 873-C4
OAKDALE PL
4200 PIT 94565 574-D7
OAKDALE RD
2200 HIL 94010 728-D7
OAKDALE ST
- RDWC 94062 769-J5
4500 UNC 94587 732-B7
4500 UNC - 752-A1
4500 UNC 94587 752-A1
OAKDELL DR
1600 MLPK 94025 790-E6
OAKDELL PL
900 SJS 95117 853-D3
21900 CPTO 95014 832-B7
OAKDENE CT
- WLCK 94596 612-E6
OAKES BLVD
- SLN 94577 671-A7
OAKES DR
2400 HAY 94542 712-C2
3800 AlaC 94542 712-D3
OAK ESTATES CT
2800 SJS 95135 855-F5
OAKFIELD AV
100 RDWC 94061 790-B2
OAKFIELD LN
500 MLPK 94025 790-E6
OAK FLAT RD
- ORIN 94563 610-J5
2300 SJS 95131 814-D5
OAKFORD RD
100 WDSD 94062 789-J3
OAK FOREST CT
- PTLV 94028 830-D2
OAK FOREST RD
- NVTO 94949 546-E4
OAK FOREST WY
6000 SJS 95120 874-D7
OAKGATE DR
100 CCCo 94506 654-C5
OAKGATE WY
3100 SJS 95148 855-E1
OAK GLEN CIR
2300 MRTZ 94553 592-A1
OAK GLEN CT
- CCCo 94526 633-C5
300 MRTZ 94553 592-A1
OAKGLEN WY
1200 SJS 95120 874-B6

OAK GLENN DR
18600 SCIC 95030 872-H5
OAK GROVE AV
- ATN 94027 790-G2
100 MLPK 94025 790-F3
500 BURL 94010 728-F6
5600 OAK 94618 629-J5
OAK GROVE CT
2000 CNCD 94518 592-F6
OAK GROVE DR
400 SCL 95054 813-E5
700 SJS 95129 853-A2
OAK GROVE PZ
700 MLPK 94025 790-F4
OAK GROVE RD
- CNCD 94520 592-F5
700 CNCD 94518 592-F5
1900 WLCK 94598 592-F5
1900 WLCK 94598 612-H1
OAK GROVE ST
- SF 94107 648-A7
OAKHAM CT
200 SRMN 94583 673-E5
OAKHAM DR
3000 SRMN 94583 673-E5
OAK HAVEN CT
1300 ANT 94509 595-E5
OAKHAVEN DR
19700 SAR 95070 852-F5
OAK HAVEN WY
1100 ANT 94509 595-E5
OAKHAVEN WY
- WDSD 94062 789-J5
OAK HILL AV
4100 PA 94306 811-B4
OAK HILL CIR
- OAK 94605 671-C3
OAK HILL CT
1200 PIN 94564 569-E5
OAKHILL CT
3400 SMTO 94403 748-J7
OAK HILL DR
- SANS 94960 566-C7
OAKHILL DR
- WDSD 94062 809-F1
OAK HILL LN
100 SMCo 94010 728-B7
OAK HILL RD
900 LFYT 94549 611-E6
3900 OAK 94605 671-C2
OAK HILL WY
- LGTS 95032 893-A1
OAKHILL WY
31000 HAY 94544 732-D2
OAK HILLS CIR
2200 PIT 94565 573-G4
OAK HILLS DR
2200 PIT 94565 573-G4
OAK HOLLOW CT
1400 PIN 94564 569-E5
OAK HOLLOW TER
- FRMT 94536 752-B4
OAK HOLLOW WY
- MLPK 94025 790-E7
OAKHURST AV
1300 LALT 94024 831-H3
1300 SCAR 94070 769-G5
OAKHURST CT
5500 SJS 95129 852-H4
OAKHURST DR
5600 CLAY 94517 593-H5
16200 MSER 95030 872-J6
OAKHURST LN
- SF 94131 667-D3
OAKHURST PL
200 MLPK 94025 770-G7
OAKHURST RD
- MrnC 94901 586-H3
OAKHURST WY
- MPS 95035 794-A6
OAK KNOLL AV
- SANS 94960 566-A6
OAK KNOLL BLVD
3300 OAK 94605 671-B4
OAK KNOLL CIR
24000 LAH 94024 831-D3
OAK KNOLL CT
- MrnC 94945 526-G3
- WLCK 94596 612-E6
15700 LGTS 95030 873-A5
15700 LGTS 95030 872-J5
OAK KNOLL DR
- MrnC 94960 566-A4
1200 SJS 95129 852-H4
1200 RDWC 94062 769-G7
1200 SMCo 94062 769-G7
1700 BLMT 94002 749-D7
1700 BLMT 94002 769-C1
3200 RDWC 94062 789-G1
3200 SMCo 94062 789-G1
15700 MSER 95030 873-A5
15700 LGTS 95030 873-A5
W OAK KNOLL DR
- MrnC 94960 566-A4
OAK KNOLL LN
500 MLPK 94025 790-E6
OAK KNOLL LP
- WLCK 94596 612-D6
OAK KNOLL PTH
2800 BERK 94705 630-A3
OAK KNOLL RD
- MrnC 94904 586-D4
- NVTO 94947 525-G3
1000 LFYT 94549 611-A6
5500 CCCo 94803 569-E7
5500 CCCo 94803 589-F1
OAK KNOLL TER
2700 BERK 94705 630-A3
OAKLAND AV
- SANS 94960 566-B6
100 OAK 94610 649-H2
100 OAK 94611 649-H2
100 SJS 95116 834-G4
700 OAK 94610 650-A1
700 PDMT 94611 650-A1
700 OAK 94611 650-A1
800 LFYT 94549 611-H7
1000 MLPK 94025 770-H7
1000 MLPK 94025 790-H1
1000 PDMT 94610 650-A1
1300 CNCD 94518 592-G2
1400 CNCD 94519 592-G2

OAKLAND AV
2000 PLE 94588 694-E7
OAKLAND BLVD
1200 WLCK 94596 612-B5
OAKLAND CT
- WLCK 94596 612-B5
OAKLAND PL
100 LGTS 95030 873-B3
OAKLAND ALAMEDA FERRY
- SF - 648-B2
- SF - 648-D4
OAKLAWN DR
- DALY 94015 687-A3
OAKLEAF CT
1000 CNCD 94521 593-D5
21900 CPTO 95014 832-B7
OAKLEAF DR
3500 SJS 95127 835-C4
OAKLEAF PL
10000 CPTO 95014 832-B7
OAKLEY AV
200 SCAR 94070 769-D4
200 SMCo 94070 769-D4
2000 SMCo 94025 790-D6
OAKLEY DR
1400 LALT 94024 831-J4
OAKLEY RD
2200 ANT 94509 575-H6
OAK MANOR CT
4000 HAY 94542 712-F3
OAK MANOR PZ
200 MRTZ 94553 591-H4
OAKMEAD DR
1700 CNCD 94520 592-F3
OAKMEAD PKWY
300 SUNV 94086 813-A7
1200 SUNV 94086 812-J6
OAK MEADOW CT
- CCCo 94507 633-A5
4600 ANT 94509 595-J3
7700 CPTO 95014 852-C4
OAK MEADOW DR
100 LGTS 95030 873-B6
OAKMEAD VILLAGE CT
2900 SCL 95051 813-A7
2900 SCL 95051 833-A1
OAKMEAD VILLAGE DR
3000 SCL 95051 813-A7
3100 SCL 95054 813-A7
OAKMILL CT
2800 SJS 95121 854-J3
OAKMONT AV
- PDMT 94610 650-B2
- PDMT 94611 650-B2
- SRFL 94901 566-F6
OAKMONT CIR
5500 LVMR 94550 696-C2
OAKMONT CT
- CCCo 94806 569-C4
- SRFL 94901 566-F6
700 DNVL 94526 653-E6
OAKMONT DR
- DALY 94015 686-J4
1000 SJS 95117 853-B3
1100 WLCK 94595 632-A2
1100 WLCK 94595 631-J1
1800 SBRN 94066 707-D5
3100 SSF 94080 707-D5
OAKMONT PL
1000 SJS 95117 853-B3
1400 PIT 94565 574-F5
OAKMONT WY
100 LGTS 95032 873-C4
2000 WLCK 94595 632-A2
30400 HAY 94544 732-D1
OAKMORE CT
100 VAL 94591 530-F4
OAKMORE DR
- SCIC 95127 815-A7
OAKMORE PL
1700 OAK 94602 650-D3
OAKMORE RD
3900 OAK 94602 650-D3
OAK MOUNTAIN CT
- MrnC 94903 546-A6
OAK MOUNTAIN DR
- MrnC 94903 546-A6
OAKNOLL CT
21900 CPTO 95014 832-B7
OAK PARK BLVD
1500 PLHL 94523 592-A7
OAK PARK CT
12100 LAH 94024 831-D3
OAKPARK CT
3700 CNCD 94519 593-A1
OAK PARK DR
- ALA 94502 670-A5
- SF 94131 667-D3
100 LGTS 95032 873-C4
5400 SJS 95129 852-H4
OAK PARK LN
100 PLHL 94523 612-A1
2500 SJS 95008 853-F7
OAK PARK WY
500 SMCo 94062 789-E2
S OAK PARK WY
500 SMCo 94062 789-F2
OAK POINT TER
1500 SUNV 94087 832-D5
OAK POINTE CT
4100 HAY 94542 712-F2
OAKPORT ST
4400 OAK 94601 670-D2
4400 OAK 94621 670-E4
OAKRAIDER DR
3000 CCCo 94507 632-H3
OAKRIDGE CT
- CCCo 94506 653-J2
- PIT 94565 574-G6
1900 CNCD 94521 593-E3
25000 HAY 94541 712-C2
OAKRIDGE DR
- DALY 94014 687-G3
100 CCCo 94506 653-J2
200 SMCo 94014 687-G3
400 RDWC 94062 789-H1
600 RDWC 94061 789-H1
600 SCIC 94024 831-F4
1000 FRMT 94539 773-H2
OAKRIDGE LN
- CCCo 94506 653-J2

STREET Block City ZIP Pg-Grid

OAKRIDGE LN
- ORIN 94563 611-A7
1800 PIT 94565 574-G5
OAK RIDGE RD
- BERK 94705 630-A4
700 PIN 94564 569-E4
OAKRIDGE RD
- MrnC 94903 566-E5
200 SCIC 95030 872-G6
OAK RIDGE TER
- MrnC 94945 526-G3
OAK RIDGE WY
15200 LGTS 95030 873-B4
OAK RIM CT
100 LGTS 95032 873-C5
OAK RIM DR
1400 HIL 94010 748-E5
OAK RIM WY
100 LGTS 95032 873-C6
OAK ROYAL DR
1500 CNCD 94521 593-C3
OAKS DR
2100 HIL 94010 728-D7
OAKSHADE CT
- PIT 94565 574-F6
OAKSHADE DR
- ALA 94502 670-A5
OAKSHADE LN
- MrnC 94945 526-D2
OAKSHIRE CT
1200 WLCK 94598 612-E2
OAKSHIRE PL
400 CCCo 94507 632-J3
400 CCCo 94507 633-A3
17700 AlaC 94546 692-A2
OAKSIDE AV
500 SMCo 94063 770-D7
OAKSIDE CT
900 PLHL 94523 592-D4
OAK SPRING CT
11500 CPTO 95014 852-C4
OAK SPRINGS DR
100 SANS 94960 566-A4
OAKTON CT
1800 SJS 95148 835-A5
OAK TRAIL CT
- CCCo 94507 633-A5
OAK TREE CT
- SRFL 94903 566-D1
OAKTREE CT
900 PIT 94565 573-J3
2700 UNC 94587 752-G1
OAKTREE DR
300 MTVW 94040 811-F4
1000 SJS 95129 852-H3
OAK TREE LN
- BLMT 94002 769-E2
OAKTREE PL
- HIL 94010 728-C7
OAK TREE FARM DR
- PLE 94566 734-D1
- PLE 94586 734-D1
OAKVALE AV
- BERK 94705 630-A4
OAKVALE CT
- WLCK 94596 612-B5
OAKVALE RD
100 CCCo 94596 612-A4
2100 WLCK 94596 612-B5
OAKVALE TER
500 WLCK 94596 612-B5
OAK VALLEY DR
- SRMN 94583 673-J6
- NVTO 94947 525-F3
- MrnC 94947 525-F3
OAK VALLEY RD
- SMTO 94402 748-H4
OAK VIEW AV
1500 CCCo 94706 609-F4
1600 CCCo 94707 609-F4
OAKVIEW AV
1100 HAY 94541 691-J7
OAK VIEW CIR
900 LFYT 94549 611-G6
OAK VIEW CT
- NVTO 94949 526-C7
OAKVIEW CT
5100 PLE 94566 714-D2
OAK VIEW DR
100 MrnC 94903 566-E5
OAKVIEW DR
100 SCAR 94070 769-G5
1900 OAK 94602 650-E3
OAKVIEW LN
21800 CPTO 95014 832-B7
OAKVIEW RD
1100 SJS 95121 855-A5
OAK VIEW TER
100 DNVL 94526 652-G2
OAKVIEW WY
600 SMCo 94062 789-G1
700 RDWC 94062 789-G1
OAKVILLE AV
10300 CPTO 95014 852-F2
OAK VISTA CT
- CCCo - 591-G5
OAKVUE CT
- PLHL 94523 592-B6
OAKVUE LN
300 PLHL 94523 592-A7
OAKVUE RD
- PLHL 94523 592-B7
OAKWOOD AV
- SANS 94960 566-A5
600 VAL 94591 530-E4
1700 SJS 95124 873-H3
OAKWOOD BLVD
- RDWC 94061 790-C1
- ATN 94027 790-C1
E OAKWOOD BLVD
200 RDWC 94061 790-C1
W OAKWOOD BLVD
200 RDWC 94061 790-C1
OAKWOOD CIR
900 MRTZ 94553 571-G5
OAKWOOD CT
- OAK 94611 630-F6
600 LALT 94024 831-G2
900 HAY 94541 711-F3
1200 PCFA 94044 726-J6
4200 CNCD 94521 593-B2
OAK WOOD DR
100 LGTS 95030 873-B2
OAKWOOD DR
- RDWC 94061 790-C1
- SRFL 94901 566-E6
200 NVTO 94949 546-H4
400 SCL 95054 813-E5
1100 MLBR 94030 727-H3
1200 AlaC 94586 734-B3
1600 SMTO 94403 748-H7
2000 EPA 94303 791-A2
6400 OAK 94611 630-F6
N OAKWOOD DR
500 NVTO 94949 546-H3
OAKWOOD LN
3100 CCCo 94507 632-J4
OAKWOOD PL
300 MLPK 94025 770-H7
300 MLPK 94025 790-H1
OAKWOOD RD
- ORIN 94563 630-J2
OAKWOOD ST
- SF 94110 667-H2
OAKWOOD TER
3500 FRMT 94536 752-A6
OAKWOOD WY
200 LGTS 95032 873-C4
OARSMAN CT
100 HER 94547 570-B6
OASIS CT
1100 FRMT 94539 773-G4
10200 CPTO 95014 832-A7
OASIS DR
900 CNCD 94518 592-F6
5500 SJS 95123 875-B4
OBERLIN AV
600 CCCo 94708 609-F3
1200 SLN 94579 691-A5
OBERLIN ST
1900 SCIC - 791-A7
1900 SCIC 94305 811-A1
2000 PA 94306 811-A1
OBERLIN WY
6400 SJS 95123 875-B7
OBERON DR
3000 CCCo 94596 592-D7
OBERT DR
100 SJS 95136 874-J2
OBERTZ LN
- NVTO 94949 546-C3
OBISPO CT
100 FRMT 94539 753-E3
11500 DBLN 94568 693-F3
OBRAD DR
12300 SAR 95070 852-H5
OBRIEN CIR
100 VAL 94589 509-J5
OBRIEN CT
1000 SJS 95126 833-G5
OBRIEN DR
- EPA 94303 771-B7
900 MLPK 94025 771-A7
OBRIEN RD
2900 RCH 94806 589-B2
OBRIEN TER
- FRMT 94538 753-C6
O BRINE LN
- PA 94303 791-D4
OBSERVATION PL
- OAK 94611 630-E5
OBSERVATORY DR
10300 SCIC 95127 815-B7
10300 SCIC 95127 835-C1
OBSIDIAN CT
100 VAL 94589 510-C6
7700 CPTO 95014 852-C3
OBSIDIAN WY
- LVMR 94550 715-C3
100 HER 94547 569-G5
400 CLAY 94517 593-J5
OBURN CT
1500 CMBL 95008 873-B2
OCALA AV
1700 SJS 95122 834-J7
2800 SJS 95148 834-J7
2800 SJS 95148 835-A5
2800 SJS 95122 835-A5
OCALA CT
2900 SJS 95148 835-B5
OCALA ST
2500 HAY 94545 711-G7
2600 HAY 94545 731-G1
OCASO CAMINO
1000 FRMT 94539 773-F1
OCASO CORTE
43500 FRMT 94539 773-G1
OCCIDENTAL AV
100 BURL 94010 728-F7
100 BURL 94010 748-G1
400 SMTO 94402 748-G1
400 HIL 94010 728-F7
OCCIDENTAL CT
- SJS 95123 874-F7
OCCIDENTAL RD
2100 HAY 94545 711-G5
2100 AlaC 94545 711-F6
OCCIDENTAL ST
5800 OAK 94608 629-F5
OCCIDENTAL WY
800 SMCo 94062 789-F2
OCEAN AV
- SF 94112 667-F7
500 RCH 94801 588-C7
900 SF 94112 667-C6
1100 OAK 94608 629-E5
1200 EMVL 94608 629-E5
1800 SF 94127 667-C6
2500 SF 94132 667-A6
4500 SF 94132 666-J6
OCEAN WY
- MLV 94941 606-C3
OCEANA BLVD
300 PCFA 94044 706-J4
OCEANA CIR
2000 ALA 94501 649-E7
OCEANA DR
300 PIT 94565 574-A3
OCEAN BREEZE TER
- FRMT 94536 753-C2
OCEAN GROVE AV
- DALY 94015 687-A5
OCEAN HILLS WY
5900 LVMR 94550 696-C2
OCEANO PL
- NVTO 94949 546-F2
OCEAN PINES LN
- CCCo 94507 632-J3
OCEANSIDE DR
- DALY 94015 687-A7
- DALY 94015 686-J7
OCEANSIDE WY
- RDWC 94065 749-J5
OCEAN VIEW AV
300 CCCo 94707 609-E4
500 SMTO 94401 729-B7
500 SMTO 94401 749-B1
OCEAN VIEW DR
- SMCo - 768-C3
5600 OAK 94618 629-J5
5600 OAK 94618 630-A5
21000 AlaC 94541 691-H7
OCHO RIOS DR
900 DNVL 94526 653-A4
6100 SJS 95123 874-G6
OCHO RIOS PL
- DNVL 94526 653-A4
OCIE WY
200 HAY 94541 711-G3
OCONNELL CT
34300 FRMT 94555 752-B2
OCONNELL LN
1100 UNC 94587 733-A4
1100 UNC 94587 732-H5
OCONNOR DR
200 SJS 95128 833-F7
200 SJS 95128 853-F1
400 CCCo 94806 569-B4
400 PIN 94806 569-B4
400 SCIC 95128 853-F1
3500 LFYT 94549 611-F7
O CONNOR ST
400 MLPK 94025 791-C2
500 EPA 94303 791-C2
OCONNOR ST
100 MLPK 94025 791-A2
W OCONNOR ST
100 MLPK 94025 791-A2
300 MLPK 94025 790-J2
OCOTILLO CT
46900 FRMT 94539 773-J6
OCTAVIA ST
- SF 94102 667-H1
- SRFL 94901 586-F2
100 SF 94102 647-H7
1600 SF 94109 647-H5
2600 OAK 94619 650-E6
2600 SF 94123 647-H4
2800 SF 94123 647-H3
OCTAVIUS DR
3200 SCL 95054 813-B7
OCTOBER DR
5500 SJS 95138 875-D4
OCTOBER WY
7900 CPTO 95014 852-C2
ODDSTAD BLVD
600 PCFA 94044 727-C5
ODDSTAD DR
100 VAL 94589 530-B1
1100 RDWC 94063 770-B5
ODDSTAD WY
600 PCFA 94044 726-J2
ODELL CT
4500 FRMT 94536 752-J5
ODELL PL
- ATN 94027 790-E2
ODELL WY
900 LALT 94024 831-H1
ODESSA AV
100 PIT 94565 574-D1
ODESSA CT
- RDWC 94063 770-F6
ODIN DR
300 PLHL 94523 592-A3
ODIN PL
300 PLHL 94523 592-A3
ODOM RD
23300 HAY 94541 711-F4
ODONNELL AV
600 SLN 94577 690-H1
ODONNELL DR
2600 CCCo 94806 569-B6
ODYSSEY CT
1100 SJS 95118 874-G3
OELLA CT
4000 SJS 95124 874-A2
OFARRELL DR
400 BEN 94510 550-J2
400 BEN 94510 551-A2
OFARRELL ST
- SF 94108 648-A6
200 SF 94102 648-A6
400 SF 94102 647-J6
600 SF 94109 647-J6
1500 SF 94115 647-F6
1900 SMTO 94403 749-A4
OFFENBACH PL
400 SUNV 94087 832-E3
OGDEN AV
- SF 94110 667-J6
OGDEN CT
- MPS 95035 793-J7
5500 CNCD 94521 593-H5
OGDEN DR
1800 BURL 94010 728-B4
4100 FRMT 94538 753-B6
OGILVIE DR
18300 AlaC 94546 691-J3
O GRADY DR
7000 SJS 95120 894-G3
OHANNESON RD
- OAK 94605 651-A7
OHARA CT
1500 CLAY 94517 593-F5
2300 SJS 95133 834-F1
OHARE AV
2600 SPAB 94806 588-H2
OHARE DR
1400 BEN 94510 551-B4
OHARRON DR
300 HAY 94544 712-B6
OHARTE RD
2500 CCCo 94806 569-B5
OHATCH DR
2400 CCCo 94806 569-B5
OHIGGINS DR
1400 SJS 95126 853-G4
OHIO
4000 ALA 94501 649-E6
OHIO AV
100 RCH 94804 589-A7
200 RCH 94801 588-F7
200 RCH 94804 588-H7
2400 RDWC 94061 790-A3
W OHIO AV
100 RCH 94801 588-E7
100 RCH 94804 588-E7
OHIO CT
100 MPS 95035 793-J7
5500 CNCD 94521 593-F6
OHIO ST
- VAL 94590 529-H4
700 VAL 94590 530-A4
OHLONE
- PTLV 94028 830-C2
OHLONE CT
100 LGTS 95030 873-B6
OHLONE DR
2500 SJS 95132 814-E6
OHLONE HTS
1800 CLAY 94517 593-H5
OHLONE LN
26400 LAH 94022 811-B5
OHLONE TR
- CCCo - 652-D1
OHLONE WY
- SF 94131 667-G6
3200 AlaC 94541 692-D7
OHLONES ST
300 FRMT 94539 753-H7
OHLSON LN
- DNVL 94526 633-A7
- DNVL 94526 632-J7
OHMAN PL
5600 CLAY 94517 593-G5
OHNA CT
4100 FRMT 94536 752-G3
OIL CANYON TR
- ANT - 595-A6
- CCCo - 595-A6
- CCCo - 594-H7
OJAI DR
18900 SCIC 95030 872-G6
18900 MSER 95030 872-G6
OJAI LP
4500 UNC - 752-B1
4500 UNC 94587 732-B7
4500 UNC 94587 752-B1
OJIBWA CT
2000 FRMT 94539 773-G3
OJO DE AGUA CT
2000 SJS 95116 834-D2
OKA LN
14300 LGTS 95030 873-D3
OKA RD
14400 LGTS 95030 873-C3
14500 SCIC 95030 873-C3
OKANOGAN CT
14200 SAR 95070 872-F2
OKANOGAN DR
14000 SAR 95070 872-F2
OKEEFE LN
24000 LAH 94022 831-C1
25000 LALT 94022 831-C1
OKEEFE ST
100 MLPK 94025 791-A2
300 MLPK 94025 790-J2
E OKEEFE ST
100 MLPK 94025 791-A2
100 EPA 94303 791-A2
OKEEFE WY
1400 VAL 94590 530-C2
OKINO CT
5400 SJS 95123 874-J3
OLAZABA TER
43800 FRMT 94539 773-J1
OLCESE CT
- DALY 94015 687-B6
OLCOTT ST
3000 SCL 95054 813-C7
OLD AV
- AlaC 94542 712-E1
OLD 1ST ST
2500 LVMR 94550 695-H7
OLD ABBEY PL
1300 SJS 95132 814-E6
OLD ADOBE RD
100 SAR 95070 872-J3
100 LGTS 95030 872-J3
900 PA 94306 811-B4
OLD ADOBE WY
100 LGTS 95030 872-J3
OLD ALAMEDA PT
1100 ALA 94502 670-A7
OLD ALMADEN RD
2800 SJS 95125 854-C7
3300 SJS 95136 854-C7
OLD ALTOS RD
13600 LALT 94022 811-D7
13600 LAH 94022 811-D7
OLD BAYSHORE HWY
- SJS 95110 833-H1
200 SJS 95112 833-H1
600 SJS 95112 834-A2
OLD BERNAL AV
100 PLE 94566 714-D4
OLD BLACKHAWK RD
3500 DNVL 94506 653-H5
OLD BLOSSOM HILL
RD
200 SCIC 95032 873-D6
200 LGTS 95032 873-D6
OLDBRIDGE RD
1800 SJS 95131 814-D7
OLDBROOK CT
500 SJS 95111 855-A7
OLD CALAVERAS RD
1900 MPS 95035 794-D5
1900 SCIC 95035 794-D5
OLD CANADA RD
- SMCo 94062 769-A7
- SMCo 94062 768-E3
OLD CANYON RD
100 FRMT 94536 753-C1
200 FRMT 94536 733-E6
OLDCASTLE LN
100 ALA 94502 669-H5
OLD CHINATOWN LN
- SF 94108 648-A5
OLD COUNTY RD
- BLMT 94002 749-D7
- BSBN 94005 688-A6
100 CCCo 94525 550-B5
100 SCAR 94070 769-G3
400 PCFA 94044 726-J2
700 BLMT 94002 769-F1
1300 SMCo 94002 769-F1
4100 SMTO 94403 749-D7
OLD CREEK CIR
2200 PIT 94565 574-E4
OLD CREEK DR
900 SJS 95120 894-G2
OLD CREEK RD
700 DNVL 94526 653-C3
OLD CREST PL
2400 SJS 95132 814-E6
OLD CROW RD
- LAH 94022 830-J1
OLD CROW CANYON RD
2300 SRMN 94583 673-B1
OLD DUBLIN RD
4200 AlaC 94552 692-D5
OLDE DR
100 LGTS 95032 873-D7
OLD ELM CT
2400 SJS 95132 814-E6
OLD ESTATES CT
2800 SJS 95135 855-G5
OLD EVANS RD
400 MPS 95035 794-D5
OLD FAIRVIEW AV
- AlaC 94542 712-E1
OLD FARM CT
500 DNVL 94526 653-B3
OLD FARM RD
400 DNVL 94526 653-B3
OLDFIELD WY
2900 SJS 95135 855-F3
OLD FOOTHILL RD
3200 PLE 94588 714-A3
3200 PLE 94588 713-J3
OLD FORGE LN
1200 SJS 95132 814-E6
OLD GATE CT
2400 SJS 95132 814-E6
OLD GLEN COVE RD
- SolC 94591 550-E1
- VAL 94591 550-E1
OLD GLORY CT
- FRMT 94539 773-H1
3600 ANT 94509 595-C3
OLD GLORY LN
2800 SCL 95054 813-B4
OLDHAM CT
300 DNVL 94526 653-C3
OLDHAM PL
35100 NWK 94560 752-E3
OLDHAM WY
600 SJS 95111 854-H4
OLD HAWTHORNE DR
900 LFYT 94549 611-H6
OLD HWY 40
20000 CCCo 94525 550-A5
20000 CCCo - 549-J5
20000 CCCo - 550-A5
OLD IRONSIDES DR
4600 SCL 95054 813-B4
OLD JONAS HILL RD
600 LFYT 94549 631-E1
700 LFYT 94549 611-F7
W OLD JULIAN ST
100 SJS 95110 834-A6
OLD KILN WY
1200 RCH 94801 608-D3
OLD KIRKER PASS RD
1800 CNCD 94521 593-F4
OLD LA HONDA RD
- WDSD 94062 809-H5
1000 PTLV 94028 809-G7
1300 SMCo 94020 809-G7
OLD LANDING RD
- MrnC 94920 607-C3
OLD LONE TREE WY
1300 ANT 94509 595-E3
OLD LUCAS VALLEY
RD
- SRFL 94903 546-C7
OLD MANOR PL
1100 SJS 95132 814-E6
OLD MASON ST
- SF 94129 647-D3
800 SF 94123 647-E3
800 SF 94129 647-E3
OLD MEADOW CT
6500 SJS 95135 855-J7
OLD MIDDLEFIELD WY
1700 MTVW 94043 811-F2
2400 PA 94043 811-F2
2400 PA 94306 811-F2
OLD MILL CT
6600 SJS 95120 894-E1
OLD MILL RD
- SRMN 94583 673-B1
OLD MILL ST
- MLV 94941 606-D3
OLD MILLSTONE LN
- LFYT 94549 611-G7
OLD MTN VIEW DR
3500 LFYT 94549 611-F7
OLD MTN
VIEW-ALVISO RD
- SCL 95002 813-A3
900 SUNV 94089 812-J3
1200 SUNV 94089 813-A3
3100 SCL 95054 813-A3
OLD OAK CT
400 LALT 94022 811-D6
OLD OAK DR
1100 SJS 95120 894-E2
1900 WLCK 94595 632-B1
OLD OAK WY
13300 SAR 95070 852-C7
13300 SAR 95070 872-C1
OLD OAKLAND RD
900 SJS 95112 834-B1
1000 SJS 95133 834-B1
1600 SJS 95112 814-A4
1700 SJS 95131 814-A4
OLD ORCHARD CT
100 LGTS 95032 873-G6
400 DNVL 94526 653-C3
OLD ORCHARD DR
100 LGTS 95032 873-G6
500 DNVL 94526 653-C3
OLD ORCHARD RD
- MRTZ 94553 571-G5
700 CMBL 95008 853-D7
800 CMBL 95008 873-D1
OLD PAGE MILL RD
2000 SCIC 94304 810-J4
2200 PA 94304 810-J4
2200 LAH 94304 810-J4
2300 LAH 94022 810-J4
OLD PARK PL
1300 SJS 95132 814-E5
OLD PIEDMONT RD
1400 SJS 95132 814-G3
1800 SCIC 95132 814-F1
2100 MPS 95035 814-F1
OLD POST WY
2300 SJS 95132 814-E6
OLD QUARRY RD
100 LKSP 94904 586-H4
600 PLHL 94523 592-B2
OLD RANCH CT
400 SRMN 94583 673-H6
OLD RANCH LN
11500 SCIC 94024 831-E4
OLD RANCH RD
- MrnC 94947 525-H6
- MrnC 94946 525-H6
3400 SRMN 94583 673-J7
11400 SCIC 94024 831-E4
OLD RANCH TR
- UNC 94587 712-G7
- UNC 94587 732-G1
OLD RANCH ESTATES
DR
1500 SRMN 94583 673-J6
OLD REDWOOD HWY
- CCCo - 631-A7
- CCCo - 630-J7
OLD REDWOOD RD
- OAK 94619 650-J5
OLD RIDGE CT
2400 SJS 95132 814-E6
OLD RIVER CT
500 VAL 94589 509-H5
OLD RIVER DR
300 VAL 94589 509-H5
OLD RODGERS RCH CT
- PLHL 94523 591-J6
OLD ROSE PL
1300 SJS 95132 814-E5
OLD SAN FRANCISCO
RD
200 SUNV 94086 832-E1
OLD SAN PABLO DAM
RD
- CCCo - 589-J6
- CCCo - 609-J1
- CCCo - 610-A2
- CCCo 94563 610-C4
OLD SANTA RITA RD
3500 PLE 94588 694-D6
OLD SCHOOL RD
5300 CCCo 94506 654-G5
5500 CCCo - 654-G5
OLD SNAKEY RD
12000 LAH 94022 831-B3
OLD SPANISH TR
100 SMCo 94028 830-D4
100 PTLV 94028 830-D4
OLD STAGE COACH RD
- SMCo 94062 769-E7
OLD STONE PL
1300 SJS 95132 814-E6
OLD STONE WY
1300 SJS 95132 814-E5
OLD SUISUN RD
2200 BEN 94510 551-C4
OLD TOWER RD
1700 LVMR 94550 715-G2
OLD TOWN CT
900 CPTO 95014 852-B2
OLD TRACE CT
4100 PA 94306 811-B4
OLD TRACE LN
900 LAH 94022 811-B5
900 PA 94306 811-B5
OLD TRACE RD
4100 PA 94306 811-B4
OLDTREE CT
1700 SJS 95131 814-D4
OLD TREE WY
13500 SAR 95070 872-F1
OLD TULLY RD
- SJS 95112 854-F4
- SJS 95111 854-F4
- SCIC 95111 854-F4
OLD TUNNEL RD
- CCCo - 630-E3
2500 OAK 94611 630-D4
3000 LFYT 94549 611-J5
3200 LFYT 94595 612-A5
3200 LFYT 94595 611-J5
3200 CCCo 94595 612-A5
3200 CCCo 94595 611-J5
OLD VINE CT
600 PLHL 94523 592-A4
OLD WARM SPRINGS
BLVD
44000 FRMT 94538 773-E3
OLDWELL CT
- SJS 95138 875-D4
OLD WILLOW PL
1200 SJS 95125 854-F5
OLDWOOD CT
3000 SJS 95148 855-E1
OLD WOOD RD
14200 SAR 95070 872-H2
OLD YERBA BUENA RD
3200 SJS 95135 855-H4
3300 SCIC 95135 855-H4
OLEAN ST
31900 HAY 94544 732-E3
OLEANDER
- FRMT 94536 753-D1
OLEANDER AV
300 ALA 94502 670-A7
16100 SCIC 95032 873-C5
16300 LGTS 95032 873-C5
OLEANDER COM
5700 FRMT 94555 752-B3
OLEANDER CT
100 VAL 94591 530-G7
1000 SUNV 94086 832-H2
3900 AlaC 94546 691-H2
OLEANDER DR
100 SRFL 94903 566-D2
1100 LFYT 94549 611-B5
5700 NWK 94560 752-H7
OLEANDER PL
800 NVTO 94945 526-D4
OLEANDER ST
4200 LVMR 94550 696-A4
14700 SLN 94578 691-C4
OLEARY LN
1800 CCCo 94521 593-E3
OLENA CT
- SJS 95127 834-J2
OLGA DR
3900 SJS 95117 853-B2
4100 SJS 95129 853-B2
OLGA ST
- FRMT 94555 732-C7
OLIMA ST
500 SAUS 94965 626-H1
OLIN ST
3100 SJS 95117 853-D1
3100 SCIC 95117 853-D1
OLINDA CT
- CCCo 94803 589-G4
2300 PIN 94564 569-F7
OLINDA RD
5400 CCCo 94803 589-F3
5700 RCH 94803 589-F3
OLINDER CT
900 SJS 95122 834-F6
OLIVA CT
100 NVTO 94945 525-H2
2000 PLE 94588 694-E7
OLIVA DR
- NVTO 94945 525-H2
OLIVAS CIR
8700 SJS 95135 855-J6
OLIVE AV
- LKSP 94939 586-E6
- PDMT 94611 650-A1
- ROSS 94957 586-B2
- SANS 94960 566-B7
- SRFL 94901 566-H7
200 PA 94306 791-B7
200 PDMT 94611 649-J1
300 FRMT 94539 753-E7
400 PA 94306 811-B1
600 SSF 94080 707-J2
1400 CCCo 94805 589-C6
21600 CPTO 95014 852-B1
W OLIVE AV
100 SUNV 94086 832-C1
1000 SUNV 94086 812-B7
OLIVE COM
43000 FRMT 94539 753-H7
OLIVE CT
- MTVW 94041 811-J6
- SMTO 94401 729-B7
100 HER 94547 569-J4
500 SLN 94578 691-D5
700 SBRN 94066 707-H7
4600 RCH 94804 609-A2
7700 PLE 94588 713-J1
42400 FRMT 94539 753-G7
OLIVE DR
4700 CNCD 94521 593-D3
7500 PLE 94588 713-J1
10500 SCIC 95127 835-B1
10500 SCIC 95127 815-B7
OLIVE LN
- PCFA 94044 706-J6
1700 ANT 94509 575-F5
OLIVE PL
- HAY 94541 692-B7
- SCIC 95127 815-B7
- SCIC 95127 835-B1
OLIVE ST
- MLV 94941 606-D3
- SF 94109 647-H6
100 LGTS 95030 873-A6
100 MrnC 94945 526-F4
200 NVTO 94945 526-C3
300 MLPK 94025 790-E5
400 SLN 94578 691-C5
500 SAUS 94965 627-A2
1100 SCAR 94070 769-G3
1800 SCIC 95128 833-G7
2200 SJS 95128 833-G7
2400 CCCo 94553 571-F4
7700 OAK 94621 670-J3
7700 OAK 94605 670-H3
9000 OAK 94603 671-A5
9100 OAK 94603 670-J4
36500 NWK 94560 752-D6
OLIVE WY
- PIT 94565 574-E7
OLIVE BRANCH CT
- BEN 94510 551-C3
6700 SJS 95120 894-E3
OLIVE BRANCH LN
1100 SJS 95120 894-E2
OLIVEGATE LN
2000 SJS 95136 874-J3
OLIVEGLEN CT
- CNCD - 613-D1
OLIVE HILL LN
100 WDSD 94062 789-F5
OLIVEIRA LN
- LFYT 94549 631-H1
OLIVER AV
2500 OAK 94605 671-A5
OLIVER CT
- MLPK 94025 790-C6
400 PIN 94564 569-C4
3500 LFYT 94549 611-F7
OLIVER DR
2400 HAY 94545 731-G1
2500 HAY 94545 711-G7
OLIVER LN
- MrnC 94941 606-H5

OLIVER ST
1998 BAY AREA STREET INDEX
OVERLAKE CT 973

Thomas Bros. Maps ®
COPYRIGHT 1997

BAY AREA

STREET
Block City ZIP Pg-Grid

OLIVER ST
- DALY 94014 687-E3
- SF 94112 687-E3
300 MPS 95035 794-A3
1100 RDWC 94061 790-A1
OLIVER WY
38500 FRMT 94536 753-D1
OLIVERA CT
2100 CNCD 94520 572-F6
OLIVERA RD
- CNCD 94519 572-E5
1900 CNCD 94520 572-E5
E OLIVERA RD
2500 CNCD 94519 572-G6
2700 CNCD 94519 592-H1
OLIVERIA PL
2100 FRMT 94539 773-G3
OLIVE SPRING CT
11600 CPTO 95014 852-A4
OLIVESTONE WY
2600 SJS 95132 814-E5
OLIVET PKWY
400 CLMA 94014 687-D6
OLIVE TREE CT
24600 LAH 94024 831-D5
OLIVETREE DR
1700 SJS 95131 814-C4
OLIVE TREE LN
24600 LAH 94024 831-C4
24700 SCIC 94024 831-C4
OLIVETTI CT
3600 SJS 95148 835-F7
OLIVEWOOD CT
700 PIT 94565 574-E5
OLIVEWOOD DR
700 PIT 94565 574-E5
OLIVEWOOD PL
3000 SJS 95148 855-E1
OLIVE WOOD ST
19900 CPTO 95014 832-F6
OLIVIAN DR
500 SJS 95123 875-B3
OLIVINA AV
200 LVMR 94550 715-D1
1400 LVMR 94550 695-G7
OLMO CT
1000 SJS 95129 852-H2
OLMO WY
1800 WLCK 94598 612-E1
OLMSTEAD CT
2500 SSF 94080 707-C4
OLMSTEAD ST
600 SF 94134 688-A1
700 SF 94134 687-J1
6700 OAK 94621 670-F3
OLMSTED RD
- SCIC 94305 810-J1
- SCIC - 791-A7
- SCIC 94305 790-J7
OLNEY CT
- DNVL 94526 653-C6
32200 UNC 94587 732-C5
OLSEN DR
3100 SJS 95117 853-D1
3100 SCIC 95117 853-D1
OLSEN WY
35500 UNC 94587 732-H6
OLSON CT
100 VAL 94589 510-D5
OLSTAD CT
5300 SJS 95111 875-C2
OLYMPIA AV
1200 SCIC 95008 873-E1
1300 SJS 95008 873-E1
OLYMPIA CIR
3600 PIT 94565 574-C4
OLYMPIA DR
200 PIT 94565 574-C5
OLYMPIA ST
1600 CNCD 94521 593-A2
OLYMPIA WY
- NVTO 94949 546-B2
- SF 94131 667-E3
OLYMPIA FIELDS CT
- SRMN 94583 673-H7
OLYMPIA FIELDS DR
9400 SRMN 94583 673-H7
OLYMPIAN WY
100 PCFA 94044 726-G4
OLYMPIC AV
100 HAY 94544 732-C1
2300 MLPK 94025 790-D7
4200 SMTO 94403 749-D6
OLYMPIC BLVD
1500 WLCK 94596 612-C6
1900 CCCo 94595 612-A7
1900 WLCK 94595 612-C6
2500 CCCo 94595 611-J7
2600 LFYT 94549 611-H7
OLYMPIC CT
100 SBRN 94066 707-D5
2200 MRTZ 94553 572-A7
8000 NWK 94560 752-C7
OLYMPIC CT N
3600 PLE 94588 714-A1
OLYMPIC CT S
3500 PLE 94588 714-A1
OLYMPIC DR
100 VAL 94589 510-B6
1100 MPS 95035 814-C1
1800 MRTZ 94553 572-A7
1800 MRTZ 94553 571-J7
2300 SSF 94080 707-D5
2500 SBRN 94066 707-D5
OLYMPIC ST
- VAL 94589 510-B5
OLYMPIC WY
100 LVMR 94550 695-D7
200 SRFL 94903 566-F2
2100 SMCo 94015 686-J3
2200 DALY 94015 686-J3
OLYMPIC OAKS DR
- LFYT 94549 611-H7
OLYMPUS
400 HER 94547 569-F3
OLYMPUS AV
- BERK 94720 610-A7
- BERK 94708 609-J7
- BERK 94708 610-A7
41700 FRMT 94539 753-F6
OLYMPUS CT
900 SUNV 94087 832-B6
OLYMPUS DR
1300 SJS 95129 853-A4
OMAHA CT
6200 SJS 95123 874-H6
OMAK ST
- FRMT 94539 773-H4
OMAR DR
- SJS 95123 875-B4
OMAR ST
4800 FRMT 94538 773-B1
OMAR WY
- SF 94127 667-E5
OMEGA AV
4100 AlaC 94546 692-B5
OMEGA CIR
3100 PLE 94588 694-C7
OMEGA CT
- SJS 95127 814-H6
OMEGA DR
45900 FRMT 94539 773-H5
OMEGA LN
14400 SAR 95070 872-H3
OMEGA RD
2000 SRMN 94583 653-B7
2100 SRMN 94583 673-C1
OMIRA DR
200 SJS 95123 875-A4
ONA CT
- SRMN 94583 673-F6
ONDINA CT
40800 FRMT 94539 753-F4
ONDINA DR
- FRMT 94539 753-F5
ONDINA PL
40700 FRMT 94539 753-F4
ONDINE CT
1000 SJS 95132 814-H5
ONEIDA AV
- SF 94112 667-F7
- SF 94112 687-F1
ONEIDA CIR
2100 DNVL 94526 653-D7
ONEIDA CT
400 DNVL 94526 653-D7
ONEIDA DR
600 SUNV 94087 832-D2
6100 SJS 95123 874-H6
ONEIL AV
24500 HAY 94544 712-A3
ONEIL CIR
100 HER 94547 569-E3
ONEIL CT
- CCCo 94806 569-C6
ONEIL TER
34100 FRMT 94555 752-C2
ONEILL AV
- BLMT 94002 749-F7
- SMCo 94002 749-F7
200 BLMT 94002 769-E1
200 SMCo 94002 769-F1
ONEILL DR
3900 SMTO 94403 749-D6
ONEL DR
2100 SJS 95131 833-H1
2100 SJS 95131 813-H7
ONE OAK LN
15400 MSER 95030 873-A5
ONEONTA AV
500 PCFA 94044 727-A1
ONEONTA DR
24900 LAH 94022 831-C2
ONIQUE LN
- SF 94131 667-F5
ONLEY DR
1600 PLHL 94523 592-B4
ONONDAGA AV
- SF 94112 667-F7
100 SF 94112 687-F1
ONONDAGA CT
1300 FRMT 94539 773-G4
ONONDAGA DR
45100 FRMT 94539 773-G4
ONONDAGA PL
1400 FRMT 94539 773-G4
ONONDAGA WY
1100 FRMT 94539 773-G4
ON ORBIT DR
15500 SCIC 95070 872-C5
ONSLOW COM
38100 FRMT 94536 752-J1
ONSLOW WY
3300 SJS 95132 814-G4
ONTARIO COM
5300 FRMT 94555 752-C3
ONTARIO CT
600 SUNV 94087 832-D5
ONTARIO DR
300 LVMR 94550 715-D3
1500 SUNV 94087 832-D5
2400 SJS 95124 853-G7
ONTARIO LN
2400 CMBL 95008 853-B5
ONTARIO PL
200 HAY 94544 732-F3
ONTARIO RD
200 MPS 95035 794-A6
ONTARIO ST
- SMTO 94401 729-B7
ONYX CT
- HER 94547 569-G5
700 SJS 95117 853-D2
20000 AlaC 94546 692-B5
ONYX PL
6700 DBLN 94568 693-J2
ONYX RD
100 LVMR 94550 715-D3
ONYX ST
- LKSP 94939 586-E6
OPAH WY
4300 UNC 94587 731-J5
OPAL AV
100 RDWC 94062 769-H6
OPAL CT
- SRMN 94583 673-F2
100 HER 94547 569-G4
20000 AlaC 94546 692-B5
44200 FRMT 94539 773-H2
OPAL DR
100 VAL 94589 510-C6
700 SJS 95117 853-D3
OPAL PL
- SF 94102 648-A6
OPAL ST
- LKSP 94939 586-E5
1900 CCCo 94596 612-D6
1900 WLCK 94596 612-D6
3800 OAK 94609 629-H7
3800 OAK 94609 649-H1
OPAL WY
200 LVMR 94550 715-D3
OPALO LN
- SF 94131 667-F5
OPALSTONE TER
2500 MrnC 94903 546-E6
OPCEN RD
- CCCo 94553 571-G3
- MRTZ 94553 571-G3
OPENMEADOW CT
4400 SJS 95129 853-A1
OPERATIONS RD
100 FRMT 94539 773-J1
OPHELIA AV
2600 SJS 95122 855-A1
OPHELIA CT
2700 SJS 95122 855-A2
OPHIR AL
- SF 94109 647-J6
OPHIR CT
- MPS 95035 793-J7
1800 MRTZ 94553 571-J7
OPTIMIST ST
22800 HAY 94541 711-H2
OPTIMO AV
600 FRMT 94539 753-E5
ORA AV
1000 LVMR 94550 695-F7
ORA ST
5400 SJS 95129 852-H3
ORA WY
- SF 94131 667-F5
ORACLE PKWY
100 RDWC 94065 749-F6
ORACLE OAK PL
800 SUNV 94086 832-G2
ORAM LN
- PLHL 94523 592-A7
ORAM WY
- CCCo 94565 573-F2
ORANDA TER
1000 FRMT 94536 753-C3
ORANGE AL
- SF 94110 667-H4
ORANGE AV
- LKSP 94939 586-E6
- SSF 94080 707-H3
400 LALT 94022 811-D7
400 LALT 94022 831-D1
600 NVTO 94945 526-G3
700 SCAR 94070 769-G3
800 SCIC 94043 812-A2
800 SUNV 94087 832-C2
1100 MLPK 94025 790-D5
1100 SMCo 94025 790-D5
10000 CPTO 95014 832-C2
10000 CPTO 95014 852-B1
21200 AlaC 94546 691-J7
W ORANGE AV
- SSF 94080 707-F3
ORANGE CT
- DALY 94014 687-D5
- HIL 94010 748-D1
- MrnC 94901 586-H3
ORANGE ST
- MrnC 94901 586-H3
100 OAK 94610 649-H2
100 VAL 94590 550-B1
500 DALY 94014 687-D5
1000 CNCD 94518 592-E6
2100 CCCo 94553 571-F4
2100 MRTZ 94553 571-F4
3100 SJS 95127 814-H7
ORANGE WY
600 LVMR 94550 715-E3
2600 ANT 94509 595-G5
ORANGE BLOSSOM CT
- DNVL 94526 653-B4
- AMCN 94589 509-J2
ORANGE BLOSSOM DR
7500 CPTO 95014 852-D4
ORANGE BLOSSOM LN
100 SRFL 94903 566-D2
15700 SCIC 95032 873-D6
ORANGE BLOSSOM WY
800 DNVL 94526 653-B4
ORANGEBRICK WY
100 SJS 95120 894-F2
ORANGE GROVE DR
1800 SJS 95124 873-G1
ORANGESTONE WY
- SJS 95132 814-E5
ORANGETREE LN
1800 MTVW 94040 831-G1
10500 CPTO 95014 832-E7
ORANGEVALE
200 PIT 94565 574-B3
ORANGEWOOD CT
4200 CNCD 94521 593-B2
4700 PLE 94588 713-J1
ORANGEWOOD DR
500 FRMT 94536 753-D1
1500 SJS 95121 855-A3
ORANGEWOOD ST
19800 CPTO 95014 832-F6
ORBEN PL
- SF 94115 647-G5
ORCA TER
1000 FRMT 94536 753-C3
ORCHARD AV
- RDWC 94061 790-B1
100 HAY 94544 712-A3
100 MTVW 94043 811-J5
100 MTVW 94043 812-A4
200 HAY 94544 711-J4
300 SUNV 94086 812-E6
1000 SolC 94591 530-E6
1000 VAL 94591 530-E6
1200 SLN 94577 690-J1
1700 SLN 94577 691-A2
3300 CNCD 94518 592-H3
5900 RCH 94804 609-C3
ORCHARD CT
- CCCo 94507 632-F5
- ORIN 94563 630-J3
22000 CPTO 95014 832-A7
ORCHARD DR
100 FRMT 94536 753-D1
3000 SJS 95134 813-F5
ORCHARD GN
200 MTVW 94043 812-A5
ORCHARD LN
- BERK 94704 630-A2
900 ANT 94509 575-E4
1600 WLCK 94595 612-C7
2400 CCCo 94553 571-F3
ORCHARD PKWY
- SJS 95131 813-G7
2600 SJS 95134 813-F5
ORCHARD RD
- ORIN 94563 630-J2
200 ORIN 94563 631-A3
1000 LFYT 94549 611-E5
20200 SAR 95070 872-E2
ORCHARD ST
- LGTS 95032 893-A1
ORCHARD TR
- CCCo 94553 591-E4
- MRTZ 94553 591-F3
ORCHARD WY
- MrnC 94904 586-D3
- NVTO 94947 526-A3
1600 PLE 94566 714-D2
1700 LVMR 94550 715-E3
ORCHARD CITY DR
- CMBL 95008 853-E6
ORCHARD ESTATES DR
- WLCK 94598 612-J4
ORCHARD HILL CT
3400 LFYT 94549 611-F6
ORCHARD HILL LN
- WDSD 94062 809-H6
26900 LAH 94022 811-C7
ORCHARD HILLS ST
- ATN 94027 790-B4
ORCHARD MEADOW DR
20000 SCIC 95070 852-A7
ORCHARD MEADOW RD
3400 OAK 94613 650-G7
ORCHARD OAK CIR
100 CMBL 95008 853-F6
ORCHARD PARK DR
5600 SJS 95123 874-J5
ORCHARD SPRING CT
11600 CPTO 95014 852-A4
ORCHARD SPRING LN
11600 CPTO 95014 852-A4
ORCHARD VALLEY CT
3300 LFYT 94549 611-G6
ORCHARD VIEW AV
300 MRTZ 94553 571-G5
ORCHARD VIEW DR
1600 SJS 95124 873-J6
ORCHID CT
100 HER 94547 570-A4
ORCHID DR
200 PIT 94565 574-E5
300 SRFL 94903 566-D2
1100 SUNV 94086 832-H2
14200 SLN 94578 691-C3
ORCHID PL
800 LALT 94024 831-E1
ORCHID WY
900 SJS 95117 853-B3
ORD CT
- SF 94114 667-F2
ORD ST
- SF 94129 647-D4
- SF 94114 667-F2
ORDEN CT
100 FRMT 94539 753-E3
ORDWAY ST
- SF 94134 688-A1
900 ALB 94706 609-F6
900 ALB 94707 609-F6
1100 BERK 94706 609-F6
1300 BERK 94702 609-E7
1300 BERK 94702 629-E1
OREGOLD PL
700 SJS 95131 814-B6
OREGON AV
- RDWC 94061 789-J2
- RDWC 94061 790-A2
100 PA 94301 791-B6
700 SMTO 94402 748-H4
700 PA 94303 791-B6
OREGON CT
900 MPS 95035 794-A5
1200 CNCD 94521 593-E6
OREGON DR
1300 CNCD 94521 593-E6
OREGON EXWY Rt#-G3
- PA 94301 791-C6
- PA 94303 791-C6
300 PA 94306 791-C6
OREGON ST
- BEN 94510 551-E2
- RCH 94801 608-D1
500 VAL 94590 530-A2
1100 BERK 94702 629-E4
1300 BERK 94703 629-F3
2100 BERK 94705 629-H3
2300 UNC 94587 732-E6
OREGON WY
1000 MPS 95035 794-A5
3500 LVMR 94550 715-J1
OREILLY AV
- SF 94129 647-E4
ORELLA CT
12600 SAR 95070 852-F6
ORESTES WY
2000 SJS 95008 853-B6
ORI AV
2700 SJS 95128 853-E2
ORICK CT
300 SJS 95123 874-J4
ORICK ST
32700 UNC 94587 732-B7
ORIENT DR
700 NVTO 94945 526-H1
ORIENTE ST
- DALY 94014 687-J4
ORILLA CT
1100 LALT 94022 811-D3
ORILLIA CT
1500 SUNV 94087 832-D5
ORIN CT
4100 SJS 95124 873-E3
ORIN DR
2400 OAK 94612 649-H2
ORIN LN
2100 PLHL 94523 592-B3
ORINDA AV
- PCFA 94044 727-A2
ORINDA CIR
- PIT 94565 574-B4
ORINDA CT
- PIT 94565 574-C4
5500 LVMR 94550 696-C2
ORINDA DR
2500 SJS 95121 855-D3
3500 SMTO 94403 749-D5
ORINDA LN
- PIT 94565 574-C4
700 WLCK 94596 612-B4
ORINDA ST
3400 PA 94306 811-C1
ORINDA WY
- ORIN 94563 610-G7
ORINDA VIEW RD
- ORIN 94563 611-A3
- ORIN 94563 610-J3
ORINDA VISTA DR
- OAK 94605 671-C3
ORINDAWOODS DR
100 ORIN 94563 610-H7
ORIOLE AV
400 LVMR 94550 695-E7
400 LVMR 94550 715-E1
1400 AlaC 94578 691-E4
1500 SUNV 94087 832-G5
ORIOLE CIR
100 NVTO 94949 546-E5
ORIOLE CT
100 HER 94547 569-H5
3800 ANT 94509 594-J1
ORIOLE DR
3100 SJS 95117 853-D3
ORIOLE PL
3400 FRMT 94555 732-D7
ORIOLE RD
- ORIN 94563 610-F5
14000 SAR 95070 872-G4
ORIOLE WY
- SF 94116 667-C3
15100 SAR 95070 872-H4
ORION
800 HER 94547 569-F3
ORION CT
100 MPS 95035 793-J7
2100 LVMR 94550 715-E4
3800 PLE 94566 714-F4
ORION DR
- VAL 94591 510-J3
ORION LN
- FCTY 94404 749-F4
7700 CPTO 95014 852-C3
ORION PL
900 CPTO 95014 852-C3
ORION ST
22600 AlaC 94541 692-C6
ORION WY
600 LVMR 94550 715-E4
ORISKANY DR
- SMCo 94402 748-G7
ORIZABA AV
- SF 94132 687-D2
ORKNEY AV
700 SCL 95054 813-E6
ORKNEY CT
5100 NWK 94560 752-E4
ORLANDO AV
27400 HAY 94545 711-H7
27700 HAY 94545 731-J1
ORLANDO CT
1500 WLCK 94596 611-J2
ORLANDO DR
1300 SJS 95122 834-H6
2000 SJS 95122 854-J1
ORLEANS CT
1700 WLCK 94598 592-E7
1700 WLCK 94598 612-F1
13700 SAR 95070 872-G1
ORLEANS DR
100 MRTZ 94553 571-G6
1200 SUNV 94089 812-G3
1600 SJS 95122 854-J1
2200 PIN 94564 569-E3
35400 NWK 94560 752-C5
ORLINE CT
10700 CPTO 95014 852-D2
ORLOFF DR
1200 PLE 94566 714-F1
ORME ST
4000 PA 94306 811-C2
ORMINDALE CT
- OAK 94611 630-E5
ORMOND AV
27700 HAY 94544 712-A7
27800 HAY 94544 732-A1
ORMOND CT
- NVTO 94947 526-A4
ORMONDE DR
700 MTVW 94043 811-H3
ORMONDE WY
1300 MTVW 94043 811-H3
ORMSBY DR
1400 SUNV 94087 832-D4
ORNELLAS DR
2000 MPS 95035 814-E1
ORO CT
- NVTO 94947 525-G4
100 VAL 94591 530-D2
ORO DR
1600 FRMT 94539 753-E5
OROFINO CT
600 PLE 94566 714-H3
OROGRANDE PL
7700 SCIC 95014 852-C3
7700 CPTO 95014 852-C3
OROLETTE PL
1900 SJS 95131 814-D6
ORONSAY CT
200 SJS 95119 875-D7
ORONSAY WY
200 SJS 95119 875-D7
OROPEZA CT
600 SJS 95133 834-G1
OROSI CT
200 SJS 95116 834-F3
OROSI WY
2000 SJS 95116 834-F3
OROURKE DR
- CCCo 94806 569-B4
ORO VALLEY CIR
1700 WLCK 94596 612-G7
ORO VALLEY CT
1800 WLCK 94596 612-H7
OROVILLE CT
4000 FRMT 94555 752-D1
OROVILLE RD
400 MPS 95035 794-A6
OROVILLE ST
3500 ANT 94509 595-H1
ORR CT
- ALA 94502 669-J6
1600 LALT 94024 831-J4
ORR RD
- ALA 94502 669-J6
ORRAL ST
7000 OAK 94621 670-G3
ORREY WY
- SSF 94080 707-E5
ORRIS TER
200 SRFL 94903 566-E3
ORSINI CT
5100 PLE 94588 694-A6
ORTEGA AV
- MTVW 94040 811-F4
1500 HAY 94544 732-A1
3200 LFYT 94549 611-H5
ORTEGA CT
- PCFA 94044 726-J4
3700 PA 94303 791-E7
ORTEGA DR
1500 MRTZ 94553 591-H1
26800 LAH 94022 811-A5
ORTEGA ST
- SF 94116 667-A3
- SF 94122 667-A3
2700 SF 94122 666-H3
2700 SF 94116 666-H3
ORTEGA WY
700 SF 94122 667-C3
700 SF 94116 667-C3
ORTHELLO WY
2800 SCL 95051 833-A4
ORTHO WY
700 RCH 94801 588-F5
ORTIZ CT
1200 SUNV 94089 813-A4
ORTO ST
400 SJS 95125 854-D3
ORVIETO CT
- PLE 94566 715-B5
5700 SJS 95138 875-G1
ORVIS AV
500 SJS 95112 834-D7
ORWELL PL
3100 FRMT 94536 752-G2
OSAGE AL
- SF 94110 667-J4
OSAGE AV
- LALT 94022 811-F7
1800 HAY 94545 731-J2
OSAGE CT
- HAY 94545 732-A2
- HAY 94545 731-J2
600 SJS 95123 874-G4
OSAGE PL
5700 CNCD 94521 593-F7
OSAGE RIVER CT
34600 FRMT 94555 752-E1
OSAGE RIVER PL
4000 FRMT 94555 752-E1
OSBORN AV
1100 SMCo 94061 790-B3
OSBORNE AV
2300 SCL 95050 833-D7
OSBORNE CT
- OAK 94611 650-G2
OSBORNE LN
500 PLHL 94523 592-B4
OSCAR AL
- SF 94105 648-B6
OSCAR AV
9300 OAK 94603 670-G6
OSCAR CT
4800 FRMT 94538 753-B7
4800 FRMT 94538 773-B1
OSCAR ST
1500 RCH 94804 609-B3
OSCEOLA CT
900 WLCK 94598 612-H4
OSCEOLA LN
- SF 94124 668-C6
OSGOOD CT
400 SJS 95111 875-B2
3000 FRMT 94539 773-F2
OSGOOD PL
- SF 94133 648-A4
OSGOOD RD
41000 FRMT 94539 773-E1
44100 FRMT 94539 753-E7
OSHAUGHNESSY BLVD
- SF 94127 667-E4
- SF 94127 667-E5
- SF 94131 667-E4
- SF 94131 667-E5
OSITOS AV
400 SUNV 94086 812-C7
400 SUNV 94086 832-C1
OSLO CT
1500 LVMR 94550 715-G3
OSLO LN
1300 SJS 95118 874-B5
OSO ST
3600 SMTO 94403 749-D5
OSO GRANDE WY
- ANT 94509 595-H2
OSPREY CT
- RDWC 94065 750-A5
1500 SJS 95127 835-C4
OSPREY DR
- RDWC 94065 750-A5
2200 UNC 94587 732-G7
OSTENBERG DR
6000 SJS 95120 874-C7
OSTRANDER RD
5800 OAK 94618 630-B6
OSTRICH CT
5200 SJS 95123 874-F7
OSTROSKY CT
- CCCo 94507 632-H3
OSUNA PL
1100 SJS 95129 852-J3
OSWALD PL
1600 SCL 95051 833-B3
OSWEGO CT
- LFYT 94549 611-G7
- LFYT 94549 631-G1
OSWEGO DR
800 SJS 95122 854-F1
OSWOSSO PL
32300 HAY 94544 732-F3
OTAY AV
- SMTO 94403 749-C5
OTEGA AV
- SF 94112 687-E1
OTHELLO AV
2600 SJS 95122 855-A2
OTHELLO DR
4200 FRMT 94555 752-C1
OTHELLO RD
33500 FRMT 94555 752-C1
OTIS AV
100 WDSD 94062 789-G5
OTIS DR
900 ALA 94501 669-G2
2500 ALA 94501 670-A3
OTIS DR Rt#-61
- ALA 94502 670-A3
OTIS ST
- SF 94103 667-H1
2900 BERK 94703 629-G4
OTIS WY
- LALT 94022 811-F6
OTONO CT
300 SJS 95111 875-A1
OTOOLE AV
1800 SJS 95131 814-A5
2400 SJS 95131 813-J5
OTOOLE LN
- SJS 95131 814-A6
OTOOLE WY
- SJS 95131 814-A6
2400 CCCo 94806 569-B5
OTSEGO AV
- SF 94112 667-F7
- SF 94112 687-F1
OTTAWA AV
- SF 94112 687-E1
1200 SLN 94579 691-A4
OTTAWA CT
1600 SUNV 94087 832-D5
OTTAWA ST
- SMTO 94401 729-A6
OTTAWA WY
100 FRMT 94539 793-J2
2400 SJS 95130 853-A7
OTTER CT
3300 HAY 94542 712-F4
OTTERSON CT
2900 PA 94303 791-D5
OTTERSON ST
500 SJS 95110 834-A7
OTTILIA ST
300 DALY 94014 687-J3
OTTO CT
900 SJS 95132 814-J5
OUR LN
2400 MTVW 94040 831-J1
OUR HILL LN
2900 WDSD 94062 789-H6
OUR LADYS WY
- SCL 95054 813-B5
OURSAN TR
- CCCo - 590-E6
- CCCo - 611-A2
- CCCo - 610-H1
OUTER CIR
200 RDWC 94062 769-H7
OUTLOOK AV
5900 OAK 94605 650-H7
6100 OAK 94605 670-H1
7700 OAK 94605 671-A3
OUTLOOK CIR
1000 PCFA 94044 707-B6
OUTLOOK CT
3400 SJS 95132 814-G3
21300 AlaC 94546 691-J6
OUTLOOK DR
- SBRN 94066 707-B6
500 SCIC 94024 831-F2
1100 PCFA 94044 707-B6
OUTRIGGER DR
- SLN 94577 690-G5
- VAL 94591 550-D1
OUTRIGGER LN
1100 FCTY 94404 749-H4
OVAL RD
- OAK 94611 630-C5
OVATION CT
700 SJS 95134 813-H4
OVELLA WY
3500 PLE 94566 715-B7
OVER ST
- LKSP 94939 586-E5
3300 OAK 94619 650-E6
OVERACKER AV
38500 FRMT 94536 753-D2
38900 FRMT 94538 753-D2
OVERACKER TER
100 FRMT 94536 753-C2
OVERBROOK DR
3200 SJS 95118 874-B1
OVERDALE AV
6100 OAK 94605 650-H7
OVEREND AV
4100 RCH 94804 609-A1
OVERHILL CT
- ORIN 94563 630-H1
OVERHILL DR
600 HAY 94544 712-D6
OVERHILL RD
- MLV 94941 606-F2
- ORIN 94563 630-H1
100 ORIN 94563 631-A1
1800 CNCD 94520 572-E6
OVERLAKE AV
5900 LVMR 94550 696-D2
OVERLAKE CT
- OAK 94611 630-E6

INDEX

BAY AREA

INDEX

STREET — Block City ZIP Pg-Grid

OVERLAKE PL
6500 NWK 94560 752-B5
OVERLAND AL
- VAL 94590 529-H4
600 VAL 94590 530-A4
OVERLAND AV
6200 EMVL 94608 629-E5
OVERLAND CT
600 SJS 95111 854-H5
OVERLAND DR
1300 SMTO 94403 748-J7
OVERLAND WY
600 SJS 95111 854-H5
S OVERLOOK
200 SRMN 94583 673-F2
OVERLOOK AV
1100 HAY 94542 712-A3
OVERLOOK CRES
- VAL 94591 510-J4
OVERLOOK CT
- WLCK 94596 612-B4
1100 SRMN 94583 673-F2
OVERLOOK DR
- CNCD 94521 593-C6
- SF - 667-B1
- VAL 94591 510-J4
1000 SRMN 94583 673-E3
2100 CCCo 94596 612-B4
2100 WLCK 94596 612-B3
15900 SCIC 95030 872-F6
OVERLOOK LN
- RCH 94803 569-C7
OVERLOOK RD
900 BERK 94708 609-J5
17900 SCIC 95030 872-H7
18300 MSER 95030 872-H7
18400 LGTS 95030 872-H7
OVERLOOK ST
800 SMTO 94403 749-A7
OVERLOOK TER
44700 FRMT 94539 773-J2
OVERMOOR ST
11000 OAK 94605 671-D5
OVERTURE CT
700 SJS 95134 813-H4
OVIEDO CT
- PCFA 94044 726-J4
OWEN ST
- SF 94129 647-D4
2300 SCL 95054 813-C7
OWENS CT
2100 PIN 94564 569-F6
5300 PLE 94588 694-B5
OWENS DR
600 NVTO 94949 546-D1
4900 PLE 94588 694-A5
OWENS ST
- SF 94107 668-B1
OWENS LAKE DR
800 SJS 95123 874-D5
OWEN SOUND DR
1400 SUNV 94087 832-D4
OWHANEE CT
700 FRMT 94539 774-A4
700 FRMT 94539 773-J4
OWL CT
- DBLN 94568 694-D4
100 FRMT 94539 773-J2
700 ANT 94509 595-F2
OWL DR
43900 FRMT 94539 773-J1
OWL PL
44100 FRMT 94539 773-J2
OWL HILL CT
- ORIN 94563 630-J2
OWL HILL RD
- ORIN 94563 630-J2
OWL RIDGE CT
1900 WLCK 94596 611-H2
OWLSWOOD LN
- TBRN 94920 607-C6
OWLSWOOD RD
- LKSP 94939 586-E7
- TBRN 94920 607-C6
OWLSWOOD WY
400 SJS 95111 854-F6
OWSLEY AV
900 SJS 95122 834-F7
OXBOW CT
1300 SUNV 94087 832-D4
5100 SJS 95124 873-F5
7900 DBLN 94568 693-G4
OXBOW LN
7800 DBLN 94568 693-G4
OXFORD
100 HER 94547 569-H3
OXFORD AV
- MLV 94941 606-F4
200 PA 94306 791-A7
1200 SUNV 94087 832-B2
1500 SMTO 94403 749-C2
2700 RCH 94806 588-J1
2800 RCH 94806 589-A2
OXFORD CIR
7400 DBLN 94568 694-A2
OXFORD COM
3600 FRMT 94536 752-J4
OXFORD CT
- VAL 94591 530-G4
- PIT 94565 574-C4
100 CCCo 94507 632-J2
3500 SCL 95051 832-J6
OXFORD DR
- MrnC 94903 566-H3
100 MRGA 94556 651-E2
900 LALT 94024 831-H5
3500 SCL 95051 832-J6
OXFORD LN
- BERK 94704 629-H2
100 SBRN 94066 727-G2
3200 SJS 95117 853-D3
OXFORD PL
1400 LVMR 94550 715-G5
3200 CNCD 94518 592-H3
4900 NWK 94560 752-E4
6500 DBLN 94568 694-A2
OXFORD RD
1100 BURL 94010 728-D5
OXFORD ST
- SF 94134 667-H7
300 AlaC 94541 711-E1
500 SF 94134 687-J1
800 BERK 94707 609-G5
1200 BERK 94709 609-H7
1300 RDWC 94061 790-A1
1600 BERK 94709 629-H1
1900 BERK 94704 629-H1
1900 BERK 94720 629-H1
OXFORD WY
100 BLMT 94002 749-F7
800 BEN 94510 530-J6
OXSEN ST
1500 PLE 94566 714-E1
OXTON DR
1100 SJS 95121 854-J3
OYAMA DR
1400 SJS 95131 814-B7
OYAMA PL
1400 SJS 95131 814-B7
OYSTER CT
500 FCTY 94404 749-F5
3500 UNC 94587 732-A4
OYSTER BAY DR
4700 SJS 95136 874-D2
OYSTER BAY TER
34800 FRMT 94555 752-E1
OYSTER POINT BLVD
- SSF 94080 708-B2
OYSTER POND RD
- ALA 94502 670-A5
OYSTER SHOALS
- ALA 94502 670-A6
OZARK RIVER WY
34800 FRMT 94555 752-E2

P

P ST
- BEN 94510 551-B4
N P ST
200 LVMR 94550 715-G1
500 LVMR 94550 695-F7
S P ST
100 LVMR 94550 715-G1
PABCO
- CCCo 94553 571-G2
PABLO VISTA AV
1700 SPAB 94806 588-H1
PACCHETTI WY
100 MTVW 94040 811-E3
PACE BLVD
- PIT 94565 574-H4
PACER CT
300 VAL 94591 530-E1
PACER DR
100 VAL 94591 530-E1
PACER LN
2600 SCIC 95111 854-G4
PACER PL
- WLCK 94596 632-F2
PACHECO AV
100 MrnC 94947 526-A5
PACHECO BLVD
1100 MRTZ 94553 571-E3
2200 CCCo 94553 571-G3
4400 CCCo 94553 572-B6
4600 MRTZ 94553 572-B6
5700 CCCo 94553 592-C1
PACHECO DR
700 MPS 95035 794-B6
2300 SJS 95133 834-F1
33600 FRMT 94555 732-D7
PACHECO ST
- MrnC 94965 626-H1
- SF 94127 667-D4
- SRFL 94901 566-G7
- SF 94116 667-D4
200 SF 94116 667-C3
1300 SCL 95051 833-A4
2000 CNCD 94520 592-F1
2700 CNCD 94519 592-G1
3000 SF 94116 666-H4
5800 CCCo 94553 592-F1
PACHECO WY
100 VAL 94591 530-D7
1400 HAY 94544 732-A2
PACHECO CREEK DR
- NVTO 94949 546-D4
PACHECO MANOR DR
5300 CCCo 94553 572-B7
PACIFIC AV
- SF 94129 647-C5
- CCCo 94572 549-H7
- PDMT 94611 650-B1
- SBRN 94066 707-J5
- SF 94111 648-A4
100 ALA 94501 649-E7
100 PCFA 94044 706-J6
200 PCFA 94044 707-J5
200 SMCo 94063 770-C7
300 RCH 94801 588-C7
300 RCH 94801 608-C1
400 SF 94133 648-A4
500 ALA 94501 669-G1
800 SCIC 95126 853-J1
1000 SF 94133 647-F5
1200 SF 94109 647-F5
1200 SLN 94577 690-J1
1300 SJS 95002 793-C7
1900 SLN 94577 691-A2
2100 ALA 94501 670-A2
2100 SF 94115 647-F5
2300 SF 94118 647-F5
2500 SF 94118 647-E5
2700 CNCD 94518 592-G2
2900 LVMR 94550 715-J2
3100 SF 94129 647-F5
W PACIFIC AV
- SF 94118 647-C5
- SF 94129 647-C5
3300 SF 94129 647-E5
3300 SF 94118 647-E5
PACIFIC BLVD
1900 SMTO 94403 749-C6
1900 SMTO 94402 749-B3
PACIFIC CT
100 VAL 94589 510-B6
200 ANT 94509 595-E1
900 WLCK 94598 612-G4
PACIFIC DR
- CCCo 94806 569-B5
- NVTO 94949 546-C1
400 MTVW 94043 812-B5
2300 SCL 95051 832-J2
PACIFIC ST
1100 UNC 94587 732-E5
28200 HAY 94544 712-B7
29100 HAY 94544 732-C1
40200 FRMT 94538 753-C6
PACIFIC WY
- MrnC 94965 626-A2
PACIFICA AV
- CCCo 94565 573-D1
PACIFICA CT
1800 BEN 94510 551-C4
PACIFICA DR
2000 SJS 95131 814-A5
20000 CPTO 95014 852-E1
PACIFICA WY
200 MPS 95035 793-J4
PACIFIC CREST DR
- SMCo - 768-D3
PACIFIC HEIGHTS BLVD
3700 SBRN 94066 707-C5
PACIFICO AV
- DALY 94015 687-A7
PACIFIC QUEEN PASG
- CMAD 94925 606-J1
PACIFIC RIM LN
2400 SJS 95121 855-E4
PACIFIC RIM WY
4400 SJS 95121 855-E4
PACIFIC VIEW DR
- SMCo - 768-D4
PACINA DR
2000 SJS 95116 834-H5
PACINI AV
- PIT 94565 574-C5
PACKARD AL
100 VAL 94590 529-J4
600 VAL 94590 530-A4
PACKARD CT
1900 CNCD 94521 593-G4
44100 FRMT 94539 773-J2
PACKET LNDG
200 ALA 94502 670-A5
PACKING PL
200 SJS 95116 834-G4
PACO DR
400 LALT 94024 811-F7
PACU TER
- FRMT 94536 753-C3
PADDINGTON CT
- BLMT 94002 769-B3
PADDINGTON WY
1200 SJS 95127 835-A4
PADDLEWHEEL DR
100 VAL 94591 550-F2
PADDOCK CT
- PLHL 94523 591-H3
5100 ANT 94509 595-G4
PADDOCK DR
2400 SRMN 94583 673-B3
PADDOCK LN
- SRMN 94583 673-B4
PADDON CIR
5800 SJS 95123 875-A5
PADERO AV
13200 SAR 95070 852-C7
PADERO CT
13200 SAR 95070 852-C7
PADILLA CT
- DNVL 94526 653-C6
PADILLA WY
3200 SJS 95148 835-D7
PADRE AV
1300 SLN 94579 691-A6
PADRE CT
12100 LAH 94022 831-B2
PADRE ST
3100 CCCo 94549 611-H1
PADRE WY
11500 DBLN 94568 693-F3
PADRES CT
1500 SJS 95125 854-C3
PADRES DR
1400 SJS 95125 854-B3
PAGANINI AV
2600 SJS 95122 855-A1
PAGANO CT
400 SLN 94578 691-C5
PAGE AV
- FRMT 94538 793-G2
PAGE CT
1200 PIN 94564 569-C5
4000 PLE 94588 694-A7
PAGE ST
- SF 94102 647-H7
300 CMBL 95008 853-F6
300 SCIC 95126 853-H1
300 SJS 95126 853-H1
400 SF 94102 667-E1
500 SF 94117 667-E1
700 BERK 94804 629-D1
1000 BERK 94702 629-D1
1000 BERK 94702 609-E7
1400 ALA 94501 669-F1
1900 SF 94117 667-E1
3000 RDWC 94063 770-E6
16500 AlaC 94578 691-G4
PAGEANT WY
- LGTS 95032 893-A1
PAGE MILL DR
100 SJS 95111 875-B2
PAGE MILL RD
100 PA 94306 791-B7
500 PA 94304 811-A2
500 PA 94305 791-B7
1000 PA 94304 830-G2
1000 SCIC 95014 830-G2
1100 PA 94305 811-A2
1200 SCIC 94305 811-A2
1600 SCIC 94305 810-H7
1600 PA 94304 810-H7
11600 LAH 94022 830-G2
11800 SCIC 94022 830-G2
12700 LAH 94022 810-H7
20800 SMCo 94028 830-F7
PAGE MILL RD Rt#-G3
1800 SCIC 94305 810-J4
1800 PA 94304 810-J4
1900 SCIC 94304 810-J4
2400 LAH 94022 810-J4
PAGODA PL
- SF 94108 648-A5
PAGODA TREE CT
800 SUNV 94086 832-G2
PAGOSA CT
700 WLCK 94596 612-B2
700 DNVL 94526 653-B3
48900 FRMT 94539 793-J2
PAGOSA WY
- FRMT 94539 793-J3
500 FRMT 94539 794-A2
PAICH CT
2500 FRMT 94539 753-F7
PAIGE CT
2100 PIT 94565 574-A3
PAINE CT
3000 FRMT 94555 732-F7
PAINTBRUSH DR
1000 SUNV 94086 832-H3
PAINTBRUSH PZ
28600 HAY 94542 712-B3
PAINTED PONY RD
3700 RCH 94803 589-G1
PAINTED ROCK DR
2400 SCL 95051 833-A1
PAISLEY CT
900 ANT 94509 575-C7
PAIUTE CT
44300 FRMT 94539 773-G3
PAIUTE LN
400 SJS 95123 874-H5
PAJARO AV
200 SUNV 94086 812-D6
PAJARO CT
100 SUNV 94086 812-D6
1400 AlaC 94578 691-F5
1600 FRMT 94539 753-E6
6500 SJS 95120 894-D1
PAJARO DR
40900 FRMT 94539 753-E5
PAJARO WY
100 VAL 94591 530-D2
6500 SJS 95120 894-D1
PALA AV
- PDMT 94611 630-B7
- SJS 95127 834-H2
- SCIC 95127 834-H2
400 SUNV 94086 832-C1
500 SLN 94577 671-B7
PALACE CT
500 ALA 94501 669-F1
900 BEN 94510 550-H1
PALACE DR
- SF 94123 647-E3
- SF 94129 647-E3
- SJS 95129 853-A1
PALACEWOOD CT
4900 SJS 95129 852-J2
PALACIO CT
- FRMT 94539 753-F4
PALACIO ESPADA CT
200 SJS 95116 834-F3
PALACIO ROYALE CIR
200 SJS 95116 834-D2
PALACIO VERDE CT
200 SJS 95116 834-D2
PALADIN DR
3900 SJS 95124 873-J2
PALADIN WY
- PLE 94566 715-C7
PALADINI RD
- NVTO 94947 525-H3
PALAMOS AV
1100 SUNV 94089 812-J4
1200 SUNV 94089 813-A4
PALAMOS CT
- SRMN 94583 673-C3
PALANA CT
- CCCo 94595 612-B6
PALANTINO WY
3200 SJS 95135 855-G3
PALATINO ST
40600 FRMT 94539 753-F4
PALATKA LN
1900 HAY 94545 711-H6
PALAZZI CT
- SANS 94960 566-A6
PALERMO CT
100 HER 94547 570-B6
13000 SAR 95070 852-F7
PALERMO DR
- PLE 94566 715-D7
PALI CT
- OAK 94611 630-C5
PALI WY
- PIT 94565 574-E5
PALINDO AV
- CNCD 94520 592-F3
PALISADE CT
1000 MRTZ 94553 571-H5
PALISADE DR
800 MRTZ 94553 571-H5
4200 SJS 95111 855-A7
PALISADE ST
900 HAY 94542 712-A3
PALISADES DR
- DALY 94015 686-J5
1300 MPS 95035 793-J4
PALISADES WY
4400 ANT 94509 595-J2
PALM
- BEN 94510 551-C5
- CNCD 94518 592-G4
PALM AV
- CCCo 94572 570-A3
- HER 94547 569-J3
- HER 94547 570-A3
- CMAD 94925 586-F7
- LGTS 95030 872-J7
- LKSP 94939 586-E6
- MLBR 94030 728-A3
- SANS 94960 566-C7
- SF 94118 647-D6
- SRFL 94901 566-H7
100 SCAR 94070 769-F3
300 MrnC 94903 586-E3
300 OAK 94610 649-J3
400 MRTZ 94553 571-F5
500 LALT 94022 811-E7
500 LALT 94022 831-E1
500 SSF 94080 707-H2
600 CCCo 94553 571-F4
700 RDWC 94061 790-A1
800 RDWC 94061 789-J2
900 SMTO 94401 749-A2
1200 BLMT 94002 769-F1
1200 SMTO 94402 749-A2
1400 CCCo 94805 589-C6
2000 SMTO 94403 749-B4
2200 LVMR 94550 715-H2
22200 CPTO 95014 852-A1
41700 FRMT 94539 753-G6
PALM CT
- MLPK 94025 790-E5
- LKSP 94939 586-F6
100 SBRN 94066 707-E7
700 SUNV 94086 832-G2
2800 BERK 94705 629-J3
4000 FRMT 94536 752-H3
7400 PLE 94588 713-J1
PALM DR
- NVTO 94949 546-H3
- UNC 94587 732-C6
- PIT 94565 574-E5
100 PA 94305 790-H6
100 PDMT 94610 650-A2
100 SCIC 94305 790-H6
400 SCL 95053 833-F4
1100 BURL 94010 728-E6
PALM PL
1900 SMTO 94403 749-B4
2100 HAY 94545 731-H1
PALM ST
400 PA 94301 791-A3
600 SJS 95110 854-B1
PALM WY
- MrnC 94965 606-B4
PALMA WY
500 MrnC 94965 606-E6
PALMA VISTA
- CCCo 94526 633-F7
PALM BEACH LN
- ALA 94502 670-A5
PALM BEACH WY
- ANT 94509 595-D1
2000 SJS 95122 854-J1
PALM CIRCLE RD
- SMCo 94062 789-E3
- WDSD 94062 789-E3
PALMCREST DR
100 DALY 94015 687-B4
PALMDALE AV
- DALY 94015 687-A5
PALMDALE CT
2500 SCL 95051 833-B2
7700 PLE 94588 693-J7
32800 UNC 94587 732-B7
PALMDALE ST
4300 UNC 94587 732-B7
PALM DESERT WY
- SJS 95123 875-G2
PALMER AV
100 MTVW 94043 811-G3
900 SPAB 94806 588-H1
2400 BLMT 94002 769-B1
3200 OAK 94602 650-C5
PALMER CT
- PLHL 94549 591-H5
- TBRN 94920 607-B5
PALMER DR
100 LGTS 95030 873-C3
1000 NVTO 94949 546-D1
1800 PLE 94588 694-F7
37800 FRMT 94536 752-H4
PALMER LN
- PTLV 94028 810-C6
200 SMCo 94043 790-E1
200 ATN 94027 790-E1
400 SMCo 94025 770-E7
PALMER PL
3400 PLE 94588 694-F7
PALMER RD
700 CCCo 94596 612-F7
800 CCCo 94596 632-F1
800 WLCK 94596 632-F1
PALMER ST
400 MPS 95035 813-J1
PALMERA CT
1700 ALA 94501 669-H2
PALMERA WY
800 MrnC 94903 566-H2
PALMETTO AV
100 PCFA 94044 706-J2
200 SF 94132 687-C2
4900 PCFA 94044 707-A2
PALMETTO CT
5000 PCFA 94044 707-A2
PALMETTO DR
400 SUNV 94086 832-G1
500 SJS 95111 854-G6
33000 UNC 94587 732-G3
PALMETTO ST
2400 OAK 94602 650-D5
PALMETTO DUNES CT
5000 SJS 95138 855-E6
PALMETTO DUNES LN
- CCCo 94507 633-B4
PALM GROVE CT
5300 SJS 95123 875-A3
PALM HAVEN AV
600 SJS 95125 854-A2
PALMIRA CT
700 SRMN 94583 673-B3
PALMIRA PL
2400 SRMN 94583 673-B3
PALMIRA WY
2200 SJS 95122 854-J1
PALMITA PL
200 MTVW 94041 811-J5
PALMITO DR
900 MLBR 94030 728-A2
PALM MEADOW LN
2000 CNCD 94518 592-F7
PALMO CT
- NVTO 94945 525-J1
PALMO WY
- NVTO 94945 525-J1
PALM RIDGE LN
100 SJS 95123 874-G7
PALMS DR
500 CCCo 94553 572-A3
PALM SPRING CT
11600 CPTO 95014 852-A4
PALM SPRINGS CIR
5900 SJS 95123 874-G6
PALMTAG DR
12300 SAR 95070 852-G6
PALM VIEW DR
5400 SJS 95123 875-B4
PALMVIEW WY
1400 SJS 95122 834-H6
PALMWELL WY
- SJS 95138 875-D5
PALMWOOD AV
27400 HAY 94545 711-H7
PALMWOOD CT
3800 CNCD 94521 592-J3
PALMWOOD DR
1400 SJS 95122 834-H6
3800 CNCD 94518 592-J3
3800 CNCD 94521 592-J3
PALO DR
- PA 94304 790-H5
200 SCIC 94305 790-H5
PALO ALTO AV
- SF 94131 667-E3
100 PA 94301 790-J3
200 MTVW 94041 811-G5
200 SF 94114 667-E3
200 SF 94114 667-E3
200 SF 94131 667-E3
600 MLPK 94025 790-J3
1000 PA 94301 791-A3
PALO ALTO CT
- PLHL 94523 592-B3
PALO ALTO DR
3800 LFYT 94549 611-C5
PALO ALTO ST
800 PA 94301 790-J3
PALO ALTO WY
1900 SMCo 94025 790-E7
PALO AMARILLO DR
47000 FRMT 94539 774-A5
47000 FRMT 94539 773-J5
PALO HILLS DR
26700 LAH 94022 811-A5
PALOMA AV
- PCFA 94044 706-J5
- SF 94127 667-C6
200 PCFA 94044 707-A5
200 SRFL 94901 566-G7
600 OAK 94610 650-B3
700 BURL 94010 728-D5
1300 BLMT 94002 769-E1
4500 SJS 95111 875-A1
PALOMA CT
300 MRTZ 94553 571-F5
2300 PIN 94564 569-F6
23700 CPTO 95014 831-G5
32000 UNC 94587 732-A6
PALOMA DR
- CMAD 94925 606-H1
3300 SCL 95051 833-A4
3300 SCL 95051 832-J4
PALOMA RD
- PTLV 94028 810-B5
11500 AlaC 94586 734-E6
PALOMA RD Rt#-84
11500 AlaC 94586 734-D6
PALOMA ST
2400 PIN 94564 569-F6
PALOMA TER
300 FRMT 94536 733-B7
PALOMA CORTE
200 WLCK 94598 612-H2
PALOMAR AV
600 SUNV 94086 812-D5
PALOMAR CT
300 SBRN 94066 727-H1
PALOMAR DR
300 DALY 94015 687-A7
700 SMCo 94062 769-E6
4000 ANT 94509 595-G1
S PALOMAR DR
- SMCo 94062 769-F6
PALOMAR LN
100 VAL 94591 530-D3
PALOMARES CT
1100 LFYT 94549 611-J5
PALOMARES RD
24200 AlaC 94542 692-G5
25900 AlaC 94542 712-H1
28800 HAY 94542 712-H1
32600 AlaC 94542 713-A3
32600 HAY 94542 713-A3
35000 AlaC 94586 733-E1
35000 UNC 94587 733-F1
35100 AlaC 94544 713-D6
35100 AlaC 94586 713-D6
PALOMARES ST
3100 LFYT 94549 611-H5
PALOMAR REAL
- CMBL 95008 853-F7
PALOMAS
- MTVW 94043 811-J2
PALOMINO CIR
- MrnC 94947 525-F4
PALOMINO COM
33200 FRMT 94555 732-C6
PALOMINO CT
700 WLCK 94596 632-G2
PALOMINO DR
600 PLE 94566 714-G4
14600 SCIC 95127 835-B2
PALOMINO PL
1900 CNCD 94521 593-F4
PALOMINO RD
- MrnC 94947 525-F4
2100 LVMR 94550 696-A3
PALOMINO WY
14000 SAR 95070 872-B2
PALO OAKS CT
18900 SAR 95070 852-H6
PALOS CT
2400 PIN 94564 589-J1
PALOS PL
- SF 94132 667-A6
PALOS WY
4700 UNC 94587 731-J6
PALO SANTO DR
1600 CMBL 95008 853-A6
PALOS VERDES CT
3200 SMTO 94403 748-J6
PALOS VERDES DR
1300 SMTO 94403 748-J6
11100 CPTO 95014 852-B3
15400 MSER 95030 873-A5
PALOS VERDES WY
3700 SSF 94080 707-C4
PALOU AV
900 SF 94124 668-A5
PALOU DR
1100 PCFA 94044 726-J6
PALOU ST
800 VAL 94591 550-D1
PALO VERDE AV
2300 EPA 94303 791-A1
PALO VERDE DR
400 SUNV 94086 832-G2
1900 CNCD 94519 572-J7
4200 PIT 94565 574-F6
PALO VERDE RD
6300 AlaC 94542 692-F5
6300 AlaC 94552 692-F5
PALO VERDE WY
100 VAL 94589 530-C1
400 SUNV 94086 832-G1
2900 ANT 94509 575-A7
PALO VISTA RD
10200 CPTO 95014 852-A1
PAM LN
1500 SJS 95120 874-A7
PAMARON WY
- NVTO 94949 546-F2
PAMELA AV
200 SJS 95116 834-G2
PAMELA COM
4600 LVMR 94550 696-B7
PAMELA CT
- DALY 94015 687-A6
- MrnC 94920 606-J4
- CCCo 94565 573-F2
200 CCCo 94803 589-G2
200 RCH 94803 589-G2
200 VAL 94589 510-C5
400 HAY 94541 711-H2
1500 CNCD 94520 592-E3
PAMELA DR
200 MTVW 94040 811-J6
400 CCCo 94565 573-F1
PAMELA PL
900 PLE 94566 714-F4
PAMELA ST
100 VAL 94589 510-C5
PAMELA WY
20700 SAR 95070 872-D3
PAMELIA WY
3300 PIT 94565 574-D4
PAMLAR AV
300 CMBL 95008 853-E4
500 SJS 95128 853-F4
PAMPAS AV
4300 OAK 94619 650-G6
PAMPAS CIR
4400 ANT 94509 595-G3
PAMPAS CT
2500 ANT 94509 595-G3
20100 SAR 95070 852-E5
PAMPAS DR
1200 SJS 95120 874-C7
PAMPAS LN
300 SCIC 94305 790-J7
PAMPAS WALL
600 SCIC 94305 790-J6
PAMPLONA CT
- SRMN 94583 673-D3
5500 CNCD 94521 593-G5
PANADERO CT
1000 CLAY 94517 593-G7
PANADERO WY
1000 CLAY 94517 593-G7
PANAMA AV
1800 SJS 95122 834-H7
2000 SJS 95122 854-H1
5100 RCH 94804 609-B4
PANAMA CIR
400 UNC 94587 732-D5
PANAMA CT
4000 OAK 94611 649-J1
PANAMA ST
100 SCIC 94305 790-G7
100 SF 94132 687-C2
2000 HAY 94545 731-H1
PANCHITA WY
400 LALT 94022 811-E5
PANCHO CT
6300 SJS 95123 874-J7
PANCHO VIA WY
3500 CNCD 94518 592-J3
PANDA CT
3800 SJS 95117 853-B3
PANDA DR
900 SJS 95117 853-B3
PANDA LN
900 SJS 95117 853-B2
PANDA PL
3800 SJS 95117 853-B3
PANDA WY
1700 HAY 94541 712-B1
PANDORA DR
1800 SJS 95124 873-G1
PANELLI PL
800 SCL 95050 833-F5
PANGBURN LN
100 CCCo 94507 632-G7
PANITZ ST
24900 AlaC 94541 712-C2
PANJON ST
300 HAY 94544 712-B7
PANMURE CT
3100 SJS 95135 855-F3
PANOCHE AV
1100 SJS 95122 834-F7
PANORAMA CT
- DNVL 94506 653-H6
- HIL 94010 748-B1
300 BEN 94510 551-A2
PANORAMA DR
- NVTO 94949 546-G5
- SF 94131 667-E3
- VAL 94589 530-C2
100 BEN 94510 551-B1
100 SF 94131 667-E3

STREET
Block City ZIP Pg-Grid

PANORAMA DR
500 SF 94131 667-E4
1200 LFYT 94549 611-C4
19100 SAR 95070 872-G4
PANORAMA TR
- FRMT 94539 754-A6
- FRMT 94539 753-J6
- FRMT 94539 774-A1
PANORAMA WY
100 LGTS 95032 873-G6
PANORAMIC AV
- PIT 94565 574-C5
PANORAMIC DR
1100 MRTZ 94553 571-D4
2200 CNCD 94520 572-G4
PANORAMIC HWY
1200 MrnC 94965 606-B3
1700 MrnC 94941 606-B3
PANORAMIC PL
- BERK 94704 630-A2
PANORAMIC WY
- BERK 94704 629-J2
- BERK 94704 630-A2
- CCCo 94595 612-A7
400 OAK 94704 630-A2
1000 OAK 94705 630-B2
16300 AlaC 94578 691-G4
PANSY ST
14400 SLN 94578 691-C3
PANTALIS CT
2500 SJS 95132 814-E6
PANTALIS DR
2500 SJS 95132 814-E6
PANTANO CIR
300 CCCo 94553 572-B7
PANTANO LN
200 CCCo 94553 572-B7
PANTON AL
- SF 94109 647-J5
PANTON TER
37100 FRMT 94536 752-H2
PAOLO CT
1900 SJS 95131 814-D6
PAPAC WY
500 SCIC 95117 853-D2
PAPAGO ST
47500 FRMT 94539 773-J7
PAPAYA CT
400 SJS 95111 854-G7
PAPAYA ST
24700 HAY 94545 711-G5
36800 NWK 94560 752-C7
36800 NWK 94560 772-C1
PAPAZIAN WY
4000 FRMT 94538 753-D7
PAPER MILL CT
- NVTO 94949 546-E4
PAPILLON TER
4000 FRMT 94538 773-E3
PAPPANI WY
- SJS 95148 855-F2
PAPPAS PL
2100 HAY 94542 712-D4
PAPPAS ST
200 PIT 94565 574-C5
PAR AV
11600 SCIC 94024 831-E4
PAR CT
8000 NWK 94560 752-C7
PAR LN
- NVTO 94949 546-C2
PARADA ST
39900 NWK 94560 772-J2
PARADISE AV
- SF 94131 667-F6
PARADISE BLVD
500 AlaC 94541 691-F7
PARADISE CT
- HIL 94402 748-G6
- NVTO 94945 526-A2
800 LFYT 94549 611-F7
3900 PA 94306 811-B3
PARADISE DR
- FRMT 94536 733-C7
- FRMT 94536 753-D1
100 PCFA 94044 707-A2
200 TBRN 94920 627-E1
1000 TBRN 94920 607-E7
1100 MRTZ 94553 571-H7
1800 MrnC 94920 607-A1
4500 MrnC 94920 607-A1
5000 CMAD - 607-A1
5100 CMAD 94925 607-A1
5400 CMAD 94925 606-H1
5800 CMAD 94925 586-H7
10300 CPTO 95014 852-D1
PARADISE LN
- PLHL 94523 592-A7
PARADISE WY
700 SMCo 94062 789-F2
900 PA 94306 811-B3
PARADISE COVE RD
- MrnC 94920 607-D5
PARADISE KNOLL
4500 AlaC 94546 692-C5
PARADISE PEAK CT
1900 ANT 94509 595-F5
PARADISE VALLEY CT
600 DNVL 94526 653-E7
PARADISE VLY CT N
700 DNVL 94526 653-E7
PARADISE VLY CT S
600 DNVL 94526 653-E7
PARAGON CIR
2600 PLE 94588 714-A4
PARAGON DR
2100 SJS 95131 813-J6
PARAISO CT
- DNVL 94526 653-B4
200 SJS 95119 875-D7
PARAISO DR
100 DNVL 94526 653-B4
PARAISO PL
- SF 94132 667-B6
PARAMOUNT DR
200 MLBR 94030 728-A2
300 MLBR 94030 727-J3
12900 SAR 95070 852-D6
PARAMOUNT RD
800 OAK 94610 650-B3
PARAMOUNT TER
- SF 94118 647-E7
PARDEE AL
- SF 94133 648-A4
PARDEE AV
4500 FRMT 94538 753-A6
PARDEE CT
700 HAY 94544 712-A6
39400 FRMT 94538 753-A6
PARDEE DR
8400 OAK 94621 670-E7
PARDEE LN
7700 OAK 94621 670-E6
PARDEE PL
- LVMR 94550 715-G5
PARDEE ST
900 BERK 94804 629-E3
PARENTE RD
- TBRN 94920 607-B2
PARFAIT LN
- ALA 94502 670-A5
PARIS LN
1800 ANT 94509 575-G5
PARIS ST
200 SF 94112 667-G7
400 SF 94112 687-F1
PARIS WY
1200 LVMR 94550 715-F3
2200 SJS 95132 814-E2
PARISH AV
3600 FRMT 94536 752-H3
PARISH CIR
37300 FRMT 94536 752-H3
PARISH CT
- ALA 94502 670-A6
PARISH PL
10100 CPTO 95014 832-E7
PARK AL
300 SF 94127 667-D5
PARK AV
- LGTS 95030 893-A1
- MLV 94941 606-E4
- MrnC 94965 606-E4
- CCCo 94595 612-B7
100 PA 94306 791-A7
300 SJS 95113 834-A7
300 SJS 95110 834-A7
400 SJS 95002 793-C7
600 SJS 95126 834-A7
700 BURL 94010 728-F6
700 SJS 95126 833-G6
800 ALA 94501 669-J3
900 ALA 94501 670-A2
1100 EMVL 94608 629-E7
1200 SBRN 94066 707-H7
1400 NVTO 94945 526-B3
1800 SCIC 95126 833-J7
2100 SCL 95050 833-F5
2100 SJS 95050 833-F5
2500 CNCD 94520 572-F7
2500 CNCD 94520 592-F1
2800 SCL 95053 833-F5
5800 CCCo 94805 589-B4
5800 RCH 94805 589-B4
S PARK AV
- SF 94107 648-B7
PARK AV E
900 ALA 94501 670-A3
PARK AV W
900 ALA 94501 670-A3
PARK BLVD
- OAK 94611 630-F7
- SF 94129 647-C4
- SF 94129 647-C5
100 MLBR 94030 728-A2
100 MLBR 94030 727-J2
200 SBRN 94066 727-J2
1600 OAK 94606 649-J4
1700 PA 94306 791-A6
2000 OAK 94606 650-C4
2800 OAK 94610 650-C4
3300 PA 94306 811-C1
3800 OAK 94602 650-C4
4700 PDMT 94610 650-D3
4800 PDMT 94611 650-D3
4900 OAK 94611 650-D3
PARK CIR
- MrnC 94965 606-H7
20600 CPTO 95014 832-D7
PARK CIR E
10100 CPTO 95014 832-D7
PARK CIR W
10100 CPTO 95014 832-D7
PARK CT
- RCH 94803 569-C7
500 SCL 95050 833-F5
800 MTVW 94040 811-H6
1500 NVTO 94945 526-B3
2900 MRTZ 94553 571-G4
E PARK CT
- CCCo 94596 612-A4
W PARK CT
- CCCo 94596 612-A4
PARK DR
- ATN 94027 790-D2
- ROSS 94957 586-B2
- SANS 94960 566-B6
800 MTVW 94022 811-G5
800 MTVW 94040 811-G5
15000 SAR 95070 872-E4
S PARK DR
500 SJS 95129 852-J1
1000 CCCo 94708 610-A6
1500 OAK 94708 610-C7
PARK GN
700 MRTZ 94553 571-E5
PARK LN
- CMAD 94925 606-G1
- MLPK 94025 790-J1
- ANT 94509 575-D4
- BSBN 94005 688-A6
- OAK 94610 650-B2
- RCH 94803 569-C7
- SJS 95123 875-B4
- PDMT 94610 650-B2
100 ATN 94027 790-D4
100 SCAR 94070 769-H5
200 AMCN 94589 509-J3
200 SANS 94960 566-C6
400 SMTO 94402 748-G1
3000 SJS 95127 835-B5
3200 LFYT 94549 611-H4
PARK PL
- RDWC 94065 749-J2
PARK PL
- TBRN 94920 607-B2
100 MLBR 94030 728-A2
100 MLBR 94030 727-J2
100 RCH 94801 588-D7
100 RCH 94801 608-D1
100 SRMN 94583 673-B2
100 SBRN 94066 728-A2
100 SBRN 94066 727-J2
1000 PLHL 94523 592-A4
3400 PLE 94588 694-G6
20300 SAR 95070 872-E2
PARK RD
- BURL 94010 728-G7
600 SMCo 94062 789-F1
2000 BEN 94510 551-F1
3000 SMCo 94063 770-D7
3200 SMCo 94025 770-D7
PARK RD S
- BEN 94510 551-D6
PARK ST
- CNCD 94518 592-G2
- CNCD 94519 592-G2
- OAK 94606 670-A2
- LKSP 94939 586-E6
- SF 94110 667-H6
- SRFL 94901 566-H7
- SRFL 94901 586-H1
- VAL 94591 530-D5
- SAUS 94965 627-B2
100 CCCo 94520 572-G2
100 RDWC 94061 770-C7
100 RDWC 94061 790-B1
200 SLN 94577 670-J7
300 ALA 94501 669-J3
300 MRGA 94556 631-E3
1100 ALA 94501 670-A2
1600 LVMR 94550 695-G7
1900 MRTZ 94553 571-D4
2200 CNCD 94520 592-G2
2200 PIN 94564 569-E4
2700 BERK 94702 629-F3
24100 HAY 94544 711-J3
W PARK ST
2900 MRTZ 94553 571-D4
PARK TER
- MLV 94941 606-E4
PARK WY
- AlaC 94586 713-J7
- AlaC 94586 733-J1
- BERK 94804 609-C7
- LKSP 94939 586-F7
- PDMT 94611 630-B7
- SANS 94960 566-C7
100 SSF 94080 707-H2
500 MrnC 94941 606-C4
800 ELCR 94530 609-E3
800 OAK 94606 649-J6
16100 SCIC 95127 815-B6
16100 SJS 95127 815-B6
20300 AlaC 94546 691-J5
24000 HAY 94541 711-H2
24000 HAY 94544 711-H2
PARK ARCADIA DR
4600 SJS 95136 874-J2
PARK ARROYO PL
2000 HAY 94545 731-H1
PARK BELMONT PL
- SJS 95136 874-J1
PARK BLVD WY
3700 OAK 94610 650-B4
PARK BOLTON PL
100 SJS 95136 874-H1
PARK BRISTOL PL
4400 SJS 95136 874-J1
PARK BROOK CT
1100 MPS 95035 794-C6
PARK CENTER LN
4000 FRMT 94538 753-B6
PARK CENTRAL
800 RCH 94803 589-C1
800 RCH 94803 569-C7
PARK CENTRAL CT
1300 RCH 94803 569-C7
PARK CHARLES CT
3900 SJS 95111 854-J6
PARK CHERRY PL
4500 SJS 95136 874-J2
PARK CONCORD PL
4600 SJS 95136 874-J2
PARK CREST CT
1100 NVTO 94947 526-D6
1500 SJS 95118 874-A6
PARK CREST DR
5600 SJS 95118 874-A6
PARKDALE DR
600 CMBL 95008 853-F7
600 SJS 95008 853-F7
PARKDALE PZ
6500 MRTZ 94553 591-H3
PARKDALE WY
- ANT 94509 595-H4
1600 SJS 95127 835-B5
1800 SJS 95148 835-B5
3100 RDWC 94061 789-H2
PARK DARTMOUTH PL
100 SJS 95136 874-H1
PARK DOUGLAS PL
4700 SJS 95136 874-J2
PARK ELLEN DR
100 SJS 95136 874-J2
PARKER AV
- ATN 94027 790-B4
- SF 94118 647-E6
- CCCo 94572 549-H7
400 CCCo 94572 569-H1
500 SF 94117 647-E6
2500 OAK 94605 670-J2
PARKER CT
900 SCL 95050 833-E3
2900 MTVW 94043 811-F3
34300 FRMT 94555 752-B2
PARKER LN
500 ANT 94509 575-E5
PARKER RD
2800 RCH 94806 589-B2
17400 AlaC 94546 691-H2
PARKER ST
700 SCL 95050 833-E3
900 BERK 94804 629-E3
1100 BERK 94702 629-E3
1300 SLN 94577 671-C7
PARKER ST
1500 BERK 94703 629-E3
1900 BERK 94704 629-J2
2400 MTVW 94043 811-F3
PARKER RANCH CT
12400 SAR 95070 852-C6
PARKER RANCH RD
12000 SAR 95070 852-C6
PARK ESSEX PL
- SJS 95136 874-J1
PARK ESTATES WY
2800 SJS 95135 855-F5
PARKFIELD AV
5000 SJS 95129 852-J3
PARK FLETCHER PL
- SJS 95136 874-J1
PARK GATE
- BERK 94708 609-J6
PARKGATE CT
2200 RCH 94806 568-J7
2200 RCH 94806 588-J1
PARK GATE RD
- LFYT 94549 631-J4
PARK GLEN CT
1100 MPS 95035 794-C6
1400 CNCD 94521 593-E5
PARKGREEN CIR
4900 ANT 94509 595-J4
PARK GROTON PL
- SJS 95136 874-J1
PARK GROVE DR
1100 MPS 95035 794-C6
PARKGROVE DR
- SSF 94014 707-H1
PARKHAVEN CT
- VAL 94591 530-E3
1400 PLHL 94523 591-J2
3300 SJS 95132 814-F2
PARKHAVEN DR
- PLHL 94523 591-J2
- VAL 94591 530-E3
100 DNVL 94506 654-A6
3200 SJS 95132 814-E3
PARK HEIGHTS DR
1100 MPS 95035 794-C6
PARK HIGHLANDS BLVD
5200 CNCD 94521 593-E5
PARK HILL AV
- SF 94117 667-F1
PARKHILL CT
- ANT 94509 595-H3
PARK HILL DR
- MPS 95035 794-C6
PARK HILL RD
600 DNVL 94526 653-C3
PARKHILLS AV
1600 LALT 94024 831-J4
PARK HILLS RD
1000 BERK 94708 609-J5
PARKHURST AL
- SF 94108 648-A5
PARKHURST DR
500 CMBL 95008 853-A7
13000 OAK 94619 651-B6
PARKHURST PL
- PLHL 94523 592-C7
PARKHURST TER
4200 FRMT 94538 753-A6
PARKINGTON AV
1100 SUNV 94087 832-B1
PARKINSON AV
1000 PA 94301 791-A4
PARKINSON CT
1000 SCIC 95126 853-J1
PARK JOHNSON PL
500 SJS 95111 854-J6
PARK LAKE CIR
100 WLCK 94598 612-F2
PARKLAND AV
3400 SJS 95117 853-C3
PARKLAND CT
2500 SCL 95051 833-A1
4700 ANT 94509 595-H4
PARK LAND DR
1400 CNCD 94521 593-E5
PARKLAND DR
- WLCK 94596 612-A2
PARKLANE DR
- ORIN 94563 631-A1
PARK LANE PZ
300 MRTZ 94553 591-H3
PARKMALL CT
3700 CNCD 94519 593-A1
PARK MANOR DR
- DALY 94015 686-J4
5600 SJS 95118 874-A6
PARKMEAD CT
100 CCCo 94595 612-B7
PARK MEADOW CT
- CCCo 94526 633-D5
500 SJS 95129 852-J1
PARKMEADOW CT
45500 FRMT 94539 773-H4
PARK MEADOW DR
400 SJS 95129 852-J2
1900 CCCo 94526 633-D5
PARKMEADOW DR
44300 FRMT 94539 773-G2
PARK MEADOW PL
2000 FRMT 94539 773-G3
PARK MILFORD PL
4600 SJS 95136 874-J2
PARKMONT COM
- FRMT 94536 753-A3
PARKMONT CT
1200 SJS 95131 814-B7
PARKMONT DR
1400 SJS 95131 814-B7
1900 CCCo 94526 633-D6
37900 FRMT 94536 753-A3
PARKMOOR AV
500 SCIC 95128 853-F1
500 SJS 95128 853-F1
1100 SJS 95126 853-H2
PARK NORTON PL
4600 SJS 95136 874-J2
PARK OAK CT
1100 MPS 95035 794-C6
PARK OXFORD PL
- SJS 95136 874-J2
PARK PACIFICA AV
900 PCFA 94044 727-B5
PARK PAXTON PL
4400 SJS 95136 874-J1
PARK PLACE COM
2800 FRMT 94536 753-A3
2800 FRMT 94536 752-J1
PARK PLACE DR
3700 PIT 94565 574-E5
PARK PLAZA DR
- DALY 94015 687-B3
200 SMCo 94015 687-B4
PARK PLEASANT CIR
1300 SJS 95127 835-B3
PARKRIDGE CIR
- SSF 94014 707-H1
- SSF 94014 687-H7
PARKRIDGE CT
- BLMT 94002 769-C3
- RCH 94803 569-C7
PARK RIDGE DR
1500 SJS 95118 874-A6
PARKRIDGE DR
- OAK - 651-B6
- SF 94131 667-F3
1100 RCH 94803 569-C7
5000 OAK 94619 651-B6
5100 AlaC - 651-B6
PARKRIDGE PL
- RCH 94803 569-C7
PARK RIDGE RD
- SRFL 94903 566-D1
PARKROSE AV
- DALY 94015 707-B2
PARKROW LN
2800 SJS 95132 814-E3
PARK ROYAL DR
1900 SJS 95125 853-J6
PARK SHARON DR
- SJS 95136 874-J2
PARKSHORE DR
35800 NWK 94560 752-E4
PARKSIDE AV
- DALY 94015 687-A3
1600 SJS 95125 854-A6
1900 HIL 94010 748-F1
PARKSIDE CIR
2700 CNCD 94519 592-G1
PARKSIDE CT
- FRMT 94536 753-A3
- SANS 94960 566-B6
600 CCCo 94708 609-G4
17300 MSER 95030 873-B4
PARKSIDE DR
- BERK 94705 630-A4
- PDMT 94611 630-A7
- PIT 94565 574-D2
100 PA 94306 811-E2
800 RCH 94803 569-C7
800 RCH 94803 589-C1
1200 WLCK 94596 612-C3
1200 CCCo 94596 612-B4
1800 CNCD 94519 592-G1
2100 FRMT 94536 753-A3
2500 UNC 94587 732-B4
3100 PLE 94588 694-C7
5900 PLE 94588 714-B1
26100 HAY 94542 712-D3
N PARKSIDE DR
500 PIT 94565 574-C2
PARKSIDE LN
- DNVL 94506 653-E4
1300 PIT 94565 574-D2
10200 CPTO 95014 852-F1
PARKSIDE PL
5700 NWK 94560 752-E5
PARKSIDE WY
- MrnC 94904 586-G4
- LKSP 94904 586-G4
500 SMTO 94403 749-A5
PARK SOMMERS WY
4400 SJS 95136 874-J2
PARK SUTTON PL
4600 SJS 95136 874-J2
PARK TERRACE CT
- CCCo 94596 612-A4
PARKTREE CT
3700 CNCD 94519 593-A1
N PARK VICTORIA DR
- MPS 95035 794-A3
S PARK VICTORIA DR
- MPS 95035 794-C6
500 MPS 95035 814-D1
PARKVIEW AV
- DALY 94014 687-C3
1500 SJS 95130 853-A5
N PARKVIEW AV
200 DALY 94014 687-C3
S PARKVIEW AV
- DALY 94014 687-C3
PARKVIEW CIR
- CMAD 94925 606-H2
600 PCFA 94044 707-B2
PARK VIEW CT
- CCCo 94596 612-A3
PARKVIEW CT
- ANT 94509 595-H4
- AMCN 94589 509-J2
100 SBRN 94066 727-H2
200 PDMT 94610 650-B2
600 PCFA 94044 707-A2
1400 PLE 94566 714-D2
PARK VIEW DR
600 SCL 95134 813-E4
1100 MPS 95035 794-C6
PARKVIEW DR
100 SBRN 94066 727-H2
PARKVIEW RD
19200 AlaC 94546 692-C4
PARK VIEW TER
200 OAK 94610 649-H3
PARKVIEW TER
100 VAL 94589 510-B7
PARKVIEW WY
2700 SMTO 94403 749-A5
PARKVIEW GREEN CIR
1600 SJS 95131 814-C7
PARKVIEW TERRACE DR
- SPAB 94806 589-B3
PARK VILLA CIR
8000 CPTO 95014 852-B2
PARK VILLAGE PL
- SJS 95136 874-J1
PARK VISTA
7400 ELCR 94530 609-D2
PARK VISTA CIR
1800 SCL 95050 833-D3
PARK WARREN PL
- SJS 95136 874-J1
PARK WATSON PL
100 SJS 95136 874-J2
PARKWAY CT
- ORIN 94563 631-A2
1200 RCH 94803 569-C7
3700 CNCD 94519 593-A1
PARKWAY DR
700 MRTZ 94553 571-G5
1200 RCH 94803 569-C7
W PARKWAY LN
500 FCTY 94404 749-E3
PARKWELL CT
100 SJS 95138 875-E4
PARKWEST DR
4500 SJS 95130 853-A5
PARK WILLOW CT
1100 MPS 95035 794-C6
PARK WILSHIRE DR
2500 SJS 95124 853-H7
2500 SJS 95124 873-H1
PARKWOOD AV
- MLV 94941 606-D3
PARK WOOD CIR
7300 DBLN 94568 694-A2
PARKWOOD DR
- ATN 94027 790-H1
- DALY 94015 687-B3
100 VAL 94591 530-E4
1200 NVTO 94947 526-C6
1400 SMTO 94403 748-H7
1800 SMTO 94403 768-H1
10100 CPTO 95014 832-C7
PARKWOOD ST
42700 FRMT 94538 773-D1
PARKWOOD WY
1000 RDWC 94061 790-B2
2100 SJS 95125 854-A6
PARLETT PL
10100 CPTO 95014 832-E7
PARLIAMENT CT
3400 SJS 95132 814-J3
PARLIN PL
- SRMN 94583 673-E6
PARLINGTON CT
- CCCo 94507 632-E3
PARMA CT
- PLE 94566 715-C7
34300 FRMT 94555 752-B6
PARMA DR
1100 SJS 95120 894-D1
PARMA ST
- DALY 94014 687-D4
PARMA WY
500 LALT 94024 831-F2
PARMER AV
200 SJS 95116 834-F4
PARNASSUS AV
- SF 94117 667-E2
100 SF 94117 667-E2
300 SF 94143 667-E2
500 SF 94122 667-E2
PARNASSUS CT
- HAY 94542 712-C3
E PARNASSUS CT
- BERK 94708 609-J7
W PARNASSUS CT
- BERK 94708 609-J7
PARNASSUS RD
- BERK 94708 609-J7
PARNELL AV
- DALY 94015 707-C2
PARNELL CT
- WLCK 94596 612-D2
PARNELL DR
2700 SJS 95121 854-J3
PARNELL PL
800 SUNV 94087 832-F6
PARODI CT
- ALA 94502 669-J6
PARQUE DR
100 SF 94134 687-H2
PARQUET CT
2400 SJS 95124 853-H7
W PARR AV
600 CMBL 95008 873-B2
700 LGTS 95030 873-B2
PARR BLVD
- SPAB 94806 588-F2
- CCCo 94801 588-F2
400 RCH 94801 588-F2
PARR LN
200 CMBL 95008 853-D6
PARRIN CT
2900 CNCD 94518 592-G7
PARRISH CT
4900 SJS 95111 875-C1
PARRISH DR
2200 WLCK 94598 612-F1
PARROT AV
1500 SUNV 94087 832-G5
PARROT CT
- WLCK 94596 612-F7
PARROT PL
- DNVL 94526 652-J1
PARROT ST
- VAL 94590 529-H2
PARROTT CT
- SMTO 94402 748-H7
PARROTT DR
200 SMTO 94402 748-H3
800 HIL 94010 748-H3
800 HIL 94402 748-G5
1100 SMCo 94402 748-G5
PARROTT ST
- SLN 94577 691-A1
500 SJS 95112 854-F3
PARSON BROWN CT
- MRGA 94556 631-D6
PARSONS AV
1300 CMBL 95008 873-E2
18700 AlaC 94546 691-J4
PARSONS CT
1300 CMBL 95008 873-E1
3600 AlaC 94546 691-J4
PARSONS LN
1800 ANT 94509 575-F6
PARSONS ST
- SF 94118 647-E7
PARSONS WY
- LALT 94022 811-E5
PAR THREE DR
10600 CPTO 95014 852-A2
PARTITION RD
3500 WDSD 94062 789-E7
3500 WDSD 94062 809-F1
PARTLET CT
44500 FRMT 94539 773-J2
PARTRIDGE AV
100 DALY 94014 687-J3
600 MLPK 94025 790-G4
1500 SUNV 94087 832-G5
2900 OAK 94605 671-A2
3300 OAK 94605 670-J2
PARTRIDGE COM
700 LVMR 94550 695-E7
PARTRIDGE CT
- NVTO 94945 526-A1
- SRFL 94901 567-D5
- CCCo 94526 633-D5
4400 SJS 95121 855-E4
PARTRIDGE DR
- NVTO 94945 526-A1
- SRFL 94901 567-D5
1400 HER 94547 569-H4
4000 SJS 95121 855-E3
PARTRIDGE LN
- DALY 94014 687-E3
23200 SCIC 94024 831-G4
PARTRIDGE WY
2200 UNC 94587 732-G7
PARU ST
700 ALA 94501 669-H2
PARVIN DR
500 MPS 95035 794-B5
PARY CT
- CCCo 94507 632-H5
PASADENA AV
- MrnC 94960 566-B5
- SANS 94960 566-B5
10000 CPTO 95014 852-B1
10000 SCIC 95014 852-B1
PASADENA DR
3500 SMTO 94403 749-D5
PASADENA ST
- DALY 94014 687-H2
- SF 94134 687-H2
PASAS ST
2100 PLE 94566 714-G1
PASATIEMPO DR
1700 SJS 95124 873-J3
PASATIEMPO ST
2100 LVMR 94550 696-C2
PASCOE AV
900 SJS 95125 854-B6
PASEITO TER
900 PCFA 94044 706-J5
PASEO WY
- LKSP 94904 586-G4
PASEO BERNAL
200 MRGA 94556 631-E7
PASEO CARMELO
16700 LGTS 95032 893-D2
PASEO CATALINA
6700 PLE 94566 714-A2
PASEO CERRO
12400 SAR 95070 852-H6
PASEO CIMA
- WLCK 94598 612-E5
PASEO DE ARBOLES
2900 SJS 95135 855-F4
PASEO DEL CAJON
1600 PLE 94566 714-C2
PASEO DEL CAMPO
400 MRGA 94556 631-D2
15700 AlaC 94580 691-C7
15900 AlaC 94580 711-D1
PASEO DEL ORO
2000 SJS 95124 873-F2
PASEO DEL RIO
100 MRGA 94556 631-D2
500 AlaC 94580 691-D7
PASEO DEL ROBLE
13500 LAH 94022 810-H6
PASEO DEL ROBLE CT
13600 LAH 94022 810-H6
PASEO DEL SOL
2000 SJS 95124 873-F2
PASEO DE PALOMAS
500 CMBL 95008 853-F6
PASEO DE SAN ANTONIO WK
- SJS 95113 834-B6
PASEO DE SOL
100 CCCo 94507 632-G3
PASEO ESTERO DR
800 SJS 95122 854-G2
PASEO FLORES
12500 SAR 95070 852-H6
PASEO GRANADA
3000 PLE 94566 714-B2
PASEO GRANDE
- AlaC 94541 691-E7
- AlaC 94580 691-D7
900 AlaC 94580 711-C1
3800 MRGA 94556 631-D2
PASEO LADO
18500 SAR 95070 852-H7
PASEO LAGUNA SECO
1600 LVMR 94550 695-F6
PASEO LARGAVISTA
15700 AlaC 94580 691-D7
PASEO LAURA
100 LGTS 95030 873-D3
PASEO LINARES
- MRGA 94556 631-E5
PASEO MARTHA AV
38000 FRMT 94536 753-A3
PASEO MIRASOL
- TBRN 94920 606-J3
- TBRN 94920 607-A3
PASEO NAVARRO
5500 PLE 94566 714-C2
PASEO NOGALES
1400 CCCo 94507 632-E3
PASEO OLIVOS
12600 SAR 95070 852-H6

STREET
Block City ZIP Pg-Grid

PASEO OLIVOS CT
2000 SJS 95130 852-J6
PASEO OLIVOS WY
4900 SJS 95130 852-J6
PASEO PADRE CT
38100 FRMT 94536 753-A3
PASEO PADRE PKWY
- NWK 94560 752-A3
3200 FRMT 94555 732-E7
3500 FRMT - 752-H2
3500 FRMT 94555 752-A3
35200 FRMT 94536 752-H2
37900 FRMT 94536 753-B4
39000 FRMT 94538 753-B4
39000 FRMT 94539 753-F6
39700 FRMT 94539 773-G1
PASEO PICO
- SAR 95070 852-H6
PASEO PRESADA
12700 SAR 95070 852-H6
PASEO PUEBLO
18500 SAR 95070 852-H6
PASEO PUEBLO CT
6100 SJS 95120 874-C7
PASEO PUEBLO DR
6000 SJS 95120 874-D7
PASEO REFUGIO
300 MPS 95035 794-B6
PASEO ROBLES
3100 PLE 94566 714-A2
PASEO SAN LEON
6700 PLE 94566 714-B2
PASEO SANTA CRUZ
6000 PLE 94566 714-A2
PASEO SANTA MARIA
6300 PLE 94566 714-B2
PASEO TIERRA
18500 SAR 95070 852-H6
PASEO TRANQUILLO
4900 SJS 95118 873-J4
PASETTA DR
2100 SCL 95050 833-C2
PASHOTE CT
1400 MPS 95035 794-A4
PASITO TER
100 SUNV 94086 812-D6
PASO DE AVILA
100 CCCo 94553 571-C6
PASO DEL ARROYO
- PTLV 94028 810-D7
PASO DEL RIO CT
5400 CNCD 94521 593-E7
PASO DEL RIO WY
5300 CNCD 94521 593-D7
PASO LOS CERRITOS
6000 SJS 95120 874-B7
6300 SJS 95120 894-B1
PASO NOGAL
100 CCCo 94523 592-B2
100 PLHL 94523 591-J3
200 PLHL 94523 592-A3
500 MRTZ 94553 591-J3
PASO NOGAL CT
- PLHL 94523 592-A3
- PLHL 94523 591-J3
PASO ROBLES AV
- LALT 94022 811-D4
PASO ROBLES DR
6700 OAK 94611 630-F7
PASQUALE CT
300 SJS 95133 834-H1
PASSAGE LN
- RDWC 94065 750-C4
PASSEGGI CT
4200 PLE 94588 694-C5
PASTEL CT
- NVTO 94947 526-C5
PASTEL LN
1400 NVTO 94947 526-C5
13300 MTVW 94040 832-A1
PASTEUR DR
100 PA 94304 790-G6
100 SCIC 94305 790-G6
PASTO CT
1800 WLCK 94595 632-B1
PASTORI AV
- FRFX 94930 566-A6
- SANS 94960 566-A6
PASTORIA AV
400 SUNV 94086 832-D1
N PASTORIA AV
200 SUNV 94086 812-D6
S PASTORIA AV
100 SUNV 94086 812-D7
PATALITA DR
700 NVTO 94945 526-H1
PATCH AV
300 SCIC 95128 853-F1
PATH WY
100 SJS 95136 874-H2
PATH 1
- LKSP 94939 586-D6
PATH 2
- LKSP 94939 586-E6
PATH 3
- LKSP 94939 586-D6
PATIO CT
1200 CMBL 95008 853-G6
PATIO DR
1600 CMBL 95008 853-G6
1700 SCIC 95125 853-H6
20200 AlaC 94546 692-A5
PATLEN DR
1200 LALT 94024 831-H3
PATOMA CT
600 FRMT 94536 753-D1
PATRA DR
2500 CCCo 94803 589-H5
PATRIC CT
20200 CPTO 95014 852-E2
PATRICIA AV
200 PIT 94565 574-F4
400 SMTO 94401 749-B1
2800 ANT 94509 575-E7
PATRICIA CT
100 MTVW 94041 811-J6
400 MPS 95035 794-E7
900 CMBL 95008 873-B1
10400 OAK 94603 670-H7
24600 AlaC 94541 712-B2
PATRICIA DR
- ATN 94027 790-C2

PATRICIA DR
100 AMCN 94589 510-A4
300 AMCN 94589 509-J4
1900 PLHL 94523 592-C5
2300 SCL 95050 833-C5
2500 SCL 95051 833-B5
PATRICIA LN
- MrnC 94941 606-F3
100 CCCo 94507 632-F6
500 PA 94303 791-C4
3100 LVMR 94550 715-H1
PATRICIA PL
- MLPK 94025 790-F5
PATRICIA RD
- ORIN 94563 630-G2
PATRICIA ST
4100 FRMT 94536 752-J4
PATRICIA WY
800 SRFL 94903 566-B1
900 SJS 95125 854-A3
PATRICK AV
26600 HAY 94544 711-J7
PATRICK CT
100 VAL 94591 530-E4
PATRICK DR
200 CCCo 94553 572-B7
800 PIN 94564 569-D4
PATRICK LN
- ORIN 94563 631-B1
PATRICK WY
400 LALT 94022 811-D5
PATRICK HENRY DR
2900 SCL 95054 813-A4
PATRIOT CT
3500 ANT 94509 595-C3
PATRIOT PL
600 FRMT 94539 773-H2
PATRIOT WY
21000 CPTO 95014 832-C7
PATROL CT
- WDSD 94062 789-D6
PATROL RD
500 WDSD 94062 789-D6
PATT AV
2800 SJS 95133 834-G1
2900 SCIC 95133 814-H7
2900 SJS 95133 814-H7
PATTEN RD
- SF 94129 647-C4
PATTERSON AV
- SMCo 94025 790-D5
3600 OAK 94619 650-F6
PATTERSON BLVD
100 PLHL 94523 592-B7
PATTERSON CIR
6200 CCCo 94805 589-B5
PATTERSON LN
- NVTO 94949 546-G4
PATTERSON ST
- SF 94124 668-A5
100 SJS 95112 834-C7
PATTERSON PASS RD
6200 LVMR 94550 696-B6
7700 AlaC 94550 696-E6
PATTERSON RANCH RD
6300 FRMT 94555 752-A4
6300 FRMT 94555 751-J4
PATTIANI WY
2700 ALA 94502 669-J6
PATTON AV
300 SCIC 95128 853-F1
14900 SLN 94578 691-D3
PATTON DR
18800 AlaC 94546 692-A3
PATTON PL
- HIL 94010 728-C7
- HIL 94010 748-C1
PATTON ST
- SF 94110 667-H5
5800 OAK 94618 630-A4
PATTON TER
41500 FRMT 94538 773-D1
PATTY WY
3100 LFYT 94549 611-J6
PAUL AV
- BSBN 94005 688-A7
- MTVW 94041 812-A6
- SF 94124 688-B1
- MTVW 94041 811-J6
200 SF 94124 668-B7
500 SF 94134 668-B7
700 PA 94306 811-C2
14200 SAR 95070 872-D2
PAUL CT
- BEN 94510 551-C1
1500 ANT 94509 575-F7
25600 AlaC 94541 712-D2
PAUL DR
- SRFL 94903 566-F2
PAUL LN
1800 CNCD 94521 593-F4
PAUL ST
- DALY 94014 687-D4
PAUL TER
3900 FRMT 94538 753-D7
PAULA CT
200 MRTZ 94553 591-H4
400 SCL 95050 833-D6
1200 LALT 94024 831-H2
4700 LVMR 94550 696-B7
PAULA DR
1100 CMBL 95008 853-B5
PAULA ST
800 SJS 95126 853-J2
1000 SCIC 95126 853-J2
PAULA WY
- VAL 94590 529-H3
PAULANELLA PL
- CCCo - 652-E3
PAULDING ST
- SF 94131 667-F7
- SF 94112 667-F7
PAULETTA CT
- DNVL 94526 653-C4
PAULETTE LN
- ANT 94509 574-J6
PAULI PL
- ORIN 94563 611-A7
PAULINE DR
1300 SUNV 94087 832-F4
2300 SJS 95124 853-G7

PAUL ROBESON CT
800 EPA 94303 791-B1
PAUL SCARLET DR
5100 CNCD 94521 593-E4
PAULSEN LN
100 CCCo 94595 612-B6
100 WLCK 94595 612-B6
200 PA 94301 790-J4
PAULSON CT
- SMTO 94403 749-B4
900 LFYT 94549 611-B6
PAVAN CT
2800 SJS 95148 855-D2
PAVAN DR
3000 SJS 95148 855-D2
PAVILLION PTH
- CMAD 94925 606-C5
PAVISO DR
20400 CPTO 95014 832-E6
PAVO CT
5000 LVMR 94550 696-B3
PAVO LN
600 FCTY 94404 749-E4
PAVON
100 HER 94547 569-E3
PAWNEE DR
2500 WLCK 94598 612-H3
5100 ANT 94509 595-H5
44900 FRMT 94539 773-H3
PAWNEE PL
200 FRMT 94539 773-H3
PAWNEE WY
- PLE 94588 694-G7
PAWTUCKET WY
7300 SJS 95139 895-F1
PAXTON AV
3300 OAK 94601 650-D6
PAXTON CT
5200 FRMT 94536 752-H6
6000 SJS 95123 874-F6
PAXTON VILLA CT
800 NVTO 94947 526-A4
PAYETTE AV
1000 SUNV 94087 832-B6
PAYETTE CT
1300 SJS 95129 852-G4
PAYNE AV
3100 SJS 95130 853-B4
3100 SJS 95117 853-B4
3400 SJS 95128 853-E4
3400 SJS 95008 853-E4
3500 CMBL 95008 853-E4
3500 CMBL 95128 853-E4
4200 SJS 95129 853-B4
PAYNE CT
700 RCH 94806 568-G6
800 SUNV 94087 832-C2
6800 PLE 94588 694-A7
PAYNE DR
500 RCH 94806 568-G6
1100 LALT 94024 831-H3
PAYNE RD
3900 PLE 94588 714-A1
4100 PLE 94588 694-A7
PAYNE ST
32200 HAY 94544 732-E3
PAYOT CT
- ALA 94502 670-B7
PAYOT LN
- ALA 94502 670-B7
PAYSON ST
- SF 94132 687-C2
PAYTON AV
14800 SCIC 95124 873-G3
PAZZI RD
400 WLCK 94598 613-A2
400 WLCK 94598 612-J2
PEABODY LN
1100 OAK 94608 629-E5
1200 EMVL 94608 629-E5
PEABODY ST
- SF 94134 688-A2
PEACE TER
33300 FRMT 94555 732-C7
PEACEFUL LN
100 LFYT 94549 611-J4
4700 PLE 94566 714-E4
PEACEFUL GLEN CT
1400 SJS 95121 855-D7
PEACEFUL VALLEY DR
600 SRMN 94583 673-J6
PEACH AV
700 SUNV 94087 832-C2
PEACH CT
1200 SJS 95116 834-E5
36700 NWK 94560 752-C7
PEACH DR
200 AlaC 94580 691-D7
PEACH PL
1200 CNCD 94518 592-E5
1700 CNCD 94520 592-E5
PEACH ST
100 VAL 94589 510-B7
600 NVTO 94945 526-C3
900 ALA 94501 670-B4
1300 CCCo 94553 571-F3
2100 PIN 94564 569-E4
9200 OAK 94603 671-A4
9300 OAK 94603 670-J4
PEACH TER
4900 SJS 95008 872-J1
PEACH BLOSSOM DR
7500 CPTO 95014 852-D4
PEACHBLOSSOM LN
15600 SCIC 95032 873-C5
15600 LGTS 95032 873-C5
PEACH GROVE CT
5200 SJS 95123 874-F7
PEACH HILL RD
15100 SAR 95070 872-E5
15300 SAR 95030 872-E5
15400 SCIC 95030 872-E5
PEACHSTONE TER
300 MrnC 94903 546-D6
PEACHTREE AV
7700 NWK 94560 752-C7
PEACHTREE CIR
2100 PIT 94565 573-J3
2300 ANT 94509 595-A2
PEACH TREE COM
1400 LVMR 94550 696-A4

PEACHTREE CT
1200 CMBL 95008 873-B2
1700 MTVW 94040 831-G1
PEACH TREE DR
2300 HAY 94545 731-H1
PEACHTREE LN
2000 SJS 95128 833-E6
20000 CPTO 95014 832-E7
PEACH WILLOW CT
100 LGTS 95030 873-B2
PEACHWILLOW LN
3000 WLCK 94598 612-H1
3000 WLCK 94598 592-H7
PEACHWILLOW ST
1700 PIT 94565 573-F3
PEACHWOOD CT
1200 SBRN 94066 707-H7
2700 SJS 95132 814-E5
PEACHWOOD DR
1600 SJS 95132 814-D4
3900 CNCD 94519 573-A7
PEACHWOOD PL
1600 SJS 95132 814-D5
PEACHWOOD ST
42600 FRMT 94538 773-D2
PEACOCK AV
1500 SUNV 94087 832-G5
1700 MTVW 94043 811-H3
PEACOCK BLVD
400 LFYT 94549 631-G3
400 LFYT 94556 631-G3
PEACOCK CT
- DBLN 94568 694-D4
- SRFL 94901 567-E5
3600 SCL 95051 832-H4
PEACOCK DR
- SRFL 94901 567-D5
PEACOCK LN
- SRFL 94901 567-D6
16300 SCIC 95032 873-D7
PEACOCK PL
2200 UNC 94587 732-G7
PEACOCK CREEK DR
1000 CLAY 94517 593-J7
1000 CLAY 94517 594-A7
PEACOCK GAP DR
4400 SJS 95127 815-C6
4400 SCIC 95127 815-C6
PEACOCK HILL DR
- AlaC 94542 692-E7
- AlaC 94542 712-E1
PEAK CT
- HER 94547 569-H4
E PEAK CT
2200 MRTZ 94553 572-A7
PEAK DR
3500 SJS 95127 835-C3
PEAK LN
- PTLV 94028 810-D5
N PEAK PL
2100 MRTZ 94553 572-B6
PEAKE PL
100 CCCo 94507 633-A5
100 CCCo 94507 632-J5
PEAK LOOP TR
- AlaC 94544 712-E6
PEAK VIEW DR
48900 FRMT 94539 793-J2
PEANUT BRITTLE DR
3000 SJS 95148 835-D7
PEAR AV
700 SUNV 94087 832-C2
1200 MTVW 94043 811-J2
PEAR CT
- HIL 94010 748-D2
PEAR DR
1200 CNCD 94518 592-E6
PEAR ST
2100 PIN 94564 569-E4
2900 ANT 94509 574-J7
24700 HAY 94545 711-G5
PEAR BLOSSOM CT
- SJS 95123 875-E2
PEARCE
100 HER 94547 569-F3
PEARCE RD
- SRFL 94901 586-F2
PEARCE ST
- SF 94129 647-D3
22200 HAY 94541 711-H1
PEARCE MITCHELL PL
- SCIC 94305 810-H1
N PEARDALE DR
3900 LFYT 94549 611-B5
S PEARDALE DR
3900 LFYT 94549 611-B5
PEARL AV
100 SCAR 94070 769-H5
1800 CNCD 94520 572-J3
1800 CCCo 94520 572-J3
3000 SJS 95136 854-D7
3500 SJS 95136 874-D1
22500 HAY 94541 692-B7
PEARL CT
- VAL 94591 530-D5
PEARL DR
200 LVMR 94550 715-D2
PEARL PL
6700 DBLN 94568 693-J2
PEARL ST
- OAK 94611 649-J2
- SAUS 94965 627-A2
- SF 94103 667-H1
100 OAK 94610 649-J2
900 ALA 94501 670-A3
PEARLGRASS CT
- SRMN 94583 653-H7
PEARLGRASS LN
- SRMN 94583 653-H7
PEARL HARBOR RD
100 ALA 94501 649-D6
PEARL RIVER TER
- FRMT 94555 732-C7
PEARLROTH DR
6300 SJS 95123 875-A7
PEARLTONE DR
3200 SJS 95117 853-D3
PEARLWOOD WY
700 SJS 95123 874-F5
PEARMAIN ST
9800 OAK 94603 670-H6

PEARSON AV
1200 SLN 94577 690-H2
PEARSON CT
1600 SJS 95122 834-G7
PEARTREE CT
- DNVL 94526 653-A1
19100 CPTO 95014 832-F7
PEARTREE LN
1700 MTVW 94040 831-G1
2600 SJS 95121 855-E4
19800 CPTO 95014 832-F7
PEARY CT
1000 LVMR 94550 715-G2
PEARY WY
1700 LVMR 94550 715-G2
PEASE AV
1200 ALA 94501 670-A3
PEBBLE CT
- SRMN 94583 673-G7
200 CCCo 94507 632-H5
700 CCCo 94803 589-D1
27800 HAY 94542 712-E4
PEBBLE DR
- SMCo 94062 769-E6
400 CCCo 94803 589-D1
1300 SCAR 94070 769-E6
2000 CCCo 94507 632-H5
3900 ANT 94509 595-E1
PEBBLE LN
100 CCCo 94507 632-H5
PEBBLE PL
100 SRMN 94583 673-G6
10600 CPTO 95014 832-C6
PEBBLE BEACH AV
8100 NWK 94560 752-C7
PEBBLE BEACH CT
1500 MPS 95035 794-D3
2400 SJS 95125 854-C6
7300 ELCR 94530 589-D7
31300 HAY 94544 732-E2
PEBBLE BEACH DR
- CLAY 94517 593-J7
- NVTO 94949 546-D2
- CLAY 94517 594-A7
200 PIT 94565 574-E1
2400 SJS 95125 854-C6
2600 SCL 95051 833-B1
7300 ELCR 94530 589-D7
10500 OAK 94605 671-D3
PEBBLE BEACH LP
200 PIT 94565 574-E1
2400 CCCo 94549 591-H4
PEBBLE BEACH WY
7300 ELCR 94530 589-D7
PEBBLEBROOK CT
1500 WLCK 94596 632-H2
PEBBLE CREEK CT
1000 SJS 95127 834-J4
PEBBLECREEK CT
200 MRTZ 94553 571-J6
PEBBLE GLEN DR
4800 SJS 95129 852-J3
5200 CNCD 94521 593-D6
PEBBLELAKE CT
800 SUNV 94089 812-H5
PEBBLETREE CT
5100 SJS 95111 875-C2
PEBBLETREE WY
5200 SJS 95111 875-C2
PEBBLEWOOD CT
900 FRMT 94539 773-J5
5000 PLE 94566 714-D2
6600 SJS 95120 894-F1
PEBBLEWOOD WY
1100 SMTO 94403 749-E6
PECAN CT
- SRMN 94583 673-F7
100 VAL 94589 510-B7
800 SUNV 94087 832-C3
1200 SJS 95131 814-D7
1600 RDWC 94061 790-A2
7400 PLE 94588 714-A1
7400 PLE 94588 713-J1
36200 FRMT 94536 752-J1
PECAN DR
- SRFL 94903 566-B2
100 HER 94547 570-A5
PECAN ST
300 VAL 94589 510-A7
2400 UNC 94587 732-C4
2400 ANT 94509 574-J7
PECAN WY
700 CMBL 95008 853-B7
PECAN BLOSSOM DR
5300 SJS 95123 875-B3
PECAN GROVE CT
100 SJS 95123 874-J3
PECHIN CIR
2400 SJS 95130 853-A7
PECK LN
12000 LAH 94022 831-B3
PECK ST
1600 SMTO 94401 729-B7
PECKS LN
100 SSF 94080 708-A2
PECO ST
34800 UNC 94587 732-G7
PECORA WY
100 SMCo 94028 810-D4
PECOS AV
4100 FRMT 94555 752-D2
PECOS CT
4500 FRMT 94555 752-D2
PECOS PT
3800 SJS 95132 814-J5
PECOS WY
1100 SUNV 94089 812-J4
PECOS RIVER CT
600 SJS 95111 854-H4
PECTEN CT
1000 MPS 95035 814-C3
PEDESTRIAN WY
- FRMT 94538 753-B6
- SF 94123 647-F3
400 OAK 94618 629-J5
PEDRICK CT
1100 SJS 95120 894-D1
PEDRINI CT
34300 FRMT 94555 752-B6
PEDRO AV
2100 MPS 95035 794-E7

PEDRO ST
900 SJS 95126 853-J2
PEDRO VIEW RD
- SCIC 95127 835-C1
PEEKSKILL DR
700 SUNV 94087 832-C2
PEERLESS AV
1800 ELCR 94530 609-B1
PEGAN COM
1300 LVMR 94550 716-B1
PEGASUS CT
7500 SJS 95139 875-H7
32300 UNC 94587 732-A6
PEGASUS LN
600 FCTY 94404 749-E3
PEGASUS WY
7300 SJS 95139 875-G7
PEGGY AV
1000 CMBL 95008 873-B1
PEGGY CT
1300 CMBL 95008 873-B1
PEGGY DR
1900 PLHL 94523 592-C5
PEGGY LN
- CCCo 94553 591-E2
900 MLPK 94025 770-G7
PEIKING DR
1200 SJS 95131 814-B7
PELADEAU ST
5700 EMVL 94608 629-E6
PELHAM CT
6400 SJS 95123 875-A7
41400 FRMT 94539 753-F6
PELHAM PL
2200 OAK 94611 650-F1
26800 HAY 94542 712-E3
PELICAN CT
- DNVL 94506 653-E4
200 FCTY 94404 749-H1
600 LVMR 94550 695-E7
5200 SJS 95123 874-F7
PELICAN DR
100 VAL 94589 509-H5
2700 UNC 94587 732-D6
PELICAN LN
- RDWC 94065 749-H6
100 NVTO 94949 546-E5
PELICAN LP
100 PIT 94565 574-E1
PELICAN ST
- DNVL 94506 653-E4
PELICAN WY
- SRFL 94901 587-A4
1200 RCH 94801 608-D3
2000 SLN 94579 690-J6
PELICAN PT RD
- BLV 94920 607-C7
- BLV 94920 627-C1
PELICAN RIDGE DR
7200 SJS 95120 894-F3
PELLEAS LN
700 SJS 95127 814-H6
PELLEGRINELLI DR
- TBRN 94920 607-B3
PELLIER CT
1300 SJS 95121 854-J2
PELLIER DR
1200 SJS 95121 854-J3
PELTON CIR
100 SLN 94577 691-A1
PELTON PL
- SF 94133 648-A4
PEMBA CT
200 SJS 95119 875-D6
PEMBA DR
6400 SJS 95119 875-D6
PEMBERTON PL
- SF 94114 667-E3
PEMBRIDGE CT
3400 SJS 95118 874-C1
PEMBRIDGE DR
1100 SJS 95118 874-C1
PEMBROKE CT
- OAK 94619 650-J5
PEMBROKE DR
100 VAL 94589 510-C5
1100 SJS 95131 814-E6
4300 CNCD 94521 593-A4
PEMBROKE PL
- MLPK 94025 790-F6
PEMBROOK CT
- MRGA 94556 651-F2
PEMENTEL CT
41100 FRMT 94539 753-G4
PENA CT
500 PA 94306 811-C2
PENA ST
- SF 94129 647-D4
- SF 94129 647-D4
PENDERGAST AV
18700 SCIC 95014 852-H2
PENDLETON AV
900 SUNV 94087 832-B6
PENDLETON DR
2800 SJS 95148 855-D1
PENDLETON WY
300 OAK 94621 670-E6
PENDRAGON LN
2500 SJS 95116 834-J4
PENHURST AV
- DALY 94015 707-B2
PENHURST CT
100 DALY 94015 707-B2
PENHURST PL
4100 SJS 95135 855-F3
PENINSULA AV
- BURL 94010 728-H7
- SMTO 94401 728-H7
200 SF 94134 688-A2
PENINSULA BLVD
10000 CPTO 95014 832-B7
PENINSULA DR
- RCH 94804 608-H3
PENINSULA RD
- AlaC - 651-D5
- AlaC 94546 651-D5
- AlaC 94546 671-F1
- BLV 94920 627-D1
- BLV 94920 607-D7
PENINSULA ST
14900 SLN 94578 691-C5

PENINSULA WY
900 SMCo 94025 790-H1
PENINSULAR AV
1000 LALT 94024 831-H4
10700 CPTO 95014 832-A6
PENINSULAR CT
1000 LALT 94024 831-H3
PENITENCIA CT
500 MPS 95035 793-J6
PENITENCIA ST
500 MPS 95035 793-J6
PENITENCIA CREEK RD
2600 SJS 95132 814-F7
2900 SJS 95133 814-F7
3100 SJS 95127 814-F7
3400 SCIC 95132 814-F7
3600 SCIC 95133 814-F7
14800 SCIC 95127 814-F7
14900 SCIC 95127 815-A5
15300 SJS 95132 815-A5
16100 SJS 95127 815-A5
PENN AV
5000 SCIC 95124 873-E4
9800 SJS 95124 873-E4
16000 AlaC 94580 691-E6
PENN DR
6800 DBLN 94568 693-J3
PENN LN
40600 FRMT 94538 753-D6
PENN PZ
- CNCD 94518 592-E6
PENN WY
200 LGTS 95032 873-D4
PENNANT CT
500 RDWC 94065 749-H7
PENNIMAN AV
3400 OAK 94602 650-E6
3500 OAK 94619 650-E6
PENNIMAN CT
3000 OAK 94619 650-E7
PENNINGTON CT
- CCCo 94525 550-E5
PENNINGTON LN
1000 CPTO 95014 852-C3
PENNINGTON PL
400 DNVL 94526 653-D3
PENNINGTON ST
- SF 94129 647-D3
PENNSYLVANIA AV
- LGTS 95030 872-J7
100 RDWC 94063 770-B6
100 SF 94107 668-B3
200 RCH 94801 588-F5
3300 FRMT 94536 753-A4
PENNSYLVANIA BLVD
1300 CNCD 94521 593-F6
PENNSYLVANIA COM
3300 FRMT 94536 753-A4
PENNSYLVANIA ST
300 VAL 94590 529-J5
400 VAL 94590 530-A5
PENNY LN
- LKSP 94939 586-D6
- SF 94131 667-G6
500 AlaC 94541 711-E2
4100 CCCo 94803 589-D2
5300 CCCo 94506 654-F7
PENNY TER
- MrnC 94964 587-B5
4000 FRMT 94538 773-D1
PENNY WY
1700 LALT 94024 832-A4
PENNYHILL DR
200 SJS 95127 834-H1
PENNY ROYAL LN
700 SRFL 94903 566-B2
PENNYROYAL TER
1200 SUNV 94087 832-C3
PENOBSCOT DR
200 RDWC 94063 770-C4
PENRITH WK
- PLHL 94523 591-B1
PENROD PL
600 SJS 95116 834-J4
PENSACOLA
100 ALA 94501 649-D6
PENSACOLA CT
- NVTO 94949 546-A3
PENSACOLA DR
1500 SJS 95122 854-H1
PENSACOLA ST
- CCCo 94565 573-H2
1000 FCTY 94404 749-F5
PENSACOLA WY
27600 HAY 94544 711-J7
27600 HAY 94544 731-J1
PENTLAND CT
3000 SJS 95148 855-C2
PENTLAND WY
2200 SJS 95148 855-C2
PENTZ WY
5800 SJS 95123 875-B5
PENWITH AV
3900 SJS 95130 853-B4
PENWOOD ST
1700 SJS 95133 834-E1
PENZANCE COM
37000 FRMT 94536 752-A6
PEONY CT
100 FRMT 94538 773-B2
PEONY DR
5100 LVMR 94550 696-B3
PEONY LN
1600 SJS 95124 873-J6
PEORIA ST
- DALY 94014 687-D3
PEPITA CT
3100 SJS 95132 814-G5
PEPITONE AV
1000 SJS 95110 854-C2
PEPPER AV
- CMAD 94925 586-F7
- LKSP 94939 586-F7
100 BURL 94010 728-F7
100 BURL 94010 748-F1
200 HIL 94010 728-F7
400 PA 94304 811-B1
400 PA 94306 791-B7
400 PA 94306 811-B1
1000 SUNV 94087 832-C2

STREET Block City ZIP Pg-Grid

PEPPER CT
100 LALT 94022 811-E7
PEPPER DR
- LALT 94022 811-E7
100 VAL 94589 510-B6
600 SBRN 94066 707-G7
2200 CNCD 94520 572-F6
PEPPER LN
- SCAR 94070 769-E2
15000 SAR 95070 872-F4
PEPPER ST
18200 AlaC 94546 692-B3
PEPPER WY
- SRFL 94901 566-E6
PEPPERCORN CT
100 VAL 94591 530-F7
PEPPERDINE ST
14700 SLN 94579 691-B4
PEPPERIDGE CT
2700 SJS 95148 835-E6
PEPPERIDGE DR
3400 SJS 95148 835-E6
PEPPERIDGE PL
5700 CNCD 94521 593-G7
PEPPERMILL CIR
3000 PIT 94565 574-F6
PEPPERMILL CT
- PIT 94565 574-F6
1000 CNCD 94518 592-H4
PEPPERMILL LN
100 PIT 94565 574-F5
PEPPERMINT DR
3000 SJS 95148 835-C7
PEPPERRIDGE WY
5700 CNCD 94521 593-F7
PEPPER TREE CT
800 SCL 95051 833-A5
PEPPERTREE CT
2400 ANT 94509 575-B6
3900 RDWC 94061 789-G3
6000 NWK 94560 752-G7
8100 DBLN 94568 693-G3
PEPPER TREE LN
- LGTS 95030 873-B5
800 SCL 95051 833-A5
3300 SCIC 95127 814-H6
3900 SCIC 95127 814-J6
3900 SJS 95127 814-J6
20800 CPTO 95014 852-C1
PEPPERTREE LN
3700 AlaC 94546 692-A3
PEPPER TREE PL
1500 PIT 94565 574-G6
PEPPERTREE PL
1000 LVMR 94550 715-G2
PEPPERTREE RD
300 WLCK 94598 592-J7
300 WLCK 94598 612-J1
7700 DBLN 94568 693-F3
PEPPERTREE WY
100 PIT 94565 574-F5
2100 ANT 94509 575-B6
PEPPERWOOD CT
- MLPK 94025 790-H2
800 CCCo - 654-A1
800 CCCo 94506 654-A1
1600 CNCD 94521 593-B2
PEPPERWOOD DR
800 CCCo - 654-A1
4800 SJS 95124 873-H4
PEPPERWOOD LN
- CMAD 94925 606-H2
2600 SCL 95051 833-B6
PEPPERWOOD PL
2600 AlaC 94541 692-C7
PEPPERWOOD ST
100 HER 94547 569-J4
PEPPERWOOD TER
3400 FRMT 94536 752-A6
PEPYS WY
- FRMT 94536 753-C3
PERADA DR
3300 WLCK 94598 612-J1
3500 WLCK 94598 592-J7
PERALES ST
1100 LFYT 94549 611-H5
PERALTA AV
- BERK 94702 609-E7
- LGTS 95030 872-J7
- SF 94110 668-A4
- SLN 94577 670-J7
- SLN 94577 690-J1
100 MrnC 94941 606-E6
400 SUNV 94086 832-D1
800 SLN 94577 671-A7
900 BERK 94707 609-F6
900 SF 94110 667-J6
1000 ALB 94706 609-F6
1200 BERK 94706 609-E7
PERALTA BLVD
4000 FRMT 94536 752-H4
PERALTA BLVD Rt#-84
1200 FRMT 94536 753-A3
2700 FRMT 94536 752-J3
PERALTA CT
- FRMT 94536 752-H3
- MRGA 94556 651-F1
1300 SJS 95120 874-C7
14100 SAR 95070 872-C2
PERALTA DR
1200 SJS 95120 874-C7
PERALTA RD
100 PCFA 94044 726-H5
900 SMCo - 726-H5
1000 CNCD 94520 572-E5
PERALTA ST
300 OAK 94607 649-D4
2800 OAK 94608 649-D4
3700 OAK 94608 629-F7
3700 EMVL 94608 629-F7
22100 HAY 94541 711-H1
PERALTA TER
- FRMT 94536 753-A3
PERALTA OAKS CT
2900 OAK 94605 671-B5
PERALTA OAKS DR
10600 OAK 94605 671-B5
PERCH WY
- UNC 94545 731-J6
PERCHERON CT
100 VAL 94591 530-D2
PERCHERON PL
- HIL 94402 748-H4
900 SMTO 94402 748-H4
PERCHERON RD
2100 LVMR 94550 696-A2
PERCHERON WY
5200 ANT 94509 595-J6
PERCIVALE DR
3100 SJS 95127 814-H7
PEREGO TER
- SF 94131 667-F4
PEREGO WY
18500 SAR 95070 872-H1
PEREGRINE CT
900 SCL 95051 832-H5
PEREGRINE WY
4000 PLE 94566 714-E1
4200 FRMT 94555 732-B7
PEREGRINO WY
1500 SJS 95125 853-J6
PEREIRA CT
33600 FRMT 94555 732-D6
PEREIRA RD
1000 CCCo 94553 590-G2
PEREZ DR
1400 PCFA 94044 726-J6
PERGOLA CT
- AlaC 94552 692-D5
PERICH CT
2300 MTVW 94040 831-J1
PERIDOT CT
100 HER 94547 569-G4
PERIDOT DR
1500 LVMR 94550 715-D3
2600 SJS 95132 814-F5
PERIDOT PL
2600 SJS 95132 814-F5
PERIE LN
3700 SJS 95132 814-J4
3800 SJS 95132 815-A4
PERIMETER RD
- LAH 94022 831-C2
- NVTO 94949 546-J4
- SMTO 94402 748-H5
5500 SJS 95193 875-C4
6300 SJS 95119 875-C5
N PERIMETER RD
- MLPK 94025 790-J1
S PERIMETER RD
600 MLPK 94025 790-J2
W PERIMETER RD
600 MLPK 94025 790-J1
600 SMCo 94025 790-J1
PERINE PL
- SF 94115 647-G5
PERITA DR
- DALY 94015 687-A7
PERIVALE CT
3100 SJS 95148 855-E2
PERIWINKLE DR
30800 UNC 94587 732-A5
PERIWINKLE LN
4700 SJS 95129 853-B2
4700 SJS 95129 852-B7
PERIWINKLE RD
29600 HAY 94544 712-D7
PERIWINKLE TER
800 SUNV 94086 832-F3
PERIWINKLE WY
1700 ANT 94509 595-E3
PERKINS AV
100 VAL 94590 530-C5
PERKINS CT
100 LGTS 95030 873-B3
600 SJS 95127 814-J6
4100 FRMT 94536 752-F3
PERKINS DR
300 AlaC 94541 711-E1
PERKINS RD
- VAL 94589 510-F4
1700 NaCo 94589 510-F4
2400 OAK 94602 650-E3
PERKINS ST
100 OAK 94610 649-J2
35900 FRMT 94536 752-F2
PERLITA CT
3700 AlaC 94541 692-C6
PERMANENTE WY
100 MTVW 94041 811-G4
PERNICH CT
1300 SJS 95120 874-C7
PEROLY CT
- OAK 94601 650-C6
PERRA WY
3100 WLCK 94598 612-H3
PERREIRA DR
900 SCL 95051 832-J5
900 SCL 95051 833-A5
PERRICH AV
2700 AlaC 94546 691-G4
PERRIN AV
8500 NWK 94560 772-C2
PERRIN CT
1500 SJS 95131 814-D6
PERRIN RD
600 MRTZ 94553 571-C6
PERRONE CIR
1800 SJS 95116 834-F3
PERRY AV
400 PCFA 94044 707-A4
1900 SMCo 94025 790-E7
PERRY COM
600 FRMT 94539 753-H5
PERRY CT
400 SCL 95054 813-E6
1600 SJS 95116 834-F4
PERRY LN
7800 PLE 94588 693-H7
PERRY RD
34100 UNC 94587 732-F6
PERRY ST
- RDWC 94063 770-A5
- SF 94107 648-B6
100 MPS 95035 794-C7
200 MrnC 94941 606-F6
PERRY WY
5000 ANT 94509 595-H4
PERRYMONT AV
200 SJS 95125 854-D4
400 SCIC 95125 854-D4
PERRY WALK AV
- SRFL 94901 586-F2
PERSEUS LN
800 FCTY 94404 749-F4
PERSHING AV
700 SJS 95126 833-J6
1200 SMTO 94403 749-C2
PERSHING DR
- OAK 94611 650-D1
100 SLN 94577 670-J7
500 PLHL 94596 592-D7
500 CCCo 94596 592-D7
800 SLN 94577 671-A7
800 SLN 94577 691-A1
1500 SF 94129 647-B5
PERSIA AV
- SF 94112 667-G7
200 SF 94112 687-G1
900 SF 94134 687-G1
PERSIAN DR
100 SUNV 94089 812-F3
PERSIANWOOD PL
5100 SJS 95111 875-C2
PERSIMMON AV
800 SUNV 94087 832-C2
PERSIMMON CT
- HIL 94010 748-C1
- WLCK 94598 592-J7
27600 HAY 94544 712-B6
PERSIMMON DR
100 VAL 94589 510-B7
27600 HAY 94544 712-B6
PERSIMMON PL
4600 SJS 95129 853-A2
8300 NWK 94560 752-C7
PERSIMMON RD
300 WLCK 94598 592-H7
PERSIMMON ST
3100 ANT 94509 574-J7
PERSIMMON GROVE CT
5300 SJS 95123 874-F7
PERTH CT
600 MPS 95035 794-A6
1300 CNCD 94521 593-A4
5000 ANT 94509 595-J2
PERTH PL
- OAK 94705 630-B3
PERTH ST
100 VAL 94591 530-G5
PERTH WY
- BEN 94510 551-B2
PERU AV
100 SF 94112 667-G7
700 SF 94134 667-G7
PERU CT
1700 PLE 94566 714-E1
PERUGIA CT
2500 SJS 95138 855-G7
PERUKA PL
300 SJS 95116 834-D4
PESCADERO CT
- DNVL 94526 633-B7
200 MPS 95035 793-J5
PESCADERO DR
700 SJS 95123 874-F5
PESCADERO ST
900 MPS 95035 793-J5
PESCADERO TER
300 SUNV 94086 812-D7
PESCARA CT
2600 SJS 95008 873-F1
PESHEL CT
16400 AlaC 94580 691-F6
PESTANA PL
300 LVMR 94550 695-J7
4000 FRMT 94538 773-E4
PESTANA WY
3300 LVMR 94550 696-A7
3300 LVMR 94550 695-J7
PETAL WY
1200 SJS 95129 852-G4
PETALUMA CT
1800 MPS 95035 794-D6
PETAR CT
- CLAY 94517 613-J2
- PIT 94565 574-B4
PETAR LN
- PIT 94565 574-B4
PETAR PL
- SRMN 94583 673-G6
2800 ANT 94509 575-A7
PETARD TER
34300 FRMT 94555 752-C2
PETER CT
- NVTO 94947 526-C5
S PETER CT
- CMBL 95008 853-G6
N PETER DR
- CMBL 95008 853-G6
S PETER DR
- CMBL 95008 853-G6
PETER ST
- DALY 94014 687-C4
PETER COUTTS CIR
- SCIC 94305 811-A2
PETER COUTTS RD
- SCIC 94305 810-J1
100 SCIC 94305 811-A2
PETERMAN AV
25800 HAY 94545 711-H6
PETERMAN LN
25800 HAY 94545 711-H6
PETER PAN AV
700 SJS 95116 834-H4
PETERS AV
- PLE 94566 714-D4
- SF 94110 667-H4
PETERS ST
1500 SLN 94578 691-D3
PETERSBURG DR
2100 MPS 95035 794-E7
PETERSEN AV
1500 SJS 95129 852-H5
PETERSEN WY
17600 AlaC 94546 691-H2
PETERSON CT
- AlaC 94541 712-B2
1200 LALT 94024 831-H3
PETERSON PL
- CCCo 94595 612-B6
PETERSON RD
- PLHL 94523 592-A6
PETERSON ST
400 OAK 94601 670-B1
PETERSON WY
3600 SCL 95054 813-A6
PETERS RANCH RD
500 DNVL 94526 653-A6
PETER YORKE WY
- SF 94109 647-H6
PETIE CT
1000 MTVW 94040 811-J6
PETITE WY
29000 HAY 94544 712-B7
PETOLA RD
700 DNVL 94526 652-H1
PETRARCH CT
3200 SJS 95135 855-F2
PETRARCH PL
- SF 94104 648-B5
PETRI PL
1600 SJS 95118 873-J5
1600 SJS 95124 873-J5
PETRIFIED FOREST CT
3900 PLE 94588 714-A1
PETRINA CT
28000 HAY 94545 731-J1
PETRINI CT
- MLBR 94030 728-A5
PETROLEUM ST
2500 OAK 94607 649-B3
PETRONI WY
1100 SJS 95120 894-F2
PETTICOAT LN
100 WLCK 94596 612-C6
PETTIGREW CT
2900 SJS 95148 855-C2
PETTIGREW DR
2200 SJS 95148 855-C2
PETTIS AV
200 MTVW 94041 811-G5
PETTIT LN
- MRTZ 94553 571-H4
PETULLA CT
4000 SJS 95124 873-J2
PETUNIA CT
2800 UNC 94587 752-F1
PEUGEOT PL
36400 NWK 94560 752-E6
PEYTON CT
2200 ANT 94509 595-A1
PEYTON DR
300 HAY 94544 712-B5
PFEFFER LN
2400 SJS 95128 853-F2
2400 SCIC 95128 853-F2
PFEIFFER CT
6600 SJS 95120 894-G1
PFEIFFER LN
2500 PIN 94564 569-J7
PFEIFFER ST
- SF 94133 648-A3
PFEIFFER WY
2500 PIN 94564 569-J7
PFEIFFER RANCH RD
6300 SCIC 95120 874-F7
6300 SJS 95120 874-E7
6400 SJS 95120 894-F1
PFEIFLE AV
12900 SCIC 95111 854-H6
PHAETON DR
7900 OAK 94605 671-C1
PHANOR DR
500 RCH 94806 568-G6
PHANTOM AV
1400 SCIC 95125 853-H5
1600 CMBL 95125 853-H5
PHARLAP AV
5000 SJS 95111 875-B2
PHARLAP DR
10000 CPTO 95014 832-B7
PHEASANT CIR
- PIT 94565 574-C6
PHEASANT CT
- DBLN 94568 694-D4
- SRFL 94901 567-D5
- PIT 94565 574-C6
6400 LVMR 94550 696-D2
PHEASANT DR
1000 PIT 94565 574-C7
1500 HER 94547 569-G4
PHEASANT RD
18000 SCIC 95032 893-H3
18600 SCIC 95030 893-H3
PHEASANT ST
33100 FRMT 94555 732-B7
PHEASANT WY
6300 LVMR 94550 696-D2
PHEASANT HILL CT
1400 SJS 95120 894-G4
PHEASANT HILL DR
1200 SJS 95120 894-F4
PHEASANT HILL WY
1300 SJS 95120 894-F4
PHEASANT RIDGE WY
- SJS 95136 854-F6
PHEASANT RUN DR
300 CCCo 94506 654-D3
PHEASANT RUN PL
- CCCo 94506 654-D3
PHEASANT RUN TER
- CCCo 94506 654-D3
PHEASANT WOODS DR
21500 AlaC 94552 692-D5
PHEBE AV
4600 FRMT 94555 752-C2
PHEBE RD
- FRMT 94555 752-C1
PHELAN AV
- SF 94112 667-E7
- SJS 95112 854-E2
100 VAL 94590 530-C5
900 SJS 95122 854-F1
2500 HAY 94545 731-H2
4700 FRMT 94538 753-A7
PHELAN CT
1800 SJS 95122 854-G1
PHELAN WY
1100 SJS 95122 854-G1
PHELAND CT
800 MPS 95035 814-D1
PHELPS AV
1000 SJS 95117 853-C4
PHELPS RD
300 SCAR 94070 769-E3
PHELPS ST
- VAL 94590 529-H2
200 SF 94124 668-B6
400 OAK 94603 670-F6
PHIL CT
600 CPTO 95014 852-G2
PHIL DR
15600 AlaC 94580 711-A2
PHIL LN
19100 SCIC 95014 852-G2
19100 CPTO 95014 852-G2
PHIL PL
10500 CPTO 95014 852-G2
PHILADELPHIA PL
42600 FRMT 94538 773-E1
PHILEO CT
4900 SJS 95118 873-J4
PHILIP CT
2900 SJS 95121 855-A3
PHILIP DR
200 DALY 94015 707-C1
PHILIP LN
- SCAR 94070 769-F3
PHILIP TER
- MrnC 94945 526-J3
PHILLIP CT
3000 RCH 94806 589-A2
PHILLIP RD
- WDSD 94062 809-H3
PHILLIP ST
400 SolC 94590 530-B6
PHILLIPS AV
2600 SCL 95051 833-B4
17100 LGTS 95032 893-C1
PHILLIPS CT
1100 SCL 95051 833-B4
5200 CNCD 94521 593-F4
PHILLIPS LN
- SLN 94577 690-G2
1800 ANT 94509 575-J6
PHILLIPS PL
5200 CNCD 94521 593-F4
PHILLIPS RD
- PA 94303 791-C3
3200 LFYT 94549 611-G7
PHILLIPS WY
900 HAY 94541 711-F4
PHINNEY PL
7500 SJS 95139 895-G1
PHINNEY WY
7300 SJS 95139 895-G1
PHLEGER RD
- SMCo 94062 789-C2
PHLOX WY
- LVMR 94550 696-C3
PHOEBE CT
3800 PLE 94566 714-F1
PHOENIX CIR
100 VAL 94589 510-B7
PHOENIX CT
- DNVL 94506 653-E4
800 FRMT 94539 773-H4
3800 SJS 95130 853-B4
PHOENIX DR
1400 SJS 95130 853-B5
1400 CMBL 95008 853-B5
PHOENIX LN
800 FCTY 94404 749-H1
3100 ALA 94502 670-A7
PHOENIX ST
- DNVL 94506 653-E4
4000 CNCD 94521 593-B2
PHOENIX TER
- SF 94133 647-J4
PHOENIX WY
1200 SLN 94577 690-H1
PHOTINIA LN
300 SCIC 95127 835-B1
PHYLIS DR
- PLHL 94523 592-C5
100 LGTS 95032 873-G6
PHYLIS PL
4800 MRTZ 94553 571-F7
PHYLIS TER
4800 MRTZ 94553 571-E7
PHYLLIS AV
900 MTVW 94040 811-J7
7000 SJS 95129 852-E3
PHYLLIS CT
- BLMT 94002 769-D1
100 VAL 94590 550-C2
1100 MTVW 94040 811-J7
4500 LVMR 94550 696-B7
PHYLLIS LN
4600 CNCD 94521 593-C3
PHYLMORE CT
- AlaC 94541 691-H7
PIAZZA CT
- SCIC 95127 815-A7
5300 PLE 94588 694-C6
PIAZZA DR
500 MTVW 94043 812-B3
PIAZZA WY
- SCIC 95127 815-A7
- SLN 94577 671-C7
100 SCIC 95127 835-A1
PICADILLY CIR
100 VAL 94591 530-H5
PICADILLY CT
- SRFL 94903 566-G5
1000 CNCD 94518 592-F5
3200 PLE 94588 694-E6
PICADILLY DR
3200 SJS 95118 874-C1
PICADILLY PL
1400 CMBL 95008 853-G5
PICARD AV
3800 PLE 94588 694-F6
PICARDO AV
- PCFA 94044 727-B4
PICARDO CT
- PCFA 94044 727-B4
PICARDY CT
- WLCK 94596 612-B2
PICARDY DR
5500 OAK 94605 670-G1
N PICARDY DR
5500 OAK 94605 670-G1
S PICARDY DR
5500 OAK 94605 670-G1
PICARDY PL
6500 NWK 94560 752-D6
PICARDY PLACE CT
3900 SJS 95121 855-B4
PICASSO CT
400 VAL 94591 530-E2
PICASSO DR
1200 SUNV 94087 832-F4
PICASSO TER
600 SUNV 94087 832-E3
PICCADILLY CT
- SCAR 94070 769-E5
PICCADILLY LN
4100 SMTO 94403 749-D6
PICCADILLY PL
100 SBRN 94066 707-G6
PICEA CT
3900 AlaC 94542 712-F3
PICKEREL DR
4200 UNC 94587 731-J5
PICKERING AV
- FRMT 94536 753-D2
W PICKERING AV
- FRMT 94536 753-D2
PICKERING CT
38600 FRMT 94536 753-D1
PICKERING PL
100 WLCK 94598 612-F3
PICKFAIR LN
2600 LVMR 94550 695-H6
PICKFORD AV
- SCIC 95127 834-J1
PICKFORD PL
2700 AlaC 94541 692-C7
PICKFORD WY
2900 AlaC 94541 692-C7
PICKWICK DR
4100 CNCD 94521 593-A3
PICNIC AV
100 SRFL 94901 586-G2
PICNIC LN
700 WLCK 94596 612-B3
PICO AV
- SF 94127 667-D7
600 SMTO 94403 749-A5
PICO BLVD
500 SCAR 94070 769-H2
PICO CT
- SRFL 94903 566-A1
- ORIN 94563 631-B5
1400 WLCK 94596 611-J2
PICO LN
800 LALT 94022 811-E4
PICO PL
100 CCCo 94565 573-D2
2100 AlaC 94578 691-G5
PICO RD
42000 FRMT 94539 753-H4
PICO TER
800 PCFA 94044 707-A5
PICO WY
1500 WLCK 94596 611-J2
PICO VISTA
- NVTO 94945 525-J2
PIDGEON CT
- LFYT 94549 611-B6
PIEDMONT AV
- BERK 94720 629-J2
- ORIN 94563 610-E6
100 SBRN 94066 727-G2
200 PCFA 94044 727-A2
2300 BERK 94704 629-J2
2700 BERK 94705 629-J3
3300 OAK 94611 649-J1
4200 OAK 94611 629-J7
4400 OAK 94611 630-A7
PIEDMONT CRES
2500 BERK 94704 629-J2
PIEDMONT CT
- LKSP 94939 586-E7
- PDMT 94611 650-B1
100 LGTS 95032 873-G6
PIEDMONT DR
1700 CNCD 94519 593-A1
PIEDMONT LN
100 PIT 94565 574-F4
PIEDMONT PL
200 RCH 94801 608-D1
PIEDMONT RD
- LKSP 94939 586-E7
- MPS 95035 794-E7
200 SCIC 95035 794-E7
700 MPS 95035 814-F1
900 SJS 95127 814-F2
1000 SJS 95132 814-F2
1100 SCIC 95035 814-F1
15000 SAR 95070 872-E4
PIEDMONT ST
- SF 94117 667-F2
PIEDMONT TER
- FRMT 94539 774-B7
PIEDMONT WY
800 RDWC 94062 789-H1
2100 PIT 94565 574-F4
PIEDRA DR
100 SUNV 94086 812-C7
1400 WLCK 94596 612-A2
PIEDRAS CIR
1800 CCCo 94526 633-D5
PIEDRAS CT
100 CCCo 94526 633-D5
PIEMONTE DR
- PLE 94566 715-B6
PIER ST
2300 OAK 94607 649-B2
PIERCE AV
- SJS 95110 834-C7
1200 SLN 94577 690-J1
PIERCE CT
1800 CNCD 94521 593-D2
3200 ANT 94509 575-C7
3200 ANT 94509 595-C1
20000 SAR 95070 852-E6
PIERCE DR
- NVTO 94947 526-B6
PIERCE LN
- NVTO 94947 526-B6
PIERCE RD
100 MLPK 94025 770-H7
400 MLPK 94025 790-J1
12800 SAR 95070 852-E7
13300 SAR 95070 872-B1
PIERCE ST
- SF 94117 667-G1
100 DALY 94015 687-B5
300 SF 94117 647-G7
500 ALB 94706 609-C5
500 RCH 94804 609-C4
600 VAL 94590 530-A3
800 ALB 94804 609-C4
1000 SF 94115 647-G5
1100 SCL 95050 833-D4
1700 SMTO 94403 749-C2
2700 SF 94123 647-G4
3100 SF 94123 647-F3
PIERCE WY
3900 FRMT 94536 752-J4
PIERCE RANCH RD
1300 SJS 95120 894-C2
PIERCY RD
300 SJS 95138 875-D3
300 SCIC 95138 875-E3
PIERINO AV
700 SUNV 94086 832-F2
PIERPOINT AV
5000 OAK 94602 650-F3
PIER POINT LN
- RDWC 94065 749-H5
PIERRE CT
100 VAL 94591 530-G3
PIERS CT
900 PA 94303 791-D6
PIERS LN
- SMCo 94025 810-E2
900 SCIC 94304 810-E2
PIERSON AV
1400 RCH 94804 608-H2
PIERSON ST
3300 OAK 94619 650-G7
PIETRO DR
1300 SJS 95131 814-C7
PIETRONAVE LN
700 PLE 94566 714-J3
PIETZ CT
6000 SJS 95123 874-F6
PIGEON HOLLOW RD
- MrnC 94901 566-J7
- MrnC 94901 586-J1
PIKE AV
1900 SLN 94577 690-J5
PIKE COM
38900 FRMT 94536 753-C3
PIKE CT
2200 CNCD 94520 572-F4
7100 DBLN 94568 693-J4
PIKE LN
- SMTO 94403 749-D5
4000 CNCD 94520 572-G4
PIKE PL
- UNC 94545 731-J6
PIKE RD
13800 SAR 95070 872-C1
PIKES CT
300 MRTZ 94553 591-H4
PIKES PEAK DR
- MrnC 94903 546-B7
PILAND DR
1300 SJS 95130 853-C4
PILAR CT
5800 SJS 95120 874-C5
PILAR PL
- PCFA 94044 727-A3
PILARCITOS CT
- HIL 94010 748-E6
PILARCITOS RD
- SMCo - 727-G6
PILARCITOS CREEK RD
- SMCo - 768-B4
PILGRIM AV
- SF 94112 667-F7
1700 MTVW 94040 811-F5
5900 SJS 95129 852-G5
PILGRIM DR
500 FCTY 94404 749-G2
PILGRIM LP
- FRMT 94539 773-J1
PILINUT CT
1000 SUNV 94087 832-C2
PILLON REAL
- PLHL 94523 591-J3
PILLSBURY CT
2500 LVMR 94550 715-G4
4000 ANT 94509 595-H1
PILLSBURY LN
- MrnC 94947 525-H4
PILOT CIR
- RDWC 94065 749-J5
- RDWC 94065 750-A5
PILOT HILL CT
100 VAL 94589 509-J5
PILOT KNOB DR
2300 SCL 95051 833-B1
PIMA DR
600 SJS 95123 874-H5
PIMA ST
47600 FRMT 94539 773-H7
PIMENTEL CT
- MRGA 94556 651-E1
- NVTO 94949 546-F1
PIMENTO AV
1100 SUNV 94087 832-C3
PIMLICO CT
500 WLCK 94596 612-C3
PIMLICO DR
100 WLCK 94596 612-C3
3500 PLE 94588 694-E5
PIMLOTT LN
- MLV 94941 606-D4
PINAR LN
- SF 94115 647-F7
PINARD ST
2100 MPS 95035 814-E1
PINCEA CT
- SAR 95070 852-B6
PINE
200 CMBL 95008 853-E6
PINE AV
- BLV 94920 627-D2
- SCAR 94070 769-F3
100 SSF 94080 708-A2
200 SSF 94080 707-J2
500 SUNV 94086 812-E5
600 SJS 95125 854-B4
700 PIN 94564 569-E4

978 PINE AV 1998 BAY AREA STREET INDEX PLYMOUTH WY

BAY AREA

STREET
Block City ZIP Pg-Grid

PINE AV
800 NVTO 94947 526-B4
1300 SPAB 94806 588-G4
2300 RCH 94806 588-H4
2900 BERK 94705 630-A3
PINE CT
- DALY 94014 687-H3
- HIL 94010 748-D2
- MrnC 94904 586-E3
700 MRTZ 94553 571-F4
6900 DBLN 94568 693-J4
43900 FRMT 94539 773-G2
PINE LN
- OAK 94618 630-B5
- LALT 94022 811-D5
700 SRFL 94903 566-C2
1000 LFYT 94549 611-C6
PINE PTH
- BERK 94705 630-A3
PINE ST
- RDWC 94063 770-B7
- SF 94111 648-A5
- SRFL 94901 566-E7
- SolC 94590 530-C6
100 FRMT 94539 773-G1
100 SANS 94960 586-B1
200 SBRN 94066 707-J7
200 SF 94104 648-A5
300 MLBR 94030 728-B2
300 SAUS 94965 627-A3
400 MrnC 94965 606-E7
500 MRTZ 94553 571-E2
500 SF 94108 648-A5
500 OAK 94607 649-C3
600 SBRN 94066 708-A6
700 LVMR 94550 695-E7
900 VAL 94590 530-C7
900 SF 94108 647-F6
1000 MLPK 94025 790-G3
1000 VAL 94590 550-C1
1100 PIT 94565 574-F3
1100 SF 94109 647-F6
1200 PA 94301 791-B5
1200 WLCK 94596 612-C4
1500 CNCD 94520 592-E2
2000 SF 94115 647-F6
2200 CCCo 94553 571-E3
3100 ANT 94509 574-J7
3400 AlaC 94546 692-A6
17000 LGTS 95032 873-B7
PINE TER
- TBRN 94920 607-B5
500 SSF 94080 707-J2
PINEAPPLE AV
800 SUNV 94087 832-C2
PINE BROOK CT
11700 CPTO 95014 852-C4
PINE BROOK LN
11700 CPTO 95014 852-C4
PINE CONE CT
17500 MSER 95030 873-A5
PINECONE CT
- SRFL 94901 567-C5
PINECONE DR
400 DNVL 94526 653-B4
PINE CREEK CT
- PIT - 573-F4
PINE CREEK DR
3300 SJS 95132 814-G3
PINE CREEK LN
200 AMCN 94589 510-B4
PINE CREEK RD
100 CCCo 94598 612-J4
400 CCCo 94598 613-A5
PINE CREEK WY
1200 CNCD 94520 592-F3
PINE CREST CT
- AlaC 94552 672-C7
PINECREST CT
2500 ANT 94509 595-F3
2800 SJS 95121 855-E4
PINE CREST DR
1200 CNCD 94521 593-B4
PINECREST DR
500 SCIC 94024 831-J5
1900 SBRN 94066 707-E6
5100 OAK 94605 671-C1
PINE CREST RD
500 MrnC 94941 606-E6
PINECREST TER
- SMTO 94402 748-G1
PINEDALE CT
700 HAY 94544 712-A2
700 HAY 94544 711-J2
7200 SJS 95139 895-F1
PINEFIELD RD
300 SJS 95134 813-C2
PINEGATE WY
3200 SJS 95148 855-E1
PINE GROVE CT
- CCCo 94596 612-D2
PINE GROVE WY
1400 SJS 95129 852-G4
PINEHAVEN DR
- DALY 94015 687-A4
PINEHAVEN PL
3700 AlaC 94546 692-B4
PINEHAVEN RD
6300 OAK 94611 630-D5
PINEHAVEN WY
200 PCFA 94044 707-A7
4900 ANT 94509 595-E4
PINE HILL CT
- SRFL 94903 566-D1
4800 SJS 95129 852-J2
PINE HILL DR
- CCCo 94803 589-F2
PINE HILL LN
400 PLE 94566 714-E4
PINE HILL RD
300 MrnC 94941 606-E6
700 SCIC 94305 810-J1
PINEHILL RD
100 HIL 94010 748-E2
PINE HILLS CT
- CCCo - 630-G7
- OAK 94611 630-G7
PINE HILLS DR
- OAK 94611 630-G7
PINE HILLS LN
- OAK 94611 630-G7

PINE HOLLOW CIR
1700 SJS 95133 834-E2
PINE HOLLOW CT
1000 CLAY 94517 593-H7
PINE HOLLOW RD
5200 CNCD 94521 593-D6
5600 CLAY 94517 593-F7
5700 CLAY 94521 593-F7
PINEHURST AV
200 LGTS 95032 873-F6
PINEHURST CT
1000 CNCD 94521 593-C6
1000 MLBR 94030 727-H3
1600 LVMR 94550 696-C3
2100 ELCR 94530 589-D7
PINEHURST CT W
1700 MPS 95035 794-D3
PINEHURST DR
1400 SJS 95118 874-B2
1600 LALT 94024 832-A3
PINEHURST PL
800 SRMN 94583 673-G6
PINEHURST RD
- AlaC - 651-C3
- CCCo - 631-A7
- CCCo - 630-G6
- CCCo - 651-A1
- OAK 94611 630-G6
PINEHURST SQ
1300 SJS 95117 853-C4
PINEHURST WY
- SF 94127 667-C7
100 SSF 94080 707-G5
2100 ELCR 94530 589-D7
PINE KNOLL DR
1500 BLMT 94002 769-D1
1700 BLMT 94002 749-D7
2000 WLCK 94595 632-A1
PINELAND AV
5900 SJS 95123 874-J5
PINE MEADOW CT
- SJS 95135 855-H7
PINEMEADOWS CT
1000 MRTZ 94553 571-H7
PINEMONT DR
4700 SJS 95008 873-A1
4700 SJS 95008 872-J1
PINENEEDLE DR
6500 OAK 94611 630-D5
PINE NUT CT
100 SUNV 94087 832-C2
PINENUT CT
400 SRMN 94583 673-G7
2200 ANT 94509 575-H6
PINENUT WY
2200 ANT 94509 575-H6
PINEO AV
500 MrnC 94965 606-E6
PINE PARK CT
400 MRTZ 94553 571-F5
PINE PASS TER
1500 SUNV 94087 832-D5
PINE RIDGE
400 SRMN 94583 673-F3
PINE RIDGE CT
3500 SJS 95127 835-C3
PINE RIDGE DR
100 SMCo - 768-D4
PINERIDGE RD
2700 AlaC 94546 691-G3
PINE RIDGE WY
- PTLV 94028 810-D5
400 MrnC 94941 606-E6
3500 SJS 95127 835-C3
PINE SHADOW LN
1200 CNCD 94521 593-F7
PINE SPRING CT
3200 SJS 95121 855-B3
PINETO PL
- PLE 94566 715-C6
PINE TOP AV
5500 OAK 94613 650-H7
PINE TREE CT
- SRFL 94903 566-E4
PINETREE CT
1700 CNCD 94521 593-B2
PINE TREE DR
1300 CCCo 94507 632-F4
PINE TREE LN
- ORIN 94563 631-B2
PINETREE TER
5000 SJS 95008 872-J1
PINE TREE TR
- CCCo 94553 591-D3
PINE TREE BRIDGE DR
- CNCD 94518 592-F4
PINE VALLEY CT
300 SRMN 94583 673-H6
PINE VALLEY RD
2800 SRMN 94583 673-F7
PINEVIEW CT
- PLHL 94523 592-A6
PINEVIEW DR
200 SCL 95050 833-D7
500 SJS 95117 833-D7
PINE VIEW LN
- NVTO 94945 526-B2
PINEVIEW LN
100 MLPK 94025 790-D5
1300 CNCD 94521 593-B4
PINEVILLE AV
10300 CPTO 95014 852-F2
PINEVILLE CIR
7600 AlaC 94552 692-G3
PINEWELL CT
5600 SJS 95138 875-D4
PINE WOOD CT
500 LGTS 95030 873-B2
PINEWOOD CT
1700 MPS 95035 814-A3
3300 HAY 94542 712-E4
4200 CNCD 94521 593-B2
4400 UNC 94587 732-A7
PINEWOOD DR
300 MrnC 94903 546-D7
600 SJS 95129 853-A3
3400 HAY 94542 712-E4
PINE WOOD LN
100 LGTS 95030 873-B2

PINEWOOD LN
- NVTO 94947 526-D6
PINEWOOD PL
1000 SJS 95129 853-A3
1500 PIT 94565 574-G6
3700 SCL 95054 813-E5
PINEWOOD RD
5800 OAK 94611 630-C6
PINEWOOD TER
1000 SPAB 94806 588-J3
3300 FRMT 94536 752-A6
PINEWOOD WY
1500 MPS 95035 814-A3
PINK AL
- SF 94103 667-H1
PINKERTON CT
- SRMN 94583 673-E4
3200 SJS 95148 835-E7
PINKERTON DR
3200 SJS 95148 835-D7
PINKSTONE CT
1600 SJS 95122 835-A5
PINMORE DR
1500 SJS 95118 874-A4
1600 SJS 95118 873-J4
PINNACLE CT
- HER 94547 569-H3
3500 SJS 95132 814-G3
19300 SAR 95070 872-G3
PINNACLE DR
2300 MRTZ 94553 572-A7
3300 SJS 95132 814-G4
PINNACLE RIDGE CT
100 DNVL 94506 654-A6
PINNACLES CT
23900 AlaC 94541 692-C7
23900 AlaC 94541 712-C1
PINNTAGE PKWY
20200 CPTO 95014 852-E1
PINO AL
- SF 94122 666-J2
PIN OAK CT
3400 SJS 95148 835-E7
PIN OAK DR
400 SUNV 94086 832-G1
PIN OAK PL
2000 CCCo 94506 653-H1
PINO CREST
- WLCK 94598 612-E4
PINOLE AV
100 CCCo 94572 549-H7
PINOLE CT
10600 CPTO 95014 852-E2
PINOLE RD
- CCCo 94803 589-F3
PINOLE ST
100 HER 94547 569-E3
PINOLE SHORES DR
600 PIN 94564 569-C3
PINOLE VALLEY RD
600 PIN 94564 589-H1
600 PIN 94564 569-F4
1100 CCCo 94803 569-G7
PINON AV
100 PIN 94564 569-D4
800 MLBR 94030 728-B5
800 BURL 94010 728-B5
PINON CT
700 SUNV 94086 832-G2
2000 LVMR 94550 696-A3
2400 MRTZ 94553 571-F4
4400 CNCD 94521 593-B5
PINON DR
100 PTLV 94028 810-B4
800 MRTZ 94553 571-F4
PINON PL
4400 SJS 95136 874-J1
PINON WY
4100 LVMR 94550 696-A3
4100 LVMR 94550 695-J3
PINON CANYON CT
- AlaC 94542 692-E6
PINOT CT
200 SJS 95119 875-E7
600 CLAY 94517 593-J7
2100 LVMR 94550 715-H3
3700 PLE 94566 714-G4
PINOTAGE CT
8300 SJS 95135 855-J7
PINOT BLANC WY
600 FRMT 94539 794-A2
3200 SJS 95135 855-G3
PINOT GRIS WY
4100 SJS 95135 855-G3
PINOT NOIR CT
8000 SJS 95135 855-H6
PINRAIL LN
600 FCTY 94404 749-J1
PINTA CT
100 LGTS 95032 873-C7
PINTA LN
700 FCTY 94404 749-G2
PINTAIL CT
1300 SJS 95118 874-C2
PINTAIL DR
- ANT 94509 594-H2
PINTO AV
- SF 94132 687-A1
PINTO CT
300 VAL 94591 530-E1
900 WLCK 94596 632-G2
33100 UNC 94587 732-F3
PINTO DR
100 VAL 94591 530-E1
600 SJS 95111 854-H5
PINTO LN
- MrnC 94947 525-F4
PINTO ST
- LVMR 94550 696-A2
PINTO WY
- WDSD 94062 789-D6
PINTO PALM TER
- SUNV 94086 832-G4
PINTO RIVER CT
4600 SJS 95136 874-G2
PINYON PL
- NVTO 94945 525-E2
PIOCHE ST
100 SF 94134 667-H7
PIOMBO PL
- SRFL 94901 587-B4

PIONEER AV
- HAY 94545 731-G2
100 WLCK 94596 612-C2
2400 SCIC 95128 853-F1
PIONEER CT
- NVTO 94945 525-J2
- SRMN 94583 673-B3
100 VAL 94589 509-H5
200 RCH 94803 589-G3
2000 SMTO 94403 749-A4
5100 ANT 94509 595-J5
PIONEER LN
6500 DBLN 94568 694-A3
6600 DBLN 94568 693-J3
PIONEER WY
- MTVW 94041 812-A6
5100 ANT 94509 595-J5
PIONEER TRAIL PL
400 PLE 94566 714-D6
PIO PICO WY
- PCFA 94044 727-C5
PIPEDREAM CT
1100 SJS 95122 834-F7
PIPER AV
800 SUNV 94087 832-C2
PIPER CT
- NVTO 94947 525-J3
4400 ANT 94509 595-J2
PIPER DR
1200 MPS 95035 814-B2
4100 SJS 95117 853-A3
4100 SJS 95129 853-A3
PIPER LP
- SF 94129 647-D4
PIPER ST
4500 FRMT 94538 753-B7
7600 OAK 94621 670-D6
PIPER RIDGE CT
1900 WLCK 94596 611-H3
PIPING ROCK RD
- NVTO 94949 546-A3
PIPIT CT
4800 PLE 94566 714-D1
PIPPIN AV
800 SUNV 94087 832-C2
PIPPIN ST
9800 OAK 94603 670-H6
PIPPIN CREEK CT
1100 SJS 95120 894-G3
PIRATE CV
- DALY 94014 687-E5
PIRATE LN
800 CCCo 94565 573-D1
PIRATES COVE CT
100 VAL 94591 550-G2
PISA CT
- SJS 95138 855-E7
- SSF 94080 707-G4
5900 FRMT 94555 752-B3
PISCES AV
5000 LVMR 94550 696-B3
PISCES DR
3400 SJS 95111 854-F7
PISCES LN
500 FCTY 94404 749-E4
PISMO CT
400 LVMR 94550 715-E3
5100 ANT 94509 595-F4
6300 SJS 95123 875-A7
PISMO TER
300 SUNV 94086 812-D7
PISTACHIO CT
2800 ANT 94509 575-H6
27700 HAY 94544 712-B6
PISTACHIO DR
3400 SJS 95111 854-G6
PISTACHIO GROVE CT
5300 SJS 95123 874-F7
PISTOIA WY
- SJS 95138 855-G7
- SJS 95138 875-G1
PISTOL CT
33600 FRMT 94555 752-B1
PITCAIRN DR
500 FCTY 94404 749-G5
PITCAIRN WY
3300 SJS 95111 854-J5
PITCH PINE CT
4300 SJS 95136 874-H1
4400 CNCD 94521 593-B5
PITMAN AV
1200 PA 94301 791-A3
1400 PA 94303 791-A3
PITNER CT
3000 SJS 95148 855-D1
PITT CT
7100 DBLN 94568 693-J4
PITT WY
- CCCo 94803 589-C3
PITTSBURG AV
300 CCCo 94801 588-E3
PITTSBURG-ANTIOCH HWY
2500 ANT 94509 575-A4
2700 ANT 94509 574-H4
2700 PIT 94565 574-H4
PITTSBURG WATERFRONT RD
300 PIT 94565 574-H2
PITTSFIELD WY
7200 SJS 95139 875-G7
PIUTE CT
900 WLCK 94598 612-H4
PIVATO CT
- NVTO 94945 526-C4
PIXANNE CT
2600 SJS 95148 835-B6
PIXIE LN
- SCAR 94070 769-C4
600 DNVL 94526 652-H1
PIXIE TR
400 MrnC 94941 606-D4
PIXLEY AV
- CMAD 94925 586-F7
PIXLEY ST
- SF 94123 647-G4
- SF 94123 647-G4
PIZARRO DR
36000 FRMT 94536 752-F3
PIZARRO LN
900 FCTY 94404 749-F3

PIZARRO WY
- SF 94112 667-D6
PIZZIMENTI CT
4700 CNCD 94521 593-D3
PLACE MOULIN
- TBRN 94920 607-D5
PLACENZA ST
800 LVMR 94550 695-E7
PLACER CIR
1600 LVMR 94550 695-E6
PLACER CT
- CCCo 94565 573-H2
600 LVMR 94550 695-E6
PLACER DR
1500 CNCD 94521 593-B3
2000 AlaC 94578 691-D2
2200 CCCo 94565 573-H2
PLACER PL
100 VAL 94591 550-C1
PLACER ST
1900 RCH 94804 609-C3
PLACER WY
- BSBN 94005 688-A7
39700 FRMT 94538 753-B6
PLACER OAKS RD
16700 LGTS 95032 873-B5
PLACER RIDGE RD
900 CCCo 94596 612-A5
PLACER SPRING CT
11800 CPTO 95014 852-C4
PLACID CT
- SJS 95135 875-J1
- SRMN 94583 653-F6
PLACIDA CT
14600 SAR 95070 872-C3
PLACITAS AV
- ATN 94027 790-E1
500 SMCo 94025 770-E7
500 SMCo 94063 790-E1
PLAID PL
- HIL 94010 748-E4
PLAINFIELD DR
4700 SJS 95111 875-B1
PLAINVIEW CT
6500 SJS 95120 894-C1
PLANET CIR
4300 UNC 94587 732-A6
PLANETREE PL
900 SUNV 94086 832-G3
PLANK AV
7100 ELCR 94530 609-C1
PLANK CT
7300 ELCR 94530 609-C1
PLANTANO WY
1100 PLE 94566 714-G2
PLATA CT
- NVTO 94947 525-G4
400 DNVL 94526 653-C3
PLATA WY
11700 DBLN 94568 693-G4
PLATEAU AV
1500 SCIC 94024 831-F3
PLATEAU CT
- HER 94547 569-H3
PLATEAU DR
600 CCCo 94708 609-G4
3300 BLMT 94002 769-A1
PLATERO PL
39500 FRMT 94539 753-E3
PLATINUM CT
100 VAL 94589 510-B6
1800 SJS 95116 834-F3
PLATINUM TER
34200 FRMT 94555 752-C2
PLATO CT
- PLHL 94523 591-J7
PLATT AV
- SAUS 94965 627-A3
1100 MPS 95035 814-D1
PLATT CT
- MrnC 94941 606-J6
100 VAL 94589 510-B7
800 MPS 95035 814-D1
PLATT CT N
3700 PLE 94588 714-A1
PLATT CT S
3600 PLE 94588 714-A1
PLATT DR
2300 MRTZ 94553 572-A7
PLATTE RIVER CT
5200 PLE 94588 693-H6
PLATT RIVER PL
34700 FRMT 94555 752-E2
PLA VADA CT
800 CNCD 94518 592-F6
PLAYA
1900 SMTO 94403 749-E5
PLAYA CT
- HER 94547 569-H4
- SRMN 94583 673-B2
PLAYA DEL REY
100 SRFL 94901 587-A2
5400 SJS 95123 874-F3
PLAYA VERDE
- MrnC 94920 607-D5
PLAYER CT
100 WLCK 94598 612-E3
PLAZA AV
800 LVMR 94550 715-E3
PLAZA CIR
100 DNVL 94526 633-D6
5000 RCH 94804 609-B1
PLAZA CT
100 DNVL 94526 633-D6
1700 MTVW 94040 831-G1
PLAZA DR
- LFYT 94549 611-F6
- PIT 94565 574-D6
- VAL 94591 510-E7
- VAL 94591 530-E1
- MrnC 94941 606-G3
100 SUNV 94089 812-F3
800 SJS 95125 854-A2
1000 CCCo 94553 571-G4
1400 AlaC 94578 691-E4
PLAZA LN
900 FCTY 94404 749-E3
1500 BURL 94010 728-C4
PLAZA ST
- SF 94116 667-D4
PLAZA WY
4900 RCH 94804 609-B1

PLAZA AMAPOLA
700 NVTO 94947 526-B4
PLAZA AMERICAS
2600 SJS 95132 814-D4
PLAZA BANDERAS
2600 SJS 95132 814-D4
PLAZA CASITAS
1700 SJS 95132 814-D4
PLAZA CLAVELES
2600 SJS 95132 814-D4
PLAZA CORONA
5000 SCL 95054 813-C3
PLAZA DE GUADALUPE
2100 SJS 95116 834-G3
PLAZA DEMIRA
- NVTO 94947 526-B4
PLAZA DE ORO
1400 BEN 94510 550-J3
PLAZA ENCINA
5500 CNCD 94521 593-E7
PLAZA ERMITA
5500 CNCD 94521 593-E7
PLAZA ESCUELA
4900 SCL 95054 813-C3
PLAZA HERMOSA
700 NVTO 94947 526-B4
PLAZA INVIERNO
600 SJS 95111 875-B1
PLAZA LA POSADA
200 LGTS 95030 872-J3
PLAZA LINDA
700 NVTO 94947 526-B4
PLAZA LOMA
- NVTO 94947 526-B4
PLAZA MONTEZ
1900 SJS 95132 814-D3
PLAZA NOGAL
5500 CNCD 94521 593-E7
PLAZOLETA
100 LGTS 95030 872-J2
PLEASANT AV
- SAR 95070 872-E4
- CMAD 94925 606-G1
PLEASANT CT
- WLCK 94596 612-C1
PLEASANT LN
- RCH 94803 589-E3
- SRFL 94901 586-F2
1500 CCCo 94549 611-J2
PLEASANT PL
100 ANT 94509 575-D4
PLEASANT ST
- FCTY 94404 749-E6
- LGTS 95032 873-B7
- LGTS 95032 893-B1
- SF 94108 647-J5
- SJS 95110 834-A6
2500 OAK 94602 650-D5
N PLEASANT ST
200 SJS 95110 834-A6
PLEASANT WY
300 SLN 94577 670-J7
700 LVMR 94550 696-D4
800 LALT 94022 811-E4
24900 HAY 94544 711-J4
PLEASANT ACRES DR
2300 SCIC 95148 835-E5
PLEASANT CREST CT
2000 SJS 95148 835-D4
PLEASANT CREST DR
3500 SJS 95148 835-D5
PLEASANT ECHO DR
3500 SJS 95148 835-D4
PLEASANT GROVE CT
- SJS 95112 854-E4
PLEASANT HILL CIR
1100 LFYT 94549 611-H5
PLEASANT HILL CT
27700 HAY 94542 712-E4
PLEASANT HILL RD
900 RDWC 94061 789-H2
1000 LFYT 94549 611-H4
1200 CCCo 94549 611-J1
1300 WLCK 94596 611-J1
1600 MRTZ 94553 591-J4
1600 PLHL 94523 591-J4
1600 PLHL 94523 611-J1
1700 PLHL 94523 592-A5
2600 CCCo 94549 591-J4
5200 PLE 94588 693-H6
PLEASANT HILL RD E
800 MRTZ 94553 571-F7
PLEASANT HILLS CT
7000 SJS 95139 895-E1
PLEASANT KNOLL DR
3500 SJS 95148 835-D4
PLEASANT OAKS CT
200 PLHL 94523 591-J5
PLEASANT OAKS DR
900 PLHL 94523 591-J5
PLEASANT OAKS PL
- PLHL 94523 591-J5
PLEASANTON AV
4200 PLE 94566 714-D3
PLEASANTON-SUNOL RD
- PLE 94566 714-C7
7900 AlaC 94566 714-C7
7900 AlaC 94566 734-D2
7900 AlaC 94586 734-D2
PLEASANT RIDGE AV
- SCIC 95127 834-H2
PLEASANT ROW CT
3500 SJS 95148 835-D5
PLEASANT VALLEY AV
1700 OAK 94611 630-A7
1800 OAK 94611 629-J7
PLEASANT VALLEY CT
- SRMN 94583 673-J6
N PLEASANT VALLEY CT
4400 OAK 94611 630-A7
S PLEASANT VALLEY CT
4400 OAK 94611 630-A7
PLEASANT VALLEY DR
- WLCK 94596 612-C1
300 MRTZ 94553 591-F1
1000 PLHL 94523 592-C7
1000 PLHL 94523 612-C1
PLEASANT VIEW AV
17300 MSER 95030 873-A5

PLEASANT VIEW DR
100 PLHL 94523 592-A7
PLEASANT VIEW LN
2100 AlaC 94550 715-H3
2100 LVMR 94550 715-H3
PLEASANT VIEW RD
- NVTO 94947 525-J3
PLEASANT VISTA DR
3700 SCIC 95148 835-E5
PLEIADES PL
4100 UNC 94587 732-B6
PLEITNER AV
3000 OAK 94602 650-D5
PLOMOSA CT
600 FRMT 94539 793-J1
PLOMOSA RD
48500 FRMT 94539 793-J2
PLOMOSA WY
- FRMT 94539 793-J1
PLOVER PL
300 PIT 94565 574-D1
PLOVER ST
800 FCTY 94404 749-H2
PLOW WY
100 VAL 94590 529-H2
PLUM AV
1100 SUNV 94087 832-C3
PLUM LN
1000 CNCD 94518 592-F5
PLUM ST
- SF 94103 667-J1
600 NVTO 94945 526-D3
1100 SJS 95110 854-C2
2100 PIN 94564 569-E4
3100 CCCo 94553 571-G4
PLUMAS AV
- SANS 94960 566-A7
1400 MLPK 94025 770-H7
5400 RCH 94804 609-B3
PLUMAS CIR
- NVTO 94947 526-E6
PLUMAS CT
- CCCo 94565 573-H2
100 SBRN 94066 707-D7
600 MRTZ 94553 571-E7
1000 LVMR 94550 695-F6
4000 HAY 94542 712-F4
39400 FRMT 94538 753-A6
PLUMAS DR
2700 SJS 95121 854-J3
2700 SJS 95121 855-A3
12000 SAR 95070 852-E5
PLUMAS ST
- BSBN 94005 688-A6
PLUMAS WY
39700 FRMT 94538 753-B6
PLUM BLOSSOM DR
7400 CPTO 95014 852-D4
PLUMERIA CT
1800 PLE 94566 714-E1
1800 PLE 94588 714-E1
PLUMERIA DR
- SJS 95134 813-F6
PLUMERIA WY
35800 FRMT 94536 732-J7
PLUM GROVE CT
5200 SJS 95123 874-F7
PLUMLEIGH AV
2800 ANT 94509 575-D7
PLUMLEIGH DR
2100 FRMT 94539 753-E6
PLUMLEIGH LN
1200 CNCD 94521 593-A5
PLUMMER AV
2200 SJS 95125 854-A6
2900 SJS 95125 874-B1
2900 SJS 95118 874-B1
6200 NWK 94560 752-E7
PLUMMER CT
24400 HAY 94545 711-E5
PLUMPOINTE LN
2000 SRMN 94583 653-J7
PLUMSTEAD CT
2200 SJS 95148 855-C2
PLUMSTEAD WY
2800 SJS 95148 855-C2
PLUM TREE LN
100 SCIC 94305 790-H6
PLUMTREE LN
900 MTVW 94040 831-G1
10200 CPTO 95014 832-E7
PLUM TREE ST
200 HAY 94544 711-J4
PLUMWOOD PL
1400 SBRN 94066 707-G7
PLUTO ST
28700 HAY 94544 712-B7
PLUTO WY
4100 UNC 94587 732-B6
PLYMOUTH AV
- MLV 94941 606-F4
- SCAR 94070 769-E4
- SF 94112 687-D2
600 FRMT 94539 753-F6
1100 SF 94112 667-D7
1600 SF 94127 667-D6
6100 CCCo 94805 589-C5
6100 SJS 95129 852-G4
PLYMOUTH CIR
- DALY 94015 707-D3
PLYMOUTH CT
- SRMN 94583 673-G5
400 BEN 94510 551-A2
PLYMOUTH CV
100 SRFL 94901 587-A2
PLYMOUTH DR
1000 SUNV 94087 832-B2
1900 PIT 94565 574-E3
12500 SAR 95070 852-F6
18100 AlaC 94546 691-J3
PLYMOUTH LN
600 FCTY 94404 749-F4
1400 ANT 94509 575-F5
PLYMOUTH RD
3100 LFYT 94549 611-J4
PLYMOUTH ST
1400 MTVW 94043 811-G1
7800 OAK 94621 670-H3
9000 OAK 94603 670-J4
PLYMOUTH WY
600 BURL 94010 728-G6
2600 SBRN 94066 707-E7

INDEX

PLYMPTON CT 1998 BAY AREA STREET INDEX PREBLE AV 979

STREET
Block City ZIP Pg-Grid

PLYMPTON CT
100 SJS 95139 875-G7
POAS CIR
- SJS 95116 834-G3
POAS CT
2000 SJS 95116 834-G3
POCATELLO AV
900 SUNV 94087 832-B6
POCATELLO CT
500 SJS 95111 854-H5
POCATELLO DR
400 SJS 95111 854-H5
POCO LN
- CCCo 94595 632-C1
POCO WY
- AMCN 94589 510-A1
1900 SJS 95116 834-H5
POCONO MANOR PL
400 SRMN 94583 673-H6
POCO PASEO
- ORIN 94563 630-J3
POCO PASO
- MrnC 94903 566-E5
PODA CT
1000 FRMT 94539 753-G7
PODVA LN
900 DNVL 94526 653-A4
PODVA RD
800 DNVL 94526 653-A4
POE LN
1300 SJS 95130 853-B4
POE ST
300 PA 94301 790-H4
1300 BERK 94702 629-E2
POETT LN
2400 SCL 95051 833-B2
POETT RD
300 HIL 94010 748-H2
POGGI ST
400 ALA 94501 649-E7
POGLIA CT
5600 SJS 95138 875-G1
POHONO ST
- MrnC 94941 606-H7
POINCIANA DR
1100 SCL 95051 832-H3
1100 SUNV 94086 832-H3
POINCIANA PL
39300 FRMT 94538 752-J6
POINCIANA ST
700 HAY 94545 711-G5
POINSETT AV
5300 ELCR 94530 589-B7
5300 RCH 94805 589-B7
POINSETTIA AV
- CCCo 94565 573-H2
- SMTO 94403 749-C5
POINSETTIA CT
4400 SJS 95136 874-H2
POINT ANDRUS CT
2600 ANT 94509 595-G2
POINT ARENA CT
2800 ANT 94509 595-H2
POINT BENICIA CIR
- BEN 94510 551-A3
POINT BENICIA WY
100 BEN 94510 551-B5
POINT CREEK CT
800 SJS 95133 814-G7
POINT CREEK DR
800 SJS 95133 814-G7
POINTDEXTER CT
2800 SJS 95133 814-G6
POINT DUME CT
2600 ANT 94509 595-G2
POINT DUNES CT
200 SJS 95139 895-H2
POINTE CLAIRE CT
1400 SUNV 94087 832-D4
POINTE CLAIRE DR
1300 SUNV 94087 832-D4
POINT EDEN WY
3900 HAY 94545 731-D1
POINTE PACIFIC DR
700 DALY 94014 687-D3
POINT GALLINAS RD
- MrnC 94903 566-J2
POINT LOBOS AV
- SF 94121 646-H6
POINT LOBOS CT
2600 ANT 94509 595-G2
POINT REYES CT
900 VAL 94591 550-E3
2800 ANT 94509 595-H2
POINT REYES WY
- PCFA 94044 727-B5
POINT SAL CT
2600 ANT 94509 595-G2
POINT SAN BRUNO BLVD
300 SSF 94080 708-C3
POINT SAN PEDRO RD
- MrnC 94901 586-H1
- SRFL 94901 586-H1
100 SRFL 94901 587-B1
100 MrnC 94901 587-A1
600 MrnC 94901 587-B1
700 MrnC 94901 567-C7
800 SRFL 94901 567-C7
POINT SUR CT
2600 ANT 94509 595-G2
POINTVIEW LN
- RCH 94806 588-F1
POIRIER ST
600 OAK 94609 629-G5
POKER FLAT PL
1200 SJS 95120 874-C6
POLARIS AV
200 MTVW 94043 811-H4
600 FCTY 94404 749-F4
4100 UNC 94587 732-B7
POLARIS CT
- MPS 95035 814-A3
100 VAL 94591 550-G3
POLARIS DR
- PIT 94565 574-A2
1500 PIT 94565 573-J3
POLARIS WY
200 DALY 94014 687-F2
200 SF 94112 687-F2
700 LVMR 94550 715-E4

POLHEMUS AV
200 ATN 94027 790-C4
POLHEMUS RD
- SMTO 94402 748-G7
200 SMCo 94402 748-G7
700 SMCo 94402 768-H1
700 SMTO 94402 768-H1
POLHEMUS WY
- LKSP 94939 586-D6
POLITZER DR
- MLPK 94025 790-E5
POLK AV
1000 SUNV 94086 812-B7
2000 SMTO 94403 749-C2
2400 SCL 95051 833-C7
POLK CT
1900 MTVW 94040 831-G1
3100 ANT 94509 575-A7
POLK LN
1100 SJS 95117 853-C3
POLK ST
- BEN 94510 551-D6
- SF 94102 647-H4
700 SF 94109 647-H4
800 ALB 94706 609-D6
1800 CNCD 94521 593-D3
2400 SF 94109 647-H3
POLK WY
300 LVMR 94550 696-A7
POLK SPRING CT
1200 SJS 95120 894-G4
POLLARD CT
2100 CMBL 95030 872-J2
POLLARD PL
- SF 94133 648-A4
- SF 94133 648-A4
POLLARD RD
700 LGTS 95030 873-A2
800 CMBL 95008 873-A2
1600 CMBL 95030 873-A2
1800 LGTS 95030 872-J2
1800 CMBL 95030 872-J2
2000 SAR 95070 872-J2
POLLARD OAKS CT
- LGTS 95030 873-B2
POLLARDSTOWN
- DBLN 94568 693-G4
POLLEN CT
2000 SJS 95131 814-D7
POLLEY LN
- PLHL 94523 612-A1
POLLUX CT
800 FCTY 94404 749-F4
32300 UNC 94587 732-A6
POLO CT
1900 SMTO 94403 749-A4
POLONIUS CIR
4000 FRMT 94555 732-C7
POLSON CIR
1100 MRTZ 94553 571-H6
POLSON CT
1100 MRTZ 94553 571-H6
POLTONHALL CT
3200 SJS 95121 855-C5
POLTON PLACE WY
3700 SJS 95121 855-B4
POLVADERO DR
6900 SJS 95119 895-E1
POLVOROSA AV
2200 SLN 94577 690-G3
POLVOROSA CT
36500 FRMT 94536 752-G3
POLYNESIA DR
1100 FCTY 94404 749-G2
POLYNESIA WY
100 UNC 94587 732-C5
POMACE CT
2400 FRMT 94539 773-G3
3200 PLE 94566 714-G4
POMACE ST
44100 FRMT 94539 773-G3
POMANDER PL
6600 SJS 95120 894-G1
POMAR WY
1800 WLCK 94598 612-E1
POMAR VISTA
2100 AlaC 94578 691-G5
2300 AlaC 94546 691-G5
POME AV
1100 SUNV 94087 832-C3
POMEGRANATE AV
6100 NWK 94560 752-F7
POMEGRANATE CT
1100 SUNV 94087 832-C3
POMEGRANATE LN
400 SJS 95134 813-C2
POMELO CT
1100 SUNV 94087 832-C3
POMERADO DR
3200 SJS 95135 855-H3
POMERADO WY
3300 SJS 95135 855-G3
POMEROY AV
500 SCL 95051 832-J6
700 SCL 95051 833-A5
3100 SJS 95121 855-C3
POMEROY CT
2500 SSF 94080 707-C4
3200 SJS 95121 855-C3
POMEROY RD
- ROSS 94957 586-D1
POMEZIA CT
2100 PLE 94566 715-B6
POMFRET WK
- PLHL 94523 591-B1
POMINO WY
- PLE 94566 715-B6
POMO CT
- CCCo 94565 573-E2
400 FRMT 94539 773-J4
POMO ST
2000 CCCo 94565 573-E2
POMONA AV
100 ELCR 94530 609-D3
400 VAL 94589 510-B6
500 ALB 94706 609-D6
900 CCCo 94553 571-F4
1400 SJS 95110 854-D2
1600 SJS 95125 854-D2
2100 MRTZ 94553 571-F4
4200 PA 94306 811-C3

POMONA CT
400 LVMR 94550 696-A7
7300 ELCR 94530 609-D3
POMONA PL
4000 PIT 94565 574-E6
POMONA ST
- CCCo 94525 550-E5
- SF 94124 668-B6
500 AlaC 94580 691-D5
POMONA WY
4000 LVMR 94550 696-A7
4300 LVMR 94550 716-A1
POMPANO AV
27600 HAY 94544 712-A7
27800 HAY 94544 732-A1
POMPANO CIR
300 FCTY 94404 749-H2
POMPANO ST
1200 SJS 95122 834-H6
POMPEI CT
5900 FRMT 94555 752-B6
POMPEY DR
1400 SJS 95128 853-E5
POMPONI ST
4400 UNC 94545 731-J6
POMPONIO
- PTLV 94028 830-C1
PONCA CT
1700 FRMT 94539 773-G4
PONCE AV
2600 BLMT 94002 769-B1
PONCE CT
5700 SJS 95120 874-C5
PONCE DR
4200 PA 94306 811-E2
PONCETTA DR
- DALY 94015 687-B3
POND CT
- MPS 95035 794-A7
N POND CT
2300 CCCo 94549 591-G4
S POND CT
2400 CCCo 94549 591-G4
POND DR
35600 FRMT 94536 732-J6
POND ISL
600 ALA 94501 669-H3
POND ST
- SF 94114 667-G2
POND WY
1900 SJS 95131 814-C4
POND DIVIDE RD
- MRTZ 94553 571-E2
PONDEREY PL
- CCCo 94521 593-E4
PONDEROSA AV
700 SUNV 94086 832-G3
PONDEROSA CT
300 RCH 94803 589-G3
400 CCCo 94549 591-G6
27400 HAY 94545 711-G7
27400 HAY 94545 731-G1
36600 NWK 94560 752-C7
PONDEROSA DR
1900 LVMR 94550 695-J3
2000 LVMR 94550 696-A3
2800 CNCD 94520 572-F7
PONDEROSA LN
100 CCCo 94595 612-A7
PONDEROSA RD
- SSF 94080 707-F4
200 SMCo 94080 707-F4
PONDEROSA TER
4900 SJS 95008 872-J1
37900 FRMT 94536 753-A3
37900 FRMT 94536 752-J1
PONDEROSA TR
3300 PIN 94564 569-F5
PONDEROSA WY
2800 SCL 95051 833-A6
3100 ANT 94509 575-A7
PONS CT
4000 PLE 94566 714-G4
PONSELLE CT
2600 SJS 95121 854-J4
PONTE FIRE RD
- NVTO 94949 546-C4
100 MrnC 94903 546-C4
PONTIAC AV
13900 SAR 95070 872-D2
PONTIAC CT
1000 WLCK 94598 612-H4
PONTIAC DR
2700 WLCK 94598 612-H4
5700 SJS 95123 874-H5
PONTIAC ST
100 SLN 94577 670-J6
100 OAK 94603 670-J6
24400 HAY 94544 711-J3
PONTIAC WY
100 FRMT 94539 773-H7
PONTIUS CT
5800 SJS 95123 875-A5
PONY CT
- SRMN 94583 673-B3
PONY PASS CIR
4800 SJS 95136 874-H2
POOLSIDE PL
- SLN 94578 691-D5
POPE CT
1700 CMBL 95008 873-D2
POPE DR
600 VAL 94591 530-F6
POPE RD
- SF 94123 647-H3
POPE ST
- DALY 94014 687-F2
- SF 94129 647-C4
- SF 94112 687-F2
100 MLPK 94025 791-A3
200 MLPK 94025 790-J2
POPE WY
900 HAY 94545 711-F4
POPEJOY CT
4800 SJS 95118 873-J4
POPLAR AV
- RDWC 94061 789-J2
- CMBL 95008 853-F6
- MLBR 94030 728-B4
- ROSS 94957 586-C2
100 AlaC 94541 711-G2
100 SBRN 94066 727-J1

POPLAR AV
100 RDWC 94061 790-B1
100 MrnC 94904 586-C2
300 SBRN 94066 707-J7
500 SSF 94080 707-H2
800 SUNV 94086 832-G3
1300 PCFA 94044 727-B5
1300 SUNV 94087 832-G3
1500 CCCo 94805 589-C6
1800 RDWC 94061 770-B7
2000 EPA 94303 791-A1
4000 CNCD 94521 593-A2
E POPLAR AV
- SMTO 94401 748-H1
100 SMTO 94401 728-J6
1100 SMTO 94401 729-A6
W POPLAR AV
- SMTO 94402 748-G1
POPLAR COM
5600 FRMT 94538 773-A1
POPLAR CT
- CCCo 94595 612-B7
100 HER 94547 569-J4
600 LVMR 94550 695-J6
900 SUNV 94086 832-G3
POPLAR DR
- MrnC 94904 586-E2
1000 NVTO 94945 525-H1
1600 CCCo 94595 612-B7
2200 SJS 95122 834-J5
2400 ANT 94509 575-C6
POPLAR ST
- BERK 94708 609-H5
- SF 94110 667-H4
300 MrnC 94965 606-E7
700 SCL 95050 833-F5
1000 OAK 94607 649-E2
2800 OAK 94608 649-E2
37000 NWK 94560 752-C7
POPLAR TER
4900 SJS 95008 872-J1
POPLAR WY
- PDMT 94611 650-C1
6700 DBLN 94568 693-J3
POPLARWOOD CT
1700 CNCD 94521 593-D3
POPLARWOOD WY
2500 SJS 95132 814-C3
POPPY AV
1700 MLPK 94025 790-E6
POPPY CIR
500 BEN 94510 530-J7
500 BEN 94510 550-J1
POPPY CT
100 CCCo 94596 612-F7
100 FRMT 94538 773-B1
100 MPS 95035 794-D6
100 VAL 94591 530-F7
100 HER 94547 569-J3
800 SUNV 94086 832-G3
POPPY DR
100 HER 94547 569-J4
2100 BURL 94010 728-C6
22500 CPTO 95014 831-J7
POPPY LN
- SCIC 95127 814-J5
- BERK 94708 609-H5
- MPS 95035 794-D6
- ORIN 94563 610-J4
- SCAR 94070 769-C4
- SF 94131 667-G5
15600 MSER 95030 873-A5
POPPY PL
400 MTVW 94043 811-H4
700 PLHL 94523 591-J3
POPPY PZ
- HAY 94542 712-B3
POPPY WY
- LVMR 94550 696-A4
1200 ANT 94509 575-B5
1200 CPTO 95014 852-D4
POPPYBANK CT
1500 PLE 94566 714-F1
POPPY BLOSSOM CT
5300 SJS 95123 875-B3
POPPY HILLS CT
5700 SJS 95138 875-G1
POPULUS PL
900 SUNV 94086 832-G3
POQUITO CT
1500 PIN 94564 569-D5
PORGY PL
1300 SJS 95128 853-F4
PORPOISE TER
500 SUNV 94089 812-G3
PORT DR
600 SMTO 94404 749-D1
PORT ST
600 CCCo 94525 550-D5
PORT WY
2100 SJS 95133 814-E7
PORTA BALLENA
1200 ALA 94501 669-E2
PORTAGE AV
400 PA 94306 811-B1
PORTAGE RD
6800 DBLN 94568 693-H4
PORTAGE MOUNTAIN DR
1500 SJS 95126 853-H4
PORTAL AV
800 OAK 94610 650-B2
10000 CPTO 95014 832-F7
10000 CPTO 95014 852-F1
W PORTAL AV
- SF 94127 667-C5
300 SF 94132 667-C5
PORTAL CT
2200 SJS 95131 814-A5
PORTAL LN
- SCL 95134 813-D5
500 FCTY 94404 749-F3
PORTAL PL
700 PA 94303 791-B6
PORTAL PTH
- SF 94127 667-C5
PORTAL PZ
19800 CPTO 95014 852-F1
PORTAL WY
2200 SJS 95148 835-D6
PORT ANCHORWOOD PL
36500 NWK 94560 752-F5

PORTA ROSSA CIR
- PLE 94588 694-D6
PORT CHICAGO HWY
200 CCCo 94565 573-E2
800 CCCo 94520 572-G3
800 CCCo 94565 572-G3
800 CCCo 94553 572-G3
1700 CNCD 94519 592-G1
2000 CNCD 94520 572-G3
2000 CNCD 94519 572-G3
4500 CNCD 94520 592-G1
PORTER DR
3100 PA 94304 811-A2
PORTER LN
- SCIC 95127 815-A7
300 SCIC 95127 835-B1
PORTER PL
200 SRMN 94583 673-A1
PORTER ST
- SF 94110 667-J6
400 VAL 94590 530-B7
900 VAL 94590 550-B1
4100 OAK 94619 650-F6
4300 FRMT 94538 753-B7
PORTERFIELD CT
2400 MTVW 94040 831-J1
PORT FOGWOOD PL
36600 NWK 94560 752-F5
PORTHOLE CT
300 HER 94547 570-B6
PORTIA AV
1000 SUNV 94086 812-C7
PORTIA TER
34300 FRMT 94555 752-D2
PORTIFINO CIR
- RDWC 94065 749-J6
PORTILLO VALLEY DR
5000 SRMN 94583 673-J7
PORTLAND AV
- BERK 94707 609-D5
300 OAK 94606 650-A4
900 LALT 94024 831-H2
1100 ALB 94706 609-D5
PORTLAND CT
- DNVL 94526 653-C4
PORTMAN DR
800 RDWC 94065 750-C6
PORTO ALEGRE CT
- SJS 95120 874-D5
PORTO ALEGRE DR
5700 SJS 95120 874-C5
PORTO ALEGRE PL
1100 SJS 95120 874-D6
PORTO BELLO DR
- SRFL 94901 586-J1
PORTOBELLO DR
1400 SJS 95118 874-A3
PORTOFINO CIR
14900 SLN 94578 691-D3
PORTOFINO CT
- SCAR 94070 769-E4
100 HER 94547 570-B6
PORTOFINO DR
300 SCAR 94070 769-E5
PORTO FINO LN
600 FCTY 94404 749-F3
PORTOFINO RD
- SRFL 94901 586-J2
PORTOFINO TER
400 MPS 95035 793-G3
PORTOLA AV
- VAL 94591 550-D1
- DALY 94015 687-A7
- MrnC 94903 566-G5
- SSF 94080 707-G4
600 RCH 94801 588-G6
800 ALA 94501 669-G2
900 VAL 94591 530-D7
1000 SJS 95126 833-G5
1000 SCL 95126 833-G5
1500 PA 94306 791-A6
2200 LVMR 94550 695-G6
PORTOLA AV Rt#-J2
1000 LVMR 94550 695-F6
E PORTOLA AV
- LALT 94022 811-E4
W PORTOLA AV
- LALT 94022 811-D4
PORTOLA CT
- CCCo 94506 654-A5
200 LALT 94022 811-E4
5100 ANT 94509 595-F4
PORTOLA DR
- SF 94114 667-E4
- SF 94114 667-F4
- SF 94131 667-E4
- SF 94131 667-F4
200 CCCo 94506 654-A5
200 SMTO 94403 749-B5
400 SF 94131 667-C5
500 SF 94127 667-C5
700 SLN 94578 691-A4
1400 MPS 95035 814-D1
4500 FRMT 94536 752-F4
6300 ELCR 94530 609-C3
PORTOLA LN
- MLV 94941 606-D2
PORTOLA RD
- SMCo - 727-F5
- SMCo - 748-A3
- PTLV 94028 810-A6
1000 WDSD 94062 809-G2
1000 PTLV 94028 809-J4
1700 SMCo 94025 809-H4
PORTOLA ST
700 SF 94129 647-E4
PORTOLA WY
- CMAD 94925 586-F7
100 SBRN 94066 727-J2
PORTOLA GREEN CIR
- PTLV 94028 810-C7
PORTOLA MEADOWS RD
1100 LVMR 94550 695-G6
PORTO MARINO DR
- TBRN 94920 607-B4
1000 SCAR 94070 769-E5
PORTO MARINO LN
- SCAR 94070 769-E5
PORTO MARINO WY
- SCAR 94070 769-E5
PORTO ROSA WY
2800 SCAR 94070 769-F5

PORTOS CT
19200 SAR 95070 852-G7
PORTOS DR
19000 SAR 95070 872-G1
PORTOS PL
19100 SAR 95070 872-G1
PORTREE DR
7500 SJS 95135 855-J6
PORT ROWAN DR
6900 SJS 95119 875-F6
PORT ROYAL AV
- FCTY 94404 749-E5
PORTRUSH CT
5600 SJS 95138 875-F1
PORT SAILWOOD DR
5200 NWK 94560 752-F5
PORTSMOUTH AV
5400 NWK 94560 752-D4
26600 HAY 94545 711-F7
27200 HAY 94545 731-G1
PORTSMOUTH CIR
- PLHL 94523 591-B1
PORTSMOUTH CT
- SRMN 94583 673-F5
2000 SJS 95132 814-J2
3600 PLE 94588 694-F5
5500 NWK 94560 752-D4
PORTSMOUTH CV
- SRFL 94901 587-A2
PORTSMOUTH LN
600 FCTY 94404 749-F5
PORTSMOUTH RD
- OAK 94610 650-B2
- PDMT 94610 650-B2
PORTSMOUTH WY
2200 SMTO 94403 749-D4
PORTSWOOD CIR
700 SJS 95120 894-H3
PORTSWOOD DR
700 SJS 95120 894-H3
PORT TIDEWOOD ST
36600 NWK 94560 752-F5
PORT WALK PL
700 RDWC 94065 749-H6
PORTWOOD AV
800 OAK 94601 670-B1
POSADA CT
100 SRMN 94583 673-C3
POSADA WY
400 FRMT 94536 753-A1
POSADA DEL SOL
100 NVTO 94949 546-F3
POSEN AV
1600 ALB 94706 609-F7
1600 BERK 94706 609-F7
1600 BERK 94707 609-F7
POSEY AV
- RCH 94801 608-D1
POSEY PL
1800 CNCD 94519 592-J1
POSHARD ST
100 PLHL 94523 592-B7
POSITANO CIR
400 RDWC 94065 749-J4
POSITANO LN
6700 SJS 95138 875-G4
POSITANO WY
400 RDWC 94065 749-J4
POSSUM LN
- PTLV 94028 810-A6
POST AV
1300 SLN 94579 691-A5
1300 SPAB 94806 588-G3
POST RD
100 CCCo 94595 632-D1
5400 OAK 94613 650-H7
6800 DBLN 94568 693-J3
POST ST
- LKSP 94939 586-E6
- SF 94108 648-A6
- SJS 95113 834-B6
- SF 94104 648-A6
100 MTVW 94040 811-J7
400 SF 94102 648-A6
400 AlaC 94580 691-D7
500 SF 94102 647-F6
600 SF 94109 647-F6
900 ALA 94501 670-B4
1600 SF 94115 647-F6
37000 FRMT 94536 752-H3
POSTGATE CT
1900 SJS 95121 855-C3
POST OAK CIR
5900 SJS 95120 874-C6
POST OFFICE CT
2400 ALA 94501 670-A2
POSTON DR
4700 SJS 95136 874-J3
POSTWOOD DR
2800 SJS 95132 814-D3
POTAWATAMI DR
45300 FRMT 94539 773-H4
POTEL COM
36100 FRMT 94536 733-B6
POTEL TER
- FRMT 94536 733-B7
POTMARNOCH CT
5000 SJS 95138 855-E6
POTOMAC CT
- ANT 94509 574-J6
600 SJS 95136 874-F2
POTOMAC DR
100 LGTS 95032 873-D5
POTOMAC ST
- SF 94117 667-G1
2400 OAK 94602 650-E4
POTOMAC WY
300 MRTZ 94553 591-H4
2000 SMTO 94403 749-C4
POTOMAC RIVER PL
34700 FRMT 94555 752-E2
POTRERO AV
- SF 94103 668-A4
300 SUNV 94086 812-D6
400 SF 94110 668-A4
700 RCH 94804 609-G1
2100 RCH 94804 609-A1
5100 ELCR 94530 609-C1
7600 ELCR 94530 589-D7
POTRERO CT
2300 PIN 94564 569-F7

POTRERO DR
- NWK 94560 772-J2
1700 SJS 95124 873-G1
POTSDAM ST
31800 HAY 94544 732-E3
POTTER CT
16700 LGTS 95032 873-C7
POTTER ST
400 BERK 94804 629-D4
1300 CCCo 94553 571-F3
2400 OAK 94601 650-E7
2400 OAK 94601 670-E1
POTTS DR
13000 SCIC 95111 854-H6
POUGHKEEPSIE RD
- SJS 95119 875-C4
- SJS 95193 875-C4
100 SJS 95123 875-B4
POULARD CT
44500 FRMT 94539 773-J2
POULOS CT
2800 PIN 94564 569-H6
POWDERBORN CT N
4500 SJS 95136 874-G2
POWDERBORN CT S
4600 SJS 95136 874-G2
POWDER BOWL CT
- RCH 94803 589-G2
POWDER RIVER PL
34700 FRMT 94555 752-E1
POWELL AV
200 PLHL 94523 592-B7
POWELL CT
300 CCCo 94565 573-C2
1600 SJS 95122 834-G7
POWELL DR
300 CCCo 94565 573-C2
3500 LFYT 94549 631-E1
POWELL ST
- SF 94102 648-A4
- SMTO 94401 729-B7
100 SF 94108 648-A4
1100 OAK 94608 629-E6
1200 SF 94133 648-A4
1200 EMVL 94608 629-B6
1500 SF 94133 648-A3
1800 SPAB 94806 588-H3
2200 ALA 94501 669-J3
2300 SF 94133 647-J3
POWER AV
- PIT 94565 574-B2
POWER CT
- SJS 95133 834-B2
POWER DR
100 VAL 94589 510-B7
100 VAL 94589 530-B1
POWERS AV
- SF 94110 667-H4
POWERS CT
- ALA 94501 669-H1
POWERS ST
- DBLN 94568 694-B3
POWERSCOURT WY
- SJS 95136 854-E6
POWHATAN PL
- SMCo 94402 768-G1
POWHATTAN AV
300 SF 94110 667-J5
1000 SF 94110 668-A5
POWHATTAN CT
200 DNVL 94526 653-D7
POWNAL AV
2800 SRMN 94583 673-F6
PRADA CT
1300 MPS 95035 794-C5
PRADA DR
400 MPS 95035 794-C5
PRADERIA CIR
500 FRMT 94539 773-H2
PRADO CT
- PTLV 94028 810-C7
PRADO LN
3200 SJS 95148 835-D6
PRADO ST
- SF 94123 647-F3
PRADO WY
- LFYT 94549 611-F3
PRADO SECOYA
- ATN 94027 790-E4
PRAGUE CT
6500 SJS 95119 875-D7
PRAGUE DR
100 SJS 95119 875-D7
PRAGUE ST
- SF 94112 687-G1
- SMTO 94401 729-A6
PRAIRIE DR
3300 PLE 94588 714-A3
PRAIRIE LN
2900 SJS 95127 834-H1
PRAIRIE CREEK DR
700 PCFA 94044 727-C5
PRAIRIE DOG LN
100 FRMT 94539 773-H3
PRAIRIE FALCON DR
- NVTO 94949 546-E5
PRAIRIE VIEW CT
200 SJS 95127 834-H1
PRAIRIE WILLOW CT
4400 CNCD 94521 593-B5
PRAIRIE WOOD CT
200 SJS 95127 834-H2
PRAM RD
- PIT 94565 574-A2
PRARIE WY
5000 ANT 94509 595-H4
PRATHER AV
5100 RCH 94805 589-B7
PRATO CT
5300 PLE 94588 694-A6
PRATT AV
2400 HAY 94587 732-B4
PRATT PL
- SF 94108 648-A5
PREAKNESS CT
300 WLCK 94596 612-C3
PREAKNESS DR
600 WLCK 94596 612-C3
PREAKNESS LN
100 VAL 94591 530-E2
PREBLE AV
2300 RCH 94804 588-H6

BAY AREA
INDEX

STREET
Block City ZIP Pg-Grid

PRECITA AV
- SF 94110 667-J4
500 SF 94110 668-A4
PREDA ST
- SLN 94577 690-J1
PRELUDE DR
1300 SJS 95131 814-C7
PREMIER PL
1700 CNCD 94520 592-E4
PRENTISS DR
1100 SJS 95120 894-F2
PRENTISS PL
- SRMN 94583 673-F6
3200 OAK 94601 650-C6
PRENTISS ST
- SF 94110 667-J6
3200 OAK 94601 650-D6
PRESCO LN
1000 RCH 94801 588-F5
PRESCOTT AV
1100 SUNV 94089 812-J4
1200 SUNV 94089 813-A4
3600 SJS 95124 873-H2
PRESCOTT CT
- SF 94133 648-A4
5300 FRMT 94536 752-G6
PRESCOTT LN
700 FCTY 94404 749-G5
PRESERVATION DR
200 SJS 95116 834-G4
PRESHER WY
1100 LFYT 94549 611-E5
PRESIDENT DR
16800 AlaC 94578 691-G5
17000 AlaC 94546 691-G5
PRESIDIO AV
- MLV 94941 606-D3
- SF 94115 647-F5
500 CMAD 94925 606-G1
PRESIDIO BLVD
- SF 94129 647-E4
- SF 94129 647-E4
- SF 94129 647-E4
100 SF 94129 647-E4
PRESIDIO BLVD Rt#-1
- SF - 647-C7
- SF 94118 647-C7
PRESIDIO CT
- CMAD 94925 606-H2
2100 DNVL 94526 653-E7
PRESIDIO DR
8000 CPTO 95014 852-B2
PRESIDIO LN
- PIT 94565 574-D4
PRESIDIO TER
- SF 94118 647-D5
PRESIDIO WY
39000 FRMT 94538 753-A5
PRESLEY WY
5700 OAK 94618 630-A5
PRESTIGE PL
900 SRMN 94583 673-B1
PRESTON AV
5000 LVMR 94550 696-B5
PRESTON CT
100 FRMT 94536 753-C2
300 LVMR 94550 696-B5
2700 MTVW 94040 831-J2
5400 CNCD 94521 593-G4
PRESTON DR
100 MTVW 94040 831-J2
5700 SJS 95124 873-J6
PRESTON PL
35200 NWK 94560 752-D3
PRESTON RD
- WDSD 94062 809-H4
PRESTWICK AV
2500 CNCD 94519 572-G6
30400 HAY 94544 732-E1
PRESTWICK CT
- NVTO 94949 546-A2
100 VAL 94591 530-G3
PRESWICK CT
700 SUNV 94087 832-F6
PRETOR WY
- SF 94112 687-F2
PRETORIA CT
800 SJS 95127 814-H6
PREVOST CT
1000 SJS 95125 854-E5
PREVOST ST
800 SJS 95125 854-B2
PREWETT RANCH DR
1100 ANT 94509 595-G5
PRICE AV
500 RDWC 94063 770-A4
19800 CPTO 95014 852-F1
PRICE CT
3000 PA 94303 791-D6
PRICE LN
- PLHL 94523 592-B6
PRICE RW
- SF 94133 648-A4
PRICE ST
- DALY 94014 687-C4
PRICE WY
500 VAL 94591 530-E5
1800 SLN 94577 690-H1
2300 SJS 95124 853-G7
PRICEWOOD CT
700 SJS 95120 894-H3
PRIDE CT
3200 SJS 95127 814-H6
PRIDE ST
700 SJS 95127 814-H6
PRIDMORE CT
3900 CNCD 94521 593-A3
3900 CNCD 94521 592-J3
PRIEST ST
- SF 94109 647-J5
PRIETA CT
10900 SCIC 95127 815-B7
PRIME AV
22700 AlaC 94541 692-C7
PRIMERA CT
2600 SJS 95148 835-D6
PRIMM AV
1400 SJS 95122 834-H6
PRIMO CT
1900 SJS 95131 814-C6
PRIMROSE AV
900 SUNV 94086 832-G3
PRIMROSE CT
- WLCK 94598 592-H7
100 VAL 94591 530-H5
2000 FRMT 94539 773-G3
PRIMROSE DR
300 PLHL 94523 591-J3
1200 SLN 94578 691-C3
PRIMROSE LN
- SCAR 94070 769-E2
100 VAL 94591 530-H5
1600 PIN 94564 569-D4
3200 WLCK 94598 592-H7
4800 LVMR 94550 696-A4
PRIMROSE PL
200 PLHL 94523 591-J3
700 HAY 94544 711-J5
PRIMROSE PTH
100 MrnC 94941 606-F5
PRIMROSE RD
100 BURL 94010 728-G7
PRIMROSE TER
600 PIN 94564 569-E4
PRIMROSE WY
- PA 94303 791-C4
- SRMN 94583 653-J7
1200 CPTO 95014 852-D4
PRINCE DR
6000 SJS 95129 852-G3
6900 DBLN 94568 693-J3
PRINCE ST
200 LGTS 95030 873-A2
400 OAK 94610 650-A2
1400 BERK 94702 629-F4
1500 BERK 94703 629-F4
2100 BERK 94705 629-H4
2700 BERK 94705 630-A4
PRINCE ALBERT CT
3400 SJS 95132 814-J2
PRINCE CHARLES CT
3400 SJS 95132 814-J2
PRINCE EDWARD WY
1400 SUNV 94087 832-D4
PRINCE ESTATES CT
5300 SJS 95135 855-H5
PRINCE GEORGE DR
1900 SJS 95116 834-F3
PRINCE OF WALES LN
3400 SJS 95132 814-J3
PRINCE PHILIP CT
3400 SJS 95132 814-J2
PRINCE ROYAL DR
- CMAD 94925 606-J2
400 CMAD 94925 607-A1
PRINCE ROYAL PASG
- CMAD 94925 606-J1
PRINCE ROYAL PL
4600 SJS 95136 874-F2
PRINCESS CT
4100 UNC 94587 732-A5
PRINCESS LN
- SAUS 94965 627-B3
200 MrnC 94941 606-E5
PRINCESS PL
600 MPS 95035 794-B4
PRINCESS ST
- SAUS 94965 627-B3
PRINCESS ANNE DR
900 SJS 95128 853-G3
PRINCESS ELLEENA CT
24000 LAH 94024 831-E3
PRINCESS MARGARET CT
3400 SJS 95132 814-J3
PRINCETON
100 VAL 94589 510-A5
PRINCETON AV
200 CCCo 94708 609-G4
200 MrnC 94941 606-F6
PRINCETON CT
- DNVL 94526 653-B3
1200 PIT 94565 574-F5
3300 SCL 95051 832-J6
PRINCETON DR
600 SUNV 94087 832-D2
1400 SJS 95118 874-A5
2200 SBRN 94066 727-F1
PRINCETON LN
300 DNVL 94526 653-B3
2500 ANT 94509 575-D1
PRINCETON PL
- AlaC 94552 692-G3
PRINCETON RD
- MLPK 94025 790-G5
400 SMTO 94402 748-H3
PRINCETON ST
- SF 94134 667-J7
2000 PA 94306 791-A7
2000 PA 94306 811-A1
5300 OAK 94601 670-E1
21500 AlaC 94541 711-G1
21900 HAY 94541 711-G1
PRINCETON TER
- FRMT 94536 753-B3
PRINCETON WY
3200 SCL 95051 832-J6
3800 LVMR 94550 715-J1
3900 LVMR 94550 716-A1
PRINDIVILLE CT
100 SJS 95138 875-G7
PRINDIVILLE DR
7300 SJS 95138 875-G7
PRINDLE RD
2600 BLMT 94002 769-B2
PRING CT
18600 SCIC 95014 852-H1
PRINGLE AV
100 WLCK 94596 612-B4
PRINTEMPO DR
600 SJS 95134 813-H4
PRINTEMPO PL
800 SJS 95134 813-H4
PRINTY AV
400 MPS 95035 794-C5
PRIOR LN
200 ATN 94027 790-F2
PRISCILLA CT
1700 MTVW 94040 811-G5
PRISCILLA DR
1200 SJS 95129 853-A4
PRISCILLA LN
12300 LAH 94022 831-D3
12300 LAH 94024 831-D3
PRITCHARD CT
700 SCL 95051 833-B6
PRITCHETT CT
1300 LALT 94024 831-J3
PRITCHETT WY
1300 LALT 94024 831-J3
PRIVADA LUISITA
100 LGTS 95030 873-B4
PRIVATEER DR
- CMAD 94925 607-A1
PRIVET CT
700 SUNV 94086 832-G2
PRIVET DR
2900 HIL 94010 748-B1
PROCTOR AV
4700 OAK 94618 630-C6
PROCTOR LN
3700 AlaC 94546 692-B2
PROCTOR RD
4600 AlaC 94546 692-A2
5100 AlaC 94546 691-J2
PRODUCE AV
100 SSF 94080 707-J4
100 SSF 94080 708-A4
PRODUCTION AV
26200 HAY 94545 711-E7
26200 HAY 94545 731-E1
PROFESSIONAL CTR PKWY
- SRFL 94903 566-E3
PROGRESS ST
- SF 94124 668-C6
PROMENADE CT
800 SJS 95138 875-G5
PROMENADE LN
200 DNVL 94506 653-J5
700 SJS 95138 875-G5
PROMENADE WY
3800 PLE 94566 714-F3
PROMETHEAN WY
100 MTVW 94043 812-A5
PROMINTORY LN
100 CCCo 94549 611-H1
PROMONTORY CT
500 RDWC 94065 749-H6
PROMONTORY DR
- RCH 94804 608-E3
- VAL 94591 510-J6
PROMONTORY LN
200 SRMN 94583 673-B1
PROMONTORY PT LN
700 FCTY 94404 749-E4
PRONGHORN CT
4400 ANT 94509 595-F3
PRONGHORN WY
4400 ANT 94509 595-F3
PRONTO DR
600 SJS 95123 874-F5
PROSPECT AV
- CCCo - 550-H6
- SANS 94960 586-C1
- SAUS 94965 627-B3
- SF 94110 667-H5
- LGTS 95032 893-A1
100 DNVL 94526 653-A2
100 SCIC 95032 893-A1
100 ROSS 94957 586-C1
100 DNVL 94526 652-J2
600 OAK 94606 650-A3
600 OAK 94610 650-A3
1500 MRTZ 94553 571-D4
2700 CNCD 94518 592-G2
24600 LAH 94024 831-C3
24600 LAH 94022 831-C3
W PROSPECT AV
- DNVL 94526 652-J3
PROSPECT CT
100 LGTS 95032 893-A1
6800 PLE 94588 694-A7
21600 HAY 94541 691-H7
PROSPECT DR
- SRFL 94901 566-G6
PROSPECT LN
- CMAD 94925 606-G1
PROSPECT PL
700 NVTO 94945 526-C3
PROSPECT PTH
- MrnC 94941 606-F5
PROSPECT RD
- PDMT 94610 650-B2
5800 SAR 95070 852-D5
7400 CPTO 95014 852-D5
18900 SJS 95129 852-F5
21300 SCIC 95070 852-B6
PROSPECT RW
600 SMTO 94401 728-G7
PROSPECT ST
- WDSD 94062 789-G6
500 SCAR 94070 769-F3
900 SJS 95110 854-C1
1600 BLMT 94002 769-F2
2100 MLPK 94025 790-D7
2100 SMCo 94025 790-D7
2200 BERK 94704 629-J2
2200 BERK 94720 629-J2
21600 HAY 94541 691-H7
22000 HAY 94541 711-H1
PROSPECT TER
22300 HAY 94541 711-J1
PROSPECT HILL RD
3100 OAK 94613 650-G7
3100 OAK 94613 670-G1
PROSPECTS WY
- ANT 94509 575-C3
PROSPECT STEPS
6000 OAK 94618 630-A5
PROSPER AV
1100 SJS 95118 874-C2
PROSPER ST
- SF 94114 667-G2
PROSPERITY CT
1500 SJS 95131 814-C6
PROSPERITY WY
2100 AlaC 94578 691-G4
PROSPERO
4700 FRMT 94555 752-B1
PROUD DR
1400 SJS 95132 814-G4
PROUTY WY
1000 SJS 95129 852-H3
PROVANCE ST
35400 NWK 94560 752-C5
PROVANMILL WY
2100 SJS 95121 855-C4
PROVENCE CT
- SJS 95135 855-F3
1300 ANT 94509 575-F7
2600 LVMR 94550 715-H3
PROVENCE DR
- FRMT 94538 753-C3
PROVIDENCE CT
900 CPTO 95014 852-B2
2400 WLCK 94596 632-H2
PROVIDENCE DR
4000 MRTZ 94553 571-J6
PROVIDENCE WY
- HAY 94544 732-B2
PROVIDENT DR
- HIL 94010 748-D2
PROVINCETOWN CT
2400 MRTZ 94553 572-A5
PROVINCETOWN DR
1500 SJS 95129 852-G5
PROVO CT
3100 SJS 95127 814-H6
PROVO LN
- CCCo 94526 633-A7
PROW WY
7200 DBLN 94568 693-F5
PROWSHEAD LN
800 FCTY 94404 749-H5
PRUNE AV
2000 FRMT 94539 773-F3
PRUNE CT
1000 SUNV 94087 832-C2
PRUNE ST
800 OAK 94603 670-H6
1900 PIN 94564 569-E4
PRUNE WY
600 SJS 95117 853-D1
PRUNE BLOSSOM DR
5300 SJS 95123 875-E2
13700 SAR 95070 872-D1
PRUNELLE CT
1100 SUNV 94087 832-C3
PRUNERIDGE AV
1800 SCL 95050 833-D7
1800 SCL 95128 833-D7
1900 SJS 95117 833-D7
2500 SCL 95051 833-A7
3200 SCL 95051 832-G6
19000 CPTO 95014 832-G6
PRUNETREE CT
2400 SJS 95121 855-E4
PRUNETREE LN
4000 SJS 95121 855-D4
10300 CPTO 95014 832-E7
PTARMIGAN CT
2200 UNC 94587 732-G7
PTARMIGAN DR
- WLCK 94595 632-A4
PUCCINI AV
2600 SJS 95122 855-A1
PUCCINI DR
500 SUNV 94087 832-E3
PUDDINGSTONE RD
200 ALA 94502 670-A5
PUEBLA CT
1400 SJS 95118 874-B3
PUEBLO AV
- CCCo 94565 573-G2
PUEBLO CT
- CCCo 94595 632-D2
- ORIN 94563 631-C5
500 VAL 94591 550-E1
PUEBLO DR
- MrnC 94903 546-E7
100 PIT 94565 574-C6
200 SJS 95131 814-A5
10800 OAK 94603 690-H1
PUEBLO ST
- DALY 94014 687-J3
100 SF 94134 687-J3
PUEBLO TER
34500 FRMT 94555 752-D2
PUEBLO WY
- PLE 94588 694-D6
- VAL 94591 550-C1
PUEBLO CALLE
27900 HAY 94545 731-G1
PUEBLO CREEK
2600 HAY 94545 731-G1
PUEBLO DEL ORO
27900 HAY 94545 731-G1
PUEBLO HILL CT
3600 SJS 95127 835-B1
PUEBLO LAKE
2600 HAY 94545 731-G1
PUEBLO SERENA
27900 HAY 94545 731-G1
PUEBLO SPRINGS
27900 HAY 94545 731-G1
PUEBLO VISTA
10300 SCIC 95127 835-B1
10300 SJS 95127 835-B1
PUENTE CT
20000 SAR 95070 852-F6
PUERTO PL
400 HAY 94541 711-G3
PUERTO GOLFITO CT
100 SJS 95116 834-D2
PUERTO LIMON CT
2000 SJS 95116 834-F3
PUERTO VALLARTA
400 PLE 94566 714-E5
PUERTO VALLARTA DR
1500 SJS 95120 874-A7
1600 SJS 95120 894-A1
1600 SJS 95120 893-J1
PUESTA DEL SOL
100 LGTS 95030 872-J3
43500 FRMT 94539 773-G1
PUFFIN CT
- CMBL 95008 853-D5
- NVTO 94949 546-E5
200 FCTY 94404 749-G1
PUGET SOUND WY
800 SJS 95133 834-E1
PULASKI DR
32000 HAY 94544 732-F3
PULASKI DR
32900 UNC 94587 732-F3
PULGAS AV
1800 EPA 94303 791-C3
2500 EPA 94303 771-C7
PULIDO CT
- DNVL 94526 633-C6
PULIDO RD
100 DNVL 94526 633-C6
PULLMAN AV
- PIT 94565 573-H1
300 CCCo 94565 573-H1
2100 BLMT 94002 769-C2
2200 RCH 94804 588-J7
PULLMAN CT
900 CNCD 94518 592-F6
PULLMAN RD
400 HIL 94010 748-D3
PULLMAN ST
200 LVMR 94550 696-D4
1800 SPAB 94806 588-H4
PULLMAN WY
- SJS 95111 854-F6
PULORA CT
1100 SUNV 94087 832-C3
PULSAR AV
1900 LVMR 94550 715-E4
PUMICE CT
200 VAL 94589 510-C6
PUMICE DR
100 VAL 94589 510-C6
PUMPHERSTON CT
2200 SJS 95148 855-C2
PUMPHERSTON WY
3200 SJS 95148 855-C2
PUMPKIN CT
7900 CPTO 95014 852-C2
PUMPKIN DR
7900 CPTO 95014 852-B2
PURCELL DR
- ALA 94502 670-A5
PURCELL PL
35300 FRMT 94536 752-F1
PURDUE AV
- CCCo 94708 609-G3
1600 EPA 94303 771-B7
PURDUE CT
700 SCL 95051 832-J6
1400 UNC 94587 732-F5
PURDUE DR
100 VAL 94589 510-A5
18200 SAR 95070 852-J7
PURDUE PL
5500 SJS 95118 874-A5
PURDUE RD
2700 SRMN 94583 653-B7
PURDUE ST
900 SLN 94579 691-A5
PURDUE WY
3900 LVMR 94550 696-A7
3900 LVMR 94550 695-J7
PURE CT
500 SJS 95136 874-G3
PURI CT
- PLE 94588 713-J3
PURISIMA CREEK RD
- SMCo 94062 789-A6
PURISSIMA AV
400 SUNV 94086 832-D1
PURISSIMA RD
26300 LAH 94022 831-B1
26600 LAH 94022 811-A6
PURITAN CT
700 SJS 95123 874-G6
PURITANI CT
2500 SJS 95121 854-H4
PURITANI WY
1400 SJS 95121 854-H4
PURLEY LN
3500 CNCD 94519 572-G5
PURPLE CLIFF CT
6500 SJS 95119 875-D7
PURPLE GLEN DR
200 SJS 95119 875-D7
PURPLE HILLS DR
6100 SJS 95119 875-D7
PURPLE KNOLL CT
6200 SJS 95119 875-C6
PURPLELEAF ST
48000 FRMT 94539 793-H1
PURPLE SAGE CT
6100 SJS 95119 875-C6
PURPLE VALE CT
6500 SJS 95119 875-D7
PURSON LN
1400 CCCo 94549 611-H2
1400 WLCK 94596 611-H2
PUSATERI WY
1100 SJS 95121 854-J4
PUTNAM BLVD
2900 PLHL 94523 612-B1
2900 WLCK 94596 612-B1
3100 WLCK 94596 592-B7
3100 PLHL 94523 592-B7
PUTNAM CT
8700 DBLN 94568 693-F2
PUTNAM ST
- SF 94110 667-J6
200 ANT 94509 575-A7
2200 ANT 94509 574-J7
PUTNEY CT
1900 SJS 95132 814-D3
PUTTENHAM WY
3100 FRMT 94536 752-G2
PUTTER AV
11500 SCIC 94024 831-E4
PUTTER WY
11600 SCIC 94024 831-E4
PYLE CT
2200 SCL 95051 833-B2
PYNE LN
1300 ALA 94502 670-A7
PYRACANTHA CT
100 VAL 94591 530-F6
PYRAMID CT
1500 SJS 95130 853-B4
PYRAMID DR
2100 RCH 94803 589-D3
PYRAMID ST
2200 LVMR 94550 715-G4
PYRENEES PL
1500 WLCK 94598 612-E2
PYRITE CT
100 ANT 94509 595-F2
1500 LVMR 94550 715-D3
PYRMONT CT
- CCCo 94553 591-C3
PYRO
3000 ALA 94501 649-E6
PYRO ST
- CNCD 94519 572-H6
PYROLA LN
- SCAR 94070 769-C5
PYRUS WY
800 SUNV 94087 832-C2

Q

S Q ST
100 LVMR 94550 715-G1
QUADRANT LN
400 FCTY 94404 749-J1
QUADRES CT
4700 FRMT 94538 752-J6
QUADROS LN
2000 SJS 95131 814-E7
QUAIL
- PTLV 94028 830-C1
QUAIL AV
- BERK 94708 609-J6
1500 SUNV 94087 832-H5
3600 AlaC 94546 691-H3
QUAIL CT
- AlaC 94566 714-A7
- AlaC 94566 734-B1
- ATN 94027 790-H1
- MrnC 94903 546-E6
- NVTO 94949 546-E5
- PIT 94565 574-F7
- WLCK 94596 612-D7
100 HER 94547 569-G4
100 VAL 94591 530-D2
200 ANT 94509 595-E1
1100 CNCD 94518 592-H3
1600 LVMR 94550 715-H3
2600 UNC 94587 732-D6
QUAIL DR
1500 MPS 95035 794-C5
2500 UNC 94587 732-D5
QUAIL LN
- CCCo 94553 591-D3
- SCAR 94070 769-D5
25900 LAH 94022 811-C7
QUAIL RDGE
- ROSS 94957 586-B3
- MrnC 94904 586-B3
QUAIL RUN
- LFYT 94549 611-G5
QUAIL WY
- MrnC 94960 566-B4
QUAIL ACRES
14100 SAR 95070 872-F2
QUAIL BUSH CT
400 SJS 95117 853-C1
QUAIL CANYON CT
2000 HAY 94542 712-C3
3800 SCIC 95148 835-F5
QUAIL CANYON RD
3800 SCIC 95148 835-F5
QUAIL CLIFF WY
7000 SJS 95120 894-G3
QUAIL COVE CT
7000 SJS 95120 894-F3
QUAIL COVE WY
7000 SJS 95120 894-F3
QUAIL CREEK CIR
1000 SJS 95120 894-F3
7600 DBLN 94568 694-A1
QUAIL CREST DR
600 CCCo 94598 613-A3
QUAIL CREST WY
7000 SJS 95120 894-F4
QUAIL DUNES WY
7000 SJS 95120 894-G3
QUAIL HILL LN
- CCCo 94803 589-C3
- RCH 94803 589-C3
QUAIL HILL RD
15900 LGTS 95032 873-D6
QUAIL HOLLOW
100 CCCo 94553 591-E2
QUAIL HOLLOW DR
- SJS 95128 853-F4
QUAIL KNOLL CT
1100 SJS 95120 894-F3
QUAIL MEADOW RD
1900 SCIC 94024 831-G5
QUAIL MEADOWS CT
- WDSD 94062 789-J6
QUAIL MEADOWS DR
- WDSD 94062 789-H6
QUAIL MEADOWS LN
- DNVL 94506 653-E4
QUAIL POINT CIR
2000 SBRN 94066 707-F6
QUAIL RIDGE CT
1100 SJS 95120 894-F3
QUAIL RIDGE RD
3700 LFYT 94549 611-C5
QUAIL RUN CT
1200 SJS 95118 874-C3
3600 FRMT 94555 732-D7
4300 CCCo 94506 654-C3
15500 SCIC 95070 872-C4
QUAIL RUN DR
4100 CCCo 94506 654-C3
QUAIL RUN LN
4200 CCCo 94506 654-C2
QUAIL RUN PL
4200 CCCo 94506 654-C3
QUAIL RUN RD
33400 FRMT 94555 732-D7
QUAIL RUN WY
4200 CCCo 94506 654-C3
QUAIL VIEW CIR
1400 WLCK 94596 611-J3
QUAIL VIEW WY
1000 SJS 95120 894-F3
QUAIL WALK CT
3400 CCCo 94506 654-C3
QUAIL WALK LN
3300 CCCo 94506 654-C3
QUAMME DR
1100 SJS 95121 854-J3
QUANDT CT
1200 LFYT 94549 611-H4
QUANDT RD
3100 LFYT 94549 611-H4
QUANE ST
- SF 94110 667-H3
QUANTAS LN
800 HAY 94545 711-G5
QUANTICO CT
2400 SJS 95128 853-F3
QUARRY CT E
1300 RCH 94801 608-D2
QUARRY CT W
1300 RCH 94801 608-D2
QUARRY LN
1100 PLE 94566 714-F2
QUARRY RD
- SF 94129 647-D5
- BERK 94708 609-J7
- MLV 94941 606-C1
- SRFL 94901 566-F7
100 PA 94304 790-H5
100 SCIC 94305 790-H5
300 SMCo 94002 769-F1
3700 AlaC 94541 692-D7
21300 SAR 95070 872-C1
N QUARRY RD
17300 LGTS 95032 893-C1
S QUARRY RD
16400 LGTS 95032 893-C2
QUARRY LAKES DR
3300 UNC 94587 732-H7
QUARRY PARK DR
4000 SJS 95136 854-E6
QUARRY PARK WY
4000 SJS 95136 854-E6
QUARTERMASTER CYN RD
1000 SRMN 94583 653-G7
QUARTUCCIO WY
4100 SCIC 95148 835-G7
QUARTZ CIR
200 LVMR 94550 715-D2
7200 DBLN 94568 693-J2
QUARTZ CT
- PIT 94565 573-F4
QUARTZ LN
100 VAL 94589 510-B6
QUARTZ PL
6200 NWK 94560 772-H1
QUARTZ ST
400 RDWC 94062 769-J7
500 RDWC 94062 789-J1
600 RDWC 94061 789-J1
QUARTZ TER
34200 FRMT 94555 752-C2
QUARTZ WY
- SF 94131 667-F4
1400 SJS 95118 874-B2
QUAY LN
300 RDWC 94065 749-H7
QUEBEC AV
1900 SLN 94579 691-A7
QUEBEC COM
5300 FRMT 94555 752-C3
QUEBEC CT
1500 SUNV 94087 832-D5
QUEBEC ST
- SMTO 94401 729-B7
2200 CNCD 94520 572-F5
QUEBEC WY
1900 SJS 95124 853-G7
QUEEN CT
21900 AlaC 94546 692-B6
QUEEN ST
22000 AlaC 94546 692-B6
QUEEN ANNE CT
- MLBR 94030 728-A2
4600 UNC 94587 731-J6
QUEEN ANNE DR
1000 SJS 95129 852-G3
1100 SUNV 94087 832-C3
4100 UNC 94587 731-J6
4200 UNC 94587 732-A6
QUEEN CHARLOTTE DR
1600 SUNV 94087 832-D5
QUEEN ELIZABETH WY
1800 SJS 95132 814-J3
QUEEN MARY CT
1900 SJS 95132 814-J2
QUEENS AV
1300 SMTO 94403 749-C3
QUEENS CT
- ATN 94027 790-C4
200 SCAR 94070 769-D4
400 CMBL 95008 853-D5
QUEENS LN
400 SJS 95112 834-A2
2000 SMCo 94402 768-H1
QUEENS RD
500 ALA 94501 669-F1
1200 BERK 94708 609-J6
1800 CNCD 94519 592-J1
1800 CNCD 94519 572-J7
QUEENS WY
200 PIT 94565 574-E5
QUEENSBORO WY
4200 UNC 94587 732-A5
4200 UNC 94587 731-J5
QUEENSBRIDGE CT
1000 SJS 95120 894-G4
QUEENSBRIDGE WY
1000 SJS 95120 894-G4
QUEENSBROOK DR
1000 SJS 95129 852-C7
QUEENSBROOK PL
- ORIN 94563 631-B3
QUEENSBURRY AV
1400 LALT 94024 832-A3
QUEENS CROSSING DR
1400 SJS 95132 814-E4
QUEENS ESTATES CT
2900 SJS 95135 855-G5
QUEENS OAK CT
22600 CPTO 95014 831-J6
QUEENS PARK CT
42600 FRMT 94538 773-C2
QUEENSTONE DR
2400 MrnC 94903 546-D6
QUEENSTONE FIRE RD
- MrnC 94903 546-B5

STREET
Block City ZIP Pg-Grid

QUEENSTOWN CT
1500 SUNV 94087 832-D5
QUEENSTOWN DR
1700 SJS 95132 814-E3
QUEENSWOOD CT
7000 SJS 95120 894-H3
QUEENSWOOD WY
6800 SJS 95120 894-H2
QUEEN VICTORIA WY
3400 SJS 95132 814-J3
QUEMA CT
1400 FRMT 94539 773-G1
QUEMA DR
1100 FRMT 94539 753-G7
1100 FRMT 94539 773-G1
QUERCUS CT
400 NVTO 94945 526-D4
900 SUNV 94086 832-H3
27900 AlaC 94542 712-F4
QUERCUS LN
- PIT 94565 574-D6
QUESADA AV
1000 SF 94124 668-B5
QUESADA CT
2000 ANT 94509 595-A1
QUESADA DR
3300 SJS 95148 835-D7
QUESADA WY
1600 BURL 94010 728-B5
QUESO CT
- FRMT 94539 753-D2
QUESO PL
100 FRMT 94539 753-D2
QUETTA AV
700 SUNV 94087 832-D2
QUETTA CT
800 SUNV 94087 832-D2
QUEVA VISTA
- NVTO 94945 525-J2
QUEVEDO WY
100 HAY 94544 712-C7
QUICKERT RD
15400 SAR 95070 872-C5
15400 SCIC 95070 872-C5
QUICKSILVER AV
6200 NWK 94560 772-H1
QUICKSILVER CT
4400 HAY 94542 712-G4
QUICKSILVER DR
1000 SJS 95136 874-D2
QUICKSTEP LN
- SF 94115 647-E5
QUIET CIR
1200 CNCD 94521 593-F7
1900 SJS 95132 814-E3
QUIET LN
- CCCo 94803 589-F2
QUIET HARBOR DR
100 VAL 94591 550-E2
QUIET LAKE PL
2100 MRTZ 94553 592-A1
QUIET MEADOW CT
1400 SJS 95121 855-D7
QUIET PATH CT
- PIT - 573-F4
QUIET PLACE CT
900 WLCK 94598 612-G4
QUIET PLACE DR
2000 WLCK 94598 612-G4
QUIETWOOD
- OAK 94605 671-D2
QUIETWOOD DR
300 MrnC 94903 546-D7
QUIETWOOD LN
- PLHL 94523 592-D4
QUIGLEY LN
3400 OAK 94602 650-E5
QUIGLEY PL
4200 OAK 94619 650-F6
QUIGLEY ST
3400 OAK 94619 650-E5
QUILEN CT
- SCIC 94305 790-J7
QUILTING LN
100 VAL 94589 510-D6
QUIMBY RD
1700 SJS 95122 835-G7
1700 SJS 95122 855-B1
2400 SJS 95148 855-B1
3600 SJS 95148 835-G7
3700 SCIC 95148 835-H7
QUINAN ST
500 PIN 94564 569-E4
QUINAULT WY
100 FRMT 94539 773-H7
QUINCE AV
800 SCL 95051 833-A6
1100 SUNV 94087 832-D3
QUINCE CT
- NVTO 94947 526-D7
QUINCE LN
500 MPS 95035 794-D5
QUINCE PL
- NWK 94560 772-H1
QUINCE ST
1200 SMTO 94402 748-J3
QUINCY AL
- VAL 94590 529-H4
500 VAL 94590 530-A4
QUINCY CT
700 SRMN 94583 673-E5
QUINCY DR
400 MTVW 94043 811-F2
1200 SJS 95132 814-G5
QUINCY ST
- SF 94108 648-A5
QUINCY WY
600 HAY 94541 711-G4
QUINLAN LN
3700 SJS 95118 874-B2
QUINN AV
500 SJS 95112 854-G3
2100 SCL 95051 833-B2
QUINN CT
2100 SCL 95051 833-B2
QUINN LN
24000 AlaC 94541 712-B1
QUINNHILL AV
200 SCIC 94024 831-E2
200 LALT 94024 831-E2
QUINT ST
- SF 94124 668-B5
QUINTANA CT
1500 FRMT 94539 753-E5
QUINTANA WY
1000 FRMT 94539 753-E5
QUINTARA ST
- SF 94116 667-A4
2500 SF 94116 666-H4
QUINTAS LN
100 MRGA 94556 631-D2
QUINTERNO CT
22200 CPTO 95014 852-A1
QUINTERRA LN
100 DNVL 94526 652-J2
QUINTINIA DR
800 SUNV 94086 832-G2
QUINTO WY
2700 SJS 95124 873-H1
QUISISANA DR
- MrnC 94904 586-E3
QUITO RD
2200 SAR 95070 872-J1
2200 SJS 95130 872-J1
QUITO RD Rt#-G2
1900 SJS 95130 852-J7
1900 SAR 95130 852-J7
1900 SAR 95070 852-J7
2200 SAR 95070 872-J1
2200 SJS 95130 872-J1
14900 LGTS 95030 872-H4
15000 MSER 95030 872-H4
15500 SCIC 95030 872-H4
QUITO OAKS WY
13900 SAR 95070 872-J2
QUIVIRA CT
500 DNVL 94526 653-B2
QUME DR
2200 SJS 95131 814-C5

R

S R ST
200 LVMR 94550 715-F1
RAAP AV
3700 MRTZ 94553 571-E6
RABBIT CT
100 FRMT 94539 773-H3
RABIA DR
5500 SJS 95123 874-H4
RABO TER
36600 FRMT 94536 752-F4
RACCOON CT
- NVTO 94949 546-D4
RACCOON DR
- SF 94114 667-F3
RACCOON RD
- NVTO 94949 546-D4
RACE ST
- SJS 95126 833-J7
200 SCIC 95126 833-J7
200 SCIC 95126 853-J1
300 SJS 95126 853-J1
RACHAEL PL
200 PLE 94566 714-E3
RACHEL CT
2500 ANT 94509 595-G4
5700 SJS 95123 874-J5
RACHEL RD
1000 CCCo 94806 569-A5
RACHELLE RD
1000 WLCK 94596 612-A3
RACHELLE ST
500 LVMR 94550 696-C6
RACHILL LN
- CCCo 94803 589-H4
RACINE AV
5100 FRMT 94536 752-H6
RACINE LN
- SF 94134 688-A2
RACINE ST
5800 OAK 94609 629-H5
RACOON CT
100 FRMT 94539 773-J3
RACOON LN
- TBRN 94920 607-E7
RACOON HOLLOW CT
- PLE 94588 713-J3
RACQUET CT
- NVTO 94947 525-G3
RACQUET CLUB DR
- SRFL 94901 566-D6
RADBURN DR
3700 SSF 94080 707-D4
RADCLIFF DR
28100 LAH 94022 810-H5
RADCLIFF LN
1200 HAY 94545 711-G5
RADCLIFF WY
800 SUNV 94087 832-C2
RADCLIFFE AV
6000 NWK 94560 752-D6
RADCLIFFE CT
400 VAL 94589 510-C5
2000 MRTZ 94553 571-H7
RADCLIFFE DR
100 VAL 94589 510-C5
400 SCL 95051 833-A7
900 SJS 95117 853-D3
RADCLIFFE RD
1500 LVMR 94550 716-A2
RADELE CT
5300 FRMT 94536 752-G6
RADFORD CT
100 SRMN 94583 673-G4
RADFORD DR
100 CMBL 95008 853-B5
RADFORD LN
700 FCTY 94404 749-G4
RADIAN DR
- SolC 94589 510-H4
- VAL 94591 510-H4
RADIANT AV
2500 CCCo 94801 588-G2
2500 RCH 94801 588-G2
RADIANT DR
6200 SJS 95123 874-J7
RADIANT LN
900 SRMN 94583 673-B1
RADIO AV
2000 SJS 95125 854-B5
RADIO RD
- SMCo 94014 687-F4
1400 RDWC 94065 750-A5
RADIO TER
- SF 94116 667-C3
RADIO INTELLIGENCE RD
- NVTO 94949 546-G3
RADKO DR
6500 SJS 95119 875-D7
RADLEY CT
2400 HAY 94545 711-C5
RADNOR CT
200 BEN 94510 551-B2
RADNOR RD
500 OAK 94606 650-A4
RADOYKA DR
12200 SAR 95070 852-H6
RAE AV
- SF 94112 687-E2
RAE CT
- ORIN 94563 631-C5
100 VAL 94591 530-E4
RAE DR
- ORIN 94563 631-C5
- PLHL 94523 592-C4
RAE LN
800 NVTO 94947 525-H3
22100 CPTO 95014 852-A2
RAE ANNE CT
1100 CNCD 94520 592-D5
RAE ANNE DR
1300 CNCD 94520 592-E5
RAEANNE DR
100 CCCo 94507 632-G7
RAEBURN CT
800 SJS 95136 874-E1
RAFAEL DR
- SRFL 94901 566-G7
1000 SJS 95120 874-E7
RAFAEL WY
- MrnC 94903 566-G3
RAFAELA ST
2500 PIN 94564 569-F4
RAFAHI WY
3000 AlaC 94541 712-C1
RAFTON DR
4900 SJS 95124 873-J4
RAGGIO AV
2300 SCL 95050 833-B3
2400 SCL 95051 833-B3
RAGLAND ST
- AlaC 94541 691-F6
RAHARA DR
1000 LFYT 94549 611-B5
RAHLVES DR
5000 AlaC 94546 692-B3
RAHN CT
- WLCK 94596 612-B2
RAHWAY DR
4700 SJS 95111 875-B1
RAICH DR
7100 SJS 95120 894-H4
RAIL CT
- FRMT 94536 753-D1
RAILROAD AV
- CCCo - 550-H5
- FRMT 94536 753-F7
- RCH 94801 588-D7
- RCH 94801 608-D1
- VAL 94592 549-J1
- CCCo 94572 549-H7
- DNVL 94526 652-J2
- HER 94547 569-E2
- PIN 94564 569-E3
- SRFL 94901 587-A2
- VAL 94592 529-H6
100 ANT 94509 575-D5
100 DNVL 94526 653-A2
200 MPS 95035 794-A7
300 PIT 94565 574-C6
300 SSF 94080 707-H3
800 NVTO 94945 526-C2
900 SCL 95050 833-F3
1300 LVMR 94550 715-G1
1500 LVMR 94550 695-H7
1700 SMTO 94402 749-B3
9000 OAK 94603 670-G6
33000 UNC 94587 732-F4
41000 FRMT 94539 753-E7
N RAILROAD AV
- SMTO 94401 748-J1
S RAILROAD AV
- SMTO 94401 748-J1
100 SMTO 94401 749-A2
400 SMTO 94402 749-A2
N RAILROAD CT
300 MPS 95035 794-A6
RAILROAD LN
- PIT 94565 574-E2
RAILROAD PL
1000 SBRN 94066 707-J5
RAILROAD ST
300 PLE 94566 714-E3
RAILROAD GRADE FIRE RD
- MLV 94941 586-B7
- MLV 94941 606-B1
- MrnC 94965 586-B7
- MrnC 94965 606-A1
RAILWAY AV
- CMBL 95008 853-E6
1100 SMTO 94401 749-A2
1100 SMTO 94402 749-A2
RAIMUNDO WY
700 SCIC 94305 810-J2
1100 SCIC 94305 811-A2
RAINBOW CIR
- DNVL 94506 653-F4
RAINBOW CT
- HAY 94542 712-C3
100 VAL 94591 530-F4
1100 MRTZ 94553 571-H7
21600 CPTO 95014 852-B4
RAINBOW DR
600 MTVW 94041 812-A7
1100 MRTZ 94553 571-H7
1300 SMCo 94402 748-G6
5800 SJS 95129 852-E4
7300 CPTO 95014 852-B4
21500 SCIC 95014 852-B4
RAINBOW LN
- MLV 94941 606-D4
200 PLHL 94523 592-A7
200 PLHL 94523 612-A1
RAINBOW PL
21000 CPTO 95014 852-A4
RAINBOW RD
- MrnC 94903 566-E5
RAINBOW TER
4100 FRMT 94555 752-E1
RAINBOW BRIDGE CT
- SRMN 94583 673-G3
RAINBOW BRIDGE WY
- SRMN 94583 673-G3
RAINBOW VIEW DR
1800 WLCK 94595 632-B1
RAIN CLOUD DR
5000 RCH 94803 589-G3
RAINDANCE CT
- SJS 95136 874-H2
RAINDANCE RD
45800 FRMT 94539 774-A5
RAINDEER CT
34400 FRMT 94555 752-D1
RAINDEER RD
4200 FRMT 94555 752-D1
RAIN DROP CIR
2100 PIT 94565 573-J2
RAINER AV
100 VAL 94589 510-B5
RAINES CT
100 VAL 94591 530-F5
RAINFIELD DR
2700 SJS 95133 834-G1
RAINFLOWER DR
5300 LVMR 94550 696-C4
RAINIER AV
- LVMR 94550 715-D1
100 SJS 95126 833-J7
200 SSF 94080 707-G4
1000 PCFA 94044 727-C5
17500 AlaC 94541 691-E7
17500 AlaC 94580 691-E7
RAINIER CT
1900 MRTZ 94553 572-A7
2600 UNC 94587 732-F7
RAINIER DR
1900 MRTZ 94553 572-A7
RAINIER LN
- ANT 94509 595-D1
RAINIER PL
4300 PIT 94565 574-E7
RAINTREE CT
- HAY 94544 712-B7
100 VAL 94589 510-B5
800 SJS 95129 852-J2
RAINTREE DR
800 SJS 95129 852-J2
RAINTREE PL
900 LFYT 94549 611-J7
RAINTREE SPRING CT
11500 CPTO 95014 852-A4
RAINVIEW DR
2700 SJS 95133 834-G1
RAINWATER CT
40700 FRMT 94539 753-E4
RAINWELL CT
2700 SJS 95133 834-G1
RAINWELL DR
400 SJS 95133 834-G1
RAINWOOD CT
2800 SJS 95148 835-D7
RAJKOVICH WY
1100 SJS 95120 894-F3
RAKE CT
1500 SLN 94578 691-D3
RAKTAD RD
21100 SCIC 95120 895-B5
RALCO RD
37800 FRMT 94536 752-H4
RALEIGH CT
100 HER 94547 570-B5
3100 FRMT 94555 732-E7
RALEIGH DR
2400 SJS 95124 853-J7
RALEIGH PL
1100 HAY 94544 711-J6
18900 SAR 95070 852-G6
RALEIGH RD
- SJS 95193 875-C5
200 SJS 95119 875-C5
RALEIGH ST
- SF 94112 667-F7
RALENE CT
1600 SJS 95131 814-D5
RALENE PL
1600 SJS 95131 814-D5
RALMAR AV
2000 EPA 94303 791-A1
2400 EPA 94303 771-A7
RALSTON AV
- RDWC 94065 749-F7
- MLV 94941 606-C1
- SF 94129 647-C3
400 BLMT 94002 749-F7
400 MLV 94941 606-C1
500 BLMT 94002 769-B2
1500 BURL 94010 728-F7
1600 HIL 94010 728-F7
1700 CCCo 94805 589-B4
1700 HIL 94010 748-E1
2800 SMCo 94070 768-J2
2900 SMTO 94402 768-J2
2900 SMCo 94402 768-J2
2900 BLMT 94002 768-J2
5800 RCH 94805 589-B4
RALSTON COM
4000 FRMT 94538 753-B5
RALSTON CT
- HIL 94010 748-D2
100 VAL 94591 530-F4
2300 SJS 95148 855-C1
2600 SCL 95051 833-B3
22200 AlaC 94541 692-C6
RALSTON DR
2300 SJS 95148 855-C2
RALSTON LN
3700 AlaC 94541 692-C6
RALSTON PL
22400 AlaC 94541 692-C6
RALSTON RD
- ATN 94027 790-C3
RALSTON ST
- SF 94132 687-C1
RALSTON WY
- AlaC 94541 692-C6
RALSTON RANCH RD
- BLMT 94002 768-J2
RALT CT
- SJS 95123 874-F7
RALYA CT
18500 SCIC 95014 852-H1
RAM CT
45100 FRMT 94539 773-J3
RAM LN
800 FCTY 94404 749-F4
RAMA DR
3100 SJS 95124 873-H2
RAMADA CT
3100 CCCo 94549 611-J1
RAMAGE PEAK TR
- AlaC 94546 652-B6
- CCCo - 652-B6
RAMBLER AL
400 VAL 94591 530-D6
RAMBLEWOOD CT
35100 FRMT 94536 752-F1
RAMBLEWOOD DR
6400 SJS 95120 894-E1
RAMBLEWOOD PL
3500 FRMT 94536 752-F1
RAMBLEWOOD WY
1100 SMTO 94403 749-E6
1500 PLE 94566 714-D2
RAMBO CT
2300 SCL 95054 813-C5
RAMBOW DR
3400 PA 94306 791-D7
3400 PA 94306 811-D1
RAMEL WY
100 LGTS 95032 893-B1
RAMER CT
1100 CNCD 94520 592-E5
RAMEY CT
200 PIN 94564 569-E3
RAMIREZ CT
3800 SJS 95121 855-D3
RAMISH DR
2100 SJS 95131 814-D6
RAMITA CT
1400 SJS 95128 853-F5
RAMKE PL
2400 SCL 95050 833-C6
RAMON CT
- DNVL 94526 652-J1
RAMON DR
200 LALT 94024 811-F7
1300 SUNV 94087 832-G4
RAMON PL
200 SRMN 94583 673-G6
RAMON TER
41000 FRMT 94539 753-E6
RAMONA AV
- OAK 94611 630-A7
100 ELCR 94530 609-E4
100 PCFA 94044 727-A2
100 PDMT 94611 630-A7
100 SSF 94080 707-G4
500 ALB 94706 609-E6
700 SUNV 94087 832-C1
900 SJS 95125 854-A2
22300 CPTO 95014 852-A1
RAMONA CIR
3600 PA 94306 811-D1
RAMONA CT
- NVTO 94945 525-J1
2800 SCL 95051 833-B6
RAMONA DR
- ORIN 94563 631-C5
2000 PLHL 94523 592-D6
2400 AlaC 94545 711-E6
RAMONA RD
- DNVL 94526 653-B2
100 SMCo 94028 830-E3
RAMONA ST
- PIT 94565 574-C5
- SF 94103 667-H1
200 PA 94301 790-H4
200 SMTO 94401 728-J7
300 SMTO 94401 748-J1
1100 PA 94301 791-B7
2300 PIN 94564 569-F6
2500 PA 94306 791-B7
3100 PA 94306 811-D1
RAMONA WY
- NVTO 94945 525-J1
- SANS 94960 566-A6
900 SLN 94577 671-A7
W RAMONA WY
1500 CCCo 94507 632-E4
RAMOS AV
400 HAY 94544 711-J3
RAMOS CT
500 MPS 95035 794-D5
2700 MTVW 94040 832-A2
RAMOS WY
2100 SJS 95128 833-F7
3100 PA 94304 811-B1
RAMOSO RD
100 PTLV 94028 810-B4
RAMPART AV
10400 CPTO 95014 852-F2
RAMPART CT
2400 HAY 94545 731-H1
RAMPART DR
11300 DBLN 94568 693-F5
RAMPART ST
2400 OAK 94602 650-E4
RAMPART WY
- DALY 94014 687-E3
RAMPO CT
- PLHL 94523 592-A6
RAMSAY CIR
1300 WLCK 94596 612-A3
1300 WLCK 94596 611-J3
RAMSDELL PL
2500 SJS 95148 855-C1
RAMSEL CT
- SF 94129 647-C3
RAMSELL ST
- SF 94132 687-C2
RAMSEY CT
3700 CCCo 94803 589-C3
RAMSGATE CT
- DNVL 94526 653-B3
RAMSGATE DR
5100 NWK 94560 752-D3
RAMSGATE LN
- PLHL 94523 592-A4
RAMSGATE PL
34400 FRMT 94555 732-E7
RAMSGATE WY
- VAL 94591 530-G4
1400 SJS 95127 835-A4
RAMSTAD DR
3300 SJS 95127 835-B3
RAMSTREE DR
1600 SJS 95131 814-C5
RANCH CT
1400 SJS 95132 814-G3
RANCH DR
- MPS 95035 813-H1
200 MPS 95035 793-H7
RANCH LN
- LKSP 94939 586-F6
RANCH PL
3500 SJS 95132 814-G3
RANCH RD
- CCCo 94553 571-J3
- ORIN 94563 610-H4
- SCIC 95135 855-J1
- WDSD 94062 809-F4
- MrnC 94903 566-E5
- SMCo 94062 809-F4
4500 SCIC 95148 835-J7
4500 SCIC 95148 855-J1
4900 MrnC 94920 607-B1
4900 TBRN 94920 607-B1
RANCHERIA RD
- MrnC 94904 586-D4
600 LKSP 94939 586-D4
RANCHERO WY
- HAY 94544 712-C7
1000 SJS 95117 853-B3
N RANCHFORD CT
3600 CNCD 94520 572-G5
S RANCHFORD CT
3600 CNCD 94520 572-G5
RANCH HOLLOW WY
4900 ANT 94509 595-E4
RANCHITA CT
1400 LALT 94024 831-J3
RANCHITA DR
1300 LALT 94024 831-J3
RANCHITO CT
- ELCR 94530 609-C2
RANCHITO DR
2200 CNCD 94520 572-G5
RANCHITOS RD
- MrnC 94903 566-F5
- SRFL 94903 566-F5
RANCHITOS DEL SOL
- CCCo 94526 633-F7
RANCHO AV
- SMCo 94063 770-F5
RANCHO CT
6700 PLE 94588 714-A1
20300 AlaC 94541 711-E2
N RANCHO CT
- PIN 94803 569-E6
RANCHO DR
- MrnC 94920 606-J4
- SANS 94960 566-A5
- SCIC 95111 854-H7
900 SJS 95111 854-H7
RANCHO PL
10200 CPTO 95014 852-A1
N RANCHO PL
- PIN 94803 569-E6
100 CCCo 94803 569-E6
RANCHO RD
2000 CCCo 94803 569-E7
2600 PIN 94564 569-E7
3900 LFYT 94549 611-B6
N RANCHO RD
- PIN 94564 569-E6
900 CCCo 94803 569-E6
1000 PIN 94803 569-E6
S RANCHO RD
800 CCCo 94803 569-F7
RANCHO WY
2100 PIT 94565 573-J3
RANCHO ARROYO PKWY
400 FRMT 94536 733-B7
500 FRMT 94536 753-A1
RANCHO BELLA VISTA
20100 SAR 95070 872-E3
RANCHO DEEP CLIFF DR
22300 CPTO 95014 852-A2
RANCHO DE LA ROSA
1400 CCCo 94553 591-A3
1400 CCCo 94553 590-J4
RANCHO DEL HAMBRE
- LFYT 94549 611-F2
RANCHO DEL LAGO RD
2200 CCCo 94553 590-H5
RANCHO DIABLO DR
- LFYT 94549 611-B4
RANCHO ESTATES CT
3700 CCCo 94598 613-A3
RANCHO HIGUERA CT
2000 FRMT 94539 774-A5
RANCHO HIGUERA RD
400 MPS 95035 794-A4
46600 FRMT 94539 774-A5
47100 FRMT 94539 773-J5
RANCHO LA BOCA RD
- CCCo - 591-A4
700 CCCo 94553 590-J3
1300 CCCo 94553 591-A4
RANCHO LAS CIMAS WY
18500 SAR 95070 872-H3
RANCHO MANOR CT
100 SJS 95111 854-H6
RANCHO MANUELLA LN
26000 LAH 94022 811-C5
RANCHO MCCORMICK BLVD
2000 SCL 95050 833-C3
RANCHO MCCORMICK CT
2100 SCL 95050 833-C3
RANCHO PALOMARES DR
- AlaC 94542 692-E6
- AlaC 94552 692-E6
RANCHO PALOMARES PL
- AlaC 94552 692-E6
RANCHO VENTURA ST
22300 CPTO 95014 852-A1
RANCHO VERDE CIR E
1900 DNVL 94526 653-D7
RANCHO VERDE CIR W
1900 DNVL 94526 653-D7
RANCHO VIEW CT
3400 SJS 95132 814-G3
RANCHO VIEW DR
1400 LFYT 94549 611-H2
RANCHO VIEW RD
1400 LFYT 94549 611-H2
RANCHO VISTA RD
- CCCo 94803 569-E7
RANCH POINT WY
1100 ANT 94509 595-E4
RAND AV
600 OAK 94610 650-A3
RAND ST
400 SMTO 94401 729-B7
500 SMTO 94401 749-B1
1600 MPS 95035 794-A4
RANDALL AV
1900 CNCD 94520 572-E6
RANDALL CT
- SMCo 94015 687-B5
6000 SJS 95123 874-G6
6400 PLE 94566 714-D6
30900 UNC 94587 732-B4
RANDALL PL
- MLPK 94025 790-F6
5200 FRMT 94538 773-C3
RANDALL RD
- WLCK 94596 612-B5
1800 SMTO 94402 748-H7
1800 SMCo 94402 748-H7
RANDALL ST
- SF 94110 667-H5
- SF 94131 667-G5
RANDALL WY
2500 AlaC 94541 712-C1
RANDERS CT
2700 PA 94303 791-C6
RANDI CT
4700 UNC 94587 731-J7
RANDICK CT
3100 PLE 94588 694-F6
RANDLESWOOD CT
5800 SJS 95129 852-G3
RANDOL AV
1100 SJS 95126 833-H6
RANDOL CREEK DR
6900 SJS 95120 894-G3
RANDOLF DR
100 NVTO 94949 546-G4
RANDOLFI PL
1100 SJS 95131 814-E7
RANDOLPH AV
- SSF 94080 708-A2
200 SSF 94080 707-J1
3200 OAK 94602 650-C4
3600 SCL 95051 832-H7
RANDOLPH CT
2100 ANT 94509 575-A7
2100 ANT 94509 595-A1
RANDOLPH DR
1900 SJS 95128 853-G2
1900 SCIC 95128 853-G2
RANDOLPH PKWY
1600 LALT 94024 831-J4
RANDOLPH PL
- PCFA 94044 727-B6
- SRMN 94583 673-F6
RANDOLPH RD
- PIT 94565 574-C5
RANDOLPH ST
- SF 94132 687-C2
RANDOM WY
100 PLHL 94523 591-J7
RANDWICK AV
- OAK 94611 649-H1
RANDY COM
4000 FRMT 94538 773-D1
RANDY CT
- SMCo 94061 790-A3
RANDY LN
900 SPAB 94806 588-G2
10000 CPTO 95014 832-E6
RANDY ST
1300 SLN 94579 691-A7
RANELAGH RD
300 HIL 94010 748-H1
RANERE CT
1000 SUNV 94087 832-C2
RANEY CT
700 SCL 95050 833-C5
RANFRE LN
19300 SAR 95070 852-G7
19300 SAR 95070 872-G1
RANGE CT
- HER 94547 569-H4
RANGE PL
2100 MRTZ 94553 572-A7
RANGE RD
- PIT 94565 574-A3
RANGEL RD
400 MRTZ 94553 571-J6
RANGER CIR
700 FCTY 94404 749-G2
RANGER CT
- CCCo 94507 632-G4
RANGER PL
300 DNVL 94526 653-B5
RANGEVIEW PL
2100 MRTZ 94553 572-B2
RANGPUR CT
1000 SUNV 94087 832-D2
RANKER PL
400 HAY 94544 712-A6
RANKIN AV
- SJS 95110 834-A5
RANKIN DR
1000 MPS 95035 794-C4
RANKIN ST
- SF 94124 668-B5
RANKIN WY
100 BEN 94510 551-C4
RANLEIGH WY
1000 PDMT 94610 650-B2

STREET
Block City ZIP Pg-Grid
RANSOM AV
2100 OAK 94601 650-D7
RANSOME DR
1100 NVTO 94949 546-C1
RANSON DR
600 SJS 95133 834-F1
RANSPOT DR
2300 AlaC 94578 691-G4
RANTOUL CIR
100 SLN 94577 671-C7
RANWICK CT
4200 SJS 95118 874-C2
RAPALLO CT
- CCCo 94565 573-D2
RAPALLO LN
300 CCCo 94565 573-D2
RAPALLO WY
2000 CCCo 94565 573-D2
RAPHAEL CT
2000 WLCK 94598 612-F2
RAPLEY RD
- WDSD 94062 809-G7
RAPLEY TR
- PTLV 94028 830-C3
- SMCo 94028 830-C3
- SMCo 94020 830-B5
RAPOSA CT
1200 SJS 95121 855-A4
RAPOSA DR
1100 SJS 95121 855-A4
RAPOSA VISTA
- NVTO 94945 525-J2
RAPP AV
37000 FRMT 94536 753-A1
RAPPAHANNOCK CT
300 DNVL 94526 653-D7
RAPPOLLA CT
5100 PLE 94588 694-A6
RAQUEL CT
400 LALT 94022 811-C5
1600 SJS 95128 853-G3
RAQUEL LN
300 LALT 94022 811-C5
RARITAN PL
2600 SJS 95148 835-E6
RASMUS CIR
3000 SJS 95148 855-E1
RASMUSSEN CT
2600 PLE 94588 694-F6
RASPBERRY PL
4700 SJS 95129 853-B2
RASSAI CT
- DNVL 94526 632-J7
RASSANI DR
100 DNVL 94506 654-A6
RATEKIN DR
30400 UNC 94587 732-A4
RATHBONE WY
3400 PLE 94588 694-F6
RATHMANN DR
2800 SJS 95148 835-E7
RATON CT
1200 CCCo 94803 569-C7
RATTAN CT
600 FRMT 94539 793-J2
RATTAN TER
800 SUNV 94086 832-G3
RATTO PL
35400 FRMT 94536 752-F2
RATTO RD
- ALA 94502 669-J6
RAU DR
- FRMT 94536 753-C1
RAUSCH ST
- SF 94103 648-A7
RAVEN CT
100 DNVL 94526 653-C4
100 HER 94547 569-H5
13800 SAR 95070 872-J1
RAVEN PL
5000 CLAY 94517 594-A5
RAVEN RD
- MrnC 94960 566-A3
2000 PLE 94566 714-D1
RAVEN TER
33800 FRMT 94555 732-D7
RAVEN WY
5000 CLAY 94517 594-A5
RAVENDALE CT
3400 SJS 95111 854-G6
RAVENDALE DR
200 MTVW 94043 812-B6
RAVEN GLASS CT
- WLCK 94598 612-H6
RAVENHILL RD
100 ORIN 94563 610-H6
RAVENNA ST
600 LVMR 94550 695-E7
RAVENNA TER
600 FRMT 94536 753-B2
RAVENSBOURNE PARK ST
42700 FRMT 94538 773-C2
RAVENSBURY AV
22500 SCIC 95014 831-E5
23000 LAH 94024 831-E4
23100 SCIC 94024 831-E5
RAVENSCOURT AV
900 SJS 95128 853-F4
1000 CMBL 95128 853-F4
RAVENSCOURT RD
500 HIL 94010 748-G2
RAVENS COVE LN
3200 ALA 94501 670-A4
RAVENS PLACE WY
1500 SJS 95121 855-B4
RAVENSWOOD AV
100 ATN 94027 790-G3
100 MLPK 94025 790-G3
RAVENSWOOD DR
1400 LALT 94024 832-A3
RAVENSWOOD WY
3100 SJS 95148 855-E1
3100 SJS 95148 835-E7
RAVENWOOD AV
5600 NWK 94560 752-D5
RAVENWOOD CT
900 ANT 94509 575-C7
RAVENWOOD DR
- SF 94127 667-D6
- CCCo 94526 612-D2
1700 CNCD 94520 592-F3

STREET
Block City ZIP Pg-Grid
RAVENWOOD DR
13700 SAR 95070 872-J1
RAVENWOOD LN
2300 OAK 94602 650-E4
RAVENWOOD PL
4100 AlaC 94546 692-B5
RAVENWOOD WY
100 SSF 94080 707-G5
RAVILLA CT
- DALY 94014 687-E2
RAVINE CT
2300 SJS 95133 834-F1
RAVINE DR
100 PIT 94565 574-C4
100 WDSD 94062 789-G5
2300 SJS 95133 834-F1
RAVINE RD
15700 SCIC 95030 872-G5
RAVINE WY
- MrnC 94904 586-B4
- MrnC 94947 525-E3
RAVIN HILL LN
- MRGA 94556 631-C5
RAVINIA WY
100 LGTS 95032 893-D2
RAVIZZA AV
1600 SCL 95051 833-B3
RAWHIDE CT
100 VAL 94589 509-J5
RAWHIDE WY
2000 AlaC 94552 692-F2
RAWLES ST
- SF 94129 647-E4
RAWLINGS DR
900 SJS 95136 874-D2
RAWLS CT
100 SJS 95139 895-F1
RAWSON ST
2400 OAK 94601 670-F1
2600 OAK 94619 650-F7
2600 OAK 94619 670-F1
RAY AV
1000 LALT 94022 811-D4
1900 ELCR 94530 589-B6
1900 CCCo 94805 589-B6
5000 AlaC 94546 692-B4
RAY CT
- BURL 94010 728-C5
- FRMT 94536 753-D2
- SRFL 94901 566-D6
- MrnC 94901 566-D6
- CCCo 94526 633-C6
RAY DR
1500 BURL 94010 728-C5
RAY ST
- PLE 94566 714-E3
RAYANNA AV
3300 SCL 95051 832-J3
RAYBAL CT
6300 SJS 95123 875-A7
RAYBURN ST
- SF 94114 667-G3
RAYCLIFF PL
700 CNCD 94518 592-J6
RAYCLIFF TER
- SF 94115 647-F5
RAYLAND CT
6800 PLE 94588 694-A6
RAYMOND
- CCCo 94595 612-C7
RAYMOND AV
- SANS 94960 586-B1
- SANS 94960 566-B7
- SF 94134 687-J2
200 SF 94134 688-A2
500 SCIC 95128 853-G1
600 SJS 95128 853-G1
RAYMOND CT
- SCAR 94070 769-G6
RAYMOND DR
200 BEN 94510 551-B4
300 HAY 94544 712-B5
1100 CCCo 94553 572-B7
1200 CCCo 94553 592-B1
RAYMOND RD
4000 AlaC 94550 696-A1
4000 AlaC 94550 695-J1
4300 LVMR 94550 696-A1
RAYMOND ST
1100 MRTZ 94553 571-D4
3000 SCL 95054 813-D7
6400 OAK 94609 629-H4
RAYMUNDO AV
700 LALT 94024 811-G6
RAYMUNDO DR
100 WDSD 94062 789-D4
RAYMUNDO TR
- SMCo 94062 789-A3
READ AV
2400 BLMT 94002 769-C2
READ DR
300 LFYT 94549 631-H3
READE LN
- SAUS 94965 627-B3
READING AV
2200 AlaC 94546 692-A6
READING PL
600 DNVL 94526 653-B5
READING WY
- PLHL 94523 591-B1
READY CT
- WLCK 94598 612-F2
READY RD
- WLCK 94598 612-F2
REAGAN CT
2800 ANT 94509 575-A7
REALM DR
7000 SJS 95119 875-E7
REAM ST
500 SolC 94590 530-C6
500 VAL 94590 530-C6
REAMER RD
18000 AlaC 94546 691-J2
REAMWOOD AV
1200 SUNV 94089 813-A4
3200 SCL 95054 813-A4
REARDON RD
- SF 94124 668-D7
REATA PL
- OAK 94618 630-A4
REBECCA CT
- AMCN 94589 509-J1

STREET
Block City ZIP Pg-Grid
REBECCA CT
- CCCo 94596 612-A5
REBECCA DR
1100 LVMR 94550 696-C7
2500 PIN 94564 569-D6
REBECCA LN
- ATN 94027 790-G2
- SF 94124 668-C6
11600 LAH 94024 831-E3
REBECCA WY
- NVTO 94945 526-D3
600 SJS 95117 853-B2
REBECCA LYNN WY
2400 SCL 95050 833-C6
REBECCA PRIVADA
800 MTVW 94040 832-A1
REBEIRO AV
2600 SCL 95051 833-B6
REBEL CT
5000 SJS 95118 874-A4
REBEL WY
1500 SJS 95118 873-J4
1500 SJS 95118 874-A4
REBELO LN
- MrnC 94947 525-E4
RECIFE WY
5800 SJS 95120 874-C5
RECINO ST
100 FRMT 94539 753-F4
RECREATION AV
- MLPK 94025 790-J1
RECREATION DR
- SUNV 94089 812-H3
RECREATION WY
1300 RDWC 94061 789-H2
RECTOR COM
4000 FRMT 94538 753-B5
RED CT
900 PLE 94566 714-H4
RED ALDER CT
- CCCo 94506 653-J3
RED ARROW CT
- RCH 94803 589-G1
RED BARK CT
- LFYT 94549 611-G2
REDBERRY CT
2300 PLE 94566 714-C1
REDBERRY DR
16300 SCIC 95030 872-F5
RED BIRCH CT
- CCCo 94506 653-J3
REDBIRD DR
800 SJS 95125 854-C6
RED BUD CT
- DNVL 94526 653-F4
REDBUD CT
- NVTO 94945 526-B1
2400 SJS 95128 853-F4
7600 NWK 94560 752-D7
7700 PLE 94588 713-J1
REDBUD DR
700 LVMR 94550 695-E7
REDBUD LN
100 VAL 94591 550-F1
200 HAY 94541 711-G3
REDBUSH TER
2000 SJS 95128 833-F6
RED CEDAR CT
- CCCo 94506 653-J3
REDCEDAR TER
- FRMT 94536 752-H3
REDCLIFF CT
22500 MTVW 94040 832-A1
REDCLIFF DR
1200 SJS 95118 854-C7
1200 SJS 95118 874-C1
RED CLIFF TER
- FRMT 94536 753-C1
REDCLOUD CT
4300 CNCD 94518 593-A5
REDCOACH LN
- ORIN 94563 610-H3
RED CREEK DR
4900 SJS 95136 874-J2
4900 SJS 95136 875-A2
RED CYPRESS CT
- CCCo 94506 653-J3
RED CYPRESS PL
- CCCo 94506 653-J3
REDDING CT
- TBRN 94920 607-B4
REDDING PL
- OAK 94619 650-F7
REDDING RD
- CMBL 95008 873-E2
300 SJS 95008 873-E2
REDDING ST
3500 OAK 94619 650-F6
REDDING WY
- SRFL 94901 586-H3
REDDINGTON CT
900 WLCK 94596 632-F1
REDDY ST
- SF 94124 668-B7
REDEN DR
4300 SJS 95130 853-A7
REDFEARN DR
- CCCo 94507 632-G4
REDFERN CT
1100 CNCD 94521 593-F7
REDFIELD AL
- SF 94133 647-J4
REDFIELD CT
1500 SJS 95121 855-A3
REDFIELD PL
300 MRGA 94556 651-E3
RED FIR CT
- CCCo 94506 653-J3
21100 CPTO 95014 852-C2
RED FIR WY
- LVMR 94550 696-A3
REDGLEN CT
3200 SJS 95135 855-E2
REDGRAVE PL
34400 FRMT 94555 752-E1
RED HAWK CIR
1400 FRMT 94538 753-C4
RED HAWK CT
- BSBN 94005 688-A5
- BSBN 94005 687-J5
RED HAWK RD
100 NVTO 94949 546-E5

STREET
Block City ZIP Pg-Grid
RED HAWK TER
1400 FRMT 94538 753-C3
REDHEAD LN
- LGTS 95032 893-B1
RED HILL AV
- SANS 94960 566-C7
RED HILL CIR
- TBRN 94920 607-D7
RED HILL CT
2400 UNC 94587 732-B4
RED HILL RD
20000 SCIC 95030 872-E5
RED HOLLY CT
7100 SJS 95120 894-C3
REDHOOK LN
3400 ALA 94502 670-A7
REDINGTON RD
2100 HIL 94010 728-D7
RED LAKE TER
- FRMT 94555 732-C6
REDLAND RD
- SMCo 94062 809-F5
REDLANDS CT
1200 CNCD 94521 593-F7
REDLANDS ST
4300 UNC 94587 732-B7
REDLANDS WY
1200 CNCD 94521 593-F7
RED LEAF CT
- DALY 94014 687-G3
3200 HAY 94542 712-E4
RED LEAF WY
1100 PIT 94565 573-J2
RED MAPLE CT
- HAY 94544 712-E7
- CCCo 94506 653-J4
4400 CNCD 94521 593-B5
RED MAPLE DR
300 CCCo 94506 653-J4
RED MAPLE PL
- CCCo 94506 653-J5
RED MAPLE ST
1700 UNC 94587 732-C4
REDMOND AV
900 SJS 95120 894-E1
900 SJS 95120 874-A7
REDMOND CT
1000 SJS 95120 874-E7
RED MOUNTAIN RD
- MrnC 94903 546-A6
REDOAK COM
4400 FRMT 94538 773-C1
RED OAK CT
- NVTO 94949 546-C1
1300 PIN 94564 569-E5
29600 HAY 94544 712-D7
RED OAK DR
- SUNV 94086 832-G1
1000 CNCD 94521 593-D6
RED OAK DR E
200 SUNV 94086 832-G1
RED OAK DR W
200 SUNV 94086 832-G1
RED OAK PL
2100 CCCo 94506 653-G1
RED OAK WY
3700 RDWC 94061 789-G2
REDOAKS DR
1100 SJS 95128 853-E4
REDONDO AV
5200 OAK 94618 629-H6
REDONDO CT
- ALA 94501 649-G7
5500 CLAY 94517 593-F6
11200 CPTO 95014 852-B3
REDONDO DR
100 PIT 94565 574-C6
1200 SJS 95125 854-B5
REDONDO ST
- SF 94124 688-B1
REDONDO TER
300 SUNV 94086 812-D7
REDONDO WY
100 DNVL 94526 653-C1
900 LVMR 94550 715-F3
RED PINE CT
- CCCo 94506 654-A3
1100 SJS 95125 854-A4
RED RIVER WY
100 SJS 95136 875-A3
REDROCK CT
1100 SUNV 94089 812-J4
REDROCK DR
300 ANT 94509 595-E2
REDROCK PL
2100 MRTZ 94553 572-B7
RED ROCK RD
800 PDMT 94618 630-C7
800 PDMT 94611 630-C7
REDROCK RD
26600 LAH 94022 830-J2
RED ROCK WY
- SRFL 94901 566-F6
- MrnC 94903 566-F6
- SF 94131 667-F4
REDSTONE CT
3900 ANT 94509 595-F1
REDSTONE DR
5000 SJS 95124 873-E4
REDSTONE PL
1000 HAY 94542 712-A3
REDSTONE TER
4100 FRMT 94555 752-B2
RED TAIL CT
3700 SCL 95051 832-H5
REDTAIL CT
5100 ANT 94509 595-H5
RED WILLOW RD
100 SRMN 94583 653-J7
REDWING AV
1600 SUNV 94087 832-H5
RED WING DR
400 CCCo 94526 633-C4
REDWING PL
- MRGA 94556 631-F5
3300 FRMT 94555 732-D7
REDWING ST
100 VAL 94589 510-B5
REDWOOD
- BEN 94510 551-C6
REDWOOD AV
- MLPK 94025 790-J2

STREET
Block City ZIP Pg-Grid
REDWOOD AV
- CMAD 94925 586-F7
- LKSP 94939 586-D6
- MrnC 94965 606-B3
- RDWC 94061 789-J2
- RDWC 94061 790-A1
200 MPS 95035 793-H6
200 SCL 95051 833-A7
200 CMAD 94925 606-F1
400 SBRN 94066 727-H1
500 SJS 95050 833-E7
500 SJS 95128 833-E7
500 SSF 94080 707-H3
900 SUNV 94086 832-H3
1100 RDWC 94061 770-B7
1500 SLN 94579 691-A5
N REDWOOD AV
- SJS 95050 833-E7
1300 SJS 95128 833-E6
S REDWOOD AV
300 SJS 95128 853-E1
REDWOOD BLVD
- NVTO 94947 546-E1
- NVTO 94949 546-E1
500 NVTO 94947 526-C6
6900 NVTO 94945 526-C2
REDWOOD CIR
- LFYT 94549 611-C4
1300 SPAB 94806 588-H1
3700 PA 94306 811-D1
REDWOOD CT
800 CCCo 94525 550-D5
3400 AlaC 94546 692-A5
3900 PLE 94588 713-J2
36500 NWK 94560 752-D6
REDWOOD DR
- HIL 94010 748-H2
- ROSS 94957 586-C2
- SRFL 94901 586-E2
200 MrnC 94904 586-C2
800 CCCo 94506 654-A2
900 SJS 95138 875-F6
1200 CNCD 94520 592-E4
1400 LALT 94024 831-J6
1800 MRTZ 94553 571-J7
2300 ANT 94509 574-J7
N REDWOOD DR
100 SRFL 94903 566-F1
REDWOOD GN
19500 AlaC 94546 692-A4
REDWOOD HTS
3700 AlaC 94546 692-A3
REDWOOD HWY
- CCCo 631-A7
- LKSP 94904 586-H6
- SRFL 94903 566-E1
1700 CMAD 94925 586-H6
1900 LKSP 94925 586-H6
REDWOOD HWY
U.S.-101
- CMAD - 586-H5
- CMAD - 606-G4
- LKSP - 586-H5
- LKSP - 586-H5
- MLV - 606-G4
- MrnC - 546-F6
- MrnC - 546-F7
- MrnC - 566-E2
- MrnC - 566-F1
- MrnC - 586-H5
- MrnC - 606-G4
- MrnC - 627-B4
- MrnC - 626-H1
- NVTO - 526-C3
- NVTO - 546-F7
- SAUS - 627-B4
- SAUS - 626-H1
- SF - 627-B4
- SRFL - 566-E1
- SRFL - 566-E2
- SRFL - 566-F5
- SRFL - 586-H5
REDWOOD LN
- CMAD 94925 606-C3
- MLV 94941 606-C3
1200 LFYT 94549 611-C4
REDWOOD PKWY
- VAL 94589 530-D2
2800 VAL 94591 530-F1
REDWOOD RD
- SANS 94960 566-A7
400 SANS 94960 586-A1
1700 HER 94547 569-J4
2000 HER 94547 570-A5
3500 AlaC - 650-J4
3500 OAK 94619 650-H5
3700 AlaC 94546 692-A1
4100 LVMR 94550 696-A4
6500 AlaC - 651-A4
7000 NVTO 94945 526-C4
15000 AlaC 94546 651-D6
15200 AlaC 94546 671-E1
16000 AlaC 94546 672-A6
REDWOOD ST
100 SF 94102 647-H7
400 VAL 94589 529-J2
400 VAL 94590 529-J2
700 VAL 94589 530-B2
700 VAL 94590 530-B2
1100 PIT 94565 574-E3
REDWOOD TER
- ORIN 94563 610-E6
38200 FRMT 94536 753-B2
REDWOOD WY
- ATN 94027 790-D2
1200 MLBR 94030 727-H3
1200 PCFA 94044 727-A5
REDWOOD CREEK TR
- MrnC 94965 606-A6
REDWOOD HIGHWAY FRONTAGE RD
- MrnC 94920 606-G5
200 MLV 94941 606-G6
500 MrnC 94941 606-G5
3500 SRFL 94903 566-E2
REDWOOD SHORES PKWY
100 RDWC 94065 749-H7
100 RDWC 94065 769-H1
600 RDWC 94065 750-A5
REECE WY
2900 SJS 95133 814-G7

STREET
Block City ZIP Pg-Grid
REED AV
700 SUNV 94086 832-F2
1300 SLN 94578 691-C3
2600 AlaC 94550 715-H5
REED BLVD
- MrnC 94941 606-H4
REED CIR
200 MrnC 94941 606-H5
REED CT
- BEN 94510 550-J2
4600 FRMT 94538 753-A6
REED DR
- MRGA 94556 651-F2
100 AMCN 94589 510-A4
REED PL
- CCCo 94707 609-F3
REED ST
- MrnC 94941 606-E5
- SF 94109 647-J5
- MLV 94941 606-E5
300 SCL 95050 833-D3
E REED ST
- SJS 95112 834-D7
W REED ST
- SJS 95110 834-C7
REED TER
1000 SUNV 94086 832-H2
REED WY
3100 CNCD 94518 592-H3
23100 HAY 94541 711-F3
REEDER CT
5200 FRMT 94536 752-H6
REEDHURST AV
3900 SJS 95118 874-A2
REEDLAND CIR
4300 SRMN 94583 653-H7
REEDLAND WOODS WY
- TBRN 94920 606-J3
REEDLEY WY
5200 AlaC 94546 692-B2
REED RANCH RD
- TBRN 94920 607-A4
REEF DR
- PIT 94565 574-E5
400 SMTO 94404 749-E1
400 FCTY 94404 749-E1
REEF POINT CT
700 CCCo 94572 569-J2
REEF POINT DR
800 CCCo 94572 569-J2
800 CCCo 94572 570-A2
REESE ST
1200 RDWC 94061 790-A1
REEVE ST
900 SCL 95050 833-E3
REEVES CT
200 SCIC 95127 835-B2
REFLECTION CIRCLE DR
- SMCo - 768-C3
REFLECTIONS CIR
300 SRMN 94583 673-F3
REFLECTIONS DR
100 SRMN 94583 673-F3
3600 PLE 94566 714-F2
REFLECTIONS LN
- MPS 95035 793-H6
REFREDI CT
21800 CPTO 95014 852-B1
REFUGIO VALLEY RD
1300 HER 94547 569-J4
1700 HER 94547 570-A5
REGABY PLACE CT
3800 SJS 95121 855-B5
REGAL AV
25900 HAY 94544 711-H6
REGAL CT
700 MLPK 94025 790-J2
4100 SCIC 95127 814-J6
4100 SCIC 95127 815-A6
REGAL DR
1700 CNCD 94521 593-B2
2400 UNC 94587 732-C4
REGAL RD
- BERK 94708 609-G5
REGALIA AV
800 PLE 94566 714-E3
REGALIA DR
- NVTO 94945 525-H2
REGAL LILY LN
2100 SRMN 94583 653-J7
REGALO CT
1400 SJS 95128 853-F4
REGAN DR
3900 SMTO 94403 749-D6
REGAN LN
12700 SAR 95070 852-E6
REGAN ST
10100 SJS 95127 835-B3
REGAN WY
800 FRMT 94539 753-G7
REGANTI DR
- CNCD 94520 592-E5
1000 CNCD 94518 592-E5
REGANTI PL
- CNCD 94518 592-E5
- CNCD 94520 592-E5
REGAS DR
600 CMBL 95008 853-F7
600 SJS 95008 853-F7
REGATTA BLVD
1100 RCH 94804 608-G2
REGATTA CT
- SLN 94579 691-F3
- VAL 94591 550-G3
N REGATTA DR
100 VAL 94591 550-F2
S REGATTA DR
100 VAL 94591 550-F3
REGATTA LN
1600 SJS 95112 833-J1
REGATTA SQ
1000 RCH 94804 608-G2
REGATTA WY
- SLN 94579 691-A7
REGELLO CT
1900 SPAB 94806 588-H3
REGENCY
100 PIT 94565 574-B6
REGENCY CT
- SRMN 94583 673-J6
200 CCCo 94803 589-F3

STREET
Block City ZIP Pg-Grid
REGENCY CT
800 CCCo 94596 612-A5
800 SCAR 94070 769-D5
1500 ELCR 94530 609-D1
REGENCY DR
- CLAY 94517 613-J2
1200 SJS 95129 852-H4
2800 PLE 94588 714-A3
REGENCY KNOLL DR
1000 SJS 95129 852-C7
REGENCY OAKS DR
6100 SJS 95129 852-C7
REGENT CT
- NVTO 94947 526-A4
200 AMCN 94589 510-A3
900 RDWC 94061 790-B1
REGENT DR
100 PIT 94565 574-E6
900 LALT 94024 831-H5
1400 SLN 94577 691-D1
REGENT PL
- PA 94301 791-A4
100 CCCo 94507 632-F6
1200 LVMR 94550 715-F5
REGENT RD
2400 LVMR 94550 715-F5
REGENT ST
- SF 94112 687-D2
800 ALA 94501 669-J3
800 SJS 95110 833-J4
900 ALA 94501 670-A3
1300 RDWC 94061 790-A1
2500 BERK 94704 629-J3
2700 BERK 94705 629-J3
2900 OAK 94618 629-J4
REGENT WY
2200 AlaC 94546 691-G6
REGENT PARK DR
700 SJS 95123 874-F4
REGENTS BLVD
- UNC 94545 731-J6
32200 UNC 94587 731-J6
32300 UNC 94587 732-A6
32700 UNC - 752-A1
32700 UNC 94587 752-A1
REGENTS PARK DR
100 VAL 94591 530-G6
REGENTS PARK LN
4800 FRMT 94538 773-C2
REGIA CT
1100 SUNV 94087 832-D3
REGINA AV
1300 SPAB 94806 588-G4
REGINA CT
2300 SCL 95054 813-C5
4600 ANT 94509 574-H5
REGINA LN
4600 CNCD 94521 593-C3
REGINA WY
- SRFL 94903 566-C3
900 PCFA 94044 726-J4
1700 CMBL 95008 873-A1
1800 SJS 95008 873-A1
REGIO CT
1000 LFYT 94549 611-H6
11600 DBLN 94568 693-F3
REGIO DR
11600 DBLN 94568 693-F3
REGIONAL ST
6500 DBLN 94568 693-G4
REGIS CT
600 BEN 94510 530-J7
3300 SCL 95051 833-A2
REGNART CT
21600 CPTO 95014 852-B3
REGNART RD
21500 CPTO 95014 852-A4
REGNART WY
2800 SCL 95051 833-B7
REGNART CANYON DR
11600 CPTO 95014 852-A4
REGO COM
400 FRMT 94536 753-E1
REGULUS CT
- ALA 94501 649-G7
500 LVMR 94550 715-E4
REGULUS RD
500 LVMR 94550 715-E4
REGULUS ST
700 FCTY 94404 749-E5
REICHERT AV
800 NVTO 94945 526-C4
REICHERT CT
- NVTO 94945 526-C4
REICHLING AV
100 PCFA 94044 727-A2
REID AV
800 SBRN 94066 707-H7
REID CT
5000 RCH 94804 609-B1
REID LN
20500 SAR 95070 872-D2
REIDS ROOST RD
- SMCo 94062 809-C3
REILLY CT
11500 DBLN 94568 693-F5
REIMCHE DR
4100 ANT 94509 574-H6
REINA PL
36400 NWK 94560 752-E5
REINA DEL MAR AV
100 PCFA 94044 727-A1
REINCLAUD CT
1100 SUNV 94087 832-C3
REINDEER CT
2300 ANT 94509 595-G2
REINELL PL
20200 CPTO 95014 832-E7
REINER LN
1100 WLCK 94596 612-B1
REINER ST
- DALY 94014 687-C5
- SMCo 94014 687-C5
REINERT AV
2100 MTVW 94043 811-G2
REINERT RD
800 MTVW 94043 811-G2
REINHARDT DR
3900 OAK 94619 650-G5
4800 OAK 94613 650-G5
REINOSO CT
3600 SJS 95136 874-D1

STREET
Block City ZIP Pg-Grid

REIS AV
- SolC 94590 530-C6
200 VAL 94591 530-D6
REISLING CT
700 CLAY 94517 593-J7
REISLING WY
8300 SJS 95135 855-H7
RELIANCE WY
800 FRMT 94539 773-G4
RELIEZ CT
3200 LFYT 94549 611-H3
RELIEZ HIGHLAND RD
3300 LFYT 94549 591-G7
RELIEZ STATION LN
900 LFYT 94549 611-J6
RELIEZ STATION RD
700 LFYT 94549 611-H7
700 LFYT 94549 631-H1
RELIEZ VALLEY CT
- LFYT 94549 591-G7
RELIEZ VALLEY RD
1500 CCCo 94549 591-G4
1600 LFYT 94549 591-G7
1700 LFYT 94549 611-G2
1900 MRTZ 94553 591-E3
2200 PLHL 94549 591-G4
2300 CCCo - 591-E3
2300 CCCo 94553 591-E3
REMBRANDT DR
1000 SUNV 94087 832-F3
REMCO ST
3400 AlaC 94546 691-H3
REMER TER
5800 FRMT 94555 752-B3
REMILLARD CT
900 SJS 95122 834-E7
4100 PLE 94566 714-G5
REMILLARD DR
400 HIL 94010 748-D3
REMINGTON CT
- DNVL 94526 652-J3
100 VAL 94590 530-B7
1200 SUNV 94087 832-A3
3000 SJS 95148 855-D1
REMINGTON DR
100 DNVL 94526 653-A3
100 DNVL 94526 652-J3
33700 UNC 94587 732-E6
E REMINGTON DR
100 SUNV 94087 832-E3
W REMINGTON DR
500 SUNV 94087 832-B2
REMINGTON LP
200 CCCo - 652-J4
200 DNVL 94526 652-J4
REMINGTON WY
2900 SJS 95148 835-D7
3000 SJS 95148 855-D1
REMMEL CT
- ALA 94502 669-J6
REMO CT
2300 SCL 95054 813-C5
REMO ST
700 SJS 95116 834-F6
REMORA DR
- UNC 94587 731-J5
REMSEN CT
1000 SUNV 94087 832-B3
REMUDA LN
1600 SJS 95112 833-J1
REMUDA WY
3600 PIN 94564 569-H7
RENA CT
- NVTO 94947 525-J3
RENADA PL
900 SRMN 94583 673-G5
RENAISSANCE DR
- SJS 95134 813-D2
RENAISSANCE RD
- MrnC 94945 526-J4
- NVTO 94945 526-J4
RENATA CT
- NVTO 94947 526-C7
RENATO CT
- RDWC 94061 790-C1
4500 FRMT 94536 752-E3
RENEE CT
100 CCCo 94803 589-E2
100 RCH 94803 589-E2
1000 SJS 95120 894-H4
RENEE WY
- CNCD 94521 593-F4
RENETTA CT
800 LALT 94024 831-E1
RENFIELD WY
2300 SJS 95148 855-C2
RENFREW CT
100 CCCo 94803 589-D1
2200 SJS 95131 814-D5
RENFREW RD
600 CCCo 94803 569-D7
600 CCCo 94803 589-D1
N RENGSTORFF AV
100 MTVW 94040 811-G3
100 MTVW 94043 811-G1
S RENGSTORFF AV
200 MTVW 94040 811-F4
RENICK CT
2900 SJS 95148 855-D2
RENIDA ST
100 SolC 94591 530-E7
RENNELLWOOD WY
4000 PLE 94566 714-E1
RENNIE AV
- SCIC 95127 815-A6
RENO DR
2300 SJS 95148 835-D6
RENO PL
4800 RCH 94803 589-J2
4800 RCH 94803 590-A2
RENOIR CT
1000 SUNV 94087 832-F3
RENOVA DR
400 SCIC 95128 853-F2
RENRAW DR
1200 SJS 95127 835-C3
RENTON CT
800 SJS 95123 874-E5
RENTON WY
2600 AlaC 94546 691-H5
RENWICK LN
2100 ANT 94509 575-F6

RENWICK PL
100 WLCK 94598 612-J1
RENWICK ST
2400 OAK 94601 650-E7
2600 OAK 94619 650-E7
RENZ RD
- MLV 94941 606-C3
RENZO CT
4700 SJS 95111 875-B1
REO AL
100 VAL 94590 529-J4
500 VAL 94590 530-B4
REPOSA WY
- SF 94127 667-E5
3600 BLMT 94002 769-A2
REPOSO DR
10900 OAK 94603 670-H7
10900 OAK 94603 690-H1
REPUBLIC AV
100 SJS 95116 834-H3
1900 SLN 94577 690-H4
REPUBLIC CT
2500 SJS 95116 834-H3
REPUBLIC PL
2500 SJS 95116 834-J3
REQUA CT
2900 SJS 95148 835-E7
REQUA PL
- PDMT 94611 650-B2
REQUA RD
100 PDMT 94611 650-B2
RERUN DR
- CCCo 94553 571-G2
RESEARCH AV
46100 FRMT 94539 773-G4
RESEARCH DR
2000 LVMR 94550 716-D1
3000 RCH 94806 569-A7
RESEARCH PL
3000 SJS 95134 813-G4
RESEARCH RD
26200 HAY 94545 731-D1
RESEDA CIR
5200 FRMT 94538 773-A1
RESEDA DR
600 SUNV 94087 832-D1
RESEDA WY
2000 ANT 94509 595-B1
RESERVA LN
- TBRN 94920 627-F1
RESERVOIR AV
- NVTO 94945 525-J2
RESERVOIR DR
- CCCo 94553 571-G3
600 NVTO 94945 526-C3
RESERVOIR LP
- CCCo 94553 571-G3
RESERVOIR RD
- BEN 94510 551-E1
- NVTO 94949 546-H2
- ATN 94027 790-B6
- LGTS 95032 893-A1
- SRFL 94901 586-E1
100 HIL 94010 748-G3
RESERVOIR ST
- CCCo - 550-G6
- SF 94114 667-H1
RESERVOIR HILL DR
- DALY 94014 687-D4
RESIDENT LN
- MLPK 94025 790-J2
RESNIK ST
- HER 94547 570-A5
RESOTA ST
700 HAY 94545 711-G5
RESSA RD
300 PCFA 94044 707-A6
RESTANI WY
- SF 94112 687-F1
RESTON CT
3900 SSF 94080 707-D4
RESULTS WY
- CPTO 95014 852-B1
RETIRO WY
- SF 94123 647-G3
RETTIG AV
4000 OAK 94602 650-F4
RETTIG PL
4000 OAK 94602 650-F4
RETTUS CT
600 SJS 95111 854-G3
REUEL CT
- SF 94124 668-C6
REUSS RD
10700 AlaC 94550 716-J4
REVA AV
200 SLN 94577 690-J1
REVA CT
10200 SCIC 95127 835-A3
REVA DR
3100 CNCD 94519 572-G7
REVELSTOKE WY
1400 SUNV 94087 832-D5
REVERE AV
- HAY 94544 732-E3
1000 SF 94124 668-B6
1400 SJS 95118 874-B1
2900 OAK 94605 671-C6
REVERE CT
800 LFYT 94549 611-A7
REVERE DR
800 SUNV 94087 832-C3
2000 CNCD 94520 572-E6
REVERE PL
44200 FRMT 94539 773-H2
REVERE RD
800 LFYT 94549 611-A7
REVERE ST
100 VAL 94591 530-D4
REVERE TER
- FRMT 94539 773-H2
REVERE WY
800 SMCo 94062 789-F2
REVEY AV
100 SJS 95128 853-F1
100 SCIC 95128 853-F1
100 SCIC 95128 833-F7
100 SJS 95128 833-F7
REVIEW WY
- HAY 94544 711-H3
REVIVAL TER
500 FRMT 94536 753-G3

REX AV
- SF 94127 667-D5
REX CIR
100 CMBL 95008 853-D5
REX RD
1100 HAY 94541 691-J7
REX ST
1700 SMTO 94403 749-C3
REXFORD WY
39800 FRMT 94538 753-B6
REXWOOD CT
3800 SJS 95121 855-C4
REY ST
- SF 94134 687-J2
REYES DR
4500 UNC 94587 731-J6
REYMOUTH DR
35400 NWK 94560 752-D4
REYNA PL
- MLPK 94025 790-F5
REYNARD LN
100 VAL 94591 530-E1
REYNAUD DR
14800 SCIC 95127 835-B1
REYNELLA CT
1100 SUNV 94087 832-D3
REYNOLDS CIR
400 SJS 95112 833-J1
REYNOLDS COM
37000 FRMT 94536 752-H2
REYNOLDS CT
- MRGA 94556 631-D6
- HIL 94010 728-D7
3000 FRMT 94536 752-H2
REYNOLDS DR
36500 FRMT 94536 752-H2
REYNOLDS PL
5700 CNCD 94521 593-G7
REYNOLDS RD
19200 SCIC 95030 894-A4
20300 SCIC 95030 893-J6
REYNOLDS ST
- DALY 94014 687-G3
500 SLN 94577 690-G1
RHAPSODY WY
4400 SJS 95111 855-A7
RHEA CT
- CCCo 94565 573-F2
100 VAL 94589 509-J6
RHEA WY
500 LVMR 94550 715-E4
RHEEM AV
2300 RCH 94801 588-G4
2800 RCH 94804 588-H4
3400 RCH 94804 589-A4
3600 SPAB 94805 589-A4
RHEEM BLVD
- ORIN 94563 631-B2
100 MRGA 94556 631-F4
RHEEM CT
1800 PLE 94588 694-E7
RHEEM DR
1900 PLE 94588 694-E7
RHEEM TR
- LFYT 94549 631-C1
- MRGA 94556 631-C1
RHINE CT
- CLAY 94517 593-G7
RHINE LN
1400 SJS 95118 874-B5
RHINE ST
- SF 94112 687-D2
200 DALY 94014 687-D2
RHINE WY
1000 PLE 94566 714-H4
RHINECASTLE WY
1100 SJS 95120 874-D6
RHINECLIFF WY
1400 SJS 95126 853-H4
RHINESTONE TER
- MrnC 94903 546-E5
RHINETTE AV
1100 BURL 94010 728-E5
RHODA AV
3400 OAK 94602 650-E5
8200 DBLN 94568 693-F2
RHODA CT
11900 DBLN 94568 693-F2
RHODA DR
3700 SJS 95117 853-B3
13200 LAH 94022 811-A6
RHODA PL
8500 DBLN 94568 693-F2
RHODA WY
1100 CNCD 94518 592-J4
RHODE ISLAND CT
1400 CNCD 94521 593-F6
RHODE ISLAND ST
- SF 94103 668-A2
400 SF 94107 668-A3
RHODES CT
100 SJS 95126 833-J7
900 PLHL 94523 592-C3
RHODES DR
500 PA 94303 791-C4
RHODESIA WY
1500 SJS 95126 853-H4
RHODODENDRON CT
100 VAL 94591 530-F6
1900 LVMR 94550 696-A3
RHODODENDRON DR
1300 LVMR 94550 696-A4
RHONDA CT
100 VAL 94589 509-J6
RHONDA DR
4800 SJS 95129 852-J4
RHONDA LN
- LVMR 94550 696-B7
RHONDA WY
200 MrnC 94941 606-E5
RHONE CT
400 MTVW 94043 811-G3
RHONE DR
- LVMR 94550 715-H4
RHUS ST
1200 SMTO 94402 748-J3
RHUS RIDGE RD
11800 LAH 94022 831-B3
12000 SCIC 94022 831-B3
RIA DR
16300 AlaC 94578 691-F5

RIALTO CT
400 MTVW 94043 811-G2
4100 PIT 94565 574-E6
RIALTO DR
- CLAY 94517 613-J2
RIALTO WY
- PLE 94588 694-C6
RIATA CT
39800 FRMT 94538 753-B6
RIBBON DR
4000 SJS 95130 853-B4
RIBBON ST
1300 FCTY 94404 749-H2
RIBCHESTER CT
5700 SJS 95123 874-J4
RIBEIRO RD
- VAL 94592 529-G7
- VAL 94592 549-G1
RIBERA CT
35500 FRMT 94536 752-E2
RIBERA ST
4200 FRMT 94536 752-E2
RIBIER CT
1100 SUNV 94087 832-D3
RIBISI CIR
1000 SJS 95131 814-E7
RIBISI WY
1800 SJS 95131 814-D7
RICARDO AV
100 PDMT 94611 650-A1
18300 AlaC 94541 711-E1
RICARDO CT
7700 ELCR 94530 609-E3
RICARDO DR
2000 CNCD 94519 592-G1
RICARDO LN
- MrnC 94941 606-H4
RICARDO RD
100 MrnC 94941 606-H5
RICA VISTA
- NVTO 94947 525-J3
RICA VISTA WY
15600 SCIC 95127 815-B7
RICE CT
5000 SJS 95111 875-A2
20600 SAR 95070 852-D7
RICE DR
- SRFL 94901 586-G2
4900 SJS 95111 875-A2
RICE LN
- LKSP 94939 586-F6
- MrnC 94941 606-H5
RICE ST
- DALY 94014 687-D2
- SF 94112 687-D2
1100 VAL 94590 530-B5
4400 LVMR 94550 716-A1
RICE WY
- WLCK 94595 612-C7
- WLCK 94595 632-C1
5000 SJS 95111 875-A2
RICH AV
900 MTVW 94022 811-G5
900 MTVW 94040 811-G5
7000 NWK 94560 752-E7
RICH PL
- MTVW 94022 811-G5
- MTVW 94040 811-G5
RICH ST
- LKSP 94904 586-H5
400 OAK 94609 629-H7
RICH ACRES CT
- ORIN 94563 610-E6
RICH ACRES RD
- ORIN 94563 610-E6
RICHARD AV
1400 SCL 95050 833-D2
2600 CNCD 94520 572-E7
2800 CNCD 94520 592-E1
RICHARD CIR
- CCCo 94565 573-F2
RICHARD CT
- ORIN 94563 631-A4
300 DNVL 94526 653-C2
2800 CNCD 94520 572-E7
RICHARD LN
100 CCCo 94595 612-A7
800 DNVL 94526 653-B1
RICHARD PL
4100 PIT 94565 574-F6
RICHARD HENREY
DANA PL
- SF 94133 647-J3
RICHARDS AV
1400 SJS 95125 853-J4
RICHARDS CIR
- SF 94124 668-C6
RICHARDS RD
5000 OAK 94613 650-G7
RICHARDSON AV
1100 LALT 94024 831-H4
RICHARDSON AV
U.S.-101
- SF 94123 647-E3
- SF 94129 647-E3
RICHARDSON CT
300 MrnC 94965 606-F7
800 PA 94303 791-D7
1600 CNCD 94519 592-H2
RICHARDSON DR
- VAL 94589 530-A1
100 MrnC 94941 606-H4
3400 SJS 95127 814-J6
41500 FRMT 94538 753-E7
41500 FRMT 94538 773-E1
RICHARDSON RD
- CCCo 94707 609-F4
RICHARDSON ST
100 MRTZ 94553 571-D3
200 SAUS 94965 627-B4
RICHARDSON WY
- PDMT 94611 650-C1
300 MrnC 94965 606-F7
RICHARDS ROAD TR
- SMCo 94062 789-B4
RICHDALE AV
400 SJS 95111 854-J6
RICHELIEU CT
300 LALT 94022 811-E5
13700 SAR 95070 872-G1
RICHELLE RD
- LFYT 94549 611-H7

RICHEY DR
15200 SCIC 95124 873-E4
RICHFIELD DR
- SJS 95129 853-A1
RICHGROVE CT
2800 SJS 95148 835-E7
RICHIE DR
- PLHL 94523 592-C6
RICHIE LN
- NVTO 94947 525-H4
RICHLAND AV
- SF 94110 667-H6
2200 SJS 95125 854-C7
RICHLAND CT
- SCAR 94070 769-H4
RICHLAND DR
2200 SJS 95125 854-B6
RICHLEE DR
300 CMBL 95008 853-G5
RICHMOND AV
300 SJS 95128 853-H2
300 SCIC 95128 853-H2
2800 OAK 94611 649-H2
4300 FRMT 94536 752-J5
6600 CCCo 94805 589-C6
E RICHMOND AV
- RCH 94801 608-D1
W RICHMOND AV
100 RCH 94801 588-C7
400 RCH 94801 608-D1
RICHMOND BLVD
3000 OAK 94611 649-H2
RICHMOND CT
1700 CCCo 94805 589-C6
RICHMOND DR
200 MLBR 94030 728-A3
400 MLBR 94030 727-J4
RICHMOND LN
- RCH 94801 588-B4
RICHMOND PKWY
1200 RCH 94801 588-F1
1500 CCCo 94801 588-E4
3000 RCH 94806 568-H7
3100 RCH 94806 569-A6
3500 CCCo 94806 569-A6
3600 PIN 94803 569-A6
RICHMOND RD
- OAK 94605 651-B7
- OAK 94619 651-B7
- SANS 94960 566-C1
200 HIL 94010 748-G2
RICHMOND ST
400 ELCR 94530 609-C1
RICHMOND-SAN
RAFAEL BRDG I-580
- MrnC - 587-C5
- RCH - 588-A6
- RCH - 587-H6
- SRFL - 587-C5
RICHTER CT
1200 MPS 95035 814-C1
RICHWOOD CT
19400 CPTO 95014 852-G1
RICHWOOD DR
10100 CPTO 95014 852-F1
RICK CT
- MRGA 94556 651-D1
RICK WY
25300 AlaC 94541 712-C2
RICKARD ST
- SF 94134 668-A6
RICKENBACKER CIR
- LVMR 94550 695-C6
RICKENBACKER PL
- LVMR 94550 695-D6
RICKENBACKER ST
1100 SJS 95128 853-F3
RICKOVER LN
1100 FCTY 94404 749-G5
RICKS AV
3100 MRTZ 94553 571-E5
RICKY CT
700 CMBL 95008 853-C6
RICKY DR
700 CMBL 95008 853-C6
RICO COM
37200 FRMT 94536 752-J2
RICO WY
- SF 94123 647-F3
RIDDELL LN
200 ALA 94502 670-A5
RIDDER PARK DR
700 SJS 95131 834-A1
700 SJS 95131 814-A6
RIDDLE RD
3100 SJS 95117 853-D2
RIDER CT
- CCCo 94595 612-B7
26000 HAY 94544 712-A5
RIDER LN
- MLV 94941 606-D2
RIDER TR
- SMCo 94062 809-C6
RIDGE AV
- MrnC 94965 606-B4
- SRFL 94901 566-H7
200 SolC 94591 530-E7
400 SolC 94591 550-E1
RIDGE CIR
- BEN 94510 551-A4
RIDGE CT
- CMAD 94925 606-H2
- WDSD 94062 789-G5
800 SSF 94080 707-G1
1200 SF 94134 687-H2
2900 SCL 95051 833-A6
6800 LVMR 94550 696-E2
S RIDGE CT
200 CCCo 94506 654-B3
RIDGE DR
800 CNCD 94518 592-G3
4200 PIT 94565 574-D6
S RIDGE DR
3300 RCH 94806 568-J7
3300 RCH 94806 588-J1
3300 RCH 94806 589-A1
RIDGE LN
- MrnC 94965 606-B4
- ORIN 94563 610-F4
- SF 94112 687-E1
- SPAB 94806 589-A3

RIDGE PL
- PLHL 94523 591-J4
RIDGE RD
- SANS 94960 566-B5
- SAUS 94965 627-A4
- MrnC 94965 627-A4
100 CCCo 94526 633-B6
300 NVTO 94947 526-A5
300 SCAR 94070 769-G5
300 NVTO 94947 525-J5
400 TBRN 94920 607-E7
500 MrnC 94920 607-E7
700 SCL 95051 833-A6
1500 BLMT 94002 749-D7
2400 BERK 94709 629-H1
2400 SPAB 94806 588-J3
2600 SPAB 94806 589-A3
3300 LFYT 94549 611-G6
RIDGE TER
- FRMT 94539 753-E2
RIDGE TR
- CCCo - 595-A5
- CCCo - 594-J5
- CCCo - 632-C7
- CCCo - 652-C1
RIDGE WY
- CMAD 94925 586-F7
2200 CCCo 94553 571-F3
2200 MRTZ 94553 571-F3
RIDGEBROOK WY
4100 SJS 95111 855-A7
RIDGECLIFF CT
2300 SJS 95131 814-D5
RIDGE CREEK CT
11700 CPTO 95014 852-C4
RIDGECREEK LN
24100 AlaC 94541 712-B1
RIDGECREST AV
16000 MSER 95030 872-H6
RIDGECREST BLVD
100 MrnC 94965 586-A7
RIDGE CREST CT
3200 AlaC 94541 692-D7
RIDGECREST CT
2200 CCCo 94549 611-H1
2200 PIT 94565 574-A4
RIDGECREST RD
- MrnC 94904 586-C5
1300 PIN 94564 569-D5
RIDGECREST TER
- SMTO 94402 748-H7
RIDGECREST WY
2200 PIT 94565 574-A4
2200 PIT 94565 573-J4
RIDGEFARM DR
400 SJS 95123 874-J5
RIDGEFIELD AV
- DALY 94015 687-A7
RIDGEGATE CT
5000 ANT 94509 595-E4
RIDGEGATE DR
2900 SJS 95133 814-G7
RIDGE GATE RD
400 ORIN 94563 610-G7
RIDGEGLEN WY
2300 SJS 95133 834-G1
RIDGELAND CIR
1800 DNVL 94526 653-B7
RIDGELAND DR
- DNVL 94526 653-B6
RIDGELEY DR
1000 CMBL 95008 853-G5
1400 SCIC 95125 853-G5
RIDGELINE CT
1200 SJS 95127 835-C3
RIDGELINE DR
- ANT 94509 595-J1
RIDGEMONT CT
4200 OAK 94619 650-J6
RIDGEMONT DR
1000 MPS 95035 814-E1
1900 SJS 95148 835-B5
2900 SJS 95127 835-B5
3300 MTVW 94040 831-J2
6000 OAK 94619 650-J7
RIDGEMONT PL
1100 CNCD 94521 593-F7
RIDGEMOOR RD
8900 OAK 94605 671-C2
RIDGE OAK CT
1200 SJS 95120 874-C7
RIDGE PARK CT
900 CNCD 94518 592-H4
RIDGE PARK DR
900 CNCD 94518 592-H3
RIDGE PARK LN
- CNCD 94518 592-G3
RIDGEPOINTE CT
2100 CCCo 94596 612-E7
RIDGEPONTE CT
- SRMN 94583 673-J6
RIDGEROCK DR
100 ANT 94509 595-D1
RIDGESTONE CT
- CCCo - 613-B3
RIDGESTONE RD
1300 LVMR 94550 696-D3
RIDGESTONE WY
1400 LVMR 94550 696-D3
RIDGETOP DR
14800 SCIC 95127 814-J6
14800 SJS 95127 814-J6
RIDGETREE WY
1600 SJS 95131 814-D4
RIDGEVALE LN
200 PLHL 94523 592-A6
RIDGEVALE RD
5300 PLE 94566 714-C2
RIDGEVALE WY
5200 PLE 94566 714-C2
RIDGEVIEW AV
- SCIC 95127 815-B7
RIDGEVIEW CIR
5300 CCCo 94803 589-F3
RIDGE VIEW CT
1200 NVTO 94947 526-C7
RIDGEVIEW CT
- MrnC 94965 606-G7
- SRMN 94583 673-E2
400 PLHL 94523 591-J2
800 SSF 94080 707-H1
10400 CPTO 95014 832-G7

RIDGEVIEW CT
10700 SCIC 95127 815-B7
RIDGE VIEW DR
- NVTO 94949 546-G5
RIDGEVIEW DR
- ATN 94027 790-A5
300 PLHL 94523 591-J2
800 MrnC 94965 606-D5
4800 ANT 94509 595-J3
RIDGE VIEW HTS
1200 NVTO 94947 526-C7
RIDGEVIEW LN
2700 WLCK 94598 612-H4
RIDGEVIEW PL
1000 PLHL 94523 591-J2
3300 AlaC 94541 712-D2
RIDGEVIEW TER
- SCIC 95127 815-B7
600 FRMT 94536 753-C3
RIDGEVIEW WY
10600 SCIC 95127 815-B7
N RIDGE VISTA AV
200 SCIC 95127 814-H7
200 SJS 95127 814-H7
11900 SCIC 95127 834-H1
S RIDGE VISTA AV
300 SCIC 95127 834-J1
300 SJS 95127 834-J1
RIDGEWAY
- LKSP 94939 586-D6
RIDGEWAY AV
100 OAK 94611 629-J7
2600 SBRN 94066 727-F1
RIDGEWAY DR
500 PCFA 94044 707-A7
RIDGEWAY LN
- CMAD 94925 606-C5
- ELCR 94530 609-F2
- LKSP 94939 586-E7
- LKSP 94939 606-C5
RIDGEWAY RD
- HIL 94010 748-G3
100 WDSD 94062 789-H4
RIDGEWOOD AV
- SF 94112 667-E6
200 SF 94127 667-E6
300 MrnC 94941 606-C4
RIDGEWOOD CT
- BLMT 94002 769-C3
- VAL 94591 530-E5
- ANT 94509 595-E2
1300 MRTZ 94553 571-J6
3500 CNCD 94518 592-H4
RIDGEWOOD DR
- SRFL 94901 566-D5
400 MRTZ 94553 571-J6
1000 MLBR 94030 727-H3
1100 CNCD 94518 592-H4
1300 SJS 95118 874-B4
4700 FRMT 94555 752-C3
6300 AlaC 94552 692-F4
6800 OAK 94611 630-F6
RIDGEWOOD LN
- OAK 94611 630-F6
25800 LAH 94022 831-B2
RIDGEWOOD RD
1200 PLE 94566 714-D2
1500 CCCo 94507 632-E4
N RIDGEWOOD RD
- MrnC 94904 586-C4
S RIDGEWOOD RD
- MrnC 94904 586-C4
RIDGEWOOD WY
- OAK 94611 630-F6
3300 RCH 94806 568-J7
RIDGEWOOD FIRE RD
- MrnC 94960 566-C5
- SANS 94960 566-C5
200 SRFL 94903 566-C5
200 MrnC 94901 566-C5
RIDING CT
6000 SJS 95124 873-J7
RIDING CLUB DR
4500 HAY 94542 712-G4
RIDLEY DR
38200 FRMT 94536 753-B2
RIDLEY WY
1200 SJS 95125 853-J4
RIDPATH ST
4600 FRMT 94538 753-B7
RIEDAL PL
10100 CPTO 95014 832-F7
RIEDEL CT
2800 SJS 95135 855-E2
RIEDEL DR
2800 SJS 95135 855-D3
RIEGER AV
1200 HAY 94544 712-A7
1200 HAY 94544 711-J7
RIELLY CT
700 SJS 95123 874-F4
RIESLING CIR
1100 LVMR 94550 715-J2
RIESLING CT
2100 PIT 94565 574-A3
2100 PIT 94565 573-J3
3700 PLE 94566 714-G4
19400 SAR 95070 872-F3
RIESLING DR
900 PLE 94566 714-G4
RIESLING ST
- FRMT 94539 793-J2
RIESLING TER
1200 SUNV 94087 832-C3
RIETZ CT
3400 CNCD 94520 572-F6
RIFFEL CT
2400 AlaC 94546 691-H5
RIFLE LN
4100 OAK 94605 671-A1
RIFLE RANGE RD
- AlaC 94546 672-A3
- AlaC 94546 671-J4
- AlaC 94552 672-A3
- OAK 94605 651-B7
- OAK 94605 671-B1
- PCFA 94044 707-A7
400 PIT 94565 574-B3
1300 ELCR 94530 609-E1
1300 ELCR 94530 589-E7
1400 RCH 94805 589-E7

STREET Block City ZIP Pg-Grid

RIFLE RANGE RD TR
- RCH 94805 589-E7
RIGATTI CIR
5000 PLE 94588 694-C6
RIGEL LN
800 FCTY 94404 749-E3
RIGGS CT
28100 HAY 94542 712-E5
RIGOLETTO DR
1700 SJS 95122 855-A2
RILEA WY
4300 OAK 94605 671-B1
RILEY AV
100 SF 94129 647-D4
RILEY CT
900 CNCD 94520 592-E4
RILEY DR
200 CCCo 94553 572-B7
700 ALB 94804 609-D6
800 ALB 94706 609-D6
RILEY WY
800 RDWC 94061 790-C2
RILEY RIDGE RD
- AlaC 94546 652-A7
- AlaC 94546 651-J7
- AlaC 94546 671-H1
RILMA CT
1000 LALT 94022 811-E4
RIM RD
2600 CCCo 94806 569-A5
RIM TR
- LFYT 94549 611-B7
- LFYT 94549 631-D1
- LFYT 94563 611-B7
- MRGA 94556 631-C2
RIMA CT
- DNVL 94526 653-C1
1000 FRMT 94539 773-H2
RIMCREST CT
- PIT 94565 573-F4
RIMER DR
1100 MRGA 94556 651-E2
RIM RIDGE CT
1900 WLCK 94596 611-H3
RIMROCK DR
1300 SJS 95120 894-D3
3900 ANT 94509 595-E1
RIMROCK RD
- LFYT 94549 631-E1
RIMWOOD DR
5200 SJS 95118 874-B4
RINALDO DR
- VAL 94589 509-J5
100 VAL 94589 510-A5
RINCON AV
100 LVMR 94550 715-F1
200 LVMR 94550 695-F7
400 SUNV 94086 832-D1
3700 CMBL 95008 853-B6
3700 SJS 95008 853-B6
4100 SJS 95130 853-B6
E RINCON AV
- CMBL 95008 853-E6
W RINCON AV
- CMBL 95008 853-D6
RINCON CIR
900 SJS 95131 813-J4
4100 PA 94306 811-C3
RINCON DR
5900 OAK 94611 650-E1
RINCON LN
400 CCCo 94803 589-D1
RINCON RD
- CCCo 94707 609-F3
400 CCCo 94803 589-D1
500 CCCo 94803 569-D7
RINCON ST
100 SF 94107 648-C6
RINCON WY
800 MrnC 94903 566-H2
RINCONADA CIR
- SMCo 94070 768-J3
- BLMT 94002 769-A3
- BLMT 94002 768-J3
RINCONADA CT
400 BEN 94510 551-C5
400 LALT 94022 811-F7
RINCONADA DR
2400 SJS 95125 854-C6
RINCONADA OAKS CT
100 LGTS 95030 872-J3
RINCONDADA AV
100 PA 94301 791-A6
RINEHART DR
2300 SJS 95133 834-G2
RING CT
5700 FRMT 94538 773-B2
RINGOLD ST
- SF 94103 648-A7
RINGROSE CT
1300 SJS 95121 855-B1
RINGWOOD AV
- SMCo 94025 790-H2
- ATN 94027 790-H1
800 MLPK 94025 790-H1
1000 MLPK 94025 770-H7
1400 SJS 95131 814-B4
1800 SCIC 95131 814-B4
RINGWOOD CT
1100 SJS 95131 814-B6
RIO CT
- BURL 94010 728-B5
- SF 94127 667-F5
4000 SJS 95134 813-D2
RIO LN
4300 CCCo 94565 573-D2
RIO BARRANCA CT
2100 SJS 95116 834-G3
RIO BLANCO DR
1600 CNCD 94521 593-C3
RIO BRAVO DR
3400 SJS 95148 835-D6
RIO CHICO DR
100 SJS 95111 854-J7
RIO DE ESMERALDA
3200 SJS 95121 855-A4
RIO DE JOYAS
3200 SJS 95121 855-A4
RIO DEL CT
- DNVL 94526 653-A4
RIO DE LATA
3200 SJS 95121 855-A4
RIO DEL MAR
- AMCN 94589 510-A1
100 AMCN 94589 509-J2
RIO DE LOS MOLINOS AV
100 SUNV 94086 812-C6
RIO DE ORO
3200 SJS 95121 855-B4
RIO DE PERLA
3200 SJS 95121 855-B4
RIO DE PLATA
3200 SJS 95121 855-A4
RIO DE PLOMO
1300 SJS 95121 855-B4
RIO GRANDE CT
200 SRMN 94583 653-G7
1200 ANT 94509 575-B7
RIO GRANDE DR
1400 AMCN 94589 509-J1
2800 ANT 94509 595-B1
3000 ANT 94509 575-B7
5200 SJS 95136 874-J3
RIO GRANDE PL
300 SRMN 94583 653-G7
300 DNVL 94506 653-G7
RIO GUACIMAL CT
2100 SJS 95116 834-G3
RIO HONDO DR
1200 SJS 95120 894-C1
RIOJA CT
40800 FRMT 94539 753-E6
RIO LOBO DR
5200 SJS 95136 875-A3
RIORDAN DR
2100 SJS 95130 853-A7
RIORDAN PL
- MLPK 94025 790-H2
RIO RITA WY
4700 SJS 95129 853-A1
RIO ROBLES
- SJS 95134 813-E3
RIO SERENA AV
- CMBL 95008 853-A5
200 SJS 95130 853-A5
RIO VERDE CT
4900 SJS 95118 874-A3
RIO VERDE DR
4900 SJS 95118 874-A3
RIO VERDE PL
200 MPS 95035 813-J1
RIO VERDE ST
- SF 94134 687-H3
- DALY 94014 687-H3
RIO VISTA
- ORIN 94563 610-G7
100 LGTS 95030 872-J2
RIO VISTA AV
- OAK 94611 649-J1
4800 SJS 95129 853-A1
4800 SJS 95129 852-J1
RIO VISTA DR
900 PCFA 94044 726-J5
RIO VISTA ST
21700 HAY 94541 691-H7
RIPLE ROUGE RD
- PIT 94565 574-A5
- PIT 94565 573-J5
RIPLEY AV
- RCH 94801 588-F6
RIPLEY DR
500 SJS 95133 834-E2
RIPLEY ST
- SF 94110 668-A5
- SF 94110 667-J5
RIPON CT
32700 UNC 94587 732-B7
RIPTIDE CT
300 PIT 94565 574-A3
RISA CT
- ORIN 94563 631-C4
RISA RD
900 LFYT 94549 611-D6
RISDON CT
900 CNCD 94518 592-F6
RISDON DR
2900 UNC 94587 732-A4
RISDON RD
1600 CNCD 94518 592-F6
RISEL AV
- DALY 94014 687-E3
E RISHELL CT
4600 CNCD 94521 593-C3
W RISHELL CT
4600 CNCD 94521 593-C3
RISHELL DR
- OAK 94619 650-H4
1600 CNCD 94521 593-C4
RISING RD
- NVTO 94945 526-A1
100 MrnC 94945 606-F5
RISING DAWN LN
1300 CNCD 94521 593-B5
RISING GLEN RD
1100 PIN 94564 569-E5
RISING HILL CT
4600 OAK 94605 651-A7
RISPIN DR
1000 OAK 94705 630-B3
RITA CT
- AMCN 94589 509-J1
- NVTO 94945 526-D3
2200 SCL 95050 833-D6
RITA DR
4100 CCCo 94553 572-A3
RITA WY
- ORIN 94563 631-A5
RITANNA CT
20600 SAR 95070 852-D5
RITCH ST
200 SF 94107 648-B7
RITCHIE ST
2400 OAK 94605 670-J3
RITTENHOUSE AV
- ATN 94027 790-D1
RITTER ST
- SRFL 94901 586-G1
RITZ CT
3600 SJS 95148 835-F7
RIVAS AV
- SF 94132 687-B1
RIVER DR
- FRMT 94536 753-C1
N RIVER ST
- SJS 95113 834-A6
- SJS 95110 834-A6
RIVERA CT
1100 LVMR 94550 696-D3
RIVERA DR
2800 BURL 94010 728-A6
RIVERA ST
- SANS 94960 566-B6
300 SF 94116 667-B4
700 MPS 95035 794-B4
1200 ELCR 94530 609-D2
2400 SF 94116 666-H4
RIVER ASH CT
- SJS 95136 874-H1
4400 CNCD 94521 593-C5
RIVERBANK AV
1800 AlaC 94546 691-J6
1800 HAY 94546 691-J6
RIVERBANK TER
38800 FRMT 94536 753-C3
RIVER BED CT
2200 SCL 95054 813-C5
RIVERBEND TER
3800 FRMT 94555 732-C7
RIVER BIRCH CT
1600 SJS 95131 834-D1
RIVER BIRCH DR
1600 SJS 95131 834-D1
RIVERBORO PL
- SJS 95123 874-D3
RIVERCREEK DR
200 FRMT 94536 732-J7
RIVERCREST CT
10300 CPTO 95014 832-A7
RIVERCREST LN
300 HAY 94544 732-E2
RIVERDALE CT
5200 PLE 94588 693-J6
13600 SAR 95070 872-H1
RIVERDALE DR
13600 SAR 95070 872-H1
RIVERDALE ST
14900 SLN 94578 691-C5
RIVER FALLS DR
700 SJS 95111 855-A7
RIVERHILL DR
- BEN 94510 551-C4
RIVERMONT CT
2600 SJS 95116 834-J4
RIVERMOUTH LN
100 VAL 94591 550-E2
RIVER OAK WY
600 HAY 94544 712-D7
RIVER OAKS CIR
300 SJS 95134 813-G4
RIVER OAKS PKWY
100 SJS 95134 813-F4
RIVER OAKS PL
- SJS 95134 813-F4
RIVER OAKS RD
- SRFL 94901 566-D6
RIVER PARK DR
700 SJS 95111 855-A7
RIVER PINES WY
100 VAL 94589 509-J5
RIVER RANCH CIR
13800 SAR 95070 872-E1
RIVER ROCK CT
400 SJS 95136 854-F7
RIVER ROCK LN
1000 DNVL 94526 653-A2
RIVERRUN DR
2700 SCIC 95127 834-H2
2700 SJS 95127 834-H2
RIVERS ST
1000 SPAB 94806 588-H1
RIVERSIDE AV
300 FRMT 94536 753-B1
5100 SPAB 94806 589-A4
RIVERSIDE CT
- CCCo 94565 573-E1
400 SCL 95134 813-F4
RIVERSIDE DR
- SBRN 94066 707-D6
100 CCCo 94565 573-D1
600 LALT 94024 831-F2
600 SJS 95125 854-A2
22300 CPTO 95014 852-A2
RIVERSIDE PL
- CCCo 94565 573-E2
W RIVERSIDE WY
1000 SJS 95129 852-E2
RIVERTON DR
- SF 94132 667-A6
700 MLBR 94030 727-J4
900 SCAR 94070 769-G2
RIVERTON PL
200 SRMN 94583 673-G7
RIVER TRAIL CT
4800 SJS 95136 874-H3
RIVERVIEW CT
3700 PIT 94565 574-C5
3800 CNCD 94520 572-G4
RIVER VIEW DR
300 SJS 95111 875-A1
600 SJS 95111 855-B7
RIVERVIEW DR
- PIT 94565 574-C5
100 VAL 94589 510-B7
2200 CNCD 94520 572-G4
RIVERVIEW PL
3800 CNCD 94520 572-G4
RIVERVIEW TER
- BEN 94510 551-B4
RIVER VISTA LN
- NVTO 94945 526-H1
RIVERWAY DR
100 PIT 94565 574-E1
RIVERWAY LN
- SolC 94589 529-F2
- VAL 94592 529-F2
RIVERWOOD CIR
200 MRTZ 94553 571-H6
RIVIERA AV
1500 WLCK 94596 612-B4
RIVIERA CIR
- LKSP 94939 586-F5
- RDWC 94065 749-J7
RIVIERA CT
- OAK 94605 671-D3
100 SBRN 94066 707-D5
RIVIERA CT
900 SJS 95129 852-J2
7900 PLE 94588 714-B5
RIVIERA DR
- SRFL 94901 567-D6
100 LGTS 95030 873-B6
200 UNC 94587 732-J5
600 LALT 94024 811-G7
36600 FRMT 94536 753-A1
RIVIERA PL
- SRFL 94901 567-D5
500 SRMN 94583 673-H6
RIVIERA RD
10300 CPTO 95014 852-A1
RIVIERA WY
3000 SRMN 94583 673-F6
RIVIERA MANOR RD
- SRFL 94901 567-E5
RIVOIR DR
4000 SJS 95118 874-A2
RIVOLI ST
- SF 94117 667-E2
- SF 94117 667-E2
RIXFORD LN
600 LALT 94024 831-F2
RIZAL CT
6400 SJS 95119 875-C7
RIZAL DR
100 HIL 94010 748-F5
RIZAL ST
- SF 94107 648-B6
RIZZO AV
21300 AlaC 94546 691-J6
ROACH ST
- SF 94133 647-J4
ROAD 20
900 SPAB 94806 588-G2
ROAD 24
4500 CCCo 94803 569-D7
4500 CCCo 94803 589-C1
4500 RCH 94803 569-D7
4500 RCH 94803 589-C1
ROAD A
- ALA 94502 670-A7
- ALA 94502 690-A1
9500 SJS 95138 875-E2
ROAD B
- ALA 94502 670-B7
- ALA 94502 690-B1
ROAD G
- SJS 95138 875-F3
ROADING DR
400 SJS 95123 874-J5
ROADRUNNER RD
- FRMT 94539 773-J5
ROADRUNNER TER
1300 SUNV 94087 832-H4
ROAN CT
- WLCK 94596 632-G2
2100 LVMR 94550 696-A2
ROAN DR
100 DNVL 94526 633-C7
ROAN LN
2200 WLCK 94596 632-F2
ROAN PL
- WDSD 94062 789-D6
ROAN ST
300 SJS 95123 874-J5
ROANOKE
4000 ALA 94501 649-F6
ROANOKE DR
400 MRTZ 94553 591-H4
ROANOKE RD
6300 OAK 94618 630-A4
6300 BERK 94705 630-A4
ROANOKE ST
- SF 94131 667-G6
28600 HAY 94544 712-B7
ROANOKE WY
38800 FRMT 94536 752-J6
ROANWOOD CT
- ANT 94509 575-F7
ROANWOOD WY
5700 CNCD 94521 593-G7
ROATAN CT
- SRMN 94583 673-D3
ROBALO CT
1100 SJS 95132 814-G5
ROBB DR
4500 SJS 95118 874-B2
ROBB RD
800 PA 94306 811-B5
800 LAH 94022 811-B5
2000 WLCK 94596 632-G1
ROBBIA CT
1200 SUNV 94087 832-F4
ROBBIA DR
1000 SUNV 94087 832-F3
ROBBIE KEITH LN
1600 WLCK 94596 612-C1
ROBBINS PL
- CCCo 94507 632-H5
ROBBLEE AV
- SF 94124 668-B6
ROBERSON LN
400 SJS 95112 833-J1
ROBERT AV
- BLMT 94002 768-J1
400 SCL 95050 833-E2
ROBERT CT
- SRFL 94901 566-E7
5700 CCCo 94803 589-G4
ROBERT PL
- MLBR 94030 728-A3
ROBERT RD
- ORIN 94563 631-A1
- LFYT 94563 611-B7
- ORIN 94563 611-B7
ROBERT ST
200 ANT 94509 575-D7
ROBERT WY
300 LVMR 94550 715-D1
4500 RCH 94803 589-E1
ROBERTA AV
- PLHL 94523 592-B7
ROBERTA CT
2900 SJS 95121 854-J4
ROBERTA DR
- WDSD 94062 809-G1
1400 SMTO 94403 749-D3
8500 ELCR 94530 609-F2
ROBERT DAVEY JR DR
- ALA 94502 669-J5
- ALA 94502 670-A5
ROBERT DOLLAR SCENIC DR
- SRFL 94901 566-F6
ROBERT FOWLER WY
2400 SJS 95148 835-A6
ROBERT H MILLER DR
2800 RCH 94806 588-J1
2800 RCH 94806 589-A1
2800 RCH 94806 569-A7
ROBERT KIRK LN
- SF 94108 648-A5
ROBERTO ST
17000 AlaC 94546 691-G5
ROBERT PEARY LN
800 FCTY 94404 749-F4
ROBERTS AV
- SRFL 94901 586-F2
5400 OAK 94619 670-G1
5500 OAK 94605 670-G1
41000 FRMT 94538 773-E1
42100 FRMT 94538 753-D7
ROBERTS CT
- DNVL 94526 652-G1
- MRGA 94556 651-D1
- SJS 95110 854-D2
800 MRTZ 94553 571-G7
800 MRTZ 94553 591-G1
1800 CCCo 94521 593-E3
ROBERTS DR
- MLPK 94025 790-E4
ROBERTS LN
3400 CNCD 94519 592-J1
ROBERTS RD
- LGTS 95030 873-A6
200 PCFA 94044 726-H3
16200 LGTS 95032 873-B6
ROBERTS ST
- CCCo 94565 573-H2
1100 SJS 95122 834-F7
1100 SJS 95122 854-F1
34800 UNC 94587 732-G7
ROBERTS WY
- HIL 94010 748-E3
ROBERTSON AV
5600 NWK 94560 752-F7
6500 NWK 94560 772-F1
ROBERTSON RD
2400 SCL 95051 833-B2
3600 LFYT 94549 611-E7
ROBERTSON TER
- MLV 94941 606-E4
ROBERTSON WY
500 RDWC 94062 789-E2
500 SMCo 94062 789-E2
ROBERTSON PARK RD
- AlaC 94550 715-J3
- LVMR 94550 716-A3
- LVMR 94550 715-H2
ROBERTSVILLE CT
500 SJS 95118 874-G3
ROBEY DR
16800 AlaC 94578 691-G5
17000 AlaC 94546 691-G5
ROBIE LN
16200 SCIC 95032 873-C7
16200 LGTS 95032 873-C7
ROBIN COM
- LVMR 94550 696-A6
ROBIN CT
100 HER 94547 569-H5
100 VAL 94591 530-E3
700 EPA 94303 791-B1
1100 SUNV 94087 832-B3
2500 UNC 94587 732-D6
4700 FRMT 94538 773-C1
6200 PLE 94588 694-A7
ROBIN DR
300 CMAD 94925 607-A1
500 SCL 95050 833-C5
1800 SJS 95124 873-H1
ROBIN LN
800 CMBL 95008 853-D7
800 CMBL 95008 873-D1
800 MLBR 94030 727-H3
1800 CNCD 94520 592-E4
3700 AlaC 94546 692-B5
ROBIN RD
- HIL 94010 748-E2
300 MrnC 94965 606-F7
ROBIN ST
15000 AlaC 94578 691-D3
40300 FRMT 94538 773-C1
40500 FRMT 94538 753-C7
ROBIN WY
- SCAR 94070 769-G6
100 LGTS 95032 873-C7
200 MLPK 94025 790-J3
900 SUNV 94087 832-B2
19800 SAR 95070 872-F4
ROBIN ANN DR
15300 MSER 95030 873-A5
ROBINDELL WY
7700 CPTO 95014 852-C3
ROBIN HOOD CT
1000 LALT 94024 831-H4
ROBIN HOOD DR
2000 LALT 94024 831-H4
5700 CNCD 94521 593-G7
ROBINHOOD DR
- SF 94127 667-D5
- SRFL 94901 567-B6
ROBINHOOD LN
- NVTO 94945 526-D3
ROBINHOOD WY
6200 OAK 94611 630-D6
ROBIN RIDGE CT
1900 WLCK 94596 611-H3
ROBINSDALE RD
- MRTZ 94553 571-H4
ROBINSON AV
- PIT 94565 574-C4
2400 SCL 95051 833-B3
ROBINSON DR
- SF 94112 687-G2
- DALY 94014 687-G2
3100 OAK 94602 650-G3
ROBINSON ST
- SF 94124 668-E7
100 MRTZ 94553 571-D4
ROBIN WHIPPLE WY
1600 BLMT 94002 769-D1
ROBINWOOD LN
200 HIL 94010 748-E3
ROBISON DR
3100 OAK 94705 630-B3
ROBLAR AV
100 HIL 94010 748-H1
300 MLBR 94030 728-C3
ROBLAR DR
100 NVTO 94949 546-F2
ROBLAR LN
2500 SCL 95051 833-B2
ROBLE AV
200 RDWC 94061 790-B1
400 PIN 94564 569-D4
600 MLPK 94025 790-F4
ROBLE CT
- BERK 94705 630-B4
- SANS 94960 566-A5
19400 SAR 95070 852-F7
ROBLE DR
500 SCIC 94305 790-G7
800 SUNV 94086 832-H3
ROBLE RD
- SRFL 94901 586-E1
- OAK 94618 630-B4
- BERK 94705 630-B4
100 CCCo 94596 612-D1
1200 MLBR 94030 728-A5
ROBLE RDGE
900 PA 94306 811-B2
ROBLE ALTO
27900 LAH 94022 810-H7
ROBLE ALTO CT
13600 LAH 94022 810-H6
ROBLE BLANCO
27900 LAH 94022 810-H7
ROBLEDA CT
26700 LAH 94022 811-C7
ROBLEDA DR
- ATN 94027 790-C2
ROBLEDA RD
12000 LAH 94022 831-C1
13000 LAH 94022 811-C7
ROBLEDO DR
10900 OAK 94603 670-H7
ROBLE LADERA RD
12500 LAH 94022 811-A7
ROBLES CT
1100 LFYT 94549 611-[illegible]
ROBLES DR
- WDSD 94062 809-G1
100 VAL 94591 530-E7
300 VAL 94591 550-F1
2100 ANT 94509 595-A1
2400 ANT 94509 594-J1
ROBLES DEL ORO
15600 SCIC 95030 872-H5
ROBLE VENENO LN
12600 LAH 94022 811-B7
ROBLEY TER
- OAK 94611 649-J1
ROBNICK CT
1300 CMBL 95008 873-A1
ROBSCOTT AV
17800 AlaC 94541 711-E1
ROBSHEAL DR
1300 SJS 95125 854-A5
1300 SJS 95125 853-J5
ROBWAY AV
1100 CMBL 95008 853-G5
ROBYN DR
1200 DNVL 94526 653-C4
ROCA CT
- NVTO 94947 525-G4
ROCA DR
35300 FRMT 94536 752-E3
ROCA ST
2400 ANT 94509 575-H6
ROCCA AV
500 SSF 94080 707-H2
ROCCA CT
- SSF 94080 707-J2
3500 PLE 94588 694-A6
ROCHDALE WY
- BERK 94708 609-H4
ROCHE DR
1500 PLHL 94523 592-B4
ROCHELLE AV
- PIT 94565 574-F6
6500 NWK 94560 752-C6
28200 HAY 94544 712-B7
ROCHELLE DR
1800 SJS 95124 873-H1
4600 UNC 94587 731-J7
ROCHESTER AV
- SJS 95123 875-B4
- SJS 95193 875-B4
ROCHESTER CT
1000 SUNV 94087 832-B3
29000 HAY 94544 732-B2
ROCHESTER ST
- SMTO 94401 729-B6
ROCHI CT
1400 AlaC 94578 691-E5
ROCHIN CT
15900 LGTS 95032 873-E5
ROCHIN TER
15900 LGTS 95032 873-D6
15900 SCIC 95032 873-D6
ROCK AL
- SF 94127 667-D5
ROCK AV
400 FRMT 94536 732-J7
700 FRMT 94536 752-J1
900 SJS 95131 814-A5
ROCK CT
900 ANT 94509 595-F2
ROCK ISL
600 ALA 94501 669-H2
ROCK LN
- BERK 94708 609-H5
ROCK RD
- ROSS 94957 586-B3
- MrnC 94904 586-B3
ROCK ST
1600 MTVW 94043 811-G2
ROCKAWAY AV
- SF 94127 667-D5
ROCKAWAY LN
22300 HAY 94541 692-A7
ROCKAWAY BEACH AV
100 PCFA 94044 726-J2
700 PCFA 94044 727-A3
ROCK CANYON CIR
900 SJS 95127 814-J5
ROCK CREEK CT
- SMCo 94062 789-F2
600 WLCK 94598 612-J3
5400 CNCD 94521 593-E7
ROCKCREEK CT
4100 CCCo 94506 654-C5
ROCKCREEK DR
4100 CCCo 94506 654-C5
ROCK CREEK PL
700 PLHL 94523 592-D4
ROCK CREEK WY
300 PLHL 94523 592-D4
1100 CNCD 94521 593-E7
ROCKDALE DR
500 SF 94127 667-E5
500 SF 94127 667-E5
900 SJS 95129 853-A3
ROCKEFELLER DR
900 SUNV 94087 832-B3
ROCKEN LN
700 NVTO 94947 525-H3
ROCKETT DR
3000 FRMT 94538 753-D6
ROCKFORD AV
- DALY 94015 707-A1
- DALY 94015 706-J1
ROCKFORD DR
3800 ANT 94509 595-F1
ROCKFORD PL
8000 PLE 94566 734-D1
8000 PLE 94586 734-D1
ROCKFORD RD
21900 HAY 94541 691-J7
ROCK HARBOR LN
- FCTY 94404 749-E6
ROCKHAVEN DR
1200 SJS 95120 894-E3
ROCK HILL DR
- TBRN 94920 607-C5
ROCKHURST CT
2000 SCL 95051 832-J2
ROCKHURST DR
17600 AlaC 94546 692-B2
ROCKINGHAM CT
- OAK 94605 651-A7
ROCKINGHAM DR
3900 PLE 94588 694-E6
ROCKING HORSE CT
600 SJS 95123 874-J7
ROCK ISLAND CIR
600 DNVL 94526 653-C5
ROCK ISLAND DR
4300 ANT 94509 595-F2
ROCKLAND ST
- SF 94109 647-H4
ROCKLEDGE LN
- WLCK 94595 632-A2
ROCKLIN CT
1400 SJS 95131 814-C7
ROCKLIN DR
4800 UNC 94587 752-A1
ROCKLYN CT
- CMAD 94925 586-F7
ROCKNE CT
900 CNCD 94518 592-G6
ROCKNE DR
2000 CNCD 94518 592-G6
ROCK OAK CT
100 WLCK 94598 612-J1
ROCK OAK RD
200 WLCK 94598 612-J1
300 WLCK 94598 592-J7
ROCK PASS PL
2100 MRTZ 94553 572-B7
ROCKPOINT LN
- LALT 94024 831-E2
- SCIC 94024 831-E2
ROCKPORT AV
3200 SJS 95132 814-G5
ROCKPORT CT
- RCH 94804 608-E3
- DNVL 94526 653-A1
5300 NWK 94560 752-E4
ROCKPORT CV
- SRFL 94901 587-A2
ROCKPORT DR
500 SUNV 94087 832-D3
ROCKPORT WY
- HAY 94544 732-B1
200 NVTO 94947 526-E6
ROCKRIDGE AV
- DALY 94015 687-A6
ROCKRIDGE BLVD N
6000 OAK 94618 630-A5
ROCKRIDGE BLVD S
6000 OAK 94618 630-A5
ROCK RIDGE CT
- DNVL 94526 653-E3
1000 PIT 94565 573-J3
ROCKRIDGE DR
- SF 94116 667-C4
2800 PLHL 94523 591-J3
ROCKRIDGE PL
6100 OAK 94618 630-A5
ROCKRIDGE RD
- HIL 94010 748-G2
100 SCAR 94070 769-F4
ROCK RIDGE WY
900 PIT 94565 573-J3
ROCKRIDGE WY
2400 SCL 95051 833-B1
ROCK RIVER CT
2900 SJS 95111 854-H4
ROCK RIVER DR
100 VAL 94589 510-B4
ROCKROSE AV
1000 SUNV 94086 832-G3
ROCKROSE CT
700 HAY 94544 712-A7
38500 NWK 94560 772-G1
ROCKROSE DR
6000 NWK 94560 772-G1
ROCK ROSE LN
600 SRMN 94583 653-J7
ROCKROSE ST
- LVMR 94550 715-D1

ROCKROSE WY 1998 BAY AREA STREET INDEX ROSS PARK CT 985

STREET Block City ZIP Pg-Grid

ROCKROSE WY
- NVTO 94945 526-B2
ROCKSPRAY ST
37600 NWK 94560 752-G6
ROCK SPRING CT
11500 CPTO 95014 852-A4
ROCKSPRING DR
1700 SJS 95112 854-F2
ROCKSPRING PL
1600 WLCK 94596 612-G7
1800 WLCK 94598 612-G7
ROCKSPRING WY
900 ANT 94509 595-D4
ROCK SPRINGS DR
1900 HAY 94545 711-F5
ROCKTON AV
6900 SJS 95119 875-F6
ROCKTON PL
- SJS 95119 875-F6
ROCKTREE CT
1700 SJS 95131 814-D4
ROCKVIEW CT
6800 SJS 95120 894-C3
ROCKVIEW DR
800 WLCK 94595 632-B2
ROCKWALL WY
5000 ANT 94509 595-E4
ROCKWAY AV
7300 ELCR 94530 609-E4
ROCKWAY CT
900 PLE 94566 714-F3
ROCKWAY DR
- SCIC 95127 835-A2
ROCKWELL ST
6000 OAK 94618 629-J4
ROCKWOOD CT
- SF 94127 667-D5
- SMTO 94403 748-J6
- VAL 94591 530-E5
ROCKWOOD DR
100 SSF 94080 707-G5
700 SJS 95129 853-A2
37400 FRMT 94536 752-G4
ROCKWOOD PL
1700 CNCD 94521 593-C2
ROCK WREN LN
- BSBN 94005 687-J5
ROCKY RD
800 ANT 94509 575-C6
4900 RCH 94803 589-G1
ROCKY WY
500 WDSD 94062 789-E2
ROCKY CREEK CT
3600 SJS 95148 835-D4
ROCKY CREEK WY
14500 SAR 95070 872-D3
ROCKY CREST DR
6500 SJS 95120 874-F7
ROCKY GLEN CT
6100 SJS 95123 874-F6
ROCKY MOUNTAIN AV
1600 MPS 95035 814-D2
ROCKY MOUNTAIN CT
3700 PLE 94588 714-A2
ROCKY MOUNTAIN DR
3000 SJS 95127 835-B5
ROCKY POINT DR
3900 ANT 94509 595-F1
ROCKY RIDGE RD
- CCCo - 652-B3
ROCKY RIDGE TR
- CCCo - 652-B2
ROCKY WATER LN
2900 SJS 95148 855-B3
ROD RD
- SF 94129 647-C3
RODEO AV
- CCCo 94572 549-H7
- SAUS 94965 626-J2
500 CCCo 94572 569-H1
RODEO CIR
5000 ANT 94509 595-J3
RODEO CT
100 CCCo 94549 591-H6
100 VAL 94589 510-E6
300 SJS 95111 854-H5
5000 ANT 94509 595-J3
RODEO DR
300 SJS 95111 854-H5
RODEO LN
2900 LVMR 94550 715-J2
RODEO PL
400 SJS 95111 854-H5
RODERICK CT
1000 LFYT 94549 611-H6
RODERICK RD
4200 OAK 94605 671-D4
RODERIGO
4500 FRMT 94555 752-C1
RODGERS ST
- SF 94103 648-A7
- VAL 94590 529-H2
RODIN CT
2000 VAL 94591 530-E2
RODLING DR
6900 SJS 95138 875-F6
RODLING WY
100 SJS 95138 875-F6
RODNEY COM
3100 FRMT 94538 753-D6
RODNEY DR
700 SLN 94577 671-B7
1100 SJS 95118 874-B2
RODONI CT
12700 SAR 95070 852-G6
RODONOVAN CT
200 SCL 95051 832-J7
RODONOVAN DR
- SCL 95051 832-J7
RODRIGUES AV
100 MPS 95035 794-C7
400 CCCo 94553 571-J3
19800 CPTO 95014 852-D1
RODRIGUES LN
- CCCo 94596 612-A5
RODRIGUEZ ST
700 SF 94129 647-E4
ROEBLING RD
300 SSF 94080 708-B3
ROEBUCK WY
4500 ANT 94509 595-H3
ROEDER CT
300 SJS 95111 875-B2
ROEDER RD
4900 SJS 95111 875-B2
ROEDING AV
1100 FRMT 94536 732-H7
ROEHAMPTON AV
10000 SCIC 95127 835-A3
ROEHAMPTON RD
400 HIL 94010 748-G2
ROELLING LN
300 ANT 94509 575-E5
ROEMER WY
- SF 94112 687-E2
ROENOKE WY
2000 SJS 95128 853-G3
ROEWILL DR
1000 SJS 95117 853-B3
ROGAN RD
12100 AlaC 94586 754-C2
ROGELL AV
1200 SMTO 94401 729-A7
ROGELL CT
400 SMTO 94401 729-A6
ROGER AV
- SANS 94960 566-C7
ROGER CT
1600 ELCR 94530 609-D1
ROGER DR
- SRFL 94901 566-G6
ROGER ST
1500 MPS 95035 794-A4
ROGERIO ST
17000 AlaC 94541 691-G6
ROGERS AV
100 SCAR 94070 769-F5
1600 SJS 95112 834-A1
1600 SJS 95112 833-J1
1600 SJS 95112 813-J7
3100 WLCK 94596 612-B1
4800 FRMT 94536 752-H6
ROGERS CT
- PLHL 94523 612-B1
700 SCL 95051 833-B6
2800 OAK 94619 650-E7
ROGERS RD
3400 CNCD 94519 592-J1
ROGERS ST
- LGTS 95032 893-A1
ROGERS WY
700 PIN 94564 569-D4
ROGGE RD
100 EPA 94303 791-C1
ROHN WY
5800 SJS 95123 875-A5
ROHRER DR
2900 LFYT 94549 631-H3
ROJO PL
1400 SJS 95128 853-F5
ROJO WY
2200 PLE 94566 714-G3
ROLAND AV
2800 SCAR 94070 769-F6
ROLAND CT
- CCCo 94803 589-E2
4000 CNCD 94521 593-B2
ROLAND DR
4000 CNCD 94521 593-B2
ROLAND WY
400 OAK 94621 670-E6
ROLANDO AV
16500 AlaC 94578 691-G5
16900 AlaC 94546 691-G5
ROLEE LN
200 PLHL 94523 592-C7
ROLEEN CT
100 VAL 94589 509-J6
ROLEEN DR
400 VAL 94589 510-A6
500 VAL 94589 509-J5
ROLEN CT
- CLAY 94517 593-G7
ROLFE CT
14900 SCIC 95127 835-B1
ROLFE DR
200 PIT 94565 574-C3
ROLINE CT
15000 SCIC 95124 873-F4
ROLISON RD
3000 MLPK 94025 770-E6
3000 RDWC 94063 770-E6
ROLL ST
1600 SCL 95050 833-C3
ROLLING LN
400 CCCo 94507 633-A4
ROLLINGDELL CT
1100 CPTO 95014 852-D3
ROLLINGDELL DR
7300 CPTO 95014 852-D3
7300 SJS 95129 852-D3
ROLLING GLEN CT
6000 SJS 95123 874-F6
ROLLING GREEN WY
- PLHL 94523 592-A5
ROLLING HILL CT
1200 MRTZ 94553 571-H7
ROLLING HILL WY
1000 MRTZ 94553 571-G7
ROLLING HILLS AV
- SMTO 94403 749-B7
ROLLING HILLS CIR
7400 DBLN 94568 693-F4
ROLLING HILLS CT
- LVMR 94550 696-E3
2500 CCCo 94507 633-A4
3700 PIT 94565 574-E5
ROLLINGHILLS CT
2500 CCCo 94507 632-J4
2500 CCCo 94507 633-A4
19200 AlaC 94546 692-C4
ROLLING HILLS DR
1900 WLCK 94595 632-A1
3700 PIT 94565 574-E5
11100 DBLN 94568 693-F3
ROLLING HILLS LN
- DNVL 94526 653-D6
ROLLING HILLS PL
11600 DBLN 94568 693-F4
ROLLING HILLS RD
- TBRN 94920 607-D6
22000 SCIC 95070 852-B5
ROLLINGHILLS WY
4700 AlaC 94546 692-C4
ROLLING MEADOW CT
3300 CNCD 94518 592-H5
6400 SJS 95135 855-J7
ROLLING OAKS CT
6500 SJS 95120 894-C2
ROLLING OAKS DR
6500 SJS 95120 894-C2
ROLLING RIDGE LN
24100 AlaC 94541 712-B1
ROLLING RIDGE WY
5100 CCCo 94553 591-D2
ROLLINGSIDE DR
3500 SJS 95148 835-F7
ROLLINGWOOD CT
3000 SJS 95148 835-F7
ROLLINGWOOD DR
- SRFL 94901 567-B6
200 VAL 94591 530-F6
2000 SBRN 94066 707-E6
2600 CCCo 94806 588-J3
2600 SPAB 94806 588-J3
2700 CCCo 94806 589-A2
ROLLING WOOD PL
1500 PIT 94565 574-G5
ROLLING WOODS WY
- CNCD 94521 613-D1
1100 CNCD 94521 593-D7
ROLLINS RD
- BURL 94010 728-D4
- MLBR 94030 728-D4
ROLLINS ST
14600 SLN 94579 691-A4
ROLLY RD
10200 SCIC 94024 831-F5
ROLPH AV
300 CCCo 94525 550-D5
ROLPH ST
- SF 94112 687-F2
ROLPH PARK CT
- CCCo 94525 550-D5
ROLPH PARK DR
- CCCo 94525 550-D5
ROMA CT
500 LVMR 94550 695-E7
2900 SCL 95051 833-A7
6000 FRMT 94555 752-B6
ROMA PL
3300 SRMN 94583 673-G5
ROMA ST
800 LVMR 94550 695-E7
ROMAE CT
300 DNVL 94526 632-J7
ROMAGNOLO ST
2800 AlaC 94541 692-C7
ROMAIN ST
- SF 94114 667-F3
200 SF 94131 667-F3
ROMAN WY
1300 MRTZ 94553 571-G6
ROMAN EAGLE CT
- PLE 94566 714-J4
ROMANO CIR
2300 PLE 94566 715-B7
ROMANY RD
5700 OAK 94618 630-B6
ROMAR CT
- NVTO 94945 526-B2
ROMBERG DR
1200 SUNV 94087 832-E3
ROME CT
2200 PIT 94565 573-J4
ROME DR
100 VAL 94589 510-A5
20500 SCIC 95120 895-A6
ROME PL
200 HAY 94544 732-F3
ROME ST
- SF 94112 687-E1
ROMEO AV
10200 SJS 95127 835-C2
ROMEO CT
600 PLE 94566 714-D6
ROMEO PL
4900 FRMT 94555 752-C2
ROMERO CIR
100 CCCo 94507 632-E5
ROMERO CT
- NVTO 94945 525-J1
ROMERO RD
100 WDSD 94062 789-G6
ROMERO ST
600 SJS 95128 853-F4
ROMEY LN
2200 HAY 94541 692-B7
ROMFORD DR
5200 SJS 95124 873-H5
ROMILLY CT
35900 FRMT 94536 752-F3
ROMILLY WY
4300 FRMT 94536 752-F3
ROMINE WY
- VAL 94591 530-D6
ROMITA CT
16000 MSER 95030 872-H6
ROMLEY LN
1500 CCCo 94507 632-E3
ROMNEY AV
100 SSF 94080 707-E2
ROMOLO ST
- SF 94133 648-A4
RON CT
100 VAL 94591 530-F3
RONADA AV
- OAK 94611 630-A7
- PDMT 94611 630-A7
RONALD AV
400 CMBL 95008 853-C7
RONALD CT
700 LALT 94024 831-G2
1600 SJS 95118 873-J4
3500 FRMT 94538 773-E1
RONALD LN
23200 HAY 94541 711-G3
RONALD ST
2000 SCL 95050 833-D2
RONALD WY
3300 CNCD 94519 572-G6
10900 CPTO 95014 852-B3
RONCO DR
2700 SJS 95132 814-F5
RONDA CT
- PIT 94565 574-A2
- WLCK 94596 612-B2
35300 FRMT 94536 752-F1
RONDA DR
14700 SCIC 95124 873-G4
14700 SJS 95124 873-G4
RONDA ST
15600 AlaC 94580 691-D6
RONDALE CT
200 AlaC 94541 711-F1
RONDEAU DR
4000 SJS 95124 873-J3
RONDEE LN
- NVTO 94945 526-A2
RONDEL PL
- SF 94110 667-H2
RONDEN CT
1600 MTVW 94040 811-G6
RONDO WY
- SMCo 94025 790-D5
RONEY AV
100 VAL 94590 530-C5
RONIE WY
1800 SJS 95124 873-H3
RONINO WY
3200 LFYT 94549 611-H4
RONNIE ST
1600 PIT 94565 574-F3
RONNIE WY
13300 SAR 95070 852-G7
13400 SAR 95070 872-G1
ROOSEVELT
- RDWC 94061 789-J1
- RDWC 94061 790-A1
ROOSEVELT AV
- DALY 94014 687-E3
- MLV 94941 606-D2
- MrnC 94903 566-G4
100 RDWC 94061 789-J2
200 SUNV 94086 812-F6
400 LVMR 94550 696-D4
1200 HAY 94544 711-J7
2000 RDWC 94061 790-A1
2100 BERK 94703 629-G2
2100 BURL 94010 728-D6
2200 RDWC 94061 770-A7
2300 RCH 94801 588-G6
2800 RCH 94804 588-H6
3300 RCH 94805 588-H6
3600 RCH 94805 589-A6
ROOSEVELT CIR
- PA 94306 811-D1
2300 SCL 95051 833-C2
ROOSEVELT CT
2300 SCL 95051 833-C2
2700 ANT 94509 575-E7
ROOSEVELT DR
2400 ALA 94501 669-J3
ROOSEVELT LN
2700 ANT 94509 575-E6
ROOSEVELT PL
5400 FRMT 94538 753-A7
5400 FRMT 94538 773-A1
5500 FRMT 94538 772-J1
ROOSEVELT ST
900 SJS 95112 834-D4
ROOSEVELT WY
- SF 94117 667-F2
- SJS 95002 793-C7
- SF 94114 667-F2
ROOSTER CT
- SJS 95136 874-J2
ROOSTER DR
5200 SJS 95136 874-J3
ROQUE MORAES CT
- MLV 94941 606-F4
ROQUE MORAES DR
- MLV 94941 606-G4
RORKE WY
800 PA 94303 791-E6
ROSA AV
1000 SUNV 94086 832-G3
ROSA CT
900 SUNV 94086 832-G3
ROSA CORTE
200 WLCK 94598 612-H2
ROSADA CT
3300 PLE 94588 694-D6
ROSADO RD
200 FRMT 94539 753-F4
ROSA FLORA CIR
100 SSF 94080 707-G4
ROSAL AV
500 OAK 94610 650-A2
S ROSAL AV
1200 CNCD 94521 593-A4
1200 CNCD 94521 592-J4
ROSAL LN
1300 CNCD 94521 593-A3
ROSAL WY
600 MrnC 94903 566-H2
ROSALEE CT
3700 AlaC 94546 691-J3
ROSALIA AV
1200 SJS 95117 853-B4
1300 SJS 95130 853-B4
1300 SUNV 94087 832-G4
ROSALIA DR
1000 NVTO 94945 526-D3
ROSALIE CT
200 LGTS 95032 873-C7
ROSALIE DR
1300 SCL 95050 833-C4
ROSALIND AV
5300 ELCR 94530 589-B5
5300 RCH 94805 589-B7
6100 CCCo 94805 589-B5
ROSALIND LN
18500 SCIC 95120 894-G1
ROSALINDA CT
2600 SJS 95121 854-J4
ROSALITA CT
4100 FRMT 94536 752-F2
ROSALITA LN
- MLBR 94030 727-J2
ROSARIO AV
21500 CPTO 95014 852-B2
ROSARIO CT
100 SRMN 94583 673-C3
2800 SJS 95132 814-D3
19100 AlaC 94541 691-F7
ROSARIO DR
2800 SJS 95132 814-D3
ROSATO CT
2900 SJS 95135 855-E3
ROSCOE ST
- SF 94110 667-H6
ROSE AV
- CCCo 94565 573-H2
- MLV 94941 606-B3
- SANS 94960 586-B1
200 DNVL 94526 653-A2
200 DNVL 94526 652-J2
200 PLE 94566 714-C3
800 MTVW 94040 831-G1
800 SMCo 94063 770-F7
900 MLPK 94025 790-F4
900 OAK 94611 650-A1
900 RDWC 94063 770-F7
900 PDMT 94611 650-A1
2800 SJS 95127 834-J3
3600 SCIC 95127 834-J2
4100 SCIC 95127 834-J2
4100 SCIC 95127 835-A2
15800 LGTS 95030 873-A6
15800 MSER 95030 873-A6
16100 MSER 95030 872-J6
E ROSE CIR
1000 LALT 94024 831-J2
W ROSE CIR
1000 LALT 94024 831-J2
ROSE CT
- SAUS 94965 627-B3
100 CMBL 95008 853-D6
100 VAL 94589 509-J6
400 PIN 94564 569-C4
900 BURL 94010 728-F5
900 SCL 95051 833-B5
3400 CNCD 94519 592-J2
3700 LFYT 94549 611-D5
3900 FRMT 94536 752-H3
5700 NWK 94560 752-D5
17900 MSER 95030 872-J6
ROSE DR
- BEN 94510 551-B1
100 MPS 95035 794-A4
600 BEN 94510 530-H7
900 BEN 94510 550-H1
13400 SLN 94577 691-B3
13400 SLN 94578 691-B3
ROSE LN
- LGTS 95030 873-A5
- ORIN 94563 610-F6
- VAL 94590 530-C3
100 BLMT 94002 769-E2
700 LALT 94024 831-F1
1200 LFYT 94549 611-D5
1500 PLE 94566 714-C3
1900 PLHL 94523 592-B5
4300 CNCD 94518 593-A5
ROSE PL
1200 SJS 95112 854-D1
ROSE ST
- NVTO 94945 526-C3
- SF 94102 647-H7
- SRFL 94901 586-H3
- MrnC 94901 586-H3
- SF 94102 667-H1
100 CCCo 94595 612-A7
300 DNVL 94526 652-J2
400 LVMR 94550 715-J1
400 LVMR 94550 695-J7
900 HAY 94541 691-H7
1200 BERK 94702 629-E1
1200 CCCo 94525 550-D5
1300 BERK 94703 609-F7
1300 BERK 94702 609-F7
1900 BERK 94709 609-G7
2300 BERK 94708 609-H7
2600 CCCo 94553 571-G4
ROSE WK
- BERK 94708 609-H7
ROSE WY
2500 SCL 95051 833-B3
4700 UNC 94587 732-A7
4700 UNC 94587 731-J7
4700 UNC 94587 751-J1
4800 UNC 94545 751-J1
ROSE ANN AV
- PIT 94565 574-C3
ROSEANN DR
1200 MRTZ 94553 571-H6
ROSE ANNA DR
1500 SJS 95118 874-A5
ROSEANNE CT
900 AlaC 94580 691-F6
ROSE ARBOR AV
5900 CCCo 94806 589-B3
ROSEBANK AV
- MrnC 94904 586-E3
ROSEBANK LN
- MrnC 94904 586-E3
ROSEBAY CT
- SJS 95127 834-J2
ROSE BLOSSOM DR
700 CPTO 95014 852-C2
ROSE BOWL DR
- SAUS 94965 627-A4
ROSEBRIAR WY
1100 SJS 95131 834-D1
1100 SJS 95131 814-D7
ROSEBROOK CT
3600 CNCD 94518 592-H4
ROSEBUD CT
1900 SJS 95128 853-G3
2700 UNC 94587 752-G1
ROSECLIFF LN
29000 HAY 94544 732-A2
ROSE COURT TER
- MrnC 94945 526-E4
ROSE CREEK DR
3000 SJS 95148 835-B5
ROSECREST DR
1800 OAK 94602 650-E2
ROSECREST TER
1400 SJS 95126 833-H7
ROSEDALE AV
800 LFYT 94549 611-F7
1100 BURL 94010 728-D5
1500 OAK 94601 670-D1
1900 OAK 94601 650-D7
ROSEDALE CT
7500 PLE 94588 693-H6
ROSEDALE DR
2000 CCCo 94806 569-B4
3200 SJS 95117 853-D2
ROSEFIELD WY
1100 MLPK 94025 790-E4
ROSEGARDEN CT
48900 FRMT 94539 794-A2
ROSEGARDEN LN
1300 CPTO 95014 852-D4
ROSEGATE TER
38700 FRMT 94536 753-C3
ROSEHILL PL
2200 AlaC 94541 692-C7
ROSELAND DR
1600 CNCD 94519 592-J2
ROSELEAF CT
16300 SCIC 95032 873-D5
ROSELEAF LN
16100 SCIC 95032 873-D5
ROSELLA CT
- SF 94112 687-F1
ROSELLE COM
- FRMT 94536 752-G5
ROSELLE LN
- ORIN 94563 630-J3
ROSELLI DR
1300 LVMR 94550 715-F3
ROSELMA PL
900 PLE 94566 714-F5
ROSELYN TER
- SF 94118 647-E7
ROSEMAR AV
3600 SJS 95127 835-B2
ROSEMAR CT
700 SJS 95127 835-C1
ROSE MARIE DR
100 CNCD 94518 592-G4
ROSEMARIE PL
300 CCCo 94565 573-D1
19400 CPTO 95014 852-G1
ROSEMARY CT
- NVTO 94945 526-B2
- SF 94116 667-B5
1700 ANT 94509 595-E3
1900 FRMT 94539 773-G3
2000 MRTZ 94553 572-A6
ROSEMARY DR
100 VAL 94589 509-J6
ROSEMARY LN
- SRMN 94583 693-F1
1300 CNCD 94518 592-E5
1700 RDWC 94061 790-A2
E ROSEMARY LN
- CMBL 95128 853-E5
- CMBL 95008 853-E5
2900 SJS 95008 853-E5
2900 SJS 95128 853-E5
W ROSEMARY LN
2900 CMBL 95008 853-D5
ROSEMARY ST
- SJS 95112 834-A3
- SJS 95110 833-J3
- SJS 95112 833-J3
ROSEMEAD CT
- DNVL 94526 653-C2
ROSEMERE CT
1500 FRMT 94539 773-G2
ROSEMERE DR
43900 FRMT 94539 773-G2
ROSEMONT AV
- BERK 94708 609-H4
- SANS 94960 566-A5
200 MrnC 94941 606-F6
1000 LALT 94024 831-H3
ROSEMONT CT
100 CCCo 94596 612-A4
1000 LALT 94024 831-H3
ROSEMONT DR
300 SCL 95051 832-J7
ROSEMONT PL
- SF 94103 667-H1
ROSEMOUNT RD
600 OAK 94610 650-A3
ROSENBAUM AV
4100 SJS 95136 874-G1
ROSENCRANS WY
7100 SJS 95139 895-F1
ROSENELFE CIR
3000 SJS 95148 835-B5
ROSENKRANZ ST
- SF 94110 667-J5
ROSE ORCHARD WY
- SCIC 95134 813-E2
- SJS 95134 813-E2
ROSE RIDGE LN
5900 SJS 95123 874-G7
ROSE ROCK CIR
3700 PLE 94588 694-E7
ROSETREE CT
1800 PLE 94566 714-D1
ROSETTE CT
900 SUNV 94086 832-G3
ROSETTE TER
800 SUNV 94086 832-G3
ROSE VIEW DR
10000 SCIC 95127 835-C1
ROSEVILLE CT
- TBRN 94920 607-B4
ROSEWELL CT
- SJS 95138 875-D4
ROSEWELL WY
- SJS 95138 875-D4
ROSEWOOD AV
300 SJS 95117 853-D1
300 SCIC 95117 853-D1
700 VAL 94591 530-E5
900 SCAR 94070 769-G3
4100 RCH 94804 609-A1
ROSEWOOD COM
42000 FRMT 94538 773-C1
ROSEWOOD CT
- CCCo - 654-A1
- SRFL 94901 567-C6
200 HAY 94544 712-B6
600 LALT 94024 831-F1
800 CCCo 94596 612-G7
900 PIT 94565 573-J3
ROSEWOOD DR
- ATN 94027 790-G1
- NVTO 94947 526-D6
- SF 94127 667-D6
- ATN 94027 770-G7
700 CCCo 94596 612-F7
700 PA 94303 791-C6
900 SMTO 94401 749-A2
2100 SBRN 94066 727-F1
2900 PLE 94588 694-D5
4200 CNCD 94521 593-B2
35900 NWK 94560 752-D5
ROSEWOOD LN
- CCCo - 654-A1
ROSEWOOD ST
10600 CPTO 95014 832-F6
ROSEWOOD WY
100 SSF 94080 707-G5
1000 ALA 94501 669-G2
ROSIE LEE LN
- SF 94124 668-D6
ROSILIE ST
100 SMTO 94403 749-E6
ROSINA CT
4300 CNCD 94518 593-A5
ROSITA AV
400 LALT 94024 831-F1
2100 SCL 95050 833-D7
ROSITA CT
2300 SCL 95050 833-D6
7100 DBLN 94568 693-J3
ROSITA CT N
1000 PCFA 94044 726-J5
ROSITA CT S
1000 PCFA 94044 726-J5
ROSITA RD
700 PCFA 94044 726-H5
1100 PCFA 94044 727-A6
ROSKELLY DR
2100 CNCD 94519 572-G7
ROSLIN CT
6200 PLE 94588 694-A7
ROSLYN AV
- SCAR 94070 769-E4
- SMCo 94070 769-E4
ROSLYN CIR
700 MTVW 94043 812-A3
ROSLYN CT
- BERK 94618 630-A4
- BERK 94705 630-A4
- DALY 94015 686-J4
2400 SJS 95121 854-J2
ROSLYN DR
100 CNCD 94518 592-H3
1400 CNCD 94519 592-H3
ROSOLI TER
4400 FRMT 94536 752-G4
ROSS AL
- SF 94108 648-A4
ROSS AV
- SANS 94960 586-B1
300 ANT 94509 575-E5
2800 SJS 95124 873-J3
ROSS CIR
- OAK 94618 630-A4
1700 SJS 95124 873-J3
ROSS COM
- ROSS 94957 586-C2
39500 FRMT 94538 753-B5
ROSS CT
800 PA 94303 791-D7
ROSS DR
- MRGA 94556 651-E1
300 MrnC 94935 606-F7
300 SUNV 94089 812-E4
ROSS LN
200 FCTY 94404 749-F5
ROSS PL
2600 WLCK 94596 612-A2
27700 HAY 94544 712-B6
ROSS RD
- ALA 94502 669-H6
- SAUS 94965 626-H1
2300 PA 94303 791-C5
ROSS ST
- OAK 94618 630-A4
- SRFL 94901 586-E1
100 VAL 94591 530-D4
1100 BLMT 94002 749-D7
ROSS TER
4200 FRMT 94538 753-A5
ROSS WY
- BSBN 94005 688-A7
- SBRN 94066 707-D6
ROSSBURN CT
1100 SJS 95121 855-B6
ROSS CREEK CT
100 LGTS 95032 873-E5
ROSS GATE CT
4500 PLE 94566 694-D7
ROSS GATE WY
4500 PLE 94566 694-D7
ROSSI AV
- ANT 94509 575-D6
- SF 94118 647-E7
ROSSI ST
3300 LFYT 94549 611-G2
ROSSI WY
1000 SMTO 94403 749-C4
ROSSMERE CT
13600 SAR 95070 872-F1
ROSSMOOR AV
400 OAK 94603 670-G6
ROSSMOOR CT
- OAK 94603 670-G6
- PIT 94565 574-B3
ROSSMOOR DR
- SF 94132 667-B6
ROSSMOOR PKWY
1200 WLCK 94595 632-B2
ROSSMORE CT
2900 SJS 95148 855-C1
ROSSMORE LN
600 HAY 94544 711-H5
2900 SJS 95148 855-C1
ROSSMORE WY
2900 SJS 95148 855-C1
ROSSMOYNE DR
14800 SCIC 95124 873-H4
ROSSO CT
- PLE 94566 715-C6
ROSSOTTO DR
2400 SJS 95130 853-A7
ROSS PARK CT
4000 SJS 95118 874-B2

BAY AREA
INDEX
COPYRIGHT 1997 Thomas Bros. Maps ®

STREET Block City ZIP Pg-Grid

ROSS PARK DR
4000 SJS 95118 874-B2
ROSS STREET TER
- SRFL 94901 586-F1
ROSS VALLEY DR
- SRFL 94901 566-D7
- SRFL 94901 586-D1
ROSSWAY CT
1300 LALT 94024 831-J4
ROSSWOOD DR
1700 SJS 95124 873-G4
ROSTI
100 HER 94547 569-E3
ROSWELL CT
300 MPS 95035 794-D7
ROSWELL DR
100 MPS 95035 794-D7
ROTARY ST
300 HAY 94541 711-H2
ROTARY WY
- VAL 94591 530-D1
ROTH PL
2000 SCL 95051 833-D1
ROTH WY
100 SCIC 94305 790-G6
ROTHBURY COM
4500 FRMT 94536 752-G4
ROTHERHAM DR
900 ANT 94509 575-B7
ROTHERHAVEN WY
4500 SJS 95111 875-A1
4500 SJS 95111 874-J1
ROTHLAND CT
1300 SJS 95131 814-D7
ROTHMAN CT
5500 AlaC 94552 692-D2
ROTHROCK DR
100 SJS 95116 834-G2
ROTHSCHILD CT
11200 DBLN 94568 693-E4
ROTHSCHILD PL
11400 DBLN 94568 693-F4
ROTTECK ST
- SF 94112 667-G6
ROTTERDAM LN
5600 SJS 95118 874-B5
ROUEN CT
- SJS 95127 834-J1
ROUGH AND READY RD
400 SJS 95133 834-G1
500 SJS 95133 814-G7
ROUNDHILL CT
100 VAL 94591 530-D2
200 CLAY 94517 613-H1
ROUND HILL DR
3200 HAY 94542 712-E4
ROUNDHILL DR
- CCCo 94507 633-A5
2300 CCCo 94507 632-J5
3700 PIT 94565 574-G6
ROUNDHILL PL
200 CLAY 94517 613-H1
200 CLAY 94517 593-H7
ROUND HILL RD
- TBRN 94920 607-D5
900 RDWC 94061 789-H2
ROUNDHILL RD
2300 CCCo 94507 632-H3
ROUND HOUSE PL
200 CLAY 94517 593-G5
ROUNDLEAF CT
1900 SJS 95131 814-C6
ROUNDS ST
100 VAL 94589 510-C6
ROUNDTABLE DR
- SJS 95111 875-B3
ROUND TOP LOOP TR
- CCCo - 630-F5
ROUNDTREE BLVD
- MrnC 94903 546-E7
ROUNDTREE COM
5500 FRMT 94538 773-A1
ROUNDTREE CT
4800 SJS 95008 872-J1
5400 CNCD 94521 593-E6
ROUNDTREE DR
4700 SJS 95008 873-A1
4700 SJS 95008 872-J1
5400 CNCD 94521 593-E6
ROUNDTREE PL
5400 CNCD 94521 593-E6
ROUNDTREE TER
5500 FRMT 94538 773-A1
ROUNDTREE WY
100 MrnC 94903 546-E7
5400 CNCD 94521 593-E6
ROUNDUP CT
5100 ANT 94509 595-J5
ROUNDUP WY
5100 ANT 94509 595-J5
ROUSE CT
100 PLHL 94523 612-B1
7100 SJS 95139 875-F7
ROUSILLON AV
4600 FRMT 94555 752-D2
ROUSILLON PL
4500 FRMT 94555 752-D2
ROUSSEAU DR
1200 SUNV 94087 832-F4
ROUSSEAU ST
- HAY 94544 732-D2
- SF 94112 667-G6
ROUX CT
1800 MRTZ 94553 572-A6
1800 MRTZ 94553 571-J6
ROVIGO CT
- DNVL 94506 653-D1
ROWAN WY
- MLV 94941 606-C1
ROWAN TREE LN
- HIL 94010 748-C2
ROWE PL
3100 FRMT 94536 752-H2
3500 LFYT 94549 611-F7
ROWELL LN
500 PLE 94566 714-F4
ROWENA CT
3500 SCL 95054 813-E6
ROWENA DR
1100 HAY 94542 712-A2
ROWLAND AV
- SANS 94960 566-B7
ROWLAND BLVD
- NVTO 94949 526-B7
300 NVTO 94947 526-D5
ROWLAND CT
- NVTO 94947 526-B6
ROWLAND DR
3300 LFYT 94549 611-G3
33800 FRMT 94555 732-D7
ROWLAND ST
- SF 94133 648-A4
ROWLAND WY
- NVTO 94945 526-D5
- NVTO 94947 526-D5
ROWLEY CIR
- TBRN 94920 607-B5
ROWLEY DR
3500 SJS 95132 814-F2
ROWNTREE WY
2400 SSF 94080 707-D4
ROXANNE AV
1100 HAY 94542 712-A2
ROXANNE CT
100 WLCK 94596 612-C1
5200 LVMR 94550 696-C7
ROXANNE DR
5200 SJS 95124 873-H5
ROXANNE LN
- LFYT 94549 611-H7
ROXANNE ST
900 LVMR 94550 696-C7
ROXBURG LN
- ALA 94502 670-A5
- ALA 94502 669-J5
ROXBURY AV
3000 OAK 94605 671-C6
ROXBURY CT
- CCCo 94507 633-A5
800 ANT 94509 575-F7
1200 SCL 95050 833-F6
1700 CNCD 94519 593-B1
ROXBURY DR
1700 CNCD 94519 593-B1
1700 CNCD 94519 573-B7
ROXBURY LN
- SMCo 94402 748-F6
500 LGTS 95030 873-A2
3600 HAY 94542 712-E3
ROXBURY ST
- SCL 95050 833-E6
ROXBURY WY
500 BLMT 94002 749-E7
ROXIE LN
1100 WLCK 94596 612-C1
ROXIE TER
5900 FRMT 94555 752-B4
ROX PLACE CT
3600 SJS 95121 855-B4
ROY AV
1000 SJS 95125 854-B6
ROY CT
- NVTO 94947 525-G2
ROY LN
- CCCo 94565 573-E2
ROYAL AV
300 SJS 95126 854-A1
1300 SMTO 94401 749-B2
19200 AlaC 94541 711-E1
21200 HAY 94541 711-E1
ROYAL CT
- SRFL 94901 586-J1
100 VAL 94591 530-G3
1800 WLCK 94595 612-C7
ROYAL DR
2000 SCL 95050 833-C3
ROYAL LN
- SF 94112 687-F2
1100 SCAR 94070 769-D6
ROYAL RD
500 LVMR 94550 695-H6
3400 CNCD 94519 572-J7
3400 CNCD 94519 592-J1
ROYAL ST
900 OAK 94603 670-J7
ROYAL ACORN PL
6000 SJS 95120 874-D7
ROYAL ACRES CT
1000 SJS 95136 874-C2
ROYAL ANN
- UNC 94587 732-F6
ROYAL ANN COM
38500 FRMT 94536 753-C2
ROYAL ANN CT
1100 SUNV 94087 832-D3
1400 SJS 95129 852-G4
2500 UNC 94587 732-F7
ROYAL ANN DR
1100 SUNV 94087 832-D3
1400 SJS 95129 852-G4
2300 UNC 94587 732-F6
ROYAL ANN LN
800 CNCD 94518 592-G7
ROYAL ANN ST
10200 OAK 94603 670-H6
ROYAL ARCH CT
4000 CNCD 94519 593-B1
ROYAL ARCH DR
3900 CNCD 94519 593-B1
ROYALBROOK CT
800 SJS 95111 855-A6
ROYAL CREST DR
1100 SJS 95131 834-D1
1100 SJS 95131 814-C7
ROYALE PARK CT
4500 SJS 95136 874-F2
ROYALE PARK DR
400 SJS 95136 874-F2
ROYAL ESTATES CT
5000 SJS 95135 855-G5
ROYAL FOREST CT
4600 SJS 95136 874-F2
ROYAL GARDEN PL
4600 SJS 95136 874-G2
ROYAL GATE PL
400 SJS 95136 874-G2
ROYAL GLEN CT
600 SJS 95133 814-H7
1800 CCCo 94595 612-C7
ROYAL GLEN DR
600 SJS 95133 814-G7
1800 CCCo 94595 612-C7
ROYAL GROVE CT
4600 SJS 95136 874-G2
ROYAL INDUSTRIAL WY
1400 CNCD 94520 592-D2
N ROYAL LINKS CIR
- ANT 94509 595-D1
S ROYAL LINKS CIR
4000 ANT 94509 595-D2
ROYAL LINKS CT
4000 ANT 94509 595-D2
ROYAL MEADOW LN
3000 SJS 95135 855-J7
ROYAL OAK CT
6200 SJS 95123 875-A6
ROYAL OAK RD
10200 OAK 94605 671-C3
ROYAL OAK TER
1200 NVTO 94947 526-D6
ROYAL OAK WY
22500 CPTO 95014 831-J6
ROYAL OAKS CT
- CCCo 94507 633-A5
ROYAL OAKS DR
2300 CCCo 94507 632-J5
2400 CCCo 94507 633-A5
ROYAL PALM DR
4900 FRMT 94538 752-J7
35100 FRMT 94538 753-A7
ROYAL PALM PL
200 DNVL 94526 653-D5
ROYAL RIDGE CT
- CCCo 94507 633-A5
7000 SJS 95120 894-E3
ROYAL RIDGE DR
7000 SJS 95120 894-E3
ROYALRIDGE WY
2500 SCL 95051 833-C1
ROYAL SAINT CT
200 DNVL 94526 653-D6
ROYALTON CT
3200 PLE 94588 694-E6
ROYALTREE CIR
2200 SJS 95131 814-C5
ROYALVALE WY
2700 SJS 95132 814-C4
ROYAL VIEW DR
1500 WLCK 94598 612-D3
ROYAL WINGS WY
2000 SLN 94579 690-J6
ROYALWOOD WY
6800 SJS 95120 894-H3
ROYCE DR
300 SJS 95133 834-E3
ROYCE ST
100 LGTS 95030 873-A7
ROYCE WY
- DALY 94014 687-D5
100 PIT 94565 574-C4
ROYCOTT WY
1100 SJS 95125 854-A5
ROYCROFT WY
5000 FRMT 94538 773-B1
ROYSHILL LN
- DBLN 94552 693-D5
ROYSTON CT
1100 SJS 95120 894-E2
8600 DBLN 94568 693-F2
ROYSTON LN
600 HAY 94544 712-D7
ROYSTON WK
- PLHL 94523 591-J4
ROYWOOD CT
100 VAL 94591 530-F5
ROZZI PL
400 SSF 94080 708-B2
RUBEN CT
- NVTO 94947 525-G3
RUBICON AV
6200 NWK 94560 772-H1
RUBICON CIR
100 DNVL 94526 652-J1
RUBICON CT
- MrnC 94903 546-A6
100 MRTZ 94553 572-B7
2300 WLCK 94598 612-G2
RUBICON DR
- MrnC 94903 546-A6
RUBICON VALLEY CT
- SRMN 94583 673-J6
RUBIDOUX TER
- SUNV 94086 812-C7
RUBIN DR
3300 OAK 94602 650-G4
RUBINO CT
- PLE 94566 715-B5
RUBIO WY
100 HAY 94544 712-C7
RUBION CT
3400 SJS 95148 835-D4
RUBION DR
3400 SJS 95148 835-C5
RUBIS DR
800 SUNV 94087 832-D2
RUBY AV
100 SCAR 94070 769-G5
2300 SJS 95148 855-E1
3000 SJS 95148 835-D5
3700 SCIC 95148 835-D5
4100 SJS 95135 855-F3
W RUBY AV
- CCCo 94801 588-F4
RUBY CT
100 HER 94547 569-G4
100 LVMR 94550 715-D2
3400 SJS 95148 835-E7
RUBY LN
100 VAL 94590 550-C2
RUBY RD
100 LVMR 94550 715-D2
RUBY ST
- RDWC 94061 790-A1
400 RDWC 94062 769-J7
500 RDWC 94062 789-J1
600 RDWC 94061 789-J1
3700 OAK 94609 649-H1
3800 OAK 94609 629-H7
22400 AlaC 94546 692-A7
RUBY TER
2700 SJS 95148 835-E6
RUBY VW
2700 SJS 95148 835-E6
RUBYE DR
1900 ANT 94509 575-E6
RUBY HILL BLVD
- PLE 94566 715-C5
E RUBY HILL DR
3000 PLE 94566 715-C5
W RUBY HILL DR
- PLE 94566 715-B5
RUCKER DR
5200 SJS 95124 873-H5
5200 SJS 95032 873-H5
21800 CPTO 95014 852-B2
RUCKMAN AV
1200 SF 94129 647-C3
RUDD CT
500 SJS 95111 854-J6
RUDDEN AV
- SF 94112 667-F7
RUDDER LN
1000 FCTY 94404 749-H4
RUDGEAR DR
- WLCK 94596 632-E1
RUDGEAR RD
1000 WLCK 94596 632-G1
1000 CCCo 94596 632-G1
RUDGEAR ST
- WLCK 94595 632-E1
1000 WLCK 94596 632-E1
RUDNICK AV
- NVTO 94945 526-D3
RUDSDALE ST
6900 OAK 94621 670-G3
RUDY CT
5700 SJS 95124 873-J6
RUDY DR
5400 SJS 95124 873-J6
RUDYARD DR
300 MPS 95035 793-J7
RUE AVATI
1300 SJS 95131 814-C6
RUE BORDEAUX
4700 SJS 95136 874-J2
RUE BOULOGNE
100 SJS 95136 874-J2
RUE CALAIS
4800 SJS 95136 874-J2
RUE CANNES
2200 SJS 95136 874-J2
RUE CHENE DOR
3500 SJS 95148 855-G1
RUE FERRARI
5800 SJS 95138 875-E4
RUE LE MANS
4700 SJS 95136 874-J2
RUE LOIRET
4800 SJS 95136 874-J2
RUE LYON CT
4700 SJS 95136 874-J2
RUE MIRASSOU
- SJS 95148 855-F1
RUE MONTAGNE
800 CMBL 95008 853-F7
RUE NICE CT
4800 SJS 95136 874-J2
RUE ORLEANS CT
4700 SJS 95136 874-J2
RUE PARIS
100 SJS 95136 874-J2
RUE TOULON CT
4800 SJS 95136 874-J2
RUE TOURS CT
4800 SJS 95136 874-J2
RUFF AV
2800 PIN 94564 569-F5
RUFF CT
2700 PIN 94564 569-F5
RUFF DR
900 SJS 95110 833-J4
RUFUS CT
900 AlaC 94541 691-H7
RUGBY AV
300 BERK 94707 609-G4
300 CCCo 94708 609-G4
RUGBY CT
1100 SJS 95120 874-C6
1500 CNCD 94518 592-E6
RUGBY PL
35100 NWK 94560 752-E3
RUGE DR
1000 SJS 95132 814-F6
RUGER ST
- SF 94129 647-F4
RUGGLES ST
15300 SLN 94579 691-B7
RUHLMAN LN
1100 NVTO 94945 525-J2
RUIZ CT
1500 SJS 95129 852-H4
RULE CT
100 CCCo 94595 612-B6
RUMFORD DR
21200 CPTO 95014 832-C7
RUMFORD TER
- UNC 94587 732-G6
RUMRILL BLVD
1100 SPAB 94806 588-H2
1800 SPAB 94801 588-G4
RUMRILL RD
2300 SPAB 94806 588-H2
RUMSEY CT
400 SJS 95111 875-C2
RUNCKEL LN
35600 FRMT 94536 752-G1
RUNNING BEAR DR
5100 SJS 95136 875-A2
RUNNING FARM LN
- SCIC 94305 790-J7
- SCIC 94305 810-J1
RUNNING HILLS AV
5700 LVMR 94550 696-C2
RUNNING SPRINGS DR
- WLCK 94595 632-A3
RUNNING SPRINGS RD
- SJS 95135 875-J1
RUNNING WATER CT
2300 SCL 95054 813-C5
RUNNINGWOOD CIR
800 MTVW 94040 832-A1
RUNNYMEAD CT
1000 LALT 94024 831-H2
RUNNYMEAD DR
1100 LALT 94024 831-H2
RUNNYMEDE CT
3200 PLE 94588 694-E6
RUNNYMEDE DR
1100 SJS 95117 853-D4
RUNNYMEDE RD
800 WDSD 94062 789-E4
RUNNYMEDE ST
400 EPA 94303 791-B1
RUNO CT
18500 SCIC 95014 852-H1
RUNSHAW PL
1200 SJS 95121 855-A5
RUPERT DR
2300 SJS 95124 873-E3
RUPPEL PL
- LFYT 94549 631-J4
RUPPELL PL
1100 CPTO 95014 852-D4
RURAL LN
300 MLPK 94025 810-E1
300 SMCo 94025 810-E1
RUSCHIN DR
35700 NWK 94560 752-E5
RUSH CREEK PL
900 NVTO 94945 526-C2
RUSH LANDING RD
100 NVTO 94945 526-C1
RUSHMORE LN
200 LGTS 95030 873-B6
RUSKIN AV
3500 FRMT 94536 752-G3
RUSKIN DR
3100 SJS 95132 814-F4
RUSKIN PL
3700 FRMT 94536 752-G2
RUSS AV
1600 SLN 94578 691-D3
RUSS ST
- SF 94103 648-A7
RUSSEL AV
- MrnC 94904 586-D3
RUSSELL AV
- PTLV 94028 809-J6
900 LALT 94024 831-G2
1800 SCL 95054 813-D6
RUSSELL CT
- CCCo 94598 612-F5
- MLPK 94025 790-J3
16500 AlaC 94578 691-G4
20700 SAR 95070 872-D1
34300 FRMT 94555 752-D1
RUSSELL DR
- ANT 94509 575-C6
100 CCCo 94598 612-F5
1900 MRGA 94556 631-G5
RUSSELL LN
700 MPS 95035 794-B4
20500 SAR 95070 872-D1
RUSSELL ST
- OAK 94605 650-J7
- OAK 94619 650-J7
- SF 94109 647-J4
400 VAL 94591 530-D6
1100 BERK 94702 629-F4
1200 BERK 94703 629-F4
2100 BERK 94705 629-H3
2700 BERK 94705 630-A3
3000 OAK 94705 630-A3
RUSSELL WY
- HAY 94541 692-A7
- HAY 94541 691-J7
- HAY 94541 711-J1
RUSSELL RIDGE TR
- CCCo - 611-C3
- LFYT 94549 611-C3
RUSSET CT
600 WLCK 94598 613-C4
RUSSET DR
800 SUNV 94087 832-D2
RUSSET ST
10500 OAK 94603 670-H7
RUSSET TER
700 SUNV 94087 832-D1
RUSSIA AV
- SF 94112 687-G1
RUSSIAN HILL PL
- SF 94133 647-J4
RUSSO CT
4700 CNCD 94521 593-C3
RUSSO DR
5300 SJS 95118 874-C3
RUSTIC AV
2700 SJS 95124 873-G1
RUSTIC DR
2700 SJS 95124 873-G1
3200 SCL 95051 833-A5
20600 AlaC 94546 692-A5
RUSTIC LN
600 MTVW 94040 811-H7
RUSTIC PL
- SRMN 94583 673-J6
RUSTIC RD
4300 CNCD 94521 593-B4
RUSTIC WY
- ORIN 94563 631-A2
- SRFL 94901 566-F6
RUSTIC RANCH CT
1100 SJS 95120 894-H3
RUSTIC RIDGE CIR
200 SJS 95123 874-G7
RUSTING AV
4000 OAK 94605 650-H7
RUTAN CT
1200 LVMR 94550 695-D6
RUTAN DR
1400 LVMR 94550 695-D6
RUTGERS CT
100 VAL 94589 510-A5
4300 LVMR 94550 716-A2
RUTGERS LN
2600 ANT 94509 575-D1
RUTGERS ST
500 AlaC 94580 691-D5
1600 EPA 94303 771-C6
RUTGERS WY
1500 LVMR 94550 716-A2
RUTH AV
300 MTVW 94043 811-F3
800 BLMT 94002 749-D7
5400 OAK 94601 670-F1
RUTH CT
- LFYT 94595 612-A6
- NVTO 94945 526-A3
400 SLN 94578 691-D4
1000 EPA 94303 791-C1
2800 SCL 95051 833-B6
32300 UNC 94587 732-A7
RUTH DR
700 PLHL 94523 592-C3
1100 SJS 95125 854-C7
RUTH ST
- SF 94112 667-F7
RUTH WY
500 LVMR 94550 715-E1
4600 UNC 94587 732-A7
4600 UNC 94587 731-J7
RUTH CABRAL WY
2400 SCL 95050 833-C5
RUTHELEN CT
14700 SLN 94578 691-C5
RUTHELMA AV
4200 PA 94306 811-D2
RUTHERDALE AV
800 SCAR 94070 769-F4
RUTHERFORD AV
- SANS 94960 566-A5
100 SMCo 94061 790-B2
6800 SJS 95129 852-E4
RUTHERFORD CT
2500 FRMT 94539 774-A3
RUTHERFORD DR
200 DNVL 94526 652-G1
RUTHERFORD LN
- CCCo 94553 572-B5
2100 FRMT 94539 774-A3
32400 UNC 94587 732-C4
RUTHERFORD PL
2600 FRMT 94539 774-A3
RUTHERFORD ST
2000 OAK 94601 650-C7
RUTHERFORD TER
45100 FRMT 94539 774-A3
RUTHERGLEN PL
5200 SJS 95136 874-F3
RUTHER PLACE CT
1600 SJS 95121 855-B4
RUTHER PLACE WY
3600 SJS 95121 855-B4
RUTHLAND RD
6100 OAK 94611 630-D5
RUTHVEN AV
400 PA 94301 790-H4
RUTHVEN LN
- DBLN 94552 693-E5
RUTLAND AV
300 SCIC 95128 853-G1
RUTLAND CT
- ALA 94502 669-H6
200 SRMN 94583 673-F5
35300 NWK 94560 752-D4
RUTLAND DR
500 PCFA 94044 707-A2
RUTLAND ST
- SF 94134 688-A2
500 DALY 94014 688-A2
500 DALY 94014 687-J3
RUTLEDGE COM
3600 FRMT 94538 753-D6
RUTLEDGE PL
1000 PLE 94566 714-F6
2000 SCL 95051 833-D2
RUTLEDGE RD
20700 AlaC 94546 691-J5
RUTLEDGE ST
- SF 94110 668-A4
300 SF 94110 667-J4
RUTTNER CT
4900 SJS 95111 875-C1
RUTTNER PL
4900 SJS 95111 875-C1
RUUS LN
28100 HAY 94544 732-A1
RUUS RD
28100 HAY 94544 712-B7
28400 HAY 94544 732-B1
RUXTON CT
6200 PLE 94588 694-A7
RYAN AV
- MLV 94941 606-F4
3000 SCL 95051 833-A6
RYAN CT
- SCIC 94305 810-J2
800 CNCD 94518 592-H6
RYAN DR
100 PLHL 94523 592-B1
10100 SJS 95127 835-B3
RYAN PL
800 PLHL 94523 592-B1
RYAN RD
2500 CNCD 94518 592-G6
RYAN ST
1000 OAK 94621 670-C6
RYAN WY
100 SSF 94080 707-H4
RYAN INDUSTRIAL CT
100 SRMN 94583 673-B1
RYANS AL
700 MLPK 94025 790-F4
RYCROFT CT
7000 SJS 95120 894-H3
RYDAL AV
300 MrnC 94941 606-D5
RYDAL CT
- OAK 94611 650-F1
- ORIN 94563 631-C5
RYDER ST
200 SMTO 94401 729-B7
400 VAL 94590 530-B5
3500 SCL 95051 812-J7
RYDIN RD
2500 RCH 94804 609-B4
RYE CT
1000 SJS 95127 835-C2
RYE TER
33700 FRMT 94555 732-E6
RYEGATE CT
300 SJS 95133 834-F2
RYEGATE PL
- SRMN 94583 673-F5
RYLAND ST
100 SJS 95110 834-A5
RYMAR CT
1000 SJS 95133 814-F6
RYMAR DR
2500 SJS 95133 814-F7
RYMAR LN
2500 SJS 95133 814-F6
RYMAR PL
1000 SJS 95133 814-F6
RYMAR TER
1000 SJS 95133 814-F7
RYMAR WY
1000 SJS 95133 814-F7

S

S ST
200 BEN 94510 551-C4
N S ST
100 LVMR 94550 715-F1
S S ST
- LVMR 94550 715-F1
SABA CT
- SRMN 94583 673-D3
SABA LN
- MrnC 94920 607-C2
SABAL CIR
2800 MRTZ 94553 571-E4
SABAL CT
1100 SJS 95132 814-G5
SABAL DR
1100 SJS 95132 814-G5
SABERCAT CT
2500 FRMT 94539 773-F1
SABERCAT PL
43000 FRMT 94539 773-F1
SABERCAT RD
2500 FRMT 94539 773-F1
SABIN AV
5100 FRMT 94536 752-H6
SABIN PL
- SF 94108 648-A5
SABINA CT
200 DNVL 94526 653-C3
17000 AlaC 94546 691-H5
SABINA WY
1500 SJS 95118 874-A4
SABIO CT
4100 FRMT 94536 752-F2
SABLE POINTE
- ALA 94502 670-A5
SABRE ST
1600 HAY 94545 711-D3
SABRINA CT
1200 RDWC 94061 790-A1
SACLAN TER
300 CLAY 94517 593-H5
SACRAMENTO
4000 ALA 94501 649-E6
SACRAMENTO AV
- MrnC 94901 566-C5
- MrnC 94960 566-C5
- SAUS 94965 626-H1
100 SANS 94960 566-C5
4200 FRMT 94538 753-A6
5100 RCH 94804 609-B4
SACRAMENTO ST
100 SF 94111 648-A5
300 VAL 94590 529-J5
400 SF 94104 648-A5
500 EPA 94303 791-B1
700 SF 94108 648-A5
1100 SF 94108 647-E5
1300 BERK 94702 609-F7
1300 SF 94109 647-E5
1300 BERK 94703 609-F7
1400 BERK 94702 629-F3
1400 BERK 94703 629-F3
2100 VAL 94589 529-H1
2200 SF 94115 647-E5
3000 OAK 94608 629-F5
3400 SF 94118 647-E5
3600 SF 94118 647-D6
4000 CNCD 94521 593-B2
SACRAMENTO TER
900 PCFA 94044 707-A5
SACRAMENTO WY
- SAUS 94965 627-B3
SACREMENTO AV
4000 SJS 95111 855-A6
SADDLE CT
27800 LAH 94022 810-J6
SADDLE DR
3100 AlaC 94541 712-D2
SADDLE LN
- MrnC 94947 525-F3
SADDLE RD
- CCCo 94595 632-C2
SADDLEBACK
- PTLV 94028 830-C1
SADDLEBACK CIR
500 LVMR 94550 695-E5
SADDLEBACK CT
- CCCo 94506 653-H2
5300 RCH 94803 590-A3
SADDLEBACK DR
- DALY 94014 687-G2
- SF 94134 687-G2
2300 CCCo 94506 653-H2
2400 DNVL 94506 653-H2
SADDLEBACK LN
- CCCo 94506 653-H2
SADDLEBACK PL
- CCCo 94506 653-H2
SADDLE BACK TER
500 FRMT 94536 753-C2
SADDLE BROOK CT
- OAK 94619 651-B6
SADDLEBROOK CT
- NVTO 94947 525-J4
SADDLE BROOK DR
- SJS 95136 874-H2
- SJS 95136 875-A2
5100 OAK 94619 651-B6
SADDLEBROOK LN
400 PLHL 94523 591-J3
SADDLE CREEK CT
500 SRMN 94583 694-B1
SADDLEHILL LN
1200 CNCD 94521 593-B4
SADDLE MOUNTAIN DR
14200 LAH 94022 810-J6
SADDLE OAKS CT
100 CCCo 94596 612-G6
SADDLE TREE CT
- SJS 95136 874-H2

Thomas Bros. Maps® COPYRIGHT 1997

STREET
Block City ZIP Pg-Grid

SADDLEVIEW CT
- LVMR 94550 696-E3
SADDLEWOOD CT
5300 CNCD 94521 593-F4
SADDLEWOOD DR
1000 SJS 95121 854-H2
1800 CNCD 94521 593-F4
SADIE CT
4000 SJS 95008 853-B7
SADOWA ST
- SF 94112 687-D2
200 SF 94132 687-D2
SAFARI DR
400 SJS 95123 874-J6
SAFARI WY
200 CCCo 94553 572-C7
SAFE HAVEN CT
- SJS 95111 854-J5
SAFFARIAN CT
2100 SJS 95121 855-C3
SAFFLE CT
1400 CMBL 95008 873-B1
SAFFOLD AV
- SF 94129 647-B4
SAFIRA LN
- SF 94131 667-F4
SAGA LN
- MLPK 94025 790-D7
- MLPK 94025 810-D1
SAGAMORE ST
200 SF 94112 687-D2
200 SF 94132 687-D2
SAGE CIR
- SRMN 94583 673-C4
SAGE CT
- NVTO 94945 526-A1
- WLCK 94596 612-B3
400 BEN 94510 551-A1
900 CPTO 95014 852-C2
1000 FRMT 94539 773-H3
2600 ANT 94509 595-G5
6800 DBLN 94568 693-J4
N SAGE CT
1100 SUNV 94087 832-D3
SAGE DR
800 MRTZ 94553 591-F3
SAGE LN
- ALA 94502 670-A7
SAGE RD
8900 OAK 94605 671-C2
8900 OAK 94627 671-C2
SAGE ST
100 VAL 94589 510-D6
1100 EPA 94303 791-C2
25600 HAY 94545 711-E7
SAGEBRUSH CT
- SRFL 94901 567-C5
SAGEBRUSH DR
3900 ANT 94509 595-H4
SAGEBRUSH PZ
- HAY 94542 712-B3
SAGE GROUSE RD
- NVTO 94949 546-E5
SAGE HEN CT
1300 SJS 95118 874-C2
SAGE HEN WY
1300 SUNV 94087 832-H4
SAGE HILL CT
- DNVL 94526 653-B6
SAGELAND DR
1700 SJS 95131 814-D6
SAGELEAF CT
700 HAY 94544 712-A7
SAGEMEADOW CT
100 MPS 95035 794-A6
SAGEMILL CT
1200 SJS 95121 854-J3
SAGEMONT AV
4500 SJS 95130 853-A5
SAGE OAK WY
6000 SJS 95120 874-D7
SAGER CT
- ORIN 94563 631-A5
SAGER WY
6200 SJS 95123 874-H7
SAGEWELL WY
5700 SJS 95138 875-D4
SAGEWOOD AV
1500 SLN 94579 691-A5
SAGEWOOD CT
1800 CNCD 94521 593-F4
SAGEWOOD LN
3200 SJS 95132 814-E2
SAGHALIE LN
- SAUS 94965 627-B3
SAGINAW CIR
- PLE 94588 694-D6
SAGINAW CT
- PLE 94588 694-D6
SAGINAW DR
100 RDWC 94063 770-C3
SAGITTARIUS LN
3200 SJS 95111 854-F6
SAGUARE COM
1100 FRMT 94539 774-A4
SAGUARE CT
1100 FRMT 94539 774-A4
SAGUARE TER
1100 FRMT 94539 774-A4
SAHARA CT
1000 HAY 94541 711-D2
SAHARA DR
100 CCCo 94553 572-C7
SAHARA RD
1000 HAY 94541 711-D2
SAHARA WY
2000 SCL 95050 833-D3
SAICH WY
10000 CPTO 95014 832-D7
SAIDEL DR
2200 SJS 95124 873-E4
SAILFISH COM
38900 FRMT 94536 753-C3
SAILFISH ISL
300 FCTY 94404 749-H3
SAILMAKER CT
- SRFL 94903 566-G2
SAILWAY DR
- FRMT 94538 753-C5
SAINT ALBANS RD
100 CCCo 94708 609-F3

SAINT ALICIA CT
100 CCCo 94507 632-H4
SAINT ALPHONSUS WY
1500 CCCo 94507 632-F5
SAINT ANDREWS AV
22300 CPTO 95014 852-A2
27100 HAY 94544 712-A6
SAINT ANDREWS CT
1700 MPS 95035 794-D3
SAINT ANDREWS DR
- NVTO 94949 546-A2
900 CCCo 94803 569-D7
1600 MRGA 94556 631-C7
SAINT ANDREWS LN
- CCCo 94507 632-J4
SAINT ANDREWS PL
- CCCo 94507 632-H4
1700 SJS 95132 814-E3
SAINT ANDREWS RD
4100 OAK 94605 671-C3
SAINT ANDREWS ST
- HAY 94544 732-D2
SAINT ANDREWS WY
4000 ANT 94509 595-D2
SAINT ANN CT
- DNVL 94526 653-C6
3200 ANT 94509 595-C3
19700 SAR 95070 852-F7
SAINT ANNES CT
5100 SJS 95138 855-F7
SAINT ANNES PL
30300 HAY 94544 732-D2
SAINT ANTHONY CT
1100 LALT 94024 831-J5
SAINT ANTHONY DR
1600 SCIC 95125 853-H5
41100 FRMT 94539 753-F5
SAINT ANTHONYS PL
1600 CMBL 95008 873-E2
SAINT AUGUSTINE CT
- BEN 94510 551-C4
SAINT AUGUSTINE DR
200 BEN 94510 551-C4
SAINT BEATRICE CT
- DNVL 94526 653-D6
SAINT BEDE LN
800 HAY 94544 712-A6
800 HAY 94544 711-J6
SAINT BENEDICT CT
- SRMN 94583 673-E5
SAINT BERNARD LN
- TBRN 94920 607-E7
SAINT BERNARD RD
- TBRN 94920 607-E7
SAINT BONAVENTURE CT
5000 CNCD 94521 593-D5
SAINT CATHERINE CT
1300 CNCD 94521 593-D5
5400 SCIC 95127 815-A7
SAINT CATHERINE DR
200 DALY 94015 687-A7
SAINT CATHERINES SQ
300 BEN 94510 551-B4
SAINT CELESTINE CT
5000 CNCD 94521 593-D5
SAINT CHARLES AV
- SF 94132 687-C2
SAINT CHARLES CT
- DNVL 94526 653-B5
1100 LALT 94024 831-H5
SAINT CHARLES PL
2200 LVMR 94550 715-G4
SAINT CHARLES ST
1100 ALA 94501 669-G2
1700 ALA 94501 649-G7
20700 SAR 95070 872-D3
SAINT CHRISTOPHER CT
3100 ANT 94509 595-A1
SAINT CHRISTOPHER DR
200 DNVL 94526 653-D5
SAINT CHRISTOPHER ST
37000 NWK 94560 752-F5
SAINT CHRISTOPHER WY
5300 NWK 94560 752-F5
SAINT CLAIRE CT
- PLHL 94523 591-J2
2200 SCL 95054 813-C5
SAINT CLAIRE DR
500 PA 94306 791-D7
1300 ANT 94509 575-G5
1300 CCCo 94509 575-G5
SAINT CLAIRE LN
- PLHL 94523 592-A2
- PLHL 94523 591-J2
SAINT CLOUD CT
4300 OAK 94619 650-J6
SAINT CLOUD DR
2500 SSF 94080 707-D5
2500 SBRN 94066 707-D5
SAINT CROIX CT
4200 SJS 95118 874-C2
SAINT CROIX DR
- SF 94127 667-E5
SAINT CROIX LN
600 FCTY 94404 749-J1
SAINT DAVID DR
1600 DNVL 94526 653-C5
SAINT DENIS CT
200 SRMN 94583 673-F5
SAINT DENIS DR
2800 SRMN 94583 673-E5
SAINT DUNSTAN CT
5000 CNCD 94521 593-D5
SAINT EDWARD CT
100 DNVL 94526 653-C5
SAINT EDWARD ST
37000 NWK 94560 752-F6
SAINT ELIZABETH CT
1200 CNCD 94518 592-J4
SAINT ELIZABETH DR
800 SCIC 95126 853-H3
800 SJS 95126 853-H3
SAINT ELMO DR
9800 OAK 94603 670-G7
SAINT ELMO WY
- SF 94127 667-D6

SAINT FLORENCE DR
400 SJS 95133 834-G1
SAINT FRANCES DR
900 ANT 94509 575-B6
SAINT FRANCIS AV
700 NVTO 94947 525-G3
27100 HAY 94544 712-A6
SAINT FRANCIS BLVD
- DALY 94015 687-B7
- SF 94127 667-C6
600 DALY 94015 707-B1
SAINT FRANCIS CT
- BEN 94510 551-C4
- LFYT 94549 611-D4
100 DNVL 94526 653-D6
500 MLPK 94025 790-F6
SAINT FRANCIS DR
- VAL 94590 529-J3
400 DNVL 94526 653-D6
1000 CNCD 94518 592-H4
1400 SCIC 95125 853-H5
2100 PA 94303 791-D4
3700 LFYT 94549 611-D4
SAINT FRANCIS LN
100 SRFL 94901 566-H7
SAINT FRANCIS PL
- SF 94107 648-B6
500 MLPK 94025 790-F6
SAINT FRANCIS RD
- HIL 94010 748-H2
26400 LAH 94022 811-A5
SAINT FRANCIS ST
- RDWC 94061 789-J1
300 RDWC 94062 769-J7
500 MLPK 94025 790-A1
600 RDWC 94061 790-A1
SAINT FRANCIS TER
- FRMT 94539 774-B7
SAINT FRANCIS WY
100 RDWC 94062 769-H7
600 PLE 94566 714-G1
600 RDWC 94061 769-H7
700 RDWC 94061 789-J1
1100 SCAR 94070 769-H5
SAINT GABRIELE CT
- TBRN 94920 607-E6
SAINT GARRETT CT
5000 CNCD 94521 593-D5
SAINT GEORGE AL
- SF 94108 648-A5
SAINT GEORGE CT
- PLHL 94523 591-J2
SAINT GEORGE DR
2200 CNCD 94520 572-G4
SAINT GEORGE LN
7200 SJS 95120 894-G5
SAINT GEORGE RD
500 DNVL 94526 653-E6
SAINT GEORGE ST
300 AlaC 94541 691-G7
500 LVMR 94550 695-H6
SAINT GERMAIN AV
- SF 94114 667-E3
100 SF 94114 667-E3
SAINT GERMAIN CT
- PLHL 94523 591-J2
SAINT GERMAIN LN
100 PLHL 94523 591-J2
100 PLHL 94523 592-A2
SAINT GERMAIN PL
- CNCD 94521 593-E4
SAINT GILES LN
2600 MTVW 94040 831-J2
SAINT HELENA CT
100 DNVL 94526 653-C6
SAINT HELENA DR
1500 DNVL 94526 653-C6
2400 HAY 94542 712-D3
SAINT HENRY DR
200 FRMT 94539 753-F5
SAINT HILL RD
- ORIN 94563 611-A6
SAINT IGNATIUS PL
3200 SCL 95051 833-A2
SAINT ISABEL AV
5200 NWK 94560 752-F6
SAINT IVES CT
600 WLCK 94598 612-E1
SAINT JAMES AL
- SF 94108 648-A4
100 SF 94133 648-A4
SAINT JAMES CIR
400 PDMT 94611 650-D2
SAINT JAMES CT
- DALY 94015 687-B6
- ORIN 94563 610-G4
100 DNVL 94526 653-C6
900 AlaC 94541 691-G7
SAINT JAMES DR
- PDMT 94611 650-C2
- PDMT 94610 650-D2
3900 CCCo 94803 589-B3
SAINT JAMES PKWY
1400 CNCD 94521 593-D5
SAINT JAMES PL
- PDMT 94610 650-C2
3200 ANT 94509 595-B1
SAINT JAMES RD
2700 BLMT 94002 769-A3
2900 BLMT 94002 768-J2
2900 SMCo 94070 768-J2
SAINT JAMES ST
37000 FRMT 94536 752-G4
E SAINT JAMES ST
- SJS 95112 834-C5
1100 SJS 95116 834-F3
W SAINT JAMES ST
100 SJS 95113 834-B6
100 SJS 95110 834-B6
SAINT JEAN CT
100 DNVL 94526 653-C5
SAINT JOAN CT
- DNVL 94526 653-C5
20700 SAR 95070 852-D5
SAINT JOAN LN
100 PLHL 94523 591-J2
SAINT JOHN CIR
700 PLE 94566 714-D3
800 CNCD 94518 592-H5
SAINT JOHN CT
- NVTO 94947 525-G3
- SMTO 94401 728-H7

SAINT JOHN CT
800 PLE 94566 714-D3
800 CNCD 94518 592-H5
SAINT JOHN LN
- CCCo 94803 589-H5
4400 PIT 94565 574-C7
SAINT JOHN ST
400 PLE 94566 714-D3
E SAINT JOHN ST
- SJS 95112 834-C5
- SJS 95113 834-C5
1100 SJS 95116 834-E4
W SAINT JOHN ST
100 SJS 95113 834-A6
100 SJS 95110 834-A6
SAINT JOHNS CT
- AlaC 94580 691-E6
- WLCK 94596 612-B4
SAINT JOHNS DR
15900 AlaC 94580 691-E6
SAINT JOHNS MINE RD
- VAL 94591 510-G7
- VAL 94591 530-H1
SAINT JOSEPH AV
900 LALT 94024 831-G5
7500 SCIC 94024 831-G5
7500 CPTO 95014 831-G5
SAINT JOSEPH CT
11400 LALT 94024 831-G4
SAINT JOSEPH DR
2800 CNCD 94518 592-G5
SAINT JOSEPHS AV
- SF 94115 647-F6
SAINT JUDE LN
- MrnC 94965 606-B3
SAINT JULIE CT
- PLHL 94523 592-A2
SAINT JULIE DR
300 SJS 95119 875-C7
SAINT KITTS CT
800 SJS 95127 814-G6
SAINT KITTS LN
1400 FCTY 94404 749-G5
SAINT LAURENT CT
5400 SCIC 95127 815-A7
SAINT LAWRENCE CT
- PLHL 94523 592-C7
700 PCFA 94044 727-C4
SAINT LAWRENCE DR
800 PCFA 94044 727-C4
1800 SCL 95051 832-J3
2400 SJS 95124 853-G7
SAINT LAWRENCE WY
1600 PLHL 94523 592-C7
SAINT LEONARDS WY
3800 FRMT 94538 753-C6
SAINT LOUIS AL
- SF 94108 648-A4
SAINT LOUIS CT
900 CNCD 94518 592-E7
SAINT LOUIS DR
1200 CNCD 94518 592-D7
SAINT LOUIS LN
- PLHL 94523 592-A2
- PLHL 94523 591-J2
SAINT LUCIA CT
800 SJS 95127 814-G6
SAINT LUCIA DR
- RDWC 94065 749-J5
SAINT LUCIA PL
- MrnC 94920 607-C2
SAINT LUKE CT
- NWK 94560 752-F6
- DNVL 94526 653-C6
24800 AlaC 94541 712-C1
SAINT MARGARET CT
2600 ALA 94501 670-A2
SAINT MARGARETS CT
2200 LVMR 94550 715-G4
SAINT MARK AV
5300 NWK 94560 752-F6
SAINT MARK CT
- DNVL 94526 653-C6
1200 LALT 94024 831-J5
SAINT MARKS CT
- DALY 94015 687-B6
SAINT MARTIN DR
- RDWC 94065 749-J5
- RDWC 94065 750-A5
SAINT MARY AV
600 SLN 94577 671-C7
SAINT MARY DR
1200 LVMR 94550 716-A2
SAINT MARY ST
300 PLE 94566 714-D3
37000 NWK 94560 752-F5
SAINT MARY ALICE CT
5000 CNCD 94521 593-D5
SAINT MARYS AV
- SF 94112 667-H6
100 SF 94131 667-H6
SAINT MARYS CT
- SMTO 94401 728-J7
100 MRTZ 94553 571-D6
SAINT MARYS PL
- RDWC 94063 770-F7
100 VAL 94589 510-B5
3300 SCL 95051 832-J2
SAINT MARYS RD
200 LFYT 94549 611-F7
200 LFYT 94549 631-G5
200 MRGA 94556 631-E6
SAINT MARYS ST
3800 MRTZ 94553 571-D6
SAINT MATTHEW DR
5600 NWK 94560 752-F6
SAINT MATTHEW PL
1100 CNCD 94518 593-A4
SAINT MATTHEW WY
1200 LALT 94024 831-J5
SAINT MATTHEWS AV
- SMTO 94401 748-J1
SAINT MAURICE CT
- DNVL 94526 653-B6
SAINT MICHAEL CIR
700 PLE 94566 714-G3
SAINT MICHAEL CT
- SRMN 94583 673-E5
3300 PA 94306 791-D7
3900 CNCD 94519 573-A7

SAINT MICHAEL DR
3300 PA 94306 791-D7
SAINT MICHAELS CT
- DALY 94015 687-A6
SAINT MORITZ AV
1200 MRTZ 94553 571-H5
SAINT MORITZ DR
3700 PIT 94565 574-E6
SAINT NICHOLAS CT
200 FRMT 94539 753-F5
SAINT NORBERT DR
300 DNVL 94526 653-D6
SAINT OLAF WY
100 VAL 94589 510-B5
SAINT PATRICIA CT
5000 CNCD 94521 593-D5
SAINT PATRICKS CT
- DNVL 94526 653-B5
SAINT PATRICKS DR
100 DNVL 94526 653-B6
SAINT PAUL CIR
- NVTO 94947 526-A3
4200 PIT 94565 574-E6
SAINT PAUL CT
5800 OAK 94618 630-C6
SAINT PAUL DR
200 CCCo 94507 632-H4
1700 CMBL 95008 853-B5
5700 NWK 94560 752-F6
SAINT PAUL WY
4200 CNCD 94518 593-A4
SAINT PETER CT
3700 CNCD 94518 592-J3
SAINT PHILIP CT
100 DNVL 94526 653-C5
1800 CNCD 94519 592-J1
SAINT PHILLIP CT
200 FRMT 94539 753-F5
SAINT PIERRE CT
- SRMN 94583 673-E5
SAINT RAMON CT
- DNVL 94526 653-C7
SAINT RAPHAEL DR
1000 CCCo 94565 573-D2
SAINT RAYMOND CT
7800 DBLN 94568 693-G3
SAINT REGIS DR
400 DNVL 94526 653-D6
1500 SJS 95124 874-A3
SAINT STEPHENS CIR
- ORIN 94563 610-J6
SAINT STEPHENS DR
- ORIN 94563 610-J6
SAINT TENNY PL
- SF 94105 648-B6
SAINT TERESA CT
- DNVL 94526 653-C5
SAINT THOMAS CT
- PLHL 94523 591-J2
SAINT THOMAS LN
- PLHL 94523 591-J2
500 FCTY 94404 749-G5
SAINT THOMAS WY
- MrnC 94920 607-C2
500 PLE 94566 714-G1
SAINT TIMOTHY CT
- DNVL 94526 653-D6
SAINT TIMOTHY PL
1100 CNCD 94518 593-A5
1100 CNCD 94518 592-J5
SAINT TROPEZ CT
- DNVL 94506 653-H5
SAINT TROPEZ DR
- CCCo 94565 573-D2
SAINT VINCENT CT
100 DNVL 94526 653-C6
SAINT VINCENT LN
500 FCTY 94404 749-J2
SAINT VINCENTS DR
- MrnC 94903 546-F6
SAIS AV
- SANS 94960 566-B7
SAJAK AV
1200 SJS 95131 814-B7
SAKLAN RD
22800 AlaC 94545 711-E5
23500 HAY 94545 711-E5
SAKLAN INDIAN DR
- WLCK 94595 632-B3
SAKURA WY
19300 CPTO 95014 852-G1
SAL CT
29400 HAY 94544 732-C1
SAL ST
- SF 94129 647-D4
SALA ST
- VAL 94589 530-A1
SALA TER
- SF 94112 687-E2
SALADA AV
100 PCFA 94044 706-J5
SALADO DR
1500 MTVW 94043 791-G7
1500 MTVW 94043 811-G1
SALAMANCA AV
1400 HAY 94544 732-A1
SALAMANCA CT
200 SRMN 94583 673-C3
1400 FRMT 94539 753-G7
SALAS CT
2100 EPA 94303 791-C2
SALAZAR CT
100 CLAY 94517 613-J1
SALBERG AV
600 SCL 95051 833-B6
SALEM AV
22300 CPTO 95014 832-A7
22500 CPTO 95014 831-J7
SALEM CT
- CCCo 94806 569-B4
300 SRMN 94583 673-E5
600 LVMR 94550 695-E6
SALEM CV
- SRFL 94901 587-A2
SALEM DR
2900 SCL 95051 833-A6
3100 SJS 95127 814-H6
SALEM RD
19600 AlaC 94546 692-A4
SALEM ST
4300 EMVL 94608 629-F6
6400 OAK 94608 629-F5

E SALEM ST
3900 CNCD 94521 593-B2
SALEM WY
43600 FRMT 94538 773-E2
SALEM TOWN CT
- DNVL 94526 653-C4
SALERNO DR
900 SCIC 95008 873-E1
SALESIAN AV
2800 RCH 94804 588-J4
SALICE WY
- CMBL 95008 853-D6
SALIDA WY
1100 CCCo 94803 569-C7
SALIDA DEL SOL
6000 SJS 95123 874-F6
SALINA DR
4500 SJS 95124 873-F3
SALINAS AV
- SANS 94960 566-B5
100 SF 94124 688-B1
SALINAS CT
3300 SJS 95132 814-G3
SALINAS PL
34400 FRMT 94555 752-D1
SALISBURY CT
3100 FRMT 94555 732-F7
3100 LVMR 94550 695-H6
SALISBURY DR
- PIT 94565 574-C3
1600 SJS 95124 873-J3
5200 NWK 94560 752-E4
SALISBURY LN
2200 CNCD 94520 572-F5
SALISBURY ST
3400 OAK 94601 650-D6
SALISBURY WY
2200 SMTO 94403 749-C4
SALLY CT
2900 SCL 95051 833-A3
4800 UNC 94587 751-J1
23200 AlaC 94541 692-D7
SALLY DR
4400 SJS 95124 873-H4
SALLY LN
- CCCo 94595 612-A6
SALLY ANN RD
- ORIN 94563 631-A2
SALLY CREEK CIR
1800 AlaC 94541 712-B2
SALLY RIDE DR
200 CCCo 94553 572-C7
200 CCCo 94520 572-C7
SALLY RIDE WY
- OAK 94621 690-C1
SALMAR AV
400 CMBL 95008 853-E5
SALMARK CT
- HIL 94402 748-G5
SALMON DR
400 SJS 95111 854-G4
SALMON RD
- ALA 94502 669-H6
SALMON ST
- SF 94133 647-J4
SALMON TER
38800 FRMT 94536 753-F3
SALMON WY
31000 HAY 94544 732-C3
SALMON CREEK CT
1500 SJS 95127 835-C3
SALOME CT
2600 SJS 95121 854-H4
SALSBURY DR
200 SCL 95051 833-B7
SALT CT
700 RDWC 94065 749-H5
SALT LNDG
- MrnC 94920 606-H3
SALTAMONTES DR
14600 LAH 94022 811-C5
SALT CREEK LN
- MLV 94941 606-G2
SALTER CT
900 PLHL 94523 592-C3
SALT LAKE CT
800 SJS 95133 814-G6
SALT LAKE DR
600 SJS 95133 814-G7
SALTON SEA LN
32400 FRMT 94555 732-B6
SALT POINT CT
200 VAL 94591 550-E2
SALUDA CT
1300 SJS 95121 854-J2
SALVADOR CT
3900 PLE 94566 714-F4
35800 FRMT 94536 752-F3
SALVADOR WY
- SRFL 94903 566-E1
SALVATIERRA ST
500 SCIC 94305 810-H1
SALVATORE CT
1300 SJS 95120 874-C6
SALVATORE DR
- NVTO 94949 546-E2
1200 SJS 95120 874-C6
SALVIA COM
5600 FRMT 94538 773-A2
SALVIA DR
- AlaC 94542 692-E7
SALVINO CT
2900 RCH 94803 589-E2
SALVIO ST
1700 CNCD 94520 592-F2
2500 CNCD 94519 592-G1
2900 CNCD 94519 572-H7
SAMANTHA CT
100 CCCo 94507 632-G2
32200 UNC 94587 731-J7
SAMAR DR
6400 SJS 95119 875-C7
SAMARIA LN
- OAK 94619 650-H5
SAMARITAN CT
2500 SJS 95124 873-D4
SAMARITAN DR
2000 SCIC 95124 873-D3
2000 SJS 95124 873-D3
15100 LGTS 95032 873-D3
SAMARITAN PL
2300 SJS 95124 873-E4

SAM CAVA LN
400 CMBL 95008 853-E6
SAMEDRA ST
1400 SUNV 94087 832-C5
SAM MCDONALD RD
- SCIC 94305 790-J6
SAMMIE AV
600 FRMT 94539 773-H6
SAMOA CIR
400 UNC 94587 732-D5
SAMOA CT
100 SRMN 94583 653-E7
100 SRMN 94583 673-E1
SAMOA LN
700 NVTO 94947 526-E6
SAMOA RD
13800 SLN 94577 690-H5
SAMOA WY
2300 SJS 95122 834-J5
SAMOSET ST
- SF 94110 668-A5
SAMROSE DR
- NVTO 94945 526-E3
100 MrnC 94945 526-E3
SAMSON CT
4500 SJS 95124 873-J3
SAMSON ST
200 RDWC 94063 770-A5
SAMSON WY
3400 AlaC 94546 692-A5
3400 AlaC 94546 691-J5
3900 SJS 95124 873-H3
SAMUEL CT
100 CLAY 94517 613-J1
SAMUEL DR
2900 SJS 95121 855-A3
SAMUEL LN
12800 LAH 94022 811-A6
SAMUEL ST
2500 PIN 94564 569-F4
SAN ALESO AV
- SF 94127 667-C6
700 SUNV 94086 812-E5
SAN ALESO WY
- NVTO 94945 525-H1
SAN ANDREAS AV
1500 SJS 95118 874-A1
SAN ANDREAS CIR
- NVTO 94945 525-H1
SAN ANDREAS CT
- NVTO 94945 525-H1
100 SUNV 94086 812-E7
300 MPS 95035 793-J5
700 CNCD 94518 592-H7
SAN ANDREAS DR
- DNVL 94506 653-F1
- NVTO 94945 525-H1
100 MLPK 94025 790-H3
200 MPS 95035 793-J5
3000 UNC 94587 732-A5
SAN ANDREAS WY
- SF 94127 667-D6
100 VAL 94589 509-H5
SAN ANGELO AV
400 SUNV 94086 812-E6
SAN ANGELO WY
3100 UNC 94587 732-B5
SAN ANSELMO AV
- SANS 94960 566-A7
- SF 94127 667-C5
100 SBRN 94066 727-J1
200 SBRN 94066 728-A1
1000 MLBR 94030 728-A1
1400 SANS 94960 586-C1
1700 ROSS 94957 586-C1
SAN ANSELMO AV N
200 SBRN 94066 727-J1
400 SBRN 94066 707-J7
SAN ANSELMO WY
200 SUNV 94086 812-E6
6300 SJS 95119 875-C7
SAN ANTONIO AV
- MTVW 94040 811-F2
100 PA 94306 811-F2
100 SBRN 94066 728-A1
100 SMCo 94128 728-A1
300 SMTO 94401 728-J7
700 PA 94043 811-F2
700 PA 94303 811-F2
1000 MTVW 94043 791-F7
1000 PA 94303 791-F7
1100 ALA 94501 669-G1
1400 MLPK 94025 790-F3
1500 MTVW 94303 791-F7
1800 BERK 94707 609-F5
2200 ALA 94501 670-A2
SAN ANTONIO CIR
- DALY 94014 687-F3
100 MTVW 94040 811-E3
SAN ANTONIO CT
- WLCK 94598 612-F3
200 SJS 95116 834-F5
SAN ANTONIO DR
2600 WLCK 94598 612-F3
SAN ANTONIO PL
- SF 94133 648-A4
- SF 94133 648-A4
2100 SCL 95051 833-A2
SAN ANTONIO RD
100 MTVW 94040 811-E4
N SAN ANTONIO RD
- LALT 94022 811-E6
S SAN ANTONIO RD
- LALT 94022 811-E7
SAN ANTONIO ST
5400 PLE 94566 714-E5
30400 HAY 94544 732-C2
E SAN ANTONIO ST
400 SJS 95112 834-D6
800 SJS 95116 834-G4
SAN ANTONIO WY
200 PA 94306 811-F2
200 WLCK 94598 612-F3
1600 OAK 94606 650-A5
37000 NWK 94560 752-F5
SAN ARDO CT
- WLCK 94598 612-F3
700 CNCD 94518 592-H7
31300 UNC 94587 732-B6
SAN ARDO DR
1500 SCIC 95125 853-H4

BAY AREA

INDEX

STREET
Block City ZIP Pg-Grid

SAN ARDO WY
800 MTVW 94043 811-J3
2800 BLMT 94002 769-B1
SAN BENITO AV
- ATN 94027 790-E1
100 SBRN 94066 728-A1
400 LGTS 95030 873-A6
500 SMCo 94025 770-E7
500 SMCo 94063 790-E1
15800 MSER 95030 873-A5
SAN BENITO CT
- WLCK 94598 612-G3
30800 HAY 94544 732-C3
SAN BENITO DR
2600 WLCK 94598 612-F3
E SAN BENITO DR
1300 FRMT 94539 794-A2
SAN BENITO RD
- BSBN 94005 688-A6
900 BERK 94707 609-G6
SAN BENITO ST
1600 RCH 94804 609-C3
3600 SMTO 94403 749-D6
30900 HAY 94544 732-C3
SAN BENITO WY
- NVTO 94945 525-H1
- SF 94127 667-C6
15800 MSER 95030 873-A5
SAN BERNARDINO CT
100 CCCo 94565 573-E2
SAN BERNARDINO WY
300 SUNV 94086 812-E6
3100 UNC 94587 732-B5
3900 SJS 95111 854-J7
SAN BLAS CT
- NVTO 94945 525-H1
SAN BLAS PL
- SRMN 94583 673-G5
SAN BLAS RD
- HAY 94541 711-G3
SANBORN AV
1400 SJS 95110 854-D2
SANBORN CT
400 BEN 94510 550-J2
SANBORN DR
- OAK 94602 650-F3
- OAK 94611 650-F3
SANBORN RD
- ORIN 94563 630-J3
15800 SCIC 95070 872-A6
SANBORN TER
38500 FRMT 94536 753-C2
SAN BRUNO AV
- SMCo 94128 708-A6
- BSBN 94005 688-A6
- SF 94103 668-A2
400 SF 94110 668-A3
500 SF 94107 668-A2
2100 SF 94110 668-A7
2100 SF 94134 668-A7
3100 SF 94134 688-A1
SAN BRUNO AV E
- SMCo 94128 708-A6
100 SBRN 94066 707-J6
700 SBRN 94066 708-A6
SAN BRUNO AV W
- SBRN 94066 707-G7
2000 SBRN 94066 727-F1
SAN BRUNO CT
700 CNCD 94518 592-J7
31300 UNC 94587 732-D4
SAN BUENA CT
6100 SJS 95119 875-C6
SAN BUENAVENTURA WY
- SF 94127 667-C6
SAN CARLO CT
- DNVL 94526 653-C7
SAN CARLOS
2400 AlaC 94546 691-H5
SAN CARLOS AV
- SAUS 94965 627-B3
100 ELCR 94530 609-E6
100 SMCo 94061 790-B3
200 PDMT 94611 650-A1
300 PDMT 94610 650-A1
500 ALB 94706 609-E6
700 MTVW 94043 812-A3
700 MTVW 94043 811-J3
1100 SCAR 94070 769-E3
1200 CNCD 94518 592-G3
2300 CCCo 94553 571-F4
4400 OAK 94601 650-E7
4400 OAK 94601 670-E1
E SAN CARLOS AV
900 SCAR 94070 769-G2
SAN CARLOS CT
- WLCK 94598 612-G4
- PIT 94565 574-C4
700 PA 94303 791-C6
700 FRMT 94539 753-E4
SAN CARLOS DR
900 ANT 94509 575-C6
2500 WLCK 94598 612-F3
2900 CCCo 94598 612-F3
N SAN CARLOS DR
300 WLCK 94598 612-E2
900 CCCo 94598 612-E2
E SAN CARLOS LN
700 SCAR 94070 769-H2
SAN CARLOS PL
- PIT 94565 574-C4
40100 FRMT 94539 753-E4
SAN CARLOS ST
- SF 94110 667-H3
900 SCIC 95126 853-F1
900 SJS 95126 853-F1
1500 SJS 95128 853-F1
1700 SCIC 95128 853-F1
E SAN CARLOS ST
- SJS 95113 834-C7
100 SJS 95112 834-D6
W SAN CARLOS ST
- SJS 95110 834-C7
- SJS 95113 834-C7
1800 SJS 95110 854-A1
1800 SJS 95126 854-A1
1900 SCIC 95126 854-A1
W SAN CARLOS ST Rt#-82
- SJS 95113 834-A7
- SJS 95110 834-A7
W SAN CARLOS ST Rt#-82
1600 SJS 95126 834-A7
SAN CARLOS WY
- NVTO 94945 525-J1
3200 UNC 94587 732-A5
5600 PLE 94566 714-D5
SAN CARRIZO WY
700 MTVW 94043 812-A3
800 MTVW 94043 811-J3
SAN CARVANTE CT
31300 UNC 94587 732-B6
SAN CARVANTE WY
3200 UNC 94587 732-B6
SANCHES ST
- SF 94129 647-E4
- SF 94129 647-E5
SANCHEZ AV
1100 BURL 94010 728-E6
1700 HIL 94010 728-E6
SANCHEZ DR
5500 SJS 95123 874-D4
5500 SJS 95136 874-D4
SANCHEZ ST
- SF 94114 667-G1
1200 SF 94131 667-G4
1300 SF 94131 667-G5
SANCHEZ WY
- MrnC 94947 525-E3
1100 RDWC 94061 790-A1
SAN CLEMENTE
1000 PLE 94566 714-H3
SAN CLEMENTE AV
3000 SJS 95118 874-A1
SAN CLEMENTE DR
- CMAD 94925 586-H7
- CMAD 94925 606-H1
200 MLPK 94025 790-H3
SAN CLEMENTE LN
600 FCTY 94404 749-G5
SAN CLEMENTE ST
30000 HAY 94544 732-C3
SAN CLEMENTE WY
700 MTVW 94043 811-H3
SAN CONRADO TER
600 SUNV 94086 812-G5
SANCTUARY WY
- SMCo - 768-D4
SAND DR
500 SJS 95125 854-D6
SAND RD
1900 FRMT 94539 773-F1
SANDALRIDGE CT
900 MPS 95035 794-A5
SANDALWOOD CT
- SRFL 94903 566-C2
100 VAL 94591 530-E4
600 MPS 95035 794-A4
1300 SJS 95127 835-A4
2000 PA 94303 791-D4
3000 LFYT 94549 631-H3
SANDALWOOD DR
1800 CNCD 94519 573-A7
1800 CNCD 94519 593-A1
4400 PLE 94588 713-J1
4400 PLE 94588 693-J7
SANDALWOOD ISL
600 ALA 94501 669-H2
SANDALWOOD LN
900 MPS 95035 794-A5
1200 LALT 94024 831-H4
SANDALWOOD PL
- PIT 94565 574-F6
SANDALWOOD ST
36000 NWK 94560 752-E4
SAND BEACH PL
1100 ALA 94501 669-G3
SAND BEACH RD
300 ALA 94501 669-G3
SAND BLOSSOM ST
100 SJS 95123 875-A3
SANDBURG CT
- MLV 94941 606-H6
SANDBURG WY
29200 HAY 94544 732-B2
SANDCREEK WY
1800 ALA 94501 669-H3
SANDDOLLAR CT
3500 UNC 94587 732-A5
SAND DOLLAR DR
- RCH 94804 608-H2
100 VAL 94591 550-E2
SAND DUNE WY
5500 SJS 95123 875-B4
SANDELIN AV
1100 SLN 94577 671-C7
SANDELIN CT
1300 SLN 94577 671-C7
SANDERLING CT
- CMBL 95008 853-D5
SANDERLING DR
2400 PLE 94566 714-D1
2400 PLE 94566 694-D7
2800 FRMT 94555 732-D6
SANDERLING ST
1000 FCTY 94404 749-H1
SANDERLING WY
2600 PLE 94566 694-D7
SANDERLING ISLAND
1200 RCH 94801 608-D3
SANDERS AV
400 SJS 95116 834-G4
SANDERS CT
- CCCo 94803 589-E3
SANDERS DR
100 MRGA 94556 631-D7
1000 MRGA 94556 651-E1
SANDERS RANCH RD
- MRGA 94556 651-F1
SAND HARBOR
- ALA 94502 670-A6
SAND HILL CIR
100 MLPK 94025 790-B7
SAND HILL CT
- WDSD 94062 809-H2
SANDHILL CT
- ORIN 94563 610-G2
SAND HILL RD
100 MLPK 94025 790-F6
500 PA 94304 790-G5
1300 SCIC 94305 790-G5
2100 SMCo 94025 790-F6
SAND HILL RD
2400 MLPK 94025 810-C1
2400 SMCo 94025 810-A1
3000 SMCo 94025 809-J2
3600 WDSD 94062 809-H3
SANDHILL RD
- ORIN 94563 610-G2
SANDHILL TER
33700 FRMT 94555 732-D7
SAND HILL WY
2500 SCL 95051 833-C1
SAND HOOK ISL
600 ALA 94501 669-G2
SANDHURST CT
- VAL 94591 530-H6
SANDHURST DR
- MPS 95035 794-A6
1000 VAL 94591 530-H6
SANDIA AV
1100 SUNV 94089 812-J5
1100 SUNV 94089 813-A5
SANDIA DR
1000 PLE 94566 714-G3
SAN DIEGO AV
- SF 94112 687-C3
100 DALY 94014 687-C3
100 SBRN 94066 728-A2
600 SUNV 94086 812-F5
SAN DIEGO CT
31300 UNC 94587 732-B6
SAN DIEGO PL
400 SRMN 94583 673-F5
SAN DIEGO RD
100 ALA 94501 649-D6
700 BERK 94707 609-G5
SAN DIEGO ST
5600 ELCR 94530 609-C4
SANDLEWOOD DR
28000 HAY 94545 731-H1
SAN DOMAR DR
1300 MTVW 94043 811-H3
SAN DOMINGO WY
- NVTO 94945 525-G1
300 LALT 94022 811-C5
SANDOVAL WY
600 HAY 94544 732-C1
SANDPEBBLE CT
- DNVL 94526 653-E4
SANDPEBBLE DR
4000 SJS 95136 854-F7
SANDPIPER CIR
- CMAD 94925 586-G6
SANDPIPER COM
700 LVMR 94550 695-E7
SANDPIPER CT
- CMBL 95008 853-D5
- SRFL 94903 566-G3
100 CCCo 94572 569-J2
100 NVTO 94949 546-F5
200 FCTY 94404 749-G1
1500 SUNV 94087 832-H5
2600 WLCK 94596 612-B2
3400 HAY 94542 712-F4
4400 FRMT 94555 752-B1
SANDPIPER DR
100 PIT 94565 574-D1
100 VAL 94589 509-H5
SANDPIPER LN
- RDWC 94065 749-G6
SANDPIPER PL
- ALA 94502 669-J5
33200 FRMT - 752-B1
33200 FRMT 94555 732-B7
33200 FRMT 94555 752-B1
SANDPIPER WY
2300 PLE 94566 714-C1
SANDPIPER SPIT
1400 RCH 94801 608-D3
SAND POINT CT
2700 SJS 95148 855-C1
SAND POINT DR
2600 SJS 95148 855-C1
9500 SRMN 94583 693-G1
SANDPOINT DR
- RCH 94804 608-H3
900 CCCo 94572 569-J2
1000 CCCo 94572 570-A1
SAND POINTE LN
100 CCCo 94565 573-D2
SANDRA CIR
4100 PIT 94565 574-F6
SANDRA CT
- AlaC 94541 691-G6
- CCCo 94507 632-G6
- WLCK 94595 612-C7
900 SSF 94080 707-G2
1600 PIN 94564 569-E6
4500 UNC 94587 732-A7
SANDRA DR
1200 SJS 95125 854-B6
SANDRA LN
- MLBR 94030 728-A3
SANDRA PL
2900 PA 94303 791-D6
SANDRA RD
- HIL 94010 748-E3
SANDRA WY
5300 LVMR 94550 716-C1
SANDRINGHAM N
200 MRGA 94556 631-E7
SANDRINGHAM S
100 MRGA 94556 631-E7
SANDRINGHAM PL
- PDMT 94611 650-D2
SANDRINGHAM RD
- PDMT 94611 650-D2
SANDRINGHAM WY
1400 SJS 95126 833-H7
SANDSTONE
- PTLV 94028 830-C1
SANDSTONE CT
- CCCo 94507 632-H4
- MrnC 94903 546-E5
1000 ANT 94509 595-D4
SANDSTONE DR
100 VAL 94589 510-B4
200 FRMT 94536 732-J6
SANDSTONE LN
1100 SJS 95132 814-F6
SANDSTONE RD
3000 CCCo 94507 632-H4
SAND WEDGE PL
100 WLCK 94598 612-E3
SANDY CT
1500 ANT 94509 575-G5
SANDY DR
- VAL 94590 550-B1
SANDY LN
- WLCK 94596 612-B3
4800 SJS 95124 873-G4
4800 SCIC 95124 873-G4
SANDY RD
3700 AlaC 94546 692-B3
SANDY WY
400 BEN 94510 551-B3
1500 ANT 94509 575-F5
3000 SRMN 94583 673-F5
SANDY BEACH RD
- VAL 94590 550-B1
SANDY BRIDGES CT
1200 AlaC 94541 691-G6
SANDY BRIDGES LN
1200 AlaC 94541 691-G6
SANDY BROOK CT
700 CCCo 94572 569-J2
SANDY COVE DR
800 CCCo 94572 569-J2
800 CCCo 94572 570-A2
SANDY COVE LN
200 CCCo 94565 573-E2
SANDY CREEK LN
1700 SJS 95125 853-J5
SANDY CREEK WY
- LKSP 94939 586-E5
SANDY HILL CT
400 ANT 94509 595-E2
SANDY HILL RD
- CLMA 94014 687-E7
SANDY HOOK CT
600 FCTY 94404 749-F5
SANDY HOOK DR
- HAY 94544 732-B1
SANDY NECK WY
100 VAL 94591 550-E1
SANDY ROCK CT
1600 SJS 95125 853-J5
SANDY ROCK LN
1600 SJS 95125 853-J5
SAN ELIJO CT
2700 ANT 94509 595-G2
SAN EMILION CT
- MTVW 94043 811-G3
SAN FELICIA WY
500 LALT 94022 811-E5
SAN FELIPE AV
- SF 94127 667-D6
- SSF 94080 707-E3
100 SBRN 94066 728-A1
200 SBRN 94066 727-J1
SAN FELIPE RD
3000 SJS 95135 855-D2
3000 SJS 95148 855-D2
3100 SJS 95121 855-D2
4900 SJS 95138 855-G5
6100 SJS 95138 875-J1
6100 SJS 95135 875-J1
6400 SCIC 95138 875-J1
SAN FELIPE WY
- NVTO 94945 525-G1
SAN FERNANDO AV
600 BERK 94707 609-F5
10200 CPTO 95014 852-B1
SAN FERNANDO CT
22000 CPTO 95014 852-A1
22000 SCIC 95014 852-A1
E SAN FERNANDO ST
- SJS 95113 834-C6
100 SJS 95192 834-C6
100 SJS 95112 834-C6
900 SJS 95116 834-F4
W SAN FERNANDO ST
100 SJS 95113 834-A7
400 SJS 95110 834-A7
700 SJS 95126 834-A7
1100 SJS 95126 833-J7
SAN FERNANDO WY
- DALY 94015 687-B6
- SF 94127 667-C6
3000 UNC 94587 732-B5
SAN FILIPPO CT
1200 SJS 95128 853-E3
SANFORD AV
- CCCo 94801 588-F4
- CMBL 95008 853-E6
100 RCH 94801 588-F4
1100 SPAB 94806 588-G4
SANFORD DR
6000 SJS 95123 874-F6
SANFORD RD
3400 LFYT 94549 611-G2
SANFORD ST
- CMAD 94925 586-G7
3400 CNCD 94520 572-F6
7800 OAK 94605 671-A1
SAN FRANCISCAN DR
17200 AlaC 94552 692-B2
SAN FRANCISCO AV
- BSBN 94005 688-A6
300 SMCo 94005 688-A6
SAN FRANCISCO BLVD
- SANS 94960 566-B6
400 MrnC 94901 566-B6
500 MrnC 94960 566-B6
SAN FRANCISCO CT
- OAK 94601 670-B1
800 SCIC 94305 810-J1
5100 SJS 95138 855-F7
SAN FRANCISCO TER
800 SCIC 94305 810-J1
4000 FRMT 94538 753-B5
SAN GABRIEL AV
- SF 94112 667-F7
600 ALB 94706 609-E5
SAN GABRIEL CT
400 PLE 94566 714-E5
700 CNCD 94518 592-H7
SAN GABRIEL DR
100 SUNV 94086 812-G7
3100 CNCD 94518 592-H7
SAN GABRIEL WY
1500 SCIC 95125 853-H5
3100 UNC 94587 732-B5
SAN GABRIL CIR
- DALY 94014 687-F3
SAN GABRIL CT
- DALY 94014 687-F3
SANGAMORE ST
1200 HAY 94545 711-F5
SANGER WY
500 SJS 95125 854-C4
SAN GERONIMO WY
200 SUNV 94086 812-G7
SAN GIORGIO CT
4000 PLE 94588 694-C6
SANGO CT
300 MPS 95035 814-B3
SAN GORGONIO AV
100 VAL 94589 530-C1
SAN GREGORIO CT
- DNVL 94526 633-B7
- NVTO 94947 525-G4
2700 ANT 94509 595-G2
SAN GREGORIO DR
2700 ANT 94509 595-H2
SAN GREGORIO WY
400 SJS 95111 854-J7
SANGRO CT
- PLE 94566 715-D6
SAN IGNACIO AV
6200 SJS 95119 875-D7
SAN JACINTO CT
31400 UNC 94587 732-B6
SAN JACINTO WY
- SF 94127 667-D6
SAN JOAQUIN AV
100 ANT 94509 575-C6
1500 SJS 95118 874-A1
SAN JOAQUIN CT
- NVTO 94947 525-F3
100 SBRN 94066 707-D7
100 CCCo 94565 573-E1
SAN JOAQUIN PL
- NVTO 94947 525-F3
SAN JOAQUIN ST
1400 RCH 94804 609-B3
SAN JOAQUIN WY
3100 UNC 94587 732-B5
SAN JOSE AV
- SF 94110 667-H4
- SF 94110 667-H4
- SJS 95110 854-D3
- SJS 95125 854-D3
100 PCFA 94044 706-J6
200 SF 94131 667-G6
300 MLBR 94030 728-B2
600 SF 94112 667-F7
1300 CNCD 94518 592-G2
1400 ALA 94501 669-H2
2200 SF 94112 687-E2
2300 ALA 94501 670-A3
5200 RCH 94804 609-C4
SAN JOSE AV Rt#-82
3200 DALY 94014 687-D3
SAN JOSE BLVD
800 NVTO 94949 546-C1
SAN JOSE CT
- WLCK 94598 612-F3
31400 UNC 94587 732-C5
SAN JOSE DR
100 NVTO 94949 546-H4
1100 ANT 94509 575-A6
5400 PLE 94566 714-E5
SAN JOSE PL
400 SRMN 94583 673-F5
SAN JOSE ST
900 SLN 94577 671-B7
1100 SLN 94577 691-B1
SAN JUAN AV
- DALY 94015 687-A7
- SF 94112 667-F7
- SMCo 94025 790-D5
100 MLBR 94030 728-A2
100 SBRN 94066 728-A2
1200 SJS 95110 833-J3
1800 BERK 94707 609-F5
2300 WLCK 94596 612-B3
3000 SCL 95051 833-A2
4100 FRMT 94536 752-F3
SAN JUAN BLVD
2800 BLMT 94002 769-A1
SAN JUAN CT
- LALT 94022 811-E4
- NVTO 94945 525-H1
300 SMTO 94402 748-G1
700 CNCD 94518 592-H7
3100 ANT 94509 575-B7
4000 FRMT 94536 752-G3
SAN JUAN DR
600 SUNV 94086 812-G6
3700 PIT 94565 574-D5
SAN JUAN PL
700 SRMN 94583 673-F5
3100 UNC 94587 732-B5
SAN JUAN ST
500 SCIC 94305 810-H1
3700 OAK 94601 650-D7
SAN JUAN WY
5400 PLE 94566 714-E5
SAN JUDE AV
700 PA 94306 811-B2
SAN JULE CT
700 SUNV 94086 812-G5
SAN JULIAN CT
900 MTVW 94043 811-G3
SAN JULIAN WY
400 MTVW 94043 811-G2
SAN JUNIPERO DR
800 SUNV 94086 812-G5
SAN JUSTO CT
700 SUNV 94086 812-G5
SANKO RD
200 PLHL 94523 592-B3
SAN LAZARO AV
100 SUNV 94086 812-G7
SAN LEANDRO AV
900 MTVW 94043 811-J2
900 MTVW 94043 812-A3
10500 CPTO 95014 852-A2
SAN LEANDRO BLVD
100 SLN 94577 691-A2
1200 SLN 94577 690-J1
1500 SLN 94577 670-J7
2500 SLN 94578 691-A2
SAN LEANDRO ST
2000 OAK 94603 670-G5
2000 SLN 94577 670-G5
3200 OAK 94601 670-C1
5300 OAK 94621 670-G5
SAN LEANDRO WY
- SF 94127 667-C6
SAN LISA CT
3600 CNCD 94520 572-G5
SAN LORENZO AV
1500 BERK 94707 609-F5
SAN LORENZO DR
5600 SJS 95123 874-F4
SAN LORENZO WY
- SF 94127 667-D5
SAN LUCAR CT
100 SUNV 94086 812-G7
100 SUNV 94086 832-G1
SAN LUCAS AV
700 MTVW 94043 811-J3
800 MTVW 94043 812-A3
SAN LUCAS CT
800 MTVW 94043 811-J3
SAN LUCES WY
3200 UNC 94587 732-A5
SAN LUIS AV
100 SBRN 94066 728-A1
100 SBRN 94066 727-J1
300 LALT 94024 811-F7
1300 OAK 94602 650-D3
1400 MTVW 94043 811-G3
9900 SRMN 94583 673-G5
SAN LUIS CIR
- DALY 94014 687-F3
SAN LUIS CT
- DALY 94014 687-F3
- NVTO 94945 525-J1
- WLCK 94596 612-B3
700 CNCD 94518 592-H7
3100 UNC 94587 732-A5
5600 PLE 94566 714-D5
SAN LUIS DR
200 MLPK 94025 790-H2
SAN LUIS RD
500 BERK 94707 609-G4
1500 WLCK 94596 612-A2
SAN LUIS ST
1600 RCH 94804 609-C4
SAN LUIS WY
100 NVTO 94945 525-J1
SAN LUISITO WY
600 SUNV 94086 812-G6
SAN LUIS OBISPO AV
1100 HAY 94544 732-C3
SAN LUIS REY AV
3000 SJS 95118 874-A1
SAN LUPPE DR
800 MTVW 94043 812-A3
W SAN MARCO AV
100 SBRN 94066 728-A1
100 SBRN 94066 727-J1
SAN MARCO CT
3300 UNC 94587 732-A5
SAN MARCO PL
- SRMN 94583 673-G5
SAN MARCO WY
- PLE 94588 694-C6
3200 UNC 94587 732-A5
SAN MARCOS AV
- SF 94116 667-C4
SAN MARCOS CIR
900 MTVW 94043 811-H3
SAN MARCOS CT
- NVTO 94945 525-H1
700 CNCD 94518 592-H7
2600 SJS 95132 814-E5
SAN MARCOS DR
- PIT 94565 574-G6
1300 SJS 95132 814-E5
SAN MARCOS PL
- SRFL 94901 567-D6
SAN MARCOS RD
19200 SAR 95070 872-F3
SAN MARCOS WY
3400 SCL 95051 832-J3
SAN MARDO AV
3300 SCIC 95127 814-H6
SAN MARIN DR
- NVTO 94945 526-A1
300 NVTO 94945 525-G1
SAN MARINO AV
100 VAL 94589 530-B1
100 VAL 94590 530-B1
3300 SCIC 95127 814-H6
SAN MARINO CT
- SRFL 94901 567-E5
- WLCK 94598 612-F3
31400 UNC 94587 732-B6
SAN MARINO DR
- SRFL 94901 567-D6
SAN MARINO PL
- SRFL 94901 567-D6
SAN MARLO WY
400 PCFA 94044 726-J2
SAN MARTIN PL
600 LALT 94024 811-G7
800 FRMT 94539 753-G6
SAN MATEO AV
- BURL 94010 728-F6
200 LGTS 95030 873-A6
400 SBRN 94066 707-J5
400 SBRN 94066 727-J1
1000 SSF 94066 707-J5
1300 SSF 94080 707-J5
2600 SMCo 94063 770-C7
SAN MATEO CT
- SRFL 94903 566-C3
700 CNCD 94518 592-H7
800 SUNV 94086 812-G5
SAN MATEO DR
- PA 94304 790-G5
- MLPK 94025 790-E4
- SJS 95111 854-H7
N SAN MATEO DR
- SMTO 94401 728-H7
400 SMTO 94401 748-J1
S SAN MATEO DR
- SMTO 94401 748-J1
SAN MATEO LN
400 BSBN 94005 688-A7
SAN MATEO RD
- BERK 94707 609-G5
SAN MATEO ST
1800 RCH 94804 609-C3
2900 ELCR 94530 609-C3
SAN MATEO WY
- NVTO 94945 525-J1
3000 UNC 94587 732-B5
SAN MICHELE CT
2300 CNCD 94520 572-G5
SAN MICHELE DR
3600 CNCD 94520 572-G5
SAN MIGUEL AV
- DALY 94015 687-A7
600 BERK 94707 609-F5
600 SCL 95050 833-C5
600 SUNV 94086 812-G6
19100 AlaC 94546 691-J4
SAN MIGUEL CIR
4300 PIT 94565 574-F7
SAN MIGUEL CT
- NVTO 94945 525-H2
300 MPS 95035 813-J1
500 PLE 94566 714-E5
3000 CNCD 94518 592-G5
3100 ANT 94509 595-B1
SAN MIGUEL DR
100 SRMN 94583 673-G5
800 LVMR 94550 715-F3
1600 WLCK 94596 612-D5
1900 CCCo 94596 612-D6
2400 CCCo 94596 632-F1
SAN MIGUEL LN
700 FCTY 94404 749-G5
SAN MIGUEL PL
- WLCK 94596 612-D6
SAN MIGUEL RD
800 CNCD 94518 592-G3
SAN MIGUEL ST
300 SF 94112 687-E1
SAN MIGUEL WY
- NVTO 94945 525-H2
- SMTO 94403 749-D5
2700 SCAR 94070 769-F5
4100 SJS 95111 854-J7
SAN MORENO CT
39800 FRMT 94539 753-E3
SAN MORENO PL
- FRMT 94539 753-E4
SAN MORITZ DR
1100 SJS 95132 814-F5
SAN NICHOLAS LN
600 FCTY 94404 749-G5
SANNITA CT
- PLE 94566 715-C7
SAN ONOFRE CT
2700 ANT 94509 595-H2
3300 SCIC 95127 814-H6
3300 SJS 95127 814-H6
SAN PABLO AV
- NVTO 94949 546-H4
- MrnC 94903 566-F5
- SF 94127 667-D5
- SRFL 94903 566-F5
- CCCo 94572 549-H7
300 MLBR 94030 728-B2
500 PIN 94564 569-F4
700 SUNV 94086 812-H5
1400 OAK 94612 649-F1
2400 OAK 94607 649-F1
2700 OAK 94608 649-F1
2700 HER 94547 569-F4
3300 SCIC 95127 814-H6
3400 SJS 95127 814-J6
4400 CCCo 94572 569-F4
11900 ELCR 94530 589-A5
11900 RCH 94805 589-A5
13000 SPAB 94805 589-A5
13200 SPAB 94806 589-A5
13300 SPAB 94806 588-J3
14800 SCIC 95127 814-J6
14800 RCH 94806 588-J3
15000 RCH 94806 568-J7
15000 SPAB 94806 568-J7
15500 RCH 94806 569-B5
15600 CCCo 94806 569-B5
16600 PIN 94806 569-B5
20000 CCCo 94525 550-A5
20000 CCCo - 550-A5
SAN PABLO AV Rt#-123
300 ALB 94706 609-D6
300 ELCR 94530 609-B1
1000 ALB 94804 609-D6
1100 BERK 94804 609-D6
1100 BERK 94706 609-D6
1300 BERK 94804 629-E1
1300 BERK 94702 609-D6
1300 BERK 94702 629-E1
2700 OAK 94608 629-E3
3500 OAK 94608 649-F1
3600 EMVL 94608 629-E3
3600 EMVL 94608 649-F1
10200 RCH 94804 609-B1
11800 ELCR 94530 589-B7
12100 RCH 94805 589-B7
SAN PABLO CT
- MRGA 94556 631-G5
3300 UNC 94587 732-A5
3700 SCIC 95127 814-J6
SAN PABLO DR
700 MTVW 94043 812-A3
700 MTVW 94043 811-J3
SAN PABLO RDGE
- RCH 94805 589-E4
SAN PABLO TER
300 PCFA 94044 707-A5
SAN PABLO WY
900 NVTO 94949 546-G2
3200 UNC 94587 732-A5
SAN PABLO DAM RD
- CCCo - 609-J1
- CCCo - 610-A2
500 CCCo 94563 610-A2
2200 SPAB 94806 589-A3
3000 SPAB 94803 589-A3
3100 CCCo 94803 589-A3
3400 RCH 94803 589-A3
5100 CCCo 94803 589-E3
7100 CCCo - 589-J6
SAN PALO CT
18600 SAR 95070 852-H5
SAN PATRICIO AV
600 SUNV 94086 812-G6

Block	City	ZIP	Pg-Grid
SAN PAULO CT			
-	DNVL	94526	653-C7
SAN PAULO WY			
400	NVTO	94949	546-F2
SAN PEDRO AV			
200	PCFA	94044	726-G4
600	SUNV	94086	812-H6
1800	BERK	94707	609-F5
SAN PEDRO CT			
-	WLCK	94598	612-F3
3300	UNC	94587	732-A5
N SAN PEDRO CT			
-	MrnC	94903	566-H3
SAN PEDRO DR			
36000	FRMT	94536	752-F4
SAN PEDRO PL			
-	SRMN	94583	673-G5
SAN PEDRO RD			
-	DALY	94014	687-C5
-	SMCo	94014	687-C5
100	ALA	94501	649-D6
300	DALY	94015	687-C5
N SAN PEDRO RD			
-	SRFL	94901	567-B3
-	SRFL	94903	566-F5
100	MrnC	94903	566-J2
400	MrnC	94903	567-B3
N SAN PEDRO ST			
-	SJS	95110	834-A4
-	SJS	95110	833-J3
S SAN PEDRO ST			
-	SJS	95113	834-B6
SAN PEDRO WY			
3200	UNC	94587	732-A5
SAN PEDRO MOUNTAIN RD			
-	PCFA	94044	726-H6
-	SMCo	-	726-H6
SAN PEDRO TERRACE RD			
700	PCFA	94044	726-H4
700	SMCo	-	726-H4
SAN PETRA CT			
300	MPS	95035	813-J1
SAN PETRONIO AV			
800	SUNV	94086	812-H5
SAN PIEDRAS PL			
-	SRMN	94583	673-G5
SAN PIER CT			
800	SUNV	94086	812-H5
SAN PIERRE WY			
500	MTVW	94043	811-H3
SAN QUENTIN TER			
-	MrnC	94964	587-B5
SAN RAFAEL AV			
-	SANS	94960	566-B7
-	SRFL	94901	586-E2
-	TBRN	94920	607-C7
-	BLV	94920	607-C7
400	BLV	94920	627-D1
800	MTVW	94043	811-J3
2100	SCL	95051	833-A2
SAN RAFAEL CT			
-	WLCK	94598	612-F3
2000	SCL	95051	833-A3
SAN RAFAEL PL			
700	SCIC	94305	810-H1
SAN RAFAEL ST			
700	SUNV	94086	812-H6
1000	SLN	94577	671-B7
1200	SLN	94577	691-C1
SAN RAFAEL WY			
-	SF	94127	667-C6
3100	UNC	94587	732-B5
SAN RAMON			
100	VAL	94589	530-B2
SAN RAMON AV			
700	SUNV	94086	812-H5
1200	MTVW	94043	811-G2
1800	BERK	94707	609-F4
SAN RAMON CT			
900	MTVW	94043	811-H3
3100	UNC	94587	732-B5
SAN RAMON DR			
100	SJS	95111	854-H7
SAN RAMON RD			
3100	CNCD	94519	572-H7
7000	DBLN	94568	693-G3
7000	PLE	94588	693-G3
8800	SRMN	94583	693-G3
SAN RAMON WY			
-	NVTO	94945	525-G1
100	SF	94112	667-D7
4000	SJS	95111	854-J7
SAN RAMON VALLEY BLVD			
2100	SRMN	94583	673-C1
19700	CCCo	94583	673-E6
20400	SRMN	94583	693-F1
SAN RAMON VLY BLVD			
500	DNVL	94526	653-B4
1700	SRMN	94583	653-B4
SAN RAYMUNDO RD			
1000	HIL	94010	748-F2
N SAN RAYMUNDO RD			
400	HIL	94010	748-F2
SAN RELIEZ CT			
1300	LFYT	94549	611-G4
SAN REMO CT			
1400	LVMR	94550	715-G4
2100	AlaC	94578	691-F4
2200	PIT	94565	574-A4
SAN REMO DR			
16200	AlaC	94578	691-F4
SAN REMO WY			
2200	PIT	94565	574-A4
SAN REMOS WY			
1000	SCAR	94070	769-F5
SAN REY AV			
300	MLBR	94030	728-B2
SAN REY PL			
200	DNVL	94526	633-B7
200	DNVL	94526	653-B1
SAN RIVAS DR			
3200	SJS	95148	835-D7
SAN ROBERTO PL			
400	SRMN	94583	673-G4
SAN SABA CT			
800	SUNV	94086	812-H5
SAN SABA DR			
3300	SJS	95148	835-D6
SAN SABANA CT			
7700	DBLN	94568	693-G4
SAN SABANA RD			
7500	DBLN	94568	693-G4
E SAN SALVADOR ST			
-	SJS	95113	834-D6
-	SJS	95112	834-D6
100	SJS	95192	834-D6
W SAN SALVADOR ST			
-	SJS	95110	834-C7
SAN SEBASTIAN			
4600	OAK	94602	650-D3
SAN SEBASTIAN DR			
300	NVTO	94949	546-F2
SAN SEBASTIAN PL			
40200	FRMT	94539	753-E4
SAN SIMEON CT			
200	FRMT	94539	753-E4
700	CNCD	94518	592-H7
2100	ANT	94509	595-A2
SAN SIMEON DR			
700	CNCD	94518	592-G5
800	MTVW	94043	811-J3
SAN SIMEON PL			
-	PIT	94565	574-D7
100	VAL	94591	550-E1
300	SRMN	94583	673-G5
5300	AlaC	94552	692-D5
SAN SIMEON ST			
600	SUNV	94086	812-H6
SAN SIMEON WY			
2800	SCAR	94070	769-F5
4000	SJS	95111	854-J7
SANSOME ST			
-	SF	94104	648-B4
400	SF	94111	648-B4
700	SF	94133	648-B4
900	SF	94111	648-A4
900	SF	94133	648-A4
SAN SOUCI			
1000	WLCK	94596	612-D4
SANTA ANA AV			
-	DALY	94015	687-A7
-	SF	94127	667-C6
400	SJS	95112	834-B3
SANTA ANA CT			
-	TBRN	94920	607-E6
SANTA ANA DR			
-	PLHL	94523	592-D3
700	PIT	94565	574-E5
SANTA ANA LN			
700	CNCD	94518	592-H7
SANTA ANA PL			
-	WLCK	94598	612-G4
SANTA ANA ST			
1000	AlaC	94580	691-E5
2200	PA	94303	791-C4
SANTA ANA WY			
31300	UNC	94587	732-B5
SANTA ANITA			
-	SLN	94579	691-A6
-	SLN	94579	690-J7
SANTA ANNA CT			
200	SUNV	94086	812-G7
SANTA BARBARA AV			
-	SANS	94960	566-B6
-	SF	94112	687-C2
-	DALY	94014	687-C2
600	MLBR	94030	727-H2
3400	SCL	95051	832-J3
SANTA BARBARA CT			
3200	UNC	94587	732-D4
SANTA BARBARA DR			
400	LALT	94022	811-F6
1600	SCIC	95125	853-H4
2500	PIN	94564	569-G6
SANTA BARBARA PL			
100	SBRN	94066	707-D6
SANTA BARBARA RD			
-	BERK	94708	609-G4
-	PLHL	94523	592-B7
500	BERK	94707	609-G4
SANTA BARBARA WY			
3200	ANT	94509	595-C3
SANTA BELLA PL			
21700	CPTO	95014	852-B3
SANTA CATALINA CT			
100	MRGA	94556	631-G5
SANTA CATALINA LN			
600	FCTY	94404	749-G5
SANTA CATALINA ST			
2300	PA	94303	791-D4
SANTA CATALINA WY			
31300	UNC	94587	732-B5
SANTA CHRISTINA CT			
700	SUNV	94086	812-F5
SANTA CLARA AV			
-	OAK	94611	649-J2
-	OAK	94610	649-J2
-	SF	94127	667-C6
100	ALA	94501	649-J2
100	ALA	94501	669-E1
100	MTVW	94043	811-J4
100	SBRN	94066	728-A2
100	SMCo	94061	790-A3
100	RDWC	94061	790-A3
500	BERK	94707	609-F5
1200	RCH	94804	609-C3
1300	CNCD	94518	592-G2
2200	ALA	94501	670-A2
2900	ELCR	94530	609-C4
10000	CPTO	95014	832-B7
SANTA CLARA CT			
-	DALY	94014	687-F3
-	SRFL	94903	566-C3
100	DNVL	94526	653-B4
3200	UNC	94587	732-A5
SANTA CLARA DR			
100	DNVL	94526	653-B4
SANTA CLARA ST			
-	BSBN	94005	688-A6
400	VAL	94590	529-J3
700	SCL	95053	833-D5
900	SCL	95050	833-D5
1200	RCH	94804	609-B2
22400	HAY	94541	711-H4
24300	HAY	94544	711-H4
E SANTA CLARA ST			
400	SJS	95113	834-C6
500	SJS	95112	834-C6
800	SJS	95116	834-C6
W SANTA CLARA ST			
-	SJS	95113	834-A7
100	SJS	95110	834-A7
W SANTA CLARA ST Rt#-82			
500	SJS	95113	834-A7
500	SJS	95126	834-A7
SANTA CLARA WY			
200	SMTO	94403	749-D5
3800	LVMR	94550	695-J7
3900	LVMR	94550	696-A7
22400	HAY	94541	711-G2
SANTA COLETA CT			
600	SUNV	94086	812-F5
SANTA CRUZ			
1700	AlaC	94541	691-G6
SANTA CRUZ AV			
-	DALY	94014	687-C2
-	SANS	94960	566-B6
-	SF	94112	687-C2
500	MLPK	94025	790-F3
1600	SCL	95051	833-A2
2000	SMCo	94025	790-E6
5400	RCH	94804	609-C4
N SANTA CRUZ AV			
-	LGTS	95030	873-A6
SANTA CRUZ CT			
-	PIT	94565	574-E2
4500	FRMT	94536	752-G4
SANTA CRUZ DR			
800	PLHL	94523	592-C4
SANTA CRUZ LN			
600	FCTY	94404	749-G5
3100	ALA	94502	670-A6
SANTA CRUZ PL			
300	SRMN	94583	673-G4
SANTA CRUZ RD			
4000	OAK	94605	671-B3
SANTA CRUZ WY			
31300	UNC	94587	732-B5
SANTA DOMINGA AV			
100	SBRN	94066	728-A1
100	SBRN	94066	727-J1
SANTA ELENA AV			
-	DALY	94015	687-B7
SANTA ELENA WY			
200	SUNV	94086	812-F7
31300	UNC	94587	732-B5
SANTA FE AV			
-	RCH	94801	608-C1
-	SF	94124	668-A6
200	RCH	94801	588-B6
400	ELCR	94530	609-E5
400	CCCo	94706	609-E5
400	ALB	94706	609-E5
800	SCIC	94305	810-J1
900	CCCo	94553	571-G4
900	MRTZ	94553	571-G4
1100	BERK	94706	609-E7
1200	HER	94547	569-F3
1300	BERK	94702	609-E7
1800	CCCo	94509	575-H4
E SANTA FE AV			
400	PIT	94565	574-E2
W SANTA FE AV			
-	PIT	94565	574-D2
SANTA FE CT			
4000	CNCD	94521	593-A2
SANTA FE DR			
200	WLCK	94598	612-F3
1300	SJS	95118	874-B3
SANTA FE ST			
17000	AlaC	94541	691-G5
SANTA FE TER			
200	SUNV	94086	812-F7
SANTA FE WY			
31300	UNC	94587	732-B5
SANTA FELICIA CT			
-	HIL	94402	748-H4
SANTA FLORITA AV			
400	MLBR	94030	727-J2
SANTA GABRIELLA CT			
-	NVTO	94945	525-G1
SANTA GINA CT			
-	HIL	94402	748-H4
SANTA HELENA AV			
100	SBRN	94066	728-A2
200	MLBR	94030	728-A2
SANTA INEZ AV			
100	SBRN	94066	728-A2
E SANTA INEZ AV			
-	SMTO	94401	748-H1
400	SMTO	94401	728-J7
1000	SMTO	94401	729-A7
W SANTA INEZ AV			
-	SMTO	94402	748-G2
100	HIL	94010	748-G2
SANTA INEZ CT			
1900	SCL	95051	832-J3
3100	UNC	94587	732-B5
SANTA INEZ DR			
1500	SCIC	95125	853-H4
SANTA ISABELA CT			
3200	UNC	94587	732-B5
SANTA LUCIA			
-	ORIN	94563	610-F5
SANTA LUCIA AV			
100	SBRN	94066	728-A1
100	SBRN	94066	727-H2
900	MLBR	94030	727-H2
SANTA LUCIA CT			
-	PLHL	94523	592-D3
SANTA LUCIA DR			
800	PLHL	94523	592-C3
1600	SCIC	95125	853-H4
3100	SCL	95051	833-A5
SANTA MARGARITA			
-	SLN	94579	691-A7
SANTA MARGARITA AV			
100	MLPK	94025	790-H3
700	MLBR	94030	727-H2
3000	SJS	95118	874-A1
SANTA MARGARITA DR			
-	SRFL	94901	566-D7
SANTA MARIA AV			
-	PTLV	94028	809-J6
-	PCFA	94044	706-J5
100	SBRN	94066	728-A2
700	SCIC	94305	810-H2
1500	SJS	95125	853-J4
3000	SCL	95051	833-A2
18800	AlaC	94546	692-A3
SANTA MARIA CT			
-	OAK	94601	670-B1
100	NVTO	94947	525-G3
3000	CNCD	94518	592-H7
3300	LFYT	94549	611-G7
3600	AlaC	94546	692-A4
SANTA MARIA DR			
-	NVTO	94947	525-G4
2200	PIT	94565	573-H4
3000	CNCD	94518	592-H7
31000	UNC	94587	732-B5
SANTA MARIA LN			
-	HIL	94010	748-G1
700	FCTY	94404	749-G2
SANTA MARIA RD			
600	CCCo	94803	589-C1
SANTA MARIA ST			
1300	SLN	94577	691-B1
SANTA MARIA WY			
-	ORIN	94563	610-G7
800	LFYT	94549	611-G7
SANTA MARINA ST			
-	SF	94110	667-H5
SANTA MARTA CT			
3100	UNC	94587	732-B5
SANTA MESA DR			
400	SJS	95123	874-J6
SANTA MONICA			
400	SLN	94579	690-J6
400	SLN	94579	691-A7
SANTA MONICA AV			
100	MLPK	94025	790-H3
1500	SJS	95118	874-A1
SANTA MONICA CT			
1000	PLHL	94523	592-C4
SANTA MONICA DR			
-	PLHL	94523	592-C3
SANTA MONICA TER			
-	FRMT	94539	794-B1
SANTA MONICA WY			
-	SF	94127	667-C5
3200	UNC	94587	732-B6
SANTANA RD			
500	NVTO	94945	526-G1
SANTANA ST			
30700	HAY	94544	732-C3
SANTANDER CT			
200	LALT	94022	811-D4
SANTANDER DR			
400	SRMN	94583	673-C3
SANTA PAULA			
300	SLN	94579	691-A7
SANTA PAULA AV			
-	MLBR	94030	728-B3
-	SF	94127	667-D5
600	SUNV	94086	812-H6
1200	SJS	95110	833-J2
22300	CPTO	95014	852-A1
SANTA PAULA CT			
700	CNCD	94518	592-H7
SANTA PAULA DR			
100	DALY	94015	687-B6
3000	CNCD	94518	592-H7
SANTA PAULA WY			
3200	UNC	94587	732-B6
SANTA RAY AV			
500	OAK	94610	650-A3
SANTA RITA AV			
-	DALY	94015	707-A1
-	SF	94116	667-D4
-	SF	94116	667-C4
100	PA	94301	791-B6
300	MLPK	94025	790-F5
700	LALT	94022	811-D4
SANTA RITA CT			
-	WLCK	94596	612-D7
1000	LALT	94022	811-D3
SANTA RITA DR			
-	WLCK	94596	612-D6
300	MPS	95035	794-B6
3700	CNCD	94519	572-J7
SANTA RITA RD			
1000	PLE	94588	694-E6
1000	PLE	94566	694-D6
2100	PLE	94566	714-E2
4100	CCCo	94803	589-D2
4200	RCH	94803	589-E2
SANTA RITA ST			
700	SUNV	94086	812-H5
3600	OAK	94601	650-D7
SANTA RITA WY			
4100	SJS	95111	854-J7
31300	UNC	94587	732-B5
SANTA ROSA AV			
-	SAUS	94965	627-A3
-	SF	94112	667-F7
-	VAL	94590	529-H3
100	MTVW	94043	811-J4
100	PCFA	94044	706-J6
100	OAK	94610	649-J2
500	BERK	94707	609-F5
10000	SRMN	94583	673-G5
SANTA ROSA CIR			
2000	ALA	94501	649-E7
SANTA ROSA CT			
1900	SCL	95051	832-J3
3200	UNC	94587	732-A5
SANTA ROSA DR			
100	SJS	95111	854-J7
300	LGTS	95032	893-G1
300	LGTS	95032	873-G7
SANTA ROSA LN			
700	FCTY	94404	749-G5
SANTA ROSA PL			
100	SRMN	94583	673-F4
SANTA ROSA ST			
700	SUNV	94086	812-H5
1200	SLN	94577	691-B1
SANTA ROSA WY			
3200	UNC	94587	732-B5
SANTA SOPHIA CT			
3200	UNC	94587	732-D4
SANTA SOPHIA WY			
3200	UNC	94587	732-B6
SANTA SUSANA			
200	SLN	94579	691-A7
SANTA SUSANA AV			
600	MLBR	94030	727-J2
SANTA SUSANA ST			
700	SUNV	94086	812-H5
SANTA SUSANA WY			
800	PIT	94565	574-A4
SANTA SUSANA WY			
800	PIT	94565	573-J4
3200	UNC	94587	732-A5
4100	SJS	95111	854-J7
SANTA SUSANNA CT			
700	CNCD	94518	592-H6
SANTA TERESA			
100	SLN	94579	691-A6
SANTA TERESA BLVD			
5400	SJS	95136	874-E5
5500	SJS	95123	874-E5
5900	SJS	95123	875-C6
6200	SJS	95119	875-C6
7000	SJS	95139	875-C6
7000	SJS	95139	895-H2
7300	SCIC	95139	895-H2
7300	SCIC	95119	895-H2
SANTA TERESA COM			
40100	FRMT	94539	753-E4
SANTA TERESA CT			
6100	SJS	95123	875-A6
SANTA TERESA DR			
10800	CPTO	95014	852-B3
12200	SRMN	94583	673-G4
SANTA TERESA ST			
100	SCIC	94305	790-G7
300	SJS	95110	834-A5
SANTA TERESA TER			
40100	FRMT	94539	753-E4
SANTA TERESA WY			
500	MLBR	94030	727-J2
SANTA TRINITA AV			
300	SUNV	94086	812-H7
SANTA VICTORIA CT			
-	NVTO	94945	525-G1
SANTA YNEZ			
500	SLN	94579	690-J6
500	SLN	94579	691-A7
SANTA YNEZ AV			
-	SF	94112	667-F7
SANTA YNEZ CIR			
-	NVTO	94947	525-G3
SANTA YNEZ CT			
-	OAK	94601	650-B7
-	OAK	94601	670-B1
700	CNCD	94518	592-H6
SANTA YNEZ ST			
600	SCIC	94305	810-H1
600	SUNV	94086	812-J6
SANTA YORMA CT			
-	NVTO	94945	525-G1
SANTA YSABEL AV			
-	SF	94112	667-F7
SANTA YSABEL WY			
6000	SJS	95123	874-F6
SANTEE DR			
1300	SJS	95122	834-G7
SANTEE RD			
4300	FRMT	94555	752-D2
SANTEE RIVER CT			
600	SJS	95111	854-H4
SANTEL CT			
-	PLE	94566	715-C5
SAN THOMAS WY			
100	DNVL	94526	653-B4
SANTIAGO AV			
-	ATN	94027	790-D4
100	SMCo	94061	790-A3
1900	SJS	95122	834-J7
SANTIAGO CT			
-	NVTO	94947	526-A3
200	DNVL	94526	653-B1
1600	ANT	94509	575-A7
SANTIAGO DR			
100	DNVL	94526	653-B1
SANTIAGO LN			
200	DNVL	94526	653-C1
SANTIAGO RD			
13800	SLN	94577	690-H5
SANTIAGO ST			
200	SF	94116	667-A4
2300	SF	94116	666-H4
3600	SMTO	94403	749-D5
35100	FRMT	94536	752-E2
SANTIAGO WY			
-	SRFL	94903	546-D7
-	SRFL	94903	566-D1
SANTO CT			
11500	DBLN	94568	693-F3
SANTO TR			
-	CCCo	-	591-A5
SANTOLINA DR			
1100	NVTO	94945	526-B2
SAN TOMAS CT			
1500	SJS	95130	853-B4
SAN TOMAS EXWY Rt#-G4			
-	CMBL	95008	853-C6
-	SCL	95051	853-C4
-	SCL	95117	853-C6
-	SCL	95117	853-C4
-	SJS	95008	853-C4
-	SJS	95130	853-C4
100	SJS	95117	853-C4
200	SCL	95051	833-C3
200	SCL	95050	833-C6
2900	SCL	95054	813-C7
2900	SCL	95054	833-C3
SAN TOMAS PL			
600	SRMN	94583	673-F5
SAN TOMAS ST			
700	SUNV	94086	812-H5
SAN TOMAS AQUINO PKWY			
-	SJS	95130	853-C4
N SAN TOMAS AQUINO RD			
-	CMBL	95008	853-B6
200	SJS	95008	853-B6
300	SJS	95130	853-B6
1200	SJS	95117	853-B6
1200	SJS	95129	853-B6
S SAN TOMAS AQUINO RD			
100	SJS	95008	853-A7
600	SJS	95130	853-A7
700	CMBL	95008	853-A7
2100	CMBL	95008	873-B1
SANTOS CT			
-	FRMT	94536	753-D2
600	MPS	95035	794-C5
SANTOS LN			
2900	CCCo	94596	612-D1
SANTOS ST			
-	SF	94134	687-H2
200	DALY	94014	687-H2
21100	AlaC	94541	691-G7
21100	AlaC	94541	711-G1
SANTOS RANCH RD			
9500	AlaC	94586	713-H3
9500	AlaC	94588	713-H3
11000	HAY	94586	713-H3
SANTUCCI CT			
20200	HAY	94544	732-C1
SAN VERON AV			
800	MTVW	94043	811-J3
SAN VICENTE AV			
22400	SCIC	95120	895-A4
22500	SJS	95120	895-B4
SAN VICENTE CT			
-	DNVL	94526	653-C7
SAN VICENTE WY			
300	SUNV	94086	812-J7
SAN VINCENTE AV			
22600	SCIC	95120	895-B4
SAN VINCENTE CT			
1900	CNCD	94519	572-J7
SAN VINCENTE DR			
1800	CNCD	94519	572-J7
SAN VITO CT			
300	SJS	95116	834-F3
SAN YSIDRO CT			
-	DNVL	94526	633-B7
SAN YSIDRO WY			
2900	SCL	95051	812-J7
2900	SCL	95051	832-J1
4000	SJS	95111	854-J7
SAN ZENO WY			
100	SUNV	94086	832-J1
SAO AUGUSTINE WY			
-	SRFL	94903	566-E4
SAPENA CT			
400	SCL	95054	813-E7
SAPLING CT			
1700	CNCD	94519	593-B1
SAPONI LN			
-	CCCo	94565	573-H2
SAPPHIRE CT			
-	SRMN	94583	673-F2
900	SJS	95136	874-E3
1200	HER	94547	569-G4
SAPPHIRE DR			
1000	LVMR	94550	715-D3
SAPPHIRE ST			
300	RDWC	94062	769-H7
500	RDWC	94062	789-J1
600	RDWC	94061	789-J1
6700	DBLN	94568	693-J2
19900	AlaC	94546	692-C5
SAPWOOD LN			
1600	SJS	95133	814-H3
SAPWOOD WY			
2300	SJS	95133	814-H3
SARA AV			
300	SUNV	94086	812-C7
SARA CT			
-	CCCo	94565	573-H2
900	SUNV	94086	812-C7
SARA LN			
-	CCCo	94507	632-E2
-	SCAR	94070	769-F5
SARABAND WY			
800	SJS	95122	854-F1
SARAGLEN CT			
19900	SAR	95070	852-F5
SARAGLEN DR			
12000	SAR	95070	852-F5
SARAH CT			
2100	PIN	94564	569-F5
4000	SJS	95136	874-E1
4600	LVMR	94550	696-B7
SARAH DR			
-	MLV	94941	606-F2
1600	PIN	94564	569-E6
SARAH LN			
-	MRGA	94556	651-E2
SARAH PL			
500	HAY	94544	732-F2
SARAHILLS CT			
21300	SAR	95070	872-C1
SARAHILLS DR			
13400	SAR	95070	872-C1
SARALYNN DR			
1600	SJS	95121	855-A2
SARANAC DR			
700	SUNV	94087	832-C3
SARANAP AV			
100	CCCo	94595	612-A5
100	LFYT	94595	612-A5
400	WLCK	94595	612-A5
SARA PARK CIR			
18800	SAR	95070	852-H6
SARASOTA LN			
2000	HAY	94545	711-H7
SARASOTA WY			
1800	SJS	95122	834-H7
2000	SJS	95122	854-H1
SARATOGA AV			
-	LGTS	95030	873-B7
-	LGTS	95032	873-B7
-	SCL	95051	833-C7
-	SCL	95051	853-B1
200	SCL	95050	833-C7
300	SJS	95129	853-B1
1100	EPA	94303	791-A1
1300	EPA	94303	771-A7
1400	SJS	95129	852-G7
1700	SAR	95070	852-G7
1700	SAR	95129	852-G7
1800	SJS	95130	852-J7
2500	CNCD	94519	572-G6
13400	SAR	95070	872-E2
SARATOGA CT			
-	CCCo	94507	633-A5
SARATOGA DR			
1300	MPS	95035	814-D1
3200	SMTO	94403	749-B4
SARATOGA ST			
16200	AlaC	94578	691-F4
SARATOGA WY			
3700	PLE	94588	694-F5
SARATOGA-SUNNYVALE RD			
800	SUNV	94087	832-E5
1600	CPTO	95014	832-E5
12000	SAR	95070	852-D7
S SARATOGA-SUNNYVALE RD			
12500	SAR	95070	852-D5
13400	SAR	95070	872-D1
SARATOGA CREEK DR			
12200	SAR	95070	852-G6
SARATOGA GLEN CT			
12700	SAR	95070	852-H6
SARATOGA GLEN PL			
18900	SAR	95070	852-G6
SARATOGA HEIGHTS CT			
14500	SAR	95070	872-B2
SARATOGA HEIGHTS DR			
21400	SAR	95070	872-B2
SARATOGA HILLS RD			
20700	SAR	95070	872-C1
SARATOGA LOS GATOS RD			
-	LGTS	95030	873-A6
100	LGTS	95032	873-B7
SARATOGA LOS GATOS RD Rt#-9			
17900	LGTS	95030	873-A6
17900	MSER	95030	873-A6
17900	MSER	95030	872-G5
18500	SCIC	95030	872-G5
18800	SAR	95070	872-E3
SARATOGA PARK ST			
42500	FRMT	94538	773-C2
S SARATOGA SUNNYVALE RD			
13500	SAR	95070	872-D2
SARATOGA VILLA PL			
12000	SAR	95070	852-D5
SARATOGA VISTA AV			
13500	SAR	95070	872-E1
SARATOGA VISTA CT			
20000	SAR	95070	872-E1
SARATOGA WOODS CIR			
12700	SAR	95070	852-E6
SARAVIEW CT			
20800	SAR	95070	852-C7
20800	SAR	95070	872-D1
SARAVIEW DR			
13400	SAR	95070	872-D1
SARAZEN AV			
3300	OAK	94605	671-A3
SARDONYX RD			
1600	LVMR	94550	715-C3
SARGENT AV			
2700	CCCo	94806	569-B5
4400	AlaC	94546	692-B4
SARGENT CT			
500	BEN	94510	550-J1
SARGENT DR			
1000	SUNV	94087	832-F3
SARGENT LN			
-	ATN	94027	790-B7
SARGENT RD			
1600	CNCD	94518	592-F6
SARGENT ST			
-	SF	94132	687-C1
SARITA CT			
-	PIN	94564	569-G7
SARITA WY			
1300	SCL	95051	832-H4
SARK CT			
400	MPS	95035	794-A6
SARK WY			
3700	SJS	95111	855-A6
SARON DR			
-	SJS	95116	834-G4
SARONI CT			
-	OAK	94611	630-F7
SARONI DR			
6500	OAK	94611	630-F6
SASKATCHEWAN DR			
1400	SUNV	94087	832-D5
SASSAFRAS CT			
8200	PLE	94566	734-C1
8200	PLE	94586	734-C1
SASSAFRAS DR			
3400	SJS	95111	854-G6
SASSAFRAS LN			
-	SRMN	94583	653-H7
SASSEL AV			
900	CNCD	94518	592-G5
SASSONE CT			
1200	MPS	95035	814-D2
SATELITE ST			
28400	HAY	94545	731-H2
SATH CT			
-	ALA	94502	669-J6
SATINWOOD DR			
3600	SJS	95148	835-F7
4200	CNCD	94521	593-C2
SATTLER DR			
3700	CNCD	94519	593-A1
SATURN AV			
-	FRMT	94539	793-J1
600	HAY	94544	712-B7
SATURN CT			
600	FCTY	94404	749-E3
1400	MPS	95035	794-D7
SATURN DR			
14500	AlaC	94578	691-D3
SATURN ST			
-	SF	94114	667-F2
SATURN TER			
300	SUNV	94086	832-E1
SATURN WY			
700	LVMR	94550	715-E4
4200	UNC	94587	732-A6
SAUNDERS AV			
-	SANS	94960	566-B6
SAUNDERS DR			
100	VAL	94591	530-F5
SAUSAL DR			
-	PTLV	94028	810-C6
SAUSAL ST			
1700	OAK	94602	650-C5
SAUSALITO BLVD			
-	SAUS	94965	627-A4
SAUSALITO RD			
13800	SLN	94577	690-H5

STREET Block City ZIP Pg-Grid

SAUSALITO ST
200 CMAD 94925 586-G7
200 CMAD 94925 606-G1
SAUSALITO TER
34800 FRMT 94555 752-B2
SAUSALITO FERRY
- BLV - 627-C3
- MrnC - 627-C3
- SAUS - 627-C3
- SF - 627-H5
- SF - 648-B1
- SF - 648-C4
- TBRN - 627-C3
SAUSALITO LATERAL
- MrnC 94965 627-B5
SAUSALITO TIBURON FERRY
- SF - 627-H6
- SF - 647-H1
SAUTERNE WY
900 PLE 94566 714-H3
SAUTNER DR
400 SJS 95123 875-B7
SAUVIGNON CT
1400 LVMR 94550 715-H3
8300 SJS 95135 855-J7
SAVAGE AV
3300 PIN 94564 569-G7
SAVAGE WY
- DALY 94015 687-B7
SAVAKER AV
800 SJS 95126 853-J2
SAVANA LN
3500 ALA 94502 670-B7
SAVANNA CIR
- NVTO 94947 526-B7
SAVANNAH CIR
700 WLCK 94598 612-G1
700 WLCK 94598 592-G7
SAVANNAH CT
900 WLCK 94598 592-G7
900 WLCK 94598 612-G1
3900 SSF 94080 707-C4
SAVANNAH DR
1100 SJS 95117 853-D3
SAVANNAH RD
- SANS 94960 566-B7
3800 FRMT 94538 773-E3
SAVENDISH CT
5200 SJS 95136 874-F3
SAVERIO CT
2100 SJS 95008 853-B6
SAVIGNON CT
800 CLAY 94517 613-J1
SAVONA CT
- DNVL 94526 653-C1
SAVONA WY
400 RDWC 94065 749-J5
SAVORY DR
800 SUNV 94087 832-D2
SAVOY CT
600 WLCK 94598 612-E2
SAVOY DR
4500 SJS 95129 853-A4
SAVOY WY
100 SLN 94577 691-B2
SAVSTROM WY
400 SJS 95111 875-B1
SAWGRASS CT
7900 PLE 94588 714-B6
SAWLEAF CT
1500 SJS 95131 814-D6
SAWLEAF ST
48200 FRMT 94539 793-J1
SAW MILL LN
- MTVW 94043 811-J3
SAWTOOTH CT
3600 SJS 95111 854-G6
SAWYER CT
2300 SCL 95054 813-C5
SAWYER ST
100 VAL 94589 510-C5
200 SF 94134 687-J2
SAXON CT
3100 FRMT 94555 732-E7
36200 NWK 94560 752-F4
SAXON ST
2200 MRTZ 94553 571-F5
SAXON WY
1100 MLPK 94025 790-F4
SAXONY CT
- VAL 94591 530-H6
5600 SJS 95123 874-G4
SAXTON CT
- WLCK 94596 612-B2
SAYBROOK PL
2400 MRTZ 94553 572-A5
SAYBROOK RD
1300 LVMR 94550 695-E6
SAYBROOK WY
100 VAL 94591 550-E1
SAYOKO CIR
4200 SJS 95136 874-H1
SAYRE AV
- SCIC 94035 812-B2
5300 FRMT 94536 752-H6
SAYRE DR
6900 OAK 94611 630-F7
SAYRE ST
1300 SLN 94579 691-B7
SCALLETTA LN
1000 SJS 95120 894-H4
SCALLY CT
2000 CNCD 94518 592-G6
SCAMMAN CT
3800 FRMT 94538 773-D1
SCANLAN PL
2400 SCL 95050 833-C6
SCANLAN WY
1000 PIN 94564 569-D4
SCARAWAY DR
3000 SJS 95132 814-F4
SCARBORO PL
100 SRMN 94583 673-E6
SCARBOROUGH DR
5000 NWK 94560 752-E3
5700 OAK 94611 650-F1
SCARFF WY
26000 LAH 94022 811-C5
SCARLET OAK CT
300 PLHL 94523 592-B1

SCARLET OAK PL
2000 CCCo 94506 653-G1
SCARLETT CT
5700 DBLN 94568 694-A4
SCARLETT DR
6100 DBLN 94568 694-B5
SCARLETT WY
4900 SJS 95111 875-C1
SCARLETWOOD TER
4800 SJS 95129 852-B7
SCARSBOROUGH WY
100 LGTS 95030 873-A3
SCARSDALE CT
1100 SJS 95120 894-G4
SCARSDALE PL
7100 SJS 95120 894-G4
SCARSDALE WY
7100 SJS 95120 894-G4
SCENERY CT
6500 SJS 95120 894-C1
SCENIC AV
- PDMT 94611 650-C1
- SANS 94960 566-A7
- SRFL 94901 566-E7
100 PDMT 94611 630-B7
1300 BERK 94708 609-H7
1500 CCCo 94805 589-C6
1600 BERK 94709 609-H7
1600 BERK 94709 629-H1
1900 MRTZ 94553 571-F3
2200 CCCo 94553 571-F3
2400 OAK 94602 650-C1
4200 PIT 94565 574-D6
4700 LVMR 94550 696-B3
E SCENIC AV
- RCH 94801 608-D1
W SCENIC AV
- RCH 94801 608-D1
SCENIC BLVD
10000 CPTO 95014 852-A1
SCENIC CIR
10300 CPTO 95014 852-A1
SCENIC CT
- DNVL 94506 653-G5
- ORIN 94563 630-J2
100 CNCD 94518 592-G4
100 SBRN 94066 727-H2
10400 CPTO 95014 852-A1
SCENIC DR
- NVTO 94949 546-G5
- ORIN 94563 630-J1
- VAL 94591 530-D6
100 SMCo 94062 769-G6
100 CNCD 94518 592-G4
N SCENIC DR
1200 LFYT 94549 611-G4
SCENIC LN
- SAUS 94965 627-A3
SCENIC PL
900 PLHL 94523 592-A4
SCENIC SQ
1900 SJS 95132 814-E3
SCENIC ST
2200 ELCR 94530 589-C7
SCENIC WY
- CCCo 94553 571-E2
- DALY 94014 687-E3
- MRTZ 94553 571-E2
- SF 94121 647-A5
- SMTO 94403 748-J6
100 VAL 94590 529-H2
200 PCFA 94044 707-A6
1100 AlaC 94541 691-G6
SCENIC HEIGHTS WY
21600 SCIC 95070 852-B5
SCENIC MEADOW CT
- SJS 95135 855-H7
SCENIC MEADOW LN
- SJS 95135 855-G7
- SJS 95138 855-G7
SCENICVIEW CT
1700 SLN 94577 691-D1
SCENICVIEW DR
1300 SLN 94577 691-D1
SCENIC VISTA DR
20700 SCIC 95120 894-J2
20800 SCIC 95120 895-A1
20800 SCIC 95119 895-A1
SCEPTER CT
1800 SJS 95132 814-G2
SCETTRINI DR
- SRFL 94903 566-E3
SCETTRINI FIRE RD
100 SRFL 94903 566-G5
200 SRFL 94901 566-G5
200 MrnC 94903 566-G5
SCHAAF CT
- SRFL 94901 566-D7
SCHAEFER RANCH RD
- AlaC 94552 693-C3
SCHAFER RD
100 HAY 94544 712-A6
700 HAY 94544 711-J6
SCHALLENBERGER RD
1500 SJS 95112 814-A7
1500 SJS 95131 814-A7
SCHARFF AV
- SJS 95116 834-G3
SCHAUPP CT
1100 CNCD 94520 592-E4
SCHELBERT TER
4800 FRMT 94555 752-C2
SCHELLING AV
800 LFYT 94549 611-G7
SCHEMBRI CT
- EPA 94303 791-B1
SCHEMBRI LN
700 EPA 94303 791-B1
SCHENONE CT
1500 CNCD 94521 593-E5
SCHERMAN CT
100 LVMR 94550 715-D2
SCHERMAN WY
200 LVMR 94550 715-D2
SCHIELE AV
700 SJS 95126 833-H6
SCHILLER CT
1300 CNCD 94521 592-J3
SCHILLER ST
1500 ALA 94501 669-J1
SCHILLINGSBURG AV
21400 SCIC 95120 895-C5

SCHIRADO PL
- MrnC 94901 586-J1
SCHLOSSER CT
4600 AlaC 94546 692-B4
SCHMIDT LN
- MrnC 94903 566-G3
6300 ELCR 94530 609-C2
SCHOFIELD CT
1100 CNCD 94520 592-E4
SCHOFIELD RD
- SF 94123 647-H3
- SF 94129 647-C4
SCHOOL AL
100 SF 94133 648-A4
SCHOOL AV
5200 ELCR 94530 609-B2
5200 RCH 94804 609-B2
SCHOOL CT
40100 FRMT 94538 753-B6
SCHOOL LN
100 WLCK 94596 612-B3
SCHOOL PTH
- RCH 94804 609-B2
SCHOOL RD
300 MrnC 94945 526-G3
SCHOOL ST
- ANT 94509 574-H5
- CCCo - 550-H6
- SJS 95002 813-C1
- DALY 94014 687-C4
- PIT 94565 574-E3
- SSF 94080 707-J2
100 DNVL 94526 653-A2
100 SUNV 94086 812-E6
200 FRMT 94536 753-A1
200 LVMR 94550 695-H7
200 LVMR 94550 715-H1
200 DALY 94015 687-C4
900 SLN 94577 691-C2
1000 MRGA 94556 631-D7
1500 SCAR 94070 769-G3
1800 MRGA 94556 651-D1
2100 PIN 94564 569-E4
2600 OAK 94602 650-D5
3400 LFYT 94549 611-F7
4000 PLE 94566 714-E2
13600 SLN 94578 691-C2
SCHOOL TER
- MrnC 94945 526-G3
SCHOOL WY
4400 AlaC 94546 691-J2
SCHOOLDALE DR
1800 SJS 95124 853-H7
SCHOOLHOUSE RD
700 SJS 95138 875-G5
SCHOONER CT
- RCH 94804 608-G2
3000 SJS 95148 855-D1
SCHOONER DR
- RCH 94804 608-G2
SCHOONER RD
13700 SLN 94577 690-H4
SCHOONER ST
800 FCTY 94404 749-G4
SCHOONER WY
100 VAL 94590 550-B2
300 PIT 94565 574-A3
600 PIT 94565 573-J3
1600 CCCo 94565 573-J3
SCHOONER BAY DR
800 RDWC 94065 750-C6
SCHOONER HILL
- OAK 94618 630-C4
- OAK 94705 630-C4
SCHOTT ST
100 SJS 95116 834-G2
SCHRADER DR
1900 SJS 95124 853-F7
SCHROEDER AV
300 SUNV 94086 812-E6
SCHUBERT AV
2400 SJS 95124 853-G7
SCHUBERT DR
700 SUNV 94087 832-F3
SCHULTE DR
1700 SJS 95133 834-E3
SCHUPP CT
- CCCo 94803 569-D6
SCHUSTER AV
19000 AlaC 94546 691-J3
SCHUYLER AV
- HAY 94544 732-E3
SCHUYLKILL AV
- HAY 94544 732-E3
SCHWEEN CT
4000 PLE 94566 714-F1
SCHWEPPES CT
1800 SJS 95132 814-J3
SCHWERIN ST
- SF 94134 687-J3
300 DALY 94014 687-J3
SCHWIE AL
- MLPK 94025 790-E6
SCHYLER ST
2900 OAK 94602 650-D5
SCIOTA AV
- SRMN 94583 673-H6
SCIOTA PL
- SRMN 94583 673-H7
SCOFIELD AV
4000 PA 94306 811-E2
SCOFIELD CT
600 EPA 94303 791-B3
43000 FRMT 94539 753-H6
SCOFIELD DR
200 MRGA 94556 631-C3
20500 CPTO 95014 852-D1
42600 FRMT 94539 753-H6
SCOLLON CT
1300 SJS 95132 814-F5
SCORPIO DR
1800 SJS 95111 854-G6
SCORPIO LN
600 FCTY 94404 749-E4
SCORPION PL
900 FRMT 94539 773-J5
SCORPION RD
1000 FRMT 94539 773-J5
SCOSSA AV
1300 SJS 95118 874-B3
SCOSSA CT
- SJS 95118 874-B3

SCOTCH CT
200 DNVL 94526 653-B2
SCOTCHBROOK PZ
- HAY 94542 712-B3
SCOTCH HEATHER CT
3100 SJS 95148 855-E2
SCOTIA AV
- SF 94124 668-A6
4600 OAK 94605 671-D4
SCOTIA CT
200 FRMT 94539 773-H2
SCOTIA LN
100 NVTO 94947 526-D7
SCOTIA ST
4800 UNC 94587 752-A1
SCOTLAND DR
1100 CPTO 95014 852-D3
19400 SAR 95070 852-F7
SCOTLAND ST
- SF 94133 647-J4
SCOTS CT
- WLCK 94596 612-E6
SCOTS LN
900 CCCo 94596 612-F6
1000 WLCK 94596 612-E6
SCOTSGLEN CT
900 SJS 95136 874-D1
SCOTT AV
500 RDWC 94063 770-C6
800 RCH 94804 608-F3
18400 MSER 95030 872-H6
SCOTT BLVD
400 SCL 95050 833-D3
2900 SCL 95054 833-D3
2900 SCL 95054 813-A7
3300 SUNV 94086 813-A7
SCOTT CIR
- NVTO 94949 546-G4
SCOTT CT
800 CMBL 95008 873-C1
3000 HIL 94010 748-B1
SCOTT DR
- MLPK 94025 770-G6
SCOTT LN
- LKSP 94939 586-E6
1900 LALT 94024 831-H5
SCOTT PL
- LKSP 94939 586-E6
1100 HAY 94544 711-J6
SCOTT RD
1800 CNCD 94519 592-J1
SCOTT ST
- SBRN 94066 707-J5
- SF 94117 667-G1
- VAL 94590 530-A5
200 LVMR 94550 695-J7
200 MrnC 94941 606-E4
300 SF 94117 647-G6
400 FRMT 94539 753-H7
700 NVTO 94945 526-C3
900 OAK 94610 650-A2
900 PA 94301 790-J5
1000 SF 94115 647-G6
1200 ELCR 94530 609-D2
1500 SJS 95126 853-G1
1600 SCIC 95126 853-G1
1600 SMTO 94403 749-D1
1700 SJS 95128 853-E1
1800 SCIC 95128 853-G1
2700 SF 94123 647-F4
3100 SF 94123 647-F3
SCOTT CREEK RD
600 FRMT 94539 794-A2
600 FRMT 94539 793-J2
2200 SCIC 95035 794-A2
SCOTTS CHUTE CT
100 RCH 94803 589-G2
SCOTTSDALE CT
2800 SJS 95148 855-C2
SCOTTSDALE DR
2400 SJS 95148 835-B7
2500 SJS 95148 855-C1
SCOTTSDALE RD
200 PLHL 94523 592-B1
SCOTTSDALE WY
- NVTO 94947 526-C6
SCOTTSFIELD DR
4300 SJS 95136 874-D2
SCOTTS MILL CT
200 DNVL 94526 653-C4
SCOTTS MILL RD
400 DNVL 94526 653-C4
SCOTTS VALLEY
- HER 94547 569-F4
SCOTTSVILLE CT
500 SJS 95133 834-F2
SCOTTY ST
1500 SJS 95122 834-G6
SCOUT CT
4800 SJS 95136 874-J2
SCOUT PL
400 DNVL 94526 653-B5
SCOUT RD
5600 OAK 94611 650-E1
SCOVILLE ST
5500 OAK 94621 670-F2
SCOWN LN
800 NVTO 94945 526-C3
SCRIPPS AV
4000 PA 94306 811-E2
SCRIPPS CT
200 PA 94306 811-E2
SCRIPPS ST
25500 HAY 94545 711-G6
SCRIPPSHAVEN DR
400 CCCo 94595 632-D1
SCULLY AV
12000 SAR 95070 852-F5
SCUPPER CT
200 HER 94547 570-B6
SEA WY
- SRFL 94901 587-A1
SEABEE PL
1900 SJS 95133 834-E1
SEABISCUIT DR
200 SJS 95111 875-B2
SEABOARD AV
2500 SJS 95131 813-F7
SEABOARD LN
25500 HAY 94545 711-D7
SEABORN CT
1600 ALA 94501 669-H1

SEABOURNE CT
1100 ANT 94509 575-F7
SEABREEZE CT
- PCFA 94044 707-A1
3600 HAY 94542 712-F4
SEA BREEZE DR
800 BEN 94510 551-A4
800 BEN 94510 550-J4
SEABREEZE DR
- RCH 94804 608-J3
SEA BRIDGE CT
100 ALA 94502 670-A5
SEABRIDGE DR
- FRMT 94538 793-F1
SEA BRIDGE WY
100 ALA 94502 670-A5
SEABROOK CT
800 SJS 95111 855-A6
SEABURY DR
800 SJS 95136 874-E2
SEABURY RD
700 HIL 94010 748-F1
SEACAPE DR
- MrnC 94965 626-A2
SEA CHASE DR
800 RDWC 94065 750-C6
SEA CLIFF AV
- SF 94121 647-A5
SEACLIFF AV
- DALY 94015 686-J5
SEA CLIFF CT
700 CCCo 94572 569-J2
SEACLIFF DR
1000 RCH 94804 608-E3
1100 RCH 94801 608-E3
2000 MPS 95035 794-E7
SEA CLIFF LN
300 RDWC 94065 749-J2
SEA CLIFF PL
- CCCo 94565 573-E2
SEACLIFF PL
100 VAL 94591 550-E1
SEA CLIFF TER
34700 FRMT 94555 752-E2
SEA CLIFF WY
2000 SBRN 94066 707-C5
SEACLIFF WY
2300 SJS 95122 854-J1
SEA CLOUD AV
2000 SLN 94579 690-J6
SEA CLOUD DR
700 FCTY 94404 749-G5
SEACOR CT
4100 OAK 94605 671-B2
SEACREEK CT
3200 SJS 95121 855-D7
SEACREEK WY
1600 SJS 95121 855-D7
SEACREST CT
- DALY 94015 706-J2
SEA CREST TER
- FRMT 94536 753-C2
SEADRIFT DR
- RCH 94804 608-H2
SEADRIFT LNDG
- MrnC 94920 606-H3
SEA EAGLE CT
2200 PLE 94566 714-D1
SEAFARER CT
100 VAL 94591 550-F2
SEAFIELD CT
3000 SJS 95148 855-C3
SEAFIRTH LN
- TBRN 94920 607-C4
SEAFIRTH PL
- TBRN 94920 607-C4
SEAFIRTH RD
- TBRN 94920 607-C4
- MrnC 94920 607-C4
SEAFORTH CT
300 PCFA 94044 707-A7
300 PCFA 94044 727-A1
SEAGATE CT
- RDWC 94065 749-J2
SEAGATE DR
100 SMTO 94403 749-E6
13700 SLN 94577 690-G5
SEAGATE PL
- BLMT 94002 749-E7
SEAGATE WY
500 BLMT 94002 749-E6
SEAGRAMS CT
3200 AlaC 94541 692-F6
SEAGRAVES WY
20100 SAR 95070 872-E2
SEA GULL CT
2100 PIT 94565 574-B3
19700 SAR 95070 852-F6
SEAGULL CT
- RCH 94804 608-J3
400 HER 94547 570-B6
SEAGULL DR
- RCH 94804 608-J3
SEAGULL RW
100 NVTO 94947 526-C4
SEA GULL WY
19800 SAR 95070 852-E5
SEA HAVEN CT
- PCFA 94044 707-A1
SEA HORSE
4000 ALA 94501 649-E6
SEA HORSE CT
300 FCTY 94404 749-H3
SEAHORSE DR
100 VAL 94591 550-D1
SEAHORSE LN
500 RDWC 94065 749-J6
SEA ISLAND LN
900 FCTY 94404 749-H1
SEA ISLE DR
- RCH 94804 608-J3
SEAL ST
- HAY 94545 711-E7
- SMTO 94403 749-D2
SEALANE CT
100 PIT 94565 574-A3
SEALE AV
100 PA 94301 791-A6
700 PA 94303 791-A6
SEALION PL
- VAL 94591 550-D2

SEAL POINTE DR
800 RDWC 94065 750-A6
SEAL ROCK DR
- SF 94121 646-H6
SEAL ROCK TER
34800 FRMT 94555 752-B2
SEAMAN PL
1000 SJS 95133 814-E7
SEAMAST PASG
- CMAD 94925 606-J1
- CMAD 94925 586-J7
SEA MIST CT
200 VAL 94591 550-G2
300 HAY 94544 712-C7
SEA MIST DR
100 VAL 94591 550-G2
SEA MIST TER
34400 FRMT 94555 752-C3
SEAN CIR
5400 SJS 95123 874-J4
SEAN CT
- PLHL 94523 592-B3
- SJS 95123 874-F6
2600 SSF 94080 707-C4
SEAN LN
5500 SJS 95123 874-J3
SEAN PL
800 CNCD 94518 592-G7
SEA PINES
- MRGA 94556 631-C7
SEA POINT WY
- PIT 94565 574-E1
SEAPORT AV
4900 RCH 94804 609-A3
SEAPORT BLVD
- RDWC 94063 770-C4
600 SMCo 94063 770-C4
SEAPORT CT
400 RDWC 94063 770-C3
SEAPORT DR
- UNC 94545 731-H5
100 VAL 94590 550-B1
31100 UNC 94587 731-H5
SEA RANCH CT
600 VAL 94591 550-E3
SEARCY DR
1300 SJS 95118 874-B2
SEAREEL LN
1400 SJS 95131 814-A4
SEARLES AV
1500 SJS 95125 854-A4
SEARLES LN
- SANS 94960 566-C6
SEARS ST
- SF 94112 687-D2
SEARS POINT HWY Rt#-37
- MrnC 94945 526-G5
- NVTO 94945 526-G5
- SonC - 526-G5
SEARS POINT RD Rt#-37
- SolC 94589 509-A7
- SolC 94589 529-B1
- SolC 94590 529-F2
- SolC 94592 529-F2
- VAL 94590 529-F2
- VAL 94592 529-F2
SEARSPORT CT
1000 ANT 94509 575-E7
SEARSVILLE CT
- HIL 94010 748-F6
SEARSVILLE RD
- SCIC 94305 790-F7
SEARVILLE RD
1500 PA 94304 810-G5
1700 SCIC 94304 810-G5
28000 LAH 94022 810-G5
SEASCAPE CIR
900 CCCo 94572 569-J1
SEASCAPE CT
1000 CCCo 94572 569-J1
SEASCAPE DR
100 VAL 94591 550-D2
500 NVTO 94947 526-D7
SEASCAPE RD
39300 FRMT 94538 752-J7
SEA SHELL DR
- RCH 94804 608-H2
SEASHORE DR
- DALY 94014 687-E5
SEASIDE CT
- UNC 94545 751-J1
SEASIDE DR
- UNC 94545 751-J1
100 MPS 95035 793-J5
200 PCFA 94044 706-J7
200 PCFA 94044 707-A7
SEASIDE WY
1100 MPS 95035 793-J5
SEASONS DR
1100 PIT 94565 573-J2
SEASONS WY
1900 PIT 94565 573-J1
SEASPRAY CT
2000 SLN 94579 690-J6
SEA SPRAY LN
700 FCTY 94404 749-E3
SEASTORM CT
- RDWC 94065 750-A5
SEASTORM DR
- RDWC 94065 750-A5
SEATON AV
20600 SAR 95070 872-D1
SEATTLE RD
100 ALA 94501 649-D6
SEAVER AV
- RCH 94804 609-A2
- RCH 94804 608-J2
SEAVER CT
1500 HAY 94545 711-G5
SEAVER DR
500 MLV 94941 606-G4
SEAVER ST
25400 HAY 94545 711-G5
SEA VIEW AV
- MrnC 94901 586-J1
SEAVIEW AV
- PDMT 94611 650-C1
100 PDMT 94610 650-C1
4800 AlaC 94546 692-A3

W SEA VIEW AV
- MrnC 94901 586-J1
- SRFL 94901 586-J1
SEA VIEW CT
- MrnC 94901 566-J7
- MrnC 94901 586-J1
- SRFL 94901 566-J7
SEAVIEW CT
100 VAL 94589 530-A1
SEAVIEW DR
- DALY 94015 686-J6
100 BEN 94510 551-B3
100 ELCR 94530 609-E2
300 SJS 95002 813-B1
1700 SJS 95122 834-H7
SEA VIEW PKWY
2500 ALA 94502 669-H5
2900 ALA 94502 670-A5
SEAVIEW PL
7400 ELCR 94530 609-D2
SEAVIEW TER
- SF 94121 647-A6
SEAVIEW TR
- CCCo 94708 610-A4
- ORIN 94563 610-C6
SEAWALL CT
100 VAL 94591 550-F1
SEAWALL DR
- BERK 94804 629-B2
SEAWAY CT
100 HER 94547 570-B6
SEAWELL CT
100 SJS 95138 875-E4
SEAWIND DR
100 VAL 94590 550-B1
SEAWITCH DR
- VAL 94590 550-B1
SEAWOLF PASG
- CMAD 94925 606-J1
SEAWOOD WY
700 SJS 95120 894-J3
SEBASIAN WY
400 SJS 95111 854-J6
SEBASTIAN CT
100 LGTS 95032 873-J6
SEBASTIAN DR
200 MLBR 94030 728-A5
1600 BURL 94010 728-A5
SEBASTIAN LN
1100 WLCK 94598 612-J5
SEBASTIAN WY
27500 HAY 94544 711-J7
SEBASTIAN BORELLO DR
2800 SJS 95148 855-D2
SEBASTOPOL LN
2400 HAY 94542 712-D4
SEBILLE RD
- DBLN 94568 694-B1
SEBREE LN
18200 MSER 95030 872-J5
SEBRING CT
29000 HAY 94544 732-A2
SECCOMBE CT
2100 WLCK 94598 612-G2
SECLUDED AV
- SMCo 94063 770-F5
SECLUDED PL
100 LFYT 94549 612-A4
100 LFYT 94549 611-J4
SECRETARIAT DR
2500 PLE 94566 714-C1
SECRET MEADOW CT
- AlaC 94542 692-E7
SECRET MEADOW DR
- AlaC 94542 692-E7
SECURITY PAC PL
- SF 94108 648-A6
SEDGE ST
4100 FRMT 94555 732-B7
SEDGEFIELD AV
7200 SRMN 94583 673-G6
SEDGEFIELD CT
100 SRMN 94583 673-G7
SEDGEMAN ST
15400 SLN 94579 691-C6
SEDLAK CT
2500 SJS 95148 855-B1
SEDUM RD
48600 FRMT 94539 793-J2
SEEBECK CT
2000 SJS 95132 814-F2
SEEBER CT
7700 CPTO 95014 852-C4
SEELEY ST
1200 SLN 94577 690-J2
SEELY AV
2600 SCIC 95134 813-H4
2600 SJS 95134 813-H4
SEEMA CIR
400 UNC 94587 732-D5
SEEMANS LN
- WLCK 94596 612-C2
SEEMAS LN
- WLCK 94596 592-D7
SEENA AV
900 LALT 94024 831-G2
SEENO AV
- PIT 94565 574-C6
SEGO CT
1600 SJS 95131 834-D1
SEGOVIA CT
100 VAL 94591 530-G7
3200 SJS 95127 814-H6
3700 SRMN 94583 673-C3
SEGOVIA PL
200 FRMT 94539 753-E3
SEGUNDO CT
2200 PLE 94588 714-B5
SEGURA CT
2900 SJS 95125 873-J1
SEIBEL ST
- SRFL 94901 586-F2
SEIFERT AV
5600 SJS 95118 874-B4
SEINE CT
- SJS 95127 834-J1
11400 DBLN 94568 693-F3
SEKI CT
- SMCo 94062 789-G2
SELBORN PL
1400 SJS 95126 833-H7

STREET
Block City ZIP Pg-Grid

SELBORNE DR
- PDMT 94611 650-D2
15900 AlaC 94578 691-F3
SELBORNE WY
- MRGA 94556 651-E2
SELBY DR
16500 AlaC 94546 691-G4
16500 AlaC 94578 691-G4
SELBY LN
- ATN 94027 790-C2
- SMCo 94063 790-C1
700 SCIC 95127 814-H6
1100 SMCo 94061 790-B3
W SELBY LN
1100 ATN 94027 790-C2
1400 SMCo 94061 790-B3
SELBY RD
- CCCo 94525 550-B4
SELBY ST
300 SF 94124 668-B5
SELDON CT
3000 FRMT 94539 773-E2
SELENA CT
- ANT 94509 595-D1
SELFRIDGE RD
- VAL 94590 529-H1
SELFRIDGE WY
- NVTO 94949 546-G4
SELIG LN
1700 LALT 94024 832-A3
SELIMA WY
100 CCCo 94553 572-C7
SELINDA LN
5000 SJS 95032 873-H4
SELINDA WY
5100 SJS 95032 873-H5
SELKIRK CT
5200 ANT 94509 595-J2
SELKIRK PL
800 SUNV 94087 832-F6
SELKIRK ST
- OAK 94619 650-G5
4600 FRMT 94538 753-B7
SELLERS CT
3500 FRMT 94536 752-F1
SELLINGS CT
- CCCo 94596 612-F6
SELMA AV
5100 FRMT 94536 752-H7
SELMA WY
- SF 94122 667-C3
SELMAC AV
- SJS 95136 874-E1
SELO DR
1300 SUNV 94087 832-D4
SELVA DR
3200 SJS 95148 835-D6
SELWYN DR
100 MPS 95035 794-C7
SEM LN
- BLMT 94002 749-F7
SEMERIA AV
2200 BLMT 94002 769-C1
SEMICIRCULAR RD
100 SMCo 94063 790-D1
SEMICONDUCTOR DR
2900 SCL 95051 812-H7
2900 SCL 95051 832-H1
2900 SCL 94086 812-H7
2900 SCL 94086 832-H1
SEMILLION DR
48800 FRMT 94539 793-J2
SEMILLON CIR
300 CLAY 94517 593-H7
SEMINARY AV
1000 OAK 94621 670-F2
1400 ALA 94502 670-B7
2200 OAK 94605 650-H7
2300 OAK 94613 650-H7
3000 OAK 94613 670-F2
3000 OAK 94605 670-F2
SEMINARY CT
5800 OAK 94605 670-F2
SEMINARY DR
- MLPK 94025 790-H2
100 MrnC 94941 606-H5
SEMINARY RD
- SANS 94960 586-B1
SEMINOLE AV
- CMAD 94925 586-G7
- SF 94112 687-F1
SEMINOLE CIR
5000 CNCD 94521 593-D5
SEMINOLE COM
900 FRMT 94539 773-H3
SEMINOLE CT
- SRMN 94583 673-D5
SEMINOLE DR
800 LVMR 94550 695-E7
SEMINOLE TER
900 FRMT 94539 773-H2
SEMINOLE WY
- PLE 94588 694-G7
700 PA 94303 811-F1
800 RDWC 94062 789-G2
1600 SJS 95122 854-J1
27600 HAY 94544 711-J7
27600 HAY 94544 731-J1
SEMPLE CRSG
200 BEN 94510 551-B5
SEMPLE CT
600 BEN 94510 551-B5
SENATE WY
10000 CPTO 95014 832-C7
SENCA CT
700 DNVL 94526 653-B3
SENECA AV
- SF 94112 687-F1
SENECA CT
600 SJS 95123 874-G4
1000 WLCK 94598 612-H4
SENECA LN
- SRMN 94583 673-C4
1500 SMCo 94402 748-F6
SENECA ST
400 PA 94301 791-A3
400 PA 94301 790-J3
8500 OAK 94605 671-A3
32100 HAY 94544 732-F3
SENECA PARK AV
4400 FRMT 94538 773-C2
SENECA PARK LP
4900 FRMT 94538 773-C2
SENIOR AV
- BERK 94708 610-A7
SENNA CT
400 SUNV 94086 832-G1
SENTER RD
- SJS 95111 854-H5
1300 SJS 95112 854-F2
SENTER CREEK CT
2600 SJS 95111 854-G4
SENTINEL CT
- SRFL 94901 566-E7
- SRFL 94901 586-E1
3500 HAY 94542 712-F4
SENTINEL DR
3400 MRTZ 94553 571-F6
46000 FRMT 94539 774-A4
46000 FRMT 94539 773-J5
SENTINEL PL
45900 FRMT 94539 774-A4
46000 FRMT 94539 773-J4
SENTINEL ST
5800 SJS 95120 874-B6
SENTRY LN
- DNVL 94506 653-E4
SENTRY PALM CT
- SJS 95133 814-J4
SEPTEMBER CT
800 CPTO 95014 852-C2
3700 AlaC 94546 691-H2
SEPTEMBER DR
800 CPTO 95014 852-C2
5500 SJS 95138 875-D4
SEPTEMBER SONG CT
1700 SJS 95131 814-D7
SEPULVEDA AV
2000 MPS 95035 794-E7
SEPULVEDA CT
200 MPS 95035 794-E7
5500 CNCD 94521 593-G5
SEPULVIDA CT
- AlaC 94541 711-G1
SEQUESTER CT
2400 SJS 95133 814-F6
SEQUIERA RD
- MrnC 94903 546-C7
- SRFL 94903 546-C7
SEQUIM COM
- FRMT 94539 773-F6
SEQUOIA AV
100 CCCo 94595 612-B7
100 SJS 95126 833-H7
100 SMCo 94061 790-A3
200 PA 94306 791-A6
200 SSF 94080 707-F2
200 VAL 94591 550-C1
600 MLBR 94030 728-B4
700 SMTO 94403 749-A5
700 SMTO 94403 748-J5
800 BURL 94010 728-B4
1300 SBRN 94066 707-E6
1400 CCCo 94805 589-C6
SEQUOIA CT
- SCAR 94070 769-D3
500 HAY 94541 711-G3
1900 MRTZ 94553 572-A7
4000 CNCD 94519 593-B1
6000 PLE 94588 714-B1
36600 NWK 94560 752-C7
SEQUOIA DR
- NVTO 94949 546-J5
- SANS 94960 566-C6
100 PIT 94565 574-D5
400 SUNV 94086 832-G2
500 MPS 95035 794-D7
600 MPS 95035 814-E1
700 LVMR 94550 695-E7
1900 MRTZ 94553 572-A7
1900 MRTZ 94553 571-J7
2300 ANT 94509 575-A7
2300 ANT 94509 574-J7
11800 SCIC 94024 831-J5
SEQUOIA LN
400 SCIC 94305 790-G7
SEQUOIA RD
100 HER 94547 569-J4
100 HER 94547 570-A4
500 HAY 94541 711-F3
37200 FRMT 94536 752-J3
SEQUOIA TER
200 CCCo 94506 654-A2
2900 FRMT 94536 752-H2
SEQUOIA WY
- CCCo 94553 591-E2
- PCFA 94044 727-B5
- SF 94127 667-E5
- SMCo 94061 790-B4
- SMCo 94062 809-F6
- MRTZ 94553 591-E2
400 SCIC 94024 831-J5
2600 BLMT 94002 749-B7
2600 BLMT 94002 769-B1
SEQUOIA GLEN LN
- NVTO 94947 526-D7
SEQUOIA VALLEY RD
600 MLV 94941 606-C3
600 MrnC 94941 606-C3
SEQUOIA WOODS PL
700 CNCD 94518 592-H6
SEQUOYAH RD
3800 OAK 94605 671-D2
SEQUOYAH VIEW CT
- OAK 94605 671-C3
SEQUOYAH VIEW DR
- OAK 94605 671-C3
SERAFIX RD
- CCCo 94507 632-J2
2000 CCCo - 633-A2
2000 CCCo 94507 633-A2
SERANA CT
- SSF 94080 707-E3
SERENA CT
7900 DBLN 94568 693-G3
SERENA DR
700 PCFA 94044 726-J4
SERENA LN
- DNVL 94526 633-B7
- DNVL 94526 653-C1
SERENA WY
100 SCL 95051 833-B7
100 SCL 95051 853-B1
SERENADE CT
600 SJS 95111 855-A7
SERENADE WY
400 SJS 95111 855-A7
SERENA VISTA CT
16200 MSER 95030 872-J6
SERENE CT
- DNVL 94526 653-C7
1100 PIN 94564 569-D4
3100 RCH 94803 589-E1
SERENE PL
- DNVL 94526 653-C7
SERENE WY
21000 SCIC 95120 894-J2
SERENE VALLEY CT
1200 SJS 95120 894-E2
SERENIDAD ST
1700 LVMR 94550 715-E3
SERENITY CT
6800 SJS 95120 894-F2
SERENITY TER
- PLE 94586 693-H7
SERENITY WY
6800 SJS 95120 894-F2
SERENITY CIRCLE DR
- SMCo - 768-C3
SERENO CIR
- OAK 94619 650-H5
SERENO COM
36400 FRMT 94536 733-A7
36400 FRMT 94536 753-A1
SERENO CT
17200 MSER 95030 873-B4
SERENO DR
500 VAL 94589 529-J1
500 VAL 94589 530-A1
23300 CPTO 95014 831-H6
SERENO PL
- VAL 94589 530-B1
SERENO WY
- NVTO 94945 526-A1
SERENO VISTA WY
200 SJS 95116 834-D2
SERGE AV
1900 SJS 95130 852-J6
SERGEANT MITCHELL ST
- SF 94129 647-E3
SERIANA CT
3000 UNC 94587 732-B4
3000 UNC 94587 731-J4
SERIANA PL
2900 UNC 94587 732-A4
SERIANA WY
2900 UNC 94587 732-A4
SERPA
200 FRMT 94536 753-E1
200 FRMT 94536 733-A7
SERPA DR
1600 MPS 95035 794-D5
3000 SJS 95148 855-C2
SERPENTINE AV
- SF 94110 668-A4
SERPENTINE CT
100 VAL 94589 510-C6
SERPENTINE DR
- UNC 94587 732-G6
100 VAL 94589 510-B6
3300 ANT 94509 575-F7
3300 ANT 94509 595-F1
SERPENTINE LN
1000 PLE 94566 714-F2
SERRA AV
- MLBR 94030 728-B3
2000 SCL 95050 833-C5
4500 FRMT 94538 753-A6
4700 FRMT 94538 752-J6
SERRA CT
- SMTO 94401 729-A7
100 SBRN 94066 727-H2
100 VAL 94590 530-B2
200 LGTS 95032 873-B6
11600 DBLN 94568 693-F3
SERRA DR
300 SSF 94080 707-E2
800 SLN 94578 691-C5
1400 PCFA 94044 726-J5
SERRA PL
39100 FRMT 94538 753-A6
39100 FRMT 94538 752-J6
SERRA ST
- CMAD 94925 586-F7
100 SCIC 94305 790-H7
700 SCIC - 791-A7
SERRA WY
- MPS 95035 793-J7
- SRFL 94903 566-B2
100 MPS 95035 794-A7
SERRAMAR DR
- OAK 94611 630-D5
SERRAMONTE BLVD
- DALY 94015 707-B1
400 CLMA 94014 687-C7
900 CLMA 94014 707-B1
SERRAMONTE CT
600 DNVL 94526 653-E6
SERRAMONTE DR
- SCIC 95030 872-H5
SERRAMONTE TER
300 FRMT 94536 753-E1
SERRANA CT
800 PIT 94565 574-A3
800 PIT 94565 573-J3
SERRANO AV
300 SCIC 95127 835-A2
SERRANO CT
1000 LFYT 94549 611-F5
SERRANO DR
- ATN 94027 790-C2
- SF 94132 687-A1
SERRANO ST
3600 MRTZ 94553 571-D5
SERRANO WY
2200 PIT 94565 573-J4
SERRAOAKS CT
13700 SAR 95070 872-H1
SERRAVISTA AV
100 DALY 94015 707-C2
SERVICE DR
1400 WLCK 94596 612-C2
SERVICE RD
- ANT 94509 575-D5
SERVICE ST
800 SJS 95112 834-B2
2200 SF 94123 647-G4
SESAME CT
1200 SUNV 94087 832-D3
2500 SJS 95148 835-A6
SESAME DR
1100 SUNV 94087 832-D3
SESSIONS DR
6800 SJS 95119 875-F6
SESSIONS RD
- LFYT 94549 611-F5
SETAREH CT
1200 SJS 95125 854-A3
SETH CT
1000 SJS 95120 894-G3
SETON LN
1100 HAY 94545 711-G6
SETTERQUIST DR
- VAL 94589 510-C7
SETTING SUN DR
4600 RCH 94803 589-F1
SETTING SUN PL
- CCCo 94803 589-F1
- RCH 94803 589-F1
SETTLE AV
1100 SJS 95125 854-A3
SETTLE CT
100 VAL 94591 530-E6
SEVA ST
- PLE 94566 714-G1
SEVELY DR
800 MTVW 94041 812-A6
SEVEN ACRES LN
14000 LAH 94022 811-C6
SEVEN HILLS RD
3400 AlaC 94546 691-H3
4000 AlaC 94546 692-A3
SEVEN HILLS RCH RD
700 WLCK 94596 612-D3
700 CCCo 94596 612-D3
800 WLCK 94598 612-D3
800 CCCo 94598 612-D3
SEVEN SPRINGS DR
11500 CPTO 95014 852-C4
SEVEN SPRINGS LN
11500 CPTO 95014 852-C4
SEVEN SPRINGS PKWY
11700 CPTO 95014 852-C4
SEVEN TREES BLVD
3800 SJS 95111 854-H6
SEVEN TREES VILLAGE WY
3300 SJS 95111 854-G6
SEVERANCE CT
5100 SJS 95136 874-E3
SEVERANCE DR
4900 SJS 95136 874-E3
SEVERINI LN
2900 AlaC 94546 691-H4
SEVERN DR
35200 NWK 94560 752-E3
SEVERN LN
400 HIL 94010 748-H1
SEVERN PL
4900 NWK 94560 752-E3
SEVERN RD
16400 AlaC 94578 691-G4
SEVERN ST
- SF 94114 667-H3
SEVERUS DR
100 VAL 94589 509-J4
1800 VAL 94589 510-A4
SEVERYNS AV
- SCIC 94035 812-B2
- SCIC 94043 812-B2
SEVIER AV
1000 MLPK 94025 790-J1
1100 MLPK 94025 770-J7
1300 MLPK 94025 771-A7
SEVILLA DR
- LALT 94022 811-E5
SEVILLA LN
20500 SAR 95070 872-D1
SEVILLA RD
22000 HAY 94541 691-J7
SEVILLE
- PIT 94565 574-C6
SEVILLE CIR
2800 ANT 94509 575-A6
SEVILLE CT
- MLBR 94030 728-A2
- CCCo 94526 633-C5
2400 PIN 94564 569-H7
40400 FRMT 94539 753-E4
SEVILLE DR
- MrnC 94903 546-E7
1100 PCFA 94044 726-J5
SEVILLE PL
100 SRMN 94583 673-G5
500 FRMT 94539 753-E4
SEVILLE ST
- SF 94112 687-F2
100 VAL 94591 530-F6
SEVILLE WY
- SMTO 94402 749-A3
- SMTO 94402 748-J3
- SSF 94080 707-E6
700 NVTO 94949 546-F2
1700 SJS 95131 814-D7
SEVYSON CT
2900 PA 94303 791-D6
SEWARD CT
10100 SCIC 95127 835-A3
SEWARD DR
1900 PIT 94565 574-E3
SEWARD ST
- SF 94114 667-F3
SEXTANT CT
300 HER 94547 570-B6
800 SMTO 94404 749-D2
SEXTUS RD
200 OAK 94603 670-F7
SEYFERTH WY
3000 SJS 95118 854-C7
SEYMORE PL
1000 HAY 94544 711-J6
SEYMOUR LN
300 MrnC 94941 606-D4
1000 MLPK 94025 790-E5
SEYMOUR PL
3000 FRMT 94555 732-E7
SEYMOUR ST
- SF 94115 647-G7
200 SJS 95110 834-A5
300 SJS 95110 833-J5
SHAD CT
300 FCTY 94404 749-H2
SHADDICK DR
400 ANT 94509 575-F7
SHADDY TER
- FRMT 94539 773-G3
SHADELAND CT
3300 CNCD 94519 592-H2
SHADELANDS DR
2400 WLCK 94598 612-G1
6100 SJS 95123 874-H7
SHADELANDS PL
500 SRMN 94583 673-J7
SHADE OAK LN
1300 CNCD 94521 593-B5
SHADE TREE LN
2200 SJS 95131 814-C5
SHADEWELL CT
- DNVL 94506 653-F2
SHADEWELL DR
- DNVL 94506 653-G3
SHADLE AV
1100 CMBL 95008 873-B1
SHADOW CT
500 SJS 95129 853-B2
2100 PIT 94565 574-B4
SHADOW DR
11700 DBLN 94568 693-F4
SHADOW GN
500 SJS 95129 853-A2
SHADOW LN
2400 ANT 94509 575-B6
SHADOW PL
7300 DBLN 94568 693-G4
SHADOW BROOK DR
900 SJS 95120 894-F2
SHADOW BROOK LN
- WDSD 94062 809-H2
SHADOWBROOKE COM
2200 FRMT 94539 753-E6
SHADOW CREEK DR
600 SJS 95136 854-E7
3400 CCCo 94506 654-C5
SHADOW CREEK LN
- ORIN 94563 631-A2
SHADOW CREEK PL
11600 SCIC 94024 831-G4
SHADOWCREST WY
5400 SJS 95123 874-G4
SHADOW DANCE DR
100 SJS 95125 854-C3
SHADOW ESTATES
5100 SJS 95135 855-G5
SHADOWFALLS CIR
300 MRTZ 94553 571-G5
SHADOWFALLS DR
4800 MRTZ 94553 571-G5
SHADOWFAX DR
1200 SJS 95121 855-A4
W SHADOWGRAPH DR
100 SJS 95125 854-C3
SHADOWHAWK CIR
- DNVL 94506 653-J6
SHADOW HILL CIR
200 PIT 94565 573-F4
SHADOWHILL LN
7400 CPTO 95014 852-D3
SHADOWHURST CT
4500 SJS 95136 874-E2
SHADOWLAKE CT
200 MPS 95035 794-A6
SHADOW LAKE PL
2100 MRTZ 94553 592-A1
SHADOW LEAF DR
3300 SJS 95132 814-G4
SHADOW MOUNTAIN
- OAK 94605 671-D2
SHADOW MOUNTAIN CT
100 PLHL 94523 592-B2
2500 SRMN 94583 673-B2
6800 SJS 95120 894-E3
SHADOW MOUNTAIN DR
2500 SRMN 94583 673-B2
13000 SAR 95070 852-E7
SHADOW MOUNTAIN PL
500 SRMN 94583 673-C2
SHADOW OAK RD
- DNVL 94526 652-G2
SHADOW OAKS WY
13900 SAR 95070 872-E2
SHADOW PARK PL
3200 SJS 95121 855-B2
SHADOW RIDGE CT
2100 SJS 95138 855-E5
SHADOW RIDGE DR
5600 AlaC 94552 692-E3
SHADOW RIDGE WY
2100 SJS 95138 855-E5
SHADOW RUN DR
400 SJS 95125 854-C3
SHADOW SPRINGS PL
3000 SJS 95121 855-B1
SHADOW TREE CT
- DNVL 94506 654-B5
SHADOWTREE DR
2100 SJS 95131 814-C5
SHADOWVALE WY
2600 SJS 95132 814-C4
SHADOW WOOD CT
- SJS 95136 874-J7
SHADOWWOOD DR
100 PLHL 94523 592-B1
SHADOW WOOD LN
- AlaC 94541 691-H6
SHADY AV
5000 SJS 95129 852-J4
SHADY GN
700 MRTZ 94553 571-E5
SHADY LN
- HIL 94010 748-E4
- LKSP 94939 586-E7
- ROSS 94957 586-C2
- WLCK 94596 612-C3
100 ANT 94509 575-D4
100 VAL 94591 550-F1
200 VAL 94591 530-F7
300 MLV 94941 606-D1
2000 NVTO 94945 525-J2
15700 LGTS 95032 873-D6
SHADYBROOK CT
11900 SAR 95070 852-H4
SHADYBROOK DR
- CNCD - 613-D1
SHADY CREEK CT
1700 SJS 95148 835-D4
SHADY CREEK DR
- DNVL 94526 653-E4
SHADY CREEK PL
1000 DNVL 94526 653-E4
SHADY CREEK RD
7600 DBLN 94568 694-A1
SHADY DALE AV
1000 CMBL 95008 853-G6
SHADY DRAW
2600 PIN 94564 569-H7
SHADY GLEN AV
1500 SCL 95050 833-F6
SHADY GLEN RD
100 CCCo 94596 612-E6
100 WLCK 94596 612-E6
SHADYGROVE CT
6200 CPTO 95014 852-G2
SHADYGROVE DR
6000 CPTO 95014 852-G2
SHADYHOLLOW CT
3600 SJS 95148 835-G7
SHADY HOLLOW DR
7400 NWK 94560 752-B6
SHADY LANE CT
- WLCK 94596 612-C3
SHADY OAK CT
- DNVL 94506 653-H5
SHADY OAK LN
20500 CPTO 95014 832-D6
SHADY OAKS CT
26700 LAH 94022 811-A5
SHADY SPRING LN
3300 MTVW 94040 831-J2
SHADYSPRINGS RD
21600 AlaC 94546 691-J7
SHADY TREE CT
100 DNVL 94526 653-E3
SHADY VALLEY CT
300 SRMN 94583 673-J6
SHADY VIEW LN
16300 LGTS 95032 873-D7
16300 SCIC 95032 873-D7
SHADYWOOD CT
1900 CNCD 94521 593-F3
SHAFER DR
1000 NVTO 94949 546-C1
3400 SCL 95051 832-J5
SHAFFER DR
1400 SJS 95132 814-F3
SHAFTER AV
1000 SF 94124 668-A5
3700 OAK 94609 649-H1
3800 OAK 94609 629-H7
5100 OAK 94618 629-J6
SHAFTER RD
- SF 94129 647-E4
SHAFTER ST
1200 SMTO 94402 748-J3
SHAHAN CT
100 ANT 94509 575-E7
SHAKER CT
1100 SJS 95120 894-C5
SHAKESPEARE DR
1200 CNCD 94521 593-A4
SHAKESPEARE ST
- DALY 94014 687-C2
100 SF 94112 687-C2
SHALE CIR
- ANT 94509 595-E1
SHALE COM
46800 FRMT 94539 773-G6
SHALEN CT
5000 SJS 95130 852-J6
SHALIMAR CIR
5000 FRMT 94555 752-D2
SHALIMAR TER
34700 FRMT 94555 752-A3
SHALLOW CT
33700 FRMT 94555 752-C1
SHAMROCK AV
1700 SCL 95051 833-B3
SHAMROCK COM
5200 FRMT 94555 752-B2
SHAMROCK CT
- MLBR 94030 728-A3
100 VAL 94589 510-C5
3800 SSF 94080 707-C4
SHAMROCK DR
300 SCIC 95008 873-E1
400 SJS 95008 873-E1
2400 CCCo 94806 569-A5
2400 WLCK 94596 632-H2
SHAMROCK LN
- ALA 94502 669-H5
SHAMROCK PL
8600 DBLN 94568 693-H1
SHAMROCK WY
1200 LVMR 94550 715-F5
4200 AlaC 94546 692-B4
SHAMROCK RANCH RD
- SMCo - 726-G5
SHAMUS CT
2600 CCCo 94806 569-B6
SHANA CT
400 DNVL 94526 653-B3
SHANA ST
5500 FRMT 94538 773-B2
SHANDELIN CT
- CCCo 94526 633-C5
SHANDON CT
4000 SJS 95136 854-E6
SHANDON ROCK CT
700 SJS 95136 854-F7
SHANDWICK CT
1000 SJS 95136 874-C1
SHANE DR
2700 RCH 94806 589-A1
SHANER DR
2700 ALA 94502 669-J6
SHANG CT
3100 SJS 95127 834-H1
SHANGHAI CIR
1500 SJS 95131 814-B7
SHANGHAI CT
1200 SJS 95131 814-B6
SHANGRILA CT
1600 LFYT 94549 611-F1
SHANGRILA RD
3400 CCCo - 611-F1
3400 LFYT 94549 611-F1
SHANGRILA WY
- SF 94127 667-D5
SHANIKO COM
- FRMT 94539 773-H6
SHANKLIN CT
- NVTO 94945 526-A2
SHANLEY LN
- ROSS 94957 586-C1
SHANNON
100 PIT 94565 574-B3
SHANNON AV
2300 CCCo 94806 569-C5
7700 DBLN 94568 693-G3
SHANNON CIR
- ALA 94502 669-H5
SHANNON CT
- MRGA 94556 651-G2
- NVTO 94949 546-C1
- NVTO 94949 526-C7
100 LVMR 94550 696-E6
1500 BEN 94510 551-B4
2900 SCL 95051 833-A6
3200 AlaC 94541 692-D7
7900 DBLN 94568 693-G3
21400 CPTO 95014 852-C2
SHANNON DR
2200 SSF 94080 707-D5
SHANNON LN
- SRFL 94901 566-D6
- MrnC 94901 566-D6
2200 WLCK 94598 612-F1
SHANNON RD
14000 SCIC 95032 893-G1
14400 LGTS 95032 893-G1
14800 SCIC 95032 873-F7
15300 LGTS 95032 873-C6
16100 SCIC 95032 873-C6
SHANNON ST
- SF 94102 647-J6
SHANNON WY
500 RDWC 94065 749-J6
SHANNONDALE CT
4800 ANT 94509 595-J3
SHANNONDALE DR
4400 ANT 94509 595-H3
SHANTILLY CT
200 CCCo 94526 633-D5
SHARAB CT
4100 PLE 94566 714-F4
SHARD CT
700 FRMT 94539 773-J7
SHARENE LN
100 WLCK 94596 612-D5
SHARI CT
- NVTO 94947 526-C7
100 VAL 94589 509-J5
SHARILYN LN
- NVTO 94947 525-H2
SHARMAR CT
- CCCo 94595 632-D1
SHARMON PALMS LN
700 CMBL 95008 853-C7
800 CMBL 95008 873-C1
SHARON AV
- PDMT 94611 650-C1
100 CCCo 94572 549-G7
600 HIL 94010 728-E7
2000 BLMT 94002 769-C1
SHARON CIR
1500 CCCo 94549 611-J2
SHARON CT
- DALY 94014 687-H3
- MLPK 94025 790-D7
- PDMT 94611 650-C1
100 LGTS 95124 873-E6
100 LGTS 95032 873-E6
200 MRTZ 94553 591-H3
800 CMBL 95008 853-C7
800 PA 94303 791-B4
3200 LFYT 94549 631-H2
3500 CCCo 94565 573-F1
7600 DBLN 94568 693-G2
SHARON DR
- CCCo 94565 573-F1
1700 CNCD 94519 593-A1
7000 SJS 95129 852-E4
SHARON LN
5400 SJS 95124 873-G6
SHARON PL
- CCCo 94565 573-F1
1500 SMTO 94401 729-A7
SHARON RD
- ALA 94502 669-J6
2000 MLPK 94025 790-D7
2000 SMCo 94025 790-D7
SHARON ST
- CCCo 94565 573-F1
- SF 94114 667-G2
8300 DBLN 94568 693-G2
15500 AlaC 94580 691-D6
SHARON WY
- CCCo 94565 573-F1
- PCFA 94044 706-J4
SHARON MANOR CT
1400 SJS 95129 852-E4
SHARON OAKS DR
2300 MLPK 94025 790-E7
SHARON PARK DR
100 MLPK 94025 790-C7
SHARP AV
200 CMBL 95008 873-E1
1400 SJS 95008 873-E1
1800 WLCK 94596 612-B5
SHARP CT
1300 CMBL 95008 873-E2
SHARP PL
- SF 94109 647-J4
- SF 94109 647-J4
SHARP PARK RD
- PCFA 94044 707-A7
700 SBRN 94066 707-A7
SHARY AV
700 MTVW 94041 811-J6
SHARY CIR
1000 CNCD 94518 592-F5

BAY AREA
INDEX

STREET Block City ZIP Pg-Grid

SHARY CT
1000 CNCD 94518 592-G5
SHASTA
3000 ALA 94501 649-E6
SHASTA AV
1100 SJS 95126 833-H7
1500 SJS 95128 833-H7
1500 SJS 95128 853-G1
5400 SPAB 94806 589-A4
SHASTA CIR
3800 PIT 94565 574-D5
SHASTA CT
- SSF 94080 707-F4
- SRMN 94583 653-F7
100 ANT 94509 575-C7
100 ANT 94509 595-C1
2200 MRTZ 94553 572-A7
4600 PLE 94566 694-D7
5600 CLAY 94517 593-F6
SHASTA DR
2100 MRTZ 94553 572-A7
3300 SMTO 94403 748-J6
3800 SCL 95051 832-H6
4100 PA 94306 811-E2
SHASTA LN
- MLPK 94025 790-C7
- PCFA 94044 707-A3
- WLCK 94596 612-B2
SHASTA RD
2600 BERK 94708 609-H6
SHASTA ST
- LVMR 94550 695-D7
- AlaC 94541 691-E7
- LALT 94022 811-D6
100 VAL 94590 530-C4
700 RDWC 94063 770-B7
1600 RCH 94804 609-C3
37000 FRMT 94536 752-G4
SHASTA WY
500 MrnC 94965 606-E6
SHASTA FIR DR
700 SUNV 94086 832-G2
SHASTA FIR WY
- SUNV 94086 832-G2
SHASTA SPRING CT
11800 CPTO 95014 852-A5
SHATO PL
100 FRMT 94539 793-H1
SHATTUCK AV
800 BERK 94707 609-G6
1200 BERK 94709 609-G7
1600 BERK 94709 629-G1
1900 BERK 94704 629-G1
2700 BERK 94705 629-H4
2700 BERK 94703 629-H4
3200 OAK 94609 629-H4
5300 FRMT 94555 752-C3
SHATTUCK DR
21800 CPTO 95014 852-B2
SHATTUCK PL
1400 BERK 94709 609-G7
SHATTUCK SQ
- BERK 94704 629-G2
SHAUNA CT
4800 AlaC 94546 692-C4
SHAUNA LN
900 PA 94306 811-B3
SHAVANO WY
300 SRMN 94583 693-H1
SHAVANO PEAK CT
4800 ANT 94509 595-D3
SHAVER ST
- SRFL 94901 586-F1
SHAVER GRADE FIRE RD
- MrnC 94904 586-A3
- MrnC 94930 586-A3
SHAVER LAKE ST
32600 FRMT 94555 732-C6
SHAW CIR
3300 ANT 94509 595-C1
SHAW CT
- RDWC 94061 789-J1
40400 FRMT 94538 753-D6
SHAW DR
- MrnC 94901 566-C7
- SANS 94960 566-C7
1500 SJS 95118 874-A1
SHAW PL
- AlaC 94541 691-G6
- SRMN 94583 673-F6
SHAW RD
- SBRN 94066 708-A5
200 SSF 94066 707-J5
200 SSF 94080 707-J5
200 SSF 94066 708-A5
200 SSF 94080 708-A5
300 CCCo 94596 592-C7
300 PLHL 94596 592-C7
SHAW ST
- SF 94105 648-B5
10200 OAK 94605 671-B5
SHAWCROFT DR
5900 SJS 95123 874-J6
SHAWN CT
- CCCo 94526 633-C5
3400 AlaC 94541 692-D7
SHAWN DR
1200 PIN 94564 569-C6
1200 CCCo 94806 569-B6
1300 SJS 95118 874-B3
SHAWN WY
3200 AlaC 94541 692-D7
SHAWNA ST
4400 LVMR 94550 696-A7
SHAWNEE AV
- SF 94112 687-E1
SHAWNEE CT
- OAK 94619 650-J4
- SRMN 94583 673-D4
700 HAY 94544 732-E1
SHAWNEE LN
- ORIN 94563 631-A1
400 SJS 95123 874-H5
SHAWNEE PASS
100 PTLV 94028 810-B6
SHAWNEE PL
400 FRMT 94539 793-J1
SHAWNEE RD
1300 LVMR 94550 695-E6
SHAWNEE WY
- PLE 94588 694-D6
300 FRMT 94539 793-J1
SHAY DR
7900 OAK 94605 671-C1
SHAYAN CT
- MrnC 94941 606-H4
SHAYNOR CT
3700 SJS 95130 853-C4
SHEA CT
7200 SJS 95139 895-F1
SHEA DR
1900 PIN 94564 569-F6
SHEA TER
1300 VAL 94591 530-G6
SHEARER DR
- ATN 94027 790-C1
SHEARTON DR
600 SJS 95117 853-C2
SHEARWATER CT
4400 PLE 94566 714-E1
SHEARWATER DR
6800 SJS 95120 894-H2
SHEARWATER ISL
200 FCTY 94404 749-G2
SHEARWATER PKWY
- RDWC 94065 749-H5
400 RDWC 94065 750-A5
SHEARWATER RD
4500 PLE 94566 714-D1
SHEARWATER TER
33600 FRMT 94555 732-D7
SHEEHAN CT
7100 SJS 95120 894-G3
SHEEPBERRY CT
4400 CNCD 94521 593-C5
SHEFFELS PEAK CT
4900 ANT 94509 595-E3
SHEFFIELD
100 HER 94547 569-J3
SHEFFIELD AV
- SPAB 94806 588-H2
300 MrnC 94941 606-F6
1500 CMBL 95008 853-G5
1600 CMBL 95125 853-G5
2900 OAK 94602 650-C5
SHEFFIELD CIR
3800 CCCo 94506 654-A5
SHEFFIELD CT
- SPAB 94806 588-H2
300 CMBL 95125 853-H5
4000 ANT 94509 595-G1
7300 DBLN 94568 693-H2
SHEFFIELD DR
- DALY 94015 687-B3
2300 LVMR 94550 715-F4
4000 ANT 94509 595-G2
SHEFFIELD LN
- PLE 94588 694-F7
200 RDWC 94061 790-B2
7200 DBLN 94568 693-H2
32300 UNC 94587 732-C4
SHEFFIELD PL
2700 AlaC 94546 691-G3
3100 CNCD 94518 592-G3
SHEFFIELD RD
100 ALA 94502 669-J5
400 ALA 94502 670-A5
18500 AlaC 94546 691-G3
SHEFFIELD WY
- ALA 94502 669-J5
200 AMCN 94589 510-A4
200 AMCN 94589 509-J4
SHEFFIELD RIDGE CT
2100 SJS 95138 855-F5
SHEILA CT
- VAL 94591 530-E3
- NVTO 94947 525-G2
- PLHL 94523 612-B1
- SANS 94960 566-A4
200 MRGA 94556 631-D7
200 MRGA 94556 651-D1
800 CMBL 95008 873-C1
32500 UNC 94587 752-A1
SHEILA LN
1100 PCFA 94044 727-A5
1200 PCFA 94044 726-J5
SHEILA ST
23100 AlaC 94541 692-D7
SHEILA WY
32500 UNC 94587 752-A1
SHELBOURNE AV
- DALY 94015 687-A7
SHELBOURNE PL
- SMCo 94402 768-G1
SHELBOURNE WY
2300 ANT 94509 595-G1
SHELBURNE RD
1200 LVMR 94550 695-E6
SHELBY CT
600 DNVL 94526 653-D7
5300 FRMT 94536 752-H6
SHELBY LN
500 LALT 94024 811-F7
SHELBY CREEK CT
1300 SJS 95120 894-F4
SHELBY CREEK LN
1200 SJS 95120 894-F4
SHELBY HILL LN
- DNVL 94526 632-J6
SHELBY HILL RD
- DNVL 94526 632-H6
SHELDON AV
- VAL 94591 530-D5
SHELDON CIR
4200 PLE 94588 713-J1
SHELDON CT
- WLCK 94596 612-B2
2700 RCH 94803 589-E2
20100 AlaC 94546 692-B5
SHELDON DR
2500 RCH 94803 589-D2
SHELDON LN
- WLCK 94596 612-B2
SHELDON PTH
2700 RCH 94803 589-F1
SHELDON RD
16700 SCIC 95030 872-H7
SHELDON ST
10500 OAK 94605 671-B5
SHELDON TER
- SF 94122 667-C3
SHELDON WY
- HIL 94010 728-D6
SHELDRAKE CT
- MrnC 94903 546-E6
SHELFORD AV
- SCAR 94070 769-E2
SHELL AV
700 MRTZ 94553 571-E4
900 CCCo 94553 571-F2
W SHELL AV
2200 CCCo 94553 571-F4
2200 MRTZ 94553 571-F4
SHELL BLVD
500 FCTY 94404 749-F2
SHELL CIR
1200 CLAY 94517 593-H6
SHELL CT
- MrnC 94941 606-G3
SHELL LN
1100 CLAY 94517 593-H6
SHELL PKWY
400 RDWC 94065 749-H5
SHELL PL
2200 AlaC 94541 692-C7
SHELL RD
- MLV 94941 606-G3
- MrnC 94941 606-G3
SHELL ST
100 PCFA 94044 706-J5
SHELLBACK PL
2000 SJS 95133 814-E7
2000 SJS 95133 834-E1
SHELLBARK CT
4300 CNCD 94521 593-B5
SHELLBARK DR
- SJS 95136 874-H1
SHELLBORNE CT
4700 FRMT 94538 773-C2
SHELLBURNE WY
17400 LGTS 95030 873-A5
SHELL DOCK
700 MRTZ 94553 571-E2
SHELLEY AV
2200 CMBL 95008 873-E2
2200 SJS 95124 873-E2
2200 SJS 95008 873-E2
SHELLEY CT
400 MPS 95035 794-B6
700 CCCo 94572 569-J3
700 CCCo 94572 570-A3
36300 NWK 94560 752-F4
SHELLEY DR
- MLV 94941 606-G4
100 VAL 94591 530-E6
SHELLEY ST
500 LVMR 94550 696-C6
800 CCCo 94572 569-J3
800 HER 94547 569-J3
800 CCCo 94572 570-A3
SHELLFLOWER CT
4400 CNCD 94518 593-A6
SHELL GATE PL
1100 ALA 94501 669-G2
SHELL GATE RD
300 ALA 94501 669-G3
SHELLIE CT
100 CCCo 94565 573-F1
SHELLMOUND ST
- OAK 94608 629-E6
5000 EMVL 94608 629-E6
SHELL RIDGE CT
- WLCK 94598 612-E3
SHELLWOOD DR
4700 CNCD 94521 593-D3
SHELLY CT
6100 SJS 95123 874-G6
SHELLY DR
500 PLHL 94523 592-B7
20600 CPTO 95014 852-D1
SHELLY LN
1000 HAY 94544 712-A7
SHELLY PL
- DNVL 94526 652-H1
SHELTER CT
- CCCo 94565 573-E2
SHELTER LN
- DALY 94014 687-E6
SHELTER BAY AV
1000 MLV 94941 606-G5
SHELTER COVE RD
- PCFA 94044 726-G4
SHELTER CREEK LN
- SBRN 94066 727-G1
100 SBRN 94066 707-G7
SHELTERWOOD DR
6400 OAK 94611 630-F7
SHELTON WY
1000 SJS 95125 853-J3
SHENADO PL
- SJS 95136 875-B3
- SJS 95123 875-B3
SHENANDOAH AV
1500 MPS 95035 794-D7
SHENANDOAH CT
3600 PLE 94588 714-A2
SHENANDOAH DR
200 MRTZ 94553 591-H4
800 SUNV 94087 832-C3
1000 SJS 95125 854-D7
SHENANDOAH PL
100 SRFL 94903 566-F1
600 HAY 94544 712-A6
34400 FRMT 94555 752-D1
SHENANDOAH WY
- PCFA 94044 727-C5
SHEPARD CT
100 HER 94547 570-B5
SHEPARD ST
100 HER 94547 570-B5
SHEPARD WY
800 RDWC 94062 789-G2
SHEPARDSON LN
- ALA 94502 670-A5
SHEPHARD PL
- SF 94108 648-A5
SHEPHERD AV
100 HAY 94544 712-A6
400 SJS 95125 854-B2
SHEPHERD ST
4400 OAK 94619 650-G6
SHEPHERD WY
- TBRN 94920 607-B3
SHEPHERD CANYON RD
5700 OAK 94611 650-E1
5800 OAK 94611 630-F7
SHEPPARD CT
1200 WLCK 94598 612-E2
SHEPPARD RD
1000 WLCK 94598 612-E1
SHEPPARD WY
2600 ANT 94509 574-H6
SHERATON DR
600 SUNV 94087 832-C3
2000 SCL 95050 833-C3
SHERATON PL
2200 SMCo 94402 768-G1
SHERBEAR DR
2700 SRMN 94583 673-C2
SHERBORNE DR
2500 BLMT 94002 769-B3
SHERBOURNE DR
4300 SJS 95124 874-A3
SHERBROOKE WY
2900 SJS 95127 835-A4
SHERBURNE CT
100 DNVL 94526 653-C6
SHERBURNE HILLS CT
- DNVL 94526 653-F5
SHERBURNE HILLS RD
- DNVL 94526 653-F4
SHEREE CT
12600 SCIC 95127 814-J5
SHEREEN PL
- CMBL 95008 853-C6
SHERI CT
- DNVL 94526 653-A3
SHERI LN
600 DNVL 94526 653-A3
SHERI ANN AV
1800 SJS 95131 814-B6
SHERIDAN AV
- SF 94129 647-D4
100 PA 94306 791-B7
100 PDMT 94611 650-C2
SHERIDAN CIR
400 LVMR 94550 695-J6
12400 SAR 95070 852-E6
SHERIDAN CT
- MLV 94941 606-E1
3600 CNCD 94518 592-H3
35600 NWK 94560 752-E4
SHERIDAN DR
300 MLPK 94025 770-H7
SHERIDAN LN
100 CCCo 94553 591-F1
100 MRTZ 94553 591-F1
1300 HAY 94544 711-J6
SHERIDAN PL
- PCFA 94044 727-B6
400 SJS 95111 854-G4
SHERIDAN RD
- OAK 94618 630-C6
1200 CNCD 94518 592-J3
4200 AlaC 94586 754-A3
SHERIDAN ST
- LALT 94022 831-D1
- SF 94103 667-J1
- VAL 94590 530-A6
1000 VAL 94590 550-C1
SHERIDAN WY
100 WDSD 94062 789-J4
SHERLAND AV
- MTVW 94043 812-A4
SHERLAND CT
300 MTVW 94043 812-B4
SHERLOCK CT
27300 LAH 94022 830-H2
SHERLOCK DR
2400 SJS 95121 854-H3
SHERLOCK RD
27000 LAH 94022 830-H2
SHERLOCK WY
4200 CNCD 94521 593-A4
SHERMAN AV
100 PA 94306 791-B7
800 MLPK 94025 790-D6
900 NVTO 94945 526-C3
1100 SMCo 94025 790-D6
1500 BURL 94010 728-D6
SHERMAN CT
- SJS 95193 875-C4
900 MPS 95035 794-B4
2200 ANT 94509 595-A1
SHERMAN DR
- AlaC 94552 692-G3
1400 BEN 94510 551-B4
1600 UNC 94587 732-E5
2000 PLHL 94523 592-D6
SHERMAN RD
- SF 94129 647-E4
SHERMAN ST
- SF 94103 648-A7
400 LALT 94022 811-D7
700 SCL 95053 833-F4
900 SJS 95110 854-D2
900 SCL 95050 833-F4
1000 ALA 94501 669-H2
1100 VAL 94591 530-E4
1700 ALA 94501 649-H7
2900 PIT 94565 574-D5
SHERMAN WY
900 PLE 94566 714-E5
SHERMAN OAKS DR
700 SJS 95128 853-G3
SHERREE CT
600 MRTZ 94553 591-G4
SHERREE DR
500 MRTZ 94553 591-G4
SHERROD CT
100 VAL 94591 530-E4
SHERRY CT
200 SJS 95119 875-E7
1000 LVMR 94550 715-H2
1200 SLN 94577 691-D2
4000 PLE 94566 714-F4
SHERRY WY
1000 LVMR 94550 715-H2
SHERWICK DR
6800 OAK 94705 630-C4
SHERWIN AV
1400 EMVL 94608 629-E7
2100 SCL 95050 833-C5
SHERWOOD AV
900 VAL 94591 530-E5
SHERWOOD AV
1000 SJS 95126 833-G5
1200 SCL 95050 833-G5
1200 SCL 95126 833-G5
SHERWOOD CT
- HIL 94010 748-H1
- MLBR 94030 727-J5
- MRGA 94556 651-D1
- MrnC 94904 586-E4
- SF 94127 667-E6
- PIT 94565 574-G6
1100 SUNV 94087 832-B3
4200 CNCD 94521 593-A4
18300 AlaC 94546 691-H3
SHERWOOD DR
400 MrnC 94965 606-G7
900 SUNV 94087 832-B3
1200 CNCD 94521 593-A4
2500 SBRN 94066 707-E6
2900 SCAR 94070 769-F5
5900 OAK 94611 630-D6
SHERWOOD LN
100 ALA 94502 669-J5
800 LALT 94022 811-E4
SHERWOOD PL
- NVTO 94945 526-D3
6400 DBLN 94568 694-A2
SHERWOOD ST
41500 FRMT 94538 773-D1
SHERWOOD WY
- CCCo 94596 612-A5
100 SSF 94080 707-G5
300 MLPK 94025 790-G4
SHERWOOD FOREST DR
5700 CCCo 94803 589-G4
SHERYL CT
- PLHL 94523 612-A1
SHERYL DR
100 CCCo 94806 569-A5
100 SBRN 94066 707-D6
SHETLAND AV
4700 OAK 94605 671-E4
SHETLAND CT
- SRMN 94583 673-E4
- OAK 94605 671-E4
100 VAL 94591 530-E2
500 MPS 95035 794-B6
700 SJS 95127 814-H6
SHETLAND DR
3000 PLHL 94523 591-J3
SHETLAND LN
- PLHL 94523 591-H3
SHETLAND PL
800 SUNV 94087 832-F6
SHETLAND RD
2000 LVMR 94550 696-A3
SHEVELIN RD
100 NVTO 94947 526-C7
SHEVLIN DR
800 ELCR 94530 609-E2
SHEVLIN PL
7800 ELCR 94530 609-E2
SHIBLEY AV
2200 SJS 95125 854-A6
SHIELD DR
2400 UNC 94587 732-C4
SHIELDS LN
- NVTO 94947 525-H4
SHIELDS ST
- SF 94132 687-C1
SHILLING CT
1800 SJS 95132 814-J2
SHILOH AV
2000 MPS 95035 794-E7
SHILSHONE WY
2400 SJS 95121 854-H3
SHIMMER CT
- MPS 95035 793-H6
SHINGLEWOOD CT
- UNC 94587 731-J5
SHINING STAR LN
15000 SLN 94579 690-J6
SHINN CT
1400 FRMT 94536 753-B2
SHINN ST
37800 FRMT 94536 753-B2
SHINN MOUNTAIN CT
5000 ANT 94509 595-F5
SHIPLEY AV
- DALY 94015 707-C2
SHIPLEY ST
100 SF 94107 648-A7
SHIRE CT
100 LGTS 95030 873-A3
2200 LVMR 94550 696-A2
SHIRE LN
3100 CCCo 94598 613-A3
SHIRECREST CT
600 SJS 95123 874-G4
SHIRE OAKS CT
300 LFYT 94549 631-H4
SHIRE OAKS DR
300 LFYT 94549 631-H4
SHIRLEE DR
400 DNVL 94526 632-J7
SHIRLEY AV
300 AlaC 94541 711-E1
800 SUNV 94086 812-D6
11700 SCIC 94024 831-F4
SHIRLEY CT
100 VAL 94590 550-C1
4800 UNC 94587 752-A1
4800 UNC 94587 751-J1
SHIRLEY DR
- OAK 94611 650-G1
100 SPAB 94806 588-J3
1100 MPS 95035 794-C7
1500 PLHL 94523 592-C4
1500 BEN 94510 551-B4
6000 OAK 94611 630-G7
SHIRLEY RD
2100 BLMT 94002 749-C7
2100 BLMT 94002 769-B1
SHIRLEY WY
400 MLPK 94025 790-J2
1200 CNCD 94520 592-F3
5000 LVMR 94550 716-B1
SHIRLEY VISTA
300 CCCo 94803 589-E1
SHIRLYNN CT
500 LALT 94022 811-E7
SHOAL CIR
- RDWC 94065 750-A5
SHOAL DR
- CCCo 94565 573-D1
- DALY 94014 687-E5
900 SMTO 94404 749-D2
SHOAL DR W
- VAL 94591 550-E2
SHOEMAKER CT
5700 LVMR 94550 696-C4
SHOEMAKER DR
700 LVMR 94550 696-C4
SHOFNER PL
3100 SJS 95111 854-F7
SHOLES CT
14200 LAH 94022 811-B6
SHON CT
- NVTO 94947 526-B7
SHON DR
- NVTO 94947 526-B7
SHONA CT
4000 SJS 95124 874-A2
SHONE AV
3600 OAK 94605 671-A2
SHOOTING STAR ISL
100 FCTY 94404 749-H3
SHOOTING STAR TER
800 SUNV 94086 832-F3
SHOPPE LN
- MLPK 94025 790-J2
SHORE DR
- PLE 94566 714-F2
SHORE WK
- ALA 94501 669-G2
SHOREBIRD CIR
100 RDWC 94065 749-H6
SHOREBIRD DR
4400 UNC 94587 731-H5
SHOREBIRD WY
1100 MTVW 94043 812-A1
1100 MTVW 94043 811-J1
SHOREHAM CT
10200 SCIC 95127 834-J3
SHOREHAM PARK CT
42600 FRMT 94538 773-C2
SHOREHAVEN AV
7700 NWK 94560 752-C7
SHOREHAVEN CIR
5500 LVMR 94550 696-C2
SHORE HAVEN CT
100 CCCo 94806 569-B4
SHOREHAVEN PL
36300 NWK 94560 752-C6
SHORELAND DR
1100 SJS 95122 854-H1
N SHORELINE BLVD
300 MTVW 94043 811-J1
1900 MTVW 94043 791-J7
S SHORELINE BLVD
100 MTVW 94041 811-H5
300 MTVW 94043 811-H5
SHORELINE CIR
- SRMN 94583 653-G7
- SRMN 94583 673-G1
SHORELINE CT
- FRMT 94538 793-G2
- SSF 94080 708-C1
- RCH 94804 608-H3
SHORE LINE DR
900 ALA 94501 669-G2
SHORELINE DR
- SRMN 94583 653-G7
- SRMN 94583 673-G1
100 PIT 94565 574-E1
100 RDWC 94065 749-G7
100 RDWC 94065 769-G1
900 SMTO 94404 749-D3
SHORELINE LP
- SRMN 94583 653-G7
- SRMN 94583 673-G1
SHORELINE PKWY
100 SRFL 94901 587-A4
SHORELINE PL
100 VAL 94591 550-F1
SHOREPOINT CT
900 ALA 94501 669-G2
SHORES CT
- SRFL 94903 566-G3
SHORESIDE CT
2300 SCL 95054 813-C5
SHORESIDE DR
- PCFA 94044 726-G4
SHORE VIEW AV
- SF 94121 646-J6
SHOREVIEW AV
100 PCFA 94044 706-J5
1500 SMTO 94401 729-B7
1500 SMTO 94401 749-C1
2000 SMTO 94404 749-C1
2000 SMTO 94403 749-C1
SHOREVIEW CT
- UNC 94545 731-H6
1000 CCCo 94565 573-F1
1300 SJS 95122 854-H1
SHOREWAY RD
- RDWC 94065 749-F7
- RDWC 94065 769-G1
- SCAR 94070 769-G1
1000 BLMT 94002 749-F7
1100 BLMT 94002 769-G1
SHOREWOOD CT
- RCH 94804 608-J3
6300 PLE 94588 694-B7
SHOREWOOD LN
400 SJS 95134 813-C2
SHOREY ST
1700 OAK 94607 649-C3
SHORT AV
900 AlaC 94586 734-B3
1100 SPAB 94806 568-H7
SHORT CT
400 HAY 94544 732-B1
SHORT LN
- LKSP 94939 586-F6
SHORT RD
15900 LGTS 95032 873-D6
SHORT ST
- PCFA 94044 707-A3
- SF 94114 667-F3
- VAL 94590 530-C5
100 DNVL 94526 653-A2
1600 BERK 94702 629-F1
SHORT ST
2100 WLCK 94596 612-B4
2600 OAK 94619 650-E6
SHORT TR
- CMAD 94925 606-C5
SHORT WY
- LKSP 94939 586-F7
SHORT HILL CT
14000 SAR 95070 872-G2
SHORTHILL RD
4300 OAK 94605 671-C3
SHORTRIDGE AV
1100 SJS 95116 834-F4
SHOSHONE CIR
2100 DNVL 94526 653-D7
SHOSHONE CT
100 DNVL 94526 653-D7
200 SJS 95127 834-H1
500 FRMT 94539 773-J5
SHOSHONE DR
200 SJS 95127 834-H1
SHOSHONE PL
- PTLV 94028 810-B6
SHOTWELL ST
- SF 94103 667-J3
200 SF 94110 667-J3
1200 SF 94110 667-J4
SHOVLER LAKE CT
3800 FRMT 94555 732-H4
SHOW TER
5900 FRMT 94555 752-B4
SHOWERS DR
- MTVW 94040 811-E4
SHRADER ST
- SF 94117 647-E7
200 SF 94117 667-E1
400 SF 94117 667-E1
SHRATTON AV
- SMCo 94002 769-D4
- SMCo 94070 769-D4
- SCAR 94070 769-D4
SHREEN CT
1600 SJS 95124 874-A2
SHREWSBURY CT
- PLHL 94523 592-A4
- PLHL 94523 591-B1
SHRIVER CT
1200 SJS 95132 814-G5
SHRIVER DR
3100 SJS 95132 814-G5
SHUBERT CT
19300 SAR 95070 852-G6
SHUBERT DR
19200 SAR 95070 852-G6
SHUCK DR
- MrnC 94941 606-H5
SHUEY AV
1500 WLCK 94596 612-B5
SHUEY DR
- MRGA 94556 651-E2
SHUKLA CT
3600 WLCK 94598 613-A3
SHULGIN RD
1400 CCCo 94549 611-H2
SHULMAN AV
900 SCL 95050 833-E2
1800 SJS 95124 853-G7
SHUMAKER WY
1500 SJS 95131 814-D6
SHYLOCK DR
33500 FRMT 94555 732-C7
33500 FRMT - 752-C1
33500 FRMT 94555 752-C1
SIBELIUS AV
2600 SJS 95122 855-A1
SIBERT CT
800 LFYT 94549 611-F7
SIBERT LP
- SF 94129 647-D4
SIBLEY RD
700 SF 94129 647-E4
SICKLES AV
100 SF 94112 687-E2
N SIDE AV
2700 SMCo 94063 770-D7
W SIDE AV
- SMCo 94063 790-C1
2800 SMCo 94063 770-C7
SIDERS CT
3500 ANT 94509 595-E1
SIDLAW CT
4500 SJS 95136 874-F2
SIDNEY AV
500 ANT 94509 575-E5
1600 SLN 94578 691-D3
SIDNEY CT
- MrnC 94903 566-H3
SIDNEY DR
38200 FRMT 94536 753-B2
SIDNEY ST
- MLV 94941 606-E3
SIEBER CT
400 SJS 95111 854-F7
SIEBER PL
500 SJS 95111 854-F7
SIEBER WY
3200 SJS 95111 854-F7
SIENA PL
100 DNVL 94506 653-H5
SIENA ST
5700 PLE 94588 694-C5
SIENNA CT
6000 FRMT 94555 752-B6
SIENNA DR
10300 SJS 95127 835-A4
SIENNA WY
- SRFL 94901 566-H6
SIERRA AV
- PDMT 94611 650-C1
- SANS 94960 566-A6
400 MTVW 94041 811-H6
500 PCFA 94044 727-A1
1000 CCCo 94553 571-F4
1100 SJS 95126 833-H7
5200 RCH 94805 589-B6
5700 CCCo 94805 589-B6
22600 AlaC 94541 692-C7
SIERRA CIR
- SRFL 94901 586-E2
SIERRA CT
- MRGA 94556 651-G2
- TBRN 94920 607-B4

STREET
Block City ZIP Pg-Grid

SIERRA CT
200 MRTZ 94553 591-H4
1100 LVMR 94550 715-F3
1200 SJS 95132 814-E5
2200 CNCD 94518 592-F5
2300 PA 94303 791-D4
6200 DBLN 94568 693-J4
6300 DBLN 94568 694-A4
SIERRA DR
- MRTZ 94553 591-H4
100 PIT 94565 574-D6
200 HIL 94010 748-G2
1000 MLPK 94025 790-C6
2800 CNCD 94518 592-H5
SIERRA LN
- DBLN 94568 693-J4
- PTLV 94028 810-C5
100 WLCK 94596 612-D5
6800 DBLN 94568 694-A4
SIERRA RD
1100 SJS 95131 834-C1
1300 SJS 95131 814-D6
2000 CNCD 94518 592-F5
2400 SJS 95132 814-G4
3500 SCIC 95132 814-J3
3700 SCIC 95132 814-J3
3900 SCIC 95132 815-A3
3900 SJS 95132 815-A3
5600 SCIC 95140 815-E3
SIERRA ST
- SF 94107 668-B3
1000 BERK 94707 609-F6
1200 RDWC 94061 790-A1
SIERRA TER
900 PCFA 94044 707-A5
SIERRA AZULE
300 LGTS 95032 873-G7
SIERRA CREEK WY
1400 SJS 95132 814-F3
SIERRA GRANDE CT
- SJS 95116 834-H3
SIERRA GRANDE WY
2500 SJS 95116 834-H3
SIERRA LINDA
100 LGTS 95030 872-J2
SIERRA MAR DR
1200 SJS 95118 874-B1
1200 SJS 95118 854-C7
SIERRA MEADOW CT
2500 SJS 95116 834-H3
SIERRA MEADOW DR
- SJS 95116 834-H3
SIERRA MESA DR
- SJS 95116 834-H3
SIERRA MONTE WY
2500 SJS 95116 834-H3
SIERRA MORENA
100 LGTS 95032 873-E5
SIERRA POINT PKWY
1000 BSBN 94005 688-B5
SIERRA POINT RD
- BSBN 94005 688-A6
SIERRA RIDGE CT
- DNVL 94506 654-A6
SIERRA RIDGE RD
- RCH 94806 569-B6
SIERRA SERENA
2500 SJS 95116 834-H3
SIERRA SPRING CT
11700 CPTO 95014 852-A5
SIERRA SPRING LN
- CPTO 95014 852-A5
SIERRA VENTURA DR
2100 LALT 94024 831-H5
SIERRA VILLAGE CT
1100 SJS 95132 814-H3
SIERRA VILLAGE PL
1200 SJS 95132 814-H3
SIERRA VILLAGE WY
1100 SJS 95132 814-H3
SIERRAVILLE AV
1300 SJS 95132 814-F4
SIERRA VISTA
- AMCN 94589 509-J2
- NVTO 94947 525-J2
SIERRA VISTA AV
- MTVW 94043 811-H1
SIERRA VISTA CT
2500 SJS 95116 834-H3
3300 CNCD 94518 592-H5
SIERRA VISTA PL
- DNVL 94526 653-A2
- SJS 95116 834-H3
SIERRA VISTA WY
1000 LFYT 94549 611-F5
SIERRAWOOD CT
3700 CNCD 94519 593-A1
SIERRA WOOD DR
2000 SJS 95132 814-C3
SIERRAWOOD LN
4400 PLE 94588 693-J7
4400 PLE 94588 713-J1
SIESTA CT
- SMCo 94028 810-D4
4200 OAK 94619 650-F6
6800 PLE 94588 714-A1
SIESTA DR
1500 LALT 94024 831-J3
SIESTA VISTA DR
15600 SCIC 95127 815-C7
SIETA CT
1400 SJS 95118 874-B1
SIGAL DR
20600 SAR 95070 872-D4
SIGERSON LN
1200 AlaC 94586 734-G3
SIGNAL CT
900 CNCD 94518 592-F6
SIGOURNEY AV
9900 OAK 94605 671-C3
SIGRID WY
5300 SJS 95136 874-J3
5300 SJS 95123 874-J3
SIINO AV
- CCCo 94565 573-H2
100 PIT 94565 573-H2
4000 CNCD 94521 593-A3
SIKORSKY ST
1000 OAK 94621 670-D6
SILACCI DR
800 CMBL 95008 853-A7
1400 CMBL 95008 873-A1

SILAS CT
- BEN 94510 551-C1
SILBERMAN DR
6100 SJS 95120 874-C7
SILBURY CT
3100 SJS 95148 855-E2
SILCREEK DR
- SJS 95116 834-F3
SILENCE DR
2000 SJS 95148 835-D4
SILENT HILLS LN
12400 LAH 94022 831-A2
SILER LN
1200 SJS 95116 834-F5
SILER PL
1000 OAK 94705 630-B3
SILICON DR
900 SJS 95126 833-H5
SILICON VALLEY BLVD
300 SJS 95138 875-F5
SILK CT
3600 SJS 95111 854-G6
36700 NWK 94560 752-D7
SILK OAK CIR
- SRFL 94901 567-C5
SILK OAK WY
700 SUNV 94086 832-G2
SILK TREE CT
2400 MRTZ 94553 572-A6
SILKTREE CT
- DNVL 94526 653-B7
- HIL 94010 748-C2
SILKTREE LN
100 VAL 94591 550-F1
SILKWOOD LN
1700 CNCD 94521 593-F4
SILLIMAN ST
- SF 94134 668-A6
400 SF 94134 667-H7
SILSBY AV
2400 UNC 94587 732-F7
SILVA AV
- MLBR 94030 728-B3
4300 MTVW 94040 811-E3
4300 SJS 95118 874-B2
4300 PA 94306 811-E3
5200 RCH 94805 589-B6
5300 ELCR 94530 589-B6
24000 HAY 94544 711-J2
SILVA CT
4300 PA 94306 811-E3
43700 FRMT 94539 773-H1
SILVA LN
- MrnC 94947 525-H4
1200 ALA 94502 670-A7
SILVA ST
4200 ANT 94509 574-H5
SILVA DALE
1400 CCCo 94507 632-E3
SILVEIRA PKWY
1500 SRFL 94903 566-G1
SILVER AV
- CCCo 94801 588-F3
200 SF 94112 667-G7
600 SF 94134 667-G7
1200 SF 94134 668-A6
1600 RDWC 94061 790-A1
1600 SF 94124 668-A6
SILVER CT
3300 PIN 94564 569-G7
SILVER ST
4000 PLE 94566 714-E2
SILVER TER
4900 FRMT 94555 752-A3
SILVERA LN
- SJS 95136 874-D2
SILVERA ST
100 MPS 95035 793-J6
SILVER ACRES CT
5100 SJS 95138 855-F7
SILVERADO AV
20200 CPTO 95014 852-E2
SILVERADO CT
- CLAY 94517 594-A7
200 OAK 94605 671-D3
300 DNVL 94526 653-D6
900 HAY 94541 711-E2
3200 LFYT 94549 631-H2
SILVERADO DR
400 LFYT 94549 631-H3
500 TBRN 94920 607-B4
1200 SJS 95120 894-D2
2100 ANT 94509 595-A2
2500 PIN 94564 569-G7
N SILVERADO DR
600 LFYT 94549 631-H2
SILVERADO RD
900 HAY 94541 711-E2
SILVERADO WY
100 LFYT 94549 631-J4
SILVER BELL DR
6900 SJS 95120 894-D4
SILVER BELT DR
1100 RCH 94803 589-H3
SILVERBERRY CT
4400 CNCD 94521 593-B5
SILVERBERRY DR
4300 SJS 95136 874-H1
SILVERBERRY ST
- ANT 94509 595-F3
SILVER BIRCH CT
- CCCo 94506 654-A3
SILVER BIRCH DR
- AlaC 94542 692-E7
SILVER BIRCH LN
- HAY 94544 712-E7
SILVER BLOSSOM CT
2200 SJS 95138 855-F7
SILVER BLUFF WY
2200 SJS 95138 855-G7
SILVER BREEZE CT
2200 SJS 95138 855-G7
SILVER BROOK CT
7000 SJS 95120 894-D4
SILVER CANYON DR
1100 SJS 95120 894-D4
SILVER CHIEF PL
400 DNVL 94526 653-B5
SILVER CHIEF WY
400 DNVL 94526 653-B5

SILVER CLIFF DR
6900 SJS 95120 894-D4
SILVER CLOUD PL
100 DNVL 94526 653-B5
SILVER CREEK CIR
2300 ANT 94509 595-A2
SILVER CREEK CT
1700 SJS 95121 855-C4
SILVER CREEK RD
2500 SJS 95121 855-B3
3300 SJS 95121 855-C4
5500 SJS 95138 875-H1
5800 SCIC 95138 875-H1
SILVER CREEK VALLEY RD
400 SJS 95138 875-D3
400 SJS 95111 875-D3
1200 SCIC 95138 875-D3
2400 SJS 95138 855-E5
5000 SJS 95121 855-E5
SILVER CREST CT
- LFYT 94549 631-F1
SILVERCREST CT
- ANT 94509 595-J3
2500 PIN 94564 569-H7
SILVERCREST DR
1600 SJS 95118 874-A2
SILVERCREST ST
2600 PIN 94564 569-J7
SILVERCREST WY
4400 ANT 94509 595-H3
SILVER DELL RD
1500 LFYT 94549 611-F1
SILVERDELL WY
400 HAY 94544 712-B7
400 HAY 94544 732-B1
SILVER ESTATES
2800 SJS 95135 855-G5
SILVER FIR LN
- CCCo 94506 654-A3
SILVER FOX DR
6900 SJS 95120 894-D4
SILVER FOX PL
- AlaC 94546 691-G4
SILVER GARDEN WY
5200 SJS 95138 855-F7
SILVERGATE CT
6900 SJS 95120 894-D4
SILVERGATE DR
11400 DBLN 94568 693-F4
11700 DBLN 94552 693-F4
SILVER GLEN CT
1700 SJS 95121 855-B4
SILVER HILL CT
4800 ANT 94509 595-J3
SILVERHILL CT
1100 CCCo 94549 591-G5
SILVER HILL DR
1100 SJS 95120 894-D4
SILVERHILL DR
1100 CCCo 94549 591-H5
SILVER HILL RD
1000 RDWC 94061 789-G3
SILVERHILL WY
- CCCo 94549 591-H5
SILVER HOLLOW CT
2100 SJS 95138 855-F7
SILVER HOLLOW DR
- CCCo - 613-B3
SILVERIA CT
2300 SCL 95054 813-C4
SILVER KNOLL CT
2200 SJS 95138 855-F7
SILVERLAKE CT
300 MPS 95035 794-A6
SILVER LAKE DR
400 DNVL 94526 653-D6
SILVERLAKE DR
100 MPS 95035 794-A6
200 SUNV 94089 812-H4
SILVER LAKE PL
2100 MRTZ 94553 592-A1
SILVER LAKE WY
2000 MRTZ 94553 592-A1
SILVERLAND CT
2900 SJS 95135 855-D3
SILVERLAND DR
2900 SJS 95135 855-E3
SILVER LEAF CT
- LFYT 94549 611-G2
SILVERLEAF DR
16000 AlaC 94580 691-E5
SILVER LEAF RD
5600 SJS 95138 875-D4
SILVERLOCK CT
34900 FRMT 94555 752-E1
SILVERLOCK RD
3500 FRMT 94555 752-E1
SILVER LODE LN
7100 SJS 95120 894-H4
SILVER MAPLE DR
3400 CCCo 94506 653-J5
3400 CCCo 94506 654-A5
SILVER MAPLE LN
- HAY 94544 712-E7
SILVER MEADOW CT
1700 SJS 95121 855-B4
4200 CCCo 94506 654-C4
SILVER MOON CT
7000 SJS 95120 894-D4
SILVER OAK CT
1100 SJS 95120 874-D7
1400 PIN 94564 569-F5
SILVER OAK LN
500 CCCo 94506 653-J5
22600 CPTO 95014 831-J7
SILVER OAK PL
3600 CCCo 94506 653-J5
SILVER OAK TER
100 ORIN 94563 611-A3
SILVER OAK WY
22500 CPTO 95014 831-J7
SILVER OAKS PL
700 WLCK 94596 612-B2
SILVER OAKS ST
- LVMR 94550 695-J7
SILVER OAKS WY
3500 LVMR 94550 695-H7
SILVER PEAK DR
6900 SJS 95120 894-D4
SILVER PINE CT
700 SUNV 94086 832-G2

SILVER PINE LN
- CCCo 94506 654-A3
SILVERPINE LN
100 VAL 94591 550-F1
SILVER POINT WY
5300 SJS 95138 855-F7
SILVER REEF DR
5000 FRMT 94538 753-A7
SILVER RIDGE CT
5100 SJS 95138 855-G6
SILVER RIDGE DR
5100 SJS 95138 855-G6
SILVER SAGE
5500 SJS 95123 875-B4
SILVER SAGE CT
5400 CNCD 94521 593-E7
SILVER SHADOW DR
1100 SJS 95120 894-D4
SILVERSPOT DR
- BSBN 94005 687-H5
SILVER SPRING CT
11500 CPTO 95014 852-A4
SILVER SPRINGS CT
3400 LFYT 94549 631-F1
SILVER SPRINGS RD
3400 LFYT 94549 631-F1
3500 LFYT 94549 611-F7
S SILVER SPRINGS RD
3400 LFYT 94549 631-F1
SILVER SPRINGS WY
- SJS 95123 875-G2
SILVER SPUR CT
3400 CNCD 94518 592-J6
SILVER STAR CT
7000 SJS 95120 894-D4
SILVERSTONE CT
6500 MRTZ 94553 591-H4
SILVERSTONE PL
1500 SJS 95122 835-A5
1700 SJS 95148 835-A5
SILVER TERRACE WY
2200 SJS 95138 855-F7
SILVERTIDE CT
- UNC 94545 731-J6
SILVERTIDE DR
4600 UNC 94545 731-J6
SILVERTIP CT
300 MPS 95035 813-J3
SILVER TIP WY
700 SUNV 94086 832-H2
SILVER TRAIL CT
5200 SJS 95138 855-F7
SILVERTREE DR
1600 SJS 95131 814-C5
SILVERTREE LN
7500 DBLN 94568 693-G4
SILVER VALE CT
2100 SJS 95138 855-F7
SILVER VIEW CT
100 VAL 94591 530-D3
SILVERVIEW DR
- SF 94124 668-B6
SILVER VISTA WY
5300 SJS 95138 855-G7
SILVERWOOD AV
1900 MTVW 94043 811-G4
3700 OAK 94602 650-F5
SILVERWOOD CT
- ORIN 94563 611-A7
300 DNVL 94526 653-D7
SILVERWOOD DR
400 LFYT 94549 611-A7
500 ORIN 94563 611-A7
1500 MRTZ 94553 571-J7
1700 SJS 95124 873-J2
1800 CNCD 94519 573-A7
1800 CNCD 94519 593-A1
SILVEY CT
1700 CNCD 94521 593-E4
SILVIA CT
- MRGA 94556 631-D7
200 LALT 94024 811-F7
800 PCFA 94044 726-H5
SILVIA DR
200 LALT 94024 811-F7
SILVO LN
300 NVTO 94947 526-D7
SIMAS AV
2200 PIN 94564 569-G7
SIMAS DR
400 MPS 95035 794-C5
SIMBERLAN DR
3100 SJS 95148 855-E1
SIMKINS CT
2900 PA 94303 791-D5
SIMM CT
5500 FRMT 94538 773-B2
SIMMONDS RD
- MrnC 94965 626-F6
SIMMONS CT
- NVTO 94945 525-J2
SIMMONS LN
900 NVTO 94945 525-J2
1000 NVTO 94945 526-A2
SIMMONS ST
1200 ANT 94509 575-F5
3300 OAK 94619 650-G7
SIMMS ST
- SRFL 94901 586-J3
SIMO LN
- CCCo 94507 632-E4
SIMON AV
2000 SJS 95122 834-J6
SIMON LN
13200 LAH 94022 810-J7
SIMON ST
500 HAY 94541 711-H1
SIMONDS LP
- SF 94129 647-E4
SIMONI CT
5100 CCCo 94803 589-G2
5100 RCH 94803 589-G2
SIMONI DR
15600 SCIC 95127 815-B7
SIMONS WY
- LGTS 95032 873-B7
SIMONSON CT
1200 SJS 95121 854-J2
SIMONSON WY
1200 SJS 95121 854-J2

SIMONTON ST
100 VAL 94589 510-D6
SIMPLE CT
33600 FRMT 94555 752-B1
SIMPSON CT
- WLCK 94596 612-E5
1400 PIT 94565 574-G4
SIMPSON DR
- CCCo 94596 612-E5
- DALY 94015 707-C2
- WLCK 94596 612-E5
SIMPSON WY
1800 SJS 95125 854-A5
SIMS AV
- VAL 94590 529-G2
SIMS CT
29100 HAY 94544 732-B1
SIMS DR
6600 OAK 94611 650-E2
SIMSBURY RD
19100 AlaC 94546 691-J4
SIMS MOUNTAIN CT
1500 ANT 94509 595-E4
SIMSON ST
6500 OAK 94605 670-H1
SINAI DR
200 CCCo 94553 572-C6
SINALOA CT
- NVTO 94947 525-H4
SINBAD AV
800 SJS 95116 834-J4
SINCLAIR AV
2600 CNCD 94519 592-G2
SINCLAIR DR
400 SJS 95116 834-G4
1800 PLE 94588 694-E7
SINCLAIR FRWY I-280
- SCIC - 853-G2
- SJS - 834-E7
- SJS - 854-A2
- SJS - 853-G2
SINCLAIR FRWY I-680
- FRMT - 794-A1
- FRMT - 793-J1
- FRMT 94539 773-F3
- MPS - 794-A1
- MPS - 814-E6
- SCIC - 814-E6
- SJS - 814-E6
- SJS - 834-F1
SINCLAIR ST
24700 HAY 94545 711-E5
SINCLAIR FRONTAGE RD
200 MPS 95035 794-C7
400 MPS 95035 814-C1
SINGALONG WY
- AlaC 94586 713-J7
SINGING HILL LN
14500 SAR 95070 872-H3
SINGING HILLS AV
5700 LVMR 94550 696-C2
SINGING HILLS RD
- CCCo 94595 632-E2
SINGING RAIN PL
2800 SJS 95127 835-A4
SINGING WOOD CT
- WLCK 94595 632-B4
SINGINGWOOD LN
- ORIN 94563 610-J3
SINGLETARY AV
1100 SJS 95126 833-H7
SINGLETON AV
- ALA 94501 649-E6
SINGLETON LN
400 SJS 95111 854-J5
SINGLETON RD
600 SCIC 95111 854-G6
3600 SJS 95111 854-J5
SINGLETREE CT
6800 PLE 94588 714-A1
SINGLETREE WY
1500 SJS 95124 874-A6
1600 SJS 95118 874-A6
6300 PLE 94588 694-A7
6400 PLE 94588 714-A1
SINGLEY DR
300 MPS 95035 794-A5
SINNET CT
1900 DNVL 94526 653-D7
SINNOTT LN
100 MPS 95035 814-A1
SINSBURY WY
33700 UNC 94587 732-E6
SIOUX CT
1000 FRMT 94539 773-H3
SIOUX DR
1600 FRMT 94539 773-G3
SIOUX LN
- LALT 94022 811-E6
- SRMN 94583 673-C4
400 SJS 95123 874-H5
SIOUX TER
44300 FRMT 94539 773-H3
SIOUX WY
- PTLV 94028 810-C6
SIPPOLA WY
1300 SJS 95121 854-J2
SIRAH CT
2100 LVMR 94550 715-H3
3600 PLE 94566 714-G4
SIRARD LN
- SRFL 94901 566-D6
SIR FRANCIS DRAKE BLVD
- LKSP 94904 586-C2
- MrnC 94904 586-C2
- LKSP 94939 586-C2
400 SANS 94960 566-A6
600 FRFX 94930 566-A6
1200 SANS 94960 586-C2
1300 ROSS 94957 586-C2
E SIR FRANCIS DRAKE BLVD
- SRFL 94901 587-A5
- SRFL 94964 587-A5
- LKSP 94904 586-J5
300 MrnC 94904 586-J5
400 MrnC 94964 587-A5
400 MrnC 94964 586-J5

E SIR FRANCIS DRAKE BLVD
400 MrnC 94904 587-A5
SIRINA CT
- SJS 95131 814-B5
SISKIYOU CT
100 SBRN 94066 707-D7
200 WLCK 94598 612-E3
3500 HAY 94542 712-F4
SISKIYOU DR
900 MLPK 94025 790-C7
1500 WLCK 94598 612-E3
SISKIYOU PL
- MLPK 94025 790-C7
SISTER CITIES BLVD
- SSF 94080 708-A1
200 SSF 94080 707-J1
SITKA CT
500 WLCK 94598 592-J7
SITKA DR
600 WLCK 94598 592-J7
SITKA ST
1900 SLN 94577 690-G3
SITKA TER
1000 SUNV 94086 832-H2
SIWARD DR
34000 FRMT 94555 752-D1
SKALL DR
400 SJS 95111 854-J6
SKANDER CT
- PLHL 94523 592-A3
SKANDER LN
300 PLHL 94523 592-A3
SKARLATOS PL
3700 AlaC 94546 692-A3
SKEET RANGE RD
- NVTO 94949 546-G3
SKELLY AV
100 HER 94547 569-F3
SKELTON AV
1300 FRMT 94536 753-B3
SKELTON CT
1500 FRMT 94536 753-B3
SKIBBEREEN LN
200 VAL 94590 530-C3
SKIFF CIR
500 RDWC 94065 749-H7
SKIMMER CT
2500 PLE 94566 714-D1
SKIPJACK LN
100 FCTY 94404 749-J1
SKIPPER RD
- CCCo 94565 573-E1
SKIPSTONE CT
400 SJS 95136 854-F7
SKIPTON CT
2800 ANT 94509 575-C6
SKOKIE LN
1200 HAY 94545 711-H6
SKOWHEGAN CT
100 SJS 95139 895-G1
SKY CT
3700 SMTO 94403 749-B6
SKY LN
3400 LFYT 94549 611-F5
14700 SCIC 95032 873-F7
SKY RD
- MrnC 94920 606-J4
2400 WLCK 94596 612-B3
SKY TER
- DNVL 94526 652-H3
SKYCREST DR
400 DNVL 94506 654-B6
1100 WLCK 94595 631-J1
SKYE RD
43600 FRMT 94539 773-G1
SKYFARM CT
6500 SJS 95120 894-B1
SKYFARM DR
2100 HIL 94010 728-D7
2100 HIL 94010 748-D2
5800 AlaC 94552 692-C1
6500 SJS 95120 894-C1
SKYHARBOUR LN
400 CCCo 94565 573-D2
SKY HAWK DR
4800 RCH 94803 589-G1
SKY-HY CIR
600 LFYT 94549 631-F1
600 MRGA 94556 631-F1
SKY-HY CT
600 LFYT 94549 631-F1
SKY-HY DR
- LFYT 94549 631-E2
- MRGA 94556 631-E2
SKYLAKE CT
1100 SUNV 94089 812-J4
SKYLAND WY
- ROSS 94957 586-D2
SKYLARK CT
- DNVL 94506 653-E5
- HAY 94544 712-E7
2100 UNC 94587 732-G6
5000 PLE 94566 694-D7
SKYLARK DR
- LKSP 94939 586-D5
2400 SJS 95125 854-C6
3500 CNCD 94520 572-G6
34600 UNC 94587 732-F6
SKYLARK LN
- DNVL 94506 653-E5
SKYLARK WY
2400 PLE 94566 694-D7
2500 PLE 94566 714-D1
SKYLAWN DR
- SMCo - 768-D4
SKY LINE
- CCCo 94806 569-A5
SKYLINE
- SANS 94960 566-A5
SKYLINE BLVD
- SF 94132 686-J1
- SMCo - 748-D4
100 MLBR 94030 727-H4
500 SBRN 94066 727-F1
1600 BURL 94010 728-A6
1600 SMCo 94010 728-A6
5800 OAK 94611 630-D4
5800 SMCo 94010 748-D4
5900 SMCo 94010 728-A6
6000 BURL 94010 748-B1
6000 SMCo 94010 748-B1

SKYLINE BLVD
6000 HIL 94010 748-B1
6700 CCCo - 630-E5
6700 CCCo 94611 630-E5
8000 OAK 94611 650-H2
11500 AlaC - 650-H2
11500 OAK 94602 650-H2
11500 OAK 94619 650-H2
12100 OAK 94619 651-A5
13700 OAK 94619 671-D1
14600 OAK 94605 671-D1
15700 AlaC 94546 671-E2
15700 AlaC 94605 671-D1
SKYLINE BLVD Rt#-35
- DALY 94015 687-A5
- DALY 94015 686-J3
- SF 94132 666-H6
- SF 94132 686-J3
- SMCo - 748-E6
500 SMCo - 727-F1
500 SBRN 94066 727-F1
900 SBRN 94066 707-D5
900 SMCo - 707-D5
1100 DALY 94015 707-B1
1200 PCFA 94044 707-B1
1900 SMCo - 768-F1
2100 SMCo 94015 686-J3
2700 SSF 94080 707-D5
7500 SMCo 94062 768-E5
13800 SMCo 94062 789-A7
14700 SMCo 94062 809-A1
17100 WDSD 94062 809-G7
17300 SMCo 94020 809-G7
17300 WDSD 94020 809-D4
18100 PTLV 94028 809-G7
19300 SMCo 94020 830-A4
19300 PTLV 94028 830-A4
19800 SMCo 94028 830-C7
SKYLINE CIR
8000 OAK 94619 671-D1
SKYLINE CT
100 VAL 94591 530-D2
SKYLINE DR
- DALY 94015 686-J4
- SMCo 94062 809-F6
100 VAL 94591 530-D2
300 DALY 94015 687-A5
600 MRTZ 94553 591-G3
900 DALY 94015 707-A1
1200 DALY 94015 706-J1
1900 MPS 95035 814-E1
3400 HAY 94542 712-F5
5800 CCCo 94803 569-F7
5900 CCCo 94803 589-F1
SKYLINE PL
4300 PIT 94565 574-E7
SKYLINE TER
- MrnC 94941 606-D5
SKYLINE TR
- AlaC - 651-C5
- AlaC 94546 651-D6
- AlaC 94546 671-E1
- OAK 94605 671-E1
- SMCo 94062 789-A6
SKYLINE FRONTAGE RD
1900 HIL 94010 748-B1
1900 SMCo 94010 748-B1
SKYLINKS CT
6100 LVMR 94550 696-C2
SKYLINKS WY
5900 LVMR 94550 696-C2
SKYLONDA DR
- SMCo 94020 809-F5
SKY MEADOW WY
6400 SJS 95135 855-J7
SKYMONT CT
- BLMT 94002 768-J1
SKYMONT DR
4100 BLMT 94002 768-J1
SKY OAKS WY
19500 SCIC 95030 872-F5
SKYPARK CIR
- SSF 94014 687-J7
- SSF 94014 707-J1
SKYPOINT CT
4200 OAK 94619 650-J6
SKYPORT DR
- SJS 95110 833-H2
SKY RANCH CT
600 LFYT 94549 631-F1
SKY RANCH LN
- PLHL 94523 592-A4
SKY TRAIL FIRE RD
- MrnC 94946 525-F7
SKY VIEW CT
- CCCo - 651-F3
SKYVIEW CT
500 PLHL 94523 591-J2
SKYVIEW DR
- RCH 94803 589-G3
- VAL 94591 530-D3
300 PLHL 94523 591-H2
1300 BURL 94010 748-B1
1700 SLN 94577 691-D1
15200 SCIC 95132 814-H4
15200 SJS 95132 814-H4
SKYVIEW PL
5700 RCH 94803 589-G3
SKYVIEW RD
- ROSS 94957 586-D2
SKYVIEW TER
- SRFL 94903 566-D1
15300 SCIC 95132 814-J4
SKYVIEW WY
- SF 94131 667-E4
SKYWAY
100 VAL 94591 530-D3
SKYWAY CT
2100 FRMT 94539 773-F3
SKYWAY DR
200 SJS 95111 874-J1
300 SJS 95111 875-A1
800 SJS 95136 874-H1
SKYWAY LN
- OAK 94619 651-C7
SKYWAY RD
600 RDWC 94065 769-H2
600 SCAR 94070 769-H2
SKYWEST DR
19900 HAY 94541 711-E2

STREET Block City ZIP Pg-Grid

SKYWOOD RD
800 LFYT 94549 611-G7
SKYWOOD WY
- WDSD 94062 809-F5
SLADKY AV
800 MTVW 94040 811-G7
SLATE CT
- UNC 94587 732-G6
SLATE DR
- UNC 94587 732-G6
SLATER AV
700 PLHL 94523 592-A5
700 PLHL 94523 591-J5
SLATER CT
1400 CNCD 94521 592-J3
3600 SJS 95132 814-F2
SLATER LN
- OAK 94705 630-A3
SLAYTON ST
40600 FRMT 94539 753-F4
SLEEPER AV
100 MTVW 94040 831-J1
2100 MTVW 94040 832-A1
SLEEPY CREEK DR
7200 SJS 95120 894-J4
SLEEPY CREEK WY
7200 SJS 95120 894-J4
SLEEPY HOLLOW AV
- SMCo 94063 770-F5
2000 HAY 94545 711-F7
SLEEPY HOLLOW AV S
27200 HAY 94545 711-G6
SLEEPY HOLLOW CT
- ORIN 94563 610-G4
SLEEPY HOLLOW DR
- MrnC 94960 566-A3
SLEEPY HOLLOW LN
- ORIN 94563 610-F4
1100 MLBR 94030 727-H4
2300 SJS 95116 834-J5
SLEEPY MEADOW CT
1400 SJS 95121 855-D7
SLEIGH LN
- CCCo 94596 612-F6
SLENDER CT
33600 FRMT 94555 752-C1
SLIDA DR
6300 SJS 95129 852-F4
SLOAN AL
- SF 94105 648-B5
SLOAN CT
5500 CNCD 94521 593-H4
SLOAN ST
2100 OAK 94602 650-D4
4600 FRMT 94538 753-A6
SLOAT BLVD
- SF 94132 667-A6
1600 SF 94132 666-J6
2300 SF 94116 666-H6
SLOAT CT
300 SCL 95051 833-A7
SLOAT RD
4300 FRMT 94538 753-A6
13700 FRMT 94538 752-J6
SLOBDNIK
- CCCo 94553 571-G2
SLOCCUM CT
32200 UNC 94587 732-C5
SLOOP CT
100 FCTY 94404 749-H4
SLOPE CREST DR
13200 OAK 94619 651-C6
SLOPEVIEW CT
6000 AlaC 94552 692-C1
SLOPEVIEW DR
3500 SJS 95148 835-E7
3700 SCIC 95148 835-E7
SLOPING MEADOW CT
6500 SJS 95135 855-J7
SLOWDOWN CT
500 MrnC 94947 525-H5
SMALLEY AV
100 AlaC 94541 711-G2
300 HAY 94541 711-H1
SMALLWOOD CT
3700 PLE 94566 714-G5
SMITH AV
- DBLN 94568 694-A3
700 PIN 94564 569-E4
900 CMBL 95008 853-B7
1700 SJS 95112 854-E2
5700 NWK 94560 752-G7
6100 NWK 94560 772-F1
SMITH CT
- ALA 94502 669-H5
38100 FRMT 94536 753-A2
SMITH DR
5100 MRTZ 94553 591-F1
SMITH LN
- SANS 94960 566-C7
2000 CNCD 94518 592-F7
SMITH RD
100 CCCo 94526 633-A6
800 MrnC 94965 606-E7
SMITH ST
3500 UNC 94587 732-A5
3700 UNC 94587 731-J5
SMITH CREEK DR
100 LGTS 95030 873-A3
SMITHERS DR
2700 SJS 95148 855-C1
SMITH GATE CT
4700 PLE 94588 694-D7
SMITH PEAK CT
2000 ANT 94509 595-F4
SMITH RANCH RD
- SRFL 94903 566-F1
400 SRFL 94903 546-H7
400 MrnC 94903 546-H7
400 MrnC 94903 566-F1
SMITHWOOD ST
- MPS 95035 793-J7
SMOKE RIVER CT
4600 SJS 95136 874-E2
SMOKE TREE COM
- PLE 94566 714-G3
SMOKE TREE CT
100 SJS 95136 874-H1
4400 CNCD 94521 593-B5
SMOKETREE CT
- CCCo 94549 591-H5

SMOKE TREE LN
- WDSD 94062 809-F1
SMOKETREE ST
2700 ANT 94509 575-J5
SMOKE TREE WY
600 SUNV 94086 832-H2
SMOKEWOOD CT
- DNVL 94526 653-B4
SMOKEY CT
500 CMBL 95008 853-A7
3300 ANT 94509 595-H2
SMOKEY HILLS DR
100 VAL 94589 510-C5
SMYRNA CT
1100 SUNV 94087 832-D3
SMYTH RD
- BERK 94704 630-A2
SNAKE RD
5500 OAK 94611 650-E1
5900 OAK 94611 630-E7
SNAKE RIVER PL
34700 FRMT 94555 752-E2
SNAPDRAGON PL
500 BEN 94510 551-A1
SNAPPER TER
- FRMT 94536 753-B2
SNEAD CT
- PLHL 94549 591-H5
SNEAD DR
4600 SCL 95054 813-D4
SNEATH LN
- PCFA 94044 727-D1
800 SBRN 94066 707-G6
3600 SBRN 94066 727-D1
3700 SMCo 94044 727-D1
SNECKNER CT
- SMCo 94025 810-F1
SNELL AV
3500 SJS 95136 854-G7
4000 SJS 95136 874-H1
4800 SCIC 95136 874-H1
5200 SJS 95123 874-J4
SNELL CT
200 SJS 95123 874-J3
26500 LAH 94022 811-B5
SNELL LN
26500 LAH 94022 811-B5
SNELL RD
16200 SCIC 95032 893-B2
16400 LGTS 95032 893-B2
SNELL ST
6900 OAK 94621 670-F4
SNELL WY
5600 SJS 95123 874-J5
SNIVELY AV
3300 SCL 95051 832-J4
SNODGRASS LN
- ANT - 595-G6
SNOW AV
37100 NWK 94560 752-D7
SNOW CT
- ORIN 94563 631-A5
- ORIN 94563 630-J5
SNOW DR
900 MRTZ 94553 571-G7
4700 SJS 95111 855-B7
4800 SJS 95111 875-B1
SNOW ST
1200 MTVW 94041 811-G5
SNOW TER
700 SJS 95111 855-B7
SNOWBALL CT
- LVMR 94550 715-D1
SNOWBANK CT
4100 SJS 95135 855-F3
SNOWBERRY CT
- ORIN 94563 610-G3
- SRFL 94901 567-C5
1100 SUNV 94087 832-D3
4400 CNCD 94521 593-B5
6100 SJS 95123 875-B6
SNOWBERRY LN
- ORIN 94563 610-G3
SNOWBERRY WK
- ALA 94501 669-H3
SNOWCLOUD CT
4300 CNCD 94518 593-A6
SNOWDEN AV
- ATN 94027 790-D1
SNOWDEN PL
5500 SJS 95138 855-H7
5600 SJS 95138 875-H1
SNOWDEN WY
5600 SJS 95138 875-H1
SNOWDON AV
6700 ELCR 94530 609-C1
SNOWDON CT
700 WLCK 94598 612-J4
SNOWDON PL
400 CCCo 94506 654-B4
SNOWDOWN AV
10700 OAK 94605 671-D4
SNOWDRIFT CT
- RCH 94803 589-G2
SNOWFLAKE COM
5600 FRMT 94538 773-A2
SNOW FLAKE WY
300 PIT 94565 573-J2
SNOWMASS PEAK CT
4800 ANT 94509 595-E3
SNOW MELT CT
- CCCo 94506 654-C4
SNOWMOUNTAIN CT
- CCCo 94506 654-C4
SNYDER AV
400 SJS 95125 854-A2
SNYDER CT
2600 WLCK 94598 612-H4
SNYDER LN
400 MTVW 94043 812-B5
700 WLCK 94598 612-H4
SNYDER WY
- FRMT 94536 733-A7
SOAPROOT CT
1800 WLCK 94595 632-B1
SOARES CT
3300 SCL 95051 832-J5
SOARES LN
4100 LFYT 94549 611-A4
SOBEY RD
14100 SAR 95070 872-H2

SOBEY MEADOWS CT
14000 SAR 95070 872-H2
SOBEY OAKS CT
14500 SAR 95070 872-G3
SOBRANTE AV
- RCH 94806 568-G5
4000 CCCo 94803 589-E1
5200 CCCo 94803 569-E7
SOBRANTE CT
100 FRMT 94536 753-D2
1800 WLCK 94595 632-B1
SOBRANTE RD
6500 OAK 94611 630-F5
SOBRANTE ST
38700 FRMT 94536 753-D2
SOBRANTE WY
200 SUNV 94086 812-D6
SOBRATO CT
600 CMBL 95008 853-C7
SOBRATO DR
600 CMBL 95008 853-C7
600 CMBL 95008 873-C1
SOBRATO LN
600 CMBL 95008 853-C7
SOBRATO WY
600 CMBL 95008 853-C7
SOCA TER
4400 FRMT 94536 752-G3
SOCCER CT
1400 CNCD 94518 592-E6
SOCORRO AV
1100 SUNV 94089 812-J5
1100 SUNV 94089 813-A5
SODA PL
100 DNVL 94526 653-B1
SODARO DR
- CCCo 94553 571-H4
SODA SPRINGS RD
15400 SCIC 95030 893-C6
SODAVILLE CT
45400 FRMT 94539 773-H4
SOELRO CT
4000 SCIC 95127 815-B7
SOFIA CT
35000 FRMT 94536 752-E2
SOFT SHADOW CT
- RCH 94803 589-G2
SOGOL CT
1900 SJS 95122 854-G2
SOGOL DR
- SJS 95122 854-G1
SOHO CIR
- BLMT 94002 769-A3
SOJOURNER TRUTH CT
2700 BERK 94702 629-F3
SOL ST
2100 AlaC 94578 691-E3
SOLA AV
- SF 94116 667-D4
SOLA ST
20800 CPTO 95014 852-D1
SOLACE PL
2500 MTVW 94040 831-J1
SOLANA CT
- BLMT 94002 769-E2
900 MTVW 94040 811-F5
3400 LFYT 94549 631-F1
SOLANA DR
- LALT 94022 811-F6
700 LFYT 94549 631-F1
700 LFYT 94549 611-F7
1000 MTVW 94040 811-F6
1400 BLMT 94002 769-E2
4000 PA 94306 811-C2
11600 DBLN 94568 693-F3
19600 SAR 95070 852-F6
SOLANA RD
100 PTLV 94028 810-B5
SOLANO AV
- VAL 94590 529-J6
- CCCo 94525 573-H2
- VAL 94590 530-B5
300 AlaC 94541 711-E1
700 ALB 94706 609-C6
1400 BERK 94707 609-E6
1500 ALB 94707 609-E6
2000 VAL 94591 530-B5
3400 RCH 94805 589-A5
5700 CCCo 94805 589-A5
SOLANO CT
- CCCo 94565 573-H2
800 CCCo 94803 589-C1
1900 CNCD 94520 572-E6
3300 SCL 95051 832-J5
SOLANO DR
400 BEN 94510 551-A1
500 BEN 94510 530-J7
500 BEN 94510 550-J1
1300 PCFA 94044 726-J5
6200 SJS 95119 875-C6
SOLANO ST
- BSBN 94005 688-A6
100 SRFL 94901 566-D6
100 TBRN 94920 607-F7
SOLANO WY
- CCCo 94553 572-B1
1400 CCCo 94520 572-D6
1400 CNCD 94520 572-D6
1500 OAK 94606 650-A6
4300 UNC 94587 731-J5
SOLAR CIR
4200 UNC 94587 732-B7
SOLAR CT
- MPS 95035 794-D6
- SRFL 94901 586-H2
SOLAR WY
4200 FRMT 94538 773-D4
SOLARI ST
1000 PIT 94565 574-E2
SOLBRAE WY
- ORIN 94563 610-E6
SOLEADO CT
11500 DBLN 94568 693-F3
SOLERA DR
8600 SJS 95135 855-J6
SOLITA CT
700 LGTS 95030 873-A4
SOLITAIRE CT
3700 AlaC 94546 692-B4
SOLITO CT
700 SJS 95123 874-G5

SOLITUDE LN
1500 RCH 94803 589-G3
SOLOMON CT
6200 SJS 95123 875-B7
SOLOMON LN
3300 ALA 94502 670-A7
SOLSTICE CT
- FRMT 94539 773-J4
SOLTERO DR
5800 SJS 95123 874-F5
SOLVEIG DR
2000 CCCo 94596 612-E7
SOMBRERO CIR
2800 SRMN 94583 673-D4
SOMERS ST
1500 PIT 94565 574-E3
SOMERSET AV
2100 AlaC 94578 691-H5
2600 AlaC 94546 692-A4
2800 AlaC 94546 691-J4
SOMERSET CT
- BLMT 94002 769-E5
100 VAL 94589 530-B1
800 SCAR 94070 769-E5
1900 LALT 94024 831-H5
10300 CPTO 95014 852-E1
SOMERSET DR
- NVTO 94945 526-A1
800 SUNV 94087 832-C3
1100 SJS 95132 814-G5
2500 BLMT 94002 769-B3
3100 LFYT 94549 631-H2
20000 CPTO 95014 852-E1
SOMERSET LN
- ATN 94027 790-D4
- MLV 94941 606-G3
600 FCTY 94404 749-G5
SOMERSET PL
- BERK 94707 609-G5
- NVTO 94945 526-A1
- PA 94301 791-A4
- WDSD 94062 789-F4
700 CNCD 94518 592-H7
1600 ANT 94509 575-F5
3100 LFYT 94549 631-J3
5200 NWK 94560 752-E4
SOMERSET RD
- OAK 94611 650-D1
- PDMT 94611 650-D1
SOMERSET ST
- SF 94134 668-A6
- SF 94134 688-A1
100 RDWC 94062 769-H5
SOMERSET TER
34500 FRMT 94555 752-B2
SOMERSET PARK CIR
2600 SJS 95132 814-F5
SOMERSVILLE RD
- PIT 94565 575-A5
- ANT 94509 575-A5
2100 ANT 94509 574-J6
3000 ANT 94509 594-G2
3000 CCCo - 574-H7
4500 CCCo - 594-G2
SOMERSWORTH DR
1900 SJS 95124 853-G7
SOMERVILLE CT
19700 SAR 95070 852-F5
SOMERVILLE DR
19500 SAR 95070 852-F5
SOMMER CT
- TBRN 94920 607-B5
SONATA WY
4500 SJS 95111 855-A7
SONDRA WY
100 CMBL 95008 853-C5
SONG CT
1100 SJS 95131 834-D1
SONGBIRD CT
- LFYT 94549 611-E6
SONGROTH WY
100 MTVW 94040 811-E3
SONI CT
600 SJS 95116 834-H4
SONIA ST
- OAK 94618 630-C6
SONIA WY
800 MTVW 94040 811-H6
SONJA RD
100 SSF 94080 707-H1
SONNET CT
1800 SJS 95131 814-C4
SONNET LN
18800 AlaC 94541 711-E1
SONOMA AV
- ATN 94027 790-H1
400 CCCo 94572 549-J7
500 LVMR 94550 715-E2
500 CCCo 94572 569-J1
1000 MLPK 94025 790-H1
1000 MLPK 94025 770-H7
1400 ALB 94706 609-E6
1600 ALB 94707 609-E6
1600 BERK 94706 609-E6
1600 BERK 94707 609-E6
2600 ELCR 94530 589-B6
2700 RCH 94805 589-B6
SONOMA BLVD Rt#-29
100 VAL 94590 529-J4
100 VAL 94590 530-A6
100 VAL 94590 550-B1
3600 VAL 94589 529-J4
3600 VAL 94589 530-A1
3900 SolC 94589 530-A1
3900 VAL 94589 510-A7
SONOMA CT
100 SBRN 94066 707-D6
600 LVMR 94550 715-E2
1400 WLCK 94596 611-J2
SONOMA DR
1400 MPS 95035 814-D1
5300 PLE 94566 714-D5
SONOMA LN
2500 ANT 94509 575-D1
SONOMA PL
- MLPK 94025 770-H7
2600 SCL 95051 833-B5
SONOMA ST
- SF 94133 648-A4
- SRFL 94901 586-J2
100 SJS 95110 834-A7
600 RCH 94805 589-B5

SONOMA ST
22300 HAY 94541 711-G3
SONOMA TER
800 SCIC 94305 810-J1
SONOMA WY
1400 OAK 94606 650-B6
2600 PIN 94564 569-H6
SONORA AV
- DNVL 94526 653-A2
- SJS 95110 833-H3
- SSF 94080 707-H4
100 DNVL 94526 652-J2
SONORA CT
- TBRN 94920 607-B4
600 MRTZ 94553 571-E7
1100 SUNV 94086 832-H1
39000 FRMT 94538 752-J6
SONORA DR
200 SMTO 94402 748-J3
SONORA PASS
100 VAL 94589 509-J6
SONORA WY
- CMAD 94925 606-J2
4500 UNC 94587 731-J6
SONTURA CT
5400 AlaC 94552 692-D3
SONUCA AV
900 CMBL 95008 873-C1
SOPHIA WY
4100 SJS 95134 813-D2
SOPHIST DR
3800 SJS 95132 815-A4
SOQUEL ST
32900 UNC 94587 752-A1
SOQUEL WY
300 SUNV 94086 812-E6
SORA COM
4100 FRMT 94555 752-D1
SORA TER
4200 FRMT 94555 752-D1
SORANI CT
17800 AlaC 94546 691-J2
SORANI WY
4700 AlaC 94546 692-A2
4700 AlaC 94546 691-J2
SORANO CT
- PLE 94566 715-B6
SORCI DR
3600 SJS 95124 874-A2
SORENSON AV
19300 CPTO 95014 852-G1
SORENSON RD
600 HAY 94544 712-B5
SORGEPARK PL
200 SJS 95127 834-H1
SORNOWAY LN
- DBLN 94552 693-E5
SORREL AV
5900 SJS 95123 874-J6
SORREL CT
- DNVL 94526 633-C7
100 VAL 94591 530-E1
500 BEN 94510 550-J1
SORREL LN
- SCAR 94070 769-C4
SORREL DOWNS CT
3300 PLE 94588 714-A2
SORRELL CT
1500 WLCK 94598 612-F4
SORRELL DR
1600 WLCK 94598 612-F4
SORRENTO CT
- DNVL 94526 652-J3
200 HER 94547 570-B6
1900 MTVW 94040 831-H1
SORRENTO PL
1600 LVMR 94550 715-G4
SORRENTO WY
- SRFL 94901 587-A1
200 SJS 95119 875-C6
2800 UNC 94587 732-A4
SORRENTO PARK CT
4600 FRMT 94538 773-C2
SOS DR
- WLCK 94596 612-C2
SOTA PL
- SRMN 94583 673-G5
SOTELLO AV
- PDMT 94611 650-D1
SOTELO AV
- SF 94116 667-D4
SOTERION DR
1600 SJS 95118 873-J5
SOTO CT
800 MRTZ 94553 571-E4
1300 SJS 95121 854-J2
SOTO RD
24100 HAY 94544 712-A4
24400 HAY 94544 711-H3
SOTO ST
300 MRTZ 94553 571-E4
1800 CCCo 94801 588-G3
SOTOCASTLE LN
100 BLMT 94002 749-F6
SOULE AV
100 PLHL 94523 592-B6
SOULE RD
- ORIN 94563 611-A5
- ORIN 94563 610-J5
SOUSA DR
900 WLCK 94596 612-A3
SOUSA LN
13300 SAR 95070 872-H1
SOUTH AV
- CCCo - 550-H6
- CCCo 94507 632-F6
SOUTH BLVD
100 SMTO 94402 749-A3
SOUTH CIR
200 NVTO 94949 546-J4
SOUTH CT
100 CCCo 94507 632-F6
2200 PA 94301 791-C7
2600 PA 94306 791-C7
3200 PA 94306 811-D1
SOUTH DR
100 MTVW 94040 831-H1
2300 SCL 95051 833-C2
SOUTH LN
- LVMR 94550 696-C4
- LFYT 94549 611-D7

SOUTH MALL
- OAK 94621 670-F4
SOUTH PL
400 RDWC 94062 769-J7
SOUTH PZ
- MLPK 94025 790-J2
SOUTH RD
- AlaC 94566 734-C1
300 BLMT 94002 749-D7
300 BLMT 94002 769-E1
SOUTH ST
- CCCo 94565 573-H3
- SAUS 94965 627-B4
300 RCH 94804 608-J1
400 RCH 94804 588-J7
1000 BURL 94010 728-G6
SOUTH TR
- CMAD 94925 606-E1
- ORIN 94563 610-F7
SOUTH WY
- CMAD 94925 606-G1
SOUTH ACRES RD
1000 LFYT 94549 611-D6
SOUTHAMPTON AV
- BERK 94707 609-G5
SOUTHAMPTON CT
3600 SJS 95148 835-G7
SOUTHAMPTON DR
700 PA 94303 791-B5
SOUTHAMPTON LN
- BERK 94707 609-G5
SOUTHAMPTON PL
- LFYT 94549 611-G4
SOUTHAMPTON RD
900 BEN 94510 551-A2
1000 BEN 94510 550-J2
SOUTHAMPTON TER
3700 FRMT - 752-D1
3700 FRMT 94555 732-D7
SOUTHAMPTON WY
2200 SMTO 94403 749-C4
SOUTHARD CT
- MRGA 94556 631-E7
SOUTHARD PL
- SF 94109 647-J4
SOUTHBAY DR
300 SJS 95134 813-D2
SOUTHBAY FRWY Rt#-237
- MPS - 813-C1
- SCL - 813-C1
- SCIC - 813-C1
- SJS - 813-C1
- SUNV - 813-C1
- SUNV - 812-D4
SOUTH BREEZE CT
5900 SJS 95138 875-E5
SOUTHBRIDGE CT
5200 SJS 95118 874-C4
SOUTHBRIDGE PL
5200 SJS 95118 874-C4
SOUTHBROOK CT
5700 CLAY 94517 593-G6
5900 SJS 95138 875-E5
SOUTHBROOK DR
- SJS 95138 875-E5
5500 CLAY 94517 593-F5
SOUTHBROOK PL
200 CLAY 94517 593-G6
SOUTHCLIFF AV
100 SSF 94080 707-E3
SOUTHCREEK CT
- SJS 95138 875-E5
SOUTHCREST WY
5500 SCIC 95123 874-G4
5500 SJS 95123 874-G4
SOUTHDALE AV
- DALY 94015 687-A7
SOUTHDALE WY
500 WDSD 94062 789-E3
SOUTHDOWN CT
- HIL 94010 748-F4
1000 WLCK 94596 632-G1
SOUTHDOWN RD
1100 HIL 94010 748-F4
SOUTHERLAND WY
43400 FRMT 94539 773-F1
SOUTHERN FRWY I-280
- DALY - 687-C2
- DALY - 687-C4
- SF - 648-C7
- SF - 668-B1
- SF - 668-B4
- SF - 667-E7
- SF - 687-E1
- SF - 687-D2
SOUTHERN HEIGHTS AV
- SF 94107 668-A3
SOUTHERN HEIGHTS BLVD
- MrnC 94904 586-F2
- SRFL 94901 586-F2
SOUTHERN MARIN LINE
100 MrnC - 586-A4
SOUTHFIELD CT
- SJS 95138 875-E5
SOUTH FORK LN
13400 LAH 94022 810-J7
SOUTHFRONT RD
4900 LVMR 94550 696-E4
SOUTH GARDEN CT
5900 SJS 95138 875-F5
SOUTHGATE AV
- DALY 94015 687-A4
400 DALY 94015 686-J4
SOUTHGATE CT
- SJS 95138 875-E5
SOUTHGATE DR
- WDSD 94062 789-J5
- WDSD 94062 790-A5
SOUTH GATE RD
2600 CCCo - 633-H3
SOUTHGATE ST
- ATN 94027 790-D2
1400 HAY 94545 711-H6
SOUTHGREEN
- LKSP 94939 586-F6
SOUTHGROVE DR
700 SJS 95133 834-F1

SOUTHGROVE DR
700 SJS 95133 814-H3
SOUTHGROVE LN
2300 SJS 95133 814-H3
SOUTH HILL CT
200 DALY 94014 687-F3
SOUTH HILL DR
- BSBN 94005 687-H5
SOUTHLAKE COM
- FRMT 94538 773-D3
SOUTHLAKE CT
- SJS 95138 875-E5
SOUTHLAKE DR
- SJS 95138 875-E5
SOUTHLAND DR
700 HAY 94545 711-F4
SOUTHLAND PL
700 HAY 94545 711-F4
SOUTH LOOP RD
1200 ALA 94502 690-A1
SOUTHMAR CT
- SJS 95138 875-E5
SOUTHMONT CT
5900 SJS 95138 875-E5
SOUTHMOOR DR
600 PCFA 94044 707-B4
SOUTHOAKS CT
5900 SJS 95138 875-E5
SOUTHPARK CT
1700 CNCD 94519 593-A1
SOUTH PARK LN
2400 SCL 95051 833-B1
SOUTHPINE CT
- SJS 95138 875-E5
SOUTHPINE DR
5700 SJS 95138 875-E5
SOUTH POINT RD
- ORIN 94563 611-A5
SOUTHPORT CT
- SJS 95138 875-E5
100 VAL 94591 530-G5
SOUTHPORT DR
800 RDWC 94065 750-A6
SOUTHPORT WY
- VAL 94591 530-G4
SOUTH RIDGE CT
1100 CNCD 94518 592-J4
SOUTHRIDGE CT
- SMTO 94402 748-H6
5900 SJS 95138 875-E5
SOUTHRIDGE DR
- TBRN 94920 607-A4
SOUTHRIDGE DR E
- TBRN 94920 607-A5
SOUTHRIDGE DR W
- TBRN 94920 607-A4
SOUTHRIDGE WY
- DALY 94014 687-G3
SOUTH SAN FRANCISCO DR
- SSF 94080 708-A1
- SSF 94014 708-A1
300 SSF 94014 707-H1
300 SSF 94080 707-H1
SOUTHSEA CT
- SJS 95138 875-E5
SOUTH SHORE E
- MrnC 94941 606-H6
SOUTH SHORE W
- MrnC 94941 606-G6
SOUTHSHORE CT
11600 CPTO 95014 852-C4
SOUTH SHORE CTR W
500 ALA 94501 669-J3
SOUTHSIDE DR
- SJS 95111 854-H5
- SJS 95111 854-H5
SOUTHSUN CT
100 SJS 95138 875-E4
SOUTH SURF CT
5900 SJS 95138 875-E5
SOUTH TERRACE CT
- SJS 95138 875-E5
SOUTH VALLEY FRWY U.S.-101
- SCIC - 875-D4
- SJS - 875-D4
SOUTHVIEW CT
100 SJS 95138 875-E4
600 BLMT 94002 769-E1
SOUTHVIEW DR
2400 CCCo 94507 632-J4
5700 SJS 95138 875-E5
SOUTHVIEW LN
100 CCCo 94507 632-J4
SOUTHVIEW TER
- SANS 94960 566-D6
SOUTHVIEW WY
700 WDSD 94062 789-F3
SOUTHWAITE CT
- ORIN 94563 631-B5
SOUTHWEST CT
2200 MRTZ 94553 572-A7
SOUTHWEST EXWY
600 SJS 95126 853-G4
1700 SJS 95128 853-G4
SOUTHWEST PL
- BERK 94704 630-A3
- BERK 94705 630-A3
SOUTHWICK CT
5100 SJS 95136 874-F3
11800 DBLN 94568 693-F2
SOUTHWICK DR
8500 DBLN 94568 693-F2
8700 SRMN 94583 693-F2
25400 HAY 94544 711-J4
SOUTHWIND CIR
- RCH 94804 608-H3
SOUTHWIND DR
- HER 94547 570-A6
- PLHL 94523 591-H2
5800 SJS 95138 875-E5
SOUTHWOOD AV
- ROSS 94957 586-B2
400 SUNV 94086 832-E1
3600 SMTO 94403 749-B6
SOUTHWOOD CT
- OAK 94611 630-F7
- ORIN 94563 630-H1
SOUTHWOOD CTR
100 SSF 94080 707-G4

STREET
Block City ZIP Pg-Grid
SOUTHWOOD DR
- ORIN 94563 610-J6
- ORIN 94563 630-H1
- SF 94112 667-D7
100 PA 94301 791-B3
600 SSF 94080 707-F3
1300 SJS 95129 853-A4
1300 SJS 95130 853-A4
2000 CCCo 94806 569-B4
2200 PIT 94565 573-G4
2900 ALA 94501 670-B2
37400 FRMT 94536 752-G5
SOUTHWYCKE TER
2900 FRMT 94536 752-H2
SOUZA AV
5600 NWK 94560 752-F6
SOUZA CT
- ALA 94502 669-J7
22700 HAY 94541 711-H2
SOUZA WY
100 VAL 94589 510-D6
SOVEREIGN CT
8800 DBLN 94568 693-H1
8800 SRMN 94583 693-H1
SOVEREIGN WY
800 RDWC 94065 750-C6
SPAATZ CT
500 ANT 94509 595-E1
SPACE PARK DR
1100 SCL 95054 813-D7
SPACE PARK WY
- MTVW 94043 812-A1
1200 MTVW 94043 811-J1
SPADAFORE AV
900 SJS 95125 854-D7
SPADAFORE CT
900 SJS 95125 854-C6
SPADY ST
40000 FRMT 94538 753-C6
SPAGNOLI CT
300 LALT 94022 811-D5
SPAICH DR
1100 SJS 95117 853-C4
SPALDING AV
- SUNV 94087 832-E3
23900 SCIC 94024 831-E3
SPANIEL CT
4800 CNCD 94521 593-C4
SPANISH BAY CT
1900 SJS 95138 855-F7
SPANISHGATE CT
2100 SJS 95132 814-D3
SPANISH OAK CT
10000 CPTO 95014 831-J6
SPANISH TRAIL DR
2400 TBRN 94920 607-F7
2400 MrnC 94920 607-F7
SPANISH TRAIL RD
2300 TBRN 94920 607-F7
2300 MrnC 94920 607-F7
SPANOS ST
1200 ANT 94509 575-B5
SPAR AV
300 SCIC 95117 853-D1
300 SJS 95117 853-D1
SPAR CT
- PLHL 94523 592-B1
SPAR DR
600 RDWC 94065 749-H7
800 SMTO 94404 749-D2
SPARGUR DR
500 LALT 94022 811-F6
SPARKLING WY
1600 SJS 95125 853-J5
SPARKS WY
2700 AlaC 94541 692-C7
SPARLING DR
300 HAY 94544 712-B6
SPARROW CT
- DBLN 94568 694-D4
- EPA 94303 791-C2
- LVMR 94550 715-D1
- MRGA 94556 651-D1
- PLHL 94523 592-A5
1600 SUNV 94087 832-H5
SPARROW DR
100 HER 94547 569-H5
2000 FRMT 94539 773-G3
SPARROW RD
28200 HAY 94545 731-J2
SPARROW ST
- LVMR 94550 715-D1
- SF 94103 667-H2
SPARTA ST
- SF 94134 688-A1
SPARTAN CT
500 SJS 95112 854-E1
SPARTAN WY
- ANT 94509 575-C7
SPAULDING AV
2100 BERK 94703 629-F2
SPAULDING ST
100 SANS 94960 566-C7
4100 ANT 94509 595-H1
SPEAK LN
4800 SJS 95118 874-C2
SPEAR AV
600 SF 94124 668-E7
900 SF 94124 668-D7
1000 SF 94124 688-D1
SPEAR ST
- SF 94105 648-B5
SPECIALE WY
1100 SJS 95125 854-C7
SPEERS AV
1300 SMTO 94403 749-C2
SPENCE AV
100 MPS 95035 793-J7
400 FRMT 94536 753-C3
SPENCER
100 VAL 94589 510-A5
SPENCER AV
- SAUS 94965 627-A3
700 SJS 95125 854-B1
16800 LGTS 95032 873-C7
SPENCER CT
- SAUS 94965 627-B3
700 MTVW 94040 831-G1
700 LALT 94024 831-G1
2500 CCCo 94806 569-B5
5200 NWK 94560 752-F5
6900 DBLN 94568 693-J3

SPENCER LN
- ATN 94027 790-E3
2600 HAY 94542 712-D4
SPENCER PL
2500 CCCo 94806 569-B5
SPENCER RD
- ALA 94501 649-J7
SPENCER ST
- SF 94103 667-H2
6900 OAK 94621 670-F3
SPENCER WY
900 LALT 94024 831-G2
SPENDER CT
35000 FRMT 94536 752-F1
SPENGLER TR
- CCCo - 591-E6
SPENO DR
3400 SJS 95117 853-C4
SPERRY AV
100 SolC 94590 530-C6
200 VAL 94590 530-C6
SPERRY LN
15000 SAR 95070 872-H4
SPETTI DR
100 FRMT 94536 753-C2
SPICEWOOD CT
700 SJS 95120 894-H3
SPILLMAN RD
- OAK 94605 671-D2
SPINDRIFT AV
700 SJS 95134 813-F2
SPINDRIFT DR
700 SJS 95134 813-F2
SPINDRIFT LN
800 SJS 95134 813-F2
SPINDRIFT PASG
- CMAD 94925 606-J1
SPINDRIFT PL
700 SJS 95134 813-F2
SPINDRIFT ST
700 SJS 95134 813-F2
SPINDRIFT WY
700 SJS 95134 813-F2
SPINEL CT
100 HER 94547 569-G4
SPINEL PL
1400 LVMR 94550 715-D3
SPINNAKER CT
- PIT 94565 574-A3
100 VAL 94590 550-B2
200 FCTY 94404 749-H4
SPINNAKER DR
- FRMT 94538 793-F1
- SAUS 94965 627-B3
5500 SJS 95123 874-J4
SPINNAKER PL
- RDWC 94065 749-H6
SPINNAKER ST
100 FCTY 94404 749-H4
SPINNAKER WY
- BERK 94804 629-B1
100 PIT 94565 574-A3
100 VAL 94590 550-B2
2500 RCH 94804 608-H3
SPINNAKER POINT DR
- SRFL 94901 587-A2
SPINNAKER WALKWAY
5400 SJS 95123 874-J4
SPINOSA DR
800 SUNV 94087 832-D3
SPINOSA WY
- NVTO 94945 526-B1
SPIRO DR
1100 SJS 95116 834-F6
SPIROS WY
- SMCo 94025 790-D5
SPLITRAIL CT
600 LVMR 94550 695-E5
SPODE WY
300 SJS 95123 875-B6
SPOFFORD LN
- SF 94108 648-A5
SPOKANE AV
500 ALB 94706 609-E5
SPOKANE CT
48500 FRMT 94539 793-J2
SPOKANE DR
1100 SJS 95122 854-H1
SPOKANE PL
48600 FRMT 94539 793-J1
SPOKANE RD
- FRMT 94539 793-J2
SPOLETO CT
5200 PLE 94588 694-C6
SPONSON CT
6300 SJS 95123 875-B7
SPONSON LN
6200 SJS 95123 875-B7
SPOONBILL COM
34600 FRMT 94555 752-D2
SPOONBILL WY
1300 SUNV 94087 832-H4
SPOONER COVE CT
4600 UNC 94545 731-J6
SPOONWOOD CT
4200 SJS 95136 874-H1
4300 CNCD 94521 593-C5
SPORTS LN
- BERK 94704 630-A2
SPORTS PARK DR
5000 PLE 94588 714-B1
5000 PLE 94588 694-C7
SPOSITO CIR
200 SJS 95136 874-G1
SPOTORNO CT
- PLE 94566 715-B6
SPRAGUE CT
19700 AlaC 94546 691-H4
SPRAGUE LN
1100 FCTY 94404 749-G4
SPRAWLING OAKS CT
20500 SCIC 95120 895-A5
SPRECKELS AV
100 LGTS 95032 893-B1
SPRECKLES AV
1200 SJS 95002 793-C6
SPRECKLES LAKE DR
- SF - 667-A1
- SF - 666-J1
SPRIERING DR
1500 CMBL 95008 873-E2

SPRIG CT
1300 SUNV 94087 832-H4
2400 CNCD 94520 572-G4
SPRIG DR
- BEN 94510 551-F3
4000 CNCD 94520 572-G3
SPRIG WY
3900 ANT 94509 594-J1
SPRING CT
- ORIN 94563 630-G1
1000 HAY 94542 712-B4
SPRING DR
100 SJS 95138 875-C4
700 WLCK 94598 612-G3
800 MrnC 94965 606-D7
25500 HAY 94542 712-B4
SPRING LN
- BLMT 94002 769-E2
- DNVL 94526 633-A7
- DNVL 94526 632-J7
- LKSP 94939 586-E5
- TBRN 94920 607-D6
SPRING PTH
- PDMT 94611 630-C7
- PDMT 94618 630-C7
SPRING RD
- FRMT 94538 772-J3
- MrnC 94904 586-B3
- ORIN 94563 630-G1
- ROSS 94957 586-C3
- VAL 94590 530-A4
SPRING ST
- PCFA 94044 727-A3
- RDWC 94063 770-B5
- PIN 94564 569-C4
- LGTS 95032 893-B1
100 PLE 94566 714-E3
100 SF 94104 648-A5
100 SRFL 94901 586-G2
300 RCH 94804 608-J1
400 SJS 95110 834-A5
500 SAUS 94965 626-J3
500 SJS 95110 833-J4
500 SAUS 94965 627-A2
1200 SCAR 94070 769-F2
1500 MTVW 94043 811-H2
2200 SMCo 94063 770-D6
SPRING TR
- CMAD 94925 606-C5
SPRING WY
- BERK 94708 609-H7
SPRING BLOSSOM CT
20500 SAR 95070 852-D6
SPRINGBROOK AV
3500 SJS 95148 835-F7
3700 SCIC 95148 835-F7
SPRINGBROOK CT
- CCCo 94596 612-A5
2900 SJS 95148 835-F7
SPRINGBROOK DR
300 VAL 94591 530-E4
SPRINGBROOK LN
16500 AlaC 94552 672-C7
19000 SAR 95070 872-H3
SPRINGBROOK RD
1200 CCCo 94596 612-A5
1200 LFYT 94549 612-A5
1600 LFYT 94549 611-J4
1600 WLCK 94596 612-A5
1700 WLCK 94595 612-A5
SPRING CREEK LN
3400 SCIC 95035 794-G5
SPRINGCREST CT
5100 ANT 94509 595-E4
SPRING CREST TER
- FRMT 94536 752-B5
SPRINGDALE AV
5100 PLE 94588 693-H6
SPRINGDALE DR
200 PCFA 94044 707-A2
4800 SJS 95129 852-J2
SPRINGDALE LN
2800 SRMN 94583 673-F6
SPRINGDALE WY
- SMCo 94062 769-E7
SPRINGER AV
14200 SAR 95070 872-D2
SPRINGER CT
3600 WLCK 94598 613-A3
14600 SAR 95070 872-D3
SPRINGER RD
- MTVW 94040 811-G7
- LALT 94024 811-G7
600 MTVW 94040 831-G1
600 LALT 94024 831-G1
SPRINGER TER
500 LALT 94024 811-F7
SPRINGER WY
6000 SJS 95123 875-B6
SPRINGFIELD CT
5100 ANT 94509 595-E4
SPRINGFIELD DR
- SF 94132 667-A6
900 MLBR 94030 727-H4
900 SCAR 94070 769-G2
900 WLCK 94598 612-G4
1000 SRMN 94583 673-F3
1000 SJS 95130 853-B5
3900 CMBL 95008 853-B5
SPRINGFIELD PL
300 MRGA 94556 651-E3
SPRINGFIELD ST
9800 OAK 94603 671-A5
SPRINGFIELD TER
800 SUNV 94087 832-C3
SPRINGFIELD WY
600 MrnC 94965 606-D7
700 VAL 94589 509-H5
2200 SMTO 94403 749-C4
3100 SJS 95111 854-H5
SPRING GARDEN CT
- SRMN 94583 673-H3
SPRING GARDEN DR
2900 SJS 95127 834-H1
SPRING GROVE AV
- SANS 94960 566-D1
- SRFL 94901 566-D7
- SRFL 94901 586-D1
- SANS 94960 566-C7
SPRING GROVE DR
900 SJS 95126 853-J3

SPRING GROVE LN
200 SRFL 94901 586-D1
SPRINGHAVEN CT
- SJS 95111 875-A1
- SRMN 94583 673-H2
SPRING HAVEN ST
1900 LVMR 94550 696-C3
SPRING HILL CIR
- SAUS 94965 626-J2
SPRINGHILL CT
3400 LFYT 94549 611-F3
13600 SAR 95070 872-H1
SPRINGHILL DR
1300 PIT 94565 574-F7
25800 LAH 94022 811-C5
SPRINGHILL LN
- LFYT 94549 611-F3
SPRINGHILL RD
3200 LFYT 94549 611-F3
SPRING HILL WY
900 SJS 95120 894-F4
SPRINGHOUSE DR
- PLE 94588 694-D6
SPRINGKNOLL CT
3000 SCIC 95127 835-G3
SPRING LAKE CT
2100 MRTZ 94553 592-A1
SPRING LAKE DR
1900 MRTZ 94553 592-A1
1900 MRTZ 94553 591-J1
SPRINGLAKE DR
4200 SLN 94578 691-C5
SPRING MEADOW CT
6400 SJS 95135 855-J7
SPRING MEADOW LN
1300 CNCD 94521 593-A4
SPRING MOUNTAIN LN
800 AMCN 94589 510-B4
SPRINGPARK CIR
300 SJS 95136 874-G1
SPRINGPATH LN
6500 SJS 95120 894-B1
SPRINGRIDGE CT
1900 CNCD 94521 593-E3
SPRINGS RD
1200 VAL 94591 530-E4
SPRINGSIDE RD
100 CCCo 94596 612-A4
SPRINGSIDE WY
300 MrnC 94941 606-E7
SPRINGSONG CT
- SRMN 94583 673-H2
SPRINGSONG DR
1700 SJS 95131 834-D1
1700 SJS 95131 814-D7
SPRINGSTONE DR
200 FRMT 94536 732-J7
SPRINGTOWN BLVD
900 LVMR 94550 696-A3
SPRINGVALE CT
2800 CNCD 94518 592-H6
SPRINGVALE WY
2800 CNCD 94518 592-H5
SPRING VALLEY COM
1000 LVMR 94550 696-A4
SPRING VALLEY LN
- MLBR 94030 728-A5
200 MPS 95035 794-D5
SPRING VALLEY WY
- SCAR 94070 769-F3
100 SRMN 94583 673-H3
4500 CNCD 94521 593-B4
SPRINGVIEW CIR
900 SRMN 94583 673-F3
SPRINGVIEW CT
- SRMN 94583 673-H2
1300 CNCD 94521 593-B4
SPRINGVIEW LN
3100 SCIC 95127 835-G3
SPRING VISTA CT
- SRMN 94583 673-H3
SPRING WATER CT
- CCCo 94506 654-B4
SPRINGWATER DR
1800 FRMT 94539 773-G2
SPRING WATER ST
900 CCCo 94506 654-B4
SPRINGWOOD CT
900 CCCo 94572 569-J1
900 CCCo 94572 570-A1
SPRINGWOOD DR
- SRMN 94583 673-H3
600 SJS 95129 852-J2
4500 UNC 94587 732-A7
SPRINGWOOD ST
- CCCo 94572 569-J1
SPRINGWOOD WY
100 SSF 94080 707-G5
1100 ANT 94509 575-B5
1200 PCFA 94044 726-J6
4600 CNCD 94521 593-C3
SPROUL CT
6400 SJS 95120 894-E1
SPROULE LN
- SF 94108 647-J5
SPRUANCE CT
1300 SJS 95128 853-F4
SPRUANCE LN
700 FCTY 94404 749-G4
SPRUANCE ST
1100 SJS 95128 853-F3
SPRUCE
900 SJS 95138 875-F6
SPRUCE AV
- ATN 94025 790-E2
- SANS 94960 566-A6
- SSF 94080 707-J2
- MLPK 94025 790-E2
N SPRUCE AV
- SSF 94080 707-J2
400 SSF 94080 708-A2
S SPRUCE AV
- SSF 94080 707-H4
SPRUCE CT
- PCFA 94044 727-A4
800 CCCo 94572 569-J1
7900 NWK 94560 752-D7
SPRUCE DR
600 SUNV 94086 832-H2
SPRUCE LN
- LFYT 94549 611-G7
6500 DBLN 94568 693-J4

SPRUCE PL
100 NVTO 94945 525-E2
SPRUCE ST
- MLBR 94030 728-B2
- RDWC 94063 770-B7
- SF 94118 647-E5
- SolC 94591 530-D6
- VAL 94591 530-D6
300 ALA 94501 649-E7
400 BERK 94708 609-G5
400 CCCo 94708 609-G5
400 MrnC 94965 606-E7
500 BERK 94707 609-G5
600 SJS 95110 834-A5
600 OAK 94610 650-A4
1000 LVMR 94550 695-F7
1200 BERK 94709 609-H7
1200 CCCo 94553 571-F4
1300 SLN 94579 691-A4
1600 BERK 94709 629-H1
1700 SLN 94579 690-J5
2600 OAK 94606 650-A4
19700 AlaC 94546 692-B5
35800 NWK 94560 752-B6
36900 NWK 94560 772-D1
SPRUCE TER
- FRMT 94536 752-H3
SPRUCEGATE CT
3200 SJS 95148 855-E1
SPRUCE HILL CT
100 LGTS 95030 873-C3
SPRUCEMONT PL
100 SJS 95139 895-F1
SPRUCE ROCK ST
3400 SJS 95121 855-D3
SPRUCEWOOD CT
400 PLHL 94523 591-H2
SPRUCEWOOD DR
1300 SJS 95118 874-B4
SPRY COM
5600 FRMT 94538 773-A1
SPUMANTE CT
- PLE 94566 715-B6
SPUR DR
25500 AlaC 94541 712-D2
SPUR WY
4900 ANT 94509 595-J3
SPURAWAY DR
100 SMTO 94403 749-A4
SPYGLASS CT
- ANT 94509 595-D2
2400 UNC 94587 732-B4
3600 AlaC 94546 691-J4
7900 PLE 94588 714-B5
SPYGLASS DR
- NVTO 94949 546-A2
1900 SBRN 94066 707-B5
3400 SMTO 94403 749-A6
SPYGLASS LN
1700 MRGA 94556 631-C7
2200 ELCR 94530 589-D7
SPYGLASS PKWY
100 VAL 94591 550-F3
SPYGLASS HILL
- OAK 94618 630-C4
SPYGLASS HILL RD
100 SJS 95127 815-B6
SPYGLASS HILLS DR
2200 LVMR 94550 696-C2
SPYROCK CT
100 WLCK 94595 612-C7
SQUAREHAVEN CT
- SJS 95111 874-J1
SQUAW CT
2500 ANT 94509 595-G4
SQUERI DR
3400 SJS 95127 835-C3
SQUIRE CT
- CCCo 94507 633-A5
- CCCo 94507 632-J5
SQUIRECREEK CIR
3300 SJS 95121 855-D7
SQUIRECREEK LN
1500 SJS 95121 855-D7
SQUIREDELL DR
6100 SJS 95129 852-F4
SQUIREHILL CT
7700 CPTO 95014 852-C3
SQUIREWOOD WY
7500 CPTO 95014 852-D3
SQUIRREL CREEK CIR
7700 DBLN 94568 694-A1
SQUIRREL HOLLOW LN
14100 SAR 95070 872-E2
SQUIRREL RIDGE WY
300 DNVL 94506 654-B5
STAATS WY
2000 SCL 95050 833-C3
STACEY COM
200 FRMT 94539 773-H6
STACEY CT
- HIL 94010 728-E7
3400 MTVW 94040 831-J2
3500 PLE 94588 694-G5
STACEY LN
24200 AlaC 94541 712-C1
STACEY WY
3400 PLE 94588 694-F5
STACIA DR
2700 SJS 95124 873-J1
STACIA ST
- LGTS 95032 893-B1
STACY CT
- NVTO 94947 525-J3
5500 LVMR 94550 696-C6
STACY ST
4700 OAK 94605 671-E4
STADIUM AV
- MrnC 94904 586-D3
100 MrnC 94941 606-F5
STADIUM WY
- MrnC 94904 586-D3
2700 LVMR 94550 715-H3
STADIUM RIMWAY
- BERK 94704 629-J1
- BERK 94720 629-J1
STADLER DR
- WDSD 94062 809-F5
STAFFORD AV
1200 CNCD 94521 592-J4
1200 CNCD 94521 593-A4
1500 HAY 94541 692-A7

STAFFORD DR
1100 CPTO 95014 852-C3
STAFFORD PL
4900 NWK 94560 752-E4
STAFFORD RD
- MRGA 94556 631-F5
STAFFORD ST
- DALY 94015 707-C3
1400 SCAR 94070 769-J4
1400 RDWC 94063 769-J4
1900 SCL 95050 833-D4
STAG AV
2000 SMCo 94402 768-H1
STAGECOACH CT
- CCCo 94549 591-G6
STAGECOACH DR
3300 CCCo 94549 591-G6
6900 DBLN 94568 694-A3
6900 DBLN 94568 693-J3
STAGECOACH RD
7000 DBLN 94568 693-J2
7500 SRMN 94583 673-J7
7500 SRMN 94583 693-J1
STAGECOACH WY
5100 ANT 94509 595-H5
STAGEHAND DR
200 SJS 95111 875-B2
STAGELINE CT
100 VAL 94591 530-D2
STAGELINE DR
100 VAL 94591 530-D2
STAGHORN CT
1600 SJS 95121 855-A3
STAGHORN LN
1500 SJS 95121 855-A3
STAGHOUND PASG
- CMAD 94925 606-J1
STAGI CT
900 LALT 94024 831-E2
STAGI LN
800 LALT 94024 831-E1
STAHL ST
1300 SJS 95122 834-H5
STAIRLEY ST
- RCH 94801 608-D1
STALLION CT
- WLCK 94596 632-F2
STALLION RD
1100 CCCo 94803 569-D6
1100 PIN 94564 569-D6
STALLION WY
2800 SJS 95121 855-A3
STAMBAUGH ST
100 RDWC 94063 770-B6
STAMFORD CT
2600 SSF 94080 707-C4
STAMM AV
600 MTVW 94040 811-H6
STAMM DR
2700 ANT 94509 575-E6
STANBRIDGE CT
200 DNVL 94526 653-A1
200 ALA 94502 669-J5
STANBRIDGE LN
200 ALA 94502 669-J5
STANCHION LN
300 FCTY 94404 749-J1
STANDARD AV
2300 SPAB 94806 588-H3
STANDARD OIL AV
- ANT 94509 574-H5
- PIT 94565 574-H5
STANDER DR
3200 SJS 95148 855-F1
STANDISH AV
- SF 94131 667-F7
- SF 94112 667-F7
18100 AlaC 94541 691-F7
STANDISH CT
- CCCo 94525 550-D6
800 PCFA 94044 726-J5
STANDISH DR
14500 SCIC 95124 873-G3
STANDISH RD
800 PCFA 94044 726-H5
STANDISH ST
200 RDWC 94063 770-A5
STANDRIDGE CT
6400 SJS 95123 875-B7
STANFIELD CT
16700 AlaC 94552 672-C7
STANFIELD DR
600 CMBL 95008 853-F7
600 SJS 95008 853-F7
STANFORD AV
- SCIC 94304 810-F2
100 CCCo 94708 609-G3
100 MrnC 94941 606-F6
100 SMCo 94025 790-E6
200 PA 94306 791-A7
400 SMCo 94063 770-D7
500 SCIC - 791-A7
600 FRMT 94539 774-A4
600 MLPK 94025 790-E6
800 BERK 94703 629-F6
800 OAK 94608 629-F6
900 FRMT 94539 773-J4
1000 SCIC 94305 811-F3
1000 PA 94306 811-F3
1100 SCIC 94305 810-J2
1100 PA 94306 810-J2
1200 EMVL 94608 629-E6
1500 SMTO 94403 749-C2
2100 MTVW 94040 811-F3
18400 AlaC 94546 692-A3
STANFORD CT
- FRMT 94539 773-J4
- LKSP 94939 586-E4
- NVTO 94947 526-A3
- NVTO 94947 525-J4
400 LVMR 94550 716-A1
900 MLPK 94025 790-E5
14100 LAH 94022 810-H5
STANFORD DR
100 VAL 94589 510-B5
STANFORD LN
- SCAR 94070 769-H5
STANFORD PL
2300 SCL 95051 833-A2
7400 CPTO 95014 852-D3
STANFORD ST
- SF 94107 648-C7

STANFORD ST
1500 CNCD 94519 592-H2
1800 ALA 94501 669-J1
2400 UNC 94587 732-E6
STANFORD WY
- SAUS 94965 626-H1
2500 ANT 94509 595-G5
3800 LVMR 94550 715-J1
3900 LVMR 94550 716-A1
STANFORD HEIGHTS AV
- SF 94127 667-E6
STANGLAND AV
- SRFL 94901 586-F2
STANHOPE CT
1500 SJS 95121 855-A3
STANHOPE DR
2800 SJS 95121 855-A3
STANHOPE LN
1200 HAY 94545 711-G5
STANISLAUS CT
100 HAY 94544 712-A5
100 SBRN 94066 707-D7
2300 SJS 95133 834-F1
STANISLAUS DR
700 SJS 95133 834-F1
STANISLAUS WY
200 HAY 94544 712-A5
STANLEY AV
100 PCFA 94044 726-G4
900 LALT 94024 831-G2
1900 SCL 95050 833-D6
4000 FRMT 94538 773-D1
9800 OAK 94605 671-B4
STANLEY BLVD
200 AlaC 94550 715-B2
1200 PLE 94566 714-E3
3100 AlaC 94566 714-F3
3100 LFYT 94549 611-H5
4100 AlaC 94566 715-B2
E STANLEY BLVD
100 AlaC 94550 715-E1
500 LVMR 94550 715-E1
STANLEY CT
- CCCo 94595 612-A7
- CCCo 94595 611-J7
100 HER 94547 570-B5
3200 CNCD 94519 572-G7
6000 SJS 95123 875-B6
STANLEY LN
600 CCCo 94803 589-G4
STANLEY PL
100 OAK 94611 649-J2
STANLEY RD
- BURL 94010 728-H6
STANLEY ST
- SF 94132 687-C2
100 RDWC 94062 769-H7
STANLEY WY
900 PA 94303 791-B4
STANLEY DOLLAR DR
- WLCK 94595 632-A3
STANMORE CIR
100 VAL 94591 530-G5
STANMORE DR
1600 PLHL 94523 592-B4
STANNAGE AV
400 ALB 94706 609-D6
1100 BERK 94706 609-D6
1300 BERK 94702 609-D6
1400 BERK 94702 629-E1
STANTON AV
- ORIN 94563 610-E6
900 SPAB 94806 568-H7
900 SPAB 94806 588-H1
18500 AlaC 94546 691-G3
STANTON CT
- DNVL 94506 653-H5
- ORIN 94563 610-E6
6500 PLE 94566 714-D6
STANTON PL
19300 AlaC 94546 691-H4
STANTON RD
800 BURL 94010 728-D4
STANTON ST
- SF 94114 667-F3
1400 ALA 94501 669-H1
2800 BERK 94702 629-F4
STANTON TER
200 ORIN 94563 610-E6
STANTON WY
- MLV 94941 606-F2
1300 SJS 95131 814-C7
STANTON HEIGHTS CT
2700 AlaC 94546 691-H4
STANTON HILL RD
2300 AlaC 94546 691-H5
STANTONVILLE CT
200 OAK 94619 650-H4
STANTONVILLE DR
- OAK 94619 650-H4
STANWELL CIR
2300 CNCD 94520 592-E1
STANWELL DR
2300 CNCD 94520 592-E1
2400 CNCD 94520 572-E7
STANWICH RD
1600 SJS 95131 814-D5
STANWIRTH CT
1200 LALT 94024 831-J3
STANWOOD AV
25800 HAY 94544 711-J6
STANWOOD DR
1300 SJS 95118 874-B4
STANWOOD LN
3100 LFYT 94549 611-J6
STANYAN ST
- SF 94117 647-E6
- SF 94118 647-E6
100 SF 94117 667-E1
1200 SF 94117 667-E2
STAOER LN
1800 ANT 94509 575-J5
STAPLES
100 HER 94547 569-F3
STAPLES AV
- SF 94131 667-F7
100 SCIC 95127 834-J1
100 SF 94112 667-F7
300 SF 94112 667-E7
300 SCIC 95127 814-J7

STREET Block City ZIP Pg-Grid
STAPLES RANCH DR
3000 PLE 94588 694-G5
STAPLETON CT
1500 SJS 95118 874-A5
STAPLETON DR
2700 ANT 94509 574-J6
STAR AV
100 SolC 94590 530-C6
2200 AlaC 94546 692-A6
3200 OAK 94619 650-E6
STAR CT
2200 AlaC 94546 692-A6
STAR WY
- BURL 94010 728-E5
STARBIRD CIR
1100 SJS 95117 853-C3
STARBOARD CT
- MrnC 94941 606-J7
STARBOARD DR
100 VAL 94590 529-H2
400 RDWC 94065 749-H7
500 SMTO 94404 749-D1
4300 FRMT 94538 773-E5
STARBRIDGE CT
400 PLHL 94523 592-D3
STARBRIGHT DR
2200 SJS 95124 873-E2
STARBUSH DR
600 SUNV 94086 832-H2
STAR BUSH LN
1300 SJS 95118 874-B5
STARCREST DR
5400 SJS 95123 874-F3
STARDUST CT
1400 SCL 95050 833-D3
STARDUST LN
500 LALT 94024 811-F7
700 SJS 95123 874-F4
STARDUST WY
1100 MPS 95035 813-J2
STARFIRE CIR
5500 FRMT 94538 773-A1
STARFISH CT
2000 SJS 95148 835-B5
STARFISH DR
200 VAL 94591 550-D2
STARFISH LN
300 RDWC 94065 749-J2
STARFISH TER
- FRMT 94536 753-F3
STARFLOWER CT
900 SUNV 94086 832-G3
5600 NWK 94560 752-G6
STARFLOWER DR
4700 MRTZ 94553 572-A6
STARFLOWER ST
37600 NWK 94560 752-G6
STARFLOWER WY
5300 LVMR 94550 696-C4
STARGLO PL
1100 SJS 95131 814-B6
STAR JASMINE CT
- SJS 95131 814-B5
STARK ST
- SF 94133 648-A4
STARK WY
1400 SJS 95118 874-B2
STARK KNOLL PL
- OAK 94618 630-C7
STARKVILLE CT
6800 CCCo 94611 630-F5
STARLIGHT CT
700 SJS 95117 853-D2
STARLIGHT LN
2400 ANT 94509 575-B5
STARLIGHT PL
100 DNVL 94526 653-C5
STARLING AV
400 LVMR 94550 695-E7
400 LVMR 94550 715-E1
STARLING CT
- WLCK 94596 612-A2
300 MrnC 94965 606-F7
2600 PLE 94566 714-C1
STARLING DR
22200 SCIC 94024 832-A6
22400 SCIC 94024 832-A6
22400 CPTO 94024 832-A6
34800 UNC 94587 732-G7
STARLING RD
300 MrnC 94965 606-F7
STARLING ST
- DNVL 94506 653-E5
STARLING WY
100 HER 94547 569-H4
STARLING RIDGE CT
1100 SJS 95120 894-F3
STARLING VALLEY DR
7000 SJS 95120 894-E3
STARLING VIEW DR
1100 SJS 95120 894-E3
STARLITE CT
- MTVW 94043 811-J3
400 MPS 95035 813-J3
48000 FRMT 94539 793-J1
STARLITE DR
100 SMCo 94402 748-G6
1000 MPS 95035 813-J3
1600 MPS 95035 814-A3
STARLITE LN
800 LALT 94024 831-E1
STARLITE ST
100 SSF 94080 707-H4
STARLITE WY
100 FRMT 94539 793-J1
STARLYN DR
100 PLHL 94523 592-A6
STAR MINE CT
4900 ANT - 595-D4
STAR MINE TR
- CCCo - 595-B6
STAR MINE WY
4800 ANT - 595-D3
STARMONT CT
400 DNVL 94526 652-G2
STARMONT LN
- DNVL 94526 652-G2
STAR PINE WY
2000 SLN 94577 690-G1
STARR AV
300 SolC 94590 530-C5
300 VAL 94590 530-C5

STREET Block City ZIP Pg-Grid
STARR CT
500 FRMT 94539 753-J6
600 SCL 95051 833-B6
STARR LN
1300 CNCD 94521 593-A3
STARR ST
1100 CCCo 94525 550-D4
42800 FRMT 94539 753-H7
STARR WY
- MTVW 94040 811-H7
STARRETT CT
18600 SCIC 95014 852-H2
STAR RIDGE CT
12600 SAR 95070 852-C6
STARR KING CIR
3700 PA 94306 811-D1
STARR KING WY
- SF 94109 647-H6
STARS & STRIPES DR
5100 SCL 95054 813-B3
STAR TREE CT
2600 MRTZ 94553 572-A6
STARVIEW CT
100 OAK 94618 630-C4
STARVIEW DR
- OAK 94618 630-C4
300 DNVL 94526 652-G2
1700 SLN 94577 691-D2
3700 SJS 95124 873-E3
STARVIEW PL
100 DNVL 94526 652-H2
STARVIEW WY
- SF 94131 667-E4
STARWARD DR
7300 DBLN 94568 693-G3
STARWOOD CT
1100 SJS 95120 874-C6
STARWOOD DR
400 SMCo 94062 809-E6
5900 SJS 95120 874-C6
STARWOOD PL
1100 SJS 95120 874-C6
STASIA CT
100 NVTO 94947 525-F2
STASIA DR
- NVTO 94947 525-F2
STATE AV
4900 RCH 94804 609-B1
STATE CT
4800 RCH 94804 609-A1
STATE DR
- SF 94132 667-A7
STATE FRWY Rt#-4
- ANT - 575-A5
STATE PL
- OAK 94704 630-A2
STATE ST
- LALT 94022 811-D7
- SMTO 94401 728-J6
700 SJS 95110 854-C1
700 VAL 94590 530-C4
1200 SJS 95002 793-B7
2400 SLN 94577 690-G4
39000 FRMT 94538 753-A4
STATE ACCESS RD
800 NVTO 94949 546-G3
STATEN AV
300 OAK 94610 649-J3
STATE PARK RD
- BEN 94510 550-G1
STATES ST
- HAY 94544 712-C7
- SF 94114 667-F2
29200 HAY 94544 732-C1
STATICE COM
5600 FRMT 94538 773-A2
STATION AV
- DALY 94014 687-C5
STATION PL
800 BERK 94707 609-F6
STAUFFER BLVD
100 SJS 95125 854-D3
STAUFFER CT
- OAK 94619 650-H5
STAUFFER LN
11200 CPTO 95014 852-C4
STAUFFER PL
4600 OAK 94619 650-H5
STAUNTON CT
2100 PA 94306 791-A7
STAYNER RD
1200 SJS 95121 855-B5
STAYSAIL CT
200 FCTY 94404 749-H4
STEAMER LN
100 VAL 94591 550-D2
STEARMAN AV
1800 HAY 94545 711-C3
STEARNS AV
1400 OAK 94603 671-A4
1400 OAK 94603 670-J4
2500 OAK 94605 671-B4
STEBBINS AV
2100 SCL 95051 833-B2
STEDING CT
- CCCo 94596 612-F6
STEED WY
4500 ANT 94509 595-G3
STEEL ST
200 HAY 94544 712-A5
STEELE CT
- CCCo 94565 573-F1
- WLCK 94595 612-C7
STEELE DR
3300 CCCo 94565 573-F1
STEELE ST
4300 OAK 94619 650-G6
STEELHEAD TER
- FRMT 94536 753-F3
STEEPLECHASE LN
1100 CPTO 95014 852-D3
STEFFA ST
700 CCCo 94565 573-C2
STEFFAN ST
200 VAL 94591 530-D6
STEGE AV
400 RCH 94804 608-J1
600 RCH 94804 609-A1
STEIN CT
3900 SSF 94080 707-C4
STEIN WY
- ORIN 94563 630-H2

STREET Block City ZIP Pg-Grid
STEIN AM RHEIN CT
- RDWC 94063 770-C5
STEINBAUGH CT
3800 SJS 95132 814-J4
STEINBECK DR
800 SJS 95123 874-E4
STEINER ST
- SF 94117 667-G1
400 SF 94117 647-G6
1100 SF 94115 647-G6
2800 SF 94123 647-G4
3100 SF 94123 647-G4
STEINHART CT
2800 SCL 95051 833-B6
STEINMETZ WY
2800 OAK 94602 650-F4
STEINWAY AV
800 CMBL 95008 873-B1
STEITZ CT
900 SJS 95116 834-H5
STELLA CT
- PLHL 94523 592-B4
800 SUNV 94087 832-D2
6000 SJS 95123 875-A6
STELLA LN
- LKSP 94939 586-D4
STELLA ST
700 VAL 94589 510-D5
10500 OAK 94605 671-C5
STELLAR CT
3600 FRMT 94538 753-C6
STELLAR WY
1100 MPS 95035 814-A2
STELLING CT
3000 PA 94303 791-D6
STELLING DR
3000 PA 94303 791-D6
STELLING RD
800 CPTO 95014 852-D1
1000 SCIC 95014 852-D1
10000 CPTO 95014 832-D7
10100 SCIC 95014 832-D7
STEMEL CT
600 MPS 95035 794-C5
STEMEL WY
1300 MPS 95035 794-C5
STEMPLE CT
2800 SJS 95121 855-A2
STENDER WY
2200 SCL 95054 813-B7
STENDHAL LN
600 CPTO 95014 852-G2
STENERSON LN
3700 FRMT 94538 753-B5
STENHAMMER DR
37900 FRMT 94536 733-D7
STEPHANIE CT
100 VAL 94589 510-A6
1200 CNCD 94521 593-A5
3200 SJS 95132 814-F3
STEPHANIE DR
4300 CNCD 94521 593-A5
STEPHANIE LN
- CCCo 94507 632-F3
STEPHANIE WY
4100 PIT 94565 574-E6
STEPHANO CT
33500 FRMT 94555 752-C1
STEPHEN CT
100 VAL 94589 510-A5
STEPHEN DR
2800 RCH 94803 589-E2
STEPHEN RD
400 SMTO 94403 749-B6
STEPHEN WY
1300 SJS 95129 852-G4
STEPHENIE LN
15900 LGTS 95032 873-D6
STEPHENS CT
- CCCo 94525 550-D5
STEPHENS WY
- OAK 94705 630-B3
STERLING AV
200 PCFA 94044 726-G4
1000 BERK 94708 609-H6
2000 SMCo 94025 790-D6
3200 ALA 94501 670-B3
STERLING BLVD
10100 SCIC 95014 852-H2
STERLING CT
4600 FRMT 94536 752-H5
4700 ANT 94509 595-J3
STERLING DR
500 SLN 94578 691-B4
600 MRTZ 94553 591-G3
4700 FRMT 94536 752-H5
7500 OAK 94605 671-A2
8000 OAK 94605 670-J1
STERLING PL
- LVMR 94550 715-G4
STERLING RD
- LVMR 94550 696-E5
STERLING ST
- SF 94107 648-B6
100 VAL 94591 530-E1
STERLING WY
- LVMR 94550 715-G4
- CCCo 94549 611-J2
3000 RDWC 94061 789-J3
STERLING GATE CT
7000 SJS 95120 894-G4
STERLING GATE DR
1000 SJS 95120 894-G4
STERLING HILL DR
4700 ANT 94509 595-J3
STERLING OAKS DR
5900 SJS 95120 874-C6
STERLING VIEW AV
500 BLMT 94002 749-D6
STERN AV
700 PA 94303 791-D6
10000 CPTO 95014 852-H1
10000 SJS 95014 852-H1
10000 SCIC 95014 852-H1
STERN CT
- SLN 94579 691-A7
STERN LN
- ATN 94027 790-C4
1000 FCTY 94404 749-G4
STERNE CT
34200 FRMT 94555 732-E7

STREET Block City ZIP Pg-Grid
STERNE PL
2800 FRMT 94555 732-E7
STETSON AV
- CMAD 94925 606-F1
- MLV 94941 606-D2
- MrnC 94904 586-D3
STETSON CT
600 LVMR 94550 695-E6
STETSON DR
- DNVL 94506 654-A6
- DNVL 94506 653-J6
- AMCN 94589 510-A4
STETSON WY
500 LVMR 94550 695-E6
STEUART ST
- SF 94111 648-C5
- SF 94105 648-C5
STEUBEN BAY
- ALA 94502 670-A5
STEUBEN CT
3800 FRMT 94538 773-D1
STEUBEN DR
700 SUNV 94087 832-C3
STEVAL PL
3500 SJS 95136 874-D1
STEVELOE PL
- SF 94102 647-J6
STEVEN CIR
200 PLHL 94523 592-A5
200 PLHL 94523 591-J5
300 BEN 94510 551-A2
STEVEN CT
300 BEN 94510 551-A2
STEVEN DR
1000 PIT 94565 574-E6
STEVEN WY
- MrnC 94903 566-G3
STEVENS AL
- SF 94111 648-B4
STEVENS AV
1700 EPA 94303 771-C7
STEVENS CIR
800 SCIC 94043 812-A2
STEVENS CT
- TBRN 94920 607-D6
200 SCAR 94070 769-E6
1300 CMBL 95008 873-C2
3100 SJS 95148 855-E1
STEVENS LN
- LFYT 94549 611-J4
2900 SJS 95148 855-D1
STEVENS PL
1600 LALT 94024 832-A5
STEVENS RD
400 SCIC 94043 812-A2
STEVENS ST
- SRFL 94901 566-G7
- SRFL 94901 586-G1
3900 AlaC 94546 692-A5
STEVENS WY
800 SCIC 94043 812-A2
STEVENS CREEK BLVD
3100 SJS 95128 853-B1
3100 SJS 95050 853-B1
3200 SCL 95050 853-B1
3400 SCL 95117 853-B1
3400 SJS 95117 853-B1
3600 SCL 95051 853-B1
3800 SJS 95129 853-B1
4900 SJS 95129 852-E1
4900 SCL 95051 852-E1
5400 SJS 95014 852-E1
18700 SCL 95014 852-E1
18900 CPTO 95014 852-E1
18900 SCIC 95014 852-E1
23200 SCIC 95014 831-H7
STEVENS CREEK FRWY Rt#-85
- CPTO - 832-A1
- LALT - 832-A1
- MTVW - 812-A7
- MTVW - 832-A1
- SCIC - 832-A1
- SUNV - 832-A1
STEVENSON AV
- BERK 94708 609-J6
STEVENSON BLVD
- FRMT 94538 772-J2
- NWK 94560 772-J2
- FRMT 94539 753-D4
200 FRMT 94538 753-D4
4900 FRMT 94538 773-A2
5500 NWK 94560 773-A2
STEVENSON COM
- FRMT 94538 753-C5
STEVENSON DR
- PLHL 94523 592-A7
STEVENSON LN
- ATN 94027 790-D3
STEVENSON PL
39400 FRMT 94539 753-D3
STEVENSON ST
- SF 94105 648-B5
100 SF 94103 648-A6
500 SF 94103 647-J7
1300 SF 94103 667-H1
2800 SCL 95051 833-A6
2900 PIT 94565 574-C4
STEVICK DR
300 ATN 94027 790-B5
STEWART AV
- SJS 95127 834-J2
- SCIC 95127 834-J2
700 SMCo 94015 687-A4
2000 CCCo 94596 632-F1
2000 WLCK 94596 632-F1
5500 FRMT 94538 773-A3
STEWART CIR
100 PLHL 94523 592-A7
STEWART CT
- MRGA 94556 631-D3
1100 SUNV 94086 812-H6
1900 ALA 94501 649-G7
13100 SAR 95070 852-D7
STEWART DR
- SRFL 94901 566-F7
- TBRN 94920 607-B4
300 HAY 94544 712-B6
800 SUNV 94086 812-G6
STEWART LN
1800 CCCo 94509 575-H5

STREET Block City ZIP Pg-Grid
STEWART ST
- ANT 94509 595-J2
- VAL 94590 530-B5
STEWARTON DR
3400 RCH 94803 589-E1
STEWARTVILLE DR
4800 ANT - 595-D3
STEWARTVILLE TR
- CCCo - 595-A7
- CCCo - 594-G5
STIERLIN CT
2000 MTVW 94043 812-A1
2000 MTVW 94043 811-J1
STIERLIN RD
100 MTVW 94043 811-J4
STILES WY
10500 SCIC 95127 815-B7
STILL ST
- SF 94112 667-G6
STILLCREEK CT
2200 MRTZ 94553 572-A7
STILL CREEK PL
1300 DNVL 94506 653-G1
STILL CREEK RD
- WDSD 94062 809-F4
200 DNVL 94506 653-G1
STILLINGS AV
- SF 94131 667-F6
STILLMAN CT
1600 CNCD 94519 593-A2
STILLMAN ST
- SF 94107 648-B7
STILLSPRING PL
2100 MRTZ 94553 572-B2
STILLWATER COM
38700 FRMT 94536 753-C2
STILLWATER CT
4600 CNCD 94521 593-C3
STILLWATER LN
100 SJS 95139 895-F1
STILLWELL CIR
- ANT 94509 575-C6
STILLWELL DR
1500 SF 94129 647-B5
2100 HAY 94545 731-H1
STILT CT
200 FCTY 94404 749-G1
STIMEL CT
1200 CNCD 94518 592-D6
STIMEL DR
900 CNCD 94518 592-D7
STIMSON WY
3100 SJS 95135 855-F3
STINGRAY TER
- FRMT 94536 753-B2
STINSON CIR
3000 WLCK 94598 612-H1
STINSON ST
100 VAL 94591 550-E2
1000 OAK 94621 670-D6
STIRLING CT
5300 NWK 94560 752-D4
STIRLING DR
- DNVL 94526 653-D3
600 MPS 95035 794-A3
1100 CCCo 94572 570-A1
1200 CCCo - 570-B1
STIRRUP CT
2400 WLCK 94596 632-F2
STIRRUP LN
- MrnC 94947 525-F3
STIRRUP WY
4900 ANT 94509 595-J3
27700 LAH 94022 810-J5
STITTS CT
- NVTO 94945 526-A3
STIVERS ST
38600 FRMT 94536 753-B3
STOAKES AV
100 SLN 94577 671-A7
100 SLN 94577 670-J7
STOCK BRDG
- CNCD 94518 592-F4
STOCKBRIDGE AV
- ATN 94027 790-C3
- SMCo 94061 790-C3
2100 WDSD 94062 790-C3
STOCKBRIDGE DR
1300 SJS 95130 853-B4
2400 OAK 94611 650-F1
STOCKER CT
300 FRMT 94539 773-H7
STOCK FARM RD
- SCIC 94305 790-F6
STOCKHOLM RD
1900 LVMR 94550 715-G4
STOCKLMEIR CT
22000 CPTO 95014 852-A1
STOCKTON AV
- SJS 95126 834-A6
100 SJS 95126 833-J5
800 SJS 95110 833-H4
6300 ELCR 94530 609-E2
STOCKTON CT
2100 PIT 94565 574-A3
STOCKTON PL
3100 PA 94303 791-E6
STOCKTON ST
- SF 94102 648-A4
- SF 94108 648-A4
1100 SF 94133 648-A4
1400 SF 94133 648-A3
STOCKTON WY
40700 FRMT 94538 753-D6
STODDARD CT
- DNVL 94526 653-C5
STODDARD PL
- DNVL 94526 653-C5
STODDARD WY
- BERK 94708 609-J6
STOESSER CT
7100 SJS 95120 894-G4
STOKES AV
2400 PIN 94564 569-H7
2400 PIN 94564 589-H1
10200 CPTO 95014 832-B6
STOKES ST
1400 CMBL 95128 853-F4
1400 SJS 95128 853-F4
1800 SJS 95126 853-G4
STONE AV
1700 SJS 95125 854-D3

STREET Block City ZIP Pg-Grid
STONE AV
2100 SCIC 95125 854-D3
STONE CT
- CCCo 94507 632-H5
- DNVL 94526 653-C6
- SANS 94960 566-B5
400 SJS 95125 854-C3
24700 HAY 94545 711-F5
STONE DR
400 NVTO 94947 526-C7
500 NVTO 94949 526-C7
STONE LN
700 PA 94303 791-E7
STONE PL
3500 ANT 94509 595-C1
STONE RD
- BEN 94510 551-E1
STONE ST
- SF 94129 647-C3
- SF 94108 648-A5
700 OAK 94603 670-H6
1900 SPAB 94806 588-H2
STONEBRIDGE CT
500 PLHL 94523 592-D4
STONEBRIDGE DR
200 FRMT 94536 732-J7
STONEBRIDGE RD
2100 LVMR 94550 715-F4
STONEBRIDGE WY
600 PLHL 94523 592-D4
STONEBROOK CT
12300 LAH 94022 831-C2
STONEBROOK DR
10900 LAH 94024 831-D3
10900 SCIC 94024 831-D3
10900 LAH 94022 831-C3
STONEBROOK LN
- HAY 94544 732-A2
STONE CANYON CT
4400 CNCD 94521 593-C5
STONE CANYON DR
- AlaC 94542 692-E7
4300 SJS 95136 874-H1
STONECREEK CT
1400 MRTZ 94553 591-H1
STONE CREEK DR
1400 SJS 95132 814-F3
1600 SCIC 95132 814-F3
STONECRESS AV
600 NWK 94560 752-G7
600 NWK 94560 772-G1
STONECREST DR
- SF 94132 667-B7
1000 ANT 94509 595-D4
4800 ANT - 595-D4
STONECREST WY
2700 SJS 95133 814-G6
STONEDALE DR
7200 PLE 94588 693-J6
STONEFIELD CT
700 SJS 95136 854-F7
STONEFIELD PL
400 MRGA 94556 651-F3
STONEFORD
100 PIT 94565 574-A3
STONEFORD AV
300 OAK 94603 670-G7
STONEGATE CIR
200 SJS 95125 854-D3
STONEGATE CT
- CCCo 94507 632-J2
STONEGATE DR
600 SSF 94080 707-G1
2100 CCCo 94507 632-J2
2600 CCCo 94507 633-A1
STONEGATE LN
3100 CCCo 94507 632-J2
STONEGATE RD
- PTLV 94028 810-B6
STONEGATE WY
- AMCN 94589 510-C3
4900 ANT 94509 595-E4
STONEGLEN N
3700 RCH 94806 569-A7
STONEGLEN S
3600 RCH 94806 569-A7
3600 RCH 94806 568-J7
STONEGLEN CT
900 SJS 95122 854-G2
STONE HARBOR
- ALA 94502 670-A5
STONE HARBOUR DR
600 PIT 94565 574-E3
STONEHAVEN CT
- NVTO 94947 525-G2
900 WLCK 94598 612-J4
STONEHAVEN DR
600 WLCK 94598 612-J3
2000 LALT 94024 831-H5
STONEHEDGE CT
10200 SCIC 95127 835-A3
STONEHEDGE DR
1300 PLHL 94523 591-H2
STONEHEDGE PL
3300 CNCD 94518 592-H6
STONEHEDGE RD
- HIL 94010 748-H2
STONEHEDGE WY
10000 SCIC 95127 835-A3
STONEHENGE RD
3000 FRMT 94555 732-E7
STONEHILL CT
6500 SJS 95120 874-F7
STONEHILL DR
- CCCo 94526 633-A5
6500 SJS 95120 874-F7
STONEHURST CT
- CCCo 94553 591-C2
7900 PLE 94588 693-H7
STONEHURST DR
800 SCIC 95008 853-F7
800 SCIC 95008 873-F1
5300 CCCo 94553 591-C2
STONEMAG WY
600 SJS 95127 814-J6
STONEMAN AV
700 PIT 94565 574-E5
STONEMAN ST
- SF 94110 667-J4
STONE PINE CT
2000 SCL 95050 833-C3

STREET Block City ZIP Pg-Grid
STONEPINE CT
- HIL 94010 748-E1
STONE PINE LN
100 MLPK 94025 790-E3
STONE PINE PT
100 SRMN 94583 673-B1
STONEPINE RD
- HIL 94010 748-E2
STONE PINE TER
- FRMT 94538 753-B3
STONE POINTE WY
3800 PLE 94588 694-E6
STONE RIDGE CT
4900 OAK 94605 651-B7
STONERIDGE CT
- HAY 94544 712-A6
STONERIDGE DR
2200 PIT 94565 574-F4
3200 PLE 94588 694-B6
3800 PLE 94566 694-E7
6700 PLE 94588 693-H6
14600 SAR 95070 872-C3
STONERIDGE MALL RD
5500 PLE 94588 693-H5
STONE VALLEY CT
- CCCo 94553 591-C2
STONE VALLEY RD
800 CCCo 94507 632-G5
2400 CCCo 94507 633-A5
2500 CCCo 94526 633-A5
2900 DNVL 94526 633-C6
STONE VALLEY RD W
3100 CCCo 94507 632-F5
STONE VALLEY WY
100 CCCo 94507 632-G4
STONE VIEW CT
- CCCo 94553 591-C2
STONEWALK CT
100 VAL 94589 510-B4
STONEWALL AV
23000 HAY 94541 711-F3
STONEWALL RD
- OAK 94705 630-A3
STONEWOOD CT
100 VAL 94591 530-F7
STONEWOOD DR
37400 FRMT 94536 752-G5
STONEWOOD LN
1900 SJS 95132 814-E2
STONEWOOD PL
1400 CNCD 94520 592-F3
STONEWOOD WY
4900 ANT 94509 595-E4
STONEY CT
900 ANT 94509 595-F1
900 MLBR 94030 727-H4
STONEYBROOK AV
- SF 94112 667-H7
STONEYBROOK CT
400 CCCo 94506 654-D5
STONEYBROOK DR
1000 MRTZ 94553 571-H6
STONEY CREEK DR
1300 SRMN 94583 694-A1
STONEYFORD AV
- SF 94112 667-H7
STONEYFORD DR
600 SMCo 94015 687-A5
700 DALY 94015 687-A5
STONEY GORGE WY
1200 ANT 94509 595-E4
STONEYHAVEN WY
4400 SJS 95111 874-J1
STONEY POINT PL
- SMCo 94402 768-G2
STONEY RIDGE PL
100 WLCK 94596 612-D5
STONEY RIDGE RD
100 VAL 94589 510-B5
STONINGTON AV
1000 SPAB 94806 588-H1
STONINGTON CT
- DNVL 94526 653-A1
STONINGTON TER
38600 FRMT 94536 753-C2
STONINGTON POINTE
- ALA 94502 670-A6
STONYBROOK RD
100 LGTS 95032 873-C7
STONYDALE DR
10100 CPTO 95014 832-A7
STONY HILL RD
800 TBRN 94920 607-C6
900 RDWC 94061 789-H2
STONYLAKE CT
1100 SUNV 94089 812-J5
STORER AV
3200 OAK 94619 650-F7
STORER DR
300 MrnC 94941 606-H5
STOREY AV
1200 SF 94129 647-C3
STOREY LN
4100 CNCD 94518 593-A4
4100 CNCD 94518 592-J4
STORRIE ST
- SF 94114 667-F2
STORY CT
1300 SJS 95127 835-C3
STORY LN
3300 SJS 95127 835-C3
3300 SCIC 95127 835-C3
STORY RD
1200 SJS 95122 834-F7
1600 SJS 95116 834-H5
2700 SJS 95127 834-H5
3500 SJS 95127 835-B2
4000 SCIC 95127 835-B2
7500 SCIC 95127 835-B2
STORY BOOK CT
700 NVTO 94947 526-A4
STORY BOOK LN
1100 SJS 95116 834-E5
STORYBOOK WK
- ALA 94501 669-G3
STORY HILL LN
28000 LAH 94022 810-H7
STOUT
100 HER 94547 569-F3
STOVER ST
500 SJS 95110 834-A7

STREET Block	City	ZIP	Pg-Grid
STOW AV			
400	OAK	94606	649-J4
1700	WLCK	94596	612-C5
STOW LN			
900	LFYT	94549	611-H6
STOWA WY			
-	DALY	94014	687-D5
STOWBRIDGE CT			
-	DNVL	94526	653-A1
STOWE AV			
1800	SJS	95116	834-F4
STOWE COM			
35600	FRMT	94536	752-F2
STOWE CT			
-	SMCo	94025	810-F1
STOWE LN			
-	SMCo	94025	810-E1
STOWELL AV			
300	SUNV	94086	812-E6
STOW LAKE DR			
-	SF	-	667-B1
STOW LAKE DR E			
-	SF	-	667-B1
STRAITS VIEW DR			
1900	TBRN	94920	607-F7
STRAITWOOD CT			
3500	ANT	94509	595-H1
STRANAHAN CIR			
200	CLAY	94517	593-H7
STRAND AV			
200	PLHL	94523	592-A5
200	PLHL	94523	591-J5
STRAND CT			
-	PLHL	94523	591-J5
300	AMCN	94589	509-J3
STRAND RD			
2000	CCCo	94596	612-D7
STRANG AV			
2000	AlaC	94578	691-F4
STRANG CT			
-	ORIN	94563	630-J1
STRASBOURG LN			
1800	ANT	94509	575-G6
STRATA DR			
-	VAL	94591	510-J5
STRATA ALMADEN			
1100	SJS	95120	874-D6
STRATFORD AV			
100	SLN	94577	671-A6
2200	SCIC	95124	873-F3
4600	FRMT	94538	773-C1
15000	SJS	95124	873-E3
STRATFORD CT			
-	AMCN	94589	510-B3
-	DNVL	94506	653-H5
-	PLHL	94523	592-A7
-	PLHL	94523	591-J7
100	MTVW	94040	831-J1
2100	ANT	94509	595-F1
3800	PLE	94588	694-F5
15000	MSER	95030	872-H4
STRATFORD DR			
-	SF	94132	667-B7
100	SF	94132	687-B1
1800	MPS	95035	794-B2
2800	SRMN	94583	673-F7
STRATFORD LP			
400	AMCN	94589	510-B3
STRATFORD PL			
200	LALT	94022	811-D6
STRATFORD RD			
-	CCCo	94707	609-F4
700	OAK	94610	650-A3
29000	HAY	94544	732-A2
STRATFORD ST			
100	RDWC	94062	769-J5
100	VAL	94591	530-H5
STRATFORD WY			
2000	SMTO	94403	749-A4
STRATFORD PK CT			
400	SJS	95136	874-F2
STRATHMOOR DR			
-	OAK	94705	630-C3
STRATHMORE CT			
1300	CNCD	94518	592-E6
STRATHMORE PL			
100	LGTS	95030	873-B3
STRATTON CIR			
1800	WLCK	94598	612-F2
STRATTON COM			
39400	FRMT	94538	753-A5
STRATTON CT			
23600	AlaC	94541	692-C7
STRATTON PL			
2100	SJS	95131	814-D6
STRATTON RD			
2000	WLCK	94598	612-F2
STRAUB WY			
1100	ALA	94502	669-J6
STRAUSS WY			
1300	SJS	95132	814-F5
STRAWBERRY CIR			
-	MrnC	94941	606-J4
STRAWBERRY CT			
1100	SUNV	94087	832-D3
1300	DNVL	94526	653-B6
2600	ANT	94509	595-G4
STRAWBERRY DR			
100	MrnC	94941	606-J5
STRAWBERRY LN			
-	MrnC	94941	606-J6
500	SJS	95129	853-B2
1300	DNVL	94526	653-B6
1700	MPS	95035	794-D6
STRAWBERRY LNDG			
-	MrnC	94941	606-J5
STRAWBERRY PARK DR			
4200	SJS	95129	853-A2
4700	SJS	95129	852-J2
STRAWFLOWER LN			
5600	SJS	95118	874-B5
STRAWFLOWER WY			
40200	FRMT	94538	773-A1
STRAYER DR			
1000	SJS	95129	852-G3
STRAYHORN RD			
1900	PLHL	94523	591-J3
STREAMBED PL			
11500	DBLN	94568	693-E4
STREAMWOOD CT			
3300	ANT	94509	595-H1

STREET Block	City	ZIP	Pg-Grid
STRELOW CT			
6100	SJS	95120	874-C7
STRENTZEL LN			
100	CCCo	94553	591-E1
STRETFORD RD			
-	CCCo	94553	571-F3
STRICKROTH DR			
700	MPS	95035	794-A5
STRIPED MAPLE CT			
4300	CNCD	94521	593-B5
STRIPER COM			
-	FRMT	94536	753-C3
STROBRIDGE AV			
1600	AlaC	94546	691-J6
1700	HAY	94546	691-J6
STROMBERG CT			
27500	HAY	94545	731-G1
STROUD PL			
400	SJS	95111	854-H6
STRYKER ST			
26100	HAY	94545	711-F6
STUART CT			
-	LALT	94022	811-E6
1700	BEN	94510	550-J2
STUART PL			
-	DNVL	94526	653-E3
STUART ST			
1000	LFYT	94549	611-G6
1500	BERK	94703	629-F3
2100	BERK	94705	629-H3
3100	OAK	94602	650-B4
STUBBINS WY			
1400	SJS	95132	814-E4
STUBBS RD			
-	PLHL	94523	592-B3
STUCKEY DR			
4900	SJS	95124	873-G4
STUDEBAKER CIR			
5300	SJS	95123	874-H3
STUDEBAKER RD			
1100	CCCo	94595	612-A6
STUDENT LN			
4500	SJS	95130	853-A5
STUDIO CIR			
400	SMTO	94401	728-H7
STUGUN CT			
-	PLHL	94523	592-A3
STULMAN DR			
300	MPS	95035	794-D7
STURBRIDGE CT			
500	WLCK	94598	612-J2
STURDIVANT AV			
-	SANS	94960	586-C1
STURGEON COM			
-	FRMT	94536	753-C3
STURGEON WY			
1300	SJS	95129	852-G4
STURLA DR			
2400	SJS	95148	855-C1
STUTZ AL			
400	VAL	94590	529-J3
500	VAL	94590	530-A3
STUTZ WY			
2900	SJS	95148	855-D1
STUYVESANT DR			
200	MrnC	94960	566-A3
SUBLETT DR			
25600	HAY	94544	712-A4
SUDAN LN			
-	SCAR	94070	769-D5
SUDAN LP			
-	CCCo	94553	572-C6
SUDBURY CT			
100	MPS	95035	794-A5
SUDBURY DR			
-	MPS	95035	794-A5
SUDDARD CT			
6300	PLE	94588	694-B7
SUE AV			
2500	SJS	95111	854-G3
SUEIRRO ST			
700	HAY	94541	711-E3
SUENEN CT			
1900	WLCK	94595	632-B1
SUENO DR			
3200	SJS	95148	835-D6
SUENO WY			
2300	FRMT	94539	753-E6
SUEZ DR			
100	CCCo	94553	572-C7
SUFFIELD AV			
-	SANS	94960	566-A5
SUFFOLK CT			
1100	LALT	94024	831-H2
SUFFOLK DR			
100	SLN	94577	670-J7
1300	SJS	95127	835-A5
SUFFOLK LN			
100	VAL	94591	530-E2
SUFFOLK WY			
1000	LALT	94024	831-H2
4000	PLE	94588	694-E6
SUFONET DR			
2100	SJS	95124	873-F4
SUGAR BEET WY			
3100	UNC	94587	732-A4
SUGARBERRY LN			
3100	WLCK	94598	592-H7
SUGARBUSH PL			
3900	AlaC	94546	691-H2
SUGAR CREEK CT			
100	CCCo	94507	633-A4
SUGARCREEK CT			
3400	SJS	95121	855-D7
SUGARCREEK DR			
3400	SJS	95121	855-D7
SUGAR CREEK LN			
100	CCCo	94507	633-A3
SUGAR HILL DR			
-	HIL	94402	748-G5
SUGARLAND CIR			
4600	CNCD	94521	593-C5
SUGARLAND CT			
4400	CNCD	94521	593-C5
SUGAR LOAF DR			
-	TBRN	94920	607-E5
SUGARLOAF DR			
1300	CCCo	94507	632-F3
1600	SMTO	94403	748-J7
1600	SMTO	94403	768-J1
SUGARLOAF LN			
-	CCCo	94507	632-F3

STREET Block	City	ZIP	Pg-Grid
SUGARLOAF TER			
-	CCCo	94507	632-F3
SUGAR MAPLE CT			
-	HAY	94544	712-E7
4300	CNCD	94521	593-C5
SUGAR MAPLE DR			
100	SJS	95136	874-H1
4000	CCCo	94506	653-J4
4000	CCCo	94506	654-A4
SUGARPINE AV			
800	SUNV	94086	832-H3
SUGAR PINE CT			
2800	SJS	95121	855-E3
36600	NWK	94560	752-C7
SUGAR PINE LN			
-	CCCo	94506	654-A3
SUGAR PINE ST			
1900	ANT	94509	575-J6
SUGAR PINE WY			
4100	LVMR	94550	696-A4
4100	LVMR	94550	695-J4
SUGARPLUM DR			
2500	SJS	95148	835-D7
SUGARTREE DR			
2100	PIT	94565	573-J3
SUISSE DR			
400	SJS	95123	874-J6
SUISUN AV			
-	CCCo	94565	573-H1
200	CCCo	94572	549-J7
500	CCCo	94572	569-H1
2500	SJS	95121	855-D3
SUISUN CT			
500	CLAY	94517	593-H6
SUISUN DR			
20000	CPTO	95014	852-E2
SULGRAVE LN			
-	SRFL	94901	567-E5
SULLIVAN AV			
-	DALY	94015	687-B5
100	SMCo	94015	687-B5
800	CNCD	94518	592-H6
1900	SJS	95122	834-H6
15300	SLN	94579	691-B6
SULLIVAN DR			
-	MRGA	94556	631-C5
500	MTVW	94041	812-A7
3700	SCL	95051	832-H7
SULLIVAN ST			
2000	SMTO	94403	749-C4
2400	CCCo	94806	569-A5
SULLIVAN UNPS			
-	FRMT	94536	733-B7
-	FRMT	94536	753-B1
SULLIVAN WY			
20900	SAR	95070	872-C2
SULLY ST			
42600	FRMT	94539	753-G7
SULPHER SPRINGS TR			
-	CCCo	-	652-F2
SULPHUR DR			
2500	AlaC	94541	712-C1
SULPHUR SPRING CT			
3000	SJS	95148	855-E1
SULTAN PL			
5400	SJS	95123	875-B3
SULTANA DR			
1000	SJS	95122	854-G1
SULU CT			
6400	SJS	95119	875-C7
SUMAC CIR			
1300	CNCD	94521	593-D5
SUMAC CT			
-	NVTO	94945	526-A1
SUMAC DR			
1000	MPS	95035	813-H2
1000	SUNV	94086	832-G3
SUMAC ST			
32700	UNC	94587	732-F3
SUMAC WY			
900	FRMT	94539	773-J5
SUMATRA AV			
1800	SJS	95122	834-H7
SUMATRA ST			
1000	HAY	94544	712-A7
1400	HAY	94544	711-J7
1400	HAY	94544	731-J1
SUMBA CT			
200	SJS	95123	874-J3
SUMMER AV			
1100	BURL	94010	728-E5
SUMMER CT			
1200	PLE	94566	714-D2
2300	SJS	95116	834-H4
SUMMER DR			
100	SJS	95138	875-D4
SUMMER PL			
-	AlaC	94546	692-A4
5600	SJS	95138	875-D4
SUMMER ST			
2200	BERK	94709	609-H7
2300	SJS	95116	834-H4
SUMMER WY			
1100	PIT	94565	573-J2
SUMMERAIN CT			
1000	SJS	95122	854-F2
SUMMERBROOK CT			
5700	SJS	95123	874-E4
SUMMERBROOK LN			
800	SJS	95123	874-E4
SUMMER CREEK DR			
3100	SJS	95136	854-D7
SUMMER CREEK LN			
400	SRMN	94583	673-F4
SUMMERCREST CT			
-	AlaC	94552	692-G2
SUMMERDALE DR			
1000	SJS	95132	814-F6
SUMMERDAYS CT			
2800	SJS	95132	814-F6
SUMMER EVE CT			
2200	SJS	95122	854-G1
SUMMERFIELD CT			
-	DNVL	94506	653-F5
SUMMERFIELD DR			
-	CMBL	95008	853-A7
200	CCCo	94565	573-G3
900	SJS	95121	854-H4
SUMMERFIELD ST			
-	DNVL	94506	653-G5
SUMMERFORD CIR			
200	SRMN	94583	673-F4

STREET Block	City	ZIP	Pg-Grid
SUMMERGARDEN CT			
1000	SJS	95132	814-G6
SUMMERGLEN PL			
-	AlaC	94552	692-G2
SUMMERGLEN TER			
-	AlaC	94552	692-G2
SUMMERHEIGHTS DR			
2700	SJS	95132	814-F6
SUMMERHILL AV			
24000	LAH	94024	831-E2
24000	SCIC	94024	831-E2
24700	LALT	94024	831-E2
SUMMER HILL CT			
-	DNVL	94526	653-B6
SUMMERHILL CT			
-	SRFL	94903	566-E4
3000	SJS	95148	855-G1
12700	SCIC	94024	831-E2
SUMMERHILL LN			
100	CCCo	94553	591-D2
100	WDSD	94062	789-J3
SUMMERHILL WY			
-	SRFL	94903	566-E4
SUMMER HOLLY COM			
-	FRMT	94536	752-G5
SUMMER HOLM PL			
-	HIL	94010	728-F7
SUMMERLAND DR			
400	SJS	95134	813-C2
SUMMERLEAF DR			
900	SJS	95120	894-G1
SUMMERLEAF PL			
900	SJS	95120	894-G1
SUMMERMIST CT			
1000	SJS	95122	854-G2
SUMMERPARK CT			
1000	SJS	95132	814-F6
SUMMERPARK PL			
-	AlaC	94552	692-G2
SUMMERPLACE DR			
900	SJS	95122	854-G1
SUMMERPOINTE PL			
-	AlaC	94552	692-G2
SUMMERRAIN DR			
100	SSF	94080	707-G2
SUMMERRIDGE DR			
-	AlaC	94552	692-G2
SUMMERS AV			
-	NVTO	94945	526-D3
SUMMERSET CT			
100	SRMN	94583	673-G4
SUMMERSHORE CT			
1000	SJS	95122	854-F2
SUMMERSIDE CIR			
100	DNVL	94526	653-C6
SUMMERSIDE DR			
900	SJS	95122	854-G2
900	SCIC	95122	854-G2
SUMMERSONG CT			
1000	SJS	95132	814-G6
SUMMERSVILLE CT			
-	VAL	94591	550-D2
SUMMERTON DR			
2100	SJS	95122	854-G2
SUMMERTREE CT			
-	LVMR	94550	715-D1
1000	SJS	95132	814-F6
SUMMERTREE DR			
-	LVMR	94550	715-D1
SUMMER VALLEY CT			
500	SRMN	94583	673-J6
SUMMERVIEW CT			
300	SRMN	94583	673-F4
SUMMERVIEW DR			
1000	SJS	95132	814-F6
SUMMERWIND CT			
1000	SJS	95132	814-F6
SUMMERWIND DR			
100	MPS	95035	793-J5
SUMMERWIND WY			
1100	MPS	95035	793-J5
SUMMERWINGS CT			
1000	SJS	95132	814-F6
SUMMERWOOD CT			
1000	SJS	95132	814-F6
SUMMERWOOD DR			
300	FRMT	94536	732-J6
SUMMERWOOD LP			
100	SRMN	94583	673-F4
SUMMERWOOD PL			
800	CNCD	94518	592-G6
SUMMIT AV			
-	MrnC	94965	606-C1
-	MLV	94941	606-C1
-	SRFL	94901	587-A1
100	MrnC	94901	587-A1
100	MrnC	94901	586-J1
200	MrnC	94901	566-J7
300	SRFL	94901	566-J7
5200	SCIC	95127	814-J7
SUMMIT CIR			
-	WLCK	94598	612-E5
SUMMIT CT			
-	PIN	94564	569-E4
-	SMCo	94062	789-F1
-	SSF	94080	707-E5
800	SUNV	94087	832-D2
18600	AlaC	94546	692-B3
SUMMIT DR			
-	VAL	94591	510-E7
-	CMAD	94925	606-E1
-	CMAD	94925	586-F7
100	SMCo	94062	789-F1
100	LKSP	94939	586-F7
300	PIN	94564	569-E4
2100	BURL	94010	728-C7
2100	SMCo	94010	728-B7
2200	HIL	94010	728-C7
2800	SMCo	94010	748-B1
2800	HIL	94010	748-B1
2900	FRMT	94555	732-D6
W SUMMIT DR			
-	SMCo	94062	789-F1
SUMMIT LN			
-	BERK	94708	610-A7
-	CMAD	94925	606-C5
-	MrnC	94945	526-H3
SUMMIT PL			
300	RCH	94801	588-C7
SUMMIT RD			
-	CCCo	-	633-J1
-	MrnC	94903	566-J3

STREET Block	City	ZIP	Pg-Grid
SUMMIT RD			
-	WDSD	94062	809-G6
-	SANS	94960	566-A7
-	FRFX	94930	566-A7
100	WLCK	94598	612-E5
1200	LFYT	94549	611-H4
1300	BERK	94708	610-A7
3100	SBRN	94066	707-C5
SUMMIT ST			
-	SF	94112	687-E1
2800	OAK	94609	649-H2
SUMMIT TR			
-	CCCo	-	652-F2
-	CMAD	94925	606-C5
-	MLV	94941	606-C5
SUMMIT WY			
500	RDWC	94062	789-F3
500	SMCo	94062	789-F3
17000	LGTS	95030	873-B4
SUMMIT PARK CT			
8400	ELCR	94530	609-E1
SUMMIT PARK LN			
8400	ELCR	94530	589-E7
8400	ELCR	94530	609-E1
SUMMIT RIDGE CT			
3600	SJS	95148	835-G7
SUMMIT RIDGE PL			
-	SMCo	94062	789-G1
SUMMIT SPRINGS RD			
400	WDSD	94062	789-E7
SUMMIT SPRINGS FIRE RD			
-	SMCo	94062	789-A6
SUMMIT VIEW DR			
1200	CNCD	94521	593-B4
3200	SRMN	94583	673-J6
SUMMIT VIEW TER			
-	FRMT	94539	794-B1
SUMMIT WOOD CT			
11500	LAH	94022	831-C3
SUMMIT WOOD RD			
11400	LAH	94022	831-B3
SUMNER DR			
12400	SAR	95070	852-E6
SUMNER PL			
-	HAY	94541	692-B7
SUMNER ST			
-	SF	94129	647-E4
-	SF	94129	647-E4
-	SF	94129	647-E4
-	SF	94103	648-A7
SUMNER MEADOWS CT			
-	CCCo	94507	632-G3
SUMTER AV			
43100	FRMT	94538	773-E2
SUN AV			
100	HAY	94544	712-B7
SUN CT			
-	MRTZ	94553	571-H6
1100	MPS	95035	814-A2
3000	RCH	94803	589-E1
SUN LN			
700	NVTO	94947	525-H3
1500	SJS	95132	814-F3
SUNBEAM CIR			
1300	SJS	95122	834-G6
SUNBEAM LN			
-	SF	94112	687-F1
SUNBERRY DR			
200	CMBL	95008	853-D5
SUN BLOSSOM DR			
100	SJS	95123	875-A3
SUNBROOK CT			
3700	SJS	95111	855-A6
SUNBURST CT			
1200	WLCK	94596	632-G1
SUNBURST DR			
200	HAY	94544	712-A5
2900	SJS	95111	854-G5
SUNBURST LN			
5100	LVMR	94550	696-B5
SUNCLIFF PL			
-	VAL	94591	550-D2
SUN CLOUD CT			
5500	CNCD	94521	593-E7
SUNCREST AV			
3300	SJS	95132	814-H5
3800	SJS	95132	815-A4
SUNCREST CT			
1600	WLCK	94596	612-C1
SUND AV			
-	SCIC	95032	893-B1
100	LGTS	95032	893-B1
SUNDALE CT			
39500	FRMT	94538	753-A6
SUNDALE DR			
39000	FRMT	94538	753-B5
40300	FRMT	94538	773-B1
SUNDALE RD			
3600	LFYT	94549	611-D7
SUNDANCE CT			
2600	WLCK	94598	612-H4
5100	ANT	94509	595-H4
SUNDANCE DR			
900	FRMT	94539	773-J5
1000	FRMT	94539	774-A5
5100	LVMR	94550	696-B5
SUNDANCE WY			
300	NVTO	94945	526-B1
5000	ANT	94509	595-H4
SUNDBERG AV			
1800	SLN	94577	690-J2
SUNDERLAND DR			
7900	CPTO	95014	852-C3
SUNDEW CT			
4300	HAY	94542	712-G4
SUNDIAL CIR			
700	LVMR	94550	696-B4
SUNDOWN LN			
1200	SJS	95127	835-A4
SUNDOWN RD			
4100	LVMR	94550	696-A3
SUNDOWN TER			
200	ORIN	94563	611-A3
200	ORIN	94563	610-J3
SUNDOWN CANYON WY			
10500	LAH	94024	831-E5
SUNDROP CT			
7400	PLE	94588	714-A2
7400	PLE	94588	713-J2

STREET Block	City	ZIP	Pg-Grid
SUNFISH COM			
-	FRMT	94536	753-C3
SUNFISH CT			
100	VAL	94591	550-D1
300	FCTY	94404	749-H3
SUNFLOWER CT			
100	HER	94547	570-A4
600	SRMN	94583	653-J7
700	CNCD	94518	592-J6
4100	UNC	94587	732-A6
5300	LVMR	94550	696-B4
SUNFLOWER DR			
2800	ANT	94509	575-G7
3000	ANT	94509	595-H1
SUNFLOWER LN			
5600	SJS	95118	874-B5
SUNFLOWER ST			
1500	SLN	94578	691-C4
SUNGLEN WY			
-	DNVL	94506	653-G2
SUN GLORY LN			
2200	SJS	95124	873-F1
SUNGLOW LN			
-	SF	94112	667-H7
SUNGOLD CIR			
800	LVMR	94550	696-B4
SUNHAVEN RD			
100	DNVL	94506	653-G2
SUNHILL			
-	PTLV	94028	830-C2
SUNHILL CIR			
-	CCCo	94803	589-D1
SUNHILL CT			
1600	MRTZ	94553	571-J6
SUNHILL LN			
400	MRTZ	94553	571-J6
SUNHILLS DR			
16400	SCIC	94024	831-F5
SUNKEN GARDENS TER			
900	SUNV	94086	832-G3
SUNKIST CT			
300	LALT	94022	811-F5
SUNKIST DR			
6800	OAK	94605	670-J1
7600	OAK	94605	671-A2
SUNKIST LN			
-	LALT	94022	811-F6
SUNLAND CT			
1400	SJS	95130	853-A4
SUNLAND ST			
-	FRMT	94538	753-C6
SUNLEAF WY			
3400	RCH	94806	568-J7
SUNLIGHT CIR			
1100	CNCD	94518	593-A5
SUNLIGHT CT			
4400	CNCD	94518	593-A5
SUNLITE DR			
800	SCL	95050	833-C5
SUNMOR AV			
1900	MTVW	94040	832-A1
SUNNY CT			
1100	SJS	95116	834-F5
1500	WLCK	94595	612-D7
SUNNY DR			
-	SANS	94960	566-C7
SUNNY LN			
400	CCCo	94803	569-E7
2400	ANT	94509	575-B6
SUNNY PL			
1600	HAY	94545	711-H6
4700	CNCD	94521	593-C3
SUNNYARBOR CT			
800	CMBL	95008	873-C1
SUNNYBANK LN			
2800	AlaC	94541	712-C1
SUNNYBANK PL			
23900	AlaC	94541	712-C1
SUNNYBRAE BLVD			
500	SMTO	94402	749-B2
SUNNYBRAE CT			
100	MRTZ	94553	591-G2
SUNNYBRAE DR			
200	MRTZ	94553	591-H2
SUNNYBRAE LN			
900	NVTO	94947	526-D7
SUNNYBROOK CT			
400	CMBL	95008	853-D7
3200	AlaC	94541	692-F6
18900	SAR	95070	852-H4
SUNNYBROOK DR			
400	CMBL	95008	853-C7
900	LFYT	94549	611-C6
SUNNYBROOK PL			
100	SRMN	94583	673-F7
SUNNYBROOK RD			
1400	CCCo	94507	632-E3
SUNNYBROOK WY			
5900	LVMR	94550	696-C3
SUNNY COVE CIR			
-	ALA	94502	670-A5
SUNNY CREEK DR			
5100	SJS	95135	855-G5
SUNNY CREEK PL			
5100	SJS	95135	855-G5
SUNNYCREST AV			
-	MLV	94941	606-C3
SUNNYCREST CIR			
1300	SJS	95122	854-H1
SUNNYCREST CT			
2600	FRMT	94539	753-F7
SUNNYDALE AV			
-	SCAR	94070	769-H5
-	SF	94134	688-A2
400	SF	94134	687-H2
2200	SF	94112	687-H2
SUNNYDALE CT			
100	HAY	94544	732-D1
3500	SJS	95117	853-C3
SUNNYDAYS LN			
3500	SCL	95051	832-J3
SUNNYGATE CT			
3500	SJS	95117	853-C3
SUNNYGLEN DR			
100	VAL	94591	530-F7
2500	SJS	95122	835-A6
SUNNYHAVEN DR			
1100	SJS	95117	853-C3
SUNNYHAVEN ST			
15300	SLN	94579	691-A7
SUNNY HILL RD			
-	SMCo	94062	789-E1

STREET Block	City	ZIP	Pg-Grid
SUNNYHILL RD			
-	NVTO	94945	526-B2
SUNNYHILL WY			
-	PIT	94565	574-C6
SUNNYHILLS CT			
100	MPS	95035	793-J4
SUNNY HILLS DR			
-	SANS	94960	566-C6
300	MrnC	94901	566-C6
SUNNYHILLS DR			
1600	MPS	95035	793-J3
SUNNY HILLS RD			
900	LFYT	94549	611-A6
SUNNYHILLS RD			
800	OAK	94610	650-B3
SUNNYLAKE CT			
3500	SJS	95117	853-C4
SUNNYMEAD CT			
3500	SJS	95117	853-C4
SUNNY MEADOW LN			
3000	SJS	95135	855-G5
SUNNY MEADOW PL			
3000	SJS	95135	855-G5
SUNNYMERE AV			
6200	OAK	94605	670-J1
6500	OAK	94605	650-H7
SUNNYMOUNT AV			
500	SUNV	94087	832-D2
E SUNNYOAKS AV			
-	CMBL	95008	873-D1
W SUNNYOAKS AV			
200	CMBL	95008	873-C1
SUNNY OAKS DR			
-	MrnC	94903	566-H3
5500	SJS	95123	874-F4
SUNNY ORCHARD LN			
5200	SJS	95135	855-G5
SUNNYPARK CT			
800	CMBL	95008	873-C1
SUNNYSIDE AV			
-	CMAD	94925	606-G1
-	CMBL	95008	853-E6
-	MLV	94941	606-D3
-	SANS	94960	586-B1
100	PDMT	94610	650-A1
100	PDMT	94611	650-A1
SUNNYSIDE CT			
-	CMAD	94925	586-F7
-	ORIN	94563	610-H2
SUNNYSIDE DR			
-	SLN	94577	671-A7
1000	SSF	94080	707-F2
19000	SAR	95070	872-G5
SUNNYSIDE LN			
-	ORIN	94563	610-G3
SUNNYSIDE PL			
-	SRMN	94583	673-J6
SUNNYSIDE RD			
3000	OAK	94613	670-G1
SUNNYSIDE ST			
9000	OAK	94603	671-A5
10200	OAK	94603	670-J4
SUNNYSIDE TER			
-	SF	94112	667-E7
SUNNY SLOPE AV			
400	OAK	94610	650-A2
SUNNYSLOPE AV			
-	SCIC	95127	835-A1
100	SJS	95127	835-A1
1300	BLMT	94002	769-E1
6000	AlaC	94552	692-F4
SUNNYSLOPE RD			
200	FRMT	94536	732-J7
SUNNYSLOPES DR			
200	MRTZ	94553	571-H5
SUNNYVALE AV			
-	SUNV	94086	812-E6
200	SUNV	94086	832-E1
600	SUNV	94087	832-E1
1500	WLCK	94596	612-B1
SUNNYVALE PL			
-	WLCK	94596	612-B1
SUNNYVIEW CT			
1100	PIN	94564	569-D4
SUNNYVIEW DR			
500	PIN	94564	569-D4
SUNNYVIEW LN			
2000	MTVW	94040	831-J1
SUNNY VISTA DR			
2100	SCL	95128	833-E6
2100	SJS	95128	833-E6
SUNOL BLVD			
5300	PLE	94566	714-D6
SUNOL CT			
1000	HAY	94541	711-D2
SUNOL RD			
17900	HAY	94541	711-D2
SUNOL ST			
-	SJS	95126	833-J7
200	SCIC	95126	833-J7
200	SJS	95126	853-J1
300	SJS	95126	853-J1
400	SJS	95126	854-A1
SUNOL RIDGE TR			
38900	AlaC	94586	713-G6
39400	AlaC	94586	733-H1
SUNPARK CT			
300	SJS	95136	874-G2
SUNPARK LN			
300	SJS	95136	874-G2
SUNPARK PL			
300	SJS	95136	874-G2
SUNRAY DR			
16600	LGTS	95032	873-C5
SUN RIDGE CT			
3100	LFYT	94549	611-J4
SUNRIDGE CT			
5600	AlaC	94552	692-D3
SUN RIDGE DR			
200	SRMN	94583	673-J6
SUNRIDGE DR			
-	LVMR	94550	696-E3
SUN RIDGE LN			
100	SJS	95123	874-G7
SUNRISE AV			
-	MLV	94941	606-E4
SUNRISE CT			
-	MLPK	94025	790-E7
-	SSF	94080	707-E5
300	BEN	94510	551-C3
1300	LALT	94024	831-H3
3500	MRTZ	94553	571-D5

BAY AREA

STREET
Block City ZIP Pg-Grid

SUNRISE CT
3600 RCH 94806 568-J7
27300 HAY 94544 712-B7
27300 HAY 94544 732-B1
SUN RISE DR
- SJS 95002 813-B1
SUNRISE DR
- WDSD 94062 809-G4
600 FRMT 94539 773-H2
2200 SJS 95124 873-E3
4800 MRTZ 94553 572-A5
5100 LVMR 94550 696-B4
20500 CPTO 95014 852-D1
SUNRISE LN
- CCCo 94549 611-J2
- LKSP 94939 586-E7
- MrnC 94965 606-B4
- CMAD 94925 586-E7
100 NVTO 94949 546-G5
SUNRISE TER
- DNVL 94526 633-C6
SUNRISE WY
100 VAL 94591 530-F3
300 SF 94134 687-J2
1100 MPS 95035 813-J2
SUNRISE FARM RD
27400 LAH 94022 830-J1
SUNRISE HILL
1100 CNCD 94518 592-J4
SUNRISE HILL CT
- ORIN 94563 630-H2
SUNRISE HILL RD
- ORIN 94563 630-H2
SUNRISE RIDGE DR
- CCCo - 591-G5
SUNRISE SPRING CT
11500 CPTO 95014 852-A4
SUNRIVER COM
33200 FRMT 94555 732-C7
SUNROSE AV
5700 NWK 94560 752-F7
SUNROSE TER
900 SUNV 94086 832-G3
SUNSET AV
- VAL 94591 530-D6
100 SUNV 94086 812-D7
400 SJS 95116 834-H5
600 SSF 94080 707-G2
2300 CNCD 94519 592-G2
2700 OAK 94601 650-D6
7600 NWK 94560 752-D7
E SUNSET AV
2600 OAK 94601 650-D6
N SUNSET AV
- SJS 95116 834-G3
S SUNSET AV
- SJS 95116 834-G4
SUNSET BLVD
- SF 94116 666-J3
- SF 94116 666-J5
- SF 94122 666-J3
100 AlaC 94541 711-G1
300 HAY 94541 711-H1
800 HAY 94541 691-H7
1800 SF 94132 666-J5
W SUNSET BLVD
400 AlaC 94541 711-E2
SUNSET CIR
100 BEN 94510 551-B3
SUNSET CT
- CCCo 94707 609-F4
- DNVL 94506 654-A6
- MLPK 94025 790-D7
- NVTO 94947 526-C6
2000 SJS 95116 834-G4
3100 SMTO 94403 749-A6
21800 AlaC 94541 711-G1
SUNSET DR
- SRMN 94583 673-E3
- ANT 94509 575-D6
- CCCo 94707 609-E3
- DALY 94015 706-J2
- PLHL 94523 592-A6
200 HER 94547 570-B6
200 NVTO 94949 546-H4
300 DNVL 94506 654-A6
700 SCAR 94070 769-F5
700 LVMR 94550 695-E6
800 SCL 95050 833-C5
3500 SBRN 94066 707-B6
5200 RCH 94803 589-E1
5200 CCCo 94803 589-E1
12700 LAH 94022 831-C1
19900 SCIC 95030 872-E5
19900 SAR 95070 872-E5
SUNSET LN
- BERK 94708 609-H5
- MLPK 94025 790-D7
- MLV 94941 606-C4
2700 ANT 94509 575-D7
3400 ANT 94509 595-D1
SUNSET LP
1100 LFYT 94595 612-A6
1100 LFYT 94595 611-J6
1500 CCCo 94595 611-J6
SUNSET PKWY
200 NVTO 94947 526-B7
800 NVTO 94949 526-B7
1000 NVTO 94949 546-B1
SUNSET RD
300 ALA 94501 669-G3
300 PLHL 94523 592-A5
SUNSET TER
- CCCo 94707 609-F3
- ORIN 94563 631-B3
2600 SMTO 94403 749-A6
4000 FRMT 94536 752-F2
SUNSET TR
- TBRN - 627-G2
- BERK 94705 630-B3
- OAK 94705 630-B3
300 MrnC 94945 526-G2
SUNSET WK
- ALB 94706 609-D6
SUNSET WY
- MrnC 94965 626-A2
- SRFL 94901 566-D7
100 PIT 94565 574-E5
300 MrnC 94941 606-E7
500 SMCo 94062 789-E2
SUNSET CIRCLE DR
- SMCo - 768-C3

SUNSET GLEN DR
700 SJS 95123 874-F6
SUNSET SPRING CT
11500 CPTO 95014 852-A4
SUNSET VIEW CT
2000 SJS 95116 834-G4
SUNSHADE LN
1400 SJS 95122 834-G6
SUNSHADOW LN
1300 SJS 95127 835-A4
SUNSHINE AV
- SAUS 94965 627-B4
SUNSHINE CIR
1000 DNVL 94506 653-F5
SUNSHINE CT
700 FRMT 94539 753-G7
700 LALT 94024 811-G7
1400 OAK 94621 670-G3
1400 SJS 95122 834-G7
SUNSHINE DR
100 PCFA 94044 707-A1
700 LALT 94024 811-G7
1300 CNCD 94520 592-E4
SUNSHINE PL
3100 AlaC 94546 691-G3
SUNSPRING CIR
5500 SJS 95138 875-C4
SUNSTAR COM
5400 FRMT 94555 752-C3
SUN STREAM CT
300 CCCo 94506 654-B5
SUNSTREAM LN
5100 LVMR 94550 696-B5
SUN TREE CT
600 CCCo 94506 654-B4
SUNTREE CT
900 SUNV 94086 832-H3
SUNTREE LN
100 PLHL 94523 592-B1
SUN VALLEY AV
3000 WLCK 94596 612-B1
SUN VALLEY CT
12600 SAR 95070 852-H6
SUN VALLEY DR
- WLCK 94596 612-C1
11100 OAK 94605 671-E4
SUNVIEW AV
- SANS 94960 566-B5
SUN VIEW CT
3600 CNCD 94520 572-G5
SUNVIEW DR
- SF 94131 667-F4
15200 LGTS 95032 873-F7
SUN VIEW PL
2400 CNCD 94520 572-G5
SUN VIEW TER
1700 CNCD 94520 572-G5
SUN VIEW WY
3600 CNCD 94520 572-G5
SUNWOOD CT
3300 ANT 94509 595-H1
SUNWOOD DR
2900 SJS 95111 854-G5
7500 DBLN 94568 693-G3
SUNWOOD MDWS PL
100 SJS 95139 875-F7
SUNYVALE CT
26500 HAY 94544 712-A6
SUPERIOR AV
400 SLN 94577 671-C7
SUPERIOR DR
- CMBL 95008 853-B6
2500 LVMR 94550 715-G5
SUPERIOR RD
600 MPS 95035 794-A5
SUPREME CT
- WLCK 94596 612-B2
SUPREME DR
1900 SJS 95148 835-A6
SURBER DR
300 SJS 95123 875-A5
SURF CT
3400 SCIC 95127 814-H6
SURF DR
- PIT 94565 574-E5
SURF ST
100 PCFA 94044 706-J5
SURF WY
- NVTO 94945 526-A2
SURF BIRD ISL
200 FCTY 94404 749-G1
SURFPERCH ST
800 FCTY 94404 749-H2
SURFSIDE CT
- CCCo 94806 569-C4
SURFWOOD CIR
- SRFL 94901 567-C7
SURIAN CT
1000 SJS 95120 894-G3
SURIGAO CT
- CNCD 94520 572-H3
SURMONT CT
- CCCo 94549 591-J7
100 LGTS 95032 873-G6
SURMONT DR
100 LGTS 95032 873-G6
3100 CCCo 94549 591-J7
3200 PLHL 94523 591-J6
SURREY AV
- MLV 94941 606-F4
SURREY CT
- DALY 94015 707-C2
- DNVL 94526 633-C7
100 MPS 95035 794-D6
1600 WLCK 94598 612-E1
5300 NWK 94560 752-E4
SURREY LN
- ATN 94027 790-F2
- SRFL 94903 566-C3
4700 RCH 94803 589-J2
7600 OAK 94605 651-C7
7600 OAK 94605 671-C1
13300 SAR 95070 852-D7
SURREY PL
200 LALT 94022 811-D6
2100 SJS 95008 853-F7
3100 CNCD 94518 592-H7
SURREY ST
- SF 94131 667-F6
SURREY WY
24500 HAY 94544 711-H4

SURRY PL
3000 FRMT 94536 752-H2
SURRYHNE ST
3200 OAK 94607 649-E1
SUR VERANO
7200 SJS 95135 855-J5
SURVEY WY
- CCCo 94596 612-A5
SUSAN AV
7400 ELCR 94530 609-E4
SUSAN CT
- CCCo 94507 632-F5
900 NVTO 94947 526-D7
1500 SMTO 94403 749-D3
1600 BEN 94510 551-B4
6000 SJS 95123 874-F6
SUSAN DR
2300 SCL 95050 833-C4
3000 SBRN 94066 707-C5
SUSAN LN
1800 PLHL 94523 592-C5
5500 LVMR 94550 716-C1
SUSAN PL
27400 HAY 94544 712-A6
SUSAN ST
100 VAL 94589 509-J6
SUSAN WY
900 NVTO 94947 526-D7
1000 SUNV 94087 832-B1
SUSANA ST
400 MRTZ 94553 571-E3
SUSAN GALE CT
- MLPK 94025 790-C6
SUSANWOOD DR
4000 CNCD 94521 593-A2
SUSIE LN
2800 SCAR 94070 769-G6
SUSIE WY
300 SSF 94080 707-G2
SUSQUEHANNA CT
900 SUNV 94087 832-B3
SUSSEX CT
- SRFL 94903 566-E4
100 SRMN 94583 673-G4
300 BLMT 94002 749-E7
1200 CNCD 94521 593-A4
SUSSEX DR
2700 SJS 95127 835-A4
2700 SJS 95127 834-J4
SUSSEX PL
700 MPS 95035 794-A3
1800 MLPK 94025 790-F2
5200 NWK 94560 752-E4
SUSSEX SQ
1100 MTVW 94040 811-J7
SUSSEX ST
- SF 94131 667-F5
100 CCCo 94520 572-G2
SUSSEX WY
- RDWC 94061 789-J3
- RDWC 94061 790-A3
200 PCFA 94044 726-G4
1200 HAY 94544 732-B1
1300 CNCD 94521 593-A4
SUSSEX PARK CT
5100 SJS 95136 874-F3
SUTCLIFF AV
4700 SJS 95118 874-B3
SUTCLIFFE CT
3400 WLCK 94598 612-J2
SUTCLIFFE PL
400 WLCK 94598 612-J2
SUTER ST
3000 OAK 94602 650-D5
3500 OAK 94619 650-F6
SUTHERLAND AV
11100 CPTO 95014 852-B3
SUTHERLAND CT
1500 CNCD 94521 593-D4
4000 PLE 94588 694-E7
SUTHERLAND DR
- ATN 94027 790-B5
100 CCCo 94596 612-F6
100 WLCK 94596 612-F6
3900 PA 94303 811-F1
5000 CNCD 94521 593-D4
SUTRO AV
700 NVTO 94947 525-G3
SUTRO CT
- NVTO 94947 525-G3
SUTRO DR
2500 SJS 95124 873-H1
SUTRO ST
1200 SPAB 94806 588-G4
22700 HAY 94541 711-J2
SUTRO HEIGHTS AV
- SF 94121 646-H7
SUTTER AV
700 PA 94303 791-C6
800 SUNV 94086 832-D1
800 SUNV 94086 812-C7
1300 SPAB 94806 588-G3
2100 SCL 95050 833-C7
5400 RCH 94804 609-C3
SUTTER CT
- CCCo 94565 573-G2
- TBRN 94920 607-B5
SUTTER DR
39000 FRMT 94538 752-J6
39300 FRMT 94538 753-A6
SUTTER ST
- SF 94104 648-A5
- SJS 95110 854-C1
100 SF 94108 648-A5
400 VAL 94590 530-A5
500 SF 94102 648-A5
600 SF 94102 647-F6
700 SF 94109 647-F6
1000 BERK 94707 609-G6
1100 BERK 94709 609-G6
1500 CNCD 94520 592-E2
1600 LVMR 94550 695-E5
1700 SF 94115 647-F6
SUTTER CREEK CIR
5000 SJS 95136 875-A2
SUTTER CREEK LN
- MTVW 94043 811-J3
SUTTER GATE AV
4400 PLE 94566 694-D7
SUTTERGATE CT
2100 SJS 95132 814-D3

SUTTERGATE WY
2900 SJS 95132 814-D3
SUTTERS MILL CT
- WLCK 94596 612-D5
SUTTERWIND DR
- MPS 95035 794-A6
SUTTON AV
- SSF 94080 707-D1
SUTTON CIR
- DNVL 94506 653-H5
SUTTON CT
- DNVL 94506 653-H5
600 WLCK 94598 612-H6
3200 FRMT 94536 752-J3
SUTTON DR
600 WLCK 94598 613-A3
14800 SCIC 95124 873-H4
SUTTON LN
- MrnC 94945 526-G2
7500 DBLN 94568 693-H3
SUTTON LP
3300 FRMT 94536 752-J3
SUTTON PARK PL
5900 CPTO 95014 852-G2
SUVA CT
- SRMN 94583 653-E7
SUZANNE CT
500 PA 94306 811-D3
1300 SJS 95129 852-H4
SUZANNE DR
4100 PIT 94565 574-E7
4200 PA 94306 811-D3
4700 CCCo - 574-E7
SUZANNE PL
100 PLHL 94523 592-D6
SUZAY CT
1400 SJS 95122 854-H1
SUZIE ST
4100 SMTO 94403 749-E6
SUZUKI CT
2700 SJS 95121 854-J4
SWAIN COM
34700 FRMT 94555 752-D2
SWAIN WY
1900 SJS 95124 873-G4
SWAINLAND RD
6100 OAK 94611 630-C5
SWALLOW CT
- ANT 94509 594-J1
400 LVMR 94550 695-D7
3600 AlaC 94546 691-J3
SWALLOW DR
500 LVMR 94550 695-D7
500 LVMR 94550 715-D1
600 SJS 95111 854-J5
1600 SUNV 94087 832-H5
SWALLOW ST
- DNVL 94506 653-E5
SWALLOW WY
- ANT 94509 594-H1
1500 HER 94547 569-H4
3700 SCL 95051 832-H4
3700 CPTO 95014 832-H6
SWALLOW TAIL RD
1300 CNCD 94521 593-C5
SWAN CT
- DNVL 94506 653-E5
- WLCK 94596 612-A2
2100 UNC 94587 732-G6
SWAN LN
200 LVMR 94550 695-D7
SWAN PL
700 LVMR 94550 695-D7
SWAN ST
- DNVL 94506 653-J6
900 FCTY 94404 749-H1
SWAN WY
- OAK 94621 670-E7
100 VAL 94589 510-A5
SWANCREEK CT
3300 SJS 95121 855-D7
SWANCREEK WY
1500 SJS 95121 855-D7
SWANGATE WY
1600 SJS 95124 873-J3
SWAN LAKE CT
2100 MRTZ 94553 592-A1
SWAN OAK LN
10000 CPTO 95014 831-J7
SWANS WY
500 RCH 94805 589-A6
SWANSEA CT
2000 SJS 95132 814-J2
SWANSEA LN
- PLHL 94523 592-A4
- PLHL 94523 591-J4
SWANSON WY
2600 MTVW 94040 831-J1
SWANSTON WY
1700 SJS 95132 814-E4
SWANSWOOD CT
700 SJS 95120 894-J3
SWANZY CT
- VAL 94591 550-C1
SWANZY DAM RD
- VAL 94591 550-C1
SWAPS DR
300 SJS 95111 875-B2
SWARTHMORE DR
18200 SAR 95070 852-J7
SWEENEY AV
800 SMCo 94063 770-C6
SWEENEY CT
- CCCo 94803 589-F2
SWEENEY RD
1100 ANT 94509 575-E7
SWEENY ST
- SF 94134 668-A6
200 SF 94134 667-J6
SWEET CT
600 LFYT 94549 631-H2
SWEET DR
900 SJS 95129 853-A3
3200 LFYT 94549 631-G1
3300 LFYT 94549 611-G7
SWEET LN
21200 AlaC 94546 691-J6
SWEET RD
- ALA 94502 669-H6
- LFYT 94595 612-A6
SWEET WY
- ALA 94502 669-H6

SWEETBAY DR
700 SUNV 94086 832-H3
SWEETBERRY CT
100 SJS 95136 874-H1
SWEETBRIAR CIR
3000 LFYT 94549 631-H3
SWEETBRIAR CT
4300 CNCD 94521 593-C5
SWEETBRIAR DR
1600 SJS 95125 853-J6
2500 SJS 95008 853-F7
2500 SCIC 95008 853-F7
2500 SCIC 95008 873-F1
SWEETBRIAR LN
- SAUS 94965 627-B3
SWEETBRIAR PL
17700 AlaC 94546 692-A2
SWEETBRIER LN
500 BEN 94510 551-A1
SWEETGUM CT
1900 SJS 95131 814-D7
SWEETLEAF CT
2800 SJS 95148 835-E7
SWEET OAK ST
10800 CPTO 95014 832-A6
10800 LALT 95014 832-A6
11000 CPTO 94024 832-A6
SWEETPEA CT
- DNVL 94506 654-B5
SWEETSER AV
700 NVTO 94945 526-C3
SWEET SHRUB CT
4400 CNCD 94521 593-B5
SWEET WATER CT
- CCCo 94506 654-C4
SWEET WATER DR
700 CCCo 94506 654-C4
SWEETWATER DR
1000 SLN 94578 691-C6
2200 MRTZ 94553 572-A7
SWEETWATER WY
700 SJS 95133 834-F1
SWEET WILLIAM LN
- SMCo 94025 770-E7
SWEETWOOD DR
1300 SMCo 94015 687-B5
1300 DALY 94015 687-B5
4900 RCH 94803 589-F2
SWEETWOOD ST
43200 FRMT 94538 773-D2
SWEIGERT RD
3400 SCIC 95132 815-C1
3400 SJS 95132 814-H2
3400 SCIC 95132 814-H2
SWENSEN CT
2000 SJS 95131 814-E7
SWENSON CT
700 SLN 94579 691-B6
SWENSON ST
14900 SLN 94579 691-C6
SWICKARD AV
- SJS 95193 875-D5
- SJS 95119 875-D5
SWIFT AV
300 SSF 94080 708-B4
2100 SJS 95148 835-A6
SWIFT CT
- ALA 94502 669-H5
- MLV 94941 606-G4
1600 SUNV 94087 832-H5
1900 HAY 94545 731-J1
36300 NWK 94560 752-F4
SWINDON CT
3100 SJS 95148 855-E2
SWINDON PL
4900 NWK 94560 752-F4
SWINGING GATE CT
1200 SJS 95120 894-E2
SWISS AV
- SF 94131 667-F5
SWISTA WY
1800 CCCo 94521 593-E3
SWORDFISH COM
38900 FRMT 94536 753-C3
SWORDFISH ST
1200 FCTY 94404 749-H3
SYBIL AV
200 SLN 94577 691-B1
24500 HAY 94542 712-A2
SYCAMORE AV
- CCCo 94572 570-A3
- LKSP 94939 586-E6
- MLV 94941 606-E3
100 SMTO 94402 728-G7
100 SMTO 94402 748-G1
100 SSF 94080 707-H4
100 SANS 94960 566-A7
300 HAY 94544 712-A3
300 HAY 94544 711-J3
700 SBRN 94066 707-H7
1500 HER 94547 569-G3
2400 CNCD 94520 572-F7
4300 RCH 94804 609-A2
SYCAMORE CIR
400 DNVL 94526 653-B4
SYCAMORE CT
- CCCo 94565 573-G2
- RDWC 94061 790-A2
100 VAL 94591 530-F4
300 LGTS 95032 873-F5
600 LVMR 94550 695-J6
2200 LALT 94024 831-J6
SYCAMORE DR
400 MPS 95035 813-H3
500 ANT 94509 575-B5
800 PA 94303 791-D6
900 NVTO 94945 525-E1
1000 MLBR 94030 727-H3
1700 PIT 94565 574-G6
SYCAMORE GN
1900 SJS 95125 853-J6
SYCAMORE RD
- ORIN 94563 610-H4
300 PLE 94566 714-D6
600 AlaC 94566 714-D6
SYCAMORE ST
- FRMT 94536 753-C1
- SF 94110 667-H2
100 SCAR 94070 769-F3
100 SLN 94579 691-D6
100 AlaC 94580 691-D6
500 OAK 94612 649-G2

SYCAMORE ST
2600 CCCo 94553 571-G4
36500 NWK 94560 752-D7
37300 NWK 94560 772-E1
SYCAMORE TER
1200 SUNV 94086 832-H4
SYCAMORE TR
- AlaC 94546 652-C5
- CCCo - 652-C4
SYCAMORE WY
2800 SCL 95051 833-A7
SYCAMORE HILL CT
300 DNVL 94526 653-C2
SYCAMORE VALLEY RD
600 DNVL 94526 653-C3
SYCAMORE VLY RD E
100 DNVL 94526 653-B3
SYCAMORE VLY RD W
100 DNVL 94526 653-A3
SYDENHAM CT
400 SJS 95111 875-C2
SYDNEY AV
1800 LVMR 94550 715-G3
SYDNEY CIR
18700 AlaC 94546 691-G3
SYDNEY CT
3600 SJS 95132 814-F2
SYDNEY DR
200 CCCo 94595 632-D2
1300 SUNV 94087 832-D4
3500 SJS 95132 814-E2
SYDNEY WY
- SF 94127 667-E4
2700 AlaC 94546 691-G3
SYDNOR DR
800 SCIC 95008 853-F7
SYKES CT
2800 SCL 95051 833-B6
SYL DOR LN
- MrnC 94947 525-H4
SYLHOWE RD
2700 OAK 94602 650-F3
SYLVAN AV
- SJS 95050 833-E7
- SJS 95128 833-E7
100 SBRN 94066 707-J7
100 SMTO 94403 749-A6
300 MTVW 94041 812-A7
3000 OAK 94602 650-F4
SYLVAN CIR
1800 SLN 94577 671-D7
SYLVAN CT
- MLBR 94030 728-A4
SYLVAN DR
- SF 94132 667-A6
900 SCAR 94070 769-G2
3100 SJS 95148 835-C5
SYLVAN LN
- ROSS 94957 586-C2
SYLVAN RD
100 CCCo 94596 632-F1
SYLVAN ST
500 SMCo 94014 687-D5
500 DALY 94014 687-D5
SYLVAN TER
- MrnC 94903 566-H3
SYLVAN WY
- CNCD 94521 593-D5
- OAK 94610 650-A2
- PDMT 94610 650-A2
200 SMCo 94062 769-E7
200 SMCo 94062 789-E1
SYLVANDALE AV
600 SCIC 95111 854-H6
700 SJS 95111 854-J6
700 SJS 95111 855-A6
10100 SCIC 95111 855-A6
SYLVANDALE WY
13200 SCIC 95111 854-H6
SYLVANER CT
900 CLAY 94517 613-J1
3200 PLE 94566 714-G4
SYLVANER DR
600 PLE 94566 714-G3
SYLVANER WY
600 FRMT 94539 794-A2
6000 SJS 95120 874-D6
SYLVAN GLEN CT
24600 HAY 94541 712-B2
SYLVESTER DR
33800 FRMT 94555 732-D7
SYLVESTER RD
100 SSF 94080 708-A3
SYLVIA AV
100 MPS 95035 813-J1
SYLVIA CIR
- NVTO 94947 525-H2
100 PLE 94566 714-F3
SYLVIA CT
100 VAL 94591 530-D3
300 MPS 95035 813-J1
3000 RCH 94803 589-E2
SYLVIA DR
- PLHL 94523 592-C4
1200 SJS 95121 854-J4
1200 SJS 95121 855-A3
SYLVIA WY
100 SRFL 94903 566-B3
14500 SLN 94578 691-D3
SYLVIAN WY
- LALT 94022 811-D6
SYMPHONY LN
4600 SJS 95111 855-A7
SYNTAX CT
- SJS 95002 813-C1
SYOSSET LN
- MrnC 94947 525-H5
SYRACUSE AV
33700 UNC 94587 732-E5
SYRACUSE DR
1000 SUNV 94087 832-B3
SYSTRON DR
2700 CNCD 94518 592-G3

T

T ST
300 BEN 94510 551-C4
T- HEAD RD
- CCCo 94553 571-H3
TAAFFE RD
26200 LAH 94022 831-A1

N TAAFFE ST
100 SUNV 94086 812-E7
S TAAFFE ST
100 SUNV 94086 812-E7
400 SUNV 94086 832-D1
TABER PL
- SF 94107 648-B7
TABLE TOP
- CCCo - 591-E7
- CCCo - 611-E1
TABORA DR
3100 ANT 94509 575-C7
3100 ANT 94509 595-B1
TABU TER
34600 FRMT 94555 752-D2
TABUA CT
20900 AlaC 94541 691-G7
20900 AlaC 94541 711-G1
TACCHELLA WY
37700 FRMT 94536 752-J3
TACOMA AV
1600 BERK 94707 609-F6
2100 MRTZ 94553 571-F4
2200 CCCo 94553 571-F4
TACOMA COM
5100 FRMT 94555 752-C3
TACOMA ST
- SF 94118 647-C6
TACOMA WY
1500 RDWC 94063 769-J4
1500 RDWC 94063 770-A4
TACONIC CT
5600 SJS 95123 874-H4
TADIN LN
1500 WDSD 94062 809-H7
TADLEY CT
300 RDWC 94061 790-B1
TAFFY CT
2600 SJS 95148 835-C7
6700 PLE 94588 694-A7
TAFFY DR
2600 SJS 95148 835-C7
TAFT AV
600 ALB 94706 609-D5
2600 SCL 95051 833-B6
4200 RCH 94804 609-A1
5400 OAK 94618 629-J6
5400 OAK 94618 630-A5
6200 CCCo 94805 589-C5
TAFT CT
- NVTO 94947 526-B5
1700 ANT 94509 575-A7
2600 SCL 95051 833-B6
TAFT DR
5200 SJS 95124 873-F5
TAFT ST
900 RDWC 94061 789-J1
1800 CNCD 94521 593-D2
26400 HAY 94544 712-A5
TAFT WY
100 VAL 94591 530-E4
TAGART DR
2600 SJS 95148 835-C7
2600 SJS 95148 855-C1
TAGLIO CT
6800 SJS 95120 894-H2
TAGUS CT
- PTLV 94028 810-D5
TAHITI CT
2000 SJS 95122 854-H1
TAHITI DR
2200 SRMN 94583 653-E7
2200 SRMN 94583 673-E1
TAHITI LN
1000 ALA 94502 670-A6
TAHITI RD
13800 SLN 94577 690-H5
TAHITI ST
2300 HAY 94545 711-G7
TAHITIAN CIR
300 UNC 94587 732-C6
TAHJA RD
- CCCo - 654-J6
TAHOE
- PLHL 94523 592-C6
TAHOE AV
2500 HAY 94545 731-H1
TAHOE CIR
- NVTO 94947 526-E7
4600 MRTZ 94553 571-F7
TAHOE CT
- SSF 94080 707-F4
- WLCK 94596 612-D5
- SRMN 94583 653-F7
1700 LVMR 94550 715-G5
2300 HAY 94545 731-H1
3300 ANT 94509 575-E7
4500 PLE 94566 694-D7
TAHOE DR
600 MRTZ 94553 571-E7
1000 BLMT 94002 769-A2
1600 MPS 95035 814-D1
2600 LVMR 94550 715-G5
TAHOE PL
- PIT 94565 574-G6
100 SRFL 94903 566-F2
3000 SRMN 94583 653-F7
6800 ELCR 94530 609-D4
TAHOE TER
500 MTVW 94041 812-B7
TAHOE WY
2900 SJS 95125 854-B7
3600 SCL 95051 812-H7
TAHOE PARK CT
4800 FRMT 94538 773-C1
TAHOS RD
300 ORIN 94563 610-J6
400 ORIN 94563 611-A7
E TAHOS RD
- ORIN 94563 611-A6
W TAHOS RD
- ORIN 94563 610-J6
TAIDA ST
1100 SJS 95131 834-D1
TAINAN CT
1200 SJS 95131 814-B7
TAINAN DR
1400 SJS 95131 814-B7
TAINAN PL
1200 SJS 95131 814-B7
TAINI CT
1900 SJS 95133 834-E1

INDEX

STREET
Block City ZIP Pg-Grid

TAINTER PTH
300 CMAD 94925 606-F1
TAIPAN CT
3700 AlaC 94541 692-C7
TAIPEI DR
1500 SJS 95131 814-B7
TAIT AV
- LGTS 95030 872-J7
100 LGTS 95030 873-A7
TAIT CT
5500 NWK 94560 752-F6
TAJI CT
900 SJS 95122 854-G2
TAJI DR
900 SJS 95122 854-G2
TAKA CT
1300 SJS 95122 854-H1
TAKENS CT
7500 PLE 94588 714-A3
TALATHY WY
3200 SJS 95135 855-E3
TALAVERA DR
2300 SRMN 94583 673-C3
TALBART ST
200 MRTZ 94553 571-D3
TALBERT CT
- SF 94134 688-A2
TALBERT ST
- SF 94134 688-A3
200 DALY 94014 688-A3
400 DALY 94014 687-J3
TALBERT TER
37100 FRMT 94536 752-H2
TALBOT AV
300 PCFA 94044 707-A5
400 ALB 94706 609-D5
1100 BERK 94706 609-D5
1300 BERK 94702 609-D5
2600 OAK 94605 671-B5
TALBOT LN
2700 AlaC 94546 691-G4
TALBOT WY
3100 ANT 94509 575-F7
TALBRYN DR
1200 BLMT 94002 769-E2
TALBRYN LN
- BLMT 94002 769-E1
TALESFORE CT
1100 SJS 95131 814-E7
TALIA AV
2100 SCL 95050 833-D7
TALISMAN CT
700 PA 94303 791-E7
TALISMAN DR
800 PA 94303 791-E7
800 SUNV 94087 832-E2
TALISMAN WY
1500 CNCD 94521 593-E5
TALLAC ST
100 VAL 94589 510-B5
TALLAC WY
17500 AlaC 94541 691-E7
TALLAHASSEE DR
1100 SJS 95122 834-J5
TALLAHASSEE ST
2200 HAY 94545 711-G7
TALLENT AV
600 SCIC 95127 814-J5
TALLEY WY
- HER 94547 569-F2
TALLMAN CT
800 SJS 95123 874-E4
5300 FRMT 94536 752-H7
TALLWOOD CT
- ATN 94027 790-C6
TALLWOOD DR
100 DALY 94014 687-D4
TALLY HO CT
700 CCCo 94517 613-G2
TALMAGE AV
- SCIC 95127 834-J1
TAMAL AV
- SANS 94960 566-B6
TAMAL PZ
100 CMAD 94925 586-G6
TAMALPAIS AV
- BLV 94920 607-C7
- LKSP 94939 586-E5
- LVMR 94550 695-D7
- MLV 94941 606-B2
- MrnC 94965 606-F7
- SANS 94960 566-B7
- TBRN 94920 627-D1
600 NVTO 94947 526-A4
800 SRFL 94901 586-G1
2000 ELCR 94530 589-C7
6300 SJS 95120 874-E7
6300 SJS 95120 894-E1
TAMALPAIS CIR
- BLV 94920 607-C7
TAMALPAIS CT
2000 ELCR 94530 589-C7
TAMALPAIS DR
100 VAL 94589 510-B7
200 CMAD 94925 586-G7
500 MrnC 94941 606-C4
2600 PIN 94564 569-G6
TAMALPAIS PL
1100 HAY 94542 712-A3
TAMALPAIS RD
- BERK 94708 609-H6
- LKSP 94939 586-F5
- MrnC 94904 586-F5
TAMALPAIS ST
2400 MTVW 94043 811-F3
TAMALPAIS TER
- SF 94118 647-E7
TAMALPAIS VW
- ORIN 94563 611-A4
- ORIN 94563 610-J4
TAMAL VISTA BLVD
- CMAD 94925 586-G6
TAMAL VISTA DR
- SANS 94960 566-D7
- SRFL 94901 566-D7
TAMAL VISTA LN
- MrnC 94904 586-F3
TAMAR CT
4700 CNCD 94521 593-C3
TAMARA CT
1400 BEN 94510 551-B4

TAMARACK AV
700 SCAR 94070 769-F4
800 SJS 95128 833-E7
TAMARACK DR
- HIL 94010 748-E1
100 HER 94547 570-A5
100 UNC 94587 732-F3
500 SRFL 94903 566-C3
7000 DBLN 94568 693-H3
TAMARACK LN
200 SSF 94080 707-G2
800 SUNV 94086 832-H3
3700 SCL 95051 832-H3
TAMARACK PL
400 NVTO 94945 525-E2
TAMARACK WY
5700 CNCD 94521 593-G7
5700 CLAY 94517 593-G7
TAMARIN LN
- MrnC 94945 526-H3
TAMARIND CT
21000 SCIC 95014 832-C6
TAMARISK
- MRGA 94556 631-C7
TAMARISK CT
200 WLCK 94598 612-J2
TAMARISK DR
200 WLCK 94598 612-J2
10500 OAK 94605 671-D2
TAMARRON WY
300 SRMN 94583 673-G3
TAMAYO ST
3700 FRMT 94536 752-F2
TAMBOUR WY
1800 SJS 95131 814-C4
TAMERA LN
- AlaC 94546 691-J3
TAMI WY
500 MTVW 94041 812-B7
TAMIE LN
2000 SJS 95130 852-J6
TAMI LEE DR
1300 SJS 95122 834-G7
TAMMY CIR
- CCCo 94565 573-F2
TAMMY CT
4800 UNC 94587 751-J1
5600 LVMR 94550 696-C6
TAMMY LN
- PLHL 94523 591-J5
1600 CNCD 94519 593-A2
TAM O SHANTER DR
6500 SJS 95120 894-D2
TAM-O-SHANTER RD
- CCCo 94507 632-J4
TAMPA AV
2000 OAK 94611 630-E7
27100 HAY 94544 712-A7
27900 HAY 94544 732-A1
TAMPA CT
300 FCTY 94404 749-F5
1600 SJS 95122 854-J1
TAMPA DR
- SRFL 94901 566-G7
TAMPA LN
- SF 94124 668-B6
TAMPA WY
1600 SJS 95122 834-H7
2000 SJS 95122 854-J1
TAMPICO
100 WLCK 94598 612-E4
TAMPICO PL
1400 WLCK 94598 612-E4
TAMPICO RD
35300 FRMT 94536 752-F2
TAMPICO WY
4500 SJS 95118 874-A3
TAMSON CT
15300 MSER 95030 872-J4
TAMUR CT
4200 PLE 94566 714-F4
TAMWORTH AV
13700 SAR 95070 872-D1
TAMWORTH CT
3200 WLCK 94598 612-H6
TANAGER AV
1700 AlaC 94578 691-E4
TANAGER CIR
2400 CNCD 94520 572-G6
TANAGER COM
4100 FRMT 94555 752-D1
TANAGER CT
- BSBN 94005 687-J5
900 SUNV 94087 832-A2
2100 PLE 94566 714-E1
2400 CNCD 94520 572-G6
TANAGER DR
2100 PLE 94566 714-E1
2300 PLE 94566 694-D7
TANAGER PL
2400 CNCD 94520 572-F6
TANAGER RD
400 LVMR 94550 695-D7
400 LVMR 94550 715-D1
TANAGER TER
4200 FRMT 94555 752-D1
TANAGER WY
100 HER 94547 569-H5
300 LVMR 94550 695-D7
TANAKA DR
1300 SJS 95131 814-C7
TANBARK CT
- NVTO 94945 526-A1
TAN BARK DR
34200 FRMT 94555 752-B3
TANBARK LN
- CCCo 94507 633-B3
TANBARK ST
4200 SJS 95129 853-A2
TANBARK TER
500 SRFL 94903 566-C2
TANBOR WY
200 CCCo 94553 572-C7
TANDANG SORA
- SF 94107 648-B6
TANDEM LN
5400 RCH 94803 589-J2
TANDERA AV
5800 SJS 95123 874-F5
TANFIELD LN
400 SJS 95111 854-F6

TANFIELD RD
- TBRN 94920 607-C4
TANFORAN AV
- SBRN 94066 707-H5
- SSF 94080 707-H5
TANGANYIKA CIR
200 ANT 94509 575-B7
TANGER CT
2200 UNC 94587 732-G7
TANGERINE CT
200 SRMN 94583 673-J7
200 SRMN 94583 693-J1
TANGERINE ST
9100 SRMN 94583 693-J1
TANGERINE WY
1100 SUNV 94087 832-D3
TANGLEWOOD
25400 HAY 94542 712-B3
TANGLEWOOD AV
- MrnC 94904 586-D5
TANGLEWOOD CT
100 VAL 94589 530-B1
1600 PLE 94566 714-D2
TANGLEWOOD DR
- LFYT 94549 611-E7
2700 SJS 95127 835-A5
21400 AlaC 94546 691-J7
TANGLEWOOD LN
- LFYT 94549 611-E7
- MrnC 94947 525-G6
400 CCCo 94595 632-D1
TANGLEWOOD PL
- LFYT 94549 611-E7
TANGLEWOOD RD
- BERK 94705 630-A3
- OAK 94705 630-A3
TANGLEWOOD WY
1100 SMTO 94403 749-E6
1700 PLE 94566 714-D2
TANGLEWOOD PARK DR
5300 FRMT 94538 773-B1
TANGO WY
4600 SJS 95111 855-A7
TANKERLAND CT
3500 SJS 95121 855-D3
TANKIT CT
2100 SJS 95008 853-B6
TANKIT DR
2100 SJS 95008 853-B6
TANKLAGE RD
900 SCAR 94070 769-H3
TANLAND DR
1000 PA 94303 791-D5
TANNAHILL DR
6600 SJS 95120 894-E1
TANNERY WY
3100 SCL 95054 813-A6
TANNET CT
500 PLE 94566 714-G3
TANNHAUSER CT
2600 SJS 95121 854-H4
TANNHAUSER WY
1400 SJS 95121 854-H4
TAN OAK CIR
- SRFL 94903 566-D1
TANOAK CT
- CMAD 94925 606-G1
TAN OAK DR
100 PTLV 94028 830-C1
5400 FRMT 94555 752-B3
TANOAK DR
400 SCL 95051 833-B7
TANTALLON CT
2900 SJS 95132 814-F4
TANTAU AV
800 CPTO 95014 852-G2
10000 SCIC 95014 852-G1
N TANTAU AV
10100 CPTO 95014 832-G7
TAORMINO AV
5800 SJS 95123 874-F5
TAOS CT
19600 SAR 95070 872-F2
TAOS DR
14000 SAR 95070 872-F2
TAOS RD
48600 FRMT 94539 793-J2
TAPER AV
100 VAL 94589 510-C6
2800 SCL 95051 833-A3
3000 SJS 95124 873-G2
TAPER CT
800 VAL 94589 510-D5
1300 SJS 95122 854-H1
TAPER LN
1800 SJS 95122 854-G1
TAPER ST
2300 PIN 94564 589-J1
TAPESTRY CT
- LVMR 94550 715-H4
TAPESTRY DR
- LVMR 94550 715-H4
TAPESTRY WY
2600 PLE 94588 714-A3
TAPIA DR
- SF 94132 667-B7
- SF 94132 687-B1
TAPIS WY
1100 PCFA 94044 726-J5
TAPPAN CT
- ORIN 94563 610-G3
TAPPAN LN
- ORIN 94563 610-F2
TAPPAN TER
300 ORIN 94563 610-F3
TAPPAN WY
- ORIN 94563 610-F2
TAPROOT CT
2300 SJS 95133 814-H3
TAPSCOTT AV
1900 ELCR 94530 589-C7
1900 ELCR 94530 609-C1
TARA CT
- UNC 94587 731-J4
1500 CLAY 94517 593-F5
TARA DR
5400 CLAY 94517 593-F5
TARA LN
- NVTO 94945 526-A2
2400 SSF 94080 707-D5
TARA RD
- ORIN 94563 630-J1

TARA RD
100 ORIN 94563 631-A1
TARA ST
100 EPA 94303 791-C1
100 SF 94112 687-E1
100 EPA 94303 771-C7
TARABROOK DR
- ORIN 94563 630-J1
TARA HILL RD
- TBRN 94920 607-D6
TARA HILLS DR
500 CCCo 94806 569-B4
800 PIN 94564 569-C5
1200 PIN 94806 569-C5
TARANGA CT
7200 SJS 95139 875-G7
TARANTINO DR
- MRTZ 94553 571-D2
TARAVAL ST
- SF 94127 667-A5
- SF 94116 667-A5
2400 SF 94116 666-H5
TARA VIEW RD
- TBRN 94920 607-D6
TAREYTON AV
9600 SRMN 94583 673-F7
TAREYTON CT
- SRMN 94583 673-F7
TARMAN AV
24900 HAY 94544 711-H4
TARN CT
- HER 94547 569-H4
TAROB CT
1800 MPS 95035 814-B3
TARPON ST
900 FCTY 94404 749-H2
TARPON WY
31300 UNC 94587 731-J5
TARRAGON DR
500 SRFL 94903 566-C2
TARRAGON ST
25900 HAY 94544 712-A5
TARRANT CT
- SRFL 94903 566-F5
TAR RIVER CT
34500 FRMT 94555 752-D2
TARRY LN
- ORIN 94563 610-G3
TARRYTON CT
1300 ANT 94509 575-F7
TARRYTON ISL
500 ALA 94501 669-G2
TARRYTOWN CT
600 SJS 95136 874-F2
600 WLCK 94598 613-A3
TARRYTOWN RD
1400 SMCo 94402 748-F7
TARTAN CT
100 WLCK 94598 612-G2
TARTAN DR
2500 SCL 95051 833-B2
TARTAN RD
- MLV 94941 606-E1
TARTAN WY
12100 OAK 94619 650-J4
TARTAN TRAIL RD
1000 HIL 94010 748-E4
TARTARIAN ST
700 OAK 94603 670-H6
TARTARIAN WY
500 SUNV 94087 832-D2
1300 SJS 95129 852-G4
34200 UNC 94587 732-F6
TARTER CT
- SJS 95136 854-E7
TARTER WY
- SJS 95136 854-E7
TAR WEED PZ
- HAY 94542 712-B3
TASCO CT
- SPAB 94806 568-H7
TASKER LN
- SCAR 94070 769-F5
TASMAN CT
- SUNV 94089 812-H4
TASMAN DR
- SJS 95134 813-D3
400 SUNV 94089 812-G3
700 MPS 95035 813-H3
1200 SUNV 94089 813-A4
2100 SCL 95054 813-A4
TASSAJARA AV
2500 ELCR 94530 589-C6
2600 CCCo 94805 589-C6
TASSAJARA LN
2400 DNVL 94526 653-E4
TASSAJARA RD
- PLE 94588 694-E4
5800 DBLN 94568 694-E4
6500 AlaC 94568 694-E4
TASSAJARA RANCH DR
- DNVL 94506 654-A6
- DNVL 94506 653-J6
TASSASARA DR
700 MPS 95035 794-B5
TASSO ST
100 PA 94301 790-J3
1300 PA 94301 791-A5
TATE TER
- OAK 94605 671-E5
TATRA CT
800 SJS 95136 874-E3
TATRA DR
5000 SJS 95136 874-E2
TAUBEH CT
3900 SJS 95136 874-F1
TAURUS AV
- OAK 94611 630-D6
TAURUS DR
- MrnC 94947 525-F2
800 FCTY 94404 749-E3
TAVAN ESTATES
900 MRTZ 94553 591-F4
900 CCCo - 591-F4
TAVIS PL
2200 FRMT 94538 773-F4
TAWNY DR
500 PLE 94566 714-G3
TAWNY TER
36500 FRMT 94536 752-G3
TAWNYGATE WY
1600 SJS 95124 873-J3

TAY AV
3900 UNC 94587 731-J5
TAYLOR AV
200 SUNV 94086 812-E6
300 ALA 94501 669-E1
300 SBRN 94066 707-J7
300 SBRN 94066 727-J1
1000 SolC 94591 530-D6
2400 OAK 94605 671-A5
29200 HAY 94544 732-C1
TAYLOR BLVD
- CCCo 94549 591-J7
- PLHL 94523 591-J6
100 MLBR 94030 728-A4
200 PLHL 94523 592-A4
1500 CCCo 94549 611-H2
1800 LFYT 94549 591-J7
1800 LFYT 94549 611-H2
TAYLOR COM
39600 FRMT 94538 753-B5
TAYLOR CT
500 MTVW 94043 812-A4
TAYLOR DR
200 SSF 94080 707-G4
400 MPS 95035 794-A3
TAYLOR LN
- CMAD 94925 586-F7
- LKSP 94939 586-F7
TAYLOR RD
- SF 94129 647-D4
- TBRN 94920 607-B2
- MrnC 94920 607-B2
TAYLOR ST
- SANS 94960 566-B6
- SF 94102 648-A6
- SRFL 94901 586-F1
400 SF 94102 647-J5
600 SF 94109 647-J5
800 SF 94108 647-J5
900 ALB 94706 609-D6
900 SJS 95002 793-B7
1400 SF 94133 647-J4
1600 SMTO 94403 749-C2
1800 SF 94133 647-J3
E TAYLOR ST
- SJS 95112 834-C3
W TAYLOR ST
- SJS 95110 834-A4
300 SJS 95110 833-H6
700 SJS 95126 833-H6
TAYLOR WY
500 SMCo 94002 769-G2
600 SCAR 94070 769-G2
TAYSIDE CT
7500 SJS 95135 855-J5
TEABERRY CT
6100 SJS 95123 875-B6
TEABERRY LN
- MrnC 94920 607-E5
S TEA GARDEN DR
- SF 94118 667-C1
TEAGARDEN ST
2300 SLN 94577 690-J2
2400 SLN 94577 691-A3
TEAK CT
600 WLCK 94598 592-H7
TEAK GROVE CT
100 SJS 95123 875-A3
TEAKWOOD AV
800 LGTS 95030 873-B2
TEAKWOOD CT
- SRFL 94901 567-C6
800 LGTS 95030 873-B2
4200 CNCD 94521 593-C2
TEAKWOOD DR
1300 SJS 95128 853-E4
1700 MRTZ 94553 571-J7
37600 FRMT 94536 752-H5
TEAKWOOD ST
2100 VAL 94591 530-E5
22600 HAY 94541 711-F3
TEAL COM
34600 FRMT 94555 752-D2
TEAL CT
- BEN 94510 551-F2
- EPA 94303 791-C2
- PIT 94565 574-B4
100 VAL 94589 509-G5
500 LVMR 94550 695-D7
TEAL DR
- BEN 94510 551-F2
1100 SUNV 94087 832-H5
1400 SCL 95051 832-H5
TEAL LN
2600 UNC 94587 732-D5
TEAL RD
- BLV 94920 627-D1
TEAL ST
600 FCTY 94404 749-G1
TEALE AV
3900 SJS 95117 853-B3
TEAL RIDGE CT
3000 SJS 95136 854-F6
TEA ROSE CIR
1100 SJS 95131 814-B6
TEA ROSE WY
1800 SJS 95131 814-B6
TEASDALE PL
500 HAY 94544 711-H5
TEA TREE CT
- DNVL 94526 653-B6
2500 MRTZ 94553 572-A6
TEATREE CT
- HIL 94010 748-C2
600 SJS 95128 853-F2
TEATRO AV
900 PIT 94565 574-F3
TECADO COM
40600 FRMT 94539 753-G2
TECADO TER
- FRMT 94539 753-G2
6400 AlaC 94586 753-G2
TECHNOLOGY CT
2900 RCH 94806 569-A6
4000 FRMT 94538 773-D3
TECHNOLOGY DR
800 MPS 95035 813-G2
1500 SJS 95110 833-H1
2400 HAY 94545 731-H2
4100 FRMT 94538 773-D4
TECHNOLOGY PL
4000 FRMT 94538 773-E3

TED AV
12300 SAR 95070 852-E5
TED CT
12300 SAR 95070 852-E5
TEDDINGTON DR
3100 SJS 95148 855-D2
TEDDY AV
- SF 94134 688-A2
- SF 94134 687-J1
TEDDY DR
100 UNC 94587 732-F3
TEERLINK WY
14100 SAR 95070 872-B2
TEHACHAPI WY
5000 ANT 94509 595-E3
TEHAMA AV
500 HAY 94541 711-F3
1000 MLPK 94025 770-H7
1000 MLPK 94025 790-H1
2100 SJS 95122 834-J6
4100 FRMT 94538 753-B6
5100 RCH 94804 609-B3
TEHAMA CT
100 SBRN 94066 727-E1
TEHAMA ST
- SF 94105 648-B6
300 SF 94103 648-A7
700 SF 94103 647-J7
TEIGLAND RD
3100 CCCo 94549 611-J1
TEKMAN DR
1000 SJS 95122 854-H2
TELEGRAPH AV
1500 OAK 94612 649-G2
2300 BERK 94704 629-H5
2700 BERK 94705 629-H5
2700 OAK 94609 649-G2
3800 OAK 94609 629-H5
TELEGRAPH DR
3500 SJS 95132 814-H4
TELEGRAPH PL
- SF 94133 648-A3
TELEGRAPH HILL
- CCCo 94806 569-A5
TELEGRAPH HILL BLVD
- SF 94133 648-A3
TELEPHONE TR
- MrnC 94965 586-A7
TELFER AV
1100 SJS 95125 854-A4
TELFORD AV
600 SSF 94080 707-J2
700 MTVW 94043 811-H2
TELLERDAY CT
100 VAL 94589 510-C5
TELLES LN
100 FRMT 94539 753-H6
TELVIN ST
1300 ALB 94706 609-E6
TEMBLOR WY
4400 ANT 94509 595-J2
TEMESCAL CIR
- EMVL 94608 629-E6
TEMESCAL TER
- SF 94118 647-E7
TEMESCAL WY
700 SMCo 94062 789-F2
TEMPE CT
600 PLHL 94523 592-B2
TEMPEST COM
4800 FRMT 94555 752-C2
TEMPEST TER
34200 FRMT 94555 752-C2
TEMPLAR AL
400 VAL 94590 529-J3
500 VAL 94590 530-A3
TEMPLAR PL
- OAK 94618 630-C7
TEMPLE CT
- CCCo 94553 572-B7
2800 EPA 94303 771-C6
3100 SCL 95051 833-A6
TEMPLE DR
900 CCCo 94553 572-B6
900 SJS 95117 853-B3
N TEMPLE DR
- MPS 95035 794-D5
S TEMPLE DR
- MPS 95035 794-D7
TEMPLE ST
- SF 94114 667-F2
TEMPLE WY
100 VAL 94591 530-E3
38000 FRMT 94536 753-A2
TEMPLEBAR WY
600 LALT 94022 811-D5
TEMPLEMAN CT
400 CMAD 94925 606-F1
TEMPLETON AV
- DALY 94014 687-E3
TEMPLETON CT
600 SUNV 94087 832-D3
TEMPLETON DR
500 SUNV 94087 832-D3
TEMPLETON PL
13800 LAH 94022 811-D7
TEMPLETON ST
22600 HAY 94541 692-B7
TEN ACRES CT
14100 SAR 95070 872-H2
TEN ACRES RD
18800 SAR 95070 872-G2
TENAKA PL
1500 SUNV 94087 832-D5
TENAYA AV
5100 NWK 94560 752-F5
TENAYA DR
500 TBRN 94920 607-B5
1300 SJS 95125 854-B7
TENAYA LN
- NVTO 94947 526-A5
TENBY TER
100 CCCo 94506 654-A5
TENDER LN
700 FCTY 94404 749-G5
TENLEY CT
3200 SJS 95148 855-D2
TENLEY DR
3200 SJS 95148 855-D2
TENNANT AV
- SJS 95138 875-F4

TENNENT AV
100 PIN 94564 569-E4
TENNENT CT
2300 PIN 94564 569-E3
TENNESSEE AV
- MrnC 94965 606-E6
300 MrnC 94941 606-E6
TENNESSEE LN
200 PA 94306 811-D2
TENNESSEE ST
- VAL 94590 529-J4
500 VAL 94590 530-A4
600 SF 94107 668-C4
1700 SF 94124 668-C4
1800 SF 94124 668-C4
2100 VAL 94591 530-D4
TENNESSEE GLEN WY
200 MrnC 94965 606-F7
TENNESSEE VALLEY RD
- MrnC 94965 606-F7
200 MrnC 94965 626-E2
TENNIS DR
800 SSF 94080 707-G3
TENNIS CLUB DR
- CCCo 94506 653-H2
TENNY DR
100 BEN 94510 551-C3
TENNYSON AV
100 PA 94301 791-A6
700 PA 94303 791-A6
TENNYSON DR
- LVMR 94550 696-A6
- MLV 94941 606-G4
1700 CNCD 94521 593-F4
TENNYSON LN
900 SJS 95116 834-G5
W TENNYSON RD
- HAY 94544 712-A7
- HAY 94544 711-G7
1900 HAY 94545 711-G7
2500 HAY 94545 731-F1
TEN OAK CT
13100 SAR 95070 852-F7
TEN OAK WY
12900 SAR 95070 852-F7
TENOR CT
4900 FRMT 94538 773-B1
TEODORA CT
- MRGA 94556 651-F1
TEOLA WY
2000 SJS 95121 855-C3
TEPA WY
12100 LAH 94022 831-B3
TEPEE CT
5100 ANT 94509 595-G4
TEPIC PL
31200 HAY 94544 732-E2
TERA CT
900 WLCK 94596 612-A1
TERACINA DR
300 SRMN 94583 673-G2
TERALBA CT
100 SJS 95139 895-G1
TERALYNN CT
- OAK 94619 650-H5
TEREDO DR
500 RDWC 94065 749-H7
TERESA PL
500 SRMN 94583 673-G4
TERESA ST
- DALY 94014 687-D5
600 MRTZ 94553 571-E5
TERESA MARIE TER
1600 MPS 95035 793-G3
TERESI CT
700 SJS 95117 853-D2
TERESI LN
600 LALT 94024 831-F1
TERESITA BLVD
- SF 94127 667-E4
200 SF 94127 667-E5
600 SF 94131 667-E5
TERESITA DR
1200 SJS 95129 852-J5
TERESITA WY
100 LGTS 95032 893-D1
TERFIDIA LN
- MPS 95035 794-D6
TERI CT
100 VAL 94589 509-J5
4600 UNC 94587 731-J7
TERILYN AV
1100 SJS 95122 834-G6
2000 SJS 95122 854-H1
TERMAN DR
4200 PA 94306 811-C3
TERMINAL AV
- MLPK 94025 770-H7
1400 SJS 95112 834-A2
TERMINAL BLVD
2500 MTVW 94043 791-F6
TERMINAL CIR
500 LVMR 94550 695-B6
TERMINAL CT
- SSF 94080 708-A4
- SSF 94080 707-J4
TERMINAL DR
- SJS 95110 833-G2
TERMINAL PL
1200 SMTO 94401 729-A7
2300 BERK 94704 629-H2
TERMINAL RD
- NVTO 94949 546-J4
TERMINAL WY
900 SCAR 94070 769-G3
TERN CT
- SRFL 94901 587-A2
TERNERS DR
800 MrnC 94965 626-H1
TERRA AV
1200 SLN 94578 691-C3
TERRA ALTA CT
2000 MPS 95035 814-E2
TERRA ALTA DR
1200 MPS 95035 814-E1
4000 SRMN 94583 673-G4
TERRA BELLA AV
900 MTVW 94043 811-H2
900 SJS 95125 854-B5
TERRA BELLA DR
- CCCo 94596 612-F6

STREET Block City ZIP Pg-Grid

TERRA BELLA DR
700 MPS 95035 794-B6
11200 CPTO 95014 852-B3
TERRABELLA PL
4300 OAK 94619 650-H5
TERRABELLA WY
4200 OAK 94619 650-H5
TERRA CALIFORNIA DR
800 WLCK 94595 632-B2
TERRACE AV
- DALY 94015 687-A4
- MrnC 94904 586-D3
- RCH 94801 608-D1
- SRFL 94901 566-D7
- SANS 94960 566-D7
100 SRFL 94901 586-D1
200 SBRN 94066 707-J7
200 SBRN 94066 727-J1
1200 HAY 94541 712-A1
TERRACE CT
- LGTS 95032 893-B1
- TBRN 94920 607-A4
- CNCD 94518 592-H4
100 HER 94547 569-H4
700 LALT 94024 811-G7
TERRACE DR
- SF 94127 667-C5
- CNCD 94518 592-G4
200 SSF 94080 707-H4
400 SJS 95112 834-D4
600 MrnC 94965 626-H1
700 SCIC 94024 831-G4
1000 AlaC 94586 734-B3
1300 MLBR 94030 727-H2
1700 BLMT 94002 769-C1
1800 ANT 94509 575-F6
7300 ELCR 94530 609-F2
21500 CPTO 95014 852-B3
35500 FRMT 94536 732-J6
TERRACE RD
- CCCo 94596 612-A4
600 SCAR 94070 769-F6
1100 WLCK 94596 612-A4
TERRACE ST
1500 ALB 94706 609-E6
4100 OAK 94611 629-J7
TERRACE WK
- BERK 94707 609-G6
200 SF 94127 667-D6
TERRACE WY
400 SMTO 94403 749-B5
1600 WLCK 94596 612-B5
2800 MRTZ 94553 571-E5
3500 LFYT 94549 611-E6
TERRACE LAKE DR
- SJS 95123 874-E5
TERRACE VIEW AV
2800 ANT 94509 595-G1
3100 ANT 94509 575-G7
TERRACE VIEW CT
- DALY 94015 687-A5
TERRACE VIEW DR
- SJS 95123 874-D5
TERRA COTTA CT
3100 SJS 95135 855-E2
TERRA COTTA DR
3100 SJS 95135 855-E2
TERRADILLO AV
- SRFL 94901 586-H1
- SRFL 94901 566-H7
TERRA GRANADA DR
- WLCK 94595 632-B4
TERRAINE ST
- SJS 95113 834-B6
- SJS 95110 834-A6
TERRA LINDA CT
- MLBR 94030 728-A5
TERRA LINDA DR
- SRFL 94903 566-C4
TERRA MESA WY
300 MPS 95035 793-H3
TERRA NOBLE WY
1000 SJS 95132 814-H5
TERRA NOVA BLVD
1000 PCFA 94044 727-A4
TERRANOVA DR
- ANT 94509 575-D7
- ANT 94509 595-D1
TERRAPIN CT
700 CNCD 94518 592-J6
TERRA TERESA
- CCCo 94549 591-J7
TERRA VILLA AV
2200 EPA 94303 791-C2
TERRA VISTA AV
- SF 94115 647-F6
TERRAZA DEL SOL
3100 CNCD 94520 572-E6
TERRAZZO CT
5800 SJS 95123 874-F5
TERRAZZO DR
700 SJS 95123 874-F5
TERREBONNE DR
1100 WLCK 94598 612-F1
TERRELL ST
900 SJS 95136 874-D1
TERRENCE AV
12100 SAR 95070 852-F5
TERRENO DE FLORES LN
14900 LGTS 95032 873-D4
TERRI WY
1800 SJS 95124 873-H3
TERRI ANN LN
- CCCo 94803 589-F4
TERRIER CT
6000 SJS 95123 875-B6
TERRIER PL
- HIL 94010 748-F5
TERRY CIR
- NVTO 94947 526-C7
- NVTO 94949 526-C7
TERRY CT
900 PIT 94565 574-E5
2700 PIN 94564 569-H6
3100 AlaC 94546 691-H3
TERRY LN
600 DNVL 94526 652-H1
700 LVMR 94550 696-C7
1900 SMCo 94061 790-B4

TERRY TER
40800 FRMT 94539 753-E5
TERRY WY
1500 PLHL 94523 592-C4
10200 CPTO 95014 852-D1
10900 SCIC 94024 831-F5
18400 AlaC 94546 691-H3
TERRY A FRANCOIS BLVD
- SF 94107 648-C7
100 SF 94107 668-C2
TERRYBROOK CT
100 VAL 94591 530-E3
TERRYBROOK LN
100 VAL 94591 530-E3
TERRY LYNN DR
1500 CNCD 94521 593-E5
TERRYWOOD CT
3100 SJS 95132 814-D2
TERSINI CT
1800 SJS 95131 814-C7
TERSTINA PL
3700 SCL 95051 832-H3
TESLA RD Rt#-J2
4500 AlaC 94550 716-A3
TESORO CT
1800 PIN 94564 569-E5
5400 SJS 95124 873-G5
TESTA ST
- SAUS 94965 626-J2
TETON CT
200 SRFL 94903 566-F2
800 LVMR 94550 695-D7
TETON PL
3400 CNCD 94518 592-H6
TEVIS PL
- HIL 94010 748-E1
- PA 94301 791-B4
TEVIS ST
5800 OAK 94621 670-E3
TEVLIN ST
1000 BERK 94706 609-E7
1200 ALB 94706 609-E7
TEWA CT
1000 FRMT 94539 774-A5
TEWKSBURY ST
- RCH 94801 588-C7
TEXAS
3000 ALA 94501 649-E6
TEXAS CT
5800 SJS 95120 874-B6
TEXAS PL
300 SBRN 94066 727-J1
TEXAS ST
- ANT 94509 575-D6
100 SF 94107 668-B3
200 VAL 94590 530-A3
3000 OAK 94602 650-D5
TEXAS WY
2000 SMTO 94403 749-B4
THACKER CT
100 VAL 94591 530-F6
THACKERAY AV
27800 HAY 94544 712-A7
28100 HAY 94544 732-A1
THACKERAY DR
2300 OAK 94611 650-F1
THACKERAY LN
900 SJS 95116 834-G5
THADDEUS DR
2400 MTVW 94043 811-G2
THAGE WY
- PTLV 94028 809-J6
THAIN WY
500 PA 94306 811-C2
THAINWOOD WY
3800 SJS 95121 855-C5
THAIS LN
1300 HAY 94544 711-J6
THALIA ST
- MLV 94941 606-E3
THAMES CT
7200 DBLN 94568 693-J3
THAMES DR
1100 SJS 95129 852-G3
1200 CNCD 94518 592-D6
THAMES LN
100 LALT 94022 811-D5
THAMES PARK CT
400 SJS 95136 874-F1
THANE ST
38500 FRMT 94536 753-C2
THARP DR
100 MRGA 94556 651-E2
THATCH LN
- ALA 94502 670-A7
THATCHER CT
900 LALT 94024 831-H2
THATCHER DR
900 LALT 94024 831-H1
900 MTVW 94040 831-H1
4900 MRTZ 94553 572-A6
THATCHER LN
100 FCTY 94404 749-F5
THAU WY
1800 ALA 94501 649-F7
THAYER AV
2100 HAY 94545 711-F6
THAYER CT
2200 SJS 95122 854-H1
THAYER WY
100 AMCN 94589 510-A3
THE ALAMEDA
- SANS 94960 566-A5
300 MrnC 94960 566-B4
500 BERK 94707 609-F5
2600 SCL 95053 833-F4
2800 CNCD 94519 592-G2
3100 SCL 95050 833-F4
THE ALAMEDA Rt#-82
700 SCL 95126 833-H5
700 SJS 95126 833-H5
2100 SJS 95126 834-A7
2200 SCL 95050 833-H5
2600 SCL 95053 833-H5
THE AMERICANA
900 MTVW 94040 812-A7
THEATER AV
43200 FRMT 94539 753-J7
THE CRESCENT
- BERK 94708 609-J5

THE CROSSWAYS
200 BERK 94708 609-J5
THE DALLES AV
700 SUNV 94087 832-A4
THE EMBARCADERO
- SF 94105 648-C6
- SF 94107 648-C6
100 SF 94111 648-C6
500 RDWC 94065 749-J4
500 RDWC 94065 750-A4
500 SF 94111 648-A3
1300 SF 94133 648-A3
1600 SF 94133 647-J3
THE GLADE
500 ORIN 94563 610-G7
THE KNOLL
200 ORIN 94563 610-H7
THELMA AV
1000 VAL 94591 530-E5
20000 SAR 95070 872-E1
THELMA DR
- CCCo 94565 573-E2
THELMA ST
21700 HAY 94541 711-F2
THELMA WY
900 SJS 95122 834-F7
900 SJS 95122 854-F1
THENDARA WY
13400 LAH 94022 811-A5
THEO DR
1500 SJS 95131 814-B7
THEO LN
100 PLHL 94523 592-B6
THEODEN CT
1100 SJS 95121 855-A4
THE PLAZA DR
- BERK 94705 630-A4
THERESA AV
- AMCN 94589 510-A1
1100 CMBL 95008 873-C2
4500 FRMT 94538 753-C7
4500 FRMT 94538 773-C1
THERESA CT
- NVTO 94947 525-H3
- TBRN 94920 607-C5
900 MLPK 94025 770-G7
3700 AlaC 94546 692-B6
THERESA DR
500 SSF 94080 707-E2
THERESA LN
2700 SJS 95124 873-F1
3200 CCCo 94549 591-H6
THERESA PTH
- RCH 94804 609-A1
THERESA ST
- SF 94112 667-G6
THERESA WY
5100 LVMR 94550 696-C6
THERMAL RD
100 AlaC 94586 734-C5
THERMAL ST
8500 OAK 94605 671-A3
THE SHORT CUT
- OAK 94705 630-A3
- BERK 94708 609-J5
THE SPIRAL
300 BERK 94708 609-J5
THE STRAND AV
1600 SJS 95120 874-B6
THETA AV
- DALY 94014 687-C3
THETA CT
400 SJS 95123 875-A7
36700 FRMT 94536 752-G4
THETA ST
4600 FRMT 94536 752-F4
THE TREES TRLER PK DR
- CNCD 94518 592-E5
- CNCD 94520 592-E5
THE TURN
6800 OAK 94611 630-E5
THE UPLANDS
- BERK 94705 630-A4
THE VILLAGES PKWY
2000 SJS 95135 855-G6
THE VILLAGES FAIRWAY DR
2000 SJS 95135 855-H6
THE WOODS DR
3900 SJS 95136 854-H7
3900 SJS 95136 874-H1
THICKET WY
6100 SJS 95119 875-D5
THIEL RD
1000 HAY 94544 732-A1
THIERS ST
- DALY 94014 687-C4
THIESSEN CT
4800 CNCD 94521 593-D4
THIMBLEBERRY LN
4600 SJS 95129 853-B2
THIMBLEHALL LN
3400 SJS 95121 855-C5
THIRTY HILL RD
- CCCo 94553 571-F2
- MRTZ 94553 571-F2
THISTLE
- PTLV 94028 830-C1
THISTLE CIR
200 MRTZ 94553 591-G2
THISTLE CT
- HAY 94542 712-C3
100 HER 94547 569-J4
1000 SUNV 94086 832-G3
THISTLE DR
4400 SJS 95136 874-F1
THISTLE WY
- SRMN 94583 653-H6
100 MRTZ 94553 591-H2
3700 PLE 94588 694-F5
THISTLEDOWN CT
3100 PLE 94588 694-F6
THISTLEWOOD CT
1300 SJS 95121 855-B1
5100 ANT 94509 595-J6
THOBURN CT
- SCIC 94305 790-J7
THOITS ST
15000 SLN 94579 691-A6
THOMAS AV
- SF 94129 647-D4

THOMAS AV
- BSBN 94005 688-B6
- SolC 94590 530-B6
1200 SF 94124 668-A6
1900 SLN 94577 691-C1
5300 OAK 94618 629-J6
5400 OAK 94618 630-A6
6100 NWK 94560 752-F7
24300 HAY 94544 712-A3
24300 HAY 94544 711-J3
THOMAS CT
- NVTO 94947 525-H3
- ROSS 94957 586-C2
- SMTO 94401 728-J7
- SRFL 94901 566-E7
700 WLCK 94596 612-B2
1000 ANT 94509 575-F7
1500 MTVW 94040 811-G6
1500 MTVW 94022 811-G6
2700 PIN 94564 569-H6
THOMAS DR
- BEN 94510 551-C1
- MrnC 94920 606-H3
200 LGTS 95032 873-G5
600 RCH 94806 568-G6
1200 MRTZ 94553 571-D3
3300 PA 94303 791-E6
THOMAS LN
700 WLCK 94596 612-B2
THOMAS RD
3300 SCL 95054 813-D6
THOMAS WY
100 PIT 94565 574-C4
THOMAS MELLON DR
- SF 94134 688-B2
THOMAS MORE WY
- SF 94132 687-B2
THOMPSON AV
100 MTVW 94043 811-F3
2900 ALA 94501 670-B3
3300 SJS 95118 874-A1
THOMPSON CT
2300 MTVW 94043 811-G3
4500 FRMT 94538 753-A6
THOMPSON DR
4100 CNCD 94518 592-J5
THOMPSON LN
2000 CCCo 94803 569-E7
2000 CCCo 94803 589-E1
THOMPSON PL
900 SUNV 94086 812-G6
2300 SCL 95050 833-C3
3400 AlaC 94541 712-E2
THOMPSON RD
1000 LFYT 94549 611-E5
S THOMPSON RD
900 LFYT 94549 611-E6
THOMPSON SQ
100 MTVW 94043 811-F3
THOMPSON ST
900 MRTZ 94553 571-E3
4500 OAK 94601 670-E1
THOMPSON CREEK CT
2700 SJS 95121 855-E3
3800 SJS 95135 855-E3
THOR AV
- SF 94131 667-G6
THOREAU DR
- MLV 94941 606-G4
THORN CT
- OAK 94611 630-F5
THORN DR
1500 CNCD 94521 593-E4
THORNALLY ST
400 SLN 94578 691-D5
THORNAPPLE DR
600 SUNV 94086 832-H2
THORNBRIAR DR
1500 SJS 95131 834-C1
THORNBURG RD
- SF 94129 647-E3
THORNBURY AV
18900 AlaC 94546 691-J3
THORNCREST DR
1500 SJS 95131 834-C1
THORNDALE CT
1000 SJS 95121 855-A5
THORNDALE DR
- SRFL 94903 566-D3
6400 OAK 94611 630-E5
THORNDALE PL
- MRGA 94556 631-C5
THORNE DR
300 HAY 94544 712-B6
THORNHAVEN WY
4500 SJS 95111 875-A1
4600 SJS 95111 874-J1
THORNHILL CT
- NVTO 94949 546-B2
- DNVL 94526 653-C2
3600 LVMR 94550 695-J5
6000 OAK 94611 630-E6
34300 FRMT 94555 732-E7
THORNHILL DR
600 LVMR 94550 695-J6
600 LVMR 94550 696-A6
700 SMCo 94015 687-A5
2600 SCAR 94070 769-F5
5500 OAK 94611 630-E6
THORNHILL PL
4300 PIT 94565 574-D7
34200 FRMT 94555 732-E7
THORNHILL RD
600 DNVL 94526 653-C2
THORNHILL WY
4200 PIT 94565 574-E7
THORNLEAF WY
1500 SJS 95131 834-C1
THORNMILL WY
1200 SJS 95121 854-J3
THORNTON AV
- SF 94124 668-B6
3600 FRMT 94536 752-E7
5400 NWK 94560 752-B6
8200 NWK 94560 772-C1
9100 FRMT 94555 752-B6
THORNTON AV Rt#-84
3900 FRMT 94555 752-H3
THORNTON COM
4500 FRMT 94536 752-G4
THORNTON CT
- NVTO 94945 526-A1

THORNTON CT
27900 HAY 94544 712-A7
THORNTON ST
- SLN 94577 691-A1
800 SLN 94577 690-J2
THORNTON WY
500 SJS 95128 853-F2
500 SCIC 95128 853-F3
THORNTREE CT
1100 SJS 95120 874-D6
THORNTREE DR
5900 SJS 95120 874-C6
THORNTREE PL
1100 SJS 95120 874-C6
THORN VALLEY CT
1200 SJS 95131 834-C1
THORNWALL LN
1200 HAY 94545 711-H6
THORNWOOD CT
4300 CNCD 94521 593-C3
THORNWOOD DR
800 PA 94303 791-E7
1500 CNCD 94521 593-B4
5300 SJS 95123 874-E3
THORNWOOD TER
500 SRFL 94903 566-C2
THORP LN
- SF 94114 667-F2
THORP PL
- SAR 95030 872-G5
THORPE CT
1200 LALT 94024 831-H3
THORS BAY RD
8600 ELCR 94530 609-E1
THORSEN CT
700 SCIC 94024 831-G4
THORUP LN
- SRMN 94583 673-C1
28100 HAY 94542 712-E5
THOUSAND OAKS
- OAK 94605 671-D2
THOUSAND OAKS BLVD
1300 ALB 94706 609-E5
1400 BERK 94707 609-F5
THOUSAND OAKS CT
1000 SJS 95136 874-D2
THOUSAND OAKS DR
3600 SJS 95136 874-D1
5700 AlaC 94552 692-C2
THOUSAND PINES CT
3200 SJS 95148 855-D2
THRASHER AV
200 LVMR 94550 715-E1
400 LVMR 94550 695-E7
THRASHER CT
2100 UNC 94587 732-G7
THRASHER LN
2600 SJS 95125 854-B7
THREADNEEDLE WY
1800 SJS 95121 855-B3
THREE FORKS LN
13400 LAH 94022 810-H7
THREE OAKS CT
14800 SAR 95070 872-F3
THREE OAKS WY
19500 SAR 95070 872-F4
THREE SPRINGS CT
3000 SCIC 95127 835-G3
THREE SPRINGS RD
3000 SCIC 95127 835-G3
THRESHER DR
100 VAL 94591 550-E1
THRIFT PL
3400 SJS 95148 835-E6
THRIFT ST
- SF 94112 687-D1
200 SF 94132 687-D1
THROCKMORTON AV
- MLV 94941 606-C2
THROCKMORTON LN
- MLV 94941 606-C2
THROCKMORTON TR
- MrnC 94965 586-A7
THRUSH CT
100 HER 94547 569-H5
1500 SCL 95051 832-H5
2600 SJS 95125 854-C6
THRUSH DR
2500 SJS 95125 854-C6
THRUSH ST
1400 AlaC 94578 691-E4
THRUSH TER
3600 FRMT 94555 732-J3
THRUSH WY
3700 SCL 95051 832-H5
THUMB MOUNTAIN CT
2000 ANT 94509 595-F5
THUNDERBIRD AV
1300 SUNV 94087 832-H5
1400 SCL 95051 832-H5
THUNDERBIRD CT
- OAK 94605 671-D3
- NVTO 94949 546-B3
3600 CNCD 94520 572-G5
THUNDERBIRD DR
- NVTO 94949 546-B3
3400 CNCD 94520 572-F6
9400 SRMN 94583 673-H6
THUNDERBIRD PL
9400 SRMN 94583 673-H7
22300 HAY 94545 711-E4
THUNDERBIRD WY
1800 SCIC 95125 853-H6
THUNDERHEAD CT
4800 RCH 94803 589-G1
THUNE AV
- MRGA 94556 651-E1
THURESON WY
5500 SJS 95124 873-H6
THURLES PL
- ALA 94502 669-J5
THURM AV
- SMTO 94403 749-B7
2200 BLMT 94002 749-B7
2200 BLMT 94002 769-B1
THURMAN DR
3000 SJS 95148 855-F1
THURSTON AV
1100 LALT 94024 831-H4
THURSTON CT
23300 AlaC 94541 692-D7

THURSTON ST
200 LGTS 95030 873-A6
41000 FRMT 94538 753-C7
41400 FRMT 94538 773-C1
THYME PL
500 SRFL 94903 566-C2
TIA PL
- MRGA 94556 651-F2
1900 SJS 95131 814-E7
TIANA LN
700 MTVW 94041 812-B7
TIARA CT
- SMCo 94010 728-B7
TIARA DR
2100 SJS 95116 834-H5
TIBER CT
1600 SJS 95138 875-F1
TIBERAN WY
5000 SJS 95130 852-J6
TIBOUCHINA LN
6200 SJS 95119 875-D5
TIBURON BLVD
100 MrnC 94901 586-H3
TIBURON BLVD Rt#-131
- MrnC 94920 606-H4
- TBRN 94920 606-H4
- MrnC 94941 606-H4
100 MrnC 94920 607-A5
100 TBRN 94920 607-A5
1500 BLV 94920 607-C6
1700 TBRN 94920 627-E1
TIBURON CT
200 CCCo 94596 612-A4
4500 ANT 94509 595-F3
TIBURON DR
4100 FRMT 94555 752-D2
TIBURON RD
14100 SLN 94577 690-H5
TIBURON ST
- SRFL 94901 586-J2
TIBURON TER
34800 FRMT 94555 752-E2
TIBURON WY
2800 BURL 94010 728-B6
TIBURON FERRY
- TBRN - 627-E1
- TBRN - 627-E1
TICE DR
1000 MPS 95035 794-B4
TICE CREEK DR
- WLCK 94595 632-B2
TICE HOLLOW CT
- CCCo 94595 632-C1
TICE VALLEY BLVD
1600 CCCo 94595 612-A7
1600 CCCo 94595 632-B1
1700 WLCK 94595 632-B1
2000 CCCo 94595 632-B1
TICE VALLEY LN
- WLCK 94595 632-B2
- CCCo 94595 632-B2
TICHENOR CT
1400 LFYT 94549 611-G3
TICINO CT
- PLE 94566 715-C7
TICONDEROGA CT
- SMCo 94402 768-H1
- SMTO 94402 768-H1
TICONDEROGA DR
800 SUNV 94087 832-B3
1900 SMCo 94402 768-G1
TIDEWATER AV
4400 OAK 94601 670-C2
TIDEWATER DR
- RDWC 94065 750-A6
100 HER 94547 570-A5
30700 UNC 94587 731-J4
30700 UNC 94587 732-A4
TIDEWAY DR
300 ALA 94501 669-E1
TIEGEN DR
1100 HAY 94542 712-A2
TIERRA ST
38700 FRMT 94536 753-D1
TIERRA BUENA DR
1400 SJS 95121 854-J2
1500 SJS 95121 855-A2
TIERRA GRANDE CT
21300 SCIC 95120 895-C5
TIERRA SOMBRA CT
21600 SCIC 95120 895-C5
TIERRA VERDE CT
- CCCo 94598 612-F4
TIERRA VISTA WY
- SRFL 94901 566-E7
TIFFANY AV
- SF 94110 667-H4
TIFFANY DR
- PIT 94565 574-C5
TIFFANY LN
- OAK 94611 630-F7
1100 PLE 94566 714-D2
TIFFANY PL
700 CNCD 94518 592-J6
TIFFANY RD
500 SLN 94577 690-G1
TIFFANY WY
1600 SJS 95125 854-A7
TIFFIN CT
- CLAY 94517 593-G7
TIFFIN DR
100 SJS 95136 874-J2
900 CLAY 94517 593-G7
TIFFIN PL
500 LVMR 94550 695-E6
TIFFIN RD
1800 OAK 94602 650-D3
TIFTON WY
4900 SJS 95118 874-B3
TIGARA CT
3700 SJS 95136 874-D1
TIGER LILY COM
- LVMR 94550 696-A4
TIGER TAIL CT
- ORIN 94563 610-H4
TIGERWOOD WY
400 SJS 95111 875-C2
TIKI LN
100 PIT 94565 574-E5
TIKI RD
2700 NVTO 94945 526-G1

TILBURY DR
4400 SJS 95130 853-A6
TILDEN CIR
- SRFL 94901 566-C6
TILDEN CT
- NVTO 94947 526-B6
TILDEN DR
4800 SJS 95124 873-G4
N TILDEN LN
4000 LFYT 94549 611-B6
S TILDEN LN
4000 LFYT 94549 611-B6
TILDEN PL
5400 FRMT 94538 752-J7
5500 FRMT 94538 772-J1
TILDEN ST
15400 SLN 94579 691-B7
TILDEN WY
300 ALA 94501 670-A2
300 OAK 94601 670-A2
24300 HAY 94545 711-F4
TILGRIM WY
2100 HAY 94545 731-H1
TILIA ST
1200 SMTO 94402 748-J3
TILLAMOOK DR
6200 SJS 95123 874-H7
TILLER DR
- SMTO 94404 749-D2
TILLER LN
- FCTY 94404 749-H4
400 RDWC 94065 749-H7
TILLER PL
- PIT 94565 574-A2
TILLEY CIR
1000 CNCD 94518 592-J5
TILLMAN AV
- SJS 95126 833-H7
TILLMAN PL
- SF 94108 648-A5
TILSON AV
18700 SCIC 95014 852-G2
19100 CPTO 95014 852-G2
TILSON DR
1100 CNCD 94520 592-E4
TILTON AV
- SMTO 94401 748-J1
700 SMTO 94401 728-J7
800 SMTO 94401 729-A7
TILTON CT
2600 SJS 95121 854-J3
TILTON DR
1100 SUNV 94087 832-E3
TILTON TER
- SMTO 94401 748-J1
TIM CT
200 DNVL 94526 652-J2
TIMBER CT
6500 SJS 95120 894-E1
TIMBER CV
- CMBL 95008 853-E7
TIMBER LN
- LFYT 94549 611-D7
TIMBER ST
37600 NWK 94560 752-G6
TIMBER WY
300 MPS 95035 813-J3
TIMBERCOVE ST
500 VAL 94591 550-E3
TIMBER CREEK DR
1500 SJS 95131 814-D5
TIMBERCREEK RD
1100 SRMN 94583 673-J7
TIMBERCREEK TER
41400 FRMT 94539 753-E7
TIMBERCREST DR
1000 SJS 95120 894-E1
TIMBERHEAD LN
300 FCTY 94404 749-G6
TIMBERLAKE AV
3400 SJS 95148 835-D6
TIMBERLAKE CT
2600 SJS 95148 835-E6
TIMBERLANE RD
1700 SMCo 94402 748-H7
1800 SMTO 94402 748-H7
TIMBERLANE WY
1700 SMTO 94402 768-H1
1700 SMCo 94402 768-H1
TIMBERLEAF CT
- CCCo - 613-B3
- CCCo 94598 613-B3
TIMBERLINE CT
100 DNVL 94526 653-B4
400 PLHL 94523 591-J6
2800 SJS 95121 855-E3
TIMBERLINE DR
3700 SJS 95121 855-E3
TIMBERLOOP DR
4200 SJS 95136 854-F7
4200 SJS 95136 874-F1
TIMBERPINE AV
600 SUNV 94086 832-H2
TIMBERPINE CT
1100 SUNV 94086 832-H2
TIMBER SPRING CT
11600 CPTO 95014 852-C4
TIMBERVIEW CT
- DNVL 94506 653-H4
6500 SJS 95120 894-C1
TIMBERVIEW DR
6500 SJS 95120 894-C2
TIMBERWOOD CT
6800 SJS 95120 894-H2
TIMCO CT
3500 AlaC 94552 692-C5
TIMCO WY
21100 AlaC 94552 692-C5
TIMES AV
18500 AlaC 94580 691-F7
18900 AlaC 94541 691-F7
18900 AlaC 94541 711-F1
TIMES WY
2300 ALA 94501 670-A2
TIMLOTT CT
3800 PA 94306 811-C2
TIMLOTT LN
800 PA 94306 811-C2
TIMOR CT
700 SJS 95127 814-H6
TIMOTEO DR
- MrnC 94941 606-H4

STREET Block City ZIP Pg-Grid

TIMOTEO TER
- MrnC 94941 606-H4
TIMOTHY CT
- NVTO 94949 546-E5
TIMOTHY DR
- SANS 94960 566-A4
900 SJS 95133 834-C2
1200 SLN 94577 690-H2
TIMOTHY LN
200 RDWC 94070 769-G6
200 SCAR 94070 769-G6
900 MLPK 94025 770-G7
1000 LFYT 94549 611-C6
TIMOTHY PL
3600 ANT 94509 595-B1
TIMPANOGAS CIR
38300 FRMT 94536 753-D1
TIMPANOGOS LN
600 DNVL 94526 633-A7
TINA CT
1300 MRTZ 94553 571-H6
TINA PL
7200 DBLN 94568 693-F5
TINA ST
- CCCo 94565 573-F2
TINA WY
600 HAY 94544 732-E2
600 LVMR 94550 715-E3
TINDER CT
5400 AlaC 94552 692-D3
TINGLEY ST
- SF 94112 667-G6
TINKER AV
- ALA 94501 649-F6
TINTERN LN
- PTLV 94028 810-B6
TINY ST
100 MPS 95035 794-A3
100 MPS 95035 793-J3
TIOGA AV
- SF 94134 688-A1
TIOGA CT
- MrnC 94903 546-A6
300 PA 94306 811-E2
400 PLE 94566 714-H2
500 SUNV 94087 832-D3
TIOGA DR
700 MLBR 94030 727-J4
2200 MLPK 94025 790-C6
24600 HAY 94544 711-J3
TIOGA LN
100 MrnC 94904 586-F4
TIOGA RD
3100 CNCD 94518 592-G4
TIOGA WY
- BLMT 94002 769-A2
- PCFA 94044 727-B5
1800 SJS 95124 853-H7
TIOGA PASS CT
6300 LVMR 94550 696-D3
TIPPAWINGO AV
3400 PA 94306 811-B1
TIPPERARY AV
2300 SSF 94080 707-D5
TIPPERARY CT
- ALA 94502 669-H5
TIPPERARY LN
100 ALA 94502 669-H5
TIPPICANOE AV
300 HAY 94544 732-F3
TIPTOE LN
- HIL 94010 748-B1
- SMCo 94010 748-B1
100 SMCo 94010 728-B7
100 HIL 94010 728-B7
1500 LALT 94024 832-A3
7400 CPTO 95014 852-D3
TIPTON CT
4800 UNC 94587 752-B1
TIROL CT
500 MPS 95035 794-A5
TIROS WY
1200 SUNV 94086 812-J6
TIRSO ST
40700 FRMT 94539 753-E4
TISBURY LN
- CCCo 94805 589-C5
TISCH WY
3000 SJS 95128 853-E2
TISDALE AV
- VAL 94592 529-G6
TISDALE WY
5000 SJS 95130 852-J7
TISSIACK CT
- FRMT 94539 773-H4
TISSIACK PL
45900 FRMT 94539 773-H5
TISSIACK WY
45900 FRMT 94539 773-H5
TITAN
- HER 94547 569-F3
TITAN WY
1200 SUNV 94086 812-J6
2500 AlaC 94546 691-G4
TITANIA CT
100 CCCo 94596 592-D7
TITLEIST CT
300 SJS 95127 815-A7
TITUS AV
12000 SAR 95070 852-G6
TITUS CT
19300 SAR 95070 852-G6
TIVERTON DR
3800 SJS 95121 855-B5
TIVOLI WY
1200 SJS 95120 894-E3
TIVOVI LN
100 DNVL 94506 653-J5
TOANO CT
1500 SJS 95131 814-D6
TOAST CT
- CCCo 94525 550-F5
TOBAGO AV
1900 SJS 95122 854-H1
TOBAGO LN
1000 ALA 94502 670-B7
TOBI CT
1800 CNCD 94521 593-D3
TOBI DR
4700 CNCD 94521 593-D3
TOBIAS DR
1500 SJS 95118 874-A4
TOBIN CT
100 VAL 94589 509-J6
TOBIN DR
600 SolC 94589 509-J6
600 VAL 94589 509-J6
2900 SJS 95132 814-E4
TOBIN CLARK DR
- HIL 94402 748-H4
TOBRUCK CT
1900 LVMR 94550 715-G3
TOBRUK ST
100 OAK 94626 649-C2
TOBY RD
9900 SRMN 94583 673-E5
TOCOLOMA AV
100 SF 94134 688-B2
TODD AV
2500 CNCD 94520 592-F3
TODD CT
- CCCo 94526 633-C5
2900 AlaC 94546 691-H4
TODD LN
- CCCo 94596 612-C2
- WLCK 94596 612-C2
25900 LAH 94022 811-C7
TODD ST
- SF 94129 647-C4
1300 MTVW 94040 811-G6
4500 FRMT 94538 753-B6
TODD WY
300 MrnC 94941 606-D4
3000 SJS 95124 873-G2
3100 SRMN 94583 673-F5
TODO EL MUNDO
100 WDSD 94062 789-J5
TOFFLEMIRE DR
- LFYT 94549 631-E1
TOFT ST
400 MTVW 94041 811-G5
TOFTS DR
1100 SJS 95131 814-E6
TOIYABE CT
100 LVMR 94550 695-D7
TOIYABE WY
2300 SJS 95133 814-F7
TOKAY COM
1100 LVMR 94550 715-H2
TOKAY CT
- PLHL 94523 592-A5
3100 PLE 94566 714-H4
3400 SJS 95148 835-C4
TOKAY WY
3400 SJS 95148 835-C4
TOKOLA DR
2600 CNCD 94518 592-G6
TOLAN WY
- LFYT 94549 611-A4
TOLAND ST
- SF 94124 668-B5
TOLBERT CT
2300 SJS 95122 854-J1
TOLBERT DR
1500 SJS 95122 854-H1
TOLEDO AV
1600 BURL 94010 728-B6
2500 SCL 95051 833-B6
TOLEDO CT
- BURL 94010 728-B6
- LFYT 94549 611-D5
100 VAL 94591 530-F6
1600 PCFA 94044 727-B6
35800 FRMT 94536 752-F2
TOLEDO DR
- LFYT 94549 611-D5
12200 SRMN 94583 673-F4
TOLEDO WY
- SF 94123 647-G4
16500 AlaC 94578 691-G4
TOLER AV
100 SLN 94577 691-A1
9800 OAK 94603 671-A5
TOLIN CT
200 SJS 95139 895-F1
TOLL GATE RD
21100 SAR 95070 872-B2
TOLLIVER DR
2900 SJS 95148 855-D2
TOLLRIDGE CT
- SMTO 94402 748-C7
TOLMAN DR
700 SCIC 94305 810-J2
TOLTEC CIR
2500 SRMN 94583 673-C3
TOLTECA CT
1200 FRMT 94539 773-H3
TOLTECA DR
1200 FRMT 94539 773-H3
TOLUCA DR
12200 SRMN 94583 673-G4
TOLWORTH DR
1000 SJS 95128 853-F3
1600 CMBL 95128 853-F3
TOM CT
- SRMN 94583 673-F6
TOMAHAWK CT
- NVTO 94949 526-B7
TOMAHAWK DR
- SANS 94960 566-B5
5100 SJS 95136 875-A3
TOMAHAWK PL
49000 FRMT 94539 793-J3
TOMALES ST
- SAUS 94965 626-J1
TOMAR CT
2400 PIN 94564 569-G7
TOMAS WY
200 PLE 94566 714-D5
TOMASINA CT
2200 SJS 95008 873-E1
TOMASO CT
- SF 94134 687-J2
TOMI LEA ST
600 LALT 94022 811-E5
TOMLEE DR
1300 BERK 94702 629-F1
TOMLIN WY
2200 SJS 95133 834-F2
TOMLINSON LN
900 SJS 95116 834-G5
TOMMY LN
7400 SCIC 95120 894-H5
TOMPKINS AV
- SF 94110 667-J6
1000 SF 94110 668-A6
4100 OAK 94619 650-G6
TOMPKINS DR
5800 SJS 95129 852-G3
TOMPKINS WY
2300 ANT 94509 595-A1
TOMRICK AV
4500 SJS 95124 873-F3
TONALEA ST
48900 FRMT 94539 793-J2
TONGA CT
700 SJS 95127 814-H6
TONGA LN
3300 ALA 94502 670-A7
TONI CT
- AlaC 94541 711-F1
- CCCo 94526 633-D5
100 VAL 94591 530-F3
10200 CPTO 95014 832-E7
TONI ANN PL
13500 SAR 95070 872-D1
TONICA RD
43600 FRMT 94539 773-H1
TONINO DR
4600 SJS 95136 874-D2
TONITA WY
10300 CPTO 95014 852-D1
TONO LN
200 CCCo 94596 592-C7
TONOPAH CIR
- PLE 94588 694-D6
TONOPAH CT
- PLE 94588 694-D6
48600 FRMT 94539 793-J2
TONOPAH DR
- FRMT 94539 793-J2
5600 SJS 95123 875-A4
TONSTAD PL
700 PLHL 94523 592-A3
TONY DR
4800 SJS 95124 873-G4
TONY TER
34100 FRMT 94555 752-B3
TOPAM GLEN CT
7400 SCIC 95120 894-J5
TOPANGA DR
10500 OAK 94603 670-H7
TOPAR AV
1400 SCIC 94024 831-G3
TOPAWA DR
600 FRMT 94539 773-H6
TOPAZ AV
1000 SJS 95117 853-B4
TOPAZ CIR
7500 DBLN 94568 693-J2
TOPAZ CT
100 HER 94547 569-G5
900 VAL 94590 550-B2
20000 AlaC 94546 692-B5
44200 FRMT 94539 773-H2
TOPAZ DR
2400 NVTO 94945 526-G1
TOPAZ LN
- PLHL 94523 591-J4
TOPAZ ST
100 MPS 95035 794-A7
100 MPS 95035 814-B1
300 RDWC 94062 769-H7
500 RDWC 94062 789-J1
600 RDWC 94061 789-J1
TOPAZ WY
- SF 94131 667-G5
100 LVMR 94550 715-D3
44200 FRMT 94539 773-H2
TOPEKA AV
- SF 94124 668-B6
- SJS 95128 853-G1
- SCIC 95128 853-G1
- SCIC 95128 833-G7
- SJS 95128 833-G7
- SJS 95126 833-G7
TOPEKA PL
300 DNVL 94526 653-C5
TOPINERA LN
- LFYT 94549 591-H7
TOPLEY CT
500 VAL 94591 530-E2
TOPLEY DR
2000 VAL 94591 530-E2
TOPOCK CT
3500 SJS 95111 854-G7
TOP OF THE HILL CT
15200 LGTS 95032 893-E1
TOP OF THE HILL RD
15200 LGTS 95032 893-F1
15200 SCIC 95032 893-F1
TOPPER CT
- LFYT 94549 611-G7
TOPPER LN
800 LFYT 94549 611-G7
TOPPING WY
16400 SCIC 95032 873-C7
TOPSAIL CT
- PLHL 94553 592-B1
- PLHL 94523 592-B1
100 VAL 94591 550-F2
200 FCTY 94404 749-G4
TOPSAIL DR
200 VAL 94591 550-F2
TOPSIDE WY
- MrnC 94941 606-J6
TORDO CT
200 FRMT 94539 753-F3
TORELLO LN
26000 LAH 94022 811-C6
TORENIA CIR
40200 FRMT 94538 773-B1
TORERO PZ
800 CMBL 95008 873-C1
TORINO CT
- DNVL 94526 653-C1
3400 CNCD 94518 592-H6
4100 PLE 94588 694-A5
TORINO DR
- SMCo 94070 769-E4
300 SCAR 94070 769-E4
TORINO WY
3500 CNCD 94518 592-J6
TORINO KNOLLS
- SCAR 94070 769-E5
TORLAND CT
500 SUNV 94087 832-D3
TORLANO CT
3400 PLE 94566 715-C6
TORMEY AV
- PIT 94565 573-H2
- CCCo 94565 573-H2
700 CCCo 94572 549-H7
TORNEY AV
- SF 94129 647-E4
TORO CT
- PTLV 94028 810-D6
TORONTO AV
2000 SLN 94579 691-A7
2000 SLN 94579 711-A1
TORONTO LN
2100 CNCD 94520 572-F5
TORRANCE AV
1200 SUNV 94089 812-J5
10000 SJS 95127 835-A3
TORRANO AV
700 HAY 94544 712-A4
900 HAY 94542 712-A4
TORRANO COM
300 FRMT 94536 732-J7
TORRE AV
10000 CPTO 95014 852-E1
TORRE CT
1500 SJS 95120 874-A6
TORREGATA LP
- SJS 95134 813-G2
TORRENS CT
- SF 94109 647-J5
TORRENZIA DR
- SJS 95134 813-D2
TORREON AV
9900 SRMN 94583 673-F5
TORRES AV
1100 MPS 95035 794-C5
4200 FRMT 94536 752-G3
TORREY CT
2600 PLE 94588 694-F6
TORREYA AV
600 SUNV 94086 832-H2
TORREYA CT
700 PA 94303 791-D7
TORREY PINE CT
100 WLCK 94598 612-J1
5600 RCH 94803 589-G4
TORREY PINE WY
4100 LVMR 94550 696-A4
4100 LVMR 94550 695-J4
TORREY PINES CT
100 VAL 94591 530-G3
TORREY PINES PL
- CLAY 94517 594-A7
TORREYS PEAK CT
4800 ANT 94509 595-D3
TORRINGTON CT
1400 SJS 95120 874-B6
2100 MRTZ 94553 572-A6
34300 FRMT 94555 732-E7
TORRINGTON DR
600 SUNV 94087 832-D3
TORRINGTON PL
34200 FRMT 94555 732-E7
TORTOISE PL
1900 WLCK 94595 632-B1
TORTOLA WY
400 SJS 95133 834-G2
TORTOSA CT
3700 SRMN 94583 673-B3
TORTUGA RD
13800 SLN 94577 690-G5
TORWOOD CT
500 LALT 94022 811-C5
TORWOOD LN
400 LALT 94022 811-D5
TORY CT
7000 DBLN 94568 693-J3
TORY WY
6700 DBLN 94568 693-J3
TORYGLEN WY
2100 SJS 95121 855-C3
TOSCA CT
1500 SJS 95121 854-J2
TOSCA WY
2500 SJS 95121 854-J2
3000 CNCD 94520 572-F6
TOSCANA CT
2900 SJS 95135 855-E3
TOSCANO CT
2000 MPS 95035 794-A2
TOTANA CT
2600 SRMN 94583 673-C3
TOTEM CT
100 FRMT 94539 773-J4
5000 ANT 94509 595-H4
TOTHERO PL
400 FRMT 94536 753-D2
TOTTEN ST
2600 AlaC 94546 692-A6
TOTTENHAM CT
5000 NWK 94560 752-E3
5000 SJS 95136 874-F3
TOTTERDELL CT
- ORIN 94563 631-B5
TOTTERDELL ST
3000 OAK 94611 650-G1
TOUCAN CT
1700 HAY 94541 712-B1
TOUCAN WY
- ANT 94509 594-J1
TOUCHARD ST
- SF 94109 647-J5
TOUCHSTONE TER
4700 FRMT 94555 752-C2
TOULON CT
1300 LVMR 94550 695-F6
1600 SJS 95138 875-F1
TOULON PL
36200 NWK 94560 752-D6
TOULOUSE ST
36000 NWK 94560 752-C6
TOURAINE DR
1400 SJS 95118 874-A6
TOURIGA CT
500 PLE 94566 714-G3
TOURIGA DR
3200 PLE 94566 714-G4
TOURIGA PL
1000 PLE 94566 714-G4
TOURMALINE AV
- LVMR 94550 715-D3
TOURMALINE CT
- LVMR 94550 715-C3
TOURNAMENT DR
700 HIL 94402 748-H4
TOURNAMENT WY
- HIL 94402 748-G5
TOURNEY DR
1200 SJS 95131 814-D6
TOURNEY LP
200 LGTS 95032 893-B2
TOURNEY RD
17500 LGTS 95032 893-B1
17600 SCIC 95032 893-B2
TOURRAINE DR
6000 NWK 94560 752-D5
TOURRAINE PL
6000 NWK 94560 752-D5
TOUSSIN AV
- MrnC 94904 586-D3
TOVAR DR
400 SJS 95123 875-A6
TOWER DR
- MrnC 94941 606-G3
TOWER LN
900 FCTY 94404 749-E3
TOWER RD
- SMCo 94402 768-H2
TOWER POINT LN
- TBRN 94920 607-F7
- TBRN 94920 627-F1
TOWERS DR
200 CCCo 94553 572-B7
TOWERS LN
2900 SJS 95121 855-A3
TOWERS ST
14800 SLN 94578 691-D3
TOWERS WY
37000 FRMT 94536 752-G4
TOWHEE CT
700 FRMT 94539 773-J7
34900 UNC 94587 732-G7
TOWHEE ST
47400 FRMT 94539 773-H7
TOWLE PL
600 PA 94306 791-D7
TOWLE WY
600 PA 94306 791-C7
TOWN AND COUNTRY DR
- DNVL 94526 653-A3
100 DNVL 94526 652-J3
TOWN AND COUNTRY LN
1900 SCL 95050 833-D6
TOWN CENTER DR
- MPS 95035 794-B6
TOWNCENTER DR
200 SUNV 94086 812-E7
TOWN CENTER LN
20300 CPTO 95014 852-E1
TOWN CLUB DR
1600 SJS 95124 873-J2
TOWNE TER
100 LGTS 95030 873-A6
TOWNS CT
3700 PIN 94564 569-J7
TOWNSEND AV
800 SJS 95112 834-B1
1300 SJS 95131 814-C7
1700 SCL 95051 833-A3
4300 OAK 94602 650-D3
24500 HAY 94544 711-G4
TOWNSEND ST
- SF 94107 648-B7
400 SF 94107 668-A1
600 SF 94103 668-A1
TOWNSEND TER
- SUNV 94087 832-B3
TOWNSEND PARK CIR
1200 SJS 95131 814-C7
TOWN SQUARE CT
- OAK 94603 670-J6
TOWNSQUARE DR
3500 SCIC 95127 835-B2
3500 SJS 95127 835-B2
TOY LN
2600 SJS 95121 855-D3
E TOYAH CT
4200 CNCD 94521 593-C2
TOYAMA DR
400 SUNV 94089 812-G4
TOYON AV
- BLV 94920 627-D1
100 SSF 94080 707-H3
300 LALT 94022 811-D6
300 SJS 95127 814-J6
600 SUNV 94086 832-H2
1300 AlaC 94586 734-B3
TOYON CT
- CMAD 94925 606-G1
- SAUS 94965 627-A3
100 HER 94547 569-J4
100 WDSD 94062 789-G5
1600 SMTO 94403 768-J1
1900 PLE 94588 714-B6
3400 SCIC 95127 814-J6
3400 SJS 95127 814-J6
5100 ANT 94509 595-H4
TOYON DR
100 VAL 94589 530-B2
100 VAL 94590 530-B2
900 BURL 94010 728-F6
1200 MLBR 94030 728-A5
1400 CNCD 94520 592-F3
2800 SCL 95051 833-A7
15500 SCIC 95030 872-H5
TOYON LN
- SAUS 94965 627-A3
- SAUS 94965 626-J3
- SF 94112 687-G2
TOYON PL
500 BEN 94510 550-J1
600 PA 94306 791-D7
4500 OAK 94619 650-G5
TOYON RD
- ATN 94027 790-G1
1700 LFYT 94549 611-G1
1700 LFYT 94549 591-G7
TOYON ST
- CCCo 94553 571-G4
TOYON TER
- ALA 94501 670-A4
- DNVL 94526 632-J7
- SANS 94960 566-B5
TOYON TR
- CCCo - 591-C4
- CCCo 94553 591-C4
TOYON WY
- NVTO 94945 526-D4
- SRFL 94901 586-E2
800 RDWC 94062 789-G1
2300 SBRN 94066 707-F6
5000 ANT 94509 595-H4
TOYONITA RD
23300 LAH 94024 831-E5
TOZIER ST
35700 NWK 94560 752-C6
TRABUCO CT
3200 SJS 95135 855-G3
TRACE AV
600 SJS 95126 833-G7
TRACEL DR
6100 SJS 95129 852-F5
TRACY CT
- CCCo 94507 632-J4
- MRGA 94556 651-G2
14000 LAH 94022 810-H6
14000 PA 94304 810-H6
TRACY DR
3200 SCL 95051 832-J7
TRACY LN
- CCCo 94507 632-J3
TRACY PL
- SF 94133 648-A4
TRACY ST
15500 AlaC 94580 691-D6
TRACY WY
300 CCCo 94507 632-J3
TRADAN DR
2400 SJS 95131 814-C4
TRADER LN
2200 SMTO 94404 749-E2
TRADE WIND LN
5100 FRMT 94538 753-A7
TRADEWIND LN
800 CCCo 94572 570-A2
TRADEWIND PASG
- CMAD 94925 606-J1
- CMAD 94925 607-A1
TRADEWINDS CT
200 SJS 95123 874-J4
TRADEWINDS DR
200 SJS 95123 874-J3
TRADEWINDS WKWY
5400 SJS 95123 874-J4
TRADE ZONE BLVD
300 MPS 95035 814-B4
300 SJS 95131 814-B4
TRADE ZONE CIR
1900 SJS 95131 814-B4
TRADE ZONE CT
1800 SJS 95131 814-B4
TRADE ZONE PL
2400 SJS 95131 814-B4
TRADE ZONE WY
1800 SJS 95131 814-B4
TRADITION CT
6600 SJS 95120 894-C5
TRAEGER AV
- SBRN 94066 707-H6
TRAFALAGAR CT
2600 CCCo 94520 572-G2
TRAFALGAR AV
2000 HAY 94545 711-G6
TRAFALGAR CIR
2600 CCCo 94520 572-G2
TRAFALGAR CT
1200 CNCD 94518 592-D6
TRAFALGAR PL
2000 OAK 94611 650-E1
3400 SJS 95132 814-J3
TRAFALGAR RD
3100 FRMT 94555 732-E7
TRAIL LN
- WDSD 94062 810-A5
TRAILCREEK CT
1700 CNCD 94521 593-D3
TRAILRIDGE CT
5000 ANT 94509 595-E4
TRAILRIDGE WY
5000 ANT 94509 595-E4
TRAIL RUN CT
4800 SJS 95136 875-A2
TRAILS END DR
800 WLCK 94598 613-A4
800 CCCo 94598 613-A4
TRAIL SIDE CT
5500 AlaC 94552 692-E3
TRAILSIDE PL
- PLHL 94523 591-H2
TRAILSIDE TER
- FRMT 94536 732-H7
TRAILVIEW CIR
300 MRTZ 94553 571-G5
TRAILVIEW CT
- SRMN 94583 673-D4
TRAIL WAY DR
31800 UNC 94587 732-A6
TRAILWAY DR
4100 SCIC 95127 835-A2
TRAINOR ST
- SF 94103 667-J1
TRALEE CT
- CCCo 94806 569-C6
TRALEE LN
300 ALA 94502 669-H5
TRALEE WY
- SRFL 94903 566-C1
TRAMANTO DR
2800 SCAR 94070 769-E6
TRAMIER CT
8300 SJS 95135 855-H7
TRAMINER CT
200 FRMT 94539 773-J4
TRAMPINI CIR
34200 FRMT 94555 752-B6
TRAMWAY DR
200 MPS 95035 794-A5
TRAMWAY PL
400 MPS 95035 794-A5
TRANSIT AV
33000 UNC 94587 732-D5
TRANSOM LN
400 FCTY 94404 749-G6
TRANSOM WY
2200 SLN 94577 690-H4
TRANSPORT ST
3900 PA 94303 791-F7
TRANSVERSE DR
- SF - 667-B1
TRAPLINE TR
- CCCo - 652-E3
TRAPPERS TR
- PA 94304 830-E2
TRASK ST
5000 OAK 94601 670-F1
5500 OAK 94605 670-F1
TRAUD CT
1300 CNCD 94518 592-E7
TRAUD DR
1400 CNCD 94518 592-E7
TRAUGHBER ST
1100 MPS 95035 794-C5
TRAVALINI CT
100 CCCo 94803 589-G2
TRAVERSO AV
300 LALT 94022 811-D4
TRAVERSO CT
400 LALT 94022 811-D4
TRAVERTINE WY
- UNC 94587 732-G6
TRAXLER RD
- SANS 94960 566-A5
TRAYNOR CT
24600 HAY 94544 711-J3
TRAYNOR RD
1200 CNCD 94520 592-E3
TRAYNOR ST
- HAY 94544 711-J4
TREADWAY DR
2300 SJS 95133 834-F1
TREADWAY LN
1900 PLHL 94523 592-C5
TREANOR ST
- SRFL 94901 586-F1
TREASURE CT
100 SRMN 94583 673-B1
TREASURE DR
700 CCCo 94565 573-D1
TREASURE HILL
- OAK 94618 630-C4
TREASURE ISLAND DR
100 BLMT 94002 749-F6
TREASURY PL
- SF 94104 648-B5
TREAT AV
200 SF 94103 667-J2
400 SF 94110 667-J2
1500 SF 94110 667-J4
TREAT BLVD
- WLCK 94596 612-D1
1300 CCCo 94596 612-D1
1400 WLCK 94598 612-D1
2400 CNCD 94518 592-F7
2400 WLCK 94598 592-F7
4000 CNCD 94518 593-A5
4200 CNCD 94521 593-A5
TREAT LN
1300 CNCD 94521 593-A4
27700 HAY 94545 731-G1
TREATY CT
5000 SJS 95136 875-A2
TREBBIANO PL
- PLE 94566 715-C6
TREBOL LN
3200 SJS 95148 835-D6
TREE LN
- NVTO 94947 525-J4
5600 AlaC 94552 692-E4
TREE CREEK PL
2300 DNVL 94506 653-F1
TREECREST PL
- WLCK 94596 612-D6
TREEFLOWER DR
5300 LVMR 94550 696-B4
TREE GARDEN PL
- CNCD 94518 592-E6
TREEHAVEN CT
- PLHL 94523 592-D4
TREEHAVEN DR
- SRFL 94901 566-E7
TREELINE PL
11500 DBLN 94568 693-E4
TREESIDE CT
- SSF 94080 707-G2
TREESIDE WY
2500 RCH 94806 568-J7
2500 RCH 94806 588-J1
TREE SWALLOW PL
3300 FRMT 94555 732-D7
TREE TOP CT
5800 SJS 95123 875-A5
TREETOP LN
- SMTO 94402 748-H4
TREE TOP WY
- MrnC 94904 586-B4
TREE TOPS CIR
3000 SBRN 94066 707-C5
TREE VIEW DR
200 DALY 94014 687-E3
TREEVIEW ST
30000 HAY 94544 712-E7
30000 HAY 94544 732-E1
TREEWOOD CT
4800 PLE 94588 713-J1
TREEWOOD LN
1900 SJS 95132 814-E2
TREFRY CT
32100 UNC 94587 732-C5
TREG LN
900 CNCD 94518 592-F6
E TREGALLAS RD
- ANT 94509 575-D6
W TREGALLAS RD
200 ANT 94509 575-C6
TREGASKIS AV
400 VAL 94591 530-D4
TREGO DR
4700 SJS 95118 874-B3
TRELANY RD
- PLHL 94523 592-C6
TRELLIS CT
900 PLE 94566 714-F3

Street	Block City ZIP	Pg-Grid
TRELLIS DR		
	- SRFL 94903	566-C3
TRELLIS LN		
	1000 ALA 94502	670-A7
TRELLIS PL		
	3200 SJS 95135	855-E3
TREMBATH CT		
	1800 ANT 94509	575-G5
TREMBATH LN		
	1300 ANT 94509	575-G5
	1300 CCCo 94509	575-G5
TREMBATH ST		
	1800 ANT 94509	575-G5
TREMONT AV		
	500 RCH 94801	588-C7
TREMONT CT		
	800 ANT 94509	575-F7
TREMONT ST		
	3000 BERK 94703	629-G4
	6500 OAK 94609	629-G4
TRENARY WY		
	5000 SJS 95118	874-C3
TRENERY DR		
	3500 AlaC 94588	694-F7
	3500 PLE 94588	694-F7
TRENOUTH ST		
	4200 FRMT 94538	753-D7
	4200 FRMT 94538	773-D1
TRENT CT		
	700 CCCo 94506	654-A5
TRENT DR		
	4800 SJS 95124	873-G4
TRENT ST		
	900 CNCD 94518	592-E7
TRENT TER		
	700 CCCo 94506	654-A5
TRENTON BLVD		
	900 SPAB 94806	588-G2
TRENTON CIR		
	100 PLE 94566	714-F3
TRENTON CT		
	1900 WLCK 94596	612-G7
	3600 FRMT 94538	773-E1
TRENTON DR		
	700 SUNV 94087	832-C3
	1900 SJS 95124	873-G1
	2200 SBRN 94066	707-G7
	2400 SBRN 94066	727-F1
	17600 AlaC 94546	692-B2
TRENTON PL		
	- SMCo 94402	748-F7
TRENTON ST		
	- SF 94108	648-A5
TRENTON WY		
	300 MLPK 94025	790-J3
	600 BURL 94010	728-G6
TRENTS FERRY CT		
	500 SJS 95133	834-E2
TRES ALMENDRAS		
	- LFYT 94549	611-J5
TRES CASAS CT		
	1000 WLCK 94598	612-G4
TRESEDER CT		
	100 LGTS 95032	873-B7
TRES MESAS		
	- ORIN 94563	610-E7
TRES PALMAS		
	900 MRTZ 94553	591-G4
TRESTLE DR		
	- HAY 94544	711-H3
TRESTLE GLEN CT		
	300 WLCK 94598	612-F2
TRESTLE GLEN DR		
	300 TBRN 94920	607-B4
	300 MrnC 94920	607-B4
TRESTLE GLEN RD		
	600 OAK 94610	650-A3
	1700 OAK 94602	650-C3
	1700 PDMT 94602	650-C3
	1700 PDMT 94610	650-C3
	2000 WLCK 94598	612-F2
TRESTLE GLEN TER		
	100 TBRN 94920	607-B4
TREVARNO RD		
	- LVMR 94550	696-A6
TREVINO TER		
	1000 SJS 95120	894-E1
TREVISO AV		
	1500 SJS 95118	874-B5
TREVISO CT		
	5900 FRMT 94555	752-B6
TREVOR AV		
	31500 HAY 94544	732-F2
	32300 UNC 94587	732-F2
TREVOR DR		
	1500 SJS 95118	874-A4
TREYBURN CIR		
	500 SRMN 94583	693-H1
TRI LN		
	6300 CCCo 94803	589-H5
	6300 RCH 94803	589-H5
TRIAD DR		
	- LVMR 94550	695-C4
TRIANA WY		
	100 SRMN 94583	693-H1
TRIANGLE CIR		
	900 RCH 94801	588-F5
TRIANON WY		
	200 LALT 94022	811-E6
TRIBOROUGH LN		
	1400 SJS 95126	853-G4
TRIBUNE AV		
	2500 HAY 94542	712-D3
TRICIA WY		
	20400 SAR 95070	852-E7
TRIDENT CT		
	100 VAL 94591	550-F2
TRIDENT DR		
	400 RDWC 94065	749-H7
E TRIDENT DR		
	- PIT 94565	574-A2
	- PIT 94565	573-J2
W TRIDENT DR		
	- PIT 94565	573-J2
TRIESTE CT		
	1600 SJS 95122	854-F1
TRIESTE WY		
	1500 SJS 95122	854-F1
	5700 PLE 94588	694-C6
TRIFARI PL		
	3200 CNCD 94518	592-J7
TRIFONE DR		
	900 SJS 95117	853-C3
TRIGGER CT		
	1200 CCCo 94572	549-J6
TRIGGER LN		
	- CCCo 94803	569-G7
	- CCCo 94803	589-F1
TRIGGER RD		
	1200 CCCo 94572	549-J6
TRILLIUM CT		
	- SCAR 94070	769-C4
TRILLIUM LN		
	1000 MrnC 94965	606-D6
TRIMAR CT		
	3900 SJS 95111	854-J6
TRIMARAN CT		
	100 FCTY 94404	749-H4
TRIMBLE CT		
	2100 SJS 95132	814-C3
	2800 HAY 94542	712-E4
TRIMBLE RD		
	200 SJS 95131	813-G6
	200 SJS 95134	813-G6
	400 SCL 95134	813-G6
	400 SCL 95054	813-G6
	2500 SJS 95131	814-C3
	2500 MPS 95035	814-C3
	2500 SJS 95132	814-C3
TRIMBOLI WY		
	41000 FRMT 94538	753-D7
TRIMINGHAM DR		
	1400 PLE 94566	714-E1
TRINA CT		
	- CCCo 94596	612-F7
TRINCULO LN		
	33500 FRMT 94555	752-B1
TRINIDAD AV		
	4800 OAK 94602	650-G4
TRINIDAD CIR		
	500 UNC 94587	732-C6
TRINIDAD CT		
	6500 SJS 95120	894-D1
TRINIDAD DR		
	- MrnC 94920	607-C2
	6400 SJS 95120	894-E1
TRINIDAD LN		
	400 FCTY 94404	749-F5
TRINIDAD RD		
	2700 SJS 95111	854-H4
	14100 SLN 94577	690-H5
TRINIDAD ST		
	26700 HAY 94545	711-F7
TRINIDAD TER		
	4100 FRMT 94555	752-E1
TRINITY AV		
	200 CCCo 94708	609-G3
	1700 WLCK 94596	612-B5
	13800 SAR 95070	872-D1
TRINITY CIR		
	- LVMR 94550	695-D7
TRINITY CT		
	- MLPK 94025	790-C7
	- PIT 94565	574-D5
	100 SBRN 94066	707-D7
	1800 ANT 94509	575-F5
	2100 MRTZ 94553	572-A7
	6400 DBLN 94568	694-A4
	13900 SAR 95070	872-D2
TRINITY DR		
	- NVTO 94947	526-D7
	1000 MLPK 94025	790-C7
TRINITY LN		
	- PTLV 94028	809-J6
TRINITY PL		
	2100 MRTZ 94553	572-A7
	3100 SJS 95124	873-F2
TRINITY RD		
	- BSBN 94005	688-A6
TRINITY ST		
	- SF 94104	648-A5
	- SF 94108	648-A5
	200 VAL 94590	529-H4
	2000 SMTO 94403	749-C4
TRINITY TER		
	- MRGA 94556	651-E2
TRINITY WY		
	- SRFL 94903	566-D3
	39500 FRMT 94538	753-B6
TRINITY RIVER CT		
	2900 SJS 95111	854-H4
TRINITY SPRING CT		
	11700 CPTO 95014	852-A5
TRINTEL CT		
	3600 WLCK 94598	613-A3
TRIO CT		
	5300 FRMT 94538	773-B1
TRIOMPHE CT		
	400 DNVL 94506	653-J5
TRIPALDI WY		
	2200 HAY 94545	731-J2
TRIPIANO CT		
	2000 MTVW 94040	831-J1
TRIPOLI		
	4000 ALA 94501	649-E6
TRIPOLI AV		
	1800 SJS 95122	854-G1
TRIPOLI CT		
	100 SRMN 94583	673-H6
	12900 LAH 94022	830-J1
TRIPP AV		
	1200 SJS 95116	834-D4
TRIPP CT		
	- WDSD 94062	789-E7
TRIPP RD		
	3300 WDSD 94062	789-E6
	3600 WDSD 94062	809-F1
TRISH CT		
	- DNVL 94506	653-G4
TRISH DR		
	- DNVL 94506	653-G4
	- NVTO 94947	525-F2
	- MrnC 94947	525-F2
TRISH LN		
	- DNVL 94506	653-G4
TRISTAN AV		
	3100 SJS 95127	814-H7
TRITON CT		
	1600 SCL 95050	833-D3
TRITON DR		
	1100 FCTY 94404	749-F2
TRITON ST		
	28400 HAY 94544	712-B7
TRIUMPH CT		
	1400 SJS 95129	852-E4
TRIUMPH DR		
	3000 ALA 94501	649-G7
TRIXIE DR		
	- LVMR 94550	696-A6
TROGLIA TER		
	100 PCFA 94044	727-A3
TROJAN AV		
	900 SLN 94579	691-B6
TROLLMAN AV		
	1400 SMTO 94401	729-A7
TROMBAS AV		
	1900 SLN 94577	691-C1
TRONA WY		
	1500 SJS 95125	854-A7
	1600 SJS 95125	873-J1
TRONSON CT		
	3600 SJS 95132	814-F2
TROON CT		
	500 MPS 95035	794-B6
TROON PL		
	30500 HAY 94544	732-D1
TROOST CT		
	5400 AlaC 94552	692-D3
TROPHY CT		
	- HIL 94402	748-H4
TROPHY DR		
	900 MTVW 94040	811-G6
TROPIC CT		
	15300 SLN 94579	691-C6
TROPIC WY		
	39200 FRMT 94538	752-J7
TROPICANA WY		
	300 UNC 94587	732-C6
TROST RD		
	- SRFL 94901	586-E1
TROTTER CT		
	800 WLCK 94596	632-G3
TROTTER DR		
	100 VAL 94591	530-E2
TROTTER WY		
	2200 WLCK 94596	632-F2
	2600 PLE 94588	714-A4
TROUN WY		
	700 LVMR 94550	695-J6
TROUSDALE DR		
	- SMCo	728-B6
	- SMCo 94010	728-B6
	1100 BURL 94010	728-B6
TROUT CT		
	44800 FRMT 94539	773-J3
TROUT FARM BRDG		
	- CNCD 94518	592-E6
TROUT FARM RD		
	- SMCo	727-B7
TROWBRIDGE WY		
	1100 CCCo 94506	654-A5
	5600 SJS 95138	855-G7
	5800 SJS 95138	875-H1
TROWVILLE LN		
	1600 HAY 94545	711-H6
TROY AL		
	- SF 94109	647-J5
TROY AV		
	5100 FRMT 94536	752-H6
TROY CT		
	300 CCCo 94803	589-E2
	900 SUNV 94087	832-C3
TROY DR		
	500 SJS 95117	853-B1
TROY PL		
	- HAY 94544	732-E3
TROY ST		
	- LVMR 94550	695-E7
TROYER AV		
	42200 FRMT 94539	753-F7
TROY PARK PL		
	1800 SJS 95124	873-G4
TRUBY ST		
	- SF 94129	647-E4
TRUCKEE CT		
	4000 SJS 95136	874-H1
	6200 NWK 94560	772-H1
TRUCKEE LN		
	100 SJS 95136	874-G1
TRUDEAN WY		
	1700 SJS 95132	814-D4
TRUDY LN		
	- SMCo 94025	790-D5
TRUETT CT		
	2900 SJS 95148	855-D4
TRUETT ST		
	- SF 94108	648-A5
	- SF 94108	647-J5
TRUFFLE CT		
	3200 SJS 95148	855-E2
TRUITT AV		
	- MRTZ 94553	571-F7
TRUITT LN		
	- OAK 94618	630-C6
TRUMAN AV		
	1400 LALT 94024	832-A3
	2400 OAK 94605	671-A5
	3300 MTVW 94040	832-A3
	3500 LALT 94040	832-A3
TRUMAN CT		
	- NVTO 94947	526-B6
	2600 ANT 94509	574-H6
TRUMAN DR		
	- NVTO 94947	526-A6
	- NVTO 94949	526-A6
TRUMAN PL		
	5400 FRMT 94538	752-J7
TRUMAN ST		
	1100 RDWC 94061	789-J1
	1500 CCCo 94801	588-F4
TRUMAN WY		
	- SJS 95002	793-C7
TRUMBULL AV		
	500 MrnC 94947	525-G4
	500 NVTO 94947	525-G4
TRUMBULL CT		
	- NVTO 94947	525-H3
	500 SUNV 94087	832-D3
TRUMBULL ST		
	- SF 94134	667-H6
	- SF 94112	667-H6
TRUMPET CT		
	4400 AlaC 94552	692-D3
TRUMPETER PL		
	1200 SJS 95131	814-B6
TRUST WY		
	3900 HAY 94545	731-D1
TRYM ST		
	1800 AlaC 94541	712-B1
TRYNA DR		
	3300 MTVW 94040	832-A2
TRYSAIL CT		
	200 FCTY 94404	749-G4
TUBAC LN		
	5600 SJS 95118	874-B5
TUBBS ST		
	- SF 94107	668-C3
TUBBY ST		
	400 CMBL 95008	853-E5
TUBMAN CT		
	500 SJS 95125	854-D5
TUCKER AV		
	- SF 94134	688-A1
TUCKER DR		
	6300 SJS 95129	852-F4
TUCSON AV		
	1100 SUNV 94089	812-J5
TUCSON DR		
	5600 SJS 95118	874-D4
TUCSON WY		
	6600 SJS 95119	875-D5
TUDOR CT		
	- CCCo 94507	632-J2
	- SRFL 94903	566-G5
	600 SLN 94577	690-G1
	1200 SJS 95127	834-J4
	1300 CNCD 94521	593-A4
	7500 PLE 94588	714-A3
TUDOR DR		
	1600 MLPK 94025	790-F2
TUDOR PL		
	36200 NWK 94560	752-E4
TUDOR RD		
	400 SLN 94577	690-G1
TUERS CT		
	1000 SJS 95121	854-J4
TUERS RD		
	2600 SJS 95121	854-H3
	3200 SJS 95121	855-A5
TUGGLE AV		
	18700 SCIC 95014	852-H2
TUGGLE PL		
	10600 SCIC 95014	852-H2
TULA CT		
	20800 CPTO 95014	852-D1
TULA LN		
	10200 CPTO 95014	852-D1
TULAGI ST		
	100 OAK 94626	649-C3
TULANE AV		
	1000 SLN 94579	691-B6
	1600 EPA 94303	771-B6
TULANE CT		
	700 SMTO 94402	748-H3
	800 MTVW 94040	811-G7
	1100 LVMR 94550	716-A1
	3400 SCL 95051	832-J6
TULANE DR		
	- LKSP 94939	586-E4
	600 SCL 95051	832-J6
	800 MTVW 94040	811-G7
	1200 WLCK 94596	632-G2
TULANE RD		
	200 SMTO 94402	748-H3
TULANE ST		
	- SF 94134	667-J7
	1600 UNC 94587	732-F6
TULARCITOS DR		
	1200 MPS 95035	794-D3
TULARE AV		
	900 ALB 94707	609-F6
	900 BERK 94707	609-F6
	1700 CCCo 94805	589-B6
	2300 ELCR 94530	589-C6
	2800 RCH 94804	588-J4
	3500 RCH 94804	589-A4
	3500 SPAB 94806	589-A4
TULARE CT		
	4100 CNCD 94521	593-A3
	4100 ANT 94509	595-J1
TULARE DR		
	100 SBRN 94066	707-E7
	3000 SJS 95132	814-F4
	4000 CNCD 94521	593-A3
	48900 FRMT 94539	794-A2
TULARE ST		
	- BSBN 94005	688-B6
	900 SF 94124	668-C4
TULARE HILL DR		
	7300 SJS 95139	875-G7
TULARE HILL LN		
	7400 SJS 95139	875-G7
TULARE HILL RD		
	7400 SJS 95139	875-G7
TULE CT		
	- CLAY 94517	593-G6
TULE LAKE LN		
	32700 FRMT 94555	732-B6
TULIP AL		
	- SF 94103	648-A7
TULIP AV		
	1700 HAY 94545	731-J1
	4400 OAK 94619	650-G6
TULIP CT		
	- SMCo 94010	748-B1
	900 SUNV 94086	832-G3
	5100 LVMR 94550	696-B4
TULIP DR		
	1000 SUNV 94086	832-G3
	1200 ANT 94509	575-B5
TULIP LN		
	- SLN 94577	690-J1
	- PA 94303	791-C4
	- SCAR 94070	769-D4
	100 MLBR 94030	727-H4
TULIP RD		
	2100 SJS 95128	833-E6
	2400 SCL 95128	833-E6
TULIP ST		
	100 HER 94547	570-B4
TULIP WY		
	1200 LVMR 94550	696-B4
TULIPAN DR		
	1000 SJS 95129	852-G3
TULIP BLOSSOM CT		
	100 SJS 95123	875-A4
TULIPTREE LN		
	2600 SCL 95051	833-B7
TULIPWOOD CIR		
	7200 PLE 94588	713-J1
TULIPWOOD CT		
	4200 PLE 94588	713-J1
TULIPWOOD LN		
	3200 SJS 95132	814-E2
TULITA CT		
	21000 SCIC 95014	832-C7
TULLAMORE PL		
	- ALA 94502	669-H4
TULLER AV		
	2500 ELCR 94530	589-B7
TULLIBEE CT		
	1200 CCCo 94572	549-J7
TULLIBEE RD		
	1200 CCCo 94572	549-J7
TULLY CT		
	3600 SJS 95148	835-F6
TULLY PL		
	3000 OAK 94605	671-A2
TULLY RD		
	- SJS 95112	854-F4
	- SJS 95122	854-H2
	- SJS 95121	854-H2
	300 SCIC 95111	854-F4
	300 SJS 95111	854-H2
	1600 SJS 95122	855-A1
	1900 SJS 95122	835-B7
	2200 SJS 95148	835-E6
	2900 SCIC 95148	835-D6
	3500 SCIC 95148	835-E6
TULLY WY		
	800 CNCD 94518	592-G6
TULSA ST		
	500 AlaC 94580	691-D5
TUMBLE WY		
	3500 SJS 95132	814-G4
TUMBLEWEED COM		
	400 FRMT 94539	773-J4
TUMBLEWEED CT		
	- SRMN 94583	673-C4
	4100 UNC 94587	732-A6
	5100 ANT 94509	595-J6
TUMBLING BROOK RD		
	- ORIN 94563	610-D6
TUM SUDEN WY		
	- RDWC 94062	789-F3
	- SMCo 94062	789-F3
	- WDSD 94062	789-F3
TUMWATER CT		
	900 WLCK 94598	612-H4
TUMWATER DR		
	2700 WLCK 94598	612-H4
TUNBRIDGE DR		
	36200 NWK 94560	752-F4
TUNBRIDGE RD		
	600 DNVL 94526	653-C3
TUNBRIDGE WY		
	6700 SJS 95120	894-G2
TUNIS AV		
	3600 SJS 95132	814-F2
TUNIS PL		
	- CCCo 94553	572-C7
TUNIS RD		
	200 OAK 94603	670-F7
TUNITAS LN		
	- SSF 94080	707-E3
TUNITAS CREEK RD		
	- SMCo 94062	789-A7
TUNNEL AV		
	100 SF 94134	688-A4
	200 RCH 94801	608-D1
	500 BSBN 94005	688-A4
TUNNEL LN		
	400 CMAD 94925	606-F1
TUNNEL RD		
	1800 OAK 94618	630-C4
	1800 OAK 94705	630-C4
	2000 OAK 94611	630-D3
TUNNEL RD Rt#-13		
	- BERK 94705	630-B4
	- OAK 94705	630-B4
	1800 OAK 94618	630-B4
TUNSTEAD AV		
	- SANS 94960	566-B7
	- SANS 94960	586-C1
TUOLOMNE CT		
	6100 SJS 95123	874-H6
TUOLUMNE AV		
	200 MRTZ 94553	571-E6
TUOLUMNE CT		
	100 MLBR 94030	727-J4
TUOLUMNE DR		
	100 FRMT 94539	793-J2
TUOLUMNE RD		
	1100 MLBR 94030	727-H4
TUOLUMNE ST		
	- VAL 94590	530-B5
	1600 VAL 94589	530-B1
	2200 VAL 94589	510-A7
TUOLUMNE WY		
	4500 CNCD 94521	593-B5
TUPELO DR		
	3400 WLCK 94598	612-J1
TUPELO ST		
	34200 FRMT 94555	752-B2
TUPELO TER		
	34400 FRMT 94555	752-C3
TUPOLO DR		
	1600 SJS 95124	873-J3
	4900 SJS 95118	873-J3
TURANDOT CT		
	1500 SJS 95121	854-H4
TURBAN CT		
	5600 FRMT 94538	773-B2
TURF CT		
	5200 ANT 94509	595-J5
TURINO ST		
	800 LVMR 94550	695-E7
TURK DR		
	- MRGA 94556	631-E5
TURK ST		
	- SF 94102	648-A6
	100 SF 94102	647-G6
	1000 SF 94115	647-G6
	2200 SF 94118	647-G6
	2700 SF 94118	647-D7
	2900 SF 94117	647-D7
TURKEY FARM LN		
	- WDSD 94062	809-G1
TURK MURPHY LN		
	- SF 94133	648-A4
TURKS HEAD CT		
	- RDWC 94065	749-H7
TURKS HEAD LN		
	- RDWC 94065	749-H7
TURLEY CT		
	1900 SJS 95116	834-H5
TURLEY DR		
	800 SJS 95116	834-G5
TURLOCK LN		
	1300 SJS 95132	814-F4
TURLOCK WY		
	100 HAY 94544	712-A5
TURNAGAIN RD		
	- MrnC 94904	586-C4
TURNBERRY DR		
	2500 SSF 94080	707-D5
	2500 SBRN 94066	707-D5
TURNBERRY PL		
	5200 SJS 95136	874-F3
TURNBERRY WY		
	- VAL 94591	530-G3
TURNER AV		
	4300 OAK 94605	671-E5
TURNER CT		
	- CCCo 94507	632-H2
	100 SJS 95139	895-F1
	800 HAY 94545	711-G5
	1200 AlaC 94545	711-G5
	3400 FRMT 94536	752-H3
	3400 CNCD 94518	592-J6
	4300 OAK 94605	671-D5
TURNER DR		
	400 BEN 94510	551-A2
	700 SCIC 95128	853-F2
	1000 NVTO 94949	546-C1
TURNER LN		
	1200 AlaC 94586	734-G3
TURNER PKWY		
	- VAL 94591	530-E1
TURNER PL		
	3700 FRMT 94536	752-G3
TURNER ST		
	- VAL 94591	530-F1
TURNER TER		
	- SF 94107	668-B3
	400 SMTO 94401	728-H7
	400 SMTO 94401	748-H1
TURNER WY		
	1200 CMBL 95008	873-B1
TURNEY ST		
	300 SAUS 94965	627-A3
TURNHOUSE LN		
	2000 SJS 95121	855-C3
TURNLEY AV		
	- OAK 94605	671-B3
TURNSTONE CT		
	200 FCTY 94404	749-H1
	400 LVMR 94550	715-D1
TURNSTONE DR		
	- SRFL 94901	587-A2
	100 LVMR 94550	715-D1
	2600 PLE 94566	714-C1
TURNSTONE LN		
	3000 FRMT 94555	732-D6
TURNSTONE PL		
	33500 FRMT 94555	732-D6
TURNSTONE WY		
	1300 SUNV 94087	832-H4
TURNSWORTH AV		
	- RDWC 94062	769-H6
TURNWOOD CT		
	3600 SJS 95130	853-C4
TURPIN CT		
	600 RCH 94801	588-F6
TURPIN ST		
	600 RCH 94801	588-F6
TURPIN WY		
	35900 FRMT 94536	732-J7
TURQUESA CT		
	200 SJS 95116	834-F3
TURQUOISE DR		
	300 HER 94547	569-G5
	900 HER 94564	569-H5
TURQUOISE ST		
	300 MPS 95035	814-B1
	7600 DBLN 94568	693-J2
	48200 FRMT 94539	793-J1
TURQUOISE WY		
	- LVMR 94550	715-D3
	- SF 94131	667-F4
TURRETT DR		
	1200 SJS 95131	814-D6
TURRIFF WY		
	1400 SJS 95132	814-E4
TURRIN DR		
	400 PLHL 94523	592-B6
TURRINI CIR		
	- DNVL 94526	653-B1
TURRINI CT		
	100 DNVL 94526	653-B1
TURRINI DR		
	700 DNVL 94526	653-B1
TURRINI PL		
	- DNVL 94526	653-B1
TURTLE BAY PL		
	- SMCo 94402	768-G1
TURTLE CREEK		
	- OAK 94605	671-D2
TURTLE CREEK CT		
	300 SJS 95125	854-D4
TURTLE CREEK RD		
	4200 CNCD 94521	593-B4
TURTLE ROCK CT		
	- TBRN 94920	607-B3
TURTLEROCK DR		
	1100 SJS 95122	854-G1
TURTLE ROCK LN		
	1100 CNCD 94521	593-B4
TUSCALOOSA AV		
	- ATN 94027	790-C3
TUSCAN PARK CT		
	3200 SJS 95135	855-F2
TUSCANY AL		
	- SF 94133	648-A3
TUSCANY CIR		
	- LVMR 94550	715-J4
TUSCANY CT		
	- FRMT 94539	773-J4
	- LVMR 94550	715-H4
	- DNVL 94506	653-H4
TUSCANY CT		
	100 HER 94547	570-B6
TUSCANY DR		
	7600 DBLN 94568	694-A1
TUSCANY PL		
	1000 CPTO 95014	852-D2
TUSCANY WY		
	- DNVL 94506	653-G5
TUSCARORA CT		
	5900 SJS 95123	874-J5
TUSCARORA DR		
	400 SJS 95123	874-H6
TUSTIN CT		
	- BEN 94510	551-B1
TUSTIN DR		
	1700 SJS 95122	855-A3
TUXEDO COM		
	34700 FRMT 94555	752-D3
TUXEDO CT		
	20700 AlaC 94552	692-C5
TUYSHTAK CT		
	- CLAY 94517	593-J5
TWAIN AV		
	- BERK 94708	609-J6
TWAIN CT		
	18800 SAR 95070	872-H1
TWAIN ST		
	600 SF 94111	648-A5
TWAINE CIR		
	2100 SLN 94577	690-G2
TWAIN HARTE LN		
	- SRFL 94901	586-G3
TWEED CT		
	19400 SAR 95070	872-F1
TWEED DR		
	100 DNVL 94526	653-C3
TWEED LN		
	- DNVL 94526	653-C3
TWEED TER		
	- SRFL 94901	567-B7
	- MrnC 94901	567-B7
TWEEDHOLM CT		
	6200 SJS 95120	894-B1
TWEEDSMUIR CT		
	2100 SJS 95121	855-C4
TWELVE ACRES DR		
	600 LALT 94022	811-C5
TWELVE OAK HILL DR		
	- SRFL 94903	546-D7
	- SRFL 94903	566-D1
TWELVE OAKS CT		
	1400 CCCo 94507	632-E3
TWELVE OAKS DR		
	- PLE 94588	714-A5
TWELVE OAKS RD		
	100 LGTS 95032	893-D1
TWIG LN		
	19100 SCIC 95014	852-G1
TWILIGHT COM		
	5300 FRMT 94555	752-C3
TWILIGHT CT		
	4200 HAY 94542	712-G4
	19900 CPTO 95014	832-F7
TWILIGHT DR		
	3700 SJS 95124	873-E3
TWINBRIDGE CIR		
	100 PLHL 94523	592-D4
TWIN BROOK CT		
	900 SJS 95126	853-J3
TWIN BROOK DR		
	900 SJS 95126	853-J3
TWIN CREEKS CT		
	23700 AlaC 94541	692-C7
	23700 AlaC 94541	712-B1
TWIN CREEKS DR		
	2500 SRMN 94583	673-C1
TWIN CREEKS RD		
	18300 MSER 95030	872-H4
	18500 SAR 95070	872-H4
TWIN DOLPHIN DR		
	- RDWC 94065	749-G7
	- RDWC 94065	769-G1
TWIN FALLS CT		
	3800 SJS 95121	855-D3
TWINFLOWER CT		
	2400 MRTZ 94553	572-A6
TWINING CT		
	600 ANT 94509	595-E1
TWINKLE CT		
	- MPS 95035	793-H6
TWINLAKE DR		
	200 SUNV 94089	812-H5
TWIN OAK CT		
	1000 RDWC 94061	789-G3
TWIN OAKS AV		
	- SRFL 94901	566-F7
TWIN OAKS DR		
	100 LGTS 95032	873-D7
TWIN OAKS LN		
	400 CCCo 94596	612-F7
	2700 SJS 95127	835-A5
TWIN OAKS WY		
	3800 OAK 94605	671-B3
TWIN PEAKS BLVD		
	- SF 94117	667-E3
	- SF 94114	667-E3
	200 SF 94131	667-E4
	300 SF 94131	667-E4
TWIN PEAKS DR		
	100 CCCo 94595	612-C7
TWIN PEAKS LN		
	300 CCCo 94507	633-A4
TWIN PEAKS TER		
	4000 FRMT 94538	753-B5
TWINVIEW DR		
	100 PLHL 94523	591-J6
TWINVIEW PL		
	700 PLHL 94523	592-A6
	700 PLHL 94523	591-J6
TWITTER CT		
	- OAK 94605	650-H6
TWYLA CT		
	2400 SJS 95008	853-B7
TWYLA LN		
	3900 SJS 95008	853-B7
TYBALT CT		
	33900 FRMT 94555	752-C2
TYBALT DR		
	800 SJS 95127	835-C1
TYBURN PL		
	300 DNVL 94526	653-C3

STREET
Block City ZIP Pg-Grid

TYEE CT
5200 AlaC 94546 691-J6
TYEE ST
21200 AlaC 94546 691-J6
TYHURST CT
5500 SJS 95123 874-J4
TYHURST WALKWAY
5400 SJS 95123 874-J4
TYLER AV
100 SCL 95117 853-D1
100 SCL 95117 833-D7
400 LVMR 94550 696-A7
TYLER CT
- AMCN 94589 510-A4
100 SCL 95051 833-A7
900 CNCD 94518 592-H5
2200 ANT 94509 575-A7
5200 AlaC 94546 692-B2
5500 FRMT 94538 752-J7
TYLER LN
4900 AlaC 94546 692-B2
TYLER PL
5400 FRMT 94538 752-J7
TYLER RD
- VAL 94592 549-H2
- VAL 94592 550-A2
TYLER ST
- BEN 94510 551-D6
- NVTO 94947 526-A5
600 OAK 94603 670-G6
1500 BERK 94703 629-F4
1800 SPAB 94806 588-H3
TYLER TER
800 PLHL 94523 591-J5
TYLER PARK WY
1400 MTVW 94040 811-J7
TYMN WY
1900 SJS 95122 834-J6
TYNAN AV
- ALA 94501 649-F6
TYNAN WY
- PTLV 94028 809-J6
TYNDALL CT
4400 CNCD 94518 593-A6
TYNDALL ST
400 LALT 94022 811-E7
TYNE CT
- BEN 94510 530-J7
6900 DBLN 94568 693-J3
TYNE PL
5000 NWK 94560 752-E4
TYNE WY
3700 SCL 95054 813-E6
TYNEBOURNE PL
100 ALA 94502 669-J5
TYR CT
- PLHL 94523 592-B3
TYR LN
21500 SCIC 95120 895-C4
TYRELLA AV
200 MTVW 94043 812-A4
TYRELLA CT
100 MTVW 94043 812-A4
TYRONE CT
2600 SSF 94080 707-C4
TYRREL CT
- DNVL 94526 653-D4
TYRRELL AV
26500 HAY 94544 712-A6
TYRRELL ST
4600 OAK 94601 650-E7
TYSON CIR
- PDMT 94611 650-D1
TYSON CT
- DNVL 94526 653-D4
TYSON LN
38500 FRMT 94536 753-C3

U

UCCELLI BLVD
- RDWC 94063 770-B4
UINTA CT
800 FRMT 94536 753-D1
UKIAH CT
100 WLCK 94595 612-C7
ULFINIAN WY
600 MRTZ 94553 571-E3
ULLMAN CT
4400 SJS 95121 855-E4
ULLOA CT
900 NVTO 94949 546-B1
ULLOA ST
- SF 94127 667-E4
1200 SF 94116 667-A5
3300 SF 94116 666-H5
ULMECA PL
- FRMT 94539 793-J1
500 FRMT 94539 773-J7
ULMER CT
300 RDWC 94061 790-C1
ULSTER DR
2000 SJS 95131 814-D6
ULSTER PL
- ALA 94502 669-J5
ULSTER WY
- SSF 94080 707-E5
ULTIMA CT
- DNVL 94526 653-B1
UMBARGER RD
- SCIC 95111 854-F5
- SJS 95111 854-F5
300 SJS 95121 854-J4
UMPQUA CT
900 FRMT 94539 773-H4
UNA CT
1800 FRMT 94539 753-E5
UNA WY
- MLV 94941 606-E4
UNDAJON DR
600 SJS 95133 834-E2
UNDERHILL DR
900 CCCo 94507 632-G7
UNDERHILL RD
- MLV 94941 606-G2
- ORIN 94563 630-H1
UNDERHILLS RD
900 OAK 94610 650-B3
UNDERWOOD AV
1200 SF 94124 668-C7
5100 OAK 94613 650-G7
25700 HAY 94544 711-J5
UNDERWOOD DR
3700 SJS 95117 853-B2
UNIFIED WY
2200 SJS 95125 854-D4
UNION AV
1500 RDWC 94061 790-A1
2000 CMBL 95008 853-F6
2300 SJS 95008 853-F6
2400 SCIC 95008 853-F6
2600 SJS 95124 853-F6
2600 SJS 95124 873-F3
2900 AlaC 94541 692-C7
3400 SCIC 95124 873-F3
14700 SJS 95032 873-F5
14700 LGTS 95032 873-F5
UNION CT
500 BEN 94510 550-J1
3700 ANT 94509 595-C3
UNION PZ
- CNCD 94518 592-E6
UNION SQ
- UNC 94587 732-G6
UNION ST
- SF 94111 648-A4
- SJS 95110 854-C1
- SRFL 94901 586-H1
100 VAL 94590 530-B6
100 SRFL 94901 566-H7
200 SF 94133 648-A4
700 OAK 94607 649-E2
700 SF 94133 647-J4
800 ALA 94501 669-H2
1000 SF 94109 647-J4
1200 SF 94109 647-H4
1500 SF 94123 647-F4
2800 OAK 94608 649-E2
3200 FRMT 94538 753-D7
UNION CITY BLVD
3900 UNC 94587 731-J4
4800 UNC 94545 751-J1
4800 UNC 94587 751-J1
28700 HAY 94545 731-J4
28700 AlaC 94545 731-J4
28800 UNC 94545 731-J7
32600 UNC 94587 752-A1
32600 UNC 94555 752-A1
32700 FRMT 94555 752-A1
UNION MINE CT
4900 ANT - 595-D3
UNION MINE DR
4800 ANT - 595-D3
UNIONSTONE DR
- MrnC 94903 546-D5
UNIONSTONE LN
- MrnC 94903 546-D5
UNITED PL
10000 CPTO 95014 832-D7
UNIVERSITY AV
- BERK 94704 629-B2
- PA 94301 790-J4
- LGTS 95030 873-B5
100 LALT 94022 811-D6
100 VAL 94591 530-D3
200 SJS 95110 833-H5
500 LALT 94022 831-E1
600 BERK 94702 629-F1
800 LALT 94024 831-E1
800 PA 94301 791-A3
800 MSER 95030 873-B5
800 BERK 94703 629-F1
900 SCIC 94024 831-E1
900 SJS 95126 833-G6
1700 SJS 95128 833-F7
1900 BERK 94704 629-F1
1900 EPA 94303 791-B2
2100 MTVW 94040 811-F4
2400 SPAB 94806 588-H3
2500 EPA 94303 771-B7
UNIVERSITY AV Rt#-109
2600 EPA 94303 771-B6
2700 MLPK 94303 771-B6
2800 MLPK 94025 771-B6
UNIVERSITY CT
25400 HAY 94542 712-C3
UNIVERSITY DR
- MLPK 94025 790-F3
33300 UNC 94587 732-F5
UNIVERSITY ST
- SF 94134 667-J7
500 SCL 95050 833-D5
500 SF 94134 687-J1
UNIVERSITY TER
500 LALT 94022 831-D1
UNIVERSITY WY
1600 SJS 95128 833-F7
1700 SJS 95126 833-F7
21500 CPTO 95014 832-B7
UNWIN CT
2400 SSF 94080 707-D4
UP ST
1500 BERK 94804 629-D1
UPENUF RD
- WDSD 94062 809-H6
UPHALL CT
1900 SJS 95121 855-C5
UPLAND AV
- DALY 94015 687-A5
- DALY 94015 686-J5
- SCAR 94070 769-F3
UPLAND CIR
100 CMAD 94925 607-A1
UPLAND CT
100 VAL 94589 530-A1
200 RDWC 94062 769-G7
2400 LVMR 94550 715-G4
11500 SCIC 95014 852-B4
UPLAND DR
- SF 94112 667-C6
- SF 94127 667-C6
800 LFYT 94549 611-E7
2200 CNCD 94520 572-F7
4600 RCH 94803 589-D3
UPLAND LN
- MLV 94941 606-D2
- NVTO 94945 526-E3
UPLAND RD
- MrnC 94904 586-B4
200 RDWC 94062 769-G7
400 SMCo 94062 769-G7
2200 AlaC 94578 691-E2
2400 SMCo 94062 789-H1
UPLAND RD
2400 RDWC 94062 789-H1
UPLAND WY
600 FRMT 94539 773-H2
11500 CPTO 95014 852-B4
11500 SCIC 95014 852-B4
22800 HAY 94541 692-C7
UPLANDS DR
200 HIL 94010 748-H2
UPPER RD
- ROSS 94957 586-B2
100 MrnC 94903 566-J2
UPPER RD W
- ROSS 94957 586-A2
UPPER TER
- SF 94117 667-F2
UPPER TR
- AlaC 94552 652-E6
- CCCo - 652-C3
- LFYT 94549 611-B7
UPPER ALCATRAZ PL
- MLV 94941 606-D2
UPPER AMES AV
- ROSS 94957 586-C2
UPPER ARDMORE
- LKSP 94939 586-E7
UPPER BRIAR RD
- MrnC 94904 586-D5
UPPER CECILIA WY
- TBRN 94920 607-A4
UPPER FREMONT DR
- SRFL 94901 586-E1
UPPER HAPPY VLY RD
1000 LFYT 94549 611-B5
UPPER HILL CT
13800 SAR 95070 872-C1
UPPER HILL DR
13800 SAR 95070 872-C1
UPPERHILL RD
- MLV 94941 606-G2
UPPER LAKE RD
- WDSD 94062 809-H5
UPPER LOCK AV
3200 BLMT 94002 769-A2
UPPER N TER
- TBRN 94920 607-A4
UPPER OAK DR
- SRFL 94903 566-C1
- SRFL 94903 546-D7
UPPER POND CT
2400 CCCo - 591-G5
UPPER SERVICE RD
- SF 94131 667-D2
- SF 94143 667-D2
UPPER TOYON DR
- SRFL 94901 586-E1
- MrnC 94904 586-E2
- ROSS 94957 586-E1
UPPER VIA CASITAS
- LKSP 94939 586-F4
UPPER VINTNERS CIR
- FRMT 94539 773-J4
UPR GOLDEN RAIN RD
2300 WLCK 94595 632-A1
2800 WLCK 94595 631-J1
UPSON CT
- PLHL 94523 592-A5
UPTON AV
- SF 94129 647-C4
15200 SLN 94578 691-D5
UPTON CT
700 SJS 95136 874-E1
UPTON RD
- CCCo 94563 630-F2
- ORIN 94563 630-F2
2900 MRTZ 94553 571-F7
UPTON ST
- SMCo 94062 789-J1
400 SF 94124 668-A5
400 SMCo 94062 769-H7
500 RDWC 94062 789-J1
600 RDWC 94061 789-J1
UPTON WY
700 SJS 95136 874-E1
URANIUM RD
100 SCL 95051 833-A1
100 SUNV 94086 833-A1
2800 SCL 95051 813-A7
URANUS AV
100 HAY 94544 712-B7
100 OAK 94611 630-D6
URANUS DR
4100 UNC 94587 732-B6
URANUS PL
32400 UNC 94587 732-B6
URANUS TER
- SF 94114 667-F2
URBAN LN
600 PA 94301 790-H5
URBAN ST
40000 FRMT 94538 753-C6
URBAN WY
400 HAY 94544 711-J3
URBANO DR N
- SF 94127 667-C7
URBANO DR S
400 SF 94127 667-C7
URIDIAS RANCH RD
2100 MPS 95035 794-E6
2100 SCIC 95035 794-E6
URLIN CT
6100 SJS 95123 875-B6
URNA AV
1700 SJS 95124 873-H1
URSA DR
48400 FRMT 94539 793-J1
URSA LN
800 FCTY 94404 749-F4
URSA WY
3200 AlaC 94541 692-D6
URSHAN CT
100 SJS 95138 875-G6
URSHAN WY
7200 SJS 95138 875-G6
URSLA ST
700 LVMR 94550 696-B7
URSULA AV
700 PCFA 94044 727-B2
URSULA LN
27200 LAH 94022 830-J1
URSULA WY
1300 EPA 94303 791-B1
URZI CT
2800 SJS 95135 855-E2
URZI DR
3200 SJS 95135 855-E2
USHER CT
- CCCo 94507 632-H2
USHER ST
15500 AlaC 94580 691-D6
USONA DR
1400 SJS 95118 874-B3
UTAH AV
100 SSF 94080 708-A4
UTAH DR
2900 RCH 94803 589-E2
UTAH ST
100 SF 94103 668-A2
400 SF 94110 668-A2
500 PLE 94566 714-G2
8100 OAK 94605 671-A2
UTAH WY
- FRMT 94536 753-A3
- RDWC 94062 789-H1
UTE CT
- SRMN 94583 673-D5
1600 FRMT 94539 773-G4
6100 SJS 95123 874-H6
UTE DR
6100 SJS 95123 874-H6
UTICA CT
300 SJS 95123 875-B7
500 SUNV 94087 832-D3
7000 DBLN 94568 693-J3
UTICA DR
500 SUNV 94087 832-D3
UTICA LN
300 SJS 95123 875-B7
UTICA ST
32300 HAY 94544 732-F3
UTOPIA PL
1100 SJS 95127 835-C2
UVAS AV
200 MPS 95035 793-J6
UVAS CT
700 SJS 95123 874-G5
25300 AlaC 94541 712-C2
UVAS RD Rt#-G8
23200 SJS 95141 895-G7
UXBRIDGE CT
- SJS 95139 875-G7

V

VACA DR
40700 FRMT 94539 753-E5
VACA CREEK RD
1000 CCCo 94553 591-D3
VACA CREEK WY
100 CCCo 94553 591-D2
VACATION DR
1100 LFYT 94549 611-J5
VACCA ST
- RCH 94801 588-B6
VAGABOND CT
200 CCCo 94526 633-D6
VAGABOND LN
28900 HAY 94544 712-B7
28900 HAY 94544 732-B1
VAGABOND WY
100 CCCo 94526 633-D6
VAI AV
21300 CPTO 95014 852-C3
VAILWOOD CT
- DNVL 94526 653-D5
1300 PLE 94566 714-D2
VAILWOOD DR
1200 DNVL 94526 653-D4
VAILWOOD PL
100 SMTO 94403 749-E6
VAILWOOD WY
1100 SMTO 94403 749-E6
VAL ST
4500 FRMT 94538 753-B7
VAL AIRE PL
900 WLCK 94596 612-E7
VALAIS CT
- FRMT 94539 753-E4
VALANT PL
- OAK 94610 650-C2
- PDMT 94610 650-C2
VALCARTIER DR
1400 SUNV 94087 832-D5
VALDEFLORES DR
100 SMCo 94010 728-B7
VALDEZ AV
- SF 94112 667-D6
200 SF 94127 667-D6
1800 BLMT 94002 769-D2
VALDEZ CT
2400 ANT 94509 595-A2
VALDEZ PL
900 SCIC 94305 810-J2
1100 FRMT 94539 753-E4
VALDEZ ST
2200 OAK 94612 649-H3
2800 OAK 94611 649-H3
VALDEZ WY
1200 FRMT 94539 753-E5
1500 PCFA 94044 727-A6
VALDIVIA CIR
100 SRMN 94583 673-C3
VALDIVIA CT
- BURL 94010 728-C6
VALDIVIA WY
2300 BURL 94010 728-B6
VALDOSTA CT
1900 PLE 94566 714-E1
VALDOSTA RD
1100 SJS 95121 855-A5
VALE AV
- SF 94132 667-A5
1400 CMBL 95008 873-C2
3300 OAK 94619 650-F6
VALE CT
6100 SJS 95123 875-A6
6800 PLE 94588 694-A7
VALE DR
300 SJS 95123 875-A6
VALE RD
1800 RCH 94804 588-J4
1800 SPAB 94806 588-J4
2400 SPAB 94806 589-A4
VALE ST
- DALY 94014 687-C5
VALELAKE CT
1100 SUNV 94089 812-J4
VALENCIA AV
- SRFL 94901 586-H1
1000 SUNV 94086 832-C1
VALENCIA CT
- NVTO 94945 526-A3
- PTLV 94028 810-D6
2300 SJS 95125 853-J6
2800 SPAB 94806 588-J2
3400 WLCK 94598 592-J7
40400 FRMT 94539 753-E4
VALENCIA DR
200 LALT 94022 811-E5
200 MLBR 94030 727-J5
200 MLBR 94030 728-A5
300 SSF 94080 707-F5
700 MPS 95035 794-B6
VALENCIA LN
300 CMAD 94925 586-F7
VALENCIA PL
2800 ANT 94509 575-A6
2800 ANT 94509 574-J6
22000 HAY 94541 691-J7
VALENCIA RD
- ORIN 94563 631-B5
VALENCIA ST
- SF 94103 667-H3
100 VAL 94591 530-F6
500 SF 94110 667-H3
1500 SF 94110 667-H4
8400 DBLN 94568 693-G2
VALENCIA WY
1000 PCFA 94044 726-J4
1000 PCFA 94044 727-A4
2800 SPAB 94806 588-J2
4700 UNC 94587 731-J7
VALENTE CIR
2100 MRTZ 94553 571-E3
VALENTE CT
2100 MRTZ 94553 571-E3
4000 LFYT 94549 611-B6
VALENTE DR
4000 LFYT 94549 611-B6
VALENTINE ST
7500 OAK 94605 671-A1
VALENZA WY
3500 PLE 94566 715-B7
VALERGA DR
2100 BLMT 94002 769-D3
VALERIAN CT
1200 SUNV 94086 832-G3
VALERIAN WY
1000 SUNV 94086 832-G3
VALERIE CT
900 CCCo 94803 569-D6
1700 BEN 94510 551-B3
2200 SJS 95008 853-B7
VALERIE DR
3900 SJS 95008 853-B7
VALERI RUTH CT
500 SCL 95050 833-C6
VALERO DR
40800 FRMT 94539 753-E6
VALERTON CT
- SF 94112 667-F7
VALESCO CT
- NVTO 94949 546-E4
VALHALLA CT
1700 SJS 95132 814-E4
VALHALLA DR
2900 SJS 95132 814-E4
VALIANT WY
2400 UNC 94587 732-C4
VALINDA DR
3700 CNCD 94518 592-H4
VALITA DR
600 SLN 94577 691-C2
VALLA CT
- WLCK 94596 612-B3
VALLA DR
1700 SJS 95124 873-H1
VALLCO PKWY
19100 CPTO 95014 832-G7
VALLECITO CT
- WLCK 94596 612-E6
1100 LFYT 94549 611-B5
VALLECITO LN
- CCCo 94596 612-E6
- ORIN 94563 610-F6
- WLCK 94596 612-E7
100 PCFA 94044 727-B2
VALLECITO PL
2700 OAK 94606 650-B4
VALLECITO RD
22000 CPTO 95014 852-A2
VALLECITO WY
2600 ANT 94509 595-G5
VALLECITOS LN
- AlaC 94586 734-E6
VALLECITOS RD Rt#-84
11000 AlaC 94586 734-F5
E VALLECITOS RD Rt#-84
800 AlaC 94550 715-E6
800 PLE 94550 715-E6
1200 PLE 94566 715-E6
1300 LVMR 94550 715-E6
11300 AlaC 94586 734-H4
VALLECITOS WY
100 LGTS 95030 872-J4
VALLE DEL LAGO
- SJS 95135 855-G4
VALLEE TER
36000 FRMT 94536 733-A7
VALLEJO AV
200 CCCo 94572 549-J7
500 CCCo 94572 569-J1
800 NVTO 94945 526-B3
VALLEJO CT
200 MLBR 94030 727-J5
600 AlaC 94541 711-H1
VALLEJO DR
- MLBR 94030 727-J5
200 MLBR 94030 728-A6
1300 SJS 95130 853-A4
VALLEJO PL
3200 SRMN 94583 673-G5
VALLEJO ST
- SF 94129 647-D3
- BERK 94707 609-F5
- SF 94111 648-B4
300 CCCo 94525 550-E4
300 SF 94133 648-A4
300 SF 94133 648-B4
800 SF 94133 647-F5
1100 SF 94109 647-F5
1600 SF 94123 647-F5
2000 SF 94115 647-F5
3900 UNC 94587 731-J5
5500 OAK 94608 629-E5
5500 EMVL 94608 629-E5
21600 AlaC 94541 691-H7
21600 AlaC 94541 711-H1
37800 FRMT 94536 753-C1
VALLEJO TER
- SF 94133 647-J4
700 PCFA 94044 707-A5
VALLEJO WY
- SRFL 94903 566-A2
37000 FRMT 94536 733-B7
VALLEJO-SAN FRANCISCO FERRY
- VAL 94590 529-J6
- VAL 94592 530-A7
- CCCo - 549-H3
- HER - 549-F7
- HER - 569-C1
- PIN - 569-C1
- PIN - 568-D3
- RCH - 568-D3
- SF - 608-A3
- VAL - 549-H3
- VAL - 550-A1
- SF - 648-C4
- SF - 648-D1
- SF - 607-J1
VALLETA CT
- SF 94131 667-F6
VALLE VERDE CT
100 DNVL 94526 633-C6
VALLE VISTA
100 DNVL 94526 633-D6
4300 PIT 94565 574-C6
VALLE VISTA AV
- VAL 94590 529-J2
100 VAL 94590 530-A2
200 HAY 94544 712-C7
400 OAK 94610 650-A2
800 VAL 94589 530-C1
VALLE VISTA CT
19200 SAR 95070 872-G4
VALLE VISTA DR
19200 SAR 95070 872-F4
VALLEY AV
- MRTZ 94553 571-F7
2500 PIN 94564 569-E4
3500 PLE 94566 714-B1
4100 CCCo 94553 571-F7
4100 CCCo 94553 572-A3
VALLEY CIR
- MLV 94941 606-F4
VALLEY CT
- ATN 94027 790-A7
- ORIN 94563 631-A2
- WDSD 94062 790-A7
200 PLHL 94523 592-A7
700 SCL 95051 833-A6
1100 CNCD 94520 592-F3
VALLEY DR
- ORIN 94563 631-A2
- ORIN 94563 630-J3
- PIT 94565 574-D6
100 BSBN 94005 688-A5
100 NVTO 94949 546-G5
200 PLHL 94523 592-A7
300 BSBN 94005 687-J5
VALLEY LN
3800 CCCo 94803 589-D3
VALLEY RD
- ATN 94027 790-A7
- MrnC 94941 606-G3
- SANS 94960 566-A5
- SCAR 94070 769-F3
1500 CCCo 94707 609-E4
VALLEY RUN
100 HER 94547 569-H4
VALLEY ST
- DALY 94014 687-C5
- SF 94110 667-G5
100 SF 94131 667-G5
200 LALT 94022 811-E7
200 SAUS 94965 627-B4
200 SMCo 94014 687-C5
1300 HAY 94541 712-A1
1500 SLN 94577 690-H2
2100 OAK 94612 649-G3
2300 BERK 94702 629-F2
VALLEY ST N
2100 BERK 94702 629-F2
VALLEY TR
- CCCo - 591-D7
- CCCo - 611-D1
- CCCo - 652-D3
VALLEY WY
100 LKSP 94939 586-D6
400 MPS 95035 793-J7
600 SCL 95051 833-B6
4800 ANT 94509 595-J4
VALLEY BROOK CT
22500 AlaC 94541 692-D6
VALLEYBROOK CT
4100 SJS 95111 855-A7
VALLEY BROOK WY
3200 AlaC 94541 692-D6
VALLEY CREEK LN
300 DNVL 94526 653-A2
VALLEY CREST CT
1500 SJS 95131 834-D1
VALLEY CREST DR
1400 SJS 95131 834-C1
5000 CNCD 94521 593-D4
VALLEY FORGE DR
1000 SUNV 94087 832-B3
VALLEY FORGE ST
31700 HAY 94544 732-E3
VALLEY FORGE WY
500 SJS 95117 853-C4
500 SCIC 95117 853-C4
600 CMBL 95008 853-C4
VALLEY GLEN CT
6200 SJS 95123 874-G7
VALLEY GLEN DR
6100 SJS 95123 874-G6
VALLEY GLEN LN
100 MRTZ 94553 591-G2
VALLEY GREEN DR
20500 CPTO 95014 832-D6
VALLEYHAVEN WY
- SJS 95111 874-J1
VALLEY HEIGHTS DR
2700 SJS 95133 814-G7
VALLEY HIGH
4000 LFYT 94549 611-B4
VALLEY HIGH DR
300 PLHL 94523 591-J2
VALLEY HILL DR
- CCCo 94549 631-H6
- MRGA 94556 631-H6
- CCCo - 631-H6
VALLEY MEADOW CT
5900 SJS 95135 855-J7
VALLEY OAK
- PTLV 94028 830-C2
VALLEY OAK CT
1200 NVTO 94947 526-C6
VALLEY OAK DR
- AlaC 94552 692-E6
3700 AlaC 94542 692-E6
17200 MSER 95030 873-B4
VALLEY OAK LN
100 VAL 94591 550-E1
200 VAL 94591 530-E7
VALLEY OAK PZ
200 MRTZ 94553 591-H3
VALLEY OAK RD
2000 PLE 94588 714-A6
VALLEY OAKS CT
- CCCo 94507 632-H5
VALLEY OAKS DR
100 CCCo 94507 632-H5
VALLEY ORCHARD CT
4900 CCCo 94553 591-C3
VALLEY PARK CIR
100 SJS 95139 895-H2
VALLEY QUAIL CIR
1100 SJS 95120 894-F3
VALLEY RIDGE LN
3700 SCIC 95148 835-E5
VALLEY SQUARE LN
3200 SJS 95117 853-D4
VALLEYSTONE DR
- MrnC 94903 546-D6
VALLEY TRAILS DR
6900 PLE 94588 714-A1
VALLEY VIEW AV
- SCIC 95127 815-A7
- SRFL 94901 566-E6
300 SCIC 95127 814-J6
1600 BLMT 94002 749-D7
1600 BLMT 94002 769-D1
VALLEY VIEW CT
- CCCo 94803 589-F2
- DNVL 94526 652-J1
- SMCo 94402 748-G6
500 MRTZ 94553 571-G5
1000 SCIC 94024 831-F2
7200 PLE 94588 693-J6
VALLEY VIEW DR
- ORIN 94563 631-A5
300 SCIC 94024 831-F2
1900 PIN 94564 569-E4
22600 AlaC 94541 692-D6
VALLEY VIEW LN
100 ORIN 94563 610-H5
900 MrnC 94941 606-E5
1900 CNCD 94521 593-F4
VALLEY VIEW RD
- LFYT 94549 611-C4
- OAK 94611 630-D5
- ORIN 94563 610-H4
300 PLHL 94523 592-A5
4100 CCCo 94803 589-F2
4200 RCH 94803 589-F2
5000 CCCo 94803 589-F2
5600 RCH 94805 589-E4
VALLEY VIEW ST
3700 LVMR 94550 695-J6
VALLEYVIEW WY
100 SSF 94080 707-E5
VALLEY VISTA CT
400 WLCK 94598 612-J2
VALLEY VISTA RD
400 WLCK 94598 612-J2
3400 WLCK 94598 613-A2
VALLEYWOOD CT
3000 SJS 95148 855-E1
VALLEYWOOD DR
- PCFA 94044 726-J6
2000 SBRN 94066 707-E6
VALMAINE CT
3000 SJS 95135 855-F3
VALMAR DR
5200 CNCD 94521 593-D6
VALMAR PL
- SCAR 94070 769-F5
VALMAR TER
- SF 94112 667-H7
- SF 94134 667-H7
VALMY ST
100 MPS 95035 794-A4
VALORIE ST
2000 FRMT 94539 753-F7
VALORY LN
3800 LFYT 94549 611-D4
VALOTA RD
600 RDWC 94061 789-J1
900 RDWC 94061 790-A2
VALPARAISO AV
- ATN 94027 790-E5
- MLPK 94025 790-C6
700 MLPK 94027 790-E5
1800 MLPK 94025 790-E5
VALPARAISO ST
- SF 94133 647-J4
600 SCIC 94305 810-H1
VALPEY PARK AV
4700 FRMT 94538 773-B2
VALPEY PARK CT
4700 FRMT 94538 773-C2
VALPICO DR
1700 SJS 95124 853-J7

STREET Block City ZIP Pg-Grid

VALROY CT
400 SJS 95123 875-A7
VALROY DR
6200 SJS 95123 875-A7
VALS LN
3200 LFYT 94549 611-H4
VALVERDE DR
300 SSF 94080 707-F5
VAL VISTA AV
- MLV 94941 606-E2
VAN AV
14700 AlaC 94578 691-E2
VAN CT
500 HAY 94544 732-B1
800 SUNV 94087 832-D2
VAN AUKEN CIR
900 PA 94303 791-D5
VAN BUREN AV
200 OAK 94610 649-H3
VAN BUREN CIR
1800 MTVW 94040 831-G1
VAN BUREN CT
- NVTO 94947 526-B6
3000 ANT 94509 575-A7
VAN BUREN DR
3000 ANT 94509 575-A7
VAN BUREN PL
500 SRMN 94583 673-F6
3100 ANT 94509 575-A7
VAN BUREN RD
100 MLPK 94025 770-H7
400 MLPK 94025 790-J1
VAN BUREN ST
- SF 94131 667-G6
300 LALT 94022 811-C4
1600 SMTO 94403 749-C2
2800 ALA 94501 670-B3
VANCE CT
3400 SJS 95132 814-G4
VANCE DR
1300 SJS 95132 814-G4
VANCE LN
- EPA 94303 791-C2
- LFYT 94549 611-H3
VANCLEAVE LN
1000 WLCK 94598 612-D5
1000 WLCK 94596 612-D5
VAN CLEAVE WY
- OAK 94619 650-H5
VAN COTT CT
- SJS 95127 834-H3
VANCOUVER AV
1100 BURL 94010 728-D6
VANCOUVER COM
38500 FRMT 94536 753-B3
VANCOUVER CT
14300 SCIC 95127 835-B3
VANCOUVER GRN
1700 FRMT 94536 753-B3
VANCOUVER WY
1200 LVMR 94550 715-F3
3500 CNCD 94520 572-F5
VANDA WY
700 FRMT 94536 732-J7
VANDELL WY
400 CMBL 95008 873-D2
VANDENBERG WY
- ANT 94509 595-F1
VANDER WY
1300 SJS 95112 834-B1
VANDERBILT CT E
1100 SUNV 94087 832-D3
VANDERBILT CT W
1100 SUNV 94087 832-D3
VANDERBILT DR
600 SUNV 94087 832-D3
4300 SJS 95130 853-A7
4300 CMBL 95008 853-A7
4800 SJS 95130 852-J7
18200 SAR 95070 852-J7
VANDERBILT ST
29500 HAY 94544 712-D7
29700 HAY 94544 732-E1
VANDERBILT WY
3300 SCL 95051 832-J6
VANDERSLICE AV
2000 CCCo 94596 612-E7
2000 WLCK 94596 612-E7
2000 WLCK 94596 632-E1
2000 CCCo 94596 632-E1
VANDERSLICE CT
2100 WLCK 94596 632-E1
VANDEWATER ST
300 SF 94133 648-A3
300 SF 94133 647-J3
VAN DE WATER WY
500 SJS 95111 854-F7
VAN DUSEN LN
1300 CMBL 95008 873-A2
VAN DYCK CT
800 SUNV 94087 832-F3
VAN DYCK DR
1200 SUNV 94087 832-F3
VAN DYKE AV
400 OAK 94606 650-A4
1200 SF 94124 668-B7
VANE COM
34400 FRMT 94555 752-B4
VANESSA DR
1100 SJS 95126 853-H3
VANESSA ST
100 VAL 94589 510-E5
VAN FLEET AV
5200 RCH 94804 609-C4
VAN GORDON PL
- DNVL 94526 652-H1
VANGORN CT
3100 SJS 95121 855-A4
VANGORN WY
3300 SJS 95121 855-A4
VAN HOOTEN CT
- MrnC 94960 566-A3
VAN KEUREN AV
- SF 94124 668-F7
VAN MOURIK AV
3900 OAK 94605 650-H7
VAN NESS AV
- SF 94103 667-J1
2700 SF 94109 647-H3
2700 SF 94123 647-H3

VAN NESS AV
U.S.-101
- SF 94102 647-H5
- SF 94103 647-H5
800 SF 94109 647-H5
2200 SF 94123 647-H5
2400 SF 94109 647-H4
2400 SF 94123 647-H4
S VAN NESS AV
200 SF 94103 667-J1
500 SF 94110 667-J1
1500 SF 94110 667-J4
S VAN NESS AV
U.S.-101
- SF 94103 667-J3
VAN NESS ST
1800 SPAB 94806 588-H3
VANNESSA DR
600 SMTO 94402 749-B3
VANNIER DR
500 BLMT 94002 749-D7
500 BLMT 94002 769-D1
VANNOY AV
4900 AlaC 94546 692-B4
VANNOY CT
3700 AlaC 94546 692-C4
VAN PATTEN DR
1300 DNVL 94526 653-C6
VANPORT CT
1700 SJS 95122 855-B3
VANPORT DR
2900 SJS 95122 855-B3
VAN RIPPER LN
- ORIN 94563 610-G3
VAN SANSUL AV
2900 SJS 95128 853-E3
VAN SICKLEN PL
- OAK 94610 650-C3
VAN TASSEL CT
- MrnC 94960 566-A2
VAN TASSEL LN
- ORIN 94563 610-G3
VANTINI WY
- PLE 94566 715-C6
VAN WINKLE LN
2400 SJS 95116 834-J4
VAQUERO CT
13600 SAR 95070 872-C1
VAQUERO DR
700 MTVW 94043 811-J3
VAQUERO WY
100 SMCo 94062 789-G1
2100 ANT 94509 595-A1
VAQUEROS AV
- CCCo 94572 549-H7
400 CCCo 94572 569-H1
600 SUNV 94086 812-E5
VARBORG TER
- SANS 94960 566-B4
VARDA LANDING RD
- SAUS 94965 626-J1
VARDEN AV
2800 SJS 95124 873-G1
VARDIN TER
1000 FRMT 94536 753-C3
VARELA AV
- SF 94132 687-B1
VARENNES ST
- SF 94133 648-A4
VARESE CT
- PLE 94566 715-C5
VARGAS CT
100 MPS 95035 794-A4
5700 SJS 95120 874-C5
VARGAS DR
1200 SJS 95120 874-C6
VARGAS PL
2300 SCL 95050 833-C3
VARGAS RD
40400 FRMT 94539 753-G2
41100 AlaC 94586 753-G2
VARGUS CT
2600 CNCD 94520 572-F6
VARIAN CT
200 SJS 95119 875-D7
VARIAN ST
1000 SCAR 94070 769-J4
VARIAN WY
22200 CPTO 95014 832-A7
VARIZ
100 HER 94547 569-E3
VARNER CT
3400 SJS 95132 814-H4
VARNEY PL
- SF 94107 648-B7
VARNI CT
1600 BEN 94510 551-C4
VARNI PL
31100 UNC 94587 731-J5
VARSI PL
700 SCL 95053 833-F5
700 SCL 95050 833-F5
VARSITY CT
1000 MTVW 94040 811-G7
VARTAN CT
- WLCK 94596 612-C2
VASCO CT
- MLV 94941 606-G2
VASCO DR
- MLV 94941 606-F3
VASCO RD
800 AlaC 94550 696-C1
N VASCO RD
700 LVMR 94550 696-C3
S VASCO RD
100 LVMR 94550 696-D5
1700 LVMR 94550 716-D2
2000 AlaC 94550 716-D2
VASCO DA GAMA
900 FCTY 94404 749-F4
VASHELL WY
- ORIN 94563 630-H1
VASILAKOS CT
- SMCo 94025 790-C5
VASILAKOS WY
- SMCo 94025 790-D5
VASONA AV
500 LGTS 95030 873-B2
VASONA CT
600 LGTS 95030 873-C2
27700 HAY 94544 712-A7

VASONA ST
600 MPS 95035 793-J6
VASONA TER
500 LGTS 95030 873-B5
VASONA OAKS DR
100 LGTS 95030 873-B5
VASONA PARK RD
- LGTS 95030 873-B6
VASQUEZ AV
- SF 94127 667-D4
1100 SUNV 94086 812-B7
VASQUEZ CT
400 SUNV 94086 812-B7
900 UNC 94587 732-F4
VASSAR AV
300 BERK 94708 609-G4
300 CCCo 94708 609-G4
300 BERK 94707 609-G4
1700 MTVW 94043 811-H3
15500 AlaC 94580 691-D5
VASSAR DR
5400 SJS 95118 874-A5
VASSAR PL
- SF 94107 648-B6
VAUGHN AV
300 SJS 95128 853-G1
300 SCIC 95128 853-G1
18900 AlaC 94546 691-J4
VAUGHN RD
3300 LFYT 94549 591-G7
VAUXHALL CIR
5300 SJS 95123 874-H3
VAVOLD ST
1700 CNCD 94519 592-J2
VEALE AV
800 MRTZ 94553 571-G4
800 CCCo 94553 571-G4
VEASY ST
31000 UNC 94587 731-H5
VECINO ST
500 BEN 94510 551-D4
VEDA DR
400 DNVL 94526 652-J2
VEGA CIR
700 FCTY 94404 749-E4
VEGA CT
- VAL 94591 510-J4
- PCFA 94044 727-B3
VEGA RD
- LVMR 94550 715-F4
VEGA ST
- SF 94115 647-F7
VEGA TER
400 FRMT 94536 753-E1
VEGAS AV
1700 MPS 95035 794-A3
2200 AlaC 94546 692-A6
2200 AlaC 94546 691-J6
VEGAS DR
6200 SJS 95120 874-E7
6300 SJS 95120 894-E1
VELARDE DR
13800 SLN 94578 691-C2
VELARDE ST
200 MTVW 94041 811-J5
VELASCO AV
- DALY 94014 687-H2
- SF 94134 687-H2
VELASCO CT
- DNVL 94526 653-C6
VELASCO DR
300 SJS 95123 874-H4
VELENZUELA CT
1400 PIT 94565 574-G5
VELVET DR
2600 WLCK 94596 632-G3
VELVET WY
2600 WLCK 94596 632-G3
VELVETLAKE DR
200 SUNV 94089 812-J5
VELVET MEADOW CT
6700 SJS 95120 894-F2
VENADO CT
5600 SJS 95123 875-B4
VENADO DR
- TBRN 94920 607-E6
VENADO WY
100 SJS 95123 875-B4
VENADO CAMINO
2500 WLCK 94598 612-G2
VENADO CORTE
100 WLCK 94598 612-H2
VENARD AL
2100 SF 94133 647-J3
VENDOLA DR
- MrnC 94903 566-G2
VENDOME AV
- DALY 94014 687-D2
VENDOME ST
400 SJS 95110 834-A5
600 SJS 95110 833-J5
VENDOR CT
1800 ANT 94509 595-F3
VENDOR WY
1800 ANT 94509 595-F3
VENDURA CT
19300 SAR 95070 852-G6
VENECIA DR
400 SJS 95133 834-G1
VENETIA RD
- OAK 94605 671-C4
VENETIA MEADOW
- MrnC 94903 566-G3
VENETO AV
- UNC 94587 732-J6
VENETO CT
- PLE 94588 694-A5
VENETO ST
34500 UNC 94587 732-H5
VENICE CT
- SLN 94577 671-A7
5100 PLE 94588 694-A6
VENICE DR
1800 CNCD 94519 593-A1
VENICE LN
1800 ANT 94509 575-G5
VENICE WY
4300 SJS 95129 853-A3
VENN AV
2300 SJS 95124 873-E4
VENNDALE AV
2300 SJS 95124 873-E4

VENNER DR
- MRTZ 94553 571-F6
VENNER RD
4800 MRTZ 94553 571-F7
VENNUM DR
1500 SJS 95131 814-C6
VENTANA DR
7200 SJS 95129 852-E2
VENTANA PL
7200 SJS 95129 852-E2
VENTNOR CT
29600 HAY 94544 732-C1
VENTRY WY
16700 AlaC 94580 691-F6
VENTURA AV
- SF 94116 667-D3
200 PA 94306 811-C1
500 SMTO 94403 749-A6
800 LVMR 94550 715-F1
900 ALB 94707 609-F6
900 ALB 94706 609-F7
1400 SPAB 94806 589-A4
4500 SJS 95111 875-A1
26200 HAY 94544 712-A5
26200 HAY 94544 711-J5
VENTURA CT
- PCFA 94044 727-A6
800 LVMR 94550 715-F1
2900 ANT 94509 575-B7
3900 PA 94306 811-C1
VENTURA DR
600 PIT 94565 574-E6
6600 DBLN 94568 694-A3
48900 FRMT 94539 794-A2
VENTURA PL
400 SRMN 94583 673-F6
2100 SCL 95051 833-A2
VENTURA ST
- VAL 94590 530-B4
600 RCH 94805 589-A5
1000 SPAB 94805 589-A5
VENTURA WY
900 MrnC 94941 606-E6
4500 UNC 94587 731-J6
VENUS CT
- TBRN 94920 607-B4
600 FRMT 94539 793-J1
600 FCTY 94404 749-E3
VENUS ST
- SF 94124 668-B6
28500 HAY 94544 712-B7
VENUS WY
- MPS 95035 813-J2
900 LVMR 94550 715-F4
VERA AV
100 RDWC 94061 770-A7
1600 RDWC 94061 789-H1
15200 SLN 94578 691-D5
VERA CT
- RDWC 94061 770-A6
VERA LN
5100 SJS 95111 875-B2
VERA CRUZ AV
500 NVTO 94949 546-F2
600 LALT 94022 811-E5
VERA CRUZ DR
5900 SJS 95120 874-A7
VERACRUZ DR
3200 SRMN 94583 673-F4
VERANO CT
400 SJS 95111 875-B1
500 HIL 94402 748-H4
500 SMTO 94402 748-H4
VERANO DR
- SSF 94080 707-E3
200 DALY 94015 687-B7
200 LALT 94022 811-F6
VERA SCHULTZ DR
- SRFL 94903 566-F4
VERBALEE LN
- HIL 94402 748-H4
VERBENA CT
400 PLHL 94523 591-H2
2000 FRMT 94539 773-G3
VERBENA DR
100 EPA 94303 791-C3
VERBENA PL
- PLHL 94523 591-H2
VERBENA WY
- SRMN 94583 653-J7
4800 SJS 95129 853-B2
4800 SJS 95129 852-B7
VERDAD WY
- NVTO 94945 525-J1
VERDA DEL CIERVO
100 CCCo 94526 633-E7
VERDANT WY
3100 SJS 95117 853-D3
VERDE AV
- CCCo 94801 588-F3
100 CCCo 94801 588-F3
VERDE CT
100 LGTS 95032 873-E5
3200 PLE 94588 694-C7
20500 SAR 95070 872-D1
VERDE DR
1000 PLE 94566 714-G3
VERDEMAR DR
1000 ALA 94502 670-A6
1000 ALA 94502 669-J7
VERDE MESA DR
100 DNVL 94526 633-C6
VERDE MOOR CT
20800 SAR 95070 852-D6
VERDES ROBLES
17200 LGTS 95030 873-B4
VERDE VISTA CT
13600 SAR 95070 872-D1
VERDE VISTA LN
20500 SAR 95070 872-D1
VERDI DR
700 SUNV 94087 832-F3
3300 SJS 95111 854-J5
VERDI RD
29000 HAY 94544 712-C7
VERDI ST
- SRFL 94901 586-J2
1500 ALA 94501 669-G1
VERDIGRIS CIR
4200 SJS 95134 813-D2
VERDITE ST
- LVMR 94550 715-D3

VERDOSA DR
4000 PA 94306 811-C2
VERDUCCI CT
400 DALY 94015 707-D3
VERDUCCI DR
400 DALY 94015 707-C3
VERDUN AV
3100 SMTO 94403 749-A6
3100 SMTO 94403 748-J6
VERDUN WY
- SF 94127 667-D5
VEREDA CT
700 SJS 95123 874-G6
VEREDA PTH
- TBRN 94920 607-F7
VERGEL TER
300 VAL 94589 509-H5
VERGIL CT
2600 AlaC 94546 692-B6
VERGIL ST
21900 AlaC 94546 692-A6
VERIL WY
31800 HAY 94544 732-F2
VERISSIMO DR
- MrnC 94947 525-E3
VERITAS WK
300 PCFA 94044 727-A1
VERJANE DR
6000 ELCR 94530 609-B1
VERLOR CT
24700 HAY 94545 711-F5
VERMEHR PL
- SF 94108 648-A5
VERMILION CT
3100 SJS 95135 855-E2
VERMONT AV
300 BERK 94707 609-G4
1300 CNCD 94521 593-F6
VERMONT LN
- ANT 94509 575-D2
VERMONT PL
3200 PLE 94588 694-G6
VERMONT ST
- SF 94103 668-A2
400 SF 94107 668-A2
400 SJS 95110 833-H5
800 OAK 94610 650-A2
900 SJS 95126 833-H5
1000 SF 94110 668-A4
22600 AlaC 94541 692-B7
22600 HAY 94541 692-B7
VERMONT WY
1100 SBRN 94066 707-E7
VERN AV
500 LVMR 94550 695-H7
VERN LN
3400 CNCD 94519 593-A1
3400 CNCD 94519 592-J1
VERNA CT
- SLN 94577 690-H3
1300 CNCD 94518 592-G3
VERNA DR
2900 SCIC 95133 834-H1
VERNA ST
- SF 94127 667-E6
VERNA WY
5600 CLAY 94517 593-F6
VERNA WY E
5800 CLAY 94517 593-G6
VERNAL AV
900 MrnC 94941 606-E5
1300 FRMT 94539 753-G6
VERNAL AV N
900 MrnC 94941 606-E5
VERNAL AV S
900 MrnC 94941 606-E5
VERNAL AV W
900 MrnC 94941 606-E5
VERNAL CT
- VAL 94591 510-J4
- CCCo 94507 632-F4
200 LALT 94022 811-D5
VERNAL DR
100 CCCo 94507 632-F3
1300 SJS 95130 853-B4
VERNAL WY
700 SMCo 94062 789-F2
VERNALIS CIR
2100 ALA 94501 649-E7
VERNE ST
40400 FRMT 94538 773-B1
VERNE ROBERTS CIR
1300 ANT 94509 575-A4
1600 ANT 94509 574-J4
VERNETTI WY
21800 AlaC 94546 692-B6
VERNICE AV
3200 SJS 95127 835-B3
VERNIE CT
900 CPTO 95014 852-D2
VERNIER DR
1700 CNCD 94519 593-A2
VERNIER PL
1000 SCIC 94305 810-J2
VERNON AV
- CCCo 94801 588-F4
100 RCH 94801 588-F4
500 SCIC 94043 812-A2
500 MTVW 94043 812-A2
1200 SJS 95125 854-B3
3100 LFYT 94549 611-H7
5100 FRMT 94536 752-H6
VERNON CIR
800 MTVW 94043 812-A3
VERNON CT
18400 AlaC 94546 692-A3
VERNON ST
- OAK 94610 649-H2
- SF 94132 687-C1
VERNON TER
100 OAK 94610 649-H2
1100 SMTO 94402 748-J4
3300 PA 94303 791-E6
VERNON WY
600 BURL 94010 728-G6
VERONA AV
100 PCFA 94044 727-A2
300 DNVL 94526 652-J1
900 LVMR 94550 715-F2
27400 HAY 94545 711-G7
27400 HAY 94545 731-G1

VERONA CT
- DNVL 94526 652-J2
100 LGTS 95030 872-J4
3200 CNCD 94518 592-H2
VERONA PL
- CMAD 94925 606-J1
VERONA PTH
- OAK 94618 630-B5
VERONA RD
- SJS 95135 855-H3
- AlaC 94566 734-D1
- PLE 94566 734-D1
VERONICA AV
4100 AlaC 94546 692-B5
VERONICA CT
1000 EPA 94303 791-C1
1300 ANT 94509 575-G5
VERONICA DR
19800 SAR 95070 852-F6
VERONICA PL
- PTLV 94028 810-C7
2000 SJS 95124 873-F1
VERRADA RD
1000 OAK 94610 650-B3
VERSAILLES AV
800 ALA 94501 670-A3
VERSAILLES CT
- SJS 95127 834-C1
- DNVL 94506 653-H5
VERSAILLES DR
- MLPK 94025 790-F3
VERSAILLES PL
100 PIT 94565 574-C7
VERSAILLES WY
19600 SAR 95070 872-F3
VERSAILLES PARK CT
4700 FRMT 94538 773-C2
VERVAIS AV
400 VAL 94591 530-D3
4200 PLE 94566 714-E3
VERWOOD DR
2400 SJS 95130 853-A7
VESCA WY
4800 SJS 95129 853-B2
VESPER AV
600 FRMT 94539 793-J1
VESPERO AV
- PCFA 94044 727-B1
VESPUCCI LN
700 FCTY 94404 749-F4
VESSING CT
18500 SAR 95070 872-H3
VESSING RD
2900 PLHL 94523 612-A1
18500 SAR 95070 872-H3
VESTA ST
- SF 94124 668-B6
VESTAL CT
2000 SLN 94577 690-H2
VESTAL ST
400 SJS 95112 834-B3
2100 AlaC 94546 692-A6
VESTE CT
34300 FRMT 94555 752-B6
VESUVIUS LN
3000 SJS 95132 814-F5
VETERAN WY
- OAK 94602 650-D4
VETERANS BLVD
400 RDWC 94063 769-J4
400 RDWC 94063 770-A5
VETERANS CT
- ALA 94502 670-A5
1000 MRTZ 94553 571-G6
VETERANS DR
900 MRTZ 94553 571-G6
VETERANS PL
- SANS 94960 566-B6
VIA ACALANES
500 AlaC 94580 691-D7
VIA AIRES
600 AlaC 94580 711-D1
VIA ALAMITOS
15800 AlaC 94580 691-C7
15800 AlaC 94580 711-D1
VIA ALAMO
600 AlaC 94580 711-D1
VIA ALAMOSA
1100 ALA 94502 669-J6
VIA ALEGRIA CT
1500 SJS 95121 855-B4
VIA ALISO
1000 ALA 94502 669-J6
VIA ALMADEN
1100 SJS 95120 874-C6
VIA ALONDRA
- CCCo 94507 632-H3
VIA ALTA
1000 LFYT 94549 611-D5
2100 BEN 94510 551-D4
VIA ALTO CT
13700 SAR 95070 872-H1
VIA AMIGOS
1500 AlaC 94580 711-B1
1700 LVMR 94550 695-E6
6300 SJS 95120 894-D1
VIA AMPARO
7200 SJS 95135 855-J6
VIA ANACAPA
7000 SJS 95139 875-F7
17000 AlaC 94580 691-E7
17000 AlaC 94580 711-E1
VIA ANADE
1300 AlaC 94580 711-C1
VIA ANDETA
16100 AlaC 94580 691-E7
16100 AlaC 94580 711-E1
VIA ANNETTE
17200 AlaC 94580 711-C2
VIA APPIA
500 WLCK 94598 612-E2
VIA ARAGON
100 FRMT 94539 753-H6
VIA ARLINE
- LAH 94022 831-B1
VIA ARRIBA
16000 AlaC 94580 691-D7
16400 AlaC 94580 711-D1
VIA ARRIBA CT
13100 SAR 95070 852-G7
VIA ARRIBA DR
13100 SAR 95070 852-G7

VIA ARROYO
15700 AlaC 94580 691-D7
VIA ASPERO
- CCCo 94526 633-A6
VIA BAHIA
- SUNV 94089 812-H3
VIA BAJA
1000 LFYT 94549 611-D5
VIA BAJA DR
700 MPS 95035 794-B5
VIA BARCELONA
- MRGA 94556 631-F4
VIA BARRANCA
- LKSP 94904 586-G4
7000 SJS 95139 875-F7
VIA BARRETT
1400 AlaC 94580 691-B7
1400 AlaC 94580 711-B1
VIA BELARDO
- LKSP 94939 586-F5
VIA BELLA
7200 SJS 95139 875-F7
VIA BELLITA
200 AlaC 94580 691-E7
VIA BELMONTE
7000 SJS 95135 855-J5
VIA BLANC CT
13100 SAR 95070 852-F7
VIA BLANCA
7000 SJS 95139 875-F7
VIA BOLSA
100 AlaC 94580 691-E7
VIA BONITA
100 CCCo 94507 632-F5
1000 ALA 94502 669-J6
18400 MSER 95030 872-J6
VIA BREGANI
800 AlaC 94580 691-C7
VIA BREZZO
7200 SJS 95120 894-G5
VIA BUENA VISTA
1400 AlaC 94580 711-C2
VIA BUFANO
- SF 94133 648-A4
VIA CABALLERO
15300 MSER 95030 872-J4
VIA CABRERA LN
100 MRTZ 94553 571-F6
VIA CALLADOS
- ORIN 94563 610-G2
VIA CALZADA
7300 SJS 95135 855-J5
VIA CAMINO CT
22100 CPTO 95014 832-A7
VIA CAMPAGNA
- SJS 95120 894-A1
- SJS 95120 893-J1
VIA CAMPINA
- SJS 95139 875-F6
VIA CAMPO AUREO
- SJS 95120 894-A1
VIA CAMPO VERDE
- SJS 95120 893-J1
VIA CANCION
1400 SJS 95128 853-F5
VIA CANON
- MLBR 94030 728-A4
VIA CANTARES
7300 SJS 95135 855-J5
VIA CAPISTRANO
- TBRN 94920 607-A3
- TBRN 94920 606-J3
VIA CAPRI
- SUNV 94089 812-H3
VIA CARMELA
7100 SJS 95139 875-G7
VIA CARMEN
2800 SJS 95124 873-F1
17200 AlaC 94580 711-C2
VIA CARRETA
1600 AlaC 94580 711-C2
VIA CARRIZO
7200 SJS 95135 855-J6
VIA CASITAS
200 LKSP 94939 586-F4
VIA CATHERINE
16000 AlaC 94580 711-B2
VIA CERRADA
- CCCo 94507 632-E4
VIA CERRO GORDO
27600 LAH 94022 830-H1
VIA CHEPARRO
- MrnC 94904 586-G4
100 LKSP 94904 586-G4
VIA CHIQUITA
16100 AlaC 94580 711-C1
VIA CHORRO
1500 AlaC 94580 711-B1
VIA CIELO
7000 SJS 95135 855-H5
17000 AlaC 94580 711-D1
VIA CIMA CT
200 DNVL 94526 633-D6
VIA CIMA LN
- DNVL 94526 633-D6
VIA CINCO DE MAYO
1700 SJS 95132 814-D4
VIA COCHES
300 AlaC 94580 711-E1
VIA CODORNIZ
1400 SJS 95128 853-F4
VIA COLINA
7100 SJS 95139 875-F7
15100 SAR 95070 872-G4
VIA COLLADO
100 LGTS 95030 872-J3
VIA COLUSA
15700 AlaC 94580 691-D7
VIA CONEJO
15800 AlaC 94580 691-D7
VIA CONIL
100 AlaC 94580 691-E7
VIA CONTENTA
1400 SJS 95128 853-F5
VIA COPLA
100 CCCo 94507 632-F7
VIA CORALLA
1000 AlaC 94580 711-C2
VIA CORDOBA
2800 CCCo 94583 673-B3
2800 SRMN 94583 673-B3
15700 AlaC 94580 691-E7

STREET
Block City ZIP Pg-Grid

VIA CORDOVA
300 MRTZ 94553 571-F6
VIA CORDURA
7000 SJS 95139 875-F6
VIA CORITA
27800 LAH 94022 831-A1
27800 LAH 94022 830-J1
VIA CORONA
7100 SJS 95139 875-G7
17000 AlaC 94580 691-E7
VIA CORTA
1100 ALA 94502 669-J6
15700 AlaC 94580 691-D7
20700 SCIC 95120 894-J2
20700 SCIC 95120 895-A1
VIA CORTE
- ORIN 94563 610-F6
VIA CORTINA
- SJS 95120 893-J1
VIA CRESCENTE CT
19200 SAR 95070 852-G7
VIA CRESPI
400 SCIC 94305 790-G7
VIA CRISTOBAL
1100 LVMR 94550 695-E5
3800 SJS 95008 853-B6
VIA DE ADRIANNA
6200 SJS 95120 874-B7
6200 SJS 95120 894-B1
VIA DE CABALLE
4700 SJS 95118 874-B3
VIA DE CIELO
5900 PLE 94566 714-B2
VIA DE FLORES
4000 CCCo 94553 571-J4
VIA DE GUADALUPE
- SJS 95116 834-G3
VIA DE LA CRUZ
- PLE 94566 714-B2
VIA DE LAS ABEJAS
6100 SJS 95120 874-B7
VIA DE LA VISTA
14000 SCIC 95127 835-F2
VIA DEL CORONADO
3000 SJS 95132 814-D3
VIA DEL GATO
1000 CCCo 94507 632-G5
VIA DELIZIA
- HIL 94010 748-G3
VIA DEL LISA CT
3700 CNCD 94518 592-J4
VIA DEL MAR
3200 SJS 95124 873-F2
VIA DEL ORO
6400 SJS 95119 875-E7
VIA DE LOS CERROS
6000 PLE 94566 714-B2
VIA DE LOS GRANDE
1300 SJS 95120 894-B1
VIA DE LOS MILAGROS
2400 PLE 94566 714-B2
VIA DE LOS REYES
1300 SJS 95120 874-B7
VIA DEL PAZ
900 LVMR 94550 715-F3
VIA DEL PLANO
400 MrnC 94949 546-E2
VIA DEL POZO
1000 LALT 94022 811-D4
VIA DEL PRADO
15800 AlaC 94580 691-C7
VIA DEL REY
400 CCCo 94507 632-E5
17000 AlaC 94580 711-C1
VIA DEL RIO
7000 SJS 95139 875-F7
VIA DEL ROBLES
16100 AlaC 94580 711-C1
VIA DEL SOL
- WLCK 94596 612-C1
200 PLHL 94523 592-C7
200 PLHL 94523 612-C1
600 LVMR 94550 715-E4
2900 SJS 95132 814-D3
15700 AlaC 94580 691-D7
15900 AlaC 94580 711-D1
VIA DEL SUR
15100 MSER 95030 873-A4
VIA DEL VERDES
1700 CNCD 94521 593-C3
VIA DE MARCOS
14500 SAR 95070 872-G3
VIA DE MERCADOS
2000 CNCD 94520 592-E1
VIADER CT
600 SCL 95050 833-D5
VIADER DR
1000 MRGA 94556 631-D7
VIA DESCANSADA
- ORIN 94563 610-G5
VIA DESCANSO
15900 AlaC 94580 691-D7
VIA DESTE
1300 LVMR 94550 695-E5
2000 SJS 95008 853-C6
VIA DE TESOROS
100 LGTS 95030 872-J4
VIA DIABLO
- CCCo 94526 633-F6
VIA DIEGO
- AlaC 94580 691-E7
VIA DI SALERNO
1000 PLE 94566 715-C6
VIA DOBLE
1100 CNCD 94521 593-E7
VIA DOLOROSA
1200 AlaC 94580 711-D2
VIA DOMINGUEZ
2800 WLCK 94596 612-A1
VIA DONDERA
1300 SCL 95051 833-A4
VIA DON JOSE
1400 CCCo 94507 632-F4
VIA DORA DR
4000 ANT 94509 595-H2
VIA EDUARDO
15800 AlaC 94580 711-B1
VIA EL CAPITAN
1800 SJS 95124 873-H1
VIA EL CERRITO
17200 AlaC 94580 711-C2

VIA EL DORADO LN
200 MRTZ 94553 571-F5
VIA ELEVADO
200 AlaC 94580 711-E1
VIA EL MONTE
1200 AlaC 94580 711-C1
VIA ELVERANO
- TBRN 94920 606-J3
VIA ENCANTADA
18100 MSER 95030 872-J4
VIA ENCINAS
17300 AlaC 94580 711-D1
VIA ENCINITAS
2700 SJS 95132 814-D3
VIA ENRICO
800 AlaC 94580 691-C7
VIA ENSENADA
5500 CNCD 94521 593-E7
VIA ENSENADA CT
1100 CNCD 94521 593-E7
VIA ESCALERA
2100 LALT 94024 831-H5
VIA ESCONDIDO
800 MrnC 94949 546-E2
1100 NVTO 94949 546-E2
1400 AlaC 94580 711-B1
VIA ESCUELA CT
13000 SAR 95070 852-F7
VIA ESCUELA DR
19500 SAR 95070 852-F7
VIA ESMOND
15700 AlaC 94580 691-B7
VIA ESPADA
2200 PLE 94566 714-B3
VIA ESPERANZA
1100 AlaC 94580 711-D2
VIA ESPLENDOR
23000 CPTO 95014 831-H5
VIA ESTRELLA
3900 CCCo 94553 571-J3
17200 AlaC 94580 711-D2
VIA FAISAN
1300 AlaC 94580 711-C1
VIA FARALLON
- ORIN 94563 610-G6
VIA FELIZ
27600 LAH 94022 810-J7
VIA FERRARI
1100 SJS 95122 834-G7
VIA FLOREADO
- ORIN 94563 610-J5
VIA FLORES
1700 SJS 95132 814-D4
17000 AlaC 94580 711-D1
VIA FORTUNA
- SJS 95120 894-A1
- SJS 95120 893-J1
VIA FRANCES
17200 AlaC 94580 711-C2
VIA GABARDO
1200 LFYT 94549 612-A4
VIA GIARAMITA
- CCCo 94803 589-F2
VIA GRANADA
- SUNV 94089 812-H3
700 LVMR 94550 715-F2
3700 LFYT 94549 631-E2
3700 MRGA 94556 631-E2
15500 AlaC 94580 691-E7
VIA GRANDE CT
13200 SAR 95070 852-F7
VIA GRANDE DR
13100 SAR 95070 852-F7
VIA GRANJA
7000 SJS 95135 855-J5
VIA HARRIET
16000 AlaC 94580 711-B2
VIA HELENA
1600 AlaC 94580 711-C2
VIA HERBOSA
400 MrnC 94949 546-F2
VIA HERMANA
1300 AlaC 94580 691-B7
1400 AlaC 94580 711-B1
VIA HERMOSA
- AlaC 94580 691-E7
- LKSP 94904 586-H4
- ORIN 94563 610-H5
700 DNVL 94526 653-B2
VIA HIDALGO
300 LKSP 94939 586-F4
VIA HOLON
- LKSP 94939 586-F4
VIA HONDA
900 AlaC 94580 711-D2
VIA HORNITOS
15800 AlaC 94580 711-B1
VIA HORQUETA
1100 SRFL 94903 566-D2
VIA HUERTA
1200 LALT 94024 831-H5
VIA JOAQUIN
100 MRGA 94556 631-E6
VIA JOSE
1100 SJS 95120 874-D7
18100 AlaC 94580 711-E2
VIA JULIA
17300 AlaC 94580 711-C2
VIA KARL
16100 AlaC 94580 711-B2
VIA LA BRISA
- LKSP 94939 586-G5
VIA LACQUA
1400 AlaC 94580 711-B1
VIA LA CUMBRE
- CCCo 94549 591-J7
- LKSP 94904 586-H4
300 MrnC 94901 586-H4
VIA LAGO
100 LGTS 95030 872-J2
VIA LAGUNA
1600 SMTO 94404 749-E3
7300 SJS 95135 855-J5
VIA LA JOLLA
17200 AlaC 94580 711-C2
VIA LA PALOMA
1300 AlaC 94580 711-C1
VIA LA PAZ
- LKSP 94904 586-G4
4500 UNC 94587 731-J6
VIA LA POSADA
200 LGTS 95030 872-J3

VIA LARGA
3100 CCCo 94507 632-E5
VIA LAS CRUCES
- ORIN 94563 610-J5
VIA LERIDA
- LKSP 94904 586-G4
VIA LINARES
- AlaC 94580 691-E7
VIA LOBOS
1500 AlaC 94580 691-B7
1500 AlaC 94580 711-B1
VIA LOMA
1400 WLCK 94598 612-E4
VIA LOMAS
7100 SJS 95139 875-F7
VIA LOMBARDI
20800 CPTO 95014 832-E6
VIA LOMITA
15100 MSER 95030 872-J4
VIA LOS ALTOS
- TBRN 94920 606-J3
- MrnC 94920 606-J3
VIA LOS COLORADOS
3500 LFYT 94549 631-H1
VIA LOS NINOS
- WLCK 94596 612-C3
VIA LOS TRANCOS
1100 AlaC 94580 711-D2
VIA LUCAS
1100 AlaC 94580 711-C1
VIA LUCERO
200 AlaC 94580 691-E7
300 AlaC 94580 711-E1
VIA LUCIA
100 CCCo 94507 632-E4
S VIA LUCIA
100 CCCo 94507 632-F6
S VIA LUCIA LN
100 CCCo 94507 632-F6
VIA LUGANO
- SJS 95120 893-J1
VIA LUNADO
15700 AlaC 94580 691-D7
VIA LUPINE
16100 AlaC 94580 711-C1
VIA MADELINE
15500 AlaC 94580 691-C7
VIA MADERA
1200 AlaC 94580 711-C2
VIA MADERO DR
5900 SJS 95120 874-A7
VIA MADEROS
2200 LALT 94024 831-H6
VIA MADRID
800 LVMR 94550 715-F2
4400 UNC 94587 731-J6
VIA MADRONAS CT
19400 SAR 95070 852-F7
VIA MADRONAS DR
13100 SAR 95070 852-F7
VIA MAGDALENA
- LFYT 94549 611-C5
17100 AlaC 94580 711-D1
VIA MAGGIORE
- SJS 95120 893-J1
VIA MALAGA
- FRMT 94539 753-H6
100 AlaC 94580 691-E7
VIA MANTILLA
100 WLCK 94598 612-H2
VIA MANZANAS
700 AlaC 94580 711-C1
VIA MARGARITA
17000 AlaC 94580 711-D1
VIA MARGARITA CT
- AlaC 94580 711-D1
VIA MARIA
7100 SJS 95139 875-F7
VIA MARIPOSA
700 AlaC 94580 711-D1
VIA MARLIN
15800 AlaC 94580 691-E7
VIA MATEO
800 LVMR 94550 695-E5
1100 SJS 95120 894-D1
VIA MATERO
- AlaC 94580 691-E7
VIA MEDIA
1000 LFYT 94549 611-D6
2100 BEN 94510 551-D4
15800 AlaC 94580 691-D7
16100 AlaC 94580 711-D1
VIA MELINA
17200 AlaC 94580 711-C2
VIA MERCADO
500 AlaC 94580 691-D7
VIA MESA
- SJS 95139 875-F6
1400 AlaC 94580 711-C2
VIA MILANO
3800 SJS 95008 853-B6
VIA MILOS
16100 AlaC 94580 711-B2
VIA MIMOSA
7200 SJS 95135 855-J6
VIA MIRABEL
500 AlaC 94580 711-D1
VIA MIRLO
16900 AlaC 94580 691-E7
VIA MONTALVO
900 LVMR 94550 695-E5
3800 SJS 95008 853-B6
VIA MONTANAS
900 CNCD 94518 592-G4
VIA MONTE
- WLCK 94598 612-H2
N VIA MONTE
- WLCK 94598 612-H1
VIA MONTE DR
5600 SJS 95118 874-C4
19400 SAR 95070 852-F7
VIA MONTEBELLO
- SRFL 94901 567-E5
VIA MONTECITOS
7200 SJS 95135 855-J5
VIA MONTEZ
3000 SJS 95132 814-D3
VIA MORAGA
43000 FRMT 94539 753-G7
43000 FRMT 94539 773-G1
VIA MORELLA
- AlaC 94580 691-E7

VIA MURIETTA
2100 AlaC 94580 711-A1
VIA NAPOLI
2100 SJS 95008 853-B6
20300 CPTO 95014 832-E6
VIA NATAL
1700 AlaC 94580 711-B2
VIA NAVARRA
42800 FRMT 94539 753-H6
VIA NAVARRO
- LKSP 94904 586-H4
VIA NIDA
- SUNV 94089 812-H3
VIANNE CT
- ORIN 94563 631-A1
VIA NUBE
1200 AlaC 94580 711-D2
VIA NUEVA
1000 LFYT 94549 611-B5
15700 AlaC 94580 711-B1
VIA OLINDA
16000 AlaC 94580 711-D1
VIA ONEG
- LFYT 94549 611-E6
VIA OPORTO
42800 FRMT 94539 753-H6
VIA ORINDA
1700 FRMT 94539 753-G7
1700 FRMT 94539 773-G1
VIA ORTEGA
400 SCIC 94305 790-G7
VIA OWEN
16100 AlaC 94580 711-B2
VIA PACHECO
500 AlaC 94580 691-D7
VIA PACIFICA
7100 SJS 95139 875-G7
VIA PAJARO
1100 LFYT 94549 611-D6
VIA PALAMOS
20300 CPTO 95014 832-E6
VIA PALMA
1000 AlaC 94580 711-D2
VIA PALOMA
- SJS 95120 893-J1
VIA PALOMINO
15200 MSER 95030 873-A4
15300 MSER 95030 872-J4
VIA PALOS
100 AlaC 94580 691-E7
VIA PALOU
400 SCIC 94305 790-G7
VIA PARAISO E
- TBRN 94920 607-C6
VIA PARAISO W
- TBRN 94920 607-C5
VIA PARO
15800 AlaC 94580 691-D7
15900 AlaC 94580 711-D1
VIA PASATIEMPO
17000 AlaC 94580 711-D1
VIA PAVISO
10700 CPTO 95014 832-E6
VIA PECORO
200 AlaC 94580 711-E1
VIA PEQUENA
18400 AlaC 94580 691-E7
VIA PERALTA
300 CCCo 94553 572-C6
5700 PLE 94566 714-C2
VIA PERDIDO
17000 AlaC 94580 711-D1
VIA PIEDRA
7300 SJS 95135 855-J5
VIA PIEDRAS
17000 AlaC 94580 711-D1
VIA PINADA LN
200 MRTZ 94553 571-F5
VIA PINALE
15800 AlaC 94580 691-D7
16000 AlaC 94580 711-D1
VIA PINTO
15200 MSER 95030 873-A4
VIA PISA
1500 SJS 95128 853-H2
VIA PLANETA
200 CCCo 94553 571-J3
VIA PORTADA
7000 SJS 95135 855-J5
VIA PORTOFINO
20300 CPTO 95014 832-E6
VIA POTRERO
7100 SJS 95135 855-J5
VIA POUDRE
600 AlaC 94580 711-D1
VIA PRADERA
800 AlaC 94580 711-E2
VIA PRADERA
7000 SJS 95139 875-F7
VIA PRADERIA
43900 FRMT 94539 773-H2
VIA PRIMAVERA CT
500 SJS 95111 875-B1
VIA PRIMAVERA DR
300 SJS 95111 875-A1
VIA PRIMERO
16000 AlaC 94580 691-E7
16500 AlaC 94580 711-E1
VIA PUEBLA
42800 FRMT 94539 753-H6
VIA PUEBLO LN
100 SCIC 94305 790-G6
VIA PUNTA
15700 AlaC 94580 691-C7
VIA QUITO
6800 PLE 94566 714-B2
VIA RAMADA
7000 SJS 95139 875-F7
VIA RANCHERO
900 CMBL 95008 873-C1
VIA RANCHERO CT
13200 SAR 95070 852-G7
VIA RANCHERO DR
13200 SAR 95070 852-G7
VIA RANCHO
1500 AlaC 94580 711-B1
VIA REAL DR
19300 SAR 95070 852-G7
VIA RECODO
300 MrnC 94965 626-F1
VIA REDONDO
1700 AlaC 94580 711-C1
VIA REGGIO CT
1900 SJS 95132 814-C4

VIA REGINA
21700 SAR 95070 872-B1
VIA REGIO
15700 AlaC 94580 691-D7
VIA REPRESA
15700 AlaC 94580 711-B1
VIA RINCON
17100 AlaC 94580 691-E7
17100 AlaC 94580 711-E1
VIA RIVERA
15700 AlaC 94580 691-D7
VIA ROBLE
1000 LFYT 94549 611-D5
VIA ROBLES
- CCCo 94595 632-D2
VIA RODRIGUEZ
300 AlaC 94580 691-D7
VIA ROMA
2100 SJS 95008 853-B6
VIA ROMERA
7100 SJS 95139 875-F7
VIA ROMERO
100 CCCo 94507 632-E5
VIA ROMERO LN
- CCCo 94507 632-E5
VIA RONCOLE
12000 SAR 95070 852-D5
VIA ROSARIO
200 FRMT 94539 753-H6
VIA ROSAS
17600 AlaC 94580 711-D1
VIA ROYAL
400 WLCK 94596 612-B3
VIA SALICE
3800 SJS 95008 853-B6
VIA SAN ARDO
17200 AlaC 94580 711-C2
VIA SAN BLAS
6500 PLE 94566 714-B2
VIA SAN CARLOS
- AlaC 94580 691-E7
41900 FRMT 94539 753-G6
VIA SAN DIMAS
- FRMT 94539 753-H6
VIA SAN FERNANDO
- TBRN 94920 606-J3
VIA SAN GABRIEL
41900 FRMT 94539 753-G5
VIA SAN INIGO
- ORIN 94563 610-E7
VIA SAN JOSE
1200 LVMR 94550 695-E5
VIA SAN JUAN
1200 AlaC 94580 711-C1
VIA SAN LUIS REY
41900 FRMT 94539 753-G6
VIA SAN MARINO
100 AlaC 94580 691-E7
20300 CPTO 95014 832-E6
VIA SAN MIGUEL
41800 FRMT 94539 753-G6
VIA SANTA MARIA
100 LGTS 95032 873-C7
VIA SANTA TERESA
20100 SCIC 95120 894-H2
VIA SARITA
1600 AlaC 94580 711-C2
VIA SARONNO
- SJS 95120 893-J1
VIA SECO
15700 AlaC 94580 691-B7
15700 AlaC 94580 711-B1
VIA SEGUNDO
16000 AlaC 94580 691-E7
17100 AlaC 94580 711-E1
VIA SENDERO
7200 SJS 95135 855-J6
VIA SERENA
100 CCCo 94507 632-F6
7000 SJS 95139 875-F7
VIA SERENO DR
17500 MSER 95030 873-A5
VIA SESSI
1300 SRFL 94901 586-F1
VIA SEVILLA
16000 AlaC 94580 691-E7
VIA SEVILLE
800 LVMR 94550 715-F2
VIA SIESTA
- SUNV 94089 812-H3
VIA SOLANA
7100 SJS 95135 855-J5
VIA SOMBRIO
1400 FRMT 94539 753-G7
VIA SONATA
2100 AlaC 94580 711-A1
VIA SONORA
16000 AlaC 94580 711-C1
VIA SONYA
1500 AlaC 94580 711-C2
VIA SORRENTO
2100 AlaC 94580 711-A1
20300 CPTO 95014 832-E6
VIA SUSANA
17300 AlaC 94580 711-C2
VIA TERESA
100 LGTS 95030 872-J4
VIA TESORO CT
19100 SAR 95070 872-G2
VIA TOLEDO
15800 AlaC 94580 691-E7
18300 AlaC 94580 711-E1
VIA TOMAR
- AlaC 94580 691-E7
VIA TOVITA
1600 AlaC 94580 711-C2
VIA TOYON
1500 AlaC 94580 711-C1
VIA VALENCIA
300 CCCo 94553 572-C6
17000 AlaC 94580 691-E7
VIA VALIENTE
900 SJS 95120 894-G2
VIA VALPARAISO
42900 FRMT 94539 753-H6
VIA VALVERDE
7000 SJS 95135 855-J5
VIA VAN DYKE
- MLV 94941 606-E2
VIA VAN VUREN
- SRFL 94903 566-E5

VIA VAQUERO
15400 MSER 95030 872-J5
VIA VAQUEROS
- CCCo 94553 591-E2
VIA VECINOS
16000 AlaC 94580 711-C1
VIA VEGA
15500 AlaC 94580 691-C7
VIA VENITO WY
1000 PIT 94565 573-J4
VIA VENTANA
1500 AlaC 94580 711-B1
12600 LAH 94022 830-H1
VIA VENTURA
23400 CPTO 95014 831-H6
VIA VERA CRUZ
400 FRMT 94539 753-H6
VIA VERDE
- AlaC 94580 691-E7
2500 WLCK 94598 612-H2
VIA VERDI
3700 RCH 94803 589-B2
VIA VICO
7200 SJS 95129 852-E3
VIA VIENTO
100 AlaC 94580 691-E7
VIA VISTA
1100 AlaC 94580 711-C1
1400 SMTO 94404 749-D3
7200 SJS 95139 875-F7
VIA VOLANTE
20300 CPTO 95014 832-E6
VIA WALTER
16000 AlaC 94580 711-B2
VIA ZAPATA
7900 DBLN 94568 693-F3
VICANNA DR
6300 SJS 95129 852-F4
VICAR LN
900 SJS 95117 853-C3
VICENTE DR
1200 SUNV 94086 812-B7
VICENTE PL
- OAK 94705 630-B3
VICENTE RD
- BERK 94705 630-B4
- OAK 94705 630-B4
VICENTE ST
- SF 94127 667-B5
200 SF 94116 667-A5
2300 SF 94116 666-H5
5600 OAK 94609 629-H5
VICENTE WY
5400 OAK 94609 629-H6
VICENZA CT
- DNVL 94506 653-D1
VICENZA WY
2300 SJS 95138 855-F6
VICEROY CT
10100 CPTO 95014 832-A7
VICEROY WY
800 SJS 95133 814-G6
900 SJS 95132 814-G6
VICKERY AV
14600 SAR 95070 872-D3
VICKERY PL
14700 SAR 95070 872-E3
VICKI DR
1800 PLHL 94523 612-A1
VICKSBURG AV
1700 OAK 94601 670-E1
VICKSBURG CT
10200 CPTO 95014 852-F1
VICKSBURG DR
10100 CPTO 95014 852-F1
VICKSBURG ST
- SF 94114 667-G4
VICTOR AV
- CMBL 95008 853-C5
1200 SLN 94579 691-A5
3300 OAK 94602 650-F4
3500 OAK 94619 650-F5
5200 ELCR 94530 609-B1
5200 RCH 94804 609-B1
VICTOR CT
- NVTO 94947 526-A4
3200 SJS 95132 814-F3
3300 SCL 95054 813-F6
VICTOR PL
14100 SAR 95070 872-D2
VICTOR ST
3200 SCL 95054 813-F6
3600 PIN 94564 569-J7
VICTOR WY
600 MTVW 94040 811-H6
VICTORIA AV
- MLBR 94030 728-B4
500 SLN 94577 671-B6
3200 SCL 95051 833-A3
3300 LFYT 94549 611-G6
3300 SCL 95051 832-J3
4300 UNC 94587 731-J6
4300 UNC 94587 732-A6
4600 FRMT 94538 773-C1
4700 FRMT 94538 753-C7
VICTORIA BAY
200 ALA 94502 670-A6
VICTORIA CT
500 SLN 94577 671-A6
600 CCCo 94565 573-J3
900 LFYT 94549 611-G6
2000 LALT 94024 832-A5
2300 LVMR 94550 715-G4
14300 SCIC 95127 835-B3
E VICTORIA CT
1200 SPAB 94806 588-G4
N VICTORIA CT
1400 SPAB 94806 588-G4
S VICTORIA CT
1400 SPAB 94806 588-G4
W VICTORIA CT
1200 SPAB 94806 588-G4
VICTORIA DR
- ATN 94027 790-F3
VICTORIA LN
5400 RCH 94803 589-J3
VICTORIA LNDG
1800 SJS 95131 814-C4
VICTORIA MNR
2700 SCAR 94070 769-G6
VICTORIA PL
300 PA 94306 811-D2

VICTORIA RD
- BURL 94010 728-H6
VICTORIA ST
- DALY 94015 707-C2
- SF 94132 687-C2
- SolC 94591 530-E7
300 ELCR 94530 609-D4
600 SF 94127 667-C7
VICTORIA TER
1300 SUNV 94087 832-D4
VICTORIA WY
- LKSP 94904 586-H5
1500 PCFA 94044 727-A4
VICTORIA MEADOW CT
2900 PLE 94566 714-H3
VICTORIAN CT
- BEN 94510 551-D5
VICTORIAN LN
300 DNVL 94526 633-A6
VICTORIA PARK CT
4600 FRMT 94538 773-C2
VICTORIA PARK DR
4000 SJS 95136 874-F1
VICTORIA RIDGE CT
2800 PLE 94566 714-H3
VICTOR PARK LN
- HIL 94010 748-F2
VICTORY AV
100 PIT 94565 574-D3
300 SSF 94080 707-H4
400 MTVW 94043 811-F2
VICTORY CIR
- SRMN 94583 673-F2
VICTORY CT
- OAK 94607 649-G5
- SRMN 94583 673-F2
VICTORY DR
21900 HAY 94541 711-F3
VICTORY LN
- LGTS 95030 873-A7
1100 CNCD 94518 592-D5
1100 CNCD 94520 592-D5
37200 FRMT 94536 753-B1
VIDA CT
100 NVTO 94947 525-G5
1600 SLN 94579 691-A7
VIDAL DR
- SF 94132 687-A1
VIDA LEON CT
300 SJS 95116 834-D2
VIDELL ST
700 AlaC 94580 691-E5
VIEBROCK WY
- HAY 94544 732-B1
VIEJO WY
- UNC 94587 731-H6
- NVTO 94945 526-A1
VIEJO VISTA
- CCCo 94595 632-D2
VIELA CT
1000 LFYT 94549 611-J5
VIENNA DR
- MPS 95035 793-J4
- MPS 95035 794-A4
1200 SUNV 94089 812-H4
VIENNA ST
- SF 94112 667-H7
300 SF 94112 687-G1
1000 LVMR 94550 715-G3
VIENTO CT
38800 FRMT 94536 753-D2
VIENTO DR
- FRMT 94536 753-D2
VIERA AV
1400 CCCo 94509 575-H5
2100 ANT 94509 575-H6
VIERA CT
2100 ANT 94509 575-H6
VIERRA CT
1300 SJS 95125 854-A5
VIERRA WY
100 HER 94547 570-B6
VIEW AV
7100 ELCR 94530 589-C7
VIEW DR
- AlaC 94566 734-B1
- AlaC 94566 714-B7
900 RCH 94803 589-C1
900 RCH 94803 569-C7
1200 SLN 94577 691-C1
1700 MPS 95035 794-D6
3000 ANT 94509 575-C7
3000 ANT 94509 595-D1
E VIEW DR
3500 LFYT 94549 611-F7
VIEW LN
- CCCo 94596 612-E6
E VIEW PL
2100 MRTZ 94553 572-B7
VIEW PT
20400 AlaC 94552 692-E4
VIEW ST
- LALT 94022 811-D6
- LKSP 94939 586-E6
- VAL 94590 529-H2
100 MTVW 94041 811-J6
4300 OAK 94611 629-J7
VIEW TR
- MLBR 94030 728-A4
VIEW WY
1000 PCFA 94044 727-A5
VIEWCREST CIR
- SSF 94080 707-H1
VIEW CREST CT
4300 OAK 94619 650-J7
VIEWCREST CT
20200 SCIC 95120 894-J2
VIEW CREST DR
6100 OAK 94619 650-J6
VIEWCREST DR
20200 SCIC 95120 894-H2
VIEWFIELD RD
15800 MSER 95030 872-J6
VIEW HAVEN RD
1200 HIL 94010 748-F4
VIEWMONT AV
- SCIC 95127 835-A2
100 VAL 94590 530-C3
VIEWMONT CT
3400 SCIC 95127 835-A2
3400 SJS 95127 835-A2

BAY AREA

INDEX

1006 VIEWMONT ST
1998 BAY AREA STREET INDEX
WAGNER RD

BAY AREA

STREET Block City ZIP Pg-Grid

VIEWMONT ST
300 BEN 94510 551-C4
VIEWMONT TER
- SSF 94080 707-H2
VIEWOAK DR
12100 SAR 95070 852-F5
VIEW OAKS WY
20600 SCIC 95120 894-J2
VIEWPARK CIR
300 SJS 95136 874-G1
VIEWPARK CT
400 MrnC 94965 606-E7
400 MrnC 94965 626-E1
VIEW POINT CIR
44200 FRMT 94539 773-J2
VIEW POINT CT
300 FRMT 94539 773-J2
VIEWPOINT CT
- DNVL 94506 654-B6
6400 MRTZ 94553 591-H3
VIEWPOINT DR
200 DNVL 94506 654-B6
VIEWPOINT LN
10000 SJS 95120 894-G4
VIEW POINT RD
700 MrnC 94965 606-E7
VIEWPOINTE BLVD
900 CCCo 94572 569-J2
1000 CCCo 94572 570-A1
VIEWRIDGE DR
800 SMTO 94403 749-A7
19700 SAR 95070 852-F5
VIKING DR
300 PLHL 94523 592-B3
VIKING PL
200 CCCo 94526 633-C4
VIKING ST
25000 HAY 94545 711-D6
VIKING WY
- PIT 94565 573-J3
VILI WY
500 PLHL 94523 592-A3
VILLA
- MTVW 94043 812-A2
- MTVW 94043 811-J2
VILLA AV
- CLMA 94014 687-D7
- LGTS 95032 893-A1
- SRFL 94901 566-G6
700 SJS 95126 833-H6
900 BLMT 94002 769-C1
VILLA CT
- MrnC 94904 586-E3
- SSF 94080 707-F2
100 CCCo 94549 611-H1
VILLA DR
- SPAB 94806 588-J4
1300 SCIC 94024 831-F3
VILLA LN
- MLBR 94030 728-A5
800 MRGA 94556 631-C6
VILLA LP
2000 PLE 94588 714-B5
VILLA PL
- NVTO 94945 526-A2
2300 SCL 95054 813-C4
VILLA ST
200 MTVW 94041 811-G4
500 SMCo 94014 687-D5
600 DALY 94014 687-D5
VILLA TER
- SF 94114 667-F2
200 SMTO 94401 728-H7
N VILLA WY
100 CCCo 94595 612-B6
S VILLA WY
1700 CCCo 94595 612-B6
VILLA CENTRE WY
- SJS 95128 853-E1
VILLA DE ANZA AV
10600 CPTO 95014 832-F6
VILLA EAST HILLS CT
3100 SJS 95127 835-A3
VILLA FELICE CT
17100 LGTS 95030 873-B4
VILLA GARDEN DR
- MrnC 94965 606-G7
VILLAGE CIR
- SRFL 94903 566-G5
100 NVTO 94947 526-D7
VILLAGE COM
38000 FRMT 94536 752-J4
VILLAGE CT
- LVMR 94550 696-E3
- SRFL 94903 566-G5
100 WLCK 94596 612-D5
200 SJS 95110 833-J4
1400 MTVW 94040 832-A1
2200 BLMT 94002 769-C2
2600 UNC 94587 732-E6
VILLAGE CTR
900 LFYT 94549 611-D7
VILLAGE DR
- LVMR 94550 696-D3
400 ELCR 94530 609-E3
1100 BLMT 94002 769-C2
3300 AlaC 94546 692-A5
12900 SAR 95070 852-G7
VILLAGE LN
- BEN 94510 551-D5
- SMCo 94015 687-B4
300 LGTS 95030 873-A7
VILLAGE LP
200 DNVL 94526 653-A3
VILLAGE PKWY
- HER 94547 569-F3
6200 DBLN 94568 693-H3
9400 SRMN 94583 693-H1
VILLAGE PL
100 MRTZ 94553 571-G5
VILLAGE RD
3500 CNCD 94519 592-J1
3600 CNCD 94519 573-A7
3600 CNCD 94519 593-A1
VILLAGE TER
3700 FRMT 94536 752-J4
VILLAGE WY
200 SSF 94080 707-J3
2500 UNC 94587 732-E6
VILLAGE CENTER DR
300 SJS 95134 813-H4

VILLAGE GATE RD
- ORIN 94563 610-G7
VILLAGE GREEN DR
- LVMR 94550 696-D3
VILLAGE HERMOSA LN
8200 SJS 95135 855-J6
VILLAGE OAKS DR
900 MRTZ 94553 571-H6
VILLAGETREE DR
2000 SJS 95131 814-D6
VILLAGE VIEW CT
- ORIN 94563 610-G6
11300 DBLN 94568 693-E3
VILLAGEWOOD WY
6800 SJS 95120 894-H3
VILLAGIO PL
- SJS 95134 813-H4
VILLA GLEN WY
3800 SJS 95136 874-D1
VILLA MARIA
- NVTO 94947 526-A4
VILLA MARIA CT
1000 SJS 95125 854-E5
21500 CPTO 95014 852-B3
VILLA MONTEREY
2600 SJS 95111 854-G5
VILLANOVA CT
3300 SCL 95051 833-A2
VILLANOVA DR
- OAK 94611 630-F6
- CCCo 94611 630-F6
VILLANOVA LN
- CCCo 94611 630-F6
- OAK 94611 630-F6
VILLANOVA RD
2100 SJS 95130 852-J7
2200 SAR 95070 852-J7
VILLA NUEVA CT
100 MTVW 94040 831-J1
VILLA NUEVA DR
1000 ELCR 94530 609-E1
VILLA NUEVA WY
2400 MTVW 94040 831-J1
VILLA OAKS LN
21700 SAR 95070 852-B7
21900 SCIC 95070 852-B7
VILLA PARK CT
500 SJS 95118 874-C3
VILLA PARK LN
- SJS 95118 874-G3
VILLA PARK WY
500 SJS 95118 874-C3
VILLA REAL
500 PA 94306 811-C2
VILLAREAL DR
3700 AlaC 94552 692-F3
VILLARITA DR
1500 CMBL 95008 853-A6
1900 SJS 95130 853-A6
VILLA ROBLEDA DR
3300 MTVW 94040 832-A2
VILLA STONE DR
1600 SJS 95125 854-D3
VILLA TERESA WY
700 SJS 95123 874-E5
VILLA VERA
4000 PA 94306 811-C2
VILLA VISTA
800 SMCo 94062 789-G1
4000 PA 94306 811-C2
VILLA VISTA CT
- MrnC 94947 525-F3
VILLA VISTA RD
- SCIC 95135 855-H4
- SJS 95135 855-H4
VILMAR AV
6000 SJS 95120 874-B7
VINCENT CT
3800 AlaC 94546 692-B5
6000 SJS 95123 875-A6
VINCENT DR
200 MTVW 94041 811-J6
2800 PIN 94564 570-A7
3300 SCL 95051 832-J1
VINCENT LN
- NVTO 94945 526-E3
VINCENT RD
3100 PLHL 94596 592-D7
VINCENT ST
1600 PIT 94565 574-E3
VINCENTE AV
400 BERK 94707 609-F5
VINCENTE CT
35000 FRMT 94536 752-E2
VINCENTE RD
1700 CNCD 94519 592-H2
VINCENTE ST
4000 FRMT 94536 752-E2
VINCI PARK WY
1100 SJS 95131 814-D7
VINE AV
- RCH 94801 608-D1
- SANS 94960 586-B1
300 SUNV 94086 832-E1
800 CCCo 94553 571-F4
2900 SJS 95148 855-F1
VINE CT
- AlaC 94546 691-J2
800 SMTO 94401 749-C1
VINE LN
- BERK 94708 609-H7
1400 CCCo 94507 632-E3
1800 CCCo 94509 575-H5
VINE ST
- BERK 94703 609-G7
- BERK 94708 609-G7
- LKSP 94939 586-E6
- SCAR 94070 769-F2
100 MLPK 94025 790-E6
100 SMCo 94025 790-E6
500 SJS 95110 834-B7
600 SJS 95110 854-C1
1400 SJS 95125 854-C1
1500 BLMT 94002 769-F2
1900 BERK 94709 609-G7
3500 AlaC 94566 714-F3
3700 PLE 94566 714-F3
14800 SAR 95070 872-E3
VINE TER
- SF 94108 648-A5
VINEDALE SQ
1900 SJS 95132 814-F3

VINEDO LN
25700 LAH 94022 831-B2
VINE HILL N
- CCCo 94553 571-J3
VINE HILL S
- CCCo 94553 571-H3
VINE HILL ARC
- CCCo 94553 571-J3
VINEHILL CIR
1700 FRMT 94539 774-A3
1700 FRMT 94539 773-J3
VINEHILL CT
1600 FRMT 94539 773-J4
1600 FRMT 94539 774-A4
VINE HILL LN
600 SRMN 94583 673-J7
VINE HILL LP
- CCCo 94553 571-H3
VINE HILL RD
- CCCo 94553 571-H3
VINEHILL TER
45700 FRMT 94539 774-A4
VINE HILL WY
400 MRTZ 94553 571-F7
500 MRTZ 94553 591-G1
VINELAND AV
17300 LGTS 95030 873-A5
17300 MSER 95030 873-A5
17900 MSER 95030 872-J4
VINELAND CT
17600 MSER 95030 873-A5
VINEMAPLE AV
600 SUNV 94086 832-J2
VINETA CT
5600 MRTZ 94553 591-G1
VINEWOOD CT
- PIT 94565 573-G4
VINEWOOD ST
35700 NWK 94560 752-D4
VINEWOOD WY
4800 ANT 94509 595-J3
VINEYARD AV
- LVMR 94550 715-A4
- SANS 94960 586-B1
- AlaC 94550 715-A4
- PLE 94550 715-A4
- PLE 94566 715-A4
100 AlaC 94566 715-A4
400 PLE 94566 714-E3
800 AlaC 94566 714-G3
45200 FRMT 94539 773-J4
E VINEYARD AV
200 AlaC 94550 715-D5
200 LVMR 94550 715-D5
VINEYARD CT
- NVTO 94947 525-H3
800 PLHL 94523 592-A4
2200 LALT 94024 831-J5
VINEYARD DR
- SRFL 94901 566-F6
200 SJS 95119 875-D7
200 SJS 95119 895-D1
1500 LALT 94024 831-J6
1500 LALT 94024 832-A5
1700 ANT 94509 575-J5
3800 RDWC 94061 789-G3
VINEYARD LN
3000 PLE 94566 715-A4
19100 SAR 95070 852-G7
VINEYARD PL
400 PLE 94566 714-F3
VINEYARD RD
2000 NVTO 94947 525-G3
2400 MrnC 94947 525-E4
17400 AlaC 94546 691-H3
VINEYARD WY
- MrnC 94904 586-D4
VINEYARD CREEK CT
8600 SJS 95135 855-J6
VINEYARD HILL RD
- WDSD 94062 809-H2
VINEYARD RIDGE CT
8600 SJS 95135 855-J6
VINEYARD RIDGE PL
8600 SJS 95135 855-J6
VINEYARD SPRING CT
11600 CPTO 95014 852-A4
VIN GRANDE CT
- SJS 95135 855-E3
VINING DR
1200 SLN 94579 691-B7
1700 SLN 94579 711-A1
VINTAGE CT
- WDSD 94062 809-H2
3800 CNCD 94518 592-J4
VINTAGE LN
2000 LVMR 94550 715-H3
21600 SAR 95070 872-B3
VINTAGE TER
36500 FRMT 94536 752-G3
VINTAGE WY
100 NVTO 94947 526-D5
800 SJS 95122 854-F1
VINTAGE ACRES WY
- SJS 95148 855-F2
VINTAGE CREST DR
3100 SJS 95148 855-E1
VINTAGE OAKS CT
3100 SJS 95148 855-F2
VINTAGE PARK DR
300 FCTY 94404 749-E2
VINTNER CT
14900 SAR 95070 872-B3
VINTNER WY
1000 PLE 94566 714-G4
1600 SJS 95124 873-H4
VINTON CT
- SF 94108 648-A5
VINYARD CT
100 LGTS 95030 872-J3
VIOLA AV
- SJS 95110 834-B7
VIOLA CT
35600 FRMT 94536 752-F3
VIOLA PL
- CNCD 94518 592-H6
700 LALT 94024 831-E1
VIOLA ST
2600 OAK 94619 650-E6
VIOLA WY
- MrnC 94965 626-F1

VIOLET AV
4800 LVMR 94550 696-A4
VIOLET CT
2700 ANT 94509 575-G7
VIOLET DR
100 VAL 94589 510-A6
VIOLET LN
- SCAR 94070 769-C4
VIOLET RD
100 HER 94547 570-A4
VIOLET ST
400 SLN 94578 691-C5
VIOLET WY
1500 PLHL 94523 592-C4
2100 SJS 95008 853-C6
VIONA AV
600 OAK 94610 650-A3
VIOX WY
- SRFL 94901 586-E1
VIRDEN AV
3600 OAK 94619 650-F5
VIREO AV
1500 SUNV 94087 832-H5
3600 SCL 95051 832-H5
VIRGIL CIR
3400 PLE 94588 714-B1
VIRGIL CT
- CCCo 94565 573-F1
VIRGIL PL
1100 SJS 95120 894-H4
VIRGIL ST
- SF 94110 667-J4
400 CCCo 94565 573-F1
VIRGIL WILLIAMS TR
- CCCo - 652-G1
- CCCo 94526 652-G1
VIRGINIA AV
- CMBL 95008 853-C7
- SF 94110 667-H5
100 BLMT 94002 749-E7
100 RCH 94804 608-F1
100 BLMT 94002 769-E1
200 SMTO 94402 748-H3
800 CMBL 95008 873-C1
1100 RDWC 94061 789-J1
1200 RDWC 94061 790-A2
1600 SJS 95116 834-G5
1700 NVTO 94945 526-A2
1800 NVTO 94945 525-J2
4300 OAK 94619 650-F7
VIRGINIA CIR
200 MRTZ 94553 591-H4
VIRGINIA CT
- CCCo 94596 612-F6
100 CCCo 94526 633-C5
800 CMBL 95008 873-C1
1100 CNCD 94520 592-E4
VIRGINIA DR
- CCCo 94565 573-F2
- ORIN 94563 631-A2
300 LVMR 94550 715-D2
500 TBRN 94920 607-B4
VIRGINIA GDNS W
- BERK 94702 629-E1
VIRGINIA LN
- ATN 94027 790-E1
100 CCCo 94526 633-C4
1100 CNCD 94520 592-E4
VIRGINIA PL
1500 SJS 95116 834-F5
VIRGINIA ST
100 HAY 94544 712-A5
200 CCCo 94525 550-C4
300 VAL 94590 529-J5
500 VAL 94590 530-A5
1100 BERK 94804 629-D1
1200 BERK 94702 629-F1
1300 CCCo 94526 633-C4
1300 SLN 94577 690-H1
1300 BERK 94703 629-F1
1900 BERK 94709 629-H1
E VIRGINIA ST
- SJS 95112 854-C1
100 SJS 95112 834-D7
W VIRGINIA ST
- SJS 95110 854-C1
300 SJS 95125 854-A1
VIRGINIA WY
300 AlaC 94566 714-G3
400 MRTZ 94553 591-H4
VIRGINIA HILLS DR
100 MRTZ 94553 591-H4
VIRGINIA SWAN PL
10200 CPTO 95014 832-E7
VIRGIN ISLANDS CT
3600 PLE 94588 714-A1
VIRGO LN
3400 SJS 95111 854-F6
VIRGO RD
6200 OAK 94611 630-D6
VIRIO COM
4500 FRMT 94536 752-A6
VIRMAR AV
5600 OAK 94618 630-A5
VISA CT
100 FRMT 94538 773-B2
VISALIA AV
1300 RCH 94801 588-G5
1500 ALB 94706 609-F5
1500 BERK 94707 609-F5
VISCAINO AV
1100 SUNV 94086 812-B7
VISCAINO CT
12600 LAH 94022 811-B7
VISCAINO DR
12600 LAH 94022 811-B7
VISCAINO PL
12800 LAH 94022 811-A7
VISCAINO RD
12600 LAH 94022 811-B6
VISCAINO WY
- SRFL 94903 566-D4
200 SJS 95119 875-C7
VISITACION AV
- BSBN 94005 688-A6
200 SF 94134 687-J2
1200 SF 94134 688-A2
VISO CT
3300 SCL 95054 813-E6
VISTA AV
- PDMT 94611 650-B1
- SMTO 94403 749-D6

VISTA AV
100 SCIC 95127 814-J7
200 SJS 95127 814-J7
400 PA 94306 811-C2
600 SCAR 94070 769-F3
3300 OAK 94619 650-F6
17600 MSER 95030 873-A5
E VISTA AV
- DALY 94014 687-D3
VISTA CIR
- SMCo - 768-D4
VISTA CT
- SF 94129 647-E5
- CMAD 94925 606-J2
- SSF 94080 707-E5
400 BEN 94510 551-B4
400 LVMR 94550 695-J7
500 MLBR 94030 727-J2
700 SMCo 94062 789-G1
3700 AlaC 94541 692-C7
20200 CPTO 95014 832-E7
S VISTA CT
2700 ANT 94509 575-B6
VISTA DR
- SMCo - 768-D4
- DNVL 94526 653-B2
- MrnC 94904 586-E2
400 SCAR 94070 769-F3
600 SMCo 94062 789-G1
800 RDWC 94062 789-G1
10100 CPTO 95014 832-E7
VISTA LN
- CCCo 94595 632-D2
- SANS 94960 566-A6
- SF 94131 667-F3
- SMCo 94010 728-B6
100 VAL 94590 530-B2
15400 LGTS 95032 873-D5
VISTA LP
5900 SJS 95124 873-J7
VISTA PL
2900 ANT 94509 575-B7
11500 DBLN 94568 693-F3
VISTA RD
- ALA 94502 669-H5
800 HIL 94010 748-G3
1400 ELCR 94530 589-E7
VISTA ST
100 LVMR 94550 695-J7
1500 OAK 94602 650-D3
VISTA TR
- CCCo - 652-E2
VISTA WY
100 MRTZ 94553 571-E5
400 MPS 95035 794-B7
400 MPS 95035 814-C1
2800 ANT 94509 575-B6
VISTA ARROYO CT
12100 SAR 95070 852-C5
VISTA BAHIA WY
27500 HAY 94542 712-E4
VISTA BELLA
- LFYT 94549 611-G4
VISTA CAY
1900 SMTO 94404 749-H1
VISTA CERRO TER
600 FRMT 94539 773-J1
VISTA CHARONOAKS
3600 WLCK 94598 613-A2
VISTA CLARA
- SAUS 94965 627-A3
VISTA CLUB CIR
1500 SCL 95054 813-D4
VISTA CREEK DR
2900 SJS 95133 814-G6
VISTA DE ALMADEN
18600 SCIC 95120 874-G7
VISTA DE ALMADEN CT
- SCIC 95120 874-G7
VISTA DEL ARBOL
200 LGTS 95032 893-C1
VISTA DEL CAMPO
100 LGTS 95032 873-C7
VISTA DEL DIABLO
100 DNVL 94526 633-C6
900 MRTZ 94553 591-F4
VISTA DEL GRANDE
- SCAR 94070 769-F4
VISTA DEL LAGO
- LGTS 95030 872-J2
VISTA DEL MAR
- OAK 94611 630-E6
- ORIN 94563 610-F5
- TBRN 94920 607-F7
100 LGTS 95032 893-C1
100 SRFL 94901 586-J2
200 SRFL 94901 587-A2
1000 SJS 95132 814-J5
1500 MrnC 94920 607-F7
1900 SMTO 94404 749-E3
43400 FRMT 94539 773-H1
VISTA DEL MAR PL
100 ORIN 94563 610-F5
VISTA DEL MONTE
100 LGTS 95032 873-C7
100 LGTS 95032 893-C1
2400 CNCD 94520 592-F4
VISTA DEL MORAGA
- ORIN 94563 630-J3
VISTA DEL ORINDA
- ORIN 94563 610-D7
VISTA DEL PLAZA LN
22100 HAY 94541 691-J7
VISTA DEL PRADO
100 LGTS 95032 893-B1
VISTA DEL RIO
300 CCCo 94553 572-C6
1800 CCCo 94525 550-B5
VISTA DEL SOL
- MrnC 94941 606-H4
1500 SMTO 94404 749-H1
2500 SJS 95116 834-H3
44800 FRMT 94539 773-J2
44800 FRMT 94539 774-A2
VISTA DEL VALLE
3500 SJS 95132 814-J5
VISTA DE SIERRA
200 LGTS 95032 893-C1
VISTA DE VALLE
300 MrnC 94965 626-E1
12900 LAH 94022 831-B1

VISTA DIABLO
- PIT 94565 574-B6
1100 PLE 94566 714-H2
VISTA DIABLO CT
2600 PLE 94566 714-H3
VISTA DIABLO WY
2700 PLE 94566 714-H3
VISTA FLORES
1100 PLE 94566 714-G2
VISTAGLEN CT
1700 SJS 95122 835-A6
VISTAGLEN DR
1700 SJS 95122 835-A6
VISTA GLEN PL
200 MRTZ 94553 591-G2
VISTA GRAND CT
2600 SLN 94577 691-D2
VISTA GRAND DR
1200 SLN 94577 691-D2
VISTA GRANDE
- LKSP 94904 586-F3
100 MrnC 94904 586-F3
300 CCCo 94553 572-C6
700 MLBR 94030 727-J4
1000 PLE 94566 714-G3
2100 CCCo 94526 633-E7
VISTA GRANDE AV
- BEN 94510 551-D4
- DALY 94014 687-C3
700 LALT 94024 811-G6
800 MTVW 94024 811-G6
800 MTVW 94040 811-G6
VISTA GRANDE ST
2100 DNVL 94526 653-B2
VISTA GRANDE TER
- FRMT 94539 774-A2
- FRMT 94539 773-J2
VISTA GREENS CT
24900 HAY 94541 712-C2
VISTA HEIGHTS RD
100 RCH 94805 589-D7
VISTA HERMOSA
- WLCK 94596 612-B4
VISTA HILL TER
600 FRMT 94539 773-J1
VISTA HILLS CT
2800 ANT 94509 595-G1
VISTA KNOLL BLVD
10200 CPTO 95014 832-A7
VISTA LINDA DR
300 MLV 94941 606-E2
VISTA LOMA
20700 SCIC 95120 894-J2
VISTA MAR AV
400 PCFA 94044 707-A4
VISTAMONT AV
500 BERK 94708 609-H4
VISTAMONT CT
500 BERK 94708 609-H4
VISTAMONT DR
3000 SJS 95118 854-B7
3000 SJS 95118 874-C1
VISTA MONTANA
- SJS 95134 813-D2
VISTA MONTARA CIR
800 PCFA 94044 726-H5
VISTA MONTE DR
- SRMN 94583 673-J7
- SRMN 94583 694-A1
- SRMN 94583 693-J1
VISTA NORTE CT
3500 MPS 95035 794-G6
3500 SCIC 95035 794-G6
VISTA OAK
1000 SJS 95132 814-J5
VISTA OAKS CT
20300 CPTO 95014 832-E7
VISTA OAKS DR
3400 MRTZ 94553 571-E6
VISTA PARK DR
4000 SJS 95136 854-F7
VISTAPARK DR
4000 SJS 95136 874-F1
VISTA POINT CT
1100 CNCD 94521 593-D7
VISTA POINT LN
1100 CNCD 94521 593-D7
VISTA POINTE CIR
1000 SRMN 94583 673-F2
VISTA POINTE DR
800 SRMN 94583 673-F2
VISTA REAL
- MrnC 94941 606-H5
VISTA REGINA
13900 SAR 95070 872-B1
VISTA RIDGE DR
200 MPS 95035 794-G6
300 SCIC 95035 794-G6
VISTA SERENA
15400 LAH 94022 831-C1
VISTA SPRING CT
500 MPS 95035 794-H6
VISTA TIBURON DR
- TBRN 94920 606-J3
VISTA VALLE CT
10100 SCIC 95127 815-C7
VISTA VERDE CT
- SF 94131 667-F6
VISTA VERDE DR
2200 SJS 95148 835-D5
2200 SCIC 95148 835-C6
VISTA VERDE WY
200 SMCo 94028 830-E5
VISTA VIA
- LFYT 94549 611-H6
VISTAVIEW CT
- SF 94124 668-B6
VISTAVIEW DR
3300 SJS 95132 814-G4
VISTA WOOD WY
- SRFL 94901 566-E6
VISTAZO EAST ST
1500 TBRN 94920 607-F7
VISTAZO WEST ST
1400 TBRN 94920 607-E6
VITA CT
- PLHL 94523 612-A1
VITERO WY
5800 SJS 95138 875-H1
VIVA LN
1300 CNCD 94518 592-J3

VIVIAN COM
100 FRMT 94536 733-B6
VIVIAN CT
- NVTO 94947 525-G3
VIVIAN DR
- PLHL 94523 592-C5
300 LGTS 95032 873-C7
300 LGTS 95032 893-C1
600 LVMR 94550 696-C6
E VIVIAN DR
- PLHL 94523 592-C5
VIVIAN LN
2800 SJS 95124 873-G1
VIVIAN PL
35800 FRMT 94536 733-B6
35800 FRMT 94536 732-J7
VIVIAN ST
- SRFL 94901 586-H2
2000 AlaC 94546 691-J6
VIZCAYA CIR
2100 SJS 95008 873-F1
2100 SJS 95008 853-F7
VIZCAYA WY
2100 SJS 95008 873-F1
VIZZOLINI CT
- PLE 94566 715-B5
VOELKER DR
400 SMTO 94403 749-B6
VOERT CT
2000 WLCK 94598 612-G3
VOGEL CT
40400 FRMT 94538 753-C6
VOGELSANG DR
- MrnC 94903 546-A6
VOGUE CT
27600 LAH 94022 831-A1
VOLANS LN
800 FCTY 94404 749-H1
VOLATILE DR
- CCCo 94553 571-H3
VOLCANIC TR
- CCCo - 630-F4
VOLCANO CT
100 VAL 94589 509-H5
VOLLMER WY
1700 SJS 95116 834-G5
VOLPEY WY
2800 UNC 94587 732-A3
VOLTAIRE AV
9900 OAK 94603 671-A5
VOLTAIRE ST
26500 HAY 94544 712-B5
VOLTERRA CT
- DNVL 94506 653-D1
5800 SJS 95138 875-G1
VOLTI LN
1100 LALT 94024 831-J2
VOLZ CT
100 CCCo 94507 632-G6
VOMAC CT
8100 DBLN 94568 693-G3
VOMAC RD
7900 DBLN 94568 693-G3
W VOMAC RD
8300 DBLN 94568 693-F2
VON DOOLEN CT
2800 PIN 94564 569-H6
VON EUW COM
- FRMT 94536 753-A2
VONNA CT
700 SJS 95123 874-G5
VOORHEES DR
24500 LAH 94024 831-D2
VOSS CT
- AlaC 94541 711-E2
VOSS PARK LN
2000 SJS 95131 814-E7
VOYAGER DR
100 VAL 94590 529-G2
VOYAGER WY
800 HAY 94544 712-A3
VUELTA OLIVOS
1000 FRMT 94539 753-G6
VULCAN STAIRWAY
- SF 94114 667-F2

W

W ST
- BEN 94510 551-D4
WABANA COM
- FRMT 94539 773-J7
WABANA ST
47700 FRMT 94539 773-J7
WABASH AV
- SJS 95128 833-G7
100 SCIC 95128 833-G7
100 SCIC 95128 853-G1
200 SJS 95128 853-G1
WABASH PL
400 DNVL 94526 653-C5
WABASH ST
1200 SJS 95002 793-B7
WABASH TER
- SF 94134 688-A2
WABASH RIVER PL
34700 FRMT 94555 752-E2
WACO ST
1000 SJS 95110 833-H4
WADDINGTON AV
400 SUNV 94086 812-F5
WADE AV
1600 SCL 95051 833-B3
WADEAN PL
5400 OAK 94601 670-E2
WADI RUN
100 HER 94547 569-H4
WADSWORTH AV
- LGTS 95030 872-J7
WADSWORTH CT
4700 FRMT 94538 773-C1
WAGMAN DR
400 SJS 95129 852-J2
WAGNER AL
- SF 94102 647-J6
WAGNER AV
1700 MTVW 94043 811-H3
WAGNER RD
- SF 94129 647-C3
- LFYT 94549 611-D5
17200 SCIC 95032 893-G3

INDEX

STREET Block City ZIP Pg-Grid

WAGNER ST
- BEN 94510 551-F1
15400 AlaC 94580 691-E5
42600 FRMT 94539 753-H6
WAGON CT
4500 ANT 94509 595-J3
WAGONER DR
700 LVMR 94550 715-F3
WAGON WHEEL WY
5000 ANT 94509 595-H4
WAGONWHEEL WY
4900 RCH 94803 590-A3
WAIKIKI CIR
300 UNC 94587 732-C6
WAIMEA CT
4400 SJS 95118 874-B2
WAINFLEET CT
900 ANT 94509 575-C7
WAINGARTH WY
800 DNVL 94526 633-C6
WAINWRIGHT AV
300 SJS 95128 853-F1
300 SCIC 95128 853-F1
1200 SLN 94577 690-J2
WAINWRIGHT COM
39500 FRMT 94538 753-A5
WAINWRIGHT CT
30700 UNC 94587 731-J4
WAINWRIGHT DR
800 SJS 95128 853-F4
WAINWRIGHT PL
- MLV 94941 606-C3
WAINWRIGHT ST
800 BEN 94510 551-A4
800 BEN 94510 550-J4
WAINWRIGHT TER
39500 FRMT 94538 753-B6
WAIT ST
400 HAY 94541 711-G3
WAITE AV
500 SUNV 94086 812-F6
WAITHMAN WY
900 SF 94127 667-D5
WAKE AV
- OAK 94626 649-D1
- OAK 94649 649-D1
2000 OAK 94607 649-C1
13500 SLN 94577 691-C2
13500 SLN 94578 691-C2
WAKE CT
100 VAL 94589 510-B7
WAKEFIELD AV
- DALY 94015 707-C2
2500 OAK 94606 650-B5
5700 CCCo 94806 589-A3
WAKEFIELD CT
- CCCo 94506 654-B4
- BLMT 94002 769-B3
WAKEFIELD DR
- ALA 94501 649-J7
- MRGA 94556 631-C5
1400 HAY 94544 732-B2
2600 BLMT 94002 769-B3
WAKEFIELD LP
4100 FRMT 94536 752-G3
WAKEFIELD TER
1500 LALT 94024 832-A3
WAKE FOREST DR
700 MTVW 94043 812-A3
WAKEROBIN LN
500 SRFL 94903 566-C2
WALAVISTA AV
500 OAK 94610 650-B2
WALBRIDGE AV
- SF 94134 687-H2
WALBROOK CT
800 WLCK 94598 612-G3
WALBROOK DR
5400 SJS 95129 852-G4
11800 SAR 95070 852-H5
W WALBROOK DR
5800 SJS 95129 852-G4
WALCOTT RD
- SCIC 94035 812-B1
- SCIC 94043 812-B1
WALDALE CT
- WLCK 94596 612-B3
WALDECK CT
- OAK 94611 650-G2
WALDEN CT
1600 FRMT 94539 753-G6
12300 SAR 95070 852-F5
WALDEN LN
- MLV 94941 606-B1
WALDEN RD
1200 WLCK 94596 612-C3
1300 CCCo 94596 612-C3
WALDEN SQ
2300 SJS 95124 853-H7
WALDEN WK
- CNCD 94518 592-E6
WALDHEIM CT
7000 SJS 95120 894-H3
WALDIE PZ
100 ANT 94509 575-C3
WALDO AL
- SF 94109 647-J4
WALDO AV
100 PDMT 94611 650-B1
6300 ELCR 94530 609-D3
WALDO CT
- MrnC 94965 626-G1
WALDO LN
7300 ELCR 94530 609-D3
WALDO RD
300 CMBL 95008 853-C7
WALES CT
- SJS 95138 875-H1
100 CCCo 94506 654-A4
1500 CNCD 94521 593-D4
WALFORD DR
100 MRGA 94556 651-E2
WALGLEN CT
900 SJS 95136 874-D1
WALGROVE WY
2900 SJS 95128 853-E3
WALHAVEN CT
700 WLCK 94598 612-G3
WALKER AV
700 OAK 94610 650-A3
1000 WLCK 94596 612-D5

WALKER CT
1800 SJS 95122 854-G1
5200 ANT 94509 595-J5
21100 AlaC 94546 691-J6
WALKER DR
200 MTVW 94043 812-A3
WALKER PL
2500 LVMR 94550 715-G5
WALKER ST
- MrnC 94920 606-H3
2700 BERK 94705 629-H3
WALKINGSHAW WY
3100 SJS 95132 814-F4
WALL AV
3300 RCH 94804 588-J7
3400 RCH 94804 589-A7
3600 RCH 94804 609-A1
5900 ELCR 94530 609-B1
WALL COM
39600 FRMT 94538 753-B5
WALL CT
400 LVMR 94550 715-E2
WALL PL
- SF 94109 647-J5
WALL ST
100 LVMR 94550 715-E1
3000 SCIC 95111 854-G5
3000 SJS 95111 854-G5
5200 ELCR 94530 589-B7
5200 ELCR 94530 609-B1
WALLABI CT
- LFYT 94549 631-G4
WALLABY CT
4300 ANT 94509 595-H3
WALLACE AV
100 VAL 94590 530-C5
1300 SF 94124 668-C7
1900 SLN 94577 690-H2
WALLACE CT
- NVTO 94947 526-B6
1400 PIN 94564 569-D5
2300 ANT 94509 574-J7
WALLACE DR
900 SJS 95120 874-E7
5900 CLAY 94517 593-G6
22000 CPTO 95014 832-A6
WALLACE LN
- DBLN 94552 693-E5
- DBLN 94568 693-E5
WALLACE PL
5400 FRMT 94538 752-J7
WALLACE RD
100 PDMT 94610 650-B2
WALLACE ST
2400 OAK 94606 650-B5
2600 SCL 95051 833-B4
2700 BERK 94702 629-E3
WALLACE WY
- SRFL 94903 566-C4
WALLEA DR
500 MLPK 94025 790-F4
WALLEN CT
- SF 94129 647-E5
WALLER AV
100 CCCo 94595 612-C6
100 WLCK 94595 612-C6
3300 RCH 94804 588-J7
3600 RCH 94804 589-A7
5100 FRMT 94536 752-H6
WALLER RD
- WLCK 94596 612-C6
WALLER ST
- SF 94102 667-H1
300 SF 94117 667-E1
1700 SF 94117 667-E1
WALLEYE COM
- FRMT 94536 753-F3
WALLIN CT
- WLCK 94596 612-C2
WALLIN DR
100 MRTZ 94553 571-D6
WALLIS CT
4100 PA 94306 811-C4
WALLYFORD CT
2500 SJS 95121 855-D4
WALLY PLACE WY
3600 SJS 95121 855-B4
WALMSLEY ST
- DBLN 94568 694-A3
WALNUT
- BEN 94510 551-B5
WALNUT AV
- ATN 94027 790-E2
- CMAD 94925 586-F7
- FRMT 94536 753-C3
- LGTS 95030 872-J7
- LKSP 94939 586-E6
- MLV 94941 606-E3
- ROSS 94957 586-B2
100 SUNV 94086 812-E6
200 WLCK 94598 612-F2
300 SSF 94080 707-J3
300 VAL 94592 529-F3
400 FRMT 94538 753-B4
500 MRTZ 94553 571-E6
700 HIL 94010 728-E6
700 BURL 94010 728-E6
1400 CCCo 94509 575-H5
1400 FRMT 94539 753-C3
3300 CNCD 94519 592-H2
3700 CNCD 94519 593-A2
20400 SAR 95070 872-D2
WALNUT BLVD
2000 WLCK 94596 612-D3
2000 WLCK 94598 612-D3
3300 CCCo 94596 612-E6
WALNUT CIR
10300 CPTO 95014 852-A1
WALNUT CT
100 HER 94547 569-J4
100 HER 94547 570-A4
500 VAL 94589 510-A7
700 NVTO 94945 525-E2
WALNUT DR
400 MPS 95035 793-J6
1000 LFYT 94549 611-G6
1200 CMBL 95008 873-C2
1500 PA 94303 791-B4
1700 MTVW 94040 831-G1
2500 SLN 94577 690-G4
4000 PLE 94566 714-E3

WALNUT LN
3200 LFYT 94549 631-G1
WALNUT PL
1600 CNCD 94519 592-J2
WALNUT RD
17500 AlaC 94546 691-J3
WALNUT ST
- SBRN 94066 707-J6
- SF 94118 647-E5
- SF 94115 647-E5
100 VAL 94589 510-A7
200 RDWC 94063 770-B5
400 SCAR 94070 769-G3
500 SJS 95110 833-J5
700 SBRN 94066 708-A6
800 ALA 94501 669-J2
1000 MRTZ 94553 571-F4
1000 CCCo 94553 571-F4
1100 BERK 94707 609-G7
1200 BERK 94709 609-G7
1500 ALA 94501 670-A2
1600 BERK 94709 629-G1
1600 LVMR 94550 695-G7
1700 ELCR 94530 609-C1
1900 BERK 94704 629-G1
3500 LFYT 94549 611-E6
3900 OAK 94619 650-E6
5300 OAK 94619 670-F1
5500 OAK 94605 670-F1
9000 OAK 94603 670-J4
36800 NWK 94560 752-D7
37200 NWK 94560 772-D1
WALNUT TER
39000 FRMT 94536 753-C3
WALNUT WY
4300 PIT 94565 574-E7
WALNUT BLOSSOM DR
5400 SJS 95123 875-A4
WALNUT CREEK CT
200 CCCo 94506 654-C5
WALNUT GROVE AV
1400 SJS 95050 833-F6
1400 SJS 95126 833-F6
1400 SCL 95050 833-F6
2000 SJS 95128 833-E6
2400 SCL 95128 833-E6
WALNUT HEIGHTS LN
1600 CNCD 94519 592-H2
WALNUT HILL CT
100 LGTS 95030 873-C3
WALNUT SHADOWS CT
2000 CNCD 94518 592-F7
WALNUT SPRING CT
11600 CPTO 95014 852-A4
WALNUT VIEW PL
- CCCo 94596 612-B5
- WLCK 94596 612-B5
WALNUT WOODS CT
1000 SJS 95122 834-F7
WALNUT WOODS DR
900 SJS 95122 834-F7
WALPERT ST
1000 HAY 94541 712-A2
WALSH AV
600 SCL 95050 833-C1
2300 SCL 95051 833-C1
WALSH CT
- SJS 95123 874-F7
800 BEN 94510 530-H6
WALSH DR
100 MrnC 94941 606-C4
100 MrnC 94965 606-C4
WALSH RD
300 ATN 94027 790-B6
WALSH WY
1700 HAY 94542 712-B3
WALTER AV
600 PIN 94564 569-C4
9200 OAK 94603 670-G6
WALTER CT
- VAL 94591 530-F3
WALTER LN
700 SRFL 94901 586-G1
WALTER PL
- SRFL 94903 566-E4
WALTER ST
- SF 94114 667-G1
WALTER WY
- ANT 94509 575-D6
WALTER COSTA TR
1000 LFYT 94549 611-C4
WALTER DINOS CT
3400 AlaC 94542 712-D1
WALTER HAYS DR
100 PA 94303 791-B4
WALTER LUM PL
- SF 94108 648-A5
WALTERMIRE ST
600 BLMT 94002 769-E1
WALTERS AV
1500 CMBL 95008 873-A1
WALTERS CT
39500 FRMT 94538 753-A6
WALTERS RD
- ROSS 94957 586-C2
WALTERS WY
2300 CNCD 94520 592-F3
2500 CNCD 94518 592-F3
WALTHAM RD
1500 CNCD 94520 592-E3
WALTHAM ST
- SF 94110 667-J5
600 MTVW 94040 831-J2
WALTHAM CROSS
2700 BLMT 94002 769-A3
WALTON AV
3900 FRMT 94536 752-H3
21700 SCIC 95120 895-C5
WALTON CT
2900 PIN 94564 570-A7
WALTON LN
- ANT 94509 575-D7
21700 SCIC 95120 895-C5
WALTON RD
600 LGTS 95030 873-B5
WALTON ST
- SCAR 94070 769-F2
WALTON WY
3200 SJS 95117 853-C3
WALTRIP LN
2600 CNCD 94518 592-G6
5600 SJS 95118 874-B5

WANDA LN
- ORIN 94563 610-J6
600 MrnC 94965 606-D6
WANDA ST
- SF 94112 667-F7
1100 CCCo 94525 550-C4
WANDA WY
- CCCo 94553 591-E2
WANDEL DR
- MRGA 94556 651-E1
- MRGA 94556 631-E7
WANFLETE CT
- ORIN 94563 631-B5
WANLASS AV
3200 SPAB 94806 588-H1
WANO ST
500 MRTZ 94553 571-E4
WANSTEAD CT
3200 WLCK 94598 612-J3
WAR ADMIRAL AV
300 SJS 95111 875-B2
WAR ADMIRAL WY
5000 SJS 95111 875-B1
WARBLER DR
3900 ANT 94509 594-J1
WARBLER LN
- BSBN 94005 687-J4
WARBLER LP
4200 FRMT 94555 732-B7
WARBLER WY
1500 SCL 95051 832-H6
1500 SUNV 94087 832-H6
WARBURTON AV
900 SCL 95050 833-C3
2400 SCL 95051 833-A3
3300 SCL 95051 832-J3
WARD AV
7400 ELCR 94530 609-E5
WARD CT
- DALY 94015 707-B1
- PLHL 94523 592-A5
100 VAL 94589 509-J5
WARD DR
2100 CCCo 94596 612-E7
WARD LN
3100 OAK 94602 650-D6
WARD ST
- LKSP 94939 586-E6
100 SF 94134 688-A1
200 MRTZ 94553 571-D3
1100 BERK 94702 629-E3
1200 BERK 94703 629-F3
1400 HAY 94541 712-A1
2100 BERK 94705 629-H3
E WARD ST
100 LKSP 94939 586-F6
WARD WY
2100 SMCo 94062 790-A4
2600 CNCD 94518 592-G6
13400 SAR 95070 852-G7
13400 SAR 95070 872-G1
WARDELL CT
12500 SAR 95070 852-D6
WARDELL RD
20500 SAR 95070 852-D6
WARDEN AV
400 SLN 94577 690-G1
WARDLOW LN
1600 CNCD 94521 593-B2
WARE CT
- BEN 94510 530-J7
WAREC WY
300 LALT 94022 811-D6
WAREHOUSE RD
- MLPK 94025 790-J1
- NVTO 94949 546-G3
WARFIELD AV
700 OAK 94610 650-A2
1100 PDMT 94610 650-A2
WARFIELD DR
- MRGA 94556 631-C4
WARFIELD WY
2200 SJS 95122 854-G2
WARFORD AV
400 VAL 94591 530-D5
WARFORD TER
- ORIN 94563 610-J7
WAR GLORY PL
8100 PLE 94566 734-C1
WARM CANYON WY
- HIL 94010 748-D3
WARMCASTLE CT
300 MRTZ 94553 571-J6
WARM SPRINGS BLVD
46600 FRMT 94539 773-G4
48000 FRMT 94539 793-H1
WARM SPRINGS CT
1900 WLCK 94595 632-B1
WARMSPRINGS CT
2000 FRMT 94539 773-F4
WARM SPRINGS DR
2800 SJS 95127 834-H1
WARMWOOD LN
2000 SJS 95132 814-D2
WARMWOOD WY
- HIL 94010 748-D3
WARNER AV
300 HAY 94544 732-F3
1300 SUNV 94087 832-C4
2000 OAK 94603 671-A5
2300 OAK 94603 670-J5
WARNER CT
- ANT 94509 595-J1
- SRFL 94901 586-F1
1200 LFYT 94549 611-J4
3600 SJS 95127 835-C3
WARNER DR
3500 SJS 95127 835-C3
WARNER LN
- PLHL 94523 592-C7
WARNER PL
- SF 94109 647-J4
WARNER RD
- SCIC 94035 812-B2
- SCIC 94043 812-B2
WARNER RANGE AV
2300 MLPK 94025 790-D7
WARREN AV
- OAK 94611 649-H1
200 SLN 94577 691-B2
1000 SJS 95125 854-B2
1100 SolC 94591 530-E7

WARREN AV
1100 VAL 94591 530-E7
E WARREN AV
100 FRMT 94539 773-G6
200 FRMT 94538 773-G6
W WARREN AV
600 FRMT 94538 773-F7
WARREN DR
- SF 94131 667-D3
100 SCL 95051 833-B7
1700 CCCo 94801 588-F3
WARREN FRWY Rt#-13
- OAK - 630-D6
- OAK - 650-F3
- OAK - 650-F3
- OAK - 650-F3
- OAK - 650-F3
- OAK - 650-F3
WARREN LN
2400 WLCK 94596 612-B3
WARREN RD
- SMTO 94402 748-G1
100 SMTO 94402 728-G7
2300 CCCo 94595 612-A6
WARREN ST
- MRTZ 94553 571-E3
300 SJS 95112 834-B3
400 RDWC 94063 770-A5
900 HAY 94541 711-J1
WARREN WY
- PIT 94565 574-C3
800 PA 94303 791-C5
E WARREN COMM
100 FRMT 94539 773-H6
WARRENS WY
- TBRN 94920 607-A4
WARRENTON CT
3000 PLE 94588 694-F6
WARRING DR
700 SJS 95123 874-F4
WARRING ST
2300 BERK 94704 629-J2
WARRINGTON AV
400 SMCo 94063 770-D7
2900 SJS 95127 835-A4
WARSAW AV
1600 LVMR 94550 715-G3
WAR WAGON CT
5200 SJS 95136 874-J3
WAR WAGON DR
5100 SJS 95136 874-J3
5100 SJS 95136 875-A3
WARWICK AV
100 SLN 94577 671-A6
300 OAK 94610 649-J3
WARWICK CT
- LFYT 94549 631-J3
100 CCCo 94507 632-J2
900 SUNV 94087 832-B3
34800 FRMT 94555 732-J4
34800 FRMT 94555 752-F1
WARWICK DR
100 CMBL 95008 853-C5
100 WLCK 94598 612-F3
100 BEN 94510 551-B3
WARWICK PL
2600 HAY 94542 712-D3
WARWICK RD
3000 FRMT 94555 732-F7
3200 FRMT 94555 752-E1
15300 SJS 95124 873-G5
WARWICK ST
- DALY 94015 707-C3
100 RDWC 94062 769-H5
300 SCAR 94070 769-H5
WASATCH DR
500 FRMT 94536 733-D7
500 FRMT 94536 753-D1
1300 MTVW 94040 832-A2
WASDEN CT
2400 WLCK 94598 592-F7
WASHBURN DR
200 FRMT 94536 753-A1
WASHBURN ST
- SF 94103 647-J7
WASHINGTON AV
- MrnC 94903 566-G4
- RCH 94801 608-D1
100 PA 94301 791-B6
100 SUNV 94086 812-B6
300 RCH 94801 588-B6
600 ALB 94706 609-E5
600 ALB 94804 609-C6
1200 SLN 94577 691-A1
1400 BERK 94707 609-E5
2000 RDWC 94061 789-J3
2400 RDWC 94061 790-A2
13700 SLN 94578 691-A1
14900 SLN 94579 691-C7
15200 AlaC 94580 691-C7
33800 UNC 94587 732-E6
WASHINGTON BLVD
- SF 94129 647-B4
100 FRMT 94539 753-E7
1300 CNCD 94521 593-E6
3600 FRMT 94538 753-E7
WASHINGTON COM
3700 FRMT 94539 753-G7
WASHINGTON CT
200 RCH 94801 608-C1
400 TBRN 94920 607-A4
3300 ALA 94501 670-B4
WASHINGTON DR
- MPS 95035 793-J4
- MPS 95035 794-A4
WASHINGTON LN
- ORIN 94563 610-F4
WASHINGTON ST
- BEN 94510 551-E6
- SJS 95002 813-B1
- CCCo 94565 573-H2
- DALY 94014 687-B5
- NVTO 94947 526-B6
- SCL 95050 833-E4
- SF 94111 648-A5
100 DALY 94015 687-B5
100 OAK 94607 649-F5
100 SJS 95112 834-B1
300 VAL 94590 530-A2
600 LALT 94022 831-E1
600 SMCo 94015 687-B5
700 SF 94108 648-A5

WASHINGTON ST
800 MTVW 94043 811-H4
800 SCAR 94070 769-J4
1100 SF 94108 647-G5
1300 SF 94109 647-G5
1400 OAK 94612 649-F5
1600 SMTO 94403 749-C2
2200 SF 94115 647-G5
2600 ALA 94501 670-A3
3400 SF 94118 647-E5
3600 PLE 94566 714-F2
3600 SF 94118 647-D5
WASHINGTON TER
3700 FRMT 94539 753-G7
WASHINGTON WY
2100 ANT 94509 575-A7
2100 ANT 94509 574-J7
WASHINGTON PARK AV
- MrnC 94965 606-B3
WASHO CT
44900 FRMT 94539 773-H3
WASHO DR
100 FRMT 94539 773-H3
WASHOE DR
1100 SJS 95120 894-D1
WASHOE PL
- SF 94133 648-A4
WASHOE WY
- PLE 94588 694-G7
WASKOW DR
400 SJS 95123 875-A6
WATCHMAN WY
- SF 94107 668-B3
WATCHWOOD CT
200 ORIN 94563 610-G7
WATCHWOOD RD
200 ORIN 94563 610-G7
WATER ST
- CCCo 94565 573-F2
- SF 94133 647-J3
200 RCH 94801 608-C1
300 OAK 94607 649-F5
3000 SCIC 95111 854-G5
5400 SJS 95111 854-G6
WATER WY
- LKSP 94939 586-D7
WATERBERRY CT
- PLHL 94523 592-A6
- PLHL 94523 591-J6
WATERBIRD WY
1000 SCL 95051 832-H5
2400 CCCo 94553 572-A2
2400 CCCo 94553 571-J2
WATERBURY CT
3600 SJS 95117 853-C3
WATERBURY LN
600 FCTY 94404 749-F5
WATERBURY PL
- SRMN 94583 673-E6
WATEREE CT
34500 FRMT 94555 752-D2
WATEREE ST
600 SAUS 94965 626-J2
WATERFALL CT
5200 SJS 95136 875-B3
WATERFALL ISL
600 ALA 94501 669-G2
WATERFALL WY
1200 CNCD 94521 593-B4
2900 SLN 94578 691-C6
WATERFLOWER DR
5800 LVMR 94550 696-C4
WATERFORD CT
- RDWC 94065 749-H5
8600 DBLN 94568 693-F2
WATERFORD DR
7500 CPTO 95014 852-D4
WATERFORD LN
3700 WLCK 94598 613-A3
WATERFORD PL
- ALA 94502 669-H5
100 PIN 94806 569-B4
20100 AlaC 94552 692-D4
WATERFORD ST
200 PCFA 94044 706-J3
300 PCFA 94044 707-A3
WATERFORD MEADOW CT
100 MPS 95035 794-C2
WATERFRONT RD
- CCCo 94553 571-H1
- MRTZ 94553 571-H1
1100 CCCo 94553 572-A1
WATERHOUSE RD
3900 OAK 94602 650-D3
WATERLILY WY
1300 CNCD 94521 593-B5
WATERLOO CT
- BLMT 94002 769-A3
1200 CNCD 94518 592-E6
3400 SJS 95132 814-J2
WATERLOO DR
- OAK 94611 650-G1
WATERLOO PL
- MRGA 94556 631-E6
WATERLOO ST
- SF 94124 668-A5
WATERMAN CIR
100 DNVL 94526 653-C6
WATERMAN CT
200 DNVL 94526 653-C6
3400 SJS 95127 814-J7
WATER OAK CT
4400 CNCD 94521 593-A5
WATERSIDE CIR
- FRMT 94538 753-B3
- RDWC 94065 750-A6
- SRFL 94903 566-F3
WATERSON CT
24600 HAY 94544 711-J3
WATERS PARK BLVD
- SMTO 94403 749-D4
WATERTON LN
1100 SJS 95131 834-D1
WATERTON ST
2800 ALA 94501 670-A4
WATERVIEW CT
3200 HAY 94542 712-E4
WATERVIEW DR
- RCH 94804 608-H3
1200 MrnC 94941 606-D5

WATERVIEW ISL
600 ALA 94501 669-H2
WATERVIEW PL
300 CCCo 94565 573-D2
WATERVIEW TER
100 VAL 94591 550-D2
WATERVIEW WY
- RCH 94804 608-H4
WATERVILLE DR
4500 SJS 95118 874-C3
WATERVILLE ST
- SF 94124 668-A6
WATER WITCH WY
500 SJS 95117 853-D2
WATERWORLD PKWY
1600 CNCD 94520 592-D2
WATKINS AV
- ATN 94027 790-E2
WATKINS CT
30600 UNC 94587 731-J4
WATKINS LN
- WLCK 94596 612-D5
WATKINS ST
1300 BERK 94706 609-E7
22500 HAY 94541 711-J1
23900 HAY 94544 711-J2
30800 UNC 94587 731-J5
WATKINS WY
4100 SJS 95135 855-F3
WATSON CT
- BEN 94510 551-B1
1500 MPS 95035 814-C3
2400 PA 94303 791-D4
WATSON CT E
2900 CNCD 94518 592-H5
WATSON CT W
2800 CNCD 94518 592-G5
WATSON DR
200 CMBL 95008 853-E5
WATSON PL
- SF 94112 667-F7
WATSON ST
2500 AlaC 94546 692-A6
WATSON CANYON CT
700 SRMN 94583 673-F2
WATT AV
- SF 94112 687-F2
- SRFL 94901 566-H7
WATTERS CT
4300 AlaC 94546 692-A3
WATTERS DR
14700 SJS 95127 835-B2
14800 SCIC 95127 835-B2
18400 AlaC 94546 692-A3
WATTIS WY
200 SSF 94080 708-A4
WATTLING ST
800 OAK 94601 670-C1
WATTS ST
3600 EMVL 94608 629-F7
3600 OAK 94608 629-F7
WAUCHULA WY
26600 HAY 94545 711-G6
WAUGH PL
3100 FRMT 94536 752-F1
WAVE PL
1900 SJS 95133 834-E1
WAVECREST DR
- DALY 94015 686-J7
WAVERLEY CT
- MLPK 94025 790-G3
WAVERLEY ST
100 PA 94301 790-J4
200 MLPK 94025 790-G4
900 PA 94301 791-A5
2600 PA 94306 791-C7
3300 PA 94306 811-D1
WAVERLEY OAKS
- PA 94301 791-B6
WAVERLY AV
1600 SJS 95122 854-J1
1800 SJS 95122 834-J7
2100 SJS 95122 835-A7
3000 SMCo 94063 790-D1
19000 AlaC 94541 711-F1
WAVERLY COM
900 LVMR 94550 695-H6
WAVERLY CT
- CCCo 94507 632-J5
- SSF 94080 707-F5
100 MRTZ 94553 591-J4
WAVERLY LN
200 LALT 94022 811-E7
WAVERLY PL
- HIL 94010 748-H1
- SF 94108 648-A5
100 MTVW 94040 831-J2
500 PCFA 94044 707-B3
WAVERLY RD
- SANS 94960 586-B1
6500 MRTZ 94553 591-H4
WAVERLY ST
100 SUNV 94086 812-D7
300 SUNV 94086 832-D1
2300 OAK 94612 649-H3
WAVERLY TER
37100 FRMT 94536 752-H2
WAVERLY WY
- DALY 94014 687-F2
- SF 94112 687-F2
1400 PIT 94565 574-F5
2600 LVMR 94550 695-H6
WAWONA AV
800 OAK 94610 650-B2
WAWONA CIR
- MRTZ 94553 571-F6
WAWONA CT
400 CLAY 94517 593-J6
WAWONA DR
1500 SJS 95125 854-A7
1500 SJS 95125 874-A1
WAWONA LN
400 CLAY 94517 593-J5
WAWONA ST
- SF 94127 667-C5
400 SF 94116 667-A5
400 SF 94132 667-A5
2300 SF 94116 666-H5
WAX LAX WY
400 LVMR 94550 696-D4
WAXWING AV
1500 SUNV 94087 832-H6

STREET
Block City ZIP Pg-Grid

WAXWING WY
- ANT 94509 594-J1
WAYCROSS CT
4200 PLE 94566 714-E1
WAYCROSS RD
1900 FRMT 94539 753-F6
3600 SJS 95121 855-A5
WAYLAND AV
4900 SJS 95118 874-C3
WAYLAND LN
100 CCCo 94507 632-F6
WAYLAND ST
- SF 94134 668-A7
700 SF 94134 667-J7
1500 SF 94134 687-J1
WAYNE AV
100 CCCo 94507 632-G7
100 CCCo 94507 652-G1
200 OAK 94606 649-J4
1100 SJS 95131 814-A6
1200 SLN 94577 690-J2
WAYNE CT
- RDWC 94063 770-F6
100 CCCo 94596 612-C1
1300 ALA 94501 670-A3
WAYNE PL
- SF 94133 648-A4
300 OAK 94606 649-J4
WAYNE ST
2300 MRTZ 94553 571-F5
WAY POINTS RD
- DNVL 94526 652-H2
WAYSIDE PZ
3100 CCCo 94596 612-D1
WAYSIDE RD
- PTLV 94028 809-J6
WAYWORD DR
1500 SJS 95122 834-H7
WEATHERLY CT
- DNVL 94506 653-H6
WEATHERLY DR
- CLAY 94517 613-J2
- MrnC 94941 606-J6
500 SJS 95134 813-D2
WEATHERLY PL
600 SRMN 94583 673-F6
WEATHERMARK CT
100 VAL 94591 550-F3
WEATHERSFIELD WY
1200 SJS 95118 874-B5
WEAVER CT
2000 CNCD 94518 592-F7
WEAVER DR
1300 SJS 95125 853-J4
WEAVER LN
800 CNCD 94518 592-F7
800 WLCK 94598 592-F7
WEAVER PL
5600 OAK 94619 651-A6
WEAVER RD
16700 SCIC 95030 893-D7
WEBB AV
2400 ALA 94501 670-A2
WEBB LN
900 LFYT 94549 611-E7
1500 WLCK 94595 612-C7
WEBB PL
- SF 94133 647-J4
WEBB ST
2700 VAL 94591 530-D5
WEBB CANYON DR
7000 SJS 95120 894-E3
7000 SCIC 95120 894-E3
WEBER LN
- MrnC 94901 586-H4
WEBER RD
6300 FRMT 94538 773-A4
WEBER ST
1200 ALA 94501 669-G2
WEBFOOT LP
34000 FRMT 94555 752-B2
WEBSTER CT
2500 PA 94301 791-C6
2500 PA 94306 791-C6
2600 SCL 95051 833-B3
WEBSTER DR
500 MRTZ 94553 591-G3
600 SJS 95133 834-F1
WEBSTER ST
- ALA 94501 649-F5
- OAK 94607 649-G4
- SF 94117 667-H1
- SF 94102 667-H1
100 PA 94301 790-J3
100 VAL 94591 530-D4
300 SF 94102 647-G6
300 SF 94117 647-G6
500 HAY 94544 712-B6
700 PA 94301 791-A4
1000 SF 94115 647-G6
1200 OAK 94612 649-H2
2300 BERK 94705 629-H4
2500 PA 94306 791-C6
2700 SF 94123 647-G4
2800 OAK 94609 649-H1
2800 OAK 94611 649-H1
2800 BERK 94705 630-A4
3000 SF 94123 647-G3
3800 OAK 94609 629-H7
WEBSTER ST Rt#-260
1300 ALA 94501 669-F1
1700 ALA 94501 649-F7
WEDDELL CT
900 SUNV 94089 812-F4
E WEDDELL DR
100 SUNV 94089 812-F4
W WEDDELL DR
100 SUNV 94089 812-E4
WEDEMEYER ST
- SF 94129 647-B5
WEDGEWOOD AV
100 LGTS 95030 873-A2
WEDGEWOOD CT
100 VAL 94591 530-F4
800 PLHL 94523 591-J7
1500 LVMR 94550 715-G4
5500 SJS 95123 874-F4
WEDGEWOOD DR
700 PIT 94565 574-A3
700 SJS 95123 874-F4
800 PIT 94565 573-J3
1500 HIL 94010 748-E5
WEDGEWOOD ST
3800 SLN 94578 691-B3
WEDGEWOOD WY
2100 LVMR 94550 715-G4
WEE BLYTHEN
- OAK 94619 650-J4
WEEDIN CT
3600 SJS 95132 814-F2
WEE DONEGAL
600 CCCo 94549 591-H4
WEEKS ST
300 EPA 94303 791-B1
WEEPING CREEK WY
3300 SJS 95121 855-D7
WEEPINGGATE LN
1000 SJS 95136 874-J3
WEEPING OAK CT
22600 CPTO 95014 831-J7
WEEPING OAKS CT
1200 SJS 95120 894-E2
WEEPINGRIDGE CT
- SMTO 94402 748-C7
WEEPING SPRUCE CT
4400 CNCD 94521 593-B5
WEETH DR
14500 SCIC 95124 873-G2
WEHNER DR
3400 SCL 95051 832-J5
WEHNER WY
6200 SJS 95135 855-H6
WEIBEL DR
45600 FRMT 94539 773-J4
WEIBEL WY
1200 SJS 95125 853-G4
WEIGAND CT
42700 FRMT 94539 753-G7
WEIMAR AV
5900 SJS 95120 874-B6
WEINER WY
2100 SRMN 94583 653-J7
WEIR DR
1800 AlaC 94541 712-B2
WEISS
300 HER 94547 569-E3
WEISS CT
100 HER 94547 569-E3
WEKIVA AV
1000 CMBL 95008 873-B1
WELBY CT
3100 SJS 95111 854-H5
WELCH AV
1000 SJS 95117 853-C3
1700 SJS 95112 854-F2
WELCH CT
- CNCD 94520 572-F6
100 VAL 94591 530-E2
WELCH RD
700 PA 94304 790-G6
1000 SCIC 94305 790-G6
WELCH ST
- SRFL 94901 586-F1
WELCH WY
4000 ANT 94509 595-G1
WELCH CREEK RD
3000 AlaC 94586 754-G7
WELCOME AV
- CNCD 94518 592-G4
2300 RCH 94804 588-H7
WELCOME LN
- SRFL 94901 566-H6
WELD ST
6900 OAK 94621 670-G2
WELDON AV
400 OAK 94610 650-A2
WELDON CT
300 BEN 94510 551-A2
WELDON LN
1100 SJS 95131 834-D1
WELDON ST
- SF 94134 668-A6
1000 CCCo 94565 573-F2
WELDWOOD AV
900 LGTS 95030 873-B2
WELDWOOD CT
900 LGTS 95030 873-B2
WELFORD LN
1800 HAY 94544 732-A2
WELK COM
- FRMT 94555 732-E6
WELK TER
33700 FRMT 94555 732-E6
WELKER CT
- CMBL 95008 853-B6
WELLBORNE CT
- WLCK 94596 612-A3
WELLBROCK HTS
- SRFL 94903 566-C4
WELLCROFT CT
3200 SJS 95148 855-C2
WELLE RD
- CCCo 94525 550-E5
WELLER CT
- PLHL 94523 592-A7
- PLHL 94523 612-A1
WELLER LN
- MPS 95035 794-A7
- MPS 95035 793-J7
- DNVL 94526 653-A1
WELLER RD
- SCIC 95035 774-G7
- SCIC 95035 794-G1
WELLER RANCH RD
- SMCo - 727-B6
WELLESLEY AV
400 MrnC 94941 606-E6
600 CCCo 94708 609-F3
1600 SMTO 94403 749-C2
WELLESLEY CRES
100 RDWC 94062 769-J5
WELLESLEY CT
- LFYT 94549 611-B3
3500 MTVW 94040 831-J2
WELLESLEY DR
- CCCo - 611-B3
- CCCo 94549 611-B3
- LFYT 94549 611-B3
WELLESLEY ST
1900 SCIC - 791-A7
2000 PA 94306 791-A7
WELLESLY CT
400 MrnC 94941 606-E6
WELLFLEET BAY
- ALA 94502 670-A6
WELLFLEET DR
100 VAL 94591 550-E1
WELLFLEET WY
6000 SJS 95129 852-G4
WELLINGHAM DR
2400 LVMR 94550 695-G6
WELLINGTON AV
- DALY 94014 687-D3
- ROSS 94957 586-C1
100 CCCo 94520 572-G1
WELLINGTON CT
2600 CCCo 94520 572-G2
19900 SAR 95070 852-E6
WELLINGTON DR
100 SCAR 94070 769-D2
1800 MPS 95035 794-B2
WELLINGTON LN
100 CCCo 94507 633-A2
100 CCCo 94507 632-J2
WELLINGTON PL
- VAL 94591 550-D2
800 CMBL 95008 853-B7
4000 CCCo 94549 611-J1
35900 FRMT 94536 752-F3
WELLINGTON SQ
3700 SJS 95136 874-C1
WELLINGTON ST
1000 OAK 94602 650-C3
1000 OAK 94610 650-C3
WELLINGTON WY
15900 AlaC 94578 691-F3
WELLINGTON PARK DR
4800 SJS 95136 874-G2
5000 SCIC 95136 874-G2
WELLMAN TER
34300 FRMT 94555 752-A3
WELLMEADOW CT
6400 SJS 95120 894-C1
WELLS AV
- PA 94301 790-J5
7300 NWK 94560 772-D1
34500 FRMT 94555 752-E1
WELLS CT
5600 SJS 95123 874-H4
WELLS ST
800 RDWC 94061 790-B1
4000 PLE 94566 714-E2
WELLSBURY CT
600 PA 94306 791-C7
WELLSBURY WY
600 PA 94306 791-D7
WELL SPRING CT
11500 CPTO 95014 852-A4
WELSH CT
2300 WLCK 94598 612-G2
WELSH ST
- SF 94107 648-B7
WELWYN PL
3000 WLCK 94598 612-J1
WEMA WY
1700 SJS 95124 873-H1
WEMBERLY DR
2700 BLMT 94002 769-A3
WEMBLEY CT
400 RDWC 94061 790-B2
1800 SJS 95132 814-E3
5000 NWK 94560 752-E4
WEMBLEY DR
- DALY 94015 707-B2
WEMBLY DR
100 DNVL 94526 653-A5
WEMBURY WY
- MrnC 94941 606-G6
WENATCHEE COM
- FRMT 94539 773-G6
WENDELL AV
500 CMBL 95008 873-C1
2300 RCH 94804 588-H5
WENDELL CT
42000 FRMT 94538 773-E1
WENDELL LN
1900 PLHL 94523 592-A7
WENDOVER LN
2100 SJS 95121 855-C4
WENDY CT
100 UNC 94587 732-E3
WENDY DR
1500 PLHL 94523 592-D5
WENDY LN
- LFYT 94563 611-B7
13500 SAR 95070 872-G1
WENDY ST
100 VAL 94589 510-D6
WENDY WY
400 MrnC 94941 606-E6
1400 SJS 95125 854-A6
1400 SMCo 94025 790-D5
WENGATE ST
15000 SLN 94579 691-A6
WENK AV
5900 RCH 94804 609-C2
WENLOCK DR
1100 SJS 95122 834-J5
WENRICK CT
1700 LALT 94024 831-J4
WENTE PL
2000 SJS 95125 853-G4
WENTE ST
2100 AlaC 94550 715-J4
2500 AlaC 94550 716-A3
2500 LVMR 94550 716-A3
WENTE WY
2000 SJS 95125 853-G4
WENTWORTH AV
5200 OAK 94601 670-E1
WENTWORTH CT
- AMCN 94589 509-H3
WENTWORTH DR
2500 SSF 94080 707-D5
2500 SBRN 94066 707-D5
WENTWORTH LN
- NVTO 94949 546-B3
WENTWORTH PL
- SF 94108 648-A4
7900 NWK 94560 752-B6
WENTWORTH ST
1000 MTVW 94043 811-H4
WENTWORTH WY
1200 SJS 95121 855-B5
WERDEN ST
- VAL 94590 529-J2
WERNER AV
- DALY 94014 687-C5
WERNER CT
- NVTO 94947 526-A4
5000 OAK 94602 650-F3
WERTH AV
1100 MLPK 94025 790-F5
WESCOAT CT
600 SCIC 94035 812-B3
600 SCIC 94043 812-B3
WESCOAT RD
400 SCIC 94035 812-B3
400 SCIC 94043 812-B3
WESLEY AV
400 OAK 94606 649-J4
500 OAK 94606 650-A3
600 OAK 94610 650-A3
1700 ELCR 94530 609-C1
WESLEY CT
1000 WLCK 94596 612-C1
1500 CNCD 94521 593-A2
1800 SJS 95148 835-A5
WESLEY WY
700 OAK 94610 650-A3
3800 CCCo 94803 589-D2
WESSEX AV
1400 LALT 94024 831-J3
WESSEX DR
4100 SJS 95136 874-E1
WESSEX PL
600 MPS 95035 794-B3
WESSEX WY
- SCAR 94070 769-E3
400 BLMT 94002 749-E7
3100 RDWC 94061 789-H1
WESSIX CT
- DALY 94015 707-C3
WEST BLVD
- PIT 94565 574-C4
WEST CIR
- OAK 94611 630-F7
WEST CT
- OAK 94603 670-G7
- SANS 94960 566-A5
- SAUS 94965 627-B4
300 SJS 95116 834-E3
1400 NVTO 94945 526-B3
3600 RCH 94806 569-A7
3600 RCH 94806 568-J7
25500 AlaC 94541 712-D2
WEST LN
- OAK 94618 630-A5
- SANS 94960 566-C7
WEST PL
1000 ALB 94706 609-F6
WEST RD
- ROSS 94957 586-B2
3600 LFYT 94549 611-E6
15900 SCIC 95030 872-G6
WEST ST
- PIT 94565 574-D2
- SRFL 94901 586-E1
100 SAUS 94965 627-B4
200 CCCo 94525 550-D4
1100 OAK 94607 649-F3
1200 HAY 94545 711-E5
1400 OAK 94612 649-G2
1400 AlaC 94545 711-E5
1500 CNCD 94521 593-A2
1600 CNCD 94519 593-A2
2100 BERK 94702 629-E2
2200 OAK 94608 649-G2
2200 OAK 94609 649-G2
3700 OAK 94608 629-G7
3700 OAK 94609 629-G7
WEST TER
3300 LFYT 94549 631-G1
WEST TR
- CMAD 94925 606-C5
WEST WY
- ORIN 94563 610-G6
WESTACRES DR
10200 CPTO 95014 852-D1
WESTAIRE BLVD
400 MRTZ 94553 571-G5
WESTAIRE CT
700 MRTZ 94553 571-G5
WESTALL AV
- OAK 94611 649-H1
WESTBAY AV
1100 SLN 94577 671-B6
WESTBERRY DR
2600 SJS 95132 814-E4
WESTBORO DR
2900 SCIC 95127 835-A3
2900 SCIC 95127 834-J3
2900 SJS 95127 835-A3
2900 SJS 95127 834-J3
WESTBOROUGH BLVD
- SSF 94080 707-C5
400 SMCo 94080 707-E4
2900 SBRN 94066 707-C5
WESTBOURNE CT
- DNVL 94506 654-A6
29000 HAY 94544 732-B2
WESTBOURNE DR
3100 ANT 94509 575-E7
WESTBRAE DR
- DALY 94015 686-J7
WESTBRANCH DR
2700 SJS 95148 855-C2
WESTBRIAR KNOLLS
900 DNVL 94526 632-H7
WESTBROOK AV
- DALY 94015 687-A4
100 DALY 94015 686-J4
11400 SCIC 94024 831-F4
WESTBROOK CT
- CLAY 94517 593-F5
- SF 94124 668-C6
700 CCCo 94506 654-D5
2300 WLCK 94598 612-G4
WESTBROOK LN
2000 LVMR 94550 715-F4
WESTBROOK PL
1200 LVMR 94550 715-F4
WESTBURY CT
5300 NWK 94560 752-D4
WESTBURY DR
1800 CNCD 94519 592-J1
WESTBURY RD
3900 AlaC 94546 691-J3
WESTCHESTER
100 MRGA 94556 651-D1
WESTCHESTER CT
2400 SSF 94080 707-D4
WESTCHESTER DR
100 SJS 95124 873-E5
100 LGTS 95124 873-E5
100 LGTS 95032 873-E5
500 CMBL 95008 853-F7
1000 SUNV 94087 832-B3
2800 SRMN 94583 673-F6
WESTCHESTER PL
1600 CNCD 94519 593-A2
WESTCHESTER ST
300 HAY 94544 732-E3
WESTCHESTER TER
34000 FRMT 94555 752-D1
WESTCLIFF CT
- PCFA 94044 707-A1
WESTCLIFFE CIR
400 WLCK 94596 612-D3
WESTCLIFFE LN
2200 WLCK 94596 612-D3
WESTCLIFFE PL
400 WLCK 94596 612-C3
WESTCOTT DR
14500 SAR 95070 872-E3
WEST CREEK CT
- LFYT 94549 611-E7
WEST CREEK DR
1600 SJS 95125 853-J6
WESTDALE AV
- DALY 94015 687-A3
WESTDALE DR
4900 SJS 95129 852-J2
WEST END AV
200 SRFL 94901 586-E1
WESTERMAN CT
16900 AlaC 94541 691-F6
WESTERN AV
100 LVMR 94550 715-F1
1000 VAL 94591 530-D5
1100 MrnC 94941 606-D5
14700 SLN 94578 691-C4
33000 UNC 94587 732-E5
WESTERN BLVD
19000 AlaC 94541 691-F7
21300 AlaC 94541 711-G1
21500 HAY 94541 711-H1
WESTERN DR
- NVTO 94947 525-H3
- RCH 94801 588-A5
- RCH 94801 587-J3
1600 RCH 94801 608-C1
10100 CPTO 95014 852-D1
WESTERN HILLS DR
- PLHL 94523 592-A6
WESTERN SHORE LN
- SF 94115 647-E5
WESTERN STAR PL
600 DNVL 94526 653-C5
WESTFIELD AV
- DALY 94015 687-A5
2700 SJS 95128 853-E3
2700 CMBL 95128 853-E3
21600 AlaC 94541 691-G7
21600 HAY 94541 691-G7
21600 HAY 94541 711-H1
WESTFIELD CIR
100 DNVL 94526 653-A4
WESTFIELD CT
6500 MRTZ 94553 591-H4
WESTFIELD DR
1100 MLPK 94025 790-F5
WESTFIELD WY
500 OAK 94619 650-H5
WESTFORD WY
2500 MTVW 94040 832-A2
WEST FORK CT
- SJS 95136 874-D2
WESTGATE AV
2200 SJS 95125 854-B6
2700 CNCD 94520 572-E7
WESTGATE CIR
100 SPAB 94806 588-G2
WESTGATE CT
2700 CNCD 94520 572-E7
WEST GATE DR
6000 LVMR 94550 696-D7
6000 AlaC 94550 696-D7
WESTGATE DR
- SF 94127 667-C6
2200 PIT 94565 574-E4
WESTGATE ST
- RDWC 94062 769-H7
WESTGROVE LN
2700 SJS 95148 855-C2
WESTHAVEN DR
- DALY 94015 687-A3
1600 SJS 95132 814-F3
WEST HILL CT
1000 CPTO 95014 852-D3
WESTHILL DR
100 LGTS 95032 873-G6
300 BSBN 94005 687-H5
WEST HILL LN
7600 CPTO 95014 852-D3
WESTHILL PL
100 BSBN 94005 687-H5
WESTINGHOUSE DR
47500 FRMT 94539 773-H7
47500 FRMT 94539 793-H1
WESTLAKE AV
- DALY 94014 687-C4
WESTLAKE DR
- VAL 94591 530-F3
400 SJS 95117 853-C2
WESTLAWN AV
- DALY 94015 687-A3
WESTLINE DR
- DALY 94015 707-A1
- DALY 94015 706-J1
100 PCFA 94044 706-J2
300 ALA 94501 669-G2
WESTLINE WK
- ALA 94501 669-G2
WEST LOOP RD
- HAY 94542 712-C3
WESTLYNN WY
900 CPTO 95014 852-D2
WESTMINISTER CT
1800 SJS 95132 814-E3
29000 HAY 94544 732-B2
WESTMINISTER LN
700 LALT 94022 811-D4
WESTMINISTER WY
100 VAL 94591 530-H6
WESTMINSTER AV
1100 EPA 94303 791-A1
1200 EPA 94303 771-A7
WESTMINSTER CT
10100 CPTO 95014 831-J7
WESTMINSTER DR
- OAK 94618 630-A6
WESTMINSTER PL
- LFYT 94595 612-A6
4000 CCCo 94506 654-A5
WESTMINSTER WY
2300 LVMR 94550 695-G6
WESTMONT AV
1200 CMBL 95008 873-A1
3000 SJS 95008 873-A1
3400 SJS 95008 872-J1
4900 SJS 95130 872-J1
WESTMONT CT
900 SJS 95117 853-C3
1000 PIT 94565 573-H4
WESTMONT DR
- DALY 94015 687-A3
- DALY 94015 686-J3
WESTMOOR AV
- DALY 94015 687-A6
300 DALY 94015 686-J5
WESTMOOR RD
1500 BURL 94010 728-C5
WESTMOOR WY
6800 SJS 95129 852-E4
WESTMOORLAND DR
100 SF 94132 667-A6
WESTMORELAND AV
2600 RDWC 94063 770-C7
2600 SMCo 94063 770-C7
2900 SMCo 94063 790-C1
WESTMORELAND CIR
1100 WLCK 94596 632-G1
WESTMORELAND CT
2200 WLCK 94596 632-G1
2300 SJS 95124 853-H6
WESTMORELAND DR
2100 SJS 95124 853-H6
7000 OAK 94705 630-C3
WESTMORLAND AV
400 SMTO 94402 748-G1
WESTON CT
2300 ANT 94509 595-F1
WESTON DR
- DALY 94015 686-J3
500 SJS 95008 853-A6
500 SJS 95130 853-A6
600 CMBL 95008 853-A6
26400 LAH 94022 811-B5
WESTOVER CIR
100 NVTO 94949 546-G4
WESTOVER CT
- ORIN 94563 631-B5
- PLHL 94523 592-A5
WESTOVER DR
1800 PLHL 94523 592-A5
5800 OAK 94611 650-F1
5900 OAK 94611 630-F7
13600 SAR 95070 872-G1
WESTOVER LN
500 PLHL 94523 592-A5
WEST PARK
700 AMCN 94589 510-B4
WESTPARK DR
- DALY 94015 687-A3
2300 SJS 95124 853-H7
WESTPARK ST
21500 HAY 94541 711-F2
WESTPOINT PL
- SMCo 94402 748-F6
WEST POINT RD
- SF 94124 668-D6
WESTPORT CT
- UNC 94545 751-J1
3300 WLCK 94598 612-J3
WESTPORT DR
400 PCFA 94044 707-A7
WESTPORT LN
100 VAL 94591 550-F1
WESTPORT WY
- UNC 94545 751-J1
WESTRIDGE AV
- DALY 94015 686-J5
1000 DNVL 94526 653-A4
WEST RIDGE CT
20100 AlaC 94546 691-H5
WESTRIDGE CT
6100 WLCK 94595 632-C5
27800 LAH 94022 830-H1
WESTRIDGE DR
100 PTLV 94028 810-B5
100 SCL 95050 833-D7
100 SCL 95117 833-D7
100 SCL 95117 853-D1
100 SJS 95117 833-D7
900 MPS 95035 814-E1
WESTRIDGE LN
- NVTO 94945 526-E3
WESTSHORE CT
11600 CPTO 95014 852-A5
WEST SHORE RD
- BLV 94920 607-C7
- BLV 94920 627-C1
WESTSIDE AV
500 SUNV 94087 832-D3
WESTSIDE CT
2600 SRMN 94583 673-E6
WESTSIDE DR
- SRMN 94583 693-F2
- SF 94130 648-D1
2600 SRMN 94583 673-E6
WESTVALE CT
200 SRMN 94583 673-C3
WEST VALLEY DR
600 CMBL 95008 853-F7
WEST VALLEY FRWY Rt#-85
- CMBL - 873-C2
- CPTO - 832-B6
- CPTO - 852-E4
WEST VALLEY FRWY Rt#-85
- LGTS - 873-C2
- SAR - 852-E4
- SAR - 872-H1
- SCIC - 852-E4
- SCIC - 873-C2
- SCIC - 874-C3
- SJS - 852-E4
- SJS - 875-A5
- SJS - 873-C2
- SJS - 874-C3
- SJS - 872-J1
- SUNV - 832-B6
WESTVIEW AV
- SF 94134 667-H6
WEST VIEW CT
3700 SCIC 95148 835-E4
WESTVIEW CT
800 MRTZ 94553 571-F5
WEST VIEW DR
1100 OAK 94705 630-B4
3500 SCIC 95148 835-D5
3500 SJS 95148 835-D5
18600 SAR 95070 852-H5
WESTVIEW DR
200 SSF 94080 707-F2
WEST VIEW PL
- OAK 94705 630-B3
WESTVIEW PL
5700 CCCo 94806 589-B4
WESTVIEW TR
- LFYT 94549 611-B7
- LFYT 94549 631-B1
WESTVIEW WY
25700 HAY 94542 712-B4
WESTWARD DR
- CMAD 94925 607-A1
WESTWARD LN
- DNVL 94506 653-G2
WESTWARD PL
2100 MRTZ 94553 572-A7
WESTWICH ST
100 DNVL 94506 653-J6
WEST WIND RD
- LFYT 94549 611-G1
WESTWIND WY
25800 LAH 94022 811-B7
WESTWOOD AV
- SRFL 94901 586-D1
800 AlaC 94586 734-B3
2800 SRMN 94583 673-F7
4600 FRMT 94536 752-H5
WESTWOOD CT
- ORIN 94563 630-H1
1500 WLCK 94595 612-C7
2200 PIT 94565 573-H4
3400 SMTO 94403 748-J7
4200 CNCD 94521 593-C2
4700 RCH 94803 589-F2
6200 OAK 94611 630-E6
WESTWOOD DR
- NVTO 94945 526-D3
- SF 94112 667-D7
- SRFL 94901 586-D1
- MrnC 94901 586-B4
1000 SJS 95125 853-J3
1000 SJS 95131 814-A4
1600 CNCD 94521 593-B2
WESTWOOD LN
2200 PIT 94565 573-H4
WESTWOOD ST
100 VAL 94591 530-E5
800 HAY 94544 712-A6
800 HAY 94544 711-J6
1100 RDWC 94061 789-J2
WESTWOOD WY
4900 ANT 94509 595-J4
6200 OAK 94611 630-E6
WETMORE DR
3000 SJS 95148 835-F7
3000 SJS 95148 855-F1
WETMORE RD
1200 AlaC 94550 715-F6
3000 OAK 94613 650-H7
3000 OAK 94613 670-G1
WETMORE ST
- SF 94108 648-A5
WETTERHORN CT
4400 CNCD 94518 593-A6
WEXFORD AV
2200 SSF 94080 707-E5
WEXFORD CT
8200 DBLN 94568 693-G2
WEXFORD DR
2700 SJS 95132 814-E4
2700 CNCD 94519 572-H6
WEXFORD PL
- ALA 94502 669-J5
WEXLER PEAK WY
4800 ANT 94509 595-D3
WEYBRIDGE CT
- OAK 94611 650-G2
WEYBRIDGE DR
500 SJS 95123 875-A7
WEYBURN LN
1000 SJS 95129 852-E3
WEYERS CT
2800 SJS 95148 855-D2
WEYLAND CT
33700 UNC 94587 732-F5
WEYMOTH DR
1200 CPTO 95014 852-C4
WEYMOUTH
300 HER 94547 569-J2
WEYMOUTH CT
100 ALA 94502 670-A5
200 SRMN 94583 673-F5
1200 HAY 94544 732-B2
3100 PLE 94588 694-E6
WEYRAUGH RD
- VAL 94592 529-G7
- VAL 94592 549-G1
WHALEBONE CT
- VAL 94591 530-G7
WHALEBONE WY
29200 HAY 94544 732-B1
WHALER CIR
100 HER 94547 570-A6
WHALEY AV
- SJS 95110 833-J4

STREET
Block City ZIP Pg-Grid

WHALEY DR
6200 SJS 95135 855-H6
WHARF CIR
- SRFL 94903 566-F2
WHARF DR
- CCCo 94565 573-D1
WHARF RW
100 RDWC 94065 749-H5
WHARF ST
- RCH 94804 608-E2
WHARF TER
34900 FRMT 94555 752-E2
WHARFSIDE RD
800 SMTO 94404 749-D2
WHARTON CT
- SJS 95132 814-G3
WHARTON RD
- SJS 95132 814-G3
WHARTON WY
1400 CNCD 94521 593-B4
WHATLEY CT
3200 ANT 94509 595-B1
WHEAT CT
1000 SJS 95127 835-C2
WHEAT ST
- SF 94124 668-B7
- SF 94124 688-A1
WHEATON DR
19600 CPTO 95014 832-F7
WHEELER AV
- RDWC 94061 790-B2
100 LGTS 95032 873-B7
200 SF 94134 688-A2
WHEELER DR
4500 FRMT 94538 753-A7
WHEELER ST
2900 BERK 94705 629-H3
6500 OAK 94609 629-H4
WHEELER WY
2100 ANT 94509 595-A1
WHEEL HOUSE LN
900 FCTY 94404 749-H4
WHEELING DR
3300 SCL 95051 832-J6
WHEELON AV
31300 HAY 94544 732-E3
WHEELSMAN PL
5700 SJS 95123 874-F4
WHELAN AV
1900 SLN 94577 691-C1
WHIMBREL CT
- FRMT 94555 732-D7
WHIMBREL RD
33400 FRMT 94555 732-D6
WHINNEY PLACE WY
3800 SJS 95121 855-B4
WHIPPLE AV
- SF 94112 687-E2
400 RDWC 94063 770-A5
800 RDWC 94063 769-H6
1000 RDWC 94062 769-H6
WHIPPLE CT
14700 SCIC 95127 835-B1
WHIPPLE RD
200 UNC 94587 732-A3
200 UNC 94587 731-J4
1100 HAY 94544 732-A3
3100 HAY 94587 732-C3
WHIPPOORWILL CT
600 WLCK 94598 613-C4
1700 LVMR 94550 696-D3
2100 PIN 94564 569-F7
WHIRLAWAY DR
100 SJS 95111 875-B2
WHIRLOW PL
1100 SJS 95131 814-D7
WHISKEY HILL RD
100 SMCo 94025 789-H7
100 WDSD 94062 789-H7
400 WDSD 94062 809-J1
400 SMCo 94025 809-J1
WHISMAN CT
200 MTVW 94043 812-B4
N WHISMAN RD
- MTVW 94043 812-B4
S WHISMAN RD
100 MTVW 94041 812-A6
WHISMAN STATION DR
400 MTVW 94043 812-B5
WHISPERING ELM CT
3200 SJS 95148 855-D2
WHISPERING HLS CIR
2500 SJS 95148 855-B1
WHISPERING HLS DR
2700 SJS 95148 855-B2
WHISPERING HLS LN
2700 SJS 95148 855-B2
WHISPERING HLS LP
2600 SJS 95148 855-B1
WHISPERING HLS RD
2700 SJS 95148 855-B2
WHISPERING HLS WY
2700 SJS 95148 855-C2
WHISPERING OAKS DR
1200 CCCo 94506 654-C4
20500 SCIC 95120 895-A5
WHISPERING OAKS LN
4100 CCCo 94506 654-C3
WHISPERING OAKS PL
1200 CCCo 94506 654-B4
WHISPERING PINE CT
5700 AlaC 94552 692-B1
WHISPERING PINES DR
6500 SJS 95120 894-C2
WHISPERING TREES LN
100 DNVL 94526 652-H2
WHITAKER AV
- BERK 94708 609-J6
WHITAKER WY
1200 MLPK 94025 790-E5
WHITBOURNE CT
1300 SJS 95120 894-C2
WHITBOURNE DR
6500 SJS 95120 894-C2
WHITBY CT
3100 SJS 95148 855-E2
WHITCLEM CT
200 PA 94306 811-E2
WHITCLEM DR
200 PA 94306 811-D2
WHITCLEM PL
300 PA 94306 811-D2
WHITCLEM WY
200 PA 94306 811-D2
WHITCOMB AV
900 LFYT 94549 611-H7
WHITCOMB CT
900 MPS 95035 814-E1
WHITE CT
- OAK 94611 630-G7
3100 SJS 95127 835-A3
WHITE DR
300 HAY 94544 712-B6
900 SCL 95051 833-B4
N WHITE RD
- SJS 95127 834-J2
- SCIC 95127 834-J2
500 SCIC 95127 814-H7
500 SJS 95133 814-H7
500 SJS 95127 814-H7
600 SJS 95133 834-J2
700 SCIC 95133 834-J2
700 SCIC 95133 814-H7
S WHITE RD
- SJS 95127 834-J2
- SCIC 95127 834-J2
300 SJS 95127 835-C6
1800 SJS 95148 835-C6
2000 SCIC 95148 835-C6
2600 SJS 95148 855-D1
WHITE ST
- SF 94109 647-J4
- SJS 95126 834-A7
700 SMCo 94015 687-B4
WHITE WY
- SANS 94960 566-A7
- SANS 94960 586-A1
600 SBRN 94066 707-H7
WHITE ACRES DR
2700 SJS 95148 855-D2
WHITEBICK DR
1000 SJS 95129 852-G3
WHITE BIRCH TER
- FRMT 94538 753-B3
WHITE CEDAR TER
- FRMT 94536 752-B5
WHITE CHAPEL DR
100 BEN 94510 551-B2
WHITE CLIFF CT
- OAK 94605 671-C4
WHITECLIFF CT
- SMTO 94402 748-H7
1900 WLCK 94596 632-G1
3100 RCH 94803 589-E1
WHITE CLIFF DR
1000 SJS 95129 852-F3
WHITECLIFF DR
100 VAL 94589 530-C1
WHITE CLIFF RD
- OAK 94605 671-C4
WHITECLIFF RD
28900 HAY 94544 732-A1
WHITECLIFF WY
- SF 94124 668-B6
1300 WLCK 94596 632-G1
1400 WLCK 94596 612-G7
1800 SMTO 94402 748-H7
2200 SBRN 94066 707-G7
4400 RCH 94803 589-E1
WHITE CREEK LN
1600 SJS 95125 853-J5
WHITECREST CT
41300 FRMT 94539 753-F6
WHITE FIR CT
10500 CPTO 95014 852-C2
WHITE FIR DR
500 SLN 94577 690-G1
WHITE FIR LN
800 SJS 95133 814-H3
WHITEGATE AV
1300 SJS 95125 854-B7
WHITE GATE RD
1000 CCCo 94526 633-C5
WHITEHALL AV
800 SJS 95128 853-F4
1000 CMBL 95128 853-F4
WHITEHALL CT
1200 WLCK 94595 632-A1
3400 PLE 94588 694-F5
WHITEHALL DR
- ORIN 94563 631-B5
WHITEHALL LN
200 RDWC 94061 790-B2
32300 UNC 94587 732-C4
WHITEHALL PL
2000 ALA 94501 669-H3
WHITEHALL RD
400 ALA 94501 669-H3
WHITEHAVEN CT
700 WLCK 94598 613-A3
800 ANT 94509 575-C7
6000 SJS 95138 875-H1
WHITEHAVEN DR
3200 WLCK 94598 613-A3
3300 WLCK 94598 612-J3
WHITEHAVEN PL
800 SRMN 94583 673-J7
WHITEHAVEN WY
5100 CCCo 94553 591-D2
WHITEHEAD CT
34200 FRMT 94555 732-E7
WHITEHEAD LN
33700 FRMT 94555 732-E6
WHITEHOOF WY
4300 ANT 94509 595-G2
WHITEHORN WY
1200 BURL 94010 728-E5
WHITEHURST CT
1300 SJS 95125 854-B3
WHITELEAF CT
3100 SJS 95148 855-E1
WHITELEAF WY
3000 SJS 95148 855-E2
WHITEMARSH CT
1100 SJS 95120 894-E2
WHITE MOUNTAIN CT
5600 MRTZ 94553 591-H2
WHITE OAK CT
- MLPK 94025 790-E6
5100 CNCD 94521 593-D6
8600 PLE 94588 714-A6
WHITE OAK DR
- LFYT 94549 611-A6
- ORIN 94563 611-A6
1000 CNCD 94521 593-D6
1800 MLPK 94025 790-E6
WHITEOAK DR
1000 SJS 95129 852-H3
WHITE OAK LN
800 SUNV 94086 832-J3
800 SCL 95051 832-J3
1700 UNC 94587 732-D4
WHITE OAK PL
200 PIT 94565 574-C5
2400 CCCo 94506 653-G1
WHITE OAK WY
1100 SCAR 94070 769-G5
WHITE OAKS AV
1200 CMBL 95008 873-E3
1700 SCIC 95008 873-E3
4100 SJS 95124 873-E3
WHITE OAKS CT
1800 CMBL 95008 873-E2
WHITE PELICAN PL
3400 FRMT 94555 732-D7
WHITE PINE CT
1100 SJS 95125 854-A4
WHITE PINE DR
100 VAL 94591 530-G4
WHITE PINE LN
- CCCo 94506 654-A3
- LFYT 94549 611-B3
WHITE PLAINS CT
- SMTO 94402 768-G2
WHITEROCK CIR
1500 SJS 95125 853-J5
WHITEROCK CT
1400 SJS 95125 853-J5
WHITE ROCK WY
1300 ANT 94509 595-E3
WHITEROSE CT
3100 SJS 95148 855-E2
WHITEROSE DR
3200 SJS 95148 855-E2
WHITESAND CT
3200 SJS 95148 855-E2
WHITESAND DR
3000 SJS 95148 855-E2
WHITE SANDS CT
4600 CCCo 94803 589-D1
WHITE SANDS PL
4700 CCCo 94803 589-D1
WHITESELL DR
25400 HAY 94545 711-D7
WHITESIDES DR
- VAL 94591 550-F2
WHITESTONE CT
2500 SJS 95122 835-A5
28000 HAY 94542 712-E4
WHITETAIL CT
2600 ANT 94509 595-G3
45300 FRMT 94539 773-J3
WHITETAIL DR
2300 ANT 94509 595-G2
WHITETHORNE DR
100 MRGA 94556 651-E2
600 SJS 95128 853-F4
900 CMBL 95128 853-F4
WHITEWOOD CT
1300 SJS 95131 814-B6
WHITEWOOD DR
500 SRFL 94903 566-D2
1600 SJS 95131 814-B6
WHITEWOOD PL
1400 CNCD 94520 592-F2
WHITFIELD AV
4800 FRMT 94536 752-H6
WHITFIELD CT
- CCCo 94549 591-J7
- PLHL 94523 591-J7
- SF 94124 668-C6
1200 SJS 95131 814-D7
WHITHAM AV
1600 SCIC 94024 831-F4
WHITHORN CT
800 LVMR 94550 695-J5
WHITING CT
- MRGA 94556 631-D6
WHITING ST
- SF 94133 648-A3
4600 PLE 94566 714-E4
WHITMAN CT
- SCAR 94070 769-E6
300 PA 94301 791-A5
WHITMAN LN
900 CNCD 94518 592-F6
WHITMAN RD
1400 CNCD 94518 592-G5
WHITMAN ST
24500 HAY 94544 712-A4
27600 HAY 94544 711-J3
WHITMAN WY
2000 SBRN 94066 727-G1
3200 SJS 95132 814-H5
WHITMER CT
1000 FRMT 94539 753-F5
WHITMORE PL
- OAK 94611 629-J7
WHITMORE ST
200 OAK 94611 629-J7
WHITNEY AV
- LGTS 95032 873-B7
- LGTS 95032 893-B1
100 VAL 94589 510-B6
WHITNEY CT
- AlaC 94541 691-E7
- MLPK 94025 790-C7
200 WLCK 94598 612-E3
2400 MTVW 94043 811-F3
WHITNEY DR
1000 MLPK 94025 790-C7
2400 MTVW 94043 811-F3
2800 PLE 94566 714-H3
WHITNEY LN
10000 SCIC 95127 835-C1
WHITNEY PL
- FRMT 94539 793-H2
WHITNEY ST
- LALT 94022 811-D7
- SF 94131 667-H5
400 SLN 94577 690-F1
5900 OAK 94609 629-H5
6500 BERK 94703 629-G4
WHITNEY WY
10500 CPTO 95014 852-E2
WHITNEY YOUNG CIR
- SF 94124 668-C6
WHITS RD
- MTVW 94040 811-F3
WHITSELL ST
3500 PA 94306 811-B1
WHITSIDE CT
- DNVL 94526 653-D3
WHITT CT
- CLAY 94517 593-G6
WHITTEN LN
- LFYT 94549 611-F6
WHITTIER AV
100 MrnC 94903 566-G4
WHITTIER CT
- MLV 94941 606-H6
WHITTIER LN
100 HAY 94544 712-A5
100 HAY 94544 711-J5
WHITTIER RD
100 PLHL 94523 592-A7
WHITTIER ST
- MPS 95035 793-J7
- SF 94112 687-E2
100 DALY 94014 687-E2
WHITTINGTON DR
2800 SJS 95148 855-D1
WHITTINGTON LN
500 AlaC 94541 711-E1
WHITTLE AV
1700 OAK 94602 650-E3
WHITTLE CT
- OAK 94602 650-D4
WHITTON AV
1100 SJS 95116 834-F4
WHITWELL RD
1000 HIL 94010 748-F3
WHITWOOD LN
1600 CMBL 95008 853-A6
1800 SJS 95130 853-A6
WHYTE PARK AV
2000 CCCo 94595 612-A7
WHY WORRY LN
- WDSD 94062 809-F1
- WDSD 94062 789-F7
WICHAM PL
- HIL 94010 748-H1
WICHITA
3000 ALA 94501 649-F6
WICHITA CT
6200 SJS 95123 874-H6
WICHITAW DR
700 FRMT 94539 773-H6
WICHKAM ST
100 VAL 94591 530-G4
WICKET CT
1500 CNCD 94518 592-E6
WICKHAM CT
1700 SJS 95132 814-E4
WICKHAM DR
200 MrnC 94941 606-D5
1000 MRGA 94556 631-F6
WICKHAM PL
2500 SCL 95051 833-B2
WICKHAM RD
1600 SJS 95132 814-E4
WICKLOW CT
1500 WLCK 94598 612-E1
8600 DBLN 94568 693-G2
WICKLOW DR
200 SSF 94080 707-D2
WICKLOW LN
8400 DBLN 94568 693-G2
WICKMAN CT
17000 AlaC 94541 691-F6
WICKMAN PL
- AlaC 94541 691-F6
WICKS BLVD
14200 SLN 94577 690-J5
14700 SLN 94579 690-J5
14900 SLN 94579 691-A6
15500 SLN 94579 711-A1
WICKSON AV
400 OAK 94610 650-A3
WIDEN CT
1700 SJS 95132 814-E4
WIDEVIEW CT
100 SMCo 94062 789-F1
WIDGEON ST
700 FCTY 94404 749-G1
WIDGET DR
700 SJS 95117 853-C2
WIDMAR CT
- CLAY 94517 613-G1
WIDMAR PL
100 CLAY 94517 613-G1
WIEGMAN RD
30700 HAY 94544 732-B3
WIESE ST
- SF 94103 667-H2
WIEUCA RD
16300 SCIC 95030 872-G6
WIGAN CT
2200 SJS 95131 814-E7
WIGET LN
100 WLCK 94598 612-H2
N WIGET LN
100 WLCK 94598 612-G1
WIGGINS CT
100 PLHL 94523 592-A4
WIGHTMAN CT
- ANT 94509 575-D6
WIGWAM CT
- SJS 95136 875-B3
WIILIAM AV
400 LKSP 94939 586-F6
WILANETA AV
400 FRMT 94539 793-J2
WILART DR
3000 CCCo 94806 589-B2
3000 RCH 94806 589-B2
WILBEAM AV
20800 AlaC 94546 692-A6
WILBER CIR
- ORIN 94563 630-J3
WILBUR AV
- ANT 94509 575-D4
1200 CCCo 94509 575-G4
2700 SJS 95127 834-J3
2800 SCIC 95127 834-J3
WILBUR DR
400 PLHL 94523 592-A4
WILBUR LN
- ANT 94509 575-H5
- CCCo 94509 575-H5
WILBUR ST
2300 OAK 94602 650-E4
WILBURN AV
- ATN 94027 790-D1
WILBURN PL
37500 FRMT 94536 752-H4
WILCOX AV
1800 SPAB 94806 588-H4
3200 SJS 95118 874-A1
4600 SCL 95054 813-C4
WILCOX LN
24000 AlaC 94541 712-B1
WILCOX WY
1700 SJS 95125 854-A5
WILDA AV
3900 OAK 94611 649-J1
WILDBERRY CT
100 VAL 94591 530-F7
4400 CNCD 94521 593-B5
WILD BERRY LN
14600 SAR 95070 872-C2
WILDBROOK CT
1800 CNCD 94521 593-D3
WILDCAT CIR
4500 ANT 94509 595-H2
WILDCAT CT
11400 DBLN 94568 693-F4
WILDCAT DR
- SAR 95070 872-E4
8400 ELCR 94530 589-E7
WILDCAT LN
4500 CNCD 94521 593-B4
WILD CAT WY
- CLAY 94517 593-J5
WILDCAT WY
1500 SJS 95118 874-A6
WILDCAT CANYON PKWY
5900 RCH 94805 589-B4
5900 CCCo 94805 589-B4
WILDCAT CANYON RD
- CCCo 94563 610-B5
500 BERK 94708 609-H4
500 CCCo 94708 609-H4
800 BERK 94708 610-B5
800 CCCo 94708 610-A4
WILDCAT CREEK RD
- RCH 94805 609-G2
500 CCCo 94708 609-G2
WILDCAT CREEK TR
- RCH 94805 589-D6
WILD CREEK DR
7200 SJS 95120 894-J4
WILDCREST DR
13300 LAH 94022 811-C7
13300 LAH 94022 831-C1
WILDCROFT DR
100 MRTZ 94553 591-H2
WILD CURRANT WY
6800 OAK 94611 630-F6
WILDE AV
- SF 94134 688-A1
2500 PLE 94588 694-F6
WILDE CT
800 PIN 94564 569-C5
WILDER AV
100 LGTS 95030 873-A7
WILDER ST
- SF 94131 667-G6
WILDERNESS LN
100 LFYT 94549 611-A7
WILDES CT
100 CCCo 94565 573-C1
WILDEWOOD DR
3000 CNCD 94518 592-G3
WILDFLOWER AV
100 VAL 94591 550-F1
WILDFLOWER COM
3800 FRMT 94538 773-D1
WILD FLOWER CT
- DNVL 94526 653-E3
200 PLE 94566 714-F3
200 AlaC 94566 714-F3
WILDFLOWER CT
- DALY 94014 687-H3
- CMAD 94925 606-H2
11600 CPTO 95014 852-D4
WILDFLOWER DR
- LVMR 94550 696-C3
- PLHL 94523 591-J3
- CMAD 94925 606-H2
2100 ANT 94509 575-G7
2900 ANT 94509 595-F1
WILD FLOWER LN
100 PLE 94566 714-F3
100 AlaC 94566 714-F3
13700 LAH 94022 811-C7
WILD FLOWER PL
500 CCCo 94526 633-C3
WILD FLOWER WY
7300 CPTO 95014 852-D4
WILDFLOWER WY
200 MRTZ 94553 571-H4
3500 CNCD 94518 592-J6
WILD FLOWER PARK LN
300 MTVW 94043 811-J4
WILDFLOWER VALLEY CT
- SRMN 94583 673-J6
WILDHORSE DR
2400 SRMN 94583 673-C3
WILD HORSE RD
- ANT 94509 595-J1
WILD HORSE VALLEY DR
- MrnC 94947 525-F5
WILDING LN
- OAK 94618 630-B6
WILDING WY
24300 HAY 94545 711-F4
WILDMAN DR
1300 SJS 95127 835-C3
WILD OAK CT
- CCCo 94506 654-B3
- CCCo 94596 612-G6
1000 CNCD 94521 593-C5
WILD OAK DR
- NVTO 94949 546-G5
WILD OAK LN
- CCCo 94506 654-B4
WILD OAK PL
- CCCo 94506 654-B3
WILD OAK WY
14500 SAR 95070 872-F3
WILDOMAR AV
- MLV 94941 606-D3
WILD PLUM LN
14100 LAH 94022 811-C6
WILDROSE CIR
300 PIN 94564 569-C3
WILDROSE CT
- CNCD - 613-D1
WILD ROSE LN
3700 AlaC 94546 692-B3
WILDROSE WY
1400 MTVW 94043 811-H4
WILDWAY
15000 LGTS 95030 873-B4
N WILDWOOD
300 HER 94547 569-G3
S WILDWOOD
100 HER 94547 569-G4
WILDWOOD AV
- CMAD 94925 606-G1
- OAK 94610 650-A2
- PDMT 94610 650-A2
- SCAR 94070 769-G5
200 PDMT 94611 650-B2
800 SMCo 94015 687-A4
900 DALY 94015 687-A4
900 DALY 94015 686-J4
1200 SUNV 94089 812-J5
1200 SUNV 94089 813-A5
WILDWOOD CT
- DNVL 94526 653-B4
- SMCo 94015 687-A4
- PLHL 94523 611-J1
2300 ANT 94509 595-A2
4600 RCH 94803 589-F1
6600 SJS 95120 894-C5
WILDWOOD DR
- ORIN 94563 630-G1
- SMTO 94402 748-H3
200 SSF 94080 707-F5
WILDWOOD GDNS
- PDMT 94611 650-B2
WILDWOOD LN
- MrnC 94947 525-H6
- SMCo 94025 810-E1
600 PA 94303 791-C4
3500 LFYT 94549 611-E6
WILDWOOD PL
- RCH 94803 589-F1
- ELCR 94530 609-C1
- PLHL 94523 611-J1
4300 AlaC 94546 691-J2
WILDWOOD RD
1000 DBLN 94568 694-A2
WILDWOOD ST
22600 HAY 94541 692-B7
WILDWOOD WY
- SRFL 94901 566-F6
100 WDSD 94062 789-H4
400 SCL 95054 813-E5
500 SF 94112 667-D7
20700 SAR 95070 872-D2
WILDWOOD PARK CT
4600 FRMT 94538 773-D2
WILEY CT
- DNVL 94526 653-C6
WILEY ST
14300 SLN 94579 691-A4
WILFORD CT
39400 FRMT 94538 753-A6
WILFORD ST
39300 FRMT 94538 753-A6
WILFRED WY
1900 SJS 95124 873-G4
WILHELMINA WY
1100 SJS 95120 894-F3
WILKE DR
5400 CNCD 94521 593-F5
WILKEY CT
2700 SJS 95127 834-J4
WILKIE CT
4100 PA 94306 811-D2
WILKIE DR
100 CCCo 94598 612-F5
WILKIE ST
4700 OAK 94619 650-G6
WILKIE WY
3900 PA 94306 811-C1
WILKINS CT
- TBRN 94920 607-C5
WILKINS LN
1600 CNCD 94519 593-A2
WILKINS PL
- MLV 94941 606-G4
WILKINS ST
- SRFL 94901 566-G7
WILKINSON AV
10700 CPTO 95014 852-B3
WILKINSON LN
3500 LFYT 94549 611-F6
WILL CT
10200 CPTO 95014 832-E7
WILLAMETTE AV
200 CCCo 94708 609-G3
WILLAMETTE DR
6300 SJS 95123 874-H7
WILLARD AV
- CCCo 94801 588-F4
200 RCH 94801 588-F4
300 SJS 95126 853-H1
300 SCIC 95126 853-H1
N WILLARD AV
- SJS 95126 853-H1
WILLARD LN
- HIL 94010 748-F3
WILLARD PL
- OAK 94705 630-B4
WILLARD ST
1200 SF 94117 667-E1
WILLARD ST N
- SF 94118 647-D7
WILLARD WY
- HAY 94545 731-J2
WILLARD GARDEN CT
1500 SJS 95126 853-H1
WILLBOROUGH PL
700 BURL 94010 728-F6
WILLBRIDGE TER
34400 FRMT 94555 752-B3
WILLCREST DR
1400 CNCD 94521 593-C5
WILLESTER AV
2000 SJS 95124 873-F2
WILLET PL
3300 FRMT 94555 732-D6
WILLET WY
2300 PLE 94566 714-D1
WILLIAM AV
- BSBN 94005 688-B6
- LKSP 94939 586-E6
3000 SMCo 94063 790-D1
WILLIAM CT
- MLPK 94025 790-E5
- SAUS 94965 626-J2
- DNVL 94526 652-J2
E WILLIAM CT
1000 SJS 95116 834-E5
WILLIAM DR
700 LVMR 94550 715-E2
2200 SCL 95050 833-C2
E WILLIAM ST
- SJS 95113 834-D7
- SJS 95112 834-D7
800 SJS 95116 834-G4
W WILLIAM ST
- SJS 95110 834-C7
400 SJS 95125 854-A1
WILLIAM WY
- PIT 94565 574-C4
1300 CNCD 94520 592-E3
WILLIAM HENRY CT
- PLHL 94523 592-A4
1600 LALT 94024 831-J4
WILLIAM HENRY WY
200 MRTZ 94553 591-F1
WILLIAM REED DR
100 ANT 94509 575-C5
WILLIAMS
100 HER 94547 569-E3
WILLIAMS AV
- SF 94124 668-B7
1200 SBRN 94066 707-H7
1500 BLMT 94002 749-D7
20300 SAR 95070 872-D2
WILLIAMS CT
- ORIN 94563 631-C5
2400 SSF 94080 707-D4
WILLIAMS DR
- MRGA 94556 631-E4
500 RCH 94806 568-G7
WILLIAMS LN
- FCTY 94404 749-F6
- SCAR 94070 769-E3
WILLIAMS PL
400 SMTO 94401 728-H7
WILLIAMS RD
2900 SJS 95117 853-B3
3700 SJS 95128 853-E3
4200 SJS 95129 853-A3
4600 SJS 95129 852-J3
WILLIAMS ST
- SLN 94577 691-B1
- SRFL 94901 566-H6
500 OAK 94612 649-G3
700 SLN 94577 690-J2
2000 PA 94306 791-A7
WILLIAMS WY
800 MTVW 94040 812-A7
WILLIAMSBURG CT
2400 SSF 94080 707-D4
WILLIAMSBURG DR
3100 SJS 95117 853-D4
WILLIAMSBURG LN
20100 SAR 95070 852-E6
WILLIAMSON CT
- NVTO 94947 525-H3
100 MRTZ 94553 571-J6
WILLIAMSON RANCH DR
5300 ANT 94509 595-J4
WILLIAMSPORT DR
1500 SJS 95131 814-C6
WILLIAR AV
200 SF 94112 687-E1
WILLIFORD DR
2500 SJS 95133 814-F7
WILLIMET WY
24100 HAY 94544 711-G4
WILLIS AV
400 SJS 95126 854-B1
500 SJS 95125 854-B1
700 HAY 94541 711-J2
WILLIS CT
3500 OAK 94619 650-F5
WILLIS DR
- MrnC 94941 606-H6
WILLIS LN
3300 ALA 94502 670-A7
WILLITS ST
- DALY 94014 687-C3
WILLKIE PL
5400 FRMT 94538 773-A1
WILLMAR DR
4100 PA 94306 811-C3
WILLO MAR DR
1200 SJS 95118 854-C7
WILLOUGHBY CT
300 LFYT 94549 611-J6
WILLOW AV
- CCCo 94595 612-B7
- CMAD 94925 586-F7
- LKSP 94939 586-E6
- MLBR 94030 728-B4
- PIT 94565 573-H4
- ROSS 94957 586-C3
- SRFL 94903 566-F4
- FRFX 94930 566-A5
100 AlaC 94541 711-G1
200 SSF 94080 707-G2
200 CMAD 94925 606-F1
400 MPS 95035 793-H6
800 CCCo 94572 569-H1
900 HER 94547 569-J3
1000 CCCo 94547 569-J3
1100 SUNV 94086 832-J1

STREET
Block City ZIP Pg-Grid

WILLOW AV
1500 BURL 94010 728-E6
1500 SLN 94579 691-A5
1700 SLN 94579 690-J5
2100 ANT 94509 575-H6
WILLOW CT
- PIT 94565 573-G4
- HIL 94010 728-E7
400 LVMR 94550 695-J7
400 NVTO 94945 526-D3
500 BEN 94510 551-A1
500 BEN 94510 550-J1
21600 AlaC 94541 711-G1
WILLOW DR
- DNVL 94526 653-A3
1000 LFYT 94549 611-G6
5000 SJS 95032 873-H5
WILLOW LN
- BLMT 94002 769-D1
- CCCo 94707 609-F4
- SAUS 94965 626-J2
E WILLOW PL
- MLPK 94025 790-H3
WILLOW RD
- EPA 94303 790-J1
- PA 94304 790-G5
- MLPK 94025 790-J1
100 SPAB 94806 589-A4
100 SPAB 94806 588-J3
1100 MLPK 94025 791-A1
1200 MLPK 94025 771-A7
1700 HIL 94010 728-E7
4400 PLE 94588 694-B7
WILLOW RD Rt#-114
- MLPK 94025 791-A1
900 EPA 94303 771-A7
900 EPA 94303 791-A1
1200 MLPK 94025 771-A7
WILLOW ST
- LFYT 94549 611-F6
- MLV 94941 606-E4
- SF 94109 647-H6
- SJS 95110 854-C2
- SRFL 94901 586-F1
100 CCCo 94553 572-C7
100 CCCo 94553 592-C1
200 VAL 94589 510-A7
300 ALA 94501 669-J2
400 RDWC 94063 770-C6
400 SJS 95125 854-A3
600 SF 94115 647-H6
700 OAK 94607 649-E2
800 MRTZ 94553 571-E3
800 SMCo 94063 770-C6
1100 PIN 94564 569-F4
1100 SJS 95125 853-J3
1700 SCIC 95125 853-H4
1900 ALA 94501 670-A1
6600 ELCR 94530 609-D4
36600 NWK 94560 752-C7
36600 NWK 94560 772-C1
WILLOW TR
- BERK 94705 630-B4
WILLOW WK
- SANS 94960 566-A6
WILLOW WY
- SANS 94960 566-A5
600 SCL 95054 813-E5
1300 CNCD 94520 592-D2
1700 SBRN 94066 707-E6
WILLOWBRAE AV
1500 SJS 95125 853-J4
WILLOWBROOK DR
100 PTLV 94028 830-B1
200 PTLV 94028 810-B7
1500 SJS 95118 874-A2
WILLOWBROOK LN
- CCCo 94595 632-C1
WILLOWBROOK WY
10700 CPTO 95014 852-F2
WILLOW CIRCLE CT
- SJS 95125 854-E5
WILLOW CREEK CT
1700 SJS 95124 873-J1
3700 CNCD 94518 592-J4
WILLOW CREEK DR
1600 SJS 95124 873-J1
6500 DBLN 94568 694-A1
WILLOW CREEK LN
- CCCo 94506 653-J4
200 MRTZ 94553 571-H6
WILLOWDALE DR
1500 SJS 95118 874-A2
WILLOW ESTATES
5000 SJS 95135 855-G5
WILLOWGATE DR
1500 SJS 95118 874-A2
WILLOWGATE ST
600 MTVW 94043 811-J5
WILLOW GLEN CT
4300 CNCD 94521 593-C5
WILLOW GLEN PL
5300 AlaC 94546 692-B2
WILLOW GLEN WY
- SCAR 94070 769-E4
400 SJS 95125 854-A4
WILLOWGROVE LN
6000 CPTO 95014 852-G2
WILLOWHAVEN CT
1500 SJS 95126 853-H3
WILLOWHAVEN DR
1100 SJS 95126 853-H3
WILLOWHAVEN WY
4900 ANT 94509 595-E4
WILLOW HILL CT
100 LGTS 95030 873-C3
WILLOW HILL RD
- ROSS 94957 586-C3
WILLOWHURST AV
1600 SCIC 95125 853-H5
1700 SJS 95125 853-H5
WILLOW LAKE CT
2100 MRTZ 94553 592-A1
WILLOW LAKE DR
2100 MRTZ 94553 592-A1
WILLOW LAKE LN
1600 SJS 95131 814-B6
WILLOWLEAF DR
900 SJS 95128 853-G3
WILLOWMERE RD
- DNVL 94526 653-B1

WILLOWMONT AV
1400 SJS 95118 874-A2
1600 SJS 95124 874-A2
1600 SJS 95124 873-J2
WILLOW OAK CT
1200 PIN 94564 569-E5
WILLOW OAKS DR
1500 SJS 95125 853-J4
WILLOWOOD CT
4400 CNCD 94521 593-C2
WILLOWOOD DR
3500 SJS 95118 874-A2
37400 FRMT 94536 752-G4
WILLOWPARK DR
3500 SJS 95118 874-A2
WILLOW PASS RD
700 CCCo 94565 574-A2
700 PIT 94565 573-E2
700 PIT 94565 574-A2
700 CCCo 94565 573-E2
1000 CCCo 94523 592-C3
1000 CNCD 94520 592-E2
1000 PLHL 94523 592-C3
2300 CNCD 94519 592-E2
3200 CNCD 94519 572-J7
3600 CNCD 94519 573-A6
3800 CNCD 94520 573-A6
5100 CCCo 94520 573-A6
WILLOW POND CT
800 SRMN 94583 653-H7
WILLOWPOND LN
25500 LAH 94022 831-B3
WILLOWREN WY
2500 PLE 94566 714-C1
WILLOW SPRING CT
- MRGA 94556 631-E5
WILLOW SPRING LN
- MRGA 94556 631-E5
WILLOW TREE CT
2400 MRTZ 94553 572-A6
WILLOWTREE CT
1400 SJS 95118 874-B1
WILLOWVIEW CT
- DNVL 94526 653-B1
5100 PLE 94588 693-J7
WILLOWVIEW DR
3500 SJS 95118 874-A2
WILLOW WREN PL
3500 FRMT 94555 732-D7
WILL ROGERS DR
3900 SJS 95117 853-B3
4200 SJS 95129 853-A3
WILLS ST
- SF 94124 668-D6
WILLWOOD CT
- SRFL 94901 567-B6
WILL WOOL DR
2200 SJS 95112 854-G2
WILLY WY
1000 CNCD 94518 592-F5
WILMA AV
6200 NWK 94560 752-E6
WILMA WY
4900 SJS 95124 873-E4
27200 AlaC 94541 712-C1
WILMAC AV
800 NVTO 94947 525-J3
WILMAC TER
- FRMT 94536 752-H2
WILMINGTON AV
1000 SJS 95129 852-J3
WILMINGTON DR
2100 WLCK 94596 632-G1
WILMINGTON RD
800 SMTO 94402 748-H4
3600 FRMT 94538 773-E3
WILMINGTON WY
900 SMCo 94062 789-F3
900 SMCo 94061 789-F3
WILMINGTON ACRES CT
- SMCo 94062 789-G3
WILMORE AV
800 CNCD 94518 592-G6
WILMORE CT
2700 CNCD 94518 592-H6
WILMOT ST
- SF 94115 647-G6
WILMS AV
- SSF 94080 707-G4
WILSHAM DR
1000 SJS 95132 814-F6
WILSHIRE AV
- VAL 94591 530-D7
- DALY 94015 687-A2
3600 SMTO 94403 749-B6
WILSHIRE BLVD
1700 SJS 95116 834-F3
4100 OAK 94602 650-F4
WILSHIRE CT
- DALY 94015 687-B3
100 DNVL 94526 653-D6
100 SCAR 94070 769-F5
WILSHIRE PL
2900 CNCD 94518 592-G5
WILSON AV
- MrnC 94947 525-H4
- SJS 95126 834-A7
- VAL 94590 529-G2
300 RCH 94805 589-A5
300 SUNV 94086 832-F1
500 NVTO 94947 525-H4
700 CCCo 94553 571-F4
700 MRTZ 94553 571-F4
900 SolC 94589 529-G2
900 SolC 94590 529-G2
3400 OAK 94602 650-D5
3800 AlaC 94546 692-A3
4000 AlaC 94546 691-J3
WILSON CIR
- BERK 94708 610-A7
WILSON COM
2800 FRMT 94538 753-D6
WILSON CT
- CCCo 94507 632-F3
- SRFL 94901 566-G6
600 SCL 95051 833-B6
1600 CNCD 94521 593-B2
1900 MTVW 94040 831-G1
21800 CPTO 95014 832-B7
WILSON LN
3900 CNCD 94521 593-B2

WILSON PL
3400 OAK 94602 650-D5
WILSON RD
- CCCo 94507 632-F3
WILSON ST
- DALY 94014 687-D2
- RDWC 94063 770-A6
100 ALB 94804 609-D7
100 SF 94112 687-D2
1200 PA 94301 791-B4
2100 ANT 94509 575-J5
WILSON WY
- MPS 95035 793-J3
- MrnC 94904 586-D6
- SJS 95002 793-C7
- SJS 95002 813-C1
100 AMCN 94589 510-A2
200 LKSP 94939 586-D6
6900 ELCR 94530 589-C7
WILSON HILL CT
- NVTO 94945 526-C4
WILTON AV
200 PA 94306 811-C1
WILTON DR
100 CMBL 95008 853-D7
6700 OAK 94611 650-G1
WILTON PL
100 SRMN 94583 673-F6
WILTON RD
1300 LVMR 94550 695-E6
WILTSHIRE AV
- LKSP 94939 586-E7
WIMBLEDON CT
- NVTO 94945 546-D2
4000 SJS 95135 855-H5
WIMBLEDON DR
14400 LGTS 95030 873-B3
WIMBLEDON LN
700 LVMR 94550 695-H6
2400 SLN 94577 691-B2
WIMBLEDON PL
1900 LALT 94024 831-J5
2200 SLN 94577 691-A4
WIMBLEDON RD
200 WLCK 94598 612-F1
WIMBLEDON WY
- SRFL 94901 566-D6
WIMPOLE ST
- MRGA 94556 631-E3
WINCHELL CT
100 VAL 94589 530-B1
N WINCHESTER BLVD
- SCL 95050 833-D5
100 SCL 95128 833-E7
S WINCHESTER BLVD
300 SJS 95117 853-E4
300 SJS 95128 853-E4
700 LGTS 95030 873-B3
900 MSER 95030 873-B3
1500 CMBL 95117 853-E4
1500 CMBL 95128 853-E4
1500 CMBL 95008 853-E4
2700 CMBL 95008 873-B3
WINCHESTER CT
- FCTY 94404 749-E5
500 CCCo 94549 591-G6
WINCHESTER DR
- ATN 94027 790-E2
700 BURL 94010 728-G6
2700 AlaC 94541 712-C2
32300 UNC 94587 732-C5
WINCHESTER LN
4600 MRTZ 94553 571-E7
WINCHESTER PL
- BURL 94010 728-G5
3600 WLCK 94598 613-A3
4900 NWK 94560 752-E3
34800 FRMT 94555 732-J4
WINCHESTER ST
100 DALY 94014 687-D3
300 VAL 94590 530-B7
WIND CAVE CT
3500 PLE 94588 714-A1
WINDCHIME CT
700 CCCo 94598 613-A3
WINDCHIME DR
300 DNVL 94506 653-J6
WINDCREST LN
- SSF 94080 707-H1
WINDELER CT
- MRGA 94556 651-E1
WINDELL CT
700 SJS 95123 874-F4
WINDEMERE ISL
600 ALA 94501 669-G2
WINDEMERE RD
- HIL 94010 748-E5
28900 HAY 94544 732-A1
WINDERMERE AV
1000 MLPK 94025 790-J1
1100 MLPK 94025 770-J7
WINDERMERE CIR
400 LVMR 94550 695-J6
WINDERMERE CT
4200 CNCD 94521 593-A4
WINDERMERE DR
35000 NWK 94560 752-D3
WINDERMERE WY
1200 CNCD 94521 593-A4
WINDFELDT RD
25200 AlaC 94541 712-C2
WINDFLOWER CT
4400 CNCD 94518 593-A6
WINDFLOWER DR
5300 LVMR 94550 696-C4
WINDFLOWER WY
5400 LVMR 94550 696-C4
WINDHAM LN
100 MTVW 94043 812-A5
WINDHAVEN CT
- PLHL 94523 591-H2
WINDHOVER WY
- CCCo 94553 571-J4
WINDIMER DR
1200 LALT 94024 831-H5
WINDING BLVD
16600 AlaC 94578 691-G4
WINDING GN
- CCCo 94526 633-A5
WINDING LN
- ANT 94509 595-H1
- ORIN 94563 610-G2

WINDING LN
44700 FRMT 94539 773-G3
WINDING WY
- CCCo 94611 630-F6
- OAK 94611 630-F6
- SCAR 94070 769-E5
- ROSS 94957 586-D1
- SF 94112 687-F2
- SMCo 94070 769-E5
100 WDSD 94062 809-H1
200 WDSD 94062 789-H7
1500 BLMT 94002 749-D7
4500 SJS 95129 853-A4
11600 SCIC 94024 831-E4
WINDING BROOK CT
- SRMN 94583 673-J7
WINDING CREEK CT
1800 SJS 95148 835-D4
WINDING STREAM CT
- LVMR 94550 696-E3
WINDING STREAM DR
1400 LVMR 94550 696-E3
WINDING TRAIL LN
- DBLN 94568 693-F4
WINDING TRAIL PL
- DBLN 94568 693-E4
WINDING VISTA COM
- FRMT 94539 794-B1
WINDINGWOOD CT
300 MTVW 94040 811-F4
WINDJAMMER CIR
1000 FCTY 94404 749-G3
WINDJAMMER CT
- RCH 94804 608-E3
WINDJAMMER DR
100 SolC 94591 530-G7
100 VAL 94591 530-G7
WINDJAMMER PL
- DALY 94014 687-D5
WINDLASS LN
500 FCTY 94404 749-J1
WINDLASS WY
2200 SLN 94577 690-H4
WINDMILL CT
600 FRMT 94539 773-J5
700 CNCD 94518 592-J6
1100 SJS 95121 854-J4
WINDMILL DR
46600 FRMT 94539 773-J5
WINDMILL LN
600 PLE 94566 714-E4
WINDMILL PL
- NVTO 94945 526-B1
WINDMILL WY
100 PLE 94566 714-E4
3500 CNCD 94518 592-J6
WINDMILL CANYON DR
3000 CLAY 94517 594-A5
3000 CLAY 94517 593-J5
3100 CCCo - 594-A5
WINDMILL CANYON PL
300 CLAY 94517 593-J5
WINDMILL PARK LN
300 MTVW 94043 811-J4
WINDOVER DR
- DNVL 94506 653-G2
WINDOVER TER
- DNVL 94506 653-G2
WIND RIDGE LN
5700 SJS 95123 874-G7
WIND ROSE PL
2100 MTVW 94043 811-G2
WINDSHADOW CT
100 VAL 94591 550-F2
WINDSONG CT
800 CCCo 94598 613-B3
WINDSONG TER
34300 FRMT 94555 752-C3
WINDSONG WY
3300 LFYT 94549 611-G2
WINDSOR
600 HER 94547 569-J2
WINDSOR AV
- CCCo 94708 609-F3
- SRFL 94901 566-E6
100 SRMN 94583 673-H7
WINDSOR CT
- DNVL 94506 653-H5
100 SBRN 94066 707-E7
100 SCAR 94070 769-E4
100 VAL 94591 530-H5
2000 AlaC 94578 691-F4
3100 LFYT 94549 611-J6
3400 PLE 94588 694-E5
12200 LAH 94022 830-J1
40100 FRMT 94538 753-B6
WINDSOR DR
- HIL 94010 728-E7
- SCAR 94070 769-E4
- DALY 94015 687-A3
200 SMCo 94070 769-E4
500 MLPK 94025 790-F4
600 BEN 94510 530-J7
1000 LFYT 94549 611-J6
2700 ANT 94509 575-E7
2800 ALA 94501 670-B2
15900 AlaC 94578 691-F3
WINDSOR LN
6300 SJS 95129 852-F3
WINDSOR PL
- SF 94133 648-A4
2400 LVMR 94550 715-F5
3000 CNCD 94518 592-G3
7600 DBLN 94568 694-B2
WINDSOR ST
1000 SJS 95129 852-E3
WINDSOR TER
600 SUNV 94087 832-D3
WINDSOR WY
100 VAL 94591 530-H5
700 RDWC 94061 789-J1
1100 MLPK 94025 790-F4
1300 LVMR 94550 715-F5
4600 RCH 94803 589-E2
6800 SJS 95129 852-E4
9900 SRMN 94583 673-F5
WINDSOR HILLS CIR
800 SJS 95123 874-E5
WINDSOR HILLS DR
5800 SJS 95123 874-E5
WINDSOR PARK DR
4200 SJS 95136 874-F1

WINDSTONE DR
- MrnC 94903 546-E6
WINDSTREAM PL
200 DNVL 94526 653-A1
200 DNVL 94526 652-J2
WINDSURFER CT
100 VAL 94591 550-F2
WINDTREE CT
2900 LFYT 94549 611-J7
WINDWARD CT
100 VAL 94591 550-F3
700 CCCo 94572 570-A2
WINDWARD DR
- CMAD 94925 606-J1
700 CCCo 94572 570-A2
900 CCCo 94572 569-J2
WINDWARD LN
1100 ALA 94502 670-A7
WINDWARD RD
- BLV 94920 607-C7
- DNVL 94526 652-H2
WINDWARD WY
- RCH 94804 608-H3
- LFYT 94549 631-J3
100 SRFL 94901 587-A3
2000 SMTO 94404 749-E3
WINDWARD HILL
- OAK 94618 630-C4
WINDWOOD CT
1400 MRTZ 94553 571-J6
WINE ST
500 RCH 94801 608-D1
WINE BARREL WY
3400 SJS 95124 873-E2
WINEBERRY WY
7000 DBLN 94568 693-H2
WINE CASK WY
3400 SJS 95124 873-E2
WINE CORK WY
3400 SJS 95124 873-E2
WINE GROWER WY
2200 SJS 95124 873-E2
3200 SJS 95008 873-E2
WINEMA COM
- FRMT 94539 773-H6
WINE MAKER WY
2200 SJS 95124 873-E2
WINERY CT
8000 SJS 95135 855-J6
WINESTONE CT
100 CCCo 94526 633-A6
300 CCCo 94598 613-A3
WINE VALLEY CIR
8800 SJS 95135 855-J6
WINFIELD BLVD
5500 SJS 95136 874-E3
5500 SJS 95123 874-D6
5900 SJS 95120 874-D6
WINFIELD DR
2700 MTVW 94040 831-J2
WINFIELD LN
- CCCo 94595 632-D2
WINFIELD ST
- SF 94110 667-H5
WING PL
900 SCIC 94305 810-J2
WINGATE AV
400 SMCo 94070 769-E4
WINGATE DR
600 SUNV 94087 832-D3
4700 PLE 94566 714-D2
WINGATE PL
4900 NWK 94560 752-E3
WINGATE WY
1900 HAY 94541 692-B7
WINGED TER
300 SRMN 94583 673-G2
WINGED FOOT CT
- SRMN 94583 673-H7
WINGEDFOOT CT
7900 PLE 94588 714-B5
WINGED FOOT DR
- NVTO 94949 546-D2
WINGED FOOT PL
100 SRMN 94583 673-H7
WINGFIELD WY
- BEN 94510 551-C5
WING FOOT
- MRGA 94556 631-C7
WINGHAM PL
4100 SJS 95135 855-F3
WINIFRED CT
- ANT 94509 575-E4
WINIFRED DR
5200 AlaC 94546 692-C3
WINIFRED WY
100 SPAB 94806 588-J3
WINKLEBLECK ST
- RDWC 94063 770-A6
WINN CT
- SRMN 94583 673-F7
28300 HAY 94544 712-B7
WINN RD
20100 SAR 95070 872-E4
WINN WY
- SF 94129 647-E4
WINNEBAGO CT
6100 SJS 95123 874-H6
WINNERS CIR
2700 CCCo 94507 632-E4
WINNIPEG COM
200 FRMT 94538 773-E2
WINNIPEG GRN
300 FRMT 94538 773-E3
WINNIPEG TER
200 FRMT 94538 773-E3
WINONA AV
100 PCFA 94044 727-A2
WINONA DR
1300 SJS 95125 854-A5
WINSFORD CT
5000 NWK 94560 752-E4
WINSHIP AV
- ROSS 94957 586-C1
WINSLOW AV
- VAL 94589 530-A2
- VAL 94590 530-A2
WINSLOW CT
- CMBL 95008 853-A6
WINSLOW DR
1000 SJS 95122 834-G7

WINSLOW PL
- SRMN 94583 673-E6
- MRGA 94556 631-D5
WINSLOW ST
- RDWC 94063 770-A5
100 CCCo 94525 550-E4
WINSLOW TER
34400 FRMT 94555 752-B4
WINSOR AV
1000 OAK 94610 650-B2
1000 PDMT 94610 650-B2
WINSOR CT
2500 UNC 94587 732-F7
WINSOR ST
- MPS 95035 794-A7
WINSTEAD TER
700 SUNV 94087 832-C3
WINSTED CT
100 SJS 95139 875-G7
WINSTON CT
500 BEN 94510 550-J1
1000 SJS 95131 834-C1
5100 FRMT 94536 752-G5
WINSTON DR
- SF 94132 667-B7
500 PLHL 94523 592-A5
WINSTON PL
700 MTVW 94043 812-A3
WINSTON ST
1700 SJS 95131 834-D1
WINSTON WY
- SMCo 94061 790-B3
WINTER CT
4500 PLE 94566 714-D3
WINTER LN
5500 SJS 95138 875-C4
19900 SAR 95070 852-E7
WINTER PL
- SF 94133 648-A4
- SF 94133 647-J4
WINTER WY
1100 PIT 94565 573-J2
WINTERBERRY CT
- SRMN 94583 673-H3
4300 CNCD 94521 593-C5
WINTERBERRY WY
500 SJS 95129 853-B2
WINTERBROOK DR
3000 CCCo 94565 573-F2
6100 SJS 95129 852-C7
WINTERBROOK RD
16000 LGTS 95032 873-D6
WINTERCREEK
- PTLV 94028 830-C2
WINTERGLEN WY
5000 ANT 94509 595-J3
WINTERGREEN CT
- NVTO 94945 526-B2
WINTERGREEN DR
5600 NWK 94560 752-H7
19700 CPTO 95014 852-F1
WINTERGREEN LN
600 WLCK 94598 592-H7
WINTERGREEN PL
4400 AlaC 94546 691-J2
WINTERGREEN TER
- SRFL 94903 566-C2
WINTERGREEN WY
800 PA 94303 791-D6
WINTER HARBOR PL
100 VAL 94591 550-F1
WINTERHAVEN CT
- SRMN 94583 693-H1
WINTER HILLS CT
- SRMN 94583 673-H3
WINTERLEAF CT
- SRMN 94583 673-H3
WINTER PARK WY
1800 SJS 95122 834-J6
WINTERRUN DR
- SRMN 94583 673-H3
WINTERSET WY
- SRMN 94583 673-H3
6500 SJS 95120 894-F1
WINTERSIDE CIR
700 SRMN 94583 673-F4
WINTERSIDE CT
- SRMN 94583 673-H3
WINTERSONG CT
1800 SJS 95131 814-D7
WINTERSPRING CT
- VAL 94591 510-J4
WINTERWIND CIR
300 SRMN 94583 673-H3
WINTERWIND CT
- SRMN 94583 673-H3
WINTERWOOD CT
- DNVL 94526 653-C6
WINTER WREN PL
3300 FRMT 94555 732-D7
WINTHROP AV
2800 SRMN 94583 673-F7
WINTHROP PL
- VAL 94591 530-F3
WINTHROP ST
- SF 94133 648-A3
3300 CNCD 94519 572-G6
WINTHROPE ST
7900 OAK 94605 671-A2
WINTON AV
- HAY 94544 711-J3
- HAY 94541 711-J3
W WINTON AV
- HAY 94544 711-G3
- HAY 94541 711-G3
600 HAY 94545 711-B4
1100 AlaC 94545 711-E4
WINTON DR
1000 WLCK 94598 612-F1
1100 CNCD 94518 592-F7
1100 CNCD 94518 612-F1
WINTON WY
4800 SJS 95124 873-E4
4800 SCIC 95124 873-E4
12100 LAH 94024 831-E4
WINWAY CIR
3500 SMTO 94403 749-C6
WINWOOD AV
200 PCFA 94044 706-J3
200 PCFA 94044 707-A3
WINWOOD CT
300 MTVW 94040 811-F4

WINWOOD PL
- MLV 94941 606-D2
WINWOOD WY
2900 SJS 95148 855-D1
WISCONSIN CT
5500 CNCD 94521 593-E6
WISCONSIN ST
- SF 94107 668-B3
- SF 94103 668-B3
3000 OAK 94602 650-F4
3500 OAK 94619 650-F5
WISNER DR
1300 ANT 94509 575-E5
WISNOM AV
400 SMTO 94401 748-H1
WISSAHICKON AV
100 LGTS 95030 872-J7
WISSER CT
- SF 94129 647-C4
WISTAR RD
200 OAK 94603 670-F7
WISTARIA CT
1500 LALT 94024 831-J5
WISTARIA LN
1500 LALT 94024 831-J5
WISTARIA WY
- PDMT 94611 650-C2
- SCL 95050 833-F5
WISTERIA CT
- NVTO 94945 526-B2
WISTERIA DR
100 EPA 94303 791-C2
700 FRMT 94539 753-G6
WISTERIA LN
2900 AlaC 94546 691-J4
WISTERIA ST
6900 SRMN 94583 693-H1
19800 AlaC 94546 691-J5
WISTERIA TR
- AlaC 94586 734-A1
- AlaC 94586 733-J1
WISTERIA WY
- ATN 94027 790-G1
100 MrnC 94941 606-F5
500 SRFL 94903 566-C2
5200 LVMR 94550 696-B4
6300 SJS 95129 852-F4
WISWALL CT
3100 RCH 94806 589-B1
WISWALL DR
2700 RCH 94806 589-B2
WITCHER ST
3100 AlaC 94546 691-J5
WITHERIDGE RD
- SCAR 94070 769-D3
- SMCo 94002 769-D3
2700 BLMT 94002 769-D3
WITHERLY LN
600 FRMT 94539 753-J7
WITHERS AV
- PLHL 94523 612-A1
- PLHL 94523 611-J1
3000 CCCo 94549 611-J1
3000 LFYT 94549 591-H7
3000 CCCo 94549 591-H7
WITHERSED LN
3300 WLCK 94598 612-J3
WITHERSPOON COM
3600 FRMT 94538 753-D6
WITHERSPOON GRN
3700 FRMT 94538 753-D6
WITHERSPOON TER
40600 FRMT 94538 753-D6
WITHEY RD
16200 MSER 95030 872-H6
WITHEY HEIGHTS RD
- MSER 95030 872-H6
- SCIC 95030 872-H6
WITHROW PL
2900 SCL 95051 833-A6
WITTENMYER CT
4900 MRTZ 94553 572-A6
WIVEN PLACE WY
3800 SJS 95121 855-B4
WIXON DR
42700 FRMT 94538 773-D2
WIZARD CT
2000 SJS 95131 814-D6
WOBURN CT
600 MTVW 94040 831-J2
WOEHL CT
21800 SCIC 95120 895-C4
WOLCOT WY
20300 SAR 95070 852-E6
WOLCOTT COM
40800 FRMT 94538 753-D6
WOLCOTT DR
40600 FRMT 94538 753-D6
WOLCOTT LN
200 CCCo 94553 571-B3
WOLCOTT PL
40600 FRMT 94538 753-D6
WOLF WY
4400 ANT 94509 595-H3
4800 CNCD 94521 593-C4
WOLFBACK RIDGE RD
- MrnC 94965 627-A4
- MrnC 94965 626-J4
- SAUS 94965 627-A4
WOLFBACK RIDGE TER
- SAUS 94965 627-A4
WOLFBERRY CT
100 SJS 95136 874-H1
WOLFE AV
- SRFL 94901 586-F2
WOLFE CT
3000 FRMT 94555 732-F7
WOLFE DR
1600 SMTO 94402 749-B2
WOLFE RD
10000 CPTO 95014 832-G7
N WOLFE RD
100 SUNV 94086 832-G1
100 SUNV 94086 812-G6
S WOLFE RD
100 SUNV 94086 832-G2
1300 SCIC 94087 832-G2
1300 SUNV 94087 832-G5
WOLFE CANYON RD
- MrnC 94904 586-F3
WOLFE GLEN WY
- MrnC 94904 586-E3

STREET Block City ZIP Pg-Grid

WOLFE GRADE
- MrnC 94904 586-E3
100 SRFL 94901 586-E3
WOLLAM AV
- CCCo 94565 573-H3
WOLLIN WY
100 LGTS 95032 873-D7
WOLSEY PL
3000 FRMT 94555 732-E7
WOLVERINE WY
4400 ANT 94509 595-G3
WOMACK CT
- NVTO 94947 525-H2
WONDERAMA DR
1900 SJS 95148 835-A5
WONDERCOLOR LN
100 SSF 94080 708-A4
WONG CT
5300 SJS 95123 874-J3
WONG DR
5300 SJS 95123 874-J3
WONG WY
100 SBRN 94066 707-G6
WOOD CT
- CCCo 94507 632-E4
- OAK 94611 650-D1
- SANS 94960 566-B6
100 VAL 94591 530-E2
WOOD DR
5900 OAK 94611 650-D1
WOOD GRN
800 MTVW 94041 811-J6
WOOD LN
- MLPK 94025 790-E5
WOOD ST
- SF 94118 647-E6
300 LVMR 94550 695-H7
300 LVMR 94550 715-H1
400 OAK 94607 649-D2
1200 OAK 94608 629-E7
1600 ALA 94501 669-G1
1700 ALA 94501 649-G7
2700 OAK 94608 649-D2
2700 OAK 94649 649-D2
WOODACRE AV
24500 HAY 94544 711-G4
WOODACRE DR
- SF 94132 667-C6
WOODACRES CT
- ORIN 94563 610-H6
WOODACRES LN
- ORIN 94563 610-H6
WOOD ACRES RD
15700 SCIC 95030 872-G6
WOODALE CT
1300 SJS 95127 835-A4
WOODALL ST
- VAL 94590 529-H2
WOODARD RD
15000 SCIC 95124 873-E2
15000 SJS 95124 873-E2
15900 SCIC 95008 873-D2
WOODBANK WY
18400 SAR 95070 872-H3
WOODBARK CT
3700 SJS 95117 853-B3
WOODBERRY AV
1300 SMTO 94403 748-J7
WOODBINE AV
2100 OAK 94602 650-D5
20100 AlaC 94546 692-A5
WOODBINE DR
- MLV 94941 606-D2
500 SRFL 94903 566-C2
WOODBINE LN
400 DNVL 94526 653-A1
WOODBINE PL
5800 NWK 94560 752-G7
WOODBINE WY
1000 SJS 95117 853-C3
3600 PLE 94588 694-F5
WOODBOROUGH PL
- PIT 94565 574-F6
WOODBOROUGH RD
1100 LFYT 94549 611-J4
WOODBOROUGH WY
2700 SRMN 94583 673-E6
WOODBRAE CT
5000 SJS 95130 852-J7
WOODBRIDGE CIR
100 SMTO 94403 749-E6
WOODBRIDGE PL
35400 FRMT 94536 752-F1
WOODBRIDGE WY
400 SCL 95054 813-F5
4600 ANT 94509 595-J3
WOODBURN WY
13500 SCIC 95127 834-J3
WOODBURY CT
1900 WLCK 94596 612-G7
WOODBURY DR
- AlaC 94542 692-E7
21800 CPTO 95014 832-B7
WOODBURY LN
- SolC 94591 530-E7
- VAL 94591 530-E7
WOODCHUCK LN
1300 CNCD 94521 593-C5
WOODCHUCK PL
600 HAY 94544 712-D7
WOODCLIFF CT
- OAK 94605 671-C5
6500 SJS 95120 894-C2
WOODCLIFF DR
6500 SJS 95120 894-C1
WOODCOCK COM
4700 FRMT 94555 752-D2
WOODCOCK CT
400 MPS 95035 794-A3
WOOD CREEK COM
100 FRMT 94539 773-H5
WOODCREEK CT
- SMCo 94402 768-H1
WOODCREEK LN
3700 SJS 95117 853-B4
WOOD CREEK TER
100 FRMT 94539 773-G5
WOODCREST CIR
- OAK 94602 650-F3
WOODCREST CT
- HIL 94010 748-F4
42200 FRMT 94538 773-D1
WOODCREST DR
- ORIN 94563 631-A3
1600 CNCD 94521 593-B2
2500 SRMN 94583 673-A1
3000 SJS 95118 874-B1
4000 FRMT 94538 773-D1
WOOD DELL CT
18700 SAR 95070 852-H6
WOOD DUCK AV
900 SCL 95051 832-H5
WOOD DUCK CT
900 SCL 95051 832-H5
WOODED CREEK LN
- LFYT 94549 611-H4
WOODED GLEN DR
2000 LALT 94024 831-G4
WOODED HILLS CT
800 FRMT 94539 773-J5
WOODED HILLS DR
1200 SJS 95120 894-E3
WOODED LAKE DR
7000 SJS 95120 894-D3
WOODED VIEW DR
100 LGTS 95032 873-E7
200 LGTS 95032 893-E1
WOODELF DR
1300 SJS 95121 855-A3
WOODFALLS CT
1000 SJS 95116 834-E6
WOODFERN
- PTLV 94028 830-C2
WOODFERN CT
- CCCo 94598 613-A2
WOODFIELD
100 HER 94547 569-E3
WOODFLOWER WY
1100 SJS 95117 853-C4
WOODFORD DR
- MRGA 94556 631-E3
3500 SJS 95124 873-J2
WOODGATE CT
- HIL 94010 748-B1
700 SLN 94579 691-C6
2900 SJS 95120 873-J1
5300 RCH 94803 590-A3
WOODGATE DR
700 SLN 94579 691-C6
WOODGATE PL
- NVTO 94945 526-B1
700 SLN 94579 691-C6
WOODGLEN DR
2000 SJS 95130 853-A6
WOODGLEN LN
100 MRTZ 94553 591-H2
WOODGREEN WY
100 BEN 94510 551-B3
WOODGROVE CT
- CNCD 94521 613-D1
WOODGROVE LN
900 SJS 95136 874-D2
WOODGROVE SQ
1400 SJS 95117 853-C4
WOODHALL WY
2800 ANT 94509 575-B7
WOODHAMS RD
- SCL 95051 833-A6
- SCL 95051 853-A1
WOODHAMS OAKS PL
800 SCL 95051 833-A6
WOODHAVEN COM
- LVMR 94550 695-F6
WOODHAVEN CT
- CCCo 94507 632-G6
- SF 94131 667-D3
WOODHAVEN DR
14000 SCIC 95127 835-A3
14000 SJS 95127 835-A3
WOODHAVEN LN
- CCCo 94595 632-C2
3300 CNCD 94519 572-G6
WOODHAVEN RD
- ROSS 94957 586-A1
- SANS 94960 586-A1
700 BERK 94708 609-H5
WOODHAVEN WY
1000 ANT 94509 595-D4
1600 OAK 94611 630-E6
WOOD HILL CT
11800 CPTO 95014 852-C4
WOODHILL DR
- RDWC 94061 789-G4
- RDWC 94062 789-G4
- WDSD 94062 789-G4
2200 PIT 94565 573-F4
2300 PIT - 573-F4
WOOD HOLLOW DR
- NVTO 94945 526-B1
WOODHUE CT
- SMCo 94062 769-G7
WOODHUE LN
- CMAD 94925 606-G1
WOODHUE TER
34700 FRMT 94555 752-D2
WOODHURST LN
5400 SJS 95123 874-F4
WOODING CT
2400 SJS 95128 853-F3
WOODLAND AV
- DALY 94015 687-A7
- MrnC 94901 586-H2
- SANS 94960 586-B1
- SF 94117 667-E2
- SRFL 94901 586-F2
400 LGTS 95030 873-A7
500 MLPK 94025 790-J3
600 HAY 94544 712-D7
600 SLN 94577 671-A7
800 SCAR 94070 769-G4
900 MLPK 94025 791-A3
1500 EPA 94303 791-B3
1800 SCL 95050 833-D7
2200 SJS 95128 833-E7
2500 SCL 95128 833-E7
WOODLAND CT
- MPS 95035 814-A3
- NVTO 94949 526-C7
- SRMN 94583 673-E2
800 MLPK 94025 790-J3
1700 CNCD 94521 593-C2
WOODLAND DR
- CCCo 94595 632-D2
900 SMTO 94402 748-H4
900 SRMN 94583 673-E2
900 HIL 94402 748-H4
1500 PIT 94565 574-G5
1800 ANT 94509 575-E6
4100 CNCD 94521 593-C2
32400 UNC 94587 732-A7
WOODLAND LN
300 MTVW 94043 811-J4
WOODLAND PK
300 SLN 94577 671-A7
WOODLAND PL
- MrnC 94904 586-B4
- SRFL 94901 586-B4
2500 SMCo 94062 789-F1
6600 OAK 94611 630-D5
WOODLAND RD
- MrnC 94904 586-B4
- ORIN 94563 631-B4
WOODLAND TER
4000 FRMT 94538 753-D7
WOODLAND WY
- PDMT 94611 650-B2
100 MPS 95035 814-A3
3300 LFYT 94549 611-G6
3800 RDWC 94062 789-G2
3800 SMCo 94062 789-G2
WOODLARK WY
7900 CPTO 95014 852-C2
WOODLAWN AV
1200 SJS 95128 853-E4
WOODLAWN DR
3000 CCCo 94596 592-D7
WOODLEAF AV
- RDWC 94061 789-G3
WOODLEAF CT
- NVTO 94945 526-A1
3700 SJS 95117 853-B3
WOODLEAF WY
2100 MTVW 94040 831-J1
WOODLEIGH CIR
18800 SAR 95070 852-B7
WOODLEY DR
3500 SJS 95148 835-F7
WOODLYN RD
100 CCCo 94507 632-F5
WOODMAN CT
1300 SJS 95121 855-B2
WOODMEADOW CT
1300 SJS 95131 814-B6
WOODMEADOW LN
1300 SJS 95131 814-B6
WOODMERE DR
4000 SJS 95136 854-F7
WOODMINSTER DR
400 MRGA 94556 631-F4
1000 SJS 95121 854-H2
WOODMINSTER LN
5000 OAK 94602 650-F3
WOODMONT AV
500 BERK 94708 609-H4
500 CCCo 94708 609-H4
WOODMONT CT
- BERK 94708 609-H4
- DNVL 94526 653-C3
WOODMONT DR
3000 SJS 95118 874-B1
12700 SAR 95070 852-E7
WOODMONT WY
- ANT 94509 595-J4
- CCCo - 630-D3
- OAK 94611 630-D3
WOODMOOR CT
1900 CNCD 94518 592-F6
WOODMOOR DR
900 CNCD 94518 592-F6
2700 SJS 95127 835-A5
WOODOAKS DR
- MrnC 94903 566-G4
WOODPECKER CT
- VAL 94591 530-F5
1900 WLCK 94595 632-B1
WOOD RANCH CIR
- DNVL 94506 653-G5
WOOD RANCH DR
- DNVL 94506 653-H5
WOODREN CT
7700 DBLN 94568 693-G3
WOODRIDGE CT
- RDWC 94061 789-G4
6300 MRTZ 94553 591-H3
WOODRIDGE DR
100 VAL 94591 530-E3
WOODRIDGE PL
- VAL 94591 530-E4
WOODRIDGE RD
- HIL 94010 748-F4
22600 HAY 94541 692-B7
WOODRIDGE WY
1600 SJS 95148 835-B5
1600 SJS 95127 835-B5
WOODROE AV
- AlaC 94552 692-C6
22600 AlaC 94541 692-C6
WOODROE CT
3000 AlaC 94541 692-C6
WOODROSE CT
- SRFL 94901 567-C5
WOODROSE WY
5600 LVMR 94550 696-C3
WOODROW AV
- SolC 94590 530-C6
100 VAL 94591 530-D6
WOODROW DR
7100 OAK 94611 630-F7
WOODROW PL
- PCFA 94044 727-B5
WOODROW ST
- DALY 94014 687-C3
1100 RDWC 94061 770-B7
WOODRUFF AV
3400 OAK 94602 650-C4
WOODRUFF DR
1200 SJS 95120 874-C7
38000 NWK 94560 752-F7
WOODRUFF LN
3600 CNCD 94519 592-J2
WOODRUFF RD
- SANS 94960 586-C1
WOODRUFF WY
200 MPS 95035 793-J4
WOODS CT
2900 SJS 95148 855-D1
WOODS LN
- LALT 94024 831-J5
- SCIC 94024 831-J5
WOODS ST
- SRFL 94901 586-E1
WOODS WY
3000 SJS 95148 835-D7
WOODSDALE CT
1800 CNCD 94521 593-C2
WOODSDALE DR
1800 CNCD 94521 593-C2
WOODSIDE AV
- DALY 94015 687-A7
- SF 94127 667-D4
- SF 94116 667-D4
200 SF 94131 667-D4
300 MrnC 94941 606-E6
WOODSIDE CT
- DNVL 94506 653-G5
- SANS 94960 566-A4
500 SSF 94080 707-G2
1700 CNCD 94519 593-A2
2600 PIN 94564 569-J7
3400 SJS 95121 855-D3
3900 LFYT 94549 611-B7
12400 SAR 95070 852-G5
WOODSIDE DR
- DNVL 94506 653-G5
- MRGA 94556 631-D6
- RDWC 94061 789-J4
- SANS 94960 566-A4
- WDSD 94062 789-J4
12100 SAR 95070 852-G5
WOODSIDE EXWY
- RDWC 94063 770-C5
WOODSIDE EXWY Rt#-84
- RDWC - 770-C6
- RDWC - 770-C6
WOODSIDE LN
- MLV 94941 606-E4
3300 SJS 95121 855-D3
WOODSIDE RD
100 VAL 94589 530-B1
1000 BERK 94708 609-J6
WOODSIDE RD Rt#-84
300 RDWC 94061 790-B2
300 SMCo 94061 790-B2
1900 RDWC 94061 770-B7
2100 WDSD 94062 790-B2
2100 SMCo 94062 790-B2
2400 WDSD 94062 789-J5
3500 WDSD 94062 809-F1
WOODSIDE TER
- FRMT 94539 774-A7
WOODSIDE WY
- OAK 94611 630-D3
- ROSS 94957 586-C3
- SRFL 94901 567-C5
600 SMTO 94401 728-H7
600 WDSD 94062 789-E3
20600 AlaC 94546 692-B5
WOODSIDE MEADOWS RD
3000 PLHL 94523 591-J6
WOODSON CT
1500 SJS 95118 874-B2
4200 CNCD 94521 593-C3
WOODSON WY
100 VAL 94591 530-E3
WOODSTOCK CT
- SRFL 94903 566-G5
100 BEN 94510 551-B2
100 RCH 94803 590-A3
1000 WLCK 94598 612-J4
WOODSTOCK LN
700 LALT 94022 831-E1
3400 MTVW 94040 831-J2
WOODSTOCK PL
- RDWC 94062 769-H6
WOODSTOCK RD
600 HIL 94010 748-F2
4000 HAY 94542 712-F3
WOODSTOCK WY
500 SCL 95054 813-E5
5200 SJS 95118 874-A4
WOODSWORTH AV
- RDWC 94062 769-H6
WOODSWORTH LN
- PLHL 94523 592-C5
WOODTHRUSH CT
700 HAY 94544 712-E7
700 HAY 94544 732-E1
900 SJS 95120 894-G2
4700 PLE 94566 694-D7
WOODTHRUSH RD
4800 PLE 94566 714-D1
4900 PLE 94566 694-D7
WOODTHRUSH WY
2300 PLE 94566 714-D1
WOODTHRUST CT
600 HAY 94544 712-E7
WOODTOWN CT
1000 SJS 95116 834-E6
WOODTREE CT
3400 SJS 95121 855-D3
WOODVALE CT
- VAL 94591 530-D3
1000 SJS 95116 834-E6
WOODVALLEY CT
- DNVL 94506 653-J5
WOODVALLEY DR
- DNVL 94506 653-J5
WOODVALLEY PL
- DNVL 94506 653-J5
WOODVIEW CIR
100 SRMN 94583 673-F3
WOOD VIEW COM
46200 FRMT 94539 773-G5
WOODVIEW CT
- SRMN 94583 673-F3
100 MRTZ 94553 591-J1
3300 LFYT 94549 631-G2
WOODVIEW DR
3200 LFYT 94549 631-G1
5500 RCH 94803 589-J3
5500 RCH 94803 590-A3
WOODVIEW LN
- MrnC 94945 526-J3
- WDSD 94062 810-A6
14100 SAR 95070 872-F2
WOODVIEW PL
900 SJS 95120 894-G3
WOODVIEW RD
1300 PIT 94565 574-D2
WOOD VIEW TER
400 FRMT 94539 773-G5
WOODVIEW TER
1200 LALT 94024 831-H5
WOODVIEW TERRACE DR
100 SRMN 94583 673-E2
WOODWARD AV
- SAUS 94965 626-J2
100 SAUS 94965 627-A2
3200 SCL 95054 813-E6
WOODWARD CT
- CCCo 94525 550-E5
20600 SAR 95070 872-D1
WOODWARD DR
- MPS 95035 794-A6
400 FRMT 94536 753-D2
WOODWARD PL
500 FRMT 94536 753-D2
WOODWARD ST
- SF 94103 667-H1
WOODWARDIA LN
19400 SCIC 95030 872-F5
WOODWIND PL
700 CCCo 94598 613-A3
WOODWORTH WY
- SCIC 95127 815-D7
WOODY CT
1900 SJS 95132 814-E2
WOODY LN
3200 SJS 95132 814-E3
WOODYEND CT
3400 SJS 95121 855-A4
WOOL AV
12900 SCIC 95111 854-H6
WOOL CT
- BEN 94510 551-C1
- SF 94129 647-C4
WOOL DR
600 MPS 95035 794-C5
WOOL ST
- SF 94110 667-J5
WOOL CREEK DR
600 SJS 95112 854-F2
WOOLSEY ST
- SF 94134 668-A7
700 SF 94134 667-J7
800 SF 94134 687-J1
1500 BERK 94703 629-G4
2100 BERK 94705 629-H4
2200 OAK 94609 629-H4
2400 OAK 94618 629-H4
WOOSLEY DR
6200 SJS 95123 875-B6
WOOSTER AV
300 SJS 95116 834-D3
2300 BLMT 94002 749-B7
2300 BLMT 94002 769-B1
4200 SMTO 94403 749-B7
WOOSTER CT
6600 AlaC 94552 692-F3
WOOTTEN DR
100 WLCK 94596 612-A3
WORCESTER
- HER 94547 569-J2
WORCESTER AV
- SF 94132 687-C2
WORCESTER LN
100 LGTS 95032 873-C7
WORCESTER LP
100 LGTS 95032 893-C1
WORCHESTER CT
1200 WLCK 94596 632-G1
WORDEN LN
14200 SAR 95070 872-E2
WORDEN ST
- SF 94133 648-A3
WORDEN WY
4400 OAK 94619 650-G6
WORDSWORTH CT
- MLV 94941 606-G4
WORFE ST
400 VAL 94590 530-B5
WORLEY AV
500 SUNV 94086 812-F6
WORN SPRINGS FIRE RD
- MrnC 94904 586-A2
- MrnC 94930 586-A2
- ROSS 94957 586-A1
WORNUM WY
- CMAD 94925 586-G6
- LKSP 94925 586-G6
WORRELL RD
- ANT 94509 575-D7
WORTH CT
3300 WLCK 94598 612-J3
WORTH ST
- SF 94114 667-F3
400 OAK 94603 670-F6
WORTHAM CT
100 MTVW 94040 831-J2
WORTHING
100 HER 94547 569-J3
WORTHING CT
3300 FRMT 94536 752-J3
6700 SJS 95120 894-G2
WORTHING DR
36200 NWK 94560 752-F4
WORTHINGTON CT
1000 ANT 94509 575-E7
WORTHINGTON LN
- SRFL 94901 566-G6
WORTHLEY DR
15600 AlaC 94580 711-A1
WOVENWOOD
400 ORIN 94563 610-H6
WOY CIR
100 PIN 94564 569-D3
WOZ WY
- SJS 95110 834-B7
WRAIGHT AV
400 LGTS 95030 873-A7
WRANGLER RD
3000 SRMN 94583 653-H6
WRAY AV
- SAUS 94965 627-A3
WREN AV
900 SCL 95051 832-J5
900 SUNV 94087 832-J5
3200 CNCD 94519 592-H1
WREN CT
- ANT 94509 594-J1
- CNCD 94519 592-J1
100 HER 94547 569-J5
100 VAL 94591 530-E2
2100 UNC 94587 732-G7
2400 SSF 94080 707-D4
28200 HAY 94545 731-J1
WREN DR
800 SJS 95125 854-C6
WREN LN
1800 CNCD 94519 592-J1
WREN WY
200 CMBL 95008 853-C6
300 SJS 95008 853-C7
WRENN ST
1900 OAK 94602 650-E3
WRIGHT AV
400 RCH 94804 608-F1
900 MTVW 94043 811-H4
1200 SUNV 94087 832-B4
2300 PIN 94564 569-H7
2700 PIN 94564 570-A7
WRIGHT CT
400 CLAY 94517 613-J1
1000 SUNV 94087 832-B4
2400 SSF 94080 707-D4
WRIGHT DR
23500 HAY 94541 711-F4
24000 HAY 94545 711-F4
WRIGHT LP
- SF 94129 647-C4
1300 SF 94129 647-C4
WRIGHT PL
3700 PA 94306 811-D1
WRIGHT ST
- SF 94110 668-A4
100 VAL 94590 529-H3
1000 OAK 94621 670-D6
WRIGHT TER
1000 SUNV 94087 832-B4
WRIGHT WY
13200 LAH 94022 811-A7
WRIGHT BROTHERS AV
100 LVMR 94550 695-D7
WRIGLEY WY
800 MPS 95035 794-C7
WRIN AV
700 SLN 94577 690-H1
WUNDERLICH DR
1000 SJS 95129 852-H3
10200 SCIC 95014 852-H1
WYANDOTTE AV
800 DALY 94014 687-D5
WYANDOTTE DR
100 SJS 95123 875-B5
WYANDOTTE ST
2100 MTVW 94043 811-F1
WYATT CIR
100 PLHL 94523 592-A7
WYATT DR
1500 SCL 95054 813-D6
WYATT LN
39800 FRMT 94538 753-B7
WYCLIFFE CT
2900 SJS 95148 855-D4
WYCOMBE AV
100 SCAR 94070 769-E2
WYCOMBE PL
35200 NWK 94560 752-D3
WYETH RD
200 HAY 94544 712-A4
WYGAL DR
- CCCo 94553 571-H3
WYLIE DR
1700 MPS 95035 794-D7
WYLIE WY
1300 SJS 95130 853-C4
WYMAN AV
- SF 94129 647-C5
14600 SLN 94578 691-D3
WYMAN PL
- OAK 94619 650-G7
WYMAN ST
3200 OAK 94619 650-G7
5900 SPAB 94806 589-B3
WYMAN WY
800 SJS 95133 814-F7
WYMORE WY
1200 ANT 94509 575-G5
1200 CCCo 94509 575-G5
WYNDALE CT
18300 AlaC 94546 691-H3
WYNDALE DR
3400 AlaC 94546 691-H3
WYNDHAM DR
- PTLV 94028 810-A6
1600 SJS 95124 873-J3
1600 SJS 95124 874-A3
3200 FRMT 94536 752-F1
WYNFAIR RIDGE WY
2100 SJS 95138 855-F5
WYNGAARD AV
- PDMT 94611 650-D2
WYNN CIR
900 LVMR 94550 716-B1
WYOMA PL
500 MPS 95035 794-B5
WYOMING ST
- PLE 94566 714-G2
700 MRTZ 94553 571-F5
WYRICK AV
1700 SJS 95124 873-G2
1800 SCIC 95124 873-G2
WYTON LN
- SF 94132 667-B7
WYWORRY CT
- NVTO 94947 525-J3

X

XANADU TER
34200 FRMT 94555 752-C2
XAVIER AV
1200 HAY 94545 711-F5
XAVIER COM
5000 FRMT 94555 752-C2
XAVIER CT
2000 SCL 95051 832-J2
3700 SJS 95008 853-B7
4100 LVMR 94550 716-A1
XAVIER PL
- CLAY 94517 593-F5
XAVIER ST
1600 EPA 94303 771-B7
XAVIER WY
1000 LVMR 94550 716-A1

Y

YACHT LN
- DALY 94014 687-E6
YACHT RD
- SF 94123 647-F3
YACHT CLUB DR
- SRFL 94901 586-H2
YACHTSMAN DR
100 VAL 94591 550-F2
YAFFE DR
2400 AlaC 94578 691-H5
YAKIMA CIR
3100 SJS 95121 855-A4
YAKIMA DR
800 FRMT 94539 773-J5
YALE AV
- LKSP 94939 586-E4
100 MrnC 94941 606-F5
200 CCCo 94708 609-G3
5700 CCCo 94805 589-B5
5700 RCH 94805 589-B5
16100 AlaC 94580 691-E6
YALE CIR
- CCCo 94708 609-G4
YALE CT
- SRMN 94583 693-F1
100 VAL 94589 510-A5
14500 LAH 94022 810-H5
YALE DR
400 SMTO 94402 748-H3
700 HIL 94402 748-H3
1600 MTVW 94040 811-G7
1800 ALA 94501 670-B2
5400 SJS 95118 874-A5
YALE LN
700 SCL 95051 832-J6
YALE RD
- MLPK 94025 790-G4
YALE ST
- SF 94134 667-J7
500 SF 94134 687-J1
1900 SCIC - 791-A7
2000 PA 94306 791-A7
2200 MRTZ 94553 571-F5
YALE WY
3400 FRMT 94538 773-E3
3800 LVMR 94550 716-A1
3800 LVMR 94550 715-J1
3800 LVMR 94550 695-J7
YAMADA DR
1300 SJS 95131 814-C7
YAMATO DR
4800 SJS 95111 875-B1
YAMPA CT
48900 FRMT 94539 793-J2
YAMPA RD
- FRMT 94539 793-J2
YAMPA WY
- FRMT 94539 793-J2
500 FRMT 94539 794-A2
YANCY DR
3000 SJS 95148 855-D2
YANEZ CT
- SMCo 94062 789-F2
YANKEE CT
2000 SLN 94579 690-J6
YANKEE HILL
- OAK 94618 630-C4
YANKEE JIM CT
100 VAL 94589 509-H4
YANKEE POINT CT
1500 SJS 95131 814-D6
YARBOROUGH LN
200 RDWC 94061 790-B2
YARD CT
1100 SJS 95133 834-C2
YARDARM CT
100 VAL 94591 550-F2
YARDIS CT
800 MTVW 94040 831-G1
YARDLEY CT
1900 CNCD 94521 593-G4
YARMOUNTH TER
1300 SUNV 94087 832-E4
YARMOUTH CT
- OAK 94619 650-J4
900 SJS 95120 894-G2
5300 NWK 94560 752-E4
YARMOUTH WY
900 SJS 95120 894-G2
2800 SRMN 94583 673-E6
YARNALL PL
- RDWC 94063 770-F6
YARO CT
600 FRMT 94539 753-G6
YARROW LN
- NVTO 94947 526-D7
YARROW VALLEY LN
- ORIN 94563 610-H3
YARWOOD CT
1000 SJS 95128 853-F2
YASOU DEMAS WY
- SJS 95119 875-D5
YASUI CT
100 SJS 95138 875-G7
YATES CT
800 SUNV 94087 832-E2
YAWL CT
100 FCTY 94404 749-G4
YEADON WY
6100 SJS 95119 875-C6
YEANDLE AV
20200 AlaC 94546 692-A5
YEARLING CT
300 PLE 94566 734-C1
YELLOWBIRD CT
6000 SJS 95120 874-B7

STREET
Block City ZIP Pg-Grid

YELLOWLEAF CT
3200 SJS 95135 855-D2
YELLOWOOD LN
4300 PIT 94565 574-C7
YELLOWOOD PL
100 PIT 94565 574-C7
YELLOWSTONE AV
1400 MPS 95035 814-D1
YELLOWSTONE CT
- SRFL 94903 566-F1
- WLCK 94598 612-H3
1900 ANT 94509 575-G5
3500 PLE 94588 714-A1
YELLOWSTONE DR
400 SSF 94080 707-F4
1400 ANT 94509 575-F5
2300 MRTZ 94553 572-A7
2300 MRTZ 94553 592-A1
3900 SJS 95130 853-B4
YELLOWSTONE TER
600 SUNV 94087 832-D3
YELLOWSTONE WY
- LVMR 94550 695-D7
- PCFA 94044 727-B5
YELLOWSTONE PARK DR
4800 FRMT 94538 773-C3
YEOMAN DR
1600 CNCD 94521 593-C2
YERBA BANK CT
- SJS 95121 855-E4
YERBA BUENA AV
- LALT 94022 811-D5
- SF 94127 667-D5
400 SCIC 94306 811-D5
900 EMVL 94608 629-F7
900 OAK 94608 629-E7
2900 SJS 95135 855-E3
3600 SJS 95121 855-E3
YERBA BUENA CT
3700 SJS 95121 855-D3
YERBA BUENA PL
200 FRMT 94536 753-D2
200 LALT 94022 811-D5
YERBA BUENA RD
800 SJS 95111 855-B5
800 SCIC 95111 855-B5
800 SCIC 95121 855-B5
900 SJS 95121 855-B5
2900 SJS 95135 855-F4
YERBA BUENA ST
200 FRMT 94536 753-D2
YERBA BUENA TR
- CCCo - 591-C7
- CCCo - 611-C1
YERBA BUENA WY
2500 SCL 95054 813-B2
YERBA CLIFF CT
- SJS 95121 855-F5
YERBA HILLS CT
- SJS 95121 855-E4
YERBA SANTA AV
- LALT 94022 811-D5
YERBA SANTA CT
13800 SAR 95070 872-F1
YERBA SANTA PZ
- HAY 94542 712-B3
YERBA VISTA CT
2600 SJS 95121 855-E4
YERMO CT
500 SJS 95111 854-G6
YESLER CT
2300 SJS 95131 814-D4
YETTA DR
- CCCo 94596 632-F1
YEW CT
7700 NWK 94560 752-D7
24600 HAY 94545 711-F5
YEW ST
1300 SMTO 94402 748-J4
YEW TREE CT
3600 SJS 95111 854-G6
YGNACIO AV
4300 OAK 94601 670-D1
YGNACIO CT
100 WLCK 94598 612-D4
YGNACIO VALLEY RD
100 WLCK 94596 612-B4
900 WLCK 94598 612-F2
3000 WLCK 94598 613-A1
3300 WLCK 94598 593-B6
4200 CCCo 94518 593-B6
4200 CCCo 94521 593-B6
4500 CNCD 94521 593-B6
YGNACIO WOODS CT
700 CNCD 94518 592-H6
YNEZ CIR
700 DNVL 94526 653-B2
YNIGO WY
4200 PA 94306 811-C3
YOLANDA CIR
1800 CLAY 94517 593-G5
YOLANDA CT
1400 SJS 95118 874-B2
YOLANDA DR
- SANS 94960 566-B6
YOLANO DR
100 VAL 94589 509-J7
YOLO AV
500 VAL 94590 529-J3
1900 BERK 94709 609-G7
1900 BERK 94707 609-G7
3000 ELCR 94530 609-C4
3000 RCH 94804 609-C4
YOLO CT
- CCCo 94565 573-E2
- SJS 95136 874-E1
100 SBRN 94066 707-D6
YOLO DR
3800 SJS 95136 874-F1
3800 SAR 95070 852-D6
YOLO ST
- CMAD 94925 606-H1
22500 HAY 94541 711-G2
YOLO TER
37200 FRMT 94536 752-G4
YOLO WY
700 LVMR 94550 695-E6
YONA VISTA
16000 SCIC 95127 815-A6
YORBA LN
2900 SF 94116 666-J6
YORBA LN
2900 SF 94132 666-J6
YORBA ST
2200 SF 94116 667-A6
2200 SF 94132 667-A6
2300 SF 94116 666-J6
2300 SF 94132 666-J6
YORK AV
100 CCCo 94708 609-F3
1300 CMBL 95008 873-A1
1500 SMTO 94401 729-A7
YORK CT
300 WLCK 94598 612-F2
7000 DBLN 94568 693-J3
YORK DR
- PDMT 94611 650-A1
- PDMT 94611 630-A7
400 BEN 94510 551-A2
400 BEN 94510 550-J2
5300 FRMT 94536 752-H7
6800 DBLN 94568 693-J4
YORK PL
- MRGA 94556 631-D6
100 HAY 94544 732-E3
YORK ST
- DALY 94015 707-C3
300 VAL 94590 529-J5
500 PIT 94565 574-D2
500 SF 94110 668-A3
500 VAL 94590 530-A5
800 OAK 94610 650-A3
1200 CCCo 94801 588-F4
1200 RCH 94801 588-F4
1500 SF 94110 668-A4
1600 SJS 95124 873-J2
YORK TR
- OAK 94605 651-A6
- OAK 94619 651-A6
YORK WY
300 LVMR 94550 695-D6
YORKSHIRE CT
100 SBRN 94066 727-F1
100 VAL 94591 530-F6
500 LVMR 94550 695-H6
900 LFYT 94549 611-G6
2900 PLE 94588 694-F6
YORKSHIRE DR
- OAK 94618 630-B6
500 LVMR 94550 695-H6
900 LALT 94024 831-H5
1100 CPTO 95014 852-C3
2300 ANT 94509 595-G1
YORKSHIRE LN
- SMCo 94062 769-G6
YORKSHIRE PL
1000 CCCo 94506 654-A5
2000 ALA 94501 669-H3
YORKSHIRE RD
400 ALA 94501 669-H3
YORKSHIRE ST
3800 SLN 94578 691-B4
YORKSHIRE WY
400 BLMT 94002 749-E7
2000 MTVW 94040 831-J1
YORKTON DR
2600 MTVW 94040 831-J2
YORKTON WY
5000 SJS 95130 852-J7
YORKTOWN DR
900 SUNV 94087 832-B3
YORKTOWN RD
1600 SMCo 94402 748-F7
1600 SMCo 94402 768-G1
3500 FRMT 94538 773-E2
YORTON LN
500 AlaC 94541 711-E1
YOSEMITE AV
- OAK 94611 649-J1
400 MTVW 94041 811-H6
1100 SJS 95126 833-H7
1200 SF 94124 668-C7
1200 SF 94124 688-C1
2800 ALA 94501 670-B2
2800 SRMN 94583 673-F7
3100 ELCR 94530 609-C4
YOSEMITE CIR
1300 CLAY 94517 593-F6
YOSEMITE CT
600 WDSD 94062 789-E3
5500 CLAY 94517 593-F7
YOSEMITE CT N
3800 PLE 94588 714-A1
YOSEMITE CT S
3700 PLE 94588 714-A1
YOSEMITE DR
100 PIT 94565 574-D5
200 LVMR 94550 715-D1
400 LVMR 94550 695-D7
500 MPS 95035 814-B1
500 SSF 94080 707-F4
900 PCFA 94044 727-B5
1400 ANT 94509 575-F6
1400 MPS 95035 794-D7
2600 BLMT 94002 769-A2
YOSEMITE PL
- LVMR 94550 695-C7
YOSEMITE RD
- ORIN 94563 611-A4
- SRFL 94903 566-F2
1800 BERK 94707 609-F5
YOSEMITE WY
100 LGTS 95032 873-B7
1200 HAY 94545 711-F5
4500 FRMT 94538 753-A6
YOSHIDA DR
24900 HAY 94545 711-F5
YOSHINO PL
10100 CPTO 95014 852-G1
YOUNG AV
3700 OAK 94619 650-G5
22000 AlaC 94546 692-A6
YOUNG CT
- CCCo 94507 632-H2
- SF 94124 668-C6
- SF 94124 688-C1
1000 NVTO 94949 546-C1
24100 SCIC 94024 831-F3
YOUNG DR
- VAL 94592 529-G7
- VAL 94592 549-G1
38000 FRMT 94536 753-A2
YOUNG ST
- SF 94129 647-E3
YOUNG ST
1400 SMTO 94401 749-B1
2700 ALA 94502 669-J6
E YOUNGER AV
- SJS 95112 834-A3
W YOUNGER AV
- SJS 95110 834-A3
YOUNGS CIR
3400 SJS 95127 814-J7
YOUNGS CT
600 SJS 95127 814-J6
2100 WLCK 94596 632-F1
YOUNGS VALLEY RD
2100 WLCK 94596 632-F1
YSABEL DR
3600 SBRN 94066 707-B6
YSC TR
- FRMT 94539 754-A7
- FRMT 94539 774-A1
YUBA AV
1200 SPAB 94806 589-A4
2500 ELCR 94530 589-B6
3200 SJS 95117 853-C3
5300 OAK 94619 670-F1
YUBA CT
- CCCo 94565 573-H2
100 SBRN 94066 707-D6
19600 SAR 95070 852-F6
39500 FRMT 94538 753-A6
YUBA DR
700 MTVW 94041 812-A6
800 MTVW 94041 811-J7
YUBA LN
27800 LAH 94022 810-J7
27800 LAH 94022 830-J1
YUBA ST
400 VAL 94590 530-B5
500 ELCR 94530 589-B5
500 RCH 94805 589-B5
1000 SPAB 94805 589-B5
1000 SPAB 94806 589-B5
YUCATAN DR
47000 FRMT 94539 773-H6
YUCATAN WY
4900 SJS 95118 874-B3
YUCCA AV
3000 SJS 95124 873-J1
YUCCA CT
- SRMN 94583 673-C4
100 FRMT 94538 773-B2
YUKON CT
- NVTO 94947 526-C5
100 VAL 94589 509-H5
34500 FRMT 94555 752-D2
YUKON DR
1400 SUNV 94087 832-D5
YUKON PL
- LVMR 94550 715-D4
YUKON ST
- SF 94114 667-F3
2200 CNCD 94520 572-G5
2300 SLN 94577 690-G4
YUKON TER
1300 SUNV 94087 832-D4
YUKON WY
- LVMR 94550 715-D4
1200 NVTO 94947 526-C5
2200 SJS 95008 853-B7
YUKON RIVER WY
- SJS 95131 814-B6
YUMA AV
1200 SUNV 94089 812-J5
YUMA CT
- PLE 94588 694-D6
2700 WLCK 94598 612-H4
YUMA DR
3100 SJS 95111 854-H5
YUMA PL
19400 AlaC 94546 691-H4
YUMA ST
19400 AlaC 94546 691-H4
19400 AlaC 94578 691-H4
YUMA WY
- PLE 94588 694-D6
YUROK CIR
500 SJS 95123 874-H5
YUROK CT
- FRMT 94539 773-H2
500 SJS 95123 874-H5
YVETTE CT
1100 SJS 95118 874-C3
YVONNE CT
1700 CNCD 94521 593-F4
15100 SCIC 95124 873-F4
YVONNE DR
1800 CNCD 94521 593-F4

Z

ZABALLOS CT
22600 HAY 94541 692-B7
ZACATE AV
39000 FRMT 94539 753-D2
ZACATE CT
100 FRMT 94539 753-D2
ZACATE PL
- FRMT 94539 753-D3
ZACHARY CT
- MLPK 94025 790-D7
1200 SJS 95121 854-H2
ZACHARY WY
2400 SJS 95121 854-J2
ZACK WY
3700 AlaC 94546 692-B5
ZAGORA DR
300 DNVL 94506 654-A6
ZAMORA CT
100 VAL 94591 530-F5
1000 MPS 95035 794-B4
1400 HAY 94544 732-A2
ZAMORA DR
300 SSF 94080 707-F5
900 PCFA 94044 727-A4
ZAMORA PL
300 DNVL 94526 653-D5
ZAMPA LN
- SF 94115 647-G6
ZANCO WY
- NVTO 94947 526-A4
ZAND LN
- CCCo 94507 632-G5
ZANDER CT
- ORIN 94563 631-C3
ZANDER DR
- ORIN 94563 631-C3
ZANDOL CT
8500 DBLN 94568 693-F2
ZANDRA CT
- CCCo 94806 569-A5
ZANDRA PL
- NVTO 94945 526-D3
ZANKER LN
- SJS 95134 793-E7
ZANKER RD
1600 SJS 95112 833-J1
1900 SJS 95112 813-H6
2000 SJS 95131 813-H6
2600 SJS 95134 813-F1
3800 SJS 95134 793-F7
ZAPATA CT
11700 DBLN 94568 693-F3
ZAPATA WY
- PTLV 94028 810-A5
ZAPOTEC DR
46900 FRMT 94539 773-J6
47100 FRMT 94539 774-A6
ZAPPETTINI CT
- LAH 94022 830-H2
ZARA AV
5300 RCH 94805 589-B6
5400 ELCR 94530 589-B6
ZARICK DR
900 SJS 95129 853-A3
ZARO CT
5200 PLE 94588 694-A6
ZATON AV
400 SJS 95117 853-C1
400 SCIC 95117 853-C1
ZEILE CREEK TR
- AlaC 94544 712-E5
- HAY 94542 712-E5
- HAY 94544 712-E5
ZEKA DR
1200 SJS 95131 814-C7
ZELMA CT
- PLHL 94523 612-A1
ZELMA ST
14800 SLN 94579 691-B5
ZENA AV
17100 MSER 95030 873-B4
17300 LGTS 95030 873-B4
ZENATO PL
- PLE 94566 715-A6
ZENITH RIDGE DR
500 DNVL 94506 654-A6
ZENNIA DR
2200 PIT 94565 573-J4
ZENO PL
- SF 94105 648-C6
ZENO ST
19700 AlaC 94546 691-H5
ZEPHYR
100 HER 94547 569-F3
ZEPHYR AV
900 HAY 94544 732-B3
ZEPHYR CIR
500 DNVL 94526 653-C5
ZEPHYR CT
- MrnC 94903 546-A7
1300 SJS 95127 835-A4
ZEPHYR PL
100 DNVL 94526 653-C5
ZEPPELIN CT
4900 SJS 95111 875-A2
ZEPPELIN DR
1000 LVMR 94550 695-D7
ZERMATT ST
600 LVMR 94550 695-E7
ZEUS
- HER 94547 569-F3
ZEVANOVE CT
4200 PLE 94588 694-C6
ZIEGLER AV
4400 OAK 94605 671-D5
ZIELE CREEK DR
28000 HAY 94542 712-E5
ZIG ZAG TR
- MrnC 94965 606-A2
ZILEMAN CT
5800 SJS 95123 875-A5
ZILEMAN DR
5800 SJS 95123 875-A5
ZINFADEL CIR
400 CLAY 94517 593-H7
400 CLAY 94517 613-H1
ZINFANDEL CT
1000 PLE 94566 714-H4
2100 LVMR 94550 715-H3
19300 SAR 95070 872-G3
ZINFANDEL ST
- FRMT 94539 793-J2
ZINFANDEL WY
1100 SJS 95120 874-D6
ZINN DR
5900 OAK 94611 630-E7
5900 OAK 94611 650-E1
ZINN ST
1600 CCCo 94805 589-C5
ZINNIA CIR
100 VAL 94591 530-G7
ZINNIA CT
2800 UNC 94587 732-G7
4700 LVMR 94550 696-A4
ZINNIA DR
15000 SLN 94578 691-C4
ZINNIA LN
1600 SJS 95124 873-J6
ZION AV
- PIT 94565 574-D7
ZION CT
300 SRFL 94903 566-F3
1300 MPS 95035 794-D7
ZION LN
2900 SJS 95132 814-F5
ZION PL
3400 CNCD 94518 592-H6
ZION CANYON CT
3400 PLE 94588 714-A1
ZIRCON CT
100 HER 94547 569-G4
100 VAL 94589 510-B6
5000 SJS 95136 874-E3
ZIRCON PL
- SF 94131 667-G5
ZIRCON TER
34300 FRMT 94555 752-C2
ZIRCON WY
500 LVMR 94550 715-D2
ZISCH DR
3300 SJS 95118 874-B1
ZITA CT
500 DNVL 94526 653-D5
ZITA DR
500 SSF 94080 707-E2
ZITA MNR
- DALY 94015 687-B5
ZOE CT
200 PIN 94564 569-E3
ZOE ST
- SF 94107 648-B7
ZOILA CT
- NVTO 94947 525-G4
ZOOK RD
- SCIC 94035 792-B7
- SCIC 94035 812-B1
- SUNV 94089 792-B7
ZORAH ST
500 OAK 94606 650-A4
ZORIA CIR
2200 SJS 95131 814-D5
ZORKA AV
20100 SAR 95070 852-E5
ZORRO CT
24100 AlaC 94541 712-B1
ZULMIDA AV
6200 NWK 94560 752-D6
ZUMWALT LN
700 FCTY 94404 749-G5
ZUNI CT
1500 SJS 95131 814-D6
ZUNI WY
- PLE 94588 694-D6
ZUNIC DR
47500 FRMT 94539 773-J7
ZURICH CT
- PLHL 94523 592-C5
1100 SJS 95132 814-G5
ZURICH TER
1300 SUNV 94087 832-D4
ZWISSIG CT
3600 PLE 94566 714-F3
ZWISSIGG WY
700 UNC 94587 732-G5

#

1ST AV
- MTVW 94043 812-B5
- SCIC 94035 812-E1
- DALY 94014 687-C5
100 PCFA 94044 706-J5
200 SMCo 94063 770-D7
200 SMCo 94063 790-D1
200 SMTO 94401 748-J1
500 CCCo 94525 550-D5
500 SBRN 94066 707-J6
500 SMTO 94401 749-A1
1000 SUNV 94089 812-E1
1300 OAK 94606 649-H5
1300 OAK 94607 649-H5
1500 WLCK 94596 612-A2
1ST AV N
100 CCCo 94553 572-C7
1ST AV S
100 CCCo 94553 592-B1
300 PLHL 94523 592-B1
1ST LN
300 SSF 94080 707-H3
1ST ST
- ALA 94501 649-A3
- AlaC 94586 734-B5
- OAK 94625 649-A3
- CMAD 94925 586-F7
- LALT 94022 811-D7
- RCH 94801 588-F6
- SF 94105 648-B5
- SF 94130 648-E2
- SRFL 94901 586-F1
- SSF 94080 707-G3
200 BEN 94510 551-C3
200 CCCo 94572 549-H7
600 SUNV 94089 812-H4
700 ANT 94509 575-C3
800 LFYT 94549 611-F6
900 NVTO 94945 526-B3
1600 SCL 95134 813-E5
1700 CNCD 94519 592-G2
3900 PLE 94566 714-E3
22700 HAY 94541 711-J1
22800 HAY 94541 712-A1
1ST ST Rt# 84
1300 LVMR 94550 715-F1
2100 LVMR 94550 695-J6
3600 LVMR 94550 696-A6
N 1ST ST
- CCCo 94801 588-F3
- CMBL 95008 853-E6
500 SJS 95112 834-A4
500 SJS 95110 834-A4
800 SJS 95113 834-A4
1000 SJS 95112 833-J2
1100 SJS 95110 833-J2
1200 SJS 95002 813-C1
2000 SJS 95131 833-J2
2100 SJS 95131 813-H7
2600 SJS 95134 813-E2
3600 SCIC 95134 813-E2
S 1ST ST
- SJS 95113 834-B6
100 RCH 94804 588-F7
300 CMBL 95008 853-E6
300 SJS 95110 834-C7
400 RCH 94804 608-F1
500 SJS 95112 834-C7
S 1ST ST Rt# 82
600 SJS 95110 834-C7
600 SJS 95112 834-C7
W 1ST ST
900 MLPK 94025 790-G2
1ST ST W
1000 SBRN 94066 707-H5
1ST AV CT
- WLCK 94596 612-B2
1ST AV PL
1400 OAK 94606 649-H4
2ND AV
- DALY 94014 687-C5
- SF 94118 647-D6
- SMTO 94401 748-J2
200 PCFA 94044 706-J5
200 RDWC 94063 770-E6
200 SLN 94577 691-B2
200 SMCo 94063 770-D7
200 SMCo 94063 790-D1
300 SMCo 94014 687-C5
400 SBRN 94066 707-J6
400 SMTO 94401 749-A1
500 CCCo 94525 550-D5
700 PIN 94564 569-D4
1000 OAK 94606 649-H5
1100 SUNV 94089 812-E2
1200 SF 94122 667-D2
1200 SMTO 94401 729-B7
1500 WLCK 94596 612-B2
2ND AV S
100 PLHL 94553 592-B1
100 CCCo 94553 592-B1
100 PLHL 94523 592-B1
300 CCCo 94523 592-C1
2ND CT
1100 ANT 94509 575-C3
2ND LN
200 SSF 94080 707-G2
2ND ST
- AlaC 94586 734-B5
- CCCo - 550-H6
- DBLN 94568 694-B4
- OAK 94625 649-A3
- SUNV 94089 812-H3
- LALT 94022 811-D6
- RCH 94801 588-F6
- SAUS 94965 627-B4
- SF 94105 648-B6
- SSF 94080 707-G3
100 CCCo 94572 549-G7
100 OAK 94607 649-F5
300 ANT 94509 575-C3
300 SF 94107 648-B6
400 SRFL 94901 586-E1
900 LFYT 94549 611-F6
900 NVTO 94945 526-B2
1000 ALB 94804 609-C7
1000 BERK 94804 609-C7
1300 LVMR 94550 715-G1
1300 BERK 94804 629-C1
1500 CCCo 94801 588-F3
1700 ALA 94501 649-E7
1700 CNCD 94519 592-G2
2000 SCL 95054 813-C5
2000 SCL 95134 813-E5
2400 LVMR 94550 695-H7
3900 PA 94306 811-D1
4300 PLE 94566 714-E4
22400 HAY 94541 711-J1
22600 HAY 94541 712-A2
24600 AlaC 94541 712-C2
33300 UNC 94587 732-G4
36800 FRMT 94536 753-B1
E 2ND ST
100 MLPK 94025 790-H3
200 BEN 94510 551-E1
N 2ND ST
- CMBL 95008 853-E6
- SJS 95113 834-A3
100 SJS 95112 834-A3
S 2ND ST
- SJS 95113 834-C7
100 RCH 94804 588-F7
300 RCH 94804 608-F1
400 SJS 95112 834-C7
700 SJS 95112 854-C1
W 2ND ST
400 PIT 94565 574-D1
600 MLPK 94025 790-G3
700 BEN 94510 551-B5
1200 CCCo 94525 550-D5
2ND ST W
1000 SBRN 94066 707-H6
3RD AV
- MTVW 94043 812-B5
- DALY 94014 687-D5
- SF 94118 647-D6
200 RDWC 94063 770-D7
200 SMCo 94063 770-D7
200 SMCo 94063 790-D1
300 PCFA 94044 706-J5
300 SMCo 94014 687-D5
400 CCCo 94525 550-D5
400 SBRN 94066 707-J6
600 PIN 94564 569-D4
700 SF 94124 688-E1
1000 SUNV 94089 812-E2
1100 OAK 94606 649-J4
1200 SF 94122 667-D2
1300 SF 94143 667-D2
1500 WLCK 94596 612-A2
E 3RD AV
- SMTO 94401 748-J2
300 SMTO 94401 749-A1
1300 SMTO 94401 729-B7
2000 FCTY 94404 749-E1
W 3RD AV
- SMTO 94402 748-J2
3RD AV S
- CCCo 94553 592-B1
- PLHL 94523 592-B1
3RD LN
200 SSF 94080 707-G2
3RD ST
- AlaC 94586 734-B5
- DBLN 94568 694-A4
- SF 94134 688-B1
- CCCo 94572 549-G7
- HER 94547 549-G7
- LALT 94022 811-D6
- RCH 94801 588-F7
- SAUS 94965 627-B4
- SF 94103 648-B6
- SF 94130 648-E1
- SRFL 94901 586-F1
- MrnC 94901 586-G1
200 ANT 94509 575-C4
200 LVMR 94550 715-G1
200 OAK 94625 649-A4
300 OAK 94607 649-D4
3RD ST
300 SF 94107 648-B6
500 VAL 94590 530-A7
900 LFYT 94549 611-F6
900 SF 94107 668-C3
1000 NVTO 94945 526-B3
1100 CCCo 94801 588-F4
1100 CCCo 94801 588-F4
1300 ALA 94501 669-E1
1500 BERK 94804 609-C7
1600 CNCD 94519 592-G1
1600 ALA 94501 649-E7
1600 BERK 94804 629-D1
2000 SCL 95054 813-C5
2000 SCL 95134 813-E5
2600 LVMR 94550 695-H7
3100 SF 94124 668-C3
3200 SF 94124 668-B7
4500 PLE 94566 714-E4
5800 SF 94124 688-B1
20600 SAR 95070 872-D3
22500 HAY 94541 712-A1
33200 UNC 94587 732-G4
37200 FRMT 94536 753-B1
E 3RD ST
- PIT 94565 574-E1
400 MLPK 94025 790-H3
800 BEN 94510 551-C4
N 3RD ST
- HAY 94541 691-J7
- CMBL 95008 853-E5
- SJS 95113 834-B5
- SJS 95112 834-A3
1900 CNCD 94519 592-G1
22200 AlaC 94546 691-J7
S 3RD ST
- SJS 95113 834-C7
100 RCH 94804 588-F7
100 CMBL 95008 853-E6
300 SJS 95112 834-C7
400 RCH 94804 608-F1
700 SJS 95112 854-D1
W 3RD ST
600 MLPK 94025 790-G3
700 BEN 94510 551-B4
3RD ST W
1000 SBRN 94066 707-H6
4TH AV
- MTVW 94043 812-B5
- SF 94118 647-D6
200 SMCo 94063 790-D1
400 PCFA 94044 706-J5
400 SMCo 94063 770-D7
500 SBRN 94066 707-J6
500 SBRN 94066 708-A7
700 PIN 94564 569-D4
700 RDWC 94063 770-E6
900 CCCo 94525 550-D4
1000 OAK 94606 649-H5
1200 SF 94122 667-D2
1400 SF 94143 667-D2
E 4TH AV
- SMTO 94401 748-J2
200 SMTO 94401 749-A1
400 SMTO 94402 749-A1
W 4TH AV
- SMTO 94402 748-J2
4TH AV S
100 PLHL 94523 592-A1
100 CCCo 94553 592-A1
4TH LN
200 SSF 94080 707-G2
4TH ST
- CCCo - 550-H6
- CCCo 94525 550-A5
- DBLN 94568 694-B4
- OAK 94625 649-B4
- SUNV 94089 812-H3
- LALT 94022 811-E6
- OAK 94607 649-F4
- RCH 94801 588-F6
- SF 94103 648-A6
- SF 94130 648-E1
100 CCCo 94572 549-H7
100 SANS 94960 566-D7
100 SAUS 94965 627-B4
300 SF 94107 648-A6
300 SRFL 94901 586-F1
800 SF 94107 668-C1
900 CCCo 94801 588-F4
900 NVTO 94945 526-B3
900 LFYT 94549 611-G6
1200 LVMR 94550 715-G1
1200 BERK 94804 609-D7
1200 BERK 94804 629-D1
1300 ALA 94501 669-E1
1600 SCL 95134 813-E5
1600 ALA 94501 649-E4
1900 SRFL 94901 566-D7
2800 LVMR 94550 695-H7
20600 SAR 95070 872-D2
22700 HAY 94541 712-A1
33200 UNC 94587 732-G4
38000 FRMT 94536 753-C1
E 4TH ST
- PIT 94565 574-E1
600 MLPK 94025 790-G3
800 BEN 94510 551-C5
N 4TH ST
- SJS 95112 834-A3
- SJS 95113 834-B5
1200 SJS 95112 833-J2
22200 AlaC 94546 692-A7
22500 HAY 94541 692-A7
22500 HAY 94541 712-A1
S 4TH ST
- SJS 95113 834-C6
- CMBL 95008 853-E6
- SJS 95112 834-C6
100 RCH 94804 588-F7
100 SJS 95192 834-C6
300 RCH 94804 608-F1
W 4TH ST
100 ANT 94509 575-C4
400 PIT 94565 574-D1
700 MLPK 94025 790-G3
900 BEN 94510 551-B4
5TH AV
- MrnC 94901 566-D6
- OAK 94606 649-H5
- RDWC 94063 770-E6
- SF 94118 647-D6

BAY AREA

INDEX

5TH AV 1998 BAY AREA STREET INDEX E 26TH ST 1013

STREET — Block City ZIP Pg-Grid

5TH AV
- \- SMCo 94063 790-D1
- 400 SMCo 94063 770-D7
- 500 PCFA 94044 706-J4
- 500 SRFL 94901 586-G1
- 500 SBRN 94066 708-A7
- 600 SBRN 94066 707-J6
- 700 PIN 94564 569-D4
- 800 CCCo 94525 550-D5
- 1200 BLMT 94002 769-F1
- 1200 SF 94122 667-D2
- 1200 CNCD 94518 592-G3
- 1400 SF 94143 667-D2
- 1400 SRFL 94901 566-D7
- 2100 OAK 94606 650-A4

E 5TH AV
- \- SMTO 94401 749-A1
- 100 SMTO 94401 748-J2
- 100 SMTO 94402 748-J2
- 200 SMTO 94402 749-A1

W 5TH AV
- \- SMTO 94402 748-J2

5TH AV S
- \- CCCo 94553 592-A1

5TH ST
- \- AlaC 94580 691-E6
- \- CCCo - 550-H6
- \- DBLN 94568 694-A3
- \- NVTO 94949 546-H3
- \- OAK 94625 649-B4
- \- VAL 94592 529-G5
- \- SF 94103 648-A6
- \- VAL 94590 530-B6
- 100 ANT 94509 575-B4
- 100 OAK 94607 649-C3
- 100 RCH 94801 588-F5
- 300 SF 94107 648-A6
- 800 SF 94107 668-B1
- 900 NVTO 94945 526-B3
- 1000 SCIC 94035 812-E2
- 1000 VAL 94590 550-C1
- 1000 SUNV 94089 812-E2
- 1100 BERK 94804 609-D7
- 1300 CCCo 94572 549-J7
- 1300 LVMR 94550 715-G1
- 1300 BERK 94804 629-D1
- 1400 ALA 94501 669-D1
- 1500 CCCo 94801 588-F4
- 1500 CNCD 94519 592-H1
- 1600 ALA 94501 649-F7
- 4100 SCL 95134 813-E5
- 20600 SAR 95070 872-D3
- 22500 HAY 94541 692-A7
- 22800 HAY 94541 712-A1
- 33100 UNC 94587 732-F4

E 5TH ST
- \- PIT 94565 574-E1
- 600 BEN 94510 551-C5

N 5TH ST
- \- HAY 94541 692-A7
- \- HAY 94541 712-A1
- \- SJS 95113 834-B5
- \- SJS 95112 834-A3
- 22100 AlaC 94546 692-A7

S 5TH ST
- \- SJS 95113 834-C7
- \- SJS 95112 834-C7
- 100 RCH 94804 588-F7
- 300 RCH 94804 608-F1
- 800 SJS 95112 854-D1

W 5TH ST
- 900 BEN 94510 551-B4

6TH AV
- \- OAK 94606 649-H5
- \- SF 94118 647-D6
- 200 SMTO 94401 749-A2
- 300 SMCo 94063 790-D1
- 400 SMCo 94025 770-D7
- 600 PCFA 94044 706-J5
- 600 SBRN 94066 708-A6
- 600 SMCo 94063 770-D7
- 700 CCCo 94525 550-D5
- 700 SBRN 94066 707-J6
- 900 RDWC 94063 770-D7
- 1000 BLMT 94002 769-E1
- 1000 SUNV 94089 812-E3
- 1200 SF 94122 667-D2
- 1300 SF 94124 668-E7
- 1300 SF 94124 688-D1

6TH LN
- 100 SSF 94080 707-J2

6TH ST
- \- CCCo - 550-H6
- \- DBLN 94568 694-A3
- \- SUNV 94089 812-H3
- \- ANT 94509 575-B4
- \- OAK 94625 649-B4
- \- RCH 94801 588-F5
- \- SF 94103 648-A7
- \- VAL 94590 530-A6
- 300 CCCo 94572 569-H1
- 300 SF 94107 648-B7
- 400 OAK 94607 649-F4
- 600 SF 94103 668-B1
- 600 SF 94107 668-B1
- 1000 NVTO 94945 526-B3
- 1100 ALB 94804 609-D7
- 1100 BERK 94804 609-D7
- 1200 CCCo 94801 588-F4
- 1300 CCCo 94572 549-J7
- 1400 ALA 94501 669-F1
- 1400 BERK 94804 629-D1
- 1500 LVMR 94550 715-H1
- 1500 SCL 95054 813-D4
- 1600 CNCD 94519 592-H1
- 14600 SAR 95070 872-D3
- 22500 HAY 94541 692-A7
- 22600 HAY 94541 712-A1
- 33100 UNC 94587 732-F4

E 6TH ST
- 100 PIT 94565 574-E1
- 700 BEN 94510 551-C5

N 6TH ST
- \- SJS 95113 834-B5
- \- SJS 95112 834-B4
- 1900 CNCD 94519 572-G7
- 2400 CNCD 94519 592-H1
- 22100 AlaC 94546 692-A7

S 6TH ST
- \- RCH 94804 588-F7
- \- SJS 95113 834-C7
- \- SJS 95112 834-C7
- 300 RCH 94804 608-F1
- 800 SJS 95112 854-D1

W 6TH ST
- \- PIT 94565 574-D1
- 700 BEN 94510 551-A4

7TH AV
- \- SF - 667-D3
- \- SF 94118 647-D6
- 200 SMTO 94401 749-A2
- 400 SMCo 94025 770-E7
- 400 SMCo 94063 790-D1
- 500 SBRN 94066 708-A6
- 500 SMTO 94402 749-A1
- 700 SMCo 94063 770-E7
- 800 CCCo 94525 550-C5
- 900 RDWC 94063 770-E7
- 1000 OAK 94606 649-J5
- 1000 SUNV 94089 812-D3
- 1200 SF 94122 667-D3
- 1600 SF 94131 667-D3
- 1600 SF 94116 667-D3
- 1900 OAK 94606 650-A5

7TH LN
- 200 SSF 94080 707-J2
- 200 SSF 94080 708-A2

7TH ST
- \- DBLN 94568 694-A3
- \- SF 94102 647-J7
- \- SUNV 94089 812-H3
- \- ANT 94509 575-C4
- \- OAK 94606 649-H5
- \- OAK 94607 649-D3
- \- RCH 94801 588-F6
- \- SF 94103 647-J7
- \- SF 94103 648-A7
- 300 VAL 94592 529-G5
- 400 CCCo 94547 569-H1
- 400 CCCo 94572 569-H1
- 500 SF 94103 668-A1
- 800 SF 94107 668-A1
- 900 NVTO 94945 526-A2
- 1100 CCCo 94572 549-J7
- 1200 BERK 94804 609-D7
- 1400 BERK 94804 629-D1
- 1700 CCCo 94801 588-G3
- 1700 SCL 95054 813-D4
- 2000 LVMR 94550 715-G1
- 2100 OAK 94626 649-C3
- 2900 OAK 94625 649-A3
- 22500 HAY 94541 692-A7
- 22800 HAY 94541 712-B1
- 33100 UNC 94587 732-F4

E 7TH ST
- 100 PIT 94565 574-E1
- 1000 BEN 94510 551-C6
- 2200 OAK 94606 670-A1
- 2400 OAK 94601 670-B1

N 7TH ST
- \- SJS 95113 834-B4
- \- SJS 95112 834-A3

S 7TH ST
- \- SJS 95113 834-D7
- \- SJS 95112 834-D7
- 100 RCH 94804 588-F7
- 300 RCH 94804 608-F1
- 500 SJS 95112 854-D1

W 7TH ST
- \- PIT 94565 574-D1
- 1200 BEN 94510 551-A4

7TH ST EXT
- 600 OAK 94607 649-B3
- 600 OAK 94626 649-B3

8TH AV
- \- SF 94118 667-D3
- \- OAK 94606 649-J5
- \- SF 94118 647-C7
- 200 SMTO 94401 749-A2
- 300 SMCo 94025 770-E7
- 300 SMCo 94063 790-D1
- 700 SMCo 94063 770-E6
- 900 RDWC 94063 770-E6
- 1000 SUNV 94089 812-E3
- 1200 SF 94122 667-D3
- 1800 OAK 94606 650-A5
- 1900 SF 94116 667-D3
- 2700 OAK 94610 650-A5

8TH LN
- 200 SSF 94080 707-J2
- 200 SSF 94080 708-A2

8TH ST
- \- OAK 94625 649-B5
- \- ANT 94509 575-C4
- \- RCH 94801 588-F5
- \- SF 94103 647-J7
- \- SolC 94590 530-B5
- \- OAK 94607 649-E4
- \- VAL 94590 530-B5
- 200 SF 94103 648-A7
- 300 SF 94103 668-A1
- 1000 NVTO 94945 526-A3
- 1100 ALB 94706 609-D7
- 1100 ALB 94804 609-D7
- 1100 BERK 94804 609-D7
- 1200 ALA 94501 669-D1
- 1200 SF 94107 668-B1
- 1400 BERK 94804 629-D1
- 1500 OAK 94626 649-C3
- 1700 ALA 94501 649-D7
- 2100 LVMR 94550 715-H1
- 5700 DBLN 94568 694-A3
- 33100 UNC 94587 732-F4

E 8TH ST
- \- OAK 94606 650-A6
- \- PIT 94565 574-E2
- 500 OAK 94606 649-H5
- 3200 OAK 94601 670-C1

N 8TH ST
- \- SJS 95113 834-C5
- \- SJS 95112 834-B3

S 8TH ST
- \- SJS 95113 834-D7
- \- SJS 95112 834-D7
- 100 RCH 94804 588-F7
- 500 RCH 94804 608-F1
- 900 SJS 95112 854-D1

W 8TH ST
- \- PIT 94565 574-D1
- 700 BEN 94510 551-A4

9TH AV
- \- OAK 94606 649-J5
- \- SF 94118 647-C7
- \- SMTO 94401 749-A2
- \- SMTO 94402 749-A2
- 300 SMCo 94025 770-E7
- 300 SMCo 94063 790-D1
- 700 SMCo 94063 770-E7
- 1000 SUNV 94089 812-E3
- 1200 SF 94122 667-C3
- 1700 OAK 94606 650-A5
- 1900 SF 94116 667-C4
- 2200 SF 94116 667-C4

9TH LN
- 200 SSF 94080 707-J2
- 200 SSF 94080 708-A2

9TH ST
- \- DBLN 94568 694-A3
- \- OAK 94625 649-B5
- \- SUNV 94089 812-H3
- \- RCH 94801 588-G6
- \- SF 94103 647-J7
- \- SF 94130 648-E1
- \- VAL 94590 530-B5
- \- ANT 94509 575-C4
- \- OAK 94607 649-F4
- 200 SolC 94590 530-B5
- 200 SF 94103 667-J1
- 300 SF 94103 668-A1
- 400 VAL 94592 529-G6
- 900 ALB 94804 609-D7
- 900 BERK 94804 609-D7
- 1100 ALA 94501 669-D1
- 1100 BERK 94804 629-D1
- 1600 ALA 94501 649-G7
- 33100 UNC 94587 732-F4

E 9TH ST
- 200 PIT 94565 574-E2
- 2500 OAK 94601 650-B7
- 2600 OAK 94601 670-B1

N 9TH ST
- \- SJS 95113 834-B4
- \- SJS 95112 834-B4

S 9TH ST
- \- SJS 95113 834-D7
- \- SJS 95112 834-D7
- 100 RCH 94804 588-F7
- 400 RCH 94804 608-F1
- 900 SJS 95112 854-D1

W 9TH ST
- \- PIT 94565 574-D1
- 800 BEN 94510 550-J4
- 1000 BEN 94510 551-A4

10TH AV
- \- SF 94118 667-C3
- \- OAK 94606 649-H6
- \- SF 94118 647-C6
- \- SMTO 94401 749-A2
- \- SMTO 94402 749-A2
- 600 SMCo 94025 770-E7
- 800 RDWC 94063 770-E6
- 800 SMCo 94063 770-E7
- 900 OAK 94606 650-A5
- 1200 SF 94122 667-C3
- 1900 SF 94116 667-C3

10TH ST
- \- DBLN 94568 694-A2
- \- OAK 94625 649-C4
- \- SUNV 94089 812-H3
- \- ALB 94804 609-D7
- \- ANT 94509 575-B4
- \- BERK 94804 609-D7
- \- SF 94103 647-J7
- \- OAK 94606 649-H5
- \- OAK 94607 649-E3
- 200 SF 94103 667-J1
- 400 SF 94103 668-A1
- 500 BERK 94804 629-D1
- 900 RCH 94801 588-G5
- 1000 CCCo 94509 575-B4
- 1900 OAK 94626 649-C2
- 2700 SPAB 94806 588-G1
- 33400 UNC 94587 732-F5

E 10TH ST
- 100 PIT 94565 574-E2
- 2400 OAK 94601 650-B7
- 2700 OAK 94601 670-B1
- 27500 HAY 94544 712-B6

N 10TH ST
- \- SJS 95113 834-B4
- \- SJS 95112 834-B2

S 10TH ST
- \- SJS 95112 834-D6
- \- SJS 95113 834-D6
- 100 SJS 95192 834-D6
- 800 SJS 95112 854-F2

W 10TH ST
- \- PIT 94565 574-D2
- 1000 BEN 94510 550-J3

11TH AV
- \- SF 94118 647-C6
- \- SMTO 94401 749-A2
- \- SMTO 94402 749-A2
- 600 SMCo 94025 770-E7
- 800 SMCo 94063 770-E7
- 1000 OAK 94606 649-J6
- 1000 SUNV 94089 812-D3
- 1200 SF 94122 667-C3
- 1600 OAK 94606 650-A5
- 1900 SF 94116 667-C3
- 2800 OAK 94610 650-A5

11TH ST
- \- ALA 94501 649-D7
- \- ALA 94501 669-D1
- \- DBLN 94568 694-A2
- \- OAK 94625 649-C5
- \- OAK 94607 649-D3
- \- OAK 94626 649-C2
- \- RCH 94801 588-G6
- \- SF 94103 647-J7
- 100 SF 94103 667-J1
- 400 ANT 94509 575-C4
- 2700 SPAB 94806 588-H1
- 3300 SPAB 94806 568-H7
- 33500 UNC 94587 732-F5

E 11TH ST
- \- OAK 94606 650-B7
- 100 OAK 94606 649-H5
- 700 PIT 94565 574-F2
- 2400 OAK 94601 650-B7
- 27500 HAY 94544 712-B6

N 11TH ST
- \- SJS 95112 834-B3

S 11TH ST
- \- RCH 94804 608-G1
- \- SJS 95112 834-D6
- 300 RCH 94804 588-G7
- 900 SJS 95112 854-E1

W 11TH ST
- \- PIT 94565 574-D2
- 1100 BEN 94510 550-J3

12TH AV
- \- SF 94118 647-C7
- \- SMTO 94402 749-A3
- 600 SMCo 94025 770-E7
- 800 SMCo 94063 770-E7
- 1100 OAK 94606 649-J6
- 1200 SF 94122 667-C2
- 1500 OAK 94606 650-A5
- 1900 SF 94116 667-C3
- 2100 SF 94116 667-C4

12TH ST
- \- OAK 94625 649-C4
- \- OAK 94607 649-D3
- \- RCH 94801 588-G6
- \- SF 94103 647-H7
- \- SF 94103 667-J1
- 100 VAL 94590 530-C5
- 400 ANT 94509 575-C4
- 800 OAK 94612 649-F4
- 1100 DBLN 94568 694-A2
- 2700 SPAB 94806 588-H1
- 33600 UNC 94587 732-F5

E 12TH ST
- \- OAK 94606 649-J5
- \- OAK 94607 649-J5
- 300 PIT 94565 574-E2
- 1300 OAK 94606 650-A6
- 2300 OAK 94606 650-A6
- 2900 OAK 94601 670-C1
- 27500 HAY 94544 712-C6

N 12TH ST
- \- SJS 95112 834-B3

S 12TH ST
- \- SJS 95112 834-D6
- 100 RCH 94804 588-G7
- 200 RCH 94804 608-G1
- 1000 SJS 95112 854-E1

W 12TH ST
- 100 PIT 94565 574-D2
- 1000 BEN 94510 550-J3

12TH ST S
- \- DBLN 94568 694-B2

E 12TH ST PL
- 4300 OAK 94601 670-D1

13TH AV
- \- SMTO 94402 749-A3
- 1100 OAK 94606 649-J6
- 1200 OAK 94606 650-A6
- 2800 OAK 94610 650-B4
- 2900 OAK 94602 650-B4

13TH ST
- \- DBLN 94568 694-A2
- \- RCH 94801 588-G5
- 100 VAL 94590 530-C5
- 100 SF 94103 667-J1
- 300 ANT 94509 575-C5
- 800 OAK 94612 649-F4
- 1100 OAK 94607 649-E3
- 1500 OAK 94625 649-C5
- 2700 SPAB 94806 588-H1
- 33200 UNC 94587 732-F5

E 13TH ST
- \- ANT 94509 575-E4
- 3000 OAK 94601 650-C7
- 3000 OAK 94601 670-C1
- 28100 HAY 94544 712-C6

N 13TH ST
- \- SJS 95112 834-B2

S 13TH ST
- \- SJS 95112 834-D6
- 100 RCH 94804 588-G7
- 200 RCH 94804 608-G1

W 13TH ST
- 300 PIT 94565 574-D2
- 1100 BEN 94510 550-J3

13TH ST W
- \- VAL 94592 529-G7

14TH AV
- \- SF 94118 647-C6
- \- SF 94129 647-C6
- \- SMTO 94402 749-A3
- 600 SMCo 94025 770-E7
- 1200 OAK 94606 650-A5
- 1200 SF 94122 667-C2
- 1700 SF 94116 667-C3
- 2100 SF 94116 667-C5
- 2700 SF 94127 667-C5
- 3000 OAK 94602 650-A5

14TH ST
- \- DBLN 94568 694-A2
- \- OAK 94625 649-C5
- \- VAL 94592 529-H6
- \- SF 94103 667-H1
- \- VAL 94590 530-C4
- \- OAK 94607 649-E3
- 100 OAK 94606 649-G4
- 600 RCH 94801 588-G5
- 600 SF 94114 667-H1
- 900 OAK 94612 649-G4
- 1000 SF 94117 667-H1
- 1600 SPAB 94806 588-H2
- 1800 OAK 94626 649-C2
- 33300 UNC 94587 732-F5

E 14TH ST
- 400 ANT 94509 575-E5
- 400 PIT 94565 574-F3

E 14TH ST Rt# 185
- \- SLN 94577 670-J6
- \- OAK 94603 670-J6
- 200 SLN 94577 671-A7
- 900 SLN 94577 691-B2
- 13600 SLN 94578 691-B2
- 14800 AlaC 94578 691-F5
- 15800 AlaC 94580 691-F5
- 17000 AlaC 94541 691-F5

N 14TH ST
- \- SJS 95112 834-C3

S 14TH ST
- \- SJS 95112 834-D6

W 14TH ST
- 500 ANT 94509 575-C5
- 1200 BEN 94510 550-H3

15TH AV
- \- SF 94129 647-C6
- \- SF 94118 647-C6
- \- SMTO 94402 749-A3
- 700 SMCo 94025 770-F7
- 900 RDWC 94063 770-F7
- 1200 OAK 94606 650-A6
- 1200 SF 94122 667-C2
- 1900 SF 94116 667-C4
- 2100 SF 94116 667-C5
- 2600 SF 94127 667-C5
- 2700 SF 94132 667-C5

15TH ST
- \- DBLN 94568 694-A2
- \- OAK 94625 649-C4
- \- RCH 94801 588-G5
- \- SF 94103 668-A1
- \- SF 94107 668-A1
- 100 OAK 94612 649-F3
- 500 ANT 94509 575-C5
- 700 OAK 94607 649-C2
- 1000 SF 94103 667-J1
- 1100 SPAB 94806 588-H2
- 1800 OAK 94626 649-C2
- 1900 SF 94114 667-G2
- 2500 SF 94117 667-G2
- 33600 UNC 94587 732-F5

E 15TH ST
- \- ANT 94509 575-D5
- \- OAK 94606 649-J5
- 100 PIT 94565 574-E3
- 1200 OAK 94606 650-A6
- 2300 OAK 94601 650-A6
- 3400 OAK 94601 670-C1
- 5500 OAK 94621 670-E2
- 27500 HAY 94544 712-C6

N 15TH ST
- \- SJS 95112 834-B2

S 15TH ST
- \- SJS 95112 834-D6
- 100 RCH 94804 588-G7
- 300 RCH 94804 608-G1

W 15TH ST
- \- ANT 94509 575-D5

16TH AV
- \- SF 94118 647-C6
- \- SMTO 94402 749-A3
- 500 SMCo 94025 770-E7
- 500 SMCo 94063 790-E1
- 1000 RDWC 94063 770-F6
- 1100 OAK 94606 650-A6
- 1200 SF 94122 667-C3
- 1900 SF 94116 667-C3
- 2100 SF 94116 667-C4

16TH ST
- \- ANT 94509 575-C5
- \- RCH 94801 588-G6
- 200 SF 94107 668-A2
- 500 OAK 94612 649-G3
- 700 OAK 94607 649-D2
- 1300 SF 94103 668-A2
- 1600 SPAB 94806 588-H2
- 2100 SF 94110 668-A2
- 2400 SF 94103 667-H2
- 2400 SF 94110 667-H2
- 3300 SF 94114 667-G2

E 16TH ST
- \- ANT 94509 575-D5
- 100 OAK 94606 649-J4
- 200 PIT 94565 574-E3
- 2300 OAK 94601 650-B7
- 3600 OAK 94601 670-D1
- 5500 OAK 94621 670-E2
- 27500 HAY 94544 712-C6

N 16TH ST
- 100 SJS 95112 834-C3

S 16TH ST
- \- SJS 95112 834-D6
- 100 RCH 94804 588-G7
- 300 RCH 94804 608-G1

17TH AV
- \- SF 94121 647-B6
- \- SMTO 94402 749-A3
- \- SF 94118 647-B6
- 500 SMCo 94025 770-F7
- 500 SMCo 94063 790-F1
- 1000 RDWC 94063 770-F7
- 1200 OAK 94606 650-A5
- 1200 SF 94122 667-B3
- 1900 SF 94116 667-B3
- 2100 SF 94116 667-C5

17TH ST
- \- ANT 94509 575-C5
- \- OAK 94612 649-F3
- \- RCH 94801 588-G5
- 400 SF 94107 668-C2
- 800 OAK 94607 649-E2
- 1100 SPAB 94806 588-H1
- 1800 SF 94103 668-A2
- 1900 OAK 94626 649-C2
- 2100 SF 94110 668-A2
- 2700 SF 94110 667-H2
- 3600 SF 94114 667-E2
- 4500 SF 94117 667-E2
- 4900 SF 94117 667-E2

E 17TH ST
- 100 PIT 94565 574-E3
- 300 OAK 94606 649-J4
- 1100 OAK 94606 650-A5
- 2300 OAK 94601 650-C7
- 4000 OAK 94601 670-D1
- 5500 OAK 94621 670-E2

N 17TH ST
- \- SJS 95112 834-C3

S 17TH ST
- \- SJS 95112 834-D5
- 100 RCH 94804 588-G7
- 300 RCH 94804 608-G1

W 17TH ST
- 200 PIT 94565 574-C3

18TH AV
- \- SF 94121 647-B6
- \- SMTO 94402 749-B3
- \- SF 94118 647-B6
- 600 SMCo 94025 770-F7
- 600 SMCo 94063 790-F1
- 1100 RDWC 94063 770-F6
- 1200 OAK 94606 650-A6
- 1200 SF 94122 667-B4
- 1900 SF 94116 667-B4
- 2100 SF 94116 667-B5

18TH ST
- \- RCH 94801 588-H5
- 500 OAK 94612 649-G3
- 500 SF 94107 668-B2
- 700 OAK 94607 649-D2
- 1100 SPAB 94806 588-H1
- 2400 SF 94110 668-A2
- 2800 SF 94110 667-J2
- 3700 SF 94114 667-F2

E 18TH ST
- \- ANT 94509 575-E5
- \- OAK 94606 649-J5
- 800 OAK 94606 650-A5
- 1600 CCCo 94509 575-H5
- 2900 OAK 94601 650-C7
- 3900 OAK 94601 670-D1

N 18TH ST
- 100 SJS 95112 834-C3

S 18TH ST
- 100 RCH 94804 588-G7
- 200 SJS 95116 834-E6
- 200 RCH 94804 608-G1

W 18TH ST
- \- ANT 94509 575-B5

19TH AV
- \- SF 94121 647-B6
- \- SMTO 94403 749-B3
- 1200 OAK 94606 650-A6
- 4000 SF 94132 687-C1

19TH AV Rt# 1
- 1100 SF 94132 687-B1
- 1200 SF 94122 667-B3
- 1900 SF 94116 667-B3
- 2100 SF 94116 667-B5
- 2700 SF 94132 667-B5

19TH ST
- \- RCH 94801 588-H6
- 100 OAK 94612 649-F3
- 500 SF 94107 668-B2
- 700 OAK 94607 649-E2
- 1200 OAK 94626 649-D2
- 1300 SPAB 94806 588-H2
- 2500 SF 94110 668-A2
- 2800 SF 94110 667-J2
- 3700 SF 94114 667-F2

E 19TH ST
- \- ANT 94509 575-D5
- 700 OAK 94606 649-J5
- 800 OAK 94606 650-A5
- 2300 OAK 94601 650-C7

N 19TH ST
- 100 SJS 95112 834-C3

S 19TH ST
- \- SJS 95116 834-D5
- 100 RCH 94804 588-H7
- 200 RCH 94804 608-G1

W 19TH ST
- 100 ANT 94509 575-C5

20TH AV
- \- SF 94121 647-B6
- 1200 OAK 94606 650-A6
- 1200 SF 94122 667-B3
- 1900 SF 94116 667-B3
- 2100 SF 94116 667-B5
- 2900 SF 94132 667-B6

E 20TH AV
- \- SMTO 94402 749-B4
- \- SMTO 94403 749-B4

W 20TH AV
- \- SMTO 94402 749-A4
- \- SMTO 94403 749-A4

20TH ST
- \- RCH 94801 588-H5
- 200 OAK 94612 649-G3
- 400 SF 94107 668-B2
- 800 OAK 94607 649-E2
- 1100 SPAB 94806 588-H1
- 2400 SF 94110 668-A2
- 2900 SF 94110 667-J3
- 3800 SF 94114 667-J3
- 3900 SF 94114 667-H3

E 20TH ST
- 500 OAK 94606 649-J4
- 600 OAK 94606 650-A5
- 2300 OAK 94601 650-B6

N 20TH ST
- \- SJS 95116 834-D5
- 100 SJS 95112 834-D3

S 20TH ST
- \- SJS 95116 834-D5
- 100 RCH 94804 588-H7
- 300 RCH 94804 608-H1

W 20TH ST
- \- ANT 94509 575-D5

21ST AV
- \- SF 94121 647-B6
- \- SMTO 94403 749-B4
- 1200 OAK 94606 650-B6
- 1200 SF 94122 667-B4
- 1900 SF 94116 667-B4
- 2100 SF 94116 667-B5
- 2900 SF 94132 667-B6

21ST ST
- 100 RCH 94801 588-H6
- 200 OAK 94612 649-G3
- 800 OAK 94607 649-E2
- 1300 OAK 94626 649-D1
- 1300 SPAB 94806 588-H2
- 2600 SF 94110 668-A3
- 2800 SF 94110 667-H3
- 3500 SF 94114 667-F3

E 21ST ST
- 400 OAK 94606 650-A5
- 2100 OAK 94601 650-B6

N 21ST ST
- \- SJS 95116 834-D4
- 300 SJS 95112 834-C3

S 21ST ST
- \- SJS 95116 834-E5
- 100 RCH 94804 588-H7
- 300 RCH 94804 608-H1

22ND AV
- \- SF 94121 647-B6
- 900 OAK 94606 650-C5
- 1200 SF 94122 667-B3
- 1900 SF 94116 667-B3
- 2100 SF 94116 667-B5
- 2900 SF 94132 667-B5
- 2900 OAK 94602 650-C5

22ND RD
- \- SMTO 94403 749-A4

22ND ST
- 100 RCH 94801 588-H6
- 300 OAK 94612 649-G3
- 500 SF 94107 668-C3
- 800 OAK 94607 649-F2
- 1800 SPAB 94806 588-H2
- 2300 SF 94110 668-A3
- 2800 SF 94110 667-G3
- 3500 SF 94114 667-G3

E 22ND ST
- 500 OAK 94606 650-A4
- 2300 OAK 94601 650-C7

N 22ND ST
- 500 SJS 95112 834-D3

S 22ND ST
- \- SJS 95116 834-E5
- 100 RCH 94804 588-H7
- 200 RCH 94804 608-H1

23RD AV
- \- SMTO 94403 749-A4
- 100 SF 94121 647-B6
- 300 OAK 94606 670-B1
- 300 OAK 94601 670-B1
- 1100 OAK 94601 650-B6
- 1100 OAK 94606 650-B6
- 1200 SF 94122 667-B4
- 1900 SF 94116 667-B4
- 2400 SF 94116 667-B5
- 2700 OAK 94602 650-B6
- 2900 SF 94132 667-B6

23RD ST
- 100 RCH 94804 588-H3
- 100 RCH 94801 588-H6
- 200 OAK 94612 649-F2
- 400 SF 94107 668-C3
- 1100 SPAB 94806 588-H3
- 1100 RCH 94806 588-H3
- 2300 SF 94110 668-A3
- 2900 SF 94110 667-J3
- 3700 SF 94114 667-G3

E 23RD ST
- 600 OAK 94606 650-A5
- 2300 OAK 94601 650-C6

N 23RD ST
- 700 SJS 95112 834-C3

S 23RD ST
- \- SJS 95116 834-E5
- 100 RCH 94804 588-H7
- 400 RCH 94804 608-H1

23RD AV OVPS
- 1100 OAK 94606 650-B7
- 1100 OAK 94601 650-B7

24TH AV
- \- SF 94121 647-B6
- \- SMTO 94403 749-A5
- 1200 SF 94122 667-B3
- 1400 OAK 94601 650-B6
- 1900 SF 94116 667-B3
- 2100 SF 94116 667-B5
- 2900 SF 94132 667-B6

24TH ST
- 100 RCH 94804 588-H5
- 200 OAK 94612 649-G2
- 500 SF 94107 668-C3
- 800 OAK 94607 649-E1
- 1300 RCH 94806 588-H4
- 1600 SPAB 94806 588-H4
- 2400 SF 94110 668-A3
- 2900 SF 94110 667-J3
- 3700 SF 94114 667-F4

E 24TH ST
- 700 OAK 94606 650-A4
- 2200 OAK 94601 650-B5

N 24TH ST
- \- SJS 95116 834-D4

S 24TH ST
- \- SJS 95116 834-E5
- 200 RCH 94804 588-H7
- 300 RCH 94804 608-H1

25TH AV
- \- SF 94121 647-A5
- 1000 OAK 94601 650-C5
- 1100 SF - 667-B3
- 1200 SF 94122 667-B3
- 2100 SF 94116 667-B3
- 2100 SF 94116 667-B5
- 2800 OAK 94602 650-C5
- 2900 SF 94132 667-B6

E 25TH AV
- \- SMTO 94403 749-B4

W 25TH AV
- \- SMTO 94403 749-B5

25TH ST
- 100 RCH 94804 588-H6
- 400 OAK 94612 649-G2
- 700 SF 94107 668-B3
- 1300 RCH 94806 588-H4
- 1600 SPAB 94806 588-H4
- 2500 SF 94110 668-A4
- 2900 SF 94110 667-J4
- 3800 SF 94114 667-G4

E 25TH ST
- 1300 OAK 94606 650-B5
- 2600 OAK 94601 650-B5

N 25TH ST
- \- SJS 95116 834-E4

S 25TH ST
- 200 RCH 94804 588-H7
- 200 RCH 94804 608-H1

26TH AV
- \- SF 94121 647-A6
- 200 SMTO 94403 749-A5
- 700 SMTO 94403 748-J5
- 900 OAK 94601 650-C6
- 1200 SF 94122 667-A3
- 2100 SF 94116 667-A3
- 2100 SF 94116 667-B6
- 2900 SF 94132 667-B6

26TH PL
- \- SMTO 94403 749-B5

26TH ST
- 200 RCH 94804 588-H5
- 200 OAK 94612 649-F2
- 700 SF 94107 668-B4
- 900 OAK 94607 649-E1
- 1300 RCH 94806 588-H4
- 1600 SPAB 94806 588-H4
- 2800 SF 94110 668-A4
- 3000 SF 94110 667-G4
- 3800 SF 94131 667-G4

E 26TH ST
- 1300 OAK 94606 650-B5
- 2300 OAK 94601 650-C6

BAY AREA INDEX

BAY AREA

Block	City	ZIP	Pg-Grid
N 26TH ST			
-	SJS	95116	834-E4
S 26TH ST			
-	SJS	95116	834-E5
300	RCH	94804	588-H7
300	RCH	94804	608-H1
27TH AV			
-	SF	94121	647-A6
-	SMTO	94403	749-B5
800	OAK	94601	650-B7
800	OAK	94601	670-B1
1200	SF	94122	667-A3
2100	SF	94116	667-A3
2100	SF	94116	667-A5
27TH ST			
-	SF	94110	667-G4
200	OAK	94612	649-F2
200	SF	94131	667-G4
300	RCH	94804	588-J6
800	OAK	94607	649-F2
1500	RCH	94806	588-J4
E 27TH ST			
1300	OAK	94606	650-B5
2300	OAK	94601	650-D6
N 27TH ST			
-	SJS	95116	834-E4
S 27TH ST			
100	RCH	94804	588-H7
300	RCH	94804	608-H1
28TH AV			
-	SMTO	94403	749-B5
100	SF	94121	647-A6
1200	SF	94122	667-A3
1400	OAK	94601	650-B7
1900	SF	94116	667-A3
2100	SF	94116	667-A5
28TH ST			
-	SF	94110	667-G4
100	SF	94131	667-G4
200	OAK	94612	649-G2
200	RCH	94804	588-J5
200	OAK	94611	649-H2
300	OAK	94609	649-G2
800	OAK	94608	649-E1
800	OAK	94607	649-E1
E 28TH ST			
800	OAK	94610	650-B4
900	OAK	94606	650-B5
2400	OAK	94602	650-C5
2400	OAK	94601	650-C5
N 28TH ST			
-	SJS	95116	834-E4
S 28TH ST			
-	SJS	95116	834-E5
300	RCH	94804	588-H7
300	RCH	94804	608-H1
29TH AV			
-	SMTO	94403	749-B5
100	SF	94121	647-A6
400	OAK	94601	670-B1
400	OAK	94606	670-B1
1000	OAK	94601	650-B7
1200	SF	94122	667-A3
1900	SF	94116	667-A3
2100	SF	94116	667-A5
29TH ST			
-	RCH	94804	588-J5
-	SF	94110	667-G5
200	OAK	94611	649-G2
200	SF	94131	667-G5
300	OAK	94609	649-G2
800	OAK	94608	649-G2
E 29TH ST			
1900	OAK	94606	650-B5
2500	OAK	94601	650-C5
2500	OAK	94602	650-C5
S 29TH ST			
100	RCH	94804	588-J7
200	RCH	94804	608-J1
30TH AV			
-	SMTO	94403	749-B5
100	SF	94121	647-A6
900	SF	-	647-A7
900	SF	-	667-A3
1200	OAK	94601	650-B7
1200	SF	94122	667-A3
1900	SF	94116	667-A3
2100	SF	94116	667-A5
30TH ST			
-	SF	94110	667-G5
200	OAK	94611	649-H2
200	SF	94131	667-G5
300	RCH	94804	588-J6
300	OAK	94609	649-H2
800	OAK	94608	649-F1
E 30TH ST			
1900	OAK	94606	650-B5
2300	OAK	94602	650-B5
N 30TH ST			
-	SJS	95116	834-E4
S 30TH ST			
-	SJS	95116	834-E5
500	RCH	94804	608-J1
31ST AV			
-	SMTO	94403	749-A6
200	SF	94121	647-A6
900	SMTO	94403	748-J6
1200	OAK	94601	670-C1
1200	SF	94122	667-A3
1300	OAK	94601	650-C7
1900	SF	94116	667-A3
2100	SF	94116	667-A5
31ST ST			
300	RCH	94804	588-J6
500	OAK	94609	649-G1
800	OAK	94608	649-F1
E 31ST ST			
1300	OAK	94606	650-B4
1300	OAK	94602	650-B4
N 31ST ST			
-	SJS	95116	834-E4
S 31ST ST			
-	SJS	95116	834-F4
100	RCH	94804	588-J7
100	RCH	94804	608-J1
32ND AV			
-	SF	94121	647-A7
1200	SF	94122	667-A3
1900	SF	94116	667-A3
2100	SF	94116	667-A5
32ND ST			
300	RCH	94804	588-J5
600	OAK	94609	649-G1
800	OAK	94608	649-F1
1600	OAK	94607	649-E1
E 32ND ST			
1300	OAK	94602	650-B4
N 32ND ST			
-	SJS	95116	834-E4
S 32ND ST			
600	RCH	94804	608-J1
33RD AV			
400	SF	94121	647-A7
800	OAK	94601	670-C1
1200	SF	94122	667-A4
1400	OAK	94601	650-C7
1900	SF	94116	667-A4
2100	SF	94116	667-A5
33RD ST			
100	RCH	94804	588-J6
200	RCH	94805	588-J6
500	OAK	94609	649-G1
800	OAK	94608	649-G1
E 33RD ST			
1000	OAK	94610	650-B4
1300	OAK	94602	650-B4
N 33RD ST			
-	SJS	95116	834-E3
200	SJS	95133	834-E3
S 33RD ST			
-	RCH	94804	588-J7
-	SJS	95116	834-F4
500	RCH	94804	608-J1
34TH AV			
400	SF	94121	646-J7
700	OAK	94601	670-C1
1200	SF	94122	666-J2
1400	OAK	94601	650-C7
1600	SF	94122	667-A4
1900	SF	94116	667-A4
2100	SF	94116	667-A5
2800	SF	94132	667-A5
34TH ST			
300	OAK	94609	649-G1
300	OAK	94611	649-G1
300	RCH	94805	588-J5
800	OAK	94608	649-F1
1000	RCH	94804	588-J5
E 34TH ST			
1000	OAK	94610	650-B4
1300	OAK	94602	650-B4
N 34TH ST			
-	SJS	95116	834-E3
S 34TH ST			
-	SJS	95116	834-F4
300	RCH	94804	608-J1
35TH AV			
400	SF	94121	646-J7
800	OAK	94601	670-C1
1200	SF	94122	666-J3
1500	OAK	94601	650-C7
1900	SF	94116	666-J3
2100	SF	94116	666-J5
2500	OAK	94619	650-E6
2600	OAK	94602	650-E6
2800	SF	94132	666-J5
35TH ST			
100	RCH	94805	588-J6
600	OAK	94609	649-F1
700	RCH	94805	589-A5
800	OAK	94608	649-F1
S 35TH ST			
100	RCH	94804	588-J7
400	RCH	94804	608-J1
36TH AV			
-	SMTO	94403	749-B6
400	SF	94121	646-J7
700	OAK	94601	670-C1
800	SF	-	666-J1
1200	SF	94122	666-J3
1400	OAK	94601	650-C7
1900	SF	94116	666-J3
2500	SF	94116	666-J5
2800	SF	94132	666-J5
36TH ST			
300	RCH	94805	588-J7
400	OAK	94609	649-H1
600	RCH	94805	589-A5
800	OAK	94608	649-F1
1000	RCH	94804	589-A5
1100	OAK	94608	629-F7
2600	OAK	94612	649-F1
E 36TH ST			
1300	OAK	94602	650-B4
S 36TH ST			
300	RCH	94804	588-J7
300	RCH	94804	608-J1
37TH AV			
-	SMTO	94403	749-B6
400	SF	94121	646-J7
600	OAK	94601	670-C1
800	SF	94121	666-J3
1200	SF	94122	666-J3
1600	OAK	94601	650-D7
1900	SF	94116	666-J3
2100	SF	94116	666-J5
2800	SF	94132	666-J5
37TH ST			
-	RCH	94805	588-J7
400	OAK	94609	649-G1
400	RCH	94805	589-A5
800	OAK	94608	649-G1
900	OAK	94608	629-F7
1000	EMVL	94608	629-F7
1000	RCH	94804	588-J7
S 37TH ST			
-	RCH	94804	588-J7
-	RCH	94804	608-J1
38TH AV			
400	SF	94121	646-J7
400	SMTO	94403	749-B7
800	SF	94121	666-J3
900	OAK	94601	670-C1
1200	SF	94122	666-J3
1400	OAK	94601	650-D7
2200	SF	94116	666-J5
2600	OAK	94619	650-E6
E 38TH AV			
-	SMTO	94403	749-D6
W 38TH AV			
-	SMTO	94403	749-C6
38TH ST			
200	OAK	94611	649-H1
300	OAK	94609	649-H1
300	RCH	94805	589-A5
E 38TH ST			
1300	OAK	94602	650-C4
S 38TH ST			
300	RCH	94804	589-A7
300	RCH	94804	609-A1
39TH AV			
400	SF	94121	646-J7
800	SF	94121	666-J2
900	OAK	94601	670-C1
1200	SF	94122	666-J2
1800	OAK	94601	650-D7
2100	SF	94116	666-J2
2100	SF	94116	666-J5
2600	OAK	94619	650-E6
2800	SF	94132	666-J5
E 39TH AV			
-	SMTO	94403	749-D6
W 39TH AV			
-	SMTO	94403	749-C6
39TH ST			
300	RCH	94805	589-A7
600	OAK	94609	629-G7
800	OAK	94608	629-F7
900	EMVL	94608	629-F7
S 39TH ST			
100	RCH	94804	589-A7
400	RCH	94804	609-A1
40TH AV			
400	SF	94121	646-J7
800	SF	94121	666-J3
900	OAK	94601	670-C1
1200	SF	94122	666-J3
1700	OAK	94601	650-D7
2100	SF	94116	666-J3
2100	SF	94116	666-J5
E 40TH AV			
-	SMTO	94403	749-D6
W 40TH AV			
-	SMTO	94403	749-C7
40TH ST			
100	OAK	94611	649-J1
300	OAK	94609	629-H7
300	OAK	94611	629-H7
300	RCH	94805	589-A7
800	OAK	94608	629-F7
1000	EMVL	94608	629-E7
S 40TH ST			
-	RCH	94804	609-A1
40TH WY			
100	OAK	94611	649-J1
41ST AV			
400	SF	94121	646-J7
800	SF	94121	666-J3
1000	OAK	94601	670-D1
1200	SF	94122	666-J3
1900	SF	94116	666-J3
2000	OAK	94601	650-D7
2100	SF	94116	666-J5
2700	SF	94132	666-J5
W 41ST AV			
-	SMTO	94403	749-C7
E 41ST PL			
-	SMTO	94403	749-D6
41ST ST			
-	OAK	94611	649-J1
100	OAK	94611	629-H7
300	OAK	94609	629-H7
300	RCH	94805	589-A7
800	OAK	94608	629-G7
1000	EMVL	94608	629-F7
S 41ST ST			
300	RCH	94804	589-A7
400	RCH	94804	609-A1
42ND AV			
-	SMTO	94403	749-B7
400	SF	94121	646-H7
800	SF	94121	666-J3
900	OAK	94601	670-D1
1200	SF	94122	666-J3
1900	SF	94116	666-J3
2000	OAK	94601	650-E7
2100	SF	94116	666-J5
42ND AV Rt# 77			
800	OAK	94601	670-C1
42ND ST			
300	OAK	94609	629-H7
300	OAK	94611	629-H7
300	RCH	94805	589-A7
800	OAK	94608	629-G7
1000	EMVL	94608	629-G7
S 42ND ST			
100	RCH	94804	589-A7
100	RCH	94804	609-A1
43RD AV			
-	SMTO	94403	749-C7
400	SF	94121	646-H7
800	SF	94121	666-H3
1200	SF	94122	666-H3
1900	SF	94116	666-H3
2100	SF	94116	666-H5
43RD ST			
300	OAK	94609	629-H7
300	RCH	94805	589-A7
800	OAK	94608	629-G7
1000	EMVL	94608	629-F7
S 43RD ST			
200	RCH	94804	589-A7
200	RCH	94804	609-A2
44TH AV			
100	SMTO	94403	749-D7
400	SF	94121	646-H7
800	SF	94121	666-H2
1000	OAK	94601	670-D1
1200	SF	94122	666-H2
1900	SF	94116	666-H2
2100	SF	94116	666-H5
44TH ST			
300	OAK	94609	629-H7
300	RCH	94805	589-A7
800	OAK	94608	629-G7
1000	EMVL	94608	629-G7
S 44TH ST			
200	RCH	94804	589-A7
200	RCH	94804	609-A1
45TH AV			
400	SF	94121	646-H7
700	OAK	94601	670-E1
800	SF	94121	666-H3
1200	SF	94122	666-H3
1900	SF	94116	666-H3
2100	SF	94116	666-H5
45TH ST			
300	OAK	94609	629-H7
300	OAK	94611	629-H7
300	RCH	94805	589-A7
800	OAK	94608	629-G6
900	EMVL	94608	629-F6
S 45TH ST			
-	RCH	94804	589-A7
100	RCH	94804	609-A1
46TH AV			
400	SF	94121	646-H7
700	OAK	94601	670-D1
800	SF	94121	666-H3
1200	SF	94122	666-H3
1900	SF	94116	666-H3
2100	SF	94116	666-H5
46TH ST			
400	RCH	94805	589-A7
500	OAK	94609	629-H7
800	OAK	94608	629-G6
900	EMVL	94608	629-G6
S 46TH ST			
-	RCH	94804	608-J3
-	RCH	94804	589-A7
-	RCH	94804	609-A2
47TH AV			
400	SF	94121	646-H7
800	OAK	94601	670-E1
800	SF	94121	666-H1
900	SF	-	666-H1
1200	SF	94122	666-H3
1900	SF	94116	666-H3
2100	SF	94116	666-H5
2200	OAK	94601	650-E7
47TH ST			
500	OAK	94609	629-H7
600	OAK	94608	629-G6
1000	EMVL	94608	629-F6
S 47TH ST			
-	RCH	94804	589-A7
-	RCH	94804	609-A1
48TH AV			
400	SF	94121	646-H7
800	SF	94121	666-H3
1200	OAK	94601	670-D2
1200	SF	94122	666-H3
1900	SF	94116	666-H3
2100	SF	94116	666-H5
48TH ST			
400	OAK	94609	629-H6
1000	EMVL	94608	629-F6
1000	OAK	94608	629-F6
49TH AV			
800	OAK	94601	670-D2
49TH ST			
300	OAK	94611	629-H6
300	OAK	94618	629-H6
300	OAK	94609	629-H6
S 49TH ST			
300	RCH	94804	609-B1
50TH AV			
600	OAK	94601	670-D2
50TH ST			
300	OAK	94609	629-H6
S 50TH ST			
300	RCH	94804	609-B1
51ST AV			
800	OAK	94601	670-E1
51ST ST			
300	OAK	94611	629-H6
300	OAK	94618	629-H6
300	OAK	94609	629-H6
800	OAK	94608	629-G6
S 51ST ST			
1300	RCH	94804	609-A3
52ND AV			
800	OAK	94601	670-E2
52ND ST			
500	OAK	94609	629-H6
800	OAK	94608	629-G6
S 52ND ST			
600	RCH	94804	609-B1
53RD AV			
800	OAK	94601	670-D2
53RD ST			
500	OAK	94609	629-H6
800	OAK	94608	629-F6
800	EMVL	94608	629-E6
S 53RD ST			
800	ELCR	94530	609-B2
54TH AV			
800	OAK	94601	670-E2
54TH ST			
500	OAK	94609	629-G6
800	OAK	94608	629-F6
1200	EMVL	94608	629-E6
S 54TH ST			
1200	RCH	94804	609-B2
55TH AV			
1400	OAK	94601	670-E2
1400	OAK	94621	670-F1
2200	OAK	94619	670-F1
2200	OAK	94605	670-F1
55TH ST			
400	OAK	94609	629-G6
800	OAK	94608	629-F6
1200	EMVL	94608	629-E6
S 55TH ST			
800	ELCR	94530	609-B2
1000	RCH	94804	609-B2
56TH AV			
1400	OAK	94621	670-E2
2600	OAK	94605	670-F1
56TH ST			
500	OAK	94609	629-G6
800	OAK	94608	629-F6
S 56TH ST			
1000	RCH	94804	609-B2
1400	ELCR	94530	609-B2
57TH AV			
1100	OAK	94605	670-F1
1100	OAK	94621	670-E2
57TH ST			
400	OAK	94609	629-H5
800	OAK	94608	629-F6
S 57TH ST			
1000	RCH	94804	609-B2
58TH AV			
1100	OAK	94621	670-E3
2900	OAK	94605	670-G1
58TH ST			
400	OAK	94609	629-G5
800	OAK	94608	629-G5
S 58TH ST			
1200	RCH	94804	609-C2
59TH ST			
400	OAK	94609	629-H5
800	OAK	94608	629-F5
1400	EMVL	94608	629-E6
S 59TH ST			
1200	RCH	94804	609-C3
60TH AV			
1100	OAK	94621	670-E3
2400	OAK	94605	670-G1
60TH ST			
300	OAK	94618	629-H5
400	OAK	94609	629-H5
800	OAK	94608	629-F5
61ST AV			
1100	OAK	94621	670-F2
2400	OAK	94605	670-G1
61ST ST			
300	OAK	94618	629-H5
300	OAK	94609	629-G5
800	OAK	94608	629-F5
1200	EMVL	94608	629-E5
62ND AV			
1100	OAK	94621	670-E3
2200	OAK	94605	670-G1
62ND ST			
300	OAK	94618	629-J5
400	OAK	94609	629-G5
900	BERK	94703	629-G5
900	OAK	94608	629-F5
1300	EMVL	94608	629-E5
63RD AV			
1300	OAK	94621	670-F3
2300	OAK	94605	670-G1
63RD ST			
300	OAK	94618	629-J4
400	OAK	94609	629-H5
1500	BERK	94703	629-G5
1500	EMVL	94608	629-E5
1600	OAK	94608	629-F5
64TH AV			
1100	OAK	94621	670-F2
2200	OAK	94605	670-H1
64TH ST			
1100	OAK	94608	629-E5
1200	EMVL	94608	629-D5
64TH AV PL			
3300	OAK	94605	670-H1
65TH AV			
1100	OAK	94621	670-F2
2200	OAK	94605	670-H1
65TH ST			
400	OAK	94609	629-H4
1000	EMVL	94608	629-D5
1200	OAK	94608	629-G4
1200	BERK	94702	629-G4
1200	BERK	94703	629-G4
66TH AV			
500	OAK	94621	670-F3
2200	OAK	94605	670-H1
66TH ST			
400	OAK	94609	629-H4
1200	EMVL	94608	629-E5
1300	OAK	94608	629-F4
1300	BERK	94702	629-F4
67TH AV			
1400	OAK	94605	670-G2
1400	OAK	94621	670-F3
67TH ST			
1200	EMVL	94608	629-E5
1200	OAK	94608	629-F4
1300	BERK	94702	629-F4
68TH AV			
1400	OAK	94621	670-G3
2400	OAK	94605	670-H2
69TH AV			
800	OAK	94605	670-H2
800	OAK	94621	670-G3
70TH AV			
800	OAK	94621	670-F3
71ST AV			
700	OAK	94621	670-G3
72ND AV			
900	OAK	94621	670-G3
3300	OAK	94605	670-H2
73RD AV			
-	OAK	94605	670-J2
-	OAK	94621	670-G3
74TH AV			
1400	OAK	94621	670-G3
2500	OAK	94605	670-H2
75TH AV			
800	OAK	94621	670-F4
2400	OAK	94605	670-H2
76TH AV			
700	OAK	94621	670-G3
2400	OAK	94605	670-H2
77TH AV			
700	OAK	94621	670-G3
2300	OAK	94605	670-J2
78TH AV			
1100	OAK	94621	670-G3
1700	OAK	94605	670-J2
79TH AV			
1100	OAK	94621	670-G3
1800	OAK	94605	670-J3
80TH AV			
1000	OAK	94621	670-H3
2000	OAK	94605	670-H3
81ST AV			
800	OAK	94621	670-H3
2000	OAK	94605	670-J3
82ND AV			
1000	OAK	94621	670-H3
1700	OAK	94605	670-H3
2600	OAK	94605	671-A3
83RD AV			
1000	OAK	94621	670-G4
1700	OAK	94605	670-J3
84TH AV			
900	OAK	94621	670-G4
1700	OAK	94605	670-J3
85TH AV			
500	OAK	94621	670-G4
1700	OAK	94605	670-J3
86TH AV			
800	OAK	94621	670-H4
1700	OAK	94605	670-J3
87TH AV			
900	OAK	94621	670-H4
1700	OAK	94605	670-J4
87TH ST			
-	DALY	94015	687-A4
-	SMCo	94015	687-A4
1000	DALY	94015	686-J4
88TH AV			
900	OAK	94621	670-J4
1800	OAK	94605	670-J4
2200	OAK	94605	671-A4
88TH ST			
-	DALY	94015	687-B4
100	SMCo	94015	687-B4
89TH AV			
900	OAK	94621	670-H4
900	OAK	94603	670-G5
1800	OAK	94605	670-J4
2400	OAK	94605	671-A4
89TH ST			
-	DALY	94015	687-B5
400	SMCo	94015	687-B5
90TH AV			
900	OAK	94603	670-G5
900	OAK	94621	670-H4
900	OAK	94605	670-J4
2400	OAK	94603	671-A4
2400	OAK	94605	671-A4
90TH ST			
-	DALY	94015	687-B5
400	SMCo	94015	687-B5
91ST AV			
900	OAK	94603	670-G5
91ST ST			
-	DALY	94015	687-B5
92ND AV			
800	OAK	94603	670-J4
92ND ST			
100	DALY	94015	687-B5
100	SMCo	94015	687-B5
93RD AV			
1200	OAK	94603	670-H5
94TH AV			
900	OAK	94603	670-H5
95TH AV			
1200	OAK	94603	670-H5
96TH AV			
1200	OAK	94603	670-H5
1400	OAK	94603	671-A4
2400	OAK	94605	671-A4
97TH AV			
1200	OAK	94603	670-H5
98TH AV			
-	OAK	94603	670-H6
200	OAK	94603	671-A5
2200	OAK	94603	690-E1
2200	OAK	94621	690-E1
2500	OAK	94605	671-A5
99TH AV			
1200	OAK	94603	670-J5
1700	OAK	94603	671-A5
2500	OAK	94605	671-B5
99TH AV CT			
9900	OAK	94603	670-J5
100TH AV			
700	OAK	94603	670-J5
1300	OAK	94603	671-A5
101ST AV			
1400	OAK	94603	670-J5
1400	OAK	94603	671-A5
102ND AV			
1200	OAK	94603	670-H6
1200	OAK	94603	671-A5
103RD AV			
1600	OAK	94603	670-H6
1600	OAK	94603	671-A5
104TH AV			
1300	OAK	94603	670-H6
1300	OAK	94603	671-A6
105TH AV			
400	OAK	94603	670-H6
400	OAK	94603	671-A6
10000	OAK	94603	690-G1
106TH AV			
200	OAK	94603	671-A6
900	OAK	94603	670-J6
2600	OAK	94605	671-B5
107TH AV			
700	OAK	94603	670-H7
1800	OAK	94603	671-A6
2900	OAK	94605	671-B5
108TH AV			
1800	OAK	94603	671-A6
2600	OAK	94605	671-A6
109TH AV			
1800	OAK	94603	671-A6
2600	OAK	94605	671-B6
W AVENUE 130TH			
2500	SLN	94577	690-G4
W AVENUE 133RD			
2000	SLN	94577	690-H4
W AVENUE 134TH			
2000	SLN	94577	690-H4
W AVENUE 135TH			
2000	SLN	94577	690-H4
135TH AV			
1200	SLN	94577	691-B2
1200	SLN	94578	691-B2
W AVENUE 136TH			
2000	SLN	94577	690-H4
136TH AV			
1100	SLN	94578	691-B3
1500	SLN	94577	691-C2
137TH AV			
-	SLN	94577	691-B3
1500	SLN	94578	691-C2
138TH AV			
1400	SLN	94578	691-C2
139TH AV			
800	SLN	94578	691-C2
W AVENUE 140TH			
1900	SLN	94577	690-J4
140TH AV			
1400	SLN	94578	691-C2
141ST AV			
1200	SLN	94578	691-C2
142ND AV			
1400	SLN	94578	691-C3
143RD AV			
900	SLN	94578	691-C2
144TH AV			
1200	SLN	94578	691-C3
145TH AV			
1200	SLN	94578	691-C3
146TH AV			
1400	SLN	94578	691-D3
147TH AV			
1100	SLN	94578	691-C4
148TH AV			
1200	SLN	94578	691-D3
149TH AV			
2000	AlaC	94578	691-E3
150TH AV			
1400	SLN	94578	691-D4
1400	AlaC	94578	691-E3
151ST AV			
1400	AlaC	94578	691-D4
152ND AV			
1400	AlaC	94578	691-D4
153RD AV			
1400	AlaC	94578	691-D4
155TH AV			
1400	AlaC	94578	691-E4
156TH AV			
1400	AlaC	94578	691-E4
159TH AV			
1300	AlaC	94580	691-E5
1300	AlaC	94578	691-E4
160TH AV			
1400	AlaC	94578	691-E5
162ND AV			
1400	AlaC	94578	691-E5
163RD AV			
1400	AlaC	94578	691-F5
164TH AV			
1400	AlaC	94578	691-F5
165TH AV			
1400	AlaC	94578	691-F5
166TH AV			
1400	AlaC	94578	691-F5
167TH AV			
1300	AlaC	94578	691-F5
168TH AV			
1400	AlaC	94578	691-F6
170TH AV			
1200	AlaC	94578	691-G5
1200	AlaC	94541	691-G5
1900	AlaC	94546	691-G5
171ST AV			
1400	AlaC	94541	691-G6
172ND AV			
1400	AlaC	94541	691-G6
173RD AV			
1400	AlaC	94541	691-G6
1900	AlaC	94546	691-G5
174TH AV			
2100	AlaC	94546	691-G5
I 80 FRWY			
-	NaCo	-	510-E4
-	OAK	-	649-C1
-	SF	-	648-B7
-	SF	-	648-E4
-	SF	-	668-A1
-	SolC	-	550-D3
-	SolC	-	510-E4
-	SolC	-	530-C6
-	VAL	-	550-C2
-	VAL	-	510-E4
-	VAL	-	530-D1
I 80 EASTSHORE FRWY			
-	ALB	-	609-C5
-	ALB	-	609-C5
-	BERK	-	609-C5
-	BERK	-	629-D3
-	CCCo	-	549-J7
-	CCCo	-	550-B6
-	CCCo	-	569-H2
-	CCCo	-	589-A3
-	ELCR	-	609-C5
-	EMVL	-	629-D3
-	EMVL	-	629-D7
-	HER	-	569-H2
-	OAK	-	629-D7
-	OAK	-	629-D7
-	OAK	-	649-D1
-	OAK	-	649-D1
-	OAK	-	649-D1
-	OAK	-	649-D1
-	PIN	-	569-B7
-	RCH	-	569-B7
-	RCH	-	589-A3
-	RCH	-	609-C5
-	SPAB	-	589-A3
I 238 FRWY			
-	AlaC	-	691-E6
-	AlaC	-	691-E6
-	AlaC	-	691-E6
-	SLN	-	691-E6
-	SLN	-	691-E6
I 280 FRWY			
-	DALY	-	687-C2
-	DALY	-	707-C1
-	SF	-	687-D2
-	SF	-	687-E1
I 280 JOHN F FORAN FRWY			
-	DALY	-	687-C2
-	DALY	-	687-C4
-	SF	-	667-E7
-	SF	-	668-A6
-	SF	-	668-B1
-	SF	-	687-D2
-	SF	-	687-E1
I 280 J SERRA FRWY			
-	DALY	-	687-C7
-	DALY	-	687-C7
-	DALY	-	707-C2
-	HIL	-	748-D4
-	HIL	-	748-D4
-	LAH	-	810-F3
-	LAH	-	811-A7
-	LAH	-	831-G5
-	LALT	-	831-G5
-	MLBR	-	727-G3
-	MLBR	-	728-A7
-	MLPK	-	810-C1
-	PA	-	810-F3
-	SBRN	-	707-C2
-	SBRN	-	727-G3

INDEX

STREET
Block City ZIP Pg-Grid

I 280 J SERRA FRWY
- SCL - 832-C6
- SCL - 852-H1
- SCIC - 810-F3
- SCIC - 831-G5
- SCIC - 832-C6
- SJS - 852-H1
- SJS - 853-A1
- SMCo - 727-G3
- SMCo - 727-G3
- SMCo - 728-A7
- SMCo - 748-D4
- SMCo - 748-D4
- SMCo - 748-D4
- SMCo - 768-F1
- SMCo - 768-F1
- SMCo - 768-F1
- SMCo - 769-A4
- SMCo - 789-D1
- SMCo - 789-D1
- SMCo - 790-A6
- SMCo - 810-C1
- SSF - 707-C2
- SUNV - 832-C6
- WDSD - 789-G4
- WDSD - 790-A6
- CPTO - 832-C6
I 280 SINCLAIR FRWY
- SCIC - 853-G2
- SJS - 834-E7
- SJS - 853-G2
- SJS - 854-A2
I 280 SOUTHERN FRWY
- DALY - 687-C2
- DALY - 687-C4
- SF - 648-C7
- SF - 667-E7
- SF - 668-B1
- SF - 668-B4
- SF - 687-D2
- SF - 687-E1
I 380 FRWY
- SBRN - 707-H6
- SBRN - 708-A6
- SMCo - 708-A6
- SSF - 708-A5
I 580 FRWY
- AlaC - 691-G6
- AlaC - 691-H6
- AlaC - 692-B6
- AlaC - 692-H4
- AlaC - 693-B5
- AlaC - 693-C5
- AlaC - 694-D5
- AlaC - 694-D5
- AlaC - 694-D5
- AlaC - 695-H5
- AlaC - 696-G2
- DBLN - 693-H5
- DBLN - 694-D5
- LVMR - 694-D5
- LVMR - 694-D5
- LVMR - 695-H5
- LVMR - 696-G2
- MrnC - 587-C5
- PLE - 693-C5
- PLE - 693-H5
- PLE - 694-D5
- SRFL - 587-A4
- SRFL - 586-H2
I 580 JOHN T KNOX FRWY
- ALB - 609-B3
- RCH - 588-C7
- RCH - 608-H1
- RCH - 609-B3
I 580 MACARTHUR FRWY
- AlaC - 691-D3
- AlaC - 691-G5
- AlaC - 691-G6
- EMVL - 629-D6
- OAK - 629-D7
- OAK - 629-E7
- OAK - 649-H1
- OAK - 649-H1
- OAK - 649-H1
- OAK - 649-H1
- OAK - 649-H1
- OAK - 650-J7
- OAK - 650-J7
- OAK - 650-J7
- OAK - 650-J7
- OAK - 671-A1
- SLN - 671-A1
- SLN - 671-A1
- SLN - 691-C1
- SLN - 691-C1
600 OAK - 649-H1
6900 OAK - 650-J7
6900 OAK - 670-J1
I 580 RICHMOND-SAN RAFAEL BR
- MrnC - 587-C5
- RCH - 587-H6
- RCH - 588-A6
- SRFL - 587-C5
I 680 FRWY
- AlaC - 714-C5
- AlaC - 714-C5
- AlaC - 714-C5
- AlaC - 714-C5
- AlaC - 714-C5
- AlaC - 734-D2
- AlaC - 734-D2
- AlaC - 753-J3
- AlaC - 754-B2
- BEN - 551-F7
- CCCo - 571-H2
- CCCo - 572-A5
- CCCo - 592-C2
- CCCo - 612-C1
- CCCo - 632-G6
- CNCD - 592-C2
- DBLN - 693-H4
- DNVL - 632-G6
- DNVL - 652-J1
- DNVL - 653-A3
- DNVL - 673-C2
- FRMT - 753-G6
- FRMT - 773-F1
- MRTZ - 551-F7
- MRTZ - 571-H2
- PLE - 693-H4
- PLE - 713-J1
- PLE - 714-C5
- PLE - 714-C5
- PLHL - 592-D6
- PLHL - 612-C1
- SRMN - 653-A3
- SRMN - 673-C2
- SRMN - 693-H4
- SolC - 551-F7
- WLCK - 612-B5
- WLCK - 632-E1
I 680 L E GIBSON FWY
- BEN - 551-E5
I 680 SINCLAIR FRWY
- FRMT - 773-F3
- FRMT - 793-J1
- FRMT - 794-A1
- MPS - 794-A1
- MPS - 814-E6
- SCIC - 814-E6
- SJS - 814-E6
- SJS - 834-F1
I 780 FRWY
- BEN - 550-H2
- BEN - 551-D5
- BEN - 530-F7
- SolC - 530-F7
- VAL - 530-F7
I 880 CYPRESS FRWY
- EMVL - 629-D7
- OAK - 629-E7
- OAK - 649-C3
- OAK - 649-C3
- OAK - 649-C3
- OAK - 649-C3
I 880 NIMITZ FRWY
- AlaC - 691-D6
- AlaC - 711-G5
- AlaC - 711-G5
- FRMT - 732-A2
- FRMT - 752-G5
- FRMT - 772-J1
- FRMT - 773-D4
- FRMT - 793-G2
- HAY - 711-G5
- HAY - 711-G5
- HAY - 711-G5
- HAY - 731-J1
- HAY - 731-J1
- HAY - 732-A2
- HAY - 732-A2
- HAY - 732-A2
- MPS - 793-H4
- MPS - 813-J1
- NWK - 752-G5
- NWK - 772-J1
- NWK - 773-D4
- OAK - 649-H5
- OAK - 649-H5
- OAK - 650-A6
- OAK - 650-A6
- OAK - 670-D3
- OAK - 670-D3
- OAK - 670-D3
- OAK - 690-H2
- SJS - 813-J1
- SJS - 814-A6
- SJS - 833-H5
- SJS - 834-A1
- SJS - 853-F1
- SLN - 690-H2
- SLN - 691-A3
- SLN - 691-A3
- SLN - 691-A4
- UNC - 732-A2
I 980 GROVE SHAFTER FRWY
- OAK - 649-G2
- OAK - 649-G2
- OAK - 649-G2
Rt# G2 LAWRENCE EXWY
- SAR 95070 852-H4
- SCL 95051 832-J6
- SCL 95051 852-H4
100 SUNV 94086 812-J7
300 SJS 95014 852-H4
300 SJS 95129 852-H4
300 SCIC 95014 852-H4
800 SUNV 94087 832-J6
1000 SUNV 94089 812-J3
1800 SAR 95129 852-H4
1900 SUNV 94086 832-J6
2900 SCL 95051 812-J7
Rt# G2 QUITO RD
1900 SJS 95130 852-J7
1900 SAR 95130 852-J7
1900 SAR 95070 852-J7
2200 SAR 95070 872-J1
2200 SJS 95130 872-J1
14900 LGTS 95030 872-H4
15000 MSER 95030 872-H4
15500 SCIC 95030 872-H4
Rt# G3 OREGON EXWY
- PA 94301 791-C6
- PA 94303 791-C6
300 PA 94306 791-C6
Rt# G3 PAGE MILL RD
1800 SCIC 94305 810-J4
1800 PA 94304 810-J4
1900 SCIC 94304 810-J4
2400 LAH 94022 810-J4
Rt# G4 MONTAGUE EXWY
- SJS 95134 813-F5
400 SCL 95054 813-D6
400 SCL 95134 813-F5
600 MPS 95035 813-F5
600 SJS 95131 813-F5
1500 SCIC 95134 813-F5
Rt# G4 SAN TOMAS EXWY
- CMBL 95008 853-C6
- SCL 95051 853-C4
- SCL 95117 833-C6
- SCL 95117 853-C4
- SJS 95008 853-C4
- SJS 95130 853-C4
100 SJS 95117 853-C4
200 SCL 95051 833-C3
200 SCL 95050 833-C6
2900 SCL 95054 813-C7
2900 SCL 95054 833-C3
Rt# G5 FOOTHILL BLVD
8100 CPTO 95014 832-A6
8100 LALT 94024 832-A6
8400 SCIC 94024 832-A6
8700 CPTO 94024 832-A6
Rt# G5 FOOTHILL EXWY
100 LALT 94022 811-C5
100 LALT 94022 831-F1
200 LALT 94024 831-F1
400 SCIC 94024 831-F1
2600 SCIC 94304 810-J3
2600 PA 94304 810-J3
2800 PA 94304 811-C5
2800 SCIC 94304 811-C5
4100 PA 94306 811-C5
4400 LALT 94024 832-A6
7100 CPTO 95014 832-A6
14000 LAH 94022 811-C5
14000 SCIC 94306 811-C5
Rt# G5 JUNIPERO SERRA BLVD
- MLPK 94025 790-F7
- SCIC 94305 790-F7
- SCIC 94304 790-F7
100 SCIC 94304 810-G1
100 SCIC 94305 810-G1
Rt# G6 CENTRAL EXWY
- MTVW 94041 812-B5
- MTVW 94043 812-B5
- MTVW 94086 812-B5
- PA 94306 811-G3
- SCL 94086 812-H7
- SCL 95051 812-H7
- SUNV 94086 812-H7
- SUNV 94086 813-A7
100 MTVW 94043 811-G3
700 SCL 95050 833-D1
700 SCL 95054 833-D1
800 MTVW 94041 811-G3
800 SCL 95054 833-D1
2000 MTVW 94040 811-G3
2400 SCL 95051 833-D1
2700 SCL 95051 813-A7
2700 SCL 95054 813-A7
3000 SUNV 95054 813-A7
Rt# G8 ALMADEN EXWY
3500 SJS 95118 874-D2
3500 SJS 95136 874-D2
4000 SJS 95118 854-C7
4000 SJS 95136 854-C7
5900 SJS 95120 874-D2
6600 SJS 95120 894-F2
8900 SJS 95123 874-D2
Rt# G8 HARRY RD
20400 SCIC 95120 894-J4
20400 SJS 95120 894-J4
Rt# G8 MCKEAN RD
19600 SJS 95120 894-J4
19600 SCIC 95120 894-J4
20000 SCIC 95120 895-A4
22200 SJS 95120 895-D6
23100 SJS 95141 895-D6
Rt# G8 UVAS RD
23200 SJS 95141 895-G7
Rt# G10 BLOSSOM HILL RD
- LGTS 95030 873-C6
- SJS 95123 874-E4
100 SJS 95111 875-A4
200 SJS 95138 875-A4
400 LGTS 95032 873-C6
400 SCIC 95123 874-E4
700 SJS 95123 875-A4
1000 SJS 95193 875-A4
1400 SJS 95124 873-F6
1400 SJS 95124 874-A6
1600 SJS 95118 874-A6
15800 SCIC 95032 873-C6
Rt# J2 N LIVERMORE AV
5100 LVMR 94550 695-G7
5800 LVMR 94550 715-G1
Rt# J2 PORTOLA AV
1000 LVMR 94550 695-F6
Rt# J2 S LIVERMORE AV
- LVMR 94550 715-J2
1400 LVMR 94550 716-A3
1700 AlaC 94550 716-A3
Rt# J2 TESLA RD
4500 AlaC 94550 716-A3
Rt# 1 19TH AV
1100 SF 94132 687-B1
1200 SF 94122 667-B3
1900 SF 94116 667-B3
2100 SF 94116 667-B5
2700 SF 94132 667-B5
Rt# 1 CABRILLO FRWY
- DALY - 687-B7
- DALY - 707-A2
- PCFA - 706-J4
100 PCFA - 707-A2
Rt# 1 CABRILLO HWY
- PCFA 94044 707-A7
- SMCo - 726-F6
100 PCFA 94044 726-H3
100 PCFA 94044 727-A1
Rt# 1 CROSS OVER DR
1000 SF - 667-B1
Rt# 1 JUNIPERO SERRA BLVD
- SF 94132 687-C4
Rt# 1 JUNIPERO SERRA FRWY
- DALY - 687-C3
- SF - 687-C3
Rt# 1 LOMBARD ST
500 SF 94133 647-J3
1000 SF 94109 647-J4
Rt# 1 PRESIDIO BLVD
- SF 94118 647-C7
Rt# 1 SHORELINE HWY
200 MrnC 94941 606-E6
200 MrnC 94965 606-E6
500 MrnC 94965 626-A2
Rt# 4 FRWY
- ANT - 574-H5
- ANT - 575-A5
- CCCo - 572-D5
- CCCo - 573-C3
- CNCD - 572-H4
- CNCD - 573-C3
- PIT - 573-C3
- PIT - 574-B3
Rt# 4 J MUIR PKWY
- CCCo - 570-C3
- CCCo - 571-A4
- CCCo - 572-A6
- HER - 570-C3
- MRTZ - 571-G6
- MRTZ - 572-A6
1500 HER 94547 569-H3
1800 CCCo 94572 569-H3
1800 CCCo 94572 570-C3
Rt# 4 STATE FRWY
- ANT - 575-A5
Rt# 9 BIG BASIN WY
14300 SAR 95070 872-D3
Rt# 9 CONGRESS SPRINGS RD
20900 SAR 95070 872-A3
21900 SCIC 95070 872-A3
Rt# 9 SARATOGA LOS GATOS RD
17900 LGTS 95030 873-A6
17900 MSER 95030 872-G5
17900 MSER 95030 873-A6
18500 SCIC 95030 872-G5
18800 SAR 95070 872-E3
Rt# 13 ASHBY AV
1200 BERK 94702 629-F4
1200 BERK 94804 629-D4
1300 BERK 94703 629-F4
2100 BERK 94705 629-F4
2800 BERK 94705 630-A3
Rt# 13 LANDVALE RD
- OAK 94611 630-B4
300 OAK 94618 630-B4
Rt# 13 TUNNEL RD
- BERK 94705 630-B4
- OAK 94705 630-B4
1800 OAK 94618 630-B4
Rt# 13 WARREN FRWY
- OAK - 630-D6
- OAK - 650-F3
- OAK - 650-F3
- OAK - 650-F3
- OAK - 650-F3
- OAK - 650-F3
- OAK - 650-F3
Rt# 17 FRWY
- CMBL - 853-F3
- CMBL - 873-D2
- LGTS - 873-D3
- LGTS - 893-A1
- SCIC - 873-D2
- SJS - 853-F3
Rt# 24 FRWY
- CCCo - 611-E6
- CCCo - 612-A5
- CCCo - 630-G2
- CCCo - 630-G2
- LFYT - 611-B6
- OAK - 629-H6
- OAK - 629-J5
- OAK - 630-B4
- OAK - 630-B4
- ORIN - 610-H6
- ORIN - 611-B6
- ORIN - 630-G2
- ORIN - 630-G2
- WLCK - 612-B5
Rt# 24 GROVE SHAFTER FRWY
- OAK - 629-G7
- OAK - 629-G7
- OAK - 649-G1
Rt#-29
2700 AMCN 94589 510-A1
2700 VAL 94589 510-A4
Rt#-29 SONOMA BLVD
100 VAL 94590 529-J4
100 VAL 94590 530-A6
100 VAL 94590 550-B1
3600 VAL 94589 529-J4
3600 VAL 94589 530-A1
3900 SolC 94589 530-A1
3900 VAL 94589 510-A7
Rt# 35 SKYLINE BLVD
- DALY 94015 687-A5
- DALY 94015 686-J3
- SF 94132 666-H6
- SF 94132 686-J3
- SMCo - 748-E6
500 SMCo - 727-F1
500 SBRN 94066 727-F1
900 SBRN 94066 707-D5
900 SMCo - 707-D5
1100 DALY 94015 707-B1
1200 PCFA 94044 707-B1
1900 SMCo - 768-F1
2100 SMCo 94015 686-J3
2700 SSF 94080 707-D5
7500 SMCo 94062 768-E5
13800 SMCo 94062 789-A7
14700 SMCo 94062 809-A1
17100 WDSD 94062 809-G7
17300 SMCo 94020 809-G7
17300 WDSD 94020 809-D4
18100 PTLV 94028 809-G7
19300 SMCo 94020 830-A4
19300 PTLV 94028 830-A4
19800 SMCo 94028 830-C7
Rt#-37 MARINE WORLD PKWY
700 SolC 94589 529-H1
700 VAL 94589 529-H1
700 VAL 94590 529-H1
700 SolC 94589 509-J7
700 VAL 94589 509-J7
1400 VAL 94589 510-A6
1600 VAL 94591 510-A6
Rt# 37 SEARS POINT HWY
- MrnC 94945 526-G5
- NVTO 94945 526-G5
- SonC - 526-G5
Rt#-37 SEARS POINT RD
- SolC 94589 509-A7
- SolC 94589 529-B1
- SolC 94590 529-F2
- SolC 94592 529-F2
- VAL 94590 529-F2
- VAL 94592 529-F2
Rt# 61 BROADWAY
900 ALA 94501 670-A3
Rt# 61 CENTRAL AV
700 ALA 94501 669-G1
Rt# 61 DOOLITTLE DR
- ALA 94502 670-B5
7200 OAK 94621 670-B5
7200 OAK 94621 690-F1
9400 SLN 94577 690-F1
10100 OAK 94603 690-F1
Rt# 61 ENCINAL AV
1300 ALA 94501 669-H2
2200 ALA 94501 670-A2
Rt# 61 OTIS DR
- ALA 94502 670-A3
2600 ALA 94501 670-A3
Rt# 77 42ND AV
800 OAK 94601 670-C1
Rt# 82 E EL CAMINO REAL
- SCL 95051 832-G4
100 SUNV 94087 832-E2
100 SUNV 94086 832-G4
800 SCIC 94087 832-G4
1100 SCL 94086 832-G4
Rt# 82 EL CAMINO REAL
- BURL 94010 728-E6
- CLMA 94014 687-C5
- MLBR 94030 728-A2
- MLPK 94025 790-C1
- PA 94301 790-H4
- SCAR 94070 769-F2
- PA 94304 790-H4
100 ATN 94027 790-C1
100 BLMT 94002 749-D7
100 MTVW 94040 811-B1
100 SBRN 94066 727-J1
100 SSF 94080 707-G4
100 MTVW 94041 811-B1
100 SBRN 94066 707-G4
100 SMCo 94063 790-C1
200 DALY 94014 687-C5
200 SCIC 94305 790-H4
200 SMCo 94014 687-C5
200 PA 94305 790-H4
300 SCL 95050 833-A4
400 SCL 95053 833-A4
500 BLMT 94002 769-F2
500 HIL 94010 728-E6
700 CLMA 94014 707-E1
800 RDWC 94062 769-H3
800 RDWC 94062 770-A6
800 RDWC 94063 769-H3
800 RDWC 94063 770-A6
800 SMTO 94402 749-D7
1300 RDWC 94061 770-A6
1300 SMCo 94080 707-E1
1300 SBRN 94066 728-A2
1400 SCIC - 791-A6
1400 PA - 790-H4
1400 PA 94306 791-A6
1500 MLPK 94027 790-C1
1700 MLBR 94030 727-J1
1700 ATN 94025 790-C1
2400 PA 94305 791-A6
2400 SCL 95051 833-A4
2600 RDWC 94061 790-C1
2600 SMCo 94063 770-A6
2700 PA 94304 811-B1
2800 PA 94306 811-B1
3300 SCL 95051 832-J4
4300 LALT 94022 811-B1
Rt# 82 MISSION ST
6300 DALY 94014 687-C4
Rt# 82 MONTEREY HWY
- SJS 95111 854-F5
- SJS 95125 854-D2
200 SCIC 95111 854-F5
700 SJS 95112 854-D2
700 SJS 95110 854-D2
3700 SJS 95136 854-F5
4100 SJS 95136 874-H1
4100 SJS 95111 874-H1
4700 SJS 95136 875-A2
4700 SJS 95111 875-A2
5100 SJS 95123 875-A2
5200 SJS 95193 875-A2
Rt# 82 MONTGOMERY ST
- SJS 95110 834-A7
200 SJS 95110 854-A1
Rt# 82 N EL CAMINO REAL
- SMTO 94401 728-G7
- SMTO 94402 728-G7
100 SMTO 94402 748-H1
100 SMTO 94401 748-H1
800 BURL 94010 728-G7
Rt# 82 S 1ST ST
600 SJS 95110 834-C7
600 SJS 95112 834-C7
Rt# 82 S AUTUMN ST
- SJS 95110 834-A7
- SJS 95113 834-A7
Rt# 82 S EL CAMINO REAL
- BLMT 94002 749-A2
- SMTO 94401 748-J2
- SMTO 94402 748-J2
500 SMTO 94402 749-A2
500 SMTO 94401 749-A2
2000 SMTO 94403 749-A2
Rt# 82 S MARKET ST
300 SJS 95110 834-B7
Rt# 82 S MONTGOMERY ST
- SJS 95110 834-A7
- SJS 95113 834-A7
Rt# 82 SAN JOSE AV
3200 DALY 94014 687-D3
Rt# 82 THE ALAMEDA
700 SCL 95126 833-H5
700 SJS 95126 833-H5
2100 SJS 95126 834-A7
2200 SCL 95050 833-H5
2600 SCL 95053 833-H5
Rt# 82 W EL CAMINO REAL
- MTVW 94040 811-F4
- MTVW 94041 811-F4
100 SUNV 94086 832-C1
100 SUNV 94087 832-C1
100 MTVW 94040 812-A7
100 MTVW 94041 812-A7
300 SCIC 94087 832-C1
900 SUNV 94086 812-A7
1100 SUNV 94087 812-A7
1700 LALT 94022 811-F4
Rt# 82 W SAN CARLOS ST
- SJS 95113 834-A7
- SJS 95110 834-A7
1600 SJS 95126 834-A7
Rt# 82 W SANTA CLARA ST
500 SJS 95113 834-A7
500 SJS 95126 834-A7
Rt# 84 FRWY
- FRMT - 752-B5
- NWK - 752-B5
4400 FRMT - 752-B5
Rt# 84 HWY
- FRMT 94555 751-J6
- LVMR 94550 715-D6
- PLE 94550 715-D6
- PLE 94566 715-D6
Rt# 84 BAYFRONT EXWY
- FRMT 94555 771-D3
- MLPK 94025 770-G6
- MLPK 94025 771-A6
- MLPK 94303 771-D3
Rt# 84 E VALLECITOS RD
800 AlaC 94550 715-E6
800 PLE 94550 715-E6
1200 PLE 94566 715-E6
1300 LVMR 94550 715-E6
11300 AlaC 94586 734-H4
Rt# 84 FREMONT BLVD
36800 FRMT 94536 752-H3
Rt# 84 HOLMES ST
300 LVMR 94550 715-F2
2200 AlaC 94550 715-F5
Rt# 84 LA HONDA RD
300 WDSD 94062 809-F5
400 SMCo 94062 809-F7
1700 SMCo 94020 809-F5
1700 WDSD 94020 809-F5
Rt# 84 LOWE RD
- WDSD 94062 789-G6
Rt# 84 MARSH RD
- MLPK 94025 770-F7
Rt# 84 MOWRY AV
- FRMT 94536 753-C2
- FRMT 94538 753-C2
Rt# 84 NILES CANYON RD
- UNC 94587 733-E5
100 FRMT 94536 733-G5
200 FRMT 94536 753-C1
500 AlaC 94586 733-G5
12000 AlaC 94586 734-A6
Rt# 84 PALOMA RD
11500 AlaC 94586 734-D6
Rt# 84 PERALTA BLVD
1200 FRMT 94536 753-A3
2700 FRMT 94536 752-J3
Rt# 84 THORNTON AV
3900 FRMT 94536 752-H3
Rt# 84 VALLECITOS RD
11000 AlaC 94586 734-F5
Rt# 84 WOODSIDE EXWY
- RDWC - 770-C6
- RDWC - 770-C6
Rt# 84 WOODSIDE RD
300 RDWC 94061 790-B2
300 SMCo 94061 790-B2
1900 RDWC 94061 770-B7
2100 WDSD 94062 790-B2
2100 SMCo 94062 790-B2
2400 WDSD 94062 789-J5
3500 WDSD 94062 809-F1
Rt# 84 1ST ST
1300 LVMR 94550 715-F1
2100 LVMR 94550 695-J6
3600 LVMR 94550 696-A6
Rt# 85 FRWY
- CPTO - 852-C1
- SAR - 852-E5
- SCIC - 852-C2
- SJS - 852-D4
Rt# 85 STEVENS CREEK FRWY
- CPTO - 832-A1
- LALT - 832-A1
- MTVW - 812-A7
- MTVW - 832-A1
- SCIC - 832-A1
- SUNV - 832-A1
Rt# 85 WEST VALLEY FRWY
- CMBL - 873-C2
- CPTO - 832-B6
- CPTO - 852-E4
- LGTS - 873-C2
- SAR - 852-E4
- SAR - 872-H1
- SCIC - 852-E4
- SCIC - 873-C2
- SCIC - 874-C3
- SJS - 852-E4
- SJS - 872-J1
- SJS - 873-C2
- SJS - 874-C3
- SJS - 875-A5
- SUNV - 832-B6
Rt# 87 GUADALUPE FRWY
- SCIC - 854-D6
- SCIC - 874-E1
- SJS - 834-A5
- SJS - 854-C3
- SJS - 874-E1
Rt# 92 FRWY
- HAY - 711-H4
- HAY - 711-H5
- HAY - 731-B1
Rt# 92 CANADA RD
- SMCo - 768-G2
- SMCo 94402 768-G2
- SMCo 94062 768-G2
Rt# 92 HALF MOON BAY RD
2900 SMCo - 768-E3
2900 SMCo 94062 768-E3
Rt# 92 J ARTHUR YOUNGER FRWY
- BLMT - 768-H2
- FCTY - 729-G7
- FCTY - 729-G7
- FCTY - 749-F2
- HIL - 748-J5
- SMCo - 748-J5
- SMCo - 768-H2
- SMCo - 768-H2
- SMTO - 748-J5
- SMTO - 748-J5
- SMTO - 749-A4
- SMTO - 749-F2
- SMTO - 749-F2
- SMTO - 768-H2
- SMTO - 768-H2
Rt# 92 JACKSON ST
- HAY 94544 711-H4
- HAY 94541 711-H4
Rt# 109 UNIVERSITY AV
2600 EPA 94303 771-B6
2700 MLPK 94303 771-B6
2800 MLPK 94025 771-B6
Rt# 112 DAVIS ST
- SLN 94577 690-J1
200 SLN 94577 691-A1
Rt# 114 ALBERNI ST
900 EPA 94303 771-A7
Rt# 114 WILLOW RD
- MLPK 94025 791-A1
900 EPA 94303 771-A7
900 EPA 94303 791-A1
1200 MLPK 94025 771-A7
Rt# 123 SAN PABLO AV
300 ALB 94706 609-D6
300 ELCR 94530 609-B1
1000 ALB 94804 609-D6
1100 BERK 94804 609-D6
1100 BERK 94706 609-D6
1300 BERK 94804 629-E1
1300 BERK 94702 609-D6
1300 BERK 94702 629-E1
2700 OAK 94608 629-E3
3500 OAK 94608 649-F1
3600 EMVL 94608 629-E3
3600 EMVL 94608 649-F1
10200 RCH 94804 609-B1
Rt# 123 SN PBLO AV
11800 ELCR 94530 589-B7
12100 RCH 94805 589-B7
Rt# 130 ALUM ROCK AV
- SJS 95116 834-H3
3400 SJS 95127 834-H3
3500 SCIC 95127 834-H3
5900 SCIC 95127 834-H3
6900 SCIC 95127 835-A1
8900 SCIC 95127 815-A7
Rt# 130 MOUNT HAMILTON RD
- SCIC 95127 815-B7
- SCIC 95127 835-D1
- SCIC 95140 835-G2
1000 SCIC 95140 815-E7
Rt# 131 TIBURON BLVD
- MrnC 94920 606-H4
- TBRN 94920 606-H4
- MrnC 94941 606-H4
100 MrnC 94920 607-A5
100 TBRN 94920 607-A5
1500 BLV 94920 607-C6
1700 TBRN 94920 627-E1
Rt#-141 MAINE ST
100 VAL 94590 529-J5
300 VAL 94590 530-A5
Rt# 185 E 14TH ST
- SLN 94577 670-J6
- OAK 94603 670-J6
200 SLN 94577 671-A7
900 SLN 94577 691-B2
13600 SLN 94578 691-B2
14800 AlaC 94578 691-F5
15800 AlaC 94580 691-F5
17000 AlaC 94541 691-F5
Rt# 185 INTERNATIONAL BLVD
3500 OAK 94601 670-C1
5500 OAK 94621 670-H4
9400 OAK 94603 670-H4
9400 SLN 94577 670-H4
Rt# 185 MSN BLVD
17300 AlaC 94541 691-G6
19800 HAY 94541 691-G6

STREET
Block City ZIP Pg-Grid

Rt# 237 CLVRS BLVD
100 MPS 95035 793-J7
100 MPS 95035 794-A7
Rt#-237 MTN VIEW-ALVISO RD
200 MTVW 94041 812-A6
500 MTVW 94043 812-A6
500 MTVW 94041 811-J6
Rt# 237 SOUTHBAY FRWY
- MPS - 813-C1
- SCL - 813-C1
- SCIC - 813-C1
- SJS - 813-C1
- SUNV - 812-D4
- SUNV - 813-C1
Rt# 238 FOOTHILL BLVD
17200 AlaC 94546 691-H6
20800 AlaC 94541 691-H6
21000 HAY 94541 691-H6
21800 HAY 94541 711-J1
Rt# 238 MISSION BLVD
20100 HAY 94541 691-H7
20100 HAY 94541 711-H1
23900 HAY 94544 711-H1
24200 HAY 94544 712-B5
24300 HAY 94542 712-A3
30100 HAY 94544 732-D1
33000 UNC 94587 732-G4
35100 FRMT 94536 732-G4
35500 FRMT 94536 733-B7
37300 FRMT 94536 753-E3
39000 FRMT 94539 753-E3
Rt# 242 FRWY
- CNCD - 572-F6
- CNCD - 592-D4
- PLHL - 592-D4
Rt# 260 WEBSTER ST
1300 ALA 94501 669-F1
1700 ALA 94501 649-F7
Rt# 262 MISSION BLVD
46000 FRMT 94539 773-G6
46600 FRMT 94538 773-G6
U.S. 101 BAYSHORE FRWY
- BLMT - 749-B1
- BLMT - 769-G1
- BSBN - 688-B3
- BSBN - 708-B1
- BURL - 728-F5
- EPA - 790-J1
- EPA - 791-E5
- MLBR - 728-B2
- MLPK - 770-C5
- MLPK - 790-J1
- MLPK - 791-E5
- MTVW - 791-E5
- MTVW - 811-G1
- MTVW - 812-C4
- PA - 791-E5
- RDWC - 769-G1
- RDWC - 769-G1
- RDWC - 770-C5
- SCAR - 769-G1
- SCL - 813-B6
- SCIC - 812-C4
- SCIC - 855-B5
- SF - 688-B3
- SJS - 813-B6
- SJS - 833-G1
- SJS - 834-C2
- SJS - 854-H1
- SJS - 855-B5
- SJS - 855-B5
- SJS - 875-C1
- SMCo - 708-A5
- SMCo - 728-B2
- SMCo - 769-G1
- SMCo - 769-G1
- SMTO - 728-F5
- SMTO - 729-A7
- SMTO - 749-B1
- SMTO - 749-B1
- SMTO - 749-B1
- SSF - 708-B1
- SUNV - 812-C4
- SUNV - 813-B6
U.S. 101 CENTRAL FRWY
- SF - 647-H7
- SF - 667-J1
- SF - 668-A1
U.S. 101 DOYLE DR
- SF 94129 647-D3
- SF 94129 647-E3
U.S. 101 GOLDEN GATE BRG FRWY
- SF - 627-B7
- SF - 647-B1
U.S. 101 JAMES LICK FRWY
- SF - 668-A2
- SF - 668-A6
- SF - 688-A1
- SF - 688-A1
U.S. 101 LOMBARD ST
1400 SF 94123 647-F4
U.S. 101 REDWOOD HWY
- CMAD - 586-H5
- CMAD - 606-G4
- LKSP - 586-H5
- MLV - 606-G4
- MrnC - 546-F6
- MrnC - 546-F7
- MrnC - 566-E2
- MrnC - 566-F1
- MrnC - 586-H5
- MrnC - 606-G4
- MrnC - 626-H1
- MrnC - 627-B4
- NVTO - 526-C3
- NVTO - 546-F7
- SAUS - 626-H1
- SAUS - 627-B4
- SF - 627-B4
- SRFL - 566-E1
- SRFL - 566-E2

STREET
Block City ZIP Pg-Grid

U.S. 101 REDWOOD HWY
- SRFL - 566-F5
- SRFL - 586-H5
U.S. 101 RICHARDSON AV
- SF 94123 647-E3
100 SF 94129 647-E3
U.S. 101 S VAN NESS AV
- SF 94103 667-J3
U.S. 101 SOUTH VALLEY FRWY
- SCIC - 875-D4
- SJS - 875-D4
U S 101 VN NESS AV
- SF 94102 647-H5
- SF 94103 647-H5
800 SF 94109 647-H5
2200 SF 94123 647-H5
2400 SF 94109 647-H4
2400 SF 94123 647-H4

AIRPORTS

FEATURE NAME Address City, ZIP Code	PAGE-GRID
BUCHANAN FIELD AIRPORT 550 SALLY RIDE DR, CCCo, 94520, (510)646-5722	572 - D6
HAYWARD AIR TERMINAL 20301 SKYWEST DR, HAY, 94541, (501)293-8678	711 - D2
LIVERMORE MUNICIPAL AIRPORT 636 TERMINAL CIR, LVMR, 94550, (510)373-5280	695 - A6
OAKLAND INTERNATIONAL AIRPORT 1 AIRPORT DR, OAK, 94621, (510)577-4000	690 - B1
PALO ALTO AIRPORT 1925 EMBARCADERO RD, PA, 94303, (650)856-7833	791 - E2
REID-HILLVIEW AIRPORT 2500 CUNNINGHAM AV, SJS, 95148, (408)929-2256	835 - A6
SAN CARLOS AIRPORT BAYSHORE FRWY, SCAR, 94070, (650)573-3700	769 - H1
SAN FRANCISCO INTERNATIONAL-AIRPORT 1799 BAYSHORE HWY, SMCo, 94128, (650)876-7809	728 - D2
SAN JOSE INTERNATIONAL AIRPORT 1661 AIRPORT BLVD, SJS, 95110, (408)277-4759	833 - F1
SKY SAILING AIRPORT 44999 CHRISTY ST, FRMT, 94538, (415)656-9900	773 - C5
SMITH RANCH AIRPORT 2173 SAN FRANCISCO BLVD, SRFL, 94903, (415)453-0212	566 - G1

BEACHES & HARBORS

FEATURE NAME Address City, ZIP Code	PAGE-GRID
BAKER BEACH GIBSON RD & BTTRY CHAMBERLAIN, SF, 94129, (415)556-0560	647 - A5
BARNHILL MARINA 2394 MARINER SQUARE DR, ALA, 94501, (408)523-7270	649 - G6
BROWNS ISLAND REGIONAL SHORELINE BROWNS ISLAND, PIT, 94565	574 - G1
CHINA BEACH EL CAMINO DEL MAR & 32ND AV, SF, 94121	647 - A5
CROWN, ROBERT MEM STATE BEACH 620 CENTRAL AV, ALA, 94501	669 - G2
FORTMANN MARINA FORTMANN WY & ALASKA PACKER ST, ALA, 94501	649 - H7
JACK LONDON MARINA 54 JACK LONDON SQ, OAK, 94607, (415)834-4591	649 - F5
KELLERS BEACH DORMAN DR, RCH, 94801	608 - C1
MCNEARS BEACH PARK PT SAN PEDRO RD, SRFL, 94901	567 - F5
MUIR BEACH SUNSET WY, MrnC, 94965, (415)388-2595	626 - A2
OCEAN BEACH GREAT HWY & JUDAH ST, SF, 94122	666 - H3
PACIFIC MARINA FOOT OF SHERMAN ST, ALA, 94501, (408)522-7300	649 - G7
PENINSULA BEACH COYOTE POINT DR, SMTO, 94401	728 - J5
PERLES BEACH TBRN	627 - G3
POINT MOLATE BEACH WESTERN DR, RCH, 94801	588 - A5
QUARRY BEACH TBRN	627 - J3
RODEO MARINA FOOT OF PACIFIC AV, CCCo, 94572, (510)799-4436	549 - H6
SAN PEDRO BEACH CABRILLO HWY, PCFA, 94044	726 - H2
SAND SPRINGS BEACH TBRN	627 - H3
SEAL ROCKS BEACH EL CAMINO DEL MAR, SF, 94121	646 - G6
SHARP PARK BEACH BEACH BLVD, PCFA, 94044	706 - J6
THORTON STATE BEACH SKYLINE BLVD & THORNTON STATE, DALY, 94015	686 - J3

BED & BREAKFAST

FEATURE NAME Address City, ZIP Code	PAGE-GRID
PANAMA HOTEL 4 BAYVIEW ST, SRFL, 94901, (415)457-3993	586 - F1
PELICAN INN BED AND BREAKFAST 10 PACIFIC WY, MrnC, 94965, (415)383-6000	626 - A1

BUILDINGS

FEATURE NAME Address City, ZIP Code	PAGE-GRID
1 HARRISON STREET 1 HARRISON ST, SF, 94105	648 - C5
49 STEVENSON ST 49 STEVENSON ST, SF, 94103	648 - A6
50 FREMONT STREET 50 FREMONT ST, SF, 94105, (415)543-5600	648 - B5
55 HAWTHORNE ST 55 HAWTHORNE ST, SF, 94105	648 - B6
60 SPEAR ST 60 SPEAR ST, SF, 94105	648 - B5
71 STEVENSON ST 71 STEVENSON ST, SF, 94103	648 - A6
75 HAWTHORNE ST PLAZA 75 HAWTHORNE ST PZ, SF, 94105	648 - B6
90 NEW MONTGOMERY 90 NEW MONTGOMERY ST, SF, 94105, (415)777-0952	648 - B6
100 CALIFORNIA ST 100 CALIFORNIA ST, SF, 94111	648 - B5
100 FIRST PLAZA 100 1ST ST, SF, 94105	648 - B5
100 PINE ST 100 PINE ST, SF, 94111, (415)986-6469	648 - B5
101 CALIFORNIA ST 101 CALIFORNIA ST, SF, 94111, (415)398-8655	648 - B5
120 MONTGOMERY STREET 120 MONTGOMERY ST, SF, 94104	648 - B5
123 MISSION ST 123 MISSION ST, SF, 94105, (415)974-1722	648 - B5
160 SPEAR ST 160 SPEAR ST, SF, 94105	648 - B5
201 CALIFORNIA ST 201 CALIFORNIA ST, SF, 94111	648 - B5
221 MAIN ST 221 MAIN ST, SF, 94105	648 - C5
301 HOWARD ST 301 HOWARD ST, SF, 94105	648 - C5
333 BUSH ST 333 BUSH ST, SF, 94108, (415)982-2278	648 - A5
333 MARKET ST 333 MARKET ST, SF, 94105, (415)546-0333	648 - B5
343 SANSOME 343 SANSOME ST, SF, 94104	648 - B5
353 SACRAMENTO ST 353 SACRAMENTO ST, SF, 94104	648 - B5
388 MARKET ST 388 MARKET ST, SF, 94111	648 - B5
425 MARKET ST 425 MARKET ST, SF, 94105	648 - B5
455 MARKET ST 455 MARKET ST, SF, 94105	648 - B5
475 SANSOME ST 475 SANSOME ST, SF, 94111	648 - B5
505 MONTGOMERY ST 505 MONTGOMERY ST, SF, 94111	648 - A5
580 CALIFORNIA ST 580 CALIFORNIA ST, SF, 94104	648 - A5
595 MARKET ST 595 MARKET ST, SF, 94108	648 - A6
601 MONTGOMERY ST 601 MONTGOMERY ST, SF, 94111	648 - A5
605 MARKET STREET 605 MARKET ST, SF, 94103, (415)495-0239	648 - A6
650 CALIFORNIA ST 650 CALIFORNIA ST, SF, 94108	648 - A5
660 MARKET ST 660 MARKET ST, SF, 94108, (415)788-4820	648 - A6
ABC 900 FRONT ST, SF, 94111, (415)954-7777	648 - B4
ADAM GRANT 114 SANSOME ST, SF, 94104, (415)981-0375	648 - B5
AEROFLOT AIRLINES 291 GEARY ST, SF, 94108, (415)434-2300	648 - A6
AIR FRANCE AIRLINES 360 POST ST, SF, 94102	648 - A5
AMERICAN AIRLINES 51 O'FARREL ST, SF, 94108, (415)433-7300	648 - A6
AMERICAN SAVINGS MARKET & KEARNY STS, SF, 94108, (415)362-8220	648 - A6
ANZA CORPORATE CENTER 433 AIRPORT BLVD, BURL, 94010, (650)342-5711	728 - G5
AT&T 795 FOLSOM ST, SF, 94107	648 - B6
BANK OF AMERICA BUILDING 1200 BROADWAY, OAK, 94612, (510)649-6600	649 - G3
BANK OF AMERICA BUILDING 1500 PARK ST, ALA, 94501, (510)649-6600	670 - A2
BANK OF AMERICA BUILDING 2129 SHATTUCK AV, BERK, 94704, (510)273-5743	629 - H2
BANK OF CA COMPUTER CENTER 640 BATTERY ST, SF, 94111	648 - B4
BANK OF CANTON 555 MONTGOMERY ST, SF, 94104	648 - A5
BANK OF SAN FRANCISCO 550 MONTGOMERY ST, SF, 94104	648 - A5
BANKERS INVESTMENT 742 MARKET ST, SF, 94108, (415)781-2836	648 - A6
BAYSIDE PLAZA 188 THE EMBARCADERO ST, SF, 94105, (415)979-2300	648 - C6
BERKELEY YACHT CLUB 1 SEAWALL DR, BERK, 94804, (510)540-9167	629 - B2
BEVATRON BUILDING 2200 UNIVERSITY AV, BERK, 94720, (510)642-6000	629 - J1
BLUE CROSS BUILDING 1950 FRANKLIN ST, OAK, 94612, (510)654-3000	649 - G3
BRITISH AIRWAYS 51 OFARRELL ST, SF, 94108, (415)247-9297	648 - A6
BROOKS BROTHERS 209 POST ST, SF, 94108	648 - A5
BUILDERS EXCHANGE 850 S VAN NESS AV, SF, 94109, (415)282-8220	647 - H6
CALIF ORIENTATION CTR FOR THE-BLIND ADAMS ST, ALB, 94706	609 - D5
CALIFORNIA SCHOOL FOR THE BLIND WALNUT AV, FRMT, 94538	753 - D3
CARMELITE MONASTERY JESSEN CT, CCCo, 94707	609 - F2
CENTRAL TOWER 703 MARKET ST, SF, 94105, (415)982-1935	648 - B5
CENTRUM III 300 ORACLE PKWY, RDWC, 94065	749 - G6
CHEVRON 225 BUSH ST, SF, 94108, (415)894-7700	648 - A5
CHINA AIRLINES 391 STOCKTON ST, SF, 94108, (415)391-3954	648 - A5
CHRONICLE 5TH ST & MISSION ST, SF, 94103, (415)777-1111	648 - A6
CITICORP 180 GRAND AV, OAK, 94612	649 - H3
CITICORP CENTER 1 SANSOME ST, SF, 94104	648 - B5
CITY CENTER 14TH ST & BROADWAY, OAK, 94612	649 - G4
CLOROX BUILDING 1221 BROADWAY, OAK, 94607, (510)271-7000	649 - G4
COMMERCIAL 833 MARKET ST, SF, 94103, (415)362-4915	648 - A6
CONTINENTAL AIRLINES 433 CALIFORNIA ST, SF, 94104, (415)397-8818	648 - B5
CONVENTION PLAZA 201 3RD ST, SF, 94103	648 - B6
COUNTY ADMINISTRATION BUILDING 1221 OAK ST, OAK, 94612, (510)272-6984	649 - H4
COUNTY BUILDING 244 W WINTON AV, HAY, 94544	711 - H3
COURT HOUSE SQUARE 1000 4TH ST, SRFL, 94901	586 - G1
DELTA AIRLINES 250 STOCKTON ST, SF, 94108, (415)552-5700	648 - A6
DIVERSIFIED FINANCIAL CENTRE 1299 4TH ST, SRFL, 94901	586 - F1
E B CENTER FOR BLIND 3834 OPAL ST, OAK, 94609, (510)450-1580	649 - H1
ECKER SQUARE 25 ECKER ST, SF, 94105	648 - B5
EDUCATIONAL SERVICES CENTER ALVARADO-NILES RD & MEYERS DR, UNC, 94587	732 - F6
EIGHT THIRTY MARKET 830 MARKET ST, SF, 94102	648 - A6
ELKS LODGE 1059 WILMINGTON WY, RDWC, 94061, (650)365-1991	789 - F3
EMBARCADERO CENTER W 275 BATTERY ST, SF, 94104, (415)772-0500	648 - B5
ENVIRONMENTAL CENTER 2581 HARBOR ST, PIT, 94565	574 - E5
EXCHANGE BLOCK 369 PINE ST, SF, 94104, (415)421-0422	648 - B5
FASHION INSTITUTE 55 STOCKTON ST, SF, 94108, (415)433-6691	648 - A6
FEDERAL HOME LOAN BANK 600 CALIFORNIA ST, SF, 94108	648 - A5
FERRY BUILDING EMBARCADERO & WASHINGTON ST, SF, 94111	648 - C4
FIFTEEN CALIFORNIA ST 15 CALIFORNIA ST, SF, 94111	648 - B5
FIFTY HAWTHORNE 50 HAWTHORNE ST, SF, 94103	648 - B6
FILBERT LANDING 201 FILBERT ST, SF, 94133	648 - A4
FINANCIAL CENTER BUILDING 405 14TH ST, OAK, 94612, (510)839-4959	649 - G4
FIRST INTERSTATE CENTER BATTERY ST & PINE ST, SF, 94104	648 - B5
FIRST MARKET TOWER 525 MARKET ST, SF, 94108	648 - A5
FIVE FREMONT CENTER 5 MISSION ST & FREMONT ST, SF, 94105	648 - B5
FLATIRON 1 SUTTER ST, SF, 94105	648 - B5
FLOOD 870 MARKET ST, SF, 94102, (415)982-3298	648 - A6
FOLGER 101 HOWARD ST, SF, 94105	648 - C5
FORTY FOUR MONTGOMERY 44 MONTGOMRERY ST, SF, 94104, (415)392-2433	648 - B5
FOUR EMBARCADERO CENTER EMBARCADERO CTR, SF, 94111, (415)772-0500	648 - B5
FOUR SEVENTEEN MONTGOMERY 417 MONTGOMERY ST, SF, 94104, (415)392-2470	648 - A5
FOURTEEN NINETY-NINE BUILDING 1499 BAYSHORE HWY, BURL, 94010, (650)348-1051	728 - E4
FOX PLAZA 1390 MARKET ST, SF, 94102, (415)626-6900	647 - J7
FRANKLIN BUILDING 1624 FRANKLIN ST, OAK, 94612, (510)763-2911	649 - G4
FREMONT CENTER 215 FREMONT ST, SF, 94105	648 - B5
FREMONT COMM DEVELOPMENT CTR 39550 LIBERTY ST, FRMT, 94538, (510)494-4620	753 - B5
GALLERIA DESIGN CENTER 101 HENRY ADAMS ST, SF, 94103, (415)863-3388	668 - A1
GOLDEN GATE 25 TAYLOR ST, SF, 94102, (415)775-3890	648 - A6
GOLDEN GATEWAY CENTER 460 DAVIS ST, SF, 94111, (415)434-2000	648 - B4
GRANT 1095 MARKET ST, SF, 94103, (415)621-8139	647 - J7
GREAT WESTERN BANK 425 CALIFORNIA ST, SF, 94104	648 - B5
GREAT WESTERN SAVINGS BUILDING 1700 BROADWAY, OAK, 94612, (510)452-6503	649 - G3
GUNST, ELKAN 323 GEARY ST, SF, 94102, (415)421-4762	648 - A6
GUZZARDO 836 MONTGOMERY ST, SF, 94133, (415)433-4672	648 - A4
HARMON GYMNASTIC 2200 UNIVERSITY AV, BERK, 94720, (510)642-6000	629 - H2
HARRISON BUILDING 1800 HARRISON ST, OAK, 94612, 510-	649 - H4
HASS 1255 SANSOME ST, SF, 94133	648 - A3
HAYWARD UNIFIED SCHOOL DISTRICT 24411 AMADOR ST, HAY, 94544, (510)784-2600	711 - H4
HEALTH CENTER 850 UNIVERSITY AV, BERK, 94804	629 - D2
HEARST 669 MARKET ST, SF, 94105, (415)777-0600	648 - B5
HILLCREST JUVENILE HOME TOWER RD, SMCo, 94402	768 - H2
HILLS PLAZA 1 345 SPEAR ST, SF, 94105	648 - C5
HILLS PLAZA 2 1 HARRISON ST, SF, 94105	648 - C5
HOBART 582 MARKET ST, SF, 94104, (415)362-8783	648 - B5
HONG KONG BANK 160 SANSOME ST, SF, 94104	648 - B5
HUMBOLDT BANK 785 MARKET ST, SF, 94103	648 - A6
IBM RESEARCH LABORATORY LOOP DR, SJS, 95120	895 - B2
INDUSTRIAL INDEMNITY 255 CALIFORNIA ST, SF, 94111	648 - B5
INSURANCE BUILDING 1404 FRANKLIN ST, OAK, 94612	649 - G4
INSURANCE EXCHANGE 433 CALIFORNIA ST, SF, 94104, (415)362-0529	648 - A5
INTERNATIONAL 601 CALIFORNIA ST, SF, 94108, (415)981-7878	648 - A5
INTERNATIONAL HOUSE 2200 UNIVERSITY AV, BERK, 94720, (510)642-6000	629 - J2
IOOF HOME SAR, 95070	872 - G3
JAPAN AIRLINES POWELL ST & OFARRELL ST, SF, 94102, (415)765-8555	648 - A6
KAISER CENTER 300 LAKESIDE DR, OAK, 94612, (510)462-1122	649 - H3
KINGS DAUGHTERS HOME BROADWAY, OAK, 94611	649 - H1
KOHL 400 MONTGOMERY ST, SF, 94104, (415)392-2470	648 - A5
KOREAN AIR 251 POST ST, SF, 94108, (415)956-6373	648 - A5
KOSHLAND 1160 BATTERY ST, SF, 94111	648 - B3
KPIX 855 BATTERY ST, SF, 94111, (415)362-5550	648 - B4
KRE RADIO STATION POTTER ST & BOLIVAR DR, BERK, 94804	629 - D4
KRESS 939 MARKET ST, SF, 94103, (415)495-8748	648 - A6
LAKE MERRITT PLAZA 1999 HARRISON AV, OAK, 94612	649 - G3
LEVI STRAUSS 1155 BATTERY ST, SF, 94111, (415)544-6000	648 - B3
LUFTHANSA 240 STOCKTON ST, SF, 94108, (415)398-7400	648 - A6
MAPLES PAVILION CAMPUS DR, SCIC, 94305, (650)723-2300	790 - J7
MARATHON PLAZA 303 2ND ST, SF, 94105	648 - B6
MARINE FIREMANS UNION 240 2ND ST, SF, 94105	648 - B6
MARITIME ADMINISTRATION 211 MAIN ST, SF, 94105, (415)744-3125	648 - B5
MASONIC HOME FOR ADULTS 34400 MISSION BLVD, UNC, 94587, (510)471-3434	732 - H4
MASTICK SENIOR CENTER 1155 SANTA CLARA AV, ALA, 94501, (510)748-4587	669 - G1
MATHEWS, MERTLE BUILDING 4301 E 14TH ST, SLN, 94577	691 - A1
MCMULLEN BUILDING 1305 FRANKLIN ST, OAK, 94612	649 - G4
MEDICO/DENTAL 490 POST ST, SF, 94102, (415)781-1427	648 - A6
MEMORIAL BUILDING BANCROFT AV & CALLAN AV, SLN, 94577	671 - B7
MERCANTILE CENTER 706 MISSION ST, SF, 94103	648 - A6
MERCHANTS EXCHANGE 465 CALIFORNIA ST, SF, 94104, (415)421-7730	648 - B5
MEXICANA AIRLINES 421 POWELL ST, SF, 94102, (415)982-1424	648 - A6
MILLS BUILDING & TOWER 220 MONTGOMERY ST, SF, 94104, (415)421-1444	648 - B5
MONADNOCK 685 MARKET ST, SF, 94103, (415)781-1361	648 - A6
MONSANTO CHEMICAL COMPANY 1778 MONSANTO WY, CCCo, 94553, (510)313-0681	572 - D2
MONTEREY CONSERVATORY MONTEREY BLVD & CONGO ST, SF, 94131	667 - F6

FEATURE NAME Address City, ZIP Code	PAGE-GRID
MONTGOMERY WASHINGTON TOWER 655 MONTGOMERY ST, SF, 94111, (415)981-2655	648 - A4
MOUNT DIABLO FAMILY BRANCH YMCA 350 CIVIC DR, PLHL, 94523, (510)687-8900	592 - B3
MUNICIPAL SAILBOAT HOUSE OAK, 94610	649 - J4
NATIVE SONS 414 MASON ST, SF, 94102, (415)392-0943	648 - A6
NEW MONTGOMERY TOWER 33 NEW MONTGOMERY ST, SF, 94105	648 - B6
NINETEEN TWENTY FOUR BUILDING 1924 BROADWAY, OAK, 94612	649 - G3
NORTHWEST 433 CALIFORNIA ST, SF, 94104, (415)225-2525	648 - B5
OAKLAND EXECUTIVE CENTER HASSLER WY, OAK, 94621	670 - E5
OAKLAND FEDERAL BUILDING 1301 CLAY ST, OAK, 94612	649 - F4
OAKLAND UNIFIED SCHOOL DIST-ADMIN BLDG 1025 2ND AV, OAK, 94606, (510)836-8100	649 - H5
OAKLAND WORLD TRADE CENTER EMBARCADERO, OAK, 94607	649 - G5
ONE BUSH ST 1 BUSH ST, SF, 94111	648 - B5
ONE CALIFORNIA ST 1 CALIFORNIA ST, SF, 94111, (415)421-4144	648 - B5
ONE ELEVEN SUTTER 111 SUTTER ST, SF, 94108, (415)477-3274	648 - A5
ONE EMBARCADERO CENTER EMBARCADERO CTR, SF, 94111, (415)772-0500	648 - B5
ONE JACKSON PLACE 633 BATTERY ST, SF, 94111, (415)362-1800	648 - B4
ONE MARITIME PLAZA 1 MARITIME PZ, SF, 94111, (415)397-2339	648 - B5
ONE MARKET PLAZA 1 MARKET PZ, SF, 94105	648 - B5
ONE POST BLDG 1 POST ST, SF, 94104, (415)546-1300	648 - B5
ORPHEUM THEATRE 1192 MARKET ST, SF, 94102, (415)474-3800	647 - J7
PACIFIC BANK 351 CALIFORNIA ST, SF, 94104	648 - B5
PACIFIC BELL 140 NEW MONTGOMERY ST, SF, 94105, (415)811-9000	648 - B6
PACIFIC BUILDING 610 16TH ST, OAK, 94612, (510)465-5455	649 - G3
PACIFIC CENTRE 22 4TH ST, SF, 94103, (415)398-7333	648 - A6
PACIFIC COAST STOCK EXCHANGE 301 PINE ST, SF, 94104, (415)393-4000	648 - B5
PACIFIC GATEWAY 201 MISSION ST, SF, 94105	648 - B5
PACIFIC TELESIS TOWER 1 MONTGOMERY ST, SF, 94108	648 - B5
PARK PLAZA BUILDING 3100 MOWRY AV, FRMT, 94538, (510)797-6606	753 - A4
PHELAN 760 MARKET ST, SF, 94108, (415)392-7552	648 - A6
PHILIPPINE AIRLINES 447 SUTTER ST, SF, 94108, (415)391-0270	648 - A5
PIERCE BUILDING 385 17TH ST, OAK, 94612	649 - G3
QANTAS AIRWAYS 360 POST ST, SF, 94102, (415)445-1461	648 - A5
RAY 181 FREMONT ST, SF, 94105, (415)392-3870	648 - B5
REDWOOD BANK 735 MONTGOMERY ST, SF, 94133, (415)788-3700	648 - A4
RIALTO 116 NEW MONTGOMERY ST, SF, 94105, (415)421-0704	648 - B6
RINCON CENTER 101 SPEAR ST, SF, 94105	648 - B5
ROBERT DOLLAR 311 CALIFORNIA ST, SF, 94104, (415)392-8454	648 - B5
ROTHSCHILD 165 POST ST, SF, 94108	648 - A5
RUCKER FULLER 731 SANSOME ST, SF, 94133, (415)627-4600	648 - B4
RUSS 235 MONTGOMERY ST, SF, 94104, (415)421-7424	648 - A5
SAILORS UNION OF PACIFIC 450 HARRISON ST, SF, 94105	648 - C6
SAINT FRANCIS MEDICAL 909 HYDE ST, SF, 94109, (415)673-1317	647 - J5
SAN FRANCISCO FEDERAL SAVINGS POST ST & KEARNY ST, SF, 94108	648 - A5
SAN JOSE CIVIC AUDITORIUM 145 W SAN CARLOS ST, SJS, 95113, (408)277-3900	834 - B7
SANDIA NATIONAL LABORATORIES EAST AV & GREENVILLE RD, AlaC, 94550, (510)294-3000	716 - F1
SEVENTY NINE NEW MONTGOMERY 79 NEW MONTGOMERY ST, SF, 94105	648 - B6
SHAKLEE TERRACES 444 MARKET ST, SF, 94104	648 - B5
SHARON 55 NEW MONTGOMERY ST, SF, 94105, (415)982-9281	648 - B6
SHELL 100 BUSH ST, SF, 94104, (415)986-0647	648 - B5
SINGAPORE AIRLINES 476 POST ST, SF, 94102, (415)781-7304	648 - A6
SIXTY FOUR PINE ST 64 PINE ST, SF, 94111	648 - B5
SOUTHERN PACIFIC 1 MARKET PZ, SF, 94105, (415)541-1000	648 - B5
SPEAR STREET TERRACE 201 SPEAR ST, SF, 94105	648 - C5
SPEAR STREET TOWER 1 MARKET PZ, SF, 94105	648 - B5
STEGE SANITARY DISTRICT 7500 SCHMIDT LN, ELCR, 94530, (510)524-4668	609 - D2
STEUART ST TOWER 1 MARKET PZ, SF, 94105	648 - B5
STOCK EXCHANGE TOWER 155 SANSOME ST, SF, 94104	648 - B5
SUMITOMO BANK 320 CALIFORNIA ST, SF, 94104	648 - B5
SUTTER MEDICAL DENTAL 450 SUTTER ST, SF, 94108, (415)421-7221	648 - A5
TACA 870 MARKET ST, SF, 94108	648 - A6
TENNYSON PROFESSIONAL BUILDING 781 W TENNYSON RD, HAY, 94544	712 - B7
THE GATEWAY 651 GATEWAY BLVD, SSF, 94080	708 - A2
THE ORDWAY 21ST ST, OAK, 94612	649 - H3
THIRTY-THIRTY BRIDGEWAY BUILDING 3030 BRIDGEWAY BLVD, SAUS, 94965, (415)332-3800	627 - B3
THREE EMBARCADERO CENTER EMBARCADERO CTR, SF, 94111, (415)772-0500	648 - B5
TOSCO OIL REFINING COMPANY SOLANO WY, CCCo, 94553, (510)228-1220	572 - C2
TRADE SHOW CENTER 2 HENRY ADAMS ST, SF, 94103, (415)864-1500	668 - A1

FEATURE NAME Address City, ZIP Code	PAGE-GRID
TRANS PACIFIC CENTER 11TH ST & WEBSTER ST, OAK, 94607	649 - G4
TRANS WORLD AIRLINES 595 MARKET ST, SF, 94104, (415)864-5731	648 - B5
TRANSAMERICA 701 MONTGOMERY ST, SF, 94133	648 - A4
TRANSAMERICA (PYRAMID) 600 MONTGOMERY ST, SF, 94111, (415)983-4000	648 - A5
TWO EMBARCADERO CENTER EMBARCADERO CTR, SF, 94111, (415)772-0500	648 - B5
TWO RINCON CENTER 121 SPEAR ST, SF, 94105	648 - B5
TWO TRANSAMERICA CENTER 505 SANSOME ST, SF, 94111	648 - B5
UNION BANK 350 CALIFORNIA ST, SF, 94104, (415)445-0224	648 - B5
UNITED AIRLINES 124 GEARY ST, SF, 94108, (415)397-2100	648 - A6
US AIRWAYS 433 CALIFORINIA ST, SF, 94104, (415)956-8636	648 - A5
VETERANS MEMORIAL AUDITORIUM AV OF THE FLAGS, SRFL, 94903	566 - F4
WATER TREATMENT PLANT OFF OLYMPIA DR, PIT, 94565	574 - B5
WELLS FARGO 464 CALIFORNIA ST, SF, 94104, (415)396-0123	648 - B5
WELLS FARGO BUILDING 1345 BROADWAY, OAK, 94612, (510)464-2040	649 - G4
WORLD SAVINGS CENTER 1901 HARRISON ST, OAK, 94612	649 - H3
YERBA BUENA WEST 150 4TH ST, SF, 94103, (415)495-3433	648 - A6
YMCA BROADWAY, OAK, 94612	649 - G3
YMCA WESTERN SHORE LN, SF, 94115	647 - H6
YOUTH GUIDANCE CENTER WOODSIDE AV & TWIN PEAKS RD, SF, 94131	667 - E4
YWCA WEBSTER ST & 15TH ST, OAK, 94612	649 - G4

BUILDINGS - GOVERNMENTAL

FEATURE NAME Address City, ZIP Code	PAGE-GRID
ALAMEDA COUNTY HEALTH DEPARTMENT 499 5TH ST, OAK, 94607, (510)268-2722	649 - F5
ALAMEDA COUNTY WELFARE BUILDING 401 BROADWAY, OAK, 94607, (510)268-2002	649 - F5
BILL GRAHAM CIVIC AUDITORIUM 99 GROVE ST AT POLK ST, SF, 94102, (415)974-4060	647 - J7
CALIFORNIA STATE BUILDING 350 MCALLISTER ST, SF, 94102	647 - H6
CITY CORPORATION YARD SCHMIDT LN, ELCR, 94530	609 - D2
CONCORD POLICE ACADEMY 5060 AVILA RD, CCCo, (510)676-8298	573 - C3
CONTRA COSTA CO MUNICIPAL-COURTHOUSE 100 37TH ST, RCH, 94805, (510)374-3137	588 - J7
CONTRA COSTA CO OFFICE OF-EDUCATION 77 SANTA BARBARA RD, PLHL, 94523, (510)942-3388	592 - B7
CONTRA COSTA COUNTY FINANCE-BUILDING COURT ST & MAIN ST, MRTZ, 94553	571 - D3
CONTRA COSTA COUNTY HEALTH-DEPARTMENT 1111 WARD ST, MRTZ, 94553, (510)313-6710	571 - E2
COUNTY ADMINISTRATION BUILDING 651 PINE ST, MRTZ, 94553, (415)646-4121	571 - E2
COUNTY COURTHOUSE 725 COURT ST, MRTZ, 94553, (510)646-2985	571 - E3
COUNTY DETENTION CENTER 725 COURT ST, MRTZ, 94553, (415)646-2985	571 - E3
COUNTY HEALTH DEPARTMENT 2060 FAIRMONT DR, AlaC, 94578	691 - E3
COUNTY OF ALAMEDA HALL OF JUSTICE 24405 AMADOR ST, HAY, 94544, (510)670-5661	711 - G3
COURTHOUSE 1225 FALLON ST, OAK, 94612, (510)272-6070	649 - H4
COURTHOUSE 2233 SHORE LINE DR, ALA, 94501, (510)268-4208	669 - J3
COURTHOUSE 39439 PAS PADRE PKWY, FRMT, 94538, (510)795-2444	753 - B4
COURTHOUSE 600 WASHINGTON ST, OAK, 94612, (510)268-7724	649 - G4
COURTHOUSE 7TH ST, OAK, 94607	649 - F4
COURTHOUSE GRANT & BIRCH, PA, 94306	791 - B7
DEPARTMENT OF ANIMAL SERVICES 651 PINOLE SHORES DR, PIN, 94564, (510)374-3966	569 - C4
ELMWOOD CORRECTIONAL FACILITY 701 ABEL ST, MPS, 95035, (408)299-2831	814 - A2
FED CORRECTIONAL INST PLEASANTON 8TH ST & GOODFELLOW AV, DBLN, 94568	694 - B2
FEDERAL BUILDING 450 GOLDEN GATE AV, SF, 94102, (415)556-6600	647 - J6
FEDERAL BUILDING MCALLISTER ST & HYDE ST, SF, 94102	647 - J7
FEDERAL RESERVE BANK 101 MARKET ST, SF, 94105, (415)974-2000	648 - B5
HALL OF JUSTICE 2600 BARRETT AV, RCH, 94804, (510)620-6513	588 - J6
HALL OF JUSTICE 3501 CIVIC CENTER DR, SRFL, 94903, (415)499-6211	566 - F4
HALL OF JUSTICE 401 MARSHALL ST, RDWC, 94063	770 - A5
HALL OF JUSTICE 850 BRYANT ST, SF, 94103, (415)553-9395	648 - A7
JUVENILE HALL 2200 FAIRMONT DR, AlaC, 94578, (510)667-4970	691 - E2
JUVENILE HALL IDYLBERRY RD, MrnC, 94903, (415)499-6705	546 - B7
JUVENILE HALL MUIR RD, MRTZ, 94553	571 - J7
LAFAYETTE TOWN HALL LFYT, 94549	611 - F7
MARE ISLAND NAVAL RES HQ 7TH ST & WALNUT AV, VAL, 94592	529 - G5
MARIN COUNTY ADMIN BUILDING 3501 CIVIC CENTER DR, SRFL, 94903, (415)499-6151	566 - F4
MARITIME COMMISSION 525 MARKET ST, SF, 94105, (415)974-9756	648 - B5
MECHANICS INSTITUTE 57 POST ST, SF, 94108, (415)956-2260	648 - A5
METRO TRANSPORT CENTER 101 8TH ST, OAK, 94607, (510)464-7700	649 - G5
MILPITAS CIVIC CENTER CALAVERAS BLVD & TOWN CENTER D, MPS, 95035	794 - B7
PORT OF OAKLAND 66 WATER ST, OAK, 94607, (510)444-3188	649 - E5
POLICE ACADEMY 350 AMBER DR, SF, 94131	667 - F4
PUBLIC WORKS ELMHURST ST, HAY, 94544, (510)293-5208	711 - H3

FEATURE NAME Address City, ZIP Code	PAGE-GRID
SF CIVIC CENTER VAN NESS AV & POLK ST, SF, 94102	647 - J7
SAN FRANCISCO JAIL COUNTY JAIL RD, SMCo, 94044	707 - D7
SAN MATEO COUNTY COURT BUILDING 1050 MISSION RD, SSF, 94080, (650)877-5705	707 - F2
SAN MATEO COUNTY COURTHOUSE 401 MARSHALL ST, RDWC, 94063	770 - A5
SAN MATEO CO GOV CENTER WINSLOW ST & BRADFORD ST, RDWC, 94063, (650)363-4711	770 - A5
SAN MATEO COUNTY HEALTH CENTER OAK AV, SSF, 94080	707 - G2
SAN QUENTIN STATE PENITENTIARY MAIN ST, MrnC, 94964	587 - A5
SANTA CLARA CIVIC CENTER 1500 WARBURTON AV, SCL, 95050	833 - D3
SANTA CLARA COUNTY COURTHOUSE 191 N 1ST ST, SJS, 95113, (408)299-2964	834 - B6
SANTA CLARA COUNTY MUNICIPAL-COURT 605 W EL CAMINO REAL, SUNV, 94086, (408)739-1503	832 - D1
SANTA CLARA COUNTY SERVICE CENTER BERGER DR, SJS, 95112	834 - B1
SANTA CLARA COURTHOUSE 1500 WARBURTON AV, SCL, 95050	833 - D3
SANTA RITA REHABILITATION CENTER 5325 DUBLIN BLVD, DBLN, 94568, (510)551-6500	694 - C2
SOLONO CO BLDG WORFE ST & VIRGINIA ST, VAL, 94590	530 - B5
U S CUSTOMS AIRPORT BLVD, SJS, 95110	833 - H3
UNITED STATES MINT 155 HERMANN ST, SF, 94102, (415)556-6704	667 - H1
US APPRAISERS BUILDING 630 SANSOME ST, SF, 94111	648 - B4
US CUSTOMS HOUSE 555 BATTERY ST, SF, 94111, (415)705-4440	648 - B5
VETERANS ADMINISTRATION 211 MAIN ST, SF, 94105	648 - C5
VETERANS BUILDING 200 GRAND AV, OAK, 94612, (510)238-3284	649 - H3
VETERANS BUILDING 2203 CENTRAL AV, ALA, 94501, (510)523-9843	669 - J2
VETERANS BUILDING CENTER ST, BERK, 94704	629 - G2
VETERANS BUILDING SALEM ST, EMVL, 94608	629 - F7
WEST COUNTY DETENTION FACILITY 5555 GIANT HWY, RCH, 94806, (510)262-4200	568 - H5
WEST VALLEY COURTHOUSE 14205 CAPRI DR, LGTS, 95030, (408)378-3227	873 - C2

CEMETERIES

FEATURE NAME Address City, ZIP Code	PAGE-GRID
ALHAMBRA CEMETERY CARQUINEZ SCENIC DR, MRTZ, 94553	571 - C3
ALTA MESA CEMETERY 695 ARASTRADERO RD, PA, 94306	811 - C4
CALVARY CATHOLIC CEMETERY 2655 MADDEN AV, SJS, 95116, (408)258-2940	834 - H2
CARQUINEZ CEMETERY BENICIA RD, VAL, 94591	530 - E7
CATHOLIC CEMETERY CARQUINEZ SCENIC DR, MRTZ, 94553	571 - C3
CATHOLIC CEMETERY STARVIEW DR, AlaC, 94578	691 - E2
CEDAR LAWN MEMORIAL CEMETERY 48800 WARM SPRINGS BLVD, FRMT, 94539, (510)656-5565	793 - J2
CEMETERY 1ST ST & P ST, BEN, 94510	551 - B4
CEMETERY 500 CANADA RD, SMCo, 94062	789 - A1
CEMETERY 6050 SUNOL BLVD, PLE, 94566	714 - D5
CEMETERY CALAVERAS RD, SCIC, 95035	794 - H5
CEMETERY DUBLIN BLVD & DONLON WY, DBLN, 94568	693 - G5
CEMETERY E LAUREL CREEK RD, SMTO, 94403	768 - J1
CEMETERY EL PORTAL & LA GONDA WY, DNVL, 94526	632 - H7
CEMETERY HESPERIAN BLVD & COLLEGE ST, AlaC, 94580	691 - D6
CEMETERY JUNIPERO SERRA BLVD, DALY, 94015	707 - C1
CEMETERY SANTA CRUZ AV, MLPK, 94025	790 - E6
CHAPEL OF THE CHIMES MEM CEMETERY 32992 MISSION BLVD, UNC, 94587, (510)538-3131	732 - F3
CHINESE CEMETERY CALLAN BLVD, DALY, 94015, (650)992-4581	707 - B1
CYPRESS LAWN CEMETERY JUNIPERO SERRA BLVD, CLMA, 94014, (415)775-0580	707 - D1
DAPHNE FERNWOOD CEMETERY 301 TENNESSEE VALLEY BLVD, MrnC, 94965, (415)383-7100	606 - G7
ETERNAL HOME CEMETERY EL CAMINO REAL & OLIVET PKWY, CLMA, 94014, (650)755-5236	687 - D6
EVERGREEN CEMETERY 6450 CAMDEN ST, OAK, 94605, (510)632-1602	670 - H1
FREMONT MEMORIAL PARK CEMETERY 4250 IRVINGTON AV, FRMT, 94538	753 - D7
GOLDEN GATE NATIONAL CEMETERY SNEATH LN, SBRN, 94066, (650)761-1646	707 - G6
GOLDEN HILLS MEMORIAL PARK HILLSIDE BL & SERRAMONTE BL, CLMA, 94014	687 - E6
GREEK ORTHODOX MEMORIAL PARK 1148 EL CAMINO REAL, CLMA, 94014, (650)755-6939	687 - D7
GREENLAWN MEMORIAL PARK 1100 EL CAMINO REAL, CLMA, 94014, (650)755-7622	687 - C7
HANS MEMORIAL PARK SKYLINE DR & REDWOOD PKWY, VAL, 94591	530 - D2
HILLS OF ETERNITY MEMORIAL PARK EL CAMINO REAL, CLMA, 94014, (650)756-3633	687 - E6
HILLSIDE CEMETERY PHELPS ST, VAL, 94590	529 - H2
HOLY CROSS CEMETERY E 18TH ST & WYMORE WY, CCCo, 94509, (510)757-4500	575 - H5
HOLY CROSS CEMETERY MISSION RD, CLMA, 94014, (650)756-2060	707 - E1
HOLY GHOST CEMETERY CENTRAL AV, FRMT, 94536	752 - G6
HOLY SEPULCHRE CEMETERY 26320 MISSION BLVD, HAY, 94544, (501)581-2488	712 - B5
HOME OF PEACE CEMETERY 4712 FAIRFAX AV, OAK, 94601, (510)482-1147	650 - E7
HOME OF PEACE CEMETERY EL CAMINO REAL, CLMA, 94014, (650)755-4700	687 - D7
HOY SUN MEMORIAL CEMETERY HILLSIDE BL & SERRAMONTE BL, CLMA, 94014, (650)757-9892	687 - E6
ITALIAN CEMETERY EL CAMINO REAL, CLMA, 94014, (650)755-1511	687 - D6
JAPANESE CEMETERY HILLSIDE BLVD & HOFFMAN ST, CLMA, 94014, (650)755-3747	687 - D6

FEATURE NAME	Address City, ZIP Code	PAGE-GRID
JEWISH CEMETERY	4550 PIEDMONT AV, OAK, 94611	630 - A7
LAFAYETTE CEMETERY	3287 MOUNT DIABLO BLVD, LFYT, 94549, (510)283-3700	611 - H5
LIVE OAK CEMETERY	DEER OAK PL, CNCD, 94521	593 - D5
LONE TREE CEMETERY	24591 FAIRVIEW AV, AlaC, 94541, (501)582-1274	712 - C1
LOS GATOS CEMETERY	2255 LOS GATOS ALMADEN RD, SJS, 95124, (408)356-4151	873 - E5
MADRONIA CEMETERY	6TH ST, SAR, 95070	872 - D3
MEMORIAL CROSS CEMETERY	DE LA CRUZ BLVD & MARTIN AV, SJS, 95050	833 - F2
MEMORY GARDENS CEMETERY	2011 ARNOLD INDUSTRIAL WY, CCCo, 94520, (510)685-3464	572 - F4
MEMORY GARDENS CEMETERY	3873 EAST AV, LVMR, 94550, (510)447-8417	715 - J1
MILITARY CEMETERY	BIRCH RD, BEN, 94510	551 - D5
MISSION CITY MEM PK CEMETERY	WINCHESTER BLVD, SCL, 95050, (408)984-3090	833 - D6
MOUNT OLIVET CEMETRY	LOS RANCHITOS RD, SRFL, 94903	566 - E4
MOUNT TAMALPAIS CEMETERY	2500 W 5TH AV, MrnC, 94901, (415)479-9020	566 - C5
MOUNTAIN VIEW CEMETERY	5000 PIEDMONT AV, OAK, 94611, (510)658-2588	630 - A7
MT EDEN CEMETERY	2200 DEPOT RD, HAY, 94545, (501)782-3266	711 - F6
OAK HILL CEMETERY	300 CURTNER AV, SJS, 95125, (408)297-2447	854 - E4
OAK VIEW MEMORIAL PARK CEMETERY	E 18TH ST & VERA AV, ANT, 94509, (510)757-4500	575 - H5
OAKMONT MEMORIAL PARK	2099 RELIEZ VALLEY RD, CCCo, 94549, (510)935-3311	591 - G5
OLIVET MEMORIAL PARK	1601 HILLSIDE BLVD, CLMA, 94014, (650)755-0322	687 - D5
PRESBYTERIAN CEMETERY	BONDE WY, FRMT, 94536	752 - H3
QUEEN OF HEAVEN CEMETERY	1965 RELIEZ VALLEY RD, CCCo, 94549, (510)932-0900	591 - G6
ROLLING HILLS MEMORIAL PARK	EASTSHORE FRWY & HILLTOP DR, RCH, 94803, (510)223-6161	589 - C1
ROSELAWN CEMETERY	1240 N LIVERMORE AV, LVMR, 94550, (510)581-1206	695 - G6
SAINT DOMINICS CEMETERY	5TH ST & HILLCREST AV, BEN, 94510	551 - D4
SAINT JOHNS CEMETERY	PARROTT DR, SMTO, 94402	748 - H4
SAINT JOSEPH CEMETERY	2560 CHURCH LN, SPAB, 94806, (510)223-1265	589 - A3
SAINT JOSEPHS CEMETERY	44200 MISSION BLVD, FRMT, 94539	773 - H2
SAINT MARYS CEMETERY	4529 HOWE ST, OAK, 94611, (510)654-0936	630 - A6
SAINT MICHAELS CEMETERY	EAST AV & DOLORES ST, LVMR, 94550	715 - J1
SAINT STEPHEN CATHOLIC CEMETERY	MONUMENT BL & MONUMENT CT, CNCD, 94520	592 - F3
SAINT VINCENT CEMETERY	BENICIA RD, VAL, 94591	530 - E7
SALEM MEMORIAL PARK	EL CM REAL & SERRAMONTE BL, CLMA, 94014	687 - D6
SAN FRANCISCO COLUMBARIUM	1 LORAINE CT, SF, 94118, (415)752-7891	647 - D6
SAN FRANCISCO NATIONAL CEMETERY	LINCOLN BLVD & SHERIDAN AV, SF, 94129	647 - D4
SANTA CLARA CATHOLIC CEMETERY	490 LINCOLN ST, SCL, 95050, (408)296-4656	833 - E5
SERBIAN CEMETERY	1801 HILLSIDE BLVD, CLMA, 94014, (650)755-2453	687 - E6
SKYLAWN MEMORIAL PARK CEMETERY	HALF MOON BAY RD, SMCo	768 - C4
SKYVIEW MEMORIAL CEMETERY	ROLLINGWOOD DR, VAL, 94591	530 - F6
SUNRISE MEMORIAL CEMETERY	SACRAMENTO ST & VALLE VISTA AV, VAL, 94590	529 - J2
SUNSET VIEW CEMETERY	101 COLUSA AV, CCCo, 94707, (510)525-5111	609 - E3
UNION CEMETERY	WOODSIDE RD, RDWC, 94061	770 - B7
VALLEY MEMORIAL PARK	650 BUGEIA LN, NVTO, 94945, (415)897-9609	526 - E1
WOODLAWN MEMORIAL PARK	1000 EL CAMINO REAL, CLMA, 94014, (650)755-1727	687 - C6

CHAMBERS OF COMMERCE

FEATURE NAME	Address City, ZIP Code	PAGE-GRID
ANTIOCH CHAMBER OF COMMERCE	301 W 10TH ST, ANT, 94509, (510)757-1800	575 - D4
BELMONT CITY CHAMBER OF COMMERCE	1365 5TH AV, BLMT, 94002, (650)595-8696	769 - F1
BELVEDERE-TIBURON PENINSULA CC	96 MAIN ST, TBRN, 94920, (415)435-5633	627 - E1
BENICIA CHAMBER OF COMMERCE	601 1ST ST, BEN, 94510, (707)745-2120	551 - B5
BERKELEY CHAMBER OF COMMERCE	1834 UNIVERSITY AV, BERK, 94703, (510)549-7000	629 - G2
BURLINGAME CHAMBER OF COMMERCE	290 CALIFORNIA DR, BURL, 94010, (650)344-1735	728 - G6
CAMPBELL CHAMBER OF COMMERCE	1628 W CAMPBELL BLVD, CMBL, 95008, (408)378-6252	853 - A6
CASTRO VALLEY CHAMBER OF COMMERCE	21096 REDWOOD RD, AlaC, 94546, (510)537-5300	692 - A6
CHAMBER OF COMMERCE	150 PARK LN, BSBN, 94005, (415)467-7283	688 - A5
CHAMBER OF COMMERCE - HAYWARD	22561 MAIN ST, HAY, 94541, (510)537-2424	711 - J1
CONCORD CHAMBER OF COMMERCE	2151 SALVIO ST, CNCD, 94520, (510)685-1181	592 - F1
CONCORD VIS & CONV BUREAU	2151 SALVIO ST, CNCD, 94520, (510)685-1184	592 - F1
CORTE MADERA CHAMBER OF COMMERCE	121 CTE MADERA TOWN CENTER, CMAD, 94925	586 - G7
CRAB COVE VISITORS CENTER	MCKAY LN, ALA, 94501	669 - F2
CUPERTINO CHAMBER OF COMMERCE	20455 SILVERADO AV, CPTO, 95014, (408)252-7054	852 - E2
DALY CITY-COLIMA CC	355 GELLERT BLVD, DALY, 94015, (415)991-5101	707 - C1
DANVILLE AREA CHAMBER OF COMMERCE	380 DIABLO RD #103, DNVL, 94526, (510)837-4400	653 - A2
DUBLIN CHAMBER OF COMMERCE	7080 DONLON WY, DBLN, 94568, (510)828-6200	693 - G5
EAST PALO ALTO CHAMBER OF COMERCE	1491 E BAYSHORE RD, EPA, 94303, (650)462-4915	791 - A2
EL CERRITO CHAMBER OF COMMERCE	10848 SAN PABLO AV, ELCR, 94530, (510)233-7040	609 - C2
EL SOBRANTE CHAMBER OF COMMERCE	3817 SAN PABLO DAM RD #330, CCCo, 94803, (510)223-0757	589 - C2
EMERYVILLE CHAMBER OF COMMERCE	2200 POWELL ST, EMVL, 94608, (510)652-5223	629 - D6
FOSTER CITY CHAMBER OF COMMERCE	1125 E HILLSDALE BLVD, FCTY, 94404, (650)573-7600	749 - F2
FREMONT C OF C & VISITORS BUREAU	2201 WALNUT STE 110 AV, FRMT, 94538, (510)759-2244	753 - B4
HERCULES CHAMBER OF COMMERCE	111 CIVIC DR, HER, 94547, (510)799-8200	569 - H3
LAFAYETTE CHAMBER OF COMMERCE	100 LAFAYETTE CIR, LFYT, 94549, (510)284-7404	611 - E6
LIVERMORE CHAMBER OF COMMERCE	2157 FIRST ST, LVMR, 94550, (510)447-1606	715 - F4
LOS ALTOS CHAMBER OF COMMERCE	321 UNIVERSITY AV, LALT, 94022, (650)948-1455	811 - D7
MARTINEZ CHAMBER OF COMMERCE	620 LAS JUNTAS ST, MRTZ, 94553, (510)228-2345	571 - D3
MENLO PARK CHAMBER OF COMMERCE	1100 MERRILL ST, MLPK, 94025, (650)325-2818	790 - F3
MILL VALLEY / LARKSPUR CC	85 THROCKMORTON AV, MLV, 94941, (415)388-9700	606 - D3
MILLBRAE CHAMBER OF COMMERCE	50 VICTORIA AV, MLBR, 94030, (650)697-7324	728 - B3
MILPITAS CHAMBER OF COMMERCE	75 S MILPITAS BLVD, MPS, 95035, (408)262-2613	794 - A7
MORAGA CHAMBER OF COMMERCE	440 CENTER ST, MRGA, 94556, (510)376-2520	631 - E3
MOUNTAIN VIEW CHAMBER OF COMMERCE	580 CASTRO ST, MTVW, 94041, (650)968-8378	811 - H5
NEWARK CHAMBER OF COMMERCE	6066 CIVIC TERRACE AV, NWK, 94560, (510)744-1000	752 - F6
NOVATO CHAMBER OF COMMERCE	807 DE LONG AV, NVTO, 94945, (415)897-1164	526 - C3
OAKLAND CHAMBER OF COMMERCE	475 14TH ST, OAK, 94612, (510)874-4800	649 - G4
ORINDA CHAMBER OF COMMERCE	2 THEATRE SQ #137, ORIN, 94563, (510)254-3909	630 - H1
PACIFICA CHAMBER OF COMMERCE	450 DONDEE WY, PCFA, 94044, (650)355-4122	726 - J2
PALO ALTO CHAMBER OF COMMERCE	325 FOREST AV, PA, 94301, (650)324-3121	790 - J5
PINOLE CHAMBER OF COMMERCE	751 BELMONT WY, PIN, 94564, (510)724-4484	569 - C4
PITTSBURG CHAMBER OF COMMERCE	2010 RAILROAD AV, PIT, 94565, (510)432-7301	574 - D3
PLEASANT HILL CHAMBER OF COMMERCE	91 GREGORY LN, PLHL, 94523, (510)687-0700	592 - C5
PLEASANTON CHAMBER OF COMMERCE	777 PETERS AV, PLE, 94566, (510)846-5858	714 - E3
REDWOOD CITY CHAMBER OF COMMERCE	1675 BROADWAY, RDWC, 94063, (650)364-1722	770 - B6
RICHMOND CHAMBER OF COMMERCE	3925 MACDONALD AV, RCH, 94805, (510)234-3512	589 - A7
RODEO CHAMBER OF COMMERCE	586 PARKER AV, CCCo, 94572, (510)799-7351	569 - H1
SAN ANSELMO CHAMBER OF COMMERCE	1000 SIR FRANCIS DRAKE BLVD, SANS, 94960, (415)454-2510	566 - B6
SAN BRUNO CHAMBER OF COMMERCE	618 SAN MATEO AV, SBRN, 94066, (650)588-0180	707 - J7
SAN CARLOS CHAMBER OF COMMERCE	1560 LAUREL ST, SCAR, 94070, (650)593-1068	769 - H4
SAN FRANCISCO CHAMBER OF COMMERCE	465 CALIFORNIA ST, SF, 94104, (415)392-4511	648 - B5
SAN FRANCISCO VISITORS BUREAU	201 3RD ST, SF, 94103, (415)974-6900	648 - B6
SAN JOSE CHAMBER OF COMMERCE	180 S MARKET ST, SJS, 95113, (408)291-5250	834 - B7
SAN JOSE CONV & VIS BUREAU	333 W SAN CARLOS ST, SJS, 95110, (408)295-9600	834 - B7
SAN LEANDRO CHAMBER OF COMMERCE	262 DAVIS ST, SLN, 94577, (510)351-1481	691 - A1
SAN MATEO CHAMBER OF COMMERCE	1021 S EL CAMINO REAL, SMTO, 94402, (650)341-5679	749 - A3
SAN MATEO COUNTY CONV & VIS BUR	111 ANZA BLVD, BURL, 94010, (650)348-7600	728 - G5
SAN PABLO CHAMBER OF COMMERCE	13880 SANN PABLO AV #D, SPAB, 94806, (510)215-3000	588 - J3
SAN RAFAEL CHAMBER OF COMMERCE	817 MISSION AV, SRFL, 94901, (415)454-4163	566 - G7
SAN RAMON CHAMBER OF COMMERCE	2355 SAN RAMON VALLEY BLVD, SRMN, 94583, (510)831-9500	673 - C1
SANTA CLARA CHAMBER OF COMMERCE	1850 WARBURTON AV, SCL, 95050, (408)244-9660	833 - D3
SARATOGA CHAMBER OF COMMERCE	20460 SARATOGA LOS GATOS RD, SAR, 95070, (408)867-0753	872 - D3
SAUSALITO CHAMBER OF COMMERCE	333 CALEDONIA AV, SAUS, 94966, (415)331-7262	627 - A2
SOUTH SAN FRANCISCO CC	213 LINDEN AV, SSF, 94080, (650)588-1911	707 - J3
SUNNYVALE CHAMBER OF COMMERCE	499 MURPHY AV, SUNV, 94086, (408)736-4971	832 - E1
UNION CITY CHAMBER OF COMMERCE	32980 ALVARADO-NILES RD, UNC, 94587, (510)471-6659	732 - D5
US CHAMBER OF COMMERCE	1901 S BASCOM AV, CMBL, 95008, (408)371-6000	853 - F5
VALLEJO CHAMBER OF COMMERCE	2 FLORIDA ST, VAL, 94590, (707)644-5551	529 - H4
WALNUT CREEK CHAMBER OF COMMERCE	1501 N BROADWAY, WLCK, 94596, (510)831-9500	612 - C5

CITY HALLS

FEATURE NAME	Address City, ZIP Code	PAGE-GRID
ALAMEDA CITY HALL	OAK ST & SANTA CLARA AV, ALA, 94501, (510)528-5710	670 - A2
ALBANY CITY HALL	1000 SAN PABLO AV, ALB, 94706, (510)644-8523	609 - D6
AMERICAN CANYON CITY HALL	2185 ELLIOT DR, AMCN, 94589, (707)647-4360	509 - J4
ANTIOCH CITY HALL	3RD ST & H ST, ANT, 94509, (510)779-7000	575 - C4
ATHERTON CITY HALL	91 ASHFIELD RD, ATN, 94027, (650)325-4457	790 - E2
BELMONT CITY HALL	1070 6TH AV, BLMT, 94002, (415)573-2790	769 - E1
BELVEDERE CITY HALL	450 SAN RAFAEL AV, BLV, 94920, (415)435-3838	607 - D7
BENICIA CITY HALL	250 E L ST, BEN, 94510, (707)746-4200	551 - C5
BERKELEY CITY HALL	2180 MILVIA ST, BERK, 94704, (510)644-6480	629 - G2
BRISBANE CITY HALL	150 PARK LN, BSBN, 94005, (650)467-1515	688 - A5
BURLINGAME CITY HALL	501 PRIMROSE RD, BURL, 94010, (650)696-7200	728 - F6
CAMPBELL CITY HALL	70 N 1ST ST, CMBL, 95008, (408)866-2100	853 - E5
CLAYTON CITY HALL	1007 OAK ST, CLAY, 94517, (510)672-3622	593 - H7
COLMA CITY HALL	235 EL CAMINO REAL, CLMA, 94014, (650)997-8300	687 - D7
CONCORD CITY HALL	1950 PARKSIDE DR, CNCD, 94519, (510)671-3000	592 - G1
CORTE MADERA CITY HALL	300 TAMALPAIS DR, CMAD, 94925, (415)924-1700	586 - F7
CUPERTINO CITY HALL	10300 TORRE AV, CPTO, 95014, (408)252-4505	852 - E1
DALY CITY HALL	90TH ST, DALY, 94015, (650)991-8000	687 - B5
DANVILLE CITY HALL	510 LA GONDA WY, DNVL, 94526, (510)820-6337	652 - J1
DUBLIN CITY HALL	100 CIVIC PZ, DBLN, 94568, (510)833-6600	693 - J4
EAST PALO ALTO CITY HALL	2415 UNIVERSITY AV, EPA, 94303, (650)853-3127	791 - B1
EL CERRITO CITY HALL	10890 SAN PABLO AV, ELCR, 94530, (510)215-4300	609 - C2
EMERYVILLE CITY HALL	2000 POWELL ST, EMVL, 94608, (510)654-6161	629 - D6
FOSTER CITY CITY HALL	610 FOSTER CITY BLVD, FCTY, 94404, (650)349-1200	749 - F2
FREMONT ADMINISTRATION CENTER	39100 LIBERTY ST, FRMT, 94538, (510)494-4620	753 - B4
HAYWARD CITY HALL	25151 CLAWITER RD, HAY, 94545, (510)293-5000	711 - E6
HERCULES CITY HALL	111 CIVIC DR, HER, 94547, (510)799-8200	569 - H3
HILLSBOROUGH CITY HALL	1600 FLORIBUNDA AV, HIL, 94010, (650)579-3800	728 - F7
LAFAYETTE CITY HALL	3675 MOUNT DIABLO BLVD, LFYT, 94549, (510)284-1968	611 - E6
LARKSPUR CITY HALL	400 MAGNOLIA AV, LKSP, 94939, (415)927-5110	586 - F6
LIVERMORE CITY OFFICES CITY HALL	1052 S LIVERMORE AV, LVMR, 94550, (510)373-5130	715 - J2
LOS ALTOS CITY HALL	1 N SAN ANTONIO RD, LALT, 94022, (650)348-1491	811 - E6
LOS ALTOS HILLS CITY HALL	26379 W FREMONT RD, LAH, 94022, (650)941-7222	811 - B6
LOS GATOS CITY HALL	110 E MAIN ST, LGTS, 95032, (408)354-6801	893 - A1
MARTINEZ CITY HALL	525 HENRIETTA ST, MRTZ, 94553, (510)372-3500	571 - D3
MENLO PARK CITY HALL	701 LAUREL ST, MLPK, 94025, (650)858-3360	790 - G3
MILL VALLEY CITY HALL	26 CTE MADERA AV, MLV, 94941, (415)388-4033	606 - D3
MILLBRAE CITY HALL	621 MAGNOLIA AV, MLBR, 94030, (650)259-2332	728 - B3
MILPITAS CITY HALL	455 CALVAVERAS BLVD, MPS, 95035, (408)942-2374	794 - B7
MONTE SERENO CITY HALL	18041 SARATOGA-LOS GATOS RD, MSER, 95030, (408)354-6834	872 - J6
MORAGA TOWN HALL	2100 DONALD DR, MRGA, 94556, (510)376-2590	631 - E4
MOUNTAIN VIEW CITY HALL	500 CASTRO ST, MTVW, 94041, (650)966-6300	811 - H5
NEWARK CITY HALL	37101 NEWARK BLVD, NWK, 94560, (510)793-1400	752 - E6
NOVATO CITY HALL	901 SHERMAN AV, NVTO, 94945, (415)897-4311	526 - C3
OAKLAND CITY HALL	1 CITY HALL PZ, OAK, 94612, (510)238-3611	649 - G3
ORINDA CITY HALL	26 ORINDA WY, ORIN, 94563, (510)254-3900	610 - G7
PACIFICA CITY HALL	170 SANTA MARIA AV, PCFA, 94044, (650)738-7300	706 - J5
PALO ALTO CITY HALL	250 HAMILTON AV, PA, 94301, (650)329-3211	790 - J5
PIEDMONT CITY HALL	120 VISTA AV, PDMT, 94611, (510)420-3040	650 - B1
PINOLE CITY HALL	2200 PEAR ST, PIN, 94564, (510)724-9000	569 - E4
PITTSBURG CITY HALL	65 CIVIC AV, PIT, 94565, (510)439-4850	574 - D3
PLEASANT HILL CITY HALL	100 GREGORY LN, PLHL, 94523, (510)671-5270	592 - C5
PLEASANTON CITY HALL	200 BERNAL AV, PLE, 94566, (510)484-8000	714 - D4
PORTOLA VALLEY TOWN HALL	765 PORTOLA RD, PTLV, 94028, (650)851-1700	810 - A6
REDWOOD CITY HALL	1017 MIDDLEFIELD RD, RDWC, 94063, (650)780-7000	770 - B6
RICHMOND CITY OFFICES	2600 BARRETT AV, RCH, 94804, (510)620-6513	588 - H6
ROSS CITY HALL	31 SIR FRANCIS DRAKE BLVD, ROSS, 94957, (415)453-1453	586 - C2
SAN ANSELMO CITY HALL	525 SAN ANSELMO AV, SANS, 94960, (415)258-4600	566 - C7
SAN BRUNO CITY HALL	567 EL CAMINO REAL, SBRN, 94066, (650)877-8897	707 - J7
SAN CARLOS CITY HALL	600 ELM ST, SCAR, 94070, (650)593-8011	769 - G3
SAN FRANCISCO CITY HALL	400 VAN NESS AV, SF, 94102, (415)554-4000	647 - J7
SAN JOSE CITY HALL	801 N 1ST ST, SJS, 95110, (408)277-4000	834 - A4
SAN LEANDRO CITY HALL	835 E 14TH ST, SLN, 94577, (510)577-3200	671 - A7
SAN MATEO CITY HALL	330 W 20TH AV, SMTO, 94403, (650)377-3420	749 - A4
SAN PABLO CITY HALL	SAN PABLO AV & CHURCH LN, SPAB, 94806, (510)215-3000	588 - J3
SAN RAFAEL CITY HALL	1400 5TH AV, SRFL, 94901, (415)485-3066	566 - F7
SAN RAMON CITY HALL	2222 CM RAMON, SRMN, 94583, (510)275-2200	673 - D1
SANTA CLARA CITY HALL	1500 WARBURTON AV, SCL, 95050, (408)984-3000	833 - D3
SARATOGA CITY HALL	13777 FRUITVALE AV, SAR, 95070, (408)868-1200	872 - F1
SAUSALITO CITY HALL	420 LITHO ST, SAUS, 94965, (415)332-0310	627 - A3
SOUTH SAN FRANCISCO CITY HALL	400 GRAND AV, SSF, 94080, (650)877-8500	707 - J3
SUNNYVALE CITY HALL	456 W OLIVE AV, SUNV, 94086, (408)738-5411	832 - D1
TIBURON CITY HALL	1505 TIBURON BLVD, TBRN, 94920, (415)435-0956	607 - D7
UNION CITY CITY HALL	34009 ALVARADO-NILES RD, UNC, 94587, (510)471-3115	732 - F6
VALLEJO CITY HALL	555 SANTA CLARA ST, VAL, 94590, (707)648-4527	529 - J5
WALNUT CREEK CITY HALL	1666 N MAIN ST, WLCK, 94596, (510)943-5800	612 - C5
WOODSIDE TOWN HALL	2955 WOODSIDE RD, WDSD, 94062, (415)851-6790	789 - H7

COLLEGES & UNIVERSITIES

FEATURE NAME	Address City, ZIP Code	PAGE-GRID
ARMSTRONG UNIVERSITY	2222 HAROLD WY, BERK, 94704, (510)848-2500	629 - G2
CSU OF HAYWARD	4700 YGNACIO VALLEY RD, CNCD, 94521, (510)602-6700	593 - C6
CSU OF HAYWARD	CARLOS BEE BL & WEST LOOP, HAY, 94542, (501)881-3000	712 - C4
CALIFORNIA COLLEGE OF ARTS & CRAFTS	BROADWAY & COLLEGE AV, OAK, 94618, (510)653-8118	629 - J6
CALIFORNIA MARITIME ACADEMY	200 MARITIME ACADEMY DR, VAL, 94590, (707)648-4200	550 - C2
CANADA COLLEGE	4200 FARM HILL BLVD, WDSD, 94062, (650)306-3100	789 - F4
CHABOT COLLEGE	25555 HESPERIAN BLVD, HAY, 94545, (510)786-6600	711 - F5

FEATURE NAME Address City, ZIP Code	PAGE-GRID
CITY COLLEGE OF SAN FRANCISCO 50 PHELAN AV, SF, 94112, (415)239-3000	667 - E7
COLLEGE OF MARIN 885 COLLEGE AV, MrnC, 94904, (415)457-8811	586 - D3
COLLEGE OF NOTRE DAME 1500 RALSTON AV, BLMT, 94002, (650)574-6444	769 - D1
COLLEGE OF SAN MATEO 1700 W HILLSDALE BLVD, SMTO, 94402, (650)574-6161	748 - H5
COLLEGE OF THE HOLY NAMES 3500 MOUNTAIN BLVD, OAK, 94602, (510)436-1000	650 - G4
CONTRA COSTA COLLEGE (W CAMPUS) 2600 MISSION BELL DR, SPAB, 94806, (510)235-7800	588 - J2
DE ANZA COLLEGE 21250 STEVENS CREEK BLVD, CPTO, 95014, (408)864-4567	852 - C1
DIABLO VALLEY COLLEGE 321 GOLF CLUB RD, PLHL, 94523, (510)685-1230	592 - B2
DOMINICAN COLLEGE 1520 GRAND AV, SRFL, 94901, (415)457-4440	566 - H7
EVERGREEN VLY COMM COLLEGE 3095 YERBA BUENA RD, SJS, 95135	855 - G4
FOOTHILL COLLEGE 12345 S EL MONTE AV, LAH, 94022, (650)949-7777	831 - C2
GOLDEN GATE UNIVERSITY 550 MISSION ST, SF, 94105, (415)442-7225	648 - B5
HOLY REDEEMER COLLEGE GOLF LINKS RD & GLENLY RD, OAK, 94605	671 - A3
INDIAN VALLEY COLLEGES 1800 IGNACIO BLVD, NVTO, 94949, (415)883-2211	526 - A7
KENNEDY, JOHN F UNIVERSITY 12 ALTARINDA RD, ORIN, 94563, (510)254-0200	610 - H7
LANEY COLLEGE 900 FALLON ST, OAK, 94607, (510)834-5740	649 - H5
LAS POSITAS COLLEGE 3033 COLLIER CANYON RD, LVMR, 94550, (510)373-5800	695 - D3
LOS MEDANOS COLLEGE 2700 E LELAND RD, PIT, 94565, (510)798-3500	574 - G5
MARYKNOLL SEMINARY 23000 CRISTO REY DR, SCIC, 94024, (650)967-3822	831 - H6
MENLO COLLEGE 1000 EL CAMINO REAL, ATN, 94027, (650)323-6141	790 - E3
MERRITT COLLEGE 12500 CAMPUS DR, OAK, 94619, (510)531-4911	650 - J6
MILLS COLLEGE 5000 MACARTHUR BLVD, OAK, 94613, (510)430-2255	650 - G7
MISSION COLLEGE 3000 MISSION COLLEGE BLVD, SCL, 95054, (408)988-2200	813 - A5
NEWARK OHLONE CTR - NEWARK CAMPUS 35753 CEDAR BLVD, NWK, 94560, (510)745-9037	752 - E4
OHLONE COLLEGE 43600 MISSION BLVD, FRMT, 94539, (501)659-6000	773 - J1
SAINT ALBERTS COLLEGE 5890 BIRCH CT, OAK, 94618, (510)596-1800	629 - J5
SAINT JOSEPHS SEMINARY CRISTO REY DR, CPTO, 95014	831 - G6
SAINT MARYS COLLEGE OF CALIFORNIA SAINT MARYS RD, MRGA, 94556, (510)376-4411	631 - G6
SAINT PATRICKS SEMINARY MIDDLEFIELD RD & SANTA MONICA, MLPK, 94025	790 - H2
SAMUEL MERRITT COLLEGE 370 HAWTHORNE AV, OAK, 94609, (510)869-6618	649 - H1
SAN FRANCISCO ART INSTITUTE 800 CHESTNUT ST, SF, 94133, (415)771-7020	647 - J3
SAN FRANCISCO STATE UNIVERSITY 1600 HOLLOWAY AV, SF, 94132, (415)469-1111	667 - B7
SAN FRANCISCO THEOLOGICAL-SEMINARY 2 KENSINGTON RD, SANS, 94960, (415)258-6500	586 - B1
SAN JOSE CHRISTIAN COLLEGE 790 S 12TH ST, SJS, 95112, (408)293-9058	834 - D7
SAN JOSE CITY COLLEGE 2100 MOORPARK AV, SJS, 95128, (408)298-2181	853 - G2
SAN JOSE STATE UNIVERSITY 125 S 7TH ST, SJS, 95192, (408)924-1000	834 - C6
SANTA CLARA UNIVERSITY 500 EL CAMINO REAL, SCL, 95053, (408)554-4000	833 - E4
SF COMM COLLEGE AIRPORT SCHOOL N ACCESS RD, SSF, 94080	708 - C6
SKYLINE COLLEGE 3300 COLLEGE DR, SBRN, 94066, (650)738-4100	707 - C6
STANFORD UNIVERSITY JUNIPERO SERRA BLVD, SCIC, 94305, (650)723-2300	790 - G6
THE COLLEGE OF ALAMEDA 555 ATLANTIC AV, ALA, 94501, (510)522-7221	649 - F7
UNIV OF CAL RICHMOND FIELD STA 1301 S 46TH ST, RCH, 94804, (510)231-9400	608 - J2
UNIV OF CALIF SAN FRANCISCO 501 PARNASSUS AV, SF, 94143, (415)476-9000	667 - D2
UNIV OF SAN FRANCISCO LAW SCHOOL STANYAN ST & HAYES ST, SF, 94117	647 - E7
UNIVERSITY OF CALIFORNIA VASCO RD & EAST GATE DR AV, AlaC, 94550, (510)422-1100	716 - D1
UNIVERSITY OF CALIFORNIA BERKELEY 2200 UNIVERSITY AV, BERK, 94720, (510)642-6000	629 - J1
UNIVERSITY OF PHOENIX 3590 N 1ST ST, SJS, 95134, (408)435-8500	813 - E3
UNIVERSITY OF SAN FRANCISCO 2130 FULTON ST, SF, 94117, (415)422-5555	647 - E7
UNIVERSITY OF THE PACIFIC 2155 WEBSTER ST, SF, 94115, (415)929-6450	647 - G5
USF LONE MOUNTAIN CAMPUS 2130 FULTON ST, SF, 94118, (415)422-5555	647 - E7
WEST VALLEY-SARATOGA COLLEGE 14000 FRUITVALE AV, SAR, 95070, (408)867-2200	872 - G2

DEPARTMENT OF MOTOR VEHICLES

FEATURE NAME Address City, ZIP Code	PAGE-GRID
CONCORD DEPT OF MOTOR VEHICLES 2075 MERIDIAN PARK BLVD, CNCD, 94520, (510)671-2876	592 - D2
DALY CITY DMV 1500 SULLIVAN AV, DALY, 94015, (650)994-5700	687 - B5
DEPARTMENT OF MOTOR VEHICLES 150 JACKSON ST, HAY, 94544, (510)537-7761	711 - J3
DEPARTMENT OF MOTOR VEHICLES 200 COUCH ST, VAL, 94590, 649-0130	530 - A2
DEPARTMENT OF MOTOR VEHICLES 75 TAMAL VISTA BLVD, CMAD, 94925, (415)924-5560	586 - G6
EL CERRITO DMV 6400 MANILA AV, ELCR, 94530, (510)235-9171	609 - C2
FREMONT DMV 4287 CENTRAL AV, FRMT, 94536, (510)797-0515	752 - H4
LOS GATOS DMV 600 N SANTA CRUZ AV, LGTS, 95030, (408)354-6541	873 - A6
MOUNTAIN VIEW DMV 595 SHOWERS DR, MTVW, 94040, (650)968-0610	811 - F4
NOVATO FIELD OFFICE DMV 936 7TH ST, NVTO, 94945, (415)897-0490	526 - A3
OAKLAND DMV 501 85TH AV, OAK, 94621, (510)568-0691	670 - F6
OAKLAND DMV 5300 CLAREMONT AV, OAK, 94618, (510)450-3670	629 - H6
PITTSBURG DMV 1399 BUCHANAN RD, PIT, 94565, (510)432-4748	574 - F6
PLEASANTON DMV 6300 W LAS POSITAS BLVD, PLE, 94588, (510)462-7042	714 - B1
REDWOOD CITY DMV 300 BREWSTER AV, RDWC, 94063, (650)368-2837	770 - A5
SAN FRANCISCO DMV 1377 FELL ST, SF, 94117, (415)557-1179	647 - F7
SAN JOSE DMV 111 W ALMA AV, SJS, 95110, (408)277-1301	854 - D2
SAN MATEO DMV 425 N AMPHLETT BLVD, SMTO, 94401, (650)342-5332	728 - J7
SANTA CLARA DMV 3665 FLORA VISTA AV, SCL, 95051, (408)277-1640	832 - J4
SANTA TERESA DMV 180 MARTINVALE LN, SJS, 95119, (408)224-4511	875 - E7
WALNUT CREEK DMV 1910 N BROADWAY, WLCK, 94596, (510)935-4464	612 - C4

ENTERTAINMENT & SPORTS

FEATURE NAME Address City, ZIP Code	PAGE-GRID
3COM PARK (CANDLESTICK PARK) GIANTS DR, SF, 94124	688 - C2
ALAMEDA COUNTY FAIRGROUNDS PLEASANTON AV & ROSE AV, PLE, 94566, (510)426-7600	714 - C3
BAY MEADOWS RACETRACK 2600 S DELAWARE ST, SMTO, 94403, (650)574-7223	749 - C4
CHILDRENS FAIRYLAND 1520 LAKESIDE DR, OAK, 94610, (510)832-3609	649 - H3
CONVENTION CENTER AV OF THE FLAGS, SRFL, 94903	566 - F3
COUNTY FAIR BUILDING 2495 S DELAWARE ST, SMTO, 94403, (650)574-3247	749 - C4
COW PALACE GENEVA & RIO VERDE, DALY, 94014, (415)469-6000	687 - H3
FREMONT DRAG STRIP 44999 CHRISTY ST, FRMT, 94538, (510)656-9900	773 - D5
FUDENNA STADIUM COUNTRY DR & FREMONT BLVD, FRMT, 94536	753 - A4
GOLDEN GATE PARK STADIUM 36TH ST & JOHN F KENNEDY DR, SF	667 - A1
GREAT AMERICA THEME PARK 1 GREAT AMERICA PKWY, SCL, 95054, (408)988-1776	813 - B4
KAISER, H J CONVENTION CENTER 10 10TH ST, OAK, 94607, (510)893-2082	649 - H5
KEZAR STADIUM FREDERICK ST, SF, 94117, (415)753-7032	667 - D1
MOSCONE CONVENTION CENTER 747 HOWARD ST, SF, 94103, (415)974-4000	648 - B6
OAKLAND ALAMEDA CO COLISEUM NIMITZ FRWY & HEGENBERGER RD, OAK, 94621, (510)569-2121	670 - E4
OAKLAND ALAMEDA COUNTY ARENA NIMITZ FRWY & HEGENBERGER RD, OAK, 94621, (510)569-2121	670 - E4
OAKLAND CONV CTR & VIS AUTHORITY 550 10TH ST, OAK, 94607, (510)839-7500	649 - G4
RACE TRACK PLE, 94566	714 - C3
RAGING WATERS 2333 WHITE RD, SJS, 95148, (408)270-8000	835 - B6
SAN JOSE ARENA W SANTA CLARA ST & AUTUMN ST, SJS, 95110, (408)287-9200	834 - A6
SAN JOSE CONVENTION CENTER 150 W SAN CARLOS ST, SJS, 95110, (408)277-3900	834 - B7
SAN JOSE MUNICIPAL BASEBALL-STADIUM E ALMA AV & SENTER RD, SJS, 95112	854 - E1
SANTA CLARA CONVENTION CENTER 5001 GREAT AMERICA PKWY, SCL, 95054, (408)748-7000	813 - B3
SANTA CLARA COUNTY FAIRGROUNDS 344 TULLY RD, SCIC, 95111, (408)295-3050	854 - F4
SCL COUNTY FAIRGROUNDS RACETRACK SANTA CLARA COUNTY FAIRGROUNDS, SCIC, 95111	854 - G4
SOLANO COUNTY FAIRGROUNDS 900 FAIRGROUNDS DR, VAL, 94589, (707)648-3247	510 - D7
SPARTAN STADIUM S 7TH ST & E ALMA AV, SJS, 95112, (408)924-6363	854 - E1
STANFORD STADIUM NELSON RD & SAM MCDONALD RD, SCIC, 94305, (650)723-2300	790 - J6
UC BERKELEY MEMORIAL STADIUM 2200 UNIVERSITY AV, BERK, 94720, (510)642-6000	629 - J1

FIRE TRAILS

FEATURE NAME Address City, ZIP Code	PAGE-GRID
1-1 OAKVALE CT, WLCK, 94596	612 - A5
1-2 461 SUMMIT RD, WLCK, 94598	612 - F5
1-4 630 LA CASA VIA, WLCK, 94598	612 - F4
1-5 MARSHAL DR, WLCK, 94598	612 - F5
2-1 3550 ECHO SPRING RD, LFYT, 94549	611 - F1
2-3 1070 CM VERDE CIR, WLCK, 94596	611 - J3
2-4 1645 GREEN HILLS DR, CCCo, 94549	611 - H1
2-5 LARKEY LN, WLCK, 94596	612 - A3
2-6 3238 GREEN HILLS DR, CCCo, 94549	611 - H1
2-7 TAYLOR BLVD, CCCo, 94549	611 - H1
3-1 KING DR, CCCo, 94595	612 - A7
3-2 ROCKVIEW DR, WLCK, 94595	632 - C2
3-3 SAKLAN INDIAN DR, WLCK, 94595	632 - C3
3-4 ROSSMOOR PKWY, WLCK, 94595	632 - C4
3-5 PTARMIGAN, WLCK, 94595	632 - A4
3-7 STANLEY DOLLAR DR, WLCK, 94595	632 - B3
3-8 HORSEMANS CANYON DR, WLCK, 94595, (510)933-2607	632 - D5
3-9 CACTUS CT, WLCK, 94595	632 - B2
4-1 WHITECLIFF WY, WLCK, 94596	612 - H7
4-2 BENHAM CT, WLCK, 94596	632 - H1
4-3 1880 ROCKSPRING PL, WLCK, 94598	612 - H6
4-4 WOODBURY CT, WLCK, 94596	612 - H7
4-5 SUTHERLAND DR, WLCK, 94598	612 - F6
4-6 RUDGEAR RD, WLCK, 94596	632 - G1
4-7 WHITECLIFF WY, WLCK, 94596	632 - G1
4-8 2086 ROBB RD, WLCK, 94596	632 - G1
4-10 60 LYMAN CT, WLCK, 94596	632 - E1
4-11 YOUNGS VALLEY RD, WLCK, 94596	632 - F2
4-12 ROCKSPRING PL, WLCK, 94596	612 - H7
4-13 BRIDLE LN, WLCK, 94596	632 - F2
4-14 I-680 NORTHBOUND, WLCK, 94595, (510)933-2607	632 - E1
5-5 STAGE COACH DR, CCCo, 94549	591 - G6
6-1 4491 EVORA RD, CCCo, 94565	573 - C2
6-2 4700 EVORA RD, CCCo, 94565	573 - C2
6-3 4690 EVORA RD, CCCo, 94565	573 - B2
6-4 AVILA RD, PIT, 94565	573 - D3
6-5 EVORA RD, CCCo, 94520	573 - A3
6-6 CANAL RD, CNCD, 94518	592 - G3
6-8 AVILA RD, PIT	573 - C3
7-2 LAS LOMAS WY, WLCK, 94598	612 - G4
7-3 DEER VALLEY LN, WLCK, 94598	612 - H5
7-4 CODORNIZ LN, WLCK, 94598	612 - H5
7-5 HANNA GROVE TR, WLCK, 94598	612 - J5
7-6 1000 CASTLE ROCK RD, CCCo, 94598	613 - A6
7-7 1600 CASTLE ROCK RD, CCCo, 94598	613 - A6
7-8 1600 CASTLE ROCK RD, CCCo	613 - A6
7-9 1600 CASTLE ROCK RD, CCCo	613 - B6
7-10 VALLEY VISTA RD, WLCK, 94598	613 - A2
7-11 VALLEY VISTA RD, WLCK, 94598	613 - A2
7-12 VALLEY VISTA RD, WLCK, 94598	613 - A2
7-13 ARBOLADO DR, CCCo	613 - B3
7-14 RIDGESTONE CT, CCCo	613 - B3
7-15 NORTH GATE RD, CCCo, 94598	613 - B5
7-16 NORTH GATE RD, CCCo	613 - B5
7-17 NORTH GATE RD, CCCo	613 - B6
7-18 NORTH GATE RD, CCCo	613 - C7
7-19 NORTH GATE RD, CCCo	613 - C7
7-20 NORTH GATE RD, CCCo	613 - C7
7-21 NORTH GATE RD, CCCo, 94598	613 - B3
7-22 DIABLO FOOTHILLS REG PK, WLCK, 94598	612 - J6
7-23 DIABLO FOOTHILLS REGIONAL PK, CCCo	613 - A7
7-24 PINECREEK RD, CCCo, 94598	612 - J5
7-25 NORTH GATE RD, CCCo, 94598	613 - A5
8-1 COURT LN, CNCD, 94518	592 - J5
10-1 YGNACIO VALLEY RD, CNCD, 94521	593 - A6
10-2 YGNACIO VALLEY RD, WLCK, 94598	613 - A1
10-17 LIME RIDGE, CNCD, 94518	592 - J5
10-18 VIA MONTANAS, CNCD, 94518	592 - H5
10-19 VIA MONTANAS, CNCD, 94518	592 - H4
10-20 CENTER LIME RIDGE, CNCD, 94518	592 - J6
10-22 FAIR WEATHER CIR, CNCD, 94518	593 - A6
10-23 NAVARONNE WY, WLCK, 94598	592 - J7
10-24 YGNACIO VALLEY RD, WLCK, 94598	593 - A7
11-2 HESS RD, CCCo	593 - J4
11-4 KIRKER PASS RD, CCCo	593 - J3
11-5 KAISER QUARRY RD, CCCo	613 - F1
11-6 555 MITCHELL CANYON RD, CCCo, 94517	613 - G1
11-7 KAISER QUARRY RD, CCCo	613 - E1
11-8 MITCHELL CANYON RD, CCCo	613 - G2
11-10 HESS RD, CCCo	593 - J4
11-11 PINE HOLLOW RD, CNCD	613 - D1
11-12 PINE HOLLOW RD, CNCD	613 - D1
11-13 PINE HOLLOW RD, CNCD	613 - D1
11-14 YGNACIO VALLEY RD, CNCD, 94521	593 - C6
11-16 247 MONTAIRE PKWY, CLAY, 94517	613 - J2
11-17 IRONWOOD WY, CNCD, 94521	593 - F7
11-18 MITCHELL CANYON RD, CCCo	613 - G3
11-19 MERRITT DR, CNCD, 94521	593 - F7
11-20 PEACOCK CREEK DR, CLAY, 94517	593 - J7
11-21 CLAYTON RD, CLAY, 94517	613 - J1
11-22 747 BLOCHING CIR, CLAY, 94517	613 - J2
11-23 157 REGENCY DR, CLAY, 94517	613 - J2
11-24 RIALTO DR, CCCo, 94517	613 - J3
11-25 1908 KIRKWOOD DR, CNCD, 94521	593 - G5
11-26 REGENCY DR, CCCo, 94517	613 - J2

FEATURE NAME	Address City, ZIP Code	PAGE-GRID
11-27	MOUNT TAMALPAIS DR, CCCo, 94517	613 - H2
11-28	AHWANEE CT, CLAY, 94517	593 - H6
11-31	BLUE OAK LN, CLAY, 94517	593 - J5
11-33	KELOK WY, CLAY, 94517	593 - J6
13-1	5550 ALHAMBRA AV, MRTZ, 94553	591 - G2
13-2	LINDSEY DR, MRTZ, 94553	591 - G2
13-3	CHRISTIE DR, MRTZ, 94553	591 - F1
13-5	2635 RELIEZ VALLEY RD, CCCo, 94553	591 - F2
13-9	FRANKLIN CANYON RD, CCCo	570 - J4
13-9	FRANKLIN CANYON RD, CCCo, 94553	571 - A4
13-10	FRANKLIN CANYON RD, CCCo	570 - J4
13-11	FRANKLIN CANYON RD, CCCo	570 - J3
13-12	MCEWEN RD, CCCo	570 - J3
13-13	MCEWEN RD, CCCo	570 - J2
13-18	FRANKLIN CANYON RD, CCCo, 94553	571 - A5
13-19	FRANKLIN CANYON RD, CCCo, 94553	571 - A5
13-20	MCHARRY RANCH RD, CCCo, 94553	571 - A5
13-21	WOLCOTT LN, CCCo, 94553	571 - B5
13-21A	WOLCOTT LN, CCCo, 94553	571 - B5
13-22	2560 FRANKLIN CANYON RD, CCCo, 94553	571 - B5
13-22A	2480 FRANKLIN CANYON RD, CCCo, 94553	571 - C6
13-23	FRANKLIN CANYON RD, CCCo, 94553	571 - A5
13-24	2785 FRANKLIN CANYON RD, CCCo, 94553	571 - B5
13-24A	FRANKLIN CANYON RD, CCCo, 94553	571 - B6
13-25	DUTRA RD, CCCo, 94553	571 - C7
13-26	FRANKLIN CANYON RD, MRTZ, 94553	571 - E7
13-27	148 GORDON WY, CCCo, 94553	591 - D2
13-28	1200 CHRISTIE RD, CCCo, 94553	570 - J7
13-30	5530 ALHAMBRA VALLEY RD, CCCo, 94553	591 - B2
13-32	1150 BRIONES RD, CCCo, 94553	591 - D4
13-33	1150 BRIONES RD, CCCo	591 - E4
13-34	5433 ALHAMBRA VALLEY RD, CCCo, 94553	591 - C3
13-35	VACA CREEK RD, CCCo, 94553	591 - D3
13-35B	2000 STONEHURST CT, CCCo, 94553	591 - C2
13-35C	1055 STONEHURST DR, CCCo, 94553	591 - C2
13-36	5355 ALHAMBRA VALLEY RD, CCCo, 94553	591 - D3
13-37	BRIONES RD, CCCo, 94553	591 - D4
13-38	4950 ALHAMBRA VALLEY RD, MRTZ, 94553	591 - E1
13-39	5026 ALHAMBRA VALLEY RD, MRTZ, 94553	591 - E1
13-40	ALHAMBRA AV, MRTZ, 94553	591 - G1
13-41	COSTANZA DR, MRTZ, 94553	591 - G1
13-42	MCHARRY RANCH RD, CCCo, 94553	570 - J6
13-43	MT KENNEDY DR, MRTZ, 94553	591 - G1
13-44	720 VINE HILL WY, MRTZ, 94553	591 - G1
13-46	ROANOKE DR, MRTZ, 94553	571 - C5
13-46	ROANOKE DR, MRTZ, 94553	591 - H3
13-47	CANYON WY, MRTZ, 94553	571 - D6
14-1	BUCKLEY ST, MRTZ, 94553	571 - C3
14-2	BUCKLEY ST, MRTZ, 94553	571 - C3
14-3	1158 PANORAMIC DR, MRTZ, 94553	571 - D4
14-4	ARABIAN HEIGHTS DR, MRTZ, 94553	571 - D4
14-5	WALLIN DR, MRTZ, 94553	571 - D6
14-6	CARQUINEZ SCENIC DR, CCCo, 94553	571 - A2
14-7	F ST, CCCo, 94553	571 - C3
14-8	1711 DUNCAN DR, MRTZ, 94553	571 - D4
14-9	DUNCAN DR, MRTZ, 94553	571 - D4
14-10	DUNCAN DR, MRTZ, 94553	571 - D4
14-11	CANYON WY, MRTZ, 94553	571 - D6
14-12	GREEN ST, MRTZ, 94553	571 - D4
15-3	BACON WY, WLCK, 94596	612 - A4
15-4	1329 SAN RELIEZ CT, LFYT, 94549	611 - H4
15-6	3475 RANCHO DEL HOMBRE, LFYT, 94549	611 - F2
15-7	SPRINGHILL RD, CCCo	611 - E3
15-8	SPRINGHILL RD, CCCo	611 - E3
15-9	VIS BELLA, LFYT, 94549	611 - F4
15-10	LAFAYETTE RDG TR, LFYT, 94549	611 - F4
15-11	SESSIONS RD, LFYT, 94549	611 - F4

FEATURE NAME	Address City, ZIP Code	PAGE-GRID
15-13	1219 MONTICELLO RD, LFYT, 94549	611 - E4
15-14	SUMMIT RD, LFYT, 94549	611 - J4
15-15	DEER HILL RD, LFYT, 94549	611 - H5
15-16	CRESTMONT DR, LFYT, 94549	611 - D5
15-17	DEER HILL RD, LFYT, 94549	611 - H5
15-18	RELIEZ VALLEY RD, WLCK, 94596	611 - J3
15-19	MONARCH RIDGE DR, WLCK, 94596	611 - H3
15-20	LAMPLIGHT CT, WLCK, 94596	611 - J3
16-5	PANORAMA DR, LFYT, 94549	611 - D3
16-11	120 CAMELIA LN, LFYT, 94549	611 - A5
16-13	LORINDA LN, LFYT, 94549	611 - A5
16-14	MT DIABLO BLVD, LFYT, 94549	611 - B6
16-15	LAFAYETTE RESERVOIR, LFYT, 94549	611 - C6
16-16	1182 ESTATES DR, LFYT, 94549	611 - B5
17-1	WOODVIEW DR, LFYT, 94549	631 - G1
17-2	MORECROFT RD, LFYT, 94549	632 - A4
17-3	HUNSAKER CANYON RD, CCCo, 94549	632 - A4
17-4	MILDRED LN, MRGA, 94556	631 - F3
17-6	788 RELIEZ STATION RD, LFYT, 94549	631 - H1
17-8	HUNSAKER CANYON RD, LFYT, 94549	632 - A5
17-9	3160 LUCAS DR, LFYT, 94549	631 - J2
17-10	DRIFTWOOD DR, LFYT, 94549	631 - H4
17-11	ROHRER DR, LFYT, 94549	631 - H3
17-12	595 SILVERADO DR, LFYT, 94549	631 - H3
17-15	OAK CANYON RD, LFYT, 94549	632 - A3
17-17	DAWKINS DR, LFYT, 94549	631 - H3
18-1	MEDBURN ST, CCCo, 94565	572 - G2
18-2	NORMAN AV, CCCo, 94565	572 - G1
18-4	NICHOLS RD, CCCo, 94565	573 - B1
19-1	ALHAMBRA VALLEY RD, CCCo, 94553	590 - J3
19-2	5895 ALHAMBRA VALLEY RD, CCCo	591 - A5
19-3	6001 ALHAMBRA VALLEY RD, CCCo, 94553	590 - H3
19-4	ALHAMBRA VALLEY RD, CCCo, 94553	590 - G3
19-5	PEREIRA RD, CCCo, 94553	590 - F2
19-6	ALHAMBRA VALLEY RD, CCCo	590 - E2
19-7	ALHAMBRA VALLEY RD, CCCo	590 - E2
19-8	ALHAMBRA VALLEY RD, CCCo	590 - E2
19-8A	ALHAMBRA VALLEY RD, CCCo	590 - D2
19-9	ALHAMBRA VALLEY RD, CCCo	590 - C1
19-10	BEAR CREEK RD, CCCo, 94553	590 - F3
19-11	BEAR CREEK RD, CCCo, 94553	590 - F4
19-12	1190 BEAR CREEK RD, CCCo, 94553	590 - G5
19-13	1220 BEAR CREEK RD, CCCo, 94553	590 - G5
19-14	BEAR OAKS LN, CCCo	590 - H5
19-17	BEARINDA LN, CCCo	590 - G7
19-18	BEAR CREEK RD, CCCo	590 - J7
19-19	BEAR CREEK RD, CCCo	590 - J7
19-20	BEAR CREEK RD, CCCo	590 - H7
19-21	BEAR CREEK RD, CCCo	611 - A1
19-22	RANCHO DEL LAGO RD, CCCo, 94553	590 - H4
19-23	ABRIGO VLY TR, CCCo	611 - B1
19-24	HOMESTEAD VLY TR, CCCo	611 - B1
19-25	BLACK OAK TR, CCCo	591 - C7
19-26	VALLEY TR, CCCo	591 - C7
19-27	BRIONES CREST TR, CCCo	591 - D6
19-28	BRIONES RD, CCCo	591 - D6
19-29	BEAR CREEK RD, CCCo	611 - A2
19-30	4935 HAPPY VALLEY RD, CCCo, 94549	611 - B2
19-31	4927 HAPPY VALLEY RD, CCCo, 94549	611 - B2
19-32	4927 HAPPY VALLEY RD, CCCo, 94549	611 - B2
19-33	RUSSEL RDG TR, LFYT, 94549	611 - B3
19-34	HAMPTON RD, CCCo	590 - F6
19-35	HAMPTON RD, CCCo	590 - F6
19-36	5799 ALHAMBRA VALLEY RD, CCCo, 94553	590 - J2
19-37	5700 ALHAMBRA VALLEY RD, CCCo, 94553	591 - A2
19-38	ALHAMBRA VALLEY RD, CCCo, 94553	591 - A2
19-39	1090 FERNDALE RD, CCCo, 94553	590 - J1

FEATURE NAME	Address City, ZIP Code	PAGE-GRID
19-40	1090 FERNDALE RD, CCCo, 94553	590 - H2
19-41	BRIONES RD, CCCo	591 - D5
21-1	6170 ALHAMBRA AV, MRTZ, 94553	591 - H3
21-2	BENHAM DR, MRTZ, 94553	591 - H3
21-3	VIEWPOINT CT, MRTZ, 94553	591 - H3
21-4	PASO NOGAL, PLHL, 94523	591 - J3
21-5	ELLINGTON TER, PLHL, 94523	591 - J2
21-6	RELIEZ VALLEY RD, CCCo, 94549	591 - G7
21-7	STAGE COACH DR, CCCo, 94549	591 - H6
21-8	SILVERHILL CT, CCCo, 94549	591 - G5
21-9	STAGE COACH DR, CCCo	591 - F7
21-10	BRIONES PK, CCCo	591 - G7
21-11	BRIONES PK, CCCo	591 - G6
21-12	1965 RELIEZ VALLEY RD, CCCo	591 - F5
21-13	RELIEZ VLY RD, CCCo	591 - G6
21-14	2099 RELIEZ VALLEY RD, CCCo, 94549	591 - H5
21-15	HIDDEN POND RD, CCCo	591 - G5
21-16	RELIEZ VALLEY RD, CCCo, 94549	591 - G4
21-17	TAVAN ESTATES DR, CCCo	591 - F4
21-18	SKYLINE DR, MRTZ, 94553	591 - H3
21-19	HORIZON DR, MRTZ, 94553	591 - G3
21-20	BOIES DR, PLHL, 94523	592 - A3
31-1	1411 SAN RAMON VALLEY BLVD, DNVL, 94526	653 - B5
31-2	MIDLAND WY, DNVL, 94526	653 - A4
31-6	CAMPBELL PL, DNVL, 94526	653 - E3
32-1	CAMILLE AV, CCCo, 94507	632 - F7
32-2	LAS TRAMPAS RD, CCCo, 94507, (510)933-2607	632 - E6
32-3	2130 LAS TRAMPAS RD, CCCo, 94507	632 - D5
32-4	RIDGEWOOD RD, CCCo, 94507, (510)933-2607	632 - D4
32-5	2600 RIDGEWOOD RD, CCCo, 94507, (510)933-2607	632 - E5
32-6	ALAMO RANCH RD, CCCo, 94507	632 - G5
32-7	SUGARLOAF DR, CCCo, 94507	632 - F3
32-8	TRACY CT, CCCo, 94507	632 - J3
32-9	HIGH EAGLE RD, CCCo, 94507	632 - H5
32-10	OAKSHIRE PL, CCCo, 94507	633 - B4
32-11	STONE VALLEY RD, CCCo, 94507	633 - B5
32-12	LIVORNA RD, CCCo, 94507	632 - H2
33-1	LA GONDA WY, DNVL, 94526	632 - H6
33-2	2900 STONE VALLEY RD, CCCo, 94526	633 - B6
33-3	GOLDEN MEADOW LN, CCCo, 94526	633 - B4
33-4	GREEN VALLEY RD, CCCo, 94526	633 - C3
33-5	MERANO ST, DNVL, 94506	653 - E1
33-6	EMMONS CYN DR & COUNTRY OAK LN, CCCo, 94526	633 - D4
33-7	LACKLAND DR, CCCo, 94526	633 - E5
33-8	VIA DIABLO, CCCo, 94526	633 - F6
33-9	MCCAULEY RD, DNVL, 94506	653 - D2
33-10	DIABLO RD W/O CLYDESDALE DR, DNVL, 94526	633 - D7
33-11	DIABLO RD E/O ALAMEDA DIABLO, DNVL, 94506	633 - D7
33-12	DIABLO RD AT AVD NUEVA, DNVL, 94506	653 - E1
33-13	2406 DIABLO LAKES LN, CCCo, 94526	633 - F6
35-1	HOLBROOK DR, DNVL, 94506	653 - G4
35-3	MAPLEWOOD DR, DNVL, 94506	653 - J3
35-5	PEPPERWOOD DR, CCCo	654 - A1
35-6	EAGLE NEST PL, CCCo, 94506	654 - B2
35-8	BLACKHAWK MEADOW LN, CCCo, 94506	654 - D2
35-9	NOTTINGHAM DR, CCCo, 94506	654 - A4
35-10	CLOVERBROOK DR AT RASSANI DR, DNVL, 94506	654 - A6
35-11	LAURELWOOD DR, DNVL, 94506	653 - H3
35-12	WEST OF LAURELWOOD DR, DNVL, 94506	653 - H4
35-13	SUNHAVEN RD, DNVL, 94506	653 - H3
35-14	BLACKHAWK RD, CCCo, 94506	653 - J2
35-16	NORTHVIEW CT, DNVL, 94506	653 - H6
35-17	RIO GRANDE PL, SRMN, 94583	653 - G7
36-1	FINLEY RD, CCCo, 94506	654 - F2
36-2	FINLEY RD, CCCo	654 - H1
36-2A	FINLEY RD, CCCo	654 - H2
36-3	JOHNSTON RD, CCCo	654 - J6

FEATURE NAME	Address City, ZIP Code	PAGE-GRID
36-4	7191 JOHNSTON RD, CCCo	654 - J7
41-1	CASA REALE, ORIN, 94563	631 - B3
41-7	ALTA MESA, MRGA, 94556	631 - F7
41-11	AUGUSTA DR, MRGA, 94556	631 - B6
41-15	OLD REDWOOD HWY, CCCo	631 - A7
41-19	SAINT MARYS COLLEGE, MRGA, 94556	631 - G6
42-1	PAS GRANDE, MRGA, 94556	631 - C2
42-2	MORAGA RD, MRGA, 94556	631 - E2
42-3	LA SALLE DR, MRGA, 94556	631 - E3
42-4	KIMBERLY DR, MRGA, 94556	631 - D3
42-7	ALICE LN, MRGA, 94556	631 - C4
42-8	RHEEM BLVD, MRGA, 94556	631 - F4
42-10	VALLEY HILL DR, MRGA, 94556	631 - H6
42-10A	CATTLE CHUTE RD, MRGA, 94556	631 - H5
42-11	BOLLINGER CANYON RD, CCCo	631 - J7
42-11	BOLLINGER CANYON RD, CCCo	632 - A7
42-13	BOLLINGER CANYON RD, CCCo	631 - J7
44-5	END OF MEADOW PARK CT, LFYT, 94549	631 - B1
44-6	RHEEM BLVD, ORIN, 94563	631 - C2
44-7	HILLCREST DR, ORIN, 94563	631 - A1
44-8	DOLORES WY, ORIN, 94563	631 - A5
59-1	SOUTH GATE RD AT ROCK CITY, CCCo	633 - H5
59-2	SOUTH GATE RD AT ROCK CITY, CCCo	633 - H6
59-3	SOUTH GATE RD AT ROCK CITY, CCCo	633 - H6
59-4	SOUTH GATE RD AT ROCK CITY, CCCo	633 - J5
59-5	SOUTH GATE RD AT ROCK CITY, CCCo	633 - H3
59-6	SUMMIT RD, CCCo	633 - H3
59-7	SUMMIT RD, CCCo	633 - J2
59-8	SUMMIT RD, CCCo	633 - J2
59-9	NORTH GATE RD, CCCo	633 - G2
59-10	SUMMIT RD AT JUNIPER, CCCo	633 - H1
59-11	NORTH GATE RD, CCCo	633 - E2
59-12	NORTH GATE RD, CCCo	633 - E2
59-13	NORTH GATE RD, CCCo	613 - C7
59-14	SOUTH GATE RD AT ROCK CITY, CCCo	633 - H5
61-2	CANAL BLVD, RCH, 94804	608 - E2
63-1	LEISURE LN, CCCo, 94803	589 - E3
63-2	TRI LN, RCH, 94803	589 - H5
63-3	SAN PABLO DAM RD, CCCo	589 - H6
63-4	SAN PABLO DAM RD, CCCo	589 - H6
63-5	SAN PABLO DAM RD, CCCo	589 - J7
63-6	HILLSIDE DR, CCCo, 94803	589 - H5
63-7	PATRA DR, CCCo, 94803	589 - H5
63-8	CASTRO RANCH RD, CCCo, 94803	589 - H3
63-9	CASTRO RANCH RD, CCCo, 94803	589 - J3
63-10	CASTRO RANCH RD, CCCo, 94803	589 - J3
63-11	CASTRO RANCH RD, CCCo	590 - A3
63-12	COACH DR, RCH, 94803	589 - J2
66-1	WILD CAT CANYON PKWY, RCH, 94805	589 - B4
68-1	GIANT HWY, RCH, 94806	568 - G6
68-2	GIANT HWY & SOBRANTE AV, RCH, 94806	568 - H5
69-1	CAPITAL HILL, RCH, 94806	589 - B4
69-2	BONITA RD, RCH, 94806	589 - B4
69-3	MONTE CRESTA AV, RCH, 94803	589 - C3
69-4	LA CRESCENTA RD, RCH, 94803	589 - C3
69-5	WESLEY WY, RCH, 94803	589 - D3
69-6	CLARK RD, RCH, 94803	589 - D3
69-7	UPLAND DR, RCH, 94803	589 - E3
71-1	TAMALPAIS CT, ELCR, 94530	589 - C7
72-1	RIFLE RANGE RD, RCH, 94805	589 - E7
73-1	END OF TENNENT AV, PIN, 94564	569 - E3
73-2	END PINOLE SHORE DR, PIN, 94564	569 - C3
73-3	END OF PEACH ST OFF TENNENT AV, PIN, 94564	569 - E4
73-5	END CANYON DR, PIN, 94564	569 - E5
74-1	END OF GARRITY CT, PIN, 94564	569 - G5
74-2A	NEXT TO 3300 PONDEROSA TR, PIN, 94564	569 - G5
74-2B	NEXT TO 3309 PONDEROSA TR, PIN, 94564	569 - G5

FEATURE NAME	Address City, ZIP Code	PAGE-GRID
74-3	2457 FARIA, PIN, 94564	569 - F5
74-4	2458 FARIA, PIN, 94564	569 - F5
74-5	END OF PALOMA ST, PIN, 94564	569 - G6
74-6	END OF CARMELITA WY, PIN, 94564	569 - G6
74-7	END OF APPALOOSA TR, PIN, 94564	569 - H6
74-8	END OF SILVERCREST, PIN, 94564	569 - J7
74-9	END OF HAMILTON, PIN, 94564	569 - J6
74-10	END OF DOIDGE AV, PIN, 94564	570 - A6
74-11	4005 MARCUS, PIN, 94564	569 - J7
74-12	4030 MARCUS, CCCo	569 - J7
74-14	END LUCAS AV, PIN, 94564	569 - G6
74-15	PFEIFFER WY, PIN, 94564	569 - J7
74-16	END OF ADOBE RD, PIN, 94564	589 - H1
74-18	'Y' ON ALHAMBRA VALLEY RD, CCCo	590 - B2
74-19	ALHAMBRA VALLEY RD, CCCo	590 - B1
74-20	ALHAMBRA VALLEY RD, CCCo	590 - B2
74-21	('Y' ON LEFT-CASTRO RANCH RD), CCCo	590 - B2
74-22	AT Y CASTRO RANCH RD, CCCo	590 - A2
74-23	ALHAMBRA VALLEY RD, CCCo	590 - A2
74-24	ALHAMBRA VALLEY RD, CCCo	590 - A2
74-25	AT MOHRING RANCH BARN, CCCo	589 - J1
74-26	AT MOHRING RANCH BARN, CCCo	589 - J1
74-29A	END OF GALBRETH, CCCo, 94803	569 - F7
74-29B	GALBRETH ON LEFT, PIN, 94564	569 - F7
74-30	END OF HOKE CT, PIN, 94564	569 - E6
74-31	ACROSS FROM 2079 SHEA DR, PIN, 94564	569 - F6
74-32	1980 SARAH DR, PIN, 94564	569 - E5
74-33	END OF DUNCAN, PIN, 94564	569 - E6
74-34	TURQUOISE DR NEAR ONYX CT, HER, 94547	569 - H5
75-1	13 PARKER AV, CCCo	549 - J6
75-2	HWY 40 AT PACIFIC RFINERY, HER, 94547	569 - H1
75-3	END OF SPRINGWOOD CT, CCCo, 94572	569 - J1
76-4	VIEWPOINTE BLVD, CCCo, 94572	569 - J2
76-5	HWY 4 AT CLAEYS RANCH, CCCo	570 - B3
76-6	HWY 4, CCCo	570 - B2
76-7	HWY 4, CCCo	570 - B3
76-8	HWY 4, CCCo	570 - B3
76-9	HWY 4, CCCo	570 - B3
76-9A	HWY 4, CCCo	570 - B3
76-10	HWY 4 AT FERNANDEZ RANCH, CCCo	570 - B3
76-11	HWY 4 AT GOLF COURSE, HER	570 - D4
76-12	HWY 4 AT GOLF COURSE, CCCo	570 - D4
76-13	CHRISTIE RD, CCCo	570 - F5
76-14	CHRISTIE RD, CCCo	570 - F5
76-15	CHRISTIE RD, CCCo	570 - G5
76-16	HWY 4 AT CHRISTIE CRSG, CCCo	570 - C3
76-17	HWY 4, CCCo	570 - F3
76-18	HWY 4 AT DANLOS KENNELS, CCCo	570 - F3
76-18A	HWY 4, CCCo	570 - F3
76-19	HWY 4, CCCo	570 - F3
76-20	BARRY HILL RD, CCCo	570 - G3
76-21	BARRY HILL CT, CCCo	570 - G3
76-22	CUMMINGS SKWY, CCCo	570 - H3
76-23	FRANKLIN CANYON RD, CCCo, 94553	570 - H3
76-24	CUMMINGS SKWY, CCCo	570 - G3
76-25	CUMMINGS SKWY, CCCo	570 - G2
76-26	CUMMINGS SKWY, CCCo	570 - G2
76-27	CUMMINGS SKWY, CCCo	570 - G2
76-29	241 SHEPARD CT, HER, 94547	570 - B4
76-30	END OF REFUGIO VALLEY RD, CCCo	570 - C6
76-31	521 FALCON WY, HER, 94547	570 - A5
76-32	END OF PHEASANT, HER, 94547	569 - J6
76-33	FALCON WY & REFUGIO VALLEY RD, HER, 94547	570 - A5
76-34	341 GRISSOM ST, HER, 94547	570 - B4
77-1	CARQUINEZ SCENIC DR, CCCo, 94553	571 - A2
77-2	CARQUINEZ SCENIC DR, CCCo	570 - J1
77-3	CARQUINEZ SCENIC DR, CCCo	550 - H7

FEATURE NAME	Address City, ZIP Code	PAGE-GRID
77-5	CARQUINEZ SCENIC DR, CCCo	550 - H6
77-6	MCEWEN RD, CCCo	570 - H1
77-7	MCEWEN RD, CCCo	570 - H2
77-8	MCEWEN RD, CCCo	570 - H1
77-9	MCEWEN RD, CCCo	570 - G1
77-10	CARQUINEZ SCENIC DR, CCCo	550 - G5
77-11	CARQUINEZ SCENIC DR, CCCo	550 - F5
78-12	DUPURU DR, CCCo, 94525	550 - F5
78-12A	CARQUINEZ SCENIC DR, CCCo, 94525	550 - F5
78-13	ROLPH PARK DR, CCCo, 94525	550 - E5
78-14	CUMMINGS SKWY, CCCo	570 - F1
78-15	CUMMINGS SKWY, CCCo	570 - F1
78-16	CROCKETT BLVD, CCCo	550 - F7
78-17	CROCKETT BLVD, CCCo	550 - E7
78-18	CUMMINGS SKWY, CCCo	550 - D6
79-19	CUMMINGS SKWY, CCCo	550 - D6
79-20	CUMMINGS SKWY, CCCo	550 - C6
79-21	CROCKETT BLVD, CCCo, 94525	550 - D5
79-22	CROCKETT BLVD, CCCo, 94525	550 - D5
79-23	2ND AND ROSE ST, CCCo, 94525	550 - D5
79-24	OLD COUNTY RD, CCCo, 94525	550 - B5
79-25	OLD COUNTY RD, CCCo, 94525	550 - B5
82-1	CONTRA LOMA BLVD, ANT, 94509	595 - B3
82-2	CONTRA LOMA BLVD, ANT	595 - B3
82-3	EMPIRE MINE RD, ANT	595 - D6
82-4	EMPIRE MINE RD, ANT	595 - D6
82-5	EMPIRE MINE RD, ANT	595 - D6
82-6	EMPIRE MINE RD, CCCo	595 - D7
84-1	W 10TH ST, PIT, 94565	574 - C2
85-2	KIRKER PASS RD, CCCo	574 - C7
86-2	EVORA RD, CCCo, 94565	573 - D2
86-7	BAILEY RD, CCCo, 94565	573 - G4
86-8	BAILEY RD, CCCo	573 - G5
86-9	BAILEY RD, CCCo	573 - F6
86-10	BAILEY RD, CCCo	573 - G7
86-11	JACQUELINE DR, PIT, 94565	573 - J5
86-13	W LELAND RD, PIT, 94565	574 - A4
86-14	POINSETTIA AV, CCCo, 94565	573 - G1
86-15	NORTH BROADWAY, CCCo, 94565	573 - H1
86-16	WILLOW PASS RD, CCCo, 94565	574 - A2

GOLF COURSES

FEATURE NAME	Address City, ZIP Code	PAGE-GRID
ALMADEN COUNTRY CLUB	6663 HAMPTON DR, SJS, 95120, (408)268-4653	894 - D2
BAY MEADOWS GOLF COURSE	2600 S DELAWARE ST, SMTO, 94403, (650)341-7204	749 - C5
BLACKBERRY FARM GOLF COURSE	22100 STEVENS CREEK BLVD, CPTO, 95014, (408)253-9200	852 - A1
BLACKHAWK CC - FALLS (WEST)	599 BLACKHAWK CLUB DR, CCCo, 94506, (510)736-6550	654 - A2
BLACKHAWK COUNTRY CLUB - LAKESIDE	599 BLACKHAWK CLUB DR, CCCo, 94506, (510)736-6565	654 - A2
BLACKHAWK COUNTRY CLUB EAST (PVT)	599 BLACKHAWK CLUB DR, CCCo, 94506, (510)736-6565	654 - C3
BLUE ROCK SPRINGS GOLF COURSE	COLUMBUS PKWY, VAL, 94591, (707)643-8476	530 - G2
BOUNDARY OAK GOLF COURSE	3800 VALLEY VISTA RD, WLCK, 94598, (510)934-6211	613 - A1
BUCHANAN FIELD GOLF COURSE	3330 CONCORD AV, CCCo, 94520, (510)682-1846	592 - C1
BURLINGAME COUNTRY CLUB	80 NEW PLACE RD, HIL, 94010, (650)342-0750	748 - E1
CALIFORNIA GOLF CLUB OF SF	844 W ORANGE AV, SMCo, 94080, (650)589-0144	707 - F4
CANYON LAKES GOLF CLUB	640 BOLLINGER CANYON WY, SRMN, 94583, (510)735-6511	673 - F1
CASTLEWOOD COUNTRY CLUB	707 CASTLEWOOD DR, AlaC, 94566, (510)846-5151	714 - B7
CLAREMONT COUNTRY CLUB	5295 BROADWAY TER, OAK, 94611, (510)653-6789	630 - A6
CONTRA COSTA COUNTRY CLUB	801 GOLF CLUB RD, CCCo, 94523, (510)685-8288	592 - A2
CORICA, CHUCK MUNI GOLF COMPLEX	CLUBHOUSE MEMORIAL RD, ALA, 94502, (510)522-4321	670 - B6
CROW CANYON COUNTRY CLUB	711 SILVER LAKE DR, DNVL, 94526, (510)735-8300	653 - E7
CRYSTAL SPRINGS GOLF COURSE	6650 GOLF COURSE DR, SMCo, (650)342-0603	748 - C3
CYPRESS GREENS GOLF COURSE	2050 WHITE RD, SCIC, 95148, (408)238-3485	835 - C5
CYPRESS HILLS GOLF COURSE	2001 HILLSIDE BLVD, CLMA, 94014, (650)992-5155	687 - E6
DEEP CLIFF GOLF COURSE	10700 CLUBHOUSE LN, CPTO, 95014, (408)253-5357	852 - A2
DELTA VIEW GOLF COURSE	2242 GOLF CLUB RD, PIT, 94565, (510)427-4940	574 - A4
DIABLO COUNTRY CLUB	1700 CLUBHOUSE RD, CCCo, 94526, (510)837-9233	633 - D6
DIABLO CREEK GOLF COURSE	4050 PORT CHICAGO HWY, CNCD, 94520, (510)686-6262	572 - H3
DIABLO HILLS GOLF COURSE	1551 MARCHBANKS DR, WLCK, 94598, (510)939-7372	612 - E3
EMERALD HILLS GOLF COURSE	1059 WILMINGTON WY, RDWC, 94061, (650)368-7820	789 - F3

FEATURE NAME Address City, ZIP Code	PAGE-GRID
FAIRWAYS GOLF COURSE ROSE AV & PLEASANTON AV, PLE, 94566, (510)462-4653	714 - D3
FRANKLIN CANYON GOLF COURSE HWY 4 PKWY, HER, (510)799-6191	570 - E4
FREMONT HILLS COUNTRY CLUB ROBLE LADERA & PURISSIMA RD, LAH, 94022	811 - A7
GLENEAGLES INTERNATIONAL GOLF-COURSE 2100 SUNNYDALE AV, SF, 94134, (415)587-2425	687 - H2
GOLDEN GATE MUNICIPAL GOLF COURSE 47TH AV & FULTON ST, SF, (415)751-8987	666 - H1
GREEN HILLS COUNTRY CLUB LUDEMAN LN & LAUREL AV, MLBR, 94030, (650)588-4616	727 - J3
HARDING PK MUNICIPAL GOLF COURSE HARDING RD & SKYLINE BLVD, SF, 94132, (415)878-4427	666 - J7
INDIAN VALLEY GOLF CLUB 3035 NOVATO BLVD, MrnC, 94947, (415)897-1118	525 - D2
JOE MORTARA VALLEJO GOLF COURSE 900 FAIRGROUNDS DR, VAL, 94589, (707)642-5146	510 - D7
LAGUNITAS COUNTRY CLUB LAGUNITAS RD & GLENWOOD AV, ROSS, 94957, (415)453-8706	586 - B3
LAKE CHABOT GOLF COURSE GOLF LINKS RD, OAK, 94605, (510)351-5812	671 - E6
LAKE MERCED GOLF & COUNTRY CLUB 2300 JUNIPERO SERRA BLVD, DALY, 94015, (650)755-2233	687 - B4
LA RINCONADA COUNTRY CLUB 14595 CLEARVIEW DR, LGTS, 95030, (408)395-4220	873 - A3
LAS POSITAS GOLF COURSE 909 CLUBHOUSE DR, LVMR, 94550, (510)443-3122	695 - A5
LEMA, TONY GOLF COURSE 13800 NEPTUNE DR, SLN, 94579, (510)895-2162	690 - H6
LINCOLN PARK GOLF COURSE 34TH AV & CLEMENT ST, SF, 94121, (415)221-9911	646 - J6
LONE TREE GOLF COURSE 4800 GOLF COURSE RD, ANT, 94509, (510)757-5200	595 - D3
LOS ALTOS GOLF & COUNTRY CLUB 1560 COUNTRY CLUB DR, SCIC, 94024, (650)948-1024	831 - G4
MARE ISLAND GOLF CLUB 1800 CLUB DR, VAL, 94592, (707)644-3888	549 - H1
MARIN COUNTRY CLUB 500 COUNTRY CLUB DR, NVTO, 94949, (415)382-6700	546 - B2
MARINA GOLF COURSE 13800 NEPTUNE DR, SLN, 94577, (510)895-2164	690 - G5
MCINNIS PARK GOLF CENTER 350 SMITH RANCH RD, SRFL, 94903, (415)492-1800	566 - G1
MENLO COUNTRY CLUB 2300 WOODSIDE RD, WDSD, 94062, (650)366-9910	790 - A4
MILL VALLEY GOLF COURSE 280 BUENA VISTA AV, MLV, 94941, (415)388-9982	606 - F2
MIRA VISTA COUNTRY CLUB & GOLF-COURSE CUTTING BL & SCENIC ST, ELCR, 94530, (510)233-7045	589 - D7
MOFFETT FIELD GOLF COURSE MACON RD & MARRIAGE RD, SCIC, 94035, (408)603-8026	812 - D1
MONTCLAIR GOLF COURSE 2477 MONTEREY BLVD, OAK, 94602, (510)482-0422	650 - E2
MORAGA COUNTRY CLUB 1600 SAINT ANDREWS DR, MRGA, 94556, (510)376-2253	631 - C6
OAKHURST COUNTRY CLUB 1001 PEACOCK CREEK DR, CLAY, 94517, (510)672-9737	593 - H5
ORINDA COUNTRY CLUB 305 CM SOBRANTE, ORIN, 94563, (510)254-4313	610 - F6
PALO ALTO HILLS GOLF & COUNTRY-CLUB 3000 ALEXIS DR, PA, 94304, (650)948-1800	810 - G7
PALO ALTO MUNICIPAL GOLF COURSE 1875 EMBARCADERO RD, PA, 94303, (415)856-0881	791 - D3
PARKWAY GOLF COURSE 3400 STEVENSON BLVD, FRMT, 94538, (510)656-6862	753 - C5
PEACOCK GAP GOLF & COUNTRY CLUB 333 BISCAYNE DR, SRFL, 94901, (415)453-3111	567 - D5
PENINSULA GOLF & COUNTRY CLUB 701 MADERA DR, SMCo, 94403, (650)638-2239	748 - J5
PINE MEADOWS GOLF COURSE 451 VINE HILL WY, MRTZ, 94553, (510)228-2881	571 - H7
PLEASANT HILLS GOLF COURSE 2050 WHITE RD, SCIC, 95148, (408)238-3485	835 - C6
POINTE GOLF CLUB 1500 COUNTRY CLUB DR, MPS, 95035, (408)262-2500	794 - D4
POPPY RIDGE GOLF COURSE 4280 GREENVILLE, AlaC, 94550, (510)447-6779	716 - H5
PRESIDIO GOLF COURSE 300 FINLEY RD, SF, 94129, (415)561-4653	647 - C5
PRUNERIDGE GOLF COURSE 400 N SARATOGA AV, SCL, 95050, (408)248-4424	833 - C7
RICHMOND COUNTRY CLUB 3900 GIANT RD, RCH, 94806, (510)232-7815	568 - H6
ROSSMOOR GOLF COURSE 1010 STANLEY DOLLAR DR, WLCK, 94595, (510)933-2607	632 - B2
ROUND HILL GOLF & COUNTRY CLUB 3169 ROUND HILL DR, CCCo, 94507, (510)837-7424	632 - J4
RUBY HILL GOLF COURSE 2001 E RUBY HILL BLVD, PLE, 94566, (510)417-5850	715 - B6
SAN FRANCISCO GOLF CLUB J SERRA BL & BROTHERHOOD WY, SF, 94132, (415)469-4100	687 - B2
SAN JOSE COUNTRY CLUB 15571 ALUM ROCK AV, SCIC, 95127, (408)258-4901	815 - A6
SAN JOSE MUNICIPAL GOLF COURSE 1560 OAKLAND RD, SJS, 95131, (408)441-4653	814 - B7
SAN MATEO MUNICIPAL GOLF COURSE 1700 COYOTE POINT DR, SMTO, 94401, (650)347-1461	728 - J6
SAN RAMON ROYAL VISTA GOLF COURSE 9430 FIRCREST LN, SRMN, 94583, (510)828-6100	673 - G6
SANTA CLARA GOLF & TENNIS CLUB 5155 STARS & STRIPES DR, SCL, 95054, (408)986-1666	813 - B3
SANTA TERESA GOLF CLUB 260 BERNAL RD, SCIC, 95119, (408)225-2650	895 - D3
SARATOGA COUNTRY CLUB 21990 PROSPECT RD, SAR, 95070, (408)253-0340	852 - B6
SEQUOYAH COUNTRY CLUB 4550 HEAFEY RD, OAK, 94605, (510)632-2900	671 - D3
SHARON HEIGHTS GOLF & COUNTRY-CLUB 2900 SAND HILL RD, MLPK, 94025, (650)854-6422	790 - B7
SHARP PARK GOLF COURSE SHARP PARK RD, PCFA, 94044, (650)359-3380	706 - J7
SHORELINE GOLF LINKS 2600 N SHORELINE BLVD, MTVW, 94043, (415)969-2041	791 - H7
SILVER CREEK VALLEY COUNTRY CLUB 5960 COUNTRY CLUB PKWY, SJS, 95138, (408)239-5775	875 - G1
SKYWEST GOLF COURSE 1401 GOLF COURSE RD, HAY, 94541, (510)278-6188	711 - C3
SPRING VALLEY GOLF COURSE 3441 CALAVERAS RD, MPS, 95035, (408)262-1722	794 - G5
SPRINGTOWN GOLF COURSE 939 LARKSPUR DR, LVMR, 94550, (510)455-5695	696 - A3
STANFORD UNIVERSITY DRIVING RANGE CAMPUS DR W & LS ARBOLES AV, SCIC, 94305, (650)323-9516	790 - G7
STANFORD UNIVERSITY GOLF COURSE 198 JUNIPERO SERRA BLVD, SCIC, 94304, (650)323-0944	790 - F7
SUNKEN GARDENS GOLF COURSE 1010 S WOLFE RD, SUNV, 94086, (408)732-2046	832 - G3
SUNNY HILLS GOLF CENTER 49055 WARM SPRINGS BLVD, FRMT, 94539	793 - J3
SUNNYVALE MUNICIPAL GOLF COURSE 605 MACARA AV, SUNV, 94086, (408)738-3666	812 - C4
SUNOL VALLEY GOLF COURSE 6900 MISSION RD, AlaC, 94586, (510)862-0414	754 - C1
THE OLYMPIC COUNTRY CLUB 599 SKYLINE BLVD, SMCo, 94015, (415)587-4800	686 - J3
THE VILLAGES GOLF & COUNTRY CLUB 5000 CRIBARI LN, SJS, 95135, (408)274-4400	855 - H6
THUNDERBIRD GOLF COURSE 221 S KING RD, SJS, 95116, (408)259-3355	834 - F5
TILDEN PARK GOLF COURSE GOLF COURSE DR & SHASTA RD, CCCo, 94708, (510)848-7373	610 - A6
WILLOW PARK GOLF COURSE 17007 REDWOOD RD, AlaC, 94546, (510)537-8989	671 - J7

HOSPITALS

FEATURE NAME Address City, ZIP Code	PAGE-GRID
AGNEWS DEVELOPMENTAL CTR (EAST) ZANKER RD, SJS, 95134, (408)432-8500	813 - G3
AGNEWS DEVELOPMENTAL CTR (WEST) MONTAGUE EXWY, SCL, 95054, (408)432-8500	813 - D4
ALAMEDA CO MED CTR- HIGHLAND-CAMPUS 1411 E 31ST ST, OAK, 94606, (510)437-5081	650 - B4
ALAMEDA HOSPITAL 2070 CLINTON AV, ALA, 94501, (510)522-3700	669 - J2
ALEXIAN BROTHERS HOSPITAL 225 N JACKSON AV, SJS, 95116, (408)259-5000	834 - G2
ALTA BATES MEDICAL CENTER 2450 ASHBY AV, BERK, 94705, (510)540-4444	629 - J4
BOOTH MEMORIAL HOSPITAL 2794 GARDEN ST, OAK, 94601, (510)535-5088	650 - C5
BROOKSIDE HOSPITAL 2000 VALE RD, SPAB, 94806, (510)235-7006	588 - J4
CALIFORNIA PACIFIC MEDICAL CENTER 2333 BUCHANAN ST, SF, 94115, (415)563-4321	647 - G5
CALIFORNIA PACIFIC MEDICAL CENTER 3700 CALIFORNIA ST, SF, 94118, (415)387-8700	647 - D6
CAMINO HEALTHCARE 2500 GRANT RD, MTVW, 94040, (650)940-7000	831 - H1
CHILDRENS HOSPITAL MEDICAL CENTER 747 52ND ST, OAK, 94609, (510)428-3000	629 - G6
CHINESE HOSPITAL 845 JACKSON ST, SF, 94108, (415)982-2400	648 - A4
COLUMBIA GOOD SAMARITAN HOSPITAL 2425 SAMARITAN DR, SJS, 95124, (408)559-2011	873 - E3
COMM HOSP OF LOS GATOS-SARATOGA 815 POLLARD, LGTS, 95030, (408)378-6131	873 - B2
CRYSTAL SPRINGS REHAB CENTER 35 TOWER RD, SMCo, 94402, (650)312-5200	768 - H2
DAVIES MEDICAL CENTER CASTRO ST & DUBOCE AV, SF, 94114, (415)565-6000	667 - G1
DOCTORS HOSPITAL-PINOLE 2151 APPIAN WY, PIN, 94564, (510)741-2401	569 - D5
EAST BAY HOSPITAL 820 23RD ST, RCH, 94804, (510)234-2525	588 - H5
EDEN HOSPITAL 20103 LAKE CHABOT RD, AlaC, 94546, (510)537-1234	691 - J5
FAIRMONT HOSPITAL 15400 FOOTHILL BLVD, AlaC, 94578, (510)667-7800	691 - E3
FIRST HOSPITAL VALLEJO 525 OREGON ST, VAL, 94590, (707)648-2200	530 - A2
HERRICK MEMORIAL HOSPITAL 2001 DWIGHT WY, BERK, 94704, (510)845-0130	629 - G2
KAISER FNDTN HOSP-E BAY CAMPUS 280 W MACARTHUR BLVD, OAK, 94611, (510)596-1000	649 - H1
KAISER FOUNDATION HOSPITAL 27400 HESPERIAN BLVD, HAY, 94545, (510)784-4343	711 - G7
KAISER FOUNDATION HOSPITAL 1150 VETERANS BLVD, RDWC, 94063, (650)299-2000	770 - B5
KAISER FOUNDATION HOSPITAL 1200 EL CAMINO REAL, SSF, 94080, (650)742-2547	707 - F2
KAISER FOUNDATION HOSPITAL 1425 S MAIN ST, WLCK, 94596, (510)295-4000	612 - C6
KAISER FOUNDATION HOSPITAL 200 MUIR RD, MRTZ, 94553, (510)372-1000	571 - G6
KAISER FOUNDATION HOSPITAL 900 KIELY DR, SCL, 95051, (408)236-6400	833 - A5
KAISER FOUNDATION HOSPITAL 901 NEVIN AV, RCH, 94801, (510)307-1500	588 - F6
KAISER FOUNDATION HOSPITAL 975 SERENO DR, VAL, 94589, (707)648-6230	530 - A1
KAISER PERMANENTE MEDICAL CENTER 2425 GEARY BLVD, SF, 94115, (405)929-4000	647 - F6
KAISER PERMANENTE MEDI HOSP 99 MONTECILLO RD, SRFL, 94903, (415)444-2000	566 - D3
LAGUNA HONDA HOSPITAL 375 LAGUNA HONDA BLVD, SF, 94116, (415)664-1580	667 - D4
LAUREL GROVE HOSPITAL 19933 LAKE CHABOT RD, AlaC, 94546, (510)537-1234	691 - H5
LETTERMAN GENERAL HOSPITAL LETTERMAN DR & DEWITT RD, SF, 94129	647 - E4
LUCILE PACKARD CHILDRENS HOSPITAL 725 WELCH RD, PA, 94304, (650)497-8000	790 - G6
MARIN GENERAL HOSPITAL 250 BON AIR RD, MrnC, 94904, (415)925-7000	586 - E4
MEDICAL CENTER 411 30TH ST, OAK, 94609, (510)451-9909	649 - H2
MERRITHEW MEMORIAL HOSPITAL 2500 ALHAMBRA AV, MRTZ, 94553, (510)370-5000	571 - E4
MILLS HOSPITAL 100 S SAN MATEO DR, SMTO, 94401, (650)696-4400	748 - J2
MOUNT DIABLO MEDICAL CENTER 2540 EAST ST, CNCD, 94520, (510)682-8200	592 - F1
MUIR, JOHN MEDICAL CENTER 1601 YGNACIO VALLEY RD, WLCK, 94598, (510)939-3000	612 - E3
NOVATO COMMUNITY HOSPITAL 1625 HILL RD, NVTO, 94947, (415)897-3111	526 - A5
OCONNOR HOSPITAL 21505 FOREST AV, SJS, 95128, (408)947-2500	833 - F7
PENINSULA HOSPITAL 1783 EL CAMINO REAL, BURL, 94010, (650)696-5400	728 - C5
RONALD MCDONALD HOUSE 520 SAND HILL RD, PA, 94304, (650)325-5113	790 - G5
SAINT FRANCIS MEMORIAL HOSPITAL 900 HYDE ST, SF, 94109, (415)353-6000	647 - J5
SAINT LUKES HOSPITAL 3555 CESAR CHAVEZ ST, SF, 94110, (415)647-8600	667 - H4
SAINT MARYS HOSPITAL 450 STANYAN ST, SF, 94117, (415)668-1000	667 - E1
SAINT ROSE HOSPITAL 27200 CALAROGA AV, HAY, 94545, (510)782-6200	711 - H7
SAN FRANCISCO GENERAL HOSPITAL 1001 POTRERO AV, SF, 94110, (415)206-8000	668 - A3
SAN JOSE MEDICAL CENTER 675 E SANTA CLARA ST, SJS, 95112, (408)998-3212	834 - D5
SAN LEANDRO HOSPITAL 13855 E 14TH ST, SLN, 94578, (510)667-4510	691 - C2
SAN MATEO COUNTY GENERAL HOSPITAL 222 W 39TH AV, SMTO, 94403, (650)573-2222	749 - C6
SAN RAMON REGIONAL MEDICAL CENTER 6001 NORRIS CANYON RD, SRMN, 94583, (510)275-9200	673 - E1
SANTA CLARA VALLEY MEDICAL CENTER 751 BASCOM AV, SCIC, 95128, (408)299-5100	853 - F2
SANTA TERESA COMMUNITY HOSPITAL 250 HOSPITAL PKWY, SJS, 95119, (408)972-7000	875 - C6
SEQUOIA HOSPITAL 170 ALAMEDA DE LAS PULGAS, RDWC, 94062, (415)367-5561	769 - H6
SETON MEDICAL CENTER 1900 SULLIVAN AV, DALY, 94015, (650)992-4000	687 - B6
SHRINERS HOSP FOR CRIPPLED-CHILDREN 1701 19TH AV, SF, 94122, (415)665-1100	667 - B3
STANFORD UNIVERSITY HOSPITAL 300 PASTEUR DR, PA, 94304, (650)723-4000	790 - G6
SUMMIT MEDICAL CENTER 400 29TH ST, OAK, 94609, (510)655-4000	649 - H2
SUMMIT MEDICAL CENTER- NORTH HAWTHORNE AV & WEBSTER ST, OAK, 94609, (510)655-4000	649 - H1
SUMMIT MEDICAL CENTER- SOUTH 3100 SUMMIT ST, OAK, 94609, (510)835-4500	649 - H2
SUMMIT MEDICAL CENTER- WEST 450 30TH ST, OAK, 94609, (510)451-4900	649 - G1
SUTTER DELTA MEDICAL CENTER 3901 LONE TREE WY, ANT, 94509, (510)779-7200	595 - D1
SUTTER SOLANO MEDICAL CENTER 300 HOSPITAL DR, VAL, 94589, (707)554-4444	530 - C1
UCSF MEDICAL CENTER 500 PARNASSUS AV, SF, 94131, (415)476-1000	667 - D2
UCSF MOUNT ZION HOSPITAL 1600 DIVISADERO ST, SF, 94115, (415)567-6600	647 - G6
VALLEY CARE MEDICAL CENTER 5555 W LAS POSITAS BLVD, PLE, 94588, (510)847-3000	694 - D6
VALLEY MEMORIAL HOSPITAL 1111 E STANLEY BLVD, LVMR, 94550, (510)447-7000	715 - F1
VENCOR HOSPITAL OF SAN LEANDRO 2800 BENEDICT DR, SLN, 94577, (510)357-8300	691 - D2
VA HOSPITAL MENLO PK 795 WILLOW RD, MLPK, 94025, (650)493-5000	790 - J1
VA HOSPITAL-PALO ALTO 3801 MIRANDA AV, PA, 94304, (650)493-5000	811 - B3
VETERANS AFFAIRS MEDICAL CENTER 150 MUIR RD, MRTZ, 94553, (510)372-2000	571 - F6
VETERANS AFFAIRS MEDICAL CENTER 4150 CLEMENT ST, SF, 94121, (415)750-2041	646 - H6
WALNUT CREEK HOSPITAL 175 LA CASA VIA, WLCK, 94598, (510)933-7990	612 - F3
WASHINGTON TOWNSHIP HLTH CARE 2000 MOWRY AV, FRMT, 94538, (510)797-1111	753 - B3

HOTELS & MOTELS

FEATURE NAME Address City, ZIP Code	PAGE-GRID
AIRPORT INN INTERNATIONAL 1355 N 4TH ST, SJS, 95112, (408)453-5340	834 - A2
AIRPORT WEST-COMFORT INN 1390 EL CAMINO REAL, MLBR, 94030, (650)952-3200	728 - A2
AMERICANA 121 7TH ST, SF, 94103, (415)626-0200	648 - A7
ANA HOTEL 50 3RD ST, SF, 94103, (415)974-6400	648 - A6
ARENA HOTEL 817 THE ALAMEDA, SJS, 95126, (408)294-6500	833 - J7
BERESFORD ARMS 701 POST ST, SF, 94102, (415)673-2600	647 - J6
BERKELEY MARINA MARRIOTT 200 MARINA BLVD, BERK, 94804, (510)548-7920	629 - C2
BEST WESTERN CANTERBURY HOTEL 750 SUTTER ST, SF, 94109, (415)474-6464	647 - J5
BEST WESTERN CORTE MADERA INN 1815 REDWOOD HWY, CMAD, 94925, (415)924-1502	586 - H7
BEST WESTERN CREEKSIDE INN 3400 EL CAMINO REAL, PA, 94306, (650)493-2411	811 - C1
BEST WESTERN DUBLIN PK HOTEL 6680 REGIONAL ST, DBLN, 94568, (510)828-7750	693 - G5
BEST WESTERN EL RANCHO INN 1100 EL CAMINO REAL, MLBR, 94030, (650)588-8500	728 - A2
BEST WESTERN GARDEN COURT INN 5400 MOWRY AV, FRMT, 94538, (510)792-4300	752 - J7
BEST WESTERN GROSVENOR HOTEL 380 S AIRPORT BLVD, SSF, 94080, (650)873-3200	708 - A4
BEST WESTERN HERITAGE INN 1955 E 2ND ST, BEN, 94510, (707)746-0401	551 - C4
BEST WESTERN HERITAGE INN 3210 DELTA FAIR BLVD, ANT, 94509, (510)778-2000	575 - A5
BEST WESTERN HERITAGE INN 4600 CLAYTON RD, CNCD, 94521, (510)686-4466	593 - C4
BEST WESTERN INN AT THE SQUARE 233 BROADWAY, OAK, 94607, (510)452-4565	649 - F5
BEST WESTERN INN MOTEL 360 W A ST, HAY, 94541, (510)785-8700	711 - F2
BEST WESTERN LOS PRADOS INN 2940 S NORFOLK ST, SMTO, 94403, (650)341-3300	749 - E4
BEST WESTERN MOUNTAIN VIEW INN 2300 EL CAMINO REAL, MTVW, 94040, (650)962-9912	811 - E4
BEST WESTERN NOVATO OAKS INN 215 ALAMEDA DEL PRADO, NVTO, 94949, (415)833-4400	546 - F4
BEST WESTERN SAN JOSE LODGE 1440 N 1ST ST, SJS, 95112, (408)453-7750	833 - J2
BEST WESTERN SUNNYVALE INN 940 W WEDDELL DR, SUNV, 94089, (408)734-3742	812 - E4
BEVERLY HERITAGE HOTEL 1820 BARBER LN, MPS, 95035, (408)943-9080	813 - J4
BILTMORE HOTEL 2151 LAURELWOOD, SCL, 95054, (408)988-8411	813 - C6
CAMPTON PLACE 340 STOCKTON ST, SF, 94108, (415)781-5555	648 - A5
CASA MADRONA 801 BRIDGEWAY BLVD, SAUS, 94965, (415)332-0502	627 - B3
CATHEDRAL HILL VAN NESS AV & GEARY ST, SF, 94109, (415)776-8200	647 - H6
CHANCELLOR HOTEL 433 POWELL ST, SF, 94102, (415)362-1403	648 - A5
CLAREMONT RESORT & SPA 41 TUNNEL RD, OAK, 94705, (510)843-3000	630 - A3
CLARION HOTEL 401 E MILLBRAE AV, MLBR, 94030, (650)692-6363	728 - D3
CLIFT HOTEL 495 GEARY ST, SF, 94102, (415)775-4700	648 - A6
COMFORT INN 1185 ADMIRAL CALLAGHAN LN, VAL, 94591, (707)648-1400	510 - E7
COMFORT SUITES 121 E GRAND AV, SSF, 94080, (650)589-7766	708 - A3
CONCORD HILTON 1970 DIAMOND BLVD, CNCD, 94520, (510)827-2000	592 - D2
CORAL REEF MOTEL 400 PARK ST, ALA, 94501, (510)521-2330	669 - J3
COURTYARD BY MARRIOTT 1050 BAYHILL DR, SBRN, 94066, (650)952-3333	707 - H6
COURTYARD BY MARRIOTT 10605 WOLFE RD, CPTO, 95014, (650)252-9100	832 - F6
COURTYARD BY MARRIOTT 1727 TECHNOLOGY DR, SJS, 95110, (408)441-6111	833 - H2
COURTYARD BY MARRIOTT 2500 LARKSPUR LANDING CIR, LKSP, 94904, (415)925-1800	586 - J4
COURTYARD BY MARRIOTT 3150 GARRITY WY, RCH, 94806, (510)262-0700	589 - B1
COURTYARD BY MARRIOTT 47000 LAKEVIEW BLVD, FRMT, 94538, (510)656-1800	773 - F7

FEATURE NAME	Address City, ZIP Code	PAGE-GRID
COURTYARD BY MARRIOTT	5059 HOPYARD RD, PLE, 94588, (510)463-1414	694 - B6
COURTYARD BY MARRIOTT	550 SHELL BLVD, FCTY, 94404, (650)377-0660	749 - F2
CROWN STERLING SUITES	150 ANZA BLVD, BURL, 94010, (650)342-4600	728 - G5
CROWNE PLAZA	600 AIRPORT BLVD, BURL, 94010, (650)340-8500	728 - G5
CUPERTINO INN	10889 DE ANZA BLVD, CPTO, 95014, (408)996-7700	832 - E6
DAYS INN	4200 GREAT AMERICAN PKWY, SCL, 95054, (408)980-1525	813 - B5
DOUBLETREE HOTEL	835 AIRPORT BLVD, BURL, 94010, (650)344-5500	728 - F5
DOWNTOWN TRAVELODGE	790 ELLIS ST, SF, 94109, (415)775-7612	647 - J6
DUNFEY SAN MATEO HOTEL	1770 AMPHLETT PL, SMTO, 94402, (650)573-7661	749 - C3
ECONOMY INNS OF AMERICA	270 S ABBOTT AV, MPS, 95035, (408)946-8889	813 - J1
EMBASSY SUITES	1345 TREAT BLVD, CCCo, 94596, (510)934-2500	612 - C1
EMBASSY SUITES	2885 LAKESIDE DR, SCL, 95054, (408)496-6400	813 - A6
EMBASSY SUITES HOTEL	101 MCINNIS PKWY, SRFL, 94903, (415)499-9223	566 - F3
EMBASSY SUITES MILPITAS	901 CALAVERAS BLVD, MPS, 95035, (408)942-0400	794 - B6
EMBASSY SUITES SSF	250 GATEWAY BLVD, SSF, 94080, (650)589-3400	708 - A3
EXECUTIVE INN	20777 HESPERIAN BLVD, AlaC, 94541, (510)732-6300	711 - E2
EXECUTIVE INN MOTEL	1755 EMBARCADERO, OAK, 94606, (510)536-6633	650 - A7
FAIRMONT	950 MASON ST, SF, 94108, (415)772-5000	648 - A5
FAIRMONT HOTEL	170 S MARKET ST, SJS, 95113, (408)998-1900	834 - C7
FOUR POINTS HOTEL	1100 N MATHILDA AV, SUNV, 94089, (408)745-6000	812 - E3
FOUR SEASONS CLIFTON	495 GEARY ST, SF, 94102, (415)775-4700	647 - J6
GALLERIA PARK HOTEL	191 SUTTER ST, SF, 94108, (415)781-3060	648 - A5
GATEWAY INN	2585 SEABOARD AV, SJS, 95131, (408)435-8800	813 - F7
GOOD NITE INN	485 VETERANS BLVD, RDWC, 94063, (415)365-5500	770 - A4
GRAND HYATT SAN FRANCISCO	345 STOCKTON ST, SF, 94108, (415)398-1234	648 - A5
GROSVENOR INN	1050 VAN NESS AV, SF, 94109, (415)673-4711	647 - H6
HAMPTON INN-OAKLAND AIRPORT	8465 ENTERPRISE WY, OAK, 94621, (510)632-8900	670 - F5
HILTON	1250 LAKSIDE DR, SUNV, 94086, (408)738-4888	812 - J6
HILTON HOTEL	39900 BALENTINE DR, NWK, 94560, (510)490-8390	773 - A1
HILTON PLEASANTON HOTEL	7050 JOHNSON DR, PLE, 94588, (510)463-8000	693 - J5
HILTON TOWERS	300 S ALMADEN BLVD, SJS, 95110, (408)287-2100	834 - B7
HOLIDAY INN	1800 POWELL ST, EMVL, 94608, (510)658-9300	629 - D6
HOLIDAY INN	720 LAS FLORES RD, LVMR, 94550, (510)443-4950	696 - B5
HOLIDAY INN EXPRESS	160 SHORELINE HWY, MrnC, 94965, (415)332-5700	606 - G7
HOLIDAY INN EXPRESS	2532 CASTRO VALLEY BLVD, AlaC, 94546, (510)538-9501	691 - H5
HOLIDAY INN EXPRESS	350 N BAYSHORE BLVD, SMTO, 94401, (650)344-6376	729 - A7
HOLIDAY INN HOTEL	11950 DUBLIN CANYON RD, PLE, 94588, (510)847-6000	693 - G6
HOLIDAY INN HOTEL	625 EL CAMINO REAL, PA, 94301, (650)328-2800	790 - H5
HOLIDAY INN MARINE WORLD AFRICA	1000 FAIRGROUNDS DR, VAL, 94589, (707)644-1200	510 - C7
HOLIDAY INN MILPITAS	777 BELLEW DR, MPS, 95035, (408)321-9500	813 - H1
HOLIDAY INN OF CONCORD	1050 BURNETT AV, CNCD, 94520, (510)687-5500	592 - C2
HOLIDAY INN OF WALNUT CREEK	2730 N MAIN ST, WLCK, 94596, (510)932-3332	612 - C2
HOLIDAY INN PARK CENTER PLAZA	282 S ALMADEN BLVD, SJS, 95113, (408)998-0400	834 - B7
HOLIDAY INN SAN FRANCISCO INTL	275 S AIRPORT BLVD, SSF, 94080, (650)873-3550	708 - A4
HOLIDAY INN SAN JOSE	399 SILICON VALLEY BLVD, SJS, 95138, (408)972-7800	875 - F4
HOLIDAY INN SAN MATEO	330 N BAYSHORE BLVD, SMTO, 94401, (650)344-3219	729 - A7
HOLIDAY INN-CIVIC CENTER	50 8TH ST, SF, 94103, (415)626-6103	647 - J7
HOLIDAY INN-FINANCIAL DISTRICT	750 KEARNY ST, SF, 94111, (415)433-6600	648 - A5
HOLIDAY INN-FISHERMANS WHARF	1300 COLUMBUS AV, SF, 94133, (415)771-9000	647 - J3
HOLIDAY INN-FOSTER CITY	1221 CHESS DR, FCTY, 94404, (650)570-5700	749 - E2
HOLIDAY INN-GOLDEN GATE	1500 VAN NESS AV, SF, 94109, (415)441-4000	647 - H5
HOLIDAY INN-OAKLAND AIRPORT	500 HEGENBERGER RD, OAK, 94621, (510)562-5311	670 - F6
HOLIDAY INN-UNION SQUARE	480 SUTTER ST, SF, 94108, (415)398-8900	648 - A5
HOMEWOOD SUITES	10 TRIMBLE RD, SJS, 95131, (408)428-9900	813 - G6
HOTEL DE ANZA	233 W SANTA CLARA ST, SJS, 95110, (408)286-1000	834 - B6
HOTEL NIKKO	222 MASON ST, SF, 94102, (415)394-1111	648 - A6
HOTEL SAINTE CLAIRE	302 S MARKET ST, SJS, 95110, (408)295-2000	834 - C7
HOTEL SOFITEL	223 TWIN DOLPHIN DR, RDWC, 94065, (650)598-9000	749 - G7
HOWARD JOHNSON	5405 STEVENS CREEK BLVD, SCL, 95014, (408)257-8600	852 - H1
HOWARD JOHNSONS	580 BEACH ST, SF, 94133, (415)775-3800	647 - J3
HUNTINGTON HOTEL - NOB HILL	1075 CALIFORNIA ST, SF, 94108, (415)474-5400	647 - J5
HYATT REGENCY SAN FRANCISCO	5 EMBARCADERO CTR, SF, 94111, (415)788-1234	648 - B5
HYATT REGENCY SF AIRPORT	1333 OLD BAYSHORE HWY, BURL, 94010, (650)347-1234	728 - E4
HYATT SAN JOSE	1740 N 1ST ST, SJS, 95112, (408)993-1234	833 - J1
HYATT-FISHERMANS WHARF	555 N POINT ST, SF, 94133, (415)563-1234	647 - J3
HYATT-RICKEYS	4219 EL CAMINO REAL, PA, 94306, (650)493-8000	811 - D2
JOHN MUIR INN	445 MUIR STATION RD, MRTZ, 94553, (510)229-1010	571 - F6
LA QUINTA INN	20 AIRPORT BLVD, SSF, 94080	707 - J4
LAFAYETTE PARK HOTEL	3287 MOUNT DIABLO BLVD, LFYT, 94549, (510)283-3700	611 - H6
LE BARON HOTEL	1350 N 1ST ST, SJS, 95112, (408)453-6200	833 - J2
MANDARIN ORIENTAL	222 SANSOME ST, SF, 94104, (415)885-0999	648 - B5
MAPLE TREE INN	711 E EL CAMINO REAL, SUNV, 94086, (408)720-9700	832 - F2
MARIANIS INN	2500 EL CAMINO REAL, SCL, 95051, (408)243-1431	833 - B4
MARINES MEMORIAL CLUB/HOTEL	609 SUTTER ST, SF, 94102, (415)673-6672	648 - A5
MARK HOPKINS	1 NOB HILL CIR, SF, 94108, (415)392-3434	648 - A5
MARRIOTT HOTEL	2355 N MAIN ST, WLCK, 94596, (510)934-2000	612 - C3
MARRIOTT-BISHOP RANCH HOTEL	2600 BISHOP DR, SRMN, 94583, (510)867-9200	673 - D3
MARRIOTT-FISHERMANS WHARF	1250 COLUMBUS AV, SF, 94133, (415)775-7555	647 - J3
MARRIOTT-MOSCONE CENTER	55 4TH ST, SF, 94103, (415)896-1600	648 - A6
MARRIOTT-OAKLAND	1001 BROADWAY, OAK, 94607, (510)451-4000	649 - G4
MCLAREN LODGE	FELL ST & STANYON ST, SF, 94117, (415)666-7200	667 - E1
MIYAKO	1625 POST ST, SF, 94115, (415)922-3200	647 - H6
MIYAKO INN	1800 SUTTER ST, SF, 94115, (415)921-4000	647 - G6
OAKLAND AIRPORT HILTON	1 HEGENBERGER RD, OAK, 94621, (510)635-5000	670 - E7
PALACE HOTEL	2 NEW MONTGOMERY ST, SF, 94105, (415)392-8600	648 - B6
PAN PACIFIC	500 POST ST, SF, 94102, (415)771-8600	648 - A6
PARC FIFTY FIVE	55 CYRL MAGNIN ST, SF, 94102, (415)392-8000	648 - A6
PARK HYATT	333 BATTERY ST, SF, 94104, (415)392-1234	648 - B5
PARK INN	5977 MOWRY AV, NWK, 94560	772 - H1
PARK PLAZA	1177 AIRPORT BLVD, BURL, 94010, (415)342-9200	728 - F5
PARK PLAZA HOTEL	150 HEGENBERGER RD, OAK, 94621, (510)635-5300	670 - F7
QUALITY SUITES	3100 LAKESIDE DR, SCL, 95054, (408)748-9800	813 - A6
RADISSON HAUS INN	1085 E EL CAMINO REAL, SUNV, 94086, (408)247-0800	832 - H4
RADISSON HOTEL-UNION CITY	32083 ALVARADO-NILES RD, UNC, 94587, (510)489-2200	732 - C5
RADISSON PLAZA HOTEL	1471 N 4TH ST, SJS, 95112, (408)452-0200	833 - J2
RAMADA INN	1000 ADMIRAL CALLAGHAN LN, VAL, 94591, (707)643-2700	510 - E7
RAMADA INN	1217 WILDWOOD AV, SUNV, 94089, (408)245-5330	812 - J5
RAMADA INN	1250 OLD BAYSHORE HWY, BURL, 94010, (650)347-2381	728 - E4
RAMADA INN	2436 MAHOGANY WY, ANT, 94509, (510)754-6600	575 - A5
RAMADA INN	920 UNIVERSITY AV, BERK, 94804, (510)849-1121	629 - D2
RAMADA INN SAN FRANCISCO NORTH	245 S AIRPORT BLVD, SSF, 94080, (650)589-7200	708 - A4
RAMADA-FISHERMANS WHARF	590 BAY ST, SF, 94133, (415)885-4700	647 - J3
RAPHAEL	386 GEARY ST, SF, 94102, (415)986-2000	648 - A6
RED LION INN	2050 GATEWAY PL, SJS, 95110, (408)453-4000	833 - H1
RED ROOF INN	777 AIRPORT BLVD, BURL, 94010, (650)342-7772	728 - G5
RENAISSANCE STANFORD COURT	905 CALIFORNIA ST, SF, 94108, (415)989-3500	648 - A5
RESIDENCE INN	1080 STEWART DR, SUNV, 94086, (408)720-8893	812 - J6
RESIDENCE INN	2000 WINDWARD WY, SMTO, 94404, (650)574-4700	749 - E3
RESIDENCE INN	2761 S BASCOM AV, SJS, 95008, (408)559-1551	873 - F1
RESIDENCE INN	750 LAKEWAY DR, SUNV, 94086, (408)720-1000	813 - A6
RESIDENCE INN BY MARRIOTT	1000 AIRWAY BLVD, LVMR, 94550, (510)373-1800	695 - B5
RESIDENCE INN BY MARRIOTT	1071 MARKET PL, SRMN, 94583, (510)277-9292	673 - E3
RESIDENCE INN BY MARRIOTT	5400 FARWELL PL, FRMT, 94536, (510)794-5900	752 - J7
RESIDENCE INN BY MARRIOTT	700 ELLINWOOD WY, PLHL, 94523, (510)689-1010	592 - D4
RESIDENCE INN HOTEL	1854 W EL CAMINO REAL, MTVW, 94041, (650)940-1300	811 - G5
RITZ CARLTON SAN FRANCISCO	600 STOCKTON ST, SF, 94108, (415)296-7465	648 - A5
ROYAL BAY INN	44 ADMIRAL CALLAGHAN LN, VAL, 94591, (707)643-1061	530 - D4
SF AIRPORT HILTON	SF INTERNATIONAL AIRPORT, SMCo, 94128, (650)589-0770	728 - B2
SF AIRPORT MARRIOTT	1800 BAYSHORE HWY, BURL, 94010, (650)692-9100	728 - D3
SAN FRANCISCO HILTON AND TOWERS	333 OFARRELL ST, SF, 94102, (415)771-1400	648 - A6
SAN LEANDRO MARINA INN MOTEL	62 SAN LEANDRO MARINA, SLN, 94577, (510)895-1311	690 - G5
SANTA CLARA MARRIOTT	2700 MISSION COLLEGE BLVD, SCL, 95054, (408)988-1500	813 - B5
SHANNON COURT HOTEL	550 GEARY ST, SF, 94102, (415)775-5000	647 - J6
SHERATON-FISHERMANS WHARF	2500 MASON ST, SF, 94133, (415)362-5500	647 - J3
SHERATON HOTEL & CONFERENCE-CENTER	45 JOHN GLENN DR, CCCo, 94520, (510)825-7700	592 - D1
SHERATON PALACE	2 NEW MONTGOMERY ST, SF, 94105, (415)392-8600	648 - B5
SHERATON PLEASANTON HOTEL	5115 HOPYARD RD, PLE, 94588, (510)460-8800	694 - B5
SHERATON SILICON VALLEY EAST	1801 BARBER LN, MPS, 95035, (408)943-0600	813 - J4
SIR FRANCIS DRAKE	450 POWELL ST, SF, 94108, (415)392-7755	648 - A5
STANFORD PARK HOTEL	100 EL CAMINO REAL, MLPK, 94025, (650)322-1234	790 - G4
STANFORD TERRACE INN	531 STANFORD AV, PA, 94306, (650)857-0333	791 - A7
SUNDOWNER INN	504 ROSS DR, SUNV, 94089, (408)734-9900	812 - E4
SUPER 8 LODGE	111 MITCHELL AV, SSF, 94080, (415)877-0770	708 - A4
SUPER 8 LODGE MOTEL	5375 OWENS CT, PLE, 94588, (510)463-1300	694 - B5
SUPER 8 MOTEL	485 S MAIN ST, MPS, 95035, (408)946-1615	814 - A1
THE DONATELLO	150 POST ST, SF, 94102, (415)441-7100	648 - A6
THE HANDLERY UNION SQUARE	351 GEARY ST, SF, 94102, (415)781-7800	648 - A6
THE PRESCOTT HOTEL	545 POST ST, SF, 94102, (415)563-0303	648 - A6
THE PRUNEYARD INN	1995 S BASCOM AV, CMBL, 95008, (408)559-4300	853 - F5
TOWN HOUSE MOTEL	1421 1ST ST, LVMR, 94550, (510)447-3865	715 - G1
TRAVELODGE AT FISHERMANS WHARF	250 BEACH ST, SF, 94133, (415)392-6700	647 - J3
TRAVELODGE BERKELEY MOTEL	1820 UNIVERSITY AV, BERK, 94703, (510)843-4262	629 - G1
TRAVELODGE-FISHERMANS WHARF	1201 COLUMBUS AV, SF, 94133, (415)776-7070	647 - J3
TRAVELODGE, GOLDEN GATE	2230 LOMBARD ST, SF, 94123, (415)922-3900	647 - G4
TRAVELODGE SAN FRANCISCO CENTRAL	1707 MARKET ST, SF, 94103, (415)621-6775	667 - H1
UNION HOTEL	401 1ST ST, BEN, 94510, (707)746-0100	551 - B5
VAGABOND INN	1640 BAYSHORE HWY, BURL, 94010, (650)692-4040	728 - E3
VAGABOND INN, MIDTOWN	2550 VAN NESS AV, SF, 94123, (415)776-7500	647 - H4
VILLA FLORENCE	225 POWELL ST, SF, 94102, (415)397-7700	648 - A6
VILLA HOTEL AIRPORT SOUTH	4000 S EL CAMINO REAL, SMTO, 94403, (650)341-0966	749 - D6
WATERFRONT PLAZA HOTEL	10 WASHINGTON ST, OAK, 94607, (510)836-3800	649 - F5
WELLEX INN	31140 ALVARADO-NILES RD, UNC, 94587, (510)475-0600	732 - A4
WESTIN HOTEL	5101 GREAT AMERICAN PKWY, SCL, 95054, (408)986-0700	813 - B4
WESTIN SAINT FRANCIS	335 POWELL ST, SF, 94102, (415)397-7000	648 - A6
WESTIN - SF AIRPORT	1 OLD BAYSHORE HWY, MLBR, 94030, (650)692-3500	728 - D3
WOODFIN SUITES	39150 CEDAR BLVD, NWK, 94560, (510)795-1200	772 - H1
WOODFIN SUITES	635 E EL CAMINO REAL, SUNV, 94086, (408)738-1700	832 - E2
WYNDHAM GARDEN HOTEL	1300 CHESAPEAKE TER, SUNV, 94089, (408)747-0999	812 - H3
WYNDHAM GARDEN HOTEL	5990 STONERIDGE MALL RD, PLE, 94588, (510)463-3330	693 - H5
WYNDHAM GARDENS HOTEL	1010 NORTHGATE DR, SRFL, 94903, (415)479-8800	566 - E3

LIBRARIES

FEATURE NAME	Address City, ZIP Code	PAGE-GRID
ALAMEDA MAIN LIBRARY	2264 SANTA CLARA AV, ALA, 94501, (510)748-4660	670 - A2
ALBANY LIBRARY	1247 MARIN AV, ALB, 94706, (510)526-3720	609 - E6
ALMADEN BRANCH	6455 CAMDEN AV, SJS, 95120, (408)268-7600	894 - D1
ALUM ROCK LIBRARY	75 S WHITE RD, SJS, 95127, (408)251-1280	834 - J2
ALVISO BRANCH LIBRARY	1060 TAYLOR ST, SJS, 95002, (650)263-3626	793 - B7
ANTIOCH LIBRARY	501 W 18TH ST, ANT, 94509, (510)757-9224	575 - D5
ANZA LIBRARY	550 37TH AV, SF, 94121, (415)666-7160	646 - J7
ASIAN BRANCH LIBRARY	388 9TH ST, OAK, 94607, (510)238-3400	649 - G4
ATHERTON	2 DINKLESPEIL STATION LN, ATN, 94027, (650)328-2422	790 - E2
BANCROFT LIBRARY	UC BERKELEY, BERK, 94720, (510)642-6000	629 - H1
BAY FARM ISLAND BRANCH LIBRARY	3221 MECARTNEY RD, ALA, 94502, (510)748-4668	670 - A6
BAY POINT LIBRARY	205 PACIFICA AV, CCCo, 94565, (510)458-2215	573 - E1
BAYSHORE LIBRARY	2960 GENEVA AV, DALY, 94014, (650)991-8074	687 - J3
BAYVIEW LIBRARY	5100 HARNETT AV, RCH, 94804, (510)620-6566	609 - B2
BAYVIEW-ANNA WARDEN LIBRARY	5075 3RD ST, SF, 94124, (415)715-4100	668 - C6
BELMONT	1110 ALAMEDA DE LAS PULGAS, BLMT, 94002, (650)591-8286	769 - C2
BELVEDERE TIBURON LIBRARY	1501 TIBURON BLVD, TBRN, 94920	607 - D7
BENICIA LIBRARY	150 E L ST, BEN, 94510, 707-	551 - C5
BERKELEY BRANCH LIBRARY CLAREMONT	2940 BENVENUE AV, BERK, 94705, (510)644-6880	629 - J4
BERKELEY BRANCH LIBRARY NORTH	1170 THE ALAMEDA, BERK, 94707, (510)644-6850	609 - G6
BERKELEY BRANCH LIBRARY SOUTH	1901 RUSSELL ST, BERK, 94703, (510)644-6860	629 - G3
BERKELEY BRANCH LIBRARY WEST	1125 UNIVERSITY AV, BERK, 94702, (510)644-6870	629 - E2
BERKELEY CENTRAL LIBRARY	2090 KITTREDGE ST, BERK, 94704, (510)644-6100	629 - G2
BERNAL HEIGHTS LIBRARY	500 CORTLAND AV, SF, 94110, (415)695-5160	667 - J5
BERRYESSA	3311 NOBLE AV, SJS, 95132, (408)272-3554	814 - H5
BIBLIOTECA LATINO AMERICANA	690 LOCUST ST, SJS, 95110, (408)294-1237	854 - C1
BRISBANE LIBRARY	250 VISITACION AV, BSBN, 94005, (650)467-2060	688 - A6
BROOKFIELD LIBRARY	9255 EDES AV, OAK, 94603, (510)615-5725	670 - G6
BURLINGAME LIBRARY	480 PRIMROSE RD, BURL, 94010, (650)342-1036	728 - G6
BUSINESS LIBRARY	2400 STEVENSON BLVD, FRMT, 94538, (510)505-7001	753 - C4
CALABAZAS BRANCH LIBRARY	1230 BLANEY AV, SJS, 95129, (408)996-1535	852 - E3
CAMBRIAN BRANCH LIBRARY	1780 HILLSDALE AV, SJS, 95124, (408)269-5062	873 - H2
CAMPBELL LIBRARY	77 HARRISON AV, CMBL, 95008, (408)378-8122	853 - E5
CASTRO VALLEY LIBRARY	20055 REDWOOD RD, AlaC, 94546, (510)670-6280	692 - A5
CENTERVILLE LIBRARY	3801 NICOLET AV, FRMT, 94536, (510)795-2629	752 - F2
CHINATOWN LIBRARY	1135 POWELL ST, SF, 94108, (415)274-0275	648 - A5
CIVIC CENTER LIBRARY	1000 N LIVERMORE AV, LVMR, 94550, (510)373-5500	715 - J2
CLAYTON LIBRARY	6125 CLAYTON RD, CLAY, 94517, (510)673-0659	593 - H6
COLLEGE TERRACE BRANCH LIBRARY	2300 WELLESLEY ST, PA, 94306, (415)329-2298	791 - A7
CONCORD LIBRARY	2900 SALVIO ST, CNCD, 94519, (510)646-5455	592 - G1

FEATURE NAME Address City, ZIP Code	PAGE-GRID
CORTE MADERA LIBRARY 707 MEADOWSWEET DR, CMAD, 94925, (415)924-4844	586 - G7
CROCKETT LIBRARY 991 LORING AV, CCCo, 94525, (510)787-2345	550 - D4
CUPERTINO LIBRARY 10400 TORRE AV, CPTO, 95014	852 - E1
DALY CITY LIBRARY 40 WEMBLEY DR, DALY, 94015, (650)991-8023	707 - B2
DALY, JOHN D LIBRARY 6351 MISSION ST, DALY, 94014, (650)991-8073	687 - D3
DANVILLE LIBRARY 400 FRONT ST, DNVL, 94526, (510)837-4889	653 - A2
DIMOND BRANCH LIBRARY 3565 FRUITVALE AV, OAK, 94602, (510)482-7844	650 - D4
DOE LIBRARY UC BERKELEY, BERK, 94720, (510)642-6000	629 - H1
DOWNTOWN BRANCH LIBRARY 270 FOREST AV, PA, 94301, (650)329-2641	790 - J5
DUBLIN LIBRARY 7606 AMADOR VALLEY BLVD, DBLN, 94568, (510)828-1315	693 - H4
EASTMONT BRANCH LIBRARY EASTMONT MALL-2ND FLOOR, OAK, 94605, (510)615-5726	670 - H2
EASTON BRANCH LIBRARY 1800 EASTON DR, BURL, 94010, (650)343-1794	728 - D6
EAST PALO ALTO BRANCH LIBRARY 2415 UNIVERSITY AV E, EPA, 94303, (650)321-7712	791 - B1
EAST SAN JOSE CARNEGIE LIBRARY 1102 E SANTA CLARA ST, SJS, 95116, (408)998-2069	834 - E5
EDUCATIONAL PARK LIBRARY 1770 EDUCATIONAL PARK DR, SJS, 95133, (408)272-3662	834 - F2
EL CERRITO LIBRARY 6510 STOCKTON AV, ELCR, 94530, (510)526-7512	609 - D3
EL SOBRANTE LIBRARY 4191 APPIAN WY, CCCo, 94803, (510)374-3991	589 - C2
ELMHURST BRANCH LIBRARY 1427 88TH AV, OAK, 94621, (510)615-5727	670 - H4
EMPIRE BRANCH LIBRARY 491 E EMPIRE ST, SJS, 95112, (408)286-5627	834 - C4
EUREKA VALLEY-HARVEY MILK LIBRARY 3555 16TH ST, SF, 94114, (415)554-9445	667 - G2
EVERGREEN BRANCH 2635 ABORN RD, SJS, 95148, (408)238-4434	855 - C2
EXCELSIOR LIBRARY 4400 MISSION ST, SF, 94112, (415)337-4735	667 - G7
FAIR OAKS BRANCH LIBRARY 2600 MIDDLEFIELD RD, RDWC, 94063, (650)780-7261	770 - C7
FOSTER CITY LIBRARY 1000 E HILLSDALE BLVD, FCTY, 94404, (650)574-4842	749 - F2
FREMONT MAIN LIBRARY 2400 STEVENSON BLVD, FRMT, 94538, (510)745-1401	753 - C4
GLEN PARK LIBRARY 653 CHENERY ST, SF, 94131, (415)337-4740	667 - G6
GOLDEN GATE BRANCH LIBRARY 5606 SAN PABLO AV, OAK, 94608, (510)597-5023	629 - F6
GOLDEN GATE VALLEY LIBRARY 1801 GREEN ST, SF, 94123, (415)292-2195	647 - H4
GRAND AVENUE LIBRARY 306 WALNUT AV, SSF, 94080, (650)877-8530	707 - J3
HAYWARD LIBRARY 835 C ST, HAY, 94541, (510)293-8685	711 - J2
HILLSDALE BRANCH LIBRARY 205 W HILLSDALE BLVD, SMTO, 94403, (650)373-4880	749 - B6
HILLVIEW BRANCH LIBRARY 2255 OCALA AV, SJS, 95122, (408)272-3100	834 - J6
INGLESIDE LIBRARY 387 ASHTON AV, SF, 94127, (415)337-4745	667 - D7
IRVINGTON LIBRARY 41825 GREENPARK DR, FRMT, 94538, (510)795-2631	773 - D1
KENNEDY JOHN F LIBRARY 505 SANTA CLARA ST, VAL, 94590, (707)553-5568	529 - J5
KENSINGTON LIBRARY 61 ARLINGTON AV, CCCo, 94708, (510)524-3043	609 - F3
KING, MARTIN LUTHER JR LIBRARY 6833 E INTERNATIONAL BLVD, OAK, 94621, (510)238-7346	670 - G3
LAFAYETTE LIBRARY 952 MORAGA RD, LFYT, 94549, (510)283-3872	611 - F6
LAKEVIEW BRANCH LIBRARY 550 EL EMBARCADERO, OAK, 94610, (510)238-7344	649 - J3
LARKSPUR LIBRARY 400 MAGNOLIA AV, LKSP, 94939, (415)927-5005	586 - F6
LATIN-AMERICAN LIBRARY 1900 FRUITVALE AV, OAK, 94601, (510)535-5620	650 - C7
LAW LIBRARY 224 W WINTON AV, HAY, 94544, (510)881-6380	711 - J3
LIBRARY GLENMOOR DR & MATTOS DR, FRMT, 94536	752 - H5
LIBRARY PERALTA BLVD & EDWARD AV, FRMT, 94536	753 - A3
LIBRARY FOR THE BLIND 3150 SACRAMENTO ST, SF, 94115, (415)292-2022	647 - F5
LOS ALTOS LIBRARY 13 S SAN ANTONIO RD, LALT, 94022, (650)948-7683	811 - E6
MANOR BRANCH LIBRARY 1307 MANOR BLVD, SLN, 94579, (510)357-6252	691 - A6
MARIN CITY LIBRARY 630 DRAKE AV ANNEX B, MrnC, 94965, (415)332-1128	626 - H1
MARIN COUNTY CIVIC CENTER LIBRARY 3501 CIVIC CENTER DR, SRFL, 94903, (415)499-6211	566 - F5
MARINA BRANCH LIBRARY 1530 SUSAN CT, SMTO, 94403, (650)377-4686	749 - D3
MARINA LIBRARY 1890 CHESTNUT ST, SF, 94123, (415)292-2150	647 - G4
MARTINEZ LIBRARY 740 COURT ST, MRTZ, 94553, (510)646-2898	571 - D3
MELROSE BRANCH LIBRARY 4805 FOOTHILL BLVD, OAK, 94601, (510)535-5623	670 - E1
MENLO PARK BRANCH ALMA ST & RAVENSWOOD AV, MLPK, 94025, (650)858-3460	790 - G3
MERCED LIBRARY 155 WINSTON DR, SF, 94132, (415)337-4780	667 - B7
MILL VALLEY LIBRARY 375 THROCKMORTON AV, MLV, 94941, (415)388-2190	606 - C3
MILLBRAE LIBRARY 1 LIBRARY AV, MLBR, 94030, (650)697-7606	728 - A3
MILPITAS COMMUNITY 40 N MILPITAS BLVD, MPS, 95035, (408)262-1171	794 - A7
MISSION BRANCH 1098 LEXINGTON ST, SCL, 95050, (408)984-3154	833 - E4
MISSION LIBRARY 3359 24TH ST, SF, 94110, (415)695-5090	667 - H4
MITCHELL PARK LIBRARY 3700 MIDDLEFIELD RD, PA, 94306, (650)329-2586	811 - E1
MOFFITT LIBRARY UC BERKELEY, BERK, 94720, (510)642-6000	629 - H1
MONTCLAIR BRANCH LIBRARY 1687 MOUNTAIN BLVD, OAK, 94611, (510)482-7810	630 - D7
MORAGA LIBRARY 1500 SAINT MARYS RD, MRGA, 94556, (510)376-6852	631 - E6
MOUNTAIN VIEW LIBRARIES 585 FRANKLIN ST, MTVW, 94041, (650)903-6887	811 - H5
MULFORD MARINA BRANCH LIBRARY 13699 AURORA DR, SLN, 94577, (510)357-3850	690 - G4
NEWARK LIBRARY 6300 CIVIC TERRACE AV, NWK, 94560, (510)795-2627	752 - E6
NILES READING CENTER 150 I ST, FRMT, 94536, (510)795-2626	753 - B1
NOE VALLEY-SALLY BURN LIBRARY 451 JERSEY ST, SF, 94114, (415)695-5095	667 - G4
NORTH BEACH LIBRARY 2000 MASON ST, SF, 94133, (415)274-0270	647 - J3
NOVATO LIBRARY 1720 S NOVATO BLVD, NVTO, 94945, (415)898-4623	526 - A3
OAKLAND MAIN LIBRARY 125 14TH ST, OAK, 94612, (510)238-3134	649 - H4
OCEAN VIEW 111 BROAD ST, SF, 94112, (415)337-4785	687 - D2
ORINDA LIBRARY 2 IRWIN WY, ORIN, 94563, (510)254-2184	610 - G7
ORTEGA LIBRARY 3223 ORTEGA ST, SF, 94116, (415)753-7120	666 - J3
PACIFICA BRANCH LIBRARY 104 HILTON WY, PCFA, 94044, (650)355-5196	706 - J6
PALO ALTO CHILDRENS LIBRARY 1276 HARRIET ST, PA, 94301, (415)329-2134	791 - A5
PALO ALTO MAIN LIBRARY 1213 NEWELL RD, PA, 94303, (415)329-2664	791 - B4
PARK LIBRARY 1833 PAGE ST, SF, 94117, (415)666-7155	667 - E1
PARKSIDE LIBRARY 1200 TARAVAL ST, SF, 94116, (415)753-7125	667 - B5
PEARL AV BRANCH 4270 PEARL AV, SJS, 95136, (408)265-7834	874 - E1
PIEDMONT AVENUE BRANCH LIBRARY 160 41ST ST, OAK, 94611, (510)597-5011	649 - J1
PINOLE LIBRARY 2935 PINOLE VALLEY RD, PIN, 94564, (510)758-2741	569 - F6
PITTSBURG LIBRARY 80 POWER AV, PIT, 94565, (510)427-8390	574 - D3
PLEASANT HILL CENTRAL LIBRARY 1750 OAK PARK BLVD, PLHL, 94523, (510)646-6434	592 - B7
PLEASANTON LIBRARY 400 OLD BERNAL AV, PLE, 94566, (510)462-3535	714 - D4
PORTOLA LIBRARY 2450 SAN BRUNO AV, SF, 94134, (415)715-4090	668 - A6
PORTOLA VALLEY BRANCH LIBRARY 765 PORTOLA RD, PTLV, 94028, (650)851-0560	810 - A6
POTRERO LIBRARY 1616 20TH ST, SF, 94107, (415)695-6640	668 - B2
PRESIDIO LIBRARY 3150 SACRAMENTO ST, SF, 94115, (415)292-2155	647 - F5
REDWOOD CITY BRANCH LIBRARY 1044 MIDDLEFIELD RD, RDWC, 94063, (650)780-7018	770 - B6
RICHMOND LIBRARY 351 9TH AV, SF, 94118, (415)666-7165	647 - C6
RICHMOND MAIN LIBRARY 325 CIVIC CENTER PZ, RCH, 94804, (510)620-6561	588 - H6
RICHMOND WEST SIDE LIBRARY 135 WASHINGTON AV, RCH, 94801, (510)620-6567	608 - D1
RINCON BRANCH LIBRARY 725 RINCON AV, LVMR, 94550, (510)373-5540	695 - F7
ROCKRIDGE BRANCH LIBRARY 5366 COLLEGE AV, OAK, 94618, (510)597-5017	629 - J6
RODEO LIBRARY 220 PACIFIC AV, CCCo, 94572, (510)799-2606	549 - H7
ROSEGARDEN BRANCH LIBRARY 1580 NAGLEE AV, SJS, 95126, (408)998-1511	833 - G6
ROSSMOOR LEISURE WORLD 1001 GOLDEN RAIN RD, WLCK, 94595, (510)939-9194	632 - B2
SAN ANSELMO LIBRARY 110 TUNSTEAD AV, SANS, 94960, (415)258-4656	566 - C7
SAN BRUNO LIBRARY 701 ANGUS AV W, SBRN, 94066, (650)877-8878	707 - J7
SAN CARLOS LIBRARY 610 WALNUT ST, SCAR, 94070, (650)591-0341	769 - G3
SAN FRANCISCO MAIN LIBRARY 100 LARKIN ST, SF, 94102, (415)557-4400	647 - J7
SAN JOSE MAIN BRANCH LIBRARY 180 W SAN CARLOS ST, SJS, 95110, (408)277-4846	834 - B7
SAN LEANDRO COMM LIB CTR 300 ESTUDILLO AV, SLN, 94577, (510)577-3490	691 - A1
SAN LORENZO LIBRARY 395 PAS GRANDE, AlaC, 94580, (510)670-6283	691 - D7
SAN MATEO COUNTY LIBRARY 25 TOWER RD, SMCo, 94402, (650)312-5258	768 - H2
SAN MATEO LIBRARY 55 W 3RD AV, SMTO, 94402, (650)373-4800	748 - J2
SAN PABLO LIBRARY 2101 MARKET AV, SPAB, 94806, (510)374-3998	588 - H3
SAN RAFAEL LIBRARY 1100 E ST, SRFL, 94901, (415)485-3320	566 - F7
SAN RAMON LIBRARY 100 MONTGOMERY ST, SRMN, 94583, (510)866-8467	673 - F3
SANCHEZ LIBRARY 1111 TERRA NOVA BLVD, PCFA, 94044, (650)359-3397	727 - B5
SANTA CLARA CENTRAL LIBRARY 2635 HOMESTEAD RD, SCL, 95051, (408)984-3097	833 - B5
SANTA TERESA LIBRARY 290 INTERNATIONAL CIR, SJS, 95119, (408)281-1878	875 - C6
SARATOGA COMMUNITY 13650 SARATOGA AV, SAR, 95070, (408)867-6126	872 - F1
SAUSALITO LIBRARY 420 LITHO ST, SAUS, 94965, (415)289-4120	627 - A2
SCHABERG, H W LIBRARY 2140 EUCLID AV, RDWC, 94061, (650)780-7010	789 - J1
SEVEN TREES BRANCH LIBRARY 3597 CAS DR, SJS, 95111, (408)629-4535	854 - H6
SOUTH BRANCH LIBRARY 14799 E 14TH ST, SLN, 94578, (510)357-5464	691 - D3
SOUTH SAN FRANCISCO LIBRARY 840 W ORANGE AV, SSF, 94080, (650)877-8525	707 - F3
SPRINGSTOWNE LIBRARY 1003 OAKWOOD AV, VAL, 94591, (707)553-5546	530 - E4
SPRINGTOWN BRANCH LIBRARY 998 BLUEBELL DR, LVMR, 94550, (510)373-5517	696 - B4
SUNNYVALE LIBRARY 665 W OLIVE AV, SUNV, 94086, (408)730-7300	832 - D1
SUNSET LIBRARY 1305 18TH AV, SF, 94122, (415)753-7130	667 - B2
TEMESCAL BRANCH LIBRARY 5205 TELEGRAPH AV, OAK, 94609, (510)597-5049	629 - H6
TERMAN PARK LIBRARY 661 ARASTRADERO RD, PA, 94306, (650)329-2606	811 - C3
UNION CITY LIBRARY 34007 ALVARADO-NILES RD, UNC, 94587, (510)745-1464	732 - F6
VISITACION VALLEY LIBRARY 45 LELAND AV, SF, 94134, (415)337-4790	688 - A2
WALNUT CREEK LIBRARY 1644 N BROADWAY, WLCK, 94596, (510)646-6773	612 - C5
WEEKES, GEORGE BRANCH LIBRARY 27300 PATRICK AV, HAY, 94544, (510)782-2155	711 - J7
WEST END BRANCH LIBRARY 788 SANTA CLARA AV, ALA, 94501, (510)748-4667	669 - G1
WESTERN ADDITION LIBRARY 1550 SCOTT ST, SF, 94115, (415)292-2160	647 - G6
WESTLAKE BRANCH LIBRARY 275 SOUTHGATE AV, DALY, 94015, (650)991-8071	687 - A4
WEST OAKLAND BRANCH LIBRARY 1801 ADELINE ST, OAK, 94607, (519)238-7352	649 - E2
WEST PORTAL LIBRARY 190 LENOX WY, SF, 94127, (415)753-7135	667 - C5
WEST VALLEY BRANCH LIBRARY 1243 SAN THOMAS AQUINO RD, SJS, 95117, (408)244-4747	853 - A4
WILLOW GLEN BRANCH LIBRARY 1157 MINNESOTA AV, SJS, 95125, (408)998-2022	854 - A4
WOODLAND LIBRARY 1975 GRANT RD, LALT, 94024, (650)969-6030	831 - J4
WOODSIDE PUBLIC LIBRARY 3140 WOODSIDE RD, WDSD, 94062, (650)851-0147	789 - G6
YGNACIO VALLEY LIBRARY 2661 OAK GROVE RD, WLCK, 94598, (510)938-1481	612 - H2

MILITARY INSTALLATIONS

FEATURE NAME Address City, ZIP Code	PAGE-GRID
AIR NATIONAL GUARD W WINTON AV, HAY, 94545	711 - E4
ALAMEDA POINT MAIN ST & ATLANTIC AV, ALA, 94501	649 - B6
EAST FORT MILEY CLEMENT ST, SF, 94121	646 - J6
FORT BAKER MrnC, 94965	627 - A6
FORT BERRY MrnC, 94965	626 - H7
FORT CRONKHITE MrnC, 94965	626 - D5
FORT FUNSTON HERBST RD, SF, 94132	666 - H6
MARE ISLAND NAVAL RESV (CLOSED) MARE ISLAND, SolC, 94547	549 - H2
MILITARY RESERVE RENAISSANCE RD, NVTO, 94945	526 - J6
MOFFETT FIELD NAVAL AIR STATION FAIRCHILD DR & DAILEY RD, SCIC, 94035	812 - D3
NATIONAL GUARD ARMORY 240 N 2ND ST, SJS, 95112	834 - B5
NATIONAL GUARD ARMORY 251 W HEDDING ST, SJS, 95110, (408)297-1974	833 - J4
NATIONAL GUARD ARMORY 624 CARLSON BLVD, RCH, 94804, (510)237-2909	608 - J1
NATIONAL GUARD ARMORY 99 POWER AV, PIT, 94565, (510)432-2757	574 - D3
NATIONAL GUARD ARMORY ALVARADO ST, SPAB, 94806	588 - J2
NAS ALAMEDA SUPPLY ANNEX SINGLETON AV, ALA, 94501	649 - E6
NAVAL RESERVATION INNES AV & DONAHUE ST, SF, 94124	668 - D7
OAKLAND ARMY BASE W GRAND AV & TULAGI ST, OAK, 94626	649 - D2
TREASURE ISLAND NAVAL RESERVATION SF-OAKLAND BAY BRIDGE, SF, 94130, (415)395-1000	648 - D1
U S ARMY RESERVE CENTER 155 W HEDDING ST, SJS, 95110, (408)292-4160	833 - J4
US COAST GUARD ALAMEDA HARBOR, ALA, 94501	649 - J6
US COAST GUARD STATION MARINE DR, SF, 94129	647 - D3
US GOVERNMENT RESERVATION HARTFORD AV & LORRAINE RD, AlaC, 94550	695 - J2
UNITED STATES MILITARY RESERVE HERBST RD & SKYLINE BLVD, SF, 94132	666 - H6
US NAVY LANDS COMMODORE DR W & 1ST ST W, SBRN, 94066	707 - H6
US NAVAL RESERVE 2101 CLEMENT AV, ALA, 94501	670 - A1
US NAVAL WEAPONS STATION CONCORD WILLOW PASS RD, CNCD, 94520, (510)246-2000	572 - B5
US NAVY FLEET INDUS SUPP CTR MIDDLE HARBOR RD, OAK, 94625	649 - A3
WEST FORT MILEY CLEMENT ST, SF, 94121	646 - H6

MOBILE HOME PARKS

FEATURE NAME Address City, ZIP Code	PAGE-GRID
ADOBE WELLS MOBILE HOME PARK 1220 TASMAN DR, SUNV, 94089, (408)734-8424	812 - J3
CASA DE AMIGOS MOBILE HOME PARK 1085 TASMAN DR, SUNV, 94089, (408)734-3379	812 - G3
CASA DE LAGO MOBILE HOME PARKS OAKLAND RD, SJS, 95131, (408)432-1323	814 - A4
FAIROAKS MOBILE HOME PARK 580 AHWANEE AV, SUNV, 94086, (408)736-6672	812 - G5
MOBILAND MOBILE HOME PARK 780 N FAIR OAKS AV, SUNV, 94086, (408)773-1210	812 - G5
PLAZA DEL REY MOBILE HOME PARK 1225 VIENNA DR, SUNV, 94089, (408)734-2746	812 - H4
VILLAGE OF THE FOUR SEASONS 200 FORD RD, SJS, 95138, (408)225-7255	875 - D4
WOODBRIDGE MOBILE HOME PARK SJS, 95121	855 - A3

MUSEUMS

FEATURE NAME Address City, ZIP Code	PAGE-GRID
AFRICAN AMERICAN MUSEUM & LIBRARY 5606 SAN PABLO AV, OAK, 94608, (510)597-5053	629 - F6
ASIAN ART MUSEUM S TEA GARDEN DR, SF, 94118, (415)668-8921	667 - C1
BAY AREA DISCOVERY MUSEUM 557 EAST RD, MrnC, 94965, (415)487-4398	627 - C6
BAYLANDS NATURE INTERPRETIVE-CENTER 2775 EMBARCADERO RD, PA, 94303, (650)329-2506	791 - F3
BEHRING AUTO MUSEUM 3750 BLACKHAWK PLAZA CIR, CCCo, 94506, (510)736-2277	653 - J5
BENICIA CAMEL BARN MUSEUM CAMEL BARN RD, BEN, 94510, 707-	551 - D5
CALIF PALACE OF THE LEGION OF-HONOR LEGION OF HONOR DR, SF, 94121, (415)750-3614	646 - J6
CALIFORNIA HIST SOCIETY MUSEUM 687 MISSION ST, SF, 94103, (415)357-1848	648 - B6
CENTER FOR THE ARTS 701 MISSION ST, SF, 94103, (415)978-2700	648 - A6
CHILDRENS DISCOVERY MUSEUM 180 WOZ WY, SJS, 95110, (408)298-5437	834 - B7
CLAYTON HISTORICAL SOCIETY MUSEUM 6101 MAIN ST, CLAY, 94517, (510)672-0240	593 - H7
COYOTE POINT MUSEUM COYOTE POINT DR, SMTO, 94401, (650)342-7755	729 - A5
DE SAISSET MUSEUM 500 EL CAMINO REAL, SCL, 95053, (408)554-4528	833 - F4
EGYPTIAN MUSEUM & PLANETARIUM 1342 NAGLEE AV, SJS, 95126, (408)947-3636	833 - G6
HAYWARD HISTORICAL MUSEUM 22701 MAIN ST, HAY, 94541, (510)581-0223	711 - J2
LINDSAY, ALEX JR MUSEUM 1901 1ST AV, WLCK, 94596, (510)935-1978	612 - B2
MARIN CO HISTORICAL SOCIETY MUS 1125 B ST, SRFL, 94901, (415)454-8538	586 - F1
MARIN MUS OF THE AMERICAN INDIAN 2200 NOVATO BLVD, NVTO, 94945, (415)897-4064	525 - H2
MARTINEZ MUSEUM 1005 ESCOBAR ST, MRTZ, 94553, (510)228-8160	571 - E2

FEATURE NAME	Address City, ZIP Code	PAGE-GRID
MH DE YOUNG MUSEUM	S TEA GARDEN DR, SF, 94118, (415)863-3330	667 - C1
MUSEUM OF AMERICAN HERITAGE	3401 EL CAMINO REAL, PA, 94306, (650)321-1004	811 - C1
NATURAL SCIENCE CENTER	BELLEVUE AV, OAK, 94610	649 - J3
NEW ALMADEN MUSEUM	21570 ALMADEN RD, SCIC, 95120, (408)268-7869	894 - J7
NOVATO HISTORY MUSEUM & ARCHIVES	815 DE LONG AV, NVTO, 94945, (415)897-4320	526 - B3
OAKLAND MUSEUM OF CALIFORNIA	1000 OAK ST, OAK, 94607, (510)834-2413	649 - H4
PALACE OF FINE ARTS EXPLORATORIUM	3601 LYON ST, SF, 94123, (415)563-7337	647 - E3
PALO ALTO JUNIOR MUSEUM & ZOO	1451 MIDDLEFIELD RD, PA, 94301, (415)329-2111	791 - B5
PARDEE HOME MUSEUM	672 11TH ST, OAK, 94607, (510)444-2187	649 - F4
PIONEER MEMORIAL MUSEUM	PRESIDIO AV & MASONIC AV, SF, 94115	647 - F6
PRESIDIO MUSEUM	LINCOLN BLVD & FUNSTON AV, SF, 94129, (415)561-4323	647 - E4
RANDALL MUSEUM	199 MUSEUM WY, SF, 94114, (415)554-9600	667 - F2
RICHMOND MUSEUM	400 NEVIN AV, RCH, 94801, (510)620-6842	588 - F6
SAN FRANCISCO NATL MARITIME MUS	HYDE ST & JEFFERSON ST, SF, 94109, (415)556-3002	647 - H3
SF PERFORMING ARTS LIBRARY	399 GROVE ST, SF, 94102, (415)255-4800	647 - H7
SAN JOSE HISTORICAL MUSEUM	1600 SENTER RD, SJS, 95112, (408)287-2290	854 - F2
SAN JOSE MUSEUM OF ART	110 S MARKET ST, SJS, 95113, (408)294-2787	834 - B6
SANCHEZ ADOBE MUSEUM	LINDA MAR BL & ADOBE DR, PCFA, 94044, (650)359-1462	726 - J5
SANTA CLARA HISTORIC MUSEUM	1509 WARBURTON AV, SCL, 95050, (408)248-2787	833 - D3
SHADELANDS RANCH HIST MUS	2660 YGNACIO VALLEY RD, WLCK, 94598, (510)935-7871	612 - G1
STOREFRONT MUSEUM	486 9TH ST, OAK, 94607, (510)835-0355	649 - G4
THE TECH MUSEUM OF INNOVATION	145 W SAN CARLOS ST, SJS, 95113, (408)279-7150	834 - B7
TREASURE ISLAND MUSEUM	AV OF THE PALMS, SF, 94130, (415)395-5067	648 - E2
TRITON MUSEUM OF ART	1505 WARBURTON AV, SCL, 95050, (408)247-3754	833 - D3
VALLEJO NAVAL & HISTORICAL MUSEUM	734 MARIN ST, VAL, 94590, (707)643-0077	529 - J5
WESTERN AEROSPACE MUSEUM	8280 BOEING ST, OAK, 94621, (510)638-7100	670 - D7

OPEN SPACE PRESERVES

FEATURE NAME	Address City, ZIP Code	PAGE-GRID
ACALANES OPEN SPACE	680 FWY, WLCK, 94596	612 - A5
ALTO BOWL PRESERVE	LOMITA DR, MLV, 94941	606 - G2
ARASTRADERO PRESERVE	ARASTRADERO RD, PA, 94304	810 - E7
BALTIMORE CANYON PRESERVE	BLUE RIDGE RD, MrnC, 94904	586 - C5
BAYLANDS NATURE PRESERVE	EMBARCADERO RD, EPA, 94303	791 - D2
BEACONSFIELD OPEN SPACE	BEACONSFIELD PL, OAK, 94611	650 - F1
BISHOP RANCH REGIONAL OPEN SPACE	MORGAN DR, CCCo, 94583	673 - C5
BLACK DIAMOND MINES REG PRESERVE	FREDDRICKSONS LN, CCCo, (510)757-2620	594 - F4
BLITHEDALE SUMMIT PRESERVE	SUMMIT DR, LKSP, 94939	586 - D7
BOTHIN MARSH OPEN SPACE PRESERVE	ALMONTE BL & ROSEMONT AV, MrnC, 94941	606 - G6
CAMINO ALTO PRESERVE	CAMINO ALTO & CORTE MADERA AV, MLV, 94941	606 - F2
CARQUINEZ STRAIT TRAIL	SAN PABLO AV, CCCo, 94525	550 - B5
CLAREMONT CYN REGNL PRSV	CLAREMONT AV, OAK, 94705	630 - A2
COAL CREEK OPEN SPACE	SKYLINE BLVD, SMCo, 94028	830 - C5
DEER ISLAND PRESERVE	DEER ISLAND LN, NVTO, 94945	526 - F5
DOW WETLANDS PRESERVE	PITTSBURG-ANTIOCH HWY, ANT, 94509	575 - B3
EAST BAY REGIONAL PARK OPEN SPACE	OFF OAKSHIRE PL, CCCo, 94507	633 - A4
EL CORTE DE MADERA OPEN SPACE	SKYLINE BLVD, SMCo, 94062	809 - B4
FOOTHILLS OPEN SPACE	PAGE MILL RD, PA, 94304	830 - G3
FRANKLIN HILLS OPEN SPACE	JOHN MUIR PKWY, MRTZ, 94553	571 - D5
FREEMONT OLDER OPEN SPACE	ROLLING HILLS RD, SCIC, 95014	852 - A4
GRIZZLY PEAK OPEN SPACE	TUNNEL RD, OAK, 94611	630 - D3
HUCKLEBERRY BOTANIC REGIONAL-RESERVE	PINEHURST RD, CCCo	630 - H6
IGNACIO VALLEY PRESERVE	CHICKEN SHACK FIRE RD, NVTO, 94949	546 - B4
INDIAN TREE PRESERVE	MrnC, 94947	525 - C5
INDIAN VALLEY PRESERVE	NVTO, 94949	546 - B2
KING ESTATE OPEN SPACE	CREST AV & FONTAINE ST, OAK, 94605	671 - A3
KING MOUNTAIN PRESERVE	EVERGREEN FIRE RD, MrnC, 94904	586 - C6
KING MOUNTAIN PRESERVE	TAMALPAIS AV & MIMOSA AV, LKSP, 94939	586 - E5
LAS TRAMPAS REGIONAL WILDERNESS	BOLLINGER CANYON RD, CCCo	652 - D1
LEONA REGIONAL OPEN SPACE	CAMPUS DR, OAK, 94605	651 - A7
LIME RIDGE OPEN SPACE	YGNACIO VALLEY RD, WLCK, 94598	593 - A7
LITTLE MTN OPEN SPACE PRSV	MrnC, 94947	525 - E2
LOMA VERDE PRESERVE	NVTO, 94949	546 - D3
LONE TREE PT REGNL SHORELINE	CCCo, 94572	549 - G7
LOS TRANCOS OPEN SPACE	PAGE MILL RD, PA, 94304	830 - F6
MARIN OPEN SPACE	REDWOOD RD, SANS, 94960	586 - A1
MISSION PEAK REGIONAL PRESERVE	OFF MILL CREEK ROAD, FRMT, 94539	794 - D1
OLD ST HILARYS OPEN SPACE PRSV	TBRN, 94920	607 - E6
OPEN SPACE	CCCo, 94553	571 - J2
OPEN SPACE	ALHAMBRA AV, MRTZ, 94553	571 - D7
ORINDA OPEN SPACE PRESERVE	HALL DR & FLEETWOOD CT, ORIN, 94563	631 - B3
PACHECO VALLE PRESERVE	NVTO, 94949	546 - D4
POINT PINOLE REGIONAL SHORELINE	GIANT HWY & SOBRANTE AV, RCH, 94806	568 - G4
PULGAS RIDGE OPEN SPACE	HASSLER RD, SMCo, 94070	769 - D6
PURISIMA CK REDWOODS OPEN SPACE	PURISIMA CREEK RD & SKYLINE BL, SMCo, 94062	789 - A6
RANCHO SAN ANTONIO OPEN SPACE	CRISTO REY DR, SCIC, 95014	831 - D5
RANKIN OPEN SPACE	PANORAMIC DR, MRTZ, 94553	571 - C3
RAVENSWOOD OPEN SPACE PRESERVE	HWY 84, MLPK, 94303	771 - D4
RAVENSWOOD OPEN SPACE PRESERVE	ILLINOIS ST & STEVENS AV, MLPK, 94303	771 - C6
REDWOOD GROVE NATURE PRESERVE	UNIVERSITY AV & SHERMAN ST, LALT, 94022	811 - D7
RING MOUNTAIN OPEN SPACE PRESERVE	MrnC, 94920	606 - J2
RUSSIAN RIDGE OPEN SPACE	SKYLINE BLVD, SMCo, 94020	830 - C7
SF BAY NATIONAL REFUGE	HARBOR BLVD, RDWC, 94063	750 - A4
SF BAY NATIONAL WILDLIFE REFUGE	HOPE ST & ELIZABETH ST, FRMT	772 - A4
SAN PABLO BAY REGIONAL SHORELINE	SAN PABLO BAY, CCCo, 94806	569 - B3
SAN PEDRO MOUNTAIN PRESERVE	WOODOAKS DR, MrnC, 94903	566 - H4
SANTA MARGARITA ISLAND PRESERVE	VENDOLA DR, MrnC, 94903	566 - G3
SANTA VENETIA MARSH PRESERVE	VENDOLA DR & SAND PEDRO RD, MrnC, 94903	566 - J2
SHELL RIDGE OPEN SPACE	MARSHALL DR, WLCK, 94598	612 - G5
SIBLEY VOLCANIC REGIONAL PRESERVE	SKYLINE BLVD, CCCo	630 - E3
SOBRANTE RIDGE REGIONAL PRESERVE	CASTRO RANCH RD, RCH, 94803	589 - H2
SUNOL REGIONAL WILDERNESS	GEARY RD & CAL GEARY RD, AlaC, 94586, (510)862-2244	774 - G2
SYCAMORE VALLEY OPEN SPACE	BLACKHAWK RD, DNVL, 94506	653 - H3
SYCAMORE VALLEY OPEN SPACE	CM TASSAJARA, DNVL, 94506	653 - F3
TERRA LINDA-SLEEPY HLW DIVIDE N-PRSV	LUCAS VALLEY RD, SRFL, 94903	566 - A1
TIBURON RIDGE PRESERVE	HWY 101 REDWOOD HWY FRONTAGE, CMAD, 94925	606 - H3
TIBURON UPLANDS NATURE RESERVE	PARADISE DR, MrnC, 94920	607 - F6
TILDEN NATURE STUDY AREA	CENTRAL PARK DR, CCCo, 94708, (510)525-2233	609 - H2
TIMBERLAND OPEN SPACE	QUEENS LN, SMTO, 94402	768 - H1
VERISSIMO HILLS PRESERVE	OAK VALLEY DR, NVTO, 94947	525 - F3
WINDY HILL OPEN SPACE	SKYLINE BLVD, PTLV, 94028	809 - H7
YOUNG, HUGH OPEN SPACE	WRIGHT AV, PIN, 94564	569 - H7

PARK & RIDE

FEATURE NAME	Address City, ZIP Code	PAGE-GRID
3RD AV PARK & RIDE	3RD AV & 101 FWY, SMTO, 94401	729 - B7
101/92 PARK & RIDE	HWY 92 & 101 FRWY, SMTO, 94403	749 - C3
ASCENSION PARK & RIDE	PROSPECT RD & MILLER AV, SAR, 95070	852 - F5
BLOCKBUSTER VIDEO PARK & RIDE	MCKEE RD & N CAPITOL AV, SJS, 95133	834 - G1
BLOSSOM HILL STATION PARK & RIDE	BLOSSOM HILL RD & HWY 85, SJS, 95123	874 - G4
BRANHAM STATION PARK & RIDE	BRANHAM LN & NARVAEZ AV LN, SJS, 95136	874 - F2
CAMDEN AV PARK & RIDE	CAMDEN AV & HWY 85, SJS, 95118	873 - J4
CAMPBELL SENIOR CTR PK & RIDE	W CAMPBELL AV & S WNCHESTER BL, CMBL, 95008	853 - D6
CAPITOL AVENUE PARK & RIDE	N CAPITOL AV & AV A, SJS, 95127	834 - H2
CAPITOL STATION PARK & RIDE	CAPITOL EXPWY & NARVAEZ AV, SJS, 95136	874 - E1
CAPITOL STATION PARK & RIDE	MONTEREY HWY & FEHREN DR, SJS, 95111	854 - G6
COTTLE STATION PARK & RIDE	COTTLE RD & 85 FWY, SJS, 95119	875 - C5
CRESPI PARK & RIDE	CRESPI DR & CABRILLO HWY, PCFA, 94044	726 - H3
CURTNER STATION PARK & RIDE	CANOAS GARDEN AV & CURTNER AV, SJS, 95125	854 - D5
EASTRIDGE MALL PARK & RIDE	TULLY RD & CAPITOL EXWY, SJS, 95122	835 - B7
EDGEWOOD PARK & RIDE	EDGEWOOD RD & 280 FWY, SMCo, 94070	789 - C1
FORD ROAD PARK & RIDE	MONTEREY HWY & FORD RD, SJS, 95138	875 - C4
HAYNE RD PARK & RIDE	HAYNE RD & I-280 FWY, SMCo, 94010	748 - D4
KMART PARK & RIDE	BOLLINGER RD & SARATOGA-SUNV, SJS, 95129	852 - D2
KMART PARK & RIDE	EL CAMINO REAL & LAWRENCE EXWY, SCL, 95051	832 - H4
KMART PARK & RIDE	FRUITDALE AV & SOUTHWEST EXWY, SJS, 95126	853 - H3
KMART PARK & RIDE	N JACKSON AV & MCKEE RD, SJS, 95116	834 - G2
MOORPARK AV PARK & RIDE	MOORPARK AV & LAWRENCE EXPWY, SJS, 95129	852 - J3
OHLONE-CHYNOWETH STA P & R	CHYNOWETH AV & HWY 87, SJS, 95136	874 - E3
PAGE MILL & ECR PARK & RIDE	EL CAMINO REAL & OREGON EXWY, PA, 94306	791 - B7
PAGE MILL & HWY 280 PARK & RIDE	PAGE MILL RD & HWY 280, LAH, 94022	810 - H5
PARK & RIDE	1100 ANDERSEN DR, SRFL, 94901	586 - J3
PARK & RIDE	1535 BOCKMAN RD, AlaC, 94580	711 - C1
PARK & RIDE	1680 RUDGEAR RD, WLCK, 94596	632 - D1
PARK & RIDE	32030 ALVARADO BLVD, UNC, 94587	732 - A6
PARK & RIDE	35080 NEWARK BLVD, NWK, 94560	752 - D4
PARK & RIDE	3RD ST & HETHERTON ST, SRFL, 94901	586 - G1
PARK & RIDE	7TH ST & UNION ST, OAK, 94607	649 - E3
PARK & RIDE	ALAMEDA DEL PRADO & HWY 101, NVTO, 94949	546 - F4
PARK & RIDE	ALHAMBRA AV & FRANKLIN CANYON, MRTZ, 94553	571 - E7
PARK & RIDE	ARDENWOOD BLVD & 84 FRWY, FRMT, 94555	752 - C4
PARK & RIDE	BAYSHORE BLVD & TUNNEL AV, BSBN, 94005	688 - B6
PARK & RIDE	BENICIA RD & LINCOLN RD E, VAL, 94591	530 - C6
PARK & RIDE	CHABOT DR & OWENS DR, PLE, 94588	694 - B5
PARK & RIDE	CLEARBROK RD & LONE TREE WY, ANT, 94509	595 - D1
PARK & RIDE	CURTOLA PKWY & LEMON ST, SolC, 94590	530 - C6
PARK & RIDE	E 12TH ST & FRUITVALE AV, OAK, 94601	670 - C1
PARK & RIDE	E AIRWAY BL & RUTAN DR, LVMR, 94550	695 - D5
PARK & RIDE	E SIR FRANCIS DRAKE BLVD, LKSP, 94904	586 - H5
PARK & RIDE	FOLGER AV, BERK, 94804	629 - E4
PARK & RIDE	FOOTHILL BLVD & JOHN DR, AlaC, 94546	691 - H6
PARK & RIDE	GATEWAY BLVD & 24 FRWY, ORIN, 94563	630 - F2
PARK & RIDE	HART ST & REDWOOD AV, CMAD, 94925	586 - F7
PARK & RIDE	HILLCREST AV & 4 FRWY, ANT, 94509	575 - G6
PARK & RIDE	HILLTOP DR & EASTSHORE FRWY, RCH, 94803	589 - C1
PARK & RIDE	HWY 1 & HWY 101, MrnC, 94965	606 - G6
PARK & RIDE	HWY 101 & ATHERTON AVE, NVTO, 94945	526 - C2
PARK & RIDE	HWY 101 & REDWOOD FRONTAGE RD, MLV, 94941	606 - G5
PARK & RIDE	HWY 101 & SMITH RANCH RD, SRFL, 94903	566 - F1
PARK & RIDE	HWY 101 & SPENCER AV, SAUS, 94965	627 - A3
PARK & RIDE	I-580 FRWY & CENTER ST, AlaC, 94546	692 - B6
PARK & RIDE	I-580 FRWY & FRUITVALE AV, OAK, 94602	650 - D5
PARK & RIDE	I-680 FRWY & MISSION BLVD, FRMT, 94539	753 - H6
PARK & RIDE	I-780 & E 2ND ST, BEN, 94510	551 - C4
PARK & RIDE	I-80 & MAGAZINE ST, VAL, 94590	530 - C7
PARK & RIDE	I-80 FRWY & TOLL PLAZA, OAK, 94649	649 - B1
PARK & RIDE	ISLAND DR & DOOLITTLE DR, ALA, 94502	670 - B5
PARK & RIDE	JUNIPERO SERRA BLVD & D ST, DALY, 94014	687 - C6
PARK & RIDE	LINCOLN AV & HWY 101, SRFL, 94901	566 - F6
PARK & RIDE	MISSION BLVD & CALLERY CT, FRMT, 94539	753 - G5
PARK & RIDE	MITCHELL DR & OAK GROVE RD, WLCK, 94598	612 - H1
PARK & RIDE	MONUMENT BLVD & 680 FRWY, PLHL, 94523	592 - D6
PARK & RIDE	PACHECO BLVD & 4 FRWY, CCCo, 94553	572 - B6
PARK & RIDE	PINOLE VLY RD & EASTSHORE FRWY, PIN, 94564	569 - F5
PARK & RIDE	PORT CHICAGO HWY AT BART STA, CNCD, 94519	572 - G5
PARK & RIDE	PORTOLA AV & ALVISO PL, LVMR, 94550	695 - F6
PARK & RIDE	REDWOOD HWY & ROWLAND BL, NVTO, 94947	526 - D5
PARK & RIDE	REDWOOD RD & MOUNTAIN BLVD, OAK, 94619	650 - H5
PARK & RIDE	RICHMOND PKWY & EASTSHORE FRWY, CCCo, 94806	569 - C6
PARK & RIDE	S MAIN ST & WELLER LN, MPS, 95035	794 - A7
PARK & RIDE	SAN PABLO AV & JOHN MUIR PKWY, HER, 94547	569 - G3
PARK & RIDE	SEARS POINT HWY & ATHERTON AV, MrnC, 94945	526 - H4
PARK & RIDE	SIR FRANCIS DRAKE & DEL MONTE, LKSP, 94939	586 - G5
PARK & RIDE	SIR FRANCIS DRAKE & LA CUESTA, LKSP, 94939	586 - G4
PARK & RIDE	THORNTON AV & CABRILLO DR, FRMT, 94536	752 - G4
PARK & RIDE	W LELAND RD & SOUTHWOOD DR, PIT, 94565	573 - G3
PARK & RIDE	WANDA ST & EASTSHORE FRWY, CCCo, 94525	550 - C4
PARK & RIDE	WILLOW AV & EASTSHORE FRWY, CCCo, 94547	569 - J2
PARK & RIDE	WILLOW PASS RD & 242 FRWY, CNCD, 94520	592 - E2
PIEDMONT HILLS CENTER PARK & RIDE	SIERRA RD & PIEDMONT RD, SJS, 95132	814 - G4
RALSTON PARK & RIDE	HWY 92 & RALSTON AV, SMCo, 94070	768 - J2
RIVER OAKS STATION PARK & RIDE	RIVER OAKS PL & N 1ST ST, SJS, 95134	813 - F4
SAMTRANS PARK & RIDE	1 ST AV & B ST, SMTO, 94401	748 - J1
SAMTRANS PARK & RIDE	LINDA MAR BLVD & CABRILLO HWY, PCFA, 94044	726 - H4
SAMTRANS PARK & RIDE	VETERANS BLVD & WHIPPLE AV, RDWC, 94063	770 - A6
SAMTRANS PARK & RIDE	WESTBOROUGH BLVD & GELLERT DR, SSF, 94080	707 - E4
SAMTRANS TRANSIT TRANSFER POINT	STANFORD SHOPPING CENTER, PA, 94304	790 - H5
SANTA TERESA STA NORTH P & R	SANTA TERESA BLVD & MIYUKI DR, SJS, 95119	875 - D6
SANTA TERESA STA SOUTH P & R	SANTA TERESA BL & SAN IGNACIO, SJS, 95119	875 - D6
SARATOGA RD PARK & RIDE	SARATOGA RD & SANTA CRUZ AV, LGTS, 95030	873 - A7
SNELL AVENUE STATION PARK & RIDE	SNELL AV & HWY 85, SJS, 95123	874 - H4
TAMIEN STATION PARK & RIDE	LELONG AV & W ALMA AV, SJS, 95110	854 - C3
TASMAN STATION PARK & RIDE	TASMAN DR & N 1ST ST, SJS, 95134	813 - F3

PARK & RIDE

FEATURE NAME	Address City, ZIP Code	PAGE-GRID
VALLCO FASHION PARK PARK & RIDE	WOLFE RD & SERRA FRWY, CPTO, 95014	832 - F7
WINFIELD STATION PARK & RIDE	COLEMAN AV & WINFIELD BLVD, SJS, 95123	874 - D5
WOODSIDE PARK & RIDE	WOODSIDE RD & I-280 FRWY, WDSD, 94062	789 - J6

PARKS & RECREATION

FEATURE NAME	Address City, ZIP Code	PAGE-GRID
7TH & WALNUT PARK	7TH AV & WALNUT ST, SBRN, 94066	708 - A6
7TH AV PARK	6TH AV & 7TH AV, SBRN, 94066	708 - A6
9TH STREET PARK	W 9TH & K STS, BEN, 94510	550 - J4
25TH ST MINI PARK	25TH ST, OAK, 94612	649 - G2
85TH AVENUE MINI PARK	85TH AV & HOLLY ST, OAK, 94621	670 - H4
88TH AVENUE MINI PARK	88TH AV & PLYMOUTH ST, OAK, 94621	670 - H4
ADAMS PARK	HARRISON ST & GRAND AV, OAK, 94612	649 - H3
ADAMS ROGERS PARK	OAKDALE AV & INGALLS ST, SF, 94124	668 - C6
ADOBE PARK	FOOTHILL RD, PLE, 94588	714 - A3
AGNEW PARK	AGNEW RD, SCL, 95054	813 - C5
AGUA VISTA PARK	100 TERRY A FRANCIOS BLVD, SF, 94107	668 - C2
ALAMEDA PARK	CENTRAL AV & LINCOLN AV, ALA, 94501	669 - D1
ALAMO CREEK PARK	DOUGHERTY RD & WILDWOOD RD, DBLN, 94568	694 - A2
ALAMO ELEMENTRY PARK	100 WILSON RD, CCCo, 94507	632 - F3
ALAMO SQUARE	FULTON ST & SCOTT ST, SF, 94117	647 - G7
ALBANY HILL PARK	BELMONT AV & LASSEN ST, ALB, 94706	609 - C5
ALBERT PARK	B ST & TREANOR ST, SRFL, 94901	586 - F1
ALBERTSON PARKWAY	PURPLE HILLS DR & DONDERO WY, SJS, 95119	875 - C6
ALCATRAZ STATE PARK	SF, (415)546-2700	627 - H7
ALEXANDER PARK	OLD COUNTY RD, BLMT, 94002	749 - E7
ALEXANDER PARK	POMONA ST, CCCo, 94525	550 - D5
ALLENDALE RECREATION CENTER	3711 SUTER ST, OAK, 94619, (510)563-1188	650 - E6
ALMADEN LAKE PARK	ALMADEN EXPWY & WINFILD BLVD, SJS, 95123	874 - D5
ALMADEN MEADOWS PARK	CAMDEN AV & MERIDIAN AV, SJS, 95120	894 - C1
ALMADEN QUICKSILVER COUNTY PARK	ALMADEN RD & ALAMITOS RD, SCIC, 95120, (408)268-3883	894 - E5
ALMOND PARK	ALMOND AV & EMORY WY, LVMR, 94550	716 - A2
ALMONDRIDGE PARK	ALMNDRDGE DR & ALMOND TREE CT, ANT, 94509	575 - J6
ALTA PLAZA	JACKSON ST & SCOTT ST, SF, 94115	647 - G5
ALUM ROCK PARK	16240 ALUM ROCK AV, SJS, 95132, (408)277-4661	815 - C5
ALVARADO PARK	PARK AV, RCH, 94806	589 - B4
ALVARADO PARK	SMITH ST, UNC, 94587	731 - J5
ALVAREZ PARK	2280 ROSITA AV, SCL, 95050	833 - D6
ALVISO PARK	WILSON WY, SJS, 95002	813 - C1
AMADOR VALLEY COMMUNITY PARK	4455 BLACK AV, PLE, 94566	714 - E2
AMBROSE PARK	MEMORIAL WY & WOLLAM AV, CCCo, 94565	573 - H3
AMERICAN CANYON COMMUNITY PARK	DONALDSON WY & W DONALDSON WY, AMCN, 94589, 707-	509 - J2
ANDREW SPINAS PARK	BROADWAY & 2ND AV, RDWC, 94063	770 - D6
ANGEL ISLAND STATE PARK	TBRN, (415)435-1915	627 - H2
ANTHONY CHABOT REGIONAL PARK	REDWOOD RD, AlaC, 94546	671 - G6
ANTIOCH COMMUNITY PARK	BLYTHE DR, ANT, 94509	595 - C2
ANTIOCH YOUTH SPORTS COMPLEX	WILBUR AV, ANT, 94509	575 - F4
APTOS PLAYGROUND	APTOS AV & OCEAN AV, SF, 94127	667 - C7
ARBOLADO PARK	ARBOLADO DR & SUTTON DR, WLCK, 94598	613 - A3
ARCTURUS PARK	ARCTURUS CIR, FCTY, 94404	749 - E4
ARDEN PARK	ALTA VISTA WY & ALTA ARDENDALE, DALY, 94014	687 - G3
ARGONNE PLAYGROUND	19TH AV, SF, 94121	647 - B7
ARGUELLO PARK	WELLINGTON DR, SCAR, 94070	769 - E3
ARLINGTON PARK	1120 ARLINGTON BLVD, ELCR, 94530, (510)234-9631	609 - E1
ARMSTRONG, NEIL SCHOOL PARK	GORHAM PL & WESTCHESTER DR, SRMN, 94583	673 - F6
ARROYO AGUA CALIENTE PARK	PARKMEADOW DR & PADRE PKWY, FRMT, 94539	773 - G3
ARROYO AVICHI PARK	HILL RD, NVTO, 94947	526 - B5
ARROYO PARK	QUARRY LAKES DR, UNC, 94587	732 - H7
ARROYO VIEJO RECREATION AREA	7701 KRAUSE AV, OAK, 94605, (510)636-0138	670 - H3
ASH STREET PARK	ENTERPRISE DR, NWK, 94560	772 - D1
ASHLAND PARK	168TH AV & CARRIAGE WY, AlaC, 94578	691 - F5
ATCHISON VILLAGE PARK	W BISSELL AV & CURRY ST, RCH, 94801	588 - E7
ATHAN DOWNS	MONTEVIDEO DR & 680 FRWY, SRMN, 94583	673 - E5
ATHOL PLAZA	LAKESHORE AV & FOOTHILL BLVD, OAK, 94606	649 - J4
AUGUSTIN-BERNAL PARK	LONGVIEW DR & LONGVIEW LN, PLE, 94586	714 - A6
AVENIDA ESPANA PARK	RAWLS CT & DOWNS DR, SJS, 95139	895 - F1
AVENUE TERRACE PARK	BENNETT PL & GUIDO ST, OAK, 94602	650 - F4
AZEVEDA PARK	ROYAL PALM DR, FRMT, 94538	752 - J7
AZULE PARK	GOLETA AV, SAR, 95070	852 - E5
BABE RUTH BASEBALL FIELD	SOMERSVILLE RD W, ANT, 94509	575 - B4
BACHMAN PARK	BACHMAN AV & BROOKS AV, LGTS, 95030	872 - J7
BACKESTO PARK	N 13TH ST & E EMPIRE ST, SJS, 95112	834 - C4
BAHIA PARKS	SANTANA RD, NVTO, 94945	526 - G1
BALBOA PARK	OCEAN AV & SAN JOSE AV, SF, 94112, (415)337-4715	667 - F7
BALDWIN, JOHN F PARK	1950 PARKSIDE DR, CNCD, 94519	592 - G1
BARBARA PRICE MARINA PARK	L ST, ANT, 94509	575 - C3
BARRETT PARK	RALSTON AV, BLMT, 94002	769 - D2
BARRIER, HARRY A MEMORIAL PARK	MOUNTAIN VIEW AV, SRFL, 94901	566 - J5
BAYFRONT PARK	BAYSHORE HWY & E MILLBRAE AV, MLBR, 94030	728 - D3
BAYFRONT PARK	MARSH RD, MLPK, 94025	770 - H5
BAYFRONT PARK	ROQUE MORAES DR & HAMILTON DR, MLV, 94941	606 - F4
BAYSHORE CIRCLE PARK	N BAYSHORE CIR, SBRN, 94066	707 - J5
BAYSHORE HEIGHTS PARK	400 MARTIN ST, DALY, 94014	687 - H3
BAYSHORE PARK	45 MIDWAY DR, DALY, 94014	687 - J3
BAYSIDE PARK	AIRPORT BLVD & BAYSHORE HWY, BURL, 94010	728 - E5
BAYSIDE PARK	KEHOE AV & MEADOW VIEW PL, SMTO, 94403	749 - C1
BAYSIDE PARK	LERIDA AV & CUARDO AV, MLBR, 94030	728 - C3
BAY TREES PARK	CULL CANYON RD & CROW CYN RD, AlaC, 94552	692 - C4
BAYVIEW CIRCLE PARK	BAYVIEW CIR, CNCD, 94520	572 - G4
BAYVIEW PARK	JAMESTOWN AV, SF, 94124	688 - B2
BAYVIEW PLAYGROUND	3RD ST & CARROLL AV, SF, 94124	668 - B7
BEACH PARK	FRANCISCO BLVD, SRFL, 94901	586 - H1
BEGIN PLAZA	21ST ST & SAN PABLO AV, OAK, 94612	649 - G3
BELAMEDA PARK	1110 ALAMEDA DE LAS PULGAS, BLMT, 94002	769 - C2
BELL STREET PARK	BELL ST & UNIVERSITY AV, EPA, 94303	791 - B2
BELLA VISTA RECREATION AREA	2450 11TH AV, OAK, 94606	650 - A4
BELMONT SPORTS COMPLEX	ISLAND PKWY, BLMT, 94002	749 - F6
BELVERON PARK	TRESTLE GLEN DR & MERCURY AV, TBRN, 94920	607 - A4
BENICIA STATE RECREATION AREA	HWY 780 & DILLON RD, BEN, 94510	550 - G2
BERCUT EQUITATION FIELD	CHAIN OF LAKES & JF KENNEDY DR, SF, (415)668-7360	666 - J1
BERESFORD PARK	28TH AV & PARKVIEW WY, SMTO, 94403	749 - A5
BERKELEY AQUATIC PARK	3RD ST & BANCROFT WY, BERK, 94804	629 - D4
BERNAL HEIGHTS PARK	BERNAL HEIGHTS BLVD, SF, 94110	667 - J5
BERNAL PARK	E HEDDING ST & N 7TH ST, SJS, 95112	834 - B3
BERRYESSA CREEK PARK	ISADORA DR, SJS, 95132	814 - F3
BEVERLY HILLS PARK	DEL SUR ST & ALTA PUNTA DR, VAL, 94591	550 - D1
BICENTENNIAL PARK	TANAGER DR & TAHOE CT, PLE, 94566	694 - E7
BIDWELL PARK	100 ROUSSEAU ST, HAY, 94544	732 - D2
BIEBRACH PARK	W VIRGINIA ST & DELMAS AV, SJS, 95125	854 - B1
BIG CANYON PARK	BRITTAN AV, SCAR, 94070	769 - D5
BIG TREES PARK	KATHY WY & IRENE WY, LVMR, 94550	716 - C1
BILLY GOAT HILL PARK	BEACON ST & LAIDLEY ST, SF, 94131	667 - G5
BIRCH GROVE PARK	ROBERTSON AV & BIRCH ST, NWK, 94560	752 - G7
BIRCHFIELD, KENNETH MEMORIAL PARK	SANTA CLARA ST & ELMHURST ST, HAY, 94544	711 - G3
BLACOW PARK	40400 SUNDALE DR, FRMT, 94538	773 - B1
BLITHEDALE PK	W BLITHEDALE AV &MARGUERITE AV, MLV, 94941	606 - C1
BLOSSOM HILL PARK	BLOSSOM HILL RD, LGTS, 95032	873 - D6
BLUE ROCK SPRINGS CORRIDOR	REDWOOD PKWY & ASCOT PKWY, VAL, 94591	530 - F3
BLUE ROCK SPRINGS PARK	COLUMBUS PKWY, VAL, 94591	530 - H2
BOAT PARK	FOSTER CITY BLVD, FCTY, 94404	749 - G3
BOEDDEKER PARK	JONES ST & EDDY ST, SF, 94102	647 - J6
BOGGINI PARK	STEVENS LN & MILLBROOK DR, SJS, 95148	855 - D1
BOL PARK	LAGUNA AV & LAGUNA CT, PA, 94306	811 - B2
BOLLINGER CANYON SCHOOL PARK	BOLLINGER CYN RD & TALAVERA DR, SRMN, 94583	673 - C4
BONAIRE PARK	JUNIPER ST & HICKORY AV, SLN, 94579	691 - A5
BON AIR LANDING PARK	S ELISEO DR & CORTE REAL, LKSP, 94939	586 - F5
BOOKER T ANDERSON JR PARK	CYPRESS AV & ELLS LN, RCH, 94804	609 - A2
BOONE ACRES PARK	DAVONA DR & WESTWOOD AV, SRMN, 94583	673 - F7
BOORMAN PARK	S 25TH ST & MAINE AV, RCH, 94804	588 - H7
BOOSTER PARK	500 GABLE DR, FRMT, 94539	773 - J7
BOOTHBAY PARK	BOOTHBAY AV, FCTY, 94404	749 - F5
BOREL PARK	BOREL AV, SMTO, 94402	748 - J4
BORGES RANCH PARK	BORGES LN & KENYON WY, VAL, 94589	510 - C5
BOULWARE PARK	390 FERNANDO AV, PA, 94306	811 - C1
BOWDEN PARK	ALMA ST & CALIFORNIA AV, PA, 94301	791 - B7
BOWERS PARK	2582 CABRILLO AV, SCL, 95051	833 - B3
BOWLING GREEN PARK	474 EMBARCADERO RD, PA, 94301	791 - A5
BOWLING GREENS	1450 ADDISON ST, BERK, 94702	629 - F2
BOYD MEMORIAL PARK	B ST & MISSION AV, SRFL, 94901	566 - F7
BOYD, NANCY PARK	PLEASANT HILL RD & CHURCH ST, MRTZ, 94553	571 - F7
BOYLE PARK	E BLITHEDALE AV & E DR, MLV, 94941	606 - E3
BRACHER PARK	2700 BOWERS AV, SCL, 95051	833 - B1
BRALY PARK	704 DAFFODIL CT, SUNV, 94086, (408)732-4891	832 - F2
BRANHAM LANE PARK	BRANHAM LN, SJS, 95124	873 - J3
BRAXTON, ABRAHAM PARK	PLAZA CIR, RCH, 94804	609 - B1
BRAZIL QUARRY PARK	KENT WY & HEATHER GLEN LN, CNCD, 94521	593 - D4
BRENTWOOD PARK	ROSEWOOD WY & BRIARWOOD DR, SSF, 94080	707 - F5
BRET HARTE PARK	DIABLO RD & CAMINO TASSAJARA, DNVL, 94526	653 - B2
BRET HARTE PARK	IRWIN ST & BAYWOOD TER, SRFL, 94901	586 - G3
BRIDGEPOINT PARK	SPRUCE ST & PAR CT, NWK, 94560	752 - C6
BRIDGEVIEW PARK	SHIRLEY DR, BEN, 94510	551 - B4
BRIGADOON PARK	BRIGADOON WY & DAN MALONEY DR, SJS, 95121	855 - C3
BRIONES PARK	MAYBELL AV & CLEMO AV, PA, 94306	811 - C3
BRIONES REGIONAL PARK	BEAR CREEK RD, CCCo, (510)223-7840	591 - C5
BRIONES REGIONAL PARK	BEAR CREEK RD, CCCo, (510)223-7840	610 - J1
BROOKDALE PARK	HIGH ST, OAK, 94601	650 - E7
BROOKFIELD VILLAGE PARK	525 JONES AV, OAK, 94603	670 - G6
BROOKGLEN PARK	BROOKGLEN DR & BROCKTON LN, SAR, 95070	852 - G6
BROOKS PARK	SHIELDS ST & ARCH ST, SF, 94132	687 - C1
BROOK STREET PARK	BROOK ST & HOUGH AV, LFYT, 94549	611 - F6
BROOKTREE PARK	FALLINGTREE DR, SJS, 95131	814 - C5
BROOKVALE PARK	NICOLET AV & ASHTON PL, FRMT, 94536	752 - G1
BROOKWOOD PARK	TAYLOR BL & WITHERS AV, CCCo, 94549	591 - H7
BUBB PARK	BARBARA AV, MTVW, 94040	811 - H7
BUCHANAN PARK	HARBOR ST & BUCHANAN RD, PIT, 94565	574 - D6
BUCKEYE PARK	ROSEWOOD DR & ALCOTT RD, SBRN, 94066	727 - G1
BUENA VISTA PARK	BUENA VISTA AV & HAIGHT ST, SF, 94117	667 - F1
BUENA VISTA PARK	MACKINTOSH ST, FRMT, 94539	753 - F4
BURCKHALTER PARK	EDWARDS AV & SAN RAMON AV, OAK, 94605	670 - J1
BURG PARK	CLINTON AV & 30TH ST, RCH, 94804	588 - J5
BURGESS PARK	LAUREL ST & MIEKLE DR, MLPK, 94025	790 - G3
BURI BURI PARK	1059 EL CAMINO REAL, SSF, 94080	707 - F3
BURTON PARK	BRITTAN AV & CEDAR ST, SCAR, 94070	769 - G4
BUSHROD PARK	560 59TH ST, OAK, 94609, (510)652-5612	629 - H5
BUTCHER PARK	CAMDEN AV & OAKWOOD AV, SJS, 95124	873 - H2
BYXBEE RECREATION AREA	EMBARCADERO RD, PA, 94303	791 - F3
CABRILLO PARK	SAN PEDRO DR & BALBOA WY, FRMT, 94536	752 - F4
CADWALLADER PARK	S 1ST ST & KEYES ST, SJS, 95112	854 - D1
CAFFODIO, AL PARK	SHAWNEE RD, LVMR, 94550	695 - F6
CAHALAN PARK	PEARLWOOD WY & CAHALAN AV, SJS, 95123	874 - F5
CALERO PARK	LEAN AV & CALERO AV, SJS, 95123	875 - A5
CALERO RESERVOIR COUNTY PARK	23201 MCKEAN RD, SCIC, 95120, (408)268-3883	895 - E7
CALLAN PARK	CARTER DR, SSF, 94080	707 - C4
CAMBRIDGE PARK	VICTORY LN, CNCD, 94520	592 - E5
CAMDEN PARK	UNION AV & CAMDEN AV, SJS, 95124	873 - F2
CAMERON PARK	210 WELLESLEY, PA, 94306	791 - A7
CAMPBELL PARK	CAMPBELL AV & GILMAN AV, CMBL, 95008	853 - F6
CANAL PARK	GENTRYTOWN DR & DIMAGGIO WY, ANT, 94509	574 - J7
CANDLESTICK POINT STATE REC AREA	JAMESTOWN AV & HARNEY WY, SF, 94124	688 - D2
CANNERY PARK	125 B ST, HAY, 94541	711 - G2
CANOAS PARK	THRUSH DR & KINGFISHER DR, SJS, 95125	854 - C6
CANYON TRAIL PARK	6757 GATTO AV, ELCR, 94530, (510)215-4370	589 - B7
CANYON VIEW PARK	FARM HILL DR, HAY, 94542	712 - E4
CAPITOL PARK	BAMBI LN & PETER PAN AV, SJS, 95116	834 - J4
CAPPY RICKS PARK	ARREBA ST, MRTZ, 94553	571 - E3
CARDOZA PARK	KENNEDY DR, MPS, 95035	794 - C6
CARLI, STEVE PARK	1045 LOS PADRES BLVD, SCL, 95050	833 - C5
CARLOS BEE PARK	GROVE WY & BAYWOOD AV, AlaC, 94546	691 - J7
CARMICHAEL, EARL J PARK	BENTON ST, SCL, 95051	832 - J4
CARNEGIE PARK	4TH ST & S K ST, LVMR, 94550	715 - G1
CARNEY, TYRONE PARK	105TH AV & CAPISTRANO DR, OAK, 94603	670 - H7
CARQUINEZ PARK	SANDY BEACH RD & PORTER ST, VAL, 94590	550 - B1
CARQUINEZ STRAIT REG SHORELINE-PARK	CARQUINEZ SCENIC DR, CCCo, 94553	571 - B3

FEATURE NAME Address City, ZIP Code	PAGE-GRID
CARRABELLE PARK CAMDEN AV & VILLAGEWOOD WY, SJS, 95120	894 - H2
CASA CERRITO PARK PORTOLA DR & NAVELLIER ST, ELCR, 94530	609 - D2
CASA VERDE PARK SAN LUIS CT, UNC, 94587	732 - B5
CASANOVA PARK CASANOVA DR, SMTO, 94403	749 - E6
CASCADE PARK LOVELL AV, MLV, 94941	606 - B2
CASSELL PARK LEEWARD DR & BRENFORD DR, SJS, 95122	834 - J5
CASTLE ROCK REGIONAL PARK 1600 CASTLE ROCK RD, CCCo	613 - A7
CASTLEWOOD PARK HEARTWOOD AV & LAMONT CT, VAL, 94591	530 - E5
CASTRO PARK 1420 NORVELL ST, ELCR, 94530, (510)215-4370	609 - C2
CASTRO SCHOOL PARK LATHAM ST & ESCUELA AV, MTVW, 94041	811 - G5
CASTRO VALLEY COMMUNITY PARK LAKE CHABOT RD & QUAIL AV, AlaC, 94546	691 - H3
CATALDI PARK MORRILL AV, SJS, 95132	814 - E4
CATAMARAN PARK CATAMARAN ST, FCTY, 94404	749 - G3
CEDAR STREET PARK CEDAR ST, SCAR, 94070	769 - F2
CENTENNIAL PARK 4TH ST & HOLMES ST, LVMR, 94550	715 - F1
CENTENNIAL PARK 5001 SUNOL BLVD, PLE, 94566	714 - D5
CENTENNIAL PARK AMADOR ST, HAY, 94541	711 - G3
CENTERVILLE PARK 38200 HASTINGS ST, FRMT, 94536	753 - A4
CENTRAL PARK 50 E 5TH AV, SMTO, 94401	748 - J2
CENTRAL PARK 969 KIELY BLVD, SCL, 95051	833 - B5
CENTRAL PARK CENTRAL AV & YOLO AV, RCH, 94804	609 - C4
CENTRAL PARK PALM AV & LINCOLN CIR, MLBR, 94030	728 - A3
CENTRAL RESERVOIR RECREATION AREA SHEFFIELD AV, OAK, 94602	650 - C5
CERRITO VISTA PARK 950 POMONA AV, ELCR, 94530, (510)526-9809	609 - D2
CESAR CHAVEZ STATE PARK SPINNAKER WY, BERK, 94804	629 - B1
CHABOT PARK ESTUDILLO AV & SYLVAN CIR, OAK, 94605	671 - D7
CHABOT RECREATION CENTER 6800 CHABOT RD, OAK, 94618	630 - A4
CHANNING CIRCLE PARK CHANNING CIR, BEN, 94510	530 - H6
CHERRY GROVE PARK LEONARD DR & WILLIAMS ST, SLN, 94577	690 - H2
CHERRY LAND PARK GROVE WY, AlaC, 94541	711 - F1
CHICHIBU PARK LONGVIEW RD & ACORN RD, ANT, 94509	595 - C1
CHILDREN OF THE RAINBOW PARK MADDEN AV & GRAMERCY PL, SJS, 95116	834 - G2
CHILDRENS WONDERLAND 360 GLENN ST, VAL, 94590	530 - B4
CHILPANCINGO PARK GOLF CLUB RD, PLHL, 94523	592 - C2
CHINA CAMP STATE PARK N SAN PEDRO RD, MrnC, 94903, (415)456-0766	567 - B4
CHRISTENSEN PARK BRIDGEPORT CIR, LVMR, 94550	696 - C2
CHRISTOPHER PLAYGROUND DIAMOND HEIGHTS BLVD, SF, 94131	667 - F5
CHYNOWETH PARK CHYNOWETH AV & EDENVALE AV, SJS, 95136	875 - A3
CIMARRON PARK ORANGE ST, SJS, 95127	814 - H6
CIPRIANI FIELD MONSERAT AV, BLMT, 94002	769 - B1
CITY HALL PARK SAN CARLOS AV & ELM ST, SCAR, 94070	769 - G3
CITY HALL PLAZA 1 CITY HALL PZ, OAK, 94612	649 - G4
CITY PARK 10TH ST & A ST, ANT, 94509	575 - D4
CITY PARK CYPRESS AV & CRYSTAL SPRINGS, SBRN, 94066	727 - J1
CITY PARK MILITARY WEST & 1ST ST, BEN, 94510, (707)746-4285	551 - B4
CITY PARK RAILROAD AV & N PARKSIDE DR, PIT, 94565	574 - D3
CITY PARK SACRAMENTO ST & ALABAMA ST, VAL, 94590	529 - J4
CITY PLAZA PARK LEXINGTON & MAIN STS, SCL, 95050	833 - E4
CIVIC CENTER POLK ST & GROVE ST, SF, 94102	647 - J7
CIVIC CENTER PARK CIVIC TERRACE AV, NWK, 94560	752 - E7
CIVIC CENTER PARK LINCOLN ST & EL CAMINO REAL, SCL, 95050	833 - D4
CIVIC CENTER PARK MILITARY W & 1ST ST, BEN, 94510	551 - B5
CIVIC CENTER PARK S MATHILDA AV & ALL AMERICA WY, SUNV, 94086	832 - D1
CIVIC PARK 101 MAIN ST, PLE, 94566	714 - D4
CIVIC PARK CIVIC DR & BROADWAY, WLCK, 94596	612 - C5
CLARK, BILL PARK BELLFLOWER ST & HILLFLOWER DR, LVMR, 94550	696 - C4
CLARK, ESTHER PARK OLD TRACE LN & OLD ADOBE RD, PA, 94306	811 - B5
CLAY AVENUE PARK CLAY AV, SSF, 94080	707 - C2
CLAYTON COMMUNITY PARK MARSH CREEK RD, CLAY, 94517	613 - J1
CLAYTON PARK CLAYTON RD, CLAY, 94517	593 - H7
CLAYTON VALLEY CENTER PARK ALBERTA WY & VALMAR DR, CNCD, 94521	593 - D6
CLEVELAND PARK MARTIN BLVD & PRICE WY, SLN, 94577	690 - H1
CLINTON SQUARE 600 E 12TH ST, OAK, 94606	649 - J5
CLOUD VIEW PARK CLOUD VIEW RD & BOOKER AV, SAUS, 94965	627 - A3
CLYDE PARK NORMAN AV & SUSSEX ST, CCCo, 94520	572 - G2
CODORNICES PLAYGROUND 1201 EUCLID AV, BERK, 94708, (510)644-6530	609 - H7
COGSWELL PLAZA BRYANT ST & LYTTON AV, PA, 94301	790 - J4

FEATURE NAME Address City, ZIP Code	PAGE-GRID
COLBY PARK 451 61ST ST, OAK, 94609	629 - H5
COLISEUM GARDENS 69TH AV & BRENTFORD ST, OAK, 94621	670 - F3
COLLEGE HEIGHTS PARK HAYWARD BLVD, HAY, 94542	712 - D4
COLUMBIA PARK GLENDALE AV & MORSE AV, SUNV, 94086	812 - F5
COLUMBIAN GARDENS KOFORD RD & EMPIRE RD, OAK, 94603	670 - G6
COLUMBUS PARK 1600 WALNUT ST, SJS, 95110	833 - J5
COMANCHE PARK SHAWNEE LN & COMANCHE DR, SJS, 95123	874 - H5
COMMODORE PARK CHERRY AV & COMMODORE DR W, SBRN, 94066	707 - G6
CONCORD BLVD PARK CONCORD BLVD & MENDOCINO DR, CNCD, 94521	593 - C2
CONCORD COMMUNITY PARK COWELL RD & HALE DR, CNCD, 94518	592 - H3
CONCORDIA PARK 64TH AV & BRANN ST, OAK, 94605	670 - G1
CONGRESS SPRINGS PARK GLEN BRAE CT, SAR, 95070	852 - G7
CONNIE PARK CONNIE AV, SMTO, 94402	749 - B3
CONRAD PARK BEACH ST & COLUMBUS AV, SF, 94133	647 - J3
CONTEMPO PARK METEOR DR, UNC, 94587	732 - A6
CONTRA LOMA PARK MAHOGANY WY & MANDARIN WY, ANT, 94509, (510)757-0404	575 - B6
CONTRA LOMA REGIONAL PARK CONTRA LOMA BLVD, ANT, 94509, (510)757-0404	595 - A3
COOPER PARK EUNICE AV & VILLA NUEVA WY, MTVW, 94040	831 - J1
CORONA HEIGHTS PLAYGROUND MUSEUM WY, SF, 94114	667 - F2
COUNTRY CLUB SCHOOL PARK BLUE FOX WY & DAVONA DR, SRMN, 94583	693 - G1
COUNTRY MANOR PARK ASILOMAR DR & PALOMAR DR, ANT, 94509	595 - G2
COVINGTON MINI PARK & POOL ROSITA AV & LA PRENDA RD, LALT, 94024	831 - F1
COY PARK COY DR & SIGRID WY, SJS, 95123	874 - J3
COYOTE CREEK PARK CHAIN MONTEREY HWY, SJS, 95111	855 - A5
COYOTE HILLS REGIONAL PARK STATE HWY 84, FRMT, 94555	751 - H4
COYOTE POINT COUNTY REC AREA 1701 COYOTE POINT DR, SMTO, 94401, (650)573-2592	728 - J5
CRAGMONT PARK REGAL RD & HILLDALE AV, BERK, 94708	609 - H6
CRANDALL CREEK PARK MERRIMAC RIVER & MOHAWK RIVER, FRMT, 94555	752 - E2
CREEK PARK CENTER BL & SIR FRANCIS DRAKE, SANS, 94960	566 - C7
CREEKSIDE PARK BELMONT AV & LASSEN ST, ELCR, 94530	609 - C5
CREEKSIDE PARK BON AIR RD, MrnC, 94904	586 - E4
CREEKSIDE PARK JAMES BLK CIR & ALA DEL PRADO, NVTO, 94949	546 - E5
CREEKSIDE PARK LA MAR CT & DAVISON AV, CPTO, 95014	852 - F2
CREIGHTON PARK CRIEGHTON CT, MPS, 95035	814 - D1
CRESCENT PARK CENTER HARTNETT AV, RCH, 94804	609 - A2
CRESTVIEW PARK CRESTVIEW DR, SCAR, 94070	769 - D6
CRITTENDEN SCHOOL PARK MIDDLEFIELD RD & BURGOYNE ST, MTVW, 94043	811 - H2
CROCKER AMAZON PLAYGROUND GENEVA AV & MOSCOW ST, SF, 94112	687 - G2
CROCKER PARK 55 HAMPTON RD, PDMT, 94611	650 - C2
CUERNAVACA PARK ALCAZAR DR & HUNT DR, BURL, 94010	728 - A6
CUESTA PARK CUESTA DR & GRANT RD, MTVW, 94040	831 - H1
CULL CANYON REGIONAL REC AREA 18627 E CASTRO VALLEY BLVD, AlaC, 94552	692 - B1
DAN FOLEY PARK LAKESIDE DR, VAL, 94589	530 - C1
DANNA ROCK PARK MILLHAVEN PL & HOUNDSHAVEN WY, SJS, 95111	874 - J1
DANRIDGE CALABAZAS PARK BLANEY AV & RAINBOW DR, SJS, 95129	852 - E3
DANVILLE SOUTH PARK CM RAMON, DNVL, 94526	653 - C7
DAVIS, JOHN HUBERT PARK FOLSOM AV & 17TH ST, SPAB, 94806	588 - H3
DAYTON PLAYGROUND 1500 DAYTON AV, SLN, 94579	691 - A6
DE ANZA PARK 1150 LIME DR, SUNV, 94087, (408)730-7506	832 - B3
DE ANZA PARK N 3RD ST, HAY, 94541	711 - J1
DE ANZA PARK NAUTILUS PL, PIT, 94565	574 - A2
DE ANZA PARK PRINCETON DR & MERIDIAN AV, SJS, 95118	874 - B5
DE ANZA HISTORICAL PARK ARROYO CT, SMTO, 94402	748 - J2
DE FREMERY PARK 1651 ADELINE ST, OAK, 94607	649 - E3
DECOTO PLAZA E ST & 6TH ST, UNC, 94587	732 - G4
DEEP CREEK PARK DEEP CREEK RD & MACBETH AV, FRMT, 94555	752 - C1
DEERFIELD PARK DEERFIELD DR & BUCKSKIN DR, ANT, 94509	595 - H3
DEERVIEW PARK COLUMBIA DR & THOUSAND OAKS DR, AlaC, 94552	692 - C2
DEL PRADO PARK PASEO SANTA CRUZ & HANSEN DR, PLE, 94566	714 - A2
DEL RAY PARK BOCKMAN RD, AlaC, 94580	711 - C2
DELTA MEADOWS PARK JACK LONDON DR & CANDY DR, VAL, 94589	509 - J6
DELUCCHI PARK 1ST ST, PLE, 94566	714 - E4
DEMONSTRATION ORCHARD HOBSON ST & SPRING ST, SJS, 95110	833 - J5
DIABLO FOOTHILLS REGIONAL PARK CASTLE ROCK RD, CCCo, 94598	613 - A6
DIABLO SHADOWS PARK DIABLO SHADOW DR & BRANDYWINE, WLCK, 94598	612 - J2
DIABLO VISTA PARK CROW CYN RD & TASSAJARA RCH RD, DNVL, 94506	653 - J6
DIMOND PARK 3860 HANLY RD, OAK, 94602, (510)531-7055	650 - D4

FEATURE NAME Address City, ZIP Code	PAGE-GRID
DINOSAUR HILL PARK TAYLOR BLVD, PLHL, 94523	591 - J7
DISNEY, WALT SCHOOL PARK PINE VALLEY RD & DEL MAR DR, SRMN, 94583	673 - G6
DIXON LANDING PARK MILMONT DR & JURGENS DR, MPS, 95035	793 - J4
DOERR PARK POTRERO DR & PARK WILSHIRE DR, SJS, 95124	873 - H1
DOGWOOD PARK OLIVINA AV & ORIOLE AV, LVMR, 94550	695 - E7
DOLAN PARK IGLESIA DR & PADRE WY, DBLN, 94568	693 - F3
DOLLIVER PARK MADRONE AV & MAGNOLIA AV, LKSP, 94939	586 - E6
DOLPHIN PARK QUAY LN & TURKS HEAD LN, RDWC, 94065	749 - H7
DON CASTRO REGIONAL RECREATION-AREA WOODROE AV, AlaC, 94552	692 - C6
DOOLAN PARK JUNCTION AV & LADD AV, LVMR, 94550	695 - H7
DOUGLASS PLAYGROUND 26TH ST & DOUGLASS ST, SF, 94131, (415)695-5017	667 - F4
DOVE BEEGER PARK WHIPPLE AV, RDWC, 94062	769 - H7
DOVE HILL PARK DOVE HILL RD & DEANS PLACE WY, SJS, 95121	855 - B4
DRACENA PARK DRACENA AV, PDMT, 94611	650 - A1
DRY CREEK PIONEER REGIONAL PARK MISSION BLVD, UNC, 94587	732 - H1
DUBLIN SPORTS GROUNDS DUBLIN BLVD & CIVIC PZ, DBLN, 94568	693 - J5
DUBLIN SWIM CENTER VILLAGE PKWY, DBLN, 94568	693 - H2
DUBOCE PARK DUBOCE AV & STEINER ST, SF, 94117	667 - G1
DUNCAN PARK BREWSTER AV & NEVADA ST, RDWC, 94062	769 - H7
DUNPHY PARK BRIDGEWAY BLVD & NAPA ST, SAUS, 94965	627 - A2
DURANT PARK 651 29TH ST, OAK, 94609	649 - G2
E HILLSDALE PARK CHESTNUT LN, SMTO, 94403	749 - B6
EAGLE PARK SHORELINE BL & HIGH SCHOOL WY, MTVW, 94041	811 - H5
EAGLESRIDGE PARK EAGLERIDGE DR & GREYSTONE DR, ANT, 94509	595 - E2
EARL WARREN PARK CROW CYN RD & E CASTRO VLY BL, AlaC, 94552	692 - C5
EARNSCLIFF CANYON PARK HAZEL AV & MONTE VISTA AV, MLV, 94941	606 - C3
EAST AVENUE PARK EAST AV, AlaC, 94541	712 - D2
EASTER BOWL CALIFORNIA WY & TUM SUDEN WY, RDWC, 94062	789 - F2
EASTSHORE STATE PARK BUCHANAN ST, ALB, 94804	609 - B5
EATON PARK EATON AV, SCAR, 94070	769 - E6
ED R LEVIN COUNTY PARK 3100 CALAVERAS RD, SCIC, 95035, (408)262-6980	774 - E7
EDENDALE PARK ASHLAND AV & BERTERO AV, AlaC, 94580	691 - E5
EDENVALE GARDEN PARK EDENVALE AV & SADDLEBROOK DR, SJS, 95136	875 - A2
EDGEHILL MOUNTAIN PARK SHANGRILA WY, SF, 94127	667 - D5
EDGEMAR PARK CLIFTON RD & WINWOOD AV, PCFA, 94044	707 - A3
EDGEWATER PARK EDGEWATER BLVD, FCTY, 94404	749 - F4
EDGEWOOD COUNTY PARK EDGEWOOD RD & J SERRA FRWY, RDWC, 94062	789 - D1
EDGEWOOD PARK SUNNY CREST AV & EDGEWOOD AV, MLV, 94941	606 - C3
EL CAMINO PARK 100 EL CAMINO REAL, PA, 94301	790 - H4
EL DIVISADERO PARK EL DIVISADERO AV & SAN CARLOS, WLCK, 94598	612 - F3
EL PADRO PARK EL PADRO DR & ONTARIO DR, LVMR, 94550	715 - E3
EL PALO ALTO PARK EL CAMION REAL & ALMA ST, PA, 94301	790 - H4
EL QUITO PARK PASEO PRESADA & COX AV, SAR, 95070	852 - H6
ELLIS LAKE PARK CLAYTON RD & ASHBURY DR, CNCD, 94520	592 - F2
ELM PARK ELM AV & 8TH ST, RCH, 94801	588 - F6
ELMHURST PLAZA 1150 98TH AV, OAK, 94603	670 - H5
ENCHANTED KNOLLS PARK ROQUE MORAES & HAMILTON DR, MLV, 94941	606 - G4
ENCINAL PARK CORTE MADERA AV & MACARA AV, SUNV, 94086	812 - D5
ERCKENBRACK PARK NIANTIC DR, FCTY, 94404	749 - G2
ERIKSON PARK CORTE DE PLATA & PEARL AV, SJS, 95136	874 - E2
ERSKINE, DOROTHY PARK MARTHA AV & BURNSIDE AV, SF, 94131	667 - F6
ESTUARY PARK EMBARCADERO, OAK, 94607	649 - G6
EUCALYPTUS GROVE PARK N MAGAZINE, NWK, 94560	772 - H1
EUREKA VALLEY RECREATION CENTER DIAMOND ST & 19TH ST, SF, 94114	667 - G2
EVERGREEN PARK YERBA BUENA RD, SJS, 95135	855 - F5
FAIR GROUNDS 10TH ST & L ST, CCCo, 94509	575 - C5
FAIRLANDS PARK W LAS POSITAS BLVD, PLE, 94588	694 - E6
FAIRMEAD PARK LOYOLA DR & DUKE PATH, RCH, 94806	589 - A2
FAIRMONT PARK 649 PARKVIEW CIR, PCFA, 94044	707 - A2
FAIRMONT PARK STOCKTON AV & LEXINGTON AV, ELCR, 94530	609 - D3
FAIRMONT PARK VIEWMONT AV, VAL, 94590	530 - C3
FAIRMONT TERRACE PARK MANCHESTER RD & WINDSOR DR, AlaC, 94578	691 - F3
FAIRMONT WEST PARK PALMETTO AV & MAGELLAN DR, PCFA, 94044	707 - A2
FAIRMOUNT PLAZA FAIRMOUNT ST & MIGUEL ST, SF, 94131	667 - G5
FAIR OAKS PARK 540 N FAIR OAKS AV, SUNV, 94086, (408)730-7506	812 - G6
FAIR OAKS PARK HAMPTON DR, PLHL, 94523	592 - D6
FAIRVIEW PARK ASTER DR & CRESTVIEW DR, ANT, 94509	575 - B4

FEATURE NAME	Address City, ZIP Code	PAGE-GRID
FAIRVIEW PARK	ROMAGNOLO ST, AlaC, 94541	692 - C7
FAIRWAY GREENS PARK	BRIERGATE WY, HAY, 94544	732 - E1
FAIRWAY PARK	CINDY WY & CULLEN DR, PCFA, 94044	707 - A7
FARRAGUT PARK	FARRAGUT BLVD, FCTY, 94404	749 - F4
FASSLER PARK	CRESPI DR, PCFA, 94044	727 - A4
FAUDE PARK	OAKLAND AV, SANS, 94960	566 - B6
FERNANDEZ PARK	TENNENT AV, PIN, 94564	569 - E4
FERNISH PARK	FERNISH DR & GULUZZO DR, SJS, 95148	835 - D5
FIESTA MEADOWS PARK	FIESTA DR & BERMUDA DR, SMTO, 94403	749 - C4
FIRTH PARK	GLEN PKWY & SIERRA POINT RD, BSBN, 94005	688 - A7
FISCHER PARK	DEEP CREEK RD & MAYBIRD CIR, FRMT, 94555	752 - C2
FITZGERALD PARK	2ND ST & H ST, BEN, 94510	551 - B5
FLEETWOOD PARK	FLEETWOOD DR, SBRN, 94066	707 - E7
FLEISHMAN PARK	MCEVOY ST ST, RDWC, 94061	790 - B1
FLICKINGER PARK	FLICKENGER AV, SJS, 95131	814 - D6
FLOOD COUNTY PARK	BAY RD, MLPK, 94025, (650)363-4022	770 - H7
FLORESTA PARK	3750 MONTEREY BLVD, SLN, 94578	691 - B5
FOLSOM PARK	FOLSOM ST & 21ST ST, SF, 94110	667 - J3
FOOTHILL MEADOWS	38TH AV, OAK, 94601	670 - D1
FOOTHILL PARK	CAHALAN AV & FOOTHILL DR, SJS, 95123	874 - F6
FOOTHILL PARK	ROSWELL DR, MPS, 95035	794 - D7
FOOTHILL PARK	SEATON AV & TAMWORTH AV, SAR, 95070	872 - D1
FOOTHILLS PARK	ALHAMBRA AV & BENHAM DR, MRTZ, 94553	591 - H3
FOREST LANE PARK	FOREST LN, SBRN, 94066	707 - H6
FOXBORO PARK	CANTERBURY DR, HER, 94547	569 - J3
FRANCESCA TERRACE PARK	HILLCREST AV, BEN, 94510	551 - D4
FRANKFORT PARK	FRANKFORT ST & OLIVER ST, DALY, 94014	687 - E3
FRANKLIN CENTER	1010 E 15TH ST, OAK, 94606, (510)451-1993	649 - J5
FRANKLIN PARK	1300 SAN ANTONIO AV, ALA, 94501	669 - H2
FRANKLIN SQUARE	17TH ST & HAMPSHIRE ST, SF, 94110	668 - A2
FREEMAN PARK	BLITHEDALE AV & RYAN AV, MLV, 94941	606 - F4
FREMONT	SANTA CRUZ AV & UNIVERSITY DR, MLPK, 94025	790 - F4
FREMONT CENTRAL PARK	40204 PAS PADRE PKWY, FRMT, 94538	753 - D4
FREMONT PARK	JEFFERSON ST & FREMONT ST, SCL, 95050	833 - E4
FRONTIERLAND PARK	YOSEMITE DR & HUMBOLDT CT, PCFA, 94044	727 - C5
FRUITVALE BRIDGE PARK	ALAMEDA AV & FRUITVALE AV, OAK, 94601	670 - B2
FRUITVALE PLAZA	4500 INTERNATIONAL BLVD, OAK, 94601	670 - D1
FULTON PLAYGROUND	28TH AV, SF, 94121	647 - A7
GABRIELSON PARK	BRIDGEWAY BLVD & ANCHOR ST, SAUS, 94965	627 - B3
GANSBERGER PARK	KAY AV & CALAROGA AV, HAY, 94545	711 - G6
GARBER PARK	CLAREMONT AV, OAK, 94705	630 - B3
GARDINER PARK	MYREN DR & PORTOS DR, SAR, 95070	872 - G1
GARFIELD MUNICIPAL PLAYGROUND	2260 FOOTHILL BLVD, OAK, 94606	650 - B6
GARFIELD SQUARE	26TH ST & HARRISON ST, SF, 94110, (415)695-5010	667 - J4
GARIN REGIONAL PARK	GARIN AV, AlaC, 94544	712 - F7
GARRETT PARK	CANYON LN & GLENWOOD AV, RDWC, 94062	789 - G1
GATEWAY PARK	S GRANT ST & E 3RD AV, SMTO, 94401	749 - A1
GELLERT PARK	50 WEMBLEY DR, DALY, 94015	707 - B1
GEMELLO PARK	SOLANA CT & MARICH WY, MTVW, 94040	811 - F5
GENTRY TOWN PARK	PALO VERGE WY & MONTEREY DR, ANT, 94509	575 - A7
GEORGE R MOSCONE REC CENTER	CHESTNUT ST & BUCHANAN ST, SF, 94123, (415)292-2006	647 - G3
GERSTLE MEMORIAL PARK	SAN RAFAEL AV & CLARK ST, SRFL, 94901	586 - E2
GIBSON PARK	FLORIDA ST & AMADOR ST, VAL, 94590	530 - B4
GILL, PETER T PARK	PASEO REFUGIO & SANTA RITA DR, MPS, 95035	794 - B6
GILMAN PARK	GILMAN AV & GIANTS DR, SF, 94124	688 - C1
GLEN CANYON PARK	OSHAUGHNESSY BLVD, SF, 94131	667 - F5
GLEN COVE PARK	GLEN COVE PKWY, VAL, 94591	550 - F2
GLEN COVE WATERFRONT PARK	S REGATTA DR, VAL, 94591	550 - F3
GLEN ECHO CREEK PARK	MONTELL ST, OAK, 94611	649 - J1
GLEN PARK RECREATION CENTER	BOSWORTH ST & ELK ST, SF, 94131, (415)337-4705	667 - F6
GLENVIEW PARK	GLENVIEW DR, SBRN, 94066	707 - F7
GLENVIEW PARK	VALLEY QUAIL CIR & QUAIL VIEW, SJS, 95120	894 - F3
GODFREY PARK	281 BEACH RD, ALA, 94502, (510)521-1551	670 - B6
GOLDEN GATE NATIONAL REC AREA	SF, 94129, (415)556-0560	647 - D2
GOLDEN GATE NATIONAL REC AREA	MrnC, 94965	626 - C3
GOLDEN GATE NATIONAL REC AREA	CABRILLO HWY, PCFA, 94044	727 - C1
GOLDEN GATE PARK	1100 61ST ST, OAK, 94608	629 - F5
GOLDEN GATE PARK	FELL ST & STANYAN ST, SF, (415)666-7200	667 - D1
GOLDEN HILLS PARK	VALLEY RD, MRTZ, 94553	591 - G3
GOLDEN OAKS PARK	ALMADEN EXPWY & OAK FOREST WY, SJS, 95120	874 - D6
GOLDEN VIEW SCHOOL PARK	CROW CANYON RD & CYN CRES DR, SRMN, 94583	653 - G7
GOMES PARK	LEMOS LN, FRMT, 94539	753 - E4
GOMEZ, LEFTY BALLFIELD COMPLEX	PARKER AV & 4TH ST, CCCo, 94572	549 - H7
GOMEZ, MARV PARK	FORBES AV & BUCHER AV, SCL, 95051	833 - C6
GRAHAM SCHOOL PARK	CASTRO ST & MIRAMONTE AV, MTVW, 94040	811 - H6
GRAHAM, DUNCAN PARK	VISTA GRANDE & LINDA VISTA AV, BEN, 94510	551 - D4
GRANADA PARK	GRANADA DR & VISTA CT, CMAD, 94925	606 - J2
GRAND VIEW PARK	14TH AV & 15TH AV, SF, 94122	667 - C3
GRANT MAHONEY PARK	MARIPOSA ST & ARKANSAS ST, VAL, 94590	530 - C3
GRANT PARK	HOLT AV & GRANT PARK LN, LALT, 94024	832 - A4
GRATTAN PLAYGROUND	STANYON ST & ALMA ST, SF, 94117	667 - E2
GRAYSTONE PARK	CAMDEN AV & WINTERSET WY, SJS, 95120	894 - F1
GREAT OAKS PARK	SNOW DR & GIUSTI DR, SJS, 95111	875 - B2
GREEN BELT PARK	CAMPUS DR, HAY, 94542	712 - E3
GREEN HILLS PARK	MAGNOLIA AV & LUDEMAN LN, MLBR, 94030	728 - A3
GREENMAN RECREATIONAL FIELD	1100 66TH AV, OAK, 94621	670 - F3
GREENRIDGE PARK	CROW CANYON RD, AlaC, 94552	692 - E2
GREENVILLE NORTH PARK	SCENIC AV & HEATHER LN, LVMR, 94550	696 - B3
GREENWOOD PARK	MIDDLE LN, HAY, 94545	711 - E5
GREER PARK	1098 AMARILLO AV, PA, 94303	791 - D5
GRIMMER PARK	PHILADELPHIA PL & MONMOUTH PL, FRMT, 94538	773 - E2
GROESBECK HILL PARK	KLEIN RD & GROESBECK HILL RD, SJS, 95148	835 - E6
GROVE RECREATION CENTER	1730 OREGON ST, BERK, 94703, (510)644-6225	629 - G4
GROVE SHAFTER PARK	34TH ST, OAK, 94609	649 - G1
GRUNDY PARK	CHESTNUT AV & PARK AV, SBRN, 94066	707 - H7
GUADALUPE GARDENS	TAYLOR ST & WALNUT ST, SJS, 95110	833 - J5
GUADALUPE OAK GROVE PARK	THORNTREE DR & PORTO ALEGRE CT, SJS, 95120	874 - C6
GUADALUPE RESERVOIR COUNTY PARK	HICKS RD, SCIC, 95120	894 - C5
GUADALUPE RIVER PARK	W SAN CARLOS ST & WOZ WY, SJS, 95110	834 - B7
GULL PARK	GULL AV, FCTY, 94404	749 - G1
GULLO PARK	WILLIAMS RD & MOORPARK AV, SJS, 95129	852 - J3
HAAS, WALTER PARK	ADDISON ST & BEACON ST, SF, 94131	667 - G5
HAGEMANN PARK	TURNSTONE DR & HUMMINGBIRD LN, LVMR, 94550	715 - E1
HAKONE GARDENS	21000 BIG BASIN WY, SAR, 95070, (408)741-1689	872 - C3
HALCYON PARK	1245 147TH AV, SLN, 94578	691 - C3
HALL MEMORIAL PARK	LA HONDA DR, MPS, 95035	793 - J5
HALL RANCH PARK	HALL RANCH PKWY, UNC, 94587	731 - J6
HALLMARK PARK	HALLMARK DR, BLMT, 94002	769 - B3
HAMANN PARK	WESTFIELD AV & CENTRAL AV, SJS, 95128	853 - E3
HAMILTON PARK	S ELISEO DR, LKSP, 94939	586 - E5
HAMILTON SQUARE	GEARY BLVD & STEINER ST, SF, 94115	647 - G6
HANNA PARK	REFUGIO VLY RD & MANDALAY AV, HER, 94547	570 - B6
HANSEN PARK	BLACK AV, PLE, 94566	714 - C2
HANSEN PARK	E STANLEY BL & S S ST, LVMR, 94550	715 - F1
HAPPY HOLLOW PARK	1300 SENTER RD, SJS, 95112, (408)292-8188	854 - E1
HARBOR VIEW PARK	MONTE DIABLO AV & ROCHESTER ST, SMTO, 94401	729 - A6
HARBOUR PARK	ASHBURTON DR & WESTBOURNE DR, ANT, 94509	575 - F7
HARDING PARK	7115 C ST, ELCR, 94530, (510)526-9866	609 - E4
HARDY PARK	HARDY ST & MILES AV, OAK, 94618	629 - J6
HARRINGTON, DOC PARK	3400 OLEANDER AV, ALA, 94502	670 - A7
HARRISON SQUARE	299 7TH ST, OAK, 94607	649 - G5
HARVEST PARK	HARVEST RD, PLE, 94566	714 - D2
HARVEY COMMUNITY PARK	LAKE ARROWHEAD AV, FRMT, 94555	732 - B6
HATHAWAY PARK	COLOMBO DR & VALLEJO DR, SJS, 95130	853 - A4
HAVENS PLAYGROUND	BONITA AV & VISTA AV, PDMT, 94611	650 - B1
HAWES PARK	OAK AV & JOHNSON ST, RDWC, 94061	770 - A7
HAWK HILL PARK	RIVERA ST & FUNSTON AV, SF, 94116	667 - C4
HAYWARD MEMORIAL PARK	24176 MISSION BLVD, HAY, 94541	712 - A2
HAYWARD PLAYGROUND	TURK ST & GOUGH ST, SF, 94102	647 - H6
HAYWARD REGIONAL SHORELINE	BREAKWATER AV, HAY, 94545	711 - A6
HEATH PARK	1220 143RD AV, SLN, 94578	691 - C3
HEATHER FARM PARK	301 N SAN CARLOS DR, WLCK, 94598, (510)935-3300	612 - E2
HEATHER PARK	MELENDY DR, SCAR, 94070	769 - E5
HEATHERLARK PARK	NORTHWAY RD, PLE, 94566	714 - C1
HEATHERWOOD PARK	HEATHER WY & MIDWAY RD, LKSP, 94939	586 - F6
HELLMAN RECREATION AREA	3500 MALCOLM AV, OAK, 94605	671 - C5
HENRY RANCH PARK	SEVERUS DR & AUBURN DR, VAL, 94589	509 - H5
HERITAGE OAKS PARK	MCKENZIE AV & PORTLAND AV, LALT, 94024	831 - H3
HERITAGE ROSE GARDEN	TAYLOR ST & VENDOME ST, SJS, 95110	833 - J5
HERMAN STREET PARK	HERMAN ST & DIAMOND ST, SBRN, 94066	707 - J6
HERMAN, JUSTIN PLAZA	MARKET ST & THE EMBARCADERO, SF, 94111	648 - B4
HESTER PARK	NAGLEE AV & DANA AV, SJS, 95126	833 - G7
HESTER, LEH PARK	HAMPTON DR & HOOKSTON RD, CNCD, 94518	592 - D6
HIDDEN LAKES PARK	MORELLO AV, MRTZ, 94553	591 - J1
HIDDEN VALLEY MEMORIAL PARK	BLUM RD & IMHOFF DR, CCCo, 94553	572 - B5
HIDDEN VALLEY PARK	CENTER AV, MRTZ, 94553	591 - J1
HIGHLANDS PARK	MELENDY DR & ABERDEEN DR, SCAR, 94070	769 - E4
HIGHLANDS PARK	PENNSYLVANIA BL & MAINE DR, CNCD, 94521	593 - F6
HIGHLANDS PARK	REGENTS PARK DR, VAL, 94591	530 - G6
HIGHLANDS PARK	SAINT PAUL CIR, PIT, 94565	574 - E6
HIGUERA ADOBE PARK	47300 RANCHO HIGUERA RD, FRMT, 94539	774 - A6
HILL PARK	HILL RD & INDIAN VALLEY RD, NVTO, 94947	526 - B5
HILLCREST CIRCLE PARK	HILLCREST RD & ARUNDEL RD, SCAR, 94070	769 - F3
HILLCREST COMMUNITY PARK	OLIVERA RD & GRANT ST, CNCD, 94520	572 - E6
HILLCREST KNOLLS PARK	VAN AV & 150TH AV, AlaC, 94578	691 - E3
HILLCREST PARK	LARKSPUR DR & VIOLET CT, ANT, 94509	575 - G7
HILLSDALE PARK	DAFFODIL DR, PIT, 94565	573 - J4
W HILLSDALE PARK	LOUISE LN, SMTO, 94403	749 - B6
HILLSIDE NATURAL AREA	MOESER LN, ELCR, 94530	609 - D2
HILLSIDE PARK	222 LAUSANNE AV, DALY, 94014	687 - D4
HILLTOP GREEN PARK	PARKWAY DR & PARK CENTRAL, RCH, 94803	569 - C7
HILLTOP LAKE PARK	HILLTOP DR & RESEARCH DR, RCH, 94806	569 - A7
HILLTOP PARK	2700 GROOM DR, RCH, 94806	588 - J1
HILLTOP PARK	LA SALLE AV & NEWCOMB AV, SF, 94124	668 - C6
HILLVIEW COMMUNITY CENTER	HILLVIEW AV & SAN ANTONIO RD, LALT, 94022	811 - E7
HILLVIEW PARK	2251 OCALA AV, SJS, 95122	834 - J6
HINKEL, J PARK	SAN DIEGO RD & SOMERSET PL, BERK, 94707	609 - G5
HOLBOOK PALMER PARK	WATKINS AV & MCCORMICK LN, ATN, 94027	790 - E2
HOLIDAY HIGHLANDS PARK	FIG TREE LN, MRTZ, 94553	571 - J6
HOLLY MINI PARK	HOLLY ST & 98TH AV, OAK, 94603	670 - J5
HOLLY PARK	HOLLY PARK CIR, SF, 94110	667 - H5
HOLM WELL PARK	CRYSTAL CIR & PERIDOT DR, LVMR, 94550	715 - D3
HOLMES PARK	HOLMES ST & LOMITAS AV, LVMR, 94550	715 - F4
HOMERIDGE PARK	2985 STEVENSON ST, SCL, 95051	833 - A6
HOOVER PARK	2901 COWPER AV, PA, 94306	791 - C7
HOOVER PARK	BARNHART PL & ASTER LN, CPTO, 95014	852 - D4
HOOVER PARK	SPRING ST & CHARTER ST, RDWC, 94063	770 - C6
HOPKINS CREEKSIDE PARK	ALMA ST & PALO ALTO AV, PA, 94301	790 - H4
HORSESHOE PARK	SEAWALL DR, BERK, 94804	629 - B2
HOUGE PARK	JACKSOL DR & BARRETT AV, SJS, 95124	873 - E3
HOWE HOMESTEAD PARK	WALNUT BLVD & HOMESTEAD AV, WLCK, 94598	612 - E5
HUBER PARK	7711 TERRACE DR, ELCR, 94530	609 - E3
HUDDART COUNTY PARK	KINGS MOUNTAIN RD & SKYLINE BL, SMCo, 94062	789 - B5
INDEPENDENCE PARK	HOLMES ST & REGENT RD, LVMR, 94550	715 - F5
INDEPENDENCE PARK	MARE ISLAND WY & MAINE ST, VAL, 94590	529 - H5
INDIA BASIN SHORELINE PARK	HUNTERS POINT BLVD, SF, 94124	668 - D6
INDIAN ROCK PARK	INDIAN ROCK AV & OXFORD ST, BERK, 94707	609 - G6
INDIAN SPRINGS PARK	W 39TH AV, SMTO, 94403	749 - B7
INTERIOR PARK BELT	STANYON ST, SF, 94117	667 - E2
IRVINGTON PARK	41800 BLACOW RD, FRMT, 94538	773 - D1
IRVINGTON PLAZA PARK	BAY ST, FRMT, 94538	753 - D7
JACK FARELL PARK	FORDHAM ST, EPA, 94303	771 - C7
JACK FISCHER PARK	POLLARD RD & ABBOTT AV, CMBL, 95008	873 - B1
JACKSON PARK	2450 ENCINAL AV, ALA, 94501	670 - A3
JACKSON PLAYGROUND	ARKANSAS ST & MARIPOSA ST, SF, 94107	668 - B2
JACOBSEN PARK	JACOBSEN ST, ANT, 94509	575 - F5
JARDIN DE NINOS PARK	MIDDLEFIELD RD & CEDAR ST, RDWC, 94063	770 - B6
JEFFERSON PLAYGROUND	14311 LARK ST, SLN, 94578	691 - C3
JEFFERSON SQUARE	TURK ST & GOUGH ST, SF, 94102	647 - H6
JEFFERSON SQUARE RECREATION-CENTER	645 7TH ST, OAK, 94607	649 - F4
JERRY RUSSOM MEMORIAL PARK	OLD LUCAS VALLEY RD, SRFL, 94903	566 - C1

FEATURE NAME / Address City, ZIP Code	PAGE-GRID
JOAQUIN MILLER PARK 3101 JOAQUIN MILLER RD, OAK, 94611, (510)232-7100	650 - G3
JOHNSON PARK EVERETT AV & WAVERLEY ST, PA, 94301	790 - H4
JOHNSON, WADE PARK 1300 12TH ST, OAK, 94607	649 - E3
JOINVILLE PARK KEHOE AV, SMTO, 94403	749 - D1
JOLLYMAN PARK JOLLYMAN LN & STELLING RD, CPTO, 95014	852 - D2
JONES, VICTOR PARK ROBINHOOD DR & MAPLEWOOD DR, SRFL, 94901	567 - B5
JOSEF HOOG PARK MARIN OAKS DR & MONTURA WY, NVTO, 94949	546 - C1
JULIUS KAHN PLAYGROUND W PACIFIC AV & SPRUCE ST, SF, 94129, (415)292-2004	647 - E5
JUNIPERO SERRA COUNTY PARK CRYSTAL SPRINGS AV, SBRN, 94066, (650)589-5708	727 - H2
JURI COMMONS PARK SAN JOSE AV & JURI ST, SF, 94110	667 - H4
KELLEY PARK KEYES ST & SENTER RD, SJS, 95122, (408)297-0778	834 - E7
KELLOCH-VELASCO PARK KELLOCH AV & VELASCO AV, DALY, 94014	687 - J2
KELLOG PARK EMBARCADERO RD & WAVERLY ST, PA, 94301	791 - A5
KELLY PARK 100 TERMINAL AV, MLPK, 94025, (650)322-4578	770 - H7
KENNEDY GROVE REGIONAL REC AREA HILLSIDE DR & PABLO DAM RD, CCCo, 94803	589 - J5
KENNEDY TRACT PARK 26TH AV, OAK, 94601	650 - B7
KENNEDY, CHARLES F PARK 1333 DECOTO RD, UNC, 94587, (510)489-0360	732 - G6
KENNEDY, JOHN F PARK 19501 HESPERIAN BLVD, HAY, 94541	711 - E2
KENNEDY, JOHN F PARK 41ST ST & CUTTING BLVD, RCH, 94804, (510)620-6792	609 - A1
KENNEY, JAMES RECREATION CENTER 901 DELAWARE ST, BERK, 94804, (510)644-8511	629 - D1
KETCH PARK KETCH CT, FCTY, 94404	749 - G4
KILLDEER PARK KILLDEER CT, FCTY, 94404	749 - G1
KIMBERLY PARK KIMBERLY DR, AMCN, 94589	509 - J4
KING, M L PARK 725 MONTE DIABLO AV, SMTO, 94401, (650)377-4714	728 - J7
KING, MARTIN LUTHER JR REG-SHORELINE OAKPORT ST, OAK, 94601	670 - D3
KING, MARTIN LUTHER MEMORIAL PARK 360 HARBOUR WY S, RCH, 94804, (510)236-7540	608 - G1
KIRK PARK 2801 BRIARWOOD DR, SJS, 95125	874 - A1
KLEIN PARK CALIFORNIA ST & ORTEGA AV, MTVW, 94040	811 - F4
KNOLL PARK KNOLLPARK WY & KNOLLPARK CIR, ANT, 94509	595 - J4
KNOLL PARK LOGAN DR, FRMT, 94538	753 - B6
KNOWLAND PARK GOLF LINKS RD, OAK, 94605	671 - C4
KOLB PARK BRIGHTON PL, DBLN, 94568	693 - H2
KOSHLAND PARK BUCHANAN ST & PAGE ST, SF, 94102	667 - H1
KOTTINGER PARK KOTTINGER DR, PLE, 94566	714 - F4
KOTTINGER VILLAGE PARK VINEYARD AV, PLE, 94566	714 - F3
KRUSI PARK 3000 CALHOUN ST, ALA, 94501	670 - A4
LA COLINA PARK LOS PINOS WY & ANSDELL WY, SJS, 95123	875 - A6
LA MOINE VALLEY VIEW PARK MORNINGSIDE DR, RCH, 94803	589 - F2
LAFAYETTE COMMUNITY PARK SAINT MARYS RD, LFYT, 94549	631 - H3
LAFAYETTE PARK EL CAMINO REAL & LAFAYETTE ST, SCL, 95050	833 - E3
LAFAYETTE PARK GOUGH ST & WASHINGTON ST, SF, 94109	647 - H5
LAFAYETTE RESERVOIR REC AREA HWY 24 & MOUNT DIABLO BL, LFYT, 94549, (510)284-9669	631 - C1
LAFAYETTE SQUARE 1000 JEFFERSON ST, OAK, 94607	649 - F4
LAGOON PARK ARMORY DR, SRFL, 94903	566 - F4
LAGUNA PARK LAGUNA AV & GROVE AV, BURL, 94010	728 - D5
LAKE CUNNINGHAM PARK TULLY RD & WHITE RD, SJS, 95148, (408)277-4319	835 - B6
LAKE DALWIGK PARK LEMON ST & 6TH ST, VAL, 94590	530 - B6
LAKE MERRITT CHANNEL PARK 7TH ST & E 8TH ST, OAK, 94606	649 - H5
LAKE SHORE PARK MACARTHUR BLVD & GRAND AV, OAK, 94610	649 - J3
LAKESHORE PARK 1550 MARINA CT, SMTO, 94403	749 - D4
LAKESHORE PARK LAKE BLVD & CHANNEL DR, NWK, 94560	752 - E4
LAKESIDE PARK 666 BELLEVUE AV, OAK, 94610, (510)238-3090	649 - H3
LAKE TEMESCAL REGIONAL REC AREA BROADWAY & WARREN FRWY, OAK, 94611	630 - C5
LAKEWOOD PARK 834 LAKECHIME DR, SUNV, 94089, (408)734-2310	812 - H4
LANDELS SCHOOL PARK 115 DANA ST, MTVW, 94041	811 - J5
LANDSDALE STATION PARK FORREST AV & GLEN RD, SANS, 94960	566 - A6
LARKEY PARK 1901 1ST AV, WLCK, 94596	612 - B2
LARSEN PARK ULLOA ST & 19TH AV, SF, 94116	667 - B5
LAS JUNTAS PARK CAMINO LAS JUNTAS, PLHL, 94523	592 - B4
LAS PALMAS PARK RUSSET DR & DANFORTH DR, SUNV, 94087	832 - D2
LAUREL ST PARK LAUREL ST, SCAR, 94070	769 - G3
LAURELWOOD PARK GLENDORA DR, SMTO, 94403	748 - J7
LAUREOLA PARK 503 OLD COUNTRY RD, SCAR, 94070	769 - G2
LAURIE MEADOWS PARK LAURIE MEADOWS DR, SMTO, 94403	749 - E6
LEE GARNER PARK NOVATO BLVD & TAMALPAIS AV, NVTO, 94945	526 - A3
LEVIN, ED R COUNTY PARK 3100 CALAVERAS RD, SCIC, 95035, (408)262-6980	794 - F3
LEWELLING PLAYGROUND 750 FARGO AV, SLN, 94579	691 - B6
LEXINGTON RESERVOIR COUNTY PARK LIMEKILN RD & ALMA BRIDGE RD, SCIC, 95030, (408)867-0190	893 - A4
LEYDECKER PARK 3225 MECARTNEY RD, ALA, 94502, (510)521-1256	670 - A6
LICK MILL PARK FAIRWAY GLEN, SCL, 95054	813 - C4
LINCOLN GLEN PARK LINCOLN AV & CURTNER AV, SJS, 95125	854 - B5
LINCOLN PARK 1450 HIGH ST, ALA, 94501	670 - B3
LINCOLN PARK 901 BRUNSWICK ST, DALY, 94014	687 - E3
LINCOLN PARK UNIVERSITY AV & MIDDLEBURY LN, LALT, 94022	811 - D7
LINCOLN PLAYGROUND 451 W JOAQUIN AV, SLN, 94577	691 - A1
LINCOLN SQUARE RECREATION CENTER 250 10TH ST, OAK, 94607, (510)893-2497	649 - G4
LINDA VISTA PARK LINDA VISTA DR, CPTO, 95014	852 - A3
LINDEN COMMUNITY PARK 950 45TH ST, OAK, 94608	629 - G7
LINDEN PARK LINDEN ST & PARK ST, RDWC, 94061	770 - C7
LIONS FIELD PARK 1ST AV, SBRN, 94066	707 - J7
LIONS PARK NOVATO BLVD, MrnC, 94947	525 - E1
LIONS PARK TIOGA DR, MLBR, 94030	727 - J4
LITTLE HILLS RANCH REGIONAL REC-AREA 18013 BOLLINGER CANYON RD, AlaC, 94552, (510)837-7076	652 - E6
LITTLE LEAGUE FIELD PARK I ST & E 3RD ST, BEN, 94510	551 - C5
LITTLEJOHN PARK 1301 BUENA VISTA AV, ALA, 94501	669 - H1
LIVE OAK MANOR PARK LONGRIDGE RD & LESTER AV, LGTS, 95032	873 - D4
LIVE OAK RECREATION CENTER 1301 SHATTUCK AV, BERK, 94709, (510)644-8513	609 - G7
LIVERMORE DOWNS PARK PAS LAGUNA SECO, LVMR, 94550	695 - F6
LIVERMORE, ROBERT PARK 4700 EAST AV, LVMR, 94550	716 - A1
LIVORNA PARK LIVORNA RD & MIRANDA AV, CCCo, 94507	632 - H3
LOMITA PARK 500 SAN ANSELMO AV, SBRN, 94066	728 - A1
LONDON, JACK PARK ROSE DR & HASTINGS DR, BEN, 94510	551 - A1
LONE HILL PARK WINTER DR & LYNN CT, SJS, 95124	873 - J4
LONE TREE CREEK PARK 500 STARLITE WY, FRMT, 94539	793 - J1
LONGFELLOW PARK 520 LINCOLN AV, ALA, 94501, (510)522-5262	669 - F1
LONGVIEW PARK WESTLINE DR, DALY, 94015	706 - J1
LONGWOOD PARK REED WY & LEONARDO WY, HAY, 94541	711 - F3
LOS ALAMITOS/CALERO CREEK PARK CAMDEN AV & HARRY RD, SJS, 95120	894 - J3
LOS CERRITOS COMMUNITY PARK NICOLET AV & ALDER AV, FRMT, 94536	752 - G2
LOS GATOS CREEK PARK DELL AV, CMBL, 95008, (408)358-3741	873 - D1
LOS PASEOS PARK VIA VISTA & AVD GRANDE, SJS, 95139	875 - F7
LOS PRADOS PARK BAHIA, SMTO, 94403	749 - E5
LOUIE FRANCIS PARK BANTRY RD & OCONNOR DR, PIN, 94806	569 - C5
LOWELL PARK 1000 12TH ST, OAK, 94607	649 - E3
LOWRY PARK LAKE MEAD DR, FRMT, 94555	732 - C7
LUCAS PARK PLGD LUCAS AV & 10TH ST, RCH, 94801	588 - G5
LYNBROOK PARK KEVIN DR, CCCo, 94565	573 - F1
LYNWOOD HILL PARK LEAFWOOD HGHTS & GREENWOOD DR, NVTO, 94947	526 - D6
LYNWOOD PARK S NOVATO BLVD & ROWLAND BLVD, NVTO, 94947	526 - C6
LYONS FIELD PARK 99TH AV & PLYMOUTH ST, OAK, 94603	670 - J5
MACGREGOR PLAY FIELDS CEDAR BLVD. & MCDONALD AV, NWK, 94560	752 - D4
MACHADO PARK 3360 CABRILLO AV, SCL, 95051	832 - J3
MADDUX PARK MADDUX ST & PALM AV DR, RDWC, 94061	790 - A3
MADEIRA PARK MADEIRA WY & SCHOOL ST, LVMR, 94550	695 - H7
MADISON PARK 150 8TH ST, OAK, 94607	649 - G5
MAGNOLIA PARK MAGNOLIA AV & ALEXANDER AV, LKSP, 94939	586 - F7
MAITLAND, R HENRY PARK ALAMEDA DR & MENDOCINO RD, LVMR, 94550	695 - E6
MANDANA PLAZA 3501 LAKESHORE AV, OAK, 94610	650 - A3
MANOR, REX PARK FARLEY ST, MTVW, 94043	811 - G4
MANZANITA RECREATION CENTER 2150 E 28TH ST, OAK, 94606	650 - B5
MAPE PARK PLATA WY, DBLN, 94568	693 - G4
MARCHBANK PARK PARKVIEW AV & WOODROW ST, DALY, 94014	687 - C3
MARCHETTI, GINO PARK END OF BELLE DR, ANT, 94509	574 - H6
MARIA B FREITAS MEMORIAL PARK MONTECILLO RD, SRFL, 94903	566 - D3
MARIN HIGHLANDS PARK BLANCA DR & SANTA MARIA DR, NVTO, 94947	525 - G4
MARINA ISLAND PARK MARINERS ISLAND BLVD, SMTO, 94404	749 - D2
MARINA PARK NEPTUNE DR & S DIKE RD, SLN, 94577	690 - G5
MARINA PARK POWELL ST, EMVL, 94608	629 - B6
MARINA PARK REGATTA BL & MARINA BAY PKWY, RCH, 94804	608 - H2
MARINA PARK W 4TH ST, PIT, 94565	574 - D1
MARINA VISTA MEMORIAL PARK MAINE ST & MARE ISLAND WY, VAL, 94590	529 - H5
MARINA VISTA PARK BAY ST & SPRUCE ST, SMCo, 94128	728 - B2
MARINER PARK TEREDO DR, RDWC, 94065	749 - H7
MARINSHIP PARK MARINSHIP AV & LIBERTY SHIP WY, SAUS, 94965	627 - A2
MARINWOOD PARK LUCAS VALLEY RD & MILLER CREEK, MrnC, 94903	546 - D7
MARION PARK GRANT AV & 8TH ST, NVTO, 94945	526 - A3
MARKHAM NATURE AREA LA VISTA WY, CNCD, 94521	592 - J4
MARLIN PARK MARLIN AV, FCTY, 94404	749 - H3
MARLIN PARK NEPTUNE DR, RDWC, 94065	749 - H7
MARSHALL PARK CURTIS ST & I-880 FRWY, FRMT, 94538	773 - B1
MARSTON CAMPBELL PARK 16TH ST & WEST ST, OAK, 94607	649 - F3
MARTIN LUTHER KING JR PARK OLIMA ST & COLOMA ST, SAUS, 94965	626 - J1
MARTIN LUTHER KING PARK DAISY LN, EPA, 94303	791 - D2
MARTIN PARK FORESTDALE AV & MELBOURNE BL, SJS, 95116	834 - E6
MARTIN, T J PARK BURCHELL AV & MEDALLION DR, SJS, 95120	874 - B6
MARTINEZ REGIONAL SHORELINE PARK FERRY ST, MRTZ, 94553	571 - C2
MARTINEZ WATERFRONT PARK FERRY ST, MRTZ, 94553	571 - D2
MARYMEADE PARK FREMONT AV & GRANT RD, LALT, 94024	831 - H3
MAX BAER PARK MURDELL LN & FONTONETT AV, LVMR, 94550	715 - D3
MAXWELL PARK FLEMING AV, OAK, 94619	650 - F7
MAYFAIR PARK SUNSET AV & KAMMERER AV, SJS, 95116	834 - G4
MAYFIELD PARK 2300 COLLEGE AV & WELLESLEY ST, PA, 94306	791 - A7
MAYHEWS LANDING PARK CHERRY ST & MONTCALM AV, NWK, 94560	752 - D6
MAYWOOD PARK 3330 PRUNERIDGE AV, SCL, 95051	832 - J7
MCCARTNEY PARK SUNNYSIDE DR & BREED AV, SLN, 94577	671 - A7
MCCLELLAN RANCH PARK MCCLELLAN RD & MIRA VISTA RD, CPTO, 95014	852 - A2
MCCLYMONDS MINI PARK 1000 26TH ST, OAK, 94607	649 - F2
MCCONAGHY PARK HESPERIAN BLVD, AlaC, 94580	711 - E2
MCCOPPIN SQUARE SANTIAGO ST & 24TH AV, SF, 94116	667 - B4
MCCREA MEMORIAL PARK CARSON ST & SHEPHERD ST, OAK, 94619	650 - G6
MCDOUGAL PARK VISTA DR, BLMT, 94002	769 - D2
MCENERY PARK W SAN FERNANDO ST & RIVER ST, SJS, 95110	834 - B7
MCGEE, HAP RANCH PARK LA GONDA WY, DNVL, 94526	632 - H6
MCINNIS, JOHN F COUNTY PARK SMITH RANCH RD, SRFL, 94903	566 - C1
MCINTYRE RANCH PARK ST JOHNS MINE RD, VAL, 94591	530 - H1
MCKELVEY PARK PARK DR & MIRAMONTE AV, MTVW, 94040	811 - H6
MCKENZIE PARK FREMONT AV & ALTOS OAKS DR, LALT, 94024	831 - G2
MCKINLEY PARK BUENA VISTA AV & WALNUT ST, ALA, 94501	670 - A1
MCKINLEY PARK KOTTINGER DR & CABERNET CT, PLE, 94566	714 - F4
MCKINLEY PLAYGROUND 2150 E 14TH ST, SLN, 94577	691 - B2
MCKINLEY SQUARE VERMONT ST & 20TH ST, SF, 94107	668 - A3
MCLAREN, JOHN PARK MANSELL ST & JOHN F SHELLEY DR, SF, 94134	687 - H1
MEADOW BROOK PARK YELLOWSTONE DR & GEYSER CIR, ANT, 94509	575 - G6
MEADOW HOMES PARK SUNSHINE DR & DETROIT AV, CNCD, 94520	592 - F3
MEADOW PARK NOB HILL AV & ROGERS WY, PIN, 94564	569 - D4
MEADOWLARK PARK PRAIRIE DR, PLE, 94588	714 - A3
MEADOWS PARK BLUEFIELD DR & BLISS CT, SJS, 95136	874 - F1
MEADOWS PARK W LAS POSITAS BLVD, PLE, 94588	694 - G6
MEEK PARK HAMPTON RD & HARVARD AV, AlaC, 94541	691 - F7
MELODY PARK LA TORRE AV & NOKOMIS DR, SJS, 95111	855 - A7
MEMORIAL PARK 1301 PORTLAND AV, ALB, 94706	609 - E5
MEMORIAL PARK BANCROFT AV & CALLAN AV, SLN, 94577	671 - B7
MEMORIAL PARK D ST, ANT, 94509	575 - D7
MEMORIAL PARK MACDONALD AV, RCH, 94801	588 - G6
MEMORIAL PARK STEVENS CREEK BL & ANTON WY, CPTO, 95014	832 - C7
MERVIN MORRIS PARK GRANT AV & NIELSON AV, AlaC, 94580	711 - C1
METCALF PARK MONTEREY HWY & FORSUM RD, SJS, 95138	875 - G6
MEZES PARK STANDISH ST & WARREN ST, RDWC, 94063, (650)780-7250	770 - A5
MICHIGAN PARK 500 SPRUCE ST, BERK, 94707	609 - G4
MIDDLE SCHOOL PARK BUCHANAN ST, ALB, 94706	609 - D6
MIDTOWN TERRACE PLAYGROUND CLARENDON AV & OLYMPIA WY, SF, 94131, (415)753-7036	667 - E3
MILL CREEK HOLLOW DEERWOOD PL & DEERWOOD DR, SRMN, 94583	673 - B1
MILL ESTATE PARK SEBASTIAN DR & LAKE ST, MLBR, 94030	728 - A5
MILLER GROVE PARK ELDRIGE AV & BLITHEDALE AV, MLV, 94941	606 - D2
MILLER-KNOX REGIONAL SHORELINE DORMAN DR, RCH, 94801	608 - D2
MILLS CANYON PARK ARGUELLO DR & SEBASTIAN DR, BURL, 94010	728 - B6
MINER PARK LEAN AV & COPCO LN, SJS, 95123	875 - A4
MIRA VISTA HILLS PARK SILVERADO DR & HILLIARD CIR, ANT, 94509	595 - A2
MIRA VISTA PARK S FRANCISCO WY & RIO GRANDE DR, ANT, 94509	575 - B7
MIRABEAU PARK HALEY ST & MIRABEAU DR, NWK, 94560	752 - C5
MISE PARK MITTY WY & PARK MEADOW DR, SJS, 95129	852 - J1

FEATURE NAME Address City, ZIP Code	PAGE-GRID
MISSION DOLORES PARK DOLORES ST & 18TH ST, SF, 94114, (415)554-9529	667 - H2
MISSION HILLS PARK FRANKFORT ST & GUTTENBERG ST, DALY, 94014	687 - F3
MISSION HILLS PARK HOPKINS WY & INDEPENDENCE DR, PLE, 94566	714 - E5
MISSION PLAYGROUND 19TH ST & VALENCIA ST, SF, 94110	667 - H2
MISSION SAN JOSE PARK 41500 MISSION BLVD, FRMT, 94539	753 - G5
MISSION SAN JOSE PARK BAUTISTA ST & BECADO PL, FRMT, 94539	773 - H1
MITCHELL CREEK PARK MITCHELL CANYON RD, CCCo	613 - G2
MITCHELL PARK 600 E MEADOW DR, PA, 94306	811 - E1
MIWOK PARK NOVATO BLVD & REGALIA DR, NVTO, 94945	525 - H2
MOCHO PARK HOLMES ST & MOCHO ST, LVMR, 94550	715 - F2
MODEL AIRPLANE FIELD DOOLITTLE DR, ALA, 94502	670 - B5
MOLINO PARK MOLINO AV, MLV, 94941	606 - E4
MOLLER PARK PLEASANT HILL RD & CHESTNUT WY, PLE, 94588	693 - H7
MONROE MINI PARK MILLER AV & MONROE DR, PA, 94306	811 - E3
MONTA LOMA SCHOOL PARK THOMPSON AV & LAURA AV, MTVW, 94043	811 - F3
MONTAGUE PARK DE LA CRUZ BLVD, SCL, 95054	813 - E6
MONTALVIN PARK LETTIA RD, CCCo, 94806	569 - A5
MONTARA BAY COMMUNITY CENTER 2250 TARA HILLS DR, CCCo, 94806, (510)724-1434	569 - A4
MONTCLAIR PARK 1160 SAINT JOSEPH AV, LALT, 94024	831 - H5
MONTCLAIR RECREATION CENTER 6300 MORAGA AV, OAK, 94611, (510)339-8919	630 - D7
MONTE VERDE PARK OAKMONT DR & EVERGREEN DR, SBRN, 94066	707 - E5
MONTEVIDEO SCHOOL PARK BROADMOOR DR, SRMN, 94583	673 - F4
MONTGOMERY HILL PARK YERBA BUENA RD, SJS, 95135	855 - H4
MOORE, PAUL PARK OVERBROOK DR & MYRTLE AV, SJS, 95118	874 - B1
MORAGA COMMONS PARK MORAGA RD & SAINT MARYS RD, MRGA, 94556	631 - E6
MORAN, KEVIN PARK SCULLY AV & SARAGLEN DR, SAR, 95070	852 - F5
MORELLO SCHOOL PARK MORELLO AV, MRTZ, 94553	571 - H5
MORGAN, JOHN D PARK RINCON AV & PARR LN, CMBL, 95008	853 - D6
MORGAN PLAZA 2600 21ST AV, OAK, 94606	650 - B5
MORGAN TERRITORY REGIONAL PARK MORGAN TERRITORY RD, CCCo	654 - J2
MOSSWOOD PARK 3612 WEBSTER ST, OAK, 94609, (510)655-4736	649 - H1
MOUNT DAVIDSON PARK MYRA WY & DALEWOOD WY, SF, 94127	667 - E5
MOUNT DIABLO STATE PARK MOUNT DIABLO AV, CCCo, (510)837-2525	633 - D2
MOUNT OLYMPUS PARK UPPER TER, SF, 94117	667 - F2
MOUNT PLEASANT PARK PARK PLEASANT CIR, SJS, 95127	835 - B3
MOUNTAIN LAKE PARK W PACIFIC BLVD, SF, 94129	647 - C5
MOUNTAIN VIEW PARK PARKWAY DR, MRTZ, 94553	571 - F5
MOUNTAIRE PARK SUNSET LN & NORTHRIDGE CT, ANT, 94509	575 - E7
MT EDEN PARK DARWIN ST & LAUDERDALE AV, HAY, 94545	711 - G7
MUIR, JOHN PARK VISTA WY, MRTZ, 94553	571 - F5
MUIRWOOD PARK MUIRWOOD DR, PLE, 94588	693 - J7
MULFORD PARK AURORA DR & WALNUT DR, SLN, 94577	690 - G4
MUNICIPAL ROSE GARDEN GARDEN DR & NAGLEE AV, SJS, 95126, (408)277-5661	833 - G7
MURDOCK PARK CASTLE GLEN AV & WUNDERLICK DR, SJS, 95129	852 - H3
MURPHY PARK YELLOWSTONE AV, MPS, 95035	814 - D1
MURPHY, MARTIN JR PARK SUNNYVALE AV & CALIFORNIA AV, SUNV, 94086	812 - E6
MUSICK PARK CEDAR BLVD & MUSICK AV, NWK, 94560	752 - E5
NATALIE COFFIN GREENE PARK LAGUNITAS RD & GLENWOOD AV, ROSS, 94957	586 - B3
NEALON PARK 802 MIDDLE AV, MLPK, 94025, (650)858-3570	790 - G4
NEIGHBORHOOD PARK LARKSPUR LANDING CIR, LKSP, 94904	586 - J4
NEPTUNE PARK 2301 WEBSTER ST, ALA, 94501	649 - F7
NEVIN CENTER & PARK 598 NEVIN AV, RCH, 94801, (510)237-0524	588 - F6
NEWARK COMMUNITY PARK NEWARK BLVD & CEDAR BLVD, NWK, 94560	752 - D4
NEWHALL COMMUNITY PARK WHARTON WY, CNCD, 94521	593 - C4
NICHOLL PARK MACDONALD AV & NICHOLL CT, RCH, 94804	588 - J7
NICOL, ROLPH PARK EUCALYPTUS DR & 25TH AV, SF, 94132	667 - B6
NIELSEN PARK STONERIDGE DR & KAMP DR, PLE, 94588	694 - E7
NILES COMMUNITY PARK 500 SCHOOL ST, FRMT, 94536	753 - B1
NISSEN, MAY PARK RINCON AV, LVMR, 94550	695 - F7
NIVEN PARK DRAKES LANDING RD, LKSP, 94939	586 - G5
NOBLE PARK NOBLE AV, SJS, 95132	814 - H5
NORDVIK PARK COMMERCE DR & TUPELO ST, FRMT, 94555	752 - B3
NORRIS, KATHLEEN MEMORIAL PARK WILDOMAR ST & FLORENCE AV, MLV, 94941	606 - D3
NORTH COYOTE PARK OLD OAKLAND RD, SJS, 95112	834 - B1
NORTH GATE COMMUNITY PARK MILTON ST & PASEO PADRE PKWY, FRMT, 94555	732 - D7
NORTH LIVERMORE PARK BLUEBELL DR & GALLOWAY ST, LVMR, 94550	696 - A3
NORTH OAKLAND REG SPORTS CTR BROADWAY, OAK, 94611	630 - D4

FEATURE NAME Address City, ZIP Code	PAGE-GRID
NORTH RICHMOND BALLPARK 3RD ST, CCCo, 94801	588 - F3
NORTH VALLEJO PARK FAIRGROUNDS DR, VAL, 94589	510 - C6
NORTHRIDGE PARK NORTHRIDGE DR & CARMEL AV, DALY, 94015	686 - J6
NORTHWOOD PARK ROYALVALE WY, SJS, 95132	814 - C3
OAK GLEN PARK RICHMOND BLVD, OAK, 94611	649 - H1
OAK MEADOW PARK BLOSSOM HLL RD & UNIVERSITY AV, LGTS, 95030	873 - B5
OAK PARK FRISBIE ST, OAK, 94611	649 - H2
OAK PARK RIDGE PARKSIDE CT, SANS, 94960	566 - B6
OAKHILL PARK MUIRWOOD DR, PLE, 94588	713 - J1
OAKHILL PARK STONE VALLEY RD & GLENWOOD CT, DNVL, 94526	633 - B6
OAKKNOLL PIONEER MEMORIAL PARK 750 E STANLEY BLVD, LVMR, 94550	715 - E1
OCEAN VIEW PLAYGROUND PLYMOUTH AV & MONTANA ST, SF, 94112	687 - D1
ODDSTAD PARK CRESPI DR & BARCELONA DR, PCFA, 94044	727 - A4
OHAIR PARK NOVATO BLVD & SUTRO AV, NVTO, 94947	525 - F2
OHLONE PARK MARTIN LUTHER WY & HEARST AV, BERK, 94703	629 - F1
OHLONE PARK TURQUOISE DR & OPAL CT, HER, 94547	569 - G4
OLD HIGHLANDS PARK PARKSIDE DR, HAY, 94542	712 - D3
OLD MILL PARK THROCKMORTON AV & LAUREL ST, MLV, 94941	606 - C3
OLD MISSION PARK PINE ST & IBERO WY, FRMT, 94539	773 - H1
OLD RANCH PARK OLD RANCH RD & VISTA MONTE DR, SRMN, 94583	673 - J7
OLEANDER PARK OLEANDER DR, SRFL, 94903	566 - D2
OLIVE PARK OLIVE ST & SUMMERS AV, NVTO, 94945	526 - D3
ORANGE MEMORIAL PARK W ORANGE AV, SSF, 94080	707 - G3
ORCHARD GARDENS PARK 238 GARNER DR, SUNV, 94089, (408)730-7506	812 - F4
ORINDA COMMUNITY PARK ALTARINDA RD, ORIN, 94563	610 - G7
ORINDA OAKS PARK MORAGA WY & HALL DR, ORIN, 94563	631 - B4
ORINDA SPORTS FIELD CM PABLO, ORIN, 94563	610 - E5
ORLOFF PARK KOLLN ST, PLE, 94566	714 - E1
ORTEGA PARK 636 HARROW WY, SUNV, 94087, (408)739-6320	832 - E5
OSAGE PARK 816 BROOKSIDE DR, DNVL, 94526	653 - C5
OSHAUGHNESSY HOLLOW PARK OSHAUGHNESSY BLVD, SF, 94127	667 - F5
OSTRANDER PARK BROADWAY TER, OAK, 94618	630 - B5
OUR PARK VAN WINKLE LN & GALAHAD AV, SJS, 95116	834 - J4
OVERFELT GARDENS PARK EDUCATIONAL PARK DR & MCKEE RD, SJS, 95133	834 - F2
OVERLOOK PARK OLIVE BRANCH CT, BEN, 94510	551 - C3
OYSTER BAY REGIONAL SHORELINE NEPTUNE DR, SLN, 94577	690 - E3
OYSTER POINT PARK OYSTER POINT BLVD & MARINA BL, SSF, 94080	708 - C2
P A L SPORTS CENTER S KING RD & VIRGINIA AV, SJS, 95116	834 - G5
PACIFIC HEIGHTS PARK LONGVIEW DR & GOODWIN DR, SBRN, 94066	707 - D6
PACIFIC RECREATION COMPLEX ALADDIN AV & TEAGARDEN ST, SLN, 94577	691 - A3
PALACE OF FINE ARTS PALACE DR & MARINA BLVD, SF, 94123	647 - F4
PALISADES PARK PALISADES DR & WESTRIDGE AV, DALY, 94015	686 - J5
PALM HAVEN PARK PLAZA DR & PALM HAVEN AV, SJS, 95125	854 - A2
PALM PARK HUDSON ST, RDWC, 94061	790 - B1
PALMA CEIA PARK MIAMI AV & DECATUR WY, HAY, 94545	711 - H7
PALMETTO PARK PALMETTO AV & BRIGHTON RD, PCFA, 94044	706 - J6
PALO ALTO FOOTHILLS PARK- (PRIVATE) 3300 PAGE MILL RD, PA, 94304	830 - F3
PALOMARES HILLS PARK VILLAREAL DR & LAURELWOOD DR, AlaC, 94552	692 - F2
PANAMA PARK DATSHIRE WY & CARLISLE WY, SUNV, 94087	832 - F4
PANHANDLE OAK ST & STANYAN ST, SF, 94117	667 - E1
PARADISE BEACH PARK PARADISE DR, MrnC, 94920	607 - E5
PARADISE VALLEY PARK HILLSIDE BLVD, SSF, 94080	707 - J2
PARCHESTER PARK & CENTER COLLINS AV & MORTON AV, RCH, 94806	568 - G7
PARDEE, ELEANOR PARK 851 CENTER ST, PA, 94301	791 - B4
PARK 1250 CAMPUS DR, BERK, 94708	609 - J7
PARK 1290 62ND ST, EMVL, 94608	629 - E5
PARK 1700 14TH AV, OAK, 94606	650 - A5
PARK 1851 HOPKINS ST, BERK, 94707	609 - G7
PARK 18TH AV, SF, 94121	647 - B6
PARK 2000 DURANT AV, BERK, 94704	629 - G2
PARK 30TH AV, SF, 94121	647 - A6
PARK 3801 BEAUMONT AV, OAK, 94602	650 - C4
PARK 401 LA SALLE AV, PDMT, 94611	650 - D2
PARK 5201 MARTIN LUTHER KING JR WY, OAK, 94608	629 - G6
PARK 798 ARLINGTON AV, BERK, 94707	609 - G5
PARK 851 CONTRA COSTA AV, BERK, 94707	609 - G5
PARK 851 SANTA BARBARA RD, BERK, 94707	609 - G5

FEATURE NAME Address City, ZIP Code	PAGE-GRID
PARK ADRIAN WY & ROSAL WY, MrnC, 94903	566 - H2
PARK ARGUELLO BLVD & MARVILLA PL, PCFA, 94044	726 - H4
PARK AVALON DR & DORADO WY, SSF, 94080	707 - F4
PARK BERRY AV, HAY, 94544	711 - J4
PARK BROOKSIDE ST, SPAB, 94806	588 - H3
PARK BUSH ST & FAIRMONT AV, MTVW, 94041	811 - H6
PARK CARIBBEAN DR & GENEVA DR, SUNV, 94089	812 - G2
PARK CENTRAL AV & RYDIN RD, RCH, 94804	609 - B4
PARK CRESTVIEW DR, SCAR, 94070	769 - C4
PARK DOYLE DR & LASSEN AV, SJS, 95129	852 - H4
PARK DUNDEE DR, SSF, 94080	707 - D2
PARK EAST AV & 6TH ST, LVMR, 94550	715 - H1
PARK EDWARDS AV & SAN RAMON AV, OAK, 94605	671 - A1
PARK EL CAMINO REAL & CASTRO ST, MTVW, 94041	811 - H6
PARK FAIRMONT DR & LARK ST, AlaC, 94578	691 - E4
PARK FAIRVIEW AV, PDMT, 94610	650 - A1
PARK FARNSWORTH ST & CORVALLIS ST, SLN, 94579	691 - B5
PARK GRAND AV, PDMT, 94611	650 - A1
PARK HACIENDA WY, MrnC, 94903	566 - H2
PARK IMPERIAL DR, PCFA, 94044	707 - B3
PARK JOHN T KNOX FRWY, RCH, 94804	609 - B4
PARK K ST & 2ND ST, BEN, 94510	551 - B5
PARK LA GONDA WY, CCCo, 94507	632 - H6
PARK LARKIN ST & MYRTLE ST, SF, 94109	647 - J6
PARK LATHROP AV & TOCOLOMA AV, SF, 94134	688 - B2
PARK LATHROP DR, SCIC, 94305	810 - J2
PARK LAUREL CREEK DR & MORGAN DR, PLE, 94586	693 - G6
PARK LINDA AV, PDMT, 94611	650 - A1
PARK LYNWOOD LN, MLBR, 94030	727 - H3
PARK MISSION BLVD, HAY, 94541	711 - J2
PARK MORAGA RD & PLAZA DR, LFYT, 94549	611 - F6
PARK MOSS WY, OAK, 94611	649 - J1
PARK N 6TH ST & ESPERANZA DR, CNCD, 94519	572 - G7
PARK OLD CNTY RD & SN FRANCISCO AV, BSBN, 94005	688 - A6
PARK OLIVERA RD & MARS ST, CNCD, 94519	572 - H7
PARK ORTEGA ST & 28TH AV, SF, 94116	667 - A3
PARK PAJARO CT & W CALIFORNIA AV, SUNV, 94086	812 - D6
PARK PARKSIDE DR, BERK, 94705	630 - A4
PARK PEAR ST & CHERRY ST, ANT, 94509	574 - J7
PARK PERALTA ST, OAK, 94608	649 - F1
PARK POMPANO CIR, FCTY, 94404	749 - H3
PARK PROMENADE WY, PLE, 94566	714 - F2
PARK PUTNAM ST & JACKSON PL, ANT, 94509	575 - A7
PARK RALSTON AV, BLMT, 94002	749 - F7
PARK REDWOOD AV & CORTE MADERA AV, CMAD, 94925	586 - F7
PARK S LIVERMORE AV & 7TH ST, LVMR, 94550	715 - H1
PARK SANTA FE AV, HER, 94547	569 - F3
PARK SARATOGA DR, SMTO, 94403	749 - C4
PARK SHIELDS ST & MONTICELLO ST, SF, 94132	687 - C1
PARK SOLANO AV & 38TH ST, RCH, 94805	589 - A5
PARK SOLANO DR & HASTINGS DR, BEN, 94510	551 - A1
PARK SOUTH G ST & 7TH ST, LVMR, 94550	715 - H1
PARK SOUTHWOOD DR, SSF, 94080	707 - F4
PARK SPALDING AV, SUNV, 94087	832 - E3
PARK SUNSET BLVD & SLOAT BLVD, SF, 94116	666 - J3
PARK TAMARACK LN & ELM CT, SSF, 94080	707 - H2
PARK TAYLOR ST & VALLEJO ST, SF, 94133	647 - J4
PARK TERRACE DR, FRMT, 94536	732 - J6
PARK THE PLAZA, BERK, 94705	630 - A4
PARK TUERS RD, SCIC, 95121	855 - B6
PARK TUNNEL RD, OAK, 94618	630 - C4
PARK VASQUEZ AV & LAGUNA HONDA BLVD, SF, 94127	667 - D4
PARK VENDOLA DR & MABRY WY, MrnC, 94903	566 - G2
PARK VIA RAMADA, SJS, 95139	875 - F7
PARK WILLOW LN, BLMT, 94002	769 - D1
PARK YOSEMITE RD, BERK, 94707	609 - F5
PARK ZAMORA DR, SSF, 94080	707 - F5

FEATURE NAME	Address City, ZIP Code	PAGE-GRID
PARK BOULEVARD PLAYGOUND	2300 PARK BLVD, OAK, 94606	649 - J4
PARKSIDE AQUATIC PARK	ROBERTA DR, SMTO, 94403	749 - D2
PARKSIDE SQUARE	VICENTE ST & 28TH AV, SF, 94116	667 - A5
PARKVIEW 1 PARK	BLUEFIELD DR & VIEWPARK CIR, SJS, 95136	874 - G1
PARKVIEW 2 PARK	SPOSITO CIR & GRANDPARK CIR, SJS, 95136	874 - G1
PARKVIEW 3 PARK	MONET PL & SAYOKO CIR, SJS, 95136	874 - H1
PARKWAY	COLLEGE AV & S S ST, LVMR, 94550	715 - F2
PARKWAY PARK	SARATOGA AV, SCL, 95117	833 - C7
PARMA PARK	CAMDEN AV & LITTLE FALLS DR, SJS, 95120	894 - D1
PARQUE DE LA AMISTAD	VOLLMER WY, SJS, 95116	834 - G5
PARQUE DE LOS POBLADORES	S MARKET ST & S 1ST ST, SJS, 95110	834 - C7
PASO NOGAL PARK	PASO NOGA & PRIMROSE DR, PLHL, 94523	591 - J3
PATTERSON PARK	CABRILLO DR & ANGELES AV, FRMT, 94536	752 - E3
PAUL PARK	CAMINO PABLO & BROOKWOOD RD, ORIN, 94563	630 - H1
PEACOCK PARK	BISCAYNE DR, SRFL, 94901	567 - D5
PEERS PARK	1899 PARK BLVD, PA, 94306	791 - A6
PELLIER PARK	W SAINT JAMES & TERRAINE ST, SJS, 95110	834 - B6
PENITENCIA CREEK COUNTY PARK	N JACKSON AV & MABURY RD, SJS, 95133	834 - E1
PENITENCIA CREEK COUNTY PARK	PENITENCIA CREEK RD, SJS, 95133, (408)356-2729	814 - G6
PENKE PARK	MISTLETOE DR, HAY, 94545	731 - H1
PERALTA HACIENDA PARK	34TH AV, OAK, 94601	650 - D6
PERALTA PARK	12TH ST & 1ST AV, OAK, 94607	649 - H5
PERSHING PARK	CRESCENT AV & NEWLANDS AV, BURL, 94010	728 - G7
PICKLE WEED PARK	SPINNAKER POINT & RAILROAD AV, SRFL, 94901	587 - A1
PIEDMONT PARK	PIEDMONT CT & HIGHLAND AV, PDMT, 94611, (510)420-3050	650 - B1
PINE GROVE SPORTS FIELD	12 ALTARINDA RD, ORIN, 94563	610 - H7
PINE LAKE PARK	WAWONA ST & 28TH AV, SF, 94132	667 - A5
PINEWOOD PARK	GREENWOOD WY & PINEWOOD WY, MPS, 95035	814 - A3
PINEWOOD PARK	MAUREEN LN & LOCKWOOD LN, PLHL, 94523	592 - A5
PINOLE PARK	PINOLE VALLEY RD, PIN, 94564	589 - H1
PINTO RANCH RECREATION AREA	REDWOOD RD & OLD REDWOOD RD, OAK, 94619	650 - H5
PIONEER MEMORIAL PARK	CHURCH ST & CASTRO ST, MTVW, 94041	811 - H5
PIONEER PARK	SIMMONS LN & SHADY LN, NVTO, 94945	525 - J2
PIONEER PARK	TELEGRAPH HILL BLVD, SF, 94133	648 - A3
PIPER PARK	DOHERTY DR, LKSP, 94939	586 - F5
PLATA ARROYO PARK	N KING RD & MCKEE RD, SJS, 95116	834 - F3
PLAYA DEL REY PARK	GLENBURRY & DUNBURRY WY, SJS, 95123	874 - F3
PLAYGROUND	1600 VIRGINIA ST, BERK, 94703	629 - F1
PLAYGROUND	BISSELL AV & 7TH ST, RCH, 94801	588 - F7
PLAYGROUND	BRUNSWICK ST & LOWELL ST, SF, 94112	687 - E2
PLAYGROUND	BYRON DR, SSF, 94080	707 - D2
PLAYGROUND	CARLSON BL & HUNTINGTON AV, RCH, 94804	609 - C3
PLAYGROUND	CAYUGA AV & NAGLEE AV, SF, 94112	687 - E2
PLAYGROUND	CRESTWOOD DR, SSF, 94080	707 - G1
PLAYGROUND	MCDONNELL DR, SSF, 94080	707 - E2
PLAYGROUND	MENDOCINO ST & BURLINGAME AV, RCH, 94804	609 - C3
PLAYGROUND	MONTEREY ST & CARL AV, RCH, 94804	609 - B3
PLAZA DE CESAR CHAVEZ	S MARKET ST & PARK AV, SJS, 95113	834 - B7
PLAZA PARK	BERK AV & 47TH ST, RCH, 94804	609 - A1
PLAZA PARK	MADERA CT, FRMT, 94536	752 - H5
PLEASANT HILL PARK	GREGORY LN & CLEAVELAND RD, PLHL, 94523	592 - C5
PLEASANT OAK PARK	MONTICELLO AV & HAWTHORNE DR, PLHL, 94523	592 - B7
PLEASANTON RIDGE REGIONAL PARK	FOOTHILL RD, PLE, 94586	713 - H1
PLEASANTON RIDGE REGIONAL PARK	SANTOS RANCH RD, HAY, 94586	713 - F3
PLEASANTON SPORTS & REC PARK	SPORTS PARK DR, PLE, 94588	714 - C1
PLEASANTON TENNIS & COMM PARK	HOPYARD RD & VALLEY AV, PLE, 94566	714 - B1
PLEASURE ISLAND PARK	PEARL DR & FLINT ST, LVMR, 94550	715 - D2
PLOMOSA PARK	SCOTT CREEK RD, FRMT, 94539	793 - J1
POINSETT PARK	5611 POINSETT AV, ELCR, 94530	589 - B7
POINT ISABEL REGIONAL SHORELINE	RYDIN RD, RCH, 94804	609 - A4
POINT SAN BRUNO PARK	FORBES BLVD & SAN BRUNO BLVD, SSF, 94080	708 - D3
POLARIS PARK	POLARIS WY & CANYON DR, DALY, 94014	687 - F3
POMO PARK	CARMEL AV & CANYON DR, PCFA, 94044	707 - A5
PONDEROSA PARK	HENDERSON AV & IRIS AV, SUNV, 94086, (408)730-7506	832 - H2
PONDEROSA PARK	SHARP PARK RD & PACIFIC HTS BL, SBRN, 94066	707 - C5
POPLAR RECREATION CENTER	3131 UNION ST, OAK, 94608	649 - F1
PORT ROYAL PARK	PORT ROYAL AV, FCTY, 94404	749 - F6
PORTAL PARK	PORTAL AV, CPTO, 95014	832 - F7
PORTOLA HIGHLANDS PARK	SNEATH LN, SBRN, 94066	707 - D7
PORTOLA PARK	PORTOLA AV, LVMR, 94550	695 - G6
PORTOLA RECREATION CENTER	SILLIMAN ST & SOMERSET ST, SF, 94134	667 - J7
PORTSIDE PARK	BRIDGE PKWY, RDWC, 94065	749 - H7
PORTSMOUTH SQUARE	WASHINGTON ST & KEARNY ST, SF, 94108	648 - A5
POSEY PARK	SAN MATEO AV & HUNTINGTON AV, SBRN, 94066	707 - J6
POTRERO DEL SOL PARK	1500 SAN BRUNO AV, SF, 94110	668 - A4
POTRERO HILL RECREATION CENTER	ARKANSAS ST & MADERA ST, SF, 94107	668 - B3
PRECITA PARK	PRECITA AV & FOLSOM ST, SF, 94110	667 - J4
PREWETT FAMILY PARK	LONE TREE WY & DEER VALLEY RD, ANT, 94509	595 - H4
PROSSERVILLE PARK	END OF 7TH ST, ANT, 94509	575 - B4
PRUSCH PARK	647 S KING RD, SJS, 95116, (408)926-5555	834 - G6
PULGAS WATER TEMPLE	CANADA RD, SMCo, 94062	769 - A6
QUARRY LAKES REGIONAL PARK	ISHERWOOD WY, FRMT, 94536	752 - H1
RAIMONDI PARK	1700 20TH ST, OAK, 94607	649 - D2
RAIN CLOUD PARK	SOLITUDE LN, RCH, 94803	589 - G3
RAINBOW PARK	JOHNSON AV & RAINBOW DR, SJS, 95129	852 - G4
RAINBOW RECREATION CENTER	5800 INTERNATIONAL BLVD, OAK, 94621	670 - F2
RAMBLEWOOD PARK	LIGHTLAND RD & DUNDALE DR, SJS, 95121	855 - B5
RAMOS PARK	800 E MEADOW DR, PA, 94303	791 - E7
RANCHO ARROYO PARK	2151 DEPOT RD, HAY, 94545	711 - F6
RANCHO ARROYO PARK	MONTECITO DR, FRMT, 94536	753 - A1
RANCHO LAGUNA PARK	CM PABLO, MRGA, 94556	651 - F3
RANCHO SAN ANTONIO COUNTY PARK	CRISTO REY DR, SCIC, 95014	831 - G6
RANKIN PARK	BUCKLEY ST, MRTZ, 94553	571 - C3
RAVENSWOOD PARK	ARROYO RD & SUPERIOR DR, LVMR, 94550	715 - G5
RAY PARK	BALBOA WY & DEVERAUX DR, BURL, 94010	728 - C5
RAYMOND KIMBELL PLAYGROUND	GEARY BLVD & STEINER ST, SF, 94115	647 - G6
RAYNOR PARK	1565 QUAIL AV, SUNV, 94087, (408)730-7506	832 - G5
RECREATION CENTER	45TH ST, OAK, 94609	629 - H7
RED MORTON COMMUNITY PARK	1400 ROOSEVELT AV, RDWC, 94061, (650)780-7250	790 - A1
RED WILLOW PARK	RED WILLOW RD & CORIANDER CT, SRMN, 94583	653 - J7
REDWOOD HEIGHTS REC AREA	REDWOOD RD & ATLAS AV, OAK, 94619	650 - G5
REDWOOD REGIONAL PARK	7861 REDWOOD RD, CCCo	650 - H2
REFUGIO VALLEY PARK	SYCAMORE AV & REFUGIO VLY RD, HER, 94547	569 - H4
REMILLARD PARK	E SIR FRANCIS DRAKE BLVD, LKSP, 94904	586 - J5
REMILLARD PARK	POPPY LN & KELLER AV, BERK, 94708	609 - H6
RENGSTORFF PARK	CRISANTO AV & RENGSTORFF AV, MTVW, 94040	811 - G4
REUTHER, WALTER PARK	JACKLIN RD, MPS, 95035	794 - B5
RICHARDSON BAY PARK	TIBURON BLVD & SILVERADO DR, TBRN, 94920	607 - B5
RICHARDSON PARK	HOBBS AV, VAL, 94589	510 - B7
RICHARDSON PARK	HOBBS AV, VAL, 94589	530 - B1
RICHMOND PLAYGROUND	19TH AV, SF, 94121	647 - B6
RINCONADA PARK	777 EMBARCADERO RD, PA, 94301	791 - B5
RITTLER PARK	GRAND ST & OTIS DR, ALA, 94501	669 - H3
RIVER GLEN PARK	PINE AV & BIRD AV, SJS, 95125	854 - B4
RIVER PARK	WILSON AV, VAL, 94590	529 - H3
RIX PARK	RAVNSBRNE PK ST & SENECA PK LP, FRMT, 94538	773 - C2
ROBERTS REGIONAL RECREATION AREA	10570 SKYLINE BLVD, AlaC, (510)635-0135	650 - J3
ROBERTSON PARK	LIVERMORE AV & WENTE ST, LVMR, 94550	715 - H2
ROBLES PARK	4116 PARK BLVD, PA, 94306	811 - D2
ROBSON PARK	RAYMOND AV & CRESCENT RD, SANS, 94960	566 - B7
ROCHAMBEAU PLAYGROUND	25TH AV, SF, 94121	647 - A6
ROCKRIDGE PARK	ROCKRIDGE BLVD, OAK, 94618	630 - A5
ROGERS, BEN PARK	CARLSBAD ST, MPS, 95035	794 - E7
ROLPH PLAYGROUND	HAMPSHIRE ST & 26TH ST, SF, 94110	668 - A4
ROOSEVELT PARK	E SANTA CLARA ST & N 19TH ST, SJS, 95116	834 - D5
ROOSEVELT PLAYGROUND	900 DOWLING BLVD, SLN, 94577	671 - B6
ROOT PARK	E 14TH ST & HAYS ST, SLN, 94577	691 - A1
ROSA MINI PARK	MINI DR & ROLEEN DR, VAL, 94589	509 - J5
ROSE GARDEN PARK	698 CHETWOOD ST, OAK, 94610	650 - A2
ROSE GARDENS	1250 EUCLID AV, BERK, 94708	609 - H6
ROSICRUCIAN PARK	PARK AV & NAGLEE AV, SJS, 95126	833 - H6
ROSS COMMON PARK	LAGUNITAS RD & ROSS COM, ROSS, 94957	586 - C2
ROSS PLAYGROUND	ARGUELLO BLVD & EDWARD ST, SF, 94118	647 - D7
ROTARY PARK	DON AV & WARBURTON AV, SCL, 95050	833 - D3
ROTARY PARK	S ASHTON AV & MILLBRAE AV, MLBR, 94030	728 - A4
ROY AVENUE MINI PARK	ALMADEN RD & ALMADEN EXWY, SJS, 95125	854 - C6
RUDGEAR PARK	RUDGEAR RD & DAPPLEGRAY LN, WLCK, 94596	632 - G1
RUSSIAN HILL PARK	LARKIN ST & CHESTNUT ST, SF, 94109	647 - H3
RUUS PARK	FOLSOM AV & DICKENS AV, HAY, 94544	732 - A1
RYAN, LEO J MEMORIAL PARK	E HILLSDALE BLVD, FCTY, 94404	749 - F3
RYDER COURT PARK	RYDER ST, SMTO, 94401	729 - B7
RYLAND PARK	N 1ST ST & FOX AV, SJS, 95110	834 - B5
SAINT JAMES PARK	E SAINT JAMES ST & N 2ND ST, SJS, 95112	834 - B6
SAINT MARYS BALLFIELD	SAINT MARYS RD, LFYT, 94549	631 - H1
SAINT MARYS PARK	CRESENT AV & AGNON AV, SF, 94112, (415)695-5006	667 - H6
SALFINGERE, FRANK PARK	TALOR BL & RUTH DR, PLHL, 94523	592 - C3
SAN ANDREAS PARK	SAN ANDREAS DR, UNC, 94587	732 - B5
SAN ANSELMO MEMORIAL PARK	VETERANS PL, SANS, 94960	566 - B6
SAN ANTONIO PARK	WRIGHT AV & ASTORIA DR, SUNV, 94087	832 - B4
SAN ANTONIO RECREATION CENTER	1701 E 19TH ST, OAK, 94606, (510)533-6505	650 - A6
SAN BRUNO MTN STATE AND CO PARK	GUADALUPE CANYON PKWY, SMCo, 94014	687 - F5
SAN CARLOS AVENUE MINI PARK	SAN CARLOS AV, SCAR, 94070	769 - E3
SAN CLEMENTE PARK	PARADISE DR & HIND PASSAGE, CMAD, 94925	606 - J1
SAN FELIPE PARK	D ST, AlaC, 94541	692 - B7
SAN LORENZO PARK	VIA CATHERINE, AlaC, 94580	711 - B2
SAN MIGUEL PARK	SAN JOSE CT & SAN CARLOS DR, WLCK, 94598	612 - F3
SAN PABLO PARK	PARK ST, BERK, 94702	629 - F4
SAN PABLO RESERVOIR REC AREA	7301 SAN PABLO DAM RD, CCCo, (510)223-1661	610 - A1
SAN PEDRO VALLEY COUNTY PARK	600 ODDSTAD BLVD, PCFA, 94044, (650)355-8289	727 - C6
SAN RAMON CENTRAL PARK	ALCOSTA BLVD & BOLLINGER CYN, SRMN, 94583	673 - E3
SAN TOMAS PARK	FENAN DR & LEMOYNE WY, SJS, 95008	853 - B7
SAN VERON PARK	MIDDLEFIELD RD & SAN VERON AV, MTVW, 94043	811 - J3
SANBORN PARK	1601 FRUITVALE AV, OAK, 94601	650 - C7
SANDLEWOOD PARK	RUSSEL LN & ESCUELA PKWY, MPS, 95035	794 - B4
SANTA MARGARITA VALLEY PARK	DE LA GUERRA RD, SRFL, 94903	566 - A1
SANTA TERESA COUNTY PARK	BERNAL RD, SCIC, 95119, (408)268-3883	895 - E3
SANTANA PARK	TISCH WY & BAYWOOD AV, SJS, 95128	853 - E1
SARAIVA, ETHEREE PARK	MILITARY E & E 6TH ST, BEN, 94510	551 - C5
SARATOGA CREEK PARK	CORDELIA AV & HOYET DR, SJS, 95129	852 - H4
SCHAFER PARK	EVERGREEN ST, HAY, 94544	711 - J5
SCHMIDT, HENRY PARK	SARATOGA AV & LOS PADRES BLVD, SCL, 95050	833 - D6
SCHULTZ PARK	BONITO WY & CAMINO ALTO, MLBR, 94030	728 - A4
SCOTT PARK	CHANNING AV & SCOTT ST, PA, 94301	790 - J5
SCOTTSDALE PARK	BRANHAM LN & TAMPICO WY, SJS, 95118	874 - A3
SEA CLOUD PARK	SEA CLOUD DR, FCTY, 94404	749 - G4
SEALE PARK	3100 STOCKTON PL, PA, 94303	791 - D6
SEARS, RICK PARK	SIERRA RD & MEADOW WY, CNCD, 94518	592 - F5
SELLICK PARK	APPIAN WY, SSF, 94080	707 - E4
SELWYN PARK	SELWYN DR, MPS, 95035	794 - C7
SENIOR CENTER PARK GARDENS	ALCOSTA BL & STAGECOACH RD, SRMN, 94583	673 - J7
SERRA PARK	730 THE DALLES AV, SUNV, 94087, (408)730-7506	832 - D5
SETTERQUIST PARK	MINI DR, VAL, 94589	510 - B5
SEVEN HILLS PARK	FLORENCE ST, UNC, 94587	732 - J5
SHAD PARK	SHAD CT, FCTY, 94404	749 - H2
SHADOW CLIFFS REGIONAL REC AREA	STANLEY BLVD, PLE, 94566, (510)846-3000	714 - H2
SHADOWOOD PARK	CAMELBACK RD & CAMELBACK PL, PLHL, 94523	592 - B1
SHADY OAK PARK	COYOTE RD & BRODERICK DR, SJS, 95111	875 - D2
SHANNON HILLS PARK	BANBRIDGE PL, PLHL, 94523	591 - H4
SHANNON PARK	DAVIT LN & SHANNON WY, RDWC, 94065	749 - J6
SHANNON PARK	SHANNON AV & PEPPERTREE RD, DBLN, 94568	693 - G3
SHARON PARK	SHARON PARK DR & KLAMATH DR, MLPK, 94025	790 - C7
SHARP PARK	SHARP PARK RD, PCFA, 94044	707 - B7
SHEFFIELD RECREATION CENTER	243 MARLOW DR, OAK, 94605	671 - D7
SHEPHERD CANYON PARK	SHEPHERD CANYON RD, OAK, 94611	650 - F1
SHEVELAND PARK	COUGHLAN ST & CRAVEN ST, VAL, 94590	529 - H3
SHIELD REID PARK	CHESLEY AV & KELSEY ST, RCH, 94801	588 - F4
SHIMADA FRIENDSHIP PARK	MARINA BAY CT, RCH, 94804	608 - H3
SHINN MEMORIAL PARK	GILBERT AV & SIDNEY DR, FRMT, 94536	753 - B2
SHOREBIRD PARK	ISLAND DR, RDWC, 94065	749 - H6
SHOREBIRD PARK	SEAWALL DR, BERK, 94710	629 - B3
SHORELINE AT MOUNTAIN VIEW	SHORELINE BLVD, MTVW, 94043	791 - H6

FEATURE NAME Address City, ZIP Code	PAGE-GRID
SHORELINE PARK INDEPENDENCE DR, ALA, 94501	649 - G6
SHORELINE PARK SAN FRANCISCO BAY, ALA, 94502	669 - H5
SHOREVIEW PARK 950 OCEAN VIEW AV, SMTO, 94401	749 - C1
SHOUP PARK 400 UNIVERSITY AV, LALT, 94022	811 - D7
SIEMPRE VERDE PARK PARK ST & CHERRYWOOD AV, SLN, 94577	670 - J7
SIGN HILL PARK ROCCA AV & POPLAR AV, SSF, 94080	707 - H2
SILLMAN, GEORGE M REC COMPLEX 6500 MOWRY AV, NWK, 94560	772 - H2
SILVER CREEK LINEAR PARK SILVER CREEK & YERBA BUENA RD, SJS, 95138	855 - C5
SILVER LEAF PARK SILVER LEAF RD & PALMWELL WY, SJS, 95138	875 - E4
SILVER TERRACE PLAYGROUND SILVER AV & ELMIRA ST, SF, 94124	668 - A6
SINNOTT PARK CLEAR LAKE AV, MPS, 95035	814 - D2
SKILMAN, FRANK PARK GALLAGHER DR & ROSE DR, BEN, 94510	551 - B1
SLADE PARK MANUEL DR & LOUIS DR, NVTO, 94945	526 - D4
SLATER SCHOOL PARK N WHISMAN RD & 3RD AV, MTVW, 94043	812 - B5
SMALL WORLD PARK HARBOR ST & LELAND LN, PIT, 94565	574 - E4
SMITH, F M PARK 200 NEWTON AV, OAK, 94606	649 - J4
SMITH, ROGERS PARK GRAYSON RD & CORTSEN RD, PLHL, 94523	591 - J5
SNOW PARK 19TH ST & HARRISON ST, OAK, 94612	649 - H3
SOBRANTE PARK BERGEDO DR & PUEBLO DR, OAK, 94603	690 - H1
SOLARI PARK CAS DR & ARBOLES AV, SJS, 95111	854 - H6
SOMERSET SQUARE PARK STOKES AV & WILSON CT, CPTO, 95014	832 - B6
SORENDALE PARK GOODWIN ST & JANE AV, HAY, 94544	712 - A5
SORICH RANCH PARK SAN FRANCISCO BLVD, SANS, 94960	566 - C5
SOUTH OF MARKET PARK FOLSOM ST & 6TH ST, SF, 94103	648 - A7
SOUTH PARK SOUTH PARK AV & LONDON AL, SF, 94107	648 - B6
SOUTH SUNSET PLAYGROUND VICENTE ST & 40TH AV, SF, 94116	666 - J5
SOUTHAMPTON PARK PANORAMA DR & CHELSEA HILLS DR, BEN, 94510	551 - B2
SOUTHGATE PARK SLEEPY HOLLOW AV & CHIPLAY AV, HAY, 94545	711 - H6
SOUTHVIEW PARK RICHARDSON ST & 4TH ST, SAUS, 94965	627 - B4
SPRING GROVE PARK CENTRAL BLVD, HAY, 94542	712 - B3
SPRUIELL, TEX PARK FELICIA AV & JESSICA DR, LVMR, 94550	696 - C7
SPUR TRAIL PARK MAGNOLIA AV & MILLBRAE AV, MLBR, 94030	728 - B4
STAFFORD GROVE PARK MARION AV, NVTO, 94945	526 - A3
STAFFORD LAKE PARK NOVATO BLVD, MrnC, 94947	525 - B3
STAFFORD PARK HOPKINS AV & LOWELL ST, RDWC, 94062	769 - H6
STAGECOACH PARK TURQUOISE ST & STAGECOACH RD, DBLN, 94568	693 - J2
STARBIRD PARK BOYNTON AV & WILLIAMS RD, SJS, 95117	853 - C3
STARLITE PARK ABBOTT AV & RUDYARD DR, MPS, 95035	793 - J7
STENZEL PARK ELVINA DR & LAVERNE DR, SLN, 94579	691 - A6
STERN, SIGMUND RECREATION GROVE WAWONA ST & 19TH AV, SF, 94132	667 - B5
STEVENSON SCHOOL PARK MONTECITO AV & BURGOYNE ST, MTVW, 94043	811 - H3
STEWART DRAW PARK HOKE CT, PIN, 94564	569 - E6
STEWART PLAYGROUND BARRETT AV & 3RD ST, RCH, 94801	588 - F6
STONEGATE PARK KENOGA DR, SJS, 95121	854 - H3
STONEHURST RECREATION AREA E ST & 103RD AV, OAK, 94603	670 - H6
STONEMAN PARK W LELAND RD, PIT, 94565	574 - A5
STONEMAN WEST PARK HARBOR ST & PRESIDIO LN, PIT, 94565	574 - D4
STONY BROOK PARK 600 WOODLAND AV, HAY, 94544	712 - D7
STONY BROOK PARK NILES CANYON RD, AlaC, 94586	733 - F5
STRAND, JENNY PARK MONO WY & HANCOCK DR, SCL, 95051	832 - H7
STRAWBERRY PARK BELVEDERE DR & RICARDO LN, MrnC, 94941	606 - J4
STRICKROTH PARK STRICKROTH DR & AARON PARK DR, MPS, 95035	794 - A5
STULSAFT PARK RECREATION WY & GOODWIN AV, RDWC, 94061	789 - H3
SUGAR LOAF OPEN SPACE REC AREA RUDGEAR RD & 680 FRWY, WLCK, 94596	632 - E2
SULPHUR CREEK PARK D ST, AlaC, 94541	712 - B1
SULPHUR SPRING PARK ASCOT DR & MASTLAND DR, OAK, 94611	650 - F2
SUN TERRACE PARK VANCOUVER WY & MONTREAL CIR, CNCD, 94520	572 - F5
SUN VALLEY PARK SOLANO ST, SRFL, 94901	566 - E6
SUNFISH PARK SUNFISH CT, FCTY, 94404	749 - H3
SUNKEN GARDENS PARK HILLCREST AV & DRAKE WY, LVMR, 94550	715 - J2
SUNNYBRAE PARK SUNNYBRAE BLVD, SMTO, 94402	749 - B2
SUNNYHILLS PARK COELHO ST & CONWAY ST, MPS, 95035	794 - A3
SUNNY RIDGE PARK GALLAGHER CIR, ANT, 94509	595 - C1
SUNNYSIDE RECREATION CENTER EDNA ST, SF, 94127	667 - E6
SUNNYVALE BAYLANDS PARK SOUTHBAY FWY & LAWRENCE EXPWY, SUNV, 94089	812 - J2
SUNSET COMMUNITY CENTER QUINTARA ST & 29TH AV, SF, 94116, (415)753-7047	666 - J4
SUNSET EAST PARK GENEVA ST & FLORENCE RD, LVMR, 94550	715 - G2

FEATURE NAME Address City, ZIP Code	PAGE-GRID
SUNSET HEIGHTS PLAYGROUND ROCKRIDGE DR, SF, 94116	667 - C4
SUNSET PLAYGROUND LAWTON ST & 29TH AV, SF, 94122	667 - A3
SUSANA PARK SUSANA ST, MRTZ, 94553	571 - E3
SUTRO HEIGHTS PARK POINT LOBOS AV & 48TH AV, SF, 94121	646 - H7
SUTTER GATE PARK SUTTER GATE AV & SANTA RITA RD, PLE, 94566	694 - D7
SUTTON PARK CENTER RD & MEYERS CT, NVTO, 94947	526 - A3
SWARTZ, AMBER PARK SAVAGE AV, PIN, 94564	569 - G7
SYCAMORE PARK PARK TER & SYCAMORE AV, MLV, 94941	606 - E4
SYCAMORE VALLEY PARK CM TASSAJARA, DNVL, 94506	653 - F4
SYLVAN PARK SYLVAN AV & GLENBOROUGH DR, MTVW, 94041	812 - A6
TANKHILL PARK TWINPEAKS BLVD, SF, 94117	667 - E2
TAPESTRY PARK SILVERLAND DR, SJS, 95135	855 - E2
TASSAFARONGA RECREATION CENTER 900 84TH AV, OAK, 94621	670 - G4
TASSAJARA CREEK REGIONAL PARK N OF 580 FY, W OF TASSAJARA RD, DBLN, 94568	694 - E1
TASSAJARA PARK 2575 TASSAJARA AV, ELCR, 94530	589 - C6
TAWNY PARK TAWNY DR, PLE, 94566	714 - G3
TENNYSON PARK PANJON ST & HUNTWOOD AV, HAY, 94544	712 - B7
TERMAN PARK 655 ARASTRADERO RD, PA, 94306	811 - D3
TERRA LINDA PARK 670 DEL GANADO RD, SRFL, 94903	566 - C2
TERRACE PARK GARDNER ST & SELFRIDGE RD, VAL, 94590	529 - H2
TERRACE PARK TERRACE ST, ALB, 94706	609 - E7
TERRACE VIEW PLAYGROUND FAIRLAWN RD & QUEENS RD, BERK, 94708, (510)644-6530	609 - J7
TERRELL PARK KENTON CT & NORMINGTON WY, SJS, 95136	874 - D1
THE OVAL PARK PALM DR & SERRA ST, SCIC, 94305	790 - H6
THOMPSON FIELD 2150 CLEMENT AV, ALA, 94501	670 - A1
THOUSAND OAKS PARK BROCKHMPTON CT & NORMINGTON WY, SJS, 95136	874 - D1
THRASHER PARK DAVIS ST & ORCHARD AV, SLN, 94577	690 - J1
THREE OAKS PARK RUPPELL PL & MOLTZEN DR, CPTO, 95014	852 - D3
TICE VALLEY PARK TICE VALLEY BL & ROSSMOOR PKWY, WLCK, 94595	632 - B1
TIDELANDS PARK J HART CLINTON DR, SMTO, 94404	749 - D1
TIFFANY PARK BRIDGEWAY BLVD & NOBLE LN, SAUS, 94965	627 - B4
TILDEN REGIONAL PARK CANON DR, CCCo, 94708, (510)652-1155	610 - A5
TILLER PARK SIERRA AV & VENTURA ST, RCH, 94805	589 - B6
TILLMAN PARK 220 AUGHINBAUGH WY, ALA, 94502, (510)521-8307	669 - J5
TODOS SANTOS PLAZA SALVIO ST & GRANT ST, CNCD, 94520	592 - F1
TOWATA PARK OTIS DR, ALA, 94501	670 - A4
TOWN ESTATES PARK CAMERON DR, UNC, 94587	732 - C4
TOWN PARK TAMALPAIS DR, CMAD, 94925	586 - G7
TOWNSEND PARK TOWNSEND PARK CIR, SJS, 95131	814 - C7
TRAP & SKEET RANGE JOHN MUIR DR & SKYLINE BLVD, SF, 94132	686 - J1
TRINTA PARK LESLIE ST, SMTO, 94402	749 - B4
TURNBULL PARK 2ND ST & E ST, BEN, 94510	551 - C6
TURNER, MATTHEW PARK K ST & W 12TH ST, BEN, 94510	550 - J3
TURNSTONE PARK TURNSTONE CT, FCTY, 94404	749 - H2
TURTLE ROCK PARK BOA VISTA DR & MALDEN AV, SJS, 95122	854 - H1
TWIN CREEKS SCHOOL PARK RIOS DR & ABRIGO CT, SRMN, 94583	673 - B2
TWIN CREEKS SPORTS COMPLEX CARIBBEAN DR & SOUTHBAY FRWY, SUNV, 94089	812 - H2
TWIN PEAKS PARK TWIN PEAKS BLVD, SF, 94131	667 - E3
TWIN PINES PARK RALSTON AV, BLMT, 94002	769 - E1
UNION SQUARE GEARY ST & POWELL ST, SF, 94108	648 - A6
UNIVERSITY PARK MONROE ST & 10TH ST, ALB, 94804	609 - D7
UPPER NOE RECREATION CENTER SANCHEZ ST & DAY ST, SF, 94131	667 - G5
VAL VISTA PARK PAYNE RD, PLE, 94588	694 - A7
VALLE VISTA PARK 350 VALLE VISTA, HAY, 94544	712 - C7
VALLEJO MILL PARK ORANGEWOOD DR, FRMT, 94536	753 - D1
VALLEY TRAILS PARK VALLEY TRAILS DR, PLE, 94588	714 - A1
VANTAGE POINT PARK 1200 E 12TH ST, OAK, 94606	650 - A6
VARIAN PARK AMELIA CT & VARIAN WY, CPTO, 95014	832 - A7
VASONA LAKE COUNTY PARK 298 GARDEN HILL DR, LGTS, 95030, (408)356-2729	873 - B5
VERDESE CARTER PARK SUNNYSIDE ST & 96TH AV, OAK, 94603	671 - A5
VICTORIA PARK VICTORIA AV & BANCROFT AV, SLN, 94577	671 - B6
VICTORIA PARK VICTORIA RD & HOWARD AV, BURL, 94010	728 - H6
VILLA MONTALVO ARBORETUM 15400 MONTALVO RD, SCIC, 95070, (408)867-0190	872 - D5
VILLAGE EAST PARK GENTRYTOWN DR, ANT, 94509	574 - J6
VILLAGE EAST PARK GENTRYTOWN DR, ANT, 94509	575 - A6
VILLAGE GREEN PARK VILLAGE PKWY & TRIANA WY, SRMN, 94583	693 - H1
VILLAGE PARK CALIFORNIA DR & EASTMOOR RD, BURL, 94010	728 - D5

FEATURE NAME Address City, ZIP Code	PAGE-GRID
VINCENT PARK PENINSULA DR, RCH, 94804	608 - G3
VINCI PARK VINCI PARK WY, SJS, 95131	814 - D7
VINTAGE HILLS PARK ARBOR DR, PLE, 94566	714 - H4
VISTA MEADOWS PARK WESTMINSTER WY & LAMBETH RD, LVMR, 94550	695 - G6
VISTA PARK CULEBRA RD & VISTA RD, HIL, 94010	748 - G3
VISTA PARK NEW COMPTON DR & HYDE PARK DR, SJS, 95136	874 - F2
WALLENBERG PARK CURTNER AV & COTTLE AV, SJS, 95125	854 - A6
WALLIS PARK GRANT AV & ASH ST, PA, 94306	791 - B7
WALNUT GROVE PARK NORTHWAY RD & HARVEST RD, PLE, 94566	714 - D1
WARBURTON PARK 2250 ROYAL DR, SCL, 95050, (408)241-6465	833 - C3
WARDEN AVENUE PARK WARDEN AV, SLN, 94577	690 - G1
WARM SPRINGS PARK FERNALD ST & QUINAULT WY, FRMT, 94539	773 - H6
WASHINGTON CITY PARK 880 W WASHINGTON AV, SUNV, 94086, (408)732-3479	812 - D7
WASHINGTON MANOR PARK PURDUE ST & CROSBY ST, SLN, 94579	691 - B5
WASHINGTON PARK 110 E RICHMOND AV, RCH, 94801, (510)620-6792	608 - D1
WASHINGTON PARK 740 CENTRAL AV, ALA, 94501, (510)521-0162	669 - F1
WASHINGTON PARK 850 BURLINGAME AV, BURL, 94010, (650)344-6386	728 - G6
WASHINGTON PARK LOUISIANA ST & NAPA ST, VAL, 94590	530 - A4
WASHINGTON PARK POPLAR ST, SCL, 95050	833 - E5
WASHINGTON SQUARE COLUMBUS AV & FILBERT ST, SF, 94133	648 - A4
WATER DOG LAKE PARK LAKE RD, BLMT, 94002	769 - B2
WATERFORD PARK VISTA PARK DR & SANDPEBBLE DR, SJS, 95136	854 - F7
WATSON PARK E JACKSON ST & N 22ND ST, SJS, 95112	834 - D3
WATTENBURGER PARK RODODENDRON DR, LVMR, 94550	696 - A4
WAUGH PARK HILLCREST BLVD & EL PASEO, MLBR, 94030	728 - A4
WAYSIDE PARK 1ST ST, PLE, 94566	714 - E4
WEEKES COMMUNITY PARK TAMPA AV, HAY, 94544	711 - J7
WEISSHARR PARK 2300 DARTMOUTH ST, PA, 94306	811 - A1
WELCH PARK 1900 SANTIAGO AV, SJS, 95122	854 - J1
WELLESLEY CRESCENT PARK WELLESLEY CRES, RDWC, 94062	769 - J5
WENDELL PARK PLAYGROUND WENDELL AV, RCH, 94804	588 - H5
WENTE PARK DARWIN AV & KINGSPORT AV, LVMR, 94550	715 - G3
WERRY PARK DARTMOUTH ST, PA, 94306	810 - J1
WESTBOROUGH PARK WESTBOROUGH BLVD & GALWAY DR, SSF, 94080	707 - D4
WESTLAKE PARK 149 LAKE MERCED BLVD, DALY, 94015	687 - A3
WESTMOOR PARK 123 EDGEMONT DR, DALY, 94015	687 - A6
WESTRIDGE PARK FREMONT BLVD & NICOLET AV, FRMT, 94536	752 - F2
WESTVIEW PARK SKYLINE BLVD, PCFA, 94044	707 - C5
WESTWOOD OAKS PARK 460 LA HERNAN DR, SCL, 95051	832 - H6
WESTWOOD PARK BRIARFIELD AV & WESTWOOD ST, RDWC, 94061	789 - H2
WHISMAN SCHOOL PARK EASY ST & WALKER DR, MTVW, 94043	812 - A4
WHITE FIELD LINDA MAR BLVD & SEVILLE DR, PCFA, 94044	726 - J5
WILCOX PARK WILCOX WY & DUKE WY, SJS, 95125	854 - A5
WILDCAT CANYON REGIONAL PARK HILL RD, RCH, 94805	609 - G1
WILDWOOD PARK 4TH ST & WILDWOOD WY, SAR, 95070	872 - D2
WILLARD PARK 2550 DERBY ST, BERK, 94705	629 - J3
WILLIAM CANN MEMORIAL PARK MARSH HAWK RD, UNC, 94587	732 - D6
WILLIAM STREET PARK E WILLIAM ST & S 16TH ST, SJS, 95112	834 - E6
WILLIAMS, JACK PARK PULSAR AV & NEPTUNE RD, LVMR, 94550	715 - E4
WILLIAMSON RANCH PARK LONE TREE WY & HILLCREST AV, ANT, 94509	595 - J4
WILLOW GLEN PARK W 7TH & K STS, BEN, 94510	551 - A4
WILLOW OAKS PARK 500 WILLOW RD, MLPK, 94025	790 - J2
WILLOW PASS COMMUNITY PARK OLIVERA RD & SALVIO ST, CNCD, 94519, (510)671-3326	572 - H7
WILLOW STREET BRAMHALL PARK WILLOW ST & CAMINO RAMON, SJS, 95125	853 - J3
WILSON PARK PORTAL AV & WINTERGREEN DR, CPTO, 95014	852 - F1
WILSON PARK SOLANO AV & SCOTT ST, VAL, 94590	530 - B6
WINDMILL SPRINGS PARK UMBARGER RD, SJS, 95121	854 - J3
WINSTON MANOR PARK ELKWOOD DR & DUVAL DR, SSF, 94080	707 - D1
WOOD PARK PENNSYLVANIA AV & 18TH ST, RCH, 94801	588 - G5
W D WOOD PARK MCKILLUP RD, OAK, 94602	650 - C5
WOODFIELD PARK LUPINE RD & VIOLET RD, HER, 94547	570 - A4
WOODLAND HILLS PARK CRESTVIEW DR & ALTA VISTA, PIT, 94565	574 - B6
WOODSTOCK PARK 300 CYPRESS ST, ALA, 94501	649 - E7
WOODTHRUSH PARK WOODTHRUSH DR, PLE, 94566	714 - D1
WUNDERLICH COUNTY PARK 4040 WOODSIDE RD, SMCo, 94062, (650)851-7570	809 - E3
YEE TOCK CHEE PARK BRIDGEWAY BLVD & PRINCESS ST, SAUS, 94965	627 - B3
YELLOWSTONE PARK 1400 YELLOWSTONE AV, MPS, 95035	814 - D1

FEATURE NAME / Address City, ZIP Code	PAGE-GRID
YGNACIO PLAZA MARTINEZ PARK ALHAMBRA AV & HENRIETTA ST, MRTZ, 94553	571 - D3
YGNACIO VALLEY PARK OAK GROVE RD & MINERT RD, CNCD, 94518	592 - G6
YOUNGBLOOD COLEMAN PLAYGROUND 1801 MENDELL ST, SF, 94124	668 - C5

PERFORMING ARTS

FEATURE NAME / Address City, ZIP Code	PAGE-GRID
ALTARENA PLAYHOUSE 1409 HIGH ST, ALA, 94501, (510)523-1553	670 - B3
ART CENTER AUDITORIUM 2600 BARRETT AV, RCH, 94804, (510)620-6513	588 - H6
BERKELEY COMMUNITY THEATER 1930 ALLSTON WY, BERK, 94703, (510)644-6893	629 - G2
BERKELEY JEWISH THEATER 1414 WALNUT ST, BERK, 94709, (510)848-0237	609 - G7
BERKELEY REPERTORY THEATRE 2025 ADDISON ST, BERK, 94704, (510)845-4700	629 - G2
BROOKS HALL 99 GROVE ST, SF, 94102, (415)974-4060	647 - J7
CALIFORNIA CONSERVATORY 999 E 14TH ST, SLN, 94577, (510)632-8850	691 - A1
CONCORD PAVILION 2000 KIRKER PASS RD, CNCD, 94521, (510)671-3100	593 - H4
CONTRA COSTA CIVIC THEATRE 951 POMONA AV, ELCR, 94530, (510)524-9132	609 - D3
CURRAN THEATER 445 GEARY ST, SF, 94102, (415)474-3800	648 - A6
FOREST MDWS PERFORMING ARTS CTR 1500 GRAND AV, SRFL, 94901, (415)457-4440	566 - H7
GEARY THEATRE 415 GEARY ST, SF, 94102, (415)749-2228	648 - A6
GOLDEN GATE THEATRE 6TH ST & MARKET ST, SF, 94103, (415)474-3800	648 - A6
HERBST THEATRE 401 VAN NESS AV & MCALLISTR ST, SF, 94102, (415)392-4400	647 - H7
LOUISE M. DAVIES SYMPHONY HALL 201 VAN NESS AV & GROVE ST, SF, 94102, (415)431-5400	647 - H7
MASQUERS PLAYHOUSE 105 PARK PL, RCH, 94801, (510)232-3888	588 - D7
MEMORIAL AUDITORIUM CIVIC CENTER & NEVIN AV, RCH, 94804	588 - H6
MUSIC CONCOURSE CONCOURSE DR, SF, 94118	667 - C1
PERFORMING ARTS CENTER 255 S ALMADEN BLVD, SJS, 95110, (408)288-7474	834 - B7
PHOENIX THEATRE 301 8TH ST, SF, 94103, (415)621-4423	648 - A7
REGIONAL CENTER FOR THE ARTS 1601 CIVIC DR, WLCK, 94596, (510)943-7469	612 - C5
RICHMOND ART CENTER CIVIC CENTER & NEVIN AV, RCH, 94804	588 - H6
SAN MATEO PERFORMING ARTS CENTER 600 N DELAWARE ST, SMTO, 94401, (650)348-8243	728 - H6
SHORELINE AMPHITHEATRE AT MTN-VIEW 1 AMPHITHEATRE PKWY, MTVW, 94043, (650)962-1000	791 - H7
SIMMONS, CALVIN THEATER 10 10TH ST, OAK, 94607, (510)893-2082	649 - H5
UC BERKELEY GREEK THEATER 2200 UNIVERSITY AV, BERK, 94720, (510)642-6000	629 - J1
UNIVERSITY ARTS BANCROFT WY & BOWDITCH ST, BERK, 94704	629 - J2
VILLA MONTALVO 15400 MONTALVO RD, SAR, 95070, (408)741-3421	872 - D4
WAR MEMORIAL OPERA HOUSE 301 VAN NESS AV & GROVE ST, SF, 94102, (415)621-6600	647 - H7
WARFIELD THEATRE 982 MARKET ST, SF, 94102, (415)775-7722	648 - A6
WOODMINSTER AMPHITHEATER 3300 JOAQUIN MILLER RD, OAK, 94611, 510-	650 - G3

POINTS OF INTEREST

FEATURE NAME / Address City, ZIP Code	PAGE-GRID
ADOBE ART CENTER ANITA AV, AlaC, 94546	691 - J5
ADOBE MOBILE LODGE ADOBE DR, CNCD, 94520	572 - F6
ALICE ARTS CENTER 1418 ALICE ST, OAK, 94612, (510)839-5510	649 - G4
ALLIED ARTS GUILD ARBOR RD & CREEK DR, MLPK, 94025, (650)325-3259	790 - G5
BAYLANDS ATHLETIC CENTER 1900 GENG RD, PA, 94303	791 - D4
BLUNT POINT LIGHTHOUSE TBRN	627 - J4
BROTHERS LIGHTHOUSE, THE POINT SAN PABLO, RCH, 94801, (510)233-2385	587 - H3
CALIFORNIA ACADEMY OF SCIENCES CONCOURSE DR, SF, 94118, (415)750-7145	667 - C1
CAMRON-STANFORD HOUSE 1418 LAKESIDE DR, OAK, 94612, (510)836-1976	649 - H4
CARQUINEZ STRAIT LIGHTHOUSE SEAWIND DR, VAL, 94590	550 - B2
CENTENNIAL CENTER BOTANY GROUNDS FOOTHILL BLVD & CITY CENTER DR, HAY, 94541	691 - J7
CENTENNIAL HALL 22292 FOOTHILL BLVD, HAY, 94541, (510)881-1911	691 - J7
CHABOT OBSERVATORY 4917 MOUNTAIN BLVD, OAK, 94605, (510)530-3480	650 - H6
CLIFF HOUSE 1066 POINT LOBOS AV, SF, 94121, (415)386-3330	646 - G7
CLOCKTOWER COMMANDANTS LN, BEN, 94510	551 - E6
CONSERVATORY OF FLOWERS CONSERVATORY DR W, SF, (415)666-7017	667 - D1
CONTRA COSTA FAIR GROUNDS 10TH & L ST, ANT, 94509, (510)757-4400	575 - C4
COUNTY OF SANTA CLARA GIRLS RANCH BERNAL RD, SCIC, 95119	895 - D2
CROW CANYON GARDENS PARK PL, SRMN, 94583	673 - B2
DAVIE TENNIS STADIUM 198 OAK RD, PDMT, 94611, (510)444-5663	650 - B2
DUNSMUIR HOUSE & GARDENS 2960 PERALTA OAKS DR, OAK, 94605, (510)615-5555	671 - C6
DUTCH WINDMILL GREAT HWY & JOHN F KENNEDY DR, SF	666 - H1
EDOFF MEMORIAL BANDSTAND BELLEVUE AV, OAK, 94610	649 - H3
EL CERRITO COMMUNITY SWIM CENTER 7007 MOESER LN, ELCR, 94530, (510)215-4370	609 - D2
FISHERMANS MEMORIAL CHAPEL THE EMBARCADERO & TAYLOR ST, SF, 94133	647 - J2
FISHERMANS WHARF JEFFERSON ST & TAYLOR ST, SF, 94133	647 - H3
GOLDEN GATE EQUESTRIAN CENTER 36TH AV & JOHN F KENNEDY DR, SF	666 - J1
GREEK ORTHODOX CHURCH 4700 LINCOLN AV, OAK, 94602, (510)531-3400	650 - E3
HAPPY HOLLOW ZOO 1300 SENTER RD, SJS, 95112, (408)292-8188	854 - E1
HAYWARD SHORELINE INTERPRETIVE-CENTER 4901 BREAKWATER DR, HAY, 94545, (510)881-6751	731 - C1
HOOVER PAVILION QUARRY RD & PALO DR, PA, 94304	790 - H5
JAPANESE FRIENDSHIP TEA GARDEN 1300 SENTER RD, SJS, 95112, (408)277-2757	854 - E1
JAPANESE TEA GARDEN MARTIN LUTHER KING JR DR, SF, 94118, (415)752-1171	667 - C1
KNOWLAND STATE ARBORETUM GOLF LINKS RD, OAK, 94605	671 - D4
LAWRENCE HALL OF SCIENCE CENTENNIAL DR, BERK, 94720	610 - A7
LAWRENCE LIVERMORE NATIONAL-LABORATORY S VASCO RD & W GATE DR AV, AlaC, 94550, (510)422-1100	696 - F7
LIME POINT LIGHTHOUSE SF	627 - B7
LONDON, JACK MARINA 54 JACK LONDON SQ, OAK, 94607, (510)834-4591	649 - F5
MARIN ART & GARDEN CENTER SIR FRANCIS DRAKE BLVD, ROSS, 94957, (415)454-5597	586 - D2
MARINE WORLD AFRICA USA MARINE WORLD PKWY, VAL, 94589, (707)643-6722	510 - C7
MAUSOLEUM LOMITA DR & CAMPUS DR, SCIC, 94305, (650)723-2300	790 - H6
MCCONAGHY ESTATE 18701 HESPERIAN BLVD, AlaC, 94541, (510)276-3010	711 - E1
MORMON TEMPLE 4700 LINCOLN AV, OAK, 94602, (510)531-1475	650 - F3
MORRISON PLANETARIUM CONCOURSE DR, SF, 94118, (415)750-7000	667 - C1
MURPHY WINDMILL M L KING JR DR & GREAT HWY, SF	666 - H1
OAKLAND ZOO GOLF LINKS RD, OAK, 94605, (510)632-9523	671 - B4
OUR LADY'S HOME 3499 FOOTHILL BLVD, OAK, 94601, (510)525-5661	650 - C7
PALO ALTO CULTURAL CENTER 1313 NEWELL RD, PA, 94303, (415)329-2366	791 - B5
PARAMOUNT THEATRE 2025 BROADWAY, OAK, 94612, (510)465-6400	649 - G3
RICHARDSON BAY AUDUBON CENTER 376 GREENWOOD BEACH RD, TBRN, 94920, (415)388-2524	606 - J5
SAN FRANCISCO ZOO SLOAT BLVD & 45TH AV, SF, 94132, (415)753-7061	666 - H6
SHERMAN HOUSE 2160 GREEN ST, SF, 94123, (415)563-3600	647 - G4
STANFORD LINEAR ACCELERATOR-CENTER 2575 SAND HILL RD, SMCo, 94025, (650)926-3300	810 - D1
STATE OF CALIFORNIA CONSERVATION-CAMP BOLLINGER CANYON RD, CCCo	652 - E3
STEAM TRAINS GRIZZLY PEAK BLVD, CCCo, 94708	610 - C7
STEINHART AQUARIUM CONCOURSE DR, SF, 94118, (415)221-5100	667 - C1
SUNSET MAGAZINE CENTER MIDDLEFIELD RD & WILLOW RD, MLPK, 94025, (650)321-3600	790 - H3
THOMAS BROTHERS MAPS STORE 550 JACKSON ST, SF, 94133, (415)981-7520	648 - A4
TIBURON MARINE LABORATORY PARADISE RD, MrnC, 94920	607 - F5
U C LEUSCHNER OBSERVATORY 4927 HAPPY VALLEY RD, CCCo, (510)284-9403	611 - B2
U S D A WESTERN REGIONAL-RESEARCH LAB BUCHANAN ST, ALB, 94706	609 - C6
UNDERWATER WORLD THE EMBARCADERO AT BEACH ST, SF, 94133, (415)623-5300	648 - A3
UNION STREET PLAZA UNION ST, SF, 94123, (415)931-2445	647 - G4
VALLEJO MUNICIPAL MARINA HARBOR WY WY, VAL, 94590	529 - H4
VISTA POINT N END GOLDEN GATE BRIDGE, MrnC, 94965	627 - B6
WATER TEMPLE AlaC, 94586	734 - C7
WINCHESTER MYSTERY HOUSE 1750 S WINCHESTER BLVD, SJS, 95117, (408)247-2101	853 - D1
YERBA BUENA GARDENS MISSION ST & 3RD ST, SF, 94103, (415)978-2787	648 - A6

POINTS OF INTEREST - HISTORIC

FEATURE NAME / Address City, ZIP Code	PAGE-GRID
ALCATRAZ ISLAND ALCATRAZ ISLAND, SF, (415)546-2700	627 - H7
BENICIA CAPITOL S H PK 1ST & G STS, BEN, 94510	551 - B5
COIT TOWER TELEGRAPH HILL BLVD, SF, 94133, (415)362-0808	648 - A4
FILOLI HOUSE & GARDENS CANADA RD, SMCo, 94062, (650)364-2880	769 - A7
FORT MASON MARINA BLVD & BUCHANAN ST, SF, 94123, (415)979-3010	647 - H3
FORT POINT NATIONAL HISTORIC SITE MARINE DR, SF, 94129, (415)556-1693	647 - C2
FORT SCOTT LINCOLN BLVD & DYNAMITE RD, SF, 94129	647 - B4
GOLDEN GATE BRIDGE HWY 101 & BATTERY EAST RD, SF, 94129, (415)921-5858	647 - B2
HAYES MANSION HISTORICAL LANDMARK EDENVALE AV & RED RIVER WY, SJS, 95136	875 - A2
HIGUERA ADOBE PARK N PARK VICTORIA DR & WESSEX PL, MPS, 95035	794 - B3
MISSION DOLORES 3321 16TH ST, SF, 94114, (415)621-8203	667 - H2
MISSION SAN JOSE DE GUADALUPE 43300 MISSION BLVD, FRMT, 94539	753 - J7
MISSION SAN RAFAEL 1104 5TH AV, SRFL, 94901, (415)454-8141	586 - F1
MISSION SANTA CLARA DE ASIS 820 ALVISO ST, SCL, 95053, (408)554-4023	833 - E4
MOUNT DAVIDSON CROSS SF, 94127	667 - E5
MUIR WOODS NATIONAL MONUMENT MUIR WOODS RD, MrnC, 94965, (415)388-2595	606 - A4
MUIR, JOHN NATIONAL HISTORIC SITE 4202 ALHAMBRA AV, MRTZ, 94553, (510)228-8860	571 - E6
OHLONE INDIAN GRAVEYARD 1500 WASHINGTON BLVD, FRMT, 94539	753 - G7
OLD FEDERAL RESERVE 400 SANSOME ST, SF, 94111	648 - B5
OLD SAINT HILARY'S HISTORIC-PRESERVE ESPERANZA ST & MAR WEST ST, TBRN, 94920	607 - E7
OLD UNITED STATES MINT 88 5TH ST, SF, 94103, (415)744-6830	648 - A6
ONEIL, EUGENE NATIONAL HISTORIC-SITE 1000 KUSS RD, CCCo, 94526, (510)838-0249	652 - G1
PACHECO, FERNANDO ADOBE 3119 GRANT ST, CNCD, 94520	572 - E6
PATTERSON HOUSE 34600 ARDENWOOD BLVD, FRMT, 94555, (510)796-0663	752 - D3
PERALTA ADOBE 175 W SAINT JOHN ST, SJS, 95110, (408)993-8182	834 - B6
PIER 39 THE EMBARCADERO & PIER 39, SF, 94133	648 - A2
PORTALS OF THE PAST CROSS OVER DR & TRANSVERSE DR, SF	667 - B1
SF BAY DISCOVERY CO HIST SITE SWEENEY RIDGE TR, PCFA, 94044	727 - D3
SF NATIONAL MARITIME HIST PARK HYDE ST & JEFFERSON ST, SF, 94109, (415)556-3002	647 - H2
SOLDIERS MONUMENT BOYD RD & MAIN ST, PLHL, 94523	592 - C6
VALLEJO MILL HISTORICAL PARK MISSION BL & NILES CANYON RD, FRMT, 94536	733 - C7
VICTORIAN ROW OLD OAKLAND BROADWAY & 9TH ST, OAK, 94607	649 - F4
WAR MEMORIAL 6655 MISSION ST, DALY, 94014, (650)991-8020	687 - D3
WILLIAMS HISTORICAL PARK 39200 FREMONT BLVD, FRMT, 94538	753 - A5
WOODSIDE COUNTRY STORE HIST SITE 471 KINGS MOUNTAIN RD, WDSD, 94062, (650)851-7615	789 - E6

POST OFFICES

FEATURE NAME / Address City, ZIP Code	PAGE-GRID
A POST OFFICE 1550 STEINER ST, SF, 94115, (415)563-5954	647 - G6
AGNEW STATION POST OFFICE 4601 LAFAYETTE ST, SCL, 95054	813 - D4
AIRPORT BRANCH POST OFFICE SF INTERNATIONAL AIRPORT, SMCo, 94128, (650)742-1431	728 - C2
AIRPORT STATION POST OFFICE 8495 PARDEE DR, OAK, 94621, (510)251-3102	670 - E7
ALAMEDA POST OFFICE 2201 SHORE LINE DR, ALA, 94501, (510)748-5366	669 - J3
ALAMO POST OFFICE 225 ALAMO PZ, CCCo, 94507, (510)935-1155	632 - F5
ALBANY BRANCH 1191 SOLANO AV, ALB, 94706, (510)649-3135	609 - D6
ALMADEN VALLEY STATION 6525 CROWN BLVD, SJS, 95120	894 - E1
ALVARADO STATION POST OFFICE 3861 SMITH ST, UNC, 94587, (510)471-4757	731 - J5
ALVISO STATION POST OFFICE 1160 TAYLOR ST, SJS, 95002	793 - B7
ANTIOCH POST OFFICE 2730 W TREGALLAS RD, ANT, 94509, (510)757-4191	575 - D6
BAYSIDE STATION 1750 LUNDY AV, SJS, 95131	814 - C6
BAYSIDE STATION POST OFFICE 2731 JUNCTION AV, SJS, 95134	813 - H5
BAYVIEW POST OFFICE 2111 LANE ST, SF, 94124, (415)822-7619	668 - B7
BELMONT POST OFFICE 640 MASONIC WY, BLMT, 94002, (650)591-9471	769 - E1
BELVEDERE - TIBURON POST OFFICE 6 BEACH RD, TBRN, 94920, (415)435-1361	627 - D1
BERKELEY MAIN POST OFFICE 2000 ALLSTON WY, BERK, 94704, (510)649-3100	629 - G2
BERNAL 30 29TH ST, SF, 94110, (415)695-1703	667 - H4
BERRYESSA STATION 1315 PIEDMONT RD, SJS, 95132	814 - G4
BLOSSOM HILL STATION 5706 CAHALAN AV, SJS, 95123, (408)225-8020	874 - G4
BLOSSOM VALLEY STATION 1776 MIRAMONTE AV, MTVW, 94040	831 - H1
BRADFORD STATION POST OFFICE 822 C ST, HAY, 94541, (510)538-7700	711 - J1
BRISBANE POST OFFICE 250 OLD COUNTY RD, BSBN, 94005, (650)467-8171	688 - A6
BROADWAY STATION POST OFFICE 1141 CAPUCHINO AV, BURL, 94010, (650)343-7861	728 - E6
BURLINGAME ANNEX POST OFFICE 820 STANTON RD, BURL, 94010, (650)697-9588	728 - D4
BURLINGAME POST OFFICE 220 PARK RD, BURL, 94010, (650)342-7694	728 - G7
C POST OFFICE 1198 S VAN NESS AV, SF, 94110, (415)285-7382	667 - J3
CAMBRIAN PARK POST OFFICE 1769 HILLSDALE AV, SJS, 95124	873 - H2
CAMBRIDGE STATION POST OFFICE 265 CAMBRIDGE AV, PA, 94306, (650)327-4174	791 - A7
CAMPBELL POST OFFICE 500 W HAMILTON AV, CMBL, 95008	853 - D5
CANYON POST OFFICE PINEHURST RD, CCCo, (510)376-5600	630 - J7
CASA CORREO STATION POST OFFICE 4494 TREAT BLVD, CNCD, 94521, (510)687-1500	593 - B3
CASTRO VALLEY BRANCH POST OFFICE 20283 SANTA MARIA AV, AlaC, 94546, (510)581-0191	692 - A5
CHESTNUT STATION POST OFFICE 36 CHESTNUT AV, SSF, 94080, (650)583-0376	707 - G3
CHINATOWN POST OFFICE 867 STOCKTON ST, SF, 94108, (415)956-3566	648 - A5
CITY HALL POST OFFICE VAN NESS AV, SF, 94102, (415)621-6325	647 - H7
CIVIC CENTER POST OFFICE 101 HYDE ST, SF, 94102, (415)441-8399	647 - J6
CLAYTON POST OFFICE 1028 DIABLO ST, CLAY, 94517, (510)672-6515	593 - H7
COLMA POST OFFICE 7373 MISSION ST, DALY, 94014, (650)755-1868	687 - C5
CONCORD MAIN POST OFFICE 2121 MERIDIAN PARK BLVD, CNCD, 94520, (510)687-1500	592 - D2
CORTE MADERA POST OFFICE 7 PIXLEY AV, CMAD, 94925, (415)924-4463	586 - F7
COUNTRY CLUB STATION POST OFFICE 1545 SCHOOL ST, MRGA, 94556, (510)376-4948	631 - D7
COURT STATION POST OFFICE 815 COURT ST, MRTZ, 94553, (510)229-2134	571 - E3
COYOTE POST OFFICE MONTEREY RD, SCIC, 95137, (408)463-0666	895 - J2
CROCKETT POST OFFICE 420 ROLPH AV, CCCo, 94525, (510)787-1000	550 - D4
CUPERTINO POST OFFICE 20850 STEVENS CREEK BLVD, CPTO, 95014, (408)252-6798	852 - D1
DALY CITY POST OFFICE 1100 SULLIVAN AV, DALY, 94015, (650)756-2303	687 - B5
DANVILLE MAIN POST OFFICE 2605 CM TASSAJARA, DNVL, 94526, (510)736-5044	653 - F4
DANVILLE SQUARE STATION POST-OFFICE 43 DANVILLE SQ, DNVL, 94526, (510)736-5044	652 - J2
DIABLO POST OFFICE 1701 EL NIDO, CCCo, 94526, (510)837-3800	633 - E7
DIAMOND HEIGHTS POST OFFICE 5262 DIAMOND HEIGHTS BLVD, SF, 94131, (415)550-6412	667 - G4
DIMOND STATION POST OFFICE 2226 MACARTHUR BLVD, OAK, 94602, (510)251-3107	650 - D4
DOLLAR RANCH STATION POST OFFICE 1221 ROSSMOOR PKWY, WLCK, 94595, (510)932-7020	632 - B1

FEATURE NAME	Address City, ZIP Code	PAGE-GRID
DOWNTOWN STATION POST OFFICE	855 JEFFERSON AV, RDWC, 94063, (650)369-5228	770 - B6
DUBLIN POST OFFICE	6937 VILLAGE PARKWAY, DBLN, 94568, (510)828-0934	693 - H4
E POST OFFICE	460 BRANNAN ST, SF, 94107, (415)543-7729	648 - B7
EASTMONT POST OFFICE	8033 MACARTHUR BLVD, OAK, 94605, (510)251-3109	670 - J3
EAST PALO ALTO POST OFFICE	2197 E BAYSHORE RD, PA, 94303, (650)452-4300	791 - D4
EL CERRITO MAIN POST OFFICE	11135 SAN PABLO AV, ELCR, 94530, (510)235-3373	609 - C2
EL SOBRANTE BRANCH POST OFFICE	535 APPIAN WY, CCCo, 94803, (510)262-1960	589 - E1
ELMWOOD STATION	2705 WEBSTER ST, BERK, 94705, (510)251-3112	629 - J4
EMERYVILLE POST OFFICE	1585 62ND ST, EMVL, 94608, (510)251-3112	629 - E5
EMPORIUM POST OFFICE	835 MARKET ST, SF, 94103, (415)543-2606	648 - A6
ENCINAL STATION POST OFFICE	526 W FREMONT AV, SUNV, 94087, (408)245-0617	832 - E3
ESTUDILLO STATION POST OFFICE	1319 WASHINGTON AV, SLN, 94577, (510)483-1636	691 - A1
FAIRMOUNT STATION POST OFFICE	6324 FAIRMOUNT AV, ELCR, 94530, (510)525-6252	609 - D4
FEDERAL BUILDING POST OFFICE	450 GOLDEN GATE AV, SF, 94102, (415)621-7505	647 - J6
FISK POST OFFICE	1317 9TH AV, SF, 94122, (415)759-1901	667 - C2
FOSTER CITY POST OFFICE	1050 SHELL BLVD, FCTY, 94404, (650)349-5529	749 - G4
FREMONT MAIN POST OFFICE	37010 DUSTERBERRY WY, FRMT, 94536, (510)792-8654	752 - G4
FRUITVILLE STATION POST OFFICE	1445 34TH AV, OAK, 94601, (510)251-3115	650 - C7
G POST OFFICE	4304 18TH ST, SF, 94114, (415)621-5317	667 - G2
GEARY POST OFFICE	5654 GEARY BLVD, SF, 94121, (415)752-0231	647 - B6
GOLDEN GATE POST OFFICE	3245 GEARY BLVD, SF, 94118, (415)751-1645	647 - E6
GRAND LAKE STATION POST OFFICE	490 LAKE PARK AV, OAK, 94610, (510)251-3084	650 - A3
HACIENDA STATION POST OFFICE	4682 CHABOT DR, PLE, 94588, (510)847-3867	694 - B6
HAYWARD MAIN POST OFFICE	24438 SANTA CLARA ST, HAY, 94544, (510)783-2400	711 - H4
HERCULES POST OFFICE	1611 SYCAMORE AV, HER, 94547, (510)799-3175	569 - H3
HILLVIEW STATION POST OFFICE	2450 ALVIN AV, SJS, 95121, (408)238-1854	854 - J1
IRVINGTON STATION POST OFFICE	41041 TRIMBOLI WY, FRMT, 94538, (510)651-0171	753 - D7
J POST OFFICE	554 CLAYTON ST, SF, 94117, (415)621-7445	667 - E1
KAISER CENTER STATION POST OFFICE	300 LAKESIDE DR, OAK, 94612, (510)251-3086	649 - H3
KENTFIELD POST OFFICE	822 COLLEGE AV, MrnC, 94904, (415)454-9627	586 - D3
LANDSCAPE STATION	1831 SOLANO AV, BERK, 94707, (510)649-3143	609 - F6
LARKSPUR POST OFFICE	120 WARD ST, LKSP, 94939, (415)924-4792	586 - E6
LAUREL STATION POST OFFICE	3521 MAYBELLE AV, OAK, 94619, (510)251-3120	650 - F6
LETTERMAN POST OFFICE	1100 LETTERMAN DR, SF, 94129, (415)563-7195	647 - E4
LINDEN AVENUE STATION POST OFFICE	322 LINDEN AV, SSF, 94080, (650)589-2242	707 - J3
LIVERMORE POST OFFICE	220 S LIVERMORE AV, LVMR, 94550, (510)447-3580	715 - H1
LOS ALTOS POST OFFICE	100 1ST ST, LALT, 94022, (650)948-6000	811 - D7
LOS GATOS POST OFFICE	101 S SANTA CRUZ AV, LGTS, 95030	893 - A1
MACYS UNION SQUARE POST OFFICE	180 OFARREL ST, SF, 94108, (415)956-3570	648 - A6
MARCUS FOSTER STATION POST OFFICE	9201 E INTERNATIONAL BLVD, OAK, 94603, (510)251-3124	670 - H5
MARINA POST OFFICE	2055 LOMBARD ST, SF, 94123, (415)563-4674	647 - G4
MARTINEZ MAIN POST OFFICE	4100 ALHAMBRA AV, MRTZ, 94553, (510)228-1000	571 - E6
MCLAREN POST OFFICE	2755 SAN BRUNO AV, SF, 94134, (415)467-3560	668 - A7
MENLO PARK POST OFFICE	3875 BOHANNON DR, MLPK, 94025, (650)323-0038	770 - F7
MILL VALLEY POST OFFICE	751 E BLITHEDALE AV, MLV, 94941, (415)388-9656	606 - F3
MILLBRAE POST OFFICE	501 BROADWAY, MLBR, 94030, (650)697-2506	728 - B3
MILLS COLLEGE POST OFFICE	POST RD, OAK, 94613, (510)430-2133	650 - H7
MILPITAS POST OFFICE	450 S ABEL ST, MPS, 95035	814 - A1
MIRA VISTA STATION POST OFFICE	12651 SAN PABLO AV, RCH, 94805, (510)232-9635	589 - A5
MISSION ANNEX POST OFFICE	1600 BRYANT ST, SF, 94103, (415)621-8646	668 - A1
MISSION RAFAEL STATION POST-OFFICE	910 D ST, SRFL, 94901, (415)453-1153	586 - F1
MISSION SAN JOSE STATION POST-OFFICE	43456 ELLSWORTH, FRMT, 94539, (510)656-3003	753 - H7
MISSION STATION	1050 KIELY BLVD, SCL, 95051	833 - B4
MORAGA MAIN POST OFFICE	460 CENTER ST, MRGA, 94556, (510)376-4948	631 - E3
MOUNT EDEN POST OFFICE	2163 ALDENGATE WY, HAY, 94545, (510)782-6434	711 - H7
MOUNTAIN VIEW POST OFFICE	211 HOPE ST, MTVW, 94041, (650)967-5721	811 - J5
NEW ALMADEN	21300 ALMADEN RD, SCIC, 95120, (408)268-7730	894 - J7
NEWARK POST OFFICE	6250 THORNTON AV, NWK, 94560, (510)797-2464	752 - E6
NILES POST OFFICE	160 J ST, FRMT, 94536, (510)793-3707	753 - B1
NOE VALLEY POST OFFICE	4083 24TH ST, SF, 94114, (415)821-0776	667 - G3
NORTH BEACH POST OFFICE	1640 STOCKTON ST, SF, 94133, (415)956-3581	648 - A4
NORTH BERKELEY STATION	1521 SHATTUCK AV, BERK, 94709, (510)649-3146	609 - G7
NORTH OAKLAND STATION POST OFFICE	4869 TELEGRAPH AV, OAK, 94609, (510)251-3126	629 - H6
NOVATO POST OFFICE	1537 S NOVATO BLVD, NVTO, 94947, (415)897-3171	526 - B5
NUMBER 40 BELL BAZAAR POST OFFICE	3030 16TH ST, SF, 94103, (415)621-6053	667 - H2
OAK GROVE STATION POST OFFICE	655 OAK GROVE AV, MLPK, 94025, (650)321-7681	790 - F3
OAKLAND CIVIC CENTER POST OFFICE	201 13TH ST, OAK, 94612, (510)255-3000	649 - G4
OAKLAND MAIN POST OFFICE	1675 7TH ST, OAK, 94607, (510)874-8200	649 - D3
ORINDA POST OFFICE	29 ORINDA WY, ORIN, 94563, (510)254-2298	610 - G7
P & DC POST OFFICE	1300 EVANS AV, SF, 94124, (415)550-5247	668 - C5
PACHECO STATION POST OFFICE	4980 PACHECO BLVD, CCCo, 94553, (510)228-1104	572 - B6
PACIFIC POST OFFICE	50 W MANOR DR, PCFA, 94044, (650)355-4000	706 - J3
PALO ALTO	380 HAMILTON AV, PA, 94301, (650)323-1361	790 - J4
PARK CENTRAL STATION POST OFFICE	1333 PARK AV, ALA, 94501, (510)748-5374	670 - A2
PARK STATION POST OFFICE	2900 SACRAMENTO ST, BERK, 94702, (510)649-3149	629 - F4
PARKMOOR STATION POST OFFICE	1545 PARKMOOR AV, SJS, 95126	853 - H1
PARKSIDE POST OFFICE	1800 TARAVAL ST, SF, 94116, (415)759-1601	667 - A5
PIEDMONT STATION POST OFFICE	195 41ST ST, OAK, 94611, (510)251-3130	649 - J1
PINE STREET POST OFFICE	1400 PINE ST, SF, 94109, (415)289-0755	647 - J5
PINOLE POST OFFICE	2101 PEAR ST, PIN, 94564, (510)741-3050	569 - E4
PITTSBURG POST OFFICE	835 RAILROAD AV, PIT, 94565, (510)432-0123	574 - E2
PLAZA STATION POST OFFICE	141 S TAAFFE AV, SUNV, 94086, (408)738-1150	812 - E7
PLEASANT HILL POST OFFICE	1945 CONTRA COSTA BLVD, PLHL, 94523, (510)687-1500	592 - C5
PLEASANTON POST OFFICE	4300 BLACK AV, PLE, 94566, (510)846-5631	714 - E2
POINT RICHMOND STATION POST-OFFICE	102 WASHINGTON AV, RCH, 94801, (510)232-9693	588 - D7
PORT COSTA POST OFFICE	3 CANYON LAKE RD, CCCo, (510)787-2980	550 - H6
POST OFFICE	1052 S LIVERMORE AV, LVMR, 94550	715 - J2
POST OFFICE	2000 ALCATRAZ AV, BERK, 94703	629 - G5
POST OFFICE	290 E L ST, BEN, 94510, (707)745-0219	551 - C5
POST OFFICE	420 W 4TH ST, ANT, 94509, (510)778-1054	575 - D4
POST OFFICE	MT DIABLO BLVD, LFYT, 94549	611 - E6
POST OFFICE	POST ST & THORNTON AV, FRMT, 94536	752 - H3
POST OFFICE	SOUTHLAND DR, HAY, 94545	711 - G4
POST OFFICE	UNIVERSITY & BAY, EPA, 94303	791 - B1
POST OFFICE F	15 ONONDAGA AV, SF, 94112, (415)334-0739	687 - F1
PRESIDIO POST OFFICE	950 LINCOLN BLVD, SF, 94129, (415)563-4975	647 - E4
REDWOOD CITY POST OFFICE	1100 BROADWAY, RDWC, 94063, (650)368-4181	770 - C5
RICHMOND MAIN POST OFFICE	1025 NEVIN AV, RCH, 94801, (510)232-9707	588 - G6
RINCON CENTER POST OFFICE	180 STEAURT ST, SF, 94105, (415)543-3340	648 - C5
ROBERTSVILLE STATION	1175 BRANHAM LN, SJS, 95118	874 - C2
RODEO POST OFFICE	499 PARKER AV, CCCo, 94572, (510)799-4583	549 - H7
ROSS POST OFFICE	1 ROSS COM, ROSS, 94957, (415)454-4123	586 - C2
SAINT JAMES PARK POST OFFICE	105 N 1ST ST, SJS, 95113	834 - B6
SAINT MARYS COLLEGE STATION PO	SAINT MARYS RD & RHEEM BLVD, MRGA, 94556, (510)376-1070	631 - G6
SAINT MATTHEWS STATION POST-OFFICE	210 S ELLSWORTH AV, SMTO, 94401, (650)343-5618	748 - J1
SAN ANSELMO POST OFFICE	121 SAN ANSELMO AV, SANS, 94960, (415)453-0830	586 - C1
SAN BRUNO POST OFFICE	1300 HUNTINGTON AV, SBRN, 94066, (650)952-2900	707 - H5
SAN CARLOS	809 LAUREL ST, SCAR, 94070, (650)591-5321	769 - G3
SAN LEANDRO MAIN POST OFFICE	1777 ABRAM CT, SLN, 94577, (510)483-0550	690 - J3
SAN LORENZO POST OFFICE	15888 HESPERIAN BLVD, AlaC, 94580, (510)317-1100	691 - D7
SAN MATEO POST OFFICE	1630 S DELAWARE ST, SMTO, 94402, (650)349-2301	749 - B3
SAN PABLO BRANCH POST OFFICE	2080 23RD ST, SPAB, 94806, (510)232-9636	588 - H3
SAN QUENTIN POST OFFICE	1 MAIN ST, MrnC, 94964, (415)456-4741	587 - B5
SAN RAFAEL CIVIC CENTER BRANCH PO	2 CIVIC CENTER DR, SRFL, 94903, (415)479-6338	566 - G4
SAN RAFAEL POST OFFICE	40 BELLAM BLVD, SRFL, 94901, (415)459-0944	586 - J3
SAN RAMON POST OFFICE	12935 ALCOSTA BLVD, SRMN, 94583, (510)277-0527	673 - D1
SANTA CLARA POST OFFICE	1200 FRANKLIN MALL ST, SCL, 95050	833 - E4
SARATOGA POST OFFICE	19630 ALLENDALE AV, SAR, 95070	872 - E2
SATHER GATE STATION	2515 DURANT AV, BERK, 94704, (510)649-3152	629 - J2
SAUSALITO POST OFFICE	150 HARBOR DR, SAUS, 94965, (415)332-4656	626 - J1
SOUTH BERKELEY STATION POST-OFFICE	3175 ADELINE ST, BERK, 94703, (510)649-3155	629 - G4
SOUTH SAN LEANDRO STATION POST-OFFICE	14811 E 14TH ST, SLN, 94578, (510)351-5316	691 - D3
STANFORD UNIVERSITY BRANCH POST-OFFICE	LAGUNITA DR & LANE W, SCIC, 94305, (650)322-0059	790 - H7
STATION A	364 WOODSIDE PZ, RDWC, 94061, (650)368-3605	790 - A3
STATION A POST OFFICE	135 W 25TH AV, SMTO, 94403, (650)345-2611	749 - B5
STATION A POST OFFICE	200 BROADWAY, RCH, 94804, (510)232-9694	588 - H7
STATION A POST OFFICE	2111 SAN PABLO AV, BERK, 94702, (510)649-3131	629 - E2
STATION A POST OFFICE	690 ROBERTS RD, PCFA, 94044	726 - H3
STATION B POST OFFICE	1074 LINCOLN AV, SJS, 95125	854 - A2
STATION B POST OFFICE	1446 FRANKLIN ST, OAK, 94612, (510)251-3080	649 - G4
STATION C POST OFFICE	20TH ST & BROADWAY, OAK, 94612, (510)891-5297	649 - G3
STATION D POST OFFICE	560 14TH ST, OAK, 94612, (510)251-3082	649 - G3
STATION D POST OFFICE	70 S JACKSON AV, SJS, 95116	834 - H3
STATION E POST OFFICE	1954 MOUNTAIN BLVD, OAK, 94611, (510)251-3100	650 - E1
STONESTOWN POST OFFICE	565 BUCKINGHAM WY, SF, 94132, (415)759-1660	667 - B7
SUNNYVALE POST OFFICE	580 N MARY AV, SUNV, 94086, (408)732-0121	812 - D5
SUNOL POST OFFICE	11925 MAIN ST, AlaC, 94586, (510)862-2130	734 - C6
SUNSET POST OFFICE	1314 22ND AV, SF, 94122, (415)759-1707	667 - B2
SUTTER POST OFFICE	150 SUTTER ST, SF, 94108, (415)956-3169	648 - A5
TERRA LINDA BRANCH POST OFFICE	603 DEL GANADO RD, SRFL, 94903, (415)479-1850	566 - C2
TODOS SANTOS STATION POST OFFICE	2043 EAST ST, CNCD, 94520, (510)687-1500	592 - F1
UNION CITY MAIN POST OFFICE	33170 ALVARADO-NILES RD, UNC, 94587, (510)471-4040	732 - D5
VISITATION POST OFFICE	68 LELAND AV, SF, 94134, (415)333-1150	688 - A2
VISTA GRANDE STATION	6025 MISSION ST, DALY, 94014, (415)334-7884	687 - D3
WALNUT CREEK MAIN POST OFFICE	2070 N BROADWAY, WLCK, 94596, (510)935-2611	612 - C4
WARM SPRINGS STATION POST OFFICE	240 FRANCISCO LN, FRMT, 94539, (510)656-3815	773 - H6
WASHINGTON MANOR STATION POST-OFFICE	921 MANOR BLVD, SLN, 94579, (510)351-6450	691 - B6
WEBSTER STATION POST OFFICE	1415 WEBSTER ST, ALA, 94501, (510)748-5376	669 - F1
WEST GRAND CARRIER ANNEX	577 W GRAND AV, OAK, 94612, (510)874-8480	649 - G3
WEST MENLO PARK BRANCH POST-OFFICE	2120 AVY AV, SMCo, 94025	790 - D6
WEST PORTAL POST OFFICE	317 W PORTAL AV, SF, 94127, (415)759-1811	667 - C5
WESTGATE STATION POST OFFICE	4285 PAYNE AV, SJS, 95117	853 - A4
WESTLAKE STATION POST OFFICE	199 SOUTHGATE AV, DALY, 94015, (650)756-1842	687 - A4
WILLOW GLEN POST OFFICE	1750 MERIDIAN AV, SJS, 95125	853 - J5
WOODSIDE POST OFFICE	2995 #200 WOODSIDE RD, WDSD, 94062, (650)851-8711	789 - H6

SCHOOLS - PRIVATE ELEMENTARY

FEATURE NAME	Address City, ZIP Code	PAGE-GRID
A CHILDS HIDEAWAY ELEM SCHOOL	37531 FREMONT BLVD, FRMT, 94536, (510)792-8415	752 - H3
ACHIEVER CHRISTIAN ELEM SCHOOL	820 IRONWOOD DR, SJS, 95125, (408)264-6789	854 - D6
ALL SAINTS ELEM SCHOOL	22870 2ND ST, HAY, 94541, (510)582-1910	712 - A1
ALL SOULS ELEM SCHOOL	479 MILLER AV, SSF, 94080, (650)583-3562	707 - J3
ALMA HEIGHTS CHRISTIAN	1030 LINDA MAR BLVD, PCFA, 94044, (650)359-0555	726 - J5
ALMADEN COUNTRY ELEM SCHOOL	6835 TRINIDAD DR, SJS, 95120, (408)997-0424	894 - F1
ALPHA BEACON CHRISTIAN	750 DARTMOUTH, SCAR, 94070, (650)592-2811	769 - D2
AMERICAN HERITAGE CHRISTIAN	425 GRESEL ST, HAY, 94544, (510)471-1010	732 - E2
ANTIOCH CHRISTIAN TUTORIAL	640 E TREGALLAS RD, ANT, 94509, (510)757-1837	575 - E6
APOSTLES LUTHERAN ELEM SCHOOL	5828 SANTA TERESA BLVD, SJS, 95123, (408)578-4800	874 - G6
ARMSTRONG, CHARLES	1405 SOLANA DR, BLMT, 94002, (650)592-7570	769 - E2
ASSUMPTION ELEM SCHOOL	1851 136TH AV, SLN, 94578, (510)357-8772	691 - C2
ATHERTON ACADEMY	8030 ATHERTON ST, OAK, 94605, (510)562-7015	670 - J3
AURORA ELEM SCHOOL	40 DULWICH RD, OAK, 94618, (510)428-2606	630 - B6
BEACON DAY ELEM SCHOOL	2101 LIVINGSTON ST, OAK, 94606, (510)436-4466	650 - A7
BEECHWOOD ELEM SCHOOL	50 TERMINAL AV, MLPK, 94025, (650)327-5052	770 - H7
BELMONT OAKS ACADEMY	2200 CARLMONT DR, BLMT, 94002, (650)593-6175	769 - C2
BENTLEY ELEM SCHOOL	1 HILLER DR, OAK, 94618, (510)843-2512	630 - B4
BERKELEY MONTESSORI ELEM SCHOOL	2030 FRANCISCO ST, BERK, 94709, (510)843-9374	629 - G1
BERKWOOD HEDGE ELEM SCHOOL	1809 BANCROFT WY, BERK, 94703, (510)843-5724	629 - G2
BETHEL CHRISTIAN ACADEMY	SC 431 RINCON LN, CCCo, 94803, (510)223-9550	589 - D1
BPC DAY	2027 7TH ST, BERK, 94804, (510)845-0876	629 - D2
BRANDEIS HILLEL DAY ELEM SCHOOL	655 BROTHERHOOD WY, SF, 94132, (415)406-1035	687 - B2
BRANDEIS-HILLEL PRIVATE SCHOOL	170 N SAN PEDRO RD, MrnC, 94903, (415)472-1833	566 - G4
CALVARY CATHEDRAL ACADEMY	2165 LUCRETIA AV, SJS, 95122, (408)298-7622	854 - G2
CALVARY CHRISTIAN ACADEMY	S 4892 SAN PABLO DAM RD, CCCo, 94803, (510)222-3828	589 - E3
CALVARY CHRISTIAN PRIVATE	2200 ARROYO RD, LVMR, 94550, (510)443-7947	715 - H4
CALVARY LUTHERAN ELEM SCHOOL	17200 VIA MAGDALENA, AlaC, 94580, (510)278-2598	711 - D1
CAMELOT ELEM SCHOOL	2330 POMAR VISTA, AlaC, 94546, (510)481-1304	691 - G5
CAMPBELL CHRISTIAN	1075 W CAMPBELL AV, CMBL, 95008, (408)374-7260	853 - B6
CANTERBURY CHRISTIAN ELEM SCHOOL	101 N EL MONTE AV, LALT, 94022, (650)949-0909	811 - F6
CANTERBURY ELEM SCHOOL	3120 SHANE DR, RCH, 94806, (510)222-5050	589 - A1
CARDEN EL ENCANTO	615 HOBART TER, SCL, 95051, (414)244-5041	833 - B6
CARDEN ELEM SCHOOL	2109 BROADWAY, BURL, 94010, (650)348-2131	728 - D6
CARDEN SCHOOL OF ALMADEN S VLY	1921 CLARINDA WY, SJS, 95124, (408)879-1000	873 - G4
CAREY ELEM SCHOOL	2101 ALAMEDA DE LAS PULGAS, SMTO, 94403, (650)345-8205	749 - A4
CATHEDRAL SCHOOL FOR BOYS	1275 SACRAMENTO ST, SF, 94108, (415)771-6600	647 - J5
CHALLENGER ELEM SCHOOL	1185 HOLLENBECK AV, SUNV, 94087, (408)245-7170	832 - D3
CHALLENGER ELEM SCHOOL	1325 BOURET DR, SJS, 95118, (408)723-0111	874 - B3
CHALLENGER ELEM SCHOOL	5301 CURTIS ST, FRMT, 94538, (510)440-0424	773 - B1
CHALLENGER ELEM SCHOOL	880 WREN DR, SJS, 95125, (408)448-3010	854 - D6

FEATURE NAME	Address City, ZIP Code	PAGE-GRID
CHINESE CHRISTIAN ELEM SCHOOL	750 FARGO AV, SLN, 94579, (510)351-4957	691 - C6
CHRIST THE KING ELEM SCHOOL	195 BRANDON RD, PLHL, 94523, (510)685-1109	592 - A5
CHRISTIAN CENTER ELEM SCHOOL	1210 STONEMAN AV, PIT, 94565, (510)439-2552	574 - F5
CHRISTIAN COMMUNITY ACADEMY	1523 MCLAUGHLIN AV, SJS, 95122, (408)279-0846	834 - G7
CHRISTIAN COMMUNITY ELEM SCHOOL	39700 MISSION BLVD, FRMT, 94539, (510)651-5437	753 - E3
CHRISTIAN HERITAGE	36060 FREMONT BLVD, FRMT, 94536, (510)797-7938	752 - G2
CHRISTIAN LIFE SCHOOL	1370 S NOVATO BLVD, NVTO, 94947, (415)892-5713	526 - C6
CLARA MOHAMMED SCHOOL	1652 47TH AV, OAK, 94601, (510)436-7755	670 - D1
COMMUNITY CHRISTIAN ELEM SCHOOL	562 LEWELLING BLVD, SLN, 94579, (510)351-3630	691 - C6
CONVENT OF THE SACRED HEART	2200 BROADWAY ST, SF, 94115, (415)563-2900	647 - G5
CORNERSTONE ACADEMY BAPTIST	801 SILVER AV, SF, 94134, (415)587-7256	667 - H7
CORPUS CHRISTI ELEM SCHOOL	1 ESTATES DR, PDMT, 94611, (510)530-4056	650 - D3
CORPUS CHRISTI ELEM SCHOOL	75 FRANCIS ST, SF, 94112, (415)587-7014	667 - G7
CROSSROADS CHRISTIAN ELEM SCHOOL	20600 JOHN DR, AlaC, 94546, (510)537-4277	691 - H5
DELMAR BURKE, KATHERINE ELEM	7070 CALIFORNIA ST, SF, 94121, (415)751-0177	647 - A6
DISCOVERY CENTER ELEM SCHOOL	65 OCEAN AV, SF, 94112, (415)333-6609	667 - F7
DORRIS-EATON ELEM SCHOOL	1847 NEWELL AV, CCCo, 94595, (510)933-5225	612 - C7
EAST BAY SIERRA ELEM SCHOOL	960 AVIS DR, ELCR, 94530, (510)527-4714	609 - D2
EAST BAY WALDORF ELEM SCHOOL	1275 61ST ST, EMVL, 94608, (510)547-1842	629 - E5
ECOLE BILINGUE	1009 HEINZ AV, BERK, 94804, (510)549-3867	629 - E4
EL SOBRANTE CHRISTIAN ELEM SCHOOL	5100 ARGYLE RD, CCCo, 94803, (510)223-2242	569 - E7
EPIPHANY ELEM SCHOOL	600 ITALY AV, SF, 94112, (415)337-4030	687 - G1
FIRST BAPTIST CHURCH SCHOOL	42 WALLER ST, SF, 94102, (415)863-1691	667 - H1
FIVE WOUNDS ELEM SCHOOL	1390 FIVE WOUNDS LN, SJS, 95116, (408)293-0425	834 - E4
FREMONT CHRISTIAN ELEM SCHOOL	4760 THORNTON AV, FRMT, 94536, (510)792-4700	752 - G4
FRENCH-AMERICAN INTL ELEM	220 BUCHANAN ST, SF, 94102, (415)626-8564	667 - H1
GOLDEN GATE ACADEMY ELEM SCHOOL	3800 MOUNTAIN BLVD, OAK, 94619, (510)531-0110	650 - G4
GOOD SHEPHERD ELEM SCHOOL	909 OCEANA BLVD, PCFA, 94044, (650)359-4544	706 - J4
GOOD SHEPHERD LUTHERAN ELEM	166 W HARDER RD, HAY, 94544, (510)783-5234	711 - J5
GRANADA ISLAMIC ELEM SCHOOL	3003 SCOTT BLVD, SCL, 95054, (408)980-1167	813 - D7
HAMLIN	2129 VALLEJO ST, SF, 94115, (415)922-0600	647 - G5
HARKER ACADEMY	500 SARATOGA AV, SJS, 95117, (408)249-2510	853 - B1
HEAD-ROYCE ELEM SCHOOL	4315 LINCOLN AV, OAK, 94602, (510)531-1300	650 - E3
HEBREW ACADEMY OF SAN FRANCISCO	645 14TH AV, SF, 94118, (415)752-7490	647 - C7
HERITAGE CHRISTIAN ACADEMY	1305 MIDDLEFIELD RD, RDWC, 94063, (650)366-3842	770 - B6
HIGHLANDS CHRISTIAN ELEM SCHOOL	1900 MONTEREY DR, SBRN, 94066, (650)873-4090	707 - E7
HILLBROOK SCHOOL	16000 MARCHMONT DR, LGTS, 95032, (408)356-6116	873 - D7
HILLTOP CHRISTIAN ELEM SCHOOL	210 LOCUST DR, VAL, 94591, (707)643-1726	530 - F4
HILLTOP CHRISTIAN ELEM SCHOOL	320 WORRELL RD, ANT, 94509, (510)778-0214	575 - E7
HIS ACADEMY	28398 CUBBERLEY CT, HAY, 94545, (510)735-3577	731 - H2
HOLY ANGELS ELEM SCHOOL	20 REINER ST, SMCo, 94014, (650)755-0220	687 - C5
HOLY FAMILY ELEM SCHOOL	4848 PEARL AV, SJS, 95136, (408)978-1355	874 - E2
HOLY NAME ELEM SCHOOL	1560 40TH AV, SF, 94122, (415)731-4077	666 - J2
HOLY ROSARY ELEM SCHOOL	25 E 15TH ST, ANT, 94509, (510)757-1270	575 - D5
HOLY SPIRIT ELEM SCHOOL	3930 PARISH AV, FRMT, 94536, (510)793-3553	752 - H3
HOPE SCHOOL OF EXCELLENCE ELEM	8411 MACARTHUR BLVD, OAK, 94605, (510)569-5888	670 - J3
IMMACULATE CONCEPTION ELEM	1550 TREAT AV, SF, 94110, (415)824-6860	667 - J4
IMMACULATE HEART OF MARY	1000 ALAMEDA DE LAS PULGAS, BLMT, 94002, (650)593-4265	769 - C2
KEYS SCHOOL	2890 MIDDLEFIELD RD, PA, 94306, (650)328-1711	791 - C6
KINGS VALLEY CHRISTIAN SCHOOL	4255 CLAYTON RD, CNCD, 94521, (510)687-2020	593 - A3
KITTREDGE SCHOOL	2355 LAKE ST, SF, 94121, (415)750-8390	647 - A6
KROUZIAN-ZEKARIAN OF ST. GREGORY	825 BROTHERHOOD WY, SF, 94132, (415)586-8686	687 - B2
LIBERTY BAPTIST ELEM SCHOOL	2790 S KING RD, SJS, 95122, (408)274-5613	855 - A2
LOS ALTOS CHRISTIAN ELEM SCHOOL	625 MAGDALENA AV, LALT, 94024, (650)948-3738	831 - F2
LOS GATOS ACADEMY	220 BELGATOS RD, LGTS, 95032, (408)358-1046	873 - H6
LOS GATOS CHRISTIAN SCHOOL	16845 HICKS RD, LGTS, 95032, (408)268-1502	873 - J7
LYCEE FRANCAIS INTL ELEM SCHOOL	330 GOLDEN HIND PASSAGE, CMAD, 94925, (415)924-4202	606 - J1
LYCEE FRANCAIS INTL-LAPEROUSE	3301 BALBOA ST, SF, 94121, (415)668-1833	646 - J7
MARIN COUNTRY DAY ELEM SCHOOL	5221 PARADISE DR, CMAD, 94925, (415)927-5900	607 - A1
MARIN HORIZON SCHOOL	305 MONTFORD AV, MrnC, 94941, (415)388-8408	606 - D4
MARIN PRIMARY ELEM SCHOOL	20 MAGNOLIA AV, LKSP, 94939, (415)924-2608	586 - F7
MARIN WALDORF ELEM SCHOOL	755 IDYLBERRY RD, MrnC, 94903, (415)479-8190	546 - B7
MATER DOLOROSA ELEM SCHOOL	1040 MILLER AV, SSF, 94080, (650)588-8175	707 - G2
MID-PENINSULA JEWISH COMM SCH	655 ARASTRADERO RD, PA, 94306, (650)424-8482	811 - C3
MILPITAS CHRISTIAN ELEM SCHOOL	3435 BIRCHWOOD LN, SJS, 95132, (408)945-6530	814 - E2
MILPITAS FOOTHILL SEVENTH-DAY-ADVNT	1991 LANDESS AV, MPS, 95035, (408)263-2568	814 - E2
MIRAMONTE ELEM SCHOOL	1175 ALTAMEAD DR, LALT, 94024, (650)967-2783	831 - H2
MISSION DOLORES ELEM SCHOOL	3371 16TH ST, SF, 94103, (415)861-7673	667 - H2
MONARCH CHRISTIAN ELEM SCHOOL	1196 LIME DR, SUNV, 94087, (408)745-7386	832 - B3
MONTESSORI CHILDRENS ELEM SCHOOL	1836 B ST, HAY, 94541, (510)537-8155	692 - B7
MONTESSORI SCHOOL OF FREMONT	155 WASHINGTON BLVD, FRMT, 94539, (510)490-0919	753 - H7
MONTESSORI SCHOOL OF SAN LEANDRO	16292 FOOTHILL BLVD, AlaC, 94578, (510)278-1115	691 - F4
MOST HOLY TRINITY ELEM SCHOOL	1940 CUNNINGHAM AV, SJS, 95122, (408)729-3431	834 - J7
MOUNT TAMALPAIS	100 HARVARD AV, MrnC, 94941, (415)383-9434	606 - F5
MULBERRY ELEM SCHOOL	1980 E HAMILTON AV, CMBL, 95125, (408)377-1595	853 - H5
NATIVITY ELEM SCHOOL	1250 LAUREL ST, MLPK, 94025, (650)325-7304	790 - F3
NEW COVENANT SCHOOL	220 BLAKE AV, SCL, 95051, (408)249-3993	833 - A7
NEW HORIZONS SCHOOL	2550 PERALTA BLVD, FRMT, 94536, (501)791-5683	753 - A3
NOMURA ELEM SCHOOL	1615 CARLSON BLVD, RCH, 94804, (510)528-1727	609 - B3
NORTH BAY CHRISTIAN ACADEMY	1055 LAS OVEJAS, SRFL, 94903, (415)492-0550	566 - B1
NORTHERN LIGHT ELEM SCHOOL	4500 REDWOOD RD, OAK, 94619, (510)530-9366	650 - H5
NORTH HILLS CHRISTIAN ELEM SCHOOL	200 ADMIRAL CALLAGHAN LN, VAL, 94591, (707)644-5284	530 - D3
NOTRE DAME	1500 RALSTON AV, BLMT, 94002, (650)591-2209	769 - E1
NOTRE DAME VICTORIES ELEM SCHOOL	659 PINE ST, SF, 94108, (415)421-0069	648 - A5
NUEVA CTR FOR LEARNING	6565 SKYLINE BLVD, HIL, 94010, (650)348-2272	748 - C2
OLD ORCHARD ELEM SCHOOL	400 W CAMPBELL AV, CMBL, 95008, (408)378-5935	853 - C6
OUR LADY OF ANGELS ELEM SCHOOL	1328 CABRILLO AV, BURL, 94010, (650)343-9200	728 - D6
OUR LADY OF GRACE ELEM SCHOOL	19920 ANITA AV, AlaC, 94546, (510)581-3155	691 - J4
OUR LADY OF LORETTO ELEM SCHOOL	1811 VIRGINIA AV, NVTO, 94945, (415)892-8621	526 - A3
OUR LADY OF LOURDES ELEM SCHOOL	515 BODEN WY, OAK, 94610, (510)444-8014	649 - J3
OUR LADY OF MERCY ELEM SCHOOL	7 ELMWOOD DR, DALY, 94015, (650)756-3395	687 - A4
OUR LADY OF MOUNT CARMEL	301 GRAND ST, RDWC, 94062, (650)366-6127	769 - J6
OUR LADY OF PERPETUAL HELP	80 WELLINGTON AV, DALY, 94014, (650)755-4438	687 - D3
OUR LADY OF THE ROSARY ELEM	678 B ST, UNC, 94587, (510)471-3765	732 - F4
OUR LADY OF THE VISITACION	785 SUNNYDALE AV, SF, 94134, (415)239-7840	687 - J2
OUR SAVIOR LUTHERAN ELEM SCHOOL	1385 S LIVERMORE AV, LVMR, 94550, (510)455-5437	715 - J2
PALMER SCHOOL FOR BOYS & GIRLS	2740 JONES RD, CCCo, 94596, (510)934-4888	612 - C2
PARK DAY ELEM SCHOOL	370 43RD ST, OAK, 94609, (510)653-0317	629 - H7
PATTEN ACADEMY OF CHRISTIAN-EDUCATION	2433 COOLIDGE AV, OAK, 94601, (510)533-8300	650 - C6
PENINSULA FRENCH AMERICAN	870 N CALIFORNIA AV, PA, 94303, (650)328-2338	791 - C5
PENINSULA SCHOOL, LTD	920 PENINSULA WY, SMCo, 94025, (650)325-1584	790 - H1
PETER PAN ACADEMY ELEM SCHOOL	3171 MECARTNEY RD, ALA, 94502, (510)523-4080	670 - A6
PHILLIPS BROOKS ELEM SCHOOL	2245 AVY AV, MLPK, 94025, (650)854-4545	790 - D7
PINEWOOD PVT SCHOOL OF LOS ALTOS	327 FREMONT AV, LALT, 94024, (650)948-5438	831 - F1
PINEWOOD-LOWER CAMPUS	477 FREMONT AV, LALT, 94024, (650)962-9076	831 - F2
PLANTATION CHRISTIAN ELEM SCHOOL	209 HERLONG AV, SJS, 95123, (408)972-8211	875 - B5
PLEASANT HILL JUNIOR ACADEMY	796 GRAYSON RD, PLHL, 94523, (510)934-9261	591 - J6
PRESIDIO HILL	3839 WASHINGTON ST, SF, 94118, (415)751-9318	647 - E5
PRIMARY PLUS	3500 AMBER DR, SJS, 95117, (408)248-2464	853 - D3
PRINCE OF PEACE LUTHERAN	38451 FREMONT BLVD, FRMT, 94536, (510)797-8186	752 - J4
PROSPECT ELEM SCHOOL	2060 TAPSCOTT AV, ELCR, 94530, (510)232-4123	589 - B7
QUARRY LANE ELEM SCHOOL	3750 BOULDER ST, PLE, 94566, (510)846-9400	714 - F2
QUEEN OF ALL SAINTS ELEM SCHOOL	2391 GRANT ST, CNCD, 94520, (510)685-8700	592 - F1
QUEEN OF APOSTLES ELEM SCHOOL	4950 MITTY WY, SJS, 95129, (408)252-3659	852 - J2
RAINBOW BRIDGE CENTER ELEM SCHOOL	1500 YOSEMITE DR, MPS, 95035, (408)945-9090	794 - D7
RAINBOW MONTESSORI ELEM SCHOOL	790 E DUANE AV, SUNV, 94086, (408)738-3261	812 - G6
REDEEMER LUTHERAN ELEM SCHOOL	468 GRAND ST, RDWC, 94062, (650)366-3466	769 - J6
REDWOOD CHRISTIAN ELEM SCHOOL	19300 REDWOOD RD, AlaC, 94546, (510)537-4288	692 - A4
REDWOOD DAY SCHOOL	3245 SHEFFIELD AV, OAK, 94602, (510)534-0800	650 - C5
REIGNIERD ELEM SCHOOL	380 CONTRA COSTA ST, VAL, 94590, (707)644-0447	530 - B5
RESURRECTION ELEM SCHOOL	1395 HOLLENBECK, SUNV, 94087, (408)245-4571	832 - D4
ROGER WILLIAMS	600 GRAND AV, SSF, 94080, (650)877-3995	707 - H2
SACRED HEART ELEM SCHOOL	13718 SARATOGA AV, SAR, 95070, (408)867-9241	872 - F1
SACRED HEART GRAMMAR ELEM SCHOOL	735 FELL ST, SF, 94117, (415)621-8035	647 - G7
SAINT AGNES ELEM SCHOOL	3886 CHESTNUT AV, CNCD, 94519, (510)689-3990	593 - A2
SAINT ANDREW MISSIONARY ELEM	2624 WEST ST, OAK, 94612, (510)465-8023	649 - G2
SAINT ANDREWS PRIVATE	13601 SARATOGA AV, SAR, 95070, (408)867-3785	872 - F1
SAINT ANNE ELEM SCHOOL	1320 14TH AV, SF, 94122, (415)664-7977	667 - C2
SAINT ANSELM ELEM SCHOOL	40 BELLE AV, SANS, 94960, (415)454-8667	586 - C1
SAINT ANTHONY ELEM SCHOOL	1500 E 15TH ST, OAK, 94606, (510)534-3334	650 - A6
SAINT ANTHONY ELEM SCHOOL	299 PRECITA AV, SF, 94110, (415)648-2008	667 - J4
SAINT APOLLINARIS ELEM SCHOOL	3700 LASSEN ST, VAL, 94591, (707)224-6525	530 - D4
SAINT AUGUSTINE ELEM SCHOOL	410 ALCATRAZ AV, OAK, 94618, (510)652-6727	629 - J4
SAINT BARNABAS ELEM SCHOOL	1400 6TH ST, ALA, 94501, (510)521-0595	669 - F1
SAINT BASIL CATHOLIC SCHOOL	1230 NEBRASKA ST, VAL, 94590, (707)642-7629	530 - C3
SAINT BEDES ELEM SCHOOL	26910 PATRICK AV, HAY, 94544, (510)782-3444	711 - J6
SAINT BERNARD ELEM SCHOOL	1630 62ND AV, OAK, 94621, (510)632-6323	670 - F2
SAINT BRENDAN ELEM SCHOOL	234 ULLOA ST, SF, 94127, (415)731-2665	667 - D5
SAINT BRIGID ELEM SCHOOL	2250 FRANKLIN ST, SF, 94109, (415)673-4523	647 - H5
SAINT CATHERINE OF SIENA	1300 BAYSWATER AV, BURL, 94010, (650)344-7176	728 - G7
SAINT CATHERINE OF SIENA	SC 604 MELLUS ST, MRTZ, 94553, (510)228-4140	571 - D3
SAINT CATHERINE OF SIENA ELEM	3460 TENNESSEE ST, VAL, 94591, (707)643-6691	530 - F4
SAINT CECILIA ELEM SCHOOL	660 VICENTE ST, SF, 94116, (415)731-8400	667 - B5
ST CHARLES ELEM SCHOOL	850 TAMARACK AV, SCAR, 94070, (650)593-1629	769 - F4
SAINT CHARLES BORROMEO SCHOOL	3250 18TH ST, SF, 94110, (415)861-7652	667 - J2
SAINT CHRISTOPHER ELEM SCHOOL	2278 BOOKSIN AV, SJS, 95125, (408)723-7223	854 - A6
SAINT CLARE ELEM SCHOOL	725 WASHINGTON ST, SCL, 95050, (408)246-6797	833 - E4
SAINT CLEMENT ELEM SCHOOL	790 CALHOUN ST, HAY, 94544, (510)538-5885	712 - C5
SAINT COLUMBA ELEM SCHOOL	1086 ALCATRAZ AV, OAK, 94608, (510)652-2956	629 - F5
SAINT CORNELIUS ELEM SCHOOL	201 28TH ST, RCH, 94804, (510)232-3326	588 - J7
SAINT CYPRIAN ELEM SCHOOL	195 LEOTA AV, SUNV, 94086, (408)738-3444	812 - C7
SAINT CYRIL ELEM SCHOOL	3200 62ND AV, OAK, 94605, (510)638-9445	670 - G1
SAINT DAVIDS ELEM SCHOOL	871 SONOMA ST, RCH, 94805, (510)232-2283	589 - B5
SAINT DOMINIC ELEM SCHOOL	2445 PINE ST, SF, 94115, (415)346-9500	647 - G5
SAINT DOMINICS CATHOLIC SCHOOL	935 5TH ST, BEN, 94510, (707)745-1266	551 - C5
SAINT DUNSTANS ELEM SCHOOL	1150 MAGNOLIA AV, MLBR, 94030, (650)697-8119	728 - A3
SAINT EDWARDS ELEM SCHOOL	5788 THORNTON AV, NWK, 94560, (510)793-7242	752 - F6
SAINT ELIZABETH ELEM SCHOOL	1516 33RD AV, OAK, 94601, (510)532-7392	650 - C7
SAINT ELIZABETHS ELEM SCHOOL	450 SOMERSET ST, SF, 94134, (415)468-3247	668 - A7
ST ELIZABETH SETON CATHOLIC COMM	1095 CHANNING AV, PA, 94301, (415)326-9004	791 - B4
SAINT EMYDIUS ELEM SCHOOL	301 DE MONTFORT AV, SF, 94112, (415)333-4877	667 - D7
SAINT FELICITAS ELEM SCHOOL	1650 MANOR BLVD, SLN, 94579, (510)357-2530	691 - A6
SAINT FINN BARR ELEM SCHOOL	419 HEARST AV, SF, 94112, (415)333-1800	667 - E6
SAINT FRANCIS CABRINI	15325 WOODWARD RD, SCIC, 95124, (408)377-6545	873 - F2
SAINT FRANCIS OF ASSISI SCHOOL	866 OAK GROVE RD, CNCD, 94518, (510)682-5414	592 - G6
SAINT GABRIEL ELEM SCHOOL	2550 41ST AV, SF, 94116, (415)566-0314	666 - J5
ST GREGORY ELEM SCHOOL	2701 HACIENDA ST, SMTO, 94403, (650)573-0111	749 - B5
ST HILARY ELEM SCHOOL	765 HILARY DR, TBRN, 94920, (415)435-2224	607 - C5
SAINT ISABELLAS PAROCHIAL	S 1 TRINITY WY, SRFL, 94903, (415)479-3727	566 - D3
SAINT ISIDORE ELEM SCHOOL	435 LA GONDA WY, DNVL, 94526, (510)837-2977	652 - J1
SAINT JAMES ELEM SCHOOL	321 FAIR OAKS ST, SF, 94110, (415)647-8972	667 - H4
SAINT JARLATH ELEM SCHOOL	2634 PLEASANT ST, OAK, 94602, (510)532-4387	650 - D5
SAINT JEROME ELEM SCHOOL	320 SAN CARLOS AV, ELCR, 94530, (510)525-9484	609 - E4
SAINT JOACHIMS ELEM SCHOOL	21250 HESPERIAN BLVD, HAY, 94541, (510)783-3177	711 - E2
SAINT JOHN ELEM SCHOOL	270 E LEWELLING BLVD, AlaC, 94580, (510)276-6632	691 - E6
SAINT JOHN ELEM SCHOOL	925 CHENERY ST, SF, 94131, (415)584-8383	667 - F6
SAINT JOHN THE BAPTIST	11156 SAN PABLO AV, ELCR, 94530, (510)234-2244	609 - C2
SAINT JOHN THE BAPTIST CATHOLIC	360 S ABEL ST, MPS, 95035, (408)262-8110	814 - A1
SAINT JOHN THE EVANGELIST	4056 MISSION ST, SF, 94112, (415)334-4646	667 - G6
SAINT JOHN VIANNEY PRIVATE	4601 HYLAND AV, SJS, 95127, (408)258-7677	834 - J1
ST JOSEPHS ELEM SCHOOL	50 EMILIE AV, ATN, 94027, (650)322-9931	790 - E4
SAINT JOSEPH ELEM SCHOOL	1910 SAN ANTONIO AV, ALA, 94501, (510)522-4457	669 - J2
SAINT JOSEPH ELEM SCHOOL	1961 PLUM ST, PIN, 94564, (510)724-0242	569 - E4
SAINT JOSEPH ELEM SCHOOL	220 10TH ST, SF, 94103, (415)431-1206	667 - J1
SAINT JOSEPH ELEM SCHOOL	43222 MISSION BLVD, FRMT, 94539, (510)656-6525	753 - J7
SAINT JOSEPH OF CUPERTINO	10120 N DE ANZA BLVD, CPTO, 95014, (650)252-6441	832 - E7
SAINT JOSEPH THE WORKER ELEM	2125 JEFFERSON AV, BERK, 94703, (510)845-6266	629 - F2
SAINT JOSEPHS ELEM SCHOOL	1120 MIRAMONTE AV, MTVW, 94040, (650)967-1839	811 - H6
SAINT JUSTIN ELEM SCHOOL	2655 HOMESTEAD RD, SCL, 95051, (408)248-1094	833 - B5
SAINT LAWRENCE ELEM SCHOOL	1971 SAINT LAWRENCE DR, SCL, 95051, (408)296-2260	832 - J3
SAINT LAWRENCE OTOOLE	3695 HIGH ST, OAK, 94619, (510)530-0266	650 - F6
SAINT LEANDER ELEM SCHOOL	451 DAVIS ST, SLN, 94577, (510)351-4144	691 - A1
SAINT LEO ELEM SCHOOL	4238 HOWE ST, OAK, 94611, (510)654-7828	629 - J7
SAINT LEO THE GREAT ELEM SCHOOL	1051 W SAN FERNANDO ST, SJS, 95126, (408)293-4846	833 - J7
SAINT LEONARD ELEM SCHOOL	3635 ST SAINT LEONARDS WY, FRMT, 94538, (510)657-1674	753 - C6
SAINT LOUIS BERTRAND ELEM SCHOOL	1445 101ST AV, OAK, 94603, (510)568-1067	670 - J5
SAINT LUCY ELEM SCHOOL	76 E KENNEDY AV, CMBL, 95008, (408)378-7454	853 - E6
SAINT MARKS ELEM SCHOOL	39 TRELLIS DR, SRFL, 94903, (415)472-8000	566 - D3
SAINT MARTIN DE PORRES SCHOOL	675 41ST ST, OAK, 94609, (510)652-2220	629 - G7
SAINT MARTIN ELEM SCHOOL	597 CENTRAL AV, SUNV, 94086, (408)736-5534	832 - E1
SAINT MARTIN OF TOURS	300 OCONNOR DR, SJS, 95128, (408)287-3630	833 - F7

FEATURE NAME	Address City, ZIP Code	PAGE-GRID
SAINT MARY CHINESE DAY ELEM	910 BROADWAY ST, SF, 94133, (415)929-4690	647 - J4
SAINT MARYS ELEM SCHOOL	1158 BONT LN, WLCK, 94596, (510)935-5054	612 - B6
SAINT MARYS ELEM SCHOOL	30 LYNDON AV, LGTS, 95030, (408)354-3944	873 - A7
ST MATTHEWS CATHOLIC ELEM SCHOOL	900 S EL CAMINO REAL, SMTO, 94402, (650)343-1373	749 - A2
SAINT MATTHEWS EPISCOPAL	16 BALDWIN AV, SMTO, 94401, (650)342-5436	748 - J1
ST MATTHIAS SCHOOL OF RELIGION	1685 CORDILLERAS RD, RDWC, 94062, (650)366-7085	769 - G7
SAINT MICHAELS ELEM SCHOOL	372 MAPLE ST, LVMR, 94550, (510)447-1888	715 - H1
SAINT MONICA ELEM SCHOOL	5920 GEARY BLVD, SF, 94121, (415)751-9564	647 - B6
SAINT NICHOLAS ELEM SCHOOL	12816 S EL MONTE AV, LAH, 94024, (650)941-4056	831 - E2
SAINT PASCHAL BAYLON ELEM SCHOOL	3710 DORISA AV, OAK, 94605, (510)635-7922	671 - B4
SAINT PATRICK ELEM SCHOOL	120 KING ST, LKSP, 94939, (415)924-0501	586 - E6
SAINT PATRICK ELEM SCHOOL	51 N 9TH ST, SJS, 95113, (408)283-5858	834 - C5
SAINT PATRICKS ELEM SCHOOL	1630 10TH ST, OAK, 94607, (510)832-1757	649 - D3
SAINT PATRICKS ELEM SCHOOL	907 7TH ST, CCCo, 94572, (510)799-2506	569 - J1
SAINT PAUL ELEM SCHOOL	180 FAIR OAKS ST, SF, 94110, (415)648-2055	667 - H3
SAINT PAUL ELEM SCHOOL	1825 CHURCH LN, SPAB, 94806, (510)233-3080	588 - J3
ST PAUL OF THE SHIPWRECK ACADEMY	1060 KEY AV, SF, 94124, (415)467-1798	688 - B1
SAINT PAULS ELEM SCHOOL	116 MONTECITO AV, OAK, 94610, (510)287-9600	649 - H3
SAINT PERPETUA ELEM SCHOOL	3445 HAMLIN RD, LFYT, 94549, (510)284-1640	611 - F7
SAINT PETER ELEM SCHOOL	1266 FLORIDA ST, SF, 94110, (415)647-8662	667 - J4
SAINT PETER MARTYR ELEM SCHOOL	425 W 4TH ST, PIT, 94565, (510)439-1014	574 - D1
SAINT PHILIP ELEM SCHOOL	665 ELIZABETH ST, SF, 94114, (415)824-8467	667 - G3
SAINT PHILIP LUTHERAN SCHOOL	8850 DAVONA DR, DBLN, 94568, (510)829-3857	693 - G2
SAINT PHILIP NERI ELEM SCHOOL	1335 HIGH ST, ALA, 94501, (510)521-0787	670 - B3
ST PIUS ELEM SCHOOL	1100 WOODSIDE RD, RDWC, 94061, (650)368-8327	790 - B2
SAINT RAPHAELS ELEM SCHOOL	1100 5TH AV, SRFL, 94901, (415)454-4455	586 - F1
SAINT RAYMOND ELEM SCHOOL	11555 SHANNON AV, DBLN, 94568, (510)828-4064	693 - G3
SAINT RAYMOND ELEM SCHOOL	1211 ARBOR RD, MLPK, 94025, (650)322-2312	790 - F4
SAINT ROBERT ELEM SCHOOL	345 OAK AV, SBRN, 94066, (650)583-5065	727 - H1
SAINT SIMON ELEM SCHOOL	1840 GRANT RD, LALT, 94024, (650)968-9952	831 - J4
SAINT STEPHEN ELEM SCHOOL	401 EUCALYPTUS DR, SF, 94132, (415)664-8331	667 - B6
SAINT STEPHENS ELEM SCHOOL	500 SHAWNEE LN, SJS, 95123, (408)365-2927	874 - H5
SAINT THERESA ELEM SCHOOL	4850 CLAREWOOD DR, OAK, 94618, (510)547-3146	630 - B6
SAINT THOMAS MORE ELEM SCHOOL	50 THOMAS MORE WY, SF, 94132, (650)377-0100	687 - C2
SAINT THOMAS THE APOSTLE	3801 BALBOA ST, SF, 94121, (415)221-2711	646 - J7
SAINT TIMOTHY ELEM SCHOOL	1515 DOLAN AV, SMTO, 94401, (650)342-6567	729 - B7
SAINT TIMOTHY ELEM SCHOOL	5100 CAMDEN AV, SJS, 95118, (408)265-0244	873 - J4
SAINT VERONICA ELEM SCHOOL	434 ALIDA WY, SSF, 94080, (650)589-3909	707 - G4
SAINT VICTOR ELEM SCHOOL	3150 SIERRA RD, SJS, 95132, (408)251-1740	814 - G5
SAINT VINCENT DE PAUL ELEM SCHOOL	2350 GREEN ST, SF, 94123, (415)346-5505	647 - G4
SAINT VINCENT FERRER	420 FLORIDA ST, VAL, 94590, (707)642-4311	529 - J4
SAINTS PETER & PAUL	600 FIBERT ST, SF, 94133, (415)421-5219	648 - A4
SAN FRANCISCO CHRISTIAN	25 WHITTIER ST, SF, 94112, (415)586-1117	687 - E2
SAN FRANCISCO DAY	350 MASONIC AV, SF, 94115, (415)931-2422	647 - F7
SAN FRANCISCO JUNIOR ACADEMY	66 GENEVA AV, SF, 94112, (415)585-5550	687 - F1
SAN FRANCISCO MONTESSORI	300 GAVEN ST, SF, 94134, (415)239-5065	667 - J6
SAN FRANCISCO WALDORF ELEM SCHOOL	2938 WASHINGTON ST, SF, 94115, (415)931-2750	647 - F5
SAN JOSE CHRISTIAN	1300 SHEFFIELD AV, CMBL, 95008, (408)371-7741	853 - G5
SAN RAMON VALLEY CHRISTIAN-ACADEMY	220 W EL PINTADO RD, DNVL, 94526, (510)838-9622	653 - A2
SCHOOL OF THE MADELEINE ELEM	1225 MILVIA ST, BERK, 94709, (510)526-4744	609 - G7
SEVEN HILLS ELEM SCHOOL	975 N SAN CARLOS DR, CCCo, 94598, (510)933-0666	612 - E2
SF CHINESE PARENT COMMUNITY ELEM	843 STOCKTON ST, SF, 94108, (415)391-5564	648 - A5
SHELTONS PRIMARY EDUCATION ELEM-SCHOOL	3339 MARTIN LUTHER KING JR WY, BERK, 94703, (510)652-6132	629 - G5
SHERWOOD FOREST CHRISTIAN SCHOOL	5570 OLINDA RD, CCCo, 94803, (510)223-6079	589 - G3
SHILOH CHILDRENS CENTER ELEM	3295 SCHOOL ST, OAK, 94602, (510)526-4744	650 - E6
SOUTH PENINSULA HEBREW DAY	1030 ASTORIA DR, SUNV, 94087, (408)738-3060	832 - B4
SOUTHBAY CHRISTIAN ELEM SCHOOL	1134 MIRAMONTE AV, MTVW, 94040, (650)961-5781	811 - H6
SPRAINGS ACADEMY	89 MORAGA WY, ORIN, 94563, (510)253-1906	630 - H1
STAR OF THE SEA ELEM SCHOOL	360 9TH AV, SF, 94118, (415)221-8558	647 - C6
STIVERS ELEM SCHOOL	1000 PAS GRANDE, AlaC, 94580, (510)278-8356	711 - C1
STUART HALL FOR BOYS ELEM SCHOOL	2252 BROADWAY ST, SF, 94115, (415)563-2900	647 - G4
SUNSHINE CHRISTIAN ELEM SCHOOL	445 S MARY AV, SUNV, 94086, (408)736-3286	812 - C7
TABERNACLE BAPTIST ELEM SCHOOL	4380 CONCORD BLVD, CNCD, 94521, (510)685-9169	593 - C2
TEHIYAH DAY ELEM SCHOOL	2603 TASSAJARA AV, ELCR, 94530, (510)233-3013	589 - C6
THE ACADEMY ELEM SCHOOL	2722 BENVENUE AV, BERK, 94705, (510)549-0605	629 - J3
TOWN SCHOOL FOR BOYS ELEM SCHOOL	2750 JACKSON ST, SF, 94115, (415)921-3747	647 - F5
TRINITY EPISCOPAL ELEM SCHOOL	2650 SAND HILL RD, MLPK, 94025, (650)854-0288	810 - D1
VALLEY CHRISTIAN ELEM SCHOOL	10800 DUBLIN BLVD, DBLN, 94568, (510)828-4850	693 - E5
VALLEY CHRISTIAN SCHOOL	220 KENSINGTON WY, LGTS, 95032, (408)559-4400	873 - G5
VALLEY MONTESSORI	460 N LIVERMORE AV, LVMR, 94550, (510)455-8021	695 - G7
VISTA CHRISTIAN ELEM SCHOOL	2354 ANDRADE AV, RCH, 94804, (510)237-4981	588 - H5
WALDORF SCHOOL OF THE PENINSULA	401 ROSITA AV, LALT, 94024, (650)948-8433	831 - F1
WALNUT CREEK CHRISTIAN ACADEMY	2336 BUENA VISTA AV, WLCK, 94596, (510)935-1587	612 - B4
WAY OF TRUTH ELEM SCHOOL	1575 7TH ST, OAK, 94607, (510)835-7866	649 - F4
WEST PORTAL LUTHERAN ELEM SCHOOL	200 SLOAT BLVD, SF, 94132, (415)665-6330	667 - C6
WEST VALLEY ELEM SCHOOL	95 DOT AV, CMBL, 95008, (408)378-4327	853 - D6
WHITE PONY & MEHER ELEM SCHOOL	999 LELAND DR, LFYT, 94549, (510)938-4826	611 - J6
WINDRUSH ELEM SCHOOL	1800 ELM ST, ELCR, 94530, (510)970-7580	609 - C1
WOODLAND ELEM SCHOOL	360 LA CUESTA DR, SMCo, 94028, (650)854-9065	810 - E3
WOODLANDS CHRISTIAN ELEM SCHOOL	2721 LARKEY LN, WLCK, 94596, (510)945-6863	612 - A2
YAVNEH DAY ELEM SCHOOL	14855 OKA RD, LGTS, 95030, (408)358-3413	873 - C3
YGNACIO VALLEY CHRISTIAN SCHOOL	4977 CONCORD BLVD, CCCo, 94521, (510)798-3131	593 - E3
ZION LUTHERAN ELEM SCHOOL	495 9TH AV, SF, 94118, (415)221-7500	647 - C7
ZION LUTHERAN ELEM SCHOOL	5201 PARK BLVD, PDMT, 94611, (510)530-7909	650 - D2

SCHOOLS - PRIVATE HIGH

FEATURE NAME	Address City, ZIP Code	PAGE-GRID
AMERICAN HERITAGE CHRISTIAN HS	425 GRESEL ST, HAY, 94544, (510)471-1010	732 - E2
ANTIOCH CHRISTIAN TUTORIAL HS	640 E TREGALLAS RD, ANT, 94509, (510)757-1837	575 - F6
ARCHBISHOP MITTY HIGH SCHOOL	5000 MITTY WY, SJS, 95129, (408)252-6610	852 - J2
ATHENIAN HIGH SCHOOL	2100 MOUNT DIABLO SCENIC BLVD, CCCo, 94506, (510)837-5375	633 - F7
BEACON HIGH SCHOOL	2101 LIVINGSTON ST, OAK, 94606, (510)436-6462	650 - A7
BELLARMINE COLLEGE PREP	850 ELM ST, SJS, 95126, (408)294-9224	833 - H5
BEREAN CHRISTIAN HIGH SCHOOL	245 EL DIVISADERO AV, WLCK, 94598, (510)945-6464	612 - F3
BISHOP ODOWD HIGH SCHOOL	9500 STEARNS AV, OAK, 94605, (510)577-9100	671 - A4
BRANSON HIGH SCHOOL	39 FERNHILL AV, ROSS, 94957, (415)454-3612	586 - B2
BRIDGEMONT HIGH SCHOOL	501 CAMBRIDGE ST, SF, 94134, (415)333-7600	667 - J7
CALVARY CHRISTIAN ACADEMY	4892 SAN PABLO DAM RD, CCCo, 94803, (501)222-3828	589 - E3
CARONDELET HIGH SCHOOL	1133 WINTON DR, CNCD, 94518, (510)686-5353	592 - F7
CHINESE CHRISTIAN HIGH SCHOOL	750 FARGO AV, SLN, 94579, (510)351-4957	691 - C6
CHRISTIAN CENTER HIGH SCHOOL	1210 STONEMAN AV, PIT, 94565, (510)439-2552	574 - F5
CHRISTIAN COMMUNITY ACADEMY	1523 MCLAUGHLIN AV, SJS, 95122, (408)279-0846	834 - F7
CHRISTIAN HERITAGE ACADEMY	36060 FREMONT BLVD, FRMT, 94536, (510)797-7938	752 - G2
COLLEGE PREPARATORY HIGH SCHOOL	6100 BROADWAY, OAK, 94618, (510)652-0111	630 - A5
CONTRA COSTA CHRISTIAN HS	2721 LARKEY LN, WLCK, 94596, (510)934-4964	612 - A2
CONVENT OF THE SACRED HEART HS	2222 BROADWAY ST, SF, 94115, (415)292-3122	647 - G5
CRYSTAL SPRINGS AND UPLANDS	400 UPLANDS DR, HIL, 94010, (650)342-4175	748 - H2
DE LA SALLE HIGH SCHOOL	1130 WINTON DR, CNCD, 94518, (510)686-3310	592 - F7
DELTA CHRISTIAN HIGH SCHOOL	625 W 4TH ST, ANT, 94509, (510)778-7700	575 - C4
DREW COLLEGE PREPARATORY HS	2901 CALIFORNIA ST, SF, 94115, (415)346-4831	647 - F5
FREMONT CHRISTIAN HIGH SCHOOL	4760 THORNTON AV, FRMT, 94536, (510)792-4700	752 - G4
FRENCH-AMERICAN INTERNATIONAL HS	220 BUCHANAN ST, SF, 94102, (415)626-8564	667 - H1
GOLDEN GATE ACADEMY HIGH SCHOOL	3800 MOUNTAIN BLVD, OAK, 94619, (510)531-0110	650 - G4
HEAD-ROYCE HIGH SCHOOL	4315 LINCOLN AV, OAK, 94602, (510)531-1300	650 - E3
HIGHLANDS CHRISTIAN HIGH SCHOOL	1900 MONTEREY DR, SBRN, 94066, (650)873-4090	707 - E7
HIS ACADEMY HIGH SCHOOL	28398 CUBBERLEY CT, HAY, 94545, (510)735-3577	731 - H2
HOLY NAMES HIGH SCHOOL	4660 HARBORD DR, OAK, 94618, (510)450-1110	630 - B6
IMMACULATE CONCEPTION ACADEMY	3625 24TH ST, SF, 94110, (415)824-2052	667 - H4
KINGS ACADEMY HIGH SCHOOL	562 N BRITTON AV, SUNV, 94086, (408)481-9900	812 - G6
LIBERTY BAPTIST HIGH SCHOOL	2790 S KING RD, SJS, 95122, (408)274-5613	855 - A2
LICK-WILMERDING HIGH SCHOOL	755 OCEAN AV, SF, 94112, (415)333-4021	667 - E7
LOS GATOS ACADEMY	220 BELGATOS RD, LGTS, 95032, (408)358-1046	873 - H6
LYCEE FRANCAIS INTL-LAPEROUSE	3301 BALBOA ST, SF, 94121, (415)668-1833	646 - J7
MARIN ACADEMY HIGH SCHOOL	1600 MISSION AV, SRFL, 94901, (415)453-4550	566 - F7
MARIN CATHOLIC HIGH SCHOOL	675 SIR FRANCIS DRAKE BLVD, MrnC, 94904, (415)461-8844	586 - E4
MAYBECK HIGH SCHOOL	2362 BANCROFT WY, BERK, 94704, (510)841-8489	629 - H2
MENLO HIGH SCHOOL	50 VALPARAISO AV, ATN, 94027, (650)688-3863	790 - F3
MERCY HIGH SCHOOL	2750 ADELINE DR, BURL, 94010, (650)343-3631	728 - C6
MERCY HIGH SCHOOL (GIRLS)	3250 19TH AV, SF, 94132, (415)334-0525	667 - B6
MID-PENINSULA EDUCATION CENTER	870 N CALIFORNIA AV, PA, 94303, (650)493-5910	791 - C5
MOREAU CATHOLIC HIGH SCHOOL	27170 MISSION BLVD, HAY, 94544, (510)582-5851	712 - C5
MOUNTAIN VIEW ACADEMY HIGH SCHOOL	360 S SHORELINE BLVD, MTVW, 94041, (650)967-2324	811 - H5
NORTH BAY ORINDA HIGH SCHOOL	19 ALTARINDA RD, ORIN, 94563, (510)254-7553	610 - H7
NORTH HILLS CHRISTIAN HIGH SCHOOL	200 ADMIRAL CALLAGHAN LN, VAL, 94591, (707)644-5284	530 - D3
NOTRE DAME HIGH SCHOOL	1540 RALSTON AV, BLMT, 94002, (650)595-1913	769 - D1
NOTRE DAME HIGH SCHOOL	596 S 2ND ST, SJS, 95112, (408)294-1113	834 - C7
PATTEN ACADEMY OF CHRISTIAN-EDUCATION	2433 COOLIDGE AV, OAK, 94601, (510)533-8300	650 - C6
PINEWOOD HIGH SCHOOL	26800 FREMONT RD, LAH, 94022, (650)941-1532	811 - B5
PLANTATION CHRISTIAN HIGH SCHOOL	209 HERLONG AV, SJS, 95123, (408)972-8211	875 - B5
PRESENTATION HIGH SCHOOL	2281 PLUMMER AV, SJS, 95125, (408)264-1664	854 - A6
REDWOOD CHRISTIAN JR & SR HS	1500 DAYTON AV, SLN, 94579, (510)352-8330	691 - A6
REIGNIERD HIGH SCHOOL	380 CONTRA COSTA ST, VAL, 94590, (707)644-0447	530 - B5
RIORDAN HIGH SCHOOL (BOYS)	175 PHELAN AV, SF, 94112, (415)586-8200	667 - E7
SACRED HEART CATHEDRAL PREP HS	1055 ELLIS ST, SF, 94109, (415)775-6626	647 - H6
SACRED HEART PREPARATORY	150 VALPARAISO AV, ATN, 94027, (650)322-1866	790 - E4
SAINT ANDREW MISSIONARY HS	2624 WEST ST, OAK, 94612, (510)465-8023	649 - G2
SAINT ELIZABETH HIGH SCHOOL	1530 34TH AV, OAK, 94601, (510)532-8947	670 - C1
SAINT FRANCIS HS OF MOUNTAIN VW	1885 MIRAMONTE AV, MTVW, 94040, (650)968-1213	831 - H1
SAINT IGNATIUS COLLEGE PREP HS	2001 37TH AV, SF, 94116, (415)731-7500	666 - J4
SAINT JOHN THE EVANGELIST HS	4056 MISSION ST, SF, 94112, (415)334-4646	667 - H6
SAINT JOSEPH NOTRE DAME HS	1011 CHESTNUT ST, ALA, 94501, (510)523-1526	669 - J2
SAINT LAWRENCE ACADEMY HS	2000 LAWRENCE CT, SCL, 95051, (408)296-3013	832 - J3
SAINT MARYS COLLEGE HIGH SCHOOL	ALBINA AV & HOPKINS ST, ALB, 94706, (510)526-9242	609 - F7
SAINT PATRICK HIGH SCHOOL	1500 BENICIA RD, VAL, 94591, (707)644-4425	530 - G7
SAINT PAUL HIGH SCHOOL	317 29TH ST, SF, 94131, (415)648-0505	667 - H4
SAINT ROSE ACADEMY	2475 PINE ST, SF, 94115, (415)921-3584	647 - G5
SALESIAN HIGH SCHOOL	2851 SALESIAN AV, RCH, 94806, (510)234-4433	588 - J4
SAN FRANCISCO UNIVERSITY HS	3065 JACKSON ST, SF, 94115, (415)346-8400	647 - F5
SERRA, JUNIPERO HIGH SCHOOL	451 W 20TH AV, SMTO, 94403, (650)345-8207	749 - A4
SHADY GROVE HIGH SCHOOL	17467 ALMOND RD, AlaC, 94546, (510)537-3088	691 - J2
SHILOH CHRISTIAN ACADEMY	3295 SCHOOL ST, OAK, 94602, (510)261-2002	650 - E6
STAR OF THE SEA ACADEMY	350 9TH AV, SF, 94118, (415)221-8558	647 - C6
URBAN HIGH SCHOOL	1563 PAGE ST, SF, 94117, (415)626-2919	667 - F1
VALLEY CHRISTIAN HIGH SCHOOL	10800 DUBLIN BLVD, DBLN, 94568, (510)828-4627	693 - E5
VALLEY CHRISTIAN HIGH SCHOOL	1570 BRANHAM LN, SJS, 95118, (408)377-5882	874 - A3
WOODSIDE PRIORY	302 PORTOLA RD, PTLV, 94028, (650)851-8221	810 - C7

SCHOOLS - PRIVATE JUNIOR HIGH

FEATURE NAME	Address City, ZIP Code	PAGE-GRID
VALLEY CHRISTIAN JR HS	1570 BRANHAM LN, SJS, 95118, (408)978-9830	874 - A3

SCHOOLS - PRIVATE MIDDLE

FEATURE NAME	Address City, ZIP Code	PAGE-GRID
ALMADEN COUNTRY MIDDLE SCHOOL	6835 TRINIDAD DR, SJS, 95120, (408)997-0424	894 - F1

SCHOOLS - PUBLIC ELEMENTARY

FEATURE NAME	Address City, ZIP Code	PAGE-GRID
ADDISON ELEM SCHOOL	650 ADDISON AV, PA, 94301, (650)322-5935	791 - A4
ALAMO ELEM SCHOOL	100 WILSON RD, CCCo, 94507, (510)938-0448	632 - F3
ALAMO ELEM SCHOOL	250 23RD AV, SF, 94121, (415)750-8456	647 - B6
ALEXANDER ROSE ELEM SCHOOL	250 ROSWELL DR, MPS, 95035, (408)495-5580	794 - D7
ALISAL ELEM SCHOOL	1454 SANTA RITA RD, PLE, 94566, (510)426-4200	714 - E2
ALLEN ELEM SCHOOL	5845 ALLEN AV, SJS, 95123, (408)935-6205	874 - F5
ALLEN, DECIMA M ELEM SCHOOL	875 ANGUS AV W, SBRN, 94066, (650)244-0165	707 - H7
ALLENDALE ELEM SCHOOL	3670 PENNIMAN AV, OAK, 94619, (510)532-6080	650 - E6
ALMADEN ELEM SCHOOL	1295 DENTWOOD DR, SJS, 95118, (408)535-6207	874 - C4
ALMOND AVENUE ELEM SCHOOL	1401 ALMOND AV, LVMR, 94550, (510)606-3350	716 - B1
ALMOND ELEM SCHOOL	550 ALMOND AV, LALT, 94022, (650)941-0470	811 - F6
ALTA VISTA ELEM SCHOOL	200 BLOSSOM VALLEY DR, LGTS, 95032, (408)356-6146	873 - E5
ALVARADO ELEM SCHOOL	31100 FREDI ST, UNC, 94587, (510)471-1039	732 - A5
ALVARADO ELEM SCHOOL	625 DOUGLASS ST, SF, 94114, (415)695-5695	667 - F3
ANDERSON, ALEX ELEM SCHOOL	5800 CALPINE DR, SJS, 95123, (408)226-3370	875 - B5
ANDERSON, LEROY ELEM SCHOOL	4000 RHODA DR, SJS, 95117, (408)243-6031	853 - B3
ARBUCKLE, CLYDE ELEM SCHOOL	1970 CINDERELLA LN, SJS, 95116, (408)259-2910	834 - H5
ARDENWOOD ELEM SCHOOL	33955 EMILIA LN, FRMT, 94555, (510)794-0392	752 - C1
ARGONAUT ELEM SCHOOL	13200 SHADOW MOUNTAIN DR, SAR, 95070, (408)867-4773	852 - E7
ARGONNE ELEM SCHOOL	3950 SACRAMENTO ST, SF, 94118, (415)750-8460	647 - D6
ARMSTRONG, NEIL A ELEM SCHOOL	2849 CALAIS DR, SRMN, 94583, (510)803-7440	673 - F6
ARROYO SECO ELEM SCHOOL	5280 IRENE WY, LVMR, 94550, (510)606-4700	696 - C7
ARTS ELEM SCHOOL	5263 BROADWAY TER, OAK, 94618, (510)658-4926	629 - J6
ARUNDEL ELEM SCHOOL	200 ARUNDEL RD, SCAR, 94070, (650)508-7311	769 - E3
ATHENOUR ELEM SCHOOL	5200 DENT AV, SJS, 95118, (408)265-8455	874 - A4
AUDUBON ELEM SCHOOL	841 GULL AV, FCTY, 94404, (650)312-7500	749 - H1
AYERS ELEM SCHOOL	5120 MYRTLE DR, CNCD, 94521, (510)682-7686	593 - E3
AZEVADA, JOSEPH ELEM SCHOOL	39450 ROYAL PALM DR, FRMT, 94538, (510)657-3900	752 - J7
BACHRODT, WALTER L ELEM SCHOOL	102 SONORA AV, SJS, 95110, (408)535-6211	833 - J2

BAY AREA
INDEX

FEATURE NAME	Address City, ZIP Code	PAGE-GRID
BACICH, ANTHONY G ELEM SCHOOL	25 MCALLISTER AV, MrnC, 94904, (415)925-2220	586 - E4
BAGBY ELEM SCHOOL	1840 HARRIS AV, SJS, 95124, (408)377-3882	853 - H7
BAHIA VISTA ELEM SCHOOL	125 BAHIA WY, SRFL, 94901, (415)485-2415	587 - A2
BAKER, GUSSIE M ELEM SCHOOL	4845 BUCKNALL RD, SJS, 95130, (408)379-2101	853 - A6
BALDWIN, JOHN ELEM SCHOOL	741 BROOKSIDE DR, DNVL, 94526, (510)552-5670	653 - B4
BALDWIN, JULIA ELEM SCHOOL	280 MARTINVALE LN, SJS, 95119, (408)229-6302	895 - E1
BANCROFT ELEM SCHOOL	2200 PARRISH DR, WLCK, 94598, (510)933-3405	612 - F1
BAY ELEM SCHOOL	2001 BOCKMAN RD, AlaC, 94580, (510)481-4652	711 - B1
BAY FARM ELEM SCHOOL	200 AUGHINBAUGH WY, ALA, 94502, (510)748-4010	669 - J5
BAYSHORE ELEM SCHOOL	155 ORIENTE ST, DALY, 94014, (415)467-0442	687 - J3
BAYSIDE ELEM SCHOOL	630 NEVADA ST, SAUS, 94965, (415)332-1024	626 - J2
BAYVIEW ELEM SCHOOL	3001 16TH ST, SPAB, 94806, (510)237-0363	588 - H1
BAYWOOD ELEM SCHOOL	600 ALAMEDA DE LAS PULGAS, SMTO, 94402, (650)312-7511	748 - H3
BEACH ELEM SCHOOL	100 LAKE AV, PDMT, 94611, (510)420-3696	650 - A1
BEL AIR ELEM SCHOOL	663 CANAL RD, CCCo, 94565, (510)458-2606	573 - H3
BEL AIRE ELEM SCHOOL	277 KAREN WY, TBRN, 94920, (415)388-7100	607 - A3
BELLA VISTA ELEM SCHOOL	1025 E 28TH ST, OAK, 94606, (510)533-1056	650 - B4
BELLE AIR ELEM SCHOOL	450 THIRD AV, SBRN, 94066, (650)244-0154	708 - A7
BELLE HAVEN ELEM SCHOOL	415 IVY DR, MLPK, 94025, (650)329-2898	770 - J7
BELSHAW ELEM SCHOOL	2801 ROOSEVELT LN, ANT, 94509, (510)706-4140	575 - E6
BERKELEY ARTS MAGNET ELEM SCHOOL	1645 MILVIA ST, BERK, 94709, (510)644-6225	629 - G1
BEVERLY HILLS ELEM SCHOOL	1450 CORONEL AV, VAL, 94591, (707)644-5557	530 - D7
BIDWELL ELEM SCHOOL	800 GARY AV, ANT, 94509, (510)706-4116	575 - F6
BISHOP ELEM SCHOOL	450 N SUNNYVALE AV, SUNV, 94086, (408)522-8229	812 - F6
BLACKFORD ELEM SCHOOL	1970 WILLOW ST, SJS, 95125, (408)364-4221	853 - H4
BLACOW, JOHN ELEM SCHOOL	40404 SUNDALE DR, FRMT, 94538, (510)656-5121	753 - B7
BLOSSOM HILL ELEM SCHOOL	16400 BLOSSOM HILL RD, LGTS, 95032, (408)356-3141	873 - D6
BLOSSOM VALLEY ELEM SCHOOL	420 ALLEGAN CIR, SJS, 95123, (408)227-4260	875 - A6
BLUE HILLS ELEM SCHOOL	12300 DE SANKA AV, SAR, 95070, (408)257-9282	852 - E5
BOLLINGER CANYON ELEM SCHOOL	2300 TALAVERA DR, SRMN, 94583, (510)824-0390	673 - D3
BOOKSIN ELEM SCHOOL	1590 DRY CREEK RD, SJS, 95125, (408)535-6213	853 - J6
BOWERS ELEM SCHOOL	2755 BARKLEY AV, SCL, 95051, (408)985-0171	833 - B3
BOWMAN ELEM SCHOOL	520 JEFFERSON ST, HAY, 94544, (510)293-8567	712 - B5
BRACHER ELEM SCHOOL	2700 CHROMITE DR, SCL, 95051, (408)984-1682	833 - B2
BRALY ELEM SCHOOL	675 GAIL AV, SUNV, 94086, (408)983-1441	832 - F2
BRENTWOOD OAKS ELEM SCHOOL	2086 CLARKE AV, EPA, 94303, (650)329-2875	791 - C2
BREWER ISLAND	1151 POLYNESIA DR, FCTY, 94404, (650)312-7532	749 - G2
BRIARWOOD ELEM SCHOOL	1930 TOWNSEND AV, SCL, 95051, (408)554-6202	833 - A3
BRIER ELEM SCHOOL	39201 SUNDALE DR, FRMT, 94538, (510)657-5020	753 - A6
BRIONES, JUANA ELEM SCHOOL	4100 ORME AV, PA, 94306, (650)856-0877	811 - C3
BRISBANE ELEM SCHOOL	500 SAN BRUNO AV, BSBN, 94005, (650)467-0120	688 - A6
BRITTAN ACRES ELEM SCHOOL	2000 BELLE AV, SCAR, 94070, (650)593-7891	769 - G4
BROOKFIELD VILLAGE ELEM SCHOOL	401 JONES AV, OAK, 94603, (510)562-5437	670 - G6
BROOKSIDE ELEM SCHOOL	116 BUTTERFIELD RD, SANS, 94960, (415)453-2948	566 - A5
BROOKSIDE UPPER CAMPUS SCHOOL	46 GREEN VALLEY CT, MrnC, 94960, (415)454-7409	566 - B3
BROOKTREE ELEM SCHOOL	1781 OLIVETREE DR, SJS, 95131, (408)923-1910	814 - C5
BROOKVALE ELEM SCHOOL	3400 NICOLET AV, FRMT, 94536, (510)797-5940	752 - G2
BROWN, MARGARET PAULINE	305 EASTMOOR AV, DALY, 94015, (650)991-1243	687 - B6
BRYANT ELEM SCHOOL	1050 YORK ST, SF, 94110, (415)695-5780	668 - A3
BUBB, BENJAMIN ELEM SCHOOL	525 HANS AV, MTVW, 94040, (650)965-9697	811 - H7
BUENA VISTA ANNEX SCHOOL	2641 25TH ST, SF, 94110, (415)695-5875	668 - A4
BUENA VISTA ELEM SCHOOL	2355 SAN JUAN AV, WLCK, 94596, (510)944-6822	612 - B3
BULLIS-PURISSIMA ELEM SCHOOL	25890 FREMONT RD, LAH, 94022, (650)941-3880	811 - C6
BUNKER, JAMES L ELEM SCHOOL	6071 SMITH AV, NWK, 94560, (510)794-2020	752 - G7
BURBANK ELEM SCHOOL	353 B ST, HAY, 94541, (510)293-8568	711 - H2
BURBANK, LUTHER ELEM SCHOOL	3550 64TH AV, OAK, 94605, (510)632-3400	670 - H1
BURCKHALTER ELEM SCHOOL	3994 BURCKHALTER AV, OAK, 94605, (510)568-5802	670 - J1
BURI BURI ELEM SCHOOL	120 EL CAMPO DR, SSF, 94080, (650)877-8776	707 - E3
BURNETT, WILLIAM ELEM SCHOOL	400 FANYON ST, MPS, 95035, (408)945-2431	794 - C5
BURTON VALLEY ELEM SCHOOL	561 MERRIEWOOD DR, LFYT, 94549, (510)284-7046	631 - J3
CABELLO, REFUGIO M ELEM SCHOOL	4500 CABELLO ST, UNC, 94587, (510)489-4141	732 - A6
CABRILLO ELEM SCHOOL	36700 SAN PEDRO DR, FRMT, 94536, (510)792-3232	752 - F4
CABRILLO ELEM SCHOOL	601 CRESPI DR, PCFA, 94044, (650)355-0414	726 - J3
CABRILLO ELEM SCHOOL	735 24TH AV, SF, 94121, (415)750-8464	647 - B7
CADWALLADER ELEM SCHOOL	3799 CADWALLADER RD, SJS, 95121, (408)270-4950	855 - D3
CAMBRIDGE ELEM SCHOOL	1135 LACEY LN, CNCD, 94520, (510)686-4749	592 - E5
CAMINO PABLO ELEM SCHOOL	1111 CM PABLO, MRGA, 94556, (510)376-4435	651 - E2
CANYON ELEM SCHOOL	PINEHURST RD, CCCo, (510)376-4671	651 - A1
CAPRI ELEM SCHOOL	850 CHAPMAN AV, CMBL, 95008, (408)364-4260	873 - C2
CARLTON ELEM SCHOOL	2421 CARLTON AV, SJS, 95124, (408)356-1141	873 - E4
CARMICHAEL, BESSIE ELEM SCHOOL	55 SHERMAN ST, SF, 94103, (415)241-6294	648 - A7
CARSON, RACHEL ELEM SCHOOL	4245 MEG DR, SJS, 95136, (408)535-6287	874 - F1
CARVER, GEORGE WASHINGTON ELEM	1360 OAKDALE AV, SF, 94124, (415)330-1540	668 - C6
CASSELL, SYLVIA ELEM SCHOOL	1300 TALLAHASSEE DR, SJS, 95122, (408)259-2653	834 - J5
CASTLEMONT ELEM SCHOOL	3040 E PAYNE AV, SJS, 95128, (408)364-4233	853 - E4
CASTRO ELEM SCHOOL	7125 DONAL AV, ELCR, 94530, (510)234-6200	609 - C2
CASTRO VALLEY ELEM SCHOOL	20185 SAN MIGUEL AV, AlaC, 94546, (510)537-1919	691 - J5
CASTRO, MARIANO ELEM SCHOOL	505 ESCUELA AV, MTVW, 94041, (650)964-7555	811 - G4
CAVE, ELMER	770 TREGASKIS AV, VAL, 94591, (707)643-8853	530 - D4
CEDAR GROVE ELEM SCHOOL	2702 SUGAR PLUM DR, SJS, 95148, (408)270-4958	835 - D7
CEIA, PALMA ELEM SCHOOL	27679 MELBOURNE AV, HAY, 94545, (510)293-8512	711 - J7
CENTRAL ELEM SCHOOL	525 MIDDLE RD, BLMT, 94002, (650)637-4820	749 - E7
CHABOT ELEM SCHOOL	19104 LAKE CHABOT RD, AlaC, 94546, (510)537-2342	691 - H4
CHABOT, ANTHONY ELEM SCHOOL	6686 CHABOT RD, OAK, 94618, (510)655-3285	630 - A4
CHADBOURNE, JOSHUA ELEM SCHOOL	801 PLYMOUTH AV, FRMT, 94539, (510)656-5242	753 - F5
CHAVEZ, CESAR ELEM SCHOOL	2000 KAMMERER AV, SJS, 95116, (408)258-5078	834 - G4
CHAVEZ, CESAR ELEM SCHOOL	2450 RALMER AV, EPA, 94303, (650)329-6700	791 - A1
CHAVEZ, CESAR ELEM SCHOOL	825 SHOTWELL ST, SF, 94110, (415)695-5765	667 - J3
CHERRY CHASE ELEM SCHOOL	1138 HEATHERSTONE WY, SUNV, 94087, (408)522-8241	832 - B1
CHERRYLAND ELEM SCHOOL	585 WILLOW AV, AlaC, 94541, (510)293-8569	711 - G1
CHERRYWOOD ELEM SCHOOL	2550 GREENGATE DR, SJS, 95132, (408)923-1915	814 - E5
CHIN, JOHN YEHALL	350 BROADWAY ST, SF, 94133, (415)291-7946	648 - A4
CHINESE EDUCATION CENTER ELEM	657 MERCHANT ST, SF, 94111, (415)291-7918	648 - B5
CHRISTENSEN, ANDREW N ELEM SCHOOL	5757 HAGGIN OAKS AV, LVMR, 94550, (510)606-4702	696 - C2
CHRISTOPHER ELEM SCHOOL	565 COYOTE RD, SJS, 95111, (408)227-8550	855 - A7
CIPRIANI	2525 BUENA VISTA AV, BLMT, 94002, (415)637-4840	769 - B1
CLARENDON ELEM SCHOOL	500 CLARENDON AV, SF, 94131, (415)759-2796	667 - D3
CLEVELAND ELEM SCHOOL	455 ATHENS ST, SF, 94112, (415)469-4709	687 - G1
CLEVELAND ELEM SCHOOL	745 CLEVELAND ST, OAK, 94606, (510)451-5931	650 - A4
CLIFFORD ELEM SCHOOL	225 CLIFFORD AV, SMCo, 94062, (650)366-8011	769 - G6
COBB, WILLIAM L ELEM SCHOOL	2725 CALIFORNIA ST, SF, 94115, (415)749-3505	647 - F6
COLE ELEM SCHOOL	1011 UNION ST, OAK, 94607, (510)444-7733	649 - E3
COLEMAN ELEM SCHOOL	140 RAFAEL DR, SRFL, 94901, (415)485-2420	566 - G7
COLLINS ELEM SCHOOL	10401 VISTA DR, CPTO, 95014, (650)252-6002	832 - E7
COLLINS ELEM SCHOOL	1224 PINOLE VALLEY RD, PIN, 94564, (510)724-3086	569 - F5
COLMA ELEM SCHOOL	444 E MARKET ST, DALY, 94014, (650)991-1211	687 - D5
COLONIAL ACRES ELEM SCHOOL	17115 MEEKLAND AV, AlaC, 94541, (510)481-4613	691 - E7
COLUMBUS, CHRISTOPHER	60 CHRISTOPHER CT, DALY, 94015, (650)991-1206	707 - A1
COMMODORE SLOAT ELEM SCHOOL	50 DARIEN WY, SF, 94127, (415)759-2807	667 - C6
COMMODORE STOCKTON ELEM SCHOOL	950 CLAY ST, SF, 94108, (415)291-7921	648 - A5
COOPER ELEM SCHOOL	612 DEL MAR AV, VAL, 94589, (707)643-8681	530 - B1
CORNELL ELEM SCHOOL	920 TALBOT AV, ALB, 94706, (510)559-6510	609 - E6
CORONADO ELEM SCHOOL	2001 VIRGINIA AV, RCH, 94804, (510)233-7800	608 - H1
CORTE MADERA	4575 ALPINE RD, PTLV, 94028, (415)851-0409	830 - C1
CORVALLIS ELEM SCHOOL	14790 CORVALLIS ST, SLN, 94579, (510)481-4655	691 - B5
CORY, BENJAMIN ELEM SCHOOL	2280 KENWOOD AV, SJS, 95128, (408)535-6219	833 - E7
COSTANO ELEM SCHOOL	2695 FORDHAM ST, EPA, 94303, (650)329-2830	771 - B7
COUNTRY CLUB ELEM SCHOOL	7534 BLUE FOX WY, SRMN, 94583, (510)803-7430	693 - G1
COUNTRY LANE ELEM SCHOOL	5140 COUNTRY LN, SJS, 95129, (408)252-3444	852 - J4
COX, E MORRIS ELEM SCHOOL	9860 SUNNYSIDE ST, OAK, 94603, (510)569-6166	671 - A5
CRAGMONT EAST-KINDERGARTEN SCHOOL	830 REGAL RD, BERK, 94708, (510)644-6408	609 - H5
CRESTMOOR ELEM SCHOOL	2322 CRESTMOOR DR, SBRN, 94066, (650)244-0152	707 - F7
CROCE, LEO R ELEM SCHOOL	5650 SCENIC AV, LVMR, 94550, (510)606-4706	696 - C3
CROCKER HIGHLANDS ELEM SCHOOL	525 MIDCREST RD, OAK, 94610, (510)832-6458	650 - C3
CUMBERLAND ELEM SCHOOL	824 CUMBERLAND AV, SUNV, 94087, (408)522-8255	832 - C1
CUMMINS, NEIL ELEM SCHOOL	58 MOHAWK AV, CMAD, 94925, (415)927-6965	586 - G7
CURETON, HORACE ELEM SCHOOL	3720 E HILLS DR, SJS, 95127, (408)258-5066	835 - B2
CURTNER ELEM SCHOOL	275 REDWOOD AV, MPS, 95035, (650)945-2434	793 - J6
DARLING, ANNE ELEM SCHOOL	333 N 33RD ST, SJS, 95133, (408)535-6209	834 - E3
DAVES AV ELEM SCHOOL	17770 DAVES AV, MSER, 95030, (408)395-6311	873 - A5
DAVIDSON, JOHN ELEM SCHOOL	436 DEL SUR ST, VAL, 94591, (707)643-8474	530 - D7
DE AVILA, WILLIAM ELEM SCHOOL	1351 HAIGHT ST, SF, 94117, (415)241-6325	667 - F1
DE VARGAS ELEM SCHOOL	5050 MOORPARK AV, SJS, 95129, (408)252-0303	852 - J2
DECOTO ELEM SCHOOL	600 G ST, UNC, 94587, (510)471-2461	732 - G4
DEL REY ELEM SCHOOL	1510 VIA SONYA, AlaC, 94580, (510)481-4644	711 - C2
DEL REY ELEM SCHOOL	25 EL CAMINO MORAGA, ORIN, 94563, (510)376-4478	631 - B5
DEL ROBLE	5345 AVD ALMENDROS, SJS, 95123, (408)225-5675	874 - H3
DILWORTH ELEM SCHOOL	1101 STRAYER DR, SJS, 95129, (408)253-2850	852 - G3
DISNEY, WALT ELEM SCHOOL	3250 PINE VALLEY RD, SRMN, 94583, (510)803-7445	673 - G6
DIXIE ELEM SCHOOL	1175 IDYLBERRY RD, MrnC, 94903, (415)479-6200	546 - C7
DONALDSON WAY	430 DONALDSON WY, AMCN, 94589, (707)644-4486	509 - J2
DONLON ELEM SCHOOL	4150 DORMAN RD, PLE, 94588, (510)426-4220	694 - A7
DORSA, ANTHONY J ELEM SCHOOL	1290 BAL HARBOR WY, SJS, 95122, (408)259-2460	834 - H6
DOVE HILL ELEM SCHOOL	1460 COLT WY, SJS, 95121, (408)270-4964	855 - B4
DOVER ELEM SCHOOL	1871 21ST ST, SPAB, 94806, (510)237-1088	588 - H3
DOWNER, EDWARD M ELEM SCHOOL	1777 SANFORD AV, SPAB, 94806, (510)234-3851	588 - G4
DREW, CHARLES R ELEM SCHOOL	50 POMONA ST, SF, 94124, (415)330-1526	668 - E6
DUBLIN ELEM SCHOOL	7997 VOMAC RD, DBLN, 94568	693 - G3
DURHAM, J HALEY ELEM SCHOOL	40292 LESLIE ST, FRMT, 94538, (510)656-6360	753 - C5
DUVENECK ELEM SCHOOL	705 ALESTER AV, PA, 94303, (650)322-5946	791 - C4
EARHART, AMELIA ELEM SCHOOL	400 PACKET LANDING RD, ALA, 94502, (510)748-4003	670 - A5
EAST AVENUE ELEM SCHOOL	2424 EAST AV, AlaC, 94541, (510)293-8570	712 - C2
EASTERBROOK ELEM SCHOOL	4660 EASTUS DR, SJS, 95129, (408)253-3424	853 - A3
EDEN GARDENS ELEM SCHOOL	2184 THAYER AV, HAY, 94545, (510)293-8501	711 - F6
EDEN, LORIN A ELEM SCHOOL	27790 PORTSMOUTH AV, HAY, 94545, (510)293-8509	731 - G1
EDENDALE ELEM SCHOOL	16160 ASHLAND AV, AlaC, 94580, (510)481-4640	691 - E5
EDENVALE ELEM SCHOOL	285 AZUCAR AV, SJS, 95111, (408)227-7060	875 - C2
EDISON ELEM SCHOOL	2700 BUENA VISTA AV, ALA, 94501, (510)748-4002	670 - B2
EDISON ELEM SCHOOL	3531 22ND ST, SF, 94114, (415)695-5848	667 - H3
EDISON, THOMAS ELEM SCHOOL	1267 SOUTHGATE AV, DALY, 94015, (650)991-1250	687 - A7
EISENHOWER ELEM SCHOOL	277 RODONOVAN DR, SCL, 95051, (408)248-4313	832 - J7
EL CARMELO ELEM SCHOOL	3024 BRYANT ST, PA, 94306, (650)856-0960	791 - C7
EL CRYSTAL ELEM SCHOOL	201 BALBOA WY, SBRN, 94066, (650)244-0149	727 - J1
EL DORADO ELEM SCHOOL	70 DELTA ST, SF, 94134, (415)330-1537	688 - A1
EL MONTE ELEM SCHOOL	1400 DINA DR, CNCD, 94518, (510)685-3113	592 - J3
EL SOBRANTE ELEM SCHOOL	1060 MANOR RD, CCCo, 94803, (510)223-4500	569 - D7
ELDRIDGE ELEM SCHOOL	26825 ELDRIDGE AV, HAY, 94544, (510)293-8503	711 - J6
ELLERHORST ELEM SCHOOL	3501 PINOLE VALLEY RD, PIN, 94564, (510)758-1000	569 - G7
ELLIS ELEM SCHOOL	550 E OLIVE AV, SUNV, 94086, (408)522-8260	832 - F1
EMERSON ELEM SCHOOL	2800 FOREST AV, BERK, 94705, (510)644-6890	629 - J3
EMERSON ELEM SCHOOL	4803 LAWTON AV, OAK, 94609, (510)658-1818	629 - H7
EMPIRE GARDENS ELEM SCHOOL	1060 E EMPIRE ST, SJS, 95112, (408)535-6211	834 - D4
ENCINAL ELEM SCHOOL	195 ENCINAL AV, ATN, 94027, (650)326-5164	790 - F2
ERIKSON ELEM SCHOOL	4849 PEARL AV, SJS, 95136, (408)535-6036	874 - E2
ESCONDIDO ELEM SCHOOL	890 ESCONDIDO RD, SCIC, 94305, (650)856-1337	810 - J1
EVERGREEN ELEM SCHOOL	3010 FOWLER RD, SJS, 95135, (408)270-4966	855 - E3
FAIR OAKS ELEM SCHOOL	2400 LISA LN, PLHL, 94523, (510)685-4494	592 - D6
FAIR OAKS ELEM SCHOOL	2950 FAIR OAKS AV, SMCo, 94063, (650)368-3953	770 - D7
FAIRLANDS ELEM SCHOOL	4151 W LAS POSITAS, PLE, 94588, (510)462-4210	694 - E6
FAIRMEADOW ELEM SCHOOL	500 E MEADOW DR, PA, 94306, (650)856-0845	811 - E1
FAIRMONT ELEM SCHOOL	290 EDGEWOOD DR, PCFA, 94044, (650)359-5473	707 - A2
FAIRMONT ELEM SCHOOL	724 KEARNEY ST, ELCR, 94530, (510)525-5235	609 - D3
FAIRMOUNT ELEM SCHOOL	65 CHENERY ST, SF, 94131, (415)695-5669	667 - H5
FAIRVIEW ELEM SCHOOL	23515 MAUD AV, AlaC, 94541, (510)293-8571	692 - D7
FAMMATRE ELEM SCHOOL	2800 NEW JERSEY AV, SJS, 95124, (408)377-5480	873 - G1
FARIA ELEM SCHOOL	10155 BARBARA LN, CPTO, 95014, (408)252-0706	852 - D1
FARMAR, MARY	901 MILITARY W, BEN, 94510, (707)747-8350	551 - A3
FARNHAM ELEM SCHOOL	15711 WOODARD RD, SJS, 95124, (408)377-3321	873 - E2
FARRAGUT	301 FARRAGUT AV, VAL, 94590, (707)642-4409	529 - J3
FEDERAL TERRACE	415 DANIELS AV, VAL, 94590, (707)643-4501	529 - H2
FIESTA GARDENS INTERNATIONAL	1001 BERMUDA DR, SMTO, 94403, (650)312-7737	749 - C3
FLOOD, JAMES ELEM SCHOOL	320 SHERIDAN DR, MLPK, 94025, (650)329-2890	770 - H7
FLYNN, LEONARD ELEM SCHOOL	3125 CESAR CHAVEZ ST, SF, 94110, (415)695-5770	667 - J4
FOOTHILL ELEM SCHOOL	1200 JENSEN DR, PIT, 94565, (510)473-4300	574 - F6
FOOTHILL ELEM SCHOOL	13919 LYNDE AV, SAR, 95070, (408)867-4036	872 - D1
FORD ELEM SCHOOL	2711 MARICOPA AV, RCH, 94804, (510)234-8336	588 - J4
FORD, HENRY ELEM SCHOOL	2498 MASSACHUSETTS AV, RDWC, 94061, (650)368-2981	790 - A3
FOREST HILL ELEM SCHOOL	4450 MCCOY AV, CMBL, 95130, (408)364-4279	853 - A7
FOREST PARK ELEM SCHOOL	34400 MAYBIRD CIR, FRMT, 94555, (510)713-0141	752 - C3
FOSTER CITY ELEM SCHOOL	461 BEACH PARK BLVD, FCTY, 94404, (650)312-7522	749 - F4
FOX ELEM SCHOOL	3100 ST JAMES RD, BLMT, 94002, (650)637-4850	768 - J2

FEATURE NAME	Address City, ZIP Code	PAGE-GRID
FRANKLIN ELEM SCHOOL	1150 VIRGINIA ST, BERK, 94702, (510)644-8810	629 - E1
FRANKLIN ELEM SCHOOL	2385 TROUSDALE DR, BURL, 94010, (650)259-3850	728 - B5
FRANKLIN ELEM SCHOOL	420 TULLY RD, SJS, 95111, (408)283-6375	854 - F3
FRANKLIN ELEM SCHOOL	915 FOOTHILL BLVD, OAK, 94606, (510)452-1031	649 - J5
FREDERIKSEN ELEM SCHOOL	7243 TAMARACK DR, DBLN, 94568, (510)828-1037	693 - J3
FREMONT ELEM SCHOOL	1413 F ST, ANT, 94509, (510)706-4101	575 - D5
FROST, EARL ELEM SCHOOL	530 GETTYSBURG DR, SJS, 95123, (408)225-1881	874 - H4
FRUITVALE ELEM SCHOOL	3200 BOSTON AV, OAK, 94602, (510)532-4231	650 - D5
GALLINAS ELEM SCHOOL	177 N SAN PEDRO RD, MrnC, 94903, (415)492-3150	566 - G4
GARDEN GATE ELEM SCHOOL	10500 ANN ARBOR AV, CPTO, 95014, (650)252-5414	832 - C6
GARDEN VILLAGE ELEM SCHOOL	208 GARDEN LN, SMCo, 94015, (650)991-1233	687 - B4
GARDNER ELEM SCHOOL	502 ILLINOIS AV, SJS, 95125, (408)535-6225	854 - B1
GARFIELD CHARTER ELEM SCHOOL	3600 MIDDLEFIELD RD, SMCo, 94063, (650)369-3759	790 - D1
GARFIELD ELEM SCHOOL	13050 AURORA DR, SLN, 94577, (510)667-3580	690 - G4
GARFIELD ELEM SCHOOL	1640 22ND AV, OAK, 94606, (510)532-4052	650 - B6
GARFIELD ELEM SCHOOL	420 FILBERT ST, SF, 94133, (415)291-7924	648 - A4
GILL, JOHN ELEM SCHOOL	555 AVE DEL ORA, RDWC, 94062, (650)365-8320	769 - J7
GLASSBROOK ELEM SCHOOL	975 SCHAFER RD, HAY, 94544, (510)293-8505	711 - J6
GLEN COVE	501 GLEN COVE PKWY, VAL, 94591, (707)556-8491	550 - F2
GLENMOOR ELEM SCHOOL	4620 MATTOS DR, FRMT, 94536, (510)797-0130	752 - H5
GLEN PARK ELEM SCHOOL	151 LIPPARD AV, SF, 94131, (415)469-4713	667 - G6
GLENVIEW ELEM SCHOOL	4215 LA CRESTA AV, OAK, 94602, (510)530-8811	650 - D4
GLENWOOD ELEM SCHOOL	25 CASTLEWOOD DR, SRFL, 94901, (415)485-2430	567 - C6
GLIDER ELEM SCHOOL	511 COZY DR, SJS, 95123, (408)227-1505	874 - J6
GLORIETTA ELEM SCHOOL	15 MARTHA RD, ORIN, 94563, (510)254-8770	631 - A2
GOLDEN GATE ELEM SCHOOL	1601 TURK ST, SF, 94115, (415)749-3509	647 - G7
GOLDEN GATE ELEM SCHOOL	6200 SAN PABLO AV, OAK, 94608, (510)652-4428	629 - F5
GOLDEN VIEW ELEM SCHOOL	5025 CANYON CREST DR, SRMN, 94583, (510)735-0555	653 - G7
GOMES, JOHN M ELEM SCHOOL	555 LEMOS LN, FRMT, 94539, (510)656-3414	753 - E4
GOSS, MILDRED ELEM SCHOOL	2475 VAN WINKLE LN, SJS, 95116, (408)258-8172	834 - J4
GRAHAM, JAMES A ELEM SCHOOL	36270 CHERRY ST, NWK, 94560, (510)794-2023	752 - D6
GRANT ELEM SCHOOL	2400 DOWNER AV, RCH, 94804, (510)232-4736	588 - H5
GRANT ELEM SCHOOL	470 E JACKSON ST, SJS, 95112, (408)535-6277	834 - B4
GRASS VALLEY ELEM SCHOOL	4720 DUNKIRK AV, OAK, 94605, (510)430-9664	671 - E4
GRATTAN ELEM SCHOOL	165 GRATTAN ST, SF, 94117, (415)759-2815	667 - E2
GRAYSTONE ELEM SCHOOL	6982 SHEARWATER DR, SJS, 95120, (408)535-6317	894 - H2
GREENBROOK ELEM SCHOOL	1475 HARLAN DR, DNVL, 94526, (510)552-5550	653 - C6
GREEN HILLS ELEM SCHOOL	401 LUDEMAN LN, MLBR, 94030, (650)588-6485	728 - A3
GREEN VALLEY ELEM SCHOOL	1001 DIABLO RD, DNVL, 94526, (510)552-5685	633 - C7
GREEN, HARVEY ELEM SCHOOL	42875 GATEWOOD ST, FRMT, 94538, (510)656-6411	773 - D2
GREGORY GARDENS ELEM SCHOOL	200 HARRIET DR, PLHL, 94523, (510)827-3770	592 - C4
GRIMMER, E M ELEM SCHOOL	43030 NEWPORT DR, FRMT, 94538, (510)656-1250	773 - E2
GUADALUPE ELEM SCHOOL	6044 VERA CRUZ DR, SJS, 95120, (408)268-1031	874 - A7
GUADALUPE ELEM SCHOOL	859 PRAGUE ST, SF, 94112, (415)469-4718	687 - G2
HACIENDA SCIENCE/ENVIRONMENTAL-MAGNET	1290 KIMBERLY DR, SJS, 95118, (408)535-6259	874 - C1
HAIGHT ELEM SCHOOL	2025 SANTA CLARA AV, ALA, 94501, (510)748-4005	669 - J1
HALL, GEORGE ELEM SCHOOL	130 SAN MIGUEL WY, SMTO, 94403, (650)312-7533	749 - D5
HAMAN, CW ELEM SCHOOL	865 LOS PADRES BLVD, SCL, 95050, (408)244-6893	833 - C5
HAMILTON ELEM SCHOOL	601 BOLLING DR, NVTO, 94949, (415)883-4691	546 - G4
HANNA RANCH	2482 REFUGIO VALLEY RD, HER, 94547, (510)245-9902	570 - B6
HAPPY VALLEY ELEM SCHOOL	3855 HAPPY VALLEY RD, LFYT, 94549, (510)284-7049	611 - C4
HARDER ELEM SCHOOL	495 WYETH RD, HAY, 94544, (510)293-8572	712 - A4
HARDING ELEM SCHOOL	7230 FAIRMOUNT AV, ELCR, 94530, (510)525-0273	609 - E4
HARTE, BRET ELEM SCHOOL	1035 GILMAN AV, SF, 94124, (415)330-1520	688 - C1
HAVENS, FRANK C ELEM SCHOOL	1800 OAKLAND AV, PDMT, 94611, (510)420-3680	650 - B1
HAWES ELEM SCHOOL	909 ROOSEVELT AV, RDWC, 94061, (650)366-3122	770 - A7
HAWTHORNE YEAR-ROUND ELEM SCHOOL	1700 28TH AV, OAK, 94601, (510)533-8362	650 - C7
HAYES ELEM SCHOOL	5035 POSTON DR, SJS, 95136, (408)227-0424	874 - J2
HAYS, WALTER ELEM SCHOOL	1525 MIDDLEFIELD RD, PA, 94301, (650)322-5956	791 - B5
HAZELWOOD ELEM SCHOOL	775 WALDO RD, CMBL, 95008, (408)364-4230	853 - C7
HEATHER ELEM SCHOOL	2757 MELENDY DR, SCAR, 94070, (650)508-7303	769 - E5
HEIGHTS ELEM SCHOOL	163 WEST BLVD, PIT, 94565, (510)473-4311	574 - C5
HELLYER, G W ELEM SCHOOL	725 HELLYER AV, SJS, 95111, (408)363-5750	855 - A6
HENDERSON, JOE	650 HASTINGS DR, BEN, 94510, (707)747-8370	551 - A1
HERCULES ELEM SCHOOL	1919 LUPINE RD, HER, 94547, (510)799-3930	569 - J4
HESPERIAN ELEM SCHOOL	620 DREW ST, AlaC, 94580, (510)481-4634	691 - E5
HESTER ELEM SCHOOL	1460 THE ALAMEDA, SJS, 95126, (408)535-6235	833 - J6
HIDDEN VALLEY ELEM SCHOOL	500 GLACIER DR, MRTZ, 94553, (510)228-9530	591 - J1
HIGHLAND ELEM SCHOOL	1309 ENSIGN AV, VAL, 94590, (707)643-7641	530 - C3
HIGHLAND ELEM SCHOOL	2021 HIGHLAND BLVD, HAY, 94542, (510)293-8573	712 - C3
HIGHLAND ELEM SCHOOL	2829 MOYERS RD, RCH, 94806, (510)223-2495	589 - A2
HIGHLAND ELEM SCHOOL	8521 A ST, OAK, 94621, (510)562-0755	670 - H4
HIGHLANDS ELEM SCHOOL	1326 PENNSYLVANIA BLVD, CNCD, 94521, (510)672-5252	593 - F6
HIGHLANDS ELEM SCHOOL	2320 NEWPORT ST, SMCo, 94402, (650)312-7544	748 - F7
HIGHLANDS ELEM SCHOOL	4141 HARBOR ST, PIT, 94565, (510)473-4320	574 - D6
HILLCREST ELEM SCHOOL	30 MARGUERITE DR, OAK, 94618, (510)547-1757	630 - B6
HILLCREST ELEM SCHOOL	810 SILVER AV, SF, 94134, (415)469-4722	667 - H7
HILLCREST ELEM SCHOOL	CALIFORNIA ST & MAHONEY ST, CCCo, (510)799-4431	549 - J7
HILLSDALE ELEM SCHOOL	3200 WATER ST, SJS, 95111, (408)363-5650	854 - H6
HILLSIDE ELEM SCHOOL	1400 HILLSIDE BLVD, SSF, 94080, (650)877-8801	707 - H1
HILLSIDE ELEM SCHOOL	15980 MARCELLA ST, AlaC, 94578, (510)481-4637	691 - F4
HILLVIEW CREST ELEM SCHOOL	31410 WHEELON AV, HAY, 94544, (510)471-5720	732 - E2
HIRSCH, O N ELEM SCHOOL	41399 CHAPEL WY, FRMT, 94538, (510)657-3537	753 - D7
HOLBROOK ELEM SCHOOL	3333 RONALD WY, CNCD, 94519, (510)685-6446	572 - G6
HOLLY OAK ELEM SCHOOL	2995 ROSSMORE WY, SJS, 95148, (408)270-4975	855 - C2
HOOVER ELEM SCHOOL	890 BROCKHURST ST, OAK, 94608, (510)658-0266	649 - F1
HOOVER PUBLIC ELEM SCHOOL	701 CHARTER ST, RDWC, 94063, (650)366-6236	770 - C6
HOOVER, HERBERT ELEM SCHOOL	1635 PARK AV, SJS, 95126, (408)535-6274	833 - H6
HOOVER, HERBERT ELEM SCHOOL	800 BARRON AV, PA, 94306, (650)856-1377	811 - B2
HORRALL, ALBION H. ELEM SCHOOL	949 OCEAN VIEW AV, SMTO, 94401, (650)312-7550	749 - C1
HOWARD, CHARLES P ELEM SCHOOL	8755 FONTAINE ST, OAK, 94605, (510)568-4355	671 - B3
HUBBARD, O S ELEM SCHOOL	1745 JUNE AV, SJS, 95122, (408)251-1296	834 - H7
HUGHES, KATHRYN ELEM SCHOOL	4949 CL DE ESCUELA, SCL, 95054, (408)988-2390	813 - C3
INDEPENDENT ELEM SCHOOL	21201 INDEPENDENT SCHOOL RD, AlaC, 94552, (510)537-9558	692 - D5
INDIAN VALLEY ELEM SCHOOL	551 MARSHALL DR, WLCK, 94598, (510)944-6828	612 - F5
JACKSON AVENUE ELEM SCHOOL	554 JACKSON AV, LVMR, 94550, (510)606-4717	696 - A7
JANSEN RANCH ELEM SCHOOL	2001 CARSON LN, AlaC, 94552, (501)537-3000	692 - F3
JEFFERSON ELEM SCHOOL	1400 ADA ST, BERK, 94702, (510)644-6298	609 - F7
JEFFERSON ELEM SCHOOL	1725 IRVING ST, SF, 94122, (415)759-2821	667 - B2
JEFFERSON YEAR-ROUND ELEM SCHOOL	2035 40TH AV, OAK, 94601, (510)532-5335	650 - D7
JEFFERSON, THOMAS ELEM SCHOOL	14311 LARK ST, SLN, 94578, (510)667-3581	691 - D3
KAISER, HENRY J JR ELEM SCHOOL	25 S HILL CT, OAK, 94618, (510)841-5547	630 - B4
KENNEDY, JOHN F ELEM SCHOOL	35430 BLACKBURN DR, NWK, 94560, (510)794-2027	752 - D4
KENNEDY, JOHN F ELEM SCHOOL	785 PRICE ST, DALY, 94014, (650)991-1239	687 - D4
KENNEDY, ROBERT F ELEM SCHOOL	1602 LUCRETIA AV, SJS, 95122, (408)283-6325	854 - F1
KENSINGTON ELEM SCHOOL	90 HIGHLAND BLVD, CCCo, 94708, (510)526-7343	609 - F3
KEY, FRANCIS SCOTT ELEM SCHOOL	1530 43RD AV, SF, 94122, (415)759-2811	666 - H2
KIMBALL ELEM SCHOOL	1310 AUGUST WY, ANT, 94509, (510)706-4130	575 - E5
KING ELEM SCHOOL	234 S 39TH ST, RCH, 94804, (510)232-0623	589 - A7
KING, MARTIN LUTHER JR ELEM-SCHOOL	960 10TH ST, OAK, 94607, (510)465-5146	649 - F3
KING, STARR ELEM SCHOOL	1215 CAROLINA ST, SF, 94107, (415)695-5797	668 - B3
LA ESCUELITA ELEM SCHOOL	1100 3RD AV, OAK, 94606, (510)763-3522	649 - H5
LAFAYETTE ELEM SCHOOL	1700 MARKET ST, OAK, 94607, (510)893-1383	649 - F3
LAFAYETTE ELEM SCHOOL	4545 ANZA ST, SF, 94121, (415)750-8543	646 - J7
LAFAYETTE ELEM SCHOOL	950 MORAGA RD, LFYT, 94549, (510)283-6231	611 - F6
LAKE ELEM SCHOOL	2700 11TH ST, SPAB, 94806, (510)234-7395	588 - G1
LAKESHORE ELEM SCHOOL	220 MIDDLEFIELD DR, SF, 94132, (415)759-2825	667 - A6
LAKEVIEW ELEM SCHOOL	746 GRAND AV, OAK, 94610, (510)893-3779	649 - J3
LAKEWOOD ELEM SCHOOL	750 LAKECHIME DR, SUNV, 94089, (408)522-8272	812 - H4
LANDELS, EDITH ELEM SCHOOL	115 DANA ST, MTVW, 94041, (650)965-4675	811 - J5
LANEVIEW ELEM SCHOOL	2095 WARMWOOD LN, SJS, 95132, (408)923-1920	814 - D2
LAS JUNTAS ELEM SCHOOL	4105 PACHECO BLVD, CCCo, 94553, (510)313-0460	571 - J4
LAS LOMITAS ELEM SCHOOL	299 ALAMEDA DE LAS PULGAS, ATN, 94027, (650)854-5900	790 - C5
LATIMER ELEM SCHOOL	4250 LATIMER AV, SJS, 95130, (408)379-2412	853 - A5
LAUREL ELEM SCHOOL	316 36TH AV, SMTO, 94403, (650)312-7555	749 - B6
LAUREL ELEM SCHOOL	3750 BROWN AV, OAK, 94619, (510)530-2200	650 - F5
LAUREL ELEM SCHOOL	95 EDGE RD, ATN, 94027, (650)324-0186	790 - H1
LAURELWOOD ELEM SCHOOL	4280 PARTRIDGE DR, SJS, 95121, (408)270-4983	855 - E4
LAURELWOOD ELEM SCHOOL	955 TEAL DR, SCL, 95051, (408)554-1390	832 - H5
LAWTON ELEM SCHOOL	1570 31ST AV, SF, 94122, (415)759-2832	667 - A2
LAZEAR ELEM SCHOOL	824 29TH AV, OAK, 94601, (510)532-3521	670 - B1
LECONTE ELEM SCHOOL	2241 RUSSELL ST, BERK, 94705, (510)644-6290	629 - H3
LEITCH, JAMES ELEM SCHOOL	47100 FERNALD ST, FRMT, 94539, (510)657-6100	773 - H6
LIETZ ELEM SCHOOL	5300 CARTER AV, SJS, 95118, (408)264-8314	874 - A5
LILIENTHAL, CLAIRE ELEM SCHOOL	3630 DIVISADERO ST, SF, 94123, (415)749-3516	647 - F3
LINCOLN	620 CAROLINA ST, VAL, 94590, (707)643-2239	529 - J4
LINCOLN ELEM SCHOOL	1801 DEVEREUX DR, BURL, 94010, (650)697-8230	728 - C5
LINCOLN ELEM SCHOOL	21710 MCCLELLAN RD, CPTO, 95014, (408)252-4798	852 - B2
LINCOLN ELEM SCHOOL	225 11TH ST, OAK, 94607, (510)451-3100	649 - G4
LINCOLN ELEM SCHOOL	29 6TH ST, RCH, 94801, (510)232-2239	588 - F7
LINCOLN ELEM SCHOOL	36111 BETTENCOURT ST, NWK, 94560, (510)794-2030	752 - C6
LINDA MAR ELEM SCHOOL	830 ROSITA RD, PCFA, 94044, (650)359-2400	726 - H5
LINDA VISTA ELEM SCHOOL	100 KIRK AV, SJS, 95127, (408)258-4938	815 - A7
LOCKWOOD ELEM SCHOOL	6701 E INTERNATIONAL BLVD, OAK, 94621, (510)569-3066	670 - F3
LOMA VERDE ELEM SCHOOL	399 ALAMEDA DE LA LOMA, MrnC, 94949, (415)883-4681	546 - E2
LOMA VISTA	146 RAINER AV, VAL, 94589, (707)643-2501	510 - B5
LOMITA PARK ELEM SCHOOL	200 SANTA HELENA AV, MLBR, 94030, (650)588-5852	728 - A2
LONDON, JACK ELEM SCHOOL	4550 COUNTRY HILLS DR, ANT, 94509, (510)706-5400	595 - G3
LONE HILL ELEM SCHOOL	4949 HARWOOD RD, SJS, 95124, (408)269-1173	873 - H4
LONGFELLOW ELEM SCHOOL	3877 LUSK ST, OAK, 94608, (510)653-5216	629 - G7
LONGFELLOW ELEM SCHOOL	500 PACIFIC AV, ALA, 94501, (510)748-4008	669 - F1
LONGFELLOW ELEM SCHOOL	755 MORSE ST, SF, 94112, (415)469-4730	687 - E2
LONGWOOD ELEM SCHOOL	850 LONGWOOD AV, HAY, 94541, (510)293-8507	711 - F3
LOS ALAMITOS ELEM SCHOOL	6130 SILBERMAN DR, SJS, 95120, (408)535-6297	874 - C7
LOS ALTOS	201 COVINGTON RD, LALT, 94024, (650)941-4010	831 - E1
LOS ARBOLES ELEM SCHOOL	455 LOS ARBOLES AV, SJS, 95111, (408)363-5675	854 - J6
LOS CERRITOS ELEM SCHOOL	210 W ORANGE AV, SSF, 94080, (650)877-8841	707 - G3
LOS MEDANOS ELEM SCHOOL	610 CROWLEY AV, PIT, 94565, (510)473-4330	574 - C3
LOS PASEOS ELEM SCHOOL	121 AVD GRANDE, SJS, 95139, (408)578-8800	875 - F7
LOS PERALES ELEM SCHOOL	22 WAKEFIELD DR, MRGA, 94556, (510)376-7452	631 - D5
LOWELL ELEM SCHOOL	625 S 7TH ST, SJS, 95112, (408)535-6243	834 - D7
LOYOLA ELEM SCHOOL	770 BERRY AV, LALT, 94024, (650)964-5165	831 - G2
LU SUTTON ELEM SCHOOL	1800 CENTER RD, NVTO, 94947, (415)897-3196	526 - A3
LUM, DONALD D ELEM SCHOOL	1801 SANDCREEK WY, ALA, 94501, (510)748-4009	669 - H3
LUTHER BURBANK ELEM SCHOOL	4 WABASH AV, SCIC, 95128, (408)295-1813	853 - G1
LYDIKSEN ELEM SCHOOL	7700 HIGHLAND OAKS DR, PLE, 94588, (510)426-4421	713 - J1
LYNDALE ELEM SCHOOL	13901 NORDYKE DR, SJS, 95127, (408)251-4010	834 - J3
LYNHAVEN ELEM SCHOOL	881 S CYPRESS AV, SJS, 95117, (498)364-4215	853 - C2
LYNWOOD ELEM SCHOOL	1320 LYNWOOD DR, NVTO, 94947, (415)897-4161	526 - C6
MACGREGOR ELEM SCHOOL	601 SAN GABRIEL AV, ALB, 94706, (510)559-6650	609 - E5
MADERA ELEM SCHOOL	8500 MADERA DR, ELCR, 94530, (510)235-4499	609 - D1
MAGUIRE, EDNA ELEM SCHOOL	80 LOMITA DR, MLV, 94941, (415)389-7733	606 - G3
MAJESTIC WAY ELEM SCHOOL	1855 MAJESTIC WY, SJS, 95132, (408)923-1925	814 - F3
MALCOLM X ELEM SCHOOL	1731 PRINCE ST, BERK, 94703, (510)644-6313	629 - G4
MALCOLM X ELEM SCHOOL	350 HARBOR RD, SF, 94124, (415)695-5950	668 - D6
MALONEY, TOM ELEM SCHOOL	38700 LOGAN DR, FRMT, 94536, (510)797-4422	752 - J5
MANN, HORACE ELEM SCHOOL	5222 YGNACIO AV, OAK, 94601, (510)532-8070	670 - E1
MANN, HORACE ELEM SCHOOL	55 N 7TH ST, SJS, 95113, (408)535-6237	834 - C6
MANOR, LORENZO ELEM SCHOOL	18250 BENGAL ST, AlaC, 94541, (510)481-4648	711 - E1
MANZANITA ELEM SCHOOL	2409 E 27TH ST, OAK, 94601, (510)532-8245	650 - C6
MARE ISLAND	9TH ST & TISDALE AV, VAL, 94592, (707)642-4020	529 - G6
MARIN ELEM SCHOOL	1001 SANTA FE AV, ALB, 94706, (510)559-6520	609 - E6
MARKHAM ELEM SCHOOL	1570 WARD ST, HAY, 94541, (510)293-8509	712 - A1
MARKHAM ELEM SCHOOL	7220 KRAUSE AV, OAK, 94605, (510)568-2523	670 - H2
MARSH ELEM SCHOOL	2304 G ST, ANT, 94509, (510)706-4110	575 - C6
MARSHALL ELEM SCHOOL	1575 15TH ST, SF, 94103, (415)241-6280	667 - J2
MARSHALL ELEM SCHOOL	20111 MARSHALL ST, AlaC, 94546, (510)537-2431	692 - B5
MARSHALL LANE ELEM SCHOOL	14114 MARILYN LN, SAR, 95070, (408)364-4259	872 - H2
MARSHALL, JOHN ELEM SCHOOL	3400 MALCOLM AV, OAK, 94605, (510)568-3112	671 - C5
MARTIN ELEM SCHOOL	35 SCHOOL ST, SSF, 94080, (650)877-3955	707 - J2
MARTINEZ ELEM SCHOOL	850 JONES ST, MRTZ, 94553, (510)313-0408	571 - E3
MARYLIN AVENUE ELEM SCHOOL	800 MARYLIN AV, LVMR, 94550, (510)606-4724	695 - F7
MATTOS, JOHN G ELEM SCHOOL	37944 FARWELL DR, FRMT, 94536, (510)793-1359	752 - G6
MAXWELL PARK ELEM SCHOOL	4730 FLEMING AV, OAK, 94619, (510)533-9558	650 - F7
MAYNE, GEORGE ELEM SCHOOL	1490 TAYLOR ST, SJS, 95002, (408)262-3600	813 - C1
MCAULIFFE, CHRISTA ELEM SCHOOL	12211 TITUS AV, SAR, 95070, (408)253-4696	852 - G5
MCCOPPIN, FRANK ELEM SCHOOL	651 6TH AV, SF, 94118, (415)750-8475	647 - D7
MCKINLEY ELEM SCHOOL	1025 14TH ST, SF, 94114, (415)241-6300	667 - G1
MCKINLEY ELEM SCHOOL	2150 E 14TH ST, SLN, 94577, (510)667-3582	691 - B2
MCKINLEY ELEM SCHOOL	651 MACREDES AV, SJS, 95116, (408)283-6350	834 - E6
MCKINLEY ELEM SCHOOL	701 PALOMA AV, BURL, 94010, (650)259-3870	728 - F6

FEATURE NAME / Address City, ZIP Code	PAGE-GRID
MEADOW HEIGHTS ELEM SCHOOL 2619 DOLORES ST, SMTO, 94403, (650)312-7566	749 - A5
MEADOW HOMES ELEM SCHOOL 1371 DETROIT AV, CNCD, 94520, (510)685-8760	592 - F3
MEADOWS ELEM SCHOOL 1101 HELEN DR, MLBR, 94030, (650)583-7590	727 - H3
MEADOWS, JEANNE R ELEM SCHOOL 1250 TAPER LN, SJS, 95122, (408)283-6300	854 - H1
MELROSE ELEM SCHOOL 1325 53RD AV, OAK, 94601, (510)533-7506	670 - E2
MENLO OAKS ELEM SCHOOL 475 POPE ST, MLPK, 94025, (650)329-2828	790 - J2
MEYER, DONALD J ELEM SCHOOL 1824 DAYTONA DR, SJS, 95122, (408)258-8208	834 - J6
MEYERHOLZ ELEM SCHOOL 6990 MELVIN DR, SJS, 95129, (408)252-7450	852 - E3
MICHELL, JOE ELEM SCHOOL 1001 ELAINE AV, LVMR, 94550, (510)606-4738	715 - F2
MILANI, LOUIS ELEM SCHOOL 37490 BIRCH ST, NWK, 94560, (510)794-2033	752 - F6
MILK, HARVEY ELEM SCHOOL 4235 19TH ST, SF, 94114, (415)241-6276	667 - G3
MILLARD MCCOLLAM ELEM SCHOOL 3311 LUCIAN AV, SJS, 95127, (408)258-1006	814 - J7
MILLARD, STEVEN ELEM SCHOOL 5200 VALPEY PK, FRMT, 94538, (510)657-2500	773 - C2
MILLBROOK ELEM SCHOOL 3200 MILLBROOK DR, SJS, 95148, (408)270-6767	855 - D2
MILLER, GEORGE P ELEM SCHOOL 250 SINGLETON AV, ALA, 94501, (510)748-4011	649 - E6
MILLER, GRANDIN ELEM SCHOOL 1250 S KING RD, SJS, 95122, (408)258-2214	834 - H6
MILLER, JOAQUIN ELEM SCHOOL 5525 ASCOT DR, OAK, 94611, (510)531-8918	650 - E2
MILLIKIN ELEM SCHOOL 2720 SONOMA PL, SCL, 95051, (408)554-6661	833 - B5
MILLS 380 E L ST, BEN, 94510, (707)747-8380	551 - C5
MINER, GEORGE ELEM SCHOOL 5629 LEAN AV, SJS, 95123, (408)225-2144	875 - A4
MINI, DAN ELEM SCHOOL 1530 LORENZO DR, VAL, 94589, (707)642-8917	509 - J5
MIRA VISTA ELEM SCHOOL 6397 HAZEL AV, CCCo, 94805, (510)232-4064	589 - C6
MIRALOMA ELEM SCHOOL 175 OMAR WY, SF, 94127, (415)469-4734	667 - E5
MISSION EDUCATION CENTER 1670 NOE ST, SF, 94131, (415)695-5313	667 - G5
MISSION ELEM SCHOOL 1711 MISSION DR, ANT, 94509, (510)706-5210	575 - A6
MISSION SAN JOSE ELEM SCHOOL 43545 BRYANT ST, FRMT, 94539, (510)656-1200	753 - H7
MISSION VALLEY ELEM SCHOOL 41700 DENISE ST, FRMT, 94539, (510)656-2000	753 - F6
MONROE ELEM SCHOOL 260 MADRID ST, SF, 94112, (415)469-4736	667 - G7
MONROE, JAMES ELEM SCHOOL 3750 MONTEREY BLVD, SLN, 94578, (510)667-3583	691 - B5
MONTA LOMA ELEM SCHOOL 460 THOMPSON AV, MTVW, 94043, (650)903-6915	811 - G3
MONTAGUE ELEM SCHOOL 750 LAURIE AV, SCL, 95054, (408)988-3052	813 - E6
MONTAIR ELEM SCHOOL 300 QUINTERRA LN, DNVL, 94526, (510)552-5656	652 - J2
MONTALVIN MANOR ELEM SCHOOL 300 CHRISTINE DR, CCCo, 94806, (510)223-6230	568 - J5
MONTCLAIR ELEM SCHOOL 1160 SAINT JOSEPH AV, LALT, 94024, (650)967-9388	831 - H5
MONTCLAIR ELEM SCHOOL 1757 MOUNTAIN BLVD, OAK, 94611, (510)339-9550	630 - D7
MONTE GARDENS ELEM SCHOOL 3841 LARKSPUR DR, CNCD, 94519, (510)685-3834	572 - J7
MONTE VERDE ELEM SCHOOL 2551 SAINT CLOUD DR, SBRN, 94066, (650)877-8838	707 - E5
MONTEVIDEO ELEM SCHOOL 13000 BROADMOOR DR, SRMN, 94583, (510)803-7450	673 - F4
MONTGOMERY, JOHN J ELEM SCHOOL 2010 DANIEL MALONEY DR, SJS, 95121, (408)270-6718	855 - C3
MORELLO PARK ELEM SCHOOL 244 MORELLO AV, MRTZ, 94553, (510)313-0391	571 - H5
MOSCONE, GEORGE R ELEM SCHOOL 2355 FOLSOM ST, SF, 94110, (415)695-5736	667 - J3
MOUNT DIABLO ELEM SCHOOL 5880 MOUNT ZION DR, CLAY, 94517, (510)672-4840	593 - G7
MOUNTAIN VIEW ELEM SCHOOL 1705 THORNWOOD DR, CNCD, 94521, (510)689-6450	593 - C3
MT PLEASANT ELEM SCHOOL 14275 CANDLER AV, SJS, 95127, (408)258-6451	835 - B4
MUIR ELEM SCHOOL 6560 HANOVER DR, SJS, 95129, (408)252-5265	852 - F4
MUIR, JOHN ELEM SCHOOL 130 CAMBRIDGE LN, SBRN, 94066, (650)244-0143	727 - F1
MUIR, JOHN ELEM SCHOOL 205 VISTA WY, MRTZ, 94553, (510)313-0470	571 - F5
MUIR, JOHN ELEM SCHOOL 24823 SOTO RD, HAY, 94544, (510)293-8575	711 - J4
MUIR, JOHN ELEM SCHOOL 2955 CLAREMONT AV, BERK, 94705, (510)644-6410	630 - A3
MUIR, JOHN ELEM SCHOOL 380 WEBSTER ST, SF, 94102, (415)241-6335	647 - H7
MUIR, JOHN ELEM SCHOOL 615 GREYSTONE DR, ANT, 94509, (510)706-4120	595 - E2
MUNCK, CARL B ELEM SCHOOL 11900 CAMPUS DR, OAK, 94619, (510)531-0611	650 - H5
MURPHY ELEM SCHOOL 4350 VALLEY VIEW RD, RCH, 94803, (510)223-2781	589 - E1
MURRAY ELEM SCHOOL 8435 DAVONA DR, DBLN, 94568, (510)828-2568	693 - H2
MURWOOD ELEM SCHOOL 2050 VANDERSLICE AV, CCCo, 94596, (510)943-2462	612 - D7
MUSICK, E L ELEM SCHOOL 5735 MUSICK AV, NWK, 94560, (510)794-2036	752 - E5
NEILSEN ELEM SCHOOL 7500 AMARILLO DR, DBLN, 94568, (510)828-2030	693 - G4
NESBIT ELEM SCHOOL 500 BIDDULPH WY, BLMT, 94002, (650)637-4860	749 - E7
NILES ELEM SCHOOL 37141 2ND ST, FRMT, 94536, (510)793-1141	753 - B1
NIMITZ ELEM SCHOOL 545 E CHEYENNE DR, SUNV, 94087, (408)736-2180	832 - D4
NIXON, LUCILLE M ELEM SCHOOL 1711 STANFORD AV, SCIC, 94305, (650)856-1622	810 - J2
NOBLE ELEM SCHOOL 3466 GROSSMONT DR, SJS, 95132, (408)923-1935	814 - H5
NODDIN ELEM SCHOOL 1755 GILDA WY, SJS, 95124, (408)356-2126	873 - H5
NORTH HILLSBOROUGH ELEM SCHOOL 545 EUCALYPTUS AV, HIL, 94010, (650)347-4175	748 - E1
NORTH SHOREVIEW ELEM SCHOOL 1301 CYPRESS AV, SMTO, 94401, (650)312-7588	729 - A7
NORTHWOOD ELEM SCHOOL 2760 TRIMBLE RD, SJS, 95132, (408)923-1940	814 - C3
NORWOOD CREEK ELEM SCHOOL 3241 REMINGTON WY, SJS, 95148, (408)270-6726	835 - D7
NYSTROM ELEM SCHOOL 230 HARBOUR WY S, RCH, 94804, (510)235-0147	588 - G7
OAK AVENUE ELEM SCHOOL 1501 OAK AV, LALT, 94024, (650)964-2187	831 - J3
OAK KNOLL ELEM SCHOOL 1895 OAK KNOLL LN, MLPK, 94025, (650)854-4433	790 - E6
OAK RIDGE ELEM SCHOOL 5920 BUFKIN DR, SJS, 95123, (408)578-5900	875 - A5
ODDSTAD ELEM SCHOOL 930 ODDSTAD BLVD, PCFA, 94044, (650)355-3638	727 - C5
OHLONE ELEM SCHOOL 1616 PHEASANT DR, HER, 94547, (510)799-0889	569 - G4
OHLONE ELEM SCHOOL 950 AMARILLO AV, PA, 94303, (650)856-1726	791 - D5
OLD MILL ELEM SCHOOL 352 THROCKMORTON AV, MLV, 94941, (415)389-7727	606 - C3
OLINDA ELEM SCHOOL 5855 OLINDA RD, RCH, 94803, (510)223-2800	589 - G4
OLINDER, SELMA ELEM SCHOOL 890 E WILLIAM ST, SJS, 95116, (408)535-6245	834 - E6
OLIVE ELEM SCHOOL 629 PLUM ST, NVTO, 94945, (415)897-2131	526 - D3
OLIVEIRA ELEM SCHOOL 4180 ALDER AV, FRMT, 94536, (510)797-1132	752 - G3
ORCHARD ELEM SCHOOL 711 E GISH RD, SJS, 95112, (408)998-2830	834 - B1
ORION ELEM SCHOOL 3150 GRANGER WY, RDWC, 94061, (650)363-0611	789 - J3
ORMONDALE ELEM SCHOOL 200 SHAWNEE PASS, PTLV, 94028, (650)851-7230	810 - B6
ORTEGA, JOSE ELEM SCHOOL 400 SARGENT ST, SF, 94132, (415)469-4726	687 - C1
OSTER ELEM SCHOOL 1855 LENCAR WY, SJS, 95124, (408)266-8121	873 - H3
OTIS, FRANK ELEM SCHOOL 3010 FILLMORE ST, ALA, 94501, (510)748-4013	670 - A4
OXFORD ELEM SCHOOL 1130 OXFORD ST, BERK, 94707, (510)644-6300	609 - G6
PADEN, WILLIAM G ELEM SCHOOL 444 CENTRAL AV, ALA, 94501, (510)748-4014	669 - E1
PAINTER, BEN ELEM SCHOOL 500 ROUGH AND READY RD, SJS, 95133, (408)258-1458	834 - G1
PALO VERDE ELEM SCHOOL 3450 LOUIS RD, PA, 94303, (650)856-1672	791 - E7
PALOMARES ELEM SCHOOL 6395 PALO VERDE RD, AlaC, 94542, (510)582-4207	692 - F5
PANORAMA ELEM SCHOOL 25 BELLEVUE AV, DALY, 94014, (415)586-6595	687 - F3
PARK ELEM SCHOOL 161 CLARK DR, SMTO, 94402, (650)312-7577	748 - G1
PARK ELEM SCHOOL 360 E BLITHEDALE AV, MLV, 94941, (415)389-7735	606 - E3
PARK ELEM SCHOOL 411 LARCHMONT ST, HAY, 94544, (510)293-8515	711 - H4
PARKER ELEM SCHOOL 7929 NEY AV, OAK, 94605, (510)568-8076	670 - J2
PARKER, JEAN ELEM SCHOOL 840 BROADWAY ST, SF, 94133, (415)291-7990	648 - A4
PARKMEAD ELEM SCHOOL 1920 MAGNOLIA WY, CCCo, 94595, (510)944-6858	612 - B7
PARKMONT ELEM SCHOOL 2601 PARKSIDE DR, FRMT, 94536, (510)793-7492	753 - B3
PARKS, ROSA ELEM SCHOOL 1501 OFARRELL ST, SF, 94115, (415)749-3519	647 - G6
PARKSIDE ELEM SCHOOL 1685 EISENHOWER ST, SMTO, 94403, (650)312-7575	749 - C2
PARKSIDE ELEM SCHOOL 985 W 17TH ST, PIT, 94565, (510)473-4341	574 - C3
PARKVIEW ELEM SCHOOL 330 BLUEFIELD DR, SJS, 95136, (408)226-4655	874 - G1
PATTERSON ELEM SCHOOL 35521 CABRILLO DR, FRMT, 94536, (510)793-3010	752 - E3
PATTERSON, GRACE 1080 PORTER ST, VAL, 94590, (707)556-8580	550 - B1
PAYNE, GEORGE C ELEM SCHOOL 3750 GLEASON AV, SJS, 95130, (408)241-1788	853 - C4
PEABODY, GEORGE ELEM SCHOOL 251 6TH AV, SF, 94118, (415)750-8480	647 - D6
PENNYCOOK, ANNIE 3620 FERNWOOD DR, VAL, 94591, (707)643-8241	530 - E5
PERALTA ELEM SCHOOL 460 63RD ST, OAK, 94609, (510)652-6344	629 - H5
PERES ELEM SCHOOL 719 5TH ST, RCH, 94801, (510)232-4543	588 - F5
PIEDMONT AVENUE ELEM SCHOOL 4314 PIEDMONT AV, OAK, 94611, (510)658-4567	629 - J7
PIONEER ELEM SCHOOL 32737 BEL AIRE ST, UNC, 94587, (510)487-4530	752 - A1
PLEASANT HILL ELEM SCHOOL 2097 OAK PARK BLVD, PLHL, 94523, (510)934-3341	592 - A7
PLEASANT VALLEY ELEM SCHOOL 755 SUTRO AV, NVTO, 94947, (415)897-5104	525 - G3
POMEROY ELEM SCHOOL 1250 POMEROY AV, SCL, 95051, (408)554-0834	833 - A4
POMEROY, MARSHALL ELEM SCHOOL 1505 ESCUELA PKWY, MPS, 95035, (408)945-2424	794 - A4
PONDEROSA ELEM SCHOOL 295 PONDEROSA RD, SMCo, 94080, (650)877-8825	707 - G4
PONDEROSA ELEM SCHOOL 804 PONDEROSA AV, SUNV, 94086, (408)245-6009	832 - G2
PORTAL, LOUIS ELEM SCHOOL 10300 N BLANEY AV, CPTO, 95014, (408)973-8191	832 - F7
PORTOLA ELEM SCHOOL 300 AMADOR AV, SBRN, 94066, (650)871-7133	707 - D7
PORTOLA, DON GASPAR DE ELEM-SCHOOL 2451 PORTOLA AV, LVMR, 94550, (510)606-4743	695 - G7
PRESCOTT ELEM SCHOOL 920 CAMPBELL ST, OAK, 94607, (510)452-4394	649 - D3
PROCTOR ELEM SCHOOL 17520 REDWOOD RD, AlaC, 94546, (510)537-0630	692 - A2
PUBLIC ELEM SCHOOL COLUSA ST & KISSELL AL, VAL, 94590	530 - B5
RANCHO ELEM SCHOOL 1430 JOHNSON ST, NVTO, 94947, (415)897-3101	526 - B5
RANCHO LAS POSITAS ELEM SCHOOL 401 E JACK LONDON BLVD, LVMR, 94550, (510)606-4748	695 - D7
RANCHO ROMERO ELEM SCHOOL 180 HEMME AV, CCCo, 94507, (510)552-5675	632 - G6
RANDALL, ROBERT ELEM SCHOOL 1300 EDSEL DR, MPS, 95035	794 - C7
RANDOL, JAMES ELEM SCHOOL 762 SUNSET GLEN DR, SJS, 95123, (408)535-6380	874 - G6
REDDING ELEM SCHOOL 1421 PINE ST, SF, 94109, (415)749-3525	647 - J5
REDWOOD HEIGHTS ELEM SCHOOL 4401 39TH AV, OAK, 94619, (510)531-1973	650 - G5
REED ELEM SCHOOL 1199 TIBURON BLVD, TBRN, 94920, (415)435-3302	607 - D7
REED ELEM SCHOOL 1524 JACOB AV, SJS, 95118, (408)535-6247	874 - B2
REGNART ELEM SCHOOL 1170 YORKSHIRE DR, CPTO, 95014, (408)253-5250	852 - C3
REVERE, PAUL ANNEX 610 TOMPKINS AV, SF, 94110, (415)695-5974	667 - J5
REVERE, PAUL ELEM SCHOOL 555 TOMPKINS AV, SF, 94110, (415)695-5656	667 - J6
RHEEM, DONALD L ELEM SCHOOL 90 LAIRD DR, MRGA, 94556, (510)376-4441	631 - D4
RIO VISTA ELEM SCHOOL 611 PACIFICA AV, CCCo, 94565, (510)458-6101	573 - D1
RIVER GLEN ELEM SCHOOL 1610 BIRD AV, SJS, 95125, (408)535-6240	854 - C4
RIVERSIDE ELEM SCHOOL 1300 AMADOR ST, SPAB, 94806, (510)237-1441	589 - A4
ROGERS, WILLIAM R ELEM SCHOOL 2999 RIDGEMONT DR, SJS, 95127, (408)258-3686	835 - B5
ROLLINGWOOD ELEM SCHOOL 2500 COTTONWOOD DR, SBRN, 94066, (650)244-0146	707 - E6
ROOFTOP ALTERNATIVE ELEM SCHOOL 443 BURNETT AV, SF, 94131, (415)695-5691	667 - F3
ROOSEVELT ELEM SCHOOL 2223 VERA AV, RDWC, 94061, (650)369-5597	789 - J1
ROOSEVELT ELEM SCHOOL 951 DOWLING BLVD, SLN, 94577, (510)667-3584	671 - B6
ROOSEVELT, FRANKLIN D 1200 SKYLINE DR, DALY, 94015, (650)991-1230	707 - A2
ROSEMARY ELEM SCHOOL 401 W HAMILTON AV, CMBL, 95008, (408)364-4254	853 - D5
ROSS ELEM SCHOOL LAGUNITAS RD & ALLEN AV, ROSS, 94957, (415)457-2705	586 - C2
ROY CLOUD ELEM SCHOOL 3790 RED OAK WY, RDWC, 94061, (650)369-2264	789 - G2
RUSKIN ELEM SCHOOL 1401 TURLOCK LN, SJS, 95132, (408)923-1950	814 - F4
RUUS ELEM SCHOOL 28027 DICKENS AV, HAY, 94544, (510)293-8517	732 - A1
SAKAMOTO ELEM SCHOOL 6280 SHADELANDS DR, SJS, 95123, (408)227-3411	874 - H7
SAN ANSELMO ELEM SCHOOL 6670 SAN ANSELMO WY, SJS, 95119, (408)578-2710	875 - D7
SAN ANTONIO ELEM SCHOOL 1855 E SAN ANTONIO ST, SJS, 95116, (408)258-8582	834 - F4
SAN FRANCISCO COMMUNITY ELEM-SCHOOL 125 EXCELSIOR AV, SF, 94112, (415)469-4739	667 - G7
SAN MIGUEL ELEM SCHOOL 777 SAN MIGUEL AV, SUNV, 94086, (408)522-8279	812 - G5
SAN PEDRO ELEM SCHOOL 498 POINT SAN PEDRO RD, SRFL, 94901, (415)485-2450	587 - B1
SAN RAMON ELEM SCHOOL 45 SAN RAMON WY, NVTO, 94945, (415)897-1196	525 - H1
SANCHEZ ELEM SCHOOL 325 SANCHEZ ST, SF, 94114, (415)241-6380	667 - G2
SANDERS, ROBERT ELEM SCHOOL 3411 ROCKY MOUNTAIN DR, SJS, 95127, (408)258-7288	835 - C4
SANTA FE ELEM SCHOOL 915 54TH ST, OAK, 94608, (510)653-1076	629 - G6
SANTA RITA ELEM SCHOOL 700 LOS ALTOS AV, LALT, 94022, (650)941-3288	811 - D5
SANTA TERESA ELEM SCHOOL 6200 ENCINAL DR, SJS, 95119, (408)227-3303	875 - C6
SANTEE ELEM SCHOOL 1313 AUDUBON DR, SJS, 95122, (408)283-6450	834 - G7
SARATOGA ELEM SCHOOL 14592 OAK ST, SAR, 95070, (408)867-3476	872 - D3
SARTORETTE ELEM SCHOOL 3850 WOODFORD DR, SJS, 95124, (408)264-4380	873 - J2
SCHAFER PARK ELEM SCHOOL 26268 FLAMINGO AV, HAY, 94544, (510)293-8520	711 - J5
SCHALLENBERGER ELEM SCHOOL 1280 KOCH LN, SJS, 95125, (408)535-6253	854 - B7
SCHILLING, AUGUST ELEM SCHOOL 36901 SPRUCE ST, NWK, 94560, (510)794-2048	752 - D7
SCOTT LANE ELEM SCHOOL 1925 SCOTT BLVD, SCL, 95050, (408)985-1050	833 - D3
SEARLES ELEM SCHOOL 33629 15TH ST, UNC, 94587, (510)471-2772	732 - F5
SEAVIEW ELEM SCHOOL 2000 SOUTHWOOD DR, CCCo, 94806, (510)724-0444	569 - B4
SEDGWICK ELEM SCHOOL 19200 PHIL LN, CPTO, 95014, (408)252-3103	852 - G2
SELBY LANE ELEM SCHOOL 170 SELBY LN, ATN, 94027, (650)368-3996	790 - B3
SEMPLE, ROBERT 2015 E 3RD ST, BEN, 94510, (707)747-8360	551 - C4
SEQUOIA ELEM SCHOOL 277 BOYD RD, PLHL, 94523, (510)935-5721	592 - C6
SEQUOIA ELEM SCHOOL 3730 LINCOLN AV, OAK, 94602, (510)531-7200	650 - D4
SERRA, JUNIPERO ELEM SCHOOL 151 VICTORIA ST, DALY, 94015, (650)877-8853	707 - C2
SERRA, JUNIPERO ELEM SCHOOL 625 HOLLY PARK CIR, SF, 94110, (415)695-5685	667 - H6
SEVEN TREES ELEM SCHOOL 3975 MIRA LOMA WY, SJS, 95111, (408)363-5775	854 - J7
SHANNON ELEM SCHOOL 685 MARLESTA RD, PIN, 94564, (510)724-0943	569 - C5
SHARP PARK ELEM SCHOOL 1427 PALMETTO AV, PCFA, 94044, (650)355-7400	706 - J5
SHELDON ELEM SCHOOL 2601 MAY RD, RCH, 94803, (510)223-0500	589 - E2
SHEPHERD ELEM SCHOOL 27211 TYRRELL AV, HAY, 94544, (510)293-8522	712 - A6
SHERIDAN ELEM SCHOOL 431 CAPITOL AV, SF, 94112, (415)469-4743	687 - D2
SHERMAN ELEM SCHOOL 1651 UNION ST, SF, 94123, (415)749-3530	647 - H4
SHERMAN, ELISABETH ELEM SCHOOL 5328 BRANN ST, OAK, 94619, (510)536-1886	650 - G7
SHIELDS, LESTER W ELEM SCHOOL 2851 GAY AV, SJS, 95127, (408)258-4916	834 - H2
SHORE ACRES ELEM SCHOOL 351 MARINA RD, CCCo, 94565, (510)458-3261	573 - D1
SILVEIRA, MARY E ELEM SCHOOL 375 BLACKSTONE DR, MrnC, 94903, (415)479-8373	546 - E6
SILVER OAKS ELEM SCHOOL FARNSWORTH DR & SAN FELIPE RD, SJS, 95138, (408)223-4515	855 - G7
SILVERWOOD ELEM SCHOOL 1649 CLAYCORD AV, CNCD, 94521, (510)687-1150	593 - D3
SIMONDS ELEM SCHOOL 6515 GRAPEVINE WY, SJS, 95120, (408)535-6251	894 - D1
SINNOTT, JOHN ELEM SCHOOL 2025 YELLOWSTONE AV, MPS, 95035, (408)945-2441	814 - E1
SKYLINE ELEM SCHOOL 55 CHRISTEN AV, DALY, 94015, (650)877-8846	707 - C3
SLATER, KENNETH N ELEM SCHOOL 325 GLADYS AV, MTVW, 94043, (650)964-7392	812 - B5
SLEEPY HOLLOW ELEM SCHOOL 20 WASHINGTON LN, ORIN, 94563, (510)254-8711	610 - F4
SLONAKER, HARRY ELEM SCHOOL 1601 CUNNINGHAM AV, SJS, 95122, (408)259-1941	834 - H7
SMITH, EMMA C ELEM SCHOOL 391 ONTARIO DR, LVMR, 94550, (510)606-4705	715 - D3
SMITH, KATHERINE R ELEM SCHOOL 2025 CLARICE DR, SJS, 95122, (408)270-6751	835 - A7
SNOW, H A ELEM SCHOOL 6580 MIRABEAU DR, NWK, 94560, (510)794-2051	752 - C5
SOBRANTE PARK ELEM SCHOOL 470 EL PASEO DR, OAK, 94603, (510)568-8711	670 - H7

FEATURE NAME	Address City, ZIP Code	PAGE-GRID
SOUTH HILLSBOROUGH ELEM SCHOOL	303 EL CERRITO AV, HIL, 94010, (650)344-0303	748 - H2
SOUTHGATE ELEM SCHOOL	26601 CALAROGA AV, HAY, 94545, (510)293-8524	711 - H6
SPANGLER, ANTHONY ELEM SCHOOL	140 N ABBOTT AV, MPS, 95035, (650)945-5592	793 - J7
SPRING VALLEY ELEM SCHOOL	1451 JACKSON ST, SF, 94109, (415)749-3535	647 - J5
SPRING VALLEY ELEM SCHOOL	817 MURCHISON DR, MLBR, 94030, (650)697-5681	728 - B5
SPRINGER ELEM SCHOOL	1120 ROSE AV, MTVW, 94040, (650)964-3374	831 - G1
SPRINGHILL ELEM SCHOOL	3301 SPRINGHILL RD, LFYT, 94549, (510)283-8281	611 - H4
SPRUCE ELEM SCHOOL	501 SPRUCE AV, SSF, 94080, (650)877-8780	707 - J2
STANTON ELEM SCHOOL	2644 SOMERSET AV, AlaC, 94546, (510)727-9192	691 - H4
STEFFAN MANOR ELEM SCHOOL	815 CEDAR ST, VAL, 94591, (707)642-7581	530 - D5
STEGE ELEM SCHOOL	4949 CYPRESS AV, RCH, 94804, (510)232-8442	609 - B2
STEVENS CREEK ELEM SCHOOL	10300 AINSWORTH DR, CPTO, 95014, (650)245-3312	832 - A7
STEVENSON, ROBERT LOUIS ELEM	2051 34TH AV, SF, 94116, (415)759-2837	666 - J4
STEWART ELEM SCHOOL	2040 HOKE DR, PIN, 94564, (510)758-1142	569 - E6
STIPE, SAMUEL ELEM SCHOOL	5000 LYNG DR, SJS, 95111, (408)227-7332	875 - B1
STOCKLMEIR, LOUIS V ELEM SCHOOL	592 DUNHOLME WY, SUNV, 94087, (408)732-3363	832 - E5
STONEGATE ELEM SCHOOL	2605 GASSMANN DR, SJS, 95121, (408)363-5625	854 - H3
STONEHURST ELEM SCHOOL	10315 E ST, OAK, 94603, (510)569-1336	670 - H6
STONEMAN ELEM SCHOOL	2929 LOVERIDGE RD, PIT, 94565, (510)473-4350	574 - F5
STRANDWOOD ELEM SCHOOL	416 GLADYS DR, PLHL, 94523, (510)685-3212	592 - B5
STROBRIDGE ELEM SCHOOL	21400 BEDFORD DR, HAY, 94546, (510)293-8576	691 - J6
SUMMERDALE	1100 SUMMERDALE DR, SJS, 95132, (408)923-1960	814 - G6
SUN TERRACE ELEM SCHOOL	2448 FLOYD LN, CNCD, 94520, (510)682-4861	572 - G5
SUN VALLEY ELEM SCHOOL	75 HAPPY LN, SRFL, 94901, (415)485-2440	566 - D6
SUNNYBRAE ELEM SCHOOL	1031 S DELAWARE ST, SMTO, 94402, (650)312-7599	749 - B2
SUNNYSIDE ELEM SCHOOL	250 FOERSTER ST, SF, 94112, (415)469-4746	667 - E6
SUNOL GLEN ELEM SCHOOL	MAIN ST & BOND ST, AlaC, 94586, (510)862-2321	734 - C6
SUNSET ELEM SCHOOL	1671 FRANKFURT WY, LVMR, 94550, (510)606-4752	715 - G3
SUNSET ELEM SCHOOL	3045 SANTIAGO, SF, 94116, (415)759-2760	666 - J4
SUNSHINE GARDENS ELEM SCHOOL	1200 MILLER AV, SSF, 94080, (650)877-8784	707 - F1
SUTRO ELEM SCHOOL	235 12TH AV, SF, 94118, (415)750-8525	647 - C6
SUTTER ELEM SCHOOL	3200 FORBES AV, SCL, 95051, (408)554-0690	832 - J6
SUTTER ELEM SCHOOL	3410 LONGVIEW RD, ANT, 94509, (510)706-4146	595 - C1
SWETT, JOHN ELEM SCHOOL	4551 STEELE ST, OAK, 94619, (510)531-5100	650 - G6
SWETT, JOHN ELEM SCHOOL	4955 ALHAMBRA VALLEY RD, MRTZ, 94553, (510)313-0400	591 - E1
SWETT, JOHN ELEM SCHOOL	727 GOLDEN GATE AV, SF, 94102, (415)241-6320	647 - H7
SYCAMORE VALLEY ELEM SCHOOL	2200 HOLBROOK DR, DNVL, 94506, (510)736-0102	653 - G4
TAFT ELEM SCHOOL	903 10TH AV, RDWC, 94063, (650)369-2589	770 - E6
TAMALPAIS VALLEY ELEM SCHOOL	350 BELL LN, MrnC, 94965, (415)389-7731	606 - F7
TARA HILLS ELEM SCHOOL	2300 DOLAN WY, CCCo, 94806, (510)724-3454	569 - C5
TAYLOR, BERTHA ELEM SCHOOL	410 SAUTNER DR, SJS, 95123, (408)226-0462	875 - B7
TAYLOR, EDWARD R ELEM SCHOOL	423 BURROWS ST, SF, 94134, (415)330-1530	668 - A7
TERRELL ELEM SCHOOL	3925 PEARL AV, SJS, 95136, (408)535-6255	874 - D1
THE DELPHI ACADEMY	445 E CHARLESTON RD, PA, 94306, (650)493-3100	811 - E1
THEUERKAUF ELEM SCHOOL	1625 SAN LUIS AV, MTVW, 94043, (650)903-6925	811 - H3
THOMAS P RYAN ELEM SCHOOL	1241 MCGINNESS AV, SJS, 95127, (408)258-4936	835 - A4
THOMAS, WADE ELEM SCHOOL	ROSS AV, SANS, 94960, (415)454-4603	586 - B1
THORNHILL ELEM SCHOOL	5880 THORNHILL DR, OAK, 94611, (510)339-1300	630 - E7
THOUSAND OAKS ELEM SCHOOL	840 COLUSA AV, BERK, 94707, (510)644-6368	609 - F6
TOBIAS, MARJORIE H ELEM SCHOOL	725 SOUTHGATE AV, DALY, 94015, (650)991-1246	687 - A5
TOLER HEIGHTS ELEM SCHOOL	9736 LAWLOR ST, OAK, 94605, (510)562-4913	671 - A4
TOYON ELEM SCHOOL	995 BARD ST, SJS, 95127, (408)923-1965	814 - H6
TRACE, MERITT ELEM SCHOOL	651 DANA AV, SJS, 95126, (408)535-6257	833 - G7
TREEVIEW ELEM SCHOOL	30565 TREEVIEW ST, HAY, 94544, (510)293-8577	732 - E1
TURNBULL LEARNING ACADEMY SCHOOL	715 INDIAN AV, SMTO, 94401, (650)312-7766	728 - J7
TURNER ELEM SCHOOL	4207 DELTA FAIR BLVD, ANT, 94509, (510)706-5200	574 - H5
TWIN CREEKS ELEM SCHOOL	2785 MARSH DR, SRMN, 94583, (510)552-5650	673 - B2
TYRRELL ELEM SCHOOL	27000 TYRRELL AV, HAY, 94544, (510)293-8526	712 - A6
ULLOA ELEM SCHOOL	2650 42ND AV, SF, 94116, (415)759-2841	666 - J5
VALHALLA ELEM SCHOOL	530 KIKI DR, PLHL, 94523, (510)687-1700	592 - A3
VALLE VERDE ELEM SCHOOL	3275 PEACHWILLOW LN, WLCK, 94598, (510)939-5700	592 - H7
VALLE VISTA ELEM SCHOOL	2400 FLINT AV, SJS, 95148, (408)238-3525	835 - D6
VALLECITO ELEM SCHOOL	50 NOVA ALBION WY, SRFL, 94903, (415)479-2032	566 - D3
VALLEJO MILL ELEM SCHOOL	38569 CANYON HEIGHTS DR, FRMT, 94536, (510)793-1441	753 - D1
VALLEMAR ELEM SCHOOL	377 REINA DEL MAR AV, PCFA, 94044, (650)359-2444	727 - A1
VALLEY VIEW ELEM SCHOOL	3416 MAYWOOD DR, RCH, 94803, (510)223-6363	589 - F1
VALLEY VIEW ELEM SCHOOL	480 ADAMS WY, PLE, 94566, (510)426-4231	714 - F3
VAN, METER LOUISE ELEM SCHOOL	16445 LOS GATOS BLVD, LGTS, 95032, (408)356-5131	873 - C6
VANNOY ELEM SCHOOL	5100 VANNOY AV, AlaC, 94546, (510)537-1832	692 - C4
VARGAS ELEM SCHOOL	1054 CARSON DR, SUNV, 94086, (408)522-8267	812 - C7
VERDE ELEM SCHOOL	2000 GIARAMITA ST, CCCo, 94801, (510)237-0166	588 - F3
VINCI PARK ELEM SCHOOL	1311 VINCI PARK WY, SJS, 95131, (408)923-1970	814 - D7
VINTAGE HILLS ELEM SCHOOL	1125 CONCORD ST, PLE, 94566, (510)426-4241	714 - G4
VISITACION VALLEY ELEM SCHOOL	55 SCHWERIN ST, SF, 94134, (415)469-4796	687 - J2
VISTA GRANDE ELEM SCHOOL	667 DIABLO RD, DNVL, 94526, (510)552-5660	653 - B1
VISTA-MACGREGOR ELEM SCHOOL	720 JACKSON ST, ALB, 94706, (510)559-6630	609 - D5
WALNUT ACRES ELEM SCHOOL	180 CEREZO DR, WLCK, 94598, (510)939-1333	612 - H3
WALNUT GROVE ELEM SCHOOL	1999 HARVEST RD, PLE, 94566, (510)426-4251	714 - D2
WALNUT HEIGHTS ELEM SCHOOL	4064 WALNUT BLVD, WLCK, 94598, (510)944-6834	612 - F6
WARDLAW, JOSEPH H ELEM SCHOOL	1698 OAKWOOD AV, VAL, 94591, (707)648-0173	530 - F2
WARM SPRINGS ELEM SCHOOL	47370 WARM SPRINGS BLVD, FRMT, 94539, (510)656-1611	773 - H7
WARWICK ELEM SCHOOL	3375 WARWICK RD, FRMT, 94555, (510)793-8660	752 - E1
WASHINGTON ELEM SCHOOL	100 OAK ST, SJS, 95110, (408)535-6261	854 - C1
WASHINGTON ELEM SCHOOL	2300 MARTIN LUTHER KING JR WY, BERK, 94703, (510)644-6310	629 - G2
WASHINGTON ELEM SCHOOL	250 DUTTON AV, SLN, 94577, (510)667-3586	671 - A7
WASHINGTON ELEM SCHOOL	565 WINE ST, RCH, 94801, (510)232-1436	608 - D1
WASHINGTON ELEM SCHOOL	581 61ST ST, OAK, 94609, (510)658-5060	629 - H5
WASHINGTON ELEM SCHOOL	801 HOWARD AV, BURL, 94010, (650)259-3880	728 - H6
WASHINGTON ELEM SCHOOL	825 TAYLOR AV, ALA, 94501, (510)748-4007	669 - G1
WASHINGTON MANOR ELEM SCHOOL	1170 FARGO AV, SLN, 94579, (510)481-4658	691 - B6
WASHINGTON, GEORGE ELEM SCHOOL	251 WHITTIER ST, DALY, 94014, (650)991-1236	687 - E2
WEBSTER ACADEMY ELEM SCHOOL	8000 BIRCH ST, OAK, 94621, (510)569-7910	670 - H3
WEBSTER, DANIEL ELEM SCHOOL	425 EL DORADO DR, DALY, 94015, (650)991-1222	687 - B7
WEBSTER, DANIEL ELEM SCHOOL	465 MISSOURI ST, SF, 94107, (415)695-5787	668 - B2
WEIBEL, FRED E ELEM SCHOOL	45135 S GRIMMER BLVD, FRMT, 94539, (510)651-6958	773 - H4
WELLER, JOSEPH ELEM SCHOOL	345 BOULDER ST, MPS, 95035, (408)945-2428	794 - A3
WEST HILLSBOROUGH ELEM SCHOOL	376 BARBARA WY, HIL, 94010, (650)344-9870	748 - D3
WEST PORTAL ELEM SCHOOL	5 LENOX WY, SF, 94127, (415)759-2846	667 - D5
WEST VALLEY ELEM SCHOOL	1635 BELLEVILLE WY, SUNV, 94087, (408)245-0148	832 - A5
WESTLAKE ELEM SCHOOL	80 FIELDCREST DR, DALY, 94015, (650)991-1252	687 - B3
WESTVIEW ELEM SCHOOL	367 GLENCOURT WY, PCFA, 94044, (650)355-6441	707 - B4
WESTWOOD ELEM SCHOOL	1748 WEST ST, CNCD, 94521, (510)685-4202	593 - B2
WESTWOOD ELEM SCHOOL	435 SARATOGA AV, SCL, 95050, (408)554-0308	833 - D6
WHALEY ELEM SCHOOL	2655 ALVIN AV, SJS, 95121, (408)270-6759	854 - J2
WHISMAN ELEM SCHOOL	310 EASY ST, MTVW, 94043, (650)903-6935	812 - A4
WHITE OAKS ELEM SCHOOL	1901 WHITE OAK WY, SCAR, 94070, (650)508-7317	769 - H5
WHITTIER ELEM SCHOOL	6328 E 17TH ST, OAK, 94621, (510)638-3963	670 - F2
WIDENMANN, ELSA	100 WHITNEY AV, VAL, 94589, (707)552-0545	510 - B5
WILDWOOD ELEM SCHOOL	301 WILDWOOD AV, PDMT, 94611, (510)420-3710	650 - B2
WILLIAMS ELEM SCHOOL	1150 RAJKOVICH WY, SJS, 95120, (408)535-6196	894 - F3
WILLOW COVE ELEM SCHOOL	1880 HANLON WY, PIT, 94565, (510)709-2000	573 - J2
WILLOW GLEN ELEM SCHOOL	1425 LINCOLN AV, SJS, 95125, (408)535-6265	854 - A4
WILLOW OAKS ELEM SCHOOL	620 WILLOW RD, MLPK, 94025, (650)329-2850	790 - J2
WILSON ELEM SCHOOL	629 42ND ST, RCH, 94805, (510)232-6852	589 - A6
WILSON, WOODROW ELEM SCHOOL	1300 WILLIAMS ST, SLN, 94577, (510)667-3587	690 - J2
WILSON, WOODROW ELEM SCHOOL	43 MIRIAM ST, DALY, 94014, (650)991-1255	687 - C3
WINDMILL SPRINGS ELEM SCHOOL	2880 AETNA WY, SJS, 95121, (408)363-5600	854 - J3
WO, YICK ELEM SCHOOL	2245 JONES ST, SF, 94133, (415)749-3540	647 - J4
WOODSIDE ELEM SCHOOL	3195 WOODSIDE RD, WDSD, 94062, (650)851-1571	789 - G7
WOODSIDE ELEM SCHOOL	761 SAN SIMEON DR, CNCD, 94518, (510)689-7671	592 - H7
WOODSTOCK ELEM SCHOOL	1900 3RD ST, ALA, 94501, (510)748-4012	649 - E7
WREN AVENUE ELEM SCHOOL	3339 WREN AV, CNCD, 94519, (510)685-7002	592 - H1
YATES, ANNA ELEM SCHOOL	1070 41ST ST, EMVL, 94608, (510)652-7137	629 - F7
YGNACIO VALLEY ELEM SCHOOL	2217 CHALOMAR RD, CNCD, 94518, (510)682-9336	592 - G5
YU, ALICE FONG ELEM SCHOOL	1541 12TH AV, SF, 94122, (415)759-2764	667 - C2
ZANKER, PEARL ELEM SCHOOL	1585 FALLEN LEAF DR, MPS, 95035, (408)945-2438	814 - A3

SCHOOLS - PUBLIC HIGH

FEATURE NAME	Address City, ZIP Code	PAGE-GRID
ACALANES HIGH SCHOOL	1200 PLEASANT HILL RD, LFYT, 94549, (510)935-2600	611 - H4
ALAMEDA HIGH SCHOOL	2201 ENCINAL AV, ALA, 94501, (510)748-4022	669 - J2
ALBANY HIGH SCHOOL	603 KEY ROUTE BLVD, ALB, 94706, (510)559-6550	609 - E5
ALHAMBRA HIGH SCHOOL	150 E ST, MRTZ, 94553, (510)313-0440	571 - D5
AMADOR VALLEY HIGH SCHOOL	1155 SANTA RITA RD, PLE, 94566, (510)846-2818	714 - E2
AMERICAN HIGH SCHOOL	36300 FREMONT BLVD, FRMT, 94536, (510)796-1776	752 - G2
ANTIOCH HIGH SCHOOL	700 W 18TH ST, ANT, 94509, (510)706-5300	575 - C5
ARAGON HIGH SCHOOL	900 ALAMEDA DE LAS PULGAS, SMTO, 94402, (650)342-7980	748 - J3
ARROYO HIGH SCHOOL	15701 LORENZO AV, AlaC, 94580, (510)481-4662	691 - C7
BADEN (CONT) HIGH SHCOOL	825 SOUTHWOOD DR, SSF, 94080, (650)877-8769	707 - H3
BALBOA HIGH SCHOOL	1000 CAYUGA AV, SF, 94112, (415)469-4090	687 - F1
BENICIA HIGH SCHOOL	1101 MILITARY W, BEN, 94510, (707)747-8325	550 - J3
BERKELEY HIGH SCHOOL	2246 MILVIA ST, BERK, 94704, (510)644-6120	629 - G2
BLACKFORD HIGH SCHOOL	3800 BLACKFORD AV, SJS, 95117, (408)241-0330	853 - C2
BOHANNON HIGH CONTINUATION	800 BOCKMON RD, AlaC, 94580, (510)317-4400	711 - D2
BRENKWITZ CONTINUATION HS	22100 PRINCETON ST, HAY, 94541, (510)293-8330	711 - G1
BROADWAY CONTINUATION HIGH SCHOOL	1088 BROADWAY AV, SJS, 95125, (408)535-6285	854 - A3
BUNCHE CENTER CONTINUATION HS	1240 18TH ST, OAK, 94607, (510)832-1656	649 - E2
BURLINGAME HIGH SCHOOL	400 CAROLAN AV, BURL, 94010, (650)342-8971	728 - G6
BURTON, PHILLIP & SALA HS	400 MANSELL ST, SF, 94134, (415)469-4550	688 - A1
CALAVERAS HILLS CONTINUATION	1331 CALAVERAS BLVD, MPS, 95035, (408)945-2398	794 - C6
CALIFORNIA HIGH SCHOOL	9870 BROADMOOR DR, SRMN, 94583, (510)803-7400	673 - F5
CAMPOLINDO HIGH SCHOOL	300 MORAGA RD, MRGA, 94556, (510)376-5986	631 - E2
CAPUCHINO HIGH SCHOOL	1501 MAGNOLIA AV, SBRN, 94066, (650)583-9977	727 - J2
CARLMONT HIGH SCHOOL	1400 ALAMEDA DE LAS PULGAS, BLMT, 94002, (650)595-0210	769 - D3
CASTLEMONT HIGH SCHOOL	8601 MACARTHUR BLVD, OAK, 94605, (510)635-8600	671 - A3
CASTRO VALLEY HIGH SCHOOL	19400 SANTA MARIA AV, AlaC, 94546, (510)537-5910	692 - A4
CLAYTON VALLEY HIGH SCHOOL	1101 ALBERTA WY, CNCD, 94521, (510)682-7474	593 - D5
COLLEGE PARK HIGH SCHOOL	201 VIKING DR, PLHL, 94523, (510)682-7670	592 - B3
CONCORD HIGH SCHOOL	4200 CONCORD BLVD, CNCD, 94521, (510)687-2030	593 - B1
CUPERTINO HIGH SCHOOL	10100 FINCH AV, CPTO, 95014, (408)366-7380	852 - G1
DE ANZA HIGH SCHOOL	5000 VALLEY VIEW RD, RCH, 94803, (510)223-3811	589 - E2
DEER VALLEY HIGH SCHOOL	4700 LONETREE DR, ANT, 94509, (510)776-5555	595 - G4
DEL AMIGO CONTINUATION HS	189 DEL AMIGO RD, DNVL, 94526, (510)552-5571	652 - H1
DEL MAR HIGH SCHOOL	1224 DEL MAR AV, SJS, 95128, (408)298-0260	853 - G3
DEL VALLE CONTINUATION HIGH	2253 5TH ST, LVMR, 94550, (510)606-4709	715 - H1
DEWEY/BAYMART CONTINUATION HS	3709 E 12TH ST, OAK, 94601, (510)534-1721	670 - C1
DOWNTOWN CONTINUATION HIGH SCHOOL	110 BARTLETT ST, SF, 94110, (415)695-5860	667 - H3
DUBLIN HIGH SCHOOL	8151 VILLAGE PKWY, DBLN, 94568, (510)833-3300	693 - J2
EAST CAMPUS CONTINUATION HS	1950 CARLETON ST, BERK, 94704, (510)664-6159	629 - G3
EAST SIDE CENTER CONTINUATION	6701 E INTERNATIONAL BLVD, OAK, 94621, (510)638-5373	670 - F3
EL CAMINO HIGH SCHOOL	1320 MISSION RD, SSF, 94080, (650)877-8806	707 - F1
EL CERRITO HIGH SCHOOL	540 ASHBURY AV, ELCR, 94530, (510)525-0234	609 - E4
EL RANCHO VERDE ALT HIGH SCHOOL	541 BLANCHE ST, HAY, 94544, (510)471-5126	732 - F2
EMERY MIDDLE ACAD/EMERY HS	1100 47TH ST, EMVL, 94608, (510)652-1056	629 - F6
ENCINAL HIGH SCHOOL	210 CENTRAL AV, ALA, 94501, (510)748-4023	669 - E1
FOOTHILL CONTINUATION HIGH SCHOOL	230 PALA AV, SJS, 95127, (408)259-4464	834 - H2
FOOTHILL HIGH SCHOOL	4375 FOOTHILL RD, PLE, 94588, (510)462-4243	713 - J2
FREMONT HIGH SCHOOL	1279 SUNNYVALE-SARATOGA RD, SUNV, 94087, (408)522-2400	832 - D3
FREMONT HIGH SCHOOL	4610 FOOTHILL BLVD, OAK, 94601, (510)261-3240	670 - D1
GALILEO HIGH SCHOOL	1150 FRANCISCO ST, SF, 94109, (415)749-3430	647 - H3
GOMPERS, SAMUEL CONT HIGH SCHOOL	157 9TH ST, RCH, 94801, (510)234-1172	588 - F7
GRANADA HIGH SCHOOL	400 WALL ST, LVMR, 94550, (510)606-4800	715 - E2
GUNDERSON HIGH SCHOOL	620 GAUNDABERT LN, SJS, 95136, (408)535-6340	874 - F3
GUNN, HENRY M HIGH SCHOOL	780 ARASTRADERO RD, PA, 94306, (650)354-8200	811 - C4
HAYWARD HIGH SCHOOL	1633 EAST AV, HAY, 94541, (510)293-8586	712 - B2
HILL, ANDREW HIGH SCHOOL	3200 SENTER RD, SJS, 95111, (408)227-8800	854 - J5
HILLSDALE HIGH SCHOOL	3115 DEL MONTE ST, SMTO, 94403, (650)574-7230	749 - A6
HOGAN HIGH SCHOOL	850 ROSEWOOD AV, VAL, 94591, (707)556-8510	530 - E5
HOMESTEAD HIGH SCHOOL	21370 HOMESTEAD RD, CPTO, 95014, (650)522-2500	832 - C6
INDEPENDENCE HIGH SCHOOL	1717 44TH AV, SF, 94122, (415)242-2528	666 - H3
INDEPENDENCE HIGH SCHOOL	1776 EDUCATIONAL PARK DR, SJS, 95133, (408)729-3911	834 - F2
INTERNATIONAL STUDIES ACADEMY	693 VERMONT ST, SF, 94107, (415)595-5866	668 - A2
IRVINGTON HIGH SCHOOL	41800 BLACOW RD, FRMT, 94538, (510)656-5711	773 - C1
ISLAND CONTINUATION HIGH SCHOOL	2437 EAGLE AV, ALA, 94501, (510)748-4024	670 - A2
JC BUTTE HIGH SCHOOL	ASCOT PKWY, VAL, 94591	530 - F2
JEFFERSON HIGH SCHOOL	6996 MISSION ST, DALY, 94014, (650)992-4050	687 - C4
KENNEDY HIGH SCHOOL	4300 CUTTING BLVD, RCH, 94804, (510)235-2291	609 - A1
KENNEDY, JOHN F HIGH SCHOOL	39999 BLACOW RD, FRMT, 94538, (510)657-4070	753 - A7
LAS LOMAS HIGH SCHOOL	1460 S MAIN ST, WLCK, 94596, (510)935-4110	612 - D6
LEIGH HIGH SCHOOL	5210 LEIGH AV, SJS, 95124, (408)377-4470	873 - G5
LELAND HIGH SCHOOL	6677 CAMDEN AV, SJS, 95120, (408)535-6290	894 - G2
LIBERTY HIGH SCHOOL	350 K ST, BEN, 94510, (707)747-8323	551 - C5
LICK, JAMES HIGH SCHOOL	57 N WHITE RD, SJS, 95127, (408)729-3580	834 - J2

FEATURE NAME / Address City, ZIP Code	PAGE-GRID
LINCOLN HIGH SCOOL 2600 TEAGARDEN ST, SLN, 94577, (510)667-3578	691 - A3
LINCOLN, ABRAHAM HIGH SCHOOL 2162 24TH AV, SF, 94116, (415)759-2700	667 - B4
LINCOLN, ABRAHAM HIGH SCHOOL 555 DANA AV, SJS, 95126, (408)535-6300	833 - G7
LIVE OAK CONTINUATION HIGH SCHOOL 1708 F ST, ANT, 94509, (510)706-5206	575 - D5
LIVERMORE HIGH SCHOOL 600 MAPLE ST, LVMR, 94550, (510)606-4812	715 - H1
LOGAN, JAMES HIGH SCHOOL 1800 H ST, UNC, 94587, (510)471-2520	732 - F6
LOS ALTOS HIGH SCHOOL 201 ALMOND AV, LALT, 94022, (650)968-6571	811 - E6
LOS GATOS HIGH SCHOOL 20 HIGH SCHOOL CT, LGTS, 95032, (408)354-2730	893 - A1
LOWELL HIGH SCHOOL 1101 EUCALYPTUS DR, SF, 94132, (415)759-2730	667 - B6
LYNBROOK HIGH SCHOOL 1280 JOHNSON AV, SJS, 95129, (408)366-7700	852 - G4
MARK TWAIN CONTINUATION HS 17421 W FARLEY RD, LGTS, 95030, (408)354-1919	873 - B5
MARSHALL, THURGOOD ACADEMIC HS 45 CONKLING ST, SF, 94124, (415)695-5612	668 - A6
MCATEER, EUGENE J HIGH SCHOOL 555 PORTOLA DR, SF, 94131, (415)695-5700	667 - E4
MCCLYMONDS HIGH SCHOOL 2607 MYRTLE ST, OAK, 94607, (510)893-6569	649 - F2
MENLO-ATHERTON HIGH SCHOOL 555 MIDDLEFIELD RD, ATN, 94027, (650)322-5311	790 - G2
MIDDLE COLLEGE HIGH SCHOOL 2600 MISSION BELL DR, SPAB, 94806, (510)235-7800	588 - J2
MILLS HIGH SCHOOL 400 MURCHISON DR, MLBR, 94030, (650)697-3344	728 - B4
MILPITAS HIGH SCHOOL 1285 ESCUELA PKWY, MPS, 95035, (408)945-5500	794 - A4
MIRAMONTE HIGH SCHOOL 750 MORAGA WY, ORIN, 94563, (510)376-4423	631 - C6
MISSION HIGH SCHOOL 3750 18TH ST, SF, 94114, (415)241-6240	667 - H2
MISSION SAN JOSE HIGH SCHOOL 41717 PALM AV, FRMT, 94539, (510)657-3600	753 - G5
MOFFETT HIGH SCHOOL 333 MOFFETT BLVD, MTVW, 94043, (650)940-1333	811 - J4
MONTA VISTA HIGH SCHOOL 21840 MCCLELLAN RD, CPTO, 95014, (408)366-7600	852 - B2
MONTE VISTA HIGH SCHOOL 3131 STONE VALLEY RD, DNVL, 94526, (510)552-5530	633 - B6
MONTECITO HIGH SCHOOL 600 F ST, MRTZ, 94553, (510)228-3276	571 - E5
MOUNT DIABLO HIGH SCHOOL 2450 GRANT ST, CNCD, 94520, (510)682-4030	592 - F1
MOUNT EDEN HIGH SCHOOL 2300 PANAMA ST, HAY, 94545, (510)293-8539	731 - H1
MOUNT PLEASANT HIGH SCHOOL 1750 S WHITE RD, SJS, 95127, (408)251-7820	835 - B5
MOUNTAIN VIEW HIGH SCHOOL 3535 TRUMAN AV, MTVW, 94040, (408)940-4600	832 - A2
NEW VALLEY CONTINUATION HS 1840 BENTON ST, SCL, 95050, (408)984-0632	833 - D5
NEWARK MEMORIAL HIGH SCHOOL 39375 CEDAR BLVD, NWK, 94560, (510)794-2145	772 - H1
NEWCOMER HIGH (LEP) SCHOOL 2340 JACKSON ST, SF, 94115, (415)241-6584	647 - G5
NORTH CAMPUS CONT HIGH SCHOOL 2465 DOLAN WY, CCCo, 94806, (510)741-2857	569 - B5
NORTHGATE HIGH SCHOOL 425 CASTLE ROCK RD, WLCK, 94598, (510)938-0900	612 - J4
NOVATO HIGH SCHOOL 625 ARTHUR ST, NVTO, 94947, (415)898-2125	526 - B6
OAK GROVE HIGH SCHOOL 285 BLOSSOM HILL RD, SJS, 95123, (408)225-9332	875 - A4
OAKLAND HIGH SCHOOL 1023 MACARTHUR BLVD, OAK, 94610, (510)451-1208	650 - B4
OAKLAND TECHNICAL HIGH SCHOOL 4351 BROADWAY, OAK, 94609, (510)658-5300	629 - J7
OCEANA HIGH SCHOOL 401 PALOMA AV, PCFA, 94044, (650)355-4131	707 - A5
OCONNELL, JOHN HIGH SCHOOL 1920 41ST AV, SF, 94116, (415)759-2724	666 - J3
OLYMPIC CONTINUATION HIGH SCHOOL 2730 SALVIO ST, CNCD, 94519, (510)687-0363	592 - G1
OVERFELT, WILLIAM C HIGH SCHOOL 1835 CUNNINGHAM AV, SJS, 95122, (408)259-0540	834 - J7
PALO ALTO HIGH SCHOOL 50 EMBARCADERO RD, PA, 94301, (650)329-3710	790 - J6
PEGASUS CONTINUATION HIGH SCHOOL 1776 EDUCATIONAL PARK DR, SJS, 95133, (408)729-3911	834 - F2
PENINSULA CONTINUATION HS 300 PIEDMONT AV, SBRN, 94066, (650)583-3016	727 - G2
PEOPLES CONT HIGH 233 HOBBS AV, VAL, 94589, (707)644-0456	530 - B1
PIEDMONT HIGH SCHOOL 800 MAGNOLIA AV, PDMT, 94611, (510)420-3626	650 - B1
PIEDMONT HILLS HIGH SCHOOL 1377 PIEDMONT RD, SJS, 95132, (408)729-3950	814 - G4
PINOLE VALLEY HIGH SCHOOL 2900 PINOLE VALLEY RD, PIN, 94564, (510)758-4664	569 - F6
PIONEER HIGH SCHOOL 1290 BLOSSOM HILL RD, SJS, 95118, (408)535-6310	874 - C4
PITTSBURG HIGH SCHOOL 250 SCHOOL ST, PIT, 94565, (510)473-4100	574 - E3
PROSPECT HIGH SCHOOL 18900 PROSPECT RD, SAR, 95070, (408)253-1662	852 - H5
PROSPECTS HIGH SCHOOL 820 W 2ND ST, ANT, 94509, (510)706-5310	575 - C3
REDWOOD ALTERNATIVE HIGH SCHOOL 18400 CLIFTON WY, AlaC, 94546, (510)537-3193	691 - H3
REDWOOD HIGH (CONT) 1968 OLD COUNTY RD, RDWC, 94063, (650)369-1411	769 - J4
REDWOOD HIGH SCHOOL 395 DOHERTY DR, LKSP, 94939, (415)924-6200	586 - G6
RICHMOND HIGH SCHOOL 1250 23RD ST, RCH, 94804, (510)237-8770	588 - H4
RIVERSIDE CONTINUATION HS 809 BLACK DIAMOND ST, PIT, 94565, (510)473-4487	574 - E2
ROBERTSON CONTINUATION HS 4455 SENECA PARK AV, FRMT, 94538, (510)657-9155	773 - C2
SAN ANDREAS CONT HIGH SCHOOL 599 WILLIAM AV, LKSP, 94939, (415)945-3770	586 - F6
SAN JOSE ACADEMY HIGH SCHOOL 275 N 24TH ST, SJS, 95116, (408)535-6320	834 - D4
SAN LEANDRO HIGH SCHOOL 2200 BANCROFT AV, SLN, 94577, (510)667-3540	691 - C2
SAN LORENZO HIGH SCHOOL 50 E LEWELLING BLVD, AlaC, 94580, (510)481-4627	691 - E6
SAN MARIN HIGH SCHOOL 15 SAN MARIN DR, NVTO, 94945, (415)898-2121	525 - G1
SAN MATEO HIGH SCHOOL 506 N DELAWARE ST, SMTO, 94401, (650)348-8050	728 - J7
SAN RAFAEL HIGH SCHOOL 185 MISSION AV, SRFL, 94901, (415)485-2330	586 - H1
SAN RAMON VALLEY HIGH SCHOOL 140 LOVE LN, DNVL, 94526, (510)552-5580	652 - J1
SANTA CLARA HIGH SCHOOL 3000 BENTON ST, SCL, 95051, (408)985-5900	833 - A5
SANTA TERESA HIGH SCHOOL 6150 SNELL RD, SJS, 95123, (408)578-9100	874 - J6
SARATOGA HIGH SCHOOL 20300 HERRIMAN AV, SAR, 95070, (408)867-3411	872 - E1
SCHOOL OF THE ARTS HIGH SCHOOL 700 FONT BLVD, SF, 94132, (415)469-4027	667 - A7
SEQUOIA HIGH SCHOOL 1201 BREWSTER AV, RDWC, 94062, (650)367-9780	770 - A6
SHORELINE CONTINUATION HS 1299 BRYANT AV, MTVW, 94040, (408)940-4656	832 - A2
SILVER CREEK HIGH SCHOOL 3434 SILVER CREEK RD, SJS, 95121, (408)274-1700	855 - B4
SIR FRANCIS DRAKE HIGH SCHOOL 1327 SIR FRANCIS DRAKE BLVD, SANS, 94960, (415)453-8770	566 - B6
SKYLINE HIGH SCHOOL 12250 SKYLINE BLVD, OAK, 94619, (510)531-9161	651 - A5
SOUTH SAN FRANCISCO HIGH SCHOOL 400 B ST, SSF, 94080, (650)877-8754	707 - G4
SOUTHWOOD HIGH SCHOOL 825 SOUTHWOOD DR, SSF, 94080, (650)877-8769	707 - F3
SWETT, JOHN HIGH SCHOOL 1098 POMONA ST, CCCo, 94525, (510)787-1088	550 - D5
TAMALPAIS HIGH SCHOOL 700 MILLER AV, MLV, 94941, (415)388-3292	606 - F5
TENNYSON HIGH SCHOOL 27035 WHITMAN RD, HAY, 94544, (510)293-8591	712 - B5
TERRA LINDA HIGH SCHOOL 320 NOVA ALBION WY, SRFL, 94903, (415)492-3100	566 - D4
TERRA NOVA HIGH SCHOOL 1450 TERRA NOVA BLVD, PCFA, 94044, (650)359-3961	727 - B4
VALLEJO HIGH SCHOOL 840 NEBRASKA ST, VAL, 94590, (707)556-8700	530 - B3
VALLEY HIGH SCHOOL CONTINUATION 6901 YORK DR, DBLN, 94568, (510)829-4322	693 - J3
VILLAGE CONTINUATION HIGH SCHOOL 4645 BERNAL AV, PLE, 94566, (510)426-4260	714 - E4
VINEYARD ALTERNATIVE HIGH SCHOOL 543 SONOMA AV, LVMR, 94550, (510)606-4756	715 - E2
WALLENBERG, RAOUL TRADITIONAL HS 40 VEGA ST, SF, 94115, (415)749-3469	647 - F7
WASHINGTON HIGH SCHOOL 38442 FREMONT BLVD, FRMT, 94536, (510)794-8866	752 - J4
WASHINGTON, GEORGE HIGH SCHOOL 600 32ND AV, SF, 94121, (415)750-8400	647 - A7
WELLS, IDA B / TWAIN, MARK HS 1099 HAYES ST, SF, 94117, (415)241-6315	647 - G7
WESTMONT HIGH SCHOOL 4805 WESTMONT AV, SJS, 95008, (408)378-1500	873 - A1
WESTMOOR HIGH SCHOOL 131 WESTMOOR AV, DALY, 94015, (650)756-3434	687 - A6
WILCOX, ADRIAN HIGH SCHOOL 3250 MONROE ST, SCL, 95051, (408)554-6300	833 - A2
WILLOW GLEN HIGH SCHOOL 2001 COTTLE AV, SJS, 95125, (408)535-6330	854 - A5
WOODSIDE HIGH SCHOOL 199 CHURCHILL AV, SMCo, 94062, (650)367-9750	790 - A4
YERBA BUENA HIGH SCHOOL 1855 LUCRETIA AV, SJS, 95122, (408)279-1500	854 - G1
YGNACIO VALLEY HIGH SCHOOL 755 OAK GROVE RD, CNCD, 94518, (510)685-8414	592 - G7

SCHOOLS - PUBLIC INTERMEDIATE

FEATURE NAME / Address City, ZIP Code	PAGE-GRID
BERNAL INTERMEDIATE SCHOOL 6610 SAN IGNACIO DR, SJS, 95119, (408)578-5731	875 - D7
BLACH, GEORGINA P INTERMEDIATE 1120 COVINGTON RD, LALT, 94024, (650)964-1196	831 - H2
BURLINGAME INTERMEDIATE SCHOOL 1715 QUESADA WY, BURL, 94010, (650)259-3830	728 - B5
DAVIS, CAROLINE INTER SCHOOL 5035 EDENVIEW DR, SJS, 95111, (408)227-8550	875 - A2
EGAN, ARDIS G INTERMEDIATE SCHOOL 100 W PORTOLA AV, LALT, 94022, (650)941-6174	811 - D4
FOOTHILL INTERMEDIATE SCHOOL 1966 FLINT AV, SJS, 95148, (408)223-3750	835 - C5
FRANKLIN, BENJAMIN INTER SCHOOL 700 STEWART AV, SMCo, 94015, (650)991-1202	687 - B4
HARTE, BRET INTERMEDIATE SCHOOL 1047 E ST, HAY, 94541, (510)293-8578	712 - A2
HARVEST PARK INTERMEDIATE SCHOOL 4900 VALLEY AV, PLE, 94566, (510)846-6828	714 - D1
HERMAN, LEONARD INTER SCHOOL 5955 BLOSSOM AV, SJS, 95123, (408)226-1886	874 - H5
HYDE INTERMEDIATE SCHOOL 19325 BOLLINGER RD, CPTO, 95014, (408)252-6290	852 - G2
KING, MARTIN LUTHER JR INTER 26890 HOLLY HILL AV, HAY, 94545, (510)293-8528	711 - H7
LA VISTA INTERMEDIATE SCHOOL 27845 WHITMAN RD, HAY, 94544, (510)293-8581	712 - B6
LEYVA, GEORGE V INTER SCHOOL 1865 MONROVIA DR, SJS, 95122, (408)270-4992	855 - B2
LIPMAN INTERMEDIATE SCHOOL 1 SOLANO ST, BSBN, 94005, (650)467-9541	687 - J6
MCKINLEY INTERMEDIATE SCHOOL 400 DUANE ST, RDWC, 94062, (650)366-3827	770 - A6
MCNAIR, RONALD INTER SCHOOL 2033 PULGAS AV, EPA, 94303, (650)329-2888	791 - C2
MORAGA, JOAQUIN INTER SCHOOL 1010 CM PABLO, MRGA, 94556, (510)376-7206	651 - D1
OCHOA, ANTHONY W INTER SCHOOL 2121 DEPOT RD, HAY, 94545, (510)293-8532	711 - F6
ORINDA INTERMEDIATE SCHOOL 80 IVY DR, ORIN, 94563, (510)376-4402	631 - C5
PARKSIDE INTERMEDIATE SCHOOL 1801 NILES AV, SBRN, 94066, (650)244-0160	727 - H1
PINE VALLEY INTERMEDIATE SCHOOL 3000 PINE VALLEY RD, SRMN, 94583, (510)803-7420	673 - G7
QUIMBY OAK INTERMEDIATE SCHOOL 3190 QUIMBY RD, SJS, 95148, (408)270-6735	855 - E1
RALSTON INTERMEDIATE 2675 RALSTON AV, BLMT, 94002, (650)637-4880	769 - A2
RIVERA, FERNANDO INTER SCHOOL 1255 SOUTHGATE AV, DALY, 94015, (650)991-1225	687 - A7
ROBERTSON, GARNET J INTER SCHOOL 1 MARTIN ST, DALY, 94014, (415)467-5443	687 - J4
STANLEY, M H INTERMEDIATE SCHOOL 3455 SCHOOL ST, LFYT, 94549, (510)283-6282	611 - F7
WALNUT CREEK INTERMEDIATE SCHOOL 2425 WALNUT BLVD, WLCK, 94596, (510)944-6840	612 - D4
WINTON INTERMEDIATE SCHOOL 119 W WINTON AV, HAY, 94544, (510)293-8583	711 - H3

SCHOOLS - PUBLIC JUNIOR HIGH

FEATURE NAME / Address City, ZIP Code	PAGE-GRID
ARTS SCHOOL 5263 BROADWAY TER, OAK, 94618, (510)658-4926	630 - A6
BOEGER,AUGUST JUNIOR HIGH SCHOOL 1944 FLINT AV, SJS, 95148, (408)223-3770	835 - C5
BREWER, EDNA JUNIOR HIGH SCHOOL 3748 13TH AV, OAK, 94602, (510)530-4550	650 - C4
CENTERVILLE JUNIOR HIGH SCHOOL 37720 FREMONT BLVD, FRMT, 94536, (510)797-2072	752 - J4
CENTRAL JUNIOR HIGH SCHOOL 1201 STONEMAN AV, PIT, 94565, (510)473-4450	574 - F5
CUPERTINO JUNIOR HIGH SCHOOL 1650 BERNARDO AV, SUNV, 94087, (408)245-0303	832 - B5
FAIR, J WILBUR JUNIOR HIGH SCHOOL 1702 MCLAUGHLIN AV, SJS, 95122, (408)283-6400	854 - G1
FRANKLIN JUNIOR HIGH SCHOOL 501 STARR AV, VAL, 94590, (707)556-8470	530 - C5
FRICK JUNIOR HIGH SCHOOL 2845 64TH AV, OAK, 94605, (510)562-6565	670 - G1
HARTE, BRET JUNIOR HIGH SCHOOL 3700 COOLIDGE AV, OAK, 94602, (510)482-5825	650 - E4
HAVENSCOURT JUNIOR HIGH SCHOOL 1390 66TH AV, OAK, 94621, (510)562-7911	670 - F3
HILLVIEW JUNIOR HIGH SCHOOL 333 YOSEMITE DR, PIT, 94565, (510)473-4401	574 - D5
HOPKINS, WILLIAM JR HS 600 DRISCOLL RD, FRMT, 94539, (510)656-3500	753 - F5
HORNER, JOHN M JUNIOR HIGH SCHOOL 41365 CHAPEL WY, FRMT, 94538, (510)656-4000	753 - D7
KENNEDY JUNIOR HIGH SCHOOL 821 BUBB RD, CPTO, 95014, (408)253-1525	852 - B2
KING ESTATES JUNIOR HIGH SCHOOL 8251 FONTAINE ST, OAK, 94605, (510)569-1569	671 - B2
MARTINEZ JUNIOR HIGH SCHOOL 1600 COURT ST, MRTZ, 94553, (510)313-0414	571 - E3
MILLER JUNIOR HIGH SCHOOL 6151 RAINBOW DR, SJS, 95129, (408)252-3755	852 - G3
MONTERA JUNIOR HIGH SCHOOL 5555 ASCOT DR, OAK, 94611, (510)531-0626	650 - F2
NEWARK JUNIOR HIGH SCHOOL 6201 LAFAYETTE AV, NWK, 94560, (510)794-2062	752 - D5
REDWOOD MIDDLE SCHOOL 13925 FRUITVALE AV, SAR, 95070, (408)867-3042	872 - F1
ROOSEVELT JUNIOR HIGH SCHOOL 1926 19TH AV, OAK, 94606, (510)261-8516	650 - B6
SIMMONS, CALVIN JR HS 2101 35TH AV, OAK, 94601, (510)534-0610	650 - D6
SOLANO JUNIOR HIGH 1025 CORCORAN AV, VAL, 94589, (707)643-8641	510 - C5
SPRINGSTOWNE JUNIOR HIGH SCHOOL 2833 TENNESSEE ST, VAL, 94591, (707)643-8471	530 - E4
SYLVANDALE JUNIOR HIGH SCHOOL 653 SYLVANDALE AV, SJS, 95111, (408)363-5700	854 - J6
THORNTON JUNIOR HIGH SCHOOL 4357 THORNTON AV, FRMT, 94536, (510)792-4700	752 - G3
VALLEJO JUNIOR HIGH SCHOOL 1347 AMADOR ST, VAL, 94590, (707)643-2341	530 - A3
WALTERS, G M JUNIOR HIGH SCHOOL 39600 LOGAN DR, FRMT, 94538, (510)656-7211	753 - A6
WESTLAKE JUNIOR HIGH SCHOOL 2629 HARRISON ST, OAK, 94612, (510)893-1045	649 - H2

SCHOOLS - PUBLIC MIDDLE

FEATURE NAME / Address City, ZIP Code	PAGE-GRID
ABBOTT MIDDLE SCHOOL 600 36TH AV, SMTO, 94403, (650)312-7600	749 - B6
ADAMS MIDDLE SCHOOL 5000 PATTERSON CIR, CCCo, 94805, (510)235-5464	589 - B5
ALBANY MIDDLE SCHOOL 1000 JACKSON ST, ALB, 94706, (510)559-6540	609 - D6
ALTA LOMA MIDDLE SCHOOL 116 ROMNEY AV, SSF, 94080, (650)877-8797	707 - E2
ALVARADO MIDDLE SCHOOL 31604 ALVARADO BLVD, UNC, 94587, (510)489-0700	732 - A5
ANTIOCH MIDDLE SCHOOL 1500 D ST, ANT, 94509, (510)706-5316	575 - D5
APTOS MIDDLE SCHOOL 105 APTOS AV, SF, 94127, (415)469-4520	667 - C6
BANCROFT MIDDLE SCHOOL 1150 BANCROFT AV, SLN, 94577, (510)667-3561	691 - B1
BARNARD-WHITE MIDDLE SCHOOL 725 WHIPPLE RD, UNC, 94587, (510)471-5363	732 - F3
BAYSIDE MIDDLE SCHOOL 2025 KEHOE AV, SMTO, 94403, (650)312-7660	749 - C1
BENICIA MIDDLE SCHOOL 1100 SOUTHAMPTON RD, BEN, 94510, (707)747-8340	550 - J2
BLACK DIAMOND MIDDLE SCHOOL 4730 STERLING HILLS DR, ANT, 94509, (510)776-5500	595 - H3
BOREL MIDDLE SCHOOL 425 BARNESON AV, SMTO, 94402, (650)312-7670	749 - A4
BOWDITCH MIDDLE SCHOOL 1450 TARPON ST, FCTY, 94404, (650)312-7680	749 - J2
BUCHSER, EMIL MIDDLE SCHOOL 1111 BELLOMY ST, SCL, 95050, (408)984-2900	833 - E5
BURBANK, LUTHER MIDDLE SCHOOL 325 LA GRANDE AV, SF, 94112, (415)469-4547	687 - H1
BURNETT, PETER MIDDLE SCHOOL 850 N 2ND ST, SJS, 95112, (408)535-6267	834 - A4
CABRILLO MIDDLE 2550 CABRILLO AV, SCL, 95051, (408)983-2660	833 - B3
CAMPBELL MIDDLE SCHOOL 295 W CHERRY LN, CMBL, 95008, (408)364-4222	853 - D6
CANYON MIDDLE SCHOOL 19600 CULL CANYON RD, AlaC, 94552, (510)538-8833	692 - D4
CARQUINEZ MIDDLE SCHOOL 1099 POMONA ST, CCCo, 94525, (510)787-1081	550 - D5
CARTER, VERDESE MIDDLE SCHOOL 4521 WEBSTER ST, OAK, 94609, (510)654-8936	629 - H7
CASTILLERO MIDDLE SCHOOL 6384 LEYLAND PARK DR, SJS, 95120, (408)535-6385	894 - C1
CASTRO, ELVIRA MIDDLE SCHOOL 4600 STUDENT LN, SJS, 95130, (408)379-3620	853 - A5
CENTRAL MIDDLE SCHOOL 828 CHESTNUT ST, SCAR, 94070, (650)508-7321	769 - G4
CESAR CHAVEZ MIDDLE SCHOOL 2801 HOP RANCH RD, UNC, 94587, (510)487-1700	732 - D6
CHABOYA MIDDLE SCHOOL 3276 FOWLER RD, SJS, 95135, (408)270-6900	855 - G3
CHIPMAN MIDDLE SCHOOL 401 PACIFIC AV, ALA, 94501, (510)748-4017	649 - E7
CLAREMONT MIDDLE SCHOOL 5750 COLLEGE AV, OAK, 94618, (510)652-3931	629 - J5
COLUMBIA MIDDLE SCHOOL MORSE AV, SUNV, 94086, (408)522-8247	812 - F5
CRESPI MIDDLE SCHOOL 1121 ALLVIEW AV, CCCo, 94803, (510)223-8611	569 - C7
CRITTENDEN MIDDLE SCHOOL 1701 ROCK ST, MTVW, 94043, (650)903-6945	811 - H2
CROCKER, WILLIAM H MIDDLE SCHOOL 2600 RALSTON AV, HIL, 94010, (650)342-6331	748 - E1
DARTMOUTH MIDDLE SCHOOL 5575 DARTMOUTH DR, SJS, 95118, (408)264-1122	874 - A5
DAVIDSON, JAMES B MIDDLE SCHOOL 280 WOODLAND AV, SRFL, 94901, (415)485-2400	586 - G2
DAVIS, GLORIA B. MIDDLE SCHOOL 1195 HUDSON ST, SF, 94124, (415)469-4547	668 - D6
DEL MAR INTERMEDIATE SCHOOL 105 AVD MIRAFLORES, TBRN, 94920, (415)435-1468	607 - B5
DENMAN, JAMES MIDDLE SCHOOL 241 ONEIDA AV, SF, 94112, (415)469-4535	687 - F1
DIABLO VIEW MIDDLE SCHOOL 300 DIABLO VW LN, CLAY, 94517, (510)672-0898	613 - J1
EAST AVENUE MIDDLE SCHOOL 3951 EAST AV, LVMR, 94550, (510)606-4709	715 - J1

FEATURE NAME	Address City, ZIP Code	PAGE-GRID
EL DORADO MIDDLE SCHOOL	1750 WEST ST, CNCD, 94521, (510)682-5700	593 - B2
ELMHURST MIDDLE SCHOOL	1800 98TH AV, OAK, 94603, (510)562-5755	670 - J5
EVERETT MIDDLE SCHOOL	450 CHURCH ST, SF, 94114, (415)241-6344	667 - G2
FISCHER, CLYDE L MIDDLE SCHOOL	1720 HOPKINS DR, SJS, 95122, (408)258-6244	834 - J6
FISHER, RAYMOND J MIDDLE SCHOOL	17000 ROBERTS RD, LGTS, 95032, (408)356-2141	873 - B6
FOOTHILL MIDDLE SCHOOL	2775 CEDRO LN, WLCK, 94598, (510)939-8600	612 - H2
FOSTER, MARCUS MIDDLE SCHOOL	2850 WEST ST, OAK, 94609, (510)763-1178	649 - G2
FRANCISCO MIDDLE SCHOOL	2190 POWELL ST, SF, 94133, (415)291-7900	648 - A3
FRANKLIN, BENJAMIN MIDDLE SCHOOL	1430 SCOTT ST, SF, 94115, (415)749-3476	647 - G6
GEORGE, JOSEPH MIDDLE SCHOOL	277 MAHONEY DR, SJS, 95127, (408)259-2402	835 - A1
GIANNINI, A P MIDDLE SCHOOL	3151 ORTEGA ST, SF, 94116, (415)759-2770	666 - J3
GLENBROOK MIDDLE SCHOOL	2351 OLIVERA RD, CNCD, 94520, (510)685-6835	572 - F6
GRAHAM, ISSAC NEWTON MIDDLE	1175 CASTRO ST, MTVW, 94040, (650)965-9292	811 - H6
HALL MIDDLE SCHOOL	200 DOHERTY DR, LKSP, 94939, (415)927-6978	586 - F5
HARTE, BRET MIDDLE SCHOOL	7050 BRET HARTE DR, SJS, 95120, (408)535-6270	894 - G2
HELMS MIDDLE SCHOOL	2500 RD 20, SPAB, 94806, (510)233-3988	588 - J3
HILL MIDDLE SCHOOL	720 DIABLO AV, NVTO, 94947, (415)899-9300	526 - B4
HILLVIEW MIDDLE SCHOOL	1100 ELDER AV, MLPK, 94025, (650)326-4341	790 - E5
HOOVER, HERBERT MIDDLE SCHOOL	2290 14TH AV, SF, 94116, (415)759-2783	667 - C4
IRON HORSE MIDDLE SCHOOL	12601 ALCOSTA BLVD, SRMN, 94583, (510)824-2820	673 - E2
JANE LATHROP STANFORD MIDDLE	480 E MEADOW DR, PA, 94306, (650)856-1713	811 - D1
JOHN MUIR MIDDLE SCHOOL	1260 BRANHAM LN, SJS, 95118, (408)535-6281	874 - C3
JORDAN, DAVID STARR MIDDLE SCHOOL	750 N CALIFORNIA AV, PA, 94303, (650)494-8120	791 - C6
JUNCTION AVENUE MIDDLE SCHOOL	298 JUNCTION AV, LVMR, 94550, (510)606-4720	695 - H7
KENNEDY, JOHN F MIDDLE SCHOOL	2521 GOODWIN AV, RDWC, 94061, (650)365-4611	789 - J2
KENT, ADALINE E MIDDLE SCHOOL	250 STADIUM WY, MrnC, 94904, (415)925-2200	586 - D3
KING, MARTIN LUTHER ACADEMIC MID	350 GIRARD ST, SF, 94134, (415)330-1500	668 - A7
KING, MARTIN LUTHER MIDDLE SCHOOL	1781 ROSE ST, BERK, 94703, (510)644-6280	609 - F7
LA ENTRADA MIDDLE SCHOOL	2200 SHARON RD, MLPK, 94025, (650)854-3962	790 - D7
LICK, JAMES MIDDLE SCHOOL	1220 NOE ST, SF, 94114, (415)695-5675	667 - G4
LINCOLN MIDDLE SCHOOL	1250 FERNSIDE BLVD, ALA, 94501, (510)748-4018	670 - B4
LONGFELLOW ARTS & TECHNOLOGY	1500 DERBY ST, BERK, 94703, (510)644-6313	629 - F3
LOS CERROS MIDDLE SCHOOL	968 BLEMER RD, DNVL, 94526, (510)552-5620	633 - C7
LOWELL MIDDLE SCHOOL	991 14TH ST, OAK, 94607, (510)832-1436	649 - F3
MADISON MIDDLE SCHOOL	400 CAPISTRANO DR, OAK, 94603, (510)568-5889	690 - H1
MANN, HORACE MIDDLE SCHOOL	3351 23RD ST, SF, 94110, (415)695-5881	667 - H3
MARINA MIDDLE SCHOOL	3500 FILLMORE ST, SF, 94123, (415)749-3495	647 - G4
MARKHAM, EDWIN MIDDLE SCHOOL	2105 COTTLE AV, SJS, 95125, (408)535-6227	854 - A5
MATHSON, LEE MIDDLE SCHOOL	2050 KAMMERER AV, SJS, 95116, (408)251-3232	834 - H4
MENDENHALL, WILLIAM MIDDLE SCHOOL	1701 EL PADRO DR, LVMR, 94550, (510)606-4731	715 - E3
MILL VALLEY MIDDLE SCHOOL	425 SYCAMORE AV, MLV, 94941, (415)389-7711	606 - F4
MILLER CREEK MIDDLE SCHOOL	2255 LAS GALLINAS AV, MrnC, 94903, (415)479-1660	546 - D7
MONROE MIDDLE SCHOOL	1055 S MONROE ST, SJS, 95128, (408)364-4232	853 - E3
MORRILL MIDDLE SCHOOL	1970 MORRILL AV, SJS, 95132, (408)923-1930	814 - E3
MUIR, JOHN MIDDLE SCHOOL	1444 WILLIAMS ST, SLN, 94577, (510)667-3570	690 - J2
MURPHY, MARTIN MIDDLE SCHOOL	141 AVD ESPANA, SJS, 95139, (408)779-8351	895 - F1
OAK GROVE MIDDLE SCHOOL	2050 MINERT RD, CNCD, 94518, (510)682-1843	592 - F7
OCALA MIDDLE SCHOOL	2800 OCALA AV, SJS, 95148, (408)923-2800	835 - B5
ORTEGA MIDDLE SCHOOL	1283 TERRA NOVA BLVD, PCFA, 94044, (650)359-3941	727 - A5
PACIFIC HEIGHTS MIDDLE SCHOOL	3791 PACIFIC HEIGHTS BLVD, SBRN, 94066, (650)355-6900	707 - C6
PALA MIDDLE SCHOOL	149 N WHITE RD, SJS, 95127, (408)258-4996	834 - J2
PARK MIDDLE SCHOOL	1 SPARTAN WY, ANT, 94509, (510)706-5314	575 - C7
PARKWAY HEIGHTS MIDDLE SCHOOL	825 PARK WY, SSF, 94080, (650)877-8788	707 - G2
PETERSON MIDDLE SCHOOL	1380 ROSALIA AV, SUNV, 94087, (408)720-8540	832 - G4
PIEDMONT MIDDLE SCHOOL	740 MAGNOLIA AV, PDMT, 94611, (510)420-3660	650 - B1
PIEDMONT MIDDLE SCHOOL	955 PIEDMONT RD, SJS, 95132, (408)923-1945	814 - G5
PINE HOLLOW MIDDLE SCHOOL	5522 PINE HOLLOW RD, CNCD, 94521, (510)672-5444	593 - F7
PINOLE MIDDLE SCHOOL	1575 MANN DR, PIN, 94564, (510)724-4042	569 - D5
PLEASANTON MIDDLE SCHOOL	5001 CASE AV, AlaC, 94566, (510)426-4390	714 - D4
POLLICITA, THOMAS R MIDDLE SCHOOL	550 E MARKET ST, DALY, 94014, (650)991-1216	687 - D5
PORTOLA MIDDLE SCHOOL	1021 NAVELLIER ST, ELCR, 94530, (510)524-0405	609 - D2
POTRERO HILL MIDDLE SCHOOL	655 DE HARO ST, SF, 94107, (415)695-5905	668 - B2
PRESIDIO MIDDLE SCHOOL	450 30TH AV, SF, 94121, (415)750-8435	647 - A6
PRICE, IDA MIDDLE SCHOOL	2650 NEW JERSEY AV, SJS, 95124, (408)377-2532	873 - G1
RANCHO MILPITAS MIDDLE SCHOOL	1915 YELLOWSTONE AV, MPS, 95035, (408)945-5561	814 - D1
RIVERVIEW MIDDLE SCHOOL	205 PACIFICA AV, CCCo, 94565, (510)458-3216	573 - E1
ROGERS, SAMUEL C MIDDLE SCHOOL	4835 DOYLE RD, SJS, 95129, (408)253-7262	852 - J3
ROLLING HILLS MIDDLE SCHOOL	1585 MORE AV, CMBL, 95030, (408)364-4235	872 - J1
ROOSEVELT MIDDLE SCHOOL	460 ARGUELLO BLVD, SF, 94118, (415)750-8446	647 - D6
RUSSEL, THOMAS MIDDLE SCHOOL	1500 ESCUELA PKWY, MPS, 95035, (408)945-2312	794 - B4
SAN JOSE MIDDLE SCHOOL	1000 SUNSET PKWY, NVTO, 94949, (415)883-7831	526 - B7
SEQUOIA MIDDLE SCHOOL	265 BOYD RD, PLHL, 94523, (510)934-8174	592 - C6
SHEPPARD, WILLIAM L MIDDLE SCHOOL	480 ROUGH AND READY RD, SJS, 95133, (408)258-4323	834 - H1
SIERRAMONT MIDDLE SCHOOL	3155 KIMLEE DR, SJS, 95132, (408)923-1955	814 - F4
SINALOA MIDDLE SCHOOL	2045 VINEYARD RD, NVTO, 94947, (415)897-2111	525 - H3
STEINBECK MIDDLE SCHOOL	820 STEINBECK DR, SJS, 95123, (408)535-6395	874 - E4
STONE VALLEY MIDDLE SCHOOL	3001 MIRANDA AV, CCCo, 94507, (510)552-5640	632 - G4
SUNNYVALE MIDDLE SCHOOL	1080 MANGO AV, SUNV, 94087, (408)522-8288	832 - B2
TAYLOR MIDDLE SCHOOL	850 TAYLOR BLVD, MLBR, 94030, (650)697-4096	728 - A4
UNION MIDDLE SCHOOL	2130 LOS GATOS-ALMADEN RD, SJS, 95124, (408)371-0366	873 - F5
VALLEY VIEW MIDDLE SCHOOL	181 VIKING DR, PLHL, 94523, (510)686-6136	592 - B3
VISITACION VALLEY MIDDLE SCHOOL	450 RAYMOND AV, SF, 94134, (415)469-4590	687 - J1
WELLS MIDDLE SCHOOL	6800 PENN DR, DBLN, 94568, (510)828-6227	693 - J3
WESTBOROUGH MIDDLE SCHOOL	2570 WESTBOROUGH BLVD, SSF, 94080, (650)877-8848	707 - D4
WILLARD MIDDLE SCHOOL	2425 STUART ST, BERK, 94705, (510)644-6330	629 - H3
WOOD, CHARLOTTE MIDDLE SCHOOL	600 EL CAPITAN DR, DNVL, 94526, (510)552-5600	653 - C5
WOOD, WILL C MIDDLE SCHOOL	420 GRAND ST, ALA, 94501, (510)748-4015	669 - H3

SHOPPING CENTERS - COMMUNITY

FEATURE NAME	Address City, ZIP Code	PAGE-GRID
280 METRO CENTER	JUNIPERO SERRA BLVD & COLA BL, CLMA, 94014	687 - C7
ABORN SQUARE	CAPITOL EXPWY & ABORN RD, SJS, 95121	855 - B3
ALAMO PLAZA	DANVILLE BL & STONE VALLEY RD, CCCo, 94507, (510)947-6633	632 - F5
ALMADEN OAKS PLAZA	REDMOND & MERIDIAN AV, SJS, 95120, (408)478-8757	874 - B7
ALMADEN PLAZA	ALMADEN EXWY $ BLOSSOM HILL RD, SJS, 95118	874 - C4
ALMADEN VIA VALIENTE PLAZA	ALMADEN EXPWY & VIA VALIENTE, SJS, 95120, (408)269-8273	894 - G3
ALVARADO PLACE CTR	ALVARADO BLVD & DYER ST, UNC, 94587	732 - A6
ALVARADO PLAZA	ALVARADO BLVD & DYER ST, UNC, 94587	732 - A6
AMADOR CENTER	SANTA RITA RD & VALLEY AV, PLE, 94566	714 - E1
ANTIOCH SQUARE	E 18TH ST & A ST, ANT, 94509	575 - D5
APPIAN 80 CENTER	APPIAN WY & EASTSHORE FRWY, PIN, 94564, (510)254-1074	569 - D5
ARGONAUT PLACE SHOPPING CENTER	SARATOGA-SUNNYVALE RD & BLAUER, SAR, 95070	852 - E6
ATLANTIC PLAZA	RAILROAD AV & ATLANTIC AV, PIT, 94565	574 - D4
BAYHILL CENTER	BAYHILL DR & CHERRY AV, SBRN, 94066	707 - G7
BEL AIR	TREAT BLVD & BEL AIR DR, CNCD, 94521	593 - B4
BEL MATEO CENTER	42ND AV & OLYMPIC AV, SMTO, 94403, (650)349-0431	749 - D7
BERESFORD SQUARE	N MILPITAS BLVD & CALAVERAS BL, MPS, 95035, (408)946-1550	794 - A7
BERRYESSA CORNERS CENTER	CAPITOL AV & BERRYESSA RD, SJS, 95132	814 - F6
BEST PLAZA	STONERIDGE DR & SPRINGDALE AV, PLE, 94588	693 - H6
BLACKHAWK PLAZA	BLACKHAWK PLAZA CIR, CCCo, 94506	653 - J5
BLOSSOM HILL SQUARE	BLOSSOM HILL RD & HARWOOD RD, LGTS, 95032	873 - H6
BLOSSOM VALLEY CENTER	1700 MIRAMONTE AV, MTVW, 94040	831 - G1
BOARDWALK SHOPPING CENTER	TIBURON BLVD & BEACH RD, TBRN, 94920, (415)435-2822	607 - D7
BON AIR CENTER	SIR FRANCIS DRAKE & LA CUESTA, LKSP, 94939, (415)461-0200	586 - G4
BOREL SQUARE	BOVET RD & S EL CAMINO REAL, SMTO, 94402	749 - A4
BRENTWOOD CENTER	EL CAMINO REAL & S SPRUCE, SSF, 94080, (415)761-2277	707 - H5
BROOKVALE	FREMONT BLVD & NICOLET AV, FRMT, 94536	752 - F2
BURI BURI	WESTBOROUGH BL & CAMARITAS AV, SSF, 94080	707 - F3
BURLINGAME PLAZA	MAGNOLIA AV & TROUSDALE DR, BURL, 94010	728 - B4
CAMBRIAN PARK PLAZA	UNION AV & CAMDEN AV, SCIC, 95124	873 - G2
CAMDEN PARK CENTER	CAMDEN AV & UNION AV, SJS, 95124	873 - F2
CAMPBELL PLAZA	WINCHESTER BLVD & BUDD AV, CMBL, 95008	853 - D7
CARIBBEES CENTER	LEWIS RD & SENTER RD, SJS, 95111, (408)225-1180	854 - H4
CARLMONT VILLAGE	AVD D L PULGAS & RALSTON AV, BLMT, 94002, (415)593-8075	769 - C2
CASTRO VILLAGE	20630 PATIO DR, AlaC, 94546, (510)538-9600	692 - A5
CASTROVALLEY MARKET PLACE	CROW CANYON RD & E CASTRO VLY, AlaC, 94552, (510)381-7310	692 - D5
CENTURY PLAZA	CENTURY BLVD & SOMERSVILLE RD, PIT, 94565	575 - A5
CHARTER SQUARE	BEACH PARK BLVD & SHELL BLVD, FCTY, 94404	749 - G4
CHARTER SQUARE	CHARTER SQUARE TER, FRMT, 94555	752 - D1
CHERRY CHASE CENTER	613 CHERRY CHASE CTR, SUNV, 94087, (408)736-4158	832 - B1
CITY SQUARE	N MILIPITAS BLVD & DIXON RD, MPS, 95035	793 - J3
CLAYTON STATION	CLAYTON RD & KIRKER PASS RD, CLAY, 94517	593 - F5
CLAYTON VALLEY CENTER	CLAYTON RD & YGNACIO VALLEY RD, CNCD, 94521	593 - E5
COLLEGE SQUARE CENTER	CONTRA COSTA BL & GOLF CLUB RD, PLHL, 94523	592 - C2
CONCORD PARK & SHOP CENTER	WILLOW PASS RD & MARKET ST, CNCD, 94520	592 - E2
CONCORD TERMINAL CENTER	CLAYTON RD & PORT CHICAGO HWY, CNCD, 94519	592 - G2
COUNTRY CLUB VILLA	TOYON AV & MCKEE RD, SJS, 95127, (408)251-3730	814 - J7
COUNTRY FAIR	MONTEVIDEO DR & ALCOSTA BLVD, SRMN, 94583	673 - G4
COUNTRY WOOD CENTER	TREAT BLVD & BANCROFT RD, WLCK, 94598	612 - F1
CREEKSIDE CENTER	MISSION BLVD & MATTOX RD, AlaC, 94541, (510)376-1011	691 - G7
CREEKSIDE CENTER	SYCAMORE AV & EASTSHORE FRWY, HER, 94547	569 - H3
CRESPI CENTER	580 CRESPI DR, PCFA, 94044	726 - H4
CROCKER GALLERIA	50 POST ST, SF, 94108, (415)393-1500	648 - A5
CROSBY COMMONS	BURLINGAME AV & PRIMROSE RD, BURL, 94010	728 - F7
CROSSINGS, THE	DEER VALLEY RD & HILLCREST AV, ANT, 94509	575 - G7
CROW CANYON COMMONS	CROW CANYON PL, SRMN, 94583, (510)930-8098	673 - D1
CRYSTAL SPRINGS CENTER	POLHEMUS RD & DE ANZA BLVD, SMTO, 94402	748 - H7
CUPERTINO CROSSROADS CENTER	STEVENS CK BLVD & DE ANZA BL, CPTO, 95014	852 - D1
CUPERTINO VILLAGE	WOLFE RD & HOMESTEAD RD, CPTO, 95014, (408)255-8157	832 - F6
DANA PLAZA	CONCORD BLVD & LANDANA DR, CNCD, 94519	593 - B1
DE ANZA CENTER	S DE ANZA BLVD & KENTWOOD AV, SJS, 95129, (408)688-4604	852 - D3
DE ANZA SQUARE	FREMONT AV & MARY AV, SUNV, 94087, (408)738-4444	832 - C4
DEER VALLEY CENTER	LONE TREE WY & DEER VALLEY RD, ANT, 94509	595 - G4
DEL PRADO SQUARE SHOPPING CENTER	HWY 101 & IGNACIO BL, NVTO, 94949	546 - F2
DELTA FAIR CENTER	DELTA FAIR BLVD & BUCHANAN RD, ANT, 94509	575 - A6
DESIN SQUARE	BRANHAM LN & INDIAN AV, SJS, 95118	874 - A3
DIABLO PLAZA	CROW CYN RD & SAN RAMON VLY BL, SRMN, 94583	673 - C1
DIAMOND HEIGHTS CENTER	DIAMOND HTS BL & GOLD MINE DR, SF, 94131	667 - F5
DIANDA PLAZA	CLAYTON RD & THORNWOOD DR, CNCD, 94521	593 - B3
DOWNER SQUARE	BLOSSOM HILL RD & SNELL RD, SJS, 95123	874 - J4
DOWNTOWN NOVATO CENTER	TAMALPAIS AVE & GRANT AVE, NVTO, 94945, (415)897-9601	526 - A3
DUBLIN PLACE CENTER	AMADOR VLY BL & REGIONAL ST, DBLN, 94568	693 - H4
DUBLIN PLAZA	AMADOR VLY BL & REGIONAL ST, DBLN, 94568	693 - G4
DUBLIN SQUARE CENTER	DUBLIN BLVD & DONLON WY, DBLN, 94568	693 - G5
DUFFEL PLAZA	STEVENSON BLVD & BALENTINE DR, NWK, 94560	773 - A2
DURANT SQUARE	14TH ST & DURANT AV, OAK, 94603	670 - J6
DVC PLAZA	OLD QUARRY RD & GOLF CLUB RD, PLHL, 94523	592 - C2
DYER STREET TRIANGLE	DYER ST & LYNCH WY, UNC, 94587	732 - B4
EAST BAY BRIDGE CENTER	HOLLIS ST & 40TH ST, EMVL, 94608	629 - F7
EASTWOOD PLAZA	A ST & W 20TH ST, ANT, 94509	575 - D5
EDGEWATER PLACE	EDGEWATER & BEACH PARK BLVD, FCTY, 94404, (650)986-0647	749 - F4
EL CAMINO CENTER	EL CAMINO REAL & SCOTT BLVD, SCL, 95050	833 - C4
EL MERCADO PLAZA	DECOTO RD & ALVARADO-NILES RD, UNC, 94587	732 - G6
EL PASEO CENTER	CAMPBELL AV & SARATOGA AV, SJS, 95130, (408)378-0247	852 - J5
EL PORTAL CENTER	114 EL PORTAL DR, SPAB, 94806, (510)235-3855	588 - J2
EMBARCADERO CENTER	4 EMBARCADERO CTR, SF, 94111, (415)772-0500	648 - B5
EMERYVILLE MARKET PLACE	BAY ST, EMVL, 94608, (510)665-6600	629 - D5
ENCINA GRANDE CENTER	YGNACIO VLY RD & OAK GROVE RD, WLCK, 94598	612 - H2
EUREKA SQUARE	EUREKA DR & OCEANA BLVD, PCFA, 94044, (650)359-9896	706 - J6
FAIRWAY PARK	MISSION BLVD & ROUSSEAU ST, HAY, 94544, (510)487-0400	732 - E2
FASHION FAIRE	HESPERIAN BLVD & FAIRMONT DR, SLN, 94578	691 - D4
FERNSIDE CENTER	BLANDING AV & BROADWAY, ALA, 94501	670 - B2
FOOTHILL SQUARE	MACARTHUR BLVD & 108TH AV, OAK, 94605	671 - B5
FOXWORTHY CENTER	FOXWORTHY AV & CHERRY AV, SJS, 95125	854 - B7
FREMONT CENTER	FREMONT BLVD & GRIMMER BLVD, FRMT, 94538	753 - C7
FREMONT CORNERS CENTER	FREMONT & SARATOGA-SUNNYVALE, SUNV, 94087	832 - E4
FREMONT PLAZA	FREMONT BLVD & MOWRY AV, FRMT, 94538	753 - A5
GATEWAY CENTER	SAN RAMON VLY BL & WESTSIDE DR, SRMN, 94583	693 - F1
GATEWAY PLAZA	MOWRY AV & PASEO PADRE PKWY, FRMT, 94538	753 - B4
GATEWAY PLAZA	PLAZA DR, VAL, 94591	510 - E7
GATEWAY PLAZA	W HARPER RD & SANTA CLARA ST, HAY, 94544	711 - H5
GATEWAY SQUARE	HOPYARD RD & STONERIDGE DR, PLE, 94588	694 - B6
GHIRARDELLI SQUARE	900 NORTH POINT ST, SF, 94109, (415)775-5500	647 - H3
GLENMOOR CENTER	4551 EGGERS DR, FRMT, 94536, (510)793-4030	752 - H5
GOULD CENTER	CAPITOL EXWY & MCLAUGHLIN AV, SJS, 95121	855 - A4
GRANT ROAD PLAZA	1040 GRANT RD, MTVW, 94040, (650)973-7180	811 - J7
GREENHOUSE MARKETPLACE	15000 WASHINGTON AV, SLN, 94579	691 - C6
GREGORY VILLAGE	CONTRA COSTA BLVD & DORIS DR, PLHL, 94523	592 - C5
HACIENDA GARDENS CENTER	MERIDIAN AV & FOXWORTHY AV, SJS, 95124	873 - J1
HAMILTON PLAZA	HAMILTON AV & BASCOM AV, CMBL, 95008, (408)255-4106	853 - G5
HARBOR BAY LANDING	885 ISLAND DR, ALA, 94502, (510)283-8262	670 - A6
HILLVIEW PLAZA	SW HILLVIEW & BLOSSOM HILL RD, SJS, 95123, (408)453-7900	874 - E4
HOMESTEAD CENTER	HOMESTEAD RD & LAWRENCE EXWY, SCL, 95051, (408)249-1590	832 - J5

FEATURE NAME Address City, ZIP Code	PAGE-GRID
HOMESTEAD SQUARE HOMESTEAD & SARATOGA-SUNNYVALE, CPTO, 95014	832 - D6
HUNTINGDON VILLAGE S DE ANZA BLVD & KENTWOOD AV, SJS, 95129, (408)287-1779	852 - E3
IGNACIO CENTER 455 ENTRADA DR, NVTO, 94949, (415)883-4012	546 - E1
JACK LONDON VILLAGE ALICE ST & EMBARCADERO, OAK, 94607	649 - G5
JACKSON-AMADOR CENTER W JACKSON ST & AMADOR ST, HAY, 94544	711 - H4
JAPAN CENTER 1737 POST ST, SF, 94115, (415)922-6776	647 - H6
K-MART CENTER THORNTON AV & CEDAR BLVD, NWK, 94560	752 - F5
KING PLAZA KING DR & CALLAN BLVD, DALY, 94015	707 - C3
KINGS COURT CENTER BLOSSOM HILL RD & LOS GATOS BL, LGTS, 95032	873 - C6
KIRKWOOD PLAZA CAMPBELL AV & SAN TOMAS AQUINO, CMBL, 95008	853 - A6
LA FIESTA SQUARE MORAGA RD & WILKINSON LN, LFYT, 94549	611 - F6
LA HACIENDA CENTER EL CAMINO REAL & MARIA LN, SUNV, 94086, (408)732-7300	832 - F3
LARKSPUR LANDING 101 FRWY & E SIR FRANCIS DRAKE, LKSP, 94904, (415)461-3424	586 - H4
LARWIN PLAZA SONOMA BL & REDWOOD ST, VAL, 94590	529 - J2
LAURELWOOD CENTER HILLSDALE BLVD & CAMPUS DR, SMTO, 94403, (650)349-0431	748 - J6
LAWRENCE SQUARE EL CAMINO REAL & LAWRENCE EXWY, SCL, 95051	832 - J3
LAWRENCE STATION CENTER LAWRENCE EXWY & HOMESTEAD RD, SCL, 95051	832 - J6
LIDO FAIRE NEWARK BLVD & JARVIS AV, NWK, 94560	752 - D5
LINCOLN SQUARE CENTER 4100 REDWOOD RD, OAK, 94619	650 - H5
LINDA MAR LINDA MAR BLVD & CABRILLO HWY, PCFA, 94044, (650)433-9300	726 - H4
LIVERMORE ARCADE RAILROAD AV & N P ST, LVMR, 94550	715 - F1
LIVERMORE CENTER RINCON AV & PINE ST, LVMR, 94550	695 - F7
LIVERY, THE SAN RAMON VALLEY BLVD, DNVL, 94526	653 - A3
LOEHMANNS PLAZA HOLLENBECK AV & HOMESTEAD RD, SUNV, 94087	832 - D5
LONGS PLAZA EL CAMINO REAL & HULL DR, SCAR, 94070	769 - F2
LORENZO MANOR CENTER HESPERIAN BL & HACIENDA AV, AlaC, 94541	711 - E1
LOS ALTOS RANCHO CENTER FOOTHILL EXPWY & SPRINGER RD, LALT, 94024	831 - F2
LOS ARBOLES MOWRY AV & BLACOW RD, FRMT, 94538	752 - J7
LUCKY LAKESHORE PLAZA 1501 SLOAT BLVD, SF, 94132	667 - A6
MACARTHUR BROADWAY CENTER MACARTHUR BLVD & BROADWAY, OAK, 94611	649 - H1
MAINSTREET AT SANTA TERESA SANTA TERESA BL & BLOSSOM HILL, SJS, 95123	874 - E4
MARIN SQUARE 75 BELLAM BLVD, SRFL, 94901, (415)563-6200	586 - J3
MARINA SQUARE MARINA BLVD & NIMITZ FRWY, SLN, 94577	690 - J3
MARINA VILLAGE CENTER MARINA VILLAGE PKWY, ALA, 94501	649 - G7
MARIPOSA GARDENS CENTER HOMESTEAD BLVD & KIELY BLVD, SCL, 95051, (650)433-9300	833 - B6
MARKETPLACE ON STEVENS CREEK STEVENS CREEK BLVD & PORTAL AV, CPTO, 95014	852 - F1
MARLIN COVE FOSTER CITY BLVD & MARLIN AV, FCTY, 94404, (650)832-1888	749 - H3
MCCARTHY RANCH MARKETPLACE MCCARTHY BLVD & RANCH DR, MPS, 95035	793 - H7
MERVYNS EAST CENTER STORY RD & MCGINNESS AV, SJS, 95127, (408)294-0868	835 - A4
MERVYNS PLAZA EL CAMINO REAL & SCOTT BLVD, SCL, 95050, (408)985-8881	833 - C4
MERVYNS PLAZA HWY 101 & WALNUT ST, RDWC, 94063	770 - B5
METRO CENTER E HILLSDALE BLVD, FCTY, 94404	749 - F3
MILLBRAE SQUARE BROADWAY & MEADOW GLEN AV, MLBR, 94030	728 - A3
MILLS PARK EL CAMINO REAL & SAN BRUNO AV, SBRN, 94066, (510)392-2780	707 - H6
MISSION CENTER MISSION BLVD & ANZA ST, FRMT, 94539	753 - H7
MISSION PLAZA 1811 SANTA RITA RD, PLE, 94566	714 - E1
MISSION VALLEY CENTER MISSION BLVD, FRMT, 94539	753 - E4
MONARCH CENTER I-880 FRWY & DAVIS ST, SLN, 94577	690 - H2
MONTECITO PLAZA 3RD ST & GRAND AV, SRFL, 94901, (415)453-2843	586 - H1
MONTEREY PLAZA MONTEREY HWY & FORD RD, SJS, 95138, (408)327-7113	875 - C3
MOONLITE CENTER EL CAMINO REAL & KIELY BLVD, SCL, 95051	833 - B4
MORAGA CENTER MORAGA RD & MORAGA WY, MRGA, 94556	631 - E7
MOUNTAIN VIEW CENTER EL CAMINO REAL & GRANT RD, MTVW, 94040	811 - J7
MOWRY EAST CENTER 5200 MOWRY AV, FRMT, 94538, (510)796-0660	752 - J7
MT PLEASANT CENTER STORY RD & WHITE RD, SJS, 95127	835 - A4
MUIR STATION MUIR STATION RD & CENTER AV, MRTZ, 94553	571 - F6
NAVE SHOPPING CENTER 1535 S NOVATO BLVD, NVTO, 94947, (415)479-8788	526 - B5
NEW PARK PLAZA BALINTINE DR & CEDAR BLVD, NWK, 94560	772 - J1
NEWARK MARKETPLACE JARVIS AV & NEWARK BLVD, NWK, 94560	752 - C4
NEWARK SQUARE THORNTON AV & CEDAR BLVD, NWK, 94560	752 - F6
NORTH PARK PLAZA CALIFORNIA AV & LOVERIDGE RD, PIT, 94565	574 - G4
NORTHGATE CENTER FREITAS PKWY & NORTHGATE DR, SRFL, 94903, (415)546-0696	566 - D3
NORTHPOINT CENTRE 2351 POWELL ST, SF, 94133, (415)391-1313	648 - A3
NORTHWOOD SQUARE LANDESS AV & MORRILL AV, SJS, 95132, (408)946-6791	814 - D2
NOVATO FAIR SHOPPING CENTER REDWOOD BLVD & DIABLO AV, NVTO, 94945	526 - B4
OAK GROVE PLAZA YGNACIO VLY RD & SAN CARLOS DR, WLCK, 94598	612 - F3
OAK HILLS CENTER SUNOL BLVD & MISSION DR, PLE, 94566	714 - D5
OAK HILLS CENTER W LELAND RD & BAILEY RD, PIT, 94565	573 - G3
OLD MILL SPECIALTY CENTER 2540 CALIFORNIA ST, MTVW, 94040, (650)941-9595	811 - F4
OLD TOWN CENTER UNIVERSITY AV & SARATOGA-LOS G, LGTS, 95030	873 - A7
OLDTOWN CENTER NEWARK BL & MAYHEWS LANDING RD, NWK, 94560	752 - E6
OLIVER CORNERS CENTER HESPERIAN BLVD & W TENNYSON RD, HAY, 94545	711 - H7
ORCHARD FARMS CENTER BOLLINGER RD & MILLER AV, SJS, 95129, (408)437-3011	852 - G2
PACHECO PLAZA IGNACIO BLVD, NVTO, 94949, (415)883-4646	546 - E2
PACIFIC MANOR MANOR PZ, PCFA, 94044	706 - J3
PALOS VERDES MALL PLEASANT HILL RD & CM VERDE, WLCK, 94596	611 - J2
PARADISE CENTER PARADISE DR & EL CAMINO DR, CMAD, 94925	606 - J1
PARK IN RHEEM VALLEY, THE CENTER ST & PARK ST, MRGA, 94556	631 - E4
PARK PLACE SONOMA BLVD, VAL, 94589	530 - A2
PARKTOWN PLAZA PARK VICTORIA DR & LANDESS AV, MPS, 95035	814 - D2
PASEO PADRE CENTER FREMONT BLVD & PAS PADRE PKWY, FRMT, 94555	752 - E1
PAVILION AT SAN JOSE S 1ST ST & E SAN FERNANDO ST, SJS, 95113, (408)286-2076	834 - C6
PAVLINA PLAZA 693 E REMINGTON DR, SUNV, 94087, (408)738-1777	832 - E2
PELTON CENTER PELTON CIR, SLN, 94577	691 - A1
PEPPERTREE PLAZA MURIETTA BLVD & E STANLEY BLVD, LVMR, 94550	715 - F1
PIEDMONT HILLS CENTER SIERRA RD & PIEDMONT RD, SJS, 95132	814 - G5
PINOLE VALLEY CENTER PINOLE VLY RD & EASTSHORE FRWY, PIN, 94564	569 - F5
PINOLE VISTA CENTER APPIAN WY & FITZGERALD DR, PIN, 94564, (510)262-9569	569 - D6
PINOLE VISTA CROSSINGS FITZGERALD DR, PIN, 94803	569 - C7
PLAZA 580 I-580 FRWY & 1ST ST, LVMR, 94550	696 - A5
PLAZA AT BISHOP RANCH BOLLINGER CANYON RD & 680 FRWY, SRMN, 94583	673 - D3
PLAZA DE SANTA TERESA SANTA TERESA BLVD & COTTLE RD, SJS, 95119	875 - B6
PLAZA DEL ROBLE CENTER 4TH ST & BIG BASIN WY, SAR, 95070, (408)371-8155	872 - D3
PLEASANT HILL PLAZA CONTRA COSTA BLVD & GREGORY LN, PLHL, 94523	592 - D5
PLEASANT HILL SHOPPING CENTER CNTRA CSTA BL & CHLPNCNGO PKWY, PLHL, 94523	592 - C1
POWELL STREET PLAZA SHELLMOUND ST & CHRISTIE AV, EMVL, 94608	629 - D6
PRINCETON PLAZA MALL BLOSSOM HILL RD & KOOSER RD, SJS, 95118, (408)275-0550	874 - B5
PRUNERIDGE CENTER SAN TOMAS EXPWY & SARATOGA AV, SCL, 95050	833 - C7
PT TIBURON PLAZA SHOPPING CENTER PARADISE DR & MAIN ST, TBRN, 94920	627 - E1
PUEBLO PLAZA ALMADEN EXPWY & BLOSSOM HLL RD, SJS, 95118	874 - D4
QUITO VILLAGE CENTER COX AV & PASEO PRESADA, SAR, 95070, (408)378-3354	852 - H6
RALEYS CENTER CLAYBURN RD & CAMBY RD, ANT, 94509	595 - D1
RALEYS CENTER JARVIS AV & NEWARK BLVD, NWK, 94560	752 - C4
RED HILL CENTER 900 SIR FRANCIS DRAKE BLVD, SANS, 94960	566 - B6
REDWOOD PLAZA BROADWAY & MAIN ST, RDWC, 94063	770 - B6
ROCKRIDGE CENTER PLEASANT VALLEY AV & BROADWAY, OAK, 94611	629 - J7
ROSE PAVILLION 4225 ROSEWOOD DR, PLE, 94588, (510)463-3939	694 - E5
ROSEMONT CENTER NEWARK BLVD & JARVIS AV, NWK, 94560	752 - D4
ROSSMOOR SHOPPING CENTER TICE VLY BLVD & ROSSMOOR PKWY, WLCK, 94595	632 - B1
SAFEWAY CENTER SAN CARLOS ST & SHASTA AV, SJS, 95128, (408)241-6641	853 - H1
SAN BRUNO TOWNE CENTER EL CAMINO REAL & NOOR AV, SBRN, 94066	707 - H5
SAN LORENZO VILLAGE PASEO GRANDE & PAS LARGAVISTA, AlaC, 94580	691 - D7
SANTA TERESA SQUARE SANTA TERESA BLVD & SNELL AV, SJS, 95123	874 - H6
SANTA TERESA VILLAGE BERNAL RD & SANTA TERESA BLVD, SJS, 95139, (408)287-1779	875 - E7
SARATOGA PLAZA DUCKETT WY & SARATOGA-SUNV RD, SJS, 95129	852 - E4
SARATOGA SQUARE SARATOGA AV & KIELY BLVD, SJS, 95129	853 - B1
SEAPORT VILLAGE NORTH SEAPORT BLVD & SEAPORT CT, RDWC, 94063	770 - C3
SEQUOIA STATION JEFFERSON AV & EL CAMINO REAL, RDWC, 94063	770 - A6
SERRA CENTER 200 SERRA WY, MPS, 95035, (408)263-1800	793 - J7
SERRA CENTER JUNIPERO SERRA & SERRAMONTE BL, CLMA, 94014	687 - C7
SERRAMONTE PLAZA SERRAMONTE BLVD & GELLERT BLVD, DALY, 94015	707 - C1
SEVEN TREES CENTER SENTER RD & SEVEN TREES BLVD, SJS, 95111	854 - H7
SHAMROCK VILLAGE AMADOR VALLEY RD, DBLN, 94568	693 - G4
SHARON HEIGHTS CENTER 325 SHARON PARK DR, MLPK, 94025, (650)854-5053	790 - E7
SILVER CREEK PLAZA CAPITOL EXPWY & SILVER CK RD, SJS, 95121	855 - B3
SKYCREST CENTER SAN BRUNO AV & GLENVIEW DR, SBRN, 94066	727 - F1
SKYLINE PLAZA SOUTHGATE AV & HIGATE DR, DALY, 94015	687 - A6
SOLANO SQUARE 1ST ST & MILITARY W, BEN, 94510	551 - B4
SOUTHAMPTON CENTER I-780 & SOUTHAMPTON RD, BEN, 94510	551 - A3
STEVENS CREEK CENTRAL STEVENS CREEK BLVD & HWY 280, SJS, 95129	852 - J1
STRAWBERRY VILLAGE SHOPPING-CENTER BELVEDERE DR & REED BL, MrnC, 94941	606 - H4
SUNRISE PLAZA BLOSSOM HILL RD & CAHALAN AV, SJS, 95123, (408)371-8770	874 - G4
SYCAMORE PLAZA SOMERSVILLE RD & SYCAMORE DR, ANT, 94509	575 - A5
SYCAMORE SQUARE SAN RAMON VALLEY BL & BOONE CT, DNVL, 94526	653 - A3
TAMALPAIS JUNCTION SHOPPING-CENTER HWY 1 & FLAMINGO RD, MrnC, 94965	606 - F6
TASSAJARA CROSSING CM TASSAJARA & CROW CANYON RD, DNVL, 94506	653 - J5
THE ANCHORAGE 2800 LEAVENWORTH ST, SF, 94133, (415)775-6000	647 - J3
THE CANNERY 2801 LEAVENWORTH ST, SF, 94133, (415)771-3112	647 - J3
THE CROSSROADS FREMONT BLVD & WALNUT AV, FRMT, 94538	753 - B5
THE MARKET PLACE 480 MARKET PL, SRMN, 94583, (510)277-3000	673 - F3
THE MARKET PLACE TAMAL VISTA BL & SANDPIPER CIR, CMAD, 94925	586 - G6
THE OAKS CENTER STEVENS CREEK BLVD & HWY 85, CPTO, 95014, (650)564-8848	832 - C7
THE PRUNEYARD BASCOM AV & CAMPBELL AV, CMBL, 95008, (408)371-0811	853 - F6
THE SQUARE SHOPPING CENTER WILSON AV & NOVATO BLVD, NVTO, 94947	525 - J2
THE STANFORD BARN SHOPPING CENTER QUARRY RD & WELCH RD, PA, 94304	790 - G5
THE VILLAGE AT LIVERMORE E STANLEY BLVD & S S ST, LVMR, 94550, (510)271-0745	715 - F1
THE VILLAGE FAIR 777 BRIDGEWAY BLVD, SAUS, 94965	627 - B3
TOWN & COUNTRY SAN RAMON VLY & TOWN & COUNTRY, DNVL, 94526	653 - A3
TOWN & COUNTRY VILLAGE EL CM REAL & EMBARCADERO RD, PA, 94301, (510)325-3266	790 - J5
TOWN & COUNTRY VILLAGE STEVENS CK BL & WINCHESTER TER, SJS, 95117	853 - D1
TOWN & COUNTRY VILLAGE W WASHINGTON AV & TAAFFE ST, SUNV, 94086, (408)736-6654	812 - D7
TOWN CENTER N MILPITAS BLVD & CALAVERAS BL, MPS, 95035	794 - B6
TOWN FAIR STATE ST & BEACON AV, FRMT, 94538	753 - B4
TREAT PLAZA CENTER TREAT BLVD & CLAYTON RD, CNCD, 94521	593 - B3
TROPICANA CENTER STORY RD & S KING RD, SJS, 95122	834 - G6
TULLY CORNERS TULLY RD & QUIMBY RD, SJS, 95122	855 - A1
UNION CITY MARKETPLACE DECOTO RD & ALVARADO-NILES RD, UNC, 94587	732 - F6
VALLEJO CORNERS TURNER PKWY & ADML CALLAGHA LN, VAL, 94591	530 - D1
VILLA CENTER LAWRENCE EXPY & STEVENS CK BL, SCL, 95051	852 - J1
VILLAGE COURT SAN ANTONIO & EL CAMINO REAL, LALT, 94022, (650)949-0960	811 - E4
VILLAGE OAKS CENTER ARNOLD DR & MORELLO AV, MRTZ, 94553	571 - H6
VINEYARD CENTER CLAYTON RD & AYERS RD, CNCD, 94521	593 - E5
VINEYARD FACTORY STORES SOUTH FRONT RD & LONGARD RD, LVMR, 94550	696 - F3
VINTAGE OAKS AT NOVATO 208 VINTAGE WY, NVTO, 94947, (415)897-9999	526 - D5
WAL-MART CENTER E LELAND RD & LOVERIDGE RD, PIT, 94565	574 - F4
WALNUT PLAZA CENTER WALNUT AV & LIBERTY ST, FRMT, 94538	753 - B4
WARM SPRINGS PLAZA MISSION BLVD & MOHAVE DR, FRMT, 94539	773 - G6
WEST PARK PLAZA PAYNE AV & WINCHESTER BLVD, SJS, 95117	853 - D4
WEST VALLEY COMPLEX 2980 STEVENS CREEK BLVD, SJS, 95128, (408)345-4670	853 - E1
WESTGATE WEST PROSPECT RD & LAWRENCE EXWY, SJS, 95129, (408)998-7399	852 - H5
WESTMOOR VILLAGE FREMONT AV & MARY AV, SUNV, 94087, (408)245-0553	832 - C3
WHITE ROAD PLAZA STORY RD & WHITE RD, SJS, 95127	835 - A3
WILLOW GLEN CENTER ALMADEN EXWY & CURTNER AV, SJS, 95125	854 - C5
WILLOWS CENTER 1975 DIAMOND BLVD, CNCD, 94520, (510)825-4000	592 - D2
WOLFE-REED CENTER REED AV & WOLFE RD, SUNV, 94086, (408)296-3042	832 - G2
WOODSIDE CENTRAL EL CAMINO REAL & REDWOOD AV, RDWC, 94061	770 - B7
WOODSIDE PLAZA WOODSIDE AV & KENTUCKY ST, RDWC, 94061, (650)772-7000	790 - A3
YGNACIO VALLEY CENTER OAK GROVE RD & TREAT BLVD, CNCD, 94518	592 - G7

SHOPPING MALLS

FEATURE NAME Address City, ZIP Code	PAGE-GRID
BAYFAIR MALL E 14TH ST & BAYFAIR DR, SLN, 94578, (510)357-6000	691 - D4
BROADWAY PLAZA 1249 BROADWAY PZ, WLCK, 94596, (510)939-7600	612 - D6
CAPITOL SQUARE MALL 390 N CAPITOL AV, SJS, 95133, (408)775-0717	834 - G1
CONTRA COSTA CENTER 2302 MONUMENT BLVD, PLHL, 94523, (510)686-4646	592 - D6
COUNTY EAST MALL 2556 SOMERSVILLE RD, ANT, 94509, (510)754-5230	574 - J5
EASTMONT MALL 7200 BANCROFT AV, OAK, 94605, (510)632-1131	670 - H2
EASTRIDGE MALL 1 EASTRIDGE CENTER, SJS, 95122, (408)238-3600	855 - A1
EL CERRITO PLAZA SAN PABLO AV & FAIRMOUNT AV, ELCR, 94530, (510)524-6535	609 - D4
FREMONT HUB CENTER 39210 FREMONT BLVD, FRMT, 94538, (510)792-1720	753 - A5
HILLSDALE CENTER 60 HILLSDALE BLVD, SMTO, 94403, (650)345-8222	749 - B5
HILLTOP REGIONAL CENTER 2200 HILLTOP MALL RD, RCH, 94806, (510)223-6900	569 - A7
ISLAND CENTER FASHION ISLAND BLVD, SMTO, 94404, (650)570-5300	749 - E2
NEWPARK MALL MOWRY AV & CEDAR BLVD, NWK, 94560, (501)794-5522	772 - H1
OAKRIDGE MALL 925 BLOSSOM HILL RD, SJS, 95123, (408)578-2910	874 - E4
SAN ANTONIO CENTER 2550 W EL CAMINO REAL, MTVW, 94040, (650)941-3794	811 - E3
SAN FRANCISCO CENTRE 5TH ST & MARKET ST, SF, 94103, (415)495-5656	648 - A6
SERRAMONTE CENTER SERRAMONTE BL & CALLAN BL, DALY, 94015, (650)992-8686	687 - C7
SOUTH SHORE CENTER 2300 SHORE LINE DR, ALA, 94501	669 - J3
SOUTHLAND MALL 1 SOUTHLAND MALL, HAY, 94545, (510)782-5050	711 - G4
STANFORD SHOPPING CENTER 180 EL CAMINO REAL, PA, 94304, (650)617-8585	790 - G5
STONERIDGE MALL STONERIDGE MALL RD, PLE, 94588	693 - H5

SHOPPING MALLS

FEATURE NAME	Address City, ZIP Code	PAGE-GRID
STONESTOWN GALLERIA	19TH AV & WINSTON DR, SF, 94132, (415)759-2623	667 - B6
SUN VALLEY SHOPPING CENTER	CONTRA COSTA BLVD, CNCD, 94520, (510)825-0400	592 - C2
SUNNYVALE TOWN CENTER	2502 TOWN CENTER LN, SUNV, 94086, (408)245-3270	812 - D7
TANFORAN PARK	EL CAMINO REAL, SBRN, 94066, (650)873-2000	707 - H5
THE GREAT MALL OF THE BAY AREA	341 E CAPITOL AV, MPS, 95035, (408)945-2033	814 - A2
THE MALL AT NORTHGATE	580 NORTHGATE DR, SRFL, 94903, (415)479-5955	566 - E3
TOWN CENTER CORTE MADERA	706 TAMALPAIS DR, CMAD, 94925, (415)924-2961	586 - G7
VALLCO FASHION PARK	10123 N WOLFE RD, CPTO, 95014, (408)255-5660	832 - F7
VALLEY FAIR	2855 STEVENS CREEK BLVD, SCL, 95050, (408)248-4450	853 - E1
VILLAGE AT CORTE MADERA	1852 REDWOOD HWY, CMAD, 94925, (415)924-8557	586 - H7
WESTGATE MALL	1600 SARATOGA AV, SJS, 95129, (408)379-9350	852 - J5
WESTLAKE CENTER	285 LAKE MERCED BLVD, DALY, 94015, (650)756-2161	687 - A3

TRANSPORTATION

FEATURE NAME	Address City, ZIP Code	PAGE-GRID
12TH STREET BART STATION	1245 BROADWAY, OAK, 94607	649 - G4
16TH ST & MISSION ST STATION	16TH ST & MISSION ST, SF, 94110	667 - J2
19TH STREET BART STATION	1900 BROADWAY, OAK, 94612	649 - G3
24TH ST & MISSION ST STATION	24TH ST & MISSION ST, SF, 94110	667 - J3
ALAMEDA GATEWAY FERRY TERMINAL	MAIN ST, ALA, 94501	649 - D5
AMTRAK BERKELEY STATION	UNIVERSITY AV & 3RD ST, BERK, 94804	629 - D2
AMTRAK EMERYVILLE STATION	59TH ST & LANDREGAN ST, EMVL, 94608	629 - E6
AMTRAK MARTINEZ STATION	401 FERRY ST, MRTZ, 94553, (510)228-4004	571 - D2
AMTRAK SAN JOSE	W SANTA CLARA ST & CAHILL ST, SJS, 95110	834 - A7
AMTRAK SANTA CLARA STATION	LAFAYETTE ST & TASMAN DR, SCL, 95054	813 - C3
ANGEL ISLAND FERRY TERMINAL	TBRN	627 - G1
ASHBY BART STATION	3100 ADELINE ST, BERK, 94703	629 - G4
BALBOA PARK STATION	OCEAN AV & SAN JOSE AV, SF, 94112	687 - E1
BART CONCORD STATION	1451 OAKLAND AV, CNCD, 94518	592 - G2
BART EL CERRITO DEL NORTE STATION	6400 CUTTING BLVD, ELCR, 94530	609 - B1
BART EL CERRITO PLAZA STATION	6699 FAIRMOUNT AV, ELCR, 94530	609 - D4
BART LAFAYETTE STATION	3601 DEER HILL RD, LFYT, 94549	611 - E6
BART NORTH CONCORD MARTINEZ-STATION	3700 PORT CHICAGO HWY, CNCD, 94519	572 - G5
BART ORINDA STATION	11 CM PABLO, ORIN, 94563	630 - H1
BART PITTSBURG/BAY POINT STATION	1600 LELAND RD, PIT, 94565	573 - G3
BART PLEASANT HILL STATION	1365 TREAT BLVD, CCCo, 94596	612 - D1
BART RICHMOND STATION	1700 NEVIN AV, RCH, 94801	588 - G6
BART WALNUT CREEK STATION	200 YGNACIO VALLEY RD, WLCK, 94596	612 - B4
BAYFAIR BART STATION	15242 HESPERIAN BLVD, SLN, 94578	691 - D5
BAYSHORE CALTRAIN STATION	TUNNEL AV & VISITACION AV, SF, 94134	688 - A2
BERKELEY BART STATION	2610 SHATTUCK AV, BERK, 94704	629 - G2
BLOSSOM HILL VTA RAIL STATION	BLOSSOM HILL RD & HWY 85, SJS, 95123	874 - G4
BNSF STATION	101 GARRARD BLVD, RCH, 94801	588 - E6
BNSF STATION	1ST ST & I ST, ANT, 94509	575 - C3
BNSF STATION	RAILROAD AV & W SANTA FE AV, PIT, 94565, (510)432-7371	574 - E2
BONAVENTURA VTA RAIL STATION	N 1ST ST & BONAVENTURA DR, SJS, 95134	813 - G6
BRANHAM VTA RAIL STATION	BRANHAM LN & HWY 87, SJS, 95136	874 - F2
CALTRAIN 22ND STREET STATION	22ND ST & PENNSYLVANIA AV, SF, 94107	668 - B3
CALTRAIN ATHERTON STATION	FAIR OAKS LN & DNKLSPEL STA LN, ATN, 94027	790 - E2
CALTRAIN BELMONT STATION	EL CAMINO REAL & RALSTON AV, BLMT, 94002	769 - E1
CALTRAIN BLOSSOM HILL STATION	MONTEREY RD & FORD RD, SJS, 95138	875 - C4
CALTRAIN BROADWAY STATION	BROADWAY & CALIFORNIA DR, BURL, 94010	728 - E5
CALTRAIN BURLINGAME STATION	BURLINGAME AV & CALIFORNIA DR, BURL, 94010	728 - G6
CALTRAIN CALIFORNIA AV STATION	PARK BLVD & CALIFORNIA AV, PA, 94306	791 - B7
CALTRAIN CAPITOL STATION	MONTEREY HWY & FEHREN DR, SJS, 95136	854 - G6
CALTRAIN CASTRO STATION	W EVELYN AV & VIEW ST, MTVW, 94041	811 - J5
CALTRAIN COLLEGE PARK STATION	STOCKTON AV & EMORY ST, SJS, 95110	833 - H5
CALTRAIN HAYWARD PARK STATION	16TH AV, SMTO, 94402	749 - B3
CALTRAIN HILLSDALE STATION	E HILLSDALE BL & EL CM REAL, SMTO, 94403	749 - C5
CALTRAIN LAWRENCE STATION	LAWRENCE STA RD& LAWRENCE EXWY, SUNV, 94086	832 - J1
CALTRAIN MENLO PARK STATION	STA CRUZ AV & MERRILL ST, MLPK, 94025	790 - F3
CALTRAIN MILLBRAE STATION	E MILLBRAE & CALIFORNIA, MLBR, 94030	728 - C4
CALTRAIN MOUNTAIN VIEW STATION	S RENGSTORFF & CRISANTO AV, MTVW, 94040	811 - G4
CALTRAIN PALO ALTO STATION	UNIVERSITY AV & MITCHELL LN, PA, 94301	790 - H5
CALTRAIN PAUL AVENUE STATION	PAUL AV & GOULD ST, SF, 94124	668 - B7
CALTRAIN REDWOOD CITY STATION	BROADWAY & WINSLOW ST, RDWC, 94063	770 - A6
CALTRAIN S SAN FRANCISCO STATION	DUBUQUE AV & GRAND AV, SSF, 94080	708 - A3
CALTRAIN SAN BRUNO STATION	HUNTINGTON AV & SYLVAN AV, SBRN, 94066	707 - J7
CALTRAIN SAN CARLOS STATION	EL CAMINO REAL & SAN CARLOS, SCAR, 94070	769 - G3
CALTRAIN SAN JOSE STATION	W SANTA CLARA ST & CAHILL ST, SJS, 95110	834 - A7
CALTRAIN SAN MATEO STATION	2ND AV & RAILROAD AV, SMTO, 94401	749 - A1
CALTRAIN SANTA CLARA STATION	RAILROAD AV & FRANKLN ST, SCL, 95050	833 - F4
CALTRAIN SUNNYVALE STATION	EVELYN AV & FRANCES AV, SUNV, 94086	812 - E7
CALTRAIN TAMIEN STATION	W ALMA AV & LICK AV, SJS, 95110	854 - C2
CALTRAIN TERMINAL	FOURTH ST & TOWNSEND ST, SF, 94107	648 - B7
CAPITOL VTA RAIL STATION	CAPITOL EXWY & HWY 87, SJS, 95136	874 - E1
CASTRO STREET STATION	CASTRO ST & MARKET ST, SF, 94114	667 - G2
CASTRO VALLEY BART STATION	NORBRIDGE AV, AlaC, 94546	692 - A6
CHAMPION VTA RAIL STATION	TASMAN DR & CHAMPION CT, SJS, 95134	813 - E3
CHURCH STREET STATION	CHURCH ST & MARKET ST, SF, 94114	667 - H1
CIVIC CENTER STATION	7TH ST & MARKET ST, SF, 94103	647 - J7
CIVIC CENTER VTA RAIL STATION	N 1ST ST & E MISSION ST, SJS, 95112	834 - A4
COLISEUM BART STATION	7200 LEANDRO ST, OAK, 94621	670 - F4
COLMA BART STATION	EL CAMINO REAL & F ST, SMCo, 94014, (650)992-4398	687 - C6
COMPONENT VTA RAIL STATION	N 1ST ST & COMPONENT DR, SJS, 95131	813 - G7
CONVENTION CENTER VTA RAIL-STATION	W SAN CARLOS ST & MARKET ST, SJS, 95110	834 - B7
COTTLE VTA RAIL STATION	COTTLE RD & HWY 85, SJS, 95119	875 - C5
CURTNER VTA RAIL STATION	GUADALUPE FRWY & CURTNER AV, SJS, 95125	854 - D5
DALY CITY STATION	JOHN DALY BLVD & DE LONG ST, DALY, 94014	687 - C3
DELLUMS TRAIN STATION (AMTRAK)	245 2ND ST, OAK, 94607	649 - G5
EAST DUBLIN/PLEASANTON BART-STATION	I-580 & DOUGHERTY RD, PLE, 94588	694 - B5
EMBARCADERO STATION	MAIN ST & MARKET ST, SF, 94105	648 - B5
FERRY TERMINAL	495 MARE ISLAND WY, VAL, 94590, (707)643-3779	529 - H5
FERRY TERMINAL	MECARTNEY DR, ALA, 94502	669 - H6
FOREST HILLS STATION	LAGUNA HONDA BLVD & DEWEY BLVD, SF, 94116	667 - D4
FREMONT BART STATION	2000 BART WY, FRMT, 94538	753 - B3
FREMONT BUS STATION	3780 BONDE WY, FRMT, 94536, (510)797-4020	752 - H3
FRUITVALE BART STATION	3401 E 12TH ST, OAK, 94601	670 - C1
GISH VTA RAIL STATION	N 1ST ST & GISH RD, SJS, 95112	833 - J2
GLEN PARK STATION	BOSWORTH ST & DIAMOND ST, SF, 94131	667 - G6
GOLDEN GATE LARKSPUR FERRY-TERMINAL	E SIR FRANCIS DRAKE BLVD, LKSP, 94904	586 - H5
GOLDEN GATE SAUSALITO FERRY-TERMINAL	ANCHOR SPINNAKER DR & PARK ST, SAUS, 94965	627 - B3
GREAT AMERICA VTA RAIL STATION	TASMAN DR & GREAT AMERICA PKWY, SCL, 95054	813 - B4
GREEN MUNI CENTER	SAN JOSE AV & GENEVA AV, SF, 94112	687 - E1
GREYHOUND BUS STATION	101 EL PORTAL DR, SPAB, 94806, (510)235-1441	588 - J2
GREYHOUND BUS STATION	145 S SANTA CRUZ AV, LGTS, 95030, (408)354-0766	873 - A7
GREYHOUND BUS STATION	2103 SAN PABLO AV, OAK, 94612	649 - G3
GREYHOUND BUS STATION	22589 WATKINS ST, HAY, 94541, (510)581-3720	711 - J1
GREYHOUND BUS STATION	70 ALMADEN AV, SJS, 95113, (408)295-4151	834 - B6
GREYHOUND BUS STATION	CENTRAL EXPWY & MAYFIELO AV, MTVW, 94043	811 - F3
GREYHOUND BUS TERMINAL	1916 2ND ST, LVMR, 94550, (510)447-2600	715 - G1
HAYWARD BART STATION	699 B ST, HAY, 94541	711 - H2
JAPANTOWN/AYER VTA RAIL STATION	N 1ST ST & AYER AV, SJS, 95112	834 - A5
KARINA VTA RAIL STATION	N 1ST ST & KARINA CT, SJS, 95131	833 - H1
LAKE MERRITT BART STATION	800 MADISON ST, OAK, 94607	649 - G5
LARKSPUR FERRY TERMINAL	E SIR FRANCIS DRAKE BLVD, LKSP, 94904	586 - H5
LICK MILL VTA RAIL STATION	TASMAN DR & LICK MILL BLVD, SCL, 95054	813 - C3
MACARTHUR BART STATION	555 40TH ST, OAK, 94609	629 - G7
METRO/AIRPORT VTA RAIL STATION	N 1ST ST & METRO DR, SJS, 95112	833 - H1
MONTGOMERY ST STATION	MONTGOMERY ST & MARKET ST, SF, 94105	648 - B5
NORTH BERKELEY BART STATION	1750 SACRAMENTO ST, BERK, 94702	629 - F1
OAKLAND WEST BART STATION	1451 7TH ST, OAK, 94607	649 - D4
OAKRIDGE VTA RAIL STATION	WINFIELD BLVD & BLOSSOM RIVER, SJS, 95123	874 - E4
OHLONE-CHYNOWETH VTA RAIL STATION	PEARL AV & CHYNOWETH AV, SJS, 95136	874 - E3
OLD IRONSIDES VTA RAIL STATION	TASMAN DR & OLD IRONSIDES DR, SCL, 95054	813 - B4
ORCHARD VTA RAIL STATION	N 1ST ST & ORCHARD PKWY, SJS, 95134	813 - G5
PAS D ANTONIO VTA RAIL STATION	N 1ST ST & PAS D SAN ANTONIO, SJS, 95113	834 - B7
PAS D ANTONIO VTA RAIL STATION	N 2ND ST & PAS D SAN ANTONIO, SJS, 95113	834 - C6
POWELL STATION	POWELL ST & MARKET ST, SF, 94103	648 - A6
RAILROAD STATION	GRANT AVE & SCOTT CT, NVTO, 94945	526 - C3
RIVER OAKS VTA RAIL STATION	N 1ST ST & RIVER OAKS PKWY, SJS, 95134	813 - F4
ROCKRIDGE BART STATION	5660 COLLEGE AV, OAK, 94618	629 - J5
SAINT JAMES VTA RAIL STATION	N 1ST ST & E SAINT JAMES ST, SJS, 95112	834 - B6
SAINT JAMES VTA RAIL STATION	N 2ND ST & E SAINT JOHN ST, SJS, 95112	834 - B6
SAMTRANS TRANSIT TRANSFER POINT	1ST AV & B ST, SMTO, 94401	748 - J1
SAMTRANS TRANSIT TRANSFER POINT	AIRPORT BL & LINDEN AV, SSF, 94080	708 - A2
SAMTRANS TRANSIT TRANSFER POINT	ARROYO DR & EL CAMINO REAL, SSF, 94080	707 - F3
SAMTRANS TRANSIT TRANSFER POINT	BAYSHORE BLVD & TUNNEL AV, BSBN, 94005	688 - B6
SAMTRANS TRANSIT TRANSFER POINT	CRESPI DR & CABRILLO HWY, PCFA, 94044	726 - H3
SAMTRANS TRANSIT TRANSFER POINT	E HILLSDALE BL & EL CM REAL, SMTO, 94403	749 - C5
SAMTRANS TRANSIT TRANSFER POINT	EL CAMINO REAL & JAMES AV, RDWC, 94063	770 - A6
SAMTRANS TRANSIT TRANSFER POINT	EL CAMINO REAL & OAK GROVE AV, MLPK, 94025	790 - F3
SAMTRANS TRANSIT TRANSFER POINT	HILLSDALE SHOPPING CENTER, SMTO, 94403	749 - C6
SAMTRANS TRANSIT TRANSFER POINT	HWY 92 & 101 FWY, SMTO, 94403	749 - C3
SAMTRANS TRANSIT TRANSFER POINT	JOHN DALY BLVD & DE LONG ST, DALY, 94014	687 - C3
SAMTRANS TRANSIT TRANSFER POINT	JUNIPERO SERRA BLVD & D ST, DALY, 94014	687 - C6
SAMTRANS TRANSIT TRANSFER POINT	LINDA MAR BLVD & CABRILLO HWY, PCFA, 94044	726 - H4
SAMTRANS TRANSIT TRANSFER POINT	MURCHISON DR & EL CAMINO REAL, MLBR, 94030	728 - B4
SAMTRANS TRANSIT TRANSFER POINT	OCEANA BLVD & MANOR DR, PCFA, 94044	706 - J3
SAMTRANS TRANSIT TRANSFER POINT	SAN CARLOS & EL CAMINO REAL, SCAR, 94070	769 - G3
SAMTRANS TRANSIT TRANSFER POINT	SERRAMONTE CENTER, DALY, 94015	707 - C1
SAMTRANS TRANSIT TRANSFER POINT	TANFORAN PARK, SBRN, 94066	707 - H5
SAMTRANS TRANSIT TRANSFER POINT	VETERANS BL & WHIPPLE AV, RDWC, 94063	770 - A4
SAMTRANS TRANSIT TRANSFER POINT	W MANOR DR & MANOR PZ, PCFA, 94044	706 - J3
SAMTRANS TRANSIT TRANSFER POINT	WESTBOROUGH BL & GELLERT BLVD, SSF, 94080	707 - D4
SAN LEANDRO BART STATION	1401 SAN LEANDRO BLVD, SLN, 94577	691 - A1
SANTA CLARA VTA RAIL STATION	N 1ST ST & E SANTA CLARA ST, SJS, 95113	834 - B6
SANTA CLARA VTA RAIL STATION	S 2ND ST & E SANTA CLARA ST, SJS, 95113	834 - B6
SANTA TERESA VTA RAIL STATION	SANTA TERESA BLVD, SJS, 95119	875 - D6
SNELL VTA RAIL STATION	SNELL AV & HWY 85, SJS, 95123	874 - J4
SOUTH HAYWARD BART STATION	28601 DIXON ST, HAY, 94544	712 - C7
SOUTHERN PACIFIC NEWARK STATION	7373 CARTER AV, NWK, 94560, (510)797-2430	752 - D7
SOUTHERN PACIFIC SAN LEANDRO-STATION	801 DAVIS ST, SLN, 94577, (510)483-0696	691 - A1
TAMIEN VTA RAIL STATION	GUADALUPE FRWY & W ALMA AV, SJS, 95110	854 - C2
TASMAN VTA RAIL STATION	TASMAN DR & N 1ST ST, SJS, 95134	813 - E3
TECHNOLOGY CENTER VTA RAIL-STATION	WOOZ WY & W SAN CARLOS ST, SJS, 95110	834 - B7
TIBURON FERRY TERMINAL	PARADISE DR, TBRN, 94920	627 - E1
TRANSBAY TRANSIT TERMINAL	1ST ST & NATOMA ST, SF, 94105	648 - B5
UNION CITY BART STATION	10 UNION SQ, UNC, 94587	732 - G6
UNION PACIFIC	2062 OAK ST, LVMR, 94550	695 - G7
UNION PACIFIC	691 C ST, HAY, 94541	711 - H2
UNION PACIFIC	RAILROAD AV, FRMT, 94536	753 - B2
UNION PACIFIC RAILROAD STATION	495 ROSE AV, PLE, 94566	714 - D3
UNION PACIFIC STATION	1011 W ESTUDILLO AV, SLN, 94577	691 - A1
VAN NESS STATION	12TH ST & MARKET ST, SF, 94103	647 - H7
VIRGINIA VTA LIGHT RAIL STATION	W VIRGINIA ST & GUADALUPE FRWY, SJS, 95125	854 - B1
WEST PORTAL STATION	W PORTAL AV & VICENTE ST, SF, 94127	667 - C5
WINFIELD VTA RAIL STATION	WINFIELD BLVD & COLEMAN RD, SJS, 95123	874 - D5

WINERIES

FEATURE NAME	Address City, ZIP Code	PAGE-GRID
ALMADEN WINERY	CHAMBERTIN RD & TOURAINE DR, SJS, 95118	874 - B6
CONCANNON VINEYARDS	4590 TESLA RD, AlaC, 94550, (510)455-7770	716 - B3
CONRAD VIANO WINERY	150 MORELLO AV, CCCo, 94553, (510)228-6465	571 - H5
LIVERMORE VALLEY CELLARS	1508 WETMORE RD, AlaC, 94550, (510)447-1751	715 - G6
LOHR, J WINERY	1000 LENZEN AV, SJS, 95126, (408)288-5057	833 - J6
MIRASSOU CHAMPAGNE CELLARS	300 COLLEGE AV, LGTS, 95032, (408)395-3790	893 - A2
MIRASSOU VINEYARDS	3000 ABORN RD, SJS, 95135, (408)274-4000	855 - F2
RETZLAFF VINEYARDS	1356 LIVERMORE AV, AlaC, 94550, (510)447-8941	716 - A2
ROSENBLUM CELLARS	2900 MAIN ST, ALA, 94501, (510)865-7007	649 - D6
STONY RIDGE WINERY	4948 TESLA RD, AlaC, 94550, (510)449-0660	716 - B3
TAKARA SAKE USA	708 ADDISON ST, BERK, 94804, (510)540-8250	629 - D2
WEIBEL BROTHERS WINERY	1250 STANFORD AV, FRMT, 94539, (510)656-2340	773 - J4
WENTE BROTHERS WINERY	5565 TESLA RD, AlaC, 94550, (510)447-3603	716 - C3

BAY AREA

INDEX

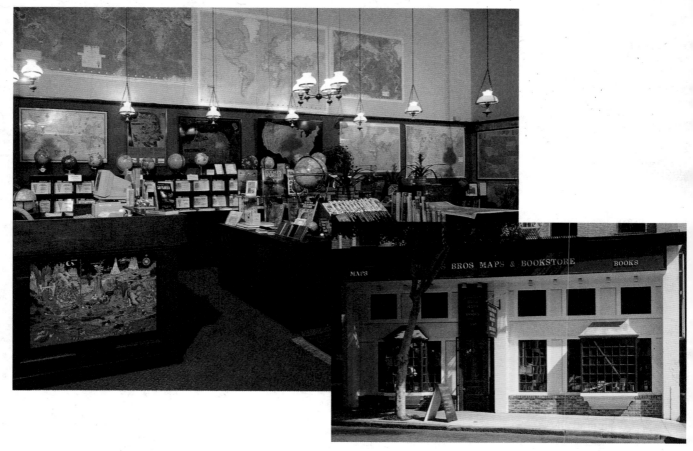

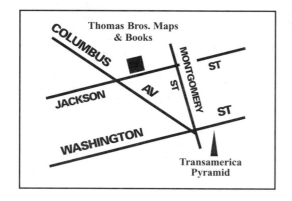